THE FORMULA ONE RECORD BOOK

Published in 2023 by Welbeck

An imprint of Welbeck Non-Fiction Limited, part of Welbeck Publishing Group.
Based in London and Sydney.

20 Mortimer Street
London
W1T 3JW

www.welbeckpublishing.com

A CIP catalogue record for this book is available from the British Library

ISBN 978 1 80279 089 4

Editor: Conor Kilgallon
Consultant editor: Peter Higham
Design: James Empringham and Russell Knowles
Database processing and typesetting: RefineCatch Ltd, www.refinecatch.com
Production: Rachel Burgess

Printed in the UK by Bell and Bain Ltd, Glasgow

10 9 8 7 6 5 4 3 2 1

The facts and stats in this book are correct as of January 2023.

THE FORMULA ONE RECORD BOOK

EVERY GRAND PRIX RESULT
TEAM & DRIVER STATS • ALL-TIME RECORDS

2023 EDITION

BRUCE JONES

CONTENTS

INTRODUCTION

It was a brave new world when the Formula 1 World Championship roared into action at Silverstone in 1950. There had been top-level single-seater racing before, with startling action between Auto Union and Mercedes in grands prix around Europe before World War II. However, the 1950 campaign was the first time that the sport had been organised into a championship, with set races and fixed rules.

Alfa Romeo's domination of the championship's first two seasons was soon over when the Italian manufacturer withdrew at the end of 1951, leaving F1 to start its cycle of change as it sought to ensure that rule changes would increase the number of teams and drivers. It has been a constant evolution ever since.

While automotive manufacturers looked for the glory that a grand prix victory could provide in terms of creating a sporting image that could boost sales, F1 began to be driven by smaller enterprises, nimble outfits whose innovation helped them to react faster than the larger factories. After all, how else would little British outfits Cooper and Lotus have managed to topple mighty Ferrari and Maserati?

The Formula One Record Book charts the extraordinary growth and development of the World Championship across 73 campaigns from 1950 to 2022, with full race results of every one of the 1,049 grands prix, allowing you to compare how good the best were and, in some cases, how far off the pace various challengers languished. Incredibly, more than 400 teams have taken part across the decades and the roll call of drivers who have started a grand prix tops 700, and their full records are contained at the back of the book.

From 1950 to 2022, you can see in the results every single driver's efforts, showing how even some of the greats grappled with uncompetitive machinery early in their careers, and those who never managed even to qualify.

Alongside each season's race results, there is an analysis of the drivers' and teams' year-at-a-glance achievements, plus the final points tables, and the stories picking out the highs, lows, novelties and talking points of each of the 73 championship seasons. These include the dogfights between rivals, the introduction of ground-breaking technology, the arrival of new talent, the introduction of new circuits, changes in the scoring system, the all-time great cars or drivers, or simply an unusual fact.

The numbers competing in F1 have fluctuated, from 21 cars for that first round at Silverstone in 1950 to just 10 at the 1958 Argentinian GP, then increasing to 34 for the 1953 German GP. In 1989, 39 cars turned up, meaning some drivers had to prequalify just for the right to qualify. Nowadays, 20 drivers going for 20 places is much simpler.

Not surprisingly, the cars have changed out of all recognition and, alongside this, the drivers' environment has been transformed, from sitting in an exposed cockpit behind the engine to being cocooned in a safety cell in front of the power unit. This ever-increasing driver safety has stemmed the driver fatalities that used to be an all-too-common feature.

The circuits have changed enormously too. Silverstone, Monaco and Monza remain from that inaugural year, but they have been constantly reshaped to keep them current, while Spa-Francorchamps and the Nurburgring have been chopped in their quest both for modernity and safety. In recent decades, these have been joined by purpose-built tracks created to host a grand prix, like Abu Dhabi's Yas Marina and Istanbul Park, as well as new temporary street circuits in Singapore, Miami and Las Vegas, taking the all-time number of F1 venues to 77.

Another huge difference is the expansion of each season. In the 1950s, each year usually contained six to eight grands prix, but that number has almost trebled as F1's owners Liberty Media push for ever more races, with 23 planned for 2023. And logistics have become ever-more complex, as the largely European-based format of the 1950s has become today's global spread.

With many more races each year, a driver in a competitive car soon exceeds the number of wins, poles or fastest laps set by even the greats of years gone by, which can lead to a skewed analysis of which driver really is the best. Likewise, a win was worth eight points from 1950 to 1957, whereas it is now 25, so you can understand how even the winners from the first three decades of F1 are sinking down any all-time list.

The history of F1 has one constant – Ferrari – which has been involved every season. Its record-topping tally includes the most starts, titles, wins, pole positions, fastest laps and points, but the story of F1 charted in this book shows how the rise of specialist racing teams, largely based in Britain, have taken the battle to them. In turn, Cooper, BRM, Lotus, McLaren, Brabham, Williams, Red Bull Racing, BAR and Mercedes have all had spells at the top. Yet, the soaring cost of competing in F1 has led to even some of these world champions failing. Others have kept going by changing ownership and often, with it, their names. Take Jordan, who started in 1991 but subsequently became Midland, Spyker, Force India, Racing Point and now Aston Martin.

This introduces another problem, as a different team had raced as Aston Martin, in 1959. Others to have had a second life include Alfa Romeo, Lotus and Renault. Confusingly, the Lotus name has been carried by three teams with no shared bloodline to the original outfit. Similarly, Renault was run from France in the 1970s, then became a name used by a British-based team from 2002 to 2011, and 2016 to 2020. If that's not complicated enough, that same team also raced as Lotus from 2012–15.

This book covers every team, driver and circuit that has ever raced in, or hosted, a round of the world championship, so the Ferraris, Fangios and Monacos, plus the McLarens, Hamiltons and Monzas share these pages with teams, drivers and circuits of whose existence only the most diligent F1 fans are aware, but they are all part of the world championship's rich history.

THE 1950s

1950

SEASON SUMMARY

Grand Prix racing was finally formalised in 1950 with the launch of a Formula One World Championship that comprised six grands prix, plus the Indianapolis 500 (see next page), after the immediate post-war years had a series of non-championship races. Alfa Romeo arrived with the fastest car and its one-two-three finish in the opening race showed how their rivals had a lot of catching up to do. The venerable Lago-Talbot was the best of the rest until Ferrari introduced its 375 racer for the final round at Monza. Across the year, Alfa Romeo stayed out in front, winning all six races, as lead driver Giuseppe "Nino" Farina beat Juan Manuel Fangio to the title.

BRITISH GRAND PRIX

SILVERSTONE • ROUND 1 • DATE: 13TH MAY 1950
Laps: 70 • Distance: 202.230miles/325.458km • Weather: Warm & bright

Pos	Driver	Team	Chassis-Engine	Result	Qual
1	Giuseppe Farina	Alfa Romeo	Alfa Romeo 158	2h13m23.600s	1
2	Luigi Fagioli	Alfa Romeo	Alfa Romeo 158	2h13m26.200s	2
3	Reg Parnell	Alfa Romeo	Alfa Romeo 158	2h14m15.600s	4
4	Yves Giraud-Cabantous	Talbot-Darracq	Talbot-Lago T26C-DA	68 laps	6
5	Louis Rosier	Ecurie Rosier	Talbot-Lago T26C	68 laps	9
6	Bob Gerard	Bob Gerard	ERA B	67 laps	13
7	Cuth Harrison	Cuth Harrison	ERA B	67 laps	15
8	Philippe Etancelin	Philippe Etancelin	Talbot-Lago T26C	65 laps	14
9	David Hampshire	Scuderia Ambrosiana	Maserati 4CLT-48	64 laps	16
10	Fry / Shawe-Taylor*	Joe Fry	Maserati 4CL	64 laps	20
11	Johnny Claes	Ecurie Belge	Talbot-Lago T26C	64 laps	21
R	Juan Manuel Fangio	Alfa Romeo	Alfa Romeo 158	62 laps/oil leak	3
NC	Joe Kelly	Joe Kelly	Alta GP	57 laps	19
R	"B Bira"	Scuderia Enrico Plate	Maserati 4CLT-48	49 laps/out of fuel	5
R	David Murray	Scuderia Ambrosiana	Maserati 4CLT-48	44 laps/engine	18
NC	Geoffrey Crossley	Geoffrey Crossley	Alta GP	43 laps	17
R	Emmanuel de Graffenried	Emmanuel de Graffenried	Maserati 4CLT-50	36 laps/engine	8
R	Louis Chiron	Maserati	Maserati 4CLT-48	24 laps/clutch	11
R	Eugene Martin	Talbot-Lago	Talbot-Lago T26C-DA	8 laps/fuel pressure	7
R	Walker / Rolt*	Peter Walker	ERA E	5 laps	10
R	Leslie Johnson	T A S O Mathieson	ERA E	2 laps/supercharger	12

*Joe Fry, Brian Shawe-Taylor, Peter Walker, Tony Rolt

Pole: Farina, 1m50.800s, 93.866mph/151.063kph. Fastest lap: Farina, 1m50.600s, 94.036mph/151.336kph on Lap 2. Race leaders: Farina 1-9, 16-37, 39-70; Fagioli 10-14, 38; Fangio 15

A ROYAL SEND-OFF

With King George VI watching from a covered scaffold platform, the 21-car British GP field powered away from the grid at Silverstone and the crowd was treated to a dominant display from the works Alfa Romeos as the Italian team locked out the four-car front row and roared to the top three places.

TECHNICAL RULE BOOK

The first ever rule book for the World Championship dictated that teams could run their pre-war single seaters with two types of engines: normally aspirated or supercharged. To balance out performance differences, the normally aspirated engines could be a maximum capacity of 4500cc, and the more complex supercharged engines up to 1500cc.

MONACO GRAND PRIX

MONTE CARLO • ROUND 2 • DATE: 21ST MAY 1950
Laps: 100 • Distance: 197.596miles/318.0km • Weather: Cool & bright

Pos	Driver	Team	Chassis-Engine	Result	Qual
1	Juan Manuel Fangio	Alfa Romeo	Alfa Romeo 158	3h13m18.700s	1
2	Alberto Ascari	Ferrari	Ferrari 125	99 laps	7
3	Louis Chiron	Maserati	Maserati 4CLT-48	98 laps	8
4	Raymond Sommer	Ferrari	Ferrari 125	97 laps	9
5	"B Bira"	Scuderia Enrico Plate	Maserati 4CLT-48	95 laps	15
6	Bob Gerard	Bob Gerard	ERA A	94 laps	16
7	Johnny Claes	Ecurie Belge	Talbot-Lago T26C	94 laps	18
R	Luigi Villoresi	Ferrari	Ferrari 125	63 laps/axle	6
R	Philippe Etancelin	Philippe Etancelin	Talbot-Lago T26C	36 laps/oil leak	4
R	Jose Froilan Gonzalez	Scuderia Achille Varzi	Maserati 4CLT-48	1 lap/accident	3
R	Giuseppe Farina	Alfa Romeo	Alfa Romeo 158	0 laps/accident	2
R	Luigi Fagioli	Alfa Romeo	Alfa Romeo 158	0 laps/accident	5
R	Louis Rosier	Ecurie Rosier	Talbot-Lago T26C	0 laps/accident	10
R	Robert Manzon	Gordini	Simca-Gordini T15	0 laps/accident	11
R	Emmanuel de Graffenried	Emmanuel de Graffenried	Maserati 4CLT-48	0 laps/accident	12
R	Maurice Trintignant	Gordini	Simca-Gordini T15	0 laps/accident	13
R	Cuth Harrison	Cuth Harrison	ERA B	0 laps/accident	14
R	Franco Rol	Maserati	Maserati 4CLT-48	0 laps/accident	17
R	Harry Schell	Horschell Racing Corporation	Cooper-JAP T12	0 laps/accident	19
NS	Alfredo Pian	Scuderia Achille Varzi	Maserati 4CLT-50	accident	18
NS	Peter Whitehead	Peter Whitehead	Ferrari 125	engine	21

Pole: Fangio, 1m50.200s, 64.549mph/103.883kph. Fastest lap: Fangio, 1m51.000s, 64.085mph/103.135kph on Lap 24. Race leaders: Fangio 1-100

INDIANAPOLIS 500

From 1950 to 1960, the Indianapolis 500 was part of the World Championship. But an entry from Ferrari for Alberto Ascari in 1952 was the F1 teams' lone bid to tackle America's greatest race. The scores for drivers in the Indianapolis 500 have been left out of the points tables in this book. No sooner had the Indianapolis 500 been dropped than the F1 teams and drivers decided to take on the roadsters with considerable success.

AIR BASE TO RACE TRACK

Silverstone was one of many air bases looking for a new purpose after World War II and making a circuit out of its perimeter roads and runways in 1948 led to a rapid expansion of racing. With the startline moved to between Woodcote and Copse corners in 1950, the basic shape was established.

SWISS GRAND PRIX

BREMGARTEN • ROUND 3 • DATE: 4TH JUNE 1950
Laps: 42 • Distance: 189.565miles/305.76km • Weather: Warm & bright

Pos	Driver	Team	Chassis-Engine	Result	Qual
1	Giuseppe Farina	Alfa Romeo	Alfa Romeo 158	2h02m53.700s	2
2	Luigi Fagioli	Alfa Romeo	Alfa Romeo 158	2h02m54.100s	3
3	Louis Rosier	Talbot-Darracq	Talbot-Lago T26C-DA	41 laps	10
4	"B Bira"	Scuderia Enrico Plate	Maserati 4CLT-48	40 laps	8
5	Felice Bonetto	Scuderia Milano	Maserati 4CLT-50	40 laps	12
6	Emmanuel de Graffenried	Scuderia Enrico Plate	Maserati 4CLT-48	40 laps	11
7	Nello Pagani	Scuderia Achille Varzi	Maserati 4CLT-48	39 laps	15
8	Harry Schell	Ecurie Bleue	Talbot-Lago T26C	39 laps	18
9	Louis Chiron	Maserati	Maserati 4CLT-48	39 laps	16
10	Johnny Claes	Ecurie Belge	Talbot-Lago T26C	38 laps	14
11	Toni Branca	Scuderia Achille Varzi	Maserati 4CL	35 laps	17
R	Juan Manuel Fangio	Alfa Romeo	Alfa Romeo 158	33 laps/engine	1
R	Philippe Etancelin	Philippe Etancelin	Talbot-Lago T26C	25 laps/gearbox	6
R	Eugene Martin	Talbot-Darracq	Talbot-Lago T26C-DA	19 laps/accident	9
R	Raymond Sommer	Ferrari	Ferrari 166F2-50	19 laps/suspension	13
R	Luigi Villoresi	Ferrari	Ferrari 125	9 laps/engine	4
R	Alberto Ascari	Ferrari	Ferrari 125	4 laps/fuel pump	5
R	Yves Giraud-Cabantous	Talbot-Darracq	Talbot-Lago T26C-DA	0 laps/accident	7

Pole: Fangio, 2m42.100s, 100.461mph/161.677kph. Fastest lap: Farina, 2m41.600s, 100.772mph/162.178kph on Lap 8. Race leaders: Fangio 1-6, 21-22; Farina 7-20, 24-42; Fagioli 23

SWISS ROLL

A Swiss GP was one of the season's six grands prix and it was held on the Bremgarten circuit in a forest outside Bern. The track caught the drivers' attention with its fast, flowing curves under overhanging trees, but it had a reputation as a dangerous place, as it had claimed the lives of Achille Varzi and Christian Kautz in 1948.

IN MEMORIAM

Joe Fry was the first F1 driver to die, in a minor race at Blandford Camp two months after his British GP debut. However, Raymond Sommer was the first big name to fall. He had raced to fourth at Monaco for Ferrari but was killed a week after the final F1 round in a minor race at Cadours.

BELGIAN GRAND PRIX

SPA-FRANCORCHAMPS • ROUND 4 • DATE: 18TH JUNE 1950
Laps: 35 • Distance: 306.958miles/494.2km • Weather: Warm & bright

Pos	Driver	Team	Chassis-Engine	Result	Qual
1	Juan Manuel Fangio	Alfa Romeo	Alfa Romeo 158	2h47m26.000s	2
2	Luigi Fagioli	Alfa Romeo	Alfa Romeo 158	2h47m40.000s	3
3	Louis Rosier	Talbot-Darracq	Talbot-Lago T26C-DA	2h49m45.000s	8
4	Giuseppe Farina	Alfa Romeo	Alfa Romeo 158	2h51m31.000s	1
5	Alberto Ascari	Ferrari	Ferrari 275	34 laps	7
6	Luigi Villoresi	Ferrari	Ferrari 125	33 laps	4
7	Pierre Levegh	Pierre Levegh	Talbot-Lago T26C	33 laps	10
8	Johnny Claes	Ecurie Belge	Talbot-Lago T26C	32 laps	14
9	Geoffrey Crossley	Geoffrey Crossley	Alta GP	30 laps	12
10	Toni Branca	Antonio Branca	Maserati 4CL	29 laps	13
R	Eugene Chaboud	Ecurie Leutitia	Talbot-Lago T26C-DA	22 laps/oil pipe	11
R	Raymond Sommer	Raymond Sommer	Talbot-Lago T26C	20 laps/fuel pressure	5
R	Philippe Etancelin	Talbot-Darracq	Talbot-Lago T26C-DA	15 laps/overheating	6
R	Yves Giraud-Cabantous	Talbot-Darracq	Talbot-Lago T26C-DA	2 laps/oil pipe	9

Pole: Farina, 4m37.000s, 114.027mph/183.509kph. Fastest lap: Farina, 4m34.100s, 115.233mph/185.450kph on Lap 18. Race leaders: Fangio 1-6, 20-35; Farina 7-11, 18-19; Sommer 13-17

NEW CONSTRUCTORS

While Alfa Romeo dominated in 1950 and Ferrari and Lago-Talbot gave chase, F1's first campaign marked the arrival of British constructor Cooper, along with other pre-war British challengers, Alta and ERA. Cooper was a growing marque, with Charles Cooper's cars' dominance in 500cc racing proving that small could be beautiful.

FRENCH GRAND PRIX

REIMS • ROUND 5 • DATE: 2ND JULY 1950
Laps: 64 • Distance: 310.695miles/500.16km • Weather: Hot & bright

Pos	Driver	Team	Chassis-Engine	Result	Qual
1	Juan Manuel Fangio	Alfa Romeo	Alfa Romeo 158	2h57m52.800s	1
2	Luigi Fagioli	Alfa Romeo	Alfa Romeo 158	2h58m18.500s	3
3	Peter Whitehead	Peter Whitehead	Ferrari 125	61 laps	18
4	Robert Manzon	Gordini	Simca-Gordini T15	61 laps	12
5	Etancelin / Chaboud*	Talbot-Darracq	Talbot-Lago T26C-DA	59 laps	4
6	Pozzi / Rosier*	Charles Pozzi	Talbot-Lago T26C	56 laps	15
7	Giuseppe Farina	Alfa Romeo	Alfa Romeo 158	55 laps/fuel pump	2
8	Yves Giraud-Cabantous	Talbot-Darracq	Talbot-Lago T26C-DA	52 laps	5
R	Pierre Levegh	Pierre Levegh	Talbot-Lago T26C	36 laps/engine	9
R	Felice Bonetto	Scuderia Milano	Maserati-Milano 4CLT-50	14 laps/engine	10
R	Johnny Claes	Ecurie Belge	Talbot-Lago T26C	11 laps/overheating	14
R	Louis Rosier	Talbot-Darracq	Talbot-Lago T26C-DA	10 laps/overheating	6
R	Reg Parnell	Vandervell Products	Maserati 4CLT-48	9 laps/engine	11
R	Franco Rol	Maserati	Maserati 4CLT-48	6 laps/engine	7
R	Louis Chiron	Maserati	Maserati 4CLT-48	6 laps/engine	13

Pos	Driver	Team	Chassis-Engine	Result	Qual
R	David Hampshire	Scuderia Ambrosiana	Maserati 4CLT-48	5 laps/engine	17
R	Raymond Sommer	Talbot-Darracq	Talbot-Lago T26C-GS	4 laps/overheating	16
R	Jose Froilan Gonzalez	Scuderia Achille Varzi	Maserati 4CLT-48	3 laps/engine	8
NS	Eugene Chaboud	Ecurie Leutitia	Lago-Talbot T26C	-	10

*Philippe Etancelin, Eugene Chaboud, Charles Pozzi, Louis Rosier

Pole: Fangio, 2m30.600s, 116.079mph/186.812kph. Fastest lap: Fangio, 2m35.600s, 112.349mph/180.809kph on Lap 52. Race leaders: Farina 1-16; Fangio 17-64

NEW DRIVERS

Beyond "The Three Fs" – Giuseppe Farina, Juan Manuel Fangio and Luigi Fagioli – who dominated for Alfa Romeo, names that stood out in F1's inaugural season included Alberto Ascari for Ferrari, Louis Rosier in both works and privately entered Lago-Talbots, and Louis Chiron for Maserati, with Briton Peter Whitehead a distant third at Reims.

ITALIAN GRAND PRIX

MONZA • ROUND 6 • DATE: 3RD SEPTEMBER 1950
Laps: 80 • Distance: 313.171miles/504.0km • Weather: Warm & bright, then dull

Pos	Driver	Team	Chassis-Engine	Result	Qual
1	Giuseppe Farina	Alfa Romeo	Alfa Romeo 159	2h51m17.400s	3
2	Serafini / Ascari*	Ferrari	Ferrari 375	2h52m36.000s	6
3	Luigi Fagioli	Alfa Romeo	Alfa Romeo 158	2h52m53.000s	5
4	Louis Rosier	Ecurie Rosier	Talbot-Lago T26C	75 laps	13
5	Philippe Etancelin	Philippe Etancelin	Talbot-Lago T26C	75 laps	16
6	Emmanuel de Graffenried	Emmanuel de Graffenried	Maserati 4CLT-48	72 laps	17
7	Peter Whitehead	Peter Whitehead	Ferrari 125	72 laps	18
R	David Murray	Scuderia Ambrosiana	Maserati 4CL	56 laps/gearbox	24
R	Cuth Harrison	Cuth Harrison	ERA B	51 laps/radiator damage	21
R	Raymond Sommer	Raymond Sommer	Talbot-Lago T26C	48 laps/oil pipe	8
R	Guy Mairesse	Guy Mairesse	Talbot-Lago T26C	42 laps/mechanical	11
R	Franco Rol	Maserati	Maserati 4CLT-48	39 laps/mechanical	9
R	Taruffi / Fangio*	Alfa Romeo	Alfa Romeo 158	34 laps/engine	7
R	Pierre Levegh	Pierre Levegh	Talbot-Lago T26C	29 laps/gearbox	20
R	Juan Manuel Fangio	Alfa Romeo	Alfa Romeo 158	23 laps/gearbox	1
R	Johnny Claes	Ecurie Belge	Talbot-Lago T26C	22 laps/overheating	22
R	Alberto Ascari	Ferrari	Ferrari 375	21 laps/engine	2
R	Clemente Biondetti	Clemente Biondetti	Ferrari-Jaguar 166T	17 laps/engine	25
R	Henri Louveau	Ecurie Rosier	Talbot-Lago T26C-GS	16 laps/brakes	14
R	Franco Comotti	Scuderia Milano	Maserati-Milano 4CLT-50	15 laps/mechanical	26
R	Maurice Trintignant	Gordini	Simca-Gordini T15	13 laps/water pipe	12
R	Louis Chiron	Maserati	Maserati 4CLT-48	13 laps/fuel pressure	19
R	Consalvo Sanesi	Alfa Romeo	Alfa Romeo 158	11 laps/engine	4
R	Robert Manzon	Gordini	Simca-Gordini T15	7 laps/transmission	10
R	"B Bira"	Scuderia Enrico Plate	Maserati 4CLT-50	1 lap/engine	15
R	Paul Pietsch	Paul Pietsch	Maserati 4CLT-48	0 laps/engine	27
NS	Felice Bonetto	Scuderia Milano	Milano	-	23

*Dorino Serafini, Alberto Ascari, Piero Taruffi, Juan Manuel Fangio

Pole: Fangio, 1m58.600s, 118.825mph/191.231kph. Fastest lap: Fangio, 2m00.000s, 117.439mph/189.000kph on Lap 7. Race leaders: Farina 1-13, 16-80; Ascari 14-15

CLASSIC CAR: ALFA ROMEO 159

Designed by Gioacchino Colombo in 1938 for the second-tier *voiturette* category, Alfa Romeo's 158 became the car to beat after World War II, as no rivals had the resources to beat it. However, Alfa Romeo's push in 1950 for more power from the straight-eight supercharged 1500cc engine, boosting it to 350bhp, meant that its Achilles heel was its thirst for fuel. Uprated to 159 spec for Farina for the Italian GP, the engine offered him 425bhp but did only 0.7km per litre (1.6 miles per gallon). But this didn't stop him from adding to the 158s' wins in the first five races.

WORLD DRIVERS' CHAMPIONSHIP FINAL RESULTS

Pos	Driver	Nat	Car-Engine	R1	R2	R3	R4	R5	R6	Total
1	Giuseppe Farina	ITA	Alfa Romeo 158	1PF	R	1F	4PF	7	-	30
			Alfa Romeo 159	-	-	-	-	-	1	
2	Juan Manuel Fangio	ARG	Alfa Romeo 158	R	1PF	RP	1	1PF	RPF/R	27
3	Luigi Fagioli	ITA	Alfa Romeo 158	2	R	2	2	2	3	24
4	Louis Rosier	FRA	Talbot-Lago T26C	5	R	-	-	6	4	13
			Talbot-Lago T26C-DA	-	-	3	3	R	-	
5	Alberto Ascari	ITA	Ferrari 125	-	2	R	-	-	-	11
			Ferrari 275	-	-	-	5	NS	-	
			Ferrari 375	-	-	-	-	-	2|R	
8	"B Bira"	THA	Maserati 4CLT-48	R	5	4	-	-	R	5
9	Reg Parnell	GBR	Alfa Romeo 158	3	-	-	-	-	-	4
			Maserati 4CLT-48	-	-	-	-	R	-	
9	Louis Chiron	MCO	Maserati 4CLT-48	R	3	9	-	R	R	4
9	Peter Whitehead	GBR	Ferrari 125	-	NS	-	-	-	7	4
13	Dorino Serafini	ITA	Ferrari 375	-	-	-	-	-	2	3
14	Yves Giraud-Cabantous	FRA	Talbot-Lago T26C-DA	4	-	R	R	8	-	3
14	Raymond Sommer	FRA	Ferrari 125	-	4	-	-	-	-	3
			Ferrari 166F2-50	-	-	R	-	-	-	
			Talbot-Lago T26C	-	-	-	R	-	R	
			Talbot-Lago T26C-GS	-	-	-	-	R	-	
14	Robert Manzon	FRA	Simca-Gordini T15	-	R	-	-	4	R	3
18	Philippe Etancelin	FRA	Talbot-Lago T26C	8	R	R	-	-	5	3
			Talbot-Lago T26C-DA	-	-	-	R	5	-	
19	Felice Bonetto	ITA	Maserati 4CLT-50	-	-	5	-	-	-	2
			Maserati-Milano 4CLT-50	-	-	-	-	R	-	
			Milano	-	-	-	-	-	NS	
20	Eugene Chaboud	FRA	Talbot-Lago T26C-DA	-	-	-	R	5/NS	-	1

SYMBOLS AND GRAND PRIX KEY

Round 1	**British GP**
Round 2	**Monaco GP**
Round 3	**Swiss GP**
Round 4	**Belgian GP**
Round 5	**French GP**
Round 6	**Italian GP**

Indianapolis 500 results not included

SCORING

1st	**8 points**
2nd	**6 points**
3rd	**4 points**
4th	**3 points**
5th	**2 points**
Fastest Lap	**1 point**

DNPQ DID NOT PRE-QUALIFY **DNQ** DID NOT QUALIFY **DQ** DISQUALIFIED **EX** EXCLUDED
F FASTEST LAP **NC** NOT CLASSIFIED **NS** NON-STARTER **P** POLE POSITION **R** RETIRED

1951

SEASON SUMMARY

Juan Manuel Fangio shifted up a gear in 1951 and assumed a dominant position in the Alfa Romeo team as he mastered the two-stop runs the thirsty 159s required to beat anything that Ferrari could throw at him. The 40-year-old Argentinian was made to fight, though, as the Ferrari challenge accelerated. Indeed, he would have been beaten to the title by Alberto Ascari had Ferrari not got its tyre choice wrong at the final round in Spain. These Italian teams reigned supreme, filling the top six places at three of the season's seven grands prix, leaving only scraps for Lago-Talbot and BRM to fight over.

SWISS GRAND PRIX

BREMGARTEN • ROUND 1 • DATE: 27TH MAY 1951
Laps: 42 • Distance: 189.565miles/305.76km • Weather: Cool with heavy rain

Pos	Driver	Team	Chassis-Engine	Result	Qual
1	Juan Manuel Fangio	Alfa Romeo	Alfa Romeo 159	2h07m53.640s	1
2	Piero Taruffi	Ferrari	Ferrari 375	2h08m48.880s	6
3	Giuseppe Farina	Alfa Romeo	Alfa Romeo 159	2h09m12.950s	2
4	Consalvo Sanesi	Alfa Romeo	Alfa Romeo 159	41 laps	4
5	Emmanuel de Graffenried	Alfa Romeo	Alfa Romeo 159	40 laps	5
6	Alberto Ascari	Ferrari	Ferrari 375	40 laps	7
7	Louis Chiron	Scuderia Enrico Plate	Maserati 4CLT-48	40 laps	19
8	Stirling Moss	HWM	HWM-Alta	40 laps	14
9	Louis Rosier	Ecurie Rosier	Talbot-Lago T26C-DA	39 laps	8
10	Philippe Etancelin	Philippe Etancelin	Talbot-Lago T26C-DA	39 laps	12
11	Rudi Fischer	Ecurie Espadon	Ferrari 212	39 laps	10
12	Harry Schell	Scuderia Enrico Plate	Maserati 4CLT-48	38 laps	17
13	Johnny Claes	Ecurie Belge	Talbot-Lago T26C-DA	35 laps	18
14	Guy Mairesse	Yves Giraud-Cabantous	Talbot-Lago T26C	31 laps	21
R	Peter Whitehead	Ferrari	Ferrari 125	36 laps/accident	9
R	Henri Louveau	Ecurie Rosier	Talbot-Lago T26C	30 laps/accident	11
R	George Abecassis	HWM	HWM-Alta	23 laps/magneto	20
R	Yves Giraud-Cabantous	Yves Giraud-Cabantous	Talbot-Lago T26C	14 laps/ignition	15
R	Luigi Villoresi	Ferrari	Ferrari 375	12 laps/accident	3
R	Jose Froilan Gonzalez	Jose Froilan Gonzalez	Talbot-Lago T26C-GS	10 laps/fuel pump	13
R	Peter Hirt	Ecurie Espadon	Veritas Meteor	0 laps/fuel system	16

Pole: Fangio, 2m35.900s, 104.457mph/168.107kph. Fastest lap: Fangio, 2m51.100s, 95.194mph/153.200kph on Lap 33. Race leaders: Fangio 1-23, 29-42; Farina 24-28

OVER AND OUT

Dominant Alfa Romeo had a hard decision to make in F1's second year: to stay on or to pull out. The Italian road car manufacturer knew that the World Championship would be run to a new set of rules in 1952, and simply didn't have the funds available to design and build a new car.

FERRARI'S FIRST

With its challenge gaining pace through 1951, Ferrari came on strong to achieve the marque's first World Championship success. This came at the fourth-round British GP, with Jose Froilan Gonzalez grabbing his Ferrari 375 by the scruff of the neck and seizing his moment when Fangio stalled at a pit stop. Team-mate Alberto Ascari won the next two.

BELGIAN GRAND PRIX

SPA-FRANCORCHAMPS • ROUND 2 • DATE: 17TH JUNE 1951
Laps: 36 • Distance: 315.676miles/508.32km • Weather: Warm & bright

Pos	Driver	Team	Chassis-Engine	Result	Qual
1	Giuseppe Farina	Alfa Romeo	Alfa Romeo 159	2h45m46.200s	2
2	Alberto Ascari	Ferrari	Ferrari 375	2h48m37.200s	4
3	Luigi Villoresi	Ferrari	Ferrari 375	2h50m08.100s	3
4	Louis Rosier	Ecurie Rosier	Talbot-Lago T26C-DA	34 laps	7
5	Yves Giraud-Cabantous	Yves Giraud-Cabantous	Talbot-Lago T26C	34 laps	8
6	Andre Pilette	Ecurie Belgique	Talbot-Lago T26C	33 laps	12
7	Johnny Claes	Ecurie Belge	Talbot-Lago T26C-DA	33 laps	11
8	Pierre Levegh	Pierre Levegh	Talbot-Lago T26C	32 laps	13
9	Juan Manuel Fangio	Alfa Romeo	Alfa Romeo 159	32 laps	1
R	Louis Chiron	Ecurie Rosier	Talbot-Lago T26C	28 laps/engine	9
R	Consalvo Sanesi	Alfa Romeo	Alfa Romeo 159	11 laps/radiator damage	6
R	Piero Taruffi	Ferrari	Ferrari 375	8 laps/transmission	5
R	Philippe Etancelin	Philippe Etancelin	Talbot-Lago T26C-DA	0 laps/transmission	10

Pole: Fangio, 4m25.000s, 119.190mph/191.818kph. Fastest lap: Fangio, 4m22.100s, 120.483mph/193.900kph on Lap 10. Race leaders: Villoresi 1-2; Farina 3-14, 16-36; Fangio 15

FRENCH GRAND PRIX

REIMS • ROUND 3 • DATE: 1ST JULY 1951
Laps: 77 • Distance: 373.913miles/601.755km • Weather: Hot & bright

Pos	Driver	Team	Chassis-Engine	Result	Qual
1	Fagioli / Fangio*	Alfa Romeo	Alfa Romeo 159	3h22m11.000s	7
2	Gonzalez / Ascari*	Ferrari	Ferrari 375	3h23m09.200s	6
3	Luigi Villoresi	Ferrari	Ferrari 375	74 laps	4
4	Reg Parnell	Vandervell Products	Ferrari 375	73 laps	9
5	Giuseppe Farina	Alfa Romeo	Alfa Romeo 159	73 laps	2
6	Louis Chiron	Ecurie Rosier	Talbot-Lago T26C	71 laps	8
7	Yves Giraud-Cabantous	Yves Giraud-Cabantous	Talbot-Lago T26C	71 laps	11
8	Eugene Chaboud	Eugene Chaboud	Talbot-Lago T26C-GS	69 laps	14
9	Guy Mairesse	Yves Giraud-Cabantous	Talbot-Lago T26C	66 laps	19
10	Consalvo Sanesi	Alfa Romeo	Alfa Romeo 159	58 laps	5
11	Fangio / Fagioli*	Alfa Romeo	Alfa Romeo 159	55 laps	1
R	Johnny Claes	Ecurie Belge	Talbot-Lago T26C-DA	54 laps/accident	12
R	Louis Rosier	Ecurie Rosier	Talbot-Lago T26C-DA	43 laps/transmission	13
R	Philippe Etancelin	Philippe Etancelin	Talbot-Lago T26C-DA	37 laps/engine	10
R	Aldo Gordini	Gordini	Simca-Gordini T11	27 laps/engine	17
R	Harry Schell	Scuderia Enrico Plate	Maserati 4CLT-48	23 laps/overheating	22

Pos	Driver	Team	Chassis-Engine	Result	Qual
R	Maurice Trintignant	Gordini	Simca-Gordini T15	11 laps/engine	18
R	Alberto Ascari	Ferrari	Ferrari 375	10 laps/gearbox	3
R	Andre Simon	Gordini	Simca-Gordini T15	7 laps/engine	21
R	Robert Manzon	Gordini	Simca-Gordini T15	3 laps/engine	23
R	Onofre Marimon	Scuderia Milano	Maserati-Milano 4CLT-50	2 laps/engine	15
R	Emmanuel de Graffenried	Scuderia Enrico Plate	Maserati 4CLT-48	1 lap/transmission	16
R	Peter Whitehead	Graham Whitehead	Ferrari 125	1 lap/engine	20
NS	Brian Shawe-Taylor	Vandervell Products	Ferrari 375	Parnell drove	

*Luigi Fagioli, Juan Manuel Fangio, Jose Froilan Gonzalez, Alberto Ascari

Pole: Fangio, 3m05.700s, 94.139mph/151.502kph. Fastest lap: Fangio, 2m27.800s, 118.309mph/190.400kph on Lap 32. Race leaders: Ascari 1-8, 45-50; Fangio 9, 51-77; Farina 10-44

BRITISH GRAND PRIX

SILVERSTONE • ROUND 4 • DATE: 14TH JULY 1951
Laps: 90 • Distance: 260.9miles/418.445km • Weather: Warm & bright

Pos	Driver	Team	Chassis-Engine	Result	Qual
1	Jose Froilan Gonzalez	Ferrari	Ferrari 375	2h42m18.200s	1
2	Juan Manuel Fangio	Alfa Romeo	Alfa Romeo 159	2h43m09.200s	2
3	Luigi Villoresi	Ferrari	Ferrari 375	88 laps	5
4	Felice Bonetto	Alfa Romeo	Alfa Romeo 159	87 laps	7
5	Reg Parnell	BRM	BRM P15	85 laps	20
6	Consalvo Sanesi	Alfa Romeo	Alfa Romeo 159	84 laps	6
7	Peter Walker	BRM	BRM P15	84 laps	19
8	Brian Shawe-Taylor	Brian Shawe-Taylor	ERA B	84 laps	12
9	Peter Whitehead	Vanwall	Ferrari 375	83 laps	8
10	Louis Rosier	Ecurie Rosier	Talbot-Lago T26C-DA	83 laps	9
11	Bob Gerard	Bob Gerard	ERA B	82 laps	10
12	Duncan Hamilton	Duncan Hamilton	Talbot-Lago T26C	81 laps	11
13	Johnny Claes	Ecurie Belge	Talbot-Lago T26C-DA	80 laps	14
R	Giuseppe Farina	Alfa Romeo	Alfa Romeo 159	75 laps/clutch	3
NC	Joe Kelly	Joe Kelly	Alta GP	75 laps/not classified	18
R	Alberto Ascari	Ferrari	Ferrari 375	56 laps/gearbox	4
R	Philip Fotheringham-Parker	Philip Fotheringham-Parker	Maserati 4CL	46 laps/oil leak	16
R	David Murray	Scuderia Ambrosiana	Maserati 4CLT-48	45 laps/engine	15
R	Louis Chiron	Ecurie Rosier	Talbot-Lago T26C	41 laps/brakes	13
R	John James	John James	Maserati 4CLT-48	23 laps/radiator	17

Pole: Gonzalez, 1m43.400s, 100.584mph/161.874kph. Fastest lap: Farina, 1m44.000s, 99.978mph/160.900kph on Lap 38. Race leaders: Bonetto 1; Gonzalez 2-9, 39-47, 49-90; Fangio 10-38, 48

RACING ON THE STREETS

Where Monaco led, others were sure to follow, and so the first time Spain hosted a round of the World Championship was on a layout of streets in Pedralbes, a western suburb of Barcelona. The track was unusually wide and fast for a street track, and Juan Manuel Fangio won at a canter to clinch the title.

GERMAN GRAND PRIX

NURBURGRING • ROUND 5 • DATE: 29TH JULY 1951
Laps: 20 • Distance: 283.346miles/456.2km • Weather: Warm & bright

Pos	Driver	Team	Chassis-Engine	Result	Qual
1	Alberto Ascari	Ferrari	Ferrari 375	3h23m03.300s	1
2	Juan Manuel Fangio	Alfa Romeo	Alfa Romeo 159	3h23m33.800s	3
3	Jose Froilan Gonzalez	Ferrari	Ferrari 375	3h27m42.300s	2
4	Luigi Villoresi	Ferrari	Ferrari 375	3h28m53.500s	5
5	Piero Taruffi	Ferrari	Ferrari 375	3h30m52.400s	6
6	Rudi Fischer	Ecurie Espadon	Ferrari 212	19 laps	8
7	Robert Manzon	Gordini	Simca-Gordini T15	19 laps	9
8	Louis Rosier	Ecurie Rosier	Talbot-Lago T26C-DA	19 laps	15
9	Pierre Levegh	Pierre Levegh	Talbot-Lago T26C	18 laps	19
10	Jacques Swaters	Ecurie Belgique	Talbot-Lago T26C	18 laps	22
11	Johnny Claes	Ecurie Belge	Talbot-Lago T26C-DA	17 laps	18
R	Yves Giraud-Cabantous	Yves Giraud-Cabantous	Talbot-Lago T26C	17 laps/accident	11
R	Maurice Trintignant	Gordini	Simca-Gordini T15	13 laps/engine	14
R	Felice Bonetto	Alfa Romeo	Alfa Romeo 159	12 laps/magneto	10
R	Duncan Hamilton	Duncan Hamilton	Talbot-Lago T26C	12 laps/fuel pressure	20
R	Paul Pietsch	Alfa Romeo	Alfa Romeo 159	11 laps/accident	7
R	Andre Simon	Gordini	Simca-Gordini T15	11 laps/engine	12
R	Giuseppe Farina	Alfa Romeo	Alfa Romeo 159	8 laps/overheating	4
R	Philippe Etancelin	Philippe Etancelin	Talbot-Lago T26C-DA	4 laps/gearbox	21
R	Louis Chiron	Ecurie Rosier	Talbot-Lago T26C	3 laps/ignition	13
R	Toni Branca	Antonio Branca	Maserati 4CLT-48	3 laps/engine	17
R	Emmanuel de Graffenried	Scuderia Enrico Plate	Maserati 4CLT-48	2 laps/engine	16
NS	David Murray	Scuderia Ambrosiana	Maserati 4CLT-48	-	-

Pole: Ascari, 9m55.800s, 85.640mph/137.824kph. Fastest lap: Fangio, 9m55.800s, 85.624mph/137.800kph on Lap 12. Race leaders: Fangio 1-4, 11-14; Ascari 5-9, 15-20; Gonzalez 10

CHAMPIONS IN THEIR 40S

Racing drivers were older in the 1950s, with many no longer in their 20s or 30s, some not even in their 40s. The concept of a teenager racing in F1 at 17, like Max Verstappen did in 2015, was unthinkable. Indeed, Farina was 43 when he won the 1950 title and Fangio 40 when he followed suit in 1951.

BRM'S EMBARRASSMENT

British Racing Motors aimed to topple the Italian constructors, but failed to do so in 1951. It most wanted to succeed at the British GP, especially as it hadn't been ready for the previous race, at Reims. The V16-powered Type 15 did venture out at Silverstone but Reg Parnell could only drive it to a distant fifth place, suffering burns for his efforts.

A DRIVER WITH HEFT

It wasn't a prerequisite in the 1950s for an F1 driver to be as slim as they are today. Indeed, the main requirement was to be fit enough, or at least strong enough, to handle the heavy cars for races that lasted three hours. The ultimate example of this was the hefty Jose Froilan Gonzalez, nicknamed the "Pampas Bull".

ITALIAN GRAND PRIX

MONZA • ROUND 6 • DATE: 16TH SEPTEMBER 1951
Laps: 80 • Distance: 313.171miles/504.0km • Weather: Hot & bright

Pos	Driver	Team	Chassis-Engine	Result	Qual
1	Alberto Ascari	Ferrari	Ferrari 375	2h42m39.300s	3
2	Jose Froilan Gonzalez	Ferrari	Ferrari 375	2h43m23.900s	4
3	Bonetto / Farina*	Alfa Romeo	Alfa Romeo 159	79 laps	7
4	Luigi Villoresi	Ferrari	Ferrari 375	79 laps	5
5	Piero Taruffi	Ferrari	Ferrari 375	78 laps	6
6	Andre Simon	Gordini	Simca-Gordini T15	74 laps	11
7	Louis Rosier	Ecurie Rosier	Talbot-Lago T26C-DA	73 laps	15
8	Yves Giraud-Cabantous	Yves Giraud-Cabantous	Talbot-Lago T26C	72 laps	14
9	Franco Rol	OSCA	OSCA 4500G	67 laps	18
R	Juan Manuel Fangio	Alfa Romeo	Alfa Romeo 159	39 laps/engine	1
R	Maurice Trintignant	Gordini	Simca-Gordini T15	29 laps/engine	12
R	Robert Manzon	Gordini	Simca-Gordini T15	29 laps/engine	13
R	Louis Chiron	Ecurie Rosier	Talbot-Lago T26C	23 laps/ignition	17
R	Pierre Levegh	Pierre Levegh	Talbot-Lago T26C	9 laps/engine	20
R	Jacques Swaters	Ecurie Belgique	Talbot-Lago T26C	7 laps/overheating	22
R	Giuseppe Farina	Alfa Romeo	Alfa Romeo 159	6 laps/engine	2
R	Johnny Claes	Ecurie Belge	Talbot-Lago T26C-DA	4 laps/fuel pump	21
R	Emmanuel de Graffenried	Alfa Romeo	Alfa Romeo 159	1 lap/compressor	9
R	Peter Whitehead	Peter Whitehead	Ferrari 125	1 lap/magneto	19
R	Chico Landi	Francisco Landi	Ferrari 375	0 laps/transmission	16
NS	Reg Parnell	BRM	BRM P15	engine	8
NS	Ken Richardson	BRM	BRM P15	wrong licence	10
NS	Rudi Fischer	Ecurie Espadon	Ferrari 212	accident	-
NS	Hans Stuck	BRM	BRM P15	engine	-

*Felice Bonetto, Giuseppe Farina

Pole: Fangio, 1m53.200s, 124.493mph/200.353kph. Fastest lap: Farina, 1m56.500s, 120.980mph/194.700kph on Lap 64. Race leaders: Fangio 1-3, 8-13; Ascari 4-7, 14-80

NEW CONSTRUCTORS

Along with BRM, HWM, OSCA and Veritas made their championship debuts. British team HWM – Hersham & Walton Motors – had a young Stirling Moss on its books, and OSCA was established by three of the Maserati brothers (although its strength was sports cars rather than F1), while Germany's Veritas marque did little of note.

BRITAIN'S ELDER STATESMAN

Reg Parnell made his reputation either side of World War II. Invited to join Alfa Romeo for the 1950 British GP, he finished third, and then raced the Thinwall Special Ferrari in 1951, winning the non-championship International Trophy and coming fourth at Reims before having a troubled time with BRM. He would later run his own F1 team.

SPANISH GRAND PRIX

PEDRALBES • ROUND 7 • DATE: 28TH OCTOBER 1951
Laps: 70 • Distance: 274.653miles/442.12km • Weather: Warm & bright

Pos	Driver	Team	Chassis-Engine	Result	Qual
1	Juan Manuel Fangio	Alfa Romeo	Alfa Romeo 159	2h46m54.100s	2
2	Jose Froilan Gonzalez	Ferrari	Ferrari 375	2h47m48.380s	3
3	Giuseppe Farina	Alfa Romeo	Alfa Romeo 159	2h48m39.640s	4
4	Alberto Ascari	Ferrari	Ferrari 375	68 laps	1
5	Felice Bonetto	Alfa Romeo	Alfa Romeo 159	68 laps	8
6	Emmanuel de Graffenried	Alfa Romeo	Alfa Romeo 159	66 laps	6
7	Louis Rosier	Ecurie Rosier	Talbot-Lago T26C-DA	64 laps	20
8	Philippe Etancelin	Philippe Etancelin	Talbot-Lago T26C-DA	63 laps	13
9	Robert Manzon	Gordini	Simca-Gordini T15	63 laps	9
10	Chico Godia-Sales	Scuderia Milano	Maserati 4CLT-48	60 laps	17
R	Luigi Villoresi	Ferrari	Ferrari 375	48 laps/ignition	5
R	Andre Simon	Gordini	Simca-Gordini T15	48 laps/engine	10
R	Johnny Claes	Ecurie Belge	Talbot-Lago T26C-DA	37 laps/accident	15
R	Piero Taruffi	Ferrari	Ferrari 375	30 laps/wheel	7
R	Maurice Trintignant	Gordini	Simca-Gordini T15	25 laps/engine	11
R	Georges Grignard	Georges Grignard	Talbot-Lago T26C-DA	23 laps/engine	16
R	Yves Giraud-Cabantous	Yves Giraud-Cabantous	Talbot-Lago T26C	7 laps/accident	14
R	Louis Chiron	Ecurie Rosier	Talbot-Lago T26C	4 laps/ignition	12
R	"B Bira"	B Bira	Maserati-OSCA 4CLT-48	1 lap/engine	19
NS	Juan Jover	Scuderia Milano	Maserati 4CLT-48	engine	18

Pole: Ascari, 2m10.590s, 108.189mph/174.114kph. Fastest lap: Fangio, 2m16.930s, 103.178mph/166.050kph on Lap 3. Race leaders: Ascari 1-3; Fangio 4-70

SHARING THE GLORY

If the lead driver in a team hit mechanical trouble, their race wasn't over, as there was a custom in the 1950s of taking over another driver's car. This is what Fangio did at Reims, when his car failed and he commandeered Alfa Romeo team-mate Luigi Fagioli's 159 and took that on to victory, taking half the points.

NEW DRIVERS

There were 19 drivers new to F1 in 1951, and the pick of these was 21-year-old Stirling Moss, who finished eighth in the Swiss GP for HWM and showed immense ability in other single-seater and sports car races. French newcomer Andre Simon finished a distant sixth at Monza, six laps down, for Gordini.

WORLD DRIVERS' CHAMPIONSHIP FINAL RESULTS

Pos	Driver	Nat	Car-Engine	R1	R2	R3	R4	R5	R6	R7	Total
1	Juan Manuel Fangio	ARG	Alfa Romeo 159	1PF	9PF	1F|11P	2	2F	RP	1F	31
2	Alberto Ascari	ITA	Ferrari 375	6	2	2|R	R	1P	1	4P	25
3	Jose Froilan Gonzalez	ARG	Talbot-Lago T26C-GS	R	-	-	-	-	-	-	24
			Ferrari 375	-	-	2	1P	3	2	2	
4	Giuseppe Farina	ITA	Alfa Romeo 159	3	1	5	RF	R	3F|R	3	19
5	Luigi Villoresi	ITA	Ferrari 375	R	3	3	3	4	4	R	15
6	Piero Taruffi	ITA	Ferrari 375	2	R	-	-	5	5	R	10
8	Felice Bonetto	ITA	Alfa Romeo 159	-	-	-	4	R	3	5	7
10	Reg Parnell	GBR	Ferrari 375	-	-	4	-	-	-	-	5
			BRM P15	-	-	-	5	-	NS	-	
11	Luigi Fagioli	ITA	Alfa Romeo 159	-	-	1|11	-	-	-	-	4
12	Consalvo Sanesi	ITA	Alfa Romeo 159	4	R	10	6	-	-	-	3
12	Louis Rosier	FRA	Talbot-Lago T26C-DA	9	4	R	10	8	7	7	3
17	Emmanuel de Graffenried	CHE	Alfa Romeo 159	5	-	-	-	-	R	6	2
			Maserati 4CLT-48	-	-	R	-	R	-	-	
17	Yves Giraud-Cabantous	FRA	Lago-Talbot T26C	R	5	7	-	R	8	R	2

SYMBOLS AND GRAND PRIX KEY

Round 1 **Swiss GP**
Round 2 **Belgian GP**
Round 3 **French GP**
Round 4 **British GP**
Round 5 **German GP**
Round 6 **Italian GP**
Round 7 **Spanish GP**

Indianapolis 500 results not included

SCORING

1st **8 points**
2nd **6 points**
3rd **4 points**
4th **3 points**
5th **2 points**
Fastest lap **1 point**

DNPQ DID NOT PRE-QUALIFY **DNQ DID NOT QUALIFY** **DQ DISQUALIFIED** **EX EXCLUDED**
F FASTEST LAP **NC NOT CLASSIFIED** **NS NON-STARTER** **P POLE POSITION** **R RETIRED**

1952

SEASON SUMMARY

In order to stop grid sizes from dwindling and more than make up for Alfa Romeo's withdrawal, it was all change for 1952 as the World Championship was run to less powerful F2 regulations to enable new constructors to be able to afford to participate. This worked, and eight new constructors joined the series. Yet none could challenge Ferrari, which had already prepared for the switch to smaller engines, and a Ferrari 500 won each of the seven grands prix. Piero Taruffi won the opening round at Bremgarten, while team leader Alberto Ascari took a shot at the Indianapolis 500. Thereafter, Ascari was unbeaten, with Guiseppe Farina usually second.

SWISS GRAND PRIX

BREMGARTEN • ROUND 1 • DATE: 18TH MAY 1952
Laps: 62 • Distance: 280.260miles/451.36km • Weather: Warm but dull

Pos	Driver	Team	Chassis-Engine	Result	Qual
1	Piero Taruffi	Ferrari	Ferrari 500	3h01m46.100s	2
2	Rudi Fischer	Ecurie Espadon	Ferrari 500	3h04m23.300s	5
3	Jean Behra	Gordini	Gordini T16	61 laps	7
4	Ken Wharton	Scuderia Franera	Frazer-Nash-Bristol FN48	60 laps	13
5	Alan Brown	Ecurie Richmond	Cooper-Bristol T20	59 laps	15
6	Emmanuel de Graffenried	Scuderia Enrico Plate	Maserati-Plate 4CLT-48	58 laps	8
7	Peter Hirt	Ecurie Espadon	Ferrari 212	56 laps	19
8	Eric Brandon	Ecurie Richmond	Cooper-Bristol T20	55 laps	17
R	"B Bira"	Gordini	Simca-Gordini T15	52 laps/engine	11
R	Simon / Farina*	Ferrari	Ferrari 500	51 laps/magneto	4
R	Harry Schell	Scuderia Enrico Plate	Maserati-Plate 4CLT-48	31 laps/engine	18
R	Stirling Moss	HWM	HWM-Alta	24 laps/withdrawn	9
R	Lance Macklin	HWM	HWM-Alta	24 laps/withdrawn	12
R	Robert Manzon	Gordini	Gordini T16	20 laps/radiator damage	3
R	Giuseppe Farina	Ferrari	Ferrari 500	16 laps/magneto	1
R	Peter Collins	HWM	HWM-Alta	12 laps/halfshaft	6
R	George Abecassis	HWM	HWM-Alta	12 laps/halfshaft	10
R	Hans Stuck	AFM	AFM-Kuchen	4 laps/engine	14
R	Toni Ulmen	Toni Ulmen	Veritas Meteor	4 laps/oil leak	16
R	Louis Rosier	Ecurie Rosier	Ferrari 500	2 laps/accident	20
R	Max de Terra	Alfred Dattner	Simca-Gordini T11	1 lap/magneto	21
NS	Maurice Trintignant	Ecurie Rosier	Ferrari 166F2-50	engine	-

*Andre Simon, Nino Farina

Pole: Farina, 2m47.500s, 97.223mph/156.465kph. Fastest lap: Taruffi, 2m49.100s, 96.312mph/155.000kph on Lap 46. Race leaders: Farina 1-16; Taruffi 17-62

FORMULA ONE BECOMES FORMULA TWO

The key change in 1952 was the move to F2 regulations, and this meant the downsizing of engines. Cars fitted with supercharged engines now had a maximum capacity of 500cc, while normally aspirated engines were downsized from 4500cc to just 2000cc, cutting power from 425bhp to 165bhp.

BELGIAN GRAND PRIX

SPA-FRANCORCHAMPS • ROUND 2 • DATE: 22ND JUNE 1952
Laps: 36 • Distance: 315.676miles/508.32km • Weather: Cool with heavy rain

Pos	Driver	Team	Chassis-Engine	Result	Qual
1	Alberto Ascari	Ferrari	Ferrari 500	3h03m46.300s	1
2	Giuseppe Farina	Ferrari	Ferrari 500	3h05m41.500s	2
3	Robert Manzon	Gordini	Gordini T16	3h08m14.700s	4
4	Mike Hawthorn	Leslie Hawthorn	Cooper-Bristol T20	35 laps	6
5	Paul Frere	HWM	HWM-Alta	34 laps	8
6	Alan Brown	Ecurie Richmond	Cooper-Bristol T20	34 laps	9
7	Charles de Tornaco	Ecurie Francorchamps	Ferrari 500	33 laps	13
8	Johnny Claes	Gordini	Gordini T16	33 laps	19
9	Eric Brandon	Ecurie Richmond	Cooper-Bristol T20	33 laps	12
10	"B Bira"	Gordini	Simca-Gordini T15	32 laps	18
11	Lance Macklin	HWM	HWM-Alta	32 laps	14
12	Roger Laurent	HWM	HWM-Alta	32 laps	20
13	Arthur Legat	Arthur Legat	Veritas Meteor	31 laps	21
14	Robert O'Brien	Robert O'Brien	Simca-Gordini T15	30 laps	22
15	Tony Gaze	Tony Gaze	HWM-Alta	30 laps	16
R	Robin M-C*	W S Aston	Aston-Butterworth	17 laps/engine	15
R	Piero Taruffi	Ferrari	Ferrari 500	13 laps/accident	3
R	Jean Behra	Gordini	Gordini T16	13 laps/accident	5
R	Ken Wharton	Scuderia Franera	Frazer-Nash-Bristol FN48	10 laps/spun off	7
R	Louis Rosier	Ecurie Rosier	Ferrari 500	6 laps/transmission	17
R	Peter Collins	HWM	HWM-Alta	3 laps/halfshaft	11
R	Stirling Moss	ERA	ERA-Bristol G	0 laps/engine	10

*Robin Montgomerie-Charrington

Pole: Ascari, 4m37.000s, 114.027mph/183.509kph. Fastest lap: Ascari, 4m55.000s, 106.875mph/172.000kph on Lap 2. Race leaders: Behra 1; Ascari 2-36

FRENCH GP ON THE MOVE

France developed a reputation for moving its grand prix around, and 1952 marked a move from the gentle undulations of Reims to one with definite gradients. The new track's downhill plunge from the start line, through the daunting Virage des Six Freres righthander to the cobbled Nouveau Monde hairpin was a notable challenge.

FRENCH GRAND PRIX

ROUEN-LES-ESSARTS • ROUND 3 • DATE: 6TH JULY 1952
Laps: 76 • Distance: 240.474miles/387.6km • Weather: Dull, rain later

Pos	Driver	Team	Chassis-Engine	Result	Qual
1	Alberto Ascari	Ferrari	Ferrari 500	3h00m20.300s	1
2	Giuseppe Farina	Ferrari	Ferrari 500	3h01m31.000s	2
3	Piero Taruffi	Ferrari	Ferrari 500	75 laps	3
4	Robert Manzon	Gordini	Gordini T16	74 laps	5
5	Maurice Trintignant	Gordini	Simca-Gordini T15	72 laps	6

Pos	Driver	Team	Chassis-Engine	Result	Qual
6	Peter Collins	HWM	HWM-Alta	70 laps	8
7	Jean Behra	Gordini	Gordini T16	70 laps	4
8	Philippe Etancelin	Escuderia Bandeirantes	Maserati A6GCM	70 laps	18
9	Lance Macklin	HWM	HWM-Alta	70 laps	14
10	Yves Giraud-Cabantous	HWM	HWM-Alta	68 laps	10
11	Fischer / Hirt*	Ecurie Espadon	Ferrari 212	66 laps	17
12	Franco Comotti	Scuderia Marzotto	Ferrari 166F2-50	63 laps	16
R	"B Bira"	Gordini	Gordini T16	56 laps/axle	7
R	Mike Hawthorn	Archie Bryde	Cooper-Bristol T20	51 laps/ignition	15
R	de Graffenried / Schell*	Scuderia Enrico Plate	Maserati-Plate 4CLT-48	34 laps/brakes	12
R	Peter Whitehead	Peter Whitehead	Alta	26 laps/clutch	13
R	Louis Rosier	Ecurie Rosier	Ferrari 500	17 laps/engine	9
R	Johnny Claes	Ecurie Belge	Simca-Gordini T15	15 laps/engine	20
R	Harry Schell	Scuderia Enrico Plate	Maserati-Plate 4CLT-48	7 laps/gearbox	11
R	Piero Carini	Scuderia Marzotto	Ferrari 166F2-50	2 laps/engine	19
NS	Rudi Fischer	Ecurie Espadon	Ferrari 500	-	-

*Rudi Fischer, Peter Hirt, Emmanuel de Graffenried, Harry Schell

Pole: Ascari, 2m14.800s, 84.631mph/136.201kph. Fastest lap: Ascari, 2m17.300s, 83.090mph/133.721kph on Lap 28. Race leaders: Ascari 1-76

A MONACO GP WITHOUT F1

Despite being part of the World Championship in 1950, the next Monaco GP, in 1952, was for sports cars instead. Won by Vittorio Marzotto in a Ferrari, it was to remain a one-off, and Monaco didn't get F1 cars back onto its streets until 1955. It was a World Championship constant until the pandemic of 2020.

BRITISH GRAND PRIX

SILVERSTONE • ROUND 4 • DATE: 19TH JULY 1952
Laps: 85 • Distance: 248.792miles/400.392km • Weather: Warm but dull

Pos	Driver	Team	Chassis-Engine	Result	Qual
1	Alberto Ascari	Ferrari	Ferrari 500	2h44m11.000s	2
2	Piero Taruffi	Ferrari	Ferrari 500	84 laps	3
3	Mike Hawthorn	Leslie Hawthorn	Cooper-Bristol T20	83 laps	7
4	Dennis Poore	Connaught	Connaught-Francis A	83 laps	8
5	Eric Thompson	Connaught	Connaught-Francis A	82 laps	9
6	Giuseppe Farina	Ferrari	Ferrari 500	82 laps	1
7	Reg Parnell	Archie Bryde	Cooper-Bristol T20	82 laps	6
8	Roy Salvadori	G Caprara	Ferrari 500	82 laps	19
9	Ken Downing	Connaught	Connaught-Francis A	82 laps	5
10	Peter Whitehead	Peter Whitehead	Ferrari 125	81 laps	20
11	"B Bira"	Gordini	Gordini T16	81 laps	10
12	Graham Whitehead	Peter Whitehead	Alta	80 laps	12
13	Rudi Fischer	Ecurie Espadon	Ferrari 500	80 laps	15
14	Johnny Claes	Ecurie Belge	Simca-Gordini T15	79 laps	23
15	Lance Macklin	HWM	HWM-Alta	79 laps	29
16	Kenneth McAlpine	Connaught	Connaught-Francis A	79 laps	17
17	Harry Schell	Scuderia Enrico Plate	Maserati 4CLT	78 laps	32
18	Gino Bianco	Escuderia Bandeirantes	Maserati A6GCM	77 laps	28

Pos	Driver	Team	Chassis-Engine	Result	Qual
19	Emmanuel de Graffenried	Scuderia Enrico Plate	Maserat-Plate 4CLT-48	76 laps	31
20	Eric Brandon	Ecurie Richmond	Cooper-Bristol T20	76 laps	18
21	Tony Crook	Tony Crook	Frazer-Nash-BMW 421	75 laps	25
22	Alan Brown	Ecurie Richmond	Cooper-Bristol T20	69 laps	13
R	Peter Collins	HWM	HWM-Alta	73 laps/ignition	14
R	Duncan Hamilton	HWM	HWM-Alta	44 laps/engine	11
R	Stirling Moss	ERA	ERA-Bristol G	36 laps/engine	16
R	Maurice Trintignant	Gordini	Gordini T16	21 laps/gearbox	21
R	Tony Gaze	Tony Gaze	HWM-Alta	19 laps/engine	26
R	David Murray	Ecurie Ecosse	Cooper-Bristol T20	14 laps/engine	22
R	Robert Manzon	Gordini	Gordini T16	9 laps/clutch	4
R	Peter Hirt	Ecurie Espadon	Ferrari 212	3 laps/brakes	24
R	Eitel Cantoni	Escuderia Bandeirantes	Maserati A6GCM	0 laps/brakes	27
NS	Bill Aston	W S Aston	Aston-Butterworth	-	30

Pole: Farina, 1m50.000s, 95.791mph/154.161kph. Fastest lap: Ascari, 1m52.000s, 93.827mph/151.000kph on Lap 9. Race leaders: Ascari 1-85

GERMAN GRAND PRIX

NURBURGRING • ROUND 5 • DATE: 3RD AUGUST 1952
Laps: 18 • Distance: 254.798miles/410.58km • Weather: Warm & bright

Pos	Driver	Team	Chassis-Engine	Result	Qual
1	Alberto Ascari	Ferrari	Ferrari 500	3h06m13.300s	1
2	Giuseppe Farina	Ferrari	Ferrari 500	3h06m27.400s	2
3	Rudi Fischer	Ecurie Espadon	Ferrari 500	3h13m23.400s	6
4	Piero Taruffi	Ferrari	Ferrari 500	17 laps	5
5	Jean Behra	Gordini	Gordini T16	17 laps	11
6	Roger Laurent	Ecurie Francorchamps	Ferrari 500	16 laps	17
7	Fritz Riess	Fritz Riess	Veritas-BMW RS	16 laps	12
8	Toni Ulmen	Toni Ulmen	Veritas Meteor	16 laps	15
9	Helmut Niedermayr	Helmut Niedermayr	AFM-BMW	15 laps	22
10	Johnny Claes	HWM	HWM-Alta	15 laps	32
11	Hans Klenk	Hans Klenk	Veritas Meteor	14 laps	8
12	Ernst Klodwig	Ernst Klodwig	BMW Heck	14 laps	29
R	Robert Manzon	Gordini	Gordini T16	8 laps/accident	4
R	Willi Heeks	Willi Heeks	AFM-BMW	7 laps/mechanical	9
R	Tony Gaze	Tony Gaze	HWM-Alta	6 laps/gearbox	14
R	Adolf Brudes	Adolf Brudes	Veritas-BMW RS	5 laps/engine	19
R	Marcel Balsa	Marcel Balsa	BMW special	5 laps/mechanical	25
R	Gunther Bechem	Bernd Nacke	BMW Eigenbau	5 laps/ignition	30
R	Eitel Cantoni	Escuderia Bandeirantes	Maserati A6GCM	4 laps/rear axle	26
R	Rudolf Krause	Rudolf Krause	BMW Greifzu	3 laps/mechanical	23

A RACING ROYAL

Prince Birabongse Bhanubanbh of Siam (now Thailand), shortened his name to "B Bira" when he raced. Starting in 1935 in an ERA given to him by his cousin Prince Chula, F1's first royal drove a Maserati in 1950, but his fourth place in Switzerland was his best result until he matched that in 1954, at Reims.

Pos	Driver	Team	Chassis-Engine	Result	Qual
R	Rudolf Schoeller	Ecurie Espadon	Ferrari 212	3 laps/suspension	24
R	Bill Aston	W S Aston	Aston-Butterworth	2 laps/fuel pressure	21
R	Maurice Trintignant	Gordini	Gordini T16	1 lap/accident	3
R	Paul Pietsch	Motor Press Verlag	Veritas Meteor	1 lap/gearbox	7
R	Paul Frere	HWM	HWM-Alta	1 lap/gearbox	13
R	Theo Helfrich	Theo Helfrich	Veritas-BMW RS	1 lap/mechanical	18
R	Josef Peters	Josef Peters	Veritas-BMW RS	1 lap/mechanical	20
R	Piero Carini	Scuderia Marzotto	Ferrari 166F2-50	1 lap/brakes	27
DQ	Felice Bonetto	Maserati	Maserati A6GCM	1 lap/push start	10
R	Gino Bianco	Escuderia Bandeirantes	Maserati A6GCM	0 laps/mechanical	16
NS	Ludwig Fischer	Ludwig Fischer	AFM-BMW	-	31
NS	Willi Krakau	Willi Krakau	AFM-BMW	-	28
NS	Harry Merkel	Willi Krakau	BMW Eigenbau	-	-
NS	Peter Collins	HWM	HWM-Alta	-	-

Pole: Ascari, 10m04.400s, 84.421mph/135.863kph. Fastest lap: Ascari, 10m05.100s, 84.320mph/135.700kph on Lap 5. Race leaders: Ascari 1-18

FANGIO MISSES SEASON

Reigning world champion Juan Manuel Fangio had been signed to lead Maserati's attack, but he broke his neck in a non-championship race at Monza. Maserati was thus left without the quality drivers to challenge Ferrari until it signed another Argentinian, Jose Froilan Gonzalez, for the final round at Monza, and he came second.

AN EXPLOSION OF GERMAN DRIVERS

The German GP at the Nurburgring had an unusual look to its grid: it was packed with local drivers turning out only for their home grand prix. Driving cars from Veritas and AFM, plus a number of BMW Specials, they boosted the grid to 30 cars. Fritz Riess was the best-placed German driver, coming seventh in a Veritas.

DUTCH GRAND PRIX

ZANDVOORT • ROUND 6 • DATE: 17TH AUGUST 1952
Laps: 90 • Distance: 234.279miles/377.37km • Weather: Cool & damp

Pos	Driver	Team	Chassis-Engine	Result	Qual
1	Alberto Ascari	Ferrari	Ferrari 500	2h53m28.500s	1
2	Giuseppe Farina	Ferrari	Ferrari 500	2h54m08.600s	2
3	Luigi Villoresi	Ferrari	Ferrari 500	2h55m02.900s	4
4	Mike Hawthorn	Leslie Hawthorn	Cooper-Bristol T20	88 laps	3
5	Robert Manzon	Gordini	Gordini T16	87 laps	6
6	Maurice Trintignant	Gordini	Gordini T16	87 laps	5
7	Duncan Hamilton	HWM	HWM-Alta	85 laps	10
8	Lance Macklin	HWM	HWM-Alta	84 laps	9
9	Landi / Flinterman*	Escuderia Bandeirantes	Maserati A6GCM	83 laps	16

Pos	Driver	Team	Chassis-Engine	Result	Qual
R	Ken Wharton	Scuderia Franera	Frazer-Nash-Bristol FN48	76 laps/wheel	7
R	Stirling Moss	ERA	ERA-Bristol G	73 laps/engine	18
NC	Dries van der Lof	HWM	HWM-Alta	70 laps/not classified	14
R	Ken Downing	Ken Downing	Connaught-Francis A	27 laps/fuel pressure	13
R	Charles de Tornaco	Ecurie Francorchamps	Ferrari 500	19 laps/engine	17
R	Paul Frere	Ecurie Belge	Simca-Gordini T15	15 laps/clutch	11
R	Jean Behra	Gordini	Gordini T16	10 laps/electrical	6
R	Jan Flinterman	Escuderia Bandeirantes	Maserati A6GCM	7 laps/differential	15
R	Gino Bianco	Escuderia Bandeirantes	Maserati A6GCM	4 laps/axle	12

*Chico Landi, Jan Flinterman

Pole: Ascari, 1m46.500s, 88.070mph/141.735kph. Fastest lap: Ascari, 1m49.800s, 85.438mph/137.500kph on Lap 89. Race leaders: Ascari 1-90

NEW CONSTRUCTORS

AFM, Aston-Butterworth, BMW, Cisitalia, Connaught, Frazer-Nash, Greifzu and Heck all made their debuts, with Ken Wharton claiming fourth place in the opening race in Switzerland, but only Connaught went on to make much of an impact, taking fourth and fifth places at the British GP, Dennis Poore ahead of Eric Thompson.

ITALIAN GRAND PRIX

MONZA • ROUND 7 • DATE: 7TH SEPTEMBER 1952
Laps: 80 • Distance: 313.171miles/504.0km • Weather: Warm & bright

Pos	Driver	Team	Chassis-Engine	Result	Qual
1	Alberto Ascari	Ferrari	Ferrari 500	2h50m45.600s	1
2	Jose Froilan Gonzalez	Maserati	Maserati A6GCM	2h51m47.400s	5
3	Luigi Villoresi	Ferrari	Ferrari 500	2h52m49.800s	2
4	Giuseppe Farina	Ferrari	Ferrari 500	2h52m57.000s	3
5	Felice Bonetto	Maserati	Maserati A6GCM	79 laps	13
6	Andre Simon	Ferrari	Ferrari 500	79 laps	8
7	Piero Taruffi	Ferrari	Ferrari 500	77 laps	6
8	Chico Landi	Escuderia Bandeirantes	Maserati A6GCM	76 laps	18
9	Ken Wharton	Scuderia Franera	Cooper-Bristol T20	76 laps	15
10	Louis Rosier	Ecurie Rosier	Ferrari 500	75 laps	17
11	Eitel Cantoni	Escuderia Bandeirantes	Maserati A6GCM	75 laps	23
12	Dennis Poore	Connaught	Connaught-Francis A	74 laps	19
13	Eric Brandon	Ecurie Richmond	Cooper-Bristol T20	73 laps	20
14	Robert Manzon	Gordini	Gordini T16	71 laps	7
15	Alan Brown	Ecurie Richmond	Cooper-Bristol T20	68 laps	21
R	Stirling Moss	Connaught	Connaught-Francis A	60 laps/suspension	9
R	Gino Bianco	Escuderia Bandeirantes	Maserati A6GCM	46 laps/engine	24
R	Jean Behra	Gordini	Gordini T16	42 laps/engine	11
NC	Mike Hawthorn	Leslie Hawthorn	Cooper-Bristol T20	38 laps /not classified	12
R	Franco Rol	Maserati	Maserati A6GCM	24 laps/engine	16
R	Maurice Trintignant	Gordini	Gordini T16	5 laps/engine	4
R	Kenneth McAlpine	Connaught	Connaught-Francis A	4 laps/suspension	22
R	Rudi Fischer	Ecurie Espadon	Ferrari 500	3 laps/engine	14

Pos	Driver	Team	Chassis-Engine	Result	Qual
R	Elie Bayol	Elie Bayol	OSCA 20	0 laps/gearbox	10
DNQ	Charles de Tornaco	Ecurie Francorchamps	Ferrari 500	-	25
DNQ	Alberto Crespo	Scuderia Enrico Plate	Maserati-Plate 4CLT-48	-	26
DNQ	Emmanuel de Graffenried	Scuderia Enrico Plate	Maserati-Plate 4CLT-48	-	27
DNQ	Peter Collins	HWM	HWM-Alta	-	28
DNQ	Peter Whitehead	Ferrari	Ferrari 125	-	29
DNQ	Tony Gaze	Tony Gaze	HWM-Alta	-	30
DNQ	Bill Aston	W S Aston	Aston-Butterworth	-	31
DNQ	Lance Macklin	HWM	HWM-Alta	-	32
DNQ	Hans Stuck	Ecurie Espadon	Ferrari 212	-	33
DNQ	Johnny Claes	Vickomtesse de Walckiers	Simca-Gordini T15	-	-
DNQ	Piero Dusio	Piero Dusio	Cisitalia-BPM D46	-	-

Pole: Ascari, 2m05.700s, 112.113mph/180.429kph. Fastest lap: Ascari, 2m06.100s, 111.758mph/179.857kph on Lap 56 Gonzalez, 2m06.100s, 111.758mph/179.857kph on Lap 57. Race leaders: Gonzalez 1-36; Ascari 37-80

NEW DRIVERS

The new F2 regs attracted 45 new drivers, including future stars Peter Collins and racing journalist Paul Frere. However, Mike Hawthorn was by far the most impressive of the new crop. Driving a privately entered Cooper, he raced to third place in the British GP and collected enough points to rank fourth-equal in the championship.

CLASSIC CAR: FERRARI 500

Ferrari was more than ready for the move to F2 rules, as Aurelio Lampredi had started developing a four-cylinder engine in 1951, both in 2.5-litre and 2-litre form. Race-ready for 1952, the smaller unit fitted to the new 500 chassis was a gem and its development programme meant that it was reliable, too. So, with bigger grids but little competitive opposition, the 500 started winning from the off, thanks to Piero Taruffi in the Swiss GP. Then Alberto Ascari returned and won the remaining six grands prix. In 1953, with power up from 165 to 180bhp, Ascari simply kept on going.

WORLD DRIVERS' CHAMPIONSHIP FINAL RESULTS

Pos	Driver	Nat	Car-Engine	R1	R2	R3	R4	R5	R6	R7	Total
1	Alberto Ascari	ITA	Ferrari 500	-	1PF	1PF	1F	1PF	1PF	1PF	36
2	Giuseppe Farina	ITA	Ferrari 500	R/RP	2	2	6P	2	2	4	24
3	Piero Taruffi	ITA	Ferrari 500	1F	R	3	2	4	-	7	22
4	Rudi Fischer	CHE	Ferrari 500	2	-	NS	13	3	-	NS	10
			Ferrari 212	-	-	11	-	-	-	-	11
5	Mike Hawthorn	GBR	Cooper-Bristol T20	-	4	R	3	-	4	NC	10
6	Robert Manzon	FRA	Gordini T16	R	3	4	R	R	5	14	9
8	Luigi Villoresi	ITA	Ferrari 500	-	-	-	-	-	3	3	8
9	Jose Froilan Gonzalez	ARG	Maserati A6GCM	-	-	-	-	-	-	2F	6.5
11	Jean Behra	FRA	Gordini T16	3	R	7	-	5	R	R	6
13	Ken Wharton	GBR	Frazer-Nash-Bristol FN48	4	R	-	-	-	R	-	3
			Cooper-Bristol T20	-	-	-	-	-	-	9	
13	Dennis Poore	GBR	Connaught-Francis A	-	-	-	4	-	-	12	3
16	Alan Brown	GBR	Cooper-Bristol T20	5	6	-	22	-	-	15	2
16	Paul Frere	BEL	HWM-Alta	-	5	-	-	R	-	-	2
			Simca-Gordini T15	-	-	-	-	-	R	-	
16	Maurice Trintignant	FRA	Ferrari 166F2-50	NS	-	-	-	-	-	-	2
			Simca-Gordini T15	-	-	5	-	-	-	-	
			Gordini T16	-	-	-	R	R	6	R	
16	Eric Thompson	GBR	Connaught-Francis A	-	-	-	5	-	-	-	2
16	Felice Bonetto	ITA	Maserati A6GCM	-	-	-	-	DQ	-	5	2

SYMBOLS AND GRAND PRIX KEY

Round 1 **Swiss GP**
Round 2 **Belgian GP**
Round 3 **French GP**
Round 4 **British GP**
Round 5 **German GP**
Round 6 **Dutch GP**
Round 7 **Italian GP**

Indianapolis 500 results not included

SCORING

1st **8 points**
2nd **6 points**
3rd **4 points**
4th **3 points**
5th **2 points**
Fastest lap **1 point**

DNPQ DID NOT PRE-QUALIFY **DNQ DID NOT QUALIFY** **DQ DISQUALIFIED** **EX EXCLUDED**
F FASTEST LAP **NC NOT CLASSIFIED** **NS NON-STARTER** **P POLE POSITION** **R RETIRED**

1953

SEASON SUMMARY

Having stormed to the 1952 World Championship title, Alberto Ascari was able to become the first driver to claim two F1 crowns in succession as Ferrari continued to rule the roost in 1953. The Italian driver didn't have it all his own way, though, as the challenge from Maserati grew stronger through the campaign, its A6GCM getting closer and closer to the Ferrari 500. Juan Manuel Fangio finally stopped Ferrari's run on the last corner of the season-closing Italian GP. Such was the domination of these two Italian marques that they locked out every podium between them, with Gordini's best being a fifth place.

ARGENTINIAN GRAND PRIX

BUENOS AIRES • ROUND 1 • DATE: 18TH JANUARY 1953
Laps: 97 • Distance: 235.811miles/379.502km • Weather: Hot & bright

Pos	Driver	Team	Chassis-Engine	Result	Qual
1	Alberto Ascari	Ferrari	Ferrari 500	3h01m04.600s	1
2	Luigi Villoresi	Ferrari	Ferrari 500	96 laps	3
3	Jose Froilan Gonzalez	Maserati	Maserati A6GCM-52	96 laps	5
4	Mike Hawthorn	Ferrari	Ferrari 500	96 laps	6
5	Oscar Galvez	Maserati	Maserati A6GCM-52	96 laps	9
6	Jean Behra	Gordini	Gordini T16	94 laps	11
7	Trintignant / Schell*	Gordini	Gordini T16	91 laps	7
8	John Barber	Cooper	Cooper-Bristol T23	90 laps	16
9	Alan Brown	Cooper	Cooper-Bristol T20	87 laps	12
R	Robert Manzon	Gordini	Gordini T16	67 laps/wheel	8
R	Juan Manuel Fangio	Maserati	Maserati A6GCM-52	36 laps/transmission	2
R	Felice Bonetto	Maserati	Maserati A6GCM-52	31 laps/transmission	15
R	Giuseppe Farina	Ferrari	Ferrari 500	30 laps/accident	4
R	Carlos Menditeguy	Gordini	Gordini T16	24 laps/gearbox	10
R	Pablo Birger	Gordini	Simca-Gordini T15	21 laps/differential	14
R	Adolfo Schwelm Cruz	Cooper	Cooper-Bristol T20	20 laps/wheel	13

*Maurice Trintignant, Harry Schell

Pole: Ascari, 3m35.400s, 40.630mph/65.388kph. Fastest lap: Ascari, 1m48.400s, 80.736mph/129.932kph on Lap 73. Race leaders: Ascari 1-97

FIRST RACE OUTSIDE EUROPE

The season-opening round of the World Championship, the Argentinian GP, was the first to be held outside Europe. Held on a new circuit in the southern suburbs of Buenos Aires, the race attracted just 16 starters. Sadly, the race itself ended in tragedy; as crowd control was poor, when Giuseppe Farina crashed, he killed nine spectators.

DUTCH GRAND PRIX

ZANDVOORT • ROUND 2 • DATE: 7TH JUNE 1953
Laps: 90 • Distance: 234.279miles/377.37km • Weather: Warm & bright

Pos	Driver	Team	Chassis-Engine	Result	Qual
1	Alberto Ascari	Ferrari	Ferrari 500	2h53m35.800s	1
2	Giuseppe Farina	Ferrari	Ferrari 500	2h53m46.200s	3
3	Bonetto/Gonzalez*	Maserati	Maserati A6GCM	89 laps	13
4	Mike Hawthorn	Ferrari	Ferrari 500	89 laps	6
5	Emmanuel de Graffenried	Emmanuel de Graffenried	Maserati A6GCM	88 laps	7
6	Maurice Trintignant	Gordini	Gordini T16	87 laps	12
7	Louis Rosier	Ecurie Rosier	Ferrari 500	86 laps	8
8	Peter Collins	HWM	HWM-Alta	84 laps	16
9	Stirling Moss	Connaught	Connaught-Francis A	83 laps	9
R	Luigi Villoresi	Ferrari	Ferrari 500	67 laps/throttle	4
R	Kenneth McAlpine	Connaught	Connaught-Francis A	63 laps/engine	14
R	Harry Schell	Gordini	Gordini T16	59 laps/transmission	10
NC	Johnny Claes	Ecurie Belge	Connaught-Francis A	52 laps	17
R	Juan Manuel Fangio	Maserati	Maserati A6GCM	36 laps/mechanical	2
R	Roberto Mieres	Gordini	Gordini T16	28 laps/transmission	19
R	Jose Froilan Gonzalez	Maserati	Maserati A6GCM	22 laps/mechanical	5
R	Ken Wharton	Ken Wharton	Cooper-Bristol T23	19 laps/physical	18
R	Roy Salvadori	Connaught	Connaught-Francis A	14 laps/engine	11
R	Lance Macklin	HWM	HWM-Alta	7 laps/throttle	15
NS	Fred Wacker	Gordini	Gordini T16	-	-

*Felice Bonetto, Jose Froilan Gonzalez

Pole: Ascari, 1m51.100s, 84.423mph/135.866kph. Fastest lap: Villoresi, 1m52.800s, 83.139mph/133.800kph on Lap 59. Race leaders: Ascari 1-90

THE FIRST WINNING STREAK

With Ascari taking win after win in 1952, it looked as though only an act of god would end his run. Winning the first three grands prix in 1953 took that run to nine in a row before team-mate Mike Hawthorn won the French GP. Ascari's record was finally equalled by Red Bull Racing's Sebastian Vettel in 2013, but has yet to be beaten.

BELGIAN GRAND PRIX

SPA-FRANCORCHAMPS • ROUND 3 • DATE: 21ST JUNE 1953
Laps: 36 • Distance: 315.676miles/508.32km • Weather: Hot & bright

Pos	Driver	Team	Chassis-Engine	Result	Qual
1	Alberto Ascari	Ferrari	Ferrari 500	2h48m30.300s	2
2	Luigi Villoresi	Ferrari	Ferrari 500	2h51m18.500s	5
3	Onofre Marimon	Maserati	Maserati A6GCM	35 laps	16
4	Emmanuel de Graffenried	Emmanuel de Graffenried	Maserati A6GCM	35 laps	9
5	Maurice Trintignant	Gordini	Gordini T16	35 laps	8
6	Mike Hawthorn	Ferrari	Ferrari 500	35 laps	7
7	Harry Schell	Gordini	Gordini T16	33 laps	12

Pos	Driver	Team	Chassis-Engine	Result	Qual
8	Louis Rosier	Ecurie Rosier	Ferrari 500	33 laps	13
9	Fred Wacker	Gordini	Gordini T16	32 laps	15
10	Paul Frere	HWM	HWM-Alta	30 laps	11
11	Andre Pilette	Ecurie Belge	Connaught-Francis A	29 laps	18
R	Claes / Fangio*	Maserati	Maserati A6GCM	35 laps/accident	10
R	Lance Macklin	HWM	HWM-Alta	19 laps/engine	17
R	Giuseppe Farina	Ferrari	Ferrari 500	16 laps/engine	4
R	Juan Manuel Fangio	Maserati	Maserati A6GCM	13 laps/engine	1
R	Jose Froilan Gonzalez	Maserati	Maserati A6GCM	11 laps/throttle	3
R	Jean Behra	Gordini	Gordini T16	9 laps/engine	14
R	Peter Collins	HWM	HWM-Alta	4 laps/clutch	16
R	Georges Berger	Georges Berger	Simca-Gordini T15	3 laps/engine	20
R	Arthur Legat	Arthur Legat	Veritas Meteor	0 laps/transmission	19
NS	Jacques Swaters	Ecurie Francorchamps	Ferrari 500	-	-
NS	Charles de Tornaco	Ecurie Francorchamps	Ferrari 500	-	-

*Johnny Claes, Juan Manuel Fangio

Pole: Fangio, 4m30.000s, 116.983mph/188.266kph. Fastest lap: Gonzalez, 4m34.000s, 115.575mph/186.000kph on Lap 2. Race leaders: Gonzalez 1-11; Fangio 12-13; Ascari 14-36

THE FIRST BRITISH WINNER

Mike Hawthorn's form in 1952 earned him a drive with Ferrari and he brought youthful zeal to a team of older drivers. After two fourth places and a sixth in the first three grands prix, he won a slipstreaming battle with Juan Manuel Fangio in the French GP to become the first Briton to win a World Championship round.

AIMING THE TRIDENT

Juan Manuel Fangio made his return to F1 after a year out with a broken neck, to join Maserati's attack. His target was Ferrari, and the Argentinian worked hard to close the gap. Finally, he won the Italian GP and then added the non-championship Modena GP a week later, showing that he was back to his best.

FRENCH GRAND PRIX

REIMS • ROUND 4 • DATE: 5TH JULY 1953
Laps: 60 • Distance: 310.736miles/500.82km • Weather: Hot & bright

Pos	Driver	Team	Chassis-Engine	Result	Qual
1	Mike Hawthorn	Ferrari	Ferrari 500	2h44m18.600s	7
2	Juan Manuel Fangio	Maserati	Maserati A6GCM	2h44m19.600s	4
3	Jose Froilan Gonzalez	Maserati	Maserati A6GCM	2h44m20.000s	5
4	Alberto Ascari	Ferrari	Ferrari 500	2h44m23.200s	1
5	Giuseppe Farina	Ferrari	Ferrari 500	2h45m26.200s	6
6	Luigi Villoresi	Ferrari	Ferrari 500	2h45m34.500s	3
7	Emmanuel de Graffenried	Emmanuel de Graffenried	Maserati A6GCM	58 laps	9

Pos	Driver	Team	Chassis-Engine	Result	Qual
8	Louis Rosier	Ecurie Rosier	Ferrari 500	56 laps	10
9	Onofre Marimon	Maserati	Maserati A6GCM	55 laps	8
10	Jean Behra	Gordini	Gordini T16	55 laps	22
11	Bob Gerard	Bob Gerard	Cooper-Bristol T23	55 laps	12
12	Johnny Claes	Ecurie Belge	Connaught-Francis A	53 laps	21
13	Peter Collins	HWM	HWM-Alta	52 laps	17
14	Yves Giraud-Cabantous	HWM	HWM-Alta	50 laps	18
15	Louis Chiron	Louis Chiron	OSCA 20	43 laps	25
R	Felice Bonetto	Maserati	Maserati A6GCM	42 laps/engine	2
R	Stirling Moss	Cooper	Cooper-Alta T24	38 laps/clutch	13
R	"B Bira"	Connaught	Connaught-Francis A	29 laps/differential	11
R	Elie Bayol	Elie Bayol	OSCA 20	18 laps/engine	15
R	Ken Wharton	Ken Wharton	Cooper-Bristol T23	17 laps/wheel	14
R	Maurice Trintignant	Gordini	Gordini T16	14 laps/transmission	23
R	Lance Macklin	HWM	HWM-Alta	9 laps/clutch	16
R	Harry Schell	Gordini	Gordini T16	4 laps/engine	20
R	Roberto Mieres	Gordini	Gordini T16	4 laps/rear axle	24
R	Roy Salvadori	Connaught	Connaught-Francis A	2 laps/ignition	19

Pole: Ascari, 2m41.200s, 115.829mph/186.409kph. Fastest lap: Fangio, 2m41.000s, 115.947mph/186.600kph on Lap 25. Race leaders: Gonzalez 1-29; Fangio 30-31, 35-36, 39-41, 45-47, 49-53, 55-56; Hawthorn 32-34, 37-38, 42-44, 48, 54, 57-60

SHORT SLEEVES, CORK HELMETS

Fire was the drivers' chief concern, but fireproof suits had yet to be invented in the 1950s, so drivers tended to drive in short-sleeved cotton shirts to keep them cool. On their heads, their pudding basin-shaped helmets, sometimes with a brim, and all worn with goggles, were made of cork. Roll hoops and safety harnesses were years away.

BRITISH GRAND PRIX

SILVERSTONE • ROUND 5 • DATE: 18TH JULY 1953
Laps: 90 • Distance: 263.427miles/423.945km • Weather: Dull with showers

Pos	Driver	Team	Chassis-Engine	Result	Qual
1	Alberto Ascari	Ferrari	Ferrari 500	2h50m00.000s	1
2	Juan Manuel Fangio	Maserati	Maserati A6GCM	2h51m00.000s	4
3	Giuseppe Farina	Ferrari	Ferrari 500	88 laps	5
4	Jose Froilan Gonzalez	Maserati	Maserati A6GCM	88 laps	2
5	Mike Hawthorn	Ferrari	Ferrari 500	87 laps	3
6	Felice Bonetto	Maserati	Maserati A6GCM	82 laps	16
7	"B Bira"	Connaught	Connaught-Francis A	82 laps	19
8	Ken Wharton	Ken Wharton	Cooper-Bristol T23	80 laps	11
9	Peter Whitehead	Atlantic Stable	Cooper-Alta T24	79 laps	14
10	Louis Rosier	Ecurie Rosier	Ferrari 500	78 laps	24
R	Jimmy Stewart	Ecurie Ecosse	Cooper-Bristol T20	79 laps/spun off	15
R	Tony Rolt	Rob Walker Racing Team	Connaught-Francis A	70 laps/halfshaft	10
R	Luigi Villoresi	Ferrari	Ferrari 500	65 laps/axle	6
R	Onofre Marimon	Maserati	Maserati A6GCM	65 laps/engine	7

Pos	Driver	Team	Chassis-Engine	Result	Qual
R	Alan Brown	R J Chase	Cooper-Bristol T23	56 laps/overheating	21
R	Peter Collins	HWM	HWM-Alta	56 laps/spun off	23
R	Jack Fairman	HWM	HWM-Alta	54 laps/clutch	27
R	Roy Salvadori	Connaught	Connaught-Francis A	50 laps/wheel	28
R	Emmanuel de Graffenried	Emmanuel de Graffenried	Maserati A6GCM	34 laps/clutch	26
R	Lance Macklin	HWM	HWM-Alta	31 laps/clutch	12
R	Jean Behra	Gordini	Gordini T16	30 laps/fuel pump	22
R	Ian Stewart	Ecurie Ecosse	Connaught-Francis A	24 laps/ignition	20
R	Maurice Trintignant	Gordini	Gordini T16	14 laps/axle	8
R	Duncan Hamilton	HWM	HWM-Alta	14 laps/clutch	17
R	Bob Gerard	Bob Gerard	Cooper-Bristol T23	8 laps/suspension	18
R	Harry Schell	Gordini	Gordini T16	5 laps/electrical	9
R	Kenneth McAlpine	Connaught	Connaught-Francis A	0 laps/mechanical	13
R	Tony Crook	Tony Crook	Cooper-Bristol T20	0 laps/fuel system	25
NS	Louis Chiron	Louis Chiron	OSCA 20	-	-

Pole: Ascari, 1m48.000s, 97.565mph/157.016kph. Fastest lap: Ascari, 1m50.000s, 95.815mph/154.200kph on Gonzalez, 1m50.000s, 95.691mph/154.000kph. Race leaders: Ascari 1-90

A CHALLENGE FROM WITHIN

While Alberto Ascari was the acknowledged Ferrari team leader, it increasingly seemed that no one had told team-mate Giuseppe Farina. World champion in 1950, he didn't see why he should not go for gold – and this led to him to refusing to heed signals to stay in front at the non-championship Marseilles GP, until he spun off.

GERMAN GRAND PRIX

NURBURGRING • ROUND 6 • DATE: 2ND AUGUST 1953
Laps: 18 • Distance: 254.798miles/410.58km • Weather: Warm & bright

Pos	Driver	Team	Chassis-Engine	Result	Qual
1	Giuseppe Farina	Ferrari	Ferrari 500	3h02m25.000s	3
2	Juan Manuel Fangio	Maserati	Maserati A6GCM	3h03m29.000s	2
3	Mike Hawthorn	Ferrari	Ferrari 500	3h04m08.600s	4
4	Felice Bonetto	Maserati	Maserati A6GCM	3h11m13.600s	7
5	Emmanuel de Graffenried	Emmanuel de Graffenried	Maserati A6GCM	17 laps	11
6	Stirling Moss	Cooper	Cooper-Alta T23	17 laps	12
7	Jacques Swaters	Ecurie Francorchamps	Ferrari 500	17 laps	19
8	Ascari / Villoresi*	Ferrari	Ferrari 500	17 laps	1
9	Hans Herrmann	Hans Herrmann	Veritas Meteor	17 laps	14
10	Louis Rosier	Ecurie Rosier	Ferrari 500	17 laps	22
11	Rodney Nuckey	Rodney Nuckey	Cooper-Bristol T23	16 laps	20
12	Theo Helfrich	Theo Helfrich	Veritas RS	16 laps	28
13	Kenneth McAlpine	Connaught	Connaught-Francis A	16 laps	16
14	Rudolf Krause	Dora Greifzu	BMW Greifzu	16 laps	26
15	Ernst Klodwig	Ernst Klodwig	BMW Heck	15 laps	32
16	Wolfgang Seidel	Wolfgang Seidel	Veritas RS	14 laps	29
R	Villoresi / Ascari*	Ferrari	Ferrari 500	15 laps/engine	6

Pos	Driver	Team	Chassis-Engine	Result	Qual
R	Alan Brown	Equipe Anglaise	Cooper-Bristol T23	15 laps/engine	17
R	Onofre Marimon	Maserati	Maserati A6GCM	13 laps/suspension	8
R	Edgar Barth	Rennkollektiv EMW	EMW-BMW	12 laps /mechanical	24
R	Johnny Claes	Ecurie Belge	Connaught-Francis A	12 laps/mechanical	25
R	Oswald Karch	Oswald Karch	Veritas RS	10 laps/mechanical	34
R	Willi Heeks	Willi Heeks	Veritas Meteor	8 laps/mechanical	18
R	Jean Behra	Gordini	Gordini T16	7 laps/gearbox	9
R	Harry Schell	Gordini	Gordini T16	6 laps/engine	10
R	"B Bira"	Connaught	Connaught-Francis A	6 laps/suspension	15
R	Theo Fitzau	Helmut Niedermayr	AFM-BMW	3 laps/mechanical	21
R	Kurt Adolff	Ecurie Espadon	Ferrari 166C	3 laps/mechanical	27
R	Gunther Bechem	Guenther Bechem	AFM-BMW	2 laps/mechanical	30
R	Maurice Trintignant	Gordini	Gordini T16	1 lap/differential	5
R	Roy Salvadori	Connaught	Connaught-Francis A	1 lap/engine	13
R	Erwin Bauer	Erwin Bauer	Veritas RS	1 lap/engine	33
R	Hans Stuck	Hans Stuck	AFM-Bristol	0 laps/mechanical	23
NS	Ernst Loof	Ernst Loof	Veritas Meteor	0 laps/fuel pump	31
NS	Helmut Glockler	Equipe Anglaise	Cooper-Bristol T23	engine	-

*Alberto Ascari, Luigi Villoresi

Pole: Ascari, 9m59.800s, 85.069mph/136.905kph. Fastest lap: Ascari, 9m56.000s, 85.624mph/137.800kph on Lap 12. Race leaders: Ascari 1-4; Hawthorn 5-7; Farina 8-18

IN MEMORIAM

With only eight grands prix, most F1 drivers filled their calendar with other events. Sadly, these too could prove fatal. Charles de Tornaco rolled his Ferrari at the Modena GP and, with no ambulance available, died on the way to hospital in someone's car. Then Felice Bonetto crashed out of second in the Carrera Panamericana road race in Mexico and lost his life.

SWISS GRAND PRIX

BREMGARTEN • ROUND 7 • DATE: 23RD AUGUST 1953
Laps: 65 • Distance: 293.909miles/473.2km • Weather: Warm & bright

Pos	Driver	Team	Chassis-Engine	Result	Qual
1	Alberto Ascari	Ferrari	Ferrari 500	3h01m34.400s	2
2	Giuseppe Farina	Ferrari	Ferrari 500	3h02m47.330s	3
3	Mike Hawthorn	Ferrari	Ferrari 500	3h03m10.360s	7
4	Fangio / Bonetto*	Maserati	Maserati A6GCM	64 laps	1
5	Hermann Lang	Maserati	Maserati A6GCM	62 laps	11
6	Luigi Villoresi	Ferrari	Ferrari 500	62 laps	6
7	Ken Wharton	Ken Wharton	Cooper-Bristol T23	62 laps	9
8	Max de Terra	Ecurie Espadon	Ferrari 166C	51 laps	19
9	Albert Scherrer	HWM	HWM-Alta	49 laps	18
R	Chico Landi	Escuderia Bandeirantes	Maserati A6GCM	54 laps/gearbox	20
R	Emmanuel de Graffenried	Emmanuel de Graffenried	Maserati A6GCM	49 laps/transmission	8
R	Onofre Marimon	Maserati	Maserati A6GCM	46 laps/engine	5
R	Maurice Trintignant	Gordini	Gordini T16	43 laps/axle	4
R	Jean Behra	Gordini	Gordini T16	37 laps/fuel pressure	12

Pos	Driver	Team	Chassis-Engine	Result	Qual
R	Bonetto / Fangio*	Maserati	Maserati A6GCM	29 laps/valve	10
R	Lance Macklin	HWM	HWM-Alta	29 laps/engine	15
R	Peter Hirt	Ecurie Espadon	Ferrari 500	17 laps/engine	17
R	Paul Frere	HWM	HWM-Alta	1 lap/engine	16
R	Jacques Swaters	Ecurie Francorchamps	Ferrari 500	0 laps/spun off	13
R	Louis Rosier	Ecurie Rosier	Ferrari 500	0 laps/spun off	14
NS	Elie Bayol	Elie Bayol	OSCA 20	-	-
NS	Louis Chiron	Louis Chiron	OSCA 20	-	-
NS	Fred Wacker	Gordini	Gordini T16	injured	-

*Juan Manuel Fangio, Felice Bonetto

Pole: Fangio, 2m40.100s, 101.717mph/163.697kph. Fastest lap: Ascari, 2m41.300s, 100.972mph/162.500kph on Lap 50. Race leaders: Ascari 1-40, 54-65; Farina 41-53

LAST RACE, LAST LAP

The Italian GP was the only grand prix run to F2 rules that was not won by Ferrari. Ascari led onto the final lap, chased by team-mate Farina and the Maseratis of Fangio and Gonzalez. Ascari got his line wrong as he tried to pass backmarkers at the final corner and spun, forcing Farina to lift off. Fangio dived by to win.

ITALIAN GRAND PRIX

MONZA • ROUND 8 • DATE: 13TH SEPTEMBER 1953
Laps: 80 • Distance: 313.171miles/504.0km • Weather: Warm & bright

Pos	Driver	Team	Chassis-Engine	Result	Qual
1	Juan Manuel Fangio	Maserati	Maserati A6GCM	2h49m45.900s	2
2	Giuseppe Farina	Ferrari	Ferrari 500	2h49m47.300s	3
3	Luigi Villoresi	Ferrari	Ferrari 500	79 laps	5
4	Mike Hawthorn	Ferrari	Ferrari 500	79 laps	6
5	Maurice Trintignant	Gordini	Gordini T16	79 laps	8
6	Roberto Mieres	Gordini	Gordini T16	77 laps	16
7	Mantovani / Musso*	Maserati	Maserati A6GCM	76 laps	12
8	Umberto Maglioli	Ferrari	Ferrari 553	75 laps	11
9	Harry Schell	Gordini	Gordini T16	75 laps	15
10	Louis Chiron	Louis Chiron	OSCA 20	72 laps	25
11	"B Bira"	Scuderia Milano	Maserati A6GCM	72 laps	23
12	Alan Brown	Equipe Anglaise	Cooper-Bristol T23	70 laps	24
13	Stirling Moss	Cooper	Cooper-Alta T24	70 laps	10
14	Hans Stuck	Hans Stuck	AFM-Bristol	67 laps	29
15	Yves Giraud-Cabantous	HWM	HWM-Alta	67 laps	28
16	Louis Rosier	Ecurie Rosier	Ferrari 500	65 laps	17
R	Alberto Ascari	Ferrari	Ferrari 500	79 laps/accident	1
R	Felice Bonetto	Maserati	Maserati A6GCM	77 laps/out of fuel	7
R	Onofre Marimon	Maserati	Maserati A6GCM	75 laps/accident	4
R	Emmanuel de Graffenried	Emmanuel de Graffenried	Maserati A6GCM	70 laps/engine	9
NC	Jack Fairman	Connaught	Connaught-Francis A	61 laps /not classified	22
NC	Ken Wharton	Ken Wharton	Cooper-Bristol T23	57 laps/not classified	19
NC	Kenneth McAlpine	Connaught	Connaught-Francis A	56 laps/not classified	18

Pos	Driver	Team	Chassis-Engine	Result	Qual
R	Piero Carini	Ferrari	Ferrari 553	40 laps/engine	20
R	Roy Salvadori	Connaught	Connaught-Francis A	33 laps/throttle	14
R	Chico Landi	Scuderia Milano	Maserati A6GCM	18 laps/engine	21
R	Elie Bayol	OSCA	OSCA 20	17 laps/engine	13
R	John Fitch	HWM	HWM-Alta	14 laps/engine	26
R	Johnny Claes	Ecurie Belge	Connaught-Francis A	7 laps/fuel system	30
R	Lance Macklin	HWM	HWM-Alta	6 laps/engine	27

*Sergio Mantovani, Luigi Musso

Pole: Ascari, 2m02.700s, 114.854mph/184.841kph. Fastest lap: Fangio, 2m04.500s, 113.194mph/182.168kph on Lap 39. Race leaders: Ascari 1-6, 9, 14-24, 29-33, 36-40, 42-45, 47-49, 53-79; Fangio 7-8, 11, 25, 27-28, 34-35, 41, 50-52, 80; Farina 10, 12-13, 26, 46

NEW CONSTRUCTOR

Only one constructor made its debut in 1953. This was EMW, short for Eisenacher Motoren Werke, its car produced at BMW's pre-war Eisenach plant, in what was newly deemed East Germany. Its car appeared only the once, fittingly for its home grand prix at the Nurburgring. Driven by Edgar Barth, it qualified 24th out of the 34 cars, but retired.

NEW DRIVERS

There was a smaller crop of new drivers, 27, than there had been in 1952, but it was a higher quality intake. Luigi Musso would go on to become a grand prix winner, while Hans Herrmann, Umberto Maglioli and Carlos Menditeguy all went on to achieve podium finishes in future seasons.

WORLD DRIVERS' CHAMPIONSHIP FINAL RESULTS

Pos	Driver	Nat	Car-Engine	R1	R2	R3
1	Alberto Ascari	ITA	Ferrari 500	1PF	1P	1
2	Juan Manuel Fangio	ARG	Maserati A6GCM-52	R	-	-
			Maserati A6GCM	-	R	R|RP
3	Giuseppe Farina	ITA	Ferrari 500	R	2	R
4	Mike Hawthorn	GBR	Ferrari 500	4	4	6
5	Luigi Villoresi	ITA	Ferrari 500	2	RF	2
6	Jose Froilan Gonzalez	ARG	Maserati A6GCM-52	3	-	-
			Maserati A6GCM	-	3|R	RF
8	Emmanuel de Graffenried	CHE	Maserati A6GCM	-	5	4
9	Felice Bonetto	ITA	Maserati A6GCM-52	R	-	-
			Maserati A6GCM	-	-	-
11	Onofre Marimon	ARG	Maserati A6GCM	-	-	3
12	Maurice Trintignant	FRA	Gordini T16	7	6	5
15	Oscar Galvez	ARG	Maserati A6GCM-52	5	-	-
15	Hermann Lang	DEU	Maserati A6GCM	-	-	-

Pos	Driver	R4	R5	R6	R7	R8	Total
1	Ascari	4P	1PF	8P|RF	1F	RP	34.5
2	Fangio	-	-	-	-		27.5
		2F	2	2	4P|R	1F	
3	Farina	5	3	1	2	2	26
4	Hawthorn	1	5	3	3	4	19
5	Villoresi	6	R	8|R	6	3	17
6	Gonzalez	-	-	-	-	-	13.5
		3	4F	-	-	-	
8	de Graffenried	7	R	5	R	R	7
9	Bonetto	-	-	-	-	-	6.5
		R	6	4	4|R	R	
11	Marimon	9	R	R	R	R	4
12	Trintignant	R	R	R	R	5	4
15	Galvez	-	-	-	-	-	2
15	Lang	-	-	-	5	-	2

SYMBOLS AND GRAND PRIX KEY

Round 1 Argentinian GP
Round 2 Dutch GP
Round 3 Belgian GP
Round 4 French GP
Round 5 British GP
Round 6 German GP
Round 7 Swiss GP
Round 8 Italian GP

Indianapolis 500 results not included

DNPQ DID NOT PRE-QUALIFY **DNQ** DID NOT QUALIFY **DQ** DISQUALIFIED **EX** EXCLUDED
F FASTEST LAP **NC** NOT CLASSIFIED **NS** NON-STARTER **P** POLE POSITION **R** RETIRED

SCORING

1st 8 points
2nd 6 points
3rd 4 points
4th 3 points
5th 2 points
Fastest lap 1 point

1954

SEASON SUMMARY

It wouldn't happen now, but Juan Manuel Fangio achieved the extraordinary feat of starting the 1954 championship with one team and ending it as champion with another. This is because Mercedes-Benz, a marque that had dominated racing in the 1930s, wasn't ready to make its F1 debut until the third round, so he had to race the first two grands prix in a works Maserati, winning both. Then, equipped with the sleek Mercedes W196, Fangio won four of the remaining races to add a second title to his one with Alfa Romeo in 1951, leaving Ferrari's lead driver, Jose Froilan Gonzalez, far behind.

ARGENTINIAN GRAND PRIX

BUENOS AIRES • ROUND 1 • DATE: 17TH JANUARY 1954
Laps: 87 • Distance: 211.501miles/340.378km • Weather: Warm & dull, rain later

Pos	Driver	Team	Chassis-Engine	Result	Qual
1	Juan Manuel Fangio	Maserati	Maserati 250F	3h00m55.800s	3
2	Giuseppe Farina	Ferrari	Ferrari 625	3h02m14.800s	1
3	Jose Froilan Gonzalez	Ferrari	Ferrari 625	3h02m56.800s	2
4	Maurice Trintignant	Ecurie Rosier	Ferrari 625	86 laps	5
5	Elie Bayol	Gordini	Gordini T16	85 laps	15
6	Harry Schell	Harry Schell	Maserati A6GCM	84 laps	11
7	"B Bira"	Maserati	Maserati A6GCM	83 laps	10
8	Emmanuel de Graffenried	Emmanuel de Graffenried	Maserati A6GCM	83 laps	13
9	Umberto Maglioli	Ferrari	Ferrari 625	82 laps	12
DQ	Jean Behra	Gordini	Gordini T16	61 laps/push start	17
DQ	Mike Hawthorn	Ferrari	Ferrari 625	51 laps/push start	4
R	Onofre Marimon	Maserati	Maserati 250F	48 laps/engine	6
R	Roberto Mieres	Roberto Mieres	Maserati A6GCM	37 laps/oil leak	8
R	Roger Loyer	Gordini	Gordini T16	19 laps/fuel pressure	16
R	Jorge Daponte	Jorge Daponte	Maserati A6GCM	19 laps/gearbox	18
R	Louis Rosier	Ecurie Rosier	Ferrari 500	1 lap/accident	14
NS	Luigi Musso	Maserati	Maserati A6GCM	engine	7
NS	Carlos Menditeguy	Onofre Marimon	Maserati A6GCM	engine	9

Pole: Farina, 1m44.800s, 83.509mph/134.395kph. Fastest lap: Gonzalez, 1m48.200s, 80.885mph/130.172kph. Race leaders: Farina 1-14, 63-64; Gonzalez 15-32, 47-58, 61-62; Hawthorn 33-34; Fangio 35-46, 59-60, 65-87

NEW SEASON, NEW RULES

The main difference for 1954 was the change from the World Championship being run to F2 rules to cars being allowed to use larger engines – up from 2000 to 2500cc, and from 500 to 750cc if supercharged – that could kick out up to 245bhp. This revision brought welcome stability, and engine capacity wouldn't be altered again until after 1960.

BELGIAN GRAND PRIX

SPA-FRANCORCHAMPS • ROUND 2 • DATE: 20TH JUNE 1954
Laps: 36 • Distance: 315.676miles/508.32km • Weather: Warm & bright

Pos	Driver	Team	Chassis-Engine	Result	Qual
1	Juan Manuel Fangio	Maserati	Maserati 250F	2h44m42.400s	1
2	Maurice Trintignant	Ferrari	Ferrari 625	2h45m06.600s	6
3	Stirling Moss	Equipe Moss	Maserati 250F	35 laps	9
4	Hawthorn/Gonzalez*	Ferrari	Ferrari 625	35 laps	5
5	Andre Pilette	Gordini	Gordini T16	35 laps	8
6	"B Bira"	"B Bira"	Maserati 250F	35 laps	13
7	Sergio Mantovani	Maserati	Maserati 250F	34 laps	11
R	Giuseppe Farina	Ferrari	Ferrari 553	14 laps/ignition	3
R	Paul Frere	Gordini	Gordini T16	14 laps/engine	10
R	Jean Behra	Gordini	Gordini T16	12 laps/suspension	7
R	Onofre Marimon	Maserati	Maserati 250F	3 laps/engine	4
R	Jose Froilan Gonzalez	Ferrari	Ferrari 625	1 lap/engine	2
R	Jacques Swaters	Ecurie Francorchamps	Ferrari 500	1 lap/engine	14
R	Roberto Mieres	Roberto Mieres	Maserati A6GCM	0 laps/fire	12

*Mike Hawthorn, Jose Froilan Gonzalez

Pole: Fangio, 4m22.100s, 120.509mph/193.941kph. Fastest lap: Fangio, 4m25.500s, 118.992mph/191.500kph on Lap 13. Race leaders: Farina 1-2, 11-13; Fangio 3-10, 14-36

A STERN FACE

Mercedes-Benz had a firm hand at the helm when the German marque returned to the sport's top category for the first time since the 1930s. This was Alfred Neubauer. A large man, who always wore a suit and hat, he had masterminded Mercedes's racing success in the 1930s and carried on in a similar vein on its return.

FRENCH GRAND PRIX

REIMS • ROUND 3 • DATE: 4TH JULY 1954
Laps: 61 • Distance: 314.676miles/506.422km • Weather: Warm & dull, rain later

Pos	Driver	Team	Chassis-Engine	Result	Qual
1	Juan Manuel Fangio	Mercedes	Mercedes W196	2h42m47.900s	1
2	Karl Kling	Mercedes	Mercedes W196	2h42m48.000s	2
3	Robert Manzon	Ecurie Rosier	Ferrari 625	60 laps	12
4	"B Bira"	"B Bira"	Maserati 250F	60 laps	6
5	Luigi Villoresi	Maserati	Maserati 250F	58 laps	14
6	Jean Behra	Gordini	Gordini T16	56 laps	17
R	Paul Frere	Gordini	Gordini T16	50 laps/rear axle	19
R	Maurice Trintignant	Ferrari	Ferrari 625	36 laps/engine	9
R	Onofre Marimon	Maserati	Maserati 250F	27 laps/gearbox	5
R	Louis Rosier	Ecurie Rosier	Ferrari 500	27 laps/engine	13
R	Roberto Mieres	Roberto Mieres	Maserati A6GCM	24 laps/engine	11
R	Ken Wharton	BRM	Maserati 250F	19 laps/transmission	16

Pos	Driver	Team	Chassis-Engine	Result	Qual
R	Harry Schell	Harry Schell	Maserati A6GCM	19 laps/fuel pump	21
R	Hans Herrmann	Mercedes	Mercedes W196	16 laps/engine	7
R	Roy Salvadori	Gilby Engineering	Maserati 250F	15 laps/halfshaft	10
R	Jose Froilan Gonzalez	Ferrari	Ferrari 553	13 laps/engine	4
R	Lance Macklin	HWM	HWM-Alta	10 laps/engine	15
R	Mike Hawthorn	Ferrari	Ferrari 553	9 laps/engine	8
R	Georges Berger	Georges Berger	Gordini T16	9 laps/engine	20
R	Jacques Pollet	Gordini	Gordini T16	8 laps/engine	18
R	Alberto Ascari	Maserati	Maserati 250F	1 lap/transmission	3
NS	Sergio Mantovani	Maserati	Maserati 250F	-	-

Pole: Fangio, 2m29.400s, 124.304mph/200.048kph. Fastest lap: Herrmann, 2m32.900s, 121.478mph/195.500kph on Lap 3. Race leaders: Kling 1-2, 29-33, 38, 54-57, 60; Fangio 3-28, 34-37, 39-53, 58-59, 61

FULL-BODIED FLAWS

The Mercedes W196 looked like no other when it made its bow with streamlined bodywork that enclosed the wheels. This worked at Reims as Juan Manuel Fangio led home a W196 one-two, but not at Silverstone, where he found that it obstructed his view of the marker barrels on some of the corners – damage from clipping them left him fourth.

BRITISH GRAND PRIX

SILVERSTONE • ROUND 4 • DATE: 17TH JULY 1954
Laps: 90 • Distance: 263.427miles/423.945km • Weather: Cool with rain

Pos	Driver	Team	Chassis-Engine	Result	Qual
1	Jose Froilan Gonzalez	Ferrari	Ferrari 625	2h56m14.000s	2
2	Mike Hawthorn	Ferrari	Ferrari 625	2h57m24.000s	3
3	Onofre Marimon	Maserati	Maserati 250F	89 laps	28
4	Juan Manuel Fangio	Mercedes	Mercedes W196	89 laps	1
5	Maurice Trintignant	Ferrari	Ferrari 625	87 laps	8
6	Roberto Mieres	Roberto Mieres	Maserati A6GCM	87 laps	32
7	Karl Kling	Mercedes	Mercedes W196	87 laps	6
8	Ken Wharton	BRM	Maserati 250F	86 laps	9
9	Andre Pilette	Gordini	Gordini T16	86 laps	12
10	Bob Gerard	Bob Gerard	Cooper-Bristol T23	85 laps	18
11	Don Beauman	Sir Jeremy Boles	Connaught-Francis A	84 laps	17
12	Harry Schell	Harry Schell	Maserati A6GCM	83 laps	16
13	Leslie Marr	Leslie Marr	Connaught-Francis A	82 laps	22
14	Leslie Thorne	Ecurie Ecosse	Connaught-Francis A	78 laps	23
15	Horace Gould	H H Gould	Cooper-Bristol T23	44 laps	20
R	Stirling Moss	A E Moss	Maserati 250F	80 laps/axle	4
R	Bill Whitehouse	W J Whitehouse	Connaught-Francis A	63 laps/fuel system	19
R	Jean Behra	Gordini	Gordini T16	54 laps/suspension	5
R	Roy Salvadori	Gilby Engineering	Maserati 250F	53 laps/transmission	7
R	"B Bira" / Flockhart*	"B Bira"	Maserati 250F	44 laps/accident	10
R	John Riseley-Prichard	Rob Walker Racing Team	Connaught-Francis A	40 laps/accident	21
R	Villoresi / Ascari*	Maserati	Maserati 250F	40 laps/engine	27

Pos	Driver	Team	Chassis-Engine	Result	Qual
R	Reg Parnell	Scuderia Ambrosiana	Ferrari 500	25 laps/engine	14
R	Alberto Ascari	Maserati	Maserati 250F	21 laps/engine	30
R	Clemar Bucci	Gordini	Gordini T16	18 laps/accident	13
R	Peter Collins	Vanwall	Vanwall	16 laps/engine	11
R	Robert Manzon	Ecurie Rosier	Ferrari 625	16 laps/engine	15
R	Peter Whitehead	Peter Whitehead	Cooper-Alta T24	4 laps/oil leak	24
R	Louis Rosier	Ecurie Rosier	Ferrari 500	2 laps/engine	31
R	Eric Brandon	Ecurie Richmond	Cooper-Bristol T23	2 laps/engine	25
NS	Alan Brown	R J Chase	Cooper-Bristol T23	-	26
NS	Rodney Nuckey	Ecurie Richmond	Cooper-Bristol T23	Brandon drove car	-

*"B Bira", Ron Flockhart, Luigi Villoresi, Alberto Ascari

Pole: Fangio, 1m45.000s, 100.353mph/161.502kph. Fastest lap: Ascari, 1m50.000s, 95.691mph/154.000kph; Behra, 1m50.000s, 95.691mph/154.000kph; Gonzalez, 1m50.000s, 95.691mph/154.000kph; Fangio, 1m50.000s, 95.691mph/154.000kph; Hawthorn, 1m50.000s, 95.691mph/154.000kph; Marimon, 1m50.000s, 95.691mph/154.000kph; Moss, 1m50.000s, 95.691mph/154.000kph. Race leaders: Gonzalez 1-90

FERRARI LOSES GROUND

Having been runaway champions in 1952 and 1953, Ferrari lost ground in 1954 as it couldn't match the pace of Maserati (with its 250F) or the incoming Mercedes. This was surprising because the marque had spent two years developing its 2.5-litre engine, but perhaps this gave Enzo Ferrari a sign that nothing stands still in F1.

GERMAN GRAND PRIX

NURBURGRING • ROUND 5 • DATE: 1ST AUGUST 1954
Laps: 22 • Distance: 311.357miles/501.82km • Weather: Warm & bright

Pos	Driver	Team	Chassis-Engine	Result	Qual
1	Juan Manuel Fangio	Mercedes	Mercedes W196	3h45m45.800s	1
2	Gonzalez / Hawthorn*	Ferrari	Ferrari 625	3h47m22.300s	5
3	Maurice Trintignant	Ferrari	Ferrari 625	3h50m54.400s	7
4	Karl Kling	Mercedes	Mercedes W196	3h51m52.300s	23
5	Sergio Mantovani	Maserati	Maserati 250F	3h54m36.300s	15
6	Piero Taruffi	Ferrari	Ferrari 625	21 laps	13
7	Harry Schell	Harry Schell	Maserati A6GCM	21 laps	14
8	Louis Rosier	Ecurie Rosier	Ferrari 500	21 laps	11
9	Robert Manzon	Ecurie Rosier	Ferrari 625	20 laps	12
10	Jean Behra	Gordini	Gordini T16	20 laps	9
R	"B Bira"	"B Bira"	Maserati 250F	18 laps/steering	19
R	Hermann Lang	Mercedes	Mercedes W196	10 laps/spun off	13
R	Clemar Bucci	Gordini	Gordini T16	8 laps/wheel	16
R	Theo Helfrich	Hans Klenk	Klen Meteor-BMW	8 laps/engine	21
R	Hans Herrmann	Mercedes	Mercedes W196	7 laps/oil leak	4
R	Paul Frere	Gordini	Gordini T16	4 laps/lost wheel	4
R	Mike Hawthorn	Ferrari	Ferrari 625	3 laps/transmission	2
R	Roberto Mieres	Roberto Mieres	Maserati A6GCM	2 laps/oil leak	17

Pos	Driver	Team	Chassis-Engine	Result	Qual
R	Stirling Moss	A E Moss	Maserati 250F	1 lap/wheel	3
R	Andre Pilette	Gordini	Gordini T16	0 laps/suspension	20
NS	Onofre Marimon	Maserati	Maserati 250F	fatal accident	8
NS	Luigi Villoresi	Maserati	Maserati 250F	-	10
NS	Ken Wharton	BRM	Maserati 250F	-	22
*Jose Froilan Gonzalez, Mike Hawthorn					

Pole: Fangio, 9m50.100s, 86.467mph/139.156kph. Fastest lap: Kling, 9m55.100s, 85.749mph/138.000kph on Lap 16. Race leaders: Fangio 1-14, 17-22; Kling 15-16

NEW CONSTRUCTORS

Mercedes-Benz stole the headlines with its immediate ability to win grands prix. However, the new rules attracted Lancia to join the World Championship as well, and the Italian manufacturer also coaxed double world champion Ascari from Ferrari, but had no car ready until the penultimate round. Vanwall and Klenk also made their first forays.

SWISS GRAND PRIX

BREMGARTEN • ROUND 6 • DATE: 22ND AUGUST 1954
Laps: 66 • Distance: 298.288miles/480.48km • Weather: Warm & damp then drying

Pos	Driver	Team	Chassis-Engine	Result	Qual
1	Juan Manuel Fangio	Mercedes	Mercedes W196	3h00m34.500s	2
2	Jose Froilan Gonzalez	Ferrari	Ferrari 625	3h01m32.300s	1
3	Hans Herrmann	Mercedes	Mercedes W196	65 laps	7
4	Roberto Mieres	Maserati	Maserati 250F	64 laps	12
5	Sergio Mantovani	Maserati	Maserati 250F	64 laps	9
6	Ken Wharton	BRM	Maserati 250F	64 laps	8
7	Umberto Maglioli	Ferrari	Ferrari 553	61 laps	11
8	Jacques Swaters	Ecurie Francorchamps	Ferrari 500	58 laps	16
R	Karl Kling	Mercedes	Mercedes W196	38 laps/fuel system	5
R	Maurice Trintignant	Ferrari	Ferrari 625	33 laps/engine	4
R	Mike Hawthorn	Ferrari	Ferrari 625	30 laps/fuel pump	6
R	Harry Schell	Maserati	Maserati 250F	23 laps/fuel pump	13
R	Stirling Moss	Maserati	Maserati 250F	21 laps/fuel pump	3
R	Fred Wacker	Gordini	Gordini T16	10 laps/transmission	15
R	Jean Behra	Gordini	Gordini T16	8 laps/clutch	14
R	Clemar Bucci	Gordini	Gordini T16	0 laps/fuel pump	10
NS	Robert Manzon	Ferrari	Ferrari 553	accident	-
NS	Roy Salvadori	Maserati	Maserati 250F	-	-

Pole: Gonzalez, 2m39.500s, 102.099mph/164.313kph. Fastest lap: Fangio, 2m39.700s, 101.967mph/164.100kph on Lap 34. Race leaders: Fangio 1-66

A SWISS FAREWELL

Although part of the inaugural World Championship in 1950, the Swiss GP at Bremgarten proved to be the last of its kind. The circuit near Bern was a test for the drivers and this time yielded a win for Fangio's Mercedes, but a huge accident in the 1955 Le Mans 24 Hours led to the F1 race being cancelled. Then Switzerland banned all motor racing.

ITALIAN GRAND PRIX

MONZA • ROUND 7 • DATE: 5TH SEPTEMBER 1954
Laps: 80 • Distance: 313.171miles/504.0km • Weather: Warm & bright

Pos	Driver	Team	Chassis-Engine	Result	Qual
1	Juan Manuel Fangio	Mercedes	Mercedes W196	2h47m47.900s	1
2	Mike Hawthorn	Ferrari	Ferrari 625	79 laps	7
3	Maglioli / Gonzalez*	Ferrari	Ferrari 625	78 laps	13
4	Hans Herrmann	Mercedes	Mercedes W196	77 laps	8
5	Maurice Trintignant	Ferrari	Ferrari 625	75 laps	11
6	Fred Wacker	Gordini	Gordini T16	75 laps	18
7	Peter Collins	Vanwall	Vanwall Special	75 laps	16
8	Louis Rosier	Maserati	Maserati 250F	74 laps	20
9	Sergio Mantovani	Maserati	Maserati 250F	74 laps	9
10	Stirling Moss	Maserati	Maserati 250F	71 laps	3
11	Jorge Daponte	Jorge Daponte	Maserati A6GCM	70 laps	19
R	Alberto Ascari	Ferrari	Ferrari 625	48 laps/engine	2
R	Luigi Villoresi	Maserati	Maserati 250F	42 laps/clutch	6
R	Karl Kling	Mercedes	Mercedes W196	36 laps/accident	4
R	Roberto Mieres	Maserati	Maserati 250F	34 laps/suspension	10
R	Luigi Musso	Maserati	Maserati 250F	32 laps/transmission	14
R	Jose Froilan Gonzalez	Ferrari	Ferrari 553	16 laps/gearbox	5
R	Robert Manzon	Ecurie Rosier	Ferrari 625	16 laps/engine	15
R	Clemar Bucci	Gordini	Gordini T16	13 laps/transmission	17
R	Jean Behra	Gordini	Gordini T16	2 laps/engine	12
DNQ	Giovanni de Riu	Giovanni de Riu	Maserati A6GCM	-	-

*Umberto Maglioli, Jose Froilan Gonzalez

Pole: Fangio, 1m59.000s, 118.425mph/190.588kph. Fastest lap: Gonzalez, 2m00.800s, 116.661mph/187.748kph on Lap 2. Race leaders: Kling 1-3; Fangio 4-5; 23, 68-80; Ascari 6-22, 24-44, 46-48; Moss 45, 49-67

NEW DRIVERS

There were just 13 new F1 drivers in 1954, not all of whom qualified for a grand prix. Karl Kling was nearly 44 when he made his F1 bow with Mercedes, and finished second on his debut at Reims. Ron Flockhart had a one-off race for Prince Bira's team, but went on to a podium finish at Monza in 1956.

CLASSIC CAR: MASERATI 250F

Renowned as one of the most striking cars ever to have contested the World Championship, the 250F was a lot more than just good looks: it won eight grands prix and helped Fangio to the 1957 drivers' title. The car raced until 1960, the last one appearing in privateer hands. Designed by Gioacchino Colombo and Vittorio Bellentani, and powered initially by a straight-six engine, before being fitted with a V12 from 1957 in an ever-slimmer body, it was a car that drivers loved for its well-balanced handling. In total, 29 250Fs were built, but the end came when rear-engined cars began to win in F1.

SPANISH GRAND PRIX

PEDRALBES • ROUND 8 • DATE: 24TH OCTOBER 1954
Laps: 80 • Distance: 313.809miles/505.28km • Weather: Warm & bright

Pos	Driver	Team	Chassis-Engine	Result	Qual
1	Mike Hawthorn	Ferrari	Ferrari 553	3h13m52.100s	3
2	Luigi Musso	Maserati	Maserati 250F	3h15m05.300s	7
3	Juan Manuel Fangio	Mercedes	Mercedes W196	79 laps	2
4	Roberto Mieres	Maserati	Maserati 250F	79 laps	11
5	Karl Kling	Mercedes	Mercedes W196	79 laps	12
6	Chico Godia-Sales	Maserati	Maserati 250F	76 laps	13
7	Louis Rosier	Ecurie Rosier	Ferrari 500	74 laps	20
8	Ken Wharton	BRM	Maserati 250F	74 laps	14
9	"B Bira"	"B Bira"	Maserati 250F	68 laps	15
R	Sergio Mantovani	Maserati	Maserati 250F	58 laps/brakes	10
R	de Graffenried/Volonterio*	Emmanuel de Graffenried	Maserati A6GCM	57 laps/engine	21
R	Hans Herrmann	Mercedes	Mercedes W196	50 laps/fuel injection	9
R	Maurice Trintignant	Ferrari	Ferrari 625	47 laps/gearbox	8
R	Jacques Pollet	Gordini	Gordini T16	37 laps/engine	16
R	Harry Schell	Harry Schell	Maserati 250F	29 laps/transmission	4
R	Stirling Moss	Maserati	Maserati 250F	20 laps/fuel pump	6
R	Jean Behra	Gordini	Gordini T16	17 laps/brakes	18
R	Jacques Swaters	Ecurie Francorchamps	Ferrari 500	16 laps/engine	19
R	Alberto Ascari	Lancia	Lancia D50	10 laps/clutch	1
R	Luigi Villoresi	Lancia	Lancia D50	2 laps/brakes	5
R	Robert Manzon	Ecurie Rosier	Ferrari 625	2 laps/engine	17
NS	Peter Collins	Vanwall	Vanwall	accident	-

*Emmanuel de Graffenried, Ottorino Volonterio

Pole: Ascari, 2m18.100s, 102.306mph/164.645kph. Fastest lap: Ascari, 2m20.400s, 100.599mph/161.900kph on Lap 3. Race leaders: Schell 1-2, 10, 13, 15-17, 19, 21, 23; Ascari 3-9; Trintignant 11-12, 14, 18, 20; Hawthorn 22, 24-80

IN MEMORIAM

Juan Manuel Fangio's protégé Onofre Marimón was one of two F1 drivers who died in 1954, the works Maserati driver being killed in practice for the German GP two weeks after he'd finished third at Silverstone. Guy Mairesse had not raced in the World Championship since 1951, but was killed in practice for the Coupe de Paris at Montlhery.

WORLD DRIVERS' CHAMPIONSHIP FINAL RESULTS

Pos	Driver	Nat	Car-Engine	R1	R2	R3	R4	R5	R6	R7	R8	Total
1	Juan Manuel Fangio	ARG	Maserati 250F	1	1PF	-	-	-	-	-	-	42
			Mercedes W196	-	-	1P	4PF	1P	1F	1P	3	
2	Jose Froilan Gonzalez	ARG	Ferrari 625	3F	4	4	1F	1F	2P	3F	-	25.14
			Ferrari 553	-	R	R	-	-	-	R	-	
3	Mike Hawthorn	GBR	Ferrari 625	DQ	4	-	2F	3F	R	2	-	24.64
			Ferrari 553	-	-	R	-	-	-	-	1	
4	Maurice Trintignant	FRA	Ferrari 625	4	2	R	5	3	R	5	R	17
5	Karl Kling	DEU	Mercedes W196	-	-	2	7	4F	R	R	5	12
7	Hans Herrmann	DEU	Mercedes W196	-	-	RF	-	R	3	4	R	8
8	Giuseppe Farina	ITA	Ferrari 625	2P	-	-	-	-	-	-	-	6
			Ferrari 553	-	R	-	-	-	-	-	-	
8	Luigi Musso	ITA	Maserati A6GCM	NS	-	-	-	-	-	-	-	6
			Maserati 250F	-	-	-	-	-	-	R	2	
11	Roberto Mieres	ARG	Maserati A6GCM	R	R	R	6	R	-	-	-	6
			Maserati 250F	-	-	-	-	-	4	R	4	
13	Stirling Moss	GBR	Maserati 250F	-	3	-	RF	-	R	10	R	4.14
13	Onofre Marimon	ARG	Maserati 250F	R	R	R	3F	NS	-	-	-	4.14
15	Robert Manzon	FRA	Ferrari 625	-	-	3	R	9	-	R	R	4
			Ferrari 553	-	-	-	-	-	NS	-	-	
16	Sergio Mantovani	ITA	Maserati 250F	-	7	NS	-	5	5	9	R	4
17	"B Bira"	THA	Maserati A6GCM	7	-	-	-	-	-	-	-	3
			Maserati 250F	-	6	4	R	R	-	-	9	
18	Umberto Maglioli	ITA	Ferrari 625	9	-	-	-	-	-	3	-	2
			Ferrari 553	-	-	-	-	-	7	-	-	
19	Elie Bayol	FRA	Gordini T16	5	-	-	-	-	-	-	-	2
19	Andre Pilette	BEL	Gordini T16	-	5	-	9	R	-	-	-	2
19	Luigi Villoresi	ITA	Maserati 250F	-	-	5	R	NS	-	R	-	2
			Lancia D50	-	-	-	-	-	-	-	R	
25	Alberto Ascari	ITA	Maserati 250F	-	-	R	RF/R	-	-	-	-	1.14
			Ferrari 625	-	-	-	-	-	-	R	-	
			Lancia D50	-	-	-	-	-	-	-	RPF	
26	Jean Behra	FRA	Gordini T16	DQ	R	6	RF	10	R	R	R	0.14

SYMBOLS AND GRAND PRIX KEY

Round 1 Argentinian GP
Round 2 Belgian GP
Round 3 French GP
Round 4 British GP
Round 5 German GP
Round 6 Swiss GP
Round 7 Italian GP
Round 8 Spanish GP

SCORING

1st 8 points
2nd 6 points
3rd 4 points
4th 3 points
5th 2 points
Fastest lap 1 point

Indianapolis 500 results not included

DNPQ DID NOT PRE-QUALIFY **DNQ** DID NOT QUALIFY **DQ** DISQUALIFIED **EX** EXCLUDED
F FASTEST LAP **NC** NOT CLASSIFIED **NS** NON-STARTER **P** POLE POSITION **R** RETIRED

1955

SEASON SUMMARY

Mercedes-Benz had near total control in its first full year of F1. However, the season was shorter than planned due to the 1955 Le Mans disaster leading to the cancellation of four of the six remaining races. Lancia quit on the spot, while Mercedes raced until the end of the year before withdrawing. Nothing should take away, though, from Fangio's third F1 title and the way he brought on young British talent Stirling Moss. Mercedes's high point was filling the first four places at the British GP. Behind them, Lancia showed good form, but their decision to quit meant that struggling Ferrari was able to take over its cars for 1956.

ARGENTINIAN GRAND PRIX

BUENOS AIRES • ROUND 1 • DATE: 16TH JANUARY 1955
Laps: 96 • Distance: 233.380miles/375.590km • Weather: Very hot & bright

Pos	Driver	Team	Chassis-Engine	Result	Qual
1	Juan Manuel Fangio	Mercedes	Mercedes W196	3h00m38.600s	3
2	Gonzalez / Farina / Trintignant*	Ferrari	Ferrari 625	3h02m08.200s	1
3	Farina / Trintignant / Maglioli*	Ferrari	Ferrari 625	94 laps	5
4	Herrmann / Kling / Moss*	Mercedes	Mercedes W196	94 laps	10
5	Roberto Mieres	Maserati	Maserati 250F	91 laps	16
6	Schell / Behra*	Maserati	Maserati 250F	88 laps	7
7	Musso / Mantovani / Schell*	Maserati	Maserati 250F	83 laps	18
R	Bucci / Menditeguy / Schell*	Maserati	Maserati 250F	55 laps/fuel pressure	20
R	Mantovani / Behra / Musso*	Maserati	Maserati 250F	55 laps/engine	19
R	Jesus Iglesias	Gordini	Gordini T16	38 laps/transmission	17
R	Maurice Trintignant	Ferrari	Ferrari 625	36 laps/engine	14
R	Castellotti / Villoresi*	Lancia	Lancia D50	35 laps/accident	12
R	Stirling Moss	Mercedes	Mercedes W196	29 laps/fuel system	8
R	Alberto Uria	A Uria	Maserati A6GCM	22 laps/out of fuel	21
R	Alberto Ascari	Lancia	Lancia D50	21 laps/accident	2
R	Elie Bayol	Gordini	Gordini T16	7 laps/transmission	15
R	Jean Behra	Maserati	Maserati 250F	2 laps/accident	4
R	Karl Kling	Mercedes	Mercedes W196	2 laps/accident	6
R	Pablo Birger	Gordini	Gordini T16	1 lap/accident	9
R	Luigi Villoresi	Lancia	Lancia D50	1 lap/oil leak	11
R	Carlos Menditeguy	Maserati	Maserati 250F	1 lap/accident	13

*Jose Froilan Gonzalez, Giuseppe Farina, Maurice Trintignant, Umberto Maglioli, Hans Herrmann, Karl Kling, Stirling Moss, Harry Schell, Jean Behra, Luigi Musso, Sergio Mantovani, Clemar Bucci, Carlos Menditeguy, Eugenio Castellotti, Luigi Villoresi

Pole: Gonzalez, 1m43.100s, 84.886mph/136.611kph. Fastest lap: Fangio, 1m48.300s, 80.810mph/130.052kph on Lap 45. Race leaders: Fangio 1-2, 26-34, 43-96; Ascari 3-5, 11-21; Gonzalez 6-10, 22-25; Schell 35-40; Mieres 41-42

MONACO GRAND PRIX

MONTE CARLO • ROUND 2 • DATE: 22ND MAY 1955
Laps: 100 • Distance: 195.113miles/314.5km • Weather: Hot & bright

Pos	Driver	Team	Chassis-Engine	Result	Qual
1	Maurice Trintignant	Ferrari	Ferrari 625	2h58m09.800s	9
2	Eugenio Castellotti	Lancia	Lancia D50	2h58m30.000s	4
3	Behra / Perdisa*	Maserati	Maserati 250F	99 laps	5
4	Giuseppe Farina	Ferrari	Ferrari 625	99 laps	14
5	Luigi Villoresi	Lancia	Lancia D50	99 laps	7
6	Louis Chiron	Lancia	Lancia D50	95 laps	19
7	Jacques Pollet	Gordini	Gordini T16	91 laps	20
8	Taruffi / Frere*	Ferrari	Ferrari 555	86 laps	15
9	Stirling Moss	Mercedes	Mercedes W196	81 laps	3
R	Perdisa / Behra*	Maserati	Maserati 250F	86 laps/spun off	11
R	Alberto Ascari	Lancia	Lancia D50	80 laps/accident	2
R	Harry Schell	Ferrari	Ferrari 555	68 laps/engine	18
R	Roberto Mieres	Maserati	Maserati 250F	64 laps/transmission	6
R	Elie Bayol	Gordini	Gordini T16	63 laps/transmission	16
R	Juan Manuel Fangio	Mercedes	Mercedes W196	49 laps/transmission	1
R	Robert Manzon	Gordini	Gordini T16	38 laps/gearbox	13
R	Andre Simon	Mercedes	Mercedes W196	24 laps/engine	10
R	Mike Hawthorn	Vanwall	Vanwall	22 laps/throttle	12
R	Louis Rosier	Ecurie Rosier	Maserati 250F	8 laps/oil leak	17
R	Luigi Musso	Maserati	Maserati 250F	7 laps/transmission	8
DNQ	Lance Macklin	Stirling Moss Ltd	Maserati 250F	-	21
DNQ	Ted Whiteaway	E N Whiteaway	HWM-Alta	-	22
NS	Hans Herrmann	Mercedes	Mercedes W196	accident	-

*Jean Behra, Cesare Perdisa, Piero Taruffi, Paul Frere

Pole: Fangio, 1m41.100s, 69.586mph/111.988kph. Fastest lap: Fangio, 1m42.400s, 68.702mph/110.566kph on Lap 27. Race leaders: Fangio 1-49; Moss 50-80; Trintignant 81-100

MOSS TAKES BREAKTHROUGH WIN

Moss refused to race any car that wasn't British until 1954, when he realised that a self-run Maserati might give him a better chance. He duly came third at Spa. In 1955, though, he raced for Mercedes and came second at Spa and Zandvoort, then chased Fangio at Aintree until getting past for his first win, never sure if Fangio had let him by.

ASCARI INTO THE MONACO HARBOUR

Alberto Ascari, world champion in 1952 and 1953, led Lancia's challenge against Mercedes dominance, but drew a blank when he spun out of the lead in Argentina. At the next grand prix, at Monaco, he qualified second but crashed into the harbour. This wasn't unusual at this street circuit, but he survived the dip, only to be killed testing a sports car at Monza four days later.

CLASSIC CAR: MERCEDES W196

Designed by Rudolf Uhlenhaut, the W196 was a landmark F1 car. Starting life with all-enveloping bodywork, the W196 was soon seen in the more usual open-wheeled F1 format and it was a winner from the outset. Having taken four wins in its partial debut season in 1954, the W196 added five more in what was a curtailed 1955 season. With its broad nose and fronted by a large radiator grille, its silver bodywork was draped over a tubular space frame. It had crisp handling from its independent suspension. Power came from one of the last straight-eight engines used in top single-seater racing, and the unit produced 275bhp, rising to 290bhp in 1955.

BELGIAN GRAND PRIX

SPA-FRANCORCHAMPS • ROUND 3 • DATE: 5TH JUNE 1955
Laps: 36 • Distance: 315.676miles/508.32km • Weather: Warm & bright

Pos	Driver	Team	Chassis-Engine	Result	Qual
1	Juan Manuel Fangio	Mercedes	Mercedes W196	2h39m29.000s	2
2	Stirling Moss	Mercedes	Mercedes W196	2h39m37.100s	3
3	Giuseppe Farina	Ferrari	Ferrari 555	2h41m09.500s	4
4	Paul Frere	Ferrari	Ferrari 555	2h42m54.500s	8
5	Mieres / Behra*	Maserati	Maserati 250F	35 laps	13
6	Maurice Trintignant	Ferrari	Ferrari 555	35 laps	10
7	Luigi Musso	Maserati	Maserati 250F	34 laps	7
8	Cesare Perdisa	Maserati	Maserati 250F	33 laps	11
9	Louis Rosier	Ecurie Rosier	Maserati 250F	33 laps	12
R	Karl Kling	Mercedes	Mercedes W196	21 laps/oil leak	6
R	Eugenio Castellotti	Lancia	Lancia D50	16 laps/gearbox	1
R	Mike Hawthorn	Vanwall	Vanwall	8 laps/gearbox	9
R	Jean Behra	Maserati	Maserati 250F	3 laps/spun off	5
NS	Harry Schell	Ferrari	Ferrari 555	Trintignant drove car	-
NS	Johnny Claes	Stirling Moss Ltd	Maserati 250F	engine	14

*Roberto Mieres, Jean Behra

Pole: Castellotti, 4m18.100s, 122.376mph/196.946kph. Fastest lap: Fangio, 4m20.600s, 121.203mph/195.057kph on Lap 18. Race leaders: Fangio 1-36

STEADY DOES IT

Maurice Trintignant chose Monaco, of all places, to make his World Championship breakthrough. The French racer qualified his Ferrari only ninth, but steadily worked his way to the front as Mercedes retired and then Ascari crashed, to take the lead on lap 81 of 100. His only other World Championship win was also at Monaco, in 1958.

DUTCH GRAND PRIX

ZANDVOORT • ROUND 4 • DATE: 19TH JUNE 1955
Laps: 100 • Distance: 260.356miles/419.3km • Weather: Cool & dull, then rain

Pos	Driver	Team	Chassis-Engine	Result	Qual
1	Juan Manuel Fangio	Mercedes	Mercedes W196	2h54m23.800s	1
2	Stirling Moss	Mercedes	Mercedes W196	2h54m24.100s	2
3	Luigi Musso	Maserati	Maserati 250F	2h55m20.900s	4
4	Roberto Mieres	Maserati	Maserati 250F	99 laps	7
5	Eugenio Castellotti	Ferrari	Ferrari 555	97 laps	9
6	Jean Behra	Maserati	Maserati 250F	97 laps	6
7	Mike Hawthorn	Ferrari	Ferrari 555	95 laps	5
8	Nano da Silva Ramos	Gordini	Gordini T16	92 laps	14
9	Louis Rosier	Ecurie Rosier	Maserati 250F	92 laps	13
10	Jacques Pollet	Gordini	Gordini T16	90 laps	12
11	Johnny Claes	Equipe Nationale Belge	Ferrari 500	88 laps	16
R	Maurice Trintignant	Ferrari	Ferrari 555	65 laps/gearbox	8
R	Robert Manzon	Gordini	Gordini T16	44 laps/transmission	11
R	Horace Gould	H H Gould	Maserati 250F	23 laps/spun off	15
R	Karl Kling	Mercedes	Mercedes W196	21 laps/spun off	3
R	Peter Walker	Stirling Moss Ltd	Maserati 250F	2 laps/wheel bearing	10

Pole: Fangio, 1m40.000s, 93.794mph/150.948kph. Fastest lap: Mieres, 1m40.900s, 92.957mph/149.600kph on Lap 3. Race leaders: Fangio 1-100

A DIFFERENT GRAND NATIONAL

Aintree, home of the Grand National horse race, found a new string to its bow when it hosted the British GP instead of Silverstone. First used for car racing in 1954 on a course laid out around the outside of the horse racing course, its main attraction was actually the giant grandstand that offered a good view across the flat terrain.

BRITISH GRAND PRIX

AINTREE • ROUND 5 • DATE: 16TH JULY 1955
Laps: 90 • Distance: 269.707miles/434.52km • Weather: Hot & bright

Pos	Driver	Team	Chassis-Engine	Result	Qual
1	Stirling Moss	Mercedes	Mercedes W196	3h07m21.200s	1
2	Juan Manuel Fangio	Mercedes	Mercedes W196	3h07m21.400s	2
3	Karl Kling	Mercedes	Mercedes W196	3h08m33.000	4
4	Piero Taruffi	Mercedes	Mercedes W196	89 laps	5
5	Luigi Musso	Maserati	Maserati 250F	89 laps	9
6	Hawthorn / Castellotti*	Ferrari	Ferrari 625	87 laps	12
7	"Mike Sparken"	Gordini	Gordini T16	81 laps	23
8	Lance Macklin	Stirling Moss Ltd	Maserati 250F	79 laps	16
9	Wharton / Schell*	Vanwall	Vanwall	72 laps	15
R	Maurice Trintignant	Ferrari	Ferrari 625	59 laps/overheating	13
R	Roberto Mieres	Maserati	Maserati 250F	47 laps/engine	6
R	Kenneth McAlpine	Connaught	Connaught-Alta B	30 laps/fuel pressure	17

Pos	Driver	Team	Chassis-Engine	Result	Qual
R	Jack Brabham	Cooper	Cooper-Bristol T40	30 laps/engine	25
R	Peter Collins	BRM	Maserati 250F	28 laps/clutch	24
R	Nano da Silva Ramos	Gordini	Gordini T16	26 laps/fuel pressure	18
R	Roy Salvadori	Gilby Engineering	Maserati 250F	23 laps/gearbox	20
R	Horace Gould	Goulds Garage	Maserati 250F	22 laps/brakes	22
R	Harry Schell	Vanwall	Vanwall	20 laps/throttle	7
R	Rolt / Walker*	Rob Walker Racing Team	Connaught-Alta B	19 laps/throttle	14
R	Leslie Marr	Leselie Marr	Connaught-Alta B	18 laps/brakes	19
R	Eugenio Castellotti	Ferrari	Ferrari 625	16 laps/transmission	10
R	Jean Behra	Maserati	Maserati 250F	9 laps/oil leak	3
R	Andre Simon	Maserati	Maserati 250F	9 laps/gearbox	8
R	Robert Manzon	Gordini	Gordini T16	4 laps/transmission	11
NS	Jack Fairman	Connaught	Connaught-Alta B	engine	21

*Mike Hawthorn, Eugenio Castellotti, Ken Wharton, Harry Schell, Tony Rolt, Peter Walker

Pole: Moss, 2m00.400s, 89.700mph/144.358kph. Fastest lap: Moss, 2m00.400s, 89.726mph/144.400kph on Lap 88. Race leaders: Fangio 1-2, 18-25; Moss 3-17, 26-90

IN MEMORIAM

The death in 1955 of Don Beauman in a sports car race was overshadowed by Ascari being killed testing at Monza. Then, even the double world champion's death was put in the shade by what happened when Pierre Levegh clipped Mike Hawthorn at Le Mans and Levegh's Mercedes flew into the crowd opposite the pits, killing him and at least 80 spectators.

ONTO THE MONZA BANKING

Built in 1922, Monza was effectively two circuits in one, with the road circuit joined to a banked oval. This two-part layout wasn't used when the World Championship made its first visit in 1950, but it was in 1955, and this extended the lap from 3.915 miles (6.3km) to 6.214 miles (10km) as Fangio led home a Mercedes one-two.

ITALIAN GRAND PRIX

MONZA • ROUND 6 • DATE: 11TH SEPTEMBER 1955
Laps: 50 • Distance: 310.685miles/500.0km • Weather: Warm & bright

Pos	Driver	Team	Chassis-Engine	Result	Qual
1	Juan Manuel Fangio	Mercedes	Mercedes W196	2h25m04.400s	1
2	Piero Taruffi	Mercedes	Mercedes W196	2h25m05.100s	9
3	Eugenio Castellotti	Ferrari	Ferrari 555	2h25m50.600s	4
4	Jean Behra	Maserati	Maserati 250F	2h29m01.900s	6
5	Carlos Menditeguy	Maserati	Maserati 250F	49 laps	16
6	Umberto Maglioli	Ferrari	Ferrari 555	49 laps	12
7	Roberto Mieres	Maserati	Maserati 250F	48 laps	7
8	Maurice Trintignant	Ferrari	Ferrari 625	47 laps	15
9	John Fitch	Stirling Moss Ltd	Maserati 250F	46 laps	20

Pos	Driver	Team	Chassis-Engine	Result	Qual
R	Mike Hawthorn	Ferrari	Ferrari 555	38 laps/gearbox	14
R	Karl Kling	Mercedes	Mercedes W196	32 laps/gearbox	3
R	Luigi Musso	Maserati	Maserati 250F	31 laps/gearbox	10
R	Horace Gould	Maserati	Maserati 250F	31 laps/suspension	21
R	Stirling Moss	Mercedes	Mercedes W196	27 laps/engine	2
R	Jacques Pollet	Gordini	Gordini T16	26 laps/engine	19
R	Nano da Silva Ramos	Gordini	Gordini T16	23 laps/fuel system	18
R	Peter Collins	Maserati	Maserati 250F	22 laps/suspension	11
R	Harry Schell	Vanwall	Vanwall	7 laps/suspension	13
R	Jean Lucas	Gordini	Gordini T32	7 laps/engine	22
R	Ken Wharton	Vanwall	Vanwall	0 laps/fuel injection	17
NS	Giuseppe Farina	Ferrari	Ferrari D50	tyres	5
NS	Luigi Villoresi	Ferrari	Ferrari D50	tyres	8

Pole: Fangio, 2m46.500s, 134.350mph/216.216kph. Fastest lap: Moss, 2m46.900s, 134.029mph/215.700kph on Lap 21. Race leaders: Fangio 1-7, 9-50; Moss 8

BROOKS WINS IN A BRITISH CAR

Mike Hawthorn became the first British F1 winner in 1953, but little-known Tony Brooks laid down another British marker when he took time off from his dental exams to travel to Sicily to contest the non-championship Syracuse GP. Driving a works Connaught, he beat the works Maseratis for the first grand prix win by a British car.

NEW DRIVERS

Of 1955's nine F1 debutants, Cesare Perdisa landed the best result, third at Monaco when he took over Jean Behra's works Maserati, but Jack Brabham would go on to be the cream of the crop. Brabham's debut in the British GP saw him qualify last in his Cooper, but he went on to become a three-time world champion.

WORLD DRIVERS' CHAMPIONSHIP FINAL RESULTS

Pos	Driver	Nat	Car-Engine	R1	R2	R3	R4	R5	R6	Total
1	Juan Manuel Fangio	ARG	Mercedes W196	1F	RPF	1F	1P	2	1P	40
2	Stirling Moss	GBR	Mercedes W196	4 | R	9	2	2	1PF	RF	23
3	Eugenio Castellotti	ITA	Lancia D50	R	2	RP	-	-	-	12
			Ferrari 555	-	-	-	5	-	3	
			Ferrari 625	-	-	-	-	6 | R	-	
4	Maurice Trintignant	FRA	Ferrari 625	2 | 3 | R	1	-	-	R	-	11.33
			Ferrari 555	-	-	6	R	-	8	
5	Giuseppe Farina	ITA	Ferrari 625	2 | 3	4	-	-	-	-	10.33
			Ferrari 555	-	-	3	-	-	-	
			Ferrari D50	-	-	-	-	-	NS	
6	Piero Taruffi	ITA	Ferrari 555	-	8	-	-	-	-	9
			Mercedes W196	-	-	-	-	4	2	
8	Roberto Mieres	ARG	Maserati 250F	5	R	5	4F	R	7	7
9	Jean Behra	FRA	Maserati 250F	6 | R | R	3 | R	5 | R	6	R	4	6
10	Luigi Musso	ITA	Maserati 250F	7 | R	R	7	3	5	R	6
11	Karl Kling	DEU	Mercedes W196	4 | R	-	R	R	3	R	5
15	Paul Frere	BEL	Ferrari 555	-	8	4	-	-	-	3
17	Jose Froilan Gonzalez	ARG	Ferrari 625	2P	-	-	-	-	-	2
18	Cesare Perdisa	ITA	Maserati 250F	-	3 | R	8	-	-	-	2
19	Luigi Villoresi	ITA	Lancia D50	R | R	5	-	-	-	-	2
			Ferrari D50	-	-	-	-	-	NS	
19	Carlos Menditeguy	ARG	Maserati 250F	R | R	-	-	-	-	5	2
21	Umberto Maglioli	ITA	Ferrari 625	3	-	-	-	-	-	1.33
			Ferrari 555	-	-	-	-	-	6	
22	Hans Herrmann	DEU	Mercedes W196	4	NS	-	-	-	-	1

SYMBOLS AND GRAND PRIX KEY

Round 1 Argentinian GP
Round 2 Monaco GP
Round 3 Belgian GP
Round 4 Dutch GP
Round 5 British GP
Round 6 Italian GP

Indianapolis 500 results not included

SCORING

1st 8 points
2nd 6 points
3rd 4 points
4th 3 points
5th 2 points
Fastest lap 1 point

DNPQ DID NOT PRE-QUALIFY **DNQ** DID NOT QUALIFY **DQ** DISQUALIFIED **EX** EXCLUDED
F FASTEST LAP **NC** NOT CLASSIFIED **NS** NON-STARTER **P** POLE POSITION **R** RETIRED

1956

SEASON SUMMARY

With Mercedes and Lancia gone, this proved to be Ferrari's year, as it abandoned its largely unsuccessful 1955 cars and concentrated on developing the more competitive D50s that Lancia left behind. Left without a drive, Juan Manuel Fangio headed to Ferrari, while Stirling Moss went to Maserati, the drivers winning the first and second grands prix, respectively. However, over the course of the seven rounds, it was Fangio who pulled ahead. But the title would have gone to Fangio's Ferrari team-mate Peter Collins – he won two rounds, but he gave up his title shot at the Monza finale, having handed his car over to Fangio, whose own D50 had failed.

ARGENTINIAN GRAND PRIX

BUENOS AIRES • ROUND 1 • DATE: 22ND JANUARY 1956
Laps: 98 • Distance: 238.243miles/383.415km • Weather: Warm but dull

Pos	Driver	Team	Chassis-Engine	Result	Qual
1	Musso / Fangio*	Ferrari	Ferrari D50	3h00m03.700s	3
2	Jean Behra	Maserati	Maserati 250F	3h00m28.100s	4
3	Mike Hawthorn	BRM	Maserati 250F	96 laps	8
4	Landi / Gerini*	Maserati	Maserati 250F	92 laps	11
5	Olivier Gendebien	Ferrari	Ferrari 555	91 laps	10
6	Uria / Gonzalez*	Alberto Uria	Maserati A6GCM	88 laps	13
R	Stirling Moss	Maserati	Maserati 250F	81 laps/engine	7
R	Peter Collins	Ferrari	Ferrari 555	58 laps/accident	9
R	Luigi Piotti	Maserati	Maserati 250F	57 laps/accident	12
R	Carlos Menditeguy	Maserati	Maserati 250F	42 laps/halfshaft	6
R	Eugenio Castellotti	Ferrari	Ferrari D50	40 laps/gearbox	2
R	Jose Froilan Gonzalez	Maserati	Maserati 250F	24 laps/engine	5
R	Juan Manuel Fangio	Ferrari	Ferrari D50	22 laps/fuel pump	1

*Luigi Musso, Juan Manuel Fangio, Chico Landi, Gerino Gerini, Alberto Uria, Oscar Gonzalez

Pole: Fangio, 1m42.500s, 85.383mph/137.411kph. Fastest lap: Fangio, 1m45.300s, 83.112mph/133.757kph on Lap 42. Race leaders: Gonzalez 1-3; Menditeguy 4-42; Moss 43-66; Fangio 67-98

FANGIO'S OFF DAY

Fangio seldom put a wheel wrong throughout his illustrious career, but the 1956 Monaco GP was one such day. He disliked the handling of the Lancia-Ferrari and spun at Ste Devote on lap two. He then clattered kerbs as he fought back from fifth, before taking over Peter Collins's less damaged car and closing to within six seconds of winner Moss.

MONACO GRAND PRIX

MONTE CARLO • ROUND 2 • DATE: 13TH MAY 1956
Laps: 100 • Distance: 195.113miles/314.5km • Weather: Warm & bright

Pos	Driver	Team	Chassis-Engine	Result	Qual
1	Stirling Moss	Maserati	Maserati 250F	3h00m32.900s	2
2	Collins / Fangio*	Ferrari	Ferrari D50	3h00m39.000s	9
3	Jean Behra	Maserati	Maserati 250F	99 laps	4
4	Fangio / Castellotti*	Ferrari	Ferrari D50	94 laps	1
5	Nano da Silva Ramos	Gordini	Gordini T16	93 laps	12
6	Bayol / Pilette*	Gordini	Gordini T32	88 laps	11
7	Perdisa / Moss*	Maserati	Maserati 250F	86 laps	7
8	Horace Gould	Goulds Garage	Maserati 250F	85 laps	14
R	Robert Manzon	Gordini	Gordini T16	90 laps/accident	12
R	Louis Rosier	Ecurie Rosier	Maserati 250F	72 laps/engine	15
R	Eugenio Castellotti	Ferrari	Ferrari D50	14 laps/clutch	3
R	Maurice Trintignant	Vanwall	Vanwall	13 laps/overheating	6
R	Harry Schell	Vanwall	Vanwall	2 laps/accident	5
R	Luigi Musso	Ferrari	Ferrari D50	2 laps/accident	8
NS	Mike Hawthorn	BRM	BRM P25	engine	10
NS	Tony Brooks	BRM	BRM P25	valve	13
NS	Louis Chiron	Scuderia Centro Sud	Maserati 250F	engine	-
DNQ	Giorgio Scarlatti	Giorgio Scarlatti	Ferrari 500	-	17

*Peter Collins, Juan Manuel Fangio, Eugenio Castellotti, Elie Bayol, Andre Pilette, Cesare Perdisa, Stirling Moss

Pole: Fangio, 1m44.000s, 67.645mph/108.865kph. Fastest lap: Collins, 1m44.400s, 67.386mph/108.448kph on Lap 100. Race leaders: Moss 1-100

TWO IN A ROW FOR COLLINS

Frustrated waiting for BRM to become competitive, Peter Collins made himself a title contender in his first campaign with Ferrari. He lapped up every bit of advice that team leader Juan Manuel Fangio could offer and, after second place at Monaco, he grabbed wins in the Belgian and French GPs at Spa-Francorchamps and Reims.

F1'S DISABLED TRAILBLAZER

Archie Scott-Brown was an amazing driver, and even more so considering his disabilities. Born with deformed legs and feet as well as a misshapen right arm, he was short in stature but determined. The Scot finished second in the non-championship International Trophy and qualified 10th for the British GP for Connaught.

BELGIAN GRAND PRIX

SPA-FRANCORCHAMPS • ROUND 3 • DATE: 3RD JUNE 1956
Laps: 36 • Distance: 315.676miles/508.32km • Weather: Warm & damp, then drying

Pos	Driver	Team	Chassis-Engine	Result	Qual
1	Peter Collins	Ferrari	Ferrari D50	2h40m00.300s	3
2	Paul Frere	Ferrari	Ferrari D50	2h41m51.600s	8
3	Perdisa / Moss*	Maserati	Maserati 250F	2h43m16.900s	9
4	Harry Schell	Vanwall	Vanwall	35 laps	6
5	Luigi Villoresi	Scuderia Centro Sud	Maserati 250F	34 laps	11
6	Andre Pilette	Ferrari	Ferrari D50	33 laps	16
7	Jean Behra	Maserati	Maserati 250F	33 laps	4
8	Louis Rosier	Ecurie Rosier	Maserati 250F	33 laps	10
R	Juan Manuel Fangio	Ferrari	Ferrari D50	23 laps/transmission	1
R	Maurice Trintignant	Vanwall	Vanwall	11 laps/fuel system	7
R	Stirling Moss	Maserati	Maserati 250F	10 laps/wheel	2
R	Eugenio Castellotti	Ferrari	Ferrari D50	10 laps/transmission	5
R	Piero Scotti	P Scotti	Connaught-Alta B	10 laps/engine	12
R	Horace Gould	H H Gould	Maserati 250F	2 laps/gearbox	15
R	Chico Godia-Sales	Maserati	Maserati 250F	0 laps/accident	14
NS	Mike Hawthorn	Maserati	Maserati 250F	-	13

*Cesare Perdisa, Stirling Moss

Pole: Fangio, 4m09.800s, 126.442mph/203.490kph. Fastest lap: Moss, 4m14.700s, 124.010mph/199.575kph on Lap 30. Race leaders: Moss 1-4; Fangio 5-23; Collins 24-36

BRINGING BRM BACK

BRM's World Championship return was brought about by industrialist Alfred Owen, who put his clout behind the outfit in 1952. But it took until 1956 for the Owen Racing Organisation to field a car of its own after running a Maserati. Three P25s entered the British GP, with Mike Hawthorn qualifying third, but all retired. Things would improve.

FRENCH GRAND PRIX

REIMS • ROUND 4 • DATE: 1ST JULY 1956
Laps: 61 • Distance: 314.676miles/506.422km • Weather: Warm but dull

Pos	Driver	Team	Chassis-Engine	Result	Qual
1	Peter Collins	Ferrari	Ferrari D50	2h34m23.400s	3
2	Eugenio Castellotti	Ferrari	Ferrari D50	2h34m23.700s	2
3	Jean Behra	Maserati	Maserati 250F	2h35m53.300s	7
4	Juan Manuel Fangio	Ferrari	Ferrari D50	2h35m58.500s	1
5	Perdisa / Moss*	Maserati	Maserati 250F	59 laps	13
6	Louis Rosier	Ecurie Rosier	Maserati 250F	58 laps	12
7	Chico Godia-Sales	Maserati	Maserati 250F	57 laps	17
8	Nano da Silva Ramos	Gordini	Gordini T32	57 laps	14
9	Robert Manzon	Gordini	Gordini T32	56 laps	15
10	Hawthorn / Schell*	Vanwall	Vanwall	56 laps	6
11	Andre Pilette	Gordini	Gordini T16	55 laps	19
R	Andre Simon	A Simon	Maserati 250F	41 laps/engine	20

Pos	Driver	Team	Chassis-Engine	Result	Qual
R	Piero Taruffi	Maserati	Maserati 250F	40 laps/engine	16
R	Olivier Gendebien	Ferrari	Ferrari D50	38 laps/clutch	11
R	Luigi Villoresi	Luigi Piotti	Maserati 250F	23 laps/brakes	10
R	Alfonso de Portago	Ferrari	Ferrari D50	20 laps/gearbox	9
R	Maurice Trintignant	Bugatti	Bugatti T251	18 laps/throttle	18
R	Stirling Moss	Maserati	Maserati 250F	12 laps/gearbox	8
R	Harry Schell	Vanwall	Vanwall	5 laps/engine	4
NS	Colin Chapman	Vanwall	Vanwall	accident	5

*Cesare Perdisa, Stirling Moss, Mike Hawthorn, Harry Schell

Pole: Fangio, 2m23.300s, 129.595mph/208.563kph. Fastest lap: Fangio, 2m25.800s, 127.381mph/205.000kph on Lap 61. Race leaders: Collins 1, 47-48, 50-61; Castellotti 2-3, 39-46, 49; Fangio 4-38

A FRENCH ENIGMA

Jean Behra was fast but often furious. Although 1956 was his best year, as he ranked fourth after finishing second in Argentina, then adding a quartet of third places in his works Maserati, he had to race as number two to Moss. In later years, his fierce temper would lead to him punching the Ferrari team manager.

BRITISH GRAND PRIX

SILVERSTONE • ROUND 5 • DATE: 14TH JULY 1956
Laps: 101 • Distance: 295.623miles/475.760km • Weather: Warm but dull

Pos	Driver	Team	Chassis-Engine	Result	Qual
1	Juan Manuel Fangio	Ferrari	Ferrari D50	2h59m47.000s	2
2	de Portago / Collins*	Ferrari	Ferrari D50	100 laps	12
3	Jean Behra	Maserati	Maserati 250F	99 laps	13
4	Jack Fairman	Connaught	Connaught-Alta B	98 laps	21
5	Horace Gould	Goulds Garage	Maserati 250F	97 laps	14
6	Luigi Villoresi	Luigi Piotti	Maserati 250F	96 laps	19
7	Cesare Perdisa	Maserati	Maserati 250F	95 laps	15
8	Chico Godia-Sales	Maserati	Maserati 250F	94 laps	25
9	Robert Manzon	Gordini	Gordini T32	94 laps	18
10	Castellotti / de Portago*	Ferrari	Ferrari D50	92 laps	8
11	Bob Gerard	Bob Gerard	Cooper-Bristol T23	88 laps	22
R	Stirling Moss	Maserati	Maserati 250F	94 laps/axle	1
R	Harry Schell	Vanwall	Vanwall	87 laps/fuel system	5
R	Desmond Titterington	Connaught	Connaught-Alta B	74 laps/engine	11
R	Nano da Silva Ramos	Gordini	Gordini T32	71 laps/axle	26
R	Maurice Trintignant	Vanwall	Vanwall	70 laps/fuel system	16
R	Peter Collins	Ferrari	Ferrari D50	64 laps/fuel pressure	4
R	Roy Salvadori	Gilby Engineering	Maserati 250F	59 laps/fuel system	7
R	Tony Brooks	BRM	BRM P25	39 laps/accident	9
R	Mike Hawthorn	BRM	BRM P25	24 laps/transmission	3
R	Louis Rosier	Ecurie Rosier	Maserati 250F	23 laps/electrical	27
R	Bruce Halford	B Halford	Maserati 250F	22 laps/engine	20
R	Umberto Maglioli	Scuderia Guastalla	Maserati 250F	21 laps/gearbox	24

Pos	Driver	Team	Chassis-Engine	Result	Qual
R	Archie Scott Brown	Connaught	Connaught-Alta B	16 laps/lost wheel	10
R	Paul Emery	Emeryson	Emeryson-Alta Emeryson	12 laps/ignition	23
R	Jack Brabham	J A Brabham	Maserati 250F	3 laps/engine	28
R	Ron Flockhart	BRM	BRM P25	2 laps/engine	17
R	Jose Froilan Gonzalez	Vanwall	Vanwall	0 laps/transmission	6

*Alfonso de Portago, Peter Collins, Eugenio Castellotti

Pole: Moss, 1m41.000s, 104.327mph/167.899kph. Fastest lap: Moss, 1m43.200s, 102.091mph/164.300kph on Lap 71. Race leaders: Hawthorn 1-15; Moss 16-68; Fangio 69-101

BUGATTI'S WOEFUL ONE-OFF

Bugatti had been famous pre-war with its beautiful and successful Type 35, but this time around, its Type 251 offering was both ugly and slow, and Maurice Trintignant could do nothing to help it fly when it turned up for the French GP at Reims. Its transversely mounted engine might have been a good idea in terms of balance, but it lacked power.

GIANT TRACKS 1: THE NURBURGRING

The Nurburgring was already an outlier by the time it hosted its first World Championship round in 1951, as its lap was a gargantuan 14.167 miles (22.799km), while the other rounds were held on tracks with lap distances of between 2.889 miles (4.649km) (Silverstone) and 8.774 miles (14.119km) (Spa-Francorchamps).

GERMAN GRAND PRIX

NURBURGRING • ROUND 6 • DATE: 5TH AUGUST 1956
Laps: 22 • Distance: 311.357miles/501.82km • Weather: Warm & bright

Pos	Driver	Team	Chassis-Engine	Result	Qual
1	Juan Manuel Fangio	Ferrari	Ferrari D50	3h38m43.700s	1
2	Stirling Moss	Maserati	Maserati 250F	3h39m30.100s	4
3	Jean Behra	Maserati	Maserati 250F	3h46m22.000s	8
4	Chico Godia-Sales	Maserati	Maserati 250F	20 laps	16
5	Louis Rosier	Ecurie Rosier	Maserati 250F	19 laps	14
DQ	Bruce Halford	B Halford	Maserati 250F	20 laps/push start	11
NC	Ottorino Volonterio	Ottorino Volonterio	Maserati A6GCM	16 laps/not classified	19
R	Andre Milhoux	Gordini	Gordini T32	15 laps/accident	21
R	de Portago / Collins*	Ferrari	Ferrari D50	14 laps/accident	10
R	Harry Schell	Scuderia Centro Sud	Maserati 250F	13 laps/overheating	12
R	Luigi Villoresi	Luigi Piotti	Maserati 250F	13 laps/engine	20
R	Musso / Castellotti*	Ferrari	Ferrari D50	11 laps/accident	5
R	Peter Collins	Ferrari	Ferrari D50	8 laps/oil leak	2
R	Eugenio Castellotti	Ferrari	Ferrari D50	5 laps/electrical	3
R	Horace Gould	Goulds Garage	Maserati 250F	3 laps/fuel pressure	13
R	Umberto Maglioli	Maserati	Maserati 250F	3 laps/accident	7
R	Roy Salvadori	Gilby Engineering	Maserati 250F	2 laps/suspension	9

Pos	Driver	Team	Chassis-Engine	Result	Qual
R	Robert Manzon	Gordini	Gordini T32	0 laps/suspension	15
R	Giorgio Scarlatti	Scuderia Centro Sud	Ferrari 500	0 laps/engine	17
NS	Cesare Perdisa	Maserati	Maserati 250F	accident	6
NS	Andre Pilette	Gordini	Gordini T32	accident	18
NS	Luigi Piotti	Luigi Piotti	Maserati 250F	Villoresi drove car	-

*Alfonso de Portago, Peter Collins, Luigi Musso, Eugenio Castellotti

Pole: Fangio, 9m59.200s, 85.154mph/137.042kph. Fastest lap: Fangio, 9m41.600s, 87.737mph/141.200kph on Lap 14. Race leaders: Fangio 1-22

NEW CONSTRUCTORS

Two constructors made their F1 bow in 1956: Bugatti and Emeryson. Bugatti's travails are told separately, but Emeryson fared little better. The British constructor's car was designed in 1953 for when the World Championship was run to F2 rules and, although upgraded to run with a 2.5-litre Alta engine, it was 13 seconds off the pace at Silverstone.

NEW DRIVERS

There were 17 new F1 drivers in 1956, including Lotus boss Colin Chapman, who did not start at Reims. Jo Bonnier, Tony Brooks and Wolfgang von Trips would all go on to become grand prix winners, while Eugenio Castellotti would immediately claim a second place at Monaco, a result matched by Alfonso de Portago at Silverstone.

ITALIAN GRAND PRIX

MONZA • ROUND 7 • DATE: 2ND SEPTEMBER 1956
Laps: 50 • Distance: 310.685miles/500.0km • Weather: Warm with showers

Pos	Driver	Team	Chassis-Engine	Result	Qual
1	Stirling Moss	Maserati	Maserati 250F	2h23m41.300s	6
2	Collins / Fangio*	Ferrari	Ferrari D50	2h23m47.000s	7
3	Ron Flockhart	Connaught	Connaught-Alta B	49 laps	24
4	Chico Godia-Sales	Maserati	Maserati 250F	49 laps	18
5	Jack Fairman	Connaught	Connaught-Alta B	47 laps	16
6	Luigi Piotti	Luigi Piotti	Maserati 250F	47 laps	15
7	Emmanuel de Graffenried	Scuderia Centro Sud	Maserati 250F	46 laps	19
8	Fangio / Castellotti*	Ferrari	Ferrari D50	46 laps	1
9	Andre Simon	Gordini	Gordini T16	45 laps	25
10	Gerino Gerini	Scuderia Guastalla	Maserati 250F	42 laps	17
11	Roy Salvadori	Gilby Engineering	Maserati 250F	41 laps	14
R	Luigi Musso	Ferrari	Ferrari D50	47 laps/steering	3
R	Maglioli / Behra*	Maserati	Maserati 250F	42 laps/steering	13
R	Harry Schell	Vanwall	Vanwall	32 laps/transmission	10

Pos	Driver	Team	Chassis-Engine	Result	Qual
R	Jean Behra	Maserati	Maserati 250F	23 laps/magneto	5
R	Bruce Halford	B Halford	Maserati 250F	16 laps/engine	22
R	Maurice Trintignant	Vanwall	Vanwall	13 laps/transmission	11
R	Piero Taruffi	Vanwall	Vanwall	12 laps/oil leak	4
R	Eugenio Castellotti	Ferrari	Ferrari D50	9 laps/tyre	2
R	Villoresi / Bonnier*	Maserati	Maserati 250F	7 laps/engine	8
R	Robert Manzon	Gordini	Gordini T32	7 laps/chassis	23
R	Alfonso de Portago	Ferrari	Ferrari D50	6 laps/puncture	9
R	Les Leston	Connaught	Connaught-Alta B	6 laps/suspension	20
R	Nano da Silva Ramos	Gordini	Gordini T32	3 laps/engine	21
NS	Wolfgang von Trips	Ferrari	Ferrari D50	-	12

*Peter Collins, Juan Manuel Fangio, Eugenio Castellotti, Umberto Maglioli, Jean Behra, Luigi Villoresi, Jo Bonnier

Pole: Fangio, 2m42.600s, 137.572mph/221.402kph. Fastest lap: Moss, 2m45.500s, 135.162mph/217.522kph on Lap 47. Race leaders: Castellotti 1-4; Moss 5-10, 12-45, 48-50; Schell 11; Musso 46-47

IN MEMORIAM

With the rate of fatalities always high, it was a relief (of sorts) when only one of the F1 flock was killed in 1956. This was Louis Rosier, who entered his own Maserati 250F, but he had become steady rather than rapid as he hit his 50s. Fifth place at the German GP was a decent return, but then he overturned his Ferrari in a sports car race at Montlhery.

WORLD DRIVERS' CHAMPIONSHIP FINAL RESULTS

Pos	Driver	Nat	Car-Engine	R1	R2	R3	R4	R5	R6	R7	Total
1	Juan Manuel Fangio	ARG	Ferrari D50	1F|RP	2F|4P	RP	4PF	1	1PF	2|8P	30
2	Stirling Moss	GBR	Maserati 250F	R	1	3F|R	5|R	RPF	2	1F	27
3	Peter Collins	GBR	Ferrari 555	R	-	-	-	-	-	-	25
			Ferrari D50	-	2F	1	1	2|R	R|R	2	
4	Jean Behra	FRA	Maserati 250F	2	3	7	3	3	3	R|R	22
6	Eugenio Castellotti	ITA	Ferrari D50	R	4|R	R	2	10	R|R	8|R	7.5
7	Paul Frere	BEL	Ferrari D50	-	-	2	-	-	-	-	6
9	Chico Godia-Sales	ESP	Maserati 250F	-	-	R	7	8	4	4	6
10	Jack Fairman	GBR	Connaught-Alta B	-	-	-	-	4	-	5	5
11	Luigi Musso	ITA	Ferrari D50	1|R	R	-	-	-	R	R	4
12	Mike Hawthorn	GBR	Maserati 250F	3	-	NS	-	-	-	-	4
			BRM P25	-	NS	-	-	R	-	-	
			Vanwall	-	-	-	10	-	-	-	
12	Ron Flockhart	GBR	BRM P25	-	-	-	-	R	-	-	4
			Connaught-Alta B	-	-	-	-	-	-	3	
15	Alfonso de Portago	ESP	Ferrari D50	-	-	-	R	2|10	R	R	3
16	Cesare Perdisa	ITA	Maserati 250F	-	7	3	5	7	NS	-	3
17	Harry Schell	USA	Vanwall	-	R	4	10|R	R	-	R	3
			Maserati 250F	-	-	-	-	-	R	-	
19	Olivier Gendebien	BEL	Ferrari 555	5	-	-	-	-	-	-	2
			Ferrari D50	-	-	-	R	-	-	-	
19	Nano da Silva Ramos	BRA	Gordini T16	-	5	-	-	-	-	-	2
			Gordini T32	-	-	-	8	R	-	R	
19	Luigi Villoresi	ITA	Maserati 250F	-	-	5	R	6	R	R	2
19	Horace Gould	GBR	Maserati 250F	-	8	R	-	5	R	-	2
19	Louis Rosier	FRA	Maserati 250F	-	R	8	6	R	5	-	2
25	Chico Landi	BRA	Maserati 250F	4	-	-	-	-	-	-	1.5
25	Gerino Gerini	ITA	Maserati 250F	4	-	-	-	-	-	10	1.5

SYMBOLS AND GRAND PRIX KEY

Round 1 Argentinian GP
Round 2 Monaco GP
Round 3 Belgian GP
Round 4 French GP
Round 5 British GP
Round 6 German GP
Round 7 Italian GP

Indianapolis 500 results not included

SCORING

1st 8 points
2nd 3 points
3rd 4 points
4th 3 points
5th 2 points
Fastest lap 1 point

DNPQ DID NOT PRE-QUALIFY **DNQ** DID NOT QUALIFY **DQ** DISQUALIFIED **EX** EXCLUDED
F FASTEST LAP **NC** NOT CLASSIFIED **NS** NON-STARTER **P** POLE POSITION **R** RETIRED

1957

SEASON SUMMARY

Juan Manuel Fangio claimed a then-record fifth F1 title, this time with Maserati, after tiring of the politics within the Ferrari camp. And he did it in imperious fashion. After a one-two-three finish for Maserati in the opening race, the writing was on the wall, especially when Fangio won the next two races. However, Vanwall led the first serious British push for gold, with Stirling Moss leading its challenge as it became the first British team to win a World Championship round. Then Ferrari upped its game too, but Fangio's consistency meant that the Argentinian took what would be his final title at the age of 46.

ARGENTINIAN GRAND PRIX

BUENOS AIRES • ROUND 1 • DATE: 13TH JANUARY 1957
Laps: 100 • Distance: 242.971miles/391.24km • Weather: Hot & bright

Pos	Driver	Team	Chassis-Engine	Result	Qual
1	Juan Manuel Fangio	Maserati	Maserati 250F	3h00m55.900s	2
2	Jean Behra	Maserati	Maserati 250F	3h01m14.200s	3
3	Carlos Menditeguy	Maserati	Maserati 250F	99 laps	8
4	Harry Schell	Scuderia Centro Sud	Maserati 250F	98 laps	9
5	Gonzalez / de Portago*	Ferrari	Ferrari D50	98 laps	10
6	Perdisa / Collins / von Trips*	Ferrari	Ferrari D50	98 laps	11
7	Jo Bonnier	Scuderia Centro Sud	Maserati 250F	95 laps	13
8	Stirling Moss	Maserati	Maserati 250F	93 laps	1
9	Alessandro de Tomaso	Scuderia Centro Sud	Ferrari 500	91 laps	12
10	Luigi Piotti	Luigi Piotti	Maserati 250F	90 laps	14
R	Eugenio Castellotti	Ferrari	Ferrari D50	75 laps/hub shaft	4
R	Mike Hawthorn	Ferrari	Ferrari D50	35 laps/clutch	7
R	Luigi Musso	Ferrari	Ferrari D50	31 laps/clutch	6
R	Peter Collins	Ferrari	Ferrari D50	26 laps/clutch	5

*Jose Froilan Gonzalez, Alfonso de Portago, Cesare Perdisa, Peter Collins, Wolfgang von Trips

Pole: Moss, 1m42.600s, 85.300mph/137.277kph. Fastest lap: Moss, 1m44.700s, 83.589mph/134.523kph on Lap 75. Race leaders: Behra 1-2, 9-12, 81, 84; Castelotti 3-8; Collins 13-25; Fangio 26-80, 82-83, 85-100

MOSS LEADS WAY FOR VANWALL

Just as Fangio joined Maserati, so Moss left Maserati to join Vanwall. Tired of BRM's failings, Tony Vandervell formed his own team and it advanced swiftly from its debut in 1954 – its sleek cars became consistent frontrunners. Tony Brooks came second at Monaco, then he and Moss shared victory at Aintree before Moss won alone at Pescara to rank second.

SHARED WINS

The results of the British GP at Aintree show that it was shared by Brooks and Moss, and this was because of Moss retiring his car and Brooks, still recuperating from burns suffered at Le Mans, handing his over. This was still the case in the mid- to late 1950s, when a lead driver was delayed or broke down, and signals from the pits made another car available. Shared drives did not receive points from 1958.

MONACO GRAND PRIX

MONTE CARLO • ROUND 2 • DATE: 19TH MAY 1957
Laps: 105 • Distance: 205.192miles/330.225km • Weather: Warm & bright

Pos	Driver	Team	Chassis-Engine	Result	Qual
1	Juan Manuel Fangio	Maserati	Maserati 250F	3h10m12.800s	1
2	Tony Brooks	Vanwall	Vanwall	3h10m38.000s	4
3	Masten Gregory	Scuderia Centro Sud	Maserati 250F	103 laps	10
4	Stuart Lewis-Evans	Connaught	Connaught-Alta B	102 laps	13
5	Maurice Trintignant	Ferrari	Ferrari D50	100 laps	6
6	Jack Brabham	Cooper	Cooper-Climax T43	100 laps	15
R	von Trips / Hawthorn*	Ferrari	Ferrari D50	95 laps/engine	9
R	Scarlatti / Schell*	Maserati	Maserati 250F	64 laps/oil leak	14
R	Ron Flockhart	BRM	BRM P25	60 laps/engine	11
R	Carlos Menditeguy	Maserati	Maserati 250F	51 laps/spun off	7
R	Ivor Bueb	Connaught	Connaught-Alta B	47 laps/oil leak	16
R	Harry Schell	Maserati	Maserati 250F	23 laps/suspension	8
R	Horace Gould	H H Gould	Maserati 250F	10 laps/accident	12
R	Peter Collins	Ferrari	Ferrari D50	4 laps/accident	2
R	Stirling Moss	Vanwall	Vanwall	4 laps/accident	3
R	Mike Hawthorn	Ferrari	Ferrari D50	4 laps/accident	5
DNQ	Roy Salvadori	BRM	BRM P25	-	17
DNQ	Hans Herrmann	Maserati	Maserati 250F	-	18
DNQ	Andre Simon	Scuderia Centro Sud	Maserati 250F	-	19
DNQ	Luigi Piotti	Luigi Piotti	Maserati 250F	-	20
DNQ	Les Leston	Cooper	Cooper-Climax T43	-	21

*Wolfgang von Trips, Mike Hawthorn, Giorgio Scarlatti, Harry Schell

Pole: Fangio, 1m42.700s, 68.501mph/110.243kph. Fastest lap: Fangio, 1m45.600s, 66.620mph/107.215kph on Lap 44. Race leaders: Moss 1-4; Fangio 5-105

ROUEN GROWS LONGER

The Rouen-les-Essarts circuit was already a tough challenge, but for the 1957 French GP it offered an extra 0.9 miles (1.4km) on each lap, extending the track to 4.065 miles (6.541km), thanks to a longer loop at its upper end. Looked at another way, it meant that the downhill sweep through the fearsome Virage des Six Freres didn't come around quite as often...

FRENCH GRAND PRIX

ROUEN-LES-ESSARTS • ROUND 3 • DATE: 7TH JULY 1957
Laps: 77 • Distance: 313.5miles/503.734km • Weather: Very hot & bright

Pos	Driver	Team	Chassis-Engine	Result	Qual
1	Juan Manuel Fangio	Maserati	Maserati 250F	3h07m46.400s	1
2	Luigi Musso	Ferrari	Ferrari D50	3h08m37.200s	3
3	Peter Collins	Ferrari	Ferrari D50	3h09m52.400s	5
4	Mike Hawthorn	Ferrari	Ferrari D50	76 laps	7
5	Harry Schell	Maserati	Maserati 250F	70 laps	4
6	Jean Behra	Maserati	Maserati 250F	69 laps	2
7	MacDowel / Brabham*	Cooper	Cooper-Climax T43	68 laps	15
R	Carlos Menditeguy	Maserati	Maserati 250F	30 laps/engine	9
R	Stuart Lewis-Evans	Vanwall	Vanwall	30 laps/steering	10
R	Roy Salvadori	Vanwall	Vanwall	25 laps/engine	6
R	Herbert MacKay-Fraser	BRM	BRM P25	24 laps/transmission	12
R	Maurice Trintignant	Ferrari	Ferrari D50	23 laps/electrical	8
R	Jack Brabham	Cooper	Cooper-Climax T43	4 laps/accident	13
R	Horace Gould	H H Gould	Maserati 250F	4 laps/halfshaft	14
R	Ron Flockhart	BRM	BRM P25	2 laps/accident	11

*Mike MacDowel, Jack Brabham

Pole: Fangio, 2m21.500s, 103.420mph/166.439kph. Fastest lap: Musso, 2m22.400s, 102.774mph/165.400kph on Lap 65. Race leaders: Musso 1-3; Fangio 4-77

FANGIO'S AMAZING PURSUIT

Fangio's victory in the 1957 German GP is still talked about with awe. He was delayed in the pits, putting the Ferraris of Peter Collins and Mike Hawthorn 50 seconds clear. No one thought he could catch them, but Fangio drove way beyond his comfort level and hunted them down with two laps to go, to win and clinch his fifth title. He said afterwards that the thought of it still made him fearful.

BRITISH GRAND PRIX

AINTREE • ROUND 4 • DATE: 20TH JULY 1957
Laps: 90 • Distance: 269.707miles/434.52km • Weather: Warm but dull

Pos	Driver	Team	Chassis-Engine	Result	Qual
1	Brooks / Moss*	Vanwall	Vanwall	3h06m37.800s	3
2	Luigi Musso	Ferrari	Ferrari D50	3h07m03.400s	10
3	Mike Hawthorn	Ferrari	Ferrari D50	3h07m20.600s	5
4	Trintignant / Collins*	Ferrari	Ferrari D50	88 laps	9
5	Roy Salvadori	Cooper	Cooper-Climax T43	85 laps	15
6	Bob Gerard	Bob Gerard	Cooper-Bristol T44	82 laps	18
7	Stuart Lewis-Evans	Vanwall	Vanwall	82 laps	6
8	Ivor Bueb	Gilby Engineering	Maserati 250F	71 laps	19
R	Jack Brabham	Rob Walker Racing Team	Cooper-Climax T43	74 laps/clutch	13
R	Jean Behra	Maserati	Maserati 250F	69 laps/clutch	2
R	Peter Collins	Ferrari	Ferrari D50	53 laps/water leak	8
R	Moss / Brooks*	Vanwall	Vanwall	51 laps/engine	1

Pos	Driver	Team	Chassis-Engine	Result	Qual
R	Juan Manuel Fangio	Maserati	Maserati 250F	49 laps/engine	4
R	Jack Fairman	BRM	BRM P25	46 laps/engine	16
R	Les Leston	BRM	BRM P25	44 laps/engine	12
R	Harry Schell	Maserati	Maserati 250F	39 laps/water pump	7
R	Carlos Menditeguy	Maserati	Maserati 250F	35 laps/transmission	11
R	Jo Bonnier	Ecurie Bonnier	Maserati 250F	18 laps/gearbox	17
NS	Horace Gould	H H Gould	Maserati 250F	accident	14

*Tony Brooks, Stirling Moss, Maurice Trintignant, Peter Collins

Pole: Moss, 2m00.200s, 89.849mph/144.599kph. Fastest lap: Moss, 1m59.200s, 90.595mph/145.800kph. Race leaders: Moss 1-22, 70-90; Behra 23-69

NEW CONSTRUCTORS

Think Porsche, and motor racing fans think of its huge success in the Le Mans 24 Hours. However, just as it started in sports car racing, it also tried F1. This wasn't the full works entry that would follow in 1960, but two full-bodied cars and one run by a privateer, in the F2 sub-class of the German GP. Edgar Barth won the class, but was only 12th overall.

NO WINS FOR FERRARI

Ferrari took its maiden win in a World Championship grand prix in 1951, dominated in 1952 and 1953, then won again in each of the following years. Then the team drew a blank in 1957, as its Lancia-Ferrari D50s, now racing as Ferrari 801s, were three years old. Pressure within the camp meant the drivers would have an all-new car for 1958.

GERMAN GRAND PRIX

NURBURGRING • ROUND 5 • DATE: 4TH AUGUST 1957
Laps: 22 • Distance: 311.357miles/501.82km • Weather: Hot & bright

Pos	Driver	Team	Chassis-Engine	Result	Qual
1	Juan Manuel Fangio	Maserati	Maserati 250F	3h30m38.300s	1
2	Mike Hawthorn	Ferrari	Ferrari D50	3h30m41.900s	2
3	Peter Collins	Ferrari	Ferrari D50	3h31m13.900s	4
4	Luigi Musso	Ferrari	Ferrari D50	3h34m15.900s	8
5	Stirling Moss	Vanwall	Vanwall	3h35m15.500s	7
6	Jean Behra	Maserati	Maserati 250F	3h35m16.800s	3
7	Harry Schell	Maserati	Maserati 250F	3h37m25.800s	6
8	Masten Gregory	Scuderia Centro Sud	Maserati 250F	21 laps	10
9	Tony Brooks	Vanwall	Vanwall	21 laps	5
10	Giorgio Scarlatti	Maserati	Maserati 250F	21 laps	13
11	Bruce Halford	B Halford	Maserati 250F	21 laps	16
12	Edgar Barth	Porsche	Porsche 550RS	21 laps	12
13	Brian Naylor	J B Naylor	Cooper-Climax T43	20 laps	17

Pos	Driver	Team	Chassis-Engine	Result	Qual
14	Carel Godin de Beaufort	Ecurie Maarsbergen	Porsche 550RS	20 laps	20
15	Tony Marsh	Ridgeway Management	Cooper-Climax T43	17 laps	22
R	Hans Herrmann	Scuderia Centro Sud	Maserati 250F	14 laps/chassis	11
R	Umberto Maglioli	Porsche	Porsche 550RS	13 laps/engine	15
R	Roy Salvadori	Cooper	Cooper-Climax T43	11 laps/suspension	14
R	Chico Godia-Sales	Francisco Godia Sales	Maserati 250F	11 laps/steering	21
R	Stuart Lewis-Evans	Vanwall	Vanwall	10 laps/gearbox	9
R	Jack Brabham	Rob Walker Racing Team	Cooper-Climax T43	6 laps/transmission	18
R	Paul England	Ridgeway Management	Cooper-Climax T41	3 laps/steering	24
R	Dick Gibson	Equipe Prideaux/Dick Gibson	Cooper-Climax T43	3 laps/steering	24
R	Horace Gould	H H Gould	Maserati 250F	2 laps/crown wheel	19

Pole: Fangio, 9m25.600s, 90.213mph/145.183kph. Fastest lap: Fangio, 9m17.400s, 91.527mph/147.300kph on Lap 20. Race leaders: Hawthorn 1-2, 15-20; Fangio 3-11, 21-22; Collins 12-14

GIANT TRACKS 2: PESCARA

While the Nurburgring is considered the big one at 14.167 miles (22.799km), its lap length was exceeded in 1957. The Pescara circuit comprised a triangular loop of public roads, with the track rising from the coastline to snake uphill as it went inland beforing returning to the coast on one of two 4-mile (6.4-km) straights. In all, its lap was F1's longest, at 16.032 miles (25.800km).

PESCARA GRAND PRIX

PESCARA • ROUND 6 • DATE: 18TH AUGUST 1957
Laps: 18 • Distance: 286.92miles/460.422km • Weather: Very hot & bright

Pos	Driver	Team	Chassis-Engine	Result	Qual
1	Stirling Moss	Vanwall	Vanwall	2h59m22.700s	2
2	Juan Manuel Fangio	Maserati	Maserati 250F	3h02m36.600s	1
3	Harry Schell	Maserati	Maserati 250F	3h06m09.500s	5
4	Masten Gregory	Scuderia Centro Sud	Maserati 250F	3h07m39.200s	7
5	Stuart Lewis-Evans	Vanwall	Vanwall	17 laps	8
6	Giorgio Scarlatti	Maserati	Maserati 250F	17 laps	10
7	Jack Brabham	Cooper	Cooper-Climax T43	15 laps	16
R	Chico Godia-Sales	Francisco Godia Sales	Maserati 250F	10 laps/engine	12
R	Luigi Musso	Ferrari	Ferrari D50	9 laps/oil leak	3
R	Bruce Halford	B Halford	Maserati 250F	9 laps/transmission	14
R	Jo Bonnier	Scuderia Centro Sud	Maserati 250F	7 laps/overheating	9
R	Jean Behra	Maserati	Maserati 250F	3 laps/oil leak	4
R	Roy Salvadori	Cooper	Cooper-Climax T43	3 laps/accident	15
R	Tony Brooks	Vanwall	Vanwall	1 lap/engine	6
R	Horace Gould	H H Gould	Maserati 250F	1 lap/accident	11
R	Luigi Piotti	Luigi Piotti	Maserati 250F	1 lap/engine	13

Pole: Fangio, 9m44.600s, 97.876mph/157.516kph. Fastest lap: Moss, 9m44.600s, 97.875mph/157.516kph on Lap 9. Race leaders: Musso 1, Moss 2-18

GERMANY'S RISING STAR

German fans found a new star to cheer in 1957 with the emergence of Wolfgang von Trips. After a few outings as Ferrari's fourth driver, "Taffy" made a name for himself at the Italian GP. This marked the day that the aristocrat outlasted the team's stars – Hawthorn, Collins and Luigi Musso – around the combined 6.214-mile (10km) lap that included the banked oval, to finish third.

ITALIAN GRAND PRIX

MONZA • ROUND 7 • DATE: 8TH SEPTEMBER 1957
Laps: 87 • Distance: 310.701miles/500.25km • Weather: Hot & bright

Pos	Driver	Team	Chassis-Engine	Result	Qual
1	Stirling Moss	Vanwall	Vanwall	2h35m03.900s	2
2	Juan Manuel Fangio	Maserati	Maserati 250F	2h35m45.100s	4
3	Wolfgang von Trips	Ferrari	Ferrari D50	85 laps	8
4	Masten Gregory	Scuderia Centro Sud	Maserati 250F	84 laps	11
5	Scarlatti / Schell*	Maserati	Maserati 250F	84 laps	12
6	Mike Hawthorn	Ferrari	Ferrari D50	83 laps	10
7	Tony Brooks	Vanwall	Vanwall	82 laps	3
8	Luigi Musso	Ferrari	Ferrari D50	82 laps	9
9	Chico Godia-Sales	Francisco Godia Sales	Maserati 250F	81 laps	15
10	Horace Gould	H H Gould	Maserati 250F	78 laps	18
11	Simon / Volonterio*	Ottorino Volonterio	Maserati 250F	72 laps	16
R	Peter Collins	Ferrari	Ferrari D50	62 laps/engine	7
R	Jean Behra	Maserati	Maserati 250F	50 laps/overheating	5
R	Stuart Lewis-Evans	Vanwall	Vanwall	49 laps/engine	1
R	Bruce Halford	B Halford	Maserati 250F	47 laps/engine	14
R	Harry Schell	Maserati	Maserati 250F	34 laps/oil leak	6
R	Jo Bonnier	Scuderia Centro Sud	Maserati 250F	31 laps/overheating	13
R	Luigi Piotti	Luigi Piotti	Maserati 250F	3 laps/engine	17

*Giorgio Scarlatti, Harry Schell, Andre Simon, Ottorino Volonterio

Pole: Lewis-Evans, 1m42.400s, 125.609mph/202.148kph. Fastest lap: Brooks, 1m43.700s, 124.034mph/199.614kph on Lap 74. Race leaders: Moss 1-3, 5, 11, 21-87; Behra 4, 6; Fangio 7-10; Brooks 12-15; Lewis-Evans 16-20

IN MEMORIAM

The ranks of drivers were depleted in a series of accidents. Ken Wharton died when he crashed in a pre-season race in New Zealand. Then, before the first round, Ferrari star Eugenio Castellotti was killed when testing. Six weeks later, Alfonso de Portago perished on the Mille Miglia road race, along with co-driver Ed Nelson and 10 spectators.

NEW DRIVERS

Masten Gregory was the most successful F1 newcomer in 1957, kicking off with an astonishing third place in a retirement-strewn Monaco GP in a Scuderia Centro Sud Maserati. He added two fourths to rank sixth. Stuart Lewis-Evans finished fourth at Monaco but the British driver peaked when taking pole for Vanwall at the Italian GP.

WORLD DRIVERS' CHAMPIONSHIP FINAL RESULTS

Pos	Driver	Nat	Car-Engine	R1	R2	R3	R4	R5	R6	R7	Total
1	Juan Manuel Fangio	ARG	Maserati 250F	1	1PF	1P	R	1PF	2P	2	40
2	Stirling Moss	GBR	Maserati 250F	8PF	-	-	-	-	-	-	25
			Vanwall	-	R	-	1F|RP	5	1F	1	
3	Luigi Musso	ITA	Ferrari D50	R	-	2F	2	4	R	8	16
4	Mike Hawthorn	GBR	Ferrari D50	R	R|R	4	3	2	-	6	13
5	Tony Brooks	GBR	Vanwall	-	2	-	1|R	9	R	7F	11
6	Masten Gregory	USA	Maserati 250F	-	3	-	-	8	4	4	10
7	Harry Schell	USA	Maserati 250F	4	R|R	5	R	7	3	5|R	10
9	Peter Collins	GBR	Ferrari D50	6|R	R	3	4|R	3	-	R	8
11	Jean Behra	FRA	Maserati 250F	2	-	6	R	6	R	R	6
12	Maurice Trintignant	FRA	Ferrari D50	-	5	R	4	-	-	-	5
12	Stuart Lewis-Evans	GBR	Connaught-Alta B	-	4	-	-	-	-	-	5
			Vanwall	-	-	R	7	R	5	RP	
14	Carlos Menditeguy	ARG	Maserati 250F	3	R	R	R	-	-	-	4
14	Wolfgang von Trips	DEU	Ferrari D50	6	R	-	-	-	-	3	4
18	Roy Salvadori	GBR	BRM P25 - DNQ	-	-	-	-	-	-	-	2
			Vanwall	-	-	R	-	-	-		
			Cooper-Climax T43	-	-	-	5	R	R	-	
20	Jose Froilan Gonzalez	ARG	Ferrari D50	5	-	-	-	-	-	-	1
20	Alfonso de Portago	ESP	Ferrari D50	5	-	-	-	-	-	-	1
20	Giorgio Scarlatti	ITA	Maserati 250F	-	R	-	-	10	6	5	1

SYMBOLS AND GRAND PRIX KEY

Round 1 **Argentinian GP**
Round 2 **Monaco GP**
Round 3 **French GP**
Round 4 **British GP**
Round 5 **German GP**
Round 6 **Pescara GP**
Round 7 **Italian GP**

Indianapolis 500 results not included

SCORING

1st **8 points**
2nd **6 points**
3rd **4 points**
4th **3 points**
5th **2 points**
Fastest lap **1 point**

DNPQ DID NOT PRE-QUALIFY **DNQ DID NOT QUALIFY** **DQ DISQUALIFIED** **EX EXCLUDED**
F FASTEST LAP **NC NOT CLASSIFIED** **NS NON-STARTER** **P POLE POSITION** **R RETIRED**

1958

SEASON SUMMARY

World Championship seasons began to become longer, moving up from seven to 10 races. This gave time for a narrative to develop, and 1958 stands out as one of F1's most dramatic. The plot: Fangio going into semi-retirement and Ferrari finding form again and having to weather an ever stronger attack from Vanwall. The British team fielded Stirling Moss – again sticking to driving for a British team – the immaculate Tony Brooks, and young charger Stuart Lewis-Evans. Between them, they won six of the races, while Ferrari team leader Mike Hawthorn won just one, but this was enough for him to sneak home as Britain's first world champion.

ARGENTINIAN GRAND PRIX

BUENOS AIRES • ROUND 1 • DATE: 19TH JANUARY 1958
Laps: 80 • Distance: 194.484miles/312.992km • Weather: Warm & bright

Pos	Driver	Team	Chassis-Engine	Result	Qual
1	Stirling Moss	Rob Walker Racing Team	Cooper-Climax T43	2h19m33.700s	7
2	Luigi Musso	Ferrari	Ferrari 246	2h19m36.400s	5
3	Mike Hawthorn	Ferrari	Ferrari 246	2h19m46.300s	2
4	Juan Manuel Fangio	Scuderia Sud Americana	Maserati 250F	2h20m26.700s	1
5	Jean Behra	Ken Kavanagh	Maserati 250F	78 laps	4
6	Harry Schell	Ecurie Bonnier	Maserati 250F	77 laps	8
7	Carlos Menditeguy	Scuderia Sud Americana	Maserati 250F	76 laps	6
8	Chico Godia-Sales	Francisco Godia Sales	Maserati 250F	75 laps	9
9	Horace Gould	H H Gould	Maserati 250F	71 laps	10
R	Peter Collins	Ferrari	Ferrari 246	0 laps/halfshaft	3

Pole: Fangio, 1m42.000s, 85.801mph/138.084kph. Fastest lap: Fangio, 1m41.800s, 85.997mph/138.400kph on Lap 30. Race leaders: Behra 1; Hawthorn 2-9; Fangio 10-34; Moss 35-80

NEW FUEL, LONGER RACES

Special alcohol-based fuels were no longer permitted when commercial fuels were made mandatory for F1 in 1958. Another change, welcomed by the drivers, was the reduction in the length of a grand prix to either 186 miles (300km) or two hours in duration, down from the epics of 1957 – the German GP lasted 3.5 hours.

ENGINES AT THE REAR

The season kicked off with just 10 cars entered for the Argentinian GP. However, it was a landmark race because it was the first one won by a car with its engine behind the driver. Stirling Moss's little Cooper T43 didn't have the pace of Fangio's Maserati, but he reckoned its lighter weight would let it run without a tyre change, and this did the trick.

MONACO GRAND PRIX

MONTE CARLO • ROUND 2 • DATE: 18TH MAY 1958
Laps: 100 • Distance: 195.113miles/314.5km • Weather: Hot & bright

Pos	Driver	Team	Chassis-Engine	Result	Qual
1	Maurice Trintignant	Rob Walker Racing Team	Cooper-Climax T45	2h52m27.900s	5
2	Luigi Musso	Ferrari	Ferrari 246	2h52m48.100s	10
3	Peter Collins	Ferrari	Ferrari 246	2h53m06.700s	9
4	Jack Brabham	Cooper	Cooper-Climax T45	97 laps	3
5	Harry Schell	BRM	BRM P25	91 laps	11
6	Cliff Allison	Lotus	Lotus-Climax 12	87 laps	13
R	Wolfgang von Trips	Ferrari	Ferrari 246	91 laps/engine	12
R	Jo Bonnier	Jo Bonnier	Maserati 250F	71 laps/accident	16
R	Graham Hill	Lotus	Lotus-Climax 12	69 laps/halfshaft	15
R	Roy Salvadori	Cooper	Cooper-Climax T45	56 laps/gearbox	4
R	Mike Hawthorn	Ferrari	Ferrari 246	47 laps/fuel pump	6
R	Stirling Moss	Vanwall	Vanwall	38 laps/engine	8
R	Jean Behra	BRM	BRM P25	29 laps/brakes	2
R	Giorgio Scarlatti	Giorgio Scarlatti	Maserati 250F	28 laps/engine	14
R	Tony Brooks	Vanwall	Vanwall	22 laps/engine	1
R	Stuart Lewis-Evans	Vanwall	Vanwall	11 laps/overheating	7
DNQ	Ron Flockhart	Rob Walker Racing Team	Cooper-Climax T43	-	17
DNQ	Chico Godia-Sales	Francisco Godia Sales	Maserati 250F	-	18
DNQ	Ken Kavanagh	Ken Kavanagh	Maserati 250F	-	19
DNQ	Gerino Gerini	Scuderia Centro Sud	Maserati 250F	-	20
DNQ	Bruce Kessler	B C Ecclestone	Connaught-Alta B	-	21
DNQ	Paul Emery	B C Ecclestone	Connaught-Alta B	-	22
DNQ	Maria Teresa de Filippis	Maria Teresa de Filippis	Maserati 250F	-	23
DNQ	Andre Testut	Andre Testut	Maserati 250F	-	24
DNQ	Giulio Cabianca	OSCA	OSCA	-	25
DNQ	Luigi Piotti	OSCA	OSCA	-	26
DNQ	Horace Gould	Scuderia Centro Sud	Maserati 250F	-	27
DNQ	Bernie Ecclestone	B C Ecclestone	Connaught-Alta B	-	28
DNQ	Luigi Taramazzo	Ken Kavanagh	Maserati 250F	-	-
DNQ	Louis Chiron	Andre Testut	Maserati 250F	-	-

Pole: Brooks, 1m39.800s, 70.492mph/113.446kph. Fastest lap: Hawthorn, 1m40.600s, 69.932mph/112.544kph on Lap 36. Race leaders: Behra 1-27; Hawthorn 28-32, 39-47; Moss 33-38; Trintignant 48-100

CLASSIC CAR: VANWALL

These sleek British Racing Green racers were designed by aerodynamicist Frank Costin, with their chassis and rear suspension penned by Colin Chapman, alongside his work on his own Lotus racers. Powered by Vanwall's own straight-four engines, the Vanwall VW racers first appeared in 1957, but they suffered a relative loss of power in 1958 with the introduction of commercial fuel, down from 285bhp to 260bhp. Fortunately, they were great to drive and the six wins collected by Moss and Brooks gave Vanwall the inaugural F1 constructors' title. However, following Lewis-Evans's death, Tony Vandervell announced the team's withdrawal from a full-time programme.

DUTCH GRAND PRIX

ZANDVOORT • ROUND 3 • DATE: 26TH MAY 1958
Laps: 75 • Distance: 195.405miles/314.475km • Weather: Cool, dull & windy

Pos	Driver	Team	Chassis-Engine	Result	Qual
1	Stirling Moss	Vanwall	Vanwall	2h04m49.200s	2
2	Harry Schell	BRM	BRM P25	2h05m37.100s	7
3	Jean Behra	BRM	BRM P25	2h06m31.500s	4
4	Roy Salvadori	Cooper	Cooper-Climax T45	74 laps	9
5	Mike Hawthorn	Ferrari	Ferrari 246	74 laps	6
6	Cliff Allison	Lotus	Lotus-Climax 12	73 laps	11
7	Luigi Musso	Ferrari	Ferrari 246	73 laps	12
8	Jack Brabham	Cooper	Cooper-Climax T45	73 laps	5
9	Maurice Trintignant	Rob Walker Racing Team	Cooper-Climax T45	72 laps	8
10	Jo Bonnier	Ecurie Bonnier	Maserati 250F	71 laps	15
11	Carel Godin de Beaufort	Ecurie Maarsbergen	Porsche RSK	69 laps	17
R	Giorgio Scarlatti	Giorgio Scarlatti	Maserati 250F	52 laps/halfshaft	16
R	Stuart Lewis-Evans	Vanwall	Vanwall	46 laps/engine	1
R	Graham Hill	Lotus	Lotus-Climax 12	40 laps/overheating	13
R	Peter Collins	Ferrari	Ferrari 246	32 laps/gearbox	10
R	Masten Gregory	H H Gould	Maserati 250F	16 laps/fuel pump	14
R	Tony Brooks	Vanwall	Vanwall	13 laps/halfshaft	3

Pole: Lewis-Evans, 1m37.100s, 96.596mph/155.456kph. Fastest lap: Moss, 1m37.600s, 96.126mph/154.700kph. Race leaders: Moss 1-75

RACING IN AFRICA
Portugal joined the World Championship with a round-the-houses course in Oporto. Complete with cobbled sections and tramlines, it kept the drivers on their toes. Apart from the Argentinian GP, F1 hadn't left Europe until it headed to Morocco for its season finale. The track used was a temporary road course at Ain Diab, outside Casablanca.

BELGIAN GRAND PRIX

SPA-FRANCORCHAMPS • ROUND 4 • DATE: 15TH JUNE 1958
Laps: 24 • Distance: 210.25miles/338.4km • Weather: Very hot & bright

Pos	Driver	Team	Chassis-Engine	Result	Qual
1	Tony Brooks	Vanwall	Vanwall	1h37m06.300s	5
2	Mike Hawthorn	Ferrari	Ferrari 246	1h37m27.000s	1
3	Stuart Lewis-Evans	Vanwall	Vanwall	1h40m07.200s	11
4	Cliff Allison	Lotus	Lotus-Climax 12	1h41m21.800s	12
5	Harry Schell	BRM	BRM P25	23 laps	7
6	Olivier Gendebien	Ferrari	Ferrari 246	23 laps	6
7	Maurice Trintignant	Scuderia Centro Sud	Maserati 250F	23 laps	16
8	Roy Salvadori	Cooper	Cooper-Climax T45	23 laps	13
9	Jo Bonnier	Jo Bonnier	Maserati 250F	22 laps	14
10	Maria Teresa de Filippis	Maria Teresa de Filippis	Maserati 250F	22 laps	19
R	Chico Godia-Sales	Francisco Godia Sales	Maserati 250F	22 laps/engine	18

Pos	Driver	Team	Chassis-Engine	Result	Qual
R	Jack Brabham	Cooper	Cooper-Climax T45	16 laps/overheating	8
R	Graham Hill	Lotus	Lotus-Climax 12	12 laps/engine	15
R	Luigi Musso	Ferrari	Ferrari 246	5 laps/accident	2
R	Peter Collins	Ferrari	Ferrari 246	5 laps/overheating	4
R	Jean Behra	BRM	BRM P25	5 laps/fuel pressure	10
R	Wolfgang Seidel	Scuderia Centro Sud	Maserati 250F	4 laps/halfshaft	17
R	Stirling Moss	Vanwall	Vanwall	0 laps/engine	3
R	Masten Gregory	Scuderia Centro Sud	Maserati 250F	0 laps/engine	9
NS	Ken Kavanagh	Ken Kavanagh	Maserati 250F	engine	20

Pole: Hawthorn, 3m57.100s, 133.026mph/214.086kph. Fastest lap: Hawthorn, 3m58.300s, 132.357mph/213.008kph on Lap 24. Race leaders: Brooks 1, 3; Collins 2, 4-24

FRENCH GRAND PRIX

REIMS • ROUND 5 • DATE: 6TH JULY 1958
Laps: 50 • Distance: 257.869miles/415.1km • Weather: Warm & bright

Pos	Driver	Team	Chassis-Engine	Result	Qual
1	Mike Hawthorn	Ferrari	Ferrari 246	2h03m21.300s	1
2	Stirling Moss	Vanwall	Vanwall	2h03m45.900s	6
3	Wolfgang von Trips	Ferrari	Ferrari 246	2h04m21.000s	21
4	Juan Manuel Fangio	Juan Manuel Fangio	Maserati 250F	2h05m51.900s	8
5	Peter Collins	Ferrari	Ferrari 246	2h08m46.200s	4
6	Jack Brabham	Cooper	Cooper-Climax T45	49 laps	12
7	Phil Hill	Ecurie Bonnier	Maserati 250F	49 laps	13
8	Jo Bonnier	Giorgio Scarlatti	Maserati 250F	48 laps	16
9	Gerino Gerini	Scuderia Centro Sud	Maserati 250F	47 laps	15
10	Troy Ruttman	Scuderia Centro Sud	Maserati 250F	45 laps	18
11	Roy Salvadori	Cooper	Cooper-Climax T45	37 laps	14
R	Harry Schell	BRM	BRM P25	41 laps/overheating	3
R	Jean Behra	BRM	BRM P25	41 laps/fuel pump	9
R	Lewis-Evans / Brooks*	Vanwall	Vanwall	35 laps/engine	10
R	Graham Hill	Lotus	Lotus-Climax 16	33 laps/overheating	19
R	Chico Godia-Sales	Francisco Godia Sales	Maserati 250F	28 laps/accident	11
R	Maurice Trintignant	BRM	BRM P25	23 laps/fuel pump	7
R	Tony Brooks	Vanwall	Vanwall	16 laps/engine	5
R	Luigi Musso	Ferrari	Ferrari 246	9 laps/accident	2
R	Carroll Shelby	Scuderia Centro Sud	Maserati 250F	9 laps/engine	17
R	Cliff Allison	Lotus	Lotus-Climax 12	6 laps/engine	20

*Stuart Lewis-Evans, Tony Brooks

Pole: Hawthorn, 2m21.700s, 131.058mph/210.918kph. Fastest lap: Hawthorn, 2m24.900s, 128.188mph/206.300kph on Lap 45. Race leaders: Hawthorn 1-50

THE PERILS OF FIRE

Stuart Lewis-Evans was clearly set for great things, and had taken two third places as he supported the Vanwall attack in 1958. However, his luck ran out at the final round, in Morocco, when he crashed after his Vanwall's transmission locked and he was badly burnt . Flown back to England, he died six days later in the country's top burns unit in East Grinstead.

BRITISH GRAND PRIX

SILVERSTONE • ROUND 6 • DATE: 19TH JULY 1958
Laps: 75 • Distance: 219.522miles/353.287km • Weather: Warm & bright

Pos	Driver	Team	Chassis-Engine	Result	Qual
1	Peter Collins	Ferrari	Ferrari 246	2h09m04.200s	6
2	Mike Hawthorn	Ferrari	Ferrari 246	2h09m28.400s	4
3	Roy Salvadori	Cooper	Cooper-Climax T45	2h09m54.800s	3
4	Stuart Lewis-Evans	Vanwall	Vanwall	2h09m55.000s	7
5	Harry Schell	BRM	BRM P25	2h10m19.000s	2
6	Jack Brabham	Cooper	Cooper-Climax T45	2h10m27.400s	10
7	Tony Brooks	Vanwall	Vanwall	74 laps	9
8	Maurice Trintignant	Rob Walker Racing Team	Cooper-Climax T43	73 laps	12
9	Carroll Shelby	Scuderia Centro Sud	Maserati 250F	72 laps	15
R	Wolfgang von Trips	Ferrari	Ferrari 246	59 laps/engine	11
R	Jo Bonnier	Jo Bonnier	Maserati 250F	49 laps/gearbox	13
R	Gerino Gerini	Scuderia Centro Sud	Maserati 250F	44 laps/gearbox	18
R	Ian Burgess	Cooper	Cooper-Climax T45	40 laps/clutch	16
R	Stirling Moss	Vanwall	Vanwall	25 laps/engine	1
R	Cliff Allison	Lotus	Lotus-Climax 12	21 laps/engine	5
R	Jean Behra	BRM	BRM P25	19 laps/suspension	8
R	Ivor Bueb	B C Ecclestone	Connaught-Alta B	19 laps/gearbox	17
R	Alan Stacey	Lotus	Lotus-Climax 16	19 laps/overheating	20
R	Graham Hill	Lotus	Lotus-Climax 16	17 laps/overheating	14
R	Jack Fairman	B C Ecclestone	Connaught-Alta B	7 laps/ignition	19
DNQ	Bernie Ecclestone	B C Ecclestone	Connaught-Alta B	Fairman drove car	21

Pole: Moss, 1m39.400s, 106.006mph/170.601kph. Fastest lap: Hawthorn, 1m40.800s, 104.534mph/168.232kph on Lap 50. Race leaders: Collins 1-75

F1'S FIRST FEMALE RACER

Maria Teresa de Filippis broke new ground when she arrived in F1 with a privately entered Maserati. Helped by Luigi Musso, she came fifth in a non-championship race in Sicily, then entered four grands prix, finishing 10th at Spa-Francorchamps. Back with a Porsche in 1959, she quit after her second mentor, Jean Behra, crashed and died at the AVUS circuit.

GERMAN GRAND PRIX

NURBURGRING • ROUND 7 • DATE: 3RD AUGUST 1958
Laps: 15 • Distance: 212.518miles/342.15km • Weather: Warm but dull

Pos	Driver	Team	Chassis-Engine	Result	Qual
1	Tony Brooks	Vanwall	Vanwall	2h21m15.000s	2
2	Roy Salvadori	Cooper	Cooper-Climax T45	2h24m44.700s	6
3	Maurice Trintignant	Rob Walker Racing Team	Cooper-Climax T45	2h26m26.200s	7
4	Wolfgang von Trips	Ferrari	Ferrari 246	2h27m31.300s	5
5	Bruce McLaren	Cooper	Cooper-Climax T45	2h27m41.300s	12
6	Edgar Barth	Porsche	Porsche RSK	2h27m47.400s	13
7	Ian Burgess	High Efficiency Motors	Cooper-Climax T43	2h28m14.300s	11
8	Tony Marsh	Tony Marsh	Cooper-Climax T45	2h28m24.900s	14
9	Phil Hill	Ferrari	Ferrari 156	2h29m00.500s	10
10	Cliff Allison	Lotus	Lotus-Climax 16	13 laps	24
11	Ivor Bueb	Ecurie Demi Litre	Lotus-Climax 12	12 laps/oil line	16
R	Mike Hawthorn	Ferrari	Ferrari 246	11 laps/clutch	1
R	Peter Collins	Ferrari	Ferrari 246	10 laps/accident	4
R	Wolfgang Seidel	Rob Walker Racing Team	Cooper-Climax T43	9 laps/suspension	17
R	Harry Schell	BRM	BRM P25	9 laps/brakes	8
R	Graham Hill	Lotus	Lotus-Climax 16	4 laps/oil line	22
R	Christian Goethals	Ecurie Eperon d'Or	Cooper-Climax T43	4 laps/fuel pump	23
R	Jean Behra	BRM	BRM P25	4 laps/suspension	9
R	Stirling Moss	Vanwall	Vanwall	3 laps/magneto	3
R	Hans Herrmann	Scuderia Centro Sud	Maserati 250F	3 laps/engine	20
R	Carel Godin de Beaufort	Ecurie Maarsbergen	Porsche 550RS	3 laps/engine	15
R	Dick Gibson	R Gibson	Cooper-Climax T43	2 laps/engine	18
R	Jack Brabham	Cooper	Cooper-Climax T45	1 lap/accident	19
R	Brian Naylor	J B Naylor	Cooper-Climax T45	1 lap/fuel pump	25
R	Jo Bonnier	Scuderia Centro Sud	Maserati 250F	1 lap/engine	21
NS	Troy Ruttman	Scuderia Centro Sud	Maserati 250F	engine	-

Pole: Hawthorn, 9m14.000s, 92.102mph/148.223kph. Fastest lap: Moss, 9m09.200s, 92.894mph/149.500kph on Lap 3. Race leaders: Moss 1-3; Hawthorn 4; Collins 5-10; Brooks 11-15

NEW DRIVERS

Two future world champions and a grand prix winner (who founded one of F1's great teams) all made their F1 debuts in 1958. These were Graham Hill and his American namesake Phil, for Lotus and Ferrari, respectively. The Cooper camp was the starting point for New Zealander Bruce McLaren and he would be the first of this trio to win a grand prix, in 1959.

IN MEMORIAM

The British contingent wasn't dulled only by the loss of Lewis-Evans, but also by the deaths of hugely popular grand prix winner Peter Collins in the German GP, and of Archie Scott-Brown, who died in a sports car race at Spa. Peter Whitehead was killed on the Tour de France road race, while Ferrari's Luigi Musso added to this sad list when he crashed fatally in the French GP.

PORTUGUESE GRAND PRIX

OPORTO • ROUND 8 • DATE: 24TH AUGUST 1958
Laps: 50 • Distance: 233.14miles/375.0km • Weather: Warm & damp then drying

Pos	Driver	Team	Chassis-Engine	Result	Qual
1	Stirling Moss	Vanwall	Vanwall	2h11m27.800s	1
2	Mike Hawthorn	Ferrari	Ferrari 246	2h16m40.550s	2
3	Stuart Lewis-Evans	Vanwall	Vanwall	49 laps	3
4	Jean Behra	BRM	BRM P25	49 laps	4
5	Wolfgang von Trips	Ferrari	Ferrari 246	49 laps	6
6	Harry Schell	BRM	BRM P25	49 laps	7
7	Jack Brabham	Cooper	Cooper-Climax T45	48 laps	8
8	Maurice Trintignant	Rob Walker Racing Team	Cooper-Climax T45	48 laps	9
9	Roy Salvadori	Cooper	Cooper-Climax T45	46 laps	11
R	Carroll Shelby	Scuderia Centro Sud	Maserati 250F	47 laps/brakes	10
R	Tony Brooks	Vanwall	Vanwall	37 laps/spun off	5
R	Graham Hill	Lotus	Lotus-Climax 16	25 laps/spun off	12
R	Cliff Allison	Scuderia Centro Sud	Maserati 250F	15 laps/engine	13
R	Jo Bonnier	Ecurie Bonnier	Maserati 250F	9 laps/physical	14
R	Maria Teresa de Filippis	Scuderia Centro Sud	Maserati 250F	6 laps/engine	15
NS	Cliff Allison	Lotus	Lotus-Climax 16	accident	-

Pole: Moss, 2m34.200s, 108.800mph/175.097kph. Fastest lap: Hawthorn, 2m32.370s, 110.106mph/177.200kph on Lap 36. Race leaders: Moss 1, 8-50; Hawthorn 2-7

NEW CONSTRUCTORS

There was just one new F1 constructor, but it would become one of the greats. It was Lotus. Founded by Colin Chapman, it ran Coventry Climax-powered Lotus 12s for Cliff Allison and Graham Hill on its Monaco debut. They both qualified and Allison finished sixth, with Hill retiring. Then, helped by retirements, Allison came fourth in Belgium. But this was just the start.

ITALIAN GRAND PRIX

MONZA • ROUND 9 • DATE: 7TH SEPTEMBER 1958
Laps: 70 • Distance: 249.794miles/402.5km • Weather: Hot & bright

Pos	Driver	Team	Chassis-Engine	Result	Qual
1	Tony Brooks	Vanwall	Vanwall	2h03m47.800s	2
2	Mike Hawthorn	Ferrari	Ferrari 246	2h04m12.000s	3
3	Phil Hill	Ferrari	Ferrari 246	2h04m16.100s	7
4	Gregory / Shelby*	Temple Buell	Maserati 250F	69 laps	11
5	Roy Salvadori	Cooper	Cooper-Climax T45	62 laps	14
6	Graham Hill	Lotus	Lotus-Climax 16	62 laps	12
7	Cliff Allison	Lotus	Lotus-Climax 12	61 laps	16
R	Maria Teresa de Filippis	Maria Teresa de Filippis	Maserati 250F	57 laps/engine	21
R	Giulio Cabianca	Ecurie Bonnier	Maserati 250F	51 laps/engine	20
R	Jean Behra	BRM	BRM P25	42 laps/clutch	8
R	Hans Herrmann	Ecurie Bonnier	Maserati 250F	32 laps/engine	18
R	Stuart Lewis-Evans	Vanwall	Vanwall	30 laps/overheating	4
R	Maurice Trintignant	Rob Walker Racing Team	Cooper-Climax T45	24 laps/gearbox	13

Pos	Driver	Team	Chassis-Engine	Result	Qual
R	Stirling Moss	Vanwall	Vanwall	17 laps/gearbox	1
R	Jo Bonnier	BRM	BRM P25	14 laps/transmission	10
R	Olivier Gendebien	Ferrari	Ferrari 246	4 laps/suspension	5
R	Gerino Gerini	Scuderia Centro Sud	Maserati 250F	2 laps/accident	19
R	Carroll Shelby	Scuderia Centro Sud	Maserati 250F	1 lap/engine	17
R	Wolfgang von Trips	Ferrari	Ferrari 246	0 laps/accident	6
R	Harry Schell	BRM	BRM P25	0 laps/accident	9
R	Jack Brabham	Cooper	Cooper-Climax T45	0 laps/suspension	15

*Masten Gregory, Carroll Shelby

Pole: Moss, 1m40.500s, 127.983mph/205.970kph. Fastest lap: Hill, 1m42.900s, 125.019mph/201.200kph on Lap 26. Race leaders: P Hill 1-4, 35-37; Hawthorn 5-6, 9, 15-34, 38-60; Moss 7-8, 10-14; Brooks 61-70

MOROCCAN GRAND PRIX

AIN DIAB • ROUND 10 • DATE: 19TH OCTOBER 1958
Laps: 53 • Distance: 250.881miles/403.754km • Weather: Warm & bright

Pos	Driver	Team	Chassis-Engine	Result	Qual
1	Stirling Moss	Vanwall	Vanwall	2h09m15.100s	2
2	Mike Hawthorn	Ferrari	Ferrari 246	2h10m39.800s	1
3	Phil Hill	Ferrari	Ferrari 246	2h10m40.600s	5
4	Jo Bonnier	BRM	BRM P25	2h11m01.800s	8
5	Harry Schell	BRM	BRM P25	2h11m48.800s	10
6	Masten Gregory	Temple Buell	Maserati 250F	52 laps	13
7	Roy Salvadori	Cooper	Cooper-Climax T45	51 laps	14
8	Jack Fairman	Cooper	Cooper-Climax T45	50 laps	11
9	Hans Herrmann	Ecurie Bonnier	Maserati 250F	50 laps	18
10	Cliff Allison	Lotus	Lotus-Climax 12	49 laps	16
11	Jack Brabham	Cooper	Cooper-Climax T45	49 laps	19
12	Gerino Gerini	Scuderia Centro Sud	Maserati 250F	48 laps	17
13	Bruce McLaren	Cooper	Cooper-Climax T45	48 laps	21
14	Robert La Caze	Robert La Caze	Cooper-Climax T45	48 laps	23
15	Andre Guelfi	Andre Guelfi	Cooper-Climax T45	48 laps	25
16	Graham Hill	Lotus	Lotus-Climax 16	45 laps	12
R	Stuart Lewis-Evans	Vanwall	Vanwall	41 laps/engine	3
R	Francois Picard	Rob Walker Racing Team	Cooper-Climax T43	31 laps/accident	24
R	Tommy Bridger	BRP	Cooper-Climax T45	30 laps/accident	22
R	Olivier Gendebien	Ferrari	Ferrari 246	29 laps/accident	6
R	Tony Brooks	Vanwall	Vanwall	29 laps/engine	7
R	Jean Behra	BRM	BRM P25	26 laps/engine	4
R	Ron Flockhart	BRM	BRM P25	15 laps/engine	15
R	Wolfgang Seidel	Scuderia Centro Sud	Maserati 250F	15 laps/accident	20
R	Maurice Trintignant	Rob Walker Racing Team	Cooper-Climax T45	9 laps/engine	9

Pole: Hawthorn, 2m23.100s, 119.084mph/191.647kph. Fastest lap: Moss, 2m22.500s, 119.613mph/192.500kph on Lap 21. Race leaders: Moss 1-53

WORLD DRIVERS' CHAMPIONSHIP FINAL RESULTS

Pos	Driver	Nat	Car-Engine	R1	R2	R3	R4	R5	R6	R7	R8	R9	R10	Total
1	Mike Hawthorn	GBR	Ferrari 246	3	RF	5	2PF	1PF	2F	RP	2F	2	2P	42
2	Stirling Moss	GBR	Cooper-Climax T43	1	-	-	-	-	-	-	-	-	-	41
			Vanwall	-	R	1F	R	2	RP	RF	1P	RP	1F	
3	Tony Brooks	GBR	Vanwall	-	RP	R	1	R | R	7	1	R	1	R	24
4	Roy Salvadori	GBR	Cooper-Climax T45	-	R	4	8	11	3	2	9	5	7	15
5	Peter Collins	GBR	Ferrari 246	R	3	R	R	5	1	R	-	-	-	14
6	Harry Schell	USA	Maserati 250F	6	-	-	-	-	-	-	-	-	-	14
			BRM P25	-	5	2	5	R	5	R	6	R	5	
7	Maurice Trintignant	FRA	Cooper-Climax T45	-	1	9	-	-	-	3	8	R	R	12
			Maserati 250F	-	-	-	7	-	-	-	-	-	-	
			BRM P25	-	-	-	-	R	-	-	-	-	-	
			Cooper-Climax T43	-	-	-	-	-	8	-	-	-	-	
8	Luigi Musso	ITA	Ferrari 246	2	2	7	R	R	-	-	-	-	-	12
9	Stuart Lewis-Evans	GBR	Vanwall	-	R	RP	3	R	4	-	3	R	R	11
10	Phil Hill	USA	Maserati 250F	-	-	-	-	7	-	-	-	-	-	9
			Ferrari 156	-	-	-	-	-	-	9	-	-	-	-
			Ferrari 246	-	-	-	-	-	-	-	-	3F	3	
11	Wolfgang von Trips	DEU	Ferrari 246	-	R	-	-	3	R	4	5	R	-	9
11	Jean Behra	FRA	Maserati 250F	5	-	-	-	-	-	-	-	-	-	9
			BRM P25	-	R	3	R	R	R	R	4	R	R	
14	Juan Manuel Fangio	ARG	Maserati 250F	4PF	-	-	-	4	-	-	-	-	-	7
18	Jack Brabham	AUS	Cooper-Climax T45	-	4	8	R	6	6	R	7	R	11	3
18	Cliff Allison	GBR	Lotus-Climax 12	-	6	6	4	R	R	-	-	7	10	3
			Lotus-Climax 16	-	-	-	-	-	-	5	-	-	-	
			Maserati 250F	-	-	-	-	-	-	-	R	-	-	
18	Jo Bonnier	SWE	Maserati 250F	-	R	10	9	8	R	R	R	-	-	3
			BRM P25	-	-	-	-	-	-	-	-	R	4	

WORLD CONSTRUCTORS' CHAMPIONSHIP FINAL RESULTS

Pos	Team-Engine	R1	R2	R3	R4	R5	R6	R7	R8	R9	R10	Total
1	Vanwall	-	-	1	1	2	4	1	1	1	1	48
2	Ferrari	2	2	5	2	1	1	4	2	2	2	40
3	Cooper-Climax	1	1	4	8	6	3	2	7	5	7	31
4	BRM	-	5	2	5	-	5	-	4	-	4	18
5	Maserati	4	-	10	7	4	9	-	-	4	6	6
6	Lotus-Climax	-	6	6	4	-	-	5	-	6	10	3

SYMBOLS AND GRAND PRIX KEY

Round 1 Argentinian GP
Round 2 Monaco GP
Round 3 Dutch GP
Round 4 Belgian GP
Round 5 French GP
Round 6 British GP
Round 7 German GP
Round 8 Portuguese GP
Round 9 Italian GP
Round 10 Moroccan GP

SCORING

1st 8 points
2nd 6 points
3rd 4 points
4th 3 points
5th 2 points
Fastest lap 1 point

Indianapolis 500 results not included

DNPQ DID NOT PRE-QUALIFY **DNQ** DID NOT QUALIFY **DQ** DISQUALIFIED **EX** EXCLUDED
F FASTEST LAP **NC** NOT CLASSIFIED **NS** NON-STARTER **P** POLE POSITION **R** RETIRED

1959

SEASON SUMMARY

The days of F1 being for front-engined cars were clearly numbered as Cooper team leader Jack Brabham landed a major blow to the establishment. While Ferrari and BRM were still running traditionally-shaped cars, Cooper continued to pioneer its smaller cars with the engine behind the driver's shoulders. More nimble, lighter, less thirsty and kinder to their tyres, Cooper's cars started the campaign with a win for Brabham in Monaco, then added another. There was also a victory for team-mate Bruce McLaren and two for Stirling Moss in a privately entered version. BRM finally took a win and Tony Brooks won twice for Ferrari, but the message was clear.

MONACO GRAND PRIX

MONTE CARLO • ROUND 1 • DATE: 10TH MAY 1959
Laps: 100 • Distance: 195.113miles/314.5km • Weather: Hot & bright

Pos	Driver	Team	Chassis-Engine	Result	Qual
1	Jack Brabham	Cooper	Cooper-Climax T51	2h55m51.300s	3
2	Tony Brooks	Ferrari	Ferrari 246	2h56m11.700s	4
3	Maurice Trintignant	Rob Walker Racing Team	Cooper-Climax T51	98 laps	6
4	Phil Hill	Ferrari	Ferrari 246	97 laps	5
5	Bruce McLaren	Cooper	Cooper-Climax T51	96 laps	13
R	Roy Salvadori	High Efficiency Motors	Cooper-Maserati T45	83 laps/transmission	8
R	Stirling Moss	Rob Walker Racing Team	Cooper-Climax T51	81 laps/transmission	1
R	Ron Flockhart	BRM	BRM P25	64 laps/spun off	10
R	Harry Schell	BRM	BRM P25	48 laps/accident	9
R	Jo Bonnier	BRM	BRM P25	44 laps/brakes	7
R	Jean Behra	Ferrari	Ferrari 246	24 laps/engine	2
R	Graham Hill	Lotus	Lotus-Climax 16	21 laps/fire	14
R	Masten Gregory	Cooper	Cooper-Climax T51	6 laps/gearbox	11
R	Wolfgang von Trips	Porsche	Porsche RSK	1 lap/collision	12
R	Cliff Allison	Ferrari	Ferrari 156	1 lap/collision	15
R	Bruce Halford	John Fisher	Lotus-Climax 16	1 lap/collision	16
DNQ	Ivor Bueb	BRP	Cooper-Climax T51	-	17
DNQ	Giorgio Scarlatti	Scuderia Ugolini	Maserati 250F	-	18
DNQ	Lucien Bianchi	Equipe Nationale Belge	Cooper-Climax T51	-	19
DNQ	Alain de Changy	Equipe Nationale Belge	Cooper-Climax T51	-	20
DNQ	Maria Teresa de Filippis	Porsche	Porsche RSK	-	21
DNQ	Pete Lovely	Lotus	Lotus-Climax 16	-	22
DNQ	Jean Lucienbonnet	Jean Lucienbonnet	Cooper-Climax T45	-	23
DNQ	Andre Testut	Monte Carlo Auto Sport	Maserati 250F	-	24

Pole: Moss, 1m39.600s, 70.633mph/113.674kph. Fastest lap: Brabham, 1m40.400s, 70.071mph/112.768kph on Lap 83. Race leaders: Behra 1-21; Moss 22-81; Brabham 82-100

DUTCH GRAND PRIX

ZANDVOORT • ROUND 2 • DATE: 31ST MAY 1959
Laps: 75 • Distance: 195.405miles/314.475km • Weather: Warm & bright

Pos	Driver	Team	Chassis-Engine	Result	Qual
1	Jo Bonnier	BRM	BRM P25	2h05m26.800s	1
2	Jack Brabham	Cooper	Cooper-Climax T51	2h05m41.000s	2
3	Masten Gregory	Cooper	Cooper-Climax T51	2h06m49.800s	7
4	Innes Ireland	Lotus	Lotus-Climax 16	74 laps	9
5	Jean Behra	Ferrari	Ferrari 156	74 laps	4
6	Phil Hill	Ferrari	Ferrari 246	73 laps	12
7	Graham Hill	Lotus	Lotus-Climax 16	73 laps	5
8	Maurice Trintignant	Rob Walker Racing Team	Cooper-Climax T51	73 laps	11
9	Cliff Allison	Ferrari	Ferrari 246	71 laps	15
10	Carel Godin de Beaufort	Ecurie Maarsbergen	Porsche RSK	68 laps	14
R	Stirling Moss	Rob Walker Racing Team	Cooper-Climax T51	62 laps/gearbox	3
R	Harry Schell	BRM	BRM P25	46 laps/gearbox	6
R	Tony Brooks	Ferrari	Ferrari 246	42 laps/oil leak	8
R	Carroll Shelby	Aston Martin	Aston Martin DBR4/250	25 laps/engine	10
R	Roy Salvadori	Aston Martin	Aston Martin DBR4/250	3 laps/engine	13

Pole: Bonnier, 1m36.000s, 97.702mph/157.237kph. Fastest lap: Moss, 1m36.600s, 97.120mph/156.300kph on Lap 42. Race leaders: Bonnier 1, 12-29, 34-59, 63-75; Gregory 2-11; Brabham 30-33; Moss 60-62

THE RISE OF THE SMALLER OUTFITS

While Britain's first constructors' title was won by Vanwall in 1958, the second was won by a small concern not blessed with the backing of British industry. This was Cooper, and in many ways it was the shape of things to come, a small British outfit showing that it could take on and beat Ferrari. To afford its racing programme, it sold cars for customer use.

FRENCH GRAND PRIX

REIMS • ROUND 3 • DATE: 5TH JULY 1959
Laps: 50 • Distance: 257.869miles/415.1km • Weather: Hot & bright

Pos	Driver	Team	Chassis-Engine	Result	Qual
1	Tony Brooks	Ferrari	Ferrari 246	2h01m26.500s	1
2	Phil Hill	Ferrari	Ferrari 246	2h01m54.000s	3
3	Jack Brabham	Cooper	Cooper-Climax T51	2h03m04.200s	2
4	Olivier Gendebien	Ferrari	Ferrari 246	2h03m14.000s	11
5	Bruce McLaren	Cooper	Cooper-Climax T51	2h03m14.200s	10
6	Ron Flockhart	BRM	BRM P25	2h03m32.200s	13
7	Harry Schell	BRM	BRM P25	47 laps	9
8	Giorgio Scarlatti	Scuderia Ugolini	Maserati 250F	41 laps	21
9	Carel Godin de Beaufort	Scuderia Ugolini	Maserati 250F	40 laps	20
10	Fritz d'Orey	Scuderia Centro Sud	Maserati 250F	40 laps	18
11	Maurice Trintignant	Rob Walker Racing Team	Cooper-Climax T51	36 laps	8
DQ	Stirling Moss	BRP	BRM P25	42 laps/push start	4
R	Jean Behra	Ferrari	Ferrari 246	31 laps/engine	5

Pos	Driver	Team	Chassis-Engine	Result	Qual
R	Roy Salvadori	High Efficiency Motors	Cooper-Maserati T45	20 laps/engine	16
R	Dan Gurney	Ferrari	Ferrari 246	19 laps/radiator damage	12
R	Innes Ireland	Lotus	Lotus-Climax 16	14 laps/wheel	15
R	Ian Burgess	Scuderia Centro Sud	Cooper-Maserati T51	13 laps/engine	19
R	Masten Gregory	Cooper	Cooper-Climax T51	8 laps/physical	7
R	Graham Hill	Lotus	Lotus-Climax 16	7 laps/radiator damage	14
R	Colin Davis	Scuderia Centro Sud	Cooper-Maserati T51	7 laps/oil leak	17
R	Jo Bonnier	BRM	BRM P25	6 laps/engine	6
NS	Asdrubal Bayardo	Scuderia Centro Sud	Maserati 250F	-	-

Pole: Brooks, 2m19.400s, 133.221mph/214.398kph. Fastest lap: Moss, 2m22.800s, 130.052mph/209.300kph on Lap 40. Race leaders: Brooks 1-50

THE FRESHEST FACE

Bruce McLaren began a trend that continues to this day by becoming the then-youngest winner of a round of the World Championship. The Kiwi's breakthrough came at the last round, the United States GP, when he took his Cooper to be first past the chequered flag, at just 22 years and three months, after team-mate Brabham's car failed on the last lap.

THE TAYLORS STEP UP

By some twist of fortune, four unrelated drivers called Taylor attempted to make their F1 debuts at the British GP at Aintree. These were Dennis and Trevor, who both failed to qualify for the race, and Mike, who started 24th but retired, and Henry, who was the pick of this pack as he qualified three places ahead of Mike and raced on to 11th place.

BRITISH GRAND PRIX

AINTREE • ROUND 4 • DATE: 18TH JULY 1959
Laps: 75 • Distance: 224.936miles/362.1km • Weather: Warm & bright

Pos	Driver	Team	Chassis-Engine	Result	Qual
1	Jack Brabham	Cooper	Cooper-Climax T51	2h30m11.600s	1
2	Stirling Moss	BRP	BRM P25	2h30m33.800s	7
3	Bruce McLaren	Cooper	Cooper-Climax T51	2h30m34.000s	8
4	Harry Schell	BRM	BRM P25	74 laps	3
5	Maurice Trintignant	Rob Walker Racing Team	Cooper-Climax T51	74 laps	4
6	Roy Salvadori	Aston Martin	Aston Martin DBR4/250	74 laps	2
7	Masten Gregory	Cooper	Cooper-Climax T51	73 laps	5
8	Alan Stacey	Lotus	Lotus-Climax 16	71 laps	12
9	Graham Hill	Lotus	Lotus-Climax 16	70 laps	9
10	Chris Bristow	BRP	Cooper-BRM T51	70 laps	16
11	Henry Taylor	Reg Parnell Racing	Cooper-Climax T51	69 laps	21
12	Peter Ashdown	Alan Brown Equipe	Cooper-Climax T45	69 laps	23
13	Ivor Bueb	BRP	Cooper-BRM T51	69 laps	18

Pos	Driver	Team	Chassis-Engine	Result	Qual
R	Carroll Shelby	Aston Martin	Aston Martin DBR4/250	69 laps/ignition	6
R	Fritz d'Orey	Scuderia Centro Sud	Maserati 250F	57 laps/accident	20
R	Ron Flockhart	BRM	BRM P25	53 laps/spun off	11
R	Jack Fairman	High Efficiency Motors	Cooper-Climax T43	39 laps/gearbox	15
R	Jo Bonnier	BRM	BRM P25	37 laps/brakes	10
R	Ian Burgess	Scuderia Centro Sud	Cooper-Maserati T51	31 laps/transmission	13
R	Hans Herrmann	Scuderia Centro Sud	Cooper-Maserati T51	21 laps/gearbox	19
R	David Piper	Dorchester Service Station	Lotus-Climax 16	19 laps/overheating	22
R	Brian Naylor	J B Naylor	JBW-Maserati	18 laps/transmission	14
R	Mike Taylor	Alan Brown Equipe	Cooper-Climax T45	17 laps/transmission	24
R	Tony Brooks	Vanwall	Vanwall	13 laps/ignition	17
NS	Innes Ireland	Lotus	Lotus-Climax 16	driver unwell	12
DNQ	Bill Moss	United Racing Stable	Cooper-Climax T51	-	25
DNQ	Mike Parkes	David Fry	Fry-Climax	-	26
DNQ	Trevor Taylor	Ace Garage - Rotherham	Cooper-Climax T51	-	27
DNQ	Keith Greene	Gilby Engineering	Gilby-Climax	-	28
DNQ	Tim Parnell	Reg Parnell Racing	Cooper-Climax T45	-	29
DNQ	Dennis Taylor	Dennis Taylor	Lotus-Climax 12	-	30

Pole: Brabham, 1m58.000s, 91.524mph/147.294kph. Fastest lap: McLaren, 1m57.000s, 92.335mph/148.600kph on Lap 75 Moss, 1m57.000s, 92.335mph/148.600kph. Race leaders: Brabham 1-75

HERRMANN'S LUCKY ESCAPE

Hans Herrmann inadvertently placed himself centre stage in one of the most evocative F1 photos of the 1950s when he crashed his British Racing Partnership BRM in the German GP at AVUS and was thrown out as the pale green P25 started a sequence of cartwheels. Incredibly, the former Mercedes driver escaped without serious injury.

THE PRECISE MR BROOKS

With F1 cars tending to break, Tony Brooks was an artist behind the wheel, not just rapid, but mechanically sympathetic too. He also avoided the risks taken by his more gung-ho rivals. In searing temperatures, he led home a Ferrari one-two in France and then won again in the German GP to go into the final race with a shot at the title.

GERMAN GRAND PRIX

AVUS • ROUND 5 • DATE: 2ND AUGUST 1959
Laps: 60 • Distance: 309.442miles/498.0km • Weather: Warm but dull

Pos	Driver	Team	Chassis-Engine	Result	Qual
1	Tony Brooks	Ferrari	Ferrari 246	2h09m31.600s	1
2	Dan Gurney	Ferrari	Ferrari 246	2h09m34.500s	3
3	Phil Hill	Ferrari	Ferrari 246	2h10m36.400s	6
4	Maurice Trintignant	Rob Walker Racing Team	Cooper-Climax T51	59 laps	12
5	Jo Bonnier	BRM	BRM P25	58 laps	7

Pos	Driver	Team	Chassis-Engine	Result	Qual
6	Ian Burgess	Scuderia Centro Sud	Cooper-Maserati T51	56 laps	15
7	Harry Schell	BRM	BRM P25	49 laps	8
R	Bruce McLaren	Cooper	Cooper-Climax T51	36 laps/transmission	9
R	Hans Herrmann	BRP	BRM P25	36 laps/accident	11
R	Masten Gregory	Cooper	Cooper-Climax T51	23 laps/engine	5
R	Jack Brabham	Cooper	Cooper-Climax T51	15 laps/transmission	4
R	Graham Hill	Lotus	Lotus-Climax 16	10 laps/gearbox	10
R	Innes Ireland	Lotus	Lotus-Climax 16	7 laps/differential	13
R	Cliff Allison	Ferrari	Ferrari 246	2 laps/clutch	14
R	Stirling Moss	Rob Walker Racing Team	Cooper-Climax T51	1 lap/transmission	2
NS	Jean Behra	Jean Behra	Behra-Porsche	killed in support race	-
NS	Wolfgang von Trips	Porsche	Porsche 718	-	-

Pole: Brooks, 2m05.900s, 147.470mph/237.331kph. Fastest lap: Brooks, 2m04.500s, 149.129mph/240.000kph on Lap 18. Race leaders: Heat 1: Brooks 1-2, 5-13, 15, 18-22, 24-30; Gregory 3-4, 23; Gurney 14, 16-17. Heat 2: P Hill 1, 6, 8-9, 15, 18-19; Brooks 2-5, 7, 10, 12, 16-17, 22-30; Gurney 11, 13-14, 20-21

THREE NEW CIRCUITS

Germany, Portugal and the USA all offered new venues in 1959. These were AVUS, Monsanto and Sebring, respectively. Berlin's AVUS was a curious track shaped like a hair clip, with the wider end sporting a banked corner. Monsanto was set in a park near Lisbon, while Sebring ran around a bumpy airfield in Florida. None were ever used by F1 again.

BRM WINS AT LONG LAST

Once the great hope for British grand prix success, BRM finally landed a win at the Dutch GP when Jo Bonnier was first to the finish after the gearbox failed on leader Stirling Moss's Cooper with a few laps to go. Although the Swede had started on pole and run at the front, it was a rare day, as his next best finish in 1959 was fifth in the German GP.

PORTUGUESE GRAND PRIX

MONSANTO • ROUND 6 • DATE: 23RD AUGUST 1959
Laps: 62 • Distance: 208.802miles/336.35km • Weather: Hot & bright

Pos	Driver	Team	Chassis-Engine	Result	Qual
1	Stirling Moss	Rob Walker Racing Team	Cooper-Climax T51	2h11m55.410s	1
2	Masten Gregory	Cooper	Cooper-Climax T51	61 laps	3
3	Dan Gurney	Ferrari	Ferrari 246	61 laps	6
4	Maurice Trintignant	Rob Walker Racing Team	Cooper-Climax T51	60 laps	4
5	Harry Schell	BRM	BRM P25	59 laps	9
6	Roy Salvadori	Aston Martin	Aston Martin DBR4/250	59 laps	12
7	Ron Flockhart	BRM	BRM P25	59 laps	11
8	Carroll Shelby	Aston Martin	Aston Martin DBR4/250	58 laps	13
9	Tony Brooks	Ferrari	Ferrari 246	57 laps	10
10	Mario Cabral	Scuderia Centro Sud	Cooper-Maserati T51	56 laps	14
R	Bruce McLaren	Cooper	Cooper-Climax T51	38 laps/transmission	8

Pos	Driver	Team	Chassis-Engine	Result	Qual
R	Jack Brabham	Cooper	Cooper-Climax T51	23 laps/accident	2
R	Jo Bonnier	BRM	BRM P25	10 laps/engine	5
R	Phil Hill	Ferrari	Ferrari 246	5 laps/accident	7
R	Graham Hill	Lotus	Lotus-Climax 16	5 laps/accident	15
R	Innes Ireland	Lotus	Lotus-Climax 16	3 laps/gearbox	16

Pole: Moss, 2m02.900s, 98.741mph/158.909kph. Fastest lap: Moss, 2m05.070s, 97.027mph/156.150kph on Lap 28. Race leaders: Moss 1-62

NEW CONSTRUCTORS

Three British constructors – Aston Martin, Fry and JBW – joined Italian Maserati 250F modifier Tec-Mec in making their F1 bow in 1959. None scored points, even though Fry and JBW had at least arrived with rear-engined machines, but Aston Martin tasted glory when its sports car team achieved its dream of winning the Le Mans 24 Hours.

ITALIAN GRAND PRIX

MONZA • ROUND 7 • DATE: 13TH SEPTEMBER 1959
Laps: 72 • Distance: 257.247miles/414.0km • Weather: Warm & bright

Pos	Driver	Team	Chassis-Engine	Result	Qual
1	Stirling Moss	Rob Walker Racing Team	Cooper-Climax T51	2h04m05.400s	1
2	Phil Hill	Ferrari	Ferrari 246	2h04m52.100s	5
3	Jack Brabham	Cooper	Cooper-Climax T51	2h05m17.900s	3
4	Dan Gurney	Ferrari	Ferrari 246	2h05m25.000s	4
5	Cliff Allison	Ferrari	Ferrari 246	71 laps	8
6	Olivier Gendebien	Ferrari	Ferrari 246	71 laps	6
7	Harry Schell	BRM	BRM P25	70 laps	7
8	Jo Bonnier	BRM	BRM P25	70 laps	11
9	Maurice Trintignant	Rob Walker Racing Team	Cooper-Climax T51	70 laps	13
10	Carroll Shelby	Aston Martin	Aston Martin DBR4/250	70 laps	19
11	Colin Davis	Scuderia Centro Sud	Cooper-Maserati T51	68 laps	18
12	Giorgio Scarlatti	Cooper	Cooper-Climax T51	68 laps	12
13	Ron Flockhart	BRM	BRM P25	67 laps	15
14	Ian Burgess	Scuderia Centro Sud	Cooper-Maserati T51	67 laps	16
15	Giulio Cabianca	Ottorino Volonterio	Maserati 250F	64 laps	21
R	Roy Salvadori	Aston Martin	Aston Martin DBR4/250	44 laps/engine	17
R	Bruce McLaren	Cooper	Cooper-Climax T51	22 laps/engine	9
R	Jack Fairman	High Efficiency Motors	Cooper-Climax T43	18 laps/engine	12
R	Innes Ireland	Lotus	Lotus-Climax 16	14 laps/brakes	14
R	Graham Hill	Lotus	Lotus-Climax 16	1 lap/clutch	10
R	Tony Brooks	Ferrari	Ferrari 246	0 laps/clutch	2

Pole: Moss, 1m39.700s, 129.010mph/207.622kph. Fastest lap: Phil Hill, 1m40.400s, 128.126mph/206.200kph on Lap 32. Race leaders: Moss 1, 4, 15, 33-72; P Hill 2-3, 5-14, 16-32

UNITED STATES GRAND PRIX

SEBRING • ROUND 8 • DATE: 12TH DECEMBER 1959
Laps: 42 • Distance: 218.400miles/351.481km • Weather: Warm & bright

Pos	Driver	Team	Chassis-Engine	Result	Qual
1	Bruce McLaren	Cooper	Cooper-Climax T51	2h12m35.700s	10
2	Maurice Trintignant	Rob Walker Racing Team	Cooper-Climax T51	2h12m36.300s	5
3	Tony Brooks	Ferrari	Ferrari 246	2h15m36.600s	4
4	Jack Brabham	Cooper	Cooper-Climax T51	2h17m33.000s	2
5	Innes Ireland	Lotus	Lotus-Climax 16	39 laps	9
6	Wolfgang von Trips	Ferrari	Ferrari 246	38 laps	6
7	Harry Blanchard	Blanchard Automobile Co	Porsche RSK	38 laps	16
R	Cliff Allison	Ferrari	Ferrari 246	23 laps/clutch	11
R	Roy Salvadori	High Efficiency Motors	Cooper-Maserati T45	23 laps/transmission	11
R	Rodger Ward	Leader Cards Inc	Watson-Offenhauser	20 laps/clutch	19
R	Alessandro de Tomaso	OSCA	Cooper-Osca T43	13 laps/brakes	14
R	Phil Hill	Ferrari	Ferrari 246	8 laps/clutch	8
R	Fritz d'Orey	Camoradi USA	Tec Mec-Maserati	6 laps/oil leak	17
R	Stirling Moss	Rob Walker Racing Team	Cooper-Climax T51	5 laps/transmission	1
R	Harry Schell	Ecurie Bleue	Cooper-Climax T51	5 laps/clutch	3
R	George Constantine	Taylor-Crawley Racing Team	Cooper-Climax T45	5 laps/overheating	15
R	Alan Stacey	Lotus	Lotus-Climax 16	2 laps/clutch	12
R	Bob Said	Connaught	Connaught-Alta C	0 laps/accident	13
NS	Phil Cade	Phil Cade	Maserati 250F	engine	18

Pole: Moss, 3m00.000s, 104.000mph/167.372kph. Fastest lap: Trintignant, 3m05.000s, 101.159mph/162.800kph on Lap 39. Race leaders: Moss 1-5; Brabham 6-41; McLaren 42

NEW DRIVERS

Fittingly for a year in which the USA hosted its first grand prix, Phil Hill was joined at Ferrari by fellow American Dan Gurney. Starting mid-season, Gurney finished second on his second appearance in Germany to rank seventh. Innes Ireland ran a full campaign with Lotus, the Scot racing to fourth on his debut at Zandvoort for the team's only points.

IN MEMORIAM

Even before the season began, reigning world champion Hawthorn was gone, dying in a road accident. He had already quit F1 and it was later revealed that he was suffering from kidney disease. Then two drivers died on the same day in August as Jean Behra flew over the banking at AVUS, and Ivor Bueb was killed in an F2 race at Clermont-Ferrand.

WORLD DRIVERS' CHAMPIONSHIP FINAL RESULTS

Pos	Driver	Nat	Car-Engine	R1	R2	R3	R4	R5	R6	R7	R8	Total
1	Jack Brabham	AUS	Cooper-Climax T51	1F	2	3	1P	R	R	3	4	31
2	Tony Brooks	GBR	Ferrari 246	2	R	1P	-	1PF	9	R	3	27
			Vanwall	-	-	-	R	-	-	-	-	
3	Stirling Moss	GBR	Cooper-Climax T51	RP	RF	-	-	R	1PF	1P	RP	25.5
			BRM P25	-	-	DQF	2F	-	-	-	-	
4	Phil Hill	USA	Ferrari 246	4	6	2	-	3	R	2F	R	20
5	Maurice Trintignant	FRA	Cooper-Climax T51	3	8	11	5	4	4	9	2F	19
6	Bruce McLaren	NZL	Cooper-Climax T51	5	-	5	3F	R	R	R	1	16.5
7	Dan Gurney	USA	Ferrari 246	-	-	R	-	2	3	4	-	13
8	Jo Bonnier	SWE	BRM P25	R	1P	R	R	5	R	8	-	10
9	Masten Gregory	USA	Cooper-Climax T51	R	3	R	7	R	2	-	-	10
10	Harry Schell	USA	BRM P25	R	R	7	4	7	5	7	-	5
			Cooper-Climax T51	-	-	-	-	-	-	-	R	
10	Innes Ireland	GBR	Lotus-Climax 16	-	4	R	-	R	R	R	5	5
12	Olivier Gendebien	BEL	Ferrari 246	-	-	4	-	-	-	6	-	3
13	Jean Behra	FRA	Ferrari 246	R	-	R	-	-	-	-	-	2
			Ferrari 156	-	5	-	-	-	-	-	-	
			Behra-Porsche	-	-	-	-	NS	-	-	-	
13	Cliff Allison	GBR	Ferrari 156	R	-	-	-	-	-	-	-	2
			Ferrari 246	-	9	-	-	R	-	5	R	

WORLD CONSTRUCTORS' CHAMPIONSHIP FINAL RESULTS

Pos	Team-Engine	R1	R2	R3	R4	R5	R6	R7	R8	Total
1	Cooper-Climax	1	2	3	1	4	1	1	1	40
2	Ferrari	2	5	1	-	1	3	2	3	32
3	BRM	-	1	6	2	5	5	7	-	18
4	Lotus-Climax	-	4	-	8	-	-	-	5	5

SYMBOLS AND GRAND PRIX KEY

Round 1	**Monaco GP**
Round 2	**Dutch GP**
Round 3	**French GP**
Round 4	**British GP**
Round 5	**German GP**
Round 6	**Portuguese GP**
Round 7	**Italian GP**
Round 8	**United States GP**

Indianapolis 500 results not included

DNPQ DID NOT PRE-QUALIFY **DNQ** DID NOT QUALIFY **DQ** DISQUALIFIED **EX** EXCLUDED
F FASTEST LAP **NC** NOT CLASSIFIED **NS** NON-STARTER **P** POLE POSITION **R** RETIRED

SCORING

1st	**8 points**
2nd	**6 points**
3rd	**4 points**
4th	**3 points**
5th	**2 points**
Fastest lap	**1 point**

THE 1960s

1960

SEASON SUMMARY

Jack Brabham made it two F1 titles on the trot, and this one was certainly less fraught for the Australian as his new, low-line Cooper T53 kept him ahead of the pack. Team-mate Bruce McLaren started the season with a win, but Brabham prevailed thanks to a run of five wins in succession during the middle of the season. Rob Walker Racing changed from Cooper cars to Lotus and Stirling Moss shone, outpacing the works Lotus attack that was led by Innes Ireland. Many teams already had their eyes on the rule changes coming in 1961, including Ferrari, who had a thin season, with Phil Hill winning the Italian GP but ranking only fifth.

ARGENTINIAN GRAND PRIX

BUENOS AIRES • ROUND 1 • DATE: 7TH FEBRUARY 1960
Laps: 80 • Distance: 194.484miles/312.992km • Weather: Very hot & bright

Pos	Driver	Team	Chassis-Engine	Result	Qual
1	Bruce McLaren	Cooper	Cooper-Climax T45	2h17m49.500s	13
2	Cliff Allison	Ferrari	Ferrari 246	2h18m15.800s	7
3	Trintignant / Moss*	Rob Walker Racing Team	Cooper-Climax T51	2h18m26.400s	8
4	Carlos Menditeguy	Scuderia Centro Sud	Cooper-Maserati T51	2h18m42.800s	12
5	Wolfgang von Trips	Ferrari	Ferrari 246	79 laps	5
6	Innes Ireland	Lotus	Lotus-Climax 18	79 laps	2
7	Jo Bonnier	BRM	BRM P25	79 laps	4
8	Phil Hill	Ferrari	Ferrari 246	77 laps	6
9	Alberto Rodriguez Larreta	Lotus	Lotus-Climax 16	77 laps	15
10	Jose Froilan Gonzalez	Ferrari	Ferrari 246	77 laps	11
11	Roberto Bonomi	Scuderia Centro Sud	Cooper-Maserati T51	76 laps	17
12	Masten Gregory	Camoradi International	Behra-Porsche	76 laps	16
13	Gino Munaron	Gino Munaron	Maserati 250F	72 laps	19
14	Nasif Estefano	Scuderia Centro Sud	Maserati 250F	70 laps	20
R	Harry Schell	Ecurie Bleue	Cooper-Climax T51	63 laps/fuel pump	9
R	Jack Brabham	Cooper	Cooper-Climax T51	42 laps/gearbox	10
R	Stirling Moss	Rob Walker Racing Team	Cooper-Climax T51	40 laps/suspension	1
R	Graham Hill	BRM	BRM P25	37 laps/overheating	3
R	Alan Stacey	Lotus	Lotus-Climax 16	24 laps/exhaustion	14
R	Ettore Chimeri	Ettore Chimeri	Maserati 250F	23 laps/exhaustion	21
R	Antonio Creus	Antonio Creus	Maserati 250F	16 laps/exhaustion	22
R	Giorgio Scarlatti	Giorgio Scarlatti	Maserati 250F	11 laps/overheating	18

*Maurice Trintignant, Stirling Moss

Pole: Moss, 1m36.900s, 90.317mph/145.352kph. Fastest lap: Moss, 1m38.9s, 88.490mph/142.411kph Moss, 1m38.900s, 88.483mph/142.400kph on Lap 37. Race leaders: Ireland 1; Bonnier 2-15, 21-36 & 41-67; Moss 16-20, 37-40; McLaren 68-80

MOSS PUTS LOTUS ON THE MAP

Lotus's breakthrough came at Monaco thanks to a brilliant drive by Stirling Moss. He put his Rob Walker Racing Lotus on pole and battled with Jo Bonnier's BRM and Brabham's Cooper before winning by 52 seconds. He missed three rounds after being thrown from his car in practice for the Belgian GP, but returned to win the United States GP.

MONACO GRAND PRIX

MONTE CARLO • ROUND 2 • DATE: 29TH MAY 1960
Laps: 100 • Distance: 195.113miles/314.5km • Weather: Warm & dull then rain

Pos	Driver	Team	Chassis-Engine	Result	Qual
1	Stirling Moss	Rob Walker Racing Team	Lotus-Climax 18	2h53m45.500s	1
2	Bruce McLaren	Cooper	Cooper-Climax T53	2h54m37.600s	11
3	Phil Hill	Ferrari	Ferrari 246	2h54m47.400s	10
4	Tony Brooks	Yeoman Credit Racign Team	Cooper-Climax T51	99 laps	3
5	Jo Bonnier	BRM	BRM P48	83 laps	5
6	Richie Ginther	Ferrari	Ferrari 246P	70 laps	9
7	Graham Hill	BRM	BRM P48	66 laps/spun off	6
8	Wolfgang von Trips	Ferrari	Ferrari 246	61 laps/clutch	8
9	Innes Ireland	Lotus	Lotus-Climax 18	56 laps	7
R	Dan Gurney	BRM	BRM P48	44 laps/suspension	14
DQ	Jack Brabham	Cooper	Cooper-Climax T53	40 laps/push start	2
R	Roy Salvadori	High Efficiency Motors	Cooper-Climax T51	29 laps/overheating	12
R	Alan Stacey	Lotus	Lotus-Climax 18	23 laps/engine mount	13
R	Chris Bristow	Yeoman Credit Racign Team	Cooper-Climax T51	17 laps/gearbox	4
R	John Surtees	Lotus	Lotus-Climax 18	17 laps/transmission	15
R	Maurice Trintignant	Scuderia Centro Sud	Cooper-Maserati T51	4 laps/gearbox	16
DNQ	Bruce Halford	Fred Tuck Cars	Cooper-Climax T45	-	17
DNQ	Cliff Allison	Ferrari	Ferrari 246	accident	18
DNQ	Brian Naylor	J B Naylor	JBW-Maserati	-	19
DNQ	Masten Gregory	Scuderia Centro Sud	Cooper-Maserati T51	-	20
DNQ	Chuck Daigh	Reventlow Automobiles Inc	Scarab	-	21
DNQ	Giorgio Scarlatti	Scuderia Castellotti	Cooper-Castellotti T51	-	22
DNQ	Lance Reventlow	Reventlow Automobiles Inc	Scarab	-	23
DNQ	Ian Burgess	Scuderia Centro Sud	Cooper-Maserati T51	-	24
DNQ	Gino Munaron	Scuderia Castellotti	Cooper-Ferrari T51	-	-

Pole: Moss, 1m36.300s, 73.054mph/117.570kph. Fastest lap: McLaren, 1m36.200s, 73.130mph/117.692kph on Lap 11. Race leaders: Bonnier 1-16 & 61-67; Moss 17-33, 41-60 & 68-100; McLaren 34-40

DUTCH GRAND PRIX

ZANDVOORT • ROUND 3 • DATE: 6TH JUNE 1960
Laps: 75 • Distance: 195.405miles/314.475km • Weather: Warm & bright

Pos	Driver	Team	Chassis-Engine	Result	Qual
1	Jack Brabham	Cooper	Cooper-Climax T53	2h01m47.200s	2
2	Innes Ireland	Lotus	Lotus-Climax 18	2h02m11.200s	3
3	Graham Hill	BRM	BRM P48	2h02m43.800s	5
4	Stirling Moss	Rob Walker Racing Team	Lotus-Climax 18	2h02m44.900s	1
5	Wolfgang von Trips	Ferrari	Ferrari 246	74 laps	15
6	Richie Ginther	Ferrari	Ferrari 246	74 laps	12
7	Henry Taylor	Yeoman Credit Racing Team	Cooper-Climax T51	78 laps	14
8	Carel Godin de Beaufort	Ecurie Maarsbergen	Cooper-Climax T51	69 laps	18
R	Alan Stacey	Lotus	Lotus-Climax 18	57 laps/transmission	8
R	Jo Bonnier	BRM	BRM P48	54 laps/engine	4
R	Phil Hill	Ferrari	Ferrari 246	54 laps/engine	13
R	Jim Clark	Lotus	Lotus-Climax 18	42 laps/transmission	11
R	Maurice Trintignant	Scuderia Centro Sud	Cooper-Maserati T51	39 laps/gearbox	17
R	Dan Gurney	BRM	BRM P48	11 laps/accident	6

Pos	Driver	Team	Chassis-Engine	Result	Qual
R	Chris Bristow	Yeoman Credit Racing Team	Cooper-Climax T51	9 laps/engine	7
R	Bruce McLaren	Cooper	Cooper-Climax T53	8 laps/transmission	9
R	Tony Brooks	Yeoman Credit Racing Team	Cooper-Climax T51	4 laps/gearbox	10
NS	Masten Gregory	Scuderia Centro Sud	Cooper-Maserati T51	start money dispute	-
NS	Chuck Daigh	Reventlow Automobiles Inc	Scarab	start money dispute	-
NS	Roy Salvadori	Aston Martin	Aston Martin DBR4/250	start money dispute	-
NS	Lance Reventlow	Reventlow Automobiles Inc	Scarab	start money dispute	-

Pole: Moss, 1m33.200s, 100.638mph/161.961kph. Fastest lap: Moss, 1m33.800s, 99.978mph/160.900kph on lap 75. Race leaders: Brabham 1-75

FERRARI MOVES ITS MOTOR

Stung into action by the rise of Cooper and Lotus, Ferrari experimented with its first rear-engined F1 racer when it entered Richie Ginther in a Dino 246P for the Monaco GP. The car was short of development and the American could only limp around, treating it like a test run as he finished 30 laps in arrears. The car made no further outings.

BELGIAN GRAND PRIX

SPA-FRANCORCHAMPS • ROUND 4 • DATE: 19TH JUNE 1960
Laps: 36 • Distance: 315.38miles/507.6km • Weather: Warm & bright

Pos	Driver	Team	Chassis-Engine	Result	Qual
1	Jack Brabham	Cooper	Cooper-Climax T53	2h21m37.300s	1
2	Bruce McLaren	Cooper	Cooper-Climax T53	2h22m40.600s	14
3	Olivier Gendebien	Yeoman Credit Racing Team	Cooper-Climax T51	35 laps	5
4	Phil Hill	Ferrari	Ferrari 246	35 laps	4
5	Jim Clark	Lotus	Lotus-Climax 18	34 laps	10
6	Lucien Bianchi	Equipe Nationale Belge	Cooper-Climax T45	28 laps	15
R	Graham Hill	BRM	BRM P48	35 laps/engine	6
R	Alan Stacey	Lotus	Lotus-Climax 18	24 laps/fatal accident	17
R	Willy Mairesse	Ferrari	Ferrari 246	23 laps/transmission	13
R	Wolfgang von Trips	Ferrari	Ferrari 246	22 laps/transmission	11
R	Chris Bristow	Yeoman Credit Racing Team	Cooper-Climax T51	19 laps/fatal accident	9
R	Chuck Daigh	Reventlow Automobiles Inc	Scarab	16 laps/engine	18
R	Jo Bonnier	BRM	BRM P48	14 laps/engine	7
R	Innes Ireland	Lotus	Lotus-Climax 18	13 laps/accident	8
R	Dan Gurney	BRM	BRM P48	4 laps/engine	12
R	Tony Brooks	Yeoman Credit Racing Team	Cooper-Climax T51	2 laps/gearbox	2
R	Lance Reventlow	Reventlow Automobiles Inc	Scarab	1 lap/engine	16
NS	Stirling Moss	Rob Walker Racing Team	Lotus-Climax 18	driver injury	3
NS	Mike Taylor	Taylor-Crawley Racing Team	Lotus-Climax 18	driver injury	-

Pole: Brabham, 3m50.000s, 137.133mph/220.695kph. Fastest lap: Ireland, 3m51.900s, 136.018mph/218.900kph Brabham, 3m51.900s, 136.018mph/218.900kph P Hill, 3m51.900s, 136.018mph/218.900kph. Race leaders: Brabham 1-36

FRENCH GRAND PRIX

REIMS • ROUND 5 • DATE: 3RD JULY 1960
Laps: 50 • Distance: 257.869miles/415.1km • Weather: Warm but dull

Pos	Driver	Team	Chassis-Engine	Result	Qual
1	Jack Brabham	Cooper	Cooper-Climax T53	1h57m24.900s	1
2	Olivier Gendebien	Yeaman Credit Racing Team	Cooper-Climax T51	1h58m13.200s	9
3	Bruce McLaren	Cooper	Cooper-Climax T53	1h58m16.800s	7
4	Henry Taylor	Yeaman Credit Racing Team	Cooper-Climax T51	49 laps	12
5	Jim Clark	Lotus	Lotus-Climax 18	49 laps	10
6	Ron Flockhart	Lotus	Lotus-Climax 18	49 laps	14
7	Innes Ireland	Lotus	Lotus-Climax 18	43 laps	4
8	Bruce Halford	Yeoman Credit Racing Team	Cooper-Climax T51	40 laps/engine	15
9	Masten Gregory	Scuderia Centro Sud	Cooper-Maserati T51	37 laps	17
10	Ian Burgess	Scuderia Centro Sud	Cooper-Maserati T51	36 laps	22
R	Wolfgang von Trips	Ferrari	Ferrari 246	30 laps/transmission	5
R	Phil Hill	Ferrari	Ferrari 246	29 laps/transmission	2
R	Jo Bonnier	BRM	BRM P48	22 laps/engine	8
R	Lucien Bianchi	Fred Tuck Cars	Cooper-Climax T45	18 laps/transmission	15
R	Dan Gurney	BRM	BRM P48	17 laps/engine	6
R	Gino Munaron	Scuderia Castellotti	Cooper-Ferrari T51	16 laps/transmission	19
R	Willy Mairesse	Ferrari	Ferrari 246	14 laps/transmission	11
R	Tony Brooks	Vanwall	Vanwall	7 laps/vibrations	13
R	Graham Hill	BRM	BRM P48	0 laps/accident	3
R	Maurice Trintignant	Scuderia Centro Sud	Cooper-Maserati T51	0 laps/accident	18
NS	Richie Ginther	Reventlow Automobiles Inc	Scarab	engine	20
NS	David Piper	Robert Bodle Ltd	Lotus-Climax 16	-	21
NS	Chuck Daigh	Reventlow Automobiles Inc	Scarab	-	23

Pole: Brabham, 2m16.800s, 135.753mph/218.473kph. Fastest lap: Brabham, 2m17.500s, 135.086mph/217.400kph on Lap 25. Race leaders: Brabham 1-3, 5, 7, 9-10,1 2, 14 & 18-50; P Hill 4-6, 11, 13 & 15-17

A DEADLY BELGIAN GP

The 1960 Belgian GP at Spa-Francorchamps was an event that everyone wanted to forget, as it was riven by disaster. After Moss and Mike Taylor were injured in practice, two rising British stars were killed in the race. Chris Bristow crashed his Yeoman Credit Cooper, then Alan Stacey was hit in the face by a bird, crashed and was thrown from his works Lotus.

FROM TWO WHEELS TO FOUR

Seven-time motorcycle world champion John Surtees showed that it was possible to transfer from two wheels to four. Indeed, he made it look easy as he won a Formula Junior race on his debut. F1 followed and in his second race, the British GP at Silverstone, he placed second behind Brabham. He would later take pole and lead in Portugal.

BRITISH GRAND PRIX

SILVERSTONE • ROUND 6 • DATE: 16TH JULY 1960
Laps: 77 • Distance: 225.376miles/362.708km • Weather: Warm but dull

Pos	Driver	Team	Chassis-Engine	Result	Qual
1	Jack Brabham	Cooper	Cooper-Climax T53	2h04m24.600s	1
2	John Surtees	Lotus	Lotus-Climax 18	2h05m14.200s	11
3	Innes Ireland	Lotus	Lotus-Climax 18	2h05m54.200s	5
4	Bruce McLaren	Cooper	Cooper-Climax T53	76 laps	3
5	Tony Brooks	Yeoman Credit Racing Team	Cooper-Climax T51	76 laps/driver injured	-
6	Wolfgang von Trips	Ferrari	Ferrari 246	75 laps	7
7	Phil Hill	Ferrari	Ferrari 246	75 laps	10
8	Henry Taylor	Yeoman Credit Racing Team	Cooper-Climax T51	74 laps	16
9	Olivier Gendebien	Yeoman Credit Racing Team	Cooper-Climax T51	74 laps	12
10	Dan Gurney	BRM	BRM P48	74 laps	6
11	Maurice Trintignant	Aston Martin	Aston Martin DBR5/250	72 laps	21
12	David Piper	Robert Bodle Ltd	Lotus-Climax 16	72 laps	24
13	Brian Naylor	J B Naylor	JBW-Maserati	72 laps	18
14	Masten Gregory	Scuderia Centro Sud	Cooper-Maserati T51	71 laps	14
15	Gino Munaron	Scuderia Castellotti	Cooper-Ferrari T51	70 laps	25
16	Jim Clark	Lotus	Lotus-Climax 18	70 laps	8
R	Graham Hill	BRM	BRM P48	71 laps/spun off	2
R	Lucien Bianchi	Fred Tuck Cars	Cooper-Climax T45	62 laps/electrical	17
R	Jo Bonnier	BRM	BRM P48	59 laps/suspension	4
R	Chuck Daigh	Cooper	Cooper-Climax T51	58 laps/overheating	19
R	Ian Burgess	Scuderia Centro Sud	Cooper-Maserati T51	58 laps/engine	20
R	Roy Salvadori	Aston Martin	Aston Martin DBR4/250	46 laps/steering	13
R	Jack Fairman	C T Atkins	Cooper-Climax T51	46 laps/fuel pump	15
R	Keith Greene	Gilby Engineering	Cooper-Maserati T45	12 laps/overheating	22
NS	Lance Reventlow	Cooper	Cooper-Climax T51	Daigh drove car	23

Pole: Brabham, 1m34.600s, 111.385mph/179.257kph. Fastest lap: G Hill, 1m34.400s, 111.598mph/179.600kph on Lap 56. Race leaders: Brabham, 1-54 & 72-77; G Hill 55-71

TEAMS OPT TO SKIP MONZA

Citing safety issues, the British teams elected to boycott the Italian GP as the organisers had decided to reintroduce the banked oval to the lap for the first time since 1956, largely to favour the more powerful but now outmoded Ferraris on the extra straights that this 6-mile (9.7km) layout provided. This left the race with just 16 starters.

PORTUGUESE GRAND PRIX

OPORTO • ROUND 7 • DATE: 14TH AUGUST 1960
Laps: 55 • Distance: 253.137miles/407.385km • Weather: Hot & bright

Pos	Driver	Team	Chassis-Engine	Result	Qual
1	Jack Brabham	Cooper	Cooper-Climax T53	2h19m00.030s	3
2	Bruce McLaren	Cooper	Cooper-Climax T53	2h19m58.000s	6
3	Jim Clark	Lotus	Lotus-Climax 18	2h20m53.260s	8
4	Wolfgang von Trips	Ferrari	Ferrari 246	2h20m58.840s	9
5	Tony Brooks	Yeoman Credit Racing Team	Cooper-Climax T51	49 laps	12
6	Innes Ireland	Lotus	Lotus-Climax 18	48 laps	7
7	Olivier Gendebien	Yeoman Credit Racing Team	Cooper-Climax T51	46 laps	14
DQ	Stirling Moss	Rob Walker Racing Team	Lotus-Climax 18	51 laps/drove wrong way	4
R	Nicha Cabral	Scuderia Centro Sud	Cooper-Maserati T51	38 laps/accident	15
R	John Surtees	Lotus	Lotus-Climax 18	37 laps/radiator damage	1
R	Phil Hill	Ferrari	Ferrari 246	30 laps/accident	10
R	Dan Gurney	BRM	BRM P48	25 laps/engine	2
R	Masten Gregory	Scuderia Centro Sud	Cooper-Maserati T51	21 laps/gearbox	11
R	Graham Hill	BRM	BRM P48	9 laps/gearbox	5
R	Jo Bonnier	BRM	BRM P48	6 laps/engine	13
NS	Henry Taylor	Yeoman Credit Racing Team	Cooper-Climax T51	-	-

Pole: Surtees, 2m25.560s, 113.829mph/183.190kph. Fastest lap: Surtees, 2m27.530s, 112.306mph/180.740kph on Lap 33. Race leaders: Gurney 1-10; Surtees 11-35; Brabham 36-55

THE END OF A LINE

A curtain came down on a chapter of F1 history at the Italian GP when Phil Hill claimed the last World Championship win for a front-engined car. Due to teams staying away (see separate story), this was a gift. Indeed, Ferrari 246s filled the top three finishing positions as Hill was followed home by Richie Ginther and, a lap down, by Willy Mairesse.

GO WEST

After Sebring had its one-off role in hosting the inaugural United States GP, the race moved to California for 1960, to Riverside. This desert circuit at the foot of the San Bernardino mountains had already hosted the US GP in 1958 when it was a sports car race, but even its challenging uphill esses after the start weren't enough to stop it being a one-hit wonder.

ITALIAN GRAND PRIX

MONZA • ROUND 8 • DATE: 4TH SEPTEMBER 1960
Laps: 50 • Distance: 310.685miles/500.0km • Weather: Warm but dull

Pos	Driver	Team	Chassis-Engine	Result	Qual
1	Phil Hill	Ferrari	Ferrari 246	2h21m09.200s	1
2	Richie Ginther	Ferrari	Ferrari 246	2h23m36.800s	2
3	Willy Mairesse	Ferrari	Ferrari 246	49 laps	3

Pos	Driver	Team	Chassis-Engine	Result	Qual
4	Giulio Cabianca	Scuderia Castellotti	Cooper-Ferrari T51	48 laps	4
5	Wolfgang von Trips	Ferrari	Ferrari 156	48 laps	6
6	Hans Herrmann	Porsche	Porsche 718	47 laps	10
7	Edgar Barth	Porsche	Porsche 718	47 laps	12
8	Piero Drogo	Scuderia Colonia	Cooper-Climax T43	45 laps	15
9	Wolfgang Seidel	Wolfgang Seidel	Cooper-Climax T45	44 laps	13
10	Fred Gamble	Camoradi International	Behra-Porsche	41 laps	14
R	Brian Naylor	J B Naylor	JBW-Maserati	41 laps/gearbox	7
R	Alfonso Thiele	Scuderia Centro Sud	Cooper-Maserati T51	32 laps/gearbox	9
R	Gino Munaron	Scuderia Castellotti	Cooper-Ferrari T51	27 laps/engine	8
R	Giorgio Scarlatti	Scuderia Centro Sud	Cooper-Maserati T51	26 laps/engine	5
R	Vic Wilson	Equipe Prideaux/Dick Gibson	Cooper-Climax T43	24 laps/engine	16
R	Arthur Owen	Arthur Owen	Cooper-Climax T45	0 laps/accident	11
NS	Horace Gould	H H Gould	Maserati 250F	crossed fuel lines	-

Pole: P Hill, 2m41.400s, 138.595mph/223.048kph. Fastest lap: P Hill, 2m43.600s, 136.732mph/220.048kph on Lap 23. Race leaders: Ginther 1-16 & 18-25; P Hill 17 & 26-50

NEW CONSTRUCTORS

Scarab was the lone constructor to break onto the scene in 1960. The American marque, financed by Woolworth's heir Lance Reventlow, was already behind the curve as its car, designed but not ready in 1959, was front-engined. Reventlow qualified just once in Europe before the car was held back until the United States GP, in which Chuck Daigh took 10th.

NEW DRIVERS

This was a good year for new drivers, with Surtees and Ginther claiming second place finishes, for Lotus and Ferrari respectively. However, both were outscored by another Team Lotus newbie, Jim Clark, who peaked with third in the Portuguese GP, but would go on to much greater things. Willy Mairesse also took a third, for Ferrari, at Monza.

UNITED STATES GRAND PRIX

RIVERSIDE • ROUND 9 • DATE: 20TH NOVEMBER 1960
Laps: 75 • Distance: 245.624miles/395.295km • Weather: Warm & bright

Pos	Driver	Team	Chassis-Engine	Result	Qual
1	Stirling Moss	Rob Walker Racing Team	Lotus-Climax 18	2h28m52.200s	1
2	Innes Ireland	Lotus	Lotus-Climax 18	2h29m30.200s	7
3	Bruce McLaren	Cooper	Cooper-Climax T53	2h29m44.200s	10
4	Jack Brabham	Cooper	Cooper-Climax T53	74 laps	2
5	Jo Bonnier	BRM	BRM P48	74 laps	4
6	Phil Hill	Yeoman Credit Racing Team	Cooper-Climax T51	74 laps	13
7	Jim Hall	Jim Hall	Lotus-Climax 18	73 laps	12
8	Roy Salvadori	High Efficiency Motors	Cooper-Climax T51	73 laps	15

Pos	Driver	Team	Chassis-Engine	Result	Qual
9	Wolfgang von Trips	Scuderia Centro Sud	Cooper-Maserati T51	72 laps	16
10	Chuck Daigh	Reventlow Automobiles Inc	Scarab	70 laps	18
11	Pete Lovely	Fred Armbruster	Cooper-Ferrari T51	69 laps	20
12	Olivier Gendebien	Yeoman Credit Racing Team	Cooper-Climax T51	69 laps	8
13	Bob Drake	Joe Lubin	Maserati 250F	68 laps	22
14	Henry Taylor	Yeoman Credit Racing Team	Cooper-Climax T51	68 laps	14
15	Maurice Trintignant	Scuderia Centro Sud	Cooper-Maserati T51	66 laps	19
16	Jim Clark	Lotus	Lotus-Climax 18	61 laps	5
R	Graham Hill	BRM	BRM P48	34 laps/gearbox	11
R	Ian Burgess	Scuderia Centro Sud	Cooper-Maserati T51	29 laps/ignition	23
R	Brian Naylor	J B Naylor	JBW-Maserati	20 laps/engine	17
R	Dan Gurney	BRM	BRM P48	18 laps/overheating	3
R	Ron Flockhart	Cooper	Cooper-Climax T51	11 laps/transmission	21
R	Tony Brooks	Yeoman Credit Racing Team	Cooper-Climax T51	6 laps/spun off	9
R	John Surtees	Lotus	Lotus-Climax 18	3 laps/accident	6

Pole: Moss, 1m55.400s, 102.166mph/164.420kph. Fastest lap: Brabham, 1m56.300s, 101.375mph/163.148kph on Lap 71. Race leaders: Brabham 1-4; Moss 5-75

IN MEMORIAM

As well as Bristow and Stacey, 1960 claimed the life of Harry Blanchard in the Buenos Aires 1000kms, then Ettore Chimeri fell a month later in practice for another sports car race in Havana. The rumbustious Harry Schell died when he crashed at Silverstone two months after that – the American was killed in practice for the International Trophy.

WORLD DRIVERS' CHAMPIONSHIP FINAL RESULTS

Pos	Driver	Nat	Car-Engine	R1	R2	R3	R4	R5	R6	R7	R8	R9	Total
1	Jack Brabham	AUS	Cooper-Climax T51	R	-	-	-	-	-	-	-	-	43
			Cooper-Climax T53	-	DQ	1	1PF	1PF	1P	1	-	4F	
2	Bruce McLaren	NZL	Cooper-Climax T45	1	-	-	-	-	-	-	-	-	34
			Cooper-Climax T53	-	2F	R	2	3	4	2	-	3	
3	Stirling Moss	GBR	Cooper-Climax T51	3 | RPF	-	-	-	-	-	-	-	-	19
			Lotus-Climax 18	-	1P	4PF	NS	-	-	DQ	-	1P	
4	Innes Ireland	GBR	Lotus-Climax 18	6	9	2	RF	7	3	6	-	2	18
5	Phil Hill	USA	Ferrari 246	8	3	R	4F	12	7	R	1PF	-	16
			Cooper-Climax T51	-	-	-	-	-	-	-	-	6	
6	Olivier Gendebien	BEL	Cooper-Climax T51	-	-	-	3	2	9	7	-	12	10
7	Wolfgang von Trips	DEU	Ferrari 246	5	8	5	R	11	6	4	-	-	10
			Ferrari 156	-	-	-	-	-	-	-	5	-	
			Cooper-Maserati T51	-	-	-	-	-	-	-	-	9	
9	Richie Ginther	USA	Ferrari 246P	-	6	-	-	-	-	-	-	-	8
			Ferrari 246	-	-	6	-	-	-	-	2	-	
			Scarab	-	-	-	-	NS	-	-	-	-	
10	Jim Clark	GBR	Lotus-Climax 18	-	-	R	5	5	16	3	-	16	8
11	Tony Brooks	GBR	Cooper-Climax T51	-	4	R	R	-	5	5	-	R	7
			Vanwall	-	-	-	-	R	-	-	-	-	
12	Cliff Allison	GBR	Ferrari 246	2	DNQ	-	-	-	-	-	-	-	6
12	John Surtees	GBR	Lotus-Climax 18	-	R	-	-	-	2	RPF	-	R	6

Pos	Driver	Nat	Car-Engine	R1	R2	R3	R4	R5	R6	R7	R8	R9	Total
15	Graham Hill	GBR	BRM P25	R	-	-	-	-	-	-	-	-	4
			BRM P48	-	7	3	R	R	RF	R	-	R	
15	Willy Mairesse	BEL	Ferrari 246	-	-	-	R	R	-	-	3	-	4
18	Jo Bonnier	SWE	BRM P25	7	-	-	-	-	-	-	-	-	4
			BRM P48	-	5	R	R	R	R	R	-	5	
19	Carlos Menditeguy	ARG	Cooper-Maserati T51	4	-	-	-	-	-	-	-	-	3
19	Henry Taylor	GBR	Cooper-Climax T51	-	-	7	-	4	8	NS	-	14	3
19	Giulio Cabianca	ITA	Cooper-Castellotti T51	-	-	-	-	-	-	-	4	-	3
24	Lucien Bianchi	BEL	Cooper-Climax T45	-	-	-	6	R	R	-	-	-	1
24	Ron Flockhart	GBR	Lotus-Climax 18	-	-	-	-	6	-	-	-	-	1
			Cooper-Climax T51	-	-	-	-	-	-	-	-	R	
24	Hans Herrmann	DEU	Porsche 718	-	-	-	-	-	-	-	6	-	1

WORLD CONSTRUCTORS' CHAMPIONSHIP FINAL RESULTS

Pos	Team-Engine	R1	R2	R3	R4	R5	R6	R7	R8	R9	Total
1	Cooper-Climax	1	2	1	1	1	1	1	8	3	48
2	Lotus-Climax	6	1	2	5	5	2	3	-	1	34
3	Ferrari	2	3	5	4	11	6	4	1	-	26
4	BRM	7	5	3	-	-	10	R	-	5	8
5	Cooper-Maserati	4	-	R	-	9	14	R	-	9	3
5	Cooper-Castellotti	-	-	-	-	-	15	-	4	-	3

SYMBOLS AND GRAND PRIX KEY

Round 1 **Argentinian GP**
Round 2 **Monaco GP**
Round 3 **Dutch GP**
Round 4 **Belgian GP**
Round 5 **French GP**
Round 6 **British GP**
Round 7 **Portuguese GP**
Round 8 **Italian GP**
Round 9 **United States GP**

SCORING

1st **8 points**
2nd **6 points**
3rd **4 points**
4th **3 points**
5th **2 points**
6th **1 point**

Indianapolis 500 results omitted

DNPQ DID NOT PRE-QUALIFY **DNQ** DID NOT QUALIFY **DQ** DISQUALIFIED **EX** EXCLUDED
F FASTEST LAP **NC** NOT CLASSIFIED **NS** NON-STARTER **P** POLE POSITION **R** RETIRED

1961

SEASON SUMMARY

Phil Hill came out on top in the first year of new regulations as Ferrari arrived ready for the new challenge. Their rivals were much less prepared after the British teams in particular had spent most of 1960 fighting to prevent the planned reduction in engine capacity. While Ferrari's new car and engine were race ready, other teams had to rely instead on F2 engines that offered notably less power, until they developed their own. To become world champion, Hill had to beat Ferrari team-mate Wolfgang von Trips, and resist flashes of brilliance from Stirling Moss. It only went the American's way, though, when the German was killed in the Italian GP.

MONACO GRAND PRIX

MONTE CARLO • ROUND 1 • DATE: 14TH MAY 1961
Laps: 100 • Distance: 195.113miles/314.5km • Weather: Warm & hazy

Pos	Driver	Team	Chassis-Engine	Result	Qual
1	Stirling Moss	Rob Walker Racing Team	Lotus-Climax 18	2h45m50.100s	1
2	Richie Ginther	Ferrari	Ferrari 156	2h45m53.700s	2
3	Phil Hill	Ferrari	Ferrari 156	2h46m31.400s	5
4	Wolfgang von Trips	Ferrari	Ferrari 156	98 laps/accident	6
5	Dan Gurney	Porsche	Porsche 718	98 laps	10
6	Bruce McLaren	Cooper	Cooper-Climax T55	95 laps	7
7	Maurice Trintignant	Scuderia Serenissima	Cooper-Maserati T51	95 laps	15
8	Cliff Allison	UDT Laystall Racing Team	Lotus-Climax 18	93 laps	14
9	Hans Herrmann	Porsche	Porsche 718	91 laps	12
10	Jim Clark	Lotus	Lotus-Climax 21	89 laps	3
11	John Surtees	Yeoman Credit Racing Team	Cooper-Climax T53	68 laps/engine	11
12	Jo Bonnier	Porsche	Porsche 787	59 laps/fuel injection	9
13	Tony Brooks	BRM	BRM-Climax P48/57	54 laps/engine	8
R	Michael May	Scuderia Colonia	Lotus-Climax 18	42 laps/gearbox	13
R	Jack Brabham	Cooper	Cooper-Climax T55	38 laps/ignition	16
R	Graham Hill	BRM	BRM-Climax P48/57	11 laps/fuel pump	4
NS	Innes Ireland	Lotus	Lotus-Climax 21	driver injured	10
DNQ	Henry Taylor	UDT Laystall Racing Team	Lotus-Climax 18	-	17
DNQ	Masten Gregory	Camoradi International	Cooper-Climax T53	-	18
DNQ	Lucien Bianchi	Equipe Nationale Belge	Emeryson-Maserati	-	19
DNQ	Olivier Gendebien	Equipe Nationale Belge	Emeryson-Maserati	-	20

Pole: Moss, 1m39.100s, 70.990mph/114.248kph. Fastest lap: Ginther, 1m36.300s, 73.054mph/117.570kph on Lap 84 Moss, 1m36.300s, 73.054mph/117.570kph on Lap 85.
Race leaders: Ginther 1-13; Moss 14-100

SHRINKING THE PACKAGE

For 1961, engines were cut from 2500cc to 1500cc. With superchargers banned, that meant that power was down, typically, to 190bhp. To prevent these smaller cars from becoming too fragile, they were given a minimum weight of 450kg (992lb). A sensible change was that rollover hoops were made mandatory to protect drivers' heads and shoulders.

DUTCH GRAND PRIX

ZANDVOORT • ROUND 2 • DATE: 22ND MAY 1961
Laps: 75 • Distance: 195.405miles/314.475km • Weather: Warm, bright & windy

Pos	Driver	Team	Chassis-Engine	Result	Qual
1	Wolfgang von Trips	Ferrari	Ferrari 156	2h01m52.100s	2
2	Phil Hill	Ferrari	Ferrari 156	2h01m53.000s	1
3	Jim Clark	Lotus	Lotus-Climax 21	2h02m05.200s	10
4	Stirling Moss	Rob Walker Racing Team	Lotus-Climax 18	2h02m14.300s	4
5	Richie Ginther	Ferrari	Ferrari 156	2h02m14.400s	3
6	Jack Brabham	Cooper	Cooper-Climax T55	2h03m12.200s	7
7	John Surtees	Yeoman Credit Racing Team	Cooper-Climax T53	2h03m18.800s	9
8	Graham Hill	BRM	BRM-Climax P48/57	2h03m21.900s	5
9	Tony Brooks	BRM	BRM-Climax P48/57	74 laps	8
10	Dan Gurney	Porsche	Porsche 787	74 laps	6
11	Jo Bonnier	Porsche	Porsche 787	73 laps	11
12	Bruce McLaren	Cooper	Cooper-Climax T55	73 laps	13
13	Trevor Taylor	Lotus	Lotus-Climax 18	73 laps	14
14	Carel Godin de Beaufort	Ecurie Maarsbergen	Porsche 718	72 laps	15
15	Hans Herrmann	Ecurie Maarsbergen	Porsche 718	72 laps	12
NS	Ian Burgess	Camoradi International	Lotus-Climax 18	reserve entry	10
NS	Masten Gregory	Camoradi International	Cooper-Climax T53	reserve entry	15

Pole: P Hill, 1m35.700s, 98.009mph/157.730kph. Fastest lap: Clark, 1m35.500s, 98.214mph/158.060kph on Lap 7. Race leaders: von Trips 1-75

WINNING ON YOUR DEBUT

Giancarlo Baghetti won on his World Championship debut. Of course, Giuseppe Farina did so by winning the first-ever World Championship race in 1950, but this was a more extraordinary feat, as the Italian was up against seasoned F1 racers when he won in a privately entered Ferrari at Reims, having already bagged two non-championship wins.

BELGIAN GRAND PRIX

SPA-FRANCORCHAMPS • ROUND 3 • DATE: 18TH JUNE 1961
Laps: 30 • Distance: 262.840miles/423.0km • Weather: Warm but dull

Pos	Driver	Team	Chassis-Engine	Result	Qual
1	Phil Hill	Ferrari	Ferrari 156	2h03m03.800s	1
2	Wolfgang von Trips	Ferrari	Ferrari 156	2h03m04.500s	2
3	Richie Ginther	Ferrari	Ferrari 156	2h03m23.300s	5
4	Olivier Gendebien	Ferrari	Ferrari 156	2h03m49.400s	3
5	John Surtees	Yeoman Credit Racing Team	Cooper-Climax T53	2h04m30.600s	4
6	Dan Gurney	Porsche	Porsche 718	2h04m34.800s	10
7	Jo Bonnier	Porsche	Porsche 718	2h05m50.900s	9
8	Stirling Moss	Rob Walker Racing Team	Lotus-Climax 18/21	2h06m59.400s	8
9	Jackie Lewis	H&L Motors	Cooper-Climax T53	29 laps	13
10	Masten Gregory	Camoradi International	Cooper-Climax T53	29 laps	12
11	Carel Godin de Beaufort	Ecurie Maarsbergen	Porsche 718	28 laps	14
12	Jim Clark	Lotus	Lotus-Climax 21	24 laps	16

Pos	Driver	Team	Chassis-Engine	Result	Qual
13	Tony Brooks	BRM	BRM-Climax P48/57	24 laps	7
R	Graham Hill	BRM	BRM-Climax P48/57	24 laps/ignition	6
R	Maurice Trintignant	Scuderia Serenissima	Cooper-Maserati T51	23 laps/gearbox	20
R	Lorenzo Bandini	Scuderia Centro Sud	Cooper-Maserati T53	20 laps/wheel	17
R	Jack Brabham	Cooper	Cooper-Climax T55	12 laps/engine	11
R	Bruce McLaren	Cooper	Cooper-Climax T55	9 laps/ignition	15
R	Innes Ireland	Lotus	Lotus-Climax 21	9 laps/engine	18
R	Lucien Bianchi	Equipe Nationale Belge	Lotus-Climax 18	9 laps/oil leak	23
R	Willy Mairesse	Equipe Nationale Belge	Lotus-Climax 18	7 laps/ignition	19
NS	Tony Marsh	Tony Marsh	Lotus-Climax 18	start money dispute	21
NS	Wolfgang Seidel	Scuderia Colonia	Lotus-Climax 18	start money dispute	22
NS	Ian Burgess	Camoradi International	Lotus-Climax 18	start money dispute	24
NS	Cliff Allison	UDT Laystall Racing Team	Lotus-Climax 18/21	driver injured	-
NS	Henry Taylor	UDT Laystall Racing Team	Lotus-Climax 18/21	Allison crashed it	-

Pole: P Hill, 3m59.300s, 131.804mph/212.118kph. Fastest lap: Ginther, 3m59.800s, 131.544mph/211.700kph on Lap 20. Race leaders: P Hill 1, 3-5, 8, 11-13, 15, 17-18, 21-23 & 25-30; Gendebien 2 & 6-7; von Trips 9-10, 14, 16, 19-20 & 24

A CLEAR ROUND

Mechanical reliability was still poor in the early 1960s, and so it was thought extraordinary when all 15 starters in the Dutch GP at Zandvoort were still running 75 laps later at the finish. Victory went, as was the norm in 1961, to a Ferrari – this time von Trips's machine – with Hill's in second. Last-placed finisher Hans Herrmann's Porsche was three laps down.

FRENCH GRAND PRIX

REIMS • ROUND 4 • DATE: 2ND JULY 1961
Laps: 52 • Distance: 268.248miles/431.704km • Weather: Hot & bright

Pos	Driver	Team	Chassis-Engine	Result	Qual
1	Giancarlo Baghetti	FISA	Ferrari 156	2h14m17.500s	12
2	Dan Gurney	Porsche	Porsche 718	2h14m17.600s	9
3	Jim Clark	Lotus	Lotus-Climax 21	2h15m18.600s	5
4	Innes Ireland	Lotus	Lotus-Climax 21	2h15m27.800s	10
5	Bruce McLaren	Cooper	Cooper-Climax T55	2h15m59.300s	8
6	Graham Hill	BRM	BRM-Climax P48/57	2h15m59.400s	6
7	Jo Bonnier	Porsche	Porsche 718	2h17m32.900s	13
8	Roy Salvadori	Yeoman Credit Racing Team	Cooper-Climax T53	51 laps	15
9	Phil Hill	Ferrari	Ferrari 156	50 laps	1
10	Henry Taylor	UDT Laystall Racing Team	Lotus-Climax 18/21	49 laps	25
11	Michael May	Scuderia Colonia	Lotus-Climax 18	48 laps	22
12	Masten Gregory	Camoradi International	Cooper-Climax T53	43 laps	16
13	Maurice Trintignant	Scuderia Serenissima	Cooper-Maserati T51	42 laps	23
14	Ian Burgess	Camoradi International	Lotus-Climax 18	42 laps	24
15	Richie Ginther	Ferrari	Ferrari 156	40 laps/fuel pressure	3
R	Stirling Moss	Rob Walker Racing Team	Lotus-Climax 18/21	31 laps/brakes	4
R	Willy Mairesse	Lotus	Lotus-Climax 21	27 laps/engine	20
R	Carel Godin de Beaufort	Ecurie Maarsbergen	Porsche 718	23 laps/overheating	17
R	Lucien Bianchi	UDT Laystall Racing Team	Lotus-Climax 18/21	21 laps/overheating	19
R	Wolfgang von Trips	Ferrari	Ferrari 156	18 laps/engine	2

Pos	Driver	Team	Chassis-Engine	Result	Qual
R	Giorgio Scarlatti	Scuderia Serenissima	De Tomaso-OSCA	15 laps/engine	26
R	Jack Brabham	Cooper	Cooper-Climax T55	14 laps/fuel pressure	14
R	Bernard Collomb	Bernard Collomb	Cooper-Climax T53	6 laps/engine	21
R	John Surtees	Yeoman Credit Racing Team	Cooper-Climax T53	4 laps/accident	7
R	Tony Brooks	BRM	BRM-Climax P48/57	4 laps/overheating	11
R	Jackie Lewis	H&L Motors	Cooper-Climax T53	4 laps/overheating	18
NS	Juan Manuel Bordeu	UDT Laystall Racing Team	Lotus-Climax 18/21	Bianchi drove car	-

Pole: P Hill, 2m44.900s, 112.620mph/181.244kph. Fastest lap: P Hill, 2m27.100s, 126.247mph/203.176kph. Race leaders: P Hill 1-12 & 18-37; von Trips 13-17; Ginther 38-40; Baghetti 41-43, 45, 47, 50 & 52; Bonnier 44; Gurney 46, 48-49 & 51

CHASING THE MONEY

There's an irony that F1 drivers ignored the Indianapolis 500 when it was part of the World Championship in the 1950s, but began to race there when it wasn't. The driver who went first was Jack Brabham, whose Cooper was dwarfed by the front-engined roadsters but raced through to ninth. It would take until 1965 before F1 racers made their breakthrough.

BRITISH GRAND PRIX

AINTREE • ROUND 5 • DATE: 15TH JULY 1961
Laps: 75 • Distance: 224.936miles/362.1km • Weather: Cool & damp then drying

Pos	Driver	Team	Chassis-Engine	Result	Qual
1	Wolfgang von Trips	Ferrari	Ferrari 156	2h40m53.600s	4
2	Phil Hill	Ferrari	Ferrari 156	2h41m39.600s	1
3	Richie Ginther	Ferrari	Ferrari 156	2h41m40.400s	2
4	Jack Brabham	Cooper	Cooper-Climax T55	2h42m02.200s	9
5	Jo Bonnier	Porsche	Porsche 718	2h42m09.800s	3
6	Roy Salvadori	Yeoman Credit Racing Team	Cooper-Climax T53	2h42m19.800s	13
7	Dan Gurney	Porsche	Porsche 718	74 laps	12
8	Bruce McLaren	Cooper	Cooper-Climax T55	74 laps	14
9	Tony Brooks	BRM	BRM-Climax P48/57	73 laps	6
10	Innes Ireland	Lotus	Lotus-Climax 21	72 laps	7
11	Masten Gregory	Camoradi International	Cooper-Climax T53	71 laps	16
12	Lorenzo Bandini	Scuderia Centro Sud	Cooper-Maserati T53	71 laps	21
13	Tony Maggs	Louise Bryden-Brown	Lotus-Climax 18	69 laps	24
14	Ian Burgess	Camoradi International	Lotus-Climax 18	69 laps	25
15	Keith Greene	Gilby Engineering	Gilby-Climax	69 laps	26
16	Carel Godin de Beaufort	Ecurie Maarsbergen	Porsche 718	69 laps	18
17	Wolfgang Seidel	Scuderia Colonia	Lotus-Climax 18	58 laps	22
R	Jim Clark	Lotus	Lotus-Climax 21	62 laps/oil leak	8
DQ	Fairman / Moss*	Rob Walker Racing Team	Ferguson-Climax P99	56 laps/push start	20
R	Lucien Bianchi	UDT Laystall Racing Team	Lotus-Climax 18/21	45 laps/gearbox	30
R	Stirling Moss	Rob Walker Racing Team	Lotus-Climax 18/21	44 laps/push start	5
R	Graham Hill	BRM	BRM-Climax P48/57	43 laps/engine	11
R	Giancarlo Baghetti	Scuderia Sant Ambroeus	Ferrari 156	27 laps/accident	19
R	Tony Marsh	Tony Marsh	Lotus-Climax 18	25 laps/ignition	27
R	John Surtees	Yeoman Credit Racing Team	Cooper-Climax T53	23 laps/differential	10
R	Tim Parnell	Tim Parnell	Lotus-Climax 18	12 laps/clutch	29

Pos	Driver	Team	Chassis-Engine	Result	Qual
R	Jackie Lewis	H&L Motors	Cooper-Climax T53	7 laps/handling	15
R	Gerry Ashmore	Gerry Ashmore	Lotus-Climax 18	7 laps/ignition	26
R	Henry Taylor	UDT Laystall Racing Team	Lotus-Climax 18/21	5 laps/accident	17
R	Massimo Natili	Scuderia Centro Sud	Cooper-Maserati T51	0 laps/gearbox	28
*Jack Fairman, Stirling Moss					

Pole: P Hill, 1m58.800s, 90.908mph/146.303kph. Fastest lap: Brooks, 1m57.800s, 91.652mph/147.500kph on Lap 72. Race leaders: P HIll 1-6; von Trips 7-75

DISASTER AT MONZA

It ought to have been a day of celebration for the Tifosi packing the spectator banking at Monza as two of their heroes diced for victory and for the F1 crown, but a clash with Clark's Lotus approaching the Parabolica on lap one sent von Trips's Ferrari into the crowd, killing him along with 14 spectators. Hill raced on to the win and the title.

THE FIRST LOTUS WORKS WIN

Colin Chapman was delighted when Moss gave Lotus its first F1 win in 1960, but was miffed that he did so with a customer team. However, he ought to have smiled when Innes Ireland won the first United States GP held at Watkins Glen in a works Lotus – the team's first victory. Except he didn't seem to be that happy, as he dropped Ireland for 1962.

GERMAN GRAND PRIX

NURBURGRING • ROUND 6 • DATE: 6TH AUGUST 1961
Laps: 15 • Distance: 212.518miles/342.15km • Weather: Cool with showers

Pos	Driver	Team	Chassis-Engine	Result	Qual
1	Stirling Moss	Rob Walker Racing Team	Lotus-Climax 18/21	2h18m12.400s	3
2	Wolfgang von Trips	Ferrari	Ferrari 156	2h18m33.800s	5
3	Phil Hill	Ferrari	Ferrari 156	2h18m34.900s	1
4	Jim Clark	Lotus	Lotus-Climax 21	2h19m29.500s	8
5	John Surtees	Yeoman Credit Racing Team	Cooper-Climax T53	2h20m05.500s	10
6	Bruce McLaren	Cooper	Cooper-Climax T55	2h20m53.800s	12
7	Dan Gurney	Porsche	Porsche 718	2h21m35.500s	7
8	Richie Ginther	Ferrari	Ferrari 156	2h23m35.500s	14
9	Jackie Lewis	H&L Motors	Cooper-Climax T53	2h23m36.100s	18
10	Roy Salvadori	Yeoman Credit Racing Team	Cooper-Climax T53	2h30m23.900s	15
11	Tony Maggs	Louise Bryden-Brown	Lotus-Climax 18	14 laps	22
12	Ian Burgess	Camoradi International	Cooper-Climax T53	14 laps	24
13	Hans Herrmann	Porsche	Porsche 718	14 laps	11
14	Carel Godin de Beaufort	Ecurie Maarsbergen	Porsche 718	14 laps	17
15	Tony Marsh	Tony Marsh	Lotus-Climax 18	13 laps	20
16	Gerry Ashmore	Gerry Ashmore	Lotus-Climax 18	13 laps	25
R	Willy Mairesse	Ferrari	Ferrari 156	13 laps/accident	13
R	Maurice Trintignant	Scuderia Serenissima	Cooper-Maserati T51	12 laps/engine	21
R	Bernard Collomb	Bernard Collomb	Cooper-Climax T53	11 laps/engine	26
R	Lorenzo Bandini	Scuderia Centro Sud	Cooper-Maserati T53	10 laps/engine	19

Pos	Driver	Team	Chassis-Engine	Result	Qual
R	Tony Brooks	BRM	BRM-Climax P48/57	6 laps/engine	9
R	Jo Bonnier	Porsche	Porsche 718	5 laps/engine	4
R	Wolfgang Seidel	Scuderia Colonia	Lotus-Climax 18	3 laps/handling	23
R	Graham Hill	BRM	BRM-Climax P48/57	1 lap/accident	6
R	Innes Ireland	Lotus	Lotus-Climax 21	1 lap/fire	16
R	Jack Brabham	Cooper	Cooper-Climax T58	0 laps/accident	2
NS	Michael May	Scuderia Colonia	Lotus-Climax 18	accident	27

Pole: P Hill, 8m55.200s, 95.337mph/153.430kph. Fastest lap: P Hill, 8m57.800s, 94.876mph/152.688kph on Lap 10. Race leaders: Moss 1-15

NEW CONSTRUCTORS
There could hardly have been more different debutants than de Tomaso and Ferguson. The former was set up by Italian-domiciled racer Alejandro de Tomaso, but building six cars was too much too soon. The latter was built to showcase the company's four-wheel drive system, as used on its tractors, and shone when Stirling Moss drove it to victory in the Oulton Park Gold Cup.

NEW DRIVERS
In addition to maiden race grand prix winner Baghetti (see separate story), 1961 also marked the first appearance of a driver who qualified second on his debut at Monza, Ferrari's hugely exciting Ricardo Rodriguez. Another hit was future Ferrari grand prix winner Lorenzo Bandini, who started off with a Scuderia Centro Sud Cooper.

ITALIAN GRAND PRIX

MONZA • ROUND 7 • DATE: 10TH SEPTEMBER 1961
Laps: 43 • Distance: 267.189miles/430.0km • Weather: Very hot & bright

Pos	Driver	Team	Chassis-Engine	Result	Qual
1	Phil Hill	Ferrari	Ferrari 156	2h03m13.000s	4
2	Dan Gurney	Porsche	Porsche 718	2h03m44.200s	12
3	Bruce McLaren	Cooper	Cooper-Climax T55	2h05m41.400s	14
4	Jackie Lewis	H&L Motors	Cooper-Climax T53	2h05m53.400s	16
5	Tony Brooks	BRM	BRM-Climax P48/57	2h05m53.500s	13
6	Roy Salvadori	Yeoman Credit Racing Team	Cooper-Climax T53	42 laps	18
7	Carel Godin de Beaufort	Ecurie Maarsbergen	Porsche 718	41 laps	15
8	Lorenzo Bandini	Scuderia Centro Sud	Cooper-Maserati T53	41 laps	21
9	Maurice Trintignant	Scuderia Serenissima	Cooper-Maserati T51	41 laps	22
10	Tim Parnell	Tim Parnell	Lotus-Climax 18	40 laps	27
11	Henry Taylor	UDT Laystall Racing Team	Lotus-Climax 18/21	39 laps	23
12	Renato Pirocchi	Pescara Racing Club	Cooper-Maserati T51	38 laps	29
R	Stirling Moss	Rob Walker Racing Team	Lotus-Climax 21	36 laps/wheel	11
R	Richie Ginther	Ferrari	Ferrari 156	23 laps/engine	3
R	Gaetano Starrabba	Prince Gaetano Starrabba	Lotus-Maserati 18	19 laps/engine	30
R	Jo Bonnier	Porsche	Porsche 718	14 laps/suspension	8
R	Ricardo Rodriguez	Ferrari	Ferrari 156	13 laps/fuel pump	2

Pos	Driver	Team	Chassis-Engine	Result	Qual
R	Giancarlo Baghetti	Scuderia Sant Ambroeus	Ferrari 156	13 laps/engine	6
R	Nino Vaccarella	Scuderia Serenissima	De Tomaso-Alfa Romeo	13 laps/engine	20
R	Masten Gregory	UDT Laystall Racing Team	Lotus-Climax 18/21	11 laps/suspension	17
R	Graham Hill	BRM	BRM-Climax P48/57	10 laps/engine	5
R	Jack Brabham	Cooper	Cooper-Climax T58	8 laps/overheating	10
R	Brian Naylor	J B Naylor	JBW-Climax	6 laps/engine	31
R	Innes Ireland	Lotus	Lotus-Climax 18/21	5 laps/chassis	9
R	Jack Fairman	Fred Tuck	Cooper-Climax T45	5 laps/engine	26
R	John Surtees	Yeoman Credit Racing Team	Cooper-Climax T53	2 laps/accident	19
R	Wolfgang von Trips	Ferrari	Ferrari 156	1 lap/fatal accident	1
R	Jim Clark	Lotus	Lotus-Climax 21	1 lap/accident	7
R	Roberto Bussinello	Isobele de Tomaso	De Tomaso-Alfa Romeo	1 lap/engine	24
R	Wolfgang Seidel	Scuderia Colonia	Lotus-Climax 18	1 lap/engine	28
R	Roberto Lippi	Scuderia Settecolli	De Tomaso-OSCA	1 lap/engine	32
R	Gerry Ashmore	Gerry Ashmore	Lotus-Climax 18	0 laps/accident	25
DNQ	Andre Pilette	Equipe Nationale Belge	Emeryson-Climax	-	33

Pole: von Trips, 2m46.300s, 134.512mph/216.476kph. Fastest lap: Baghetti, 2m48.400s, 132.834mph/213.776kph on Lap 2. Race leaders: P Hill 1-3, 5, 7, 10 & 14-43; Ginther 4, 6, 8-9, 11-13

CLASSIC CAR: FERRARI DINO 156

The Dino 156 was known as the "Sharknose" for its distinctive pointed, nostrilled nose. However, its place among the great cars of F1 was earned thanks to its prodigious win rate, before being superseded by rival marques in 1962. Designed by Carlo Chiti, the 156 started life with the best engine for the new 1.5-litre formula and this V6 was its strongest point. Enjoying a power advantage over its rivals helped its drivers to win five of 1961's eight grands prix. Unfortunately, Ferrari's first true rear-engined chassis, as opposed to the 246P conversion of the Dino 246, was not the best at handling.

UNITED STATES GRAND PRIX

WATKINS GLEN • ROUND 8 • DATE: 8TH OCTOBER 1961
Laps: 100 • Distance: 229.916miles/370.15km • Weather: Warm & bright

Pos	Driver	Team	Chassis-Engine	Result	Qual
1	Innes Ireland	Lotus	Lotus-Climax 21	2h13m45.800s	8
2	Dan Gurney	Porsche	Porsche 718	2h13m50.100s	7
3	Tony Brooks	BRM	BRM-Climax P48/57	2h14m34.800s	5
4	Bruce McLaren	Cooper	Cooper-Climax T55	2h14m43.800s	4
5	Graham Hill	BRM	BRM-Climax P48/57	99 laps	2
6	Jo Bonnier	Porsche	Porsche 718	98 laps	10
7	Jim Clark	Lotus	Lotus-Climax 21	96 laps	6
8	Roger Penske	John M Wyatt III	Cooper-Climax T53	96 laps	16
9	Peter Ryan	J Wheeler Autosport	Lotus-Climax 18/21	96 laps	13
10	Hap Sharp	Hap Sharp	Cooper-Climax T53	93 laps	17
11	Gendebien / Gregory*	UDT Laystall Racing Team	Lotus-Climax 18/21	92 laps	15
R	Roy Salvadori	Yeoman Credit Racing Team	Cooper-Climax T53	96 laps/engine	12
R	Jim Hall	Jim Hall	Lotus-Climax 18/21	76 laps/oil leak	18

Pos	Driver	Team	Chassis-Engine	Result	Qual
R	Lloyd Ruby	J Frank Harrison	Lotus-Climax 18	76 laps/magneto	19
R	Stirling Moss	Rob Walker Racing Team	Lotus-Climax 18/21	58 laps/engine	3
R	Jack Brabham	Cooper	Cooper-Climax T58	57 laps/overheating	1
R	Masten Gregory	UDT Laystall Racing Team	Lotus-Climax 18/21	23 laps/gearbox	11
R	Walt Hansgen	Momo Corporation	Cooper-Climax T53	14 laps/accident	14
R	John Surtees	Yeoman Credit Racing Team	Cooper-Climax T53	0 laps/engine	9

*Olivier Gendebien, Masten Gregory

Pole: Brabham, 1m17.000s, 107.532mph/173.057kph. Fastest lap: Brabham, 1m18.200s, 105.881mph/170.400kph on Lap 28. Race leaders: Moss 1-5, 16, 24-25, 34-35 & 39-58; Brabham 6-15, 17-23, 26-33 & 36-38; Ireland 59-100

WORLD DRIVERS' CHAMPIONSHIP FINAL RESULTS

Pos	Driver	Nat	Car-Engine	R1	R2	R3	R4	R5	R6	R7	R8	Total
1	Phil Hill	USA	Ferrari 156	3	2P	1P	9PF	2P	3PF	1	-	34
2	Wolfgang von Trips	DEU	Ferrari 156	4	1	2	R	1	2	RP	-	33
3	Stirling Moss	GBR	Lotus-Climax 18	1PF	4	-	-	-	-	-	-	21
			Lotus-Climax 18/21	-	-	8	R	R	1	-	R	
			Ferguson-Climax P99	-	-	-	-	DQ	-	-	-	
			Lotus-Climax 21	-	-	-	-	-	-	R	-	
4	Dan Gurney	USA	Porsche 718	5	-	6	2	7	7	2	2	21
			Porsche 787	-	10	-	-	-	-	-	-	
5	Richie Ginther	USA	Ferrari 156	2F	5	3F	15	3	8	R	-	16
6	Innes Ireland	GBR	Lotus-Climax 21	NS	-	R	4	10	R	-	1	12
			Lotus-Climax 18/21	-	-	-	-	-	-	R	-	
7	Jim Clark	GBR	Lotus-Climax 21	10	3F	12	3	R	4	R	7	11
8	Bruce McLaren	NZL	Cooper-Climax T55	6	12	R	5	8	6	3	4	11
9	Giancarlo Baghetti	ITA	Ferrari 156	-	-	-	1	R	-	RF	-	9
10	Tony Brooks	GBR	BRM-Climax P48/57	13	9	13	R	9F	R	5	3	6
11	Jack Brabham	AUS	Cooper-Climax T55	R	6	R	R	4	-	-	-	4
			Cooper-Climax T58	-	-	-	-	-	R	R	RPF	
12	John Surtees	GBR	Cooper-Climax T53	11	7	5	R	R	5	R	R	4
13	Olivier Gendebien	BEL	Ferrari 156	-	-	4	-	-	-	-	-	3
			Emeryson-Maserati	NQ	-	-	-	-	-	-	-	
			Lotus-Climax 18/21	-	-	-	-	-	-	-	11	
13	Jackie Lewis	GBR	Cooper-Climax T53	-	-	9	R	R	9	4	-	3
15	Jo Bonnier	SWE	Porsche 787	12	11	-	-	-	-	-	-	3
			Porsche 718	-	-	7	7	5	R	R	6	
15	Graham Hill	GBR	BRM-Climax P48/57	R	8	R	6	R	R	R	5	3
17	Roy Salvadori	GBR	Cooper-Climax T53	-	-	-	8	6	10	6	R	2

WORLD CONSTRUCTORS' CHAMPIONSHIP FINAL RESULTS

Pos	Team-Engine	R1	R2	R3	R4	R5	R6	R7	R8	Total
1	Ferrari	2	1	1	1	1	2	1	-	40
2	Lotus-Climax	1	3	8	3	10	4	10	1	32
3	Porsche	5	10	6	2	5	7	2	2	22
4	Cooper-Climax	6	6	5	5	4	5	3	4	14
5	BRM-Climax	-	-	-	6	-	-	-	-	7

SYMBOLS AND GRAND PRIX KEY

Round 1 **Monaco GP**
Round 2 **Dutch GP**
Round 3 **Belgian GP**
Round 4 **French GP**
Round 5 **British GP**
Round 6 **German GP**
Round 7 **Italian GP**
Round 8 **United States GP**

SCORING

1st **9 points**
2nd **6 points**
3rd **4 points**
4th **3 points**
5th **2 points**
6th **1 point**

DNPQ DID NOT PRE-QUALIFY **DNQ DID NOT QUALIFY** **DQ DISQUALIFIED** **EX EXCLUDED**
F FASTEST LAP **NC NOT CLASSIFIED** **NS NON-STARTER** **P POLE POSITION** **R RETIRED**

SEASON SUMMARY

This World Championship boiled down to a two-way fight between two British drivers: Graham Hill and Jim Clark. It ought to have been between three British drivers, but Stirling Moss was fortunate to survive a pre-season accident and so spent the year on the sidelines with head injuries. So, it was Hill for BRM, a team perhaps facing its last year before backing was withdrawn, versus Clark for burgeoning Lotus. Hill drew first blood at Zandvoort, but they would swap wins through the season until they travelled to South Africa for the final round. Clark's car broke and so Hill secured what would be BRM's only F1 title.

DUTCH GRAND PRIX

ZANDVOORT • ROUND 1 • DATE: 20TH MAY 1962
Laps: 80 • Distance: 208.186miles/335.44km • Weather: Warm & bright

Pos	Driver	Team	Chassis-Engine	Result	Qual
1	Graham Hill	BRM	BRM P57	2h11m02.100s	2
2	Trevor Taylor	Lotus	Lotus-Climax 24	2h11m29.300s	10
3	Phil Hill	Ferrari	Ferrari 156	2h12m23.200s	9
4	Giancarlo Baghetti	Ferrari	Ferrari 156	79 laps	12
5	Tony Maggs	Cooper	Cooper-Climax T55	78 laps	15
6	Carel Godin de Beaufort	Ecurie Maarsbergen	Porsche 718	76 laps	14
7	Jo Bonnier	Porsche	Porsche 804	75 laps	13
8	Jackie Lewis	Ecurie Galloise	Cooper-Climax T53	70 laps	7
9	Jim Clark	Lotus	Lotus-Climax 25	70 laps	3
R	Ricardo Rodriguez	Ferrari	Ferrari 156	73 laps/accident	11
R	Richie Ginther	BRM	BRM P48/57	71 laps/accident	7
R	Innes Ireland	UDT Laystall Racing Team	Lotus-Climax 24	61 laps/accident	6
R	Masten Gregory	UDT Laystall Racing Team	Lotus-Climax 18/21	54 laps/halfshaft	16
NC	Wolfgang Seidel	Ecurie Maarsbergen	Emeryson-Climax	52 laps	20
R	Dan Gurney	Porsche	Porsche 804	47 laps/gearbox	8
R	Bruce McLaren	Cooper	Cooper-Climax T60	21 laps/gearbox	5
R	Roy Salvadori	Bowmaker Racing Team	Lola-Climax 4	12 laps/withdrawn	17
R	John Surtees	Bowmaker Racing Team	Lola-Climax 4	8 laps/accident	1
R	Jack Brabham	Brabham	Lotus-Climax 24	4 laps/accident	4
R	Ben Pon	Ecurie Maarsbergen	Porsche 787	2 laps/accident	10

Pole: Surtees, 1m32.500s, 101.399mph/163.187kph. Fastest lap: McLaren, 1m34.400s, 99.357mph/159.900kph on Lap 5. Race leaders: Clark 1-11, G Hill 12-54 & 56-80; P Hill 55

OVER AND OUT

Stirling Moss, Mr Motor Racing, suffered an unexplained crash in a non-championship race at Goodwood that ended his F1 career. What was not known at the time was that Ferrari had done a deal with Rob Walker Racing to build a car for him for 1962. It was a year before Moss tested again and he decided that he would never regain his previous world-leading level, so quit.

PRIVATE PURSUITS

One feature of the second year of the 1.5-litre formula was that the number of privateer teams was on the increase. This was thanks to the availability of customer chassis from Cooper and Lotus, plus competitive engines from Coventry Climax. In the German GP, for example, half of the 30 cars entered came from 11 privateer teams.

MONACO GRAND PRIX

MONTE CARLO • ROUND 2 • DATE: 3RD JUNE 1962
Laps: 100 • Distance: 195.113miles/314.5km • Weather: Warm but dull

Pos	Driver	Team	Chassis-Engine	Result	Qual
1	Bruce McLaren	Cooper	Cooper-Climax T60	2h46m29.700s	3
2	Phil Hill	Ferrari	Ferrari 156	2h46m31.000s	9
3	Lorenzo Bandini	Ferrari	Ferrari 156	2h47m53.800s	10
4	John Surtees	Bowmaker Racing Team	Lola-Climax 4	99 laps	11
5	Jo Bonnier	Porsche	Porsche 718	93 laps	18
6	Graham Hill	BRM	BRM P57	92 laps/engine	2
7	Willy Mairesse	Ferrari	Ferrari 156	90 laps/fuel pressure	4
8	Jack Brabham	Brabham	Lotus-Climax 24	77 laps/accident	6
R	Innes Ireland	UDT Laystall Racing Team	Lotus-Climax 24	64 laps/fuel pump	8
R	Jim Clark	Lotus	Lotus-Climax 25	55 laps/clutch	1
R	Roy Salvadori	Bowmaker Racing Team	Lola-Climax 4	44 laps/suspension	12
R	Tony Maggs	Cooper	Cooper-Climax T55	43 laps/gearbox	19
R	Trevor Taylor	Lotus	Lotus-Climax 24	24 laps/oil leak	17
R	Dan Gurney	Porsche	Porsche 804	0 laps/accident	5
R	Maurice Trintignant	Rob Walker Racing Team	Lotus-Climax 24	0 laps/accident	7
R	Richie Ginther	BRM	BRM P48/57	0 laps/accident	14
NS	Ricardo Rodriguez	Ferrari	Ferrari 156	Mairesse drove car	15
DNQ	Jo Siffert	Ecurie Nationale Suisse	Lotus-Climax 21	reserve	13
DNQ	Jackie Lewis	Ecurie Galloise	BRM P48/57	reserve	15
DNQ	Masten Gregory	UDT Laystall Racing Team	Lotus-BRM 24	reserve	16
DNQ	Carel Godin de Beaufort	Ecurie Maarsbergen	Porsche 718	-	20
DNQ	Nino Vaccarella	Scuderia SSS Republica di Venezia	Lotus-Climax 18/21	-	21

Pole: Clark, 1m35.400s, 73.743mph/118.679kph. Fastest lap: Clark, 1m35.500s, 73.694mph/118.600kph on Lap 42. Race leaders: McLaren 106 & 93-100, G Hill 7-92

FROM FIRST TO FIFTH

Enzo Ferrari was seldom other than angry in 1962, as Ferrari's runaway success in 1961 showed scant chance of being repeated. Indeed, Phil Hill's second place at the season's second race was to be the team's top result and so the Italian constructor ended the year ranked behind four British marques: BRM, Lotus, Cooper and Lola.

BELGIAN GRAND PRIX

SPA-FRANCORCHAMPS • ROUND 3 • DATE: 17TH JUNE 1962
Laps: 32 • Distance: 280.239miles/451.2km • Weather: Warm & bright

Pos	Driver	Team	Chassis-Engine	Result	Qual
1	Jim Clark	Lotus	Lotus-Climax 25	2h07m32.300s	13
2	Graham Hill	BRM	BRM P57	2h08m16.400s	1
3	Phil Hill	Ferrari	Ferrari 156	2h09m38.800s	4
4	Ricardo Rodriguez	Ferrari	Ferrari 156	2h09m38.900s	7
5	John Surtees	Bowmaker Racing Team	Lola-Climax 4	31 laps	11
6	Jack Brabham	Brabham	Lotus-Climax 24	30 laps	15
7	Carel Godin de Beaufort	Ecurie Maarsbergen	Porsche 718	30 laps	13
8	Maurice Trintignant	Rob Walker Racing Team	Lotus-Climax 24	30 laps	16
9	Lucien Bianchi	Equipe Nationale Belge	Lotus-Climax 18/21	29 laps	18
10	Jo Siffert	Ecurie Filipinetti	Lotus-Climax 21	29 laps	17
NC	John Campbell-Jones	Emeryson	Lotus-Climax 18	16 laps/not classified	19
R	Trevor Taylor	Lotus	Lotus-Climax 24	25 laps/accident	3
R	Willy Mairesse	Ferrari	Ferrari 156	25 laps/accident	6
R	Richie Ginther	BRM	BRM P57	22 laps/gearbox	9
R	Tony Maggs	Cooper	Cooper-Climax T60	22 laps/gearbox	10
R	Bruce McLaren	Cooper	Cooper-Climax T60	19 laps/wheel	2
R	Masten Gregory	UDT Laystall Racing Team	Lotus-BRM 24	13 laps/withdrawn	8
R	Innes Ireland	UDT Laystall Racing Team	Lotus-Climax 24	8 laps/suspension	5
R	Giancarlo Baghetti	Ferrari	Ferrari 156	3 laps/ignition	14
NS	Dan Gurney	Wolfgang Seidel	Lotus-BRM 24	car not ready	20

Pole: G Hill, 3m57.000s, 133.083mph/214.177kph. Fastest lap: Clark, 3m55.600s, 133.843mph/215.400kph on Lap 15. Race leaders: G Hill 1, Taylor 2-3, 5 & 8; Mairesse 4 & 6-7, Clark 9-32

PORSCHE'S BIG DAY

The fourth round at Rouen produced a result that few found surprising: a win for Porsche. Dan Gurney had shone in 1961, twice finishing second in what was little more than an open-wheeled sports car. For 1962, the team introduced its flat-eight-powered 804 and this was lower, sleeker and notably superior. It was to remain Porsche's only F1 win as a chassis constructor.

FRENCH GRAND PRIX

ROUEN-LES-ESSARTS • ROUND 4 • DATE: 8TH JULY 1962
Laps: 54 • Distance: 219.510miles/353.268km • Weather: Warm & bright

Pos	Driver	Team	Chassis-Engine	Result	Qual
1	Dan Gurney	Porsche	Porsche 804	2h07m35.500s	6
2	Tony Maggs	Cooper	Cooper-Climax T60	53 laps	11
3	Richie Ginther	BRM	BRM P57	52 laps	10
4	Bruce McLaren	Cooper	Cooper-Climax T60	51 laps	3
5	John Surtees	Bowmaker Racing Team	Lola-Climax 4	51 laps	5
6	Carel Godin de Beaufort	Ecurie Maarsbergen	Porsche 718	51 laps	17
7	Maurice Trintignant	Rob Walker Racing Team	Lotus-Climax 24	50 laps	13

Pos	Driver	Team	Chassis-Engine	Result	Qual
8	Trevor Taylor	Lotus	Lotus-Climax 25	48 laps	12
9	Graham Hill	BRM	BRM P57	44 laps	2
R	Jo Bonnier	Porsche	Porsche 804	42 laps/fuel system	9
R	Jim Clark	Lotus	Lotus-Climax 25	33 laps/suspension	1
R	Jackie Lewis	Ecurie Galloise	Cooper-Climax T53	27 laps/accident	16
R	Roy Salvadori	Bowmaker Racing Team	Lola-Climax 4	20 laps/fuel pressure	14
R	Masten Gregory	UDT Laystall Racing Team	Lotus-BRM 24	14 laps/overheating	7
R	Jack Brabham	Brabham	Lotus-Climax 24	10 laps/suspension	4
R	Jo Siffert	Ecurie Filipinetti	Lotus-BRM 24	5 laps/clutch	15
R	Innes Ireland	UDT Laystall Racing Team	Lotus-Climax 24	1 lap/puncture	8

Pole: Clark, 2m14.800s, 108.561mph/174.712kph. Fastest lap: G Hill, 2m16.900s, 106.895mph/172.032kph on Lap 32. Race leaders: G Hill 1-29 & 33-41; Clark 30-32, Gurney 42-54

NURBURGRING'S BIZARRE PERILS

Failing cars were often the cause of accidents, but Graham Hill had a different reason for crashing out of qualifying at the German GP. He was flat-out down the Fuchsrohre when he came across something lying in the track. It was a television camera, extremely rare in the 1960s, that had fallen off Carel de Beaufort's Porsche, and he was unable to avoid it…

SKIRTING DISASTER

Just as Trevor Taylor joined the works Lotus line-up and finished second in the Dutch GP, his life seemed to become one crash after another. First came a clash with Ferrari's Willy Mairesse at the Belgian GP, then he hit the back of Maurice Trintignant's stalled Lotus at Rouen, before a seized engine sent him into a hedge in the German GP.

BRITISH GRAND PRIX

AINTREE • ROUND 5 • DATE: 21ST JULY 1962
Laps: 75 • Distance: 224.936miles/362.1km • Weather: Warm & bright

Pos	Driver	Team	Chassis-Engine	Result	Qual
1	Jim Clark	Lotus	Lotus-Climax 25	2h26m20.800s	1
2	John Surtees	Bowmaker Racing Team	Lola-Climax 4	2h27m10.000s	2
3	Bruce McLaren	Cooper	Cooper-Climax T60	2h28m05.600s	4
4	Graham Hill	BRM	BRM P57	2h28m17.600s	5
5	Jack Brabham	Brabham	Lotus-Climax 24	74 laps	9
6	Tony Maggs	Cooper	Cooper-Climax T60	74 laps	13
7	Masten Gregory	UDT Laystall Racing Team	Lotus-Climax 24	74 laps	14
8	Trevor Taylor	Lotus	Lotus-Climax 24	74 laps	10
9	Dan Gurney	Porsche	Porsche 804	73 laps	6
10	Jackie Lewis	Ecurie Galloise	Cooper-Climax T53	72 laps	15
11	Tony Settember	Emeryson	Emeryson-Climax	71 laps	19
12	Ian Burgess	Anglo-American Equipe	Cooper-Climax T53	71 laps	16

Pos	Driver	Team	Chassis-Engine	Result	Qual
13	Richie Ginther	BRM	BRM P57	70 laps	8
14	Carel Godin de Beaufort	Ecurie Maarsbergen	Porsche 718	69 laps	17
15	Jay Chamberlain	Ecurie Excelsior	Lotus-Climax 18	64 laps	20
16	Innes Ireland	UDT Laystall Racing Team	Lotus-Climax 24	61 laps	3
R	Phil Hill	Ferrari	Ferrari 156	46 laps/engine	12
R	Roy Salvadori	Bowmaker Racing Team	Lola-Climax 4	34 laps/battery	11
R	Jo Bonnier	Porsche	Porsche 804	26 laps/differential	7
R	Wolfgang Seidel	Wolfgang Seidel	Lotus-BRM 24	10 laps/brakes	21
R	Tony Shelly	John Dalton	Lotus-Climax 18/21	5 laps/engine	18
NS	Keith Greene	John Dalton	Lotus-Climax 18/21	Shelly drove car	-

Pole: Clark, 1m53.600s, 95.069mph/153.000kph. Fastest lap: Clark, 1m55.000s, 93.912mph/151.137kph on Lap 36. Race leaders: Clark 1-75

A BRIGHT LIGHT EXTINGUISHED

One of the saddest moments of the 1962 season was when rising star Ricardo Rodriguez was killed at the end of a part-season with Ferrari when he returned home for a non-championship grand prix in Mexico City. With Ferrari not attending, the 20-year-old was entered in a Rob Walker Racing Lotus, but crashed to his death in qualifying.

GERMAN GRAND PRIX

NURBURGRING • ROUND 6 • DATE: 5TH AUGUST 1962
Laps: 15 • Distance: 212.518miles/342.15km • Weather: Cool with heavy rain

Pos	Driver	Team	Chassis-Engine	Result	Qual
1	Graham Hill	BRM	BRM P57	2h38m45.300s	2
2	John Surtees	Bowmaker Racing Team	Lola-Climax 4	2h38m47.800s	4
3	Dan Gurney	Porsche	Porsche 804	2h38m49.700s	1
4	Jim Clark	Lotus	Lotus-Climax 25	2h39m27.400s	3
5	Bruce McLaren	Cooper	Cooper-Climax T60	2h40m04.900s	5
6	Ricardo Rodriguez	Ferrari	Ferrari 156	2h40m09.100s	10
7	Jo Bonnier	Porsche	Porsche 804	2h43m22.600s	6
8	Richie Ginther	BRM	BRM P57	2h43m45.400s	7
9	Tony Maggs	Cooper	Cooper-Climax T55	2h43m52.300s	23
10	Giancarlo Baghetti	Ferrari	Ferrari 156	2h47m00.000s	13
11	Ian Burgess	Anglo-American Equipe	Cooper-Climax T53	2h47m00.600s	16
12	Jo Siffert	Ecurie Filipinetti	Lotus-Climax 21	2h47m00.800s	17
13	Carel Godin de Beaufort	Ecurie Maarsbergen	Porsche 718	2h47m57.100s	8
14	Heini Walter	Ecurie Filipinetti	Porsche 718	14 laps	14
15	Nino Vaccarella	Scuderia SSS Republica di Venezia	Porsche 718	14 laps	15
16	Lucien Bianchi	Equipe Nationale Belge	ENB-Maserati	14 laps	25
R	Jackie Lewis	Ecurie Galloise	Cooper-Climax T53	10 laps/suspension	21
R	Phil Hill	Ferrari	Ferrari 156	9 laps/suspension	12
R	Jack Brabham	Brabham	Brabham-Climax BT3	9 laps/throttle	24
R	Keith Greene	Gilby Engineering	Gilby-BRM	7 laps/suspension	19
R	Roy Salvadori	Bowmaker Racing Team	Lola-Climax 4	4 laps/gearbox	9
R	Maurice Trintignant	Rob Walker Racing Team	Lotus-Climax 24	4 laps/gearbox	11
R	Lorenzo Bandini	Ferrari	Ferrari 158	4 laps/accident	18

Pos	Driver	Team	Chassis-Engine	Result	Qual
R	Heinz Schiller	Ecurie Filipinetti	Lotus-BRM 24	4 laps/fuel pressure	20
R	Bernard Collomb	Bernard Collomb	Cooper-Climax T53	2 laps/gearbox	22
R	Trevor Taylor	Lotus	Lotus-Climax 24	0 laps/accident	26
DNQ	Tony Shelly	John Dalton	Lotus-Climax 18/21	-	27
DNQ	Wolfgang Seidel	Wolfgang Seidel	Lotus-BRM 24	-	28
DNQ	Jay Chamberlain	Ecurie Excelsior	Lotus-Climax 18	-	29
DNQ	Gunther Seiffert	Wolfgang Seidel	Lotus-BRM 24	-	30

Pole: Gurney, 8m47.200s, 96.783mph/155.758kph. Fastest lap: G Hill, 10m12.200s, 83.325mph/134.100kph on Lap 3. Race leaders: Gurney 1-2, G Hill 3-15

RACING ON THE EDGE

The first South African GP to be part of the World Championship was kept until last, being run on 29 December. The circuit was perched above a cliff overlooking the Indian Ocean near East London. Jim Clark had won a non-championship race there in 1962 but could not repeat that result as his engine failed, handing victory and the title to Graham Hill.

ITALIAN GRAND PRIX

MONZA • ROUND 7 • DATE: 16TH SEPTEMBER 1962
Laps: 86 • Distance: 306.960miles/494.5km • Weather: Warm & dull then showers

Pos	Driver	Team	Chassis-Engine	Result	Qual
1	Graham Hill	BRM	BRM P57	2h29m08.400s	2
2	Richie Ginther	BRM	BRM P57	2h29m38.200s	3
3	Bruce McLaren	Cooper	Cooper-Climax T60	2h30m06.200s	4
4	Willy Mairesse	Ferrari	Ferrari 156	2h30m06.600s	10
5	Giancarlo Baghetti	Ferrari	Ferrari 156	2h30m39.700s	18
6	Jo Bonnier	Porsche	Porsche 804	85 laps	9
7	Tony Maggs	Cooper	Cooper-Climax T60	85 laps	12
8	Lorenzo Bandini	Ferrari	Ferrari 156	84 laps	17
9	Nino Vaccarella	Scuderia SSS Republica di Venezia	Lotus-Climax 18/21	84 laps	14
10	Carel Godin de Beaufort	Ecurie Maarsbergen	Porsche 718	81 laps	20
11	Phil Hill	Ferrari	Ferrari 156	81 laps	15
12	Masten Gregory	UDT Laystall Racing Team	Lotus-BRM 24	77 laps	6
13	Dan Gurney	Porsche	Porsche 804	66 laps/differential	7
14	Ricardo Rodriguez	Ferrari	Ferrari 156	63 laps/ignition	11
R	Innes Ireland	UDT Laystall Racing Team	Lotus-Climax 24	45 laps/suspension	5
R	John Surtees	Bowmaker Racing Team	Lola-Climax 4	42 laps/engine	8
R	Roy Salvadori	Bowmaker Racing Team	Lola-Climax 4	41 laps/engine	13
R	Trevor Taylor	Lotus	Lotus-Climax 25	25 laps/gearbox	16
R	Tony Settember	Emeryson	Emeryson-Climax	18 laps/engine	21
R	Maurice Trintignant	Rob Walker Racing Team	Lotus-Climax 24	17 laps/electrical	19
R	Jim Clark	Lotus	Lotus-Climax 25	12 laps/gearbox	1
DNQ	Tony Shelly	Wolfgang Seidel	Emeryson-Climax	-	22
DNQ	Keith Greene	Gilby Engineering	Gilby-BRM	-	23
DNQ	Gerry Ashmore	Gerry Ashmore	Lotus-Climax 18/21	-	24
DNQ	Ian Burgess	Anglo-American Equipe	Cooper-Climax T53	-	25
DNQ	Jo Siffert	Ecurie Filipinetti	Lotus-BRM 24	-	26

Pos	Driver	Team	Chassis-Engine	Result	Qual
DNQ	Ernesto Prinoth	Scuderia Jolly Club	Lotus-Climax 18	-	27
DNQ	Roberto Lippi	Scuderia Settecolli	De Tomaso-OSCA	-	28
DNQ	Jay Chamberlain	Ecurie Excelsior	Lotus-Climax 18	-	29
DNQ	Nasif Estefano	De Tomaso	De Tomaso 801	-	30

Pole: Clark, 1m40.350s, 128.175mph/206.278kph. Fastest lap: G Hill, 1m42.300s, 125.703mph/202.300kph on Lap 3. Race leaders: G Hill 1-86

NEW CONSTRUCTORS

Jack Brabham was the first F1 driver to become a constructor when he combined with designer Ron Tauranac to build single-seaters to finance his own F1 team. He twice finished fourth. ENB and LDS achieved little, but Lola shone when its F1 car was run by the Bowmaker team under Reg Parnell, with John Surtees taking two second places.

UNITED STATES GRAND PRIX

WATKINS GLEN • ROUND 8 • DATE: 7TH OCTOBER 1962
Laps: 100 • Distance: 229.916miles/370.15km • Weather: Cool & dull

Pos	Driver	Team	Chassis-Engine	Result	Qual
1	Jim Clark	Lotus	Lotus-Climax 25	2h07m13.000s	1
2	Graham Hill	BRM	BRM P57	2h07m22.200s	3
3	Bruce McLaren	Cooper	Cooper-Climax T60	99 laps	6
4	Jack Brabham	Brabham	Brabham-Climax BT3	99 laps	5
5	Dan Gurney	Porsche	Porsche 804	99 laps	4
6	Masten Gregory	UDT Laystall Racing Team	Lotus-BRM 24	99 laps	7
7	Tony Maggs	Cooper	Cooper-Climax T60	97 laps	10
8	Innes Ireland	UDT Laystall Racing Team	Lotus-Climax 24	96 laps	15
9	Roger Penske	Dupont Team Zerex	Lotus-Climax 24	96 laps	12
10	Rob Schroeder	John Mecom	Lotus-Climax 24	93 laps	16
11	Hap Sharp	Hap Sharp	Cooper-Climax T53	91 laps	14
12	Trevor Taylor	Lotus	Lotus-Climax 25	85 laps	8
13	Jo Bonnier	Porsche	Porsche 804	79 laps	9
R	Richie Ginther	BRM	BRM P57	35 laps/engine	2
R	Maurice Trintignant	Rob Walker Racing Team	Lotus-Climax 24	32 laps/brakes	17
R	Timmy Mayer	Cooper	Cooper-Climax T53	31 laps/ignition	11
R	John Surtees	Bowmaker Racing Team	Lola-Climax 4	19 laps/engine	18
R	Carel Godin de Beaufort	Ecurie Maarsbergen	Porsche 718	9 laps/accident	13
NS	Roy Salvadori	Bowmaker Racing Team	Lola-Climax 4	Surtees drove car	11
NS	Jim Hall	Jim Hall	Lotus-Climax 21	valve	18
NS	Phil Hill	Porsche	Porsche 804	driver unwell	-

Pole: Clark, 1m15.800s, 109.235mph/175.796kph. Fastest lap: Clark, 1m15.000s, 110.400mph/177.672kph on Lap 70. Race leaders: Clark 1-11 & 19-100; G Hill 12-18

SOUTH AFRICAN GRAND PRIX

EAST LONDON • ROUND 9 • DATE: 29TH DECEMBER 1962
Laps: 82 • Distance: 199.718miles/321.415km • Weather: Warm, dull & windy

Pos	Driver	Team	Chassis-Engine	Result	Qual
1	Graham Hill	BRM	BRM P57	2h08m03.300s	2
2	Bruce McLaren	Cooper	Cooper-Climax T60	2h08m53.100s	8
3	Tony Maggs	Cooper	Cooper-Climax T60	2h08m53.600s	6
4	Jack Brabham	Brabham	Brabham-Climax BT3	2h08m57.100s	3
5	Innes Ireland	UDT Laystall Racing Team	Lotus-Climax 24	81 laps	4
6	Neville Lederle	Neville Lederle	Lotus-Climax 21	78 laps	10
7	Richie Ginther	BRM	BRM P57	78 laps	7
8	John Love	John Love	Cooper-Climax T55	78 laps	12
9	Bruce Johnstone	BRM	BRM P48/57	76 laps	17
10	Ernest Pieterse	Ernest Pieterse	Lotus-Climax 21	71 laps	13
11	Carel Godin de Beaufort	Ecurie Maarsbergen	Porsche 718	70 laps/fuel pump	16
R	Doug Serrurier	Otelle Nucci	LDS-Alfa Romeo	62 laps/radiator damage	14
R	Jim Clark	Lotus	Lotus-Climax 25	61 laps/oil leak	1
R	Roy Salvadori	Bowmaker Racing Team	Lola-Climax 4	56 laps/oil leak	11
R	Mike Harris	Mike Harris	Cooper-Alfa Romeo T53	31 laps/wheel	15
R	John Surtees	Bowmaker Racing Team	Lola-Climax 4	26 laps/engine	5
R	Trevor Taylor	Lotus	Lotus-Climax 25	11 laps/gearbox	9

Pole: Clark, 1m29.300s, 98.187mph/158.017kph. Fastest lap: Clark, 1m31.000s, 96.352mph/155.065kph on Lap 3. Race leaders: Clark 1-61; G Hill 62-82

NEW DRIVERS

Jo Siffert would eventually prove to be the pick of a thin crop of new drivers, but his first year with an Ecurie Filipinetti Lotus wasn't great. Young gun Neville Lederle and 38-year-old John Love finished sixth and eighth in the South African GP, but it was rising star Tim Mayer who caught the eye, only to be killed when racing in Tasmania before he had a chance to make his name.

WORLD DRIVERS' CHAMPIONSHIP FINAL RESULTS

Pos	Driver	Nat	Car-Engine	R1	R2	R3	R4	R5	R6	R7	R8	R9	Total
1	Graham Hill	GBR	BRM P57	1	6	2P	9F	4	1F	1F	2	1	42
2	Jim Clark	GBR	Lotus-Climax 25	9	RPF	1F	RP	1PF	4	RP	1PF	RPF	30
3	Bruce McLaren	NZL	Cooper-Climax T60	RF	1	R	4	3	5	3	3	2	27
4	John Surtees	GBR	Lola-Climax 4	RP	4	5	5	2	2	R	R	R	19
5	Dan Gurney	USA	Porsche 804	R	R	-	1	9	3P	13	5	-	15
			Lotus-BRM 24	-	-	NS	-	-	-	-	-	-	
6	Phil Hill	USA	Ferrari 156	3	2	3	-	R	R	11	-	-	14
7	Tony Maggs	ZAF	Cooper-Climax T55	5	R	-	-	-	9	-	-	-	13
			Cooper-Climax T60	-	-	R	2	6	-	7	7	3	
8	Richie Ginther	USA	BRM P48/57	R	R	-	-	-	-	-	-	-	10
			BRM P57	-	-	R	3	13	8	2	R	7	
9	Jack Brabham	AUS	Lotus-Climax 24	R	8	6	R	5	-	-	-	-	9
			Brabham-Climax BT3	-	-	-	-	-	R	-	4	4	

Pos	Driver	Nat	Car-Engine	R1	R2	R3	R4	R5	R6	R7	R8	R9	Total
10	Trevor Taylor	GBR	Lotus-Climax 24	2	R	R	-	8	R	-	-	-	6
			Lotus-Climax 25	-	-	-	8	-	-	R	12	R	
11	Giancarlo Baghetti	ITA	Ferrari 156	4	-	R	-	-	10	5	-	-	5
12	Lorenzo Bandini	ITA	Ferrari 156	-	3	-	-	-	R	8	-	-	4
13	Ricardo Rodriguez	MEX	Ferrari 156	R	NS	4	-	-	6	14	-	-	4
14	Willy Mairesse	BEL	Ferrari 156	-	7	R	-	-	-	4	-	-	3
15	Jo Bonnier	SWE	Porsche 804	7	-	-	R	R	7	6	13	-	3
			Porsche 718	-	5	-	-	-	-	-	-	-	
16	Innes Ireland	GBR	Lotus-Climax 24	R	R	R	R	16	-	R	8	5	2
17	Carel Godin de Beaufort	NLD	Porsche 718	6	DNQ	7	6	14	13	10	R	11	2
18	Masten Gregory	USA	Lotus-Climax 18/21	R	-	-	-	-	-	-	-	-	1
			Lotus-BRM 24	-	DNQ	R	R	-	-	12	6	-	
			Lotus-Climax 24	-	-	-	-	7	-	-	-	-	
18	Neville Lederle	ZAF	Lotus-Climax 21	-	-	-	-	-	-	-	-	6	1

WORLD CONSTRUCTORS' CHAMPIONSHIP FINAL RESULTS

Pos	Team-Engine	R1	R2	R3	R4	R5	R6	R7	R8	R9	Total
1	BRM	1	6	2	3	4	1	1	2	1	42
2	Lotus-Climax	2	R	1	7	1	4	9	1	5	36
3	Cooper-Climax	5	1	-	2	3	5	3	3	2	29
4	Lola-Climax	-	4	5	5	2	2	-	-	-	19
5	Porsche	6	5	7	1	9	3	6	5	11	18
5	Ferrari	3	2	3	-	-	6	4	-	-	18
7	Brabham-Climax	-	-	-	-	-	-	-	4	4	6
8	Lotus-BRM	-	DNQ	-	-	-	-	12	6	-	1

SYMBOLS AND GRAND PRIX KEY

Round 1 Dutch GP
Round 2 Monaco GP
Round 3 Belgian GP
Round 4 French GP
Round 5 British GP
Round 6 German GP
Round 7 Italian GP
Round 8 United States GP
Round 9 South African GP

SCORING

1st 9 points
2nd 6 points
3rd 4 points
4th 3 points
5th 2 points
6th 1 point

DNPQ DID NOT PRE-QUALIFY **DNQ** DID NOT QUALIFY **DQ** DISQUALIFIED **EX** EXCLUDED
F FASTEST LAP **NC** NOT CLASSIFIED **NS** NON-STARTER **P** POLE POSITION **R** RETIRED

1963

SEASON SUMMARY

After finishing second in the drivers' and constructors' championships in 1962, it was clear that Jim Clark and Lotus were going to be the combination to beat. Lotus continued to lead the technical advances in F1, with the Lotus 25 still the class of the field, but it was Clark's level of performance, which put him on a different plane to his rivals, that really made the difference. BRM's Graham Hill and Richie Ginther tried their best and John Surtees impressed for Ferrari. After leading but retiring in Monaco, Clark ended up on the podium at the remaining nine grands prix, winning seven of them.

MONACO GRAND PRIX

MONTE CARLO • ROUND 1 • DATE: 26TH MAY 1963
Laps: 100 • Distance: 195.113miles/314.5km • Weather: Warm & bright

Pos	Driver	Team	Chassis-Engine	Result	Qual
1	Graham Hill	BRM	BRM P57	2h41m49.700s	2
2	Richie Ginther	BRM	BRM P57	2h41m54.300s	4
3	Bruce McLaren	Cooper	Cooper-Climax T66	2h42m02.500s	8
4	John Surtees	Ferrari	Ferrari 156/63	2h42m03.800s	3
5	Tony Maggs	Cooper	Cooper-Climax T66	98 laps	10
6	Trevor Taylor	Lotus	Lotus-Climax 25	98 laps	9
7	Jo Bonnier	Rob Walker Racing Team	Cooper-Climax T60	94 laps	11
8	Jim Clark	Lotus	Lotus-Climax 25	78 laps/gearbox	1
9	Jack Brabham	Brabham	Lotus-Climax 25	77 laps/gearbox	15
R	Innes Ireland	BRP	Lotus-BRM 24	40 laps/accident	5
R	Willy Mairesse	Ferrari	Ferrari 156/63	37 laps/gearbox	7
R	Maurice Trintignant	Reg Parnell Racing	Lola-Climax 4A	34 laps/clutch	14
R	Dan Gurney	Brabham	Brabham-Climax BT7	25 laps/differential	6
R	Jim Hall	BRP	Lotus-BRM 24	20 laps/gearbox	13
R	Jo Siffert	Siffert Racing Team	Lotus-BRM 24	3 laps/engine	12
NS	Chris Amon	Reg Parnell Racing	Lola-Climax 4A	Trintignant drove car	-
DNQ	Bernard Collomb	Bernard Collomb	Lotus-Climax 24	-	17

Pole: Clark, 1m34.300s, 74.604mph/120.063kph. Fastest lap: Surtees, 1m34.500s, 74.446mph/119.809kph on Lap 100. Race leaders: G Hill 1-17 & 79-100, Clark 18-78

F1'S DESIGN PIONEER

Colin Chapman built cars so that he could go racing. Then he built cars to make money. Then he built cars to win grands prix and his constant inventiveness was a thorn in the side of the traditional teams. The first to introduce a monocoque chassis, he went on to pioneer ground effects and many other ideas that led to seven constructors' titles.

FERRARI GETS BACK ON TRACK

John Surtees had two jobs after joining Ferrari. One was to try and take his first win and the other, increasingly, was to quash internal team squabbling. He achieved the former at the German GP, but the second part of the equation was harder to achieve as the team struggled to get back to its 1961 form, although his technical input was invaluable.

BELGIAN GRAND PRIX

SPA-FRANCORCHAMPS • ROUND 2 • DATE: 9TH JUNE 1963
Laps: 32 • Distance: 280.239miles/451.2km • Weather: Cool & wet

Pos	Driver	Team	Chassis-Engine	Result	Qual
1	Jim Clark	Lotus	Lotus-Climax 25	2h27m47.600s	8
2	Bruce McLaren	Cooper	Cooper-Climax T66	2h32m41.600s	5
3	Dan Gurney	Brabham	Brabham-Climax BT7	31 laps	2
4	Richie Ginther	BRM	BRM P57	31 laps	9
5	Jo Bonnier	Rob Walker Racing Team	Cooper-Climax T60	30 laps	13
6	Carel Godin de Beaufort	Ecurie Maarsbergen	Porsche 718	30 laps	18
7	Tony Maggs	Cooper	Cooper-Climax T66	27 laps/accident	4
8	Tony Settember	Scirocco	Scirocco-BRM SP	25 laps/accident	19
R	John Surtees	Ferrari	Ferrari 156/63	19 laps/fuel pressure	10
R	Graham Hill	BRM	BRM P57	17 laps/gearbox	1
R	Lucien Bianchi	Reg Parnell Racing	Lola-Climax 4	17 laps/accident	16
R	Jim Hall	BRP	Lotus-BRM 24	16 laps/accident	12
R	Jo Siffert	Siffert Racing Team	Lotus-BRM 24	16 laps/accident	14
R	Phil Hill	Automobili Turismo e Sport	ATS 100	13 laps/gearbox	17
R	Jack Brabham	Brabham	Brabham-Climax BT3	12 laps/fuel injection	6
R	Chris Amon	Reg Parnell Racing	Lola-Climax 4A	10 laps/oil leak	15
R	Innes Ireland	BRP	BRP-BRM 1	9 laps/gearbox	7
R	Willy Mairesse	Ferrari	Ferrari 156/63	7 laps/dropped valve	3
R	Giancarlo Baghetti	Automobili Turismo e Sport	ATS 100	7 laps/gearbox	20
R	Trevor Taylor	Lotus	Lotus-Climax 25	5 laps/physical	11

Pole: Hill, 3m54.100s, 134.732mph/216.830kph. Fastest lap: Clark, 3m58.100s, 132.468mph/213.187kph on Lap 16. Race leaders: Clark 1-32

DUTCH GRAND PRIX

ZANDVOORT • ROUND 3 • DATE: 23RD JUNE 1963
Laps: 80 • Distance: 208.186miles/335.44km • Weather: Warm & bright

Pos	Driver	Team	Chassis-Engine	Result	Qual
1	Jim Clark	Lotus	Lotus-Climax 25	2h08m13.700s	1
2	Dan Gurney	Brabham	Brabham-Climax BT7	79 laps	14
3	John Surtees	Ferrari	Ferrari 156/63	79 laps	5
4	Innes Ireland	BRP	BRP-BRM 1	79 laps	7
5	Richie Ginther	BRM	BRM P57	79 laps	6
6	Ludovico Scarfiotti	Ferrari	Ferrari 156/63	78 laps	11
7	Jo Siffert	Siffert Racing Team	Lotus-BRM 24	77 laps	17
8	Jim Hall	BRP	Lotus-BRM 24	77 laps	18
9	Carel Godin de Beaufort	Ecurie Maarsbergen	Porsche 718	75 laps	19

Pos	Driver	Team	Chassis-Engine	Result	Qual
10	Trevor Taylor	Lotus	Lotus-Climax 25	66 laps	10
11	Jo Bonnier	Rob Walker Racing Team	Cooper-Climax T60	56 laps	8
R	Graham Hill	BRM	BRM P57	69 laps/overheating	2
R	Jack Brabham	Brabham	Brabham-Climax BT7	68 laps/accident	4
R	Chris Amon	Reg Parnell Racing	Lola-Climax 4A	29 laps/water pump	12
R	Giancarlo Baghetti	Automobili Turismo e Sport	ATS 100	17 laps/ignition	15
R	Phil Hill	Automobili Turismo e Sport	ATS 100	15 laps/suspension	13
R	Tony Maggs	Cooper	Cooper-Climax T66	14 laps/overheating	9
R	Bruce McLaren	Cooper	Cooper-Climax T66	7 laps/gearbox	3
R	Gerhard Mitter	Ecurie Maarsbergen	Porsche 718	2 laps/clutch	16

Pole: Clark, 1m31.600s, 102.396mph/164.790kph. Fastest lap: Clark, 1m33.700s, 100.101mph/161.097kph on Lap 56. Race leaders: Clark 1-80

FRENCH GRAND PRIX

REIMS • ROUND 4 • DATE: 30TH JUNE 1963
Laps: 53 • Distance: 273.407miles/440.006km • Weather: Warm with showers

Pos	Driver	Team	Chassis-Engine	Result	Qual
1	Jim Clark	Lotus	Lotus-Climax 25	2h10m54.300s	1
2	Tony Maggs	Cooper	Cooper-Climax T66	2h11m59.200s	8
3	Graham Hill	BRM	BRM P61	2h13m08.200s*	2
4	Jack Brabham	Brabham	Brabham-Climax BT7	2h13m09.500s	5
5	Dan Gurney	Brabham	Brabham-Climax BT7	2h13m27.700s	3
6	Jo Siffert	Siffert Racing Team	Lotus-BRM 24	52 laps	10
7	Chris Amon	Reg Parnell Racing	Lola-Climax 4A	51 laps	15
8	Maurice Trintignant	Reg Parnell Racing	Lotus-Climax 24	50 laps	14
9	Innes Ireland	BRP	BRP-BRM 1	49 laps	9
10	Lorenzo Bandini	Scuderia Centro Sud	BRM P57	45 laps	19
11	Jim Hall	BRP	Lotus-BRM 24	45 laps	16
12	Bruce McLaren	Cooper	Cooper-Climax T66	42 laps/ignition	6
13	Trevor Taylor	Lotus	Lotus-Climax 25	41 laps/suspension	7
NC	Phil Hill	Ecurie Filipinetti	Lotus-BRM 24	34 laps/not classified	13
NC	Jo Bonnier	Rob Walker Racing Team	Cooper-Climax T60	32 laps/not classified	11
R	Masten Gregory	Tim Parnell	Lotus-BRM 24	30 laps/gearbox	17
R	John Surtees	Ferrari	Ferrari 156/63	12 laps/fuel pump	4
R	Tony Settember	Scirocco	Scirocco-BRM SP	5 laps/wheel	18
R	Richie Ginther	BRM	BRM P57	4 laps/radiator damage	12
NS	Ludovico Scarfiotti	Ferrari	Ferrari 156/63	driver injured	14
NS	Peter Arundell	Lotus	Lotus-Climax 25	withdrew	16

*G Hill was penalised 1 minute for being given a push start. No points were awarded

Pole: Clark, 2m20.200s, 132.461mph/213.175kph. Fastest lap: Clark, 2m21.600s, 131.151mph/211.067kph on Lap 12. Race leaders: Clark 1-53

POWER TO THE PEOPLE

Ferrari dominated the first year of F1's 1.5-litre formula, but the Coventry Climax was most teams's engine of choice. Cooper and Lotus had used the company's FPF four-cylinder engine in 1961, but they needed more power, so Climax developed the FWMV V8, which offered 186bhp. By 1963, a shortstroke version offered 195bhp and was good for the title.

BRITISH GRAND PRIX

SILVERSTONE • ROUND 5 • DATE: 20TH JULY 1963
Laps: 82 • Distance: 240.11miles/386.261km • Weather: Warm & bright

Pos	Driver	Team	Chassis-Engine	Result	Qual
1	Jim Clark	Lotus	Lotus-Climax 25	2h14m09.600s	1
2	John Surtees	Ferrari	Ferrari 156/63	2h14m35.400s	5
3	Graham Hill	BRM	BRM P57	2h14m47.200s	3
4	Richie Ginther	BRM	BRM P57	81 laps	9
5	Lorenzo Bandini	Scuderia Centro Sud	BRM P57	81 laps	8
6	Jim Hall	BRP	Lotus-BRM 24	80 laps	13
7	Chris Amon	Reg Parnell Racing	Lola-Climax 4A	80 laps	14
8	Mike Hailwood	Reg Parnell Racing	Lotus-Climax 24	78 laps	17
9	Tony Maggs	Cooper	Cooper-Climax T66	78 laps	7
10	Carel Godin de Beaufort	Ecurie Maarsbergen	Porsche 718	76 laps	21
11	Masten Gregory	Reg Parnell Racing	Lotus-BRM 24	75 laps	22
12	Bob Anderson	DW Racing Enterprises	Lola-Climax 4	75 laps	16
13	John Campbell-Jones	Tim Parnell	Lola-Climax 4	74 laps	23
R	Jo Siffert	Siffert Racing Team	Lotus-BRM 24	66 laps/gearbox	15
R	Jo Bonnier	Rob Walker Racing Team	Cooper-Climax T66	65 laps/fuel pressure	12
R	Dan Gurney	Brabham	Brabham-Climax BT7	59 laps/engine	2
R	Ian Raby	Ian Raby Racing	Gilby-BRM	59 laps/gearbox	19
R	Ian Burgess	Scirocco	Scirocco-BRM SP	36 laps/ignition	20
R	Jack Brabham	Brabham	Brabham-Climax BT7	27 laps/engine	4
DQ	Innes Ireland	BRP	BRP-BRM 1	26 laps/push start	11
DQ	Trevor Taylor	Lotus	Lotus-Climax 25	23 laps/push start	10
R	Tony Settember	Scirocco	Scirocco-BRM SP	20 laps/ignition	18
R	Bruce McLaren	Cooper	Cooper-Climax T66	6 laps/engine	6

Pole: Clark, 1m34.400s, 111.621mph/179.637kph. Fastest lap: Surtees, 1m36.000s, 109.761mph/176.643kph on Lap 3. Race leaders: Brabham 1-3, Clark 4-82

HOW NOT TO GO RACING

The first ATS team to grace F1, formed by Carlo Chiti when he quit Ferrari, made a disastrous debut at the Belgian GP. Based in the nearby town of Malmedy rather than at the track, none of their rivals knew that they were there until the car hit the circuit. Even in the hands of 1961 world champion Phil Hill, it was clear that the car would scare no one, apart from the driver...

GERMAN GRAND PRIX

NURBURGRING • ROUND 6 • DATE: 4TH AUGUST 1963
Laps: 15 • Distance: 212.518miles/342.15km • Weather: Warm & bright

Pos	Driver	Team	Chassis-Engine	Result	Qual
1	John Surtees	Ferrari	Ferrari 156/63	2h13m06.800s	2
2	Jim Clark	Lotus	Lotus-Climax 25	2h14m24.300s	1
3	Richie Ginther	BRM	BRM P57	2h15m51.700s	6
4	Gerhard Mitter	Ecurie Maarsbergen	Porsche 718	2h21m18.300s	15
5	Jim Hall	BRP	Lotus-BRM 24	14 laps	16

Pos	Driver	Team	Chassis-Engine	Result	Qual
6	Jo Bonnier	Rob Walker Racing Team	Cooper-Climax T66	14 laps	12
7	Jack Brabham	Brabham	Brabham-Climax BT7	14 laps	8
8	Trevor Taylor	Lotus	Lotus-Climax 25	14 laps	18
9	Jo Siffert	Siffert Racing Team	Lotus-BRM 24	10 laps/differential	9
10	Bernard Collomb	Bernard Collomb	Lotus-Climax 24	10 laps	21
R	Carel Godin de Beaufort	Ecurie Maarsbergen	Porsche 718	9 laps/wheel	17
R	Tony Maggs	Cooper	Cooper-Climax T66	7 laps/engine	10
R	Dan Gurney	Brabham	Brabham-Climax BT7	6 laps/gearbox	13
R	Mario Cabral	Scuderia Centro Sud	Cooper-Climax T60	6 laps/gearbox	20
R	Ian Burgess	Scirocco	Scirocco-BRM SP	5 laps/steering	19
R	Tony Settember	Scirocco	Scirocco-BRM SP	5 laps/accident	22
R	Bruce McLaren	Cooper	Cooper-Climax T66	3 laps/accident	5
R	Graham Hill	BRM	BRM P57	2 laps/gearbox	4
R	Chris Amon	Reg Parnell Racing	Lola-Climax 4A	2 laps/accident	14
R	Willy Mairesse	Ferrari	Ferrari 156/63	1 lap/accident	7
R	Innes Ireland	BRP	Lotus-BRM 24	1 lap/accident	11
R	Lorenzo Bandini	Scuderia Centro Sud	BRM P57	0 laps/accident	3
DNQ	Andre Pilette	Tim Parnell	Lotus-Climax 18/21	-	23
DNQ	Ian Raby	Ian Raby Racing	Gilby-BRM	-	24
DNQ	Tim Parnell	Tim Parnell	Lotus-Climax 18/21	-	25
DNQ	Kurt Kuhnke	Kurt Kuhnke	Lotus-Borgward 18	-	26

Pole: Clark, 8m45.800s, 97.041mph/156.173kph. Fastest lap: Surtees, 8m47.000s, 96.820mph/155.817kph on Lap 9. Race leaders: Ginther 1, Surtees 2-3 & 5-15, Clark 4

KEPT BACK IN SECOND

Only the refusal of officials to show leader Parnelli Jones a black flag for leaking oil around the track denied Jim Clark the honour of becoming the first F1 driver to win the Indy 500. The Scot was gracious in defeat, but Eddie Sachs, who along with Roger McCluskey spun on the oil, was not. But when Sachs confronted Jones, Jones just punched him in the face…

ITALIAN GRAND PRIX

MONZA • ROUND 7 • DATE: 8TH SEPTEMBER 1963
Laps: 86 • Distance: 306.960miles/494.5km • Weather: Warm & bright

Pos	Driver	Team	Chassis-Engine	Result	Qual
1	Jim Clark	Lotus	Lotus-Climax 25	2h24m19.600s	3
2	Richie Ginther	BRM	BRM P57	2h25m54.600s	4
3	Bruce McLaren	Cooper	Cooper-Climax T66	85 laps	8
4	Innes Ireland	BRP	BRP-BRM 1	84 laps/engine	10
5	Jack Brabham	Brabham	Brabham-Climax BT3	84 laps	7
6	Tony Maggs	Cooper	Cooper-Climax T66	84 laps	13
7	Jo Bonnier	Rob Walker Racing Team	Cooper-Climax T66	84 laps	11
8	Jim Hall	BRP	Lotus-BRM 24	84 laps	16
9	Maurice Trintignant	Scuderia Centro Sud	BRM P57	83 laps	19
10	Mike Hailwood	Reg Parnell Racing	Lola-Climax 4	82 laps	17
11	Phil Hill	Automobili Turismo e Sport	ATS 100	79 laps	14
12	Bob Anderson	DW Racing Enterprises	Lola-Climax 4	79 laps	18
13	Mike Spence	Lotus	Lotus-Climax 25	73 laps/fuel pressure	9

Pos	Driver	Team	Chassis-Engine	Result	Qual
14	Dan Gurney	Brabham	Brabham-Climax BT7	64 laps/fuel system	5
15	Giancarlo Baghetti	Automobili Turismo e Sport	ATS 100	63 laps	20
16	Graham Hill	BRM	BRM P61	59 laps/clutch	2
R	Jo Siffert	Siffert Racing Team	Lotus-BRM 24	40 laps/fuel pressure	15
R	Lorenzo Bandini	Ferrari	Ferrari 156/63	37 laps/gearbox	6
R	Masten Gregory	Tim Parnell	Lotus-BRM 24	26 laps/engine	12
R	John Surtees	Ferrari	Ferrari 156 Aero	16 laps/engine	1
NS	Chris Amon	Reg Parnell Racing	Lola-Climax 4A	driver injured	15
DNQ	Mario Cabral	Scuderia Centro Sud	Cooper-Climax T60	-	21
DNQ	Ian Raby	Ian Raby Racing	Gilby-BRM	-	22
DNQ	Tony Settember	Scirocco	Scirocco-BRM SP	-	23
DNQ	Carel Godin de Beaufort	Ecurie Maarsbergen	Porsche 718	-	24
DNQ	Ernesto Brambilla	Scuderia Centro Sud	Cooper-Maserati T53	-	26
DNQ	Andre Pilette	Tim Parnell	Lotus-Climax 18/21	-	-
DNQ	Roberto Lippi	Scuderia Settecolli	De Tomaso-Ferrari F1	-	28

Pole: Surtees, 1m37.300s, 132.193mph/212.744kph. Fastest lap: Clark, 1m38.900s, 130.054mph/209.302kph on Lap 60. Race leaders: G Hill 1-3, 24-26, 29-30, 32, 34-35, 37 & 39-41, Surtees 4-16, Clark 17-23, 28, 36, 42-45, 48-51, 53-54 & 56-86, Gurney 27, 31, 46-47, 52 & 55

A WELCOME ADDITION

Circuits seeking to host a round of the World Championship were expected to hold a non-championship race first. So Mexico did just that in 1962 before the capital city's parkland circuit was granted a date for 1963. The track earned praise for its long, wide main straight and tricky esses, but not for its crowd control, which failed to keep fans off the track.

NEW CONSTRUCTORS

As well as ATS, there were three other new constructors in 1963. BRP – British Racing Partnership – had run other chassis from 1959 before this time building a copy of the Lotus 25 in which Innes Ireland twice finished fourth. Scirocco was an update of the Emeryson funded by Hugh Powell, while Stebro was an uprated Formula Junior car.

UNITED STATES GRAND PRIX

WATKINS GLEN • ROUND 8 • DATE: 6TH OCTOBER 1963
Laps: 110 • Distance: 253.0miles/407.165km • Weather: Hot & bright

Pos	Driver	Team	Chassis-Engine	Result	Qual
1	Graham Hill	BRM	BRM P57	2h19m22.100s	1
2	Richie Ginther	BRM	BRM P57	2h19m56.400s	4
3	Jim Clark	Lotus	Lotus-Climax 25	109 laps	2
4	Jack Brabham	Brabham	Brabham-Climax BT7	108 laps	5
5	Lorenzo Bandini	Ferrari	Ferrari 156/63	106 laps	9
6	Carel Godin de Beaufort	Ecurie Maarsbergen	Porsche 718	99 laps	19
7	Peter Broeker	Stebro	Stebro-Ford Cosworth 4	88 laps	21

Pos	Driver	Team	Chassis-Engine	Result	Qual
8	Jo Bonnier	Rob Walker Racing Team	Cooper-Climax T66	85 laps	12
9	John Surtees	Ferrari	Ferrari 156/63	82 laps/engine	3
10	Jim Hall	BRP	Lotus-BRM 24	76 laps/gearbox	16
11	Bruce McLaren	Cooper	Cooper-Climax T66	74 laps/fuel pump	11
R	Jo Siffert	Siffert Racing Team	Lotus-BRM 24	56 laps/gearbox	14
R	Tony Maggs	Cooper	Cooper-Climax T66	44 laps/ignition	10
R	Rodger Ward	Reg Parnell Racing	Lotus-BRM 24	44 laps/gearbox	17
R	Dan Gurney	Brabham	Brabham-Climax BT7	42 laps/chassis	6
R	Pedro Rodriguez	Lotus	Lotus-Climax 25	36 laps/engine	13
R	Trevor Taylor	Lotus	Lotus-Climax 25	24 laps/electrical	7
R	Masten Gregory	Reg Parnell Racing	Lola-Climax 4A	14 laps/engine	8
R	Hap Sharp	Reg Parnell Racing	Lotus-BRM 24	6 laps/engine	18
R	Phil Hill	Automobili Turismo e Sport	ATS 100	4 laps/fuel pump	15
R	Giancarlo Baghetti	Automobili Turismo e Sport	ATS 100	0 laps/fuel pump	20

Pole: Hill, 1m13.400s, 112.806mph/181.544kph. Fastest lap: Clark, 1m14.500s, 111.141mph/178.864kph on Lap 50. Race leaders: G Hill 1-6, 32, 35 & 83-100, Surtees 7-31, 33-34 & 36-82

CLASSIC CAR: LOTUS 25

The looks on the faces of the Lotus customer teams said it all when they first saw the Lotus 25 at the start of 1962. The previous Lotus 24s, like all other F1 cars, had a spaceframe chassis made of tubes, but the 25 had a monocoque inspired by aviation technology. This was effectively a bathtub shape made of two D-section booms covered with a stressed metal skin. Together, they made the chassis lighter and stiffer, with the latter improving handling. Lotus boss Colin Chapman had played his first blinder. Incredibly, the 25 remained competitive until Clark changed to the Lotus 33 midway through 1965.

MEXICAN GRAND PRIX

MEXICO CITY • ROUND 9 • DATE: 27TH OCTOBER 1963
Laps: 65 • Distance: 201.945miles/325.0km • Weather: Warm but dull

Pos	Driver	Team	Chassis-Engine	Result	Qual
1	Jim Clark	Lotus	Lotus-Climax 25	2h09m52.100s	1
2	Jack Brabham	Brabham	Brabham-Climax BT7	2h11m33.200s	10
3	Richie Ginther	BRM	BRM P57	2h11m46.800s	5
4	Graham Hill	BRM	BRM P57	64 laps	3
5	Jo Bonnier	Rob Walker Racing Team	Cooper-Climax T66	62 laps	8
6	Dan Gurney	Brabham	Brabham-Climax BT7	62 laps	4
7	Hap Sharp	Reg Parnell Racing	Lotus-BRM 24	61 laps	16
8	Jim Hall	BRP	Lotus-BRM 24	61 laps	15
9	Jo Siffert	Siffert Racing Team	Lotus-BRM 24	59 laps	9
10	Carel Godin de Beaufort	Ecurie Maarsbergen	Porsche 718	58 laps	18
11	Moises Solana	Scuderia Centro Sud	BRM P57	57 laps/engine	11
R	Phil Hill	Automobili Turismo e Sport	ATS 100	40 laps/suspension	17
R	Lorenzo Bandini	Ferrari	Ferrari 156 Aero	36 laps/ignition	7
R	Bruce McLaren	Cooper	Cooper-Climax T66	30 laps/engine	6
R	Pedro Rodriguez	Lotus	Lotus-Climax 25	26 laps/suspension	20
R	Masten Gregory	Reg Parnell Racing	Lola-Climax 4A	23 laps/suspension	14

Pos	Driver	Team	Chassis-Engine	Result	Qual
R	Trevor Taylor	Lotus	Lotus-Climax 25	19 laps/engine	12
DQ	John Surtees	Ferrari	Ferrari 156 Aero	19 laps/push start	2
R	Giancarlo Baghetti	Automobili Turismo e Sport	ATS 100	12 laps/engine	21
R	Chris Amon	Reg Parnell Racing	Lotus-BRM 24	9 laps/gearbox	19
R	Tony Maggs	Cooper	Cooper-Climax T66	7 laps/engine	13
DNQ	Frank Dochnal	Frank Dochnal	Cooper-Climax T51	accident	-

Pole: Clark, 1m58.800s, 94.147mph/151.515kph. Fastest lap: Clark, 1m58.100s, 94.705mph/152.413kph. Race leaders: Clark 1-65

NEW DRIVERS

Highest ranked of 1963's new drivers was Gerhard Mitter, who raced to fourth in the German GP in a privateer Porsche. However, Ferrari's Ludovico Scarfiotti would go on to become a grand prix winner in 1966 and Pedro Rodriguez would follow that in 1967, while Chris Amon would do everything except win in a luckless F1 career.

SOUTH AFRICAN GRAND PRIX

EAST LONDON • ROUND 10 • DATE: 28TH DECEMBER 1963
Laps: 85 • Distance: 207.24miles/333.174km • Weather: Hot, bright & windy

Pos	Driver	Team	Chassis-Engine	Result	Qual
1	Jim Clark	Lotus	Lotus-Climax 25	2h10m36.900s	1
2	Dan Gurney	Brabham	Brabham-Climax BT7	2h11m43.700s	3
3	Graham Hill	BRM	BRM P57	84 laps	6
4	Bruce McLaren	Cooper	Cooper-Climax T66	84 laps	9
5	Lorenzo Bandini	Ferrari	Ferrari 156 Aero	84 laps	5
6	Jo Bonnier	Rob Walker Racing Team	Cooper-Climax T66	83 laps	11
7	Tony Maggs	Cooper	Cooper-Climax T66	82 laps	10
8	Trevor Taylor	Lotus	Lotus-Climax 25	81 laps	8
9	John Love	John Love	Cooper-Climax T55	80 laps	13
10	Carel Godin de Beaufort	Ecurie Maarsbergen	Porsche 718	79 laps	20
11	Doug Serrurier	Otelle Nucci	LDS-Alfa Romeo 2	78 laps	18
12	Trevor Blokdyk	Scuderia Lupini	Cooper-Maserati T51	77 laps	19
13	Jack Brabham	Brabham	Brabham-Climax BT7	70 laps/accident	2
14	Brausch Niemann	Ted Lanfear	Lotus-Ford 22	66 laps	15
R	Peter de Klerk	Otelle Nucci	Alfa Special-Alfa Romeo	53 laps/gearbox	16
R	David Prophet	David Prophet	Brabham-Ford BT6	49 laps/fuel pressure	14
R	John Surtees	Ferrari	Ferrari 156 Aero	43 laps/engine	4
R	Richie Ginther	BRM	BRM P57	43 laps/halfshaft	7
R	Ernie Pieterse	Lawson Organisation	Lotus-Climax 21	3 laps/engine	12
R	Sam Tingle	Sam Tingle	LDS-Alfa Romeo 2	2 laps/halfshaft	17
NS	Paddy Driver	Selby Auto Spares	Lotus-BRM 24	accident	21

Pole: Clark, 1m28.900s, 98.629mph/158.728kph. Fastest lap: Gurney, 1m29.100s, 98.407mph/158.371kph on Lap 33. Race leaders: Clark 1-85

WORLD DRIVERS' CHAMPIONSHIP FINAL RESULTS

Pos	Driver	Nat	Car-Engine	R1	R2	R3	R4	R5	R6	R7	R8	R9	R10	Total
1	Jim Clark	GBR	Lotus-Climax 25	8P	1F	1PF	1PF	1P	2P	1F	3F	1PF	1P	54
2	Graham Hill	GBR	BRM P57	1	RP	R	-	3	R	-	1P	4	3	29
			BRM P61	-	-	-	3	-	-	16	-	-	-	
2	Richie Ginther	USA	BRM P57	2	4	5	R	4	3	2	2	3	R	29
4	John Surtees	GBR	Ferrari 156/63	4F	R	3	R	2F	1F	-	9	-	-	22
			Ferrari 156 Aero	-	-	-	-	-	-	RP	-	DQ	R	
5	Dan Gurney	USA	Brabham-Climax BT7	R	3	2	5	R	R	14	R	6	2F	19
6	Bruce McLaren	NZL	Cooper-Climax T66	3	2	R	12	R	R	3	11	R	4	17
7	Jack Brabham	AUS	Lotus-Climax 25	9	-	-	-	-	-	-	-	-	-	14
			Brabham-Climax BT7	-	-	R	4	R	7	-	4	2	13	
			Brabham-Climax BT3	-	R	-	-	-	-	5	-	-	-	
8	Tony Maggs	ZAF	Cooper-Climax T66	5	7	R	2	9	R	6	R	R	7	9
9	Innes Ireland	GBR	Lotus-BRM 24	R	-	-	-	-	R	-	-	-	-	6
			BRP-BRM 1	-	R	4	9	R	-	4	-	-	-	
10	Lorenzo Bandini	ITA	BRM P57	-	-	-	10	5	R	-	-	-	-	6
			Ferrari 156/63	-	-	-	-	-	-	R	5	-	-	
			Ferrari 156 Aero	-	-	-	-	-	-	-	-	R	5	
11	Jo Bonnier	SWE	Cooper-Climax T60	7	5	11	NC	-	-	-	-	-	-	6
			Cooper-Climax T66	-	-	-	-	R	6	7	8	5	6	
12	Gerhard Mitter	DEU	Porsche 718	-	-	R	-	-	4	-	-	-	-	3
13	Jim Hall	USA	Lotus-BRM 24	R	R	8	11	6	5	8	10	8	-	3
14	Carel Godin de Beaufort	NLD	Porsche 718	-	6	9	-	10	R	DNQ	6	10	10	2
15	Trevor Taylor	GBR	Lotus-Climax 25	6	R	10	13	DQ	8	-	R	R	8	1
15	Ludovico Scarfiotti	ITA	Ferrari 156/63	-	-	6	NS	-	-	-	-	-	-	1
15	Jo Siffert	CHE	Lotus-BRM 24	R	R	7	6	R	9	R	R	9	-	1

WORLD CONSTRUCTORS' CHAMPIONSHIP FINAL RESULTS

Pos	Team-Engine	R1	R2	R3	R4	R5	R6	R7	R8	R9	R10	Total
1	Lotus-Climax	6	1	1	1	1	2	1	3	1	1	54
2	BRM	1	4	5	3	3	3	2	1	3	3	36
3	Brabham-Climax	9	3	2	4	-	7	5	4	2	2	28
4	Ferrari	4	-	3	-	2	1	-	5	-	5	26
5	Cooper-Climax	3	2	11	2	9	6	3	8	5	4	25
6	BRP-BRM	-	-	-	-	-	-	-	-	-	-	6
7	Porsche	-	6	9	-	10	4	-	6	10	10	5
8	Lotus-BRM	-	-	4	6	6	5	4	10	7	-	4

SYMBOLS AND GRAND PRIX KEY

Round 1	Monaco GP
Round 2	Belgian GP
Round 3	Dutch GP
Round 4	French GP
Round 5	British GP
Round 6	German GP
Round 7	Italian GP
Round 8	United States GP
Round 9	Mexican GP
Round 10	South African GP

SCORING

1st	9 points
2nd	6 points
3rd	4 points
4th	3 points
5th	2 points
6th	1 point

DNPQ DID NOT PRE-QUALIFY **DNQ** DID NOT QUALIFY **DQ** DISQUALIFIED **EX** EXCLUDED
F FASTEST LAP **NC** NOT CLASSIFIED **NS** NON-STARTER **P** POLE POSITION **R** RETIRED

SEASON SUMMARY

John Surtees made history in 1964 when he became the only person to date to win world championship titles on both two wheels and four. His second year with Ferrari was marked by clear progress and his two wins set him up to be part of a three-way shoot-out at the final round. It was there that he pipped fellow British drivers Graham Hill and Jim Clark to the crown. Even more thrilling for Ferrari, especially after its double title success in 1961 was followed by an atrocious year in 1962, was the fact that it also landed the constructors' championship.

MONACO GRAND PRIX

MONTE CARLO • ROUND 1 • DATE: 10TH MAY 1964
Laps: 100 • Distance: 195.113miles/314.5km • Weather: Hot & bright

Pos	Driver	Team	Chassis-Engine	Result	Qual
1	Graham Hill	BRM	BRM P261	2h41m19.500s	3
2	Richie Ginther	BRM	BRM P261	99 laps	8
3	Peter Arundell	Lotus	Lotus-Climax 25	97 laps	6
4	Jim Clark	Lotus	Lotus-Climax 25	96 laps/engine	1
5	Jo Bonnier	Rob Walker Racing Team	Cooper-Climax T66	96 laps	11
6	Mike Hailwood	Reg Parnell Racing	Lotus-BRM 25	96 laps	15
7	Bob Anderson	DW Racing Enterprises	Brabham-Climax BT11	86 laps/gearbox	12
8	Jo Siffert	Siffert Racing Team	Lotus-BRM 24	78 laps	16
9	Phil Hill	Cooper	Cooper-Climax T73	70 laps/suspension	9
10	Lorenzo Bandini	Ferrari	Ferrari 156 Aero	68 laps/gearbox	7
R	Dan Gurney	Brabham	Brabham-Climax BT7	62 laps/gearbox	5
R	Maurice Trintignant	Maurice Trintignant	BRM P57	53 laps/overheating	13
R	Jack Brabham	Brabham	Brabham-Climax BT7	29 laps/fuel injection	2
R	Bruce McLaren	Cooper	Cooper-Climax T66	17 laps/wheel	10
R	John Surtees	Ferrari	Ferrari 158	15 laps/gearbox	4
R	Trevor Taylor	BRP	BRP-BRM 1	8 laps/oil leak	14
NS	Innes Ireland	BRP	Lotus-BRM 24	driver injured	17
DNQ	Chris Amon	Reg Parnell Racing	Lotus-BRM 25	-	18
DNQ	Peter Revson	Reg Parnell Racing	Lotus-BRM 24	-	19
DNQ	Bernard Collomb	Bernard Collomb	Lotus-Climax 24	-	20

Pole: Clark, 1m34.000s, 74.842mph/120.446kph. Fastest lap: G Hill, 1m33.900s, 74.921mph/120.575kph on Lap 53. Race leaders: Clark 1-36, Gurney 37-52; G Hill 53-100

DUTCH GRAND PRIX

ZANDVOORT • ROUND 2 • DATE: 24TH MAY 1964
Laps: 80 • Distance: 208.186miles/335.44km • Weather: Hot & bright

Pos	Driver	Team	Chassis-Engine	Result	Qual
1	Jim Clark	Lotus	Lotus-Climax 25	2h07m35.400s	2
2	John Surtees	Ferrari	Ferrari 158	2h08m29.000s	4
3	Peter Arundell	Lotus	Lotus-Climax 25	79 laps	6
4	Graham Hill	BRM	BRM P261	79 laps	3
5	Chris Amon	Reg Parnell Racing	Lotus-BRM 25	79 laps	13
6	Bob Anderson	DW Racing Enterprises	Brabham-Climax BT11	78 laps	11
7	Bruce McLaren	Cooper	Cooper-Climax T73	78 laps	5

Pos	Driver	Team	Chassis-Engine	Result	Qual
8	Phil Hill	Cooper	Cooper-Climax T73	76 laps	9
9	Jo Bonnier	Rob Walker Racing Team	Brabham-BRM BT11	76 laps	12
10	Giancarlo Baghetti	Scuderia Centro Sud	BRM P57	74 laps	16
11	Richie Ginther	BRM	BRM P261	64 laps	8
12	Mike Hailwood	Reg Parnell Racing	Lotus-BRM 25	57 laps/differential	14
13	Jo Siffert	Siffert Racing Team	Brabham-BRM BT11	55 laps	18
R	Jack Brabham	Brabham	Brabham-Climax BT7	44 laps/ignition	7
R	Lorenzo Bandini	Ferrari	Ferrari 158	25 laps/fuel injection	10
R	Dan Gurney	Brabham	Brabham-Climax BT7	23 laps/steering	1
R	Carel Godin de Beaufort	Ecurie Maarsbergen	Porsche 718	8 laps/engine	17
NS	Tony Maggs	Scuderia Centro Sud	BRM P57	accident	15

Pole: Gurney, 1m31.200s, 102.845mph/165.513kph. Fastest lap: Clark, 1m32.800s, 101.071mph/162.659kph on Lap 6. Race leaders: Clark 1-80

CHANGING OF THE GUARD

The sudden death of Britain's leading post-war racer Reg Parnell in January at the age of just 53 left his son Tim in charge of the family team. Tim had had a handful of grand prix outings between 1959 and 1963 but had to change roles immediately. The team would run Chris Amon, Mike Hailwood and Peter Revson in BRM-engined Lotuses.

BELGIAN GRAND PRIX

SPA-FRANCORCHAMPS • ROUND 3 • DATE: 14TH JUNE 1964
Laps: 32 • Distance: 280.239miles/451.2km • Weather: Warm but dull

Pos	Driver	Team	Chassis-Engine	Result	Qual
1	Jim Clark	Lotus	Lotus-Climax 25	2h06m40.500s	6
2	Bruce McLaren	Cooper	Cooper-Climax T73	2h06m43.900s	7
3	Jack Brabham	Brabham	Brabham-Climax BT7	2h07m28.600s	3
4	Richie Ginther	BRM	BRM P261	2h08m39.100s	8
5	Graham Hill	BRM	BRM P261	31 laps/fuel pump	2
6	Dan Gurney	Brabham	Brabham-Climax BT7	31 laps/out of fuel	1
7	Trevor Taylor	BRP	BRP-BRM 2	31 laps	12
8	Giancarlo Baghetti	Scuderia Centro Sud	BRM P57	31 laps	17
9	Peter Arundell	Lotus	Lotus-Climax 25	28 laps/overheating	4
10	Innes Ireland	BRP	BRP-BRM 1	28 laps	16
DQ	Peter Revson	Reg Parnell Racing	Lotus-BRM 24	27 laps/push start	10
R	Jo Siffert	Siffert Racing Team	Brabham-BRM BT11	14 laps/engine	13
R	Phil Hill	Cooper	Cooper-Climax T73	13 laps/engine	15
R	Lorenzo Bandini	Ferrari	Ferrari 158	12 laps/engine	9
R	Andre Pilette	Scirocco	Scirocco-Climax SP	11 laps/engine	20
R	Jo Bonnier	Rob Walker Racing Team	Brabham-BRM BT11	8 laps/driver unwell	14
R	John Surtees	Ferrari	Ferrari 158	4 laps/engine	5
R	Chris Amon	Reg Parnell Racing	Lotus-BRM 25	3 laps/engine	11
NS	Tony Maggs	Scuderia Centro Sud	BRM P57	engine	18
NS	Bob Anderson	DW Racing Enterprises	Brabham-Climax BT11	ignition	19

Pole: Gurney, 3m50.900s, 136.599mph/219.835kph. Fastest lap: Gurney, 3m49.200s, 137.633mph/221.500kph on Lap 27. Race leaders: Gurney 1-2 & 4-29; Surtees 3; G Hill 30-31; Clark 32

CONSTRUCTOR AND DRIVER

Jack Brabham already had two F1 drivers' titles to his name when he elected to start building cars bearing his name. That was in 1962, and it took only two years for the cars designed by fellow Australian Ron Tauranac to start winning, with Dan Gurney being first to the chequered flag in the French GP at Rouen-les-Essarts.

NOT ALWAYS IN RED

It was a shock when the Ferraris turned up for the United States GP in the white-over-blue livery of Luigi Chinetti's North American Racing Team, rather than their regular red. This was because Enzo Ferrari was angered by a homologation problem for his 250LM sports cars and so made this gesture to the FIA. They also raced in NART colours in Mexico.

FRENCH GRAND PRIX

ROUEN-LES-ESSARTS • ROUND 4 • DATE: 28TH JUNE 1964
Laps: 57 • Distance: 231.705miles/372.894km • Weather: Warm but dull

Pos	Driver	Team	Chassis-Engine	Result	Qual
1	Dan Gurney	Brabham	Brabham-Climax BT7	2h07m49.100s	2
2	Graham Hill	BRM	BRM P261	2h08m13.200s	6
3	Jack Brabham	Brabham	Brabham-Climax BT7	2h08m14.000s	5
4	Peter Arundell	Lotus	Lotus-Climax 25	2h08m59.700s	4
5	Richie Ginther	BRM	BRM P261	2h10m01.200s	9
6	Bruce McLaren	Cooper	Cooper-Climax T73	56 laps	7
7	Phil Hill	Cooper	Cooper-Climax T73	56 laps	10
8	Mike Hailwood	Reg Parnell Racing	Lotus-BRM 25	56 laps	13
9	Lorenzo Bandini	Ferrari	Ferrari 158	55 laps	8
10	Chris Amon	Reg Parnell Racing	Lotus-BRM 25	53 laps	14
11	Maurice Trintignant	Maurice Trintignant	BRM P57	52 laps	16
12	Bob Anderson	DW Racing Enterprises	Brabham-Climax BT11	50 laps	15
R	Innes Ireland	BRP	BRP-BRM 1	32 laps/accident	11
R	Jim Clark	Lotus	Lotus-Climax 25	31 laps/engine	1
R	John Surtees	Ferrari	Ferrari 158	6 laps/engine	3
R	Trevor Taylor	BRP	BRP-BRM 2	6 laps/accident	12
R	Jo Siffert	Siffert Racing Team	Brabham-BRM BT11	4 laps/clutch	17
NS	Peter Revson	Reg Parnell Racing	Lotus-BRM 25	Hailwood drove car	-

Pole: Clark, 2m09.600s, 112.916mph/181.722kph. Fastest lap: Brabham, 2m11.400s, 111.370mph/179.232kph on Lap 44. Race leaders: Clark 1-30; Gurney 31-57

BRITISH GRAND PRIX

BRANDS HATCH • ROUND 5 • DATE: 11TH JULY 1964
Laps: 80 • Distance: 212.1miles/341.184km • Weather: Warm but dull

Pos	Driver	Team	Chassis-Engine	Result	Qual
1	Jim Clark	Lotus	Lotus-Climax 25	2h15m07.000s	1
2	Graham Hill	BRM	BRM P261	2h15m09.800s	2
3	John Surtees	Ferrari	Ferrari 158	2h16m27.600s	5
4	Jack Brabham	Brabham	Brabham-Climax BT7	79 laps	4
5	Lorenzo Bandini	Ferrari	Ferrari 156 Aero	78 laps	8
6	Phil Hill	Cooper	Cooper-Climax T73	78 laps	15
7	Bob Anderson	DW Racing Enterprises	Brabham-Climax BT11	78 laps	7
8	Richie Ginther	BRM	BRM P261	77 laps	14
9	Mike Spence	Lotus	Lotus-Climax 25	77 laps	13
10	Innes Ireland	BRP	BRP-BRM 2	77 laps	10
11	Jo Siffert	Siffert Racing Team	Brabham-BRM BT11	76 laps	16
12	Giancarlo Baghetti	Scuderia Centro Sud	BRM P57	76 laps	21
13	Dan Gurney	Brabham	Brabham-Climax BT7	75 laps	3
14	John Taylor	Bob Gerard Racing	Cooper-Ford T71/73	56 laps	20
R	Jo Bonnier	Rob Walker Racing Team	Brabham-BRM BT11	45 laps/brakes	9
R	Peter Revson	Revson Racing	Lotus-BRM 24	43 laps/differential	22
R	Ian Raby	Ian Raby Racing	Brabham-BRM BT3	37 laps/accident	17
R	Tony Maggs	Scuderia Centro Sud	BRM P57	37 laps/gearbox	23
R	Trevor Taylor	BRP	Lotus-BRM 24	23 laps/physical	18
R	Mike Hailwood	Reg Parnell Racing	Lotus-BRM 25	17 laps/oil line	12
R	Chris Amon	Reg Parnell Racing	Lotus-BRM 25	9 laps/clutch	11
R	Bruce McLaren	Cooper	Cooper-Climax T73	7 laps/gearbox	6
R	Frank Gardner	John Willment Automobiles	Brabham-Ford BT10	0 laps/accident	19
NS	Richard Attwood	BRM	BRM P67	withdrew	24
DNQ	Maurice Trintignant	Maurice Trintignant	BRM P57	-	25

Pole: Clark, 1m38.100s, 97.248mph/156.506kph. Fastest lap: Clark, 1m38.800s, 96.559mph/155.397kph on Lap 73. Race leaders: Clark 1-80

HILLY AND FLAT

The two circuits that were new to the World Championship, Brands Hatch and Zeltweg, could not have been more different, as the former, set in an amphitheatre in rolling hills south-east of London, offered gradient changes galore, while the latter was pancake flat, its layout marked out at a military airfield by straw bales.

SECOND IS ENOUGH FOR SUCCESS

Hill had a five-point lead over Surtees going to the final round in Mexico, with the fragility of Clark's Lotus leaving him nine points down. Hill's BRM had its exhausts squashed by Ferrari's Lorenzo Bandini, leaving Clark leading easily until his Lotus hit engine trouble with two laps to go and Bandini let Surtees past to take second place and the title.

NEW CONSTRUCTORS
There were language and cultural barriers to be overcome when Honda made its debut. The Japanese manufacturer entrusted its white car with rising sun motif to American sports car racer Ronnie Bucknum, perhaps so that it was hard to gauge their performance. He qualified ninth at Monza but retired from all three races.

GERMAN GRAND PRIX

NURBURGRING • ROUND 6 • DATE: 2ND AUGUST 1964
Laps: 15 • Distance: 212.518miles/342.15km • Weather: Warm but dull

Pos	Driver	Team	Chassis-Engine	Result	Qual
1	John Surtees	Ferrari	Ferrari 158	2h12m04.800s	1
2	Graham Hill	BRM	BRM P261	2h13m20.400s	5
3	Lorenzo Bandini	Ferrari	Ferrari 156 Aero	2h16m57.600s	4
4	Jo Siffert	Siffert Racing Team	Brabham-BRM BT11	2h17m27.900s	10
5	Maurice Trintignant	Maurice Trintignant	BRM P57	14 laps/battery	14
6	Tony Maggs	Scuderia Centro Sud	BRM P57	14 laps	16
7	Richie Ginther	BRM	BRM P261	14 laps	11
8	Mike Spence	Lotus	Lotus-Climax 33	14 laps	17
9	Gerhard Mitter	Lotus	Lotus-Climax 25	14 laps	19
10	Dan Gurney	Brabham	Brabham-Climax BT7	14 laps	3
11	Chris Amon	Reg Parnell Racing	Lotus-BRM 25	12 laps/suspension	9
12	Jack Brabham	Brabham	Brabham-Climax BT7	11 laps/differential	6
13	Ronnie Bucknum	Honda	Honda RA271	11 laps/accident	22
14	Peter Revson	Revson Racing	Lotus-BRM 24	10 laps/accident	18
R	Jim Clark	Lotus	Lotus-Climax 33	7 laps/engine	2
R	Bruce McLaren	Cooper	Cooper-Climax T73	4 laps/engine	7
R	Bob Anderson	DW Racing Enterprises	Brabham-Climax BT11	4 laps/suspension	15
R	Edgar Barth	Rob Walker Racing Team	Cooper-Climax T66	3 laps/clutch	20
R	Giancarlo Baghetti	Scuderia Centro Sud	BRM P57	2 laps/throttle	21
R	Phil Hill	Cooper	Cooper-Climax T73	1 lap/engine	8
R	Jo Bonnier	Rob Walker Racing Team	Brabham-BRM BT11	0 laps/electrical	12
R	Mike Hailwood	Reg Parnell Racing	Lotus-BRM 25	0 laps/engine	13
NS	Carel Godin de Beaufort	Ecurie Maarsbergen	Porsche 718	fatal accident	23
DNQ	Andre Pilette	Scirocco	Scirocco-Climax SP	-	24

Pole: Surtees, 8m38.400s, 98.426mph/158.402kph. Fastest lap: Surtees, 8m39.000s, 98.313mph/158.219kph on Lap 11. Race leaders: Clark 1; Surtees 2-3 & 5-15; Gurney 4

NEW DRIVERS
The pick of 1964's crop of new drivers would prove to be Jochen Rindt, who had a one-off in a Rob Walker Racing Brabham. Rindt went on to become World Champion in 1970. Future grand prix winner Peter Revson dipped his toe in the water with a Lotus run by Reg Parnell Racing, but would achieve more when he returned in 1971.

AUSTRIAN GRAND PRIX

ZELTWEG • ROUND 7 • DATE: 23RD AUGUST 1964
Laps: 105 • Distance: 208.780miles/336.0km • Weather: Warm but dull

Pos	Driver	Team	Chassis-Engine	Result	Qual
1	Lorenzo Bandini	Ferrari	Ferrari 156 Aero	2h06m18.230s	7
2	Richie Ginther	BRM	BRM P261	2h06m24.410s	5
3	Bob Anderson	DW Racing Enterprises	Brabham-Climax BT11	102 laps	14
4	Tony Maggs	Scuderia Centro Sud	BRM P57	102 laps	19
5	Innes Ireland	BRP	BRP-BRM 2	102 laps	11
6	Jo Bonnier	Rob Walker Racing Team	Brabham-Climax BT7	101 laps	10
7	Giancarlo Baghetti	Scuderia Centro Sud	BRM P57	98 laps	15
8	Mike Hailwood	Reg Parnell Racing	Lotus-BRM 25	95 laps	18
9	Jack Brabham	Brabham	Brabham-Climax BT11	73 laps	6
R	Jochen Rindt	Rob Walker Racing Team	Brabham-BRM BT11	58 laps/steering	13
R	Phil Hill	Cooper	Cooper-Climax T66	58 laps/accident	20
R	Dan Gurney	Brabham	Brabham-Climax BT7	47 laps/suspension	4
R	Bruce McLaren	Cooper	Cooper-Climax T73	43 laps/engine	9
R	Mike Spence	Lotus	Lotus-Climax 33	41 laps/halfshaft	8
R	Jim Clark	Lotus	Lotus-Climax 33	40 laps/halfshaft	3
R	Trevor Taylor	BRP	BRP-BRM 1	21 laps/suspension	16
R	Jo Siffert	Siffert Racing Team	Brabham-BRM BT11	18 laps/accident	12
R	John Surtees	Ferrari	Ferrari 158	9 laps/suspension	2
R	Chris Amon	Reg Parnell Racing	Lotus-Climax 25	7 laps/engine	17
R	Graham Hill	BRM	BRM P261	5 laps/distributor	1

Pole: G Hill, 1m09.840s, 102.494mph/164.948kph. Fastest lap: Gurney, 1m10.560s, 101.448mph/163.265kph on Lap 32. Race leaders: Gurney 1 & 8-46; Surtees 2-7; Bandini 47-105

IN MEMORIAM

F1 lost one of its most entertaining protagonists when tall Dutch aristocrat Carel Godin de Beaufort crashed his privately entered orange Porsche in practice at the Nurburgring and was thrown from the car. Up-and-coming American Timmy Mayer met his end in practice for a Tasman Series race at Tasmania's fearsome Longford circuit.

ITALIAN GRAND PRIX

MONZA • ROUND 8 • DATE: 6TH SEPTEMBER 1964
Laps: 78 • Distance: 278.377miles/448.5km • Weather: Warm but dull

Pos	Driver	Team	Chassis-Engine	Result	Qual
1	John Surtees	Ferrari	Ferrari 158	2h10m51.800s	1
2	Bruce McLaren	Cooper	Cooper-Climax T73	2h11m57.800s	5
3	Lorenzo Bandini	Ferrari	Ferrari 158	77 laps	7
4	Richie Ginther	BRM	BRM P261	77 laps	9
5	Innes Ireland	BRP	BRP-BRM 2	77 laps	13
6	Mike Spence	Lotus	Lotus-Climax 33	77 laps	8
7	Jo Siffert	Siffert Racing Team	Brabham-BRM BT11	77 laps	6
8	Giancarlo Baghetti	Scuderia Centro Sud	BRM P57	77 laps	15
9	Ludovico Scarfiotti	Ferrari	Ferrari 156 Aero	77 laps	16

Pos	Driver	Team	Chassis-Engine	Result	Qual
10	Dan Gurney	Brabham	Brabham-Climax BT7	75 laps/battery	2
11	Bob Anderson	DW Racing Enterprises	Brabham-Climax BT11	75 laps	14
12	Jo Bonnier	Rob Walker Racing Team	Brabham-Climax BT7	74 laps	12
13	Peter Revson	Revson Racing	Lotus-BRM 24	72 laps	18
14	Jack Brabham	Brabham	Brabham-Climax BT11	59 laps/engine	11
R	Jim Clark	Lotus	Lotus-Climax 25	27 laps/engine	4
R	Mario Cabral	Derrington-Francis	Derrington-Francis-ATS	24 laps/ignition	19
R	Maurice Trintignant	Maurice Trintignant	BRM P57	21 laps/fuel injection	20
R	Ronnie Bucknum	Honda	Honda RA271	12 laps/brakes	10
R	Mike Hailwood	Reg Parnell Racing	Lotus-BRM 25	4 laps/engine	17
R	Graham Hill	BRM	BRM P261	0 laps/clutch	3
NS	Jean-Claude Rudaz	Fabre Urbain	Cooper-Climax T60	piston	20
DNQ	Trevor Taylor	BRP	BRP-BRM 1	-	22
DNQ	Giacomo'Geki' Russo	Rob Walker Racing Team	Brabham-BRM BT11	-	23
DNQ	John Love	Cooper	Cooper-Climax T73	-	24
DNQ	Ian Raby	Ian Raby Racing	Brabham-BRM BT3	-	25

Pole: Surtees, 1m37.400s, 132.057mph/212.525kph. Fastest lap: Surtees, 1m38.800s, 130.186mph/209.514kph on Lap 63. Race leaders: Gurney 1, 6-7, 10, 12-14, 16, 22,25-26, 29, 32, 37-38, 45, 47-48, 50-52 & 55; Surtees 2-5, 8-9, 11, 15, 17-21, 23-24, 27-28, 30-31, 33-36, 39-44, 46, 49, 53-54 56-78

CLASSIC CAR: FERRARI 158

Ferrari knew that it had to try every trick in the book to match the Lotus 25 and so raced with three different engines, trying V6, V8 and flat-12 formats. John Surtees won the 1963 German GP with V6 power but, under internal pressure, raced with Ferrari's V8 engine in 1964, combining well with chief engineer Mauro Forghieri as he won the German and Italian GPs with a 158. The car took its name from its 1.5-litre, eight-cylinder engine. However, despite Surtees and Forghieri pushing Ferrari beyond its traditionally cautious approach, it still couldn't match the Climax engine's mid-range punch.

UNITED STATES GRAND PRIX

WATKINS GLEN • ROUND 9 • DATE: 4TH OCTOBER 1964
Laps: 110 • Distance: 253.0miles/407.165km • Weather: Warm & b right

Pos	Driver	Team	Chassis-Engine	Result	Qual
1	Graham Hill	BRM	BRM P261	2h16m38.000s	4
2	John Surtees	Ferrari	Ferrari 158	2h17m08.500s	2
3	Jo Siffert	Rob Walker Racing Team	Brabham-BRM BT11	109 laps	12
4	Richie Ginther	BRM	BRM P261	107 laps	13
5	Walt Hansgen	Lotus	Lotus-Climax 33	107 laps	17
6	Trevor Taylor	BRP	BRP-BRM 2	106 laps	15
7	Spence / Clark*	Lotus	Lotus-Climax 33	102 laps/out of fuel	6
8	Mike Hailwood	Reg Parnell Racing	Lotus-BRM 25	101 laps/oil line	16
R	Dan Gurney	Brabham	Brabham-Climax BT7	69 laps/fuel pressure	3
NC	Hap Sharp	Rob Walker Racing Team	Brabham-BRM BT11	65 laps/not classified	18
R	Lorenzo Bandini	Ferrari	Ferrari 1512	58 laps/engine	8
R	Clark / Spence*	Lotus	Lotus-Climax 33	54 laps/fuel injection	1

Pos	Driver	Team	Chassis-Engine	Result	Qual
R	Ronnie Bucknum	Honda	Honda RA271	50 laps/overheating	14
R	Chris Amon	Reg Parnell Racing	Lotus-BRM 25	47 laps/engine	11
R	Jo Bonnier	Rob Walker Racing Team	Brabham-Climax BT7	37 laps/wheel	9
R	Bruce McLaren	Cooper	Cooper-Climax T73	27 laps/engine	5
R	Jack Brabham	Brabham	Brabham-Climax BT11	14 laps/engine	7
R	Phil Hill	Cooper	Cooper-Climax T73	4 laps/ignition	19
R	Innes Ireland	BRP	BRP-BRM 2	2 laps/gearbox	10
*Mike Spence, Jim Clark					

Pole: Clark, 1m12.650s, 116.450mph/187.408kph. Fastest lap: Clark, 1m12.700s, 116.370mph/187.280kph on lap 81. Race leaders: Surtees 1-12 & 44; Clark 13-43; G Hill 45-100

MEXICAN GRAND PRIX

MEXICO CITY • ROUND 10 • DATE: 25TH OCTOBER 1964
Laps: 65 • Distance: 201.945miles/325.0km • Weather: Warm & bright

Pos	Driver	Team	Chassis-Engine	Result	Qual
1	Dan Gurney	Brabham	Brabham-Climax BT7	2h09m50.320s	2
2	John Surtees	Ferrari	Ferrari 158	2h10m59.260s	4
3	Lorenzo Bandini	Ferrari	Ferrari 1512	2h10m59.950s	3
4	Mike Spence	Lotus	Lotus-Climax 25	2h11m12.180s	5
5	Jim Clark	Lotus	Lotus-Climax 33	64 laps/engine	1
6	Pedro Rodriguez	Ferrari	Ferrari 156 Aero	64 laps	9
7	Bruce McLaren	Cooper	Cooper-Climax T73	64 laps	10
8	Richie Ginther	BRM	BRM P261	64 laps	11
9	Phil Hill	Cooper	Cooper-Climax T73	63 laps/engine	15
10	Moises Solana	Lotus	Lotus-Climax 33	63 laps	14
11	Graham Hill	BRM	BRM P261	63 laps	6
12	Innes Ireland	BRP	BRP-BRM 2	61 laps	16
13	Hap Sharp	Rob Walker Racing Team	Brabham-BRM BT11	60 laps	19
R	Chris Amon	Reg Parnell Racing	Lotus-BRM 25	46 laps/gearbox	12
R	Jack Brabham	Brabham	Brabham-Climax BT11	44 laps/electrical	7
R	Mike Hailwood	Reg Parnell Racing	Lotus-BRM 25	12 laps/overheating	17
R	Jo Siffert	Rob Walker Racing Team	Brabham-BRM BT11	11 laps/fuel pump	13
R	Jo Bonnier	Rob Walker Racing Team	Brabham-Climax BT7	9 laps/suspension	8
R	Trevor Taylor	BRP	BRP-BRM 2	6 laps/overheating	18

Pole: Clark, 1m57.240s, 95.399mph/153.531kph. Fastest lap: Clark, 1m58.370s, 94.489mph/152.065kph. Race leaders: Clark 1-63; Gurney 64-65

WORLD DRIVERS' CHAMPIONSHIP FINAL RESULTS

Pos	Driver	Nat	Car-Engine	R1	R2	R3	R4	R5	R6	R7	R8	R9	R10	Total
1	John Surtees	GBR	Ferrari 158	R	2	R	R	3	1PF	R	1PF	2	2	40
2	Graham Hill	GBR	BRM P261	1F	4	5	2	2	2	RP	R	1	11	39
3	Jim Clark	GBR	Lotus-Climax 25	4P	1F	1	RP	1PF	-	-	R	R	-	32
			Lotus-Climax 33	-	-	-	-	-	R	R	-	7F	5PF	
4	Lorenzo Bandini	ITA	Ferrari 156 Aero	10	-	-	-	5	3	1	-	-	-	23
			Ferrari 158	-	R	R	9	-	-	-	3	-	-	
			Ferrari 1512	-	-	-	-	-	-	-	-	R	3	
4	Richie Ginther	USA	BRM P261	2	11	4	5	8	7	2	4	4	8	23
6	Dan Gurney	USA	Brabham-Climax BT7	R	RP	6PF	1	13	10	RF	10	R	1	19

Pos	Driver	Nat	Car-Engine	R1	R2	R3	R4	R5	R6	R7	R8	R9	R10	Total
7	Bruce McLaren	NZL	Cooper-Climax T66	R	-	-	-	-	-	-	-	-	-	13
			Cooper-Climax T73	-	7	2	6	R	R	R	2	R	7	
8	Peter Arundell	GBR	Lotus-Climax 25	3	3	9	4	-	-	-	-	-	-	11
8	Jack Brabham	AUS	Brabham-Climax BT7	R	R	3	3F	4	12	-	-	-	-	11
			Brabham-Climax BT11	-	-	-	-	-	-	9	14	R	R	
10	Jo Siffert	CHE	Lotus-BRM 24	8	-	-	-	-	-	-	-	-	-	7
			Brabham-BRM BT11	-	13	R	R	11	4	R	7	3	R	
11	Bob Anderson	GBR	Brabham-Climax BT11	7	6	NS	12	7	R	3	11	-	-	5
12	Tony Maggs	ZAF	BRM P57	-	NS	NS	-	R	6	4	-	-	-	4
12	Mike Spence	GBR	Lotus-Climax 25	-	-	-	-	9	-	-	-	R	4	4
			Lotus-Climax 33	-	-	-	-	-	8	R	6	7	-	
12	Innes Ireland	GBR	Lotus-BRM 24	NS	-	-	-	-	-	-	-	-	-	4
			BRP-BRM 1	-	-	10	R	-	-	-	-	-	-	
			BRP-BRM 2	-	-	-	-	10	-	5	5	R	12	
15	Jo Bonnier	SWE	Cooper-Climax T66	5	-	-	-	-	-	-	-	-	-	3
			Brabham-BRM BT11	-	9	R	-	R	R	-	-	-	-	
			Brabham-Climax BT7	-	-	-	-	-	-	6	12	R	R	
16	Chris Amon	NZL	Lotus-BRM 25	DNQ	5	R	10	R	11	-	-	R	R	2
			Lotus-Climax 25	-	-	-	-	-	-	R	-	-	-	
16	Maurice Trintignant	FRA	BRM P57	R	-	-	11	DNQ	5	-	R	-	-	2
16	Walt Hansgen	USA	Lotus-Climax 33	-	-	-	-	-	-	-	-	5	-	2
19	Mike Hailwood	GBR	Lotus-BRM 25	6	12	-	8	R	R	8	R	8	R	1
19	Phil Hill	USA	Cooper-Climax T73	9	8	R	7	6	R	-	-	R	9	1
			Cooper-Climax T66	-	-	-	-	-	-	R	-	-	-	
19	Trevor Taylor	GBR	BRP-BRM 1	R	-	-	-	-	-	R	DNQ	-	-	1
			BRP-BRM 2	-	-	7	R	-	-	-	-	6	R	
			Lotus-BRM 24	-	-	-	-	R	-	-	-	-	-	
19	Pedro Rodriguez	MEX	Ferrari 156 Aero	-	-	-	-	-	-	-	-	-	6	1

WORLD CONSTRUCTORS' CHAMPIONSHIP FINAL RESULTS

Pos	Team-Engine	R1	R2	R3	R4	R5	R6	R7	R8	R9	R10	Total
1	Ferrari	10	2	R	9	3	1	1	1	2	2	45
2	BRM	1	4	4	2	2	2	2	4	1	8	42
3	Lotus-Climax	3	1	1	4	1	8		6	5	4	37
4	Brabham-Climax	7	6	3	1	4	10	3	10	-	1	30
5	Cooper-Climax	5	7	2	6	6	-	-	2	-	7	16
6	Brabham-BRM	-	9	R	-	-	-	-	-	3	13	7
7	BRP-BRM	R	-	7	R	10	-	5	5	6	12	5
8	Lotus-BRM	6	5	7	8	10	4	8	6	5	12	3

SYMBOLS AND GRAND PRIX KEY

Round 1 Monaco GP
Round 2 Dutch GP
Round 3 Belgian GP
Round 4 French GP
Round 5 British GP
Round 6 German GP
Round 7 Austrian GP
Round 8 Italian GP
Round 9 United States GP
Round 10 Mexican GP

SCORING

1st 9 points
2nd 6 points
3rd 4 points
4th 3 points
5th 2 points
6th 1 point

DNPQ DID NOT PRE-QUALIFY **DNQ** DID NOT QUALIFY **DQ** DISQUALIFIED **EX** EXCLUDED
F FASTEST LAP **NC** NOT CLASSIFIED **NS** NON-STARTER **P** POLE POSITION **R** RETIRED

1965

SEASON SUMMARY

If Jim Clark had felt frustrated by losing the 1964 title battle due to mechanical failure, he bounced back in style in 1965. The Scot stormed to the final title of F1's 1.5-litre age at a canter by winning six of the nine grands prix he contested in his Lotus. BRM proved to be the best of the rest and Graham Hill won twice to end the year as runner-up, while his impressive new team-mate Jackie Stewart ranked an impressive third overall. Then, in the final race of the year, Honda showed its remarkable progress as its driver Richie Ginther was first to the chequered flag in Mexico.

SOUTH AFRICAN GRAND PRIX

EAST LONDON • ROUND 1 • DATE: 1ST JANUARY 1965
Laps: 85 • Distance: 207.24miles/333.174km • Weather: Warm but dull

Pos	Driver	Team	Chassis-Engine	Result	Qual
1	Jim Clark	Lotus	Lotus-Climax 33	2h06m46.000s	1
2	John Surtees	Ferrari	Ferrari 158	2h07m15.000s	2
3	Graham Hill	BRM	BRM P261	2h07m17.800s	5
4	Mike Spence	Lotus	Lotus-Climax 33	2h07m40.400s	4
5	Bruce McLaren	Cooper	Cooper-Climax T73	84 laps	8
6	Jackie Stewart	BRM	BRM P261	83 laps	11
7	Jo Siffert	Rob Walker Racing Team	Brabham-BRM BT11	83 laps	14
8	Jack Brabham	Brabham	Brabham-Climax BT11	81 laps	3
9	Paul Hawkins	John Willment Automobiles	Brabham-Ford BT10	81 laps	16
10	Peter de Klerk	Otello Nucci	Alfa Special-Alfa Romeo	79 laps	17
11	Tony Maggs	Reg Parnell Racing	Lotus-BRM 25	77 laps	13
12	Frank Gardner	John Willment Automobiles	Brabham-BRM BT11	75 laps	15
13	Sam Tingle	Sam Tingle	LDS-Alfa Romeo 1	73 laps	20
14	David Prophet	David Prophet	Brabham-Ford BT10	71 laps	19
15	Lorenzo Bandini	Ferrari	Ferrari 1512	66 laps/ignition	6
NC	Bob Anderson	DW Racing Enterprises	Brabham-Climax BT11	50 laps/not classified	12
R	Jo Bonnier	Rob Walker Racing Team	Brabham-Climax BT7	42 laps/clutch	7
R	Jochen Rindt	Cooper	Cooper-Climax T73	39 laps/electrical	10
R	John Love	John Love	Cooper-Climax T55	20 laps/halfshaft	18
R	Dan Gurney	Brabham	Brabham-Climax BT11	11 laps/ignition	9
DNQ	Trevor Blokdyk	Trevor Blokdyk	Cooper-Ford T59	-	21
DNQ	Neville Lederle	Scuderia Scribante	Lotus-Climax 21	-	22
DNQ	Doug Serrurier	Otelle Nucci	LDS-Climax 2	-	23
DNQ	Brausch Niemann	Ted Lanfear	Lotus-Ford 22	-	24
DNQ	Ernest Pieterse	Lawson Organisation	Lotus-Climax 21	-	25
DNPQ	Clive Puzey	Clive Puzey	Lotus-Climax 18/21	-	-
DNPQ	Jackie Pretorius	Jackie Pretorius	LDS-Alfa Romeo 1	-	-
DNPQ	Dave Charlton	Ecurie Tomahawk	Lotus-Ford 20	-	-

Pole: Clark, 1m27.200s, 100.551mph/161.822kph. Fastest lap: Clark, 1m27.600s, 100.092mph/161.083kph on Lap 80. Race leaders: Clark 1-85

ONE TO WATCH

Jackie Stewart was a talent to watch when he rose from dominating British F3 to drive for BRM. He opened the season by winning the non-championship International Trophy at Silverstone, then went increasingly well in the World Championship to triumph at the Italian GP, where he led home team-mate Graham Hill.

MONACO GRAND PRIX

MONTE CARLO • ROUND 2 • DATE: 30TH MAY 1965
Laps: 100 • Distance: 195.113miles/314.5km • Weather: Warm but dull

Pos	Driver	Team	Chassis-Engine	Result	Qual
1	Graham Hill	BRM	BRM P261	2h37m39.600s	1
2	Lorenzo Bandini	Ferrari	Ferrari 1512	2h38m43.600s	4
3	Jackie Stewart	BRM	BRM P261	2h39m21.500s	3
4	John Surtees	Ferrari	Ferrari 158	99 laps/out of fuel	5
5	Bruce McLaren	Cooper	Cooper-Climax T77	98 laps	7
6	Jo Siffert	Rob Walker Racing Team	Brabham-BRM BT11	98 laps	10
7	Jo Bonnier	Rob Walker Racing Team	Brabham-Climax BT7	97 laps	13
8	Denny Hulme	Brabham	Brabham-Climax BT7	92 laps	8
9	Bob Anderson	DW Racing Enterprises	Brabham-Climax BT11	85 laps	9
10	Paul Hawkins	DW Racing Enterprises	Lotus-Climax 33	79 laps/accident	14
R	Jack Brabham	Brabham	Brabham-Climax BT11	43 laps/engine	2
R	Richard Attwood	Reg Parnell Racing	Lotus-BRM 25	43 laps/wheel	6
R	Ronnie Bucknum	Honda	Honda RA272	33 laps/gearbox	15
R	Frank Gardner	John Willment Automobiles	Brabham-BRM BT11	29 laps/engine	11
R	Mike Hailwood	Reg Parnell Racing	Lotus-BRM 25	11 laps/gearbox	12
R	Richie Ginther	Honda	Honda RA272	1 lap/halfshaft	17
DNQ	Jochen Rindt	Cooper	Cooper-Climax T77	-	16

Pole: Hill, 1m32.500s, 76.055mph/122.400kph. Fastest lap: Hill, 1m31.700s, 76.719mph/123.467kph on Lap 82. Race leaders: G Hill 1-24 & 65-100; Stewart 25-29; Bandini 30-33 & 43-64; Brabham 34-42

BELGIAN GRAND PRIX

SPA-FRANCORCHAMPS • ROUND 3 • DATE: 13TH JUNE 1965
Laps: 32 • Distance: 280.239miles/451.2km • Weather: Warm with heavy rain

Pos	Driver	Team	Chassis-Engine	Result	Qual
1	Jim Clark	Lotus	Lotus-Climax 33	2h23m34.800s	2
2	Jackie Stewart	BRM	BRM P261	2h24m19.600s	3
3	Bruce McLaren	Cooper	Cooper-Climax T77	31 laps	9
4	Jack Brabham	Brabham	Brabham-Climax BT11	31 laps	10
5	Graham Hill	BRM	BRM P261	31 laps	1
6	Richie Ginther	Honda	Honda RA272	31 laps	4
7	Mike Spence	Lotus	Lotus-Climax 33	31 laps	12
8	Jo Siffert	Rob Walker Racing Team	Brabham-BRM BT11	31 laps	8
9	Lorenzo Bandini	Ferrari	Ferrari 1512	30 laps	15
10	Dan Gurney	Brabham	Brabham-Climax BT11	30 laps	5
11	Jochen Rindt	Cooper	Cooper-Climax T77	29 laps	14
12	Lucien Bianchi	Scuderia Centro Sud	BRM P57	29 laps	17

Pos	Driver	Team	Chassis-Engine	Result	Qual
13	Innes Ireland	Reg Parnell Racing	Lotus-BRM 25	27 laps	16
14	Richard Attwood	Reg Parnell Racing	Lotus-BRM 25	26 laps/accident	13
R	Masten Gregory	Scuderia Centro Sud	BRM P57	12 laps/fuel pump	19
R	Jo Bonnier	Rob Walker Racing Team	Brabham-Climax BT7	9 laps/ignition	7
R	Ronnie Bucknum	Honda	Honda RA272	9 laps/gearbox	11
R	John Surtees	Ferrari	Ferrari 158	5 laps/engine	6
R	Frank Gardner	John Willment Automobiles	Brabham-BRM BT11	3 laps/ignition	18
NS	Bob Anderson	DW Racing Enterprises	Brabham-Climax BT11	withdrew	19
NS	Willy Mairesse	Scuderia Centro Sud	BRM P57	-	21

Pole: Hill, 3m45.400s, 139.932mph/225.199kph. Fastest lap: Clark, 4m12.900s, 124.716mph/200.711kph on Lap 23. Race leaders: Clark 1-32

STREET SUPREMACY

Monaco remained the race from which drivers were most likely to retire. Yet Graham Hill had the Midas touch here, and even a scare when he had to take the escape road by the harbourfront chicane didn't prevent him from clinching a remarkable Monaco hat-trick, something that seemed unlikely when he had to restart his stalled car.

A GREAT YEAR FOR BRITAIN

With British teams winning nine of the year's 10 races, there was even better news for British drivers as they filled the top three places in the drivers' championship, with Lotus star Jim Clark beating BRM's Graham Hill and Jackie Stewart. Indeed, at two grands prix, the South African and the British, there were five British drivers in the top six.

FRENCH GRAND PRIX

CLERMONT-FERRAND • ROUND 4 • DATE: 27TH JUNE 1965
Laps: 40 • Distance: 200.82miles/322.2km • Weather: Warm & bright

Pos	Driver	Team	Chassis-Engine	Result	Qual
1	Jim Clark	Lotus	Lotus-Climax 25	2h14m38.400s	1
2	Jackie Stewart	BRM	BRM P261	2h15m04.700s	2
3	John Surtees	Ferrari	Ferrari 158	2h17m11.900s	4
4	Denny Hulme	Brabham	Brabham-Climax BT11	2h17m31.500s	6
5	Graham Hill	BRM	BRM P261	39 laps	13
6	Jo Siffert	Rob Walker Racing Team	Brabham-BRM BT11	39 laps	14
7	Mike Spence	Lotus	Lotus-Climax 33	39 laps	10
8	Lorenzo Bandini	Ferrari	Ferrari 1512	36 laps/accident	3
9	Bob Anderson	DW Racing Enterprises	Brabham-Climax BT11	34 laps/fuel system	15
R	Bruce McLaren	Cooper	Cooper-Climax T77	23 laps/suspension	9
R	Jo Bonnier	Rob Walker Racing Team	Brabham-Climax BT7	21 laps/alternator	11
R	Chris Amon	Reg Parnell Racing	Lotus-BRM 25	20 laps/fuel system	8
R	Innes Ireland	Reg Parnell Racing	Lotus-BRM 25	18 laps/gearbox	17

Pos	Driver	Team	Chassis-Engine	Result	Qual
R	Dan Gurney	Brabham	Brabham-Climax BT11	16 laps/engine	5
R	Richie Ginther	Honda	Honda RA272	9 laps/ignition	7
R	Ronnie Bucknum	Honda	Honda RA272	4 laps/ignition	16
R	Jochen Rindt	Cooper	Cooper-Climax T77	3 laps/accident	12

Pole: Clark, 3m18.300s, 90.864mph/146.232kph. Fastest lap: Clark, 3m18.900s, 90.590mph/145.791kph on Lap 34. Race leaders: Clark 1-40

INDIANAPOLIS GLORY AT LAST

After a few false starts, an F1 driver won the Indianapolis 500. Fittingly, it was the peerless Clark. Lotus was extremely keen to land the jewel in American racing's crown to help its road car sales. Clark, who was second in 1963 and started on pole in 1964 but retired, won by two laps. Showing the change in era, 27 of the 33 cars were now rear-engined.

BRITISH GRAND PRIX

SILVERSTONE • ROUND 5 • DATE: 10TH JULY 1965
Laps: 80 • Distance: 233.687miles/376.84km • Weather: Warm but dull

Pos	Driver	Team	Chassis-Engine	Result	Qual
1	Jim Clark	Lotus	Lotus-Climax 33	2h05m25.400s	1
2	Graham Hill	BRM	BRM P261	2h05m28.600s	2
3	John Surtees	Ferrari	Ferrari 1512	2h05m53.000s	5
4	Mike Spence	Lotus	Lotus-Climax 33	2h06m05.000s	6
5	Jackie Stewart	BRM	BRM P261	2h06m40.000s	4
6	Dan Gurney	Brabham	Brabham-Climax BT11	79 laps	7
7	Jo Bonnier	Rob Walker Racing Team	Brabham-Climax BT7	79 laps	14
8	Frank Gardner	John Willment Automobiles	Brabham-BRM BT11	78 laps	13
9	Jo Siffert	Rob Walker Racing Team	Brabham-BRM BT11	78 laps	18
10	Bruce McLaren	Cooper	Cooper-Climax T77	77 laps	11
11	Ian Raby	Ian Raby Racing	Brabham-BRM BT3	73 laps	20
12	Masten Gregory	Scuderia Centro Sud	BRM P57	70 laps	19
13	Richard Attwood	Reg Parnell Racing	Lotus-BRM 25	63 laps	16
14	Jochen Rindt	Cooper	Cooper-Climax T77	62 laps/engine	12
R	Innes Ireland	Reg Parnell Racing	Lotus-BRM 25	41 laps/engine	15
R	John Rhodes	Bob Gerard Racing	Cooper-Climax T60	38 laps/ignition	21
R	Bob Anderson	DW Racing Enterprises	Brabham-Climax BT11	33 laps/gearbox	17
R	Denny Hulme	Brabham	Brabham-Climax BT7	29 laps/alternator	10
R	Richie Ginther	Honda	Honda RA272	26 laps/mechanical	3
R	Lorenzo Bandini	Ferrari	Ferrari 158	2 laps/engine	9
NS	Jack Brabham	Brabham	Brabham-Climax BT11	Gurney drove car	8
NS	Chris Amon	Ian Raby Racing	Brabham-BRM BT3	Raby drove car	-
DNQ	Alan Rollinson	Bob Gerard Racing	Cooper-Ford T71/73	-	22
DNQ	Brian Gubby	Brian Gubby	Lotus-Climax 24	-	23

Pole: Clark, 1m30.800s, 116.047mph/186.759kph. Fastest lap: Hill, 1m32.200s, 114.285mph/183.924kph on Lap 80. Race leaders: Clark 1-80

DUTCH GRAND PRIX

ZANDVOORT • ROUND 6 • DATE: 18TH JULY 1965
Laps: 80 • Distance: 208.186miles/335.44km • Weather: Warm but dull

Pos	Driver	Team	Chassis-Engine	Result	Qual
1	Jim Clark	Lotus	Lotus-Climax 33	2h03m59.100s	2
2	Jackie Stewart	BRM	BRM P261	2h04m07.100s	6
3	Dan Gurney	Brabham	Brabham-Climax BT11	2h04m12.100s	5
4	Graham Hill	BRM	BRM P261	2h04m44.200s	1
5	Denny Hulme	Brabham	Brabham-Climax BT11	79 laps	7
6	Richie Ginther	Honda	Honda RA272	79 laps	3
7	John Surtees	Ferrari	Ferrari 1512	79 laps	4
8	Mike Spence	Lotus	Lotus-Climax 25	79 laps	8
9	Lorenzo Bandini	Ferrari	Ferrari 158	79 laps	12
10	Innes Ireland	Reg Parnell Racing	Lotus-BRM 25	78 laps	13
11	Frank Gardner	John Willment Automobiles	Brabham-BRM BT11	77 laps	11
12	Richard Attwood	Reg Parnell Racing	Lotus-BRM 25	77 laps	17
13	Jo Siffert	Rob Walker Racing Team	Brabham-BRM BT11	55 laps	10
R	Jochen Rindt	Cooper	Cooper-Climax T77	48 laps/fuel pressure	14
R	Bruce McLaren	Cooper	Cooper-Climax T77	36 laps/differential	9
R	Jo Bonnier	Rob Walker Racing Team	Brabham-Climax BT7	16 laps/oil leak	15
R	Bob Anderson	DW Racing Enterprises	Brabham-Climax BT11	11 laps/engine	16

Pole: Hill, 1m30.700s, 103.412mph/166.425kph. Fastest lap: Clark, 1m30.600s, 103.526mph/166.609kph on Lap 5. Race leaders: Ginther 1-2; G Hill 3-5; Clark 6-80

AN EXCEEDINGLY BUSY LAP CHART

Monza was famous for producing fierce, multi-car slipstreaming battles and the 1965 Italian GP was a classic of this genre. In all, the lead changed hands a record 42 times between Clark, who led the first two laps of the race, and BRM's Stewart, who led the last two. The two other drivers to lead, Hill and Surtees, were also British.

GERMAN GRAND PRIX

NURBURGRING • ROUND 7 • DATE: 1ST AUGUST 1965
Laps: 15 • Distance: 212.518miles/342.15km • Weather: Warm but dull

Pos	Driver	Team	Chassis-Engine	Result	Qual
1	Jim Clark	Lotus	Lotus-Climax 33	2h07m52.400s	1
2	Graham Hill	BRM	BRM P261	2h08m08.300s	3
3	Dan Gurney	Brabham	Brabham-Climax BT11	2h08m13.800s	5
4	Jochen Rindt	Cooper	Cooper-Climax T77	2h11m22.000s	8
5	Jack Brabham	Brabham	Brabham-Climax BT11	2h12m33.600s	14
6	Lorenzo Bandini	Ferrari	Ferrari 158	2h13m01.000s	7
7	Jo Bonnier	Rob Walker Racing Team	Brabham-Climax BT7	2h13m50.900s	9
8	Masten Gregory	Scuderia Centro Sud	BRM P57	14 laps	18
R	John Surtees	Ferrari	Ferrari 1512	11 laps/gearbox	4
R	Jo Siffert	Rob Walker Racing Team	Brabham-BRM BT11	9 laps/engine	11
R	Mike Spence	Lotus	Lotus-Climax 33	8 laps/transmission	6
R	Gerhard Mitter	Lotus	Lotus-Climax 25	8 laps/water leak	12

Pos	Driver	Team	Chassis-Engine	Result	Qual
R	Bruce McLaren	Cooper	Cooper-Climax T77	7 laps/gearbox	10
R	Richard Attwood	Reg Parnell Racing	Lotus-BRM 25	7 laps/water leak	16
R	Denny Hulme	Brabham	Brabham-Climax BT7	5 laps/oil leak	13
R	Chris Amon	Reg Parnell Racing	Lotus-BRM 25	3 laps/electrical	15
R	Paul Hawkins	DW Racing Enterprises	Lotus-Climax 33	3 laps/oil leak	19
R	Jackie Stewart	BRM	BRM P261	2 laps/suspension	2
R	Frank Gardner	John Willment Automobiles	Brabham-BRM BT11	0 laps/gearbox	17
NS	Bob Anderson	DW Racing Enterprises	Brabham-Climax BT11	accident	15
DNQ	Roberto Bussinello	Scuderia Centro Sud	BRM P57	-	21
DNQ	Ian Raby	Ian Raby Racing	Brabham-BRM BT3	-	22

Pole: Clark, 8m22.700s, 101.500mph/163.349kph. Fastest lap: Clark, 8m24.100s, 101.219mph/162.896kph on Lap 10. Race leaders: Clark 1-15

ROCKY MOUNTAIN HIGH

There was a new challenge when the French GP moved venue for 1965, as the race's new home was the twisting and undulating Charade circuit at Clermont-Ferrand in the rocky Massif Central. Built in 1958, it would go on to host three more French GPs until 1972, after which it was no longer considered safe for F1.

A DRIVER IN TROUBLE

Innes Ireland was hugely entertaining company, but the hard-living Scot's lifestyle sometimes got him into trouble. By the end of the season, with his focus firmly on sports car racing as his F1 ride was uncompetitive, he turned up late for one of the practice sessions for the Mexican GP. His team, Reg Parnell Racing, fired him on the spot.

ITALIAN GRAND PRIX

MONZA • ROUND 8 • DATE: 12TH SEPTEMBER 1965
Laps: 76 • Distance: 271.539miles/437.0km • Weather: Warm & bright

Pos	Driver	Team	Chassis-Engine	Result	Qual
1	Jackie Stewart	BRM	BRM P261	2h04m52.800s	3
2	Graham Hill	BRM	BRM P261	2h04m56.100s	4
3	Dan Gurney	Brabham	Brabham-Climax BT11	2h05m09.300s	9
4	Lorenzo Bandini	Ferrari	Ferrari 1512	2h06m08.700s	5
5	Bruce McLaren	Cooper	Cooper-Climax T77	75 laps	11
6	Richard Attwood	Reg Parnell Racing	Lotus-BRM 25	75 laps	13
7	Jo Bonnier	Rob Walker Racing Team	Brabham-Climax BT7	74 laps	14
8	Jochen Rindt	Cooper	Cooper-Climax T73	74 laps	7
9	Innes Ireland	Reg Parnell Racing	Lotus-BRM 33	74 laps	18
10	Jim Clark	Lotus	Lotus-Climax 33	63 laps/fuel pump	1
11	Mike Spence	Lotus	Lotus-Climax 33	62 laps/alternator	8
12	Nino Vaccarella	Ferrari	Ferrari 158	58 laps/engine	15

Pos	Driver	Team	Chassis-Engine	Result	Qual
13	Roberto Bussinello	Scuderia Centro Sud	BRM P57	58 laps/fuel pressure	21
14	Richie Ginther	Honda	Honda RA272	56 laps/ignition	17
R	Denny Hulme	Brabham	Brabham-Climax BT11	46 laps/suspension	12
R	Frank Gardner	John Willment Automobiles	Brabham-BRM BT11	45 laps/engine	16
R	Jo Siffert	Rob Walker Racing Team	Brabham-BRM BT11	43 laps/gearbox	10
R	Giacomo'Geki' Russo	Lotus	Lotus-Climax 25	37 laps/gearbox	20
R	John Surtees	Ferrari	Ferrari 1512	34 laps/clutch	2
R	Ronnie Bucknum	Honda	Honda RA272	27 laps/ignition	6
R	Masten Gregory	Scuderia Centro Sud	BRM P57	22 laps/gearbox	23
R	Giancarlo Baghetti	Brabham	Brabham-Climax BT7	12 laps/engine	19
R	Giorgio Bassi	Scuderia Centro Sud	BRM P57	8 laps/engine	22

Pole: Clark, 1m35.900s, 134.122mph/215.849kph. Fastest lap: Clark, 1m36.400s, 133.427mph/214.730kph on Lap 46. Race leaders: Clark 1-2, 4, 6-7, 18, 21-24, 27, 33-35, 38, 44, 46, 51, 53-54 & 57; G Hill 3, 25-26, 28, 40, 43, 45, 50, 55-56, 64, 70-71 & 73-74; Stewart 5, 8-10, 12, 14, 17, 19-20, 29-32, 36-37, 39, 41-42, 47-49, 52, 58-63, 65-69, 72 & 75-76; Surtees 11, 13 & 15-16

UNITED STATES GRAND PRIX

WATKINS GLEN • ROUND 9 • DATE: 3RD OCTOBER 1965
Laps: 110 • Distance: 253.0miles/407.165km • Weather: Warm with wind & showers

Pos	Driver	Team	Chassis-Engine	Result	Qual
1	Graham Hill	BRM	BRM P261	2h20m36.100s	1
2	Dan Gurney	Brabham	Brabham-Climax BT11	2h20m48.600s	8
3	Jack Brabham	Brabham	Brabham-Climax BT11	2h21m33.600s	7
4	Lorenzo Bandini	Ferrari	Ferrari 1512	109 laps	5
5	Pedro Rodriguez	Ferrari	Ferrari 1512	109 laps	15
6	Jochen Rindt	Cooper	Cooper-Climax T77	108 laps	13
7	Richie Ginther	Honda	Honda RA272	108 laps	3
8	Jo Bonnier	Rob Walker Racing Team	Brabham-Climax BT7	107 laps	10
9	Bob Bondurant	Ferrari	Ferrari 158	106 laps	14
10	Richard Attwood	Reg Parnell Racing	Lotus-BRM 25	101 laps	16
11	Jo Siffert	Rob Walker Racing Team	Brabham-BRM BT11	99 laps	11
12	Moises Solana	Lotus	Lotus-Climax 25	95 laps	17
13	Ronnie Bucknum	Honda	Honda RA272	92 laps	12
R	Jackie Stewart	BRM	BRM P261	12 laps/suspension	6
R	Bruce McLaren	Cooper	Cooper-Climax T77	11 laps/fuel pressure	2
R	Jim Clark	Lotus	Lotus-Climax 33	11 laps/engine	9
R	Mike Spence	Lotus	Lotus-Climax 33	9 laps/engine	4
R	Innes Ireland	Reg Parnell Racing	Lotus-BRM 33	9 laps/physical	18

Pole: Hill, 1m11.250s, 116.210mph/187.023kph. Fastest lap: Hill, 1m11.900s, 115.140mph/185.300kph on Lap 105. Race leaders: G Hill 1, 5-10 & 12-110; Clark 3-4, 11

HONDA'S BREAKTHROUGH

Honda was determined to advance and so based its team in Europe, in the Netherlands. Its V12 was the most powerful in F1 and improved reliability resulted in its first win in the final round in Mexico. American driver Richie Ginther, who had previously finished second eight times, was the driver to achieve this, beating fellow American Dan Gurney into second place.

AN AMERICAN CHALLENGE

The tyre war in F1 heated up with the arrival of the American Goodyear outfit. The company took the battle to the previously dominant Dunlop and earned considerable plaudits by rounding out its maiden season in F1 with Ginther's Honda winning in Mexico. Goodyear would go on to become the dominant F1 tyre supplier through the 1970s.

MEXICAN GRAND PRIX

MEXICO CITY • ROUND 10 • DATE: 24TH OCTOBER 1965
Laps: 65 • Distance: 201.945miles/325.0km • Weather: Warm & bright

Pos	Driver	Team	Chassis-Engine	Result	Qual
1	Richie Ginther	Honda	Honda RA272	2h08m32.100s	3
2	Dan Gurney	Brabham	Brabham-Climax BT11	2h08m34.990s	2
3	Mike Spence	Lotus	Lotus-Climax 33	2h09m32.250s	6
4	Jo Siffert	Rob Walker Racing Team	Brabham-BRM BT11	2h10m26.520s	11
5	Ronnie Bucknum	Honda	Honda RA272	64 laps	10
6	Richard Attwood	Reg Parnell Racing	Lotus-BRM 25	64 laps	17
7	Pedro Rodriguez	Ferrari	Ferrari 1512	62 laps	14
8	Lorenzo Bandini	Ferrari	Ferrari 1512	62 laps	7
R	Graham Hill	BRM	BRM P261	56 laps/engine	5
R	Moises Solana	Lotus	Lotus-Climax 25	55 laps/ignition	9
R	Jo Bonnier	Rob Walker Racing Team	Brabham-Climax BT7	43 laps/suspension	12
R	Jochen Rindt	Cooper	Cooper-Climax T77	39 laps/ignition	16
R	Jack Brabham	Brabham	Brabham-Climax BT11	38 laps/oil leak	14
R	Jackie Stewart	BRM	BRM P261	35 laps/clutch	8
R	Bob Bondurant	Reg Parnell Racing	Lotus-BRM 33	29 laps/suspension	18
R	Bruce McLaren	Cooper	Cooper-Climax T77	25 laps/gearbox	15
R	Jim Clark	Lotus	Lotus-Climax 33	8 laps/engine	1
NS	Innes Ireland	Reg Parnell Racing	Lotus-BRM 33	driver fired	19
NS	Ludovico Scarfiotti	Ferrari	Ferrari 1512	Rodriguez drove car	13

Pole: Clark, 1m56.170s, 96.278mph/154.945kph. Fastest lap: Gurney, 1m55.840s, 96.554mph/155.390kph on Lap 57. Race leaders: Ginther 1-65

NEW DRIVERS

While Stewart stood out among the season's 12 F1 rookies, honourable mentions should go to Richard Attwood and Denny Hulme. The former impressed with a pair of sixth place finishes in a Reg Parnell Racing Lotus; the latter, a Kiwi, came fourth on his second outing in the French GP in a works Brabham, then was fifth in Holland.

WORLD DRIVERS' CHAMPIONSHIP FINAL RESULTS

Pos	Driver	Nat	Car-Engine	R1	R2	R3	R4	R5	R6	R7	R8	R9	R10	Total
1	Jim Clark	GBR	Lotus-Climax 33	1PF	-	1F	-	1P	1F	1PF	10PF	R	RP	54
			Lotus-Climax 25	-	-	-	1PF	-	-	-	-	-	-	
2	Graham Hill	GBR	BRM P261	3	1PF	5P	5	2F	4P	2	2	1PF	R	40
3	Jackie Stewart	GBR	BRM P261	6	3	2	2	5	2	R	1	R	R	33
4	Dan Gurney	USA	Brabham-Climax BT11	R	-	10	R	6	3	3	3	2	2F	25
5	John Surtees	GBR	Ferrari 158	2	4	R	3	-	-	-	-	-	-	17
			Ferrari 1512	-	-	-	-	3	7	R	R	-	-	
6	Lorenzo Bandini	ITA	Ferrari 1512	15	2	9	8	-	-	-	4	4	8	13
			Ferrari 158	-	-	-	-	R	9	6	-	-	-	
7	Richie Ginther	USA	Honda RA272	-	R	6	R	R	6	-	14	7	1	11
8	Mike Spence	GBR	Lotus-Climax 33	4	-	7	7	4	-	R	11	R	3	10
			Lotus-Climax 25	-	-	-	-	-	8	-	-	-	-	
8	Bruce McLaren	NZL	Cooper-Climax T73	5	-	-	-	-	-	-	-	-	-	10
			Cooper-Climax T77	-	5	3	R	10	R	R	5	R	R	
10	Jack Brabham	AUS	Brabham-Climax BT11	8	R	4	-	NS	-	5	-	3	R	9
11	Denny Hulme	NZL	Brabham-Climax BT7	-	8	-	-	R	-	R	-	-	-	5
			Brabham-Climax BT11	-	-	-	4	-	5	-	R	-	-	
11	Jo Siffert	CHE	Brabham-BRM BT11	7	6	8	6	9	13	R	R	11	4	5
13	Jochen Rindt	AUT	Cooper-Climax T73	R	-	-	-	-	-	-	8	-	-	4
			Cooper-Climax T77	-	DNQ	11	R	14	R	4	-	6	R	
14	Pedro Rodriguez	MEX	Ferrari 1512	-	-	-	-	-	-	-	-	5	7	2
14	Ronnie Bucknum	USA	Honda RA272	-	R	R	R	-	-	-	R	13	5	2
14	Richard Attwood	GBR	Lotus-BRM 25	-	R	14	-	13	12	R	6	10	6	2

WORLD CONSTRUCTORS' CHAMPIONSHIP FINAL RESULTS

Pos	Team-Engine	R1	R2	R3	R4	R5	R6	R7	R8	R9	R10	Total
1	Lotus-Climax	1	10	1	1	1	1	1	10	12	3	54
2	BRM	3	1	2	2	2	2	2	1	1	-	45
3	Brabham-Climax	8	7	4	4	6	3	3	3	2	2	27
4	Ferrari	2	2	9	3	3	7	6	4	4	7	26
5	Cooper-Climax	5	5	3	-	10	-	4	5	6	-	14
6	Honda	-	-	6	-	-	6	-	14	7	1	11
7	Brabham-BRM	7	6	8	6	8	11	-	-	11	4	5
8	Lotus-BRM	11	-	13	-	13	10	-	6	10	6	2

SYMBOLS AND GRAND PRIX KEY

Round 1 South African GP
Round 2 Monaco GP
Round 3 Belgian GP
Round 4 French GP
Round 5 British GP
Round 6 Dutch GP
Round 7 German GP
Round 8 Italian GP
Round 9 United States GP
Round 10 Mexican GP

SCORING

1st 9 points
2nd 6 points
3rd 4 points
4th 3 points
5th 2 points
6th 1 point

DNPQ DID NOT PRE-QUALIFY **DNQ** DID NOT QUALIFY **DQ** DISQUALIFIED **EX** EXCLUDED
F FASTEST LAP **NC** NOT CLASSIFIED **NS** NON-STARTER **P** POLE POSITION **R** RETIRED

1966

SEASON SUMMARY

It was all change for 1966, as the maximum size for engines was doubled to three litres and Jack Brabham's team was the one that reacted best to the return of power. It could easily have been Ferrari's year, as the team had new engines ready to go, but internal politics led to lead driver John Surtees leaving. This cleared the way for Brabham to win four races in a row and so land his third F1 drivers' title. Lotus struggled with a 2-litre Climax engine until it upgraded to a 3-litre BRM, but that came too late to save Jim Clark's year.

A DOUBLING OF CAPACITY

Although the upgrade to 3-litre engines and an increased minimum weight of 500kg (1,102lb) had been announced in 1963, few teams were ready, with the British teams holding out for a change only to 2 litres. Power rose from 210 to 350bhp. Brabham's Repco engine wasn't as powerful as Ferrari's V12, but it was torquier and more reliable.

MONACO GRAND PRIX

MONTE CARLO • ROUND 1 • DATE: 22ND MAY 1966
Laps: 100 • Distance: 195.113miles/314.5km • Weather: Warm & hazy

Pos	Driver	Team	Chassis-Engine	Result	Qual
1	Jackie Stewart	BRM	BRM P261	2h33m10.500s	3
2	Lorenzo Bandini	Ferrari	Ferrari 246	2h33m50.700s	5
3	Graham Hill	BRM	BRM P261	99 laps	4
4	Bob Bondurant	Team Chamaco Collect	BRM P261	95 laps	16
R	Richie Ginther	Cooper	Cooper-Maserati T81	80 laps/transmission	9
NC	Guy Ligier	Guy Ligier	Cooper-Maserati T81	75 laps/not classified	15
NC	Jo Bonnier	Ecurie Bonnier	Cooper-Maserati T81	73 laps/not classified	14
R	Jim Clark	Lotus	Lotus-Climax 33	60 laps/suspension	1
R	Jochen Rindt	Cooper	Cooper-Maserati T81	56 laps/engine	7
R	Jo Siffert	Rob Walker Racing Team	Brabham-BRM BT11	35 laps/clutch	13
R	Mike Spence	Reg Parnell Racing	Lotus-BRM 25	34 laps/suspension	12
R	Jack Brabham	Brabham	Brabham-Repco BT19	17 laps/gearbox	11
R	John Surtees	Ferrari	Ferrari 312	16 laps/transmission	2
R	Denny Hulme	Brabham	Brabham-Climax BT22	15 laps/transmission	6
R	Bruce McLaren	McLaren	McLaren-Ford M2B	9 laps/oil leak	10
R	Bob Anderson	DW Racing Enterprises	Brabham-Climax BT11	3 laps/engine	8
NS	Phil Hill	Phil Hill	Lotus-Climax 25	camera car only	-

Pole: Clark, 1m29.900s, 78.255mph/125.939kph. Fastest lap: Bandini, 1m29.800s, 78.342mph/126.080kph on Lap 90. Race leaders: Surtees 1-14; Stewart 15-100

A BELGIAN WATERSHED

Sudden rain wreaked havoc at Spa-Francorchamps when Jo Bonnier spun and four others took evasive action. Further on, Jackie Stewart's BRM hit a telegraph pole and a house, leaving him trapped upside down in his car, with the cockpit filling with fuel. Unsurprisingly, Stewart went on to lead the campaign to make F1 safer.

BELGIAN GRAND PRIX

SPA-FRANCORCHAMPS • ROUND 2 • DATE: 12TH JUNE 1966
Laps: 28 • Distance: 244.825miles/394.8km • Weather: Wet & dull

Pos	Driver	Team	Chassis-Engine	Result	Qual
1	John Surtees	Ferrari	Ferrari 312	2h09m11.300s	1
2	Jochen Rindt	Cooper	Cooper-Maserati T81	2h09m53.400s	2
3	Lorenzo Bandini	Ferrari	Ferrari 246	27 laps	5
4	Jack Brabham	Brabham	Brabham-Repco BT19	26 laps	4
5	Richie Ginther	Cooper	Cooper-Maserati T81	25 laps	8
NC	Guy Ligier	Guy Ligier	Cooper-Maserati T81	24 laps/not classified	12
NC	Dan Gurney	Anglo American Racers	Eagle-Climax T1G	23 laps/not classified	15
R	Phil Hill	Phil Hill	McLaren-Ford M3A	1 lap/camera car	17
R	Jackie Stewart	BRM	BRM P261	0 laps/accident	3
R	Jo Bonnier	Ecurie Bonnier	Cooper-Maserati T81	0 laps/accident	6
R	Mike Spence	Reg Parnell Racing	Lotus-BRM 25	0 laps/accident	7
R	Graham Hill	BRM	BRM P261	0 laps/accident	9
R	Jim Clark	Lotus	Lotus-Climax 33	0 laps/engine	10
R	Bob Bondurant	Team Chamaco Collect	BRM P261	0 laps/accident	11
R	Denny Hulme	Brabham	Brabham-Climax BT22	0 laps/accident	13
R	Jo Siffert	Rob Walker Racing Team	Cooper-Maserati T81	0 laps/accident	14
NS	Bruce McLaren	McLaren	McLaren-Serenissima M2B	bearings	16
NS	Vic Wilson	Team Chamaco Collect	BRM P261	Bondurant drove car	18
NS	Peter Arundell	Lotus	Lotus-BRM 43	engine	19

Pole: Surtees, 3m38.000s, 144.682mph/232.844kph. Fastest lap: Surtees, 4m18.700s, 121.920mph/196.211kph on Lap 18. Race leaders: Surtees 1, 3, 24-28; Bandini 2; Rindt 4-23

THE BIRTH OF A CHAMPION TEAM

Bruce McLaren added a second string to his bow in 1964 when he started building racing cars. Just two years later, he left the Cooper team and appeared on the grid at Monaco with the first McLaren F1 car, the M2B. Finding a competitive engine was a problem shared with other teams, but it was the first step in an incredible success story.

FRENCH GRAND PRIX

REIMS • ROUND 3 • DATE: 3RD JULY 1966
Laps: 48 • Distance: 247.613miles/398.496km • Weather: Very hot & bright

Pos	Driver	Team	Chassis-Engine	Result	Qual
1	Jack Brabham	Brabham	Brabham-Repco BT19	1h48m31.300s	4
2	Mike Parkes	Ferrari	Ferrari 312	1h48m40.800s	3
3	Denny Hulme	Brabham	Brabham-Repco BT20	46 laps	9
4	Jochen Rindt	Cooper	Cooper-Maserati T81	46 laps	5
5	Dan Gurney	Anglo American Racers	Eagle-Climax T1G	45 laps	14
6	John Taylor	David Bridges	Brabham-BRM BT11	45 laps	15
7	Bob Anderson	DW Racing Enterprises	Brabham-Climax BT11	44 laps	12
8	Chris Amon	Cooper	Cooper-Maserati T81	44 laps	7
NC	Guy Ligier	Guy Ligier	Cooper-Maserati T81	42 laps/not classified	11
R	Pedro Rodriguez	Lotus	Lotus-Climax 33	40 laps/oil leak	13
NC	Lorenzo Bandini	Ferrari	Ferrari 312	37 laps/not classified	1
NC	Jo Bonnier	Brabham	Brabham-Climax BT22	32 laps/not classified	17
R	Graham Hill	BRM	BRM P261	13 laps/engine	8
R	Jo Siffert	Rob Walker Racing Team	Cooper-Maserati T81	10 laps/fuel system	6
R	Mike Spence	Reg Parnell Racing	Lotus-BRM 33	8 laps/clutch	10
R	John Surtees	Cooper	Cooper-Maserati T81	5 laps/fuel system	2
R	Peter Arundell	Lotus	Lotus-BRM 43	3 laps/gearbox	16
NS	Jim Clark	Lotus	Lotus-Climax 33	driver injured	-

Pole: Bandini, 2m07.800s, 145.313mph/233.859kph. Fastest lap: Bandini, 2m11.300s, 141.439mph/227.625kph on Lap 30. Race leaders: Bandini 1-31; Brabham 32-48

BOLSTERING THE GRID

With grid sizes averaging 18 cars, it was decided that the approximately 14-mile (22.5km) Nurburgring had ample space for more entrants for the German GP, and so allowed 11 F2 cars to join. The best of these, Jean-Pierre Beltoise's Matra, finished eighth, after the best-qualified one, Jacky Ickx's own Matra, which started 17th, crashed out of the race on lap two.

REIMS' LAST ROLL OF THE DICE

The French GP turned another page in its history as it was the 11th and last to be held at Reims (plus four between 1932 and 1948). Victory went to Jack Brabham, after John Surtees (now at Cooper) and Lorenzo Bandini (Ferrari) had led early on. Brabham's victory marked the start of a four-race winning streak that landed him the title.

BRITISH GRAND PRIX

BRANDS HATCH • ROUND 4 • DATE: 16TH JULY 1966
Laps: 80 • Distance: 212.1miles/341.184km • Weather: Warm, drizzle then drying

Pos	Driver	Team	Chassis-Engine	Result	Qual
1	Jack Brabham	Brabham	Brabham-Repco BT19	2h13m13.400s	1
2	Denny Hulme	Brabham	Brabham-Repco BT20	2h13m23.000s	2
3	Graham Hill	BRM	BRM P261	79 laps	4
4	Jim Clark	Lotus	Lotus-Climax 33	79 laps	5
5	Jochen Rindt	Cooper	Cooper-Maserati T81	79 laps	7
6	Bruce McLaren	McLaren	McLaren-Serenissima M2B	78 laps	13
7	Chris Irwin	Brabham	Brabham-Climax BT22	78 laps	12
8	John Taylor	David Bridges	Brabham-BRM BT11	76 laps	16
9	Bob Bondurant	Team Chamaco Collect	BRM P261	76 laps	14
10	Guy Ligier	Guy Ligier	Cooper-Maserati T81	75 laps	17
11	Chris Lawrence	JA Pearce Engineering	Cooper-Ferrari T73	73 laps	19
NC	Bob Anderson	DW Racing Enterprises	Brabham-Climax BT11	70 laps/not classified	10
NC	Jo Siffert	Rob Walker Racing Team	Cooper-Maserati T81	70 laps/not classified	11
R	John Surtees	Cooper	Cooper-Maserati T81	67 laps/transmission	6
R	Jo Bonnier	Ecurie Bonnier	Brabham-Climax BT7	42 laps/clutch	15
R	Peter Arundell	Lotus	Lotus-BRM 33	32 laps/gearbox	20
R	Jackie Stewart	BRM	BRM P261	17 laps/engine	8
R	Mike Spence	Reg Parnell Racing	Lotus-BRM 25	15 laps/oil leak	9
R	Dan Gurney	Anglo American Racers	Eagle-Climax T1G	9 laps/engine	3
R	Trevor Taylor	Shannon	Shannon-Climax SH1	0 laps/engine	18

Pole: Brabham, 1m34.500s, 100.953mph/162.468kph. Fastest lap: Brabham, 1m37.000s, 98.351mph/158.281kph on Lap 60. Race leaders: Brabham 1-80

DUTCH GRAND PRIX

ZANDVOORT • ROUND 5 • DATE: 24TH JULY 1966
Laps: 90 • Distance: 234.279miles/377.37km • Weather: Warm & bright

Pos	Driver	Team	Chassis-Engine	Result	Qual
1	Jack Brabham	Brabham	Brabham-Repco BT20	2h20m32.500s	1
2	Graham Hill	BRM	BRM P261	89 laps	7
3	Jim Clark	Lotus	Lotus-Climax 33	88 laps	3
4	Jackie Stewart	BRM	BRM P261	88 laps	8
5	Mike Spence	Reg Parnell Racing	Lotus-BRM 25	87 laps	12
6	Lorenzo Bandini	Ferrari	Ferrari 312	87 laps	9
7	Jo Bonnier	Ecurie Bonnier	Cooper-Maserati T81	84 laps	13
8	John Taylor	David Bridges	Brabham-BRM BT11	84 laps	18
9	Guy Ligier	Guy Ligier	Cooper-Maserati T81	84 laps	17
R	Jo Siffert	Rob Walker Racing Team	Cooper-Maserati T81	79 laps/engine	11
R	Bob Anderson	DW Racing Enterprises	Brabham-Climax BT11	73 laps/suspension	15
R	John Surtees	Cooper	Cooper-Maserati T81	44 laps/electrical	10
R	Denny Hulme	Brabham	Brabham-Repco BT19	37 laps/ignition	2
R	Peter Arundell	Lotus	Lotus-BRM 33	28 laps/ignition	16
R	Dan Gurney	Anglo American Racers	Eagle-Climax T1G	26 laps/oil leak	4
R	Mike Parkes	Ferrari	Ferrari 312	10 laps/accident	5
R	Jochen Rindt	Cooper	Cooper-Maserati T81	2 laps/accident	6
NS	Bruce McLaren	McLaren	McLaren-Serenissima M2B	engine	14

Pole: Brabham, 1m28.100s, 106.463mph/171.337kph. Fastest lap: Hulme, 1m30.600s, 103.526mph/166.609kph on Lap 2. Race leaders: Brabham 1-26 & 76-90; Clark 27-75

GERMAN GRAND PRIX

NURBURGRING • ROUND 6 • DATE: 7TH AUGUST 1966
Laps: 15 • Distance: 212.518miles/342.15km • Weather: Warm & wet

Pos	Driver	Team	Chassis-Engine	Result	Qual
1	Jack Brabham	Brabham	Brabham-Repco BT19	2h27m03.000s	5
2	John Surtees	Cooper	Cooper-Maserati T81	2h27m47.400s	2
3	Jochen Rindt	Cooper	Cooper-Maserati T81	2h29m35.600s	9
4	Graham Hill	BRM	BRM P261	2h33m44.400s	10
5	Jackie Stewart	BRM	BRM P261	2h35m31.900s	3
6	Lorenzo Bandini	Ferrari	Ferrari 312	2h37m59.400s	6
7	Dan Gurney	Anglo American Racers	Eagle-Climax T1G	14 laps/electrical	8
8	Jean-Pierre Beltoise	Matra	Matra-Ford MS5/F2	14 laps	19
9	Hubert Hahne	Ken Tyrrell Racing	Matra-Ford MS5/F2	14 laps	28
10	Jo Schlesser	Matra	Matra-Ford MS5/F2	14 laps	20
11	Hans Herrmann	Roy Winkelmann Racing	Brabham-Ford BT18/F2	14 laps	23
12	Peter Arundell	Lotus	Lotus-BRM 33	14 laps	16
R	Mike Spence	Reg Parnell Racing	Lotus-BRM 25	12 laps/alternator	13
R	Jim Clark	Lotus	Lotus-Climax 33	11 laps/accident	1
R	Chris Lawrence	JA Pearce Engineering	Cooper-Ferrari T73	10 laps/suspension	18
R	Ludovico Scarfiotti	Ferrari	Ferrari 246	9 laps/electrical	4
R	Mike Parkes	Ferrari	Ferrari 312	9 laps/accident	7
R	Denny Hulme	Brabham	Brabham-Repco BT20	8 laps/ignition	15
R	Pedro Rodriguez	Ron Harris Team Lotus	Lotus-Ford 44/F2	7 laps/engine	21
R	Alan Rees	Roy Winkelmann Racing	Brabham-Ford BT18/F2	4 laps/engine	25
R	Jo Bonnier	Ecurie Bonnier	Cooper-Maserati T81	4 laps/clutch	12
R	Piers Courage	Ron Harris Team Lotus	Lotus-Ford 44/F2	3 laps/accident	24
R	Bob Bondurant	Team Chamaco Collect	BRM P261	3 laps/engine	11
R	Kurt Ahrens Jr	Caltex Racing	Brabham-Ford BT18/F2	3 laps/gearbox	22
R	Bob Anderson	DW Racing Enterprises	Brabham-Climax BT11	2 laps/transmission	14
R	Jacky Ickx	Tyrrell	Matra-Ford MS5/F2	1 lap/accident	17
R	John Taylor	David Bridges	Brabham-BRM BT11	0 laps/fatal accident	17
NS	Guy Ligier	Guy Ligier	Cooper-Maserati T81	driver injured	-
NS	Gerhard Mitter	Ron Harris Team Lotus	Lotus-Ford 44/F2	driver injured	11
NS	Silvio Moser	Silvio Moser	Brabham-Ford BT18/F2	engine	29

Pole: Clark, 4m56.500s, 172.089mph/276.951kph. Fastest lap: Surtees, 8m49.000s, 96.454mph/155.228kph on Lap 4. Race leaders: Brabham 1-15

CAPTURING THE ACTION

World champion for Ferrari in 1961, Phil Hill had a very different role in 1966 as he was tasked with driving a camera car during practice in Monaco and for the opening lap of the Belgian GP to capture footage that would be used in John Frankenheimer's movie *Grand Prix*. He used a Lotus 25 and McLaren M3A respectively, with cameras mounted to film the action sequences.

ITALIAN GRAND PRIX

MONZA • ROUND 7 • DATE: 4TH SEPTEMBER 1966
Laps: 68 • Distance: 242.956miles/391.0km • Weather: Warm & bright

Pos	Driver	Team	Chassis-Engine	Result	Qual
1	Ludovico Scarfiotti	Ferrari	Ferrari 312	1h47m14.800s	2
2	Mike Parkes	Ferrari	Ferrari 312	1h47m20.600s	1

Pos	Driver	Team	Chassis-Engine	Result	Qual
3	Denny Hulme	Brabham	Brabham-Repco BT20	1h47m20.900s	10
4	Jochen Rindt	Cooper	Cooper-Maserati T81	67 laps	8
5	Mike Spence	Reg Parnell Racing	Lotus-BRM 25	67 laps	14
6	Bob Anderson	DW Racing Enterprises	Brabham-Climax BT11	66 laps	15
7	Bob Bondurant	Team Chamaco Collect	BRM P261	65 laps	18
8	Peter Arundell	Lotus	Lotus-BRM 33	63 laps/engine	13
9	Giacomo 'Geki' Russo	Lotus	Lotus-Climax 33	63 laps	20
NC	Giancarlo Baghetti	Reg Parnell Racing	Ferrari 246	59 laps/not classified	16
R	Jim Clark	Lotus	Lotus-BRM 43	58 laps/gearbox	3
R	Jo Siffert	Rob Walker Racing Team	Cooper-Maserati T81	46 laps/engine	17
R	Lorenzo Bandini	Ferrari	Ferrari 312	33 laps/ignition	5
R	John Surtees	Cooper	Cooper-Maserati T81	31 laps/oil leak	4
R	Richie Ginther	Honda	Honda RA273	16 laps/accident	7
R	Jack Brabham	Brabham	Brabham-Repco BT19	7 laps/oil leak	6
R	Dan Gurney	Anglo American Racers	Eagle-Weslake T1G	7 laps/engine	19
R	Jackie Stewart	BRM	BRM P83	5 laps/oil leak	9
R	Jo Bonnier	Ecurie Bonnier	Cooper-Maserati T81	3 laps/throttle	12
R	Graham Hill	BRM	BRM P83	0 laps/engine	11
DNQ	Chris Amon	Chris Amon	Brabham-BRM BT11	-	21
DNQ	Phil Hill	Anglo American Racers	Eagle-Climax T1G	-	22

Pole: Parkes, 1m31.300s, 140.880mph/226.725kph. Fastest lap: Scarfiotti, 1m32.400s, 139.203mph/224.025kph on Lap 49. Race leaders: Bandini 1; Parkes, 2, 8-12 & 27; Surtees 3; Brabham 4-7; Scarfiotti 13-26 & 26-68

AN ITALIAN WINS AT HOME

Ferrari's heavy engine hampered its form, so it was a relief when Ludovico Scarfiotti, who was brought in mid-season, stepped up to win the team's home race at Monza. Team-mates Lorenzo Bandini and Mike Parkes led early on, but Scarfiotti was in front at the end, to become the first Italian winner of the Italian GP since Alberto Ascari in 1952.

NEW CONSTRUCTORS

McLaren would become the most important of the four new arrivals in 1966, while Matra would land the title in 1969. Shannon was destined to only ever be a makeweight. Dan Gurney's Eagle marque would be the most successful at its first attempt, and the team ranked seventh thanks to the American racer finishing fifth twice.

UNITED STATES GRAND PRIX

WATKINS GLEN • ROUND 8 • DATE: 2ND OCTOBER 1966
Laps: 108 • Distance: 248.400miles/399.762km • Weather: Cool & dull

Pos	Driver	Team	Chassis-Engine	Result	Qual
1	Jim Clark	Lotus	Lotus-BRM 43	2h09m40.110s	2
2	Jochen Rindt	Cooper	Cooper-Maserati T81	107 laps/out of fuel	9
3	John Surtees	Cooper	Cooper-Maserati T81	107 laps	4
4	Jo Siffert	Rob Walker Racing Team	Cooper-Maserati T81	105 laps	13

Pos	Driver	Team	Chassis-Engine	Result	Qual
5	Bruce McLaren	McLaren	McLaren-Ford M2B	105 laps	11
6	Peter Arundell	Lotus	Lotus-Climax 33	101 laps	19
R	Innes Ireland	Bernard White Racing	BRM P261	96 laps/alternator	17
NC	Richie Ginther	Honda	Honda RA273	81 laps/not classified	8
R	Mike Spence	Reg Parnell Racing	Lotus-BRM 25	74 laps/ignition	12
R	Ronnie Bucknum	Honda	Honda RA273	58 laps/engine	18
NC	Jo Bonnier	Ecurie Bonnier	Cooper-Maserati T81	57 laps/not classified	15
R	Jack Brabham	Brabham	Brabham-Repco BT20	55 laps/engine	1
R	Jackie Stewart	BRM	BRM P83	53 laps/engine	6
R	Graham Hill	BRM	BRM P83	52 laps/differential	5
R	Lorenzo Bandini	Ferrari	Ferrari 312	34 laps/engine	3
R	Denny Hulme	Brabham	Brabham-Repco BT20	18 laps/engine	7
R	Pedro Rodriguez	Lotus	Lotus-BRM 33	13 laps/starter motor	10
R	Dan Gurney	Anglo American Racers	Eagle-Weslake T1G	13 laps/clutch	14
DQ	Bob Bondurant	Anglo American Racers	Eagle-Climax T1G	5 laps/push start	16

Pole: Brabham, 1m08.420s, 121.017mph/194.758kph. Fastest lap: Surtees, 1m09.670s, 118.846mph/191.264kph on Lap 31. Race leaders: Bandini 1-9 & 20-34; Brabham 10-19 & 35-55; Clark 56-108

NEW DRIVERS

Of the 11 new drivers, Jacky Ickx and Jean-Pierre Beltoise impressed with their F2 outings in the German GP. Unusually, two drivers who dipped their toe in the F1 pond went on to set up F1 teams in the late 1970s. These were Guy Ligier, who created his eponymous team in 1976, and Alan Rees, who was one of the five founders of Arrows.

MEXICAN GRAND PRIX

MEXICO CITY • ROUND 9 • DATE: 23RD OCTOBER 1966
Laps: 65 • Distance: 201.945miles/325.0km • Weather: Warm & bright

Pos	Driver	Team	Chassis-Engine	Result	Qual
1	John Surtees	Cooper	Cooper-Maserati T81	2h06m35.340s	1
2	Jack Brabham	Brabham	Brabham-Repco BT20	2h06m43.220s	4
3	Denny Hulme	Brabham	Brabham-Repco BT20	64 laps	6
4	Richie Ginther	Honda	Honda RA273	64 laps	3
5	Dan Gurney	Anglo American Racers	Eagle-Climax T1G	64 laps	9
6	Jo Bonnier	Ecurie Bonnier	Cooper-Maserati T81	63 laps	13
7	Peter Arundell	Lotus	Lotus-BRM 43	61 laps	18
8	Ronnie Bucknum	Honda	Honda RA273	60 laps	14
R	Pedro Rodriguez	Lotus	Lotus-BRM 33	49 laps/differential	9
R	Bruce McLaren	McLaren	McLaren-Ford M2B	40 laps/engine	15
R	Jo Siffert	Rob Walker Racing Team	Cooper-Maserati T81	33 laps/suspension	12
R	Jochen Rindt	Cooper	Cooper-Maserati T81	32 laps/suspension	6
R	Innes Ireland	Bernard White Racing	BRM P261	28 laps/transmission	17
R	Jackie Stewart	BRM	BRM P83	26 laps/oil leak	11
R	Bob Bondurant	Anglo American Racers	Eagle-Weslake T1G	24 laps/fuel system	19
R	Graham Hill	BRM	BRM P83	18 laps/engine	7
R	Jim Clark	Lotus	Lotus-BRM 43	9 laps/gearbox	2
R	Moises Solana	Cooper	Cooper-Maserati T81	9 laps/overheating	15
NS	Mike Spence	Reg Parnell Racing	Lotus-BRM 25	accident	12

Pole: Surtees, 1m53.180s, 98.822mph/159.038kph. Fastest lap: Ginther, 1m53.750s, 98.326mph/158.241kph on Lap 58. Race leaders: Ginther 1; Brabham 2-5; Surtees 6-65

IN MEMORIAM
John Taylor had impressed in the first three grands prix, but collided with Jacky Ickx in the German GP and his David Bridges Brabham burst into flames, leaving him terribly burned. The other F1 driver to die was American sports car ace Walt Hansgen, whose best result was fifth in the 1964 United States GP, who fatally crashed in a test at Le Mans.

WORLD DRIVERS' CHAMPIONSHIP FINAL RESULTS

Pos	Driver	Nat	Car-Engine	R1	R2	R3	R4	R5	R6	R7	R8	R9	Total
1	Jack Brabham	AUS	Brabham-Repco BT19	R	4	1	1PF	1P	1	R	-	-	42
			Brabham-Repco BT20	-	-	-	-	-	-	-	RP	2	
2	John Surtees	GBR	Ferrari 312	R	1PF	-	-	-	-	-	-	-	28
			Cooper-Maserati T81	-	-	R	R	R	2F	R	3F	1P	
3	Jochen Rindt	AUT	Cooper-Maserati T81	R	2	4	5	R	3	4	2	R	22
4	Denny Hulme	NZL	Brabham-Climax BT22	R	R	-	-	-	-	-	-	-	18
			Brabham-Repco BT20	-	-	3	2	RF	R	3	R	3	
5	Graham Hill	GBR	BRM P261	3	R	R	3	2	4	-	-	-	17
			BRM P83	-	-	-	-	-	-	R	R	R	
6	Jim Clark	GBR	Lotus-Climax 33	RP	R	NS	4	3	RP	-	-	-	16
			Lotus-BRM 43	-	-	-	-	-	-	R	1	R	
7	Jackie Stewart	GBR	BRM P261	1	R	-	R	4	5	-	-	-	14
			BRM P83	-	-	-	-	-	-	R	R	R	
8	Mike Parkes	GBR	Ferrari 312	-	-	2	-	R	R	2P	-	-	12
8	Lorenzo Bandini	ITA	Ferrari 246	2F	3	-	-	-	-	-	-	-	12
			Ferrari 312	-	-	NCPF	-	6	6	R	R	-	
10	Ludovico Scarfiotti	ITA	Ferrari 246	-	-	-	-	-	R	-	-	-	9
			Ferrari 312	-	-	-	-	-	-	1F	-	-	
11	Richie Ginther	USA	Cooper-Maserati T81	R	5	-	-	-	-	-	-	-	5
			Honda RA273	-	-	-	-	-	-	R	NC	4F	
12	Mike Spence	GBR	Lotus-BRM 33	R	R	R	R	5	R	5	-	-	4
			Lotus-BRM 25	-	-	-	-	-	-	-	R	NS	
12	Dan Gurney	USA	Eagle-Climax T1G	-	NC	5	R	R	7	-	-	5	4
			Eagle-Weslake T1G	-	-	-	-	-	-	R	R	-	
14	Bob Bondurant	USA	BRM P261	4	R	-	9	-	R	7	-	-	3
			Eagle-Climax T1G	-	-	-	-	-	-	-	DQ	-	
			Eagle-Weslake T1G	-	-	-	-	-	-	-	-	R	
14	Jo Siffert	CHE	Brabham-BRM BT11	R	-	-	-	-	-	-	-	-	3
			Cooper-Maserati T81	-	R	R	NC	R	-	R	4	R	
14	Bruce McLaren	NZL	McLaren-Ford M2B	R	-	-	-	-	-	-	5	R	3
			McLaren-Serenissima M2B	-	NS	-	6	NS	-	-	-	-	
17	John Taylor	GBR	Brabham-BRM BT11	-	-	6	8	8	R	-	-	-	1
17	Bob Anderson	GBR	Brabham-Climax BT11	R	-	7	NC	R	R	6	-	-	1
17	Peter Arundell	GBR	Lotus-BRM 43	-	NS	R	-	-	-	-	-	-	1
			Lotus-BRM 33	-	-	-	R	R	8	8	-	7	
			Lotus-Climax 33	-	-	-	-	-	-	-	6	-	
17	Jo Bonnier	SWE	Cooper-Maserati T81	NC	R	-	-	7	R	R	NC	6	1
			Brabham-Climax BT22	-	-	NC	-	-	-	-	-	-	
			Brabham-Climax BT7	-	-	-	R	-	-	-	-	-	

WORLD CONSTRUCTORS' CHAMPIONSHIP FINAL RESULTS

Pos	Team-Engine	R1	R2	R3	R4	R5	R6	R7	R8	R9	Total
1	Brabham-Repco	-	4	1	1	1	1	3	-	2	42
2	Ferrari	2	1	2		6	6	1	-	-	31
3	Cooper-Maserati	-	2	4	5	7	2	4	2	1	30
4	BRM	1	-	-	3	2	4	7	-	-	22
5	Lotus-BRM	-	-	-	-	5	-	5	1	-	13
6	Lotus-Climax	-	-	-	4	3	8	9	6	7	8
7	Eagle-Climax	-	-	5	R	R	7	-	5	-	4
8	Honda	-	-	-	-	-	-	-	-	4	3
9	McLaren-Ford	-	-	-	-	-	-	-	5	-	2
10	Brabham-BRM	-	-	6	8	8	-	-	-	-	1
10	McLaren-Serenissima	-	-	-	6	-	-	-	-	-	1
10	Brabham-Climax	-	-	7	7	-	-	6	-	-	1

SYMBOLS AND GRAND PRIX KEY

Round 1 Monaco GP
Round 2 Belgian GP
Round 3 French GP
Round 4 British GP
Round 5 Dutch GP
Round 6 German GP
Round 7 Italian GP
Round 8 United States GP
Round 9 Mexican GP

SCORING

1st 9 points
2nd 6 points
3rd 4 points
4th 3 points
5th 2 points
6th 1 point

DNPQ DID NOT PRE-QUALIFY **DNQ** DID NOT QUALIFY **DQ** DISQUALIFIED **EX** EXCLUDED
F FASTEST LAP **NC** NOT CLASSIFIED **NS** NON-STARTER **P** POLE POSITION **R** RETIRED

1967

SEASON SUMMARY

Denny Hulme continued the Antipodean run of success by winning for the Brabham team. However, a new world order became apparent as Lotus shone from the moment that the Ford Cosworth DFV engine broke cover, at the third of the season's 11 rounds. New Zealander Hulme had gathered too many points before then to be overhauled by Jim Clark, who lost out as his Lotus 49 was at first unreliable. Indeed, Brabham designer Ron Tauranac's simple BT24 was good enough for Jack Brabham to rank second overall ahead of the Scot. Ferrari's year was both winless and spoilt by the death of its lead driver, Lorenzo Bandini.

SOUTH AFRICAN GRAND PRIX

KYALAMI • ROUND 1 • DATE: 2ND JANUARY 1967
Laps: 80 • Distance: 203.220miles/327.52km • Weather: Hot & bright

Pos	Driver	Team	Chassis-Engine	Result	Qual
1	Pedro Rodriguez	Cooper	Cooper-Maserati T81	2h05m45.900s	4
2	John Love	John Love	Cooper-Climax T79	2h06m12.300s	5
3	John Surtees	Honda	Honda RA273	79 laps	6
4	Denny Hulme	Brabham	Brabham-Repco BT20	78 laps	2
5	Bob Anderson	DW Racing Enterprises	Brabham-Climax BT11	78 laps	10
6	Jack Brabham	Brabham	Brabham-Repco BT20	76 laps	1
NC	Dave Charlton	Scuderia Scribante	Brabham-Climax BT11	63 laps/not classified	8
NC	Luki Botha	Luki Botha	Brabham-Climax BT11	60 laps/not classified	17
R	Sam Tingle	Sam Tingle	LDS-Climax 3	56 laps/accident	14
R	Piers Courage	Reg Parnell Racing	Lotus-BRM 25	51 laps/fuel system	18
R	Dan Gurney	Anglo American Racers	Eagle-Climax T1G	44 laps/suspension	11
R	Jo Siffert	Rob Walker Racing Team	Cooper-Maserati T81	41 laps/engine	16
R	Jochen Rindt	Cooper	Cooper-Maserati T81	38 laps/engine	7
R	Mike Spence	BRM	BRM P83	31 laps/oil leak	13
R	Jo Bonnier	Ecurie Bonnier	Cooper-Maserati T81	30 laps/engine	12
R	Jim Clark	Lotus	Lotus-BRM 43	22 laps/engine	3
R	Graham Hill	Lotus	Lotus-BRM 43	6 laps/accident	15
R	Jackie Stewart	BRM	BRM P83	2 laps/engine	9

Pole: Brabham, 1m28.300s, 103.714mph/166.912kph. Fastest lap: Hulme, 1m29.900s, 101.868mph/163.942kph on Lap 3. Race leaders: Hulme 1-60; Love 61-73; Rodriguez 74-80

THE RISK OF FIRE

Drivers feared fire almost more than anything else and its horrors became all too apparent at Monaco when Lorenzo Bandini was trapped in his Ferrari after crashing at the harbourfront chicane while chasing Denny Hulme's Brabham for the lead. The charismatic Italian died of his burns three days later. There were calls for better marshalling and a ban on straw bales being used around the perimeter of circuits.

A PAIR OF FIRSTS

The season-opening South African GP should have been won by Denny Hulme, but his Brabham's brakes needed attention. This put Zimbabwean driver John Love into the lead in a four-cylinder Cooper. Then, with seven laps to go, normality was restored as he had to pit for more fuel, allowing Pedro Rodriguez to come through to win in his works Cooper.

MONACO GRAND PRIX

MONTE CARLO • ROUND 2 • DATE: 7TH MAY 1967
Laps: 100 • Distance: 195.113miles/314.5km • Weather: Warm & bright

Pos	Driver	Team	Chassis-Engine	Result	Qual
1	Denny Hulme	Brabham	Brabham-Repco BT20	2h34m34.300s	4
2	Graham Hill	Lotus	Lotus-BRM 33	99 laps	8
3	Chris Amon	Ferrari	Ferrari 312	98 laps	14
4	Bruce McLaren	McLaren	McLaren-BRM M4B	97 laps	10
5	Pedro Rodriguez	Cooper	Cooper-Maserati T81	96 laps	16
6	Mike Spence	BRM	BRM P83	96 laps	12
R	Lorenzo Bandini	Ferrari	Ferrari 312	81 laps/accident	2
R	Piers Courage	Reg Parnell Racing	BRM P261	64 laps/spun off	13
R	Jim Clark	Lotus	Lotus-Climax 33	42 laps/suspension	5
R	John Surtees	Honda	Honda RA273	32 laps/engine	3
R	Jo Siffert	Rob Walker Racing Team	Cooper-Maserati T81	31 laps/fuel pressure	9
R	Jackie Stewart	BRM	BRM P261	14 laps/differential	6
R	Jochen Rindt	Cooper	Cooper-Maserati T81B	14 laps/gearbox	15
R	Dan Gurney	Anglo American Racers	Eagle-Weslake T1G	4 laps/fuel pump	7
R	Johnny Servoz-Gavin	Matra	Matra-Ford MS7/F2	4 laps/mechanical	11
R	Jack Brabham	Brabham	Brabham-Repco BT19	0 laps/engine	1
DNQ	Bob Anderson	DW Racing Enterprises	Brabham-Climax BT11	-	14
DNQ	Jean-Pierre Beltoise	Matra	Matra-Ford MS7/F2	-	18
DNQ	Richie Ginther	Anglo American Racers	Eagle-Weslake T1G	-	19

Pole: Brabham, 1m27.600s, 80.310mph/129.246kph. Fastest lap: Clark, 1m29.500s, 78.605mph/126.502kph on Lap 38. Race leaders: Bandini 1; Hulme 2-5 & 15-100; Stewart 6-14

THE EAGLE SOARS

After Jack Brabham's success racing a car bearing his name, Dan Gurney became the second driver to claim a grand prix in his own car, the Eagle. He'd won a non-championship race at Brands Hatch but his day of days came at the Belgian GP at Spa-Francorchamps when he passed Jackie Stewart as gearbox problems hit the Scot's BRM.

DUTCH GRAND PRIX

ZANDVOORT • ROUND 3 • DATE: 4TH JUNE 1967
Laps: 90 • Distance: 234.279miles/377.37km • Weather: Warm but dull

Pos	Driver	Team	Chassis-Engine	Result	Qual
1	Jim Clark	Lotus	Lotus-Ford Cosworth 49	2h14m45.100s	8
2	Jack Brabham	Brabham	Brabham-Repco BT19	2h15m08.700s	3
3	Denny Hulme	Brabham	Brabham-Repco BT20	2h15m10.800s	7
4	Chris Amon	Ferrari	Ferrari 312	2h15m12.400s	9
5	Mike Parkes	Ferrari	Ferrari 312	89 laps	10
6	Ludovico Scarfiotti	Ferrari	Ferrari 312	89 laps	15
7	Chris Irwin	Reg Parnell Racing	Lotus-BRM 25	88 laps	13
8	Mike Spence	BRM	BRM P83	87 laps	12
9	Bob Anderson	DW Racing Enterprises	Brabham-Climax BT11	86 laps	17
10	Jo Siffert	Rob Walker Racing Team	Cooper-Maserati T81	83 laps	16
R	John Surtees	Honda	Honda RA273	73 laps/throttle	6
R	Jackie Stewart	BRM	BRM P83	51 laps/brakes	11
R	Jochen Rindt	Cooper	Cooper-Maserati T81B	41 laps/suspension	4
R	Pedro Rodriguez	Cooper	Cooper-Maserati T81	39 laps/gearbox	5
R	Graham Hill	Lotus	Lotus-Ford Cosworth 49	11 laps/engine	1
R	Dan Gurney	Anglo American Racers	Eagle-Weslake T1G	8 laps/injection	2
R	Bruce McLaren	McLaren	McLaren-BRM M4B	1 lap/accident	14

Pole: Hill, 1m24.600s, 110.868mph/178.425kph. Fastest lap: Clark, 1m28.080s, 106.488mph/171.376kph on Lap 67. Race leaders: Hill 1-10; Brabham 11-15; Clark 16-90

JUMPIN' JACKY FLASH

For the second year, Jacky Ickx entered the German GP in an F2 car, again a Matra entered by Ken Tyrrell. This time, he shocked onlookers by outqualifying all but two of the F1 runners. Rules dictated that he had to start behind all the F1 cars, in 18th place, but he rose to fourth before his suspension broke. This performance earned him an F1 ride with Cooper.

BELGIAN GRAND PRIX

SPA-FRANCORCHAMPS • ROUND 4 • DATE: 18TH JUNE 1967
Laps: 28 • Distance: 244.825miles/394.8km • Weather: Warm & bright

Pos	Driver	Team	Chassis-Engine	Result	Qual
1	Dan Gurney	Anglo American Racers	Eagle-Weslake T1G	1h40m49.400s	2
2	Jackie Stewart	BRM	BRM P83	1h41m52.400s	6
3	Chris Amon	Ferrari	Ferrari 312	1h42m29.400s	5
4	Jochen Rindt	Cooper	Cooper-Maserati T81B	1h43m03.300s	4
5	Mike Spence	BRM	BRM P83	27 laps	11
6	Jim Clark	Lotus	Lotus-Ford Cosworth 49	27 laps	1
7	Jo Siffert	Rob Walker Racing Team	Cooper-Maserati T81	27 laps	16
8	Bob Anderson	DW Racing Enterprises	Brabham-Climax BT11	26 laps	17
9	Pedro Rodriguez	Cooper	Cooper-Maserati T81	25 laps/engine	13
10	Guy Ligier	Guy Ligier	Cooper-Maserati T81	25 laps	18
NC	Ludovico Scarfiotti	Ferrari	Ferrari 312	24 laps/not classified	9
R	Jack Brabham	Brabham	Brabham-Repco BT24	15 laps/engine	7

Pos	Driver	Team	Chassis-Engine	Result	Qual
R	Denny Hulme	Brabham	Brabham-Repco BT19	14 laps/engine	14
R	Jo Bonnier	Ecurie Bonnier	Cooper-Maserati T81	10 laps/engine	12
R	Graham Hill	Lotus	Lotus-Ford Cosworth 49	3 laps/clutch	3
R	John Surtees	Honda	Honda RA273	1 lap/engine	10
R	Chris Irwin	Reg Parnell Racing	BRM P261	1 lap/engine	15
R	Mike Parkes	Ferrari	Ferrari 312	0 laps/accident	8

Pole: Clark, 3m28.100s, 151.565mph/243.921kph. Fastest lap: Gurney, 3m31.900s, 148.847mph/239.546kph on Lap 19. Race leaders: Clark 1-12; Stewart 13-20; Gurney 21-28

NEW CIRCUITS

Le Mans is famous for the 8-mile (12.9-km) circuit on which it hosts its 24-hour sports car race. In 1967, it landed a round of the World Championship on the Bugatti circuit that used its pit straight and an infield loop. South Africa's Kyalami and Canada's Mosport Park also made their debuts. Use of the Bugatti track, though, was just a one-off.

FRENCH GRAND PRIX

LE MANS BUGATTI CIRCUIT • ROUND 5 • DATE: 2ND JULY 1967
Laps: 80 • Distance: 220.609miles/355.36km • Weather: Warm & bright

Pos	Driver	Team	Chassis-Engine	Result	Qual
1	Jack Brabham	Brabham	Brabham-Repco BT24	2h13m21.300s	2
2	Denny Hulme	Brabham	Brabham-Repco BT24	2h14m10.800s	6
3	Jackie Stewart	BRM	BRM P261	79 laps	10
4	Jo Siffert	Rob Walker Racing Team	Cooper-Maserati T81	77 laps	11
5	Chris Irwin	Reg Parnell Racing	BRM P83	76 laps/engine	9
6	Pedro Rodriguez	Cooper	Cooper-Maserati T81	76 laps	13
NC	Guy Ligier	Guy Ligier	Cooper-Maserati T81	68 laps/not classified	15
R	Chris Amon	Ferrari	Ferrari 312	47 laps/throttle	7
R	Dan Gurney	Anglo American Racers	Eagle-Weslake T1G	40 laps/oil leak	3
R	Jochen Rindt	Cooper	Cooper-Maserati T81B	33 laps/engine	8
R	Bruce McLaren	Anglo American Racers	Eagle-Weslake T1G	26 laps/ignition	5
R	Jim Clark	Lotus	Lotus-Ford Cosworth 49	23 laps/differential	4
R	Bob Anderson	DW Racing Enterprises	Brabham-Climax BT11	16 laps/ignition	14
R	Graham Hill	Lotus	Lotus-Ford Cosworth 49	13 laps/differential	1
R	Mike Spence	BRM	BRM P83	9 laps/halfshaft	12

Pole: Hill, 1m36.200s, 103.289mph/166.228kph. Fastest lap: Hill, 1m36.700s, 102.755mph/165.369kph on Lap 7. Race leaders: Hill 1 & 11-13; Brabham 2-4 & 24-80; Clark 5-10 & 14-23

NEW CONSTRUCTORS

Just one new constructor entered the World Championship in 1967. This was Protos, and it brought a pair of its Ron Harris-run F2 cars to the German GP. Unusual in appearance thanks to its part-enveloping windscreen, these sleek cars were designed by Frank Costin and were entered for Kurt Ahrens and Brian Hart. Neither finished.

BRITISH GRAND PRIX

SILVERSTONE • ROUND 6 • DATE: 15TH JULY 1967
Laps: 80 • Distance: 233.687miles/376.84km • Weather: Warm & bright

Pos	Driver	Team	Chassis-Engine	Result	Qual
1	Jim Clark	Lotus	Lotus-Ford Cosworth 49	1h59m25.600s	1
2	Denny Hulme	Brabham	Brabham-Repco BT24	1h59m38.400s	4
3	Chris Amon	Ferrari	Ferrari 312	1h59m42.200s	6
4	Jack Brabham	Brabham	Brabham-Repco BT24	1h59m47.400s	3
5	Pedro Rodriguez	Cooper	Cooper-Maserati T81B	79 laps	9
6	John Surtees	Honda	Honda RA273	78 laps	7
7	Chris Irwin	Reg Parnell Racing	BRM P261	77 laps	13
8	David Hobbs	Bernard White Racing	BRM P261	77 laps	14
9	Alan Rees	Cooper	Cooper-Maserati T81	76 laps	15
10	Guy Ligier	Guy Ligier	Brabham-Repco BT20	76 laps	21
R	Bob Anderson	DW Racing Enterprises	Brabham-Climax BT11	67 laps/engine	17
R	Graham Hill	Lotus	Lotus-Ford Cosworth 49	64 laps/engine	2
R	Mike Spence	BRM	BRM P83	44 laps/ignition	11
R	Dan Gurney	Anglo American Racers	Eagle-Weslake T1G	34 laps/clutch	5
R	Silvio Moser	Charles Vogele Racing	Cooper-ATS T77	29 laps/fuel pressure	20
R	Jochen Rindt	Cooper	Cooper-Maserati T86	26 laps/engine	8
R	Jackie Stewart	BRM	BRM P83	20 laps/transmission	12
R	Bruce McLaren	Anglo American Racers	Eagle-Weslake T1G	14 laps/engine	10
R	Jo Siffert	Rob Walker Racing Team	Cooper-Maserati T81	10 laps/engine	18
R	Jo Bonnier	Ecurie Bonnier	Cooper-Maserati T81	0 laps/engine	19
NS	Piers Courage	Reg Parnell Racing	BRM P261	Irwin drove car	16

Pole: Clark, 1m25.300s, 123.529mph/198.801kph. Fastest lap: Hulme, 1m27.000s, 121.115mph/194.917kph on Lap 3. Race leaders: Clark 1-25 & 55-80; Hill 26-54

GERMAN GRAND PRIX

NURBURGRING • ROUND 7 • DATE: 6TH AUGUST 1967
Laps: 15 • Distance: 212.835miles/342.525km • Weather: Warm & bright

Pos	Driver	Team	Chassis-Engine	Result	Qual
1	Denny Hulme	Brabham	Brabham-Repco BT24	2h05m55.700s	2
2	Jack Brabham	Brabham	Brabham-Repco BT24	2h06m34.200s	7
3	Chris Amon	Ferrari	Ferrari 312	2h06m34.700s	8
4	John Surtees	Honda	Honda RA273	2h08m21.400s	6
5	Jackie Oliver	Lotus Components Ltd	Lotus-Ford 48/F2	2h12m04.900s	19
6	Jo Bonnier	Ecurie Bonnier	Cooper-Maserati T81	2h14m37.800s	16
7	Alan Rees	Roy Winkelmann Racing	Brabham-Ford BT23/F2	2h14m43.600s	20
8	Guy Ligier	Guy Ligier	Brabham-Repco BT20	14 laps	17
9	Chris Irwin	Reg Parnell Racing	BRM P83	13 laps	15
10	David Hobbs	Lola Cars Ltd	Lola-BMW T100/F2	13 laps	22
11	Pedro Rodriguez	Cooper	Cooper-Maserati T81	13 laps	10
R	Dan Gurney	Anglo American Racers	Eagle-Weslake T1G	12 laps/halfshaft	4
R	Jacky Ickx	Ken Tyrrell Racing	Matra-Ford MS7/F2	12 laps/suspension	18
NC	Brian Hart	Ron Harris	Protos-Ford/F2	12 laps/not classified	25
NC	Jo Siffert	Rob Walker Racing Team	Cooper-Maserati T81	11 laps/not classified	12
R	Graham Hill	Lotus	Lotus-Ford Cosworth 49	8 laps/suspension	13
R	Hubert Hahne	BMW	Lola-BMW T100/F2	6 laps/suspension	14
R	Jackie Stewart	BRM	BRM P115	5 laps/differential	3
R	Jim Clark	Lotus	Lotus-Ford Cosworth 49	4 laps/suspension	1
R	Kurt Ahrens	Ron Harris	Protos-Ford/F2	4 laps/radiator	23
R	Jochen Rindt	Cooper	Cooper-Maserati T86	4 laps/handling	9
R	Bruce McLaren	Anglo American Racers	Eagle-Weslake T1G	3 laps/oil leak	5
R	Mike Spence	BRM	BRM P83	3 laps/differential	11

Pos	Driver	Team	Chassis-Engine	Result	Qual
R	Jo Schlesser	Ecurie Ford France	Matra-Ford MS7/F2	2 laps/clutch	21
R	Gerhard Mitter	Gerhard Mitter	Brabham-Ford BT23/F2	0 laps/engine	24
NS	Brian Redman	Lola Cars Ltd	Lola-BMW T100/F2	-	26

Pole: Clark, 8m04.100s, 105.516mph/169.812kph. Fastest lap: Gurney, 8m15.100s, 103.171mph/166.039kph on Lap 6. Race leaders: Clark 1-3; Gurney 4-12; Hulme 13-15

CANADIAN GRAND PRIX

MOSPORT PARK • ROUND 8 • DATE: 27TH AUGUST 1967
Laps: 90 • Distance: 221.216miles/356.13km • Weather: Warm but wet

Pos	Driver	Team	Chassis-Engine	Result	Qual
1	Jack Brabham	Brabham	Brabham-Repco BT24	2h40m40.000s	7
2	Denny Hulme	Brabham	Brabham-Repco BT24	2h41m41.900s	3
3	Dan Gurney	Anglo American Racers	Eagle-Weslake T1G	89 laps	5
4	Graham Hill	Lotus	Lotus-Ford Cosworth 49	88 laps	2
5	Mike Spence	BRM	BRM P83	87 laps	10
6	Chris Amon	Ferrari	Ferrari 312	87 laps	4
7	Bruce McLaren	McLaren	McLaren-BRM M5A	86 laps	6
8	Jo Bonnier	Ecurie Bonnier	Cooper-Maserati T81	85 laps	14
9	David Hobbs	Bernard White Racing	BRM P261	85 laps	12
10	Richard Attwood	Cooper	Cooper-Maserati T81B	84 laps	13
11	Mike Fisher	Mike Fisher	Lotus-BRM 33	81 laps	17
R	Jim Clark	Lotus	Lotus-Ford Cosworth 49	69 laps/ignition	1
R	Eppie Wietzes	Lotus	Lotus-Ford Cosworth 49	69 laps/ignition	16
R	Jackie Stewart	BRM	BRM P115	65 laps/throttle	9
NC	Al Pease	Castrol Oils Ltd	Eagle-Climax T1G	47 laps/not classified	15
R	Chris Irwin	Reg Parnell Racing	BRM P83	18 laps/spun off	11
R	Jochen Rindt	Cooper	Cooper-Maserati T81	4 laps/ignition	8
NS	Jo Siffert	Rob Walker Racing Team	Cooper-Maserati T81	starter motor	13
DNQ	Tom Jones	Tom Jones	Cooper-Climax T82	-	19

Pole: Clark, 1m22.400s, 107.421mph/172.878kph. Fastest lap: Clark, 1m23.100s, 106.516mph/171.422kph on Lap 54. Race leaders: Clark 1-3 & 58-67; Hulme 4-57; Brabham 68-90

NEW DRIVERS

There were nine new faces in 1967, with French star Johnny Servoz-Gavin entering the Monaco GP in an F2 Matra. He would go on to finish second at Monza in 1968. Jackie Oliver had the longer F1 career and he made his bow in an F2 Lotus. After starring in Italian F3, British racer Jonathan Williams made his debut with Ferrari, but was then dropped.

ITALIAN GRAND PRIX

MONZA • ROUND 9 • DATE: 10TH SEPTEMBER 1967
Laps: 68 • Distance: 242.956miles/391.0km • Weather: Warm & bright

Pos	Driver	Team	Chassis-Engine	Result	Qual
1	John Surtees	Honda	Honda RA300	1h43m45.000s	9
2	Jack Brabham	Brabham	Brabham-Repco BT24	1h43m45.200s	2
3	Jim Clark	Lotus	Lotus-Ford Cosworth 49	1h44m08.100s	1
4	Jochen Rindt	Cooper	Cooper-Maserati T86	1h44m41.600s	11
5	Mike Spence	BRM	BRM P83	67 laps	12
6	Jacky Ickx	Cooper	Cooper-Maserati T81B	66 laps	15
7	Chris Amon	Ferrari	Ferrari 312	64 laps	4

Pos	Driver	Team	Chassis-Engine	Result	Qual
R	Graham Hill	Lotus	Lotus-Ford Cosworth 49	58 laps/engine	8
R	Jo Siffert	Rob Walker Racing Team	Cooper-Maserati T81	50 laps/accident	13
R	Giancarlo Baghetti	Lotus	Lotus-Ford Cosworth 49	50 laps/engine	17
R	Bruce McLaren	McLaren	McLaren-BRM M5A	46 laps/engine	3
R	Jo Bonnier	Ecurie Bonnier	Cooper-Maserati T81	46 laps/overheating	14
R	Jackie Stewart	BRM	BRM P115	45 laps/engine	7
R	Denny Hulme	Brabham	Brabham-Repco BT24	30 laps/overheating	6
R	Guy Ligier	Guy Ligier	Brabham-Repco BT20	26 laps/engine	18
R	Chris Irwin	Reg Parnell Racing	BRM P83	16 laps/mechanical	16
R	Ludovico Scarfiotti	Anglo American Racers	Eagle-Weslake T1G	5 laps/engine	10
R	Dan Gurney	Anglo American Racers	Eagle-Weslake T1G	4 laps/engine	5

Pole: Clark, 1m28.500s, 145.337mph/233.898kph. Fastest lap: Clark, 1m28.500s, 145.337mph/233.898kph on Lap 26. Race leaders: Gurney 1-2; Clark 3-9, 11-12 & 61-67; Hulme 10, 13-15, 17 & 24-27; Brabham 16 & 59-60; Hill 18-23 & 28-58; Surtees 68

CLASSIC ENGINE: FORD COSWORTH DFV

When the Ford Cosworth DFV hit F1 in June 1967, it took the sport to a new level. Granted only to Lotus, this engine broke new ground by being used as a stressed member of the chassis, meaning that the suspension could be mounted directly onto it. Ford liked the simplicity of a V8 rather than 12- and 16-cylinder options, and its smaller size and lighter weight were key. Demand for the engine was immediate and other teams were able to use them from 1968, enabling the best of them to propel themselves towards the front of the field. Its 16-year F1 run would set a record 155 wins.

UNITED STATES GRAND PRIX

WATKINS GLEN • ROUND 10 • DATE: 1ST OCTOBER 1967
Laps: 108 • Distance: 248.400miles/399.762km • Weather: Warm & bright

Pos	Driver	Team	Chassis-Engine	Result	Qual
1	Jim Clark	Lotus	Lotus-Ford Cosworth 49	2h03m13.200s	2
2	Graham Hill	Lotus	Lotus-Ford Cosworth 49	2h03m19.500s	1
3	Denny Hulme	Brabham	Brabham-Repco BT24	107 laps	6
4	Jo Siffert	Rob Walker Racing Team	Cooper-Maserati T81	106 laps	12
5	Jack Brabham	Brabham	Brabham-Repco BT24	104 laps	5
6	Jo Bonnier	Ecurie Bonnier	Cooper-Maserati T81	101 laps	15
7	Jean-Pierre Beltoise	Matra	Matra-Ford MS7/F2	101 laps	18
R	John Surtees	Honda	Honda RA300	96 laps/alternator	11
R	Chris Amon	Ferrari	Ferrari 312	95 laps/engine	4
R	Jackie Stewart	BRM	BRM P115	72 laps/fuel injection	10
R	Jacky Ickx	Cooper	Cooper-Maserati T86	45 laps/overheating	16
R	Guy Ligier	Guy Ligier	Brabham-Repco BT20	43 laps/engine	17
R	Chris Irwin	Reg Parnell Racing	BRM P83	41 laps/engine	14
R	Mike Spence	BRM	BRM P83	35 laps/engine	13
R	Jochen Rindt	Cooper	Cooper-Maserati T81B	33 laps/engine	8
R	Dan Gurney	Anglo American Racers	Eagle-Weslake T1G	24 laps/suspension	3
R	Bruce McLaren	McLaren	McLaren-BRM M5A	16 laps/water leak	9
R	Moises Solana	Lotus	Lotus-Ford Cosworth 49	7 laps/ignition	7

Pole: Hill, 1m05.480s, 126.451mph/203.503kph. Fastest lap: Hill, 1m06.000s, 125.454mph/201.900kph on Lap 81. Race leaders: Hill 1-40; Clark 41-108

MEXICAN GRAND PRIX

MEXICO CITY • ROUND 11 • DATE: 22ND OCTOBER 1967
Laps: 65 • Distance: 201.945miles/325.0km • Weather: Warm & bright

Pos	Driver	Team	Chassis-Engine	Result	Qual
1	Jim Clark	Lotus	Lotus-Ford Cosworth 49	1h59m28.700s	1
2	Jack Brabham	Brabham	Brabham-Repco BT24	2h00m54.060s	5
3	Denny Hulme	Brabham	Brabham-Repco BT24	64 laps	6
4	John Surtees	Honda	Honda RA300	64 laps	7
5	Mike Spence	BRM	BRM P83	63 laps	11
6	Pedro Rodriguez	Cooper	Cooper-Maserati T81B	63 laps	13
7	Jean-Pierre Beltoise	Matra	Matra-Ford MS7/F2	63 laps	14
8	Jonathan Williams	Ferrari	Ferrari 312	63 laps	16
9	Chris Amon	Ferrari	Ferrari 312	62 laps/out of fuel	2
10	Jo Bonnier	Ecurie Bonnier	Cooper-Maserati T81	61 laps	17
11	Guy Ligier	Guy Ligier	Brabham-Repco BT20	61 laps	19
12	Jo Siffert	Rob Walker Racing Team	Cooper-Maserati T81	59 laps/overheating	10
R	Bruce McLaren	McLaren	McLaren-BRM M5A	45 laps/fuel pressure	8
R	Chris Irwin	Reg Parnell Racing	BRM P83	33 laps/oil leak	15
R	Jackie Stewart	BRM	BRM P115	24 laps/engine	12
R	Graham Hill	Lotus	Lotus-Ford Cosworth 49	18 laps/halfshaft	4
R	Moises Solana	Lotus	Lotus-Ford Cosworth 49	12 laps/suspension	9
R	Dan Gurney	Anglo American Racers	Eagle-Weslake T1G	4 laps/radiator damage	3
R	Mike Fisher	Mike Fisher	Lotus-BRM 33	1 lap/fuel metering unit	18

Pole: Clark, 1m47.560s, 103.985mph/167.348kph. Fastest lap: Clark, 1m48.130s, 103.437mph/166.466kph on Lap 52. Race leaders: Hill 1-2; Clark 3-65

IN MEMORIAM

In addition to Lorenzo Bandini, 1967 saw the death of privateer Bob Anderson in a testing accident at Silverstone, as well as 1950s F1 racer Georges Berger in an 84-hour endurance race at the Nurburgring. 'Geki' died in an Italian F3 race at Caserta (after his F1 drives dried up), and Ian Raby succumbed to his injuries in an F2 race at Zandvoort.

WORLD DRIVERS' CHAMPIONSHIP FINAL RESULTS

Pos	Driver	Nat	Car-Engine	R1	R2	R3	R4
1	Denny Hulme	NZL	Brabham-Repco BT20	4F	1	3	-
			Brabham-Repco BT19	-	-	-	R
			Brabham-Repco BT24	-	-	-	-
2	Jack Brabham	AUS	Brabham-Repco BT20	6P	-	-	-
			Brabham-Repco BT19	-	RP	2	-
			Brabham-Repco BT24	-	-	-	R
3	Jim Clark	GBR	Lotus-BRM 43	R	-	-	-
			Lotus-Climax 33	-	RF	-	-
			Lotus-Ford Cosworth 49	-	-	1F	6P
4	John Surtees	GBR	Honda RA273	3	R	R	R
			Honda RA300	-	-	-	-
4	Chris Amon	NZL	Ferrari 312	-	3	4	3

Pos	Driver	Nat	Car-Engine	R1	R2	R3	R4
6	Pedro Rodriguez	MEX	Cooper-Maserati T81	1	5	R	9
			Cooper-Maserati T81B	-	-	-	-
6	Graham Hill	GBR	Lotus-BRM 43	R	-	-	-
			Lotus-BRM 33	-	2	-	-
			Lotus-Ford Cosworth 49	-	-	RP	R
8	Dan Gurney	USA	Eagle-Climax T1G	R	-	-	-
			Eagle-Weslake T1G	-	R	R	1F
9	Jackie Stewart	GBR	BRM P83	R	-	R	2
			BRM P261	-	R	-	-
			BRM P115	-	-	-	-
10	Mike Spence	GBR	BRM P83	R	6	8	5
11	John Love	ZWE	Cooper-Climax T79	2	-	-	-
11	Jochen Rindt	AUT	Cooper-Maserati T81	R	-	-	-
			Cooper-Maserati T81B	-	R	R	4
			Cooper-Maserati T86	-	-	-	-
11	Jo Siffert	CHE	Cooper-Maserati T81	R	R	10	7
14	Bruce McLaren	NZL	McLaren-BRM M4B	-	4	R	-
			Eagle-Weslake T1G	-	-	-	-
			McLaren-BRM M5A	-	-	-	-
14	Jo Bonnier	SWE	Cooper-Maserati T81	R	-	-	R
16	Bob Anderson	GBR	Brabham-Climax BT11	5	DNQ	9	8
16	Mike Parkes	GBR	Ferrari 312	-	-	5	R
16	Chris Irwin	GBR	Lotus-BRM 25	-	-	7	-
			BRM P261	-	-	-	R
			BRM P83	-	-	-	-
19	Ludovico Scarfiotti	ITA	Ferrari 312	-	-	6	NC
			Eagle-Weslake T1G	-	-	-	-
19	Guy Ligier	FRA	Cooper-Maserati T81	-	-	-	10
			Brabham-Repco BT20	-	-	-	-
19	Jacky Ickx	BEL	Cooper-Maserati T81B	-	-	-	-
			Cooper-Maserati T86	-	-	-	-

Pos	Driver	R5	R6	R7	R8	R9	R10	R11	Total
1	Hulme	-	-	-	-	-	-	-	51
		-	-	-	-	-	-	-	
		2	2F	1	2	R	3	3	
2	Brabham	-	-	-	-	-	-	-	46
		-	-	-	-	-	-	-	
		1	4	2	1	2	5	2	
3	Clark	-	-	-	-	-	-	-	41
		-	-	-	-	-	-	-	
		R	1P	RP	RPF	3PF	1	1PF	
4	Surtees	-	6	4	-				20
		-	-	-	-	1	R	4	
4	Amon	R	3	3	6	7	R	9	20
6	Rodriguez	6	-	8	-	-	-	-	15
		-	5	-	-	-	-	6	
6	Hill	-	-	-	-	-	-	-	15
		-	-	-	-	-	-	-	
		RPF	R	R	4	R	2PF	R	
8	Gurney	-	-	-	-	-	-	-	13
		R	R	RF	3	R	R	R	
9	Stewart	-	R	-	-	-	-	-	10
		3	-	-	-	-	-	-	
		-	-	R	R	R	R	R	
10	Spence	R	R	R	5	5	R	5	9
11	Love	-	-	-	-	-	-	-	6

Pos	Driver	R5	R6	R7	R8	R9	R10	R11	Total
11	Rindt	-	-	-	R	-	-	-	6
		R	-	-	-	-	R	-	
		-	R	R	-	4	-	-	
11	Siffert	4	R	NC	NS	R	4	12	6
14	McLaren	-	-	-	-	-	-	-	3
		R	R	R	-	-	-	-	
		-	-	-	7	R	R	R	
14	Bonnier	-	R	5	8	R	6	10	3
16	Anderson	R	R	-	-	-	-	-	2
16	Parkes	-	-	-	-	-	-	-	2
16	Irwin	-	-	-	-	-	-	-	2
		-	7	-	-	-	-	-	
		5	-	7	R	R	R	R	
19	Scarfiotti	-	-	-	-	-	-	-	1
		-	-	-	-	R	-	-	
19	Ligier	NC	-	-	-	-	-	-	1
		-	10	6	-	R	R	11	
19	Ickx	-	-	-	-	6	-	-	1
		-	-	-	-	-	R	-	

WORLD CONSTRUCTORS' CHAMPIONSHIP FINAL RESULTS

Pos	Team-Engine	R1	R2	R3	R4	R5	R6	R7	R8	R9	R10	R11	Total
1	Brabham-Repco	4	1	2	10	1	2	1	1	2	3	2	63
2	Lotus-Ford	-	-	1	6	-	1	-	4	3	1	1	44
3	Cooper-Maserati	1	5	10	4	4	5	5	8	4	4	6	28
4	Honda	3	-	-	-	-	6	4	-	1	-	4	20
4	Ferrari	-	3	4	3	-	3	3	6	7	-	8	20
6	BRM	-	6	8	2	3	7	7	5	5	-	5	17
7	Eagle-Weslake	-	-	-	1	-	-	-	3	-	-	-	13
8	Cooper-Climax	2	-	-	-	-	-	-	-	-	-	-	6
8	Lotus-BRM	-	2	7	-	-	-	-	11	-	-	-	6
10	McLaren-BRM	-	4	-	-	-	-	-	7	-	-	-	3
11	Brabham-Climax	5	-	9	8	-	-	-	-	-	-	-	2

SYMBOLS AND GRAND PRIX KEY

Round 1 South African GP
Round 2 Monaco GP
Round 3 Dutch GP
Round 4 Belgian GP
Round 5 French GP
Round 6 British GP
Round 7 German GP
Round 8 Canadian GP
Round 9 Italian GP
Round 10 United States GP
Round 11 Mexican GP

SCORING

1st 9 points
2nd 6 points
3rd 4 points
4th 3 points
5th 2 points
6th 1 point

DNPQ DID NOT PRE-QUALIFY **DNQ** DID NOT QUALIFY **DQ** DISQUALIFIED **EX** EXCLUDED
F FASTEST LAP **NC** NOT CLASSIFIED **NS** NON-STARTER **P** POLE POSITION **R** RETIRED

1968

SEASON SUMMARY

The motor racing world was rocked when Jim Clark was killed competing in a F2 race. This left Graham Hill to move up to become team leader at Lotus from the second round onwards and he responded by winning the next two races to set up a title push that led to him taking his second F1 crown. In a year in which the cars sprouted wings, Jackie Stewart moved from BRM to race a Ken Tyrrell-run Matra and equalled Hill's haul of three wins. Jochen Rindt starred for Brabham, but seldom finished, and Bruce McLaren took his marque's first win, at Spa-Francorchamps.

SOUTH AFRICAN GRAND PRIX

KYALAMI • ROUND 1 • DATE: 1ST JANUARY 1968
Laps: 80 • Distance: 203.829miles/328.32km • Weather: Hot & bright

Pos	Driver	Team	Chassis-Engine	Result	Qual
1	Jim Clark	Lotus	Lotus-Ford Cosworth 49	1h53m56.600s	1
2	Graham Hill	Lotus	Lotus-Ford Cosworth 49	1h54m21.900s	2
3	Jochen Rindt	Brabham	Brabham-Repco BT24	1h54m27.000s	4
4	Chris Amon	Ferrari	Ferrari 312	78 laps	8
5	Denny Hulme	McLaren	McLaren-BRM M5A	78 laps	9
6	Jean-Pierre Beltoise	Matra	Matra-Ford MS7/F2	77 laps	18
7	Jo Siffert	Rob Walker Racing Team	Cooper-Maserati T81	77 laps	16
8	John Surtees	Honda	Honda RA301	75 laps	6
9	John Love	Team Gunston	Brabham-Repco BT20	75 laps	17
NC	Jackie Pretorius	Team Pretoria	Brabham-Climax BT11	71 laps/not classified	23
R	Dan Gurney	Anglo American Racers	Eagle-Weslake T1G	58 laps/oil leak	12
R	Jacky Ickx	Ferrari	Ferrari 312	51 laps/oil leak	11
R	Jo Bonnier	Ecurie Bonnier	Cooper-Maserati T81	46 laps/overheating	19
R	Jackie Stewart	Tyrrell	Matra-Ford Cosworth MS9	43 laps/engine	3
R	Sam Tingle	Team Gunston	LDS-Repco 3	35 laps/overheating	22
R	Basil van Rooyen	John Love	Cooper-Climax T79	22 laps/engine	20
R	Pedro Rodriguez	BRM	BRM P126	20 laps/fuel system	10
R	Jack Brabham	Brabham	Brabham-Repco BT24	16 laps/engine	5
R	Andrea de Adamich	Ferrari	Ferrari 312	13 laps/accident	7
R	Mike Spence	BRM	BRM P126	7 laps/fuel system	14
R	Brian Redman	Cooper	Cooper-Maserati T81B	4 laps/oil leak	21
R	Dave Charlton	Scuderia Scribante	Brabham-Repco BT11	3 laps/differential	14
R	Ludovico Scarfiotti	Cooper	Cooper-Maserati T86	2 laps/accident	15

Pole: Clark, 1m21.600s, 112.504mph/181.058kph. Fastest lap: Clark, 1m23.700s, 109.681mph/176.516kph on Lap 73. Race leaders: Stewart 1; Clark 2-80

THE BIGGEST SHOCK

The death of Jim Clark sent a shock wave around the racing world, emphasising that if the best of the best could be killed, then so could anyone. Typical of the time, Clark was competing in events beyond the 12 World Championship grands prix and he crashed into the trees when it's believed that a tyre failed suddenly on his Lotus in an F2 race at Hockenheim.

SPANISH GRAND PRIX

JARAMA • ROUND 2 • DATE: 12TH MAY 1968
Laps: 90 • Distance: 190.380miles/306.387km • Weather: Hot & bright

Pos	Driver	Team	Chassis-Engine	Result	Qual
1	Graham Hill	Lotus	Lotus-Ford Cosworth 49	2h15m20.100s	6
2	Denny Hulme	McLaren	McLaren-Ford Cosworth M7A	2h15m36.000s	3
3	Brian Redman	Cooper	Cooper-BRM T86B	89 laps	13
4	Ludovico Scarfiotti	Cooper	Cooper-BRM T86B	89 laps	12
5	Jean-Pierre Beltoise	Tyrrell	Matra-Ford Cosworth MS10	81 laps	5
R	Bruce McLaren	McLaren	McLaren-Ford Cosworth M7A	77 laps/oil leak	4
R	John Surtees	Honda	Honda RA301	74 laps/gearbox	7
R	Jo Siffert	Rob Walker Racing Team	Lotus-Ford Cosworth 49	62 laps/transmission	10
R	Chris Amon	Ferrari	Ferrari 312	57 laps/fuel pump	1
R	Piers Courage	Reg Parnell Racing	BRM P126	52 laps/fuel system	11
R	Pedro Rodriguez	BRM	BRM P133	27 laps/accident	2
R	Jacky Ickx	Ferrari	Ferrari 312	13 laps/ignition	8
R	Jochen Rindt	Brabham	Brabham-Repco BT24	10 laps/fuel pressure	9
NS	Jack Brabham	Brabham	Brabham-Repco BT26	engine	14

Pole: Amon, 1m27.900s, 86.634mph/139.425kph. Fastest lap: Beltoise, 1m28.300s, 86.242mph/138.793kph on Lap 47. Race leaders: Rodriguez 1-11; Beltoise 12-15; Amon 16-57; Hill 58-90

WINGS AND THINGS

F1 cars had looked much the same since 1961, but they morphed into new shapes in 1968. These were first seen when kicked-up rear bodywork was added by Lotus at Monaco, then Ferrari introduced an aerofoil mounted on stalks at Spa. By year's end, these were twice the height and Lotus even ran a pedal-operated rear wing in Mexico.

MONACO GRAND PRIX

MONTE CARLO • ROUND 3 • DATE: 26TH MAY 1968
Laps: 80 • Distance: 155.967miles/251.6km • Weather: Warm & bright

Pos	Driver	Team	Chassis-Engine	Result	Qual
1	Graham Hill	Lotus	Lotus-Ford Cosworth 49B	2h00m32.300s	1
2	Richard Attwood	BRM	BRM P126	2h00m34.500s	6
3	Lucien Bianchi	Cooper	Cooper-BRM T86B	76 laps	14
4	Ludovico Scarfiotti	Cooper	Cooper-BRM T86B	76 laps	15
5	Denny Hulme	McLaren	McLaren-Ford Cosworth M7A	73 laps	10
R	John Surtees	Honda	Honda RA301	16 laps/gearbox	4
R	Pedro Rodriguez	BRM	BRM P133	16 laps/accident	9
R	Piers Courage	Reg Parnell Racing	BRM P126	12 laps/chassis	11
R	Jo Siffert	Rob Walker Racing Team	Lotus-Ford Cosworth 49	11 laps/differential	3
R	Jean-Pierre Beltoise	Matra	Matra MS11	11 laps/accident	8
R	Dan Gurney	Anglo American Racers	Eagle-Weslake T1G	9 laps/engine	16
R	Jochen Rindt	Brabham	Brabham-Repco BT24	8 laps/accident	5
R	Jack Brabham	Brabham	Brabham-Repco BT26	7 laps/suspension	12
R	Johnny Servoz-Gavin	Tyrrell	Matra-Ford Cosworth MS10	3 laps/halfshaft	2

Pos	Driver	Team	Chassis-Engine	Result	Qual
R	Bruce McLaren	McLaren	McLaren-Ford Cosworth M7A	0 laps/accident	7
R	Jackie Oliver	Lotus	Lotus-Ford Cosworth 49	0 laps/accident	13
DNQ	Jo Bonnier	Ecurie Bonnier	McLaren-BRM M5A	not seeded	15
DNQ	Silvio Moser	Charles Vogele Racing	Brabham-Repco BT20	not seeded	16

Pole: Hill, 1m28.200s, 79.763mph/128.367kph. Fastest lap: Attwood, 1m28.100s, 79.854mph/128.513kph on Lap 80. Race leaders: Servoz-Gavin 1-3; Hill 4-80

BROKEN WRIST, NO PROBLEM

Jackie Stewart had to miss the second and third rounds after breaking a wrist in an accident in an F2 race, but he hit the winning trail for Matra in the second race after his return. This was at the Dutch GP, but he then exceeded that by winning the German GP by four minutes in a race made perilous by rain and fog to rank second overall.

BELGIAN GRAND PRIX

SPA-FRANCORCHAMPS • ROUND 4 • DATE: 9TH JUNE 1968
Laps: 28 • Distance: 244.825miles/394.8km • Weather: Warm but dull

Pos	Driver	Team	Chassis-Engine	Result	Qual
1	Bruce McLaren	McLaren	McLaren-Ford Cosworth M7A	1h40m02.100s	6
2	Pedro Rodriguez	BRM	BRM P133	1h40m14.200s	8
3	Jacky Ickx	Ferrari	Ferrari 312	1h40m41.700s	3
4	Jackie Stewart	Tyrrell	Matra-Ford Cosworth MS10	27 laps/out of fuel	2
5	Jackie Oliver	Lotus	Lotus-Ford Cosworth 49B	26 laps/transmission	15
6	Lucien Bianchi	Cooper	Cooper-BRM T86B	26 laps	12
7	Jo Siffert	Rob Walker Racing Team	Lotus-Ford Cosworth 49	25 laps/fuel pressure	9
8	Jean-Pierre Beltoise	Matra	Matra MS11	25 laps	13
R	Piers Courage	Reg Parnell Racing	BRM P126	22 laps/engine	7
R	Denny Hulme	McLaren	McLaren-Ford Cosworth M7A	18 laps/halfshaft	5
R	John Surtees	Honda	Honda RA301	11 laps/suspension	4
R	Chris Amon	Ferrari	Ferrari 312	8 laps/radiator damage	1
R	Jack Brabham	Brabham	Brabham-Repco BT26	6 laps/throttle	10
R	Brian Redman	Cooper	Cooper-BRM T86B	6 laps/spun off	10
R	Richard Attwood	BRM	BRM P126	6 laps/oil line	11
R	Graham Hill	Lotus	Lotus-Ford Cosworth 49B	5 laps/halfshaft	14
R	Jochen Rindt	Brabham	Brabham-Repco BT26	5 laps/engine	17
R	Jo Bonnier	Ecurie Bonnier	McLaren-BRM M5A	1 lap/wheel	16

Pole: Amon, 3m28.600s, 151.202mph/243.336kph. Fastest lap: Surtees, 3m30.500s, 149.837mph/241.140kph on Lap 6. Race leaders: Amon 1; Surtees 2-10; Hulme 11 & 15; Stewart 12-14 & 16-27; McLaren 28

TO FINISH FIRST...

...first you must finish. This is an old racing adage that Johnny Servoz-Gavin ought to have considered as he hared clear in the opening laps of the Monaco GP in a Tyrrell-run Matra made available by Stewart's injury. The French ace rocketed clear and kept pulling away from Hill until he thumped a barrier on lap four and broke the driveshaft.

DUTCH GRAND PRIX

ZANDVOORT • ROUND 5 • DATE: 23RD JUNE 1968
Laps: 90 • Distance: 234.279miles/377.37km • Weather: Warm with heavy rain

Pos	Driver	Team	Chassis-Engine	Result	Qual
1	Jackie Stewart	Tyrrell	Matra-Ford Cosworth MS10	2h46m11.200s	5
2	Jean-Pierre Beltoise	Matra	Matra MS11	2h47m45.130s	16
3	Pedro Rodriguez	BRM	BRM P133	89 laps	11
4	Jacky Ickx	Ferrari	Ferrari 312	88 laps	6
5	Silvio Moser	Charles Vogele Racing	Brabham-Repco BT20	87 laps	7
6	Chris Amon	Ferrari	Ferrari 312	85 laps	1
7	Richard Attwood	BRM	BRM P126	85 laps	15
8	Jo Bonnier	Ecurie Bonnier	McLaren-BRM M5A	82 laps	19
9	Graham Hill	Lotus	Lotus-Ford Cosworth 49B	81 laps/accident	3
NC	Jackie Oliver	Lotus	Lotus-Ford Cosworth 49B	80 laps/not classified	10
R	Dan Gurney	Brabham	Brabham-Repco BT24	63 laps/throttle	12
R	Jo Siffert	Rob Walker Racing Team	Lotus-Ford Cosworth 49	55 laps/gearbox	13
R	John Surtees	Honda	Honda RA301	50 laps/alternator	9
R	Piers Courage	Reg Parnell Racing	BRM P126	50 laps/spun off	14
R	Jochen Rindt	Brabham	Brabham-Repco BT26	39 laps/ignition	2
R	Jack Brabham	Brabham	Brabham-Repco BT26	22 laps/spun off	4
R	Bruce McLaren	McLaren	McLaren-Ford Cosworth M7A	19 laps/accident	8
R	Denny Hulme	McLaren	McLaren-Ford Cosworth M7A	10 laps/ignition	7
R	Lucien Bianchi	Cooper	Cooper-BRM T86B	9 laps/accident	18

Pole: Amon, 1m23.540s, 112.275mph/180.689kph. Fastest lap: Beltoise, 1m45.910s, 88.560mph/142.524kph on Lap 6. Race leaders: Hill 1-3; Stewart 4-90

FRENCH GRAND PRIX

ROUEN-LES-ESSARTS • ROUND 6 • DATE: 7TH JULY 1968
Laps: 60 • Distance: 243.609miles/392.52km • Weather: Warm but wet

Pos	Driver	Team	Chassis-Engine	Result	Qual
1	Jacky Ickx	Ferrari	Ferrari 312	2h25m40.900s	3
2	John Surtees	Honda	Honda RA301	2h27m39.500s	7
3	Jackie Stewart	Tyrrell	Matra-Ford Cosworth MS10	59 laps	2
4	Vic Elford	Cooper	Cooper-BRM T86B	58 laps	17
5	Denny Hulme	McLaren	McLaren-Ford Cosworth M7A	58 laps	4
6	Piers Courage	Reg Parnell Racing	BRM P126	57 laps	14
7	Richard Attwood	BRM	BRM P126	57 laps	12
8	Bruce McLaren	McLaren	McLaren-Ford Cosworth M7A	56 laps	6
9	Jean-Pierre Beltoise	Matra	Matra MS11	56 laps	8
10	Chris Amon	Ferrari	Ferrari 312	55 laps	5
11	Jo Siffert	Rob Walker Racing Team	Lotus-Ford Cosworth 49	54 laps	11
NC	Pedro Rodriguez	BRM	BRM P133	53 laps/not classified	10
R	Jochen Rindt	Brabham	Brabham-Repco BT26	45 laps/oil leak	1
R	Jack Brabham	Brabham	Brabham-Repco BT26	15 laps/fuel pump	13
R	Graham Hill	Lotus	Lotus-Ford Cosworth 49B	14 laps/halfshaft	9
R	Johnny Servoz-Gavin	Cooper	Cooper-BRM T86B	14 laps/accident	15
R	Jo Schlesser	Honda	Honda RA302	2 laps/accident	16
NS	Jackie Oliver	Lotus	Lotus-Ford Cosworth 49B	accident	11

Pole: Rindt, 1m56.100s, 126.046mph/202.852kph. Fastest lap: Rodriguez, 2m11.500s, 111.285mph/179.096kph on Lap 19. Race leaders: Ickx 1-18 & 20-60; Rodriguez 19

BRITISH GRAND PRIX

BRANDS HATCH • ROUND 7 • DATE: 20TH JULY 1968
Laps: 80 • Distance: 212.1miles/341.184km • Weather: Warm & bright

Pos	Driver	Team	Chassis-Engine	Result	Qual
1	Jo Siffert	Rob Walker Racing Team	Lotus-Ford Cosworth 49B	2h01m20.300s	4
2	Chris Amon	Ferrari	Ferrari 312	2h01m24.700s	3
3	Jacky Ickx	Ferrari	Ferrari 312	79 laps	12
4	Denny Hulme	McLaren	McLaren-Ford Cosworth M7A	79 laps	11
5	John Surtees	Honda	Honda RA301	78 laps	9
6	Jackie Stewart	Tyrrell	Matra-Ford Cosworth MS10	78 laps	7
7	Bruce McLaren	McLaren	McLaren-Ford Cosworth M7A	77 laps	10
8	Piers Courage	Reg Parnell Racing	BRM P126	72 laps	16
R	Jochen Rindt	Brabham	Brabham-Repco BT26	55 laps/oil leak	5
R	Pedro Rodriguez	BRM	BRM P133	52 laps/engine	13
NC	Silvio Moser	Charles Vogele Racing	Brabham-Repco BT20	52 laps/not classified	19
R	Jackie Oliver	Lotus	Lotus-Ford Cosworth 49B	43 laps/transmission	2
R	Robin Widdows	Cooper	Cooper-BRM T86B	34 laps/ignition	18
R	Graham Hill	Lotus	Lotus-Ford Cosworth 49B	26 laps/halfshaft	1
R	Vic Elford	Cooper	Cooper-BRM T86B	26 laps/engine	7
R	Jean-Pierre Beltoise	Matra	Matra MS11	11 laps/engine	14
R	Richard Attwood	BRM	BRM P126	10 laps/radiator damage	15
R	Dan Gurney	Anglo American Racers	Eagle-Weslake T1G	8 laps/fuel pump	6
R	Jo Bonnier	Ecurie Bonnier	McLaren-BRM M5A	6 laps/engine	20
R	Jack Brabham	Brabham	Brabham-Repco BT26	0 laps/engine	8

Pole: Hill, 1m28.900s, 107.312mph/172.702kph. Fastest lap: Siffert, 1m29.700s, 106.355mph/171.162kph on Lap 42. Race leaders: Oliver 1-3 & 27-43; Hill 4-26; Surtees 44-80

THE FINAL PRIVATEER VICTORY

Jo Siffert made history when he won the British GP at Brands Hatch in his Rob Walker Racing-run Lotus, as this would be the final World Championship win for a privateer entry. The Swiss driver followed the works Lotuses in the early stages, but they both retired and that left Siffert to fend off Ferrari's Chris Amon.

GERMAN GRAND PRIX

NURBURGRING • ROUND 8 • DATE: 4TH AUGUST 1968
Laps: 14 • Distance: 198.260miles/319.69km • Weather: Foggy with heavy rain

Pos	Driver	Team	Chassis-Engine	Result	Qual
1	Jackie Stewart	Tyrrell	Matra-Ford Cosworth MS10	2h19m03.200s	6
2	Graham Hill	Lotus	Lotus-Ford Cosworth 49B	2h23m06.400s	4
3	Jochen Rindt	Brabham	Brabham-Repco BT26	2h23m12.600s	3
4	Jacky Ickx	Ferrari	Ferrari 312	2h24m58.400s	1
5	Jack Brabham	Brabham	Brabham-Repco BT26	2h25m24.300s	15
6	Pedro Rodriguez	BRM	BRM P133	2h25m28.200s	14
7	Denny Hulme	McLaren	McLaren-Ford Cosworth M7A	2h25m34.200s	11
8	Piers Courage	Reg Parnell Racing	BRM P126	2h26m59.600s	8
9	Dan Gurney	Anglo American Racers	Eagle-Weslake T1G	2h27m16.900s	10

Pos	Driver	Team	Chassis-Engine	Result	Qual
10	Hubert Hahne	BMW	Lola-BMW T102/F2	2h29m14.600s	18
11	Jackie Oliver	Lotus	Lotus-Ford Cosworth 49B	13 laps	13
12	Kurt Ahrens	Caltex Racing Team	Brabham-Repco BT24	13 laps	17
13	Bruce McLaren	McLaren	McLaren-Ford Cosworth M7A	13 laps	16
14	Richard Attwood	BRM	BRM P126	13 laps	20
R	Chris Amon	Ferrari	Ferrari 312	11 laps/accident	2
R	Jean-Pierre Beltoise	Matra	Matra MS11	8 laps/accident	12
R	Jo Siffert	Rob Walker Racing Team	Lotus-Ford Cosworth 49B	6 laps/ignition	9
R	Lucien Bianchi	Cooper	Cooper-BRM T86B	6 laps/oil leak	19
R	John Surtees	Honda	Honda RA301	3 laps/ignition	7
R	Vic Elford	Cooper	Cooper-BRM T86B	0 laps/accident	5
DNQ	Silvio Moser	Charles Vogele Racing	Brabham-Repco BT20	oil pump	-

Pole: Ickx, 9m04.000s, 93.897mph/151.113kph. Fastest lap: Stewart, 9m36.000s, 88.680mph/142.718kph on Lap 8. Race leaders: Stewart 1-14

NEW CIRCUITS

The World Championship added a couple more circuits to its roster, starting with the Jarama circuit outside Madrid, which was chosen for the first Spanish GP since 1954. Then the second World Championship Canadian GP was moved to the hilly Mont Tremblant circuit at St Jovite, 113km (70 miles) north-west of Montreal, but this was the first of only two visits.

NEW DRIVERS

Incredibly, among the 11 drivers who made their F1 debuts in 1968 were future world champion Mario Andretti, multiple Le Mans 24 Hours winners Derek Bell and Henri Pescarolo, two-time Indycar champion Bobby Unser, and the winner of that year's Monte Carlo Rally, Vic Elford.

ITALIAN GRAND PRIX

MONZA • ROUND 9 • DATE: 8TH SEPTEMBER 1968
Laps: 68 • Distance: 242.956miles/391.0km • Weather: Hot & bright

Pos	Driver	Team	Chassis-Engine	Result	Qual
1	Denny Hulme	McLaren	McLaren-Ford Cosworth M7A	1h40m14.800s	7
2	Johnny Servoz-Gavin	Tyrrell	Matra-Ford Cosworth MS10	1h41m43.200s	13
3	Jacky Ickx	Ferrari	Ferrari 312	1h41m43.400s	4
4	Piers Courage	Reg Parnell Racing	BRM P126	67 laps	17
5	Jean-Pierre Beltoise	Matra	Matra MS11	66 laps	18
6	Jo Bonnier	Ecurie Bonnier	McLaren-BRM M5A	64 laps	19
R	Jo Siffert	Rob Walker Racing Team	Lotus-Ford Cosworth 49B	58 laps/suspension	9
R	Jack Brabham	Brabham	Brabham-Repco BT26	56 laps/fuel pressure	16
R	Jackie Stewart	Tyrrell	Matra-Ford Cosworth MS10	42 laps/engine	6
R	David Hobbs	Honda	Honda RA301	42 laps/engine	14
R	Jackie Oliver	Lotus	Lotus-Ford Cosworth 49B	38 laps/transmission	11

Pos	Driver	Team	Chassis-Engine	Result	Qual
R	Bruce McLaren	McLaren	McLaren-Ford Cosworth M7A	34 laps/oil leak	2
R	Jochen Rindt	Brabham	Brabham-Repco BT26	33 laps/engine	10
R	Pedro Rodriguez	BRM	BRM P138	22 laps/engine	15
R	Dan Gurney	Anglo American Racers	Eagle-Weslake T1G	19 laps/engine	12
R	Graham Hill	Lotus	Lotus-Ford Cosworth 49B	10 laps/wheel	5
R	John Surtees	Honda	Honda RA301	8 laps/accident	1
R	Chris Amon	Ferrari	Ferrari 312	8 laps/accident	3
R	Derek Bell	Ferrari	Ferrari 312	4 laps/fuel system	8
R	Vic Elford	Cooper	Cooper-BRM T86B	2 laps/accident	20
EX	Mario Andretti	Lotus	Lotus-Ford Cosworth 49B	raced in USA	11
EX	Bobby Unser	BRM	BRM P126	raced in USA	20
DNQ	Frank Gardner	Bernard White Racing	BRM P261	-	23
DNQ	Silvio Moser	Charles Vogele Racing	Brabham-Repco BT20	-	24

Pole: Surtees, 1m26.070s, 149.440mph/240.501kph. Fastest lap: Oliver, 1m26.500s, 148.694mph/239.300kph on Lap 7. Race leaders: McLaren 1-6, 8-12 & 14; Surtees 7; Stewart 13, 17-18, 27, 30, 33 & 40; Siffert 15-16; Hulme 19-26, 28-29, 31-32, 34-39 & 41-68

CANADIAN GRAND PRIX

ST JOVITE • ROUND 10 • DATE: 22ND SEPTEMBER 1968
Laps: 90 • Distance: 238.37miles/383.85km • Weather: Warm & bright

Pos	Driver	Team	Chassis-Engine	Result	Qual
1	Denny Hulme	McLaren	McLaren-Ford Cosworth M7A	2h27m11.200s	6
2	Bruce McLaren	McLaren	McLaren-Ford Cosworth M7A	89 laps	8
3	Pedro Rodriguez	BRM	BRM P133	88 laps	12
4	Graham Hill	Lotus	Lotus-Ford Cosworth 49B	86 laps	5
5	Vic Elford	Cooper	Cooper-BRM T86B	86 laps	16
6	Jackie Stewart	Tyrrell	Matra-Ford Cosworth MS10	83 laps	11
R	Jean-Pierre Beltoise	Matra	Matra MS11	77 laps/gearbox	15
R	Chris Amon	Ferrari	Ferrari 312	72 laps/transmission	2
R	Johnny Servoz-Gavin	Tyrrell	Matra-Ford Cosworth MS10	71 laps/accident	13
NC	Lucien Bianchi	Cooper	Cooper-BRM T86B	56 laps/not classified	18
R	Henri Pescarolo	Matra	Matra MS11	54 laps/fuel pressure	19
R	Jochen Rindt	Brabham	Brabham-Repco BT26	39 laps/engine	1
R	Jackie Oliver	Lotus	Lotus-Ford Cosworth 49B	32 laps/halfshaft	19
R	Jack Brabham	Brabham	Brabham-Repco BT26	31 laps/suspension	10
R	Jo Siffert	Rob Walker Racing Team	Lotus-Ford Cosworth 49B	29 laps/oil leak	3
R	Dan Gurney	Anglo American Racers	McLaren-Ford Cosworth M7A	29 laps/radiator damage	4
R	Piers Courage	Reg Parnell Racing	BRM P126	22 laps/gearbox	14
R	Bill Brack	Lotus	Lotus-Ford Cosworth 49	18 laps/halfshaft	20
R	John Surtees	Honda	Honda RA301	10 laps/gearbox	7
R	Jo Bonnier	Ecurie Bonnier	McLaren-BRM M5A	0 laps/fuel system	17
NS	Jacky Ickx	Ferrari	Ferrari 312	driver injured	14
NS	Al Pease	Castrol Oils Ltd	Eagle-Climax T1G	engine	22

Pole: Rindt, 1m33.800s, 101.711mph/163.688kph. Fastest lap: Siffert, 1m35.100s, 100.321mph/161.451kph on lap 22. Race leaders: Amon 1-72; Hulme 73-90

IN MEMORIAM

In addition to Jim Clark's death, 1968 marked the end for Mike Spence who took over the injured Stewart's Indy 500 drive, and crashed in practice. A month later, this was followed by 1966 Italian GP winner Ludovico Scarfiotti crashing fatally in a hillclimb. Jo Schlesser burned to death when he crashed his Honda in the French GP.

UNITED STATES GRAND PRIX

WATKINS GLEN • ROUND 11 • DATE: 6TH OCTOBER 1968
Laps: 108 • Distance: 248.400miles/399.762km • Weather: Warm but dull

Pos	Driver	Team	Chassis-Engine	Result	Qual
1	Jackie Stewart	Tyrrell	Matra-Ford Cosworth MS10	1h59m20.290s	2
2	Graham Hill	Lotus	Lotus-Ford Cosworth 49B	1h59m44.970s	3
3	John Surtees	Honda	Honda RA301	107 laps	9
4	Dan Gurney	Anglo American Racers	McLaren-Ford Cosworth M7A	107 laps	7
5	Jo Siffert	Rob Walker Racing Team	Lotus-Ford Cosworth 49B	105 laps	12
6	Bruce McLaren	McLaren	McLaren-Ford Cosworth M7A	103 laps	10
R	Piers Courage	Reg Parnell Racing	BRM P126	93 laps/out of fuel	14
R	Denny Hulme	McLaren	McLaren-Ford Cosworth M7A	92 laps/accident	5
NC	Lucien Bianchi	Cooper	Cooper-BRM T86B	88 laps	20
R	Jack Brabham	Brabham	Brabham-Repco BT26	77 laps/engine	8
R	Jochen Rindt	Brabham	Brabham-Repco BT26	73 laps/engine	6
R	Vic Elford	Cooper	Cooper-BRM T86B	71 laps/engine	17
R	Pedro Rodriguez	BRM	BRM P133	66 laps/suspension	11
NC	Jo Bonnier	Ecurie Bonnier	McLaren-BRM M5A	62 laps/not classified	18
R	Chris Amon	Ferrari	Ferrari 312	59 laps/mechanical	4
R	Jean-Pierre Beltoise	Matra	Matra MS11	44 laps/transmission	13
R	Bobby Unser	BRM	BRM P138	35 laps/engine	19
R	Mario Andretti	Lotus	Lotus-Ford Cosworth 49B	32 laps/clutch	1
R	Derek Bell	Ferrari	Ferrari 312	14 laps/engine	15
NS	Jackie Oliver	Lotus	Lotus-Ford Cosworth 49B	accident	16
NS	Henri Pescarolo	Matra	Matra MS11	engine	21

Pole: Andretti, 1m04.200s, 128.972mph/207.560kph. Fastest lap: Stewart, 1m05.220s, 126.954mph/204.314kph on Lap 52. Race leaders: Stewart 1-108

MEXICAN GRAND PRIX

MEXICO CITY • ROUND 12 • DATE: 3RD NOVEMBER 1968
Laps: 65 • Distance: 201.945miles/325.0km • Weather: Warm & bright

Pos	Driver	Team	Chassis-Engine	Result	Qual
1	Graham Hill	Lotus	Lotus-Ford Cosworth 49B	1h56m43.950s	3
2	Bruce McLaren	McLaren	McLaren-Ford Cosworth M7A	1h58m03.270s	9
3	Jackie Oliver	Lotus	Lotus-Ford Cosworth 49B	1h58m24.600s	14
4	Pedro Rodriguez	BRM	BRM P133	1h58m25.040s	12
5	Jo Bonnier	Ecurie Bonnier	Honda RA301	64 laps	18
6	Jo Siffert	Rob Walker Racing Team	Lotus-Ford Cosworth 49B	64 laps	1
7	Jackie Stewart	Tyrrell	Matra-Ford Cosworth MS10	64 laps	7
8	Vic Elford	Cooper	Cooper-BRM T86B	63 laps	17

Pos	Driver	Team	Chassis-Engine	Result	Qual
9	Henri Pescarolo	Matra	Matra MS11	62 laps	20
10	Jack Brabham	Brabham	Brabham-Repco BT26	59 laps/fuel pressure	8
R	Johnny Servoz-Gavin	Tyrrell	Matra-Ford Cosworth MS10	57 laps/ignition	16
R	Dan Gurney	Anglo American Racers	McLaren-Ford Cosworth M7A	28 laps/suspension	5
R	Piers Courage	Reg Parnell Racing	BRM P126	25 laps/engine	19
R	Lucien Bianchi	Cooper	Cooper-BRM T86B	21 laps/engine	21
R	John Surtees	Honda	Honda RA301	17 laps/overheating	6
R	Chris Amon	Ferrari	Ferrari 312	16 laps/transmission	2
R	Moises Solana	Lotus	Lotus-Ford Cosworth 49	14 laps/wing	11
R	Denny Hulme	McLaren	McLaren-Ford Cosworth M7A	10 laps/suspension	4
R	Jean-Pierre Beltoise	Matra	Matra MS11	10 laps/suspension	13
R	Jacky Ickx	Ferrari	Ferrari 312	3 laps/ignition	15
R	Jochen Rindt	Brabham	Brabham-Repco BT26	2 laps/ignition	10

Pole: Siffert, 1m45.220s, 106.298mph/171.070kph. Fastest lap: Siffert, 1m44.230s, 107.307mph/172.695kph on Lap 52. Race leaders: Hill 1-4, 9-21 & 25-26; Stewart 5-8; Siffert 22-24

CLASSIC CAR: LOTUS 49

The Lotus 49 first hit the track with the arrival of the Ford Cosworth DFV engine in 1967, winning first time out, and it would go on to win 11 more races across the next three seasons. Designed by Colin Chapman and aerodynamicist Maurice Phillippe, its simple cigar tube shape took packaging to a new level as the engine was used as part of the chassis and had the suspension mounted directly onto it, adding rigidity and saving weight. The 49, through its 49B and 49C derivatives, became ever-more augmented by wings, both front and back, as Lotus developed its wedge-shaped 72.

WORLD DRIVERS' CHAMPIONSHIP FINAL RESULTS

Pos	Driver	Nat	Car-Engine	R1	R2	R3	R4
1	Graham Hill	GBR	Lotus-Ford Cosworth 49	2	1	-	-
			Lotus-Ford Cosworth 49B	-	-	1P	R
2	Jackie Stewart	GBR	Matra-Ford Cosworth MS9	R	-	-	-
			Matra-Ford Cosworth MS10	-	-	-	4
3	Denny Hulme	NZL	McLaren-BRM M5A	5	-	-	-
			McLaren-Ford Cosworth M7A	-	2	5	R
4	Jacky Ickx	BEL	Ferrari 312	R	R	-	3
5	Bruce McLaren	NZL	McLaren-Ford Cosworth M7A	-	R	R	1
6	Pedro Rodriguez	MEX	BRM P126	R	-	-	-
			BRM P133	-	R	R	2
			BRM P138	-	-	-	-
7	Jo Siffert	CHE	Cooper-Maserati T81	7	-	-	-
			Lotus-Ford Cosworth 49	-	R	R	7
			Lotus-Ford Cosworth 49B	-	-	-	-
8	John Surtees	GBR	Honda RA301	8	R	R	RF
9	Jean-Pierre Beltoise	FRA	Matra-Ford MS7/F2	6	-	-	-
			Matra-Ford Cosworth MS10	-	5F	-	-
			Matra MS11	-	-	R	8
10	Chris Amon	NZL	Ferrari 312	4	RP	-	RP

Pos	Driver	Nat	Car-Engine	R1	R2	R3	R4
11	Jim Clark	GBR	Lotus-Ford Cosworth 49	1PF	-	-	-
12	Jochen Rindt	AUT	Brabham-Repco BT24	3	R	R	-
			Brabham-Repco BT26	-	-	-	R
13	Richard Attwood	GBR	BRM P126	-	-	2F	R
13	Johnny Servoz-Gavin	FRA	Matra-Ford Cosworth MS10	-	-	R	-
			Cooper-BRM T86B	-	-	-	-
15	Jackie Oliver	GBR	Lotus-Ford Cosworth 49	-	-	R	-
			Lotus-Ford Cosworth 49B	-	-	-	5
16	Ludovico Scarfiotti	ITA	Cooper-Maserati T86	R	-	-	-
			Cooper-BRM T86B	-	4	4	-
17	Lucien Bianchi	BEL	Cooper-BRM T86B	-	-	3	6
18	Vic Elford	GBR	Cooper-BRM T86B	-	-	-	-
19	Brian Redman	GBR	Cooper-Maserati T81B	R	-	-	-
			Cooper-BRM T86B	-	3	-	R
20	Piers Courage	GBR	BRM P126	-	R	R	R
21	Dan Gurney	USA	Eagle-Weslake T1G	R	-	R	-
			Brabham-Repco BT24	-	-	-	-
			McLaren-Ford Cosworth M7A	-	-	-	-
21	Jo Bonnier	SWE	McLaren-BRM M5A	R	-	DNQ	R
23	Silvio Moser	CHE	Brabham-Repco BT20	-	-	-	-
23	Jack Brabham	AUS	Brabham-Repco BT24	R	-	-	-
			Brabham-Repco BT26	-	-	R	R

Pos	Driver	R5	R6	R7	R8	R9	R10	R11	R12	Total
1	Hill	-	-	-	-	-	-	-	-	48
		9	R	RP	2	R	4	2	1	
2	Stewart	-	-	-	-	-	-	-	-	36
		1	3	6	1F	R	6	1F	7	
3	Hulme	-	-	-	-	-	-	-	-	33
		R	5	4	7	1	1	R	R	
4	Ickx	4	1	3	4P	3	NS	-	R	27
5	McLaren	R	8	7	13	R	2	6	2	22
6	Rodriguez	-	-	-	-	-	-	-	-	18
		3	NCF	R	6	-	3	R	4	
		-	-	-	-	R	-	-	-	
7	Siffert	-	-	-	-	-	-	-	-	12
		R	11	-	-	-	-	-	-	
		-	-	1F	R	R	RF	5	6PF	
8	Surtees	R	2	5	R	RP	R	3	R	12
9	Beltoise	-	-	-	-	-	-	-	-	11
		-	-	-	-	-	-	-	-	
		2F	9	R	R	5	R	R	R	
10	Amon	6P	10	2	R	R	RF	R	R	10
11	Clark	-	-	-	-	-	-	-	-	9
12	Rindt	-	-	-	-	-	-	-	-	8
		R	RP	R	3	R	RP	R	R	
13	Attwood	7	7	R	14	-	-	-	-	6
13	Servoz-Gavin	-	-	-	-	2	R	-	R	6
		-	R	-	-	-	-	-	-	
13	Oliver	-	-	-	-	-	-	-	-	6
		NC	NS	R	11	RF	R	NS	3	
13	Scarfiotti	-	-	-	-	-	-	-	-	6
		-	-	-	-	-	-	-	-	
17	Bianchi	R	-	-	R	-	NC	NC	R	5
17	Elford	-	4	R	R	R	5	R	8	5
19	Redman	-	-	-	-	-	-	-	-	4
		-	-	-	-	-	-	-	-	

Pos	Driver	R5	R6	R7	R8	R9	R10	R11	R12	Total
19	Courage	R	6	8	8	4	R	R	R	4
21	Gurney	-	-	R	9	R	-	-	-	3
		R	-	-	-	-	-	-	-	
		-	-	-	-	-	R	4	R	
21	Bonnier	8	-	R	-	6	R	NC	5	3
23	Moser	5	-	NC	-	DNQ	-	-	-	2
23	Brabham	-	-	-	-	-	-	-	-	2
		R	R	R	5	R	R	R	10	

WORLD CONSTRUCTORS' CHAMPIONSHIP FINAL RESULTS

Pos	Team-Engine	R1	R2	R3	R4	R5	R6	R7	R8	R9	R10	R11	R12	Total
1	Lotus-Ford	1	1	1	5	9	11	1	2		4	2	1	62
2	McLaren-Ford	-	2	5	1	-	5	4	7	1	1	6	2	49
3	Matra-Ford	6	-	-	4	1	3	6	1	2	6	1	7	45
4	Ferrari	4	-	-	3	4	1	2	4	3	-	-	-	32
5	BRM	-	-	2	2	3	6	8	6	4	3	-	4	28
6	Honda	8	-	-	-	-	2	5	-	-	-	3	-	14
6	Cooper-BRM	-	3	3	6	-	4	-	-	-	5	-	8	14
8	Brabham-Repco	3	-	-	-	5	-	-	3	-	-	-	10	10
9	Matra	-	5	-	8	2	9	-	-	5	-	-	9	8
10	McLaren-BRM	5	-	-	-	-	-	-	-	-	-	-	-	3

SYMBOLS AND GRAND PRIX KEY

Round 1 **South African GP**
Round 2 **Spanish GP**
Round 3 **Monaco GP**
Round 4 **Belgian GP**
Round 5 **Dutch GP**
Round 6 **French GP**
Round 7 **British GP**
Round 8 **German GP**
Round 9 **Italian GP**
Round 10 **Canadian GP**
Round 11 **United States GP**
Round 12 **Mexican GP**

SCORING

1st **9 points**
2nd **6 points**
3rd **4 points**
4th **3 points**
5th **2 points**
6th **1 point**

DNPQ DID NOT PRE-QUALIFY **DNQ DID NOT QUALIFY** **DQ DISQUALIFIED** **EX EXCLUDED**
F FASTEST LAP **NC NOT CLASSIFIED** **NS NON-STARTER** **P POLE POSITION** **R RETIRED**

1969

SEASON SUMMARY

Jackie Stewart claimed the first of his three F1 titles when he won six of the season's 11 grands prix in his nimble, Ford-powered Matra MS80. The Scot was a dominant champion, his feat all the more impressive as more of the teams gained a degree of parity by adopting Ford Cosworth DFV engines. It was also a year in which aerodynamic advancements had to be kept in check because of wing failures. There also seemed to be a changing of the guard, with Jacky Ickx making marked progress with Ferrari in his second full campaign to end the year as runner-up.

SOUTH AFRICAN GRAND PRIX

KYALAMI • ROUND 1 • DATE: 1ST MARCH 1969
Laps: 80 • Distance: 203.829miles/328.32km • Weather: Hot & bright

Pos	Driver	Team	Chassis-Engine	Result	Qual
1	Jackie Stewart	Tyrrell	Matra-Ford Cosworth MS10	1h50m39.100s	4
2	Graham Hill	Lotus	Lotus-Ford Cosworth 49B	1h50m57.900s	7
3	Denny Hulme	McLaren	McLaren-Ford Cosworth M7A	1h51m10.900s	3
4	Jo Siffert	Rob Walker Racing Team	Lotus-Ford Cosworth 49B	1h51m28.300s	12
5	Bruce McLaren	McLaren	McLaren-Ford Cosworth M7B	79 laps	8
6	Jean-Pierre Beltoise	Tyrrell	Matra-Ford Cosworth MS10	78 laps	11
7	Jackie Oliver	BRM	BRM P133	77 laps	14
8	Sam Tingle	Team Gunston	Brabham-Repco BT24	73 laps	17
NC	Piet de Klerk	Jack Holme	Brabham-Repco BT20	67 laps/not classified	16
R	Jochen Rindt	Lotus	Lotus-Ford Cosworth 49B	44 laps/fuel pump	2
R	John Surtees	BRM	BRM P138	40 laps/engine	18
R	Pedro Rodriguez	Reg Parnell Racing	BRM P126	38 laps/water leak	15
R	Chris Amon	Ferrari	Ferrari 312/69	34 laps/engine	5
R	Jack Brabham	Brabham	Brabham-Ford Cosworth BT26A	32 laps/handling	1
R	Mario Andretti	Lotus	Lotus-Ford Cosworth 49B	31 laps/gearbox	6
R	John Love	Team Gunston	Lotus-Ford Cosworth 49	31 laps/ignition	10
R	Jacky Ickx	Brabham	Brabham-Ford Cosworth BT26A	20 laps/ignition	13
R	Basil van Rooyen	Team Lawson	McLaren-Ford Cosworth M7A	12 laps/brakes	9

Pole: Brabham, 1m20.000s, 114.754mph/184.680kph. Fastest lap: Stewart, 1m21.600s, 112.530mph/181.100kph on Lap 50. Race leaders: Stewart 1-80

SPANISH GRAND PRIX

MONTJUICH PARK • ROUND 2 • DATE: 4TH MAY 1969
Laps: 90 • Distance: 211.888miles/341.1km • Weather: Warm & bright

Pos	Driver	Team	Chassis-Engine	Result	Qual
1	Jackie Stewart	Tyrrell	Matra-Ford Cosworth MS80	2h16m54.000s	4
2	Bruce McLaren	McLaren	McLaren-Ford Cosworth M7C	88 laps	13
3	Jean-Pierre Beltoise	Tyrrell	Matra-Ford Cosworth MS80	87 laps	12
4	Denny Hulme	McLaren	McLaren-Ford Cosworth M7A	87 laps	8
5	John Surtees	BRM	BRM P138	84 laps	9
6	Jacky Ickx	Brabham	Brabham-Ford Cosworth BT26A	83 laps/suspension	7
R	Pedro Rodriguez	Reg Parnell Racing	BRM P126	73 laps/engine	14
R	Chris Amon	Ferrari	Ferrari 312/69	56 laps/engine	2

Pos	Driver	Team	Chassis-Engine	Result	Qual
R	Jack Brabham	Brabham	Brabham-Ford Cosworth BT26A	51 laps/engine	5
R	Jo Siffert	Rob Walker Racing Team	Lotus-Ford Cosworth 49B	30 laps/oil leak	6
R	Jochen Rindt	Lotus	Lotus-Ford Cosworth 49B	19 laps/accident	1
R	Piers Courage	Frank Williams Racing Cars	Brabham-Ford Cosworth BT26A	18 laps/engine	11
R	Graham Hill	Lotus	Lotus-Ford Cosworth 49B	8 laps/accident	3
R	Jackie Oliver	BRM	BRM P133	1 lap/oil pipe	10

Pole: Rindt, 1m25.700s, 98.926mph/159.206kph. Fastest lap: Rindt, 1m28.300s, 96.001mph/154.500kph on Lap 15. Race leaders: Rindt 1-19; Amon 20-56; Stewart 57-90

PACE FIRST, RESULTS SECOND

Jochen Rindt was excited to join Lotus and get his hands on Cosworth DFV power after his 1968 campaign with Brabham was held back by his BT26's Repco engine. It didn't all go smoothly, though, and it was only after he started from his fifth pole of the year that he took his first win, this coming in the United States GP at Watkins Glen.

MONACO GRAND PRIX

MONTE CARLO • ROUND 3 • DATE: 18TH MAY 1969
Laps: 80 • Distance: 155.967miles/251.6km • Weather: Warm but dull

Pos	Driver	Team	Chassis-Engine	Result	Qual
1	Graham Hill	Lotus	Lotus-Ford Cosworth 49B	1h56m59.400s	4
2	Piers Courage	Frank Williams Racing Cars	Brabham-Ford Cosworth BT26A	1h57m16.700s	9
3	Jo Siffert	Rob Walker Racing Team	Lotus-Ford Cosworth 49B	1h57m34.000s	5
4	Richard Attwood	Lotus	Lotus-Ford Cosworth 49B	1h57m52.300s	10
5	Bruce McLaren	McLaren	McLaren-Ford Cosworth M7C	79 laps	11
6	Denny Hulme	McLaren	McLaren-Ford Cosworth M7A	78 laps	12
7	Vic Elford	Colin Crabbe Racing	Cooper-Maserati T86B	74 laps	16
R	Jacky Ickx	Brabham	Brabham-Ford Cosworth BT26A	48 laps/suspension	7
R	Jackie Stewart	Tyrrell	Matra-Ford Cosworth MS80	22 laps/halfshaft	1
R	Jean-Pierre Beltoise	Tyrrell	Matra-Ford Cosworth MS80	20 laps/halfshaft	3
R	Chris Amon	Ferrari	Ferrari 312/69	16 laps/differential	2
R	Pedro Rodriguez	Reg Parnell Racing	BRM P126	15 laps/engine	14
R	Silvio Moser	Silvio Moser Racing Team	Brabham-Ford Cosworth BT24	15 laps/halfshaft	15
R	John Surtees	BRM	BRM P138	9 laps/gearbox	6
R	Jack Brabham	Brabham	Brabham-Ford Cosworth BT26A	9 laps/accident	8
R	Jackie Oliver	BRM	BRM P133	0 laps/accident	13

Pole: Stewart, 1m24.600s, 83.157mph/133.829kph. Fastest lap: Stewart, 1m25.100s, 82.642mph/133.000kph on Lap 16. Race leaders: Stewart 1-22; Hill 23-80

ON A WING AND A PRAYER

One of the most dramatic races of 1968 came in the second round, the Spanish GP at Montjuich Park. Rindt led the early laps, then team-mate Graham Hill had a wing buckle as his Lotus crested a brow and hit the barriers. He noticed Rindt's wing was failing too, but couldn't warn him before it did and he crashed into Hill's car, breaking his own nose.

DUTCH GRAND PRIX

ZANDVOORT • ROUND 4 • DATE: 21ST JUNE 1969
Laps: 90 • Distance: 234.279miles/377.37km • Weather: Warm & bright

Pos	Driver	Team	Chassis-Engine	Result	Qual
1	Jackie Stewart	Tyrrell	Matra-Ford Cosworth MS80	2h06m42.080s	2
2	Jo Siffert	Rob Walker Racing Team	Lotus-Ford Cosworth 49B	2h07m06.600s	10
3	Chris Amon	Ferrari	Ferrari 312/69	2h07m12.590s	4
4	Denny Hulme	McLaren	McLaren-Ford Cosworth M7A	2h07m19.240s	7
5	Jacky Ickx	Brabham	Brabham-Ford Cosworth BT26A	2h07m19.750s	5
6	Jack Brabham	Brabham	Brabham-Ford Cosworth BT26A	2h07m52.890s	8
7	Graham Hill	Lotus	Lotus-Ford Cosworth 49B	88 laps	3
8	Jean-Pierre Beltoise	Tyrrell	Matra-Ford Cosworth MS80	87 laps	11
9	John Surtees	BRM	BRM P138	87 laps	12
10	Vic Elford	Colin Crabbe Racing	McLaren-Ford Cosworth M7B	84 laps	15
R	Silvio Moser	Silvio Moser Racing Team	Brabham-Ford Cosworth BT24	54 laps/ignition	14
R	Bruce McLaren	McLaren	McLaren-Ford Cosworth M7C	24 laps/suspension	6
R	Jochen Rindt	Lotus	Lotus-Ford Cosworth 49B	16 laps/halfshaft	1
R	Piers Courage	Frank Williams Racing Cars	Brabham-Ford Cosworth BT26A	12 laps/clutch	9
R	Jackie Oliver	BRM	BRM P133	9 laps/gearbox	13

Pole: Rindt, 1m20.850s, 116.010mph/186.701kph. Fastest lap: Stewart, 1m22.940s, 113.089mph/182.000kph on Lap 5. Race leaders: Hill 1-2; Rindt 3-16; Stewart 17-90

ALWAYS THE BRIDESMAID
Chris Amon was perpetually unlucky in F1. The New Zealander should have won many races, but was always denied. The Spanish GP was a typical example as he took the lead when the Lotuses ahead of him crashed out and was 45 seconds up on Jackie Stewart when his Ferrari's engine seized. Expecting that he might have to walk back to the pits, he kept a pack of cigarettes in his cockpit.

IT'S GOOD TO TALK
Rindt and Lotus boss Colin Chapman didn't always see eye-to-eye, often with the Austrian questioning the strength and reliability of his car, especially after he had to retire from the first three grands prix. When it looked as though he might not stay for 1970, they resolved their differences at the German GP.

FRENCH GRAND PRIX

CLERMONT-FERRAND • ROUND 5 • DATE: 6TH JULY 1969
Laps: 38 • Distance: 190.145miles/306.09km • Weather: Warm & bright

Pos	Driver	Team	Chassis-Engine	Result	Qual
1	Jackie Stewart	Tyrrell	Matra-Ford Cosworth MS80	1h56m47.400s	1
2	Jean-Pierre Beltoise	Tyrrell	Matra-Ford Cosworth MS80	1h57m44.500s	5
3	Jacky Ickx	Brabham	Brabham-Ford Cosworth BT26A	1h57m44.700s	4
4	Bruce McLaren	McLaren	McLaren-Ford Cosworth M7C	37 laps	7

Pos	Driver	Team	Chassis-Engine	Result	Qual
5	Vic Elford	Colin Crabbe Racing	McLaren-Ford Cosworth M7B	37 laps	10
6	Graham Hill	Lotus	Lotus-Ford Cosworth 49B	37 laps	8
7	Silvio Moser	Silvio Moser Racing Team	Brabham-Ford Cosworth BT24	36 laps	13
8	Denny Hulme	McLaren	McLaren-Ford Cosworth M7A	35 laps	2
9	Jo Siffert	Rob Walker Racing Team	Lotus-Ford Cosworth 49B	34 laps	9
R	Chris Amon	Ferrari	Ferrari 312/69	30 laps/engine	6
R	Jochen Rindt	Lotus	Lotus-Ford Cosworth 49B	22 laps/physical	3
R	Piers Courage	Frank Williams Racing Cars	Brabham-Ford Cosworth BT26A	21 laps/chassis	11
R	John Miles	Lotus	Lotus-Ford Cosworth 63	1 lap/fuel pump	12

Pole: Stewart, 3m00.600s, 99.770mph/160.564kph. Fastest lap: Stewart, 3m02.700s, 98.611mph/158.700kph on Lap 27. Race leaders: Stewart 1-38

THE RACE OF THE YEAR

The 1969 British GP was one of the great races as it pitched the two top drivers against each other, as Stewart took on Rindt. The latter led from pole, desperate to score his first points of the year, but Stewart lapped within a few feet of him for 60 laps, trading places until Rindt pitted as part of his rear wing was touching a tyre.

BRITISH GRAND PRIX

SILVERSTONE • ROUND 6 • DATE: 19TH JULY 1969
Laps: 84 • Distance: 245.865miles/395.682km • Weather: Warm but dull

Pos	Driver	Team	Chassis-Engine	Result	Qual
1	Jackie Stewart	Tyrrell	Matra-Ford Cosworth MS80	1h55m55.600s	2
2	Jacky Ickx	Brabham	Brabham-Ford Cosworth BT26A	83 laps	4
3	Bruce McLaren	McLaren	McLaren-Ford Cosworth M7C	83 laps	7
4	Jochen Rindt	Lotus	Lotus-Ford Cosworth 49B	83 laps	1
5	Piers Courage	Frank Williams Racing Cars	Brabham-Ford Cosworth BT26A	83 laps	10
6	Vic Elford	Colin Crabbe Racing	McLaren-Ford Cosworth M7B	82 laps	11
7	Graham Hill	Lotus	Lotus-Ford Cosworth 49B	82 laps	12
8	Jo Siffert	Rob Walker Racing Team	Lotus-Ford Cosworth 49B	81 laps	9
9	Jean-Pierre Beltoise	Tyrrell	Matra-Ford Cosworth MS84	78 laps	17
10	John Miles	Lotus	Lotus-Ford Cosworth 63	75 laps	14
R	Pedro Rodriguez	Ferrari	Ferrari 312/69	61 laps/engine	8
R	Chris Amon	Ferrari	Ferrari 312/69	45 laps/gearbox	5
R	Denny Hulme	McLaren	McLaren-Ford Cosworth M7A	27 laps/ignition	3
R	Jackie Oliver	BRM	BRM P133	19 laps/transmission	13
R	Jo Bonnier	Ecurie Bonnier	Lotus-Ford Cosworth 63	6 laps/engine	16
R	Derek Bell	McLaren	McLaren-Ford Cosworth M9A	5 laps/suspension	15
R	John Surtees	BRM	BRM P139	1 lap/suspension	6

Pole: Rindt, 1m20.800s, 130.409mph/209.873kph. Fastest lap: Stewart, 1m21.300s, 129.618mph/208.600kph on Lap 57. Race leaders: Rindt 1-5 & 16-61; Stewart 6-15 & 62-84

TRACTION TROUBLES

Lotus was determined to get four-wheel drive to work in F1 and was keen for Rindt and Hill to race its Lotus 63 in the British GP, but neither reckoned that it would work so stuck with their Lotus 49s. Also at Silverstone, the Matra MS84 and McLaren M9A 4WD machines were similarly unloved, both also weighing far more than the 2WD cars.

GERMAN GRAND PRIX

NURBURGRING • ROUND 7 • DATE: 3RD AUGUST 1969
Laps: 14 • Distance: 198.260miles/319.69km • Weather: Warm & bright

Pos	Driver	Team	Chassis-Engine	Result	Qual
1	Jacky Ickx	Brabham	Brabham-Ford Cosworth BT26A	1h49m55.400s	1
2	Jackie Stewart	Tyrrell	Matra-Ford Cosworth MS80	1h50m53.100s	2
3	Bruce McLaren	McLaren	McLaren-Ford Cosworth M7C	1h53m17.000s	8
4	Graham Hill	Lotus	Lotus-Ford Cosworth 49B	1h53m54.200s	9
5	Henri Pescarolo	Matra	Matra-Ford MS7/F2	1h58m06.400s	13
6	Richard Attwood	Frank Williams Racing	Brabham-Ford BT30/F2	13 laps	20
7	Kurt Ahrens Jr	Ahrens Racing	Brabham-Ford BT30/F2	13 laps	19
8	Rolf Stommelen	Roy Winkelmann Racing	Lotus-Ford 59B/F2	13 laps	22
9	Peter Westbury	Felday Engineering	Brabham-Ford BT30/F2	13 laps	18
10	Xavier Perrot	Squadra Tartaruga	Brabham-Ford BT23C/F2	13 laps	24
11	Jo Siffert	Rob Walker Racing Team	Lotus-Ford Cosworth 49B	12 laps/suspension	4
12	Jean-Pierre Beltoise	Tyrrell	Matra-Ford Cosworth MS80	12 laps/suspension	10
R	Denny Hulme	McLaren	McLaren-Ford Cosworth M7A	11 laps/transmission	5
R	Jackie Oliver	BRM	BRM P138	11 laps/oil leak	16
R	Jochen Rindt	Lotus	Lotus-Ford Cosworth 49B	10 laps/ignition	3
R	Francois Cevert	Tecno	Tecno-Ford/F2	9 laps/crown wheel	14
R	Johmmy Servoz-Gavin	Matra	Matra-Ford MS7/F2	6 laps/engine	12
R	Jo Bonnier	Ecurie Bonnier	Lotus-Ford Cosworth 49B	4 laps/oil leak	23
R	Piers Courage	Frank Williams Racing Cars	Brabham-Ford Cosworth BT26A	1 lap/accident	7
R	Vic Elford	Colin Crabbe Racing	McLaren-Ford Cosworth M7B	0 laps/accident	6
R	Mario Andretti	Lotus	Lotus-Ford Cosworth 63	0 laps/accident	15
NS	John Surtees	BRM	BRM P139	suspension	11
NS	Hubert Hahne	BMW	BMW 269/F2	withdrew	17
NS	Dieter Quester	BMW	BMW 269/F2	withdrew	21
NS	Gerhard Mitter	BMW	BMW 269/F2	fatal accident	25
NS	Hans Herrmann	Roy Winkelmann Racing	Lotus-Ford 59B/F2	withdrew	-

Pole: Ickx, 7m42.100s, 110.539mph/177.896kph. Fastest lap: Ickx, 7m43.800s, 110.106mph/177.200kph on Lap 7. Race leaders: Stewart 1-6; Ickx 7-14

NEW CIRCUITS

Montjuich Park was the only circuit to make its World Championship bow in 1969. The undulating circuit was laid out on roads within Montjuich Park on a hilltop in Barcelona. It had first been used in 1933 before hosting a Barcelona GP for F2 cars from 1966 to 1968. Montjuich Park and Jarama would host the Spanish GP alternately until 1975.

ITALIAN GRAND PRIX

MONZA • ROUND 8 • DATE: 7TH SEPTEMBER 1969
Laps: 68 • Distance: 242.956miles/391.0km • Weather: Warm & bright

Pos	Driver	Team	Chassis-Engine	Result	Qual
1	Jackie Stewart	Tyrrell	Matra-Ford Cosworth MS80	1h39m11.260s	3
2	Jochen Rindt	Lotus	Lotus-Ford Cosworth 49B	1h39m11.340s	1
3	Jean-Pierre Beltoise	Tyrrell	Matra-Ford Cosworth MS80	1h39m11.430s	6
4	Bruce McLaren	McLaren	McLaren-Ford Cosworth M7C	1h39m11.450s	5
5	Piers Courage	Frank Williams Racing Cars	Brabham-Ford Cosworth BT26A	1h39m44.700s	4
6	Pedro Rodriguez	Ferrari	Ferrari 312/69	66 laps	12
7	Denny Hulme	McLaren	McLaren-Ford Cosworth M7A	66 laps	2
8	Jo Siffert	Rob Walker Racing Team	Lotus-Ford Cosworth 49B	64 laps/engine	8
9	Graham Hill	Lotus	Lotus-Ford Cosworth 49B	63 laps	9
10	Jacky Ickx	Brabham	Brabham-Ford Cosworth BT26A	61 laps/out of fuel	15
NC	John Surtees	BRM	BRM P139	60 laps/not classified	10
R	Jackie Oliver	BRM	BRM P133	48 laps/fuel pressure	11
R	Silvio Moser	Silvio Moser Racing Team	Brabham-Ford Cosworth BT24	9 laps/oil leak	13
R	Jack Brabham	Brabham	Brabham-Ford Cosworth BT26A	6 laps/oil leak	7
R	John Miles	Lotus	Lotus-Ford Cosworth 63	3 laps/engine	14
NS	Ernesto Brambilla	Ferrari	Ferrari 312/69	Rodriguez drove car	-

Pole: Rindt, 1m25.480s, 150.472mph/242.161kph. Fastest lap: Beltoise, 1m25.200s, 150.993mph/243.000kph on Lap 64. Race leaders: Stewart 1-6, 9-17, 19-24, 28-30, 33, 35-36 & 38-68; Rindt 7, 25-27, 31, 34 & 37; Hulme 8; Courage 18 & 32

CANADIAN GRAND PRIX

MOSPORT PARK • ROUND 9 • DATE: 20TH SEPTEMBER 1969
Laps: 90 • Distance: 221.216miles/356.13km • Weather: Warm & bright

Pos	Driver	Team	Chassis-Engine	Result	Qual
1	Jacky Ickx	Brabham	Brabham-Ford Cosworth BT26A	1h59m25.700s	1
2	Jack Brabham	Brabham	Brabham-Ford Cosworth BT26A	2h00m11.900s	6
3	Jochen Rindt	Lotus	Lotus-Ford Cosworth 49B	2h00m17.700s	3
4	Jean-Pierre Beltoise	Tyrrell	Matra-Ford Cosworth MS80	89 laps	2
5	Bruce McLaren	McLaren	McLaren-Ford Cosworth M7C	87 laps	9
6	Johnny Servoz-Gavin	Tyrrell	Matra-Ford Cosworth MS84	84 laps	15
7	Pete Lovely	Pete Lovely Volkswagen Inc	Lotus-Ford Cosworth 49B	81 laps	16
NC	Bill Brack	BRM	BRM P138	80 laps/not classified	18
R	Graham Hill	Lotus	Lotus-Ford Cosworth 49B	42 laps/engine	7
R	Jo Siffert	Rob Walker Racing Team	Lotus-Ford Cosworth 49B	40 laps/halfshaft	8
R	John Miles	Lotus	Lotus-Ford Cosworth 63	40 laps/gearbox	11
R	Pedro Rodriguez	Ferrari	Ferrari 312/69	37 laps/fuel pressure	13
R	Jackie Stewart	Tyrrell	Matra-Ford Cosworth MS80	32 laps/collision	4
DQ	Al Pease	John Maryon	Eagle-Climax T1G	22 laps/too slow	17
R	John Surtees	BRM	BRM P139	15 laps/engine	14
R	Piers Courage	Frank Williams Racing Cars	Brabham-Ford Cosworth BT26A	13 laps/oil leak	10
R	John Cordts	Paul Seitz	Brabham-Climax BT23B	10 laps/oil leak	19
R	Denny Hulme	McLaren	McLaren-Ford Cosworth M7A	9 laps/mechanical	5
R	Jackie Oliver	BRM	BRM P139	2 laps/engine	12
R	Silvio Moser	Silvio Moser Racing Team	Brabham-Ford Cosworth BT24	0 laps/accident	20

Pole: Ickx, 1m17.400s, 114.361mph/184.046kph. Fastest lap: Brabham, 1m18.100s, 113.338mph/182.400kph on lap 62 & Ickx, 1m18.100s, 113.338mph/182.400kph on Lap 30. Race leaders: Rindt 1-5; Stewart 6-32; Ickx 33-90

NEW CONSTRUCTOR

Tecno was new in F1 in 1969. Formed by brothers Luciano and Gianfranco Pederzani as a company to build racing karts, Tecno started building F3 cars in 1966. It was with its F2 car that it joined the World Championship, entering one for Francois Cevert in the German GP. Its F1 cars followed from 1971.

UNITED STATES GRAND PRIX

WATKINS GLEN • ROUND 10 • DATE: 5TH OCTOBER 1969
Laps: 108 • Distance: 248.400miles/399.762km • Weather: Hot & bright

Pos	Driver	Team	Chassis-Engine	Result	Qual
1	Jochen Rindt	Lotus	Lotus-Ford Cosworth 49B	1h57m56.840s	1
2	Piers Courage	Frank Williams Racing Cars	Brabham-Ford Cosworth BT26A	1h58m43.830s	9
3	John Surtees	BRM	BRM P139	106 laps	11
4	Jack Brabham	Brabham	Brabham-Ford Cosworth BT26A	106 laps	10
5	Pedro Rodriguez	Ferrari	Ferrari 312/69	101 laps	12
6	Silvio Moser	Silvio Moser Racing Team	Brabham-Ford Cosworth BT24	98 laps	17
NC	Johnny Servoz-Gavin	Tyrrell	Matra-Ford Cosworth MS84	92 laps/not classified	15
R	Graham Hill	Lotus	Lotus-Ford Cosworth 49B	90 laps/accident	4
R	Jacky Ickx	Brabham	Brabham-Ford Cosworth BT26A	77 laps/engine	8
R	George Eaton	BRM	BRM P138	76 laps/engine	9
R	Jean-Pierre Beltoise	Tyrrell	Matra-Ford Cosworth MS80	72 laps/engine	7
R	Denny Hulme	McLaren	McLaren-Ford Cosworth M7A	52 laps/gearbox	2
R	Jackie Stewart	Tyrrell	Matra-Ford Cosworth MS80	35 laps/engine	3
R	Pete Lovely	Pete Lovely Volkswagen Inc	Lotus-Ford Cosworth 49B	25 laps/halfshaft	16
R	Jackie Oliver	BRM	BRM P139	23 laps/engine	14
R	Mario Andretti	Lotus	Lotus-Ford Cosworth 63	3 laps/suspension	5
R	Jo Siffert	Rob Walker Racing Team	Lotus-Ford Cosworth 49B	3 laps/fuel system	5
NS	Bruce McLaren	McLaren	McLaren-Ford Cosworth M7C	engine	6

Pole: Rindt, 1m03.620s, 130.148mph/209.453kph. Fastest lap: Rindt, 1m04.340s, 128.691mph/207.109kph on lap 69. Race leaders: Rindt 1-11 & 21-108; Stewart 12-20

MEXICAN GRAND PRIX

MEXICO CITY • ROUND 11 • DATE: 19TH OCTOBER 1969
Laps: 65 • Distance: 201.945miles/325.0km • Weather: Warm & bright

Pos	Driver	Team	Chassis-Engine	Result	Qual
1	Denny Hulme	McLaren	McLaren-Ford Cosworth M7A	1h54m08.800s	4
2	Jacky Ickx	Brabham	Brabham-Ford Cosworth BT26A	1h54m11.360s	2
3	Jack Brabham	Brabham	Brabham-Ford Cosworth BT26A	1h54m47.280s	1
4	Jackie Stewart	Tyrrell	Matra-Ford Cosworth MS80	1h54m55.840s	3
5	Jean-Pierre Beltoise	Tyrrell	Matra-Ford Cosworth MS80	1h55m47.320s	8
6	Jackie Oliver	BRM	BRM P139	63 laps	12
7	Pedro Rodriguez	Ferrari	Ferrari 312/69	63 laps	15
8	Johnny Servoz-Gavin	Tyrrell	Matra-Ford Cosworth MS84	63 laps	14
9	Pete Lovely	Pete Lovely Volkswagen Inc	Lotus-Ford Cosworth 49B	62 laps	16
10	Piers Courage	Frank Williams Racing Cars	Brabham-Ford Cosworth BT26A	61 laps	9
11	Silvio Moser	Silvio Moser Racing Team	Brabham-Ford Cosworth BT24	60 laps/oil leak	13

Pos	Driver	Team	Chassis-Engine	Result	Qual
R	John Surtees	BRM	BRM P139	53 laps/gearbox	10
R	Jochen Rindt	Lotus	Lotus-Ford Cosworth 49B	21 laps/suspension	6
R	George Eaton	BRM	BRM P139	6 laps/gearbox	17
R	Jo Siffert	Rob Walker Racing Team	Lotus-Ford Cosworth 49B	4 laps/accident	5
R	John Miles	Lotus	Lotus-Ford Cosworth 63	3 laps/fuel pump	11
NS	Bruce McLaren	McLaren	McLaren-Ford Cosworth M7C	fuel injection	7

Pole: Brabham, 1m42.900s, 108.694mph/174.927kph. Fastest lap: Ickx, 1m43.050s, 108.534mph/174.670kph on Lap 64. Race leaders: Stewart 1-5; Ickx 6-9; Hulme 10-65

NEW DRIVERS

Rolf Stommelen was the most promising of seven F1 novices. The German finished eighth overall (fourth in the F2 class) at the German GP but would go on to greater things. He was followed home in the F2 class by novices Peter Westbury and Xavier Perrot. John Miles had five outings in the tricky 4WD Lotus, finishing 10th in the British GP.

IN MEMORIAM

Gerhard Mitter was one of five F1 drivers to die, crashing at the German GP. Former Cooper works driver Lucien Bianchi was killed testing for Alfa Romeo at Le Mans. Then Paul Hawkins died in a sports car race at Oulton Park and Moises Solana in a hillclimb, while Willy Mairesse committed suicide after failing to recover from injuries.

WORLD DRIVERS' CHAMPIONSHIP FINAL RESULTS

Pos	Driver	Nat	Car-Engine	R1	R2	R3	R4	R5
1	Jackie Stewart	GBR	Matra-Ford Cosworth MS10	1F	-	-	-	-
			Matra-Ford Cosworth MS80	-	1	RPF	1F	1PF
2	Jacky Ickx	BEL	Brabham-Ford Cosworth BT26A	R	6	R	5	3
3	Bruce McLaren	NZL	McLaren-Ford Cosworth M7B	5	-	-	-	-
			McLaren-Ford Cosworth M7C	-	2	5	R	4
4	Jochen Rindt	AUT	Lotus-Ford Cosworth 49B	R	RPF	-	RP	R
5	Jean-Pierre Beltoise	FRA	Matra-Ford Cosworth MS10	6	-	-	-	-
			Matra-Ford Cosworth MS80	-	3	R	8	2
			Matra-Ford Cosworth MS84	-	-	-	-	-
6	Denny Hulme	NZL	McLaren-Ford Cosworth M7A	3	4	6	4	8
7	Graham Hill	GBR	Lotus-Ford Cosworth 49B	2	R	1	7	6
8	Piers Courage	GBR	Brabham-Ford Cosworth BT26A	-	R	2	R	R
9	Jo Siffert	CHE	Lotus-Ford Cosworth 49B	4	R	3	2	9
10	Jack Brabham	AUS	Brabham-Ford Cosworth BT26A	RP	R	R	6	-
11	John Surtees	GBR	BRM P138	R	5	R	9	-
			BRM P139	-	-	-	-	-
12	Chris Amon	NZL	Ferrari 312/69	R	R	R	3	R
13	Richard Attwood	GBR	Lotus-Ford Cosworth 49B	-	-	4	-	-
13	Vic Elford	GBR	Cooper-Maserati T86B	-	-	7	-	-
			McLaren-Ford Cosworth M7B	-	-	-	10	5
13	Pedro Rodriguez	MEX	BRM P126	R	R	R	-	-
			Ferrari 312/69	-	-	-	-	-

Pos	Driver	Nat	Car-Engine	R1	R2	R3	R4	R5
16	Johnny Servoz-Gavin	FRA	Matra-Ford Cosworth MS84	-	-	-	-	-
16	Silvio Moser	CHE	Brabham-Ford Cosworth BT24	-	-	R	R	7
16	Jackie Oliver	GBR	BRM P133	7	R	R	R	-
			BRM P138	-	-	-	-	-
			BRM P139	-	-	-	-	-

Pos	Driver	R6	R7	R8	R9	R10	R11	Total
1	Stewart	-	-	-	-	-	-	63
		1F	2	1	R	R	4	
2	Ickx	2	1PF	10	1PF	RF	2F	37
3	McLaren	-	-	-	-	-	-	26
		3	3	4	5	NS	NS	
4	Rindt	4P	R	2P	3	1PF	R	22
5	Beltoise	-	-	-	-	-	-	21
		-	6	3F	4	R	5	
		9	-	-	-	-	-	
6	Hulme	R	R	7	R	R	1	20
7	Hill	7	4	9	R	R	-	19
8	Courage	5	R	5	R	2	10	16
9	Siffert	8	5	8	R	R	R	15
10	Brabham	-	-	R	2F	4	3P	14
11	Surtees	-	-	-	-	-	-	6
		R	NS	NC	R	3	R	
12	Amon	R	-	-	-	-	-	4
13	Attwood	-	-	-	-	-	-	3
13	Elford	-	-	-	-	-	-	3
		6	R	-	-	-	-	
13	Rodriguez	-	-	-	-	-	-	3
		R	-	6	R	5	7	
16	Servoz-Gavin	-	-	-	6	NC	8	1
16	Moser	-	-	R	R	6	11	1
16	Oliver	R	-	-	-	-	-	1
		-	R	-	-	-	-	
		-	-	-	R	R	6	

WORLD CONSTRUCTORS' CHAMPIONSHIP FINAL RESULTS

Pos	Team-Engine	R1	R2	R3	R4	R5	R6	R7	R8	R9	R10	R11	Total
1	Matra-Ford	1	1	-	1	1	1	2	1	4	-	4	66
2	Brabham-Ford	-	6	2	5	3	2	1	5	1	2	2	49
3	Lotus-Ford	2	-	1	2	6	4	4	2	3	1	9	47
4	McLaren-Ford	3	2	5	4	4	3	3	4	5	-	1	38
5	Ferrari	-	-	-	3	-	-	-	6	-	5	7	7
5	BRM	7	5	-	9	-	-	-	-	-	3	6	7

SYMBOLS AND GRAND PRIX KEY

Round 1 South African GP
Round 2 Spanish GP
Round 3 Monaco GP
Round 4 Dutch GP
Round 5 French GP
Round 6 British GP
Round 7 German GP
Round 8 Italian GP
Round 9 Canadian GP
Round 10 United States GP
Round 11 Mexican GP

SCORING

1st 9 points
2nd 6 points
3rd 4 points
4th 3 points
5th 2 points
6th 1 point

DNPQ DID NOT PRE-QUALIFY **DNQ** DID NOT QUALIFY **DQ** DISQUALIFIED **EX** EXCLUDED
F FASTEST LAP **NC** NOT CLASSIFIED **NS** NON-STARTER **P** POLE POSITION **R** RETIRED

THE 1970s

SEASON SUMMARY

The 1970 World Championship produced a terrific scrap between Jochen Rindt for Lotus and Ferrari's Jacky Ickx. Tragically, Rindt didn't survive an accident in qualifying for the Italian GP and so became F1's only posthumous world champion as Ickx failed to overhaul his points tally, despite winning two of the remaining three races. Newcomer Clay Regazzoni became a name to watch as he scored his first win, for Ferrari at Monza no less, and ranked third despite missing the first four grands prix. Emerson Fittipaldi also laid down his first marker by winning the United States GP, while Jackie Stewart showed late-season pace in the first Tyrrell.

SOUTH AFRICAN GRAND PRIX

KYALAMI • ROUND 1 • DATE: 7TH MARCH 1970
Laps: 80 • Distance: 203.829miles/328.32km • Weather: Very hot & bright

Pos	Driver	Team	Chassis-Engine	Result	Qual
1	Jack Brabham	Brabham	Brabham-Ford Cosworth BT33	1h49m34.600s	3
2	Denny Hulme	McLaren	McLaren-Ford Cosworth M14A	1h49m42.700s	6
3	Jackie Stewart	Tyrrell	March-Ford Cosworth 701	1h49m51.700s	1
4	Jean-Pierre Beltoise	Matra	Matra MS120	1h50m47.700s	8
5	John Miles	Lotus	Lotus-Ford Cosworth 49C	79 laps	14
6	Graham Hill	Rob Walker Racing Team	Lotus-Ford Cosworth 49C	79 laps	19
7	Henri Pescarolo	Matra	Matra MS120	78 laps	18
8	John Love	Team Gunston	Lotus-Ford Cosworth 49	78 laps	22
9	Pedro Rodriguez	BRM	BRM P153	76 laps	16
10	Jo Siffert	March	March-Ford Cosworth 701	75 laps	9
11	Peter de Klerk	Team Gunston	Brabham-Ford Cosworth BT26	75 laps	21
12	Dave Charlton	Scuderia Scribante	Lotus-Ford Cosworth 49C	73 laps/engine	13
13	Jochen Rindt	Lotus	Lotus-Ford Cosworth 49C	72 laps/engine	4
R	Jacky Ickx	Ferrari	Ferrari 312B	60 laps/engine	5
R	John Surtees	Surtees	McLaren-Ford Cosworth M7C	60 laps/engine	7
R	George Eaton	BRM	BRM P139	58 laps/engine	23
R	Johnny Servoz-Gavin	Tyrrell	March-Ford Cosworth 701	57 laps/engine	17
R	Bruce McLaren	McLaren	McLaren-Ford Cosworth M14A	39 laps/engine	10
R	Piers Courage	Frank Williams Racing Cars	De Tomaso-Ford Cosworth 505	39 laps/accident	20
R	Mario Andretti	STP Corporation	March-Ford Cosworth 701	26 laps/overheating	11
R	Rolf Stommelen	Brabham	Brabham-Ford Cosworth BT33	23 laps/engine	15
R	Jackie Oliver	BRM	BRM P153	22 laps/gearbox	12
R	Chris Amon	March	March-Ford Cosworth 701	14 laps/overheating	2

Pole: Stewart, 1m19.300s, 115.767mph/186.310kph. Fastest lap: Brabham, 1m20.800s, 113.618mph/182.851kph on Lap 71. Race leaders: Stewart 1-19, Brabham 20-80

STARTING AT THE FRONT

The opening race, at Kyalami, witnessed newcomers March making a huge splash. There were five of its 701s on the grid, with Jackie Stewart on pole in a Tyrrell-run 701 and Chris Amon second fastest in a works machine. Stewart won the second race, but Tyrrell replaced its March after the first 10 races with the team's first homegrown car, the 001.

SPANISH GRAND PRIX

JARAMA • ROUND 2 • DATE: 19TH APRIL 1970
Laps: 90 • Distance: 190.380miles/306.387km • Weather: Warm & bright

Pos	Driver	Team	Chassis-Engine	Result	Qual
1	Jackie Stewart	Tyrrell	March-Ford Cosworth 701	2h10m58.200s	3
2	Bruce McLaren	McLaren	McLaren-Ford Cosworth M14A	89 laps	12
3	Mario Andretti	STP Corporation	March-Ford Cosworth 701	89 laps	19
4	Graham Hill	Rob Walker Racing Team	Lotus-Ford Cosworth 49C	89 laps	18
5	Johnny Servoz-Gavin	Tyrrell	March-Ford Cosworth 701	88 laps	17
R	John Surtees	Surtees	McLaren-Ford Cosworth M7C	76 laps/gearbox	14
R	Jack Brabham	Brabham	Brabham-Ford Cosworth BT33	61 laps/engine	1
R	Rolf Stommelen	Brabham	Brabham-Ford Cosworth BT33	43 laps/engine	20
R	Henri Pescarolo	Matra	Matra MS120	33 laps/engine	10
R	Jean-Pierre Beltoise	Matra	Matra MS120	31 laps/engine	4
R	Denny Hulme	McLaren	McLaren-Ford Cosworth M14A	10 laps/ignition	2
R	Chris Amon	March	March-Ford Cosworth 701	10 laps/engine	6
R	Jochen Rindt	Lotus	Lotus-Ford Cosworth 72	9 laps/ignition	9
R	Pedro Rodriguez	BRM	BRM P153	4 laps/withdrawn	5
R	Jacky Ickx	Ferrari	Ferrari 312B	0 laps/accident	7
R	Jackie Oliver	BRM	BRM P153	0 laps/accident	11
NS	Piers Courage	Frank Williams Racing Cars	De Tomaso-Ford Cosworth 505	accident	8
DNQ	Andrea de Adamich	McLaren	McLaren-Alfa Romeo M7D	reserve	13
DNQ	John Miles	Lotus	Lotus-Ford Cosworth 72	-	15
DNQ	Jo Siffert	March	March-Ford Cosworth 701	reserve	16
DNQ	Alex Soler-Roig	Garvey Team Lotus	Lotus-Ford Cosworth 49C	-	21
DNQ	George Eaton	BRM	BRM P153	-	22

Pole: Brabham, 1m23.900s, 90.765mph/146.072kph. Fastest lap: Brabham, 1m24.300s, 90.334mph/145.379kph on Lap 19. Race leaders: Stewart 1-90

A LAST LAP SLIP-UP

Jack Brabham took the lead at Monaco when Jackie Stewart's engine failed and was set for his second Monaco win. However, Jochen Rindt, back in the Lotus 49C, reduced the gap from 14 seconds to just 1.5 seconds going into the last lap. Distracted by backmarkers, Brabham missed his braking point for the final turn, Gasworks Hairpin, and slid wide into the barriers.

MONACO GRAND PRIX

MONTE CARLO • ROUND 3 • DATE: 10TH MAY 1970
Laps: 80 • Distance: 155.967miles/251.6km • Weather: Warm & bright

Pos	Driver	Team	Chassis-Engine	Result	Qual
1	Jochen Rindt	Lotus	Lotus-Ford Cosworth 49C	1h54m36.600s	8
2	Jack Brabham	Brabham	Brabham-Ford Cosworth BT33	1h54m59.700s	4
3	Henri Pescarolo	Matra	Matra MS120	1h55m28.000s	7
4	Denny Hulme	McLaren	McLaren-Ford Cosworth M14A	1h56m04.900s	3
5	Graham Hill	Rob Walker Racing Team	Lotus-Ford Cosworth 49C	79 laps	12
6	Pedro Rodriguez	BRM	BRM P153	78 laps	20
7	Ronnie Peterson	Colin Crabbe Racing	March-Ford Cosworth 701	78 laps	13

Pos	Driver	Team	Chassis-Engine	Result	Qual
8	Jo Siffert	March	March-Ford Cosworth 701	76 laps/fuel injection	11
R	Chris Amon	March	March-Ford Cosworth 701	60 laps/suspension	2
NC	Piers Courage	Frank Williams Racing Cars	De Tomaso-Ford Cosworth 505	58 laps	9
R	Jackie Stewart	Tyrrell	March-Ford Cosworth 701	57 laps/engine	1
R	Jackie Oliver	BRM	BRM P153	42 laps/engine	17
R	Jean-Pierre Beltoise	Matra	Matra MS120	21 laps/differential	6
R	Bruce McLaren	McLaren	McLaren-Ford Cosworth M14A	19 laps/suspension	10
R	John Surtees	Surtees	McLaren-Ford Cosworth M7C	14 laps/fuel pressure	16
R	Jacky Ickx	Ferrari	Ferrari 312B	11 laps/halfshaft	5
DNQ	Johnny Servoz-Gavin	Tyrrell	March-Ford Cosworth 701	reserve	14
DNQ	Rolf Stommelen	Brabham	Brabham-Ford Cosworth BT33	reserve	15
DNQ	Andrea de Adamich	McLaren	McLaren-Alfa Romeo M7D	-	18
DNQ	John Miles	Lotus	Lotus-Ford Cosworth 49C	-	19
DNQ	George Eaton	BRM	BRM P153	-	21

Pole: Stewart, 1m24.000s, 83.751mph/134.785kph. Fastest lap: Rindt, 1m23.200s, 84.557mph/136.081kph on Lap 80. Race leaders: Stewart 1-27, Brabham 28-79, Rindt 80

FLYING IN THE ARDENNES

The original Spa-Francorchamps circuit was exceedingly fast, effectively a series of straights joined by open curves. In 1970, Pedro Rodriguez set a record average speed of 149.95mph (241.31kph) after a fabulous battle with Chris Amon's March. It was BRM's first win of the 3-litre era and ended a long run of failures for its V12 engine.

BELGIAN GRAND PRIX

SPA-FRANCORCHAMPS • ROUND 4 • DATE: 7TH JUNE 1970
Laps: 28 • Distance: 244.825miles/394.8km • Weather: Warm & bright

Pos	Driver	Team	Chassis-Engine	Result	Qual
1	Pedro Rodriguez	BRM	BRM P153	1h38m09.900s	6
2	Chris Amon	March	March-Ford Cosworth 701	1h38m11.000s	3
3	Jean-Pierre Beltoise	Matra	Matra MS120	1h39m53.600s	11
4	Ignazio Giunti	Ferrari	Ferrari 312B	1h40m48.400s	8
5	Rolf Stommelen	Brabham	Brabham-Ford Cosworth BT33	1h41m41.700s	7
6	Henri Pescarolo	Matra	Matra MS120	27 laps/electrical	17
7	Jo Siffert	March	March-Ford Cosworth 701	26 laps/fuel pressure	10
8	Jacky Ickx	Ferrari	Ferrari 312B	26 laps	4
NC	Ronnie Peterson	Colin Crabbe Racing	March-Ford Cosworth 701	20 laps	9
R	Jack Brabham	Brabham	Brabham-Ford Cosworth BT33	19 laps/clutch	5
R	Graham Hill	Rob Walker Racing Team	Lotus-Ford Cosworth 49C	19 laps/engine	16
R	Jackie Stewart	Tyrrell	March-Ford Cosworth 701	14 laps/engine	1
R	John Miles	Lotus	Lotus-Ford Cosworth 72B	13 laps/gearbox	13
R	Jochen Rindt	Lotus	Lotus-Ford Cosworth 49C	10 laps/engine	2
R	Jackie Oliver	BRM	BRM P153	7 laps/engine	14
R	Piers Courage	Frank Williams Racing Cars	De Tomaso-Ford Cosworth 505	4 laps/fuel pressure	12
R	Derek Bell	Tom Wheatcroft Racing	Brabham-Ford Cosworth BT26	1 lap/gearbox	15
DNQ	Alex Soler-Roig	Lotus	Lotus-Ford Cosworth 72	-	18

Pole: Stewart, 3m28.000s, 151.638mph/244.038kph. Fastest lap: Amon, 3m27.400s, 152.077mph/244.744kph on Lap 27. Race leaders: Amon 1 & 3-4, Stewart 2, Rodriguez 5-28

THE LOSS OF A TITAN

Bruce McLaren was a grand prix winner, an engineer and an inspirational team leader. So when he was killed testing his latest Can Am sports car at Goodwood, he left a massive void as he had filled so many roles. It was a massive blow, but Teddy Mayer and Tyler Alexander stepped into the breach and kept McLaren stable.

DUTCH GRAND PRIX

ZANDVOORT • ROUND 5 • DATE: 21ST JUNE 1970
Laps: 80 • Distance: 208.186miles/335.44km • Weather: Warm but dull

Pos	Driver	Team	Chassis-Engine	Result	Qual
1	Jochen Rindt	Lotus	Lotus-Ford Cosworth 72C	1h50m43.410s	1
2	Jackie Stewart	Tyrrell	March-Ford Cosworth 701	1h51m13.410s	2
3	Jacky Ickx	Ferrari	Ferrari 312B	79 laps	3
4	Clay Regazzoni	Ferrari	Ferrari 312B	79 laps	6
5	Jean-Pierre Beltoise	Matra	Matra MS120	79 laps	10
6	John Surtees	Surtees	McLaren-Ford Cosworth M7C	79 laps	14
7	John Miles	Lotus	Lotus-Ford Cosworth 72B	78 laps	8
8	Henri Pescarolo	Matra	Matra MS120	78 laps	13
9	Ronnie Peterson	Colin Crabbe Racing	March-Ford Cosworth 701	78 laps	16
10	Pedro Rodriguez	BRM	BRM P153	77 laps	7
11	Jack Brabham	Brabham	Brabham-Ford Cosworth BT33	76 laps	12
NC	Graham Hill	Rob Walker Racing Team	Lotus-Ford Cosworth 49C	71 laps	20
R	Francois Cevert	Tyrrell	March-Ford Cosworth 701	31 laps/engine	15
R	George Eaton	BRM	BRM P153	26 laps/oil leak	18
R	Jackie Oliver	BRM	BRM P153	23 laps/engine	5
R	Piers Courage	Frank Williams Racing Cars	De Tomaso-Ford Cosworth 505	22 laps/accident	9
R	Jo Siffert	March	March-Ford Cosworth 701	22 laps/engine	17
R	Peter Gethin	McLaren	McLaren-Ford Cosworth M14A	18 laps/accident	11
R	Dan Gurney	McLaren	McLaren-Ford Cosworth M14A	2 laps/engine	19
R	Chris Amon	March	March-Ford Cosworth 701	1 lap/clutch	4
DNQ	Andrea de Adamich	McLaren	McLaren-Alfa Romeo M14D	reserve	19
DNQ	Rolf Stommelen	Brabham	Brabham-Ford Cosworth BT33	-	22
DNQ	Pete Lovely	Pete Lovely Volkswagen Inc	Lotus-Ford Cosworth 49B	-	23
DNQ	Silvio Moser	Silvio Moser Racing Team	Bellasi-Ford Cosworth F170	-	24

Pole: Rindt, 1m18.500s, 119.483mph/192.290kph. Fastest lap: Ickx, 1m19.230s, 118.382mph/190.518kph on Lap 22. Race leaders: Ickx 1-2, Rindt 3-80

FROM WORKS TO PRIVATE

Graham Hill had been a works driver since he entered F1 with newcomers Lotus in 1958. A move to BRM in 1960 was followed by a return to Lotus in 1967, but he was replaced for 1970 and so joined the ranks of private teams. Longstanding privateers Rob Walker Racing fielded him in a Lotus, with a best result of fourth in Spain.

FRENCH GRAND PRIX

CLERMONT-FERRAND • ROUND 6 • DATE: 5TH JULY 1970
Laps: 38 • Distance: 190.145miles/306.09km • Weather: Warm & bright

Pos	Driver	Team	Chassis-Engine	Result	Qual
1	Jochen Rindt	Lotus	Lotus-Ford Cosworth 72C	1h55m57.000s	6
2	Chris Amon	March	March-Ford Cosworth 701	1h56m04.610s	3
3	Jack Brabham	Brabham	Brabham-Ford Cosworth BT33	1h56m41.830s	5
4	Denny Hulme	McLaren	McLaren-Ford Cosworth M14A	1h56m42.660s	7
5	Henri Pescarolo	Matra	Matra MS120	1h57m16.420s	8
6	Dan Gurney	McLaren	McLaren-Ford Cosworth M14A	1h57m16.650s	17
7	Rolf Stommelen	Brabham	Brabham-Ford Cosworth BT33	1h58m17.160s	14
8	John Miles	Lotus	Lotus-Ford Cosworth 72B	1h58m44.170s	18
9	Jackie Stewart	Tyrrell	March-Ford Cosworth 701	1h59m06.610s	4
10	Graham Hill	Rob Walker Racing Team	Lotus-Ford Cosworth 49C	37 laps	20
11	Francois Cevert	Tyrrell	March-Ford Cosworth 701	37 laps	13
12	George Eaton	BRM	BRM P153	36 laps	19
13	Jean-Pierre Beltoise	Matra	Matra MS120	35 laps/fuel pressure	2
14	Ignazio Giunti	Ferrari	Ferrari 312B	35 laps	11
NC	Andrea de Adamich	McLaren	McLaren-Alfa Romeo M7D	29 laps	15
R	Jo Siffert	March	March-Ford Cosworth 701	23 laps/accident	16
R	Ronnie Peterson	Colin Crabbe Racing	March-Ford Cosworth 701	17 laps/differential	9
R	Jacky Ickx	Ferrari	Ferrari 312B	16 laps/engine	1
R	Pedro Rodriguez	BRM	BRM P153	6 laps/gearbox	10
R	Jackie Oliver	BRM	BRM P153	5 laps/engine	12
DNQ	Silvio Moser	Silvio Moser Racing Team	Bellasi-Ford Cosworth F170	-	21
DNQ	Pete Lovely	Pete Lovely Volkswagen Inc	Lotus-Ford Cosworth 49B	-	22
DNQ	Alex Soler-Roig	Lotus	Lotus-Ford Cosworth 49C	-	23

Pole: Ickx, 2m58.220s, 101.102mph/162.709kph. Fastest lap: Brabham, 3m00.750s, 99.686mph/160.430kph on Lap 29. Race leaders: Ickx 1-14, Beltoise 15-25, Rindt 26-38

OVER AND OUT

Johnny Servoz-Gavin was France's great hope and, after a year spent winning the F2 title, he was back in F1 in 1970 to atone for his 1968 Monaco mishap. Racing a Tyrrell-run March, he finished fifth in the Spanish GP, but hit the chicane at Monaco and failed to qualify. He quit on the spot later after it was revealed that he had reduced sight in one eye, after an off-season off-road incident.

BRITISH GRAND PRIX

BRANDS HATCH • ROUND 7 • DATE: 18TH JULY 1970
Laps: 80 • Distance: 212.1miles/341.184km • Weather: Warm & bright

Pos	Driver	Team	Chassis-Engine	Result	Qual
1	Jochen Rindt	Lotus	Lotus-Ford Cosworth 72C	1h57m02.000s	1
2	Jack Brabham	Brabham	Brabham-Ford Cosworth BT33	1h57m34.900s	2
3	Denny Hulme	McLaren	McLaren-Ford Cosworth M14A	1h57m56.400s	5
4	Clay Regazzoni	Ferrari	Ferrari 312B	1h57m56.800s	6
5	Chris Amon	March	March-Ford Cosworth 701	79 laps	17
6	Graham Hill	Rob Walker Racing Team	Lotus-Ford Cosworth 49C	79 laps	22

Pos	Driver	Team	Chassis-Engine	Result	Qual
7	Francois Cevert	Tyrrell	March-Ford Cosworth 701	79 laps	14
8	Emerson Fittipaldi	Lotus	Lotus-Ford Cosworth 49C	78 laps	21
9	Ronnie Peterson	Colin Crabbe Racing	March-Ford Cosworth 701	72 laps	13
NC	Pete Lovely	Pete Lovely Volkswagen Inc	Lotus-Ford Cosworth 49B	69 laps	23
R	Dan Gurney	McLaren	McLaren-Ford Cosworth M14A	60 laps/fuel pressure	11
R	Pedro Rodriguez	BRM	BRM P153	58 laps/accident	15
R	Jackie Oliver	BRM	BRM P153	54 laps/engine	4
R	Jackie Stewart	Tyrrell	March-Ford Cosworth 701	52 laps/clutch	8
R	John Surtees	Surtees	Surtees-Ford Cosworth TS7	51 laps/fuel pressure	19
R	Henri Pescarolo	Matra	Matra MS120	41 laps/accident	12
R	Jean-Pierre Beltoise	Matra	Matra MS120	24 laps/wheel	10
R	Mario Andretti	STP Corporation	March-Ford Cosworth 701	21 laps/suspension	9
R	Jo Siffert	March	March-Ford Cosworth 701	19 laps/suspension	20
R	John Miles	Lotus	Lotus-Ford Cosworth 72B	15 laps/engine	7
R	George Eaton	BRM	BRM P153	10 laps/fuel pressure	16
R	Jacky Ickx	Ferrari	Ferrari 312B	6 laps/transmission	3
NS	Rolf Stommelen	Brabham	Brabham-Ford Cosworth BT33	accident	10
NS	Andrea de Adamich	McLaren	McLaren-Alfa Romeo M7D	fuel tank	19
NS	Brian Redman	Frank Williams Racing Cars	De Tomaso-Ford Cosworth 505	hub	25

Pole: Rindt, 1m24.800s, 112.501mph/181.052kph. Fastest lap: Brabham, 1m25.900s, 111.039mph/178.700kph on Lap 70. Race leaders: Ickx 1-6, Rindt 7-68 & 80, Brabham 69-79

NEW CIRCUITS

Pressure from the Grand Prix Drivers' Association led to the German GP moving from the Nurburgring to Hockenheim, citing concerns about the safety of its 172-turn Nordschleife lap. Fully 200,000 fans turned out to watch Jochen Rindt win, dubbing it "Jochenheim". The next venue, the Osterreichring, was also new and it was a huge improvement on Zeltweg.

GERMAN GRAND PRIX

HOCKENHEIM • ROUND 8 • DATE: 2ND AUGUST 1970
Laps: 50 • Distance: 210.672miles/339.45km • Weather: Hot & bright

Pos	Driver	Team	Chassis-Engine	Result	Qual
1	Jochen Rindt	Lotus	Lotus-Ford Cosworth 72C	1h42m00.300s	2
2	Jacky Ickx	Ferrari	Ferrari 312B	1h42m01.000s	1
3	Denny Hulme	McLaren	McLaren-Ford Cosworth M14A	1h43m22.100s	16
4	Emerson Fittipaldi	Lotus	Lotus-Ford Cosworth 49C	1h43m55.400s	13
5	Rolf Stommelen	Brabham	Brabham-Ford Cosworth BT33	49 laps	11
6	Henri Pescarolo	Matra	Matra MS120	49 laps	5
7	Francois Cevert	Tyrrell	March-Ford Cosworth 701	49 laps	14
8	Jo Siffert	March	March-Ford Cosworth 701	47 laps/ignition	4
9	John Surtees	Surtees	Surtees-Ford Cosworth TS7	46 laps/engine	15
R	Graham Hill	Rob Walker Racing Team	Lotus-Ford Cosworth 49C	37 laps/engine	20
R	Chris Amon	March	March-Ford Cosworth 701	34 laps/engine	6
R	Clay Regazzoni	Ferrari	Ferrari 312B	30 laps/engine	3
R	John Miles	Lotus	Lotus-Ford Cosworth 72C	24 laps/engine	10
R	Jackie Stewart	Tyrrell	March-Ford Cosworth 701	20 laps/engine	7
R	Mario Andretti	STP Corporation	March-Ford Cosworth 701	15 laps/gearbox	9
R	Ronnie Peterson	Colin Crabbe Racing	March-Ford Cosworth 701	11 laps/engine	19
R	Pedro Rodriguez	BRM	BRM P153	7 laps/ignition	8

Pos	Driver	Team	Chassis-Engine	Result	Qual
R	Jackie Oliver	BRM	BRM P153	5 laps/engine	18
R	Jack Brabham	Brabham	Brabham-Ford Cosworth BT33	4 laps/oil leak	12
R	Jean-Pierre Beltoise	Matra	Matra MS120	4 laps/suspension	21
R	Peter Gethin	McLaren	McLaren-Ford Cosworth M14A	3 laps/throttle	17
DNQ	Brian Redman	Frank Williams Racing Cars	De Tomaso-Ford Cosworth 505	reserve	20
DNQ	Andrea de Adamich	McLaren	McLaren-Alfa Romeo M14D	-	22
DNQ	Silvio Moser	Silvio Moser Racing Team	Bellasi-Ford Cosworth F170	-	24
DNQ	Hubert Hahne	Hubert Hahne	March-Ford Cosworth 701	-	25

Pole: Ickx, 1m59.500s, 127.084mph/204.522kph. Fastest lap: Ickx, 2m00.500s, 126.014mph/202.800kph on Lap 50. Race leaders: Ickx 1-6 & 10-17 & 26-31 & 36-43 & 45-46 & 48, Rindt 7-9 & 18-21 & 24-25 & 32-35 & 44 & 47 & 49-50, Regazzoni 22-23

AUSTRIAN GRAND PRIX

OSTERREICHRING • ROUND 9 • DATE: 16TH AUGUST 1970
Laps: 60 • Distance: 220.6miles/354.66km • Weather: Warm & bright

Pos	Driver	Team	Chassis-Engine	Result	Qual
1	Jacky Ickx	Ferrari	Ferrari 312B	1h42m17.320s	3
2	Clay Regazzoni	Ferrari	Ferrari 312B	1h42m17.930s	2
3	Rolf Stommelen	Brabham	Brabham-Ford Cosworth BT33	1h43m45.200s	17
4	Pedro Rodriguez	BRM	BRM P153	59 laps	22
5	Jackie Oliver	BRM	BRM P153	59 laps	14
6	Jean-Pierre Beltoise	Matra	Matra MS120	59 laps	7
7	Ignazio Giunti	Ferrari	Ferrari 312B	59 laps	5
8	Chris Amon	March	March-Ford Cosworth 701	59 laps	6
9	Jo Siffert	March	March-Ford Cosworth 701	59 laps	20
10	Peter Gethin	McLaren	McLaren-Ford Cosworth M14A	59 laps	21
11	George Eaton	BRM	BRM P153	58 laps	23
12	Andrea de Adamich	McLaren	McLaren-Alfa Romeo M14D	57 laps	15
13	Jack Brabham	Brabham	Brabham-Ford Cosworth BT33	56 laps	8
14	Henri Pescarolo	Matra	Matra MS120	56 laps	13
15	Emerson Fittipaldi	Lotus	Lotus-Ford Cosworth 49C	55 laps	16
R	Denny Hulme	McLaren	McLaren-Ford Cosworth M14A	30 laps/engine	11
R	John Surtees	Surtees	Surtees-Ford Cosworth TS7	27 laps/engine	12
R	Tim Schenken	Frank Williams Racing Cars	De Tomaso-Ford Cosworth 505	25 laps/engine	19
R	Jochen Rindt	Lotus	Lotus-Ford Cosworth 72C	21 laps/engine	1
R	Mario Andretti	STP Corporation	March-Ford Cosworth 701	13 laps/accident	18
R	Silvio Moser	Silvio Moser Racing Team	Bellasi-Ford Cosworth F170	13 laps/radiator	24
R	Jackie Stewart	Tyrrell	March-Ford Cosworth 701	7 laps/mechanical	4
R	John Miles	Lotus	Lotus-Ford Cosworth 72C	4 laps/brakes	10
R	Francois Cevert	Tyrrell	March-Ford Cosworth 701	0 laps/engine	9

Pole: Rindt, 1m39.230s, 133.251mph/214.447kph. Fastest lap: Regazzoni, 1m40.390s, 131.712mph/211.970kph on Lap 51. Race leaders: Regazzoni 1, Ickx 2-60

NEW CONSTRUCTORS

March had only started making F3 cars in 1969, but stepped up in style, with John Surtees's team advancing just as fast, having taken over the Leda F5000 project. Having ended his connection with Matra, Ken Tyrrell became a constructor in 1970, while Bellasi had built F3 cars since 1966 before being asked by Silvio Moser to build an F1 car.

ITALIAN GRAND PRIX

MONZA • ROUND 10 • DATE: 6TH SEPTEMBER 1970
Laps: 68 • Distance: 242.956miles/391.0km • Weather: Hot & bright

Pos	Driver	Team	Chassis-Engine	Result	Qual
1	Clay Regazzoni	Ferrari	Ferrari 312B	1h39m06.880s	3
2	Jackie Stewart	Tyrrell	March-Ford Cosworth 701	1h39m12.610s	4
3	Jean-Pierre Beltoise	Matra	Matra MS120	1h39m12.680s	14
4	Denny Hulme	McLaren	McLaren-Ford Cosworth M14A	1h39m13.030s	9
5	Rolf Stommelen	Brabham	Brabham-Ford Cosworth BT33	1h39m13.290s	17
6	Francois Cevert	Tyrrell	March-Ford Cosworth 701	1h40m10.340s	11
7	Chris Amon	March	March-Ford Cosworth 701	67 laps	18
8	Andrea de Adamich	McLaren	McLaren-Alfa Romeo M14D	61 laps	12
NC	Peter Gethin	McLaren	McLaren-Ford Cosworth M14A	60 laps	16
R	Jackie Oliver	BRM	BRM P153	36 laps/engine	6
R	Ronnie Peterson	Colin Crabbe Racing	March-Ford Cosworth 701	35 laps/engine	13
R	Jack Brabham	Brabham	Brabham-Ford Cosworth BT33	31 laps/accident	8
R	Jacky Ickx	Ferrari	Ferrari 312B	25 laps/clutch	1
R	George Eaton	BRM	BRM P153	21 laps/overheating	20
R	Tim Schenken	Frank Williams Racing Cars	De Tomaso-Ford Cosworth 505	17 laps/engine	19
R	Ignazio Giunti	Ferrari	Ferrari 312B	14 laps/fuel system	5
R	Henri Pescarolo	Matra	Matra MS120	14 laps/engine	15
R	Pedro Rodriguez	BRM	BRM P153	12 laps/engine	2
R	Jo Siffert	March	March-Ford Cosworth 701	3 laps/engine	7
R	John Surtees	Surtees	Surtees-Ford Cosworth TS7	0 laps/electrical	10
NS	Jochen Rindt	Lotus	Lotus-Ford Cosworth 72C	fatal accident	12
NS	Graham Hill	Rob Walker Racing Team	Lotus-Ford Cosworth 72C	withdrew	16
NS	John Miles	Lotus	Lotus-Ford Cosworth 72C	withdrew	19
NS	Emerson Fittipaldi	Lotus	Lotus-Ford Cosworth 72C	withdrew	25
DNQ	Jo Bonnier	Ecurie Bonnier	McLaren-Ford Cosworth M7C	-	24
DNQ	Nanni Galli	McLaren	McLaren-Alfa Romeo M7D	-	26
DNQ	Silvio Moser	Silvio Moser Racing Team	Bellasi-Ford Cosworth F170	-	27

Pole: Ickx, 1m24.140s, 152.868mph/246.018kph. Fastest lap: Regazzoni, 1m25.200s, 150.966mph/242.957kph on Lap 65. Race leaders: Ickx 1-3 & 19-20, Rodriguez 4 & 7-8, Stewart 5-6 & 9 & 11 & 14-17 & 26-27 & 31 & 35 & 37 & 42-43 & 51 & 53, Regazzoni 10 & 12 & 32-34 & 36 & 38-41 & 44-50 & 52 & 54-68, Oliver 13 & 18 & 21-25 & 28 & 30, Hulme 29

CANADIAN GRAND PRIX

ST JOVITE • ROUND 11 • DATE: 20TH SEPTEMBER 1970
Laps: 90 • Distance: 238.37miles/383.85km • Weather: Warm & bright

Pos	Driver	Team	Chassis-Engine	Result	Qual
1	Jacky Ickx	Ferrari	Ferrari 312B	2h21m18.400s	2
2	Clay Regazzoni	Ferrari	Ferrari 312B	2h21m33.200s	3
3	Chris Amon	March	March-Ford Cosworth 701	2h22m16.300s	6
4	Pedro Rodriguez	BRM	BRM P153	89 laps	7
5	John Surtees	Surtees	Surtees-Ford Cosworth TS7	89 laps	5
6	Peter Gethin	McLaren	McLaren-Ford Cosworth M14A	88 laps	11
7	Henri Pescarolo	Matra	Matra MS120	87 laps	8
8	Jean-Pierre Beltoise	Matra	Matra MS120	85 laps/clutch	13
9	Francois Cevert	Tyrrell	March-Ford Cosworth 701	85 laps	4
10	George Eaton	BRM	BRM P153	85 laps	9
NC	Tim Schenken	Frank Williams Racing Cars	De Tomaso-Ford Cosworth 505	79 laps	17
NC	Graham Hill	Rob Walker Racing Team	Lotus-Ford Cosworth 72C	77 laps	20

Pos	Driver	Team	Chassis-Engine	Result	Qual
R	Andrea de Adamich	McLaren	McLaren-Alfa Romeo M14D	69 laps/fuel pressure	12
NC	Ronnie Peterson	Colin Crabbe Racing	March-Ford Cosworth 701	65 laps	16
R	Denny Hulme	McLaren	McLaren-Ford Cosworth M14A	59 laps/engine	15
R	Jack Brabham	Brabham	Brabham-Ford Cosworth BT33	57 laps/oil leak	19
NC	Jackie Oliver	BRM	BRM P153	52 laps	10
R	Jackie Stewart	Tyrrell	Tyrrell-Ford Cosworth 001	31 laps/mechanical	1
R	Rolf Stommelen	Brabham	Brabham-Ford Cosworth BT33	23 laps/handling	18
R	Jo Siffert	March	March-Ford Cosworth 701	22 laps/engine	14

Pole: Stewart, 1m31.500s, 104.268mph/167.803kph. Fastest lap: Regazzoni, 1m32.200s, 103.476mph/166.529kph on Lap 75. Race leaders: Stewart 1-31, Ickx 32-90

UNITED STATES GRAND PRIX

WATKINS GLEN • ROUND 12 • DATE: 4TH OCTOBER 1970
Laps: 108 • Distance: 248.400miles/399.762km • Weather: Cool & dull

Pos	Driver	Team	Chassis-Engine	Result	Qual
1	Emerson Fittipaldi	Lotus	Lotus-Ford Cosworth 72C	1h57m32.790s	3
2	Pedro Rodriguez	BRM	BRM P153	1h58m09.180s	4
3	Reine Wisell	Lotus	Lotus-Ford Cosworth 72C	1h58m17.960s	9
4	Jacky Ickx	Ferrari	Ferrari 312B	107 laps	1
5	Chris Amon	March	March-Ford Cosworth 701	107 laps	5
6	Derek Bell	Surtees	Surtees-Ford Cosworth TS7	107 laps	13
7	Denny Hulme	McLaren	McLaren-Ford Cosworth M14A	106 laps	11
8	Henri Pescarolo	Matra	Matra MS120	105 laps	12
9	Jo Siffert	March	March-Ford Cosworth 701	105 laps	23
10	Jack Brabham	Brabham	Brabham-Ford Cosworth BT33	105 laps	16
11	Ronnie Peterson	Colin Crabbe Racing	March-Ford Cosworth 701	104 laps	15
12	Rolf Stommelen	Brabham	Brabham-Ford Cosworth BT33	104 laps	19
13	Clay Regazzoni	Ferrari	Ferrari 312B	101 laps	6
14	Peter Gethin	McLaren	McLaren-Ford Cosworth M14A	100 laps	21
R	Jackie Stewart	Tyrrell	Tyrrell-Ford Cosworth 001	82 laps/oil leak	2
R	Graham Hill	Rob Walker Racing Team	Lotus-Ford Cosworth 72C	72 laps/clutch	10
R	Francois Cevert	Tyrrell	March-Ford Cosworth 701	62 laps/wheel	17
R	Tim Schenken	Frank Williams Racing Cars	De Tomaso-Ford Cosworth 505	61 laps/suspension	20
R	Jo Bonnier	Ecurie Bonnier	McLaren-Ford Cosworth M7C	50 laps/mechanical	24
R	Jean-Pierre Beltoise	Matra	Matra MS120	27 laps/handling	18
R	Gus Hutchison	Gus Hutchison	Brabham-Ford Cosworth BT26	21 laps/oil leak	22
R	Jackie Oliver	BRM	BRM P153	14 laps/engine	7
R	George Eaton	BRM	BRM P153	10 laps/engine	14
R	John Surtees	Surtees	Surtees-Ford Cosworth TS7	6 laps/engine	8
DNQ	Peter Westbury	BRM	BRM P153	-	25
DNQ	Pete Lovely	Pete Lovely Volkswagen Inc	Lotus-Ford Cosworth 49B	-	26
DNQ	Andrea de Adamich	McLaren	McLaren-Alfa Romeo M14D	-	27

Pole: Ickx, 1m03.070s, 131.283mph/211.279kph. Fastest lap: Ickx, 1m02.740s, 131.973mph/212.390kph on Lap 105. Race leaders: Stewart 1-82, Rodriguez 83-100, Fittipaldi 101-108

MEXICAN GRAND PRIX

MEXICO CITY • ROUND 13 • DATE: 25TH OCTOBER 1970
Laps: 65 • Distance: 201.945miles/325.0km • Weather: Warm & bright

Pos	Driver	Team	Chassis-Engine	Result	Qual
1	Jacky Ickx	Ferrari	Ferrari 312B	1h53m28.360s	3
2	Clay Regazzoni	Ferrari	Ferrari 312B	1h53m53.000s	1
3	Denny Hulme	McLaren	McLaren-Ford Cosworth M14A	1h54m14.330s	14
4	Chris Amon	March	March-Ford Cosworth 701	1h54m15.410s	5
5	Jean-Pierre Beltoise	Matra	Matra MS120	1h54m18.470s	6
6	Pedro Rodriguez	BRM	BRM P153	1h54m53.120s	7
7	Jackie Oliver	BRM	BRM P153	64 laps	13
8	John Surtees	Surtees	Surtees-Ford Cosworth TS7	64 laps	15
9	Henri Pescarolo	Matra	Matra MS120	61 laps	11
NC	Reine Wisell	Lotus	Lotus-Ford Cosworth 72C	56 laps	12
R	Jack Brabham	Brabham	Brabham-Ford Cosworth BT33	52 laps/engine	4
R	Jackie Stewart	Tyrrell	Tyrrell-Ford Cosworth 001	33 laps/suspension	2
R	Peter Gethin	McLaren	McLaren-Ford Cosworth M14A	27 laps/engine	10
R	Rolf Stommelen	Brabham	Brabham-Ford Cosworth BT33	15 laps/fuel system	17
R	Francois Cevert	Tyrrell	March-Ford Cosworth 701	8 laps/engine	9
R	Graham Hill	Rob Walker Racing Team	Lotus-Ford Cosworth 72C	4 laps/overheating	8
R	Jo Siffert	March	March-Ford Cosworth 701	3 laps/engine	16
R	Emerson Fittipaldi	Lotus	Lotus-Ford Cosworth 72C	1 lap/engine	18

Pole: Regazzoni, 1m41.860s, 109.804mph/176.713kph. Fastest lap: Ickx, 1m43.110s, 108.473mph/174.570kph on Lap 46. Race leaders: Regazzoni 1, Ickx 2-65

NEW DRIVERS

Of the 10 F1 newcomers, Emerson Fittipaldi and Clay Regazzoni made an equal splash as each won on their fifth outing, for Lotus and Ferrari respectively. By his third season, Fittipaldi would win the first of his two world championship titles. Ronnie Peterson and Peter Gethin would become winners, while Tim Schenken would impress.

IN MEMORIAM

Not only was Bruce McLaren killed when testing, and Jochen Rindt killed in an accident in practice at the Italian GP, but Frank Williams' protege Piers Courage also lost his life at the Dutch GP at Zandvoort, when he crashed his de Tomaso out of seventh place. The heir to the brewing fortune perished when trapped underneath his burning car.

WORLD DRIVERS' CHAMPIONSHIP FINAL RESULTS

Pos	Driver	Nat	Car-Engine	R1	R2	R3	R4	R5
1	Jochen Rindt	AUT	Lotus-Ford Cosworth 49C	13	-	1F	R	-
			Lotus-Ford Cosworth 72	-	R	-	-	-
			Lotus-Ford Cosworth 72C	-	-	-	-	1P
2	Jacky Ickx	BEL	Ferrari 312B	R	R	R	8	3F
3	Clay Regazzoni	CHE	Ferrari 312B	-	-	-	-	4
4	Denny Hulme	NZL	McLaren-Ford Cosworth M14A	2	R	4	-	-
5	Jack Brabham	AUS	Brabham-Ford Cosworth BT33	1F	RPF	2	R	11
5	Jackie Stewart	GBR	March-Ford Cosworth 701	3P	1	RP	RP	2
			Tyrrell-Ford Cosworth 001	-	-	-	-	-
7	Pedro Rodriguez	MEX	BRM P153	9	R	6	1	10
7	Chris Amon	NZL	March-Ford Cosworth 701	R	R	R	2F	R
9	Jean-Pierre Beltoise	FRA	Matra MS120	4	R	R	3	5
10	Emerson Fittipaldi	BRA	Lotus-Ford Cosworth 49C	-	-	-	-	-
			Lotus-Ford Cosworth 72C	-	-	-	-	-
11	Rolf Stommelen	DEU	Brabham-Ford Cosworth BT33	R	R	DNQ	5	DNQ
12	Henri Pescarolo	FRA	Matra MS120	7	R	3	6	8
13	Graham Hill	GBR	Lotus-Ford Cosworth 49C	6	4	5	R	NC
			Lotus-Ford Cosworth 72C	-	-	-	-	-
14	Bruce McLaren	NZL	McLaren-Ford Cosworth M14A	R	2	R	-	-
15	Mario Andretti	USA	March-Ford Cosworth 701	R	3	-	-	-
15	Reine Wisell	SWE	Lotus-Ford Cosworth 72C	-	-	-	-	-
17	Ignazio Giunti	ITA	Ferrari 312B	-	-	-	4	-
17	John Surtees	GBR	McLaren-Ford Cosworth M7C	R	-	-	-	-
			Surtees-Ford Cosworth TS7	-	R	R	-	6
19	John Miles	GBR	Lotus-Ford Cosworth 49C	5	-	DNQ	-	-
			Lotus-Ford Cosworth 72	-	DNQ	-	-	-
			Lotus-Ford Cosworth 72B	-	-	-	R	7
			Lotus-Ford Cosworth 72C	-	-	-	-	-
19	Johnny Servoz-Gavin	FRA	March-Ford Cosworth 701	R	5	DNQ	-	-
19	Jackie Oliver	GBR	BRM P153	R	R	R	R	R
22	Dan Gurney	USA	McLaren-Ford Cosworth M14A	-	-	-	-	R
22	Francois Cevert	FRA	March-Ford Cosworth 701	-	-	-	-	R
22	Peter Gethin	GBR	McLaren-Ford Cosworth M14A	-	-	-	-	R
22	Derek Bell	GBR	Brabham-Ford Cosworth BT26	-	-	-	R	-
			Surtees-Ford Cosworth TS7	-	-	-	-	-

Pos	Driver	R6	R7	R8	R9	R10	R11	R12	R13	Total
1	Rindt	-	-	-	-	-	-	-	-	45
		-	-	-	-	-	-	-	-	
		1	1P	1	RP	NS	-	-	-	
2	Ickx	RP	R	2PF	1	RP	1	4PF	1F	40
3	Regazzoni	-	4	R	2F	1F	2F	13	2P	33
4	Hulme	4	3	3	R	4	R	7	3	27
5	Brabham	3F	2F	R	13	R	R	10	R	25
5	Stewart	9	R	R	R	2	-	-	-	25
		-	-	-	-	-	RP	R	R	
7	Rodriguez	R	R	R	4	R	4	2	6	23
7	Amon	2	5	R	8	7	3	5	4	23
9	Beltoise	13	R	R	6	3	8	R	5	16
10	Fittipaldi	-	8	4	15	-	-	-	-	12
		-	-	-	-	NS	-	1	R	
11	Stommelen	7	NS	5	3	5	R	12	R	10

Pos	Driver	R6	R7	R8	R9	R10	R11	R12	R13	Total
12	Pescarolo	5	R	6	14	R	7	8	9	8
13	Hill	10	6	R	-	-	-	-	-	7
		-	-	-	-	NS	NC	R	R	
14	McLaren	-	-	-	-	-	-	-	-	6
15	Andretti	-	R	R	R	-	-	-	-	4
15	Wisell	-	-	-	-	-	-	3	NC	4
17	Giunti	14	-	-	7	R	-	-	-	3
17	Surtees	-	-	-	-	-	-	-	-	3
		-	R	9	R	R	5	R	8	
19	Miles	-	-	-	-	-	-	-	-	2
		-	-	-	-	-	-	-	-	-
		8	R	-	-	-	-	-	-	
		-	-	R	R	NS	-	-	-	
19	Servoz-Gavin	-	-	-	-	-	-	-	-	2
19	Oliver	R	R	R	5	R	NC	R	7	2
22	Gurney	6	R	-	-	-	-	-	-	1
22	Cevert	11	7	7	R	6	9	R	R	1
22	Gethin	-	-	R	10	NC	6	14	R	1
22	Bell	-	-	-	-	-	-	-	-	1
		-	-	-	-	-	-	6	-	

WORLD CONSTRUCTORS' CHAMPIONSHIP FINAL RESULTS

Pos	Team-Engine	R1	R2	R3	R4	R5	R6	R7	R8	R9	R10	R11	R12	R13	Total
1	Lotus-Ford	5	4	1	-	1	1	1	1	15	-	-	1	-	59
2	Ferrari	-	-	-	4	3	14	4	2	1	1	1	4	1	52
3	March-Ford	3	1	7	2	2	2	5	7	8	2	3	5	4	48
4	Brabham-Ford	1	-	2	5	11	3	2	5	3	5	-	10	-	35
4	McLaren-Ford	2	2	4	-	-	4	3	3	10	4	6	7	3	35
6	BRM	9	-	6	1	10	12	-	-	4	-	4	2	6	23
6	Matra	4	-	3	3	5	5	-	6	6	3	7	8	5	23
8	Surtees-Ford	-	-	-	-	6	-	-	9	-	-	5	6	8	3

SYMBOLS AND GRAND PRIX KEY

Round 1 South African GP
Round 2 Spanish GP
Round 3 Monaco GP
Round 4 Belgian GP
Round 5 Dutch GP
Round 6 French GP
Round 7 British GP
Round 8 German GP
Round 9 Austrian GP
Round 10 Italian GP
Round 11 Canadian GP
Round 12 United States GP
Round 13 Mexican GP

DNPQ DID NOT PRE-QUALIFY **DNQ** DID NOT QUALIFY **DQ** DISQUALIFIED **EX** EXCLUDED
F FASTEST LAP **NC** NOT CLASSIFIED **NS** NON-STARTER **P** POLE POSITION **R** RETIRED

SCORING

1st 9 points
2nd 6 points
3rd 4 points
4th 3 points
5th 2 points
6th 1 point

1971

SEASON SUMMARY

Ken Tyrrell's first full season as a constructor was a phenomenal one as not only did he help driver Jackie Stewart to collect the title, but his second driver, Francois Cevert, ranked third as Tyrrell scored more than double the points of closest challenger BRM in the constructors' championship. With Ferrari's challenge fading, it was left to Ronnie Peterson to shine in his second year of F1. Although he failed to win, four second places for March were enough for him to end the season as runner-up. Lotus fell from being champions in 1970 to fifth overall, failing to win a race for the first time since 1959.

SOUTH AFRICAN GRAND PRIX

KYALAMI • ROUND 1 • DATE: 6TH MARCH 1971
Laps: 79 • Distance: 201.458miles/324.216km • Weather: Hot & bright

Pos	Driver	Team	Chassis-Engine	Result	Qual
1	Mario Andretti	Ferrari	Ferrari 312B	1h47m35.500s	4
2	Jackie Stewart	Tyrrell	Tyrrell-Ford Cosworth 001	1h47m56.400s	1
3	Clay Regazzoni	Ferrari	Ferrari 312B	1h48m06.900s	3
4	Reine Wisell	Lotus	Lotus-Ford Cosworth 72C	1h48m44.900s	14
5	Chris Amon	Matra	Matra MS120	78 laps	2
6	Denny Hulme	McLaren	McLaren-Ford Cosworth M19A	78 laps	7
7	Brian Redman	Surtees	Surtees-Ford Cosworth TS7	78 laps	17
8	Jacky Ickx	Ferrari	Ferrari 312B	78 laps	8
9	Graham Hill	Brabham	Brabham-Ford Cosworth BT33	77 laps	19
10	Ronnie Peterson	March	March-Ford Cosworth 711	77 laps	13
11	Henri Pescarolo	Frank Williams Racing Cars	March-Ford Cosworth 711	77 laps	18
12	Rolf Stommelen	Surtees	Surtees-Ford Cosworth TS7	77 laps	15
13	Andrea de Adamich	March	March-Alfa Romeo 711	75 laps	22
R	Emerson Fittipaldi	Lotus	Lotus-Ford Cosworth 72C	58 laps/engine	5
R	John Surtees	Surtees	Surtees-Ford Cosworth TS9	56 laps/gearbox	6
R	Francois Cevert	Tyrrell	Tyrrell-Ford Cosworth 002	45 laps/accident	9
R	Howden Ganley	BRM	BRM P153	42 laps/engine	24
R	Pedro Rodriguez	BRM	BRM P160	33 laps/overheating	10
R	Dave Charlton	Brabham	Brabham-Ford Cosworth BT33	31 laps/engine	12
R	Jo Siffert	BRM	BRM P153	31 laps/overheating	16
R	John Love	Team Gunston	March-Ford Cosworth 701	30 laps/differential	21
R	Jackie Pretorius	Team Gunston	Brabham-Ford Cosworth BT26A	22 laps/engine	20
R	Peter Gethin	McLaren	McLaren-Ford Cosworth M14A	7 laps/oil leak	11
R	Jo Bonnier	Ecurie Bonnier	McLaren-Ford Cosworth M7C	5 laps/suspension	23
R	Alex Soler-Roig	March	March-Ford Cosworth 711	5 laps/engine	25

Pole: Stewart, 1m17.800s, 117.999mph/189.902kph. Fastest lap: Andretti, 1m20.300s, 114.326mph/183.990kph on Lap 73. Race leaders: Regazzoni 1-16, Hulme 17-75, Andretti 76-79

LESS TREAD, MORE GRIP

A radical arrival in 1971 was the slick tyre, introduced for the Spanish GP by Firestone. Goodyear soon followed suit. F1 also saw the arrival of airboxes, used to force air into the engines to give them more power. A technology that didn't last was the gas turbine engine, raced just once for Lotus by Emerson Fittipaldi to eighth place at Monza.

SPANISH GRAND PRIX

MONTJUICH PARK • ROUND 2 • DATE: 18TH APRIL 1971
Laps: 75 • Distance: 176.484miles/284.25km • Weather: Hot & bright

Pos	Driver	Team	Chassis-Engine	Result	Qual
1	Jackie Stewart	Tyrrell	Tyrrell-Ford Cosworth 003	1h49m03.400s	4
2	Jacky Ickx	Ferrari	Ferrari 312B	1h49m06.800s	1
3	Chris Amon	Matra	Matra MS120	1h50m01.500s	3
4	Pedro Rodriguez	BRM	BRM P160	1h50m21.300s	5
5	Denny Hulme	McLaren	McLaren-Ford Cosworth M19A	1h50m30.400s	9
6	Jean-Pierre Beltoise	Matra	Matra MS120B	74 laps	6
7	Francois Cevert	Tyrrell	Tyrrell-Ford Cosworth 002	74 laps	12
8	Peter Gethin	McLaren	McLaren-Ford Cosworth M14A	73 laps	7
9	Tim Schenken	Brabham	Brabham-Ford Cosworth BT33	72 laps	21
10	Howden Ganley	BRM	BRM P153	71 laps	17
11	John Surtees	Surtees	Surtees-Ford Cosworth TS9	67 laps	22
NC	Reine Wisell	Lotus	Lotus-Ford Cosworth 72C	58 laps	16
R	Emerson Fittipaldi	Lotus	Lotus-Ford Cosworth 72C	54 laps/suspension	14
R	Henri Pescarolo	Frank Williams Racing Cars	March-Ford Cosworth 711	53 laps/engine	11
R	Mario Andretti	Ferrari	Ferrari 312B	50 laps/engine	8
R	Alex Soler-Roig	March	March-Ford Cosworth 711	46 laps/mechanical	20
R	Andrea de Adamich	March	March-Alfa Romeo 711	26 laps/transmission	18
R	Ronnie Peterson	March	March-Ford Cosworth 711	24 laps/ignition	13
R	Clay Regazzoni	Ferrari	Ferrari 312B	13 laps/engine	2
R	Rolf Stommelen	Surtees	Surtees-Ford Cosworth TS9	9 laps/fuel pressure	19
R	Jo Siffert	BRM P160	BRM P160	5 laps/gearbox	10
R	Graham Hill	Brabham	Brabham-Ford Cosworth BT34	5 laps/steering	15

Pole: Ickx, 1m25.900s, 98.696mph/158.835kph. Fastest lap: Ickx, 1m25.100s, 99.623mph/160.329kph on Lap 69. Race leaders: Ickx 1-5, Stewart 6-75

FIVE, IN THE BLINK OF AN EYE

The 1971 Italian GP was one of the closest ever. Ronnie Peterson led onto the final lap from Francois Cevert. On reaching the last corner, Peterson slid wide, Cevert went for the inside and was blocked by Peter Gethin. Mike Hailwood and Howden Ganley were right there too, but Gethin won for BRM, by 0.01 from Peterson, with all five covered by just 0.61 seconds.

MONACO GRAND PRIX

MONTE CARLO • ROUND 3 • DATE: 23RD MAY 1971
Laps: 80 • Distance: 155.967miles/251.6km • Weather: Warm but dull

Pos	Driver	Team	Chassis-Engine	Result	Qual
1	Jackie Stewart	Tyrrell	Tyrrell-Ford Cosworth 003	1h52m21.300s	1
2	Ronnie Peterson	March	March-Ford Cosworth 711	1h52m46.900s	8
3	Jacky Ickx	Ferrari	Ferrari 312B2	1h53m14.600s	2
4	Denny Hulme	McLaren	McLaren-Ford Cosworth M19A	1h53m28.000s	6
5	Emerson Fittipaldi	Lotus	Lotus-Ford Cosworth 72D	79 laps	17
6	Rolf Stommelen	Surtees	Surtees-Ford Cosworth TS9	79 laps	16
7	John Surtees	Surtees	Surtees-Ford Cosworth TS9	79 laps	10
8	Henri Pescarolo	Frank Williams Racing Cars	March-Ford Cosworth 711	77 laps	13
9	Pedro Rodriguez	BRM	BRM P160	76 laps	5
10	Tim Schenken	Brabham	Brabham-Ford Cosworth BT33	76 laps	18
R	Jo Siffert	BRM	BRM P160	58 laps/oil line	3
R	Jean-Pierre Beltoise	Matra	Matra MS120B	47 laps/differential	7
R	Chris Amon	Matra	Matra MS120B	45 laps/differential	4
R	Clay Regazzoni	Ferrari	Ferrari 312B2	24 laps/accident	11
R	Peter Gethin	McLaren	McLaren-Ford Cosworth M14A	22 laps/accident	14
R	Reine Wisell	Lotus	Lotus-Ford Cosworth 72C	21 laps/wheel	12
R	Francois Cevert	Tyrrell	Tyrrell-Ford Cosworth 002	5 laps/accident	15
R	Graham Hill	Brabham	Brabham-Ford Cosworth BT34	1 lap/accident	9
DNQ	Howden Ganley	BRM	BRM P153	-	19
DNQ	Mario Andretti	Ferrari	Ferrari 312B	-	20
DNQ	Nanni Galli	March	March-Alfa Romeo 711	-	21
DNQ	Alex Soler-Roig	March	March-Ford Cosworth 711	-	22
DNQ	Skip Barber	Gene Mason Racing	March-Ford Cosworth 711	-	23

Pole: Stewart, 1m23.200s, 84.557mph/136.081kph. Fastest lap: Stewart, 1m22.200s, 85.585mph/137.737kph on Lap 57. Race leaders: Stewart 1-80

EVERYTHING BUT A WIN

Stepping up from a privately run March to the works team for his second year in F1, Ronnie Peterson starred and became Jackie Stewart's chief rival as the Ferrari challenge wilted. Second place at Monaco was followed by another at Silverstone, then two more in the Italian and Canadian GPs. For good measure, he also won the F2 title.

DUTCH GRAND PRIX

ZANDVOORT • ROUND 4 • DATE: 20TH JUNE 1971
Laps: 70 • Distance: 182.93miles/293.51km • Weather: Warm but wet

Pos	Driver	Team	Chassis-Engine	Result	Qual
1	Jacky Ickx	Ferrari	Ferrari 312B2	1h56m20.090s	1
2	Pedro Rodriguez	BRM	BRM P160	1h56m28.080s	2
3	Clay Regazzoni	Ferrari	Ferrari 312B2	69 laps	4
4	Ronnie Peterson	March	March-Ford Cosworth 711	68 laps	13
5	John Surtees	Surtees	Surtees-Ford Cosworth TS9	68 laps	7

Pos	Driver	Team	Chassis-Engine	Result	Qual
6	Jo Siffert	BRM	BRM P160	68 laps	8
7	Howden Ganley	BRM	BRM P153	66 laps	9
8	Gijs van Lennep	Stichting Autoraces*	Surtees-Ford Cosworth TS7	65 laps	21
9	Jean-Pierre Beltoise	Matra	Matra MS120B	65 laps	11
10	Graham Hill	Brabham	Brabham-Ford Cosworth BT34	65 laps	16
11	Jackie Stewart	Tyrrell	Tyrrell-Ford Cosworth 003	65 laps	3
12	Denny Hulme	McLaren	McLaren-Ford Cosworth M19A	63 laps	14
NC	Henri Pescarolo	Frank Williams*	March-Ford Cosworth 711	62 laps	15
NC	Peter Gethin	McLaren	McLaren-Ford Cosworth M19A	60 laps	23
NC	Skip Barber	Gene Mason Racing	March-Ford Cosworth 711	60 laps	24
R	Alex Soler-Roig	March	March-Ford Cosworth 711	57 laps/engine	17
R	Tim Schenken	Brabham	Brabham-Ford Cosworth BT33	39 laps/suspension	19
R	Francois Cevert	Tyrrell	Tyrrell-Ford Cosworth 002	29 laps/accident	12
DQ	Rolf Stommelen	Surtees	Surtees-Ford Cosworth TS9	19 laps/push start	18
DQ	Reine Wisell	Lotus	Lotus-Ford Cosworth 72D	17 laps/reversed into pits	6
R	Nanni Galli	March	March-Alfa Romeo 711	7 laps/accident	20
R	Dave Walker	Lotus	Lotus-Pratt & Whitney 56B	6 laps/accident	22
R	Mario Andretti	Ferrari	Ferrari 312B	5 laps/fuel pump	16
R	Chris Amon	Matra	Matra MS120B	2 laps/spun off	5

*Stichting Autoraces Nederland, Frank Williams Racing Cars

Pole: Ickx, 1m17.420s, 121.150mph/194.972kph. Fastest lap: Ickx, 1m34.950s, 98.785mph/158.980kph on Lap 49. Race leaders: Ickx 1-8 & 30 & 32-70, Rodriguez 9-29 & 31

STEWART'S RACE, SIFFERT'S WIN

Jackie Stewart was heading for a win in the Austrian GP that would wrap up the title three races early, but his Tyrrell broke a driveshaft and Jo Siffert found himself leading for BRM. Siffert was chased by Stewart's team-mate Francois Cevert until his gearbox broke and then won from Emerson Fittipaldi. With Jacky Ickx retiring, Stewart was crowned anyway.

FRENCH GRAND PRIX

CIRCUIT PAUL RICARD • ROUND 5 • DATE: 4TH JULY 1971
Laps: 55 • Distance: 198.251miles/319.55km • Weather: Hot & bright

Pos	Driver	Team	Chassis-Engine	Result	Qual
1	Jackie Stewart	Tyrrell	Tyrrell-Ford Cosworth 003	1h46m41.680s	1
2	Francois Cevert	Tyrrell	Tyrrell-Ford Cosworth 002	1h47m09.800s	7
3	Emerson Fittipaldi	Lotus	Lotus-Ford Cosworth 72D	1h47m15.750s	17
4	Jo Siffert	BRM	BRM P160	1h47m18.850s	6
5	Chris Amon	Matra	Matra MS120B	1h47m22.760s	9
6	Reine Wisell	Lotus	Lotus-Ford Cosworth 72D	1h47m57.700s	15
7	Jean-Pierre Beltoise	Matra	Matra MS120B	1h47m58.610s	8
8	John Surtees	Surtees	Surtees-Ford Cosworth TS9	1h48m06.590s	13
9	Peter Gethin	McLaren	McLaren-Ford Cosworth M19A	54 laps	19
10	Howden Ganley	BRM	BRM P153	54 laps	16
11	Rolf Stommelen	Surtees	Surtees-Ford Cosworth TS9	53 laps	10
12	Tim Schenken	Brabham	Brabham-Ford Cosworth BT33	50 laps/fuel pressure	14
13	Francois Mazet	Jo Siffert Automobiles	March-Ford Cosworth 701	50 laps	23
NC	Max Jean	Frank Williams Racing Cars	March-Ford Cosworth 711	46 laps	22

Pos	Driver	Team	Chassis-Engine	Result	Qual
R	Henri Pescarolo	Frank Williams Racing Cars	March-Ford Cosworth 711	45 laps/gearbox	18
R	Graham Hill	Brabham	Brabham-Ford Cosworth BT34	34 laps/oil line	4
R	Andrea de Adamich	March	March-Alfa Romeo 711	31 laps/engine	21
R	Pedro Rodriguez	BRM	BRM P160	27 laps/ignition	5
R	Clay Regazzoni	Ferrari	Ferrari 312B2	20 laps/accident	2
R	Ronnie Peterson	March	March-Alfa Romeo 711	19 laps/engine	12
R	Denny Hulme	McLaren	McLaren-Ford Cosworth M19A	16 laps/ignition	11
R	Jacky Ickx	Ferrari	Ferrari 312B2	4 laps/engine	3
R	Alex Soler-Roig	March	March-Ford Cosworth 711	4 laps/fuel pump	22
NS	Nanni Galli	March	March-Ford Cosworth 711	Soler-Roig drove car	20

Pole: Stewart, 1m50.710s, 117.393mph/188.926kph. Fastest lap: Stewart, 1m54.090s, 113.915mph/183.328kph on Lap 3. Race leaders: Stewart 1-55

BRM'S DOUBLE DISASTER

In a year that brought joy to BRM racers Pedro Rodriguez and Jo Siffert, with strong form for the Mexican and a win in Austria for the Swiss, both also paid the ultimate price. Rodríguez was killed in an Interserie sports car race at the Norisring, then three months later Siffert suffered suspension failure in the Rothmans Victory Race at Brands Hatch.

SAME TEAM, DIFFERENT NAME

Glance down the entry list for the Italian GP and it looks as though Emerson Fittipaldi had swapped teams, as he was entered in a Lotus fielded by World Wide Racing, rather than John Player Team Lotus. This was due to the legal ramifications that continued after Jochen Rindt's death at Monza in 1970, with Lotus fearing prosecution from the Italian authorities.

BRITISH GRAND PRIX

SILVERSTONE • ROUND 6 • DATE: 17TH JULY 1971
Laps: 68 • Distance: 199.33miles/320.314km • Weather: Warm & bright

Pos	Driver	Team	Chassis-Engine	Result	Qual
1	Jackie Stewart	Tyrrell	Tyrrell-Ford Cosworth 003	1h31m31.500s	2
2	Ronnie Peterson	March	March-Ford Cosworth 711	1h32m07.600s	5
3	Emerson Fittipaldi	Lotus	Lotus-Ford Cosworth 72D	1h32m22.000s	4
4	Henri Pescarolo	Frank Williams Racing Cars	March-Ford Cosworth 711	67 laps	17
5	Rolf Stommelen	Surtees	Surtees-Ford Cosworth TS9	67 laps	12
6	John Surtees	Surtees	Surtees-Ford Cosworth TS9	67 laps	18
7	Jean-Pierre Beltoise	Matra	Matra MS120B	66 laps	15
8	Howden Ganley	BRM	BRM P153	66 laps	11
9	Jo Siffert	BRM	BRM P160	66 laps	3
10	Francois Cevert	Tyrrell	Tyrrell-Ford Cosworth 002	65 laps	10
11	Nanni Galli	March	March-Ford Cosworth 711	65 laps	21
12	Tim Schenken	Brabham	Brabham-Ford Cosworth BT33	63 laps/gearbox	7
NC	Reine Wisell	Lotus	Lotus-Pratt & Whitney 56B	57 laps	19

Pos	Driver	Team	Chassis-Engine	Result	Qual
NC	Andrea de Adamich	March	March-Alfa Romeo 711	56 laps	24
R	Peter Gethin	McLaren	McLaren-Ford Cosworth M19A	53 laps/engine	14
R	Jacky Ickx	Ferrari	Ferrari 312B2	51 laps/engine	6
R	Clay Regazzoni	Ferrari	Ferrari 312B2	48 laps/fuel pressure	1
R	Chris Amon	Matra	Matra MS120B	35 laps/engine	9
R	Denny Hulme	McLaren	McLaren-Ford Cosworth M19A	32 laps/engine	8
R	Derek Bell	Surtees	Surtees-Ford Cosworth TS9	23 laps/suspension	23
R	Mike Beuttler	C-M-G Racing*	March-Ford Cosworth 711	21 laps/fuel pressure	20
R	Dave Charlton	Lotus	Lotus-Ford Cosworth 72D	1 lap/engine	13
R	Graham Hill	Brabham	Brabham-Ford Cosworth BT34	0 laps/accident	16
R	Jackie Oliver	McLaren	McLaren-Ford Cosworth M14A	0 laps/accident	22

*Clarke-Mordaunt-Guthrie Racing

Pole: Regazzoni, 1m18.100s, 134.917mph/217.129kph. Fastest lap: Stewart, 1m19.900s, 131.878mph/212.237kph on Lap 45. Race leaders: Regazzoni 1-3, Stewart 4-68

GERMAN GRAND PRIX

NURBURGRING • ROUND 7 • DATE: 1ST AUGUST 1971
Laps: 12 • Distance: 170.256miles/274.02km • Weather: Warm & bright

Pos	Driver	Team	Chassis-Engine	Result	Qual
1	Jackie Stewart	Tyrrell	Tyrrell-Ford Cosworth 003	1h29m15.700s	1
2	Francois Cevert	Tyrrell	Tyrrell-Ford Cosworth 002	1h29m45.800s	5
3	Clay Regazzoni	Ferrari	Ferrari 312B2	1h29m52.800s	4
4	Mario Andretti	Ferrari	Ferrari 312B2	1h31m20.700s	11
5	Ronnie Peterson	March	March-Ford Cosworth 711	1h31m44.800s	7
6	Tim Schenken	Brabham	Brabham-Ford Cosworth BT33	1h32m14.300s	9
7	John Surtees	Surtees	Surtees-Ford Cosworth TS9	1h32m34.700s	15
8	Reine Wisell	Lotus	Lotus-Ford Cosworth 72D	1h35m47.400s	17
9	Graham Hill	Brabham	Brabham-Ford Cosworth BT34	1h35m52.700s	13
10	Rolf Stommelen	Surtees	Surtees-Ford Cosworth TS9	11 laps	12
11	Vic Elford	BRM	BRM P160	11 laps	18
12	Nanni Galli	March	March-Alfa Romeo 711	10 laps	21
R	Emerson Fittipaldi	Lotus	Lotus-Ford Cosworth 72D	8 laps/oil leak	8
R	Chris Amon	Matra	Matra MS120B	6 laps/accident	16
R	Jo Siffert	BRM	BRM P160	6 laps/coil	3
R	Henri Pescarolo	Frank Williams*	March-Ford Cosworth 711	5 laps/suspension	10
R	Peter Gethin	McLaren	McLaren-Ford Cosworth M19A	5 laps/accident	19
R	Denny Hulme	McLaren	McLaren-Ford Cosworth M19A	3 laps/oil leak	6
DQ	Mike Beuttler	C-M-G Racing*	March-Ford Cosworth 711	3 laps/wrong way to pits	22
R	Howden Ganley	BRM	BRM P153	2 laps/engine	14
R	Andrea de Adamich	March	March-Alfa Romeo 711	2 laps/injection	20
R	Jacky Ickx	Ferrari	Ferrari 312B2	1 lap/accident	2
DNQ	Jo Bonnier	Ecurie Bonnier	McLaren-Ford Cosworth M7C	-	23
DNQ	Helmut Marko	Ecurie Bonnier	McLaren-Ford Cosworth M7C	out of fuel	-

*Clarke-Mordaunt-Guthrie Racing, Frank Williams Racing Cars

Pole: Stewart, 7m19.000s, 116.356mph/187.257kph. Fastest lap: Cevert, 7m20.100s, 116.065mph/186.789kph on Lap 10. Race leaders: Stewart 1-12

AUSTRIAN GRAND PRIX

OSTERREICHRING • ROUND 8 • DATE: 15TH AUGUST 1971
Laps: 54 • Distance: 198.337miles/319.194km • Weather: Warm & bright

Pos	Driver	Team	Chassis-Engine	Result	Qual
1	Jo Siffert	BRM	BRM P160	1h30m23.910s	1
2	Emerson Fittipaldi	Lotus	Lotus-Ford Cosworth 72D	1h30m28.030s	5
3	Tim Schenken	Brabham	Brabham-Ford Cosworth BT33	1h30m43.680s	7
4	Reine Wisell	Lotus	Lotus-Ford Cosworth 72D	1h30m55.780s	10
5	Graham Hill	Brabham	Brabham-Ford Cosworth BT34	1h31m12.340s	8
6	Henri Pescarolo	Frank Williams Racing Cars	March-Ford Cosworth 711	1h31m48.420s	13
7	Rolf Stommelen	Surtees	Surtees-Ford Cosworth TS9	1h32m01.330s	12
8	Ronnie Peterson	March	March-Ford Cosworth 711	53 laps	11
9	Jackie Oliver	McLaren	McLaren-Ford Cosworth M19A	53 laps	22
10	Peter Gethin	BRM	BRM P160	52 laps	16
11	Helmut Marko	BRM	BRM P153	52 laps	17
12	Nanni Galli	March	March-Alfa Romeo 711	51 laps	15
NC	Mike Beuttler	C-M-G Racing*	March-Ford Cosworth 711	47 laps	19
R	Francois Cevert	Tyrrell	Tyrrell-Ford Cosworth 002	42 laps/engine	3
R	Jackie Stewart	Tyrrell	Tyrrell-Ford Cosworth 003	35 laps/halfshaft	2
R	Jacky Ickx	Ferrari	Ferrari 312B2	31 laps/engine	6
R	Niki Lauda	March	March-Ford Cosworth 711	20 laps/handling	21
R	John Surtees	Surtees	Surtees-Ford Cosworth TS9	12 laps/engine	18
R	Clay Regazzoni	Ferrari	Ferrari 312B2	8 laps/engine	4
R	Howden Ganley	BRM	BRM P160	6 laps/ignition	14
R	Denny Hulme	McLaren	McLaren-Ford Cosworth M19A	4 laps/engine	9
NS	Jo Bonnier	Ecurie Bonnier	McLaren-Ford Cosworth M7C	fuel leak	20

*Clarke-Mordaunt-Guthrie Racing

Pole: Siffert, 1m37.440s, 135.699mph/218.386kph. Fastest lap: Siffert, 1m38.470s, 134.279mph/216.102kph on Lap 29. Race leaders: Siffert 1-54

TWO RIGHTS, TWO LEFTS

Used to host the United States GP since 1961, Watkins Glen offered more of a challenge in 1971 as it was given an extra loop that added 1.027 miles (1.652km) to its lap. This addition, known as The Anvil, was added after The Loop and offered a downhill left-hander and then a pair of right-handers, The Toe and The Heel, and then an uphill left.

ITALIAN GRAND PRIX

MONZA • ROUND 9 • DATE: 5TH SEPTEMBER 1971
Laps: 55 • Distance: 196.368miles/316.25km • Weather: Hot & bright

Pos	Driver	Team	Chassis-Engine	Result	Qual
1	Peter Gethin	BRM	BRM P160	1h18m12.600s	11
2	Ronnie Peterson	March	March-Ford Cosworth 711	1h18m12.610s	6
3	Francois Cevert	Tyrrell	Tyrrell-Ford Cosworth 002	1h18m12.690s	5
4	Mike Hailwood	Surtees	Surtees-Ford Cosworth TS9	1h18m12.780s	17
5	Howden Ganley	BRM	BRM P160	1h18m13.210s	4

Pos	Driver	Team	Chassis-Engine	Result	Qual
6	Chris Amon	Matra	Matra MS120B	1h18m44.960s	1
7	Jackie Oliver	McLaren	McLaren-Ford Cosworth M14A	1h19m37.430s	13
8	Emerson Fittipaldi	World Wide Racing	Lotus-Pratt & Whitney 56B	54 laps	18
9	Jo Siffert	BRM	BRM P160	53 laps	3
10	Jo Bonnier	Ecurie Bonnier	McLaren-Ford Cosworth M7C	51 laps	21
R	Graham Hill	Brabham	Brabham-Ford Cosworth BT34	47 laps/gearbox	14
NC	Jean-Pierre Jarier	Shell Arnold	March-Ford Cosworth 701	47 laps	24
R	Mike Beuttler	C-M-G Racing*	March-Ford Cosworth 711	41 laps/engine	16
R	Henri Pescarolo	Frank Williams Racing Cars	March-Ford Cosworth 711	40 laps/suspension	10
R	Andrea de Adamich	March	March-Alfa Romeo 711	33 laps/engine	20
R	Clay Regazzoni	Ferrari	Ferrari 312B2	17 laps/engine	8
R	Jacky Ickx	Ferrari	Ferrari 312B	15 laps/engine	2
R	Jackie Stewart	Tyrrell	Tyrrell-Ford Cosworth 003	15 laps/engine	7
R	Nanni Galli	March	March-Ford Cosworth 711	11 laps/electrical	19
R	Tim Schenken	Brabham	Brabham-Ford Cosworth BT33	5 laps/suspension	9
R	Silvio Moser	Jolly Club Switzerland	Bellasi-Ford Cosworth F170	5 laps/suspension	22
R	Helmut Marko	BRM	BRM P153	3 laps/engine	12
R	John Surtees	Surtees	Surtees-Ford Cosworth TS9A	3 laps/engine	15
NS	Rolf Stommelen	Surtees	Surtees-Ford Cosworth TS9	accident	23

*Clarke-Mordaunt-Guthrie Racing

Pole: Amon, 1m22.400s, 156.096mph/251.213kph. Fastest lap: Pescarolo, 1m23.800s, 153.489mph/247.016kph on Lap 9. Race leaders: Regazzoni 1-3 & 9, Peterson 4-7 & 10-14 & 17-22 & 24 & 26 & 33 & 47-50 & 54, Stewart 8, Cevert 15-16 & 23 & 31-32 & 34 & 36, Hailwood 25 & 27 & 35 & 42 & 51, Siffert 28-30, Amon 37-41 & 43-46, Gethin 52-53 & 55

NEW CIRCUITS

The French GP moved to a new home when it swapped old school and hilly Clermont-Ferrand for Paul Ricard, an ultra-modern circuit in the south of France. Its key feature was its 1-mile (1.6km) Mistral Straight, with the Signes corner at its far end a challenging high-speed right-hander that tested a car's handling as well as the driver's bravery.

CANADIAN GRAND PRIX

MOSPORT PARK • ROUND 10 • DATE: 19TH SEPTEMBER 1971
Laps: 64 • Distance: 157.361miles/253.248km • Weather: Warm but wet

Pos	Driver	Team	Chassis-Engine	Result	Qual
1	Jackie Stewart	Tyrrell	Tyrrell-Ford Cosworth 003	1h55m12.900s	1
2	Ronnie Peterson	March	March-Ford Cosworth 711	1h55m51.200s	6
3	Mark Donohue	Penske	McLaren-Ford Cosworth M19A	1h56m48.700s	8
4	Denny Hulme	McLaren	McLaren-Ford Cosworth M19A	63 laps	10
5	Reine Wisell	Lotus	Lotus-Ford Cosworth 72D	63 laps	7
6	Francois Cevert	Tyrrell	Tyrrell-Ford Cosworth 002	62 laps	3
7	Emerson Fittipaldi	Lotus	Lotus-Ford Cosworth 72D	62 laps	4
8	Jacky Ickx	Ferrari	Ferrari 312B2	62 laps	12
9	Jo Siffert	BRM	BRM P160	61 laps	2
10	Chris Amon	Matra	Matra MS120B	61 laps	5
11	John Surtees	Surtees	Surtees-Ford Cosworth TS9	60 laps	14
12	Helmut Marko	BRM	BRM P153	60 laps	19
13	Mario Andretti	Ferrari	Ferrari 312B2	60 laps	13
14	Peter Gethin	BRM	BRM P160	59 laps	16

Pos	Driver	Team	Chassis-Engine	Result	Qual
15	George Eaton	BRM	BRM P160	59 laps	21
16	Nanni Galli	March	March-Ford Cosworth 711	57 laps	20
NC	Mike Beuttler	March	March-Ford Cosworth 711	56 laps	22
NC	Pete Lovely	Pete Lovely Volkswagen Inc	Lotus-Ford Cosworth 69	55 laps	25
R	Rolf Stommelen	Surtees	Surtees-Ford Cosworth TS9	26 laps/overheating	23
R	Jean-Pierre Beltoise	Matra	Matra MS120B	15 laps/accident	11
R	Skip Barber	Gene Mason Racing	March-Ford Cosworth 711	13 laps/fuel pressure	24
R	Clay Regazzoni	Ferrari	Ferrari 312B	7 laps/accident	18
R	Graham Hill	Brabham	Brabham-Ford Cosworth BT34	2 laps/accident	15
R	Tim Schenken	Brabham	Brabham-Ford Cosworth BT33	1 lap/ignition	17
NS	Howden Ganley	BRM	BRM P160	accident	9
NS	Chris Craft	Ecurie Evergreen	Brabham-Ford Cosworth BT33	engine	25
NS	Henri Pescarolo	Frank Williams Racing Cars	March-Ford Cosworth 711	accident	27

Pole: Stewart, 1m15.300s, 117.550mph/189.179kph. Fastest lap: Hulme, 1m43.500s, 85.500mph/137.600kph on Lap 57. Race leaders: Stewart 1-17 & 31-64, Peterson 18-30

NEW DRIVERS

The most spectacular debut from any of 1971's 13 F1 debutants came from Mark Donohue when he turned up for the Canadian GP in a Penske-entered McLaren and came third. One race later, Howden Ganley who had a good first year with BRM took a fourth. Niki Lauda had a one-off for March but showed no sign that he'd become a three-time world champion

UNITED STATES GRAND PRIX

WATKINS GLEN • ROUND 11 • DATE: 3RD OCTOBER 1971
Laps: 59 • Distance: 199.251miles/320.665km • Weather: Warm & bright

Pos	Driver	Team	Chassis-Engine	Result	Qual
1	Francois Cevert	Tyrrell	Tyrrell-Ford Cosworth 002	1h43m51.991s	5
2	Jo Siffert	BRM	BRM P160	1h44m32.053s	6
3	Ronnie Peterson	March	March-Ford Cosworth 711	1h44m36.061s	11
4	Howden Ganley	BRM	BRM P160	1h44m48.740s	12
5	Jackie Stewart	Tyrrell	Tyrrell-Ford Cosworth 003	1h44m51.994s	1
6	Clay Regazzoni	Ferrari	Ferrari 312B2	1h45m08.417s	4
7	Graham Hill	Brabham	Brabham-Ford Cosworth BT34	58 laps	18
8	Jean-Pierre Beltoise	Matra	Matra MS120B	58 laps	10
9	Peter Gethin	BRM	BRM P160	58 laps	21
10	David Hobbs	Penske	McLaren-Ford Cosworth M19A	58 laps	22
11	Andrea de Adamich	March	March-Alfa Romeo 711	57 laps	26
12	Chris Amon	Matra	Matra MS120B	57 laps	8
13	Helmut Marko	BRM	BRM P160	57 laps	16
14	John Cannon	BRM	BRM P153	56 laps	24
15	Mike Hailwood	Surtees	Surtees-Ford Cosworth TS9	54 laps/accident	14
16	Jo Bonnier	Ecurie Bonnier	McLaren-Ford Cosworth M7C	54 laps/out of fuel	28
17	John Surtees	Surtees	Surtees-Ford Cosworth TS9A	54 laps	13
NC	Skip Barber	Gene Mason Racing	March-Ford Cosworth 711	52 laps	25
R	Jacky Ickx	Ferrari	Ferrari 312B	49 laps/alternator	7
NC	Emerson Fittipaldi	Lotus	Lotus-Ford Cosworth 72D	49 laps	2
NC	Pete Lovely	Pete Lovely Volkswagen Inc	Lotus-Ford Cosworth 69	49 laps	29

Pos	Driver	Team	Chassis-Engine	Result	Qual
R	Denny Hulme	McLaren	McLaren-Ford Cosworth M19A	47 laps/accident	3
R	Tim Schenken	Brabham	Brabham-Ford Cosworth BT33	41 laps/engine	15
R	Chris Craft	Ecurie Evergreen	Brabham-Ford Cosworth BT33	30 laps/suspension	27
R	Henri Pescarolo	Frank Williams Racing Cars	March-Ford Cosworth 711	23 laps/engine	20
R	Sam Posey	Surtees	Surtees-Ford Cosworth TS9	15 laps/engine	17
R	Nanni Galli	March	March-Ford Cosworth 711	11 laps/wheel	23
R	Reine Wisell	Lotus	Lotus-Ford Cosworth 72D	5 laps/brakes	9
R	Peter Revson	Tyrrell	Tyrrell-Ford Cosworth 001	1 lap/clutch	19
NS	Mario Andretti	Ferrari	Ferrari 312B2	raced at Trenton	6
NS	Mark Donohue	Penske	McLaren-Ford Cosworth M19A	raced at Trenton	19
NS	Gijs Van Lennep	Surtees	Surtees-Ford Cosworth TS9	Posey drove car	29

Pole: Stewart, 1m42.642s, 118.448mph/190.623kph. Fastest lap: Ickx, 1m43.474s, 117.495mph/189.090kph on Lap 43. Race leaders: Stewart 1-13, Cevert 14-59

IN MEMORIAM

The year was already a sad one before the deaths of Pedro Rodriguez and Jo Siffert, as Ignazio Giunti didn't get to add to the four outings he'd had for Ferrari in 1970 (his best result was fourth at Spa) as he was killed in a sports car race in Buenos Aires when he ploughed into Jean-Pierre Beltoise's stricken Matra as it was being pushed back to the pits.

WORLD DRIVERS' CHAMPIONSHIP FINAL RESULTS

Pos	Driver	Nat	Car-Engine	R1	R2	R3	R4
1	Jackie Stewart	GBR	Tyrrell-Ford Cosworth 001	2P	-	-	-
			Tyrrell-Ford Cosworth 003	-	1	1PF	11
2	Ronnie Peterson	SWE	March-Ford Cosworth 711	10	R	2	4
			March-Alfa Romeo 711	-	-	-	-
3	Francois Cevert	FRA	Tyrrell-Ford Cosworth 002	R	7	R	R
4	Jacky Ickx	BEL	Ferrari 312B	8	2PF	-	-
			Ferrari 312B2	-	-	3	1PF
4	Jo Siffert	CHE	BRM P153	R	-	-	-
			BRM P160	-	R	R	6
6	Emerson Fittipaldi	BRA	Lotus-Ford Cosworth 72C	R	R	-	-
			Lotus-Ford Cosworth 72D	-	-	5	-
			Lotus-Pratt & Whitney 56B	-	-	-	-
7	Clay Regazzoni	CHE	Ferrari 312B	3	R	-	-
			Ferrari 312B2	-	-	R	3
8	Mario Andretti	USA	Ferrari 312B	1F	R	DNQ	R
			Ferrari 312B2	-	-	-	-
9	Peter Gethin	GBR	McLaren-Ford Cosworth M14A	R	8	R	-
			McLaren-Ford Cosworth M19A	-	-	-	NC
			BRM P160	-	-	-	-
9	Pedro Rodriguez	MEX	BRM P160	R	4	9	2
9	Chris Amon	NZL	Matra MS120	5	3	-	-
			Matra MS120B	-	-	R	R
9	Reine Wisell	SWE	Lotus-Ford Cosworth 72C	4	NC	R	-
			Lotus-Ford Cosworth 72D	-	-	-	DQ
			Lotus-Pratt & Whitney 56B	-	-	-	-
9	Denny Hulme	NZL	McLaren-Ford Cosworth M19A	6	5	4	12

Pos	Driver	Nat	Car-Engine	R1	R2	R3	R4
14	Tim Schenken	AUS	Brabham-Ford Cosworth BT33	-	9	10	R
14	Howden Ganley	NZL	BRM P153	R	10	DNQ	7
			BRM P160	-	-	-	-
16	Mark Donohue	USA	McLaren-Ford Cosworth M19A	-	-	-	-
16	Henri Pescarolo	FRA	March-Ford Cosworth 711	11	R	8	NC
18	Mike Hailwood	GBR	Surtees-Ford Cosworth TS9	-	-	-	-
18	John Surtees	GBR	Surtees-Ford Cosworth TS9	R	11	7	5
			Surtees-Ford Cosworth TS9A	-	-	-	-
18	Rolf Stommelen	DEU	Surtees-Ford Cosworth TS7	12	-	-	-
			Surtees-Ford Cosworth TS9	-	R	6	DQ
21	Graham Hill	GBR	Brabham-Ford Cosworth BT33	9	-	-	-
			Brabham-Ford Cosworth BT34	-	R	R	10
22	Jean-Pierre Beltoise	FRA	Matra MS120B	-	6	R	9

Pos	Driver	R5	R6	R7	R8	R9	R10	R11	Total
1	Stewart	-	-	-	-	-	-	-	62
		1PF	1F	1P	R	R	1P	5P	
2	Peterson	-	2	5	8	2	2	3	33
		R	-	-	-	-	-	-	-
3	Cevert	2	10	2F	R	3	6	1	26
4	Ickx	-	-	-	-	R	-	RF	19
		R	R	R	R	-	8	-	
4	Siffert	-	-	-	-	-	-	-	19
		4	9	R	1PF	9	9	2	
6	Fittipaldi	-	-	-	-	-	-	-	16
		3	3	R	2	-	7	NC	
		-	-	-	-	8	-	-	
7	Regazzoni	-	-	-	-	-	-	-	13
		R	RP	3	R	R	R	6	
8	Andretti	-	-	-	-	-	-	-	12
		-	-	4	-	-	13	NS	
9	Gethin	-	-	-	-	-	-	-	9
		9	R	R	-	-	-	-	
		-	-	-	10	1	14	9	
9	Rodriguez	R	-	-	-	-	-	-	9
9	Amon	-	-	-	-	-	-	-	9
		5	R	R	-	6P	10	12	
9	Wisell	-	-	-	-	-	-	-	9
		6	-	8	4	-	5	R	
		-	NC	-	-	-	-	-	
9	Hulme	R	R	R	R	-	4F	R	9
14	Schenken	12	12	6	3	R	R	R	5
14	Ganley	10	8	R	-	-	-	-	5
		-	-	-	R	5	NS	4	
16	Donohue	-	-	-	-	-	3	NS	4
16	Pescarolo	R	4	R	6	RF	NS	R	4
18	Hailwood	-	-	-	-	4	-	15	3
18	Surtees	8	6	7	R	-	11	-	3
		-	-	-	-	R	-	17	
18	Stommelen	-	-	-	-	-	-	-	3
		11	5	10	7	NS	R	-	
21	Hill	-	-	-	-	-	-	-	2
		R	R	9	5	R	R	7	
22	Beltoise	7	7	-	-	-	R	8	1

WORLD CONSTRUCTORS' CHAMPIONSHIP FINAL RESULTS

Pos	Team-Engine	R1	R2	R3	R4	R5	R6	R7	R8	R9	R10	R11	Total
1	Tyrrell-Ford	2	1	1	11	1	1	1	-	3	1	1	73
2	BRM	-	4	9	2	4	8	11	1	1	9	2	36
3	Ferrari	1	2	3	1	-	-	3	-	-	8	6	33
4	March-Ford	11	-	8	NC	13	4	-	6	-	R	R	33
5	Lotus-Ford	4	-	5	DQ	3	3	8	2	-	5	NC	21
6	McLaren-Ford	6	5	4	12	9	-	-	9	7	4	10	10
7	Matra	5	3	-	9	5	7	-	-	6	10	8	9
8	Surtees-Ford	7	11	6	5	8	5	7	7	4	11	15	8
9	Brabham-Ford	9	9	10	10	12	12	6	3	-	R	7	5

SYMBOLS AND GRAND PRIX KEY

Round 1 South African GP
Round 2 Spanish GP
Round 3 Monaco GP
Round 4 Dutch GP
Round 5 French GP
Round 6 British GP
Round 7 German GP
Round 8 Austrian GP
Round 9 Italian GP
Round 10 Canadian GP
Round 11 United States GP

SCORING

1st 9 points
2nd 6 points
3rd 4 points
4th 3 points
5th 2 points
6th 1 point

DNPQ DID NOT PRE-QUALIFY **DNQ** DID NOT QUALIFY **DQ** DISQUALIFIED **EX** EXCLUDED
F FASTEST LAP **NC** NOT CLASSIFIED **NS** NON-STARTER **P** POLE POSITION **R** RETIRED

1972

SEASON SUMMARY

Two years after his F1 debut, Emerson Fittipaldi became the then youngest world champion to that date at the age of 25, dominating the European part of the season in his Lotus 72. With reigning champion Jackie Stewart forced to miss the Belgian GP because of a stomach ulcer, the Brazilian ace was crowned with two races still to run. In the first season in which F1 ran to an increased minimum weight of 550kg (1,212lb), with engines of no more than 12 cylinders, cars powered by Ford Cosworth DFV V8s continued to dominate. McLaren's Denny Hulme was a consistent third while Jacky Ickx's Ferrari proved fragile. A tyre war between Firestone and Goodyear led to F1's first qualifying tyres.

ARGENTINIAN GRAND PRIX

BUENOS AIRES • ROUND 1 • DATE: 23RD JANUARY 1972
Laps: 95 • Distance: 197.485miles/317.822km • Weather: Very hot & bright

Pos	Driver	Team	Chassis-Engine	Result	Qual
1	Jackie Stewart	Tyrrell	Tyrrell-Ford Cosworth 003	1h57m58.820s	2
2	Denny Hulme	McLaren	McLaren-Ford Cosworth M19A	1h58m24.780s	4
3	Jacky Ickx	Ferrari	Ferrari 312B2-72	1h58m58.210s	8
4	Clay Regazzoni	Ferrari	Ferrari 312B2-72	1h59m05.540s	6
5	Tim Schenken	Surtees	Surtees-Ford Cosworth TS9B	1h59m07.930s	11
6	Ronnie Peterson	March	March-Ford Cosworth 721	94 laps	10
7	Carlos Reutemann	Brabham	Brabham-Ford Cosworth BT34	93 laps	1
8	Henri Pescarolo	Frank Williams*	March-Ford Cosworth 721	93 laps	15
9	Howden Ganley	BRM	BRM P160B	93 laps	13
10	Helmut Marko	BRM	BRM P153	93 laps	19
11	Niki Lauda	March	March-Ford Cosworth 721	93 laps	22
R	Emerson Fittipaldi	Lotus	Lotus-Ford Cosworth 72D	61 laps/suspension	5
R	Francois Cevert	Tyrrell	Tyrrell-Ford Cosworth 002	59 laps/gearbox	7
R	Reine Wisell	BRM	BRM P153	59 laps/water leak	17
R	Peter Revson	McLaren	McLaren-Ford Cosworth M19A	49 laps/engine	3
R	Mario Andretti	Ferrari	Ferrari 312B2-72	20 laps/engine	9
R	Andrea de Adamich	Surtees	Surtees-Ford Cosworth TS9B	11 laps/fuel system	14
R	Graham Hill	Brabham	Brabham-Ford Cosworth BT33	11 laps/fuel pump	16
DQ	Dave Walker	Lotus	Lotus-Ford Cosworth 72D	8 laps/used tools on car	20
R	Peter Gethin	BRM	BRM P160B	1 lap/oil leak	18
R	Alex Soler-Roig	BRM	BRM P160B	1 lap/accident	21
R	Chris Amon	Matra	Matra MS120C	0 laps/gearbox	12

*Frank Williams Racing Cars

Pole: Reutemann, 1m12.460s, 103.280mph/166.213kph. Fastest lap: Stewart, 1m13.660s, 101.597mph/163.505kph on Lap 25. Race leaders: Stewart 1-95

COLLECTING THE GREATS

When Graham Hill raced to victory for Matra with Henri Pescarolo in the Le Mans 24 Hours, he was acknowledged as the first winner of what was described as motor racing's triple crown, as he had already won the Monaco GP (a then-record five times) as well as the Indianapolis 500 that he won in a John Mecom-owned Lola in 1966.

SOUTH AFRICAN GRAND PRIX

KYALAMI • ROUND 2 • DATE: 4TH MARCH 1972
Laps: 79 • Distance: 201.458miles/324.216km • Weather: Hot & bright

Pos	Driver	Team	Chassis-Engine	Result	Qual
1	Denny Hulme	McLaren	McLaren-Ford Cosworth M19A	1h45m49.100s	5
2	Emerson Fittipaldi	Lotus	Lotus-Ford Cosworth 72D	1h46m03.200s	3
3	Peter Revson	McLaren	McLaren-Ford Cosworth M19A	1h46m14.900s	12
4	Mario Andretti	Ferrari	Ferrari 312B2-72	1h46m27.600s	6
5	Ronnie Peterson	March	March-Ford Cosworth 721	1h46m38.100s	9
6	Graham Hill	Brabham	Brabham-Ford Cosworth BT33	78 laps	14
7	Niki Lauda	March	March-Ford Cosworth 721	78 laps	21
8	Jacky Ickx	Ferrari	Ferrari 312B2-72	78 laps	7
9	Francois Cevert	Tyrrell	Tyrrell-Ford Cosworth 002	78 laps	8
10	Dave Walker	Lotus	Lotus-Ford Cosworth 72D	78 laps	19
11	Henri Pescarolo	Frank Williams Racing Cars	March-Ford Cosworth 721	78 laps	22
12	Clay Regazzoni	Ferrari	Ferrari 312B2-72	77 laps	2
13	Rolf Stommelen	Eifelland	Eifelland-Ford Cosworth 21	77 laps	25
14	Helmut Marko	BRM	BRM P153	76 laps	23
15	Chris Amon	Matra	Matra MS120C	76 laps	13
16	John Love	Team Gunston	Surtees-Ford Cosworth TS9	73 laps/spun off	26
17	Carlos Pace	Frank Williams Racing Cars	March-Ford Cosworth 711	73 laps	24
NC	Howden Ganley	BRM	BRM P160B	70 laps	16
NC	Andrea de Adamich	Surtees	Surtees-Ford Cosworth TS9B	69 laps	20
NC	Peter Gethin	BRM	BRM P160B	65 laps	18
R	Jean-Pierre Beltoise	BRM	BRM P160B	61 laps/engine	11
R	Jackie Stewart	Tyrrell	Tyrrell-Ford Cosworth 003	45 laps/gearbox	1
R	Mike Hailwood	Surtees	Surtees-Ford Cosworth TS9B	28 laps/suspension	4
R	Carlos Reutemann	Brabham	Brabham-Ford Cosworth BT34	27 laps/fuel system	15
R	Tim Schenken	Surtees	Surtees-Ford Cosworth TS9B	9 laps/engine	10
R	Dave Charlton	Scuderia Scribante	Lotus-Ford Cosworth 72D	2 laps/fuel pump	17
NS	Willie Ferguson	Team Gunston	Brabham-Ford Cosworth BT33	engine	27

Pole: Stewart, 1m17.000s, 119.225mph/191.875kph. Fastest lap: Hailwood, 1m18.900s, 116.354mph/187.254kph on Lap 20. Race leaders: Hulme 1 & 57-79, Stewart 2-44, Fittipaldi 45-56

BRM'S FINAL GRAND PRIX WIN

It took BRM years to take its first F1 win, before title success came with Graham Hill in 1962 and an upturn in form in the early 1970s. But the 1972 Monaco GP was the team's last win. This was an unexpected victory, but Jean-Pierre Beltoise starred in the wet. He powered into the lead from the second row and led all the way to win by 38 seconds.

SOME GUYS HAVE NONE OF THE LUCK

Chris Amon did everything in an F1 car except win a World Championship round. That looked set to change at Clermont-Ferrand when the New Zealander led comfortably for Matra from Denny Hulme and Jackie Stewart. Then, at half-distance, he collected a puncture, fell to eighth and raced back to third, but another win had escaped him.

SPANISH GRAND PRIX

JARAMA • ROUND 3 • DATE: 1ST MAY 1972
Laps: 90 • Distance: 190.380miles/306.387km • Weather: Cool with showers

Pos	Driver	Team	Chassis-Engine	Result	Qual
1	Emerson Fittipaldi	Lotus	Lotus-Ford Cosworth 72D	2h03m41.230s	3
2	Jacky Ickx	Ferrari	Ferrari 312B2-72	2h04m00.150s	1
3	Clay Regazzoni	Ferrari	Ferrari 312B2-72	89 laps	8
4	Andrea de Adamich	Surtees	Surtees-Ford Cosworth TS9B	89 laps	13
5	Peter Revson	McLaren	McLaren-Ford Cosworth M19A	89 laps	11
6	Carlos Pace	Frank Williams Racing Cars	March-Ford Cosworth 711	89 laps	16
7	Wilson Fittipaldi	Brabham	Brabham-Ford Cosworth BT33	88 laps	14
8	Tim Schenken	Surtees	Surtees-Ford Cosworth TS9B	88 laps	18
9	Dave Walker	Lotus	Lotus-Ford Cosworth 72D	87 laps/out of fuel	24
10	Graham Hill	Brabham	Brabham-Ford Cosworth BT37	86 laps	23
11	Henri Pescarolo	Frank Williams Racing Cars	March-Ford Cosworth 721	86 laps	19
R	Jackie Stewart	Tyrrell	Tyrrell-Ford Cosworth 003	69 laps/accident	4
R	Chris Amon	Matra	Matra MS120C	66 laps/gearbox	6
R	Francois Cevert	Tyrrell	Tyrrell-Ford Cosworth 002	65 laps/ignition	12
R	Peter Gethin	BRM	BRM P180	65 laps/engine	21
R	Denny Hulme	McLaren	McLaren-Ford Cosworth M19A	48 laps/gearbox	2
R	Howden Ganley	BRM	BRM P160B	38 laps/engine	20
R	Reine Wisell	BRM	BRM P160B	24 laps/accident	10
R	Mario Andretti	Ferrari	Ferrari 312B2-72	23 laps/fuel pressure	5
R	Mike Hailwood	Surtees	Surtees-Ford Cosworth TS9B	20 laps/electrical	15
R	Ronnie Peterson	March	March-Ford Cosworth 721X	16 laps/oil leak	9
R	Rolf Stommelen	Eifelland	Eifelland-Ford Cosworth 21	15 laps/accident	17
R	Jean-Pierre Beltoise	BRM	BRM P160B	9 laps/gearbox	7
R	Niki Lauda	March	March-Ford Cosworth 721X	7 laps/differential	25
R	Alex Soler-Roig	BRM	BRM P160B	6 laps/accident	22
DNQ	Mike Beuttler	C-M-G Racing*	March-Ford Cosworth 721G	-	26

*Clarke-Mordaunt-Guthrie Racing

Pole: Ickx, 1m18.430s, 97.095mph/156.260kph. Fastest lap: Ickx, 1m21.010s, 94.003mph/151.283kph on Lap 52. Race leaders: Hulme 1-4, Stewart 5-8, Fittipaldi 9-90

MONACO GRAND PRIX

MONTE CARLO • ROUND 4 • DATE: 14TH MAY 1972
Laps: 80 • Distance: 155.967miles/251.6km • Weather: Cool and very wet

Pos	Driver	Team	Chassis-Engine	Result	Qual
1	Jean-Pierre Beltoise	BRM	BRM P160B	2h26m54.700s	4
2	Jacky Ickx	Ferrari	Ferrari 312B2-72	2h27m32.900s	2
3	Emerson Fittipaldi	Lotus	Lotus-Ford Cosworth 72D	79 laps	1
4	Jackie Stewart	Tyrrell	Tyrrell-Ford Cosworth 004	78 laps	8
5	Brian Redman	McLaren	McLaren-Ford Cosworth M19A	77 laps	10
6	Chris Amon	Matra	Matra MS120C	77 laps	6
7	Andrea de Adamich	Surtees	Surtees-Ford Cosworth TS9B	77 laps	18
8	Helmut Marko	BRM	BRM P153B	77 laps	17
9	Wilson Fittipaldi	Brabham	Brabham-Ford Cosworth BT33	77 laps	21
10	Rolf Stommelen	Eifelland	Eifelland-Ford Cosworth 21	77 laps	25
11	Ronnie Peterson	March	March-Ford Cosworth 721X	76 laps	15
12	Graham Hill	Brabham	Brabham-Ford Cosworth BT37	76 laps	19
13	Mike Beuttler	C-M-G Racing*	March-Ford Cosworth 721G	76 laps	23

Pos	Driver	Team	Chassis-Engine	Result	Qual
14	Dave Walker	Lotus	Lotus-Ford Cosworth 72D	75 laps	14
15	Denny Hulme	McLaren	McLaren-Ford Cosworth M19C	74 laps	7
16	Niki Lauda	March	March-Ford Cosworth 721X	74 laps	22
17	Carlos Pace	Frank Williams*	March-Ford Cosworth 711	72 laps	24
NC	Francois Cevert	Tyrrell	Tyrrell-Ford Cosworth 002	70 laps	12
R	Henri Pescarolo	Frank Williams*	March-Ford Cosworth 721	58 laps/accident	9
R	Clay Regazzoni	Ferrari	Ferrari 312B2-72	51 laps/accident	3
R	Mike Hailwood	Surtees	Surtees-Ford Cosworth TS9B	48 laps/accident	11
R	Howden Ganley	BRM	BRM P180	47 laps/accident	20
R	Tim Schenken	Surtees	Surtees-Ford Cosworth TS9B	31 laps/accident	13
DQ	Peter Gethin	BRM	BRM P160B	27 laps/reversed into pits	5
R	Reine Wisell	BRM	BRM P160B	16 laps/engine	16

*Clarke-Mordaunt-Guthrie Racing, Frank Williams Racing Cars

Pole: Fittipaldi, 1m21.400s, 86.427mph/139.090kph. Fastest lap: Beltoise, 1m40.000s, 70.351mph/113.220kph on Lap 9. Race leaders: Beltoise 1-80

BELGIAN GRAND PRIX

NIVELLES • ROUND 5 • DATE: 4TH JUNE 1972
Laps: 85 • Distance: 196.386miles/316.54km • Weather: Warm & bright

Pos	Driver	Team	Chassis-Engine	Result	Qual
1	Emerson Fittipaldi	Lotus	Lotus-Ford Cosworth 72D	1h44m06.700s	1
2	Francois Cevert	Tyrrell	Tyrrell-Ford Cosworth 002	1h44m33.300s	5
3	Denny Hulme	McLaren	McLaren-Ford Cosworth M19C	1h45m04.800s	3
4	Mike Hailwood	Surtees	Surtees-Ford Cosworth TS9B	1h45m18.700s	8
5	Carlos Pace	Frank Williams*	March-Ford Cosworth 711	84 laps	11
6	Chris Amon	Matra	Matra MS120C	84 laps	13
7	Peter Revson	McLaren	McLaren-Ford Cosworth M19A	83 laps	7
8	Howden Ganley	BRM	BRM P160B	83 laps	15
9	Ronnie Peterson	March	March-Ford Cosworth 721X	83 laps	14
10	Helmut Marko	BRM	BRM P153B	83 laps	23
11	Rolf Stommelen	Eifelland	Eifelland-Ford Cosworth 21	83 laps	20
12	Niki Lauda	March	March-Ford Cosworth 721X	82 laps	25
13	Carlos Reutemann	Brabham	Brabham-Ford Cosworth BT37	81 laps	9
14	Dave Walker	Lotus	Lotus-Ford Cosworth 72D	79 laps	12
R	Graham Hill	Brabham	Brabham-Ford Cosworth BT37	73 laps/suspension	16
NC	Henri Pescarolo	Frank Williams*	March-Ford Cosworth 721	59 laps	19
R	Clay Regazzoni	Ferrari	Ferrari 312B2-72	57 laps/accident	2
R	Andrea de Adamich	Surtees	Surtees-Ford Cosworth TS9B	55 laps/engine	10
R	Nanni Galli	Tecno	Tecno PA123	54 laps/accident	24
R	Jacky Ickx	Ferrari	Ferrari 312B2-72	47 laps/fuel injection	4
R	Mike Beuttler	C-M-G Racing*	March-Ford Cosworth 721G	31 laps/halfshaft	22
R	Wilson Fittipaldi	Brabham	Brabham-Ford Cosworth BT34	28 laps/gearbox	18
R	Peter Gethin	BRM	BRM P160B	27 laps/fuel pump	17
R	Jean-Pierre Beltoise	BRM	BRM P160B	15 laps/overheating	6
R	Tim Schenken	Surtees	Surtees-Ford Cosworth TS9B	11 laps/overheating	21
NS	Vern Schuppan	BRM	BRM P153B	Marko drove car	26

*Clarke-Mordaunt-Guthrie Racing, Frank Williams Racing Cars

Pole: Fittipaldi, 1m11.430s, 116.622mph/187.685kph. Fastest lap: Amon, 1m12.120s, 115.506mph/185.890kph on Lap 66. Race leaders: Regazzoni 1-8, Fittipaldi 9-85

BLINDED IN ONE EYE

Austrian fans looked set for a double treat in 1972 as Niki Lauda and Helmut Marko became more competitive in their second year of F1. Then, in a flash, it all ended for BRM driver Marko as a stone was flicked up at Clermont-Ferrand, pierced his visor and left him blind in one eye. In recent years, he has run Red Bull's development drivers.

FRENCH GRAND PRIX

CLERMONT-FERRAND • ROUND 6 • DATE: 2ND JULY 1972
Laps: 38 • Distance: 190.145miles/306.09km • Weather: Warm & bright

Pos	Driver	Team	Chassis-Engine	Result	Qual
1	Jackie Stewart	Tyrrell	Tyrrell-Ford Cosworth 003	1h52m21.500s	3
2	Emerson Fittipaldi	Lotus	Lotus-Ford Cosworth 72D	1h52m49.200s	8
3	Chris Amon	Matra	Matra MS120D	1h52m53.400s	1
4	Francois Cevert	Tyrrell	Tyrrell-Ford Cosworth 002	1h53m10.800s	7
5	Ronnie Peterson	March	March-Ford Cosworth 721G	1h53m18.300s	9
6	Mike Hailwood	Surtees	Surtees-Ford Cosworth TS9B	1h53m57.600s	10
7	Denny Hulme	McLaren	McLaren-Ford Cosworth M19C	1h54m09.600s	2
8	Wilson Fittipaldi	Brabham	Brabham-Ford Cosworth BT34	1h54m46.600s	14
9	Brian Redman	McLaren	McLaren-Ford Cosworth M19A	1h55m17.000s	13
10	Graham Hill	Brabham	Brabham-Ford Cosworth BT37	1h55m21.000s	20
11	Jacky Ickx	Ferrari	Ferrari 312B2-72	37 laps	4
12	Carlos Reutemann	Brabham	Brabham-Ford Cosworth BT37	37 laps	17
13	Nanni Galli	Ferrari	Ferrari 312B2-72	37 laps	19
14	Andrea de Adamich	Surtees	Surtees-Ford Cosworth TS9B	37 laps	12
15	Jean-Pierre Beltoise	BRM	BRM P160B	37 laps	24
16	Rolf Stommelen	Eifelland	Eifelland-Ford Cosworth 21	37 laps	15
17	Tim Schenken	Surtees	Surtees-Ford Cosworth TS9B	36 laps	5
18	Dave Walker	Lotus	Lotus-Ford Cosworth 72D	34 laps/halfshaft	22
19	Mike Beuttler	C-M-G Racing*	March-Ford Cosworth 721G	33 laps/out of fuel	23
NC	Patrick Depailler	Tyrrell	Tyrrell-Ford Cosworth 004	33 laps	16
R	Reine Wisell	BRM	BRM P160B	25 laps/gearbox	18
R	Carlos Pace	Frank Williams Racing Cars	March-Ford Cosworth 711	18 laps/engine	11
R	Helmut Marko	BRM	BRM P160B	8 laps/physical	6
R	Niki Lauda	March	March-Ford Cosworth 721G	4 laps/halfshaft	21
NS	Henri Pescarolo	Frank Williams Racing Cars	March-Ford Cosworth 721	accident	12
NS	Howden Ganley	BRM	BRM P160B	Beltoise drove car	22
NS	Peter Gethin	BRM	BRM P160B	accident	23
NS	Derek Bell	Tecno	Tecno PA123	cracked chassis	28
NS	Dave Charlton	Scuderia Scribante	Lotus-Ford Cosworth 72D	car not ready	29

*Clarke-Mordaunt-Guthrie Racing

Pole: Amon, 2m53.400s, 103.913mph/167.231kph. Fastest lap: Amon, 2m53.900s, 103.614mph/166.751kph on Lap 32. Race leaders: Amon 1-19, Stewart 20-38

BRITISH GRAND PRIX

BRANDS HATCH • ROUND 7 • DATE: 15TH JULY 1972
Laps: 76 • Distance: 201.401miles/324.124km • Weather: Warm & bright

Pos	Driver	Team	Chassis-Engine	Result	Qual
1	Emerson Fittipaldi	Lotus	Lotus-Ford Cosworth 72D	1h47m50.200s	2
2	Jackie Stewart	Tyrrell	Tyrrell-Ford Cosworth 003	1h47m54.300s	4
3	Peter Revson	McLaren	McLaren-Ford Cosworth M19A	1h49m02.700s	3
4	Chris Amon	Matra	Matra MS120C	75 laps	17
5	Denny Hulme	McLaren	McLaren-Ford Cosworth M19C	75 laps	11
6	Arturo Merzario	Ferrari	Ferrari 312B2-72	75 laps	9
7	Ronnie Peterson	March	March-Ford Cosworth 721G	74 laps/spun off	8
8	Carlos Reutemann	Brabham	Brabham-Ford Cosworth BT37	73 laps	10
9	Niki Lauda	March	March-Ford Cosworth 721G	73 laps	19
10	Rolf Stommelen	Eifelland	Eifelland-Ford Cosworth 21	71 laps	25
11	Jean-Pierre Beltoise	BRM	BRM P160C	70 laps	6
12	Wilson Fittipaldi	Brabham	Brabham-Ford Cosworth BT34	69 laps/suspension	22
13	Mike Beuttler	C-M-G Racing*	March-Ford Cosworth 721G	69 laps	23
R	Tim Schenken	Surtees	Surtees-Ford Cosworth TS9B	64 laps/suspension	5
R	Francois Cevert	Tyrrell	Tyrrell-Ford Cosworth 002	60 laps/spun off	12
R	Dave Walker	Lotus	Lotus-Ford Cosworth 72D	59 laps/suspension	15
R	Jacky Ickx	Ferrari	Ferrari 312B2-72	49 laps/fuel pressure	1
R	Graham Hill	Brabham	Brabham-Ford Cosworth BT37	47 laps/spun off	21
R	Carlos Pace	Frank Williams Racing Cars	March-Ford Cosworth 711	39 laps/differential	13
R	Jackie Oliver	BRM	BRM P160B	36 laps/suspension	14
R	Mike Hailwood	Surtees	Surtees-Ford Cosworth TS9B	31 laps/gearbox	7
R	Dave Charlton	Scribante Racing	Lotus-Ford Cosworth 72D	21 laps/gearbox	24
R	Nanni Galli	Tecno	Tecno PA123	9 laps/spun off	18
R	Henri Pescarolo	Frank Williams Racing Cars	Politoys-Ford Cosworth FX3	7 laps/accident	26
R	Peter Gethin	BRM	BRM P160B	5 laps/engine	16
R	Andrea de Adamich	Surtees	Surtees-Ford Cosworth TS9B	3 laps/accident	20
DNQ	Francois Migault	Connew	Connew-Ford Cosworth PC1	suspension	27

*Clarke-Mordaunt-Guthrie Racing

Pole: Ickx, 1m22.200s, 116.059mph/186.779kph. Fastest lap: Stewart, 1m24.000s, 113.572mph/182.777kph on Lap 58. Race leaders: Ickx 1-48, Fittipaldi 49-76

NEW CIRCUITS

From the sublime to the ridiculous was the feeling when the Belgian GP moved from Spa-Francorchamps to a new circuit, Nivelles. Built just outside the capital Brussels, this unchallenging track was unpopular with the drivers. The insertion of three chicanes to break up the slipstreaming packs of cars at Monza made the Italian track feel like a new circuit too.

NEW CONSTRUCTORS

Of the constructors new to F1 in 1972, Williams would start very slowly with its Politoys car, named after its sponsor, before working its way to nine constructors' titles from 1980. Eifelland was a caravan manufacturer that elected to reclothe a March with unusual bodywork, while Connew built its car in a lock-up garage and qualified just once.

GERMAN GRAND PRIX

NURBURGRING • ROUND 8 • DATE: 30TH JULY 1972
Laps: 14 • Distance: 198.260miles/319.69km • Weather: Warm & bright

Pos	Driver	Team	Chassis-Engine	Result	Qual
1	Jacky Ickx	Ferrari	Ferrari 312B2-72	1h42m12.300s	1
2	Clay Regazzoni	Ferrari	Ferrari 312B2-72	1h43m00.600s	7
3	Ronnie Peterson	March	March-Ford Cosworth 721G	1h43m19.000s	4
4	Howden Ganley	BRM	BRM P160C	1h44m32.500s	18
5	Brian Redman	McLaren	McLaren-Ford Cosworth M19A	1h44m48.000s	19
6	Graham Hill	Brabham	Brabham-Ford Cosworth BT37	1h45m11.900s	15
7	Wilson Fittipaldi	Brabham	Brabham-Ford Cosworth BT34	1h45m12.400s	21
8	Mike Beuttler	C-M-G Racing*	March-Ford Cosworth 721G	1h47m23.000s	27
9	Jean-Pierre Beltoise	BRM	BRM P160C	1h47m32.500s	13
10	Francois Cevert	Tyrrell	Tyrrell-Ford Cosworth 002	1h47m56.000s	5
11	Jackie Stewart	Tyrrell	Tyrrell-Ford Cosworth 003	13 laps/collision	2
12	Arturo Merzario	Ferrari	Ferrari 312B2-72	13 laps	22
13	Andrea de Adamich	Surtees	Surtees-Ford Cosworth TS9B	13 laps	20
14	Tim Schenken	Surtees	Surtees-Ford Cosworth TS9B	13 laps	12
15	Chris Amon	Matra	Matra MS120D	13 laps	8
NC	Carlos Pace	Frank Williams Racing Cars	March-Ford Cosworth 711	11 laps	11
R	Emerson Fittipaldi	Lotus	Lotus-Ford Cosworth 72D	10 laps/gearbox	3
R	Henri Pescarolo	Frank Williams Racing Cars	March-Ford Cosworth 721	10 laps/accident	9
R	Denny Hulme	McLaren	McLaren-Ford Cosworth M19C	8 laps/engine	10
R	Mike Hailwood	Surtees	Surtees-Ford Cosworth TS9B	8 laps/suspension	16
R	Carlos Reutemann	Brabham	Brabham-Ford Cosworth BT37	6 laps/differential	6
R	Rolf Stommelen	Eifelland	Eifelland-Ford Cosworth 21	6 laps/electrical	14
R	Dave Walker	Lotus	Lotus-Ford Cosworth 72D	6 laps/oil leak	23
R	Niki Lauda	March	March-Ford Cosworth 721G	4 laps/oil leak	24
R	Derek Bell	Tecno	Tecno PA123	4 laps/engine	25
R	Dave Charlton	Scuderia Scribante	Lotus-Ford Cosworth 72D	4 laps/physical	26
R	Reine Wisell	BRM	BRM P160C	3 laps/engine	17

*Clarke-Mordaunt-Guthrie Racing

Pole: Ickx, 7m07.000s, 119.626mph/192.519kph. Fastest lap: Ickx, 7m13.600s, 117.805mph/189.589kph on Lap 10. Race leaders: Ickx 1-14

NEW DRIVERS

The new drivers in 1972 included Carlos Reutemann, who came fourth in Canada for the now Bernie Ecclestone-owned Brabham team. Carlos Pace took fifth in Belgium in a Williams-run March, Arturo Merzario came sixth at Brands Hatch for Ferrari, with Patrick Depailler and Wilson Fittipaldi taking seventh places at the US and German GPs, respectively. Of this intake, only Jody Scheckter would become champion.

AUSTRIAN GRAND PRIX

OSTERREICHRING • ROUND 9 • DATE: 13TH AUGUST 1972
Laps: 54 • Distance: 198.337miles/319.194km • Weather: Hot & bright

Pos	Driver	Team	Chassis-Engine	Result	Qual
1	Emerson Fittipaldi	Lotus	Lotus-Ford Cosworth 72D	1h29m16.660s	1
2	Denny Hulme	McLaren	McLaren-Ford Cosworth M19C	1h29m17.840s	7
3	Peter Revson	McLaren	McLaren-Ford Cosworth M19C	1h29m53.190s	4
4	Mike Hailwood	Surtees	Surtees-Ford Cosworth TS9B	1h30m01.420s	12
5	Chris Amon	Matra	Matra MS120D	1h30m02.300s	6
6	Howden Ganley	BRM	BRM P160C	1h30m17.850s	10
7	Jackie Stewart	Tyrrell	Tyrrell-Ford Cosworth 005	1h30m25.750s	3
8	Jean-Pierre Beltoise	BRM	BRM P160C	1h30m38.110s	21
9	Francois Cevert	Tyrrell	Tyrrell-Ford Cosworth 002	53 laps	20
10	Niki Lauda	March	March-Ford Cosworth 721G	53 laps	22
11	Tim Schenken	Surtees	Surtees-Ford Cosworth TS9B	52 laps	8
12	Ronnie Peterson	March	March-Ford Cosworth 721G	52 laps	11
13	Peter Gethin	BRM	BRM P160C	51 laps	16
14	Andrea de Adamich	Surtees	Surtees-Ford Cosworth TS9B	51 laps	13
NC	Rolf Stommelen	Eifelland	Eifelland-Ford Cosworth 21	48 laps/engine	17
NC	Carlos Pace	Frank Williams Racing Cars	March-Ford Cosworth 711	46 laps	18
NC	Nanni Galli	Tecno	Tecno PA123	45 laps/oil leak	23
R	Graham Hill	Brabham	Brabham-Ford Cosworth BT37	36 laps/fuel metering	14
R	Wilson Fittipaldi	Brabham	Brabham-Ford Cosworth BT34	31 laps/brakes	15
R	Mike Beuttler	C-M-G Racing*	March-Ford Cosworth 721G	24 laps/fuel system	24
R	Francois Migault	Connew	Connew-Ford Cosworth PC1	22 laps/suspension	25
R	Jacky Ickx	Ferrari	Ferrari 312B2-72	20 laps/fuel system	9
R	Carlos Reutemann	Brabham	Brabham-Ford Cosworth BT37	14 laps/mechanical	5
R	Clay Regazzoni	Ferrari	Ferrari 312B2-72	13 laps/fuel system	2
R	Dave Walker	Lotus	Lotus-Ford Cosworth 72D	6 laps/engine	19
NS	Henri Pescarolo	Frank Williams Racing Cars	March-Ford Cosworth 721	accident	23

*Clarke-Mordaunt-Guthrie Racing

Pole: Fittipaldi, 1m35.970s, 137.777mph/221.731kph. Fastest lap: Hulme, 1m38.320s, 134.484mph/216.432kph on Lap 47. Race leaders: Stewart 1-23, Fittipaldi 24-54

ITALIAN GRAND PRIX

MONZA • ROUND 10 • DATE: 10TH SEPTEMBER 1972
Laps: 55 • Distance: 197.363miles/317.625km • Weather: Warm but dull

Pos	Driver	Team	Chassis-Engine	Result	Qual
1	Emerson Fittipaldi	Lotus	Lotus-Ford Cosworth 72D	1h29m58.400s	6
2	Mike Hailwood	Surtees	Surtees-Ford Cosworth TS9B	1h30m12.900s	9
3	Denny Hulme	McLaren	McLaren-Ford Cosworth M19C	1h30m22.200s	5
4	Peter Revson	McLaren	McLaren-Ford Cosworth M19C	1h30m34.100s	8
5	Graham Hill	Brabham	Brabham-Ford Cosworth BT37	1h31m04.000s	13
6	Peter Gethin	BRM	BRM P160C	1h31m20.300s	12
7	Mario Andretti	Ferrari	Ferrari 312B2-72	54 laps	7
8	Jean-Pierre Beltoise	BRM	BRM P180	54 laps	16
9	Ronnie Peterson	March	March-Ford Cosworth 721G	54 laps	24
10	Mike Beuttler	C-M-G Racing*	March-Ford Cosworth 721G	54 laps	25
11	Howden Ganley	BRM	BRM P160C	52 laps	17
12	Reine Wisell	BRM	BRM P160C	51 laps	10
13	Niki Lauda	March	March-Ford Cosworth 721G	50 laps	20
R	Jacky Ickx	Ferrari	Ferrari 312B2-72	46 laps/electrical	1

Pos	Driver	Team	Chassis-Engine	Result	Qual
R	Chris Amon	Matra	Matra MS120D	38 laps/brakes	2
R	Andrea de Adamich	Surtees	Surtees-Ford Cosworth TS9B	33 laps/brakes	21
R	Tim Schenken	Surtees	Surtees-Ford Cosworth TS9B	20 laps/spun off	15
R	Wilson Fittipaldi	Brabham	Brabham-Ford Cosworth BT34	20 laps/suspension	19
R	John Surtees	Surtees	Surtees-Ford Cosworth TS14	20 laps/fuel system	22
R	Clay Regazzoni	Ferrari	Ferrari 312B2-72	16 laps/collision	4
R	Carlos Pace	Frank Williams Racing Cars	March-Ford Cosworth 711	15 laps/collision	18
R	Carlos Reutemann	Brabham	Brabham-Ford Cosworth BT37	14 laps/suspension	11
R	Francois Cevert	Tyrrell	Tyrrell-Ford Cosworth 002	14 laps/engine	14
R	Nanni Galli	Tecno	Tecno PA123	6 laps/engine	23
R	Jackie Stewart	Tyrrell	Tyrrell-Ford Cosworth 005	0 laps/clutch	3
DNQ	Henri Pescarolo	Frank Williams Racing Cars	March-Ford Cosworth 721	-	26
DNQ	Derek Bell	Tecno	Tecno PA123	-	27

*Clarke-Mordaunt-Guthrie Racing

Pole: Ickx, 1m35.650s, 135.058mph/217.354kph. Fastest lap: Ickx, 1m36.300s, 134.154mph/215.900kph on Lap 44. Race leaders: Ickx 1-13 & 17-45, Regazzoni 14-16, Fittipaldi 46-55

IN MEMORIAM

The popular but seldom successful driver Jo Bonnier, who was the driver behind BRM's first success at Zandvoort in 1959 but was never a podium visitor again over the next 12 seasons, was the only driver with an F1 connection to die in 1972. With his F1 days behind him after 1971, he focused on sports car racing but this came to an end when he was pitched into the trees at Le Mans.

CANADIAN GRAND PRIX

MOSPORT PARK • ROUND 11 • DATE: 24TH SEPTEMBER 1972
Laps: 80 • Distance: 196.388miles/316.56km • Weather: Cool & misty

Pos	Driver	Team	Chassis-Engine	Result	Qual
1	Jackie Stewart	Tyrrell	Tyrrell-Ford Cosworth 005	1h43m16.900s	5
2	Peter Revson	McLaren	McLaren-Ford Cosworth M19C	1h44m05.100s	1
3	Denny Hulme	McLaren	McLaren-Ford Cosworth M19C	1h44m11.500s	2
4	Carlos Reutemann	Brabham	Brabham-Ford Cosworth BT37	1h44m17.600s	9
5	Clay Regazzoni	Ferrari	Ferrari 312B2-72	1h44m23.800s	7
6	Chris Amon	Matra	Matra MS120D	79 laps	10
7	Tim Schenken	Surtees	Surtees-Ford Cosworth TS9B	79 laps	13
8	Graham Hill	Brabham	Brabham-Ford Cosworth BT37	79 laps	17
9	Carlos Pace	Frank Williams*	March-Ford Cosworth 711	78 laps/out of fuel	18
10	Howden Ganley	BRM	BRM P160C	78 laps	14
11	Emerson Fittipaldi	Lotus	Lotus-Ford Cosworth 72D	78 laps	4
12	Jacky Ickx	Ferrari	Ferrari 312B2-72	76 laps	8
13	Henri Pescarolo	Frank Williams*	March-Ford Cosworth 721	73 laps	21
R	Reine Wisell	Lotus	Lotus-Ford Cosworth 72D	65 laps/engine	16
DQ	Niki Lauda	March	March-Ford Cosworth 721G	64 laps/outside assistance	19
DQ	Ronnie Peterson	March	March-Ford Cosworth 721G	61 laps/pushed wrong way	3
NC	Mike Beuttler	C-M-G Racing*	March-Ford Cosworth 721G	59 laps	24
R	Francois Cevert	Tyrrell	Tyrrell-Ford Cosworth 006	51 laps/gearbox	6
R	Peter Gethin	BRM	BRM P160C	25 laps/suspension	12
NC	Skip Barber	Gene Mason Racing	March-Ford Cosworth 711	24 laps	22

Pos	Driver	Team	Chassis-Engine	Result	Qual
R	Jean-Pierre Beltoise	BRM	BRM P180	21 laps/oil leak	20
R	Bill Brack	BRM	BRM P180	20 laps/spun off	23
R	Wilson Fittipaldi	Brabham	Brabham-Ford Cosworth BT34	5 laps/gearbox	11
R	Andrea de Adamich	Surtees	Surtees-Ford Cosworth TS9B	2 laps/gearbox	15
NS	Derek Bell	Tecno	Tecno PA123	accident	25

*Clarke-Mordaunt-Guthrie Racing, Frank Williams Racing Cars

Pole: Revson, 1m13.600s, 120.265mph/193.548kph. Fastest lap: Stewart, 1m15.700s, 116.929mph/188.179kph on Lap 25. Race leaders: Peterson 1-3, Stewart 4-80

CLASSIC CAR: LOTUS 72

The Lotus 72 was a wedge shape that changed the appearance of F1 cars as it moved its radiator from its nose to its flanks in order to reduce the frontal profile. Colin Chapman had the inspiration for the shape and Maurice Phillippe refined the idea. Although it made its debut in 1970, it broke too often for Jochen Rindt's liking, forcing him to revert to the 49C at one stage. By 1972, it had been sorted and, in its new black and gold John Player Special livery, the car looked sleeker than its rivals in the third year of its five-year run. The 72 would earn Lotus three constructors' and two drivers' titles.

UNITED STATES GRAND PRIX

WATKINS GLEN • ROUND 12 • DATE: 8TH OCTOBER 1972
Laps: 59 • Distance: 199.251miles/320.665km • Weather: Cool & dull then rain

Pos	Driver	Team	Chassis-Engine	Result	Qual
1	Jackie Stewart	Tyrrell	Tyrrell-Ford Cosworth 005	1h41m45.354s	1
2	Francois Cevert	Tyrrell	Tyrrell-Ford Cosworth 006	1h42m17.622s	4
3	Denny Hulme	McLaren	McLaren-Ford Cosworth M19C	1h42m22.882s	3
4	Ronnie Peterson	March	March-Ford Cosworth 721G	1h43m07.870s	26
5	Jacky Ickx	Ferrari	Ferrari 312B2-72	1h43m08.473s	12
6	Mario Andretti	Ferrari	Ferrari 312B2-72	58 laps	10
7	Patrick Depailler	Tyrrell	Tyrrell-Ford Cosworth 004	58 laps	11
8	Clay Regazzoni	Ferrari	Ferrari 312B2-72	58 laps	6
9	Jody Scheckter	McLaren	McLaren-Ford Cosworth M19A	58 laps	8
10	Reine Wisell	Lotus	Lotus-Ford Cosworth 72D	57 laps	16
11	Graham Hill	Brabham	Brabham-Ford Cosworth BT37	57 laps	27
12	Sam Posey	Champcarr Inc.	Surtees-Ford Cosworth TS9B	57 laps	23
13	Mike Beuttler	C-M-G Racing*	March-Ford Cosworth 721G	57 laps	21
14	Henri Pescarolo	Frank Williams Racing Cars	March-Ford Cosworth 721	57 laps	22
15	Chris Amon	Matra	Matra MS120D	57 laps	7
16	Skip Barber	Gene Mason Racing	March-Ford Cosworth 711	57 laps	20
17	Mike Hailwood	Surtees	Surtees-Ford Cosworth TS9B	56 laps/collision	14
18	Peter Revson	McLaren	McLaren-Ford Cosworth M19C	54 laps/electrical	2
NC	Niki Lauda	March	March-Ford Cosworth 721G	49 laps	25
R	Carlos Pace	Frank Williams Racing Cars	March-Ford Cosworth 711	48 laps/fuel system	15
R	Peter Gethin	BRM	BRM P160C	47 laps/engine	28
R	Howden Ganley	BRM	BRM P160C	44 laps/engine	17
R	Dave Walker	Lotus	Lotus-Ford Cosworth 72D	44 laps/engine	30
R	Wilson Fittipaldi	Brabham	Brabham-Ford Cosworth BT34	43 laps/engine	13
R	Jean-Pierre Beltoise	BRM	BRM P180	40 laps/ignition	18

Pos	Driver	Team	Chassis-Engine	Result	Qual
R	Brian Redman	BRM	BRM P180	34 laps/engine	24
R	Carlos Reutemann	Brabham	Brabham-Ford Cosworth BT37	31 laps/engine	5
R	Andrea de Adamich	Surtees	Surtees-Ford Cosworth TS9B	25 laps/collision	19
R	Tim Schenken	Surtees	Surtees-Ford Cosworth TS14	22 laps/suspension	31
R	Emerson Fittipaldi	Lotus	Lotus-Ford Cosworth 72D	17 laps/suspension	9
R	Derek Bell	Tecno	Tecno PA123	8 laps/engine	29
NS	John Surtees	Surtees	Surtees-Ford Cosworth TS14	no engine	25

*Clarke-Mordaunt-Guthrie Racing

Pole: Stewart, 1m40.481s, 120.995mph/194.723kph. Fastest lap: Stewart, 1m41.644s, 119.611mph/192.495kph on Lap 33. Race leaders: Stewart 1-59

WORLD DRIVERS' CHAMPIONSHIP FINAL RESULTS

Pos	Driver	Nat	Car-Engine	R1	R2	R3	R4
1	Emerson Fittipaldi	BRA	Lotus-Ford Cosworth 72D	R	2	1	3P
2	Jackie Stewart	GBR	Tyrrell-Ford Cosworth 003	1F	RP	R	-
			Tyrrell-Ford Cosworth 004	-	-	-	4
			Tyrrell-Ford Cosworth 005	-	-	-	-
3	Denny Hulme	NZL	McLaren-Ford Cosworth M19A	2	1	R	-
			McLaren-Ford Cosworth M19C	-	-	-	15
4	Jacky Ickx	BEL	Ferrari 312B2-72	3	8	2PF	2
5	Peter Revson	GBR USA	McLaren-Ford Cosworth M19A	R	3	5	-
			McLaren-Ford Cosworth M19C	-	-	-	-
6	Francois Cevert	FRA	Tyrrell-Ford Cosworth 002	R	9	R	NC
			Tyrrell-Ford Cosworth 006	-	-	-	-
6	Clay Regazzoni	CHE	Ferrari 312B2-72	4	12	3	R
8	Mike Hailwood	GBR	Surtees-Ford Cosworth TS9B	-	RF	R	R
9	Ronnie Peterson	SWE	March-Ford Cosworth 721	6	5	-	-
			March-Ford Cosworth 721X	-	-	R	11
			March-Ford Cosworth 721G	-	-	-	-
9	Chris Amon	NZL	Matra MS120C	NS	15	R	6
			Matra MS120D	-	-	-	-
11	Jean-Pierre Beltoise	FRA	BRM P160B	-	R	R	-
			BRM P160C	-	-	-	-
			BRM P180	-	-	-	-
12	Howden Ganley	NZL	BRM P160B	9	NC	R	-
			BRM P180	-	-	-	R
			BRM P160C	-	-	-	-
12	Mario Andretti	USA	Ferrari 312B2-72	R	4	R	-
12	Brian Redman	GBR	McLaren-Ford Cosworth M19A	-	-	-	5
			BRM P180	-	-	-	-
12	Graham Hill	GBR	Brabham-Ford Cosworth BT33	R	6	-	-
			Brabham-Ford Cosworth BT37	-	-	10	12
16	Andrea de Adamich	ITA	Surtees-Ford Cosworth TS9B	R	NC	4	7
16	Carlos Reutemann	ARG	Brabham-Ford Cosworth BT34	7P	R	-	-
			Brabham-Ford Cosworth BT37	-	-	-	-
16	Carlos Pace	BRA	March-Ford Cosworth 711	-	17	6	17
19	Tim Schenken	AUS	Surtees-Ford Cosworth TS9B	5	R	8	R
			Surtees-Ford Cosworth TS14	-	-	-	-
20	Arturo Merzario	ITA	Ferrari 312B2-72	-	-	-	-
20	Peter Gethin	GBR	BRM P160B	R	NC	-	R
			BRM P180	-	-	R	-
			BRM P160C	-	-	-	-

Pos	Driver	R5	R6	R7	R8	R9	R10	R11	R12	Total
1	Fittipaldi	1P	2	1	R	1P	1	11	R	61
2	Stewart	-	1	2F	11	-	-	-	-	45
		-	-	-	-	-	-	-	-	
		-	-	-	-	7	R	1F	1PF	
3	Hulme	-	-	-	-	-	-	-	-	39
		3	7	5	R	2F	3	3	3	
4	Ickx	R	11	RP	1PF	R	RPF	12	5	27
5	Revson	7	-	3	-	-	-	-	-	23
		-	-	-	-	3	4	2P	18	
6	Cevert	2	4	R	10	9	R	-	-	15
		-	-	-	-	-	-	R	2	
6	Regazzoni	R	-	-	2	R	R	5	8	15
8	Hailwood	4	6	R	R	4	2	-	17	13
9	Peterson	-	-	-	-	-	-	-	-	12
		9	-	-	-	-	-	-	-	
		-	5	7	3	12	9	DQ	4	
9	Amon	6F	-	4	-	-	-	-	-	12
		-	3PF	-	15	5	R	6	15	
11	Beltoise	R	15	-	-	-	-	-	-	9
		-	-	11	9	8	-	-	-	
		-	-	-	-	-	8	R	R	
12	Ganley	8	NS	-	-	-	-	-	-	4
		-	-	-	-	-	-	-	-	
		-	-	-	4	6	11	10	R	
12	Andretti	-	-	-	-	-	7	-	6	4
12	Redman	-	9	-	5	-	-	-	-	4
		-	-	-	-	-	-	-	R	
12	Hill	-	-	-	-	-	-	-	-	4
		R	10	R	6	R	5	8	11	
16	de Adamich	R	14	R	13	14	R	R	R	3
16	Reutemann	-	-	-	-	-	-	-	-	3
		13	12	8	R	R	R	4	R	
16	Pace	5	R	R	NC	NC	R	9	R	3
19	Schenken	R	17	R	14	11	R	7	-	2
		-	-	-	-	-	-	-	R	
20	Merzario	-	-	6	12	-	-	-	-	1
20	Gethin	R	NS	R	-	-	-	R	-	1
		-	-	-	-	-	-	-	-	
		-	-	-	-	13	6	R	R	

SYMBOLS AND GRAND PRIX KEY

Round 1 Argentinian GP
Round 2 South African GP
Round 3 Spanish GP
Round 4 Monaco GP
Round 5 Belgian GP
Round 6 French GP
Round 7 British GP
Round 8 German GP
Round 9 Austrian GP
Round 10 Italian GP
Round 11 Canadian GP
Round 12 United States GP

DNPQ DID NOT PRE-QUALIFY **DNQ** DID NOT QUALIFY **DQ** DISQUALIFIED **EX** EXCLUDED
F FASTEST LAP **NC** NOT CLASSIFIED **NS** NON-STARTER **P** POLE POSITION **R** RETIRED

SCORING

1st 9 points
2nd 6 points
3rd 4 points
4th 3 points
5th 2 points
6th 1 point

WORLD CONSTRUCTORS' CHAMPIONSHIP FINAL RESULTS

Pos	Team-Engine	R1	R2	R3	R4	R5	R6	R7	R8	R9	R10	R11	R12	Total
1	Lotus-Ford	-	2	1	3	1	2	1	-	1	-	11	10	61
2	Tyrrell-Ford	1	9	-	4	2	1	2	10	7	R	1	1	51
3	McLaren-Ford	2	1	5	5	3	7	3	5	2	3	2	3	47
4	Ferrari	3	4	2	2	-	11	6	1	-	7	5	5	33
5	Surtees-Ford	5	16	4	7	4	6	-	13	4	2	7	12	18
6	March-Ford	6	5	6	10	5	5	7	3	10	9	9	4	15
7	BRM	9	14	-	1	8	15	11	4	6	6	10	-	14
8	Matra	-	15	-	6	6	3	4	15	5	R	6	15	12
9	Brabham-Ford	7	6	7	9	13	8	8	6	-	5	4	11	7

1973

SEASON SUMMARY

Jackie Stewart wanted to end his F1 career with a third title and did precisely that, with a record of 27 career wins, but his achievement was spoiled by the death of his Tyrrell team-mate, Francois Cevert, in qualifying for the season-ending United States GP. Stewart's tally of five wins was enough for the title, but it seemed after winning three of the first four races that Emerson Fittipaldi would make it two titles on the trot with Lotus, before Stewart's consistency started to tell and Fittipaldi faced a challenge from within as Ronnie Peterson started winning. But the Lotus drivers had done enough to land the team the constructors' title.

ARGENTINIAN GRAND PRIX

BUENOS AIRES • ROUND 1 • DATE: 28TH JANUARY 1973
Laps: 96 • Distance: 199.564miles/321.168km • Weather: Hot & bright

Pos	Driver	Team	Chassis-Engine	Result	Qual
1	Emerson Fittipaldi	Lotus	Lotus-Ford Cosworth 72D	1h56m18.220s	2
2	Francois Cevert	Tyrrell	Tyrrell-Ford Cosworth 006	1h56m22.910s	6
3	Jackie Stewart	Tyrrell	Tyrrell-Ford Cosworth 005	1h56m51.410s	4
4	Jacky Ickx	Ferrari	Ferrari 312B2	1h57m00.790s	3
5	Denny Hulme	McLaren	McLaren-Ford Cosworth M19C	95 laps	8
6	Wilson Fittipaldi	Brabham	Brabham-Ford Cosworth BT37	95 laps	13
7	Clay Regazzoni	BRM	BRM P160D	93 laps	1
8	Peter Revson	McLaren	McLaren-Ford Cosworth M19C	92 laps	11
9	Arturo Merzario	Ferrari	Ferrari 312B2	92 laps	14
10	Mike Beuttler	C-M-G-D Racing*	March-Ford Cosworth 721G	90 laps/suspension	18
R	Jean-Pierre Jarier	March	March-Ford Cosworth 721G	84 laps	17
R	Jean-Pierre Beltoise	BRM	BRM 160D	79 laps/engine	7
NC	Howden Ganley	Frank Williams Racing Cars	Williams-Ford Cosworth FX3B	79 laps	19
R	Ronnie Peterson	Lotus	Lotus-Ford Cosworth 72D	67 laps/fuel pressure	5
R	Niki Lauda	BRM	BRM P160C	66 laps/fuel pressure	13
R	Carlos Reutemann	Brabham	Brabham-Ford Cosworth BT37	16 laps/gearbox	9
R	Mike Hailwood	Surtees	Surtees-Ford Cosworth TS14A	10 laps/halfshaft	10
R	Carlos Pace	Surtees	Surtees-Ford Cosworth TS14A	10 laps/suspension	15
R	Nanni Galli	Frank Williams Racing Cars	Williams-Ford Cosworth FX3B	0 laps/engine	16

*Clarke-Mordaunt-Guthrie-Durlacher Racing

Pole: Regazzoni, 1m10.540s, 106.091mph/170.737kph. Fastest lap: E Fittipaldi, 1m11.220s, 105.080mph/169.110kph on Lap 79. Race leaders: Regazzoni 1-28, Cevert 29-85, E Fittipaldi 86-96

MORE THAN A CHAMPION

At the conclusion of his career, with his third title wrapped up with two races remaining, Jackie Stewart left F1 as a driver who also saved lives. His campaign for greater safety made him unpopular with the establishment, but it made them think. One change that occurred in 1973 was the decision that grids would be two-by-two after the Dutch GP.

BRAZILIAN GRAND PRIX

INTERLAGOS • ROUND 2 • DATE: 11TH FEBRUARY 1973
Laps: 40 • Distance: 197.598miles/318.4km • Weather: Hot & bright

Pos	Driver	Team	Chassis-Engine	Result	Qual
1	Emerson Fittipaldi	Lotus	Lotus-Ford Cosworth 72D	1h43m55.600s	2
2	Jackie Stewart	Tyrrell	Tyrrell-Ford Cosworth 005	1h44m09.100s	8
3	Denny Hulme	McLaren	McLaren-Ford Cosworth M19C	1h45m42.000s	5
4	Arturo Merzario	Ferrari	Ferrari 312B2	39 laps	17
5	Jacky Ickx	Ferrari	Ferrari 312B2	39 laps	3
6	Clay Regazzoni	BRM	BRM P160D	39 laps	4
7	Howden Ganley	Frank Williams Racing Cars	Williams-Ford Cosworth FX3B	39 laps	14
8	Niki Lauda	BRM	BRM P160C	38 laps	13
9	Nanni Galli	Frank Williams Racing Cars	Williams-Ford Cosworth FX3B	38 laps	18
10	Francois Cevert	Tyrrell	Tyrrell-Ford Cosworth 006	38 laps	9
11	Carlos Reutemann	Brabham	Brabham-Ford Cosworth BT37	38 laps	7
12	Luiz Bueno	Surtees	Surtees-Ford Cosworth TS9B	36 laps	20
R	Jean-Pierre Beltoise	BRM	BRM P160D	23 laps/electrical	10
R	Mike Beuttler	C-M-G-D Racing*	March-Ford Cosworth 721G	18 laps/overheating	19
R	Carlos Pace	Surtees	Surtees-Ford Cosworth TS14A	9 laps/suspension	6
R	Mike Hailwood	Surtees	Surtees-Ford Cosworth TS14A	6 laps/gearbox	14
R	Jean-Pierre Jarier	March	March-Ford Cosworth 721G	6 laps/gearbox	15
R	Ronnie Peterson	Lotus	Lotus-Ford Cosworth 72D	5 laps/wheel	1
R	Wilson Fittipaldi	Brabham	Brabham-Ford Cosworth BT37	5 laps/overheating	11
R	Peter Revson	McLaren	McLaren-Ford Cosworth M19C	3 laps/gearbox	12

*Clarke-Mordaunt-Guthrie-Durlacher Racing

Pole: Peterson, 2m30.500s, 118.312mph/190.405kph. Fastest lap: Hulme, 2m35.000s, 114.891mph/184.900kph on Lap 20 E Fittipaldi, 2m35.000s, 114.891mph/184.900kph. Race leaders: E Fittipaldi 1-40

ONE SLIP, NINE CARS ELIMINATED

Jody Scheckter was seen as fast but wild when he arrived in F1 with McLaren. Having qualified third for his fourth grand prix, at Silverstone, the South African ran wide at Woodcote at the end of the opening lap, looped his M23 around and hit the pit wall. The cars behind scattered and forced a restart, with nine cars eliminated.

SOUTH AFRICAN GRAND PRIX

KYALAMI • ROUND 3 • DATE: 3RD MARCH 1973
Laps: 79 • Distance: 201.458miles/324.216km • Weather: Warm but dull

Pos	Driver	Team	Chassis-Engine	Result	Qual
1	Jackie Stewart	Tyrrell	Tyrrell-Ford Cosworth 006	1h43m11.070s	16
2	Peter Revson	McLaren	McLaren-Ford Cosworth M19C	1h43m35.620s	6
3	Emerson Fittipaldi	Lotus	Lotus-Ford Cosworth 72D	1h43m36.130s	2
4	Arturo Merzario	Ferrari	Ferrari 312B2	78 laps	15
5	Denny Hulme	McLaren	McLaren-Ford Cosworth M23	77 laps	1
6	George Follmer	Shadow	Shadow-Ford Cosworth DN1	77 laps	21
7	Carlos Reutemann	Brabham	Brabham-Ford Cosworth BT37	77 laps	8

Pos	Driver	Team	Chassis-Engine	Result	Qual
8	Andrea de Adamich	Surtees	Surtees-Ford Cosworth TS9B	77 laps	20
9	Jody Scheckter	McLaren	McLaren-Ford Cosworth M19C	75 laps/engine	3
10	Howden Ganley	Frank Williams Racing Cars	Williams-Ford Cosworth FX3B	73 laps	19
11	Ronnie Peterson	Lotus	Lotus-Ford Cosworth 72D	73 laps	4
R	Carlos Pace	Surtees	Surtees-Ford Cosworth TS14A	69 laps/accident	9
NC	Eddie Keizan	Blignaut Racing	Tyrrell-Ford Cosworth 004	67 laps	22
NC	Jean-Pierre Jarier	March	March-Ford Cosworth 721G	66 laps	18
NC	Francois Cevert	Tyrrell	Tyrrell-Ford Cosworth 005	66 laps	25
NC	Mike Beuttler	C-M-G-D Racing*	March-Ford Cosworth 721G	65 laps	23
R	Wilson Fittipaldi	Brabham	Brabham-Ford Cosworth BT37	52 laps/gearbox	17
R	Jackie Pretorius	Frank Williams Racing Cars	Williams-Ford Cosworth FX3B	35 laps/overheating	24
R	Niki Lauda	BRM	BRM P160D	26 laps/engine	10
R	Jackie Oliver	Shadow	Shadow-Ford Cosworth DN1	14 laps/engine	14
R	Jean-Pierre Beltoise	BRM	BRM P160D	4 laps/clutch	7
R	Dave Charlton	Scuderia Scribante	Lotus-Ford Cosworth 72D	3 laps/accident	13
R	Clay Regazzoni	BRM	BRM P160D	2 laps/accident	5
R	Jacky Ickx	Ferrari	Ferrari 312B2	2 laps/accident	11
R	Mike Hailwood	Surtees	Surtees-Ford Cosworth TS14A	2 laps/accident	12

*Clarke-Mordaunt-Guthrie-Durlacher Racing

Pole: Hulme, 1m16.280s, 120.351mph/193.686kph. Fastest lap: E Fittipaldi, 1m17.100s, 119.073mph/191.630kph on Lap 76. Race leaders: Hulme 1-4, Scheckter 5-6, Stewart 7-79

SPANISH GRAND PRIX

MONTJUICH PARK • ROUND 4 • DATE: 29TH APRIL 1973
Laps: 75 • Distance: 176.484miles/284.25km • Weather: Warm & bright

Pos	Driver	Team	Chassis-Engine	Result	Qual
1	Emerson Fittipaldi	Lotus	Lotus-Ford Cosworth 72E	1h48m18.700s	7
2	Francois Cevert	Tyrrell	Tyrrell-Ford Cosworth 006	1h49m01.400s	3
3	George Follmer	Shadow	Shadow-Ford Cosworth DN1	1h49m31.800s	14
4	Peter Revson	McLaren	McLaren-Ford Cosworth M23	74 laps	5
5	Jean-Pierre Beltoise	BRM	BRM P160E	74 laps	10
6	Denny Hulme	McLaren	McLaren-Ford Cosworth M23	74 laps	2
7	Mike Beuttler	C-M-G-D Racing*	March-Ford Cosworth 731	74 laps	19
8	Henri Pescarolo	March	March-Ford Cosworth 731	73 laps	18
9	Clay Regazzoni	BRM	BRM P160E	69 laps	8
10	Wilson Fittipaldi	Brabham	Brabham-Ford Cosworth BT42	69 laps	12
11	Nanni Galli	Frank Williams Racing Cars	Williams-Ford Cosworth IR	69 laps	20
12	Jacky Ickx	Ferrari	Ferrari 312B3	69 laps	6
R	Carlos Reutemann	Brabham	Brabham-Ford Cosworth BT42	66 laps/halfshaft	15
R	Howden Ganley	Frank Williams Racing Cars	Williams-Ford Cosworth IR	63 laps/out of fuel	21
R	Ronnie Peterson	Lotus	Lotus-Ford Cosworth 72E	56 laps/gearbox	1
R	Jackie Stewart	Tyrrell	Tyrrell-Ford Cosworth 006	47 laps/brakes	4
R	Niki Lauda	BRM	BRM P160E	28 laps/tyre	11
R	Graham Hill	Embassy Racing	Shadow-Ford Cosworth DN1	27 laps/brakes	22
R	Mike Hailwood	Surtees	Surtees-Ford Cosworth TS14A	25 laps/oil leak	9
R	Jackie Oliver	Shadow	Shadow-Ford Cosworth DN1	23 laps/engine	13
R	Andrea de Adamich	Brabham	Brabham-Ford Cosworth BT37	17 laps/wheel	17
R	Carlos Pace	Surtees	Surtees-Ford Cosworth TS14A	13 laps/halfshaft	16

*Clarke-Mordaunt-Guthrie-Durlacher Racing

Pole: Peterson, 1m21.800s, 103.642mph/166.797kph. Fastest lap: Peterson, 1m23.800s, 101.169mph/162.816kph on Lap 13. Race leaders: Peterson 1-56, E Fittipaldi 57-75

BELGIAN GRAND PRIX

ZOLDER • ROUND 5 • DATE: 20TH MAY 1973
Laps: 70 • Distance: 183.306miles/295.4km • Weather: Warm & bright

Pos	Driver	Team	Chassis-Engine	Result	Qual
1	Jackie Stewart	Tyrrell	Tyrrell-Ford Cosworth 006	1h42m13.430s	6
2	Francois Cevert	Tyrrell	Tyrrell-Ford Cosworth 006	1h42m45.270s	4
3	Emerson Fittipaldi	Lotus	Lotus-Ford Cosworth 72E	1h44m16.220s	9
4	Andrea de Adamich	Brabham	Brabham-Ford Cosworth BT37	69 laps	18
5	Niki Lauda	BRM	BRM P160E	69 laps	14
6	Chris Amon	Tecno	Tecno PA123B	67 laps	15
7	Denny Hulme	McLaren	McLaren-Ford Cosworth M23	67 laps	2
8	Carlos Pace	Surtees	Surtees-Ford Cosworth TS14A	66 laps	8
9	Graham Hill	Embassy Racing	Shadow-Ford Cosworth DN1	65 laps	23
10	Clay Regazzoni	BRM	BRM P160E	63 laps/accident	12
11	Mike Beuttler	C-M-G-D Racing*	March-Ford Cosworth 731	63 laps/accident	20
R	Jean-Pierre Jarier	March	March-Ford Cosworth 731	60 laps/accident	16
R	Jean-Pierre Beltoise	BRM	BRM P160E	56 laps	5
R	Wilson Fittipaldi	Brabham	Brabham-Ford Cosworth BT42	46 laps/engine	19
R	Ronnie Peterson	Lotus	Lotus-Ford Cosworth 72E	42 laps/accident	1
R	Peter Revson	McLaren	McLaren-Ford Cosworth M23	33 laps/accident	10
R	Howden Ganley	Frank Williams Racing Cars	Williams-Ford Cosworth IR	16 laps/accident	21
R	Carlos Reutemann	Brabham	Brabham-Ford Cosworth BT42	14 laps/engine	7
R	George Follmer	Shadow	Shadow-Ford Cosworth DN1	13 laps/throttle	11
R	Jackie Oliver	Shadow	Shadow-Ford Cosworth DN1	11 laps/accident	22
R	Jacky Ickx	Ferrari	Ferrari 312B3	6 laps/fuel pump	3
R	Nanni Galli	Frank Williams Racing Cars	Williams-Ford Cosworth IR	6 laps/engine	17
R	Mike Hailwood	Surtees	Surtees-Ford Cosworth TS14A	4 laps/accident	13

*Clarke-Mordaunt-Guthrie-Durlacher Racing

Pole: Peterson, 1m22.460s, 114.478mph/184.234kph. Fastest lap: Cevert, 1m25.420s, 110.510mph/177.850kph on Lap 28. Race leaders: Peterson 1, Cevert 2-19, E Fittipaldi 20-24, Stewart 25-70

AN UNNECCESSARY DEATH

One of F1's darkest days resulted in the death of British hope Roger Williamson at the Dutch GP. It's thought tyre failure pitched his March off the track and it came to rest upside down and on fire. There was a fire tender nearby, but it wouldn't go against the flow of the cars on the track and it was left to fellow racer David Purley to try to pull him out as marshals stood by.

MONACO GRAND PRIX

MONTE CARLO • ROUND 6 • DATE: 3RD JUNE 1973
Laps: 78 • Distance: 158.874miles/255.684km • Weather: Warm & bright

Pos	Driver	Team	Chassis-Engine	Result	Qual
1	Jackie Stewart	Tyrrell	Tyrrell-Ford Cosworth 006	1h57m44.300s	1
2	Emerson Fittipaldi	Lotus	Lotus-Ford Cosworth 72E	1h57m45.600s	5
3	Ronnie Peterson	Lotus	Lotus-Ford Cosworth 72E	77 laps	2
4	Francois Cevert	Tyrrell	Tyrrell-Ford Cosworth 006	77 laps	4

Pos	Driver	Team	Chassis-Engine	Result	Qual
5	Peter Revson	McLaren	McLaren-Ford Cosworth M23	76 laps	15
6	Denny Hulme	McLaren	McLaren-Ford Cosworth M23	76 laps	3
7	Andrea de Adamich	Brabham	Brabham-Ford Cosworth BT37	75 laps	25
8	Mike Hailwood	Surtees	Surtees-Ford Cosworth TS14A	75 laps	13
9	James Hunt	Hesketh	March-Ford Cosworth 731	73 laps/engine	18
10	Jackie Oliver	Shadow	Shadow-Ford Cosworth DN1	72 laps	22
11	Wilson Fittipaldi	Brabham	Brabham-Ford Cosworth BT42	71 laps/fuel system	9
R	Jean-Pierre Jarier	March	March-Ford Cosworth 731	67 laps/gearbox	14
R	Graham Hill	Embassy Racing	Shadow-Ford Cosworth DN1	62 laps/suspension	24
R	Arturo Merzario	Ferrari	Ferrari 312B3	58 laps/fuel pressure	16
R	Carlos Reutemann	Brabham	Brabham-Ford Cosworth BT42	46 laps/gearbox	19
R	Jacky Ickx	Ferrari	Ferrari 312B3	44 laps/halfshaft	7
R	Howden Ganley	Frank Williams Racing Cars	Williams-Ford Cosworth IR	41 laps/halfshaft	10
R	Jean-Pierre Beltoise	BRM	BRM P160E	39 laps/accident	11
R	Carlos Pace	Surtees	Surtees-Ford Cosworth TS14A	31 laps/halfshaft	17
R	David Purley	LEC	March-Ford Cosworth 731	31 laps/oil leak	23
R	Nanni Galli	Frank Williams Racing Cars	Williams-Ford Cosworth IR	30 laps/halfshaft	21
R	Niki Lauda	BRM	BRM P160E	24 laps/gearbox	6
R	Chris Amon	Tecno	Tecno PA123B	22 laps/overheating	12
R	Clay Regazzoni	BRM	BRM P160E	15 laps/brakes	8
R	Mike Beuttler	C-M-G-D Racing*	March-Ford Cosworth 731	3 laps/engine	21
NS	George Follmer	Shadow	Shadow-Ford Cosworth DN1	accident	20

*Clarke-Mordaunt-Guthrie-Durlacher Racing

Pole: Stewart, 1m27.500s, 83.802mph/134.866kph. Fastest lap: E Fittipaldi, 1m28.100s, 83.201mph/133.900kph on Lap 78. Race leaders: Cevert 1, Peterson 2-7, Stewart 8-78

DENIED VICTORY AT HOME

Ronnie Peterson had a frustrating start to his time with Lotus, with technical problems at five of the first six grands prix. Then, on home ground at the Swedish GP, he was heading for victory only to be denied by a puncture with just two laps to go. He would go on to win the following race, the French GP, and won three of the last four to rank third.

SWEDISH GRAND PRIX

ANDERSTORP • ROUND 7 • DATE: 17TH JUNE 1973
Laps: 80 • Distance: 199.487miles/321.44km • Weather: Warm & bright

Pos	Driver	Team	Chassis-Engine	Result	Qual
1	Denny Hulme	McLaren	McLaren-Ford Cosworth M23	1h56m46.049s	6
2	Ronnie Peterson	Lotus	Lotus-Ford Cosworth 72E	1h56m50.088s	1
3	Francois Cevert	Tyrrell	Tyrrell-Ford Cosworth 006	1h57m00.716s	2
4	Carlos Reutemann	Brabham	Brabham-Ford Cosworth BT42	1h57m04.117s	5
5	Jackie Stewart	Tyrrell	Tyrrell-Ford Cosworth 006	1h57m12.047s	3
6	Jacky Ickx	Ferrari	Ferrari 312B3	79 laps	8
7	Peter Revson	McLaren	McLaren-Ford Cosworth M23	79 laps	7
8	Mike Beuttler	C-M-G-D Racing*	March-Ford Cosworth 731	78 laps	21
9	Clay Regazzoni	BRM	BRM P160E	77 laps	12
10	Carlos Pace	Surtees	Surtees-Ford Cosworth TS14A	77 laps	16
11	Howden Ganley	Frank Williams Racing Cars	Williams-Ford Cosworth IR	77 laps	11

Pos	Driver	Team	Chassis-Engine	Result	Qual
12	Emerson Fittipaldi	Lotus	Lotus-Ford Cosworth 72E	76 laps/gearbox	4
13	Niki Lauda	BRM	BRM P160E	75 laps	15
14	George Follmer	Shadow	Shadow-Ford Cosworth DN1	74 laps	19
R	Jean-Pierre Beltoise	BRM	BRM P160E	57 laps/engine	9
R	Jackie Oliver	Shadow	Shadow-Ford Cosworth DN1	50 laps/suspension	17
R	Mike Hailwood	Surtees	Surtees-Ford Cosworth TS14A	41 laps/tyre	10
R	Jean-Pierre Jarier	March	March-Ford Cosworth 731	38 laps/throttle	20
R	Graham Hill	Embassy Racing	Shadow-Ford Cosworth DN1	16 laps/ignition	18
R	Wilson Fittipaldi	Brabham	Brabham-Ford Cosworth BT42	0 laps/accident	12
NS	Reine Wisell	Team Pierre Robert	March-Ford Cosworth 731	suspension	14
NS	Tom Belso	Frank Williams Racing Cars	Williams-Ford Cosworth IR	Ganley drove car	22

*Clarke-Mordaunt-Guthrie-Durlacher Racing

Pole: Peterson, 1m23.810s, 107.242mph/172.590kph. Fastest lap: Hulme, 1m26.146s, 104.334mph/167.910kph on Lap 7. Race leaders: Peterson 1-78, Hulme 79-80

FRENCH GRAND PRIX

CIRCUIT PAUL RICARD • ROUND 8 • DATE: 1ST JULY 1973
Laps: 54 • Distance: 194.535miles/313.74km • Weather: Very hot & bright

Pos	Driver	Team	Chassis-Engine	Result	Qual
1	Ronnie Peterson	Lotus	Lotus-Ford Cosworth 72E	1h41m36.520s	5
2	Francois Cevert	Tyrrell	Tyrrell-Ford Cosworth 006	1h42m17.440s	4
3	Carlos Reutemann	Brabham	Brabham-Ford Cosworth BT42	1h42m23.000s	8
4	Jackie Stewart	Tyrrell	Tyrrell-Ford Cosworth 006	1h42m23.450s	1
5	Jacky Ickx	Ferrari	Ferrari 312B3	1h42m25.420s	12
6	James Hunt	Hesketh	March-Ford Cosworth 731	1h42m59.060s	14
7	Arturo Merzario	Ferrari	Ferrari 312B3	1h43m05.710s	10
8	Denny Hulme	McLaren	McLaren-Ford Cosworth M23	1h43m06.050s	6
9	Niki Lauda	BRM	BRM P160E	1h43m22.280s	17
10	Graham Hill	Embassy Racing	Shadow-Ford Cosworth DN1	53 laps	16
11	Jean-Pierre Beltoise	BRM	BRM P160E	53 laps	15
12	Clay Regazzoni	BRM	BRM P160E	53 laps	9
13	Carlos Pace	Surtees	Surtees-Ford Cosworth TS14A	51 laps	18
14	Howden Ganley	Frank Williams Racing Cars	Williams-Ford Cosworth IR	51 laps	24
15	Rikky von Opel	Ensign	Ensign-Ford Cosworth N173	51 laps	25
16	Wilson Fittipaldi	Brabham	Brabham-Ford Cosworth BT42	50 laps/throttle	19
R	Jody Scheckter	McLaren	McLaren-Ford Cosworth M23	43 laps/accident	2
R	Emerson Fittipaldi	Lotus	Lotus-Ford Cosworth 72E	41 laps/accident	3
R	Mike Hailwood	Surtees	Surtees-Ford Cosworth TS14A	29 laps/oil leak	11
R	Andrea de Adamich	Brabham	Brabham-Ford Cosworth BT37	28 laps/halfshaft	13
R	Reine Wisell	C-M-G-D Racing*	March-Ford Cosworth 731	20 laps/overheating	22
R	George Follmer	Shadow	Shadow-Ford Cosworth DN1	16 laps/fuel system	20
R	Henri Pescarolo	Frank Williams Racing Cars	Williams-Ford Cosworth IR	16 laps/overheating	23
R	Jean-Pierre Jarier	March	March-Ford Cosworth 731	7 laps/halfshaft	7
R	Jackie Oliver	Shadow	Shadow-Ford Cosworth DN1	0 laps/clutch	21

*Clarke-Mordaunt-Guthrie-Durlacher Racing

Pole: Stewart, 1m48.370s, 119.928mph/193.005kph. Fastest lap: Hulme, 1m50.990s, 117.097mph/188.450kph on Lap 52. Race leaders: Scheckter 1-41, Peterson 42-54

BRITISH GRAND PRIX

SILVERSTONE • ROUND 9 • DATE: 14TH JULY 1973
Laps: 67 • Distance: 196.106miles/315.603km • Weather: Warm but dull

Pos	Driver	Team	Chassis-Engine	Result	Qual
1	Peter Revson	McLaren	McLaren-Ford Cosworth M23	1h29m18.500s	3
2	Ronnie Peterson	Lotus	Lotus-Ford Cosworth 72E	1h29m21.300s	1
3	Denny Hulme	McLaren	McLaren-Ford Cosworth M23	1h29m21.500s	2
4	James Hunt	Hesketh	March-Ford Cosworth 731	1h29m21.900s	11
5	Francois Cevert	Tyrrell	Tyrrell-Ford Cosworth 006	1h29m55.100s	7
6	Carlos Reutemann	Brabham	Brabham-Ford Cosworth BT42	1h30m03.200s	8
7	Clay Regazzoni	BRM	BRM P160E	1h30m30.200s	10
8	Jacky Ickx	Ferrari	Ferrari 312B3	1h30m35.900s	19
9	Howden Ganley	Frank Williams Racing Cars	Williams-Ford Cosworth IR	66 laps	18
10	Jackie Stewart	Tyrrell	Tyrrell-Ford Cosworth 006	66 laps	4
11	Mike Beuttler	C-M-G-D Racing*	March-Ford Cosworth 731	65 laps	24
12	Niki Lauda	BRM	BRM P160E	63 laps	9
13	Rikky von Opel	Ensign	Ensign-Ford Cosworth N173	61 laps	21
R	Wilson Fittipaldi	Brabham	Brabham-Ford Cosworth BT42	44 laps/oil leak	13
R	Emerson Fittipaldi	Lotus	Lotus-Ford Cosworth 72E	36 laps/transmission	5
R	John Watson	Brabham	Brabham-Ford Cosworth BT37	36 laps/fuel system	23
R	Graham Hill	Embassy Racing	Shadow-Ford Cosworth DN1	24 laps/chassis	27
R	Chris Amon	Tecno	Tecno PA123B	6 laps/fuel system	29
R	Graham McRae	Frank Williams Racing Cars	Williams-Ford Cosworth IR	0 laps/throttle	28
NS **	Jody Scheckter	McLaren	McLaren-Ford Cosworth M23	0 laps/accident	6
NS **	Mike Hailwood	Surtees	Surtees-Ford Cosworth TS14A	0 laps/accident	12
NS **	Jochen Mass	Surtees	Surtees-Ford Cosworth TS14A	0 laps/accident	14
NS **	Carlos Pace	Surtees	Surtees-Ford Cosworth TS14A	0 laps/accident	15
NS **	Jean-Pierre Beltoise	BRM	BRM P160E	0 laps/accident	17
NS **	Andrea de Adamich	Brabham	Brabham-Ford Cosworth BT42	0 laps/accident	20
NS **	Roger Williamson	March	March-Ford Cosworth 731	0 laps/accident	22
NS **	George Follmer	Shadow	Shadow-Ford Cosworth DN1	0 laps/accident	25
NS **	Jackie Oliver	Shadow	Shadow-Ford Cosworth DN1	0 laps/accident	26
NS	David Purley	LEC	March-Ford Cosworth 731	accident	16

*Clarke-Mordaunt-Guthrie-Durlacher Racing **nine drivers failed to take the restart

Pole: Peterson, 1m16.300s, 138.100mph/222.251kph. Fastest lap: Hunt, 1m18.600s, 134.091mph/215.800kph on Lap 63. Race leaders: Peterson 1-38, Revson 39-67

FIRST SAFETY CAR DEPLOYMENT

The 1973 Canadian GP was Peter Revson's second win, but more notably it was the first grand prix in which a safety car was used. This was called out just after everyone pitted for slicks and Scheckter hit Cevert's car and partly blocked the track, but it failed to pick up the leader. This meant that Fittipaldi lost nearly a lap and Revson took the day.

FRANCE'S FUTURE CHAMPION KILLED

Francois Cevert really was the prince in waiting up to his death in qualifying at Watkins Glen. After four years as Jackie Stewart's understudy at Tyrrell, with one win but, tellingly, five second places in 1973, his grooming was complete. For 1974, with Stewart retired, he would become team leader. Out of respect, Tyrrell declined to start the race.

DUTCH GRAND PRIX

ZANDVOORT • ROUND 10 • DATE: 29TH JULY 1973
Laps: 72 • Distance: 189.65miles/304.272km • Weather: Warm but dull

Pos	Driver	Team	Chassis-Engine	Result	Qual
1	Jackie Stewart	Tyrrell	Tyrrell-Ford Cosworth 006	1h39m12.450s	2
2	Francois Cevert	Tyrrell	Tyrrell-Ford Cosworth 006	1h39m28.280s	3
3	James Hunt	Hesketh	March-Ford Cosworth 731	1h40m15.460s	7
4	Peter Revson	McLaren	McLaren-Ford Cosworth M23	1h40m21.580s	6
5	Jean-Pierre Beltoise	BRM	BRM P160E	1h40m25.820s	9
6	Gijs van Lennep	Frank Williams*	Williams-Ford Cosworth IR	70 laps	20
7	Carlos Pace	Surtees	Surtees-Ford Cosworth TS14A	69 laps	8
8	Clay Regazzoni	BRM	BRM P160E	68 laps	12
9	Howden Ganley	Frank Williams*	Williams-Ford Cosworth IR	68 laps	15
10	George Follmer	Shadow	Shadow-Ford Cosworth DN1	67 laps	22
11	Ronnie Peterson	Lotus	Lotus-Ford Cosworth 72E	66 laps/engine	1
NC	Graham Hill	Embassy Racing	Shadow-Ford Cosworth DN1	56 laps	17
R	Niki Lauda	BRM	BRM P160E	52 laps/fuel pump	11
R	Mike Hailwood	Surtees	Surtees-Ford Cosworth TS14A	52 laps/electrical	24
R	Denny Hulme	McLaren	McLaren-Ford Cosworth M23	31 laps/engine	4
R	Wilson Fittipaldi	Brabham	Brabham-Ford Cosworth BT42	27 laps/accident	13
R	Chris Amon	Tecno	Tecno PA123B	22 laps/fuel system	19
R	Carlos Reutemann	Brabham	Brabham-Ford Cosworth BT42	9 laps/tyre	5
R	David Purley	LEC	March-Ford Cosworth 731	8 laps/stopped to help	21
R	Roger Williamson	March	March-Ford Cosworth 731	7 laps/fatal accident	18
R	Emerson Fittipaldi	Lotus	Lotus-Ford Cosworth 72E	2 laps/driver in pain	16
R	Mike Beuttler	C-M-G-D Racing*	March-Ford Cosworth 731	2 laps/electrical	23
R	Jackie Oliver	Shadow	Shadow-Ford Cosworth DN1	1 lap/accident	10
NS	Rikky von Opel	Ensign	Ensign-Ford Cosworth N173	suspension	14

*Clarke-Mordaunt-Guthrie-Durlacher Racing, Frank Williams Racing Cars

Pole: Peterson, 1m19.470s, 118.954mph/191.438kph. Fastest lap: Peterson, 1m20.310s, 117.712mph/189.440kph on Lap 42. Race leaders: Peterson 1-63, Stewart 64-72

NEW CIRCUITS

Heralding exciting change, Belgium's Zolder circuit replaced unloved Nivelles, and Sweden joined the World Championship circus with a grand prix at Anderstorp. However, the greatest addition was Interlagos, for the first Brazilian GP. The track in Sao Paulo had held a non-championship race in 1972 and the fans went wild when home-town hero Fittipaldi won.

GERMAN GRAND PRIX

NURBURGRING • ROUND 11 • DATE: 5TH AUGUST 1973
Laps: 14 • Distance: 198.260miles/319.69km • Weather: Warm & bright

Pos	Driver	Team	Chassis-Engine	Result	Qual
1	Jackie Stewart	Tyrrell	Tyrrell-Ford Cosworth 006	1h42m03.000s	1
2	Francois Cevert	Tyrrell	Tyrrell-Ford Cosworth 006	1h42m04.600s	3
3	Jacky Ickx	McLaren	McLaren-Ford Cosworth M23	1h42m44.200s	4
4	Carlos Pace	Surtees	Surtees-Ford Cosworth TS14A	1h42m56.800s	11
5	Wilson Fittipaldi	Brabham	Brabham-Ford Cosworth BT42	1h43m22.900s	13
6	Emerson Fittipaldi	Lotus	Lotus-Ford Cosworth 72E	1h43m27.300s	14
7	Jochen Mass	Surtees	Surtees-Ford Cosworth TS14A	1h43m28.200s	15
8	Jackie Oliver	Shadow	Shadow-Ford Cosworth DN1	1h43m28.700s	17
9	Peter Revson	McLaren	McLaren-Ford Cosworth M23	1h44m14.800s	7
10	Henri Pescarolo	Frank Williams Racing Cars	Williams-Fod Cosworth IR	1h44m25.500s	12
11	Rolf Stommelen	Brabham	Brabham-Ford Cosworth BT42	1h45m30.300s	16
12	Denny Hulme	McLaren	McLaren-Ford Cosworth M23	1h45m41.700s	8
13	Graham Hill	Embassy Racing	Shadow-Ford Cosworth DN1	1h45m52.000s	20
14	Mike Hailwood	Surtees	Surtees-Ford Cosworth TS14A	13 laps	18
15	David Purley	LEC	March-Ford Cosworth 731	13 laps	22
16	Mike Beuttler	C-M-G-D Racing*	March-Ford Cosworth 731	13 laps	19
R	Carlos Reutemann	Brabham	Brabham-Ford Cosworth BT42	7 laps/engine	6
R	Clay Regazzoni	BRM	BRM P160E	7 laps/engine	10
R	George Follmer	Shadow	Shadow-Ford Cosworth DN1	5 laps/accident	21
R	Jean-Pierre Beltoise	BRM	BRM P160E	4 laps/gearbox	9
R	Niki Lauda	BRM	BRM P160E	1 lap/accident	5
R	Ronnie Peterson	Lotus	Lotus-Ford Cosworth 72E	0 laps/ignition	2
NS	Howden Ganley	Frank Williams Racing Cars	Williams-Fod Cosworth IR	accident	19

*Clarke-Mordaunt-Guthrie-Durlacher Racing

Pole: Stewart, 7m07.800s, 119.402mph/192.159kph. Fastest lap: Pace, 7m11.400s, 118.433mph/190.600kph on Lap 13. Race leaders: Stewart 1-14

AUSTRIAN GRAND PRIX

OSTERREICHRING • ROUND 12 • DATE: 19TH AUGUST 1973
Laps: 54 • Distance: 198.337miles/319.194km • Weather: Hot & bright

Pos	Driver	Team	Chassis-Engine	Result	Qual
1	Ronnie Peterson	Lotus	Lotus-Ford Cosworth 72E	1h28m48.780s	2
2	Jackie Stewart	Tyrrell	Tyrrell-Ford Cosworth 006	1h28m57.790s	7
3	Carlos Pace	Surtees	Surtees-Ford Cosworth TS14A	1h29m35.420s	8
4	Carlos Reutemann	Brabham	Brabham-Ford Cosworth BT42	1h29m36.690s	5
5	Jean-Pierre Beltoise	BRM	BRM P160E	1h30m10.080s	13
6	Clay Regazzoni	BRM	BRM P160E	1h30m27.180s	14
7	Arturo Merzario	Ferrari	Ferrari 312B3	53 laps	6
8	Denny Hulme	McLaren	McLaren-Ford Cosworth M23	53 laps	3
9	Gijs van Lennep	Frank Williams Racing Cars	Williams-Ford Cosworth IR	52 laps	23
10	Mike Hailwood	Surtees	Surtees-Ford Cosworth TS14A	49 laps	15
R	Emerson Fittipaldi	Lotus	Lotus-Ford Cosworth 72E	48 laps/fuel system	1
NC	Howden Ganley	Frank Williams Racing Cars	Williams-Ford Cosworth IR	44 laps	21
R	Jean-Pierre Jarier	March	March-Ford Cosworth 731	37 laps/engine	12
R	Rikky von Opel	Ensign	Ensign-Ford Cosworth N173	34 laps/fuel system	19
R	Wilson Fittipaldi	Brabham	Brabham-Ford Cosworth BT42	31 laps/fuel system	16
R	Graham Hill	Embassy Racing	Shadow-Ford Cosworth DN1	28 laps/suspension	22
R	George Follmer	Shadow	Shadow-Ford Cosworth DN1	23 laps/differential	20

Pos	Driver	Team	Chassis-Engine	Result	Qual
R	Rolf Stommelen	Brabham	Brabham-Ford Cosworth BT42	21 laps/wheel	17
R	Jackie Oliver	Shadow	Shadow-Ford Cosworth DN1	9 laps/oil leak	18
R	Francois Cevert	Tyrrell	Tyrrell-Ford Cosworth 006	6 laps/suspension	10
R	James Hunt	Hesketh	March-Ford Cosworth 731	3 laps/fuel metering	9
R	Peter Revson	McLaren	McLaren-Ford Cosworth M23	0 laps/clutch	4
R	Mike Beuttler	C-M-G-D Racing*	March-Ford Cosworth 731	0 laps/collision	11
NS	Chris Amon	Tecno	Tecno PA123B	no engine	23
NS	Niki Lauda	BRM	BRM P160E	driver injured	25

*Clarke-Mordaunt-Guthrie-Durlacher Racing

Pole: E Fittipaldi, 1m34.980s, 139.213mph/224.042kph. Fastest lap: Pace, 1m37.290s, 135.906mph/218.720kph on Lap 46. Race leaders: Peterson 1-16 & 49-54, E Fittipaldi 17-48

NEW CONSTRUCTORS

Two constructors entered F1 in 1973. Former racer Mo Nunn's Ensign marque advanced from F2 after Rikki von Opel asked Nunn to build an F1 car. The other arrival was Shadow, a marque that started in the Can Am sports car series for founder Don Nichols, and it fared better, with George Follmer and Jackie Oliver each taking a third.

NEW DRIVERS

Of the 11 newcomers, James Hunt would go on to win the title in 1976, John Watson would rank second in 1982 and Jochen Mass would win a grand prix in 1975. Hunt, driving a March for aristocrat Lord Hesketh, finished third in Zandvoort, then second in the last race of the year at Watkins Glen to rank eighth. Follmer took third in Spain.

ITALIAN GRAND PRIX

MONZA • ROUND 13 • DATE: 9TH SEPTEMBER 1973
Laps: 55 • Distance: 197.363miles/317.625km • Weather: Hot & bright

Pos	Driver	Team	Chassis-Engine	Result	Qual
1	Ronnie Peterson	Lotus	Lotus-Ford Cosworth 72E	1h29m17.000s	1
2	Emerson Fittipaldi	Lotus	Lotus-Ford Cosworth 72E	1h29m17.800s	4
3	Peter Revson	McLaren	McLaren-Ford Cosworth M23	1h29m45.800s	2
4	Jackie Stewart	Tyrrell	Tyrrell-Ford Cosworth 006	1h29m50.200s	6
5	Francois Cevert	Tyrrell	Tyrrell-Ford Cosworth 006	1h30m03.200s	11
6	Carlos Reutemann	Brabham	Brabham-Ford Cosworth BT42	1h30m16.800s	10
7	Mike Hailwood	Surtees	Surtees-Ford Cosworth TS14A	1h30m45.700s	8
8	Jacky Ickx	Ferrari	Ferrari 312B3	54 laps	14
9	David Purley	LEC	March-Ford Cosworth 731	54 laps	24
10	George Follmer	Shadow	Shadow-Ford Cosworth DN1	54 laps	21
11	Jackie Oliver	Shadow	Shadow-Ford Cosworth DN1	54 laps	19
12	Rolf Stommelen	Brabham	Brabham-Ford Cosworth BT42	54 laps	9
13	Jean-Pierre Beltoise	BRM	BRM P160E	54 laps	13

Pos	Driver	Team	Chassis-Engine	Result	Qual
14	Graham Hill	Embassy Racing	Shadow-Ford Cosworth DN1	54 laps	22
15	Denny Hulme	McLaren	McLaren-Ford Cosworth M23	53 laps	3
NC	Howden Ganley	Frank Williams Racing Cars	Williams-Ford Cosworth IR	44 laps	20
R	Mike Beuttler	C-M-G-D Racing*	March-Ford Cosworth 731	34 laps/gearbox	12
R	Niki Lauda	BRM	BRM P160E	33 laps/accident	15
R	Clay Regazzoni	BRM	BRM P160E	30 laps/ignition	18
R	Carlos Pace	Surtees	Surtees-Ford Cosworth TS14A	17 laps/tyre	5
R	Gijs van Lennep	Frank Williams Racing Cars	Williams-Ford Cosworth IR	14 laps/overheating	23
R	Rikky von Opel	Ensign	Ensign-Ford Cosworth N173	10 laps/overheating	17
R	Wilson Fittipaldi	Brabham	Brabham-Ford Cosworth BT42	6 laps/brakes	16
R	Arturo Merzario	Ferrari	Ferrari 312B3	2 laps/suspension	7
NS	James Hunt	Hesketh	March-Ford Cosworth 731	accident	25

*Clarke-Mordaunt-Guthrie-Durlacher Racing

Pole: Peterson, 1m34.800s, 136.269mph/219.303kph. Fastest lap: Stewart, 1m35.300s, 135.583mph/218.200kph on Lap 51. Race leaders: Peterson 1-55

CANADIAN GRAND PRIX

MOSPORT PARK • ROUND 14 • DATE: 23RD SEPTEMBER 1973
Laps: 80 • Distance: 196.388miles/316.56km • Weather: Warm & wet then drying

Pos	Driver	Team	Chassis-Engine	Result	Qual
1	Peter Revson	McLaren	McLaren-Ford Cosworth M23	1h59m04.083s	2
2	Emerson Fittipaldi	Lotus	Lotus-Ford Cosworth 72E	1h59m36.817s	5
3	Jackie Oliver	Shadow	Shadow-Ford Cosworth DN1	1h59m38.588s	14
4	Jean-Pierre Beltoise	BRM	BRM P160E	1h59m40.597s	16
5	Jackie Stewart	Tyrrell	Tyrrell-Ford Cosworth 006	79 laps	9
6	Howden Ganley	Frank Williams Racing Cars	Williams-Ford Cosworth IR	79 laps	22
7	James Hunt	Hesketh	March-Ford Cosworth 731	78 laps	15
8	Carlos Reutemann	Brabham	Brabham-Ford Cosworth BT42	78 laps	4
9	Mike Hailwood	Surtees	Surtees-Ford Cosworth TS14A	78 laps	12
10	Chris Amon	Tyrrell	Tyrrell-Ford Cosworth 005	77 laps	11
11	Wilson Fittipaldi	Brabham	Brabham-Ford Cosworth BT42	77 laps	10
12	Rolf Stommelen	Brabham	Brabham-Ford Cosworth BT42	76 laps	18
13	Denny Hulme	McLaren	McLaren-Ford Cosworth M23	75 laps	7
14	Tim Schenken	Frank Williams Racing Cars	Williams-Ford Cosworth IR	75 laps	24
15	Arturo Merzario	Ferrari	Ferrari 312B3	75 laps	20
16	Graham Hill	Embassy Racing	Shadow-Ford Cosworth DN1	73 laps	17
17	George Follmer	Shadow	Shadow-Ford Cosworth DN1	73 laps	13
18	Carlos Pace	Surtees	Surtees-Ford Cosworth TS14A	72 laps/wheel	19
NC	Jean-Pierre Jarier	March	March-Ford Cosworth 731	71 laps	23
NC	Rikky von Opel	Ensign	Ensign-Ford Cosworth N173	68 laps	26
R	Niki Lauda	BRM	BRM P160E	62 laps/transmission	8
R	Jody Scheckter	McLaren	McLaren-Ford Cosworth M23	32 laps/accident	3
R	Francois Cevert	Tyrrell	Tyrrell-Ford Cosworth 006	32 laps/accident	6
R	Mike Beuttler	C-M-G-D Racing*	March-Ford Cosworth 731	20 laps/engine	21
R	Ronnie Peterson	Lotus	Lotus-Ford Cosworth 72E	16 laps/suspension	1
R	Peter Gethin	BRM	BRM P160E	5 laps/fuel pump	25

*Clarke-Mordaunt-Guthrie-Durlacher Racing

Pole: Peterson, 1m13.697s, 120.107mph/193.294kph. Fastest lap: E Fittipaldi, 1m15.496s, 117.245mph/188.688kph. Race leaders: Peterson 1-2, Lauda 3-19, E Fittipaldi 20-32, Stewart 33, Beltoise 34-39, Oliver 40-46, Revson 47-80

UNITED STATES GRAND PRIX

WATKINS GLEN • ROUND 15 • DATE: 7TH OCTOBER 1973
Laps: 59 • Distance: 199.251miles/320.665km • Weather: Cool & dull

Pos	Driver	Team	Chassis-Engine	Result	Qual
1	Ronnie Peterson	Lotus	Lotus-Ford Cosworth 72E	1h41m15.779s	1
2	James Hunt	Hesketh	March-Ford Cosworth 731	1h41m16.447s	4
3	Carlos Reutemann	Brabham	Brabham-Ford Cosworth BT42	1h41m38.709s	2
4	Denny Hulme	McLaren	McLaren-Ford Cosworth M23	1h42m06.005s	8
5	Peter Revson	McLaren	McLaren-Ford Cosworth M23	1h42m36.146s	7
6	Emerson Fittipaldi	Lotus	Lotus-Ford Cosworth 72E	1h43m03.724s	3
7	Jacky Ickx	Frank Williams Racing Cars	Williams-Ford Cosworth IR	58 laps	23
8	Clay Regazzoni	BRM	BRM P160E	58 laps	15
9	Jean-Pierre Beltoise	BRM	BRM P160E	58 laps	14
10	Mike Beuttler	C-M-G-D Racing*	March-Ford Cosworth 731	58 laps	26
11	Jean-Pierre Jarier	March	March-Ford Cosworth 731	57 laps/accident	17
12	Howden Ganley	Frank Williams Racing Cars	Williams-Ford Cosworth IR	57 laps	19
13	Graham Hill	Embassy Racing	Shadow-Ford Cosworth DN1	57 laps	18
14	George Follmer	Shadow	Shadow-Ford Cosworth DN1	57 laps	20
15	Jackie Oliver	Shadow	Shadow-Ford Cosworth DN1	55 laps	22
16	Arturo Merzario	Ferrari	Ferrari 312B3	55 laps	11
NC	Wilson Fittipaldi	Brabham	Brabham-Ford Cosworth BT42	52 laps	25
R	Jody Scheckter	McLaren	McLaren-Ford Cosworth M23	39 laps/suspension	10
R	Jochen Mass	Surtees	Surtees-Ford Cosworth TS14A	35 laps/engine	16
R	Niki Lauda	BRM	BRM P160E	35 laps/fuel pump	21
R	Mike Hailwood	Surtees	Surtees-Ford Cosworth TS14A	34 laps/suspension	6
R	Carlos Pace	Surtees	Surtees-Ford Cosworth TS14A	32 laps/suspension	9
R	John Watson	Brabham	Brabham-Ford Cosworth BT42	7 laps/engine	24
DQ	Brian Redman	Shadow	Shadow-Ford Cosworth DN1	5 laps/push start	13
NS	Rikky von Opel	Ensign	Ensign-Ford Cosworth N173	0 laps/throttle	27
NS	Francois Cevert	Tyrrell	Tyrrell-Ford Cosworth 006	fatal accident	4
NS	Jackie Stewart	Tyrrell	Tyrrell-Ford Cosworth 006	withdrawn	6
NS	Chris Amon	Tyrrell	Tyrrell-Ford Cosworth 005	withdrawn	13

*Clarke-Mordaunt-Guthrie-Durlacher Racing

Pole: Peterson, 1m39.657s, 121.995mph/196.333kph. Fastest lap: Hunt, 1m41.652s, 119.601mph/192.480kph on Lap 58. Race leaders: Peterson 1-59

IN MEMORIAM

The loss of Roger Williamson and then Francois Cevert robbed F1 of two drivers who could both have gone on to become world champions. The third F1 driver to die in 1973 was Nasif Estefano, who had quit F1 after failing to qualify his de Tomaso at the 1962 Italian GP. Still racing 11 years on, he was thrown from his car in a long-distance road race in his native Argentina.

WORLD DRIVERS' CHAMPIONSHIP FINAL RESULTS

Pos	Driver	Nat	Car-Engine	R1	R2	R3	R4	R5
1	Jackie Stewart	GBR	Tyrrell-Ford Cosworth 005	3	2	-	-	-
			Tyrrell-Ford Cosworth 006	-	-	1	R	1
2	Emerson Fittipaldi	BRA	Lotus-Ford Cosworth 72D	1F	1F	3F	-	-
			Lotus-Ford Cosworth 72E	-	-	-	1	3
3	Ronnie Peterson	SWE	Lotus-Ford Cosworth 72D	R	RP	11	-	-
			Lotus-Ford Cosworth 72E	-	-	-	RPF	RP
4	Francois Cevert	FRA	Tyrrell-Ford Cosworth 006	2	10	-	2	2F
			Tyrrell-Ford Cosworth 005	-	-	NC	-	-
5	Peter Revson	USA	McLaren-Ford Cosworth M19C	8	R	2	-	-
			McLaren-Ford Cosworth M23	-	-	-	4	R
6	Denny Hulme	NZL	McLaren-Ford Cosworth M19C	5	3F	-	-	-
			McLaren-Ford Cosworth M23	-	-	5P	6	7
7	Carlos Reutemann	ARG	Brabham-Ford Cosworth BT37	R	11	7	-	-
			Brabham-Ford Cosworth BT42	-	-	-	R	R
8	James Hunt	GBR	March-Ford Cosworth 731	-	-	-	-	-
9	Jacky Ickx	BEL	Ferrari 312B2	4	5	R	-	-
			Ferrari 312B3	-	-	-	12	R
			McLaren-Ford Cosworth M23	-	-	-	-	-
			Williams-Ford Cosworth IR	-	-	-	-	-
10	Jean-Pierre Beltoise	FRA	BRM P160D	R	R	R	-	-
			BRM P160E	-	-	-	5	R
11	Carlos Pace	BRA	Surtees-Ford Cosworth TS14A	R	R	R	R	8
12	Arturo Merzario	ITA	Ferrari 312B2	9	4	4	-	-
			Ferrari 312B3	-	-	-	-	-
13	George Follmer	USA	Shadow-Ford Cosworth DN1	-	-	6	3	R
14	Jackie Oliver	GBR	Shadow-Ford Cosworth DN1	-	-	R	R	R
15	Andrea de Adamich	ITA	Surtees-Ford Cosworth TS9B	-	-	8	-	-
			Brabham-Ford Cosworth BT37	-	-	-	R	4
			Brabham-Ford Cosworth BT42	-	-	-	-	-
15	Wilson Fittipaldi	BRA	Brabham-Ford Cosworth BT37	6	R	R	-	-
			Brabham-Ford Cosworth BT42	-	-	-	10	R
17	Niki Lauda	AUT	BRM P160C	R	8	-	-	-
			BRM P160D	-	-	R	-	-
			BRM P160E	-	-	-	R	5
17	Clay Regazzoni	CHE	BRM P160D	7P	6	R	-	-
			BRM P160E	-	-	-	9	10
19	Chris Amon	NZL	Tecno PA123B	-	-	-	-	6
			Tyrrell-Ford Cosworth 005	-	-	-	-	-
19	Gijs van Lennep	NLD	Williams-Ford Cosworth IR	-	-	-	-	-
19	Howden Ganley	NZL	Williams-Ford Cosworth FX3B	NC	7	10	-	-
			Williams-Ford Cosworth IR	-	-	-	R	R

Pos	Driver	R6	R7	R8	R9	R10	R11	R12	R13	R14	R15	Total
1	Stewart	-	-	-	-	-	-	-	-	-	-	71
		1P	5	4P	10	1	1P	2	4F	5	NS	
2	E Fittipaldi	-	-	-	-	-	-	-	-	-	-	55
		2F	12	R	R	R	6	RP	2	2F	6	
3	Peterson	-	-	-	-	-	-	-	-	-	-	52
		3	2P	1	2P	11PF	R	1	1P	RP	1P	
4	Cevert	4	3	2	5	2	2	R	5	R	NS	47
		-	-	-	-	-	-	-	-	-	-	
5	Revson	-	-	-	-	-	-	-	-	-	-	38
		5	7	-	1	4	9	R	3	1	5	

Pos	Driver	R6	R7	R8	R9	R10	R11	R12	R13	R14	R15	Total
6	Hulme	-	-	-	-	-	-	-	-	-	-	26
		6	1F	8F	3	R	12	8	15	13	4	
7	Reutemann	-	-	-	-	-	-	-	-	-	-	16
		R	4	3	6	R	R	4	6	8	3	
8	Hunt	9	-	6	4F	3	-	R	NS	7	2F	14
9	Ickx	-	-	-	-	-	-	-	-	-	-	12
		R	6	5	8	-	-	-	8	-	-	
		-	-	-	-	-	3	-	-	-	-	
		-	-	-	-	-	-	-	-	-	7	
10	Beltoise	-	-	-	-	-	-	-	-	-	-	9
		R	R	11	R	5	R	5	13	4	9	
11	Pace	R	10	13	R	7	4F	3F	R	18	R	7
12	Merzario	-	-	-	-	-	-	-	-	-	-	6
		R	-	7	-	-	-	7	R	15	16	
13	Follmer	NS	14	R	R	10	R	R	10	17	14	5
14	Oliver	10	R	R	R	R	8	R	11	3	15	4
15	de Adamich	-	-	-	-	-	-	-	-	-	-	3
		7	-	R	-	-	-	-	-	-	-	
		-	-	-	R	-	-	-	-	-	-	
15	W Fittipaldi	-	-	-	-	-	-	-	-	-	-	3
		11	R	16	R	R	5	R	R	11	NC	
17	Lauda	-	-	-	-	-	-	-	-	-	-	2
		-	-	-	-	-	-	-	-	-	-	
		R	13	9	12	R	R	NS	R	R	R	
17	Regazzoni	-	-	-	-	-	-	-	-	-	-	2
		R	9	12	7	8	R	6	R	-	8	
19	Amon	R	-	-	R	R	-	NS	-	-	-	1
		-	-	-	-	-	-	-	-	10	NS	
19	van Lennep	-	-	-	-	6	-	9	R	-	-	1
19	Ganley	-	-	-	-	-	-	-	-	-	-	1
		R	11	14	9	9	NS	NC	NC	6	12	

SYMBOLS AND GRAND PRIX KEY

Round 1 **Argentinian GP**
Round 2 **Brazilian GP**
Round 3 **South African GP**
Round 4 **Spanish GP**
Round 5 **Belgian GP**
Round 6 **Monaco GP**
Round 7 **Swedish GP**
Round 8 **French GP**
Round 9 **British GP**
Round 10 **Dutch GP**
Round 11 **German GP**
Round 12 **Austrian GP**
Round 13 **Italian GP**
Round 14 **Canadian GP**
Round 15 **United States GP**

DNPQ **DID NOT PRE-QUALIFY** **DNQ** **DID NOT QUALIFY** **DQ** **DISQUALIFIED** **EX** **EXCLUDED**
F **FASTEST LAP** **NC** **NOT CLASSIFIED** **NS** **NON-STARTER** **P** **POLE POSITION** **R** **RETIRED**

SCORING

1st **9 points**
2nd **6 points**
3rd **4 points**
4th **3 points**
5th **2 points**
6th **1 point**

WORLD CONSTRUCTORS' CHAMPIONSHIP FINAL RESULTS

Pos	Team-Engine	R1	R2	R3	R4	R5	R6	R7	R8	R9	R10	R11	R12	R13	R14	R15	Total
1	Lotus-Ford	1	1	3	1	3	2	2	1	2	11	6	1	1	2	1	92
2	Tyrrell-Ford	2	2	1	2	1	1	3	2	5	1	1	2	4	5	-	82
3	McLaren-Ford	5	3	2	4	7	5	1	8	1	4	3	8	3	1	4	58
4	Brabham-Ford	6	11	7	10	4	7	4	3	6	-	5	4	6	8	3	22
5	March-Ford	10	-	-	7	11	9	8	6	4	3	16	-	9	7	2	14
6	Ferrari	4	4	4	12	-	-	6	5	8	-	-	7	8	15	16	12
6	BRM	7	6	-	5	5	-	9	9	7	5	-	5	13	4	8	12
8	Shadow-Ford	-	-	6	3	9	10	14	10	-	10	8	-	10	3	13	9
9	Surtees-Ford	-	12	8	-	8	8	10	13	-	7	4	3	7	9	-	7
10	Iso Marlboro-Ford	-	-	-	-	-	-	-	-	-	-	-	-	-	-	7	2
11	Tecno	-	-	-	-	6	-	-	-	-	-	-	-	-	-	-	1

SEASON SUMMARY

McLaren enjoyed two arrivals for 1974. The first was Marlboro and the cigarette brand started an illustrious 23-year spell with the team. The second was Emerson Fittipaldi joining from Lotus. He raced to three wins and the title, also helping McLaren to its first constructors' crown. Ferrari had its best result for years as Clay Regazzoni ran Fittipaldi close, and Niki Lauda helped guide the Italian team to second overall. Jody Scheckter joined Tyrrell and began to calm down, taking his first win in Sweden and even having a last-round shot at the title as the team adjusted to life without Jackie Stewart.

ARGENTINIAN GRAND PRIX

BUENOS AIRES • ROUND 1 • DATE: 13TH JANUARY 1974
Laps: 53 • Distance: 196.548miles/316.314km • Weather: Hot & bright

Pos	Driver	Team	Chassis-Engine	Result	Qual
1	Denny Hulme	McLaren	McLaren-Ford Cosworth M23	1h41m02.010s	10
2	Niki Lauda	Ferrari	Ferrari 312B3	1h41m11.280s	8
3	Clay Regazzoni	Ferrari	Ferrari 312B3	1h41m22.420s	2
4	Mike Hailwood	McLaren	McLaren-Ford Cosworth M23	1h41m33.800s	9
5	Jean-Pierre Beltoise	BRM	BRM P160E	1h41m53.850s	14
6	Patrick Depailler	Tyrrell	Tyrrell-Ford Cosworth 005	1h42m54.490s	15
7	Carlos Reutemann	Brabham	Brabham-Ford Cosworth BT44	52 laps/out of fuel	6
8	Howden Ganley	March	March-Ford Cosworth 741	52 laps/out of fuel	19
9	Henri Pescarolo	BRM	BRM P160E	52 laps	21
10	Emerson Fittipaldi	McLaren	McLaren-Ford Cosworth M23	52 laps	3
11	Guy Edwards	Embassy Racing	Lola-Ford Cosworth T370	51 laps	25
12	John Watson	Goldie Hexagon Racing	Brabham-Ford Cosworth BT42	49 laps	20
13	Ronnie Peterson	Lotus	Lotus-Ford Cosworth 72E	48 laps	1
R	Graham Hill	Embassy Racing	Lola-Ford Cosworth T370	45 laps/engine	17
R	Jacky Ickx	Lotus	Lotus-Ford Cosworth 72E	36 laps/clutch	7
R	Richard Robarts	Brabham	Brabham-Ford Cosworth BT44	36 laps/gearbox	22
R	Hans-Joachim Stuck	March	March-Ford Cosworth 741	31 laps/clutch	23
R	Francois Migault	BRM	BRM P160E	31 laps/water leak	24
R	Jody Scheckter	Tyrrell	Tyrrell-Ford Cosworth 006	25 laps/engine	12
R	Carlos Pace	Surtees	Surtees-Ford Cosworth TS16	21 laps/suspension	11
R	Arturo Merzario	Frank Williams Racing Cars	Williams-Ford Cosworth FW01	19 laps/overheating	13
R	James Hunt	Hesketh	March-Ford Cosworth 731	11 laps/overheating	5
R	Jochen Mass	Surtees	Surtees-Ford Cosworth TS16	10 laps/engine	18
R	Peter Revson	Shadow	Shadow-Ford Cosworth DN3	1 lap/accident	4
R	Jean-Pierre Jarier	Shadow	Shadow-Ford Cosworth DN1	0 laps/accident	16
NS	Rikky von Opel	Ensign	Ensign-Ford Cosworth N174	handling	26

Pole: Peterson, 1m50.780s, 120.513mph/193.947kph. Fastest lap: Regazzoni, 1m52.100s, 119.094mph/191.663kph on Lap 38. Race leaders: Peterson 1-2, Reutemann 3-51, Hulme 52-53

BRAZILIAN GRAND PRIX

INTERLAGOS • ROUND 2 • DATE: 27TH JANUARY 1974
Laps: 32 • Distance: 157.873miles/254.72km • Weather: Warm & dull then rain

Pos	Driver	Team	Chassis-Engine	Result	Qual
1	Emerson Fittipaldi	McLaren	McLaren-Ford Cosworth M23	1h24m37.060s	1
2	Clay Regazzoni	Ferrari	Ferrari 312B3	1h24m50.630s	8
3	Jacky Ickx	Lotus	Lotus-Ford Cosworth 72E	31 laps	5
4	Carlos Pace	Surtees	Surtees-Ford Cosworth TS16	31 laps	12
5	Mike Hailwood	McLaren	McLaren-Ford Cosworth M23	31 laps	7
6	Ronnie Peterson	Lotus	Lotus-Ford Cosworth 72E	31 laps	4
7	Carlos Reutemann	Brabham	Brabham-Ford Cosworth BT44	31 laps	2
8	Patrick Depailler	Tyrrell	Tyrrell-Ford Cosworth 005	31 laps	16
9	James Hunt	Hesketh	March-Ford Cosworth 731	31 laps	18
10	Jean-Pierre Beltoise	BRM	BRM P160E	31 laps	17
11	Graham Hill	Embassy Racing	Lola-Ford Cosworth T370	31 laps	21
12	Denny Hulme	McLaren	McLaren-Ford Cosworth M23	31 laps	11
13	Jody Scheckter	Tyrrell	Tyrrell-Ford Cosworth 006	31 laps	14
14	Henri Pescarolo	BRM	BRM P160E	30 laps	22
15	Richard Robarts	Brabham	Brabham-Ford Cosworth BT44	30 laps	24
16	Francois Migault	BRM	BRM P160E	30 laps	23
17	Jochen Mass	Surtees	Surtees-Ford Cosworth TS16	30 laps	10
R	John Watson	Goldie Hexagon Racing	Brabham-Ford Cosworth BT42	27 laps/clutch	15
R	Hans-Joachim Stuck	March	March-Ford Cosworth 741	24 laps/transmission	13
R	Jean-Pierre Jarier	Shadow	Shadow-Ford Cosworth DN1	21 laps/brakes	19
R	Arturo Merzario	Frank Williams Racing Cars	Williams-Ford Cosworth FW01	20 laps/throttle	9
R	Peter Revson	Shadow	Shadow-Ford Cosworth DN3	10 laps/overheating	6
R	Howden Ganley	March	March-Ford Cosworth 741	8 laps/ignition	20
R	Niki Lauda	Ferrari	Ferrari 312B3	2 laps/engine	3
R	Guy Edwards	Embassy Racing	Lola-Ford Cosworth T370	2 laps/chassis	25

Pole: Fittipaldi, 3m12.970s, 92.273mph/148.499kph. Fastest lap: Regazzoni, 2m36.050s, 114.104mph/183.633kph on Lap 26. Race leaders: Reutemann 1-3, Peterson 4-15, Fittipaldi 16-32

FORZA FERRARI AGAIN

Ferrari had been in the doldrums since 1970 when it was pipped by Jochen Rindt-led Lotus. For 1974, Niki Lauda and Clay Regazzoni came in and the Austrian, in particular, gelled with new team manager Luca di Montezemolo and gave the team much needed focus. Both drivers won races, although Lauda was held back by retirements.

SOUTH AFRICAN GRAND PRIX

KYALAMI • ROUND 3 • DATE: 30TH MARCH 1974
Laps: 78 • Distance: 198.908miles/320.112km • Weather: Warm & bright

Pos	Driver	Team	Chassis-Engine	Result	Qual
1	Carlos Reutemann	Brabham	Brabham-Ford Cosworth BT44	1h42m40.960s	4
2	Jean-Pierre Beltoise	BRM	BRM P201	1h43m14.900s	11
3	Mike Hailwood	McLaren	McLaren-Ford Cosworth M23	1h43m23.120s	12
4	Patrick Depailler	Tyrrell	Tyrrell-Ford Cosworth 005	1h43m25.150s	15

Pos	Driver	Team	Chassis-Engine	Result	Qual
5	Hans-Joachim Stuck	March	March-Ford Cosworth 741	1h43m27.190s	7
6	Arturo Merzario	Frank Williams Racing Cars	Williams-Ford Cosworth FW02	1h43m37.000s	3
7	Emerson Fittipaldi	McLaren	McLaren-Ford Cosworth M23	1h43m49.350s	5
8	Jody Scheckter	Tyrrell	Tyrrell-Ford Cosworth 006	1h43m51.500s	8
9	Denny Hulme	McLaren	McLaren-Ford Cosworth M23	77 laps	9
10	Vittorio Brambilla	March	March-Ford Cosworth 741	77 laps	19
11	Carlos Pace	Surtees	Surtees-Ford Cosworth TS16	77 laps	2
12	Graham Hill	Embassy Racing	Lola-Ford Cosworth T370	77 laps	18
13	Ian Scheckter	Team Gunston	Lotus-Ford Cosworth 72E	76 laps	22
14	Eddie Keizan	Blignaut Racing	Tyrrell-Ford Cosworth 004	76 laps	24
15	Francois Migault	BRM	BRM P160E	75 laps	25
16	Niki Lauda	Ferrari	Ferrari 312B3	74 laps/ignition	1
17	Richard Robarts	Brabham	Brabham-Ford Cosworth BT44	74 laps	23
18	Henri Pescarolo	BRM	BRM P160E	72 laps	21
19	Dave Charlton	Scuderia Scribante	McLaren-Ford Cosworth M23	71 laps	20
R	Clay Regazzoni	Ferrari	Ferrari 312B3	65 laps/fuel pressure	6
R	John Watson	Goldie Hexagon Racing	Brabham-Ford Cosworth BT42	54 laps/fuel system	13
R	Jacky Ickx	Lotus	Lotus-Ford Cosworth 76	31 laps/brakes	10
R	James Hunt	Hesketh	Hesketh-Ford Cosworth 308	13 laps/transmission	14
R	Jochen Mass	Surtees	Surtees-Ford Cosworth TS16	11 laps/suspension	17
R	Paddy Driver	Team Gunston	Lotus-Ford Cosworth 72E	6 laps/clutch	26
R	Ronnie Peterson	Lotus	Lotus-Ford Cosworth 76	2 laps/collision	16
R	Tom Belso	Frank Williams Racing Cars	Williams-Ford Cosworth FW01	0 laps/clutch	27

Pole: Lauda, 1m16.580s, 119.879mph/192.927kph. Fastest lap: Reutemann, 1m18.160s, 117.457mph/189.030kph on Lap 58. Race leaders: Lauda 1-9, Reutemann 10-78

ARGENTINA HAS ANOTHER WINNER

Argentinian fans, starved of F1 success since Juan Manuel Fangio's retirement in 1958, had a winner again when Carlos Reutemann lived up to the promise he'd shown in 1973 to take his first win at Kyalami, after cruelly failing to win the season-opener on home ground when his Brabham ran out of fuel just two laps from the finish.

SPANISH GRAND PRIX

JARAMA • ROUND 4 • DATE: 28TH APRIL 1974
Laps: 84 • Distance: 177.687miles/285.961km • Weather: Warm & wet then drying

Pos	Driver	Team	Chassis-Engine	Result	Qual
1	Niki Lauda	Ferrari	Ferrari 312B3	2h00m29.560s	1
2	Clay Regazzoni	Ferrari	Ferrari 312B3	2h01m05.170s	3
3	Emerson Fittipaldi	McLaren	McLaren-Ford Cosworth M23	83 laps	4
4	Hans-Joachim Stuck	March	March-Ford Cosworth 741	82 laps	13
5	Jody Scheckter	Tyrrell	Tyrrell-Ford Cosworth 007	82 laps	9
6	Denny Hulme	McLaren	McLaren-Ford Cosworth M23	82 laps	8
7	Brian Redman	Shadow	Shadow-Ford Cosworth DN3	81 laps	21
8	Patrick Depailler	Tyrrell	Tyrrell-Ford Cosworth 006	81 laps	16
9	Mike Hailwood	McLaren	McLaren-Ford Cosworth M23	81 laps	17
10	James Hunt	Hesketh	Hesketh-Ford Cosworth 308	81 laps	10
11	John Watson	Goldie Hexagon Racing	Brabham-Ford Cosworth BT42	80 laps	15

Pos	Driver	Team	Chassis-Engine	Result	Qual
12	Henri Pescarolo	BRM	BRM P160E	80 laps	20
13	Carlos Pace	Surtees	Surtees-Ford Cosworth TS16	78 laps	14
14	Tim Schenken	Trojan	Trojan-Ford Cosworth T103	76 laps/spun off	25
NC	Jean-Pierre Jarier	Shadow	Shadow-Ford Cosworth DN3	73 laps	12
R	Graham Hill	Embassy Racing	Lola-Ford Cosworth T370	43 laps/engine	19
R	Arturo Merzario	Frank Williams Racing Cars	Williaqms-Ford Cosworth FW03	37 laps/accident	7
R	Jochen Mass	Surtees	Surtees-Ford Cosworth TS16	35 laps/gearbox	18
R	Francois Migault	BRM	BRM P160E	27 laps/engine	22
R	Jacky Ickx	Lotus	Lotus-Ford Cosworth 76	26 laps/brakes	5
R	Ronnie Peterson	Lotus	Lotus-Ford Cosworth 76	23 laps/engine	2
R	Chris Amon	Amon	Amon-Ford Cosworth AF1	22 laps/brakes	23
R	Rikky von Opel	Brabham	Brabham-Ford Cosworth BT44	14 laps/oil leak	24
R	Carlos Reutemann	Brabham	Brabham-Ford Cosworth BT44	12 laps/spun off	6
R	Jean-Pierre Beltoise	BRM	BRM P201	2 laps/engine	11
NS	Vittorio Brambilla	March	March-Ford Cosworth 741	accident	10
DNQ	Guy Edwards	Embassy Racing	Lola-Ford Cosworth T370	-	27
DNQ	Tom Belso	Frank Williams Racing Cars	Williams-Ford Cosworth FW02	-	28

Pole: Lauda, 1m18.440s, 97.083mph/156.240kph. Fastest lap: Lauda, 1m20.830s, 94.212mph/151.620kph on Lap 47. Race leaders: Peterson 1-20, Lauda 21-22 & 25-84, Ickx 23-24

BUCKING THE TREND

It seemed an anachronism when he did it, but Finnish F1 racer Leo Kinnunen set a record in 1974 when he became the last driver to compete in F1 wearing an open-faced helmet. He did this when driving a AAW Racing Team-entered Surtees in the one grand prix he qualified for (from six attempts), the Swedish GP. He preferred the open face in wet conditions.

BELGIAN GRAND PRIX

NIVELLES • ROUND 5 • DATE: 12TH MAY 1974
Laps: 85 • Distance: 196.386miles/316.54km • Weather: Warm & bright

Pos	Driver	Team	Chassis-Engine	Result	Qual
1	Emerson Fittipaldi	McLaren	McLaren-Ford Cosworth M23	1h44m20.570s	4
2	Niki Lauda	Ferrari	Ferrari 312B3	1h44m20.920s	3
3	Jody Scheckter	Tyrrell	Tyrrell-Ford Cosworth 007	1h45m06.180s	2
4	Clay Regazzoni	Ferrari	Ferrari 312B3	1h45m12.590s	1
5	Jean-Pierre Beltoise	BRM	BRM P201	1h45m28.620s	7
6	Denny Hulme	McLaren	McLaren-Ford Cosworth M23	1h45m31.110s	12
7	Mike Hailwood	McLaren	McLaren-Ford Cosworth M23	84 laps	13
8	Graham Hill	Embassy Racing	Lola-Ford Cosworth T370	83 laps	29
9	Vittorio Brambilla	March	March-Ford Cosworth 741	83 laps	31
10	Tim Schenken	Trojan	Trojan-Ford Cosworth T103	83 laps	23
11	John Watson	Goldie Hexagon Racing	Brabham-Ford Cosworth BT42	83 laps	19
12	Guy Edwards	Embassy Racing	Lola-Ford Cosworth T370	82 laps	21
13	Jean-Pierre Jarier	Shadow	Shadow-Ford Cosworth DN3	82 laps	17
14	Gijs van Lennep	Frank Williams Racing Cars	Williams-Ford Cosworth FW02	82 laps	30
15	Vern Schuppan	Ensign	Ensign-Ford Cosworth N174	82 laps	14
16	Francois Migault	BRM	BRM P160E	82 laps	25
17	Teddy Pilette	Brabham	Brabham-Ford Cosworth BT42	81 laps	27

Pos	Driver	Team	Chassis-Engine	Result	Qual
18	Brian Redman	Shadow	Shadow-Ford Cosworth DN3	80 laps/engine	18
R	Jacky Ickx	Lotus	Lotus-Ford Cosworth 76	72 laps/overheating	16
R	Tom Pryce	Token	Token-Ford Cosworth RJ02	66 laps/collision	20
R	Carlos Reutemann	Brabham	Brabham-Ford Cosworth BT44	62 laps/engine	24
R	Ronnie Peterson	Lotus	Lotus-Ford Cosworth 76	56 laps/oil leak	5
R	Patrick Depailler	Tyrrell	Tyrrell-Ford Cosworth 007	53 laps/brakes	11
R	Jochen Mass	Surtees	Surtees-Ford Cosworth TS16	53 laps/suspension	26
R	Gerard Larrousse	Scuderia Finotto	Brabham-Ford Cosworth BT42	53 laps/tyre	28
R	Carlos Pace	Surtees	Surtees-Ford Cosworth TS16	50 laps/handling	8
R	Rikky von Opel	Brabham	Brabham-Ford Cosworth BT44	49 laps/engine	22
R	James Hunt	Hesketh	Hesketh-Ford Cosworth 308	45 laps/accident	9
R	Arturo Merzario	Frank Williams Racing Cars	Williams-Ford Cosworth FW03	29 laps/transmission	6
R	Henri Pescarolo	BRM	BRM P160E	12 laps/collision	15
R	Hans-Joachim Stuck	March	March-Ford Cosworth 741	6 laps/clutch	10
DNQ	Leo Kinnunen	AAW Racing Team	Surtees-Ford Cosworth TS16	-	32

Pole: Regazzoni, 1m09.820s, 119.311mph/192.013kph. Fastest lap: Hulme, 1m11.310s, 116.818mph/188.001kph on Lap 37. Race leaders: Regazzoni 1-38, Fittipaldi 39-85

MONACO GRAND PRIX

MONTE CARLO • ROUND 6 • DATE: 26TH MAY 1974
Laps: 78 • Distance: 158.874miles/255.684km • Weather: Warm & bright

Pos	Driver	Team	Chassis-Engine	Result	Qual
1	Ronnie Peterson	Lotus	Lotus-Ford Cosworth 72E	1h58m03.700s	3
2	Jody Scheckter	Tyrrell	Tyrrell-Ford Cosworth 007	1h58m32.500s	5
3	Jean-Pierre Jarier	Shadow	Shadow-Ford Cosworth DN3	1h58m52.600s	6
4	Clay Regazzoni	Ferrari	Ferrari 312B3	1h59m06.800s	2
5	Emerson Fittipaldi	McLaren	McLaren-Ford Cosworth M23	77 laps	13
6	John Watson	Goldie Hexagon Racing	Brabham-Ford Cosworth BT42	77 laps	21
7	Graham Hill	Embassy Racing	Lola-Ford Cosworth T370	76 laps	19
8	Guy Edwards	Embassy Racing	Lola-Ford Cosworth T370	75 laps	24
9	Patrick Depailler	Tyrrell	Tyrrell-Ford Cosworth 006	74 laps	4
R	Henri Pescarolo	BRM	BRM P160E	62 laps/gearbox	25
R	Jacky Ickx	Lotus	Lotus-Ford Cosworth 72E	34 laps/engine	18
R	Niki Lauda	Ferrari	Ferrari 312B3	32 laps/ignition	1
R	James Hunt	Hesketh	Hesketh-Ford Cosworth 308	28 laps/halfshaft	7
R	Mike Hailwood	McLaren	McLaren-Ford Cosworth M23	11 laps/accident	10
R	Carlos Reutemann	Brabham	Brabham-Ford Cosworth BT44	5 laps/suspension	8
R	Francois Migault	BRM	BRM P160E	4 laps/accident	20
R	Vern Schuppan	Ensign	Ensign-Ford Cosworth N174	4 laps/accident	23
R	Hans-Joachim Stuck	March	March-Ford Cosworth 741	3 laps/collision	9
R	Jean-Pierre Beltoise	BRM	BRM P201	0 laps/collision	11
R	Denny Hulme	McLaren	McLaren-Ford Cosworth M23	0 laps/collision	12
R	Arturo Merzario	Frank Williams Racing Cars	Williams-Ford Cosworth FW03	0 laps/collision	14
R	Vittorio Brambilla	March	March-Ford Cosworth 741	0 laps/collision	15
R	Brian Redman	Shadow	Shadow-Ford Cosworth DN3	0 laps/collision	16
R	Carlos Pace	Surtees	Surtees-Ford Cosworth TS16	0 laps/collision	17
R	Tim Schenken	Trojan	Trojan-Ford Cosworth T103	0 laps/collision	22
NS	Jochen Mass	Surtees	Surtees-Ford Cosworth TS16	no spares	17
NS	Chris Amon	Amon	Amon-Ford Cosworth AF1	hub	20
DNQ	Rikky von Opel	Brabham	Brabham-Ford Cosworth BT44	-	28

Pole: Lauda, 1m26.300s, 84.967mph/136.741kph. Fastest lap: Peterson, 1m27.900s, 83.420mph/134.252kph on Lap 57. Race leaders: Regazzoni 1-20, Lauda 21-32, Peterson 33-78

NO LONGER A NOVELTY

Hesketh had been seen as party animals rather than serious racers when they arrived in F1 in 1973, but they returned with their own car in 1974 and began to consolidate their reputation as James Hunt finished third at Anderstorp, the Osterreichring and Watkins Glen, proving that the Harvey Postlethwaite-designed 308 had become more effective.

SWEDISH GRAND PRIX

ANDERSTORP • ROUND 7 • DATE: 9TH JUNE 1974
Laps: 80 • Distance: 199.487miles/321.44km • Weather: Warm & bright

Pos	Driver	Team	Chassis-Engine	Result	Qual
1	Jody Scheckter	Tyrrell	Tyrrell-Ford Cosworth 007	1h58m31.391s	2
2	Patrick Depailler	Tyrrell	Tyrrell-Ford Cosworth 007	1h58m31.771s	1
3	James Hunt	Hesketh	Hesketh-Ford Cosworth 308	1h58m34.716s	6
4	Emerson Fittipaldi	McLaren	McLaren-Ford Cosworth M23	1h59m24.898s	9
5	Jean-Pierre Jarier	Shadow	Shadow-Ford Cosworth DN3	1h59m47.794s	8
6	Graham Hill	Embassy Racing	Lola-Ford Cosworth T370	79 laps	15
7	Guy Edwards	Embassy Racing	Lola-Ford Cosworth T370	79 laps	18
8	Tom Belso	Frank Williams*	Williams-Ford Cosworth FW02	79 laps	21
9	Rikky von Opel	Brabham	Brabham-Ford Cosworth BT44	79 laps	20
10	Vittorio Brambilla	March	March-Ford Cosworth 741	78 laps/engine	17
11	John Watson	Goldie Hexagon*	Brabham-Ford Cosworth BT42	77 laps	14
DQ	Vern Schuppan	Ensign	Ensign-Ford Cosworth N174	77 laps/started unofficially	26
R	Niki Lauda	Ferrari	Ferrari 312B3	70 laps/gearbox	3
R	Reine Wisell	March	March-Ford Cosworth 741	59 laps/suspension	16
R	Denny Hulme	McLaren	McLaren-Ford Cosworth M23	56 laps/suspension	12
R	Jochen Mass	Surtees	Surtees-Ford Cosworth TS16	53 laps/suspension	22
R	Carlos Reutemann	Brabham	Brabham-Ford Cosworth BT44	30 laps/oil leak	10
R	Jacky Ickx	Lotus	Lotus-Ford Cosworth 72E	27 laps/engine	7
R	Clay Regazzoni	Ferrari	Ferrari 312B3	24 laps/gearbox	4
R	Carlos Pace	Surtees	Surtees-Ford Cosworth TS16	15 laps/handling	24
R	Ronnie Peterson	Lotus	Lotus-Ford Cosworth 72E	8 laps/halfshaft	5
R	Leo Kinnunen	AAW Racing Team	Surtees-Ford Cosworth TS16	8 laps/engine	25
R	Mike Hailwood	McLaren	McLaren-Ford Cosworth M23	5 laps/oil leak	11
R	Jean-Pierre Beltoise	BRM	BRM P201	3 laps/engine	13
R	Bertil Roos	Shadow	Shadow-Ford Cosworth DN3	2 laps/gearbox	23
R	Henri Pescarolo	BRM	BRM P201	0 laps/fire	19
NS	Richard Robarts	Frank Williams*	Williams-Ford Cosworth FW02	Belso drove car	25
NS	Arturo Merzario	Frank Williams*	Williams-Ford Cosworth FW02	driver unwell	28

*Frank Williams Racing Cars, Goldie Hexagon Racing

Pole: Depailler, 1m24.758s, 106.043mph/170.659kph. Fastest lap: Depailler, 1m27.262s, 103.000mph/165.762kph on Lap 72. Race leaders: Scheckter 1-80

HISTORY REPEATS ITSELF

Austrian racer Helmuth Koinigg was killed at Watkins Glen in a near repeat of Francois Cevert's accident in the 1973 United States GP. Koinigg was having his second outing for Surtees after failing to qualifying a Brabham for his home grand prix, when a suspension breakage pitched his car into the barriers and he didn't survive the impact.

DUTCH GRAND PRIX

ZANDVOORT • ROUND 8 • DATE: 23RD JUNE 1974
Laps: 75 • Distance: 196.412miles/316.95km • Weather: Warm & bright

Pos	Driver	Team	Chassis-Engine	Result	Qual
1	Niki Lauda	Ferrari	Ferrari 312B3	1h43m00.350s	1
2	Clay Regazzoni	Ferrari	Ferrari 312B3	1h43m08.600s	2
3	Emerson Fittipaldi	McLaren	McLaren-Ford Cosworth M23	1h43m30.620s	3
4	Mike Hailwood	McLaren	McLaren-Ford Cosworth M23	1h43m31.640s	4
5	Jody Scheckter	Tyrrell	Tyrrell-Ford Cosworth 007	1h43m34.630s	5
6	Patrick Depailler	Tyrrell	Tyrrell-Ford Cosworth 007	1h43m51.870s	8
7	John Watson	Goldie Hexagon Racing	Brabham-Ford Cosworth BT42	1h44m14.300s	13
8	Ronnie Peterson	Lotus	Lotus-Ford Cosworth 72E	73 laps	10
9	Rikky von Opel	Brabham	Brabham-Ford Cosworth BT44	73 laps	23
10	Vittorio Brambilla	March	March-Ford Cosworth 741	72 laps	15
11	Jacky Ickx	Lotus	Lotus-Ford Cosworth 72E	71 laps	18
12	Carlos Reutemann	Brabham	Brabham-Ford Cosworth BT44	71 laps	12
DQ	Vern Schuppan	Ensign	Ensign-Ford Cosworth N174	69 laps/tyre change	17
R	Denny Hulme	McLaren	McLaren-Ford Cosworth M23	65 laps/ignition	9
R	Francois Migault	BRM	BRM P201	60 laps/gearbox	25
R	Arturo Merzario	Frank Williams Racing Cars	Williams-Ford Cosworth FW02	54 laps/gearbox	21
R	Guy Edwards	Embassy Racing	Lola-Ford Cosworth T370	36 laps/fuel system	14
R	Jean-Pierre Jarier	Shadow	Shadow-Ford Cosworth DN3	28 laps/clutch	7
R	Jean-Pierre Beltoise	BRM	BRM P201	18 laps/gearbox	16
R	Graham Hill	Embassy Racing	Lola-Ford Cosworth T370	16 laps/gearbox	19
R	Henri Pescarolo	BRM	BRM P160E	15 laps/handling	24
R	Jochen Mass	Surtees	Surtees-Ford Cosworth TS16	8 laps/transmission	20
R	James Hunt	Hesketh	Hesketh-Ford Cosworth 308	2 laps/collision	6
R	Tom Pryce	Shadow	Shadow-Ford Cosworth DN3	0 laps/collision	11
R	Hans-Joachim Stuck	March	March-Ford Cosworth 741	0 laps/accident	22
DNQ	Tim Schenken	Trojan	Trojan-Ford Cosworth T103	-	26
DNQ	Gijs van Lennep	Frank Williams Racing Cars	Williams-Ford Cosworth FW01	-	27

Pole: Lauda, 1m18.310s, 120.716mph/194.274kph. Fastest lap: Peterson, 1m21.440s, 116.076mph/186.807kph on Lap 63. Race leaders: Lauda 1-75

FRENCH GRAND PRIX

DIJON-PRENOIS • ROUND 9 • DATE: 7TH JULY 1974
Laps: 80 • Distance: 163.428miles/263.12km • Weather: Warm & bright

Pos	Driver	Team	Chassis-Engine	Result	Qual
1	Ronnie Peterson	Lotus	Lotus-Ford Cosworth 72E	1h21m55.020s	2
2	Niki Lauda	Ferrari	Ferrari 312B3	1h22m15.380s	1
3	Clay Regazzoni	Ferrari	Ferrari 312B3	1h22m22.860s	4
4	Jody Scheckter	Tyrrell	Tyrrell-Ford Cosworth 007	1h22m23.130s	7
5	Jacky Ickx	Lotus	Lotus-Ford Cosworth 72E	1h22m32.560s	13
6	Denny Hulme	McLaren	McLaren-Ford Cosworth M23	1h22m33.160s	11
7	Mike Hailwood	McLaren	McLaren-Ford Cosworth M23	79 laps	6
8	Patrick Depailler	Tyrrell	Tyrrell-Ford Cosworth 006	79 laps	9
9	Arturo Merzario	Frank Williams Racing Cars	Williams-Ford Cosworth FW02	79 laps	15
10	Jean-Pierre Beltoise	BRM	BRM P201	79 laps	17
11	Vittorio Brambilla	March	March-Ford Cosworth 741	79 laps	16
12	Jean-Pierre Jarier	Shadow	Shadow-Ford Cosworth DN3	79 laps	12
13	Graham Hill	Embassy Racing	Lola-Ford Cosworth T370	78 laps	21

Pos	Driver	Team	Chassis-Engine	Result	Qual
14	Francois Migault	BRM	BRM P160E	78 laps	22
15	Guy Edwards	Embassy Racing	Lola-Ford Cosworth T370	77 laps	20
16	John Watson	Goldie Hexagon Racing	Brabham-Ford Cosworth BT42	76 laps	14
R	Emerson Fittipaldi	McLaren	McLaren-Ford Cosworth M23	27 laps/engine	5
R	Carlos Reutemann	Brabham	Brabham-Ford Cosworth BT44	24 laps/handling	8
R	Jochen Mass	Surtees	Surtees-Ford Cosworth TS16	4 laps/clutch	18
R	Tom Pryce	Shadow	Shadow-Ford Cosworth DN3	1 lap/collision	3
R	Henri Pescarolo	BRM	BRM P201	1 lap/clutch	19
R	James Hunt	Hesketh	Hesketh-Ford Cosworth 308	0 laps/collision	10
DNQ	Vern Schuppan	Ensign	Ensign-Ford Cosworth N174	-	23
DNQ	Carlos Pace	Goldie Hexagon Racing	Brabham-Ford Cosworth BT42	-	24
DNQ	Jean-Pierre Jabouille	Frank Williams Racing Cars	Iso Marlboro-Ford Cosworth FW	-	25
DNQ	Hans-Joachim Stuck	March	March-Ford Cosworth 741	-	26
DNQ	Jose Dolhem	Surtees	Surtees-Ford Cosworth TS16	-	27
DNQ	Rikky von Opel	Brabham	Brabham-Ford Cosworth BT44	-	28
DNQ	Leo Kinnunen	AAW Racing Team	Surtees-Ford Cosworth TS16	-	29
DNQ	Gerard Larrousse	Scuderia Finotto	Brabham-Ford Cosworth BT42	-	30

Pole: Lauda, 0m58.790s, 125.145mph/201.401kph. Fastest lap: Scheckter, 1m00.000s, 122.621mph/197.340kph on Lap 10. Race leaders: Lauda 1-16, Peterson 17-80

NEW FACES IN NEW PLACES

There were 20 new drivers and seven new teams in F1 in 1974, showing how the availability of the Ford Cosworth DFV made F1 an attainable dream in a record year for F1 debuts. Not all would prosper at the sport's top level and only three of the newcomers would win, but it added to the fans' interest as 34 cars turned up for the British GP.

BRITISH GRAND PRIX

BRANDS HATCH • ROUND 10 • DATE: 20TH JULY 1974
Laps: 75 • Distance: 198.270miles/319.86km • Weather: Warm & bright

Pos	Driver	Team	Chassis-Engine	Result	Qual
1	Jody Scheckter	Tyrrell	Tyrrell-Ford Cosworth 007	1h43m02.200s	3
2	Emerson Fittipaldi	McLaren	McLaren-Ford Cosworth M23	1h43m17.500s	8
3	Jacky Ickx	Lotus	Lotus-Ford Cosworth 72E	1h44m03.700s	12
4	Clay Regazzoni	Ferrari	Ferrari 312B3	1h44m09.400s	7
5	Niki Lauda	Ferrari	Ferrari 312B3	74 laps	1
6	Carlos Reutemann	Brabham	Brabham-Ford Cosworth BT44	74 laps	4
7	Denny Hulme	McLaren	McLaren-Ford Cosworth M23	74 laps	19
8	Tom Pryce	Shadow	Shadow-Ford Cosworth DN3	74 laps	5
9	Carlos Pace	Brabham	Brabham-Ford Cosworth BT44	74 laps	20
10	Ronnie Peterson	Lotus	Lotus-Ford Cosworth 72E	73 laps	2
11	John Watson	Goldie Hexagon Racing	Brabham-Ford Cosworth BT42	73 laps	13
12	Jean-Pierre Beltoise	BRM	BRM P201	72 laps	23
13	Graham Hill	Embassy Racing	Lola-Ford Cosworth T370	69 laps	22
14	Jochen Mass	Surtees	Surtees-Ford Cosworth TS16	68 laps	17
R	Henri Pescarolo	BRM	BRM P201	64 laps/engine	24
NC	Francois Migault	BRM	BRM P160E	62 laps	14
R	Mike Hailwood	McLaren	McLaren-Ford Cosworth M23	57 laps/spun off	11

Pos	Driver	Team	Chassis-Engine	Result	Qual
R	Jean-Pierre Jarier	Shadow	Shadow-Ford Cosworth DN3	45 laps/suspension	16
R	Hans-Joachim Stuck	March	March-Ford Cosworth 741	36 laps/accident	9
R	Patrick Depailler	Tyrrell	Tyrrell-Ford Cosworth 007	35 laps/engine	10
R	Arturo Merzario	Frank Williams Racing Cars	Williams-Ford Cosworth FW03	25 laps/engine	15
R	Vittorio Brambilla	March	March-Ford Cosworth 741	17 laps/fuel system	18
R	Tim Schenken	Trojan	Trojan-Ford Cosworth T103	6 laps/suspension	25
R	James Hunt	Hesketh	Hesketh-Ford Cosworth 308	2 laps/suspension	6
R	Peter Gethin	Embassy Racing	Lola-Ford Cosworth T370	0 laps/physical	21
DNQ	David Purley	Token	Token-Ford Cosworth RJ02	-	26
DNQ	Derek Bell	Surtees	Surtees-Ford Cosworth TS16	-	27
DNQ	Tom Belso	Frank Williams Racing Cars	Williams-Ford Cosworth FW01	-	28
DNQ	Lella Lombardi	Allied Polymer Group	Brabham-Ford Cosworth BT42	-	29
DNQ	Vern Schuppan	Ensign	Ensign-Ford Cosworth N174	-	30
DNQ	John Nicholson	Lyncar	Lyncar-Ford Cosworth 006	-	31
DNQ	Howden Ganley	Maki	Maki-Ford Cosworth F101	-	32
DNQ	Mike Wilds	Dempster International	March-Ford Cosworth 731	-	33
DNQ	Leo Kinnunen	AAW Racing Team	Surtees-Ford Cosworth TS16	-	34
DNQ	Guy Edwards	Embassy Racing	Lola-Ford Cosworth T370	driver injured	-

Pole: Lauda, 1m19.700s, 119.699mph/192.638kph. Fastest lap: Lauda, 1m21.100s, 117.633mph/189.312kph on Lap 25. Race leaders: Lauda 1-69, Scheckter 70-75

STRETCHING THE LAYOUT

Opened for racing in 1952, when Juan Manuel Fangio was in his pomp, the Buenos Aires circuit was extended for 1974 by the addition of an appreciable loop that took its lap length from 2.079 to 3.709 miles (3.346 to 5.969km). It turned the track left after its first corner, then a straight led to two rights, a longer straight and an esse before rejoining the old layout.

GERMAN GRAND PRIX

NURBURGRING • ROUND 11 • DATE: 4TH AUGUST 1974
Laps: 14 • Distance: 198.260miles/319.69km • Weather: Warm but dull with showers

Pos	Driver	Team	Chassis-Engine	Result	Qual
1	Clay Regazzoni	Ferrari	Ferrari 312B3	1h41m35.000s	2
2	Jody Scheckter	Tyrrell	Tyrrell-Ford Cosworth 007	1h42m25.700s	4
3	Carlos Reutemann	Brabham	Brabham-Ford Cosworth BT44	1h42m58.300s	6
4	Ronnie Peterson	Lotus	Lotus-Ford Cosworth 76	1h42m59.200s	8
5	Jacky Ickx	Lotus	Lotus-Ford Cosworth 72E	1h43m00.000s	9
6	Tom Pryce	Shadow	Shadow-Ford Cosworth DN3	1h43m53.100s	11
7	Hans-Joachim Stuck	March	March-Ford Cosworth 741	1h44m33.700s	19
8	Jean-Pierre Jarier	Shadow	Shadow-Ford Cosworth DN3	1h45m00.900s	18
9	Graham Hill	Embassy Racing	Lola-Ford Cosworth T370	1h45m01.400s	20
10	Henri Pescarolo	BRM	BRM P201	1h45m52.700s	24
11	Derek Bell	Surtees	Surtees-Ford Cosworth TS16	1h46m52.700s	25
12	Carlos Pace	Brabham	Brabham-Ford Cosworth BT44	1h48m01.300s	17
13	Vittorio Brambilla	March	March-Ford Cosworth 741	1h50m18.100s	23
14	Ian Ashley	Token	Token-Ford Cosworth RJ02	13 laps	26
15	Mike Hailwood	McLaren	McLaren-Ford Cosworth M23	12 laps/accident	12
R	Jochen Mass	Surtees	Surtees-Ford Cosworth TS16	10 laps/engine	10
R	James Hunt	Hesketh	Hesketh-Ford Cosworth 308	10 laps/gearbox	13

Pos	Driver	Team	Chassis-Engine	Result	Qual
R	Patrick Depailler	Tyrrell	Tyrrell-Ford Cosworth 007	5 laps/accident	5
R	Arturo Merzario	Frank Williams*	Williams-Ford Cosworth FW03	5 laps/throttle	16
R	Jean-Pierre Beltoise	BRM	BRM P201	4 laps/fuel system	15
R	Vern Schuppan	Ensign	Ensign-Ford Cosworth N174	4 laps/gearbox	22
R	Emerson Fittipaldi	McLaren	McLaren-Ford Cosworth M23	2 laps/suspension	3
R	Jacques Laffite	Frank Williams*	Williams-Ford Cosworth FW02	2 laps/suspension	21
R	John Watson	Goldie Hexagon Racing	Brabham-Ford Cosworth BT44	1 lap/suspension	14
R	Niki Lauda	Ferrari	Ferrari 312B3	0 laps/accident	1
DQ	Denny Hulme	McLaren	McLaren-Ford Cosworth M23	0 laps/ used spare car	7
DNQ	Francois Migault	BRM	BRM P160E	-	27
DNQ	Tim Schenken	Trojan	Trojan-Ford Cosworth T103	-	28
DNQ	Guy Edwards	Embassy Racing	Lola-Ford Cosworth T370	-	29
DNQ	Larry Perkins	Amon	Amon-Ford Cosworth AF1	-	30
DNQ	Chris Amon	Amon	Amon-Ford Cosworth AF1	driver unwell	31
DNQ	Howden Ganley	Maki	Maki-Ford Cosworth F101	accident	32

*Frank Williams Racing Cars

Pole: Lauda, 7m00.800s, 121.388mph/195.356kph. Fastest lap: Scheckter, 7m11.100s, 118.488mph/190.688kph on Lap 11. Race leaders: Regazzoni 1-14

NEW CONSTRUCTORS

Two American teams were among those seeking grand prix glory in 1974. They were Parnelli and Penske, both of whom entered cars for the final two rounds in Canada and the USA. But it was Hesketh that fared best, while Chris Amon's eponymous team, Token Racing and Trojan all had a go. Maki became the second Japanese team after Honda's bid in the 1960s.

AUSTRIAN GRAND PRIX

OSTERREICHRING • ROUND 12 • DATE: 18TH AUGUST 1974
Laps: 54 • Distance: 198.337miles/319.194km • Weather: Hot & bright

Pos	Driver	Team	Chassis-Engine	Result	Qual
1	Carlos Reutemann	Brabham	Brabham-Ford Cosworth BT44	1h28m44.720s	2
2	Denny Hulme	McLaren	McLaren-Ford Cosworth M23	1h29m27.640s	10
3	James Hunt	Hesketh	Hesketh-Ford Cosworth 308	1h29m46.260s	7
4	John Watson	Goldie Hexagon Racing	Brabham-Ford Cosworth BT44	1h29m54.110s	11
5	Clay Regazzoni	Ferrari	Ferrari 312B3	1h29m57.800s	8
6	Vittorio Brambilla	March	March-Ford Cosworth 741	1h29m58.540s	20
7	David Hobbs	McLaren	McLaren-Ford Cosworth M23	53 laps	17
8	Jean-Pierre Jarier	Shadow	Shadow-Ford Cosworth DN3	52 laps	23
9	Dieter Quester	Surtees	Surtees-Ford Cosworth TS16	51 laps	25
10	Tim Schenken	Trojan	Trojan-Ford Cosworth T103	50 laps	19
11	Hans-Joachim Stuck	March	March-Ford Cosworth 741	48 laps/suspension	15
12	Graham Hill	Embassy Racing	Lola-Ford Cosworth T370	48 laps	21
NC	Ian Ashley	Token	Token-Ford Cosworth RJ02	46 laps	24
R	Ronnie Peterson	Lotus	Lotus-Ford Cosworth 72E	45 laps/halfshaft	6
R	Jacky Ickx	Lotus	Lotus-Ford Cosworth 76	43 laps/collision	22
R	Patrick Depailler	Tyrrell	Tyrrell-Ford Cosworth 007	42 laps/collision	14
R	Carlos Pace	Brabham	Brabham-Ford Cosworth BT44	41 laps/oil leak	4
R	Emerson Fittipaldi	McLaren	McLaren-Ford Cosworth M23	37 laps/engine	3

Pos	Driver	Team	Chassis-Engine	Result	Qual
NC	Jacques Laffite	Frank Williams Racing Cars	Williams-Ford Cosworth FW02	37 laps	12
R	Arturo Merzario	Frank Williams Racing Cars	Williams-Ford Cosworth FW03	24 laps/fuel system	9
R	Tom Pryce	Shadow	Shadow-Ford Cosworth DN3	22 laps/spun off	16
R	Jean-Pierre Beltoise	BRM	BRM P201	22 laps/engine	18
R	Niki Lauda	Ferrari	Ferrari 312B3	17 laps/engine	1
R	Rolf Stommelen	Embassy Racing	Lola-Ford Cosworth T370	14 laps/accident	13
R	Jody Scheckter	Tyrrell	Tyrrell-Ford Cosworth 007	8 laps/engine	5
DNQ	Ian Scheckter	Hesketh	Hesketh-Ford Cosworth 308	-	26
DNQ	Leo Kinnunen	AAW Racing Team	Surtees-Ford Cosworth TS16	-	27
DNQ	Derek Bell	Surtees	Surtees-Ford Cosworth TS16	-	28
DNQ	Mike Wilds	Ensign	Ensign-Ford Cosworth N174	-	29
DNQ	Jean-Pierre Jabouille	Surtees	Surtees-Ford Cosworth TS16	-	30
DNQ	Helmuth Koinigg	Scuderia Finotto	Brabham-Ford Cosworth BT42	-	31

Pole: Lauda, 1m35.400s, 138.600mph/223.056kph. Fastest lap: Regazzoni, 1m37.220s, 136.005mph/218.880kph on Lap 46. Race leaders: Reutemann 1-54

NEW DRIVERS

Hans-Joachim Stuck made the biggest splash by finishing fourth in the Spanish GP for March. Tom Pryce came sixth for Shadow in the German GP, with Vittorio Brambilla matching that for March in Austria. Guy Edwards came home seventh in Sweden for the Embassy Racing team. Jacques Laffite, who would go on to win six grands prix, had a slow start with Frank Williams's Iso Marlboro.

ITALIAN GRAND PRIX

MONZA • ROUND 13 • DATE: 8TH SEPTEMBER 1974
Laps: 52 • Distance: 186.446miles/300.56km • Weather: Hot & bright

Pos	Driver	Team	Chassis-Engine	Result	Qual
1	Ronnie Peterson	Lotus	Lotus-Ford Cosworth 72E	1h22m56.600s	7
2	Emerson Fittipaldi	McLaren	McLaren-Ford Cosworth M23	1h22m57.400s	6
3	Jody Scheckter	Tyrrell	Tyrrell-Ford Cosworth 007	1h23m21.300s	12
4	Arturo Merzario	Frank Williams Racing Cars	Williams-Ford Cosworth FW03	1h24m24.300s	15
5	Carlos Pace	Brabham	Brabham-Ford Cosworth BT44	51 laps	3
6	Denny Hulme	McLaren	McLaren-Ford Cosworth M23	51 laps	19
7	John Watson	Goldie Hexagon Racing	Brabham-Ford Cosworth BT44	51 laps	4
8	Graham Hill	Embassy Racing	Lola-Ford Cosworth T370	51 laps	21
9	David Hobbs	McLaren	McLaren-Ford Cosworth M23	51 laps	23
10	Tom Pryce	Shadow	Shadow-Ford Cosworth DN3	50 laps	22
11	Patrick Depailler	Tyrrell	Tyrrell-Ford Cosworth 007	50 laps	10
R	Clay Regazzoni	Ferrari	Ferrari 312B3	40 laps/engine	5
R	Niki Lauda	Ferrari	Ferrari 312B3	32 laps/engine	1
R	Jacky Ickx	Lotus	Lotus-Ford Cosworth 76	30 laps/throttle	16
R	Rolf Stommelen	Embassy Racing	Lola-Ford Cosworth T370	25 laps/suspension	14
R	Jacques Laffite	Frank Williams Racing Cars	Williams-Ford Cosworth FW02	22 laps/engine	17
R	Jean-Pierre Jarier	Shadow	Shadow-Ford Cosworth DN3	19 laps/engine	9
R	Vittorio Brambilla	March	March-Ford Cosworth 741	16 laps/accident	13
R	Tim Schenken	Trojan	Trojan-Ford Cosworth T103	15 laps/gearbox	20
R	Carlos Reutemann	Brabham	Brabham-Ford Cosworth BT44	12 laps/gearbox	2

Pos	Driver	Team	Chassis-Engine	Result	Qual
R	Hans-Joachim Stuck	March	March-Ford Cosworth 741	11 laps/chassis	18
R	Henri Pescarolo	BRM	BRM P201	3 laps/engine	25
R	James Hunt	Hesketh	Hesketh-Ford Cosworth 308	2 laps/engine	8
R	Francois Migault	BRM	BRM P201	1 lap/gearbox	24
R	Jean-Pierre Beltoise	BRM	BRM P201	0 laps/electrical	11
DNQ	Jose Dolhem	Surtees	Surtees-Ford Cosworth TS16	-	26
DNQ	Carlo Facetti	Scuderia Finotto	Brabham-Ford Cosworth BT42	-	27
DNQ	Derek Bell	Surtees	Surtees-Ford Cosworth TS16	-	28
DNQ	Mike Wilds	Ensign	Ensign-Ford Cosworth N174	-	29
DNQ	Chris Amon	Amon	Amon-Ford Cosworth AF1	-	30
DNQ	Leo Kinnunen	AAW Racing Team	Surtees-Ford Cosworth TS16	-	31

Pole: Lauda, 1m33.160s, 138.788mph/223.357kph. Fastest lap: Pace, 1m34.200s, 137.255mph/220.891kph on Lap 46. Race leaders: Lauda 1-29, Regazzoni 30-40, Peterson 41-52

CANADIAN GRAND PRIX

MOSPORT PARK • ROUND 14 • DATE: 22ND SEPTEMBER 1974
Laps: 80 • Distance: 196.388miles/316.56km • Weather: Cool & dull

Pos	Driver	Team	Chassis-Engine	Result	Qual
1	Emerson Fittipaldi	McLaren	McLaren-Ford Cosworth M23	1h40m26.136s	1
2	Clay Regazzoni	Ferrari	Ferrari 312B3	1h40m39.170s	6
3	Ronnie Peterson	Lotus	Lotus-Ford Cosworth 72E	1h40m40.630s	10
4	James Hunt	Hesketh	Hesketh-Ford Cosworth 308	1h40m41.805s	8
5	Patrick Depailler	Tyrrell	Tyrrell-Ford Cosworth 007	1h41m21.458s	7
6	Denny Hulme	McLaren	McLaren-Ford Cosworth M23	79 laps	14
7	Mario Andretti	Parnelli	Parnelli-Ford Cosworth VPJ4	79 laps	16
8	Carlos Pace	Brabham	Brabham-Ford Cosworth BT44	79 laps	9
9	Carlos Reutemann	Brabham	Brabham-Ford Cosworth BT44	79 laps	4
10	Helmuth Koinigg	Surtees	Surtees-Ford Cosworth TS16	78 laps	22
11	Rolf Stommelen	Embassy Racing	Lola-Ford Cosworth T370	78 laps	11
12	Mark Donohue	Penske	Penske-Ford Cosworth PC1	78 laps	24
13	Jacky Ickx	Lotus	Lotus-Ford Cosworth 72E	78 laps	21
14	Graham Hill	Embassy Racing	Lola-Ford Cosworth T370	77 laps	20
15	Jacques Laffite	Frank Williams Racing Cars	Williams-Ford Cosworth FW02	74 laps/puncture	18
16	Jochen Mass	McLaren	McLaren-Ford Cosworth M23	72 laps	12
NC	Chris Amon	BRM	BRM P201	70 laps	25
R	Niki Lauda	Ferrari	Ferrari 312B3	67 laps/accident	2
R	Tom Pryce	Shadow	Shadow-Ford Cosworth DN3	65 laps/engine	13
R	John Watson	Goldie Hexagon Racing	Brabham-Ford Cosworth BT44	61 laps/suspension	15
NC	Jean-Pierre Beltoise	BRM	BRM P201	60 laps	17
R	Jody Scheckter	Tyrrell	Tyrrell-Ford Cosworth 007	48 laps/brakes	3
R	Jean-Pierre Jarier	Shadow	Shadow-Ford Cosworth DN3	46 laps/halfshaft	5
R	Arturo Merzario	Frank Williams Racing Cars	Williams-Ford Cosworth FW03	40 laps/handling	19
R	Eppie Wietzes	Team Canada	Brabham-Ford Cosworth BT42	33 laps/engine	26
R	Hans-Joachim Stuck	March	March-Ford Cosworth 741	12 laps/fuel system	23
DNQ	Derek Bell	Surtees	Surtees-Ford Cosworth TS16	-	27
DNQ	Mike Wilds	Ensign	Ensign-Ford Cosworth N174	-	28
DNQ	Vittorio Brambilla	March	March-Ford Cosworth 741	accident	29
DNQ	Ian Ashley	Chequered Flag	Brabham-Ford Cosworth BT42	-	30

Pole: Fittipaldi, 1m13.188s, 120.942mph/194.638kph. Fastest lap: Lauda, 1m13.659s, 120.169mph/193.393kph on Lap 60. Race leaders: Lauda 1-67, Fittipaldi 68-80

UNITED STATES GRAND PRIX

WATKINS GLEN • ROUND 15 • DATE: 6TH OCTOBER 1974
Laps: 59 • Distance: 199.251miles/320.665km • Weather: Warm & bright

Pos	Driver	Team	Chassis-Engine	Result	Qual
1	Carlos Reutemann	Brabham	Brabham-Ford Cosworth BT44	1h40m21.439s	1
2	Carlos Pace	Brabham	Brabham-Ford Cosworth BT44	1h40m32.174s	4
3	James Hunt	Hesketh	Hesketh-Ford Cosworth 308	1h41m31.823s	2
4	Emerson Fittipaldi	McLaren	McLaren-Ford Cosworth M23	1h41m39.192s	8
5	John Watson	Goldie Hexagon Racing	Brabham-Ford Cosworth BT44	1h41m47.243s	7
6	Patrick Depailler	Tyrrell	Tyrrell-Ford Cosworth 007	1h41m48.945s	13
7	Jochen Mass	McLaren	McLaren-Ford Cosworth M23	1h41m51.451s	20
8	Graham Hill	Embassy Racing	Lola-Ford Cosworth T370	58 laps	24
9	Chris Amon	BRM	BRM P201	57 laps	12
10	Jean-Pierre Jarier	Shadow	Shadow-Ford Cosworth DN3	57 laps	10
11	Clay Regazzoni	Ferrari	Ferrari 312B3	55 laps	9
12	Rolf Stommelen	Embassy Racing	Lola-Ford Cosworth T370	54 laps	21
R	Ronnie Peterson	Lotus	Lotus-Ford Cosworth 72E	52 laps/fuel system	19
NC	Mike Wilds	Ensign	Ensign-Ford Cosworth N174	50 laps	22
NC	Tom Pryce	Shadow	Shadow-Ford Cosworth DN3	47 laps	18
R	Jody Scheckter	Tyrrell	Tyrrell-Ford Cosworth 007	44 laps/fuel system	6
R	Arturo Merzario	Frank Williams*	Williams-Ford Cosworth FW03	43 laps/electrical	15
R	Niki Lauda	Ferrari	Ferrari 312B3	38 laps/suspension	5
R	Jacques Laffite	Frank Williams*	Williams-Ford Cosworth FW02	31 laps/engine	11
R	Mark Donohue	Penske	Penske-Ford Cosworth PC1	27 laps/suspension	14
R	Jose Dolhem	Surtees	Surtees-Ford Cosworth TS16	25 laps/withdrawn	26
R	Vittorio Brambilla	March	March-Ford Cosworth 741	21 laps/fuel system	25
R	Helmuth Koinigg	Surtees	Surtees-Ford Cosworth TS16	9 laps/fatal accident	23
R	Jacky Ickx	Lotus	Lotus-Ford Cosworth 72E	7 laps/suspension	16
DQ	Tim Schenken	Lotus	Lotus-Ford Cosworth 76	6 laps/started illegally	27
R	Denny Hulme	McLaren	McLaren-Ford Cosworth M23	4 laps/engine	17
DQ	Mario Andretti	Parnelli	Parnelli-Ford Cosworth VPJ4	4 laps/push start	3
DNQ	Hans-Joachim Stuck	March	March-Ford Cosworth 741	-	28
DNQ	Ian Ashley	Chequered Flag	Brabham-Ford Cosworth BT42	-	29
DNQ	Jean-Pierre Beltoise	BRM	BRM P201	accident	30

*Frank Williams Racing Cars

Pole: Reutemann, 1m38.978s, 122.832mph/197.680kph. Fastest lap: Pace, 1m40.608s, 120.842mph/194.477kph on Lap 54. Race leaders: Reutemann 1-59

IN MEMORIAM

In addition to Helmuth Koinigg's death, which brought the 1974 season to a tragic end, it also got off to a terrible start when Peter Revson crashed his Shadow with fatal results in pre-event practice at the South African GP. Swiss racer Silvio Moser had dropped out of F1 after 1971 and was killed when he crashed his Lola in the Monza 1000km sports car race.

WORLD DRIVERS' CHAMPIONSHIP FINAL RESULTS

Pos	Driver	Nat	Car-Engine	R1	R2	R3	R4	R5
1	Emerson Fittipaldi	BRA	McLaren-Ford Cosworth M23	10	1P	7	3	1
2	Clay Regazzoni	CHE	Ferrari 312B3	3F	2F	R	2	4P
3	Jody Scheckter	ZAF	Tyrrell-Ford Cosworth 006	R	13	8	-	-
			Tyrrell-Ford Cosworth 007	-	-	-	5	3
4	Niki Lauda	AUT	Ferrari 312B3	2	R	16P	1PF	2
5	Ronnie Peterson	SWE	Lotus-Ford Cosworth 72E	13P	6	-	-	-
			Lotus-Ford Cosworth 76	-	-	R	R	R
6	Carlos Reutemann	ARG	Brabham-Ford Cosworth BT44	7	7	1F	R	R
7	Denny Hulme	NZL	McLaren-Ford Cosworth M23	1	12	9	6	6F
8	James Hunt	GBR	March-Ford Cosworth 731	R	9	-	-	-
			Hesketh-Ford Cosworth 308	-	-	R	10	R
9	Patrick Depailler	FRA	Tyrrell-Ford Cosworth 005	6	8	4	-	-
			Tyrrell-Ford Cosworth 006	-	-	-	8	-
			Tyrrell-Ford Cosworth 007	-	-	-	-	R
10	Jacky Ickx	BEL	Lotus-Ford Cosworth 72E	R	3	-	-	-
			Lotus-Ford Cosworth 76	-	-	R	R	R
10	Mike Hailwood	GBR	McLaren-Ford Cosworth M23	4	5	3	9	7
12	Carlos Pace	BRA	Surtees-Ford Cosworth TS16	R	4	11	13	R
			Brabham-Ford Cosworth BT42	-	-	-	-	-
			Brabham-Ford Cosworth BT44	-	-	-	-	-
13	Jean-Pierre Beltoise	FRA	BRM P160E	5	10	-	-	-
			BRM P201	-	-	2	R	5
14	Jean-Pierre Jarier	FRA	Shadow-Ford Cosworth DN1	R	R	-	-	-
			Shadow-Ford Cosworth DN3	-	-	-	NC	13
14	John Watson	GBR	Brabham-Ford Cosworth BT42	12	R	R	11	11
			Brabham-Ford Cosworth BT44	-	-	-	-	-
16	Hans-Joachim Stuck	DEU	March-Ford Cosworth 741	R	R	5	4	R
17	Arturo Merzario	ITA	Williams-Ford Cosworth FW03	R	R	6	R	R
18	Graham Hill	GBR	Lola-Ford Cosworth T370	R	11	12	R	8
18	Tom Pryce	GBR	Token-Ford Cosworth RJ02	-	-	-	-	R
			Shadow-Ford Cosworth DN3	-	-	-	-	-
18	Vittorio Brambilla	ITA	March-Ford Cosworth 741	-	-	10	NS	9

Pos	Driver	R6	R7	R8	R9	R10	R11	R12	R13	R14	R15	Total
1	Fittipaldi	5	4	3	R	2	R	R	2	1P	4	55
2	Regazzoni	4	R	2	3	4	1	5F	R	2	11	52
3	J Scheckter	-	-	-	-	-	-	-	-	-	-	45
		2	1	5	4F	1	2F	R	3	R	R	
4	Lauda	RP	R	1P	2P	5PF	RP	RP	RP	RF	R	38
5	Peterson	1F	R	8F	1	10	-	R	1	3	R	35
		-	-	-	-	-	4	-	-	-	-	
6	Reutemann	R	R	12	R	6	3	1	R	9	1P	32
7	Hulme	R	R	R	6	7	R	2	6	6	R	20
8	Hunt	-	-	-	-	-	-	-	-	-	-	15
		R	3	R	R	R	R	3	R	4	3	
9	Depailler	-	-	-	-	-	-	-	-	-	-	14
		9	-	-	8	-	-	-	-	-	-	
		-	2PF	6	-	R	R	R	11	5	6	
10	Ickx	R	R	11	5	3	5	-	-	13	R	12
		-	-	-	-	-	-	R	R	-	-	
10	Hailwood	R	R	4	7	R	15	-	-	-	-	12
12	Pace	R	R	-	-	-	-	-	-	-	-	11
		-	-	-	DNQ	-	-	-	-	-	-	
		-	-	-	-	9	12	R	5F	8	2F	

Pos	Driver	R6	R7	R8	R9	R10	R11	R12	R13	R14	R15	Total
13	Beltoise	-	-	-	-	-	-	-	-	-	-	10
		R	R	R	10	12	R	R	R	NC	NS	
14	Jarier	-	-	-	-	-	-	-	-	-	-	6
		3	5	R	12	R	8	8	R	R	10	
14	Watson	6	11	7	16	11	-	-	-	-	-	6
		-	-	-	-	-	R	4	7	R	5	
16	Stuck	R	-	R	DNQ	R	7	11	R	R	DNQ	5
17	Merzario	R	NS	R	9	R	R	R	4	R	R	4
18	Hill	7	6	R	13	13	9	12	8	14	8	1
18	Pryce	-	-	-	-	-	-	-	-	-	-	1
		-	-	R	R	8	6	R	10	R	NC	
18	Brambilla	R	10	10	11	R	13	6	R	DNQ	R	1

WORLD CONSTRUCTORS' CHAMPIONSHIP FINAL RESULTS

Pos	Team-Engine	R1	R2	R3	R4	R5	R6	R7	R8	R9	R10	R11	R12	R13	R14	R15	Total
1	McLaren-Ford	1	1	3	3	1	5	4	3	6	2	15	2	2	1	4	73
2	Ferrari	2	2	16	1	2	4	-	1	2	4	1	5	-	2	11	65
3	Tyrrell-Ford	6	8	4	5	3	2	1	5	4	1	2	-	3	5	6	52
4	Lotus-Ford	13	3	13	-	-	1	-	8	1	3	4	-	1	3	-	42
5	Brabham-Ford	7	7	1	11	11	6	9	7	16	6	3	1	5	8	1	35
6	Hesketh-Ford	-	-	-	-	-	-	-	-	-	-	-	-	-	-	-	15
7	BRM	5	10	2	12	5	-	-	-	10	12	10	-	-	-	9	10
8	Shadow-Ford	-	-	-	7	13	3	5	-	12	8	6	8	10	-	10	7
9	March-Ford	8	9	5	4	9	-	3	10	11	-	7	3	-	4	3	6
10	Williams-Ford	-	-	6	-	14	-	8	-	9	-	-	-	4	15	-	4
11	Surtees-Ford	-	4	11	13	-	-	-	-	-	14	11	9	-	10	-	3
12	Lola-Ford	11	11	12	-	8	7	6	-	13	13	9	12	8	11	8	1

SYMBOLS AND GRAND PRIX KEY

Round 1 Argentinian GP
Round 2 Brazilian GP
Round 3 South African GP
Round 4 Spanish GP
Round 5 Belgian GP
Round 6 Monaco GP
Round 7 Swedish GP
Round 8 Dutch GP
Round 9 French GP
Round 10 British GP
Round 11 German GP
Round 12 Austrian GP
Round 13 Italian GP
Round 14 Canadian GP
Round 15 United States GP

SCORING

1st 9 points
2nd 6 points
3rd 4 points
4th 3 points
5th 2 points
6th 1 point

DNPQ DID NOT PRE-QUALIFY **DNQ** DID NOT QUALIFY **DQ** DISQUALIFIED **EX** EXCLUDED
F FASTEST LAP **NC** NOT CLASSIFIED **NS** NON-STARTER **P** POLE POSITION **R** RETIRED

1975

SEASON SUMMARY

Niki Lauda allied his speed, intelligence and the team's new 312T to put Ferrari back on top and become the team's first world champion since John Surtees in 1964. Among his rivals, McLaren's Emerson Fittipaldi ended the year as runner-up, while Carlos Reutemann ran increasingly well for Brabham. James Hunt scored Hesketh's only win by resisting a stern challenge from Lauda in the Dutch GP. Lord Hesketh then announced that he would quit running a team at the end of the year. There was mayhem at the British GP when a deluge hit Silverstone and only two of the top six managed to stay on the track.

ARGENTINIAN GRAND PRIX

BUENOS AIRES • ROUND 1 • DATE: 12TH JANUARY 1975
Laps: 53 • Distance: 196.548miles/316.314km • Weather: Hot & bright

Pos	Driver	Team	Chassis-Engine	Result	Qual
1	Emerson Fittipaldi	McLaren	McLaren-Ford Cosworth M23	1h39m26.290s	5
2	James Hunt	Hesketh	Hesketh-Ford Cosworth 308B	1h39m32.200s	6
3	Carlos Reutemann	Brabham	Brabham-Ford Cosworth BT44B	1h39m43.350s	3
4	Clay Regazzoni	Ferrari	Ferrari 312B3	1h40m02.080s	7
5	Patrick Depailler	Tyrrell	Tyrrell-Ford Cosworth 007	1h40m20.540s	8
6	Niki Lauda	Ferrari	Ferrari 312B3	1h40m45.940s	4
7	Mark Donohue	Penske	Penske-Ford Cosworth PC1	52 laps	16
8	Jacky Ickx	Lotus	Lotus-Ford Cosworth 72E	52 laps	18
9	Vittorio Brambilla	March	March-Ford Cosworth 741	52 laps	12
10	Graham Hill	Embassy Racing	Lola-Ford Cosworth T370	52 laps	21
11	Jody Scheckter	Tyrrell	Tyrrell-Ford Cosworth 007	52 laps	9
12	Tom Pryce	Shadow	Shadow-Ford Cosworth DN3B	51 laps/transmission	14
13	Rolf Stommelen	Embassy Racing	Lola-Ford Cosworth T370	51 laps	19
14	Jochen Mass	McLaren	McLaren-Ford Cosworth M23	50 laps	13
R	Carlos Pace	Brabham	Brabham-Ford Cosworth BT44B	46 laps/engine	2
NC	Arturo Merzario	Frank Williams Racing Cars	Williams-Ford Cosworth FW03	44 laps	20
R	Mario Andretti	Parnelli	Parnelli-Ford Cosworth VPJ4	27 laps/transmission	10
R	Mike Wilds	BRM	BRM P201	24 laps/engine	22
R	Ronnie Peterson	Lotus	Lotus-Ford Cosworth 72E	15 laps/engine	11
R	Jacques Laffite	Frank Williams Racing Cars	Williams-Ford Cosworth FW02	15 laps/gearbox	17
R	Wilson Fittipaldi	Fittipaldi	Fittipaldi-Ford Cosworth FD01	12 laps/accident	23
DQ	John Watson	Surtees	Surtees-Ford Cosworth TS16	6 laps/illegal repair	15
NS	Jean-Pierre Jarier	Shadow	Shadow-Ford Cosworth DN5	crown wheel	1

Pole: Jarier, 1m49.210s, 122.245mph/196.735kph. Fastest lap: Hunt, 1m50.910s, 120.372mph/193.720kph on Lap 34. Race leaders: Reutemann 1-25, Hunt 26-34, Fittipaldi 35-53

HUGE PACE, BUT NO REWARD

Jean-Pierre Jarier dominated the season-opening races in Argentina and Brazil for Shadow, but came away empty-handed. He qualified on pole in Buenos Aires but stripped his clutch so failed to start. On pole again at Interlagos, he passed Reutemann then rocketed clear until a fuel metering unit failed. He was never as competitive again and his best finish of 1975 was a fourth place.

BRAZILIAN GRAND PRIX

INTERLAGOS • ROUND 2 • DATE: 26TH JANUARY 1975
Laps: 40 • Distance: 197.598miles/318.4km • Weather: Very hot & bright

Pos	Driver	Team	Chassis-Engine	Result	Qual
1	Carlos Pace	Brabham	Brabham-Ford Cosworth BT44B	1h44m41.170s	6
2	Emerson Fittipaldi	McLaren	McLaren-Ford Cosworth M23	1h44m46.960s	2
3	Jochen Mass	McLaren	McLaren-Ford Cosworth M23	1h45m07.830s	10
4	Clay Regazzoni	Ferrari	Ferrari 312B3	1h45m24.450s	5
5	Niki Lauda	Ferrari	Ferrari 312B3	1h45m43.050s	4
6	James Hunt	Hesketh	Hesketh-Ford Cosworth 308B	1h45m46.290s	7
7	Mario Andretti	Parnelli	Parnelli-Ford Cosworth VPJ4	1h45m47.980s	18
8	Carlos Reutemann	Brabham	Brabham-Ford Cosworth BT44B	1h46m20.790s	3
9	Jacky Ickx	Lotus	Lotus-Ford Cosworth 72E	1h46m33.010s	12
10	John Watson	Surtees	Surtees-Ford Cosworth TS16	1h47m10.770s	13
11	Jacques Laffite	Frank Williams Racing Cars	Williams-Ford Cosworth FW02	39 laps	19
12	Graham Hill	Embassy Racing	Lola-Ford Cosworth T370	39 laps	20
13	Wilson Fittipaldi	Fittipaldi	Fittipaldi-Ford Cosworth FD02	39 laps	21
14	Rolf Stommelen	Embassy Racing	Lola-Ford Cosworth T370	39 laps	23
15	Ronnie Peterson	Lotus	Lotus-Ford Cosworth 72E	38 laps	16
R	Jean-Pierre Jarier	Shadow	Shadow-Ford Cosworth DN5	32 laps/fuel system	1
R	Patrick Depailler	Tyrrell	Tyrrell-Ford Cosworth 007	31 laps/suspension	9
R	Tom Pryce	Shadow	Shadow-Ford Cosworth DN3B	31 laps/accident	14
R	Arturo Merzario	Frank Williams Racing Cars	Williams-Ford Cosworth FW03	24 laps/fuel system	11
R	Mark Donohue	Penske	Penske-Ford Cosworth PC1	22 laps/handling	15
R	Mike Wilds	BRM	BRM P201	22 laps/electrical	22
R	Jody Scheckter	Tyrrell	Tyrrell-Ford Cosworth 007	18 laps/oil leak	8
R	Vittorio Brambilla	March	March-Ford Cosworth 741	1 lap/engine	17

Pole: Jarier, 2m29.880s, 118.801mph/191.192kph. Fastest lap: Jarier, 2m34.160s, 115.503mph/185.884kph on Lap 10. Race leaders: Reutemann 1-4, Jarier 5-32, Pace 33-40

SOUTH AFRICAN GRAND PRIX

KYALAMI • ROUND 3 • DATE: 1ST MARCH 1975
Laps: 78 • Distance: 198.908miles/320.112km • Weather: Warm & bright

Pos	Driver	Team	Chassis-Engine	Result	Qual
1	Jody Scheckter	Tyrrell	Tyrrell-Ford Cosworth 007	1h43m16.900s	3
2	Carlos Reutemann	Brabham	Brabham-Ford Cosworth BT44B	1h43m20.640s	2
3	Patrick Depailler	Tyrrell	Tyrrell-Ford Cosworth 007	1h43m33.820s	5
4	Carlos Pace	Brabham	Brabham-Ford Cosworth BT44B	1h43m34.210s	1
5	Niki Lauda	Ferrari	Ferrari 312T	1h43m45.540s	4
6	Jochen Mass	McLaren	McLaren-Ford Cosworth M23	1h44m20.240s	16
7	Rolf Stommelen	Embassy Racing	Lola-Ford Cosworth T370	1h44m29.810s	14
8	Mark Donohue	Penske	Penske-Ford Cosworth PC1	77 laps	18
9	Tom Pryce	Shadow	Shadow-Ford Cosworth DN5	77 laps	19
10	Ronnie Peterson	Lotus	Lotus-Ford Cosworth 72E	77 laps	8
11	Guy Tunmer	Team Gunston	Lotus-Ford Cosworth 72E	76 laps	25
12	Jacky Ickx	Lotus	Lotus-Ford Cosworth 72E	76 laps	21
13	Eddie Keizan	Team Gunston	Lotus-Ford Cosworth 72E	76 laps	22
14	Dave Charlton	Lucky Strike Racing	McLaren-Ford Cosworth M23	76 laps	20
15	Bob Evans	BRM	BRM P201	76 laps	24
16	Clay Regazzoni	Ferrari	Ferrari 312T	71 laps/throttle	9
17	Mario Andretti	Parnelli	Parnelli-Ford Cosworth VPJ4	70 laps/transmission	6

Pos	Driver	Team	Chassis-Engine	Result	Qual
NC	Jacques Laffite	Frank Williams Racing Cars	Williams-Ford Cosworth FW02	69 laps	23
NC	Emerson Fittipaldi	McLaren	McLaren-Ford Cosworth M23	65 laps	11
R	Ian Scheckter	Lexington Racing	Tyrrell-Ford Cosworth 007	55 laps/accident	17
R	James Hunt	Hesketh	Hesketh-Ford Cosworth 308B	53 laps/fuel system	12
R	Jean-Pierre Jarier	Shadow	Shadow-Ford Cosworth DN5	37 laps/overheating	13
R	Lella Lombardi	March	March-Ford Cosworth 741	23 laps/fuel system	26
R	Arturo Merzario	Frank Williams Racing Cars	Williams-Ford Cosworth FW03	22 laps/engine	15
R	John Watson	Surtees	Surtees-Ford Cosworth TS16	19 laps/clutch	10
R	Vittorio Brambilla	March	March-Ford Cosworth 751	16 laps/radiator	7
DQ	Wilson Fittipaldi	Fittipaldi	Fittipaldi-Ford Cosworth FD02	0 laps/started illegally	27
DNQ	Graham Hill	Embassy Racing	Lola-Ford Cosworth T370	accident	28

Pole: Pace, 1m16.410s, 120.146mph/193.356kph. Fastest lap: Pace, 1m17.200s, 118.916mph/191.378kph on Lap 11. Race leaders: Pace 1-2, Scheckter 3-78

SPANISH GRAND PRIX

MONTJUICH PARK • ROUND 4 • DATE: 27TH APRIL 1975
Laps: 29 • Distance: 67.786miles/109.91km • Weather: Warm & bright

Pos	Driver	Team	Chassis-Engine	Result	Qual
1	Jochen Mass	McLaren	McLaren-Ford Cosworth M23	42m53.700s	11
2	Jacky Ickx	Lotus	Lotus-Ford Cosworth 72E	42m54.800s	16
3	Carlos Reutemann	Brabham	Brabham-Ford Cosworth BT44B	28 laps	15
4	Jean-Pierre Jarier	Shadow	Shadow-Ford Cosworth DN5	28 laps	10
5	Vittorio Brambilla	March	March-Ford Cosworth 751	28 laps	5
6	Lella Lombardi	March	March-Ford Cosworth 751	27 laps	24
7	Tony Brise	Frank Williams Racing Cars	Williams-Ford Cosworth FW03	27 laps	18
8	John Watson	Surtees	Surtees-Ford Cosworth TS16	26 laps	6
R	Rolf Stommelen	Embassy Racing	Hill-Ford Cosworth GH1	25 laps/accident	9
R	Carlos Pace	Brabham	Brabham-Ford Cosworth BT44B	25 laps/accident	14
NC	Clay Regazzoni	Ferrari	Ferrari 312T	25 laps	2
R	Tom Pryce	Shadow	Shadow-Ford Cosworth DN5	23 laps/accident	8
R	Ronnie Peterson	Lotus	Lotus-Ford Cosworth 72E	23 laps/suspension	12
R	Roelof Wunderink	Ensign	Ensign-Ford Cosworth N174	20 laps/transmission	19
NC	Francois Migault	Embassy Racing	Hill-Ford Cosworth GH1	18 laps	22
R	Mario Andretti	Parnelli	Parnelli-Ford Cosworth VPJ4	16 laps/suspension	4
R	Bob Evans	BRM	BRM P201	7 laps/fuel system	23
R	James Hunt	Hesketh	Hesketh-Ford Cosworth 308B	6 laps/accident	3
R	Jody Scheckter	Tyrrell	Tyrrell-Ford Cosworth 007	3 laps/engine	13
R	Mark Donohue	Penske	Penske-Ford Cosworth PC1	3 laps/accident	17
R	Alan Jones	Harry Stiller Racing	Hesketh-Ford Cosworth 308B	3 laps/accident	20
R	Patrick Depailler	Tyrrell	Tyrrell-Ford Cosworth 007	1 lap/accident	7
R	Wilson Fittipaldi	Fittipaldi	Fittipaldi-Ford Cosworth FD02	1 lap/withdrawn	21
R	Arturo Merzario	Frank Williams Racing Cars	Williams-Ford Cosworth FW04	1 lap/withdrawn	25
R	Niki Lauda	Ferrari	Ferrari 312T	0 laps/accident	1
NS	Emerson Fittipaldi	McLaren	McLaren-Ford Cosworth M23	safety protest	26

Pole: Lauda, 1m23.400s, 101.654mph/163.597kph. Fastest lap: Andretti, 1m25.100s, 99.623mph/160.329kph on Lap 14. Race leaders: Hunt 1-6, Andretti 7-16, Stommelen 17-21 & 23-25, Pace 22, Mass 26-27 & 29, Ickx 28

AN UNSATISFACTORY GRAND PRIX

The Spanish GP proved controversial as the Grand Prix Drivers' Association refused to race unless the barriers at Montjuich Park were made safe. Emerson Fittipaldi boycotted the race, then Rolf Stommelen led but crashed his Hill over the barriers when its rear wing came loose, killing four spectators. McLaren's Jochen Mass went on to claim what would prove to be his only grand prix win.

MONACO GRAND PRIX

MONTE CARLO • ROUND 5 • DATE: 11TH MAY 1975
Laps: 75 • Distance: 152.288miles/245.85km • Weather: Warm & wet then drying

Pos	Driver	Team	Chassis-Engine	Result	Qual
1	Niki Lauda	Ferrari	Ferrari 312T	2h01m21.310s	1
2	Emerson Fittipaldi	McLaren	McLaren-Ford Cosworth M23	2h01m24.090s	9
3	Carlos Pace	Brabham	Brabham-Ford Cosworth BT44B	2h01m39.120s	8
4	Ronnie Peterson	Lotus	Lotus-Ford Cosworth 72E	2h01m59.760s	4
5	Patrick Depailler	Tyrrell	Tyrrell-Ford Cosworth 007	2h02m02.170s	12
6	Jochen Mass	McLaren	McLaren-Ford Cosworth M23	2h02m03.380s	15
7	Jody Scheckter	Tyrrell	Tyrrell-Ford Cosworth 007	74 laps	7
8	Jacky Ickx	Lotus	Lotus-Ford Cosworth 72E	74 laps	14
9	Carlos Reutemann	Brabham	Brabham-Ford Cosworth BT44B	73 laps	10
R	Mark Donohue	Penske	Penske-Ford Cosworth PC1	66 laps/accident	16
R	James Hunt	Hesketh	Hesketh-Ford Cosworth 308B	63 laps/accident	11
R	Alan Jones	Harry Stiller Racing	Hesketh-Ford Cosworth 308B	61 laps/wheel	18
R	Vittorio Brambilla	March	March-Ford Cosworth 751	48 laps/accident	5
R	Tom Pryce	Shadow	Shadow-Ford Cosworth DN5	39 laps/accident	2
R	Clay Regazzoni	Ferrari	Ferrari 312T	36 laps/accident	6
R	John Watson	Surtees	Surtees-Ford Cosworth TS16	36 laps/spun off	17
R	Mario Andretti	Parnelli	Parnelli-Ford Cosworth VPJ4	9 laps/oil leak	13
R	Jean-Pierre Jarier	Shadow	Shadow-Ford Cosworth DN5	0 laps/accident	3
DNQ	Jacques Laffite	Frank Williams Racing Cars	Williams-Ford Cosworth FW04	-	19
DNQ	Arturo Merzario	Frank Williams Racing Cars	Williams-Ford Cosworth FW03	-	20
DNQ	Graham Hill	Embassy Racing	Hill-Ford Cosworth GH1	-	21
DNQ	Bob Evans	BRM	BRM P201	-	22
DNQ	Roelof Wunderink	Ensign	Ensign-Ford Cosworth N174	-	23
DNQ	Torsten Palm	Hesketh	Hesketh-Ford Cosworth 308B	-	24
DNQ	Lella Lombardi	March	March-Ford Cosworth 751	-	25
DNQ	Wilson Fittipaldi	Fittipaldi	Fittipaldi-Ford Cosworth FD02	-	26

Pole: Lauda, 1m26.400s, 84.868mph/136.583kph. Fastest lap: Depailler, 1m28.670s, 82.696mph/133.086kph on Lap 68. Race leaders: Lauda 1-23 & 25-75, Peterson 24

LELLA PROVES HER POINT

Maria-Teresa de Fillipis was the first woman to race in F1, but Lella Lombardi became the first and, so far, the only female F1 driver to register in the points. This was achieved at the shortened Spanish GP when points only went to the top six finishers, not the top 10 like today. Lella also finished seventh in the German GP in her works March.

BELGIAN GRAND PRIX

ZOLDER • ROUND 6 • DATE: 25TH MAY 1975
Laps: 70 • Distance: 185.189miles/298.34km • Weather: Warm but dull

Pos	Driver	Team	Chassis-Engine	Result	Qual
1	Niki Lauda	Ferrari	Ferrari 312T	1h43m53.980s	1
2	Jody Scheckter	Tyrrell	Tyrrell-Ford Cosworth 007	1h44m13.200s	9
3	Carlos Reutemann	Brabham	Brabham-Ford Cosworth BT44B	1h44m35.800s	6
4	Patrick Depailler	Tyrrell	Tyrrell-Ford Cosworth 007	1h44m54.060s	12
5	Clay Regazzoni	Ferrari	Ferrari 312T	1h44m57.840s	4
6	Tom Pryce	Shadow	Shadow-Ford Cosworth DN5	1h45m22.430s	5
7	Emerson Fittipaldi	McLaren	McLaren-Ford Cosworth M23	69 laps	8
8	Carlos Pace	Brabham	Brabham-Ford Cosworth BT44B	69 laps	2
9	Bob Evans	BRM	BRM P201	68 laps	20
10	John Watson	Surtees	Surtees-Ford Cosworth TS16	68 laps	18
11	Mark Donohue	Penske	Penske-Ford Cosworth PC1	67 laps	21
12	Wilson Fittipaldi	Fittipaldi	Fittipaldi-Ford Cosworth FD02	67 laps	24
R	Francois Migault	Embassy Racing	Hill-Ford Cosworth GH1	57 laps/suspension	22
R	Vittorio Brambilla	March	March-Ford Cosworth 751	54 laps/brakes	3
R	Jacky Ickx	Lotus	Lotus-Ford Cosworth 72E	52 laps/brakes	16
R	Ronnie Peterson	Lotus	Lotus-Ford Cosworth 72E	36 laps/brakes	14
R	Jacques Laffite	Frank Williams Racing Cars	Williams-Ford Cosworth FW04	18 laps/gearbox	17
R	Lella Lombardi	March	March-Ford Cosworth 751	18 laps/engine	23
R	Tony Brise	Embassy Racing	Hill-Ford Cosworth GH1	17 laps/engine	7
R	James Hunt	Hesketh	Hesketh-Ford Cosworth 308B	15 laps/transmission	11
R	Jean-Pierre Jarier	Shadow	Shadow-Ford Cosworth DN5	13 laps/spun off	10
R	Arturo Merzario	Frank Williams Racing Cars	Williams-Ford Cosworth FW03	2 laps/clutch	19
R	Alan Jones	Harry Stiller Racing	Hesketh-Ford Cosworth 308B	1 lap/accident	13
R	Jochen Mass	McLaren	McLaren-Ford Cosworth M23	0 laps/accident	15

Pole: Lauda, 1m25.430s, 111.598mph/179.599kph. Fastest lap: Regazzoni, 1m26.760s, 109.887mph/176.846kph on Lap 11. Race leaders: Pace 1-3, Brambilla 4-5, Lauda 6-70

WIN THEN SPIN

Torrential rain at the Österreichring led to the Austrian GP being brought to a premature halt after 29 of the planned 54 laps. Vittorio Brambilla was in the lead at this time and he went so wild with his celebrations, waving his arms about after seeing the chequered flag waved at him, that he lost control in the wet and wiped the nose off his March.

SWEDISH GRAND PRIX

ANDERSTORP • ROUND 7 • DATE: 8TH JUNE 1975
Laps: 80 • Distance: 199.487miles/321.44km • Weather: Warm & bright

Pos	Driver	Team	Chassis-Engine	Result	Qual
1	Niki Lauda	Ferrari	Ferrari 312T	1h59m18.319s	5
2	Carlos Reutemann	Brabham	Brabham-Ford Cosworth BT44B	1h59m24.607s	4
3	Clay Regazzoni	Ferrari	Ferrari 312T	1h59m47.414s	12
4	Mario Andretti	Parnelli	Parnelli-Ford Cosworth VPJ4	2h00m02.699s	15

Pos	Driver	Team	Chassis-Engine	Result	Qual
5	Mark Donohue	Penske	Penske-Ford Cosworth PC1	2h00m49.082s	16
6	Tony Brise	Embassy Racing	Hill-Ford Cosworth GH1	79 laps	17
7	Jody Scheckter	Tyrrell	Tyrrell-Ford Cosworth 007	79 laps	8
8	Emerson Fittipaldi	McLaren	McLaren-Ford Cosworth M23	79 laps	11
9	Ronnie Peterson	Lotus	Lotus-Ford Cosworth 72E	79 laps	9
10	Torsten Palm	Hesketh	Hesketh-Ford Cosworth 308B	78 laps/out of fuel	21
11	Alan Jones	Harry Stiller Racing	Hesketh-Ford Cosworth 308B	78 laps	19
12	Patrick Depailler	Tyrrell	Tyrrell-Ford Cosworth 007	78 laps	2
13	Bob Evans	BRM	BRM P201	78 laps	23
14	Damien Magee	Frank Williams Racing Cars	Williams-Ford Cosworth FW03	78 laps	22
15	Jacky Ickx	Lotus	Lotus-Ford Cosworth 72E	77 laps	18
16	John Watson	Surtees	Surtees-Ford Cosworth TS16	77 laps	10
17	Wilson Fittipaldi	Fittipaldi	Fittipaldi-Ford Cosworth FD02	74 laps	25
R	Tom Pryce	Shadow	Shadow-Ford Cosworth DN5	53 laps/spun off	7
R	Ian Scheckter	Frank Williams Racing Cars	Williams-Ford Cosworth FW04	49 laps/tyre	20
R	Vern Schuppan	Embassy Racing	Hill-Ford Cosworth GH1	47 laps/transmission	26
R	Carlos Pace	Brabham	Brabham-Ford Cosworth BT44B	41 laps/spun off	6
R	Jean-Pierre Jarier	Shadow	Shadow-Ford Cosworth DN5	38 laps/engine	3
R	Vittorio Brambilla	March	March-Ford Cosworth 751	36 laps/transmission	1
R	Jochen Mass	McLaren	McLaren-Ford Cosworth M23	34 laps/overheating	14
R	James Hunt	Hesketh	Hesketh-Ford Cosworth 308B	21 laps/brakes	13
R	Lella Lombardi	March	March-Ford Cosworth 751	10 laps/fuel system	24

Pole: Brambilla, 1m24.630s, 106.203mph/170.918kph. Fastest lap: Lauda, 1m28.267s, 101.827mph/163.875kph on Lap 61. Race leaders: Brambilla 1-15, Reutemann 16-69, Lauda 70-80

GRAHAM HILL'S TEAM WIPED OUT

When it felt as though the season had had its fair share of woe, F1 was dealt a major hit a month after the final round when 1962 and 1968 World Champion Graham Hill and five of his Embassy Racing team, including star driver Tony Brise, were killed in a light aircraft crash as they flew back to England in fog after a test at Paul Ricard.

DUTCH GRAND PRIX

ZANDVOORT • ROUND 8 • DATE: 22ND JUNE 1975
Laps: 75 • Distance: 196.412miles/316.95km • Weather: Warm & wet then drying

Pos	Driver	Team	Chassis-Engine	Result	Qual
1	James Hunt	Hesketh	Hesketh-Ford Cosworth 308B	1h46m57.400s	3
2	Niki Lauda	Ferrari	Ferrari 312T	1h46m58.460s	1
3	Clay Regazzoni	Ferrari	Ferrari 312T	1h47m52.460s	2
4	Carlos Reutemann	Brabham	Brabham-Ford Cosworth BT44B	74 laps	5
5	Carlos Pace	Brabham	Brabham-Ford Cosworth BT44B	74 laps	9
6	Tom Pryce	Shadow	Shadow-Ford Cosworth DN5	74 laps	12
7	Tony Brise	Embassy Racing	Hill-Ford Cosworth GH1	74 laps	7
8	Mark Donohue	Penske	Penske-Ford Cosworth PC1	74 laps	18
9	Patrick Depailler	Tyrrell	Tyrrell-Ford Cosworth 007	73 laps	13
10	Gijs van Lennep	Ensign	Ensign-Ford Cosworth N174	71 laps	22
11	Wilson Fittipaldi	Fittipaldi	Fittipaldi-Ford Cosworth FD03	71 laps	24

Pos	Driver	Team	Chassis-Engine	Result	Qual
12	Ian Scheckter	Frank Williams Racing Cars	Williams-Ford Cosworth FW03	70 laps	19
13	Alan Jones	Embassy Racing	Hill-Ford Cosworth GH1	70 laps	17
14	Lella Lombardi	March	March-Ford Cosworth 751	70 laps	23
15	Ronnie Peterson	Lotus	Lotus-Ford Cosworth 72F	69 laps/out of fuel	16
16	Jody Scheckter	Tyrrell	Tyrrell-Ford Cosworth 007	67 laps/engine	4
R	Jacques Laffite	Frank Williams Racing Cars	Williams-Ford Cosworth FW04	64 laps/engine	15
R	Jochen Mass	McLaren	McLaren-Ford Cosworth M23	61 laps/accident	8
R	Jean-Pierre Jarier	Shadow	Shadow-Ford Cosworth DN5	44 laps/tyre	10
R	John Watson	Surtees	Surtees-Ford Cosworth TS16	43 laps/vibrations	14
R	Emerson Fittipaldi	McLaren	McLaren-Ford Cosworth M23	40 laps/engine	6
R	Bob Evans	BRM	BRM P201	23 laps/differential	20
R	Jacky Ickx	Lotus	Lotus-Ford Cosworth 72F	6 laps/engine	21
R	Vittorio Brambilla	March	March-Ford Cosworth 751	0 laps/suspension	11
NS	Hiroshi Fushida	Maki	Maki-Ford Cosworth F101C	engine	25

Pole: Lauda, 1m20.290s, 117.739mph/189.483kph. Fastest lap: Lauda, 1m21.540s, 115.934mph/186.578kph on Lap 55. Race leaders: Lauda 1-12, Regazzoni 13-14, Hunt 15-75

FRENCH GRAND PRIX

CIRCUIT PAUL RICARD • ROUND 9 • DATE: 6TH JULY 1975
Laps: 54 • Distance: 194.535miles/313.74km • Weather: Hot & bright

Pos	Driver	Team	Chassis-Engine	Result	Qual
1	Niki Lauda	Ferrari	Ferrari 312T	1h40m18.840s	1
2	James Hunt	Hesketh	Hesketh-Ford Cosworth 308B	1h40m20.430s	3
3	Jochen Mass	McLaren	McLaren-Ford Cosworth M23	1h40m21.150s	7
4	Emerson Fittipaldi	McLaren	McLaren-Ford Cosworth M23	1h40m58.610s	10
5	Mario Andretti	Parnelli	Parnelli-Ford Cosworth VPJ4	1h41m20.920s	15
6	Patrick Depailler	Tyrrell	Tyrrell-Ford Cosworth 007	1h41m26.240s	13
7	Tony Brise	Embassy Racing	Hill-Ford Cosworth GH1	1h41m28.450s	12
8	Jean-Pierre Jarier	Shadow	Shadow-Ford Cosworth DN5	1h41m38.620s	4
9	Jody Scheckter	Tyrrell	Tyrrell-Ford Cosworth 007	1h41m50.520s	2
10	Ronnie Peterson	Lotus	Lotus-Ford Cosworth 72F	1h41m54.860s	17
11	Jacques Laffite	Frank Williams Racing Cars	Williams-Ford Cosworth FW04	1h41m55.610s	16
12	Jean-Pierre Jabouille	Tyrrell	Tyrrell-Ford Cosworth 007	1h41m55.970s	21
13	John Watson	Surtees	Surtees-Ford Cosworth TS16	53 laps	14
14	Carlos Reutemann	Brabham	Brabham-Ford Cosworth BT44B	53 laps	11
15	Gijs van Lennep	Ensign	Ensign-Ford Cosworth N175	53 laps	22
16	Alan Jones	Embassy Racing	Hill-Ford Cosworth GH1	53 laps	20
17	Bob Evans	BRM	BRM P201	52 laps	25
18	Lella Lombardi	March	March-Ford Cosworth 751	50 laps	26
R	Carlos Pace	Brabham	Brabham-Ford Cosworth BT44B	26 laps/transmission	5
R	Jacky Ickx	Lotus	Lotus-Ford Cosworth 72F	17 laps/brakes	19
R	Wilson Fittipaldi	Fittipaldi	Fittipaldi-Ford Cosworth FD03	14 laps/engine	23
R	Vittorio Brambilla	March	March-Ford Cosworth 751	6 laps/chassis	8
R	Clay Regazzoni	Ferrari	Ferrari 312T	6 laps/engine	9
R	Mark Donohue	Penske	Penske-Ford Cosworth PC1	6 laps/transmission	18
R	Tom Pryce	Shadow	Shadow-Ford Cosworth DN5	2 laps/transmission	6
NS	Francois Migault	Frank Williams Racing Cars	Williams-Ford Cosworth FW03	engine	24

Pole: Lauda, 1m47.820s, 120.539mph/193.989kph. Fastest lap: Mass, 1m50.600s, 117.509mph/189.113kph on Lap 38. Race leaders: Lauda 1-54

NEW CONSTRUCTORS

Two world champions were behind new teams. Graham Hill's Embassy Racing had run Shadow then Lola chassis, but built its own for 1975, while Emerson Fittipaldi and brother Wilson used backing from the Copersucar sugar co-operative to finance their ambition. The third new team was John Nicholson's small Lyncar outfit.

BRITISH GRAND PRIX

SILVERSTONE • ROUND 10 • DATE: 19TH JULY 1975
Laps: 56 • Distance: 164.191miles/264.241km • Weather: Warm & wet then heavy rain

Pos	Driver	Team	Chassis-Engine	Result	Qual
1	Emerson Fittipaldi	McLaren	McLaren-Ford Cosworth M23	1h22m05.000s	7
2	Carlos Pace	Brabham	Brabham-Ford Cosworth BT44B	55 laps/accident	2
3	Jody Scheckter	Tyrrell	Tyrrell-Ford Cosworth 007	55 laps/accident	6
4	James Hunt	Hesketh	Hesketh-Ford Cosworth 308B	55 laps/accident	9
5	Mark Donohue	Penske	March-Ford Cosworth 751	55 laps/accident	15
6	Vittorio Brambilla	March	March-Ford Cosworth 751	55 laps	5
7	Jochen Mass	McLaren	McLaren-Ford Cosworth M23	55 laps/accident	10
8	Niki Lauda	Ferrari	Ferrari 312T	54 laps	3
9	Patrick Depailler	Tyrrell	Tyrrell-Ford Cosworth 007	54 laps/accident	17
10	Alan Jones	Embassy Racing	Hill-Ford Cosworth GH1	54 laps	20
11	John Watson	Surtees	Surtees-Ford Cosworth TS16	54 laps/accident	18
12	Mario Andretti	Parnelli	Parnelli-Ford Cosworth VPJ4	54 laps	12
13	Clay Regazzoni	Ferrari	Ferrari 312T	54 laps	4
14	Jean-Pierre Jarier	Shadow	Shadow-Ford Cosworth DN5	53 laps/accident	11
15	Tony Brise	Embassy Racing	Hill-Ford Cosworth GH1	53 laps/accident	13
16	Brian Henton	Lotus	Lotus-Ford Cosworth 72F	53 laps/accident	21
17	John Nicholson	Lyncar	Lyncar-Ford Cosworth 007	51 laps/accident	26
18	Dave Morgan	Surtees	Surtees-Ford Cosworth TS16	50 laps/accident	23
19	Wilson Fittipaldi	Fittipaldi	Fittipaldi-Ford Cosworth FD03	50 laps/accident	24
R	Hans-Joachim Stuck	March	March-Ford Cosworth 751	45 laps/accident	14
R	Jim Crawford	Lotus	Lotus-Ford Cosworth 72F	28 laps/accident	25
R	Tom Pryce	Shadow	Shadow-Ford Cosworth DN5	20 laps/accident	1
R	Lella Lombardi	March	March-Ford Cosworth 751	18 laps/engine	22
R	Ronnie Peterson	Lotus	Lotus-Ford Cosworth 72F	7 laps/engine	16
R	Jacques Laffite	Frank Williams Racing Cars	Williams-Ford Cosworth FW04	5 laps/gearbox	19
R	Carlos Reutemann	Brabham	Brabham-Ford Cosworth BT44B	4 laps/engine	8
DNQ	Roelof Wunderink	Ensign	Ensign-Ford Cosworth N175	-	27
DNQ	Hiroshi Fushida	Maki	Maki-Ford Cosworth F101C	-	28

Pole: Pryce, 1m19.360s, 133.004mph/214.049kph. Fastest lap: Regazzoni, 1m20.900s, 130.472mph/209.974kph on Lap 16. Race leaders: Pace 1-12 & 22-26, Regazzoni 13-18, Pryce 19-20, Scheckter 21 & 27-32, Jarier 33-34, Hunt 35-42, Fittipaldi 43-56

GERMAN GRAND PRIX

NURBURGRING • ROUND 11 • DATE: 3RD AUGUST 1975
Laps: 14 • Distance: 198.260miles/319.69km • Weather: Warm & bright

Pos	Driver	Team	Chassis-Engine	Result	Qual
1	Carlos Reutemann	Brabham	Brabham-Ford Cosworth BT44B	1h41m14.100s	10
2	Jacques Laffite	Frank Williams Racing Cars	Williams-Ford Cosworth FW04	1h42m51.800s	15
3	Niki Lauda	Ferrari	Ferrari 312T	1h43m37.400s	1
4	Tom Pryce	Shadow	Shadow-Ford Cosworth DN5	1h44m45.500s	16
5	Alan Jones	Embassy Racing	Hill-Ford Cosworth GH1	1h45m04.400s	21
6	Gijs van Lennep	Ensign	Ensign-Ford Cosworth N175	1h46m19.600s	24
7	Lella Lombardi	March	March-Ford Cosworth 751	1h48m44.500s	25
8	Harald Ertl	Warsteiner Brewery	Hesketh-Ford Cosworth 308B	1h48m55.000s	23
9	Patrick Depailler	Tyrrell	Tyrrell-Ford Cosworth 007	13 laps	4
10	Mario Andretti	Parnelli	Parnelli-Ford Cosworth VPJ4	12 laps/fuel leak	13
R	James Hunt	Hesketh	Hesketh-Ford Cosworth 308B	10 laps/rear hub	9
R	Clay Regazzoni	Ferrari	Ferrari 312T	9 laps/engine	5
R	Tony Brise	Embassy Racing	Hill-Ford Cosworth GH1	9 laps/accident	17
R	Jody Scheckter	Tyrrell	Tyrrell-Ford Cosworth 007	7 laps/accident	3
R	Jean-Pierre Jarier	Shadow	Shadow-Ford Cosworth DN5	7 laps/puncture	12
R	Carlos Pace	Brabham	Brabham-Ford Cosworth BT44B	5 laps/suspension	2
R	Wilson Fittipaldi	Fittipaldi	Fittipaldi-Ford Cosworth FD03	4 laps/engine	22
R	Hans-Joachim Stuck	March	March-Ford Cosworth 751	3 laps/engine	7
R	Emerson Fittipaldi	McLaren	McLaren-Ford Cosworth M23	3 laps/suspension	8
R	Vittorio Brambilla	March	March-Ford Cosworth 751	3 laps/suspension	11
R	John Watson	Lotus	Lotus-Ford Cosworth 72F	2 laps/suspension	14
R	Ronnie Peterson	Lotus	Lotus-Ford Cosworth 72E	1 lap/clutch	18
R	Mark Donohue	Penske	March-Ford Cosworth 751	1 lap/tyre	19
R	Jochen Mass	McLaren	McLaren-Ford Cosworth M23	0 laps/accident	6
NS	Ian Ashley	Frank Williams Racing Cars	Williams-Ford Cosworth FW03	driver injured	20
DNQ	Tony Trimmer	Maki	Maki-Ford Cosworth F101C	-	30

Pole: Lauda, 6m58.600s, 122.026mph/196.383kph. Fastest lap: Regazzoni, 7m06.400s, 119.794mph/192.790kph on Lap 7. Race leaders: Lauda 1-9, Reutemann 10-14

NEW DRIVERS

Tony Brise was the outstanding debutant from a batch of 17 rookies. He finished sixth in Sweden and took two seventh-place finishes as well in the little-fancied Hill, while future champion Alan Jones joined the team for several races and came home fifth in Germany. Harald Ertl ran strongly for the Hesketh camp.

AUSTRIAN GRAND PRIX

OSTERREICHRING • ROUND 12 • DATE: 17TH AUGUST 1975
Laps: 29 • Distance: 106.514miles/171.419km • Weather: Warm but very wet

Pos	Driver	Team	Chassis-Engine	Result	Qual
1	Vittorio Brambilla	March	March-Ford Cosworth 751	57m56.690s	8
2	James Hunt	Hesketh	Hesketh-Ford Cosworth 308B	58m23.720s	2
3	Tom Pryce	Shadow	Shadow-Ford Cosworth DN5	58m31.540s	15

Pos	Driver	Team	Chassis-Engine	Result	Qual
4	Jochen Mass	McLaren	McLaren-Ford Cosworth M23	59m09.350s	9
5	Ronnie Peterson	Lotus	Lotus-Ford Cosworth 72E	59m20.020s	13
6	Niki Lauda	Ferrari	Ferrari 312T	59m26.970s	1
7	Clay Regazzoni	Ferrari	Ferrari 312T	59m35.760s	5
8	Jody Scheckter	Tyrrell	Tyrrell-Ford Cosworth 007	28 laps	10
9	Emerson Fittipaldi	McLaren	McLaren-Ford Cosworth M23	28 laps	3
10	John Watson	Surtees	Surtees-Ford Cosworth TS16	28 laps	18
11	Patrick Depailler	Tyrrell	Tyrrell-Ford Cosworth 007	28 laps	7
12	Chris Amon	Ensign	Ensign-Ford Cosworth N175	28 laps	24
13	Brett Lunger	Hesketh	Hesketh-Ford Cosworth 308B	28 laps	17
14	Carlos Reutemann	Brabham	Brabham-Ford Cosworth BT44B	28 laps	11
15	Tony Brise	Embassy Racing	Hill-Ford Cosworth GH1	28 laps	16
16	Rolf Stommelen	Embassy Racing	Hill-Ford Cosworth GH1	27 laps	26
17	Lella Lombardi	March	March-Ford Cosworth 751	26 laps	22
NC	Roelof Wunderink	Ensign	Ensign-Ford Cosworth N174	25 laps	28
R	Harald Ertl	Warsteiner Brewery	Hesketh-Ford Cosworth 308B	23 laps/electrical	27
R	Jacques Laffite	Frank Williams Racing Cars	Williams-Ford Cosworth FW04	21 laps/handling	12
R	Carlos Pace	Brabham	Brabham-Ford Cosworth BT44B	17 laps/engine	6
R	Jo Vonlanthen	Frank Williams Racing Cars	Williams-Ford Cosworth FW01	14 laps/engine	29
R	Hans-Joachim Stuck	March	March-Ford Cosworth 751	10 laps/accident	4
R	Jean-Pierre Jarier	Shadow	Shadow-Matra DN7	10 laps/fuel injection	14
R	Bob Evans	BRM	BRM P201	2 laps/engine	25
R	Mario Andretti	Parnelli	Parnelli-Ford Cosworth VPJ4	1 lap/accident	19
NS	Mark Donohue	Penske	March-Ford Cosworth 751	fatal accident	21
NS	Brian Henton	Lotus	Lotus-Ford Cosworth 72F	acident	23
NS	Wilson Fittipaldi	Fittipaldi	Fittipaldi-Ford Cosworth FD03	driver injured	20
DNQ	Tony Trimmer	Maki	Maki-Ford Cosworth F101C	-	30

Pole: Lauda, 1m34.850s, 139.404mph/224.350kph. Fastest lap: Brambilla, 1m53.900s, 116.088mph/186.827kph. Race leaders: Lauda 1-14, Hunt 15-18, Brambilla 19-29

IN MEMORIAM

Mark Donohue had won practically everything in American racing – three TransAm titles, one Can Am title and one IROC title as well as the Daytona 24 Hours and the Indianapolis 500. Brought to Europe by Penske, he sadly crashed in the warm-up for the Austrian GP, hitting a TV tower, and died of his injuries two days later.

ITALIAN GRAND PRIX

MONZA • ROUND 13 • DATE: 7TH SEPTEMBER 1975
Laps: 52 • Distance: 186.446miles/300.56km • Weather: Warm but dull

Pos	Driver	Team	Chassis-Engine	Result	Qual
1	Clay Regazzoni	Ferrari	Ferrari 312T	1h22m42.600s	2
2	Emerson Fittipaldi	McLaren	McLaren-Ford Cosworth M23	1h22m59.200s	3
3	Niki Lauda	Ferrari	Ferrari 312T	1h23m05.800s	1
4	Carlos Reutemann	Brabham	Brabham-Ford Cosworth BT44B	1h23m37.700s	7
5	James Hunt	Hesketh	Hesketh-Ford Cosworth 308C	1h23m39.700s	8
6	Tom Pryce	Shadow	Shadow-Ford Cosworth DN5	1h23m58.500s	14
7	Patrick Depailler	Tyrrell	Tyrrell-Ford Cosworth 007	51 laps	12
8	Jody Scheckter	Tyrrell	Tyrrell-Ford Cosworth 007	51 laps	4

Pos	Driver	Team	Chassis-Engine	Result	Qual
9	Harald Ertl	Warsteiner Brewery	Hesketh-Ford Cosworth 308B	51 laps	17
10	Brett Lunger	Hesketh	Hesketh-Ford Cosworth 308B	50 laps	21
11	Arturo Merzario	Fittipaldi	Fittipaldi-Ford Cosworth FD03	48 laps	26
12	Chris Amon	Ensign	Ensign-Ford Cosworth N175	48 laps	19
13	Jim Crawford	Lotus	Lotus-Ford Cosworth 72F	46 laps	25
14	Renzo Zorzi	Frank Williams Racing Cars	Williams-Ford Cosworth FW01	46 laps	22
R	Jean-Pierre Jarier	Shadow	Shadow-Matra DN7	32 laps/fuel pump	13
R	Lella Lombardi	March	March-Ford Cosworth 751	21 laps/accident	24
R	Hans-Joachim Stuck	March	March-Ford Cosworth 751	15 laps/accident	16
R	Jacques Laffite	Frank Williams Racing Cars	Williams-Ford Cosworth FW04	7 laps/gearbox	18
R	Carlos Pace	Brabham	Brabham-Ford Cosworth BT44B	6 laps/throttle	10
R	Rolf Stommelen	Embassy Racing	Hill-Ford Cosworth GH1	3 laps/accident	23
R	Jochen Mass	McLaren	McLaren-Ford Cosworth M23	2 laps/accident	5
R	Tony Brise	Embassy Racing	Hill-Ford Cosworth GH1	1 lap/accident	6
R	Vittorio Brambilla	March	March-Ford Cosworth 751	1 lap/clutch	9
R	Ronnie Peterson	Lotus	Lotus-Ford Cosworth 72E	1 lap/engine	11
R	Mario Andretti	Parnelli	Parnelli-Ford Cosworth VPJ4	1 lap/accident	15
R	Bob Evans	BRM	BRM P201	0 laps/electrical	20
DNQ	Roelof Wunderink	Ensign	Ensign-Ford Cosworth N174	-	27
DNQ	Tony Trimmer	Maki	Maki-Ford Cosworth F101C	-	28

Pole: Lauda, 1m32.240s, 140.172mph/225.585kph. Fastest lap: Regazzoni, 1m33.100s, 138.877mph/223.501kph on Lap 47. Race leaders: Regazzoni 1-52

CLASSIC CAR: FERRARI 312T

Mauro Forghieri designed a gem in the sleek form of the Ferrari 312T. Its major step forwards over its predecessor, the 312B3, was the way that the transverse-mounted gearbox behind its flat-12 engine made the car's weight distribution more efficient, aided by its radiators and oil coolers being within the wheelbase to improve its polar moment of inertia, and so gave it superior handling. It took until the fifth round, at Monaco, for Niki Lauda to make it a winner. He then added four more wins and the drivers' title, while Clay Regazzoni added one, to give Ferrari its first constructors' title since 1964.

UNITED STATES GRAND PRIX

WATKINS GLEN • ROUND 14 • DATE: 5TH OCTOBER 1975
Laps: 59 • Distance: 199.251miles/320.665km • Weather: Cool & dull

Pos	Driver	Team	Chassis-Engine	Result	Qual
1	Niki Lauda	Ferrari	Ferrari 312T	1h42m58.175s	1
2	Emerson Fittipaldi	McLaren	McLaren-Ford Cosworth M23	1h43m03.118s	2
3	Jochen Mass	McLaren	McLaren-Ford Cosworth M23	1h43m45.812s	9
4	James Hunt	Hesketh	Hesketh-Ford Cosworth 308C	1h43m47.650s	15
5	Ronnie Peterson	Lotus	Lotus-Ford Cosworth 72E	1h43m48.161s	14
6	Jody Scheckter	Tyrrell	Tyrrell-Ford Cosworth 007	1h43m48.496s	10
7	Vittorio Brambilla	March	March-Ford Cosworth 751	1h44m42.206s	6
8	Hans-Joachim Stuck	March	March-Ford Cosworth 751	58 laps	13
9	John Watson	Penske	Penske-Ford Cosworth PC1	57 laps	12
10	Wilson Fittipaldi	Fittipaldi	Fittipaldi-Ford Cosworth FD03	55 laps	23
NC	Tom Pryce	Shadow	Shadow-Ford Cosworth DN5	52 laps	7

Pos	Driver	Team	Chassis-Engine	Result	Qual
NC	Brian Henton	Lotus	Lotus-Ford Cosworth 72F	49 laps	19
R	Brett Lunger	Hesketh	Hesketh-Ford Cosworth 308B	46 laps/accident	18
R	Roelof Wunderink	Ensign	Ensign-Ford Cosworth N175	41 laps/gearbox	22
R	Clay Regazzoni	Ferrari	Ferrari 312T	28 laps/withdrawn	11
R	Jean-Pierre Jarier	Shadow	Shadow-Ford Cosworth DN5	19 laps/wheel	4
R	Carlos Reutemann	Brabham	Brabham-Ford Cosworth BT44B	9 laps/engine	3
R	Mario Andretti	Parnelli	Parnelli-Ford Cosworth VPJ4	9 laps/suspension	5
R	Tony Brise	Embassy Racing	Hill-Ford Cosworth GH1	5 laps/accident	17
R	Michel Leclere	Tyrrell	Tyrrell-Ford Cosworth 007	5 laps/engine	20
R	Patrick Depailler	Tyrrell	Tyrrell-Ford Cosworth 007	2 laps/accident	8
R	Carlos Pace	Brabham	Brabham-Ford Cosworth BT44B	2 laps/accident	16
NS	Jacques Laffite	Frank Williams Racing Cars	Williams-Ford Cosworth FW04	driver injured	21
NS	Lella Lombardi	Frank Williams Racing Cars	Williams-Ford Cosworth FW04	ignition	24

Pole: Lauda, 1m42.003s, 119.190mph/191.817kph. Fastest lap: Fittipaldi, 1m43.374s, 117.609mph/189.273kph on Lap 43. Race leaders: Lauda 1-59

WORLD DRIVERS' CHAMPIONSHIP FINAL RESULTS

Pos	Driver	Nat	Car-Engine	R1	R2	R3	R4	R5
1	Niki Lauda	AUT	Ferrari 312B3	6	5	-	-	-
			Ferrari 312T	-	-	5	RP	1P
2	Emerson Fittipaldi	BRA	McLaren-Ford Cosworth M23	1	2	NC	NS	2
3	Carlos Reutemann	ARG	Brabham-Ford Cosworth BT44B	3	8	2	3	9
4	James Hunt	GBR	Hesketh-Ford Cosworth 308B	2F	6	R	R	R
			Hesketh-Ford Cosworth 308C	-	-	-	-	-
5	Clay Regazzoni	CHE	Ferrari 312B3	4	4	-	-	-
			Ferrari 312T	-	-	16	NC	R
6	Carlos Pace	BRA	Brabham-Ford Cosworth BT44B	R	1	4PF	R	3
7	Jody Scheckter	ZAF	Tyrrell-Ford Cosworth 007	11	R	1	R	7
7	Jochen Mass	DEU	McLaren-Ford Cosworth M23	14	3	6	1	6
9	Patrick Depailler	FRA	Tyrrell-Ford Cosworth 007	5	R	3	R	5F
10	Tom Pryce	GBR	Shadow-Ford Cosworth DN3	12	R	-	-	-
			Shadow-Ford Cosworth DN5	-	-	9	R	R
11	Vittorio Brambilla	ITA	March-Ford Cosworth 741	9	R	-	-	-
			March-Ford Cosworth 751	-	-	R	5	R
12	Jacques Laffite	FRA	Williams-Ford Cosworth FW01	R	11	NC	-	-
			Williams-Ford Cosworth FW04	-	-	-	-	-
12	Ronnie Peterson	SWE	Lotus-Ford Cosworth 72E	R	15	10	R	4
14	Mario Andretti	USA	Parnelli-Ford Cosworth VPJ4	R	7	17	RF	R
15	Mark Donohue	USA	Penske-Ford Cosworth PC1	7	R	8	R	R
			March-Ford Cosworth 751	-	-	-	-	-
16	Jacky Ickx	BEL	Lotus-Ford Cosworth 72E	8	9	12	2	8
17	Alan Jones	AUS	Hesketh-Ford Cosworth 308B	-	-	-	R	R
			Hill-Ford Cosworth GH1	-	-	-	-	-
18	Jean-Pierre Jarier	FRA	Shadow-Ford Cosworth DN5	NSP	RPF	R	4	R
			Shadow-Matra DN7	-	-	-	-	-
19	Tony Brise	GBR	Williams-Ford Cosworth FW03	-	-	-	7	-
			Hill-Ford Cosworth GH1	-	-	-	-	-
19	Gijs van Lennep	NLD	Ensign-Ford Cosworth N174	-	-	-	-	-
			Ensign-Ford Cosworth N175	-	-	-	-	-
21	Lella Lombardi	ITA	March-Ford Cosworth 741	-	-	R	-	-
			March-Ford Cosworth 751	-	-	-	6	DNQ
			Williams-Ford Cosworth FW04	-	-	-	-	-

Pos	Driver	R6	R7	R8	R9	R10	R11	R12	R13	R14	Total
1	Lauda	-	-	-	-	-	-	-	-	-	64.5
		1P	1F	2PF	1P	8	3P	6P	3P	1P	
2	E Fittipaldi	7	8	R	4	1	R	9	2	2F	45
3	Reutemann	3	2	4	14	R	1	14	4	R	37
4	Hunt	R	R	1	2	4	R	2	-	-	33
		-	-	-	-	-	-	-	5	4	
5	Regazzoni	-	-	-	-	-	-	-	-	-	25
		5F	3	3	R	13F	RF	7	1F	R	
6	Pace	8	R	5	R	2	R	R	R	R	24
7	J Scheckter	2	7	16	9	3	R	8	8	6	20
7	Mass	R	R	R	3F	7	R	4	R	3	20
9	Depailler	4	12	9	6	9	9	11	7	R	12
10	Pryce	-	-	-	-	-	-	-	-	-	8
		6	R	6	R	RP	4	3	6	NC	
11	Brambilla	-	-	-	-	-	-	-	-	-	6.5
		RP	R	R	R	6	R	1F	R	7	
12	Laffite	-	-	-	-	-	-	-	-	-	6
		R	-	R	11	R	2	R	R	NS	
12	Peterson	R	9	15	10	R	R	5	R	5	6
14	Andretti	-	4	-	5	12	10	R	R	R	5
15	Donohue	11	5	8	R	-	-	-	-	-	4
		-	-	-	-	5	R	NS	-	-	
16	Ickx	R	15	R	R	-	-	-	-	-	3
17	Jones	R	11	-	-	-	-	-	-	-	2
		-	-	13	16	10	5	-	-	-	
18	Jarier	R	R	R	8	14	R	-	-	R	1.5
		-	-	-	-	-	-	R	R	-	
19	Brise	-	-	-	-	-	-	-	-	-	1
		R	6	7	7	15	R	15	R	R	
19	van Lennep	-	-	10	-	-	-	-	-	-	1
		-	-	-	15	-	6	-	-	-	
21	Lombardi	-	-	-	-	-	-	-	-	-	0.5
		R	R	14	18	R	7	17	R	-	
		-	-	-	-	-	-	-	-	NS	

SYMBOLS AND GRAND PRIX KEY

Round 1 Argentinian GP
Round 2 Brazilian GP
Round 3 South African GP
Round 4 Spanish GP
Round 5 Monaco GP
Round 6 Belgian GP
Round 7 Swedish GP
Round 8 Dutch GP
Round 9 French GP
Round 10 British GP
Round 11 German GP
Round 12 Austrian GP
Round 13 Italian GP
Round 14 United States GP

SCORING

1st 9 points
2nd 6 points
3rd 4 points
4th 3 points
5th 2 points
6th 1 point

DNPQ DID NOT PRE-QUALIFY **DNQ** DID NOT QUALIFY **DQ** DISQUALIFIED **EX** EXCLUDED
F FASTEST LAP **NC** NOT CLASSIFIED **NS** NON-STARTER **P** POLE POSITION **R** RETIRED

WORLD CONSTRUCTORS' CHAMPIONSHIP FINAL RESULTS

Pos	Team-Engine	R1	R2	R3	R4	R5	R6	R7	R8	R9	R10	R11	R12	R13	R14	Total
1	Ferrari	4	4	5	-	1	1	1	2	1	8	3	6	1	1	72.5
2	Brabham-Ford	3	1	2	3	3	3	2	4	14	2	1	14	4	-	54
3	McLaren-Ford	1	2	6	1	2	7	8	-	3	1	-	4	2	2	53
4	Hesketh-Ford	2	6	-	-	-	-	10	1	2	4	8	2	5	4	33
5	Tyrrell-Ford	5	-	1	-	5	2	7	9	6	3	9	8	7	6	25
6	Shadow-Ford	12	-	9	4	-	6	-	6	8	14	4	3	6	-	9.5
7	Lotus-Ford	8	9	10	2	4	-	9	15	10	16	-	5	13	5	9
8	March-Ford	9	-	-	5	-	-	-	14	18	6	7	1	-	7	7.5
9	Williams-Ford	-	11	-	7	-	-	14	12	11	-	2	-	14	-	6
10	Parnelli-Ford	-	7	17	-	-	-	4	-	5	12	10	-	-	-	5
11	Hill-Ford	10	12	7	-	-	-	6	7	7	10	5	15	-	-	3
12	Penske-Ford	7	-	8	-	-	11	5	8	-	5	-	-	-	9	2
13	Ensign-Ford	-	-	-	-	-	-	-	10	15	-	6	12	12	-	1

1976

SEASON SUMMARY

This extraordinary season was such box office entertainment as new McLaren team leader James Hunt took on Ferrari's reigning champion Niki Lauda that they made a film about it. There were twists and turns from the first race to the last, with victories annulled and Lauda fortunate to survive a fiery crash at the German GP. The title outcome only became clear to Hunt after the last race in Japan, when he couldn't believe that he had won. Tyrrell was close to the action too, shocking the world by entering a six-wheeled car in its quest to find a performance advantage, while Brabham's decision to run Alfa Romeo engines left them uncompetitive.

BRAZILIAN GRAND PRIX

INTERLAGOS • ROUND 1 • DATE: 25TH JANUARY 1976
Laps: 40 • Distance: 197.598miles/318.4km • Weather: Very hot & bright

Pos	Driver	Team	Chassis-Engine	Result	Qual
1	Niki Lauda	Ferrari	Ferrari 312T	1h45m16.780s	2
2	Patrick Depailler	Tyrrell	Tyrrell-Ford Cosworth 007	1h45m38.250s	9
3	Tom Pryce	Shadow	Shadow-Ford Cosworth DN5B	1h45m40.620s	12
4	Hans-Joachim Stuck	March	March-Ford Cosworth 761	1h46m44.950s	14
5	Jody Scheckter	Tyrrell	Tyrrell-Ford Cosworth 007	1h47m13.240s	13
6	Jochen Mass	McLaren	McLaren-Ford Cosworth M23	1h47m15.050s	6
7	Clay Regazzoni	Ferrari	Ferrari 312T	1h47m32.020s	4
8	Jacky Ickx	Frank Williams	Williams-Ford Cosworth FW05	39 laps	19
9	Renzo Zorzi	Frank Williams	Williams-Ford Cosworth FW04	39 laps	17
10	Carlos Pace	Brabham	Brabham-Alfa Romeo BT45	39 laps	10
11	Ingo Hoffmann	Fittipaldi	Fittipaldi-Ford Cosworth FD03	39 laps	20
12	Carlos Reutemann	Brabham	Brabham-Alfa Romeo BT45	37 laps/out of fuel	15
13	Emerson Fittipaldi	Fittipaldi	Fittipaldi-Ford Cosworth FD04	37 laps	5
14	Lella Lombardi	March	March-Ford Cosworth 761	36 laps	22
R	Jean-Pierre Jarier	Shadow	Shadow-Ford Cosworth DN5B	33 laps/accident	3
R	James Hunt	McLaren	McLaren-Ford Cosworth M23	32 laps/accident	1
R	Vittorio Brambilla	March	March-Ford Cosworth 761	15 laps/oil leak	7
R	Jacques Laffite	Ligier	Ligier-Matra JS5	14 laps/transmission	11
R	Ronnie Peterson	Lotus	Lotus-Ford Cosworth 77	10 laps/accident	18
R	Mario Andretti	Lotus	Lotus-Ford Cosworth 77	6 laps/accident	16
R	John Watson	Penske	Penske-Ford Cosworth PC3	2 laps/fuel system	8
R	Ian Ashley	BRM	BRM P201B	2 laps/fuel pump	21

Pole: Hunt, 2m32.500s, 116.760mph/187.908kph. Fastest lap: Jarier, 2m35.070s, 114.825mph/184.793kph on Lap 31. Race leaders: Regazzoni 1-8, Lauda 9-40

A SETBACK FOR SPONSORS

A rule change made before the first race of the European season was extremely unpopular with sponsors. This was the banning of tall airboxes, with the new ones not allowed to extend above the rollhoop behind the driver's head, thus depriving advertisers of a large and very visible area for their logos.

FAMILY TIES FOR FITTIPALDI
The Fittipaldi team didn't make many waves in its debut season, so it was a surprise when Emerson Fittipaldi announced that he was quitting McLaren to head its second-year attack. Instead of challenging for wins, he had to make do with a trio of sixth places, while James Hunt took over the McLaren seat and became champion.

SOUTH AFRICAN GRAND PRIX

KYALAMI • ROUND 2 • DATE: 6TH MARCH 1976
Laps: 78 • Distance: 198.908miles/320.112km • Weather: Warm & bright

Pos	Driver	Team	Chassis-Engine	Result	Qual
1	Niki Lauda	Ferrari	Ferrari 312T	1h42m18.400s	2
2	James Hunt	McLaren	McLaren-Ford Cosworth M23	1h42m19.700s	1
3	Jochen Mass	McLaren	McLaren-Ford Cosworth M23	1h43m04.300s	4
4	Jody Scheckter	Tyrrell	Tyrrell-Ford Cosworth 007	1h43m26.800s	12
5	John Watson	Penske	Penske-Ford Cosworth PC3	77 laps	3
6	Mario Andretti	Parnelli	Parnelli-Ford Cosworth VPJ4B	77 laps	13
7	Tom Pryce	Shadow	Shadow-Ford Cosworth DN5B	77 laps	7
8	Vittorio Brambilla	March	March-Ford Cosworth 761	77 laps	5
9	Patrick Depailler	Tyrrell	Tyrrell-Ford Cosworth 007	77 laps	6
10	Bob Evans	Lotus	Lotus-Ford Cosworth 77	77 laps	23
11	Brett Lunger	Surtees	Surtees-Ford Cosworth TS19	77 laps	20
12	Hans-Joachim Stuck	March	March-Ford Cosworth 761	76 laps	17
13	Michel Leclere	Frank Williams	Williams-Ford Cosworth FW05	76 laps	22
14	Chris Amon	Ensign	Ensign-Ford Cosworth N174	76 laps	18
15	Harald Ertl	Hesketh	Hesketh-Ford Cosworth 308D	74 laps	24
16	Jacky Ickx	Frank Williams	Williams-Ford Cosworth FW05	73 laps	19
17	Emerson Fittipaldi	Fittipaldi	Fittipaldi-Ford Cosworth FD04	70 laps/engine	21
R	Clay Regazzoni	Ferrari	Ferrari 312T	52 laps/engine	9
R	Jacques Laffite	Ligier	Ligier-Matra JS5	49 laps/engine	8
R	Jean-Pierre Jarier	Shadow	Shadow-Ford Cosworth DN5B	28 laps/radiator damage	15
R	Carlos Pace	Brabham	Brabham-Alfa Romeo BT45	22 laps/fuel pressure	14
R	Gunnar Nilsson	Lotus	Lotus-Ford Cosworth 77	18 laps/clutch	25
R	Carlos Reutemann	Brabham	Brabham-Alfa Romeo BT45	16 laps/fuel pressure	11
R	Ronnie Peterson	March	March-Ford Cosworth 761	15 laps/accident	10
R	Ian Scheckter	Lexington Racing	Tyrrell-Ford Cosworth 007	0 laps/accident	16

Pole: Hunt, 1m16.100s, 120.635mph/194.144kph. Fastest lap: Lauda, 1m17.970s, 117.742mph/189.488kph on Lap 6. Race leaders: Lauda 1-78

MOB RULE DOESN'T WIN THE DAY
After Hunt's McLaren was damaged by hitting Clay Regazzoni's spinning Ferrari at Brands Hatch, he was told that he couldn't take the restart because he had returned to the pits via the back entrance. Then the partisan crowd went wild and the officials buckled. He duly won the race but was later disqualified. To balance that, his exclusion from the Spanish GP for his car being too wide had been overturned.

UNITED STATES GRAND PRIX WEST

LONG BEACH • ROUND 3 • DATE: 28TH MARCH 1976
Laps: 80 • Distance: 161.561miles/260.08km • Weather: Warm & bright

Pos	Driver	Team	Chassis-Engine	Result	Qual
1	Clay Regazzoni	Ferrari	Ferrari 312T	1h53m18.471s	1
2	Niki Lauda	Ferrari	Ferrari 312T	1h54m00.885s	4
3	Patrick Depailler	Tyrrell	Tyrrell-Ford Cosworth 007	1h54m08.443s	2
4	Jacques Laffite	Ligier	Ligier-Matra JS5	1h54m31.299s	12
5	Jochen Mass	McLaren	McLaren-Ford Cosworth M23	1h54m40.763s	14
6	Emerson Fittipaldi	Fittipaldi	Fittipaldi-Ford Cosworth FD04	79 laps	16
7	Jean-Pierre Jarier	Shadow	Shadow-Ford Cosworth DN5B	79 laps	7
8	Chris Amon	Ensign	Ensign-Ford Cosworth N174	78 laps	17
9	Carlos Pace	Brabham	Brabham-Alfa Romeo BT45	77 laps	13
10	Ronnie Peterson	March	March-Ford Cosworth 761	77 laps	6
NC	Alan Jones	Surtees	Surtees-Ford Cosworth TS19	70 laps	19
NC	John Watson	Penske	Penske-Ford Cosworth PC3	69 laps	9
R	Jody Scheckter	Tyrrell	Tyrrell-Ford Cosworth 007	34 laps/suspension	11
R	Tom Pryce	Shadow	Shadow-Ford Cosworth DN5B	32 laps/halfshaft	5
R	Mario Andretti	Parnelli	Parnelli-Ford Cosworth VPJ4B	15 laps/water leak	15
R	James Hunt	McLaren	McLaren-Ford Cosworth M23	3 laps/accident	3
R	Hans-Joachim Stuck	March	March-Ford Cosworth 761	2 laps/accident	18
R	Gunnar Nilsson	Lotus	Lotus-Ford Cosworth 77	0 laps/suspension	8
R	Carlos Reutemann	Brabham	Brabham-Alfa Romeo BT45	0 laps/accident	10
R	Vittorio Brambilla	March	March-Ford Cosworth 761	0 laps/accident	20
DNQ	Michel Leclere	Frank Williams	Williams-Ford Cosworth FW05	-	21
DNQ	Ingo Hoffmann	Fittipaldi	Fittipaldi-Ford Cosworth FD04	-	22
DNQ	Arturo Merzario	March	March-Ford Cosworth 761	-	23
DNQ	Bob Evans	Lotus	Lotus-Ford Cosworth 77	-	24
DNQ	Jacky Ickx	Frank Williams	Williams-Ford Cosworth FW05	-	25
DNQ	Harald Ertl	Hesketh	Hesketh-Ford Cosworth 308D	-	26
DNQ	Brett Lunger	Surtees	Surtees-Ford Cosworth TS19	-	27

Pole: Regazzoni, 1m23.099s, 87.513mph/140.839kph. Fastest lap: Regazzoni, 1m23.076s, 87.537mph/140.878kph on Lap 61. Race leaders: Regazzoni 1-80

SPANISH GRAND PRIX

JARAMA • ROUND 4 • DATE: 2ND MAY 1976
Laps: 75 • Distance: 158.649miles/255.322km • Weather: Warm & bright

Pos	Driver	Team	Chassis-Engine	Result	Qual
1	James Hunt	McLaren	McLaren-Ford Cosworth M23	1h42m20.430s	1
2	Niki Lauda	Ferrari	Ferrari 312T2	1h42m51.400s	2
3	Gunnar Nilsson	Lotus	Lotus-Ford Cosworth 77	1h43m08.450s	7
4	Carlos Reutemann	Brabham	Brabham-Alfa Romeo BT45	74 laps	12
5	Chris Amon	Ensign	Ensign-Ford Cosworth N176	74 laps	10
6	Carlos Pace	Brabham	Brabham-Alfa Romeo BT45	74 laps	11
7	Jacky Ickx	Walter Wolf Racing	Williams-Ford Cosworth FW05	74 laps	21
8	Tom Pryce	Shadow	Shadow-Ford Cosworth DN5B	74 laps	22
9	Alan Jones	Surtees	Surtees-Ford Cosworth TS19	74 laps	20
10	Michel Leclere	Walter Wolf Racing	Williams-Ford Cosworth FW05	73 laps	23
11	Clay Regazzoni	Ferrari	Ferrari 312T2	72 laps	5
12	Jacques Laffite	Ligier	Ligier-Matra JS5	72 laps	8

Pos	Driver	Team	Chassis-Engine	Result	Qual
13	Larry Perkins	Boro	Boro-Ford Cosworth N175	72 laps	24
R	Jochen Mass	McLaren	McLaren-Ford Cosworth M23	65 laps/engine	4
R	Jean-Pierre Jarier	Shadow	Shadow-Ford Cosworth DN5B	61 laps/electrical	15
R	Jody Scheckter	Tyrrell	Tyrrell-Ford Cosworth 007	53 laps/engine	14
R	John Watson	Penske	Penske-Ford Cosworth PC3	51 laps/engine	13
R	Arturo Merzario	March	March-Ford Cosworth 761	36 laps/gearbox	18
R	Mario Andretti	Lotus	Lotus-Ford Cosworth 77	34 laps/gearbox	9
R	Patrick Depailler	Tyrrell	Tyrrell-Ford Cosworth P34	25 laps/accident	3
R	Vittorio Brambilla	March	March-Ford Cosworth 761	21 laps/suspension	6
R	Hans-Joachim Stuck	March	March-Ford Cosworth 761	16 laps/gearbox	17
R	Ronnie Peterson	March	March-Ford Cosworth 761	11 laps/transmission	16
R	Emerson Fittipaldi	Fittipaldi	Fittipaldi-Ford Cosworth FD04	3 laps/transmission	19
DNQ	Brett Lunger	Surtees	Surtees-Ford Cosworth TS19	-	25
DNQ	Loris Kessel	RAM Racing	Brabham-Ford Cosworth BT44B	-	26
DNQ	Emilio Zapico	Frank Williams	Williams-Ford Cosworth FW04	-	27
DNQ	Emilio de Villota	RAM Racing	Brabham-Ford Cosworth BT44B	-	28
DNQ	Harald Ertl	Hesketh	Hesketh-Ford Cosworth 308D	-	29
DNQ	Ingo Hoffmann	Fittipaldi	Fittipaldi-Ford Cosworth FD04	-	30

Pole: Hunt, 1m18.520s, 96.984mph/156.080kph. Fastest lap: Mass, 1m20.930s, 94.094mph/151.430kph on Lap 52. Race leaders: Lauda 1-31, Hunt 32-75

NIKI'S LUCKY ESCAPE

The drivers no longer considered the 14-mile (22.5km) Nurburgring Nordschleife safe for hosting the German GP. Yet they raced anyway and Niki Lauda very nearly paid with his life. He crashed at Bergwerk on lap one and had to be pulled from his burning Ferrari by Guy Edwards, Harald Ertl, Brett Lunger and Arturo Merzario. Given the last rites, he lived and was racing again just five weeks later.

BELGIAN GRAND PRIX

ZOLDER • ROUND 5 • DATE: 16TH MAY 1976
Laps: 70 • Distance: 185.189miles/298.34km • Weather: Warm & bright

Pos	Driver	Team	Chassis-Engine	Result	Qual
1	Niki Lauda	Ferrari	Ferrari 312T2	1h42m53.230s	1
2	Clay Regazzoni	Ferrari	Ferrari 312T2	1h42m56.690s	2
3	Jacques Laffite	Ligier	Ligier-Matra JS5	1h43m28.610s	6
4	Jody Scheckter	Tyrrell	Tyrrell-Ford Cosworth P34	1h44m24.230s	7
5	Alan Jones	Surtees	Surtees-Ford Cosworth TS19	69 laps	16
6	Jochen Mass	McLaren	McLaren-Ford Cosworth M23	69 laps	18
7	John Watson	Penske	Penske-Ford Cosworth PC3	69 laps	17
8	Larry Perkins	Boro	Boro-Ford Cosworth N175	69 laps	20
9	Jean-Pierre Jarier	Shadow	Shadow-Ford Cosworth DN5B	69 laps	14
10	Tom Pryce	Shadow	Shadow-Ford Cosworth DN5B	68 laps	13
11	Michel Leclere	Walter Wolf Racing	Williams-Ford Cosworth FW05	68 laps	25
12	Loris Kessel	RAM Racing	Brabham-Ford Cosworth BT44B	63 laps	23
R	Brett Lunger	Surtees	Surtees-Ford Cosworth TS19	62 laps/electrical	26

Pos	Driver	Team	Chassis-Engine	Result	Qual
R	Carlos Pace	Brabham	Brabham-Alfa Romeo BT45	58 laps/electrical	9
R	Chris Amon	Ensign	Ensign-Ford Cosworth N176	51 laps/accident	8
R	James Hunt	McLaren	McLaren-Ford Cosworth M23	35 laps/gearbox	3
R	Hans-Joachim Stuck	March	March-Ford Cosworth 761	33 laps/suspension	15
R	Harald Ertl	Hesketh	Hesketh-Ford Cosworth 308D	31 laps/engine	24
R	Patrick Depailler	Tyrrell	Tyrrell-Ford Cosworth P34	29 laps/engine	4
R	Mario Andretti	Lotus	Lotus-Ford Cosworth 77	28 laps/halfshaft	11
R	Patrick Neve	RAM Racing	Brabham-Ford Cosworth BT44B	26 laps/halfshaft	19
R	Arturo Merzario	March	March-Ford Cosworth 761	21 laps/engine	21
R	Carlos Reutemann	Brabham	Brabham-Alfa Romeo BT45	17 laps/engine	12
R	Ronnie Peterson	March	March-Ford Cosworth 761	16 laps/accident	10
R	Gunnar Nilsson	Lotus	Lotus-Ford Cosworth 77	7 laps/accident	22
R	Vittorio Brambilla	March	March-Ford Cosworth 761	6 laps/halfshaft	5
DNQ	Emerson Fittipaldi	Fittipaldi	Fittipaldi-Ford Cosworth FD04	-	27
DNQ	Jacky Ickx	Walter Wolf Racing	Williams-Ford Cosworth FW05	-	28
DNQ	Guy Edwards	Hesketh	Hesketh-Ford Cosworth 308D	-	29

Pole: Lauda, 1m26.550s, 110.153mph/177.275kph. Fastest lap: Lauda, 1m25.980s, 110.883mph/178.450kph. Race leaders: Lauda 1-70

MONACO GRAND PRIX

MONTE CARLO • ROUND 6 • DATE: 30TH MAY 1976
Laps: 78 • Distance: 160.522miles/258.336km • Weather: Warm & bright

Pos	Driver	Team	Chassis-Engine	Result	Qual
1	Niki Lauda	Ferrari	Ferrari 312T2	1h59m51.470s	1
2	Jody Scheckter	Tyrrell	Tyrrell-Ford Cosworth P34	2h00m02.600s	5
3	Patrick Depailler	Tyrrell	Tyrrell-Ford Cosworth P34	2h00m56.310s	4
4	Hans-Joachim Stuck	March	March-Ford Cosworth 761	77 laps	6
5	Jochen Mass	McLaren	McLaren-Ford Cosworth M23	77 laps	11
6	Emerson Fittipaldi	Fittipaldi	Fittipaldi-Ford Cosworth FD04	77 laps	7
7	Tom Pryce	Shadow	Shadow-Ford Cosworth DN5B	77 laps	15
8	Jean-Pierre Jarier	Shadow	Shadow-Ford Cosworth DN5B	76 laps	10
9	Carlos Pace	Brabham	Brabham-Alfa Romeo BT45	76 laps	13
10	John Watson	Penske	Penske-Ford Cosworth PC3	76 laps	17
11	Michel Leclere	Walter Wolf Racing	Williams-Ford Cosworth FW05	76 laps	18
12	Jacques Laffite	Ligier	Ligier-Matra JS5	75 laps/accident	8
13	Chris Amon	Ensign	Ensign-Ford Cosworth N176	74 laps	12
14	Clay Regazzoni	Ferrari	Ferrari 312T2	73 laps/accident	2
R	Gunnar Nilsson	Lotus	Lotus-Ford Cosworth 77	39 laps/engine	16
R	Ronnie Peterson	March	March-Ford Cosworth 761	26 laps/accident	3
R	James Hunt	McLaren	McLaren-Ford Cosworth M23	24 laps/engine	14
R	Vittorio Brambilla	March	March-Ford Cosworth 761	9 laps/suspension	9
R	Alan Jones	Surtees	Surtees-Ford Cosworth TS19	1 lap/collision	19
R	Carlos Reutemann	Brabham	Brabham-Alfa Romeo BT45	0 laps/accident	20
DNQ	Jacky Ickx	Walter Wolf Racing	Williams-Ford Cosworth FW05	-	21
DNQ	Henri Pescarolo	BS Fabrications	Surtees-Ford Cosworth TS19	-	22
DNQ	Larry Perkins	Boro	Boro-Ford Cosworth 001	-	23
DNQ	Harald Ertl	Hesketh	Hesketh-Ford Cosworth 308D	-	24
DNQ	Arturo Merzario	March	March-Ford Cosworth 761	-	25

Pole: Lauda, 1m29.650s, 82.640mph/132.997kph. Fastest lap: Regazzoni, 1m30.280s, 82.063mph/132.069kph on Lap 60. Race leaders: Lauda 1-78

SWEDISH GRAND PRIX

ANDERSTORP • ROUND 7 • DATE: 13TH JUNE 1976
Laps: 72 • Distance: 179.760miles/289.296km • Weather: Warm but dull

Pos	Driver	Team	Chassis-Engine	Result	Qual
1	Jody Scheckter	Tyrrell	Tyrrell-Ford Cosworth P34	1h46m53.729s	1
2	Patrick Depailler	Tyrrell	Tyrrell-Ford Cosworth P34	1h47m13.495s	4
3	Niki Lauda	Ferrari	Ferrari 312T2	1h47m27.595s	5
4	Jacques Laffite	Ligier	Ligier-Matra JS5	1h47m49.548s	7
5	James Hunt	McLaren	McLaren-Ford Cosworth M23	1h47m53.212s	8
6	Clay Regazzoni	Ferrari	Ferrari 312T2	1h47m54.095s	11
7	Ronnie Peterson	March	March-Ford Cosworth 761	1h47m57.222s	9
8	Carlos Pace	Brabham	Brabham-Alfa Romeo BT45	1h48m05.342s	10
9	Tom Pryce	Shadow	Shadow-Ford Cosworth DN5B	71 laps	12
10	Vittorio Brambilla	March	March-Ford Cosworth 761	71 laps	15
11	Jochen Mass	McLaren	McLaren-Ford Cosworth M23	71 laps	13
12	Jean-Pierre Jarier	Shadow	Shadow-Ford Cosworth DN5B	71 laps	14
13	Alan Jones	Surtees	Surtees-Ford Cosworth TS19	71 laps	18
14	Arturo Merzario	March	March-Ford Cosworth 761	70 laps/engine	19
15	Brett Lunger	Surtees	Surtees-Ford Cosworth TS19	70 laps	24
R	Harald Ertl	Hesketh	Hesketh-Ford Cosworth 308D	54 laps/spun off	23
R	Hans-Joachim Stuck	March	March-Ford Cosworth 761	52 laps/engine	20
R	Mario Andretti	Lotus	Lotus-Ford Cosworth 77	45 laps/engine	2
R	Chris Amon	Ensign	Ensign-Ford Cosworth N176	38 laps/accident	3
R	Michel Leclere	Walter Wolf Racing	Williams-Ford Cosworth FW05	20 laps/engine	25
R	Larry Perkins	Boro	Boro-Ford Cosworth N175	18 laps/engine	22
R	Emerson Fittipaldi	Fittipaldi	Fittipaldi-Ford Cosworth FD04	10 laps/handling	21
R	Loris Kessel	RAM Racing	Brabham-Ford Cosworth BT44B	5 laps/accident	26
R	Gunnar Nilsson	Lotus	Lotus-Ford Cosworth 77	2 laps/accident	6
R	Carlos Reutemann	Brabham	Brabham-Alfa Romeo BT45	2 laps/engine	16
R	John Watson	Penske	Penske-Ford Cosworth PC4	0 laps/accident	17
DNQ	Jac Nelleman	RAM Racing	Brabham-Ford Cosworth BT44B	-	27

Pole: Scheckter, 1m25.659s, 104.927mph/168.864kph. Fastest lap: Andretti, 1m28.002s, 102.133mph/164.368kph on Lap 11. Race leaders: Andretti 1-45, Scheckter 46-72

FRENCH GRAND PRIX

CIRCUIT PAUL RICARD • ROUND 8 • DATE: 4TH JULY 1976
Laps: 54 • Distance: 194.535miles/313.74km • Weather: Hot & bright

Pos	Driver	Team	Chassis-Engine	Result	Qual
1	James Hunt	McLaren	McLaren-Ford Cosworth M23	1h40m58.600s	1
2	Patrick Depailler	Tyrrell	Tyrrell-Ford Cosworth P34	1h41m11.300s	3
3	John Watson	Penske	Penske-Ford Cosworth PC4	1h41m22.150s	8
4	Carlos Pace	Brabham	Brabham-Alfa Romeo BT45	1h41m23.420s	5
5	Mario Andretti	Lotus	Lotus-Ford Cosworth 77	1h41m42.520s	7
6	Jody Scheckter	Tyrrell	Tyrrell-Ford Cosworth P34	1h41m53.670s	9
7	Hans-Joachim Stuck	March	March-Ford Cosworth 761	1h42m20.150s	17
8	Tom Pryce	Shadow	Shadow-Ford Cosworth DN5B	1h42m29.270s	16
9	Arturo Merzario	March	March-Ford Cosworth 761	1h42m52.170s	20
10	Jacky Ickx	Walter Wolf Racing	Williams-Ford Cosworth FW05	53 laps	19
11	Carlos Reutemann	Brabham	Brabham-Alfa Romeo BT45	53 laps	10
12	Jean-Pierre Jarier	Shadow	Shadow-Ford Cosworth DN5B	53 laps	15
13	Michel Leclere	Walter Wolf Racing	Williams-Ford Cosworth FW05	53 laps	22

Pos	Driver	Team	Chassis-Engine	Result	Qual
14	Jacques Laffite	Ligier	Ligier-Matra JS5	53 laps	13
15	Jochen Mass	McLaren	McLaren-Ford Cosworth M23	53 laps	14
16	Brett Lunger	Surtees	Surtees-Ford Cosworth TS19	53 laps	23
17	Guy Edwards	Hesketh	Hesketh-Ford Cosworth 308D	53 laps	25
18	Patrick Neve	Ensign	Ensign-Ford Cosworth N176	53 laps	26
19	Ronnie Peterson	March	March-Ford Cosworth 761	51 laps/fuel system	6
R	Alan Jones	Surtees	Surtees-Ford Cosworth TS19	44 laps/suspension	18
R	Vittorio Brambilla	March	March-Ford Cosworth 761	28 laps/fuel pressure	11
R	Emerson Fittipaldi	Fittipaldi	Fittipaldi-Ford Cosworth FD04	21 laps/fuel pressure	21
R	Henri Pescarolo	BS Fabrications	Surtees-Ford Cosworth TS19	19 laps/suspension	24
R	Clay Regazzoni	Ferrari	Ferrari 312T2	17 laps/engine	4
R	Niki Lauda	Ferrari	Ferrari 312T2	8 laps/engine	2
R	Gunnar Nilsson	Lotus	Lotus-Ford Cosworth 77	8 laps/gearbox	12
R	Harald Ertl	Hesketh	Hesketh-Ford Cosworth 308D	4 laps/differential	29
DNQ	Damien Magee	RAM Racing	Brabham-Ford Cosworth BT44B	-	27
DNQ	Ingo Hoffmann	Fittipaldi	Fittipaldi-Ford Cosworth FD04	-	28
DNQ	Loris Kessel	RAM Racing	Brabham-Ford Cosworth BT44B	-	30

Pole: Hunt, 1m47.890s, 120.461mph/193.864kph. Fastest lap: Lauda, 1m51.000s, 117.066mph/188.400kph on Lap 4. Race leaders: Lauda 1-8, Hunt 9-54

THE WINNER SHAVES IT ALL

John Watson had a long-running bet with team owner Roger Penske that if ever he won a grand prix in the American team's cars, he would shave off his beard. This became a possibility with thirds in France and Britain, but then reality when the Ulsterman triumphed in the Austrian GP in what would prove to be Penske's only F1 success.

BRITISH GRAND PRIX

BRANDS HATCH • ROUND 9 • DATE: 18TH JULY 1976
Laps: 76 • Distance: 198.629miles/319.663km • Weather: Warm & bright

Pos	Driver	Team	Chassis-Engine	Result	Qual
1	Niki Lauda	Ferrari	Ferrari 312T2	1h44m19.660s	1
2	Jody Scheckter	Tyrrell	Tyrrell-Ford Cosworth P34	1h44m35.840s	8
3	John Watson	Penske	Penske-Ford Cosworth PC4	75 laps	11
4	Tom Pryce	Shadow	Shadow-Ford Cosworth DN5B	75 laps	20
5	Alan Jones	Surtees	Surtees-Ford Cosworth TS19	75 laps	19
6	Emerson Fittipaldi	Fittipaldi	Fittipaldi-Ford Cosworth FD04	74 laps	21
7	Harald Ertl	Hesketh	Hesketh-Ford Cosworth 308D	73 laps	23
8	Carlos Pace	Brabham	Brabham-Alfa Romeo BT45	73 laps	16
9	Jean-Pierre Jarier	Shadow	Shadow-Ford Cosworth DN5B	70 laps	24
DQ	James Hunt	McLaren	McLaren-Ford Cosworth M23	76 laps/illegal pit entry	2
R	Gunnar Nilsson	Lotus	Lotus-Ford Cosworth 77	67 laps/engine	14
R	Ronnie Peterson	March	March-Ford Cosworth 761	60 laps/fuel system	7
R	Brett Lunger	Surtees	Surtees-Ford Cosworth TS19	55 laps/gearbox	18
R	Patrick Depailler	Tyrrell	Tyrrell-Ford Cosworth P34	47 laps/engine	5
R	Carlos Reutemann	Brabham	Brabham-Alfa Romeo BT45	46 laps/fuel pressure	15
R	Arturo Merzario	March	March-Ford Cosworth 761	39 laps/engine	9
DQ	Clay Regazzoni	Ferrari	Ferrari 312T2	36 laps/used spare car	4
DQ	Jacques Laffite	Ligier	Ligier-Matra JS5	31 laps/used spare car	13

Pos	Driver	Team	Chassis-Engine	Result	Qual
R	Bob Evans	RAM Racing	Brabham-Ford Cosworth BT44B	24 laps/gearbox	22
R	Vittorio Brambilla	March	March-Ford Cosworth 761	22 laps/accident	10
R	Henri Pescarolo	BS Fabrications	Surtees-Ford Cosworth TS19	16 laps/fuel system	26
R	Chris Amon	Ensign	Ensign-Ford Cosworth N176	8 laps/water leak	6
R	Mario Andretti	Lotus	Lotus-Ford Cosworth 77	4 laps/ignition	3
R	Jochen Mass	McLaren	McLaren-Ford Cosworth M23	1 lap/clutch	12
R	Hans-Joachim Stuck	March	March-Ford Cosworth 761	0 laps/accident	17
R	Guy Edwards	Hesketh	Hesketh-Ford Cosworth 308D	0 laps/accident	25
DNQ	Jacky Ickx	Walter Wolf Racing	Williams-Ford Cosworth FW05	-	27
DNQ	Divina Galica	Shellsport/Whiting	Surtees-Ford Cosworth TS16	-	28
DNQ	Mike Wilds	Team P R Reilly	Shadow-Ford Cosworth DN3B	-	29
DNQ	Lella Lombardi	RAM Racing	Brabham-Ford Cosworth BT44B	-	30

Pole: Lauda, 1m19.350s, 118.573mph/190.824kph. Fastest lap: Hunt, 1m19.820s, 117.874mph/189.700kph on Lap 44. Race leaders: Lauda 1-44, Hunt 45-76

GERMAN GRAND PRIX

NURBURGRING • ROUND 10 • DATE: 1ST AUGUST 1976
Laps: 14 • Distance: 198.260miles/319.69km • Weather: Warm & wet then drying

Pos	Driver	Team	Chassis-Engine	Result	Qual
1	James Hunt	McLaren	McLaren-Ford Cosworth M23	1h41m42.700s	1
2	Jody Scheckter	Tyrrell	Tyrrell-Ford Cosworth P34	1h42m10.400s	8
3	Jochen Mass	McLaren	McLaren-Ford Cosworth M23	1h42m35.100s	9
4	Carlos Pace	Brabham	Brabham-Alfa Romeo BT45	1h42m36.900s	7
5	Gunnar Nilsson	Lotus	Lotus-Ford Cosworth 77	1h43m40.000s	16
6	Rolf Stommelen	Brabham	Brabham-Alfa Romeo BT45	1h44m13.000s	15
7	John Watson	Penske	Penske-Ford Cosworth PC4	1h44m16.600s	19
8	Tom Pryce	Shadow	Shadow-Ford Cosworth DN5B	1h44m30.900s	18
9	Clay Regazzoni	Ferrari	Ferrari 312T2	1h45m28.700s	5
10	Alan Jones	Surtees	Surtees-Ford Cosworth TS19	0m00.000s	14
11	Jean-Pierre Jarier	Shadow	Shadow-Ford Cosworth DN5B	1h46m34.400s	23
12	Mario Andretti	Lotus	Lotus-Ford Cosworth 77	1h46m40.800s	12
13	Emerson Fittipaldi	Fittipaldi	Fittipaldi-Ford Cosworth FD04	1h47m07.900s	20
14	Alessandro Pesenti-Rossi	Scuderia Gulf Rondini	Tyrrell-Ford Cosworth 007	13 laps	26
15	Guy Edwards	Hesketh	Hesketh-Ford Cosworth 308D	13 laps	25
R	Arturo Merzario	Walter Wolf Racing	Williams-Ford Cosworth FW05	3 laps/brakes	21
R	Vittorio Brambilla	March	March-Ford Cosworth 761	1 lap/accident	13
R	Niki Lauda	Ferrari	Ferrari 312T2	0 laps/accident	2
R	Patrick Depailler	Tyrrell	Tyrrell-Ford Cosworth P34	0 laps/accident	3
R	Hans-Joachim Stuck	March	March-Ford Cosworth 761	0 laps/clutch	4
R	Jacques Laffite	Ligier	Ligier-Matra JS5	0 laps/gearbox	6
R	Carlos Reutemann	Brabham	Brabham-Alfa Romeo BT45	0 laps/fuel system	10
R	Ronnie Peterson	March	March-Ford Cosworth 761	0 laps/accident	11
R	Chris Amon	Ensign	Ensign-Ford Cosworth N176	0 laps/withdrawn	17
R	Harald Ertl	Hesketh	Hesketh-Ford Cosworth 308D	0 laps/accident	22
R	Brett Lunger	Surtees	Surtees-Ford Cosworth TS19	0 laps/accident	24
DNQ	Lella Lombardi	RAM Racing	Brabham-Ford Cosworth BT44B	-	27
DNQ	Henri Pescarolo	BS Fabrications	Surtees-Ford Cosworth TS19	-	28

Pole: Hunt, 7m06.500s, 119.766mph/192.745kph. Fastest lap: Scheckter, 7m10.800s, 118.557mph/190.800kph on Lap 13. Race leaders: Hunt 1-14

AUSTRIAN GRAND PRIX

OSTERREICHRING • ROUND 11 • DATE: 15TH AUGUST 1976
Laps: 54 • Distance: 198.287miles/319.113km • Weather: Warm but dull

Pos	Driver	Team	Chassis-Engine	Result	Qual
1	John Watson	Penske	Penske-Ford Cosworth PC4	1h30m07.860s	2
2	Jacques Laffite	Ligier	Ligier-Matra JS5	1h30m18.650s	5
3	Gunnar Nilsson	Lotus	Lotus-Ford Cosworth 77	1h30m19.840s	4
4	James Hunt	McLaren	McLaren-Ford Cosworth M23	1h30m20.300s	1
5	Mario Andretti	Lotus	Lotus-Ford Cosworth 77	1h30m29.350s	9
6	Ronnie Peterson	March	March-Ford Cosworth 761	1h30m42.200s	3
7	Jochen Mass	McLaren	McLaren-Ford Cosworth M23	1h31m07.310s	12
8	Harald Ertl	Hesketh	Hesketh-Ford Cosworth 308D	53 laps	20
9	Henri Pescarolo	BS Fabrications	Surtees-Ford Cosworth TS19	52 laps	22
10	Brett Lunger	Surtees	Surtees-Ford Cosworth TS19	51 laps/accident	16
11	Alessandro Pesenti-Rossi	Scuderia Gulf Rondini	Tyrrell-Ford Cosworth 007	51 laps	23
12	Lella Lombardi	RAM Racing	Brabham-Ford Cosworth BT44B	50 laps	24
R	Hans Binder	Ensign	Ensign-Ford Cosworth N176	47 laps/throttle	19
NC	Loris Kessel	RAM Racing	Brabham-Ford Cosworth BT44B	44 laps	25
R	Vittorio Brambilla	March	March-Ford Cosworth 761	43 laps/accident	7
R	Emerson Fittipaldi	Fittipaldi	Fittipaldi-Ford Cosworth FD04	43 laps/accident	17
R	Carlos Pace	Brabham	Brabham-Alfa Romeo BT45	40 laps/accident	8
R	Jean-Pierre Jarier	Shadow	Shadow-Ford Cosworth DN5B	40 laps/fuel pump	18
R	Alan Jones	Surtees	Surtees-Ford Cosworth TS19	30 laps/accident	15
R	Hans-Joachim Stuck	March	March-Ford Cosworth 761	26 laps/fuel system	11
R	Patrick Depailler	Tyrrell	Tyrrell-Ford Cosworth P34	24 laps/suspension	13
R	Arturo Merzario	Walter Wolf Racing	Williams-Ford Cosworth FW05	17 laps/accident	21
R	Tom Pryce	Shadow	Shadow-Ford Cosworth DN5B	14 laps/brakes	6
R	Jody Scheckter	Tyrrell	Tyrrell-Ford Cosworth P34	14 laps/suspension	10
R	Carlos Reutemann	Brabham	Brabham-Alfa Romeo BT45	0 laps/clutch	14

Pole: Hunt, 1m35.020s, 139.119mph/223.891kph. Fastest lap: Hunt, 1m35.910s, 137.828mph/221.814kph. Race leaders: Watson 1-2 & 12-54, Peterson 3-9 & 11, Scheckter 10

NEW CIRCUITS

The USA landed a second grand prix with the introduction of a spring race in California. This was held on a undulating street circuit in Long Beach, where Ferrari revelled in a one-two finish. The second new circuit, Fuji Speedway, offered dreadful weather for the first Japanese GP where the Hunt v Lauda title battle was settled.

NEW CONSTRUCTORS

Despite inventing the sport, France was wholly unrepresented in F1 after Matra's withdrawal at the end of the 1972 season. So when former F1 racer Guy Ligier turned from sports cars to F1 the fans were delighted, especially when Jacques Laffite came second in Austria. The Kojima team made its bow at its home race at Fuji.

DUTCH GRAND PRIX

ZANDVOORT • ROUND 12 • DATE: 29TH AUGUST 1976
Laps: 75 • Distance: 196.412miles/316.95km • Weather: Warm & bright

Pos	Driver	Team	Chassis-Engine	Result	Qual
1	James Hunt	McLaren	McLaren-Ford Cosworth M23	1h44m52.090s	2
2	Clay Regazzoni	Ferrari	Ferrari 312T2	1h44m53.010s	5
3	Mario Andretti	Lotus	Lotus-Ford Cosworth 77	1h44m54.180s	6
4	Tom Pryce	Shadow	Shadow-Ford Cosworth DN8	1h44m59.030s	3
5	Jody Scheckter	Tyrrell	Tyrrell-Ford Cosworth P34	1h45m14.550s	8
6	Vittorio Brambilla	March	March-Ford Cosworth 761	1h45m37.120s	7
7	Patrick Depailler	Tyrrell	Tyrrell-Ford Cosworth P34	1h45m48.370s	14
8	Alan Jones	Surtees	Surtees-Ford Cosworth TS19	74 laps	16
9	Jochen Mass	McLaren	McLaren-Ford Cosworth M26	74 laps	15
10	Jean-Pierre Jarier	Shadow	Shadow-Ford Cosworth DN5B	74 laps	20
11	Henri Pescarolo	BS Fabrications	Surtees-Ford Cosworth TS19	74 laps	22
12	Rolf Stommelen	Hesketh	Hesketh-Ford Cosworth 308D	72 laps	25
R	Jacky Ickx	Ensign	Ensign-Ford Cosworth N176	66 laps/electrical	11
R	Boy Hayje	F&S Properties	Penske-Ford Cosworth PC3	63 laps/halfshaft	21
R	Carlos Pace	Brabham	Brabham-Alfa Romeo BT45	53 laps/oil leak	9
R	Jacques Laffite	Ligier	Ligier-Matra JS5	53 laps/fuel pressure	10
R	Ronnie Peterson	March	March-Ford Cosworth 761	52 laps/fuel pressure	1
R	Harald Ertl	Hesketh	Hesketh-Ford Cosworth 308D	49 laps/spun off	24
R	John Watson	Penske	Penske-Ford Cosworth PC4	47 laps/gearbox	4
R	Larry Perkins	Boro	Boro-Ford Cosworth N175	44 laps/accident	19
R	Emerson Fittipaldi	Fittipaldi	Fittipaldi-Ford Cosworth FD04	40 laps/electrical	17
R	Carlos Reutemann	Brabham	Brabham-Alfa Romeo BT45	11 laps/clutch	12
R	Gunnar Nilsson	Lotus	Lotus-Ford Cosworth 77	10 laps/accident	13
R	Conny Andersson	Surtees	Surtees-Ford Cosworth TS19	9 laps/engine	18
R	Hans-Joachim Stuck	March	March-Ford Cosworth 761	9 laps/engine	18
R	Arturo Merzario	Walter Wolf Racing	Williams-Ford Cosworth FW05	5 laps/accident	23
DNQ	Alessandro Pesenti-Rossi	Scuderia Gulf Rondini	Tyrrell-Ford Cosworth 007	-	27

Pole: Peterson, 1m21.310s, 116.262mph/187.106kph. Fastest lap: Regazzoni, 1m22.590s, 114.462mph/184.210kph on Lap 49. Race leaders: Peterson 1-11, Hunt 12-75

ITALIAN GRAND PRIX

MONZA • ROUND 13 • DATE: 12TH SEPTEMBER 1976
Laps: 52 • Distance: 187.36miles/301.6km • Weather: Warm & bright

Pos	Driver	Team	Chassis-Engine	Result	Qual
1	Ronnie Peterson	March	March-Ford Cosworth 761	1h30m35.600s	8
2	Clay Regazzoni	Ferrari	Ferrari 312T2	1h30m37.900s	9
3	Jacques Laffite	Ligier	Ligier-Matra JS5	1h30m38.600s	1
4	Niki Lauda	Ferrari	Ferrari 312T2	1h30m55.000s	5
5	Jody Scheckter	Tyrrell	Tyrrell-Ford Cosworth P34	1h30m55.100s	2
6	Patrick Depailler	Tyrrell	Tyrrell-Ford Cosworth P34	1h31m11.300s	4
7	Vittorio Brambilla	March	March-Ford Cosworth 761	1h31m19.500s	16
8	Tom Pryce	Shadow	Shadow-Ford Cosworth DN8	1h31m28.500s	15
9	Carlos Reutemann	Ferrari	Ferrari 312T2	1h31m33.100s	7
10	Jacky Ickx	Ensign	Ensign-Ford Cosworth N176	1h31m48.000s	10
11	John Watson	Penske	Penske-Ford Cosworth PC4	1h32m17.800s	27
12	Alan Jones	Surtees	Surtees-Ford Cosworth TS19	51 laps	18
13	Gunnar Nilsson	Lotus	Lotus-Ford Cosworth 77	51 laps	12

Pos	Driver	Team	Chassis-Engine	Result	Qual
14	Brett Lunger	Surtees	Surtees-Ford Cosworth TS19	50 laps	24
15	Emerson Fittipaldi	Fittipaldi	Fittipaldi-Ford Cosworth FD04	50 laps	20
16	Harald Ertl	Hesketh	Hesketh-Ford Cosworth 308D	49 laps/halfshaft	19
17	Henri Pescarolo	BS Fabrications	Surtees-Ford Cosworth TS19	49 laps	22
18	Alessandro Pesenti-Rossi	Scuderia Gulf Rondini	Tyrrell-Ford Cosworth 007	49 laps	21
19	Jean-Pierre Jarier	Shadow	Shadow-Ford Cosworth DN5B	47 laps	17
R	Rolf Stommelen	Brabham	Brabham-Alfa Romeo BT45	41 laps/fuel system	11
R	Hans-Joachim Stuck	March	March-Ford Cosworth 761	23 laps/accident	6
R	Mario Andretti	Lotus	Lotus-Ford Cosworth 77	23 laps/accident	14
R	James Hunt	McLaren	McLaren-Ford Cosworth M23	11 laps/spun off	25
R	Larry Perkins	Boro	Boro-Ford Cosworth N175	8 laps/engine	13
R	Carlos Pace	Brabham	Brabham-Alfa Romeo BT45	4 laps/engine	3
R	Jochen Mass	McLaren	McLaren-Ford Cosworth M26	2 laps/ignition	26
NS	Guy Edwards	Hesketh	Hesketh-Ford Cosworth 308D	let Watson race	23
DNQ	Arturo Merzario	Walter Wolf Racing	Williams-Ford Cosworth FW05	withdrew	25
DNQ	Otto Stuppacher*	OASC Racing Team	Tyrrell-Ford Cosworth 007	went home	26

*didn't know he'd qualified

Pole: Laffite, 1m41.350s, 128.014mph/206.018kph. Fastest lap: Peterson, 1m41.300s, 128.064mph/206.100kph on Lap 50. Race leaders: Scheckter 1-10, Peterson 11-52

NEW DRIVERS

Gunnar Nilsson shone for Lotus in his maiden season after winning in British F3. This was enough to land him a drive with Lotus and the Swede took a pair of thirds. None of the 19 other novices came close to his level, although Masahiro Hasemi was credited with fastest lap in the appallingly wet Japanese GP in his Dunlop-shod Kojima.

CANADIAN GRAND PRIX

MOSPORT PARK • ROUND 14 • DATE: 3RD OCTOBER 1976
Laps: 80 • Distance: 196.388miles/316.56km • Weather: Warm & bright

Pos	Driver	Team	Chassis-Engine	Result	Qual
1	James Hunt	McLaren	McLaren-Ford Cosworth M23	1h40m09.626s	1
2	Patrick Depailler	Tyrrell	Tyrrell-Ford Cosworth P34	1h40m15.957s	4
3	Mario Andretti	Lotus	Lotus-Ford Cosworth 77	1h40m19.992s	5
4	Jody Scheckter	Tyrrell	Tyrrell-Ford Cosworth P34	1h40m29.371s	7
5	Jochen Mass	McLaren	McLaren-Ford Cosworth M23	1h40m51.437s	11
6	Clay Regazzoni	Ferrari	Ferrari 312T2	1h40m55.882s	12
7	Carlos Pace	Brabham	Brabham-Alfa Romeo BT45	1h40m56.098s	10
8	Niki Lauda	Ferrari	Ferrari 312T2	1h41m22.583s	6
9	Ronnie Peterson	March	March-Ford Cosworth 761	79 laps	2
10	John Watson	Penske	Penske-Ford Cosworth PC4	79 laps	14
11	Tom Pryce	Shadow	Shadow-Ford Cosworth DN8	79 laps	13
12	Gunnar Nilsson	Lotus	Lotus-Ford Cosworth 77	79 laps	15
13	Jacky Ickx	Ensign	Ensign-Ford Cosworth N176	79 laps	16
14	Vittorio Brambilla	March	March-Ford Cosworth 761	79 laps	3
15	Brett Lunger	Surtees	Surtees-Ford Cosworth TS19	78 laps	22
16	Alan Jones	Surtees	Surtees-Ford Cosworth TS19	78 laps	20
17	Larry Perkins	Brabham	Brabham-Alfa Romeo BT45	78 laps	19

Pos	Driver	Team	Chassis-Engine	Result	Qual
18	Jean-Pierre Jarier	Shadow	Shadow-Ford Cosworth DN5B	77 laps	18
19	Henri Pescarolo	BS Fabrications	Surtees-Ford Cosworth TS19	77 laps	21
20	Guy Edwards	Hesketh	Hesketh-Ford Cosworth 308D	75 laps	23
R	Jacques Laffite	Ligier	Ligier-Matra JS5	43 laps/fuel pressure	9
R	Emerson Fittipaldi	Fittipaldi	Fittipaldi-Ford Cosworth FD04	41 laps/exhaust	17
R	Hans-Joachim Stuck	March	March-Ford Cosworth 761	36 laps/handling	8
R	Arturo Merzario	Walter Wolf Racing	Williams-Ford Cosworth FW05	11 laps/accident	24
DNQ	Harald Ertl	Hesketh	Hesketh-Ford Cosworth 308D	accident	23
DNQ	Chris Amon	Walter Wolf Racing	Williams-Ford Cosworth FW05	accident	26
DNQ	Otto Stuppacher	OASC Racing Team	Tyrrell-Ford Cosworth 007	-	27

Pole: Hunt, 1m12.389s, 122.277mph/196.786kph. Fastest lap: Depailler, 1m13.817s, 119.912mph/192.979kph on Lap 60. Race leaders: Peterson 1-8, Hunt 9-80

UNITED STATES GRAND PRIX

WATKINS GLEN • ROUND 15 • DATE: 10TH OCTOBER 1976
Laps: 59 • Distance: 199.251miles/320.665km • Weather: Cool & dull

Pos	Driver	Team	Chassis-Engine	Result	Qual
1	James Hunt	McLaren	McLaren-Ford Cosworth M23	1h42m40.741s	1
2	Jody Scheckter	Tyrrell	Tyrrell-Ford Cosworth P34	1h42m48.771s	2
3	Niki Lauda	Ferrari	Ferrari 312T2	1h43m43.065s	5
4	Jochen Mass	McLaren	McLaren-Ford Cosworth M23	1h43m43.199s	17
5	Hans-Joachim Stuck	March	March-Ford Cosworth 761	1h43m48.719s	6
6	John Watson	Penske	Penske-Ford Cosworth PC4	1h43m48.931s	8
7	Clay Regazzoni	Ferrari	Ferrari 312T2	58 laps	14
8	Alan Jones	Surtees	Surtees-Ford Cosworth TS19	58 laps	18
9	Emerson Fittipaldi	Fittipaldi	Fittipaldi-Ford Cosworth FD04	57 laps	15
10	Jean-Pierre Jarier	Shadow	Shadow-Ford Cosworth DN5B	57 laps	16
11	Brett Lunger	Surtees	Surtees-Ford Cosworth TS19	57 laps	24
12	Alex Ribeiro	Hesketh	Hesketh-Ford Cosworth 308D	57 laps	22
13	Harald Ertl	Hesketh	Hesketh-Ford Cosworth 308D	54 laps	21
14	Warwick Brown	Walter Wolf Racing	Williams-Ford Cosworth FW05	54 laps	23
NC	Henri Pescarolo	BS Fabrications	Surtees-Ford Cosworth TS19	48 laps	26
R	Tom Pryce	Shadow	Shadow-Ford Cosworth DN8	45 laps/engine	9
R	Vittorio Brambilla	March	March-Ford Cosworth 761	34 laps/tyre	4
R	Jacques Laffite	Ligier	Ligier-Matra JS5	34 laps/tyre	12
R	Carlos Pace	Brabham	Brabham-Alfa Romeo BT45	31 laps/collision	10
R	Larry Perkins	Brabham	Brabham-Alfa Romeo BT45	30 laps/suspension	13
R	Mario Andretti	Lotus	Lotus-Ford Cosworth 77	23 laps/suspension	11
R	Jacky Ickx	Ensign	Ensign-Ford Cosworth N176	14 laps/accident	19
R	Gunnar Nilsson	Lotus	Lotus-Ford Cosworth 77	13 laps/engine	20
R	Ronnie Peterson	March	March-Ford Cosworth 761	12 laps/suspension	3
R	Arturo Merzario	Walter Wolf Racing	Williams-Ford Cosworth FW05	9 laps/accident	25
R	Patrick Depailler	Tyrrell	Tyrrell-Ford Cosworth P34	7 laps/fuel line	7
DNQ	Otto Stuppacher	OASC Racing Team	Tyrrell-Ford Cosworth 007	-	27

Pole: Hunt, 1m43.622s, 117.327mph/188.820kph. Fastest lap: Hunt, 1m42.851s, 118.207mph/190.236kph on Lap 53. Race leaders: Scheckter 1-36 & 41-45, Hunt 37-40 & 46-59

JAPANESE GRAND PRIX

FUJI SPEEDWAY • ROUND 16 • DATE: 24TH OCTOBER 1976
Laps: 73 • Distance: 197.724miles/318.207km • Weather: Cool, very wet & misty

Pos	Driver	Team	Chassis-Engine	Result	Qual
1	Mario Andretti	Lotus	Lotus-Ford Cosworth 77	1h43m58.860s	1
2	Patrick Depailler	Tyrrell	Tyrrell-Ford Cosworth P34	72 laps	13
3	James Hunt	McLaren	McLaren-Ford Cosworth M23	72 laps	2
4	Alan Jones	Surtees	Surtees-Ford Cosworth TS19	72 laps	20
5	Clay Regazzoni	Ferrari	Ferrari 312T2	72 laps	7
6	Gunnar Nilsson	Lotus	Lotus-Ford Cosworth 77	72 laps	16
7	Jacques Laffite	Ligier	Ligier-Matra JS5	72 laps	11
8	Harald Ertl	Hesketh	Hesketh-Ford Cosworth 308D	72 laps	22
9	Noritake Takahara	Surtees	Surtees-Ford Cosworth TS19	70 laps	24
10	Jean-Pierre Jarier	Shadow	Shadow-Ford Cosworth DN5B	69 laps	15
11	Masahiro Hasemi	Kojima	Kojima-Ford Cosworth KE007	66 laps	10
R	Jody Scheckter	Tyrrell	Tyrrell-Ford Cosworth P34	58 laps/overheating	5
R	Hans Binder	Walter Wolf Racing	Williams-Ford Cosworth FW05	49 laps/wheel bearing	25
R	Tom Pryce	Shadow	Shadow-Ford Cosworth DN8	46 laps/engine	14
R	Vittorio Brambilla	March	March-Ford Cosworth 761	38 laps/electrical	8
R	Hans-Joachim Stuck	March	March-Ford Cosworth 761	37 laps/electrical	18
R	Jochen Mass	McLaren	McLaren-Ford Cosworth M23	35 laps/accident	12
R	John Watson	Penske	Penske-Ford Cosworth PC4	33 laps/engine	4
R	Kazuyoshi Hoshino	Heros Racing	Tyrrell-Ford Cosworth 007	27 laps/tyre	21
R	Arturo Merzario	Walter Wolf Racing	Williams-Ford Cosworth FW05	23 laps/gearbox	19
R	Emerson Fittipaldi	Fittipaldi	Fittipaldi-Ford Cosworth FD04	9 laps/withdrawn	23
R	Carlos Pace	Brabham	Brabham-Alfa Romeo BT45	7 laps/withdrawn	6
R	Niki Lauda	Ferrari	Ferrari 312T2	2 laps/withdrawn	3
R	Larry Perkins	Brabham	Brabham-Alfa Romeo BT45	1 lap/withdrawn	17
R	Ronnie Peterson	March	March-Ford Cosworth 761	0 laps/engine	9
NS	Masami Kuwashima	Walter Wolf Racing	Williams-Ford Cosworth FW05	Binder raced car	26
DNQ	Tony Trimmer	Maki	Maki-Ford Cosworth F102A	-	27

Pole: Andretti, 1m12.770s, 133.994mph/215.643kph. Fastest lap: Laffite, 1m19.970s, 121.930mph/196.228kph (Hasemi, 1m18.23, officially credited but thought to be an error). Race leaders: Hunt 1-61, Depailler 62-63, Andretti 64-73

CLASSIC CAR: TYRRELL P34

The Tyrrell 007 was a winning car, but its replacement was unexpectedly different as Derek Gardner designed it so that it had two regular-sized wheels at the back and four small ones at the front, both to reduce frontal area and to increase the amount of tyre contact with the track. Jody Scheckter took to it well and won on his third outing, at the Swedish GP, and augmented that with four second places, as did Patrick Depailler. Looking at this radical concept from a different angle, March and Williams later tried four wheels at the back, but they never raced them.

WORLD DRIVERS' CHAMPIONSHIP FINAL RESULTS

Pos	Driver	Nat	Car-Engine	R1	R2	R3	R4	R5	R6
1	James Hunt	GBR	McLaren-Ford Cosworth M23	RP	2P	R	1P	R	R
2	Niki Lauda	AUT	Ferrari 312T	1	1F	2	-	-	-
			Ferrari 312T2	-	-	-	2	1PF	1P
3	Jody Scheckter	ZAF	Tyrrell-Ford Cosworth 007	5	4	R	R	-	-
			Tyrrell-Ford Cosworth P34	-	-	-	-	4	2
4	Patrick Depailler	FRA	Tyrrell-Ford Cosworth 007	2	9	3	-	-	-
			Tyrrell-Ford Cosworth P34	-	-	-	R	R	3
5	Clay Regazzoni	CHE	Ferrari 312T	7	R	1PF	-	-	-
			Ferrari 312T2	-	-	-	11	2	14F
6	Mario Andretti	USA	Lotus-Ford Cosworth 77	R	-	-	R	R	-
			Parnelli-Ford Cosworth VPJ4B	-	6	R	-	-	-
7	John Watson	GBR	Penske-Ford Cosworth PC3	R	5	NC	R	7	10
			Penske-Ford Cosworth PC4	-	-	-	-	-	-
7	Jacques Laffite	FRA	Ligier-Matra JS5	R	R	4	12	3	12
9	Jochen Mass	DEU	McLaren-Ford Cosworth M23	6	3	5	RF	6	5
			McLaren-Ford Cosworth M26	-	-	-	-	-	-
10	Gunnar Nilsson	SWE	Lotus-Ford Cosworth 77	-	R	R	3	R	R
11	Ronnie Peterson	SWE	Lotus-Ford Cosworth 77	R	-	-	-	-	-
			March-Ford Cosworth 761	-	R	10	R	R	R
11	Tom Pryce	GBR	Shadow-Ford Cosworth DN5B	3	7	R	8	10	7
			Shadow-Ford Cosworth DN8	-	-	-	-	-	-
13	Hans-Joachim Stuck	DEU	March-Ford Cosworth 761	4	12	R	R	R	4
14	Carlos Pace	BRA	Brabham-Alfa Romeo BT45	10	R	9	6	R	9
14	Alan Jones	AUS	Surtees-Ford Cosworth TS19	-	-	NC	9	5	R
16	Carlos Reutemann	ARG	Brabham-Alfa Romeo BT45	12	R	R	4	R	R
			Ferrari 312T2	-	-	-	-	-	-
16	Emerson Fittipaldi	BRA	Fittipaldi-Ford Cosworth FD04	13	17	6	R	DNQ	6
18	Chris Amon	NZL	Ensign-Ford Cosworth N174	-	14	8	-	-	-
			Ensign-Ford Cosworth N176	-	-	-	5	R	13
19	Rolf Stommelen	DEU	Brabham-Alfa Romeo BT45	-	-	-	-	-	-
			Hesketh-Ford Cosworth 308D	-	-	-	-	-	-
19	Vittorio Brambilla	ITA	March-Ford Cosworth 761	R	8	R	R	R	R

Pos	Driver	R7	R8	R9	R10	R11	R12	R13	R14	R15	R16	Total
1	Hunt	5	1P	DQF	1P	4PF	1	R	1P	1PF	3	69
2	Lauda	-	-	-	-	-	-	-	-	-	-	68
		3	RF	1P	R	-	-	4	8	3	R	
3	Scheckter	-	-	-	-	-	-	-	-	-	-	49
		1P	6	2	2F	R	5	5	4	2	R	
4	Depailler	-	-	-	-	-	-	-	-	-	-	39
		2	2	R	R	R	7	6	2F	R	2	
5	Regazzoni	-	-	-	-	-	-	-	-	-	-	31
		6	R	DQ	9	-	2F	2	6	7	5	
6	Andretti	RF	5	R	12	5	3	R	3	R	1P	22
		-	-	-	-	-	-	-	-	-	-	
7	Watson	-	-	-	-	-	-	-	-	-	-	20
		R	3	3	7	1	R	11	10	6	R	
7	Laffite	4	14	DQ	R	2	R	3P	R	R	7F	20
9	Mass	11	15	R	3	7	-	-	5	4	R	19
		-	-	-	-	-	9	R	-	-	-	
10	Nilsson	R	R	R	5	3	R	13	12	R	6	11
11	Peterson	-	-	-	-	-	-	-	-	-	-	10
		7	19	R	R	6	RP	1F	9	R	R	
11	Pryce	9	8	4	8	R	-	-	-	-	-	10
		-	-	-	-	-	4	8	11	R	R	

Pos	Driver	R7	R8	R9	R10	R11	R12	R13	R14	R15	R16	Total
13	Stuck	R	7	R	R	R	R	R	R	5	R	8
14	Pace	8	4	8	4	R	R	R	7	R	R	7
14	Jones	13	R	5	10	R	8	12	16	8	4	7
16	Reutemann	R	11	R	R	R	R	-	-	-	-	3
		-	-	-	-	-	-	9	-	-	-	
16	Fittipaldi	R	R	6	13	R	R	15	R	9	R	3
18	Amon	-	-	-	-	-	-	-	-	-	-	2
		R	-	R	R	-	-	-	-	-	-	
19	Stommelen	-	-	-	6	-	-	R	-	-	-	1
		-	-	-	-	-	12	-	-	-	-	
19	Brambilla	10	R	R	R	R	6	7	14	R	R	1

WORLD CONSTRUCTORS' CHAMPIONSHIP FINAL RESULTS

Pos	Team-Engine	R1	R2	R3	R4	R5	R6	R7	R8	R9
1	Ferrari	1	1	1	2	1	1	3	-	1
2	McLaren-Ford	6	2	5	1	6	5	5	1	-
3	Tyrrell-Ford	2	4	3	-	4	2	1	2	2
4	Lotus-Ford	-	10	R	3	-	-	-	5	-
5	Penske-Ford	-	5	-	-	7	10	-	3	3
5	Ligier-Matra	-	-	4	12	3	12	4	14	-
7	March-Ford	4	8	10	R	R	4	7	7	-
8	Shadow-Ford	3	7	7	8	9	7	9	8	4
9	Brabham-Alfa Romeo	10	-	9	4	-	9	8	4	8
10	Surtees-Ford	-	11	NC	9	5	-	13	16	5
11	Fittipaldi-Ford	11	17	6	DNQ	-	6	-	-	6
12	Ensign-Ford	-	14	8	5	-	13	-	18	-
13	Parnelli-Ford	-	6	-	-	-	-	-	-	-

Pos	Team-Engine	R10	R11	R12	R13	R14	R15	R16	Total
1	Ferrari	9	-	2	2	6	3	5	83
2	McLaren-Ford	1	4	1	-	1	1	3	74
3	Tyrrell-Ford	2	11	5	5	2	2	2	71
4	Lotus-Ford	5	3	3	13	3	-	1	29
5	Penske-Ford	7	1	-	11	10	6	-	20
5	Ligier-Matra	-	2	-	3	-	-	7	20
7	March-Ford	-	6	6	1	9	5	-	19
8	Shadow-Ford	8	-	4	8	11	10	10	10
9	Brabham-Alfa Romeo	4	-	-	-	7	-	R	9
10	Surtees-Ford	10	9	8	12	15	8	4	7
11	Fittipaldi-Ford	13	-	-	15	-	9	-	3
12	Ensign-Ford	-	-	-	10	13	-	-	2
13	Parnelli-Ford	-	-	-	-	-	-	-	1

SYMBOLS AND GRAND PRIX KEY

Round 1 Brazilian GP
Round 2 South African GP
Round 3 United States GP West
Round 4 Spanish GP
Round 5 Belgian GP
Round 6 Monaco GP
Round 7 Swedish GP
Round 8 French GP
Round 9 British GP
Round 10 German GP
Round 11 Austrian GP
Round 12 Dutch GP
Round 13 Italian GP
Round 14 Canadian GP
Round 15 United States GP
Round 16 Japanese GP

SCORING

1st 9 points
2nd 6 points
3rd 4 points
4th 3 points
5th 2 points
6th 1 point

DNPQ DID NOT PRE-QUALIFY **DNQ** DID NOT QUALIFY **DQ** DISQUALIFIED **EX** EXCLUDED
F FASTEST LAP **NC** NOT CLASSIFIED **NS** NON-STARTER **P** POLE POSITION **R** RETIRED

1977

SEASON SUMMARY

The endless drama of 1976 was going to be a hard act to follow, but the amazing feat of the still burnt Niki Lauda completing his comeback to take a second title is a remarkable tale. That he ended the year clear of the rest is testament to his doggedness. Jody Scheckter moved from Tyrrell to a new team, Wolf, and impressively ended the year as runner-up, proof of how the Ford Cosworth DFV engine gave new outfits a competitive chance. The season marked the DFV's 100th win. Lotus started even more of a revolution by introducing ground effects, with its 78 winning five of the rounds.

ARGENTINIAN GRAND PRIX

BUENOS AIRES • ROUND 1 • DATE: 9TH JANUARY 1977
Laps: 53 • Distance: 196.548miles/316.314km • Weather: Very hot & bright

Pos	Driver	Team	Chassis-Engine	Result	Qual
1	Jody Scheckter	Wolf	Wolf-Ford Cosworth WR1	1h40m11.190s	11
2	Carlos Pace	Brabham	Brabham-Alfa Romeo BT45	1h40m54.430s	6
3	Carlos Reutemann	Ferrari	Ferrari 312T2	1h40m57.210s	7
4	Emerson Fittipaldi	Fittipaldi	Fittipaldi-Ford Cosworth FD04	1h41m06.670s	16
5	Mario Andretti	Lotus	Lotus-Ford Cosworth 78	51 laps/wheel	8
6	Clay Regazzoni	Ensign	Ensign-Ford Cosworth N177	51 laps	12
7	Vittorio Brambilla	Surtees	Surtees-Ford Cosworth TS19	48 laps/fuel injection	13
R	Ian Scheckter	March	March-Ford Cosworth 761B	45 laps/electrical	17
NC	Tom Pryce	Shadow	Shadow-Ford Cosworth DN8	45 laps	9
R	John Watson	Brabham	Brabham-Alfa Romeo BT45	41 laps/suspension	2
R	Alex Ribeiro	March	March-Ford Cosworth 761B	39 laps/gear lever	20
NC	Jacques Laffite	Ligier	Ligier-Matra JS7	37 laps	15
R	Patrick Depailler	Tyrrell	Tyrrell-Ford Cosworth P34	32 laps/overheating	3
R	James Hunt	McLaren	McLaren-Ford Cosworth M23	31 laps/suspension	1
R	Jochen Mass	McLaren	McLaren-Ford Cosworth M23	28 laps/spun off	5
R	Ronnie Peterson	Tyrrell	Tyrrell-Ford Cosworth P34	28 laps/spun off	14
R	Ingo Hoffmann	Fittipaldi	Fittipaldi-Ford Cosworth FD04	22 laps/engine	19
R	Niki Lauda	Ferrari	Ferrari 312T2	20 laps/fuel system	4
R	Hans Binder	Surtees	Surtees-Ford Cosworth TS19	18 laps/accident	18
R	Renzo Zorzi	Shadow	Shadow-Ford Cosworth DN5B	2 laps/gearbox	21
NS	Gunnar Nilsson	Lotus	Lotus-Ford Cosworth 78	Andretti drove car	10

Pole: Hunt, 1m48.680s, 122.842mph/197.695kph. Fastest lap: Hunt, 1m51.060s, 120.209mph/193.458kph on Lap 21. Race leaders: Watson 1-10 & 32-34, Hunt 11-31, Pace 35-47, Scheckter 48-53

STARTING WITH A BANG

Oil trader Walter Wolf had a lot of money and wanted success in F1. He had been a difficult partner for Frank Williams in 1976, so formed his own team for 1977, with a car designed by Harvey Postlethwaite and powered by a Cosworth DFV. Jody Scheckter was straight on the pace with it and won the opening race in Argentina, then twice more.

ANOTHER UNNECESSARY DEATH

Any death caused by stupidity is hard to take, yet this is what befell Tom Pryce at Kyalami. His Shadow team-mate Renzo Zorzi pulled off and had an engine fire. A marshal then ran across the straight with an extinguisher and was hit by unsighted Pryce, killing both. A fortnight later, Brabham's Carlos Pace was killed in a plane crash.

BRAZILIAN GRAND PRIX

INTERLAGOS • ROUND 2 • DATE: 23RD JANUARY 1977
Laps: 40 • Distance: 197.598miles/318.4km • Weather: Very hot & bright

Pos	Driver	Team	Chassis-Engine	Result	Qual
1	Carlos Reutemann	Ferrari	Ferrari 312T2	1h45m07.720s	2
2	James Hunt	McLaren	McLaren-Ford Cosworth M23	1h45m18.430s	1
3	Niki Lauda	Ferrari	Ferrari 312T2	1h46m55.230s	13
4	Emerson Fittipaldi	Fittipaldi	Fittipaldi-Ford Cosworth FD04	39 laps	16
5	Gunnar Nilsson	Lotus	Lotus-Ford Cosworth 78	39 laps	10
6	Renzo Zorzi	Shadow	Shadow-Ford Cosworth DN5B	39 laps	18
7	Ingo Hoffmann	Fittipaldi	Fittipaldi-Ford Cosworth FD04	38 laps	19
R	Tom Pryce	Shadow	Shadow-Ford Cosworth DN8	33 laps/engine	5
R	Carlos Pace	Brabham	Brabham-Alfa Romeo BT45	33 laps/accident	12
R	Hans Binder	Surtees	Surtees-Ford Cosworth TS19	32 laps/suspension	20
R	John Watson	Brabham	Brabham-Alfa Romeo BT45	30 laps/accident	7
R	Jacques Laffite	Ligier	Ligier-Matra JS7	26 laps/accident	14
R	Patrick Depailler	Tyrrell	Tyrrell-Ford Cosworth P34	23 laps/accident	6
R	Mario Andretti	Lotus	Lotus-Ford Cosworth 78	19 laps/ignition	3
R	Alex Ribeiro	March	March-Ford Cosworth 761B	16 laps/engine	21
R	Jochen Mass	McLaren	McLaren-Ford Cosworth M23	12 laps/accident	4
R	Ronnie Peterson	Tyrrell	Tyrrell-Ford Cosworth P34	12 laps/accident	8
R	Clay Regazzoni	Ensign	Ensign-Ford Cosworth N177	12 laps/accident	9
R	Vittorio Brambilla	Surtees	Surtees-Ford Cosworth TS19	11 laps/accident	11
R	Jody Scheckter	Wolf	Wolf-Ford Cosworth WR1	11 laps/engine	15
R	Ian Scheckter	March	March-Ford Cosworth 761B	1 lap/transmission	17
R	Larry Perkins	BRM	BRM P207	1 lap/overheating	22

Pole: Hunt, 2m30.110s, 118.619mph/190.900kph. Fastest lap: Hunt, 2m34.550s, 115.214mph/185.420kph on Lap 33. Race leaders: Pace 1-6, Hunt 7-22, Reutemann 23-40

SOUTH AFRICAN GRAND PRIX

KYALAMI • ROUND 3 • DATE: 5TH MARCH 1977
Laps: 78 • Distance: 198.908miles/320.112km • Weather: Warm but dull

Pos	Driver	Team	Chassis-Engine	Result	Qual
1	Niki Lauda	Ferrari	Ferrari 312T2	1h42m21.600s	3
2	Jody Scheckter	Wolf	Wolf-Ford Cosworth WR1	1h42m26.800s	5
3	Patrick Depailler	Tyrrell	Tyrrell-Ford Cosworth P34	1h42m27.300s	4
4	James Hunt	McLaren	McLaren-Ford Cosworth M23	1h42m31.100s	1
5	Jochen Mass	McLaren	McLaren-Ford Cosworth M23	1h42m41.500s	12
6	John Watson	Brabham	Brabham-Alfa Romeo BT45	1h42m41.800s	11
7	Vittorio Brambilla	Surtees	Surtees-Ford Cosworth TS19	1h42m45.200s	14

Pos	Driver	Team	Chassis-Engine	Result	Qual
8	Carlos Reutemann	Ferrari	Ferrari 312T2	1h42m48.300s	8
9	Clay Regazzoni	Ensign	Ensign-Ford Cosworth N177	1h43m07.800s	16
10	Emerson Fittipaldi	Fittipaldi	Fittipaldi-Ford Cosworth FD04	1h43m33.300s	9
11	Hans Binder	Surtees	Surtees-Ford Cosworth TS19	77 laps	19
12	Gunnar Nilsson	Lotus	Lotus-Ford Cosworth 78	77 laps	10
13	Carlos Pace	Brabham	Brabham-Alfa Romeo BT45B	76 laps	2
14	Brett Lunger	BS Fabrications	March-Ford Cosworth 761	76 laps	23
15	Larry Perkins	BRM	BRM P201B	73 laps	22
R	Alex Ribeiro	March	March-Ford Cosworth 761B	66 laps/engine	17
R	Hans-Joachim Stuck	March	March-Ford Cosworth 761B	55 laps/engine	18
R	Mario Andretti	Lotus	Lotus-Ford Cosworth 78	43 laps/accident	6
R	Boy Hayje	RAM Racing	March-Ford Cosworth 761	33 laps/gearbox	21
R	Jacques Laffite	Ligier	Ligier-Matra JS7	22 laps/accident	12
R	Tom Pryce	Shadow	Shadow-Ford Cosworth DN8	22 laps/fatal accident	15
R	Renzo Zorzi	Shadow	Shadow-Ford Cosworth DN8	21 laps/oil leak	20
R	Ronnie Peterson	Tyrrell	Tyrrell-Ford Cosworth P34	5 laps/fuel system	7

Pole: Hunt, 1m15.960s, 120.858mph/194.502kph. Fastest lap: Watson, 1m17.630s, 118.259mph/190.320kph on Lap 7. Race leaders: Hunt 1-6, Lauda 7-78

UNITED STATES GRAND PRIX WEST

LONG BEACH • ROUND 4 • DATE: 3RD APRIL 1977
Laps: 80 • Distance: 161.561miles/260.08km • Weather: Warm & bright

Pos	Driver	Team	Chassis-Engine	Result	Qual
1	Mario Andretti	Lotus	Lotus-Ford Cosworth 78	1h51m35.470s	2
2	Niki Lauda	Ferrari	Ferrari 312T2	1h51m36.243s	1
3	Jody Scheckter	Wolf	Wolf-Ford Cosworth WR1	1h51m40.327s	3
4	Patrick Depailler	Tyrrell	Tyrrell-Ford Cosworth P34	1h52m49.957s	12
5	Emerson Fittipaldi	Fittipaldi	Fittipaldi-Ford Cosworth FD04	1h52m56.378s	7
6	Jean-Pierre Jarier	ATS	Penske-Ford Cosworth PC4	79 laps	9
7	James Hunt	McLaren	McLaren-Ford Cosworth M23	79 laps	8
8	Gunnar Nilsson	Lotus	Lotus-Ford Cosworth 78	79 laps	16
9	Jacques Laffite	Ligier	Ligier-Matra JS7	78 laps/electrical	5
10	Brian Henton	March	March-Ford Cosworth 761B	77 laps	18
11	Hans Binder	Surtees	Surtees-Ford Cosworth TS19	77 laps	19
R	Ronnie Peterson	Tyrrell	Tyrrell-Ford Cosworth P34	62 laps/fuel system	10
R	Clay Regazzoni	Ensign	Ensign-Ford Cosworth N177	57 laps/gearbox	13
R	Hans-Joachim Stuck	Brabham	Brabham-Alfa Romeo BT45B	53 laps/brakes	17
R	Alan Jones	Shadow	Shadow-Ford Cosworth DN8	40 laps/gearbox	14
R	Jochen Mass	McLaren	McLaren-Ford Cosworth M23	39 laps/handling	15
DQ	John Watson	Brabham	Brabham-Alfa Romeo BT45B	33 laps/outside assistance	6
R	Renzo Zorzi	Shadow	Shadow-Ford Cosworth DN8	27 laps/gearbox	20
R	Alex Ribeiro	March	March-Ford Cosworth 761B	15 laps/gearbox	22
R	Carlos Reutemann	Ferrari	Ferrari 312T2	5 laps/accident	4
R	Brett Lunger	BS Fabrications	March-Ford Cosworth 761	4 laps/accident	21
R	Vittorio Brambilla	Surtees	Surtees-Ford Cosworth TS19	0 laps/accident	11

Pole: Lauda, 1m21.630s, 89.088mph/143.373kph. Fastest lap: Lauda, 1m22.753s, 87.879mph/141.428kph on Lap 62. Race leaders: Scheckter 1-76, Andretti 77-80

SPANISH GRAND PRIX

JARAMA • ROUND 5 • DATE: 8TH MAY 1977
Laps: 75 • Distance: 158.649miles/255.322km • Weather: Warm & bright

Pos	Driver	Team	Chassis-Engine	Result	Qual
1	Mario Andretti	Lotus	Lotus-Ford Cosworth 78	1h42m52.220s	1
2	Carlos Reutemann	Ferrari	Ferrari 312T2	1h43m08.070s	4
3	Jody Scheckter	Wolf	Wolf-Ford Cosworth WR2	1h43m16.730s	5
4	Jochen Mass	McLaren	McLaren-Ford Cosworth M23	1h43m17.090s	9
5	Gunnar Nilsson	Lotus	Lotus-Ford Cosworth 78	1h43m58.050s	12
6	Hans-Joachim Stuck	Brabham	Brabham-Alfa Romeo BT45B	74 laps	13
7	Jacques Laffite	Ligier	Ligier-Matra JS7	74 laps	2
8	Ronnie Peterson	Tyrrell	Tyrrell-Ford Cosworth P34	74 laps	15
9	Hans Binder	Surtees	Surtees-Ford Cosworth TS19	73 laps	20
10	Brett Lunger	BS Fabrications	March-Ford Cosworth 761	72 laps	28
11	Ian Scheckter	March	March-Ford Cosworth 761B	72 laps	17
12	Patrick Neve	Williams	March-Ford Cosworth 761	71 laps	22
13	Emilio de Villota	Iberia Airlines	McLaren-Ford Cosworth M23	70 laps	23
14	Emerson Fittipaldi	Fittipaldi	Fittipaldi-Ford Cosworth FD04	70 laps	19
R	John Watson	Brabham	Brabham-Alfa Romeo BT45B	64 laps/fuel system	6
R	Alan Jones	Shadow	Shadow-Ford Cosworth DN8	56 laps/accident	14
R	Rupert Keegan	Hesketh	Hesketh-Ford Cosworth 308E	32 laps/accident	16
R	Harald Ertl	Hesketh	Hesketh-Ford Cosworth 308E	29 laps/radiator	10
R	Renzo Zorzi	Shadow	Shadow-Ford Cosworth DN8	25 laps/engine	24
R	Arturo Merzario	Merzario	March-Ford Cosworth 761B	16 laps/suspension	21
R	Patrick Depailler	Tyrrell	Tyrrell-Ford Cosworth P34	12 laps/engine	10
R	James Hunt	McLaren	McLaren-Ford Cosworth M26	10 laps/engine	7
R	Clay Regazzoni	Ensign	Ensign-Ford Cosworth N177	9 laps/accident	8
R	Vittorio Brambilla	Surtees	Surtees-Ford Cosworth TS19	9 laps/accident	11
NS	Niki Lauda	Ferrari	Ferrari 312T2	driver injured	3
DNQ	Jean-Pierre Jarier	ATS	Penske-Ford Cosworth PC4	-	26
DNQ	Alex Ribeiro	March	March-Ford Cosworth 761B	-	27
DNQ	Boy Hayje	RAM Racing	March-Ford Cosworth 761	-	28
DNQ	Brian Henton	British F1 Racing	March-Ford Cosworth 761	-	29
DNQ	David Purley	LEC	Lec-Ford Cosworth CRP1	-	30
DNQ	Conny Andersson	BRM	BRM P207	-	31

Pole: Andretti, 1m18.700s, 96.762mph/155.724kph. Fastest lap: Laffite, 1m20.810s, 94.237mph/151.660kph on Lap 5. Race leaders: Andretti 1-75

FLYING THE TRICOLORE

The Ligier team became a winning outfit in only its second year in F1. This day of days for the French team came at the Swedish GP at Anderstorp when Jacques Laffite was heading for second when, with three laps to go, Mario Andretti's dominant Lotus pitted. It was the first win for a French driver in a French car with a French engine.

MONACO GRAND PRIX

MONTE CARLO • ROUND 6 • DATE: 22ND MAY 1977
Laps: 76 • Distance: 156.406miles/251.712km • Weather: Warm & bright

Pos	Driver	Team	Chassis-Engine	Result	Qual
1	Jody Scheckter	Wolf	Wolf-Ford Cosworth WR1	1h57m52.770s	2
2	Niki Lauda	Ferrari	Ferrari 312T2	1h57m52.860s	6
3	Carlos Reutemann	Ferrari	Ferrari 312T2	1h58m25.570s	3
4	Jochen Mass	McLaren	McLaren-Ford Cosworth M23	1h58m27.370s	9
5	Mario Andretti	Lotus	Lotus-Ford Cosworth 78	1h58m28.320s	10
6	Alan Jones	Shadow	Shadow-Ford Cosworth DN8	1h58m29.380s	11
7	Jacques Laffite	Ligier	Ligier-Matra JS7	1h58m57.210s	16
8	Vittorio Brambilla	Surtees	Surtees-Ford Cosworth TS19	1h59m01.410s	14
9	Riccardo Patrese	Shadow	Shadow-Ford Cosworth DN8	75 laps	15
10	Jacky Ickx	Ensign	Ensign-Ford Cosworth N177	75 laps	17
11	Jean-Pierre Jarier	ATS	Penske-Ford Cosworth PC4	74 laps	12
12	Rupert Keegan	Hesketh	Hesketh-Ford Cosworth 308E	73 laps	20
R	Gunnar Nilsson	Lotus	Lotus-Ford Cosworth 78	51 laps/gearbox	13
R	John Watson	Brabham	Brabham-Alfa Romeo BT45B	48 laps/gearbox	1
R	Patrick Depailler	Tyrrell	Tyrrell-Ford Cosworth P34	46 laps/gearbox	8
R	Hans Binder	Surtees	Surtees-Ford Cosworth TS19	41 laps/fuel system	19
R	Emerson Fittipaldi	Fittipaldi	Fittipaldi-Ford Cosworth FD04	37 laps/engine	18
R	James Hunt	McLaren	McLaren-Ford Cosworth M23	25 laps/engine	7
R	Hans-Joachim Stuck	Brabham	Brabham-Alfa Romeo BT45B	19 laps/electrical	5
R	Ronnie Peterson	Tyrrell	Tyrrell-Ford Cosworth P34	10 laps/brakes	4
DNQ	Arturo Merzario	Merzario	March-Ford Cosworth 761B	-	21
DNQ	Boy Hayje	RAM Racing	March-Ford Cosworth 761	-	22
DNQ	Harald Ertl	Hesketh	Hesketh-Ford Cosworth 308E	-	23
DNQ	Clay Regazzoni	Ensign	Ensign-Ford Cosworth N177	-	24
DNQ	Alex Ribeiro	March	March-Ford Cosworth 761B	-	25
DNQ	Ian Scheckter	March	March-Ford Cosworth 761B	driver injured	26

Pole: Watson, 1m29.860s, 82.447mph/132.686kph. Fastest lap: Scheckter, 1m31.070s, 81.349mph/130.920kph on Lap 35. Race leaders: Scheckter 1-76

BELGIAN GRAND PRIX

ZOLDER • ROUND 7 • DATE: 5TH JUNE 1977
Laps: 70 • Distance: 185.189miles/298.34km • Weather: Cool & wet

Pos	Driver	Team	Chassis-Engine	Result	Qual
1	Gunnar Nilsson	Lotus	Lotus-Ford Cosworth 78	1h55m05.710s	3
2	Niki Lauda	Ferrari	Ferrari 312T2	1h55m19.900s	11
3	Ronnie Peterson	Tyrrell	Tyrrell-Ford Cosworth P34	1h55m25.660s	8
4	Vittorio Brambilla	Surtees	Surtees-Ford Cosworth TS19	1h55m30.690s	12
5	Alan Jones	Shadow	Shadow-Ford Cosworth DN8	1h56m21.180s	17
6	Hans-Joachim Stuck	Brabham	Brabham-Alfa Romeo BT45B	69 laps	18
7	James Hunt	McLaren	McLaren-Ford Cosworth M26	69 laps	9
8	Patrick Depailler	Tyrrell	Tyrrell-Ford Cosworth P34	69 laps	5
9	Harald Ertl	Hesketh	Hesketh-Ford Cosworth 308E	69 laps	25
10	Patrick Neve	Williams	March-Ford Cosworth 761	68 laps	24
11	Jean-Pierre Jarier	ATS	Penske-Ford Cosworth PC4	68 laps	26
12	Larry Perkins	Surtees	Surtees-Ford Cosworth TS19	67 laps	23
13	David Purley	LEC	Lec-Ford Cosworth CRP1	67 laps	20
14	Arturo Merzario	Merzario	March-Ford Cosworth 761B	65 laps	14

Pos	Driver	Team	Chassis-Engine	Result	Qual
15	Boy Hayje	RAM Racing	March-Ford Cosworth 761	63 laps	27
R	Jody Scheckter	Wolf	Wolf-Ford Cosworth WR3	62 laps/engine	4
R	Jochen Mass	McLaren	McLaren-Ford Cosworth M23	39 laps/accident	6
R	Jacques Laffite	Ligier	Ligier-Matra JS7	32 laps/engine	10
R	Clay Regazzoni	Ensign	Ensign-Ford Cosworth N177	29 laps/engine	13
R	Carlos Reutemann	Ferrari	Ferrari 312T2	14 laps/accident	7
R	Rupert Keegan	Hesketh	Hesketh-Ford Cosworth 308E	14 laps/accident	19
R	Riccardo Patrese	Shadow	Shadow-Ford Cosworth DN8	12 laps/accident	15
R	Ian Scheckter	March	March-Ford Cosworth 761B	8 laps/accident	21
R	Emerson Fittipaldi	Fittipaldi	Fittipaldi-Ford Cosworth F5	2 laps/electrical	16
R	Mario Andretti	Lotus	Lotus-Ford Cosworth 78	0 laps/accident	1
R	John Watson	Brabham	Brabham-Alfa Romeo BT45B	0 laps/accident	2
NS	Brett Lunger	BS Fabrications	McLaren-Ford Cosworth M23	car not ready	22
DNQ	Emilio de Villota	Iberia Airlines	McLaren-Ford Cosworth M23	-	28
DNQ	Conny Andersson	BRM	BRM P207	-	29
DNQ	Alex Ribeiro	March	March-Ford Cosworth 761B	-	30
DNQ	Bernard de Dryver	British F1 Racing	March-Ford Cosworth 761	-	31
DNQ	Hector Rebaque	Hesketh	Hesketh-Ford Cosworth 308E	-	32

Pole: Andretti, 1m24.640s, 112.639mph/181.275kph. Fastest lap: Nilsson, 1m27.360s, 109.131mph/175.630kph on Lap 53. Race leaders: Scheckter 1-16, Mass 17-18, Brambilla 19-22, Lauda 23-49, Nilsson 50-70

FALLNG JUST SHORT

John Watson was wholly in control of the French GP at Dijon-Prenois, poised to give Brabham its first win since changing to Alfa Romeo engines for 1976. But then, shortly after starting the final lap, his Italian flat-12 engine spluttered and then spluttered again as it sought fuel. In a flash, Mario Andretti's Lotus drove past to victory.

SWEDISH GRAND PRIX

ANDERSTORP • ROUND 8 • DATE: 19TH JUNE 1977
Laps: 72 • Distance: 179.760miles/289.296km • Weather: Warm & bright

Pos	Driver	Team	Chassis-Engine	Result	Qual
1	Jacques Laffite	Ligier	Ligier-Matra JS7	1h46m55.520s	8
2	Jochen Mass	McLaren	McLaren-Ford Cosworth M23	1h47m03.969s	9
3	Carlos Reutemann	Ferrari	Ferrari 312T2	1h47m09.889s	12
4	Patrick Depailler	Tyrrell	Tyrrell-Ford Cosworth P34	1h47m11,828s	6
5	John Watson	Brabham	Brabham-Alfa Romeo BT45B	1h47m14.255s	2
6	Mario Andretti	Lotus	Lotus-Ford Cosworth 78	1h47m20.797s	1
7	Clay Regazzoni	Ensign	Ensign-Ford Cosworth N177	1h47m26.786s	14
8	Jean-Pierre Jarier	ATS	Penske-Ford Cosworth PC4	1h48m00.087s	17
9	Jackie Oliver	Shadow	Shadow-Ford Cosworth DN8	1h48m18.879s	16
10	Hans-Joachim Stuck	Brabham	Brabham-Alfa Romeo BT45B	71 laps	5
11	Brett Lunger	BS Fabrications	McLaren-Ford Cosworth M23	71 laps	22
12	James Hunt	McLaren	McLaren-Ford Cosworth M26	71 laps	3
13	Rupert Keegan	Hesketh	Hesketh-Ford Cosworth 308E	71 laps	24
14	David Purley	LEC	Lec-Ford Cosworth CRP1	70 laps	19

Pos	Driver	Team	Chassis-Engine	Result	Qual
15	Patrick Neve	Williams	March-Ford Cosworth 761	69 laps	20
16	Harald Ertl	Hesketh	Hesketh-Ford Cosworth 308E	68 laps	23
17	Alan Jones	Shadow	Shadow-Ford Cosworth DN8	67 laps	11
18	Emerson Fittipaldi	Fittipaldi	Fittipaldi-Ford Cosworth FD04	66 laps	18
19	Gunnar Nilsson	Lotus	Lotus-Ford Cosworth 78	64 laps/wheel	7
R	Ian Scheckter	March	March-Ford Cosworth 761B	61 laps/transmission	21
R	Vittorio Brambilla	Surtees	Surtees-Ford Cosworth TS19	52 laps/fuel pressure	13
R	Niki Lauda	Ferrari	Ferrari 312T2	47 laps/handling	15
R	Jody Scheckter	Wolf	Wolf-Ford Cosworth WR1	29 laps/accident	4
R	Ronnie Peterson	Tyrrell	Tyrrell-Ford Cosworth P34	7 laps/ignition	10
DNQ	Alex Ribeiro	March	March-Ford Cosworth 761B	-	25
DNQ	Emilio de Villota	Iberia Airlines	McLaren-Ford Cosworth M23	-	26
DNQ	Larry Perkins	Surtees	Surtees-Ford Cosworth TS19	-	27
DNQ	Boy Hayje	RAM Racing	March-Ford Cosworth 761	-	28
DNQ	Hector Rebaque	Hesketh	Hesketh-Ford Cosworth 308E	-	29
DNQ	Conny Andersson	BRM	BRM P207	-	30
DNQ	Mikko Kozarowitzky	RAM Racing	March-Ford Cosworth 761	-	31

Pole: Andretti, 1m25.404s, 105.241mph/169.369kph. Fastest lap: Andretti, 1m27.607s, 102.594mph/165.110kph. Race leaders: Watson 1, Andretti 2-69, Laffite 70-72

RENAULT INTRODUCES TURBOS

Superchargers were permitted from 1950 until 1960, used to add power. In 1977, 11 years after forced induction was allowed again, Renault brought in a different sort of technology: turbocharging. This recirculated the exhaust gases through a turbine that forced fresh air back into the engine cylinders, adding power but not, at first, reliability.

FRENCH GRAND PRIX

DIJON-PRENOIS • ROUND 9 • DATE: 3RD JULY 1977
Laps: 80 • Distance: 188.896miles/304.0km • Weather: Hot & bright

Pos	Driver	Team	Chassis-Engine	Result	Qual
1	Mario Andretti	Lotus	Lotus-Ford Cosworth 78	1h39m40.130s	1
2	John Watson	Brabham	Brabham-Alfa Romeo BT45B	1h39m41.680s	4
3	James Hunt	McLaren	McLaren-Ford Cosworth M26	1h40m14.000s	2
4	Gunnar Nilsson	Lotus	Lotus-Ford Cosworth 78	1h40m51.210s	3
5	Niki Lauda	Ferrari	Ferrari 312T2	1h40m54.280s	9
6	Carlos Reutemann	Ferrari	Ferrari 312T2	79 laps	6
7	Clay Regazzoni	Ensign	Ensign-Ford Cosworth N177	79 laps	16
8	Jacques Laffite	Ligier	Ligier-Matra JS7	78 laps	5
9	Jochen Mass	McLaren	McLaren-Ford Cosworth M23	78 laps	7
10	Rupert Keegan	Hesketh	Hesketh-Ford Cosworth 308E	78 laps	14
11	Emerson Fittipaldi	Fittipaldi	Fittipaldi-Ford Cosworth F5	77 laps	22
12	Ronnie Peterson	Tyrrell	Tyrrell-Ford Cosworth P34	77 laps	17
13	Vittorio Brambilla	Surtees	Surtees-Ford Cosworth TS19	77 laps	11
NC	Ian Scheckter	March	March-Ford Cosworth 761B	69 laps	20
R	Jody Scheckter	Wolf	Wolf-Ford Cosworth WR3	66 laps/accident	8
R	Hans-Joachim Stuck	Brabham	Brabham-Alfa Romeo BT45B	64 laps/accident	13
R	Alan Jones	Shadow	Shadow-Ford Cosworth DN8	60 laps/transmission	10

Pos	Driver	Team	Chassis-Engine	Result	Qual
R	Arturo Merzario	Merzario	March-Ford Cosworth 761B	27 laps/gearbox	18
R	Patrick Depailler	Tyrrell	Tyrrell-Ford Cosworth P34	21 laps/accident	12
R	Riccardo Patrese	Shadow	Shadow-Ford Cosworth DN8	6 laps/engine	15
R	David Purley	LEC	Lec-Ford Cosworth CRP1	5 laps/accident	21
R	Jean-Pierre Jarier	ATS	Penske-Ford Cosworth PC4	4 laps/accident	19
DNQ	Alex Ribeiro	March	March-Ford Cosworth 761B	-	23
DNQ	Patrick Neve	Williams	March-Ford Cosworth 761	-	24
DNQ	Brett Lunger	BS Fabrications	McLaren-Ford Cosworth M23	-	25
DNQ	Harald Ertl	Hesketh	Hesketh-Ford Cosworth 308E	-	26
DNQ	Larry Perkins	Surtees	Surtees-Ford Cosworth TS19	-	27
DNQ	Hector Rebaque	Hesketh	Hesketh-Ford Cosworth 308E	-	28
DNQ	Patrick Tambay	Surtees	Surtees-Ford Cosworth TS19	-	29
DNQ	Conny Andersson	BRM	BRM P207	-	30

Pole: Andretti, 1m12.210s, 117.717mph/189.447kph. Fastest lap: Andretti, 1m13.750s, 115.258mph/185.490kph on Lap 76. Race leaders: Hunt 1-4, Watson 5-79, Andretti 80

NOT QUALIFIED, NO PROBLEM...

So, you have failed to qualify for your home grand prix in Germany. Do you go home? Not if your name is Hans Heyer and you fancy a race. He arranged for someone to leave a gate open and simply drove his ATS-run Penske through it and onto the grid. He was last by a distance, but organisers' blushes were spared when his gear linkage broke.

BRITISH GRAND PRIX

SILVERSTONE • ROUND 10 • DATE: 16TH JULY 1977
Laps: 68 • Distance: 199.375miles/320.864km • Weather: Warm & bright

Pos	Driver	Team	Chassis-Engine	Result	Qual
1	James Hunt	McLaren	McLaren-Ford Cosworth M26	1h31m46.060s	1
2	Niki Lauda	Ferrari	Ferrari 312T2	1h32m04.370s	3
3	Gunnar Nilsson	Lotus	Lotus-Ford Cosworth 78	1h32m05.630s	5
4	Jochen Mass	McLaren	McLaren-Ford Cosworth M26	1h32m33.820s	11
5	Hans-Joachim Stuck	Brabham	Brabham-Alfa Romeo BT45B	1h32m57.790s	7
6	Jacques Laffite	Ligier	Ligier-Matra JS7	67 laps	15
7	Alan Jones	Shadow	Shadow-Ford Cosworth DN8	67 laps	12
8	Vittorio Brambilla	Surtees	Surtees-Ford Cosworth TS19	67 laps	8
9	Jean-Pierre Jarier	ATS	Penske-Ford Cosworth PC4	67 laps	20
10	Patrick Neve	Williams	March-Ford Cosworth 761	66 laps	26
11	Gilles Villeneuve	McLaren	McLaren-Ford Cosworth M23	66 laps	9
12	Vern Schuppan	Surtees	Surtees-Ford Cosworth TS19	66 laps	23
13	Brett Lunger	BS Fabrications	McLaren-Ford Cosworth M23	64 laps	19
14	Mario Andretti	Lotus	Lotus-Ford Cosworth 78	62 laps/engine	6
15	Carlos Reutemann	Ferrari	Ferrari 312T2	62 laps	14
R	John Watson	Brabham	Brabham-Alfa Romeo BT45B	60 laps/fuel system	2
R	Jody Scheckter	Wolf	Wolf-Ford Cosworth WR1	59 laps/engine	4
R	Emerson Fittipaldi	Fittipaldi	Fittipaldi-Ford Cosworth F5	42 laps/throttle	22
R	Arturo Merzario	Merzario	March-Ford Cosworth 761B	28 laps/transmission	17
R	Riccardo Patrese	Shadow	Shadow-Ford Cosworth DN8	20 laps/fuel pressure	25
R	Patrick Depailler	Tyrrell	Tyrrell-Ford Cosworth P34	16 laps/brakes	18

Pos	Driver	Team	Chassis-Engine	Result	Qual
R	Jean-Pierre Jabouille	Renault	Renault RS01	16 laps/turbo	21
R	Ian Scheckter	March	March-Ford Cosworth 761B	6 laps/accident	24
R	Patrick Tambay	Theodore	Ensign-Ford Cosworth N177	3 laps/electrical	10
R	Ronnie Peterson	Tyrrell	Tyrrell-Ford Cosworth P34	3 laps/engine	16
R	Rupert Keegan	Hesketh	Hesketh-Ford Cosworth 308E	0 laps/accident	13
DNQ	Alex Ribeiro	March	March-Ford Cosworth 761B	-	27
DNQ	Clay Regazzoni	Ensign	Ensign-Ford Cosworth N177	-	28
DNQ	Brian Henton	British F1 Racing	March-Ford Cosworth 761	-	28
DNQ	Emilio de Villota	Iberia Airlines	McLaren-Ford Cosworth M23	-	30
DNPQ	David Purley	LEC	Lec-Ford Cosworth CRP1	driver injured	31
DNPQ	Andy Sutcliffe	RAM Racing	March-Ford Cosworth 761	-	32
DNPQ	Guy Edwards	BRM	BRM P207	-	33
DNPQ	Tony Trimmer	Melchester Racing	Surtees-Ford Cosworth TS19	-	34
DNPQ	Brian McGuire	Brian McGuire	McGuire-Ford Cosworth BM1	-	35
DNPQ	Mikko Kozarowitzky	RAM Racing	March-Ford Cosworth 761	-	36

Pole: Hunt, 1m18.490s, 134.478mph/216.421kph. Fastest lap: Hunt, 1m19.600s, 132.600mph/213.400kph on Lap 48. Race leaders: Watson 1-49, Hunt 50-68

CIRCUIT CHANGES

The World Championship didn't include any new circuits in 1977, but the Osterreichring sported a chicane at the previously sweeping first corner, the Hella-Licht, as a result of Mark Donohue's accident there in 1975. Meanwhile, Dijon-Prenois was augmented by the addition of a loop that added 0.33 miles (0.5km) to its meagre track length.

GERMAN GRAND PRIX

HOCKENHEIM • ROUND 11 • DATE: 31ST JULY 1977
Laps: 47 • Distance: 198.268miles/319.083km • Weather: Warm & bright

Pos	Driver	Team	Chassis-Engine	Result	Qual
1	Niki Lauda	Ferrari	Ferrari 312T2	1h31m48.620s	3
2	Jody Scheckter	Wolf	Wolf-Ford Cosworth WR2	1h32m02.950s	1
3	Hans-Joachim Stuck	Brabham	Brabham-Alfa Romeo BT45B	1h32m09.520s	5
4	Carlos Reutemann	Ferrari	Ferrari 312T2	1h32m48.890s	8
5	Vittorio Brambilla	Surtees	Surtees-Ford Cosworth TS19	1h33m15.990s	10
6	Patrick Tambay	Theodore	Ensign-Ford Cosworth N177	1h33m18.430s	11
7	Vern Schuppan	Surtees	Surtees-Ford Cosworth TS19	46 laps	19
8	Alex Ribeiro	March	March-Ford Cosworth 761B	46 laps	20
9	Ronnie Peterson	Tyrrell	Tyrrell-Ford Cosworth P34	42 laps/engine	14
10	Riccardo Patrese	Shadow	Shadow-Ford Cosworth DN8	42 laps/wheel	16
R	Rupert Keegan	Hesketh	Hesketh-Ford Cosworth 308E	40 laps/accident	23
R	Mario Andretti	Lotus	Lotus-Ford Cosworth 78	34 laps/engine	7
R	James Hunt	McLaren	McLaren-Ford Cosworth M26	32 laps/fuel pump	4
R	Gunnar Nilsson	Lotus	Lotus-Ford Cosworth 78	31 laps/engine	9
R	Jochen Mass	McLaren	McLaren-Ford Cosworth M26	26 laps/gearbox	13
R	Patrick Depailler	Tyrrell	Tyrrell-Ford Cosworth P34	22 laps/engine	15
R	Jacques Laffite	Ligier	Ligier-Matra JS7	21 laps/engine	6
R	Hector Rebaque	Hesketh	Hesketh-Ford Cosworth 308E	20 laps/engine	24

Pos	Driver	Team	Chassis-Engine	Result	Qual
R	Brett Lunger	BS Fabrications	McLaren-Ford Cosworth M23	14 laps/accident	21
R	Ian Scheckter	March	March-Ford Cosworth 761B	9 laps/clutch	19
R	Hans Heyer	ATS	Penske-Ford Cosworth PC4	9 laps/transmission	25
R	John Watson	Brabham	Brabham-Alfa Romeo BT45B	8 laps/engine	2
R	Jean-Pierre Jarier	ATS	Penske-Ford Cosworth PC4	5 laps/transmission	12
R	Alan Jones	Shadow	Shadow-Ford Cosworth DN8	0 laps/accident	17
R	Clay Regazzoni	Ensign	Ensign-Ford Cosworth N177	0 laps/accident	22
DNQ	Patrick Neve	Williams	March-Ford Cosworth 761	-	25
DNQ	Emilio de Villota	Iberia Airlines	McLaren-Ford Cosworth M23	-	26
DNQ	Emerson Fittipaldi	Fittipaldi	Fittipaldi-Ford Cosworth F5	-	28
DNQ	Arturo Merzario	Merzario	March-Ford Cosworth 761B	-	29
DNQ	Teddy Pilette	BRM	BRM P207	-	30

Pole: Scheckter, 1m53.070s, 134.311mph/216.152kph. Fastest lap: Lauda, 1m55.990s, 130.929mph/210.710kph on Lap 28. Race leaders: Scheckter 1-12, Lauda 13-47

AUSTRIAN GRAND PRIX

OSTERREICHRING • ROUND 12 • DATE: 14TH AUGUST 1977
Laps: 54 • Distance: 199.391miles/320.889km • Weather: Warm & bright

Pos	Driver	Team	Chassis-Engine	Result	Qual
1	Alan Jones	Shadow	Shadow-Ford Cosworth DN8	1h37m16.490s	14
2	Niki Lauda	Ferrari	Ferrari 312T2	1h37m36.620s	1
3	Hans-Joachim Stuck	Brabham	Brabham-Alfa Romeo BT45B	1h37m50.990s	4
4	Carlos Reutemann	Ferrari	Ferrari 312T2	1h37m51.240s	5
5	Ronnie Peterson	Tyrrell	Tyrrell-Ford Cosworth P34	1h38m28.580s	15
6	Jochen Mass	McLaren	McLaren-Ford Cosworth M26	53 laps	9
7	Rupert Keegan	Hesketh	Hesketh-Ford Cosworth 308E	53 laps	20
8	John Watson	Brabham	Brabham-Alfa Romeo BT45B	53 laps	12
9	Patrick Neve	Williams	March-Ford Cosworth 761	53 laps	22
10	Brett Lunger	BS Fabrications	McLaren-Ford Cosworth M23	53 laps	17
11	Emerson Fittipaldi	Fittipaldi	Fittipaldi-Ford Cosworth F5	53 laps	23
12	Hans Binder	ATS	Penske-Ford Cosworth PC4	53 laps	19
13	Patrick Depailler	Tyrrell	Tyrrell-Ford Cosworth P34	53 laps	10
14	Jean-Pierre Jarier	ATS	Penske-Ford Cosworth PC4	52 laps	18
15	Vittorio Brambilla	Surtees	Surtees-Ford Cosworth TS19	52 laps	13
16	Vern Schuppan	Surtees	Surtees-Ford Cosworth TS19	52 laps	25
17	Emilio de Villota	Iberia Airlines	McLaren-Ford Cosworth M23	50 laps/accident	26
R	Jody Scheckter	Wolf	Wolf-Ford Cosworth WR3	45 laps/spun off	8
R	James Hunt	McLaren	McLaren-Ford Cosworth M26	43 laps/engine	2
R	Patrick Tambay	Theodore	Ensign-Ford Cosworth N177	41 laps/engine	7
R	Gunnar Nilsson	Lotus	Lotus-Ford Cosworth 78	38 laps/engine	16
R	Arturo Merzario	Shadow	Shadow-Ford Cosworth DN8	29 laps/gearbox	21
R	Jacques Laffite	Ligier	Ligier-Matra JS7	21 laps/oil leak	6
R	Mario Andretti	Lotus	Lotus-Ford Cosworth 78	11 laps/engine	3
R	Ian Scheckter	March	March-Ford Cosworth 761B	2 laps/accident	24
R	Clay Regazzoni	Ensign	Ensign-Ford Cosworth N177	0 laps/accident	11
DNQ	Brian Henton	British F1 Racing	March-Ford Cosworth 761	-	27
DNQ	Ian Ashley	Hesketh	Hesketh-Ford Cosworth 308E	-	28
DNQ	Hector Rebaque	Hesketh	Hesketh-Ford Cosworth 308E	-	29
DNQ	Alex Ribeiro	March	March-Ford Cosworth 761B	-	30

Pole: Lauda, 1m39.320s, 133.837mph/215.391kph. Fastest lap: Watson, 1m40.960s, 131.663mph/211.892kph on Lap 52. Race leaders: Andretti 1-11, Hunt 12-43, Jones 44-54

DUTCH GRAND PRIX

ZANDVOORT • ROUND 13 • DATE: 28TH AUGUST 1977
Laps: 75 • Distance: 196.412miles/316.95km • Weather: Warm but damp then drying

Pos	Driver	Team	Chassis-Engine	Result	Qual
1	Niki Lauda	Ferrari	Ferrari 312T2	1h41m45.930s	4
2	Jacques Laffite	Ligier	Ligier-Matra JS7	1h41m47.820s	2
3	Jody Scheckter	Wolf	Wolf-Ford Cosworth WR2	74 laps	15
4	Emerson Fittipaldi	Fittipaldi	Fittipaldi-Ford Cosworth F5	74 laps	17
5	Patrick Tambay	Theodore	Ensign-Ford Cosworth N177	73 laps/out of fuel	12
6	Carlos Reutemann	Ferrari	Ferrari 312T2	73 laps	6
7	Hans-Joachim Stuck	Brabham	Brabham-Alfa Romeo BT45B	73 laps	19
8	Hans Binder	ATS	Penske-Ford Cosworth PC4	73 laps	18
9	Brett Lunger	BS Fabrications	McLaren-Ford Cosworth M23	73 laps	20
10	Ian Scheckter	March	March-Ford Cosworth 771	73 laps	25
11	Alex Ribeiro	March	March-Ford Cosworth 761B	72 laps	24
12	Vittorio Brambilla	Surtees	Surtees-Ford Cosworth TS19	67 laps/accident	22
13	Riccardo Patrese	Shadow	Shadow-Ford Cosworth DN8	67 laps/engine	16
DQ	Brian Henton	HB Bewaking	Boro-Ford Cosworth N175	52 laps/push start	23
R	Jean-Pierre Jabouille	Renault	Renault RS01	39 laps/suspension	10
R	Gunnar Nilsson	Lotus	Lotus-Ford Cosworth 78	34 laps/accident	5
R	Alan Jones	Shadow	Shadow-Ford Cosworth DN8	32 laps/engine	13
R	Patrick Depailler	Tyrrell	Tyrrell-Ford Cosworth P34	31 laps/engine	11
R	Ronnie Peterson	Tyrrell	Tyrrell-Ford Cosworth P34	18 laps/ignition	7
R	Clay Regazzoni	Ensign	Ensign-Ford Cosworth N177	17 laps/throttle	9
R	Mario Andretti	Lotus	Lotus-Ford Cosworth 78	14 laps/engine	1
R	Rupert Keegan	Hesketh	Hesketh-Ford Cosworth 308E	8 laps/accident	26
R	James Hunt	McLaren	McLaren-Ford Cosworth M26	5 laps/accident	3
R	Jean-Pierre Jarier	ATS	Penske-Ford Cosworth PC4	4 laps/ignition	21
R	John Watson	Brabham	Brabham-Alfa Romeo BT45B	2 laps/oil leak	8
R	Jochen Mass	McLaren	McLaren-Ford Cosworth M26	0 laps/accident	14
DNQ	Patrick Neve	Williams	March-Ford Cosworth 761	-	27
DNQ	Arturo Merzario	Merzario	March-Ford Cosworth 761B	-	28
DNQ	Vern Schuppan	Surtees	Surtees-Ford Cosworth TS19	-	29
DNQ	Ian Ashley	Hesketh	Hesketh-Ford Cosworth 308E	-	30
DNQ	Boy Hayje	RAM Racing	March-Ford Cosworth 761	-	31
DNQ	Hector Rebaque	Hesketh	Hesketh-Ford Cosworth 308E	-	32
DNQ	Teddy Pilette	BRM	BRM P207	-	33
DNQ	Michael Bleekemolen	RAM Racing	March-Ford Cosworth 761	-	34

Pole: Andretti, 1m18.650s, 120.194mph/193.434kph. Fastest lap: Lauda, 1m19.990s, 118.178mph/190.190kph on Lap 72. Race leaders: Hunt 1-5, Laffite 6-19, Lauda 20-75

NEW CONSTRUCTORS

In addition to Renault, which arrived mid-season with its turbocharged RS01, and the Wolf WR1 that immediately hit winning form, the British Lec marque made its entrance. Named after the refrigeration company owned by David Purley's family, its Mike Pilbeam-penned CRP1 ran as high as second in a wet/dry Belgian GP.

ITALIAN GRAND PRIX

MONZA • ROUND 14 • DATE: 11TH SEPTEMBER 1977
Laps: 52 • Distance: 187.36miles/301.6km • Weather: Warm & bright

Pos	Driver	Team	Chassis-Engine	Result	Qual
1	Mario Andretti	Lotus	Lotus-Ford Cosworth 78	1h27m50.300s	4
2	Niki Lauda	Ferrari	Ferrari 312T2	1h28m07.260s	5
3	Alan Jones	Shadow	Shadow-Ford Cosworth DN8	1h28m13.930s	16
4	Jochen Mass	McLaren	McLaren-Ford Cosworth M26	1h28m18.780s	9
5	Clay Regazzoni	Ensign	Ensign-Ford Cosworth N177	1h28m20.410s	7
6	Ronnie Peterson	Tyrrell	Tyrrell-Ford Cosworth P34	1h29m09.520s	12
7	Patrick Neve	Williams	March-Ford Cosworth 761	50 laps	24
8	Jacques Laffite	Ligier	Ligier-Matra JS7	50 laps	8
9	Rupert Keegan	Hesketh	Hesketh-Ford Cosworth 308E	48 laps	23
R	Ian Scheckter	March	March-Ford Cosworth 771	41 laps/transmission	17
R	Carlos Reutemann	Ferrari	Ferrari 312T2	39 laps/spun off	2
R	Riccardo Patrese	Shadow	Shadow-Ford Cosworth DN8	39 laps/spun off	6
R	Bruno Giacomelli	McLaren	McLaren-Ford Cosworth M23	38 laps/engine	15
R	Hans-Joachim Stuck	Brabham	Brabham-Alfa Romeo BT45B	31 laps/engine	11
R	James Hunt	McLaren	McLaren-Ford Cosworth M26	26 laps/spun off	1
R	Patrick Depailler	Tyrrell	Tyrrell-Ford Cosworth P34	24 laps/engine	13
R	Jody Scheckter	Wolf	Wolf-Ford Cosworth WR1	23 laps/engine	3
R	Jean-Pierre Jabouille	Renault	Renault RS01	23 laps/engine	20
R	Jean-Pierre Jarier	ATS	Penske-Ford Cosworth PC4	19 laps/engine	18
R	Patrick Tambay	Theodore	Ensign-Ford Cosworth N177	9 laps/engine	21
R	Vittorio Brambilla	Surtees	Surtees-Ford Cosworth TS19	5 laps/accident	10
R	Brett Lunger	BS Fabrications	McLaren-Ford Cosworth M23	4 laps/engine	19
R	Gunnar Nilsson	Lotus	Lotus-Ford Cosworth 78	4 laps/suspension	22
R	John Watson	Brabham	Brabham-Alfa Romeo BT45B	3 laps/accident	14
DNQ	Alex Ribeiro	March	March-Ford Cosworth 761B	-	25
DNQ	Emerson Fittipaldi	Fittipaldi	Fittipaldi-Ford Cosworth F5	-	26
DNQ	Lamberto Leoni	Surtees	Surtees-Ford Cosworth TS19	-	27
DNQ	Brian Henton	HB Bewaking	Boro-Ford Cosworth N175	-	28
DNQ	Emilio de Villota	Iberia Airlines	McLaren-Ford Cosworth M23	-	29
DNQ	Ian Ashley	Hesketh	Hesketh-Ford Cosworth 308E	-	30
DNQ	Teddy Pilette	BRM	BRM P207	-	31
DNQ	Hans Binder	ATS	Penske-Ford Cosworth PC4	-	32
DNQ	Loris Kessel	Jolly Club Switzerland	Williams-Ford Cosworth FW03	-	33
DNQ	Giorgio Francia	Brabham	Brabham-Alfa Romeo BT45B	-	34

Pole: Hunt, 1m38.080s, 132.282mph/212.887kph. Fastest lap: Andretti, 1m39.100s, 130.922mph/210.700kph on Lap 31. Race leaders: Scheckter 1-9, Andretti 10-52

NEW DRIVERS

This season had a notably good intake, with Gilles Villeneuve being the best of the 14 rookies as he made a spectacular debut that could have yielded points for McLaren but for a faulty temperature gauge. He was then signed by Ferrari. Patrick Tambay also impressed, taking a fifth in a Theodore-entered Ensign, while Riccardo Patrese was sixth for Shadow.

UNITED STATES GRAND PRIX

WATKINS GLEN • ROUND 15 • DATE: 2ND OCTOBER 1977
Laps: 59 • Distance: 199.251miles/320.665km • Weather: Warm & bright

Pos	Driver	Team	Chassis-Engine	Result	Qual
1	James Hunt	McLaren	McLaren-Ford Cosworth M26	1h58m23.267s	1
2	Mario Andretti	Lotus	Lotus-Ford Cosworth 78	1h58m25.293s	4
3	Jody Scheckter	Wolf	Wolf-Ford Cosworth WR2	1h59m42.146s	9
4	Niki Lauda	Ferrari	Ferrari 312T2	2h00m03.882s	7
5	Clay Regazzoni	Ensign	Ensign-Ford Cosworth N177	2h00m11.405s	19
6	Carlos Reutemann	Ferrari	Ferrari 312T2	58 laps	6
7	Jacques Laffite	Ligier	Ligier-Matra JS7	58 laps	10
8	Rupert Keegan	Hesketh	Hesketh-Ford Cosworth 308E	58 laps	20
9	Jean-Pierre Jarier	Shadow	Shadow-Ford Cosworth DN8	58 laps	16
10	Brett Lunger	BS Fabrications	McLaren-Ford Cosworth M23	57 laps	17
11	Hans Binder	Surtees	Surtees-Ford Cosworth TS19	57 laps	25
12	John Watson	Brabham	Brabham-Alfa Romeo BT45B	57 laps	3
13	Emerson Fittipaldi	Fittipaldi	Fittipaldi-Ford Cosworth F5	57 laps	18
14	Patrick Depailler	Tyrrell	Tyrrell-Ford Cosworth P34	56 laps	8
15	Alex Ribeiro	March	March-Ford Cosworth 761B	56 laps	23
16	Ronnie Peterson	Tyrrell	Tyrrell-Ford Cosworth P34	56 laps	5
17	Ian Ashley	Hesketh	Hesketh-Ford Cosworth 308E	55 laps	22
18	Patrick Neve	Williams	March-Ford Cosworth 761	55 laps	24
19	Vittorio Brambilla	Surtees	Surtees-Ford Cosworth TS19	54 laps	11
R	Jean-Pierre Jabouille	Renault	Renault RS01	30 laps/alternator	14
R	Gunnar Nilsson	Lotus	Lotus-Ford Cosworth 78	17 laps/accident	12
R	Hans-Joachim Stuck	Brabham	Brabham-Alfa Romeo BT45B	14 laps/accident	2
R	Ian Scheckter	March	March-Ford Cosworth 771	10 laps/accident	21
R	Jochen Mass	McLaren	McLaren-Ford Cosworth M26	8 laps/fuel pump	15
R	Danny Ongais	Interscope Racing	Penske-Ford Cosworth PC4	6 laps/accident	26
R	Alan Jones	Shadow	Shadow-Ford Cosworth DN8	3 laps/accident	13
DNQ	Patrick Tambay	Theodore	Ensign-Ford Cosworth N177	-	27

Pole: Hunt, 1m40.863s, 120.537mph/193.985kph. Fastest lap: Peterson, 1m51.854s, 108.692mph/174.924kph on Lap 56. Race leaders: Stuck 1-14, Hunt 15-59

CANADIAN GRAND PRIX

MOSPORT PARK • ROUND 16 • DATE: 9TH OCTOBER 1977
Laps: 80 • Distance: 196.388miles/316.56km • Weather: Cool & wet

Pos	Driver	Team	Chassis-Engine	Result	Qual
1	Jody Scheckter	Wolf	Wolf-Ford Cosworth WR1	1h40m00.000s	9
2	Patrick Depailler	Tyrrell	Tyrrell-Ford Cosworth P34	1h40m06.770s	6
3	Jochen Mass	McLaren	McLaren-Ford Cosworth M26	1h40m15.760s	5
4	Alan Jones	Shadow	Shadow-Ford Cosworth DN8	1h40m46.690s	7
5	Patrick Tambay	Theodore	Ensign-Ford Cosworth N177	1h41m03.260s	16
6	Vittorio Brambilla	Surtees	Surtees-Ford Cosworth TS19	78 laps/accident	15
7	Danny Ongais	Interscope Racing	Penske-Ford Cosworth PC4	78 laps	22
8	Alex Ribeiro	March	March-Ford Cosworth 761B	78 laps	23
9	Mario Andretti	Lotus	Lotus-Ford Cosworth 78	77 laps/engine	1
10	Riccardo Patrese	Shadow	Shadow-Ford Cosworth DN8	76 laps/spun off	8
11	Brett Lunger	BS Fabrications	McLaren-Ford Cosworth M23	76 laps/engine	20
12	Gilles Villeneuve	Ferrari	Ferrari 312T2	76 laps/transmission	17
R	James Hunt	McLaren	McLaren-Ford Cosworth M26	61 laps/accident	2

Pos	Driver	Team	Chassis-Engine	Result	Qual
R	Patrick Neve	Williams	March-Ford Cosworth 761	56 laps/engine	21
R	Ronnie Peterson	Tyrrell	Tyrrell-Ford Cosworth P34	34 laps/oil leak	3
R	Rupert Keegan	Hesketh	Hesketh-Ford Cosworth 308E	32 laps/accident	25
R	Hans Binder	Surtees	Surtees-Ford Cosworth TS19	31 laps/accident	24
R	Ian Scheckter	March	March-Ford Cosworth 771	29 laps/engine	18
R	Emerson Fittipaldi	Fittipaldi	Fittipaldi-Ford Cosworth F5	29 laps/engine	19
R	Carlos Reutemann	Ferrari	Ferrari 312T2	20 laps/fuel system	12
R	Hans-Joachim Stuck	Brabham	Brabham-Alfa Romeo BT45B	19 laps/engine	13
R	Gunnar Nilsson	Lotus	Lotus-Ford Cosworth 78	17 laps/accident	4
R	Jacques Laffite	Ligier	Ligier-Matra JS7	12 laps/transmission	11
R	John Watson	Brabham	Brabham-Alfa Romeo BT45B	1 lap/suspension	10
R	Clay Regazzoni	Ensign	Ensign-Ford Cosworth N177	0 laps/accident	14
NS	Ian Ashley	Hesketh	Hesketh-Ford Cosworth 308E	driver injured	25
DNQ	Jean-Pierre Jabouille	Renault	Renault RS01	-	27

Pole: Andretti, 1m11.385s, 123.997mph/199.554kph. Fastest lap: Andretti, 1m13.299s, 120.759mph/194.343kph on Lap 56. Race leaders: Andretti 1-60 & 62-77, Hunt 61, Scheckter 78-80

IN MEMORIAM

Carlos Pace, who won just once but could have had more with Brabham, started 1977 with second in Argentina before his light aircraft accident. Tom Pryce's death in the South African GP was profoundly shocking, while former Ferrari racer Mike Parkes died in a road accident. Brian McGuire was killed at a national meeting at Brands Hatch.

JAPANESE GRAND PRIX

FUJI SPEEDWAY • ROUND 17 • DATE: 23RD OCTOBER 1977
Laps: 73 • Distance: 197.724miles/318.207km • Weather: Cool & dull

Pos	Driver	Team	Chassis-Engine	Result	Qual
1	James Hunt	McLaren	McLaren-Ford Cosworth M26	1h31m51.680s	2
2	Carlos Reutemann	Ferrari	Ferrari 312T2	1h32m54.130s	7
3	Patrick Depailler	Tyrrell	Tyrrell-Ford Cosworth P34	1h32m58.070s	15
4	Alan Jones	Shadow	Shadow-Ford Cosworth DN8	1h32m58.290s	12
5	Jacques Laffite	Ligier	Ligier-Matra JS7	72 laps/out of fuel	5
6	Riccardo Patrese	Shadow	Shadow-Ford Cosworth DN8	72 laps	13
7	Hans-Joachim Stuck	Brabham	Brabham-Alfa Romeo BT45B	72 laps	4
8	Vittorio Brambilla	Surtees	Surtees-Ford Cosworth TS19	71 laps	9
9	Kunimitsu Takahashi	Meiritsu Racing Team	Tyrrell-Ford Cosworth 007	71 laps	22
10	Jody Scheckter	Wolf	Wolf-Ford Cosworth WR3	71 laps	6
11	Kazuyoshi Hoshino	Heros Racing	Kojima-Ford Cosworth KE009	71 laps	11
12	Alex Ribeiro	March	March-Ford Cosworth 761B	69 laps	23
R	Gunnar Nilsson	Lotus	Lotus-Ford Cosworth 78	63 laps/gearbox	14
R	Clay Regazzoni	Ensign	Ensign-Ford Cosworth N177	43 laps/engine	10
R	John Watson	Brabham	Brabham-Alfa Romeo BT45B	29 laps/gearbox	3
R	Jochen Mass	McLaren	McLaren-Ford Cosworth M26	28 laps/engine	8
R	Patrick Tambay	Theodore	Ensign-Ford Cosworth N177	14 laps/engine	16
R	Ronnie Peterson	Tyrrell	Tyrrell-Ford Cosworth P34	5 laps/accident	18
R	Gilles Villeneuve	Ferrari	Ferrari 312T2	5 laps/accident	20

Pos	Driver	Team	Chassis-Engine	Result	Qual
R	Jean-Pierre Jarier	Ligier	Ligier-Matra JS7	3 laps/engine	17
R	Mario Andretti	Lotus	Lotus-Ford Cosworth 78	1 lap/collision	1
R	Noritake Takahara	Kojima	Kojima-Ford Cosworth KE009	1 lap/collision	19
R	Hans Binder	Surtees	Surtees-Ford Cosworth TS19	1 lap/collision	21

Pole: Andretti, 1m12.230s, 134.996mph/217.255kph. Fastest lap: Scheckter, 1m14.300s, 131.233mph/211.200kph on Lap 71. Race leaders: Hunt 1-73

WORLD DRIVERS' CHAMPIONSHIP FINAL RESULTS

Pos	Driver	Nat	Car-Engine	R1	R2	R3	R4	R5	R6
1	Niki Lauda	AUT	Ferrari 312T2	R	3	1	2PF	NS	2
2	Jody Scheckter	ZAF	Wolf-Ford Cosworth WR1	1	R	2	3	3	1F
3	Mario Andretti	USA	Lotus-Ford Cosworth 78	5	R	R	1	1P	5
4	Carlos Reutemann	ARG	Ferrari 312T2	3	1	8	R	2	3
5	James Hunt	GBR	McLaren-Ford Cosworth M23	RPF	2PF	4P	7	-	R
			McLaren-Ford Cosworth M26	-	-	-	-	R	-
6	Jochen Mass	DEU	McLaren-Ford Cosworth M23	R	R	5	R	4	4
			McLaren-Ford Cosworth M26	-	-	-	-	-	-
7	Alan Jones	AUS	Shadow-Ford Cosworth DN8	-	-	-	R	R	6
8	Gunnar Nilsson	SWE	Lotus-Ford Cosworth 78	NS	5	12	8	5	R
8	Patrick Depailler	FRA	Tyrrell-Ford Cosworth P34	R	R	3	4	R	R
10	Jacques Laffite	FRA	Ligier-Matra JS7	NC	R	R	9	7F	7
11	Hans-Joachim Stuck	DEU	March-Ford Cosworth 761B	-	-	R	-	-	-
			Brabham-Alfa Romeo BT45B	-	-	-	R	6	R
12	Emerson Fittipaldi	BRA	Fittipaldi-Ford Cosworth FD04	4	4	10	5	14	R
			Fittipaldi-Ford Cosworth F5	-	-	-	-	-	-
13	John Watson	GBR	Brabham-Alfa Romeo BT45	R	R	6F	-	-	-
			Brabham-Alfa Romeo BT45B	-	-	-	DQ	R	RP
14	Ronnie Peterson	SWE	Tyrrell-Ford Cosworth P34	R	R	R	R	8	R
15	Carlos Pace	BRA	Brabham-Alfa Romeo BT45	2	R	-	-	-	-
			Brabham-Alfa Romeo BT45B	-	-	13	-	-	-
15	Vittorio Brambilla	ITA	Surtees-Ford Cosworth TS19	7	R	7	R	R	8
17	Clay Regazzoni	CHE	Ensign-Ford Cosworth N177	6	R	9	R	R	DNQ
17	Patrick Tambay	FRA	Surtees-Ford Cosworth TS19	-	-	-	-	-	-
			Ensign-Ford Cosworth N177	-	-	-	-	-	-
19	Renzo Zorzi	ITA	Shadow-Ford Cosworth DN5B	R	6	-	-	-	-
			Shadow-Ford Cosworth DN8	-	-	R	R	R	-
19	Jean-Pierre Jarier	FRA	Penske-Ford Cosworth PC4	-	-	-	6	DNQ	11
			Shadow-Ford Cosworth DN8	-	-	-	-	-	-
			Ligier-Matra JS7	-	-	-	-	-	-
19	Riccardo Patrese	ITA	Shadow-Ford Cosworth DN8	-	-	-	-	-	9

Pos	Driver	R7	R8	R9	R10	R11	R12	R13	R14	R15	R16	R17	Total
1	Lauda	2	R	5	2	1F	2P	1F	2	4	-	-	72
2	Scheckter	R	R	R	R	2P	R	3	R	3	1	10F	55
3	Andretti	RP	6PF	1PF	14	R	R	RP	1F	2	9PF	RP	47
4	Reutemann	R	3	6	15	4	4	6	R	6	R	2	42
5	Hunt	-	-	-	-	-	-	-	-	-	-	-	40
		7	12	3	1PF	R	R	R	RP	1P	R	1	
6	Mass	R	2	9	-	-	-	-	-	-	-	-	25
		-	-	-	4	R	6	R	4	R	3	R	
7	Jones	5	17	R	7	R	1	R	3	R	4	4	22
8	Nilsson	1F	19	4	3	R	R	R	R	R	R	R	20
8	Depailler	8	4	R	R	R	13	R	R	14	2	3	20

Pos	Driver	R7	R8	R9	R10	R11	R12	R13	R14	R15	R16	R17	Total
10	Laffite	R	1	8	6	R	R	2	8	7	R	5	18
11	Stuck	-	-	-	-	-	-	-	-	-	-	-	12
		6	10	R	5	3	3	7	R	R	R	7	
12	Fittipaldi	-	18	-	-	-	-	-	-	-	-	-	11
		R	-	11	R	DNQ	11	4	DNQ	13	R	-	
13	Watson	-	-	-	-	-	-	-	-	-	-	-	9
		R	5	2	R	R	8F	R	R	12	R	R	
14	Peterson	3	R	12	R	9	5	R	6	16F	R	R	7
15	Pace	-	-	-	-	-	-	-	-	-	-	-	6
		-	-	-	-	-	-	-	-	-	-	-	
15	Brambilla	4	R	13	8	5	15	12	R	19	6	8	6
17	Regazzoni	R	7	7	DNQ	R	R	R	5	5	R	R	5
17	Tambay	-	-	DNQ	-	-	-	-	-	-	-	-	5
		-	-	-	R	6	R	5	R	DNQ	5	R	
19	Zorzi	-	-	-	-	-	-	-	-	-	-	-	1
		-	-	-	-	-	-	-	-	-	-	-	
19	Jarier	11	8	R	9	R	14	R	R	-	-	-	1
		-	-	-	-	-	-	-	-	9	-	-	
		-	-	-	-	-	-	-	-	-	-	R	
19	Patrese	R	-	R	R	10	-	13	R	-	10	6	1

SYMBOLS AND GRAND PRIX KEY

Round 1 **Argentinian GP**
Round 2 **Brazilian GP**
Round 3 **South African GP**
Round 4 **United States GP West**
Round 5 **Spanish GP**
Round 6 **Monaco GP**
Round 7 **Belgian GP**
Round 8 **Swedish GP**
Round 9 **French GP**
Round 10 **British GP**
Round 11 **German GP**
Round 12 **Austrian GP**
Round 13 **Dutch GP**
Round 14 **Italian GP**
Round 15 **United States GP**
Round 16 **Canadian GP**
Round 17 **Japanese GP**

SCORING

1st **9 points**
2nd **6 points**
3rd **4 points**
4th **3 points**
5th **2 points**
6th **1 point**

DNPQ DID NOT PRE-QUALIFY **DNQ DID NOT QUALIFY** **DQ DISQUALIFIED** **EX EXCLUDED**
F FASTEST LAP **NC NOT CLASSIFIED** **NS NON-STARTER** **P POLE POSITION** **R RETIRED**

WORLD CONSTRUCTORS' CHAMPIONSHIP FINAL RESULTS

Pos	Team-Engine	R1	R2	R3	R4	R5	R6	R7	R8	R9
1	Ferrari	3	1	1	2	2	2	2	3	5
2	Lotus-Ford	5	5	12	1	1	5	1	6	1
3	McLaren-Ford	-	2	4	7	4	4	7	2	3
4	Wolf-Ford	1	R	2	3	3	1	R	-	-
5	Brabham-Alfa Romeo	2	R	6	-	6	R	6	5	2
5	Tyrrell-Ford	-	R	3	4	8	R	3	4	12
7	Shadow-Ford	-	6	-	-	-	6	5	9	-
8	Ligier-Matra	-	R	-	9	7	7	R	1	8
9	Fittipaldi-Ford	4	4	10	5	14	R	R	18	11
10	Ensign-Ford	6	R	9	-	-	10	R	7	7
11	Surtees-Ford	7	R	7	11	9	8	4	-	13
12	Penske-Ford	-	-	-	6	-	11	11	8	-

Pos	Team-Engine	R10	R11	R12	R13	R14	R15	R16	R17	Total
1	Ferrari	2	1	2	1	2	4	12	2	95
2	Lotus-Ford	3	-	-	-	1	2	9	R	62
3	McLaren-Ford	1	-	6	-	4	1	3	1	60
4	Wolf-Ford	-	2	-	3	-	3	1	10	55
5	Brabham-Alfa Romeo	5	3	3	7	-	12	-	7	27
5	Tyrrell-Ford	-	9	5	-	6	14	2	3	27
7	Shadow-Ford	7	10	1	13	3	9	4	4	23
8	Ligier-Matra	6	-	-	2	8	7	-	5	18
9	Fittipaldi-Ford	-	-	11	4	-	13	-	-	11
10	Ensign-Ford	-	6	-	5	5	5	5	R	10
11	Surtees-Ford	8	5	15	12	-	11	6	8	6
12	Penske-Ford	9	-	12	8	-	-	7	-	1

1978

SEASON SUMMARY

This was the season in which Lotus struck back. Armed with its second-generation ground-effect car, it was far superior to the machines run by its rivals, who started to realise that Colin Chapman's team was doing something clever with its undercar aerodynamics. Mario Andretti won six rounds and became the second American to become world champion. He was supported faithfully by team-mate Ronnie Peterson, who sadly was killed after a crash at the start of the Italian GP. Carlos Reutemann ranked third for Ferrari, while Niki Lauda ended up fourth in his first year since leaving the Italian team.

ARGENTINIAN GRAND PRIX

BUENOS AIRES • ROUND 1 • DATE: 15TH JANUARY 1978
Laps: 52 • Distance: 192.840miles/310.346km • Weather: Hot & bright

Pos	Driver	Team	Chassis-Engine	Result	Qual
1	Mario Andretti	Lotus	Lotus-Ford Cosworth 78	1h37m04.470s	1
2	Niki Lauda	Brabham	Brabham-Alfa Romeo BT45C	1h37m17.680s	5
3	Patrick Depailler	Tyrrell	Tyrrell-Ford Cosworth 008	1h37m18.110s	10
4	James Hunt	McLaren	McLaren-Ford Cosworth M26	1h37m20.520s	6
5	Ronnie Peterson	Lotus	Lotus-Ford Cosworth 78	1h38m19.320s	3
6	Patrick Tambay	McLaren	McLaren-Ford Cosworth M26	1h38m24.370s	9
7	Carlos Reutemann	Ferrari	Ferrari 312T2	1h38m27.070s	2
8	Gilles Villeneuve	Ferrari	Ferrari 312T2	1h38m43.350s	7
9	Emerson Fittipaldi	Fittipaldi	Fittipaldi-Ford Cosworth F5A	1h38m45.070s	17
10	Jody Scheckter	Wolf	Wolf-Ford Cosworth WR4	1h38m47.970s	15
11	Jochen Mass	ATS	ATS-Ford Cosworth HS1	1h38m53.540s	13
12	Jean-Pierre Jarier	ATS	ATS-Ford Cosworth HS1	51 laps	11
13	Brett Lunger	BS Fabrications	McLaren-Ford Cosworth M23	51 laps	24
14	Didier Pironi	Tyrrell	Tyrrell-Ford Cosworth 008	51 laps	23
15	Clay Regazzoni	Shadow	Shadow-Ford Cosworth DN8	51 laps	16
16	Jacques Laffite	Ligier	Ligier-Matra JS7	50 laps/engine	8
17	Hans-Joachim Stuck	Shadow	Shadow-Ford Cosworth DN8	50 laps	18
18	Vittorio Brambilla	Surtees	Surtees-Ford Cosworth TS19	50 laps	12
R	John Watson	Brabham	Brabham-Alfa Romeo BT45C	41 laps/engine	4
R	Alan Jones	Williams	Williams-Ford Cosworth FW06	36 laps/fuel system	14
R	Danny Ongais	Ensign	Ensign-Ford Cosworth N177	35 laps/mechanical	21
R	Lamberto Leoni	Ensign	Ensign-Ford Cosworth N177	28 laps/engine	22
R	Arturo Merzario	Merzario	Merzario-Ford Cosworth A1	9 laps/differential	20
R	Rupert Keegan	Surtees	Surtees-Ford Cosworth TS19	4 laps/overheating	19
DNQ	Hector Rebaque	Rebaque	Lotus-Ford Cosworth 78	-	25
DNQ	Eddie Cheever	Theodore	Theodore-Ford Cosworth TR1	-	26
DNQ	Divina Galica	Hesketh	Hesketh-Ford Cosworth 308E	-	27

Pole: Andretti, 1m47.750s, 123.902mph/199.401kph. Fastest lap: Villeneuve, 1m49.760s, 121.633mph/195.750kph on Lap 3. Race leaders: Andretti 1-52

BRAZILIAN GRAND PRIX

JACAREPAGUA • ROUND 2 • DATE: 29TH JANUARY 1978
Laps: 63 • Distance: 196.945miles/316.953km • Weather: Very hot & bright

Pos	Driver	Team	Chassis-Engine	Result	Qual
1	Carlos Reutemann	Ferrari	Ferrari 312T2	1h49m59.860s	4
2	Emerson Fittipaldi	Fittipaldi	Fittipaldi-Ford Cosworth F5A	1h50m48.990s	7
3	Niki Lauda	Brabham	Brabham-Alfa Romeo BT45C	1h50m56.880s	10
4	Mario Andretti	Lotus	Lotus-Ford Cosworth 78	1h51m32.980s	3
5	Clay Regazzoni	Shadow	Shadow-Ford Cosworth DN8	62 laps	15
6	Didier Pironi	Tyrrell	Tyrrell-Ford Cosworth 008	62 laps	19
7	Jochen Mass	ATS	ATS-Ford Cosworth HS1	62 laps	20
8	John Watson	Brabham	Brabham-Alfa Romeo BT45C	61 laps	21
9	Jacques Laffite	Ligier	Ligier-Matra JS7	61 laps	14
10	Riccardo Patrese	Arrows	Arrows-Ford Cosworth FA1	59 laps	18
11	Alan Jones	Williams	Williams-Ford Cosworth FW06	58 laps	8
R	Hector Rebaque	Rebaque	Lotus-Ford Cosworth 78	40 laps/physical	22
R	Gilles Villeneuve	Ferrari	Ferrari 312T2	35 laps/spun off	6
R	Patrick Tambay	McLaren	McLaren-Ford Cosworth M26	34 laps/spun off	5
R	James Hunt	McLaren	McLaren-Ford Cosworth M26	25 laps/spun off	2
R	Hans-Joachim Stuck	Shadow	Shadow-Ford Cosworth DN8	25 laps/fuel system	9
R	Jody Scheckter	Wolf	Wolf-Ford Cosworth WR1	16 laps/accident	12
R	Ronnie Peterson	Lotus	Lotus-Ford Cosworth 78	15 laps/collision	1
R	Danny Ongais	Ensign	Ensign-Ford Cosworth N177	13 laps/brakes	23
R	Brett Lunger	BS Fabrications	McLaren-Ford Cosworth M23	11 laps/overheating	13
R	Patrick Depailler	Tyrrell	Tyrrell-Ford Cosworth 008	8 laps/accident	11
R	Rupert Keegan	Surtees	Surtees-Ford Cosworth TS19	5 laps/accident	24
R	Lamberto Leoni	Ensign	Ensign-Ford Cosworth N177	0 laps/driveshaft	17
NS	Jean-Pierre Jarier	ATS	ATS-Ford Cosworth HS1	Mass drove car	16
DNQ	Arturo Merzario	Merzario	Merzario-Ford Cosworth A1	-	25
DNQ	Eddie Cheever	Theodore	Theodore-Ford Cosworth TR1	-	26
DNQ	Vittorio Brambilla	Surtees	Surtees-Ford Cosworth TS19	-	27
DNQ	Divina Galica	Hesketh	Hesketh-Ford Cosworth 308E	-	28

Pole: Peterson, 1m40.450s, 112.036mph/180.304kph. Fastest lap: Reutemann, 1m43.070s, 109.188mph/175.721kph on Lap 35. Race leaders: Reutemann 1-63

ARROWS MISSES THE TOP

In 1977, Wolf won on its debut and, 12 months later, the new Arrows team – formed by a breakaway of personnel from Shadow – came close to repeating that feat in its second outing. Kyalami was the setting and Riccardo Patrese was leading with 15 laps to go when his engine failed.

NO MORE THE BRIDESMAID

In the first four full seasons of his F1 career, Patrick Depailler showed speed aplenty for Tyrrell but no wins, just eight second places. That got corrected at Monaco when it all came right at last. The Frenchman started fifth and fought the Brabhams en route to victory.

SOUTH AFRICAN GRAND PRIX

KYALAMI • ROUND 3 • DATE: 4TH MARCH 1978
Laps: 78 • Distance: 198.908miles/320.112km • Weather: Hot & bright

Pos	Driver	Team	Chassis-Engine	Result	Qual
1	Ronnie Peterson	Lotus	Lotus-Ford Cosworth 78	1h42m15.767s	11
2	Patrick Depailler	Tyrrell	Tyrrell-Ford Cosworth 008	1h42m16.233s	12
3	John Watson	Brabham	Brabham-Alfa Romeo BT46	1h42m20.209s	10
4	Alan Jones	Williams	Williams-Ford Cosworth FW06	1h42m54.753s	18
5	Jacques Laffite	Ligier	Ligier-Matra JS7/9	1h43m24.985s	14
6	Didier Pironi	Tyrrell	Tyrrell-Ford Cosworth 008	77 laps	13
7	Mario Andretti	Lotus	Lotus-Ford Cosworth 78	77 laps	2
8	Jean-Pierre Jarier	ATS	ATS-Ford Cosworth HS1	77 laps	17
9	Rolf Stommelen	Arrows	Arrows-Ford Cosworth FA1	77 laps	21
10	Hector Rebaque	Rebaque	Lotus-Ford Cosworth 78	77 laps	22
11	Brett Lunger	BS Fabrications	McLaren-Ford Cosworth M23	76 laps	19
12	Vittorio Brambilla	Surtees	Surtees-Ford Cosworth TS19	76 laps	20
R	Riccardo Patrese	Arrows	Arrows-Ford Cosworth FA1	63 laps/engine	7
R	Jody Scheckter	Wolf	Wolf-Ford Cosworth WR1	59 laps/spun off	5
R	Patrick Tambay	McLaren	McLaren-Ford Cosworth M26	56 laps/accident	4
R	Gilles Villeneuve	Ferrari	Ferrari 312T3	55 laps/oil leak	8
R	Carlos Reutemann	Ferrari	Ferrari 312T3	55 laps/spun off	9
R	Niki Lauda	Brabham	Brabham-Alfa Romeo BT46	52 laps/engine	1
R	Rupert Keegan	Surtees	Surtees-Ford Cosworth TS19	52 laps/engine	23
R	Jochen Mass	ATS	ATS-Ford Cosworth HS1	43 laps/engine	16
R	Arturo Merzario	Merzario	Merzario-Ford Cosworth A1	39 laps/suspension	26
R	Jean-Pierre Jabouille	Renault	Renault RS01	38 laps/engine	6
R	Keke Rosberg	Theodore	Theodore-Ford Cosworth TR1	15 laps/clutch	24
R	Emerson Fittipaldi	Fittipaldi	Fittipaldi-Ford Cosworth F5A	9 laps/transmission	15
R	Eddie Cheever	Hesketh	Hesketh-Ford Cosworth 308E	8 laps/oil leak	25
R	James Hunt	McLaren	McLaren-Ford Cosworth M26	5 laps/engine	3
DNQ	Rene Arnoux	Automobiles Martini	Martini-Ford Cosworth MK23	-	27
DNQ	Clay Regazzoni	Shadow	Shadow-Ford Cosworth DN8	-	28
DNQ	Lamberto Leoni	Ensign	Ensign-Ford Cosworth N177	-	29
DNQ	Hans-Joachim Stuck	Shadow	Shadow-Ford Cosworth DN8	-	30

Pole: Lauda, 1m14.650s, 122.979mph/197.915kph. Fastest lap: Andretti, 1m17.090s, 119.086mph/191.651kph on Lap 2. Race leaders: Andretti 1-20, Scheckter 21-26, Patrese 27-63, Depailler 64-77, Peterson 78

UNITED STATES GRAND PRIX WEST

LONG BEACH • ROUND 4 • DATE: 2ND APRIL 1978
Laps: 80 • Distance: 161.561miles/260.08km • Weather: Warm & bright

Pos	Driver	Team	Chassis-Engine	Result	Qual
1	Carlos Reutemann	Ferrari	Ferrari 312T3	1h52m01.301s	1
2	Mario Andretti	Lotus	Lotus-Ford Cosworth 78	1h52m12.362s	4
3	Patrick Depailler	Tyrrell	Tyrrell-Ford Cosworth 008	1h52m30.252s	12
4	Ronnie Peterson	Lotus	Lotus-Ford Cosworth 78	1h52m46.904s	6
5	Jacques Laffite	Ligier	Ligier-Matra JS7	1h53m24.185s	14
6	Riccardo Patrese	Arrows	Arrows-Ford Cosworth FA1	79 laps	9
7	Alan Jones	Williams	Williams-Ford Cosworth FW06	79 laps	8
8	Emerson Fittipaldi	Fittipaldi	Fittipaldi-Ford Cosworth F5A	79 laps	15
9	Rolf Stommelen	Arrows	Arrows-Ford Cosworth FA1	79 laps	18

Pos	Driver	Team	Chassis-Engine	Result	Qual
10	Clay Regazzoni	Shadow	Shadow-Ford Cosworth DN8	79 laps	20
11	Jean-Pierre Jarier	ATS	ATS-Ford Cosworth HS1	75 laps	19
12	Patrick Tambay	McLaren	McLaren-Ford Cosworth M26	74 laps/accident	11
R	Jody Scheckter	Wolf	Wolf-Ford Cosworth WR3	59 laps/accident	10
R	Vittorio Brambilla	Surtees	Surtees-Ford Cosworth TS19	50 laps/transmission	17
R	Jean-Pierre Jabouille	Renault	Renault RS01	43 laps/turbo	13
R	Gilles Villeneuve	Ferrari	Ferrari 312T3	38 laps/accident	2
R	Niki Lauda	Brabham	Brabham-Alfa Romeo BT46	27 laps/ignition	3
R	Didier Pironi	Tyrrell	Tyrrell-Ford Cosworth 008	25 laps/gearbox	22
R	Arturo Merzario	Merzario	Merzario-Ford Cosworth A1	17 laps/gearbox	21
R	Jochen Mass	ATS	ATS-Ford Cosworth HS1	11 laps/brakes	16
R	John Watson	Brabham	Brabham-Alfa Romeo BT46	9 laps/gearbox	5
R	James Hunt	McLaren	McLaren-Ford Cosworth M26	5 laps/accident	7
NS	Rupert Keegan	Surtees	Surtees-Ford Cosworth TS19	accident	22
NS	Hans-Joachim Stuck	Shadow	Shadow-Ford Cosworth DN9	accident	23
DNQ	Brett Lunger	BS Fabrications	McLaren-Ford Cosworth M23	-	25
DNQ	Lamberto Leoni	Ensign	Ensign-Ford Cosworth N177	-	26
DNPQ	Keke Rosberg	Theodore	Theodore-Ford Cosworth TR1	-	27
DNPQ	Hector Rebaque	Rebaque	Lotus-Ford Cosworth 78	-	28
DNPQ	Danny Ongais	Interscope Racing	Shadow-Ford Cosworth DN9	-	29
DNPQ	Derek Daly	Hesketh	Hesketh-Ford Cosworth 308E	-	30

Pole: Reutemann, 1m20.636s, 90.186mph/145.141kph. Fastest lap: Jones, 1m22.215s, 88.454mph/142.353kph on Lap 27. Race leaders: Villeneuve 1-38, Reutemann 39-80

A STARTLINE DISASTER

The most perilous part of a race is the start, and so it proved at the Italian GP when Ronnie Peterson's Lotus was caught up in a 10-car melee that was caused largely by the starting signal being given before the cars at the back of the grid had come to a halt. Peterson was expected to survive, but died during surgery on his broken legs.

MONACO GRAND PRIX

MONTE CARLO • ROUND 5 • DATE: 7TH MAY 1978
Laps: 75 • Distance: 154.102miles/248.4km • Weather: Warm & bright

Pos	Driver	Team	Chassis-Engine	Result	Qual
1	Patrick Depailler	Tyrrell	Tyrrell-Ford Cosworth 008	1h55m14.660s	5
2	Niki Lauda	Brabham	Brabham-Alfa Romeo BT46	1h55m37.110s	3
3	Jody Scheckter	Wolf	Wolf-Ford Cosworth WR1	1h55m46.950s	9
4	John Watson	Brabham	Brabham-Alfa Romeo BT46	1h55m48.190s	2
5	Didier Pironi	Tyrrell	Tyrrell-Ford Cosworth 008	1h56m22.720s	13
6	Riccardo Patrese	Arrows	Arrows-Ford Cosworth FA1	1h56m23.430s	14
7	Patrick Tambay	McLaren	McLaren-Ford Cosworth M26	74 laps	11
8	Carlos Reutemann	Ferrari	Ferrari 312T3	74 laps	1
9	Emerson Fittipaldi	Fittipaldi	Fittipaldi-Ford Cosworth F5A	74 laps	20
10	Jean-Pierre Jabouille	Renault	Renault RS01	71 laps	12
11	Mario Andretti	Lotus	Lotus-Ford Cosworth 78	69 laps	4
R	Gilles Villeneuve	Ferrari	Ferrari 312T3	62 laps/accident	8

Pos	Driver	Team	Chassis-Engine	Result	Qual
R	Ronnie Peterson	Lotus	Lotus-Ford Cosworth 78	56 laps/gearbox	7
R	James Hunt	McLaren	McLaren-Ford Cosworth M26	43 laps/anti-roll bar	6
R	Rolf Stommelen	Arrows	Arrows-Ford Cosworth FA1	38 laps/driver ill	19
R	Alan Jones	Williams	Williams-Ford Cosworth FW06	29 laps/oil leak	10
R	Jacky Ickx	Ensign	Ensign-Ford Cosworth N177	27 laps/brakes	16
R	Hans-Joachim Stuck	Shadow	Shadow-Ford Cosworth DN9	24 laps/accident	17
R	Jacques Laffite	Ligier	Ligier-Matra JS9	13 laps/gearbox	15
R	Rupert Keegan	Surtees	Surtees-Ford Cosworth TS19	8 laps/transmission	18
DNQ	Jochen Mass	ATS	ATS-Ford Cosworth HS1	-	21
DNQ	Clay Regazzoni	Shadow	Shadow-Ford Cosworth DN9	-	22
DNQ	Jean-Pierre Jarier	ATS	ATS-Ford Cosworth HS1	-	23
DNQ	Vittorio Brambilla	Surtees	Surtees-Ford Cosworth TS20	-	24
DNPQ	Keke Rosberg	Theodore	Theodore-Ford Cosworth TR1	-	25
DNPQ	Derek Daly	Hesketh	Hesketh-Ford Cosworth 308E	-	26
DNPQ	Rene Arnoux	Automobiles Martini	Martini-Ford Cosworth MK23	-	27
DNPQ	Hector Rebaque	Rebaque	Lotus-Ford Cosworth 78	-	28
DNPQ	Brett Lunger	BS Fabrications	McLaren-Ford Cosworth M26	-	29
DNPQ	Arturo Merzario	Merzario	Merzario-Ford Cosworth A1	-	30

Pole: Reutemann, 1m28.340s, 83.866mph/134.969kph. Fastest lap: Lauda, 1m28.650s, 83.572mph/134.497kph on Lap 72. Race leaders: Watson 1-37, Depailler 38-75

JARIER COMES CLOSE AGAIN

Signed by Lotus for the final two races of the year after Peterson's death, Jean-Pierre Jarier came extremely close to taking a maiden win. Robbed of third in the US GP by running out of fuel, he then rocketed clear from pole in the Canadian GP and was fully half a minute clear before he was denied by a holed brake line.

BELGIAN GRAND PRIX

ZOLDER • ROUND 6 • DATE: 21ST MAY 1978
Laps: 70 • Distance: 185.189miles/298.34km • Weather: Warm but dull

Pos	Driver	Team	Chassis-Engine	Result	Qual
1	Mario Andretti	Lotus	Lotus-Ford Cosworth 79	1h39m52.020s	1
2	Ronnie Peterson	Lotus	Lotus-Ford Cosworth 78	1h40m01.920s	7
3	Carlos Reutemann	Ferrari	Ferrari 312T3	1h40m16.360s	2
4	Gilles Villeneuve	Ferrari	Ferrari 312T3	1h40m39.060s	4
5	Jacques Laffite	Ligier	Ligier-Matra JS7/9	69 laps/accident	14
6	Didier Pironi	Tyrrell	Tyrrell-Ford Cosworth 008	69 laps	23
7	Brett Lunger	BS Fabrications	McLaren-Ford Cosworth M26	69 laps	24
8	Bruno Giacomelli	McLaren	McLaren-Ford Cosworth M26	69 laps	21
9	Rene Arnoux	Automobiles Martini	Martini-Ford Cosworth MK23	68 laps	19
10	Alan Jones	Williams	Williams-Ford Cosworth FW06	68 laps	11
11	Jochen Mass	ATS	ATS-Ford Cosworth HS1	68 laps	16
12	Jacky Ickx	Ensign	Ensign-Ford Cosworth N177	64 laps	22
13	Vittorio Brambilla	Surtees	Surtees-Ford Cosworth TS20	63 laps/engine	12
R	Hans-Joachim Stuck	Shadow	Shadow-Ford Cosworth DN9	56 laps/spun off	20

Pos	Driver	Team	Chassis-Engine	Result	Qual
NC	Jean-Pierre Jabouille	Renault	Renault RS01	56 laps	10
R	Jody Scheckter	Wolf	Wolf-Ford Cosworth WR5	53 laps/spun off	5
R	Patrick Depailler	Tyrrell	Tyrrell-Ford Cosworth 008	51 laps/gearbox	13
R	Clay Regazzoni	Shadow	Shadow-Ford Cosworth DN9	40 laps/transmission	18
R	Riccardo Patrese	Arrows	Arrows-Ford Cosworth FA1	31 laps/suspension	8
R	Rolf Stommelen	Arrows	Arrows-Ford Cosworth FA1	26 laps/spun off	17
R	John Watson	Brabham	Brabham-Alfa Romeo BT46	18 laps/accident	9
R	Niki Lauda	Brabham	Brabham-Alfa Romeo BT46	0 laps/accident	3
R	James Hunt	McLaren	McLaren-Ford Cosworth M26	0 laps/accident	6
R	Emerson Fittipaldi	Fittipaldi	Fittipaldi-Ford Cosworth F5A	0 laps/accident	15
DNQ	Rupert Keegan	Surtees	Surtees-Ford Cosworth TS20	-	25
DNQ	Derek Daly	Hesketh	Hesketh-Ford Cosworth 308E	-	26
DNQ	Keke Rosberg	Theodore	Theodore-Ford Cosworth TR1	-	27
DNQ	Alberto Colombo	ATS	ATS-Ford Cosworth HS1	-	28
DNPQ	Hector Rebaque	Rebaque	Lotus-Ford Cosworth 78	-	29
DNPQ	Arturo Merzario	Merzario	Merzario-Ford Cosworth A1	-	30
DNPQ	Patrick Neve	Patrick Neve	March-Ford Cosworth 781S	-	-
DNPQ	Bernard de Dryver	Bernard de Dryver	Ensign-Ford Cosworth N177	-	-

Pole: Andretti, 1m20.900s, 117.847mph/189.656kph. Fastest lap: Peterson, 1m23.130s, 114.685mph/184.568kph on Lap 66. Race leaders: Andretti 1-70

NEW CIRCUITS

The World Championship's first five visits to Brazil were to Interlagos, but 1978 marked a move to the Jacarepagua circuit built on reclaimed marshland near Rio de Janeiro. The Canadian GP made a move too, from Mosport Park to a circuit built on an island opposite Montreal. Gilles Villeneuve won that race, and it was named after him following his death in 1982.

SPANISH GRAND PRIX

JARAMA • ROUND 7 • DATE: 4TH JUNE 1978
Laps: 75 • Distance: 158.649miles/255.322km • Weather: Warm & bright

Pos	Driver	Team	Chassis-Engine	Result	Qual
1	Mario Andretti	Lotus	Lotus-Ford Cosworth 79	1h41m47.060s	1
2	Ronnie Peterson	Lotus	Lotus-Ford Cosworth 79	1h42m06.620s	2
3	Jacques Laffite	Ligier	Ligier-Matra JS9	1h42m24.300s	10
4	Jody Scheckter	Wolf	Wolf-Ford Cosworth WR5	1h42m47.120s	9
5	John Watson	Brabham	Brabham-Alfa Romeo BT46	1h42m52.990s	7
6	James Hunt	McLaren	McLaren-Ford Cosworth M26	74 laps	4
7	Vittorio Brambilla	Surtees	Surtees-Ford Cosworth TS20	74 laps	16
8	Alan Jones	Williams	Williams-Ford Cosworth FW06	74 laps	18
9	Jochen Mass	ATS	ATS-Ford Cosworth HS1	74 laps	17
10	Gilles Villeneuve	Ferrari	Ferrari 312T3	74 laps	5
11	Rupert Keegan	Surtees	Surtees-Ford Cosworth TS20	73 laps	23
12	Didier Pironi	Tyrrell	Tyrrell-Ford Cosworth 008	71 laps	13
13	Jean-Pierre Jabouille	Renault	Renault RS01	71 laps	11
14	Rolf Stommelen	Arrows	Arrows-Ford Cosworth FA1	71 laps	19
15	Clay Regazzoni	Shadow	Shadow-Ford Cosworth DN9	67 laps/fuel union	22
R	Jacky Ickx	Ensign	Ensign-Ford Cosworth N177	64 laps/engine	21
R	Emerson Fittipaldi	Fittipaldi	Fittipaldi-Ford Cosworth F5A	62 laps/throttle	15

Pos	Driver	Team	Chassis-Engine	Result	Qual
R	Carlos Reutemann	Ferrari	Ferrari 312T3	57 laps/accident	3
R	Niki Lauda	Brabham	Brabham-Alfa Romeo BT46	56 laps/engine	6
R	Patrick Depailler	Tyrrell	Tyrrell-Ford Cosworth 008	51 laps/engine	12
R	Hans-Joachim Stuck	Shadow	Shadow-Ford Cosworth DN9	45 laps/suspension	24
R	Riccardo Patrese	Arrows	Arrows-Ford Cosworth FA1	21 laps/engine	8
R	Hector Rebaque	Rebaque	Lotus-Ford Cosworth 78	21 laps/exhaust	20
R	Patrick Tambay	McLaren	McLaren-Ford Cosworth M26	16 laps/spun off	14
DNQ	Arturo Merzario	Merzario	Merzario-Ford Cosworth A1	-	25
DNQ	Brett Lunger	BS Fabrications	McLaren-Ford Cosworth M26	-	26
DNQ	Emilio de Villota	Centro Asegurador F1	McLaren-Ford Cosworth M23	-	27
DNQ	Alberto Colombo	ATS	ATS-Ford Cosworth HS1	-	28
DNPQ	Keke Rosberg	Theodore	Theodore-Ford Cosworth TR1	-	29

Pole: Andretti, 1m16.390s, 99.688mph/160.433kph. Fastest lap: Andretti, 1m20.060s, 95.118mph/153.078kph on Lap 5. Race leaders: Hunt 1-5, Andretti 6-75

SWEDISH GRAND PRIX

ANDERSTORP • ROUND 8 • DATE: 17TH JUNE 1978
Laps: 70 • Distance: 175.237miles/282.17km • Weather: Warm & bright

Pos	Driver	Team	Chassis-Engine	Result	Qual
1	Niki Lauda	Brabham	Brabham-Alfa Romeo BT46B	1h41m00.606s	3
2	Riccardo Patrese	Arrows	Arrows-Ford Cosworth FA1	1h41m34.625s	5
3	Ronnie Peterson	Lotus	Lotus-Ford Cosworth 79	1h41m34.711s	4
4	Patrick Tambay	McLaren	McLaren-Ford Cosworth M26	69 laps	15
5	Clay Regazzoni	Shadow	Shadow-Ford Cosworth DN9	69 laps	16
6	Emerson Fittipaldi	Fittipaldi	Fittipaldi-Ford Cosworth F5A	69 laps	13
7	Jacques Laffite	Ligier	Ligier-Matra JS9	69 laps	11
8	James Hunt	McLaren	McLaren-Ford Cosworth M26	69 laps	14
9	Gilles Villeneuve	Ferrari	Ferrari 312T3	69 laps	7
10	Carlos Reutemann	Ferrari	Ferrari 312T3	69 laps	8
11	Hans-Joachim Stuck	Shadow	Shadow-Ford Cosworth DN9	68 laps	20
12	Hector Rebaque	Rebaque	Lotus-Ford Cosworth 78	68 laps	21
13	Jochen Mass	ATS	ATS-Ford Cosworth HS1	68 laps	19
14	Rolf Stommelen	Arrows	Arrows-Ford Cosworth FA1	67 laps	24
15	Keke Rosberg	ATS	ATS-Ford Cosworth HS1	63 laps	23
NC	Arturo Merzario	Merzario	Merzario-Ford Cosworth A1	62 laps	22
R	Mario Andretti	Lotus	Lotus-Ford Cosworth 79	46 laps/engine	1
R	Alan Jones	Williams	Williams-Ford Cosworth FW06	46 laps/wheel	9
R	Patrick Depailler	Tyrrell	Tyrrell-Ford Cosworth 008	42 laps/suspension	12
R	Jean-Pierre Jabouille	Renault	Renault RS01	28 laps/engine	10
R	John Watson	Brabham	Brabham-Alfa Romeo BT46B	19 laps/spun off	2
R	Jody Scheckter	Wolf	Wolf-Ford Cosworth WR5	16 laps/overheating	6
R	Didier Pironi	Tyrrell	Tyrrell-Ford Cosworth 008	8 laps/accident	17
R	Vittorio Brambilla	Surtees	Surtees-Ford Cosworth TS20	7 laps/accident	18
DNQ	Rupert Keegan	Surtees	Surtees-Ford Cosworth TS20	-	25
DNQ	Brett Lunger	BS Fabrications	McLaren-Ford Cosworth M26	-	26
DNQ	Jacky Ickx	Ensign	Ensign-Ford Cosworth N177	-	27

Pole: Andretti, 1m22.058s, 109.886mph/176.845kph. Fastest lap: Lauda, 1m24.836s, 106.288mph/171.054kph on Lap 33. Race leaders: Andretti 1-38, Lauda 39-70

FRENCH GRAND PRIX

CIRCUIT PAUL RICARD • ROUND 9 • DATE: 2ND JULY 1978
Laps: 54 • Distance: 194.535miles/313.74km • Weather: Hot & bright

Pos	Driver	Team	Chassis-Engine	Result	Qual
1	Mario Andretti	Lotus	Lotus-Ford Cosworth 79	1h38m51.920s	2
2	Ronnie Peterson	Lotus	Lotus-Ford Cosworth 79	1h38m54.850s	5
3	James Hunt	McLaren	McLaren-Ford Cosworth M26	1h39m11.720s	4
4	John Watson	Brabham	Brabham-Alfa Romeo BT46	1h39m28.800s	1
5	Alan Jones	Williams	Williams-Ford Cosworth FW06	1h39m33.730s	14
6	Jody Scheckter	Wolf	Wolf-Ford Cosworth WR5	1h39m46.450s	7
7	Jacques Laffite	Ligier	Ligier-Matra JS7/9	1h39m46.660s	10
8	Riccardo Patrese	Arrows	Arrows-Ford Cosworth FA1	1h40m16.800s	12
9	Patrick Tambay	McLaren	McLaren-Ford Cosworth M26	1h40m18.980s	6
10	Didier Pironi	Tyrrell	Tyrrell-Ford Cosworth 008	1h40m21.900s	16
11	Hans-Joachim Stuck	Shadow	Shadow-Ford Cosworth DN9	53 laps	20
12	Gilles Villeneuve	Ferrari	Ferrari 312T3	53 laps	9
13	Jochen Mass	ATS	ATS-Ford Cosworth HS1	53 laps	25
14	Rene Arnoux	Automobiles Martini	Martini-Ford Cosworth MK23	53 laps	18
15	Rolf Stommelen	Arrows	Arrows-Ford Cosworth FA1	53 laps	21
16	Keke Rosberg	ATS	ATS-Ford Cosworth HS1	52 laps	26
17	Vittorio Brambilla	Surtees	Surtees-Ford Cosworth TS20	52 laps	19
18	Carlos Reutemann	Ferrari	Ferrari 312T3	49 laps	8
R	Brett Lunger	BS Fabrications	McLaren-Ford Cosworth M26	45 laps/engine	24
R	Emerson Fittipaldi	Fittipaldi	Fittipaldi-Ford Cosworth F5A	43 laps/suspension	15
R	Rupert Keegan	Surtees	Surtees-Ford Cosworth TS20	40 laps/engine	23
R	Bruno Giacomelli	McLaren	McLaren-Ford Cosworth M26	28 laps/engine	22
R	Niki Lauda	Brabham	Brabham-Alfa Romeo BT46	10 laps/engine	3
R	Patrick Depailler	Tyrrell	Tyrrell-Ford Cosworth 008	10 laps/engine	13
R	Clay Regazzoni	Shadow	Shadow-Ford Cosworth DN9	4 laps/electrical	17
R	Jean-Pierre Jabouille	Renault	Renault RS01	1 lap/engine	11
DNQ	Arturo Merzario	Merzario	Merzario-Ford Cosworth A1	-	27
DNQ	Derek Daly	Ensign	Ensign-Ford Cosworth N177	-	28
DNQ	Hector Rebaque	Rebaque	Lotus-Ford Cosworth 78	-	29

Pole: Watson, 1m44.410s, 124.476mph/200.325kph. Fastest lap: Reutemann, 1m48.560s, 119.718mph/192.667kph on Lap 48. Race leaders: Andretti 1-54

BRITISH GRAND PRIX

BRANDS HATCH • ROUND 10 • DATE: 16TH JULY 1978
Laps: 76 • Distance: 198.629miles/319.663km • Weather: Warm & bright

Pos	Driver	Team	Chassis-Engine	Result	Qual
1	Carlos Reutemann	Ferrari	Ferrari 312T3	1h42m12.390s	8
2	Niki Lauda	Brabham	Brabham-Alfa Romeo BT46	1h42m13.620s	4
3	John Watson	Brabham	Brabham-Alfa Romeo BT46	1h42m49.640s	9
4	Patrick Depailler	Tyrrell	Tyrrell-Ford Cosworth 008	1h43m25.660s	10
5	Hans-Joachim Stuck	Shadow	Shadow-Ford Cosworth DN9	75 laps	18
6	Patrick Tambay	McLaren	McLaren-Ford Cosworth M26	75 laps	20
7	Bruno Giacomelli	McLaren	McLaren-Ford Cosworth M26	75 laps	16
8	Brett Lunger	BS Fabrications	McLaren-Ford Cosworth M26	75 laps	24
9	Vittorio Brambilla	Surtees	Surtees-Ford Cosworth TS20	75 laps	25
10	Jacques Laffite	Ligier	Ligier-Matra JS7/9	73 laps	7
NC	Jochen Mass	ATS	ATS-Ford Cosworth HS1	66 laps	26
R	Keke Rosberg	ATS	ATS-Ford Cosworth HS1	59 laps/suspension	22

Pos	Driver	Team	Chassis-Engine	Result	Qual
R	Clay Regazzoni	Shadow	Shadow-Ford Cosworth DN9	49 laps/gearbox	17
R	Jean-Pierre Jabouille	Renault	Renault RS01	46 laps/turbo	12
R	Riccardo Patrese	Arrows	Arrows-Ford Cosworth FA1	40 laps/suspension	5
R	Didier Pironi	Tyrrell	Tyrrell-Ford Cosworth 008	40 laps/gearbox	19
R	Jody Scheckter	Wolf	Wolf-Ford Cosworth WR5	36 laps/gearbox	3
R	Emerson Fittipaldi	Fittipaldi	Fittipaldi-Ford Cosworth F5A	32 laps/engine	11
R	Arturo Merzario	Merzario	Merzario-Ford Cosworth A1	32 laps/fuel pump	23
R	Derek Daly	Ensign	Ensign-Ford Cosworth N177	30 laps/wheel	15
R	Mario Andretti	Lotus	Lotus-Ford Cosworth 79	28 laps/engine	2
R	Alan Jones	Williams	Williams-Ford Cosworth FW06	26 laps/transmission	6
R	Gilles Villeneuve	Ferrari	Ferrari 312T3	19 laps/transmission	13
R	Hector Rebaque	Rebaque	Lotus-Ford Cosworth 78	15 laps/gearbox	21
R	James Hunt	McLaren	McLaren-Ford Cosworth M26	8 laps/accident	14
R	Ronnie Peterson	Lotus	Lotus-Ford Cosworth 79	6 laps/fuel system	1
DNQ	Rolf Stommelen	Arrows	Arrows-Ford Cosworth FA1	-	27
DNQ	Geoff Lees	Mario Deliotti Racing	Ensign-Ford Cosworth N175	-	28
DNQ	Rupert Keegan	Surtees	Surtees-Ford Cosworth TS20	-	29
DNQ	Tony Trimmer	Melchester Racing	McLaren-Ford Cosworth M23	-	30

Pole: Peterson, 1m16.800s, 122.510mph/197.160kph. Fastest lap: Lauda, 1m18.600s, 119.704mph/192.645kph on Lap 72. Race leaders: Andretti 1-23, Scheckter 24-33, Lauda 34-59, Reutemann 60-76

NEW CONSTRUCTORS

In addition to Arrows, four other marques made their bow. ATS arrived with its own car, after running Penske chassis in 1977, with Teddy Yip's Theodore team replacing the Ensign it ran in 1977 with a car of its own design. Racer Arturo Merzario remodelled a March, while F2 and F3 car builder Tico Martini had his only shot at F1.

GERMAN GRAND PRIX

HOCKENHEIM • ROUND 11 • DATE: 30TH JULY 1978
Laps: 45 • Distance: 189.832miles/305.505km • Weather: Very hot & bright

Pos	Driver	Team	Chassis-Engine	Result	Qual
1	Mario Andretti	Lotus	Lotus-Ford Cosworth 79	1h28m00.900s	1
2	Jody Scheckter	Wolf	Wolf-Ford Cosworth WR5	1h28m16.250s	4
3	Jacques Laffite	Ligier	Ligier-Matra JS9	1h28m28.910s	7
4	Emerson Fittipaldi	Fittipaldi	Fittipaldi-Ford Cosworth F5A	1h28m37.780s	10
5	Didier Pironi	Tyrrell	Tyrrell-Ford Cosworth 008	1h28m58.160s	16
6	Hector Rebaque	Rebaque	Lotus-Ford Cosworth 78	1h29m38.760s	18
7	John Watson	Brabham	Brabham-Alfa Romeo BT46	1h29m40.430s	5
8	Gilles Villeneuve	Ferrari	Ferrari 312T3	1h29m57.770s	15
9	Riccardo Patrese	Arrows	Arrows-Ford Cosworth FA1	44 laps	14
10	Keke Rosberg	Theodore	Wolf-Ford Cosworth WR3	42 laps	19
11	Harald Ertl	Ensign	Ensign-Ford Cosworth N177	41 laps/engine	23
DQ	Rolf Stommelen	Arrows	Arrows-Ford Cosworth FA1	42 laps/illegal pit entry	17
R	Ronnie Peterson	Lotus	Lotus-Ford Cosworth 79	36 laps/gearbox	2
DQ	James Hunt	McLaren	McLaren-Ford Cosworth M26	34 laps/illegal pit entry	8

Pos	Driver	Team	Chassis-Engine	Result	Qual
R	Alan Jones	Williams	Williams-Ford Cosworth FW06	31 laps/fuel system	6
R	Nelson Piquet	Ensign	Ensign-Ford Cosworth N177	31 laps/engine	21
R	Vittorio Brambilla	Surtees	Surtees-Ford Cosworth TS20	24 laps/fuel system	20
R	Patrick Tambay	McLaren	McLaren-Ford Cosworth M26	16 laps/accident	11
R	Carlos Reutemann	Ferrari	Ferrari 312T3	14 laps/fuel system	12
R	Niki Lauda	Brabham	Brabham-Alfa Romeo BT46	11 laps/engine	3
R	Jean-Pierre Jabouille	Renault	Renault RS01	5 laps/engine	9
R	Jochen Mass	ATS	ATS-Ford Cosworth HS1	1 lap/accident	22
R	Hans-Joachim Stuck	Shadow	Shadow-Ford Cosworth DN9	1 lap/accident	24
R	Patrick Depailler	Tyrrell	Tyrrell-Ford Cosworth 008	0 laps/accident	13
DNQ	Clay Regazzoni	Shadow	Shadow-Ford Cosworth DN9	-	25
DNQ	Jean-Pierre Jarier	ATS	ATS-Ford Cosworth HS1	-	26
DNQ	Rupert Keegan	Surtees	Surtees-Ford Cosworth TS20	-	27
DNQ	Arturo Merzario	Merzario	Merzario-Ford Cosworth A1	-	28
DNPQ	Rene Arnoux	Automobiles Martini	Martini-Ford Cosworth MK23	-	29
DNPQ	Brett Lunger	BS Fabrications	McLaren-Ford Cosworth M26	-	30

Pole: Andretti, 1m51.900s, 135.715mph/218.412kph. Fastest lap: Peterson, 1m55.620s, 131.348mph/211.385kph on Lap 26. Race leaders: Peterson 1-4, Andretti 5-45

NEW DRIVERS

Future world champions Keke Rosberg and Nelson Piquet were among 11 newcomers in 1978. Rosberg won the non-championship International Trophy but then failed to score in a Theodore, while Piquet did well enough to land a Brabham drive for 1979. Didier Pironi got the best results, taking two fifths for Tyrrell. Derek Daly took a sixth for Ensign.

AUSTRIAN GRAND PRIX

OSTERREICHRING • ROUND 12 • DATE: 13TH AUGUST 1978
Laps: 54 • Distance: 199.391miles/320.889km • Weather: Warm with heavy rain

Pos	Driver	Team	Chassis-Engine	Result	Qual
1	Ronnie Peterson	Lotus	Lotus-Ford Cosworth 79	1h41m21.570s	1
2	Patrick Depailler	Tyrrell	Tyrrell-Ford Cosworth 008	1h42m09.010s	13
3	Gilles Villeneuve	Ferrari	Ferrari 312T3	1h43m01.330s	11
4	Emerson Fittipaldi	Fittipaldi	Fittipaldi-Ford Cosworth F5A	53 laps	6
5	Jacques Laffite	Ligier	Ligier-Matra JS9	53 laps	5
6	Vittorio Brambilla	Surtees	Surtees-Ford Cosworth TS20	53 laps	21
7	John Watson	Brabham	Brabham-Alfa Romeo BT46	53 laps	10
8	Brett Lunger	BS Fabrications	McLaren-Ford Cosworth M26	52 laps	17
9	Rene Arnoux	Automobiles Martini	Martini-Ford Cosworth MK23	52 laps	26
NC	Clay Regazzoni	Shadow	Shadow-Ford Cosworth DN9	50 laps	22
NC	Keke Rosberg	Theodore	Wolf-Ford Cosworth WR3	49 laps	25
DQ	Derek Daly	Ensign	Ensign-Ford Cosworth N177	41 laps/push start	19
R	Patrick Tambay	McLaren	McLaren-Ford Cosworth M26	40 laps/accident	14
R	Hans-Joachim Stuck	Shadow	Shadow-Ford Cosworth DN9	33 laps/accident	23
R	Jean-Pierre Jabouille	Renault	Renault RS01	31 laps/gearbox	3

Pos	Driver	Team	Chassis-Engine	Result	Qual
R	Niki Lauda	Brabham	Brabham-Alfa Romeo BT46	28 laps/accident	12
DQ	Carlos Reutemann	Ferrari	Ferrari 312T3	27 laps/push start	4
R	Didier Pironi	Tyrrell	Tyrrell-Ford Cosworth 008	20 laps/accident	9
R	James Hunt	McLaren	McLaren-Ford Cosworth M26	8 laps/accident	8
R	Alan Jones	Williams	Williams-Ford Cosworth FW06	7 laps/accident	15
R	Riccardo Patrese	Arrows	Arrows-Ford Cosworth A1	7 laps/accident	16
R	Harald Ertl	Ensign	Ensign-Ford Cosworth N177	7 laps/accident	24
R	Jody Scheckter	Wolf	Wolf-Ford Cosworth WR5	3 laps/accident	7
R	Nelson Piquet	BS Fabrications	McLaren-Ford Cosworth M23	2 laps/accident	20
R	Hector Rebaque	Rebaque	Lotus-Ford Cosworth 78	1 lap/clutch	18
R	Mario Andretti	Lotus	Lotus-Ford Cosworth 79	0 laps/accident	2
DNQ	Arturo Merzario	Merzario	Merzario-Ford Cosworth A1	-	27
DNQ	Jochen Mass	ATS	ATS-Ford Cosworth HS1	-	28
DNQ	Rupert Keegan	Surtees	Surtees-Ford Cosworth TS20	-	29
DNQ	Hans Binder	ATS	ATS-Ford Cosworth HS1	-	30
DNPQ	Rolf Stommelen	Arrows	Arrows-Ford Cosworth A1	-	31
DNPQ	Brian Henton	Surtees	Surtees-Ford Cosworth TS20	-	NT

Pole: Peterson, 1m37.710s, 136.043mph/218.940kph. Fastest lap: Peterson, 1m43.120s, 128.905mph/207.453kph. Race leaders: Peterson 1-18 & 29-54, Reutemann 19-22, Villeneuve 23-28

IN MEMORIAM

It was a truly awful year for Swedish racing fans, as not only did Peterson die from his injuries at the Italian GP, but Gunnar Nilsson succumbed to cancer after a year on the sidelines fighting the disease. He had signed to lead the new Arrows team after two years at Lotus, but was too unwell to ever drive the car.

DUTCH GRAND PRIX

ZANDVOORT • ROUND 13 • DATE: 27TH AUGUST 1978
Laps: 75 • Distance: 196.412miles/316.95km • Weather: Warm but windy

Pos	Driver	Team	Chassis-Engine	Result	Qual
1	Mario Andretti	Lotus	Lotus-Ford Cosworth 79	1h41m04.230s	1
2	Ronnie Peterson	Lotus	Lotus-Ford Cosworth 79	1h41m04.550s	2
3	Niki Lauda	Brabham	Brabham-Alfa Romeo BT46	1h41m16.440s	3
4	John Watson	Brabham	Brabham-Alfa Romeo BT46	1h41m25.150s	8
5	Emerson Fittipaldi	Fittipaldi	Fittipaldi-Ford Cosworth F5A	1h41m25.730s	10
6	Gilles Villeneuve	Ferrari	Ferrari 312T3	1h41m50.180s	5
7	Carlos Reutemann	Ferrari	Ferrari 312T3	1h42m04.750s	4
8	Jacques Laffite	Ligier	Ligier-Matra JS9	74 laps	6
9	Patrick Tambay	McLaren	McLaren-Ford Cosworth M26	74 laps	14
10	James Hunt	McLaren	McLaren-Ford Cosworth M26	74 laps	7
11	Hector Rebaque	Rebaque	Lotus-Ford Cosworth 78	74 laps	20
12	Jody Scheckter	Wolf	Wolf-Ford Cosworth WR6	73 laps	15
R	Bruno Giacomelli	McLaren	McLaren-Ford Cosworth M26	60 laps/spun off	19
R	Hans-Joachim Stuck	Shadow	Shadow-Ford Cosworth DN9	56 laps/transmission	18
R	Rene Arnoux	Automobiles Martini	Martini-Ford Cosworth MK23	40 laps/chassis	23

Pos	Driver	Team	Chassis-Engine	Result	Qual
R	Arturo Merzario	Merzario	Merzario-Ford Cosworth A1	40 laps/engine	27
DQ	Vittorio Brambilla	Surtees	Surtees-Ford Cosworth TS20	37 laps/push start	22
R	Jean-Pierre Jabouille	Renault	Renault RS01	35 laps/engine	9
R	Brett Lunger	BS Fabrications	McLaren-Ford Cosworth M26	35 laps/engine	21
R	Keke Rosberg	Theodore	Wolf-Ford Cosworth WR4	21 laps/accident	24
R	Alan Jones	Williams	Williams-Ford Cosworth FW06	17 laps/throttle	11
R	Nelson Piquet	BS Fabrications	McLaren-Ford Cosworth M23	16 laps/transmission	26
R	Patrick Depailler	Tyrrell	Tyrrell-Ford Cosworth 008	13 laps/engine	12
R	Derek Daly	Ensign	Ensign-Ford Cosworth N177	10 laps/transmission	16
R	Riccardo Patrese	Arrows	Arrows-Ford Cosworth A1	0 laps/accident	13
R	Didier Pironi	Tyrrell	Tyrrell-Ford Cosworth 008	0 laps/accident	17
NS	Rupert Keegan	Surtees	Surtees-Ford Cosworth TS20	broken hand	25
DNQ	Clay Regazzoni	Shadow	Shadow-Ford Cosworth DN9	-	28
DNQ	Michael Bleekemolen	ATS	ATS-Ford Cosworth HS1	-	29
DNQ	Jochen Mass	ATS	ATS-Ford Cosworth HS1	-	30
DNPQ	Harald Ertl	Ensign	Ensign-Ford Cosworth N177	-	31
DNPQ	Danny Ongais	Interscope Racing	Shadow-Ford Cosworth DN9	-	32
DNPQ	Rolf Stommelen	Arrows	Arrows-Ford Cosworth A1	-	33

Pole: Andretti, 1m16.360s, 123.799mph/199.235kph. Fastest lap: Lauda, 1m19.570s, 118.804mph/191.197kph on Lap 57. Race leaders: Andretti 1-75

ITALIAN GRAND PRIX

MONZA • ROUND 14 • DATE: 10TH SEPTEMBER 1978
Laps: 40 • Distance: 144.158miles/232.0km • Weather: Warm & bright

Pos	Driver	Team	Chassis-Engine	Result	Qual
1	Niki Lauda	Brabham	Brabham-Alfa Romeo BT46	1h07m04.540s	4
2	John Watson	Brabham	Brabham-Alfa Romeo BT46	1h07m06.020s	7
3	Carlos Reutemann	Ferrari	Ferrari 312T3	1h07m25.010s	11
4	Jacques Laffite	Ligier	Ligier-Matra JS9	1h07m42.070s	8
5	Patrick Tambay	McLaren	McLaren-Ford Cosworth M26	1h07m44.930s	19
6	Mario Andretti	Lotus	Lotus-Ford Cosworth 79	1h07m50.870s	1
7	Gilles Villeneuve	Ferrari	Ferrari 312T3	1h07m53.020s	2
8	Emerson Fittipaldi	Fittipaldi	Fittipaldi-Ford Cosworth F5A	1h07m59.780s	13
9	Nelson Piquet	BS Fabrications	McLaren-Ford Cosworth M23	1h08m11.370s	24
10	Derek Daly	Ensign	Ensign-Ford Cosworth N177	1h08m13.650s	18
11	Patrick Depailler	Tyrrell	Tyrrell-Ford Cosworth 008	1h08m21.110s	16
12	Jody Scheckter	Wolf	Wolf-Ford Cosworth WR6	39 laps	9
13	Alan Jones	Williams	Williams-Ford Cosworth FW06	39 laps	6
14	Bruno Giacomelli	McLaren	McLaren-Ford Cosworth M26	39 laps	20
NC	Clay Regazzoni	Shadow	Shadow-Ford Cosworth DN9	33 laps	15
R	Riccardo Patrese	Arrows	Arrows-Ford Cosworth A1	28 laps/engine	12
R	James Hunt	McLaren	McLaren-Ford Cosworth M26	19 laps/mechanical	10
R	Arturo Merzario	Merzario	Merzario-Ford Cosworth A1	14 laps/engine	22
R	Jean-Pierre Jabouille	Renault	Renault RS01	6 laps/engine	3
R	Ronnie Peterson	Lotus	Lotus-Ford Cosworth 78	0 laps/fatal accident	5
R	Didier Pironi	Tyrrell	Tyrrell-Ford Cosworth 008	0 laps/accident	14
R	Hans-Joachim Stuck	Shadow	Shadow-Ford Cosworth DN9	0 laps/accident	17
R	Brett Lunger	BS Fabrications	McLaren-Ford Cosworth M26	0 laps/accident	21
R	Vittorio Brambilla	Surtees	Surtees-Ford Cosworth TS20	0 laps/accident	23
DNQ	Hector Rebaque	Rebaque	Lotus-Ford Cosworth 78	-	25
DNQ	Harald Ertl	ATS	ATS-Ford Cosworth HS1	-	26
DNQ	Michael Bleekemolen	ATS	ATS-Ford Cosworth HS1	-	27

Pos	Driver	Team	Chassis-Engine	Result	Qual
DNQ	Carlo 'Gimax' Franchi	Surtees	Surtees-Ford Cosworth TS20	-	28
DNPQ	Keke Rosberg	Theodore	Wolf-Ford Cosworth WR4	-	29
DNPQ	Rolf Stommelen	Arrows	Arrows-Ford Cosworth A1	-	30
DNPQ	Alberto Colombo	Merzario	Merzario-Ford Cosworth A1	-	31

Pole: Andretti, 1m37.520s, 133.041mph/214.109kph. Fastest lap: Andretti, 1m38.230s, 132.080mph/212.562kph on Lap 33. Race leaders: Villeneuve 1-34, Andretti 35-40

UNITED STATES GRAND PRIX

WATKINS GLEN • ROUND 15 • DATE: 1ST OCTOBER 1978
Laps: 59 • Distance: 199.251miles/320.665km • Weather: Cool & dull

Pos	Driver	Team	Chassis-Engine	Result	Qual
1	Carlos Reutemann	Ferrari	Ferrari 312T3	1h40m48.800s	2
2	Alan Jones	Williams	Williams-Ford Cosworth FW06	1h41m08.539s	3
3	Jody Scheckter	Wolf	Wolf-Ford Cosworth WR6	1h41m34.501s	11
4	Jean-Pierre Jabouille	Renault	Renault RS01	1h42m13.807s	9
5	Emerson Fittipaldi	Fittipaldi	Fittipaldi-Ford Cosworth F5A	1h42m16.889s	13
6	Patrick Tambay	McLaren	McLaren-Ford Cosworth M26	1h42m39.010s	18
7	James Hunt	McLaren	McLaren-Ford Cosworth M26	58 laps	6
8	Derek Daly	Ensign	Ensign-Ford Cosworth N177	58 laps	19
9	Rene Arnoux	Surtees	Surtees-Ford Cosworth TS20	58 laps	21
10	Didier Pironi	Tyrrell	Tyrrell-Ford Cosworth 008	58 laps	16
11	Jacques Laffite	Ligier	Ligier-Matra JS9	58 laps	10
12	Bobby Rahal	Wolf	Wolf-Ford Cosworth WR5	58 laps	20
13	Brett Lunger	Ensign	Ensign-Ford Cosworth N177	58 laps	24
14	Clay Regazzoni	Shadow	Shadow-Ford Cosworth DN9	56 laps	17
15	Jean-Pierre Jarier	Lotus	Lotus-Ford Cosworth 79	55 laps/out of fuel	8
16	Rolf Stommelen	Arrows	Arrows-Ford Cosworth A1	54 laps	22
R	Arturo Merzario	Merzario	Merzario-Ford Cosworth A1	46 laps/gearbox	26
R	Michael Bleekemolen	ATS	ATS-Ford Cosworth HS1	43 laps/oil leak	25
R	Niki Lauda	Brabham	Brabham-Alfa Romeo BT46	28 laps/engine	5
R	Mario Andretti	Lotus	Lotus-Ford Cosworth 79	27 laps/engine	1
R	John Watson	Brabham	Brabham-Alfa Romeo BT46	25 laps/engine	7
R	Patrick Depailler	Tyrrell	Tyrrell-Ford Cosworth 008	23 laps/wheel	12
R	Gilles Villeneuve	Ferrari	Ferrari 312T3	22 laps/engine	4
R	Keke Rosberg	ATS	ATS-Ford Cosworth D1	21 laps/transmission	15
R	Hans-Joachim Stuck	Shadow	Shadow-Ford Cosworth DN9	1 lap/fuel system	14
R	Hector Rebaque	Rebaque	Lotus-Ford Cosworth 78	0 laps/clutch	23
DNQ	Beppe Gabbiani	Surtees	Surtees-Ford Cosworth TS20	-	27

Pole: Andretti, 1m38.114s, 123.914mph/199.421kph. Fastest lap: Jarier, 1m39.557s, 122.118mph/196.530kph on Lap 55. Race leaders: Andretti 1-2, Reutemann 3-59

CANADIAN GRAND PRIX

MONTREAL • ROUND 16 • DATE: 8TH OCTOBER 1978
Laps: 70 • Distance: 195.731miles/315.0km • Weather: Cool & dull

Pos	Driver	Team	Chassis-Engine	Result	Qual
1	Gilles Villeneuve	Ferrari	Ferrari 312T3	1h57m49.196s	3
2	Jody Scheckter	Wolf	Wolf-Ford Cosworth WR6	1h58m02.568s	2
3	Carlos Reutemann	Ferrari	Ferrari 312T3	1h58m08.604s	11
4	Riccardo Patrese	Arrows	Arrows-Ford Cosworth A1	1h58m13.863s	12
5	Patrick Depailler	Tyrrell	Tyrrell-Ford Cosworth 008	1h58m17.754s	13
6	Derek Daly	Ensign	Ensign-Ford Cosworth N177	1h58m43.672s	15
7	Didier Pironi	Tyrrell	Tyrrell-Ford Cosworth 008	1h59m10.446s	18
8	Patrick Tambay	McLaren	McLaren-Ford Cosworth M26	1h59m15.756s	17
9	Alan Jones	Williams	Williams-Ford Cosworth FW06	1h59m18.138s	5
10	Mario Andretti	Lotus	Lotus-Ford Cosworth 79	69 laps	9
11	Nelson Piquet	Brabham	Brabham-Alfa Romeo BT46	69 laps	14
12	Jean-Pierre Jabouille	Renault	Renault RS01	65 laps	22
NC	Keke Rosberg	ATS	ATS-Ford Cosworth D1	58 laps	21
R	Jacques Laffite	Ligier	Ligier-Matra JS9	52 laps/transmission	10
R	James Hunt	McLaren	McLaren-Ford Cosworth M26	51 laps/spun off	19
R	Jean-Pierre Jarier	Lotus	Lotus-Ford Cosworth 79	49 laps/oil leak	1
R	Rene Arnoux	Surtees	Surtees-Ford Cosworth TS20	37 laps/engine	16
R	Bobby Rahal	Wolf	Wolf-Ford Cosworth WR1	16 laps/fuel system	20
R	John Watson	Brabham	Brabham-Alfa Romeo BT46	8 laps/accident	4
R	Niki Lauda	Brabham	Brabham-Alfa Romeo BT46	5 laps/brakes	7
R	Hans-Joachim Stuck	Shadow	Shadow-Ford Cosworth DN9	1 lap/accident	8
R	Emerson Fittipaldi	Fittipaldi	Fittipaldi-Ford Cosworth F5A	0 laps/accident	6
DNQ	Clay Regazzoni	Shadow	Shadow-Ford Cosworth DN9	-	23
DNQ	Beppe Gabbiani	Surtees	Surtees-Ford Cosworth TS20	-	24
DNQ	Arturo Merzario	Merzario	Merzario-Ford Cosworth A1	-	25
DNQ	Hector Rebaque	Rebaque	Lotus-Ford Cosworth 78	-	26
DNQ	Rolf Stommelen	Arrows	Arrows-Ford Cosworth A1	-	27
DNQ	Michael Bleekemolen	ATS	ATS-Ford Cosworth HS1	-	27

Pole: Jarier, 1m38.015s, 102.700mph/165.280kph. Fastest lap: Jones, 1m38.072s, 102.641mph/165.184kph on Lap 70. Race leaders: Jarier 1-49, Villeneuve 50-70

CLASSIC CAR: LOTUS 79

The Lotus 78 introduced ground effects to F1, but no rival team realised that at the time. For 1978, Colin Chapman's ideas were translated by Martin Ogilvie and Geoff Aldridge into a more sophisticated machine, the 79, that harnessed the venturi effect created by skirts on the bottom edges of the intentionally broad sidepods. This sealed airflow all the way under the car from front to back, creating a low-pressure zone that sucked the car to the track to boost cornering speeds. It was soon superior to the Lotus 78, a car that Mario Andretti described as being "painted to the road".

WORLD DRIVERS' CHAMPIONSHIP FINAL RESULTS

Pos	Driver	Nat	Car-Engine	R1	R2	R3	R4	R5	R6
1	Mario Andretti	USA	Lotus-Ford Cosworth 78	1P	4	7F	2	11	-
			Lotus-Ford Cosworth 79	-	-	-	-	-	1P
2	Ronnie Peterson	SWE	Lotus-Ford Cosworth 78	5	RP	1	4	R	2F
			Lotus-Ford Cosworth 79	-	-	-	-	-	-
3	Carlos Reutemann	ARG	Ferrari 312T2	7	1F	-	-	-	-
			Ferrari 312T3	-	-	R	1P	8P	3
4	Niki Lauda	AUT	Brabham-Alfa Romeo BT45C	2	3	-	-	-	-
			Brabham-Alfa Romeo BT46	-	-	RP	R	2F	R
			Brabham-Alfa Romeo BT46B	-	-	-	-	-	-
5	Patrick Depailler	FRA	Tyrrell-Ford Cosworth 008	3	R	2	3	1	R
6	John Watson	GBR	Brabham-Alfa Romeo BT45C	R	8	-	-	-	-
			Brabham-Alfa Romeo BT46	-	-	3	R	4	R
			Brabham-Alfa Romeo BT46B	-	-	-	-	-	-
7	Jody Scheckter	ZAF	Wolf-Ford Cosworth WR1	10	R	R	R	3	-
			Wolf-Ford Cosworth WR5	-	-	-	-	-	R
8	Jacques Laffite	FRA	Ligier-Matra JS7	16	9	-	5	-	-
			Ligier-Matra JS7/9	-	-	5	-	-	5
			Ligier-Matra JS9	-	-	-	-	R	-
9	Gilles Villeneuve	CAN	Ferrari 312T2	8F	R	-	-	-	-
			Ferrari 312T3	-	-	R	R	R	4
9	Emerson Fittipaldi	BRA	Fittipaldi-Ford Cosworth F5A	9	2	R	8	9	R
11	Alan Jones	AUS	Williams-Ford Cosworth FW06	R	11	4	7F	R	10
11	Riccardo Patrese	ITA	Arrows-Ford Cosworth FA1	-	10	R	6	6	R
			Arrows-Ford Cosworth A1	-	-	-	-	-	-
13	James Hunt	GBR	McLaren-Ford Cosworth M26	4	R	R	R	R	R
13	Patrick Tambay	FRA	McLaren-Ford Cosworth M26	6	R	R	12	7	-
15	Didier Pironi	FRA	Tyrrell-Ford Cosworth 008	14	6	6	R	5	6
16	Clay Regazzoni	CHE	Shadow-Ford Cosworth DN8	15	5	DNQ	10	-	-
			Shadow-Ford Cosworth DN9	-	-	-	-	DNQ	R
17	Jean-Pierre Jabouille	FRA	Renault RS01	-	-	R	R	10	NC
18	Hans-Joachim Stuck	DEU	Shadow-Ford Cosworth DN8	17	R	DNQ	-	-	-
			Shadow-Ford Cosworth DN9	-	-	-	NS	R	R
19	Hector Rebaque	MEX	Lotus-Ford Cosworth 78	DNQ	R	10	DNPQ	DNPQ	DNPQ
19	Vittorio Brambilla	ITA	Surtees-Ford Cosworth TS19	18	DNQ	12	R	-	-
			Surtees-Ford Cosworth TS20	-	-	-	-	DNQ	13
19	Derek Daly	IRL	Ensign-Ford Cosworth N177	-	-	-	-	-	-

Pos	Driver	R7	R8	R9	R10	R11	R12	R13	R14	R15	R16	Total
1	Andretti	-	-	-	-	-	-	-	-	-	-	64
		1PF	RP	1	R	1P	R	1P	6PF	RP	10	
2	Peterson	-	-	-	-	-	-	-	R	-	-	51
		2	3	2	RP	RF	1PF	2	-	-	-	
3	Reutemann	-	-	-	-	-	-	-	-	-	-	48
		R	10	18F	1	R	DQ	7	3	1	3	
4	Lauda	-	-	-	-	-	-	-	-	-	-	44
		R	-	R	2F	R	R	3F	1	R	R	
		-	1F	-	-	-	-	-	-	-	-	
5	Depailler	R	R	R	4	R	2	R	11	R	5	34
6	Watson	-	-	-	-	-	-	-	-	-	-	25
		5	-	4P	3	7	7	4	2	R	R	
		-	R	-	-	-	-	-	-	-	-	
7	Scheckter	-	-	-	-	-	-	-	-	-	-	24
		4	R	6	R	2	R	12	12	3	2	

Pos	Driver	R7	R8	R9	R10	R11	R12	R13	R14	R15	R16	Total
8	Laffite	-	-	-	-	-	-	-	-	-	-	19
		-	-	7	10	-	-	-	-	-	-	
		3	7	-	-	3	5	8	4	11	R	
9	Villeneuve	-	-	-	-	-	-	-	-	-	-	17
		10	9	12	R	8	3	6	7	R	1	
9	Fittipaldi	R	6	R	R	4	4	5	8	5	R	17
11	Jones	8	R	5	R	R	R	R	13	2	9F	11
11	Patrese	R	2	8	R	9	-	-	-	-	-	11
		-	-	-	-	-	R	R	R	-	4	
13	Hunt	6	8	3	R	DQ	R	10	R	7	R	8
13	Tambay	R	4	9	6	R	R	9	5	6	8	8
15	Pironi	12	R	10	R	5	R	R	R	10	7	7
16	Regazzoni	-	-	-	-	-	-	-	-	-	-	4
		15	5	R	R	DNQ	NC	DNQ	NC	14	DNQ	
17	Jabouille	13	R	R	R	R	R	R	R	4	12	3
18	Stuck	-	-	-	-	-	-	-	-	-	-	2
		R	11	11	5	R	R	R	R	R	R	
19	Rebaque	R	12	DNQ	R	6	R	11	DNQ	R	DNQ	1
19	Brambilla	-	-	-	-	-	-	-	-	-	-	1
		7	R	17	9	R	6	DQ	R	-	-	
19	Daly	-	-	DNQ	R	-	DQ	R	10	8	6	1

SYMBOLS AND GRAND PRIX KEY

Round 1 Argentinian GP
Round 2 Brazilian GP
Round 3 South African GP
Round 4 United States GP West
Round 5 Monaco GP
Round 6 Belgian GP
Round 7 Spanish GP
Round 8 Swedish GP
Round 9 French GP
Round 10 British GP
Round 11 German GP
Round 12 Austrian GP
Round 13 Dutch GP
Round 14 Italian GP
Round 15 United States GP
Round 16 Canadian GP

SCORING

1st 9 points
2nd 6 points
3rd 4 points
4th 3 points
5th 2 points
6th 1 point

DNPQ DID NOT PRE-QUALIFY **DNQ** DID NOT QUALIFY **DQ** DISQUALIFIED **EX** EXCLUDED
F FASTEST LAP **NC** NOT CLASSIFIED **NS** NON-STARTER **P** POLE POSITION **R** RETIRED

WORLD CONSTRUCTORS' CHAMPIONSHIP FINAL RESULTS

Pos	Team-Engine	R1	R2	R3	R4	R5	R6	R7	R8	R9
1	Lotus-Ford	1	4	1	2	11	1	1	3	1
2	Ferrari	7	1	-	1	8	3	10	9	12
3	Brabham-Alfa Romeo	2	3	3	-	2	-	5	1	4
4	Tyrrell-Ford	3	6	2	3	1	6	12	-	10
5	Wolf-Ford	10	-	-	-	3	-	4	-	6
6	Ligier-Matra	16	9	5	5	-	5	3	7	7
7	Fittipaldi-Ford	9	2	-	8	9	-	-	6	-
8	McLaren-Ford	4	-	11	12	7	7	6	4	3
9	Williams-Ford	-	11	4	7	-	10	8	-	5
9	Arrows-Ford		10	9	6	6	-	14	2	8
11	Shadow-Ford	15	5	-	10	-	-	15	5	11
12	Renault	-	-	-	-	10	-	13	-	-
13	Surtees-Ford	18	-	12	-	-	13	7	-	17
13	Ensign-Ford	-	-	-	-	-	12	-	-	-

Pos	Team-Engine	R10	R11	R12	R13	R14	R15	R16	Total
1	Lotus-Ford	-	1	1	1	6	15	10	86
2	Ferrari	1	8	3	6	3	1	1	58
3	Brabham-Alfa Romeo	2	7	7	3	1	-	11	53
4	Tyrrell-Ford	4	5	2	-	11	10	5	38
5	Wolf-Ford	-	2	-	12	12	3	2	24
6	Ligier-Matra	10	3	5	8	4	11	-	19
7	Fittipaldi-Ford	-	4	4	5	8	5	-	17
8	McLaren-Ford	6	-	8	9	5	6	8	15
9	Williams-Ford	-	-	-	-	13	2	9	11
9	Arrows-Ford	-	9	-	-	-	16	4	11
11	Shadow-Ford	5	-	-	-	-	14	-	6
12	Renault	-	-	-	-	-	4	12	3
13	Surtees-Ford	9	-	6	-	-	9	-	1
13	Ensign-Ford	-	11	-	-	10	8	6	1

1979

SEASON SUMMARY

It seems extraordinary, but Lotus went from domination in 1978 to rank only fourth in 1979. It was a mark of how the outfit got it wrong as the other teams really got the hang of ground effects. Ligier started the season at a gallop before its challenge faded. Renault's turbocharged racers then hit the front and Williams ended the year with the best package of all as Alan Jones won four of the last six races, but it was Ferrari that won the day, with Jody Scheckter and Gilles Villeneuve finishing first and second in the championship largely due to a consistent accumulation of points.

ARGENTINIAN GRAND PRIX

BUENOS AIRES • ROUND 1 • DATE: 21ST JANUARY 1979
Laps: 53 • Distance: 196.548miles/316.314km • Weather: Very hot & bright

Pos	Driver	Team	Chassis-Engine	Result	Qual
1	Jacques Laffite	Ligier	Ligier-Ford Cosworth JS11	1h36m03.210s	1
2	Carlos Reutemann	Lotus	Lotus-Ford Cosworth 79	1h36m18.150s	3
3	John Watson	McLaren	McLaren-Ford Cosworth M28	1h37m32.020s	6
4	Patrick Depailler	Ligier	Ligier-Ford Cosworth JS11	1h37m44.930s	2
5	Mario Andretti	Lotus	Lotus-Ford Cosworth 79	52 laps	7
6	Emerson Fittipaldi	Fittipaldi	Fittipaldi-Ford Cosworth F5A	52 laps	11
7	Elio de Angelis	Shadow	Shadow-Ford Cosworth DN9B	52 laps	16
8	Jochen Mass	Arrows	Arrows-Ford Cosworth A1B	51 laps	14
9	Alan Jones	Williams	Williams-Ford Cosworth FW06	51 laps	15
10	Clay Regazzoni	Williams	Williams-Ford Cosworth FW06	51 laps	17
11	Derek Daly	Ensign	Ensign-Ford Cosworth N177	51 laps	24
R	Gilles Villeneuve	Ferrari	Ferrari 312T3	48 laps/engine	10
R	Hector Rebaque	Rebaque	Lotus-Ford Cosworth 79	46 laps/suspension	19
R	James Hunt	Wolf	Wolf-Ford Cosworth WR7	42 laps/electrical	18
R	Jan Lammers	Shadow	Shadow-Ford Cosworth DN9B	42 laps/transmission	21
R	Jean-Pierre Jarier	Tyrrell	Tyrrell-Ford Cosworth 009	15 laps/engine	4
R	Jean-Pierre Jabouille	Renault	Renault RS01	15 laps/engine	12
R	Niki Lauda	Brabham	Brabham-Alfa Romeo BT48	8 laps/fuel system	23
R	Rene Arnoux	Renault	Renault RS01	6 laps/engine	25
R	Jody Scheckter	Ferrari	Ferrari 312T3	0 laps/collision	5
R	Didier Pironi	Tyrrell	Tyrrell-Ford Cosworth 009	0 laps/collision	8
R	Patrick Tambay	McLaren	McLaren-Ford Cosworth M28	0 laps/collision	9
R	Nelson Piquet	Brabham	Brabham-Alfa Romeo BT46	0 laps/collision	20
R	Arturo Merzario	Merzario	Merzario-Ford Cosworth A1B	0 laps/collision	22
NS	Riccardo Patrese	Arrows	Arrows-Ford Cosworth A1B	accident	13
NS	Hans-Joachim Stuck	ATS	ATS-Ford Cosworth D2	car not ready	25

Pole: Laffite, 1m44.200s, 128.123mph/206.195kph. Fastest lap: Laffite, 1m46.910s, 124.875mph/200.968kph on Lap 42. Race leaders: Depailler 1-10, Laffite 11-53

JABOUILLE TAKES FIRST TURBO WIN

First seen in 1977, turbocharged engines took a while to become reliable, but Renault not only squeezed ever more power out of their 1500cc units, they developed a car to harness it. Their RE10 had its day of days at the 1979 French GP and, although Jean-Pierre Jabouille didn't score again, team-mate Rene Arnoux twice finished second.

BRAZILIAN GRAND PRIX

INTERLAGOS • ROUND 2 • DATE: 4TH FEBRUARY 1979
Laps: 40 • Distance: 195.702miles/314.952km • Weather: Very hot & bright

Pos	Driver	Team	Chassis-Engine	Result	Qual
1	Jacques Laffite	Ligier	Ligier-Ford Cosworth JS11	1h40m09.640s	1
2	Patrick Depailler	Ligier	Ligier-Ford Cosworth JS11	1h40m14.920s	2
3	Carlos Reutemann	Lotus	Lotus-Ford Cosworth 79	1h40m53.780s	3
4	Didier Pironi	Tyrrell	Tyrrell-Ford Cosworth 009	1h41m35.520s	8
5	Gilles Villeneuve	Ferrari	Ferrari 312T3	39 laps	5
6	Jody Scheckter	Ferrari	Ferrari 312T3	39 laps	6
7	Jochen Mass	Arrows	Arrows-Ford Cosworth A1B	39 laps	19
8	John Watson	McLaren	McLaren-Ford Cosworth M28	39 laps	14
9	Riccardo Patrese	Arrows	Arrows-Ford Cosworth A1B	39 laps	16
10	Jean-Pierre Jabouille	Renault	Renault RS01	39 laps	7
11	Emerson Fittipaldi	Fittipaldi	Fittipaldi-Ford Cosworth F5A	39 laps	9
12	Elio de Angelis	Shadow	Shadow-Ford Cosworth DN9B	39 laps	20
13	Derek Daly	Ensign	Ensign-Ford Cosworth N177	39 laps	23
14	Jan Lammers	Shadow	Shadow-Ford Cosworth DN9B	39 laps	21
15	Clay Regazzoni	Williams	Williams-Ford Cosworth FW06	38 laps	17
R	Alan Jones	Williams	Williams-Ford Cosworth FW06	33 laps/fuel system	13
R	Hans-Joachim Stuck	ATS	ATS-Ford Cosworth D2	31 laps/steering	24
R	Rene Arnoux	Renault	Renault RS01	28 laps/spun off	11
R	James Hunt	Wolf	Wolf-Ford Cosworth WR7	7 laps/steering	10
R	Patrick Tambay	McLaren	McLaren-Ford Cosworth M26	7 laps/collision	18
R	Niki Lauda	Brabham	Brabham-Alfa Romeo BT48	5 laps/gearbox	12
R	Nelson Piquet	Brabham	Brabham-Alfa Romeo BT48	5 laps/accident	22
R	Mario Andretti	Lotus	Lotus-Ford Cosworth 79	2 laps/oil leak	4
NS	Jean-Pierre Jarier	Tyrrell	Tyrrell-Ford Cosworth 009	electrics	15
DNQ	Hector Rebaque	Rebaque	Lotus-Ford Cosworth 79	-	25
DNQ	Arturo Merzario	Merzario	Merzario-Ford Cosworth A1B	-	26

Pole: Laffite, 2m23.070s, 123.108mph/198.124kph. Fastest lap: Laffite, 2m28.760s, 118.400mph/190.546kph on Lap 23. Race leaders: Laffite 1-40

SOUTH AFRICAN GRAND PRIX

KYALAMI • ROUND 3 • DATE: 3RD MARCH 1979
Laps: 78 • Distance: 198.908miles/320.112km • Weather: Warm with heavy rain

Pos	Driver	Team	Chassis-Engine	Result	Qual
1	Gilles Villeneuve	Ferrari	Ferrari 312T4	1h41m49.960s	3
2	Jody Scheckter	Ferrari	Ferrari 312T4	1h41m53.380s	2
3	Jean-Pierre Jarier	Tyrrell	Tyrrell-Ford Cosworth 009	1h42m12.070s	9

Pos	Driver	Team	Chassis-Engine	Result	Qual
4	Mario Andretti	Lotus	Lotus-Ford Cosworth 79	1h42m17.840s	8
5	Carlos Reutemann	Lotus	Lotus-Ford Cosworth 79	1h42m56.930s	11
6	Niki Lauda	Brabham	Brabham-Alfa Romeo BT48	77 laps	4
7	Nelson Piquet	Brabham	Brabham-Alfa Romeo BT48	77 laps	12
8	James Hunt	Wolf	Wolf-Ford Cosworth WR7	77 laps	13
9	Clay Regazzoni	Williams	Williams-Ford Cosworth FW06	76 laps	22
10	Patrick Tambay	McLaren	McLaren-Ford Cosworth M28	75 laps	17
11	Riccardo Patrese	Arrows	Arrows-Ford Cosworth A1B	75 laps	16
12	Jochen Mass	Arrows	Arrows-Ford Cosworth A1B	74 laps	20
13	Emerson Fittipaldi	Fittipaldi	Fittipaldi-Ford Cosworth F6	74 laps	18
R	Hector Rebaque	Rebaque	Lotus-Ford Cosworth 79	71 laps/engine	23
R	Rene Arnoux	Renault	Renault RS01	67 laps/tyre	10
R	Alan Jones	Williams	Williams-Ford Cosworth FW06	63 laps/suspension	19
R	John Watson	McLaren	McLaren-Ford Cosworth M28	61 laps/ignition	14
R	Hans-Joachim Stuck	ATS	ATS-Ford Cosworth D2	57 laps/accident	24
R	Jean-Pierre Jabouille	Renault	Renault RS01	47 laps/engine	1
R	Jacques Laffite	Ligier	Ligier-Ford Cosworth JS11	45 laps/accident	6
R	Didier Pironi	Tyrrell	Tyrrell-Ford Cosworth 009	25 laps/throttle	7
R	Elio de Angelis	Shadow	Shadow-Ford Cosworth DN9B	16 laps/accident	15
R	Patrick Depailler	Ligier	Ligier-Ford Cosworth JS11	4 laps/accident	5
R	Jan Lammers	Shadow	Shadow-Ford Cosworth DN9B	2 laps/accident	21
DNQ	Derek Daly	Ensign	Ensign-Ford Cosworth N179	-	25
DNQ	Arturo Merzario	Merzario	Merzario-Ford Cosworth A1B	-	26

Pole: Jabouille, 1m11.800s, 127.860mph/205.771kph. Fastest lap: Villeneuve, 1m14.412s, 123.372mph/198.548kph on Lap 23. Race leaders: Jabouille 1, Villeneuve 2-14 & 53-78, Scheckter 15-52

UNITED STATES GRAND PRIX WEST

LONG BEACH • ROUND 4 • DATE: 8TH APRIL 1979
Laps: 80 • Distance: 161.561miles/260.08km • Weather: Warm & bright

Pos	Driver	Team	Chassis-Engine	Result	Qual
1	Gilles Villeneuve	Ferrari	Ferrari 312T4	1h50m25.400s	1
2	Jody Scheckter	Ferrari	Ferrari 312T4	1h50m54.780s	3
3	Alan Jones	Williams	Williams-Ford Cosworth FW06	1h51m25.090s	10
4	Mario Andretti	Lotus	Lotus-Ford Cosworth 79	1h51m29.730s	6
5	Patrick Depailler	Ligier	Ligier-Ford Cosworth JS11	1h51m48.920s	4
6	Jean-Pierre Jarier	Tyrrell	Tyrrell-Ford Cosworth 009	79 laps	7
7	Elio de Angelis	Shadow	Shadow-Ford Cosworth DN9B	78 laps	20
8	Nelson Piquet	Brabham	Brabham-Alfa Romeo BT48	78 laps	12
9	Jochen Mass	Arrows	Arrows-Ford Cosworth A1B	78 laps	13
DQ	Didier Pironi	Tyrrell	Tyrrell-Ford Cosworth 009	72 laps/push start	17
R	Hector Rebaque	Rebaque	Lotus-Ford Cosworth 79	71 laps/accident	23
R	Derek Daly	Ensign	Ensign-Ford Cosworth N179	69 laps/accident	24
R	John Watson	McLaren	McLaren-Ford Cosworth M28	62 laps/injection	18
DQ	Hans-Joachim Stuck	ATS	ATS-Ford Cosworth D2	49 laps/outside assistance	21
R	Clay Regazzoni	Williams	Williams-Ford Cosworth FW06	48 laps/engine	15
R	Jan Lammers	Shadow	Shadow-Ford Cosworth DN9B	47 laps/suspension	14
R	Riccardo Patrese	Arrows	Arrows-Ford Cosworth A1B	40 laps/brakes	9
R	Carlos Reutemann	Lotus	Lotus-Ford Cosworth 79	21 laps/transmission	2
R	Emerson Fittipaldi	Fittipaldi	Fittipaldi-Ford Cosworth F5A	19 laps/transmission	16
R	Arturo Merzario	Merzario	Merzario-Ford Cosworth A1B	13 laps/engine	22
R	Jacques Laffite	Ligier	Ligier-Ford Cosworth JS11	8 laps/brakes	5
R	James Hunt	Wolf	Wolf-Ford Cosworth WR8	1 lap/transmission	8

Pos	Driver	Team	Chassis-Engine	Result	Qual
R	Niki Lauda	Brabham	Brabham-Alfa Romeo BT48	0 laps/accident	11
R	Patrick Tambay	McLaren	McLaren-Ford Cosworth M28	0 laps/collision	19
NS	Jean-Pierre Jabouille	Renault	Renault RS01	sprained wrist	20
NS	Rene Arnoux	Renault	Renault RS01	cv joint	22

Pole: Villeneuve, 1m18.825s, 92.258mph/148.475kph. Fastest lap: Villeneuve, 1m21.200s, 89.560mph/144.133kph on Lap 63. Race leaders: Villeneuve 1-80

SPANISH GRAND PRIX

JARAMA • ROUND 5 • DATE: 29TH APRIL 1979
Laps: 75 • Distance: 158.649miles/255.322km • Weather: Warm but dull

Pos	Driver	Team	Chassis-Engine	Result	Qual
1	Patrick Depailler	Ligier	Ligier-Ford Cosworth JS11	1h39m11.840s	2
2	Carlos Reutemann	Lotus	Lotus-Ford Cosworth 79	1h39m32.780s	8
3	Mario Andretti	Lotus	Lotus-Ford Cosworth 80	1h39m39.150s	4
4	Jody Scheckter	Ferrari	Ferrari 312T4	1h39m40.520s	5
5	Jean-Pierre Jarier	Tyrrell	Tyrrell-Ford Cosworth 009	1h39m42.230s	12
6	Didier Pironi	Tyrrell	Tyrrell-Ford Cosworth 009	1h40m00.270s	10
7	Gilles Villeneuve	Ferrari	Ferrari 312T4	1h40m04.150s	3
8	Jochen Mass	Arrows	Arrows-Ford Cosworth A1B	1h40m26.680s	17
9	Rene Arnoux	Renault	Renault RS01	74 laps	11
10	Riccardo Patrese	Arrows	Arrows-Ford Cosworth A1B	74 laps	16
11	Emerson Fittipaldi	Fittipaldi	Fittipaldi-Ford Cosworth F5A	74 laps	19
12	Jan Lammers	Shadow	Shadow-Ford Cosworth DN9B	73 laps	24
13	Patrick Tambay	McLaren	McLaren-Ford Cosworth M28	72 laps	20
14	Hans-Joachim Stuck	ATS	ATS-Ford Cosworth D2	69 laps	21
R	Niki Lauda	Brabham	Brabham-Alfa Romeo BT48	63 laps/water leak	6
R	Hector Rebaque	Rebaque	Lotus-Ford Cosworth 79	58 laps/engine	23
R	Alan Jones	Williams	Williams-Ford Cosworth FW07	54 laps/gearbox	13
R	Elio de Angelis	Shadow	Shadow-Ford Cosworth DN9B	52 laps/engine	22
R	Clay Regazzoni	Williams	Williams-Ford Cosworth FW07	32 laps/engine	14
R	James Hunt	Wolf	Wolf-Ford Cosworth WR7	26 laps/brakes	15
R	Jean-Pierre Jabouille	Renault	Renault RS10	21 laps/turbo	9
R	John Watson	McLaren	McLaren-Ford Cosworth M28B	21 laps/engine	18
R	Jacques Laffite	Ligier	Ligier-Ford Cosworth JS11	15 laps/engine	1
R	Nelson Piquet	Brabham	Brabham-Alfa Romeo BT48	15 laps/fuel metering	7
DNQ	Derek Daly	Ensign	Ensign-Ford Cosworth N177	-	25
DNQ	Arturo Merzario	Merzario	Merzario-Ford Cosworth A2	-	26
DNQ	Gianfranco Brancatelli	Kauhsen	Kauhsen-Ford Cosworth WK	-	27

Pole: Laffite, 1m14.500s, 102.217mph/164.503kph. Fastest lap: Villeneuve, 1m16.440s, 99.623mph/160.328kph on Lap 72. Race leaders: Depailler 1-75

BACK WITHOUT A BANG

Alfa Romeo dominated the first two years of the World Championship, in 1950 and 1951, then quit. Its return in 1979 was less glorious, at first with the portly 177 and then, near the season's end, with the still chunky-looking 179. Sadly, even with its great-sounding Alfa Romeo V12 engine, Bruno Giacomelli couldn't make it fly.

BELGIAN GRAND PRIX

ZOLDER • ROUND 6 • DATE: 13TH MAY 1979
Laps: 70 • Distance: 185.189miles/298.34km • Weather: Hot & bright

Pos	Driver	Team	Chassis-Engine	Result	Qual
1	Jody Scheckter	Ferrari	Ferrari 312T4	1h39m59.530s	7
2	Jacques Laffite	Ligier	Ligier-Ford Cosworth JS11	1h40m14.890s	1
3	Didier Pironi	Tyrrell	Tyrrell-Ford Cosworth 009	1h40m34.700s	12
4	Carlos Reutemann	Lotus	Lotus-Ford Cosworth 79	1h40m46.020s	10
5	Riccardo Patrese	Arrows	Arrows-Ford Cosworth A1B	1h41m03.840s	16
6	John Watson	McLaren	McLaren-Ford Cosworth M28B	1h41m05.380s	19
7	Gilles Villeneuve	Ferrari	Ferrari 312T4	69 laps/out of fuel	6
8	Hans-Joachim Stuck	ATS	ATS-Ford Cosworth D2	69 laps	20
9	Emerson Fittipaldi	Fittipaldi	Fittipaldi-Ford Cosworth F5A	68 laps	23
10	Jan Lammers	Shadow	Shadow-Ford Cosworth DN9B	68 laps	21
11	Jean-Pierre Jarier	Tyrrell	Tyrrell-Ford Cosworth 009	67 laps	11
R	Patrick Depailler	Ligier	Ligier-Ford Cosworth JS11	46 laps/accident	2
R	James Hunt	Wolf	Wolf-Ford Cosworth WR8	40 laps/accident	9
R	Alan Jones	Williams	Williams-Ford Cosworth FW07	39 laps/electrical	4
R	Mario Andretti	Lotus	Lotus-Ford Cosworth 79	27 laps/brakes	5
R	Nelson Piquet	Brabham	Brabham-Alfa Romeo BT48	23 laps/engine	3
R	Niki Lauda	Brabham	Brabham-Alfa Romeo BT48	23 laps/engine	13
R	Rene Arnoux	Renault	Renault RS01	22 laps/turbo	18
R	Bruno Giacomelli	Alfa Romeo	Alfa Romeo 177	21 laps/accident	14
R	Elio de Angelis	Shadow	Shadow-Ford Cosworth DN9B	21 laps/accident	24
R	Jochen Mass	Arrows	Arrows-Ford Cosworth A1B	17 laps/spun off	22
R	Hector Rebaque	Rebaque	Lotus-Ford Cosworth 79	13 laps/transmission	15
R	Jean-Pierre Jabouille	Renault	Renault RE10	13 laps/turbo	17
R	Clay Regazzoni	Williams	Williams-Ford Cosworth FW07	1 lap/accident	8
DNQ	Patrick Tambay	McLaren	McLaren-Ford Cosworth M26	-	25
DNQ	Arturo Merzario	Merzario	Merzario-Ford Cosworth A2	-	26
DNQ	Derek Daly	Ensign	Ensign-Ford Cosworth N177	-	27
DNQ	Gianfranco Brancatelli	Kauhsen	Kauhsen-Ford Cosworth WK	-	28

Pole: Laffite, 1m21.130s, 117.512mph/189.118kph. Fastest lap: Villeneuve, 1m23.090s, 114.740mph/184.657kph on Lap 63. Race leaders: Depailler 1-18 & 40-46, Laffite 19-23 & 47-53, Jones 24-39, Scheckter 54-70

MONACO GRAND PRIX

MONTE CARLO • ROUND 7 • DATE: 27TH MAY 1979
Laps: 76 • Distance: 156.406miles/251.712km • Weather: Warm & bright

Pos	Driver	Team	Chassis-Engine	Result	Qual
1	Jody Scheckter	Ferrari	Ferrari 312T4	1h55m22.480s	1
2	Clay Regazzoni	Williams	Williams-Ford Cosworth FW07	1h55m22.920s	16
3	Carlos Reutemann	Lotus	Lotus-Ford Cosworth 79	1h55m31.050s	11
4	John Watson	McLaren	McLaren-Ford Cosworth M28C	1h56m03.790s	14
5	Patrick Depailler	Ligier	Ligier-Ford Cosworth JS11	75 laps/engine	3
6	Jochen Mass	Arrows	Arrows-Ford Cosworth A1B	69 laps	8
R	Nelson Piquet	Brabham	Brabham-Alfa Romeo BT48	68 laps/driveshaft	18
NC	Jean-Pierre Jabouille	Renault	Renault RE10	68 laps	20
R	Jacques Laffite	Ligier	Ligier-Ford Cosworth JS11	55 laps/gearbox	5
R	Gilles Villeneuve	Ferrari	Ferrari 312T4	54 laps/transmission	2
R	Alan Jones	Williams	Williams-Ford Cosworth FW07	43 laps/steering	9
R	Jean-Pierre Jarier	Tyrrell	Tyrrell-Ford Cosworth 009	34 laps/suspension	6

Pos	Driver	Team	Chassis-Engine	Result	Qual
R	Hans-Joachim Stuck	ATS	ATS-Ford Cosworth D2	30 laps/wheel	12
R	Niki Lauda	Brabham	Brabham-Alfa Romeo BT48	21 laps/accident	4
R	Didier Pironi	Tyrrell	Tyrrell-Ford Cosworth 009	21 laps/accident	7
R	Mario Andretti	Lotus	Lotus-Ford Cosworth 80	21 laps/suspension	13
R	Emerson Fittipaldi	Fittipaldi	Fittipaldi-Ford Cosworth F5A	17 laps/engine	17
R	Rene Arnoux	Renault	Renault RE10	8 laps/accident	19
R	James Hunt	Wolf	Wolf-Ford Cosworth WR7	4 laps/transmission	10
R	Riccardo Patrese	Arrows	Arrows-Ford Cosworth A1B	4 laps/suspension	15
DNQ	Elio de Angelis	Shadow	Shadow-Ford Cosworth DN9B	-	21
DNQ	Patrick Tambay	McLaren	McLaren-Ford Cosworth M28B	-	22
DNQ	Jan Lammers	Shadow	Shadow-Ford Cosworth DN9B	-	23
DNQ	Derek Daly	Ensign	Ensign-Ford Cosworth N179	-	24
DNPQ	Gianfranco Brancatelli	Merzario	Merzario-Ford Cosworth A2	-	25

Pole: Scheckter, 1m26.450s, 85.699mph/137.920kph. Fastest lap: Depailler, 1m28.820s, 83.412mph/134.240kph on Lap 69. Race leaders: Scheckter 1-76

LET DOWN BY HIS MACHINERY

Mario Andretti did not become a poor driver overnight, but the 1978 World Champion's points tally in his title defence was sufficient only for equal 10th place in the championship. His wingless Lotus 80 was too complex and not fast enough. And when he reverted to the 79 from the British GP onwards, it was too unreliable.

HUNT HAS HAD ENOUGH

If Andretti thought his season a poor one, that was nothing compared to 1976 world champion James Hunt, who didn't even see the year out. Demotivated by the lack of pace that he could wring from his Wolf, with his best result eighth at Kyalami, he decided that he would quit not just the team, but the whole sport after the Monaco GP.

FRENCH GRAND PRIX

DIJON-PRENOIS • ROUND 8 • DATE: 1ST JULY 1979
Laps: 80 • Distance: 188.896miles/304.0km • Weather: Warm but dull

Pos	Driver	Team	Chassis-Engine	Result	Qual
1	Jean-Pierre Jabouille	Renault	Renault RE10	1h35m20.420s	1
2	Gilles Villeneuve	Ferrari	Ferrari 312T4	1h35m35.010s	3
3	Rene Arnoux	Renault	Renault RE10	1h35m35.250s	2
4	Alan Jones	Williams	Williams-Ford Cosworth FW07	1h35m57.030s	7
5	Jean-Pierre Jarier	Tyrrell	Tyrrell-Ford Cosworth 009	1h36m24.930s	10
6	Clay Regazzoni	Williams	Williams-Ford Cosworth FW07	1h36m25.930s	9
7	Jody Scheckter	Ferrari	Ferrari 312T4	79 laps	5
8	Jacques Laffite	Ligier	Ligier-Ford Cosworth JS11	79 laps	8
9	Keke Rosberg	Wolf	Wolf-Ford Cosworth WR8	79 laps	16
10	Patrick Tambay	McLaren	McLaren-Ford Cosworth M28C	78 laps	20
11	John Watson	McLaren	McLaren-Ford Cosworth M28C	78 laps	15

Pos	Driver	Team	Chassis-Engine	Result	Qual
12	Hector Rebaque	Rebaque	Lotus-Ford Cosworth 79	78 laps	23
13	Carlos Reutemann	Lotus	Lotus-Ford Cosworth 79	77 laps	13
14	Riccardo Patrese	Arrows	Arrows-Ford Cosworth A2	77 laps	19
15	Jochen Mass	Arrows	Arrows-Ford Cosworth A2	75 laps	22
16	Elio de Angelis	Shadow	Shadow-Ford Cosworth DN9B	75 laps	24
17	Bruno Giacomelli	Alfa Romeo	Alfa Romeo 177	75 laps	17
18	Jan Lammers	Shadow	Shadow-Ford Cosworth DN9B	73 laps	21
R	Didier Pironi	Tyrrell	Tyrrell-Ford Cosworth 009	71 laps/suspension	11
R	Emerson Fittipaldi	Fittipaldi	Fittipaldi-Ford Cosworth F5A	53 laps/engine	18
R	Nelson Piquet	Brabham	Brabham-Alfa Romeo BT48	52 laps/accident	4
R	Mario Andretti	Lotus	Lotus-Ford Cosworth 80	51 laps/brakes	12
R	Jacky Ickx	Ligier	Ligier-Ford Cosworth JS11	45 laps/engine	14
R	Niki Lauda	Brabham	Brabham-Alfa Romeo BT48	23 laps/spun off	6
NS	Hans-Joachim Stuck	ATS	ATS-Ford Cosworth D2	tyre dispute	25
DNQ	Patrick Gaillard	Ensign	Ensign-Ford Cosworth N179	-	26
DNQ	Arturo Merzario	Merzario	Merzario-Ford Cosworth A2	-	27

Pole: Jabouille, 1m07.190s, 126.512mph/203.601kph. Fastest lap: Arnoux, 1m09.160s, 122.908mph/197.802kph on Lap 71. Race leaders: Villeneuve 1-45, Jabouille 46-80

BRITISH GRAND PRIX

SILVERSTONE • ROUND 9 • DATE: 14TH JULY 1979
Laps: 68 • Distance: 199.375miles/320.864km • Weather: Warm & bright

Pos	Driver	Team	Chassis-Engine	Result	Qual
1	Clay Regazzoni	Williams	Williams-Ford Cosworth FW07	1h26m11.170s	4
2	Rene Arnoux	Renault	Renault RE10	1h26m35.450s	5
3	Jean-Pierre Jarier	Tyrrell	Tyrrell-Ford Cosworth 009	67 laps	16
4	John Watson	McLaren	McLaren-Ford Cosworth M29	67 laps	7
5	Jody Scheckter	Ferrari	Ferrari 312T4	67 laps	11
6	Jacky Ickx	Ligier	Ligier-Ford Cosworth JS11	67 laps	17
7	Patrick Tambay	McLaren	McLaren-Ford Cosworth M28C	66 laps/out of fuel	18
8	Carlos Reutemann	Lotus	Lotus-Ford Cosworth 79	66 laps	8
9	Hector Rebaque	Rebaque	Lotus-Ford Cosworth 79	66 laps	24
10	Didier Pironi	Tyrrell	Tyrrell-Ford Cosworth 009	66 laps	15
11	Jan Lammers	Shadow	Shadow-Ford Cosworth DN9B	65 laps	21
12	Elio de Angelis	Shadow	Shadow-Ford Cosworth DN9B	65 laps	12
13	Patrick Gaillard	Ensign	Ensign-Ford Cosworth N179	65 laps	23
14	Gilles Villeneuve	Ferrari	Ferrari 312T4	63 laps/fuel system	13
R	Riccardo Patrese	Arrows	Arrows-Ford Cosworth A2	45 laps/gearbox	19
R	Jacques Laffite	Ligier	Ligier-Ford Cosworth JS11	44 laps/engine	10
R	Keke Rosberg	Wolf	Wolf-Ford Cosworth WR7	44 laps/fuel system	14
R	Alan Jones	Williams	Williams-Ford Cosworth FW07	38 laps/water pump	1
R	Jochen Mass	Arrows	Arrows-Ford Cosworth A2	37 laps/gearbox	20
R	Emerson Fittipaldi	Fittipaldi	Fittipaldi-Ford Cosworth F5A	25 laps/engine	22
R	Jean-Pierre Jabouille	Renault	Renault RE10	21 laps/turbo	2
R	Niki Lauda	Brabham	Brabham-Alfa Romeo BT48	12 laps/brakes	6
R	Mario Andretti	Lotus	Lotus-Ford Cosworth 79	3 laps/wheel	9
R	Nelson Piquet	Brabham	Brabham-Alfa Romeo BT48	1 lap/spun off	3
DNQ	Hans-Joachim Stuck	ATS	ATS-Ford Cosworth D2	-	25
DNQ	Arturo Merzario	Merzario	Merzario-Ford Cosworth A2	-	26

Pole: Jones, 1m11.880s, 146.844mph/236.323kph. Fastest lap: Regazzoni, 1m14.400s, 141.871mph/228.319kph on Lap 39. Race leaders: Jones 1-38, Regazzoni 39-68

THE RACE OF THE DECADE

As Jean-Pierre Jabouille headed towards Renault's first win at Dijon-Prenois, all attention was focused on who would finish second. This might seem odd, but the battle between Rene Arnoux in the second Renault and Ferrari's Gilles Villeneuve was phenomenal as they banged wheels, swapped places and slid off countless times in the final three laps.

GERMAN GRAND PRIX

HOCKENHEIM • ROUND 10 • DATE: 29TH JULY 1979
Laps: 45 • Distance: 189.832miles/305.505km • Weather: Very hot & bright

Pos	Driver	Team	Chassis-Engine	Result	Qual
1	Alan Jones	Williams	Williams-Ford Cosworth FW07	1h24m48.830s	2
2	Clay Regazzoni	Williams	Williams-Ford Cosworth FW07	1h24m51.740s	6
3	Jacques Laffite	Ligier	Ligier-Ford Cosworth JS11	1h25m07.220s	3
4	Jody Scheckter	Ferrari	Ferrari 312T4	1h25m20.030s	5
5	John Watson	McLaren	McLaren-Ford Cosworth M29	1h26m26.630s	12
6	Jochen Mass	Arrows	Arrows-Ford Cosworth A2	44 laps	18
7	Geoff Lees	Tyrrell	Tyrrell-Ford Cosworth 009	44 laps	16
8	Gilles Villeneuve	Ferrari	Ferrari 312T4	44 laps	9
9	Didier Pironi	Tyrrell	Tyrrell-Ford Cosworth 009	44 laps	8
10	Jan Lammers	Shadow	Shadow-Ford Cosworth DN9B	44 laps	20
11	Elio de Angelis	Shadow	Shadow-Ford Cosworth DN9B	43 laps	21
12	Nelson Piquet	Brabham	Brabham-Alfa Romeo BT48	42 laps/engine	4
R	Riccardo Patrese	Arrows	Arrows-Ford Cosworth A2	34 laps/tyre	19
R	Patrick Tambay	McLaren	McLaren-Ford Cosworth M29	30 laps/suspension	15
R	Keke Rosberg	Wolf	Wolf-Ford Cosworth WR8	29 laps/engine	17
R	Niki Lauda	Brabham	Brabham-Alfa Romeo BT48	27 laps/engine	7
R	Jacky Ickx	Ligier	Ligier-Ford Cosworth JS11	24 laps/tyre	14
R	Hector Rebaque	Rebaque	Lotus-Ford Cosworth 79	22 laps/handling	24
R	Mario Andretti	Lotus	Lotus-Ford Cosworth 79	16 laps/transmission	11
R	Rene Arnoux	Renault	Renault RE10	9 laps/tyre	10
R	Jean-Pierre Jabouille	Renault	Renault RE10	7 laps/spun off	1
R	Emerson Fittipaldi	Fittipaldi	Fittipaldi-Ford Cosworth F6A	4 laps/electrical	22
R	Carlos Reutemann	Lotus	Lotus-Ford Cosworth 79	1 lap/accident	13
R	Hans-Joachim Stuck	ATS	ATS-Ford Cosworth D2	0 laps/suspension	23
DNQ	Patrick Gaillard	Ensign	Ensign-Ford Cosworth N179	-	25
DNQ	Arturo Merzario	Merzario	Merzario-Ford Cosworth A2	-	26

Pole: Jabouille, 1m48.480s, 139.994mph/225.298kph. Fastest lap: Villeneuve, 1m51.890s, 135.727mph/218.432kph on Lap 40. Race leaders: Jones 1-45

WILLIAMS WINS AT LAST

It was a day that many said would never happen, but Frank Williams' team matured to the point that by mid-1979 it had became a winning outfit. Victory at the British GP went to Clay Regazzoni after team-mate Alan Jones had led the first half of the race before retiring. The Silverstone crowd roared in appreciation.

AUSTRIAN GRAND PRIX

OSTERREICHRING • ROUND 11 • DATE: 12TH AUGUST 1979
Laps: 54 • Distance: 199.391miles/320.889km • Weather: Warm & bright

Pos	Driver	Team	Chassis-Engine	Result	Qual
1	Alan Jones	Williams	Williams-Ford Cosworth FW07	1h27m38.010s	2
2	Gilles Villeneuve	Ferrari	Ferrari 312T4	1h28m14.060s	5
3	Jacques Laffite	Ligier	Ligier-Ford Cosworth JS11	1h28m24.780s	8
4	Jody Scheckter	Ferrari	Ferrari 312T4	1h28m25.220s	9
5	Clay Regazzoni	Williams	Williams-Ford Cosworth FW07	1h28m26.930s	6
6	Rene Arnoux	Renault	Renault RE10	53 laps	1
7	Didier Pironi	Tyrrell	Tyrrell-Ford Cosworth 009	53 laps	10
8	Derek Daly	Tyrrell	Tyrrell-Ford Cosworth 009	53 laps	11
9	John Watson	McLaren	McLaren-Ford Cosworth M29	53 laps	16
10	Patrick Tambay	McLaren	McLaren-Ford Cosworth M29	53 laps	14
R	Niki Lauda	Brabham	Brabham-Alfa Romeo BT48	45 laps/engine	4
R	Patrick Gaillard	Ensign	Ensign-Ford Cosworth N179	42 laps/suspension	24
R	Riccardo Patrese	Arrows	Arrows-Ford Cosworth A2	34 laps/suspension	13
R	Elio de Angelis	Shadow	Shadow-Ford Cosworth DN9B	34 laps/engine	22
R	Nelson Piquet	Brabham	Brabham-Alfa Romeo BT48	32 laps/engine	7
R	Hans-Joachim Stuck	ATS	ATS-Ford Cosworth D3	28 laps/engine	18
R	Jacky Ickx	Ligier	Ligier-Ford Cosworth JS11	26 laps/engine	21
R	Carlos Reutemann	Lotus	Lotus-Ford Cosworth 79	22 laps/handling	17
R	Jean-Pierre Jabouille	Renault	Renault RE10	16 laps/gearbox	3
R	Keke Rosberg	Wolf	Wolf-Ford Cosworth WR9	15 laps/electrical	12
R	Emerson Fittipaldi	Fittipaldi	Fittipaldi-Ford Cosworth F6A	15 laps/brakes	19
R	Jan Lammers	Shadow	Shadow-Ford Cosworth DN9B	3 laps/accident	23
R	Jochen Mass	Arrows	Arrows-Ford Cosworth A2	1 lap/engine	20
R	Mario Andretti	Lotus	Lotus-Ford Cosworth 79	0 laps/clutch	15
DNQ	Hector Rebaque	Rebaque	Lotus-Ford Cosworth 79	-	25
DNQ	Arturo Merzario	Merzario	Merzario-Ford Cosworth A2	-	26

Pole: Arnoux, 1m34.070s, 141.307mph/227.411kph. Fastest lap: Arnoux, 1m35.770s, 138.798mph/223.375kph on Lap 40. Race leaders: Villeneuve 1-3, Jones 4-54

WET AT WATKINS GLEN

Watkins Glen in autumn can be beautiful, but is often just wet and cold. In 1979, conditions were so bad that few bothered to go out for practice in the deluge. Ferrari decided that since it might be as wet for the race, their drivers needed to get used to it, so sent its drivers out. Scheckter could hardly believe it when told that Villeneuve had lapped almost 11 seconds faster than him.

DUTCH GRAND PRIX

ZANDVOORT • ROUND 12 • DATE: 26TH AUGUST 1979
Laps: 75 • Distance: 196.412miles/316.95km • Weather: Cool & dull

Pos	Driver	Team	Chassis-Engine	Result	Qual
1	Alan Jones	Williams	Williams-Ford Cosworth FW07	1h41m19.775s	2
2	Jody Scheckter	Ferrari	Ferrari 312T4	1h41m41.558s	5
3	Jacques Laffite	Ligier	Ligier-Ford Cosworth JS11	1h42m23.028s	7

Pos	Driver	Team	Chassis-Engine	Result	Qual
4	Nelson Piquet	Brabham	Brabham-Alfa Romeo BT48	74 laps	11
5	Jacky Ickx	Ligier	Ligier-Ford Cosworth JS11	74 laps	20
6	Jochen Mass	Arrows	Arrows-Ford Cosworth A2	73 laps	18
7	Hector Rebaque	Rebaque	Lotus-Ford Cosworth 79	73 laps	24
R	Didier Pironi	Tyrrell	Tyrrell-Ford Cosworth 009	51 laps/suspension	10
R	Gilles Villeneuve	Ferrari	Ferrari 312T4	49 laps/tyre	6
R	Elio de Angelis	Shadow	Shadow-Ford Cosworth DN9B	40 laps/transmission	22
R	Keke Rosberg	Wolf	Wolf-Ford Cosworth WR9	33 laps/engine	8
R	Jean-Pierre Jabouille	Renault	Renault RE10	26 laps/clutch	4
R	John Watson	McLaren	McLaren-Ford Cosworth M29	22 laps/engine	12
R	Jean-Pierre Jarier	Tyrrell	Tyrrell-Ford Cosworth 009	20 laps/spun off	16
R	Hans-Joachim Stuck	ATS	ATS-Ford Cosworth D3	19 laps/transmission	15
R	Jan Lammers	Shadow	Shadow-Ford Cosworth DN9B	12 laps/gearbox	23
R	Mario Andretti	Lotus	Lotus-Ford Cosworth 79	9 laps/suspension	17
R	Riccardo Patrese	Arrows	Arrows-Ford Cosworth A2	7 laps/brakes	19
R	Patrick Tambay	McLaren	McLaren-Ford Cosworth M29	6 laps/engine	14
R	Niki Lauda	Brabham	Brabham-Alfa Romeo BT48	4 laps/injured wrist	9
R	Emerson Fittipaldi	Fittipaldi	Fittipaldi-Ford Cosworth F6A	2 laps/electrical	21
R	Rene Arnoux	Renault	Renault RE10	1 lap/suspension	1
R	Carlos Reutemann	Lotus	Lotus-Ford Cosworth 79	1 lap/suspension	13
R	Clay Regazzoni	Williams	Williams-Ford Cosworth FW07	0 laps/accident	3
DNQ	Patrick Gaillard	Ensign	Ensign-Ford Cosworth N179	-	25
DNQ	Arturo Merzario	Merzario	Merzario-Ford Cosworth A2	-	26

Pole: Arnoux, 1m15.461s, 125.273mph/201.608kph. Fastest lap: Villeneuve, 1m19.438s, 119.002mph/191.515kph on Lap 39. Race leaders: Jones 1-10 & 47-75, Villeneuve 11-46

SEEKING A HIGHER CALLING

Double world champion Niki Lauda was so frustrated by the numerous retirements that peppered his second year with Brabham that he elected to end his F1 career. Instead of putting his feet up, he announced that he would go off to start his own airline. However, McLaren tempted him back two years later to aim for a third title.

ITALIAN GRAND PRIX

MONZA • ROUND 13 • DATE: 9TH SEPTEMBER 1979
Laps: 50 • Distance: 180.197miles/290.0km • Weather: Warm & bright

Pos	Driver	Team	Chassis-Engine	Result	Qual
1	Jody Scheckter	Ferrari	Ferrari 312T4	1h22m00.220s	3
2	Gilles Villeneuve	Ferrari	Ferrari 312T4	1h22m00.680s	5
3	Clay Regazzoni	Williams	Williams-Ford Cosworth FW07	1h22m05.000s	6
4	Niki Lauda	Brabham	Brabham-Alfa Romeo BT48	1h22m54.620s	9
5	Mario Andretti	Lotus	Lotus-Ford Cosworth 79	1h22m59.920s	10
6	Jean-Pierre Jarier	Tyrrell	Tyrrell-Ford Cosworth 009	1h23m01.770s	16
7	Carlos Reutemann	Lotus	Lotus-Ford Cosworth 79	1h23m24.360s	13
8	Emerson Fittipaldi	Fittipaldi	Fittipaldi-Ford Cosworth F6A	49 laps	20
9	Alan Jones	Williams	Williams-Ford Cosworth FW07	49 laps	4
10	Didier Pironi	Tyrrell	Tyrrell-Ford Cosworth 009	49 laps	12
11	Hans-Joachim Stuck	ATS	ATS-Ford Cosworth D3	49 laps	15

Pos	Driver	Team	Chassis-Engine	Result	Qual
12	Vittorio Brambilla	Alfa Romeo	Alfa Romeo 177	49 laps	22
13	Riccardo Patrese	Arrows	Arrows-Ford Cosworth A2	47 laps	17
14	Jean-Pierre Jabouille	Renault	Renault RE10	45 laps/engine	1
R	Jacques Laffite	Ligier	Ligier-Ford Cosworth JS11	41 laps/engine	7
R	Keke Rosberg	Wolf	Wolf-Ford Cosworth WR8	41 laps/engine	23
R	Jacky Ickx	Ligier	Ligier-Ford Cosworth JS11	40 laps/engine	11
R	Elio de Angelis	Shadow	Shadow-Ford Cosworth DN9B	33 laps/clutch	24
R	Bruno Giacomelli	Alfa Romeo	Alfa Romeo 179	28 laps/spun off	18
R	Rene Arnoux	Renault	Renault RE10	13 laps/engine	2
R	John Watson	McLaren	McLaren-Ford Cosworth M29	13 laps/accident	19
R	Patrick Tambay	McLaren	McLaren-Ford Cosworth M29	3 laps/engine	14
R	Jochen Mass	Arrows	Arrows-Ford Cosworth A2	3 laps/suspension	21
R	Nelson Piquet	Brabham	Brabham-Alfa Romeo BT48	1 lap/accident	8
DNQ	Jan Lammers	Shadow	Shadow-Ford Cosworth DN9B	-	25
DNQ	Marc Surer	Ensign	Ensign-Ford Cosworth N179	-	26
DNQ	Arturo Merzario	Merzario	Merzario-Ford Cosworth A2	-	27
DNQ	Hector Rebaque	Rebaque	Rebaque-Ford Cosworth HR100	-	28

Pole: Jabouille, 1m34.580s, 137.177mph/220.765kph. Fastest lap: Regazzoni, 1m35.600s, 135.713mph/218.410kph on Lap 46. Race leaders: Scheckter 1 & 13-50, Arnoux 2-12

NEW CONSTRUCTORS

The 1979 season wasn't a classic one for constructors trying to break into F1. The first newbie was entered by German sports car racer Willi Kauhsen, but his angular car was an aerodynamic dud. Then Mexican racer Hector Rebaque elected no longer to run a Lotus 79 and developed his own car. That didn't work either.

CANADIAN GRAND PRIX

MONTREAL • ROUND 14 • DATE: 30TH SEPTEMBER 1979
Laps: 72 • Distance: 197.6miles/317.52km • Weather: Warm & bright

Pos	Driver	Team	Chassis-Engine	Result	Qual
1	Alan Jones	Williams	Williams-Ford Cosworth FW07	1h52m06.892s	1
2	Gilles Villeneuve	Ferrari	Ferrari 312T4	1h52m07.972s	2
3	Clay Regazzoni	Williams	Williams-Ford Cosworth FW07	1h53m20.548s	3
4	Jody Scheckter	Ferrari	Ferrari 312T4	71 laps	9
5	Didier Pironi	Tyrrell	Tyrrell-Ford Cosworth 009	71 laps	6
6	John Watson	McLaren	McLaren-Ford Cosworth M29	70 laps	17
7	Ricardo Zunino	Brabham	Brabham-Ford Cosworth BT49	68 laps	19
8	Emerson Fittipaldi	Fittipaldi	Fittipaldi-Ford Cosworth F6A	67 laps	15
9	Jan Lammers	Shadow	Shadow-Ford Cosworth DN9B	67 laps	21
10	Mario Andretti	Lotus	Lotus-Ford Cosworth 79	66 laps/out of fuel	10
R	Nelson Piquet	Brabham	Brabham-Ford Cosworth BT49	61 laps/gearbox	4
R	Vittorio Brambilla	Alfa Romeo	Alfa Romeo 179	52 laps/fuel system	18
R	Jacky Ickx	Ligier	Ligier-Ford Cosworth JS11	47 laps/gearbox	16
R	Jean-Pierre Jarier	Tyrrell	Tyrrell-Ford Cosworth 009	33 laps/engine	13
R	Derek Daly	Tyrrell	Tyrrell-Ford Cosworth 009	28 laps/engine	24
R	Hector Rebaque	Rebaque	Rebaque-Ford Cosworth HR100	26 laps/chassis	22
R	Jean-Pierre Jabouille	Renault	Renault RE10	24 laps/brakes	7

Pos	Driver	Team	Chassis-Engine	Result	Qual
R	Elio de Angelis	Shadow	Shadow-Ford Cosworth DN9B	24 laps/ignition	23
R	Carlos Reutemann	Lotus	Lotus-Ford Cosworth 79	23 laps/suspension	11
R	Riccardo Patrese	Arrows	Arrows-Ford Cosworth A1B	20 laps/spun off	14
R	Patrick Tambay	McLaren	McLaren-Ford Cosworth M29	19 laps/engine	20
R	Rene Arnoux	Renault	Renault RE10	14 laps/accident	8
R	Hans-Joachim Stuck	ATS	ATS-Ford Cosworth D3	14 laps/accident	12
R	Jacques Laffite	Ligier	Ligier-Ford Cosworth JS11	10 laps/engine	5
DNQ	Jochen Mass	Arrows	Arrows-Ford Cosworth A2	-	25
DNQ	Marc Surer	Ensign	Ensign-Ford Cosworth N179	-	26
DNQ	Keke Rosberg	Wolf	Wolf-Ford Cosworth WR9	-	27
DNQ	Alex Ribeiro	Fittipaldi	Fittipaldi-Ford Cosworth F6A	-	28
DNQ	Arturo Merzario	Merzario	Merzario-Ford Cosworth A2	-	29
NS	Niki Lauda	Brabham	Brabham-Ford Cosworth BT49	quit the sport	-
NS	Bruno Giacomelli	Alfa Romeo	Alfa Romeo 179	withdrawn	-

Pole: Jones, 1m29.892s, 109.741mph/176.611kph. Fastest lap: Jones, 1m31.272s, 108.082mph/173.941kph on Lap 65. Race leaders: Villeneuve 1-50, Jones 51-72

NEW DRIVERS

Of 1979's five F1 newcomers, Shadow pairing Elio de Angelis and Jan Lammers showed promise, with the Italian ending the year with fourth in the United States GP. Patrick Gaillard and Marc Surer both found it hard to qualify the Ensign, while Ricardo Zunino took over Lauda's Brabham in Canada and came seventh.

UNITED STATES GRAND PRIX

WATKINS GLEN • ROUND 15 • DATE: 7TH OCTOBER 1979
Laps: 59 • Distance: 199.251miles/320.665km • Weather: Cold & wet

Pos	Driver	Team	Chassis-Engine	Result	Qual
1	Gilles Villeneuve	Ferrari	Ferrari 312T4	1h52m17.734s	3
2	Rene Arnoux	Renault	Renault RE10	1h53m06.521s	7
3	Didier Pironi	Tyrrell	Tyrrell-Ford Cosworth 009	1h53m10.933s	10
4	Elio de Angelis	Shadow	Shadow-Ford Cosworth DN9B	1h53m48.246s	20
5	Hans-Joachim Stuck	ATS	ATS-Ford Cosworth D3	1h53m58.993s	14
6	John Watson	McLaren	McLaren-Ford Cosworth M29	58 laps	13
7	Emerson Fittipaldi	Fittipaldi	Fittipaldi-Ford Cosworth F6A	54 laps	23
R	Nelson Piquet	Brabham	Brabham-Ford Cosworth BT49	53 laps/transmission	2
R	Derek Daly	Tyrrell	Tyrrell-Ford Cosworth 009	52 laps/spun off	15
R	Jody Scheckter	Ferrari	Ferrari 312T4	48 laps/tyre	16
R	Riccardo Patrese	Arrows	Arrows-Ford Cosworth A2	44 laps/suspension	19
R	Alan Jones	Williams	Williams-Ford Cosworth FW07	36 laps/wheel	1
R	Marc Surer	Ensign	Ensign-Ford Cosworth N179	32 laps/engine	21
R	Clay Regazzoni	Williams	Williams-Ford Cosworth FW07	29 laps/accident	5
R	Ricardo Zunino	Brabham	Brabham-Ford Cosworth BT49	25 laps/spun off	9
R	Jean-Pierre Jabouille	Renault	Renault RE10	24 laps/engine	8
R	Keke Rosberg	Wolf	Wolf-Ford Cosworth WR8/9	20 laps/accident	12
R	Patrick Tambay	McLaren	McLaren-Ford Cosworth M29	20 laps/engine	22
R	Jean-Pierre Jarier	Tyrrell	Tyrrell-Ford Cosworth 009	18 laps/accident	11
R	Mario Andretti	Lotus	Lotus-Ford Cosworth 79	16 laps/gearbox	17
R	Carlos Reutemann	Lotus	Lotus-Ford Cosworth 79	6 laps/spun off	6

Pos	Driver	Team	Chassis-Engine	Result	Qual
R	Jacques Laffite	Ligier	Ligier-Ford Cosworth JS11	3 laps/spun off	4
R	Jacky Ickx	Ligier	Ligier-Ford Cosworth JS11	2 laps/spun off	24
R	Bruno Giacomelli	Alfa Romeo	Alfa Romeo 179	0 laps/spun off	18
DNQ	Vittorio Brambilla	Alfa Romeo	Alfa Romeo 179	-	25
DNQ	Jochen Mass	Arrows	Arrows-Ford Cosworth A2	-	26
DNQ	Jan Lammers	Shadow	Shadow-Ford Cosworth DN9B	-	27
DNQ	Hector Rebaque	Rebaque	Rebaque-Ford Cosworth HR100	-	28
DNQ	Alex Ribeiro	Fittipaldi	Fittipaldi-Ford Cosworth F6A	-	29
DNQ	Arturo Merzario	Merzario	Merzario-Ford Cosworth A2	-	30

Pole: Jones, 1m35.615s, 127.153mph/204.633kph. Fastest lap: Piquet, 1m40.054s, 121.511mph/195.554kph on Lap 51. Race leaders: Villeneuve 1-31 & 37-59, Jones 32-36

WORLD DRIVERS' CHAMPIONSHIP FINAL RESULTS

Pos	Driver	Nat	Car-Engine	R1	R2	R3	R4	R5
1	Jody Scheckter	ZAF	Ferrari 312T3	R	6	-	-	-
			Ferrari 312T4	-	-	2	2	4
2	Gilles Villeneuve	CAN	Ferrari 312T3	R	5	-	-	-
			Ferrari 312T4	-	-	1F	1PF	7F
3	Alan Jones	AUS	Williams-Ford Cosworth FW06	9	R	R	3	-
			Williams-Ford Cosworth FW07	-	-	-	-	R
4	Jacques Laffite	FRA	Ligier-Ford Cosworth JS11	1PF	1PF	R	R	RP
5	Clay Regazzoni	CHE	Williams-Ford Cosworth FW06	10	15	9	R	-
			Williams-Ford Cosworth FW07	-	-	-	-	R
6	Patrick Depailler	FRA	Ligier-Ford Cosworth JS11	4	2	R	5	1
6	Carlos Reutemann	ARG	Lotus-Ford Cosworth 79	2	3	5	R	2
8	Rene Arnoux	FRA	Renault RS01	R	R	R	NS	9
			Renault RE10	-	-	-	-	-
9	John Watson	GBR	McLaren-Ford Cosworth M28	3	8	R	R	-
			McLaren-Ford Cosworth M28B	-	-	-	-	R
			McLaren-Ford Cosworth M28C	-	-	-	-	-
			McLaren-Ford Cosworth M29	-	-	-	-	-
10	Didier Pironi	FRA	Tyrrell-Ford Cosworth 009	R	4	R	DQ	6
10	Jean-Pierre Jarier	FRA	Tyrrell-Ford Cosworth 009	R	NS	3	6	5
10	Mario Andretti	USA	Lotus-Ford Cosworth 79	5	R	4	4	-
			Lotus-Ford Cosworth 80	-	-	-	-	3
13	Jean-Pierre Jabouille	FRA	Renault RS01	R	10	RP	NS	-
			Renault RE10	-	-	-	-	R
14	Niki Lauda	AUT	Brabham-Alfa Romeo BT48	R	R	6	R	R
			Brabham-Ford Cosworth BT49	-	-	-	-	-
15	Nelson Piquet	BRA	Brabham-Alfa Romeo BT46	R	-	-	-	-
			Brabham-Alfa Romeo BT48	-	R	7	8	R
			Brabham-Ford Cosworth BT49	-	-	-	-	-
15	Elio de Angelis	ITA	Shadow-Ford Cosworth DN9B	7	12	R	7	R
15	Jacky Ickx	BEL	Ligier-Ford Cosworth JS11	-	-	-	-	-
15	Jochen Mass	DEU	Arrows-Ford Cosworth A1B	8	7	12	9	8
			Arrows-Ford Cosworth A2	-	-	-	-	-
19	Riccardo Patrese	ITA	Arrows-Ford Cosworth A1B	NS	9	11	R	10
			Arrows-Ford Cosworth A2	-	-	-	-	-
19	Hans-Joachim Stuck	DEU	ATS-Ford Cosworth D2	NS	R	R	DQ	14
			ATS-Ford Cosworth D3	-	-	-	-	-
21	Emerson Fittipaldi	BRA	Fittipaldi-Ford Cosworth F5A	6	11	-	R	11
			Fittipaldi-Ford Cosworth F6	-	-	13	-	-
			Fittipaldi-Ford Cosworth F6A	-	-	-	-	-

Pos	Driver	R6	R7	R8	R9	R10	R11	R12	R13	R14	R15	Total
1	Scheckter	-	-	-	-	-	-	-	-	-	-	51
		1	1P	7	5	4	4	2	1	4	R	
2	Villeneuve	-	-	-	-	-	-	-	-	-	-	47
		7F	R	2	14	8F	2	RF	2	2	1	
3	Jones	-	-	-	-	-	-	-	-	-	-	40
		R	R	4	RP	1	1	1	9	1PF	RP	
4	Laffite	2P	R	8	R	3	3	3	R	R	R	36
5	Regazzoni	-	-	-	-	-	-	-	-	-	-	29
		R	2	6	1F	2	5	R	3F	3	R	
6	Depailler	R	5F	-	-	-	-	-	-	-	-	20
6	Reutemann	4	3	13	8	R	R	R	7	R	R	20
8	Arnoux	R	-	-	-	-	-	-	-	-	-	17
		-	R	3F	2	R	6PF	RP	R	R	2	
9	Watson	-	-	-	-	-	-	-	-	-	-	15
		6	-	-	-	-	-	-	-	-	-	
		-	4	11	-	-	-	-	-	-	-	
		-	-	-	4	5	9	R	R	6	6	
10	Pironi	3	R	R	10	9	7	R	10	5	3	14
10	Jarier	11	R	5	3	-	-	R	6	R	R	14
10	Andretti	R	-	-	R	R	R	R	5	10	R	14
		-	R	R	-	-	-	-	-	-	-	
13	Jabouille	-	-	-	-	-	-	-	-	-	-	9
		R	NC	1P	R	RP	R	R	14P	R	R	
14	Lauda	R	R	R	R	R	R	R	4	-	-	4
		-	-	-	-	-	-	-	-	NS	-	
15	Piquet	-	-	-	-	-	-	-	-	-	-	3
		R	R	R	R	12	R	4	R	-	-	
		-	-	-	-	-	-	-	-	R	RF	
15	de Angelis	R	DNQ	16	12	11	R	R	R	R	4	3
15	Ickx	-	-	R	6	R	R	5	R	R	R	3
15	Mass	R	6	-	-	-	-	-	-	-	-	3
		-	-	15	R	6	R	6	R	DNQ	DNQ	
19	Patrese	5	R	-	-	-	-	-	-	R	-	2
		-	-	14	R	R	R	R	13	-	R	
19	Stuck	8	R	NS	DNQ	R	-	-	-	-	-	2
		-	-	-	-	-	R	R	11	R	5	
21	Fittipaldi	9	R	R	R	-	-	-	-	-	-	1
		-	-	-	-	-	-	-	-	-	-	
		-	-	-	-	R	R	R	8	8	7	

SYMBOLS AND GRAND PRIX KEY

Round 1 **Argentinian GP**
Round 2 **Brazilian GP**
Round 3 **South African GP**
Round 4 **United States GP West**
Round 5 **Spanish GP**
Round 6 **Belgian GP**
Round 7 **Monaco GP**
Round 8 **French GP**
Round 9 **British GP**
Round 10 **German GP**
Round 11 **Austrian GP**
Round 12 **Dutch GP**
Round 13 **Italian GP**
Round 14 **Canadian GP**
Round 15 **United States GP**

SCORING

1st **9 points**
2nd **6 points**
3rd **4 points**
4th **3 points**
5th **2 points**
6th **1 point**

DNPQ DID NOT PRE-QUALIFY **DNQ DID NOT QUALIFY** **DQ DISQUALIFIED** **EX EXCLUDED**
F FASTEST LAP **NC NOT CLASSIFIED** **NS NON-STARTER** **P POLE POSITION** **R RETIRED**

WORLD CONSTRUCTORS' CHAMPIONSHIP FINAL RESULTS

Pos	Team-Engine	R1	R2	R3	R4	R5	R6	R7	R8
1	Ferrari	R/R	5/6	1/2	1/2	4/7	1/7	1/R	2/7
2	Williams-Ford	9/10	15/R	9/R	3/R	R/R	R/R	2/R	4/6
3	Ligier-Ford	1/4	1/2	R/R	5/R	1/R	2/R	5/R	8/R
4	Lotus-Ford	2/5	3/R	4/5	4/R	2/3	4/R	3/R	13/R
5	Tyrrell-Ford	R/R	4/NS	3/R	6/DQ	5/6	3/11	R/R	5/R
6	Renault	R/R	10/R	R/R	NS/NS	9/R	R/R	NC/R	1/3
7	McLaren-Ford	3/R	8/R	10/R	R/R	13/R	6/DNQ	4/DNQ	10/11
8	Brabham-Alfa Romeo	R/R	R/R	6/7	8/R	R/R	R/R	R/R	R/R
9	Arrows-Ford	8/NS	7/9	11/12	9/R	8/10	5/R	6/R	14/15
10	Shadow-Ford	7/R	12/14	R/R	7/R	12/R	10/R	DNQ/DNQ	16/18
11	ATS-Ford	NS	R	R	DQ	14	8	R	DNQ
12	Fittipaldi-Ford	6	11	13	R	11	9	R	R

Pos	Team-Engine	R9	R10	R11	R12	R13	R14	R15	Total
1	Ferrari	5/14	4/8	2/4	2/R	1/2	2/4	1/R	113
2	Williams-Ford	1/R	1/2	1/5	1/R	3/9	1/3	R/R	75
3	Ligier-Ford	6/R	3/R	3/R	3/5	R/R	R/R	R/R	61
4	Lotus-Ford	8/R	R/R	R/R	R/R	5/7	10/R	R/R	39
5	Tyrrell-Ford	3/10	7/9	7/8	R/R	6/10	5/R/R	3/R/R	28
6	Renault	2/R	R/R	6/R	R/R	14/R	R/R	2/R	26
7	McLaren-Ford	4/7	5/R	9/10	R/R	R/R	6/R	6/R	15
8	Brabham-Alfa Romeo	R/R	12/R	R/R	4/R	4/R	-	-	7
9	Arrows-Ford	R/R	6/R	R/R	6/R	13/R	R/DNQ	R/DNQ	5
10	Shadow-Ford	11/12	10/11	R/R	R/R	R/DNQ	9/R	4/DNQ	3
11	ATS-Ford	DNQ	R	R	R	11	R	5	2
12	Fittipaldi-Ford	R	R	R	R	8	8	7	1

THE 1980s

1980

SEASON SUMMARY

Having ended the 1979 season in dominant form, Alan Jones picked up where he left off for Williams. He resisted an early challenge from Renault's Rene Arnoux, then fended off his new team-mate Carlos Reutemann and Brabham's Nelson Piquet. There were also cameo roles from Ligier drivers Didier Pironi and Jacques Laffite. McLaren wasn't on the pace but its new signing Alain Prost showed huge promise by finishing in the top six in his first two outings. It was a disastrous year for 1979 champions Ferrari as they ranked just 10th, their points haul falling from 113 in 1979 to just eight, as the 312T5 was extremely hard on its tyres.

F1 PLAYS POWER GAMES

Sports fans will tell you that sport and politics don't mix, and this was the case in 1980 as the sport's governing body, FISA, and the teams' body, FOCA, spent the year scrapping. The fall-out was that the Spanish GP lost its World Championship status as FISA-aligned Alfa Romeo, Ferrari and Renault withdrew. For the record, Jones won the race.

ARGENTINIAN GRAND PRIX

BUENOS AIRES • ROUND 1 • DATE: 13TH JANUARY 1980
Laps: 53 • Distance: 196.548miles/316.314km • Weather: Hot & bright

Pos	Driver	Team	Chassis-Engine	Result	Qual
1	Alan Jones	Williams	Williams-Ford Cosworth FW07	1h43m24.380s	1
2	Nelson Piquet	Brabham	Brabham-Ford Cosworth BT49	1h43m48.970s	4
3	Keke Rosberg	Fittipaldi	Fittipaldi-Ford Cosworth F7	1h44m43.020s	13
4	Derek Daly	Tyrrell	Tyrrell-Ford Cosworth 009	1h44m47.860s	22
5	Bruno Giacomelli	Alfa Romeo	Alfa Romeo 179B	52 laps	20
6	Alain Prost	McLaren	McLaren-Ford Cosworth M29B	52 laps	12
7	Ricardo Zunino	Brabham	Brabham-Ford Cosworth BT49	51 laps	16
R	Patrick Depailler	Alfa Romeo	Alfa Romeo 179B	46 laps/engine	23
R	Jody Scheckter	Ferrari	Ferrari 312T5	45 laps/engine	11
NC	Clay Regazzoni	Ensign	Ensign-Ford Cosworth N180	44 laps	15
NC	Emerson Fittipaldi	Fittipaldi	Fittipaldi-Ford Cosworth F7	37 laps	24
R	Gilles Villeneuve	Ferrari	Ferrari 312T5	36 laps/accident	8
R	Jacques Laffite	Ligier	Ligier-Ford Cosworth JS11/15	30 laps/engine	2
R	Riccardo Patrese	Arrows	Arrows-Ford Cosworth A3	27 laps/engine	7
R	Marc Surer	ATS	ATS-Ford Cosworth D3	27 laps/fire	21
R	Mario Andretti	Lotus	Lotus-Ford Cosworth 81	20 laps/fuel system	6
R	Jochen Mass	Arrows	Arrows-Ford Cosworth A3	20 laps/gearbox	14
R	Carlos Reutemann	Williams	Williams-Ford Cosworth FW07B	12 laps/engine	10
R	Elio de Angelis	Lotus	Lotus-Ford Cosworth 81	7 laps/suspension	5
R	John Watson	McLaren	McLaren-Ford Cosworth M29B	5 laps/gearbox	17
R	Jean-Pierre Jabouille	Renault	Renault RE20	3 laps/gearbox	9
R	Rene Arnoux	Renault	Renault RE20	2 laps/suspension	19
R	Didier Pironi	Ligier	Ligier-Ford Cosworth JS11/15	1 lap/engine	3
R	Jean-Pierre Jarier	Tyrrell	Tyrrell-Ford Cosworth 009	1 lap/collision	18

Pos	Driver	Team	Chassis-Engine	Result	Qual
DNQ	David Kennedy	Shadow	Shadow-Ford Cosworth DN11	-	25
DNQ	Jan Lammers	ATS	ATS-Ford Cosworth D3	-	26
DNQ	Stefan Johansson	Shadow	Shadow-Ford Cosworth DN11	-	27
DNQ	Eddie Cheever	Osella	Osella-Ford Cosworth FA1	-	28

Pole: Jones, 1m44.170s, 128.160mph/206.254kph. Fastest lap: Jones, 1m50.450s, 120.873mph/194.527kph on Lap 5. Lap leaders: Jones 1-17 & 30-53, Laffite 18-29

BRAZILIAN GRAND PRIX

INTERLAGOS • ROUND 2 • DATE: 27TH JANUARY 1980
Laps: 40 • Distance: 195.702miles/314.952km • Weather: Hot & bright

Pos	Driver	Team	Chassis-Engine	Result	Qual
1	Rene Arnoux	Renault	Renault RE20	1h40m01.330s	6
2	Elio de Angelis	Lotus	Lotus-Ford Cosworth 81	1h40m23.190s	7
3	Alan Jones	Williams	Williams-Ford Cosworth FW07B	1h41m07.440s	10
4	Didier Pironi	Ligier	Ligier-Ford Cosworth JS11/15	1h41m41.460s	2
5	Alain Prost	McLaren	McLaren-Ford Cosworth M29B	1h42m26.740s	13
6	Riccardo Patrese	Arrows	Arrows-Ford Cosworth A3	39 laps	14
7	Marc Surer	ATS	ATS-Ford Cosworth D3	39 laps	20
8	Ricardo Zunino	Brabham	Brabham-Ford Cosworth BT49	39 laps	18
9	Keke Rosberg	Fittipaldi	Fittipaldi-Ford Cosworth F7	39 laps	15
10	Jochen Mass	Arrows	Arrows-Ford Cosworth A3	39 laps	16
11	John Watson	McLaren	McLaren-Ford Cosworth M29B	39 laps	23
12	Jean-Pierre Jarier	Tyrrell	Tyrrell-Ford Cosworth 009	39 laps	22
13	Bruno Giacomelli	Alfa Romeo	Alfa Romeo 179B	39 laps	17
14	Derek Daly	Tyrrell	Tyrrell-Ford Cosworth 009	38 laps	24
15	Emerson Fittipaldi	Fittipaldi	Fittipaldi-Ford Cosworth F7	38 laps	19
16	Gilles Villeneuve	Ferrari	Ferrari 312T5	36 laps/throttle	3
R	Patrick Depailler	Alfa Romeo	Alfa Romeo 179B	33 laps/electrical	21
R	Jean-Pierre Jabouille	Renault	Renault RE20	25 laps/turbo	1
R	Nelson Piquet	Brabham	Brabham-Ford Cosworth BT49	14 laps/suspension	9
R	Jacques Laffite	Ligier	Ligier-Ford Cosworth JS11/15	13 laps/electrical	5
R	Clay Regazzoni	Ensign	Ensign-Ford Cosworth N180	13 laps/engine	12
R	Jody Scheckter	Ferrari	Ferrari 312T5	10 laps/engine	8
R	Carlos Reutemann	Williams	Williams-Ford Cosworth FW07B	1 lap/halfshaft	4
R	Mario Andretti	Lotus	Lotus-Ford Cosworth 81	1 lap/spun off	11
DNQ	David Kennedy	Shadow	Shadow-Ford Cosworth DN11	-	25
DNQ	Jan Lammers	ATS	ATS-Ford Cosworth D3	-	26
DNQ	Stefan Johansson	Shadow	Shadow-Ford Cosworth DN11	-	27
DNQ	Eddie Cheever	Osella	Osella-Ford Cosworth FA1	-	28

Pole: Jabouille, 2m21.400s, 124.562mph/200.464kph. Fastest lap: Arnoux, 2m27.310s, 119.565mph/192.421kph on Lap 22. Race leaders: Villeneuve 1, Jabouille 2-24, Arnoux 25-40

FRENCH BLUE ON THE CHARGE

Since turning to Ford power in 1979, Ligier had made giant strides. In 1980, Didier Pironi took the team to new heights, shown by the way that he beat Jones's Williams by 47 seconds at the Belgian GP. He dominated at Brands Hatch, but his car ate tyres. Team-mate Jacques Laffite led the French, British and German GPs, but only won the last of these three.

SOUTH AFRICAN GRAND PRIX

KYALAMI • ROUND 3 • DATE: 1ST MARCH 1980
Laps: 78 • Distance: 198.908miles/320.112km • Weather: Warm & bright

Pos	Driver	Team	Chassis-Engine	Result	Qual
1	Rene Arnoux	Renault	Renault RE20	1h36m52.540s	2
2	Jacques Laffite	Ligier	Ligier-Ford Cosworth JS11/15	1h37m26.610s	4
3	Didier Pironi	Ligier	Ligier-Ford Cosworth JS11/15	1h37m45.030s	5
4	Nelson Piquet	Brabham	Brabham-Ford Cosworth BT49	1h37m53.560s	3
5	Carlos Reutemann	Williams	Williams-Ford Cosworth FW07B	77 laps	6
6	Jochen Mass	Arrows	Arrows-Ford Cosworth A3	77 laps	19
7	Jean-Pierre Jarier	Tyrrell	Tyrrell-Ford Cosworth 010	77 laps	13
8	Emerson Fittipaldi	Fittipaldi	Fittipaldi-Ford Cosworth F7	77 laps	18
9	Clay Regazzoni	Ensign	Ensign-Ford Cosworth N180	77 laps	20
10	Ricardo Zunino	Brabham	Brabham-Ford Cosworth BT49	77 laps	17
11	John Watson	McLaren	McLaren-Ford Cosworth M29B	76 laps	21
12	Mario Andretti	Lotus	Lotus-Ford Cosworth 81	76 laps	15
13	Geoff Lees	Shadow	Shadow-Ford Cosworth DN11	70 laps/suspension	24
R	Bruno Giacomelli	Alfa Romeo	Alfa Romeo 179B	69 laps/engine	12
R	Jean-Pierre Jabouille	Renault	Renault RE20	61 laps/puncture	1
R	Derek Daly	Tyrrell	Tyrrell-Ford Cosworth 010	61 laps/puncture	16
R	Keke Rosberg	Fittipaldi	Fittipaldi-Ford Cosworth F7	58 laps/accident	23
NC	Patrick Depailler	Alfa Romeo	Alfa Romeo 179B	53 laps	7
R	Alan Jones	Williams	Williams-Ford Cosworth FW07B	34 laps/gearbox	8
R	Gilles Villeneuve	Ferrari	Ferrari 312T5	31 laps/transmission	10
R	Jody Scheckter	Ferrari	Ferrari 312T5	14 laps/engine	9
R	Riccardo Patrese	Arrows	Arrows-Ford Cosworth A3	10 laps/spun off	11
R	Eddie Cheever	Osella	Osella-Ford Cosworth FA1	8 laps/spun off	22
R	Elio de Angelis	Lotus	Lotus-Ford Cosworth 81	1 lap/spun off	14
DNQ	Marc Surer	ATS	ATS-Ford Cosworth D4	-	25
DNQ	David Kennedy	Shadow	Shadow-Ford Cosworth DN11	-	26
DNQ	Jan Lammers	ATS	ATS-Ford Cosworth D3	-	27
DNQ	Alain Prost	McLaren	McLaren-Ford Cosworth M29C	-	28

Pole: Jabouille, 1m10.000s, 131.148mph/211.062kph. Fastest lap: Arnoux, 1m13.150s, 125.500mph/201.974kph on Lap 51. Race leaders: Jabouille 1-61, Arnoux 62-78

UNITED STATES GRAND PRIX WEST

LONG BEACH • ROUND 4 • DATE: 30TH MARCH 1980
Laps: 80 • Distance: 161.561miles/260.08km • Weather: Warm & bright

Pos	Driver	Team	Chassis-Engine	Result	Qual
1	Nelson Piquet	Brabham	Brabham-Ford Cosworth BT49	1h50m18.550s	1
2	Riccardo Patrese	Arrows	Arrows-Ford Cosworth A3	1h51m07.762s	8
3	Emerson Fittipaldi	Fittipaldi	Fittipaldi-Ford Cosworth F7	1h51m37.113s	24
4	John Watson	McLaren	McLaren-Ford Cosworth M29C	79 laps	21
5	Jody Scheckter	Ferrari	Ferrari 312T5	79 laps	16
6	Didier Pironi	Ligier	Ligier-Ford Cosworth JS11/15	79 laps	9
7	Jochen Mass	Arrows	Arrows-Ford Cosworth A3	79 laps	17
8	Derek Daly	Tyrrell	Tyrrell-Ford Cosworth 010	79 laps	14
9	Rene Arnoux	Renault	Renault RE20	78 laps	2
10	Jean-Pierre Jabouille	Renault	Renault RE20	71 laps	11
R	Keke Rosberg	Fittipaldi	Fittipaldi-Ford Cosworth F7	58 laps/overheating	22
R	Clay Regazzoni	Ensign	Ensign-Ford Cosworth N180	50 laps/accident	23

Pos	Driver	Team	Chassis-Engine	Result	Qual
R	Bruno Giacomelli	Alfa Romeo	Alfa Romeo 179B	49 laps/accident	6
R	Alan Jones	Williams	Williams-Ford Cosworth FW07B	47 laps/accident	5
R	Gilles Villeneuve	Ferrari	Ferrari 312T5	46 laps/transmission	10
R	Patrick Depailler	Alfa Romeo	Alfa Romeo 179B	40 laps/suspension	3
R	Jacques Laffite	Ligier	Ligier-Ford Cosworth JS11/15	36 laps/puncture	13
R	Eddie Cheever	Osella	Osella-Ford Cosworth FA1	11 laps/transmission	19
R	Carlos Reutemann	Williams	Williams-Ford Cosworth FW07B	3 laps/transmission	7
R	Jean-Pierre Jarier	Tyrrell	Tyrrell-Ford Cosworth 010	3 laps/accident	12
R	Elio de Angelis	Lotus	Lotus-Ford Cosworth 81	3 laps/accident	20
R	Jan Lammers	ATS	ATS-Ford Cosworth D4	0 laps/transmission	4
R	Mario Andretti	Lotus	Lotus-Ford Cosworth 81	0 laps/accident	15
R	Ricardo Zunino	Brabham	Brabham-Ford Cosworth BT49	0 laps/accident	18
DNQ	David Kennedy	Shadow	Shadow-Ford Cosworth DN11	-	25
DNQ	Geoff Lees	Shadow	Shadow-Ford Cosworth DN11	-	26
DNQ	Stephen South	McLaren	McLaren-Ford Cosworth M29C	-	27

Pole: Piquet, 1m17.694s, 93.601mph/150.637kph. Fastest lap: Piquet, 1m19.830s, 91.097mph/146.606kph on Lap 38. Race leaders: Piquet 1-80

PERSISTENCE REWARDED

Frank Williams' desire to succeed in F1 led to him forming Williams Grand Prix Engineering with designer Patrick Head in 1977. Sponsorship from Saudia Airlines gave them the backing they required and they pushed towards the top of F1's pile. Winning both the drivers' and constructors' titles in 1980 was very special for the pair.

BELGIAN GRAND PRIX

ZOLDER • ROUND 5 • DATE: 4TH MAY 1980
Laps: 72 • Distance: 190.676miles/306.864km • Weather: Warm but dull

Pos	Driver	Team	Chassis-Engine	Result	Qual
1	Didier Pironi	Ligier	Ligier-Ford Cosworth JS11/15	1h38m46.510s	2
2	Alan Jones	Williams	Williams-Ford Cosworth FW07B	1h39m33.880s	1
3	Carlos Reutemann	Williams	Williams-Ford Cosworth FW07B	1h40m10.630s	4
4	Rene Arnoux	Renault	Renault RE20	71 laps	6
5	Jean-Pierre Jarier	Tyrrell	Tyrrell-Ford Cosworth 010	71 laps	9
6	Gilles Villeneuve	Ferrari	Ferrari 312T5	71 laps	12
7	Keke Rosberg	Fittipaldi	Fittipaldi-Ford Cosworth F7	71 laps	21
8	Jody Scheckter	Ferrari	Ferrari 312T5	70 laps	14
9	Derek Daly	Tyrrell	Tyrrell-Ford Cosworth 010	70 laps	11
10	Elio de Angelis	Lotus	Lotus-Ford Cosworth 81	69 laps/spun off	8
11	Jacques Laffite	Ligier	Ligier-Ford Cosworth JS11/15	68 laps	3
12	Jan Lammers	ATS	ATS-Ford Cosworth D4	64 laps/engine	15
NC	John Watson	McLaren	McLaren-Ford Cosworth M29C	61 laps	20
R	Riccardo Patrese	Arrows	Arrows-Ford Cosworth A3	58 laps/spun off	16
R	Mario Andretti	Lotus	Lotus-Ford Cosworth 81	41 laps/gearbox	17
R	Patrick Depailler	Alfa Romeo	Alfa Romeo 179B	38 laps/exhaust	10
R	Nelson Piquet	Brabham	Brabham-Ford Cosworth BT49	32 laps/spun off	7
R	Alain Prost	McLaren	McLaren-Ford Cosworth M29C	29 laps/transmission	19
R	Emerson Fittipaldi	Fittipaldi	Fittipaldi-Ford Cosworth F7	16 laps/electrical	24
R	Tiff Needell	Ensign	Ensign-Ford Cosworth N180	12 laps/engine	23

Pos	Driver	Team	Chassis-Engine	Result	Qual
R	Bruno Giacomelli	Alfa Romeo	Alfa Romeo 179B	11 laps/suspension	18
R	Ricardo Zunino	Brabham	Brabham-Ford Cosworth BT49	5 laps/gearbox	22
R	Jean-Pierre Jabouille	Renault	Renault RE20	1 lap/clutch	5
R	Jochen Mass	Arrows	Arrows-Ford Cosworth A3	1 lap/spun off	13
DNQ	Geoff Lees	Shadow	Shadow-Ford Cosworth DN12	-	25
DNQ	David Kennedy	Shadow	Shadow-Ford Cosworth DN11	-	26
DNQ	Eddie Cheever	Osella	Osella-Ford Cosworth FA1	-	27

Pole: Jones, 1m19.120s, 120.498mph/193.923kph. Fastest lap: Laffite, 1m20.880s, 117.876mph/189.703kph on Lap 57. Race leaders: Pironi 1-72

WELCOME TO F1, NIGEL

Nigel Mansell was so determined to impress on his F1 debut that he kept on racing despite fuel leaking into the cockpit and burning him. He had been chosen by Lotus to contest the Austrian GP in its third car and didn't want to waste the opportunity. Team boss Colin Chapman rewarded him with a full-time ride in 1981.

UP, UP AND AWAY

Monaco's confines make the dash to the first corner enthralling. In 1980, the excitement went to new heights – literally. Starting from 12th, Derek Daly had just passed Riccardo Patrese's Arrows when he hit Bruno Giacomelli's Alfa Romeo, took the rear wing off Alain Prost's McLaren then landed on team-mate Jean-Pierre Jarier's car.

MONACO GRAND PRIX

MONTE CARLO • ROUND 6 • DATE: 18TH MAY 1980
Laps: 76 • Distance: 156.406miles/251.712km • Weather: Warm with showers

Pos	Driver	Team	Chassis-Engine	Result	Qual
1	Carlos Reutemann	Williams	Williams-Ford Cosworth FW07B	1h55m34.365s	2
2	Jacques Laffite	Ligier	Ligier-Ford Cosworth JS11/15	1h56m47.994s	5
3	Nelson Piquet	Brabham	Brabham-Ford Cosworth BT49	1h56m52.091s	4
4	Jochen Mass	Arrows	Arrows-Ford Cosworth A3	75 laps	15
5	Gilles Villeneuve	Ferrari	Ferrari 312T5	75 laps	6
6	Emerson Fittipaldi	Fittipaldi	Fittipaldi-Ford Cosworth F7	74 laps	18
7	Mario Andretti	Lotus	Lotus-Ford Cosworth 81	73 laps	19
8	Riccardo Patrese	Arrows	Arrows-Ford Cosworth A3	73 laps	11
9	Elio de Angelis	Lotus	Lotus-Ford Cosworth 81	68 laps/accident	14
NC	Jan Lammers	ATS	ATS-Ford Cosworth D4	64 laps	13
R	Didier Pironi	Ligier	Ligier-Ford Cosworth JS11/15	54 laps/accident	1
R	Rene Arnoux	Renault	Renault RE20	53 laps/accident	20
R	Patrick Depailler	Alfa Romeo	Alfa Romeo 179B	50 laps/engine	7
R	Jody Scheckter	Ferrari	Ferrari 312T5	27 laps/handling	17
R	Alan Jones	Williams	Williams-Ford Cosworth FW07B	25 laps/differential	3
R	Jean-Pierre Jabouille	Renault	Renault RE20	25 laps/gearbox	16

Pos	Driver	Team	Chassis-Engine	Result	Qual
R	Bruno Giacomelli	Alfa Romeo	Alfa Romeo 179B	0 laps/accident	8
R	Jean-Pierre Jarier	Tyrrell	Tyrrell-Ford Cosworth 010	0 laps/accident	9
R	Alain Prost	McLaren	McLaren-Ford Cosworth M29C	0 laps/accident	10
R	Derek Daly	Tyrrell	Tyrrell-Ford Cosworth 010	0 laps/accident	12
DNQ	John Watson	McLaren	McLaren-Ford Cosworth M29C	-	21
DNQ	Eddie Cheever	Osella	Osella-Ford Cosworth FA1	-	22
DNQ	Geoff Lees	Shadow	Shadow-Ford Cosworth DN12	-	23
DNQ	Keke Rosberg	Fittipaldi	Fittipaldi-Ford Cosworth F7	-	24
DNQ	Ricardo Zunino	Brabham	Brabham-Ford Cosworth BT49	-	25
DNQ	Tiff Needell	Ensign	Ensign-Ford Cosworth N180	-	26
DNQ	David Kennedy	Shadow	Shadow-Ford Cosworth DN11	-	27

Pole: Pironi, 1m24.813s, 87.353mph/140.582kph. Fastest lap: Reutemann, 1m27.418s, 84.750mph/136.392kph on Lap 40. Race leaders: Pironi 1-54, Reutemann 55-76

FRENCH GRAND PRIX

CIRCUIT PAUL RICARD • ROUND 7 • DATE: 29TH JUNE 1980
Laps: 54 • Distance: 194.535miles/313.74km • Weather: Warm, dull & windy

Pos	Driver	Team	Chassis-Engine	Result	Qual
1	Alan Jones	Williams	Williams-Ford Cosworth FW07B	1h32m43.420s	4
2	Didier Pironi	Ligier	Ligier-Ford Cosworth JS11/15	1h32m47.940s	3
3	Jacques Laffite	Ligier	Ligier-Ford Cosworth JS11/15	1h33m13.680s	1
4	Nelson Piquet	Brabham	Brabham-Ford Cosworth BT49	1h33m58.300s	8
5	Rene Arnoux	Renault	Renault RE20	1h33m59.570s	2
6	Carlos Reutemann	Williams	Williams-Ford Cosworth FW07B	1h34m00.160s	5
7	John Watson	McLaren	McLaren-Ford Cosworth M29C	53 laps	13
8	Gilles Villeneuve	Ferrari	Ferrari 312T5	53 laps	17
9	Riccardo Patrese	Arrows	Arrows-Ford Cosworth A3	53 laps	18
10	Jochen Mass	Arrows	Arrows-Ford Cosworth A3	53 laps	15
11	Derek Daly	Tyrrell	Tyrrell-Ford Cosworth 010	52 laps	20
12	Jody Scheckter	Ferrari	Ferrari 312T5	52 laps	19
13	Emerson Fittipaldi	Fittipaldi	Fittipaldi-Ford Cosworth F7	50 laps/engine	24
14	Jean-Pierre Jarier	Tyrrell	Tyrrell-Ford Cosworth 010	50 laps	16
R	Eddie Cheever	Osella	Osella-Ford Cosworth FA1	43 laps/engine	21
R	Marc Surer	ATS	ATS-Ford Cosworth D4	26 laps/gearbox	11
R	Patrick Depailler	Alfa Romeo	Alfa Romeo 179B	25 laps/handling	10
R	Mario Andretti	Lotus	Lotus-Ford Cosworth 81	18 laps/gearbox	12
R	Bruno Giacomelli	Alfa Romeo	Alfa Romeo 179B	8 laps/handling	9
R	Keke Rosberg	Fittipaldi	Fittipaldi-Ford Cosworth F7	8 laps/spun off	23
R	Alain Prost	McLaren	McLaren-Ford Cosworth M29C	6 laps/transmission	7
R	Elio de Angelis	Lotus	Lotus-Ford Cosworth 81	3 laps/clutch	14
R	Jean-Pierre Jabouille	Renault	Renault RE20	0 laps/transmission	6
R	Ricardo Zunino	Brabham	Brabham-Ford Cosworth BT49	0 laps/clutch	22
DNQ	Geoff Lees	Shadow	Shadow-Ford Cosworth DN12	-	25
DNQ	Jan Lammers	Ensign	Ensign-Ford Cosworth N180	-	26
DNQ	David Kennedy	Shadow	Shadow-Ford Cosworth DN12	-	27

Pole: Laffite, 1m38.880s, 131.438mph/211.529kph. Fastest lap: Jones, 1m41.450s, 128.108mph/206.170kph on Lap 48. Race leaders: Laffite 1-34, Jones 35-54

BRITISH GRAND PRIX

BRANDS HATCH • ROUND 8 • DATE: 13TH JULY 1980
Laps: 76 • Distance: 198.629miles/319.663km • Weather: Warm but dull

Pos	Driver	Team	Chassis-Engine	Result	Qual
1	Alan Jones	Williams	Williams-Ford Cosworth FW07B	1h34m49.228s	3
2	Nelson Piquet	Brabham	Brabham-Ford Cosworth BT49	1h35m00.235s	5
3	Carlos Reutemann	Williams	Williams-Ford Cosworth FW07B	1h35m02.513s	4
4	Derek Daly	Tyrrell	Tyrrell-Ford Cosworth 010	75 laps	10
5	Jean-Pierre Jarier	Tyrrell	Tyrrell-Ford Cosworth 010	75 laps	11
6	Alain Prost	McLaren	McLaren-Ford Cosworth M29C	75 laps	7
7	Hector Rebaque	Brabham	Brabham-Ford Cosworth BT49	74 laps	17
8	John Watson	McLaren	McLaren-Ford Cosworth M29C	74 laps/engine	12
9	Riccardo Patrese	Arrows	Arrows-Ford Cosworth A3	73 laps	21
10	Jody Scheckter	Ferrari	Ferrari 312T5	73 laps	23
11	Rupert Keegan	RAM Racing	Williams-Ford Cosworth FW07	73 laps	18
12	Emerson Fittipaldi	Fittipaldi	Fittipaldi-Ford Cosworth F8	72 laps	22
13	Jochen Mass	Arrows	Arrows-Ford Cosworth A3	69 laps	24
NC	Rene Arnoux	Renault	Renault RE20	67 laps	16
R	Didier Pironi	Ligier	Ligier-Ford Cosworth JS11/15	63 laps/tyre	1
R	Marc Surer	ATS	ATS-Ford Cosworth D4	59 laps/engine	15
R	Mario Andretti	Lotus	Lotus-Ford Cosworth 81	57 laps/gearbox	9
R	Bruno Giacomelli	Alfa Romeo	Alfa Romeo 179B	42 laps/spun off	6
R	Gilles Villeneuve	Ferrari	Ferrari 312T5	35 laps/engine	19
R	Jacques Laffite	Ligier	Ligier-Ford Cosworth JS11/15	30 laps/tyre	2
R	Patrick Depailler	Alfa Romeo	Alfa Romeo 179B	27 laps/engine	8
R	Eddie Cheever	Osella	Osella-Ford Cosworth FA1	17 laps/suspension	20
R	Elio de Angelis	Lotus	Lotus-Ford Cosworth 81	16 laps/suspension	14
R	Jean-Pierre Jabouille	Renault	Renault RE20	6 laps/engine	13
DNQ	Jan Lammers	Ensign	Ensign-Ford Cosworth N180	-	25
DNQ	Keke Rosberg	Fittipaldi	Fittipaldi-Ford Cosworth F7	-	26
DNQ	Desire Wilson	RAM Racing	Williams-Ford Cosworth FW07	-	27

Pole: Pironi, 1m11.004s, 132.510mph/213.255kph. Fastest lap: Pironi, 1m12.368s, 130.012mph/209.235kph on Lap 54. Race leaders: Pironi 1-18, Laffite 19-30, Jones 31-76

GERMAN GRAND PRIX

HOCKENHEIM • ROUND 9 • DATE: 10TH AUGUST 1980
Laps: 45 • Distance: 189.832miles/305.505km • Weather: Warm but dull

Pos	Driver	Team	Chassis-Engine	Result	Qual
1	Jacques Laffite	Ligier	Ligier-Ford Cosworth JS11/15	1h22m59.730s	5
2	Carlos Reutemann	Williams	Williams-Ford Cosworth FW07B	1h23m02.920s	4
3	Alan Jones	Williams	Williams-Ford Cosworth FW07B	1h23m43.260s	1
4	Nelson Piquet	Brabham	Brabham-Ford Cosworth BT49	1h23m44.210s	6
5	Bruno Giacomelli	Alfa Romeo	Alfa Romeo 179B	1h24m16.220s	19
6	Gilles Villeneuve	Ferrari	Ferrari 312T5	1h24m28.450s	16
7	Mario Andretti	Lotus	Lotus-Ford Cosworth 81	1h24m32.740s	9
8	Jochen Mass	Arrows	Arrows-Ford Cosworth A3	1h24m47.480s	17
9	Riccardo Patrese	Arrows	Arrows-Ford Cosworth A3	44 laps	10
10	Derek Daly	Tyrrell	Tyrrell-Ford Cosworth 010	44 laps	22
11	Alain Prost	McLaren	McLaren-Ford Cosworth M29C	44 laps	14
12	Marc Surer	ATS	ATS-Ford Cosworth D4	44 laps	13
13	Jody Scheckter	Ferrari	Ferrari 312T5	44 laps	21

Pos	Driver	Team	Chassis-Engine	Result	Qual
14	Jan Lammers	Ensign	Ensign-Ford Cosworth N180	44 laps	24
15	Jean-Pierre Jarier	Tyrrell	Tyrrell-Ford Cosworth 010	44 laps	23
16	Elio de Angelis	Lotus	Lotus-Ford Cosworth 81	43 laps/wheel	11
R	John Watson	McLaren	McLaren-Ford Cosworth M29C	39 laps/engine	20
R	Jean-Pierre Jabouille	Renault	Renault RE20	27 laps/engine	2
R	Rene Arnoux	Renault	Renault RE20	26 laps/engine	3
R	Eddie Cheever	Osella	Osella-Ford Cosworth FA1	23 laps/gearbox	18
R	Didier Pironi	Ligier	Ligier-Ford Cosworth JS11/15	18 laps/transmission	7
R	Emerson Fittipaldi	Fittipaldi	Fittipaldi-Ford Cosworth F8	18 laps/brakes	12
R	Keke Rosberg	Fittipaldi	Fittipaldi-Ford Cosworth F8	8 laps/wheel	8
R	Hector Rebaque	Brabham	Brabham-Ford Cosworth BT49	4 laps/gearbox	15
DNQ	Rupert Keegan	RAM Racing	Williams-Ford Cosworth FW07B	-	25
DNQ	Harald Ertl	ATS	ATS-Ford Cosworth D4	-	26

Pole: Jones, 1m45.850s, 143.472mph/230.896kph. Fastest lap: Jones, 1m48.490s, 139.981mph/225.277kph on Lap 43. Race leaders: Jabouille 1-26, Jones 27-40, Laffite 41-45

THE END OF THE ROAD

Former Ferrari favourite Clay Regazzoni suffered career-ending spinal injuries when he crashed at Long Beach. The five-time grand prix winner had lost his ride at Williams and was snapped up by Ensign. It was a definite step backwards, but the Swiss driver gave it his all, only to have his brake pedal snap. He died in a road accident in 2006.

NEW CIRCUITS

Monza had been the home of the Italian GP since its inception, apart from when tracks in Brescia, Livorno, Milan and Turin hosted the race in the inaugural 1921 event, 1937, 1947 and 1948 respectively. In 1980, Imola became the race's sixth home. The circuit held a non-championship race in 1979 and then, with Monza still out of favour after Ronnie Peterson's death there in 1978, it was offered this second chance.

AUSTRIAN GRAND PRIX

OSTERREICHRING • ROUND 10 • DATE: 17TH AUGUST 1980
Laps: 54 • Distance: 199.391miles/320.889km • Weather: Warm & bright

Pos	Driver	Team	Chassis-Engine	Result	Qual
1	Jean-Pierre Jabouille	Renault	Renault RE20	1h26m15.730s	2
2	Alan Jones	Williams	Williams-Ford Cosworth FW07B	1h26m16.550s	3
3	Carlos Reutemann	Williams	Williams-Ford Cosworth FW07B	1h26m35.090s	4
4	Jacques Laffite	Ligier	Ligier-Ford Cosworth JS11/15	1h26m57.750s	5
5	Nelson Piquet	Brabham	Brabham-Ford Cosworth BT49	1h27m18.540s	7
6	Elio de Angelis	Lotus	Lotus-Ford Cosworth 81	1h27m30.700s	9
7	Alain Prost	McLaren	McLaren-Ford Cosworth M29C	1h27m49.140s	12
8	Gilles Villeneuve	Ferrari	Ferrari 312T5	53 laps	15
9	Rene Arnoux	Renault	Renault RE20	53 laps	1

Pos	Driver	Team	Chassis-Engine	Result	Qual
10	Hector Rebaque	Brabham	Brabham-Ford Cosworth BT49	53 laps	14
11	Emerson Fittipaldi	Fittipaldi	Fittipaldi-Ford Cosworth F8	53 laps	23
12	Marc Surer	ATS	ATS-Ford Cosworth D4	53 laps	16
13	Jody Scheckter	Ferrari	Ferrari 312T5	53 laps	22
14	Riccardo Patrese	Arrows	Arrows-Ford Cosworth A3	53 laps	18
15	Rupert Keegan	RAM Racing	Williams-Ford Cosworth FW07B	52 laps	20
16	Keke Rosberg	Fittipaldi	Fittipaldi-Ford Cosworth F8	52 laps	11
R	Nigel Mansell	Lotus	Lotus-Ford Cosworth 81B	40 laps/engine	24
R	John Watson	McLaren	McLaren-Ford Cosworth M29C	34 laps/engine	21
R	Bruno Giacomelli	Alfa Romeo	Alfa Romeo 179B	28 laps/wheel	8
R	Didier Pironi	Ligier	Ligier-Ford Cosworth JS11/15	25 laps/handling	6
R	Jean-Pierre Jarier	Tyrrell	Tyrrell-Ford Cosworth 010	25 laps/electrical	13
R	Eddie Cheever	Osella	Osella-Ford Cosworth FA1	23 laps/wheel	19
R	Derek Daly	Tyrrell	Tyrrell-Ford Cosworth 010	12 laps/brakes	10
R	Mario Andretti	Lotus	Lotus-Ford Cosworth 81	6 laps/engine	17
DNQ	Jan Lammers	Ensign	Ensign-Ford Cosworth N180	-	25
NS	Jochen Mass	Arrows	Arrows-Ford Cosworth A3	-	26

Pole: Arnoux, 1m30.270s, 147.255mph/236.985kph. Fastest lap: Arnoux, 1m32.530s, 143.659mph/231.196kph on Lap 50. Race leaders: Jones 1-2, Arnoux 3-20, Jabouille 21-54

NEW CONSTRUCTORS

Osella was the lone constructor that moved up to F1 in 1980. The Italian team was spawned by former sports car racer Enzo Osella building sports cars and, from 1974, single-seaters, mainly for F2. Its Ford-powered FA1 designed by Giorgio Stirano was overweight and fragile, as driver Eddie Cheever retired in all but one of his 11 starts.

DUTCH GRAND PRIX

ZANDVOORT • ROUND 11 • DATE: 31ST AUGUST 1980
Laps: 72 • Distance: 190.229miles/306.144km • Weather: Warm & bright

Pos	Driver	Team	Chassis-Engine	Result	Qual
1	Nelson Piquet	Brabham	Brabham-Ford Cosworth BT49	1h38m13.830s	5
2	Rene Arnoux	Renault	Renault RE20	1h38m26.760s	1
3	Jacques Laffite	Ligier	Ligier-Ford Cosworth JS11/15	1h38m27.260s	6
4	Carlos Reutemann	Williams	Williams-Ford Cosworth FW07B	1h38m29.120s	3
5	Jean-Pierre Jarier	Tyrrell	Tyrrell-Ford Cosworth 010	1h39m13.850s	17
6	Alain Prost	McLaren	McLaren-Ford Cosworth M30	1h39m36.450s	18
7	Gilles Villeneuve	Ferrari	Ferrari 312T5	71 laps	7
8	Mario Andretti	Lotus	Lotus-Ford Cosworth 81	70 laps/out of fuel	10
9	Jody Scheckter	Ferrari	Ferrari 312T5	70 laps	12
10	Marc Surer	ATS	ATS-Ford Cosworth D4	69 laps	20
11	Alan Jones	Williams	Williams-Ford Cosworth FW07B	69 laps	4
R	Derek Daly	Tyrrell	Tyrrell-Ford Cosworth 010	60 laps/brakes	23
R	Bruno Giacomelli	Alfa Romeo	Alfa Romeo 179B	58 laps/accident	8
R	Eddie Cheever	Osella	Osella-Ford Cosworth FA1	38 laps/engine	19
R	Riccardo Patrese	Arrows	Arrows-Ford Cosworth A3	29 laps/engine	14
R	Jean-Pierre Jabouille	Renault	Renault RE20	23 laps/handling	2
R	Vittorio Brambilla	Alfa Romeo	Alfa Romeo 179B	21 laps/accident	22

Pos	Driver	Team	Chassis-Engine	Result	Qual
R	Geoff Lees	Ensign	Ensign-Ford Cosworth N180	21 laps/accident	24
R	John Watson	McLaren	McLaren-Ford Cosworth M29C	18 laps/engine	9
R	Emerson Fittipaldi	Fittipaldi	Fittipaldi-Ford Cosworth F8	16 laps/brakes	21
R	Nigel Mansell	Lotus	Lotus-Ford Cosworth 81B	15 laps/brakes	16
R	Elio de Angelis	Lotus	Lotus-Ford Cosworth 81	2 laps/accident	11
R	Didier Pironi	Ligier	Ligier-Ford Cosworth JS11/15	2 laps/accident	15
R	Hector Rebaque	Brabham	Brabham-Ford Cosworth BT49	1 lap/gearbox	13
DNQ	Rupert Keegan	RAM Racing	Williams-Ford Cosworth FW07B	-	25
DNQ	Jan Lammers	Ensign	Ensign-Ford Cosworth N180	-	26
DNQ	Mike Thackwell	Arrows	Arrows-Ford Cosworth A3	-	27
DNQ	Keke Rosberg	Fittipaldi	Fittipaldi-Ford Cosworth F8	-	28
NS	Jochen Mass	Arrows	Arrows-Ford Cosworth A3	driver injured	29

Pole: Arnoux, 1m17.440s, 122.823mph/197.665kph. Fastest lap: Arnoux, 1m19.350s, 119.867mph/192.907kph on Lap 67. Race leaders: Jones 1, Arnoux 2, Laffite 3-12, Piquet 13-72

ITALIAN GRAND PRIX

IMOLA • ROUND 12 • DATE: 14TH SEPTEMBER 1980
Laps: 60 • Distance: 186.411miles/300.0km • Weather: Warm & bright

Pos	Driver	Team	Chassis-Engine	Result	Qual
1	Nelson Piquet	Brabham	Brabham-Ford Cosworth BT49	1h38m07.520s	5
2	Alan Jones	Williams	Williams-Ford Cosworth FW07B	1h38m36.450s	6
3	Carlos Reutemann	Williams	Williams-Ford Cosworth FW07B	1h39m21.190s	3
4	Elio de Angelis	Lotus	Lotus-Ford Cosworth 81	59 laps	18
5	Keke Rosberg	Fittipaldi	Fittipaldi-Ford Cosworth F8	59 laps	11
6	Didier Pironi	Ligier	Ligier-Ford Cosworth JS11/15	59 laps	13
7	Alain Prost	McLaren	McLaren-Ford Cosworth M30	59 laps	24
8	Jody Scheckter	Ferrari	Ferrari 312T5	59 laps	16
9	Jacques Laffite	Ligier	Ligier-Ford Cosworth JS11/15	59 laps	20
10	Rene Arnoux	Renault	Renault RE20	58 laps	1
11	Rupert Keegan	RAM Racing	Williams-Ford Cosworth FW07B	58 laps	21
12	Eddie Cheever	Osella	Osella-Ford Cosworth FA1B	57 laps	17
13	Jean-Pierre Jarier	Tyrrell	Tyrrell-Ford Cosworth 010	54 laps/brakes	12
R	Jean-Pierre Jabouille	Renault	Renault RE20	53 laps/gearbox	2
R	Marc Surer	ATS	ATS-Ford Cosworth D4	45 laps/engine	23
R	Mario Andretti	Lotus	Lotus-Ford Cosworth 81	40 laps/engine	10
R	Riccardo Patrese	Arrows	Arrows-Ford Cosworth A3	38 laps/engine	7
R	Derek Daly	Tyrrell	Tyrrell-Ford Cosworth 010	33 laps/accident	22
R	John Watson	McLaren	McLaren-Ford Cosworth M29C	20 laps/wheel	14
R	Hector Rebaque	Brabham	Brabham-Ford Cosworth BT49	18 laps/suspension	9
R	Emerson Fittipaldi	Fittipaldi	Fittipaldi-Ford Cosworth F8	17 laps/accident	15
R	Bruno Giacomelli	Alfa Romeo	Alfa Romeo 179B	5 laps/puncture	4
R	Gilles Villeneuve	Ferrari	Ferrari 312T5	5 laps/puncture	8
R	Vittorio Brambilla	Alfa Romeo	Alfa Romeo 179B	4 laps/spun off	19
DNQ	Nigel Mansell	Lotus	Lotus-Ford Cosworth 81	-	25
DNQ	Manfred Winkelhock	Arrows	Arrows-Ford Cosworth A3	-	26
DNQ	Jan Lammers	Ensign	Ensign-Ford Cosworth N180	-	27
DNQ	Geoff Lees	Ensign	Ensign-Ford Cosworth N180	-	28

Pole: Arnoux, 1m33.988s, 119.001mph/191.513kph. Fastest lap: Jones, 1m36.089s, 116.399mph/187.326kph on Lap 47. Race leaders: Arnoux 1-2, Jabouille 3, Piquet 4-60

CANADIAN GRAND PRIX

MONTREAL • ROUND 13 • DATE: 28TH SEPTEMBER 1980
Laps: 70 • Distance: 191.386miles/308.7km • Weather: Cool & dull

Pos	Driver	Team	Chassis-Engine	Result	Qual
1	Alan Jones	Williams	Williams-Ford Cosworth FW07B	1h46m45.530s	2
2	Carlos Reutemann	Williams	Williams-Ford Cosworth FW07B	1h47m01.070s	5
3	Didier Pironi*	Ligier	Ligier-Ford Cosworth JS11/15	1h47m04.600s	3
4	John Watson	McLaren	McLaren-Ford Cosworth M29C	1h47m16.510s	7
5	Gilles Villeneuve	Ferrari	Ferrari 312T5	1h47m40.760s	22
6	Hector Rebaque	Brabham	Brabham-Ford Cosworth BT49	69 laps	10
7	Jean-Pierre Jarier	Tyrrell	Tyrrell-Ford Cosworth 010	69 laps	15
8	Jacques Laffite	Ligier	Ligier-Ford Cosworth JS11/15	68 laps/out of fuel	9
9	Keke Rosberg	Fittipaldi	Fittipaldi-Ford Cosworth F8	68 laps	6
10	Elio de Angelis	Lotus	Lotus-Ford Cosworth 81	68 laps	17
11	Jochen Mass	Arrows	Arrows-Ford Cosworth A3	67 laps	21
12	Jan Lammers	Ensign	Ensign-Ford Cosworth N180	66 laps	19
R	Alain Prost	McLaren	McLaren-Ford Cosworth M30	41 laps/suspension	12
R	Rene Arnoux	Renault	Renault RE20	39 laps/brakes	23
R	Jean-Pierre Jabouille	Renault	Renault RE20	25 laps/suspension	13
R	Nelson Piquet	Brabham	Brabham-Ford Cosworth BT49	23 laps/engine	1
R	Mario Andretti	Lotus	Lotus-Ford Cosworth 81	11 laps/engine	18
R	Andrea de Cesaris	Alfa Romeo	Alfa Romeo 179B	8 laps/engine	8
R	Eddie Cheever	Osella	Osella-Ford Cosworth FA1B	8 laps/fuel system	14
R	Emerson Fittipaldi	Fittipaldi	Fittipaldi-Ford Cosworth F8	8 laps/gearbox	16
R	Bruno Giacomelli	Alfa Romeo	Alfa Romeo 179B	7 laps/skirt	4
R	Riccardo Patrese	Arrows	Arrows-Ford Cosworth A3	6 laps/accident	11
R	Derek Daly	Tyrrell	Tyrrell-Ford Cosworth 010	0 laps/accident	20
R	Mike Thackwell	Tyrrell	Tyrrell-Ford Cosworth 010	0 laps/accident	24
DNQ	Marc Surer	ATS	ATS-Ford Cosworth D4	-	25
DNQ	Jody Scheckter	Ferrari	Ferrari 312T5	-	26
DNQ	Rupert Keegan	RAM Racing	Williams-Ford Cosworth FW07B	-	27
DNQ	Kevin Cogan	RAM Racing	Williams-Ford Cosworth FW07B	-	28

*penalised 1m for jumped start

Pole: Piquet, 1m27.328s, 112.963mph/181.797kph. Fastest lap: Pironi, 1m28.769s, 111.129mph/178.846kph on Lap 62. Race leaders: Jones 1-2 & 24-43, Piquet 3-23, Pironi 44-70

NEW DRIVERS

Two future champions, Alain Prost and Nigel Mansell, were among F1's 12-strong intake. Prost did best, pushing John Watson hard at McLaren, while 19-year-old Mike Thackwell became the youngest driver to qualify. Desire Wilson failed in her attempt to become the first female F1 racer to make the qualifying cut since Lella Lombardi in 1976.

UNITED STATES GRAND PRIX

WATKINS GLEN • ROUND 14 • DATE: 5TH OCTOBER 1980
Laps: 59 • Distance: 199.251miles/320.665km • Weather: Cool & dull

Pos	Driver	Team	Chassis-Engine	Result	Qual
1	Alan Jones	Williams	Williams-Ford Cosworth FW07B	1h34m36.050s	5
2	Carlos Reutemann	Williams	Williams-Ford Cosworth FW07B	1h34m40.260s	3
3	Didier Pironi	Ligier	Ligier-Ford Cosworth JS11/15	1h34m48.620s	7
4	Elio de Angelis	Lotus	Lotus-Ford Cosworth 81	1h35m05.740s	4
5	Jacques Laffite	Ligier	Ligier-Ford Cosworth JS11/15	58 laps	12
6	Mario Andretti	Lotus	Lotus-Ford Cosworth 81	58 laps	11
7	Rene Arnoux	Renault	Renault RE20	58 laps	6
8	Marc Surer	ATS	ATS-Ford Cosworth D4	57 laps	17
9	Rupert Keegan	RAM Racing	Williams-Ford Cosworth FW07B	57 laps	15
10	Keke Rosberg	Fittipaldi	Fittipaldi-Ford Cosworth F8	57 laps	14
11	Jody Scheckter	Ferrari	Ferrari 312T5	56 laps	23
NC	John Watson	McLaren	McLaren-Ford Cosworth M29C	50 laps	9
R	Gilles Villeneuve	Ferrari	Ferrari 312T5	49 laps/accident	18
NC	Jean-Pierre Jarier	Tyrrell	Tyrrell-Ford Cosworth 010	40 laps	22
R	Jochen Mass	Arrows	Arrows-Ford Cosworth A3	36 laps/transmission	24
R	Bruno Giacomelli	Alfa Romeo	Alfa Romeo 179B	31 laps/electrical	1
R	Nelson Piquet	Brabham	Brabham-Ford Cosworth BT49	25 laps/spun off	2
R	Hector Rebaque	Brabham	Brabham-Ford Cosworth BT49	20 laps/engine	8
R	Eddie Cheever	Osella	Osella-Ford Cosworth FA1B	20 laps/suspension	16
R	Riccardo Patrese	Arrows	Arrows-Ford Cosworth A3	16 laps/spun off	20
R	Jan Lammers	Ensign	Ensign-Ford Cosworth N180	16 laps/steering	25
R	Emerson Fittipaldi	Fittipaldi	Fittipaldi-Ford Cosworth F8	15 laps/suspension	19
R	Derek Daly	Tyrrell	Tyrrell-Ford Cosworth 010	3 laps/spun off	21
R	Andrea de Cesaris	Alfa Romeo	Alfa Romeo 179B	2 laps/accident	10
NS	Alain Prost	McLaren	McLaren-Ford Cosworth M30	Driver injured	13
DNQ	Mike Thackwell	Tyrrell	Tyrrell-Ford Cosworth 010	-	26
DNQ	Geoff Lees	RAM Racing	Williams-Ford Cosworth FW07B	-	27

Pole: Giacomelli, 1m33.291s, 130.320mph/209.730kph. Fastest lap: Jones, 1m34.068s, 129.244mph/207.998kph on Lap 44. Race leaders: Giacomelli 1-31, Jones 32-59

IN MEMORIAM

The enigmatic Patrick Depailler lost his life just as his team, Alfa Romeo, was making progress in its second year back in F1. The Alfa Romeo was fast – he qualified third at Long Beach – but unreliable, as it lasted through just one of the first eight races. Looking for improvements, Depailler was testing at Hockenheim when he crashed.

WORLD DRIVERS' CHAMPIONSHIP FINAL RESULTS

Pos	Driver	Nat	Car-Engine	R1	R2	R3	R4	R5
1	Alan Jones	AUS	Williams-Ford Cosworth FW07	1PF	-	-	-	-
			Williams-Ford Cosworth FW07B	-	3	R	R	2P
2	Nelson Piquet	BRA	Brabham-Ford Cosworth BT49	2	R	4	1PF	R
3	Carlos Reutemann	ARG	Williams-Ford Cosworth FW07B	R	R	5	R	3
4	Jacques Laffite	FRA	Ligier-Ford Cosworth JS11/15	R	R	2	R	11F
5	Didier Pironi	FRA	Ligier-Ford Cosworth JS11/15	R	4	3	6	1
6	Rene Arnoux	FRA	Renault RE20	R	1F	1F	9	4
7	Elio de Angelis	ITA	Lotus-Ford Cosworth 81	R	2	R	R	10
8	Jean-Pierre Jabouille	FRA	Renault RE20	R	RP	RP	10	R
9	Riccardo Patrese	ITA	Arrows-Ford Cosworth A3	R	6	R	2	R
10	Keke Rosberg	FIN	Fittipaldi-Ford Cosworth F7	3	9	R	R	7
			Fittipaldi-Ford Cosworth F8	-	-	-	-	-
10	Derek Daly	IRL	Tyrrell-Ford Cosworth 009	4	14	-	-	-
			Tyrrell-Ford Cosworth 010	-	-	R	8	9
11	John Watson	GBR	McLaren-Ford Cosworth M29B	R	11	11	-	-
			McLaren-Ford Cosworth M29C	-	-	-	4	NC
13	Jean-Pierre Jarier	FRA	Tyrrell-Ford Cosworth 009	R	12	-	-	-
			Tyrrell-Ford Cosworth 010	-	-	7	R	5
14	Gilles Villeneuve	CAN	Ferrari 312T5	R	16	R	R	6
15	Emerson Fittipaldi	BRA	Fittipaldi-Ford Cosworth F7	NC	15	8	3	R
			Fittipaldi-Ford Cosworth F8	-	-	-	-	-
15	Alain Prost	FRA	McLaren-Ford Cosworth M29B	6	5	-	-	-
			McLaren-Ford Cosworth M29C	-	-	NS	-	R
			McLaren-Ford Cosworth M30	-	-	-	-	-
17	Jochen Mass	DEU	Arrows-Ford Cosworth A3	R	10	6	7	R
17	Bruno Giacomelli	ITA	Alfa Romeo 179B	5	13	R	R	R
19	Jody Scheckter	ZAF	Ferrari 312T5	R	R	R	5	8
20	Hector Rebaque	MEX	Brabham-Ford Cosworth BT49	-	-	-	-	-
20	Mario Andretti	USA	Lotus-Ford Cosworth 81	R	R	12	R	R

Pos	Driver	R6	R7	R8	R9	R10	R11	R12	R13	R14	Total
1	Jones	-	-	-	-	-	-	-	-	-	67
		R	1F	1	3PF	2	11	2F	1	1F	
2	Piquet	3	4	2	4	5	1	1	RP	R	54
3	Reutemann	1F	6	3	2	3	4	3	2	2	42
4	Laffite	2	3P	R	1	4	3	9	8	5	34
5	Pironi	RP	2	RPF	R	R	R	6	3F	3	32
6	Arnoux	R	5	NC	R	9PF	2PF	10P	R	7	29
7	de Angelis	9	R	R	16	6	R	4	10	4	13
8	Jabouille	R	R	R	R	1	R	R	R	-	9
9	Patrese	8	9	9	9	14	R	R	R	R	7
10	Rosberg	DNQ	R	DNQ	-	-	-	-	-	-	6
		-	-	-	R	16	DNQ	5	9	10	
10	Daly	-	-	-	-	-	-	-	-	-	6
		R	11	4	10	R	R	R	R	R	
10	Watson	-	-	-	-	-	-	-	-	-	6
		DNQ	7	8	R	R	R	R	4	NC	
10	Jarier	-	-	-	-	-	-	-	-	-	6
		R	14	5	15	R	5	13	7	NC	
10	Villeneuve	5	8	R	6	8	7	R	5	R	6
15	Fittipaldi	6	13	-	-	-	-	-	-	-	5
		-	-	12	R	11	R	R	R	R	

Pos	Driver	R6	R7	R8	R9	R10	R11	R12	R13	R14	Total
15	Prost	-	-	-	-	-	-	-	-	-	5
		R	R	6	11	7	-	-	-	-	
		-	-	-	-	-	6	7	R	NS	
17	Mass	4	10	13	8	NS	NS	-	11	R	4
17	Giacomelli	R	R	R	5	R	R	R	R	RP	4
19	Scheckter	R	12	10	13	13	9	8	DNQ	11	2
20	Rebaque	-	-	7	R	10	R	R	6	R	1
20	Andretti	7	R	R	7	R	8	R	R	6	1

WORLD CONSTRUCTORS' CHAMPIONSHIP FINAL RESULTS

Pos	Team-Engine	R1	R2	R3	R4	R5	R6	R7	R8
1	Williams-Ford	1/R	3/R	5/R	R/R	2/3	1/R	1/6	1/3
2	Ligier-Ford	R/R	4/R	2/3	6/R	1/11	2/R	2/3	R/R
3	Brabham-Ford	2/7	8/R	4/10	1/R	R/R	3/DNQ	4/R	2/7
4	Renault	R/R	1/R	1/R	9/10	4/R	R/R	5/R	NC/R
5	Lotus-Ford	R/R	2/R	12/R	R/R	10/R	7/9	R/R	R/R
6	Tyrrell-Ford	4/R	12/14	7/R	8/R	5/9	R/R	11/14	4/5
7	Arrows-Ford	R/R	6/10	6/R	2/7	R/R	4/8	9/10	9/13
7	Fittipaldi-Ford	3/NC	9/15	8/R	3/R	7/R	6/DNQ	13/R	12/DNQ
7	McLaren-Ford	6/R	5/11	11/NS	4/DNQ	NC/R	R/DNQ	7/R	6/8
10	Ferrari	R/R	16/R	R/R	5/R	6/8	5/R	8/12	10/R
11	Alfa Romeo	5/R	13/R	R/NC	R/R	R/R	R/R	R/R	R/R

Pos	Team-Engine	R9	R10	R11	R12	R13	R14	Total
1	Williams-Ford	2/3/DNQ	2/3/15	4/11/DNQ	2/3/11	1/2/DNQ/DNQ	1/2/9/DNQ	120
2	Ligier-Ford	1/R	4/R	3/R	6/9	3/8	3/5	66
3	Brabham-Ford	4/R	5/10	1/R	1/R	6/R	R/R	55
4	Renault	R/R	1/9	2/R	10/R	R/R	7	38
5	Lotus-Ford	7/16	6/R/R	8/R/R	4/R/DNQ	10/R	4/6	14
6	Tyrrell-Ford	10/15	R/R	5/R	13/R	7/R/R	NC/R/DNQ	12
7	Arrows-Ford	8/9	14/NS	R/DNQ	R/DNQ	11/R	R/R	11
7	Fittipaldi-Ford	R/R	11/16	R/DNQ	5/R	9/R	10/R	11
7	McLaren-Ford	11/R	7/R	6/R	7/R	4/R	NC/NS	11
10	Ferrari	6/13	8/13	7/9	8/R	5/DNQ	11/R	8
11	Alfa Romeo	5	R	R/R	R/R	R/R	R/R	4

SYMBOLS AND GRAND PRIX KEY

Round 1 **Argentinian GP**
Round 2 **Brazilian GP**
Round 3 **South African GP**
Round 4 **United States GP West**
Round 5 **Belgian GP**
Round 6 **Monaco GP**
Round 7 **French GP**
Round 8 **British GP**
Round 9 **German GP**
Round 10 **Austrian GP**
Round 11 **Dutch GP**
Round 12 **Italian GP**
Round 13 **Canadian GP**
Round 14 **United States GP**

SCORING

1st **9 points**
2nd **6 points**
3rd **4 points**
4th **3 points**
5th **2 points**
6th **1 point**

DNPQ DID NOT PRE-QUALIFY **DNQ DID NOT QUALIFY** **DQ DISQUALIFIED** **EX EXCLUDED**
F FASTEST LAP **NC NOT CLASSIFIED** **NS NON-STARTER** **P POLE POSITION** **R RETIRED**

SEASON SUMMARY

After an aborted start when the South African GP wasn't recognised as a World Championship race while FISA and FOCA continued their scrap for power, the season started at Long Beach with a Williams one-two. However, by year's end, it was a Brabham driver who was crowned world champion. This was Nelson Piquet and his three-win tally was enough to give the team its first drivers' title since 1967. Much of this success was down to Brabham designer Gordon Murray finding a way around the new 6cm (2.4in) ground clearance rule, with the BT49C's hydraulic suspension lowering it after it left the pits then reverting to the minimum height on their return.

UNITED STATES GRAND PRIX WEST

LONG BEACH • ROUND 1 • DATE: 15TH MARCH 1981
Laps: 80 • Distance: 161.561miles/260.08km • Weather: Warm & bright

Pos	Driver	Team	Chassis-Engine	Result	Qual
1	Alan Jones	Williams	Williams-Ford Cosworth FW07C	1h50m41.330s	2
2	Carlos Reutemann	Williams	Williams-Ford Cosworth FW07C	1h50m50.520s	3
3	Nelson Piquet	Brabham	Brabham-Ford Cosworth BT49C	1h51m16.250s	4
4	Mario Andretti	Alfa Romeo	Alfa Romeo 179C	1h51m30.640s	6
5	Eddie Cheever	Tyrrell	Tyrrell-Ford Cosworth 010	1h51m48.030s	8
6	Patrick Tambay	Theodore	Theodore-Ford Cosworth TY01	79 laps	17
7	Chico Serra	Fittipaldi	Fittipaldi-Ford Cosworth F8C	78 laps	18
8	Rene Arnoux	Renault	Renault RE20B	77 laps	20
R	Marc Surer	Ensign	Ensign-Ford Cosworth N180B	70 laps/electrical	19
R	Didier Pironi	Ferrari	Ferrari 126CK	67 laps/fuel system	11
R	Jean-Pierre Jarier	Ligier	Ligier-Matra JS17	64 laps/fuel pump	10
R	Hector Rebaque	Brabham	Brabham-Ford Cosworth BT49C	49 laps/accident	15
R	Bruno Giacomelli	Alfa Romeo	Alfa Romeo 179C	41 laps/collision	9
R	Jacques Laffite	Ligier	Ligier-Matra JS17	41 laps/collision	12
R	Keke Rosberg	Fittipaldi	Fittipaldi-Ford Cosworth F8C	41 laps/engine	16
R	Jan Lammers	ATS	ATS-Ford Cosworth D4	41 laps/collision	21
R	Riccardo Patrese	Arrows	Arrows-Ford Cosworth A3	33 laps/fuel system	1
R	Beppe Gabbiani	Osella	Osella-Ford Cosworth FA1B	26 laps/accident	24
R	Nigel Mansell	Lotus	Lotus-Ford Cosworth 81	25 laps/accident	7
R	Gilles Villeneuve	Ferrari	Ferrari 126CK	17 laps/halfshaft	5
R	John Watson	McLaren	McLaren-Ford Cosworth M29F	16 laps/brakes	23
R	Elio de Angelis	Lotus	Lotus-Ford Cosworth 81	13 laps/accident	13
R	Alain Prost	Renault	Renault RE20B	0 laps/collision	14
R	Andrea de Cesaris	McLaren	McLaren-Ford Cosworth M29F	0 laps/collision	22
DNQ	Kevin Cogan	Tyrrell	Tyrrell-Ford Cosworth 010	-	25
DNQ	Derek Daly	March	March-Ford Cosworth 811	-	26
DNQ	Miguel Angel Guerra	Osella	Osella-Ford Cosworth FA1B	-	27
DNQ	Siegfried Stohr	Arrows	Arrows-Ford Cosworth A3	-	28
DNQ	Eliseo Salazar	March	March-Ford Cosworth 811	-	29

Pole: Patrese, 1m19.399s, 91.591mph/147.402kph. Fastest lap: Jones, 1m20.901s, 89.891mph/144.665kph on Lap 31. Race leaders: Patrese 1-24, Reutemann 25-31, Jones 32-80

BRAZILIAN GRAND PRIX

JACAREPAGUA • ROUND 2 • DATE: 29TH MARCH 1981
Laps: 62 • Distance: 193.819miles/311.922km • Weather: Warm & wet

Pos	Driver	Team	Chassis-Engine	Result	Qual
1	Carlos Reutemann	Williams	Williams-Ford Cosworth FW07C	2h00m23.660s	2
2	Alan Jones	Williams	Williams-Ford Cosworth FW07C	2h00m28.100s	3
3	Riccardo Patrese	Arrows	Arrows-Ford Cosworth A3	2h01m26.740s	4
4	Marc Surer	Ensign	Ensign-Ford Cosworth N180B	2h01m40.690s	18
5	Elio de Angelis	Lotus	Lotus-Ford Cosworth 81	2h01m50.080s	10
6	Jacques Laffite	Ligier	Ligier-Matra JS17	2h01m50.490s	16
7	Jean-Pierre Jarier	Ligier	Ligier-Matra JS17	2h01m53.910s	23
8	John Watson	McLaren	McLaren-Ford Cosworth M29F	61 laps	15
9	Keke Rosberg	Fittipaldi	Fittipaldi-Ford Cosworth F8C	61 laps	12
10	Patrick Tambay	Theodore	Theodore-Ford Cosworth TY01	61 laps	19
11	Nigel Mansell	Lotus	Lotus-Ford Cosworth 81	61 laps	13
12	Nelson Piquet	Brabham	Brabham-Ford Cosworth BT49C	60 laps	1
13	Ricardo Zunino	Tyrrell	Tyrrell-Ford Cosworth 010	57 laps	24
NC	Eddie Cheever	Tyrrell	Tyrrell-Ford Cosworth 010	49 laps	14
NC	Bruno Giacomelli	Alfa Romeo	Alfa Romeo 179C	40 laps	6
R	Gilles Villeneuve	Ferrari	Ferrari 126CK	25 laps/turbo	7
R	Hector Rebaque	Brabham	Brabham-Ford Cosworth BT49C	22 laps/spun off	11
R	Alain Prost	Renault	Renault RE20B	20 laps/collision	5
R	Siegfried Stohr	Arrows	Arrows-Ford Cosworth A3	20 laps/accident	21
R	Didier Pironi	Ferrari	Ferrari 126CK	19 laps/collision	17
R	Andrea de Cesaris	McLaren	McLaren-Ford Cosworth M29F	9 laps/engine	20
R	Rene Arnoux	Renault	Renault RE20B	0 laps/collision	8
R	Mario Andretti	Alfa Romeo	Alfa Romeo 179C	0 laps/collision	9
R	Chico Serra	Fittipaldi	Fittipaldi-Ford Cosworth F8C	0 laps/collision	22
DNQ	Jan Lammers	ATS	ATS-Ford Cosworth D4	-	25
DNQ	Beppe Gabbiani	Osella	Osella-Ford Cosworth FA1B	-	26
DNQ	Miguel Angel Guerra	Osella	Osella-Ford Cosworth FA1B	-	27
DNQ	Eliseo Salazar	March	March-Ford Cosworth 811	-	28
DNQ	Derek Daly	March	March-Ford Cosworth 811	-	30
DNQ	Jean-Pierre Jabouille	Ligier	Ligier-Matra JS17	injured ankle	-

Pole: Piquet, 1m35.079s, 118.365mph/190.490kph. Fastest lap: Surer, 1m54.302s, 98.458mph/158.453kph on Lap 36. Race leaders: Reutemann 1-62

FALLING AT THE LAST

The final round of the year was the Caesars Palace GP in Las Vegas, and Williams' Carlos Reutemann held a one-point lead over Piquet, with Ligier's Jacques Laffite having an outside chance. In the race, Reutemann started from pole but was out of sorts, fell to eighth and was lapped, as a tiring Piquet just held on to fifth and so took the title.

ARGENTINIAN GRAND PRIX

BUENOS AIRES • ROUND 3 • DATE: 12TH APRIL 1981
Laps: 53 • Distance: 196.548miles/316.314km • Weather: Hot & bright

Pos	Driver	Team	Chassis-Engine	Result	Qual
1	Nelson Piquet	Brabham	Brabham-Ford Cosworth BT49C	1h34m32.740s	1
2	Carlos Reutemann	Williams	Williams-Ford Cosworth FW07C	1h34m59.350s	4
3	Alain Prost	Renault	Renault RE20B	1h35m22.720s	2
4	Alan Jones	Williams	Williams-Ford Cosworth FW07C	1h35m40.620s	3
5	Rene Arnoux	Renault	Renault RE20B	1h36m04.590s	5
6	Elio de Angelis	Lotus	Lotus-Ford Cosworth 81	52 laps	10
7	Riccardo Patrese	Arrows	Arrows-Ford Cosworth A3	52 laps	9
8	Mario Andretti	Alfa Romeo	Alfa Romeo 179C	52 laps	17
9	Siegfried Stohr	Arrows	Arrows-Ford Cosworth A3	52 laps	19
10	Bruno Giacomelli	Alfa Romeo	Alfa Romeo 179C	51 laps/out of fuel	22
11	Andrea de Cesaris	McLaren	McLaren-Ford Cosworth M29F	51 laps	18
12	Jan Lammers	ATS	ATS-Ford Cosworth D4	51 laps	23
13	Ricardo Zunino	Tyrrell	Tyrrell-Ford Cosworth 010	51 laps	24
R	Gilles Villeneuve	Ferrari	Ferrari 126CK	40 laps/transmission	7
R	John Watson	McLaren	McLaren-Ford Cosworth MP4/1	36 laps/transmission	11
R	Patrick Tambay	Theodore	Theodore-Ford Cosworth TY01	36 laps/oil leak	14
R	Hector Rebaque	Brabham	Brabham-Ford Cosworth BT49C	32 laps/electrical	6
R	Chico Serra	Fittipaldi	Fittipaldi-Ford Cosworth F8C	28 laps/gearbox	20
R	Jacques Laffite	Ligier	Ligier-Matra JS17	19 laps/handling	21
R	Marc Surer	Ensign	Ensign-Ford Cosworth N180B	14 laps/engine	16
R	Keke Rosberg	Fittipaldi	Fittipaldi-Ford Cosworth F8C	4 laps/fuel pump	8
R	Didier Pironi	Ferrari	Ferrari 126CK	3 laps/engine	12
R	Nigel Mansell	Lotus	Lotus-Ford Cosworth 81	3 laps/engine	15
R	Eddie Cheever	Tyrrell	Tyrrell-Ford Cosworth 010	1 lap/clutch	13
DNQ	Miguel Angel Guerra	Osella	Osella-Ford Cosworth FA1B	-	25
DNQ	Beppe Gabbiani	Osella	Osella-Ford Cosworth FA1B	-	26
DNQ	Derek Daly	March	March-Ford Cosworth 811	-	27
DNQ	Jean-Pierre Jabouille	Ligier	Ligier-Matra JS17	-	28
DNQ	Eliseo Salazar	March	March-Ford Cosworth 811	-	29

Pole: Piquet, 1m42.665s, 130.039mph/209.277kph. Fastest lap: Piquet, 1m45.287s, 126.800mph/204.066kph on Lap 6. Race leaders: Piquet 1-53

SAN MARINO GRAND PRIX

IMOLA • ROUND 4 • DATE: 3RD MAY 1981
Laps: 60 • Distance: 187.656miles/302.4km • Weather: Cool & wet

Pos	Driver	Team	Chassis-Engine	Result	Qual
1	Nelson Piquet	Brabham	Brabham-Ford Cosworth BT49C	1h51m23.970s	5
2	Riccardo Patrese	Arrows	Arrows-Ford Cosworth A3	1h51m28.550s	9
3	Carlos Reutemann	Williams	Williams-Ford Cosworth FW07C	1h51m30.310s	2
4	Hector Rebaque	Brabham	Brabham-Ford Cosworth BT49C	1h51m46.860s	13
5	Didier Pironi	Ferrari	Ferrari 126CK	1h51m49.840s	6
6	Andrea de Cesaris	McLaren	McLaren-Ford Cosworth M29F	1h52m30.580s	14
7	Gilles Villeneuve	Ferrari	Ferrari 126CK	1h53m05.940s	1
8	Rene Arnoux	Renault	Renault RE20B	59 laps	3
9	Marc Surer	Ensign	Ensign-Ford Cosworth N180B	59 laps	21
10	John Watson	McLaren	McLaren-Ford Cosworth MP4/1	58 laps	7
11	Patrick Tambay	Theodore	Theodore-Ford Cosworth TY01	58 laps	16
12	Alan Jones	Williams	Williams-Ford Cosworth FW07C	58 laps	8

Pos	Driver	Team	Chassis-Engine	Result	Qual
13	Slim Borgudd	ATS	ATS-Ford Cosworth D4	57 laps	24
NC	Jean-Pierre Jabouille	Ligier	Ligier-Matra JS17	45 laps	18
R	Eliseo Salazar	March	March-Ford Cosworth 811	38 laps/spun off	23
R	Michele Alboreto	Tyrrell	Tyrrell-Ford Cosworth 010	31 laps/collision	17
R	Beppe Gabbiani	Osella	Osella-Ford Cosworth FA1B	31 laps/collision	20
R	Bruno Giacomelli	Alfa Romeo	Alfa Romeo 179C	28 laps/collision	11
R	Eddie Cheever	Tyrrell	Tyrrell-Ford Cosworth 010	28 laps/collision	19
R	Mario Andretti	Alfa Romeo	Alfa Romeo 179C	26 laps/gearbox	12
R	Keke Rosberg	Fittipaldi	Fittipaldi-Ford Cosworth F8C	14 laps/engine	15
R	Jacques Laffite	Ligier	Ligier-Matra JS17	7 laps/suspension	10
R	Alain Prost	Renault	Renault RE20B	3 laps/gearbox	4
R	Miguel Angel Guerra	Osella	Osella-Ford Cosworth FA1B	0 laps/accident	22
DNQ	Siegfried Stohr	Arrows	Arrows-Ford Cosworth A3	-	25
DNQ	Derek Daly	March	March-Ford Cosworth 811	-	26
DNQ	Jan Lammers	ATS	ATS-Ford Cosworth D4	-	27
DNQ	Chico Serra	Fittipaldi	Fittipaldi-Ford Cosworth F8C	-	28
DNQ	Derek Warwick	Toleman	Toleman-Hart TG181	-	29
DNQ	Brian Henton	Toleman	Toleman-Hart TG181	-	30

Pole: Villeneuve, 1m34.523s, 119.274mph/191.953kph. Fastest lap: Villeneuve, 1m48.064s, 104.328mph/167.900kph on Lap 46. Race leaders: Villeneuve 1-14, Pironi 15-46, Piquet 47-60

NOT QUITE IN SAN MARINO

With Italy captivated by F1, it was decided that there could be a way to give the Tifosi a chance to see their beloved Ferraris twice each year by creating a courtesy title for a second race in Italy. Thus Imola was kept on the agenda after hosting the Italian GP in 1980, with its race given the new title of San Marino GP.

BELGIAN GRAND PRIX

ZOLDER • ROUND 5 • DATE: 17TH MAY 1981
Laps: 54 • Distance: 143.7miles/230.148km • Weather: Warm & bright, then rain

Pos	Driver	Team	Chassis-Engine	Result	Qual
1	Carlos Reutemann	Williams	Williams-Ford Cosworth FW07C	1h16m31.610s	1
2	Jacques Laffite	Ligier	Ligier-Matra JS17	1h17m07.670s	9
3	Nigel Mansell	Lotus	Lotus-Ford Cosworth 81	1h17m15.300s	10
4	Gilles Villeneuve	Ferrari	Ferrari 126CK	1h17m19.250s	7
5	Elio de Angelis	Lotus	Lotus-Ford Cosworth 81	1h17m20.810s	14
6	Eddie Cheever	Tyrrell	Tyrrell-Ford Cosworth 010	1h17m24.120s	8
7	John Watson	McLaren	McLaren-Ford Cosworth MP4/1	1h17m33.270s	5
8	Didier Pironi	Ferrari	Ferrari 126CK	1h18m03.650s	3
9	Bruno Giacomelli	Alfa Romeo	Alfa Romeo 179C	1h18m07.190s	17
10	Mario Andretti	Alfa Romeo	Alfa Romeo 179C	53 laps	18
11	Marc Surer	Ensign	Ensign-Ford Cosworth N180B	52 laps	15
12	Michele Alboreto	Tyrrell	Tyrrell-Ford Cosworth 010	52 laps	19
13	Piercarlo Ghinzani	Osella	Osella-Ford Cosworth FA1B	50 laps	24
R	Hector Rebaque	Brabham	Brabham-Ford Cosworth BT49C	39 laps/accident	21
R	Jean-Pierre Jabouille	Ligier	Ligier-Matra JS17	35 laps/transmission	16

Pos	Driver	Team	Chassis-Engine	Result	Qual
R	Chico Serra	Fittipaldi	Fittipaldi-Ford Cosworth F8C	29 laps/engine	20
R	Beppe Gabbiani	Osella	Osella-Ford Cosworth FA1B	22 laps/engine	22
R	Alan Jones	Williams	Williams-Ford Cosworth FW07C	19 laps/accident	6
R	Andrea de Cesaris	McLaren	McLaren-Ford Cosworth M29F	11 laps/gearbox	23
R	Nelson Piquet	Brabham	Brabham-Ford Cosworth BT49C	10 laps/accident	2
R	Keke Rosberg	Fittipaldi	Fittipaldi-Ford Cosworth F8C	10 laps/gearbox	11
R	Alain Prost	Renault	Renault RE20B	2 laps/clutch	12
R	Riccardo Patrese	Arrows	Arrows-Ford Cosworth A3	0 laps/collision	4
R	Siegfried Stohr	Arrows	Arrows-Ford Cosworth A3	0 laps/collision	13
DNQ	Rene Arnoux	Renault	Renault RE30	-	25
DNQ	Eliseo Salazar	March	March-Ford Cosworth 811	-	26
DNQ	Slim Borgudd	ATS	ATS-Ford Cosworth HGS1	-	27
DNQ	Patrick Tambay	Theodore	Theodore-Ford Cosworth TY01	-	28
DNQ	Derek Warwick	Toleman	Toleman-Hart TG181	-	29
DNQ	Brian Henton	Toleman	Toleman-Hart TG181	-	30
DNQ	Derek Daly	March	March-Ford Cosworth 811	-	31

Pole: Reutemann, 1m22.280s, 115.870mph/186.475kph. Fastest lap: Reutemann, 1m23.300s, 114.451mph/184.192kph on Lap 37. Race leaders: Pironi 1-12, Jones 13-19, Reutemann 20-54

RUNNING A WIDE CAR

Having inherited victory at Monaco when Jones slowed, Gilles Villeneuve was made to fight for it next time out. This was at the Spanish GP at Jarama and he inherited the lead again when Jones slid off, but then had to spend 66 laps with one eye on his mirrors as he held up four rivals. At the chequered flag, the first five cars were covered by just 1.24 seconds.

MONACO GRAND PRIX

MONTE CARLO • ROUND 6 • DATE: 31ST MAY 1981
Laps: 76 • Distance: 156.406miles/251.712km • Weather: Warm & bright

Pos	Driver	Team	Chassis-Engine	Result	Qual
1	Gilles Villeneuve	Ferrari	Ferrari 126CK	1h54m23.380s	2
2	Alan Jones	Williams	Williams-Ford Cosworth FW07C	1h55m03.290s	7
3	Jacques Laffite	Ligier	Ligier-Matra JS17	1h55m52.620s	8
4	Didier Pironi	Ferrari	Ferrari 126CK	75 laps	17
5	Eddie Cheever	Tyrrell	Tyrrell-Ford Cosworth 010	74 laps	15
6	Marc Surer	Ensign	Ensign-Ford Cosworth N180B	74 laps	19
7	Patrick Tambay	Theodore	Theodore-Ford Cosworth TY01	72 laps	16
R	Nelson Piquet	Brabham	Brabham-Ford Cosworth BT49C	53 laps/spun off	1
R	John Watson	McLaren	McLaren-Ford Cosworth MP4/1	52 laps/engine	10
R	Bruno Giacomelli	Alfa Romeo	Alfa Romeo 179C	50 laps/collision	18
R	Michele Alboreto	Tyrrell	Tyrrell-Ford Cosworth 010	50 laps/collision	20
R	Alain Prost	Renault	Renault RE30	45 laps/engine	9
R	Carlos Reutemann	Williams	Williams-Ford Cosworth FW07C	33 laps/gearbox	4
R	Elio de Angelis	Lotus	Lotus-Ford Cosworth 87	32 laps/engine	6
R	Rene Arnoux	Renault	Renault RE20B	32 laps/spun off	13
R	Riccardo Patrese	Arrows	Arrows-Ford Cosworth A3	29 laps/gearbox	5
R	Nigel Mansell	Lotus	Lotus-Ford Cosworth 87	15 laps/suspension	3

Pos	Driver	Team	Chassis-Engine	Result	Qual
R	Siegfried Stohr	Arrows	Arrows-Ford Cosworth A3	14 laps/fuel system	14
R	Andrea de Cesaris	McLaren	McLaren-Ford Cosworth MP4/1	0 laps/collision	11
R	Mario Andretti	Alfa Romeo	Alfa Romeo 179C	0 laps/collision	12
DNQ	Keke Rosberg	Fittipaldi	Fittipaldi-Ford Cosworth F8C	-	21
DNQ	Jean-Pierre Jabouille	Ligier	Ligier-Matra JS17	-	22
DNQ	Hector Rebaque	Brabham	Brabham-Ford Cosworth BT49C	-	23
DNQ	Chico Serra	Fittipaldi	Fittipaldi-Ford Cosworth F8C	-	24
DNQ	Piercarlo Ghinzani	Osella	Osella-Ford Cosworth FA1B	-	25
DNQ	Beppe Gabbiani	Osella	Osella-Ford Cosworth FA1B	-	26
DNPQ	Slim Borgudd	ATS	ATS-Ford Cosworth HGS1	-	27
DNPQ	Derek Daly	March	March-Ford Cosworth 811	-	28
DNPQ	Eliseo Salazar	March	March-Ford Cosworth 811	-	29
DNPQ	Brian Henton	Toleman	Toleman-Hart TG181	-	30
DNPQ	Derek Warwick	Toleman	Toleman-Hart TG181	-	31

Pole: Piquet, 1m25.710s, 86.439mph/139.110kph. Fastest lap: Jones, 1m27.470s, 84.700mph/136.311kph on Lap 48. Race leaders: Piquet 1-53, Jones 54-72, Villeneuve 73-76

PROST SETTLES IN

As a result of his impressive maiden F1 season with McLaren, Alain Prost was snapped up to lead Renault's attack. He finished third on his third outing, in Argentina. Then he advanced further once the RE30 was ready, collecting a trio of wins in the French, Dutch and Italian GPs to end the year ranked fifth as he outperformed team-mate Rene Arnoux.

SPANISH GRAND PRIX

JARAMA • ROUND 7 • DATE: 21ST JUNE 1981
Laps: 80 • Distance: 164.101miles/264.96km • Weather: Hot & bright

Pos	Driver	Team	Chassis-Engine	Result	Qual
1	Gilles Villeneuve	Ferrari	Ferrari 126CK	1h46m35.010s	7
2	Jacques Laffite	Ligier	Ligier-Matra JS17	1h46m35.230s	1
3	John Watson	McLaren	McLaren-Ford Cosworth MP4/1	1h46m35.590s	4
4	Carlos Reutemann	Williams	Williams-Ford Cosworth FW07C	1h46m36.020s	3
5	Elio de Angelis	Lotus	Lotus-Ford Cosworth 87	1h46m36.250s	10
6	Nigel Mansell	Lotus	Lotus-Ford Cosworth 87	1h47m03.590s	11
7	Alan Jones	Williams	Williams-Ford Cosworth FW07C	1h47m31.590s	2
8	Mario Andretti	Alfa Romeo	Alfa Romeo 179C	1h47m35.810s	8
9	Rene Arnoux	Renault	Renault RE30	1h47m42.090s	17
10	Bruno Giacomelli	Alfa Romeo	Alfa Romeo 179C	1h47m48.660s	6
11	Chico Serra	Fittipaldi	Fittipaldi-Ford Cosworth F8C	79 laps	21
12	Keke Rosberg	Fittipaldi	Fittipaldi-Ford Cosworth F8C	78 laps	15
13	Patrick Tambay	Theodore	Theodore-Ford Cosworth TY01	78 laps	16
14	Eliseo Salazar	Ensign	Ensign-Ford Cosworth N180B	77 laps	24
15	Didier Pironi	Ferrari	Ferrari 126CK	76 laps	13
16	Derek Daly	March	March-Ford Cosworth 811	75 laps	22
NC	Eddie Cheever	Tyrrell	Tyrrell-Ford Cosworth 010	62 laps	20
R	Jean-Pierre Jabouille	Ligier	Ligier-Matra JS17	51 laps/brakes	19
R	Hector Rebaque	Brabham	Brabham-Ford Cosworth BT49C	46 laps/gearbox	18
R	Nelson Piquet	Brabham	Brabham-Ford Cosworth BT49C	43 laps/accident	9

Pos	Driver	Team	Chassis-Engine	Result	Qual
R	Siegfried Stohr	Arrows	Arrows-Ford Cosworth A3	43 laps/ignition	23
R	Alain Prost	Renault	Renault RE30	28 laps/spun off	5
R	Riccardo Patrese	Arrows	Arrows-Ford Cosworth A3	21 laps/brakes	12
R	Andrea de Cesaris	McLaren	McLaren-Ford Cosworth MP4/1	9 laps/accident	14
DNQ	Michele Alboreto	Tyrrell	Tyrrell-Ford Cosworth 010	-	25
DNQ	Beppe Gabbiani	Osella	Osella-Ford Cosworth FA1B	-	26
DNQ	Slim Borgudd	ATS	ATS-Ford Cosworth HGS1	-	27
DNQ	Brian Henton	Toleman	Toleman-Hart TG181	-	28
DNQ	Derek Warwick	Toleman	Toleman-Hart TG181	-	29
DNQ	Giorgio Francia	Osella	Osella-Ford Cosworth FA1B	-	30
W	Emilio de Villota	Equipe Banco Occidental	Williams-Ford Cosworth FW07	Entry refused	-

Pole: Laffite, 1m13.754s, 100.451mph/161.661kph. Fastest lap: Jones, 1m17.818s, 95.205mph/153.219kph on Lap 5. Race leaders: Jones 1-13, Villeneuve 14-80

FRENCH GRAND PRIX

DIJON-PRENOIS • ROUND 8 • DATE: 5TH JULY 1981
Laps: 80 • Distance: 188.896miles/304.0km • Weather: Cool, rain later

Pos	Driver	Team	Chassis-Engine	Result	Qual
1	Alain Prost	Renault	Renault RE30	1h35m48.130s	3
2	John Watson	McLaren	McLaren-Ford Cosworth MP4/1	1h35m50.420s	2
3	Nelson Piquet	Brabham	Brabham-Ford Cosworth BT49C	1h36m12.350s	4
4	Rene Arnoux	Renault	Renault RE30	1h36m30.430s	1
5	Didier Pironi	Ferrari	Ferrari 126CK	79 laps	14
6	Elio de Angelis	Lotus	Lotus-Ford Cosworth 87	79 laps	8
7	Nigel Mansell	Lotus	Lotus-Ford Cosworth 87	79 laps	13
8	Mario Andretti	Alfa Romeo	Alfa Romeo 179B	79 laps	10
9	Hector Rebaque	Brabham	Brabham-Ford Cosworth BT49C	78 laps	15
10	Carlos Reutemann	Williams	Williams-Ford Cosworth FW07C	78 laps	7
11	Andrea de Cesaris	McLaren	McLaren-Ford Cosworth MP4/1	78 laps	5
12	Marc Surer	Theodore	Theodore-Ford Cosworth TY01	78 laps	21
13	Eddie Cheever	Tyrrell	Tyrrell-Ford Cosworth 010	77 laps	19
14	Riccardo Patrese	Arrows	Arrows-Ford Cosworth A3	77 laps	18
15	Bruno Giacomelli	Alfa Romeo	Alfa Romeo 179B	77 laps	12
16	Michele Alboreto	Tyrrell	Tyrrell-Ford Cosworth 010	77 laps	23
17	Alan Jones	Williams	Williams-Ford Cosworth FW07C	76 laps	9
R	Jacques Laffite	Ligier	Ligier-Matra JS17	57 laps/collision	6
R	Derek Daly	March	March-Ford Cosworth 811	55 laps/engine	20
R	Gilles Villeneuve	Ferrari	Ferrari 126CK	41 laps/electrical	11
R	Patrick Tambay	Ligier	Ligier-Matra JS17	30 laps/wheel	16
R	Keke Rosberg	Fittipaldi	Fittipaldi-Ford Cosworth F8C	11 laps/suspension	17
R	Eliseo Salazar	Ensign	Ensign-Ford Cosworth N180B	6 laps/suspension	22
NS	Chico Serra	Fittipaldi	Fittipaldi-Ford Cosworth F8C	Accident	24
DNQ	Siegfried Stohr	Arrows	Arrows-Ford Cosworth A3	-	25
DNQ	Brian Henton	Toleman	Toleman-Hart TG181	-	26
DNQ	Slim Borgudd	ATS	ATS-Ford Cosworth HGS1	-	27
DNQ	Beppe Gabbiani	Osella	Osella-Ford Cosworth FA1B	-	28
DNQ	Derek Warwick	Toleman	Toleman-Hart TG181	-	29

Pole: Arnoux, 1m05.950s, 128.890mph/207.429kph. Fastest lap: Prost, 1m09.140s, 122.944mph/197.859kph on Lap 64. Race leaders: Piquet 1-58, Prost 59-80

BRITISH GRAND PRIX

SILVERSTONE • ROUND 9 • DATE: 18TH JULY 1981
Laps: 68 • Distance: 199.375miles/320.864km • Weather: Warm & bright

Pos	Driver	Team	Chassis-Engine	Result	Qual
1	John Watson	McLaren	McLaren-Ford Cosworth MP4/1	1h26m54.801s	5
2	Carlos Reutemann	Williams	Williams-Ford Cosworth FW07C	1h27m35.453s	9
3	Jacques Laffite	Ligier	Ligier-Matra JS17	67 laps	14
4	Eddie Cheever	Tyrrell	Tyrrell-Ford Cosworth 010	67 laps	23
5	Hector Rebaque	Brabham	Brabham-Ford Cosworth BT49C	67 laps	13
6	Slim Borgudd	ATS	ATS-Ford Cosworth HGS1	67 laps	21
7	Derek Daly	March	March-Ford Cosworth 811	66 laps	17
8	Jean-Pierre Jarier	Osella	Osella-Ford Cosworth FA1B	65 laps	20
9	Rene Arnoux	Renault	Renault RE30	64 laps/engine	1
10	Riccardo Patrese	Arrows	Arrows-Ford Cosworth A3	64 laps/engine	10
11	Marc Surer	Theodore	Theodore-Ford Cosworth TY01	61 laps/out of fuel	24
R	Mario Andretti	Alfa Romeo	Alfa Romeo 179C	59 laps/throttle	11
R	Keke Rosberg	Fittipaldi	Fittipaldi-Ford Cosworth F8C	56 laps/suspension	16
DQ	Elio de Angelis	Lotus	Lotus-Ford Cosworth 87	25 laps/flag infringement	22
R	Alain Prost	Renault	Renault RE30	17 laps/engine	2
R	Patrick Tambay	Ligier	Ligier-Matra JS17	15 laps/clutch	15
R	Didier Pironi	Ferrari	Ferrari 126CK	13 laps/turbo	4
R	Nelson Piquet	Brabham	Brabham-Ford Cosworth BT49C	11 laps/tyre	3
R	Bruno Giacomelli	Alfa Romeo	Alfa Romeo 179C	5 laps/transmission	12
R	Gilles Villeneuve	Ferrari	Ferrari 126CK	4 laps/spun off	8
R	Andrea de Cesaris	McLaren	McLaren-Ford Cosworth MP4/1	3 laps/spun off	6
R	Alan Jones	Williams	Williams-Ford Cosworth FW07C	3 laps/collision	7
R	Michele Alboreto	Tyrrell	Tyrrell-Ford Cosworth 010	0 laps/clutch	19
R	Siegfried Stohr	Arrows	Arrows-Ford Cosworth A3	0 laps/spun off	18
DNQ	Chico Serra	Fittipaldi	Fittipaldi-Ford Cosworth F8C	-	25
DNQ	Brian Henton	Toleman	Toleman-Hart TG181	-	26
DNQ	Nigel Mansell	Lotus	Lotus-Ford Cosworth 87	-	27
DNQ	Eliseo Salazar	Ensign	Ensign-Ford Cosworth N180B	-	28
DNQ	Derek Warwick	Toleman	Toleman-Hart TG181	-	29
DNQ	Beppe Gabbiani	Osella	Osella-Ford Cosworth FA1B	-	30

Pole: Arnoux, 1m11.000s, 148.664mph/239.252kph. Fastest lap: Arnoux, 1m15.067s, 140.610mph/226.290kph on Lap 50. Race leaders: Prost 1-16, Arnoux 17-60, Watson 61-68

LOTUS FLOUNDERS

Champions in 1978, then fourth, then fifth, Lotus looked to bounce back with a radical design, but the twin-chassis 88 – with the upper one carrying the bodywork – was judged to be outside the rules, so Lotus had to scramble to build a more conventional car, the 87. This peaked with third place at Zolder and Lotus ended up seventh overall.

GERMAN GRAND PRIX

HOCKENHEIM • ROUND 10 • DATE: 2ND AUGUST 1981
Laps: 45 • Distance: 189.832miles/305.505km • Weather: Hot & bright

Pos	Driver	Team	Chassis-Engine	Result	Qual
1	Nelson Piquet	Brabham	Brabham-Ford Cosworth BT49C	1h25m55.600s	6
2	Alain Prost	Renault	Renault RE30	1h26m07.120s	1
3	Jacques Laffite	Ligier	Ligier-Matra JS17	1h27m00.200s	7
4	Hector Rebaque	Brabham	Brabham-Ford Cosworth BT49C	1h27m35.290s	16
5	Eddie Cheever	Tyrrell	Tyrrell-Ford Cosworth 011	1h27m46.120s	18
6	John Watson	McLaren	McLaren-Ford Cosworth MP4/1	44 laps	9
7	Elio de Angelis	Lotus	Lotus-Ford Cosworth 87	44 laps	14
8	Jean-Pierre Jarier	Osella	Osella-Ford Cosworth FA1B	44 laps	17
9	Mario Andretti	Alfa Romeo	Alfa Romeo 179B	44 laps	12
10	Gilles Villeneuve	Ferrari	Ferrari 126CK	44 laps	8
11	Alan Jones	Williams	Williams-Ford Cosworth FW07C	44 laps	4
12	Siegfried Stohr	Arrows	Arrows-Ford Cosworth A3	44 laps	24
13	Rene Arnoux	Renault	Renault RE30	44 laps	2
14	Marc Surer	Theodore	Theodore-Ford Cosworth TY01	43 laps/suspension	22
15	Bruno Giacomelli	Alfa Romeo	Alfa Romeo 179B	43 laps	19
NC	Eliseo Salazar	Ensign	Ensign-Ford Cosworth N180B	39 laps	23
R	Slim Borgudd	ATS	ATS-Ford Cosworth HGS1	35 laps/engine	20
R	Carlos Reutemann	Williams	Williams-Ford Cosworth FW07C	27 laps/engine	3
R	Patrick Tambay	Ligier	Ligier-Matra JS17	27 laps/transmission	11
R	Riccardo Patrese	Arrows	Arrows-Ford Cosworth A3	27 laps/engine	13
R	Derek Daly	March	March-Ford Cosworth 811	15 laps/suspension	21
R	Nigel Mansell	Lotus	Lotus-Ford Cosworth 87	12 laps/oil leak	15
R	Andrea de Cesaris	McLaren	McLaren-Ford Cosworth MP4/1	4 laps/collision	10
R	Didier Pironi	Ferrari	Ferrari 126CK	1 lap/electrical	5
DNQ	Keke Rosberg	Fittipaldi	Fittipaldi-Ford Cosworth F8C	-	25
DNQ	Brian Henton	Toleman	Toleman-Hart TG181	-	26
DNQ	Beppe Gabbiani	Osella	Osella-Ford Cosworth FA1B	-	27
DNQ	Derek Warwick	Toleman	Toleman-Hart TG181	-	28
DNQ	Michele Alboreto	Tyrrell	Tyrrell-Ford Cosworth 010	-	29
DNQ	Chico Serra	Fittipaldi	Fittipaldi-Ford Cosworth F8C	-	30

Pole: Prost, 1m47.500s, 141.270mph/227.352kph. Fastest lap: Jones, 1m52.420s, 135.087mph/217.402kph on Lap 4. Race leaders: Prost 1-20, Jones 21-38, Piquet 39-45

AUSTRIAN GRAND PRIX

OSTERREICHRING • ROUND 11 • DATE: 16TH AUGUST 1981
Laps: 53 • Distance: 195.698miles/314.947km • Weather: Hot & bright

Pos	Driver	Team	Chassis-Engine	Result	Qual
1	Jacques Laffite	Ligier	Ligier-Matra JS17	1h27m36.470s	4
2	Rene Arnoux	Renault	Renault RE30	1h27m41.640s	1
3	Nelson Piquet	Brabham	Brabham-Ford Cosworth BT49C	1h27m43.810s	7
4	Alan Jones	Williams	Williams-Ford Cosworth FW07C	1h27m48.510s	6
5	Carlos Reutemann	Williams	Williams-Ford Cosworth FW07C	1h28m08.320s	5
6	John Watson	McLaren	McLaren-Ford Cosworth MP4/1	1h29m07.610s	12
7	Elio de Angelis	Lotus	Lotus-Ford Cosworth 87	52 laps	9
8	Andrea de Cesaris	McLaren	McLaren-Ford Cosworth MP4/1	52 laps	18
9	Didier Pironi	Ferrari	Ferrari 126CK	52 laps	8
10	Jean-Pierre Jarier	Osella	Osella-Ford Cosworth FA1B	51 laps	14

Pos	Driver	Team	Chassis-Engine	Result	Qual
11	Derek Daly	March	March-Ford Cosworth 811	47 laps	19
R	Mario Andretti	Alfa Romeo	Alfa Romeo 179D	46 laps/engine	13
R	Slim Borgudd	ATS	ATS-Ford Cosworth HGS1	44 laps/brakes	21
R	Riccardo Patrese	Arrows	Arrows-Ford Cosworth A3	43 laps/engine	10
R	Eliseo Salazar	Ensign	Ensign-Ford Cosworth N180B	43 laps/fuel pressure	20
R	Michele Alboreto	Tyrrell	Tyrrell-Ford Cosworth 010	40 laps/gearbox	22
R	Bruno Giacomelli	Alfa Romeo	Alfa Romeo 179B	35 laps/fire	16
R	Hector Rebaque	Brabham	Brabham-Ford Cosworth BT49C	32 laps/clutch	15
R	Siegfried Stohr	Arrows	Arrows-Ford Cosworth A3	27 laps/overheating	24
R	Alain Prost	Renault	Renault RE30	26 laps/suspension	2
R	Patrick Tambay	Ligier	Ligier-Matra JS17	26 laps/engine	17
R	Nigel Mansell	Lotus	Lotus-Ford Cosworth 87	23 laps/engine	11
R	Gilles Villeneuve	Ferrari	Ferrari 126CK	11 laps/accident	3
NS	Marc Surer	Theodore	Theodore-Ford Cosworth TY01	0 laps/distributor	23
DNQ	Eddie Cheever	Tyrrell	Tyrrell-Ford Cosworth 011	-	25
DNQ	Derek Warwick	Toleman	Toleman-Hart TG181	-	26
DNQ	Brian Henton	Toleman	Toleman-Hart TG181	-	27
DNQ	Beppe Gabbiani	Osella	Osella-Ford Cosworth FA1B	-	28

Pole: Arnoux, 1m32.018s, 144.458mph/232.483kph. Fastest lap: Laffite, 1m37.620s, 136.168mph/219.141kph on Lap 47. Race leaders: Villeneuve 1, Prost 2-26, Arnoux 27-38, Laffite 39-53

NEW CIRCUITS

Building a circuit in a car park is unlikely to work, yet this is what FISA agreed to in order to take F1 to a new crowd in Las Vegas, having the temporary venue set up next to Caesars Palace casino. The track took up very little space as its 2.268-mile (3.650km) length snaked backwards and forwards through five hairpins within the car park's square perimeter.

DUTCH GRAND PRIX

ZANDVOORT • ROUND 12 • DATE: 30TH AUGUST 1981
Laps: 72 • Distance: 190.229miles/306.144km • Weather: Warm & bright

Pos	Driver	Team	Chassis-Engine	Result	Qual
1	Alain Prost	Renault	Renault RE30	1h40m22.430s	1
2	Nelson Piquet	Brabham	Brabham-Ford Cosworth BT49C	1h40m30.670s	3
3	Alan Jones	Williams	Williams-Ford Cosworth FW07C	1h40m57.930s	4
4	Hector Rebaque	Brabham	Brabham-Ford Cosworth BT49C	71 laps	15
5	Elio de Angelis	Lotus	Lotus-Ford Cosworth 87	71 laps	9
6	Eliseo Salazar	Ensign	Ensign-Ford Cosworth N180B	70 laps	24
7	Siegfried Stohr	Arrows	Arrows-Ford Cosworth A3	69 laps	21
8	Marc Surer	Theodore	Theodore-Ford Cosworth TY01	69 laps	20
9	Michele Alboreto	Tyrrell	Tyrrell-Ford Cosworth 011	68 laps/engine	25
10	Slim Borgudd	ATS	ATS-Ford Cosworth HGS1	68 laps	23
R	Mario Andretti	Alfa Romeo	Alfa Romeo 179D	62 laps/accident	7
R	John Watson	McLaren	McLaren-Ford Cosworth MP4/1	50 laps/ignition	8
R	Eddie Cheever	Tyrrell	Tyrrell-Ford Cosworth 011	46 laps/suspension	22

Pos	Driver	Team	Chassis-Engine	Result	Qual
R	Jean-Pierre Jarier	Osella	Osella-Ford Cosworth FA1B	29 laps/transmission	18
R	Rene Arnoux	Renault	Renault RE30	21 laps/engine	2
R	Bruno Giacomelli	Alfa Romeo	Alfa Romeo 179B	19 laps/tyre	14
R	Carlos Reutemann	Williams	Williams-Ford Cosworth FW07C	18 laps/collision	5
R	Jacques Laffite	Ligier	Ligier-Matra JS17	18 laps/collision	6
R	Riccardo Patrese	Arrows	Arrows-Ford Cosworth A3	16 laps/suspension	10
R	Derek Daly	March	March-Ford Cosworth 811	5 laps/suspension	19
R	Didier Pironi	Ferrari	Ferrari 126CK	4 laps/collision	12
R	Nigel Mansell	Lotus	Lotus-Ford Cosworth 87	1 lap/engine	17
R	Patrick Tambay	Ligier	Ligier-Matra JS17	0 laps/collision	11
R	Gilles Villeneuve	Ferrari	Ferrari 126CK	0 laps/collision	16
NS	Andrea de Cesaris	McLaren	McLaren-Ford Cosworth MP4/1	Multiple crashes	13
DNQ	Brian Henton	Toleman	Toleman-Hart TG181	-	26
DNQ	Keke Rosberg	Fittipaldi	Fittipaldi-Ford Cosworth F8C	-	27
DNQ	Chico Serra	Fittipaldi	Fittipaldi-Ford Cosworth F8C	-	28
DNQ	Beppe Gabbiani	Osella	Osella-Ford Cosworth FA1B	-	29
DNQ	Derek Warwick	Toleman	Toleman-Hart TG181	-	30

Pole: Prost, 1m18.176s, 121.667mph/195.804kph. Fastest lap: Jones, 1m21.830s, 116.234mph/187.060kph on Lap 15. Race leaders: Prost 1-21 & 23-72, Jones 22

NEW CONSTRUCTORS

Ted Toleman made his fortune by transporting cars, set up a team in club racing, advanced to F2, then built his own cars and won that formula in 1980. The next step was F1 in 1981 but this came with less success as Brian Henton and Derek Warwick failed to qualify until the late-season races. By 1984, though, the team was a challenger.

ITALIAN GRAND PRIX

MONZA • ROUND 13 • DATE: 13TH SEPTEMBER 1981
Laps: 52 • Distance: 187.36miles/301.6km • Weather: Warm with showers

Pos	Driver	Team	Chassis-Engine	Result	Qual
1	Alain Prost	Renault	Renault RE30	1h26m33.897s	3
2	Alan Jones	Williams	Williams-Ford Cosworth FW07C	1h26m56.072s	5
3	Carlos Reutemann	Williams	Williams-Ford Cosworth FW07C	1h27m24.484s	2
4	Elio de Angelis	Lotus	Lotus-Ford Cosworth 87	1h28m06.799s	11
5	Didier Pironi	Ferrari	Ferrari 126CK	1h28m08.419s	8
6	Nelson Piquet	Brabham	Brabham-Ford Cosworth BT49C	51 laps/engine	6
7	Andrea de Cesaris	McLaren	McLaren-Ford Cosworth MP4/1	51 laps/puncture	16
8	Bruno Giacomelli	Alfa Romeo	Alfa Romeo 179C	50 laps	10
9	Jean-Pierre Jarier	Osella	Osella-Ford Cosworth FA1C	50 laps	18
10	Brian Henton	Toleman	Toleman-Hart TG181	49 laps	23
R	Mario Andretti	Alfa Romeo	Alfa Romeo 179D	40 laps/engine	13
R	Derek Daly	March	March-Ford Cosworth 811	36 laps/gearbox	19
R	Patrick Tambay	Ligier	Ligier-Matra JS17	22 laps/puncture	15
R	Nigel Mansell	Lotus	Lotus-Ford Cosworth 87	20 laps/suspension	12
R	John Watson	McLaren	McLaren-Ford Cosworth MP4/1	19 laps/accident	7
R	Riccardo Patrese	Arrows	Arrows-Ford Cosworth A3	18 laps/gearbox	20
R	Michele Alboreto	Tyrrell	Tyrrell-Ford Cosworth 011	17 laps/accident	22

Pos	Driver	Team	Chassis-Engine	Result	Qual
R	Eliseo Salazar	Ensign	Ensign-Ford Cosworth N180B	13 laps/spun off	24
R	Rene Arnoux	Renault	Renault RE30	12 laps/spun off	1
R	Jacques Laffite	Ligier	Ligier-Matra JS17	11 laps/puncture	4
R	Eddie Cheever	Tyrrell	Tyrrell-Ford Cosworth 011	11 laps/spun off	17
R	Slim Borgudd	ATS	ATS-Ford Cosworth HGS1	10 laps/spun off	21
R	Gilles Villeneuve	Ferrari	Ferrari 126CK	5 laps/engine	9
R	Hector Rebaque	Brabham	Brabham-Ford Cosworth BT49C	0 laps/electrical	14
DNQ	Marc Surer	Theodore	Theodore-Ford Cosworth TY01	-	25
DNQ	Beppe Gabbiani	Osella	Osella-Ford Cosworth FA1B	-	26
DNQ	Derek Warwick	Toleman	Toleman-Hart TG181	-	27
DNQ	Siegfried Stohr	Arrows	Arrows-Ford Cosworth A3	-	28
DNQ	Keke Rosberg	Fittipaldi	Fittipaldi-Ford Cosworth F8C	-	29
DNQ	Chico Serra	Fittipaldi	Fittipaldi-Ford Cosworth F8C	-	30

Pole: Arnoux, 1m33.467s, 138.810mph/223.394kph. Fastest lap: Reutemann, 1m37.528s, 133.030mph/214.092kph on Lap 48. Race leaders: Prost 1-52

NEW DRIVERS

Two of the nine newcomers scored points – then awarded as far as sixth place – with Slim Borgudd achieving that for ATS at Silverstone, and Eliseo Salazar doing the same for Ensign at Zandvoort. Chico Serra (Fittipaldi) and Siegfried Stohr (Arrows) took a seventh place each, while future race winner Michele Alboreto was ninth at Zandvoort for Tyrrell.

CANADIAN GRAND PRIX

MONTREAL • ROUND 14 • DATE: 27TH SEPTEMBER 1981
Laps: 63 • Distance: 172.171miles/277.83km • Weather: Cool & wet

Pos	Driver	Team	Chassis-Engine	Result	Qual
1	Jacques Laffite	Ligier	Ligier-Matra JS17	2h01m25.205s	10
2	John Watson	McLaren	McLaren-Ford Cosworth MP4/1	2h01m31.438s	9
3	Gilles Villeneuve	Ferrari	Ferrari 126CK	2h03m15.480s	11
4	Bruno Giacomelli	Alfa Romeo	Alfa Romeo 179C	62 laps	15
5	Nelson Piquet	Brabham	Brabham-Ford Cosworth BT49C	62 laps	1
6	Elio de Angelis	Lotus	Lotus-Ford Cosworth 87	62 laps	7
7	Mario Andretti	Alfa Romeo	Alfa Romeo 179D	62 laps	16
8	Derek Daly	March	March-Ford Cosworth 811	61 laps	20
9	Marc Surer	Theodore	Theodore-Ford Cosworth TY01	61 laps	19
10	Carlos Reutemann	Williams	Williams-Ford Cosworth FW07C	60 laps	2
11	Michele Alboreto	Tyrrell	Tyrrell-Ford Cosworth 011	59 laps	22
12	Eddie Cheever	Tyrrell	Tyrrell-Ford Cosworth 011	56 laps/engine	14
R	Andrea de Cesaris	McLaren	McLaren-Ford Cosworth MP4/1	51 laps/spun off	13
R	Alain Prost	Renault	Renault RE30	48 laps/collision	4
R	Nigel Mansell	Lotus	Lotus-Ford Cosworth 87	45 laps/collision	5
R	Slim Borgudd	ATS	ATS-Ford Cosworth HGS1	40 laps/spun off	21
R	Hector Rebaque	Brabham	Brabham-Ford Cosworth BT49C	35 laps/spun off	6
R	Jean-Pierre Jarier	Osella	Osella-Ford Cosworth FA1C	26 laps/collision	23
R	Alan Jones	Williams	Williams-Ford Cosworth FW07C	24 laps/handling	3
R	Didier Pironi	Ferrari	Ferrari 126CK	24 laps/ignition	12
R	Eliseo Salazar	Ensign	Ensign-Ford Cosworth N180B	8 laps/spun off	24

Pos	Driver	Team	Chassis-Engine	Result	Qual
R	Patrick Tambay	Ligier	Ligier-Matra JS17	6 laps/spun off	17
R	Riccardo Patrese	Arrows	Arrows-Ford Cosworth A3	6 laps/spun off	18
R	Rene Arnoux	Renault	Renault RE30	0 laps/collision	8
DNQ	Keke Rosberg	Fittipaldi	Fittipaldi-Ford Cosworth F8C	-	25
DNQ	Chico Serra	Fittipaldi	Fittipaldi-Ford Cosworth F8C	-	26
DNQ	Brian Henton	Toleman	Toleman-Hart TG181	-	27
DNQ	Jacques Villeneuve Sr.	Arrows	Arrows-Ford Cosworth A3	-	28
DNQ	Derek Warwick	Toleman	Toleman-Hart TG181	-	29
DNQ	Beppe Gabbiani	Osella	Osella-Ford Cosworth FA1B	-	30

Pole: Piquet, 1m29.211s, 110.579mph/177.960kph. Fastest lap: Watson, 1m49.475s, 90.110mph/145.019kph on Lap 43. Race leaders: Jones 1-6, Prost 7-12, Laffite 13-63

CLASSIC CAR: McLAREN MP4/1

This was the car that took F1 forward in a single leap as it was the sport's first carbon fibre monocoque. Designed by John Barnard, it was lighter and more rigid than its rivals, thus offering superior handling. The MP4/1 was a huge improvement on the disappointing M29F and M30. John Watson brought a smile to the camp, fittingly at the British GP at Silverstone, when the Renaults failed and he held on to give McLaren its first win of new owner Ron Dennis' reign. Team-mate Andrea de Cesaris achieved far less with it, largely because he spent much of the year throwing his at the scenery.

CAESARS PALACE GRAND PRIX

CAESARS PALACE • ROUND 15 • DATE: 17TH OCTOBER 1981
Laps: 75 • Distance: 169.680miles/273.75km • Weather: Hot & bright

Pos	Driver	Team	Chassis-Engine	Result	Qual
1	Alan Jones	Williams	Williams-Ford Cosworth FW07C	1h44m09.077s	2
2	Alain Prost	Renault	Renault RE30	1h44m29.125s	5
3	Bruno Giacomelli	Alfa Romeo	Alfa Romeo 179C	1h44m29.505s	8
4	Nigel Mansell	Lotus	Lotus-Ford Cosworth 87	1h44m56.550s	9
5	Nelson Piquet	Brabham	Brabham-Ford Cosworth BT49C	1h45m25.515s	4
6	Jacques Laffite	Ligier	Ligier-Matra JS17	1h45m27.252s	12
7	John Watson	McLaren	McLaren-Ford Cosworth MP4/1	1h45m27.574s	6
8	Carlos Reutemann	Williams	Williams-Ford Cosworth FW07C	74 laps	1
9	Didier Pironi	Ferrari	Ferrari 126CK	73 laps	18
10	Keke Rosberg	Fittipaldi	Fittipaldi-Ford Cosworth F8C	73 laps	20
11	Riccardo Patrese	Arrows	Arrows-Ford Cosworth A3	71 laps	11
12	Andrea de Cesaris	McLaren	McLaren-Ford Cosworth MP4/1	69 laps	14
13	Michele Alboreto	Tyrrell	Tyrrell-Ford Cosworth 011	67 laps/engine	17
NC	Eliseo Salazar	Ensign	Ensign-Ford Cosworth N180B	61 laps	24
R	Derek Warwick	Toleman	Toleman-Hart TG181	43 laps/gearbox	22
R	Mario Andretti	Alfa Romeo	Alfa Romeo 179C	29 laps/suspension	10
DQ	Gilles Villeneuve	Ferrari	Ferrari 126CK	22 laps/grid error	3
R	Hector Rebaque	Brabham	Brabham-Ford Cosworth BT49C	20 laps/spun off	16
R	Marc Surer	Theodore	Theodore-Ford Cosworth TY01	19 laps/suspension	23
R	Rene Arnoux	Renault	Renault RE30	10 laps/electrical	13

Pos	Driver	Team	Chassis-Engine	Result	Qual
R	Eddie Cheever	Tyrrell	Tyrrell-Ford Cosworth 011	10 laps/engine	19
R	Patrick Tambay	Ligier	Ligier-Matra JS17	2 laps/accident	7
R	Elio de Angelis	Lotus	Lotus-Ford Cosworth 87	2 laps/water leak	15
R	Jean-Pierre Jarier	Osella	Osella-Ford Cosworth FA1C	0 laps/transmission	21
DNQ	Slim Borgudd	ATS	ATS-Ford Cosworth HGS1	-	25
DNQ	Chico Serra	Fittipaldi	Fittipaldi-Ford Cosworth F8C	-	26
DNQ	Derek Daly	March	March-Ford Cosworth 811	-	27
DNQ	Jacques Villeneuve Sr.	Arrows	Arrows-Ford Cosworth A3	-	28
DNQ	Brian Henton	Toleman	Toleman-Hart TG181	-	29
DNQ	Beppe Gabbiani	Osella	Osella-Ford Cosworth FA1B	-	30

Pole: Reutemann, 1m17.821s, 104.917mph/168.849kph. Fastest lap: Pironi, 1m20.156s, 101.861mph/163.930kph on Lap 49. Race leaders: Jones 1-75

WORLD DRIVERS' CHAMPIONSHIP FINAL RESULTS

Pos	Driver	Nat	Car-Engine	R1	R2	R3	R4	R5
1	Nelson Piquet	BRA	Brabham-Ford Cosworth BT49C	3	12P	1PF	1	R
2	Carlos Reutemann	ARG	Williams-Ford Cosworth FW07C	2	1	2	3	1PF
3	Alan Jones	AUS	Williams-Ford Cosworth FW07C	1F	2	4	12	R
4	Jacques Laffite	FRA	Ligier-Matra JS17	R	6	R	R	2
5	Alain Prost	FRA	Renault RE20B	R	R	3	R	-
			Renault RE30	-	-	-	-	R
6	John Watson	GBR	McLaren-Ford Cosworth M29F	R	8	-	-	-
			McLaren-Ford Cosworth MP4/1	-	-	R	10	7
7	Gilles Villeneuve	CAN	Ferrari 126CK	R	R	R	7PF	4
8	Elio de Angelis	ITA	Lotus-Ford Cosworth 81	R	5	6	-	5
			Lotus-Ford Cosworth 87	-	-	-	-	-
9	Rene Arnoux	FRA	Renault RE20B	8	R	5	8	-
			Renault RE30	-	-	-	-	DNQ
10	Hector Rebaque	MEX	Brabham-Ford Cosworth BT49C	R	R	R	4	R
11	Riccardo Patrese	ITA	Arrows-Ford Cosworth A3	RP	3	7	2	R
12	Eddie Cheever	USA	Tyrrell-Ford Cosworth 010	5	NC	R	R	6
			Tyrrell-Ford Cosworth 011	-	-	-	-	-
13	Didier Pironi	FRA	Ferrari 126CK	R	R	R	5	8
14	Nigel Mansell	GBR	Lotus-Ford Cosworth 81	R	11	R	-	3
			Lotus-Ford Cosworth 87	-	-	-	-	-
15	Bruno Giacomelli	ITA	Alfa Romeo 179C	R	NC	10	R	9
			Alfa Romeo 179B	-	-	-	-	-
16	Marc Surer	CHE	Ensign-Ford Cosworth N180B	R	4F	R	9	11
			Theodore-Ford Cosworth TY01	-	-	-	-	-
17	Mario Andretti	USA	Alfa Romeo 179C	4	R	8	R	10
			Alfa Romeo 179B	-	-	-	-	-
			Alfa Romeo 179D	-	-	-	-	-
18	Patrick Tambay	FRA	Theodore-Ford Cosworth TY01	6	10	R	11	DNQ
			Ligier-Matra JS17	-	-	-	-	-
18	Andrea de Cesaris	ITA	McLaren-Ford Cosworth M29F	R	R	11	6	R
			McLaren-Ford Cosworth MP4/1	-	-	-	-	-
18	Slim Borgudd	SWE	ATS-Ford Cosworth D4	-	-	-	13	-
			ATS-Ford Cosworth HGS1	-	-	-	-	DNQ
18	Eliseo Salazar	CHL	March-Ford Cosworth 811	DNQ	DNQ	DNQ	R	DNQ
			Ensign-Ford Cosworth N180B	-	-	-	-	-

Pos	Driver	R6	R7	R8	R9	R10	R11	R12	R13	R14	R15	Total
1	Piquet	RP	R	3	R	1	3	2	6	5P	5	50
2	Reutemann	R	4	10	2	R	5	R	3F	10	8P	49
3	Jones	2F	7F	17	R	11F	4	3F	2	R	1	46
4	Laffite	3	2P	R	3	3	1F	R	R	1	6	44
5	Prost	-	-	-	-	-	-	-	-	-	-	43
		R	R	1F	R	2P	R	1P	1	R	2	
6	Watson	-	-	-	-	-	-	-	-	-	-	27
		R	3	2	1	6	6	R	R	2F	7	
7	Villeneuve	1	1	R	R	10	R	R	R	3	DQ	25
8	de Angelis	-	-	-	-	-	-	-	-	-	-	14
		R	5	6	DQ	7	7	5	4	6	R	
9	Arnoux	R	-	-	-	-	-	-	-	-	-	11
		-	9	4P	9PF	13	2P	R	RP	R	R	
10	Rebaque	DNQ	R	9	5	4	R	4	R	R	R	11
11	Patrese	R	R	14	10	R	R	R	R	R	11	10
12	Cheever	5	NC	13	4	-	-	-	-	-	-	10
		-	-	-	-	5	DNQ	R	R	12	R	
13	Pironi	4	15	5	R	R	9	R	5	R	9F	9
14	Mansell	-	-	-	-	-	-	-	-	-	-	8
		R	6	7	DNQ	R	R	R	R	R	4	
15	Giacomelli	R	10	-	R	-	-	-	8	4	3	7
		-	-	15	-	15	R	R	-	-	-	
16	Surer	6	-	-	-	-	-	-	-	-	-	4
		-	-	12	11	14	NS	8	DNQ	9	R	
17	Andretti	R	8	-	R	-	-	-	-	-	R	3
		-	-	8	-	9	-	-	-	-	-	
		-	-	-	-	-	R	R	R	7	-	
18	Tambay	7	13	-	-	-	-	-	-	-	-	1
		-	-	R	R	R	R	R	R	R	R	
18	de Cesaris	-	-	-	-	-	-	-	-	-	-	1
		R	R	11	R	R	8	NS	7	R	12	
18	Borgudd	-	-	-	-	-	-	-	-	-	-	1
		DNPQ	DNQ	DNQ	6	R	R	10	R	R	DNQ	
18	Salazar	DNPQ	-	-	-	-	-	-	-	-	-	1
		-	14	R	DNQ	NC	R	6	R	R	NC	

SYMBOLS AND GRAND PRIX KEY

Round 1	**United States GP West**
Round 2	**Brazilian GP**
Round 3	**Argentinian GP**
Round 4	**San Marino GP**
Round 5	**Belgian GP**
Round 6	**Monaco GP**
Round 7	**Spanish GP**
Round 8	**French GP**
Round 9	**British GP**
Round 10	**German GP**
Round 11	**Austrian GP**
Round 12	**Dutch GP**
Round 13	**Italian GP**
Round 14	**Canadian GP**
Round 15	**Caesars Palace GP**

SCORING

1st	**9 points**
2nd	**6 points**
3rd	**4 points**
4th	**3 points**
5th	**2 points**
6th	**1 point**

DNPQ DID NOT PRE-QUALIFY **DNQ** DID NOT QUALIFY **DQ** DISQUALIFIED **EX** EXCLUDED
F FASTEST LAP **NC** NOT CLASSIFIED **NS** NON-STARTER **P** POLE POSITION **R** RETIRED

WORLD CONSTRUCTORS' CHAMPIONSHIP FINAL RESULTS

Pos	Team-Engine	R1	R2	R3	R4	R5	R6	R7	R8
1	Williams-Ford	1/2	1/2	2/4	3/12	1/R	2/R	4/7	10/17
2	Brabham-Ford	3/R	12/R	1/R	1/4	R/R	R/DNQ	R/R	3/9
3	Renault	8/R	R/R	3/5	8/R	R/DNQ	R/R	9/R	1/4
4	Ligier-Matra	R/R	6/7	R/DNQ	NC/R	2/R	3/DNQ	2/R	R/R
5	Ferrari	R/R	R/R	R/R	5/7	4/8	1/4	1/15	5/R
6	McLaren-Ford	R/R	8/R	11/R	6/10	7/R	R/R	3/R	2/11
7	Lotus-Ford	R/R	5/11	6/R	-/-	3/5	R/R	5/6	6/7
8	Arrows-Ford	R/DNQ	3/R	7/9	2/DNQ	R/R	R/R	R/R	14/DNQ
9	Alfa Romeo	4/R	NC/R	8/10	R/R	9/10	R/R	8/10	8/15
10	Tyrrell-Ford	5/DNQ	13/NC	13/R	R/R	6/12	5/R	NC/DNQ	13/16
11	Ensign-Ford	R	4	R	9	11	6	14	R
12	Theodore-Ford	6	10	R	11	DNQ	7	13	12
12	ATS-Ford	R	DNQ	12	13	DNQ	DNPQ	DNQ	DNQ

Pos	Team-Engine	R9	R10	R11	R12	R13	R14	R15	Total
1	Williams-Ford	2/R	11/R	4/5	3/R	2/3	10/R	1/8	95
2	Brabham-Ford	5/R	1/4	3/R	2/4	6/R	5/R	5/R	61
3	Renault	9/R	2/13	2/R	1/R	1/R	R/R	2/R	54
4	Ligier-Matra	3/R	3/R	1/R	R/R	R/R	1/R	6/R	44
5	Ferrari	R/R	10/R	9/R	R/R	5/R	3/R	9/DQ	34
6	McLaren-Ford	1/R	6/R	6/8	R/NS	7/R	2/R	7/12	28
7	Lotus-Ford	DQ/DNQ	7/R	7/R	5/R	4/R	6/R	4/R	22
8	Arrows-Ford	10/R	12/R	R/R	7/R	R/DNQ	R/DNQ	11/DNQ	10
9	Alfa Romeo	R/R	9/15	R/R	R/R	8/R	4/7	3/R	10
10	Tyrrell-Ford	4/R	5/DNQ	R/DNQ	9/R	R/R	11/12	13/R	10
11	Ensign-Ford	DNQ	NC	R	6	R	R	NC	5
12	Theodore-Ford	11	14	NS	8	DNQ	9	R	1
12	ATS-Ford	6	R	R	10	R	R	DNQ	1

1982

SEASON SUMMARY

This was an extraordinary year as Keke Rosberg took the title despite winning just once for Williams in a season that produced a record 11 winners across its 16 grands prix. Politics spoiled the season, with the San Marino GP boycotted by the 10 FOCA-affiliated teams, leaving just 14 cars in the race. Worse still, Gilles Villeneuve and Riccardo Paletti were both killed in action, while Didier Pironi's career was ended when he broke his legs. The cars were also considered the most physical ever produced in F1, with huge downforce allied to rock hard suspension that shook and rattled the drivers.

SOUTH AFRICAN GRAND PRIX

KYALAMI • ROUND 1 • DATE: 23RD JANUARY 1982
Laps: 77 • Distance: 196.358miles/316.008km • Weather: Hot & bright

Pos	Driver	Team	Chassis-Engine	Result	Qual
1	Alain Prost	Renault	Renault RE30B	1h32m08.401s	5
2	Carlos Reutemann	Williams	Williams-Ford Cosworth FW07C	1h32m23.347s	8
3	Rene Arnoux	Renault	Renault RE30B	1h32m36.301s	1
4	Niki Lauda	McLaren	McLaren-Ford Cosworth MP4/1	1h32m40.514s	13
5	Keke Rosberg	Williams	Williams-Ford Cosworth FW07C	1h32m54.540s	7
6	John Watson	McLaren	McLaren-Ford Cosworth MP4/1B	1h32m59.394s	9
7	Michele Alboreto	Tyrrell	Tyrrell-Ford Cosworth 011	76 laps	10
8	Elio de Angelis	Lotus	Lotus-Ford Cosworth 87B	76 laps	15
9	Eliseo Salazar	ATS	ATS-Ford Cosworth D5	75 laps	12
10	Manfred Winkelhock	ATS	ATS-Ford Cosworth D5	75 laps	20
11	Bruno Giacomelli	Alfa Romeo	Alfa Romeo 179D	74 laps	19
12	Jochen Mass	March	March-Ford Cosworth 821	74 laps	22
13	Andrea de Cesaris	Alfa Romeo	Alfa Romeo 179D	73 laps	16
14	Derek Daly	Theodore	Theodore-Ford Cosworth TY01	73 laps	24
15	Raul Boesel	March	March-Ford Cosworth 821	72 laps	21
16	Slim Borgudd	Tyrrell	Tyrrell-Ford Cosworth 011	72 laps	23
17	Chico Serra	Fittipaldi	Fittipaldi-Ford Cosworth F8D	72 laps	25
18	Didier Pironi	Ferrari	Ferrari 126C2	71 laps	6
R	Jacques Laffite	Ligier	Ligier-Matra JS17	54 laps/fuel system	11
R	Derek Warwick	Toleman	Toleman-Hart TG181C	43 laps/accident	14
R	Riccardo Patrese	Brabham	Brabham-BMW BT50	18 laps/turbo	4
R	Eddie Cheever	Ligier	Ligier-Matra JS17	11 laps/fuel system	17
R	Gilles Villeneuve	Ferrari	Ferrari 126C2	6 laps/turbo	3
R	Nelson Piquet	Brabham	Brabham-BMW BT50	3 laps/spun off	2
R	Nigel Mansell	Lotus	Lotus-Ford Cosworth 87B	0 laps/electrical	18
R	Jean-Pierre Jarier	Osella	Osella-Ford Cosworth FA1C	0 laps/collision	26
DNQ	Mauro Baldi	Arrows	Arrows-Ford Cosworth A4	-	27
DNQ	Riccardo Paletti	Osella	Osella-Ford Cosworth FA1C	-	28
DNQ	Brian Henton	Arrows	Arrows-Ford Cosworth A4	-	29
DNQ	Teo Fabi	Toleman	Toleman-Hart TG181B	-	30
NS	Roberto Guerrero	Ensign	Ensign-Ford Cosworth N180B	injunction	-
NS	Patrick Tambay	Arrows	Arrows-Ford Cosworth A4	-	-

Pole: Arnoux, 1m06.351s, 138.360mph/222.670kph. Fastest lap: Prost, 1m08.278s, 134.455mph/216.385kph on Lap 49. Race leaders: Arnoux 1-13 & 41-67, Prost 14-40 & 68-77

FILL HER UP, PLEASE

Brabham introduced refuelling stops in 1982 so that they could run the first half of the race carrying just half a load of fuel. The first of these was performed at the Austrian GP when Riccardo Patrese was given four new tyres and 24 gallons of fuel in 14 seconds. However, it didn't lead to victory as he retired four laps later with engine failure.

BRAZILIAN GRAND PRIX

JACAREPAGUA • ROUND 2 • DATE: 21ST MARCH 1982
Laps: 63 • Distance: 196.945miles/316.953km • Weather: Hot & bright

Pos	Driver	Team	Chassis-Engine	Result	Qual
DQ	Nelson Piquet	Brabham	Brabham-Ford Cosworth BT49D	63 laps/car underweight	7
DQ	Keke Rosberg	Williams	Williams-Ford Cosworth FW07C	63 laps/car underweight	3
1	Alain Prost	Renault	Renault RE30B	1h44m33.134s	1
2	John Watson	McLaren	McLaren-Ford Cosworth MP4/1B	1h44m36.124s	12
3	Nigel Mansell	Lotus	Lotus-Ford Cosworth 91	1h45m09.993s	14
4	Michele Alboreto	Tyrrell	Tyrrell-Ford Cosworth 011	1h45m23.895s	13
5	Manfred Winkelhock	ATS	ATS-Ford Cosworth D5	62 laps	15
6	Didier Pironi	Ferrari	Ferrari 126C2	62 laps	8
7	Slim Borgudd	Tyrrell	Tyrrell-Ford Cosworth 011	61 laps	21
8	Jochen Mass	March	March-Ford Cosworth 821	61 laps	22
9	Jean-Pierre Jarier	Osella	Osella-Ford Cosworth FA1C	60 laps	23
10	Mauro Baldi	Arrows	Arrows-Ford Cosworth A4	57 laps	19
R	Eliseo Salazar	ATS	ATS-Ford Cosworth D5	38 laps/engine	18
R	Chico Serra	Fittipaldi	Fittipaldi-Ford Cosworth F8D	36 laps/suspension	25
R	Riccardo Patrese	Brabham	Brabham-Ford Cosworth BT49D	34 laps/physical	9
R	Gilles Villeneuve	Ferrari	Ferrari 126C2	29 laps/spun off	2
R	Niki Lauda	McLaren	McLaren-Ford Cosworth MP4/1B	22 laps/collision	5
R	Rene Arnoux	Renault	Renault RE30B	21 laps/collision	4
R	Carlos Reutemann	Williams	Williams-Ford Cosworth FW07C	21 laps/collision	6
R	Elio de Angelis	Lotus	Lotus-Ford Cosworth 91	21 laps/collision	11
R	Eddie Cheever	Ligier	Ligier-Matra JS17	19 laps/water leak	26
R	Bruno Giacomelli	Alfa Romeo	Alfa Romeo 182	16 laps/clutch	16
R	Jacques Laffite	Ligier	Ligier-Matra JS17	15 laps/misfire	24
R	Andrea de Cesaris	Alfa Romeo	Alfa Romeo 182	14 laps/undertray	10
R	Derek Daly	Theodore	Theodore-Ford Cosworth TY02	12 laps/spun off	20
R	Raul Boesel	March	March-Ford Cosworth 821	11 laps/spun off	17
DNQ	Teo Fabi	Toleman	Toleman-Hart TG181B	-	27
DNQ	Roberto Guerrero	Ensign	Ensign-Ford Cosworth N181	-	28
DNQ	Brian Henton	Arrows	Arrows-Ford Cosworth A4	-	29
DNQ	Derek Warwick	Toleman	Toleman-Hart TG181C	-	30
DNPQ	Riccardo Paletti	Osella	Osella-Ford Cosworth FA1C	-	31

Pole: Prost, 1m28.808s, 126.723mph/203.941kph. Fastest lap: Prost, 1m37.016s, 116.001mph/186.686kph on Lap 36. Race leaders: Villeneuve 1-29, Piquet 30-63

UNITED STATES GRAND PRIX WEST

LONG BEACH • ROUND 3 • DATE: 4TH APRIL 1982
Laps: 75 • Distance: 159.693miles/257.1km • Weather: Hot & bright

Pos	Driver	Team	Chassis-Engine	Result	Qual
1	Niki Lauda	McLaren	McLaren-Ford Cosworth MP4/1B	1h58m25.318s	2
2	Keke Rosberg	Williams	Williams-Ford Cosworth FW07C	1h58m39.978s	8
DQ	Gilles Villeneuve	Ferrari	Ferrari 126C2	75 laps/illegal wing	7
3	Riccardo Patrese	Brabham	Brabham-Ford Cosworth BT49C	1h59m44.461s	18
4	Michele Alboreto	Tyrrell	Tyrrell-Ford Cosworth 011	1h59m46.265s	12
5	Elio de Angelis	Lotus	Lotus-Ford Cosworth 91	74 laps	16
6	John Watson	McLaren	McLaren-Ford Cosworth MP4/1B	74 laps	11
7	Nigel Mansell	Lotus	Lotus-Ford Cosworth 91	73 laps	17
8	Jochen Mass	March	March-Ford Cosworth 821	73 laps	21
9	Raul Boesel	March	March-Ford Cosworth 821	70 laps	23
10	Slim Borgudd	Tyrrell	Tyrrell-Ford Cosworth 011	68 laps	24
R	Eddie Cheever	Ligier	Ligier-Matra JS17B	59 laps/gearbox	13
R	Andrea de Cesaris	Alfa Romeo	Alfa Romeo 182	33 laps/spun off	1
R	Brian Henton	Arrows	Arrows-Ford Cosworth A4	32 laps/spun off	20
R	Roberto Guerrero	Ensign	Ensign-Ford Cosworth N181	27 laps/spun off	19
R	Jean-Pierre Jarier	Osella	Osella-Ford Cosworth FA1C	26 laps/transmission	10
R	Jacques Laffite	Ligier	Ligier-Matra JS17B	26 laps/spun off	15
R	Nelson Piquet	Brabham	Brabham-Ford Cosworth BT49D	25 laps/spun off	6
R	Derek Daly	Theodore	Theodore-Ford Cosworth TY02	23 laps/spun off	22
R	Mario Andretti	Williams	Williams-Ford Cosworth FW07C	19 laps/collision	14
R	Alain Prost	Renault	Renault RE30B	10 laps/spun off	4
R	Didier Pironi	Ferrari	Ferrari 126C2	6 laps/spun off	9
R	Rene Arnoux	Renault	Renault RE30B	5 laps/collision	3
R	Bruno Giacomelli	Alfa Romeo	Alfa Romeo 182	5 laps/collision	5
R	Eliseo Salazar	ATS	ATS-Ford Cosworth D5	3 laps/collision	26
R	Manfred Winkelhock	ATS	ATS-Ford Cosworth D5	1 lap/collision	25
DNQ	Teo Fabi	Toleman	Toleman-Hart TG181C	-	27
DNQ	Riccardo Paletti	Osella	Osella-Ford Cosworth FA1C	-	28
DNQ	Chico Serra	Fittipaldi	Fittipaldi-Ford Cosworth F8D	-	29
DNQ	Mauro Baldi	Arrows	Arrows-Ford Cosworth A4	-	30
DNPQ	Derek Warwick	Toleman	Toleman-Hart TG181C	-	31

Pole: de Cesaris, 1m27.316s, 87.821mph/141.334kph. Fastest lap: Lauda, 1m30.831s, 84.422mph/135.865kph on Lap 12. Race leaders: de Cesaris 1-14, Lauda 15-75

RUNNING UNDERWEIGHT

The trick used by Ford-powered teams to stay competitive with the turbo-engined cars was to fit 'water-cooled brakes'. They replenished the water tanks after the race to pass scrutineering, as they were allowed to top these up afterwards and so run the race underweight. When the top two finishers were disqualified from the Brazilian GP for being underweight, the 10 FOCA-affiliated teams boycotted the San Marino GP.

A BREACH OF TRUST

There was little love lost between Ferrari's Didier Pironi and Gilles Villeneuve after the San Marino GP. Villeneuve took the lead when Rene Arnoux retired, then both Ferrari drivers were told to slow. But they swapped places many times to put on a show for the fans, only for Pironi to go ahead and stay ahead on the final lap.

SAN MARINO GRAND PRIX

IMOLA • ROUND 4 • DATE: 25TH APRIL 1982
Laps: 60 • Distance: 187.656miles/302.4km • Weather: Warm & bright

Pos	Driver	Team	Chassis-Engine	Result	Qual
1	Didier Pironi	Ferrari	Ferrari 126C2	1h36m38.887s	4
2	Gilles Villeneuve	Ferrari	Ferrari 126C2	1h36m39.253s	3
3	Michele Alboreto	Tyrrell	Tyrrell-Ford Cosworth 011	1h37m46.571s	5
4	Jean-Pierre Jarier	Osella	Osella-Ford Cosworth FA1C	59 laps	9
5	Eliseo Salazar	ATS	ATS-Ford Cosworth D5	57 laps	14
DQ	Manfred Winkelhock	ATS	ATS-Ford Cosworth D5	54 laps/car underweight	12
NC	Teo Fabi	Toleman	Toleman-Hart TG181C	52 laps	10
R	Rene Arnoux	Renault	Renault RE30B	44 laps/turbo	1
R	Bruno Giacomelli	Alfa Romeo	Alfa Romeo 182	24 laps/engine	6
R	Riccardo Paletti	Osella	Osella-Ford Cosworth FA1C	7 laps/suspension	13
R	Alain Prost	Renault	Renault RE30B	6 laps/engine	2
R	Andrea de Cesaris	Alfa Romeo	Alfa Romeo 182	4 laps/electrical	7
R	Brian Henton	Tyrrell	Tyrrell-Ford Cosworth 011	0 laps/transmission	11
NS	Derek Warwick	Toleman	Toleman-Hart TG181C	Electrics	8

Pole: Arnoux, 1m29.765s, 125.596mph/202.127kph. Fastest lap: Pironi, 1m35.036s, 118.630mph/190.917kph on Lap 44. Race leaders: Arnoux 1-26 & 31-43, Villeneuve 27-30 & 44-45 & 49-52 & 59, Pironi 46-48 & 53-58 & 60

BELGIAN GRAND PRIX

ZOLDER • ROUND 5 • DATE: 9TH MAY 1982
Laps: 70 • Distance: 185.189miles/298.34km • Weather: Warm but dull

Pos	Driver	Team	Chassis-Engine	Result	Qual
1	John Watson	McLaren	McLaren-Ford Cosworth MP4/1B	1h35m41.995s	12
2	Keke Rosberg	Williams	Williams-Ford Cosworth FW08	1h35m49.263s	3
DQ	Niki Lauda	McLaren	McLaren-Ford Cosworth MP4/1B	70 laps/car underweight	4
3	Eddie Cheever	Ligier	Ligier-Matra JS17B	69 laps	16
4	Elio de Angelis	Lotus	Lotus-Ford Cosworth 91	68 laps	13
5	Nelson Piquet	Brabham	Brabham-BMW BT50	67 laps	10
6	Chico Serra	Fittipaldi	Fittipaldi-Ford Cosworth F8D	67 laps	25
7	Marc Surer	Arrows	Arrows-Ford Cosworth A4	66 laps	24
8	Raul Boesel	March	March-Ford Cosworth 821	66 laps	26
9	Jacques Laffite	Ligier	Ligier-Matra JS17B	66 laps	19
R	Derek Daly	Williams	Williams-Ford Cosworth FW08	60 laps/spun off	15
R	Jochen Mass	March	March-Ford Cosworth 821	60 laps/engine	27
R	Alain Prost	Renault	Renault RE30B	59 laps/spun off	1
R	Riccardo Patrese	Brabham	Brabham-BMW BT50	52 laps/spun off	11
R	Mauro Baldi	Arrows	Arrows-Ford Cosworth A4	51 laps/throttle	28

Pos	Driver	Team	Chassis-Engine	Result	Qual
R	Jean-Pierre Jarier	Osella	Osella-Ford Cosworth FA1C	37 laps/wing	18
R	Andrea de Cesaris	Alfa Romeo	Alfa Romeo 182	34 laps/gearbox	7
R	Brian Henton	Tyrrell	Tyrrell-Ford Cosworth 011	33 laps/engine	22
R	Michele Alboreto	Tyrrell	Tyrrell-Ford Cosworth 011	29 laps/engine	5
R	Derek Warwick	Toleman	Toleman-Hart TG181C	29 laps/transmission	21
R	Teo Fabi	Toleman	Toleman-Hart TG181C	13 laps/brakes	23
R	Nigel Mansell	Lotus	Lotus-Ford Cosworth 91	9 laps/clutch	9
R	Rene Arnoux	Renault	Renault RE30B	7 laps/turbo	2
R	Manfred Winkelhock	ATS	ATS-Ford Cosworth D5	0 laps/clutch	14
R	Bruno Giacomelli	Alfa Romeo	Alfa Romeo 182	0 laps/collision	17
R	Eliseo Salazar	ATS	ATS-Ford Cosworth D5	0 laps/collision	20
DNQ	Roberto Guerrero	Ensign	Ensign-Ford Cosworth N181	-	28
DNQ	Jan Lammers	Theodore	Theodore-Ford Cosworth TY02	-	29
DNPQ	Riccardo Paletti	Osella	Osella-Ford Cosworth FA1C	-	30
DNPQ	Emilio de Villota	Onyx	March-Ford Cosworth 821	-	31
NS	Didier Pironi	Ferrari	Ferrari 126C2	withdrew	6
NS	Gilles Villeneuve	Ferrari	Ferrari 126C2	fatal accident	8

Pole: Prost, 1m15.701s, 125.940mph/202.681kph. Fastest lap: Watson, 1m20.214s, 118.854mph/191.278kph on Lap 67. Race leaders: Arnoux 1-4, Rosberg 5-68, Watson 69-70

THE MOST REMARKABLE FINISH

What happened in the closing laps at Monaco was too bizarre even to be a film script. Prost was in control for Renault but crashed, so Patrese took over in his Brabham but also went off the slippery track. Pironi led onto the last lap, but stopped and de Cesaris would have taken over, but he stopped too. Patrese came back through to win.

MONACO GRAND PRIX

MONTE CARLO • ROUND 6 • DATE: 23RD MAY 1982
Laps: 76 • Distance: 156.406miles/251.712km • Weather: Warm & dry, rain later

Pos	Driver	Team	Chassis-Engine	Result	Qual
1	Riccardo Patrese	Brabham	Brabham-Ford Cosworth BT49D	1h54m11.259s	2
2	Didier Pironi	Ferrari	Ferrari 126C2	75 laps/electrical	5
3	Andrea de Cesaris	Alfa Romeo	Alfa Romeo 182	75 laps/out of fuel	7
4	Nigel Mansell	Lotus	Lotus-Ford Cosworth 91	75 laps	11
5	Elio de Angelis	Lotus	Lotus-Ford Cosworth 91	75 laps	15
6	Derek Daly	Williams	Williams-Ford Cosworth FW08	74 laps/accident	8
7	Alain Prost	Renault	Renault RE30B	73 laps/spun off	4
8	Brian Henton	Tyrrell	Tyrrell-Ford Cosworth 011	72 laps	17
9	Marc Surer	Arrows	Arrows-Ford Cosworth A4	70 laps	19
10	Michele Alboreto	Tyrrell	Tyrrell-Ford Cosworth 011	69 laps/suspension	9
R	Keke Rosberg	Williams	Williams-Ford Cosworth FW08	64 laps/collision	6
R	Niki Lauda	McLaren	McLaren-Ford Cosworth MP4/1B	56 laps/engine	12
R	Nelson Piquet	Brabham	Brabham-BMW BT50	49 laps/turbo	13
R	John Watson	McLaren	McLaren-Ford Cosworth MP4/1B	35 laps/electrical	10
R	Manfred Winkelhock	ATS	ATS-Ford Cosworth D5	31 laps/differential	14
R	Jacques Laffite	Ligier	Ligier-Matra JS19	29 laps/handling	18
R	Eddie Cheever	Ligier	Ligier-Matra JS19	27 laps/oil leak	16

Pos	Driver	Team	Chassis-Engine	Result	Qual
R	Eliseo Salazar	ATS	ATS-Ford Cosworth D5	22 laps/extinguisher	20
R	Rene Arnoux	Renault	Renault RE30B	14 laps/spun off	1
R	Bruno Giacomelli	Alfa Romeo	Alfa Romeo 182	4 laps/halfshaft	3
DNQ	Mauro Baldi	Arrows	Arrows-Ford Cosworth A4	-	21
DNQ	Jan Lammers	Theodore	Theodore-Ford Cosworth TY02	-	22
DNQ	Jochen Mass	March	March-Ford Cosworth 821	-	23
DNQ	Derek Warwick	Toleman	Toleman-Hart TG181C	-	24
DNQ	Jean-Pierre Jarier	Osella	Osella-Ford Cosworth FA1C	-	25
DNQ	Roberto Guerrero	Ensign	Ensign-Ford Cosworth N181	-	26
DNPQ	Teo Fabi	Toleman	Toleman-Hart TG181C	-	27
DNPQ	Riccardo Paletti	Osella	Osella-Ford Cosworth FA1C	-	28
DNPQ	Raul Boesel	March	March-Ford Cosworth 821	-	29
DNPQ	Chico Serra	Fittipaldi	Fittipaldi-Ford Cosworth F8D	-	30
DNPQ	Emilio de Villota	Onyx	March-Ford Cosworth 821	-	31

Pole: Arnoux, 1m23.281s, 88.960mph/143.168kph. Fastest lap: Patrese, 1m26.354s, 85.794mph/138.073kph on Lap 69. Race leaders: Arnoux 1-14, Prost 15-73, Patrese 74 & 76, Pironi 75

DETROIT GRAND PRIX

DETROIT • ROUND 7 • DATE: 6TH JUNE 1982
Laps: 62 • Distance: 154.566miles/248.750km • Weather: Warm & bright

Pos	Driver	Team	Chassis-Engine	Result	Qual
1	John Watson	McLaren	McLaren-Ford Cosworth MP4/1B	1h58m41.043s	17
2	Eddie Cheever	Ligier	Ligier-Matra JS17B	1h58m56.769s	9
3	Didier Pironi	Ferrari	Ferrari 126C2	1h59m09.120s	4
4	Keke Rosberg	Williams	Williams-Ford Cosworth FW08	1h59m53.019s	3
5	Derek Daly	Williams	Williams-Ford Cosworth FW08	2h00m04.800s	12
6	Jacques Laffite	Ligier	Ligier-Matra JS17B	61 laps	13
7	Jochen Mass	March	March-Ford Cosworth 821	61 laps	18
8	Marc Surer	Arrows	Arrows-Ford Cosworth A4	61 laps	19
9	Brian Henton	Tyrrell	Tyrrell-Ford Cosworth 011	60 laps	20
10	Rene Arnoux	Renault	Renault RE30B	59 laps	15
11	Chico Serra	Fittipaldi	Fittipaldi-Ford Cosworth F8D	59 laps	26
NC	Alain Prost	Renault	Renault RE30B	54 laps	1
R	Nigel Mansell	Lotus	Lotus-Ford Cosworth 91	44 laps/engine	7
R	Niki Lauda	McLaren	McLaren-Ford Cosworth MP4/1B	40 laps/collision	10
R	Michele Alboreto	Tyrrell	Tyrrell-Ford Cosworth 011	40 laps/spun off	16
R	Bruno Giacomelli	Alfa Romeo	Alfa Romeo 182	30 laps/collision	6
R	Elio de Angelis	Lotus	Lotus-Ford Cosworth 91	17 laps/gearbox	8
R	Eliseo Salazar	ATS	ATS-Ford Cosworth D5	13 laps/spun off	25
R	Roberto Guerrero	Ensign	Ensign-Ford Cosworth N181	6 laps/collision	11
R	Riccardo Patrese	Brabham	Brabham-Ford Cosworth BT49D	6 laps/collision	14
R	Andrea de Cesaris	Alfa Romeo	Alfa Romeo 182	2 laps/transmission	2
R	Jean-Pierre Jarier	Osella	Osella-Ford Cosworth FA1C	2 laps/ignition	22
R	Manfred Winkelhock	ATS	ATS-Ford Cosworth D5	1 lap/spun off	5
R	Raul Boesel	March	March-Ford Cosworth 821	0 laps/collision	21
R	Mauro Baldi	Arrows	Arrows-Ford Cosworth A4	0 laps/collision	24
NS	Riccardo Paletti	Osella	Osella-Ford Cosworth FA1C	accident	23
DNQ	Emilio de Villota	Onyx	March-Ford Cosworth 821	-	27
DNQ	Nelson Piquet	Brabham	Brabham-BMW BT50	-	28
NS	Jan Lammers	Theodore	Theodore-Ford Cosworth TY02	driver injured	29

Pole: Prost, 1m48.537s, 82.688mph/133.074kph. Fastest lap: Prost, 1m50.438s, 81.265mph/130.784kph on Lap 45. Race leaders: Prost 1-23, Rosberg 24-41, Watson 42-62

CANADIAN GRAND PRIX

MONTREAL • ROUND 8 • DATE: 13TH JUNE 1982
Laps: 70 • Distance: 191.386miles/308.7km • Weather: Cool & dull

Pos	Driver	Team	Chassis-Engine	Result	Qual
1	Nelson Piquet	Brabham	Brabham-BMW BT50	1h46m39.577s	4
2	Riccardo Patrese	Brabham	Brabham-Ford Cosworth BT49D	1h46m53.376s	8
3	John Watson	McLaren	McLaren-Ford Cosworth MP4/1B	1h47m41.413s	6
4	Elio de Angelis	Lotus	Lotus-Ford Cosworth 91	69 laps	10
5	Marc Surer	Arrows	Arrows-Ford Cosworth A4	69 laps	16
6	Andrea de Cesaris	Alfa Romeo	Alfa Romeo 182	68 laps/out of fuel	9
7	Derek Daly	Williams	Williams-Ford Cosworth FW08	68 laps/out of fuel	13
8	Mauro Baldi	Arrows	Arrows-Ford Cosworth A4	68 laps	17
9	Didier Pironi	Ferrari	Ferrari 126C2	67 laps	1
10	Eddie Cheever	Ligier	Ligier-Matra JS17B	66 laps/out of fuel	12
11	Jochen Mass	March	March-Ford Cosworth 821	66 laps	22
NC	Brian Henton	Tyrrell	Tyrrell-Ford Cosworth 011	59 laps	26
R	Keke Rosberg	Williams	Williams-Ford Cosworth FW08	52 laps/gearbox	7
R	Raul Boesel	March	March-Ford Cosworth 821	47 laps/engine	21
R	Michele Alboreto	Tyrrell	Tyrrell-Ford Cosworth 011	41 laps/engine	15
R	Alain Prost	Renault	Renault RE30B	30 laps/engine	3
R	Rene Arnoux	Renault	Renault RE30B	28 laps/spun off	2
R	Eliseo Salazar	ATS	ATS-Ford Cosworth D5	20 laps/engine	24
R	Niki Lauda	McLaren	McLaren-Ford Cosworth MP4/1B	17 laps/clutch	11
R	Jacques Laffite	Ligier	Ligier-Matra JS17B	8 laps/fuel system	19
R	Roberto Guerrero	Ensign	Ensign-Ford Cosworth N181	2 laps/clutch	20
R	Bruno Giacomelli	Alfa Romeo	Alfa Romeo 182	1 lap/collision	5
R	Nigel Mansell	Lotus	Lotus-Ford Cosworth 91	1 lap/collision	14
R	Jean-Pierre Jarier	Osella	Osella-Ford Cosworth FA1C	0 laps/withdrawn	18
R	Riccardo Paletti	Osella	Osella-Ford Cosworth FA1C	0 laps/fatal accident	23
R	Geoff Lees	Theodore	Theodore-Ford Cosworth TY02	0 laps/collision	25
DNQ	Manfred Winkelhock	ATS	ATS-Ford Cosworth D5	-	27
DNQ	Emilio de Villota	Onyx	March-Ford Cosworth 821	-	28
DNQ	Chico Serra	Fittipaldi	Fittipaldi-Ford Cosworth F8D	-	29

Pole: Pironi, 1m27.509s, 112.729mph/181.421kph. Fastest lap: Pironi, 1m28.323s, 111.691mph/179.749kph on Lap 66. Race leaders: Pironi 1, Arnoux 2-8, Piquet 9-70

DUTCH GRAND PRIX

ZANDVOORT • ROUND 9 • DATE: 3RD JULY 1982
Laps: 72 • Distance: 190.229miles/306.144km • Weather: Warm & bright

Pos	Driver	Team	Chassis-Engine	Result	Qual
1	Didier Pironi	Ferrari	Ferrari 126C2	1h38m03.254s	4
2	Nelson Piquet	Brabham	Brabham-BMW BT50	1h38m24.903s	3
3	Keke Rosberg	Williams	Williams-Ford Cosworth FW08	1h38m25.619s	7
4	Niki Lauda	McLaren	McLaren-Ford Cosworth MP4/1B	1h39m26.974s	5
5	Derek Daly	Williams	Williams-Ford Cosworth FW08	71 laps	12
6	Mauro Baldi	Arrows	Arrows-Ford Cosworth A4	71 laps	16
7	Michele Alboreto	Tyrrell	Tyrrell-Ford Cosworth 011	71 laps	14
8	Patrick Tambay	Ferrari	Ferrari 126C2	71 laps	6
9	John Watson	McLaren	McLaren-Ford Cosworth MP4/1B	71 laps	11
10	Marc Surer	Arrows	Arrows-Ford Cosworth A4	71 laps	17
11	Bruno Giacomelli	Alfa Romeo	Alfa Romeo 182	70 laps	8
12	Manfred Winkelhock	ATS	ATS-Ford Cosworth D5	70 laps	18

Pos	Driver	Team	Chassis-Engine	Result	Qual
13	Eliseo Salazar	ATS	ATS-Ford Cosworth D5	70 laps	25
14	Jean-Pierre Jarier	Osella	Osella-Ford Cosworth FA1C	69 laps	23
15	Riccardo Patrese	Brabham	Brabham-BMW BT50	69 laps	10
R	Jochen Mass	March	March-Ford Cosworth 821	60 laps/engine	24
R	Jan Lammers	Theodore	Theodore-Ford Cosworth TY02	41 laps/engine	26
R	Elio de Angelis	Lotus	Lotus-Ford Cosworth 91	40 laps/handling	15
R	Andrea de Cesaris	Alfa Romeo	Alfa Romeo 182	35 laps/electrical	9
R	Alain Prost	Renault	Renault RE30B	33 laps/engine	2
R	Rene Arnoux	Renault	Renault RE30B	21 laps/spun off	1
R	Brian Henton	Tyrrell	Tyrrell-Ford Cosworth 011	21 laps/throttle	20
R	Raul Boesel	March	March-Ford Cosworth 821	21 laps/engine	22
R	Chico Serra	Fittipaldi	Fittipaldi-Ford Cosworth F8D	18 laps/fuel system	19
R	Derek Warwick	Toleman	Toleman-Hart TG181C	15 laps/oil leak	13
R	Jacques Laffite	Ligier	Ligier-Matra JS17	4 laps/handling	21
DNQ	Roberto Guerrero	Ensign	Ensign-Ford Cosworth N181	-	27
DNQ	Teo Fabi	Toleman	Toleman-Hart TG181C	-	28
DNQ	Eddie Cheever	Ligier	Ligier-Matra JS19	-	29
DNQ	Roberto Moreno	Lotus	Lotus-Ford Cosworth 91	-	30
DNPQ	Emilio de Villota	Onyx	March-Ford Cosworth 821	-	31

Pole: Arnoux, 1m14.233s, 128.129mph/206.204kph. Fastest lap: Warwick, 1m19.780s, 119.221mph/191.867kph on Lap 13. Race leaders: Prost 1-4, Pironi 5-72

BACK IN THE SADDLE

Having two world titles to his name was not enough for Niki Lauda and he returned to F1 in 1982 after two years away setting up his airline. He came back with McLaren and showed that he had lost none of his ability by winning on his third race back, at Long Beach. The Austrian ace won again at Brands Hatch to rank fifth.

BY A (ROMAN) NOSE

Rome's finest driver of the 1980s, Elio de Angelis, took the first of his two F1 wins during this season. Despite starting seventh at the Osterreichring, he rose to the lead as the Brabhams, then Prost's Renault, failed, leaving de Angelis to resist Williams' Keke Rosberg, keeping his Lotus in front by just 0.05 seconds. Lotus founder Colin Chapman died in December of a heart attack.

BRITISH GRAND PRIX

BRANDS HATCH • ROUND 10 • DATE: 18TH JULY 1982
Laps: 76 • Distance: 198.629miles/319.663km • Weather: Hot & bright

Pos	Driver	Team	Chassis-Engine	Result	Qual
1	Niki Lauda	McLaren	McLaren-Ford Cosworth MP4/1B	1h35m33.812s	5
2	Didier Pironi	Ferrari	Ferrari 126C2	1h35m59.538s	4
3	Patrick Tambay	Ferrari	Ferrari 126C2	1h36m12.248s	13
4	Elio de Angelis	Lotus	Lotus-Ford Cosworth 91	1h36m15.054s	7
5	Derek Daly	Williams	Williams-Ford Cosworth FW08	1h36m15.242s	10

Pos	Driver	Team	Chassis-Engine	Result	Qual
6	Alain Prost	Renault	Renault RE30B	1h36m15.448s	8
7	Bruno Giacomelli	Alfa Romeo	Alfa Romeo 182	75 laps	14
8	Brian Henton	Tyrrell	Tyrrell-Ford Cosworth 011	75 laps	17
9	Mauro Baldi	Arrows	Arrows-Ford Cosworth A4	74 laps	26
10	Jochen Mass	March	March-Ford Cosworth 821	73 laps	25
R	Andrea de Cesaris	Alfa Romeo	Alfa Romeo 182	66 laps/electrical	11
R	Eddie Cheever	Ligier	Ligier-Matra JS17	60 laps/engine	24
R	Marc Surer	Arrows	Arrows-Ford Cosworth A4	59 laps/engine	22
R	Keke Rosberg	Williams	Williams-Ford Cosworth FW08	50 laps/fuel system	1
R	Michele Alboreto	Tyrrell	Tyrrell-Ford Cosworth 011	44 laps/engine	9
R	Jacques Laffite	Ligier	Ligier-Matra JS19	41 laps/gearbox	20
R	Derek Warwick	Toleman	Toleman-Hart TG181C	40 laps/halfshaft	16
R	Nigel Mansell	Lotus	Lotus-Ford Cosworth 91	29 laps/discomfort	23
R	Nelson Piquet	Brabham	Brabham-BMW BT50	9 laps/fuel system	3
R	Roberto Guerrero	Ensign	Ensign-Ford Cosworth N181	3 laps/engine	19
R	John Watson	McLaren	McLaren-Ford Cosworth MP4/1B	2 laps/spun off	12
R	Jean-Pierre Jarier	Osella	Osella-Ford Cosworth FA1C	2 laps/collision	18
R	Chico Serra	Fittipaldi	Fittipaldi-Ford Cosworth F8D	2 laps/collision	21
R	Riccardo Patrese	Brabham	Brabham-BMW BT50	0 laps/collision	2
R	Rene Arnoux	Renault	Renault RE30B	0 laps/collision	6
R	Teo Fabi	Toleman	Toleman-Hart TG181C	0 laps/collision	15
DNQ	Manfred Winkelhock	ATS	ATS-Ford Cosworth D5	-	27
DNQ	Jan Lammers	Theodore	Theodore-Ford Cosworth TY02	-	28
DNQ	Eliseo Salazar	ATS	ATS-Ford Cosworth D5	-	29
DNQ	Raul Boesel	March	March-Ford Cosworth 821	-	30

Pole: Rosberg, 1m09.540s, 135.300mph/217.744kph. Fastest lap: Henton, 1m13.028s, 128.837mph/207.344kph on Lap 63. Race leaders: Piquet 1-9, Lauda 10-76

FROM FURY TO FISTICUFFS

The 1982 season was one of development for Brabham as it took a while to get used to BMW's new turbocharged engine. A number of retirements left reigning champion Nelson Piquet frustrated. So when he crashed out of the lead at Hockenheim by colliding with Eliseo Salazar as he lapped him, he punched the Chilean.

FRENCH GRAND PRIX

CIRCUIT PAUL RICARD • ROUND 11 • DATE: 25TH JULY 1982
Laps: 54 • Distance: 194.535miles/313.74km • Weather: Hot & bright

Pos	Driver	Team	Chassis-Engine	Result	Qual
1	Rene Arnoux	Renault	Renault RE30B	1h33m33.217s	1
2	Alain Prost	Renault	Renault RE30B	1h33m50.525s	2
3	Didier Pironi	Ferrari	Ferrari 126C2	1h34m15.345s	3
4	Patrick Tambay	Ferrari	Ferrari 126C2	1h34m49.458s	5
5	Keke Rosberg	Williams	Williams-Ford Cosworth FW08	1h35m04.211s	10
6	Michele Alboreto	Tyrrell	Tyrrell-Ford Cosworth 011	1h35m05.556s	15
7	Derek Daly	Williams	Williams-Ford Cosworth FW08	53 laps	11
8	Niki Lauda	McLaren	McLaren-Ford Cosworth MP4/1B	53 laps	9
9	Bruno Giacomelli	Alfa Romeo	Alfa Romeo 182	53 laps	8

Pos	Driver	Team	Chassis-Engine	Result	Qual
10	Brian Henton	Tyrrell	Tyrrell-Ford Cosworth 011	53 laps	23
11	Manfred Winkelhock	ATS	ATS-Ford Cosworth D5	52 laps	18
12	Geoff Lees	Lotus	Lotus-Ford Cosworth 91	52 laps	24
13	Marc Surer	Arrows	Arrows-Ford Cosworth A4	52 laps	20
14	Jacques Laffite	Ligier	Ligier-Matra JS19	51 laps	16
15	Derek Warwick	Toleman	Toleman-Hart TG181C	50 laps	14
16	Eddie Cheever	Ligier	Ligier-Matra JS19	49 laps	19
R	Andrea de Cesaris	Alfa Romeo	Alfa Romeo 182	25 laps/spun off	7
R	Nelson Piquet	Brabham	Brabham-BMW BT50	23 laps/engine	6
R	Elio de Angelis	Lotus	Lotus-Ford Cosworth 91	17 laps/fuel system	13
R	John Watson	McLaren	McLaren-Ford Cosworth MP4/1B	13 laps/electrical	12
R	Mauro Baldi	Arrows	Arrows-Ford Cosworth A4	10 laps/collision	25
R	Jochen Mass	March	March-Ford Cosworth 821	10 laps/spun off	26
R	Riccardo Patrese	Brabham	Brabham-BMW BT50	8 laps/engine	4
R	Eliseo Salazar	ATS	ATS-Ford Cosworth D5	2 laps/spun off	22
R	Jean-Pierre Jarier	Osella	Osella-Ford Cosworth FA1C	0 laps/halfshaft	17
R	Teo Fabi	Toleman	Toleman-Hart TG181C	0 laps/oil pump	21
DNQ	Jan Lammers	Theodore	Theodore-Ford Cosworth TY02	-	27
DNQ	Roberto Guerrero	Ensign	Ensign-Ford Cosworth N181	-	28
DNQ	Chico Serra	Fittipaldi	Fittipaldi-Ford Cosworth F9	-	29
DNQ	Raul Boesel	March	March-Ford Cosworth 821	-	30

Pole: Arnoux, 1m34.406s, 137.667mph/221.553kph. Fastest lap: Patrese, 1m40.075s, 129.868mph/209.003kph on Lap 4. Race leaders: Arnoux 1-2 & 24-54, Patrese 3-7, Piquet 8-23

NEW CIRCUITS

The USA increased its World Championship involvement with a third grand prix held on a street circuit in America's Motor City, Detroit. Switzerland landed its first grand prix since 1954, with a race held in… France. This was because racing was banned within its borders, and so it was a courtesy title for a race held at Dijon-Prenois.

GERMAN GRAND PRIX

HOCKENHEIM • ROUND 12 • DATE: 8TH AUGUST 1982
Laps: 45 • Distance: 190.55miles/305.865km • Weather: Hot & bright

Pos	Driver	Team	Chassis-Engine	Result	Qual
1	Patrick Tambay	Ferrari	Ferrari 126C2	1h27m25.178s	5
2	Rene Arnoux	Renault	Renault RE30B	1h27m41.557s	3
3	Keke Rosberg	Williams	Williams-Ford Cosworth FW08	44 laps	9
4	Michele Alboreto	Tyrrell	Tyrrell-Ford Cosworth 011	44 laps	7
5	Bruno Giacomelli	Alfa Romeo	Alfa Romeo 182	44 laps	11
6	Marc Surer	Arrows	Arrows-Ford Cosworth A4	44 laps	26
7	Brian Henton	Tyrrell	Tyrrell-Ford Cosworth 011	44 laps	17
8	Roberto Guerrero	Ensign	Ensign-Ford Cosworth N181	44 laps	21
9	Nigel Mansell	Lotus	Lotus-Ford Cosworth 91	43 laps	18
10	Derek Warwick	Toleman	Toleman-Hart TG181C	43 laps	14
11	Chico Serra	Fittipaldi	Fittipaldi-Ford Cosworth F9	43 laps	25
R	John Watson	McLaren	McLaren-Ford Cosworth MP4/1B	36 laps/spun off	10
R	Jacques Laffite	Ligier	Ligier-Matra JS19	36 laps/handling	15

Pos	Driver	Team	Chassis-Engine	Result	Qual
R	Derek Daly	Williams	Williams-Ford Cosworth FW08	25 laps/engine	19
R	Raul Boesel	March	March-Ford Cosworth 821	22 laps/tyre	24
R	Elio de Angelis	Lotus	Lotus-Ford Cosworth 91	21 laps/handling	13
R	Nelson Piquet	Brabham	Brabham-BMW BT50	18 laps/collision	4
R	Eliseo Salazar	ATS	ATS-Ford Cosworth D5	17 laps/collision	22
R	Alain Prost	Renault	Renault RE30B	14 laps/fuel injection	2
R	Riccardo Patrese	Brabham	Brabham-BMW BT50	13 laps/engine	6
R	Andrea de Cesaris	Alfa Romeo	Alfa Romeo 182	9 laps/gearbox	8
R	Eddie Cheever	Ligier	Ligier-Matra JS19	8 laps/fuel system	12
R	Mauro Baldi	Arrows	Arrows-Ford Cosworth A4	6 laps/fuel system	23
R	Manfred Winkelhock	ATS	ATS-Ford Cosworth D5	3 laps/clutch	16
R	Jean-Pierre Jarier	Osella	Osella-Ford Cosworth FA1D	3 laps/steering	20
NS	Didier Pironi	Ferrari	Ferrari 126C2	driver injured	1
NS	Niki Lauda	McLaren	McLaren-Ford Cosworth MP4/1B	driver injured	8
DNQ	Tommy Byrne	Theodore	Theodore-Ford Cosworth TY02	-	28
DNQ	Rupert Keegan	March	March-Ford Cosworth 821	-	29
DNQ	Teo Fabi	Toleman	Toleman-Hart TG181C	-	30

Pole: Pironi, 1m47.947s, 140.851mph/226.677kph. Fastest lap: Piquet, 1m54.035s, 133.331mph/214.576kph on Lap 7. Race leaders: Arnoux 1, Piquet 2-18, Tambay 19-45

NEW DRIVERS

Mauro Baldi was the most successful of the seven rookies, twice finishing sixth for Arrows. Raul Boesel and Roberto Guerrero claimed an eighth place apiece for March and Ensign respectively. Despite having starred in a test for McLaren, Tommy Byrne didn't get a ride with the team and turned out instead for tail-end Theodore, qualifying just twice.

AUSTRIAN GRAND PRIX

OSTERREICHRING • ROUND 13 • DATE: 15TH AUGUST 1982
Laps: 53 • Distance: 195.698miles/314.947km • Weather: Hot & bright

Pos	Driver	Team	Chassis-Engine	Result	Qual
1	Elio de Angelis	Lotus	Lotus-Ford Cosworth 91	1h25m02.212s	7
2	Keke Rosberg	Williams	Williams-Ford Cosworth FW08	1h25m02.262s	6
3	Jacques Laffite	Ligier	Ligier-Matra JS19	52 laps	14
4	Patrick Tambay	Ferrari	Ferrari 126C2	52 laps	4
5	Niki Lauda	McLaren	McLaren-Ford Cosworth MP4/1B	52 laps	10
6	Mauro Baldi	Arrows	Arrows-Ford Cosworth A4	52 laps	23
7	Chico Serra	Fittipaldi	Fittipaldi-Ford Cosworth F9	51 laps	20
8	Alain Prost	Renault	Renault RE30B	48 laps/fuel injection	3
R	John Watson	McLaren	McLaren-Ford Cosworth MP4/1B	44 laps/engine	18
R	Brian Henton	Tyrrell	Tyrrell-Ford Cosworth 011	32 laps/engine	19
R	Nelson Piquet	Brabham	Brabham-BMW BT50	31 laps/engine	1
R	Marc Surer	Arrows	Arrows-Ford Cosworth A4	28 laps/engine	21
R	Tommy Byrne	Theodore	Theodore-Ford Cosworth TY02	28 laps/spun off	26
R	Riccardo Patrese	Brabham	Brabham-BMW BT50	27 laps/engine	2
R	Eddie Cheever	Ligier	Ligier-Matra JS19	22 laps/engine	22
R	Nigel Mansell	Lotus	Lotus-Ford Cosworth 91	17 laps/engine	12
R	Rene Arnoux	Renault	Renault RE30B	16 laps/turbo	5

Pos	Driver	Team	Chassis-Engine	Result	Qual
R	Manfred Winkelhock	ATS	ATS-Ford Cosworth D5	15 laps/spun off	25
R	Derek Warwick	Toleman	Toleman-Hart TG181C	7 laps/suspension	15
R	Teo Fabi	Toleman	Toleman-Hart TG181C	7 laps/transmission	17
R	Roberto Guerrero	Ensign	Ensign-Ford Cosworth N181	6 laps/spun off	16
R	Michele Alboreto	Tyrrell	Tyrrell-Ford Cosworth 011	1 lap/spun off	8
R	Rupert Keegan	March	March-Ford Cosworth 821	1 lap/steering	24
R	Derek Daly	Williams	Williams-Ford Cosworth FW08	0 laps/collision	9
R	Andrea de Cesaris	Alfa Romeo	Alfa Romeo 182	0 laps/collision	11
R	Bruno Giacomelli	Alfa Romeo	Alfa Romeo 182	0 laps/collision	13
DNQ	Raul Boesel	March	March-Ford Cosworth 821	-	27
DNQ	Jean-Pierre Jarier	Osella	Osella-Ford Cosworth FA1D	-	28
DNQ	Eliseo Salazar	ATS	ATS-Ford Cosworth D5	-	29

Pole: Piquet, 1m27.612s, 151.723mph/244.174kph. Fastest lap: Piquet, 1m33.699s, 141.866mph/228.312kph on Lap 5. Race leaders: Piquet 1, Patrese 2-27, Prost 28-48, de Angelis 49-53

SWISS GRAND PRIX

DIJON-PRENOIS • ROUND 14 • DATE: 29TH AUGUST 1982
Laps: 80 • Distance: 188.896miles/304.0km • Weather: Hot & bright

Pos	Driver	Team	Chassis-Engine	Result	Qual
1	Keke Rosberg	Williams	Williams-Ford Cosworth FW08	1h32m41.087s	8
2	Alain Prost	Renault	Renault RE30B	1h32m45.529s	1
3	Niki Lauda	McLaren	McLaren-Ford Cosworth MP4/1B	1h33m41.430s	4
4	Nelson Piquet	Brabham	Brabham-BMW BT50	79 laps	6
5	Riccardo Patrese	Brabham	Brabham-BMW BT50	79 laps	3
6	Elio de Angelis	Lotus	Lotus-Ford Cosworth 91	79 laps	15
7	Michele Alboreto	Tyrrell	Tyrrell-Ford Cosworth 011	79 laps	12
8	Nigel Mansell	Lotus	Lotus-Ford Cosworth 91	79 laps	26
9	Derek Daly	Williams	Williams-Ford Cosworth FW08	79 laps	7
10	Andrea de Cesaris	Alfa Romeo	Alfa Romeo 182	78 laps	5
11	Brian Henton	Tyrrell	Tyrrell-Ford Cosworth 011	78 laps	18
12	Bruno Giacomelli	Alfa Romeo	Alfa Romeo 182	78 laps	9
13	John Watson	McLaren	McLaren-Ford Cosworth MP4/1B	77 laps	11
14	Eliseo Salazar	ATS	ATS-Ford Cosworth D5	77 laps	25
15	Marc Surer	Arrows	Arrows-Ford Cosworth A5	76 laps	14
16	Rene Arnoux	Renault	Renault RE30B	75 laps/fuel injection	2
R	Eddie Cheever	Ligier	Ligier-Matra JS19	70 laps/handling	16
R	Manfred Winkelhock	ATS	ATS-Ford Cosworth D5	55 laps/chassis	20
R	Jean-Pierre Jarier	Osella	Osella-Ford Cosworth FA1D	44 laps/engine	17
R	Jacques Laffite	Ligier	Ligier-Matra JS19	33 laps/handling	13
R	Teo Fabi	Toleman	Toleman-Hart TG181C	31 laps/engine	23
R	Raul Boesel	March	March-Ford Cosworth 821	31 laps/water leak	24
R	Rupert Keegan	March	March-Ford Cosworth 821	25 laps/spun off	22
R	Derek Warwick	Toleman	Toleman-Hart TG181C	24 laps/engine	21
R	Roberto Guerrero	Ensign	Ensign-Ford Cosworth N181	4 laps/engine	19
NS	Patrick Tambay	Ferrari	Ferrari 126C2	Driver unwell	10
DNQ	Chico Serra	Fittipaldi	Fittipaldi-Ford Cosworth F9	-	27
DNQ	Tommy Byrne	Theodore	Theodore-Ford Cosworth TY02	-	28
DNQ	Mauro Baldi	Arrows	Arrows-Ford Cosworth A4	-	29

Pole: Prost, 1m01.380s, 138.487mph/222.873kph. Fastest lap: Prost, 1m07.477s, 125.974mph/202.735kph on Lap 2. Race leaders: Arnoux 1, Prost 2-78, Rosberg 79-80

ITALIAN GRAND PRIX

MONZA • ROUND 15 • DATE: 12TH SEPTEMBER 1982
Laps: 52 • Distance: 187.36miles/301.6km • Weather: Hot & bright

Pos	Driver	Team	Chassis-Engine	Result	Qual
1	Rene Arnoux	Renault	Renault RE30B	1h22m25.734s	6
2	Patrick Tambay	Ferrari	Ferrari 126C2	1h22m39.798s	3
3	Mario Andretti	Ferrari	Ferrari 126C2	1h23m14.186s	1
4	John Watson	McLaren	McLaren-Ford Cosworth MP4/1B	1h23m53.579s	12
5	Michele Alboreto	Tyrrell	Tyrrell-Ford Cosworth 011	51 laps	11
6	Eddie Cheever	Ligier	Ligier-Matra JS19	51 laps	14
7	Nigel Mansell	Lotus	Lotus-Ford Cosworth 91	51 laps	23
8	Keke Rosberg	Williams	Williams-Ford Cosworth FW08	50 laps	7
9	Eliseo Salazar	ATS	ATS-Ford Cosworth D5	50 laps	25
10	Andrea de Cesaris	Alfa Romeo	Alfa Romeo 182	50 laps	9
11	Chico Serra	Fittipaldi	Fittipaldi-Ford Cosworth F9	49 laps	26
12	Mauro Baldi	Arrows	Arrows-Ford Cosworth A5	49 laps	24
NC	Roberto Guerrero	Ensign	Ensign-Ford Cosworth N181	40 laps	18
R	Elio de Angelis	Lotus	Lotus-Ford Cosworth 91	33 laps/throttle	17
R	Bruno Giacomelli	Alfa Romeo	Alfa Romeo 182	32 laps/handling	8
R	Marc Surer	Arrows	Arrows-Ford Cosworth A4	28 laps/ignition	19
R	Alain Prost	Renault	Renault RE30B	27 laps/fuel injection	5
R	Niki Lauda	McLaren	McLaren-Ford Cosworth MP4/1B	21 laps/brakes	10
R	Jean-Pierre Jarier	Osella	Osella-Ford Cosworth FA1D	10 laps/wheel	15
R	Nelson Piquet	Brabham	Brabham-BMW BT50	7 laps/engine	2
R	Riccardo Patrese	Brabham	Brabham-BMW BT50	6 laps/clutch	4
R	Jacques Laffite	Ligier	Ligier-Matra JS19	5 laps/gearbox	21
R	Teo Fabi	Toleman	Toleman-Hart TG181C	2 laps/engine	22
R	Derek Daly	Williams	Williams-Ford Cosworth FW08	0 laps/collision	13
R	Derek Warwick	Toleman	Toleman-Hart TG183	0 laps/collision	16
R	Brian Henton	Tyrrell	Tyrrell-Ford Cosworth 011	0 laps/collision	20
DNQ	Rupert Keegan	March	March-Ford Cosworth 821	-	27
DNQ	Manfred Winkelhock	ATS	ATS-Ford Cosworth D5	-	28
DNQ	Raul Boesel	March	March-Ford Cosworth 821	-	29
DNQ	Tommy Byrne	Theodore	Theodore-Ford Cosworth TY02	-	30

Pole: Andretti, 1m28.473s, 146.646mph/236.004kph. Fastest lap: Arnoux, 1m33.619s, 138.585mph/223.031kph on Lap 25. Race leaders: Arnoux 1-52

CAESARS PALACE GRAND PRIX

CAESARS PALACE • ROUND 16 • DATE: 25TH SEPTEMBER 1982
Laps: 75 • Distance: 169.680miles/273.75km • Weather: Hot & bright

Pos	Driver	Team	Chassis-Engine	Result	Qual
1	Michele Alboreto	Tyrrell	Tyrrell-Ford Cosworth 011	1h41m56.888s	3
2	John Watson	McLaren	McLaren-Ford Cosworth MP4/1B	1h42m24.180s	9
3	Eddie Cheever	Ligier	Ligier-Matra JS19	1h42m53.338s	4
4	Alain Prost	Renault	Renault RE30B	1h43m05.536s	1
5	Keke Rosberg	Williams	Williams-Ford Cosworth FW08	1h43m08.263s	6
6	Derek Daly	Williams	Williams-Ford Cosworth FW08	74 laps	14
7	Marc Surer	Arrows	Arrows-Ford Cosworth A5	74 laps	17
8	Brian Henton	Tyrrell	Tyrrell-Ford Cosworth 011	74 laps	19
9	Andrea de Cesaris	Alfa Romeo	Alfa Romeo 182	73 laps	18
10	Bruno Giacomelli	Alfa Romeo	Alfa Romeo 182	73 laps	16
11	Mauro Baldi	Arrows	Arrows-Ford Cosworth A5	73 laps	24

Pos	Driver	Team	Chassis-Engine	Result	Qual
12	Rupert Keegan	March	March-Ford Cosworth 821	73 laps	26
13	Raul Boesel	March	March-Ford Cosworth 821	69 laps	25
NC	Manfred Winkelhock	ATS	ATS-Ford Cosworth D5	62 laps	23
R	Niki Lauda	McLaren	McLaren-Ford Cosworth MP4/1B	53 laps/engine	13
R	Tommy Byrne	Theodore	Theodore-Ford Cosworth TY02	39 laps/spun off	27
R	Derek Warwick	Toleman	Toleman-Hart TG183	32 laps/ignition	10
R	Elio de Angelis	Lotus	Lotus-Ford Cosworth 91	28 laps/engine	21
R	Mario Andretti	Ferrari	Ferrari 126C2	26 laps/spun off	7
R	Nelson Piquet	Brabham	Brabham-BMW BT50	26 laps/engine	12
R	Rene Arnoux	Renault	Renault RE30B	20 laps/engine	2
R	Riccardo Patrese	Brabham	Brabham-BMW BT50	17 laps/clutch	5
R	Nigel Mansell	Lotus	Lotus-Ford Cosworth 91	8 laps/collision	22
R	Jacques Laffite	Ligier	Ligier-Matra JS19	5 laps/ignition	11
NS	Patrick Tambay	Ferrari	Ferrari 126C2	driver unwell	8
NS	Roberto Guerrero	Ensign	Ensign-Ford Cosworth N181	engine	15
NS	Jean-Pierre Jarier	Osella	Osella-Ford Cosworth FA1D	accident	20
DNQ	Teo Fabi	Toleman	Toleman-Hart TG181C	-	28
DNQ	Eliseo Salazar	ATS	ATS-Ford Cosworth D5	-	29
DNQ	Chico Serra	Fittipaldi	Fittipaldi-Ford Cosworth F9	-	30

Pole: Prost, 1m16.356s, 106.930mph/172.088kph. Fastest lap: Alboreto, 1m19.639s, 102.522mph/164.994kph on Lap 59. Race leaders: Prost 1 & 15-51, Arnoux 2-14, Alboreto 52-75

IN MEMORIAM

F1's most flamboyant driver, Gilles Villenueve, died in qualifying at Zolder when his Ferrari hit Jochen Mass's March and cartwheeled. Patrick Tambay stepped in at Ferrari and took his first win at the German GP. Riccardo Paletti also died in action when, unsighted, he ran into the back of Didier Pironi's stalled Ferrari at the start of the Canadian GP.

WORLD DRIVERS' CHAMPIONSHIP FINAL RESULTS

Pos	Driver	Nat	Car-Engine	R1	R2	R3	R4	R5
1	Keke Rosberg	FIN	Williams-Ford Cosworth FW07C	5	DQ	2	-	-
			Williams-Ford Cosworth FW08	-	-	-	-	2
2	Didier Pironi	FRA	Ferrari 126C2	18	6	R	1F	NS
3	John Watson	GBR	McLaren-Ford Cosworth MP4/1B	6	2	6	-	1F
4	Alain Prost	FRA	Renault RE30B	1F	1PF	R	R	RP
5	Niki Lauda	AUT	McLaren-Ford Cosworth MP4/1	4	-	-	-	-
			McLaren-Ford Cosworth MP4/1B	-	R	1F	-	DQ
6	Rene Arnoux	FRA	Renault RE30B	3P	R	R	RP	R
7	Patrick Tambay	FRA	Ferrari 126C2	-	-	-	-	-
			Arrows-Ford Cosworth A4	NS	-	-	-	-
8	Michele Alboreto	ITA	Tyrrell-Ford Cosworth 011	7	4	4	3	R
9	Elio de Angelis	ITA	Lotus-Ford Cosworth 87B	8	-	-	-	-
			Lotus-Ford Cosworth 91	-	R	5	-	4
10	Riccardo Patrese	ITA	Brabham-BMW BT50	R	-	-	-	R
			Brabham-Ford Cosworth BT49D	-	R	-	-	-
			Brabham-Ford Cosworth BT49C	-	-	3	-	-
11	Nelson Piquet	BRA	Brabham-BMW BT50	R	-	-	-	5
			Brabham-Ford Cosworth BT49D	-	DQ	R	-	-

Pos	Driver	Nat	Car-Engine	R1	R2	R3	R4	R5
12	Eddie Cheever	USA	Ligier-Matra JS17B	R	R	R	-	3
			Ligier-Matra JS19	-	-	-	-	-
13	Derek Daly	IRL	Theodore-Ford Cosworth TY01	14	-	-	-	-
			Theodore-Ford Cosworth TY02	-	R	R	-	-
			Williams-Ford Cosworth FW08	-	-	-	-	R
14	Nigel Mansell	GBR	Lotus-Ford Cosworth 87B	R	-	-	-	-
			Lotus-Ford Cosworth 91	-	3	7	-	R
15	Carlos Reutemann	ARG	Williams-Ford Cosworth FW07C	2	R	-	-	-
15	Gilles Villeneuve	CAN	Ferrari 126C2	R	R	DQ	2	NS
17	Andrea de Cesaris	ITA	Alfa Romeo 179D	13	-	-	-	-
			Alfa Romeo 182	-	R	RP	R	R
17	Jacques Laffite	FRA	Ligier-Matra JS17B	R	R	R	-	9
			Ligier-Matra JS19	-	-	-	-	-
19	Mario Andretti	USA	Williams-Ford Cosworth FW07C	-	-	R	-	-
			Ferrari 126C2	-	-	-	-	-
20	Jean-Pierre Jarier	FRA	Osella-Ford Cosworth FA1C	R	9	R	4	R
			Osella-Ford Cosworth FA1D	-	-	-	-	-
21	Marc Surer	CHE	Arrows-Ford Cosworth A4	-	-	-	-	7
			Arrows-Ford Cosworth A5	-	-	-	-	-
22	Manfred Winkelhock	DEU	ATS-Ford Cosworth D5	10	5	R	DQ	R
22	Eliseo Salazar	CHL	ATS-Ford Cosworth D5	9	R	R	5	R
22	Bruno Giacomelli	ITA	Alfa Romeo 179D	11	-	-	-	-
			Alfa Romeo 182	-	R	R	R	R
25	Mauro Baldi	ITA	Arrows-Ford Cosworth A4	DNQ	10	DNQ	-	R
			Arrows-Ford Cosworth A5	-	-	-	-	-
26	Chico Serra	BRA	Fittipaldi-Ford Cosworth F8D	17	R	DNQ	-	6
			Fittipaldi-Ford Cosworth F9	-	-	-	-	-

Pos	Driver	R6	R7	R8	R9	R10	R11	R12	R13	R14	R15	R16	Total
1	Rosberg	-	-	-	-	-	-	-	-	-	-	-	44
		R	4	R	3	RP	5	3	2	1	8	5	
2	Pironi	2	3	9PF	1	2	3	NSP	-	-	-	-	39
3	Watson	R	1	3	9	R	R	R	R	13	4	2	39
4	Prost	7	NCPF	R	R	6	2	R	8	2PF	R	4P	34
5	Lauda	-	-	-	-	-	-	-	-	-	-	-	30
		R	R	R	4	1	8	NS	5	3	R	R	
6	Arnoux	RP	10	R	RP	R	1P	2	R	16	1F	R	28
7	Tambay	-	-	-	-	-	-	-	-	-	-	-	25
8	Alboreto	10	R	R	7	R	6	4	R	7	5	1F	25
9	de Angelis	-	-	-	-	-	-	-	-	-	-	-	23
		5	R	4	R	4	R	R	1	6	R	R	
10	Patrese	-	-	-	15	R	RF	R	R	5	R	R	21
		1F	R	2	-	-	-	-	-	-	-	-	
		-	-	-	-	-	-	-	-	-	-	-	-
11	Piquet	R	DNQ	1	2	R	R	RF	RPF	4	R	R	20
		-	-	-	-	-	-	-	-	-	-	-	
12	Cheever	-	2	10	-	R	-	-	-	-	-	-	15
		R	-	-	DNQ	-	16	R	R	R	6	3	
13	Daly	-	-	-	-	-	-	-	-	-	-	-	8
		-	-	-	-	-	-	-	-	-	-	-	-
		6	5	7	5	5	7	R	R	9	R	6	
14	Mansell	-	-	-	-	-	-	-	-	-	-	-	7
		4	R	R	-	R	-	9	R	8	7	R	
15	Reutemann	-	-	-	-	-	-	-	-	-	-	-	6
15	Villeneuve	-	-	-	-	-	-	-	-	-	-	-	6

Pos	Driver	R6	R7	R8	R9	R10	R11	R12	R13	R14	R15	R16	Total
17	de Cesaris	-	-	-	-	-	-	-	-	-	-	-	5
		3	R	6	R	R	R	R	R	10	10	9	
17	Laffite	-	6	R	R	-	-	-	-	-	-	-	5
		R	-	-	-	R	14	R	3	R	R	R	
19	Andretti	-	-	-	-	-	-	-	-	-	-	-	4
		-	-	-	-	-	-	-	-	-	3P	R	
20	Jarier	DNQ	R	R	14	R	R	-	-	-	-	-	3
		-	-	-	-	-	-	R	DNQ	R	R	NS	
21	Surer	9	8	5	10	R	13	6	R	-	R	-	3
		-	-	-	-	-	-	-	-	15	-	7	
22	Winkelhock	R	R	DNQ	12	DNQ	11	R	R	R	DNQ	NC	2
22	Salazar	R	R	R	13	DNQ	R	R	DNQ	14	9	DNQ	2
22	Giacomelli	-	-	-	-	-	-	-	-	-	-	-	2
		R	R	R	11	7	9	5	R	12	R	10	
25	Baldi	DNQ	R	8	6	9	R	R	6	DNQ	-	11	2
		-	-	-	-	-	-	-	-	-	12	-	
26	Serra	DNPQ	11	DNQ	R	R	-	-	-	-	-	-	1
		-	-	-	-	-	DNQ	11	7	DNQ	11	DNQ	

SYMBOLS AND GRAND PRIX KEY

Round 1	**South African GP**	**Round 9**	**Dutch GP**
Round 2	**Brazilian GP**	**Round 10**	**British GP**
Round 3	**United States GP West**	**Round 11**	**French GP**
Round 4	**San Marino GP**	**Round 12**	**German GP**
Round 5	**Belgian GP**	**Round 13**	**Austrian GP**
Round 6	**Monaco GP**	**Round 14**	**Swiss GP**
Round 7	**Detroit GP**	**Round 15**	**Italian GP**
Round 8	**Canadian GP**	**Round 16**	**Caesars Palace GP**

DNPQ DID NOT PRE-QUALIFY **DNQ** DID NOT QUALIFY **DQ** DISQUALIFIED **EX** EXCLUDED
F FASTEST LAP **NC** NOT CLASSIFIED **NS** NON-STARTER **P** POLE POSITION **R** RETIRED

SCORING

1st	**9 points**
2nd	**6 points**
3rd	**4 points**
4th	**3 points**
5th	**2 points**
6th	**1 point**

WORLD CONSTRUCTORS' CHAMPIONSHIP FINAL RESULTS

Pos	Team-Engine	R1	R2	R3	R4	R5	R6	R7	R8	R9
1	Ferrari	18/R	6/R	DQ/R	1/2	NS/NS	2	3	9	1/8
2	McLaren-Ford	4/6	2/R	1/6	-/-	1/DQ	R/R	1/R	3/R	4/9
3	Renault	1/3	1/R	R/R	R/R	R/R	7/R	10/NC	R/R	R/R
4	Williams-Ford	2/5	DQ/R	2/R	-/-	2/R	6/R	4/5	7/R	3/5
5	Lotus-Ford	8/R	3/R	5/7	-/-	4/R	4/5	R/R	4/R	R/DNQ
6	Tyrrell-Ford	7/16	4/7	4/10	3/R	R/R	8/10	9/R	NC/R	7/R
7	Brabham-BMW	R/R	-/-	-/-	-/-	5/R	R	DNQ	1	2/15
8	Ligier-Matra	R/R	R/R	R/R	-/-	3/9	R/R	2/6	10/R	R/DNQ
9	Brabham-Ford	-/-	DQ/R	3/R	-/-	-/-	1	R	2	-/-
10	Alfa Romeo	11/13	R/R	R/R	R/R	R/R	3/R	R/R	6/R	11/R
11	Arrows-Ford	DNQ/DNQ	10/DNQ	R/DNQ	-/-	7/R	9/DNQ	8/R	5/8	6/10
12	ATS-Ford	9/10	5/R	R/R	5/DQ	R/R	R/R	R/R	R/DNQ	12/13
13	Osella-Ford	R/DNQ	9/DNPQ	R/DNQ	4/R	R/DNPQ	DNQ/DNPQ	R/NS	R/R	14
14	Fittipaldi-Ford	17	R	DNQ	-	6	DNPQ	11	DNQ	R

Pos	Team-Engine	R10	R11	R12	R13	R14	R15	R16	Total
1	Ferrari	2/3	3/4	1/NS	4	NS	2/3	R/NS	74
2	McLaren-Ford	1/R	8/R	R/NS	5/R	3/13	4/R	2/R	69
3	Renault	6/R	1/2	2/R	8/R	2/16	1/R	4/R	62
4	Williams-Ford	5/R	5/7	3/R	2/R	1/9	8/R	5/6	58
5	Lotus-Ford	4/R	12/R	9/R	1/R	6/8	7/R	R/R	30
6	Tyrrell-Ford	8/R	6/10	4/7	R/R	7/11	5/R	1/8	25
7	Brabham-BMW	R/R	R/R	R/R	R/R	4/5	R/R	R/R	22
8	Ligier-Matra	R/R	14/16	R/R	3/R	R/R	6/R	3/R	20
9	Brabham-Ford	-/-	-/-	-/-	-/-	-/-	-/-	-/-	19
10	Alfa Romeo	7/R	9/R	5/R	R/R	10/12	10/R	9/10	7
11	Arrows-Ford	9/R	13/R	6/R	6/R	15/DNQ	12/R	7/11	5
12	ATS-Ford	DNQ/DNQ	11/R	R/R	R/DNQ	14/R	9/DNQ	NC/DNQ	4
13	Osella-Ford	R	R	R	DNQ	R	R	NS	3
14	Fittipaldi-Ford	R	DNQ	11	7	DNQ	11	DNQ	1

1983

SEASON SUMMARY

Having been frustrated through 1982, Nelson Piquet bounced back to claim a second world title with Brabham, making history as it was the first won with a turbocharged engine. This was the year when turbo power really began to take hold of F1 as BMW and Renault were joined by Alfa Romeo, Honda and Porsche, all offering considerable horsepower. Following a change to the aerodynamic rules, the designers went for larger wings to claw back the downforce lost and the cars became less brutal to drive. Alain Prost led for a while for Renault, and this was the season that the Ford Cosworth DFV claimed its final three wins.

BRAZILIAN GRAND PRIX

JACAREPAGUA • ROUND 1 • DATE: 13TH MARCH 1983
Laps: 63 • Distance: 196.945miles/316.953km • Weather: Hot & bright

Pos	Driver	Team	Chassis-Engine	Result	Qual
1	Nelson Piquet	Brabham	Brabham-BMW BT52	1h48m27.731s	4
DQ	Keke Rosberg*	Williams	Williams-Ford Cosworth FW08C	63 laps/push start	1
3	Niki Lauda	McLaren	McLaren-Ford Cosworth MP4/1C	1h49m19.614s	9
4	Jacques Laffite	Williams	Williams-Ford Cosworth FW08C	1h49m41.682s	18
5	Patrick Tambay	Ferrari	Ferrari 126C2B	1h49m45.848s	3
6	Marc Surer	Arrows	Arrows-Ford Cosworth A6	1h49m45.938s	20
7	Alain Prost	Renault	Renault RE30C	62 laps	2
8	Derek Warwick	Toleman	Toleman-Hart TG183B	62 laps	5
9	Chico Serra	Arrows	Arrows-Ford Cosworth A6	62 laps	23
10	Rene Arnoux	Ferrari	Ferrari 126C2B	62 laps	6
11	Danny Sullivan	Tyrrell	Tyrrell-Ford Cosworth 011	62 laps	21
12	Nigel Mansell	Lotus	Lotus-Ford Cosworth 92	61 laps	22
DQ	Elio de Angelis	Lotus	Lotus-Ford Cosworth 91	60 laps/changed car	13
13	Johnny Cecotto	Theodore	Theodore-Ford Cosworth N183	60 laps	19
14	Eliseo Salazar	RAM Racing	RAM-March-Ford Cosworth 01	59 laps	26
15	Manfred Winkelhock	ATS	ATS-BMW D6	59 laps	25
NC	Roberto Guerrero	Theodore	Theodore-Ford Cosworth N183	53 laps	14
R	Eddie Cheever	Renault	Renault RE30C	41 laps/turbo	8
R	John Watson	McLaren	McLaren-Ford Cosworth MP4/1C	34 laps/engine	16
R	Raul Boesel	Ligier	Ligier-Ford Cosworth JS21	25 laps/engine	17
R	Mauro Baldi	Alfa Romeo	Alfa Romeo 183T	23 laps/collision	10
R	Jean-Pierre Jarier	Ligier	Ligier-Ford Cosworth JS21	22 laps/suspension	12
R	Riccardo Patrese	Brabham	Brabham-BMW BT52	19 laps/exhaust	7
R	Corrado Fabi	Osella	Osella-Ford Cosworth FA1D	17 laps/engine	24
R	Bruno Giacomelli	Toleman	Toleman-Hart TG183B	16 laps/spun off	15
R	Michele Alboreto	Tyrrell	Tyrrell-Ford Cosworth 011	7 laps/engine	11
DNQ	Piercarlo Ghinzani	Osella	Osella-Ford Cosworth FA1D	-	27
EX	Andrea de Cesaris	Alfa Romeo	Alfa Romeo 183T	missed weight check	-

*second position officially not awarded

Pole: Rosberg, 1m34.526s, 119.057mph/191.604kph. Fastest lap: Piquet, 1m39.829s, 112.733mph/181.426kph on Lap 4. Race leaders: Rosberg 1-6, Piquet 7-63

UNITED STATES GRAND PRIX WEST

LONG BEACH • ROUND 2 • DATE: 27TH MARCH 1983
Laps: 75 • Distance: 152.624miles/245.625km • Weather: Hot & bright

Pos	Driver	Team	Chassis-Engine	Result	Qual
1	John Watson	McLaren	McLaren-Ford Cosworth MP4/1C	1h53m34.889s	22
2	Niki Lauda	McLaren	McLaren-Ford Cosworth MP4/1C	1h54m02.882s	23
3	Rene Arnoux	Ferrari	Ferrari 126C2B	1h54m48.527s	2
4	Jacques Laffite	Williams	Williams-Ford Cosworth FW08C	74 laps	4
5	Marc Surer	Arrows	Arrows-Ford Cosworth A6	74 laps	16
6	Johnny Cecotto	Theodore	Theodore-Ford Cosworth N183	74 laps	17
7	Raul Boesel	Ligier	Ligier-Ford Cosworth JS21	73 laps	26
8	Danny Sullivan	Tyrrell	Tyrrell-Ford Cosworth 011	73 laps	9
9	Michele Alboreto	Tyrrell	Tyrrell-Ford Cosworth 011	73 laps	7
10	Riccardo Patrese	Brabham	Brabham-BMW BT52	72 laps/distributor	11
11	Alain Prost	Renault	Renault RE40	72 laps	8
12	Nigel Mansell	Lotus	Lotus-Ford Cosworth 92	72 laps	13
R	Eddie Cheever	Renault	Renault RE30C	67 laps/gearbox	15
R	Alan Jones	Arrows	Arrows-Ford Cosworth A6	58 laps/discomfort	12
R	Nelson Piquet	Brabham	Brabham-BMW BT52	51 laps/throttle	20
R	Andrea de Cesaris	Alfa Romeo	Alfa Romeo 183T	48 laps/gearbox	19
R	Elio de Angelis	Lotus	Lotus-Renault 93T	29 laps/handling	5
R	Roberto Guerrero	Theodore	Theodore-Ford Cosworth N183	27 laps/gearbox	18
R	Jean-Pierre Jarier	Ligier	Ligier-Ford Cosworth JS21	26 laps/collision	10
R	Bruno Giacomelli	Toleman	Toleman-Hart TG183B	26 laps/battery	14
R	Mauro Baldi	Alfa Romeo	Alfa Romeo 183T	26 laps/spun off	21
R	Patrick Tambay	Ferrari	Ferrari 126C2B	25 laps/collision	1
R	Keke Rosberg	Williams	Williams-Ford Cosworth FW08C	25 laps/collision	3
R	Eliseo Salazar	RAM Racing	RAM-March-Ford Cosworth 01	25 laps/gearbox	25
R	Derek Warwick	Toleman	Toleman-Hart TG183B	11 laps/spun off	6
R	Manfred Winkelhock	ATS	ATS-BMW D6	3 laps/spun off	24
DNQ	Corrado Fabi	Osella	Osella-Ford Cosworth FA1D	-	27
DNQ	Piercarlo Ghinzani	Osella	Osella-Ford Cosworth FA1D	-	28

Pole: Tambay, 1m26.117s, 85.069mph/136.906kph. Fastest lap: Lauda, 1m28.330s, 82.938mph/133.476kph on Lap 42. Race leaders: Tambay 1-25, Laffite 26-44, Watson 45-75

FRENCH GRAND PRIX

CIRCUIT PAUL RICARD • ROUND 3 • DATE: 17TH APRIL 1983
Laps: 54 • Distance: 194.535miles/313.74km • Weather: Cool & dull

Pos	Driver	Team	Chassis-Engine	Result	Qual
1	Alain Prost	Renault	Renault RE40	1h34m13.913s	1
2	Nelson Piquet	Brabham	Brabham-BMW BT52	1h34m43.633s	6
3	Eddie Cheever	Renault	Renault RE40	1h34m54.145s	2
4	Patrick Tambay	Ferrari	Ferrari 126C2B	1h35m20.793s	11
5	Keke Rosberg	Williams	Williams-Ford Cosworth FW08C	53 laps	16
6	Jacques Laffite	Williams	Williams-Ford Cosworth FW08C	53 laps	19
7	Rene Arnoux	Ferrari	Ferrari 126C2B	53 laps	4
8	Michele Alboreto	Tyrrell	Tyrrell-Ford Cosworth 011	53 laps	15
9	Jean-Pierre Jarier	Ligier	Ligier-Ford Cosworth JS21	53 laps	20
10	Marc Surer	Arrows	Arrows-Ford Cosworth A6	53 laps	21
11	Johnny Cecotto	Theodore	Theodore-Ford Cosworth N183	52 laps	17
12	Andrea de Cesaris	Alfa Romeo	Alfa Romeo 183T	50 laps	7

Pos	Driver	Team	Chassis-Engine	Result	Qual
13	Bruno Giacomelli	Toleman	Toleman-Hart TG183B	49 laps/gearbox	13
R	Raul Boesel	Ligier	Ligier-Ford Cosworth JS21	47 laps/engine	25
R	Manfred Winkelhock	ATS	ATS-BMW D6	36 laps/turbo	10
R	Corrado Fabi	Osella	Osella-Ford Cosworth FA1D	36 laps/engine	23
R	Niki Lauda	McLaren	McLaren-Ford Cosworth MP4/1C	29 laps/wheel	12
R	Mauro Baldi	Alfa Romeo	Alfa Romeo 183T	28 laps/spun off	8
R	Chico Serra	Arrows	Arrows-Ford Cosworth A6	26 laps/gearbox	26
R	Roberto Guerrero	Theodore	Theodore-Ford Cosworth N183	23 laps/engine	22
R	Danny Sullivan	Tyrrell	Tyrrell-Ford Cosworth 011	21 laps/clutch	24
R	Elio de Angelis	Lotus	Lotus-Renault 93T	20 laps/electrical	5
R	Riccardo Patrese	Brabham	Brabham-BMW BT52	19 laps/water leak	3
R	Derek Warwick	Toleman	Toleman-Hart TG183B	14 laps/engine	9
R	Nigel Mansell	Lotus	Lotus-Ford Cosworth 92	6 laps/discomfort	18
R	John Watson	McLaren	McLaren-Ford Cosworth MP4/1C	3 laps/engine	14
DNQ	Eliseo Salazar	RAM Racing	RAM-March-Ford Cosworth 01	-	27
DNQ	Piercarlo Ghinzani	Osella	Osella-Ford Cosworth FA1D	-	28
DNQ	Jean-Louis Schlesser	RAM Racing	RAM-March-Ford Cosworth 01	-	29

Pole: Prost, 1m36.672s, 134.440mph/216.360kph. Fastest lap: Prost, 1m42.695s, 126.555mph/203.671kph on Lap 34. Race leaders: Prost 1-29 & 33-54, Piquet 30-32

LESS OF A LOAD

With the drivers having suffered through 1982 from the extreme forces that were exerted on them by the rock hard suspension and incredible handling capabilities of their cars, ground effects were eradicated by the cars now having flat undersides between the front and rear axles. This slashed their cornering capabilities, thus making life less physical for the drivers.

SAN MARINO GRAND PRIX

IMOLA • ROUND 4 • DATE: 1ST MAY 1983
Laps: 60 • Distance: 187.656miles/302.4km • Weather: Warm & bright

Pos	Driver	Team	Chassis-Engine	Result	Qual
1	Patrick Tambay	Ferrari	Ferrari 126C2B	1h37m52.460s	3
2	Alain Prost	Renault	Renault RE40	1h38m41.241s	4
3	Rene Arnoux	Ferrari	Ferrari 126C2B	59 laps	1
4	Keke Rosberg	Williams	Williams-Ford Cosworth FW08C	59 laps	11
5	John Watson	McLaren	McLaren-Ford Cosworth MP4/1C	59 laps	24
6	Marc Surer	Arrows	Arrows-Ford Cosworth A6	59 laps	12
7	Jacques Laffite	Williams	Williams-Ford Cosworth FW08C	59 laps	16
8	Chico Serra	Arrows	Arrows-Ford Cosworth A6	58 laps	20
9	Raul Boesel	Ligier	Ligier-Ford Cosworth JS21	58 laps	25
10	Mauro Baldi	Alfa Romeo	Alfa Romeo 183T	57 laps/engine	10
11	Manfred Winkelhock	ATS	ATS-BMW D6	57 laps	7
12	Nigel Mansell	Lotus	Lotus-Ford Cosworth 92	56 laps/spun off	15
R	Riccardo Patrese	Brabham	Brabham-BMW BT52	54 laps/spun off	5
R	Andrea de Cesaris	Alfa Romeo	Alfa Romeo 183T	45 laps/ignition	8
R	Elio de Angelis	Lotus	Lotus-Renault 93T	43 laps/handling	9
R	Nelson Piquet	Brabham	Brabham-BMW BT52	41 laps/engine	2
R	Jean-Pierre Jarier	Ligier	Ligier-Ford Cosworth JS21	39 laps/radiator damage	19

Pos	Driver	Team	Chassis-Engine	Result	Qual
R	Danny Sullivan	Tyrrell	Tyrrell-Ford Cosworth 011	37 laps/collision	22
R	Derek Warwick	Toleman	Toleman-Hart TG183B	27 laps/spun off	14
R	Bruno Giacomelli	Toleman	Toleman-Hart TG183B	20 laps/suspension	17
R	Corrado Fabi	Osella	Osella-Ford Cosworth FA1D	20 laps/spun off	26
R	Niki Lauda	McLaren	McLaren-Ford Cosworth MP4/1C	11 laps/spun off	18
R	Johnny Cecotto	Theodore	Theodore-Ford Cosworth N183	11 laps/spun off	23
R	Michele Alboreto	Tyrrell	Tyrrell-Ford Cosworth 011	10 laps/collision	13
R	Roberto Guerrero	Theodore	Theodore-Ford Cosworth N183	3 laps/spun off	21
R	Eddie Cheever	Renault	Renault RE40	1 lap/turbo	6
DNQ	Eliseo Salazar	RAM Racing	RAM-March-Ford Cosworth 01	-	27
DNQ	Piercarlo Ghinzani	Osella	Osella-Alfa Romeo FA1E	-	28

Pole: Arnoux, 1m31.238s, 123.568mph/198.864kph. Fastest lap: Patrese, 1m34.437s, 119.382mph/192.128kph on Lap 47. Race leaders: Arnoux 1-5, Patrese 6-33, Tambay 34-60

FROM THE BACK TO THE FRONT

It's extremely rare in F1 history for a driver to come through from the rear of the field to win, yet this is what John Watson did in 1983. He and McLaren team-mate Niki Lauda had no grip from their Michelins at Long Beach, leaving John 22nd. Although helped by a few clashes ahead of him and a change of tyres, his drive to the front was incredible.

MONACO GRAND PRIX

MONTE CARLO • ROUND 5 • DATE: 15TH MAY 1983
Laps: 76 • Distance: 156.406miles/251.712km • Weather: Warm & damp, then drying

Pos	Driver	Team	Chassis-Engine	Result	Qual
1	Keke Rosberg	Williams	Williams-Ford Cosworth FW08C	1h56m38.121s	5
2	Nelson Piquet	Brabham	Brabham-BMW BT52	1h56m56.596s	6
3	Alain Prost	Renault	Renault RE40	1h57m09.487s	1
4	Patrick Tambay	Ferrari	Ferrari 126C2B	1h57m42.418s	4
5	Danny Sullivan	Tyrrell	Tyrrell-Ford Cosworth 011	74 laps	20
6	Mauro Baldi	Alfa Romeo	Alfa Romeo 183T	74 laps	13
7	Chico Serra	Arrows	Arrows-Ford Cosworth A6	74 laps	15
R	Riccardo Patrese	Brabham	Brabham-BMW BT52	64 laps/electrical	17
R	Jacques Laffite	Williams	Williams-Ford Cosworth FW08C	53 laps/gearbox	8
R	Derek Warwick	Toleman	Toleman-Hart TG183B	50 laps/collision	10
R	Elio de Angelis	Lotus	Lotus-Renault 93T	50 laps/halfshaft	19
R	Marc Surer	Arrows	Arrows-Ford Cosworth A6	49 laps/collision	12
R	Jean-Pierre Jarier	Ligier	Ligier-Ford Cosworth JS21	32 laps/suspension	9
R	Eddie Cheever	Renault	Renault RE40	30 laps/engine	3
R	Andrea de Cesaris	Alfa Romeo	Alfa Romeo 183T	13 laps/gearbox	7
R	Rene Arnoux	Ferrari	Ferrari 126C2B	6 laps/suspension	2
R	Manfred Winkelhock	ATS	ATS-BMW D6	3 laps/collision	16
R	Raul Boesel	Ligier	Ligier-Ford Cosworth JS21	3 laps/collision	18
R	Michele Alboreto	Tyrrell	Tyrrell-Ford Cosworth 011	0 laps/collision	11
R	Nigel Mansell	Lotus	Lotus-Ford Cosworth 92	0 laps/collision	14
DNQ	Bruno Giacomelli	Toleman	Toleman-Hart TG183B	-	21
DNQ	Niki Lauda	McLaren	McLaren-Ford Cosworth MP4/1C	-	22
DNQ	John Watson	McLaren	McLaren-Ford Cosworth MP4/1C	-	23

Pos	Driver	Team	Chassis-Engine	Result	Qual
DNQ	Corrado Fabi	Osella	Osella-Ford Cosworth FA1D	-	24
DNQ	Eliseo Salazar	RAM Racing	RAM-March-Ford Cosworth 01	-	25
DNQ	Piercarlo Ghinzani	Osella	Osella-Alfa Romeo FA1E	-	26
DNPQ	Johnny Cecotto	Theodore	Theodore-Ford Cosworth N183	-	27
DNPQ	Roberto Guerrero	Theodore	Theodore-Ford Cosworth N183	-	28

Pole: Prost, 1m24.840s, 87.325mph/140.537kph. Fastest lap: Piquet, 1m27.283s, 84.881mph/136.603kph on Lap 69. Race leaders: Rosberg 1-76

BELGIAN GRAND PRIX

SPA-FRANCORCHAMPS • ROUND 6 • DATE: 22ND MAY 1983
Laps: 40 • Distance: 172.179miles/277.96km • Weather: Warm & bright

Pos	Driver	Team	Chassis-Engine	Result	Qual
1	Alain Prost	Renault	Renault RE40	1h27m11.502s	1
2	Patrick Tambay	Ferrari	Ferrari 126C2B	1h27m34.684s	2
3	Eddie Cheever	Renault	Renault RE40	1h27m51.371s	8
4	Nelson Piquet	Brabham	Brabham-BMW BT52	1h27m53.797s	4
5	Keke Rosberg	Williams	Williams-Ford Cosworth FW08C	1h28m01.982s	9
6	Jacques Laffite	Williams	Williams-Ford Cosworth FW08C	1h28m44.609s	11
7	Derek Warwick	Toleman	Toleman-Hart TG183B	1h29m10.041s	22
8	Bruno Giacomelli	Toleman	Toleman-Hart TG183B	1h29m49.775s	16
9	Elio de Angelis	Lotus	Lotus-Renault 93T	39 laps	13
10	Johnny Cecotto	Theodore	Theodore-Ford Cosworth N183	39 laps	25
11	Marc Surer	Arrows	Arrows-Ford Cosworth A6	39 laps	10
12	Danny Sullivan	Tyrrell	Tyrrell-Ford Cosworth 011	39 laps	23
13	Raul Boesel	Ligier	Ligier-Ford Cosworth JS21	39 laps	26
14	Michele Alboreto	Tyrrell	Tyrrell-Ford Cosworth 011	38 laps	17
R	Niki Lauda	McLaren	McLaren-Ford Cosworth MP4/1C	33 laps/engine	15
R	Nigel Mansell	Lotus	Lotus-Ford Cosworth 92	30 laps/gearbox	19
R	Andrea de Cesaris	Alfa Romeo	Alfa Romeo 183T	25 laps/engine	3
R	Roberto Guerrero	Theodore	Theodore-Ford Cosworth N183	23 laps/engine	14
R	Rene Arnoux	Ferrari	Ferrari 126C2B	22 laps/engine	5
R	Corrado Fabi	Osella	Osella-Ford Cosworth FA1D	19 laps/wheel	24
R	Manfred Winkelhock	ATS	ATS-BMW D6	18 laps/spun off	7
R	John Watson	McLaren	McLaren-Ford Cosworth MP4/1C	8 laps/collision	20
R	Jean-Pierre Jarier	Ligier	Ligier-Ford Cosworth JS21	8 laps/collision	21
R	Thierry Boutsen	Arrows	Arrows-Ford Cosworth A6	4 laps/suspension	18
R	Mauro Baldi	Alfa Romeo	Alfa Romeo 183T	3 laps/throttle	12
R	Riccardo Patrese	Brabham	Brabham-BMW BT52	0 laps/engine	6
DNQ	Piercarlo Ghinzani	Osella	Osella-Alfa Romeo FA1E	-	27
DNQ	Eliseo Salazar	RAM Racing	RAM-March-Ford Cosworth 01	-	28

Pole: Prost, 2m04.615s, 124.739mph/200.749kph. Fastest lap: de Cesaris, 2m07.493s, 121.924mph/196.217kph on Lap 17. Race leaders: de Cesaris 1-18, Prost 19-22 & 24-40, Piquet 23

FORD COMPLETES ITS RECORD

The winning days of the Ford Cosworth V8 came to an end after 16 years and a record 155 wins, fittingly in Ford's HQ, Detroit. Michele Alboreto was the driver who rounded out this extraordinary run, winning for Tyrrell against the might of their turbocharged rivals. John Watson and Keke Rosberg had also won with Cosworth power earlier in the year.

DETROIT GRAND PRIX

DETROIT • ROUND 7 • DATE: 5TH JUNE 1983
Laps: 60 • Distance: 150.1miles/241.404km • Weather: Warm & bright

Pos	Driver	Team	Chassis-Engine	Result	Qual
1	Michele Alboreto	Tyrrell	Tyrrell-Ford Cosworth 011	1h50m53.669s	6
2	Keke Rosberg	Williams	Williams-Ford Cosworth FW08C	1h51m01.371s	12
3	John Watson	McLaren	McLaren-Ford Cosworth MP4/1C	1h51m02.952s	21
4	Nelson Piquet	Brabham	Brabham-BMW BT52	1h52m05.854s	2
5	Jacques Laffite	Williams	Williams-Ford Cosworth FW08C	1h52m26.272s	20
6	Nigel Mansell	Lotus	Lotus-Ford Cosworth 92	59 laps	14
7	Thierry Boutsen	Arrows	Arrows-Ford Cosworth A6	59 laps	10
8	Alain Prost	Renault	Renault RE40	59 laps	13
9	Bruno Giacomelli	Toleman	Toleman-Hart TG183B	59 laps	17
10	Raul Boesel	Ligier	Ligier-Ford Cosworth JS21	58 laps	23
11	Marc Surer	Arrows	Arrows-Ford Cosworth A6	58 laps	5
12	Mauro Baldi	Alfa Romeo	Alfa Romeo 183T	56 laps	25
R	Niki Lauda	McLaren	McLaren-Ford Cosworth MP4/1C	49 laps/suspension	18
NC	Roberto Guerrero	Theodore	Theodore-Ford Cosworth N183	38 laps	11
R	Johnny Cecotto	Theodore	Theodore-Ford Cosworth N183	34 laps/gearbox	26
R	Andrea de Cesaris	Alfa Romeo	Alfa Romeo 183T	33 laps/turbo	8
R	Rene Arnoux	Ferrari	Ferrari 126C2B	31 laps/electrical	1
R	Danny Sullivan	Tyrrell	Tyrrell-Ford Cosworth 011	30 laps/electrical	16
R	Jean-Pierre Jarier	Ligier	Ligier-Ford Cosworth JS21	29 laps/wheel	19
R	Manfred Winkelhock	ATS	ATS-BMW D6	26 laps/collision	22
R	Derek Warwick	Toleman	Toleman-Hart TG183B	25 laps/engine	9
R	Riccardo Patrese	Brabham	Brabham-BMW BT52	24 laps/brakes	15
R	Elio de Angelis	Lotus	Lotus-Renault 93T	5 laps/gearbox	4
R	Eddie Cheever	Renault	Renault RE40	4 laps/distributor	7
R	Piercarlo Ghinzani	Osella	Osella-Alfa Romeo FA1E	4 laps/overheating	24
R	Patrick Tambay	Ferrari	Ferrari 126C2B	0 laps/engine	3
DNQ	Corrado Fabi	Osella	Osella-Ford Cosworth FA1D	-	27

Pole: Arnoux, 1m44.734s, 85.932mph/138.295kph. Fastest lap: Watson, 1m47.668s, 83.591mph/134.526kph on Lap 55. Race leaders: Piquet 1-9 & 32-50, Arnoux 10-31, Alboreto 51-60

CANADIAN GRAND PRIX

MONTREAL • ROUND 8 • DATE: 12TH JUNE 1983
Laps: 70 • Distance: 191.386miles/308.7km • Weather: Hot & bright

Pos	Driver	Team	Chassis-Engine	Result	Qual
1	Rene Arnoux	Ferrari	Ferrari 126C2B	1h48m31.838s	1
2	Eddie Cheever	Renault	Renault RE40	1h49m13.867s	6
3	Patrick Tambay	Ferrari	Ferrari 126C2B	1h49m24.448s	4
4	Keke Rosberg	Williams	Williams-Ford Cosworth FW08C	1h49m48.886s	9
5	Alain Prost	Renault	Renault RE40	69 laps	2
6	John Watson	McLaren	McLaren-Ford Cosworth MP4/1C	69 laps	20
7	Thierry Boutsen	Arrows	Arrows-Ford Cosworth A6	69 laps	15
8	Michele Alboreto	Tyrrell	Tyrrell-Ford Cosworth 011	68 laps	17
DQ	Danny Sullivan	Tyrrell	Tyrrell-Ford Cosworth 011	68 laps/car underweight	22
9	Manfred Winkelhock	ATS	ATS-BMW D6	67 laps	7
10	Mauro Baldi	Alfa Romeo	Alfa Romeo 183T	67 laps	26
R	Riccardo Patrese	Brabham	Brabham-BMW BT52	56 laps/gearbox	5
R	Derek Warwick	Toleman	Toleman-Hart TG183B	47 laps/turbo	12

Pos	Driver	Team	Chassis-Engine	Result	Qual
R	Bruno Giacomelli	Toleman	Toleman-Hart TG183B	43 laps/engine	10
R	Nigel Mansell	Lotus	Lotus-Ford Cosworth 92	43 laps/handling	18
R	Andrea de Cesaris	Alfa Romeo	Alfa Romeo 183T	42 laps/engine	8
R	Jacques Laffite	Williams	Williams-Ford Cosworth FW08C	37 laps/gearbox	13
R	Raul Boesel	Ligier	Ligier-Ford Cosworth JS21	32 laps/halfshaft	24
R	Roberto Guerrero	Theodore	Theodore-Ford Cosworth N183	27 laps/engine	21
R	Corrado Fabi	Osella	Osella-Ford Cosworth FA1D	26 laps/engine	25
R	Johnny Cecotto	Theodore	Theodore-Ford Cosworth N183	17 laps/differential	23
R	Nelson Piquet	Brabham	Brabham-BMW BT52	15 laps/throttle	3
R	Niki Lauda	McLaren	McLaren-Ford Cosworth MP4/1C	11 laps/spun off	19
R	Elio de Angelis	Lotus	Lotus-Renault 93T	1 lap/throttle	11
R	Marc Surer	Arrows	Arrows-Ford Cosworth A6	0 laps/transmission	14
R	Jean-Pierre Jarier	Ligier	Ligier-Ford Cosworth JS21	0 laps/gearbox	16
DNQ	Jacques Villeneuve Sr.	RAM Racing	RAM-March-Ford Cosworth 01	-	27
DNQ	Piercarlo Ghinzani	Osella	Osella-Alfa Romeo FA1E	-	28

Pole: Arnoux, 1m28.729s, 111.179mph/178.926kph. Fastest lap: Tambay, 1m30.851s, 108.583mph/174.747kph on Lap 42. Race leaders: Arnoux 1-34 & 39-70, Patrese 35-37, Tambay 38

SPA MADE SHORTER BUT SAFER

Spa-Francochamps returned to the World Championship for the first time since 1970, but not in a form that the previous generation of racers would have recognised, as it was halved in length. The new layout followed the original course, but turned sharp right at Les Combes rather than going into the neighbouring valley, then rejoined the old layout at Blanchimont.

ROSBERG ENDS A RUN

Through the 1950s and 60s, non-championship races outnumbered the rounds of the World Championship, providing prestige rather than points and, most importantly, prize money. In 1983, though, these came to an end with the Race of Champions held at Brands Hatch. This finale was won by Keke Rosberg for Williams.

BRITISH GRAND PRIX

SILVERSTONE • ROUND 9 • DATE: 16TH JULY 1983
Laps: 67 • Distance: 196.444miles/316.146km • Weather: Hot & bright

Pos	Driver	Team	Chassis-Engine	Result	Qual
1	Alain Prost	Renault	Renault RE40	1h24m39.780s	3
2	Nelson Piquet	Brabham	Brabham-BMW BT52B	1h24m58.941s	6
3	Patrick Tambay	Ferrari	Ferrari 126C3	1h25m06.026s	2
4	Nigel Mansell	Lotus	Lotus-Renault 94T	1h25m18.732s	18
5	Rene Arnoux	Ferrari	Ferrari 126C3	1h25m38.654s	1
6	Niki Lauda	McLaren	McLaren-Ford Cosworth MP4/1C	66 laps	15
7	Mauro Baldi	Alfa Romeo	Alfa Romeo 183T	66 laps	11
8	Andrea de Cesaris	Alfa Romeo	Alfa Romeo 183T	66 laps	9

Pos	Driver	Team	Chassis-Engine	Result	Qual
9	John Watson	McLaren	McLaren-Ford Cosworth MP4/1C	66 laps	24
10	Jean-Pierre Jarier	Ligier	Ligier-Ford Cosworth JS21	65 laps	25
11	Keke Rosberg	Williams	Williams-Ford Cosworth FW08C	65 laps	13
12	Jacques Laffite	Williams	Williams-Ford Cosworth FW08C	65 laps	20
13	Michele Alboreto	Tyrrell	Tyrrell-Ford Cosworth 011	65 laps	16
14	Danny Sullivan	Tyrrell	Tyrrell-Ford Cosworth 011	65 laps	23
15	Thierry Boutsen	Arrows	Arrows-Ford Cosworth A6	65 laps	17
16	Roberto Guerrero	Theodore	Theodore-Ford Cosworth N183	64 laps	21
17	Marc Surer	Arrows	Arrows-Ford Cosworth A6	64 laps	19
R	Manfred Winkelhock	ATS	ATS-BMW D6	49 laps/engine	8
R	Raul Boesel	Ligier	Ligier-Ford Cosworth JS21	48 laps/suspension	22
R	Piercarlo Ghinzani	Osella	Osella-Alfa Romeo FA1E	46 laps/fuel system	26
R	Derek Warwick	Toleman	Toleman-Hart TG183B	27 laps/gearbox	10
R	Riccardo Patrese	Brabham	Brabham-BMW BT52B	9 laps/turbo	5
R	Stefan Johansson	Spirit	Spirit-Honda 201	5 laps/fuel pump	14
R	Eddie Cheever	Renault	Renault RE40	3 laps/engine	7
R	Bruno Giacomelli	Toleman	Toleman-Hart TG183B	3 laps/turbo	12
R	Elio de Angelis	Lotus	Lotus-Renault 94T	1 lap/turbo	4
DNQ	Johnny Cecotto	Theodore	Theodore-Ford Cosworth N183	-	27
DNQ	Corrado Fabi	Osella	Osella-Alfa Romeo FA1E	-	28
DNQ	Kenny Acheson	RAM Racing	RAM-March-Ford Cosworth 01	-	29

Pole: Arnoux, 1m09.462s, 151.956mph/244.550kph. Fastest lap: Prost, 1m14.212s, 142.230mph/228.897kph on Lap 32. Race leaders: Tambay 1-19, Prost 20-36 & 42-67, Piquet 37-41

NEW CONSTRUCTORS

Having run cars in F5000, then entered cars in F1 made by Brabham, Williams and March, RAM built its own for 1983, albeit run with the March name before being called RAM in 1984. The other new marque was Spirit, which had shone in F2 in partnership with Honda and brought Honda's turbo engine to F1 for the second half of the year.

GERMAN GRAND PRIX

HOCKENHEIM • ROUND 10 • DATE: 7TH AUGUST 1983
Laps: 45 • Distance: 190.55miles/305.865km • Weather: Warm & bright

Pos	Driver	Team	Chassis-Engine	Result	Qual
1	Rene Arnoux	Ferrari	Ferrari 126C3	1h27m10.319s	2
2	Andrea de Cesaris	Alfa Romeo	Alfa Romeo 183T	1h28m20.971s	3
3	Riccardo Patrese	Brabham	Brabham-BMW BT52B	1h28m54.412s	8
4	Alain Prost	Renault	Renault RE40	1h29m11.069s	5
DQ	Niki Lauda	McLaren	McLaren-Ford Cosworth MP4/1C	44 laps/pit error	18
5	John Watson	McLaren	McLaren-Ford Cosworth MP4/1C	44 laps	23
6	Jacques Laffite	Williams	Williams-Ford Cosworth FW08C	44 laps	15
7	Marc Surer	Arrows	Arrows-Ford Cosworth A6	44 laps	20
8	Jean-Pierre Jarier	Ligier	Ligier-Ford Cosworth JS21	44 laps	19
9	Thierry Boutsen	Arrows	Arrows-Ford Cosworth A6	44 laps	14
10	Keke Rosberg	Williams	Williams-Ford Cosworth FW08C	44 laps	12
11	Johnny Cecotto	Theodore	Theodore-Ford Cosworth N183	44 laps	22
12	Danny Sullivan	Tyrrell	Tyrrell-Ford Cosworth 011	43 laps	21

Pos	Driver	Team	Chassis-Engine	Result	Qual
13	Nelson Piquet	Brabham	Brabham-BMW BT52B	42 laps/fire	4
R	Eddie Cheever	Renault	Renault RE40	38 laps/fuel system	6
R	Piercarlo Ghinzani	Osella	Osella-Alfa Romeo FA1E	34 laps/oil leak	26
R	Raul Boesel	Ligier	Ligier-Ford Cosworth JS21	27 laps/engine	25
R	Mauro Baldi	Alfa Romeo	Alfa Romeo 183T	24 laps/turbo	7
R	Bruno Giacomelli	Toleman	Toleman-Hart TG183B	19 laps/turbo	10
R	Derek Warwick	Toleman	Toleman-Hart TG183B	17 laps/engine	9
R	Patrick Tambay	Ferrari	Ferrari 126C3	11 laps/engine	1
R	Stefan Johansson	Spirit	Spirit-Honda 201C	11 laps/engine	13
R	Elio de Angelis	Lotus	Lotus-Renault 94T	10 laps/engine	11
R	Michele Alboreto	Tyrrell	Tyrrell-Ford Cosworth 011	4 laps/fuel pump	16
R	Nigel Mansell	Lotus	Lotus-Renault 94T	1 lap/engine	17
R	Roberto Guerrero	Theodore	Theodore-Ford Cosworth N183	0 laps/engine	24
DNQ	Kenny Acheson	RAM Racing	RAM-March-Ford Cosworth 01	-	27
DNQ	Corrado Fabi	Osella	Osella-Alfa Romeo FA1E	-	28
DNQ	Manfred Winkelhock	ATS	ATS-BMW D6	-	29

Pole: Tambay, 1m49.328s, 139.071mph/223.814kph. Fastest lap: Arnoux, 1m53.938s, 133.444mph/214.758kph on Lap 12. Race leaders: Tambay 1, Arnoux 2-23 & 31-45, Piquet 24-30

NEW DRIVERS

As in 1982, there were seven new F1 drivers. Danny Sullivan was the most successful, coming second in the Race of Champions and fifth at Monaco for Tyrrell. Johnny Cecotto was next best with a sixth-place finish at Long Beach for Theodore, while Arrows' Thierry Boutsen claimed two sevenths at Detroit, then Montreal.

AUSTRIAN GRAND PRIX

OSTERREICHRING • ROUND 11 • DATE: 14TH AUGUST 1983
Laps: 53 • Distance: 195.685miles/314.926km • Weather: Hot & bright

Pos	Driver	Team	Chassis-Engine	Result	Qual
1	Alain Prost	Renault	Renault RE40	1h24m32.745s	5
2	Rene Arnoux	Ferrari	Ferrari 126C3	1h24m39.580s	2
3	Nelson Piquet	Brabham	Brabham-BMW BT52B	1h25m00.404s	4
4	Eddie Cheever	Renault	Renault RE40	1h25m01.140s	8
5	Nigel Mansell	Lotus	Lotus-Renault 94T	52 laps	3
6	Niki Lauda	McLaren	McLaren-Ford Cosworth MP4/1C	51 laps	14
7	Jean-Pierre Jarier	Ligier	Ligier-Ford Cosworth JS21	51 laps	20
8	Keke Rosberg	Williams	Williams-Ford Cosworth FW08C	51 laps	15
9	John Watson	McLaren	McLaren-Ford Cosworth MP4/1C	51 laps	17
10	Corrado Fabi	Osella	Osella-Alfa Romeo FA1E	50 laps	26
11	Piercarlo Ghinzani	Osella	Osella-Alfa Romeo FA1E	49 laps	25
12	Stefan Johansson	Spirit	Spirit-Honda 201	48 laps	16
13	Thierry Boutsen	Arrows	Arrows-Ford Cosworth A6	48 laps	19
R	Manfred Winkelhock	ATS	ATS-BMW D6	33 laps/water leak	13
R	Andrea de Cesaris	Alfa Romeo	Alfa Romeo 183T	31 laps/out of fuel	11
R	Patrick Tambay	Ferrari	Ferrari 126C3	30 laps/ignition	1
R	Riccardo Patrese	Brabham	Brabham-BMW BT52B	29 laps/engine	6
R	Roberto Guerrero	Theodore	Theodore-Ford Cosworth N183	25 laps/gearbox	21

Pos	Driver	Team	Chassis-Engine	Result	Qual
R	Jacques Laffite	Williams	Williams-Ford Cosworth FW08C	21 laps/handling	24
R	Mauro Baldi	Alfa Romeo	Alfa Romeo 183T	13 laps/oil leak	9
R	Michele Alboreto	Tyrrell	Tyrrell-Ford Cosworth 011	8 laps/collision	18
R	Derek Warwick	Toleman	Toleman-Hart TG183B	2 laps/turbo	10
R	Bruno Giacomelli	Toleman	Toleman-Hart TG183B	1 lap/radiator damage	7
R	Elio de Angelis	Lotus	Lotus-Renault 94T	0 laps/collision	12
R	Marc Surer	Arrows	Arrows-Ford Cosworth A6	0 laps/collision	22
R	Danny Sullivan	Tyrrell	Tyrrell-Ford Cosworth 011	0 laps/collision	23
DNQ	Raul Boesel	Ligier	Ligier-Ford Cosworth JS21	-	27
DNQ	Johnny Cecotto	Theodore	Theodore-Ford Cosworth N183	-	28
DNQ	Kenny Acheson	RAM Racing	RAM-March-Ford Cosworth 01	-	29

Pole: Tambay, 1m29.871s, 147.899mph/238.021kph. Fastest lap: Prost, 1m33.961s, 141.461mph/227.660kph on Lap 20. Race leaders: Tambay 1-21, Arnoux 22-27 & 38-47, Piquet 28-37, Prost 48-53

DUTCH GRAND PRIX

ZANDVOORT • ROUND 12 • DATE: 28TH AUGUST 1983
Laps: 72 • Distance: 190.229miles/306.144km • Weather: Cool & dull

Pos	Driver	Team	Chassis-Engine	Result	Qual
1	Rene Arnoux	Ferrari	Ferrari 126C3	1h38m41.950s	10
2	Patrick Tambay	Ferrari	Ferrari 126C3	1h39m02.789s	2
3	John Watson	McLaren	McLaren-Ford Cosworth MP4/1C	1h39m25.691s	15
4	Derek Warwick	Toleman	Toleman-Hart TG183B	1h39m58.789s	7
5	Mauro Baldi	Alfa Romeo	Alfa Romeo 183T	1h40m06.242s	12
6	Michele Alboreto	Tyrrell	Tyrrell-Ford Cosworth 012	71 laps	18
7	Stefan Johansson	Spirit	Spirit-Honda 201C	70 laps	16
8	Marc Surer	Arrows	Arrows-Ford Cosworth A6	70 laps	14
9	Riccardo Patrese	Brabham	Brabham-BMW BT52B	70 laps	6
10	Raul Boesel	Ligier	Ligier-Ford Cosworth JS21	70 laps	24
11	Corrado Fabi	Osella	Osella-Alfa Romeo FA1E	68 laps/engine	25
12	Roberto Guerrero	Theodore	Theodore-Ford Cosworth N183	68 laps	20
13	Bruno Giacomelli	Toleman	Toleman-Hart TG183B	68 laps/spun off	13
14	Thierry Boutsen	Arrows	Arrows-Ford Cosworth A6	65 laps/engine	21
R	Keke Rosberg	Williams	Williams-Ford Cosworth FW08C	53 laps/ignition	23
DQ	Manfred Winkelhock	ATS	ATS-BMW D6	50 laps/illegal pass	9
R	Nelson Piquet	Brabham	Brabham-BMW BT52B	41 laps/collision	1
R	Alain Prost	Renault	Renault RE40	41 laps/spun off	4
R	Eddie Cheever	Renault	Renault RE40	39 laps/electrical	11
R	Jacques Laffite	Williams	Williams-Ford Cosworth FW08C	37 laps/handling	17
R	Nigel Mansell	Lotus	Lotus-Renault 94T	26 laps/spun off	5
R	Niki Lauda	McLaren	McLaren-TAG MP4/1E	25 laps/brakes	19
R	Danny Sullivan	Tyrrell	Tyrrell-Ford Cosworth 011	20 laps/engine	26
R	Elio de Angelis	Lotus	Lotus-Renault 94T	12 laps/electrical	3
R	Andrea de Cesaris	Alfa Romeo	Alfa Romeo 183T	5 laps/engine	8
R	Jean-Pierre Jarier	Ligier	Ligier-Ford Cosworth JS21	3 laps/suspension	22
DNQ	Piercarlo Ghinzani	Osella	Osella-Alfa Romeo FA1E	-	27
DNQ	Johnny Cecotto	Theodore	Theodore-Ford Cosworth N183	-	28
DNQ	Kenny Acheson	RAM Racing	RAM-March-Ford Cosworth 01	-	29

Pole: Piquet, 1m15.630s, 125.762mph/202.395kph. Fastest lap: Arnoux, 1m19.863s, 119.097mph/191.668kph on Lap 33. Race leaders: Piquet 1-41, Arnoux 42-72

IN MEMORIAM

Considered Germany's great hope in the early 1970s – he claimed a third place in his first full season and later crashed out of the lead of the 1975 Spanish GP – Rolf Stommelen was one of the casualties of 1983. By now a very successful sports car racer, he lost his life when he crashed a Porsche in an IMSA race at Riverside in California.

ITALIAN GRAND PRIX

MONZA • ROUND 13 • DATE: 11TH SEPTEMBER 1983
Laps: 52 • Distance: 187.36miles/301.6km • Weather: Warm & bright

Pos	Driver	Team	Chassis-Engine	Result	Qual
1	Nelson Piquet	Brabham	Brabham-BMW BT52B	1h23m10.880s	4
2	Rene Arnoux	Ferrari	Ferrari 126C3	1h23m21.092s	3
3	Eddie Cheever	Renault	Renault RE40	1h23m29.492s	7
4	Patrick Tambay	Ferrari	Ferrari 126C3	1h23m39.903s	2
5	Elio de Angelis	Lotus	Lotus-Renault 94T	1h24m04.560s	8
6	Derek Warwick	Toleman	Toleman-Hart TG183B	1h24m24.228s	12
7	Bruno Giacomelli	Toleman	Toleman-Hart TG183B	1h24m44.802s	14
8	Nigel Mansell	Lotus	Lotus-Renault 94T	1h24m46.915s	11
9	Jean-Pierre Jarier	Ligier	Ligier-Ford Cosworth JS21	51 laps	19
10	Marc Surer	Arrows	Arrows-Ford Cosworth A6	51 laps	20
11	Keke Rosberg*	Williams	Williams-Ford Cosworth FW08C	51 laps	16
12	Johnny Cecotto	Theodore	Theodore-Ford Cosworth N183	50 laps	26
13	Roberto Guerrero	Theodore	Theodore-Ford Cosworth N183	50 laps	21
R	Corrado Fabi	Osella	Osella-Alfa Romeo FA1E	45 laps/engine	25
R	Danny Sullivan	Tyrrell	Tyrrell-Ford Cosworth 011	44 laps/fuel pump	22
R	Thierry Boutsen	Arrows	Arrows-Ford Cosworth A6	41 laps/engine	18
R	Manfred Winkelhock	ATS	ATS-BMW D6	35 laps/exhaust	9
R	Michele Alboreto	Tyrrell	Tyrrell-Ford Cosworth 012	28 laps/clutch	24
R	Alain Prost	Renault	Renault RE40	26 laps/turbo	5
R	Niki Lauda	McLaren	McLaren-TAG MP4/1E	24 laps/electrical	13
R	John Watson	McLaren	McLaren-TAG MP4/1E	13 laps/electrical	15
R	Piercarlo Ghinzani	Osella	Osella-Alfa Romeo FA1E	10 laps/gearbox	23
R	Mauro Baldi	Alfa Romeo	Alfa Romeo 183T	4 laps/turbo	10
R	Stefan Johansson	Spirit	Spirit-Honda 201	4 laps/distributor	17
R	Riccardo Patrese	Brabham	Brabham-BMW BT52B	2 laps/engine	1
R	Andrea de Cesaris	Alfa Romeo	Alfa Romeo 183T	2 laps/collision	6
DNQ	Raul Boesel	Ligier	Ligier-Ford Cosworth JS21	-	27
DNQ	Jacques Laffite	Williams	Williams-Ford Cosworth FW08C	-	28
DNQ	Kenny Acheson	RAM Racing	RAM-March-Ford Cosworth 01	-	29

*including a 1m penalty for a start infringement, dropping him from ninth

Pole: Patrese, 1m29.122s, 145.578mph/234.285kph. Fastest lap: Piquet, 1m34.431s, 137.393mph/221.113kph on Lap 20. Race leaders: Patrese 1-2, Piquet 3-52

EUROPEAN GRAND PRIX

BRANDS HATCH • ROUND 14 • DATE: 25TH SEPTEMBER 1983
Laps: 76 • Distance: 198.634miles/319.671km • Weather: Hot & bright

Pos	Driver	Team	Chassis-Engine	Result	Qual
1	Nelson Piquet	Brabham	Brabham-BMW BT52B	1h36m45.865s	4
2	Alain Prost	Renault	Renault RE40	1h36m52.436s	8
3	Nigel Mansell	Lotus	Lotus-Renault 94T	1h37m16.180s	3
4	Andrea de Cesaris	Alfa Romeo	Alfa Romeo 183T	1h37m20.261s	14
5	Derek Warwick	Toleman	Toleman-Hart TG183B	1h37m30.780s	11
6	Bruno Giacomelli	Toleman	Toleman-Hart TG183B	1h37m38.055s	12
7	Riccardo Patrese	Brabham	Brabham-BMW BT52B	1h37m58.549s	2
8	Manfred Winkelhock	ATS	ATS-BMW D6	75 laps	9
9	Rene Arnoux	Ferrari	Ferrari 126C3	75 laps	5
10	Eddie Cheever	Renault	Renault RE40	75 laps	7
11	Thierry Boutsen	Arrows	Arrows-Ford Cosworth A6	75 laps	18
12	Roberto Guerrero	Theodore	Theodore-Ford Cosworth N183	75 laps	21
13	Jonathan Palmer	Williams	Williams-Ford Cosworth FW08C	74 laps	25
14	Stefan Johansson	Spirit	Spirit-Honda 201	74 laps	19
15	Raul Boesel	Ligier	Ligier-Ford Cosworth JS21	73 laps	23
R	Patrick Tambay	Ferrari	Ferrari 126C3	67 laps/spun off	6
R	Michele Alboreto	Tyrrell	Tyrrell-Ford Cosworth 012	64 laps/engine	26
R	Piercarlo Ghinzani	Osella	Osella-Alfa Romeo FA1E	63 laps/throttle	24
R	Marc Surer	Arrows	Arrows-Ford Cosworth A6	50 laps/engine	17
R	Keke Rosberg	Williams	Williams-Ford Cosworth FW08C	43 laps/engine	16
R	Mauro Baldi	Alfa Romeo	Alfa Romeo 183T	39 laps/clutch	15
R	John Watson	McLaren	McLaren-TAG MP4/1E	36 laps/spun off	10
R	Danny Sullivan	Tyrrell	Tyrrell-Ford Cosworth 012	27 laps/oil leak	20
R	Niki Lauda	McLaren	McLaren-TAG MP4/1E	25 laps/engine	13
R	Elio de Angelis	Lotus	Lotus-Renault 94T	12 laps/fuel pump	1
R	Jean-Pierre Jarier	Ligier	Ligier-Ford Cosworth JS21	0 laps/clutch	22
DNQ	Kenny Acheson	RAM Racing	RAM-March-Ford Cosworth 01	-	27
DNQ	Corrado Fabi	Osella	Osella-Alfa Romeo FA1E	-	28
DNQ	Jacques Laffite	Williams	Williams-Ford Cosworth FW08C	-	29

Pole: de Angelis, 1m12.092s, 130.513mph/210.041kph. Fastest lap: Mansell, 1m14.342s, 126.563mph/203.684kph on Lap 70. Race leaders: Patrese 1-10, Piquet 11-76

CLASSIC CAR: BRABHAM BT52

BMW supplied the power to the 1983 title-winning Brabham, and Gordon Murray designed its arrow-shape that was so pronounced as it ran without sidepods. With its dark blue and white livery, it was the crispest-looking car on the Qual and it was effective first time out, Nelson Piquet winning in Brazil. BMW's straight-four turbocharged engine gave it 640bhp. For qualifying, though, the boost could be wound up to offer a whacking 750bhp for Piquet and Riccardo Patrese to harness. From the British GP on, it was upgraded to BT52B spec, with smoother bodywork and changes to its suspension. In all, it won four grands prix.

SOUTH AFRICAN GRAND PRIX

KYALAMI • ROUND 15 • DATE: 15TH OCTOBER 1983
Laps: 77 • Distance: 196.358miles/316.008km • Weather: Hot & bright

Pos	Driver	Team	Chassis-Engine	Result	Qual
1	Riccardo Patrese	Brabham	Brabham-BMW BT52B	1h33m25.708s	3
2	Andrea de Cesaris	Alfa Romeo	Alfa Romeo 183T	1h33m35.027s	9
3	Nelson Piquet	Brabham	Brabham-BMW BT52B	1h33m47.677s	2
4	Derek Warwick	Toleman	Toleman-Hart TG183B	76 laps	13
5	Keke Rosberg	Williams	Williams-Honda FW09	76 laps	6
6	Eddie Cheever	Renault	Renault RE40	76 laps	14
7	Danny Sullivan	Tyrrell	Tyrrell-Ford Cosworth 012	75 laps	19
8	Marc Surer	Arrows	Arrows-Ford Cosworth A6	75 laps	22
9	Thierry Boutsen	Arrows	Arrows-Ford Cosworth A6	74 laps	20
10	Jean-Pierre Jarier	Ligier	Ligier-Ford Cosworth JS21	73 laps	21
11	Niki Lauda	McLaren	McLaren-TAG MP4/1E	71 laps/electrical	12
12	Kenny Acheson	RAM Racing	RAM-March-Ford Cosworth 01	71 laps	24
NC	Nigel Mansell	Lotus	Lotus-Renault 94T	68 laps	7
NC	Raul Boesel	Ligier	Ligier-Ford Cosworth JS21	66 laps	23
R	Michele Alboreto	Tyrrell	Tyrrell-Ford Cosworth 012	60 laps/engine	18
R	Patrick Tambay	Ferrari	Ferrari 126C3	56 laps/turbo	1
R	Bruno Giacomelli	Toleman	Toleman-Hart TG183B	56 laps/turbo	16
R	Alain Prost	Renault	Renault RE40	35 laps/turbo	5
R	Corrado Fabi	Osella	Osella-Alfa Romeo FA1E	28 laps/engine	25
R	Elio de Angelis	Lotus	Lotus-Renault 94T	20 laps/engine	11
DQ	John Watson	McLaren	McLaren-TAG MP4/1E	18 laps/illegal pass	15
R	Rene Arnoux	Ferrari	Ferrari 126C3	9 laps/engine	4
R	Mauro Baldi	Alfa Romeo	Alfa Romeo 183T	5 laps/engine	17
R	Manfred Winkelhock	ATS	ATS-BMW D6	1 lap/engine	8
R	Jacques Laffite	Williams	Williams-Honda FW09	1 lap/spun off	10
R	Piercarlo Ghinzani	Osella	Osella-Alfa Romeo FA1E	1 lap/engine	26

Pole: Tambay, 1m06.554s, 137.938mph/221.991kph. Fastest lap: Piquet, 1m09.948s, 131.245mph/211.219kph on Lap 6. Race leaders: Piquet 1-59, Patrese 60-77

WORLD DRIVERS' CHAMPIONSHIP FINAL RESULTS

Pos	Driver	Nat	Car-Engine	R1	R2	R3	R4	R5
1	Nelson Piquet	BRA	Brabham-BMW BT52	1F	R	2	R	2F
			Brabham-BMW BT52B	-	-	-	-	-
2	Alain Prost	FRA	Renault RE30C	7	-	-	-	-
			Renault RE40	-	11	1PF	2	3P
3	Rene Arnoux	FRA	Ferrari 126C2B	10	3	7	3P	R
			Ferrari 126C3	-	-	-	-	-
4	Patrick Tambay	FRA	Ferrari 126C2B	5	RP	4	1	4
			Ferrari 126C3	-	-	-	-	-
5	Keke Rosberg	FIN	Williams-Ford Cosworth FW08C	DQP	R	5	4	1
			Williams-Honda FW09	-	-	-	-	-
6	John Watson	GBR	McLaren-Ford Cosworth MP4/1C	R	1	R	5	DNQ
			McLaren-TAG MP4/1E	-	-	-	-	-
7	Eddie Cheever	USA	Renault RE30C	R	R	-	-	-
			Renault RE40	-	-	3	R	R
8	Andrea de Cesaris	ITA	Alfa Romeo 183T	DNQ	R	12	R	R
9	Riccardo Patrese	ITA	Brabham-BMW BT52	R	10	R	RF	R
			Brabham-BMW BT52B	-	-	-	-	-

Pos	Driver	Nat	Car-Engine	R1	R2	R3	R4	R5
10	Niki Lauda	AUT	McLaren-Ford Cosworth MP4/1C	3	2F	R	R	DNQ
			McLaren-TAG MP4/1E	-	-	-	-	-
11	Jacques Laffite	FRA	Williams-Ford Cosworth FW08C	4	4	6	7	R
			Williams-Honda FW09	-	-	-	-	-
12	Michele Alboreto	ITA	Tyrrell-Ford Cosworth 011	R	9	8	R	R
			Tyrrell-Ford Cosworth 012	-	-	-	-	-
13	Nigel Mansell	GBR	Lotus-Ford Cosworth 92	12	12	R	12	R
			Lotus-Renault 94T	-	-	-	-	-
14	Derek Warwick	GBR	Toleman-Hart TG183B	8	R	R	R	R
15	Marc Surer	CHE	Arrows-Ford Cosworth A6	6	5	10	6	R
16	Mauro Baldi	ITA	Alfa Romeo 183T	R	R	R	10	6
17	Danny Sullivan	USA	Tyrrell-Ford Cosworth 011	11	8	R	R	5
			Tyrrell-Ford Cosworth 012	-	-	-	-	-
17	Elio de Angelis	ITA	Lotus-Ford Cosworth 92	DQ	-	-	-	-
			Lotus-Renault 93T	-	R	R	R	R
			Lotus-Renault 94T	-	-	-	-	-
19	Johnny Cecotto	VEN	Theodore-Ford Cosworth N183	13	6	11	R	DNPQ
19	Bruno Giacomelli	ITA	Toleman-Hart TG183B	R	R	13	R	DNQ

Pos	Driver	R6	R7	R8	R9	R10	R11	R12	R13	R14	R15	Total
1	Piquet	4	4	R	-	-	-	-	-	-	-	59
		-	-	-	2	13	3	RP	1F	1	3F	
2	Prost	-	-	-	-	-	-	-	-	-	-	57
		1P	8	5	1F	4	1F	R	R	2	R	-
3	Arnoux	R	RP	1P	-	-	-	-	-	-	-	49
		-	-	-	5P	1F	2	1F	2	9	R	
4	Tambay	2	R	3F	-	-	-	-	-	-	-	40
		-	-	-	3	RP	RP	2	4	R	RP	
5	Rosberg	5	2	4	11	10	8	R	11	R	-	27
		-	-	-	-	-	-	-	-	-	5	
6	Watson	R	3F	6	9	5	9	3	-	-	-	22
		-	-	-	-	-	-	-	R	R	DQ	
7	Cheever	-	-	-	-	-	-	-	-	-	-	22
		3	R	2	R	R	4	R	3	10	6	-
8	de Cesaris	RF	R	R	8	2	R	R	R	4	2	15
9	Patrese	R	R	R	-	-	-	-	-	-	-	13
		-	-	-	R	3	R	9	RP	7	1	
10	Lauda	R	R	R	6	DQ	6	-	-	-	-	12
		-	-	-	-	-	-	R	R	R	11	
11	Laffite	6	5	R	12	6	R	R	DNQ	DNQ	-	11
		-	-	-	-	-	-	-	-	-	R	
12	Alboreto	14	1	8	13	R	R	-	-	-	-	10
		-	-	-	-	-	-	6	R	R	R	
13	Mansell	R	6	R	-	-	-	-	-	-	-	10
		-	-	-	4	R	5	R	8	3F	NC	
14	Warwick	7	R	R	R	R	R	4	6	5	4	9
15	Surer	11	11	R	17	7	R	8	10	R	8	4
16	Baldi	R	12	10	7	R	R	5	R	R	R	3
17	Sullivan	12	R	DQ	14	12	R	R	R	-	-	2
		-	-	-	-	-	-	-	-	R	7	
17	de Angelis	-	-	-	-	-	-	-	-	-	-	2
		9	R	R	-	-	-	-	-	-	-	
		-	-	-	R	R	R	R	5	RP	R	
19	Cecotto	10	R	R	DNQ	11	DNQ	DNQ	12	-	-	1
19	Giacomelli	8	9	R	R	R	R	13	7	6	R	1

WORLD CONSTRUCTORS' CHAMPIONSHIP FINAL RESULTS

Pos	Team-Engine	R1	R2	R3	R4	R5	R6	R7	R8
1	Ferrari	5/10	3/R	4/7	1/3	4/R	2/R	R/R	1/3
2	Renault	7/R	11/R	1/3	2/R	3/R	1/3	8/R	2/5
3	Brabham-BMW	1/R	10/R	2/R	R/R	2/R	4/R	4/R	R/R
4	Williams-Ford	4/DQ	4/R	5/6	4/7	1/R	5/6	2/5	4/R
5	McLaren-Ford	3/R	1/2	R/R	5/R	DNQ/DNQ	R/R	3/R	6/R
6	Alfa Romeo	R/DNQ	R/R	12/R	10/R	6/R	R/R	12/R	10/R
7	Tyrrell-Ford	11/R	8/9	8/R	R/R	5/R	12/14	1/R	8/DQ
8	Lotus-Renault	-	R	R	R	R	9	R	R
9	Toleman-Hart	8/R	R/R	13/R	R/R	R/DNQ	7/8	9/R	R/R
10	Arrows-Ford	6/9	5/R	10/R	6/8	7/R	11/R	7/11	7/R
11	Williams-Honda	-	-	-	-	-	-	-	-
12	Theodore-Ford	13/NC	6/R	11/R	R/R	DNPQ/DNPQ	10/R	NC/R	R/R
12	Lotus-Ford	12/DQ	12	R	12	R	R	6	R

Pos	Team-Engine	R9	R10	R11	R12	R13	R14	R15	Total
1	Ferrari	3/5	1/R	2/R	1/2	2/4	9/R	R/R	89
2	Renault	1/R	4/R	1/4	R/R	3/R	2/10	6/R	79
3	Brabham-BMW	2/R	3/13	3/R	9/R	1/R	1/7	1/3	72
4	Williams-Ford	11/12	6/10	8/R	R/R	11	13/R	-/-	36
5	McLaren-Ford	6/9	5/DQ	6/9	3	-/-	-/-	-/-	34
6	Alfa Romeo	7/8	2/R	R/R	5/R	R/R	4/R	2/R	18
7	Tyrrell-Ford	13/14	12/R	R/R	6/R	R/R	R/R	7/R	12
8	Lotus-Renault	4/R	R/R	5/R	R/R	5/8	3/R	NC/R	11
9	Toleman-Hart	R/R	R/R	R/R	4/13	6/7	5/6	4/R	10
10	Arrows-Ford	15/17	7/9	13/R	8/14	10/R	11/R	8/9	4
11	Williams-Honda	-	-	-	-	-	-	5/R	2
12	Theodore-Ford	16/DNQ	11/R	R/DNQ	12/DNQ	12/13	12	-	1
12	Lotus-Ford	-	-	-	-	-	-	-	1

SYMBOLS AND GRAND PRIX KEY

Round 1 Brazilian GP
Round 2 United States GP West
Round 3 French GP
Round 4 San Marino GP
Round 5 Monaco GP
Round 6 Belgian GP
Round 7 Detroit GP
Round 8 Canadian GP
Round 9 British GP
Round 10 German GP
Round 11 Austrian GP
Round 12 Dutch GP
Round 13 Italian GP
Round 14 European GP
Round 15 South African GP

SCORING

1st 9 points
2nd 6 points
3rd 4 points
4th 3 points
5th 2 points
6th 1 point

DNPQ DID NOT PRE-QUALIFY **DNQ** DID NOT QUALIFY **DQ** DISQUALIFIED **EX** EXCLUDED
F FASTEST LAP **NC** NOT CLASSIFIED **NS** NON-STARTER **P** POLE POSITION **R** RETIRED

SEASON SUMMARY

If winning the 1977 F1 title a year after nearly dying of his burns was a fairy tale, then Niki Lauda's third crown was a triumph for doggedness. He had to work really hard for it as Renault had fired Alain Prost at the end of 1983 and the Frenchman took to his new McLaren like a duck to water. After 16 grands prix, the difference between the team-mates was half a point in the team's first full year with turbocharged engines. Another driver to have a successful move was Michele Alboreto, who joined Ferrari from Tyrrell to become the team's first Italian driver since 1973, and did well enough to rank fourth.

ONE BLOW LEADS TO ANOTHER

Derek Warwick would never win a grand prix in his 146-race F1 career, but the opening race of the 1984 season was one that got away. Having his first outing for Renault after joining from Toleman, he was leading with 10 laps to go when his front-left wishbone broke, probably a legacy of Niki Lauda hitting him earlier in the race.

BRAZILIAN GRAND PRIX

JACAREPAGUA • ROUND 1 • DATE: 25TH MARCH 1984
Laps: 61 • Distance: 190.693miles/306.891km • Weather: Hot & bright

Pos	Driver	Team	Chassis-Engine	Result	Qual
1	Alain Prost	McLaren	McLaren-TAG MP4/2	1h42m34.492s	4
2	Keke Rosberg	Williams	Williams-Honda FW09	1h43m15.006s	9
3	Elio de Angelis	Lotus	Lotus-Renault 95T	1h43m33.620s	1
4	Eddie Cheever	Alfa Romeo	Alfa Romeo 184T	60 laps	12
DQ	Martin Brundle*	Tyrrell	Tyrrell-Ford Cosworth 012	60 laps	18
5	Patrick Tambay	Renault	Renault RE50	59 laps/out of fuel	8
6	Thierry Boutsen	Arrows	Arrows-Ford Cosworth A6	59 laps	20
7	Marc Surer	Arrows	Arrows-Ford Cosworth A6	59 laps	24
8	Jonathan Palmer	RAM Racing	RAM-Hart 01	58 laps	26
R	Derek Warwick	Renault	Renault RE50	51 laps/suspension	3
R	Andrea de Cesaris	Ligier	Ligier-Renault JS23	42 laps/gearbox	14
R	Riccardo Patrese	Alfa Romeo	Alfa Romeo 184T	41 laps/gearbox	11
R	Niki Lauda	McLaren	McLaren-TAG MP4/2	38 laps/electrical	6
R	Nigel Mansell	Lotus	Lotus-Renault 95T	35 laps/accident	5
R	Nelson Piquet	Brabham	Brabham-BMW BT53	32 laps/engine	7
R	Teo Fabi	Brabham	Brabham-BMW BT53	32 laps/turbo	15
R	Rene Arnoux	Ferrari	Ferrari 126C4	30 laps/battery	10
R	Piercarlo Ghinzani	Osella	Osella-Alfa Romeo FA1F	28 laps/gearbox	21
R	Francois Hesnault	Ligier	Ligier-Renault JS23	25 laps/overheating	19
R	Philippe Alliot	RAM Racing	RAM-Hart 02	24 laps/battery	25
R	Johnny Cecotto	Toleman	Toleman-Hart TG183B	18 laps/turbo	17
R	Jacques Laffite	Williams	Williams-Honda FW09	15 laps/electrical	13
R	Michele Alboreto	Ferrari	Ferrari 126C4	14 laps/brakes	2

Pos	Driver	Team	Chassis-Engine	Result	Qual
R	Mauro Baldi	Spirit	Spirit-Hart 101B	12 laps/distributor	23
DQ	Stefan Bellof*	Tyrrell	Tyrrell-Ford Cosworth 012	11 laps/throttle cable	22
R	Ayrton Senna	Toleman	Toleman-Hart TG183B	8 laps/turbo	16
EX	Manfred Winkelhock	ATS	ATS-BMW D7	push start	15

*Tyrrell was found at the ninth round, in Detroit, to be using illegal fuel and had all of its results annulled

Pole: de Angelis, 1m28.392s, 127.319mph/204.900kph. Fastest lap: Prost, 1m36.499s, 116.623mph/187.686kph on Lap 42. Race leaders: Alboreto 1-11, Lauda 12-37, Prost 38 & 51-61, Warwick 39-50

SOUTH AFRICAN GRAND PRIX

KYALAMI • ROUND 2 • DATE: 7TH APRIL 1984
Laps: 75 • Distance: 190.765miles/307.8km • Weather: Hot & bright

Pos	Driver	Team	Chassis-Engine	Result	Qual
1	Niki Lauda	McLaren	McLaren-TAG MP4/2	1h29m23.430s	8
2	Alain Prost	McLaren	McLaren-TAG MP4/2	1h30m29.380s	5
3	Derek Warwick	Renault	Renault RE50	74 laps	9
4	Riccardo Patrese	Alfa Romeo	Alfa Romeo 184T	73 laps	18
5	Andrea de Cesaris	Ligier	Ligier-Renault JS23	73 laps	14
6	Ayrton Senna	Toleman	Toleman-Hart TG183B	72 laps	13
7	Elio de Angelis	Lotus	Lotus-Renault 95T	71 laps	7
8	Mauro Baldi	Spirit	Spirit-Hart 101B	71 laps	20
9	Marc Surer	Arrows	Arrows-Ford Cosworth A6	71 laps	23
10	Francois Hesnault	Ligier	Ligier-Renault JS23	71 laps	17
DQ*	Martin Brundle	Tyrrell	Tyrrell-Ford Cosworth 012	71 laps/illegal fuel	25
11	Michele Alboreto	Ferrari	Ferrari 126C4	70 laps/ignition	10
12	Thierry Boutsen	Arrows	Arrows-Ford Cosworth A6	70 laps	26
R	Patrick Tambay	Renault	Renault RE50	66 laps/out of fuel	4
R	Jacques Laffite	Williams	Williams-Honda FW09	60 laps/transmission	11
DQ*	Stefan Bellof	Tyrrell	Tyrrell-Ford Cosworth 012	59 laps/hub	24
R	Manfred Winkelhock	ATS	ATS-BMW D7	53 laps/engine	12
R	Keke Rosberg	Williams	Williams-Honda FW09	51 laps/wheel	2
R	Nigel Mansell	Lotus	Lotus-Renault 95T	51 laps/turbo	3
R	Rene Arnoux	Ferrari	Ferrari 126C4	40 laps/fuel injection	15
R	Nelson Piquet	Brabham	Brabham-BMW BT53	29 laps/turbo	1
R	Johnny Cecotto	Toleman	Toleman-Hart TG183B	26 laps/tyre	19
R	Philippe Alliot	RAM Racing	RAM-Hart 02	24 laps/engine	22
R	Jonathan Palmer	RAM Racing	RAM-Hart 01	22 laps/gearbox	21
R	Teo Fabi	Brabham	Brabham-BMW BT53	18 laps/turbo	6
R	Eddie Cheever	Alfa Romeo	Alfa Romeo 184T	4 laps/radiator damage	16
NS	Piercarlo Ghinzani	Osella	Osella-Alfa Romeo FA1F	accident	27

Pole: Piquet, 1m04.871s, 141.517mph/227.750kph. Fastest lap: Tambay, 1m08.877s, 133.286mph/214.504kph on Lap 65. Race leaders: Rosberg 1, Piquet 2-20, Lauda 21-75

A SHORT RACE OF MUCH DRAMA

Nigel Mansell was heading for his first grand prix win, in Monaco of all places, when his Lotus got away from him on a wet track. He was out, but the race was far from over as Alain Prost was being caught fast by Ayrton Senna's Toleman as conditions worsened, with Stefan Bellof catching both. The race was stopped just as Senna caught Prost.

BELGIAN GRAND PRIX

ZOLDER • ROUND 3 • DATE: 29TH APRIL 1984
Laps: 70 • Distance: 185.189miles/298.34km • Weather: Warm & bright

Pos	Driver	Team	Chassis-Engine	Result	Qual
1	Michele Alboreto	Ferrari	Ferrari 126C4	1h36m32.048s	1
2	Derek Warwick	Renault	Renault RE50	1h37m14.434s	4
3	Rene Arnoux	Ferrari	Ferrari 126C4	1h37m41.851s	2
4	Keke Rosberg	Williams	Williams-Honda FW09	69 laps/out of fuel	3
5	Elio de Angelis	Lotus	Lotus-Renault 95T	69 laps	5
DQ*	Stefan Bellof	Tyrrell	Tyrrell-Ford Cosworth 012	69 laps/illegal fuel	21
6	Ayrton Senna	Toleman	Toleman-Hart TG183B	68 laps	19
7	Patrick Tambay	Renault	Renault RE50	68 laps	12
8	Marc Surer	Arrows	Arrows-Ford Cosworth A6	68 laps	24
9	Nelson Piquet	Brabham	Brabham-BMW BT53	66 laps/engine	9
10	Jonathan Palmer	RAM Racing	RAM-Hart 02	64 laps	26
R	Mauro Baldi	Spirit	Spirit-Hart 101B	53 laps/suspension	25
DQ*	Martin Brundle	Tyrrell	Tyrrell-Ford Cosworth 012	51 laps/illegal fuel	22
R	Andrea de Cesaris	Ligier	Ligier-Renault JS23	42 laps/accident	13
R	Teo Fabi	Brabham	Brabham-BMW BT53	42 laps/spun off	18
R	Manfred Winkelhock	ATS	ATS-BMW D7	39 laps/exhaust	6
R	Niki Lauda	McLaren	McLaren-TAG MP4/2	35 laps/water pump	14
R	Eddie Cheever	Alfa Romeo	Alfa Romeo 184T	28 laps/engine	11
R	Jacques Laffite	Williams	Williams-Honda FW09	15 laps/electrical	15
R	Thierry Boutsen	Arrows	Arrows-BMW A7	15 laps/engine	17
R	Francois Hesnault	Ligier	Ligier-Renault JS23	15 laps/radiator damage	23
R	Nigel Mansell	Lotus	Lotus-Renault 95T	14 laps/clutch	10
R	Piercarlo Ghinzani	Osella	Osella-Alfa Romeo FA1F	14 laps/transmission	20
R	Alain Prost	McLaren	McLaren-TAG MP4/2	5 laps/distributor	8
R	Riccardo Patrese	Alfa Romeo	Alfa Romeo 184T	2 laps/ignition	7
R	Johnny Cecotto	Toleman	Toleman-Hart TG183B	1 lap/clutch	16
DNQ	Philippe Alliot	RAM Racing	RAM-Hart 02	-	27

Pole: Alboreto, 1m14.846s, 127.379mph/204.996kph. Fastest lap: Arnoux, 1m19.294s, 120.233mph/193.497kph on Lap 64. Race leaders: Alboreto 1-70

SAN MARINO GRAND PRIX

IMOLA • ROUND 4 • DATE: 6TH MAY 1984
Laps: 60 • Distance: 187.656miles/302.4km • Weather: Warm & bright

Pos	Driver	Team	Chassis-Engine	Result	Qual
1	Alain Prost	McLaren	McLaren-TAG MP4/2	1h36m53.679s	2
2	Rene Arnoux	Ferrari	Ferrari 126C4	1h37m07.095s	6
3	Elio de Angelis	Lotus	Lotus-Renault 95T	59 laps/out of fuel	11
4	Derek Warwick	Renault	Renault RE50	59 laps	4
DQ*	Stefan Bellof	Tyrrell	Tyrrell-Ford Cosworth 012	59 laps/illegal fuel	21
5	Thierry Boutsen	Arrows	Arrows-Ford Cosworth A6	59 laps	20
6	Andrea de Cesaris	Ligier	Ligier-Renault JS23	58 laps/out of fuel	12
7	Eddie Cheever	Alfa Romeo	Alfa Romeo 184T	58 laps/out of fuel	8
8	Mauro Baldi	Spirit	Spirit-Hart 101B	58 laps	24
9	Jonathan Palmer	RAM Racing	RAM-Hart 02	57 laps	25
DQ*	Martin Brundle	Tyrrell	Tyrrell-Ford Cosworth 012	55 laps/fuel feed	22
R	Philippe Alliot	RAM Racing	RAM-Hart 02	53 laps/turbo	23
NC	Johnny Cecotto	Toleman	Toleman-Hart TG183B	52 laps	19

Pos	Driver	Team	Chassis-Engine	Result	Qual
R	Nelson Piquet	Brabham	Brabham-BMW BT53	48 laps/turbo	1
R	Teo Fabi	Brabham	Brabham-BMW BT53	48 laps/turbo	9
R	Jo Gartner	Osella	Osella-Alfa Romeo FA1E	46 laps/engine	26
R	Marc Surer	Arrows	Arrows-BMW A7	40 laps/turbo	16
R	Manfred Winkelhock	ATS	ATS-BMW D7	31 laps/turbo	7
R	Michele Alboreto	Ferrari	Ferrari 126C4	23 laps/exhaust	13
R	Niki Lauda	McLaren	McLaren-TAG MP4/2	15 laps/engine	5
R	Jacques Laffite	Williams	Williams-Honda FW09	11 laps/engine	15
R	Riccardo Patrese	Alfa Romeo	Alfa Romeo 184T	6 laps/electrical	10
R	Keke Rosberg	Williams	Williams-Honda FW09	2 laps/electrical	3
R	Nigel Mansell	Lotus	Lotus-Renault 95T	2 laps/spun off	18
R	Patrick Tambay	Renault	Renault RE50	0 laps/collision	14
R	Francois Hesnault	Ligier	Ligier-Renault JS23	0 laps/collision	17
DNQ	Piercarlo Ghinzani	Osella	Osella-Alfa Romeo FA1F	-	27
DNQ	Ayrton Senna	Toleman	Toleman-Hart TG183B	-	28

Pole: Piquet, 1m28.517s, 127.367mph/204.977kph. Fastest lap: Piquet, 1m33.275s, 120.870mph/194.521kph on Lap 48. Race leaders: Prost 1-60

FRENCH GRAND PRIX

DIJON-PRENOIS • ROUND 5 • DATE: 20TH MAY 1984
Laps: 79 • Distance: 190.806miles/307.073km • Weather: Warm & bright

Pos	Driver	Team	Chassis-Engine	Result	Qual
1	Niki Lauda	McLaren	McLaren-TAG MP4/2	1h31m11.951s	9
2	Patrick Tambay	Renault	Renault RE50	1h31m19.105s	1
3	Nigel Mansell	Lotus	Lotus-Renault 95T	1h31m35.920s	6
4	Rene Arnoux	Ferrari	Ferrari 126C4	1h31m55.657s	11
5	Elio de Angelis	Lotus	Lotus-Renault 95T	1h32m18.076s	2
6	Keke Rosberg	Williams	Williams-Honda FW09	78 laps	4
7	Alain Prost	McLaren	McLaren-TAG MP4/2	78 laps	5
8	Jacques Laffite	Williams	Williams-Honda FW09	78 laps	12
9	Teo Fabi	Brabham	Brabham-BMW BT53	78 laps	17
10	Andrea de Cesaris	Ligier	Ligier-Renault JS23	77 laps	26
11	Thierry Boutsen	Arrows	Arrows-BMW A7	77 laps	14
DQ*	Martin Brundle	Tyrrell	Tyrrell-Ford Cosworth 012	76 laps/illegal fuel	23
12	Piercarlo Ghinzani	Osella	Osella-Alfa Romeo FA1F	74 laps	25
13	Jonathan Palmer	RAM Racing	RAM-Hart 02	72 laps	21
R	Mauro Baldi	Spirit	Spirit-Hart 101B	61 laps/engine	24
R	Derek Warwick	Renault	Renault RE50	53 laps/accident	7
R	Eddie Cheever	Alfa Romeo	Alfa Romeo 184T	51 laps/engine	16
R	Marc Surer	Arrows	Arrows-Ford Cosworth A6	51 laps/accident	19
R	Ayrton Senna	Toleman	Toleman-Hart TG184	35 laps/turbo	13
R	Michele Alboreto	Ferrari	Ferrari 126C4	33 laps/engine	10
R	Johnny Cecotto	Toleman	Toleman-Hart TG184	22 laps/turbo	18
R	Riccardo Patrese	Alfa Romeo	Alfa Romeo 184T	15 laps/engine	15
R	Nelson Piquet	Brabham	Brabham-BMW BT53	11 laps/turbo	3
DQ*	Stefan Bellof	Tyrrell	Tyrrell-Ford Cosworth 012	11 laps/engine noise	20
R	Manfred Winkelhock	ATS	ATS-BMW D7	5 laps/clutch	8
R	Philippe Alliot	RAM Racing	RAM-Hart 02	4 laps/electrical	22
NS	Francois Hesnault	Ligier	Ligier-Renault JS23	De Cesaris took car	-

Pole: Tambay, 1m02.200s, 139.790mph/224.971kph. Fastest lap: Prost, 1m05.257s, 133.241mph/214.432kph on Lap 59. Race leaders: Tambay 1-38 & 40 & 54-61, Lauda 39 & 41-53 & 62-79

MONACO GRAND PRIX

MONTE CARLO • ROUND 6 • DATE: 3RD JUNE 1984
Laps: 31 • Distance: 63.797miles/102.672km • Weather: Cool with heavy rain

Pos	Driver	Team	Chassis-Engine	Result	Qual
1	Alain Prost	McLaren	McLaren-TAG MP4/2	1h01m07.740s	1
2	Ayrton Senna	Toleman	Toleman-Hart TG184	1h01m15.186s	13
DQ*	Stefan Bellof	Tyrrell	Tyrrell-Ford Cosworth 012	31 laps/illegal fuel	20
3	Rene Arnoux	Ferrari	Ferrari 126C4	1h01m36.817s	3
4	Keke Rosberg	Williams	Williams-Honda FW09	1h01m42.986s	10
5	Elio de Angelis	Lotus	Lotus-Renault 95T	1h01m52.179s	11
6	Michele Alboreto	Ferrari	Ferrari 126C4	30 laps	4
7	Piercarlo Ghinzani	Osella	Osella-Alfa Romeo FA1F	30 laps	19
8	Jacques Laffite	Williams	Williams-Honda FW09	30 laps	16
R	Riccardo Patrese	Alfa Romeo	Alfa Romeo 184T	24 laps/steering	14
R	Niki Lauda	McLaren	McLaren-TAG MP4/2	23 laps/spun off	8
R	Manfred Winkelhock	ATS	ATS-BMW D7	22 laps/spun off	12
R	Nigel Mansell	Lotus	Lotus-Renault 95T	15 laps/spun off	2
R	Nelson Piquet	Brabham	Brabham-BMW BT53	14 laps/electrical	9
R	Francois Hesnault	Ligier	Ligier-Renault JS23	12 laps/electrical	17
R	Corrado Fabi	Brabham	Brabham-BMW BT53	9 laps/electrical	15
R	Johnny Cecotto	Toleman	Toleman-Hart TG184	1 lap/spun off	18
R	Andrea de Cesaris	Ligier	Ligier-Renault JS23	1 lap/accident	7
R	Derek Warwick	Renault	Renault RE50	0 laps/collision	5
R	Patrick Tambay	Renault	Renault RE50	0 laps/collision	6
DNQ	Marc Surer	Arrows	Arrows-Ford Cosworth A6	-	21
DNQ	Martin Brundle	Tyrrell	Tyrrell-Ford Cosworth 012	accident	22
DNQ	Eddie Cheever	Alfa Romeo	Alfa Romeo 184T	-	23
DNQ	Thierry Boutsen	Arrows	Arrows-BMW A7	-	24
DNQ	Jonathan Palmer	RAM Racing	RAM-Hart 02	-	25
DNQ	Mauro Baldi	Spirit	Spirit-Hart 101B	-	26
DNQ	Philippe Alliot	RAM Racing	RAM-Hart 02	-	27

Pole: Prost, 1m22.661s, 89.627mph/144.242kph. Fastest lap: Senna, 1m54.334s, 64.799mph/104.283kph on Lap 24. Race leaders: Prost 1-10 & 16-31, Mansell 11-15

TYRRELL GETS THROWN OUT

Stefan Bellof and Martin Brundle took third at Monaco and second at Detroit, but Tyrrell was excluded from the season after samples taken from a water tank at Detroit were found to contain lead balls that FISA declared to be movable ballast and/or illegal contaminants. Many felt it was because Tyrrell was blocking an increase in fuel allowance.

A SLIPPERY SURFACE

The Dallas GP was a disaster that was thankfully never repeated. The Fair Park circuit was a typical street circuit, surrounded by concrete barriers, and Brundle hit one in practice, breaking a leg and an ankle to end his season. In searing temperatures, the track surface broke up and Keke Rosberg won as his rivals slid into the walls.

CANADIAN GRAND PRIX

MONTREAL • ROUND 7 • DATE: 17TH JUNE 1984
Laps: 70 • Distance: 191.386miles/308.7km • Weather: Hot & bright

Pos	Driver	Team	Chassis-Engine	Result	Qual
1	Nelson Piquet	Brabham	Brabham-BMW BT53	1h46m23.748s	1
2	Niki Lauda	McLaren	McLaren-TAG MP4/2	1h46m26.360s	8
3	Alain Prost	McLaren	McLaren-TAG MP4/2	1h47m51.780s	2
4	Elio de Angelis	Lotus	Lotus-Renault 95T	69 laps	3
5	Rene Arnoux	Ferrari	Ferrari 126C4	68 laps	5
6	Nigel Mansell	Lotus	Lotus-Renault 95T	68 laps	7
7	Ayrton Senna	Toleman	Toleman-Hart TG184	68 laps	9
8	Manfred Winkelhock	ATS	ATS-BMW D7	68 laps	12
9	Johnny Cecotto	Toleman	Toleman-Hart TG184	68 laps	20
DQ*	Martin Brundle	Tyrrell	Tyrrell-Ford Cosworth 012	68 laps/illegal fuel	21
10	Philippe Alliot	RAM Racing	RAM-Hart 02	65 laps	26
11	Eddie Cheever	Alfa Romeo	Alfa Romeo 184T	63 laps/out of fuel	11
R	Marc Surer	Arrows	Arrows-Ford Cosworth A6	59 laps/engine	23
R	Derek Warwick	Renault	Renault RE50	57 laps/chassis	4
NC	Huub Rothengatter	Spirit	Spirit-Hart 101B	56 laps	24
DQ*	Stefan Bellof	Tyrrell	Tyrrell-Ford Cosworth 012	52 laps/driveshaft	22
R	Andrea de Cesaris	Ligier	Ligier-Renault JS23	40 laps/brakes	10
R	Corrado Fabi	Brabham	Brabham-BMW BT53	39 laps/turbo	16
R	Thierry Boutsen	Arrows	Arrows-BMW A7	38 laps/engine	18
R	Riccardo Patrese	Alfa Romeo	Alfa Romeo 184T	37 laps/accident	14
R	Keke Rosberg	Williams	Williams-Honda FW09	32 laps/fuel system	15
R	Jacques Laffite	Williams	Williams-Honda FW09	31 laps/turbo	17
R	Mike Thackwell	RAM Racing	RAM-Hart 02	29 laps/turbo	25
R	Piercarlo Ghinzani	Osella	Osella-Alfa Romeo FA1F	11 laps/gearbox	19
R	Michele Alboreto	Ferrari	Ferrari 126C4	10 laps/engine	6
R	Francois Hesnault	Ligier	Ligier-Renault JS23	7 laps/turbo	13
NS	Patrick Tambay	Renault	Renault RE50	leg injuries	-

Pole: Piquet, 1m25.442s, 115.457mph/185.810kph. Fastest lap: Piquet, 1m28.763s, 111.137mph/178.858kph on Lap 55. Race leaders: Piquet 1-70

DETROIT GRAND PRIX

DETROIT • ROUND 8 • DATE: 24TH JUNE 1984
Laps: 63 • Distance: 157.501miles/253.474km • Weather: Hot & bright

Pos	Driver	Team	Chassis-Engine	Result	Qual
1	Nelson Piquet	Brabham	Brabham-BMW BT53	1h55m41.842s	1
DQ*	Martin Brundle	Tyrrell	Tyrrell-Ford Cosworth 012	63 laps/illegal fuel	11
2	Elio de Angelis	Lotus	Lotus-Renault 95T	1h56m14.480s	5
3	Teo Fabi	Brabham	Brabham-BMW BT53	1h57m08.370s	23
4	Alain Prost	McLaren	McLaren-TAG MP4/2	1h57m37.100s	2
5	Jacques Laffite	Williams	Williams-Honda FW09	62 laps	19
R	Michele Alboreto	Ferrari	Ferrari 126C4	49 laps/engine	4
R	Keke Rosberg	Williams	Williams-Honda FW09	47 laps/turbo	21
R	Derek Warwick	Renault	Renault RE50	40 laps/gearbox	6
R	Patrick Tambay	Renault	Renault RE50	33 laps/transmission	9
R	Niki Lauda	McLaren	McLaren-TAG MP4/2	33 laps/electrical	10
R	Philippe Alliot	RAM Racing	RAM-Hart 02	33 laps/brakes	20
DQ*	Stefan Bellof	Tyrrell	Tyrrell-Ford Cosworth 012	33 laps/accident	16

Pos	Driver	Team	Chassis-Engine	Result	Qual
R	Nigel Mansell	Lotus	Lotus-Renault 95T	27 laps/gearbox	3
R	Thierry Boutsen	Arrows	Arrows-BMW A7	27 laps/engine	13
R	Andrea de Cesaris	Ligier	Ligier-Renault JS23	24 laps/overheating	12
R	Johnny Cecotto	Toleman	Toleman-Hart TG184	23 laps/clutch	17
R	Ayrton Senna	Toleman	Toleman-Hart TG184	21 laps/accident	7
R	Eddie Cheever	Alfa Romeo	Alfa Romeo 184T	21 laps/engine	8
R	Riccardo Patrese	Alfa Romeo	Alfa Romeo 184T	20 laps/spun off	25
R	Francois Hesnault	Ligier	Ligier-Renault JS23	3 laps/accident	18
R	Piercarlo Ghinzani	Osella	Osella-Alfa Romeo FA1F	3 laps/accident	26
R	Rene Arnoux	Ferrari	Ferrari 126C4	2 laps/accident	15
R	Jonathan Palmer	RAM Racing	RAM-Hart 02	2 laps/tyre	24
R	Manfred Winkelhock	ATS	ATS-BMW D7	0 laps/engine	14
R	Marc Surer	Arrows	Arrows-Ford Cosworth A6	0 laps/accident	22
DNQ	Huub Rothengatter	Spirit	Spirit-Ford Cosworth 101C	-	27

Pole: Piquet, 1m40.980s, 89.127mph/143.436kph. Fastest lap: Warwick, 1m46.221s, 84.729mph/136.359kph on Lap 32. Race leaders: Piquet 1-63

DALLAS GRAND PRIX

FAIR PARK • ROUND 9 • DATE: 8TH JULY 1984
Laps: 67 • Distance: 162.405miles/261.367km • Weather: Very hot & bright

Pos	Driver	Team	Chassis-Engine	Result	Qual
1	Keke Rosberg	Williams	Williams-Honda FW09	2h01m22.617s	8
2	Rene Arnoux	Ferrari	Ferrari 126C4	2h01m45.081s	4
3	Elio de Angelis	Lotus	Lotus-Renault 95T	66 laps	2
4	Jacques Laffite	Williams	Williams-Honda FW09	65 laps	25
5	Piercarlo Ghinzani	Osella	Osella-Alfa Romeo FA1F	65 laps	18
6	Nigel Mansell	Lotus	Lotus-Renault 95T	64 laps/gearbox	1
7	Corrado Fabi	Brabham	Brabham-BMW BT53	64 laps	11
8	Manfred Winkelhock	ATS	ATS-BMW D7	64 laps	13
R	Niki Lauda	McLaren	McLaren-TAG MP4/2	60 laps/spun off	5
R	Alain Prost	McLaren	McLaren-TAG MP4/2	56 laps/spun off	7
R	Thierry Boutsen	Arrows	Arrows-BMW A7	55 laps/spun off	20
R	Michele Alboreto	Ferrari	Ferrari 126C4	54 laps/spun off	9
R	Marc Surer	Arrows	Arrows-BMW A7	54 laps/spun off	22
R	Ayrton Senna	Toleman	Toleman-Hart TG184	47 laps/clutch	6
R	Jonathan Palmer	RAM Racing	RAM-Hart 02	46 laps/electrical	26
R	Nelson Piquet	Brabham	Brabham-BMW BT53	45 laps/spun off	12
R	Patrick Tambay	Renault	Renault RE50	25 laps/spun off	10
R	Johnny Cecotto	Toleman	Toleman-Hart TG184	25 laps/spun off	15
R	Andrea de Cesaris	Ligier	Ligier-Renault JS23	15 laps/spun off	16
R	Huub Rothengatter	Spirit	Spirit-Hart 101B	15 laps/oil leak	23
R	Riccardo Patrese	Alfa Romeo	Alfa Romeo 184T	12 laps/spun off	21
R	Derek Warwick	Renault	Renault RE50	10 laps/spun off	3
DQ*	Stefan Bellof	Tyrrell	Tyrrell-Ford Cosworth 012	9 laps/accident	17
R	Eddie Cheever	Alfa Romeo	Alfa Romeo 184T	8 laps/spun off	14
R	Francois Hesnault	Ligier	Ligier-Renault JS23	0 laps/accident	19
NS	Philippe Alliot	RAM Racing	RAM-Hart 02	Accident	24
DNQ	Martin Brundle	Tyrrell	Tyrrell-Ford Cosworth 012	Broken ankles	-

Pole: Mansell, 1m37.041s, 89.923mph/144.718kph. Fastest lap: Lauda, 1m45.353s, 82.829mph/133.300kph on Lap 22. Race leaders: Mansell 1-35, Rosberg 36-48 & 57-67, Prost 49-56

A CAREER CUT SHORT

A 350cc motorcycle World Champion before he turned to cars, Johnny Cecotto was better than his F1 record suggests, but he didn't get to complete his second year at the top level of four-wheeled motorsport as he crashed his Toleman in practice at Brands Hatch, which left him with leg and ankle injuries. The Venezuelan racer went on to become a touring car star.

ZOLDER BOWS OUT

Cramped Zolder was never a circuit loved by F1, from its introduction in 1973 while Spa-Francorchamps was out of favour, until this, its final hosting of the Belgian GP. The winner was Michele Alboreto for Ferrari and his win had special resonance as, incredibly, his was the first for an Italian driver since the 1966 Italian GP.

BRITISH GRAND PRIX

BRANDS HATCH • ROUND 10 • DATE: 22ND JULY 1984
Laps: 71 • Distance: 185.561miles/298.633km • Weather: Hot & bright

Pos	Driver	Team	Chassis-Engine	Result	Qual
1	Niki Lauda	McLaren	McLaren-TAG MP4/2	1h29m28.532s	3
2	Derek Warwick	Renault	Renault RE50	1h30m10.655s	6
3	Ayrton Senna	Toleman	Toleman-Hart TG184	1h30m31.860s	7
4	Elio de Angelis	Lotus	Lotus-Renault 95T	70 laps	4
5	Michele Alboreto	Ferrari	Ferrari 126C4	70 laps	9
6	Rene Arnoux	Ferrari	Ferrari 126C4	70 laps	13
7	Nelson Piquet	Brabham	Brabham-BMW BT53	70 laps	1
8	Patrick Tambay	Renault	Renault RE50	69 laps/turbo	10
9	Piercarlo Ghinzani	Osella	Osella-Alfa Romeo FA1F	68 laps	21
10	Andrea de Cesaris	Ligier	Ligier-Renault JS23	68 laps	19
DQ*	Stefan Bellof	Tyrrell	Tyrrell-Ford Cosworth 012	68 laps/illegal fuel	26
11	Marc Surer	Arrows	Arrows-BMW A7	67 laps	15
12	Riccardo Patrese	Alfa Romeo	Alfa Romeo 184T	66 laps/out of fuel	17
NC	Huub Rothengatter	Spirit	Spirit-Hart 101B	62 laps	22
R	Francois Hesnault	Ligier	Ligier-Renault JS23	43 laps/electrical	20
R	Alain Prost	McLaren	McLaren-TAG MP4/2	37 laps/gearbox	2
R	Nigel Mansell	Lotus	Lotus-Renault 95T	24 laps/gearbox	8
R	Thierry Boutsen	Arrows	Arrows-BMW A7	24 laps/electrical	12
R	Jacques Laffite	Williams	Williams-Honda FW09B	14 laps/water pump	16
R	Jonathan Palmer	RAM Racing	RAM-Hart 02	10 laps/accident	23
R	Teo Fabi	Brabham	Brabham-BMW BT53	9 laps/electrical	14
R	Manfred Winkelhock	ATS	ATS-BMW D7	8 laps/spun off	11
R	Keke Rosberg	Williams	Williams-Honda FW09B	5 laps/engine	5
R	Eddie Cheever	Alfa Romeo	Alfa Romeo 184T	1 lap/accident	18
DQ*	Stefan Johansson	Tyrrell	Tyrrell-Ford Cosworth 012	1 lap/accident	25
R	Philippe Alliot	RAM Racing	RAM-Hart 02	0 laps/accident	24
R	Jo Gartner	Osella	Osella-Alfa Romeo FA1F	0 laps/accident	27
DNQ	Johnny Cecotto	Toleman	Toleman-Hart TG184	Broken legs	-

Pole: Piquet, 1m10.869s, 132.762mph/213.661kph. Fastest lap: Lauda, 1m13.191s, 128.551mph/206.882kph on Lap 57. Race leaders: Piquet 1-11, Prost 12-37, Lauda 38-71

GERMAN GRAND PRIX

HOCKENHEIM • ROUND 11 • DATE: 5TH AUGUST 1984
Laps: 44 • Distance: 185.832miles/299.068km • Weather: Warm & bright

Pos	Driver	Team	Chassis-Engine	Result	Qual
1	Alain Prost	McLaren	McLaren-TAG MP4/2	1h24m43.210s	1
2	Niki Lauda	McLaren	McLaren-TAG MP4/2	1h24m46.359s	7
3	Derek Warwick	Renault	Renault RE50	1h25m19.633s	3
4	Nigel Mansell	Lotus	Lotus-Renault 95T	1h25m34.873s	16
5	Patrick Tambay	Renault	Renault RE50	1h25m55.159s	4
6	Rene Arnoux	Ferrari	Ferrari 126C4	43 laps	10
7	Andrea de Cesaris	Ligier	Ligier-Renault JS23	43 laps	11
8	Francois Hesnault	Ligier	Ligier-Renault JS23	43 laps	17
DQ*	Stefan Johansson	Tyrrell	Tyrrell-Ford Cosworth 012	42 laps/illegal fuel	26
9	Huub Rothengatter	Spirit	Spirit-Hart 101B	40 laps	24
R	Manfred Winkelhock	ATS	ATS-BMW D7	31 laps/gearbox	13
R	Eddie Cheever	Alfa Romeo	Alfa Romeo 184T	29 laps/engine	18
R	Teo Fabi	Brabham	Brabham-BMW BT53	28 laps/turbo	8
R	Nelson Piquet	Brabham	Brabham-BMW BT53	23 laps/gearbox	5
R	Riccardo Patrese	Alfa Romeo	Alfa Romeo 184T	16 laps/fuel system	20
R	Piercarlo Ghinzani	Osella	Osella-Alfa Romeo FA1F	14 laps/electrical	21
R	Michele Alboreto	Ferrari	Ferrari 126C4	13 laps/engine	6
R	Jo Gartner	Osella	Osella-Alfa Romeo FA1F	13 laps/turbo	23
R	Jonathan Palmer	RAM Racing	RAM-Hart 02	11 laps/turbo	25
R	Jacques Laffite	Williams	Williams-Honda FW09B	10 laps/engine	12
R	Keke Rosberg	Williams	Williams-Honda FW09B	10 laps/electrical	19
R	Elio de Angelis	Lotus	Lotus-Renault 95T	8 laps/turbo	2
R	Thierry Boutsen	Arrows	Arrows-BMW A7	8 laps/engine	15
R	Philippe Alliot	RAM Racing	RAM-Hart 02	7 laps/overheating	22
R	Ayrton Senna	Toleman	Toleman-Hart TG184	4 laps/accident	9
R	Marc Surer	Arrows	Arrows-BMW A7	1 lap/turbo	14
DNQ	Mike Thackwell	Tyrrell	Tyrrell-Ford Cosworth 012	-	27

Pole: Prost, 1m47.012s, 142.081mph/228.658kph. Fastest lap: Prost, 1m53.538s, 133.915mph/215.515kph on Lap 31. Race leaders: de Angelis 1-7, Piquet 8-21, Prost 22-44

AUSTRIAN GRAND PRIX

OSTERREICHRING • ROUND 12 • DATE: 19TH AUGUST 1984
Laps: 51 • Distance: 188.301miles/303.042km • Weather: Warm & bright

Pos	Driver	Team	Chassis-Engine	Result	Qual
1	Niki Lauda	McLaren	McLaren-TAG MP4/2	1h21m12.851s	4
2	Nelson Piquet	Brabham	Brabham-BMW BT53	1h21m36.376s	1
3	Michele Alboreto	Ferrari	Ferrari 126C4	1h22m01.849s	12
4	Teo Fabi	Brabham	Brabham-BMW BT53	1h22m09.163s	7
5	Thierry Boutsen	Arrows	Arrows-BMW A7	50 laps	17
6	Marc Surer	Arrows	Arrows-BMW A7	50 laps	19
7	Rene Arnoux	Ferrari	Ferrari 126C4	50 laps	15
8	Francois Hesnault	Ligier	Ligier-Renault JS23	49 laps	21
9	Jonathan Palmer	RAM Racing	RAM-Hart 02	49 laps	24
10	Riccardo Patrese	Alfa Romeo	Alfa Romeo 184T	48 laps/out of fuel	13
11	Philippe Alliot	RAM Racing	RAM-Hart 02	48 laps	25
12	Gerhard Berger	ATS	ATS-BMW D7	48 laps/gearbox	20
R	Patrick Tambay	Renault	Renault RE50	42 laps/engine	5

Pos	Driver	Team	Chassis-Engine	Result	Qual
R	Ayrton Senna	Toleman	Toleman-Hart TG184	35 laps/fuel pressure	10
R	Nigel Mansell	Lotus	Lotus-Renault 95T	32 laps/engine	8
R	Alain Prost	McLaren	McLaren-TAG MP4/2	28 laps/spun off	2
R	Elio de Angelis	Lotus	Lotus-Renault 95T	28 laps/engine	3
NC	Huub Rothengatter	Spirit	Spirit-Hart 101B	23 laps	26
R	Eddie Cheever	Alfa Romeo	Alfa Romeo 184T	18 laps/engine	16
R	Derek Warwick	Renault	Renault RE50	17 laps/engine	6
R	Keke Rosberg	Williams	Williams-Honda FW09B	15 laps/handling	9
R	Andrea de Cesaris	Ligier	Ligier-Renault JS23	15 laps/fuel injection	18
R	Jacques Laffite	Williams	Williams-Honda FW09B	12 laps/engine	11
R	Jo Gartner	Osella	Osella-Alfa Romeo FA1F	6 laps/engine	22
R	Piercarlo Ghinzani	Osella	Osella-Alfa Romeo FA1F	4 laps/gearbox	23
NS	Manfred Winkelhock	ATS	ATS-BMW D7	gearbox	14
DNQ	Stefan Johansson	Tyrrell	Tyrrell-Ford Cosworth 012	-	27
EX	Stefan Bellof	Tyrrell	Tyrrell-Ford Cosworth 012	car underweight	28

Pole: Piquet, 1m26.173s, 154.246mph/248.235kph. Fastest lap: Lauda, 1m32.882s, 143.104mph/230.305kph on Lap 23. Race leaders: Piquet 1-39, Lauda 40-51

BEING CONSISTENT PAYS

With McLaren winning 12 of the season's 16 grands prix, the best that Elio de Angelis could hope for was to be the best of the rest as he led the Lotus charge. Even though he didn't claim one of the other four wins – they went to Alboreto, Nelson Piquet (twice) and Keke Rosberg – he was so consistent that he ended up third.

DUTCH GRAND PRIX

ZANDVOORT • ROUND 13 • DATE: 26TH AUGUST 1984
Laps: 71 • Distance: 187.586miles/301.892km • Weather: Warm & bright

Pos	Driver	Team	Chassis-Engine	Result	Qual
1	Alain Prost	McLaren	McLaren-TAG MP4/2	1h37m21.468s	1
2	Niki Lauda	McLaren	McLaren-TAG MP4/2	1h37m31.751s	6
3	Nigel Mansell	Lotus	Lotus-Renault 95T	1h38m41.012s	12
4	Elio de Angelis	Lotus	Lotus-Renault 95T	70 laps	3
5	Teo Fabi	Brabham	Brabham-BMW BT53	70 laps	10
6	Patrick Tambay	Renault	Renault RE50	70 laps	5
7	Francois Hesnault	Ligier	Ligier-Renault JS23	69 laps	20
DQ*	Stefan Bellof	Tyrrell	Tyrrell-Ford Cosworth 012	69 laps/illegal fuel	24
DQ*	Stefan Johansson	Tyrrell	Tyrrell-Ford Cosworth 012	69 laps/illegal fuel	25
8	Keke Rosberg	Williams	Williams-Honda FW09B	68 laps/out of fuel	7
9	Jonathan Palmer	RAM Racing	RAM-Hart 02	67 laps	22
10	Philippe Alliot	RAM Racing	RAM-Hart 02	67 laps	26
11	Rene Arnoux	Ferrari	Ferrari 126C4	66 laps/electrical	15
12	Jo Gartner	Osella	Osella-Alfa Romeo FA1F	66 laps	23
13	Eddie Cheever	Alfa Romeo	Alfa Romeo 184T	65 laps/out of fuel	17
R	Thierry Boutsen	Arrows	Arrows-BMW A7	59 laps/accident	11
R	Huub Rothengatter	Spirit	Spirit-Hart 101B	53 laps/throttle	27
R	Riccardo Patrese	Alfa Romeo	Alfa Romeo 184T	51 laps/engine	18

Pos	Driver	Team	Chassis-Engine	Result	Qual
R	Andrea de Cesaris	Ligier	Ligier-Renault JS23	31 laps/engine	14
R	Derek Warwick	Renault	Renault RE50	23 laps/spun off	4
R	Jacques Laffite	Williams	Williams-Honda FW09B	23 laps/engine	8
R	Manfred Winkelhock	ATS	ATS-BMW D7	22 laps/spun off	16
R	Ayrton Senna	Toleman	Toleman-Hart TG184	19 laps/engine	13
R	Marc Surer	Arrows	Arrows-BMW A7	17 laps/wheel	19
R	Nelson Piquet	Brabham	Brabham-BMW BT53	10 laps/fuel pressure	2
R	Piercarlo Ghinzani	Osella	Osella-Alfa Romeo FA1F	8 laps/fuel pump	21
R	Michele Alboreto	Ferrari	Ferrari 126C4	7 laps/engine	9

Pole: Prost, 1m13.567s, 129.289mph/208.071kph. Fastest lap: Arnoux, 1m19.465s, 119.693mph/192.628kph on Lap 64. Race leaders: Piquet 1-10, Prost 11-71

NO STOPS, NO FINISH?

Refuelling pit stops were banned on safety grounds and this led to panic among the teams and several drivers coasting before they reached the finish as their engines weren't efficient enough to go the distance unless the drivers backed off. At the European GP, the cars heading for second and third places ran out of fuel on the dash to the line.

NEW CIRCUITS

Far more impressive than the fiasco at Dallas was the introduction of Estoril to host the first World Championship Portuguese GP since 1960. This was a proper circuit for the championship shoot-out between the McLaren drivers. And the Nurburgring was back for the first time since 1976, not just modernised, but cut from 14.189 to 2.822 miles (22.799 to 4.541km).

ITALIAN GRAND PRIX

MONZA • ROUND 14 • DATE: 9TH SEPTEMBER 1984
Laps: 51 • Distance: 183.309miles/295.8km • Weather: Hot & bright

Pos	Driver	Team	Chassis-Engine	Result	Qual
1	Niki Lauda	McLaren	McLaren-TAG MP4/2	1h20m29.065s	4
2	Michele Alboreto	Ferrari	Ferrari 126C4	1h20m53.314s	11
3	Riccardo Patrese	Alfa Romeo	Alfa Romeo 184T	50 laps	9
4	Stefan Johansson	Toleman	Toleman-Hart TG184	49 laps	17
5	Jo Gartner*	Osella	Osella-Alfa Romeo FA1F	49 laps	24
6	Gerhard Berger*	ATS	ATS-BMW D7	49 laps	20
7	Piercarlo Ghinzani	Osella	Osella-Alfa Romeo FA1F	48 laps/out of fuel	22
8	Huub Rothengatter	Spirit	Spirit-Hart 101B	48 laps	25
9	Eddie Cheever	Alfa Romeo	Alfa Romeo 184T	45 laps/out of fuel	10
10	Thierry Boutsen	Arrows	Arrows-BMW A7	45 laps	19
R	Teo Fabi	Brabham	Brabham-BMW BT53	43 laps/engine	5
R	Patrick Tambay	Renault	Renault RE50	43 laps/throttle	8
R	Marc Surer	Arrows	Arrows-BMW A7	43 laps/engine	15

Pos	Driver	Team	Chassis-Engine	Result	Qual
R	Derek Warwick	Renault	Renault RE50	31 laps/fuel pressure	12
R	Jonathan Palmer	RAM Racing	RAM-Hart 02	20 laps/fuel pressure	26
R	Nelson Piquet	Brabham	Brabham-BMW BT53	15 laps/engine	1
R	Elio de Angelis	Lotus	Lotus-Renault 95T	14 laps/gearbox	3
R	Nigel Mansell	Lotus	Lotus-Renault 95T	13 laps/spun off	7
R	Jacques Laffite	Williams	Williams-Honda FW09B	10 laps/turbo	13
R	Keke Rosberg	Williams	Williams-Honda FW09B	8 laps/turbo	6
R	Andrea de Cesaris	Ligier	Ligier-Renault JS23	7 laps/engine	16
R	Francois Hesnault	Ligier	Ligier-Renault JS23	7 laps/spun off	18
R	Philippe Alliot	RAM Racing	RAM-Hart 02	6 laps/electrical	23
R	Rene Arnoux	Ferrari	Ferrari 126C4	5 laps/gearbox	14
R	Alain Prost	McLaren	McLaren-TAG MP4/2	3 laps/engine	2
NS	Manfred Winkelhock	ATS	ATS-BMW D7	gearbox	21
DNQ	Pierluigi Martini	Toleman	Toleman-Hart TG184	-	27

*ineligible for points, not entered in the World Championship

Pole: Piquet, 1m26.584s, 149.845mph/241.153kph. Fastest lap: Lauda, 1m31.912s, 141.159mph/227.173kph on Lap 42. Race leaders: Piquet 1-15, Tambay 16-42, Lauda 43-51

EUROPEAN GRAND PRIX

NURBURGRING • ROUND 15 • DATE: 7TH OCTOBER 1984
Laps: 67 • Distance: 189.91miles/304.314km • Weather: Cold & dull

Pos	Driver	Team	Chassis-Engine	Result	Qual
1	Alain Prost	McLaren	McLaren-TAG MP4/2	1h35m13.284s	2
2	Michele Alboreto	Ferrari	Ferrari 126C4	1h35m37.195s	5
3	Nelson Piquet	Brabham	Brabham-BMW BT53	1h35m38.206s	1
4	Niki Lauda	McLaren	McLaren-TAG MP4/2	1h35m56.370s	15
5	Rene Arnoux	Ferrari	Ferrari 126C4	1h36m14.714s	6
6	Riccardo Patrese	Alfa Romeo	Alfa Romeo 184T	66 laps	9
7	Andrea de Cesaris	Ligier	Ligier-Renault JS23	65 laps	17
8	Mauro Baldi	Spirit	Spirit-Hart 101B	65 laps	24
9	Thierry Boutsen	Arrows	Arrows-BMW A7	64 laps/ignition	11
10	Francois Hesnault	Ligier	Ligier-Renault JS23	64 laps	19
11	Derek Warwick	Renault	Renault RE50	61 laps/overheating	7
R	Jo Gartner	Osella	Osella-Alfa Romeo FA1F	60 laps/fuel system	22
R	Teo Fabi	Brabham	Brabham-BMW BT53	57 laps/gearbox	10
R	Nigel Mansell	Lotus	Lotus-Renault 95T	51 laps/engine	8
R	Patrick Tambay	Renault	Renault RE50	47 laps/fuel system	3
R	Eddie Cheever	Alfa Romeo	Alfa Romeo 184T	37 laps/fuel pump	13
R	Philippe Alliot	RAM Racing	RAM-Hart 02	37 laps/turbo	25
R	Jonathan Palmer	RAM Racing	RAM-Hart 02	35 laps/turbo	21
R	Jacques Laffite	Williams	Williams-Honda FW09B	27 laps/engine	14
R	Elio de Angelis	Lotus	Lotus-Renault 95T	25 laps/turbo	23
R	Stefan Johansson	Toleman	Toleman-Hart TG184	17 laps/overheating	26
R	Keke Rosberg	Williams	Williams-Honda FW09B	0 laps/accident	4
R	Ayrton Senna	Toleman	Toleman-Hart TG184	0 laps/accident	12
R	Marc Surer	Arrows	Arrows-BMW A7	0 laps/accident	16
R	Gerhard Berger	ATS	ATS-BMW D7	0 laps/accident	18
R	Piercarlo Ghinzani	Osella	Osella-Alfa Romeo FA1F	0 laps/accident	20

Pole: Piquet, 1m18.871s, 128.820mph/207.315kph. Fastest lap: Alboreto, 1m23.146s, 122.196mph/196.656kph on Lap 62 & Piquet, 1m23.146s, 122.196mph/196.656kph on Lap 62. Race leaders: Prost 1-67

PORTUGUESE GRAND PRIX

AUTODROMO DO ESTORIL • ROUND 16 • DATE: 21ST OCTOBER 1984
Laps: 70 • Distance: 188.899miles/304.5km • Weather: Hot & bright

Pos	Driver	Team	Chassis-Engine	Result	Qual
1	Alain Prost	McLaren	McLaren-TAG MP4/2	1h41m11.753s	2
2	Niki Lauda	McLaren	McLaren-TAG MP4/2	1h41m25.178s	11
3	Ayrton Senna	Toleman	Toleman-Hart TG184	1h41m31.795s	3
4	Michele Alboreto	Ferrari	Ferrari 126C4	1h41m32.070s	8
5	Elio de Angelis	Lotus	Lotus-Renault 95T	1h42m43.922s	5
6	Nelson Piquet	Brabham	Brabham-BMW BT53	69 laps	1
7	Patrick Tambay	Renault	Renault RE50	69 laps	7
8	Riccardo Patrese	Alfa Romeo	Alfa Romeo 184T	69 laps	12
9	Rene Arnoux	Ferrari	Ferrari 126C4	69 laps	17
10	Manfred Winkelhock	Brabham	Brabham-BMW BT53	69 laps	19
11	Stefan Johansson	Toleman	Toleman-Hart TG184	69 laps	10
12	Andrea de Cesaris	Ligier	Ligier-Renault JS23	69 laps	20
13	Gerhard Berger	ATS	ATS-BMW D7	68 laps	23
14	Jacques Laffite	Williams	Williams-Honda FW09B	67 laps	15
15	Mauro Baldi	Spirit	Spirit-Hart 101B	66 laps	25
16	Jo Gartner	Osella	Osella-Alfa Romeo FA1F	65 laps/out of fuel	24
17	Eddie Cheever	Alfa Romeo	Alfa Romeo 184T	64 laps	14
R	Piercarlo Ghinzani	Osella	Osella-Alfa Romeo FA1F	60 laps/engine	22
R	Nigel Mansell	Lotus	Lotus-Renault 95T	52 laps/spun off	6
R	Derek Warwick	Renault	Renault RE50	51 laps/gearbox	9
R	Philippe Streiff	Renault	Renault RE50	48 laps/transmission	13
R	Keke Rosberg	Williams	Williams-Honda FW09B	39 laps/engine	4
R	Francois Hesnault	Ligier	Ligier-Renault JS23	31 laps/electrical	21
R	Thierry Boutsen	Arrows	Arrows-BMW A7	24 laps/transmission	18
R	Jonathan Palmer	RAM Racing	RAM-Hart 02	19 laps/gearbox	26
R	Marc Surer	Arrows	Arrows-BMW A7	8 laps/electrical	16
R	Philippe Alliot	RAM Racing	RAM-Hart 02	2 laps/engine	27

Pole: Piquet, 1m21.703s, 119.098mph/191.669kph. Fastest lap: Lauda, 1m22.996s, 117.242mph/188.683kph on Lap 51. Race leaders: Rosberg 1-8, Prost 9-70

NEW DRIVERS

Senna aside, Tyrrell drivers Bellof and Brundle also both took podium finishes for Tyrrell before those results were expunged. Of the seven other F1 novices, Austrian pair Jo Gartner and Gerhard Berger took a fifth and a sixth for Osella and ATS respectively, although neither scored points as they were not entered in the World Championship, while Phillipe Hesnault bagged a seventh for Ligier, and Huub Rothengatter an eighth for Spirit.

WORLD DRIVERS' CHAMPIONSHIP FINAL RESULTS

Pos	Driver	Nat	Car-Engine	R1	R2	R3	R4	R5	R6
1	Niki Lauda	AUT	McLaren-TAG MP4/2	R	1	R	R	1	R
2	Alain Prost	FRA	McLaren-TAG MP4/2	1F	2	R	1	7F	1P
3	Elio de Angelis	ITA	Lotus-Renault 95T	3P	7	5	3	5	5
4	Michele Alboreto	ITA	Ferrari 126C4	R	11	1P	R	R	6
5	Nelson Piquet	BRA	Brabham-BMW BT53	R	RP	9	RPF	R	R
6	Rene Arnoux	FRA	Ferrari 126C4	R	R	3F	2	4	3
7	Derek Warwick	GBR	Renault RE50	R	3	2	4	R	R
8	Keke Rosberg	FIN	Williams-Honda FW09	2	R	4	R	6	4
			Williams-Honda FW09B	-	-	-	-	-	-
9	Ayrton Senna	BRA	Toleman-Hart TG183B	R	6	6	DNQ	-	-
			Toleman-Hart TG184	-	-	-	-	R	2F
10	Nigel Mansell	GBR	Lotus-Renault 95T	R	R	R	R	3	R
11	Patrick Tambay	FRA	Renault RE50	5	RF	7	R	2P	R
12	Teo Fabi	ITA	Brabham-BMW BT53	R	R	R	R	9	-
13	Riccardo Patrese	ITA	Alfa Romeo 184T	R	4	R	R	R	R
14	Jacques Laffite	FRA	Williams-Honda FW09	R	R	R	R	8	8
			Williams-Honda FW09B	-	-	-	-	-	-
15	Thierry Boutsen	BEL	Arrows-Ford Cosworth A6	6	12	-	5	-	-
			Arrows-BMW A7	-	-	R	-	11	DNQ
16	Eddie Cheever	USA	Alfa Romeo 184T	4	R	R	7	R	DNQ
16	Stefan Johansson	SWE	Tyrrell-Ford Cosworth 012	-	-	-	-	-	-
			Toleman-Hart TG184	-	-	-	-	-	-
18	Andrea de Cesaris	ITA	Ligier-Renault JS23	R	5	R	6	10	R
19	Piercarlo Ghinzani	ITA	Osella-Alfa Romeo FA1F	R	NS	R	DNQ	12	7
20	Marc Surer	CHE	Arrows-Ford Cosworth A6	7	9	8	-	R	DNQ
			Arrows-BMW A7	-	-	-	R	-	-

Pos	Driver	R7	R8	R9	R10	R11	R12	R13	R14	R15	R16	Total
1	Lauda	2	R	RF	1F	2	1F	2	1F	4	2F	72
2	Prost	3	4	R	R	1PF	R	1P	R	1	1	71.5
3	de Angelis	4	2	3	4	R	R	4	R	R	5	34
4	Alboreto	R	R	R	5	R	3	R	2	2F	4	30.5
5	Piquet	1PF	1P	R	7P	R	2P	R	RP	3PF	6P	29
6	Arnoux	5	R	2	6	6	7	11F	R	5	9	27
7	Warwick	R	RF	R	2	3	R	R	R	11	R	23
8	Rosberg	R	R	1	-	-	-	-	-	-	-	20.5
		-	-	-	R	R	R	8	R	R	R	
9	Senna	-	-	-	-	-	-	-	-	-	-	13
		7	R	R	3	R	R	R	-	R	3	
10	Mansell	6	R	6P	R	4	R	3	R	R	R	13
11	Tambay	NS	R	R	8	5	R	6	R	R	7	11
12	Fabi	-	3	-	R	R	4	5	R	R	-	9
13	Patrese	R	R	R	12	R	10	R	3	6	8	8
14	Laffite	R	5	4	-	-	-	-	-	-	-	5
		-	-	-	R	R	R	R	R	R	14	
15	Boutsen	-	-	-	-	-	-	-	-	-	-	5
		R	R	R	R	R	5	R	10	9	R	
16	Cheever	11	R	R	R	R	R	13	9	R	17	3
16	Johansson	-	-	-	DQ	DQ	DNQ	DQ	-	-	-	3
		-	-	-	-	-	-	-	4	R	11	
18	de Cesaris	R	R	R	10	7	R	R	R	7	12	3
19	Ghinzani	R	R	5	9	R	R	R	7	R	R	2
20	Surer	R	R	-	-	-	-	-	-	-	-	1
		-	-	R	11	R	6	R	R	R	R	

WORLD CONSTRUCTORS' CHAMPIONSHIP FINAL RESULTS

Pos	Team-Engine	R1	R2	R3	R4	R5	R6	R7	R8
1	McLaren-TAG	1/R	1/2	R/R	1/R	1/7	1/R	2/3	4/R
2	Ferrari	R/R	11/R	1/3	2/R	4/R	3/6	5/R	R/R
3	Lotus-Renault	3/R	7/R	5/R	3/R	3/5	5/R	4/6	2/R
4	Brabham-BMW	R/R	R/R	9/R	R/R	9/R	R/R	1/R	1/3
5	Renault	5/R	3/R	2/7	4/R	2/R	R/R	R/NS	R/R
6	Williams-Honda	2/R	R/R	4/R	R/R	6/8	4/8	R/R	5/R
7	Toleman-Hart	R/R	6/R	6/R	NC/DNQ	R/R	2/R	7/9	R/R
8	Alfa Romeo	4/R	4/R	R/R	7/R	R/R	R/DNQ	11/R	R/R
9	Ligier-Renault	R/R	5/10	R/R	6/R	10/NS	R/R	R/R	R/R
9	Arrows-Ford	6/7	9/12	8	5	R	DNQ	R	R
9	Arrows-BMW	-/-	-/-	R	R	11	DNQ	R	R
12	Osella-Alfa Romeo	R	NS	R	R/DNQ	12	7	R	R

Pos	Team-Engine	R9	R10	R11	R12	R13	R14	R15	R16	Total
1	McLaren-TAG	R/R	1/R	1/2	1/R	1/2	1/R	1/4	1/2	143.5
2	Ferrari	2/R	5/6	6/R	3/7	11/R	2/R	2/5	4/9	57.5
3	Lotus-Renault	3/6	4/R	4/R	R/R	3/4	R/R	R/R	5/R	47
4	Brabham-BMW	7/R	7/R	R/R	2/4	5/R	R/R	3/R	6/10	38
5	Renault	R/R	2/8	3/5	R/R	6/R	R/R	11/R	7/R/R	34
6	Williams-Honda	1/4	R/R	R/R	R/R	8/R	R/R	R/R	14/R	25.5
7	Toleman-Hart	R/R	3/DNQ	R	R	R	4/DNQ	R/R	3/11	16
8	Alfa Romeo	R/R	12/R	R/R	10/R	13/R	3/9	6/R	8/17	11
9	Ligier-Renault	R/R	10/R	7/8	8/R	7/R	R/R	7/10	12/R	3
9	Arrows-Ford	-/-	-/-	-/-	-/-	-/-	-/-	-/-	-/-	3
9	Arrows-BMW	R/R	11/R	R/R	5/6	R/R	10/R	9/R	R/R	3
12	Osella-Alfa Romeo	5	9/R	R/R	R/R	12/R	5/7	R/R	16/R	2

*Tyrrell was adjudged to have used illegal fuel in the first 9 rounds and so had their 13 points removed and were barred from competing after the Dutch GP.

SYMBOLS AND GRAND PRIX KEY

Round 1 **Brazilian GP**
Round 2 **South African GP**
Round 3 **Belgian GP**
Round 4 **San Marino GP**
Round 5 **French GP**
Round 6 **Monaco GP**
Round 7 **Canadian GP**
Round 8 **Detroit GP**
Round 9 **Dallas GP**
Round 10 **British GP**
Round 11 **German GP**
Round 12 **Austrian GP**
Round 13 **Dutch GP**
Round 14 **Italian GP**
Round 15 **European GP**
Round 16 **Portuguese GP**

SCORING

1st **9 points**
2nd **6 points**
3rd **4 points**
4th **3 points**
5th **2 points**
6th **1 point**

DNPQ DID NOT PRE-QUALIFY **DNQ DID NOT QUALIFY** **DQ DISQUALIFIED** **EX EXCLUDED**
F FASTEST LAP **NC NOT CLASSIFIED** **NS NON-STARTER** **P POLE POSITION** **R RETIRED**

1985

SEASON SUMMARY

Alain Prost dominated the 1985 season to become France's first world champion. Having been pipped in both of the previous two seasons, he controlled this campaign and easily outscored his illustrious McLaren team-mate Niki Lauda. Michele Alboreto gave Ferrari hope, but a run of retirements left him short. The biggest talent for the years ahead showed his hand at Estoril, as Ayrton Senna became a winner in his second race for Lotus. He became the team's lead driver as he won again at Spa, to outscore Elio de Angelis. Then Nigel Mansell ended the year with a bang as he won two of the last three races for Williams.

BRAZILIAN GRAND PRIX

JACAREPAGUA • ROUND 1 • DATE: 7TH APRIL 1985
Laps: 61 • Distance: 190.693miles/306.891km • Weather: Hot & bright

Pos	Driver	Team	Chassis-Engine	Result	Qual
1	Alain Prost	McLaren	McLaren-TAG MP4/2B	1h41m26.115s	6
2	Michele Alboreto	Ferrari	Ferrari 156/85	1h41m29.374s	1
3	Elio de Angelis	Lotus	Lotus-Renault 97T	60 laps	3
4	Rene Arnoux	Ferrari	Ferrari 156/85	59 laps	7
5	Patrick Tambay	Renault	Renault RE60	59 laps	11
6	Jacques Laffite	Ligier	Ligier-Renault JS25	59 laps	15
7	Stefan Johansson	Tyrrell	Tyrrell-Ford Cosworth 012	58 laps	23
8	Martin Brundle	Tyrrell	Tyrrell-Ford Cosworth 012	58 laps	21
9	Philippe Alliot	RAM Racing	RAM-Hart 03	58 laps	20
10	Derek Warwick	Renault	Renault RE60	57 laps	10
11	Thierry Boutsen	Arrows	Arrows-BMW A8	57 laps	12
12	Piercarlo Ghinzani	Osella	Osella-Alfa Romeo FA1F	57 laps	22
13	Manfred Winkelhock	RAM Racing	RAM-Hart 03	57 laps	16
R	Gerhard Berger	Arrows	Arrows-BMW A8	51 laps/suspension	19
R	Ayrton Senna	Lotus	Lotus-Renault 97T	48 laps/electrical	4
R	Eddie Cheever	Alfa Romeo	Alfa Romeo 185T	42 laps/engine	18
R	Pierluigi Martini	Minardi	Minardi-Motori Moderni M185	41 laps/engine	25
R	Niki Lauda	McLaren	McLaren-TAG MP4/2B	27 laps/fuel system	9
R	Andrea de Cesaris	Ligier	Ligier-Renault JS25	26 laps/accident	13
R	Riccardo Patrese	Alfa Romeo	Alfa Romeo 185T	20 laps/puncture	14
R	Keke Rosberg	Williams	Williams-Honda FW10	10 laps/turbo	2
R	Francois Hesnault	Brabham	Brabham-BMW BT54	9 laps/accident	17
R	Nigel Mansell	Williams	Williams-Honda FW10	8 laps/exhaust	5
R	Mauro Baldi	Spirit	Spirit-Hart 101D	7 laps/turbo	24
R	Nelson Piquet	Brabham	Brabham-BMW BT54	2 laps/transmission	8

Pole: Alboreto, 1m27.768s, 128.224mph/206.357kph. Fastest lap: Prost, 1m36.702s, 116.378mph/187.292kph on Lap 34. Race leaders: Rosberg 1-9, Alboreto 10-17, Prost 18-61

SENNA MAKES A SPLASH

Ayrton Senna was the first to admit that he rode his luck in the Portuguese GP at a very wet Estoril to take his first F1 win. Certainly, he survived a slide across the grass in his Lotus, but his speed was so astonishing as his rivals fumbled that he won by more than a minute from Alboreto's Ferrari, with no other cars on the lead lap.

PORTUGUESE GRAND PRIX

AUTODROMO DO ESTORIL • ROUND 2 • DATE: 21ST APRIL 1985
Laps: 67 • Distance: 180.846miles/291.45km • Weather: Cold with heavy rain

Pos	Driver	Team	Chassis-Engine	Result	Qual
1	Ayrton Senna	Lotus	Lotus-Renault 97T	2h00m28.006s	1
2	Michele Alboreto	Ferrari	Ferrari 156/85	2h01m30.984s	5
3	Patrick Tambay	Renault	Renault RE60	66 laps	12
4	Elio de Angelis	Lotus	Lotus-Renault 97T	66 laps	4
5	Nigel Mansell	Williams	Williams-Honda FW10	65 laps	9
6	Stefan Bellof	Tyrrell	Tyrrell-Ford Cosworth 012	65 laps	21
7	Derek Warwick	Renault	Renault RE60	65 laps	6
8	Stefan Johansson	Ferrari	Ferrari 156/85	62 laps	11
9	Piercarlo Ghinzani	Osella	Osella-Alfa Romeo FA1F	61 laps	26
NC	Manfred Winkelhock	RAM Racing	RAM-Hart 03	50 laps	15
R	Niki Lauda	McLaren	McLaren-TAG MP4/2B	49 laps/engine	7
R	Eddie Cheever	Alfa Romeo	Alfa Romeo 185T	36 laps/engine	14
R	Alain Prost	McLaren	McLaren-TAG MP4/2B	30 laps/spun off	2
R	Andrea de Cesaris	Ligier	Ligier-Renault JS25	29 laps/tyre	8
R	Nelson Piquet	Brabham	Brabham-BMW BT54	28 laps/tyre	10
R	Thierry Boutsen	Arrows	Arrows-BMW A8	28 laps/electrical	16
R	Martin Brundle	Tyrrell	Tyrrell-Ford Cosworth 012	20 laps/transmission	22
R	Mauro Baldi	Spirit	Spirit-Hart 101D	19 laps/spun off	24
R	Keke Rosberg	Williams	Williams-Honda FW10	16 laps/spun off	3
R	Jacques Laffite	Ligier	Ligier-Renault JS25	15 laps/tyre	18
R	Gerhard Berger	Arrows	Arrows-BMW A8	12 laps/spun off	17
R	Pierluigi Martini	Minardi	Minardi-Motori Moderni M185	12 laps/spun off	25
R	Riccardo Patrese	Alfa Romeo	Alfa Romeo 185T	4 laps/spun off	13
R	Francois Hesnault	Brabham	Brabham-BMW BT54	3 laps/electrical	19
R	Philippe Alliot	RAM Racing	RAM-Hart 03	3 laps/spun off	20
R	Jonathan Palmer	Zakspeed	Zakspeed 841	2 laps/suspension	23

Pole: Senna, 1m21.007s, 120.121mph/193.316kph. Fastest lap: Senna, 1m44.121s, 93.455mph/150.401kph on Lap 15. Race leaders: Senna 1-67

RENAULT BOWS OUT

People didn't know what to expect when Renault introduced turbocharged engines to F1 in 1977. They became more competitive and race wins followed. But, despite Derek Warwick and Patrick Tambay's best efforts, there were no titles for the works team and it closed at the end of 1985 to focus on being an engine supplier.

SAN MARINO GRAND PRIX

IMOLA • ROUND 3 • DATE: 5TH MAY 1985
Laps: 60 • Distance: 187.656miles/302.4km • Weather: Warm & bright

Pos	Driver	Team	Chassis-Engine	Result	Qual
DQ	Alain Prost	McLaren	McLaren-TAG MP4/2B	60 laps/car underweight	6
1	Elio de Angelis	Lotus	Lotus-Renault 97T	1h34m35.955s	3
2	Thierry Boutsen	Arrows	Arrows-BMW A8	59 laps	5
3	Patrick Tambay	Renault	Renault RE60	59 laps	11
4	Niki Lauda	McLaren	McLaren-TAG MP4/2B	59 laps	8
5	Nigel Mansell	Williams	Williams-Honda FW10	58 laps	7
6	Stefan Johansson	Ferrari	Ferrari 156/85	57 laps/out of fuel	15
7	Ayrton Senna	Lotus	Lotus-Renault 97T	57 laps/out of fuel	1
8	Nelson Piquet	Brabham	Brabham-BMW BT54	57 laps/out of fuel	9
9	Martin Brundle	Tyrrell	Tyrrell-Ford Cosworth 012	56 laps	25
10	Derek Warwick	Renault	Renault RE60	56 laps	14
R	Eddie Cheever	Alfa Romeo	Alfa Romeo 185T	50 laps/engine	12
NC	Piercarlo Ghinzani	Osella	Osella-Alfa Romeo FA1G	46 laps	22
R	Michele Alboreto	Ferrari	Ferrari 156/85	29 laps/electrical	4
R	Manfred Winkelhock	RAM Racing	RAM-Hart 03	27 laps/engine	23
R	Philippe Alliot	RAM Racing	RAM-Hart 03	24 laps/engine	21
R	Keke Rosberg	Williams	Williams-Honda FW10	23 laps/brakes	2
R	Jacques Laffite	Ligier	Ligier-Renault JS25	22 laps/turbo	16
R	Pierluigi Martini	Minardi	Minardi-Motori Moderni M185	14 laps/turbo	19
R	Andrea de Cesaris	Ligier	Ligier-Renault JS25	11 laps/spun off	13
R	Mauro Baldi	Spirit	Spirit-Hart 101D	9 laps/electrical	26
R	Francois Hesnault	Brabham	Brabham-BMW BT54	5 laps/engine	20
R	Stefan Bellof	Tyrrell	Tyrrell-Ford Cosworth 012	5 laps/engine	24
R	Gerhard Berger	Arrows	Arrows-BMW A8	4 laps/engine	10
R	Riccardo Patrese	Alfa Romeo	Alfa Romeo 185T	4 laps/engine	18
NS	Jonathan Palmer	Zakspeed	Zakspeed 841	Misfire	17

Pole: Senna, 1m27.327s, 129.102mph/207.770kph. Fastest lap: Alboreto, 1m30.961s, 123.944mph/199.470kph on Lap 29. Race leaders: Senna 1-56, Johansson 57, Prost 58-60

MONACO GRAND PRIX

MONTE CARLO • ROUND 4 • DATE: 19TH MAY 1985
Laps: 78 • Distance: 160.522miles/258.336km • Weather: Cool & dull

Pos	Driver	Team	Chassis-Engine	Result	Qual
1	Alain Prost	McLaren	McLaren-TAG MP4/2B	1h51m58.034s	5
2	Michele Alboreto	Ferrari	Ferrari 156/85	1h52m05.575s	3
3	Elio de Angelis	Lotus	Lotus-Renault 97T	1h53m25.205s	9
4	Andrea de Cesaris	Ligier	Ligier-Renault JS25	77 laps	8
5	Derek Warwick	Renault	Renault RE60	77 laps	10
6	Jacques Laffite	Ligier	Ligier-Renault JS25	77 laps	16
7	Nigel Mansell	Williams	Williams-Honda FW10	77 laps	2
8	Keke Rosberg	Williams	Williams-Honda FW10	76 laps	7
9	Thierry Boutsen	Arrows	Arrows-BMW A8	76 laps	6
10	Martin Brundle	Tyrrell	Tyrrell-Ford Cosworth 012	74 laps	18
11	Jonathan Palmer	Zakspeed	Zakspeed 841	74 laps	19
R	Niki Lauda	McLaren	McLaren-TAG MP4/2B	17 laps/spun off	14
R	Riccardo Patrese	Alfa Romeo	Alfa Romeo 185T	16 laps/accident	12
R	Nelson Piquet	Brabham	Brabham-BMW BT54	16 laps/accident	13

Pos	Driver	Team	Chassis-Engine	Result	Qual
R	Teo Fabi	Toleman	Toleman-Hart TG185	16 laps/turbo	20
R	Ayrton Senna	Lotus	Lotus-Renault 97T	13 laps/engine	1
R	Eddie Cheever	Alfa Romeo	Alfa Romeo 185T	10 laps/alternator	4
R	Stefan Johansson	Ferrari	Ferrari 156/85	1 lap/accident	15
R	Gerhard Berger	Arrows	Arrows-BMW A8	0 laps/accident	11
R	Patrick Tambay	Renault	Renault RE60	0 laps/accident	17
DNQ	Piercarlo Ghinzani	Osella	Osella-Alfa Romeo FA1G	-	21
DNQ	Stefan Bellof	Tyrrell	Tyrrell-Ford Cosworth 012	-	22
DNQ	Philippe Alliot	RAM Racing	RAM-Hart 03	-	23
DNQ	Manfred Winkelhock	RAM Racing	RAM-Hart 03	-	24
DNQ	Francois Hesnault	Brabham	Brabham-BMW BT54	-	25
DNQ	Pierluigi Martini	Minardi	Minardi-Motori Moderni M185	knee injury	26

Pole: Senna, 1m20.450s, 92.091mph/148.206kph. Fastest lap: Alboreto, 1m22.637s, 89.653mph/144.284kph on Lap 60. Race leaders: Senna 1-13, Alboreto 14-17 & 24-31, Prost 18-23 & 32-78

MANSELL'S BRILLIANT BREAKTHROUGH

After earlier setbacks, Nigel Mansell scored his first win, at Brands Hatch. This was just reward for helping to develop the Williams-Honda combination and then, with the "monkey off his back", Mansell won next time out as well, at Kyalami, before Rosberg made it three wins in a row for Williams with victory in Adelaide.

CANADIAN GRAND PRIX

MONTREAL • ROUND 5 • DATE: 16TH JUNE 1985
Laps: 70 • Distance: 191.386miles/308.7km • Weather: Cool & dull

Pos	Driver	Team	Chassis-Engine	Result	Qual
1	Michele Alboreto	Ferrari	Ferrari 156/85	1h46m01.813s	3
2	Stefan Johansson	Ferrari	Ferrari 156/85	1h46m03.770s	4
3	Alain Prost	McLaren	McLaren-TAG MP4/2B	1h46m06.154s	5
4	Keke Rosberg	Williams	Williams-Honda FW10	1h46m29.634s	8
5	Elio de Angelis	Lotus	Lotus-Renault 97T	1h46m45.162s	1
6	Nigel Mansell	Williams	Williams-Honda FW10	1h47m19.691s	16
7	Patrick Tambay	Renault	Renault RE60	69 laps	10
8	Jacques Laffite	Ligier	Ligier-Renault JS25	69 laps	19
9	Thierry Boutsen	Arrows	Arrows-BMW A8	68 laps	7
10	Riccardo Patrese	Alfa Romeo	Alfa Romeo 185T	68 laps	13
11	Stefan Bellof	Tyrrell	Tyrrell-Ford Cosworth 012	68 laps	23
12	Martin Brundle	Tyrrell	Tyrrell-Ford Cosworth 012	68 laps	24
13	Gerhard Berger	Arrows	Arrows-BMW A8	67 laps	12
14	Andrea de Cesaris	Ligier	Ligier-Renault JS25	67 laps	15
15	Marc Surer	Brabham	Brabham-BMW BT54	67 laps	20
16	Ayrton Senna	Lotus	Lotus-Renault 97T	65 laps	2
17	Eddie Cheever	Alfa Romeo	Alfa Romeo 185T	64 laps	11
R	Pierluigi Martini	Minardi	Minardi-Motori Moderni M185	57 laps/accident	25
R	Niki Lauda	McLaren	McLaren-TAG MP4/2B	37 laps/engine	17
R	Piercarlo Ghinzani	Osella	Osella-Alfa Romeo FA1G	35 laps/engine	22
R	Philippe Alliot	RAM Racing	RAM-Hart 03	28 laps/accident	21

Pos	Driver	Team	Chassis-Engine	Result	Qual
R	Derek Warwick	Renault	Renault RE60	25 laps/accident	6
R	Manfred Winkelhock	RAM Racing	RAM-Hart 03	5 laps/accident	14
R	Teo Fabi	Toleman	Toleman-Hart TG185	3 laps/turbo	18
R	Nelson Piquet	Brabham	Brabham-BMW BT54	0 laps/transmission	9

Pole: de Angelis, 1m24.567s, 116.651mph/187.732kph. Fastest lap: Senna, 1m27.445s, 112.812mph/181.554kph on Lap 45. Race leaders: de Angelis 1-15, Alboreto 16-70

DETROIT GRAND PRIX

DETROIT • ROUND 6 • DATE: 23RD JUNE 1985
Laps: 63 • Distance: 157.501miles/253.474km • Weather: Hot & bright

Pos	Driver	Team	Chassis-Engine	Result	Qual
1	Keke Rosberg	Williams	Williams-Honda FW10	1h55m39.851s	5
2	Stefan Johansson	Ferrari	Ferrari 156/85	1h56m37.400s	9
3	Michele Alboreto	Ferrari	Ferrari 156/85	1h56m43.021s	3
4	Stefan Bellof	Tyrrell	Tyrrell-Ford Cosworth 012	1h56m46.076s	19
5	Elio de Angelis	Lotus	Lotus-Renault 97T	1h57m06.817s	8
6	Nelson Piquet	Brabham	Brabham-BMW BT54	62 laps	10
7	Thierry Boutsen	Arrows	Arrows-BMW A8	62 laps	21
8	Marc Surer	Brabham	Brabham-BMW BT54	62 laps	11
9	Eddie Cheever	Alfa Romeo	Alfa Romeo 185T	61 laps	7
10	Andrea de Cesaris	Ligier	Ligier-Renault JS25	61 laps	17
11	Gerhard Berger	Arrows	Arrows-BMW A8	60 laps	24
12	Jacques Laffite	Ligier	Ligier-Renault JS25	58 laps	16
R	Ayrton Senna	Lotus	Lotus-Renault 97T	51 laps/accident	1
R	Martin Brundle	Tyrrell	Tyrrell-Ford Cosworth 012	30 laps/accident	18
R	Philippe Alliot	RAM Racing	RAM-Hart 03	27 laps/accident	23
R	Nigel Mansell	Williams	Williams-Honda FW10	26 laps/accident	2
R	Alain Prost	McLaren	McLaren-TAG MP4/2B	19 laps/brakes	4
R	Riccardo Patrese	Alfa Romeo	Alfa Romeo 185T	19 laps/electrical	14
R	Derek Warwick	Renault	Renault RE60	18 laps/transmission	6
R	Patrick Tambay	Renault	Renault RE60	15 laps/accident	15
R	Pierluigi Martini	Minardi	Minardi-Motori Moderni M185	11 laps/engine	25
R	Niki Lauda	McLaren	McLaren-TAG MP4/2B	10 laps/brakes	12
R	Teo Fabi	Toleman	Toleman-Hart TG185	4 laps/clutch	13
R	Manfred Winkelhock	RAM Racing	RAM-Hart 03	3 laps/turbo	20
R	Piercarlo Ghinzani	Osella	Osella-Alfa Romeo FA1G	0 laps/accident	22

Pole: Senna, 1m42.051s, 88.192mph/141.931kph. Fastest lap: Senna, 1m45.612s, 85.218mph/137.145kph on Lap 51. Race leaders: Senna 1-7, Rosberg 8-63

BLASTING INTO HISTORY

As the turbocharged Honda engine gained driveability after the throttle being something of an on-off switch in its early days, Keke Rosberg drew plaudits the length of the Silverstone pit lane when he said, "OK, let's do it," and set an amazing qualifying record average speed of 160.925mph (258.976kph).

FRENCH GRAND PRIX

CIRCUIT PAUL RICARD • ROUND 7 • DATE: 7TH JULY 1985
Laps: 53 • Distance: 190.818miles/307.93km • Weather: Hot & bright

Pos	Driver	Team	Chassis-Engine	Result	Qual
1	Nelson Piquet	Brabham	Brabham-BMW BT54	1h31m46.266s	5
2	Keke Rosberg	Williams	Williams-Honda FW10	1h31m52.926s	1
3	Alain Prost	McLaren	McLaren-TAG MP4/2B	1h31m55.551s	4
4	Stefan Johansson	Ferrari	Ferrari 156/85	1h32m39.757s	15
5	Elio de Angelis	Lotus	Lotus-Renault 97T	1h32m39.956s	7
6	Patrick Tambay	Renault	Renault RE60B	1h33m01.433s	9
7	Derek Warwick	Renault	Renault RE60	1h33m30.478s	10
8	Marc Surer	Brabham	Brabham-BMW BT54	52 laps	13
9	Thierry Boutsen	Arrows	Arrows-BMW A8	52 laps	11
10	Eddie Cheever	Alfa Romeo	Alfa Romeo 185T	52 laps	17
11	Riccardo Patrese	Alfa Romeo	Alfa Romeo 185T	52 laps	16
12	Manfred Winkelhock	RAM Racing	RAM-Hart 03	50 laps	19
13	Stefan Bellof	Tyrrell	Tyrrell-Ford Cosworth 012	50 laps	25
14	Teo Fabi	Toleman	Toleman-Hart TG185	49 laps/fuel system	18
15	Piercarlo Ghinzani	Osella	Osella-Alfa Romeo FA1G	49 laps	23
R	Martin Brundle	Tyrrell	Tyrrell-Renault 014	32 laps/gearbox	20
R	Niki Lauda	McLaren	McLaren-TAG MP4/2B	30 laps/gearbox	6
R	Ayrton Senna	Lotus	Lotus-Renault 97T	26 laps/engine	2
R	Gerhard Berger	Arrows	Arrows-BMW A8	20 laps/accident	9
R	Pierluigi Martini	Minardi	Minardi-Motori Moderni M185	19 laps/accident	25
R	Philippe Alliot	RAM Racing	RAM-Hart 03	8 laps/fuel system	23
R	Jonathan Palmer	Zakspeed	Zakspeed 841	6 laps/engine	22
R	Michele Alboreto	Ferrari	Ferrari 156/85	5 laps/turbo	4
R	Andrea de Cesaris	Ligier	Ligier-Renault JS25	4 laps/halfshaft	13
R	Jacques Laffite	Ligier	Ligier-Renault JS25	2 laps/turbo	15
NS	Nigel Mansell	Williams	Williams-Honda FW10	Accident	8

Pole: Rosberg, 1m32.462s, 140.561mph/226.211kph. Fastest lap: Rosberg, 1m39.914s, 130.077mph/209.340kph on Lap 46. Race leaders: Rosberg 1-10, Piquet 11-53

DE CESARIS DOES IT AGAIN

Andrea de Cesaris was always acknowledged as a quick driver, but he was also seen as one who was prone to crashing. His maiden season with McLaren was littered with bent cars. In 1985, the Ligier mechanics were given a major rebuild to do when he crashed out of the Austrian GP, cartwheeling his car in a violent trail of destruction.

BRITISH GRAND PRIX

SILVERSTONE • ROUND 8 • DATE: 21ST JULY 1985
Laps: 65 • Distance: 190.580miles/306.709km • Weather: Warm & bright

Pos	Driver	Team	Chassis-Engine	Result	Qual
1	Alain Prost	McLaren	McLaren-TAG MP4/2B	1h18m10.436s	3
2	Michele Alboreto	Ferrari	Ferrari 156/85	64 laps	6
3	Jacques Laffite	Ligier	Ligier-Renault JS25	64 laps	16

Pos	Driver	Team	Chassis-Engine	Result	Qual
4	Nelson Piquet	Brabham	Brabham-BMW BT54	64 laps	2
5	Derek Warwick	Renault	Renault RE60	64 laps	12
6	Marc Surer	Brabham	Brabham-BMW BT54	63 laps	15
7	Martin Brundle	Tyrrell	Tyrrell-Renault 014	63 laps	20
8	Gerhard Berger	Arrows	Arrows-BMW A8	63 laps	17
9	Riccardo Patrese	Alfa Romeo	Alfa Romeo 185T	62 laps	14
10	Ayrton Senna	Lotus	Lotus-Renault 97T	60 laps/fuel injection	4
11	Stefan Bellof	Tyrrell	Tyrrell-Ford Cosworth 012	59 laps	26
R	Niki Lauda	McLaren	McLaren-TAG MP4/2B	57 laps/electrical	10
R	Thierry Boutsen	Arrows	Arrows-BMW A8	57 laps/spun off	19
R	Andrea de Cesaris	Ligier	Ligier-Renault JS25	41 laps/clutch	7
R	Pierluigi Martini	Minardi	Minardi-Motori Moderni M185	38 laps/transmission	23
NC	Elio de Angelis	Lotus	Lotus-Renault 97T	37 laps	8
R	Manfred Winkelhock	RAM Racing	RAM-Hart 03	28 laps/turbo	18
R	Keke Rosberg	Williams	Williams-Honda FW10	21 laps/exhaust	1
R	Nigel Mansell	Williams	Williams-Honda FW10	17 laps/clutch	5
R	Eddie Cheever	Alfa Romeo	Alfa Romeo 184T	17 laps/turbo	22
R	Jonathan Palmer	Zakspeed	Zakspeed 841	6 laps/engine	24
R	Teo Fabi	Toleman	Toleman-Hart TG185	4 laps/transmission	9
R	Stefan Johansson	Ferrari	Ferrari 156/85	1 lap/accident	11
R	Patrick Tambay	Renault	Renault RE60	0 laps/spun off	13
R	Philippe Alliot	RAM Racing	RAM-Hart 03	0 laps/accident	21
R	Piercarlo Ghinzani	Osella	Osella-Alfa Romeo FA1G	0 laps/accident	25

Pole: Rosberg, 1m05.591s, 160.924mph/258.983kph. Fastest lap: Prost, 1m09.886s, 151.034mph/243.066kph on Lap 43. Race leaders: Senna 1-57 & 59, Prost 58 & 60-65

THE LAST FOR A WHILE

The 1985 Dutch GP proved to be Zandvoort's last one until 2021. Bringing a 34-year run to a close, McLaren dominated, with Lauda taking what would be his 25th and final grand prix win, heading team-mate Prost to the finish for the only time in Prost's title-winning season. The only Dutch driver, Huub Rothengatter, came last.

GERMAN GRAND PRIX

NURBURGRING • ROUND 9 • DATE: 4TH AUGUST 1985
Laps: 67 • Distance: 189.91miles/304.314km • Weather: Cool & dull

Pos	Driver	Team	Chassis-Engine	Result	Qual
1	Michele Alboreto	Ferrari	Ferrari 156/85	1h35m31.337s	8
2	Alain Prost	McLaren	McLaren-TAG MP4/2B	1h35m42.998s	3
3	Jacques Laffite	Ligier	Ligier-Renault JS25	1h36m22.491s	13
4	Thierry Boutsen	Arrows	Arrows-BMW A8	1h36m26.616s	15
5	Niki Lauda	McLaren	McLaren-TAG MP4/2B	1h36m45.309s	12
6	Nigel Mansell	Williams	Williams-Honda FW10	1h36m48.157s	10
7	Gerhard Berger	Arrows	Arrows-BMW A8	66 laps	17
8	Stefan Bellof	Tyrrell	Tyrrell-Renault 014	66 laps	19
9	Stefan Johansson	Ferrari	Ferrari 156/85	66 laps	2
10	Martin Brundle	Tyrrell	Tyrrell-Ford Cosworth 012	63 laps	26
11	Pierluigi Martini	Minardi	Minardi-Motori Moderni M185	62 laps/engine	27

Pos	Driver	Team	Chassis-Engine	Result	Qual
12	Keke Rosberg	Williams	Williams-Honda FW10	61 laps/brakes	4
R	Eddie Cheever	Alfa Romeo	Alfa Romeo 184T	45 laps/turbo	18
R	Elio de Angelis	Lotus	Lotus-Renault 97T	40 laps/engine	7
R	Huub Rothengatter	Osella	Osella-Alfa Romeo FA1G	32 laps/gearbox	25
R	Teo Fabi	Toleman	Toleman-Hart TG185	29 laps/clutch	1
R	Ayrton Senna	Lotus	Lotus-Renault 97T	27 laps/transmission	5
R	Derek Warwick	Renault	Renault RE60B	25 laps/ignition	20
R	Nelson Piquet	Brabham	Brabham-BMW BT54	23 laps/turbo	6
R	Patrick Tambay	Renault	Renault RE60B	19 laps/spun off	16
R	Marc Surer	Brabham	Brabham-BMW BT54	15 laps/engine	11
R	Riccardo Patrese	Alfa Romeo	Alfa Romeo 184T	8 laps/gearbox	9
R	Philippe Alliot	RAM Racing	RAM-Hart 03	8 laps/fuel pressure	21
R	Manfred Winkelhock	RAM Racing	RAM-Hart 03	8 laps/engine	22
R	Francois Hesnault	Renault	Renault RE60	8 laps/clutch	23
R	Jonathan Palmer	Zakspeed	Zakspeed 841	7 laps/alternator	24
R	Andrea de Cesaris	Ligier	Ligier-Renault JS25	0 laps/collision	14

Pole: Fabi, 1m17.429s, 131.219mph/211.176kph. Fastest lap: Lauda, 1m22.806s, 122.698mph/197.463kph on Lap 53. Race leaders: Rosberg 1-15 & 27-44, Senna 16-26, Alboreto 45-67

AUSTRIAN GRAND PRIX

OSTERREICHRING • ROUND 10 • DATE: 18TH AUGUST 1985
Laps: 52 • Distance: 191.993miles/308.984km • Weather: Warm & bright

Pos	Driver	Team	Chassis-Engine	Result	Qual
1	Alain Prost	McLaren	McLaren-TAG MP4/2B	1h20m12.583s	1
2	Ayrton Senna	Lotus	Lotus-Renault 97T	1h20m42.585s	14
3	Michele Alboreto	Ferrari	Ferrari 156/85	1h20m46.939s	9
4	Stefan Johansson	Ferrari	Ferrari 156/85	1h20m51.656s	12
5	Elio de Angelis	Lotus	Lotus-Renault 97T	1h21m34.675s	7
6	Marc Surer	Brabham	Brabham-BMW BT54	51 laps	11
7	Stefan Bellof	Tyrrell	Tyrrell-Renault 014	49 laps/out of fuel	22
8	Thierry Boutsen	Arrows	Arrows-BMW A8	49 laps	16
9	Huub Rothengatter	Osella	Osella-Alfa Romeo FA1G	48 laps	24
10	Patrick Tambay	Renault	Renault RE60B	46 laps/engine	8
R	Jacques Laffite	Ligier	Ligier-Renault JS25	43 laps/accident	15
R	Pierluigi Martini	Minardi	Minardi-Motori Moderni M185	40 laps/suspension	26
R	Niki Lauda	McLaren	McLaren-TAG MP4/2B	39 laps/engine	3
R	Gerhard Berger	Arrows	Arrows-BMW A8	33 laps/turbo	17
R	Teo Fabi	Toleman	Toleman-Hart TG185	31 laps/electrical	6
R	Derek Warwick	Renault	Renault RE60B	29 laps/engine	13
R	Kenny Acheson	RAM Racing	RAM-Hart 03	28 laps/engine	23
R	Nelson Piquet	Brabham	Brabham-BMW BT54	26 laps/exhaust	5
R	Nigel Mansell	Williams	Williams-Honda FW10	25 laps/engine	2
R	Riccardo Patrese	Alfa Romeo	Alfa Romeo 184T	25 laps/engine	10
R	Jonathan Palmer	Zakspeed	Zakspeed 841	17 laps/engine	25
R	Philippe Alliot	RAM Racing	RAM-Hart 03	16 laps/engine	21
R	Andrea de Cesaris	Ligier	Ligier-Renault JS25	13 laps/accident	18
R	Eddie Cheever	Alfa Romeo	Alfa Romeo 184T	6 laps/turbo	20
R	Keke Rosberg	Williams	Williams-Honda FW10	4 laps/fuel pressure	4
R	Piercarlo Ghinzani	Toleman	Toleman-Hart TG185	Engine	19
DNQ	Martin Brundle	Tyrrell	Tyrrell-Ford Cosworth 012	-	27

Pole: Prost, 1m25.490s, 155.478mph/250.218kph. Fastest lap: Prost, 1m29.241s, 148.943mph/239.701kph on Lap 39. Race leaders: Prost 1-25 & 40-52, Lauda 26-39

DUTCH GRAND PRIX

ZANDVOORT • ROUND 11 • DATE: 25TH AUGUST 1985
Laps: 70 • Distance: 184.587miles/297.64km • Weather: Cool & dull

Pos	Driver	Team	Chassis-Engine	Result	Qual
1	Niki Lauda	McLaren	McLaren-TAG MP4/2B	1h32m29.263s	10
2	Alain Prost	McLaren	McLaren-TAG MP4/2B	1h32m29.495s	3
3	Ayrton Senna	Lotus	Lotus-Renault 97T	1h33m17.754s	4
4	Michele Alboreto	Ferrari	Ferrari 156/85	1h33m18.100s	16
5	Elio de Angelis	Lotus	Lotus-Renault 97T	69 laps	11
6	Nigel Mansell	Williams	Williams-Honda FW10	69 laps	7
7	Martin Brundle	Tyrrell	Tyrrell-Renault 014	69 laps	21
8	Nelson Piquet	Brabham	Brabham-BMW BT54	69 laps	1
9	Gerhard Berger	Arrows	Arrows-BMW A8	68 laps	14
10	Marc Surer	Brabham	Brabham-BMW BT54	65 laps/exhaust	9
NC	Huub Rothengatter	Osella	Osella-Alfa Romeo FA1G	56 laps	26
R	Thierry Boutsen	Arrows	Arrows-BMW A8	54 laps/suspension	8
R	Philippe Alliot	RAM Racing	RAM-Hart 03	52 laps/engine	25
R	Stefan Bellof	Tyrrell	Tyrrell-Renault 014	39 laps/engine	22
R	Derek Warwick	Renault	Renault RE60B	27 laps/gearbox	12
R	Andrea de Cesaris	Ligier	Ligier-Renault JS25	25 laps/turbo	18
R	Patrick Tambay	Renault	Renault RE60B	22 laps/transmission	6
R	Keke Rosberg	Williams	Williams-Honda FW10	20 laps/engine	2
R	Teo Fabi	Toleman	Toleman-Hart TG185	18 laps/wheel	5
R	Jacques Laffite	Ligier	Ligier-Renault JS25	17 laps/electrical	13
R	Jonathan Palmer	Zakspeed	Zakspeed 841	13 laps/fuel pressure	23
R	Piercarlo Ghinzani	Toleman	Toleman-Hart TG185	12 laps/engine	15
R	Stefan Johansson	Ferrari	Ferrari 156/85	9 laps/engine	17
R	Riccardo Patrese	Alfa Romeo	Alfa Romeo 184T	1 lap/turbo	19
R	Eddie Cheever	Alfa Romeo	Alfa Romeo 184T	1 lap/turbo	20
R	Pierluigi Martini	Minardi	Minardi-Motori Moderni M185	1 lap/accident	24
DNQ	Kenny Acheson	RAM Racing	RAM-Hart 03	-	27

Pole: Piquet, 1m11.074s, 133.824mph/215.369kph. Fastest lap: Prost, 1m16.538s, 124.270mph/199.994kph on Lap 57. Race leaders: Rosberg 1-19, Prost 20-33, Lauda 34-70

NEW CIRCUITS

Australia had run a grand prix since 1928, but until 1985 it had never been a World Championship round. Adelaide stole a march on rival cities Sydney and Melbourne to land the race. Its circuit ran on public roads, through parkland and across a horse racing track, and won plaudits as the best street circuit.

NEW CONSTRUCTORS

There were two new teams in 1985, Minardi and Zakspeed. The former had advanced after winning in F2, but its first car, the M185, was both overweight and underpowered as it was designed around the uncompetitive Motori Moderni V6. Having run Ford touring cars then Group C sports cars, Zakspeed entered F1, but was held back by using its own engines.

ITALIAN GRAND PRIX

MONZA • ROUND 12 • DATE: 8TH SEPTEMBER 1985
Laps: 51 • Distance: 183.309miles/295.8km • Weather: Hot & bright

Pos	Driver	Team	Chassis-Engine	Result	Qual
1	Alain Prost	McLaren	McLaren-TAG MP4/2B	1h17m59.451s	5
2	Nelson Piquet	Brabham	Brabham-BMW BT54	1h18m51.086s	4
3	Ayrton Senna	Lotus	Lotus-Renault 97T	1h18m59.841s	1
4	Marc Surer	Brabham	Brabham-BMW BT54	1h19m00.060s	9
5	Stefan Johansson	Ferrari	Ferrari 156/85	50 laps/out of fuel	10
6	Elio de Angelis	Lotus	Lotus-Renault 97T	50 laps	6
7	Patrick Tambay	Renault	Renault RE60B	50 laps	8
8	Martin Brundle	Tyrrell	Tyrrell-Renault 014	50 laps	18
9	Thierry Boutsen	Arrows	Arrows-BMW A8	50 laps	14
10	Philippe Streiff	Ligier	Ligier-Renault JS25	49 laps	19
11	Nigel Mansell	Williams	Williams-Honda FW10	47 laps/engine	3
12	Teo Fabi	Toleman	Toleman-Hart TG185	47 laps	15
13	Michele Alboreto	Ferrari	Ferrari 156/85	45 laps/engine	7
R	Keke Rosberg	Williams	Williams-Honda FW10	44 laps/engine	2
R	Jacques Laffite	Ligier	Ligier-Renault JS25	40 laps/engine	20
R	Niki Lauda	McLaren	McLaren-TAG MP4/2B	33 laps/transmission	16
R	Riccardo Patrese	Alfa Romeo	Alfa Romeo 184T	31 laps/exhaust	13
R	Huub Rothengatter	Osella	Osella-Alfa Romeo FA1G	26 laps/engine	22
R	Philippe Alliot	RAM Racing	RAM-Hart 03	19 laps/turbo	26
R	Gerhard Berger	Arrows	Arrows-BMW A8	13 laps/engine	11
R	Derek Warwick	Renault	Renault RE60B	9 laps/transmission	12
R	Alan Jones	Haas USA	Lola-Hart THL-1	6 laps/engine	25
R	Eddie Cheever	Alfa Romeo	Alfa Romeo 184T	3 laps/engine	17
R	Kenny Acheson	RAM Racing	RAM-Hart 03	2 laps/clutch	24
R	Pierluigi Martini	Minardi	Minardi-Motori Moderni M185	0 laps/fuel pump	23
R	Piercarlo Ghinzani	Toleman	Toleman-Hart TG185	0 laps/stalled	-

Pole: Senna, 1m25.084s, 152.487mph/245.404kph. Fastest lap: Mansell, 1m28.283s, 146.961mph/236.512kph on Lap 38. Race leaders: Rosberg 1-27 & 40-44, Prost 28-39 & 45-51

NEW DRIVERS

There were just two new drivers in 1985, with Ivan Capelli contesting two late-season races for Tyrrell, finishing fourth in the Adelaide finale, up from 22nd on the Qual as half of the field retired. Christian Danner was the other new face and the tall German had two outings for Zakspeed, finishing neither.

BELGIAN GRAND PRIX

SPA-FRANCORCHAMPS • ROUND 13 • DATE: 15TH SEPTEMBER 1985
Laps: 43 • Distance: 185.194miles/298.42km • Weather: Cool & wet, then drying

Pos	Driver	Team	Chassis-Engine	Result	Qual
1	Ayrton Senna	Lotus	Lotus-Renault 97T	1h34m19.893s	2
2	Nigel Mansell	Williams	Williams-Honda FW10	1h34m48.315s	7
3	Alain Prost	McLaren	McLaren-TAG MP4/2B	1h35m15.002s	1

Pos	Driver	Team	Chassis-Engine	Result	Qual
4	Keke Rosberg	Williams	Williams-Honda FW10	1h35m35.183s	10
5	Nelson Piquet	Brabham	Brabham-BMW BT54	42 laps	3
6	Derek Warwick	Renault	Renault RE60B	42 laps	14
7	Gerhard Berger	Arrows	Arrows-BMW A8	42 laps	8
8	Marc Surer	Brabham	Brabham-BMW BT54	42 laps	12
9	Philippe Streiff	Ligier	Ligier-Renault JS25	42 laps	18
10	Thierry Boutsen	Arrows	Arrows-BMW A8	40 laps/transmission	6
11	Jacques Laffite	Ligier	Ligier-Renault JS25	38 laps/accident	17
12	Pierluigi Martini	Minardi	Minardi-Motori Moderni M185	38 laps	24
13	Martin Brundle	Tyrrell	Tyrrell-Renault 014	38 laps	21
NC	Huub Rothengatter	Osella	Osella-Alfa Romeo FA1G	37 laps	23
R	Riccardo Patrese	Alfa Romeo	Alfa Romeo 184T	31 laps/engine	15
R	Eddie Cheever	Alfa Romeo	Alfa Romeo 184T	26 laps/gearbox	19
R	Patrick Tambay	Renault	Renault RE60B	24 laps/gearbox	13
R	Teo Fabi	Toleman	Toleman-Hart TG185	23 laps/throttle	11
R	Elio de Angelis	Lotus	Lotus-Renault 97T	17 laps/turbo	9
R	Christian Danner	Zakspeed	Zakspeed 841	16 laps/gearbox	22
R	Philippe Alliot	RAM Racing	RAM-Hart 03	10 laps/accident	20
R	Stefan Johansson	Ferrari	Ferrari 156/85	7 laps/spun off	5
R	Piercarlo Ghinzani	Toleman	Toleman-Hart TG185	7 laps/accident	16
R	Michele Alboreto	Ferrari	Ferrari 156/85	3 laps/clutch	4
NS	Niki Lauda	McLaren	McLaren-TAG MP4/2B	Wrist injury	-

Pole: Prost, 1m55.306s, 134.635mph/216.675kph. Fastest lap: Prost, 2m01.730s, 127.530mph/205.241kph on Lap 38. Race leaders: Senna 1-8 & 10-43, de Angelis 9

EUROPEAN GRAND PRIX

BRANDS HATCH • ROUND 14 • DATE: 6TH OCTOBER 1985
Laps: 75 • Distance: 196.15miles/315.457km • Weather: Warm & bright

Pos	Driver	Team	Chassis-Engine	Result	Qual
1	Nigel Mansell	Williams	Williams-Honda FW10	1h32m58.109s	3
2	Ayrton Senna	Lotus	Lotus-Renault 97T	1h33m19.505s	1
3	Keke Rosberg	Williams	Williams-Honda FW10	1h33m56.642s	4
4	Alain Prost	McLaren	McLaren-TAG MP4/2B	1h34m04.230s	6
5	Elio de Angelis	Lotus	Lotus-Renault 97T	74 laps	9
6	Thierry Boutsen	Arrows	Arrows-BMW A8	73 laps	12
7	John Watson	McLaren	McLaren-TAG MP4/2B	73 laps	21
8	Philippe Streiff	Ligier	Ligier-Renault JS25	73 laps	5
9	Riccardo Patrese	Alfa Romeo	Alfa Romeo 184T	73 laps	11
10	Gerhard Berger	Arrows	Arrows-BMW A8	73 laps	19
11	Eddie Cheever	Alfa Romeo	Alfa Romeo 184T	73 laps	18
12	Patrick Tambay	Renault	Renault RE60B	72 laps	17
R	Marc Surer	Brabham	Brabham-BMW BT54	62 laps/turbo	7
R	Stefan Johansson	Ferrari	Ferrari 156/85	59 laps/electrical	13
R	Jacques Laffite	Ligier	Ligier-Renault JS25	58 laps/engine	18
R	Christian Danner	Zakspeed	Zakspeed 841	55 laps/engine	25
R	Ivan Capelli	Tyrrell	Tyrrell-Renault 014	44 laps/accident	24
R	Martin Brundle	Tyrrell	Tyrrell-Renault 014	40 laps/water leak	16
R	Teo Fabi	Toleman	Toleman-Hart TG185	33 laps/engine	20
R	Philippe Alliot	RAM Racing	RAM-Hart 03	31 laps/engine	23
R	Piercarlo Ghinzani	Toleman	Toleman-Hart TG185	16 laps/engine	14
R	Michele Alboreto	Ferrari	Ferrari 156/85	13 laps/turbo	15

Pos	Driver	Team	Chassis-Engine	Result	Qual
R	Alan Jones	Haas USA	Lola-Hart THL-1	13 laps/radiator damage	22
R	Nelson Piquet	Brabham	Brabham-BMW BT54	6 laps/accident	2
R	Derek Warwick	Renault	Renault RE60B	4 laps/fuel injection	8
R	Pierluigi Martini	Minardi	Minardi-Motori Moderni M185	3 laps/accident	26
DNQ	Huub Rothengatter	Osella	Osella-Alfa Romeo FA1G	-	27

Pole: Senna, 1m07.169s, 140.076mph/225.430kph. Fastest lap: Laffite, 1m11.526s, 131.543mph/211.698kph on Lap 55. Race leaders: Senna 1-8, Mansell 9-75

SOUTH AFRICAN GRAND PRIX

KYALAMI • ROUND 15 • DATE: 19TH OCTOBER 1985
Laps: 75 • Distance: 190.765miles/307.8km • Weather: Hot & bright

Pos	Driver	Team	Chassis-Engine	Result	Qual
1	Nigel Mansell	Williams	Williams-Honda FW10	1h28m22.866s	1
2	Keke Rosberg	Williams	Williams-Honda FW10	1h28m30.438s	3
3	Alain Prost	McLaren	McLaren-TAG MP4/2B	1h30m14.660s	9
4	Stefan Johansson	Ferrari	Ferrari 156/85	74 laps	16
5	Gerhard Berger	Arrows	Arrows-BMW A8	74 laps	11
6	Thierry Boutsen	Arrows	Arrows-BMW A8	74 laps	10
7	Martin Brundle	Tyrrell	Tyrrell-Renault 014	73 laps	17
R	Elio de Angelis	Lotus	Lotus-Renault 97T	52 laps/engine	6
R	Pierluigi Martini	Minardi	Minardi-Motori Moderni M185	45 laps/radiator damage	20
R	Niki Lauda	McLaren	McLaren-TAG MP4/2B	37 laps/turbo	8
R	Philippe Streiff	Tyrrell	Tyrrell-Renault 014	16 laps/accident	19
R	Ayrton Senna	Lotus	Lotus-Renault 97T	8 laps/engine	4
R	Michele Alboreto	Ferrari	Ferrari 156/85	8 laps/turbo	15
R	Nelson Piquet	Brabham	Brabham-BMW BT54	6 laps/engine	2
R	Piercarlo Ghinzani	Toleman	Toleman-Hart TG185	4 laps/engine	13
R	Marc Surer	Brabham	Brabham-BMW BT54	3 laps/engine	5
R	Teo Fabi	Toleman	Toleman-Hart TG185	3 laps/engine	7
R	Huub Rothengatter	Osella	Osella-Alfa Romeo FA1G	1 lap/electrical	21
R	Riccardo Patrese	Alfa Romeo	Alfa Romeo 184T	0 laps/accident	12
R	Eddie Cheever	Alfa Romeo	Alfa Romeo 184T	0 laps/accident	14
NS	Alan Jones	Haas USA	Lola-Hart THL-1	Driver unwell	18

Pole: Mansell, 1m02.366s, 147.201mph/236.898kph. Fastest lap: Rosberg, 1m08.149s, 134.710mph/216.795kph on Lap 74. Race leaders: Mansell 1-7 & 9-75, Rosberg 8

IN MEMORIAM

Germany lost two of its most popular drivers when Stefan Bellof and Manfred Winkelhock were killed in World Endurance Championship sports car races. Winkelhock crashed his Kremer Porsche at Mosport Park and died of head injuries. Three weeks later, Bellof died too, crashing his works Porsche at Spa-Francorchamps' Eau Rouge bend.

AUSTRALIAN GRAND PRIX

ADELAIDE • ROUND 16 • DATE: 3RD NOVEMBER 1985
Laps: 82 • Distance: 192.498miles/309.796km • Weather: Hot & bright

Pos	Driver	Team	Chassis-Engine	Result	Qual
1	Keke Rosberg	Williams	Williams-Honda FW10	2h00m40.473s	3
2	Jacques Laffite	Ligier	Ligier-Renault JS25	2h01m23.603s	20
3	Philippe Streiff	Ligier	Ligier-Renault JS25	2h02m09.009s	18
4	Ivan Capelli	Tyrrell	Tyrrell-Renault 014	81 laps	22
5	Stefan Johansson	Ferrari	Ferrari 156/85	81 laps	15
6	Gerhard Berger	Arrows	Arrows-BMW A8	81 laps	7
7	Huub Rothengatter	Osella	Osella-Alfa Romeo FA1G	78 laps	25
8	Pierluigi Martini	Minardi	Minardi-Motori Moderni M185	78 laps	23
R	Ayrton Senna	Lotus	Lotus-Renault 97T	62 laps/engine	1
R	Michele Alboreto	Ferrari	Ferrari 156/85	61 laps/transmission	5
R	Derek Warwick	Renault	Renault RE60B	57 laps/transmission	12
R	Niki Lauda	McLaren	McLaren-TAG MP4/2B	57 laps/accident	16
R	Martin Brundle	Tyrrell	Tyrrell-Renault 014	49 laps	17
R	Marc Surer	Brabham	Brabham-BMW BT54	42 laps/engine	6
R	Riccardo Patrese	Alfa Romeo	Alfa Romeo 184T	42 laps/exhaust	14
R	Teo Fabi	Toleman	Toleman-Hart TG185	40 laps/engine	24
R	Thierry Boutsen	Arrows	Arrows-BMW A8	37 laps/oil leak	11
R	Piercarlo Ghinzani	Toleman	Toleman-Hart TG185	28 laps/clutch	21
R	Alain Prost	McLaren	McLaren-TAG MP4/2B	26 laps/engine	4
R	Patrick Tambay	Renault	Renault RE60B	20 laps/transmission	8
R	Alan Jones	Haas USA	Lola-Hart THL-1	20 laps/electrical	19
DQ	Elio de Angelis	Lotus	Lotus-Renault 97T	18 laps/grid error	10
R	Nelson Piquet	Brabham	Brabham-BMW BT54	14 laps/fire	9
R	Eddie Cheever	Alfa Romeo	Alfa Romeo 184T	5 laps/engine	13
R	Nigel Mansell	Williams	Williams-Honda FW10	1 lap/transmission	2

Pole: Senna, 1m19.843s, 105.847mph/170.344kph. Fastest lap: Rosberg, 1m23.758s, 100.899mph/162.382kph on Lap 57. Race leaders: Rosberg 1-41 & 44-52 & 62-82, Senna 42-43 & 53-55 & 58-61, Lauda 56-57

WORLD DRIVERS' CHAMPIONSHIP FINAL RESULTS

Pos	Driver	Nat	Car-Engine	R1	R2	R3	R4	R5	R6
1	Alain Prost	FRA	McLaren-TAG MP4/2B	1F	R	DQ	1	3	R
2	Michele Alboreto	ITA	Ferrari 156/85	2P	2	RF	2F	1	3
3	Keke Rosberg	FIN	Williams-Honda FW10	R	R	R	8	4	1
4	Ayrton Senna	BRA	Lotus-Renault 97T	R	1PF	7P	RP	16F	RPF
5	Elio de Angelis	ITA	Lotus-Renault 97T	3	4	1	3	5P	5
6	Nigel Mansell	GBR	Williams-Honda FW10	R	5	5	7	6	R
7	Stefan Johansson	SWE	Tyrrell-Ford Cosworth 012	7	-	-	-	-	-
			Ferrari 156/85	-	8	6	R	2	2
8	Nelson Piquet	BRA	Brabham-BMW BT54	R	R	8	R	R	6
9	Jacques Laffite	FRA	Ligier-Renault JS25	6	R	R	6	8	12
10	Niki Lauda	AUT	McLaren-TAG MP4/2B	R	R	4	R	R	R
11	Thierry Boutsen	BEL	Arrows-BMW A8	11	R	2	9	9	7
12	Patrick Tambay	FRA	Renault RE60	5	3	3	R	7	R
			Renault RE60B	-	-	-	-	-	-
13	Marc Surer	CHE	Brabham-BMW BT54	-	-	-	-	15	8

Pos	Driver	Nat	Car-Engine	R1	R2	R3	R4	R5	R6
14	Derek Warwick	GBR	Renault RE60	10	7	10	5	R	R
			Renault RE60B	-	-	-	-	-	-
15	Philippe Streiff	FRA	Ligier-Renault JS25	-	-	-	-	-	-
			Tyrrell-Renault 014	-	-	-	-	-	-
16	Stefan Bellof	DEU	Tyrrell-Ford Cosworth 012	-	6	R	DNQ	11	4
			Tyrrell-Renault 014	-	-	-	-	-	-
17	Rene Arnoux	FRA	Ferrari 156/85	4	-	-	-	-	-
17	Andrea de Cesaris	ITA	Ligier-Renault JS25	R	R	R	4	14	10
17	Ivan Capelli	ITA	Tyrrell-Renault 014	-	-	-	-	-	-
20	Gerhard Berger	AUT	Arrows-BMW A8	R	R	R	R	13	11

Pos	Driver	R7	R8	R9	R10	R11	R12	R13	R14	R15	R16	Total
1	Prost	3	1F	2	1PF	2F	1	3PF	4	3	R	73
2	Alboreto	R	2	1	3	4	13	R	R	R	R	53
3	Rosberg	2PF	RP	12	R	R	R	4	3	2F	1F	40
4	Senna	R	10	R	2	3	3P	1	2P	R	RP	38
5	de Angelis	5	NC	R	5	5	6	R	5	R	DQ	33
6	Mansell	NS	R	6	R	6	11F	2	1	1P	R	31
7	Johansson	-	-	-	-	-	-	-	-	-	-	26
		4	R	9	4	R	5	R	R	4	5	
8	Piquet	1	4	R	R	8P	2	5	R	R	R	21
9	Laffite	R	3	3	R	R	R	11	RF	-	2	16
10	Lauda	R	R	5F	R	1	R	NS	-	R	R	14
11	Boutsen	9	R	4	8	R	9	10	6	6	R	11
12	Tambay	-	-	-	-	-	-	-	-	-	-	11
		6	R	R	10	R	7	R	12	-	R	
13	Surer	8	6	R	6	10	4	8	R	R	R	5
14	Warwick	7	-	-	-	-	-	-	-	-	-	5
		-	5	R	R	R	R	6	R	-	R	
15	Streiff	-	-	-	-	-	10	9	8	-	3	4
		-	-	-	-	-	-	-	-	R	-	
16	Bellof	13	11	-	-	-	-	-	-	-	-	4
		-	-	8	7	R	-	-	-	-	-	
17	Arnoux	-	-	-	-	-	-	-	-	-	-	3
17	de Cesaris	R	R	R	R	R	-	-	-	-	-	3
17	Capelli	-	-	-	-	-	-	-	R	-	4	3
20	Berger	R	8	7	R	9	R	7	10	5	6	3

WORLD CONSTRUCTORS' CHAMPIONSHIP FINAL RESULTS

Pos	Team-Engine	R1	R2	R3	R4	R5	R6	R7	R8
1	McLaren-TAG	1/R	R/R	4/DQ	1/R	3/R	R/R	3/R	1/R
2	Ferrari	2/4	2/8	6/R	2/R	1/2	2/3	4/R	2/R
3	Williams-Honda	R/R	5/R	5/R	7/8	4/6	1/R	2/NS	R/R
4	Lotus-Renault	3/R	1/4	1/7	3/R	5/16	5/R	5/R	10/NC
5	Brabham-BMW	R/R	R/R	8/R	R/DNQ	15/R	6/8	1/8	4/6
6	Ligier-Renault	6/R	R/R	R/R	4/6	8/14	10/12	R/R	3/R
7	Renault	5/10	3/7	3/10	5/R	7/R	R/R	6/7	5/R
8	Arrows-BMW	11/R	R/R	2/R	9/R	9/13	7/11	9/R	8/R
9	Tyrrell-Ford	7/8	6/R	9/R	10/DNQ	11/12	4/R	13	11
10	Tyrrell-Renault	-/-	-/-	-/-	-/-	-/-	-/-	R	7

Pos	Team-Engine	R9	R10	R11	R12	R13	R14	R15	R16	Total
1	McLaren-TAG	2/5	1/R	1/2	1/R	3/NS	4/7	3/R	R/R	90
2	Ferrari	1/9	3/4	4/R	5/13	R/R	R/R	4/R	5/R	82
3	Williams-Honda	6/12	R/R	6/R	11/R	2/4	1/3	1/2	1/R	71
4	Lotus-Renault	R/R	2/5	3/5	3/6	1/R	2/5	R/R	R/DQ	71
5	Brabham-BMW	R/R	6/R	8/10	2/4	5/8	R/R	R/R	R/R	26
6	Ligier-Renault	3/R	R/R	R/R	10/R	9/11	8/R	-/-	2/3	23
7	Renault	R/R/R	10/R	R/R	7/R	6/R	12/R	-/-	R/R	16
8	Arrows-BMW	4/7	8/R	9/R	9/R	7/10	6/10	5/6	6/R	14
9	Tyrrell-Ford	10	DNQ	-	-	-	-	-	-	4
10	Tyrrell-Renault	8	7	7/R	8	13	R/R	7/R	4/R	3

SYMBOLS AND GRAND PRIX KEY

Round 1 **Brazilian GP**
Round 2 **Portuguese GP**
Round 3 **San Marino GP**
Round 4 **Monaco GP**
Round 5 **Canadian GP**
Round 6 **Detroit GP**
Round 7 **French GP**
Round 8 **British GP**
Round 9 **German GP**
Round 10 **Austrian GP**
Round 11 **Dutch GP**
Round 12 **Italian GP**
Round 13 **Belgian GP**
Round 14 **European GP**
Round 15 **South African GP**
Round 16 **Australian GP**

SCORING

1st **9 points**
2nd **6 points**
3rd **4 points**
4th **3 points**
5th **2 points**
6th **1 point**

DNPQ DID NOT PRE-QUALIFY **DNQ DID NOT QUALIFY** **DQ DISQUALIFIED** **EX EXCLUDED**
F FASTEST LAP **NC NOT CLASSIFIED** **NS NON-STARTER** **P POLE POSITION** **R RETIRED**

1986

SEASON SUMMARY

The season came down to a dramatic final race in Adelaide, where a blow-out cost Nigel Mansell the title for Williams, and Alain Prost came through to become the first driver to defend a World Championship title since Jack Brabham did so in 1960. For Williams, this year was a double disaster after team founder Frank Williams was paralysed in a road accident on the way back from a pre-season test. This was also the first year in which every team ran turbocharged engines – the Renault unit looked very effective as Ayrton Senna bagged eight poles with one in his Lotus.

STRAIGHT TO THE TOP

Nelson Piquet took maximum points in his first race for Williams after moving across from Brabham when he won the Brazilian GP at Jacarepagua. Senna had been faster in qualifying, but he knew his Renault engine would be too thirsty to match Piquet over the race distance – and so it proved. There was contrast for Williams team-mate Nigel Mansell, who crashed with Senna on lap one.

BRAZILIAN GRAND PRIX

JACAREPAGUA • ROUND 1 • DATE: 23RD MARCH 1986
Laps: 61 • Distance: 190.693miles/306.891km • Weather: Hot & bright

Pos	Driver	Team	Chassis-Engine	Result	Qual
1	Nelson Piquet	Williams	Williams-Honda FW11	1h39m32.583s	2
2	Ayrton Senna	Lotus	Lotus-Renault 98T	1h40m07.410s	1
3	Jacques Laffite	Ligier	Ligier-Renault JS27	1h40m32.342s	5
4	Rene Arnoux	Ligier	Ligier-Renault JS27	1h41m01.012s	4
5	Martin Brundle	Tyrrell	Tyrrell-Renault 014	60 laps	17
6	Gerhard Berger	Benetton	Benetton-BMW B186	59 laps	16
7	Philippe Streiff	Tyrrell	Tyrrell-Renault 014	59 laps	18
8	Elio de Angelis	Brabham	Brabham-BMW BT55	58 laps	14
9	Johnny Dumfries	Lotus	Lotus-Renault 98T	58 laps	11
10	Teo Fabi	Benetton	Benetton-BMW B186	56 laps	12
R	Thierry Boutsen	Arrows	Arrows-BMW A8	37 laps/exhaust	15
R	Michele Alboreto	Ferrari	Ferrari F1/86	35 laps/fuel system	6
R	Alain Prost	McLaren	McLaren-TAG MP4/2C	30 laps/engine	9
R	Christian Danner	Osella	Osella-Alfa Romeo FA1F	29 laps/engine	24
R	Stefan Johansson	Ferrari	Ferrari F1/86	26 laps/brakes	8
R	Patrick Tambay	Haas USA	Lola-Hart THL-1	24 laps/battery	13
R	Riccardo Patrese	Brabham	Brabham-BMW BT55	21 laps/water leak	10
R	Jonathan Palmer	Zakspeed	Zakspeed 861	20 laps/engine	21
R	Marc Surer	Arrows	Arrows-BMW A8	19 laps/engine	20
R	Alessandro Nannini	Minardi	Minardi-Motori Moderni M185B	18 laps/clutch	25
R	Andrea de Cesaris	Minardi	Minardi-Motori Moderni M185B	16 laps/turbo	22

Pos	Driver	Team	Chassis-Engine	Result	Qual
R	Piercarlo Ghinzani	Osella	Osella-Alfa Romeo FA1G	16 laps/engine	23
R	Keke Rosberg	McLaren	McLaren-TAG MP4/2C	6 laps/engine	7
R	Alan Jones	Haas USA	Lola-Hart THL-1	5 laps/distributor	19
R	Nigel Mansell	Williams	Williams-Honda FW11	0 laps/spun off	3

Pole: Senna, 1m25.501s, 131.624mph/211.829kph. Fastest lap: Piquet, 1m33.546s, 120.304mph/193.611kph on Lap 46. Race leaders: Senna 1-2 & 19 & 41, Piquet 3-18 & 27-40 & 42-61, Prost 20-26

SPANISH GRAND PRIX

JEREZ • ROUND 2 • DATE: 13TH APRIL 1986
Laps: 72 • Distance: 188.707miles/303.696km • Weather: Warm & bright

Pos	Driver	Team	Chassis-Engine	Result	Qual
1	Ayrton Senna	Lotus	Lotus-Renault 98T	1h48m47.735s	1
2	Nigel Mansell	Williams	Williams-Honda FW11	1h48m47.749s	3
3	Alain Prost	McLaren	McLaren-TAG MP4/2C	1h49m09.287s	4
4	Keke Rosberg	McLaren	McLaren-TAG MP4/2C	71 laps	5
5	Teo Fabi	Benetton	Benetton-BMW B186	71 laps	9
6	Gerhard Berger	Benetton	Benetton-BMW B186	71 laps	7
7	Thierry Boutsen	Arrows	Arrows-BMW A8	68 laps	19
8	Patrick Tambay	Haas USA	Lola-Hart THL-1	66 laps	18
R	Johnny Dumfries	Lotus	Lotus-Renault 98T	52 laps/gearbox	10
R	Martin Brundle	Tyrrell	Tyrrell-Renault 014	41 laps/engine	12
R	Jacques Laffite	Ligier	Ligier-Renault JS27	40 laps/halfshaft	8
R	Nelson Piquet	Williams	Williams-Honda FW11	39 laps/engine	2
R	Marc Surer	Arrows	Arrows-BMW A8	39 laps/fuel system	22
R	Rene Arnoux	Ligier	Ligier-Renault JS27	29 laps/halfshaft	6
R	Elio de Angelis	Brabham	Brabham-BMW BT55	29 laps/gearbox	15
R	Michele Alboreto	Ferrari	Ferrari F1/86	22 laps/wheel	13
R	Philippe Streiff	Tyrrell	Tyrrell-Renault 014	22 laps/engine	20
R	Christian Danner	Osella	Osella-Alfa Romeo FA1F	14 laps/engine	23
R	Stefan Johansson	Ferrari	Ferrari F1/86	11 laps/brakes	11
R	Piercarlo Ghinzani	Osella	Osella-Alfa Romeo FA1G	10 laps/engine	21
R	Riccardo Patrese	Brabham	Brabham-BMW BT55	8 laps/gearbox	14
R	Andrea de Cesaris	Minardi	Minardi-Motori Moderni M185B	1 lap/differential	24
R	Jonathan Palmer	Zakspeed	Zakspeed 861	0 laps/collision	16
R	Alan Jones	Haas USA	Lola-Hart THL-1	0 laps/collision	17
R	Alessandro Nannini	Minardi	Minardi-Motori Moderni M185B	0 laps/differential	25

Pole: Senna, 1m21.605s, 115.622mph/186.076kph. Fastest lap: Mansell, 1m27.176s, 108.233mph/174.185kph on Lap 65. Race leaders: Senna 1-39 & 63-72, Mansell 40-62

A CHANGE OF COLOURS

The Benetton knitwear brand entered F1 as a sponsor of Tyrrell in 1983, then put its colours on Alfa Romeo and Toleman. For 1986, it was a team in its own right after taking over Toleman, and its cars were the most colourful on the Qual. They were quick too, with their BMW engines, and Gerhard Berger shone when he won in Mexico.

SAN MARINO GRAND PRIX

IMOLA • ROUND 3 • DATE: 27TH APRIL 1986
Laps: 60 • Distance: 187.656miles/302.4km • Weather: Warm & bright

Pos	Driver	Team	Chassis-Engine	Result	Qual
1	Alain Prost	McLaren	McLaren-TAG MP4/2C	1h32m28.408s	4
2	Nelson Piquet	Williams	Williams-Honda FW11	1h32m36.053s	2
3	Gerhard Berger	Benetton	Benetton-BMW B186	59 laps	9
4	Stefan Johansson	Ferrari	Ferrari F1/86	59 laps	7
5	Keke Rosberg	McLaren	McLaren-TAG MP4/2C	58 laps/out of fuel	6
6	Riccardo Patrese	Brabham	Brabham-BMW BT55	58 laps/out of fuel	16
7	Thierry Boutsen	Arrows	Arrows-BMW A8	58 laps	12
8	Martin Brundle	Tyrrell	Tyrrell-Renault 014	58 laps	13
9	Marc Surer	Arrows	Arrows-BMW A8	57 laps	15
10	Michele Alboreto	Ferrari	Ferrari F1/86	56 laps/turbo	5
R	Piercarlo Ghinzani	Osella	Osella-Alfa Romeo FA1G	52 laps/out of fuel	26
R	Rene Arnoux	Ligier	Ligier-Renault JS27	46 laps/wheel	8
R	Philippe Streiff	Tyrrell	Tyrrell-Renault 014	41 laps/transmission	22
R	Teo Fabi	Benetton	Benetton-BMW B186	39 laps/engine	10
R	Jonathan Palmer	Zakspeed	Zakspeed 861	38 laps/brakes	20
R	Christian Danner	Osella	Osella-Alfa Romeo FA1F	31 laps/electrical	25
R	Alan Jones	Haas USA	Lola-Ford THL-2	28 laps/overheating	21
R	Andrea de Cesaris	Minardi	Minardi-Motori Moderni M185B	20 laps/engine	23
R	Elio de Angelis	Brabham	Brabham-BMW BT55	19 laps/engine	19
R	Jacques Laffite	Ligier	Ligier-Renault JS27	14 laps/transmission	14
R	Ayrton Senna	Lotus	Lotus-Renault 98T	11 laps/wheel	1
R	Nigel Mansell	Williams	Williams-Honda FW11	8 laps/engine	3
R	Johnny Dumfries	Lotus	Lotus-Renault 98T	8 laps/wheel	17
R	Huub Rothengatter	Zakspeed	Zakspeed 861	7 laps/turbo	24
R	Patrick Tambay	Haas USA	Lola-Hart THL-1	5 laps/engine	11
R	Alessandro Nannini	Minardi	Minardi-Motori Moderni M185B	0 laps/accident	18

Pole: Senna, 1m25.050s, 132.559mph/213.333kph. Fastest lap: Piquet, 1m28.667s, 127.151mph/204.630kph on Lap 57. Race leaders: Piquet 1-28, Rosberg 29-32, Prost 33-60

MORE POWER, LESS FUEL

With turbocharged engines growing ever more powerful, full boost was for qualifying only as fuel economy became a major consideration as each car's allowance for a grand prix was down from 220 to 195 litres (48 to 42 gallons). Engine management systems had become more advanced, but teams still used the radio to check that their drivers were laying off the boost.

MONACO GRAND PRIX

MONTE CARLO • ROUND 4 • DATE: 11TH MAY 1986
Laps: 78 • Distance: 161.298miles/259.584km • Weather: Warm & bright

Pos	Driver	Team	Chassis-Engine	Result	Qual
1	Alain Prost	McLaren	McLaren-TAG MP4/2C	1h55m41.060s	1
2	Keke Rosberg	McLaren	McLaren-TAG MP4/2C	1h56m06.082s	9
3	Ayrton Senna	Lotus	Lotus-Renault 98T	1h56m34.706s	3

Pos	Driver	Team	Chassis-Engine	Result	Qual
4	Nigel Mansell	Williams	Williams-Honda FW11	1h56m52.462s	2
5	Rene Arnoux	Ligier	Ligier-Renault JS27	77 laps	12
6	Jacques Laffite	Ligier	Ligier-Renault JS27	77 laps	7
7	Nelson Piquet	Williams	Williams-Honda FW11	77 laps	11
8	Thierry Boutsen	Arrows	Arrows-BMW A8	75 laps	14
9	Marc Surer	Arrows	Arrows-BMW A8	75 laps	17
10	Stefan Johansson	Ferrari	Ferrari F1/86	75 laps	15
11	Philippe Streiff	Tyrrell	Tyrrell-Renault 015	74 laps	13
12	Jonathan Palmer	Zakspeed	Zakspeed 861	74 laps	19
R	Patrick Tambay	Haas USA	Lola-Ford THL-2	67 laps/accident	8
R	Martin Brundle	Tyrrell	Tyrrell-Renault 015	67 laps/accident	10
R	Gerhard Berger	Benetton	Benetton-BMW B186	42 laps/steering	5
R	Michele Alboreto	Ferrari	Ferrari F1/86	38 laps/turbo	4
R	Riccardo Patrese	Brabham	Brabham-BMW BT55	38 laps/fuel pump	6
R	Elio de Angelis	Brabham	Brabham-BMW BT55	31 laps/engine	20
R	Teo Fabi	Benetton	Benetton-BMW B186	17 laps/brakes	16
R	Alan Jones	Haas USA	Lola-Ford THL-2	2 laps/accident	18
DNQ	Piercarlo Ghinzani	Osella	Osella-Alfa Romeo FA1G	-	21
DNQ	Johnny Dumfries	Lotus	Lotus-Renault 98T	-	22
DNQ	Huub Rothengatter	Zakspeed	Zakspeed 861	-	23
DNQ	Christian Danner	Osella	Osella-Alfa Romeo FA1F	-	24
DNQ	Andrea de Cesaris	Minardi	Minardi-Motori Moderni M185B	-	25
DNQ	Alessandro Nannini	Minardi	Minardi-Motori Moderni M185B	-	26

Pole: Prost, 1m22.627s, 90.097mph/144.998kph. Fastest lap: Prost, 1m26.607s, 85.957mph/138.335kph on Lap 51. Race leaders: Prost 1-34 & 42-78, Senna 35-41

HOLD ON TIGHT

A sight we will surely never see again in F1 is a car spitting flame from its exhausts as it bucks and lurches, the driver hanging on for dear life on a one-shot qualifying run. Yet 1986 stands out as the year when this madness was at its height. It's reckoned that BMW's engines could be boosted from 900 to 1,100bhp for these blasts.

BELGIAN GRAND PRIX

SPA-FRANCORCHAMPS • ROUND 5 • DATE: 25TH MAY 1986
Laps: 43 • Distance: 185.194miles/298.42km • Weather: Hot & bright

Pos	Driver	Team	Chassis-Engine	Result	Qual
1	Nigel Mansell	Williams	Williams-Honda FW11	1h27m57.925s	5
2	Ayrton Senna	Lotus	Lotus-Renault 98T	1h28m17.752s	4
3	Stefan Johansson	Ferrari	Ferrari F1/86	1h28m24.517s	11
4	Michele Alboreto	Ferrari	Ferrari F1/86	1h28m27.559s	9
5	Jacques Laffite	Ligier	Ligier-Renault JS27	1h29m08.615s	17
6	Alain Prost	McLaren	McLaren-TAG MP4/2C	1h30m15.697s	3
7	Teo Fabi	Benetton	Benetton-BMW B186	42 laps	6
8	Riccardo Patrese	Brabham	Brabham-BMW BT55	42 laps	15
9	Marc Surer	Arrows	Arrows-BMW A8	41 laps	21
10	Gerhard Berger	Benetton	Benetton-BMW B186	41 laps	2
11	Alan Jones	Haas USA	Lola-Ford THL-2	40 laps/out of fuel	16

Pos	Driver	Team	Chassis-Engine	Result	Qual
12	Philippe Streiff	Tyrrell	Tyrrell-Renault 015	40 laps	18
13	Jonathan Palmer	Zakspeed	Zakspeed 861	37 laps	20
R	Andrea de Cesaris	Minardi	Minardi-Motori Moderni M185B	35 laps/out of fuel	19
R	Martin Brundle	Tyrrell	Tyrrell-Renault 015	25 laps/gearbox	12
R	Huub Rothengatter	Zakspeed	Zakspeed 861	25 laps/electrical	23
R	Alessandro Nannini	Minardi	Minardi-Motori Moderni M185B	24 laps/gearbox	22
R	Rene Arnoux	Ligier	Ligier-Renault JS27	23 laps/engine	7
R	Nelson Piquet	Williams	Williams-Honda FW11	16 laps/turbo	1
R	Johnny Dumfries	Lotus	Lotus-Renault 98T	7 laps/spun off	13
R	Thierry Boutsen	Arrows	Arrows-BMW A8	7 laps/electrical	14
R	Keke Rosberg	McLaren	McLaren-TAG MP4/2C	6 laps/engine	8
R	Piercarlo Ghinzani	Osella	Osella-Alfa Romeo FA1G	3 laps/engine	24
R	Christian Danner	Osella	Osella-Alfa Romeo FA1F	2 laps/engine	25
R	Patrick Tambay	Haas USA	Lola-Ford THL-2	0 laps/accident	10

Pole: Piquet, 1m54.331s, 135.784mph/218.523kph. Fastest lap: Prost, 1m59.282s, 130.148mph/209.453kph on Lap 31. Race leaders: Piquet 1-16, Senna 17-21, Johansson 22-23, Mansell 24-43

CANADIAN GRAND PRIX

MONTREAL • ROUND 6 • DATE: 15TH JUNE 1986
Laps: 69 • Distance: 188.914miles/304.29km • Weather: Hot but dull

Pos	Driver	Team	Chassis-Engine	Result	Qual
1	Nigel Mansell	Williams	Williams-Honda FW11	1h42m26.415s	1
2	Alain Prost	McLaren	McLaren-TAG MP4/2C	1h42m47.074s	4
3	Nelson Piquet	Williams	Williams-Honda FW11	1h43m02.677s	3
4	Keke Rosberg	McLaren	McLaren-TAG MP4/2C	1h44m02.088s	6
5	Ayrton Senna	Lotus	Lotus-Renault 98T	68 laps	2
6	Rene Arnoux	Ligier	Ligier-Renault JS27	68 laps	5
7	Jacques Laffite	Ligier	Ligier-Renault JS27	68 laps	8
8	Michele Alboreto	Ferrari	Ferrari F1/86	68 laps	11
9	Martin Brundle	Tyrrell	Tyrrell-Renault 015	67 laps	19
10	Alan Jones	Haas USA	Lola-Ford THL-2	66 laps	13
11	Philippe Streiff	Tyrrell	Tyrrell-Renault 014	65 laps	17
12	Huub Rothengatter	Zakspeed	Zakspeed 861	63 laps	24
R	Riccardo Patrese	Brabham	Brabham-BMW BT55	44 laps/turbo	9
R	Piercarlo Ghinzani	Osella	Osella-Alfa Romeo FA1G	43 laps/gearbox	23
R	Andrea de Cesaris	Minardi	Minardi-Motori Moderni M185B	40 laps/gearbox	21
R	Thierry Boutsen	Arrows	Arrows-BMW A8	38 laps/electrical	12
R	Gerhard Berger	Benetton	Benetton-BMW B186	34 laps/turbo	7
R	Stefan Johansson	Ferrari	Ferrari F1/86	29 laps/accident	18
R	Johnny Dumfries	Lotus	Lotus-Renault 98T	28 laps/accident	16
R	Jonathan Palmer	Zakspeed	Zakspeed 861	24 laps/engine	22
R	Derek Warwick	Brabham	Brabham-BMW BT55	20 laps/engine	10
R	Alessandro Nannini	Minardi	Minardi-Motori Moderni M185B	17 laps/turbo	20
R	Teo Fabi	Benetton	Benetton-BMW B186	13 laps/battery	15
R	Christian Danner	Osella	Osella-Alfa Romeo FA1F	6 laps/turbo	25
NS	Patrick Tambay	Haas USA	Lola-Ford THL-2	-	14

Pole: Mansell, 1m24.118s, 117.274mph/188.734kph. Fastest lap: Piquet, 1m25.443s, 115.455mph/185.808kph on Lap 63. Race leaders: Mansell 1-16 & 22-29 & 31-69, Rosberg 17-21, Prost 30

DETROIT GRAND PRIX

DETROIT • ROUND 7 • DATE: 22ND JUNE 1986
Laps: 63 • Distance: 157.501miles/253.474km • Weather: Hot but windy

Pos	Driver	Team	Chassis-Engine	Result	Qual
1	Ayrton Senna	Lotus	Lotus-Renault 98T	1h51m12.847s	1
2	Jacques Laffite	Ligier	Ligier-Renault JS27	1h51m43.864s	6
3	Alain Prost	McLaren	McLaren-TAG MP4/2C	1h51m44.671s	7
4	Michele Alboreto	Ferrari	Ferrari F1/86	1h52m43.783s	11
5	Nigel Mansell	Williams	Williams-Honda FW11	62 laps	2
6	Riccardo Patrese	Brabham	Brabham-BMW BT55	62 laps	8
7	Johnny Dumfries	Lotus	Lotus-Renault 98T	61 laps	14
8	Jonathan Palmer	Zakspeed	Zakspeed 861	61 laps	20
9	Philippe Streiff	Tyrrell	Tyrrell-Renault 015	61 laps	18
10	Derek Warwick	Brabham	Brabham-BMW BT55	60 laps	15
R	Christian Danner	Arrows	Arrows-BMW A8	51 laps/electrical	19
R	Rene Arnoux	Ligier	Ligier-Renault JS27	46 laps/accident	4
R	Thierry Boutsen	Arrows	Arrows-BMW A8	44 laps/accident	13
R	Andrea de Cesaris	Minardi	Minardi-Motori Moderni M185B	43 laps/gearbox	23
R	Nelson Piquet	Williams	Williams-Honda FW11	41 laps/accident	3
R	Stefan Johansson	Ferrari	Ferrari F1/86	40 laps/electrical	5
R	Teo Fabi	Benetton	Benetton-BMW B186	38 laps/gearbox	17
R	Eddie Cheever	Haas USA	Lola-Ford THL-2	37 laps/steering	10
R	Alan Jones	Haas USA	Lola-Ford THL-2	33 laps/steering	21
R	Allen Berg	Osella	Osella-Alfa Romeo FA1F	28 laps/electrical	25
R	Martin Brundle	Tyrrell	Tyrrell-Renault 015	15 laps/electrical	16
R	Piercarlo Ghinzani	Osella	Osella-Alfa Romeo FA1G	14 laps/turbo	22
R	Keke Rosberg	McLaren	McLaren-TAG MP4/2C	12 laps/transmission	9
R	Gerhard Berger	Benetton	Benetton-BMW B186	8 laps/engine	12
R	Alessandro Nannini	Minardi	Minardi-Motori Moderni M185B	3 laps/turbo	24
NS	Huub Rothengatter	Zakspeed	Zakspeed 861	Electrical	26

Pole: Senna, 1m38.301s, 91.556mph/147.345kph. Fastest lap: Piquet, 1m41.233s, 88.903mph/143.076kph on Lap 41. Race leaders: Senna 1 & 8-13 & 39-63, Mansell 2-7, Arnoux 14-17, Laffite 18-30, Piquet 31-38

TWO CAREERS COME TO AN END

Jacques Laffite's illustrious F1 career – 176 grands prix and six wins – came to a sudden end at the start of the British GP at Brands Hatch. Thierry Boutsen got out of shape going into the first corner and Laffite's attempt to avoid it led to him going right into the barriers, breaking his legs. Later in the year, Marc Surer was badly burnt in a rally crash.

OUT WITH A BANG

Arriving in Adelaide with a six-point advantage over Prost, the stage was set for Nigel Mansell to turn from winner to champion. After 63 laps, he was on target then he had a blow-out at 180mph (290kph). Worried about tyre wear, team-mate Piquet was brought in for fresh tyres, and this was enough for Prost to take the win and the title.

FRENCH GRAND PRIX

CIRCUIT PAUL RICARD • ROUND 8 • DATE: 6TH JULY 1986
Laps: 80 • Distance: 189.520miles/305.04km • Weather: Warm & bright

Pos	Driver	Team	Chassis-Engine	Result	Qual
1	Nigel Mansell	Williams	Williams-Honda FW11	1h37m19.272s	2
2	Alain Prost	McLaren	McLaren-TAG MP4/2C	1h37m36.400s	5
3	Nelson Piquet	Williams	Williams-Honda FW11	1h37m56.817s	3
4	Keke Rosberg	McLaren	McLaren-TAG MP4/2C	1h38m07.975s	7
5	Rene Arnoux	Ligier	Ligier-Renault JS27	79 laps	4
6	Jacques Laffite	Ligier	Ligier-Renault JS27	79 laps	11
7	Riccardo Patrese	Brabham	Brabham-BMW BT55	78 laps	16
8	Michele Alboreto	Ferrari	Ferrari F1/86	78 laps	9
9	Derek Warwick	Brabham	Brabham-BMW BT55	77 laps	14
10	Martin Brundle	Tyrrell	Tyrrell-Renault 015	77 laps	15
11	Christian Danner	Arrows	Arrows-BMW A8	76 laps	18
NC	Thierry Boutsen	Arrows	Arrows-BMW A8	67 laps	21
R	Patrick Tambay	Haas USA	Lola-Ford THL-2	64 laps/brakes	13
R	Johnny Dumfries	Lotus	Lotus-Renault 98T	56 laps/engine	12
R	Jonathan Palmer	Zakspeed	Zakspeed 861	46 laps/engine	22
R	Philippe Streiff	Tyrrell	Tyrrell-Renault 015	43 laps/fire	17
R	Huub Rothengatter	Zakspeed	Zakspeed 861	32 laps/accident	24
R	Allen Berg	Osella	Osella-Alfa Romeo FA1G	25 laps/turbo	26
R	Gerhard Berger	Benetton	Benetton-BMW B186	22 laps/gearbox	8
R	Teo Fabi	Benetton	Benetton-BMW B186	7 laps/engine	6
R	Stefan Johansson	Ferrari	Ferrari F1/86	5 laps/turbo	10
R	Ayrton Senna	Lotus	Lotus-Renault 98T	3 laps/accident	1
R	Alessandro Nannini	Minardi	Minardi-Motori Moderni M185B	3 laps/accident	19
R	Andrea de Cesaris	Minardi	Minardi-Motori Moderni M185B	3 laps/turbo	23
R	Piercarlo Ghinzani	Osella	Osella-Alfa Romeo FA1H	3 laps/accident	25
R	Alan Jones	Haas USA	Lola-Ford THL-2	2 laps/accident	20

Pole: Senna, 1m06.526s, 128.212mph/206.337kph. Fastest lap: Mansell, 1m09.993s, 121.860mph/196.116kph on Lap 57. Race leaders: Mansell 1-25 & 37-53 & 59-80, Prost 26-36 & 54-58

BRITISH GRAND PRIX

BRANDS HATCH • ROUND 9 • DATE: 13TH JULY 1986
Laps: 75 • Distance: 196.15miles/315.457km • Weather: Warm & bright

Pos	Driver	Team	Chassis-Engine	Result	Qual
1	Nigel Mansell	Williams	Williams-Honda FW11	1h30m38.471s	2
2	Nelson Piquet	Williams	Williams-Honda FW11	1h30m44.045s	1
3	Alain Prost	McLaren	McLaren-TAG MP4/2C	74 laps	6
4	Rene Arnoux	Ligier	Ligier-Renault JS27	73 laps	8
5	Martin Brundle	Tyrrell	Tyrrell-Renault 015	72 laps	11
6	Philippe Streiff	Tyrrell	Tyrrell-Renault 015	72 laps	16
7	Johnny Dumfries	Lotus	Lotus-Renault 98T	72 laps	10
8	Derek Warwick	Brabham	Brabham-BMW BT55	72 laps	9
9	Jonathan Palmer	Zakspeed	Zakspeed 861	69 laps	22
NC	Thierry Boutsen	Arrows	Arrows-BMW A8	62 laps	13
R	Patrick Tambay	Haas USA	Lola-Ford THL-2	60 laps/gearbox	17
R	Michele Alboreto	Ferrari	Ferrari F1/86	51 laps/turbo	12
R	Alessandro Nannini	Minardi	Minardi-Motori Moderni M185B	50 laps/steering	20

Pos	Driver	Team	Chassis-Engine	Result	Qual
R	Teo Fabi	Benetton	Benetton-BMW B186	45 laps/fuel system	7
R	Riccardo Patrese	Brabham	Brabham-BMW BT54	39 laps/engine	15
R	Ayrton Senna	Lotus	Lotus-Renault 98T	27 laps/gearbox	3
R	Huub Rothengatter	Zakspeed	Zakspeed 861	24 laps/engine	25
R	Andrea de Cesaris	Minardi	Minardi-Motori Moderni M185B	23 laps/electrical	21
R	Gerhard Berger	Benetton	Benetton-BMW B186	22 laps/electrical	4
R	Alan Jones	Haas USA	Lola-Ford THL-2	22 laps/throttle	14
R	Stefan Johansson	Ferrari	Ferrari F1/86	20 laps/engine	18
R	Keke Rosberg	McLaren	McLaren-TAG MP4/2C	7 laps/gearbox	5
R	Jacques Laffite	Ligier	Ligier-Renault JS27	0 laps/collision	19
R	Christian Danner	Arrows	Arrows-BMW A8	0 laps/collision	23
R	Piercarlo Ghinzani	Osella	Osella-Alfa Romeo FA1G	0 laps/collision	24
R	Allen Berg	Osella	Osella-Alfa Romeo FA1H	0 laps/collision	26

Pole: Piquet, 1m06.961s, 140.511mph/226.131kph. Fastest lap: Mansell, 1m09.593s, 135.196mph/217.578kph on Lap 69. Race leaders: Piquet 1-22, Mansell 23-75

GERMAN GRAND PRIX

HOCKENHEIM • ROUND 10 • DATE: 27TH JULY 1986
Laps: 44 • Distance: 185.832miles/299.068km • Weather: Hot & bright

Pos	Driver	Team	Chassis-Engine	Result	Qual
1	Nelson Piquet	Williams	Williams-Honda FW11	1h22m08.263s	5
2	Ayrton Senna	Lotus	Lotus-Renault 98T	1h22m23.700s	3
3	Nigel Mansell	Williams	Williams-Honda FW11	1h22m52.843s	6
4	Rene Arnoux	Ligier	Ligier-Renault JS27	1h23m23.439s	8
5	Keke Rosberg	McLaren	McLaren-TAG MP4/2C	43 laps/out of fuel	1
6	Alain Prost	McLaren	McLaren-TAG MP4/2C	43 laps/out of fuel	2
7	Derek Warwick	Brabham	Brabham-BMW BT55	43 laps	20
8	Patrick Tambay	Haas USA	Lola-Ford THL-2	43 laps	13
9	Alan Jones	Haas USA	Lola-Ford THL-2	42 laps	19
10	Gerhard Berger	Benetton	Benetton-BMW B186	42 laps	4
11	Stefan Johansson	Ferrari	Ferrari F1/86	41 laps/wing	11
12	Allen Berg	Osella	Osella-Alfa Romeo FA1F	40 laps	26
R	Christian Danner	Arrows	Arrows-BMW A8	38 laps/turbo	17
R	Huub Rothengatter	Zakspeed	Zakspeed 861	38 laps/gearbox	24
R	Jonathan Palmer	Zakspeed	Zakspeed 861	37 laps/engine	16
R	Martin Brundle	Tyrrell	Tyrrell-Renault 015	34 laps/electrical	15
R	Riccardo Patrese	Brabham	Brabham-BMW BT55	22 laps/turbo	7
R	Andrea de Cesaris	Minardi	Minardi-Motori Moderni M185B	20 laps/gearbox	23
R	Alessandro Nannini	Minardi	Minardi-Motori Moderni M185B	19 laps/overheating	22
R	Johnny Dumfries	Lotus	Lotus-Renault 98T	17 laps/radiator damage	12
R	Thierry Boutsen	Arrows	Arrows-BMW A9	13 laps/turbo	21
R	Philippe Alliot	Ligier	Ligier-Renault JS27	11 laps/engine	14
R	Piercarlo Ghinzani	Osella	Osella-Alfa Romeo FA1G	10 laps/clutch	25
R	Philippe Streiff	Tyrrell	Tyrrell-Renault 015	7 laps/engine	18
R	Michele Alboreto	Ferrari	Ferrari F1/86	6 laps/transmission	10
R	Teo Fabi	Benetton	Benetton-BMW B186	0 laps/accident	9

Pole: Rosberg, 1m42.013s, 149.044mph/239.863kph. Fastest lap: Berger, 1m46.604s, 142.625mph/229.533kph on Lap 35. Race leaders: Senna 1, Rosberg 2-5 & 15-19 & 27-38, Piquet 6-14 & 21-26 & 39-44, Prost 20

NEW CIRCUITS

The introduction of a race in a communist-run country was novel and the twisting and turning Hungaroring offered great viewing for a huge crowd as it criss-crossed a valley. After a five-year break, the Spanish GP returned, using the Jerez circuit that had great facilities but always suffered from being too far from Spain's major cities.

HUNGARIAN GRAND PRIX

HUNGARORING • ROUND 11 • DATE: 10TH AUGUST 1986
Laps: 76 • Distance: 189.557miles/305.064km • Weather: Hot & bright

Pos	Driver	Team	Chassis-Engine	Result	Qual
1	Nelson Piquet	Williams	Williams-Honda FW11	2h00m34.508s	2
2	Ayrton Senna	Lotus	Lotus-Renault 98T	2h00m52.181s	1
3	Nigel Mansell	Williams	Williams-Honda FW11	75 laps	4
4	Stefan Johansson	Ferrari	Ferrari F1/86	75 laps	7
5	Johnny Dumfries	Lotus	Lotus-Renault 98T	74 laps	8
6	Martin Brundle	Tyrrell	Tyrrell-Renault 015	74 laps	16
7	Patrick Tambay	Haas USA	Lola-Ford THL-2	74 laps	6
8	Philippe Streiff	Tyrrell	Tyrrell-Renault 015	74 laps	18
9	Philippe Alliot	Ligier	Ligier-Renault JS27	73 laps	12
10	Jonathan Palmer	Zakspeed	Zakspeed 861	70 laps	24
R	Rene Arnoux	Ligier	Ligier-Renault JS27	48 laps/engine	9
R	Alan Jones	Haas USA	Lola-Ford THL-2	46 laps/differential	10
R	Gerhard Berger	Benetton	Benetton-BMW B186	44 laps/transmission	11
R	Thierry Boutsen	Arrows	Arrows-BMW A8	40 laps/electrical	22
R	Keke Rosberg	McLaren	McLaren-TAG MP4/2C	34 laps/suspension	5
R	Teo Fabi	Benetton	Benetton-BMW B186	32 laps/transmission	13
R	Alessandro Nannini	Minardi	Minardi-Motori Moderni M186	30 laps/engine	17
R	Michele Alboreto	Ferrari	Ferrari F1/86	29 laps/accident	15
R	Derek Warwick	Brabham	Brabham-BMW BT55	28 laps/accident	19
R	Alain Prost	McLaren	McLaren-TAG MP4/2C	23 laps/accident	3
R	Piercarlo Ghinzani	Osella	Osella-Alfa Romeo FA1G	15 laps/suspension	23
R	Christian Danner	Arrows	Arrows-BMW A9	7 laps/suspension	21
R	Riccardo Patrese	Brabham	Brabham-BMW BT55	5 laps/gearbox	14
R	Andrea de Cesaris	Minardi	Minardi-Motori Moderni M186	5 laps/engine	20
R	Huub Rothengatter	Zakspeed	Zakspeed 861	2 laps/radiator damage	25
R	Allen Berg	Osella	Osella-Alfa Romeo FA1F	1 lap/turbo	26

Pole: Senna, 1m29.450s, 100.380mph/161.547kph. Fastest lap: Piquet, 1m31.001s, 98.669mph/158.793kph on Lap 73. Race leaders: Senna 1-11 & 36-56, Piquet 12-35 & 57-76

NEW CONSTRUCTORS

In addition to Benetton's transformation from Toleman, AGS entered F1 in 1986 after years of running with some success in F2, with Philippe Streiff winning the last-ever F2 race at the end of 1984. Henri Julien's squad continued in the new F3000 before ending 1986 by entering F1 with an overweight Motori Moderni-powered JH21C for Ivan Capelli.

AUSTRIAN GRAND PRIX

OSTERREICHRING • ROUND 12 • DATE: 17TH AUGUST 1986
Laps: 52 • Distance: 191.993miles/308.984km • Weather: Hot & bright

Pos	Driver	Team	Chassis-Engine	Result	Qual
1	Alain Prost	McLaren	McLaren-TAG MP4/2C	1h21m22.531s	5
2	Michele Alboreto	Ferrari	Ferrari F1/86	51 laps	9
3	Stefan Johansson	Ferrari	Ferrari F1/86	50 laps	14
4	Alan Jones	Haas USA	Lola-Ford THL-2	50 laps	16
5	Patrick Tambay	Haas USA	Lola-Ford THL-2	50 laps	13
6	Christian Danner	Arrows	Arrows-BMW A8	49 laps	22
7	Gerhard Berger	Benetton	Benetton-BMW B186	49 laps	2
8	Huub Rothengatter	Zakspeed	Zakspeed 861	48 laps	24
9	Keke Rosberg	McLaren	McLaren-TAG MP4/2C	47 laps/electrical	3
10	Rene Arnoux	Ligier	Ligier-Renault JS27	47 laps	12
11	Piercarlo Ghinzani	Osella	Osella-Alfa Romeo FA1G	46 laps	25
R	Nigel Mansell	Williams	Williams-Honda FW11	32 laps/halfshaft	6
R	Nelson Piquet	Williams	Williams-Honda FW11	29 laps/engine	7
R	Thierry Boutsen	Arrows	Arrows-BMW A9	25 laps/turbo	18
R	Teo Fabi	Benetton	Benetton-BMW B186	17 laps/engine	1
R	Philippe Alliot	Ligier	Ligier-Renault JS27	16 laps/engine	11
R	Ayrton Senna	Lotus	Lotus-Renault 98T	13 laps/engine	8
R	Alessandro Nannini	Minardi	Minardi-Motori Moderni M186	13 laps/suspension	19
R	Andrea de Cesaris	Minardi	Minardi-Motori Moderni M186	13 laps/clutch	23
R	Martin Brundle	Tyrrell	Tyrrell-Renault 015	12 laps/turbo	17
R	Philippe Streiff	Tyrrell	Tyrrell-Renault 015	10 laps/engine	20
R	Johnny Dumfries	Lotus	Lotus-Renault 98T	9 laps/engine	15
R	Jonathan Palmer	Zakspeed	Zakspeed 861	8 laps/engine	21
R	Allen Berg	Osella	Osella-Alfa Romeo FA1F	6 laps/electrical	26
R	Riccardo Patrese	Brabham	Brabham-BMW BT55	2 laps/engine	4
NS	Derek Warwick	Brabham	Brabham-BMW BT55	Patrese took car	10

Pole: Fabi, 1m23.549s, 159.090mph/256.031kph. Fastest lap: Berger, 1m29.444s, 148.605mph/239.157kph on Lap 49. Race leaders: Berger 1-25, Mansell 26-28, Prost 29-52

ITALIAN GRAND PRIX

MONZA • ROUND 13 • DATE: 7TH SEPTEMBER 1986
Laps: 51 • Distance: 183.309miles/295.8km • Weather: Hot & bright

Pos	Driver	Team	Chassis-Engine	Result	Qual
1	Nelson Piquet	Williams	Williams-Honda FW11	1h17m42.889s	6
2	Nigel Mansell	Williams	Williams-Honda FW11	1h17m52.717s	3
3	Stefan Johansson	Ferrari	Ferrari F1/86	1h18m05.804s	12
4	Keke Rosberg	McLaren	McLaren-TAG MP4/2C	1h18m36.698s	8
5	Gerhard Berger	Benetton	Benetton-BMW B186	50 laps	4
6	Alan Jones	Haas USA	Lola-Ford THL-2	49 laps	18
7	Thierry Boutsen	Arrows	Arrows-BMW A8	49 laps	13
8	Christian Danner	Arrows	Arrows-BMW A8	49 laps	16
9	Philippe Streiff	Tyrrell	Tyrrell-Renault 015	49 laps	23
10	Martin Brundle	Tyrrell	Tyrrell-Renault 015	49 laps	20
NC	Alex Caffi	Osella	Osella-Alfa Romeo FA1F	45 laps	27
R	Teo Fabi	Benetton	Benetton-BMW B186	44 laps/puncture	1
R	Michele Alboreto	Ferrari	Ferrari F1/86	33 laps/engine	9

Pos	Driver	Team	Chassis-Engine	Result	Qual
R	Andrea de Cesaris	Minardi	Minardi-Motori Moderni M186	33 laps/engine	21
R	Ivan Capelli	AGS	AGS-Motori Moderni JH21C	31 laps/puncture	25
R	Rene Arnoux	Ligier	Ligier-Renault JS27	30 laps/gearbox	11
R	Jonathan Palmer	Zakspeed	Zakspeed 861	27 laps/engine	22
DQ	Alain Prost	McLaren	McLaren-TAG MP4/2C	27 laps/car change	2
R	Philippe Alliot	Ligier	Ligier-Renault JS27	22 laps/engine	14
R	Johnny Dumfries	Lotus	Lotus-Renault 98T	18 laps/gearbox	17
R	Derek Warwick	Brabham	Brabham-BMW BT55	16 laps/spun off	7
R	Alessandro Nannini	Minardi	Minardi-Motori Moderni M185B	15 laps/electrical	19
R	Piercarlo Ghinzani	Osella	Osella-Alfa Romeo FA1G	12 laps/suspension	26
R	Riccardo Patrese	Brabham	Brabham-BMW BT55	2 laps/accident	10
R	Patrick Tambay	Haas USA	Lola-Ford THL-2	2 laps/accident	15
R	Huub Rothengatter	Zakspeed	Zakspeed 861	1 lap/engine	24
R	Ayrton Senna	Lotus	Lotus-Renault 98T	0 laps/transmission	5

Pole: Fabi, 1m24.078s, 154.311mph/248.340kph. Fastest lap: Fabi, 1m28.099s, 147.268mph/237.006kph on Lap 35. Race leaders: Berger 1-6 & 25-26, Mansell 7-24 & 27-37, Piquet 38-51

PORTUGUESE GRAND PRIX

AUTODROMO DO ESTORIL • ROUND 14 • DATE: 21ST SEPTEMBER 1986
Laps: 70 • Distance: 188.899miles/304.5km • Weather: Hot & bright

Pos	Driver	Team	Chassis-Engine	Result	Qual
1	Nigel Mansell	Williams	Williams-Honda FW11	1h37m21.900s	2
2	Alain Prost	McLaren	McLaren-TAG MP4/2C	1h37m40.672s	3
3	Nelson Piquet	Williams	Williams-Honda FW11	1h38m11.174s	6
4	Ayrton Senna	Lotus	Lotus-Renault 98T	69 laps/out of fuel	1
5	Michele Alboreto	Ferrari	Ferrari F1/86	69 laps	13
6	Stefan Johansson	Ferrari	Ferrari F1/86	69 laps	8
7	Rene Arnoux	Ligier	Ligier-Renault JS27	69 laps	10
8	Teo Fabi	Benetton	Benetton-BMW B186	68 laps	5
9	Johnny Dumfries	Lotus	Lotus-Renault 98T	68 laps	15
10	Thierry Boutsen	Arrows	Arrows-BMW A8	67 laps	21
11	Christian Danner	Arrows	Arrows-BMW A8	67 laps	22
12	Jonathan Palmer	Zakspeed	Zakspeed 861	67 laps	20
13	Allen Berg	Osella	Osella-Alfa Romeo FA1F	63 laps	27
R	Riccardo Patrese	Brabham	Brabham-BMW BT55	62 laps/engine	9
NC	Patrick Tambay	Haas USA	Lola-Ford THL-2	62 laps	14
NC	Alessandro Nannini	Minardi	Minardi-Motori Moderni M185B	60 laps	18
R	Gerhard Berger	Benetton	Benetton-BMW B186	44 laps/spun off	4
R	Andrea de Cesaris	Minardi	Minardi-Motori Moderni M186	43 laps/spun off	16
R	Keke Rosberg	McLaren	McLaren-TAG MP4/2C	41 laps/electrical	7
R	Derek Warwick	Brabham	Brabham-BMW BT55	41 laps/electrical	12
R	Philippe Alliot	Ligier	Ligier-Renault JS27	39 laps/engine	11
R	Philippe Streiff	Tyrrell	Tyrrell-Renault 015	28 laps/engine	23
R	Martin Brundle	Tyrrell	Tyrrell-Renault 015	18 laps/engine	19
R	Alan Jones	Haas USA	Lola-Ford THL-2	10 laps/spun off	17
R	Huub Rothengatter	Zakspeed	Zakspeed 861	9 laps/transmission	26
R	Piercarlo Ghinzani	Osella	Osella-Alfa Romeo FA1G	8 laps/engine	24
R	Ivan Capelli	AGS	AGS-Motori Moderni JH21C	6 laps/transmission	25

Pole: Senna, 1m16.673s, 126.911mph/204.243kph. Fastest lap: Mansell, 1m20.943s, 120.216mph/193.469kph on Lap 53. Race leaders: Mansell 1-70

MEXICAN GRAND PRIX

MEXICO CITY • ROUND 15 • DATE: 12TH OCTOBER 1986
Laps: 68 • Distance: 186.801miles/300.628km • Weather: Hot but dull

Pos	Driver	Team	Chassis-Engine	Result	Qual
1	Gerhard Berger	Benetton	Benetton-BMW B186	1h33m18.700s	4
2	Alain Prost	McLaren	McLaren-TAG MP4/2C	1h33m44.138s	6
3	Ayrton Senna	Lotus	Lotus-Renault 98T	1h34m11.213s	1
4	Nelson Piquet	Williams	Williams-Honda FW11	67 laps	2
5	Nigel Mansell	Williams	Williams-Honda FW11	67 laps	3
6	Philippe Alliot	Ligier	Ligier-Renault JS27	67 laps	10
7	Thierry Boutsen	Arrows	Arrows-BMW A8	66 laps	21
8	Andrea de Cesaris	Minardi	Minardi-Motori Moderni M186	66 laps	22
9	Christian Danner	Arrows	Arrows-BMW A8	66 laps	20
10	Jonathan Palmer	Zakspeed	Zakspeed 861	65 laps/out of fuel	18
11	Martin Brundle	Tyrrell	Tyrrell-Renault 015	65 laps	16
12	Stefan Johansson	Ferrari	Ferrari F1/86	64 laps/turbo	14
13	Riccardo Patrese	Brabham	Brabham-BMW BT55	64 laps/spun off	5
14	Alessandro Nannini	Minardi	Minardi-Motori Moderni M185B	64 laps	24
15	Rene Arnoux	Ligier	Ligier-Renault JS27	63 laps/engine	13
16	Allen Berg	Osella	Osella-Alfa Romeo FA1F	61 laps	26
R	Johnny Dumfries	Lotus	Lotus-Renault 98T	53 laps/electrical	17
R	Derek Warwick	Brabham	Brabham-BMW BT55	37 laps/engine	7
R	Alan Jones	Haas USA	Lola-Ford THL-2	35 laps/tyre	15
R	Keke Rosberg	McLaren	McLaren-TAG MP4/2C	32 laps/puncture	11
R	Michele Alboreto	Ferrari	Ferrari F1/86	10 laps/turbo	12
R	Philippe Streiff	Tyrrell	Tyrrell-Renault 015	8 laps/turbo	19
R	Piercarlo Ghinzani	Osella	Osella-Alfa Romeo FA1G	8 laps/turbo	25
R	Teo Fabi	Benetton	Benetton-BMW B186	4 laps/engine	9
R	Patrick Tambay	Haas USA	Lola-Ford THL-2	0 laps/accident	8
NS	Huub Rothengatter	Zakspeed	Zakspeed 861	Accident	23

Pole: Senna, 1m16.990s, 128.451mph/206.722kph. Fastest lap: Piquet, 1m19.360s, 124.615mph/200.549kph on Lap 64. Race leaders: Piquet 1-31, Senna 32-35, Berger 36-68

NEW DRIVERS

Johnny Dumfries was the pick of the novices and had the hardest task, starting as Senna's team-mate at Lotus. The Scottish aristocrat's best result was fifth in Hungary in what would be his only F1 season. Alessandro Nannini retired 13 times from 15 starts for Minardi, while Allen Berg and Alex Caffi ran at the back with Osella.

IN MEMORIAM

Grand prix winner Elio de Angelis was four races into the season after joining Brabham from Lotus when he was killed testing at Paul Ricard. A fortnight later, F1 lost underrated Austrian Jo Gartner when he crashed in the Le Mans 24 Hours. Despite taking fifth in the 1984 Italian GP, he was never credited with points as Osella had only registered one car.

AUSTRALIAN GRAND PRIX

ADELAIDE • ROUND 16 • DATE: 26TH OCTOBER 1986
Laps: 82 • Distance: 192.549miles/309.878km • Weather: Warm & bright

Pos	Driver	Team	Chassis-Engine	Result	Qual
1	Alain Prost	McLaren	McLaren-TAG MP4/2C	1h54m20.388s	4
2	Nelson Piquet	Williams	Williams-Honda FW11	1h54m24.593s	2
3	Stefan Johansson	Ferrari	Ferrari F1/86	81 laps	12
4	Martin Brundle	Tyrrell	Tyrrell-Renault 015	81 laps	16
5	Philippe Streiff	Tyrrell	Tyrrell-Renault 015	80 laps/out of fuel	10
6	Johnny Dumfries	Lotus	Lotus-Renault 98T	80 laps	14
7	Rene Arnoux	Ligier	Ligier-Renault JS27	79 laps	5
8	Philippe Alliot	Ligier	Ligier-Renault JS27	79 laps	8
9	Jonathan Palmer	Zakspeed	Zakspeed 861	77 laps	21
10	Teo Fabi	Benetton	Benetton-BMW B186	77 laps	13
NC	Patrick Tambay	Haas USA	Lola-Ford THL-2	70 laps	17
R	Nigel Mansell	Williams	Williams-Honda FW11	63 laps/tyre	1
R	Riccardo Patrese	Brabham	Brabham-BMW BT55	63 laps/electrical	19
R	Keke Rosberg	McLaren	McLaren-TAG MP4/2C	62 laps/tyre	7
NC	Allen Berg	Osella	Osella-Alfa Romeo FA1F	61 laps	26
R	Derek Warwick	Brabham	Brabham-BMW BT55	57 laps/brakes	20
R	Christian Danner	Arrows	Arrows-BMW A8	52 laps/engine	24
R	Thierry Boutsen	Arrows	Arrows-BMW A8	50 laps/engine	22
R	Ayrton Senna	Lotus	Lotus-Renault 98T	43 laps/engine	3
R	Gerhard Berger	Benetton	Benetton-BMW B186	40 laps/engine	6
R	Andrea de Cesaris	Minardi	Minardi-Motori Moderni M186	40 laps/extinguisher	11
R	Huub Rothengatter	Zakspeed	Zakspeed 861	29 laps/suspension	23
R	Alan Jones	Haas USA	Lola-Ford THL-2	16 laps/engine	15
R	Alessandro Nannini	Minardi	Minardi-Motori Moderni M185B	10 laps/accident	18
R	Piercarlo Ghinzani	Osella	Osella-Alfa Romeo FA1G	2 laps/transmission	25
R	Michele Alboreto	Ferrari	Ferrari F1/86	0 laps/accident	9

Pole: Mansell, 1m18.403s, 107.819mph/173.518kph. Fastest lap: Piquet, 1m20.787s, 104.637mph/168.398kph on Lap 82. Race leaders: Piquet 1-6 & 63-64, Rosberg 7-62, Prost 65-82

WORLD DRIVERS' CHAMPIONSHIP FINAL RESULTS

Pos	Driver	Nat	Car-Engine	R1	R2	R3	R4	R5	R6
1	Alain Prost	FRA	McLaren-TAG MP4/2C	R	3	1	1PF	6F	2
2	Nigel Mansell	GBR	Williams-Honda FW11	R	2F	R	4	1	1P
3	Nelson Piquet	BRA	Williams-Honda FW11	1F	R	2F	7	RP	3F
4	Ayrton Senna	BRA	Lotus-Renault 98T	2P	1P	RP	3	2	5
5	Stefan Johansson	SWE	Ferrari F1/86	R	R	4	10	3	R
6	Keke Rosberg	FIN	McLaren-TAG MP4/2C	R	4	5	2	R	4
7	Gerhard Berger	AUT	Benetton-BMW B186	6	6	3	R	10	R
8	Jacques Laffite	FRA	Ligier-Renault JS27	3	R	R	6	5	7
9	Michele Alboreto	ITA	Ferrari F1/86	R	R	10	R	4	8
10	Rene Arnoux	FRA	Ligier-Renault JS27	4	R	R	5	R	6
11	Martin Brundle	GBR	Tyrrell-Renault 014	5	R	8	-	-	-
			Tyrrell-Renault 015	-	-	-	R	R	9
12	Alan Jones	AUS	Lola-Hart THL-1	R	R	-	-	-	-
			Lola-Ford THL-2	-	-	R	R	11	10
13	Johnny Dumfries	GBR	Lotus-Renault 98T	9	R	R	DNQ	R	R
13	Philippe Streiff	FRA	Tyrrell-Renault 014	7	R	R	-	-	11
			Tyrrell-Renault 015	-	-	-	11	12	-

Pos	Driver	Nat	Car-Engine	R1	R2	R3	R4	R5	R6
15	Teo Fabi	ITA	Benetton-BMW B186	10	5	R	R	7	R
15	Patrick Tambay	FRA	Lola-Hart THL-1	R	8	R	-	-	-
			Lola-Ford THL-2	-	-	-	R	R	NS
17	Riccardo Patrese	ITA	Brabham-BMW BT55	R	R	6	R	8	R
			Brabham-BMW BT54	-	-	-	-	-	-
18	Christian Danner	DEU	Osella-Alfa Romeo FA1F	R	R	R	DNQ	R	R
			Arrows-BMW A8	-	-	-	-	-	-
			Arrows-BMW A9	-	-	-	-	-	-
18	Philippe Alliot	FRA	Ligier-Renault JS27	-	-	-	-	-	-

Pos	Driver	R7	R8	R9	R10	R11	R12	R13	R14	R15	R16	Total
1	Prost	3	2	3	6	R	1	DQ	2	2	1	72
2	Mansell	5	1F	1F	3	3	R	2	1F	5	RP	70
3	Piquet	RF	3	2P	1	1F	R	1	3	4F	2F	69
4	Senna	1P	RP	R	2	2P	R	R	4P	3P	R	55
5	Johansson	R	R	R	11	4	3	3	6	12	3	23
6	Rosberg	R	4	R	5P	R	9	4	R	R	R	22
7	Berger	R	R	R	10F	R	7F	5	R	1	R	17
8	Laffite	2	6	R	-	-	-	-	-	-	-	14
9	Alboreto	4	8	R	R	R	2	R	5	R	R	14
10	Arnoux	R	5	4	4	R	10	R	7	15	7	14
11	Brundle	-	-	-	-	-	-	-	-	-	-	8
		R	10	5	R	6	R	10	R	11	4	
12	Jones	-	-	-	-	-	-	-	-	-	-	4
		R	R	R	9	R	4	6	R	R	R	
13	Dumfries	7	R	7	R	5	R	R	9	R	6	3
13	Streiff	-	-	-	-	-	-	-	-	-	-	3
		9	R	6	R	8	R	9	R	R	5	
15	Fabi	R	R	R	R	R	RP	RPF	8	R	10	2
15	Tambay	-	-	-	-	-	-	-	-	-	-	2
		-	R	R	8	7	5	R	NC	R	NC	
17	Patrese	6	7	-	R	R	R	R	R	13	R	2
		-	-	R	-	-	-	-	-	-	-	
18	Danner	-	-	-	-	-	-	-	-	-	-	1
		R	11	R	R	-	6	8	11	9	R	
		-	-	-	-	R	-	-	-	-	-	
18	Alliot	-	-	-	R	9	R	R	R	6	8	1

SYMBOLS AND GRAND PRIX KEY

Round 1 Brazilian GP
Round 2 Spanish GP
Round 3 San Marino GP
Round 4 Monaco GP
Round 5 Belgian GP
Round 6 Canadian GP
Round 7 Detroit GP
Round 8 French GP
Round 9 British GP
Round 10 German GP
Round 11 Hungarian GP
Round 12 Austrian GP
Round 13 Italian GP
Round 14 Portuguese GP
Round 15 Mexican GP
Round 16 Australian GP

SCORING

1st 9 points
2nd 6 points
3rd 4 points
4th 3 points
5th 2 points
6th 1 point

DNPQ DID NOT PRE-QUALIFY **DNQ** DID NOT QUALIFY **DQ** DISQUALIFIED **EX** EXCLUDED
F FASTEST LAP **NC** NOT CLASSIFIED **NS** NON-STARTER **P** POLE POSITION **R** RETIRED

WORLD CONSTRUCTORS' CHAMPIONSHIP FINAL RESULTS

Pos	Team-Engine	R1	R2	R3	R4	R5	R6	R7	R8
1	Williams-Honda	1/R	2/R	2/R	4/7	1/R	1/3	5/R	1/3
2	McLaren-TAG	R/R	3/4	1/5	1/2	6/R	2/4	3/R	2/4
3	Lotus-Renault	2/9	1/R	R/R	3/DNQ	2/R	5/R	1/7	R/R
4	Ferrari	R/R	R/R	4/10	10/R	3/4	8/R	4/R	8/R
5	Ligier-Renault	3/4	R/R	R/R	5/6	5/R	6/7	2/R	5/6
6	Benetton-BMW	6/10	5/6	3/R	R/R	7/10	R/R	R/R	R/R
7	Tyrrell-Renault	5/7	R/R	8/R	11/R	12/R	9/11	9/R	10/R
8	Lola-Ford	-/-	-/-	R	R/R	11/R	10/NS	R/R	R/R
9	Brabham-BMW	8/R	R/R	6/R	R/R	8	R/R	6/10	7/9
10	Arrows-BMW	R/R	7/R	7/9	8/9	9/R	R	R/R	11/NC

Pos	Team-Engine	R9	R10	R11	R12	R13	R14	R15	R16	Total
1	Williams-Honda	1/2	1/3	1/3	R/R	1/2	1/3	4/5	2/R	141
2	McLaren-TAG	3/R	5/6	R/R	1/9	4/DQ	2/R	2/R	1/R	96
3	Lotus-Renault	7/R	2/R	2/5	R/R	R/R	4/9	3/R	6/R	58
4	Ferrari	R/R	11/R	4/R	2/3	3/R	5/6	12/R	3/R	37
5	Ligier-Renault	4/R	4/R	9/R	10/R	R/R	7/R	6/15	7/8	29
6	Benetton-BMW	R/R	10/R	R/R	7/R	5/R	8/R	1/R	10/R	19
7	Tyrrell-Renault	5/6	R/R	6/8	R/R	9/10	R/R	11/R	4/5	11
8	Lola-Ford	R/R	8/9	7/R	4/5	6/R	NC/R	R/R	NC/R	6
9	Brabham-BMW	8/R	7/R	R/R	R/NS	R/R	R/R	13/R	R/R	2
10	Arrows-BMW	NC/R	R/R	R/R	6/R	7/8	10/11	7/9	R/R	1

1987

SEASON SUMMARY

Nelson Piquet moved team for 1987 after seven years with Brabham and he chose well – the Williams-Honda FW11B was the dominant car and the season came down to a straight battle with his new team-mate Nigel Mansell. This was settled in the Brazilian's favour when Mansell's challenge ended with a spectacular accident in practice at the Japanese GP. Piquet too had a shunt in 1987, when he crashed at Imola and missed the race, later admitting to suffering for a while after that with headaches. Ayrton Senna was the best of the rest for Lotus, with the team experimenting with computer-controlled "active suspension".

BRAZILIAN GRAND PRIX

JACAREPAGUA • ROUND 1 • DATE: 12TH APRIL 1987
Laps: 61 • Distance: 190.693miles/306.891km • Weather: Hot but dull

Pos	Driver	Team	Chassis-Engine	Result	Qual
1	Alain Prost	McLaren	McLaren-TAG MP4/3	1h39m45.141s	5
2	Nelson Piquet	Williams	Williams-Honda FW11B	1h40m25.688s	2
3	Stefan Johansson	McLaren	McLaren-TAG MP4/3	1h40m41.899s	10
4	Gerhard Berger	Ferrari	Ferrari F187	1h41m24.376s	7
5	Thierry Boutsen	Benetton	Benetton-Ford B187	60 laps	6
6	Nigel Mansell	Williams	Williams-Honda FW11B	60 laps	1
7	Satoru Nakajima	Lotus	Lotus-Honda 99T	59 laps	12
8	Michele Alboreto	Ferrari	Ferrari F187	58 laps/spun off	9
9	Christian Danner	Zakspeed	Zakspeed 861	58 laps	17
10	Jonathan Palmer	Tyrrell	Tyrrell-Ford Cosworth DG016	58 laps	18
11	Philippe Streiff	Tyrrell	Tyrrell-Ford Cosworth DG016	57 laps	20
12	Pascal Fabre	AGS	AGS-Ford Cosworth JH22	55 laps	22
R	Eddie Cheever	Arrows	Arrows-Megatron A10	52 laps/overheating	14
R	Ayrton Senna	Lotus	Lotus-Honda 99T	50 laps/engine	3
R	Riccardo Patrese	Brabham	Brabham-BMW BT56	48 laps/electrical	11
R	Andrea de Cesaris	Brabham	Brabham-BMW BT56	21 laps/differential	13
R	Derek Warwick	Arrows	Arrows-Megatron A10	20 laps/engine	8
R	Alex Caffi	Osella	Osella-Alfa Romeo FA1I	20 laps/exhaustion	21
R	Alessandro Nannini	Minardi	Minardi-Motori Moderni M187	17 laps/suspension	15
R	Martin Brundle	Zakspeed	Zakspeed 861	15 laps/turbo	19
R	Teo Fabi	Benetton	Benetton-Ford B187	9 laps/turbo	4
DQ	Adrian Campos	Minardi	Minardi-Motori Moderni M187	3 laps/grid error	16
NS	Ivan Capelli	March	March-Ford Cosworth 87P	Engine	23

Pole: Mansell, 1m26.128s, 130.666mph/210.287kph. Fastest lap: Piquet, 1m33.861s, 119.900mph/192.961kph on Lap 42. Race leaders: Piquet 1-7 & 17-20, Senna 8-12, Prost 13-16 & 21-61

LOOKING TO THE FUTURE

As a step towards the banning of turbocharged engines in 1989, the sport's governing body introduced 3500cc normally aspirated units alongside the turbos. The non-turbo Ford Cosworth DFZ suffered a huge power disadvantage, usually around 300bhp. But at least it was reliable.

SAN MARINO GRAND PRIX

IMOLA • ROUND 2 • DATE: 3RD MAY 1987
Laps: 59 • Distance: 184.569miles/297.36km • Weather: Warm but dull

Pos	Driver	Team	Chassis-Engine	Result	Qual
1	Nigel Mansell	Williams	Williams-Honda FW11B	1h31m24.076s	2
2	Ayrton Senna	Lotus	Lotus-Honda 99T	1h31m51.621s	1
3	Michele Alboreto	Ferrari	Ferrari F187	1h32m03.220s	6
4	Stefan Johansson	McLaren	McLaren-TAG MP4/3	1h32m24.664s	8
5	Martin Brundle	Zakspeed	Zakspeed 861	57 laps	14
6	Satoru Nakajima	Lotus	Lotus-Honda 99T	57 laps	12
7	Christian Danner	Zakspeed	Zakspeed 861	57 laps	17
8	Philippe Streiff	Tyrrell	Tyrrell-Ford Cosworth DG016	57 laps	20
9	Riccardo Patrese	Brabham	Brabham-BMW BT56	57 laps	7
10	Philippe Alliot	Larrousse	Lola-Ford Cosworth LC87	56 laps	21
11	Derek Warwick	Arrows	Arrows-Megatron A10	55 laps/out of fuel	10
12	Alex Caffi	Osella	Osella-Alfa Romeo FA1I	54 laps/out of fuel	19
13	Pascal Fabre	AGS	AGS-Ford Cosworth JH22	53 laps	24
R	Teo Fabi	Benetton	Benetton-Ford B187	51 laps/turbo	4
R	Eddie Cheever	Arrows	Arrows-Megatron A10	48 laps/clutch	9
R	Thierry Boutsen	Benetton	Benetton-Ford B187	48 laps/engine	11
R	Jonathan Palmer	Tyrrell	Tyrrell-Ford Cosworth DG016	48 laps/clutch	23
R	Andrea de Cesaris	Brabham	Brabham-BMW BT56	39 laps/spun off	13
R	Adrian Campos	Minardi	Minardi-Motori Moderni M187	30 laps/gearbox	16
R	Gabriele Tarquini	Osella	Osella-Alfa Romeo FA1G	26 laps/gearbox	25
R	Alessandro Nannini	Minardi	Minardi-Motori Moderni M187	25 laps/turbo	15
R	Ivan Capelli	March	March-Ford Cosworth 871	18 laps/engine	22
R	Gerhard Berger	Ferrari	Ferrari F187	16 laps/electrical	5
R	Alain Prost	McLaren	McLaren-TAG MP4/3	14 laps/electrical	3
R	Piercarlo Ghinzani	Ligier	Ligier-Megatron JS29C	7 laps/handling	18
NS	Rene Arnoux	Ligier	Ligier-Megatron JS29C	-	-
NS	Nelson Piquet	Williams	Williams-Honda FW11B	-	-

Pole: Senna, 1m25.826s, 131.360mph/211.404kph. Fastest lap: Fabi, 1m29.246s, 126.326mph/203.303kph on Lap 51. Race leaders: Senna 1 & 25-26, Mansell 2-21 & 27-59, Alboreto 22-24

BELGIAN GRAND PRIX

SPA-FRANCORCHAMPS • ROUND 3 • DATE: 17TH MAY 1987
Laps: 43 • Distance: 185.194miles/298.42km • Weather: Cool & dull

Pos	Driver	Team	Chassis-Engine	Result	Qual
1	Alain Prost	McLaren	McLaren-TAG MP4/3	1h27m03.217s	6
2	Stefan Johansson	McLaren	McLaren-TAG MP4/3	1h27m27.981s	10
3	Andrea de Cesaris	Brabham	Brabham-BMW BT56	42 laps/out of fuel	13
4	Eddie Cheever	Arrows	Arrows-Megatron A10	42 laps	11
5	Satoru Nakajima	Lotus	Lotus-Honda 99T	42 laps	15
6	Rene Arnoux	Ligier	Ligier-Megatron JS29C	41 laps	16
7	Piercarlo Ghinzani	Ligier	Ligier-Megatron JS29C	40 laps/out of fuel	17
8	Philippe Alliot	Larrousse	Lola-Ford Cosworth LC87	40 laps	22
9	Philippe Streiff	Tyrrell	Tyrrell-Ford Cosworth DG016	39 laps	23
10	Pascal Fabre	AGS	AGS-Ford Cosworth JH22	38 laps/electrical	25
R	Teo Fabi	Benetton	Benetton-Ford B187	34 laps/engine	9
R	Martin Brundle	Zakspeed	Zakspeed 871	19 laps/overheating	18
R	Thierry Boutsen	Benetton	Benetton-Ford B187	18 laps/wheel	7

Pos	Driver	Team	Chassis-Engine	Result	Qual
R	Nigel Mansell	Williams	Williams-Honda FW11B	17 laps/accident	1
R	Ivan Capelli*	March	March-Ford Cosworth	14 laps/engine	21
R	Nelson Piquet	Williams	Williams-Honda FW11B	11 laps/exhaust	2
R	Alex Caffi	Osella	Osella-Alfa Romeo FA1I	11 laps/oil leak	26
R	Michele Alboreto	Ferrari	Ferrari F187	9 laps/transmission	5
R	Christian Danner	Zakspeed	Zakspeed 871	9 laps/brakes	20
R	Derek Warwick	Arrows	Arrows-Megatron A10	8 laps/radiator damage	12
R	Riccardo Patrese	Brabham	Brabham-BMW BT56	5 laps/clutch	8
R	Gerhard Berger	Ferrari	Ferrari F187	2 laps/engine	4
R	Alessandro Nannini	Minardi	Minardi-Motori Moderni M187	1 lap/turbo	14
R	Ayrton Senna	Lotus	Lotus-Honda 99T	0 laps/accident	3
R	Adrian Campos	Minardi	Minardi-Motori Moderni M187	0 laps/clutch	19
R	Jonathan Palmer	Tyrrell	Tyrrell-Ford Cosworth DG016	0 laps/accident	24

*drove March-Ford Cosworth 87P at original start, switched to March-Ford Cosworth 871 for restart

Pole: Mansell, 1m52.026s, 138.577mph/223.019kph. Fastest lap: Prost, 1m57.153s, 132.513mph/213.259kph on Lap 26. Race leaders: Piquet 1-9, Prost 10-43

TROUBLE IN AUSTRIA

Increasingly considered no longer safe for F1, the Osterreichring bowed out with a near disaster when Stefan Johansson's McLaren hit a deer in practice. This was followed by a pair of startline shunts that proved that its pit straight was too narrow for F1. The first blocked the track and the second, involving 10 cars, did the same.

MONACO GRAND PRIX

MONTE CARLO • ROUND 4 • DATE: 31ST MAY 1987
Laps: 78 • Distance: 161.298miles/259.584km • Weather: Warm & bright

Pos	Driver	Team	Chassis-Engine	Result	Qual
1	Ayrton Senna	Lotus	Lotus-Honda 99T	1h57m54.085s	2
2	Nelson Piquet	Williams	Williams-Honda FW11B	1h58m27.297s	3
3	Michele Alboreto	Ferrari	Ferrari F187	1h59m06.924s	5
4	Gerhard Berger	Ferrari	Ferrari F187	77 laps	8
5	Jonathan Palmer	Tyrrell	Tyrrell-Ford Cosworth DG016	76 laps	15
6	Ivan Capelli	March	March-Ford Cosworth 871	76 laps	19
7	Martin Brundle	Zakspeed	Zakspeed 871	76 laps	14
8	Teo Fabi	Benetton	Benetton-Ford B187	76 laps	12
9	Alain Prost	McLaren	McLaren-TAG MP4/3	75 laps/engine	4
10	Satoru Nakajima	Lotus	Lotus-Honda 99T	75 laps	17
11	Rene Arnoux	Ligier	Ligier-Megatron JS29C	74 laps	22
12	Piercarlo Ghinzani	Ligier	Ligier-Megatron JS29C	74 laps	20
13	Pascal Fabre	AGS	AGS-Ford Cosworth JH22	71 laps	24
R	Eddie Cheever	Arrows	Arrows-Megatron A10	59 laps/overheating	6
R	Derek Warwick	Arrows	Arrows-Megatron A10	58 laps/gearbox	11
R	Stefan Johansson	McLaren	McLaren-TAG MP4/3	57 laps/engine	7
R	Philippe Alliot	Larrousse	Lola-Ford Cosworth LC87	42 laps/engine	18
R	Riccardo Patrese	Brabham	Brabham-BMW BT56	41 laps/electrical	10
R	Alex Caffi	Osella	Osella-Alfa Romeo FA1I	39 laps/electrical	16
R	Andrea de Cesaris	Brabham	Brabham-BMW BT56	38 laps/suspension	21
R	Nigel Mansell	Williams	Williams-Honda FW11B	29 laps/turbo	1

Pos	Driver	Team	Chassis-Engine	Result	Qual
R	Alessandro Nannini	Minardi	Minardi-Motori Moderni M187	21 laps/electrical	13
R	Philippe Streiff	Tyrrell	Tyrrell-Ford Cosworth DG016	9 laps/accident	23
R	Thierry Boutsen	Benetton	Benetton-Ford B187	5 laps/transmission	9
NS	Adrian Campos	Minardi	Minardi-Motori Moderni M187	driver injured	25
EX	Christian Danner	Zakspeed	Zakspeed 871	dangerous driving	-

Pole: Mansell, 1m23.039s, 89.650mph/144.279kph. Fastest lap: Senna, 1m27.685s, 84.900mph/136.634kph on Lap 72. Race leaders: Mansell 1-29, Senna 30-78

DETROIT GRAND PRIX

DETROIT • ROUND 5 • DATE: 21ST JUNE 1987
Laps: 63 • Distance: 157.501miles/253.474km • Weather: Warm but dull

Pos	Driver	Team	Chassis-Engine	Result	Qual
1	Ayrton Senna	Lotus	Lotus-Honda 99T	1h50m16.358s	2
2	Nelson Piquet	Williams	Williams-Honda FW11B	1h50m50.177s	3
3	Alain Prost	McLaren	McLaren-TAG MP4/3	1h51m01.685s	5
4	Gerhard Berger	Ferrari	Ferrari F187	1h51m18.959s	12
5	Nigel Mansell	Williams	Williams-Honda FW11B	62 laps	1
6	Eddie Cheever	Arrows	Arrows-Megatron A10	60 laps/out of fuel	6
7	Stefan Johansson	McLaren	McLaren-TAG MP4/3	60 laps	11
8	Christian Danner	Zakspeed	Zakspeed 871	60 laps	16
9	Riccardo Patrese	Brabham	Brabham-BMW BT56	60 laps	9
10	Rene Arnoux	Ligier	Ligier-Megatron JS29C	60 laps	21
11	Jonathan Palmer	Tyrrell	Tyrrell-Ford Cosworth DG016	60 laps	13
12	Pascal Fabre	AGS	AGS-Ford Cosworth JH22	58 laps	26
R	Thierry Boutsen	Benetton	Benetton-Ford B187	52 laps/brakes	4
R	Piercarlo Ghinzani	Ligier	Ligier-Megatron JS29C	51 laps/clutch	23
R	Philippe Streiff	Tyrrell	Tyrrell-Ford Cosworth DG016	44 laps/wheel	14
R	Philippe Alliot	Larrousse	Lola-Ford Cosworth LC87	38 laps/accident	20
R	Michele Alboreto	Ferrari	Ferrari F187	25 laps/gearbox	7
R	Alessandro Nannini	Minardi	Minardi-Motori Moderni M187	22 laps/gearbox	18
R	Martin Brundle	Zakspeed	Zakspeed 861B	16 laps/turbo	15
R	Derek Warwick	Arrows	Arrows-Megatron A10	12 laps/accident	10
R	Ivan Capelli	March	March-Ford Cosworth 871	9 laps/electrical	22
R	Teo Fabi	Benetton	Benetton-Ford B187	6 laps/accident	8
R	Alex Caffi	Osella	Osella-Alfa Romeo FA1I	3 laps/transmission	19
R	Andrea de Cesaris	Brabham	Brabham-BMW BT56	2 laps/gearbox	17
R	Adrian Campos	Minardi	Minardi-Motori Moderni M187	1 lap/accident	25
R	Satoru Nakajima	Lotus	Lotus-Honda 99T	0 laps/accident	24

Pole: Mansell, 1m39.264s, 90.668mph/145.916kph. Fastest lap: Senna, 1m40.464s, 89.584mph/144.172kph on Lap 39. Race leaders: Mansell 1-33, Senna 34-63

GOING CLEAR AT THE TOP

Alain Prost rose to the top of the all-time F1 winners' list when he scored his 28th win. This came for the McLaren driver at the Portuguese GP, moving him ahead of Jackie Stewart who had held the record since winning at the German GP at the Nurburgring for Tyrrell in 1973. Before Stewart, Jim Clark held the record, on 25 wins.

F1'S DEVELOPMENT CLASS

There was a new trophy to be fought for following the introduction of normally-aspirated 3.5-litre engines. Known as the Jim Clark Cup, this was fought out between AGS, Larrousse, March and Tyrrell, with Jonathan Palmer winning it for Tyrrell after being the first non-turbo runner on seven occasions, to team-mate Philippe Streiff's four.

FRENCH GRAND PRIX

CIRCUIT PAUL RICARD • ROUND 6 • DATE: 5TH JULY 1987
Laps: 80 • Distance: 189.520miles/305.04km • Weather: Hot & bright

Pos	Driver	Team	Chassis-Engine	Result	Qual
1	Nigel Mansell	Williams	Williams-Honda FW11B	1h37m03.839s	1
2	Nelson Piquet	Williams	Williams-Honda FW11B	1h37m11.550s	4
3	Alain Prost	McLaren	McLaren-TAG MP4/3	1h37m59.094s	2
4	Ayrton Senna	Lotus	Lotus-Honda 99T	79 laps	3
5	Teo Fabi	Benetton	Benetton-Ford B187	77 laps/halfshaft	7
6	Philippe Streiff	Tyrrell	Tyrrell-Ford Cosworth DG016	76 laps	25
7	Jonathan Palmer	Tyrrell	Tyrrell-Ford Cosworth DG016	76 laps	24
8	Stefan Johansson	McLaren	McLaren-TAG MP4/3	74 laps/electrical	9
9	Pascal Fabre	AGS	AGS-Ford Cosworth JH22	74 laps	26
R	Gerhard Berger	Ferrari	Ferrari F187	71 laps/suspension	6
NC	Satoru Nakajima	Lotus	Lotus-Honda 99T	71 laps	16
R	Michele Alboreto	Ferrari	Ferrari F187	64 laps/engine	8
R	Derek Warwick	Arrows	Arrows-Megatron A10	62 laps/turbo	10
R	Philippe Alliot	Larrousse	Lola-Ford Cosworth LC87	57 laps/gearbox	23
R	Adrian Campos	Minardi	Minardi-Motori Moderni M187	52 laps/turbo	21
R	Ivan Capelli	March	March-Ford Cosworth 871	52 laps/engine	22
R	Rene Arnoux	Ligier	Ligier-Megatron JS29C	33 laps/exhaust	13
R	Thierry Boutsen	Benetton	Benetton-Ford B187	31 laps/engine	5
R	Christian Danner	Zakspeed	Zakspeed 871	26 laps/overheating	19
R	Piercarlo Ghinzani	Ligier	Ligier-Megatron JS29C	24 laps/engine	17
R	Alessandro Nannini	Minardi	Minardi-Motori Moderni M187	23 laps/turbo	15
R	Riccardo Patrese	Brabham	Brabham-BMW BT56	19 laps/differential	12
R	Martin Brundle	Zakspeed	Zakspeed 871	18 laps/wheel	18
R	Alex Caffi	Osella	Osella-Alfa Romeo FA1I	11 laps/engine	20
R	Andrea de Cesaris	Brabham	Brabham-BMW BT56	2 laps/turbo	11
R	Eddie Cheever	Arrows	Arrows-Megatron A10	0 laps/electrical	14

Pole: Mansell, 1m06.454s, 128.351mph/206.560kph. Fastest lap: Piquet, 1m09.548s, 122.640mph/197.371kph on Lap 68. Race leaders: Mansell 1-35 & 46-80, Piquet 36-45

A PREMATURE END

Nigel Mansell had been the dominant driver for much of 1987, winning three times before Williams' team-mate Nelson Piquet inherited victory from him in Hungary. However, five retirements hurt Mansell's title bid and he went to the penultimate race at Suzuka 12 points down. Then, in practice, he crashed and suffered a back injury that ended his year.

BRITISH GRAND PRIX

SILVERSTONE • ROUND 7 • DATE: 12TH JULY 1987
Laps: 65 • Distance: 192.982miles/310.576km • Weather: Warm & bright

Pos	Driver	Team	Chassis-Engine	Result	Qual
1	Nigel Mansell	Williams	Williams-Honda FW11B	1h19m11.780s	2
2	Nelson Piquet	Williams	Williams-Honda FW11B	1h19m13.698s	1
3	Ayrton Senna	Lotus	Lotus-Honda 99T	64 laps	3
4	Satoru Nakajima	Lotus	Lotus-Honda 99T	63 laps	12
5	Derek Warwick	Arrows	Arrows-Megatron A10	63 laps	13
6	Teo Fabi	Benetton	Benetton-Ford B187	63 laps	6
7	Thierry Boutsen	Benetton	Benetton-Ford B187	62 laps	5
8	Jonathan Palmer	Tyrrell	Tyrrell-Ford Cosworth DG016	60 laps	23
9	Pascal Fabre	AGS	AGS-Ford Cosworth JH22	59 laps	25
R	Philippe Streiff	Tyrrell	Tyrrell-Ford Cosworth DG016	57 laps/engine	22
NC	Martin Brundle	Zakspeed	Zakspeed 871	54 laps	17
R	Alain Prost	McLaren	McLaren-TAG MP4/3	53 laps/clutch	4
R	Michele Alboreto	Ferrari	Ferrari F187	52 laps/suspension	7
R	Eddie Cheever	Arrows	Arrows-Megatron A10	45 laps/engine	14
R	Adrian Campos	Minardi	Minardi-Motori Moderni M187	34 laps/fuel system	19
R	Christian Danner	Zakspeed	Zakspeed 871	32 laps/gearbox	18
R	Alex Caffi	Osella	Osella-Alfa Romeo FA1I	32 laps/engine	20
R	Riccardo Patrese	Brabham	Brabham-BMW BT56	28 laps/turbo	11
R	Stefan Johansson	McLaren	McLaren-TAG MP4/3	18 laps/engine	10
R	Alessandro Nannini	Minardi	Minardi-Motori Moderni M187	10 laps/engine	15
R	Andrea de Cesaris	Brabham	Brabham-BMW BT56	8 laps/turbo	9
R	Gerhard Berger	Ferrari	Ferrari F187	7 laps/accident	8
R	Philippe Alliot	Larrousse	Lola-Ford Cosworth LC87	7 laps/gearbox	21
R	Rene Arnoux	Ligier	Ligier-Megatron JS29C	3 laps/electrical	16
R	Ivan Capelli	March	March-Ford Cosworth 871	3 laps/accident	24
EX	Piercarlo Ghinzani	Ligier	Ligier-Megatron JS29C	driving standards	19

Pole: Piquet, 1m07.110s, 159.265mph/256.312kph. Fastest lap: Mansell, 1m09.832s, 153.053mph/246.316kph on Lap 58. Race leaders: Piquet 1-62, Mansell 63-65

GERMAN GRAND PRIX

HOCKENHEIM • ROUND 8 • DATE: 26TH JULY 1987
Laps: 44 • Distance: 185.832miles/299.068km • Weather: Warm & bright

Pos	Driver	Team	Chassis-Engine	Result	Qual
1	Nelson Piquet	Williams	Williams-Honda FW11B	1h21m25.091s	4
2	Stefan Johansson	McLaren	McLaren-TAG MP4/3	1h23m04.682s	8
3	Ayrton Senna	Lotus	Lotus-Honda 99T	43 laps	2
4	Philippe Streiff	Tyrrell	Tyrrell-Ford Cosworth DG016	43 laps	22
5	Jonathan Palmer	Tyrrell	Tyrrell-Ford Cosworth DG016	43 laps	23
6	Philippe Alliot	Larrousse	Lola-Ford Cosworth LC87	42 laps	21
7	Alain Prost	McLaren	McLaren-TAG MP4/3	39 laps/electrical	3
NC	Martin Brundle	Zakspeed	Zakspeed 871	34 laps	19
R	Piercarlo Ghinzani	Ligier	Ligier-Megatron JS29C	32 laps/engine	17
R	Adrian Campos	Minardi	Minardi-Motori Moderni M187	28 laps/engine	18
R	Thierry Boutsen	Benetton	Benetton-Ford B187	26 laps/engine	6
R	Nigel Mansell	Williams	Williams-Honda FW11B	25 laps/engine	1
R	Alessandro Nannini	Minardi	Minardi-Motori Moderni M187	25 laps/engine	16

Pos	Driver	Team	Chassis-Engine	Result	Qual
R	Derek Warwick	Arrows	Arrows-Megatron A10	23 laps/turbo	13
R	Christian Danner	Zakspeed	Zakspeed 871	21 laps/halfshaft	20
R	Gerhard Berger	Ferrari	Ferrari F187	19 laps/turbo	10
R	Teo Fabi	Benetton	Benetton-Ford B187	18 laps/engine	9
R	Alex Caffi	Osella	Osella-Alfa Romeo FA1I	17 laps/engine	26
R	Andrea de Cesaris	Brabham	Brabham-BMW BT56	12 laps/engine	7
R	Michele Alboreto	Ferrari	Ferrari F187	10 laps/turbo	5
R	Pascal Fabre	AGS	AGS-Ford Cosworth JH22	10 laps/engine	25
R	Satoru Nakajima	Lotus	Lotus-Honda 99T	9 laps/suspension	14
R	Eddie Cheever	Arrows	Arrows-Megatron A10	9 laps/throttle	15
R	Ivan Capelli	March	March-Ford Cosworth 871	7 laps/engine	24
R	Rene Arnoux	Ligier	Ligier-Megatron JS29C	6 laps/ignition	12
R	Riccardo Patrese	Brabham	Brabham-BMW BT56	5 laps/ignition	11

Pole: Mansell, 1m42.616s, 148.168mph/238.454kph. Fastest lap: Mansell, 1m45.716s, 143.823mph/231.461kph on Lap 24. Race leaders: Senna 1, Mansell 2-7 & 19-22, Prost 8-18 & 23-39, Piquet 40-44

HUNGARIAN GRAND PRIX

HUNGARORING • ROUND 9 • DATE: 9TH AUGUST 1987
Laps: 76 • Distance: 189.557miles/305.064km • Weather: Hot & bright

Pos	Driver	Team	Chassis-Engine	Result	Qual
1	Nelson Piquet	Williams	Williams-Honda FW11B	1h59m26.793s	3
2	Ayrton Senna	Lotus	Lotus-Honda 99T	2h00m04.520s	6
3	Alain Prost	McLaren	McLaren-TAG MP4/3	2h00m54.249s	4
4	Thierry Boutsen	Benetton	Benetton-Ford B187	75 laps	7
5	Riccardo Patrese	Brabham	Brabham-BMW BT56	75 laps	10
6	Derek Warwick	Arrows	Arrows-Megatron A10	74 laps	9
7	Jonathan Palmer	Tyrrell	Tyrrell-Ford Cosworth DG016	74 laps	16
8	Eddie Cheever	Arrows	Arrows-Megatron A10	74 laps	11
9	Philippe Streiff	Tyrrell	Tyrrell-Ford Cosworth DG016	74 laps	14
10	Ivan Capelli	March	March-Ford Cosworth 871	74 laps	18
11	Alessandro Nannini	Minardi	Minardi-Motori Moderni M187	73 laps	20
12	Piercarlo Ghinzani	Ligier	Ligier-Megatron JS29C	73 laps	25
13	Pascal Fabre	AGS	AGS-Ford Cosworth JH22	71 laps	26
14	Nigel Mansell	Williams	Williams-Honda FW11B	70 laps/wheel	1
R	Alex Caffi	Osella	Osella-Alfa Romeo FA1I	64 laps/fuel system	21
R	Rene Arnoux	Ligier	Ligier-Megatron JS29C	57 laps/electrical	19
R	Philippe Alliot	Larrousse	Lola-Ford Cosworth LC87	48 laps/accident	15
R	Martin Brundle	Zakspeed	Zakspeed 871	45 laps/turbo	22
R	Michele Alboreto	Ferrari	Ferrari F187	43 laps/engine	5
R	Andrea de Cesaris	Brabham	Brabham-BMW BT56	43 laps/gearbox	13
R	Stefan Johansson	McLaren	McLaren-TAG MP4/3	14 laps/gearbox	8
R	Teo Fabi	Benetton	Benetton-Ford B187	14 laps/gearbox	12
R	Adrian Campos	Minardi	Minardi-Motori Moderni M187	14 laps/spun off	24
R	Gerhard Berger	Ferrari	Ferrari F187	13 laps/differential	2
R	Christian Danner	Zakspeed	Zakspeed 871	3 laps/engine	23
R	Satoru Nakajima	Lotus	Lotus-Honda 99T	1 lap/gearbox	17

Pole: Mansell, 1m28.047s, 101.980mph/164.121kph. Fastest lap: Piquet, 1m30.149s, 99.602mph/160.294kph on Lap 63. Race leaders: Mansell 1-70, Piquet 71-76

NEW CIRCUITS
After a 10-year break, the Japanese GP was back on the calendar, albeit now at Suzuka rather than Fuji Speedway. Opened in 1962 as a test circuit for Honda, it provided a big challenge for the drivers and has been popular ever since, although the race briefly returned to Fuji in 2007-08. Silverstone was revamped with the addition of the Luffield complex before Woodcote.

AUSTRIAN GRAND PRIX

OSTERREICHRING • ROUND 10 • DATE: 16TH AUGUST 1987
Laps: 52 • Distance: 191.993miles/308.984km • Weather: Hot but dull

Pos	Driver	Team	Chassis-Engine	Result	Qual
1	Nigel Mansell	Williams	Williams-Honda FW11B	1h18m44.898s	2
2	Nelson Piquet	Williams	Williams-Honda FW11B	1h19m40.602s	1
3	Teo Fabi	Benetton	Benetton-Ford B187	51 laps	5
4	Thierry Boutsen	Benetton	Benetton-Ford B187	51 laps	4
5	Ayrton Senna	Lotus	Lotus-Honda 99T	50 laps	7
6	Alain Prost	McLaren	McLaren-TAG MP4/3	50 laps	9
7	Stefan Johansson	McLaren	McLaren-TAG MP4/3	50 laps	14
8	Piercarlo Ghinzani	Ligier	Ligier-Megatron JS29C	50 laps	18
9	Christian Danner	Zakspeed	Zakspeed 871	49 laps	20
10	Rene Arnoux	Ligier	Ligier-Megatron JS29C	49 laps	16
11	Ivan Capelli	March	March-Ford Cosworth 871	49 laps	23
12	Philippe Alliot	Larrousse	Lola-Ford Cosworth LC87	49 laps	22
13	Satoru Nakajima	Lotus	Lotus-Honda 99T	49 laps	13
14	Jonathan Palmer	Tyrrell	Tyrrell-Ford Cosworth DG016	47 laps	24
DQ	Martin Brundle	Zakspeed	Zakspeed 871	48 laps/bodywork	17
NC	Pascal Fabre	AGS	AGS-Ford Cosworth JH22	45 laps	26
R	Riccardo Patrese	Brabham	Brabham-BMW BT56	43 laps/engine	8
R	Michele Alboreto	Ferrari	Ferrari F187	42 laps/turbo	6
R	Andrea de Cesaris	Brabham	Brabham-BMW BT56	35 laps/engine	10
R	Derek Warwick	Arrows	Arrows-Megatron A10	35 laps/engine	11
R	Eddie Cheever	Arrows	Arrows-Megatron A10	31 laps/tyre	12
R	Gerhard Berger	Ferrari	Ferrari F187	5 laps/turbo	3
R	Adrian Campos	Minardi	Minardi-Motori Moderni M187	3 laps/electrical	19
R	Alessandro Nannini	Minardi	Minardi-Motori Moderni M187	1 lap/engine	15
R	Alex Caffi	Osella	Osella-Alfa Romeo FA1I	0 laps/electrical	21
R	Philippe Streiff	Tyrrell	Tyrrell-Ford Cosworth DG016	0 laps/accident	25

Pole: Piquet, 1m23.357s, 159.457mph/256.621kph. Fastest lap: Mansell, 1m28.318s, 150.499mph/242.206kph on Lap 31. Race leaders: Piquet 1-20, Mansell 21-52

NEW CONSTRUCTORS
1982 Italian F3 Champion Enzo Coloni then ran cars for others that decade helping Ivan Capelli, Alessandro Santin and Nicola Larini all win the national title. The team tried F3000 in 1986 before stepping up to F1 for two outings in 1987 with a Roberto Ori-designed chassis, a Ford DFZ engine and a meagre budget. Unsurprisingly, the results were poor.

ITALIAN GRAND PRIX

MONZA • ROUND 11 • DATE: 6TH SEPTEMBER 1987
Laps: 50 • Distance: 180.197miles/290.0km • Weather: Hot & bright

Pos	Driver	Team	Chassis-Engine	Result	Qual
1	Nelson Piquet	Williams	Williams-Honda FW11B	1h14m47.707s	1
2	Ayrton Senna	Lotus	Lotus-Honda 99T	1h14m49.513s	4
3	Nigel Mansell	Williams	Williams-Honda FW11B	1h15m36.743s	2
4	Gerhard Berger	Ferrari	Ferrari F187	1h15m45.686s	3
5	Thierry Boutsen	Benetton	Benetton-Ford B187	1h16m09.026s	6
6	Stefan Johansson	McLaren	McLaren-TAG MP4/3	1h16m16.494s	11
7	Teo Fabi	Benetton	Benetton-Ford B187	49 laps	7
8	Piercarlo Ghinzani	Ligier	Ligier-Megatron JS29C	48 laps	19
9	Christian Danner	Zakspeed	Zakspeed 871	48 laps	16
10	Rene Arnoux	Ligier	Ligier-Megatron JS29C	48 laps	15
11	Satoru Nakajima	Lotus	Lotus-Honda 99T	47 laps	14
12	Philippe Streiff	Tyrrell	Tyrrell-Ford Cosworth DG016	47 laps	24
13	Ivan Capelli	March	March-Ford Cosworth 871	47 laps	25
14	Jonathan Palmer	Tyrrell	Tyrrell-Ford Cosworth DG016	47 laps	22
15	Alain Prost	McLaren	McLaren-TAG MP4/3	46 laps	5
16	Alessandro Nannini	Minardi	Minardi-Motori Moderni M187	45 laps/engine	18
R	Martin Brundle	Zakspeed	Zakspeed 871	43 laps/gearbox	17
R	Philippe Alliot	Larrousse	Lola-Ford Cosworth LC87	37 laps/spun off	23
R	Adrian Campos	Minardi	Minardi-Motori Moderni M187	34 laps/engine	20
R	Eddie Cheever	Arrows	Arrows-Megatron A10	27 laps/halfshaft	13
R	Franco Forini	Osella	Osella-Alfa Romeo FA1I	27 laps/turbo	26
R	Alex Caffi	Osella	Osella-Alfa Romeo FA1I	16 laps/suspension	21
R	Michele Alboreto	Ferrari	Ferrari F187	13 laps/turbo	8
R	Derek Warwick	Arrows	Arrows-Megatron A10	9 laps/electrical	12
R	Andrea de Cesaris	Brabham	Brabham-BMW BT56	7 laps/suspension	10
R	Riccardo Patrese	Brabham	Brabham-BMW BT56	5 laps/engine	9
DNQ	Nicola Larini	Coloni	Coloni-Ford Cosworth FC187	-	27
DNQ	Pascal Fabre	AGS	AGS-Ford Cosworth JH22	-	28

Pole: Piquet, 1m23.460s, 155.454mph/250.179kph. Fastest lap: Senna, 1m26.796s, 149.479mph/240.564kph on Lap 49. Race leaders: Piquet 1-23 & 43-50, Senna 24-42

PORTUGUESE GRAND PRIX

AUTODROMO DO ESTORIL • ROUND 12 • DATE: 20TH SEPTEMBER 1987
Laps: 70 • Distance: 188.899miles/304.5km • Weather: Hot & bright

Pos	Driver	Team	Chassis-Engine	Result	Qual
1	Alain Prost	McLaren	McLaren-TAG MP4/3	1h37m03.906s	3
2	Gerhard Berger	Ferrari	Ferrari F187	1h37m24.399s	1
3	Nelson Piquet	Williams	Williams-Honda FW11B	1h38m07.201s	4
4	Teo Fabi	Benetton	Benetton-Ford B187	69 laps/out of fuel	10
5	Stefan Johansson	McLaren	McLaren-TAG MP4/3	69 laps	8
6	Eddie Cheever	Arrows	Arrows-Megatron A10	68 laps	11
7	Ayrton Senna	Lotus	Lotus-Honda 99T	68 laps	5
8	Satoru Nakajima	Lotus	Lotus-Honda 99T	68 laps	15
9	Ivan Capelli	March	March-Ford Cosworth 871	67 laps	22
10	Jonathan Palmer	Tyrrell	Tyrrell-Ford Cosworth DG016	67 laps	24
11	Alessandro Nannini	Minardi	Minardi-Motori Moderni M187	66 laps/out of fuel	14
12	Philippe Streiff	Tyrrell	Tyrrell-Ford Cosworth DG016	66 laps	21

Pos	Driver	Team	Chassis-Engine	Result	Qual
13	Derek Warwick	Arrows	Arrows-Megatron A10	66 laps	12
14	Thierry Boutsen	Benetton	Benetton-Ford B187	64 laps	9
R	Andrea de Cesaris	Brabham	Brabham-BMW BT56	54 laps/engine	13
R	Michele Alboreto	Ferrari	Ferrari F187	38 laps/gearbox	6
R	Martin Brundle	Zakspeed	Zakspeed 871	35 laps/gearbox	17
R	Franco Forini	Osella	Osella-Alfa Romeo FA1G	32 laps/suspension	26
R	Philippe Alliot	Larrousse	Lola-Ford Cosworth LC87	31 laps/engine	19
R	Rene Arnoux	Ligier	Ligier-Megatron JS29C	29 laps/radiator damage	18
R	Alex Caffi	Osella	Osella-Alfa Romeo FA1I	27 laps/turbo	25
R	Adrian Campos	Minardi	Minardi-Motori Moderni M187	24 laps/intercooler	20
R	Piercarlo Ghinzani	Ligier	Ligier-Megatron JS29C	24 laps/ignition	23
R	Nigel Mansell	Williams	Williams-Honda FW11B	13 laps/electrical	2
R	Riccardo Patrese	Brabham	Brabham-BMW BT56	13 laps/engine	7
R	Christian Danner	Zakspeed	Zakspeed 871	0 laps/accident	16
DNQ	Pascal Fabre	AGS	AGS-Ford Cosworth JH22	-	27

Pole: Berger, 1m17.620s, 125.362mph/201.752kph. Fastest lap: Berger, 1m19.282s, 122.734mph/197.522kph on Lap 66. Race leaders: Mansell 1, Berger 2-33 & 36-67, Alboreto 34-35, Prost 68-70

SPANISH GRAND PRIX

JEREZ • ROUND 13 • DATE: 27TH SEPTEMBER 1987
Laps: 72 • Distance: 188.707miles/303.696km • Weather: Hot & bright

Pos	Driver	Team	Chassis-Engine	Result	Qual
1	Nigel Mansell	Williams	Williams-Honda FW11B	1h49m12.692s	2
2	Alain Prost	McLaren	McLaren-TAG MP4/3	1h49m34.917s	7
3	Stefan Johansson	McLaren	McLaren-TAG MP4/3	1h49m43.510s	11
4	Nelson Piquet	Williams	Williams-Honda FW11B	1h49m44.142s	1
5	Ayrton Senna	Lotus	Lotus-Honda 99T	1h50m26.199s	5
6	Philippe Alliot	Larrousse	Lola-Ford Cosworth LC87	71 laps	17
7	Philippe Streiff	Tyrrell	Tyrrell-Ford Cosworth DG016	71 laps	15
8	Eddie Cheever	Arrows	Arrows-Megatron A10	70 laps/out of fuel	13
9	Satoru Nakajima	Lotus	Lotus-Honda 99T	70 laps	18
10	Derek Warwick	Arrows	Arrows-Megatron A10	70 laps	12
11	Martin Brundle	Zakspeed	Zakspeed 871	70 laps	20
12	Ivan Capelli	March	March-Ford Cosworth 871	70 laps	19
13	Riccardo Patrese	Brabham	Brabham-BMW BT56	68 laps	9
14	Adrian Campos	Minardi	Minardi-Motori Moderni M187	68 laps	24
15	Michele Alboreto	Ferrari	Ferrari F187	67 laps/engine	4
16	Thierry Boutsen	Benetton	Benetton-Ford B187	66 laps/accident	8
R	Gerhard Berger	Ferrari	Ferrari F187	62 laps/engine	3
R	Rene Arnoux	Ligier	Ligier-Megatron JS29C	55 laps/collision	14
R	Jonathan Palmer	Tyrrell	Tyrrell-Ford Cosworth DG016	55 laps/collision	16
R	Christian Danner	Zakspeed	Zakspeed 871	50 laps/transmission	22
R	Alessandro Nannini	Minardi	Minardi-Motori Moderni M187	45 laps/turbo	21
R	Teo Fabi	Benetton	Benetton-Ford B187	40 laps/brakes	6
R	Andrea de Cesaris	Brabham	Brabham-BMW BT56	26 laps/gearbox	10
R	Piercarlo Ghinzani	Ligier	Ligier-Megatron JS29C	24 laps/ignition	23
R	Pascal Fabre	AGS	AGS-Ford Cosworth JH22	10 laps/clutch	25
R	Nicola Larini	Coloni	Coloni-Ford Cosworth FC187	8 laps/suspension	26
DNQ	Alex Caffi	Osella	Osella-Alfa Romeo FA1I	-	27
DNQ	Franco Forini	Osella	Osella-Alfa Romeo FA1G	-	28

Pole: Piquet, 1m22.461s, 114.422mph/184.145kph. Fastest lap: Berger, 1m26.986s, 108.470mph/174.566kph on Lap 49. Race leaders: Mansell 1-72

MEXICAN GRAND PRIX

MEXICO CITY • ROUND 14 • DATE: 18TH OCTOBER 1987
Laps: 63 • Distance: 173.66miles/278.523km • Weather: Hot & bright

Pos	Driver	Team	Chassis-Engine	Result	Qual
1	Nigel Mansell	Williams	Williams-Honda FW11B	1h26m24.207s	1
2	Nelson Piquet	Williams	Williams-Honda FW11B	1h26m50.383s	3
3	Riccardo Patrese	Brabham	Brabham-BMW BT56	1h27m51.086s	8
4	Eddie Cheever	Arrows	Arrows-Megatron A10	1h28m05.559s	13
5	Teo Fabi	Benetton	Benetton-Ford B187	61 laps	6
6	Philippe Alliot	Larrousse	Lola-Ford Cosworth LC87	60 laps	24
7	Jonathan Palmer	Tyrrell	Tyrrell-Ford Cosworth DG016	60 laps	22
8	Philippe Streiff	Tyrrell	Tyrrell-Ford Cosworth DG016	60 laps	25
9	Yannick Dalmas	Larrousse	Lola-Ford Cosworth LC87	59 laps	23
R	Ayrton Senna	Lotus	Lotus-Honda 99T	54 laps/spun off	7
R	Ivan Capelli	March	March-Ford Cosworth 871	51 laps/water leak	20
R	Alex Caffi	Osella	Osella-Alfa Romeo FA1I	50 laps/engine	26
R	Piercarlo Ghinzani	Ligier	Ligier-Megatron JS29C	43 laps/water leak	21
R	Adrian Campos	Minardi	Minardi-Motori Moderni M187	32 laps/transmission	19
R	Rene Arnoux	Ligier	Ligier-Megatron JS29C	29 laps/overheating	18
R	Derek Warwick	Arrows	Arrows-Megatron A10	26 laps/accident	11
R	Andrea de Cesaris	Brabham	Brabham-BMW BT56	22 laps/accident	10
R	Gerhard Berger	Ferrari	Ferrari F187	20 laps/turbo	2
R	Thierry Boutsen	Benetton	Benetton-Ford B187	15 laps/electrical	4
R	Alessandro Nannini	Minardi	Minardi-Motori Moderni M187	13 laps/turbo	14
R	Michele Alboreto	Ferrari	Ferrari F187	12 laps/engine	9
R	Martin Brundle	Zakspeed	Zakspeed 871	3 laps/turbo	13
R	Stefan Johansson	McLaren	McLaren-TAG MP4/3	1 lap/accident	15
R	Satoru Nakajima	Lotus	Lotus-Honda 99T	1 lap/accident	16
R	Christian Danner	Zakspeed	Zakspeed 871	1 lap/accident	17
R	Alain Prost	McLaren	McLaren-TAG MP4/3	0 laps/collision	5
DNQ	Pascal Fabre	AGS	AGS-Ford Cosworth JH22	-	27

Pole: Mansell, 1m18.383s, 126.168mph/203.049kph. Fastest lap: Piquet, 1m19.132s, 124.974mph/201.127kph on Lap 57. Race leaders: Berger 1 & 15-20, Boutsen 2-14, Mansell 21-63

CLASSIC CAR: WILLIAMS FW11B

The FW11 was an outstanding car. Designed by Patrick Head and Frank Dernie, it used its turbocharged Honda horsepower well and dominated the 1986 constructors' title. For 1987, it was upgraded to FW11B specification, with a more reclined seating angle to lower the driver's headline and thus improve aerodynamics, plus more refined water radiators. The other new ingredient that improved the chassis was active suspension that was used to maintain constant ride height. Honda played its part in the new car's success, with its revised V6 turbo engine both more powerful and more fuel-efficient. Between them, Mansell and Piquet took eight wins with it.

JAPANESE GRAND PRIX

SUZUKA • ROUND 15 • DATE: 1ST NOVEMBER 1987
Laps: 51 • Distance: 185.671miles/298.809km • Weather: Cool & dull

Pos	Driver	Team	Chassis-Engine	Result	Qual
1	Gerhard Berger	Ferrari	Ferrari F187	1h32m58.072s	1
2	Ayrton Senna	Lotus	Lotus-Honda 99T	1h33m15.456s	8
3	Stefan Johansson	McLaren	McLaren-TAG MP4/3	1h33m15.766s	10
4	Michele Alboreto	Ferrari	Ferrari F187	1h34m18.513s	4
5	Thierry Boutsen	Benetton	Benetton-Ford B187	1h34m23.648s	3
6	Satoru Nakajima	Lotus	Lotus-Honda 99T	1h34m34.551s	12
7	Alain Prost	McLaren	McLaren-TAG MP4/3	50 laps	2
8	Jonathan Palmer	Tyrrell	Tyrrell-Ford Cosworth DG016	50 laps	20
9	Eddie Cheever	Arrows	Arrows-Megatron A10	50 laps	13
10	Derek Warwick	Arrows	Arrows-Megatron A10	50 laps	14
11	Riccardo Patrese	Brabham	Brabham-BMW BT56	49 laps/engine	9
12	Philippe Streiff	Tyrrell	Tyrrell-Ford Cosworth DG016	49 laps	26
13	Piercarlo Ghinzani	Ligier	Ligier-Megatron JS29C	48 laps/out of fuel	25
14	Yannick Dalmas	Larrousse	Lola-Ford Cosworth LC87	47 laps/electrical	23
15	Nelson Piquet	Williams	Williams-Honda FW11B	46 laps/engine	5
R	Rene Arnoux	Ligier	Ligier-Megatron JS29C	44 laps/out of fuel	18
R	Alex Caffi	Osella	Osella-Alfa Romeo FA1I	43 laps/out of fuel	24
R	Roberto Moreno	AGS	AGS-Ford Cosworth JH22	38 laps/electrical	27
R	Alessandro Nannini	Minardi	Minardi-Motori Moderni M187	35 laps/engine	15
R	Martin Brundle	Zakspeed	Zakspeed 871	32 laps/engine	16
R	Andrea de Cesaris	Brabham	Brabham-BMW BT56	26 laps/engine	11
R	Teo Fabi	Benetton	Benetton-Ford B187	16 laps/engine	6
R	Christian Danner	Zakspeed	Zakspeed 871	13 laps/engine	17
R	Ivan Capelli	March	March-Ford Cosworth 871	13 laps/accident	21
R	Adrian Campos	Minardi	Minardi-Motori Moderni M187	2 laps/engine	22
R	Philippe Alliot	Larrousse	Lola-Ford Cosworth LC87	0 laps/accident	19
NS	Nigel Mansell	Williams	Williams-Honda FW11B	back injury	7

Pole: Berger, 1m40.042s, 131.007mph/210.835kph. Fastest lap: Prost, 1m43.844s, 126.210mph/203.116kph on Lap 35. Race leaders: Berger 1-24 & 26-51, Senna 25

AUSTRALIAN GRAND PRIX

ADELAIDE • ROUND 16 • DATE: 15TH NOVEMBER 1987
Laps: 82 • Distance: 192.549miles/309.878km • Weather: Hot & bright

Pos	Driver	Team	Chassis-Engine	Result	Qual
1	Gerhard Berger	Ferrari	Ferrari F187	1h52m56.144s	1
DQ	Ayrton Senna	Lotus	Lotus-Honda 99T	brake ducts	4
2	Michele Alboreto	Ferrari	Ferrari F187	1h54m04.028s	6
3	Thierry Boutsen	Benetton	Benetton-Ford B187	81 laps	5
4	Jonathan Palmer	Tyrrell	Tyrrell-Ford Cosworth DG016	80 laps	19
5	Yannick Dalmas*	Larrousse	Lola-Ford Cosworth LC87	79 laps	21
6	Roberto Moreno	AGS	AGS-Ford Cosworth JH22	79 laps	25
7	Christian Danner	Zakspeed	Zakspeed 871	79 laps	24
8	Andrea de Cesaris	Brabham	Brabham-BMW BT56	78 laps/spun off	10
9	Riccardo Patrese	Williams	Williams-Honda FW11B	76 laps/oil leak	7
R	Nelson Piquet	Williams	Williams-Honda FW11B	58 laps/brakes	3
R	Ivan Capelli	March	March-Ford Cosworth	58 laps/spun off	23

Pos	Driver	Team	Chassis-Engine	Result	Qual
R	Alain Prost	McLaren	McLaren-TAG MP4/3	53 laps/brakes	2
R	Eddie Cheever	Arrows	Arrows-Megatron A10	53 laps/overheating	11
R	Stefan Johansson	McLaren	McLaren-TAG MP4/3	48 laps/brakes	8
R	Teo Fabi	Benetton	Benetton-Ford B187	46 laps/brakes	9
R	Adrian Campos	Minardi	Minardi-Motori Moderni M187	46 laps/transmission	26
R	Philippe Alliot	Larrousse	Lola-Ford Cosworth LC87	45 laps/electrical	17
R	Rene Arnoux	Ligier	Ligier-Megatron JS29C	41 laps/ignition	20
R	Stefano Modena	Brabham	Brabham-BMW BT56	31 laps/exhaustion	15
R	Piercarlo Ghinzani	Ligier	Ligier-Megatron JS29C	26 laps/ignition	22
R	Satoru Nakajima	Lotus	Lotus-Honda 99T	22 laps/suspension	14
R	Derek Warwick	Arrows	Arrows-Megatron A10	19 laps/transmission	12
R	Martin Brundle	Zakspeed	Zakspeed 871	18 laps/engine	16
R	Philippe Streiff	Tyrrell	Tyrrell-Ford Cosworth DG016	6 laps/spun off	18
R	Alessandro Nannini	Minardi	Minardi-Motori Moderni M187	0 laps/accident	13
DNQ	Alex Caffi	Osella	Osella-Alfa Romeo FA1I	-	27

*ineligible for points, not entered in the World Championship

Pole: Berger, 1m17.267s, 109.404mph/176.069kph. Fastest lap: Berger, 1m20.416s, 105.120mph/169.175kph on Lap 72. Race leaders: Berger 1-82

NEW DRIVERS

Satoru Nakajima took the best result of any of the year's seven newcomers, with a fourth place for Lotus in the British GP. Next best was Yannick Dalmas who only entered the last three races but collected a fifth place in Adelaide for the Larrousse team. F3000 champion Stefano Modena qualified mid-Qual on his debut at the final round for Brabham.

WORLD DRIVERS' CHAMPIONSHIP FINAL RESULTS

Pos	Driver	Nat	Car-Engine	R1	R2	R3	R4	R5	R6
1	Nelson Piquet	BRA	Williams-Honda FW11B	2F	NS	R	2	2	2F
2	Nigel Mansell	GBR	Williams-Honda FW11B	6P	1	RP	RP	5P	1P
3	Ayrton Senna	BRA	Lotus-Honda 99T	R	2P	R	1F	1F	4
4	Alain Prost	FRA	McLaren-TAG MP4/3	1	R	1F	9	3	3
5	Gerhard Berger	AUT	Ferrari F187	4	R	R	4	4	R
6	Stefan Johansson	SWE	McLaren-TAG MP4/3	3	4	2	R	7	8
7	Michele Alboreto	ITA	Ferrari F187	8	3	R	3	R	R
8	Thierry Boutsen	BEL	Benetton-Ford B187	5	R	R	R	R	R
9	Teo Fabi	ITA	Benetton-Ford B187	R	RF	R	8	R	5
10	Eddie Cheever	USA	Arrows-Megatron A10	R	R	4	R	6	R
11	Jonathan Palmer	GBR	Tyrrell-Ford Cosworth DG016	10	R	R	5	11	7
12	Satoru Nakajima	JPN	Lotus-Honda 99T	7	6	5	10	R	NC
13	Riccardo Patrese	ITA	Brabham-BMW BT56	R	9	R	R	9	R
			Williams-Honda FW11B	-	-	-	-	-	-
14	Andrea de Cesaris	ITA	Brabham-BMW BT56	R	R	3	R	R	R
15	Philippe Streiff	FRA	Tyrrell-Ford Cosworth DG016	11	8	9	R	R	6
16	Derek Warwick	GBR	Arrows-Megatron A10	R	11	R	R	R	R
17	Philippe Alliot	FRA	Lola-Ford Cosworth LC87	-	10	8	R	R	R

Pos	Driver	Nat	Car-Engine	R1	R2	R3	R4	R5	R6
18	Martin Brundle	GBR	Zakspeed 861	R	-	-	-	R	-
			Zakspeed 871	-	5	R	7	-	R
19	Rene Arnoux	FRA	Ligier-Megatron JS29C	-	NS	6	11	10	-
			Ligier-Megatron JS29C	-	-	-	-	-	R
19	Ivan Capelli	ITA	March-Ford Cosworth 87P	NS	-	-	-	-	-
			March-Ford Cosworth 871	-	R	R*	6	R	R
19	Roberto Moreno	BRA	AGS-Ford Cosworth JH22	-	-	-	-	-	-

*drove March-Ford Cosworth 87P at original start, switched to March-Ford Cosworth 871 for restart

Pos	Driver	R7	R8	R9	R10	R11	R12	R13	R14	R15	R16	Total
1	Piquet	2P	1	1F	2P	1P	3	4P	2F	15	R	73
2	Mansell	1F	RPF	14P	1F	3	R	1	1P	NS	-	61
3	Senna	3	3	2	5	2F	7	5	R	2	DQ	57
4	Prost	R	7	3	6	15	1	2	R	7F	R	46
5	Berger	R	R	R	R	4	2PF	RF	R	1P	1PF	36
6	Johansson	R	2	R	7	6	5	3	R	3	R	30
7	Alboreto	R	R	R	R	R	R	15	R	4	2	17
8	Boutsen	7	R	4	4	5	14	16	R	5	3	16
9	Fabi	6	R	R	3	7	4	R	5	R	R	12
10	Cheever	R	R	8	R	R	6	8	4	9	R	8
11	Palmer	8	5	7	14	14	10	R	7	8	4	7
12	Nakajima	4	R	R	13	11	8	9	R	6	R	7
13	Patrese	R	R	5	R	R	R	13	3	11	-	6
		-	-	-	-	-	-	-	-	-	9	
14	de Cesaris	R	R	R	R	R	R	R	R	R	8	4
15	Streiff	R	4	9	R	12	12	7	8	12	R	4
16	Warwick	5	R	6	R	R	13	10	R	10	R	3
17	Alliot	R	6	R	12	R	R	6	6	R	R	3
18	Brundle	-	-	-	-	-	-	-	-	-	-	2
		NC	NC	R	DQ	R	R	11	R	R	R	
19	Arnoux	-	-	-	-	-	-	-	-	-	-	1
		R	R	R	10	10	R	R	R	R	R	
19	Capelli	-	-	-	-	-	-	-	-	-	-	1
		R	R	10	11	13	9	12	R	R	R	
19	Moreno	-	-	-	-	-	-	-	-	R	6	1

SYMBOLS AND GRAND PRIX KEY

Round 1	**Brazilian GP**
Round 2	**San Marino GP**
Round 3	**Belgian GP**
Round 4	**Monaco GP**
Round 5	**Detroit GP**
Round 6	**French GP**
Round 7	**British GP**
Round 8	**German GP**
Round 9	**Hungarian GP**
Round 10	**Austrian GP**
Round 11	**Italian GP**
Round 12	**Portuguese GP**
Round 13	**Spanish GP**
Round 14	**Mexican GP**
Round 15	**Japanese GP**
Round 16	**Australian GP**

SCORING

1st	**9 points**
2nd	**6 points**
3rd	**4 points**
4th	**3 points**
5th	**2 points**
6th	**1 point**

DNPQ DID NOT PRE-QUALIFY **DNQ** DID NOT QUALIFY **DQ** DISQUALIFIED **EX** EXCLUDED
F FASTEST LAP **NC** NOT CLASSIFIED **NS** NON-STARTER **P** POLE POSITION **R** RETIRED

WORLD CONSTRUCTORS' CHAMPIONSHIP FINAL RESULTS

Pos	Team-Engine	R1	R2	R3	R4	R5	R6	R7	R8
1	Williams-Honda	2/6	1/NS	R/R	2/R	2/5	1/2	1/2	1/R
2	McLaren-TAG	1/3	4/R	1/2	9/R	3/7	3/8	R/R	2/7
3	Lotus-Honda	7/R	2/6	5/R	1/10	1/R	4/NC	3/4	3/R
4	Ferrari	4/8	3/R	R/R	3/4	4/R	R/R	R/R	R/R
5	Benetton-Ford	5/R	R/R	R/R	8/R	R/R	5/R	6/7	R/R
6	Tyrrell-Ford	10/11	8/R	9/R	5/R	11/R	6/7	8/R	4/5
7	Arrows-Megatron	R/R	11/R	4/R	R/R	6/R	R/R	5/R	R/R
8	Brabham-BMW	R/R	9/R	3/R	R/R	9/R	R/R	R/R	R/R
9	Lola-Ford	-	10	8	R	R	R	R	6
10	Zakspeed	9/R	5/7	R/R	7/DNQ	8/R	R/R	NC/R	NC/R
11	Ligier-Megatron	-/-	R/NS	6/7	11/12	10/R	R/R	R/DNQ	R/R
11	March-Ford	NS	R	R	6	R	R	R	R
11	AGS-Ford	12	13	10	13	12	9	9	R

Pos	Team-Engine	R9	R10	R11	R12	R13	R14	R15	R16	Total
1	Williams-Honda	1/14	1/2	1/3	3/R	1/4	1/2	15/NS	9/R	137
2	McLaren-TAG	3/R	6/7	6/15	1/5	2/3	R/R	3/7	R/R	76
3	Lotus-Honda	2/R	5/13	2/11	7/8	5/9	R/R	2/6	DQ/R	64
4	Ferrari	R/R	R/R	4/R	2/R	15/R	R/R	1/4	1/2	53
5	Benetton-Ford	4/R	3/4	5/7	4/14	16/R	5/R	5/R	3/R	28
6	Tyrrell-Ford	7/9	14/R	12/14	10/12	7/R	7/8	8/12	4/R	11
7	Arrows-Megatron	6/8	R/R	R/R	6/13	8/10	4/R	9/10	R/R	11
8	Brabham-BMW	5/R	R/R	R/R	R/R	13/R	3/R	11/R	8/R	10
9	Lola-Ford	R	12	R	R	6	6/9	14/R	5*/R	3
10	Zakspeed	R/R	9/DQ	9/R	R/R	11/R	R/R	R/R	7/R	2
11	Ligier-Megatron	12/R	8/10	8/10	R/R	R/R	R/R	13/R	R/R	1
11	March-Ford	10	11	13	9	12	R	R	R	1
11	AGS-Ford	13	NC	DNQ	DNQ	R	DNQ	R	6	1

*ineligible for points, not entered in the World Championship

1988

SEASON SUMMARY

It was Ayrton Senna versus team-mate Alain Prost as McLaren dominated the final year for three decades in which the World Championship was open to turbocharged engines. Even though Williams had won two titles on the trot, it had lost its engine supply deal to McLaren and its drivers had to make do with Judd engines instead, dropping down to seventh overall as neither Nigel Mansell nor Riccardo Patrese could conjure a win. Only one other team managed to take the chequered flag out in front, and that was Ferrari, fittingly, for its home grand prix just weeks after Enzo Ferrari had died, when Gerhard Berger was handed victory with two laps to go.

BRAZILIAN GRAND PRIX

JACAREPAGUA • ROUND 1 • DATE: 3RD APRIL 1988
Laps: 60 • Distance: 187.86miles/301.86km • Weather: Hot but dull

Pos	Driver	Team	Chassis-Engine	Result	Qual
1	Alain Prost	McLaren	McLaren-Honda MP4/4	1h36m06.857s	3
2	Gerhard Berger	Ferrari	Ferrari F187/88C	1h36m16.730s	4
3	Nelson Piquet	Lotus	Lotus-Honda 100T	1h37m15.438s	5
4	Derek Warwick	Arrows	Arrows-Megatron A10B	1h37m20.205s	11
5	Michele Alboreto	Ferrari	Ferrari F187/88C	1h37m21.413s	6
6	Satoru Nakajima	Lotus	Lotus-Honda 100T	59 laps	10
7	Thierry Boutsen	Benetton	Benetton-Ford B188	59 laps	7
8	Eddie Cheever	Arrows	Arrows-Megatron A10B	59 laps	15
9	Stefan Johansson	Ligier	Ligier-Judd JS31	57 laps	21
R	Andrea de Cesaris	Rial	Rial-Ford Cosworth ARC1	53 laps/engine	14
R	Jonathan Palmer	Tyrrell	Tyrrell-Ford Cosworth 017	47 laps/transmission	22
R	Luis Perez Sala	Minardi	Minardi-Ford Cosworth M188	46 laps/chassis	20
R	Philippe Alliot	Larrousse	Lola-Ford Cosworth LC88	40 laps/suspension	16
R	Philippe Streiff	AGS	AGS-Ford Cosworth JH23	35 laps/brakes	19
R	Gabriele Tarquini	Coloni	Coloni-Ford Cosworth FC188	35 laps/suspension	25
R	Yannick Dalmas	Larrousse	Lola-Ford Cosworth LC88	32 laps/engine	17
DQ	Ayrton Senna	McLaren	McLaren-Honda MP4/4	31 laps/changed car	1
R	Rene Arnoux	Ligier	Ligier-Judd JS31	23 laps/clutch	18
R	Stefano Modena	Euro Brun	EuroBrun-Ford Cosworth ER188	20 laps/engine	24
R	Nigel Mansell	Williams	Williams-Judd FW12	18 laps/engine	2
R	Alessandro Nannini	Benetton	Benetton-Ford B188	7 laps/engine	12
R	Riccardo Patrese	Williams	Williams-Judd FW12	6 laps/engine	8
R	Ivan Capelli	March	March-Judd 881	6 laps/engine	9
R	Adrian Campos	Minardi	Minardi-Ford Cosworth M188	5 laps/chassis	23
R	Mauricio Gugelmin	March	March-Judd 881	0 laps/gearbox	13
NS	Oscar Larrauri	Euro Brun	EuroBrun-Ford Cosworth ER188	-	26
DNQ	Julian Bailey	Tyrrell	Tyrrell-Ford Cosworth 017	-	27
DNQ	Piercarlo Ghinzani	Zakspeed	Zakspeed 881	-	28
DNQ	Nicola Larini	Osella	Osella-Alfa Romeo FA1I	-	29
DNQ	Bernd Schneider	Zakspeed	Zakspeed 881	-	30
DNPQ	Alex Caffi	BMS Scuderia Italia	Dallara-Ford Cosworth 3087	-	31

Pole: Senna, 1m28.096s, 127.747mph/205.589kph. Fastest lap: Berger, 1m32.943s, 121.084mph/194.867kph on Lap 45. Race leaders: Prost 1-60

CLEAN SWEEP DENIED

McLaren achieved a record 15 wins from 16 grands prix, but a clean sweep was denied them at Monza when Williams stand-in Jean-Louis Schlesser tripped up Senna. Prost had retired, but Senna was in front, albeit under pressure from Ferrari's Gerhard Berger and Michele Alboreto, when he tangled with Schlesser at the chicane.

SAN MARINO GRAND PRIX

IMOLA • ROUND 2 • DATE: 1ST MAY 1988
Laps: 60 • Distance: 187.656miles/302.4km • Weather: Warm but dull

Pos	Driver	Team	Chassis-Engine	Result	Qual
1	Ayrton Senna	McLaren	McLaren-Honda MP4/4	1h32m41.264s	1
2	Alain Prost	McLaren	McLaren-Honda MP4/4	1h32m43.598s	2
3	Nelson Piquet	Lotus	Lotus-Honda 100T	59 laps	3
4	Thierry Boutsen	Benetton	Benetton-Ford B188	59 laps	8
5	Gerhard Berger	Ferrari	Ferrari F187/88C	59 laps	5
6	Alessandro Nannini	Benetton	Benetton-Ford B188	59 laps	4
7	Eddie Cheever	Arrows	Arrows-Megatron A10B	59 laps	7
8	Satoru Nakajima	Lotus	Lotus-Honda 100T	59 laps	12
9	Derek Warwick	Arrows	Arrows-Megatron A10B	58 laps	14
10	Philippe Streiff	AGS	AGS-Ford Cosworth JH23	58 laps	13
11	Luis Perez Sala	Minardi	Minardi-Ford Cosworth M188	58 laps	18
12	Yannick Dalmas	Larrousse	Lola-Ford Cosworth LC88	58 laps	19
13	Riccardo Patrese	Williams	Williams-Judd FW12	58 laps	6
14	Jonathan Palmer	Tyrrell	Tyrrell-Ford Cosworth 017	58 laps	23
15	Mauricio Gugelmin	March	March-Judd 881	58 laps	20
16	Adrian Campos	Minardi	Minardi-Ford Cosworth M188	57 laps	22
17	Philippe Alliot	Larrousse	Lola-Ford Cosworth LC88	57 laps	15
18	Michele Alboreto	Ferrari	Ferrari F187/88C	54 laps/engine	10
NC	Stefano Modena	Euro Brun	EuroBrun-Ford Cosworth ER188	52 laps	26
R	Julian Bailey	Tyrrell	Tyrrell-Ford Cosworth 017	48 laps/gearbox	21
R	Nigel Mansell	Williams	Williams-Judd FW12	42 laps/engine	11
R	Gabriele Tarquini	Coloni	Coloni-Ford Cosworth FC188	40 laps/fuel system	17
R	Alex Caffi	BMS Scuderia Italia	Dallara-Ford Cosworth BMS-188	38 laps/gearbox	24
R	Piercarlo Ghinzani	Zakspeed	Zakspeed 881	36 laps/gearbox	25
R	Ivan Capelli	March	March-Judd 881	2 laps/gearbox	9
R	Andrea de Cesaris	Rial	Rial-Ford Cosworth ARC1	1 lap/suspension	16
EX	Nicola Larini	Osella	Osella-Alfa Romeo FA1L	failed scrutineering	-
DNQ	Oscar Larrauri	Euro Brun	EuroBrun-Ford Cosworth ER188	-	27
DNQ	Stefan Johansson	Ligier	Ligier-Judd JS31	-	28
DNQ	Rene Arnoux	Ligier	Ligier-Judd JS31	-	29
DNQ	Bernd Schneider	Zakspeed	Zakspeed 881	-	30

Pole: Senna, 1m27.148s, 129.367mph/208.197kph. Fastest lap: Prost, 1m29.685s, 125.708mph/202.308kph on Lap 53. Race leaders: Senna 1-60

MONACO GRAND PRIX

MONTE CARLO • ROUND 3 • DATE: 15TH MAY 1988
Laps: 78 • Distance: 161.298miles/259.584km • Weather: Warm but dull

Pos	Driver	Team	Chassis-Engine	Result	Qual
1	Alain Prost	McLaren	McLaren-Honda MP4/4	1h57m17.077s	2
2	Gerhard Berger	Ferrari	Ferrari F187/88C	1h57m37.530s	3
3	Michele Alboreto	Ferrari	Ferrari F187/88C	1h57m58.306s	4
4	Derek Warwick	Arrows	Arrows-Megatron A10B	77 laps	7
5	Jonathan Palmer	Tyrrell	Tyrrell-Ford Cosworth 017	77 laps	10
6	Riccardo Patrese	Williams	Williams-Judd FW12	77 laps	8
7	Yannick Dalmas	Larrousse	Lola-Ford Cosworth LC88	77 laps	21
8	Thierry Boutsen	Benetton	Benetton-Ford B188	76 laps	16
9	Nicola Larini	Osella	Osella-Alfa Romeo FA1L	75 laps	25
10	Ivan Capelli	March	March-Judd 881	72 laps	22
R	Ayrton Senna	McLaren	McLaren-Honda MP4/4	66 laps/spun off	1
R	Philippe Alliot	Larrousse	Lola-Ford Cosworth LC88	50 laps/collision	13
R	Mauricio Gugelmin	March	March-Judd 881	45 laps/fuel pump	14
R	Piercarlo Ghinzani	Zakspeed	Zakspeed 881	43 laps/gearbox	23
R	Alessandro Nannini	Benetton	Benetton-Ford B188	38 laps/gearbox	6
R	Luis Perez Sala	Minardi	Minardi-Ford Cosworth M188	36 laps/halfshaft	15
R	Nigel Mansell	Williams	Williams-Judd FW12	32 laps/collision	5
R	Andrea de Cesaris	Rial	Rial-Ford Cosworth ARC1	28 laps/engine	19
R	Rene Arnoux	Ligier	Ligier-Judd JS31	17 laps/engine	20
R	Oscar Larrauri	Euro Brun	EuroBrun-Ford Cosworth ER188	14 laps/brakes	18
R	Eddie Cheever	Arrows	Arrows-Megatron A10B	8 laps/engine	9
R	Stefan Johansson	Ligier	Ligier-Judd JS31	6 laps/engine	26
R	Gabriele Tarquini	Coloni	Coloni-Ford Cosworth FC188	5 laps/suspension	24
R	Nelson Piquet	Lotus	Lotus-Honda 100T	1 lap/collision	11
R	Alex Caffi	BMS Scuderia Italia	Dallara-Ford Cosworth BMS-188	0 laps/spun off	17
NS	Philippe Streiff	AGS	AGS-Ford Cosworth JH23	0 laps/throttle linkage	12
DNQ	Satoru Nakajima	Lotus	Lotus-Honda 100T	-	27
DNQ	Bernd Schneider	Zakspeed	Zakspeed 881	-	28
DNQ	Adrian Campos	Minardi	Minardi-Ford Cosworth M188	-	29
DNQ	Julian Bailey	Tyrrell	Tyrrell-Ford Cosworth 017	-	30
EX	Stefano Modena	Euro Brun	EuroBrun-Ford Cosworth ER188	missed weight check	-

Pole: Senna, 1m23.998s, 88.627mph/142.631kph. Fastest lap: Senna, 1m26.321s, 86.241mph/138.793kph on Lap 59. Race leaders: Senna 1-66, Prost 67-78

BENETTON ON THE RISE

Benetton's third season was a step forward as the team ranked third overall. Thierry Boutsen and Alessandro Nannini enjoyed a good Rory Byrne-designed chassis, but its normally aspirated Ford DFR was down on power. That said, Boutsen ranked fourth by recording six third-place finishes, while Nannini took two thirds.

THE DEATH OF MR FERRARI

Enzo Ferrari's death in August wasn't unexpected as he was 90 but it still rocked F1 as he had shaped the sport for half a century as he built F1's top team. A racer in his early days, he ran Alfa Romeo's attack in the 1930s before entering his own cars. Masked by sunglasses, he had a Machiavellian image as he thought more of his engines than he did of his cars or drivers.

MEXICAN GRAND PRIX

MEXICO CITY • ROUND 4 • DATE: 29TH MAY 1988
Laps: 67 • Distance: 184.54miles/296.207km • Weather: Hot & bright

Pos	Driver	Team	Chassis-Engine	Result	Qual
1	Alain Prost	McLaren	McLaren-Honda MP4/4	1h30m15.737s	2
2	Ayrton Senna	McLaren	McLaren-Honda MP4/4	1h30m22.841s	1
3	Gerhard Berger	Ferrari	Ferrari F187/88C	1h31m13.051s	3
4	Michele Alboreto	Ferrari	Ferrari F187/88C	66 laps	5
5	Derek Warwick	Arrows	Arrows-Megatron A10B	66 laps	9
6	Eddie Cheever	Arrows	Arrows-Megatron A10B	66 laps	7
7	Alessandro Nannini	Benetton	Benetton-Ford B188	65 laps	8
8	Thierry Boutsen	Benetton	Benetton-Ford B188	64 laps	11
9	Yannick Dalmas	Larrousse	Lola-Ford Cosworth LC88	64 laps	22
10	Stefan Johansson	Ligier	Ligier-Judd JS31	63 laps	24
11	Luis Perez Sala	Minardi	Minardi-Ford Cosworth M188	63 laps	25
12	Philippe Streiff	AGS	AGS-Ford Cosworth JH23	63 laps	19
13	Oscar Larrauri	Euro Brun	EuroBrun-Ford Cosworth ER188	63 laps	26
14	Gabriele Tarquini	Coloni	Coloni-Ford Cosworth FC188	62 laps	21
15	Piercarlo Ghinzani	Zakspeed	Zakspeed 881	61 laps	18
16	Ivan Capelli	March	March-Judd 881	61 laps	10
R	Nelson Piquet	Lotus	Lotus-Honda 100T	58 laps/engine	4
R	Andrea de Cesaris	Rial	Rial-Ford Cosworth ARC1	52 laps/gearbox	12
R	Satoru Nakajima	Lotus	Lotus-Honda 100T	27 laps/turbo	6
R	Nigel Mansell	Williams	Williams-Judd FW12	20 laps/engine	14
R	Bernd Schneider	Zakspeed	Zakspeed 881	16 laps/engine	15
R	Riccardo Patrese	Williams	Williams-Judd FW12	16 laps/engine	17
R	Rene Arnoux	Ligier	Ligier-Judd JS31	13 laps/collision	20
R	Alex Caffi	BMS Scuderia Italia	Dallara-Ford Cosworth BMS-188	13 laps/brakes	23
R	Mauricio Gugelmin	March	March-Judd 881	10 laps/electrical	16
R	Philippe Alliot	Larrousse	Lola-Ford Cosworth LC88	0 laps/suspension	13
DNQ	Jonathan Palmer	Tyrrell	Tyrrell-Ford Cosworth 017	-	27
DNQ	Nicola Larini	Osella	Osella-Alfa Romeo FA1L	-	28
DNQ	Julian Bailey	Tyrrell	Tyrrell-Ford Cosworth 017	-	29
DNQ	Adrian Campos	Minardi	Minardi-Ford Cosworth M188	-	30
EX	Stefano Modena	Euro Brun	EuroBrun-Ford Cosworth ER188	illegal rear wing	-

Pole: Senna, 1m17.468s, 127.659mph/205.447kph. Fastest lap: Prost, 1m18.608s, 125.807mph/202.467kph on Lap 52. Race leaders: Prost 1-67

CANADIAN GRAND PRIX

MONTREAL • ROUND 5 • DATE: 12TH JUNE 1988
Laps: 69 • Distance: 187.710miles/302.91km • Weather: Hot & bright

Pos	Driver	Team	Chassis-Engine	Result	Qual
1	Ayrton Senna	McLaren	McLaren-Honda MP4/4	1h39m46.618s	1
2	Alain Prost	McLaren	McLaren-Honda MP4/4	1h39m52.552s	2
3	Thierry Boutsen	Benetton	Benetton-Ford B188	1h40m38.027s	7
4	Nelson Piquet	Lotus	Lotus-Honda 100T	68 laps	6
5	Ivan Capelli	March	March-Judd 881	68 laps	14
6	Jonathan Palmer	Tyrrell	Tyrrell-Ford Cosworth 017	67 laps	19
7	Derek Warwick	Arrows	Arrows-Megatron A10B	67 laps	16
8	Gabriele Tarquini	Coloni	Coloni-Ford Cosworth FC188	67 laps	26
9	Andrea de Cesaris	Rial	Rial-Ford Cosworth ARC1	66 laps/out of fuel	12
10	Philippe Alliot	Larrousse	Lola-Ford Cosworth LC88	66 laps/electrical	17
11	Satoru Nakajima	Lotus	Lotus-Honda 100T	66 laps	13
12	Stefano Modena	Euro Brun	EuroBrun-Ford Cosworth ER188	66 laps	15
13	Luis Perez Sala	Minardi	Minardi-Ford Cosworth M188	64 laps	21
14	Piercarlo Ghinzani	Zakspeed	Zakspeed 881	63 laps/engine	22
R	Mauricio Gugelmin	March	March-Judd 881	54 laps/gearbox	18
R	Philippe Streiff	AGS	AGS-Ford Cosworth JH23	41 laps/suspension	10
R	Rene Arnoux	Ligier	Ligier-Judd JS31	36 laps/transmission	20
R	Michele Alboreto	Ferrari	Ferrari F187/88C	33 laps/engine	4
R	Riccardo Patrese	Williams	Williams-Judd FW12	32 laps/engine	11
R	Eddie Cheever	Arrows	Arrows-Megatron A10B	31 laps/throttle	8
R	Nigel Mansell	Williams	Williams-Judd FW12	28 laps/engine	9
R	Stefan Johansson	Ligier	Ligier-Judd JS31	24 laps/engine	25
R	Gerhard Berger	Ferrari	Ferrari F187/88C	22 laps/electrical	3
R	Alessandro Nannini	Benetton	Benetton-Ford B188	15 laps/ignition	5
R	Oscar Larrauri	Euro Brun	EuroBrun-Ford Cosworth ER188	8 laps/accident	24
R	Julian Bailey	Tyrrell	Tyrrell-Ford Cosworth 017	0 laps/collision	23
DNQ	Adrian Campos	Minardi	Minardi-Ford Cosworth M188	-	27
DNQ	Nicola Larini	Osella	Osella-Alfa Romeo FA1L	-	28
DNQ	Yannick Dalmas	Larrousse	Lola-Ford Cosworth LC88	-	29
DNQ	Bernd Schneider	Zakspeed	Zakspeed 881	-	30
DNPQ	Alex Caffi	BMS Scuderia Italia	Dallara-Ford Cosworth BMS-188	-	31

Pole: Senna, 1m21.681s, 120.225mph/193.484kph. Fastest lap: Senna, 1m24.973s, 115.567mph/185.988kph on Lap 53. Race leaders: Prost 1-18, Senna 19-69

DETROIT GRAND PRIX

DETROIT • ROUND 6 • DATE: 19TH JUNE 1988
Laps: 63 • Distance: 157.501miles/253.474km • Weather: Hot & bright

Pos	Driver	Team	Chassis-Engine	Result	Qual
1	Ayrton Senna	McLaren	McLaren-Honda MP4/4	1h54m56.035s	1
2	Alain Prost	McLaren	McLaren-Honda MP4/4	1h55m34.748s	4
3	Thierry Boutsen	Benetton	Benetton-Ford B188	62 laps	5
4	Andrea de Cesaris	Rial	Rial-Ford Cosworth ARC1	62 laps	12
5	Jonathan Palmer	Tyrrell	Tyrrell-Ford Cosworth 017	62 laps	17
6	Pierluigi Martini	Minardi	Minardi-Ford Cosworth M188	62 laps	16
7	Yannick Dalmas	Larrousse	Lola-Ford Cosworth LC88	61 laps	25
8	Alex Caffi	BMS Scuderia Italia	Dallara-Ford Cosworth BMS-188	61 laps	22
9	Julian Bailey	Tyrrell	Tyrrell-Ford Cosworth 017	59 laps/spun off	23

Pos	Driver	Team	Chassis-Engine	Result	Qual
R	Luis Perez Sala	Minardi	Minardi-Ford Cosworth M188	54 laps/gearbox	26
R	Philippe Alliot	Larrousse	Lola-Ford Cosworth LC88	46 laps/halfshaft	14
R	Stefano Modena	Euro Brun	EuroBrun-Ford Cosworth ER188	46 laps/spun off	19
R	Michele Alboreto	Ferrari	Ferrari F187/88C	45 laps/collision	3
R	Rene Arnoux	Ligier	Ligier-Judd JS31	45 laps/overheating	20
R	Mauricio Gugelmin	March	March-Judd 881	34 laps/engine	13
R	Nelson Piquet	Lotus	Lotus-Honda 100T	26 laps/spun off	8
R	Riccardo Patrese	Williams	Williams-Judd FW12	26 laps/engine	10
R	Oscar Larrauri	Euro Brun	EuroBrun-Ford Cosworth ER188	26 laps/gearbox	24
R	Derek Warwick	Arrows	Arrows-Megatron A10B	24 laps/spun off	9
R	Nigel Mansell	Williams	Williams-Judd FW12	18 laps/engine	6
R	Philippe Streiff	AGS	AGS-Ford Cosworth JH23	15 laps/suspension	11
R	Alessandro Nannini	Benetton	Benetton-Ford B188	14 laps/suspension	7
R	Eddie Cheever	Arrows	Arrows-Megatron A10B	14 laps/electrical	15
R	Nicola Larini	Osella	Osella-Alfa Romeo FA1L	7 laps/engine	27
R	Gerhard Berger	Ferrari	Ferrari F187/88C	6 laps/puncture	2
R	Stefan Johansson	Ligier	Ligier-Judd JS31	2 laps/overheating	18
NS	Ivan Capelli	March	March-Judd 881	broken foot	21
DNQ	Satoru Nakajima	Lotus	Lotus-Honda 100T	-	28
DNQ	Bernd Schneider	Zakspeed	Zakspeed 881	-	29
DNQ	Piercarlo Ghinzani	Zakspeed	Zakspeed 881	-	30
DNPQ	Gabriele Tarquini	Coloni	Coloni-Ford Cosworth FC188	-	31

Pole: Senna, 1m40.606s, 89.458mph/143.969kph. Fastest lap: Prost, 1m44.836s, 85.848mph/138.159kph on Lap 4. Race leaders: Senna 1-63

HONDA HORSES WIN AGAIN

Honda power continued to dominate, albeit this time with McLaren as the team to lead the Japanese manufacturer's attack, leaving Williams to make do with normally aspirated Judd units. For the final year of Honda turbo units, Lotus was also supplied with engines but Nelson Piquet could do no better than a trio of thirds.

FRENCH GRAND PRIX

CIRCUIT PAUL RICARD • ROUND 7 • DATE: 3RD JULY 1988
Laps: 80 • Distance: 189.520miles/305.04km • Weather: Hot & bright

Pos	Driver	Team	Chassis-Engine	Result	Qual
1	Alain Prost	McLaren	McLaren-Honda MP4/4	1h37m37.328s	1
2	Ayrton Senna	McLaren	McLaren-Honda MP4/4	1h38m09.080s	2
3	Michele Alboreto	Ferrari	Ferrari F187/88C	1h38m43.833s	4
4	Gerhard Berger	Ferrari	Ferrari F187/88C	79 laps	3
5	Nelson Piquet	Lotus	Lotus-Honda 100T	79 laps	7
6	Alessandro Nannini	Benetton	Benetton-Ford B188	79 laps	6
7	Satoru Nakajima	Lotus	Lotus-Honda 100T	79 laps	8
8	Mauricio Gugelmin	March	March-Judd 881	79 laps	16
9	Ivan Capelli	March	March-Judd 881	79 laps	10
10	Andrea de Cesaris	Rial	Rial-Ford Cosworth ARC1	78 laps	12
11	Eddie Cheever	Arrows	Arrows-Megatron A10B	78 laps	13
12	Alex Caffi	BMS Scuderia Italia	Dallara-Ford Cosworth BMS-188	78 laps	14

Pos	Driver	Team	Chassis-Engine	Result	Qual
13	Yannick Dalmas	Larrousse	Lola-Ford Cosworth LC88	78 laps	19
14	Stefano Modena	Euro Brun	EuroBrun-Ford Cosworth ER188	77 laps	20
15	Pierluigi Martini	Minardi	Minardi-Ford Cosworth M188	77 laps	23
NC	Luis Perez Sala	Minardi	Minardi-Ford Cosworth M188	70 laps	26
R	Oscar Larrauri	Euro Brun	EuroBrun-Ford Cosworth ER188	64 laps/clutch	27
R	Nicola Larini	Osella	Osella-Alfa Romeo FA1L	56 laps/halfshaft	25
R	Bernd Schneider	Zakspeed	Zakspeed 881	55 laps/gearbox	21
R	Nigel Mansell	Williams	Williams-Judd FW12	48 laps/suspension	9
R	Philippe Alliot	Larrousse	Lola-Ford Cosworth LC88	46 laps/electrical	18
R	Jonathan Palmer	Tyrrell	Tyrrell-Ford Cosworth 017	40 laps/engine	24
R	Riccardo Patrese	Williams	Williams-Judd FW12	35 laps/brakes	15
R	Thierry Boutsen	Benetton	Benetton-Ford B188	28 laps/engine	5
R	Philippe Streiff	AGS	AGS-Ford Cosworth JH23	20 laps/oil leak	17
R	Derek Warwick	Arrows	Arrows-Megatron A10B	11 laps/spun off	11
DNQ	Rene Arnoux	Ligier	Ligier-Judd JS31	-	28
DNQ	Julian Bailey	Tyrrell	Tyrrell-Ford Cosworth 017	-	29
DNQ	Stefan Johansson	Ligier	Ligier-Judd JS31	-	30
DNPQ	Gabriele Tarquini	Coloni	Coloni-Ford Cosworth FC188	-	31
EX	Piercarlo Ghinzani	Zakspeed	Zakspeed 881	missed weight check	22

Pole: Prost, 1m07.589s, 126.195mph/203.092kph. Fastest lap: Prost, 1m11.737s, 118.898mph/191.348kph on Lap 45. Race leaders: Prost 1-36 & 61-80, Senna 37-60

ATTENTION TO DETAIL

After Enzo Ferrari's death, Ron Dennis took over as the most influential team owner in F1. He had run McLaren since 1980 and taken the constructors' title in 1984 and 1985, but 1988 was the year in which his attention to detail was rewarded – Honda chose to supply his team with engines rather than Williams. This would be the first of four titles in a row.

BRITISH GRAND PRIX

SILVERSTONE • ROUND 8 • DATE: 10TH JULY 1988
Laps: 65 • Distance: 192.982miles/310.576km • Weather: Cool & wet

Pos	Driver	Team	Chassis-Engine	Result	Qual
1	Ayrton Senna	McLaren	McLaren-Honda MP4/4	1h33m16.367s	3
2	Nigel Mansell	Williams	Williams-Judd FW12	1h33m39.711s	11
3	Alessandro Nannini	Benetton	Benetton-Ford B188	1h34m07.581s	8
4	Mauricio Gugelmin	March	March-Judd 881	1h34m27.745s	5
5	Nelson Piquet	Lotus	Lotus-Honda 100T	1h34m37.202s	7
6	Derek Warwick	Arrows	Arrows-Megatron A10B	64 laps	9
7	Eddie Cheever	Arrows	Arrows-Megatron A10B	64 laps	13
8	Riccardo Patrese	Williams	Williams-Judd FW12	64 laps	15
9	Gerhard Berger	Ferrari	Ferrari F187/88C	64 laps	1
10	Satoru Nakajima	Lotus	Lotus-Honda 100T	64 laps	10
11	Alex Caffi	BMS Scuderia Italia	Dallara-Ford Cosworth BMS-188	64 laps	21
12	Stefano Modena	Euro Brun	EuroBrun-Ford Cosworth ER188	64 laps	20
13	Yannick Dalmas	Larrousse	Lola-Ford Cosworth LC88	63 laps	23
14	Philippe Alliot	Larrousse	Lola-Ford Cosworth LC88	63 laps	22

Pos	Driver	Team	Chassis-Engine	Result	Qual
15	Pierluigi Martini	Minardi	Minardi-Ford Cosworth M188	63 laps	19
16	Julian Bailey	Tyrrell	Tyrrell-Ford Cosworth 017	63 laps	24
17	Michele Alboreto	Ferrari	Ferrari F187/88C	62 laps/out of fuel	2
18	Rene Arnoux	Ligier	Ligier-Judd JS31	62 laps	25
19	Nicola Larini	Osella	Osella-Alfa Romeo FA1L	60 laps/out of fuel	26
R	Thierry Boutsen	Benetton	Benetton-Ford B188	38 laps/transmission	12
R	Ivan Capelli	March	March-Judd 881	34 laps/alternator	6
R	Alain Prost	McLaren	McLaren-Honda MP4/4	24 laps/handling	4
R	Jonathan Palmer	Tyrrell	Tyrrell-Ford Cosworth 017	14 laps/engine	17
R	Andrea de Cesaris	Rial	Rial-Ford Cosworth ARC1	9 laps/clutch	14
R	Philippe Streiff	AGS	AGS-Ford Cosworth JH23	8 laps/wing	16
R	Luis Perez Sala	Minardi	Minardi-Ford Cosworth M188	0 laps/suspension	18
DNQ	Oscar Larrauri	Euro Brun	EuroBrun-Ford Cosworth ER188	-	27
DNQ	Piercarlo Ghinzani	Zakspeed	Zakspeed 881	-	28
DNQ	Stefan Johansson	Ligier	Ligier-Judd JS31	-	29
DNQ	Bernd Schneider	Zakspeed	Zakspeed 881	-	30
DNPQ	Gabriele Tarquini	Coloni	Coloni-Ford Cosworth FC188	-	31

Pole: Berger, 1m10.133s, 152.400mph/245.264kph. Fastest lap: Mansell, 1m23.308s, 128.295mph/206.472kph on Lap 48. Race leaders: Berger 1-13, Senna 14-65

MONTREAL MAKES CHANGES

There were no new circuits for F1 to visit in 1988 and the only change facing the drivers was the modification of Montreal's Circuit Gilles Villeneuve. The shape of the circuit remained the same, but the pits (and with it the start line) were moved from after the Virage du Casino to after the chicane, further along the rowing lake.

GERMAN GRAND PRIX

HOCKENHEIM • ROUND 9 • DATE: 24TH JULY 1988
Laps: 44 • Distance: 185.832miles/299.068km • Weather: Cool & wet

Pos	Driver	Team	Chassis-Engine	Result	Qual
1	Ayrton Senna	McLaren	McLaren-Honda MP4/4	1h32m54.188s	1
2	Alain Prost	McLaren	McLaren-Honda MP4/4	1h33m07.797s	2
3	Gerhard Berger	Ferrari	Ferrari F187/88C	1h33m46.283s	3
4	Michele Alboreto	Ferrari	Ferrari F187/88C	1h34m35.100s	4
5	Ivan Capelli	March	March-Judd 881	1h34m43.794s	7
6	Thierry Boutsen	Benetton	Benetton-Ford B188	43 laps	9
7	Derek Warwick	Arrows	Arrows-Megatron A10B	43 laps	12
8	Mauricio Gugelmin	March	March-Judd 881	43 laps	10
9	Satoru Nakajima	Lotus	Lotus-Honda 100T	43 laps	8
10	Eddie Cheever	Arrows	Arrows-Megatron A10B	43 laps	15
11	Jonathan Palmer	Tyrrell	Tyrrell-Ford Cosworth 017	43 laps	24
12	Bernd Schneider	Zakspeed	Zakspeed 881	43 laps	22
13	Andrea de Cesaris	Rial	Rial-Ford Cosworth ARC1	42 laps	14
14	Piercarlo Ghinzani	Zakspeed	Zakspeed 881	42 laps	23
15	Alex Caffi	BMS Scuderia Italia	Dallara-Ford Cosworth BMS-188	42 laps	19
16	Oscar Larrauri	Euro Brun	EuroBrun-Ford Cosworth ER188	42 laps	26
17	Rene Arnoux	Ligier	Ligier-Judd JS31	41 laps	17

Pos	Driver	Team	Chassis-Engine	Result	Qual
18	Alessandro Nannini	Benetton	Benetton-Ford B188	40 laps	6
19	Yannick Dalmas	Larrousse	Lola-Ford Cosworth LC88	39 laps/clutch	21
R	Philippe Streiff	AGS	AGS-Ford Cosworth JH23	38 laps/throttle	16
R	Riccardo Patrese	Williams	Williams-Judd FW12	34 laps/spun off	13
R	Nicola Larini	Osella	Osella-Alfa Romeo FA1L	27 laps/engine	18
R	Nigel Mansell	Williams	Williams-Judd FW12	16 laps/spun off	11
R	Stefano Modena	Euro Brun	EuroBrun-Ford Cosworth ER188	15 laps/engine	25
R	Philippe Alliot	Larrousse	Lola-Ford Cosworth LC88	8 laps/spun off	20
R	Nelson Piquet	Lotus	Lotus-Honda 100T	1 lap/spun off	5
DNQ	Luis Perez Sala	Minardi	Minardi-Ford Cosworth M188	-	27
DNQ	Stefan Johansson	Ligier	Ligier-Judd JS31	-	28
DNQ	Julian Bailey	Tyrrell	Tyrrell-Ford Cosworth 017	-	29
DNQ	Pierluigi Martini	Minardi	Minardi-Ford Cosworth M188	-	30
DNPQ	Gabriele Tarquini	Coloni	Coloni-Ford Cosworth FC188	-	31

Pole: Senna, 1m44.596s, 145.363mph/233.940kph. Fastest lap: Nannini, 2m03.032s, 123.580mph/198.884kph on Lap 40. Race leaders: Senna 1-44

NEW CONSTRUCTORS

Three teams entered F1 in 1988. Giampaolo Dallara had been in F1 before, designing the de Tomaso entered in 1970. He came back with a car for BMS Scuderia Italia. Walter Brun's EuroBrun was a handful for Oscar Larrauri and Stefano Modena, while the Rial entered by former ATS boss Gunther Schmid was driven to fourth in Detroit by Andrea de Cesaris.

HUNGARIAN GRAND PRIX

HUNGARORING • ROUND 10 • DATE: 7TH AUGUST 1988
Laps: 76 • Distance: 189.557miles/305.064km • Weather: Hot & bright

Pos	Driver	Team	Chassis-Engine	Result	Qual
1	Ayrton Senna	McLaren	McLaren-Honda MP4/4	1h57m47.081s	1
2	Alain Prost	McLaren	McLaren-Honda MP4/4	1h57m47.610s	7
3	Thierry Boutsen	Benetton	Benetton-Ford B188	1h58m18.491s	3
4	Gerhard Berger	Ferrari	Ferrari F187/88C	1h59m15.751s	9
5	Mauricio Gugelmin	March	March-Judd 881	75 laps	8
6	Riccardo Patrese	Williams	Williams-Judd FW12	75 laps	6
7	Satoru Nakajima	Lotus	Lotus-Honda 100T	73 laps	19
8	Nelson Piquet	Lotus	Lotus-Honda 100T	73 laps	13
9	Yannick Dalmas	Larrousse	Lola-Ford Cosworth LC88	73 laps	17
10	Luis Perez Sala	Minardi	Minardi-Ford Cosworth M188	72 laps	11
11	Stefano Modena	Euro Brun	EuroBrun-Ford Cosworth ER188	72 laps	26
12	Philippe Alliot	Larrousse	Lola-Ford Cosworth LC88	72 laps	20
13	Gabriele Tarquini	Coloni	Coloni-Ford Cosworth FC188	71 laps	22
R	Derek Warwick	Arrows	Arrows-Megatron A10B	65 laps/brakes	12
R	Nigel Mansell	Williams	Williams-Judd FW12	60 laps/physical	2
R	Eddie Cheever	Arrows	Arrows-Megatron A10B	55 laps/brakes	14
R	Michele Alboreto	Ferrari	Ferrari F187/88C	40 laps/electrical	15
R	Rene Arnoux	Ligier	Ligier-Judd JS31	32 laps/engine	25
R	Andrea de Cesaris	Rial	Rial-Ford Cosworth ARC1	28 laps/halfshaft	18
R	Alessandro Nannini	Benetton	Benetton-Ford B188	24 laps/overheating	5

Pos	Driver	Team	Chassis-Engine	Result	Qual
R	Alex Caffi	BMS Scuderia Italia	Dallara-Ford Cosworth BMS-188	22 laps/engine	10
R	Stefan Johansson	Ligier	Ligier-Judd JS31	19 laps/throttle	24
R	Pierluigi Martini	Minardi	Minardi-Ford Cosworth M188	8 laps/collision	16
R	Philippe Streiff	AGS	AGS-Ford Cosworth JH23	8 laps/collision	23
R	Ivan Capelli	March	March-Judd 881	5 laps/engine	4
R	Jonathan Palmer	Tyrrell	Tyrrell-Ford Cosworth 017	3 laps/engine	21
DNQ	Oscar Larrauri	Euro Brun	EuroBrun-Ford Cosworth ER188	-	27
DNQ	Bernd Schneider	Zakspeed	Zakspeed 881	-	28
DNQ	Julian Bailey	Tyrrell	Tyrrell-Ford Cosworth 017	-	29
DNQ	Piercarlo Ghinzani	Zakspeed	Zakspeed 881	-	30
DNPQ	Nicola Larini	Osella	Osella-Alfa Romeo FA1L	-	31

Pole: Senna, 1m27.635s, 102.459mph/164.893kph. Fastest lap: Prost, 1m30.639s, 99.063mph/159.428kph on Lap 51. Race leaders: Senna 1-76

BELGIAN GRAND PRIX

SPA-FRANCORCHAMPS • ROUND 11 • DATE: 28TH AUGUST 1988
Laps: 43 • Distance: 185.194miles/298.42km • Weather: Warm but dull

Pos	Driver	Team	Chassis-Engine	Result	Qual
1	Ayrton Senna	McLaren	McLaren-Honda MP4/4	1h28m00.549s	1
2	Alain Prost	McLaren	McLaren-Honda MP4/4	1h28m31.019s	2
DQ	Thierry Boutsen	Benetton	Benetton-Ford B188	Illegal fuel	6
DQ	Alessandro Nannini	Benetton	Benetton-Ford B188	Illegal fuel	7
3	Ivan Capelli	March	March-Judd 881	1h29m16.317s	14
4	Nelson Piquet	Lotus	Lotus-Honda 100T	1h29m24.177s	9
5	Derek Warwick	Arrows	Arrows-Megatron A10B	1h29m25.904s	10
6	Eddie Cheever	Arrows	Arrows-Megatron A10B	42 laps	11
7	Martin Brundle	Williams	Williams-Judd FW12	42 laps	12
8	Alex Caffi	BMS Scuderia Italia	Dallara-Ford Cosworth BMS-188	42 laps	15
9	Philippe Alliot	Larrousse	Lola-Ford Cosworth LC88	42 laps	16
10	Philippe Streiff	AGS	AGS-Ford Cosworth JH23	42 laps	18
11	Stefan Johansson	Ligier	Ligier-Judd JS31	39 laps/engine	20
12	Jonathan Palmer	Tyrrell	Tyrrell-Ford Cosworth 017	39 laps/throttle	21
13	Bernd Schneider	Zakspeed	Zakspeed 881	38 laps/gearbox	25
R	Gabriele Tarquini	Coloni	Coloni-Ford Cosworth FC188	36 laps/steering	22
R	Michele Alboreto	Ferrari	Ferrari F187/88C	35 laps/engine	4
R	Riccardo Patrese	Williams	Williams-Judd FW12	30 laps/engine	5
R	Mauricio Gugelmin	March	March-Judd 881	29 laps/spun off	13
R	Piercarlo Ghinzani	Zakspeed	Zakspeed 881	25 laps/oil leak	24
R	Satoru Nakajima	Lotus	Lotus-Honda 100T	22 laps/engine	8
R	Nicola Larini	Osella	Osella-Alfa Romeo FA1L	14 laps/fuel system	26
R	Gerhard Berger	Ferrari	Ferrari F187/88C	11 laps/electronics	3
R	Yannick Dalmas	Larrousse	Lola-Ford Cosworth LC88	9 laps/engine	23
R	Rene Arnoux	Ligier	Ligier-Judd JS31	2 laps/collision	17
R	Andrea de Cesaris	Rial	Rial-Ford Cosworth ARC1	2 laps/collision	19
DNQ	Luis Perez Sala	Minardi	Minardi-Ford Cosworth M188	-	27
DNQ	Pierluigi Martini	Minardi	Minardi-Ford Cosworth M188	-	28
DNQ	Stefano Modena	Euro Brun	EuroBrun-Ford Cosworth ER188	-	29
DNQ	Julian Bailey	Tyrrell	Tyrrell-Ford Cosworth 017	-	30
DNPQ	Oscar Larrauri	Euro Brun	EuroBrun-Ford Cosworth ER188	-	31

Pole: Senna, 1m53.718s, 136.516mph/219.701kph. Fastest lap: Berger, 2m00.772s, 128.542mph/206.869kph on Lap 10. Race leaders: Senna 1-43

ITALIAN GRAND PRIX

MONZA • ROUND 12 • DATE: 11TH SEPTEMBER 1988
Laps: 51 • Distance: 183.309miles/295.8km • Weather: Hot & bright

Pos	Driver	Team	Chassis-Engine	Result	Qual
1	Gerhard Berger	Ferrari	Ferrari F187/88C	1h17m39.744s	3
2	Michele Alboreto	Ferrari	Ferrari F187/88C	1h17m40.246s	4
3	Eddie Cheever	Arrows	Arrows-Megatron A10B	1h18m15.276s	5
4	Derek Warwick	Arrows	Arrows-Megatron A10B	1h18m15.858s	6
5	Ivan Capelli	March	March-Judd 881	1h18m32.266s	11
6	Thierry Boutsen	Benetton	Benetton-Ford B188	1h18m39.622s	8
7	Riccardo Patrese	Williams	Williams-Judd FW12	1h18m54.487s	10
8	Mauricio Gugelmin	March	March-Judd 881	1h19m12.310s	13
9	Alessandro Nannini	Benetton	Benetton-Ford B188	50 laps	9
10	Ayrton Senna	McLaren	McLaren-Honda MP4/4	49 laps/collision	1
11	Jean-Louis Schlesser	Williams	Williams-Judd FW12	49 laps	22
12	Julian Bailey	Tyrrell	Tyrrell-Ford Cosworth 017	49 laps	26
13	Rene Arnoux	Ligier	Ligier-Judd JS31	49 laps	24
R	Alain Prost	McLaren	McLaren-Honda MP4/4	34 laps/engine	2
R	Philippe Alliot	Larrousse	Lola-Ford Cosworth LC88	33 laps/engine	20
R	Philippe Streiff	AGS	AGS-Ford Cosworth JH23	31 laps/clutch	23
R	Bernd Schneider	Zakspeed	Zakspeed 881	28 laps/engine	15
R	Andrea de Cesaris	Rial	Rial-Ford Cosworth ARC1	27 laps/chassis	18
R	Piercarlo Ghinzani	Zakspeed	Zakspeed 881	25 laps/engine	16
R	Alex Caffi	BMS Scuderia Italia	Dallara-Ford Cosworth BMS-188	24 laps/engine	21
R	Yannick Dalmas	Larrousse	Lola-Ford Cosworth LC88	17 laps/radiator	25
R	Pierluigi Martini	Minardi	Minardi-Ford Cosworth M188	15 laps/engine	14
R	Satoru Nakajima	Lotus	Lotus-Honda 100T	14 laps/engine	12
R	Luis Perez Sala	Minardi	Minardi-Ford Cosworth M188	12 laps/gearbox	19
R	Nelson Piquet	Lotus	Lotus-Honda 100T	11 laps/clutch	7
R	Nicola Larini	Osella	Osella-Alfa Romeo FA1L	2 laps/engine	17
DNQ	Jonathan Palmer	Tyrrell	Tyrrell-Ford Cosworth 017	-	27
DNQ	Stefan Johansson	Ligier	Ligier-Judd JS31	-	28
DNQ	Gabriele Tarquini	Coloni	Coloni-Ford Cosworth FC188	-	29
DNQ	Stefano Modena	Euro Brun	EuroBrun-Ford Cosworth ER188	-	30
DNPQ	Oscar Larrauri	Euro Brun	EuroBrun-Ford Cosworth ER188	-	31

Pole: Senna, 1m25.974s, 150.908mph/242.864kph. Fastest lap: Alboreto, 1m29.070s, 145.663mph/234.422kph on Lap 44. Race leaders: Senna 1-49, Berger 50-51

PORTUGUESE GRAND PRIX

AUTODROMO DO ESTORIL • ROUND 13 • DATE: 25TH SEPTEMBER 1988
Laps: 70 • Distance: 188.899miles/304.5km • Weather: Hot & bright

Pos	Driver	Team	Chassis-Engine	Result	Qual
1	Alain Prost	McLaren	McLaren-Honda MP4/4	1h37m40.958s	1
2	Ivan Capelli	March	March-Judd 881	1h37m50.511s	3
3	Thierry Boutsen	Benetton	Benetton-Ford B188	1h38m25.577s	13
4	Derek Warwick	Arrows	Arrows-Megatron A10B	1h38m48.377s	10
5	Michele Alboreto	Ferrari	Ferrari F187/88C	1h38m52.842s	7
6	Ayrton Senna	McLaren	McLaren-Honda MP4/4	1h38m59.227s	2
7	Alex Caffi	BMS Scuderia Italia	Dallara-Ford Cosworth BMS-188	69 laps	17
8	Luis Perez Sala	Minardi	Minardi-Ford Cosworth M188	68 laps	19
9	Philippe Streiff	AGS	AGS-Ford Cosworth JH23	68 laps	21

Pos	Driver	Team	Chassis-Engine	Result	Qual
10	Rene Arnoux	Ligier	Ligier-Judd JS31	68 laps	23
11	Gabriele Tarquini	Coloni	Coloni-Ford Cosworth FC188	65 laps	26
12	Nicola Larini	Osella	Osella-Alfa Romeo FA1L	63 laps	25
R	Mauricio Gugelmin	March	March-Judd 881	59 laps/engine	5
R	Nigel Mansell	Williams	Williams-Judd FW12	54 laps/spun off	6
R	Jonathan Palmer	Tyrrell	Tyrrell-Ford Cosworth 017	53 laps/overheating	22
R	Alessandro Nannini	Benetton	Benetton-Ford B188	52 laps/handling	9
R	Gerhard Berger	Ferrari	Ferrari F187/88C	35 laps/spun off	4
R	Nelson Piquet	Lotus	Lotus-Honda 100T	34 laps/clutch	8
R	Riccardo Patrese	Williams	Williams-Judd FW12	29 laps/radiator	11
R	Pierluigi Martini	Minardi	Minardi-Ford Cosworth M188	27 laps/engine	14
R	Yannick Dalmas	Larrousse	Lola-Ford Cosworth LC88	20 laps/alternator	15
R	Satoru Nakajima	Lotus	Lotus-Honda 100T	16 laps/spun off	16
R	Andrea de Cesaris	Rial	Rial-Ford Cosworth ARC1	11 laps/halfshaft	12
R	Eddie Cheever	Arrows	Arrows-Megatron A10B	10 laps/turbo	18
R	Philippe Alliot	Larrousse	Lola-Ford Cosworth LC88	7 laps/engine	20
R	Stefan Johansson	Ligier	Ligier-Judd JS31	4 laps/engine	24
DNQ	Julian Bailey	Tyrrell	Tyrrell-Ford Cosworth 017	-	27
DNQ	Piercarlo Ghinzani	Zakspeed	Zakspeed 881	-	28
DNQ	Stefano Modena	Euro Brun	EuroBrun-Ford Cosworth ER188	-	29
DNQ	Bernd Schneider	Zakspeed	Zakspeed 881	-	30
DNPQ	Oscar Larrauri	Euro Brun	EuroBrun-Ford Cosworth ER188	-	31

Pole: Prost, 1m17.411s, 125.701mph/202.296kph. Fastest lap: Berger, 1m21.961s, 118.722mph/191.066kph on Lap 31. Race leaders: Senna 1, Prost 2-70

NEW DRIVERS

Mauricio Gugelmin had the best result achieved by any of the seven rookies, finishing fourth for March at Silverstone. Gabriele Tarquini (Coloni) and Luis Sala (Minardi) grabbed an eighth place apiece, at Montreal and Estoril respectively, while Julian Bailey finished ninth at Detroit for Tyrrell.

SPANISH GRAND PRIX

JEREZ • ROUND 14 • DATE: 2ND OCTOBER 1988
Laps: 72 • Distance: 188.707miles/303.696km • Weather: Hot & bright

Pos	Driver	Team	Chassis-Engine	Result	Qual
1	Alain Prost	McLaren	McLaren-Honda MP4/4	1h48m43.851s	2
2	Nigel Mansell	Williams	Williams-Judd FW12	1h49m10.083s	3
3	Alessandro Nannini	Benetton	Benetton-Ford B188	1h49m19.297s	5
4	Ayrton Senna	McLaren	McLaren-Honda MP4/4	1h49m30.561s	1
5	Riccardo Patrese	Williams	Williams-Judd FW12	1h49m31.281s	7
6	Gerhard Berger	Ferrari	Ferrari F187/88C	1h49m35.664s	8
7	Mauricio Gugelmin	March	March-Judd 881	1h49m59.815s	11
8	Nelson Piquet	Lotus	Lotus-Honda 100T	1h50m01.160s	9
9	Thierry Boutsen	Benetton	Benetton-Ford B188	1h50m01.506s	4
10	Alex Caffi	BMS Scuderia Italia	Dallara-Ford Cosworth BMS-188	71 laps	18
11	Yannick Dalmas	Larrousse	Lola-Ford Cosworth LC88	71 laps	16
12	Luis Perez Sala	Minardi	Minardi-Ford Cosworth M188	70 laps	24
13	Stefano Modena	Euro Brun	EuroBrun-Ford Cosworth ER188	70 laps	26

Pos	Driver	Team	Chassis-Engine	Result	Qual
14	Philippe Alliot	Larrousse	Lola-Ford Cosworth LC88	69 laps	12
R	Stefan Johansson	Ligier	Ligier-Judd JS31	62 laps/wheel	21
R	Eddie Cheever	Arrows	Arrows-Megatron A10B	60 laps/chassis	25
R	Ivan Capelli	March	March-Judd 881	45 laps/engine	6
R	Derek Warwick	Arrows	Arrows-Megatron A10B	41 laps/chassis	17
R	Andrea de Cesaris	Rial	Rial-Ford Cosworth ARC1	37 laps/engine	23
R	Philippe Streiff	AGS	AGS-Ford Cosworth JH23	16 laps/engine	13
R	Michele Alboreto	Ferrari	Ferrari F187/88C	15 laps/engine	10
R	Pierluigi Martini	Minardi	Minardi-Ford Cosworth M188	15 laps/gearbox	20
R	Satoru Nakajima	Lotus	Lotus-Honda 100T	14 laps/spun off	15
R	Nicola Larini	Osella	Osella-Alfa Romeo FA1L	9 laps/suspension	14
R	Jonathan Palmer	Tyrrell	Tyrrell-Ford Cosworth 017	4 laps/chassis	22
R	Rene Arnoux	Ligier	Ligier-Judd JS31	0 laps/throttle	19
DNQ	Bernd Schneider	Zakspeed	Zakspeed 881	-	27
DNQ	Oscar Larrauri	Euro Brun	EuroBrun-Ford Cosworth ER188	-	28
DNQ	Julian Bailey	Tyrrell	Tyrrell-Ford Cosworth 017	-	29
DNQ	Piercarlo Ghinzani	Zakspeed	Zakspeed 881	-	30
DNPQ	Gabriele Tarquini	Coloni	Coloni-Ford Cosworth FC188	-	31

Pole: Senna, 1m24.067s, 112.236mph/180.627kph. Fastest lap: Prost, 1m27.845s, 107.409mph/172.859kph on Lap 60. Race leaders: Prost 1-72

CLASSIC CAR: McLAREN MP4/4

The McLaren MP4/4 was one of F1's all-time greats. Designed along low-line principals by Gordon Murray and Steve Nichols, it was a design good for one year only as they incorporated the Honda V6 for the last year in which turbocharged engines were permitted. Allied to a new six-speed gearbox, albeit with turbo boost reduced from 4 to 2.5 bar, the car was good enough to win every race bar one, even though drivers Prost and Senna had to back off to achieve fuel economy. The MP4/4 was so good that McLaren scored 199 points, seven more than the next six teams in the championship table between them.

JAPANESE GRAND PRIX

SUZUKA • ROUND 15 • DATE: 30TH OCTOBER 1988
Laps: 51 • Distance: 185.671miles/298.809km • Weather: Cool, with drizzle

Pos	Driver	Team	Chassis-Engine	Result	Qual
1	Ayrton Senna	McLaren	McLaren-Honda MP4/4	1h33m26.173s	1
2	Alain Prost	McLaren	McLaren-Honda MP4/4	1h33m39.536s	2
3	Thierry Boutsen	Benetton	Benetton-Ford B188	1h34m02.282s	10
4	Gerhard Berger	Ferrari	Ferrari F187/88C	1h34m52.887s	3
5	Alessandro Nannini	Benetton	Benetton-Ford B188	1h34m56.776s	12
6	Riccardo Patrese	Williams	Williams-Judd FW12	1h35m03.788s	11
7	Satoru Nakajima	Lotus	Lotus-Honda 100T	50 laps	6
8	Philippe Streiff	AGS	AGS-Ford Cosworth JH23	50 laps	18
9	Philippe Alliot	Larrousse	Lola-Ford Cosworth LC88	50 laps	19
10	Mauricio Gugelmin	March	March-Judd 881	50 laps	13
11	Michele Alboreto	Ferrari	Ferrari F187/88C	50 laps	9

Pos	Driver	Team	Chassis-Engine	Result	Qual
12	Jonathan Palmer	Tyrrell	Tyrrell-Ford Cosworth 017	50 laps	16
13	Pierluigi Martini	Minardi	Minardi-Ford Cosworth M188	49 laps	17
14	Julian Bailey	Tyrrell	Tyrrell-Ford Cosworth 017	49 laps	26
15	Luis Perez Sala	Minardi	Minardi-Ford Cosworth M188	49 laps	22
16	Aguri Suzuki	Larrousse	Lola-Ford Cosworth LC88	48 laps	20
17	Rene Arnoux	Ligier	Ligier-Judd JS31	48 laps	23
R	Andrea de Cesaris	Rial	Rial-Ford Cosworth ARC1	36 laps/overheating	14
R	Eddie Cheever	Arrows	Arrows-Megatron A10B	35 laps/ignition	15
R	Nelson Piquet	Lotus	Lotus-Honda 100T	34 laps/driver unwell	5
R	Nicola Larini	Osella	Osella-Alfa Romeo FA1L	34 laps/brakes	24
R	Nigel Mansell	Williams	Williams-Judd FW12	24 laps/collision	8
R	Alex Caffi	BMS Scuderia Italia	Dallara-Ford Cosworth BMS-188	22 laps/spun off	21
R	Ivan Capelli	March	March-Judd 881	19 laps/electrical	4
R	Derek Warwick	Arrows	Arrows-Megatron A10B	16 laps/spun off	7
R	Bernd Schneider	Zakspeed	Zakspeed 881	14 laps/physical	25
DNQ	Stefan Johansson	Ligier	Ligier-Judd JS31	-	27
DNQ	Oscar Larrauri	Euro Brun	EuroBrun-Ford Cosworth ER188	-	28
DNQ	Piercarlo Ghinzani	Zakspeed	Zakspeed 881	-	29
DNQ	Stefano Modena	Euro Brun	EuroBrun-Ford Cosworth ER188	-	30
DNPQ	Gabriele Tarquini	Coloni	Coloni-Ford Cosworth FC188	-	31

Pole: Senna, 1m41.853s, 128.677mph/207.086kph. Fastest lap: Senna, 1m46.326s, 123.263mph/198.374kph on Lap 33. Race leaders: Prost 1-15 & 17-27, Capelli 16, Senna 28-51

AUSTRALIAN GRAND PRIX

ADELAIDE • ROUND 16 • DATE: 13TH NOVEMBER 1988
Laps: 82 • Distance: 192.63miles/309.96km • Weather: Hot but dull

Pos	Driver	Team	Chassis-Engine	Result	Qual
1	Alain Prost	McLaren	McLaren-Honda MP4/4	1h53m14.676s	2
2	Ayrton Senna	McLaren	McLaren-Honda MP4/4	1h53m51.463s	1
3	Nelson Piquet	Lotus	Lotus-Honda 100T	1h54m02.222s	5
4	Riccardo Patrese	Williams	Williams-Judd FW12	1h54m34.764s	6
5	Thierry Boutsen	Benetton	Benetton-Ford B188	81 laps	10
6	Ivan Capelli	March	March-Judd 881	81 laps	9
7	Pierluigi Martini	Minardi	Minardi-Ford Cosworth M188	80 laps	14
8	Andrea de Cesaris	Rial	Rial-Ford Cosworth ARC1	77 laps/out of fuel	15
9	Stefan Johansson	Ligier	Ligier-Judd JS31	76 laps/out of fuel	22
10	Philippe Alliot	Larrousse	Lola-Ford Cosworth LC88	75 laps/out of fuel	24
11	Philippe Streiff	AGS	AGS-Ford Cosworth JH23	73 laps/electrical	16
R	Piercarlo Ghinzani	Zakspeed	Zakspeed 881	69 laps/fuel system	26
R	Nigel Mansell	Williams	Williams-Judd FW12	65 laps/spun off	3
R	Alessandro Nannini	Benetton	Benetton-Ford B188	63 laps/spun off	8
R	Stefano Modena	Euro Brun	EuroBrun-Ford Cosworth ER188	63 laps/halfshaft	20
R	Derek Warwick	Arrows	Arrows-Megatron A10B	52 laps/engine	7
R	Eddie Cheever	Arrows	Arrows-Megatron A10B	51 laps/engine	18
R	Mauricio Gugelmin	March	March-Judd 881	46 laps/collision	19
R	Satoru Nakajima	Lotus	Lotus-Honda 100T	45 laps/collision	13
R	Luis Perez Sala	Minardi	Minardi-Ford Cosworth M188	41 laps/engine	21
R	Alex Caffi	BMS Scuderia Italia	Dallara-Ford Cosworth BMS-188	32 laps/clutch	11
R	Gerhard Berger	Ferrari	Ferrari F187/88C	25 laps/collision	4
R	Rene Arnoux	Ligier	Ligier-Judd JS31	24 laps/collision	23
R	Jonathan Palmer	Tyrrell	Tyrrell-Ford Cosworth 017	16 laps/transmission	17
R	Oscar Larrauri	Euro Brun	EuroBrun-Ford Cosworth ER188	12 laps/halfshaft	25

Pos	Driver	Team	Chassis-Engine	Result	Qual
R	Michele Alboreto	Ferrari	Ferrari F187/88C	0 laps/collision	12
DNQ	Gabriele Tarquini	Coloni	Coloni-Ford Cosworth FC188	-	27
DNQ	Julian Bailey	Tyrrell	Tyrrell-Ford Cosworth 017	-	28
DNQ	Pierre-Henri Raphanel	Larrousse	Lola-Ford Cosworth LC88	-	29
DNQ	Bernd Schneider	Zakspeed	Zakspeed 881	-	30
DNPQ	Nicola Larini	Osella	Osella-Alfa Romeo FA1L	-	31

Pole: Senna, 1m17.748s, 108.756mph/175.027kph. Fastest lap: Prost, 1m21.216s, 104.112mph/167.553kph on Lap 59. Race leaders: Prost 1-13 & 26-82, Berger 14-25

WORLD DRIVERS' CHAMPIONSHIP FINAL RESULTS

Pos	Driver	Nat	Car-Engine	R1	R2	R3	R4	R5	R6
1	Ayrton Senna	BRA	McLaren-Honda MP4/4	DQP	1P	RPF	2P	1PF	1P
2	Alain Prost	FRA	McLaren-Honda MP4/4	1	2F	1	1F	2	2F
3	Gerhard Berger	AUT	Ferrari F187/88C	2F	5	2	3	R	R
4	Thierry Boutsen	BEL	Benetton-Ford B188	7	4	8	8	3	3
5	Michele Alboreto	ITA	Ferrari F187/88C	5	18	3	4	R	R
6	Nelson Piquet	BRA	Lotus-Honda 100T	3	3	R	R	4	R
7	Ivan Capelli	ITA	March-Judd 881	R	R	10	16	5	NS
8	Derek Warwick	GBR	Arrows-Megatron A10B	4	9	4	5	7	R
9	Nigel Mansell	GBR	Williams-Judd FW12	R	R	R	R	R	R
10	Alessandro Nannini	ITA	Benetton-Ford B188	R	6	R	7	R	R
11	Riccardo Patrese	ITA	Williams-Judd FW12	R	13	6	R	R	R
12	Eddie Cheever	USA	Arrows-Megatron A10B	8	7	R	6	R	R
13	Mauricio Gugelmin	BRA	March-Judd 881	R	15	R	R	R	R
14	Jonathan Palmer	GBR	Tyrrell-Ford Cosworth 017	R	14	5	DNQ	6	5
15	Andrea de Cesaris	ITA	Rial-Ford Cosworth ARC1	R	R	R	R	9	4
16	Satoru Nakajima	JPN	Lotus-Honda 100T	6	8	DNQ	R	11	DNQ
16	Pierluigi Martini	ITA	Minardi-Ford Cosworth M188	-	-	-	-	-	6

Pos	Driver	R7	R8	R9	R10	R11	R12	R13	R14	R15	R16	Total
1	Senna	2	1	1P	1P	1P	10P	6	4P	1PF	2P	90
2	Prost	1PF	R	2	2F	2	R	1P	1F	2	1F	87
3	Berger	4	9P	3	4	RF	1	RF	6	4	R	41
4	Boutsen	R	R	6	3	DQ	6	3	9	3	5	27
5	Alboreto	3	17	4	R	R	2F	5	R	11	R	24
6	Piquet	5	5	R	8	4	R	R	8	R	3	22
7	Capelli	9	R	5	R	3	5	2	R	R	6	17
8	Warwick	R	6	7	R	5	4	4	R	R	R	17
9	Mansell	R	2F	R	R	-	-	R	2	R	R	12
10	Nannini	6	3	18F	R	DQ	9	R	3	5	R	12
11	Patrese	R	8	R	6	R	7	R	5	6	4	8
12	Cheever	11	7	10	R	6	3	R	R	R	R	6
13	Gugelmin	8	4	8	5	R	8	R	7	10	R	5
14	Palmer	R	R	11	R	12	DNQ	R	R	12	R	5
15	de Cesaris	10	R	13	R	R	R	R	R	R	8	3
16	Nakajima	7	10	9	7	R	R	R	R	7	R	1
16	Martini	15	15	DNQ	R	DNQ	R	R	R	13	7	1

WORLD CONSTRUCTORS' CHAMPIONSHIP FINAL RESULTS

Pos	Team-Engine	R1	R2	R3	R4	R5	R6	R7	R8
1	McLaren-Honda	1/DQ	1/2	1/R	1/2	1/2	1/2	1/2	1/R
2	Ferrari	2/5	5/18	2/3	3/4	R/R	R/R	3/4	9/17
3	Benetton-Ford	7/R	4/6	8/R	7/8	3/R	3/R	6/R	3/R
4	Lotus-Honda	3/6	3/8	R/DNQ	R/R	4/11	R/DNQ	5/7	5/10
5	Arrows-Megatron	4/8	7/9	4/R	5/6	7/R	R/R	11/R	6/7
6	March-Judd	R/R	15/R	10/R	16/R	5/R	R/NS	8/9	4/R
7	Williams-Judd	R/R	13/R	6/R	R/R	R/R	R/R	R/R	2/8
8	Tyrrell-Ford	R/DNQ	14/R	5/DNQ	DNQ/DNQ	6/R	5/9	R/DNQ	16/R
9	Rial-Ford	R	R	R	R	9	4	10	R
10	Minardi-Ford	R/R	11/16	R/DNQ	11/DNQ	13/DNQ	6/R	15/NC	15/R

Pos	Team-Engine	R9	R10	R11	R12	R13	R14	R15	R16	Total
1	McLaren-Honda	1/2	1/2	1/2	10/R	1/6	1/4	1/2	1/2	199
2	Ferrari	3/4	4/R	R/R	1/2	5/R	6/R	4/11	R/R	65
3	Benetton-Ford	6/18	3/R	DQ/DQ	6/9	3/R	3/9	3/5	5/R	39
4	Lotus-Honda	9/R	7/8	4/R	R/R	R/R	8/R	7/R	3/R	23
5	Arrows-Megatron	7/10	R/R	5/6	3/4	4/R	R/R	R/R	R/R	23
6	March-Judd	5/8	5/R	3/R	5/8	2/R	7/R	10/R	6/R	22
7	Williams-Judd	R/R	6/R	7/R	7/11	R/R	2/5	6/R	4/R	20
8	Tyrrell-Ford	11/DNQ	R/DNQ	12/DNQ	12/DNQ	R/DNQ	R/DNQ	12/14	R/DNQ	5
9	Rial-Ford	13	R	R	R	R	R	R	8	3
10	Minardi-Ford	DNQ/DNQ	10/R	DNQ/DNQ	R/R	8/R	12/R	13/15	7/R	1

SYMBOLS AND GRAND PRIX KEY

Round 1 **Brazilian GP**
Round 2 **San Marino GP**
Round 3 **Monaco GP**
Round 4 **Mexican GP**
Round 5 **Canadian GP**
Round 6 **Detroit GP**
Round 7 **French GP**
Round 8 **British GP**
Round 9 **German GP**
Round 10 **Hungarian GP**
Round 11 **Belgian GP**
Round 12 **Italian GP**
Round 13 **Portuguese GP**
Round 14 **Spanish GP**
Round 15 **Japanese GP**
Round 16 **Australian GP**

SCORING

1st **9 points**
2nd **6 points**
3rd **4 points**
4th **3 points**
5th **2 points**
6th **1 point**

DNPQ DID NOT PRE-QUALIFY **DNQ DID NOT QUALIFY** **DQ DISQUALIFIED** **EX EXCLUDED**
F FASTEST LAP **NC NOT CLASSIFIED** **NS NON-STARTER** **P POLE POSITION** **R RETIRED**

SEASON SUMMARY

Alain Prost took his third title and then quit McLaren to join Ferrari after the atmosphere in the team soured as he and Ayrton Senna spent the year at loggerheads. This came to a conclusion at the Japanese GP when they clashed at the chicane as they scrapped for the title. Second place went to Williams, with Riccardo Patrese also third in the drivers' standings through consistent scoring rather than winning. Thierry Boutsen became a grand prix winner, twice, while Nigel Mansell led the Ferrari attack and easily outstripped team-mate Gerhard Berger, but both were held back by the car's troublesome semi-automatic gearbox.

EIGHT ENGINES GO FOR GLORY

For the first time since 1977, there were no turbocharged engines admitted to the World Championship. In their place, all 20 teams ran the 3.5-litre normally aspirated units that had been introduced in 1987. There were eight different engine builders: Cosworth, Ferrari, Ford, Honda, Judd, Lamborghini, Renault and Yamaha.

BRAZILIAN GRAND PRIX

JACAREPAGUA • ROUND 1 • DATE: 26TH MARCH 1989
Laps: 61 • Distance: 190.693miles/306.891km • Weather: Very hot & bright

Pos	Driver	Team	Chassis-Engine	Result	Qual
1	Nigel Mansell	Ferrari	Ferrari 640	1h38m58.744s	6
2	Alain Prost	McLaren	McLaren-Honda MP4/5	1h39m06.553s	5
3	Mauricio Gugelmin	March	March-Judd 881	1h39m08.114s	12
4	Johnny Herbert	Benetton	Benetton-Ford B188	1h39m09.237s	10
5	Derek Warwick	Arrows	Arrows-Ford Cosworth A11	1h39m16.610s	8
6	Alessandro Nannini	Benetton	Benetton-Ford B188	1h39m16.985s	11
7	Jonathan Palmer	Tyrrell	Tyrrell-Ford Cosworth 017B	60 laps	18
8	Satoru Nakajima	Lotus	Lotus-Judd 101	60 laps	21
9	Olivier Grouillard	Ligier	Ligier-Ford Cosworth JS33	60 laps	22
10	Michele Alboreto	Tyrrell	Tyrrell-Ford Cosworth 017B	59 laps	20
11	Ayrton Senna	McLaren	McLaren-Honda MP4/5	59 laps	1
12	Philippe Alliot	Larrousse	Lola-Lamborghini LC88B	58 laps	26
13	Andrea de Cesaris	BMS Scuderia Italia	Dallara-Ford Cosworth 189	57 laps/engine	15
14	Christian Danner	Rial	Rial-Ford Cosworth ARC2	56 laps/gearbox	17
R	Riccardo Patrese	Williams	Williams-Renault FW12C	51 laps/alternator	2
R	Eddie Cheever	Arrows	Arrows-Ford Cosworth A11	37 laps/collision	24
R	Bernd Schneider	Zakspeed	Zakspeed-Yamaha 891	36 laps/collision	25
R	Martin Brundle	Brabham	Brabham-Judd BT58	27 laps/halfshaft	13
R	Ivan Capelli	March	March-Judd 881	22 laps/suspension	7
R	Nelson Piquet	Lotus	Lotus-Judd 101	10 laps/fuel system	9
DQ	Nicola Larini	Osella	Osella-Ford Cosworth FA1M	10 laps/wrong grid	19
R	Stefano Modena	Brabham	Brabham-Judd BT58	9 laps/halfshaft	14
R	Thierry Boutsen	Williams	Williams-Renault FW12C	3 laps/engine	4

Pos	Driver	Team	Chassis-Engine	Result	Qual
R	Pierluigi Martini	Minardi	Minardi-Ford Cosworth M188B	2 laps/chassis	16
R	Gerhard Berger	Ferrari	Ferrari 640	0 laps/collision	3
R	Luis Perez Sala	Minardi	Minardi-Ford Cosworth M188B	0 laps/collision	23
DNQ	Yannick Dalmas	Larrousse	Lola-Lamborghini LC88B	-	27
DNQ	Rene Arnoux	Ligier	Ligier-Ford Cosworth JS33	-	28
DNQ	Gregor Foitek	Euro Brun	EuroBrun-Judd ER188B	-	29
DNQ	Roberto Moreno	Coloni	Coloni-Ford Cosworth FC188B	-	30
DNPQ	Alex Caffi	BMS Scuderia Italia	Dallara-Ford Cosworth 189	-	31
DNPQ	Piercarlo Ghinzani	Osella	Osella-Ford Cosworth FA1M	-	32
DNPQ	Volker Weidler	Rial	Rial-Ford Cosworth ARC2	-	33
DNPQ	Pierre-Henri Raphanel	Coloni	Coloni-Ford Cosworth FC188B	-	34
DNPQ	Joachim Winkelhock	AGS	AGS-Ford Cosworth JH23B	-	35
DNPQ	Aguri Suzuki	Zakspeed	Zakspeed-Yamaha 891	-	36
DNPQ	Stefan Johansson	Onyx	Onyx-Ford Cosworth ORE-1	-	37
DNPQ	Bertrand Gachot	Onyx	Onyx-Ford Cosworth ORE-1	-	38

Pole: Senna, 1m25.302s, 131.931mph/212.323kph. Fastest lap: Patrese, 1m32.507s, 121.655mph/195.786kph on Lap 47. Race leaders: Patrese 1-15 & 21-22, Mansell 16-20 & 28-44 & 47-61, Prost 23-27 & 45-46

STREIFF IS LEFT PARALYSED

Even before the season got underway, Philippe Streiff had been gravely injured when he broke his neck in pre-season testing when he crashed his AGS at Jacarepagua. The Frenchman was left a tetraplegic and AGS struggled through the year, although Gabriele Tarquini started well with sixth in Mexico.

SAN MARINO GRAND PRIX

IMOLA • ROUND 2 • DATE: 23RD APRIL 1989
Laps: 58 • Distance: 181.460miles/292.32km • Weather: Warm & bright

Pos	Driver	Team	Chassis-Engine	Result	Qual
1	Ayrton Senna	McLaren	McLaren-Honda MP4/5	1h26m51.245s	1
2	Alain Prost	McLaren	McLaren-Honda MP4/5	1h27m31.470s	2
3	Alessandro Nannini	Benetton	Benetton-Ford B188	57 laps	7
4	Thierry Boutsen	Williams	Williams-Renault FW12C	57 laps	6
5	Derek Warwick	Arrows	Arrows-Ford Cosworth A11	57 laps	12
6	Jonathan Palmer	Tyrrell	Tyrrell-Ford Cosworth 018	57 laps	25
7	Alex Caffi	BMS Scuderia Italia	Dallara-Ford Cosworth 189	57 laps	9
8	Gabriele Tarquini	AGS	AGS-Ford Cosworth JH23B	57 laps	18
9	Eddie Cheever	Arrows	Arrows-Ford Cosworth A11	56 laps	21
10	Andrea de Cesaris	BMS Scuderia Italia	Dallara-Ford Cosworth 189	56 laps	16
11	Johnny Herbert	Benetton	Benetton-Ford B188	56 laps	23
12	Nicola Larini	Osella	Osella-Ford Cosworth FA1M	52 laps/spun off	14
R	Martin Brundle	Brabham	Brabham-Judd BT58	51 laps/fuel system	22
NC	Satoru Nakajima	Lotus	Lotus-Judd 101	46 laps	24
R	Luis Perez Sala	Minardi	Minardi-Ford Cosworth M188B	43 laps/spun off	15
R	Mauricio Gugelmin	March	March-Judd 881	39 laps/transmission	19
R	Nelson Piquet	Lotus	Lotus-Judd 101	29 laps/engine	8
R	Nigel Mansell	Ferrari	Ferrari 640	23 laps/gearbox	3

Pos	Driver	Team	Chassis-Engine	Result	Qual
R	Riccardo Patrese	Williams	Williams-Renault FW12C	21 laps/engine	4
R	Stefano Modena	Brabham	Brabham-Judd BT58	19 laps/spun off	17
R	Pierluigi Martini	Minardi	Minardi-Ford Cosworth M188B	6 laps/gearbox	11
DQ	Olivier Grouillard	Ligier	Ligier-Ford Cosworth JS33	parc ferme breach	10
R	Gerhard Berger	Ferrari	Ferrari 640	3 laps/spun off	5
R	Ivan Capelli	March	March-Judd 881	1 lap/spun off	13
R	Philippe Alliot	Larrousse	Lola-Lamborghini LC89	0 laps/electrical	20
NS	Yannick Dalmas	Larrousse	Lola-Lamborghini LC89	engine	26
DNQ	Michele Alboreto	Tyrrell	Tyrrell-Ford Cosworth 018	-	27
DNQ	Rene Arnoux	Ligier	Ligier-Ford Cosworth JS33	-	28
DNQ	Christian Danner	Rial	Rial-Ford Cosworth ARC2	-	29
DNQ	Roberto Moreno	Coloni	Coloni-Ford Cosworth FC188B	-	30
DNPQ	Bertrand Gachot	Onyx	Onyx-Ford Cosworth ORE-1	-	31
DNPQ	Gregor Foitek	Euro Brun	EuroBrun-Judd ER188B	-	32
DNPQ	Piercarlo Ghinzani	Osella	Osella-Ford Cosworth FA1M	-	33
DNPQ	Stefan Johansson	Onyx	Onyx-Ford Cosworth ORE-1	-	34
DNPQ	Joachim Winkelhock	AGS	AGS-Ford Cosworth JH23B	-	35
DNPQ	Pierre-Henri Raphanel	Coloni	Coloni-Ford Cosworth FC188B	-	36
DNPQ	Aguri Suzuki	Zakspeed	Zakspeed-Yamaha 891	-	37
DNPQ	Bernd Schneider	Zakspeed	Zakspeed-Yamaha 891	-	38
DNPQ	Volker Weidler	Rial	Rial-Ford Cosworth ARC2	-	39

Pole: Senna, 1m26.010s, 131.079mph/210.952kph. Fastest lap: Prost, 1m26.795s, 129.894mph/209.044kph on Lap 45. Race leaders: Senna 1-58

MONACO GRAND PRIX

MONTE CARLO • ROUND 3 • DATE: 7TH MAY 1989
Laps: 77 • Distance: 159.230miles/256.256km • Weather: Warm & bright

Pos	Driver	Team	Chassis-Engine	Result	Qual
1	Ayrton Senna	McLaren	McLaren-Honda MP4/5	1h53m33.251s	1
2	Alain Prost	McLaren	McLaren-Honda MP4/5	1h54m25.780s	2
3	Stefano Modena	Brabham	Brabham-Judd BT58	76 laps	8
4	Alex Caffi	BMS Scuderia Italia	Dallara-Ford Cosworth 189	75 laps	9
5	Michele Alboreto	Tyrrell	Tyrrell-Ford Cosworth 018	75 laps	12
6	Martin Brundle	Brabham	Brabham-Judd BT58	75 laps	4
7	Eddie Cheever	Arrows	Arrows-Ford Cosworth A11	75 laps	20
8	Alessandro Nannini	Benetton	Benetton-Ford B188	74 laps	15
9	Jonathan Palmer	Tyrrell	Tyrrell-Ford Cosworth 018	74 laps	23
10	Thierry Boutsen	Williams	Williams-Renault FW12C	74 laps	3
11	Ivan Capelli	March	March-Judd CG891	73 laps	22
12	Rene Arnoux	Ligier	Ligier-Ford Cosworth JS33	73 laps	21
13	Andrea de Cesaris	BMS Scuderia Italia	Dallara-Ford Cosworth 189	73 laps	10
14	Johnny Herbert	Benetton	Benetton-Ford B188	73 laps	24
15	Riccardo Patrese	Williams	Williams-Renault FW12C	73 laps	7
R	Luis Perez Sala	Minardi	Minardi-Ford Cosworth M188B	48 laps/overheating	26
R	Gabriele Tarquini	AGS	AGS-Ford Cosworth JH23B	46 laps/electrical	13
R	Roberto Moreno	Coloni	Coloni-Ford Cosworth FC188B	44 laps/gearbox	25
R	Philippe Alliot	Larrousse	Lola-Lamborghini LC89	38 laps/engine	17
R	Mauricio Gugelmin	March	March-Judd 881	36 laps/engine	14
R	Nelson Piquet	Lotus	Lotus-Judd 101	32 laps/collision	19
R	Nigel Mansell	Ferrari	Ferrari 640	30 laps/gearbox	5
R	Pierre-Henri Raphanel	Coloni	Coloni-Ford Cosworth FC188B	19 laps/gearbox	18
R	Olivier Grouillard	Ligier	Ligier-Ford Cosworth JS33	4 laps/gearbox	16
R	Pierluigi Martini	Minardi	Minardi-Ford Cosworth M188B	3 laps/clutch	11

Pos	Driver	Team	Chassis-Engine	Result	Qual
R	Derek Warwick	Arrows	Arrows-Ford Cosworth A11	2 laps/electrical	6
DNQ	Christian Danner	Rial	Rial-Ford Cosworth ARC2	-	27
DNQ	Yannick Dalmas	Larrousse	Lola-Lamborghini LC89	-	28
DNQ	Satoru Nakajima	Lotus	Lotus-Judd 101	-	29
DNPQ	Piercarlo Ghinzani	Osella	Osella-Ford Cosworth FA1M	-	30
DNPQ	Stefan Johansson	Onyx	Onyx-Ford Cosworth ORE-1	-	31
DNPQ	Nicola Larini	Osella	Osella-Ford Cosworth FA1M	-	32
DNPQ	Bernd Schneider	Zakspeed	Zakspeed-Yamaha 891	-	33
DNPQ	Bertrand Gachot	Onyx	Onyx-Ford Cosworth ORE-1	-	34
DNPQ	Gregor Foitek	Euro Brun	EuroBrun-Judd ER188B	-	35
DNPQ	Volker Weidler	Rial	Rial-Ford Cosworth ARC2	-	36
DNPQ	Aguri Suzuki	Zakspeed	Zakspeed-Yamaha 891	-	37
DNPQ	Joachim Winkelhock	AGS	AGS-Ford Cosworth JH23B	-	38

Pole: Senna, 1m22.308s, 90.447mph/145.560kph. Fastest lap: Prost, 1m25.501s, 87.069mph/140.124kph on Lap 59. Race leaders: Senna 1-77

MANSELL BECOMES "IL LEONE"

Nigel Mansell was seen as an enemy by the Tifosi when he starred for Williams, but he became their hero when he joined Ferrari and won on his debut in the Brazilian GP. This earned him the nickname "Il Leone" for his lion-hearted approach to his driving, never giving less than his all, and adding another win in Hungary.

MEXICAN GRAND PRIX

MEXICO CITY • ROUND 4 • DATE: 28TH MAY 1989
Laps: 69 • Distance: 189.548miles/305.049km • Weather: Hot & bright

Pos	Driver	Team	Chassis-Engine	Result	Qual
1	Ayrton Senna	McLaren	McLaren-Honda MP4/5	1h35m21.431s	1
2	Riccardo Patrese	Williams	Williams-Renault FW12C	1h35m36.991s	5
3	Michele Alboreto	Tyrrell	Tyrrell-Ford Cosworth 018	1h35m52.685s	7
4	Alessandro Nannini	Benetton	Benetton-Ford B188	1h36m06.926s	13
5	Alain Prost	McLaren	McLaren-Honda MP4/5	1h36m17.544s	2
6	Gabriele Tarquini	AGS	AGS-Ford Cosworth JH23B	68 laps	17
7	Eddie Cheever	Arrows	Arrows-Ford Cosworth A11	68 laps	24
8	Olivier Grouillard	Ligier	Ligier-Ford Cosworth JS33	68 laps	11
9	Martin Brundle	Brabham	Brabham-Judd BT58	68 laps	20
10	Stefano Modena	Brabham	Brabham-Judd BT58	68 laps	9
11	Nelson Piquet	Lotus	Lotus-Judd 101	68 laps	26
12	Christian Danner	Rial	Rial-Ford Cosworth ARC2	67 laps	23
13	Alex Caffi	BMS Scuderia Italia	Dallara-Ford Cosworth 189	67 laps	19
14	Rene Arnoux	Ligier	Ligier-Ford Cosworth JS33	66 laps	25
15	Johnny Herbert	Benetton	Benetton-Ford B188	66 laps	18
R	Pierluigi Martini	Minardi	Minardi-Ford Cosworth M189	53 laps/engine	22
R	Nigel Mansell	Ferrari	Ferrari 640	43 laps/gearbox	3
R	Derek Warwick	Arrows	Arrows-Ford Cosworth A11	35 laps/electrical	10
R	Satoru Nakajima	Lotus	Lotus-Judd 101	35 laps/spun off	15
NC	Philippe Alliot	Larrousse	Lola-Lamborghini LC89	28 laps	16
R	Andrea de Cesaris	BMS Scuderia Italia	Dallara-Ford Cosworth 189	20 laps/suspension	12

Pos	Driver	Team	Chassis-Engine	Result	Qual
R	Gerhard Berger	Ferrari	Ferrari 640	16 laps/gearbox	6
R	Stefan Johansson	Onyx	Onyx-Ford Cosworth ORE-1	16 laps/transmission	21
R	Thierry Boutsen	Williams	Williams-Renault FW12C	15 laps/electrical	8
R	Jonathan Palmer	Tyrrell	Tyrrell-Ford Cosworth 018	9 laps/throttle	14
R	Ivan Capelli	March	March-Judd CG891	1 lap/transmission	4
DNQ	Luis Perez Sala	Minardi	Minardi-Ford Cosworth M189	-	27
DNQ	Mauricio Gugelmin	March	March-Judd CG891	-	28
DNQ	Yannick Dalmas	Larrousse	Lola-Lamborghini LC89	-	29
DNQ	Roberto Moreno	Coloni	Coloni-Ford Cosworth FC188B	-	30
DNPQ	Bertrand Gachot	Onyx	Onyx-Ford Cosworth ORE-1	-	31
DNPQ	Gregor Foitek	Euro Brun	EuroBrun-Judd ER188B	-	32
DNPQ	Nicola Larini	Osella	Osella-Ford Cosworth FA1M	-	33
DNPQ	Volker Weidler	Rial	Rial-Ford Cosworth ARC2	-	34
DNPQ	Bernd Schneider	Zakspeed	Zakspeed-Yamaha 891	-	35
DNPQ	Aguri Suzuki	Zakspeed	Zakspeed-Yamaha 891	-	36
DNPQ	Piercarlo Ghinzani	Osella	Osella-Ford Cosworth FA1M	-	37
DNPQ	Joachim Winkelhock	AGS	AGS-Ford Cosworth JH23B	-	38
DNPQ	Pierre-Henri Raphanel	Coloni	Coloni-Ford Cosworth FC188B	-	39

Pole: Senna, 1m17.876s, 126.990mph/204.371kph. Fastest lap: Mansell, 1m20.420s, 122.973mph/197.905kph on Lap 41. Race leaders: Senna 1-69

HERBERT STARTS IN STYLE

A major accident that seriously injured his legs in F3000 in 1988 didn't stop Johnny Herbert from graduating to F1 with Benetton. His first outing, in Brazil, was remarkable as Johnny finished fourth, just three seconds behind Prost's second-placed McLaren. But his injuries hampered his year and he was replaced midway through the season by Emanuele Pirro.

UNITED STATES GRAND PRIX

PHOENIX • ROUND 5 • DATE: 4TH JUNE 1989
Laps: 75 • Distance: 176.522miles/284.85km • Weather: Hot & bright

Pos	Driver	Team	Chassis-Engine	Result	Qual
1	Alain Prost	McLaren	McLaren-Honda MP4/5	2h01m33.133s	2
2	Riccardo Patrese	Williams	Williams-Renault FW12C	2h02m12.829s	14
3	Eddie Cheever	Arrows	Arrows-Ford Cosworth A11	2h02m16.343s	17
4	Christian Danner	Rial	Rial-Ford Cosworth ARC2	74 laps	26
5	Johnny Herbert	Benetton	Benetton-Ford B188	74 laps	25
6	Thierry Boutsen	Williams	Williams-Renault FW12C	74 laps	16
7	Gabriele Tarquini	AGS	AGS-Ford Cosworth JH23B	73 laps/engine	24
8	Andrea de Cesaris	BMS Scuderia Italia	Dallara-Ford Cosworth 189	70 laps/fuel pump	13
9	Jonathan Palmer	Tyrrell	Tyrrell-Ford Cosworth 018	69 laps/fuel system	21
R	Gerhard Berger	Ferrari	Ferrari 640	61 laps/alternator	8
R	Alex Caffi	BMS Scuderia Italia	Dallara-Ford Cosworth 189	52 laps/collision	6
R	Nelson Piquet	Lotus	Lotus-Judd 101	52 laps/spun off	22
R	Stefan Johansson	Onyx	Onyx-Ford Cosworth ORE-1	50 laps/suspension	19
R	Luis Perez Sala	Minardi	Minardi-Ford Cosworth M189	46 laps/engine	20
R	Ayrton Senna	McLaren	McLaren-Honda MP4/5	44 laps/electrical	1
R	Martin Brundle	Brabham	Brabham-Judd BT58	43 laps/brakes	5

Pos	Driver	Team	Chassis-Engine	Result	Qual
R	Stefano Modena	Brabham	Brabham-Judd BT58	37 laps/brakes	7
R	Nigel Mansell	Ferrari	Ferrari 640	31 laps/alternator	4
R	Pierluigi Martini	Minardi	Minardi-Ford Cosworth M189	26 laps/engine	15
R	Satoru Nakajima	Lotus	Lotus-Judd 101	24 laps/throttle	23
R	Ivan Capelli	March	March-Judd CG891	22 laps/transmission	11
DQ	Mauricio Gugelmin	March	March-Judd CG891	20 laps/illegal top-up	18
R	Michele Alboreto	Tyrrell	Tyrrell-Ford Cosworth 018	17 laps/gearbox	9
R	Alessandro Nannini	Benetton	Benetton-Ford B188	10 laps/exhaustion	3
R	Derek Warwick	Arrows	Arrows-Ford Cosworth A11	7 laps/collision	10
R	Philippe Alliot	Larrousse	Lola-Lamborghini LC89	3 laps/spun off	12
DNQ	Olivier Grouillard	Ligier	Ligier-Ford Cosworth JS33	-	27
DNQ	Roberto Moreno	Coloni	Coloni-Ford Cosworth FC188B	-	28
DNQ	Rene Arnoux	Ligier	Ligier-Ford Cosworth JS33	-	29
DNQ	Yannick Dalmas	Larrousse	Lola-Lamborghini LC89	-	30
DNPQ	Piercarlo Ghinzani	Osella	Osella-Ford Cosworth FA1M	-	31
DNPQ	Pierre-Henri Raphanel	Coloni	Coloni-Ford Cosworth FC188B	-	32
DNPQ	Gregor Foitek	Euro Brun	EuroBrun-Judd ER188B	-	33
DNPQ	Nicola Larini	Osella	Osella-Ford Cosworth FA1M	-	34
DNPQ	Joachim Winkelhock	AGS	AGS-Ford Cosworth JH23B	-	35
DNPQ	Volker Weidler	Rial	Rial-Ford Cosworth ARC2	-	36
DNPQ	Bernd Schneider	Zakspeed	Zakspeed-Yamaha 891	-	37
DNPQ	Aguri Suzuki	Zakspeed	Zakspeed-Yamaha 891	-	38
DNPQ	Bertrand Gachot	Onyx	Onyx-Ford Cosworth ORE-1	-	39

Pole: Senna, 1m30.108s, 94.285mph/151.737kph. Fastest lap: Senna, 1m33.969s, 90.411mph/145.503kph on Lap 38. Race leaders: Senna 1-33, Prost 34-75

BERGER'S LUCKY ESCAPE

Gerhard Berger endured the largest accident of the season when he crashed during the San Marino GP. The Austrian hit the barriers at Tamburello on lap four and his Ferrari caught fire, but was fortunately reached quickly by a fire tender, although he suffered burnt hands as well as a broken rib. He then missed the Monaco GP while his burns healed.

CANADIAN GRAND PRIX

MONTREAL • ROUND 6 • DATE: 18TH JUNE 1989
Laps: 69 • Distance: 187.710miles/302.91km • Weather: Cool & wet

Pos	Driver	Team	Chassis-Engine	Result	Qual
1	Thierry Boutsen	Williams	Williams-Renault FW12C	2h01m24.073s	6
2	Riccardo Patrese	Williams	Williams-Renault FW12C	2h01m54.080s	3
3	Andrea de Cesaris	BMS Scuderia Italia	Dallara-Ford Cosworth 189	2h03m00.722s	9
4	Nelson Piquet	Lotus	Lotus-Judd 101	2h03m05.557s	19
5	Rene Arnoux	Ligier	Ligier-Ford Cosworth JS33	68 laps	22
6	Alex Caffi	BMS Scuderia Italia	Dallara-Ford Cosworth 189	67 laps	8
7	Ayrton Senna	McLaren	McLaren-Honda MP4/5	66 laps/engine	2
8	Christian Danner	Rial	Rial-Ford Cosworth ARC2	66 laps	23
R	Roberto Moreno	Coloni	Coloni-Ford Cosworth C3	57 laps/differential	26
R	Derek Warwick	Arrows	Arrows-Ford Cosworth A11	40 laps/engine	12
R	Jonathan Palmer	Tyrrell	Tyrrell-Ford Cosworth 018	35 laps/spun off	14

Pos	Driver	Team	Chassis-Engine	Result	Qual
R	Nicola Larini	Osella	Osella-Ford Cosworth FA1M	33 laps/electrical	15
R	Ivan Capelli	March	March-Judd CG891	28 laps/spun off	21
R	Philippe Alliot	Larrousse	Lola-Lamborghini LC89	26 laps/spun off	10
DQ	Stefan Johansson	Onyx	Onyx-Ford Cosworth ORE-1	13 laps/ignored flag	18
R	Mauricio Gugelmin	March	March-Judd CG891	11 laps/electrical	17
R	Luis Perez Sala	Minardi	Minardi-Ford Cosworth M189	11 laps/spun off	24
R	Gerhard Berger	Ferrari	Ferrari 640	6 laps/gearbox	4
R	Gabriele Tarquini	AGS	AGS-Ford Cosworth JH23B	6 laps/spun off	25
R	Eddie Cheever	Arrows	Arrows-Ford Cosworth A11	3 laps/electrical	16
R	Alain Prost	McLaren	McLaren-Honda MP4/5	2 laps/suspension	1
R	Stefano Modena	Brabham	Brabham-Judd BT58	0 laps/collision	7
R	Pierluigi Martini	Minardi	Minardi-Ford Cosworth M189	0 laps/collision	11
R	Michele Alboreto	Tyrrell	Tyrrell-Ford Cosworth 018	0 laps/electrical	20
DQ	Nigel Mansell	Ferrari	Ferrari 640	illegal pit lane exit	5
DQ	Alessandro Nannini	Benetton	Benetton-Ford B188	illegal pit lane exit	13
DNQ	Satoru Nakajima	Lotus	Lotus-Judd 101	-	27
DNQ	Yannick Dalmas	Larrousse	Lola-Lamborghini LC89	-	28
DNQ	Johnny Herbert	Benetton	Benetton-Ford B188	-	29
DNQ	Olivier Grouillard	Ligier	Ligier-Ford Cosworth JS33	-	30
DNPQ	Martin Brundle	Brabham	Brabham-Judd BT58	-	31
DNPQ	Bertrand Gachot	Onyx	Onyx-Ford Cosworth ORE-1	-	32
DNPQ	Gregor Foitek	Euro Brun	EuroBrun-Judd ER188B	-	33
DNPQ	Piercarlo Ghinzani	Osella	Osella-Ford Cosworth FA1M	-	34
DNPQ	Bernd Schneider	Zakspeed	Zakspeed-Yamaha 891	-	35
DNPQ	Joachim Winkelhock	AGS	AGS-Ford Cosworth JH23B	-	36
DNPQ	Volker Weidler	Rial	Rial-Ford Cosworth ARC2	-	37
DNPQ	Aguri Suzuki	Zakspeed	Zakspeed-Yamaha 891	-	38
DNPQ	Pierre-Henri Raphanel	Coloni	Coloni-Ford Cosworth C3	-	39

Pole: Prost, 1m20.973s, 121.276mph/195.176kph. Fastest lap: Palmer, 1m31.925s, 106.827mph/171.922kph on Lap 11. Race leaders: Prost 1, Senna 2-3 & 39-66, Patrese 4-34, Warwick 35-38, Boutsen 67-69

FRENCH GRAND PRIX

CIRCUIT PAUL RICARD • ROUND 7 • DATE: 9TH JULY 1989
Laps: 80 • Distance: 189.520miles/305.04km • Weather: Hot & bright

Pos	Driver	Team	Chassis-Engine	Result	Qual
1	Alain Prost	McLaren	McLaren-Honda MP4/5	1h38m29.411s	1
2	Nigel Mansell	Ferrari	Ferrari 640	1h39m13.428s	3
3	Riccardo Patrese	Williams	Williams-Renault FW12C	1h39m36.332s	8
4	Jean Alesi	Tyrrell	Tyrrell-Ford Cosworth 018	1h39m42.643s	16
5	Stefan Johansson	Onyx	Onyx-Ford Cosworth ORE-1	79 laps	13
6	Olivier Grouillard	Ligier	Ligier-Ford Cosworth JS33	79 laps	17
7	Eddie Cheever	Arrows	Arrows-Ford Cosworth A11	79 laps	25
8	Nelson Piquet	Lotus	Lotus-Judd 101	78 laps	20
9	Emanuele Pirro	Benetton	Benetton-Ford B188	78 laps	24
10	Jonathan Palmer	Tyrrell	Tyrrell-Ford Cosworth 018	78 laps	9
11	Eric Bernard	Larrousse	Lola-Lamborghini LC89	77 laps/engine	15
12	Martin Donnelly	Arrows	Arrows-Ford Cosworth A11	77 laps	14
13	Bertrand Gachot	Onyx	Onyx-Ford Cosworth ORE-1	76 laps/engine	11
NC	Mauricio Gugelmin	March	March-Judd CG891	71 laps	10
R	Stefano Modena	Brabham	Brabham-Judd BT58	67 laps/engine	22
R	Thierry Boutsen	Williams	Williams-Renault FW12C	50 laps/gearbox	5
R	Satoru Nakajima	Lotus	Lotus-Judd 101	49 laps/engine	19

Pos	Driver	Team	Chassis-Engine	Result	Qual
R	Ivan Capelli	March	March-Judd CG891	43 laps/engine	12
R	Alessandro Nannini	Benetton	Benetton-Ford B189	40 laps/suspension	4
R	Pierluigi Martini	Minardi	Minardi-Ford Cosworth M189	31 laps/engine	23
R	Philippe Alliot	Larrousse	Lola-Lamborghini LC89	30 laps/engine	7
R	Gabriele Tarquini	AGS	AGS-Ford Cosworth JH23B	30 laps/engine	21
R	Gerhard Berger	Ferrari	Ferrari 640	29 laps/clutch	6
R	Alex Caffi	BMS Scuderia Italia	Dallara-Ford Cosworth 189	27 laps/clutch	26
R	Rene Arnoux	Ligier	Ligier-Ford Cosworth JS33	14 laps/gearbox	18
R	Ayrton Senna	McLaren	McLaren-Honda MP4/5	0 laps/differential	2
DNQ	Andrea de Cesaris	BMS Scuderia Italia	Dallara-Ford Cosworth 189	-	27
DNQ	Luis Perez Sala	Minardi	Minardi-Ford Cosworth M189	-	28
DNQ	Christian Danner	Rial	Rial-Ford Cosworth ARC2	-	29
DNQ	Roberto Moreno	Coloni	Coloni-Ford Cosworth C3	-	30
DNPQ	Nicola Larini	Osella	Osella-Ford Cosworth FA1M	-	31
DNPQ	Martin Brundle	Brabham	Brabham-Judd BT58	-	32
DNPQ	Volker Weidler	Rial	Rial-Ford Cosworth ARC2	-	33
DNPQ	Bernd Schneider	Zakspeed	Zakspeed-Yamaha 891	-	34
DNPQ	Piercarlo Ghinzani	Osella	Osella-Ford Cosworth FA1M	-	35
DNPQ	Pierre-Henri Raphanel	Coloni	Coloni-Ford Cosworth C3	-	36
DNPQ	Aguri Suzuki	Zakspeed	Zakspeed-Yamaha 891	-	37
DNPQ	Gregor Foitek	Euro Brun	EuroBrun-Judd ER188B	-	38
DNPQ	Joachim Winkelhock	AGS	AGS-Ford Cosworth JH23B	-	39

Pole: Prost, 1m07.203s, 126.920mph/204.258kph. Fastest lap: Gugelmin, 1m12.090s, 118.316mph/190.411kph on Lap 29. Race leaders: Prost 1-80

THE McLAREN DRIVERS COME TO BLOWS

Alain Prost refused to yield to a lunge by Ayrton Senna late in the Japanese GP. This came at the chicane and Prost knew that Senna had to win to keep his title hopes alive and closed the door. After the collision, a push from the marshals to move his car, Senna got going again and was first to the finish, but later disqualified for receiving outside assistance and missing the chicane.

BRITISH GRAND PRIX

SILVERSTONE • ROUND 8 • DATE: 16TH JULY 1989
Laps: 64 • Distance: 190.14miles/305.798km • Weather: Warm & bright

Pos	Driver	Team	Chassis-Engine	Result	Qual
1	Alain Prost	McLaren	McLaren-Honda MP4/5	1h19m22.131s	2
2	Nigel Mansell	Ferrari	Ferrari 640	1h19m41.500s	3
3	Alessandro Nannini	Benetton	Benetton-Ford B189	1h20m10.150s	9
4	Nelson Piquet	Lotus	Lotus-Judd 101	1h20m28.866s	10
5	Pierluigi Martini	Minardi	Minardi-Ford Cosworth M189	63 laps	11
6	Luis Perez Sala	Minardi	Minardi-Ford Cosworth M189	63 laps	15
7	Olivier Grouillard	Ligier	Ligier-Ford Cosworth JS33	63 laps	24
8	Satoru Nakajima	Lotus	Lotus-Judd 101	63 laps	16
9	Derek Warwick	Arrows	Arrows-Ford Cosworth A11	62 laps	19
10	Thierry Boutsen	Williams	Williams-Renault FW12C	62 laps	7
11	Emanuele Pirro	Benetton	Benetton-Ford Cosworth B188	62 laps	26
12	Bertrand Gachot	Onyx	Onyx-Ford Cosworth ORE-1	62 laps	21

Pos	Driver	Team	Chassis-Engine	Result	Qual
R	Mauricio Gugelmin	March	March-Judd CG891	54 laps/gearbox	6
R	Gerhard Berger	Ferrari	Ferrari 640	49 laps/gearbox	4
R	Martin Brundle	Brabham	Brabham-Judd BT58	49 laps/engine	20
R	Eric Bernard	Larrousse	Lola-Lamborghini LC89	46 laps/engine	13
R	Philippe Alliot	Larrousse	Lola-Lamborghini LC89	39 laps/engine	12
R	Jonathan Palmer	Tyrrell	Tyrrell-Ford Cosworth 018	32 laps/spun off	18
R	Stefano Modena	Brabham	Brabham-Judd BT58	31 laps/engine	14
R	Jean Alesi	Tyrrell	Tyrrell-Ford Cosworth 018	28 laps/spun off	22
R	Nicola Larini	Osella	Osella-Ford Cosworth FA1M	23 laps/handling	17
R	Riccardo Patrese	Williams	Williams-Renault FW12C	19 laps/spun off	5
R	Ivan Capelli	March	March-Judd CG891	15 laps/transmission	8
R	Andrea de Cesaris	BMS Scuderia Italia	Dallara-Ford Cosworth 189	14 laps/engine	25
R	Ayrton Senna	McLaren	McLaren-Honda MP4/5	11 laps/spun off	1
R	Roberto Moreno	Coloni	Coloni-Ford Cosworth C3	2 laps/gearbox	23
DNQ	Rene Arnoux	Ligier	Ligier-Ford Cosworth JS33	-	27
DNQ	Eddie Cheever	Arrows	Arrows-Ford Cosworth A11	-	28
DNQ	Gabriele Tarquini	AGS	AGS-Ford Cosworth JH24	-	29
DNQ	Christian Danner	Rial	Rial-Ford Cosworth ARC2	-	30
DNPQ	Stefan Johansson	Onyx	Onyx-Ford Cosworth ORE-1	-	31
DNPQ	Alex Caffi	BMS Scuderia Italia	Dallara-Ford Cosworth 189	-	32
DNPQ	Gregor Foitek	Euro Brun	EuroBrun-Judd ER188B	-	33
DNPQ	Piercarlo Ghinzani	Osella	Osella-Ford Cosworth FA1M	-	34
DNPQ	Yannick Dalmas	AGS	AGS-Ford Cosworth JH23B	-	35
DNPQ	Bernd Schneider	Zakspeed	Zakspeed-Yamaha 891	-	36
DNPQ	Pierre-Henri Raphanel	Coloni	Coloni-Ford Cosworth C3	-	37
DNPQ	Aguri Suzuki	Zakspeed	Zakspeed-Yamaha 891	-	38
DNPQ	Volker Weidler	Rial	Rial-Ford Cosworth ARC2	-	39

Pole: Senna, 1m09.099s, 154.681mph/248.935kph. Fastest lap: Mansell, 1m12.017s, 148.413mph/238.848kph on Lap 57. Race leaders: Senna 1-11, Prost 12-64

MODENA GETS A DECENT RIDE

For the first time, former F3000 champion Stefano Modena had a drive worthy of his talents and he impressed enormously for Brabham by finishing on the podium with third place in Monaco. The rest of his year was held back by a lack of reliability from the Judd engine and the Italian never scored again.

GERMAN GRAND PRIX

HOCKENHEIM • ROUND 9 • DATE: 30TH JULY 1989
Laps: 45 • Distance: 190.55miles/305.865km • Weather: Warm but dull

Pos	Driver	Team	Chassis-Engine	Result	Qual
1	Ayrton Senna	McLaren	McLaren-Honda MP4/5	1h21m43.302s	1
2	Alain Prost	McLaren	McLaren-Honda MP4/5	1h22m01.453s	2
3	Nigel Mansell	Ferrari	Ferrari 640	1h23m06.556s	3
4	Riccardo Patrese	Williams	Williams-Renault FW12C	44 laps	5
5	Nelson Piquet	Lotus	Lotus-Judd 101	44 laps	8
6	Derek Warwick	Arrows	Arrows-Ford Cosworth A11	44 laps	17
7	Andrea de Cesaris	BMS Scuderia Italia	Dallara-Ford Cosworth 189	44 laps	21
8	Martin Brundle	Brabham	Brabham-Judd BT58	44 laps	12

Pos	Driver	Team	Chassis-Engine	Result	Qual
9	Pierluigi Martini	Minardi	Minardi-Ford Cosworth M189	44 laps	13
10	Jean Alesi	Tyrrell	Tyrrell-Ford Cosworth 018	43 laps	10
11	Rene Arnoux	Ligier	Ligier-Ford Cosworth JS33	42 laps	23
12	Eddie Cheever	Arrows	Arrows-Ford Cosworth A11	40 laps/fuel system	25
R	Stefano Modena	Brabham	Brabham-Judd BT58	37 laps/engine	16
R	Satoru Nakajima	Lotus	Lotus-Judd 101	36 laps/spun off	18
R	Ivan Capelli	March	March-Judd CG891	32 laps/electrical	22
R	Mauricio Gugelmin	March	March-Judd CG891	28 laps/gearbox	14
R	Emanuele Pirro	Benetton	Benetton-Ford B189	26 laps/spun off	9
R	Philippe Alliot	Larrousse	Lola-Lamborghini LC89	20 laps/oil leak	15
R	Jonathan Palmer	Tyrrell	Tyrrell-Ford Cosworth 018	16 laps/engine	19
R	Gerhard Berger	Ferrari	Ferrari 640	13 laps/spun off	4
R	Stefan Johansson	Onyx	Onyx-Ford Cosworth ORE-1	8 laps/overheating	24
R	Alessandro Nannini	Benetton	Benetton-Ford B189	6 laps/electrical	7
R	Thierry Boutsen	Williams	Williams-Renault FW12C	4 laps/collision	6
R	Alex Caffi	BMS Scuderia Italia	Dallara-Ford Cosworth 189	2 laps/engine	20
R	Michele Alboreto	Larrousse	Lola-Lamborghini LC89	1 lap/electrical	26
R	Olivier Grouillard	Ligier	Ligier-Ford Cosworth JS33	0 laps/gearbox	11
DNQ	Luis Perez Sala	Minardi	Minardi-Ford Cosworth M189	-	27
DNQ	Bertrand Gachot	Onyx	Onyx-Ford Cosworth ORE-1	-	28
DNQ	Christian Danner	Rial	Rial-Ford Cosworth ARC2	-	29
EX	Volker Weidler	Rial	Rial-Ford Cosworth ARC2	push start	30
DNPQ	Yannick Dalmas	AGS	AGS-Ford Cosworth JH23B	-	31
DNPQ	Nicola Larini	Osella	Osella-Ford Cosworth FA1M	-	32
DNPQ	Gabriele Tarquini	AGS	AGS-Ford Cosworth JH23B	-	33
DNPQ	Piercarlo Ghinzani	Osella	Osella-Ford Cosworth FA1M	-	34
DNPQ	Roberto Moreno	Coloni	Coloni-Ford Cosworth C3	-	35
DNPQ	Pierre-Henri Raphanel	Coloni	Coloni-Ford Cosworth C3	-	36
DNPQ	Gregor Foitek	Euro Brun	EuroBrun-Judd ER189	-	37
DNPQ	Aguri Suzuki	Zakspeed	Zakspeed-Yamaha 891	-	38
DNPQ	Bernd Schneider	Zakspeed	Zakspeed-Yamaha 891	-	39

Pole: Senna, 1m42.300s, 148.626mph/239.190kph. Fastest lap: Senna, 1m45.884s, 143.595mph/231.094kph on Lap 43. Race leaders: Senna 1-19 & 43-45, Prost 20-42

HUNGARIAN GRAND PRIX

HUNGARORING • ROUND 10 • DATE: 13TH AUGUST 1989
Laps: 77 • Distance: 189.851miles/305.536km • Weather: Hot & bright

Pos	Driver	Team	Chassis-Engine	Result	Qual
1	Nigel Mansell	Ferrari	Ferrari 640	1h49m38.650s	12
2	Ayrton Senna	McLaren	McLaren-Honda MP4/5	1h50m04.617s	2
3	Thierry Boutsen	Williams	Williams-Renault FW12C	1h50m17.004s	4
4	Alain Prost	McLaren	McLaren-Honda MP4/5	1h50m22.827s	5
5	Eddie Cheever	Arrows	Arrows-Ford Cosworth A11	1h50m23.756s	16
6	Nelson Piquet	Lotus	Lotus-Judd 101	1h50m50.689s	17
7	Alex Caffi	BMS Scuderia Italia	Dallara-Ford Cosworth 189	1h51m02.875s	3
8	Emanuele Pirro	Benetton	Benetton-Ford B189	76 laps	25
9	Jean Alesi	Tyrrell	Tyrrell-Ford Cosworth 018	76 laps	11
10	Derek Warwick	Arrows	Arrows-Ford Cosworth A11	76 laps	9
11	Stefano Modena	Brabham	Brabham-Judd BT58	76 laps	8
12	Martin Brundle	Brabham	Brabham-Judd BT58	75 laps	15
13	Jonathan Palmer	Tyrrell	Tyrrell-Ford Cosworth 018	73 laps	19
R	Luis Perez Sala	Minardi	Minardi-Ford Cosworth M189	57 laps/collision	23
R	Gerhard Berger	Ferrari	Ferrari 640	56 laps/gearbox	6

Pos	Driver	Team	Chassis-Engine	Result	Qual
R	Riccardo Patrese	Williams	Williams-Renault FW12C	54 laps/water leak	1
R	Stefan Johansson	Onyx	Onyx-Ford Cosworth ORE-1	48 laps/gearbox	24
R	Alessandro Nannini	Benetton	Benetton-Ford B189	46 laps/gearbox	7
R	Bertrand Gachot	Onyx	Onyx-Ford Cosworth ORE-1	38 laps/gearbox	21
R	Satoru Nakajima	Lotus	Lotus-Judd 101	33 laps/accident	20
R	Mauricio Gugelmin	March	March-Judd CG891	27 laps/electrical	13
R	Ivan Capelli	March	March-Judd CG891	26 laps/wheel	14
R	Michele Alboreto	Larrousse	Lola-Lamborghini LC89	26 laps/engine	26
R	Piercarlo Ghinzani	Osella	Osella-Ford Cosworth FA1M	20 laps/electrical	22
R	Pierluigi Martini	Minardi	Minardi-Ford Cosworth M189	19 laps/wheel	10
R	Andrea de Cesaris	BMS Scuderia Italia	Dallara-Ford Cosworth 189	0 laps/clutch	18
DNQ	Rene Arnoux	Ligier	Ligier-Ford Cosworth JS33	-	27
DNQ	Olivier Grouillard	Ligier	Ligier-Ford Cosworth JS33	-	28
DNQ	Christian Danner	Rial	Rial-Ford Cosworth ARC2	-	29
DNQ	Volker Weidler	Rial	Rial-Ford Cosworth ARC2	-	30
DNPQ	Nicola Larini	Osella	Osella-Ford Cosworth FA1M	-	31
DNPQ	Philippe Alliot	Larrousse	Lola-Lamborghini LC89	-	32
DNPQ	Yannick Dalmas	AGS	AGS-Ford Cosworth JH23B	-	33
DNPQ	Bernd Schneider	Zakspeed	Zakspeed-Yamaha 891	-	34
DNPQ	Gabriele Tarquini	AGS	AGS-Ford Cosworth JH24	-	35
DNPQ	Roberto Moreno	Coloni	Coloni-Ford Cosworth C3	-	36
DNPQ	Gregor Foitek	Euro Brun	EuroBrun-Judd ER189	-	37
DNPQ	Aguri Suzuki	Zakspeed	Zakspeed-Yamaha 891	-	38
DNPQ	Pierre-Henri Raphanel	Coloni	Coloni-Ford Cosworth C3	-	39

Pole: Patrese, 1m19.726s, 111.333mph/179.173kph. Fastest lap: Mansell, 1m22.637s, 107.411mph/172.862kph on Lap 66. Race leaders: Patrese 1-52, Senna 53-57, Mansell 58-77

BELGIAN GRAND PRIX

SPA-FRANCORCHAMPS • ROUND 11 • DATE: 27TH AUGUST 1989
Laps: 44 • Distance: 189.540miles/305.36km • Weather: Cool & wet

Pos	Driver	Team	Chassis-Engine	Result	Qual
1	Ayrton Senna	McLaren	McLaren-Honda MP4/5	1h40m54.196s	1
2	Alain Prost	McLaren	McLaren-Honda MP4/5	1h40m55.500s	2
3	Nigel Mansell	Ferrari	Ferrari 640	1h40m56.020s	6
4	Thierry Boutsen	Williams	Williams-Renault FW12C	1h41m48.614s	4
5	Alessandro Nannini	Benetton	Benetton-Ford B189	1h42m03.001s	7
6	Derek Warwick	Arrows	Arrows-Ford Cosworth A11	1h42m12.512s	10
7	Mauricio Gugelmin	March	March-Judd CG891	43 laps	9
8	Stefan Johansson	Onyx	Onyx-Ford Cosworth ORE-1	43 laps	15
9	Pierluigi Martini	Minardi	Minardi-Ford Cosworth M189	43 laps	14
10	Emanuele Pirro	Benetton	Benetton-Ford B189	43 laps	13
11	Andrea de Cesaris	BMS Scuderia Italia	Dallara-Ford Cosworth 189	43 laps	18
12	Ivan Capelli	March	March-Judd CG891	43 laps	19
13	Olivier Grouillard	Ligier	Ligier-Ford Cosworth JS33	43 laps	26
14	Jonathan Palmer	Tyrrell	Tyrrell-Ford Cosworth 018	42 laps	21
15	Luis Perez Sala	Minardi	Minardi-Ford Cosworth M189	41 laps	25
16	Philippe Alliot	Larrousse	Lola-Lamborghini LC89	39 laps/engine	11
R	Eddie Cheever	Arrows	Arrows-Ford Cosworth A11	38 laps/wheel	24
R	Bertrand Gachot	Onyx	Onyx-Ford Cosworth ORE-1	21 laps/spun off	23
R	Riccardo Patrese	Williams	Williams-Renault FW12C	20 laps/collision	5
R	Michele Alboreto	Larrousse	Lola-Lamborghini LC89	19 laps/collision	22
R	Alex Caffi	BMS Scuderia Italia	Dallara-Ford Cosworth 189	13 laps/spun off	12
R	Martin Brundle	Brabham	Brabham-Judd BT58	12 laps/brakes	20

Pos	Driver	Team	Chassis-Engine	Result	Qual
R	Gerhard Berger	Ferrari	Ferrari 640	9 laps/spun off	3
R	Stefano Modena	Brabham	Brabham-Judd BT58	9 laps/handling	8
R	Rene Arnoux	Ligier	Ligier-Ford Cosworth JS33	4 laps/collision	17
R	Johnny Herbert	Tyrrell	Tyrrell-Ford Cosworth 018	3 laps/spun off	16
DNQ	Satoru Nakajima	Lotus	Lotus-Judd 101	-	27
DNQ	Nelson Piquet	Lotus	Lotus-Judd 101	-	28
DNQ	Christian Danner	Rial	Rial-Ford Cosworth ARC2	-	29
DNQ	Pierre-Henri Raphanel	Rial	Rial-Ford Cosworth ARC2	-	30
DNPQ	Nicola Larini	Osella	Osella-Ford Cosworth FA1M	-	31
DNPQ	Piercarlo Ghinzani	Osella	Osella-Ford Cosworth FA1M	-	32
DNPQ	Roberto Moreno	Coloni	Coloni-Ford Cosworth C3	-	33
DNPQ	Gabriele Tarquini	AGS	AGS-Ford Cosworth JH24	-	34
DNPQ	Bernd Schneider	Zakspeed	Zakspeed-Yamaha 891	-	35
DNPQ	Aguri Suzuki	Zakspeed	Zakspeed-Yamaha 891	-	36
DNPQ	Yannick Dalmas	AGS	AGS-Ford Cosworth JH24	-	37
DNPQ	Gregor Foitek	Euro Brun	EuroBrun-Judd ER188B	-	38
DNPQ	Enrico Bertaggia	Coloni	Coloni-Ford Cosworth C3	-	39

Pole: Senna, 1m50.867s, 140.026mph/225.351kph. Fastest lap: Prost, 2m11.571s, 117.992mph/189.889kph on Lap 44. Race leaders: Senna 1-44

NEW CIRCUITS

America introduced F1's first new street circuit in years when it held a race at Phoenix in Arizona. Typically, the circuit contained a number of right-angled turns and a hairpin, with a bumpy surface that made it hard to drive. The other change for 1989 was the modification of the Hungaroring with the loop after Turn 3 removed.

ITALIAN GRAND PRIX

MONZA • ROUND 12 • DATE: 10TH SEPTEMBER 1989
Laps: 53 • Distance: 190.763miles/307.4km • Weather: Hot & bright

Pos	Driver	Team	Chassis-Engine	Result	Qual
1	Alain Prost	McLaren	McLaren-Honda MP4/5	1h19m27.550s	4
2	Gerhard Berger	Ferrari	Ferrari 640	1h19m34.876s	2
3	Thierry Boutsen	Williams	Williams-Renault FW12C	1h19m42.525s	6
4	Riccardo Patrese	Williams	Williams-Renault FW12C	1h20m06.272s	5
5	Jean Alesi	Tyrrell	Tyrrell-Ford Cosworth 018	52 laps	10
6	Martin Brundle	Brabham	Brabham-Judd BT58	52 laps	12
7	Pierluigi Martini	Minardi	Minardi-Ford Cosworth M189	52 laps	15
8	Luis Perez Sala	Minardi	Minardi-Ford Cosworth M189	51 laps	26
9	Rene Arnoux	Ligier	Ligier-Ford Cosworth JS33	51 laps	23
10	Satoru Nakajima	Lotus	Lotus-Judd 101	51 laps	19
11	Alex Caffi	BMS Scuderia Italia	Dallara-Ford Cosworth 189	47 laps/engine	20
R	Andrea de Cesaris	BMS Scuderia Italia	Dallara-Ford Cosworth 189	45 laps/engine	17
R	Ayrton Senna	McLaren	McLaren-Honda MP4/5	44 laps/engine	1
R	Nigel Mansell	Ferrari	Ferrari 640	41 laps/gearbox	3
R	Bertrand Gachot	Onyx	Onyx-Ford Cosworth ORE-1	38 laps/radiator	22
R	Alessandro Nannini	Benetton	Benetton-Ford B189	33 laps/brakes	8
R	Ivan Capelli	March	March-Judd CG891	30 laps/engine	18

Pos	Driver	Team	Chassis-Engine	Result	Qual
R	Olivier Grouillard	Ligier	Ligier-Ford Cosworth JS33	30 laps/exhaust	21
R	Nelson Piquet	Lotus	Lotus-Judd 101	23 laps/spun off	11
R	Jonathan Palmer	Tyrrell	Tyrrell-Ford Cosworth 018	18 laps/engine	14
R	Derek Warwick	Arrows	Arrows-Ford Cosworth A11	18 laps/fuel system	16
R	Nicola Larini	Osella	Osella-Ford Cosworth FA1M	16 laps/gearbox	24
R	Michele Alboreto	Larrousse	Lola-Lamborghini LC89	14 laps/electrical	13
R	Mauricio Gugelmin	March	March-Judd CG891	14 laps/throttle	25
R	Philippe Alliot	Larrousse	Lola-Lamborghini LC89	1 lap/spun off	7
R	Emanuele Pirro	Benetton	Benetton-Ford B189	0 laps/transmission	9
DNQ	Eddie Cheever	Arrows	Arrows-Ford Cosworth A11	-	27
DNQ	Christian Danner	Rial	Rial-Ford Cosworth ARC2	-	28
DNQ	Pierre-Henri Raphanel	Rial	Rial-Ford Cosworth ARC2	-	29
EX	Stefano Modena	Brabham	Brabham-Judd BT58	missed weight check	30
DNPQ	Stefan Johansson	Onyx	Onyx-Ford Cosworth ORE-1	-	31
DNPQ	Gabriele Tarquini	AGS	AGS-Ford Cosworth JH24	-	32
DNPQ	Roberto Moreno	Coloni	Coloni-Ford Cosworth C3	-	33
DNPQ	Piercarlo Ghinzani	Osella	Osella-Ford Cosworth FA1M	-	34
DNPQ	Bernd Schneider	Zakspeed	Zakspeed-Yamaha 891	-	35
DNPQ	Aguri Suzuki	Zakspeed	Zakspeed-Yamaha 891	-	36
DNPQ	Oscar Larrauri	Euro Brun	EuroBrun-Judd ER189	-	37
DNPQ	Yannick Dalmas	AGS	AGS-Ford Cosworth JH24	-	38
DNPQ	Enrico Bertaggia	Coloni	Coloni-Ford Cosworth C3	-	39

Pole: Senna, 1m23.720s, 154.971mph/249.402kph. Fastest lap: Prost, 1m28.107s, 147.255mph/236.984kph on Lap 43. Race leaders: Senna 1-44, Prost 45-53

PORTUGUESE GRAND PRIX

AUTODROMO DO ESTORIL • ROUND 13 • DATE: 24TH SEPTEMBER 1989
Laps: 71 • Distance: 191.435miles/308.85km • Weather: Hot & bright

Pos	Driver	Team	Chassis-Engine	Result	Qual
1	Gerhard Berger	Ferrari	Ferrari 640	1h36m48.546s	2
2	Alain Prost	McLaren	McLaren-Honda MP4/5	1h37m21.183s	4
3	Stefan Johansson	Onyx	Onyx-Ford Cosworth ORE-1	1h37m43.871s	12
4	Alessandro Nannini	Benetton	Benetton-Ford B189	1h38m10.915s	13
5	Pierluigi Martini	Minardi	Minardi-Ford Cosworth M189	70 laps	5
6	Jonathan Palmer	Tyrrell	Tyrrell-Ford Cosworth 018	70 laps	18
7	Satoru Nakajima	Lotus	Lotus-Judd 101	70 laps	25
8	Martin Brundle	Brabham	Brabham-Judd BT58	70 laps	10
9	Philippe Alliot	Larrousse	Lola-Lamborghini LC89	70 laps	17
10	Mauricio Gugelmin	March	March-Judd CG891	69 laps	14
11	Michele Alboreto	Larrousse	Lola-Lamborghini LC89	69 laps	21
12	Luis Perez Sala	Minardi	Minardi-Ford Cosworth M189	69 laps	9
13	Rene Arnoux	Ligier	Ligier-Ford Cosworth JS33	69 laps	23
14	Stefano Modena	Brabham	Brabham-Judd BT58	69 laps	11
R	Riccardo Patrese	Williams	Williams-Renault FW13	60 laps/overheating	6
R	Thierry Boutsen	Williams	Williams-Renault FW13	60 laps/overheating	8
R	Ayrton Senna	McLaren	McLaren-Honda MP4/5	48 laps/collision	1
DQ*	Nigel Mansell	Ferrari	Ferrari 640	48 laps/collision	3
R	Derek Warwick	Arrows	Arrows-Ford Cosworth A11	37 laps/accident	22
R	Alex Caffi	BMS Scuderia Italia	Dallara-Ford Cosworth 189	33 laps/collision	7
R	Nelson Piquet	Lotus	Lotus-Judd 101	33 laps/collision	20
R	Emanuele Pirro	Benetton	Benetton-Ford B189	29 laps/suspension	16
R	Ivan Capelli	March	March-Judd CG891	25 laps/engine	24
R	Eddie Cheever	Arrows	Arrows-Ford Cosworth A11	24 laps/spun off	26

Pos	Driver	Team	Chassis-Engine	Result	Qual
R	Andrea de Cesaris	BMS Scuderia Italia	Dallara-Ford Cosworth 189	17 laps/electrical	19
R	Roberto Moreno	Coloni	Coloni-Ford Cosworth C3	11 laps/electrical	15
DNQ	Johnny Herbert	Tyrrell	Tyrrell-Ford Cosworth 018	-	27
EX	Yannick Dalmas	AGS	AGS-Ford Cosworth JH24	illegal tyres	28
DNQ	Olivier Grouillard	Ligier	Ligier-Ford Cosworth JS33	-	29
DNQ	Pierre-Henri Raphanel	Rial	Rial-Ford Cosworth ARC2	-	30
DNQ	Christian Danner	Rial	Rial-Ford Cosworth ARC2	-	31
DNPQ	JJ Lehto	Onyx	Onyx-Ford Cosworth ORE-1	-	32
DNPQ	Piercarlo Ghinzani	Osella	Osella-Ford Cosworth FA1M	-	33
DNPQ	Oscar Larrauri	Euro Brun	EuroBrun-Judd ER189	-	34
DNPQ	Gabriele Tarquini	AGS	AGS-Ford Cosworth JH24	-	35
DNPQ	Nicola Larini	Osella	Osella-Ford Cosworth FA1M	missed weight check	36
DNPQ	Aguri Suzuki	Zakspeed	Zakspeed-Yamaha 891	-	37
DNPQ	Bernd Schneider	Zakspeed	Zakspeed-Yamaha 891	-	38
DNPQ	Enrico Bertaggia	Coloni	Coloni-Ford Cosworth C3	-	39

*Mansell was disqualified for reversing in the pits & ignoring black flags

Pole: Senna, 1m15.468s, 128.937mph/207.505kph. Fastest lap: Berger, 1m18.986s, 123.194mph/198.262kph on Lap 49. Race leaders: Berger 1-23 & 41-71, Mansell 24-39, Martini 40

NEW CONSTRUCTORS

Onyx was the new kid on the block. This British team was created by Mike Earle, who ran the March team in F2, then F3000. Stefan Johansson and Bertrand Gachot struggled even to pre-qualify at the start of the year but the Swede went on to finish fifth at Paul Ricard and then third at Estoril to help the team rank 10th.

SPANISH GRAND PRIX

JEREZ • ROUND 14 • DATE: 1ST OCTOBER 1989
Laps: 73 • Distance: 191.328miles/307.914km • Weather: Hot & bright

Pos	Driver	Team	Chassis-Engine	Result	Qual
1	Ayrton Senna	McLaren	McLaren-Honda MP4/5	1h47m48.264s	1
2	Gerhard Berger	Ferrari	Ferrari 640	1h48m15.315s	2
3	Alain Prost	McLaren	McLaren-Honda MP4/5	1h48m42.052s	3
4	Jean Alesi	Tyrrell	Tyrrell-Ford Cosworth 018	72 laps	9
5	Riccardo Patrese	Williams	Williams-Renault FW12C	72 laps	6
6	Philippe Alliot	Larrousse	Lola-Lamborghini LC89	72 laps	5
7	Andrea de Cesaris	BMS Scuderia Italia	Dallara-Ford Cosworth 189	72 laps	15
8	Nelson Piquet	Lotus	Lotus-Judd 101	71 laps	7
9	Derek Warwick	Arrows	Arrows-Ford Cosworth A11	71 laps	16
10	Jonathan Palmer	Tyrrell	Tyrrell-Ford Cosworth 018	71 laps	13
R	Eddie Cheever	Arrows	Arrows-Ford Cosworth A11	61 laps/engine	22
R	Emanuele Pirro	Benetton	Benetton-Ford B189	59 laps/spun off	10
R	Alex Caffi	BMS Scuderia Italia	Dallara-Ford Cosworth 189	55 laps/engine	23
R	Martin Brundle	Brabham	Brabham-Judd BT58	51 laps/spun off	8
R	Luis Perez Sala	Minardi	Minardi-Ford Cosworth M189	47 laps/spun off	20
R	Mauricio Gugelmin	March	March-Judd CG891	47 laps/collision	26
R	Thierry Boutsen	Williams	Williams-Renault FW13	40 laps/fuel pump	21
R	Olivier Grouillard	Ligier	Ligier-Ford Cosworth JS33	34 laps/engine	24

Pos	Driver	Team	Chassis-Engine	Result	Qual
R	Pierluigi Martini	Minardi	Minardi-Ford Cosworth M189	27 laps/spun off	4
R	Ivan Capelli	March	March-Judd CG891	23 laps/transmission	19
R	JJ Lehto	Onyx	Onyx-Ford Cosworth ORE-1	20 laps/gearbox	17
R	Piercarlo Ghinzani	Osella	Osella-Ford Cosworth FA1M	17 laps/gearbox	25
R	Alessandro Nannini	Benetton	Benetton-Ford B189	14 laps/spun off	14
R	Stefano Modena	Brabham	Brabham-Judd BT58	11 laps/electrical	12
R	Nicola Larini	Osella	Osella-Ford Cosworth FA1M	6 laps/suspension	11
R	Satoru Nakajima	Lotus	Lotus-Judd 101	0 laps/collision	18
DNQ	Rene Arnoux	Ligier	Ligier-Ford Cosworth JS33	-	27
DNQ	Pierre-Henri Raphanel	Rial	Rial-Ford Cosworth ARC2	-	28
DNQ	Gregor Foitek	Rial	Rial-Ford Cosworth ARC2	-	29
DNPQ	Gabriele Tarquini	AGS	AGS-Ford Cosworth JH24	-	30
DNPQ	Stefan Johansson	Onyx	Onyx-Ford Cosworth ORE-1	-	31
DNPQ	Roberto Moreno	Coloni	Coloni-Ford Cosworth C3	-	32
DNPQ	Michele Alboreto	Larrousse	Lola-Lamborghini LC89	-	33
DNPQ	Bernd Schneider	Zakspeed	Zakspeed-Yamaha 891	-	34
DNPQ	Yannick Dalmas	AGS	AGS-Ford Cosworth JH24	-	35
DNPQ	Aguri Suzuki	Zakspeed	Zakspeed-Yamaha 891	-	36
DNPQ	Oscar Larrauri	Euro Brun	EuroBrun-Judd ER189	-	37
DNPQ	Enrico Bertaggia	Coloni	Coloni-Ford Cosworth C3	-	38

Pole: Senna, 1m20.291s, 117.515mph/189.122kph. Fastest lap: Senna, 1m25.779s, 109.996mph/177.022kph on Lap 55. Race leaders: Senna 1-73

NEW DRIVERS

Of the 14 new faces, Jean Alesi made the biggest splash by finishing fourth in both his debut at Paul Ricard and at Jerez, matching Herbert's result in round one. Herbert's replacement, Pirro, grabbed fifth at the Adelaide finale, while Olivier Grouillard took sixth at Paul Ricard for Ligier. Four drivers failed even to qualify.

JAPANESE GRAND PRIX

SUZUKA • ROUND 15 • DATE: 22ND OCTOBER 1989
Laps: 53 • Distance: 192.952miles/310.527km • Weather: Warm & bright

Pos	Driver	Team	Chassis-Engine	Result	Qual
DQ	Ayrton Senna	McLaren	McLaren-Honda MP4/5	53 laps/cutting the chicane	1
1	Alessandro Nannini	Benetton	Benetton-Ford B189	1h35m06.777s	6
2	Riccardo Patrese	Williams	Williams-Renault FW13	1h35m18.181s	5
3	Thierry Boutsen	Williams	Williams-Renault FW13	1h35m19.723s	7
4	Nelson Piquet	Lotus	Lotus-Judd 101	1h36m50.502s	11
5	Martin Brundle	Brabham	Brabham-Judd BT58	52 laps	13
6	Derek Warwick	Arrows	Arrows-Ford Cosworth A11	52 laps	25
7	Mauricio Gugelmin	March	March-Judd CG891	52 laps	20
8	Eddie Cheever	Arrows	Arrows-Ford Cosworth A11	52 laps	24
9	Alex Caffi	BMS Scuderia Italia	Dallara-Ford Cosworth 189	52 laps	15
10	Andrea de Cesaris	BMS Scuderia Italia	Dallara-Ford Cosworth 189	51 laps	16
R	Alain Prost	McLaren	McLaren-Honda MP4/5	46 laps/collision	2
R	Stefano Modena	Brabham	Brabham-Judd BT58	46 laps/engine	9
R	Nigel Mansell	Ferrari	Ferrari 640	43 laps/engine	4
R	Satoru Nakajima	Lotus	Lotus-Judd 101	41 laps/engine	12

Pos	Driver	Team	Chassis-Engine	Result	Qual
R	Jean Alesi	Tyrrell	Tyrrell-Ford Cosworth 018	37 laps/gearbox	18
R	Philippe Alliot	Larrousse	Lola-Lamborghini LC89	36 laps/engine	8
R	Gerhard Berger	Ferrari	Ferrari 640	34 laps/gearbox	3
R	Emanuele Pirro	Benetton	Benetton-Ford B189	33 laps/collision	22
R	Olivier Grouillard	Ligier	Ligier-Ford Cosworth JS33	31 laps/engine	23
R	Ivan Capelli	March	March-Judd CG891	27 laps/suspension	17
R	Nicola Larini	Osella	Osella-Ford Cosworth FA1M	21 laps/brakes	10
R	Jonathan Palmer	Tyrrell	Tyrrell-Ford Cosworth 018	20 laps/oil leak	26
R	Bernd Schneider	Zakspeed	Zakspeed-Yamaha 891	1 lap/gearbox	21
R	Luis Perez Sala	Minardi	Minardi-Ford Cosworth M189	0 laps/collision	14
R	Paolo Barilla	Minardi	Minardi-Ford Cosworth M189	0 laps/clutch	19
DNQ	Rene Arnoux	Ligier	Ligier-Ford Cosworth JS33	-	27
DNQ	Michele Alboreto	Larrousse	Lola-Lamborghini LC89	-	28
DNQ	Pierre-Henri Raphanel	Rial	Rial-Ford Cosworth ARC2	-	29
DNQ	Bertrand Gachot	Rial	Rial-Ford Cosworth ARC2	-	30
DNPQ	Piercarlo Ghinzani	Osella	Osella-Ford Cosworth FA1M	-	31
DNPQ	Roberto Moreno	Coloni	Coloni-Ford Cosworth C3	-	32
DNPQ	Stefan Johansson	Onyx	Onyx-Ford Cosworth ORE-1	-	33
DNPQ	Aguri Suzuki	Zakspeed	Zakspeed-Yamaha 891	-	34
DNPQ	Oscar Larrauri	Euro Brun	EuroBrun-Judd ER189	-	35
DNPQ	JJ Lehto	Onyx	Onyx-Ford Cosworth ORE-1	-	36
DNPQ	Gabriele Tarquini	AGS	AGS-Ford Cosworth JH24	-	37
DNPQ	Yannick Dalmas	AGS	AGS-Ford Cosworth JH24	-	38
DNPQ	Enrico Bertaggia	Coloni	Coloni-Ford Cosworth C3	-	39

Pole: Senna, 1m38.041s, 133.680mph/215.138kph. Fastest lap: Prost, 1m43.506s, 126.622mph/203.779kph on Lap 43. Race leaders: Prost 1-20 & 24-46, Senna 21-23 & 47-48 & 51-53, Nannini 49-50

AUSTRALIAN GRAND PRIX

ADELAIDE • ROUND 16 • DATE: 5TH NOVEMBER 1989
Laps: 70 • Distance: 164.45miles/264.6km • Weather: Cool & wet

Pos	Driver	Team	Chassis-Engine	Result	Qual
1	Thierry Boutsen	Williams	Williams-Renault FW13	2h00m17.421s	5
2	Alessandro Nannini	Benetton	Benetton-Ford B189	2h00m46.079s	4
3	Riccardo Patrese	Williams	Williams-Renault FW13	2h00m55.104s	6
4	Satoru Nakajima	Lotus	Lotus-Judd 101	2h00m59.752s	23
5	Emanuele Pirro	Benetton	Benetton-Ford B189	68 laps	13
6	Pierluigi Martini	Minardi	Minardi-Ford Cosworth M189	67 laps	3
7	Mauricio Gugelmin	March	March-Judd CG891	66 laps	25
8	Stefano Modena	Brabham	Brabham-Judd BT58	64 laps	8
R	Eddie Cheever	Arrows	Arrows-Ford Cosworth A11	42 laps/spun off	22
R	JJ Lehto	Onyx	Onyx-Ford Cosworth ORE-1	27 laps/electrical	17
R	Olivier Grouillard	Ligier	Ligier-Ford Cosworth JS33	22 laps/spun off	24
R	Nelson Piquet	Lotus	Lotus-Judd 101	19 laps/collision	18
R	Piercarlo Ghinzani	Osella	Osella-Ford Cosworth FA1M	18 laps/collision	21
R	Nigel Mansell	Ferrari	Ferrari 640	17 laps/spun off	7
R	Ayrton Senna	McLaren	McLaren-Honda MP4/5	13 laps/collision	1
R	Alex Caffi	BMS Scuderia Italia	Dallara-Ford Cosworth 189	13 laps/spun off	10
R	Ivan Capelli	March	March-Judd CG891	13 laps/radiator	16
R	Andrea de Cesaris	BMS Scuderia Italia	Dallara-Ford Cosworth 189	12 laps/spun off	9
R	Martin Brundle	Brabham	Brabham-Judd BT58	12 laps/collision	12
R	Derek Warwick	Arrows	Arrows-Ford Cosworth A11	7 laps/spun off	20
R	Gerhard Berger	Ferrari	Ferrari 640	6 laps/collision	14

Pos	Driver	Team	Chassis-Engine	Result	Qual
R	Philippe Alliot	Larrousse	Lola-Lamborghini LC89	6 laps/collision	19
R	Jean Alesi	Tyrrell	Tyrrell-Ford Cosworth 018	5 laps/electrical	15
R	Rene Arnoux	Ligier	Ligier-Ford Cosworth JS33	4 laps/collision	26
R	Alain Prost	McLaren	McLaren-Honda MP4/5	0 laps/withdrawn	2
R	Nicola Larini	Osella	Osella-Ford Cosworth FA1M	0 laps/electrical	11
DNQ	Jonathan Palmer	Tyrrell	Tyrrell-Ford Cosworth 018	-	27
DNQ	Luis Perez Sala	Minardi	Minardi-Ford Cosworth M189	-	28
DNQ	Bertrand Gachot	Rial	Rial-Ford Cosworth ARC2	-	29
DNQ	Pierre-Henri Raphanel	Rial	Rial-Ford Cosworth ARC2	-	30
DNPQ	Stefan Johansson	Onyx	Onyx-Ford Cosworth ORE-1	-	31
DNPQ	Michele Alboreto	Larrousse	Lola-Lamborghini LC89	-	32
DNPQ	Bernd Schneider	Zakspeed	Zakspeed-Yamaha 891	-	33
DNPQ	Roberto Moreno	Coloni	Coloni-Ford Cosworth C3	-	34
DNPQ	Oscar Larrauri	Euro Brun	EuroBrun-Judd ER189	-	35
DNPQ	Aguri Suzuki	Zakspeed	Zakspeed-Yamaha 891	-	36
DNPQ	Yannick Dalmas	AGS	AGS-Ford Cosworth JH24	-	37
DNPQ	Gabriele Tarquini	AGS	AGS-Ford Cosworth JH24	-	38
DNPQ	Enrico Bertaggia	Coloni	Coloni-Ford Cosworth C3	-	39

Pole: Senna, 1m16.665s, 110.293mph/177.499kph. Fastest lap: Nakajima, 1m38.480s, 85.861mph/138.180kph on Lap 64. Race leaders: Senna 1-13, Boutsen 14-70

WORLD DRIVERS' CHAMPIONSHIP FINAL RESULTS

Pos	Driver	Nat	Car-Engine	R1	R2	R3	R4	R5
1	Alain Prost	FRA	McLaren-Honda MP4/5	2	2F	2F	5	1
2	Ayrton Senna	BRA	McLaren-Honda MP4/5	11P	1P	1P	1P	RPF
3	Riccardo Patrese	ITA	Williams-Renault FW12C	RF	R	15	2	2
			Williams-Renault FW13	-	-	-	-	-
4	Nigel Mansell	GBR	Ferrari 640	1	R	R	RF	R
5	Thierry Boutsen	BEL	Williams-Renault FW12C	R	4	10	R	6
			Williams-Renault FW13	-	-	-	-	-
6	Alessandro Nannini	ITA	Benetton-Ford B188	6	3	8	4	R
			Benetton-Ford B189	-	-	-	-	-
7	Gerhard Berger	AUT	Ferrari 640	R	R	-	R	R
8	Nelson Piquet	BRA	Lotus-Judd 101	R	R	R	11	R
9	Jean Alesi	FRA	Tyrrell-Ford Cosworth 018	-	-	-	-	-
10	Derek Warwick	GBR	Arrows-Ford Cosworth A11	5	5	R	R	R
11	Michele Alboreto	ITA	Tyrrell-Ford Cosworth 017B	10	-	-	-	-
			Tyrrell-Ford Cosworth 018	-	DNQ	5	3	R
			Lola-Lamborghini LC89	-	-	-	-	-
11	Eddie Cheever	USA	Arrows-Ford Cosworth A11	R	9	7	7	3
11	Stefan Johansson	SWE	Onyx-Ford Cosworth ORE-1	DNPQ	DNPQ	DNPQ	R	R
14	Johnny Herbert	GBR	Benetton-Ford B188	4	11	14	15	5
			Tyrrell-Ford Cosworth 018	-	-	-	-	-
15	Pierluigi Martini	ITA	Minardi-Ford Cosworth M188B	R	R	R	-	-
			Minardi-Ford Cosworth M189	-	-	-	R	R
16	Mauricio Gugelmin	BRA	March-Judd 881	3	R	R	-	-
			March-Judd CG891	-	-	-	DNQ	DQ
16	Stefano Modena	ITA	Brabham-Judd BT58	R	R	3	10	R
16	Andrea de Cesaris	ITA	Dallara-Ford Cosworth 189	13	10	13	R	8
19	Alex Caffi	ITA	Dallara-Ford Cosworth 189	DNPQ	7	4	13	R
20	Martin Brundle	GBR	Brabham-Judd BT58	R	R	6	9	R
21	Christian Danner	DEU	Rial-Ford Cosworth ARC2	14	DNQ	DNQ	12	4
21	Satoru Nakajima	JPN	Lotus-Judd 101	8	NC	DNQ	R	R

Pos	Driver	Nat	Car-Engine	R1	R2	R3	R4	R5
23	Rene Arnoux	FRA	Ligier-Ford Cosworth JS33	DNQ	DNQ	12	14	DNQ
23	Emanuele Pirro	ITA	Benetton-Ford B188	-	-	-	-	-
			Benetton-Ford B189	-	-	-	-	-
25	Jonathan Palmer	GBR	Tyrrell-Ford Cosworth 017B	7	-	-	-	-
			Tyrrell-Ford Cosworth 018	-	6	9	R	9
26	Gabriele Tarquini	ITA	AGS-Ford Cosworth JH23B	-	8	R	6	7
			AGS-Ford Cosworth JH24	-	-	-	-	-
26	Olivier Grouillard	FRA	Ligier-Ford Cosworth JS33	9	DQ	R	8	DNQ
26	Luis Perez Sala	ESP	Minardi-Ford Cosworth M188B	R	R	R	-	-
			Minardi-Ford Cosworth M189	-	-	-	DNQ	R
26	Philippe Alliot	FRA	Lola-Lamborghini LC88B	12	-	-	-	-
			Lola-Lamborghini LC89	-	R	R	NC	R

Pos	Driver	R6	R7	R8	R9	R10	R11	R12	R13	R14	R15	R16	Total
1	Prost	RP	1P	1	2	4	2F	1F	2	3	RF	R	76
2	Senna	7	R	RP	1PF	2	1P	RP	RP	1PF	DQP	RP	60
3	Patrese	2	3	R	4	RP	R	4	-	5	-	-	40
		-	-	-	-	-	-	-	R	-	2	3	
4	Mansell	DQ	2	2F	3	1F	3	R	DQ	-	R	R	38
5	Boutsen	1	R	10	R	3	4	3	-	-	-	-	37
		-	-	-	-	-	-	-	R	R	3	1	
6	Nannini	DQ	-	-	-	-	-	-	-	-	-	-	32
		-	R	3	R	R	5	R	4	R	1	2	
7	Berger	R	R	R	R	R	R	2	1F	2	R	R	21
8	Piquet	4	8	4	5	6	DNQ	R	R	8	4	R	12
9	Alesi	-	4	R	10	9	-	5	-	4	R	R	8
10	Warwick	R	-	9	6	10	6	R	R	9	6	R	7
11	Alboreto	-	-	-	-	-	-	-	-	-	-	-	6
		R	-	-	-	-	-	-	-	-	-	-	
		-	-	-	R	R	R	R	11	DNPQ	DNQ	DNPQ	
11	Cheever	R	7	DNQ	12	5	R	DNQ	R	R	8	R	6
11	Johansson	DQ	5	DNPQ	R	R	8	DNPQ	3	DNPQ	DNPQ	DNPQ	6
14	Herbert	DNQ	-	-	-	-	-	-	-	-	-	-	5
		-	-	-	-	-	R	-	DNQ	-	-	-	
15	Martini	-	-	-	-	-	-	-	-	-	-	-	5
		R	R	5	9	R	9	7	5	R	-	6	
16	Gugelmin	-	-	-	-	-	-	-	-	-	-	-	4
		R	NCF	R	R	R	7	R	10	R	7	7	
16	Modena	R	R	R	R	11	R	DNQ	14	R	R	8	4
16	de Cesaris	3	DNQ	R	7	R	11	R	R	7	10	R	4
19	Caffi	6	R	DNPQ	R	7	R	11	R	R	9	R	4
20	Brundle	DNPQ	DNPQ	R	8	12	R	6	8	R	5	R	4
21	Danner	8	DNQ	DNQ	DNQ	DNQ	DNQ	DNQ	DNQ	-	-	-	3
21	Nakajima	DNQ	R	8	R	R	DNQ	10	7	R	R	4F	3
23	Arnoux	5	R	DNQ	11	DNQ	R	9	13	DNQ	DNQ	R	2
23	Pirro	-	9	11	-	-	-	-	-	-	-	-	2
		-	-	-	R	8	10	R	R	R	R	5	
25	Palmer	-	-	-	-	-	-	-	-	-	-	-	2
		RF	10	R	R	13	14	R	6	10	R	DNQ	
26	Tarquini	R	R	-	DNPQ	-	-	-	-	-	-	-	1
		-	-	DNQ	-	DNPQ	DNPQ	DNPQ	DNPQ	DNPQ	DNPQ	DNPQ	
26	Grouillard	DNQ	6	7	R	DNQ	13	R	DNQ	R	R	R	1
26	Perez Sala	-	-	-	-	-	-	-	-	-	-	-	1
		R	DNQ	6	DNQ	R	15	8	12	R	R	DNQ	
26	Alliot	-	-	-	-	-	-	-	-	-	-	-	1
		R	R	R	R	DNPQ	16	R	9	6	R	R	

WORLD CONSTRUCTORS' CHAMPIONSHIP FINAL RESULTS

Pos	Team-Engine	R1	R2	R3	R4	R5	R6	R7	R8
1	McLaren-Honda	2/11	1/2	1/2	1/5	1/R	7/R	1/R	1/R
2	Williams-Renault	R/R	4/R	10/15	2/R	2/6	1/2	3/R	10/R
3	Ferrari	1/R	R/R	R	R/R	R/R	R/DQ	2/R	2/R
4	Benetton-Ford	4/6	3/11	8/14	4/15	5/R	DQ/DNQ	9/R	3/11
5	Tyrrell-Ford	7/10	6/DNQ	5/9	3/R	9/R	R/R	4/10	R/R
6	Lotus-Judd	8/R	NC/R	R/DNQ	11/R	R/R	4/DNQ	8/R	4/8
7	Arrows-Ford	5/R	5/9	7/R	7/R	3/R	R/R	7/12	9/DNQ
8	Dallara-Ford	13/DNPQ	7/10	4/13	13/R	8/R	3/6	R/DNQ	R/DNPQ
9	Brabham-Judd	R/R	R/R	3/6	9/10	R/R	R/DNPQ	R/DNPQ	R/R
10	Onyx-Ford	DNPQ/ DNPQ	DNPQ/ DNPQ	DNPQ/ DNPQ	R/DNPQ	R/DNPQ	DQ/DNPQ	5/13	12/DNPQ
11	Minardi-Ford	R/R	R/R	R/R	R/DNQ	R/R	R/R	R/DNQ	5/6
12	March-Judd CG891	3/R	R/R	11/R	R/DNQ	R/DQ	R/R	NC/R	R/R
13	Rial-Ford	14/DNPQ	DNQ/ DNPQ	DNQ/ DNPQ	12/DNPQ	4/DNPQ	8/DNPQ	DNQ/ DNPQ	DNQ/ DNPQ
14	Ligier-Ford	9/DNQ	DQ/DNQ	12/R	8/14	DNQ/DNQ	5/DNQ	6/R	7/DNQ
15	AGS-Ford	DNPQ	8/DNPQ	R/DNPQ	6/DNPQ	7/DNPQ	R/DNPQ	R/DNPQ	DNQ/DNPQ
15	Lola-Lamborghini	12/DNQ	R/NS	R/DNQ	NC/DNQ	R/DNQ	R/DNQ	11/R	R/R

Pos	Team-Engine	R9	R10	R11	R12	R13	R14	R15	R16	Total
1	McLaren-Honda	1/2	2/4	1/2	1/R	2/R	1/3	DQ/R	R/R	141
2	Williams-Renault	4/R	3/R	4/R	3/4	R/R	5/R	2/3	1/3	77
3	Ferrari	3/R	1/R	3/R	2/R	1/DQ	2	R/R	R/R	59
4	Benetton-Ford	R/R	8/R	5/10	R/R	4/R	R/R	1/R	2/5	39
5	Tyrrell-Ford	10/R	9/13	14/R	5/R	6/DNQ	4/10	R/R	R/DNQ	16
6	Lotus-Judd	5/R	6/R	DNQ/DNQ	10/R	7/R	8/R	4/R	4/R	15
7	Arrows-Ford	6/12	5/10	6/R	R/DNQ	R/R	9/R	6/8	R/R	13
8	Dallara-Ford	7/R	7/R	11/R	11/R	R/R	7/R	9/10	R/R	8
9	Brabham-Judd	8/R	11/12	R/R	6/DNQ	8/14	R/R	5/R	8/R	8
10	Onyx-Ford	R/DNQ	R/R	8/R	R/DNPQ	3/DNPQ	R/DNPQ	DNPQ/ DNPQ	R/DNPQ	6
11	Minardi-Ford	9/DNQ	R/R	9/15	7/8	5/12	R/R	R/R	6/DNQ	6
12	March-Judd CG891	R/R	R/R	7/12	R/R	10/R	R/R	7/R	7/R	4
13	Rial-Ford	DNQ/DNQ	DNQ/DNQ	DNQ/DNQ	DNQ/DNQ	DNQ/DNQ	DNQ/DNQ	DNQ/DNQ	DNQ/DNQ	3
14	Ligier-Ford	11/R	DNQ/DNQ	13/R	9/R	13/DNQ	R/DNQ	R/DNQ	R/R	3
15	AGS-Ford	DNPQ/ DNPQ	DNPQ/ DNPQ	DNPQ/ DNPQ	DNPQ/ DNPQ	DNPQ/ DNPQ	DNPQ/ DNPQ	DNPQ/ DNPQ	DNPQ/ DNPQ	1
15	Lola-Lamborghini	R/R	R/DNPQ	16/R	R/R	9/11	6/DNPQ	R/DNQ	R/DNPQ	1

SYMBOLS AND GRAND PRIX KEY

Round 1	Brazilian GP	Round 9	German GP
Round 2	San Marino GP	Round 10	Hungarian GP
Round 3	Monaco GP	Round 11	Belgian GP
Round 4	Mexican GP	Round 12	Italian GP
Round 5	United States GP	Round 13	Portuguese GP
Round 6	Canadian GP	Round 14	Spanish GP
Round 7	French GP	Round 15	Japanese GP
Round 8	British GP	Round 16	Australian GP

SCORING

1st	9 points
2nd	6 points
3rd	4 points
4th	3 points
5th	2 points
6th	1 point

DNPQ DID NOT PRE-QUALIFY DNQ DID NOT QUALIFY DQ DISQUALIFIED EX EXCLUDED
F FASTEST LAP NC NOT CLASSIFIED NS NON-STARTER P POLE POSITION R RETIRED

THE 1990s

1990

SEASON SUMMARY

After another titanic season of intense competition between the sport's two top drivers, Ayrton Senna defeated Alain Prost, but only after another clash at the Japanese GP. This time they were no longer team-mates, with Prost having left McLaren to lead Ferrari's attack. The move was one of the most blatant in F1 history, with Senna simply driving Prost off the circuit at the first corner. Every other driver was merely in the supporting cast, with Nelson Piquet winning the final two rounds to end up equal-third with the new McLaren number two, Gerhard Berger, while Jean Alesi really impressed for Tyrrell.

MINARDI'S MAGIC MOMENT

Six years into its unrequited bid for F1 glory, Minardi had a huge fillip for the opening race when Pierluigi Martini shocked everyone by qualifying on the front row on the streets of Phoenix. Pirelli provided a qualifying tyre superior to Goodyear's, leaving him just 0.067 seconds behind Senna. In the race, Martini fell to a lapped seventh.

UNITED STATES GRAND PRIX

PHOENIX • ROUND 1 • DATE: 11TH MARCH 1990
Laps: 72 • Distance: 169.917miles/273.456km • Weather: Cool & dull

Pos	Driver	Team	Chassis-Engine	Result	Qual
1	Ayrton Senna	McLaren	McLaren-Honda MP4/5B	1h52m32.829s	5
2	Jean Alesi	Tyrrell	Tyrrell-Ford Cosworth 018	1h52m41.514s	4
3	Thierry Boutsen	Williams	Williams-Renault FW13B	1h53m26.909s	9
4	Nelson Piquet	Benetton	Benetton-Ford Cosworth B189B	1h53m41.187s	6
5	Stefano Modena	Brabham	Brabham-Judd BT58	1h53m42.332s	10
6	Satoru Nakajima	Tyrrell	Tyrrell-Ford Cosworth 018	71 laps	11
7	Pierluigi Martini	Minardi	Minardi-Ford Cosworth M189	71 laps	2
8	Eric Bernard	Larrousse	Lola-Lamborghini LC89	71 laps	15
9	Riccardo Patrese	Williams	Williams-Renault FW13B	71 laps	12
10	Michele Alboreto	Arrows	Arrows-Ford Cosworth A11B	70 laps	21
11	Alessandro Nannini	Benetton	Benetton-Ford Cosworth B189B	70 laps	22
12	Bernd Schneider	Arrows	Arrows-Ford Cosworth A11	70 laps	20
13	Roberto Moreno	EuroBrun	EuroBrun-Judd ER189	67 laps	16
14	Mauricio Gugelmin	Leyton House	Leyton House-Judd CG901	66 laps	25
R	Paolo Barilla	Minardi	Minardi-Ford Cosworth M189	54 laps/physical	14
R	Aguri Suzuki	Larrousse	Lola-Lamborghini LC89	53 laps/brakes	18
R	Nigel Mansell	Ferrari	Ferrari 641	49 laps/engine	17
R	Gerhard Berger	McLaren	McLaren-Honda MP4/5B	44 laps/clutch	1
R	Olivier Grouillard	Osella	Osella-Ford Cosworth FA1M	39 laps/collision	8
R	Gregor Foitek	Brabham	Brabham-Judd BT58	39 laps/accident	23
R	Andrea de Cesaris	BMS Scuderia Italia	Dallara-Ford Cosworth 190	25 laps/engine	3
R	Alain Prost	Ferrari	Ferrari 641	21 laps/oil leak	7
R	Ivan Capelli	Leyton House	Leyton House-Judd CG901	20 laps/electrical	26

Pos	Driver	Team	Chassis-Engine	Result	Qual
R	Derek Warwick	Lotus	Lotus-Lamborghini 102	6 laps/suspension	24
R	Nicola Larini	Ligier	Ligier-Ford Cosworth JS33B	4 laps/throttle	13
NS	Martin Donnelly	Lotus	Lotus-Lamborghini 102	gearbox	19
DNQ	Stefan Johansson	Onyx	Onyx-Ford Cosworth ORE-1	-	27
DNQ	Gianni Morbidelli	BMS Scuderia Italia	Dallara-Ford Cosworth 190	-	28
DNQ	JJ Lehto	Onyx	Onyx-Ford Cosworth ORE-1	-	29
DNPQ	Gabriele Tarquini	AGS	AGS-Ford Cosworth JH24	-	30
DNPQ	Yannick Dalmas	AGS	AGS-Ford Cosworth JH24	-	31
DNPQ	Claudio Langes	EuroBrun	EuroBrun-Judd ER189	-	32
DNPQ	Gary Brabham	Life	Life F190	-	33
DNPQ	Bertrand Gachot	Coloni	Coloni-Subaru C3B	-	34
EX	Philippe Alliot*	Ligier	Ligier-Ford Cosworth JS33B	outside assistance	-

*disqualified from qualifying

Pole: Berger, 1m28.664s, 95.821mph/154.209kph. Fastest lap: Berger, 1m31.050s, 93.310mph/150.168kph on Lap 34. Race leaders: Alesi 1-34, Senna 35-72

NEW-LOOK INTERLAGOS IMPRESSES

The first Brazilian GP at Interlagos since 1980 had a new look as the circuit had been modernised and its lap cut back from 4.893 to 2.667 miles (7.874 to 4.292km). Instead of starting the lap on a lightly banked left beneath the grandstands, it dropped left then right through the Senna S and ran a simpler course around its sloping site.

BRAZILIAN GRAND PRIX

INTERLAGOS • ROUND 2 • DATE: 25TH MARCH 1990
Laps: 71 • Distance: 190.807miles/307.075km • Weather: Hot & bright

Pos	Driver	Team	Chassis-Engine	Result	Qual
1	Alain Prost	Ferrari	Ferrari 641	1h37m21.258s	6
2	Gerhard Berger	McLaren	McLaren-Honda MP4/5B	1h37m34.822s	2
3	Ayrton Senna	McLaren	McLaren-Honda MP4/5B	1h37m58.980s	1
4	Nigel Mansell	Ferrari	Ferrari 641	1h38m08.524s	5
5	Thierry Boutsen	Williams	Williams-Renault FW13B	70 laps	3
6	Nelson Piquet	Benetton	Benetton-Ford Cosworth B189B	70 laps	13
7	Jean Alesi	Tyrrell	Tyrrell-Ford Cosworth 018	70 laps	7
8	Satoru Nakajima	Tyrrell	Tyrrell-Ford Cosworth 018	70 laps	19
9	Pierluigi Martini	Minardi	Minardi-Ford Cosworth M189	69 laps	8
10	Alessandro Nannini	Benetton	Benetton-Ford Cosworth B189B	68 laps/puncture	15
11	Nicola Larini	Ligier	Ligier-Ford Cosworth JS33B	68 laps	20
12	Philippe Alliot	Ligier	Ligier-Ford Cosworth JS33B	68 laps	10
13	Riccardo Patrese	Williams	Williams-Renault FW13B	65 laps/fuel pressure	4
14	Gianni Morbidelli	BMS Scuderia Italia	Dallara-Ford Cosworth 190	64 laps	16
R	Alex Caffi	Arrows	Arrows-Ford Cosworth A11B	49 laps/clutch	25
R	Martin Donnelly	Lotus	Lotus-Lamborghini 102	43 laps/spun off	14
R	Stefano Modena	Brabham	Brabham-Judd BT58	39 laps/spun off	12
R	Paolo Barilla	Minardi	Minardi-Ford Cosworth M189	38 laps/engine	17
R	Yannick Dalmas	AGS	AGS-Ford Cosworth JH24	28 laps/suspension	26
R	Derek Warwick	Lotus	Lotus-Lamborghini 102	25 laps/electrical	24
R	Aguri Suzuki	Larrousse	Lola-Lamborghini LC89	24 laps/suspension	18

Pos	Driver	Team	Chassis-Engine	Result	Qual
R	Michele Alboreto	Arrows	Arrows-Ford Cosworth A11B	24 laps/suspension	23
R	Gregor Foitek	Brabham	Brabham-Judd BT58	14 laps/transmission	22
R	Eric Bernard	Larrousse	Lola-Lamborghini LC89	13 laps/gearbox	11
R	Olivier Grouillard	Osella	Osella-Ford Cosworth FA1M	8 laps/collision	21
R	Andrea de Cesaris	BMS Scuderia Italia	Dallara-Ford Cosworth 190	0 laps/collision	9
DNQ	Stefan Johansson	Onyx	Onyx-Ford Cosworth ORE-1	-	27
DNQ	JJ Lehto	Onyx	Onyx-Ford Cosworth ORE-1	-	28
DNQ	Ivan Capelli	Leyton House	Leyton House-Judd CG901	-	29
DNQ	Mauricio Gugelmin	Leyton House	Leyton House-Judd CG901	-	30
DNPQ	Gabriele Tarquini	AGS	AGS-Ford Cosworth JH24	-	31
DNPQ	Roberto Moreno	EuroBrun	EuroBrun-Judd ER189	-	32
DNPQ	Bertrand Gachot	Coloni	Coloni-Subaru C3B	-	33
DNPQ	Claudio Langes	EuroBrun	EuroBrun-Judd ER189	-	34
DNPQ	Gary Brabham	Life	Life F190	-	35

Pole: Senna, 1m17.277s, 125.195mph/201.482kph. Fastest lap: Berger, 1m19.899s, 121.087mph/194.871kph on Lap 55. Race leaders: Senna 1-32 & 35-40, Berger 33-34, Prost 41-71

HUGE LEAP FORWARDS

Leyton House hadn't scored in the first six races, but Adrian Newey's aero changes transformed its hopes for the French GP. The team was set for a one-two at Paul Ricard, as Ivan Capelli led for 45 laps, with Mauricio Gugelmin second until his engine failed. Cruelly, Capelli was hit by a fuel pick-up problem with three laps to go, so Alain Prost won for Ferrari.

SAN MARINO GRAND PRIX

IMOLA • ROUND 3 • DATE: 13TH MAY 1990
Laps: 61 • Distance: 190.788miles/307.44km • Weather: Warm & bright

Pos	Driver	Team	Chassis-Engine	Result	Qual
1	Riccardo Patrese	Williams	Williams-Renault FW13B	1h30m55.478s	3
2	Gerhard Berger	McLaren	McLaren-Honda MP4/5B	1h31m00.595s	2
3	Alessandro Nannini	Benetton	Benetton-Ford Cosworth B190	1h31m01.718s	9
4	Alain Prost	Ferrari	Ferrari 641/2	1h31m02.321s	6
5	Nelson Piquet	Benetton	Benetton-Ford Cosworth B190	1h31m48.590s	8
6	Jean Alesi	Tyrrell	Tyrrell-Ford Cosworth 019	60 laps	7
7	Derek Warwick	Lotus	Lotus-Lamborghini 102	60 laps	11
8	Martin Donnelly	Lotus	Lotus-Lamborghini 102	60 laps	12
9	Philippe Alliot	Ligier	Ligier-Ford Cosworth JS33B	60 laps	17
10	Nicola Larini	Ligier	Ligier-Ford Cosworth JS33B	59 laps	21
11	Paolo Barilla	Minardi	Minardi-Ford Cosworth M190	59 laps	27
12	JJ Lehto	Onyx	Onyx-Ford Cosworth ORE-2	59 laps	26
13	Eric Bernard	Larrousse	Lola-Lamborghini 90	56 laps/clutch	14
R	Olivier Grouillard	Osella	Osella-Ford Cosworth FA1M-E	52 laps/wheel	23
R	Nigel Mansell	Ferrari	Ferrari 641/2	38 laps/engine	5
R	Gregor Foitek	Onyx	Onyx-Ford Cosworth ORE-2	35 laps/engine	24
R	Stefano Modena	Brabham	Brabham-Judd BT59	31 laps/brakes	15
R	Andrea de Cesaris	BMS Scuderia Italia	Dallara-Ford Cosworth 190	29 laps/wheel	18
R	Mauricio Gugelmin	Leyton House	Leyton House-Judd CG901	24 laps/electrical	13

Pos	Driver	Team	Chassis-Engine	Result	Qual
R	Thierry Boutsen	Williams	Williams-Renault FW13B	17 laps/engine	4
R	Aguri Suzuki	Larrousse	Lola-Lamborghini 90	17 laps/clutch	16
R	Ayrton Senna	McLaren	McLaren-Honda MP4/5B	3 laps/wheel	1
R	Emanuele Pirro	BMS Scuderia Italia	Dallara-Ford Cosworth 190	2 laps/spun off	22
R	Ivan Capelli	Leyton House	Leyton House-Judd CG901	0 laps/collision	19
R	Satoru Nakajima	Tyrrell	Tyrrell-Ford Cosworth 019	0 laps/collision	20
R	Roberto Moreno	EuroBrun	EuroBrun-Judd ER189B	0 laps/throttle	25
NS	Pierluigi Martini	Minardi	Minardi-Ford Cosworth M190	Driver injured	10
DNQ	Alex Caffi	Arrows	Arrows-Ford Cosworth A11B	-	28
DNQ	Michele Alboreto	Arrows	Arrows-Ford Cosworth A11B	-	29
DNQ	David Brabham	Brabham	Brabham-Judd BT59	-	30
DNPQ	Bertrand Gachot	Coloni	Coloni-Subaru C3B	-	31
DNPQ	Claudio Langes	EuroBrun	EuroBrun-Judd ER189B	-	32
DNPQ	Bruno Giacomelli	Life	Life F190	-	33
DNPQ	Gabriele Tarquini	AGS	AGS-Ford Cosworth JH25	-	34

Pole: Senna, 1m23.220s, 135.474mph/218.024kph. Fastest lap: Nannini, 1m27.156s, 129.356mph/208.178kph on Lap 60. Race leaders: Senna 1-3, Boutsen 4-17, Berger 18-50, Patrese 51-61

UNDER PRESSURE

Thierry Boutsen was an underrated talent, but he showed that he was made of stern stuff when he resisted intense pressure to win the Hungarian GP. The Belgian led from pole, initially from Gerhard Berger before the other McLaren driver, Ayrton Senna, knocked Alessandro Nannini off to lead the chase for the final 14 laps.

MONACO GRAND PRIX

MONTE CARLO • ROUND 4 • DATE: 27TH MAY 1990
Laps: 78 • Distance: 161.298miles/259.584km • Weather: Warm & bright

Pos	Driver	Team	Chassis-Engine	Result	Qual
1	Ayrton Senna	McLaren	McLaren-Honda MP4/5B	1h52m46.982s	1
2	Jean Alesi	Tyrrell	Tyrrell-Ford Cosworth 019	1h52m48.069s	3
3	Gerhard Berger	McLaren	McLaren-Honda MP4/5B	1h52m49.055s	5
4	Thierry Boutsen	Williams	Williams-Renault FW13B	77 laps	6
5	Alex Caffi	Arrows	Arrows-Ford Cosworth A11B	76 laps	22
6	Eric Bernard	Larrousse	Lola-Lamborghini 90	76 laps	24
7	Gregor Foitek	Onyx	Onyx-Ford Cosworth ORE-2	72 laps/collision	20
R	Derek Warwick	Lotus	Lotus-Lamborghini 102	66 laps/spun off	13
R	Nigel Mansell	Ferrari	Ferrari 641/2	63 laps/battery	7
R	Paolo Barilla	Minardi	Minardi-Ford Cosworth M190	52 laps/gearbox	19
R	JJ Lehto	Onyx	Onyx-Ford Cosworth ORE-2	52 laps/gearbox	26
R	Philippe Alliot	Ligier	Ligier-Ford Cosworth JS33B	47 laps/gearbox	18
R	Riccardo Patrese	Williams	Williams-Renault FW13B	41 laps/engine	4
R	Andrea de Cesaris	BMS Scuderia Italia	Dallara-Ford Cosworth 190	38 laps/engine	12
R	Satoru Nakajima	Tyrrell	Tyrrell-Ford Cosworth 019	36 laps/spun off	21
DQ	Nelson Piquet*	Benetton	Benetton-Ford Cosworth B190	36 laps/push start	10
R	Alain Prost	Ferrari	Ferrari 641/2	30 laps/battery	2
R	Alessandro Nannini	Benetton	Benetton-Ford Cosworth B190	20 laps/gearbox	16
R	David Brabham	Brabham	Brabham-Judd BT59	16 laps/transmission	25

Pos	Driver	Team	Chassis-Engine	Result	Qual
R	Ivan Capelli	Leyton House	Leyton House-Judd CG901	13 laps/brakes	23
R	Nicola Larini	Ligier	Ligier-Ford Cosworth JS33B	12 laps/differential	17
R	Aguri Suzuki	Larrousse	Lola-Lamborghini 90	11 laps/steering	15
R	Pierluigi Martini	Minardi	Minardi-Ford Cosworth M190	7 laps/electrical	8
R	Martin Donnelly	Lotus	Lotus-Lamborghini 102	6 laps/gearbox	11
R	Stefano Modena	Brabham	Brabham-Judd BT59	3 laps/transmission	14
NS	Emanuele Pirro	BMS Scuderia Italia	Dallara-Ford Cosworth 190	stalled	9
DNQ	Michele Alboreto	Arrows	Arrows-Ford Cosworth A11B	-	27
DNQ	Olivier Grouillard	Osella	Osella-Ford Cosworth FA1M-E	-	28
DNQ	Mauricio Gugelmin	Leyton House	Leyton House-Judd CG901	-	29
DNQ	Roberto Moreno	EuroBrun	EuroBrun-Judd ER189B	-	30
DNPQ	Gabriele Tarquini	AGS	AGS-Ford Cosworth JH25	-	31
DNPQ	Yannick Dalmas	AGS	AGS-Ford Cosworth JH25	-	32
DNPQ	Claudio Langes	EuroBrun	EuroBrun-Judd ER189B	-	33
DNPQ	Bertrand Gachot	Coloni	Coloni-Subaru C3B	-	34
DNPQ	Bruno Giacomelli	Life	Life F190	-	35

*disqualified – outside assistance

Pole: Senna, 1m21.314s, 91.552mph/147.339kph. Fastest lap: Senna, 1m24.468s, 88.134mph/141.838kph on Lap 59. Race leaders: Senna 1-78

CANADIAN GRAND PRIX

MONTREAL • ROUND 5 • DATE: 10TH JUNE 1990
Laps: 70 • Distance: 190.762miles/307.3km • Weather: Warm, drying track

Pos	Driver	Team	Chassis-Engine	Result	Qual
1	Ayrton Senna	McLaren	McLaren-Honda MP4/5B	1h42m56.400s	1
2	Nelson Piquet	Benetton	Benetton-Ford Cosworth B190	1h43m06.897s	5
3	Nigel Mansell	Ferrari	Ferrari 641/2	1h43m09.785s	7
4	Gerhard Berger	McLaren	McLaren-Honda MP4/5B	1h43m11.254s	2
5	Alain Prost	Ferrari	Ferrari 641/2	1h43m12.220s	3
6	Derek Warwick	Lotus	Lotus-Lamborghini 102	68 laps	11
7	Stefano Modena	Brabham	Brabham-Judd BT59	68 laps	10
8	Alex Caffi	Arrows	Arrows-Ford Cosworth A11B	68 laps	26
9	Eric Bernard	Larrousse	Lola-Lamborghini 90	67 laps	23
10	Ivan Capelli	Leyton House	Leyton House-Judd CG901	67 laps	24
11	Satoru Nakajima	Tyrrell	Tyrrell-Ford Cosworth 019	67 laps	13
12	Aguri Suzuki	Larrousse	Lola-Lamborghini 90	66 laps	18
13	Olivier Grouillard	Osella	Osella-Ford Cosworth FA1M-E	65 laps	15
R	Martin Donnelly	Lotus	Lotus-Lamborghini 102	57 laps/engine	12
R	Gregor Foitek	Onyx	Onyx-Ford Cosworth ORE-2	53 laps/engine	21
R	Andrea de Cesaris	BMS Scuderia Italia	Dallara-Ford Cosworth 190	50 laps/gearbox	25
R	JJ Lehto	Onyx	Onyx-Ford Cosworth ORE-2	46 laps/engine	22
R	Riccardo Patrese	Williams	Williams-Renault FW13B	44 laps/brakes	9
R	Philippe Alliot	Ligier	Ligier-Ford Cosworth JS33B	34 laps/engine	17
R	Jean Alesi	Tyrrell	Tyrrell-Ford Cosworth 019	26 laps/spun off	8
R	Alessandro Nannini	Benetton	Benetton-Ford Cosworth B190	21 laps/spun off	4
R	Thierry Boutsen	Williams	Williams-Renault FW13B	19 laps/collision	6
R	Nicola Larini	Ligier	Ligier-Ford Cosworth JS33B	18 laps/collision	20
R	Michele Alboreto	Arrows	Arrows-Ford Cosworth A11B	11 laps/collision	14
R	Emanuele Pirro	BMS Scuderia Italia	Dallara-Ford Cosworth 190	11 laps/collision	19
R	Pierluigi Martini	Minardi	Minardi-Ford Cosworth M190	0 laps/spun off	16
DNQ	Roberto Moreno	EuroBrun	EuroBrun-Judd ER189B	-	27
DNQ	Mauricio Gugelmin	Leyton House	Leyton House-Judd CG901	-	28
DNQ	Paolo Barilla	Minardi	Minardi-Ford Cosworth M190	-	29

Pos	Driver	Team	Chassis-Engine	Result	Qual
DNQ	David Brabham	Brabham	Brabham-Judd BT59	-	30
DNPQ	Gabriele Tarquini	AGS	AGS-Ford Cosworth JH25	-	31
DNPQ	Yannick Dalmas	AGS	AGS-Ford Cosworth JH25	-	32
DNPQ	Bertrand Gachot	Coloni	Coloni-Subaru C3B	-	33
DNPQ	Claudio Langes	EuroBrun	EuroBrun-Judd ER189B	-	34
DNPQ	Bruno Giacomelli	Life	Life F190	-	35

Pole: Senna, 1m20.399s, 122.142mph/196.569kph. Fastest lap: Berger, 1m22.077s, 119.645mph/192.550kph on Lap 70. Race leaders: Senna 1-11 & 15-70, Nannini 12-14

MEXICAN GRAND PRIX

MEXICO CITY • ROUND 6 • DATE: 24TH JUNE 1990
Laps: 69 • Distance: 189.548miles/305.049km • Weather: Warm but dull

Pos	Driver	Team	Chassis-Engine	Result	Qual
1	Alain Prost	Ferrari	Ferrari 641/2	1h32m35.783s	13
2	Nigel Mansell	Ferrari	Ferrari 641/2	1h33m01.134s	4
3	Gerhard Berger	McLaren	McLaren-Honda MP4/5B	1h33m01.313s	1
4	Alessandro Nannini	Benetton	Benetton-Ford Cosworth B190	1h33m16.882s	14
5	Thierry Boutsen	Williams	Williams-Renault FW13B	1h33m22.452s	5
6	Nelson Piquet	Benetton	Benetton-Ford Cosworth B190	1h33m22.726s	8
7	Jean Alesi	Tyrrell	Tyrrell-Ford Cosworth 019	1h33m24.860s	6
8	Martin Donnelly	Lotus	Lotus-Lamborghini 102	1h33m41.925s	12
9	Riccardo Patrese	Williams	Williams-Renault FW13B	1h33m45.701s	2
10	Derek Warwick	Lotus	Lotus-Lamborghini 102	68 laps	11
11	Stefano Modena	Brabham	Brabham-Judd BT59	68 laps	10
12	Pierluigi Martini	Minardi	Minardi-Ford Cosworth M190	68 laps	7
13	Andrea de Cesaris	BMS Scuderia Italia	Dallara-Ford Cosworth 190	68 laps	15
14	Paolo Barilla	Minardi	Minardi-Ford Cosworth M190	67 laps	16
15	Gregor Foitek	Onyx	Onyx-Ford Cosworth ORE-2	67 laps	23
16	Nicola Larini	Ligier	Ligier-Ford Cosworth JS33B	67 laps	24
17	Michele Alboreto	Arrows	Arrows-Ford Cosworth A11B	66 laps	17
18	Philippe Alliot	Ligier	Ligier-Ford Cosworth JS33B	66 laps	22
19	Olivier Grouillard	Osella	Osella-Ford Cosworth FA1M-E	65 laps	20
20	Ayrton Senna	McLaren	McLaren-Honda MP4/5B	63 laps/puncture	3
R	JJ Lehto	Onyx	Onyx-Ford Cosworth ORE-2	26 laps/engine	27
R	Eric Bernard	Larrousse	Lola-Lamborghini 90	12 laps/brakes	26
R	Satoru Nakajima	Tyrrell	Tyrrell-Ford Cosworth 019	11 laps/collision	9
R	Aguri Suzuki	Larrousse	Lola-Lamborghini 90	11 laps/collision	19
R	David Brabham	Brabham	Brabham-Judd BT59	11 laps/electrical	21
R	Emanuele Pirro	BMS Scuderia Italia	Dallara-Ford Cosworth 190	10 laps/engine	18
EX	Roberto Moreno*	EuroBrun	EuroBrun-Judd ER189B	push start	25
DNQ	Ivan Capelli	Leyton House	Leyton House-Judd CG901	-	28
DNQ	Mauricio Gugelmin	Leyton House	Leyton House-Judd CG901	-	29
DNQ	Alex Caffi	Arrows	Arrows-Ford Cosworth A11B	-	30
DNPQ	Yannick Dalmas	AGS	AGS-Ford Cosworth JH25	-	31
DNPQ	Gabriele Tarquini	AGS	AGS-Ford Cosworth JH25	-	32
DNPQ	Bertrand Gachot	Coloni	Coloni-Subaru C3B	-	33
DNPQ	Claudio Langes	EuroBrun	EuroBrun-Judd ER189B	-	34
DNPQ	Bruno Giacomelli	Life	Life F190	-	35

*disqualified from qualifying

Pole: Berger, 1m17.227s, 128.057mph/206.088kph. Fastest lap: Prost, 1m17.958s, 126.856mph/204.156kph on Lap 58. Race leaders: Senna 1-60, Prost 61-69

FRENCH GRAND PRIX

CIRCUIT PAUL RICARD • ROUND 7 • DATE: 8TH JULY 1990
Laps: 80 • Distance: 189.520miles/305.04km • Weather: Hot & bright

Pos	Driver	Team	Chassis-Engine	Result	Qual
1	Alain Prost	Ferrari	Ferrari 641/2	1h33m29.606s	4
2	Ivan Capelli	Leyton House	Leyton House-Judd CG901	1h33m38.232s	7
3	Ayrton Senna	McLaren	McLaren-Honda MP4/5B	1h33m41.212s	3
4	Nelson Piquet	Benetton	Benetton-Ford Cosworth B190	1h34m10.813s	9
5	Gerhard Berger	McLaren	McLaren-Honda MP4/5B	1h34m11.825s	2
6	Riccardo Patrese	Williams	Williams-Renault FW13B	1h34m38.957s	6
7	Aguri Suzuki	Larrousse	Lola-Lamborghini 90	79 laps	14
8	Eric Bernard	Larrousse	Lola-Lamborghini 90	79 laps	11
9	Philippe Alliot	Ligier	Ligier-Ford Cosworth JS33B	79 laps	12
10	Michele Alboreto	Arrows	Arrows-Ford Cosworth A11B	79 laps	18
11	Derek Warwick	Lotus	Lotus-Lamborghini 102	79 laps	16
12	Martin Donnelly	Lotus	Lotus-Lamborghini 102	79 laps	17
13	Stefano Modena	Brabham	Brabham-Judd BT59	78 laps	20
14	Nicola Larini	Ligier	Ligier-Ford Cosworth JS33B	78 laps	19
DQ	Andrea de Cesaris*	BMS Scuderia Italia	Dallara-Ford Cosworth 190	78 laps/underweight	21
15	David Brabham	Brabham	Brabham-Judd BT59	77 laps	25
16	Alessandro Nannini	Benetton	Benetton-Ford Cosworth B190	75 laps/electrical	5
17	Yannick Dalmas	AGS	AGS-Ford Cosworth JH25	75 laps	26
18	Nigel Mansell	Ferrari	Ferrari 641/2	72 laps/engine	1
R	Satoru Nakajima	Tyrrell	Tyrrell-Ford Cosworth 019	63 laps/gearbox	15
R	Mauricio Gugelmin	Leyton House	Leyton House-Judd CG901	58 laps/engine	10
R	Pierluigi Martini	Minardi	Minardi-Ford Cosworth M190	40 laps/electrical	23
R	Jean Alesi	Tyrrell	Tyrrell-Ford Cosworth 019	23 laps/differential	13
R	Alex Caffi	Arrows	Arrows-Ford Cosworth A11B	22 laps/suspension	22
R	Thierry Boutsen	Williams	Williams-Renault FW13B	8 laps/engine	8
R	Emanuele Pirro	BMS Scuderia Italia	Dallara-Ford Cosworth 190	7 laps/brakes	24
DNQ	Paolo Barilla	Minardi	Minardi-Ford Cosworth M190	-	27
DNQ	Gabriele Tarquini	AGS	AGS-Ford Cosworth JH25	-	28
DNQ	Gregor Foitek	Onyx	Onyx-Ford Cosworth ORE-2	-	29
DNQ	JJ Lehto	Onyx	Onyx-Ford Cosworth ORE-2	-	30
DNPQ	Olivier Grouillard	Osella	Osella-Ford Cosworth FA1M-E	-	31
DNPQ	Roberto Moreno	EuroBrun	EuroBrun-Judd ER189B	-	32
DNPQ	Claudio Langes	EuroBrun	EuroBrun-Judd ER189B	-	33
DNPQ	Bertrand Gachot	Coloni	Coloni-Subaru C3B	-	34
DNPQ	Bruno Giacomelli	Life	Life F190	-	35

*disqualified - car underweight

Pole: Mansell, 1m04.402s, 132.440mph/213.142kph. Fastest lap: Mansell, 1m08.012s, 125.410mph/201.829kph on Lap 64. Race leaders: Berger 1-27, Senna 28-29, Mansell 30-31, Patrese 32, Capelli 33-77, Prost 78-80

LIKE A PLANE CRASH

Martin Donnelly had a monumental accident in qualifying for the Spanish GP at Jerez and it almost defied belief that he survived when his Lotus speared off into the barriers at a sixth-gear corner behind the pits and disintegrated, leaving him lying unconscious in the track. Rules were passed before the end of the year to make the cars stronger.

BRITISH GRAND PRIX

SILVERSTONE • ROUND 8 • DATE: 15TH JULY 1990
Laps: 64 • Distance: 190.14miles/305.798km • Weather: Hot & bright

Pos	Driver	Team	Chassis-Engine	Result	Qual
1	Alain Prost	Ferrari	Ferrari 641/2	1h18m30.999s	5
2	Thierry Boutsen	Williams	Williams-Renault FW13B	1h19m10.091s	4
3	Ayrton Senna	McLaren	McLaren-Honda MP4/5B	1h19m14.087s	2
4	Eric Bernard	Larrousse	Lola-Lamborghini 90	1h19m46.301s	8
5	Nelson Piquet	Benetton	Benetton-Ford Cosworth B190	1h19m55.002s	11
6	Aguri Suzuki	Larrousse	Lola-Lamborghini 90	63 laps	9
7	Alex Caffi	Arrows	Arrows-Ford Cosworth A11b	63 laps	17
8	Jean Alesi	Tyrrell	Tyrrell-Ford Cosworth 019	63 laps	6
9	Stefano Modena	Brabham	Brabham-Judd BT59	62 laps	20
10	Nicola Larini	Ligier	Ligier-Ford Cosworth JS33B	62 laps	21
11	Emanuele Pirro	BMS Scuderia Italia	Dallara-Ford Cosworth 190	62 laps	19
12	Paolo Barilla	Minardi	Minardi-Ford Cosworth M190	62 laps	24
13	Philippe Alliot	Ligier	Ligier-Ford Cosworth JS33B	61 laps	22
14	Gerhard Berger	McLaren	McLaren-Honda MP4/5B	60 laps/throttle	3
R	Nigel Mansell	Ferrari	Ferrari 641/2	55 laps/gearbox	1
R	Ivan Capelli	Leyton House	Leyton House-Judd CG901	48 laps/oil leak	10
R	Martin Donnelly	Lotus	Lotus-Lamborghini 102	48 laps/engine	14
R	Derek Warwick	Lotus	Lotus-Lamborghini 102	46 laps/engine	16
R	Gabriele Tarquini	AGS	AGS-Ford Cosworth JH25	41 laps/engine	26
R	Michele Alboreto	Arrows	Arrows-Ford Cosworth A11B	37 laps/engine	25
R	Riccardo Patrese	Williams	Williams-Renault FW13B	26 laps/chassis	7
R	Satoru Nakajima	Tyrrell	Tyrrell-Ford Cosworth 019	20 laps/electrical	12
R	Alessandro Nannini	Benetton	Benetton-Ford Cosworth B190	15 laps/collision	13
R	Andrea de Cesaris	BMS Scuderia Italia	Dallara-Ford Cosworth 190	12 laps/fuel system	23
R	Pierluigi Martini	Minardi	Minardi-Ford Cosworth M190	3 laps/alternator	18
NS	Mauricio Gugelmin	Leyton House	Leyton House-Judd CG901	Fuel pump drive	15
DNQ	Olivier Grouillard	Osella	Osella-Ford Cosworth FA1ME	-	27
DNQ	David Brabham	Brabham	Brabham-Judd BT59	-	28
DNQ	JJ Lehto	Onyx	Onyx-Ford Cosworth ORE-2	-	29
DNQ	Gregor Foitek	Onyx	Onyx-Ford Cosworth ORE-2	-	30
DNPQ	Roberto Moreno	EuroBrun	EuroBrun-Judd ER189B	-	31
DNPQ	Yannick Dalmas	AGS	AGS-Ford Cosworth JH25	-	32
DNPQ	Claudio Langes	EuroBrun	EuroBrun-Judd ER189B	-	33
DNPQ	Bertrand Gachot	Coloni	Coloni-Subaru C3B	-	34
DNPQ	Bruno Giacomelli	Life	Life F190	-	35

Pole: Mansell, 1m07.428s, 158.514mph/255.104kph. Fastest lap: Mansell, 1m11.291s, 149.925mph/241.280kph on Lap 51. Race leaders: Senna 1-11, Mansell 12-21 & 28-42, Berger 22-27, Prost 43-64

DENIED BY INJURY

Alessandro Nannini's sparkling form through 1990 – with second place at Hockenheim for Benetton – led to him being talked of as a possible Ferrari driver for 1991, but he then suffered severe arm injuries in a helicopter accident and his chance was gone. He did race again though, starring in touring cars in 1992.

GERMAN GRAND PRIX

HOCKENHEIM • ROUND 9 • DATE: 29TH JULY 1990
Laps: 45 • Distance: 190.145miles/306.09km • Weather: Hot & bright

Pos	Driver	Team	Chassis-Engine	Result	Qual
1	Ayrton Senna	McLaren	McLaren-Honda MP4/5B	1h20m47.164s	1
2	Alessandro Nannini	Benetton	Benetton-Ford Cosworth B190	1h20m53.684s	9
3	Gerhard Berger	McLaren	McLaren-Honda MP4/5B	1h20m55.717s	2
4	Alain Prost	Ferrari	Ferrari 641/2	1h21m32.434s	3
5	Riccardo Patrese	Williams	Williams-Renault FW13B	1h21m35.192s	5
6	Thierry Boutsen	Williams	Williams-Renault FW13B	1h22m08.655s	6
7	Ivan Capelli	Leyton House	Leyton House-Judd CG901	44 laps	10
8	Derek Warwick	Lotus	Lotus-Lamborghini 102	44 laps	16
9	Alex Caffi	Arrows	Arrows-Ford Cosworth A11B	44 laps	18
10	Nicola Larini	Ligier	Ligier-Ford Cosworth JS33B	43 laps	22
11	Jean Alesi	Tyrrell	Tyrrell-Ford Cosworth 019	40 laps/transmission	8
NC	JJ Lehto	Monteverdi	Monteverdi-Ford Cosworth ORE-2	39 laps	25
R	Eric Bernard	Larrousse	Lola-Lamborghini 90	35 laps/fuel pump	12
R	Aguri Suzuki	Larrousse	Lola-Lamborghini 90	33 laps/clutch	11
R	Satoru Nakajima	Tyrrell	Tyrrell-Ford Cosworth 019	24 laps/engine	13
R	Nelson Piquet	Benetton	Benetton-Ford Cosworth B190	23 laps/engine	7
R	Pierluigi Martini	Minardi	Minardi-Ford Cosworth M190	20 laps/engine	15
R	Gregor Foitek	Monteverdi	Monteverdi-Ford Cosworth ORE-2	19 laps/spun off	26
DQ	Philippe Alliot*	Ligier	Ligier-Ford Cosworth JS33B	16 laps/push start	24
R	Nigel Mansell	Ferrari	Ferrari 641/2	15 laps/wing	4
R	Mauricio Gugelmin	Leyton House	Leyton House-Judd CG901	12 laps/engine	14
R	David Brabham	Brabham	Brabham-Judd BT59	12 laps/engine	21
R	Michele Alboreto	Arrows	Arrows-Ford Cosworth A11B-	10 laps/engine	19
R	Martin Donnelly	Lotus	Lotus-Lamborghini 102	1 lap/clutch	20
R	Stefano Modena	Brabham	Brabham-Judd BT59	0 laps/clutch	17
R	Emanuele Pirro	BMS Scuderia Italia	Dallara-Ford Cosworth 190	0 laps/collision	23
DNQ	Olivier Grouillard	Osella	Osella-Ford Cosworth FA1M-E	-	27
DNQ	Paolo Barilla	Minardi	Minardi-Ford Cosworth M190	-	28
DNQ	Yannick Dalmas	AGS	AGS-Ford Cosworth JH25	-	29
DNQ	Andrea de Cesaris	BMS Scuderia Italia	Dallara-Ford Cosworth 190	-	30
DNPQ	Gabriele Tarquini	AGS	AGS-Ford Cosworth JH25	-	31
DNPQ	Roberto Moreno	EuroBrun	EuroBrun-Judd ER189B	-	32
DNPQ	Bertrand Gachot	Coloni	Coloni-Ford Cosworth C3C	-	33
DNPQ	Claudio Langes	EuroBrun	EuroBrun-Judd ER189B	-	34
DNPQ	Bruno Giacomelli	Life	Life F190	-	35

*disqualified - outside assistance

Pole: Senna, 1m40.198s, 151.855mph/244.388kph. Fastest lap: Boutsen, 1m45.602s, 144.084mph/231.881kph on Lap 31. Race leaders: Senna 1-17 & 34-45, Nannini 18-33

TAKING THE OPPORTUNITY

Undoubtedly rapid in the junior categories, Roberto Moreno realised how important his stint with Benetton was as he stood in for the injured Alessandro Nannini. He moved across from tail-end EuroBrun to race to second in the Japanese GP, assisted by the first lap collision between title challengers Ayrton Senna and Alain Prost.

HUNGARIAN GRAND PRIX

HUNGARORING • ROUND 10 • DATE: 12TH AUGUST 1990
Laps: 77 • Distance: 189.851miles/305.536km • Weather: Hot & bright

Pos	Driver	Team	Chassis-Engine	Result	Qual
1	Thierry Boutsen	Williams	Williams-Renault FW13B	1h49m30.597s	1
2	Ayrton Senna	McLaren	McLaren-Honda MP4/5B	1h49m30.885s	4
3	Nelson Piquet	Benetton	Benetton-Ford Cosworth B190	1h49m58.490s	9
4	Riccardo Patrese	Williams	Williams-Renault FW13B	1h50m02.430s	2
5	Derek Warwick	Lotus	Lotus-Lamborghini 102	1h50m44.841s	11
6	Eric Bernard	Larrousse	Lola-Lamborghini 90	1h50m54.905s	12
7	Martin Donnelly	Lotus	Lotus-Lamborghini 102	76 laps	18
8	Mauricio Gugelmin	Leyton House	Leyton House-Judd CG901	76 laps	17
9	Alex Caffi	Arrows	Arrows-Ford Cosworth A11B	76 laps	26
10	Emanuele Pirro	BMS Scuderia Italia	Dallara-Ford Cosworth 190	76 laps	13
11	Nicola Larini	Ligier	Ligier-Ford Cosworth JS33B	76 laps	25
12	Michele Alboreto	Arrows	Arrows-Ford Cosworth A11B	75 laps	22
13	Gabriele Tarquini	AGS	AGS-Ford Cosworth JH25	74 laps	24
14	Philippe Alliot	Ligier	Ligier-Ford Cosworth JS33B	74 laps	21
15	Paolo Barilla	Minardi	Minardi-Ford Cosworth M190	74 laps	23
16	Gerhard Berger	McLaren	McLaren-Honda MP4/5B	72 laps/collision	3
17	Nigel Mansell	Ferrari	Ferrari 641/2	71 laps/collision	5
R	Alessandro Nannini	Benetton	Benetton-Ford Cosworth B190	64 laps/collision	7
R	Ivan Capelli	Leyton House	Leyton House-Judd CG901	56 laps/gearbox	16
R	Aguri Suzuki	Larrousse	Lola-Lamborghini 90	37 laps/engine	19
R	Jean Alesi	Tyrrell	Tyrrell-Ford Cosworth 019	36 laps/collision	6
R	Alain Prost	Ferrari	Ferrari 641/2	36 laps/gearbox	8
R	Pierluigi Martini	Minardi	Minardi-Ford Cosworth M190	35 laps/collision	14
R	Stefano Modena	Brabham	Brabham-Judd BT59	35 laps/engine	20
R	Andrea de Cesaris	BMS Scuderia Italia	Dallara-Ford Cosworth 190	22 laps/engine	10
R	Satoru Nakajima	Tyrrell	Tyrrell-Ford Cosworth 019	9 laps/brakes	15
DNQ	Yannick Dalmas	AGS	AGS-Ford Cosworth JH25	-	27
DNQ	David Brabham	Brabham	Brabham-Judd BT59	-	28
DNQ	JJ Lehto	Monteverdi	Monteverdi-Ford Cosworth ORE-2	-	29
DNQ	Gregor Foitek	Monteverdi	Monteverdi-Ford Cosworth ORE-2	-	30
DNPQ	Olivier Grouillard	Osella	Osella-Ford Cosworth FA1M-E	-	31
DNPQ	Bertrand Gachot	Coloni	Coloni-Ford Cosworth C3C	-	32
DNPQ	Roberto Moreno	EuroBrun	EuroBrun-Judd ER189B	-	33
DNPQ	Claudio Langes	EuroBrun	EuroBrun-Judd ER189B	-	34
DNPQ	Bruno Giacomelli	Life	Life F190	-	35

Pole: Boutsen, 1m17.919s, 113.915mph/183.328kph. Fastest lap: Patrese, 1m22.058s, 108.169mph/174.081kph on Lap 63. Race leaders: Boutsen 1-77

BELGIAN GRAND PRIX

SPA-FRANCORCHAMPS • ROUND 11 • DATE: 26TH AUGUST 1990
Laps: 44 • Distance: 189.540miles/305.36km • Weather: Warm but dull

Pos	Driver	Team	Chassis-Engine	Result	Qual
1	Ayrton Senna	McLaren	McLaren-Honda MP4/5B	1h26m31.997s	1
2	Alain Prost	Ferrari	Ferrari 641/2	1h26m35.547s	3
3	Gerhard Berger	McLaren	McLaren-Honda MP4/5B	1h27m00.459s	2
4	Alessandro Nannini	Benetton	Benetton-Ford Cosworth B190	1h27m21.334s	6
5	Nelson Piquet	Benetton	Benetton-Ford Cosworth B190	1h28m01.647s	8

Pos	Driver	Team	Chassis-Engine	Result	Qual
6	Mauricio Gugelmin	Leyton House	Leyton House-Judd CG901	1h28m20.848s	14
7	Ivan Capelli	Leyton House	Leyton House-Judd CG901	43 laps	12
8	Jean Alesi	Tyrrell	Tyrrell-Ford Cosworth 019	43 laps	9
9	Eric Bernard	Larrousse	Lola-Lamborghini 90	43 laps	15
10	Alex Caffi	Arrows	Arrows-Ford Cosworth A11B	43 laps	19
11	Derek Warwick	Lotus	Lotus-Lamborghini 102	43 laps	18
12	Martin Donnelly	Lotus	Lotus-Lamborghini 102	43 laps	22
13	Michele Alboreto	Arrows	Arrows-Ford Cosworth A11B	43 laps	26
14	Nicola Larini	Ligier	Ligier-Ford Cosworth JS33B	42 laps	21
15	Pierluigi Martini	Minardi	Minardi-Ford Cosworth M190	42 laps	16
16	Olivier Grouillard	Osella	Osella-Ford Cosworth FA1M-E	42 laps	23
17	Stefano Modena	Brabham	Brabham-Judd BT59	39 laps/engine	13
R	David Brabham	Brabham	Brabham-Judd BT59	36 laps/electrical	24
R	Andrea de Cesaris	BMS Scuderia Italia	Dallara-Ford Cosworth 190	27 laps/engine	20
R	Thierry Boutsen	Williams	Williams-Renault FW13B	21 laps/transmission	4
R	Nigel Mansell	Ferrari	Ferrari 641/2	19 laps/handling	5
R	Riccardo Patrese	Williams	Williams-Renault FW13B	18 laps/gearbox	7
R	Emanuele Pirro	BMS Scuderia Italia	Dallara-Ford Cosworth 190	5 laps/water leak	17
R	Satoru Nakajima	Tyrrell	Tyrrell-Ford Cosworth 019	4 laps/engine	10
R	Aguri Suzuki	Larrousse	Lola-Lamborghini 90	0 laps/collision	11
R	Paolo Barilla	Minardi	Minardi-Ford Cosworth M190	0 laps/collision	25
DNQ	Philippe Alliot	Ligier	Ligier-Ford Cosworth JS33B	-	27
DNQ	Gabriele Tarquini	AGS	AGS-Ford Cosworth JH25	-	28
DNQ	Yannick Dalmas	AGS	AGS-Ford Cosworth JH25	-	29
DNQ	Bertrand Gachot	Coloni	Coloni-Ford Cosworth C3C	-	30
DNPQ	Roberto Moreno	EuroBrun	EuroBrun-Judd ER189B	-	31
DNPQ	Claudio Langes	EuroBrun	EuroBrun-Judd ER189B	-	32
DNPQ	Bruno Giacomelli	Life	Life F190	-	33

Pole: Senna, 1m50.365s, 140.663mph/226.376kph. Fastest lap: Prost, 1m55.087s, 134.892mph/217.087kph on Lap 38. Race leaders: Senna 1-44

ITALIAN GRAND PRIX

MONZA • ROUND 12 • DATE: 9TH SEPTEMBER 1990
Laps: 53 • Distance: 190.763miles/307.4km • Weather: Hot & bright

Pos	Driver	Team	Chassis-Engine	Result	Qual
1	Ayrton Senna	McLaren	McLaren-Honda MP4/5B	1h17m57.878s	1
2	Alain Prost	Ferrari	Ferrari 641/2	1h18m03.932s	2
3	Gerhard Berger	McLaren	McLaren-Honda MP4/5B	1h18m05.282s	3
4	Nigel Mansell	Ferrari	Ferrari 641/2	1h18m54.097s	4
5	Riccardo Patrese	Williams	Williams-Renault FW13B	1h19m23.152s	7
6	Satoru Nakajima	Tyrrell	Tyrrell-Ford Cosworth 019	52 laps	14
7	Nelson Piquet	Benetton	Benetton-Ford Cosworth B190	52 laps	9
8	Alessandro Nannini	Benetton	Benetton-Ford Cosworth B190	52 laps	8
9	Alex Caffi	Arrows	Arrows-Ford Cosworth A11B	51 laps	21
10	Andrea de Cesaris	BMS Scuderia Italia	Dallara-Ford Cosworth 190	51 laps	25
11	Nicola Larini	Ligier	Ligier-Ford Cosworth JS33B	51 laps	26
12	Michele Alboreto	Arrows	Arrows-Ford Cosworth A11B	50 laps/spun off	22
13	Philippe Alliot	Ligier	Ligier-Ford Cosworth JS33B	50 laps	20
NC	Yannick Dalmas	AGS	AGS-Ford Cosworth JH25	45 laps	24
R	Ivan Capelli	Leyton House	Leyton House-Judd CG901	36 laps/engine	16
R	Aguri Suzuki	Larrousse	Lola-Lamborghini 90	36 laps/electrical	18
R	Olivier Grouillard	Osella	Osella-Ford Cosworth FA1M-E	27 laps/wheel	23

Pos	Driver	Team	Chassis-Engine	Result	Qual
R	Mauricio Gugelmin	Leyton House	Leyton House-Judd CG901	24 laps/engine	10
R	Stefano Modena	Brabham	Brabham-Judd BT59	21 laps/engine	17
R	Thierry Boutsen	Williams	Williams-Renault FW13B	18 laps/suspension	6
R	Derek Warwick	Lotus	Lotus-Lamborghini 102	15 laps/clutch	12
R	Emanuele Pirro	BMS Scuderia Italia	Dallara-Ford Cosworth 190	14 laps/spun off	19
R	Martin Donnelly	Lotus	Lotus-Lamborghini 102	13 laps/engine	11
R	Eric Bernard	Larrousse	Lola-Lamborghini 90	10 laps/clutch	13
R	Pierluigi Martini	Minardi	Minardi-Ford Cosworth M190	7 laps/suspension	15
R	Jean Alesi	Tyrrell	Tyrrell-Ford Cosworth 019	4 laps/spun off	5
DNQ	Gabriele Tarquini	AGS	AGS-Ford Cosworth JH25	-	27
DNQ	Paolo Barilla	Minardi	Minardi-Ford Cosworth M190	-	28
DNQ	David Brabham	Brabham	Brabham-Judd BT59	-	29
DNQ	Bertrand Gachot	Coloni	Coloni-Ford Cosworth C3C	-	30
DNPQ	Roberto Moreno	EuroBrun	EuroBrun-Judd ER189B	-	31
DNPQ	Claudio Langes	EuroBrun	EuroBrun-Judd ER189B	-	32
DNPQ	Bruno Giacomelli	Life	Life F190	-	33

Pole: Senna, 1m22.533s, 157.200mph/252.989kph. Fastest lap: Senna, 1m26.254s, 150.418mph/242.075kph on Lap 46. Race leaders: Senna 1-53

JAPANESE BREAKTHROUGH

Japanese driver Hiroshi Fushida had attempted to qualify a Maki in 1975 but it was only when Satoru Nakajima arrived in 1987 that there was a regular Japanese driver on the grid at races other than the Japanese GP. However, it took until the 1990 Japanese GP for a Japanese driver to appear on a podium, with Aguri Suzuki advancing from ninth on the grid to third in his Larrousse Lola.

PORTUGUESE GRAND PRIX

AUTODROMO DO ESTORIL • ROUND 13 • DATE: 23RD SEPTEMBER 1990
Laps: 61 • Distance: 164.685miles/265.35km • Weather: Hot & bright

Pos	Driver	Team	Chassis-Engine	Result	Qual
1	Nigel Mansell	Ferrari	Ferrari 641/2	1h22m11.014s	1
2	Ayrton Senna	McLaren	McLaren-Honda MP4/5B	1h22m13.822s	3
3	Alain Prost	Ferrari	Ferrari 641/2	1h22m15.203s	2
4	Gerhard Berger	McLaren	McLaren-Honda MP4/5B	1h22m16.910s	4
5	Nelson Piquet	Benetton	Benetton-Ford Cosworth B190	1h23m08.432s	6
6	Alessandro Nannini	Benetton	Benetton-Ford Cosworth B190	1h23m09.263s	9
7	Riccardo Patrese	Williams	Williams-Renault FW13B	60 laps	5
8	Jean Alesi	Tyrrell	Tyrrell-Ford Cosworth 019	60 laps	8
9	Michele Alboreto	Arrows	Arrows-Ford Cosworth A11B	60 laps	19
10	Nicola Larini	Ligier	Ligier-Ford Cosworth JS33B	59 laps	23
11	Pierluigi Martini	Minardi	Minardi-Ford Cosworth M190	59 laps	16
12	Mauricio Gugelmin	Leyton House	Leyton House-Judd CG901	59 laps	14
13	Alex Caffi	Arrows	Arrows-Ford Cosworth A11B	58 laps/accident	17
14	Aguri Suzuki	Larrousse	Lola-Lamborghini 90	58 laps/accident	11
15	Emanuele Pirro	BMS Scuderia Italia	Dallara-Ford Cosworth 190	58 laps	13
R	Philippe Alliot	Ligier	Ligier-Ford Cosworth JS33B	52 laps/accident	21
R	David Brabham	Brabham	Brabham-Judd BT59	52 laps/gearbox	26

Pos	Driver	Team	Chassis-Engine	Result	Qual
R	Ivan Capelli	Leyton House	Leyton House-Judd CG901	51 laps/engine	12
R	Thierry Boutsen	Williams	Williams-Renault FW13B	30 laps/engine	7
R	Eric Bernard	Larrousse	Lola-Lamborghini 90	24 laps/gearbox	10
R	Stefano Modena	Brabham	Brabham-Judd BT59	21 laps/gearbox	24
R	Martin Donnelly	Lotus	Lotus-Lamborghini 102	14 laps/alternator	15
R	Derek Warwick	Lotus	Lotus-Lamborghini 102	5 laps/throttle	22
R	Yannick Dalmas	AGS	AGS-Ford Cosworth JH25	3 laps/halfshaft	25
R	Andrea de Cesaris	BMS Scuderia Italia	Dallara-Ford Cosworth 190	0 laps/spun off	18
NS	Satoru Nakajima	Tyrrell	Tyrrell-Ford Cosworth 019	driver unwell	20
DNQ	Olivier Grouillard	Osella	Osella-Ford Cosworth FA1M-E	-	27
DNQ	Paolo Barilla	Minardi	Minardi-Ford Cosworth M190	-	28
DNQ	Gabriele Tarquini	AGS	AGS-Ford Cosworth JH25	-	29
DNQ	Bertrand Gachot	Coloni	Coloni-Ford Cosworth C3C	-	30
DNPQ	Roberto Moreno	EuroBrun	EuroBrun-Judd ER189B	-	31
DNPQ	Claudio Langes	EuroBrun	EuroBrun-Judd ER189B	-	32
DNPQ	Bruno Giacomelli	Life	Life F190	-	33

Pole: Mansell, 1m13.557s, 132.287mph/212.896kph. Fastest lap: Patrese, 1m18.306s, 124.264mph/199.984kph on Lap 56. Race leaders: Senna 1-28 & 32-49, Berger 29-31, Mansell 50-61

NEW CONSTRUCTORS

Of the hundreds of constructors who tried F1, Life – headed by Ernesto Vita – was one of the least successful. The Italian constructor's decision to run its own W12 engine gave it no chance. Gary Brabham tried twice and Bruno Giacomelli 12 times, but neither of them got close to even getting through pre-qualifying in order to have a shot at qualifying.

SPANISH GRAND PRIX

JEREZ • ROUND 14 • DATE: 30TH SEPTEMBER 1990
Laps: 73 • Distance: 191.328miles/307.914km • Weather: Hot & bright

Pos	Driver	Team	Chassis-Engine	Result	Qual
1	Alain Prost	Ferrari	Ferrari 641/2	1h48m01.461s	2
2	Nigel Mansell	Ferrari	Ferrari 641/2	1h48m23.525s	3
3	Alessandro Nannini	Benetton	Benetton-Ford Cosworth B190	1h48m36.335s	9
4	Thierry Boutsen	Williams	Williams-Renault FW13B	1h48m44.757s	7
5	Riccardo Patrese	Williams	Williams-Renault FW13B	1h48m58.991s	6
6	Aguri Suzuki	Larrousse	Lola-Lamborghini 90	1h49m05.189s	15
7	Nicola Larini	Ligier	Ligier-Ford Cosworth JS33B	72 laps	20
8	Mauricio Gugelmin	Leyton House	Leyton House-Judd CG901	72 laps	12
9	Yannick Dalmas	AGS	AGS-Ford Cosworth JH25	72 laps	24
10	Michele Alboreto	Arrows	Arrows-Ford Cosworth A11B	71 laps	26
R	Derek Warwick	Lotus	Lotus-Lamborghini 102	63 laps/gearbox	10
R	Ivan Capelli	Leyton House	Leyton House-Judd CG901	59 laps/physical	19
R	Gerhard Berger	McLaren	McLaren-Honda MP4/5B	56 laps/collision	5
R	Ayrton Senna	McLaren	McLaren-Honda MP4/5B	53 laps/radiator	1
R	Nelson Piquet	Benetton	Benetton-Ford Cosworth B190	47 laps/battery	8
R	Andrea de Cesaris	BMS Scuderia Italia	Dallara-Ford Cosworth 190	47 laps/engine	17
R	Olivier Grouillard	Osella	Osella-Ford Cosworth FA1M-E	45 laps/wheel	21

Pos	Driver	Team	Chassis-Engine	Result	Qual
R	Pierluigi Martini	Minardi	Minardi-Ford Cosworth M190	41 laps/spun off	11
R	Philippe Alliot	Ligier	Ligier-Ford Cosworth JS33B	22 laps/spun off	13
R	Eric Bernard	Larrousse	Lola-Lamborghini 90	20 laps/gearbox	18
R	Satoru Nakajima	Tyrrell	Tyrrell-Ford Cosworth 019	13 laps/spun off	14
R	Gabriele Tarquini	AGS	AGS-Ford Cosworth JH25	5 laps/engine	22
R	Stefano Modena	Brabham	Brabham-Judd BT59	5 laps/collision	25
R	Jean Alesi	Tyrrell	Tyrrell-Ford Cosworth 019	0 laps/spun off	4
R	Emanuele Pirro	BMS Scuderia Italia	Dallara-Ford Cosworth 190	0 laps/throttle	16
NS	Martin Donnelly	Lotus	Lotus-Lamborghini 102	driver injured	23
DNQ	David Brabham	Brabham	Brabham-Judd BT59	-	27
DNQ	Paolo Barilla	Minardi	Minardi-Ford Cosworth M190	-	28
DNQ	Bernd Schneider	Arrows	Arrows-Ford Cosworth A11	-	29
DNQ	Bertrand Gachot	Coloni	Coloni-Ford Cosworth C3C	-	30
DNPQ	Roberto Moreno	EuroBrun	EuroBrun-Judd ER189B	-	31
DNPQ	Claudio Langes	EuroBrun	EuroBrun-Judd ER189B	-	32
DNPQ	Bruno Giacomelli	Life	Life F190	-	33

Pole: Senna, 1m18.387s, 120.369mph/193.715kph. Fastest lap: Patrese, 1m24.513s, 111.644mph/179.674kph on Lap 53. Race leaders: Senna 1-26, Piquet 27-28, Prost 29-73

NEW DRIVERS

Two brothers tried to break onto the F1 scene in 1990 in the hope of emulating the feat of their three-time world champion father, Jack Brabham. David had an unproductive year with a Brabham team that had left family ownership in 1971. Gary failed with Life. Meanwhile, Claudio Langes failed with EuroBrun, while Gianni Morbidelli tried both Dallara and Minardi.

JAPANESE GRAND PRIX

SUZUKA • ROUND 15 • DATE: 21ST OCTOBER 1990
Laps: 53 • Distance: 192.952miles/310.527km • Weather: Hot & bright

Pos	Driver	Team	Chassis-Engine	Result	Qual
1	Nelson Piquet	Benetton	Benetton-Ford Cosworth B190	1h34m36.824s	6
2	Roberto Moreno	Benetton	Benetton-Ford Cosworth B190	1h34m44.047s	8
3	Aguri Suzuki	Larrousse	Lola-Lamborghini 90	1h34m59.293s	9
4	Riccardo Patrese	Williams	Williams-Renault FW13B	1h35m13.082s	8
5	Thierry Boutsen	Williams	Williams-Renault FW13B	1h35m23.708s	6
6	Satoru Nakajima	Tyrrell	Tyrrell-Ford Cosworth 019	1h35m49.174s	14
7	Nicola Larini	Ligier	Ligier-Ford Cosworth JS33B	52 laps	18
8	Pierluigi Martini	Minardi	Minardi-Ford Cosworth M190	52 laps	11
9	Alex Caffi	Arrows	Arrows-Ford Cosworth A11B	52 laps	24
10	Philippe Alliot	Ligier	Ligier-Ford Cosworth JS33B	52 laps	21
R	Derek Warwick	Lotus	Lotus-Lamborghini 102	38 laps/gearbox	12
R	Johnny Herbert	Lotus	Lotus-Lamborghini 102	31 laps/engine	15
R	Michele Alboreto	Arrows	Arrows-Ford Cosworth A11B	28 laps/engine	25
R	Nigel Mansell	Ferrari	Ferrari 641/2	26 laps/transmission	4
R	Eric Bernard	Larrousse	Lola-Lamborghini 90	24 laps/engine	17
R	Emanuele Pirro	BMS Scuderia Italia	Dallara-Ford Cosworth 190	24 laps/alternator	19
R	Gianni Morbidelli	Minardi	Minardi-Ford Cosworth M190	18 laps/spun off	20

Pos	Driver	Team	Chassis-Engine	Result	Qual
R	Ivan Capelli	Leyton House	Leyton House-Judd CG901	16 laps/ignition	13
R	Andrea de Cesaris	BMS Scuderia Italia	Dallara-Ford Cosworth 190	13 laps/spun off	26
R	Mauricio Gugelmin	Leyton House	Leyton House-Judd CG901	5 laps/engine	16
R	David Brabham	Brabham	Brabham-Judd BT59	2 laps/clutch	23
R	Gerhard Berger	McLaren	McLaren-Honda MP4/5B	1 lap/spun off	5
R	Ayrton Senna	McLaren	McLaren-Honda MP4/5B	0 laps/collision	21
R	Alain Prost	Ferrari	Ferrari 641/2	0 laps/collision	3
R	Stefano Modena	Brabham	Brabham-Judd BT59	0 laps/collision	22
NS	Jean Alesi	Tyrrell	Tyrrell-Ford Cosworth 019	driver injured	7
DNQ	Olivier Grouillard	Osella	Osella-Ford Cosworth FA1ME	-	27
DNQ	Gabriele Tarquini	AGS	AGS-Ford Cosworth JH25	-	28
DNQ	Yannick Dalmas	AGS	AGS-Ford Cosworth JH25	-	29
DNQ	Bertrand Gachot	Coloni	Coloni-Ford Cosworth C3C	-	30

Pole: Senna, 1m36.996s, 135.121mph/217.456kph. Fastest lap: Patrese, 1m44.233s, 125.739mph/202.358kph on Lap 40. Race leaders: Berger 1, Mansell 2-26, Piquet 27-53

AUSTRALIAN GRAND PRIX

ADELAIDE • ROUND 16 • DATE: 4TH NOVEMBER 1990
Laps: 81 • Distance: 190.150miles/306.18km • Weather: Hot & bright

Pos	Driver	Team	Chassis-Engine	Result	Qual
1	Nelson Piquet	Benetton	Benetton-Ford Cosworth B190	1h49m44.570s	7
2	Nigel Mansell	Ferrari	Ferrari 641/2	1h49m47.699s	3
3	Alain Prost	Ferrari	Ferrari 641/2	1h50m21.829s	4
4	Gerhard Berger	McLaren	McLaren-Honda MP4/5B	1h50m31.432s	2
5	Thierry Boutsen	Williams	Williams-Renault FW13B	1h51m35.730s	9
6	Riccardo Patrese	Williams	Williams-Renault FW13B	80 laps	6
7	Roberto Moreno	Benetton	Benetton-Ford Cosworth B190	80 laps	8
8	Jean Alesi	Tyrrell	Tyrrell-Ford Cosworth 019	80 laps	5
9	Pierluigi Martini	Minardi	Minardi-Ford Cosworth M190	79 laps	10
10	Nicola Larini	Ligier	Ligier-Ford Cosworth JS33B	79 laps	12
11	Philippe Alliot	Ligier	Ligier-Ford Cosworth JS33B	78 laps	19
12	Stefano Modena	Brabham	Brabham-Judd BT59	77 laps	17
13	Olivier Grouillard	Osella	Osella-Ford Cosworth FA1M-E	74 laps	22
R	Emanuele Pirro	BMS Scuderia Italia	Dallara-Ford Cosworth 190	68 laps/engine	21
R	Ayrton Senna	McLaren	McLaren-Honda MP4/5B	61 laps/spun off	1
R	Gabriele Tarquini	AGS	AGS-Ford Cosworth JH25	58 laps/engine	26
R	Johnny Herbert	Lotus	Lotus-Lamborghini 102	57 laps/clutch	18
R	Satoru Nakajima	Tyrrell	Tyrrell-Ford Cosworth 019	53 laps/spun off	13
R	Ivan Capelli	Leyton House	Leyton House-Judd CG901	46 laps/throttle	14
R	Derek Warwick	Lotus	Lotus-Lamborghini 102	43 laps/gearbox	11
R	Mauricio Gugelmin	Leyton House	Leyton House-Judd CG901	27 laps/brakes	16
R	Andrea de Cesaris	BMS Scuderia Italia	Dallara-Ford Cosworth 190	23 laps/electrical	15
R	Eric Bernard	Larrousse	Lola-Lamborghini 90	21 laps/gearbox	23
R	Gianni Morbidelli	Minardi	Minardi-Ford Cosworth M190	20 laps/gearbox	20
R	David Brabham	Brabham	Brabham-Judd BT59	18 laps/spun off	25
R	Aguri Suzuki	Larrousse	Lola-Lamborghini 90	6 laps/transmission	24
DNQ	Michele Alboreto	Arrows	Arrows-Ford Cosworth A11B	-	27
DNQ	Yannick Dalmas	AGS	AGS-Ford Cosworth JH25	-	28
DNQ	Alex Caffi	Arrows	Arrows-Ford Cosworth A11B	-	29
DNQ	Bertrand Gachot	Coloni	Coloni-Ford Cosworth C3C	-	30

Pole: Senna, 1m15.671s, 111.741mph/179.831kph. Fastest lap: Mansell, 1m18.203s, 108.123mph/174.008kph on Lap 75. Race leaders: Senna 1-61, Piquet 62-81

WORLD DRIVERS' CHAMPIONSHIP FINAL RESULTS

Pos	Driver	Nat	Car-Engine	R1	R2	R3	R4	R5	R6
1	Ayrton Senna	BRA	McLaren-Honda MP4/5B	1	3P	RP	1PF	1P	20
2	Alain Prost	FRA	Ferrari 641	R	1	4	R	5	1F
3	Nelson Piquet	BRA	Benetton-Ford Cosworth B189B	4	6	-	-	-	-
			Benetton-Ford Cosworth B190	-	-	5	DQ	2	6
4	Gerhard Berger	AUT	McLaren-Honda MP4/5B	RPF	2F	2	3	4F	3P
5	Nigel Mansell	GBR	Ferrari 641	R	4	R	R	3	2
6	Thierry Boutsen	BEL	Williams-Renault FW13B	3	5	R	4	R	5
7	Riccardo Patrese	ITA	Williams-Renault FW13B	9	13	1	R	R	9
8	Alessandro Nannini	ITA	Benetton-Ford Cosworth B189B	11	10	-	-	-	-
			Benetton-Ford Cosworth B190	-	-	3F	R	R	4
9	Jean Alesi	FRA	Tyrrell-Ford Cosworth 018	2	7	-	-	-	-
			Tyrrell-Ford Cosworth 019	-	-	6	2	R	7
10	Ivan Capelli	ITA	Leyton House-Judd CG901	R	DNQ	R	R	10	DNQ
10	Roberto Moreno	BRA	EuroBrun-Judd ER189	13	DNPQ	-	-	-	-
			EuroBrun-Judd ER189B	-	-	R	DNQ	DNQ	DNQ
			Benetton-Ford Cosworth B190	-	-	-	-	-	-
12	Aguri Suzuki	JPN	Lola-Lamborghini LC89	R	R	-	-	-	-
			Lola-Lamborghini 90	-	-	R	R	12	R
13	Eric Bernard	FRA	Lola-Lamborghini LC89	8	R	-	-	-	-
			Lola-Lamborghini 90	-	-	13	6	9	R
14	Derek Warwick	GBR	Lotus-Lamborghini 102	R	R	7	R	6	10
15	Satoru Nakajima	JPN	Tyrrell-Ford Cosworth 018	6	8	-	-	-	-
			Tyrrell-Ford Cosworth 019	-	-	R	R	11	R
16	Stefano Modena	ITA	Brabham-Judd BT58	5	R	-	-	-	-
			Brabham-Judd BT59	-	-	R	R	7	11
16	Alex Caffi	ITA	Arrows-Ford Cosworth A11B	-	R	DNQ	5	8	DNQ
18	Mauricio Gugelmin	BRA	Leyton House-Judd CG901	14	DNQ	R	DNQ	DNQ	DNQ

Pos	Driver	R7	R8	R9	R10	R11	R12	R13	R14	R15	R16	Total
1	Senna	3	3	1P	2	1P	1PF	2	RP	RP	RP	78
2	Prost	1	1	4	R	2F	2	3	1	R	3	71
3	Piquet	-	-	-	-	-	-	-	-	-	-	43
		4	5	R	3	5	7	5	R	1	1	
4	Berger	5	14	3	16	3	3	4	R	R	4	43
5	Mansell	18PF	RPF	R	17	R	4	1P	2	R	2F	37
6	Boutsen	R	2	6F	1P	R	R	R	4	5	5	34
7	Patrese	6	R	5	4F	R	5	7F	5F	4F	6	23
8	Nannini	-	-	-	-	-	-	-	-	-	-	21
		16	R	2	R	4	8	6	3	-	-	
9	Alesi	-	-	-	-	-	-	-	-	-	-	13
		R	8	11	R	8	R	8	R	NS	8	
10	Capelli	2	R	7	R	7	R	R	R	R	R	6
10	Moreno	-	-	-	-	-	-	-	-	-	-	6
		DNPQ	DNPQ	DNPQ	DNPQ	DNPQ	DNPQ	DNPQ	DNPQ	-	-	
		-	-	-	-	-	-	-	-	2	7	
12	Suzuki	-	-	-	-	-	-	-	-	-	-	6
		7	6	R	R	R	R	14	6	3	R	
13	Bernard	-	-	-	-	-	-	-	-	-	-	5
		8	4	R	6	9	R	R	R	R	R	
14	Warwick	11	R	8	5	11	R	R	R	R	R	3
15	Nakajima	-	-	-	-	-	-	-	-	-	-	3
		R	R	R	R	R	6	NS	R	6	R	
16	Modena	-	-	-	-	-	-	-	-	-	-	2
		13	9	R	R	17	R	R	R	R	12	

Pos	Driver	R7	R8	R9	R10	R11	R12	R13	R14	R15	R16	Total
16	Caffi	R	7	9	9	10	9	13	-	9	DNQ	2
18	Gugelmin	R	NS	R	8	6	R	12	8	R	R	1

WORLD CONSTRUCTORS' CHAMPIONSHIP FINAL RESULTS

Pos	Team-Engine	R1	R2	R3	R4	R5	R6	R7	R8
1	McLaren-Honda	1/R	2/3	2/R	1/3	1/4	3/20	3/5	3/14
2	Ferrari	R/R	1/4	4/R	R/R	3/5	1/2	1/18	1/R
3	Benetton-Ford	4/11	6/10	3/5	DQ/R	2/R	4/6	4/16	5/R
4	Williams-Renault	3/9	5/13	1/R	4/R	R/R	5/9	6/R	2/R
5	Tyrrell-Ford	2/6	7/8	6/R	2/R	11/R	7/R	R/R	8/R
6	Lola-Lamborghini	8/R	R/R	13/R	6/R	9/12	R/R	7/8	4/6
7	Leyton House-Judd	14/R	DNQ/DNQ	R/R	R/DNQ	10/DNQ	DNQ/DNQ	2/R	R/NS
8	Lotus-Lamborghini	R/NS	R/R	7/8	R/R	6/R	8/10	11/12	R/R
9	Brabham-Judd	5/R	R/R	R/DNQ	R/R	7/DNQ	11/R	13/15	9/DNQ
9	Arrows-Ford	10/12	R/R	DNQ/DNQ	5/DNQ	8/R	17/DNQ	10/R	7/R

Pos	Team-Engine	R9	R10	R11	R12	R13	R14	R15	R16	Total
1	McLaren-Honda	1/3	2/16	1/3	1/3	2/4	R/R	R/R	4/R	121
2	Ferrari	4/R	17/R	2/R	2/4	1/3	1/2	R/R	2/3	110
3	Benetton-Ford	2/R	3/R	4/5	7/8	5/6	3/R	1/2	1/7	71
4	Williams-Renault	5/6	1/4	R/R	5/R	7/R	4/5	4/5	5/6	57
5	Tyrrell-Ford	11/R	R/R	8/R	6/R	8	R/R	6/NS	8/R	16
6	Lola-Lamborghini	R/R	6/R	9/NS	R/R	14/R	6/R	3/R	R/R	11
7	Leyton House-Judd	7/R	8/R	6/7	R/R	12/R	8/R	R/R	R/R	7
8	Lotus-Lamborghini	8/R	5/7	11/12	R/R	R/R	R/NS	R/R	R/R	3
9	Brabham-Judd	R/R	R/DNQ	17/R	R/DNQ	R/R	R/DNQ	R/R	12/R	2
9	Arrows-Ford	9/R	9/12	10/13	9/12	9/13	10/DNQ	9/R	DNQ/DNQ	2

SYMBOLS AND GRAND PRIX KEY

Round 1 United States GP
Round 2 Brazilian GP
Round 3 San Marino GP
Round 4 Monaco GP
Round 5 Canadian GP
Round 6 Mexican GP
Round 7 French GP
Round 8 British GP
Round 9 German GP
Round 10 Hungarian GP
Round 11 Belgian GP
Round 12 Italian GP
Round 13 Portuguese GP
Round 14 Spanish GP
Round 15 Japanese GP
Round 16 Australian GP

SCORING

1st 9 points
2nd 6 points
3rd 4 points
4th 3 points
5th 2 points
6th 1 point

DNPQ DID NOT PRE-QUALIFY **DNQ** DID NOT QUALIFY **DQ** DISQUALIFIED **EX** EXCLUDED
F FASTEST LAP **NC** NOT CLASSIFIED **NS** NON-STARTER **P** POLE POSITION **R** RETIRED

1991

SEASON SUMMARY

Ayrton Senna made it two F1 titles in a row in another powerful season with McLaren. His main opponent wasn't Alain Prost, who had a frustrating year with Ferrari, but Nigel Mansell, who led the attack for a resurgent Williams. Their cars were powered by excellent Renault V10s mounted to the first Williams chassis in which Adrian Newey added his design skills to Patrick Head's engineering excellence. Mansell retired on the last lap of the Canadian GP and this let Nelson Piquet win for Benetton, while Riccardo Patrese won twice for Williams. Senna let team-mate Gerhard Berger win in Japan.

UNITED STATES GRAND PRIX

PHOENIX • ROUND 1 • DATE: 10TH MARCH 1991
Laps: 81 • Distance: 187.271miles/301.384km • Weather: Warm but dull

Pos	Driver	Team	Chassis-Engine	Result	Qual
1	Ayrton Senna	McLaren	McLaren-Honda MP4/6	2h00m47.828s	1
2	Alain Prost	Ferrari	Ferrari 642	2h01m04.150s	2
3	Nelson Piquet	Benetton	Benetton-Ford Cosworth B190B	2h01m05.204s	5
4	Stefano Modena	Tyrrell	Tyrrell-Honda 020	2h01m13.237s	11
5	Satoru Nakajima	Tyrrell	Tyrrell-Honda 020	80 laps	16
6	Aguri Suzuki	Larrousse	Lola-Ford Cosworth 91	79 laps	21
7	Nicola Larini	Modena Team	Lambo-Lamborghini 291	78 laps	17
8	Gabriele Tarquini	AGS	AGS-Ford Cosworth JH25	77 laps	22
9	Pierluigi Martini	Minardi	Minardi-Ferrari M191	75 laps/engine	15
10	Bertrand Gachot	Jordan	Jordan-Ford Cosworth 191	75 laps/engine	14
11	Martin Brundle	Brabham	Brabham-Yamaha BT59Y	73 laps	12
12	Jean Alesi	Ferrari	Ferrari 642	72 laps/gearbox	6
R	Mika Hakkinen	Lotus	Lotus-Judd 102B	59 laps/engine	13
R	Riccardo Patrese	Williams	Williams-Renault FW14	49 laps/gearbox	3
R	Roberto Moreno	Benetton	Benetton-Ford Cosworth B190B	49 laps/collision	8
R	Michele Alboreto	Footwork	Footwork-Porsche A11C	41 laps/engine	25
R	Ivan Capelli	Leyton House	Leyton House-Ilmor CG911	40 laps/gearbox	18
R	Thierry Boutsen	Ligier	Ligier-Lamborghini JS35	40 laps/engine	20
R	Gerhard Berger	McLaren	McLaren-Honda MP4/6	36 laps/fuel pump	7
R	Nigel Mansell	Williams	Williams-Renault FW14	35 laps/gearbox	4
R	Mauricio Gugelmin	Leyton House	Leyton House-Ilmor CG911	34 laps/gearbox	23
R	Mark Blundell	Brabham	Brabham-Yamaha BT59Y	32 laps/spun off	24
R	Emanuele Pirro	BMS Scuderia Italia	Dallara-Judd 191	16 laps/gearbox	9
R	Gianni Morbidelli	Minardi	Minardi-Ferrari M191	15 laps/gearbox	26
R	JJ Lehto	BMS Scuderia Italia	Dallara-Judd 191	12 laps/gearbox	10
R	Eric Bernard	Larrousse	Lola-Ford Cosworth 91	4 laps/engine	19
DNQ	Erik Comas	Ligier	Ligier-Lamborghini JS35	-	27
DNQ	Alex Caffi	Footwork	Footwork-Porsche A11C	-	28
DNQ	Stefan Johansson	AGS	AGS-Ford Cosworth JH25	-	29
DNQ	Julian Bailey	Lotus	Lotus-Judd 102B	-	30
DNPQ	Andrea de Cesaris	Jordan	Jordan-Ford Cosworth 191	-	31
DNPQ	Pedro Chaves	Coloni	Coloni-Ford Cosworth C4	-	32
DNPQ	Olivier Grouillard	Fondmetal	Fondmetal-Ford Cosworth FA1M-E	-	33
DNPQ	Eric van de Poele	Modena Team	Lambo-Lamborghini 291	-	34

Pole: Senna, 1m21.434s, 102.207mph/164.487kph. Fastest lap: Alesi, 1m26.758s, 95.935mph/154.393kph on Lap 49. Race leaders: Senna 1-81

BRAZILIAN GRAND PRIX

INTERLAGOS • ROUND 2 • DATE: 24TH MARCH 1991
Laps: 71 • Distance: 190.807miles/307.075km • Weather: Warm, rain later

Pos	Driver	Team	Chassis-Engine	Result	Qual
1	Ayrton Senna	McLaren	McLaren-Honda MP4/6	1h38m28.128s	1
2	Riccardo Patrese	Williams	Williams-Renault FW14	1h38m31.119s	2
3	Gerhard Berger	McLaren	McLaren-Honda MP4/6	1h38m33.544s	4
4	Alain Prost	Ferrari	Ferrari 642	1h38m47.497s	6
5	Nelson Piquet	Benetton	Benetton-Ford Cosworth B190B	1h38m50.088s	7
6	Jean Alesi	Ferrari	Ferrari 642	1h38m51.769s	5
7	Roberto Moreno	Benetton	Benetton-Ford Cosworth B190B	70 laps	14
8	Gianni Morbidelli	Minardi	Minardi-Ferrari M191	69 laps	21
9	Mika Hakkinen	Lotus	Lotus-Judd 102B	68 laps	22
10	Thierry Boutsen	Ligier	Ligier-Lamborghini JS35	68 laps	18
11	Emanuele Pirro	BMS Scuderia Italia	Dallara-Judd 191	68 laps	12
12	Martin Brundle	Brabham	Brabham-Yamaha BT59Y	67 laps	26
13	Bertrand Gachot	Jordan	Jordan-Ford Cosworth 191	63 laps/fuel system	10
R	Nigel Mansell	Williams	Williams-Renault FW14	59 laps/gearbox	3
R	Erik Comas	Ligier	Ligier-Lamborghini JS35	50 laps/engine	23
R	Pierluigi Martini	Minardi	Minardi-Ferrari M191	47 laps/spun off	20
R	Mark Blundell	Brabham	Brabham-Yamaha BT59Y	34 laps/engine	25
R	Eric Bernard	Larrousse	Lola-Ford Cosworth 91	33 laps/radiator	11
R	JJ Lehto	BMS Scuderia Italia	Dallara-Judd 191	22 laps/electrical	19
R	Andrea de Cesaris	Jordan	Jordan-Ford Cosworth 191	20 laps/engine	13
R	Stefano Modena	Tyrrell	Tyrrell-Honda 020	19 laps/gearbox	9
R	Ivan Capelli	Leyton House	Leyton House-Ilmor CG911	16 laps/transmission	15
R	Satoru Nakajima	Tyrrell	Tyrrell-Honda 020	12 laps/spun off	16
R	Mauricio Gugelmin	Leyton House	Leyton House-Ilmor CG911	9 laps/physical	8
R	Gabriele Tarquini	AGS	AGS-Ford Cosworth JH25	0 laps/suspension	24
NS	Aguri Suzuki	Larrousse	Lola-Ford Cosworth 91	Fuel pressure	17
DNQ	Alex Caffi	Footwork	Footwork-Porsche A11C	-	27
DNQ	Stefan Johansson	AGS	AGS-Ford Cosworth JH25	-	28
DNQ	Michele Alboreto	Footwork	Footwork-Porsche A11C	-	29
DNQ	Julian Bailey	Lotus	Lotus-Judd 102B	-	30
DNPQ	Eric van de Poele	Modena Team	Lambo-Lamborghini 291	-	31
DNPQ	Nicola Larini	Modena Team	Lambo-Lamborghini 291	-	32
DNPQ	Pedro Chaves	Coloni	Coloni-Ford Cosworth C4	-	33
DNPQ	Olivier Grouillard	Fondmetal	Fondmetal-Ford Cosworth F1	-	34

Pole: Senna, 1m16.392s, 126.646mph/203.817kph. Fastest lap: Mansell, 1m20.436s, 120.278mph/193.570kph on Lap 35. Race leaders: Senna 1-71

A RARE ROOKIE SUCCESS

The all-new Jordan team made a huge impression in its debut campaign in the World Championship after evolving from the successful F3000 Eddie Jordan Racing team. The outfit showed promise when Andrea de Cesaris and Bertrand Gachot came fourth and fifth in Canada, while Gachot took a fastest lap in Hungary and ranked fifth.

SAN MARINO GRAND PRIX

IMOLA • ROUND 3 • DATE: 28TH APRIL 1991
Laps: 61 • Distance: 190.788miles/307.44km • Weather: Warm, drying track

Pos	Driver	Team	Chassis-Engine	Result	Qual
1	Ayrton Senna	McLaren	McLaren-Honda MP4/6	1h35m14.750s	1
2	Gerhard Berger	McLaren	McLaren-Honda MP4/6	1h35m16.425s	5
3	JJ Lehto	BMS Scuderia Italia	Dallara-Judd 191	60 laps	16
4	Pierluigi Martini	Minardi	Minardi-Ferrari M191	59 laps	9
5	Mika Hakkinen	Lotus	Lotus-Judd 102B	58 laps	25
6	Julian Bailey	Lotus	Lotus-Judd 102B	58 laps	26
7	Thierry Boutsen	Ligier	Ligier-Lamborghini JS35	58 laps	24
8	Mark Blundell	Brabham	Brabham-Yamaha BT60Y	58 laps	23
9	Eric van de Poele	Modena Team	Lambo-Lamborghini 291	57 laps/fuel pump	21
10	Erik Comas	Ligier	Ligier-Lamborghini JS35	57 laps	19
11	Martin Brundle	Brabham	Brabham-Yamaha BT60Y	57 laps	18
12	Mauricio Gugelmin	Leyton House	Leyton House-Ilmor CG911	55 laps/engine	15
13	Roberto Moreno	Benetton	Benetton-Ford Cosworth B191	54 laps/engine	13
R	Stefano Modena	Tyrrell	Tyrrell-Honda 020	41 laps/transmission	6
R	Andrea de Cesaris	Jordan	Jordan-Ford Cosworth 191	37 laps/gearbox	11
R	Bertrand Gachot	Jordan	Jordan-Ford Cosworth 191	37 laps/suspension	12
R	Ivan Capelli	Leyton House	Leyton House-Ilmor CG911	24 laps/spun off	22
R	Riccardo Patrese	Williams	Williams-Renault FW14	17 laps/electrical	2
R	Eric Bernard	Larrousse	Lola-Ford Cosworth 91	17 laps/engine	17
R	Satoru Nakajima	Tyrrell	Tyrrell-Honda 020	15 laps/transmission	10
R	Gianni Morbidelli	Minardi	Minardi-Ferrari M191	10 laps/gearbox	8
R	Jean Alesi	Ferrari	Ferrari 642	2 laps/spun off	7
R	Aguri Suzuki	Larrousse	Lola-Ford Cosworth 91	2 laps/spun off	20
R	Nelson Piquet	Benetton	Benetton-Ford Cosworth B191	1 lap/spun off	14
R	Nigel Mansell	Williams	Williams-Renault FW14	0 laps/collision	4
NS	Alain Prost	Ferrari	Ferrari 642	spun off	3
DNQ	Gabriele Tarquini	AGS	AGS-Ford Cosworth JH25	-	27
DNQ	Fabrizio Barbazza	AGS	AGS-Ford Cosworth JH25	-	28
DNQ	Alex Caffi	Footwork	Footwork-Porsche FA12	-	29
DNQ	Michele Alboreto	Footwork	Footwork-Porsche A11C	-	30
DNPQ	Emanuele Pirro	BMS Scuderia Italia	Dallara-Judd 191	-	31
DNPQ	Olivier Grouillard	Fondmetal	Fondmetal-Ford Cosworth F1	-	32
DNPQ	Nicola Larini	Modena Team	Lambo-Lamborghini 291	-	33
DNPQ	Pedro Chaves	Coloni	Coloni-Ford Cosworth C4	-	34

Pole: Senna, 1m21.877s, 137.696mph/221.600kph. Fastest lap: Berger, 1m26.531s, 130.290mph/209.682kph on Lap 55. Race leaders: Patrese 1-9, Senna 10-61

LEHTO SCORES TEAM'S BEST

The Tifosi fell silent at Imola when both Ferraris were out after three laps, with Nigel Mansell already out and Riccardo Patrese retiring from an early lead, leaving the way clear for a McLaren one-two. No other driver finished on the lead lap but, behind them, JJ Lehto gave Scuderia Italia a podium finish by rising from 16th on the grid to finish third.

MONACO GRAND PRIX

MONTE CARLO • ROUND 4 • DATE: 12TH MAY 1991
Laps: 78 • Distance: 161.298miles/259.584km • Weather: Warm & bright

Pos	Driver	Team	Chassis-Engine	Result	Qual
1	Ayrton Senna	McLaren	McLaren-Honda MP4/6	1h53m02.334s	1
2	Nigel Mansell	Williams	Williams-Renault FW14	1h53m20.682s	5
3	Jean Alesi	Ferrari	Ferrari 642	1h53m49.789s	9
4	Roberto Moreno	Benetton	Benetton-Ford Cosworth B191	77 laps	8
5	Alain Prost	Ferrari	Ferrari 642	77 laps	7
6	Emanuele Pirro	BMS Scuderia Italia	Dallara-Judd 191	77 laps	12
7	Thierry Boutsen	Ligier	Ligier-Lamborghini JS35	76 laps	16
8	Bertrand Gachot	Jordan	Jordan-Ford Cosworth 191	76 laps	24
9	Eric Bernard	Larrousse	Lola-Ford Cosworth 91	76 laps	21
10	Erik Comas	Ligier	Ligier-Lamborghini JS35	76 laps	23
11	JJ Lehto	BMS Scuderia Italia	Dallara-Judd 191	75 laps	13
12	Pierluigi Martini	Minardi	Minardi-Ferrari M191	72 laps	14
R	Mika Hakkinen	Lotus	Lotus-Judd 102B	64 laps/oil leak	26
R	Gianni Morbidelli	Minardi	Minardi-Ferrari M191	49 laps/gearbox	17
R	Mauricio Gugelmin	Leyton House	Leyton House-Ilmor CG911	43 laps/throttle	15
R	Stefano Modena	Tyrrell	Tyrrell-Honda 020	42 laps/engine	2
R	Riccardo Patrese	Williams	Williams-Renault FW14	42 laps/spun off	3
R	Mark Blundell	Brabham	Brabham-Yamaha BT60Y	41 laps/spun off	22
R	Michele Alboreto	Footwork	Footwork-Porsche FA12	39 laps/engine	25
R	Satoru Nakajima	Tyrrell	Tyrrell-Honda 020	35 laps/spun off	11
R	Aguri Suzuki	Larrousse	Lola-Ford Cosworth 91	24 laps/spun off	19
R	Andrea de Cesaris	Jordan	Jordan-Ford Cosworth 191	21 laps/throttle	10
R	Ivan Capelli	Leyton House	Leyton House-Ilmor CG911	12 laps/brakes	18
R	Gerhard Berger	McLaren	McLaren-Honda MP4/6	9 laps/spun off	6
R	Gabriele Tarquini	AGS	AGS-Ford Cosworth JH25	9 laps/gearbox	20
R	Nelson Piquet	Benetton	Benetton-Ford Cosworth B191	0 laps/suspension	4
DNQ	Julian Bailey	Lotus	Lotus-Judd 102B	-	27
DNQ	Fabrizio Barbazza	AGS	AGS-Ford Cosworth JH25	-	28
DNQ	Alex Caffi	Footwork	Footwork-Porsche FA12	-	29
EX	Martin Brundle	Brabham	Brabham-Yamaha BT60Y	missed weight check	30
DNPQ	Nicola Larini	Modena Team	Lambo-Lamborghini 291	-	31
DNPQ	Eric van de Poele	Modena Team	Lambo-Lamborghini 291	-	32
DNPQ	Pedro Chaves	Coloni	Coloni-Ford Cosworth C4	-	33
DNPQ	Olivier Grouillard	Fondmetal	Fondmetal-Ford Cosworth F1	-	34

Pole: Senna, 1m20.344s, 92.658mph/149.118kph. Fastest lap: Prost, 1m24.368s, 88.238mph/142.006kph on Lap 77. Race leaders: Senna 1-78

CANADIAN GRAND PRIX

MONTREAL • ROUND 5 • DATE: 2ND JUNE 1991
Laps: 69 • Distance: 189.559miles/305.67km • Weather: Warm & bright

Pos	Driver	Team	Chassis-Engine	Result	Qual
1	Nelson Piquet	Benetton	Benetton-Ford Cosworth B191	1h38m51.490s	8
2	Stefano Modena	Tyrrell	Tyrrell-Honda 020	1h39m23.322s	9
3	Riccardo Patrese	Williams	Williams-Renault FW14	1h39m33.707s	1
4	Andrea de Cesaris	Jordan	Jordan-Ford Cosworth 191	1h40m11.700s	11
5	Bertrand Gachot	Jordan	Jordan-Ford Cosworth 191	1h40m13.841s	14
6	Nigel Mansell	Williams	Williams-Renault FW14	68 laps/ignition	2
7	Pierluigi Martini	Minardi	Minardi-Ferrari M191	68 laps	18

Pos	Driver	Team	Chassis-Engine	Result	Qual
8	Erik Comas	Ligier	Ligier-Lamborghini JS35	68 laps	26
9	Emanuele Pirro	BMS Scuderia Italia	Dallara-Judd 191	68 laps	10
10	Satoru Nakajima	Tyrrell	Tyrrell-Honda 020	67 laps	12
R	Mauricio Gugelmin	Leyton House	Leyton House-Ilmor CG911	61 laps/engine	23
R	JJ Lehto	BMS Scuderia Italia	Dallara-Judd 191	50 laps/engine	17
R	Stefan Johansson	Footwork	Footwork-Porsche FA12	48 laps/throttle	25
R	Ivan Capelli	Leyton House	Leyton House-Ilmor CG911	42 laps/engine	13
R	Jean Alesi	Ferrari	Ferrari 642	34 laps/engine	7
R	Eric Bernard	Larrousse	Lola-Ford Cosworth 91	29 laps/gearbox	19
R	Alain Prost	Ferrari	Ferrari 642	27 laps/gearbox	4
R	Thierry Boutsen	Ligier	Ligier-Lamborghini JS35	27 laps/engine	16
R	Ayrton Senna	McLaren	McLaren-Honda MP4/6	25 laps/alternator	3
R	Martin Brundle	Brabham	Brabham-Yamaha BT60Y	21 laps/engine	20
R	Mika Hakkinen	Lotus	Lotus-Judd 102B	21 laps/spun off	24
R	Gianni Morbidelli	Minardi	Minardi-Ferrari M191	20 laps/spun off	15
R	Roberto Moreno	Benetton	Benetton-Ford Cosworth B191	10 laps/suspension	5
R	Gerhard Berger	McLaren	McLaren-Honda MP4/6	4 laps/mechanical	6
R	Aguri Suzuki	Larrousse	Lola-Ford Cosworth 91	3 laps/oil leak	22
R	Michele Alboreto	Footwork	Footwork-Porsche FA12	2 laps/throttle	21
DNQ	Fabrizio Barbazza	AGS	AGS-Ford Cosworth JH25	-	27
DNQ	Gabriele Tarquini	AGS	AGS-Ford Cosworth JH25	-	28
DNQ	Mark Blundell	Brabham	Brabham-Yamaha BT60Y	-	29
DNQ	Johnny Herbert	Lotus	Lotus-Judd 102B	-	30
DNPQ	Olivier Grouillard	Fondmetal	Fondmetal-Ford Cosworth F1	-	31
DNPQ	Nicola Larini	Modena Team	Lambo-Lamborghini 291	-	32
DNPQ	Eric van de Poele	Modena Team	Lambo-Lamborghini 291	-	33
DNPQ	Pedro Chaves	Coloni	Coloni-Ford Cosworth C4	-	34

Pole: Patrese, 1m19.837s, 124.123mph/199.757kph. Fastest lap: Mansell, 1m22.385s, 120.284mph/193.578kph on Lap 65. Race leaders: Mansell 1-68, Piquet 69

LOTUS HITS HARD TIMES

Despite having the rapid driver line-up of Mika Hakkinen and Johnny Herbert, the fall from grace for Team Lotus continued as this once pace-setting team hit financial trouble, even under new management. At season's end, with Hakkinen's fifth place at Imola its highlight, it ranked ninth with another former title-winning team: Brabham.

MEXICAN GRAND PRIX

MEXICO CITY • ROUND 6 • DATE: 16TH JUNE 1991
Laps: 67 • Distance: 184.54miles/296.207km • Weather: Warm & bright

Pos	Driver	Team	Chassis-Engine	Result	Qual
1	Riccardo Patrese	Williams	Williams-Renault FW14	1h29m52.205s	1
2	Nigel Mansell	Williams	Williams-Renault FW14	1h29m53.541s	2
3	Ayrton Senna	McLaren	McLaren-Honda MP4/6	1h30m49.561s	3
4	Andrea de Cesaris	Jordan	Jordan-Ford Cosworth 191	66 laps/throttle	11
5	Roberto Moreno	Benetton	Benetton-Ford Cosworth B191	66 laps	9
6	Eric Bernard	Larrousse	Lola-Ford Cosworth 91	66 laps	18

Pos	Driver	Team	Chassis-Engine	Result	Qual
7	Gianni Morbidelli	Minardi	Minardi-Ferrari M191	66 laps	23
8	Thierry Boutsen	Ligier	Ligier-Lamborghini JS35	65 laps	14
9	Mika Hakkinen	Lotus	Lotus-Judd 102B	65 laps	24
10	Johnny Herbert	Lotus	Lotus-Judd 102B	65 laps	25
11	Stefano Modena	Tyrrell	Tyrrell-Honda 020	65 laps	8
12	Satoru Nakajima	Tyrrell	Tyrrell-Honda 020	64 laps	13
R	Mark Blundell	Brabham	Brabham-Yamaha BT60Y	54 laps/engine	12
R	Bertrand Gachot	Jordan	Jordan-Ford Cosworth 191	51 laps/spun off	20
R	Aguri Suzuki	Larrousse	Lola-Ford Cosworth 91	48 laps/gearbox	19
R	Nelson Piquet	Benetton	Benetton-Ford Cosworth B191	44 laps/wheel	6
R	Jean Alesi	Ferrari	Ferrari 642	42 laps/clutch	4
R	JJ Lehto	BMS Scuderia Italia	Dallara-Judd 191	30 laps/engine	16
R	Michele Alboreto	Footwork	Footwork-Porsche FA12	24 laps/engine	26
R	Martin Brundle	Brabham	Brabham-Yamaha BT60Y	20 laps/wheel	17
R	Ivan Capelli	Leyton House	Leyton House-Ilmor CG911	19 laps/engine	22
R	Alain Prost	Ferrari	Ferrari 642	16 laps/alternator	7
R	Mauricio Gugelmin	Leyton House	Leyton House-Ilmor CG911	15 laps/engine	21
R	Olivier Grouillard	Fondmetal	Fondmetal-Ford Cosworth F1	13 laps/engine	10
R	Gerhard Berger	McLaren	McLaren-Honda MP4/6	5 laps/engine	5
R	Pierluigi Martini	Minardi	Minardi-Ferrari M191	4 laps/spun off	15
DNQ	Erik Comas	Ligier	Ligier-Lamborghini JS35	-	27
DNQ	Gabriele Tarquini	AGS	AGS-Ford Cosworth JH25	-	28
DNQ	Stefan Johansson	Footwork	Footwork-Porsche FA12	-	29
DNQ	Fabrizio Barbazza	AGS	AGS-Ford Cosworth JH25	-	30
DNPQ	Nicola Larini	Modena Team	Lambo-Lamborghini 291	illegal rear wing	31
DNPQ	Eric van de Poele	Modena Team	Lambo-Lamborghini 291	-	32
DNPQ	Pedro Chaves	Coloni	Coloni-Ford Cosworth C4	-	33
DNPQ	Emanuele Pirro	BMS Scuderia Italia	Dallara-Judd 191	-	34

Pole: Patrese, 1m16.696s, 128.944mph/207.515kph. Fastest lap: Mansell, 1m16.788s, 128.789mph/207.266kph on Lap 61. Race leaders: Mansell 1-14, Patrese 15-67

FRENCH GRAND PRIX

MAGNY-COURS • ROUND 7 • DATE: 7TH JULY 1991
Laps: 72 • Distance: 191.79miles/307.512km • Weather: Warm but dull

Pos	Driver	Team	Chassis-Engine	Result	Qual
1	Nigel Mansell	Williams	Williams-Renault FW14	1h38m00.056s	4
2	Alain Prost	Ferrari	Ferrari 643	1h38m05.059s	2
3	Ayrton Senna	McLaren	McLaren-Honda MP4/6	1h38m34.990s	3
4	Jean Alesi	Ferrari	Ferrari 643	1h38m35.976s	6
5	Riccardo Patrese	Williams	Williams-Renault FW14	71 laps	1
6	Andrea de Cesaris	Jordan	Jordan-Ford Cosworth 191	71 laps	13
7	Mauricio Gugelmin	Leyton House	Leyton House-Ilmor CG911	70 laps	9
8	Nelson Piquet	Benetton	Benetton-Ford Cosworth B191	70 laps	7
9	Pierluigi Martini	Minardi	Minardi-Ferrari M191	70 laps	12
10	Johnny Herbert	Lotus	Lotus-Judd 102B	70 laps	20
11	Erik Comas	Ligier	Ligier-Lamborghini JS35	70 laps	14
12	Thierry Boutsen	Ligier	Ligier-Lamborghini JS35	69 laps	16
R	Roberto Moreno	Benetton	Benetton-Ford Cosworth B191	63 laps/driver unwell	8
R	Stefano Modena	Tyrrell	Tyrrell-Honda 020	57 laps/gearbox	11
R	Olivier Grouillard	Fondmetal	Fondmetal-Ford Cosworth F1	47 laps/oil leak	21
R	Eric Bernard	Larrousse	Lola-Ford Cosworth 91	43 laps/transmission	23
R	JJ Lehto	BMS Scuderia Italia	Dallara-Judd 191	39 laps/tyre	26

Pos	Driver	Team	Chassis-Engine	Result	Qual
R	Mark Blundell	Brabham	Brabham-Yamaha BT60Y	36 laps/spun off	17
R	Aguri Suzuki	Larrousse	Lola-Ford Cosworth 91	32 laps/transmission	22
R	Michele Alboreto	Footwork	Footwork-Ford Cosworth FA12C	31 laps/gearbox	25
R	Martin Brundle	Brabham	Brabham-Yamaha BT60Y	21 laps/gearbox	24
R	Satoru Nakajima	Tyrrell	Tyrrell-Honda 020	12 laps/spun off	18
R	Gianni Morbidelli	Minardi	Minardi-Ferrari M191	8 laps/collision	10
R	Ivan Capelli	Leyton House	Leyton House-Ilmor CG911	7 laps/spun off	15
R	Gerhard Berger	McLaren	McLaren-Honda MP4/6	6 laps/engine	5
R	Bertrand Gachot	Jordan	Jordan-Ford Cosworth 191	0 laps/spun off	19
DNQ	Mika Hakkinen	Lotus	Lotus-Judd 102B	-	27
DNQ	Fabrizio Barbazza	AGS	AGS-Ford Cosworth JH25B	-	28
DNQ	Gabriele Tarquini	AGS	AGS-Ford Cosworth JH25B	-	29
DNQ	Stefan Johansson	Footwork	Footwork-Ford Cosworth FA12C	-	30
DNPQ	Emanuele Pirro	BMS Scuderia Italia	Dallara-Judd 191	-	31
DNPQ	Nicola Larini	Modena Team	Lambo-Lamborghini 291	-	32
DNPQ	Eric van de Poele	Modena Team	Lambo-Lamborghini 291	-	33
DNPQ	Pedro Chaves	Coloni	Coloni-Ford Cosworth C4	-	34

Pole: Patrese, 1m14.559s, 128.139mph/206.220kph. Fastest lap: Mansell, 1m19.168s, 120.679mph/194.214kph on Lap 49. Race leaders: Prost 1-21 & 32-54, Mansell 22-31 & 55-72

FIRING A CHAMPION

Ferrari wasn't a happy camp in 1991 as its 643 chassis was no match for either the McLaren MP4/6 or the Williams FW14, and this led to a management reshuffle. Then, having failed to win a race and so ranked only fifth overall at the end of the season, Alain Prost was critical of the team manager Cesare Fiorio, and the team fired him.

BRITISH GRAND PRIX

SILVERSTONE • ROUND 8 • DATE: 14TH JULY 1991
Laps: 59 • Distance: 191.571miles/308.304km • Weather: Hot & bright

Pos	Driver	Team	Chassis-Engine	Result	Qual
1	Nigel Mansell	Williams	Williams-Renault FW14	1h27m35.479s	1
2	Gerhard Berger	McLaren	McLaren-Honda MP4/6	1h28m17.772s	4
3	Alain Prost	Ferrari	Ferrari 643	1h28m35.629s	5
4	Ayrton Senna	McLaren	McLaren-Honda MP4/6	58 laps/out of fuel	2
5	Nelson Piquet	Benetton	Benetton-Ford Cosworth B191	58 laps	8
6	Bertrand Gachot	Jordan	Jordan-Ford Cosworth 191	58 laps	17
7	Stefano Modena	Tyrrell	Tyrrell-Honda 020	58 laps	10
8	Satoru Nakajima	Tyrrell	Tyrrell-Honda 020	58 laps	15
9	Pierluigi Martini	Minardi	Minardi-Ferrari M191	58 laps	23
10	Emanuele Pirro	BMS Scuderia Italia	Dallara-Judd 191	57 laps	18
11	Gianni Morbidelli	Minardi	Minardi-Ferrari M191	57 laps	20
12	Mika Hakkinen	Lotus	Lotus-Judd 102B	57 laps	25
13	JJ Lehto	BMS Scuderia Italia	Dallara-Judd 191	56 laps	11
14	Johnny Herbert	Lotus	Lotus-Judd 102B	55 laps/fuel pressure	24
R	Mark Blundell	Brabham	Brabham-Yamaha BT60Y	52 laps/engine	12
R	Andrea de Cesaris	Jordan	Jordan-Ford Cosworth 191	41 laps/spun off	13
R	Jean Alesi	Ferrari	Ferrari 643	31 laps/collision	6

Pos	Driver	Team	Chassis-Engine	Result	Qual
R	Thierry Boutsen	Ligier	Ligier-Lamborghini JS35	29 laps/engine	19
R	Aguri Suzuki	Larrousse	Lola-Ford Cosworth 91	29 laps/collision	22
R	Martin Brundle	Brabham	Brabham-Yamaha BT60Y	28 laps/throttle	14
R	Michele Alboreto	Footwork	Footwork-Ford Cosworth FA12C	25 laps/transmission	26
R	Mauricio Gugelmin	Leyton House	Leyton House-Ilmor CG911	24 laps/chassis	9
R	Roberto Moreno	Benetton	Benetton-Ford Cosworth B191	21 laps/gearbox	7
R	Eric Bernard	Larrousse	Lola-Ford Cosworth 91	21 laps/transmission	21
R	Ivan Capelli	Leyton House	Leyton House-Ilmor CG911	16 laps/spun off	16
R	Riccardo Patrese	Williams	Williams-Renault FW14	1 lap/collision	3
DNQ	Erik Comas	Ligier	Ligier-Lamborghini JS35	-	27
DNQ	Stefan Johansson	Footwork	Footwork-Ford Cosworth FA12C	-	28
DNQ	Fabrizio Barbazza	AGS	AGS-Ford Cosworth JH25B	-	29
DNQ	Gabriele Tarquini	AGS	AGS-Ford Cosworth JH25B	-	30
DNPQ	Olivier Grouillard	Fondmetal	Fondmetal-Ford Cosworth F1	-	31
DNPQ	Nicola Larini	Modena Team	Lambo-Lamborghini 291	-	32
DNPQ	Eric van de Poele	Modena Team	Lambo-Lamborghini 291	-	33
DNPQ	Pedro Chaves	Coloni	Coloni-Ford Cosworth C4	-	34

Pole: Mansell, 1m20.939s, 144.418mph/232.419kph. Fastest lap: Mansell, 1m26.379s, 135.323mph/217.782kph on Lap 43. Race leaders: Mansell 1-59

DRIVER GOES TO JAIL

Bertrand Gachot's career took an unexpected turn when he wasn't able to continue the promising progress he had been making with Jordan, as he was jailed for assaulting a taxi driver with CS gas after an altercation at London's Hyde Park Corner. This opened the way for Michael Schumacher to be signed as his replacement, and the rest is history.

GERMAN GRAND PRIX

HOCKENHEIM • ROUND 9 • DATE: 28TH JULY 1991
Laps: 45 • Distance: 190.145miles/306.09km • Weather: Hot & bright

Pos	Driver	Team	Chassis-Engine	Result	Qual
1	Nigel Mansell	Williams	Williams-Renault FW14	1h19m29.661s	1
2	Riccardo Patrese	Williams	Williams-Renault FW14	1h19m43.440s	4
3	Jean Alesi	Ferrari	Ferrari 643	1h19m47.279s	6
4	Gerhard Berger	McLaren	McLaren-Honda MP4/6	1h20m02.312s	3
5	Andrea de Cesaris	Jordan	Jordan-Ford Cosworth 191	1h20m47.198s	7
6	Bertrand Gachot	Jordan	Jordan-Ford Cosworth 191	1h21m10.266s	11
7	Ayrton Senna	McLaren	McLaren-Honda MP4/6	44 laps/out of fuel	2
8	Roberto Moreno	Benetton	Benetton-Ford Cosworth B191	44 laps	9
9	Thierry Boutsen	Ligier	Ligier-Lamborghini JS35	44 laps	17
10	Emanuele Pirro	BMS Scuderia Italia	Dallara-Judd 191	44 laps	18
11	Martin Brundle	Brabham	Brabham-Yamaha BT60Y	43 laps	15
12	Mark Blundell	Brabham	Brabham-Yamaha BT60Y	43 laps	21
13	Stefano Modena	Tyrrell	Tyrrell-Honda 020	41 laps	14
R	Alain Prost	Ferrari	Ferrari 643	37 laps/spun off	5
R	Ivan Capelli	Leyton House	Leyton House-Ilmor CG911	36 laps/engine	12
R	JJ Lehto	BMS Scuderia Italia	Dallara-Judd 191	35 laps/engine	20
R	Nelson Piquet	Benetton	Benetton-Ford Cosworth B191	27 laps/engine	8

Pos	Driver	Team	Chassis-Engine	Result	Qual
R	Satoru Nakajima	Tyrrell	Tyrrell-Honda 020	26 laps/gearbox	13
R	Erik Comas	Ligier	Ligier-Lamborghini JS35	22 laps/engine	26
R	Mauricio Gugelmin	Leyton House	Leyton House-Ilmor CG911	21 laps/gearbox	16
R	Mika Hakkinen	Lotus	Lotus-Judd 102B	19 laps/engine	23
R	Aguri Suzuki	Larrousse	Lola-Ford Cosworth 91	15 laps/engine	22
R	Gianni Morbidelli	Minardi	Minardi-Ferrari M191	14 laps/differential	19
R	Pierluigi Martini	Minardi	Minardi-Ferrari M191	11 laps/differential	10
R	Eric Bernard	Larrousse	Lola-Ford Cosworth 91	9 laps/transmission	25
R	Nicola Larini	Modena Team	Lambo-Lamborghini 291	0 laps/spun off	24
DNQ	Michele Alboreto	Footwork	Footwork-Ford Cosworth FA12C	-	27
DNQ	Michael Bartels	Lotus	Lotus-Judd 102B	-	28
DNQ	Gabriele Tarquini	AGS	AGS-Ford Cosworth JH25B	-	29
DNQ	Eric van de Poele	Modena Team	Lambo-Lamborghini 291	-	30
DNPQ	Olivier Grouillard	Fondmetal	Fondmetal-Ford Cosworth F1	-	31
DNPQ	Alex Caffi	Footwork	Footwork-Ford Cosworth FA12C	-	32
DNPQ	Fabrizio Barbazza	AGS	AGS-Ford Cosworth JH25B	-	33
DNPQ	Pedro Chaves	Coloni	Coloni-Ford Cosworth C4	-	34

Pole: Mansell, 1m37.087s, 156.721mph/252.219kph. Fastest lap: Patrese, 1m43.569s, 146.913mph/236.433kph on Lap 35. Race leaders: Mansell 1-18 & 21-45, Alesi 19-20

STARTING IN STYLE

Following his impressive F1 debut at the Belgian GP, when he qualified his Jordan seventh, Michael Schumacher triggered a shuffle for the following race at Monza, as he was signed by Benetton for the rest of the year, meaning that Roberto Moreno was transferred in the opposite direction. Schumacher came fifth in his first race for Benetton.

HUNGARIAN GRAND PRIX

HUNGARORING • ROUND 10 • DATE: 11TH AUGUST 1991
Laps: 77 • Distance: 189.851miles/305.536km • Weather: Hot & bright

Pos	Driver	Team	Chassis-Engine	Result	Qual
1	Ayrton Senna	McLaren	McLaren-Honda MP4/6	1h49m12.796s	1
2	Nigel Mansell	Williams	Williams-Renault FW14	1h49m17.395s	3
3	Riccardo Patrese	Williams	Williams-Renault FW14	1h49m28.390s	2
4	Gerhard Berger	McLaren	McLaren-Honda MP4/6	1h49m34.652s	5
5	Jean Alesi	Ferrari	Ferrari 643	1h49m44.185s	6
6	Ivan Capelli	Leyton House	Leyton House-Ilmor CG911	76 laps	9
7	Andrea de Cesaris	Jordan	Jordan-Ford Cosworth 191	76 laps	17
8	Roberto Moreno	Benetton	Benetton-Ford Cosworth B191	76 laps	15
9	Bertrand Gachot	Jordan	Jordan-Ford Cosworth 191	76 laps	16
10	Erik Comas	Ligier	Ligier-Lamborghini JS35	75 laps	25
11	Mauricio Gugelmin	Leyton House	Leyton House-Ilmor CG911	75 laps	13
12	Stefano Modena	Tyrrell	Tyrrell-Honda 020	75 laps	8
13	Gianni Morbidelli	Minardi	Minardi-Ferrari M191	75 laps	23
14	Mika Hakkinen	Lotus	Lotus-Judd 102B	74 laps	26
15	Satoru Nakajima	Tyrrell	Tyrrell-Honda 020	74 laps	14
16	Nicola Larini	Modena Team	Lambo-Lamborghini 291	74 laps	24
17	Thierry Boutsen	Ligier	Ligier-Lamborghini JS35	71 laps/engine	19

Pos	Driver	Team	Chassis-Engine	Result	Qual
R	Pierluigi Martini	Minardi	Minardi-Ferrari M191	65 laps/engine	18
R	Mark Blundell	Brabham	Brabham-Yamaha BT60Y	62 laps/spun off	20
R	Martin Brundle	Brabham	Brabham-Yamaha BT60Y	59 laps/cramp	10
R	JJ Lehto	BMS Scuderia Italia	Dallara-Judd 191	49 laps/engine	12
R	Nelson Piquet	Benetton	Benetton-Ford Cosworth B191	38 laps/gearbox	11
R	Eric Bernard	Larrousse	Lola-Ford Cosworth 91	38 laps/engine	21
R	Aguri Suzuki	Larrousse	Lola-Ford Cosworth 91	38 laps/engine	22
R	Emanuele Pirro	BMS Scuderia Italia	Dallara-Judd 191	37 laps/engine	7
R	Alain Prost	Ferrari	Ferrari 643	28 laps/engine	4
DNQ	Olivier Grouillard	Fondmetal	Fondmetal-Ford Cosworth F1	-	27
DNQ	Michele Alboreto	Footwork	Footwork-Ford Cosworth FA12C	-	28
DNQ	Eric van de Poele	Modena Team	Lambo-Lamborghini 291	-	29
DNQ	Michael Bartels	Lotus	Lotus-Judd 102B	-	30
DNPQ	Gabriele Tarquini	AGS	AGS-Ford Cosworth JH25B	-	31
DNPQ	Alex Caffi	Footwork	Footwork-Ford Cosworth FA12C	-	32
DNPQ	Fabrizio Barbazza	AGS	AGS-Ford Cosworth JH25B	-	33
DNPQ	Pedro Chaves	Coloni	Coloni-Ford Cosworth C4	-	34

Pole: Senna, 1m16.147s, 116.566mph/187.595kph. Fastest lap: Gachot, 1m21.547s, 108.847mph/175.172kph on Lap 71. Race leaders: Senna 1-77

RAIN STOPS PLAY

The season-closing Australian GP was stopped by torrential rain that made driving conditions extremely perilous – five cars collided and Mansell hit a wall. Ayrton Senna was declared the winner when it was decided not to restart the race. As only 14 of the scheduled 81 laps had been run, half points were awarded.

BELGIAN GRAND PRIX

SPA-FRANCORCHAMPS • ROUND 11 • DATE: 25TH AUGUST 1991
Laps: 44 • Distance: 189.540miles/305.36km • Weather: Hot & bright

Pos	Driver	Team	Chassis-Engine	Result	Qual
1	Ayrton Senna	McLaren	McLaren-Honda MP4/6	1h27m17.669s	1
2	Gerhard Berger	McLaren	McLaren-Honda MP4/6	1h27m19.570s	4
3	Nelson Piquet	Benetton	Benetton-Ford Cosworth B191	1h27m49.845s	6
4	Roberto Moreno	Benetton	Benetton-Ford Cosworth B191	1h27m54.979s	8
5	Riccardo Patrese	Williams	Williams-Renault FW14	1h28m14.856s	17
6	Mark Blundell	Brabham	Brabham-Yamaha BT60Y	1h28m57.704s	13
7	Johnny Herbert	Lotus	Lotus-Judd 102B	1h29m02.268s	21
8	Emanuele Pirro	BMS Scuderia Italia	Dallara-Judd 191	43 laps	25
9	Martin Brundle	Brabham	Brabham-Yamaha BT60Y	43 laps	16
10	Olivier Grouillard	Fondmetal	Fondmetal-Ford Cosworth F1	43 laps	23
11	Thierry Boutsen	Ligier	Ligier-Lamborghini JS35	43 laps	18
12	Pierluigi Martini	Minardi	Minardi-Ferrari M191	42 laps	9
13	Andrea de Cesaris	Jordan	Jordan-Ford Cosworth 191	41 laps/engine	11
R	Stefano Modena	Tyrrell	Tyrrell-Honda 020	33 laps/oil leak	10
R	JJ Lehto	BMS Scuderia Italia	Dallara-Judd 191	33 laps/fuel pressure	14
R	Jean Alesi	Ferrari	Ferrari 643	30 laps/engine	5
R	Gianni Morbidelli	Minardi	Minardi-Ferrari M191	29 laps/gearbox	19

Pos	Driver	Team	Chassis-Engine	Result	Qual
R	Mika Hakkinen	Lotus	Lotus-Judd 102B	25 laps/engine	24
R	Erik Comas	Ligier	Ligier-Lamborghini JS35	25 laps/engine	26
R	Nigel Mansell	Williams	Williams-Renault FW14	22 laps/electrical	3
R	Eric Bernard	Larrousse	Lola-Ford Cosworth 91	21 laps/gearbox	20
R	Ivan Capelli	Leyton House	Leyton House-Ilmor CG911	13 laps/engine	12
R	Satoru Nakajima	Tyrrell	Tyrrell-Honda 020	7 laps/spun off	22
R	Alain Prost	Ferrari	Ferrari 643	2 laps/oil leak	2
R	Mauricio Gugelmin	Leyton House	Leyton House-Ilmor CG911	1 lap/engine	15
R	Michael Schumacher	Jordan	Jordan-Ford Cosworth 191	0 laps/clutch	7
DNQ	Aguri Suzuki	Larrousse	Lola-Ford Cosworth 91	-	27
DNQ	Nicola Larini	Modena Team	Lambo-Lamborghini 291	-	28
DNQ	Alex Caffi	Footwork	Footwork-Ford Cosworth FA12C	-	29
DNQ	Eric van de Poele	Modena Team	Lambo-Lamborghini 291	-	30
DNPQ	Michele Alboreto	Footwork	Footwork-Ford Cosworth FA12C	-	31
DNPQ	Gabriele Tarquini	AGS	AGS-Ford Cosworth JH25B	-	32
DNPQ	Pedro Chaves	Coloni	Coloni-Ford Cosworth C4	-	33
DNPQ	Fabrizio Barbazza	AGS	AGS-Ford Cosworth JH25B	-	34

Pole: Senna, 1m47.811s, 143.995mph/231.738kph. Fastest lap: Moreno, 1m55.161s, 134.805mph/216.948kph on Lap 40. Race leaders: Senna 1-14 & 31-44, Mansell 15-16 & 18-21, Piquet 17, Alesi 22-30

ITALIAN GRAND PRIX

MONZA • ROUND 12 • DATE: 8TH SEPTEMBER 1991
Laps: 53 • Distance: 190.763miles/307.4km • Weather: Warm but hazy

Pos	Driver	Team	Chassis-Engine	Result	Qual
1	Nigel Mansell	Williams	Williams-Renault FW14	1h17m54.319s	2
2	Ayrton Senna	McLaren	McLaren-Honda MP4/6	1h18m10.581s	1
3	Alain Prost	Ferrari	Ferrari 643	1h18m11.148s	5
4	Gerhard Berger	McLaren	McLaren-Honda MP4/6	1h18m22.038s	3
5	Michael Schumacher	Benetton	Benetton-Ford Cosworth B191	1h18m28.782s	7
6	Nelson Piquet	Benetton	Benetton-Ford Cosworth B191	1h18m39.919s	8
7	Andrea de Cesaris	Jordan	Jordan-Ford Cosworth 191	1h18m45.455s	14
8	Ivan Capelli	Leyton House	Leyton House-Ilmor CG911	1h19m09.338s	12
9	Gianni Morbidelli	Minardi	Minardi-Ferrari M191	52 laps	17
10	Emanuele Pirro	BMS Scuderia Italia	Dallara-Judd 191	52 laps	16
11	Erik Comas	Ligier	Ligier-Lamborghini JS35	52 laps	22
12	Mark Blundell	Brabham	Brabham-Yamaha BT60Y	52 laps	11
13	Martin Brundle	Brabham	Brabham-Yamaha BT60Y	52 laps	19
14	Mika Hakkinen	Lotus	Lotus-Judd 102B	49 laps	25
15	Mauricio Gugelmin	Leyton House	Leyton House-Ilmor CG911	49 laps	18
16	Nicola Larini	Modena Team	Lambo-Lamborghini 291	48 laps	23
R	Olivier Grouillard	Fondmetal	Fondmetal-Ford Cosworth F1	46 laps/engine	26
R	JJ Lehto	BMS Scuderia Italia	Dallara-Judd 191	35 laps/overheating	20
R	Stefano Modena	Tyrrell	Tyrrell-Honda 020	32 laps/engine	13
R	Jean Alesi	Ferrari	Ferrari 643	29 laps/engine	6
R	Riccardo Patrese	Williams	Williams-Renault FW14	27 laps/gearbox	4
R	Satoru Nakajima	Tyrrell	Tyrrell-Honda 020	24 laps/throttle	15
R	Eric Bernard	Larrousse	Lola-Ford Cosworth 91	21 laps/engine	24
R	Pierluigi Martini	Minardi	Minardi-Ferrari M191	8 laps/spun off	10
R	Roberto Moreno	Jordan	Jordan-Ford Cosworth 191	2 laps/spun off	9
R	Thierry Boutsen	Ligier	Ligier-Lamborghini JS35	1 lap/spun off	21
DNQ	Michele Alboreto	Footwork	Footwork-Ford Cosworth FA12C	-	27

Pos	Driver	Team	Chassis-Engine	Result	Qual
DNQ	Michael Bartels	Lotus	Lotus-Judd 102B	-	28
DNQ	Eric van de Poele	Modena Team	Lambo-Lamborghini 291	-	29
DNQ	Aguri Suzuki	Larrousse	Lola-Ford Cosworth 91	-	30
DNPQ	Fabrizio Barbazza	AGS	AGS-Ford Cosworth JH25B	-	31
DNPQ	Gabriele Tarquini	AGS	AGS-Ford Cosworth JH27	-	32
DNPQ	Alex Caffi	Footwork	Footwork-Ford Cosworth FA12C	-	33
DNPQ	Pedro Chaves	Coloni	Coloni-Ford Cosworth C4	-	34

Pole: Senna, 1m21.114s, 159.950mph/257.415kph. Fastest lap: Senna, 1m26.061s, 150.756mph/242.618kph on Lap 41. Race leaders: Senna 1-25 & 27-33, Patrese 26, Mansell 34-53

PORTUGUESE GRAND PRIX

AUTODROMO DO ESTORIL • ROUND 13 • DATE: 22ND SEPTEMBER 1991
Laps: 71 • Distance: 191.435miles/308.85km • Weather: Warm & bright

Pos	Driver	Team	Chassis-Engine	Result	Qual
1	Riccardo Patrese	Williams	Williams-Renault FW14	1h35m42.304s	1
2	Ayrton Senna	McLaren	McLaren-Honda MP4/6	1h36m03.245s	3
3	Jean Alesi	Ferrari	Ferrari 643	1h36m35.858s	6
4	Pierluigi Martini	Minardi	Minardi-Ferrari M191	1h36m45.802s	8
5	Nelson Piquet	Benetton	Benetton-Ford Cosworth B191	1h36m52.337s	11
6	Michael Schumacher	Benetton	Benetton-Ford Cosworth B191	1h36m58.886s	10
7	Mauricio Gugelmin	Leyton House	Leyton House-Ilmor CG911	70 laps	7
8	Andrea de Cesaris	Jordan	Jordan-Ford Cosworth 191	70 laps	14
9	Gianni Morbidelli	Minardi	Minardi-Ferrari M191	70 laps	13
10	Roberto Moreno	Jordan	Jordan-Ford Cosworth 191	70 laps	16
11	Erik Comas	Ligier	Ligier-Lamborghini JS35	70 laps	23
12	Martin Brundle	Brabham	Brabham-Yamaha BT60Y	69 laps	19
13	Satoru Nakajima	Tyrrell	Tyrrell-Honda 020	68 laps	21
14	Mika Hakkinen	Lotus	Lotus-Judd 102B	68 laps	26
15	Michele Alboreto	Footwork	Footwork-Ford Cosworth FA12C	68 laps	24
16	Thierry Boutsen	Ligier	Ligier-Lamborghini JS35	68 laps	20
17	Ivan Capelli	Leyton House	Leyton House-Ilmor CG911	64 laps/spun off	9
R	Stefano Modena	Tyrrell	Tyrrell-Honda 020	56 laps/engine	12
DQ	Nigel Mansell	Williams	Williams-Renault FW14	51 laps/pit-lane breach	4
R	Aguri Suzuki	Larrousse	Lola-Ford Cosworth 91	40 laps/transmission	25
R	Alain Prost	Ferrari	Ferrari 643	39 laps/engine	5
R	Gerhard Berger	McLaren	McLaren-Honda MP4/6	37 laps/engine	2
R	Emanuele Pirro	BMS Scuderia Italia	Dallara-Judd 191	18 laps/engine	17
R	JJ Lehto	BMS Scuderia Italia	Dallara-Judd 191	14 laps/gearbox	18
R	Mark Blundell	Brabham	Brabham-Yamaha BT60Y	12 laps/suspension	15
R	Johnny Herbert	Lotus	Lotus-Judd 102B	1 lap/engine	22
DNQ	Eric Bernard	Larrousse	Lola-Ford Cosworth 91	-	27
DNQ	Gabriele Tarquini	AGS	AGS-Ford Cosworth JH27	-	28
DNQ	Nicola Larini	Modena Team	Lambo-Lamborghini 291	-	29
DNQ	Eric van de Poele	Modena Team	Lambo-Lamborghini 291	-	30
DNPQ	Fabrizio Barbazza	AGS	AGS-Ford Cosworth JH27	-	31
DNPQ	Olivier Grouillard	Fondmetal	Fondmetal-Ford Cosworth F1	-	32
DNPQ	Alex Caffi	Footwork	Footwork-Ford Cosworth FA12C	-	33
DNPQ	Pedro Chaves	Coloni	Coloni-Ford Cosworth C4	-	34

Pole: Patrese, 1m13.001s, 133.295mph/214.517kph. Fastest lap: Mansell, 1m18.179s, 124.466mph/200.309kph on Lap 36. Race leaders: Patrese 1-17 & 30-71, Mansell 18-29

SPANISH GRAND PRIX

BARCELONA-CATALUNYA • ROUND 14 • DATE: 29TH SEPTEMBER 1991
Laps: 65 • Distance: 191.727miles/308.555km • Weather: Warm, drying track

Pos	Driver	Team	Chassis-Engine	Result	Qual
1	Nigel Mansell	Williams	Williams-Renault FW14	1h38m41.541s	2
2	Alain Prost	Ferrari	Ferrari 643	1h38m52.872s	6
3	Riccardo Patrese	Williams	Williams-Renault FW14	1h38m57.450s	4
4	Jean Alesi	Ferrari	Ferrari 643	1h39m04.313s	7
5	Ayrton Senna	McLaren	McLaren-Honda MP4/6	1h39m43.943s	3
6	Michael Schumacher	Benetton	Benetton-Ford Cosworth B191	1h40m01.009s	5
7	Mauricio Gugelmin	Leyton House	Leyton House-Ilmor CG911	64 laps	13
8	JJ Lehto	BMS Scuderia Italia	Dallara-Judd 191	64 laps	15
9	Alessandro Zanardi	Jordan	Jordan-Ford Cosworth 191	64 laps	20
10	Martin Brundle	Brabham	Brabham-Yamaha BT60Y	63 laps	11
11	Nelson Piquet	Benetton	Benetton-Ford Cosworth B191	63 laps	10
12	Gabriele Tarquini	Fondmetal	Fondmetal-Ford Cosworth F1	63 laps	22
13	Pierluigi Martini	Minardi	Minardi-Ferrari M191	63 laps	19
14	Gianni Morbidelli	Minardi	Minardi-Ferrari M191	62 laps/spun off	16
15	Emanuele Pirro	BMS Scuderia Italia	Dallara-Judd 191	62 laps	9
16	Stefano Modena	Tyrrell	Tyrrell-Honda 020	62 laps	14
17	Satoru Nakajima	Tyrrell	Tyrrell-Honda 020	62 laps	18
R	Mark Blundell	Brabham	Brabham-Yamaha BT60Y	49 laps/engine	12
R	Erik Comas	Ligier	Ligier-Lamborghini JS35	36 laps/electrical	25
R	Gerhard Berger	McLaren	McLaren-Honda MP4/6	33 laps/electrical	1
R	Michele Alboreto	Footwork	Footwork-Ford Cosworth FA12C	23 laps/engine	24
R	Andrea de Cesaris	Jordan	Jordan-Ford Cosworth 191	22 laps/electrical	17
R	Mika Hakkinen	Lotus	Lotus-Judd 102B	5 laps/spun off	21
R	Ivan Capelli	Leyton House	Leyton House-Ilmor CG911	1 lap/collision	8
R	Eric Bernard	Larrousse	Lola-Ford Cosworth 91	0 laps/collision	23
R	Thierry Boutsen	Ligier	Ligier-Lamborghini JS35	0 laps/collision	26
DNQ	Aguri Suzuki	Larrousse	Lola-Ford Cosworth 91	-	27
DNQ	Nicola Larini	Modena Team	Lambo-Lamborghini 291	-	28
DNQ	Michael Bartels	Lotus	Lotus-Judd 102B	-	29
DNQ	Eric van de Poele	Modena Team	Lambo-Lamborghini 291	-	30
DNPQ	Alex Caffi	Footwork	Footwork-Ford Cosworth FA12C	-	31
DNPQ	Fabrizio Barbazza	AGS	AGS-Ford Cosworth JH27	-	32
DNPQ	Olivier Grouillard	AGS	AGS-Ford Cosworth JH27	-	33

Pole: Berger, 1m18.751s, 134.839mph/217.002kph. Fastest lap: Patrese, 1m22.837s, 128.188mph/206.299kph on Lap 63. Race leaders: Berger 1-8 & 12-20, Mansell 9 & 21-65, Patrese 10, Senna 11

NEW CIRCUITS

Two circuits made their debuts in 1991. The first was Circuit de Catalunya, set in hills to the north of Barcelona. The second was the hugely upgraded Magny-Cours circuit in the middle of France. The Phoenix circuit was modified, while Silverstone had a major revamp, with Becketts being turned into esses and the addition of Vale and the Brooklands loop.

JAPANESE GRAND PRIX

SUZUKA • ROUND 15 • DATE: 20TH OCTOBER 1991
Laps: 53 • Distance: 193.117miles/310.792km • Weather: Warm & bright

Pos	Driver	Team	Chassis-Engine	Result	Qual
1	Gerhard Berger	McLaren	McLaren-Honda MP4/6	1h32m10.695s	1
2	Ayrton Senna	McLaren	McLaren-Honda MP4/6	1h32m11.039s	2
3	Riccardo Patrese	Williams	Williams-Renault FW14	1h33m07.426s	5
4	Alain Prost	Ferrari	Ferrari 643	1h33m31.456s	4
5	Martin Brundle	Brabham	Brabham-Yamaha BT60Y	52 laps	19
6	Stefano Modena	Tyrrell	Tyrrell-Honda 020	52 laps	14
7	Nelson Piquet	Benetton	Benetton-Ford Cosworth B191	52 laps	10
8	Mauricio Gugelmin	Leyton House	Leyton House-Ilmor CG911	52 laps	18
9	Thierry Boutsen	Ligier	Ligier-Lamborghini JS35	52 laps	17
10	Alex Caffi	Footwork	Footwork-Ford Cosworth FA12C	51 laps	26
11	Gabriele Tarquini	Fondmetal	Fondmetal-Ford Cosworth F1	50 laps	24
R	Erik Comas	Ligier	Ligier-Lamborghini JS35	41 laps/alternator	20
R	Pierluigi Martini	Minardi	Minardi-Ferrari M191	39 laps/electrical	7
R	Michael Schumacher	Benetton	Benetton-Ford Cosworth B191	34 laps/engine	9
R	Johnny Herbert	Lotus	Lotus-Judd 102B	31 laps/engine	23
R	Satoru Nakajima	Tyrrell	Tyrrell-Honda 020	30 laps/spun off	15
R	Aguri Suzuki	Larrousse	Lola-Ford Cosworth 91	26 laps/engine	25
R	Gianni Morbidelli	Minardi	Minardi-Ferrari M191	15 laps/wheel	8
R	Nigel Mansell	Williams	Williams-Renault FW14	9 laps/spun off	3
R	Alessandro Zanardi	Jordan	Jordan-Ford Cosworth 191	7 laps/gearbox	13
R	Mika Hakkinen	Lotus	Lotus-Judd 102B	4 laps/engine	21
R	Andrea de Cesaris	Jordan	Jordan-Ford Cosworth 191	1 lap/collision	11
R	JJ Lehto	BMS Scuderia Italia	Dallara-Judd 191	1 lap/collision	12
R	Emanuele Pirro	BMS Scuderia Italia	Dallara-Judd 191	1 lap/collision	16
R	Karl Wendlinger	Leyton House	Leyton House-Ilmor CG911	1 lap/collision	22
R	Jean Alesi	Ferrari	Ferrari 643	0 laps/engine	6
DNQ	Michele Alboreto	Footwork	Footwork-Ford Cosworth FA12C	-	27
DNQ	Nicola Larini	Modena Team	Lambo-Lamborghini 291	-	28
DNQ	Eric van de Poele	Modena Team	Lambo-Lamborghini 291	-	29
DNQ	Eric Bernard	Larrousse	Lola-Ford Cosworth 91	broken ankle	30
DNPQ	Mark Blundell	Brabham	Brabham-Yamaha BT60Y	-	31
DNPQ	Naoki Hattori	Coloni	Coloni-Ford Cosworth C4	-	32

Pole: Berger, 1m34.700s, 138.515mph/222.918kph. Fastest lap: Senna, 1m41.532s, 129.194mph/207.918kph on Lap 39. Race leaders: Berger 1-17 & 53, Senna 18-21 & 24-52, Patrese 22-23

NEW CONSTRUCTORS

Jordan stood out among the three newcomers, taking a pair of fourth places. The other two new teams were Fondmetal and Modena Team SpA. The first was a continuation of Osella after it was taken over by Gabriele Rumi, but it achieved little; Eric van de Poele was heading for fifth at Imola for the latter until his Lambo ran out of fuel.

NEW DRIVERS

The 1991 season marked the debut of another future world champion, in addition to Michael Schumacher. This was Mika Hakkinen, who showed immediate promise for Lotus. Mark Blundell (sixth at Spa for Brabham) and Erik Comas (eighth at Montreal for Ligier) were the pick of the other nine that also included future IndyCar star Alessandro Zanardi.

AUSTRALIAN GRAND PRIX

ADELAIDE • ROUND 16 • DATE: 3RD NOVEMBER 1991
Laps: 14 • Distance: 32.368miles/52.92km • Weather: Cool & very wet

Pos	Driver	Team	Chassis-Engine	Result	Qual
1	Ayrton Senna	McLaren	McLaren-Honda MP4/6	24m34.899s	1
2	Nigel Mansell	Williams	Williams-Renault FW14	24m36.158s	3
3	Gerhard Berger	McLaren	McLaren-Honda MP4/6	24m40.019s	2
4	Nelson Piquet	Benetton	Benetton-Ford Cosworth B191	25m05.002s	5
5	Riccardo Patrese	Williams	Williams-Renault FW14	25m25.436s	4
6	Gianni Morbidelli	Ferrari	Ferrari 643	25m25.968s	8
7	Emanuele Pirro	BMS Scuderia Italia	Dallara-Judd 191	25m27.260s	13
8	Andrea de Cesaris	Jordan	Jordan-Ford Cosworth 191	25m35.330s	12
9	Alessandro Zanardi	Jordan	Jordan-Ford Cosworth 191	25m50.466s	16
10	Stefano Modena	Tyrrell	Tyrrell-Honda 020	25m55.269s	9
11	Johnny Herbert	Lotus	Lotus-Judd 102B	25m56.972s	21
12	JJ Lehto	BMS Scuderia Italia	Dallara-Judd 191	26m13.418s	11
13	Michele Alboreto	Footwork	Footwork-Ford Cosworth FA12C	26m14.202s	15
14	Mauricio Gugelmin	Leyton House	Leyton House-Ilmor CG911	13 laps/accident	14
15	Alex Caffi	Footwork	Footwork-Ford Cosworth FA12C	13 laps	23
16	Roberto Moreno	Minardi	Minardi-Ferrari M191	13 laps	18
17	Mark Blundell	Brabham	Brabham-Yamaha BT60Y	13 laps	17
18	Erik Comas	Ligier	Ligier-Lamborghini JS35	13 laps	22
19	Mika Hakkinen	Lotus	Lotus-Judd 102B	13 laps	25
20	Karl Wendlinger	Leyton House	Leyton House-Ilmor CG911	12 laps	26
R	Pierluigi Martini	Minardi	Minardi-Ferrari M191	8 laps/spun off	10
R	Michael Schumacher	Benetton	Benetton-Ford Cosworth B191	5 laps/collision	6
R	Jean Alesi	Ferrari	Ferrari 643	5 laps/collision	7
R	Nicola Larini	Modena Team	Lambo-Lamborghini 291	5 laps/spun off	19
R	Thierry Boutsen	Ligier	Ligier-Lamborghini JS35	5 laps/collision	20
R	Satoru Nakajima	Tyrrell	Tyrrell-Honda 020	4 laps/spun off	24
DNQ	Aguri Suzuki	Larrousse	Lola-Ford Cosworth 91	-	27
DNQ	Martin Brundle	Brabham	Brabham-Yamaha BT60Y	-	28
DNQ	Eric van de Poele	Modena Team	Lambo-Lamborghini 291	-	29
DNQ	Bertrand Gachot	Larrousse	Lola-Ford Cosworth 91	-	30
DNPQ	Gabriele Tarquini	Fondmetal	Fondmetal-Ford Cosworth F1	-	31
DNPQ	Naoki Hattori	Coloni	Coloni-Ford Cosworth C4	-	32

Pole: Senna, 1m14.041s, 114.201mph/183.790kph. Fastest lap: Berger, 1m41.141s, 83.602mph/134.544kph on Lap 14. Race leaders: Senna 1-14

WORLD DRIVERS' CHAMPIONSHIP FINAL RESULTS

Pos	Driver	Nat	Car-Engine	R1	R2	R3	R4	R5	R6
1	Ayrton Senna	BRA	McLaren-Honda MP4/6	1P	1P	1P	1P	R	3
2	Nigel Mansell	GBR	Williams-Renault FW14	R	RF	R	2	6F	2F
3	Riccardo Patrese	ITA	Williams-Renault FW14	R	2	R	R	3P	1P
4	Gerhard Berger	AUT	McLaren-Honda MP4/6	R	3	2F	R	R	R
5	Alain Prost	FRA	Ferrari 642	2	4	NS	5F	R	R
			Ferrari 643	-	-	-	-	-	-
6	Nelson Piquet	BRA	Benetton-Ford Cosworth B190B	3	5	-	-	-	-
			Benetton-Ford Cosworth B191	-	-	R	R	1	R
7	Jean Alesi	FRA	Ferrari 642	12F	6	R	3	R	R
			Ferrari 643	-	-	-	-	-	-
8	Stefano Modena	ITA	Tyrrell-Honda 020	4	R	R	R	2	11
9	Andrea de Cesaris	ITA	Jordan-Ford Cosworth 191	DNPQ	R	R	R	4	4
10	Roberto Moreno	BRA	Benetton-Ford Cosworth B190B	R	7	-	-	-	-
			Benetton-Ford Cosworth B191	-	-	13	4	R	5
			Jordan-Ford Cosworth 191	-	-	-	-	-	-
			Minardi-Ferrari M191	-	-	-	-	-	-
11	Pierluigi Martini	ITA	Minardi-Ferrari M191	9	R	4	12	7	R
12	JJ Lehto	FIN	Dallara-Judd 191	R	R	3	11	R	R
13	Bertrand Gachot	FRA	Jordan-Ford Cosworth 191	10	13	R	8	5	R
			Lola-Ford Cosworth 91	-	-	-	-	-	-
13	Michael Schumacher	DEU	Jordan-Ford Cosworth 191	-	-	-	-	-	-
			Benetton-Ford Cosworth B191	-	-	-	-	-	-
15	Satoru Nakajima	JPN	Tyrrell-Honda 020	5	R	R	R	10	12
15	Mika Hakkinen	FIN	Lotus-Judd 102B	R	9	5	R	R	9
15	Martin Brundle	GBR	Brabham-Yamaha BT59Y	11	12	-	-	-	-
			Brabham-Yamaha BT60Y	-	-	11	DNQ	R	R
18	Aguri Suzuki	JPN	Lola-Ford Cosworth 91	6	NS	R	R	R	R
18	Julian Bailey	GBR	Lotus-Judd 102B	DNQ	DNQ	6	DNQ	-	-
18	Emanuele Pirro	ITA	Dallara-Judd 191	R	11	DNPQ	6	9	DNPQ
18	Eric Bernard	FRA	Lola-Ford Cosworth 91	R	R	R	9	R	6
18	Ivan Capelli	ITA	Leyton House-Ilmor CG911	R	R	R	R	R	R
18	Mark Blundell	GBR	Brabham-Yamaha BT59Y	R	R	-	-	-	-
			Brabham-Yamaha BT60Y	-	-	8	R	DNQ	R
24	Gianni Morbidelli	ITA	Minardi-Ferrari M191	R	8	R	R	R	7
			Ferrari 643	-	-	-	-	-	-

Pos	Driver	R7	R8	R9	R10	R11	R12	R13	R14	R15	R16	Total
1	Senna	3	4	7	1P	1P	2PF	2	5	2F	1P	96
2	Mansell	1F	1PF	1P	2	R	1	DQF	1	R	2	72
3	Patrese	5P	R	2F	3	5	R	1P	3F	3	5	53
4	Berger	R	2	4	4	2	4	R	RP	1P	3F	43
5	Prost	-	-	-	-	-	-	-	-	-	-	34
		2	3	R	R	R	3	R	2	4	-	
6	Piquet	-	-	-	-	-	-	-	-	-	-	26.5
		8	5	R	R	3	6	5	11	7	4	
7	Alesi	-	-	-	-	-	-	-	-	-	-	21
		4	R	3	5	R	R	3	4	R	R	
8	Modena	R	7	13	12	R	R	R	16	6	10	10
9	de Cesaris	6	R	5	7	13	7	8	R	R	8	9
10	Moreno	-	-	-	-	-	-	-	-	-	-	8
		R	R	8	8	4F	-	-	-	-	-	
		-	-	-	-	-	R	10	-	-	-	
		-	-	-	-	-	-	-	-	-	16	

Pos	Driver	R7	R8	R9	R10	R11	R12	R13	R14	R15	R16	Total
11	Martini	9	9	R	R	12	R	4	13	R	R	6
12	Lehto	R	13	R	R	R	R	R	8	R	12	4
13	Gachot	R	6	6	9F	-	-	-	-	-	-	4
		-	-	-	-	-	-	-	-	-	DNQ	
13	Schumacher	-	-	-	-	R	-	-	-	-	-	4
		-	-	-	-	-	5	6	6	R	R	
15	Nakajima	R	8	R	15	R	R	13	17	R	R	2
15	Hakkinen	DNQ	12	R	14	R	14	14	R	R	19	2
15	Brundle	-	-	-	-	-	-	-	-	-	-	2
		R	R	11	R	9	13	12	10	5	DNQ	
18	Suzuki	R	R	R	R	DNQ	DNQ	R	DNQ	R	DNQ	1
18	Bailey	-	-	-	-	-	-	-	-	-	-	1
18	Pirro	DNQ	10	10	R	8	10	R	15	R	7	1
18	Bernard	R	R	R	R	R	R	DNQ	R	NS	-	1
18	Capelli	R	R	R	6	R	8	17	R	-	-	1
18	Blundell	-	-	-	-	-	-	-	-	-	-	1
		R	R	12	R	6	12	R	R	DNPQ	17	
24	Morbidelli	R	11	R	13	R	9	9	14	R	-	0.5
		-	-	-	-	-	-	-	-	-	6	

SYMBOLS AND GRAND PRIX KEY

Round 1 United States GP
Round 2 Brazilian GP
Round 3 San Marino GP
Round 4 Monaco GP
Round 5 Canadian GP
Round 6 Mexican GP
Round 7 French GP
Round 8 British GP
Round 9 German GP
Round 10 Hungarian GP
Round 11 Belgian GP
Round 12 Italian GP
Round 13 Portuguese GP
Round 14 Spanish GP
Round 15 Japanese GP
Round 16 Australian GP

SCORING

1st 10 points
2nd 6 points
3rd 4 points
4th 3 points
5th 2 points
6th 1 point

DNPQ DID NOT PRE-QUALIFY **DNQ** DID NOT QUALIFY **DQ** DISQUALIFIED **EX** EXCLUDED
F FASTEST LAP **NC** NOT CLASSIFIED **NS** NON-STARTER **P** POLE POSITION **R** RETIRED

WORLD CONSTRUCTORS' CHAMPIONSHIP FINAL RESULTS

Pos	Team-Engine	R1	R2	R3	R4	R5	R6	R7	R8
1	McLaren-Honda	1/R	1/3	1/2	1/R	R/R	3/R	3/R	2/4
2	Williams-Renault	R/R	2/R	R/R	2/R	3/6	1/2	1/5	1/R
3	Ferrari	2/12	4/6	R/NS	3/5	R/R	R/R	2/4	3/R
4	Benetton-Ford	3/R	5/7	13/R	4/R	1/R	5/R	8/R	5/R
5	Jordan-Ford	10	13/R	R/R	8/R	4/5	4/R	6/R	6/R
6	Tyrrell-Honda	4/5	R/R	R/R	R/R	2/10	11/12	R/R	7/8
7	Minardi-Ferrari	9/R	8/R	4/R	12/R	7/R	7/R	9/R	9/11
8	Dallara-Judd	R/R	11/R	3/DNPQ	6/11	9/R	R/DNPQ	R/DNPQ	10/13
9	Lotus-Judd	R/DNQ	9/DNQ	5/6	R/DNQ	R/DNQ	9/10	10/DNQ	12/14
9	Brabham-Yamaha	11/R	12/R	8/11	R/DNQ	R/DNQ	R/R	R/R	R/R
11	Lola-Ford	6/R	R/NS	R/R	9/R	R/R	6/R	R/R	R/R
12	Leyton House-Ilmor	R/R	R/R	12/R	R/R	R/R	R/R	7/R	R/R

Pos	Team-Engine	R9	R10	R11	R12	R13	R14	R15	R16	Total
1	McLaren-Honda	4/7	1/4	1/2	2/4	2/R	5/R	1/2	1/3	139
2	Williams-Renault	1/2	2/3	5/R	1/R	1/DQ	1/3	3/R	2/5	125
3	Ferrari	3/R	5/R	R/R	3/R	3/R	2/4	4/R	6/R	55.5
4	Benetton-Ford	8/R	8/R	3/4	5/6	5/6	6/11	7/R	4/R	38.5
5	Jordan-Ford	5/6	7/9	13/R	7/R	8/10	9/R	R/R	8/9	13
6	Tyrrell-Honda	13/R	12/15	R/R	R/R	13/R	16/17	6/R	10/R	12
7	Minardi-Ferrari	R/R	13/R	12/R	9/R	4/9	13/14	R/R	16/R	6
8	Dallara-Judd	10/R	R/R	8/R	10/R	R/R	8/15	R/R	7/12	5
9	Lotus-Judd	R/DNQ	14/DNQ	7/R	14/DNQ	14/R	R/DNQ	R/R	11/19	3
9	Brabham-Yamaha	11/12	R/R	6/9	12/13	12/R	10/R	5/DNPQ	17/DNPQ	3
11	Lola-Ford	R/R	R/R	R/DNQ	R/DNQ	R/DNQ	R/DNQ	R/NS	DNQ/DNQ	2
12	Leyton House-Ilmor	R/R	6/11	R/R	8/15	7/17	7/R	8/R	14/20	1

1992

SEASON SUMMARY

Nigel Mansell was dominant for Williams at the zenith of the driver aids era, breaking Ayrton Senna's record by landing nine wins in a season. Then, showing the team's hard-headed approach, he was dropped when Alain Prost was hired for 1993 following his one-year sabbatical after being fired by Ferrari. Mansell used the FW14B to incredible effect to win the first five rounds before Senna resisted his recovery drive at Monaco. He wrapped the title up with five rounds to go, and Riccardo Patrese took another win for Williams. With Michael Schumacher becoming a winner and ranking third for Benetton ahead of Senna, Ferrari fell to a distant fourth.

A WINNING ANNIVERSARY

Michael Schumacher became a winner one year on from his debut at Spa-Francorchamps. It was a somewhat fortunate win in tricky conditions, as a spin dropped him behind Martin Brundle on lap 30 of 44. He noticed that his Benetton team-mate's tyres were blistering, so he pitted – and timed this perfectly on a drying track.

SOUTH AFRICAN GRAND PRIX

KYALAMI • ROUND 1 • DATE: 1ST MARCH 1992

Laps: 72 • Distance: 190.631miles/306.792km • Weather: Warm but dull

Pos	Driver	Team	Chassis-Engine	Result	Qual
1	Nigel Mansell	Williams	Williams-Renault FW14B	1h36m45.320s	1
2	Riccardo Patrese	Williams	Williams-Renault FW14B	1h37m09.680s	4
3	Ayrton Senna	McLaren	McLaren Honda MP4/6B	1h37m19.995s	2
4	Michael Schumacher	Benetton	Benetton-Ford Cosworth B191B	1h37m33.183s	6
5	Gerhard Berger	McLaren	McLaren Honda MP4/6B	1h37m58.954s	3
6	Johnny Herbert	Lotus	Lotus-Ford Cosworth 102D	71 laps	11
7	Erik Comas	Ligier	Ligier-Renault JS37	71 laps	13
8	Aguri Suzuki	Footwork	Footwork-Mugen Honda FA13	70 laps	16
9	Mika Hakkinen	Lotus	Lotus-Ford Cosworth 102D	70 laps	21
10	Michele Alboreto	Footwork	Footwork-Mugen Honda FA13	70 laps	17
11	Mauricio Gugelmin	Jordan	Jordan-Yamaha 192	70 laps	23
12	Ukyo Katayama	Larrousse	Venturi-Lamborghini LC92	68 laps	18
13	Eric van de Poele	Brabham	Brabham-Judd BT60B	68 laps	26
R	Olivier Grouillard	Tyrrell	Tyrrell-Ilmor 020B	62 laps/engine	12
R	Thierry Boutsen	Ligier	Ligier-Renault JS37	60 laps/fuel system	14
R	Pierluigi Martini	BMS Scuderia Italia	Dallara-Ferrari 192	56 laps/clutch	25
R	Gianni Morbidelli	Minardi	Minardi-Lamborghini M191B	55 laps/engine	19
R	JJ Lehto	BMS Scuderia Italia	Dallara-Ferrari 192	46 laps/gearbox	24
R	Christian Fittipaldi	Minardi	Minardi-Lamborghini M191B	43 laps/alternator	20
R	Andrea de Cesaris	Tyrrell	Tyrrell-Ilmor 020B	41 laps/engine	10
R	Jean Alesi	Ferrari	Ferrari F92A	40 laps/engine	5
R	Ivan Capelli	Ferrari	Ferrari F92A	28 laps/engine	9
R	Gabriele Tarquini	Fondmetal	Fondmetal-Ford Cosworth GR02	23 laps/engine	15

Pos	Driver	Team	Chassis-Engine	Result	Qual
R	Karl Wendlinger	March	March-Ilmor CG911	13 laps/overheating	7
R	Bertrand Gachot	Larrousse	Venturi-Lamborghini LC92	8 laps/steering	22
R	Martin Brundle	Benetton	Benetton-Ford Cosworth B191B	1 lap/clutch	8
DNQ	Paul Belmondo	March	March-Ilmor CG911	-	27
DNQ	Andrea Chiesa	Fondmetal	Fondmetal-Ford Cosworth GR01	-	28
DNQ	Stefano Modena	Jordan	Jordan-Yamaha 192	-	29
DNQ	Giovanna Amati	Brabham	Brabham-Judd BT60B	-	30
EX	Enrico Bertaggia	Andrea Moda	Coloni-Judd C4B	unpaid deposit	-
EX	Alex Caffi	Andrea Moda	Coloni-Judd C4B	unpaid deposit	-

Pole: Mansell, 1m15.486s, 126.269mph/203.211kph. Fastest lap: Mansell, 1m17.578s, 122.864mph/197.731kph on Lap 70. Race leaders: Mansell 1-72

MEXICAN GRAND PRIX

MEXICO CITY • ROUND 2 • DATE: 22ND MARCH 1992
Laps: 69 • Distance: 189.548miles/305.049km • Weather: Hot & bright

Pos	Driver	Team	Chassis-Engine	Result	Qual
1	Nigel Mansell	Williams	Williams-Renault FW14B	1h31m53.587s	1
2	Riccardo Patrese	Williams	Williams-Renault FW14B	1h32m06.558s	2
3	Michael Schumacher	Benetton	Benetton-Ford Cosworth B191B	1h32m15.016s	3
4	Gerhard Berger	McLaren	McLaren-Honda MP4/6B	1h32m26.934s	5
5	Andrea de Cesaris	Tyrrell	Tyrrell-Ilmor 020B	68 laps	11
6	Mika Hakkinen	Lotus	Lotus-Ford Cosworth 102D	68 laps	18
7	Johnny Herbert	Lotus	Lotus-Ford Cosworth 102D	68 laps	12
8	JJ Lehto	BMS Scuderia Italia	Dallara-Ferrari 192	68 laps	7
9	Erik Comas	Ligier	Ligier-Renault JS37	67 laps	26
10	Thierry Boutsen	Ligier	Ligier-Renault JS37	67 laps	22
11	Bertrand Gachot	Larrousse	Venturi-Lamborghini LC92	66 laps	13
12	Ukyo Katayama	Larrousse	Venturi-Lamborghini LC92	66 laps	24
13	Michele Alboreto	Footwork	Footwork-Mugen Honda FA13	65 laps	25
R	Martin Brundle	Benetton	Benetton-Ford Cosworth B191B	47 laps/engine	4
R	Gabriele Tarquini	Fondmetal	Fondmetal-Ford Cosworth GR02	45 laps/clutch	14
R	Andrea Chiesa	Fondmetal	Fondmetal-Ford Cosworth GR01	37 laps/spun off	23
R	Pierluigi Martini	BMS Scuderia Italia	Dallara-Ferrari 192	36 laps/handling	9
R	Jean Alesi	Ferrari	Ferrari F92A	31 laps/engine	10
R	Gianni Morbidelli	Minardi	Minardi-Lamborghini M191B	29 laps/spun off	21
R	Stefano Modena	Jordan	Jordan-Yamaha 192	17 laps/gearbox	15
R	Olivier Grouillard	Tyrrell	Tyrrell-Ilmor 020B	12 laps/engine	16
R	Ayrton Senna	McLaren	McLaren-Honda MP4/6B	11 laps/transmission	6
R	Christian Fittipaldi	Minardi	Minardi-Lamborghini M191B	2 laps/spun off	17
R	Mauricio Gugelmin	Jordan	Jordan-Yamaha 192	0 laps/engine	8
R	Karl Wendlinger	March	March-Ilmor CG911	0 laps/collision	19
R	Ivan Capelli	Ferrari	Ferrari F92A	0 laps/collision	20
DNQ	Aguri Suzuki	Footwork	Footwork-Mugen Honda FA13	-	27
DNQ	Paul Belmondo	March	March-Ilmor CG911	-	28
DNQ	Eric van de Poele	Brabham	Brabham-Judd BT60B	-	29
DNQ	Giovanna Amati	Brabham	Brabham-Judd BT60B	-	30

Pole: Mansell, 1m16.346s, 129.535mph/208.466kph. Fastest lap: Berger, 1m17.711s, 127.259mph/204.804kph on Lap 60. Race leaders: Mansell 1-69

BRAZILIAN GRAND PRIX

INTERLAGOS • ROUND 3 • DATE: 5TH APRIL 1992
Laps: 71 • Distance: 190.807miles/307.075km • Weather: Hot & bright

Pos	Driver	Team	Chassis-Engine	Result	Qual
1	Nigel Mansell	Williams	Williams-Renault FW14B	1h36m51.856s	1
2	Riccardo Patrese	Williams	Williams-Renault FW14B	1h37m21.186s	2
3	Michael Schumacher	Benetton	Benetton-Ford Cosworth B191B	70 laps	5
4	Jean Alesi	Ferrari	Ferrari F92A	70 laps	6
5	Ivan Capelli	Ferrari	Ferrari F92A	70 laps	11
6	Michele Alboreto	Footwork	Footwork-Mugen Honda FA13	70 laps	14
7	Gianni Morbidelli	Minardi	Minardi-Lamborghini M191B	69 laps	23
8	JJ Lehto	BMS Scuderia Italia	Dallara-Ferrari 192	69 laps	16
9	Ukyo Katayama	Larrousse	Venturi-Lamborghini LC92	68 laps	25
10	Mika Hakkinen	Lotus	Lotus-Ford Cosworth 102D	67 laps	24
R	Gabriele Tarquini	Fondmetal	Fondmetal-Ford Cosworth GR02	62 laps/engine	19
R	Karl Wendlinger	March	March-Ilmor CG911	55 laps/clutch	9
R	Christian Fittipaldi	Minardi	Minardi-Lamborghini M191B	54 laps/gearbox	20
R	Olivier Grouillard	Tyrrell	Tyrrell-Ilmor 020B	52 laps/engine	17
R	Erik Comas	Ligier	Ligier-Renault JS37	42 laps/gearbox	15
R	Thierry Boutsen	Ligier	Ligier-Renault JS37	36 laps/collision	10
R	Mauricio Gugelmin	Jordan	Jordan-Yamaha 192	36 laps/gearbox	21
R	Johnny Herbert	Lotus	Lotus-Ford Cosworth 102D	36 laps/spun off	26
R	Martin Brundle	Benetton	Benetton-Ford Cosworth B191B	30 laps/collision	7
R	Pierluigi Martini	BMS Scuderia Italia	Dallara-Ferrari 192	24 laps/clutch	8
R	Bertrand Gachot	Larrousse	Venturi-Lamborghini LC92	23 laps/suspension	18
R	Andrea de Cesaris	Tyrrell	Tyrrell-Ilmor 020B	21 laps/engine	13
R	Ayrton Senna	McLaren	McLaren-Honda MP4/7A	17 laps/engine	3
R	Gerhard Berger	McLaren	McLaren-Honda MP4/7A	4 laps/electrical	4
R	Aguri Suzuki	Footwork	Footwork-Mugen Honda FA13	2 laps/engine	22
R	Stefano Modena	Jordan	Jordan-Yamaha 192	1 lap/gearbox	12
DNQ	Andrea Chiesa	Fondmetal	Fondmetal-Ford Cosworth GR01	-	27
DNQ	Paul Belmondo	March	March-Ilmor CG911	-	28
DNQ	Eric van de Poele	Brabham	Brabham-Judd BT60B	-	29
DNQ	Giovanna Amati	Brabham	Brabham-Judd BT60B	-	30
DNPQ	Roberto Moreno	Andrea Moda	Moda-Judd S921	-	31
W	Perry McCarthy	Andrea Moda	Moda-Judd S921	-	-

Pole: Mansell, 1m15.703s, 127.798mph/205.672kph. Fastest lap: Patrese, 1m19.490s, 121.710mph/195.873kph on Lap 34. Race leaders: Patrese 1-31, Mansell 32-71

SPANISH GRAND PRIX

BARCELONA-CATALUNYA • ROUND 4 • DATE: 3RD MAY 1992
Laps: 65 • Distance: 191.727miles/308.555km • Weather: Cool & wet

Pos	Driver	Team	Chassis-Engine	Result	Qual
1	Nigel Mansell	Williams	Williams-Renault FW14B	1h56m10.674s	1
2	Michael Schumacher	Benetton	Benetton-Ford Cosworth B192	1h56m34.588s	2
3	Jean Alesi	Ferrari	Ferrari F92A	1h56m37.136s	8
4	Gerhard Berger	McLaren	McLaren-Honda MP4/7A	1h57m31.321s	7
5	Michele Alboreto	Footwork	Footwork-Mugen Honda FA13	64 laps	16
6	Pierluigi Martini	BMS Scuderia Italia	Dallara-Ferrari 192	63 laps	13
7	Aguri Suzuki	Footwork	Footwork-Mugen Honda FA13	63 laps	19
8	Karl Wendlinger	March	March-Ilmor CG911	63 laps	9
9	Ayrton Senna	McLaren	McLaren-Honda MP4-7A	62 laps/spun off	3

Pos	Driver	Team	Chassis-Engine	Result	Qual
10	Ivan Capelli	Ferrari	Ferrari F92A	62 laps/spun off	5
11	Christian Fittipaldi	Minardi	Minardi-Lamborghini M191B	61 laps	22
12	Paul Belmondo	March	March-Ilmor CG911	61 laps	23
R	JJ Lehto	BMS Scuderia Italia	Dallara-Ferrari 192	56 laps/spun off	12
R	Gabriele Tarquini	Fondmetal	Fondmetal-Ford Cosworth GR01	56 laps/spun off	18
R	Mika Hakkinen	Lotus	Lotus-Ford Cosworth 102D	56 laps/spun off	21
R	Erik Comas	Ligier	Ligier-Renault JS37	55 laps/spun off	10
R	Bertrand Gachot	Larrousse	Venturi-Lamborghini LC92	35 laps/engine	24
R	Olivier Grouillard	Tyrrell	Tyrrell-Ilmor 020B	30 laps/spun off	15
R	Gianni Morbidelli	Minardi	Minardi-Lamborghini M191B	26 laps/handling	25
R	Mauricio Gugelmin	Jordan	Jordan-Yamaha 192	24 laps/spun off	17
R	Andrea Chiesa	Fondmetal	Fondmetal-Ford Cosworth GR01	22 laps/spun off	20
R	Riccardo Patrese	Williams	Williams-Renault FW14B	19 laps/spun off	4
R	Johnny Herbert	Lotus	Lotus-Ford Cosworth 102D	13 laps/spun off	26
R	Thierry Boutsen	Ligier	Ligier-Renault JS37	11 laps/engine	14
R	Martin Brundle	Benetton	Benetton-Ford Cosworth B192	4 laps/spun off	6
R	Andrea de Cesaris	Tyrrell	Tyrrell-Ilmor 020B	2 laps/engine	11
DNQ	Ukyo Katayama	Larrousse	Venturi-Lamborghini LC92	-	27
DNQ	Eric van de Poele	Brabham	Brabham-Judd BT60B	-	28
DNQ	Stefano Modena	Jordan	Jordan-Yamaha 192	-	29
DNQ	Damon Hill	Brabham	Brabham-Judd BT60B	-	30
DNPQ	Roberto Moreno	Andrea Moda	Moda-Judd S921	-	31
DNPQ	Perry McCarthy	Andrea Moda	Moda-Judd S921	-	32

Pole: Mansell, 1m20.190s, 132.419mph/213.108kph. Fastest lap: Mansell, 1m42.503s, 103.594mph/166.719kph on Lap 10. Race leaders: Mansell 1-65

A DREAM THAT SOURED

It should have been the peak of his F1 career, but Ivan Capelli had a torrid time at Ferrari and ended the year ranked only 12th, with a best result of fifth at Interlagos. He was replaced by Nicola Larini for the final two races. The Ferrari F92A was certainly not the best, and even team-mate Jean Alesi could do no better than a pair of thirds.

SAN MARINO GRAND PRIX

IMOLA • ROUND 5 • DATE: 17TH MAY 1992
Laps: 60 • Distance: 187.656miles/302.4km • Weather: Hot & bright

Pos	Driver	Team	Chassis-Engine	Result	Qual
1	Nigel Mansell	Williams	Williams-Renault FW14B	1h28m40.927s	1
2	Riccardo Patrese	Williams	Williams-Renault FW14B	1h28m50.378s	2
3	Ayrton Senna	McLaren	McLaren-Honda MP4-7A	1h29m29.911s	3
4	Martin Brundle	Benetton	Benetton-Ford Cosworth B192	1h29m33.934s	6
5	Michele Alboreto	Footwork	Footwork-Mugen Honda FA13	59 laps	9
6	Pierluigi Martini	BMS Scuderia Italia	Dallara-Ferrari 192	59 laps	15
7	Mauricio Gugelmin	Jordan	Jordan-Yamaha 192	58 laps	18
8	Olivier Grouillard	Tyrrell	Tyrrell-Ilmor 020B	58 laps	20
9	Erik Comas	Ligier	Ligier-Renault JS37	58 laps	13
10	Aguri Suzuki	Footwork	Footwork-Mugen Honda FA13	58 laps	11
11	JJ Lehto	BMS Scuderia Italia	Dallara-Ferrari 192	57 laps/engine	16
12	Karl Wendlinger	March	March-Ilmor CG911	57 laps	12

Pos	Driver	Team	Chassis-Engine	Result	Qual
13	Paul Belmondo	March	March-Ilmor CG911	57 laps	24
14	Andrea de Cesaris	Tyrrell	Tyrrell-Ilmor 020B	55 laps/fuel pressure	14
R	Ukyo Katayama	Larrousse	Venturi-Lamborghini LC92	40 laps/spun off	17
R	Gerhard Berger	McLaren	McLaren-Honda MP4-7A	39 laps/collision	4
R	Jean Alesi	Ferrari	Ferrari F92A	39 laps/collision	7
R	Bertrand Gachot	Larrousse	Venturi-Lamborghini LC92	32 laps/spun off	19
R	Thierry Boutsen	Ligier	Ligier-Renault JS37	29 laps/engine	10
R	Stefano Modena	Jordan	Jordan-Yamaha 192	25 laps/gearbox	23
R	Gianni Morbidelli	Minardi	Minardi-Lamborghini M192	24 laps/engine	21
R	Gabriele Tarquini	Fondmetal	Fondmetal-Ford Cosworth GR01	24 laps/engine	22
R	Michael Schumacher	Benetton	Benetton-Ford Cosworth B192	20 laps/spun off	5
R	Ivan Capelli	Ferrari	Ferrari F92A	11 laps/spun off	8
R	Christian Fittipaldi	Minardi	Minardi-Lamborghini M192	8 laps/gearbox	25
R	Johnny Herbert	Lotus	Lotus-Ford Cosworth 107	8 laps/gearbox	26
DNQ	Mika Hakkinen	Lotus	Lotus-Ford Cosworth 102D	-	27
DNQ	Andrea Chiesa	Fondmetal	Fondmetal-Ford Cosworth GR01	-	28
DNQ	Damon Hill	Brabham	Brabham-Judd BT60B	-	29
DNQ	Eric van de Poele	Brabham	Brabham-Judd BT60B	-	30
DNPQ	Roberto Moreno	Andrea Moda	Moda-Judd S921	-	31
DNPQ	Perry McCarthy	Andrea Moda	Moda-Judd S921	-	32

Pole: Mansell, 1m21.842s, 137.755mph/221.695kph. Fastest lap: Patrese, 1m26.100s, 130.942mph/210.731kph on Lap 60. Race leaders: Mansell 1-60

SIMPLY NOT GOOD ENOUGH

One of the weakest attempts to make an impact in F1 was put up by Andrea Moda, a team entered by shoe manufacturer Andrea Sassetti after he bought the remains of the Coloni team. Roberto Moreno secured its only qualification and, amazingly, did so at Monaco, while Perry McCarthy struggled and the team was kicked out after the Belgian GP.

MONACO GRAND PRIX

MONTE CARLO • ROUND 6 • DATE: 31ST MAY 1992
Laps: 78 • Distance: 161.298miles/259.584km • Weather: Warm & bright

Pos	Driver	Team	Chassis-Engine	Result	Qual
1	Ayrton Senna	McLaren	McLaren-Honda MP4-7A	1h50m59.372s	3
2	Nigel Mansell	Williams	Williams-Renault FW14B	1h50m59.587s	1
3	Riccardo Patrese	Williams	Williams-Renault FW14B	1h51m31.215s	2
4	Michael Schumacher	Benetton	Benetton-Ford Cosworth B192	1h51m38.666s	6
5	Martin Brundle	Benetton	Benetton-Ford Cosworth B192	1h52m20.719s	7
6	Bertrand Gachot	Larrousse	Venturi-Lamborghini LC92	77 laps	15
7	Michele Alboreto	Footwork	Footwork-Mugen Honda FA13	77 laps	11
8	Christian Fittipaldi	Minardi	Minardi-Lamborghini M192	77 laps	17
9	JJ Lehto	BMS Scuderia Italia	Dallara-Ferrari 192	76 laps	20
10	Erik Comas	Ligier	Ligier-Renault JS37	76 laps	23
11	Aguri Suzuki	Footwork	Footwork-Mugen Honda FA13	76 laps	19
12	Thierry Boutsen	Ligier	Ligier-Renault JS37	75 laps	22
R	Ivan Capelli	Ferrari	Ferrari F92A	60 laps/spun off	8
R	Gerhard Berger	McLaren	McLaren-Honda MP4-7A	32 laps/gearbox	5
R	Mika Hakkinen	Lotus	Lotus-Ford Cosworth 107	30 laps/gearbox	14

Pos	Driver	Team	Chassis-Engine	Result	Qual
R	Jean Alesi	Ferrari	Ferrari F92A	28 laps/gearbox	4
R	Mauricio Gugelmin	Jordan	Jordan-Yamaha 192	18 laps/gearbox	13
R	Johnny Herbert	Lotus	Lotus Ford Cosworth 107	17 laps/spun off	9
R	Roberto Moreno	Andrea Moda	Moda-Judd S921	11 laps/engine	26
R	Andrea de Cesaris	Tyrrell	Tyrrell-Ilmor 020B	9 laps/gearbox	10
R	Gabriele Tarquini	Fondmetal	Fondmetal-Ford Cosworth GR01	9 laps/engine	25
R	Stefano Modena	Jordan	Jordan-Yamaha 192	6 laps/spun off	21
R	Olivier Grouillard	Tyrrell	Tyrrell-Ilmor 020B	4 laps/transmission	24
R	Gianni Morbidelli	Minardi	Minardi-Lamborghini M192	1 lap/gearbox	12
R	Karl Wendlinger	March	March-Ilmor CG911	1 lap/gearbox	16
R	Pierluigi Martini	BMS Scuderia Italia	Dallara-Ferrari 192	0 laps/spun off	18
DNQ	Eric van de Poele	Brabham	Brabham-Judd BT60B	-	27
DNQ	Damon Hill	Brabham	Brabham-Judd BT60B	-	28
DNQ	Andrea Chiesa	Fondmetal	Fondmetal-Ford Cosworth GR01	-	29
DNQ	Paul Belmondo	March	March-Ilmor CG911	-	30
DNPQ	Ukyo Katayama	Larrousse	Venturi-Lamborghini LC92	-	31
DNPQ	Perry McCarthy	Andrea Moda	Moda-Judd S921	-	32

Pole: Mansell, 1m19.495s, 93.647mph/150.711kph. Fastest lap: Mansell, 1m21.598s, 91.234mph/146.827kph on Lap 74. Race leaders: Mansell 1-70, Senna 71-78

BACK FOR MORE

Irrepressible Dutch racer Jan Lammers set the record for the longest F1 career gap when he made his return with March at the age of 36 at the Japanese GP. This was 162 grands prix after his last outing, when he failed to qualify his Theodore at the French GP at Paul Ricard in 1982. This, and the final round in Adelaide, were his last F1 outings.

CANADIAN GRAND PRIX

MONTREAL • ROUND 7 • DATE: 14TH JUNE 1992
Laps: 69 • Distance: 189.559miles/305.67km • Weather: Hot & bright

Pos	Driver	Team	Chassis-Engine	Result	Qual
1	Gerhard Berger	McLaren	McLaren-Honda MP4-7A	1h37m08.299s	4
2	Michael Schumacher	Benetton	Benetton-Ford Cosworth B192	1h37m20.700s	5
3	Jean Alesi	Ferrari	Ferrari F92A	1h38m15.626s	8
4	Karl Wendlinger	March	March-Ilmor CG911	68 laps	12
5	Andrea de Cesaris	Tyrrell	Tyrrell-Ilmor 020B	68 laps	14
6	Erik Comas	Ligier	Ligier-Renault JS37	68 laps	22
7	Michele Alboreto	Footwork	Footwork-Mugen Honda FA13	68 laps	16
8	Pierluigi Martini	BMS Scuderia Italia	Dallara-Ferrari 192	68 laps	15
9	JJ Lehto	BMS Scuderia Italia	Dallara-Ferrari 192	68 laps	23
10	Thierry Boutsen	Ligier	Ligier-Renault JS37	67 laps	21
11	Gianni Morbidelli	Minardi	Minardi-Lamborghini M192	67 laps	13
12	Olivier Grouillard	Tyrrell	Tyrrell-Ilmor 020B	67 laps	26
13	Christian Fittipaldi	Minardi	Minardi-Lamborghini M192	65 laps	25
14	Paul Belmondo	March	March-Ilmor CG911	64 laps	20
R	Ukyo Katayama	Larrousse	Venturi-Lamborghini LC92	61 laps/engine	11
R	Martin Brundle	Benetton	Benetton-Ford Cosworth B192	45 laps/transmission	7
R	Riccardo Patrese	Williams	Williams-Renault FW14B	43 laps/gearbox	2
R	Ayrton Senna	McLaren	McLaren-Honda MP4-7A	37 laps/electrical	1
R	Stefano Modena	Jordan	Jordan-Yamaha 192	36 laps/transmission	17

Pos	Driver	Team	Chassis-Engine	Result	Qual
R	Mika Hakkinen	Lotus	Lotus-Ford Cosworth 107	35 laps/gearbox	10
R	Johnny Herbert	Lotus	Lotus-Ford Cosworth 107	34 laps/clutch	6
R	Ivan Capelli	Ferrari	Ferrari F92A	18 laps/spun off	9
R	Nigel Mansell	Williams	Williams-Renault FW14B	14 laps/spun off	3
R	Mauricio Gugelmin	Jordan	Jordan-Yamaha 192	14 laps/transmission	24
DQ	Bertrand Gachot	Larrousse	Venturi-Lamborghini LC92	14 laps/push start	19
R	Gabriele Tarquini	Fondmetal	Fondmetal-Ford Cosworth GR02	0 laps/transmission	18
DNQ	Aguri Suzuki	Footwork	Footwork-Mugen Honda FA13	-	27
DNQ	Eric van de Poele	Brabham	Brabham-Judd BT60B	-	28
DNQ	Andrea Chiesa	Fondmetal	Fondmetal-Ford Cosworth GR02	-	29
DNQ	Damon Hill	Brabham	Brabham-Judd BT60B	-	30
DNPQ	Roberto Moreno	Andrea Moda	Moda-Judd S921	-	31
DNPQ	Perry McCarthy	Andrea Moda	Moda-Judd S921	-	32

Pole: Senna, 1m19.775s, 124.219mph/199.912kph. Fastest lap: Berger, 1m22.325s, 120.372mph/193.720kph on Lap 61. Race leaders: Senna 1-37, Berger 38-69

FRENCH GRAND PRIX

MAGNY-COURS • ROUND 8 • DATE: 5TH JULY 1992
Laps: 69 • Distance: 182.77miles/293.25km • Weather: Warm but dull, then wet

Pos	Driver	Team	Chassis-Engine	Result	Qual
1	Nigel Mansell	Williams	Williams-Renault FW14B	1h38m08.459s	1
2	Riccardo Patrese	Williams	Williams-Renault FW14B	1h38m54.906s	2
3	Martin Brundle	Benetton	Benetton-Ford Cosworth B192	1h39m21.038s	7
4	Mika Hakkinen	Lotus	Lotus-Ford Cosworth 107	68 laps	11
5	Erik Comas	Ligier	Ligier-Renault JS37	68 laps	10
6	Johnny Herbert	Lotus	Lotus-Ford Cosworth 107	68 laps	12
7	Michele Alboreto	Footwork	Footwork-Mugen Honda FA13	68 laps	14
8	Gianni Morbidelli	Minardi	Minardi-Lamborghini M192	68 laps	16
9	JJ Lehto	BMS Scuderia Italia	Dallara-Ferrari 192	67 laps	17
10	Pierluigi Martini	BMS Scuderia Italia	Dallara-Ferrari 192	67 laps	25
11	Olivier Grouillard	Tyrrell	Tyrrell-Ilmor 020B	66 laps	22
R	Jean Alesi	Ferrari	Ferrari F92A	61 laps/engine	6
R	Andrea de Cesaris	Tyrrell	Tyrrell-Ilmor 020B	51 laps/spun off	19
R	Ukyo Katayama	Larrousse	Venturi-Lamborghini LC92	49 laps/engine	18
R	Thierry Boutsen	Ligier	Ligier-Renault JS37	46 laps/spun off	9
R	Ivan Capelli	Ferrari	Ferrari F92A	38 laps/engine	8
R	Karl Wendlinger	March	March-Ilmor CG911	33 laps/gearbox	21
R	Stefano Modena	Jordan	Jordan-Yamaha 192	25 laps/engine	20
R	Aguri Suzuki	Footwork	Footwork-Mugen Honda FA13	20 laps/collision	15
R	Michael Schumacher	Benetton	Benetton-Ford Cosworth B192	17 laps/collision	5
R	Gerhard Berger	McLaren	McLaren-Honda MP4-7A	10 laps/engine	4
R	Gabriele Tarquini	Fondmetal	Fondmetal-Ford Cosworth GR02	6 laps/throttle	23
R	Ayrton Senna	McLaren	McLaren-Honda MP4-7A	0 laps/collision	3
R	Bertrand Gachot	Larrousse	Venturi-Lamborghini LC92	0 laps/collision	13
R	Mauricio Gugelmin	Jordan	Jordan-Yamaha 192	0 laps/collision	24
R	Andrea Chiesa	Fondmetal	Fondmetal-Ford Cosworth GR02	0 laps/collision	26
DNQ	Paul Belmondo	March	March-Ilmor CG911	-	27
DNQ	Christian Fittipaldi	Minardi	Minardi-Lamborghini M192	-	28
DNQ	Eric van de Poele	Brabham	Brabham-Judd BT60B	-	29
DNQ	Damon Hill	Brabham	Brabham-Judd BT60B	-	30

Pole: Mansell, 1m13.864s, 128.709mph/207.137kph. Fastest lap: Mansell, 1m17.070s, 123.355mph/198.520kph on Lap 37. Race leaders: Patrese 1-20, Mansell 21-69

BRITISH GRAND PRIX

SILVERSTONE • ROUND 9 • DATE: 12TH JULY 1992
Laps: 59 • Distance: 191.589miles/308.334km • Weather: Hot & bright

Pos	Driver	Team	Chassis-Engine	Result	Qual
1	Nigel Mansell	Williams	Williams-Renault FW14B	1h25m42.991s	1
2	Riccardo Patrese	Williams	Williams-Renault FW14B	1h26m22.085s	2
3	Martin Brundle	Benetton	Benetton-Ford Cosworth B192	1h26m31.386s	6
4	Michael Schumacher	Benetton	Benetton-Ford Cosworth B192	1h26m36.258s	4
5	Gerhard Berger	McLaren	McLaren-Honda MP4-7A	1h26m38.786s	5
6	Mika Hakkinen	Lotus	Lotus-Ford Cosworth 107	1h27m03.129s	9
7	Michele Alboreto	Footwork	Footwork-Mugen Honda FA13	58 laps	12
8	Erik Comas	Ligier	Ligier-Renault JS37	58 laps	10
9	Ivan Capelli	Ferrari	Ferrari F92A	58 laps	14
10	Thierry Boutsen	Ligier	Ligier-Renault JS37	57 laps	13
11	Olivier Grouillard	Tyrrell	Tyrrell-Ilmor 020B	57 laps	20
12	Aguri Suzuki	Footwork	Footwork-Mugen Honda FA13	57 laps	17
13	JJ Lehto	BMS Scuderia Italia	Dallara-Ferrari 192	57 laps	19
14	Gabriele Tarquini	Fondmetal	Fondmetal-Ford Cosworth GR02	57 laps	15
15	Pierluigi Martini	BMS Scuderia Italia	Dallara-Ferrari 192	56 laps	22
16	Damon Hill	Brabham	Brabham-Judd BT60B	55 laps	26
17	Gianni Morbidelli	Minardi	Minardi-Lamborghini M192	53 laps/engine	25
R	Ayrton Senna	McLaren	McLaren-Honda MP4-7A	52 laps/transmission	3
R	Andrea de Cesaris	Tyrrell	Tyrrell-Ilmor 020B	46 laps/spun off	18
R	Jean Alesi	Ferrari	Ferrari F92A	43 laps/fire extinguisher	8
R	Stefano Modena	Jordan	Jordan-Yamaha 192	43 laps/engine	23
R	Mauricio Gugelmin	Jordan	Jordan-Yamaha 192	37 laps/engine	24
R	Bertrand Gachot	Larrousse	Venturi-Lamborghini LC92	32 laps/wheel	11
R	Johnny Herbert	Lotus	Lotus-Ford Cosworth 107	31 laps/transmission	7
R	Ukyo Katayama	Larrousse	Venturi-Lamborghini LC92	27 laps/transmission	16
R	Karl Wendlinger	March	March-Ilmor CG911	27 laps/gearbox	21
DNQ	Alessandro Zanardi	Minardi	Minardi-Lamborghini M192	-	27
DNQ	Paul Belmondo	March	March-Ilmor CG911	-	28
DNQ	Andrea Chiesa	Fondmetal	Fondmetal-Ford Cosworth GR01	-	29
DNQ	Eric van de Poele	Brabham	Brabham-Judd BT60B	-	30
DNPQ	Roberto Moreno	Andrea Moda	Moda-Judd S921	-	31
DNPQ	Perry McCarthy	Andrea Moda	Moda-Judd S921	-	32

Pole: Mansell, 1m18.965s, 148.043mph/238.252kph. Fastest lap: Mansell, 1m22.539s, 141.632mph/227.935kph on Lap 57. Race leaders: Mansell 1-59

AN UNHAPPY LANDING

Three-time world champion Nelson Piquet didn't have any luck in his new career as an IndyCar driver after his illustrious time in F1, as the Brazilian broke his feet and his legs when he crashed while testing at Indianapolis Motor Speedway in May 1992. He would spend months on the sidelines and vowed never to race again at Indianapolis, but then did so in 1993.

GERMAN GRAND PRIX

HOCKENHEIM • ROUND 10 • DATE: 26TH JULY 1992
Laps: 45 • Distance: 190.559miles/306.675km • Weather: Hot & bright

Pos	Driver	Team	Chassis-Engine	Result	Qual
1	Nigel Mansell	Williams	Williams-Renault FW14B	1h18m22.032s	1
2	Ayrton Senna	McLaren	McLaren-Honda MP4-7A	1h18m26.532s	3
3	Michael Schumacher	Benetton	Benetton-Ford Cosworth B192	1h18m56.494s	6
4	Martin Brundle	Benetton	Benetton-Ford Cosworth B192	1h18m58.991s	9
5	Jean Alesi	Ferrari	Ferrari F92A	1h19m34.639s	5
6	Erik Comas	Ligier	Ligier-Renault JS37	1h19m58.530s	7
7	Thierry Boutsen	Ligier	Ligier-Renault JS37	1h19m59.212s	8
8	Riccardo Patrese	Williams	Williams-Renault FW14B	44 laps/spun off	2
9	Michele Alboreto	Footwork	Footwork-Mugen Honda FA13	44 laps	17
10	JJ Lehto	BMS Scuderia Italia	Dallara-Ferrari 192	44 laps	21
11	Pierluigi Martini	BMS Scuderia Italia	Dallara-Ferrari 192	44 laps	18
12	Gianni Morbidelli	Minardi	Minardi-Lamborghini M192	44 laps	26
13	Paul Belmondo	March	March-Ilmor CG911	44 laps	22
14	Bertrand Gachot	Larrousse	Venturi-Lamborghini LC92	44 laps	25
15	Mauricio Gugelmin	Jordan	Jordan-Yamaha 192	43 laps	23
16	Karl Wendlinger	March	March-Ilmor CG911	42 laps	10
R	Gabriele Tarquini	Fondmetal	Fondmetal-Ford Cosworth GR02	33 laps/engine	19
R	Andrea de Cesaris	Tyrrell	Tyrrell-Ilmor 020B	25 laps/engine	20
R	Johnny Herbert	Lotus	Lotus-Ford Cosworth 107	23 laps/engine	11
R	Ivan Capelli	Ferrari	Ferrari F92A	21 laps/engine	12
R	Mika Hakkinen	Lotus	Lotus-Ford Cosworth 107	21 laps/engine	13
R	Gerhard Berger	McLaren	McLaren-Honda MP4-7A	16 laps/electrical	4
R	Olivier Grouillard	Tyrrell	Tyrrell-Ilmor 020B	8 laps/engine	14
R	Ukyo Katayama	Larrousse	Venturi-Lamborghini LC92	8 laps/spun off	16
R	Aguri Suzuki	Footwork	Footwork-Mugen Honda FA13	1 lap/spun off	15
R	Alessandro Zanardi	Minardi	Minardi-Lamborghini M192	1 lap/gearbox	24
DNQ	Stefano Modena	Jordan	Jordan-Yamaha 192	-	27
DNQ	Eric van de Poele	Brabham	Brabham-Judd BT60B	-	28
DNQ	Andrea Chiesa	Fondmetal	Fondmetal-Ford Cosworth GR01	-	29
DNQ	Damon Hill	Brabham	Brabham-Judd BT60B	-	30
DNPQ	Roberto Moreno	Andrea Moda	Moda-Judd S921	-	31
EX	Perry McCarthy	Andrea Moda	Moda-Judd S921	missed weight check	-

Pole: Mansell, 1m37.960s, 155.621mph/250.449kph. Fastest lap: Patrese, 1m41.591s, 150.059mph/241.497kph on Lap 36. Race leaders: Mansell 1-14 & 20-45, Patrese 15-19

NEW CIRCUITS

Kyalami returned to the World Championship after a seven-year break with a new layout that only used part of the original track. The long back straight had been enveloped by an industrial estate in a previous rejig in 1987 that forced the owners to add a loop further down the hillside. The 1992 remodelling added half a kilometre (a third of a mile) to the lap.

HUNGARIAN GRAND PRIX

HUNGARORING • ROUND 11 • DATE: 16TH AUGUST 1992
Laps: 77 • Distance: 189.851miles/305.536km • Weather: Hot & bright

Pos	Driver	Team	Chassis-Engine	Result	Qual
1	Ayrton Senna	McLaren	McLaren-Honda MP4-7A	1h46m19.216s	3
2	Nigel Mansell	Williams	Williams-Renault FW14B	1h46m59.355s	2
3	Gerhard Berger	McLaren	McLaren-Honda MP4-7A	1h47m09.998s	5
4	Mika Hakkinen	Lotus	Lotus-Ford Cosworth 107	1h47m13.529s	16
5	Martin Brundle	Benetton	Benetton-Ford Cosworth B192	1h47m16.714s	6
6	Ivan Capelli	Ferrari	Ferrari F92A	76 laps	10
7	Michele Alboreto	Footwork	Footwork-Mugen Honda FA13	75 laps	7
8	Andrea de Cesaris	Tyrrell	Tyrrell-Ilmor 020B	75 laps	19
9	Paul Belmondo	March	March-Ilmor CG911	74 laps	17
10	Mauricio Gugelmin	Jordan	Jordan-Yamaha 192	73 laps	21
11	Damon Hill	Brabham	Brabham-Judd BT60B	73 laps	25
R	Michael Schumacher	Benetton	Benetton-Ford Cosworth B192	63 laps/wing	4
R	Riccardo Patrese	Williams	Williams-Renault FW14B	55 laps/engine	1
R	Pierluigi Martini	BMS Scuderia Italia	Dallara-Ferrari 192	40 laps/gearbox	26
R	Ukyo Katayama	Larrousse	Venturi-Lamborghini LC92	35 laps/engine	20
R	Jean Alesi	Ferrari	Ferrari F92A	14 laps/halfshaft	9
R	Aguri Suzuki	Footwork	Footwork-Mugen Honda FA13	13 laps/collision	14
R	Bertrand Gachot	Larrousse	Venturi-Lamborghini LC92	13 laps/wing	15
R	Olivier Grouillard	Tyrrell	Tyrrell-Ilmor 020B	13 laps/collision	22
R	Karl Wendlinger	March	March-Ilmor CG911	13 laps/collision	23
R	Stefano Modena	Jordan	Jordan-Yamaha 192	13 laps/collision	24
R	Eric van de Poele	Fondmetal	Fondmetal-Ford Cosworth GR02	2 laps/spun off	18
R	Thierry Boutsen	Ligier	Ligier-Renault JS37	0 laps/collision	8
R	Erik Comas	Ligier	Ligier-Renault JS37	0 laps/collision	11
R	Gabriele Tarquini	Fondmetal	Fondmetal-Ford Cosworth GR02	0 laps/collision	12
R	Johnny Herbert	Lotus	Lotus-Ford Cosworth 107	0 laps/collision	13
DNQ	Gianni Morbidelli	Minardi	Minardi-Lamborghini M192	-	27
DNQ	JJ Lehto	BMS Scuderia Italia	Dallara-Ferrari 192	-	28
DNQ	Alessandro Zanardi	Minardi	Minardi-Lamborghini M192	-	29
DNQ	Roberto Moreno	Andrea Moda	Moda-Judd S921	-	30
DNPQ	Perry McCarthy	Andrea Moda	Moda-Judd S921	-	31

Pole: Patrese, 1m15.476s, 117.602mph/189.262kph. Fastest lap: Mansell, 1m18.308s, 113.349mph/182.418kph on Lap 63. Race leaders: Patrese 1-38, Senna 39-77

BELGIAN GRAND PRIX

SPA-FRANCORCHAMPS • ROUND 12 • DATE: 30TH AUGUST 1992
Laps: 44 • Distance: 190.671miles/306.856km • Weather: Warm, passing rain

Pos	Driver	Team	Chassis-Engine	Result	Qual
1	Michael Schumacher	Benetton	Benetton-Ford Cosworth B192	1h36m10.721s	3
2	Nigel Mansell	Williams	Williams-Renault FW14B	1h36m47.316s	1
3	Riccardo Patrese	Williams	Williams-Renault FW14B	1h36m54.618s	4
4	Martin Brundle	Benetton	Benetton-Ford Cosworth B192	1h36m56.780s	9
5	Ayrton Senna	McLaren	McLaren-Honda MP4-7A	1h37m19.090s	2
6	Mika Hakkinen	Lotus	Lotus-Ford Cosworth 107	1h37m20.751s	8
7	JJ Lehto	BMS Scuderia Italia	Dallara-Ferrari 192	1h37m48.958s	16
8	Andrea de Cesaris	Tyrrell	Tyrrell-Ilmor 020B	43 laps	13
9	Aguri Suzuki	Footwork	Footwork-Mugen Honda FA13	43 laps	25
10	Eric van de Poele	Fondmetal	Fondmetal-Ford Cosworth GR02	43 laps	15

Pos	Driver	Team	Chassis-Engine	Result	Qual
11	Karl Wendlinger	March	March-Ilmor CG911	43 laps	18
12	Emanuele Naspetti	March	March-Ilmor CG911	43 laps	21
13	Johnny Herbert	Lotus	Lotus-Ford Cosworth 107	42 laps/engine	10
14	Mauricio Gugelmin	Jordan	Jordan-Yamaha 192	42 laps	24
15	Stefano Modena	Jordan	Jordan-Yamaha 192	42 laps	17
16	Gianni Morbidelli	Minardi	Minardi-Lamborghini M192	42 laps	23
17	Ukyo Katayama	Larrousse	Venturi-Lamborghini LC92	42 laps	26
18	Bertrand Gachot	Larrousse	Venturi-Lamborghini LC92	40 laps/spun off	20
R	Thierry Boutsen	Ligier	Ligier-Renault JS37	27 laps/spun off	7
R	Gabriele Tarquini	Fondmetal	Fondmetal-Ford Cosworth GR02	25 laps/engine	11
R	Ivan Capelli	Ferrari	Ferrari F92A	25 laps/engine	12
R	Michele Alboreto	Footwork	Footwork-Mugen Honda FA13	20 laps/gearbox	14
R	Jean Alesi	Ferrari	Ferrari F92AT	7 laps/puncture	5
R	Olivier Grouillard	Tyrrell	Tyrrell-Ilmor 020B	1 lap/collision	22
R	Gerhard Berger	McLaren	McLaren-Honda MP4-7A	0 laps/transmission	6
R	Pierluigi Martini	BMS Scuderia Italia	Dallara-Ferrari 192	0 laps/spun off	19
DNQ	Christian Fittipaldi	Minardi	Minardi-Lamborghini M192	-	27
DNQ	Roberto Moreno	Andrea Moda	Moda-Judd S921	-	28
DNQ	Perry McCarthy	Andrea Moda	Moda-Judd S921	-	29
DNQ	Erik Comas*	Ligier	Ligier-Renault JS37	driver injured	30

*Comas didn't try to qualify after crashing in first practice

Pole: Mansell, 1m50.545s, 141.122mph/227.114kph. Fastest lap: Schumacher, 1m53.791s, 137.096mph/220.636kph on Lap 39. Race leaders: Senna 1 & 7-10, Mansell 2-3 & 11-33, Patrese 4-6, Schumacher 34-44

NEW CONSTRUCTORS

Alongside hapless Andrea Moda, Larrousse also made its debut. Founded by former sports car racer Gerard Larrousse after his split with Lola, the team used a chassis designed by Robin Herd. It was badged as a Venturi after a deal with a French sports car manufacturer and was powered by a Lamborghini V12. Bertrand Gachot managed a best result of sixth at Monaco.

ITALIAN GRAND PRIX

MONZA • ROUND 13 • DATE: 13TH SEPTEMBER 1992
Laps: 53 • Distance: 190.763miles/307.4km • Weather: Hot & bright

Pos	Driver	Team	Chassis-Engine	Result	Qual
1	Ayrton Senna	McLaren	McLaren-Honda MP4-7A	1h18m15.349s	2
2	Martin Brundle	Benetton	Benetton-Ford Cosworth B192	1h18m32.399s	9
3	Michael Schumacher	Benetton	Benetton-Ford Cosworth B192	1h18m39.722s	6
4	Gerhard Berger	McLaren	McLaren-Honda MP4-7A	1h19m40.839s	5
5	Riccardo Patrese	Williams	Williams-Renault FW14B	1h19m48.507s	4
6	Andrea de Cesaris	Tyrrell	Tyrrell-Ilmor 020B	52 laps	21
7	Michele Alboreto	Footwork	Footwork-Mugen Honda FA13	52 laps	16
8	Pierluigi Martini	BMS Scuderia Italia	Dallara-Ferrari 192	52 laps	22
9	Ukyo Katayama	Larrousse	Venturi-Lamborghini LC92	50 laps/transmission	23
10	Karl Wendlinger	March	March-Ilmor CG911	50 laps	17
11	JJ Lehto	BMS Scuderia Italia	Dallara-Ferrari 192	47 laps/engine	14
R	Mauricio Gugelmin	Jordan	Jordan-Yamaha 192	46 laps/transmission	26
R	Nigel Mansell	Williams	Williams-Renault FW14B	41 laps/electrical	1
R	Thierry Boutsen	Ligier	Ligier-Renault JS37	41 laps/throttle	8

Pos	Driver	Team	Chassis-Engine	Result	Qual
R	Erik Comas	Ligier	Ligier-Renault JS37	35 laps/spun off	15
R	Gabriele Tarquini	Fondmetal	Fondmetal-Ford Cosworth GR02	30 laps/gearbox	20
R	Olivier Grouillard	Tyrrell	Tyrrell-Ilmor 020B	26 laps/engine	18
R	Johnny Herbert	Lotus	Lotus-Ford Cosworth 107	18 laps/engine	13
R	Emanuele Naspetti	March	March-Ilmor CG911	17 laps/spun off	24
R	Jean Alesi	Ferrari	Ferrari F92AT	12 laps/fuel system	3
R	Ivan Capelli	Ferrari	Ferrari F92AT	12 laps/spun off	7
R	Gianni Morbidelli	Minardi	Minardi-Lamborghini M192	12 laps/engine	12
R	Bertrand Gachot	Larrousse	Venturi-Lamborghini LC92	11 laps/engine	10
R	Mika Hakkinen	Lotus	Lotus-Ford Cosworth 107	5 laps/engine	11
R	Aguri Suzuki	Footwork	Footwork-Mugen Honda FA13	2 laps/suspension	19
R	Eric van de Poele	Fondmetal	Fondmetal-Ford Cosworth GR02	0 laps/clutch	25
DNQ	Christian Fittipaldi	Minardi	Minardi-Lamborghini M192	-	27
DNQ	Stefano Modena	Jordan	Jordan-Yamaha 192	-	28

Pole: Mansell, 1m22.221s, 157.797mph/253.949kph. Fastest lap: Mansell, 1m26.119s, 150.654mph/242.455kph on Lap 39. Race leaders: Mansell 1-19, Patrese 20-47, Senna 48-53

CLASSIC CAR: WILLIAMS FW14B

The FW14B was one of the all-time great F1 cars, a car that seemingly could do everything a driver asked of it. This was the second Williams designed by the partnership of Patrick Head and Adrian Newey. One of its strengths was the finesse of its active ride, a system that Williams had first tried in 1987. The FW14B also used an improved electro-hydraulic gearchange and, late in the season, an automatic clutch to speed up-shifts. And so, after four years of McLaren-Hondas winning the constructors' title, it was the start of three years of a Williams-Renault doing the same.

PORTUGUESE GRAND PRIX

AUTODROMO DO ESTORIL • ROUND 14 • DATE: 27TH SEPTEMBER 1992
Laps: 71 • Distance: 191.435miles/308.85km • Weather: Warm & bright

Pos	Driver	Team	Chassis-Engine	Result	Qual
1	Nigel Mansell	Williams	Williams-Renault FW14B	1h34m46.659s	1
2	Gerhard Berger	McLaren	McLaren-Honda MP4-7A	1h35m24.192s	4
3	Ayrton Senna	McLaren	McLaren-Honda MP4-7A	70 laps	3
4	Martin Brundle	Benetton	Benetton-Ford Cosworth B192	70 laps	6
5	Mika Hakkinen	Lotus	Lotus-Ford Cosworth 107	70 laps	7
6	Michele Alboreto	Footwork	Footwork-Mugen Honda FA13	70 laps	8
7	Michael Schumacher	Benetton	Benetton-Ford Cosworth B192	69 laps	5
8	Thierry Boutsen	Ligier	Ligier-Renault JS37	69 laps	11
9	Andrea de Cesaris	Tyrrell	Tyrrell-Ilmor 020B	69 laps	12
10	Aguri Suzuki	Footwork	Footwork-Mugen Honda FA13	68 laps	17
11	Emanuele Naspetti	March	March-Ilmor CG911	68 laps	23
12	Christian Fittipaldi	Minardi	Minardi-Lamborghini M192	68 laps	26
13	Stefano Modena	Jordan	Jordan-Yamaha 192	68 laps	24
14	Gianni Morbidelli	Minardi	Minardi-Lamborghini M192	68 laps	18
R	JJ Lehto	BMS Scuderia Italia	Dallara-Ferrari 192	51 laps/physical	19
R	Karl Wendlinger	March	March-Ilmor CG911	48 laps/gearbox	22
R	Erik Comas	Ligier	Ligier-Renault JS37	47 laps/engine	14
R	Ukyo Katayama	Larrousse	Venturi-Lamborghini LC92	46 laps/spun off	25

Pos	Driver	Team	Chassis-Engine	Result	Qual
R	Riccardo Patrese	Williams	Williams-Renault FW14B	43 laps/collision	2
R	Pierluigi Martini	BMS Scuderia Italia	Dallara-Ferrari 192	43 laps/puncture	21
R	Ivan Capelli	Ferrari	Ferrari F92AT	34 laps/engine	16
R	Olivier Grouillard	Tyrrell	Tyrrell-Ilmor 020B	27 laps/gearbox	15
R	Bertrand Gachot	Larrousse	Venturi-Lamborghini LC92	25 laps/engine	13
R	Mauricio Gugelmin	Jordan	Jordan-Yamaha 192	19 laps/electrical	20
R	Jean Alesi	Ferrari	Ferrari F92AT	12 laps/spun off	10
R	Johnny Herbert	Lotus	Lotus-Ford Cosworth 107	2 laps/collision	9

Pole: Mansell, 1m13.041s, 133.222mph/214.400kph. Fastest lap: Senna, 1m16.272s, 127.578mph/205.317kph on Lap 66. Race leaders: Mansell 1-71

JAPANESE GRAND PRIX

SUZUKA • ROUND 15 • DATE: 25TH OCTOBER 1992
Laps: 53 • Distance: 193.117miles/310.792km • Weather: Warm but dull

Pos	Driver	Team	Chassis-Engine	Result	Qual
1	Riccardo Patrese	Williams	Williams-Renault FW14B	1h33m09.553s	2
2	Gerhard Berger	McLaren	McLaren-Honda MP4-7A	1h33m23.282s	4
3	Martin Brundle	Benetton	Benetton-Ford Cosworth B192	1h34m25.056s	13
4	Andrea de Cesaris	Tyrrell	Tyrrell-Ilmor 020B	52 laps	9
5	Jean Alesi	Ferrari	Ferrari F92AT	52 laps	15
6	Christian Fittipaldi	Minardi	Minardi-Lamborghini M192	52 laps	12
7	Stefano Modena	Jordan	Jordan-Yamaha 192	52 laps	17
8	Aguri Suzuki	Footwork	Footwork-Mugen Honda FA13	52 laps	16
9	JJ Lehto	BMS Scuderia Italia	Dallara-Ferrari 192	52 laps	22
10	Pierluigi Martini	BMS Scuderia Italia	Dallara-Ferrari 192	52 laps	19
11	Ukyo Katayama	Larrousse	Venturi-Lamborghini LC92	52 laps	20
12	Nicola Larini	Ferrari	Ferrari F92A	52 laps	11
13	Emanuele Naspetti	March	March-Ilmor CG911	51 laps	26
14	Gianni Morbidelli	Minardi	Minardi-Lamborghini M192	51 laps	14
15	Michele Alboreto	Footwork	Footwork-Mugen Honda FA13	51 laps	24
R	Nigel Mansell	Williams	Williams-Renault FW14B	44 laps/engine	1
R	Mika Hakkinen	Lotus	Lotus-Ford Cosworth 107	44 laps/engine	7
R	Bertrand Gachot	Larrousse	Venturi-Lamborghini LC92	39 laps/collision	18
R	Erik Comas	Ligier	Ligier-Renault JS37	36 laps/engine	8
R	Jan Lammers	March	March-Ilmor CG911	27 laps/clutch	23
R	Mauricio Gugelmin	Jordan	Jordan-Yamaha 192	22 laps/spun off	25
R	Johnny Herbert	Lotus	Lotus-Ford Cosworth 107	15 laps/gearbox	6
R	Michael Schumacher	Benetton	Benetton-Ford Cosworth B192	13 laps/gearbox	5
R	Olivier Grouillard	Tyrrell	Tyrrell-Ilmor 020B	6 laps/spun off	21
R	Thierry Boutsen	Ligier	Ligier-Renault JS37	3 laps/gearbox	10
R	Ayrton Senna	McLaren	McLaren-Honda MP4-7A	2 laps/engine	3

Pole: Mansell, 1m37.360s, 134.730mph/216.828kph. Fastest lap: Mansell, 1m40.646s, 130.332mph/209.749kph on Lap 44. Race leaders: Mansell 1-35, Patrese 36-53

NEW DRIVERS

The son and nephew of former world champions Graham Hill and Emerson Fittipaldi made their F1 debuts. Damon Hill had a hard time with struggling Brabham, but Christian Fittipaldi came good with sixth at Suzuka for Minardi. Ukyo Katayama finished ninth twice for Larrousse, while Paul Belmondo also finished ninth for March in Hungary.

AUSTRALIAN GRAND PRIX

ADELAIDE • ROUND 16 • DATE: 8TH NOVEMBER 1992
Laps: 81 • Distance: 190.150miles/306.18km • Weather: Warm but dull

Pos	Driver	Team	Chassis-Engine	Result	Qual
1	Gerhard Berger	McLaren	McLaren-Honda MP4-7A	1h46m54.786s	4
2	Michael Schumacher	Benetton	Benetton-Ford Cosworth B192	1h46m55.527s	5
3	Martin Brundle	Benetton	Benetton-Ford Cosworth B192	1h47m48.942s	8
4	Jean Alesi	Ferrari	Ferrari F92AT	80 laps	6
5	Thierry Boutsen	Ligier	Ligier-Renault JS37	80 laps	22
6	Stefano Modena	Jordan	Jordan-Yamaha 192	80 laps	15
7	Mika Hakkinen	Lotus	Lotus-Ford Cosworth 107	80 laps	10
8	Aguri Suzuki	Footwork	Footwork-Mugen Honda FA13	79 laps	18
9	Christian Fittipaldi	Minardi	Minardi-Lamborghini M192	79 laps	17
10	Gianni Morbidelli	Minardi	Minardi-Lamborghini M192	79 laps	16
11	Nicola Larini	Ferrari	Ferrari F92A	79 laps	19
12	Jan Lammers	March	March-Ilmor CG911	78 laps	25
13	Johnny Herbert	Lotus	Lotus-Ford Cosworth 107	77 laps	12
R	JJ Lehto	BMS Scuderia Italia	Dallara-Ferrari 192	70 laps/gearbox	24
R	Emanuele Naspetti	March	March-Ilmor CG911	55 laps/gearbox	23
R	Bertrand Gachot	Larrousse	Venturi-Lamborghini LC92	51 laps/fuel system	21
R	Riccardo Patrese	Williams	Williams-Renault FW14B	50 laps/engine	3
R	Ukyo Katayama	Larrousse	Venturi-Lamborghini LC92	35 laps/differential	26
R	Andrea de Cesaris	Tyrrell	Tyrrell-Ilmor 020B	29 laps/engine	7
R	Nigel Mansell	Williams	Williams-Renault FW14B	18 laps/collision	1
R	Ayrton Senna	McLaren	McLaren-Honda MP4-7A	18 laps/collision	2
R	Mauricio Gugelmin	Jordan	Jordan-Yamaha 192	7 laps/spun off	20
R	Erik Comas	Ligier	Ligier-Renault JS37	4 laps/engine	9
R	Michele Alboreto	Footwork	Footwork-Mugen Honda FA13	0 laps/spun off	11
R	Olivier Grouillard	Tyrrell	Tyrrell-Ilmor 020B	0 laps/collision	13
R	Pierluigi Martini	BMS Scuderia Italia	Dallara-Ferrari 192	0 laps/collision	14

Pole: Mansell, 1m13.732s, 114.680mph/184.560kph. Fastest lap: Schumacher, 1m16.078s, 111.144mph/178.869kph on Lap 68. Race leaders: Mansell 1-18, Patrese 19-50, Berger 51-81

WORLD DRIVERS' CHAMPIONSHIP FINAL RESULTS

Pos	Driver	Nat	Car-Engine	R1	R2	R3	R4	R5	R6
1	Nigel Mansell	GBR	Williams-Renault FW14B	1PF	1P	1P	1PF	1P	2PF
2	Riccardo Patrese	ITA	Williams-Renault FW14B	2	2	2F	R	2F	3
3	Michael Schumacher	DEU	Benetton-Ford Cosworth B191B	4	3	3	-	-	-
			Benetton-Ford Cosworth B192	-	-	-	2	R	4
4	Ayrton Senna	BRA	McLaren-Honda MP4/6B	3	R	-	-	-	-
			McLaren-Honda MP4/7A	-	-	R	9	3	1
5	Gerhard Berger	AUT	McLaren-Honda MP4/6B	5	4F	-	-	-	-
			McLaren-Honda MP4/7A	-	-	R	4	R	R
6	Martin Brundle	GBR	Benetton-Ford Cosworth B191B	R	R	R	-	-	-
			Benetton-Ford Cosworth B192	-	-	-	R	4	5
7	Jean Alesi	FRA	Ferrari F92A	R	R	4	3	R	R
			Ferrari F92AT	-	-	-	-	-	-
8	Mika Hakkinen	FIN	Lotus-Ford Cosworth 102D	9	6	10	R	DNQ	-
			Lotus-Ford Cosworth 107	-	-	-	-	-	R
9	Andrea de Cesaris	ITA	Tyrrell-Ilmor 020B	R	5	R	R	14	R
10	Michele Alboreto	ITA	Footwork-Mugen Honda FA13	10	13	6	5	5	7
11	Erik Comas	FRA	Ligier-Renault JS37	7	9	R	R	9	10

Pos	Driver	Nat	Car-Engine	R1	R2	R3	R4	R5	R6
12	Karl Wendlinger	AUT	March-Ilmor CG911	R	R	R	8	12	R
13	Ivan Capelli	ITA	Ferrari F92A	R	R	5	10	R	R
			Ferrari F92AT	-	-	-	-	-	-
14	Thierry Boutsen	BEL	Ligier-Renault JS37	R	10	R	R	R	12
15	Pierluigi Martini	ITA	Dallara-Ferrari 192	R	R	R	6	6	R
15	Johnny Herbert	GBR	Lotus-Ford Cosworth 102D	6	7	R	R	-	-
			Lotus-Ford Cosworth 107	-	-	-	-	R	R
17	Bertrand Gachot	FRA	Venturi-Lamborghini LC92	R	11	R	R	R	6
17	Christian Fittipaldi	BRA	Minardi-Lamborghini M191B	R	R	R	11	-	-
			Minardi-Lamborghini M192	-	-	-	-	R	8
17	Stefano Modena	ITA	Jordan-Yamaha 192	DNQ	R	R	DNQ	R	R

Pos	Driver	R7	R8	R9	R10	R11	R12	R13	R14	R15	R16	Total
1	Mansell	R	1PF	1PF	1P	2F	2P	RPF	1P	RPF	RP	108
2	Patrese	R	2	2	8F	RP	3	5	R	1	R	56
3	Schumacher	-	-	-	-	-	-	-	-	-	-	53
		2	R	4	3	R	1F	3	7	R	2F	
4	Senna	-	-	-	-	-	-	-	-	-	-	50
		RP	R	R	2	1	5	1	3F	R	R	
5	Berger	-	-	-	-	-	-	-	-	-	-	49
		1F	R	5	R	3	R	4	2	2	1	
6	Brundle	-	-	-	-	-	-	-	-	-	-	38
		R	3	3	4	5	4	2	4	3	3	
7	Alesi	3	R	R	5	R	-	-	-	-	-	18
		-	-	-	-	-	R	R	R	5	4	
8	Hakkinen	-	-	-	-	-	-	-	-	-	-	11
		R	4	6	R	4	6	R	5	R	7	
9	de Cesaris	5	R	R	R	8	8	6	9	4	R	8
10	Alboreto	7	7	7	9	7	R	7	6	15	R	6
11	Comas	6	5	8	6	R	NS	R	R	R	R	4
12	Wendlinger	4	R	R	16	R	11	10	R	-	-	3
13	Capelli	R	R	9	R	6	R	-	-	-	-	3
		-	-	-	-	-	-	R	R	-	-	
14	Boutsen	10	R	10	7	R	R	R	8	R	5	2
15	Martini	8	10	15	11	R	R	8	R	10	R	2
15	Herbert	-	-	-	-	-	-	-	-	-	-	2
		R	6	R	R	R	13	R	R	R	13	
17	Gachot	DQ	R	R	14	R	18	R	R	R	R	1
17	Fittipaldi	-	-	-	-	-	-	-	-	-	-	1
		13	DNQ	-	-	-	DNQ	DNQ	12	6	9	
17	Modena	R	R	R	DNQ	R	15	DNQ	13	7	6	1

SYMBOLS AND GRAND PRIX KEY

Round 1	**South African GP**	**Round 9**	**British GP**
Round 2	**Mexican GP**	**Round 10**	**German GP**
Round 3	**Brazilian GP**	**Round 11**	**Hungarian GP**
Round 4	**Spanish GP**	**Round 12**	**Belgian GP**
Round 5	**San Marino GP**	**Round 13**	**Italian GP**
Round 6	**Monaco GP**	**Round 14**	**Portuguese GP**
Round 7	**Canadian GP**	**Round 15**	**Japanese GP**
Round 8	**French GP**	**Round 16**	**Australian GP**

SCORING

1st	**10 points**
2nd	**6 points**
3rd	**4 points**
4th	**3 points**
5th	**2 points**
6th	**1 point**

DNPQ DID NOT PRE-QUALIFY DNQ DID NOT QUALIFY DQ DISQUALIFIED EX EXCLUDED
F FASTEST LAP NC NOT CLASSIFIED NS NON-STARTER P POLE POSITION R RETIRED

WORLD CONSTRUCTORS' CHAMPIONSHIP FINAL RESULTS

Pos	Team-Engine	R1	R2	R3	R4	R5	R6	R7	R8
1	Williams-Renault	1/2	1/2	1/2	1/R	1/2	2/3	R/R	1/2
2	McLaren-Honda	3/5	4/R	R/R	4/9	3/R	1/R	1/R	R/R
3	Benetton-Ford	4/R	3/R	3/R	2/R	4/R	4/5	2/R	3/R
4	Ferrari	R/R	R/R	4/5	3/10	R/R	R/R	3/R	R/R
5	Lotus-Ford	6/9	6/7	10/R	R/R	R/DNQ	R/R	R/R	4/6
6	Tyrrell-Ilmor	R/R	5/R	R/R	R/R	8/14	R/R	5/12	11/R
7	Footwork-Mugen Honda	8/10	13	6/R	5/7	5/10	7/11	7/DNQ	7/R
7	Ligier-Renault	7/R	9/10	R/R	R/R	9/R	10/12	6/10	5/R
9	March-Ilmor	R/DNQ	R/DNQ	R/DNQ	8/12	12/13	R/DNQ	4/14	R/DNQ
10	Dallara-Ferrari	R/R	8/R	8/R	6/R	6/11	9/R	8/9	9/10
11	Venturi-Lamborghini	12/R	11/12	9/R	R/DNQ	R/R	6/DNPQ	R/DQ	R/R
11	Minardi-Lamborghini	R/R	R/R	7/R	11/R	R/R	8/R	11/13	8/DNQ
11	Jordan-Yamaha	11/DNQ	R/R	R/R	R/DNQ	7/R	R/R	R/R	R/R

Pos	Team-Engine	R9	R10	R11	R12	R13	R14	R15	R16	Total
1	Williams-Renault	1/2	1/8	2/R	2/3	5/R	1/R	1/R	R/R	164
2	McLaren-Honda	5/R	2/R	1/3	5/R	1/4	2/3	2/R	1/R	99
3	Benetton-Ford	3/4	3/4	5/R	1/4	2/3	4/7	3/R	2/3	91
4	Ferrari	9/R	5/R	6/R	R/R	R/R	R/R	5/12	4/11	21
5	Lotus-Ford	6/R	R/R	4/R	6/13	R/R	5/R	R/R	7/13	13
6	Tyrrell-Ilmor	11/R	R/R	8/R	8/R	6/R	9/R	4/R	R/R	8
7	Footwork-Mugen Honda	7/12	9/R	7/R	9/R	7/R	6/10	8/15	8/R	6
7	Ligier-Renault	8/10	6/7	R/R	R/NS	R/R	8/R	R/R	5/R	6
9	March-Ilmor	R/DNQ	13/16	9/R	11/12	10/R	11/R	13/R	12/R	3
10	Dallara-Ferrari	13/15	10/11	R/DNQ	7/R	8/11	R/R	9/10	R/R	2
11	Venturi-Lamborghini	R/R	14/R	R/R	17/18	9/R	R/R	11/R	R/R	1
11	Minardi-Lamborghini	17/DNQ	12/R	DNQ/DNQ	16/DNQ	R/DNQ	12/14	6/14	9/10	1
11	Jordan-Yamaha	R/R	15/DNQ	10/R	14/15	R/DNQ	13/R	7/R	6/R	1

1993

SEASON SUMMARY

Alain Prost returned from a year off to take Nigel Mansell's ride at Williams and he used it to good effect to become world champion for a fourth time. His bitter rival, Ayrton Senna, was usually unable to match him as McLaren struggled in its first year after Honda quit F1 and it had to make do with Ford power. Damon Hill blossomed as number two at Williams and not only pressed Prost but started to beat him. Benetton became a rising force and it easily eclipsed Ferrari, which had another winless year. Then, with his title claimed, Prost announced his retirement.

SOUTH AFRICAN GRAND PRIX

KYALAMI • ROUND 1 • DATE: 14TH MARCH 1993
Laps: 72 • Distance: 190.631miles/306.792km • Weather: Hot, rain later on

Pos	Driver	Team	Chassis-Engine	Result	Qual
1	Alain Prost	Williams	Williams-Renault FW15C	1h38m45.082s	1
2	Ayrton Senna	McLaren	McLaren-Ford Cosworth MP4/8	1h40m04.906s	2
3	Mark Blundell	Ligier	Ligier-Renault JS39	71 laps	8
4	Christian Fittipaldi	Minardi	Minardi-Ford Cosworth M193	71 laps	13
5	JJ Lehto	Sauber	Sauber-Ilmor C12	70 laps	6
6	Gerhard Berger	Ferrari	Ferrari F93A	69 laps/engine	15
7	Derek Warwick	Footwork	Footwork-Mugen Honda FA13B	69 laps/spun off	22
R	Martin Brundle	Ligier	Ligier-Renault JS39	57 laps/spun off	12
R	Michele Alboreto	BMS Scuderia Italia	Lola-Ferrari T93/30	55 laps/overheating	25
R	Erik Comas	Larrousse	Larrousse-Lamborghini LH93	51 laps/engine	19
R	Riccardo Patrese	Benetton	Benetton-Ford Cosworth B192B	46 laps/spun off	7
R	Michael Schumacher	Benetton	Benetton-Ford Cosworth B192B	39 laps/spun off	3
R	Johnny Herbert	Lotus	Lotus-Ford Cosworth 107B	38 laps/fuel system	17
R	Karl Wendlinger	Sauber	Sauber-Ilmor C12	33 laps/engine	10
R	Rubens Barrichello	Jordan	Jordan-Hart 193	31 laps/gearbox	14
R	Jean Alesi	Ferrari	Ferrari F93A	30 laps/suspension	5
R	Philippe Alliot	Larrousse	Larrousse-Lamborghini LH93	27 laps/spun off	11
R	Aguri Suzuki	Footwork	Footwork-Mugen Honda FA13B	21 laps/collision	20
R	Fabrizio Barbazza	Minardi	Minardi-Ford Cosworth M193	21 laps/collision	24
R	Luca Badoer	BMS Scuderia Italia	Lola-Ferrari T93/30	20 laps/gearbox	26
R	Damon Hill	Williams	Williams-Renault FW15C	16 laps/collision	4
R	Alessandro Zanardi	Lotus	Lotus-Ford Cosworth 107B	16 laps/collision	16
R	Michael Andretti	McLaren	McLaren-Ford Cosworth MP4/8	4 laps/collision	9
R	Ivan Capelli	Jordan	Jordan-Hart 193	2 laps/spun off	18
R	Ukyo Katayama	Tyrrell	Tyrrell-Yamaha 020C	1 lap/transmission	21
R	Andrea de Cesaris	Tyrrell	Tyrrell-Yamaha 020C	0 laps/transmission	23

Pole: Prost, 1m15.696s, 125.919mph/202.647kph. Fastest lap: Prost, 1m19.492s, 119.906mph/192.970kph on Lap 40. Race leaders: Senna 1-23, Prost 24-72

ONE OF THE GREAT LAPS

Donington Park held grands prix in the 1930s, when Auto Union and Mercedes annihilated the opposition, but it finally had a one-off World Championship visit when it hosted the European GP. It produced a wet/dry classic as Ayrton Senna advanced from fifth out of the first corner in his McLaren to lead by the end of lap one, trouncing Prost in his Williams.

McLAREN CHANGES TO FORD

McLaren's long run with Honda engines came to a close at the end of 1992, and the team switched to Ford power for 1993. Despite losing out in the power stakes, Ayrton Senna was still able to win five rounds and end the year as runner-up to Mansell. Team-mate Michael Andretti was less successful, peaking with third at Monza, and was replaced by Mika Hakkinen.

BRAZILIAN GRAND PRIX

INTERLAGOS • ROUND 2 • DATE: 28TH MARCH 1993
Laps: 71 • Distance: 190.807miles/307.075km • Weather: Warm, rain later

Pos	Driver	Team	Chassis-Engine	Result	Qual
1	Ayrton Senna	McLaren	McLaren-Ford Cosworth MP4/8	1h51m15.485s	3
2	Damon Hill	Williams	Williams-Renault FW15C	1h51m32.110s	2
3	Michael Schumacher	Benetton	Benetton-Ford Cosworth B193A	1h52m00.921s	4
4	Johnny Herbert	Lotus	Lotus-Ford Cosworth 107B	1h52m02.042s	12
5	Mark Blundell	Ligier	Ligier-Renault JS39	1h52m07.612s	10
6	Alessandro Zanardi	Lotus	Lotus-Ford Cosworth 107B	70 laps	15
7	Philippe Alliot	Larrousse	Larrousse-Lamborghini LH93	70 laps	11
8	Jean Alesi	Ferrari	Ferrari F93A	70 laps	9
9	Derek Warwick	Footwork	Footwork-Mugen Honda FA13B	69 laps	18
10	Erik Comas	Larrousse	Larrousse-Lamborghini LH93	69 laps	17
11	Michele Alboreto	BMS Scuderia Italia	Lola-Ferrari T93/30	68 laps	25
12	Luca Badoer	BMS Scuderia Italia	Lola-Ferrari T93/30	68 laps	21
R	Karl Wendlinger	Sauber	Sauber-Ilmor C12	61 laps/engine	8
R	JJ Lehto	Sauber	Sauber-Ilmor C12	52 laps/electrical	7
R	Andrea de Cesaris	Tyrrell	Tyrrell-Yamaha 020C	48 laps/fuel system	23
R	Alain Prost	Williams	Williams-Renault FW15C	29 laps/collision	1
R	Christian Fittipaldi	Minardi	Minardi-Ford Cosworth M193	28 laps/collision	20
R	Aguri Suzuki	Footwork	Footwork-Mugen Honda FA13B	27 laps/spun off	19
R	Ukyo Katayama	Tyrrell	Tyrrell-Yamaha 020C	26 laps/spun off	22
R	Rubens Barrichello	Jordan	Jordan-Hart 193	13 laps/gearbox	14
R	Riccardo Patrese	Benetton	Benetton-Ford Cosworth B193A	3 laps/suspension	6
R	Michael Andretti	McLaren	McLaren-Ford Cosworth MP4/8	0 laps/collision	5
R	Gerhard Berger	Ferrari	Ferrari F93A	0 laps/collision	13
R	Martin Brundle	Ligier	Ligier-Renault JS39	0 laps/collision	16
R	Fabrizio Barbazza	Minardi	Minardi-Ford Cosworth M193	0 laps/collision	24
DNQ	Ivan Capelli	Jordan	Jordan-Hart 193	-	26

Pole: Prost, 1m15.866s, 127.524mph/205.230kph. Fastest lap: Schumacher, 1m20.024s, 120.898mph/194.566kph on Lap 61. Race leaders: Prost 1-29, Hill 30-41, Senna 42-71

EUROPEAN GRAND PRIX

DONINGTON PARK • ROUND 3 • DATE: 11TH APRIL 1993
Laps: 76 • Distance: 189.983miles/305.748km • Weather: Cool & wet

Pos	Driver	Team	Chassis-Engine	Result	Qual
1	Ayrton Senna	McLaren	McLaren-Ford Cosworth MP4/8	1h50m46.570s	4
2	Damon Hill	Williams	Williams-Renault FW15C	1h52m09.769s	2
3	Alain Prost	Williams	Williams-Renault FW15C	75 laps	1

Pos	Driver	Team	Chassis-Engine	Result	Qual
4	Johnny Herbert	Lotus	Lotus-Ford Cosworth 107B	75 laps	11
5	Riccardo Patrese	Benetton	Benetton-Ford Cosworth B193B	74 laps	10
6	Fabrizio Barbazza	Minardi	Minardi-Ford Cosworth M193	74 laps	20
7	Christian Fittipaldi	Minardi	Minardi-Ford Cosworth M193	73 laps	16
8	Alessandro Zanardi	Lotus	Lotus-Ford Cosworth 107B	72 laps	13
9	Erik Comas	Larrousse	Larrousse-Lamborghini LH93	72 laps	17
10	Rubens Barrichello	Jordan	Jordan-Hart 193	70 laps/out of fuel	12
11	Michele Alboreto	BMS Scuderia Italia	Lola-Ferrari T93/30	70 laps	24
R	Derek Warwick	Footwork	Footwork-Mugen Honda FA14	66 laps/gearbox	14
R	Thierry Boutsen	Jordan	Jordan-Hart 193	61 laps/throttle	19
R	Andrea de Cesaris	Tyrrell	Tyrrell-Yamaha 020C	55 laps/gearbox	25
R	Jean Alesi	Ferrari	Ferrari F93A	36 laps/gearbox	9
R	Aguri Suzuki	Footwork	Footwork-Mugen Honda FA14	29 laps/gearbox	23
R	Philippe Alliot	Larrousse	Larrousse-Lamborghini LH93	27 laps/collision	15
R	Michael Schumacher	Benetton	Benetton-Ford Cosworth B193B	22 laps/spun off	3
R	Mark Blundell	Ligier	Ligier-Renault JS39	20 laps/spun off	21
R	Gerhard Berger	Ferrari	Ferrari F93A	19 laps/suspension	8
R	JJ Lehto	Sauber	Sauber-Ilmor C12	13 laps/handling	7
R	Ukyo Katayama	Tyrrell	Tyrrell-Yamaha 020C	11 laps/clutch	18
R	Martin Brundle	Ligier	Ligier-Renault JS39	7 laps/spun off	22
R	Karl Wendlinger	Sauber	Sauber-Ilmor C12	0 laps/collision	5
R	Michael Andretti	McLaren	McLaren-Ford Cosworth MP4/8	0 laps/collision	6
DNQ	Luca Badoer	BMS Scuderia Italia	Lola-Ferrari T93/30	-	26

Pole: Prost, 1m10.458s, 127.724mph/205.552kph. Fastest lap: Senna, 1m18.029s, 115.331mph/185.607kph on Lap 57. Race leaders: Senna 1-18 & 20-34 & 39-76, Prost 19 & 35-38

A REAL HIT ON HIS DEBUT

Eddie Irvine made an impact on his debut for Jordan at Suzuka, as he qualified eighth then finished a remarkable sixth on a circuit he knew well from racing in Japan. He ended up being punched by Ayrton Senna in a post-race altercation after Irvine had got in the Brazilian's way by unlapping himself so he could concentrate on dicing with Damon Hill.

SAN MARINO GRAND PRIX

IMOLA • ROUND 4 • DATE: 25TH APRIL 1993
Laps: 61 • Distance: 190.788miles/307.44km • Weather: Cool & damp, then drying

Pos	Driver	Team	Chassis-Engine	Result	Qual
1	Alain Prost	Williams	Williams-Renault FW15C	1h33m20.413s	1
2	Michael Schumacher	Benetton	Benetton-Ford Cosworth B193B	1h33m52.823s	3
3	Martin Brundle	Ligier	Ligier-Renault JS39	60 laps	10
4	JJ Lehto	Sauber	Sauber-Ilmor C12	59 laps/engine	16
5	Philippe Alliot	Larrousse	Larrousse-Lamborghini LH93	59 laps	14
6	Fabrizio Barbazza	Minardi	Minardi-Ford Cosworth M193	59 laps	25
7	Luca Badoer	BMS Scuderia Italia	Lola-Ferrari T93/30	58 laps	24
8	Johnny Herbert	Lotus	Lotus-Ford Cosworth 107B	57 laps/engine	12
9	Aguri Suzuki	Footwork	Footwork-Mugen Honda FA14	54 laps	21
R	Alessandro Zanardi	Lotus	Lotus-Ford Cosworth 107B	53 laps/spun off	20
R	Karl Wendlinger	Sauber	Sauber-Ilmor C12	48 laps/engine	5

Pos	Driver	Team	Chassis-Engine	Result	Qual
R	Ayrton Senna	McLaren	McLaren-Ford Cosworth MP4/8	42 laps/hydraulics	4
R	Jean Alesi	Ferrari	Ferrari F93A	40 laps/clutch	9
R	Christian Fittipaldi	Minardi	Minardi-Ford Cosworth M193	36 laps/steering	23
R	Michael Andretti	McLaren	McLaren-Ford Cosworth MP4/8	32 laps/spun off	6
R	Derek Warwick	Footwork	Footwork-Mugen Honda FA14	29 laps/spun off	15
R	Ukyo Katayama	Tyrrell	Tyrrell-Yamaha 020C	22 laps/engine	22
R	Damon Hill	Williams	Williams-Renault FW15C	20 laps/brakes	2
R	Erik Comas	Larrousse	Larrousse-Lamborghini LH93	18 laps/engine	17
R	Andrea de Cesaris	Tyrrell	Tyrrell-Yamaha 020C	18 laps/gearbox	18
R	Rubens Barrichello	Jordan	Jordan-Hart 193	17 laps/spun off	13
R	Gerhard Berger	Ferrari	Ferrari F93A	8 laps/gearbox	8
R	Thierry Boutsen	Jordan	Jordan-Hart 193	1 lap/gearbox	19
R	Mark Blundell	Ligier	Ligier-Renault JS39	0 laps/spun off	7
R	Riccardo Patrese	Benetton	Benetton-Ford Cosworth B193B	0 laps/spun off	11
DNQ	Michele Alboreto	BMS Scuderia Italia	Lola-Ferrari T93/30	-	26

Pole: Prost, 1m22.070s, 137.372mph/221.079kph. Fastest lap: Prost, 1m26.128s, 130.900mph/210.663kph on Lap 42. Race leaders: Hill 1-11, Prost 12-61

SPANISH GRAND PRIX

BARCELONA-CATALUNYA • ROUND 5 • DATE: 9TH MAY 1993
Laps: 65 • Distance: 191.727miles/308.555km • Weather: Hot & bright

Pos	Driver	Team	Chassis-Engine	Result	Qual
1	Alain Prost	Williams	Williams-Renault FW15C	1h32m27.685s	1
2	Ayrton Senna	McLaren	McLaren-Ford Cosworth MP4/8	1h32m44.558s	3
3	Michael Schumacher	Benetton	Benetton-Ford Cosworth B193B	1h32m54.810s	4
4	Riccardo Patrese	Benetton	Benetton-Ford Cosworth B193B	64 laps	5
5	Michael Andretti	McLaren	McLaren-Ford Cosworth MP4/8	64 laps	7
6	Gerhard Berger	Ferrari	Ferrari F93A	63 laps	11
7	Mark Blundell	Ligier	Ligier-Renault JS39	63 laps	12
8	Christian Fittipaldi	Minardi	Minardi-Ford Cosworth M193	63 laps	20
9	Erik Comas	Larrousse	Larrousse-Lamborghini LH93	63 laps	14
10	Aguri Suzuki	Footwork	Footwork-Mugen Honda FA14	63 laps	19
11	Thierry Boutsen	Jordan	Jordan-Hart 193	62 laps	21
12	Rubens Barrichello	Jordan	Jordan-Hart 193	62 laps	17
13	Derek Warwick	Footwork	Footwork-Mugen Honda FA14	62 laps	16
14	Alessandro Zanardi	Lotus	Lotus-Ford Cosworth 107B	60 laps/engine	15
R	JJ Lehto	Sauber	Sauber-Ilmor C12	53 laps/engine	9
R	Luca Badoer	BMS Scuderia Italia	Lola-Ferrari T93/30	43 laps/overheating	22
R	Karl Wendlinger	Sauber	Sauber-Ilmor C12	42 laps/fuel system	6
DQ	Andrea de Cesaris	Tyrrell	Tyrrell-Yamaha 020C	42 laps/outside help	24
R	Damon Hill	Williams	Williams-Renault FW15C	41 laps/engine	2
R	Jean Alesi	Ferrari	Ferrari F93A	40 laps/engine	8
R	Fabrizio Barbazza	Minardi	Minardi-Ford Cosworth M193	37 laps/spun off	25
R	Philippe Alliot	Larrousse	Larrousse-Lamborghini LH93	26 laps/transmission	13
R	Martin Brundle	Ligier	Ligier-Renault JS39	11 laps/spun off	18
R	Ukyo Katayama	Tyrrell	Tyrrell-Yamaha 020C	11 laps/spun off	23
R	Johnny Herbert	Lotus	Lotus-Ford Cosworth 107B	2 laps/suspension	10
DNQ	Michele Alboreto	BMS Scuderia Italia	Lola-Ferrari T93/30	-	26

Pole: Prost, 1m17.809s, 136.471mph/219.630kph. Fastest lap: Schumacher, 1m20.989s, 131.113mph/211.006kph on Lap 61. Race leaders: Hill 1-10, Prost 11-65

MONACO GRAND PRIX

MONTE CARLO • ROUND 6 • DATE: 23RD MAY 1993
Laps: 78 • Distance: 161.298miles/259.584km • Weather: Warm but dull

Pos	Driver	Team	Chassis-Engine	Result	Qual
1	Ayrton Senna	McLaren	McLaren-Ford Cosworth MP4/8	1h52m10.947s	3
2	Damon Hill	Williams	Williams-Renault FW15C	1h53m03.065s	4
3	Jean Alesi	Ferrari	Ferrari F93A	1h53m14.309s	5
4	Alain Prost	Williams	Williams-Renault FW15C	77 laps	1
5	Christian Fittipaldi	Minardi	Minardi-Ford Cosworth M193	76 laps	17
6	Martin Brundle	Ligier	Ligier-Renault JS39	76 laps	13
7	Alessandro Zanardi	Lotus	Lotus-Ford Cosworth 107B	76 laps	20
8	Michael Andretti	McLaren	McLaren-Ford Cosworth MP4/8	76 laps	9
9	Rubens Barrichello	Jordan	Jordan-Hart 193	76 laps	16
10	Andrea de Cesaris	Tyrrell	Tyrrell-Yamaha 020C	76 laps	19
11	Fabrizio Barbazza	Minardi	Minardi-Ford Cosworth M193	75 laps	25
12	Philippe Alliot	Larrousse	Larrousse-Lamborghini LH93	75 laps	15
13	Karl Wendlinger	Sauber	Sauber-Ilmor C12	74 laps	8
14	Gerhard Berger	Ferrari	Ferrari F93A	70 laps/collision	7
R	Johnny Herbert	Lotus	Lotus-Ford Cosworth 107B	61 laps/gearbox	14
R	Riccardo Patrese	Benetton	Benetton-Ford Cosworth B193B	53 laps/engine	6
R	Erik Comas	Larrousse	Larrousse-Lamborghini LH93	51 laps/collision	10
R	Aguri Suzuki	Footwork	Footwork-Mugen Honda FA14	46 laps/spun off	18
R	Derek Warwick	Footwork	Footwork-Mugen Honda FA14	43 laps/throttle	12
R	Michael Schumacher	Benetton	Benetton-Ford Cosworth B193B	32 laps/hydraulics	2
R	Ukyo Katayama	Tyrrell	Tyrrell-Yamaha 020C	31 laps/engine	22
R	Michele Alboreto	BMS Scuderia Italia	Lola-Ferrari T93/30	28 laps/gearbox	24
R	JJ Lehto	Sauber	Sauber-Ilmor C12	23 laps/collision	11
R	Thierry Boutsen	Jordan	Jordan-Hart 193	12 laps/suspension	23
R	Mark Blundell	Ligier	Ligier-Renault JS39	3 laps/spun off	21
DNQ	Luca Badoer	BMS Scuderia Italia	Lola-Ferrari T93/30	-	26

Pole: Prost, 1m20.557s, 92.413mph/148.724kph. Fastest lap: Prost, 1m23.604s, 89.045mph/143.304kph on Lap 52. Race leaders: Prost 1-11, Schumacher 12-32, Senna 33-78

MANSELL'S NEW CAREER

Nigel Mansell made an instant impact in his IndyCar career after his shock departure from Williams. The reigning world champion kicked off by winning the opening race at Surfers Paradise for Newman-Haas Racing, had a huge accident while practising for his first oval race at Phoenix, then bounced back to be pipped in the Indy 500 before winning four more races and being crowned champion.

HILL'S GIANT LEAP FORWARD

Damon Hill had a tough start to his F1 career with struggling Brabham. Being a test driver with Williams bore fruit, though, landing him the second race seat, an opportunity he grabbed with both hands. He kept closing the gap to Alain Prost, coming close to winning several times before breaking through in Hungary.

CANADIAN GRAND PRIX

MONTREAL • ROUND 7 • DATE: 13TH JUNE 1993
Laps: 69 • Distance: 189.559miles/305.67km • Weather: Hot & bright

Pos	Driver	Team	Chassis-Engine	Result	Qual
1	Alain Prost	Williams	Williams-Renault FW15C	1h36m41.822s	1
2	Michael Schumacher	Benetton	Benetton-Ford Cosworth B193B	1h36m56.349s	3
3	Damon Hill	Williams	Williams-Renault FW15C	1h37m34.507s	2
4	Gerhard Berger	Ferrari	Ferrari F93A	68 laps	5
5	Martin Brundle	Ligier	Ligier-Renault JS39	68 laps	7
6	Karl Wendlinger	Sauber	Sauber-Ilmor C12	68 laps	9
7	JJ Lehto	Sauber	Sauber-Ilmor C12	68 laps	11
8	Erik Comas	Larrousse	Larrousse-Lamborghini LH93	68 laps	13
9	Christian Fittipaldi	Minardi	Minardi-Ford Cosworth M193	67 laps	17
10	Johnny Herbert	Lotus	Lotus-Ford Cosworth 107B	67 laps	20
11	Alessandro Zanardi	Lotus	Lotus-Ford Cosworth 107B	67 laps	21
12	Thierry Boutsen	Jordan	Jordan-Hart 193	67 laps	24
13	Aguri Suzuki	Footwork	Footwork-Mugen Honda FA14	66 laps	16
14	Michael Andretti	McLaren	McLaren-Ford Cosworth MP4/8	66 laps	12
15	Luca Badoer	BMS Scuderia Italia	Lola-Ferrari T93/30	65 laps	25
16	Derek Warwick	Footwork	Footwork-Mugen Honda FA14	65 laps	18
17	Ukyo Katayama	Tyrrell	Tyrrell-Yamaha 020C	64 laps	22
18	Ayrton Senna	McLaren	McLaren-Ford Cosworth MP4/8	62 laps/electrical	8
R	Riccardo Patrese	Benetton	Benetton-Ford Cosworth B193B	52 laps/physical	4
R	Andrea de Cesaris	Tyrrell	Tyrrell-Yamaha 020C	45 laps/spun off	19
R	Fabrizio Barbazza	Minardi	Minardi-Ford Cosworth M193	33 laps/gearbox	23
R	Jean Alesi	Ferrari	Ferrari F93A	23 laps/engine	6
R	Mark Blundell	Ligier	Ligier-Renault JS39	13 laps/spun off	10
R	Rubens Barrichello	Jordan	Jordan-Hart 193	10 laps/electrical	14
R	Philippe Alliot	Larrousse	Larrousse-Lamborghini LH93	8 laps/engine	15
DNQ	Michele Alboreto	BMS Scuderia Italia	Lola-Ferrari T93/30	-	26

Pole: Prost, 1m18.987s, 125.458mph/201.906kph. Fastest lap: Schumacher, 1m21.500s, 121.590mph/195.680kph on Lap 57. Race leaders: Hill 1-5, Prost 6-69

A FLYING FINISH

Christian Fittipaldi flipped his Minardi on the dash to the finish of the Italian GP at Monza, after clipping the tail of Minardi team-mate Pierluigi Martini's car as they fought over seventh place. The Brazilian said he knew that something was wrong when all he could see was sky, but fortunately the car did a full rotation and landed back on its wheels.

FRENCH GRAND PRIX

MAGNY-COURS • ROUND 8 • DATE: 4TH JULY 1993
Laps: 72 • Distance: 190.139miles/306.0km • Weather: Warm but dull

Pos	Driver	Team	Chassis-Engine	Result	Qual
1	Alain Prost	Williams	Williams-Renault FW15C	1h38m35.241s	2
2	Damon Hill	Williams	Williams-Renault FW15C	1h38m35.583s	1
3	Michael Schumacher	Benetton	Benetton-Ford Cosworth B193B	1h38m56.450s	7

Pos	Driver	Team	Chassis-Engine	Result	Qual
4	Ayrton Senna	McLaren	McLaren-Ford Cosworth MP4/8	1h39m07.646s	5
5	Martin Brundle	Ligier	Ligier-Renault JS39	1h39m09.036s	3
6	Michael Andretti	McLaren	McLaren-Ford Cosworth MP4/8	71 laps	16
7	Rubens Barrichello	Jordan	Jordan-Hart 193	71 laps	8
8	Christian Fittipaldi	Minardi	Minardi-Ford Cosworth M193	71 laps	23
9	Philippe Alliot	Larrousse	Larrousse-Lamborghini LH93	70 laps	10
10	Riccardo Patrese	Benetton	Benetton-Ford Cosworth B193B	70 laps	12
11	Thierry Boutsen	Jordan	Jordan-Hart 193	70 laps	20
12	Aguri Suzuki	Footwork	Footwork-Mugen Honda FA14	70 laps	13
13	Derek Warwick	Footwork	Footwork-Mugen Honda FA14	70 laps	15
14	Gerhard Berger	Ferrari	Ferrari F93A	70 laps	14
15	Andrea de Cesaris	Tyrrell	Tyrrell-Yamaha 020C	68 laps	25
16	Erik Comas	Larrousse	Larrousse-Lamborghini LH93	66 laps/gearbox	9
R	Jean Alesi	Ferrari	Ferrari F93A	47 laps/engine	6
R	Luca Badoer	BMS Scuderia Italia	Lola-Ferrari T93/30	28 laps/suspension	22
R	Karl Wendlinger	Sauber	Sauber-Ilmor C12	25 laps/gearbox	11
R	JJ Lehto	Sauber	Sauber-Ilmor C12	22 laps/gearbox	18
R	Mark Blundell	Ligier	Ligier-Renault JS39	20 laps/spun off	4
R	Johnny Herbert	Lotus	Lotus-Ford Cosworth 107B	16 laps/spun off	19
R	Fabrizio Barbazza	Minardi	Minardi-Ford Cosworth M193	16 laps/gearbox	24
R	Ukyo Katayama	Tyrrell	Tyrrell-Yamaha 020C	9 laps/engine	21
R	Alessandro Zanardi	Lotus	Lotus-Ford Cosworth 107B	3 laps/suspension	17
DNQ	Michele Alboreto	BMS Scuderia Italia	Lola-Ferrari T93/30	-	26

Pole: Hill, 1m14.382s, 127.812mph/205.694kph. Fastest lap: Schumacher, 1m19.256s, 119.952mph/193.045kph on Lap 47. Race leaders: Hill 1-26, Prost 27-72

DEATH OF A CHAMPION

James Hunt, world champion for McLaren in 1976 and latterly sidekick to Murray Walker in the BBC commentary box, died a premature death from a heart attack at the age of just 45. Fellow F1 hell-raiser Innes Ireland also passed away, the Scot having been the first Lotus works driver to win a grand prix, at Watkins Glen in 1961.

BRITISH GRAND PRIX

SILVERSTONE • ROUND 9 • DATE: 11TH JULY 1993
Laps: 59 • Distance: 191.589miles/308.334km • Weather: Cool & dull

Pos	Driver	Team	Chassis-Engine	Result	Qual
1	Alain Prost	Williams	Williams-Renault FW15C	1h25m38.189s	1
2	Michael Schumacher	Benetton	Benetton-Ford Cosworth B193B	1h25m45.849s	3
3	Riccardo Patrese	Benetton	Benetton-Ford Cosworth B193B	1h26m55.671s	5
4	Johnny Herbert	Lotus	Lotus-Ford Cosworth 107B	1h26m56.596s	7
5	Ayrton Senna	McLaren	McLaren-Ford Cosworth MP4/8	58 laps/out of fuel	4
6	Derek Warwick	Footwork	Footwork-Mugen Honda FA14	58 laps	8
7	Mark Blundell	Ligier	Ligier-Renault JS39	58 laps	9
8	JJ Lehto	Sauber	Sauber-Ilmor C12	58 laps	16
9	Jean Alesi	Ferrari	Ferrari F93A	58 laps	12
10	Rubens Barrichello	Jordan	Jordan-Hart 193	58 laps	15
11	Philippe Alliot	Larrousse	Larrousse-Lamborghini LH93	57 laps	24
12	Christian Fittipaldi	Minardi	Minardi-Ford Cosworth M193	56 laps/gearbox	19

Pos	Driver	Team	Chassis-Engine	Result	Qual
13	Ukyo Katayama	Tyrrell	Tyrrell-Yamaha 020C	55 laps	22
14	Martin Brundle	Ligier	Ligier-Renault JS39	53 laps/gearbox	6
NC	Andrea de Cesaris	Tyrrell	Tyrrell-Yamaha 021	43 laps	21
R	Damon Hill	Williams	Williams-Renault FW15C	41 laps/engine	2
R	Alessandro Zanardi	Lotus	Lotus-Ford Cosworth 107B	41 laps/suspension	14
R	Thierry Boutsen	Jordan	Jordan-Hart 193	41 laps/wheel	23
R	Luca Badoer	BMS Scuderia Italia	Lola-Ferrari T93/30	32 laps/electrical	25
R	Pierluigi Martini	Minardi	Minardi-Ford Cosworth M193	31 laps/physical	20
R	Karl Wendlinger	Sauber	Sauber-Ilmor C12	24 laps/spun off	18
R	Gerhard Berger	Ferrari	Ferrari F93A	10 laps/suspension	13
R	Aguri Suzuki	Footwork	Footwork-Mugen Honda FA14	8 laps/spun off	10
R	Michael Andretti	McLaren	McLaren-Ford Cosworth MP4/8	0 laps/spun off	11
R	Erik Comas	Larrousse	Larrousse-Lamborghini LH93	0 laps/halfshaft	17
DNQ	Michele Alboreto	BMS Scuderia Italia	Lola-Ferrari T93/30	-	26

Pole: Prost, 1m19.006s, 147.966mph/238.128kph. Fastest lap: Hill, 1m22.515s, 141.673mph/228.002kph on Lap 41. Race leaders: Hill 1-41, Prost 42-59

GERMAN GRAND PRIX

HOCKENHEIM • ROUND 10 • DATE: 25TH JULY 1993
Laps: 45 • Distance: 190.559miles/306.675km • Weather: Warm & bright

Pos	Driver	Team	Chassis-Engine	Result	Qual
1	Alain Prost	Williams	Williams-Renault FW15C	1h18m40.885s	1
2	Michael Schumacher	Benetton	Benetton-Ford Cosworth B193B	1h18m57.549s	3
3	Mark Blundell	Ligier	Ligier-Renault JS39	1h19m40.234s	5
4	Ayrton Senna	McLaren	McLaren-Ford Cosworth MP4/8	1h19m49.114s	4
5	Riccardo Patrese	Benetton	Benetton-Ford Cosworth B193B	1h20m12.401s	7
6	Gerhard Berger	Ferrari	Ferrari F93A	1h20m15.639s	9
7	Jean Alesi	Ferrari	Ferrari F93A	1h20m16.726s	10
8	Martin Brundle	Ligier	Ligier-Renault JS39	44 laps	6
9	Karl Wendlinger	Sauber	Sauber-Ilmor C12	44 laps	14
10	Johnny Herbert	Lotus	Lotus-Ford Cosworth 107B	44 laps	13
11	Christian Fittipaldi	Minardi	Minardi-Ford Cosworth M193	44 laps	20
12	Philippe Alliot	Larrousse	Larrousse-Lamborghini LH93	44 laps	23
13	Thierry Boutsen	Jordan	Jordan-Hart 193	44 laps	24
14	Pierluigi Martini	Minardi	Minardi-Ford Cosworth M193	44 laps	22
15	Damon Hill	Williams	Williams-Renault FW15C	43 laps/tyre	2
16	Michele Alboreto	BMS Scuderia Italia	Lola-Ferrari T93/30	43 laps	26
17	Derek Warwick	Footwork	Footwork-Mugen Honda FA14	42 laps	11
R	Rubens Barrichello	Jordan	Jordan-Hart 193	34 laps/wheel	17
R	Ukyo Katayama	Tyrrell	Tyrrell-Yamaha 021	28 laps/halfshaft	21
R	JJ Lehto	Sauber	Sauber-Ilmor C12	22 laps/spun off	18
R	Alessandro Zanardi	Lotus	Lotus-Ford Cosworth 107B	19 laps/spun off	15
R	Aguri Suzuki	Footwork	Footwork-Mugen Honda FA14	9 laps/collision	8
R	Michael Andretti	McLaren	McLaren-Ford Cosworth MP4/8	4 laps/collision	12
R	Luca Badoer	BMS Scuderia Italia	Lola-Ferrari T93/30	4 laps/suspension	25
R	Andrea de Cesaris	Tyrrell	Tyrrell-Yamaha 021	1 lap/gearbox	19
R	Erik Comas	Larrousse	Larrousse-Lamborghini LH93	0 laps/gearbox	16

Pole: Prost, 1m38.748s, 154.380mph/248.450kph. Fastest lap: Schumacher, 1m41.859s, 149.664mph/240.862kph on Lap 40. Race leaders: Hill 1-7 & 10-43, Prost 8-9 & 44-45

HUNGARIAN GRAND PRIX

HUNGARORING • ROUND 11 • DATE: 15TH AUGUST 1993
Laps: 77 • Distance: 189.851miles/305.536km • Weather: Hot & bright

Pos	Driver	Team	Chassis-Engine	Result	Qual
1	Damon Hill	Williams	Williams-Renault FW15C	1h47m39.098s	2
2	Riccardo Patrese	Benetton	Benetton-Ford Cosworth B193B	1h48m51.013s	5
3	Gerhard Berger	Ferrari	Ferrari F93A	1h48m57.140s	6
4	Derek Warwick	Footwork	Footwork-Mugen Honda FA14	76 laps	9
5	Martin Brundle	Ligier	Ligier-Renault JS39	76 laps	13
6	Karl Wendlinger	Sauber	Sauber-Ilmor C12	76 laps	17
7	Mark Blundell	Ligier	Ligier-Renault JS39	76 laps	12
8	Philippe Alliot	Larrousse	Larrousse-Lamborghini LH93	75 laps	19
9	Thierry Boutsen	Jordan	Jordan-Hart 193	75 laps	24
10	Ukyo Katayama	Tyrrell	Tyrrell-Yamaha 021	73 laps	23
11	Andrea de Cesaris	Tyrrell	Tyrrell-Yamaha 021	72 laps	22
12	Alain Prost	Williams	Williams-Renault FW15C	70 laps	1
R	Pierluigi Martini	Minardi	Minardi-Ford Cosworth M193	59 laps/spun off	7
R	Erik Comas	Larrousse	Larrousse-Lamborghini LH93	54 laps/engine	18
R	Alessandro Zanardi	Lotus	Lotus-Ford Cosworth 107B	45 laps/gearbox	21
R	Aguri Suzuki	Footwork	Footwork-Mugen Honda FA14	41 laps/spun off	10
R	Michele Alboreto	BMS Scuderia Italia	Lola-Ferrari T93/30	39 laps/overheating	25
R	Johnny Herbert	Lotus	Lotus-Ford Cosworth 107B	38 laps/spun off	20
R	Luca Badoer	BMS Scuderia Italia	Lola-Ferrari T93/30	37 laps/spun off	26
R	Michael Schumacher	Benetton	Benetton-Ford Cosworth B193B	26 laps/fuel pump	3
R	Jean Alesi	Ferrari	Ferrari F93A	22 laps/spun off	8
R	Christian Fittipaldi	Minardi	Minardi-Ford Cosworth M193	22 laps/suspension	14
R	JJ Lehto	Sauber	Sauber-Ilmor C12	18 laps/engine	15
R	Ayrton Senna	McLaren	McLaren-Ford Cosworth MP4/8	17 laps/throttle	4
R	Michael Andretti	McLaren	McLaren-Ford Cosworth MP4/8	15 laps/throttle	11
R	Rubens Barrichello	Jordan	Jordan-Hart 193	0 laps/collision	16

Pole: Prost, 1m14.631s, 118.933mph/191.405kph. Fastest lap: Prost, 1m19.633s, 111.463mph/179.382kph on Lap 52. Race leaders: Hill 1-77

PATRESE PARKS UP

Riccardo Patrese retired from F1 at the end of his 17th season, becoming the World Championship's most experienced driver. His tally of 256 grands prix started with Shadow in 1977 and concluded at Adelaide, when he was classified eighth for Benetton after his car's fuel pressure plummeted on the final lap. His career produced six victories.

BELGIAN GRAND PRIX

SPA-FRANCORCHAMPS • ROUND 12 • DATE: 29TH AUGUST 1993
Laps: 44 • Distance: 190.671miles/306.856km • Weather: Hot & bright

Pos	Driver	Team	Chassis-Engine	Result	Qual
1	Damon Hill	Williams	Williams-Renault FW15C	1h24m32.124s	2
2	Michael Schumacher	Benetton	Benetton-Ford Cosworth B193B	1h24m35.792s	3
3	Alain Prost	Williams	Williams-Renault FW15C	1h24m47.112s	1

Pos	Driver	Team	Chassis-Engine	Result	Qual
4	Ayrton Senna	McLaren	McLaren-Ford Cosworth MP4/8	1h26m11.887s	5
5	Johnny Herbert	Lotus	Lotus-Ford Cosworth 107B	43 laps	10
6	Riccardo Patrese	Benetton	Benetton-Ford Cosworth B193B	43 laps	8
7	Martin Brundle	Ligier	Ligier-Renault JS39	43 laps	11
8	Michael Andretti	McLaren	McLaren-Ford Cosworth MP4/8	43 laps	14
9	JJ Lehto	Sauber	Sauber-Ilmor C12	43 laps	9
10	Gerhard Berger	Ferrari	Ferrari F93A	42 laps/collision	16
11	Mark Blundell	Ligier	Ligier-Renault JS39	42 laps/collision	15
12	Philippe Alliot	Larrousse	Larrousse-Lamborghini LH93	42 laps	18
13	Luca Badoer	BMS Scuderia Italia	Lola-Ferrari T93/30	42 laps	24
14	Michele Alboreto	BMS Scuderia Italia	Lola-Ferrari T93/30	41 laps	25
15	Ukyo Katayama	Tyrrell	Tyrrell-Yamaha 021	40 laps	23
R	Erik Comas	Larrousse	Larrousse-Lamborghini LH93	37 laps/fuel pump	19
R	Derek Warwick	Footwork	Footwork-Mugen Honda FA14	28 laps/engine	7
R	Karl Wendlinger	Sauber	Sauber-Ilmor C12	27 laps/engine	12
R	Andrea de Cesaris	Tyrrell	Tyrrell-Yamaha 021	24 laps/engine	17
R	Pierluigi Martini	Minardi	Minardi-Ford Cosworth M193	15 laps/spun off	21
R	Christian Fittipaldi	Minardi	Minardi-Ford Cosworth M193	15 laps/spun off	22
R	Aguri Suzuki	Footwork	Footwork-Mugen Honda FA14	14 laps/gearbox	6
R	Rubens Barrichello	Jordan	Jordan-Hart 193	11 laps/wheel	13
R	Jean Alesi	Ferrari	Ferrari F93A	4 laps/suspension	4
R	Thierry Boutsen	Jordan	Jordan-Hart 193	0 laps/gearbox	20
NS	Alessandro Zanardi	Lotus	Lotus-Ford Cosworth 107B	Driver injured	-

Pole: Prost, 1m47.571s, 145.024mph/233.393kph. Fastest lap: Prost, 1m51.095s, 140.423mph/225.990kph on Lap 41. Race leaders: Prost 1-30, Hill 31-44

NEW CONSTRUCTORS

A Swiss sports car team was the only new outfit in 1993, with Peter Sauber's squad making the change to F1. Previous engine partner Mercedes lent support but did not officially badge its Ilmor engines. The Leo Ress-designed car was good enough to achieve fourth-place finishes for JJ Lehto at Imola and Karl Wendlinger at Monza.

ITALIAN GRAND PRIX

MONZA • ROUND 13 • DATE: 12TH SEPTEMBER 1993
Laps: 53 • Distance: 190.763miles/307.4km • Weather: Hot & bright

Pos	Driver	Team	Chassis-Engine	Result	Qual
1	Damon Hill	Williams	Williams-Renault FW15C	1h17m07.509s	2
2	Jean Alesi	Ferrari	Ferrari F93A	1h17m47.521s	3
3	Michael Andretti	McLaren	McLaren-Ford Cosworth MP4/8	52 laps	9
4	Karl Wendlinger	Sauber	Sauber C12	52 laps	15
5	Riccardo Patrese	Benetton	Benetton-Ford Cosworth B193B	52 laps	10
6	Erik Comas	Larrousse	Larrousse-Lamborghini LH93	51 laps	20
7	Pierluigi Martini	Minardi	Minardi-Ford Cosworth M193	51 laps	22
8	Christian Fittipaldi	Minardi	Minardi-Ford Cosworth M193	51 laps	24
9	Philippe Alliot	Larrousse	Larrousse-Lamborghini LH93	51 laps	16
10	Luca Badoer	BMS Scuderia Italia	Lola-Ferrari T93/30	51 laps	25
11	Pedro Lamy	Lotus	Lotus-Ford Cosworth 107B	49 laps/electrical	26

Pos	Driver	Team	Chassis-Engine	Result	Qual
12	Alain Prost	Williams	Williams-Renault FW15C	48 laps/engine	1
13	Andrea de Cesaris	Tyrrell	Tyrrell-Yamaha 021	47 laps/fuel pressure	18
14	Ukyo Katayama	Tyrrell	Tyrrell-Yamaha 021	47 laps	17
R	Michele Alboreto	BMS Scuderia Italia	Lola-Ferrari T93/30	23 laps/suspension	21
R	Michael Schumacher	Benetton	Benetton-Ford Cosworth B193B	21 laps/engine	5
R	Mark Blundell	Ligier	Ligier-Renault JS39	20 laps/spun off	14
R	Gerhard Berger	Ferrari	Ferrari F93A	15 laps/suspension	6
R	Johnny Herbert	Lotus	Lotus-Ford Cosworth 107B	14 laps/spun off	7
R	Ayrton Senna	McLaren	McLaren-Ford Cosworth MP4/8	8 laps/collision	4
R	Martin Brundle	Ligier	Ligier-Renault JS39	8 laps/collision	12
R	Aguri Suzuki	Footwork	Footwork-Mugen Honda FA14	0 laps/collision	8
R	Derek Warwick	Footwork	Footwork-Mugen Honda FA14	0 laps/collision	11
R	JJ Lehto	Sauber	Sauber C12	0 laps/collision	13
R	Rubens Barrichello	Jordan	Jordan-Hart 193	0 laps/collision	19
R	Marco Apicella	Jordan	Jordan-Hart 193	0 laps/collision	23

Pole: Prost, 1m21.179s, 159.822mph/257.209kph. Fastest lap: Hill, 1m23.575s, 155.240mph/249.835kph on Lap 45. Race leaders: Prost 1-48, Hill 49-53

PORTUGUESE GRAND PRIX

AUTODROMO DO ESTORIL • ROUND 14 • DATE: 26TH SEPTEMBER 1993
Laps: 71 • Distance: 191.435miles/308.85km • Weather: Warm & bright

Pos	Driver	Team	Chassis-Engine	Result	Qual
1	Michael Schumacher	Benetton	Benetton-Ford Cosworth B193B	1h32m46.309s	6
2	Alain Prost	Williams	Williams-Renault FW15C	1h32m47.291s	2
3	Damon Hill	Williams	Williams-Renault FW15C	1h32m54.515s	1
4	Jean Alesi	Ferrari	Ferrari F93A	1h33m53.914s	5
5	Karl Wendlinger	Sauber	Sauber C12	70 laps	13
6	Martin Brundle	Ligier	Ligier-Renault JS39	70 laps	11
7	JJ Lehto	Sauber	Sauber C12	69 laps	12
8	Pierluigi Martini	Minardi	Minardi-Ford Cosworth M193	69 laps	19
9	Christian Fittipaldi	Minardi	Minardi-Ford Cosworth M193	69 laps	24
10	Philippe Alliot	Larrousse	Larrousse-Lamborghini LH93	69 laps	20
11	Erik Comas	Larrousse	Larrousse-Lamborghini LH93	68 laps	22
12	Andrea de Cesaris	Tyrrell	Tyrrell-Yamaha 021	68 laps	17
13	Rubens Barrichello	Jordan	Jordan-Hart 193	68 laps	15
14	Luca Badoer	BMS Scuderia Italia	Lola-Ferrari T93/30	68 laps	26
15	Derek Warwick	Footwork	Footwork-Mugen Honda FA14	63 laps/collision	9
16	Riccardo Patrese	Benetton	Benetton-Ford Cosworth B193B	63 laps/collision	7
R	Pedro Lamy	Lotus	Lotus-Ford Cosworth 107B	61 laps/spun off	18
R	Johnny Herbert	Lotus	Lotus-Ford Cosworth 107B	60 laps/spun off	14
R	Mark Blundell	Ligier	Ligier-Renault JS39	51 laps/collision	10
R	Michele Alboreto	BMS Scuderia Italia	Lola-Ferrari T93/30	38 laps/gearbox	25
R	Gerhard Berger	Ferrari	Ferrari F93A	35 laps/spun off	8
R	Mika Hakkinen	McLaren	McLaren-Ford Cosworth MP4/8	32 laps/spun off	3
R	Aguri Suzuki	Footwork	Footwork-Mugen Honda FA14	27 laps/gearbox	16
R	Ayrton Senna	McLaren	McLaren-Ford Cosworth MP4/8	19 laps/engine	4
R	Ukyo Katayama	Tyrrell	Tyrrell-Yamaha 021	12 laps/spun off	21
R	Emanuele Naspetti	Jordan	Jordan-Hart 193	8 laps/engine	23

Pole: Hill, 1m11.494s, 136.104mph/219.039kph. Fastest lap: Hill, 1m14.859s, 129.986mph/209.193kph on Lap 68. Race leaders: Alesi 1-19, Prost 20-29, Schumacher 30-71

JAPANESE GRAND PRIX

SUZUKA • ROUND 15 • DATE: 24TH OCTOBER 1993
Laps: 53 • Distance: 193.117miles/310.792km • Weather: Dry, wet later

Pos	Driver	Team	Chassis-Engine	Result	Qual
1	Ayrton Senna	McLaren	McLaren-Ford Cosworth MP4/8	1h40m27.912s	2
2	Alain Prost	Williams	Williams-Renault FW15C	1h40m39.347s	1
3	Mika Hakkinen	McLaren	McLaren-Ford Cosworth MP4/8	1h40m54.041s	3
4	Damon Hill	Williams	Williams-Renault FW15C	1h41m51.450s	6
5	Rubens Barrichello	Jordan	Jordan-Hart 193	1h42m03.013s	12
6	Eddie Irvine	Jordan	Jordan-Hart 193	1h42m14.333s	8
7	Mark Blundell	Ligier	Ligier-Renault JS39	52 laps	17
8	JJ Lehto	Sauber	Sauber C12	52 laps	11
9	Martin Brundle	Ligier	Ligier-Renault JS39	51 laps	15
10	Pierluigi Martini	Minardi	Minardi-Ford Cosworth M193	51 laps	22
11	Johnny Herbert	Lotus	Lotus-Ford Cosworth 107B	51 laps	19
12	Toshio Suzuki	Larrousse	Larrousse-Lamborghini LH93	51 laps	23
13	Pedro Lamy	Lotus	Lotus-Ford Cosworth 107B	49 laps/spun off	20
14	Derek Warwick	Footwork	Footwork-Mugen Honda FA14	48 laps/collision	7
R	Riccardo Patrese	Benetton	Benetton-Ford Cosworth B193B	45 laps/spun off	10
R	Gerhard Berger	Ferrari	Ferrari F93A	40 laps/engine	5
R	Aguri Suzuki	Footwork	Footwork-Mugen Honda FA14	28 laps/spun off	9
R	Ukyo Katayama	Tyrrell	Tyrrell-Yamaha 021	26 laps/engine	13
R	Jean-Marc Gounon	Minardi	Minardi-Ford Cosworth M193	26 laps/engine	24
R	Karl Wendlinger	Sauber	Sauber C12	25 laps/engine	16
R	Erik Comas	Larrousse	Larrousse-Lamborghini LH93	17 laps/engine	21
R	Michael Schumacher	Benetton	Benetton-Ford Cosworth B193B	10 laps/collision	4
R	Jean Alesi	Ferrari	Ferrari F93A	7 laps/engine	14
R	Andrea de Cesaris	Tyrrell	Tyrrell-Yamaha 021	0 laps/collision	18

Pole: Prost, 1m37.154s, 135.016mph/217.288kph. Fastest lap: Prost, 1m41.176s, 129.649mph/208.650kph on Lap 53. Race leaders: Senna 1-13 & 21-53, Prost 14-20

NEW DRIVERS

In addition to Michael Andretti and Eddie Irvine, Marco Apicella, Luca Badoer, Rubens Barrichello, Jean-Marc Gounon, Pedro Lamy and Toshio Suzuki all made their F1 debuts. Barrichello achieved a best result of fifth for Jordan at Suzuka and would finish as World Championship runner-up when driving for Ferrari alongside Michael Schumacher in 2002 and 2004.

AUSTRALIAN GRAND PRIX

ADELAIDE • ROUND 16 • DATE: 7TH NOVEMBER 1993
Laps: 79 • Distance: 185.207miles/298.62km • Weather: Warm & bright

Pos	Driver	Team	Chassis-Engine	Result	Qual
1	Ayrton Senna	McLaren	McLaren-Ford Cosworth MP4/8	1h43m27.476s	1
2	Alain Prost	Williams	Williams-Renault FW15C	1h43m36.735s	2
3	Damon Hill	Williams	Williams-Renault FW15C	1h44m01.378s	3
4	Jean Alesi	Ferrari	Ferrari F93A	78 laps	7
5	Gerhard Berger	Ferrari	Ferrari F93A	78 laps	6

Pos	Driver	Team	Chassis-Engine	Result	Qual
6	Martin Brundle	Ligier	Ligier-Renault JS39	78 laps	8
7	Aguri Suzuki	Footwork	Footwork-Mugen Honda FA14	78 laps	10
8	Riccardo Patrese	Benetton	Benetton-Ford Cosworth B193B	77 laps/fuel system	9
9	Mark Blundell	Ligier	Ligier-Renault JS39	77 laps	14
10	Derek Warwick	Footwork	Footwork-Mugen Honda FA14	77 laps	17
11	Rubens Barrichello	Jordan	Jordan-Hart 193	76 laps	13
12	Erik Comas	Larrousse	Larrousse-Lamborghini LH93	76 laps	21
13	Andrea de Cesaris	Tyrrell	Tyrrell-Yamaha 021	75 laps	15
14	Toshio Suzuki	Larrousse	Larrousse-Lamborghini LH93	74 laps	24
15	Karl Wendlinger	Sauber	Sauber C12	73 laps/brakes	11
R	JJ Lehto	Sauber	Sauber C12	56 laps/spun off	12
R	Jean-Marc Gounon	Minardi	Minardi-Ford Cosworth M193	34 laps/spun off	22
R	Mika Hakkinen	McLaren	McLaren-Ford Cosworth MP4/8	28 laps/brakes	5
R	Michael Schumacher	Benetton	Benetton-Ford Cosworth B193B	19 laps/engine	4
R	Ukyo Katayama	Tyrrell	Tyrrell-Yamaha 021	11 laps/spun off	18
R	Eddie Irvine	Jordan	Jordan-Hart 193	10 laps/spun off	19
R	Johnny Herbert	Lotus	Lotus-Ford Cosworth 107B	9 laps/suspension	20
R	Pierluigi Martini	Minardi	Minardi-Ford Cosworth M193	5 laps/gearbox	16
R	Pedro Lamy	Lotus	Lotus-Ford Cosworth 107B	0 laps/collision	23

Pole: Senna, 1m13.371s, 115.244mph/185.468kph. Fastest lap: Hill, 1m15.381s, 112.171mph/180.522kph on Lap 64. Race leaders: Senna 1-23 & 29-79, Prost 24-28

WORLD DRIVERS' CHAMPIONSHIP FINAL RESULTS

Pos	Driver	Nat	Car-Engine	R1	R2	R3	R4	R5	R6
1	Alain Prost	FRA	Williams-Renault FW15C	1PF	RP	3P	1PF	1P	4PF
2	Ayrton Senna	BRA	McLaren-Ford Cosworth MP4/8	2	1	1F	R	2	1
3	Damon Hill	GBR	Williams-Renault FW15C	R	2	2	R	R	2
4	Michael Schumacher	DEU	Benetton-Ford Cosworth B192B	R	3F	-	-	-	-
			Benetton-Ford Cosworth B193B	-	-	R	2	3F	R
5	Riccardo Patrese	ITA	Benetton-Ford Cosworth B192B	R	R	-	-	-	-
			Benetton-Ford Cosworth B193B	-	-	5	R	4	R
6	Jean Alesi	FRA	Ferrari F93A	R	8	R	R	R	3
7	Martin Brundle	GBR	Ligier-Renault JS39	R	R	R	3	R	6
8	Gerhard Berger	AUT	Ferrari F93A	6	R	R	R	6	14
9	Johnny Herbert	GBR	Lotus-Ford Cosworth 107B	R	4	4	8	R	R
10	Mark Blundell	GBR	Ligier-Renault JS39	3	5	R	R	7	R
11	Michael Andretti	USA	McLaren-Ford Cosworth MP4/8	R	R	R	R	5	8
12	Karl Wendlinger	AUT	Sauber-Ilmor C12	R	R	R	R	R	13
			Sauber C12	-	-	-	-	-	-
13	JJ Lehto	FIN	Sauber-Ilmor C12	5	R	R	4	R	R
			Sauber C12	-	-	-	-	-	-
13	Christian Fittipaldi	BRA	Minardi-Ford Cosworth M193	4	R	7	R	8	5
15	Mika Hakkinen	FIN	McLaren-Ford Cosworth MP4/8	-	-	-	-	-	-
16	Derek Warwick	GBR	Footwork-Mugen Honda FA13B	7	9	-	-	-	-
			Footwork-Mugen Honda FA14	-	-	R	R	13	R
17	Philippe Alliot	FRA	Larrousse-Lamborghini LH93	R	7	R	5	R	12
17	Rubens Barrichello	BRA	Jordan-Hart 193	R	R	10	R	12	9
19	Fabrizio Barbazza	ITA	Minardi-Ford Cosworth M193	R	R	6	6	R	11
20	Alessandro Zanardi	ITA	Lotus-Ford Cosworth 107B	R	6	8	R	14	7
20	Erik Comas	FRA	Larrousse-Lamborghini LH93	R	10	9	R	9	R
20	Eddie Irvine	GBR	Jordan-Hart 193	-	-	-	-	-	-

Pos	Driver	R7	R8	R9	R10	R11	R12	R13	R14	R15	R16	Total
1	Prost	1P	1	1P	1P	12PF	3PF	12P	2	2PF	2	99
2	Senna	18	4	5	4	R	4	R	R	1	1P	73
3	Hill	3	2P	RF	15	1	1	1F	3PF	4	3F	69
4	Schumacher	-	-	-	-	-	-	-	-	-	-	52
		2F	3F	2	2F	R	2	R	1	R	R	
5	Patrese	-	-	-	-	-	-	-	-	-	-	20
		R	10	3	5	2	6	5	16	R	8	
6	Alesi	R	R	9	7	R	R	2	4	R	4	16
7	Brundle	5	5	14	8	5	7	R	6	9	6	13
8	Berger	4	14	R	6	3	10	R	R	R	5	12
9	Herbert	10	R	4	10	R	5	R	R	11	R	11
10	Blundell	R	R	7	3	7	11	R	R	7	9	10
11	Andretti	14	6	R	R	R	8	3	-	-	-	7
12	Wendlinger	6	R	R	9	6	R	-	-	-	-	7
		-	-	-	-	-	-	4	5	R	15	
13	Lehto	7	R	8	R	R	9	-	-	-	-	5
		-	-	-	-	-	-	R	7	8	R	
13	Fittipaldi	9	8	12	11	R	R	8	9	-	-	5
15	Hakkinen	-	-	-	-	-	-	-	R	3	R	4
16	Warwick	-	-	-	-	-	-	-	-	-	-	4
		16	13	6	17	4	R	R	15	14	10	
17	Alliot	R	9	11	12	8	12	9	10	-	-	2
17	Barrichello	R	7	10	R	R	R	R	13	5	11	2
19	Barbazza	R	R	-	-	-	-	-	-	-	-	2
20	Zanardi	11	R	R	R	R	NS	-	-	-	-	1
20	Comas	8	16	R	R	R	R	6	11	R	12	1
20	Irvine	-	-	-	-	-	-	-	-	6	R	1

SYMBOLS AND GRAND PRIX KEY

Round 1 South African GP
Round 2 Brazilian GP
Round 3 European GP
Round 4 San Marino GP
Round 5 Spanish GP
Round 6 Monaco GP
Round 7 Canadian GP
Round 8 French GP
Round 9 British GP
Round 10 German GP
Round 11 Hungarian GP
Round 12 Belgian GP
Round 13 Italian GP
Round 14 Portuguese GP
Round 15 Japanese GP
Round 16 Australian GP

DNPQ DID NOT PRE-QUALIFY **DNQ** DID NOT QUALIFY **DQ** DISQUALIFIED **EX** EXCLUDED
F FASTEST LAP **NC** NOT CLASSIFIED **NS** NON-STARTER **P** POLE POSITION **R** RETIRED

SCORING

1st 10 points
2nd 6 points
3rd 4 points
4th 3 points
5th 2 points
6th 1 point

WORLD CONSTRUCTORS' CHAMPIONSHIP FINAL RESULTS

Pos	Team-Engine	R1	R2	R3	R4	R5	R6	R7	R8
1	Williams-Renault	1/R	2/R	2/3	1/R	1/R	2/4	1/3	1/2
2	McLaren-Ford	2/R	1/R	1/R	R/R	2/5	1/8	14/18	4/6
3	Benetton-Ford	R/R	3/R	5/R	2/R	3/4	R/R	2/R	3/10
4	Ferrari	6/R	8/R	R/R	R/R	6/R	3/14	4/R	14/R
5	Ligier-Renault	3/R	5/R	R/R	3/R	7/R	6/R	5/R	5/R
6	Lotus-Ford	R/R	4/6	4/8	8/R	14/R	7/R	10/11	R/R
7	Sauber-Ilmor	5/R	R/R	R/R	4/R	R/R	13/R	6/7	R/R
8	Minardi-Ford	4/R	R/R	6/7	6/R	8/R	5/11	9/R	8/R
9	Footwork-Mugen Honda	7/R	9/R	R/R	9/R	10/13	R/R	13/16	12/13
10	Larrousse-Lamborghini	R/R	7/10	9/R	5/R	9/R	12/R	8/R	9/16
10	Jordan-Hart	R/R	R/DNQ	10/R	R/R	11/12	9/R	12/R	7/11

Pos	Team-Engine	R9	R10	R11	R12	R13	R14	R15	R16	Total
1	Williams-Renault	1/R	1/15	1/12	1/3	1/12	2/3	2/4	2/3	168
2	McLaren-Ford	5/R	4/R	R/R	4/8	3/R	R/R	1/3	1/R	84
3	Benetton-Ford	2/3	2/5	2/R	2/6	5/R	1/16	R/R	8/R	72
4	Ferrari	9/R	6/7	3/R	10/R	2/R	4/R	R/R	4/5	28
5	Ligier-Renault	7/14	3/8	5/7	7/11	R/R	6/R	7/9	6/9	23
6	Lotus-Ford	4/R	10/R	R/R	5/NS	11/R	R/R	11/13	R/R	12
7	Sauber	8/R	9/R	6/R	9/R	4/R	5/7	8/R	15/R	12
8	Minardi-Ford	12/R	11/14	R/R	R/R	7/8	8/9	10/R	R/R	7
9	Footwork-Mugen Honda	6/R	17/R	4/R	R/R	R/R	15/R	14/R	7/10	4
10	Larrousse-Lamborghini	11/R	12/R	8/R	12/R	6/9	10/11	12/R	12/14	3
10	Jordan-Hart	10/R	13/R	9/R	R/R	R/R	13/R	5/6	11/R	3

1994

SEASON SUMMARY

This was an extraordinarily dramatic season that is remembered principally for the deaths of Ayrton Senna and Roland Ratzenberger, fortunate escapes for Rubens Barrichello, Karl Wendlinger, Jean Alesi, Andrea Montermini and Pedro Lamy, plus Jos Verstappen's pit stop fire. It was also the year in which Michael Schumacher's title victory was achieved in a controversial manner: he damaged his car in the final race in Australia, then collided with Damon Hill's Williams to stop Hill beating his points tally. Adding to the bad feeling, his team, Benetton, was found to have fitted outlawed driver aids. However, it couldn't be proved that they used them, so he kept the title.

MAKING F1 SLOWER AND SAFER

Electronic driver aids were banned for 1994, and there were also safety changes made to both cars and circuits in the fallout from the double fatalities at the San Marino GP. Front wings were raised, diffusers were shortened and then, at the German GP, 10mm (0.4in) wooden skidblocks were fitted under the cars to ensure a minimum clearance from the track.

BRAZILIAN GRAND PRIX

INTERLAGOS • ROUND 1 • DATE: 27TH MARCH 1994
Laps: 71 • Distance: 190.807miles/307.075km • Weather: Warm but dull

Pos	Driver	Team	Chassis-Engine	Result	Qual
1	Michael Schumacher	Benetton	Benetton-Ford Cosworth B194	1h35m38.759s	2
2	Damon Hill	Williams	Williams-Renault FW16	70 laps	4
3	Jean Alesi	Ferrari	Ferrari 412T1	70 laps	3
4	Rubens Barrichello	Jordan	Jordan-Hart 194	70 laps	14
5	Ukyo Katayama	Tyrrell	Tyrrell-Yamaha 022	69 laps	10
6	Karl Wendlinger	Sauber	Sauber-Mercedes C13	69 laps	7
7	Johnny Herbert	Lotus	Lotus-Mugen Honda 107C	69 laps	21
8	Pierluigi Martini	Minardi	Minardi-Ford Cosworth M193B	69 laps	15
9	Erik Comas	Larrousse	Larrousse-Ford Cosworth LH94	68 laps	13
10	Pedro Lamy	Lotus	Lotus-Mugen Honda 107C	68 laps	24
11	Olivier Panis	Ligier	Ligier-Renault JS39B	68 laps	19
12	David Brabham	Simtek	Simtek-Ford Cosworth S941	67 laps	26
R	Ayrton Senna	Williams	Williams-Renault FW16	55 laps/spun off	1
R	Jos Verstappen	Benetton	Benetton-Ford Cosworth B194	34 laps/collision	9
R	Eddie Irvine	Jordan	Jordan-Hart 194	34 laps/collision	16
R	Martin Brundle	McLaren	McLaren-Peugeot MP4/9	34 laps/collision	18
R	Eric Bernard	Ligier	Ligier-Renault JS39B	33 laps/collision	20
R	Christian Fittipaldi	Footwork	Footwork-Ford Cosworth FA15	21 laps/gearbox	11
R	Mark Blundell	Tyrrell	Tyrrell-Yamaha 022	21 laps/spun off	12
R	Heinz-Harald Frentzen	Sauber	Sauber-Mercedes C13	15 laps/spun off	5
R	Mika Hakkinen	McLaren	McLaren-Peugeot MP4/9	13 laps/engine	8
R	Michele Alboreto	Minardi	Minardi-Ford Cosworth M193B	7 laps/engine	22
R	Gianni Morbidelli	Footwork	Footwork-Ford Cosworth FA15	5 laps/gearbox	6
R	Gerhard Berger	Ferrari	Ferrari 412T1	5 laps/engine	17

Pos	Driver	Team	Chassis-Engine	Result	Qual
R	Olivier Beretta	Larrousse	Larrousse-Ford Cosworth LH94	2 laps/collision	23
R	Bertrand Gachot	Pacific	Pacific-Ilmor PR01	1 lap/collision	25
DNQ	Roland Ratzenberger	Simtek	Simtek-Ford Cosworth S941	-	27
DNQ	Paul Belmondo	Pacific	Pacific-Ilmor PR01	-	28

Pole: Senna, 1m15.962s, 127.363mph/204.970kph. Fastest lap: Schumacher, 1m18.455s, 123.315mph/198.457kph on Lap 7. Race leaders: Senna 1-21, Schumacher 22-71

PACIFIC GRAND PRIX

TI CIRCUIT • ROUND 2 • DATE: 17TH APRIL 1994
Laps: 83 • Distance: 190.977miles/307.349km • Weather: Warm & bright

Pos	Driver	Team	Chassis-Engine	Result	Qual
1	Michael Schumacher	Benetton	Benetton-Ford Cosworth B194	1h46m01.693s	2
2	Gerhard Berger	Ferrari	Ferrari 412T1	1h47m16.993s	5
3	Rubens Barrichello	Jordan	Jordan-Hart 194	82 laps	8
4	Christian Fittipaldi	Footwork	Footwork-Ford Cosworth FA15	82 laps	9
5	Heinz-Harald Frentzen	Sauber	Sauber-Mercedes C13	82 laps	11
6	Erik Comas	Larrousse	Larrousse-Ford Cosworth LH94	80 laps	16
7	Johnny Herbert	Lotus	Lotus-Mugen Honda 107C	80 laps	23
8	Pedro Lamy	Lotus	Lotus-Mugen Honda 107C	79 laps	24
9	Olivier Panis	Ligier	Ligier-Renault JS39B	78 laps	22
10	Eric Bernard	Ligier	Ligier-Renault JS39B	78 laps	18
11	Roland Ratzenberger	Simtek	Simtek-Ford Cosworth S941	78 laps	26
R	Gianni Morbidelli	Footwork	Footwork-Ford Cosworth FA15	69 laps/engine	13
R	Michele Alboreto	Minardi	Minardi-Ford Cosworth M193B	69 laps/collision	15
R	Karl Wendlinger	Sauber	Sauber-Mercedes C13	69 laps/collision	19
R	Martin Brundle	McLaren	McLaren-Peugeot MP4/9	67 laps/overheating	6
R	Pierluigi Martini	Minardi	Minardi-Ford Cosworth M193B	63 laps/spun off	17
R	Jos Verstappen	Benetton	Benetton-Ford Cosworth B194	54 laps/spun off	10
R	Damon Hill	Williams	Williams-Renault FW16	49 laps/transmission	3
R	Aguri Suzuki	Jordan	Jordan-Hart 194	44 laps/steering	20
R	Ukyo Katayama	Tyrrell	Tyrrell-Yamaha 022	42 laps/engine	14
R	Mika Hakkinen	McLaren	McLaren-Peugeot MP4/9	19 laps/gearbox	4
R	Olivier Beretta	Larrousse	Larrousse-Ford Cosworth LH94	14 laps/electrical	21
R	David Brabham	Simtek	Simtek-Ford Cosworth S941	2 laps/electrical	25
R	Ayrton Senna	Williams	Williams-Renault FW16	0 laps/collision	1
R	Nicola Larini	Ferrari	Ferrari 412T1	0 laps/collision	7
R	Mark Blundell	Tyrrell	Tyrrell-Yamaha 022	0 laps/collision	12
DNQ	Bertrand Gachot	Pacific	Pacific-Ilmor PR01	-	27
DNQ	Paul Belmondo	Pacific	Pacific-Ilmor PR01	-	28

Pole: Senna, 1m10.218s, 117.966mph/189.848kph. Fastest lap: Schumacher, 1m14.023s, 111.902mph/180.089kph on Lap 10. Race leaders: Schumacher 1-83

F1'S DARKEST WEEKEND

In an age in which death had become a stranger due to ever safer cars and circuits, F1 was rocked to its core when both Ayrton Senna and Roland Ratzenberger were killed at Imola. The Austrian crashed his Simtek in qualifying after damaging its front wing. Then the Brazilian's Williams snapped away from him early in the race and hit the wall.

SAN MARINO GRAND PRIX

IMOLA • ROUND 3 • DATE: 1ST MAY 1994
Laps: 58 • Distance: 181.460miles/292.32km • Weather: Hot & bright

Pos	Driver	Team	Chassis-Engine	Result	Qual
1	Michael Schumacher	Benetton	Benetton-Ford Cosworth B194	1h28m28.642s	2
2	Nicola Larini	Ferrari	Ferrari 412T1	1h29m23.584s	6
3	Mika Hakkinen	McLaren	McLaren-Peugeot MP4/9	1h29m39.321s	8
4	Karl Wendlinger	Sauber	Sauber-Mercedes C13	1h29m42.300s	10
5	Ukyo Katayama	Tyrrell	Tyrrell-Yamaha 022	57 laps	9
6	Damon Hill	Williams	Williams-Renault FW16	57 laps	4
7	Heinz-Harald Frentzen	Sauber	Sauber-Mercedes C13	57 laps	7
8	Martin Brundle	McLaren	McLaren-Peugeot MP4/9	57 laps	13
9	Mark Blundell	Tyrrell	Tyrrell-Yamaha 022	56 laps	12
10	Johnny Herbert	Lotus	Lotus-Mugen Honda 107C	56 laps	20
11	Olivier Panis	Ligier	Ligier-Renault JS39B	56 laps	19
12	Eric Bernard	Ligier	Ligier-Renault JS39B	55 laps	17
13	Christian Fittipaldi	Footwork	Footwork-Ford Cosworth FA15	54 laps/brakes	16
R	Andrea de Cesaris	Jordan	Jordan-Hart 194	49 laps/spun off	21
R	Michele Alboreto	Minardi	Minardi-Ford Cosworth M193B	44 laps/wheel	15
R	Gianni Morbidelli	Footwork	Footwork-Ford Cosworth FA15	40 laps/engine	11
R	Pierluigi Martini	Minardi	Minardi-Ford Cosworth M193B	37 laps/spun off	14
R	David Brabham	Simtek	Simtek-Ford Cosworth S941	27 laps/spun off	24
R	Bertrand Gachot	Pacific	Pacific-Ilmor PR01	23 laps/engine	25
R	Olivier Beretta	Larrousse	Larrousse-Ford Cosworth LH94	17 laps/engine	23
R	Gerhard Berger	Ferrari	Ferrari 412T1	16 laps/suspension	3
R	Ayrton Senna	Williams	Williams-Renault FW16	5 laps/fatal accident	1
R	Erik Comas	Larrousse	Larrousse-Ford Cosworth LH94	5 laps/vibrations	18
R	JJ Lehto	Benetton	Benetton-Ford Cosworth B194	0 laps/collision	5
R	Pedro Lamy	Lotus	Lotus-Mugen Honda 107C	0 laps/collision	22
DNQ	Roland Ratzenberger	Simtek	Simtek-Ford Cosworth S941	fatal accident	26
DNQ	Paul Belmondo	Pacific	Pacific-Ilmor PR01	-	27
DNQ	Rubens Barrichello	Jordan	Jordan-Hart 194	driver injured	28

Pole: Senna, 1m21.548s, 138.251mph/222.494kph. Fastest lap: Hill, 1m24.335s, 133.683mph/215.141kph on Lap 10. Race leaders: Senna 1-5, Schumacher 6-12 & 19-58, Berger 13-15, Hakkinen 16-18

MONACO GRAND PRIX

MONTE CARLO • ROUND 4 • DATE: 15TH MAY 1994
Laps: 78 • Distance: 161.298miles/259.584km • Weather: Hot & bright

Pos	Driver	Team	Chassis-Engine	Result	Qual
1	Michael Schumacher	Benetton	Benetton-Ford Cosworth B194	1h49m55.372s	1
2	Martin Brundle	McLaren	McLaren-Peugeot MP4/9	1h50m32.650s	8
3	Gerhard Berger	Ferrari	Ferrari 412T1	1h51m12.196s	3
4	Andrea de Cesaris	Jordan	Jordan-Hart 194	77 laps	14
5	Jean Alesi	Ferrari	Ferrari 412T1	77 laps	5
6	Michele Alboreto	Minardi	Minardi-Ford Cosworth M193B	77 laps	12
7	JJ Lehto	Benetton	Benetton-Ford Cosworth B194	77 laps	17
8	Olivier Beretta	Larrousse	Larrousse-Ford Cosworth LH94	76 laps	18
9	Olivier Panis	Ligier	Ligier-Renault JS39B	76 laps	20
10	Erik Comas	Larrousse	Larrousse-Ford Cosworth LH94	75 laps	13
11	Pedro Lamy	Lotus	Lotus-Mugen Honda 107C	73 laps	19
R	Johnny Herbert	Lotus	Lotus-Mugen Honda 107C	68 laps/gearbox	16

Pos	Driver	Team	Chassis-Engine	Result	Qual
R	Paul Belmondo	Pacific	Pacific-Ilmor PR01	53 laps/physical	24
R	Bertrand Gachot	Pacific	Pacific-Ilmor PR01	49 laps/gearbox	23
R	Christian Fittipaldi	Footwork	Footwork-Ford Cosworth FA15	47 laps/gearbox	6
R	David Brabham	Simtek	Simtek-Ford Cosworth S941	45 laps/collision	22
R	Mark Blundell	Tyrrell	Tyrrell-Yamaha 022	40 laps/engine	10
R	Ukyo Katayama	Tyrrell	Tyrrell-Yamaha 022	38 laps/gearbox	11
R	Eric Bernard	Ligier	Ligier-Renault JS39B	34 laps/spun off	21
R	Rubens Barrichello	Jordan	Jordan-Hart 194	27 laps/electrical	15
R	Mika Hakkinen	McLaren	McLaren-Peugeot MP4/9	0 laps/collision	2
R	Damon Hill	Williams	Williams-Renault FW16	0 laps/collision	4
R	Gianni Morbidelli	Footwork	Footwork-Ford Cosworth FA15	0 laps/collision	7
R	Pierluigi Martini	Minardi	Minardi-Ford Cosworth M193B	0 laps/collision	9
NS	Heinz-Harald Frentzen	Sauber	Sauber-Mercedes C13	withdrew	25
NS	Karl Wendlinger	Sauber	Sauber-Mercedes C13	driver injured	26

Pole: Schumacher, 1m18.560s, 94.762mph/152.505kph. Fastest lap: Schumacher, 1m21.076s, 91.821mph/147.772kph on Lap 35. Race leaders: Schumacher 1-78

GRABBING HIS OPPORTUNITY

When Jean Alesi was injured testing at Mugello before the Pacific GP, Nicola Larini was plucked from the sidelines to become a Ferrari driver after a year of what he thought was his post-F1 life competing in the DTM touring car series. On his second outing, at Imola, he finished second, but there was no smiling in the post-race gloom.

SPANISH GRAND PRIX

BARCELONA-CATALUNYA • ROUND 5 • DATE: 29TH MAY 1994
Laps: 65 • Distance: 191.727miles/308.555km • Weather: Hot & bright

Pos	Driver	Team	Chassis-Engine	Result	Qual
1	Damon Hill	Williams	Williams-Renault FW16	1h36m14.374s	2
2	Michael Schumacher	Benetton	Benetton-Ford Cosworth B194	1h36m38.540s	1
3	Mark Blundell	Tyrrell	Tyrrell-Yamaha 022	1h37m41.343s	11
4	Jean Alesi	Ferrari	Ferrari 412T1	64 laps	6
5	Pierluigi Martini	Minardi	Minardi-Ford Cosworth M193B	64 laps	18
6	Eddie Irvine	Jordan	Jordan-Hart 194	64 laps	13
7	Olivier Panis	Ligier	Ligier-Renault JS39B	63 laps	19
8	Eric Bernard	Ligier	Ligier-Renault JS39B	62 laps	20
9	Alessandro Zanardi	Lotus	Lotus-Mugen Honda 107C	62 laps	23
10	David Brabham	Simtek	Simtek-Ford Cosworth S941	61 laps	24
11	Martin Brundle	McLaren	McLaren-Peugeot MP4/9	59 laps/transmission	8
R	JJ Lehto	Benetton	Benetton-Ford Cosworth B194	53 laps/engine	4
R	Mika Hakkinen	McLaren	McLaren-Peugeot MP4/9	48 laps/engine	3
R	Johnny Herbert	Lotus	Lotus-Mugen Honda 109	41 laps/spun off	22
R	Rubens Barrichello	Jordan	Jordan-Hart 194	39 laps/spun off	5
R	Christian Fittipaldi	Footwork	Footwork-Ford Cosworth FA15	35 laps/engine	21
R	David Coulthard	Williams	Williams-Renault FW16	32 laps/electrical	9
R	Bertrand Gachot	Pacific	Pacific-Ilmor PR01	32 laps/wing	25
R	Gerhard Berger	Ferrari	Ferrari 412T1	27 laps/gearbox	7
R	Gianni Morbidelli	Footwork	Footwork-Ford Cosworth FA15	24 laps/fuel system	15

Pos	Driver	Team	Chassis-Engine	Result	Qual
R	Heinz-Harald Frentzen	Sauber	Sauber-Mercedes C13	21 laps/gearbox	12
R	Erik Comas	Larrousse	Larrousse-Ford Cosworth LH94	19 laps/radiator damage	16
R	Ukyo Katayama	Tyrrell	Tyrrell-Yamaha 022	16 laps/engine	10
R	Michele Alboreto	Minardi	Minardi-Ford Cosworth M193B	4 laps/engine	14
R	Paul Belmondo	Pacific	Pacific-Ilmor PR01	2 laps/spun off	26
NS	Olivier Beretta	Larrousse	Larrousse-Ford Cosworth LH94	-	17
DNQ	Andrea Montermini	Simtek	Simtek-Ford Cosworth S941	driver injured	27

Pole: Schumacher, 1m21.908s, 129.642mph/208.638kph. Fastest lap: Schumacher, 1m25.155s, 124.698mph/200.683kph on Lap 18. Race leaders: Schumacher 1-22 & 41-45, Hakkinen 23-30, Hill 31-40 & 46-65

THE BAD YEAR CONTINUES

As if the disastrous San Marino GP wasn't enough, the shocks continued at Monaco when Karl Wendlinger crashed and had to be put into an induced coma for three weeks. Later in the year, Pedro Lamy flipped his Lotus into a pedestrian tunnel at Silverstone, then Jos Verstappen was lucky to survive a refuelling blaze at the German GP.

THE END FOR LOTUS

Lotus was thwarted from landing team-saving points in the Italian GP at Monza when Johnny Herbert started fourth but was hit at the first corner. With money owed to Landhurst Leasing and to Cosworth Engineering, the administrators were appointed before the next race and paying drivers were used for the team's final three races.

CANADIAN GRAND PRIX

MONTREAL • ROUND 6 • DATE: 12TH JUNE 1994
Laps: 69 • Distance: 190.764miles/307.05km • Weather: Hot but dull

Pos	Driver	Team	Chassis-Engine	Result	Qual
1	Michael Schumacher	Benetton	Benetton-Ford Cosworth B194	1h44m31.887s	1
2	Damon Hill	Williams	Williams-Renault FW16	1h45m11.547s	4
3	Jean Alesi	Ferrari	Ferrari 412T1	1h45m45.275s	2
4	Gerhard Berger	Ferrari	Ferrari 412T1	1h45m47.496s	3
5	David Coulthard	Williams	Williams-Renault FW16	68 laps	5
6	JJ Lehto	Benetton	Benetton-Ford Cosworth B194	68 laps	20
7	Rubens Barrichello	Jordan	Jordan-Hart 194	68 laps	6
8	Johnny Herbert	Lotus	Lotus-Mugen Honda 109	68 laps	17
9	Pierluigi Martini	Minardi	Minardi-Ford Cosworth M194	68 laps	15
10	Mark Blundell	Tyrrell	Tyrrell-Yamaha 022	67 laps/spun off	13
11	Michele Alboreto	Minardi	Minardi-Ford Cosworth M194	67 laps	18
12	Olivier Panis	Ligier	Ligier-Renault JS39B	67 laps	19
13	Eric Bernard	Ligier	Ligier-Renault JS39B	66 laps	24
14	David Brabham	Simtek	Simtek-Ford Cosworth S941	65 laps	25

Pos	Driver	Team	Chassis-Engine	Result	Qual
15	Alessandro Zanardi	Lotus	Lotus-Mugen Honda 107C	62 laps/engine	23
DQ	Christian Fittipaldi	Footwork	Footwork-Ford Cosworth FA15	68 laps/car underweight	16
R	Mika Hakkinen	McLaren	McLaren-Peugeot MP4/9	61 laps/engine	7
R	Olivier Beretta	Larrousse	Larrousse-Ford Cosworth LH94	57 laps/engine	22
R	Gianni Morbidelli	Footwork	Footwork-Ford Cosworth FA15	50 laps/transmission	11
R	Bertrand Gachot	Pacific	Pacific-Ilmor PR01	47 laps/fuel pressure	26
R	Erik Comas	Larrousse	Larrousse-Ford Cosworth LH94	45 laps/clutch	21
R	Ukyo Katayama	Tyrrell	Tyrrell-Yamaha 022	44 laps/collision	9
R	Eddie Irvine	Jordan	Jordan-Hart 194	40 laps/spun off	8
R	Andrea de Cesaris	Sauber	Sauber-Mercedes C13	24 laps/fuel pressure	14
R	Heinz-Harald Frentzen	Sauber	Sauber-Mercedes C13	5 laps/spun off	10
R	Martin Brundle	McLaren	McLaren-Peugeot MP4/9	3 laps/electrical	12
DNQ	Paul Belmondo	Pacific	Pacific-Ilmor PR01	-	27

Pole: Schumacher, 1m26.178s, 115.509mph/185.894kph. Fastest lap: Schumacher, 1m28.927s, 111.938mph/180.147kph on Lap 31. Race leaders: Schumacher 1-69

FRENCH GRAND PRIX

MAGNY-COURS • ROUND 7 • DATE: 3RD JULY 1994
Laps: 72 • Distance: 190.139miles/306.0km • Weather: Hot & bright

Pos	Driver	Team	Chassis-Engine	Result	Qual
1	Michael Schumacher	Benetton	Benetton-Ford Cosworth B194	1h38m35.704s	3
2	Damon Hill	Williams	Williams-Renault FW16	1h38m48.346s	1
3	Gerhard Berger	Ferrari	Ferrari 412T1B	1h39m28.469s	5
4	Heinz-Harald Frentzen	Sauber	Sauber-Mercedes C13	71 laps	10
5	Pierluigi Martini	Minardi	Minardi-Ford Cosworth M194	70 laps	16
6	Andrea de Cesaris	Sauber	Sauber-Mercedes C13	70 laps	11
7	Johnny Herbert	Lotus	Lotus-Mugen Honda 109	70 laps	19
8	Christian Fittipaldi	Footwork	Footwork-Ford Cosworth FA15	70 laps	18
9	Jean-Marc Gounon	Simtek	Simtek-Ford Cosworth S941	68 laps	26
10	Mark Blundell	Tyrrell	Tyrrell-Yamaha 022	67 laps	17
11	Erik Comas	Larrousse	Larrousse-Ford Cosworth LH94	66 laps/engine	20
R	Ukyo Katayama	Tyrrell	Tyrrell-Yamaha 022	53 laps/spun off	14
R	Mika Hakkinen	McLaren	McLaren-Peugeot MP4/9	48 laps/engine	9
R	Nigel Mansell	Williams	Williams-Renault FW16	45 laps/gearbox	2
R	Jean Alesi	Ferrari	Ferrari 412T1B	41 laps/collision	4
R	Rubens Barrichello	Jordan	Jordan-Hart 194	41 laps/collision	7
R	Eric Bernard	Ligier	Ligier-Renault JS39B	40 laps/gearbox	15
R	Olivier Beretta	Larrousse	Larrousse-Ford Cosworth LH94	36 laps/engine	25
R	Martin Brundle	McLaren	McLaren-Peugeot MP4/9	29 laps/engine	12
R	Olivier Panis	Ligier	Ligier-Renault JS39B	28 laps/collision	13
R	Gianni Morbidelli	Footwork	Footwork-Ford Cosworth FA15	28 laps/collision	22
R	David Brabham	Simtek	Simtek-Ford Cosworth S941	28 laps/transmission	24
R	Jos Verstappen	Benetton	Benetton-Ford Cosworth B194	25 laps/spun off	8
R	Eddie Irvine	Jordan	Jordan-Hart 194	24 laps/gearbox	6
R	Michele Alboreto	Minardi	Minardi-Ford Cosworth M194	21 laps/engine	21
R	Alessandro Zanardi	Lotus	Lotus-Mugen Honda 109	20 laps/engine	23
DNQ	Bertrand Gachot	Pacific	Pacific-Ilmor PR01	-	27
DNQ	Paul Belmondo	Pacific	Pacific-Ilmor PR01	-	28

Pole: Hill, 1m16.282s, 124.629mph/200.571kph. Fastest lap: Hill, 1m19.678s, 119.316mph/192.022kph on Lap 4. Race leaders: Schumacher 1-37 & 45-72, Hill 38-44

BRITISH GRAND PRIX

SILVERSTONE • ROUND 8 • DATE: 10TH JULY 1994
Laps: 60 • Distance: 188.301miles/303.42km • Weather: Hot & bright

Pos	Driver	Team	Chassis-Engine	Result	Qual
1	Damon Hill	Williams	Williams-Renault FW16	1h30m03.640s	1
DQ	Michael Schumacher	Benetton	Benetton-Ford Cosworth B194	Ignoring black flag	2
2	Jean Alesi	Ferrari	Ferrari 412T1B	1h31m11.768s	4
3	Mika Hakkinen	McLaren	McLaren-Peugeot MP4/9	1h31m44.299s	5
4	Rubens Barrichello	Jordan	Jordan-Hart 194	1h31m45.391s	6
5	David Coulthard	Williams	Williams-Renault FW16	59 laps	7
6	Ukyo Katayama	Tyrrell	Tyrrell-Yamaha 022	59 laps	8
7	Heinz-Harald Frentzen	Sauber	Sauber-Mercedes C13	59 laps	13
8	Jos Verstappen	Benetton	Benetton-Ford Cosworth B194	59 laps	10
9	Christian Fittipaldi	Footwork	Footwork-Ford Cosworth FA15	58 laps	20
10	Pierluigi Martini	Minardi	Minardi-Ford Cosworth M194	58 laps	14
11	Johnny Herbert	Lotus	Lotus-Mugen Honda 109	58 laps	21
12	Olivier Panis	Ligier	Ligier-Renault JS39B	58 laps	15
13	Eric Bernard	Ligier	Ligier-Renault JS39B	58 laps	23
14	Olivier Beretta	Larrousse	Larrousse-Ford Cosworth LH94	58 laps	24
15	David Brabham	Simtek	Simtek-Ford Cosworth S941	57 laps	25
16	Jean-Marc Gounon	Simtek	Simtek-Ford Cosworth S941	57 laps	26
R	Michele Alboreto	Minardi	Minardi-Ford Cosworth M194	48 laps/engine	17
R	Gerhard Berger	Ferrari	Ferrari 412T1B	32 laps/engine	3
R	Mark Blundell	Tyrrell	Tyrrell-Yamaha 022	20 laps/gearbox	11
R	Erik Comas	Larrousse	Larrousse-Ford Cosworth LH94	12 laps/engine	22
R	Andrea de Cesaris	Sauber	Sauber-Mercedes C13	11 laps/engine	18
R	Gianni Morbidelli	Footwork	Footwork-Ford Cosworth FA15	5 laps/engine	16
R	Alessandro Zanardi	Lotus	Lotus-Mugen Honda 109	4 laps/engine	19
R	Martin Brundle	McLaren	McLaren-Peugeot MP4/9	0 laps/engine	9
NS	Eddie Irvine	Jordan	Jordan-Hart 194	Engine	12
DNQ	Bertrand Gachot	Pacific	Pacific-Ilmor PR01	-	27
DNQ	Paul Belmondo	Pacific	Pacific-Ilmor PR01	-	28

Pole: Hill, 1m24.960s, 133.147mph/214.279kph. Fastest lap: Hill, 1m27.100s, 129.875mph/209.014kph on Lap 11. Race leaders: Hill 1-14 & 27-60, Schumacher 15-17 & 22-26, Berger 18-21

GERMAN GRAND PRIX

HOCKENHEIM • ROUND 9 • DATE: 31ST JULY 1994
Laps: 45 • Distance: 190.782miles/307.035km • Weather: Hot & bright

Pos	Driver	Team	Chassis-Engine	Result	Qual
1	Gerhard Berger	Ferrari	Ferrari 412T1B	1h22m37.272s	1
2	Olivier Panis	Ligier	Ligier-Renault JS39B	1h23m32.051s	12
3	Eric Bernard	Ligier	Ligier-Renault JS39B	1h23m42.314s	14
4	Christian Fittipaldi	Footwork	Footwork-Ford Cosworth FA15	1h23m58.881s	17
5	Gianni Morbidelli	Footwork	Footwork-Ford Cosworth FA15	1h24m07.816s	16
6	Erik Comas	Larrousse	Larrousse-Ford Cosworth LH94	1h24m22.717s	22
7	Olivier Beretta	Larrousse	Larrousse-Ford Cosworth LH94	44 laps	24
8	Damon Hill	Williams	Williams-Renault FW16B	44 laps	3
R	Jean-Marc Gounon	Simtek	Simtek-Ford Cosworth S941	39 laps/engine	26
R	David Brabham	Simtek	Simtek-Ford Cosworth S941	37 laps/clutch	25
R	Michael Schumacher	Benetton	Benetton-Ford Cosworth B194	20 laps/engine	4
R	Martin Brundle	McLaren	McLaren-Peugeot MP4/9	19 laps/engine	13

Pos	Driver	Team	Chassis-Engine	Result	Qual
R	David Coulthard	Williams	Williams-Renault FW16B	17 laps/electrical	6
R	Jos Verstappen	Benetton	Benetton-Ford Cosworth B194	15 laps/fire	19
R	Ukyo Katayama	Tyrrell	Tyrrell-Yamaha 022	6 laps/throttle	5
R	Jean Alesi	Ferrari	Ferrari 412T1B	1 lap/engine	2
R	Mark Blundell	Tyrrell	Tyrrell-Yamaha 022	0 laps/collision	7
R	Mika Hakkinen	McLaren	McLaren-Peugeot MP4/9	0 laps/collision	8
R	Heinz-Harald Frentzen	Sauber	Sauber-Mercedes C13	0 laps/collision	9
R	Eddie Irvine	Jordan	Jordan-Hart 194	0 laps/collision	10
R	Rubens Barrichello	Jordan	Jordan-Hart 194	0 laps/collision	11
R	Johnny Herbert	Lotus	Lotus-Mugen Honda 109	0 laps/collision	15
R	Andrea de Cesaris	Sauber	Sauber-Mercedes C13	0 laps/collision	18
R	Pierluigi Martini	Minardi	Minardi-Ford Cosworth M194	0 laps/collision	20
R	Alessandro Zanardi	Lotus	Lotus-Mugen Honda 109	0 laps/collision	21
R	Michele Alboreto	Minardi	Minardi-Ford Cosworth M194	0 laps/collision	23
DNQ	Paul Belmondo	Pacific	Pacific-Ilmor PR01	-	27
DNQ	Bertrand Gachot	Pacific	Pacific-Ilmor PR01	-	28

Pole: Berger, 1m43.582s, 147.348mph/237.133kph. Fastest lap: Coulthard, 1m46.211s, 143.700mph/231.264kph on Lap 11. Race leaders: Berger 1-45

MANSELL'S FINAL WIN

In the wake of Senna's death, Williams brought Nigel Mansell back from IndyCar racing for the French GP and the last three rounds. The last of these resulted in victory in Adelaide after he recovered from a mistake on lap one, and the leading duo of Michael Schumacher and Damon Hill came to blows. It was to be Mansell's 31st and final win.

HUNGARIAN GRAND PRIX

HUNGARORING • ROUND 10 • DATE: 14TH AUGUST 1994
Laps: 77 • Distance: 189.851miles/305.536km • Weather: Hot & bright

Pos	Driver	Team	Chassis-Engine	Result	Qual
1	Michael Schumacher	Benetton	Benetton-Ford Cosworth B194	1h48m00.185s	1
2	Damon Hill	Williams	Williams-Renault FW16B	1h48m21.012s	2
3	Jos Verstappen	Benetton	Benetton-Ford Cosworth B194	1h49m10.514s	12
4	Martin Brundle	McLaren	McLaren-Peugeot MP4/9	76 laps/engine	6
5	Mark Blundell	Tyrrell	Tyrrell-Yamaha 022	76 laps	11
6	Olivier Panis	Ligier	Ligier-Renault JS39B	76 laps	9
7	Michele Alboreto	Minardi	Minardi-Ford Cosworth M194	75 laps	20
8	Erik Comas	Larrousse	Larrousse-Ford Cosworth LH94	75 laps	21
9	Olivier Beretta	Larrousse	Larrousse-Ford Cosworth LH94	75 laps	25
10	Eric Bernard	Ligier	Ligier-Renault JS39B	75 laps	18
11	David Brabham	Simtek	Simtek-Ford Cosworth S941	74 laps	23
12	Gerhard Berger	Ferrari	Ferrari 412T1B	72 laps/engine	4
13	Alessandro Zanardi	Lotus	Lotus-Mugen Honda 109	72 laps	22
14	Christian Fittipaldi	Footwork	Footwork-Ford Cosworth FA15	69 laps/transmission	16
R	David Coulthard	Williams	Williams-Renault FW16B	59 laps/spun off	3
R	Jean Alesi	Ferrari	Ferrari 412T1B	58 laps/gearbox	13
R	Pierluigi Martini	Minardi	Minardi-Ford Cosworth M194	58 laps/spun off	15
R	Heinz-Harald Frentzen	Sauber	Sauber-Mercedes C13	39 laps/gearbox	8

Pos	Driver	Team	Chassis-Engine	Result	Qual
R	Johnny Herbert	Lotus	Lotus-Mugen Honda 109	34 laps/electrical	24
R	Andrea de Cesaris	Sauber	Sauber-Mercedes C13	30 laps/collision	17
R	Gianni Morbidelli	Footwork	Footwork-Ford Cosworth FA15	30 laps/collision	19
R	Philippe Alliot	McLaren	McLaren-Peugeot MP4/9	21 laps/water leak	14
R	Jean-Marc Gounon	Simtek	Simtek-Ford Cosworth S941	9 laps/handling	26
R	Ukyo Katayama	Tyrrell	Tyrrell-Yamaha 022	0 laps/collision	5
R	Eddie Irvine	Jordan	Jordan-Hart 194	0 laps/collision	7
R	Rubens Barrichello	Jordan	Jordan-Hart 194	0 laps/collision	10
DNQ	Bertrand Gachot	Pacific	Pacific-Ilmor PR01	-	27
DNQ	Paul Belmondo	Pacific	Pacific-Ilmor PR01	-	28

Pole: Schumacher, 1m18.258s, 113.421mph/182.534kph. Fastest lap: Schumacher, 1m20.881s, 109.743mph/176.615kph on Lap 5. Race leaders: Schumacher 1-16 & 26-77, Hill 17-25

NEW CIRCUITS

A new Japanese circuit arrived on the calendar in 1994. This was the TI Circuit in the south of the country. It was used for the Pacific GP (the Japanese GP was still held at Suzuka) and was won by Schumacher for Benetton. Estoril and Silverstone both featured changes, with the former gaining the Saca Rolhas hairpin and the latter a chicane at Abbey.

BELGIAN GRAND PRIX

SPA-FRANCORCHAMPS • ROUND 11 • DATE: 28TH AUGUST 1994
Laps: 44 • Distance: 191.409miles/308.044km • Weather: Warm & bright

Pos	Driver	Team	Chassis-Engine	Result	Qual
DQ	Michael Schumacher	Benetton	Benetton-Ford Cosworth B194	44 laps/skidblock wear	2
1	Damon Hill	Williams	Williams-Renault FW16B	1h28m47.170s	3
2	Mika Hakkinen	McLaren	McLaren-Peugeot MP4/9	1h29m38.551s	8
3	Jos Verstappen	Benetton	Benetton-Ford Cosworth B194	1h29m57.623s	6
4	David Coulthard	Williams	Williams-Renault FW16B	1h30m32.957s	7
5	Mark Blundell	Tyrrell	Tyrrell-Yamaha 022	43 laps	12
6	Gianni Morbidelli	Footwork	Footwork-Ford Cosworth FA15	43 laps	14
7	Olivier Panis	Ligier	Ligier-Renault JS39B	43 laps	17
8	Pierluigi Martini	Minardi	Minardi-Ford Cosworth M194	43 laps	10
9	Michele Alboreto	Minardi	Minardi-Ford Cosworth M194	43 laps	18
10	Eric Bernard	Ligier	Ligier-Renault JS39B	42 laps	16
11	Jean-Marc Gounon	Simtek	Simtek-Ford Cosworth S941	42 laps	25
12	Johnny Herbert	Lotus	Lotus-Mugen Honda 109	41 laps	20
13	Eddie Irvine	Jordan	Jordan-Hart 194	40 laps/alternator	4
R	Christian Fittipaldi	Footwork	Footwork-Ford Cosworth FA15	33 laps/engine	24
R	David Brabham	Simtek	Simtek-Ford Cosworth S941	29 laps/wheel	21
R	Andrea de Cesaris	Sauber	Sauber-Mercedes C13	27 laps/throttle	15
R	Martin Brundle	McLaren	McLaren-Peugeot MP4/9	24 laps/spun off	13
R	Rubens Barrichello	Jordan	Jordan-Hart 194	19 laps/spun off	1
R	Ukyo Katayama	Tyrrell	Tyrrell-Yamaha 022	18 laps/engine	23
R	Philippe Adams	Lotus	Lotus-Mugen Honda 109	15 laps/spun off	26
R	Gerhard Berger	Ferrari	Ferrari 412T1B	11 laps/engine	11
R	Philippe Alliot	Larrousse	Larrousse-Ford Cosworth LH94	11 laps/engine	19

Pos	Driver	Team	Chassis-Engine	Result	Qual
R	Heinz-Harald Frentzen	Sauber	Sauber-Mercedes C13	10 laps/spun off	9
R	Erik Comas	Larrousse	Larrousse-Ford Cosworth LH94	3 laps/engine	22
R	Jean Alesi	Ferrari	Ferrari 412T1B	2 laps/engine	5
DNQ	Bertrand Gachot	Pacific	Pacific-Ilmor PR01	-	27
DNQ	Paul Belmondo	Pacific	Pacific-Ilmor PR01	-	28

Pole: Barrichello, 2m21.163s, 110.941mph/178.542kph. Fastest lap: Hill, 1m57.117s, 133.719mph/215.200kph on Lap 41. Race leaders: Schumacher 1-28 & 30-44, Coulthard 29

ITALIAN GRAND PRIX

MONZA • ROUND 12 • DATE: 11TH SEPTEMBER 1994
Laps: 53 • Distance: 190.763miles/307.4km • Weather: Hot & bright

Pos	Driver	Team	Chassis-Engine	Result	Qual
1	Damon Hill	Williams	Williams-Renault FW16B	1h18m02.754s	3
2	Gerhard Berger	Ferrari	Ferrari 412T1B	1h18m07.684s	2
3	Mika Hakkinen	McLaren	McLaren-Peugeot MP4/9	1h18m28.394s	7
4	Rubens Barrichello	Jordan	Jordan-Hart 194	1h18m53.388s	16
5	Martin Brundle	McLaren	McLaren-Peugeot MP4/9	1h19m28.329s	15
6	David Coulthard	Williams	Williams-Renault FW16B	52 laps/out of fuel	5
7	Eric Bernard	Ligier	Ligier-Renault JS39B	52 laps	12
8	Erik Comas	Larrousse	Larrousse-Ford Cosworth LH94	52 laps	24
9	JJ Lehto	Benetton	Benetton-Ford Cosworth B194	52 laps	20
10	Olivier Panis	Ligier	Ligier-Renault JS39B	51 laps	6
R	David Brabham	Simtek	Simtek-Ford Cosworth S941	46 laps/puncture	26
R	Ukyo Katayama	Tyrrell	Tyrrell-Yamaha 022	45 laps/spun off	14
R	Christian Fittipaldi	Footwork	Footwork-Ford Cosworth FA15	43 laps/engine	19
R	Eddie Irvine	Jordan	Jordan-Hart 194	41 laps/engine	9
R	Mark Blundell	Tyrrell	Tyrrell-Yamaha 022	39 laps/spun off	21
R	Pierluigi Martini	Minardi	Minardi-Ford Cosworth M194	30 laps/spun off	18
R	Michele Alboreto	Minardi	Minardi-Ford Cosworth M194	28 laps/gearbox	22
R	Heinz-Harald Frentzen	Sauber	Sauber-Mercedes C13	22 laps/engine	11
R	Andrea de Cesaris	Sauber	Sauber-Mercedes C13	20 laps/engine	8
R	Jean-Marc Gounon	Simtek	Simtek-Ford Cosworth S941	20 laps/gearbox	25
R	Yannick Dalmas	Larrousse	Larrousse-Ford Cosworth LH94	18 laps/spun off	23
R	Jean Alesi	Ferrari	Ferrari 412T1B	14 laps/gearbox	1
R	Johnny Herbert	Lotus	Lotus-Mugen Honda 109	13 laps/alternator	4
R	Jos Verstappen	Benetton	Benetton-Ford Cosworth B194	0 laps/collision	10
R	Alessandro Zanardi	Lotus	Lotus-Mugen Honda 109	0 laps/collision	13
R	Gianni Morbidelli	Footwork	Footwork-Ford Cosworth FA15	0 laps/collision	17
DNQ	Bertrand Gachot	Pacific	Pacific-Ilmor PR01	-	27
DNQ	Paul Belmondo	Pacific	Pacific-Ilmor PR01	-	28

Pole: Alesi, 1m23.844s, 154.742mph/249.033kph. Fastest lap: Hill, 1m25.930s, 150.985mph/242.988kph on Lap 24. Race leaders: Alesi 1-14, Berger 15-23, Hill 24 & 29-53, Coulthard 25 & 27-28, Hakkinen 26

PORTUGUESE GRAND PRIX

AUTODROMO DO ESTORIL • ROUND 13 • DATE: 25TH SEPTEMBER 1994
Laps: 71 • Distance: 192.38miles/309.56km • Weather: Warm & bright

Pos	Driver	Team	Chassis-Engine	Result	Qual
1	Damon Hill	Williams	Williams-Renault FW16B	1h41m10.165s	2
2	David Coulthard	Williams	Williams-Renault FW16B	1h41m10.768s	3
3	Mika Hakkinen	McLaren	McLaren-Peugeot MP4/9	1h41m30.358s	4
4	Rubens Barrichello	Jordan	Jordan-Hart 194	1h41m38.168s	8
5	Jos Verstappen	Benetton	Benetton-Ford Cosworth B194	1h41m39.550s	10
6	Martin Brundle	McLaren	McLaren-Peugeot MP4/9	1h42m02.867s	7
7	Eddie Irvine	Jordan	Jordan-Hart 194	70 laps	13
8	Christian Fittipaldi	Footwork	Footwork-Ford Cosworth FA15	70 laps	11
DQ	Olivier Panis	Ligier	Ligier-Renault JS39B	skidblock wear	15
9	Gianni Morbidelli	Footwork	Footwork-Ford Cosworth FA15	70 laps	16
10	Eric Bernard	Ligier	Ligier-Renault JS39B	70 laps	21
11	Johnny Herbert	Lotus	Lotus-Mugen Honda 109	70 laps	20
12	Pierluigi Martini	Minardi	Minardi-Ford Cosworth M194	69 laps	18
13	Michele Alboreto	Minardi	Minardi-Ford Cosworth M194	69 laps	19
14	Yannick Dalmas	Larrousse	Larrousse-Ford Cosworth LH94	69 laps	23
15	Jean-Marc Gounon	Simtek	Simtek-Ford Cosworth S941	67 laps	26
16	Philippe Adams	Lotus	Lotus-Mugen Honda 109	67 laps	25
R	Mark Blundell	Tyrrell	Tyrrell-Yamaha 022	61 laps/engine	12
R	JJ Lehto	Benetton	Benetton-Ford Cosworth B194	60 laps/spun off	14
R	Andrea de Cesaris	Sauber	Sauber-Mercedes C13	54 laps/spun off	17
R	Jean Alesi	Ferrari	Ferrari 412T1B	38 laps/collision	5
R	David Brabham	Simtek	Simtek-Ford Cosworth S941	36 laps/collision	24
R	Heinz-Harald Frentzen	Sauber	Sauber-Mercedes C13	31 laps/differential	9
R	Erik Comas	Larrousse	Larrousse-Ford Cosworth LH94	27 laps/suspension	22
R	Ukyo Katayama	Tyrrell	Tyrrell-Yamaha 022	26 laps/gearbox	6
R	Gerhard Berger	Ferrari	Ferrari 412T1B	7 laps/gearbox	1
DNQ	Bertrand Gachot	Pacific	Pacific-Ilmor PR01	-	27
DNQ	Paul Belmondo	Pacific	Pacific-Ilmor PR01	-	28

Pole: Berger, 1m20.608s, 120.993mph/194.720kph. Fastest lap: Coulthard, 1m22.446s, 118.296mph/190.379kph on Lap 12. Race leaders: Berger 1-7, Coulthard 8-17 & 26-27, Hill 18 & 28-71, Alesi 19-22, Barrichello 23-25

NEW CONSTRUCTORS

Both the teams new to F1 in 1994 were based in England. Pacific evolved from Keith Wiggins's successful F3000 outfit, but it struggled at the sport's top level, with Paul Belmondo and Bertrand Gachot seldom qualifying. Simtek was created from scratch by Nick Wirth, and driver Jean-Marc Gounon took its best result, a ninth in the French GP.

NEW DRIVERS

In addition to the unfortunate Roland Ratzenberger, David Coulthard, Heinz-Harald Frentzen, Olivier Panis and Jos Verstappen stood out from the crop of 14 F1 rookies. Verstappen grabbed two third places for Benetton, while Coulthard peaked with fourth at Spa for Williams, equalling Frentzen's best for Sauber, with Panis fifth in Adelaide for Ligier.

EUROPEAN GRAND PRIX

JEREZ • ROUND 14 • DATE: 16TH OCTOBER 1994
Laps: 69 • Distance: 189.848miles/305.532km • Weather: Hot & bright

Pos	Driver	Team	Chassis-Engine	Result	Qual
1	Michael Schumacher	Benetton	Benetton-Ford Cosworth B194	1h40m26.689s	1
2	Damon Hill	Williams	Williams-Renault FW16B	1h40m51.378s	2
3	Mika Hakkinen	McLaren	McLaren-Peugeot MP4/9	1h41m36.337s	9
4	Eddie Irvine	Jordan	Jordan-Hart 194	1h41m45.135s	10
5	Gerhard Berger	Ferrari	Ferrari 412T1B	68 laps	6
6	Heinz-Harald Frentzen	Sauber	Sauber-Mercedes C13	68 laps	4
7	Ukyo Katayama	Tyrrell	Tyrrell-Yamaha 022	68 laps	13
8	Johnny Herbert	Ligier	Ligier-Renault JS39B	68 laps	7
9	Olivier Panis	Ligier	Ligier-Renault JS39B	68 laps	11
10	Jean Alesi	Ferrari	Ferrari 412T1B	68 laps	16
11	Gianni Morbidelli	Footwork	Footwork-Ford Cosworth FA15	68 laps	8
12	Rubens Barrichello	Jordan	Jordan-Hart 194	68 laps	5
13	Mark Blundell	Tyrrell	Tyrrell-Yamaha 022	68 laps	14
14	Michele Alboreto	Minardi	Minardi-Ford Cosworth M194	67 laps	20
15	Pierluigi Martini	Minardi	Minardi-Ford Cosworth M194	67 laps	17
16	Alessandro Zanardi	Lotus	Lotus-Mugen Honda 109	67 laps	21
17	Christian Fittipaldi	Footwork	Footwork-Ford Cosworth FA15	66 laps	19
18	Eric Bernard	Lotus	Lotus-Mugen Honda 109	66 laps	22
19	Domenico Schiattarella	Simtek	Simtek-Ford Cosworth S941	64 laps	26
R	Nigel Mansell	Williams	Williams-Renault FW16B	47 laps/spun off	3
R	David Brabham	Simtek	Simtek-Ford Cosworth S941	42 laps/engine	25
R	Andrea de Cesaris	Sauber	Sauber-Mercedes C13	37 laps/throttle	18
R	Erik Comas	Larrousse	Larrousse-Ford Cosworth LH94	37 laps/alternator	23
R	Jos Verstappen	Benetton	Benetton-Ford Cosworth B194	15 laps/spun off	12
R	Hideki Noda	Larrousse	Larrousse-Ford Cosworth LH94	10 laps/gearbox	24
R	Martin Brundle	McLaren	McLaren-Peugeot MP4/9	8 laps/engine	15
DNQ	Bertrand Gachot	Pacific	Pacific-Ilmor PR01	-	27
DNQ	Paul Belmondo	Pacific	Pacific-Ilmor PR01	-	28

Pole: Schumacher, 1m22.762s, 119.682mph/192.610kph. Fastest lap: Schumacher, 1m25.040s, 116.476mph/187.450kph on Lap 17. Race leaders: Hill 1-17 & 33-34, Schumacher 18-32 & 35-69

JAPANESE GRAND PRIX

SUZUKA • ROUND 15 • DATE: 6TH NOVEMBER 1994
Laps: 50 • Distance: 182.63miles/293.2km • Weather: Cool & very wet

Pos	Driver	Team	Chassis-Engine	Result	Qual
1	Damon Hill	Williams	Williams-Renault FW16B	1h55m53.532s	2
2	Michael Schumacher	Benetton	Benetton-Ford Cosworth B194	1h55m56.897s	1
3	Jean Alesi	Ferrari	Ferrari 412T1B	1h56m45.577s	7
4	Nigel Mansell	Williams	Williams-Renault FW16B	1h56m49.606s	4
5	Eddie Irvine	Jordan	Jordan-Hart 194	1h57m35.639s	6
6	Heinz-Harald Frentzen	Sauber	Sauber-Mercedes C13	1h57m53.395s	3
7	Mika Hakkinen	McLaren	McLaren-Peugeot MP4/9	1h57m56.517s	8
8	Christian Fittipaldi	Footwork	Footwork-Ford Cosworth FA15	49 laps	18
9	Erik Comas	Larrousse	Larrousse-Ford Cosworth LH94	49 laps	22
10	Mika Salo	Lotus	Lotus-Mugen Honda 109	49 laps	25
11	Olivier Panis	Ligier	Ligier-Renault JS39B	49 laps	19
12	David Brabham	Simtek	Simtek-Ford Cosworth S941	48 laps	24

Pos	Driver	Team	Chassis-Engine	Result	Qual
13	Alessandro Zanardi	Lotus	Lotus-Mugen Honda 109	48 laps	17
R	Mark Blundell	Tyrrell	Tyrrell-Yamaha 022	26 laps/engine	13
R	Rubens Barrichello	Jordan	Jordan-Hart 194	16 laps/gearbox	10
R	Martin Brundle	McLaren	McLaren-Peugeot MP4/9	13 laps/spun off	9
R	Gianni Morbidelli	Footwork	Footwork-Ford Cosworth FA15	13 laps/spun off	12
R	Gerhard Berger	Ferrari	Ferrari 412T1B	10 laps/ignition	11
R	Pierluigi Martini	Minardi	Minardi-Ford Cosworth M194	10 laps/collision	16
R	Franck Lagorce	Ligier	Ligier-Renault JS39B	10 laps/collision	20
R	Michele Alboreto	Minardi	Minardi-Ford Cosworth M194	10 laps/spun off	21
R	Johnny Herbert	Benetton	Benetton-Ford Cosworth B194	3 laps/spun off	5
R	Ukyo Katayama	Tyrrell	Tyrrell-Yamaha 022	3 laps/spun off	14
R	Taki Inoue	Simtek	Simtek-Ford Cosworth S941	3 laps/spun off	26
R	JJ Lehto	Sauber	Sauber-Mercedes C13	0 laps/engine	15
R	Hideki Noda	Larrousse	Larrousse-Ford Cosworth LH94	0 laps/spun off	23
DNQ	Bertrand Gachot	Pacific	Pacific-Ilmor PR01	-	27
DNQ	Paul Belmondo	Pacific	Pacific-Ilmor PR01	-	28

Pole: Schumacher, 1m37.209s, 134.940mph/217.165kph. Fastest lap: Hill, 1m56.597s, 112.501mph/181.054kph on Lap 24. Race leaders: Schumacher 1-18 & 36-40, Hill 19-35 & 41-50

IN MEMORIAM

Ayrton Senna's death transcended the sport, and Brazil had a day of mourning as the three-time world champion's coffin was paraded around Sao Paulo. Roland Ratzenberger, with just one grand prix start to his name, was less well known, but his death was no less sad after he had fought for so long to be a grand prix driver.

AUSTRALIAN GRAND PRIX

ADELAIDE • ROUND 16 • DATE: 13TH NOVEMBER 1994
Laps: 81 • Distance: 190.150miles/306.18km • Weather: Warm but dull

Pos	Driver	Team	Chassis-Engine	Result	Qual
1	Nigel Mansell	Williams	Williams-Renault FW16B	1h47m51.480s	1
2	Gerhard Berger	Ferrari	Ferrari 412T1B	1h47m53.991s	11
3	Martin Brundle	McLaren	McLaren-Peugeot MP4/9	1h48m43.967s	9
4	Rubens Barrichello	Jordan	Jordan-Hart 194	1h49m02.010s	5
5	Olivier Panis	Ligier	Ligier-Renault JS39B	80 laps	12
6	Jean Alesi	Ferrari	Ferrari 412T1B	80 laps	8
7	Heinz-Harald Frentzen	Sauber	Sauber-Mercedes C13	80 laps	10
8	Christian Fittipaldi	Footwork	Footwork-Ford Cosworth FA15	80 laps	19
9	Pierluigi Martini	Minardi	Minardi-Ford Cosworth M194	79 laps	18
10	JJ Lehto	Sauber	Sauber-Mercedes C13	79 laps	17
11	Franck Lagorce	Ligier	Ligier-Renault JS39B	79 laps	20
12	Mika Hakkinen	McLaren	McLaren-Peugeot MP4/9	76 laps/spun off	4
R	Michele Alboreto	Minardi	Minardi-Ford Cosworth M194	69 laps/suspension	16
R	Mark Blundell	Tyrrell	Tyrrell-Yamaha 022	66 laps/collision	13
R	Jean-Denis Deletraz	Larrousse	Larrousse-Ford Cosworth LH94	56 laps/gearbox	25
R	Mika Salo	Lotus	Lotus-Mugen Honda 109	49 laps/electrical	22
R	David Brabham	Simtek	Simtek-Ford Cosworth S941	49 laps/engine	24

Pos	Driver	Team	Chassis-Engine	Result	Qual
R	Alessandro Zanardi	Lotus	Lotus-Mugen Honda 109	40 laps/throttle	14
R	Michael Schumacher	Benetton	Benetton-Ford Cosworth B194	35 laps/collision	2
R	Damon Hill	Williams	Williams-Renault FW16B	35 laps/collision	3
R	Domenico Schiattarella	Simtek	Simtek-Ford Cosworth S941	21 laps/gearbox	26
R	Ukyo Katayama	Tyrrell	Tyrrell-Yamaha 022	19 laps/spun off	15
R	Hideki Noda	Larrousse	Larrousse-Ford Cosworth LH94	18 laps/oil leak	23
R	Gianni Morbidelli	Footwork	Footwork-Ford Cosworth FA15	17 laps/oil leak	21
R	Eddie Irvine	Jordan	Jordan-Hart 194	15 laps/spun off	6
R	Johnny Herbert	Benetton	Benetton-Ford Cosworth B194	13 laps/gearbox	7
DNQ	Paul Belmondo	Pacific	Pacific-Ilmor PR01	-	27
DNQ	Bertrand Gachot	Pacific	Pacific-Ilmor PR01	-	28

Pole: Mansell, 1m16.179s, 110.996mph/178.631kph. Fastest lap: Schumacher, 1m17.140s, 109.613mph/176.406kph on Lap 29. Race leaders: Schumacher 1-35, Mansell 36-53 & 64-81, Berger 54-63

WORLD DRIVERS' CHAMPIONSHIP FINAL RESULTS

Pos	Driver	Nat	Car-Engine	R1	R2	R3	R4	R5	R6
1	Michael Schumacher	DEU	Benetton-Ford Cosworth B194	1F	1F	1	1PF	2PF	1PF
2	Damon Hill	GBR	Williams-Renault FW16	2	R	6F	R	1	2
			Williams-Renault FW16B	-	-	-	-	-	-
3	Gerhard Berger	AUT	Ferrari 412T1	R	2	R	3	R	4
			Ferrari 412T1B	-	-	-	-	-	-
4	Mika Hakkinen	FIN	McLaren-Peugeot MP4/9	R	R	3	R	R	R
5	Jean Alesi	FRA	Ferrari 412T1	3	-	-	5	4	3
			Ferrari 412T1B	-	-	-	-	-	-
6	Rubens Barrichello	BRA	Jordan-Hart 194	4	3	NS	R	R	7
7	Martin Brundle	GBR	McLaren-Peugeot MP4/9	R	R	8	2	11	R
8	David Coulthard	GBR	Williams-Renault FW16	-	-	-	-	R	5
			Williams-Renault FW16B	-	-	-	-	-	-
9	Nigel Mansell	GBR	Williams-Renault FW16	-	-	-	-	-	-
			Williams-Renault FW16B	-	-	-	-	-	-
10	Jos Verstappen	NLD	Benetton-Ford Cosworth B194	R	R	-	-	-	-
11	Olivier Panis	FRA	Ligier-Renault JS39B	11	9	11	9	7	12
12	Mark Blundell	GBR	Tyrrell-Yamaha 022	R	R	9	R	3	10
13	Heinz-Harald Frentzen	DEU	Sauber-Mercedes C13	R	5	7	NS	R	R
14	Nicola Larini	ITA	Ferrari 412T1	-	R	2	-	-	-
15	Christian Fittipaldi	BRA	Footwork-Ford Cosworth FA15	R	4	13	R	R	DQ
16	Eddie Irvine	GBR	Jordan-Hart 194	R	-	-	-	6	R
17	Ukyo Katayama	JPN	Tyrrell-Yamaha 022	5	R	5	R	R	R
18	Eric Bernard	FRA	Ligier-Renault JS39B	R	10	12	R	8	13
			Lotus-Mugen Honda 109	-	-	-	-	-	-
19	Karl Wendlinger	AUT	Sauber-Mercedes C13	6	R	4	NS	-	-
19	Andrea de Cesaris	ITA	Jordan-Hart 194	-	-	R	4	-	-
			Sauber-Mercedes C13	-	-	-	-	-	R
21	Pierluigi Martini	ITA	Minardi-Ford Cosworth M193B	8	R	R	R	5	-
			Minardi-Ford Cosworth M194	-	-	-	-	-	9
22	Gianni Morbidelli	ITA	Footwork-Ford Cosworth FA15	R	R	R	R	R	R
23	Erik Comas	FRA	Larrousse-Ford Cosworth LH94	9	6	R	10	R	R
24	Michele Alboreto	ITA	Minardi-Ford Cosworth M193B	R	R	R	6	R	-
			Minardi-Ford Cosworth M194	-	-	-	-	-	11
24	JJ Lehto	FIN	Benetton-Ford Cosworth B194	-	-	R	7	R	6
			Sauber-Mercedes C13	-	-	-	-	-	-

Pos	Driver	R7	R8	R9	R10	R11	R12	R13	R14	R15	R16	Total
1	Schumacher	1	DQ	R	1PF	DQ	-	-	1PF	2P	RF	92
2	Hill	2PF	1PF	-	-	-	-	-	-	-	-	91
		-	-	8	2	1F	1F	1	2	1F	R	
3	Berger	-	-	-	-	-	-	-	-	-	-	41
		3	R	1P	12	R	2	RP	5	R	2	
4	Hakkinen	R	3	R	-	2	3	3	3	7	12	26
5	Alesi	-	-	-	-	-	-	-	-	-	-	24
		R	2	R	R	R	RP	R	10	3	6	
6	Barrichello	R	4	R	R	RP	4	4	12	R	4	19
7	Brundle	R	R	R	4	R	5	6	R	R	3	16
8	Coulthard	-	5	-	-	-	-	-	-	-	-	14
		-	-	RF	R	4	6	2F	-	-	-	
9	Mansell	R	-	-	-	-	-	-	-	-	-	13
		-	-	-	-	-	-	-	R	4	1P	
10	Verstappen	R	8	R	3	3	R	5	R	-	-	10
11	Panis	R	12	2	6	7	10	DQ	9	11	5	9
12	Blundell	10	R	R	5	5	R	R	13	R	R	8
13	Frentzen	4	7	R	R	R	R	R	6	6	7	7
14	Larini	-	-	-	-	-	-	-	-	-	-	6
15	Fittipaldi	8	9	4	14	R	R	8	17	8	8	6
16	Irvine	R	NS	R	R	13	R	7	4	5	R	6
17	Katayama	R	6	R	R	R	R	R	7	R	R	5
18	Bernard	R	13	3	10	10	7	10	-	-	-	4
		-	-	-	-	-	-	-	18	-	-	
19	Wendlinger	-	-	-	-	-	-	-	-	-	-	4
19	de Cesaris	-	-	-	-	-	-	-	-	-	-	4
		6	R	R	R	R	R	R	R	-	-	
21	Martini	-	-	-	-	-	-	-	-	-	-	4
		5	10	R	R	8	R	12	15	R	9	
22	Morbidelli	R	R	5	R	6	R	9	11	R	R	3
23	Comas	11	R	6	8	R	8	R	R	9	-	2
24	Alboreto	-	-	-	-	-	-	-	-	-	-	1
		R	R	R	7	9	R	13	14	R	R	
24	Lehto	-	-	-	-	-	9	R	-	-	-	1
		-	-	-	-	-	-	-	-	R	10	

SYMBOLS AND GRAND PRIX KEY

Round 1 **Brazilian GP**
Round 2 **Pacific GP**
Round 3 **San Marino GP**
Round 4 **Monaco GP**
Round 5 **Spanish GP**
Round 6 **Canadian GP**
Round 7 **French GP**
Round 8 **British GP**
Round 9 **German GP**
Round 10 **Hungarian GP**
Round 11 **Belgian GP**
Round 12 **Italian GP**
Round 13 **Portuguese GP**
Round 14 **European GP**
Round 15 **Japanese GP**
Round 16 **Australian GP**

SCORING

1st **10 points**
2nd **6 points**
3rd **4 points**
4th **3 points**
5th **2 points**
6th **1 point**

DNPQ DID NOT PRE-QUALIFY **DNQ DID NOT QUALIFY** **DQ DISQUALIFIED** **EX EXCLUDED**
F FASTEST LAP **NC NOT CLASSIFIED** **NS NON-STARTER** **P POLE POSITION** **R RETIRED**

WORLD CONSTRUCTORS' CHAMPIONSHIP FINAL RESULTS

Pos	Team-Engine	R1	R2	R3	R4	R5	R6	R7	R8
1	Williams-Renault	2/R	R/R	6/R	R	1/R	2/5	2/R	1/5
2	Benetton-Ford	1/R	1/R	1/R	1/7	2/R	1/6	1/R	8/DQ
3	Ferrari	3/R	2/R	2/R	3/5	4/R	3/4	3/R	2/R
4	McLaren-Peugeot	R/R	R/R	3/8	2/R	11/R	R/R	R/R	3/R
5	Jordan-Hart	4/R	3/R	R/NS	4/R	6/R	7/R	R/R	4/R
6	Ligier-Renault	11/R	9/10	11/12	9/R	7/8	12/13	R/R	12/13
7	Tyrrell-Yamaha	5/R	R/R	5/9	R/R	3/R	10/R	10/R	6/R
8	Sauber-Mercedes	6/R	5/R	4/7	NS/NS	R	R/R	4/6	7/R
9	Footwork-Ford	R/R	4/R	13/R	R/R	R/R	DQ/R	8/R	9/R
10	Minardi-Ford	8/R	R/R	R/R	6/R	5/R	9/11	5/R	10/R
11	Larrousse-Ford	9/R	6/R	R/R	8/10	R/R	R/R	11/R	14/R

Pos	Team-Engine	R9	R10	R11	R12	R13	R14	R15	R16	Total
1	Williams-Renault	8/R	2/R	1/4	1/6	1/2	2/R	1/4	1/R	118
2	Benetton-Ford	R/R	1/3	3/DQ	9/R	5/R	1/R	2/R	R/R	103
3	Ferrari	1/R	12/R	R/R	2/R	R/R	5/10	3/R	2/6	71
4	McLaren-Peugeot	R/R	4/R	2/R	3/5	3/6	3/R	7/R	3/12	42
5	Jordan-Hart	R/R	R/R	13/R	4/R	4/7	4/12	5/R	4/R	28
6	Ligier-Renault	2/3	6/10	7/10	7/10	10/DQ	8/9	11/R	5/11	13
7	Tyrrell-Yamaha	R/R	5/R	5/R	R/R	R/R	7/13	R/R	R/R	13
8	Sauber-Mercedes	R/R	R/R	R/R	R/R	R/R	6/R	6/R	7/10	12
9	Footwork-Ford	4/5	14/R	6/R	R/R	8/9	11/17	8/R	8/R	9
10	Minardi-Ford	R/R	7/R	8/9	R/R	12/13	14/15	R/R	9/R	5
11	Larrousse-Ford	6/7	8/9	R/R	8/R	14/R	R/R	9/R	R/R	2

SEASON SUMMARY

Benetton showed its ambition to keep improving by replacing its Ford engines with Renault V10s, taking the battle straight to Williams. The result was a triumph for Michael Schumacher as he displayed precision and speed to win nine rounds and comfortably clinch his second world title. Damon Hill was runner-up for the second year in a row, but was generally outmuscled in a frequently physical season, with their clash at Silverstone allowing Johnny Herbert to take his first win in the second Benetton. Nigel Mansell was brought back to F1, but his full-season drive with McLaren was hampered when he couldn't fit into the car.

SMALLER ENGINES, SLOWER CARS?

With the aim of slowing the cars to avoid having another fatality, engine size was cut from a maximum of 3500cc to 3000cc, taking power output down from 820 to 675bhp for the best units. To reduce downforce, the cars had to be fitted with a 50mm (2in) stepped flat bottom in addition to the 10mm (0.4in) plank, while front and rear wings were reduced in size.

BRAZILIAN GRAND PRIX

INTERLAGOS • ROUND 1 • DATE: 26TH MARCH 1995
Laps: 71 • Distance: 190.807miles/307.075km • Weather: Warm but dull

Pos	Driver	Team	Chassis-Engine	Result	Qual
1	Michael Schumacher	Benetton	Benetton-Renault B195	1h38m34.154s	2
2	David Coulthard	Williams	Williams-Renault FW17	1h38m42.214s	3
3	Gerhard Berger	Ferrari	Ferrari 412T2	70 laps	5
4	Mika Hakkinen	McLaren	McLaren-Mercedes MP4/10	70 laps	7
5	Jean Alesi	Ferrari	Ferrari 412T2	70 laps	6
6	Mark Blundell	McLaren	McLaren-Mercedes MP4/10	70 laps	9
7	Mika Salo	Tyrrell	Tyrrell-Yamaha 023	69 laps	12
8	Aguri Suzuki	Ligier	Ligier-Mugen Honda JS41	69 laps	15
9	Andrea Montermini	Pacific	Pacific-Ford Cosworth PR02	65 laps	22
10	Pedro Diniz	Forti	Forti-Ford Cosworth FG01	64 laps	25
R	Gianni Morbidelli	Footwork	Footwork-Hart FA16	62 laps/engine	13
R	Taki Inoue	Footwork	Footwork-Hart FA16	48 laps/engine	21
R	Luca Badoer	Minardi	Minardi-Ford Cosworth M195	47 laps/gearbox	18
R	Roberto Moreno	Forti	Forti-Ford Cosworth FG01	47 laps/spun off	23
R	Karl Wendlinger	Sauber	Sauber-Ford Cosworth C14	41 laps/electrical	19
R	Damon Hill	Williams	Williams-Renault FW17	30 laps/gearbox	1
R	Johnny Herbert	Benetton	Benetton-Renault B195	30 laps/collision	4
R	Bertrand Gachot	Pacific	Pacific-Ford Cosworth PR02	23 laps/gearbox	20
R	Rubens Barrichello	Jordan	Jordan-Peugeot 195	16 laps/gearbox	16
R	Jos Verstappen	Simtek	Simtek-Ford Cosworth S951	16 laps/gearbox	24
R	Eddie Irvine	Jordan	Jordan-Peugeot 195	15 laps/clutch	8
R	Ukyo Katayama	Tyrrell	Tyrrell-Yamaha 023	15 laps/spun off	11
R	Domenico Schiattarella	Simtek	Simtek-Ford Cosworth S951	12 laps/steering	26

Pos	Driver	Team	Chassis-Engine	Result	Qual
R	Heinz-Harald Frentzen	Sauber	Sauber-Ford Cosworth C14	10 laps/electrical	14
R	Olivier Panis	Ligier	Ligier-Mugen Honda JS41	0 laps/collision	10
NS	Pierluigi Martini	Minardi	Minardi-Ford Cosworth M195	-	17

Pole: Hill, 1m20.081s, 120.812mph/194.428kph. Fastest lap: Schumacher, 1m20.921s, 119.557mph/192.409kph on Lap 51. Race leaders: Schumacher 1-17 & 31-35 & 47-71, Hill 18-21 & 23-30, Coulthard 22 & 36-46

ARGENTINIAN GRAND PRIX

BUENOS AIRES • ROUND 2 • DATE: 9TH APRIL 1995
Laps: 72 • Distance: 190.542miles/306.648km • Weather: Warm but dull

Pos	Driver	Team	Chassis-Engine	Result	Qual
1	Damon Hill	Williams	Williams-Renault FW17	1h53m14.532s	2
2	Jean Alesi	Ferrari	Ferrari 412T2	1h53m20.939s	6
3	Michael Schumacher	Benetton	Benetton-Renault B195	1h53m47.908s	3
4	Johnny Herbert	Benetton	Benetton-Renault B195	71 laps	11
5	Heinz-Harald Frentzen	Sauber	Sauber-Ford Cosworth C14	70 laps	9
6	Gerhard Berger	Ferrari	Ferrari 412T2	70 laps	8
7	Olivier Panis	Ligier	Ligier-Mugen Honda JS41	70 laps	18
8	Ukyo Katayama	Tyrrell	Tyrrell-Yamaha 023	69 laps	15
9	Domenico Schiattarella	Simtek	Simtek-Ford Cosworth S951	68 laps	20
NC	Roberto Moreno	Forti	Forti-Ford Cosworth FG01	63 laps	24
NC	Pedro Diniz	Forti	Forti-Ford Cosworth FG01	63 laps	25
R	Mika Salo	Tyrrell	Tyrrell-Yamaha 023	48 laps/collision	7
R	Aguri Suzuki	Ligier	Ligier-Mugen Honda JS41	47 laps/collision	19
R	Pierluigi Martini	Minardi	Minardi-Ford Cosworth M195	44 laps/spun off	16
R	Gianni Morbidelli	Footwork	Footwork-Hart FA16	43 laps/electrical	12
R	Taki Inoue	Footwork	Footwork-Hart FA16	40 laps/spun off	26
R	Rubens Barrichello	Jordan	Jordan-Peugeot 195	33 laps/fuel pressure	10
R	Jos Verstappen	Simtek	Simtek-Ford Cosworth S951	23 laps/gearbox	14
R	David Coulthard	Williams	Williams-Renault FW17	16 laps/electrical	1
R	Mark Blundell	McLaren	McLaren-Mercedes MP4/10	9 laps/oil leak	17
R	Eddie Irvine	Jordan	Jordan-Peugeot 195	6 laps/engine	4
R	Andrea Montermini	Pacific	Pacific-Ford Cosworth PR02	1 lap/collision	22
R	Mika Hakkinen	McLaren	McLaren-Mercedes MP4/10	0 laps/collision	5
R	Karl Wendlinger	Sauber	Sauber-Ford Cosworth C14	0 laps/collision	21
R	Bertrand Gachot	Pacific	Pacific-Ford Cosworth PR02	0 laps/collision	23
R	Luca Badoer	Minardi	Minardi-Ford Cosworth M195	0 laps/collision	13

Pole: Coulthard, 1m53.241s, 84.131mph/135.396kph. Fastest lap: Schumacher, 1m30.522s, 105.245mph/169.377kph on Lap 55. Race leaders: Coulthard 1-5, Schumacher 6-10 & 17, Hill 11-16 & 26-72, Alesi 18-25

A WINNING NUMBER TWO

Johnny Herbert took two wins against the odds when Benetton treated him very much as the number two to Michael Schumacher. His breakthrough win in his home grand prix at Silverstone was an extremely popular one, and it came his way when Hill tried to pass Schumacher at Priory with 15 laps to go and took both out. His second win came at Monza.

SAN MARINO GRAND PRIX

IMOLA • ROUND 3 • DATE: 30TH APRIL 1995
Laps: 63 • Distance: 191.621miles/308.385km • Weather: Cool & dull

Pos	Driver	Team	Chassis-Engine	Result	Qual
1	Damon Hill	Williams	Williams-Renault FW17	1h41m42.522s	4
2	Jean Alesi	Ferrari	Ferrari 412T2	1h42m01.062s	5
3	Gerhard Berger	Ferrari	Ferrari 412T2	1h42m25.668s	2
4	David Coulthard	Williams	Williams-Renault FW17	1h42m34.442s	3
5	Mika Hakkinen	McLaren	McLaren-Mercedes MP4/10	62 laps	6
6	Heinz-Harald Frentzen	Sauber	Sauber-Ford Cosworth C14	62 laps	14
7	Johnny Herbert	Benetton	Benetton-Renault B195	61 laps	8
8	Eddie Irvine	Jordan	Jordan-Peugeot 195	61 laps	7
9	Olivier Panis	Ligier	Ligier-Mugen Honda JS41	61 laps	12
10	Nigel Mansell	McLaren	McLaren-Mercedes MP4/10	61 laps	9
11	Aguri Suzuki	Ligier	Ligier-Mugen Honda JS41	60 laps	16
12	Pierluigi Martini	Minardi	Minardi-Ford Cosworth M195	59 laps	18
13	Gianni Morbidelli	Footwork	Footwork-Hart FA16	59 laps	11
14	Luca Badoer	Minardi	Minardi-Ford Cosworth M195	59 laps	20
NC	Roberto Moreno	Forti	Forti-Ford Cosworth FG01	56 laps	25
NC	Pedro Diniz	Forti	Forti-Ford Cosworth FG01	56 laps	26
R	Karl Wendlinger	Sauber	Sauber-Ford Cosworth C14	43 laps/wheel	21
R	Bertrand Gachot	Pacific	Pacific-Ford Cosworth PR02	36 laps/gearbox	22
R	Domenico Schiattarella	Simtek	Simtek-Ford Cosworth S951	35 laps/suspension	23
R	Rubens Barrichello	Jordan	Jordan-Peugeot 195	31 laps/transmission	10
R	Ukyo Katayama	Tyrrell	Tyrrell-Yamaha 023	23 laps/spun off	15
R	Mika Salo	Tyrrell	Tyrrell-Yamaha 023	19 laps/engine	13
R	Andrea Montermini	Pacific	Pacific-Ford Cosworth PR02	15 laps/gearbox	24
R	Jos Verstappen	Simtek	Simtek-Ford Cosworth S951	14 laps/gearbox	17
R	Taki Inoue	Footwork	Footwork-Hart FA16	12 laps/spun off	19
R	Michael Schumacher	Benetton	Benetton-Renault B195	10 laps/spun off	1

Pole: Schumacher, 1m27.274s, 125.464mph/201.915kph. Fastest lap: Berger, 1m29.568s, 122.251mph/196.744kph on Lap 57. Race leaders: Schumacher 1-9, Coulthard 10, Berger 11-21, Hill 22-63

SPANISH GRAND PRIX

BARCELONA-CATALUNYA • ROUND 4 • DATE: 14TH MAY 1995
Laps: 65 • Distance: 190.919miles/307.255km • Weather: Warm & bright

Pos	Driver	Team	Chassis-Engine	Result	Qual
1	Michael Schumacher	Benetton	Benetton-Renault B195	1h34m20.507s	1
2	Johnny Herbert	Benetton	Benetton-Renault B195	1h35m12.495s	7
3	Gerhard Berger	Ferrari	Ferrari 412T2	1h35m25.744s	3
4	Damon Hill	Williams	Williams-Renault FW17	1h36m22.256s	5
5	Eddie Irvine	Jordan	Jordan-Peugeot 195	64 laps	6
6	Olivier Panis	Ligier	Ligier-Mugen Honda JS41	64 laps	15
7	Rubens Barrichello	Jordan	Jordan-Peugeot 195	64 laps	8
8	Heinz-Harald Frentzen	Sauber	Sauber-Ford Cosworth C14	64 laps	12
9	Martin Brundle	Ligier	Ligier-Mugen Honda JS41	64 laps	11
10	Mika Salo	Tyrrell	Tyrrell-Yamaha 023	64 laps	13
11	Gianni Morbidelli	Footwork	Footwork-Hart FA16	63 laps	14
12	Jos Verstappen	Simtek	Simtek-Ford Cosworth S951	63 laps	16
13	Karl Wendlinger	Sauber	Sauber-Ford Cosworth C14	63 laps	20

Pos	Driver	Team	Chassis-Engine	Result	Qual
14	Pierluigi Martini	Minardi	Minardi-Ford Cosworth M195	62 laps	19
15	Domenico Schiattarella	Simtek	Simtek-Ford Cosworth S951	61 laps	22
R	Ukyo Katayama	Tyrrell	Tyrrell-Yamaha 023	56 laps/engine	17
R	David Coulthard	Williams	Williams-Renault FW17	54 laps/gearbox	4
R	Mika Hakkinen	McLaren	McLaren-Mercedes MP4/10	53 laps/fuel system	9
R	Taki Inoue	Footwork	Footwork-Hart FA16	43 laps/fire	18
R	Bertrand Gachot	Pacific	Pacific-Ford Cosworth PR02	43 laps/fire	24
R	Roberto Moreno	Forti	Forti-Ford Cosworth FG01	39 laps/overheating	25
R	Jean Alesi	Ferrari	Ferrari 412T2	25 laps/engine	2
R	Luca Badoer	Minardi	Minardi-Ford Cosworth M195	21 laps/gearbox	21
R	Nigel Mansell	McLaren	McLaren-Mercedes MP4/10	18 laps/handling	10
R	Pedro Diniz	Forti	Forti-Ford Cosworth FG01	17 laps/gearbox	26
NS	Andrea Montermini	Pacific	Pacific-Ford Cosworth PR02	gearbox	23

Pole: Schumacher, 1m21.452s, 129.818mph/208.923kph. Fastest lap: Hill, 1m24.531s, 125.090mph/201.313kph on Lap 46. Race leaders: Schumacher 1-65

MIKA'S LUCKY ESCAPE

Mika Hakkinen had a brush with death in Adelaide when his McLaren had a sudden deflation of its left rear tyre as he turned onto the Brabham Straight at 110mph (177kph) in the first qualifying session and was pitched into tyres in front of the surrounding wall. He survived only thanks to a tracheotomy performed by F1 doctor Sid Watkins.

MONACO GRAND PRIX

MONTE CARLO • ROUND 5 • DATE: 28TH MAY 1995
Laps: 78 • Distance: 161.298miles/259.584km • Weather: Warm & bright

Pos	Driver	Team	Chassis-Engine	Result	Qual
1	Michael Schumacher	Benetton	Benetton-Renault B195	1h53m11.258s	2
2	Damon Hill	Williams	Williams-Renault FW17	1h53m46.075s	1
3	Gerhard Berger	Ferrari	Ferrari 412T2	1h54m22.705s	4
4	Johnny Herbert	Benetton	Benetton-Renault B195	77 laps	7
5	Mark Blundell	McLaren	McLaren-Mercedes MP4/10B	77 laps	10
6	Heinz-Harald Frentzen	Sauber	Sauber-Ford Cosworth C14	76 laps	14
7	Pierluigi Martini	Minardi	Minardi-Ford Cosworth M195	76 laps	18
8	Jean-Christophe Boullion	Sauber	Sauber-Ford Cosworth C14	74 laps	19
9	Gianni Morbidelli	Footwork	Footwork-Hart FA16	74 laps	13
10	Pedro Diniz	Forti	Forti-Ford Cosworth FG01	72 laps	22
R	Luca Badoer	Minardi	Minardi-Ford Cosworth M195	68 laps/suspension	16
R	Olivier Panis	Ligier	Ligier-Mugen Honda JS41	65 laps/spun off	12
R	Mika Salo	Tyrrell	Tyrrell-Yamaha 023	63 laps/gearbox	17
R	Rubens Barrichello	Jordan	Jordan-Peugeot 195	60 laps/throttle	11
R	Bertrand Gachot	Pacific	Pacific-Ford Cosworth PR02	42 laps/gearbox	21
R	Jean Alesi	Ferrari	Ferrari 412T2	41 laps/spun off	5
R	Martin Brundle	Ligier	Ligier-Mugen Honda JS41	40 laps/spun off	8
R	Taki Inoue	Footwork	Footwork-Hart FA16	27 laps/gearbox	26
R	Ukyo Katayama	Tyrrell	Tyrrell-Yamaha 023	26 laps/spun off	15
DQ	Andrea Montermini	Pacific	Pacific-Ford Cosworth PR02	Ignored black flag	25
R	Eddie Irvine	Jordan	Jordan-Peugeot 195	22 laps/spun off	9

Pos	Driver	Team	Chassis-Engine	Result	Qual
R	David Coulthard	Williams	Williams-Renault FW17	16 laps/gearbox	3
R	Roberto Moreno	Forti	Forti-Ford Cosworth FG01	9 laps/brakes	24
R	Mika Hakkinen	McLaren	McLaren-Mercedes MP4/10B	8 laps/engine	6
R	Jos Verstappen	Simtek	Simtek-Ford Cosworth S951	0 laps/gearbox	23
R	Domenico Schiattarella	Simtek	Simtek-Ford Cosworth S951	0 laps/accident	20

Pole: Hill, 1m21.952s, 90.840mph/146.192kph. Fastest lap: Alesi, 1m24.621s, 87.974mph/141.581kph on Lap 36. Race leaders: Hill 1-23, Schumacher 24-35 & 37-78, Alesi 36

CANADIAN GRAND PRIX

MONTREAL • ROUND 6 • DATE: 11TH JUNE 1995
Laps: 68 • Distance: 187.47miles/301.24km • Weather: Warm but dull

Pos	Driver	Team	Chassis-Engine	Result	Qual
1	Jean Alesi	Ferrari	Ferrari 412T2	1h44m54.171s	5
2	Rubens Barrichello	Jordan	Jordan-Peugeot 195	1h45m25.648s	9
3	Eddie Irvine	Jordan	Jordan-Peugeot 195	1h45m30.151s	8
4	Olivier Panis	Ligier	Ligier-Mugen Honda JS41	1h45m35.485s	11
5	Michael Schumacher	Benetton	Benetton-Renault B195	1h45m38.847s	1
6	Gianni Morbidelli	Footwork	Footwork-Hart FA16	67 laps	13
7	Mika Salo	Tyrrell	Tyrrell-Yamaha 023	67 laps	15
8	Luca Badoer	Minardi	Minardi-Ford Cosworth M195	67 laps	19
9	Taki Inoue	Footwork	Footwork-Hart FA16	66 laps	22
10	Martin Brundle	Ligier	Ligier-Mugen Honda JS41	61 laps/collision	14
11	Gerhard Berger	Ferrari	Ferrari 412T2	61 laps/collision	4
R	Pierluigi Martini	Minardi	Minardi-Ford Cosworth M195	60 laps/throttle	17
R	Roberto Moreno	Forti	Forti-Ford Cosworth FG01	54 laps/fuel system	23
R	Damon Hill	Williams	Williams-Renault FW17	50 laps/gearbox	2
R	Mark Blundell	McLaren	McLaren-Mercedes MP4/10B	47 laps/engine	10
R	Ukyo Katayama	Tyrrell	Tyrrell-Yamaha 023	42 laps/engine	16
R	Bertrand Gachot	Pacific	Pacific-Ford Cosworth PR02	36 laps/battery	20
R	Heinz-Harald Frentzen	Sauber	Sauber-Ford Cosworth C14	26 laps/engine	12
R	Pedro Diniz	Forti	Forti-Ford Cosworth FG01	26 laps/gearbox	24
R	Jean-Christophe Boullion	Sauber	Sauber-Ford Cosworth C14	19 laps/spun off	18
R	Andrea Montermini	Pacific	Pacific-Ford Cosworth PR02	5 laps/gearbox	21
R	David Coulthard	Williams	Williams-Renault FW17	1 lap/spun off	3
R	Johnny Herbert	Benetton	Benetton-Renault B195	0 laps/collision	6
R	Mika Hakkinen	McLaren	McLaren-Mercedes MP4/10B	0 laps/collision	7

Pole: Schumacher, 1m27.661s, 113.044mph/181.928kph. Fastest lap: Schumacher, 1m29.174s, 111.126mph/178.841kph on Lap 67. Race leaders: Schumacher 1-57, Alesi 58-68

INOUE'S DOUBLE BAD LUCK

Japansese racer Taki Inoue had the most extraordinary of bad days when not only did his Footwork pull off early with engine failure in the Hungarian GP, but he was then knocked over by a course vehicle when he climbed out. Luckily, he escaped injury, and even grew to see the funny side of this sequence of events.

A BIG WIN, BUT FEW FINISHERS

The last grand prix held in Adelaide wasn't the greatest advertisement for F1 as the 1995 season came to a close. Damon Hill was a worthy winner for Williams but, in a race that had just eight of the 23 starters finishing after a string of accidents depleted the field, his winning margin of fully two laps over Olivier Panis's Ligier was bizarre.

FRENCH GRAND PRIX

MAGNY-COURS • ROUND 7 • DATE: 2ND JULY 1995
Laps: 72 • Distance: 190.139miles/306.0km • Weather: Warm but hazy

Pos	Driver	Team	Chassis-Engine	Result	Qual
1	Michael Schumacher	Benetton	Benetton-Renault B195	1h38m28.429s	2
2	Damon Hill	Williams	Williams-Renault FW17	1h38m59.738s	1
3	David Coulthard	Williams	Williams-Renault FW17	1h39m31.255s	3
4	Martin Brundle	Ligier	Ligier-Mugen Honda JS41	1h39m31.722s	9
5	Jean Alesi	Ferrari	Ferrari 412T2	1h39m46.298s	4
6	Rubens Barrichello	Jordan	Jordan-Peugeot 195	71 laps	5
7	Mika Hakkinen	McLaren	McLaren-Mercedes MP4/10B	71 laps	8
8	Olivier Panis	Ligier	Ligier-Mugen Honda JS41	71 laps	6
9	Eddie Irvine	Jordan	Jordan-Peugeot 195	71 laps	11
10	Heinz-Harald Frentzen	Sauber	Sauber-Ford Cosworth C14	71 laps	12
11	Mark Blundell	McLaren	McLaren-Mercedes MP4/10B	70 laps	13
12	Gerhard Berger	Ferrari	Ferrari 412T2	70 laps	7
13	Luca Badoer	Minardi	Minardi-Ford Cosworth M195	69 laps	17
14	Gianni Morbidelli	Footwork	Footwork-Hart FA16	69 laps	16
15	Mika Salo	Tyrrell	Tyrrell-Yamaha 023	69 laps	14
16	Roberto Moreno	Forti	Forti-Ford Cosworth FG01	66 laps	24
NC	Andrea Montermini	Pacific	Pacific-Ford Cosworth PR02	62 laps	21
R	Jean-Christophe Boullion	Sauber	Sauber-Ford Cosworth C14	48 laps/gearbox	15
R	Bertrand Gachot	Pacific	Pacific-Ford Cosworth PR02	24 laps/gearbox	22
R	Pierluigi Martini	Minardi	Minardi-Ford Cosworth M195	23 laps/gearbox	20
R	Johnny Herbert	Benetton	Benetton-Renault B195	2 laps/spun off	10
R	Taki Inoue	Footwork	Footwork-Hart FA16	0 laps/collision	18
R	Ukyo Katayama	Tyrrell	Tyrrell-Yamaha 023	0 laps/collision	19
R	Pedro Diniz	Forti	Forti-Ford Cosworth FG01	0 laps/spun off	23

Pole: Hill, 1m17.225s, 123.107mph/198.122kph. Fastest lap: Schumacher, 1m20.218s, 118.514mph/190.730kph on Lap 51. Race leaders: Hill 1-21, Schumacher 22-72

BRITISH GRAND PRIX

SILVERSTONE • ROUND 8 • DATE: 16TH JULY 1995
Laps: 61 • Distance: 191.678miles/308.477km • Weather: Warm but dull

Pos	Driver	Team	Chassis-Engine	Result	Qual
1	Johnny Herbert	Benetton	Benetton-Renault B195	1h34m35.093s	5
2	Jean Alesi	Ferrari	Ferrari 412T2	1h34m51.572s	6
3	David Coulthard	Williams	Williams-Renault FW17	1h34m58.981s	3
4	Olivier Panis	Ligier	Ligier-Mugen Honda JS41	1h36m08.261s	13
5	Mark Blundell	McLaren	McLaren-Mercedes MP4/10B	1h36m23.265s	10

Pos	Driver	Team	Chassis-Engine	Result	Qual
6	Heinz-Harald Frentzen	Sauber	Sauber-Ford Cosworth C14	60 laps	12
7	Pierluigi Martini	Minardi	Minardi-Ford Cosworth M195	60 laps	15
8	Mika Salo	Tyrrell	Tyrrell-Yamaha 023	60 laps	23
9	Jean-Christophe Boullion	Sauber	Sauber-Ford Cosworth C14	60 laps	16
10	Luca Badoer	Minardi	Minardi-Ford Cosworth M195	60 laps	18
11	Rubens Barrichello	Jordan	Jordan-Peugeot 195	59 laps/collision	9
12	Bertrand Gachot	Pacific	Pacific-Ford Cosworth PR02	58 laps	21
R	Roberto Moreno	Forti	Forti-Ford Cosworth FG01	48 laps/engine	22
R	Damon Hill	Williams	Williams-Renault FW17	45 laps/collision	1
R	Michael Schumacher	Benetton	Benetton-Renault B195	45 laps/collision	2
R	Massimiliano Papis	Footwork	Footwork-Hart FA16	28 laps/spun off	17
R	Ukyo Katayama	Tyrrell	Tyrrell-Yamaha 023	22 laps/out of fuel	14
R	Andrea Montermini	Pacific	Pacific-Ford Cosworth PR02	21 laps/spun off	24
R	Gerhard Berger	Ferrari	Ferrari 412T2	20 laps/wheel	4
R	Mika Hakkinen	McLaren	McLaren-Mercedes MP4/10B	20 laps/electrical	8
R	Martin Brundle	Ligier	Ligier-Mugen Honda JS41	16 laps/spun off	11
R	Taki Inoue	Footwork	Footwork-Hart FA16	16 laps/spun off	19
R	Pedro Diniz	Forti	Forti-Ford Cosworth FG01	13 laps/gearbox	20
R	Eddie Irvine	Jordan	Jordan-Peugeot 195	2 laps/electrical	7

Pole: Hill, 1m28.124s, 128.366mph/206.586kph. Fastest lap: Hill, 1m29.752s, 126.037mph/202.838kph on Lap 37. Race leaders: Hill 1-22 & 32-41, Schumacher 23-31 & 42-45, Herbert 46-48 & 51-61, Coulthard 49-50

GERMAN GRAND PRIX

HOCKENHEIM • ROUND 9 • DATE: 30TH JULY 1995
Laps: 45 • Distance: 190.782miles/307.035km • Weather: Hot & bright

Pos	Driver	Team	Chassis-Engine	Result	Qual
1	Michael Schumacher	Benetton	Benetton-Renault B195	1h22m56.043s	2
2	David Coulthard	Williams	Williams-Renault FW17	1h23m02.031s	3
3	Gerhard Berger	Ferrari	Ferrari 412T2	1h24m04.140s	4
4	Johnny Herbert	Benetton	Benetton-Renault B195	1h24m19.479s	9
5	Jean-Christophe Boullion	Sauber	Sauber-Ford Cosworth C14	44 laps	14
6	Aguri Suzuki	Ligier	Ligier-Mugen Honda JS41	44 laps	18
7	Ukyo Katayama	Tyrrell	Tyrrell-Yamaha 023	44 laps	17
8	Andrea Montermini	Pacific	Pacific-Ford Cosworth PR02	42 laps	23
9	Eddie Irvine	Jordan	Jordan-Peugeot 195	41 laps/engine	6
R	Mika Hakkinen	McLaren	McLaren-Mercedes MP4/10B	33 laps/engine	7
R	Heinz-Harald Frentzen	Sauber	Sauber-Ford Cosworth C14	32 laps/engine	11
R	Luca Badoer	Minardi	Minardi-Ford Cosworth M195	28 laps/oil leak	16
R	Roberto Moreno	Forti	Forti-Ford Cosworth FG01	27 laps/halfshaft	22
R	Giovanni Lavaggi	Pacific	Pacific-Ford Cosworth PR02	27 laps/gearbox	24
R	Rubens Barrichello	Jordan	Jordan-Peugeot 195	20 laps/engine	5
R	Mark Blundell	McLaren	McLaren-Mercedes MP4/10B	17 laps/engine	8
R	Olivier Panis	Ligier	Ligier-Mugen Honda JS41	13 laps/water leak	12
R	Jean Alesi	Ferrari	Ferrari 412T2	12 laps/engine	10
R	Pierluigi Martini	Minardi	Minardi-Ford Cosworth M195	11 laps/engine	20
R	Taki Inoue	Footwork	Footwork-Hart FA16	9 laps/gearbox	19
R	Pedro Diniz	Forti	Forti-Ford Cosworth FG01	8 laps/brakes	21
R	Damon Hill	Williams	Williams-Renault FW17	1 lap/spun off	1
R	Mika Salo	Tyrrell	Tyrrell-Yamaha 023	0 laps/clutch	13
R	Massimiliano Papis	Footwork	Footwork-Hart FA16	0 laps/gearbox	15

Pole: Hill, 1m44.385s, 146.214mph/235.309kph. Fastest lap: Schumacher, 1m48.824s, 140.250mph/225.711kph on Lap 22. Race leaders: Hill 1, Schumacher 2-19 & 24-45, Coulthard 20-23

HUNGARIAN GRAND PRIX

HUNGARORING • ROUND 10 • DATE: 13TH AUGUST 1995
Laps: 77 • Distance: 189.851miles/305.536km • Weather: Hot & bright

Pos	Driver	Team	Chassis-Engine	Result	Qual
1	Damon Hill	Williams	Williams-Renault FW17	1h46m25.721s	1
2	David Coulthard	Williams	Williams-Renault FW17	1h46m59.119s	2
3	Gerhard Berger	Ferrari	Ferrari 412T2	76 laps	4
4	Johnny Herbert	Benetton	Benetton-Renault B195	76 laps	9
5	Heinz-Harald Frentzen	Sauber	Sauber-Ford Cosworth C14	76 laps	11
6	Olivier Panis	Ligier	Ligier-Mugen Honda JS41	76 laps	10
7	Rubens Barrichello	Jordan	Jordan-Peugeot 195	76 laps	14
8	Luca Badoer	Minardi	Minardi-Ford Cosworth M195	75 laps	12
9	Pedro Lamy	Minardi	Minardi-Ford Cosworth M195	74 laps	15
10	Jean-Christophe Boullion	Sauber	Sauber-Ford Cosworth C14	74 laps	19
11	Michael Schumacher	Benetton	Benetton-Renault B195	73 laps/fuel pump	3
12	Andrea Montermini	Pacific	Pacific-Ford Cosworth PR02	73 laps	22
13	Eddie Irvine	Jordan	Jordan-Peugeot 195	70 laps/clutch	7
R	Martin Brundle	Ligier	Ligier-Mugen Honda JS41	67 laps/engine	8
R	Mika Salo	Tyrrell	Tyrrell-Yamaha 023	58 laps/throttle	16
R	Mark Blundell	McLaren	McLaren-Mercedes MP4/10B	54 laps/oil leak	13
R	Ukyo Katayama	Tyrrell	Tyrrell-Yamaha 023	46 laps/spun off	17
R	Massimiliano Papis	Footwork	Footwork-Hart FA16	45 laps/brakes	20
R	Jean Alesi	Ferrari	Ferrari 412T2	42 laps/engine	6
R	Pedro Diniz	Forti	Forti-Ford Cosworth FG01	32 laps/engine	23
R	Taki Inoue	Footwork	Footwork-Hart FA16	13 laps/engine	18
R	Roberto Moreno	Forti	Forti-Ford Cosworth FG01	8 laps/gearbox	21
R	Giovanni Lavaggi	Pacific	Pacific-Ford Cosworth PR02	5 laps/spun off	24
R	Mika Hakkinen	McLaren	McLaren-Mercedes MP4/10B	3 laps/engine	5

Pole: Hill, 1m16.982s, 115.301mph/185.560kph. Fastest lap: Hill, 1m20.247s, 110.610mph/178.010kph on Lap 34. Race leaders: Hill 1-77

NEW CIRCUITS

After 14 years away, Buenos Aires returned to the World Championship with a layout that cut out the run up to Curvon, and reduced the lap from 3.7 to 2.6 miles (5.9km to 4.2km). Not surprisingly, the 1994 disasters at Imola led to changes at the Italian circuit, with chicanes inserted at Tamburello and Villeneuve, while Piratella was tightened and Variante Bassa straightened.

BELGIAN GRAND PRIX

SPA-FRANCORCHAMPS • ROUND 11 • DATE: 27TH AUGUST 1995
Laps: 44 • Distance: 190.671miles/306.856km • Weather: Warm, rain later

Pos	Driver	Team	Chassis-Engine	Result	Qual
1	Michael Schumacher	Benetton	Benetton-Renault B195	1h36m47.875s	16
2	Damon Hill	Williams	Williams-Renault FW17	1h37m07.368s	8
3	Martin Brundle	Ligier	Ligier-Mugen Honda JS41	1h37m12.873s	13
4	Heinz-Harald Frentzen	Sauber	Sauber-Ford Cosworth C14	1h37m14.847s	10
5	Mark Blundell	McLaren	McLaren-Mercedes MP4/10B	1h37m21.647s	6
6	Rubens Barrichello	Jordan	Jordan-Peugeot 195	1h37m27.549s	12

Pos	Driver	Team	Chassis-Engine	Result	Qual
7	Johnny Herbert	Benetton	Benetton-Renault B195	1h37m41.923s	4
8	Mika Salo	Tyrrell	Tyrrell-Yamaha 023	1h37m42.423s	11
9	Olivier Panis	Ligier	Ligier-Mugen Honda JS41	1h37m54.045s	9
10	Pedro Lamy	Minardi	Minardi-Ford Cosworth M195	1h38m07.664s	17
11	Jean-Christophe Boullion	Sauber	Sauber-Ford Cosworth C14	43 laps	14
12	Taki Inoue	Footwork	Footwork-Hart FA16	43 laps	18
13	Pedro Diniz	Forti	Forti-Ford Cosworth FG01	42 laps	24
14	Roberto Moreno	Forti	Forti-Ford Cosworth FG01	42 laps	22
R	Ukyo Katayama	Tyrrell	Tyrrell-Yamaha 023	28 laps/spun off	15
R	Giovanni Lavaggi	Pacific	Pacific-Ford Cosworth PR02	27 laps/gearbox	23
R	Luca Badoer	Minardi	Minardi-Ford Cosworth M195	23 laps/spun off	19
R	Gerhard Berger	Ferrari	Ferrari 412T2	22 laps/electrical	1
R	Eddie Irvine	Jordan	Jordan-Peugeot 195	21 laps/fire	7
R	Massimiliano Papis	Footwork	Footwork-Hart FA16	20 laps/spun off	20
R	Andrea Montermini	Pacific	Pacific-Ford Cosworth PR02	18 laps/out of fuel	21
R	David Coulthard	Williams	Williams-Renault FW17	13 laps/gearbox	5
R	Jean Alesi	Ferrari	Ferrari 412T2	4 laps/suspension	2
R	Mika Hakkinen	McLaren	McLaren-Mercedes MP4/10B	1 lap/spun off	3

Pole: Berger, 1m54.392s, 136.376mph/219.476kph. Fastest lap: Coulthard, 1m53.412s, 137.554mph/221.373kph on Lap 11. Race leaders: Herbert 1 & 4-5, Alesi 2-3, Coulthard 6-13, Hill 14-15 & 19-21 & 24, Schumacher 16-18 & 22-23 & 25-44

NEW CONSTRUCTORS

After dominating Italian F3 and then competing in F3000, Guido Forti's eponymous team made it to F1 thanks to financial input from Pedro Diniz's father, a supermarket magnate. And here the success stopped, as neither Diniz nor fellow Brazilian Roberto Moreno could make the initially overweight FG01 finish higher than Diniz's ninth at Monza.

ITALIAN GRAND PRIX

MONZA • ROUND 12 • DATE: 10TH SEPTEMBER 1995
Laps: 53 • Distance: 189.568miles/305.81km • Weather: Warm & bright

Pos	Driver	Team	Chassis-Engine	Result	Qual
1	Johnny Herbert	Benetton	Benetton-Renault B195	1h18m27.916s	8
2	Mika Hakkinen	McLaren	McLaren-Mercedes MP4/10B	1h18m45.695s	7
3	Heinz-Harald Frentzen	Sauber	Sauber-Ford Cosworth C14	1h18m52.237s	10
4	Mark Blundell	McLaren	McLaren-Mercedes MP4/10B	1h18m56.139s	9
5	Mika Salo	Tyrrell	Tyrrell-Yamaha 023	52 laps	16
6	Jean-Christophe Boullion	Sauber	Sauber-Ford Cosworth C14	52 laps	14
7	Massimiliano Papis	Footwork	Footwork-Hart FA16	52 laps	15
8	Taki Inoue	Footwork	Footwork-Hart FA16	52 laps	20
9	Pedro Diniz	Forti	Forti-Ford Cosworth FG01	50 laps	23
10	Ukyo Katayama	Tyrrell	Tyrrell-Yamaha 023	47 laps	17
R	Jean Alesi	Ferrari	Ferrari 412T2	45 laps/wheel	5
R	Rubens Barrichello	Jordan	Jordan-Peugeot 195	43 laps/clutch	6
R	Eddie Irvine	Jordan	Jordan-Peugeot 195	40 laps/engine	12

Pos	Driver	Team	Chassis-Engine	Result	Qual
R	Gerhard Berger	Ferrari	Ferrari 412T2	32 laps/suspension	3
R	Luca Badoer	Minardi	Minardi-Ford Cosworth M195	26 laps/spun off	18
R	Michael Schumacher	Benetton	Benetton-Renault B195	23 laps/collision	2
R	Damon Hill	Williams	Williams-Renault FW17	23 laps/collision	4
R	Olivier Panis	Ligier	Ligier-Mugen Honda JS41	20 laps/spun off	13
R	David Coulthard	Williams	Williams-Renault FW17	13 laps/spun off	1
R	Martin Brundle	Ligier	Ligier-Mugen Honda JS41	10 laps/puncture	11
R	Giovanni Lavaggi	Pacific	Pacific-Ford Cosworth PR02	6 laps/spun off	24
R	Pedro Lamy	Minardi	Minardi-Ford Cosworth M195	0 laps/transmission	19
R	Andrea Montermini	Pacific	Pacific-Ford Cosworth PR02	0 laps/accident	21
R	Roberto Moreno	Forti	Forti-Ford Cosworth FG01	0 laps/accident	22

Pole: Coulthard, 1m24.462s, 152.815mph/245.933kph. Fastest lap: Berger, 1m26.419s, 149.354mph/240.363kph on Lap 24. Race leaders: Coulthard 1-13, Berger 14-24, Alesi 25 & 30-45, Barrichello 26, Hakkinen 27, Herbert 28-29 & 46-53

NEW DRIVERS

Outperforming Forti's novice Diniz, Jean-Christophe Boullion achieved the best result of any of the five rookies, coming home fifth for Sauber in the German GP. Max Papis did next best, with seventh for Footwork at Monza, while Jan Magnussen raced once for McLaren and finished 10th. Giovanni Lavaggi started but never finished for Pacific.

PORTUGUESE GRAND PRIX

AUTODROMO DO ESTORIL • ROUND 13 • DATE: 24TH SEPTEMBER 1995
Laps: 71 • Distance: 192.38miles/309.56km • Weather: Warm & bright

Pos	Driver	Team	Chassis-Engine	Result	Qual
1	David Coulthard	Williams	Williams-Renault FW17	1h41m52.145s	1
2	Michael Schumacher	Benetton	Benetton-Renault B195	1h41m59.393s	3
3	Damon Hill	Williams	Williams-Renault FW17	1h42m14.266s	2
4	Gerhard Berger	Ferrari	Ferrari 412T2	1h43m17.024s	4
5	Jean Alesi	Ferrari	Ferrari 412T2	1h43m17.574s	7
6	Heinz-Harald Frentzen	Sauber	Sauber-Ford Cosworth C14	70 laps	5
7	Johnny Herbert	Benetton	Benetton-Renault B195	70 laps	6
8	Martin Brundle	Ligier	Ligier-Mugen Honda JS41	70 laps	9
9	Mark Blundell	McLaren	McLaren-Mercedes MP4/10C	70 laps	12
10	Eddie Irvine	Jordan	Jordan-Peugeot 195	70 laps	10
11	Rubens Barrichello	Jordan	Jordan-Peugeot 195	70 laps	8
12	Jean-Christophe Boullion	Sauber	Sauber-Ford Cosworth C14	70 laps	14
13	Mika Salo	Tyrrell	Tyrrell-Yamaha 023	69 laps	15
14	Luca Badoer	Minardi	Minardi-Ford Cosworth M195	68 laps	18
15	Taki Inoue	Footwork	Footwork-Hart FA16	68 laps	19
16	Pedro Diniz	Forti	Forti-Ford Cosworth FG01	66 laps	22
17	Roberto Moreno	Forti	Forti-Ford Cosworth FG01	64 laps	23
R	Andrea Montermini	Pacific	Pacific-Ford Cosworth PR02	53 laps/gearbox	21
R	Mika Hakkinen	McLaren	McLaren-Mercedes MP4/10B	44 laps/engine	13
R	Jean-Denis Deletraz	Pacific	Pacific-Ford Cosworth PR02	14 laps/cramp	24

Pos	Driver	Team	Chassis-Engine	Result	Qual
R	Olivier Panis	Ligier	Ligier-Mugen Honda JS41	10 laps/spun off	11
R	Pedro Lamy	Minardi	Minardi-Ford Cosworth M195	7 laps/gearbox	17
R	Ukyo Katayama	Tyrrell	Tyrrell-Yamaha 023	0 laps/collision	16
R	Massimiliano Papis	Footwork	Footwork-Hart FA16	0 laps/gearbox	20

Pole: Coulthard, 1m20.537s, 121.100mph/194.891kph. Fastest lap: Coulthard, 1m23.220s, 117.195mph/188.608kph on Lap 2. Race leaders: Coulthard 1-38 & 44-71, Hill 39-43

EUROPEAN GRAND PRIX

NURBURGRING • ROUND 14 • DATE: 1ST OCTOBER 1995
Laps: 67 • Distance: 189.674miles/305.252km • Weather: Cool & damp

Pos	Driver	Team	Chassis-Engine	Result	Qual
1	Michael Schumacher	Benetton	Benetton-Renault B195	1h39m59.044s	3
2	Jean Alesi	Ferrari	Ferrari 412T2	1h40m01.728s	6
3	David Coulthard	Williams	Williams-Renault FW17B	1h40m34.426s	1
4	Rubens Barrichello	Jordan	Jordan-Peugeot 195	66 laps	11
5	Johnny Herbert	Benetton	Benetton-Renault B195	66 laps	7
6	Eddie Irvine	Jordan	Jordan-Peugeot 195	66 laps	5
7	Martin Brundle	Ligier	Ligier-Mugen Honda JS41	66 laps	12
8	Mika Hakkinen	McLaren	McLaren-Mercedes MP4/10C	65 laps	9
9	Pedro Lamy	Minardi	Minardi-Ford Cosworth M195	64 laps	16
10	Mika Salo	Tyrrell	Tyrrell-Yamaha 023	64 laps	15
11	Luca Badoer	Minardi	Minardi-Ford Cosworth M195	64 laps	18
12	Massimiliano Papis	Footwork	Footwork-Hart FA16	64 laps	17
13	Pedro Diniz	Forti	Forti-Ford Cosworth FG01	62 laps	22
14	Gabriele Tarquini	Tyrrell	Tyrrell-Yamaha 023	61 laps	19
15	Jean-Denis Deletraz	Pacific	Pacific-Ford Cosworth PR02	60 laps	24
R	Damon Hill	Williams	Williams-Renault FW17B	58 laps/spun off	2
R	Andrea Montermini	Pacific	Pacific-Ford Cosworth PR02	45 laps/out of fuel	20
R	Jean-Christophe Boullion	Sauber	Sauber-Ford Cosworth C14	44 laps/collision	13
R	Gerhard Berger	Ferrari	Ferrari 412T2	40 laps/electrical	4
R	Roberto Moreno	Forti	Forti-Ford Cosworth FG01	22 laps/halfshaft	23
R	Heinz-Harald Frentzen	Sauber	Sauber-Ford Cosworth C14	17 laps/spun off	8
R	Mark Blundell	McLaren	McLaren-Mercedes MP4/10C	14 laps/accident	10
R	Olivier Panis	Ligier	Ligier-Mugen Honda JS41	14 laps/spun off	14
R	Taki Inoue	Footwork	Footwork-Hart FA16	0 laps/electrical	21

Pole: Coulthard, 1m18.738s, 129.435mph/208.306kph. Fastest lap: Schumacher, 1m21.180s, 125.541mph/202.039kph on Lap 57. Race leaders: Coulthard 1-12, Alesi 13-64, Schumacher 65-67

PACIFIC GRAND PRIX

TI CIRCUIT • ROUND 15 • DATE: 22ND OCTOBER 1995
Laps: 83 • Distance: 190.977miles/307.349km • Weather: Warm & bright

Pos	Driver	Team	Chassis-Engine	Result	Qual
1	Michael Schumacher	Benetton	Benetton-Renault B195	1h48m49.972s	3
2	David Coulthard	Williams	Williams-Renault FW17B	1h49m04.892s	1
3	Damon Hill	Williams	Williams-Renault FW17B	1h49m38.305s	2
4	Gerhard Berger	Ferrari	Ferrari 412T2	82 laps	5
5	Jean Alesi	Ferrari	Ferrari 412T2	82 laps	4
6	Johnny Herbert	Benetton	Benetton-Renault B195	82 laps	7
7	Heinz-Harald Frentzen	Sauber	Sauber-Ford Cosworth C14	82 laps	8

Pos	Driver	Team	Chassis-Engine	Result	Qual
8	Olivier Panis	Ligier	Ligier-Mugen Honda JS41	81 laps	9
9	Mark Blundell	McLaren	McLaren-Mercedes MP4/10B	81 laps	10
10	Jan Magnussen	McLaren	McLaren-Mercedes MP4/10B	81 laps	12
11	Eddie Irvine	Jordan	Jordan-Peugeot 195	81 laps	6
12	Mika Salo	Tyrrell	Tyrrell-Yamaha 023	80 laps	18
13	Pedro Lamy	Minardi	Minardi-Ford Cosworth M195	80 laps	14
14	Ukyo Katayama	Tyrrell	Tyrrell-Yamaha 023	80 laps	17
15	Luca Badoer	Minardi	Minardi-Ford Cosworth M195	80 laps	16
16	Roberto Moreno	Forti	Forti-Ford Cosworth FG01	78 laps	22
17	Pedro Diniz	Forti	Forti-Ford Cosworth FG01	77 laps	21
R	Rubens Barrichello	Jordan	Jordan-Peugeot 195	67 laps/electrical	11
R	Gianni Morbidelli	Footwork	Footwork-Hart FA16	63 laps/engine	19
R	Taki Inoue	Footwork	Footwork-Hart FA16	38 laps/electrical	20
R	Andrea Montermini	Pacific	Pacific-Ford Cosworth PR02	14 laps/gearbox	23
R	Aguri Suzuki	Ligier	Ligier-Mugen Honda JS41	10 laps/spun off	13
R	Jean-Christophe Boullion	Sauber	Sauber-Ford Cosworth C14	7 laps/spun off	15
R	Bertrand Gachot	Pacific	Pacific-Ford Cosworth PR02	2 laps/gearbox	24

Pole: Coulthard, 1m14.013s, 111.917mph/180.114kph. Fastest lap: Schumacher, 1m16.374s, 108.457mph/174.546kph on Lap 40. Race leaders: Coulthard 1-49, Schumacher 50-83

JAPANESE GRAND PRIX

SUZUKA • ROUND 16 • DATE: 29TH OCTOBER 1995
Laps: 53 • Distance: 193.117miles/310.792km • Weather: Cool & wet, drying later

Pos	Driver	Team	Chassis-Engine	Result	Qual
1	Michael Schumacher	Benetton	Benetton-Renault B195	1h36m52.930s	1
2	Mika Hakkinen	McLaren	McLaren-Mercedes MP4/10B	1h37m12.267s	3
3	Johnny Herbert	Benetton	Benetton-Renault B195	1h38m16.734s	9
4	Eddie Irvine	Jordan	Jordan-Peugeot 195	1h38m35.066s	7
5	Olivier Panis	Ligier	Ligier-Mugen Honda JS41	52 laps	11
6	Mika Salo	Tyrrell	Tyrrell-Yamaha 023	52 laps	12
7	Mark Blundell	McLaren	McLaren-Mercedes MP4/10B	52 laps	24
8	Heinz-Harald Frentzen	Sauber	Sauber-Ford Cosworth C14	52 laps	8
9	Luca Badoer	Minardi	Minardi-Ford Cosworth M195	51 laps	17
10	Karl Wendlinger	Sauber	Sauber-Ford Cosworth C14	51 laps	15
11	Pedro Lamy	Minardi	Minardi-Ford Cosworth M195	51 laps	16
12	Taki Inoue	Footwork	Footwork-Hart FA16	51 laps	18
R	Damon Hill	Williams	Williams-Renault FW17B	40 laps/spun off	4
R	David Coulthard	Williams	Williams-Renault FW17B	39 laps/spun off	6
R	Pedro Diniz	Forti	Forti-Ford Cosworth FG01	32 laps/spun off	20
R	Jean Alesi	Ferrari	Ferrari 412T2	24 laps/transmission	2
R	Andrea Montermini	Pacific	Pacific-Ford Cosworth PR02	23 laps/spun off	19
R	Gerhard Berger	Ferrari	Ferrari 412T2	16 laps/electrical	5
R	Rubens Barrichello	Jordan	Jordan-Peugeot 195	15 laps/spun off	10
R	Ukyo Katayama	Tyrrell	Tyrrell-Yamaha 023	12 laps/spun off	14
R	Bertrand Gachot	Pacific	Pacific-Ford Cosworth PR02	6 laps/halfshaft	23
R	Roberto Moreno	Forti	Forti-Ford Cosworth FG01	1 lap/gearbox	22
R	Gianni Morbidelli	Footwork	Footwork-Hart FA16	0 laps/spun off	15
NS	Aguri Suzuki	Ligier	Ligier-Mugen Honda JS41	Accident	13

Pole: Schumacher, 1m38.023s, 133.819mph/215.361kph. Fastest lap: Schumacher, 1m42.976s, 127.382mph/205.003kph on Lap 33. Race leaders: Schumacher 1-10 & 12-31 & 36-53, Hakkinen 11, Hill 32-35

AUSTRALIAN GRAND PRIX

ADELAIDE • ROUND 17 • DATE: 12TH NOVEMBER 1995
Laps: 81 • Distance: 190.150miles/306.18km • Weather: Warm & bright

Pos	Driver	Team	Chassis-Engine	Result	Qual
1	Damon Hill	Williams	Williams-Renault FW17B	1h49m15.946s	1
2	Olivier Panis	Ligier	Ligier-Mugen Honda JS41	79 laps	12
3	Gianni Morbidelli	Footwork	Footwork-Hart FA16	79 laps	13
4	Mark Blundell	McLaren	McLaren-Mercedes MP4/10B	79 laps	10
5	Mika Salo	Tyrrell	Tyrrell-Yamaha 023	78 laps	14
6	Pedro Lamy	Minardi	Minardi-Ford Cosworth M195	78 laps	17
7	Pedro Diniz	Forti	Forti-Ford Cosworth FG01	77 laps	21
8	Bertrand Gachot	Pacific	Pacific-Ford Cosworth PR02	76 laps	23
R	Ukyo Katayama	Tyrrell	Tyrrell-Yamaha 023	70 laps/engine	16
R	Johnny Herbert	Benetton	Benetton-Renault B195	69 laps/transmission	8
R	Eddie Irvine	Jordan	Jordan-Peugeot 195	62 laps/engine	9
R	Heinz-Harald Frentzen	Sauber	Sauber-Ford Cosworth C14	39 laps/gearbox	6
R	Gerhard Berger	Ferrari	Ferrari 412T2	34 laps/engine	4
R	Martin Brundle	Ligier	Ligier-Mugen Honda JS41	29 laps/spun off	11
R	Michael Schumacher	Benetton	Benetton-Renault B195	25 laps/collision	3
R	Jean Alesi	Ferrari	Ferrari 412T2	23 laps/collision	5
R	Roberto Moreno	Forti	Forti-Ford Cosworth FG01	21 laps/spun off	20
R	Rubens Barrichello	Jordan	Jordan-Peugeot 195	20 laps/spun off	7
R	David Coulthard	Williams	Williams-Renault FW17B	19 laps/spun off	2
R	Taki Inoue	Footwork	Footwork-Hart FA16	15 laps/spun off	19
R	Karl Wendlinger	Sauber	Sauber-Ford Cosworth C14	8 laps/physical	18
R	Andrea Montermini	Pacific	Pacific-Ford Cosworth PR02	2 laps/gearbox	22
NS	Luca Badoer	Minardi	Minardi-Ford Cosworth M195	Electrical	15
NS	Mika Hakkinen	McLaren	McLaren-Mercedes MP4/10B	Driver injured	24

Pole: Hill, 1m15.505s, 111.987mph/180.226kph. Fastest lap: Hill, 1m17.943s, 108.484mph/174.589kph on Lap 16. Race leaders: Coulthard 1-19, Schumacher 20-21, Hill 22-81

CLASSIC ENGINE: RENAULT V10

The first Renault F1 engine was the RS01 that introduced turbocharging in 1977. However, the French marque's greatest F1 engines were used by other teams, with Nigel Mansell using a RS03 in 1992 to take the first of three consecutive constructors' titles for Williams. The RS07 was built to the new 3000cc maximum capacity for 1995, and this 67-degree V10 was used by both Williams and their chief rivals, Benetton. It pushed out 675bhp at 15,200rpm and won every race bar one. Becoming more confident in pushing it harder, the RS08 that was used by Williams to land the 1996 title pushed out 700bhp at 16,000rpm.

WORLD DRIVERS' CHAMPIONSHIP FINAL RESULTS

Pos	Driver	Nat	Car-Engine	R1	R2	R3	R4	R5	R6
1	Michael Schumacher	DEU	Benetton-Renault B195	1F	3F	RP	1P	1	5PF
2	Damon Hill	GBR	Williams-Renault FW17	RP	1	1	4F	2P	R
			Williams-Renault FW17B	-	-	-	-	-	-
3	David Coulthard	GBR	Williams-Renault FW17	2	RP	4	R	R	R
			Williams-Renault FW17B	-	-	-	-	-	-
4	Johnny Herbert	GBR	Benetton-Renault B195	R	4	7	2	4	R
5	Jean Alesi	FRA	Ferrari 412T2	5	2	2	R	RF	1
6	Gerhard Berger	AUT	Ferrari 412T2	3	6	3F	3	3	11
7	Mika Hakkinen	FIN	McLaren-Mercedes MP4/10	4	R	5	R	-	-
			McLaren-Mercedes MP4/10B	-	-	-	-	R	R
			McLaren-Mercedes MP4/10C	-	-	-	-	-	-
8	Olivier Panis	FRA	Ligier-Mugen Honda JS41	R	7	9	6	R	4
9	Heinz-Harald Frentzen	DEU	Sauber-Ford Cosworth C14	R	5	6	8	6	R
10	Mark Blundell	GBR	McLaren-Mercedes MP4/10	6	R	-	-	-	-
			McLaren-Mercedes MP4/10B	-	-	-	-	5	R
			McLaren-Mercedes MP4/10C	-	-	-	-	-	-
11	Rubens Barrichello	BRA	Jordan-Peugeot 195	R	R	R	7	R	2
12	Eddie Irvine	GBR	Jordan-Peugeot 195	R	R	8	5	R	3
13	Martin Brundle	GBR	Ligier-Mugen Honda JS41	-	-	-	9	R	10
14	Gianni Morbidelli	ITA	Footwork-Hart FA16	R	R	13	11	9	6
15	Mika Salo	FIN	Tyrrell-Yamaha 023	7	R	R	10	R	7
16	Jean-Christophe Boullion	FRA	Sauber-Ford Cosworth C14	-	-	-	-	8	R
17	Aguri Suzuki	JPN	Ligier-Mugen Honda JS41	8	R	11	-	-	-
17	Pedro Lamy	PRT	Minardi-Ford Cosworth M195	-	-	-	-	-	-

Pos	Driver	R7	R8	R9	R10	R11	R12	R13	R14	R15	R16	R17	Total
1	Schumacher	1F	R	1F	11	1	R	2	1F	1F	1PF	R	102
2	Hill	2P	RPF	RP	1PF	2	R	3	-	-	-	-	69
		-	-	-	-	-	-	-	R	3	R	1PF	
3	Coulthard	3	3	2	2	RF	RP	1PF	-	-	-	-	49
		-	-	-	-	-	-	-	3P	2P	R	R	
4	Herbert	R	1	4	4	7	1	7	5	6	3	R	45
5	Alesi	5	2	R	R	R	R	5	2	5	R	R	42
6	Berger	12	R	3	3	RP	RF	4	R	4	R	R	31
7	Hakkinen	-	-	-	-	-	-	-	-	-	-	-	17
		7	R	R	R	R	2	R	-	-	2	NS	
		-	-	-	-	-	-	-	8	-	-	-	
8	Panis	8	4	R	6	9	R	R	R	8	5	2	16
9	Frentzen	10	6	R	5	4	3	6	R	7	8	R	15
10	Blundell	-	-	-	-	-	-	-	-	-	-	-	13
		11	5	R	R	5	4	-	-	9	7	4	
		-	-	-	-	-	-	9	R	-	-	-	
11	Barrichello	6	11	R	7	6	R	11	4	R	R	R	11
12	Irvine	9	R	9	13	R	R	10	6	11	4	R	10
13	Brundle	4	R	-	R	3	R	8	7	-	-	R	7
14	Morbidelli	14	-	-	-	-	-	-	-	R	R	3	5
15	Salo	15	8	R	R	8	5	13	10	12	6	5	5
16	Boullion	R	9	5	10	11	6	12	R	R	-	-	3
17	Suzuki	-	-	6	-	-	-	-	-	R	NS	-	1
17	Lamy	-	-	-	9	10	R	R	9	13	11	6	1

WORLD CONSTRUCTORS' CHAMPIONSHIP FINAL RESULTS

Pos	Team-Engine	R1	R2	R3	R4	R5	R6	R7	R8	R9
1	Benetton-Renault	1/R	3/4	7/R	1/2	1/4	5/R	1/R	1/R	1/4
2	Williams-Renault	2/R	1/R	1/4	4/R	2/R	R/R	2/3	3/R	2/R
3	Ferrari	3/5	2/6	2/3	3/R	3/R	1/11	5/12	2/R	3/R
4	McLaren-Mercedes	4/6	R/R	5/10	R/R	5/R	R/R	7/11	5/R	R/R
5	Ligier-Mugen Honda	8/R	7/R	9/11	6/9	R/R	4/10	4/8	4/R	6/R
6	Jordan-Peugeot	R/R	R/R	8/R	5/7	R/R	2/3	6/9	11/R	9/R
7	Sauber-Ford	R/R	5/R	6/R	8/13	6/8	R/R	10/R	6/9	5/R
8	Footwork-Hart	R/R	R/R	13/R	11/R	9/R	6/9	14/R	R/R	R/R
9	Tyrrell-Yamaha	7/R	8/R	R/R	10/R	R/R	7/R	15/R	8/R	7/R
10	Minardi-Ford	R/R	R/NS	12/14	14/R	7/R	8/R	13/R	7/10	R/R

Pos	Team-Engine	R10	R11	R12	R13	R14	R15	R16	R17	Total
1	Benetton-Renault	4/11	1/7	1/R	2/7	1/5	1/6	1/3	R/R	137
2	Williams-Renault	1/2	2/R	R/R	1/3	3/R	2/3	R/R	1/R	112
3	Ferrari	3/R	R/R	R/R	4/5	2/R	4/5	R/R	R/R	73
4	McLaren-Mercedes	R/R	5/R	2/4	9/R	8/R	9/10	2/7	4/NS	30
5	Ligier-Mugen Honda	6/R	3/9	R/R	8/R	7/R	8/R	5/NS	2/R	24
6	Jordan-Peugeot	7/13	6/R	R/R	10/11	4/6	11/R	4/R	R/R	21
7	Sauber-Ford	5/10	4/11	3/6	6/12	R/R	7/R	8/10	R/R	18
8	Footwork-Hart	R/R	12/R	7/8	15/R	12/R	R/R	12/R	3/R	5
9	Tyrrell-Yamaha	R/R	8/R	5/10	13/R	10/14	12/14	6/R	5/R	5
10	Minardi-Ford	8/9	10/R	R/R	14/R	9/11	13/15	9/11	6/R	1

SYMBOLS AND GRAND PRIX KEY

Round 1 Brazilian GP
Round 2 Argentinian GP
Round 3 San Marino GP
Round 4 Spanish GP
Round 5 Monaco GP
Round 6 Canadian GP
Round 7 French GP
Round 8 British GP
Round 9 German GP
Round 10 Hungarian GP
Round 11 Belgian GP
Round 12 Italian GP
Round 13 Portuguese GP
Round 14 European GP
Round 15 Pacific GP
Round 16 Japanese GP
Round 17 Australian GP

SCORING

1st 10 points
2nd 6 points
3rd 4 points
4th 3 points
5th 2 points
6th 1 point

DNPQ DID NOT PRE-QUALIFY **DNQ** DID NOT QUALIFY **DQ** DISQUALIFIED **EX** EXCLUDED
F FASTEST LAP **NC** NOT CLASSIFIED **NS** NON-STARTER **P** POLE POSITION **R** RETIRED

1996

SEASON SUMMARY

Damon Hill became the first second-generation world champion by winning the F1 title for Williams. Sadly, his father Graham, world champion in 1962 and 1968, wasn't around to witness this historic moment, having been killed in a light aircraft crash in late 1975. Hill not only had to outperform Michael Schumacher – although that wasn't too hard as the reigning champion had moved to Ferrari – but his own team-mate too, as Jacques Villeneuve proved competitive in his first year in F1. Benetton missed Schumacher and slipped to third overall, as neither Jean Alesi nor Gerhard Berger managed to win a race.

AUSTRALIAN GRAND PRIX

ALBERT PARK • ROUND 1 • DATE: 10TH MARCH 1996
Laps: 58 • Distance: 191.81miles/307.516km • Weather: Warm & bright

Pos	Driver	Team	Chassis-Engine	Result	Qual
1	Damon Hill	Williams	Williams-Renault FW18	1h32m50.491s	2
2	Jacques Villeneuve	Williams	Williams-Renault FW18	1h33m28.511s	1
3	Eddie Irvine	Ferrari	Ferrari F310	1h33m53.062s	3
4	Gerhard Berger	Benetton	Benetton-Renault B196	1h34m07.528s	7
5	Mika Hakkinen	McLaren	McLaren-Mercedes MP4/11	1h34m25.562s	5
6	Mika Salo	Tyrrell	Tyrrell-Yamaha 024	57 laps	10
7	Olivier Panis	Ligier	Ligier-Mugen Honda JS43	57 laps	11
8	Heinz-Harald Frentzen	Sauber	Sauber-Ford Cosworth C15	57 laps	9
9	Ricardo Rosset	Footwork	Footwork-Hart FA17	56 laps	18
10	Pedro Diniz	Ligier	Ligier-Mugen Honda JS43	56 laps	20
11	Ukyo Katayama	Tyrrell	Tyrrell-Yamaha 024	55 laps	15
R	Pedro Lamy	Minardi	Minardi-Ford Cosworth M195B	42 laps/safety belt	17
R	Michael Schumacher	Ferrari	Ferrari F310	32 laps/brakes	4
R	Giancarlo Fisichella	Minardi	Minardi-Ford Cosworth M195B	32 laps/clutch	16
R	Rubens Barrichello	Jordan	Jordan-Peugeot 196	29 laps/engine	8
R	David Coulthard	McLaren	McLaren-Mercedes MP4/11	24 laps/throttle	13
R	Jos Verstappen	Footwork	Footwork-Hart FA17	15 laps/engine	12
R	Jean Alesi	Benetton	Benetton-Renault B196	9 laps/collision	6
R	Martin Brundle	Jordan	Jordan-Peugeot 196	1 lap/spun off	19
R	Johnny Herbert	Sauber	Sauber-Ford Cosworth C15	Crash damage	14
DNQ	Luca Badoer	Forti	Forti-Ford Cosworth FG01B	-	21
DNQ	Andrea Montermini	Forti	Forti-Ford Cosworth FG01B	-	22

Pole: Villeneuve, 1m32.371s, 128.397mph/206.636kph. Fastest lap: Villeneuve, 1m33.421s, 126.954mph/204.313kph on Lap 27. Race leaders: Villeneuve 1-29 & 33-53, Hill 30-32 & 54-58

ALMOST THE PERFECT START

Jacques Villeneuve took pole and almost won on his debut for Williams at the Australian GP. The Canadian arrived as IndyCar champion and had clearly learned well in pre-season testing, as he was right on the pace of team-mate Damon Hill, but his oil pressure fell and so he dropped to second. He won the fourth round, then added three more.

BRAZILIAN GRAND PRIX

INTERLAGOS • ROUND 2 • DATE: 31ST MARCH 1996
Laps: 71 • Distance: 190.807miles/307.075km • Weather: Heavy rain, drying later

Pos	Driver	Team	Chassis-Engine	Result	Qual
1	Damon Hill	Williams	Williams-Renault FW18	1h49m52.976s	1
2	Jean Alesi	Benetton	Benetton-Renault B196	1h50m10.958s	5
3	Michael Schumacher	Ferrari	Ferrari F310	70 laps	4
4	Mika Hakkinen	McLaren	McLaren-Mercedes MP4/11	70 laps	7
5	Mika Salo	Tyrrell	Tyrrell-Yamaha 024	70 laps	11
6	Olivier Panis	Ligier	Ligier-Mugen Honda JS43	70 laps	15
7	Eddie Irvine	Ferrari	Ferrari F310	70 laps	10
8	Pedro Diniz	Ligier	Ligier-Mugen Honda JS43	69 laps	22
9	Ukyo Katayama	Tyrrell	Tyrrell-Yamaha 024	69 laps	16
10	Pedro Lamy	Minardi	Minardi-Ford Cosworth M195B	68 laps	18
11	Luca Badoer	Forti	Forti-Ford Cosworth FG01B	67 laps	19
12	Martin Brundle	Jordan	Jordan-Peugeot 196	64 laps/spun off	6
R	Rubens Barrichello	Jordan	Jordan-Peugeot 196	59 laps/spun off	2
R	Heinz-Harald Frentzen	Sauber	Sauber-Ford Cosworth C15	36 laps/engine	9
R	David Coulthard	McLaren	McLaren-Mercedes MP4/11	29 laps/spun off	14
R	Johnny Herbert	Sauber	Sauber-Ford Cosworth C15	28 laps/engine	12
R	Jacques Villeneuve	Williams	Williams-Renault FW18	26 laps/spun off	3
R	Gerhard Berger	Benetton	Benetton-Renault B196	26 laps/hydraulics	8
R	Andrea Montermini	Forti	Forti-Ford Cosworth FG01B	26 laps/spun off	20
R	Ricardo Rosset	Footwork	Footwork-Hart FA17	24 laps/spun off	17
R	Jos Verstappen	Footwork	Footwork-Hart FA17	19 laps/engine	13
R	Tarso Marques	Minardi	Minardi-Ford Cosworth M195B	0 laps/spun off	21

Pole: Hill, 1m18.111s, 123.858mph/199.331kph. Fastest lap: Hill, 1m21.547s, 118.640mph/190.932kph on Lap 65. Race leaders: Hill 1-39 & 43-71, Alesi 40-42

WALKING ON WATER

Michael Schumacher joined Ferrari and suggested a revival of the Italian team's fortunes when he got it back to winning ways by the seventh round at Spain's Barcelona circuit. The race was held in atrociously wet conditions that highlighted his exceptional driving skills rather than any merits of the F310 chassis. He also won in the dry at Spa-Francorchamps and Monza.

ARGENTINIAN GRAND PRIX

BUENOS AIRES • ROUND 3 • DATE: 7TH APRIL 1996
Laps: 72 • Distance: 190.542miles/306.648km • Weather: Warm & bright

Pos	Driver	Team	Chassis-Engine	Result	Qual
1	Damon Hill	Williams	Williams-Renault FW18	1h54m55.322s	1
2	Jacques Villeneuve	Williams	Williams-Renault FW18	1h55m07.489s	3
3	Jean Alesi	Benetton	Benetton-Renault B196	1h55m10.076s	4
4	Rubens Barrichello	Jordan	Jordan-Peugeot 196	1h55m50.453s	6
5	Eddie Irvine	Ferrari	Ferrari F310	1h56m00.313s	10
6	Jos Verstappen	Footwork	Footwork-Hart FA17	1h56m04.235s	7
7	David Coulthard	McLaren	McLaren-Mercedes MP4/11	1h56m08.722s	9

Pos	Driver	Team	Chassis-Engine	Result	Qual
8	Olivier Panis	Ligier	Ligier-Mugen Honda JS43	1h56m09.617s	12
9	Johnny Herbert	Sauber	Sauber-Ford Cosworth C15	71 laps	17
10	Andrea Montermini	Forti	Forti-Ford Cosworth FG01B	69 laps	22
R	Gerhard Berger	Benetton	Benetton-Renault B196	56 laps/suspension	5
R	Michael Schumacher	Ferrari	Ferrari F310	46 laps/wing	2
R	Pedro Lamy	Minardi	Minardi-Ford Cosworth M195B	39 laps/transmission	19
R	Mika Salo	Tyrrell	Tyrrell-Yamaha 024	36 laps/throttle	16
R	Martin Brundle	Jordan	Jordan-Peugeot 196	34 laps/collision	15
R	Tarso Marques	Minardi	Minardi-Ford Cosworth M195B	33 laps/collision	14
R	Heinz-Harald Frentzen	Sauber	Sauber-Ford Cosworth C15	32 laps/spun off	11
R	Pedro Diniz	Ligier	Ligier-Mugen Honda JS43	29 laps/fire	18
R	Ukyo Katayama	Tyrrell	Tyrrell-Yamaha 024	28 laps/transmission	13
R	Ricardo Rosset	Footwork	Footwork-Hart FA17	24 laps/fuel pump	20
R	Luca Badoer	Forti	Forti-Ford Cosworth FG01B	24 laps/collision	21
R	Mika Hakkinen	McLaren	McLaren-Mercedes MP4/11	19 laps/throttle	8

Pole: Hill, 1m30.346s, 105.451mph/169.707kph. Fastest lap: Alesi, 1m29.413s, 106.551mph/171.478kph on Lap 66. Race leaders: Hill 1-72

F1'S RINGLEADER

Bernie Ecclestone had his first involvement in F1 back in 1958 when he tried to qualify a Connaught at Monaco. From then on, it was all about management, first of drivers and then with team ownership of Brabham from 1972. His commercial acumen led to him becoming CEO of the teams' association in 1978, and he remained as F1's supremo until 2017.

EUROPEAN GRAND PRIX

NURBURGRING • ROUND 4 • DATE: 28TH APRIL 1996
Laps: 67 • Distance: 189.674miles/305.252km • Weather: Warm but dull

Pos	Driver	Team	Chassis-Engine	Result	Qual
1	Jacques Villeneuve	Williams	Williams-Renault FW18	1h33m26.473s	2
2	Michael Schumacher	Ferrari	Ferrari F310	1h33m27.235s	3
3	David Coulthard	McLaren	McLaren-Mercedes MP4/11	1h33m59.307s	6
4	Damon Hill	Williams	Williams-Renault FW18	1h33m59.984s	1
5	Rubens Barrichello	Jordan	Jordan-Peugeot 196	1h34m00.186s	5
6	Martin Brundle	Jordan	Jordan-Peugeot 196	1h34m22.040s	11
7	Johnny Herbert	Sauber	Sauber-Ford Cosworth C15	1h34m44.500s	12
8	Mika Hakkinen	McLaren	McLaren-Mercedes MP4/11	1h34m44.911s	9
9	Gerhard Berger	Benetton	Benetton-Renault B196	1h34m47.534s	8
DQ	Mika Salo	Tyrrell	Tyrrell-Yamaha 024	66 laps/underweight	14
10	Pedro Diniz	Ligier	Ligier-Mugen Honda JS43	66 laps	17
DQ	Ukyo Katayama	Tyrrell	Tyrrell-Yamaha 024	65 laps/push start	16
11	Ricardo Rosset	Footwork	Footwork-Hart FA17	65 laps	20
12	Pedro Lamy	Minardi	Minardi-Ford Cosworth M195B	65 laps	19
13	Giancarlo Fisichella	Minardi	Minardi-Ford Cosworth M195B	65 laps	18
R	Heinz-Harald Frentzen	Sauber	Sauber-Ford Cosworth C15	59 laps/brakes	10
R	Jos Verstappen	Footwork	Footwork-Hart FA17	38 laps/engine	13
R	Eddie Irvine	Ferrari	Ferrari F310	6 laps/electrical	7

Pos	Driver	Team	Chassis-Engine	Result	Qual
R	Olivier Panis	Ligier	Ligier-Mugen Honda JS43	6 laps/collision	15
R	Jean Alesi	Benetton	Benetton-Renault B196	1 lap/collision	4
DNQ	Andrea Montermini	Forti	Forti-Ford Cosworth FG01B	-	21
DNQ	Luca Badoer	Forti	Forti-Ford Cosworth FG01B	-	22

Pole: Hill, 1m18.941s, 129.102mph/207.770kph. Fastest lap: Hill, 1m21.363s, 125.259mph/201.585kph on Lap 55. Race leaders: Villeneuve 1-67

SAN MARINO GRAND PRIX

IMOLA • ROUND 5 • DATE: 5TH MAY 1996
Laps: 63 • Distance: 191.504miles/308.196km • Weather: Warm & bright

Pos	Driver	Team	Chassis-Engine	Result	Qual
1	Damon Hill	Williams	Williams-Renault FW18	1h35m26.156s	2
2	Michael Schumacher	Ferrari	Ferrari F310	1h35m42.616s	1
3	Gerhard Berger	Benetton	Benetton-Renault B196	1h36m13.047s	7
4	Eddie Irvine	Ferrari	Ferrari F310	1h36m27.739s	6
5	Rubens Barrichello	Jordan	Jordan-Peugeot 196	1h36m44.646s	9
6	Jean Alesi	Benetton	Benetton-Renault B196	62 laps	5
7	Pedro Diniz	Ligier	Ligier-Mugen Honda JS43	62 laps	17
8	Mika Hakkinen	McLaren	McLaren-Mercedes MP4/11	61 laps/engine	11
9	Pedro Lamy	Minardi	Minardi-Ford Cosworth M195B	61 laps	18
10	Luca Badoer	Forti	Forti-Ford Cosworth FG03	59 laps	21
11	Jacques Villeneuve	Williams	Williams-Renault FW18	57 laps/suspension	3
R	Olivier Panis	Ligier	Ligier-Mugen Honda JS43	54 laps/engine	13
R	Ukyo Katayama	Tyrrell	Tyrrell-Yamaha 024	45 laps/spun off	16
R	David Coulthard	McLaren	McLaren-Mercedes MP4/11	44 laps/hydraulics	4
R	Ricardo Rosset	Footwork	Footwork-Hart FA17	40 laps/engine	20
R	Jos Verstappen	Footwork	Footwork-Hart FA17	38 laps/fuelling error	14
R	Martin Brundle	Jordan	Jordan-Peugeot 196	36 laps/spun off	12
R	Heinz-Harald Frentzen	Sauber	Sauber-Ford Cosworth C15	32 laps/brakes	10
R	Giancarlo Fisichella	Minardi	Minardi-Ford Cosworth M195B	30 laps/engine	19
R	Johnny Herbert	Sauber	Sauber-Ford Cosworth C15	25 laps/electrical	15
R	Mika Salo	Tyrrell	Tyrrell-Yamaha 024	23 laps/engine	8
DNQ	Andrea Montermini	Forti	Forti-Ford Cosworth FG03	-	22

Pole: Schumacher, 1m26.890s, 125.941mph/202.683kph. Fastest lap: Hill, 1m28.931s, 123.051mph/198.032kph on Lap 49. Race leaders: Coulthard 1-19, Schumacher 20, Hill 21-63

WILLIAMS'S REVOLVING DOOR POLICY

Williams dropped another champion in 1996. This time, it was Damon Hill, who found out his fate as early in the season as the end of July, when rumours strengthened that Heinz-Harald Frentzen had signed a contract to be his replacement for 1997. That Hill was leading the title race at the time showed how Williams thought others might lead by more.

PERSEVERANCE PAYS OFF

To win at Monaco, you need to start at the front. That Olivier Panis won was most unexpected, as he started his Ligier from 14th. However, when pole-sitter Schumacher crashed on lap one, it set the tone. Hill retired from the lead, and then so did Alesi's Benetton. Panis came through changeable conditions for the first F1 success for the French team since 1981.

MONACO GRAND PRIX

MONTE CARLO • ROUND 6 • DATE: 19TH MAY 1996
Laps: 75 • Distance: 154.725miles/249.6km • Weather: Warm & wet, drying later

Pos	Driver	Team	Chassis-Engine	Result	Qual
1	Olivier Panis	Ligier	Ligier-Mugen Honda JS43	2h00m45.629s	14
2	David Coulthard	McLaren	McLaren-Mercedes MP4/11	2h00m50.457s	5
3	Johnny Herbert	Sauber	Sauber-Ford Cosworth C15	2h01m23.132s	13
4	Heinz-Harald Frentzen	Sauber	Sauber-Ford Cosworth C15	74 laps	9
5	Mika Salo	Tyrrell	Tyrrell-Yamaha 024	70 laps/collision	11
6	Mika Hakkinen	McLaren	McLaren-Mercedes MP4/11	70 laps/collision	8
7	Eddie Irvine	Ferrari	Ferrari F310	68 laps/collision	7
R	Jacques Villeneuve	Williams	Williams-Renault FW18	66 laps/collision	10
R	Jean Alesi	Benetton	Benetton-Renault B196	60 laps/suspension	3
R	Luca Badoer	Forti	Forti-Ford Cosworth FG03	60 laps/collision	21
R	Damon Hill	Williams	Williams-Renault FW18	40 laps/engine	2
R	Martin Brundle	Jordan	Jordan-Peugeot 196	30 laps/spun off	16
R	Gerhard Berger	Benetton	Benetton-Renault B196	9 laps/gearbox	4
R	Pedro Diniz	Ligier	Ligier-Mugen Honda JS43	5 laps/transmission	17
R	Ricardo Rosset	Footwork	Footwork-Hart FA17	3 laps/spun off	20
R	Ukyo Katayama	Tyrrell	Tyrrell-Yamaha 024	2 laps/spun off	15
R	Michael Schumacher	Ferrari	Ferrari F310	0 laps/spun off	1
R	Rubens Barrichello	Jordan	Jordan-Peugeot 196	0 laps/spun off	6
R	Jos Verstappen	Footwork	Footwork-Hart FA17	0 laps/spun off	12
R	Giancarlo Fisichella	Minardi	Minardi-Ford Cosworth M195B	0 laps/collision	18
R	Pedro Lamy	Minardi	Minardi-Ford Cosworth M195B	0 laps/collision	19
NS	Andrea Montermini	Forti	Forti-Ford Cosworth FG03	Accident	22

Pole: Schumacher, 1m20.356s, 92.644mph/149.096kph. Fastest lap: Alesi, 1m25.205s, 87.371mph/140.611kph on Lap 59. Race leaders: Hill 1-27 & 30-40, Alesi 28-29 & 41-59, Panis 60-75

SPANISH GRAND PRIX

BARCELONA-CATALUNYA • ROUND 7 • DATE: 2ND JUNE 1996
Laps: 65 • Distance: 190.919miles/307.255km • Weather: Warm but heavy rain

Pos	Driver	Team	Chassis-Engine	Result	Qual
1	Michael Schumacher	Ferrari	Ferrari F310	1h59m49.307s	3
2	Jean Alesi	Benetton	Benetton-Renault B196	2h00m34.609s	4
3	Jacques Villeneuve	Williams	Williams-Renault FW18	2h00m37.695s	2
4	Heinz-Harald Frentzen	Sauber	Sauber-Ford Cosworth C15	64 laps	11
5	Mika Hakkinen	McLaren	McLaren-Mercedes MP4/11	64 laps	10
6	Pedro Diniz	Ligier	Ligier-Mugen Honda JS43	63 laps	17
R	Jos Verstappen	Footwork	Footwork-Hart FA17	47 laps/spun off	13

Pos	Driver	Team	Chassis-Engine	Result	Qual
R	Rubens Barrichello	Jordan	Jordan-Peugeot 196	45 laps/differential	7
R	Gerhard Berger	Benetton	Benetton-Renault B196	44 laps/spun off	5
R	Johnny Herbert	Sauber	Sauber-Ford Cosworth C15	20 laps/spun off	9
R	Martin Brundle	Jordan	Jordan-Peugeot 196	17 laps/differential	15
DQ	Mika Salo	Tyrrell	Tyrrell-Yamaha 024	16 laps/used spare car	12
R	Damon Hill	Williams	Williams-Renault FW18	10 laps/spun off	1
R	Ukyo Katayama	Tyrrell	Tyrrell-Yamaha 024	8 laps/electrical	16
R	Eddie Irvine	Ferrari	Ferrari F310	1 lap/spun off	6
R	Olivier Panis	Ligier	Ligier-Mugen Honda JS43	1 lap/collision	8
R	Giancarlo Fisichella	Minardi	Minardi-Ford Cosworth M195B	1 lap/collision	19
R	David Coulthard	McLaren	McLaren-Mercedes MP4/11	0 laps/collision	14
R	Pedro Lamy	Minardi	Minardi-Ford Cosworth M195B	0 laps/collision	18
R	Ricardo Rosset	Footwork	Footwork-Hart FA17	0 laps/collision	20
DNQ	Luca Badoer	Forti	Forti-Ford Cosworth FG03	-	21
DNQ	Andrea Montermini	Forti	Forti-Ford Cosworth FG03	-	22

Pole: Hill, 1m20.650s, 131.109mph/211.000kph. Fastest lap: Schumacher, 1m45.517s, 100.211mph/161.274kph on Lap 14. Race leaders: Villeneuve 1-11, Schumacher 12-65

SWAPPING WITH SCHUMACHER

Jean Alesi moved to Benetton after five years at Ferrari, with Schumacher moving in the opposite direction. Although he failed to take a win, Alesi ended the year as the team's better-placed driver by outscoring Gerhard Berger, 47 points to 21. This was good enough for him to rank fourth, thanks to coming second in Brazil, Spain, Germany and Italy.

CANADIAN GRAND PRIX

MONTREAL • ROUND 8 • DATE: 16TH JUNE 1996
Laps: 69 • Distance: 189.548miles/305.049km • Weather: Warm & bright

Pos	Driver	Team	Chassis-Engine	Result	Qual
1	Damon Hill	Williams	Williams-Renault FW18	1h36m03.465s	1
2	Jacques Villeneuve	Williams	Williams-Renault FW18	1h36m07.648s	2
3	Jean Alesi	Benetton	Benetton-Renault B196	1h36m58.121s	4
4	David Coulthard	McLaren	McLaren-Mercedes MP4/11	1h37m07.138s	10
5	Mika Hakkinen	McLaren	McLaren-Mercedes MP4/11	68 laps	6
6	Martin Brundle	Jordan	Jordan-Peugeot 196	68 laps	9
7	Johnny Herbert	Sauber	Sauber-Ford Cosworth C15	68 laps	15
8	Giancarlo Fisichella	Minardi	Minardi-Ford Cosworth M195B	67 laps	16
R	Pedro Lamy	Minardi	Minardi-Ford Cosworth M195B	44 laps/collision	19
R	Luca Badoer	Forti	Forti-Ford Cosworth FG03	44 laps/gearbox	20
R	Gerhard Berger	Benetton	Benetton-Renault B196	42 laps/spun off	7
R	Michael Schumacher	Ferrari	Ferrari F310	41 laps/halfshaft	3
R	Olivier Panis	Ligier	Ligier-Mugen Honda JS43	39 laps/engine	11
R	Mika Salo	Tyrrell	Tyrrell-Yamaha 024	39 laps/engine	14
R	Pedro Diniz	Ligier	Ligier-Mugen Honda JS43	38 laps/engine	18
R	Rubens Barrichello	Jordan	Jordan-Peugeot 196	22 laps/clutch	8
R	Andrea Montermini	Forti	Forti-Ford Cosworth FG03	22 laps/electrical	22
R	Heinz-Harald Frentzen	Sauber	Sauber-Ford Cosworth C15	19 laps/gearbox	12

Pos	Driver	Team	Chassis-Engine	Result	Qual
R	Jos Verstappen	Footwork	Footwork-Hart FA17	10 laps/engine	13
R	Ukyo Katayama	Tyrrell	Tyrrell-Yamaha 024	6 laps/collision	17
R	Ricardo Rosset	Footwork	Footwork-Hart FA17	6 laps/collision	21
R	Eddie Irvine	Ferrari	Ferrari F310	1 lap/suspension	5

Pole: Hill, 1m21.059s, 122.003mph/196.345kph. Fastest lap: Villeneuve, 1m21.916s, 120.727mph/194.291kph on Lap 67. Race leaders: Hill 1-27 & 36-69, Villeneuve 28-35

FRENCH GRAND PRIX

MAGNY-COURS • ROUND 9 • DATE: 30TH JUNE 1996
Laps: 72 • Distance: 190.139miles/306.0km • Weather: Warm & bright

Pos	Driver	Team	Chassis-Engine	Result	Qual
1	Damon Hill	Williams	Williams-Renault FW18	1h36m28.795s	2
2	Jacques Villeneuve	Williams	Williams-Renault FW18	1h36m36.922s	6
3	Jean Alesi	Benetton	Benetton-Renault B196	1h37m15.237s	3
4	Gerhard Berger	Benetton	Benetton-Renault B196	1h37m15.654s	4
5	Mika Hakkinen	McLaren	McLaren-Mercedes MP4/11	1h37m31.569s	5
6	David Coulthard	McLaren	McLaren-Mercedes MP4/11	71 laps	7
7	Olivier Panis	Ligier	Ligier-Mugen Honda JS43	71 laps	9
8	Martin Brundle	Jordan	Jordan-Peugeot 196	71 laps	8
9	Rubens Barrichello	Jordan	Jordan-Peugeot 196	71 laps	10
10	Mika Salo	Tyrrell	Tyrrell-Yamaha 024	70 laps	13
DQ	Johnny Herbert	Sauber	Sauber-Ford Cosworth C15	70 laps/deflectors	16
11	Ricardo Rosset	Footwork	Footwork-Hart FA17	69 laps	19
12	Pedro Lamy	Minardi	Minardi-Ford Cosworth M195B	69 laps	18
R	Heinz-Harald Frentzen	Sauber	Sauber-Ford Cosworth C15	56 laps/throttle	12
R	Ukyo Katayama	Tyrrell	Tyrrell-Yamaha 024	33 laps/engine	14
R	Luca Badoer	Forti	Forti-Ford Cosworth FG03	29 laps/fuel system	20
R	Pedro Diniz	Ligier	Ligier-Mugen Honda JS43	28 laps/engine	11
R	Jos Verstappen	Footwork	Footwork-Hart FA17	10 laps/steering	15
R	Eddie Irvine	Ferrari	Ferrari F310	5 laps/gearbox	22
R	Giancarlo Fisichella	Minardi	Minardi-Ford Cosworth M195B	2 laps/fuel pump	17
R	Andrea Montermini	Forti	Forti-Ford Cosworth FG03	2 laps/electrical	21
NS	Michael Schumacher	Ferrari	Ferrari F310	Engine	1

Pole: Schumacher, 1m15.989s, 125.109mph/201.344kph. Fastest lap: Villeneuve, 1m18.610s, 120.938mph/194.631kph on Lap 48. Race leaders: Hill 1-27 & 31-72, Villeneuve 28-30

FINNS ARE GETTING BETTER

Mika Hakkinen assumed the upper hand at McLaren over the incoming David Coulthard, proving that he had bounced back from the injuries he suffered at Adelaide at the end of 1995. With improving power from Mercedes, the Finn finished third in four races, each time on one of F1's classic circuits, namely Silverstone, Spa-Francorchamps, Monza and Suzuka.

BRITISH GRAND PRIX

SILVERSTONE • ROUND 10 • DATE: 14TH JULY 1996
Laps: 61 • Distance: 192.247miles/309.392km • Weather: Hot & bright

Pos	Driver	Team	Chassis-Engine	Result	Qual
1	Jacques Villeneuve	Williams	Williams-Renault FW18	1h33m00.874s	2
2	Gerhard Berger	Benetton	Benetton-Renault B196	1h33m19.900s	7
3	Mika Hakkinen	McLaren	McLaren-Mercedes MP4/11	1h33m51.704s	4
4	Rubens Barrichello	Jordan	Jordan-Peugeot 196	1h34m07.590s	6
5	David Coulthard	McLaren	McLaren-Mercedes MP4/11	1h34m23.381s	9
6	Martin Brundle	Jordan	Jordan-Peugeot 196	60 laps	8
7	Mika Salo	Tyrrell	Tyrrell-Yamaha 024	60 laps	14
8	Heinz-Harald Frentzen	Sauber	Sauber-Ford Cosworth C15	60 laps	11
9	Johnny Herbert	Sauber	Sauber-Ford Cosworth C15	60 laps	13
10	Jos Verstappen	Footwork	Footwork-Hart FA17	60 laps	15
11	Giancarlo Fisichella	Minardi	Minardi-Ford Cosworth M195B	59 laps	18
R	Jean Alesi	Benetton	Benetton-Renault B196	44 laps/brakes	5
R	Olivier Panis	Ligier	Ligier-Mugen Honda JS43	40 laps/handling	16
R	Pedro Diniz	Ligier	Ligier-Mugen Honda JS43	38 laps/engine	17
R	Damon Hill	Williams	Williams-Renault FW18	26 laps/wheel	1
R	Pedro Lamy	Minardi	Minardi-Ford Cosworth M195B	21 laps/gearbox	19
R	Ricardo Rosset	Footwork	Footwork-Hart FA17	13 laps/electrical	20
R	Ukyo Katayama	Tyrrell	Tyrrell-Yamaha 024	12 laps/engine	12
R	Eddie Irvine	Ferrari	Ferrari F310	5 laps/differential	10
R	Michael Schumacher	Ferrari	Ferrari F310	3 laps/hydraulics	3
DNQ	Andrea Montermini	Forti	Forti-Ford Cosworth FG03	-	21
DNQ	Luca Badoer	Forti	Forti-Ford Cosworth FG03	-	22

Pole: Hill, 1m26.875s, 130.598mph/210.177kph. Fastest lap: Villeneuve, 1m29.288s, 127.069mph/204.497kph on Lap 21. Race leaders: Villeneuve 1-23 & 31-61, Alesi 24-30

A NEW WAY TO ADVANCE

F3000, the final step on the single-seater ladder before F1, had a new look for 1996, as it no longer entertained battles between manufacturers but became a "spec" formula, with all of the cars built by Lola and powered by Zytek engines. Jorg Muller was crowned after clashing with Kenny Brack in the final round. Unusually, neither would go on to F1.

GERMAN GRAND PRIX

HOCKENHEIM • ROUND 11 • DATE: 28TH JULY 1996
Laps: 45 • Distance: 190.782miles/307.035km • Weather: Warm & bright

Pos	Driver	Team	Chassis-Engine	Result	Qual
1	Damon Hill	Williams	Williams-Renault FW18	1h21m43.417s	1
2	Jean Alesi	Benetton	Benetton-Renault B196	1h21m54.869s	5
3	Jacques Villeneuve	Williams	Williams-Renault FW18	1h22m17.343s	6
4	Michael Schumacher	Ferrari	Ferrari F310	1h22m24.934s	3
5	David Coulthard	McLaren	McLaren-Mercedes MP4/11	1h22m25.613s	7
6	Rubens Barrichello	Jordan	Jordan-Peugeot 196	1h23m25.516s	9
7	Olivier Panis	Ligier	Ligier-Mugen Honda JS43	1h23m27.329s	12
8	Heinz-Harald Frentzen	Sauber	Sauber-Ford Cosworth C15	44 laps	13

Pos	Driver	Team	Chassis-Engine	Result	Qual
9	Mika Salo	Tyrrell	Tyrrell-Yamaha 024	44 laps	15
10	Martin Brundle	Jordan	Jordan-Peugeot 196	44 laps	10
11	Ricardo Rosset	Footwork	Footwork-Hart FA17	44 laps	19
12	Pedro Lamy	Minardi	Minardi-Ford Cosworth M195B	43 laps	18
13	Gerhard Berger	Benetton	Benetton-Renault B196	42 laps/engine	2
R	Eddie Irvine	Ferrari	Ferrari F310	34 laps/engine	8
R	Johnny Herbert	Sauber	Sauber-Ford Cosworth C15	25 laps/vibrations	14
R	Pedro Diniz	Ligier	Ligier-Mugen Honda JS43	19 laps/engine	11
R	Ukyo Katayama	Tyrrell	Tyrrell-Yamaha 024	19 laps/spun off	16
R	Mika Hakkinen	McLaren	McLaren-Mercedes MP4/11	13 laps/gearbox	4
R	Jos Verstappen	Footwork	Footwork-Hart FA17	0 laps/collision	17
DNQ	Giovanni Lavaggi	Minardi	Minardi-Ford Cosworth M195B	-	20

Pole: Hill, 1m43.912s, 146.880mph/236.380kph. Fastest lap: Hill, 1m46.504s, 143.305mph/230.627kph on Lap 26. Race leaders: Berger 1-23 & 35-42, Hill 24-34 & 43-45

HUNGARIAN GRAND PRIX

HUNGARORING • ROUND 12 • DATE: 11TH AUGUST 1996
Laps: 77 • Distance: 189.851miles/305.536km • Weather: Warm & bright

Pos	Driver	Team	Chassis-Engine	Result	Qual
1	Jacques Villeneuve	Williams	Williams-Renault FW18	1h46m21.134s	3
2	Damon Hill	Williams	Williams-Renault FW18	1h46m21.905s	2
3	Jean Alesi	Benetton	Benetton-Renault B196	1h47m45.346s	5
4	Mika Hakkinen	McLaren	McLaren-Mercedes MP4/11	76 laps	7
5	Olivier Panis	Ligier	Ligier-Mugen Honda JS43	76 laps	11
6	Rubens Barrichello	Jordan	Jordan-Peugeot 196	75 laps	13
7	Ukyo Katayama	Tyrrell	Tyrrell-Yamaha 024	74 laps	14
8	Ricardo Rosset	Footwork	Footwork-Hart FA17	74 laps	18
9	Michael Schumacher	Ferrari	Ferrari F310	70 laps/throttle	1
10	Giovanni Lavaggi	Minardi	Minardi-Ford Cosworth M195B	69 laps/spun off	20
R	Gerhard Berger	Benetton	Benetton-Renault B196	64 laps/engine	6
R	Heinz-Harald Frentzen	Sauber	Sauber-Ford Cosworth C15	50 laps/electrical	10
R	Johnny Herbert	Sauber	Sauber-Ford Cosworth C15	35 laps/engine	8
R	Eddie Irvine	Ferrari	Ferrari F310	31 laps/gearbox	4
R	Pedro Lamy	Minardi	Minardi-Ford Cosworth M195B	24 laps/suspension	19
R	David Coulthard	McLaren	McLaren-Mercedes MP4/11	23 laps/engine	9
R	Jos Verstappen	Footwork	Footwork-Hart FA17	10 laps/spun off	17
R	Martin Brundle	Jordan	Jordan-Peugeot 196	5 laps/spun off	12
R	Pedro Diniz	Ligier	Ligier-Mugen Honda JS43	1 lap/collision	15
R	Mika Salo	Tyrrell	Tyrrell-Yamaha 024	0 laps/collision	16

Pole: Schumacher, 1m17.129s, 115.082mph/185.206kph. Fastest lap: Hill, 1m20.093s, 110.823mph/178.352kph on Lap 67. Race leaders: Schumacher 1-18, Villeneuve 19-21 & 25-58 & 64-77, Hill 22-24 & 59-63

NEW CIRCUITS

Melbourne had hosted Australian grands prix in Albert Park in 1953 and 1956, but they were non-championship affairs, and the city had to wait until it had wrested the race from Adelaide to take its World Championship bow. The track was laid out around a lake and alongside a golf course in the city's Albert Park, just a short tram ride from the city centre.

BELGIAN GRAND PRIX

SPA-FRANCORCHAMPS • ROUND 13 • DATE: 25TH AUGUST 1996
Laps: 44 • Distance: 190.507miles/306.592km • Weather: Warm & bright

Pos	Driver	Team	Chassis-Engine	Result	Qual
1	Michael Schumacher	Ferrari	Ferrari F310	1h28m15.125s	3
2	Jacques Villeneuve	Williams	Williams-Renault FW18	1h28m20.727s	1
3	Mika Hakkinen	McLaren	McLaren-Mercedes MP4/11	1h28m30.835s	6
4	Jean Alesi	Benetton	Benetton-Renault B196	1h28m34.250s	7
5	Damon Hill	Williams	Williams-Renault FW18	1h28m44.304s	2
6	Gerhard Berger	Benetton	Benetton-Renault B196	1h28m45.021s	5
7	Mika Salo	Tyrrell	Tyrrell-Yamaha 024	1h29m15.879s	13
8	Ukyo Katayama	Tyrrell	Tyrrell-Yamaha 024	1h29m55.352s	17
9	Ricardo Rosset	Footwork	Footwork-Hart FA17	43 laps	18
10	Pedro Lamy	Minardi	Minardi-Ford Cosworth M195B	43 laps	19
R	David Coulthard	McLaren	McLaren-Mercedes MP4/11	37 laps/spun off	4
R	Martin Brundle	Jordan	Jordan-Peugeot 196	34 laps/engine	8
R	Eddie Irvine	Ferrari	Ferrari F310	29 laps/gearbox	9
R	Rubens Barrichello	Jordan	Jordan-Peugeot 196	29 laps/suspension	10
R	Pedro Diniz	Ligier	Ligier-Mugen Honda JS43	22 laps/electrical	15
R	Jos Verstappen	Footwork	Footwork-Hart FA17	11 laps/spun off	16
R	Heinz-Harald Frentzen	Sauber	Sauber-Ford Cosworth C15	0 laps/collision	11
R	Johnny Herbert	Sauber	Sauber-Ford Cosworth C15	0 laps/collision	12
R	Olivier Panis	Ligier	Ligier-Mugen Honda JS43	0 laps/collision	14
DNQ	Giovanni Lavaggi	Minardi	Minardi-Ford Cosworth M195B	-	20

Pole: Villeneuve, 1m50.574s, 140.964mph/226.859kph. Fastest lap: Berger, 1m53.067s, 137.856mph/221.857kph on Lap 42. Race leaders: Villeneuve 1-14 & 30-32, Coulthard 15-21, Hakkinen 22-23, Schumacher 24-29 & 33-44

NEW DRIVERS

While Jacques Villeneuve made an instant impact, Giancarlo Fisichella was the best of 1996's other three F1 novices, finishing eighth in Canada for Minardi before being replaced by a paying driver. Ricardo Rosset did a full season with Footwork, peaking with eighth in Hungary, while fellow Brazilian Tarso Marques retired twice in two races for Minardi.

ITALIAN GRAND PRIX

MONZA • ROUND 14 • DATE: 8TH SEPTEMBER 1996
Laps: 53 • Distance: 189.568miles/305.81km • Weather: Hot & bright

Pos	Driver	Team	Chassis-Engine	Result	Qual
1	Michael Schumacher	Ferrari	Ferrari F310	1h17m43.632s	3
2	Jean Alesi	Benetton	Benetton-Renault B196	1h18m01.897s	6
3	Mika Hakkinen	McLaren	McLaren-Mercedes MP4/11	1h18m50.267s	4
4	Martin Brundle	Jordan	Jordan-Peugeot 196	1h19m08.849s	9
5	Rubens Barrichello	Jordan	Jordan-Peugeot 196	1h19m09.107s	10
6	Pedro Diniz	Ligier	Ligier-Mugen Honda JS43	52 laps	14
7	Jacques Villeneuve	Williams	Williams-Renault FW18	52 laps	2
8	Jos Verstappen	Footwork	Footwork-Hart FA17	52 laps	15

Pos	Driver	Team	Chassis-Engine	Result	Qual
9	Johnny Herbert	Sauber	Sauber-Ford Cosworth C15	51 laps/engine	12
10	Ukyo Katayama	Tyrrell	Tyrrell-Yamaha 024	51 laps	16
R	Ricardo Rosset	Footwork	Footwork-Hart FA17	36 laps/spun off	19
R	Eddie Irvine	Ferrari	Ferrari F310	23 laps/spun off	7
R	Pedro Lamy	Minardi	Minardi-Ford Cosworth M195B	12 laps/engine	18
R	Mika Salo	Tyrrell	Tyrrell-Yamaha 024	9 laps/engine	17
R	Heinz-Harald Frentzen	Sauber	Sauber-Ford Cosworth C15	7 laps/spun off	13
R	Damon Hill	Williams	Williams-Renault FW18	5 laps/spun off	1
R	Giovanni Lavaggi	Minardi	Minardi-Ford Cosworth M195B	5 laps/engine	20
R	Gerhard Berger	Benetton	Benetton-Renault B196	4 laps/hydraulics	8
R	Olivier Panis	Ligier	Ligier-Mugen Honda JS43	2 laps/spun off	11
R	David Coulthard	McLaren	McLaren-Mercedes MP4/11	1 lap/spun off	5

Pole: Hill, 1m24.204s, 153.283mph/246.686kph. Fastest lap: Schumacher, 1m26.110s, 149.891mph/241.226kph on Lap 50. Race leaders: Hill 1-5, Alesi 6-30, Schumacher 31-53

PORTUGUESE GRAND PRIX

AUTODROMO DO ESTORIL • ROUND 15 • DATE: 22ND SEPTEMBER 1996
Laps: 70 • Distance: 189.519miles/305.2km • Weather: Warm & bright

Pos	Driver	Team	Chassis-Engine	Result	Qual
1	Jacques Villeneuve	Williams	Williams-Renault FW18	1h40m22.915s	2
2	Damon Hill	Williams	Williams-Renault FW18	1h40m42.881s	1
3	Michael Schumacher	Ferrari	Ferrari F310	1h41m16.680s	4
4	Jean Alesi	Benetton	Benetton-Renault B196	1h41m18.024s	3
5	Eddie Irvine	Ferrari	Ferrari F310	1h41m50.304s	6
6	Gerhard Berger	Benetton	Benetton-Renault B196	1h41m56.056s	5
7	Heinz-Harald Frentzen	Sauber	Sauber-Ford Cosworth C15	69 laps	11
8	Johnny Herbert	Sauber	Sauber-Ford Cosworth C15	69 laps	12
9	Martin Brundle	Jordan	Jordan-Peugeot 196	69 laps	10
10	Olivier Panis	Ligier	Ligier-Mugen Honda JS43	69 laps	15
11	Mika Salo	Tyrrell	Tyrrell-Yamaha 024	69 laps	13
12	Ukyo Katayama	Tyrrell	Tyrrell-Yamaha 024	68 laps	14
13	David Coulthard	McLaren	McLaren-Mercedes MP4/11	68 laps	8
14	Ricardo Rosset	Footwork	Footwork-Hart FA17	67 laps	17
15	Giovanni Lavaggi	Minardi	Minardi-Ford Cosworth M195B	65 laps	20
16	Pedro Lamy	Minardi	Minardi-Ford Cosworth M195B	65 laps	19
R	Mika Hakkinen	McLaren	McLaren-Mercedes MP4/11	52 laps/collision	7
R	Jos Verstappen	Footwork	Footwork-Hart FA17	47 laps/engine	16
R	Pedro Diniz	Ligier	Ligier-Mugen Honda JS43	46 laps/collision	18
R	Rubens Barrichello	Jordan	Jordan-Peugeot 196	41 laps/spun off	9

Pole: Hill, 1m20.330s, 121.412mph/195.393kph. Fastest lap: Villeneuve, 1m22.873s, 117.686mph/189.398kph on Lap 37. Race leaders: Hill 1-17 & 22-33 & 36-48, Alesi 18-21, Villeneuve 34-35 & 49-70

JAPANESE GRAND PRIX

SUZUKA • ROUND 16 • DATE: 13TH OCTOBER 1996
Laps: 52 • Distance: 189.473miles/304.928km • Weather: Warm & bright

Pos	Driver	Team	Chassis-Engine	Result	Qual
1	Damon Hill	Williams	Williams-Renault FW18	1h32m33.791s	2
2	Michael Schumacher	Ferrari	Ferrari F310	1h32m35.674s	3
3	Mika Hakkinen	McLaren	McLaren-Mercedes MP4/11	1h32m37.003s	5
4	Gerhard Berger	Benetton	Benetton-Renault B196	1h33m00.317s	4
5	Martin Brundle	Jordan	Jordan-Peugeot 196	1h33m40.911s	10
6	Heinz-Harald Frentzen	Sauber	Sauber-Ford Cosworth C15	1h33m54.977s	7
7	Olivier Panis	Ligier	Ligier-Mugen Honda JS43	1h33m58.301s	12
8	David Coulthard	McLaren	McLaren-Mercedes MP4/11	1h33m59.024s	8
9	Rubens Barrichello	Jordan	Jordan-Peugeot 196	1h34m14.856s	11
10	Johnny Herbert	Sauber	Sauber-Ford Cosworth C15	1h34m15.590s	13
11	Jos Verstappen	Footwork	Footwork-Hart FA17	51 laps	17
12	Pedro Lamy	Minardi	Minardi-Ford Cosworth M195B	50 laps	18
13	Ricardo Rosset	Footwork	Footwork-Hart FA17	50 laps	19
R	Eddie Irvine	Ferrari	Ferrari F310	39 laps/collision	6
R	Ukyo Katayama	Tyrrell	Tyrrell-Yamaha 024	37 laps/engine	14
R	Jacques Villeneuve	Williams	Williams-Renault FW18	36 laps/wheel	1
R	Mika Salo	Tyrrell	Tyrrell-Yamaha 024	20 laps/engine	15
R	Pedro Diniz	Ligier	Ligier-Mugen Honda JS43	13 laps/spun off	16
R	Jean Alesi	Benetton	Benetton-Renault B196	0 laps/spun off	9
DNQ	Giovanni Lavaggi	Minardi	Minardi-Ford Cosworth M195B	-	20

Pole: Villeneuve, 1m38.909s, 132.620mph/213.432kph. Fastest lap: Villeneuve, 1m44.043s, 126.076mph/202.900kph on Lap 34. Race leaders: Hill 1-52

WORLD DRIVERS' CHAMPIONSHIP FINAL RESULTS

Pos	Driver	Nat	Car-Engine	R1	R2	R3	R4	R5	R6
1	Damon Hill	GBR	Williams-Renault FW18	1	1PF	1P	4PF	1F	R
2	Jacques Villeneuve	CAN	Williams-Renault FW18	2PF	R	2	1	11	R
3	Michael Schumacher	DEU	Ferrari F310	R	3	R	2	2P	RP
4	Jean Alesi	FRA	Benetton-Renault B196	R	2	3F	R	6	RF
5	Mika Hakkinen	FIN	McLaren-Mercedes MP4/11	5	4	R	8	8	6
6	Gerhard Berger	AUT	Benetton-Renault B196	4	R	R	9	3	R
7	David Coulthard	GBR	McLaren-Mercedes MP4/11	R	R	7	3	R	2
8	Rubens Barrichello	BRA	Jordan-Peugeot 196	R	R	4	5	5	R
9	Olivier Panis	FRA	Ligier-Mugen Honda JS43	7	6	8	R	R	1
10	Eddie Irvine	GBR	Ferrari F310	3	7	5	R	4	7
11	Martin Brundle	GBR	Jordan-Peugeot 196	R	12	R	6	R	R
12	Heinz-Harald Frentzen	DEU	Sauber-Ford Cosworth C15	8	R	R	R	R	4
13	Mika Salo	FIN	Tyrrell-Yamaha 024	6	5	R	DQ	R	5
14	Johnny Herbert	GBR	Sauber-Ford Cosworth C15	R	R	9	7	R	3
15	Pedro Diniz	BRA	Ligier-Mugen Honda JS43	10	8	R	10	7	R
16	Jos Verstappen	NLD	Footwork-Hart FA17	R	R	6	R	R	R

Pos	Driver	R7	R8	R9	R10	R11	R12	R13	R14	R15	R16	Total
1	Hill	RP	1P	1	RP	1PF	2F	5	RP	2P	1	97
2	Villeneuve	3	2F	2F	1F	3	1	2P	7	1F	RPF	78
3	Schumacher	1F	R	NSP	R	4	9P	1	1F	3	2	59
4	Alesi	2	3	3	R	2	3	4	2	4	R	47
5	Hakkinen	5	5	5	3	R	4	3	3	R	3	31

Pos	Driver	R7	R8	R9	R10	R11	R12	R13	R14	R15	R16	Total
6	Berger	R	R	4	2	13	R	6F	R	6	4	21
7	Coulthard	R	4	6	5	5	R	R	R	13	8	18
8	Barrichello	R	R	9	4	6	6	R	5	R	9	14
9	Panis	R	R	7	R	7	5	R	R	10	7	13
10	Irvine	R	R	R	R	R	R	R	R	5	R	11
11	Brundle	R	6	8	6	10	R	R	4	9	5	8
12	Frentzen	4	R	R	8	8	R	R	R	7	6	7
13	Salo	DQ	R	10	7	9	R	7	R	11	R	5
14	Herbert	R	7	DQ	9	R	R	R	9	8	10	4
15	Diniz	6	R	R	R	R	R	R	6	R	R	2
16	Verstappen	R	R	R	10	R	R	R	8	R	11	1

WORLD CONSTRUCTORS' CHAMPIONSHIP FINAL RESULTS

Pos	Team-Engine	R1	R2	R3	R4	R5	R6	R7	R8
1	Williams-Renault	1/2	1/R	1/2	1/4	1/11	R/R	3/R	1/2
2	Ferrari	3/R	3/7	5/R	2/R	2/4	7/R	1/R	R/R
3	Benetton-Renault	4/R	2/R	3/R	9/R	3/6	R/R	2/R	3/R
4	McLaren-Mercedes	5/R	4/R	7/R	3/8	8/R	2/6	5/R	4/5
5	Jordan-Peugeot	R/R	12/R	4/R	5/6	5/R	R/R	R/R	6/R
6	Ligier-Mugen Honda	7/10	6/8	8/R	10/R	7/R	1/R	6/R	R/R
7	Sauber-Ford	8/NS	R/R	9/R	7/R	R/R	3/4	4/R	7/R
8	Tyrrell-Yamaha	6/11	5/9	R/R	DQ/DQ	R/R	5/R	DQ/R	R/R
9	Footwork-Hart	9/R	R/R	6/R	11/R	R/R	R/R	R/R	R/R

Pos	Team-Engine	R9	R10	R11	R12	R13	R14	R15	R16	Total
1	Williams-Renault	1/2	1/R	1/3	1/2	2/5	7/R	1/2	1/R	175
2	Ferrari	R/NS	R/R	4/R	9/R	1/R	1/R	3/5	2/R	70
3	Benetton-Renault	3/4	2/R	2/13	3/R	4/6	2/R	4/6	4/R	68
4	McLaren-Mercedes	5/6	3/5	5/R	4/R	3/R	3/R	13/R	3/8	49
5	Jordan-Peugeot	8/9	4/6	6/10	6/R	R/R	4/5	9/R	5/9	22
6	Ligier-Mugen Honda	7/R	R/R	7/R	5/R	R/R	6/R	10/R	7/R	15
7	Sauber-Ford	DQ/R	8/9	8/R	R/R	R/R	9/R	7/8	6/10	11
8	Tyrrell-Yamaha	10/R	7/R	9/R	7/R	7/8	10/R	11/12	R/R	5
9	Footwork-Hart	11/R	10/R	11/R	8/R	9/R	8/R	14/R	11/13	1

SYMBOLS AND GRAND PRIX KEY

Round 1 Australian GP
Round 2 Brazilian GP
Round 3 Argentinian GP
Round 4 European GP
Round 5 San Marino GP
Round 6 Monaco GP
Round 7 Spanish GP
Round 8 Canadian GP
Round 9 French GP
Round 10 British GP
Round 11 German GP
Round 12 Hungarian GP
Round 13 Belgian GP
Round 14 Italian GP
Round 15 Portuguese GP
Round 16 Japanese GP

SCORING

1st 10 points
2nd 6 points
3rd 4 points
4th 3 points
5th 2 points
6th 1 point

DNPQ DID NOT PRE-QUALIFY **DNQ** DID NOT QUALIFY **DQ** DISQUALIFIED **EX** EXCLUDED
F FASTEST LAP **NC** NOT CLASSIFIED **NS** NON-STARTER **P** POLE POSITION **R** RETIRED

1997

SEASON SUMMARY

Jacques Villeneuve became the latest in the impressive line of Williams drivers to be crowned world champion, and it was another great year for the team, as team-mate Heinz-Harald Frentzen ended the year ranked second. This was only, though, after Michael Schumacher, who had been in the title fight for Ferrari until the final round, drove into Villeneuve at Jerez and subsequently had all of his points removed. McLaren ended a 49-race run without a win at the final round, while there was nearly a shock when reigning champion Damon Hill led to within a lap of victory in Hungary in his unfancied Arrows.

AUSTRALIAN GRAND PRIX

ALBERT PARK • ROUND 1 • DATE: 9TH MARCH 1997
Laps: 58 • Distance: 191.81miles/307.516km • Weather: Warm & bright

Pos	Driver	Team	Chassis-Engine	Result	Qual
1	David Coulthard	McLaren	McLaren-Mercedes MP4-12	1h30m28.718s	4
2	Michael Schumacher	Ferrari	Ferrari F310B	1h30m48.764s	3
3	Mika Hakkinen	McLaren	McLaren-Mercedes MP4-12	1h30m50.895s	6
4	Gerhard Berger	Benetton	Benetton-Renault B197	1h30m51.559s	10
5	Olivier Panis	Prost	Prost-Mugen Honda JS45	1h31m29.026s	9
6	Nicola Larini	Sauber	Sauber-Petronas C16	1h32m04.758s	13
7	Shinji Nakano	Prost	Prost-Mugen Honda JS45	56 laps	16
8	Heinz-Harald Frentzen	Williams	Williams-Renault FW19	55 laps/brakes	2
9	Jarno Trulli	Minardi	Minardi-Hart M197	55 laps	17
10	Pedro Diniz	Arrows	Arrows-Yamaha A18	54 laps	22
R	Rubens Barrichello	Stewart	Stewart-Ford Cosworth SF1	49 laps/engine	11
R	Mika Salo	Tyrrell	Tyrrell-Ford Cosworth 025	42 laps/engine	18
R	Jan Magnussen	Stewart	Stewart-Ford Cosworth SF1	36 laps/suspension	19
R	Jean Alesi	Benetton	Benetton-Renault B197	34 laps/out of fuel	8
R	Ukyo Katayama	Minardi	Minardi-Hart M197	32 laps/electrical	15
R	Giancarlo Fisichella	Jordan	Jordan-Peugeot 197	14 laps/spun off	14
R	Jos Verstappen	Tyrrell	Tyrrell-Ford Cosworth 025	2 laps/spun off	21
R	Ralf Schumacher	Jordan	Jordan-Peugeot 197	1 lap/gearbox	12
R	Jacques Villeneuve	Williams	Williams-Renault FW19	0 laps/collision	1
R	Eddie Irvine	Ferrari	Ferrari F310B	0 laps/collision	5
R	Johnny Herbert	Sauber	Sauber-Petronas C16	0 laps/collision	7
NS	Damon Hill	Arrows	Arrows-Yamaha A18	throttle sensor	20
DNQ	Vincenzo Sospiri	Lola	Lola-Ford Cosworth T97/30	-	23
DNQ	Ricardo Rosset	Lola	Lola-Ford Cosworth T97/30	-	24

Pole: Villeneuve, 1m29.369s, 132.710mph/213.577kph. Fastest lap: Frentzen, 1m30.585s, 130.929mph/210.710kph on Lap 36. Race leaders: Frentzen 1-17 & 33-39, Coulthard 18-32 & 40-58

A CHAMPION'S TEAM

Three-time world champion Jackie Stewart made a break from F1 when he retired at the end of the 1973 season, but he stayed involved by being an ambassador to key sponsors. Then, he set up his own team when elder son Paul started in Formula Ford, and this grew through F3 and F3000 to become Stewart GP, operating out of Milton Keynes.

BRAZILIAN GRAND PRIX

INTERLAGOS • ROUND 2 • DATE: 30TH MARCH 1997
Laps: 72 • Distance: 192.18miles/309.024km • Weather: Warm but dull

Pos	Driver	Team	Chassis-Engine	Result	Qual
1	Jacques Villeneuve	Williams	Williams-Renault FW19	1h36m06.990s	1
2	Gerhard Berger	Benetton	Benetton-Renault B197	1h36m11.180s	3
3	Olivier Panis	Prost	Prost-Mugen Honda JS45	1h36m22.860s	5
4	Mika Hakkinen	McLaren	McLaren-Mercedes MP4-12	1h36m40.023s	4
5	Michael Schumacher	Ferrari	Ferrari F310B	1h36m40.721s	2
6	Jean Alesi	Benetton	Benetton-Renault B197	1h36m41.010s	6
7	Johnny Herbert	Sauber	Sauber-Petronas C16	1h36m57.902s	13
8	Giancarlo Fisichella	Jordan	Jordan-Peugeot 197	1h37m07.629s	7
9	Heinz-Harald Frentzen	Williams	Williams-Renault FW19	1h37m22.392s	8
10	David Coulthard	McLaren	McLaren-Mercedes MP4-12	71 laps	12
11	Nicola Larini	Sauber	Sauber-Petronas C16	71 laps	19
12	Jarno Trulli	Minardi	Minardi-Hart M197	71 laps	17
13	Mika Salo	Tyrrell	Tyrrell-Ford Cosworth 025	71 laps	22
14	Shinji Nakano	Prost	Prost-Mugen Honda JS45	71 laps	15
15	Jos Verstappen	Tyrrell	Tyrrell-Ford Cosworth 025	70 laps	21
16	Eddie Irvine	Ferrari	Ferrari F310B	70 laps	14
17	Damon Hill	Arrows	Arrows-Yamaha A18	68 laps/engine	9
18	Ukyo Katayama	Minardi	Minardi-Hart M197	67 laps	18
R	Ralf Schumacher	Jordan	Jordan-Peugeot 197	52 laps/electrical	10
R	Rubens Barrichello	Stewart	Stewart-Ford Cosworth SF1	16 laps/suspension	11
R	Pedro Diniz	Arrows	Arrows-Yamaha A18	15 laps/suspension	16
R	Jan Magnussen	Stewart	Stewart-Ford Cosworth SF1	0 laps/accident	20

Pole: Villeneuve, 1m16.004s, 126.321mph/203.294kph. Fastest lap: Villeneuve, 1m18.397s, 122.465mph/197.089kph on Lap 28. Race leaders: Villeneuve 1-45 & 49-72, Berger 46-48

MICHAEL'S DARK SIDE

Perhaps it was down to his extreme desire to win, but Michael Schumacher revealed an unsporting streak not befitting a champion in years when his equipment wasn't the very best. It resurfaced in the final round at Jerez when he simply drove into title rival Villeneuve as they fought for the lead. He remained unrepentant, until he was shown the replay…

ARGENTINIAN GRAND PRIX

BUENOS AIRES • ROUND 3 • DATE: 13TH APRIL 1997
Laps: 72 • Distance: 190.542miles/306.648km • Weather: Hot & bright

Pos	Driver	Team	Chassis-Engine	Result	Qual
1	Jacques Villeneuve	Williams	Williams-Renault FW19	1h52m01.715s	1
2	Eddie Irvine	Ferrari	Ferrari F310B	1h52m02.694s	7
3	Ralf Schumacher	Jordan	Jordan-Peugeot 197	1h52m13.804s	6
4	Johnny Herbert	Sauber	Sauber-Petronas C16	1h52m31.634s	8
5	Mika Hakkinen	McLaren	McLaren-Mercedes MP4-12	1h52m32.066s	17
6	Gerhard Berger	Benetton	Benetton-Renault B197	1h52m33.108s	12
7	Jean Alesi	Benetton	Benetton-Renault B197	1h52m48.074s	11

Pos	Driver	Team	Chassis-Engine	Result	Qual
8	Mika Salo	Tyrrell	Tyrrell-Ford Cosworth 025	71 laps	19
9	Jarno Trulli	Minardi	Minardi-Hart M197	71 laps	18
10	Jan Magnussen	Stewart	Stewart-Ford Cosworth SF1	66 laps/engine	15
R	Nicola Larini	Sauber	Sauber-Petronas C16	63 laps/spun off	14
R	Pedro Diniz	Arrows	Arrows-Yamaha A18	50 laps/engine	22
R	Shinji Nakano	Prost	Prost-Mugen Honda JS45	49 laps/engine	20
R	Jos Verstappen	Tyrrell	Tyrrell-Ford Cosworth 025	43 laps/engine	16
R	Ukyo Katayama	Minardi	Minardi-Hart M197	37 laps/spun off	21
R	Damon Hill	Arrows	Arrows-Yamaha A18	33 laps/engine	13
R	Rubens Barrichello	Stewart	Stewart-Ford Cosworth SF1	24 laps/hydraulics	5
R	Giancarlo Fisichella	Jordan	Jordan-Peugeot 197	24 laps/collision	9
R	Olivier Panis	Prost	Prost-Mugen Honda JS45	18 laps/electrical	3
R	Heinz-Harald Frentzen	Williams	Williams-Renault FW19	5 laps/clutch	2
R	Michael Schumacher	Ferrari	Ferrari F310B	0 laps/collision	4
R	David Coulthard	McLaren	McLaren-Mercedes MP4-12	0 laps/collision	10

Pole: Villeneuve, 1m24.473s, 112.782mph/181.506kph. Fastest lap: Berger, 1m27.981s, 108.286mph/174.269kph on Lap 63. Race leaders: Villeneuve 1-38 & 45-72, Irvine 39-44

SAN MARINO GRAND PRIX

IMOLA • ROUND 4 • DATE: 27TH APRIL 1997
Laps: 62 • Distance: 189.559miles/305.66km • Weather: Warm & bright

Pos	Driver	Team	Chassis-Engine	Result	Qual
1	Heinz-Harald Frentzen	Williams	Williams-Renault FW19	1h31m00.673s	2
2	Michael Schumacher	Ferrari	Ferrari F310B	1h31m01.910s	3
3	Eddie Irvine	Ferrari	Ferrari F310B	1h32m19.016s	9
4	Giancarlo Fisichella	Jordan	Jordan-Peugeot 197	1h32m24.061s	6
5	Jean Alesi	Benetton	Benetton-Renault B197	61 laps	14
6	Mika Hakkinen	McLaren	McLaren-Mercedes MP4-12	61 laps	8
7	Nicola Larini	Sauber	Sauber-Petronas C16	61 laps	12
8	Olivier Panis	Prost	Prost-Mugen Honda JS45	61 laps	4
9	Mika Salo	Tyrrell	Tyrrell-Ford Cosworth 025	60 laps	19
10	Jos Verstappen	Tyrrell	Tyrrell-Ford Cosworth 025	60 laps	21
11	Ukyo Katayama	Minardi	Minardi-Hart M197	59 laps	22
R	Pedro Diniz	Arrows	Arrows-Yamaha A18	53 laps/gearbox	17
R	Jacques Villeneuve	Williams	Williams-Renault FW19	40 laps/gearbox	1
R	David Coulthard	McLaren	McLaren-Mercedes MP4-12	38 laps/engine	10
R	Rubens Barrichello	Stewart	Stewart-Ford Cosworth SF1	32 laps/engine	13
R	Johnny Herbert	Sauber	Sauber-Petronas C16	18 laps/electrical	7
R	Ralf Schumacher	Jordan	Jordan-Peugeot 197	17 laps/transmission	5
R	Damon Hill	Arrows	Arrows-Yamaha A18	11 laps/collision	15
R	Shinji Nakano	Prost	Prost-Mugen Honda JS45	11 laps/collision	18
R	Gerhard Berger	Benetton	Benetton-Renault B197	4 laps/spun off	11
R	Jan Magnussen	Stewart	Stewart-Ford Cosworth SF1	2 laps/spun off	16
NS	Jarno Trulli	Minardi	Minardi-Hart M197	hydraulics	20

Pole: Villeneuve, 1m23.303s, 132.385mph/213.053kph. Fastest lap: Frentzen, 1m25.531s, 128.936mph/207.503kph on Lap 42. Race leaders: Villeneuve 1-25, Frentzen 26-43 & 45-62, M Schumacher 44

MONACO GRAND PRIX

MONTE CARLO • ROUND 5 • DATE: 11TH MAY 1997
Laps: 62 • Distance: 129.675miles/208.692km • Weather: Warm & wet

Pos	Driver	Team	Chassis-Engine	Result	Qual
1	Michael Schumacher	Ferrari	Ferrari F310B	2h00m05.654s	2
2	Rubens Barrichello	Stewart	Stewart-Ford Cosworth SF1	2h00m58.960s	10
3	Eddie Irvine	Ferrari	Ferrari F310B	2h01m27.762s	15
4	Olivier Panis	Prost	Prost-Mugen Honda JS45	2h01m50.056s	12
5	Mika Salo	Tyrrell	Tyrrell-Ford Cosworth 025	61 laps	14
6	Giancarlo Fisichella	Jordan	Jordan-Peugeot 197	61 laps	4
7	Jan Magnussen	Stewart	Stewart-Ford Cosworth SF1	61 laps	19
8	Jos Verstappen	Tyrrell	Tyrrell-Ford Cosworth 025	60 laps	22
9	Gerhard Berger	Benetton	Benetton-Renault B197	60 laps	17
10	Ukyo Katayama	Minardi	Minardi-Hart M197	60 laps	20
R	Heinz-Harald Frentzen	Williams	Williams-Renault FW19	39 laps/spun off	1
R	Shinji Nakano	Prost	Prost-Mugen Honda JS45	36 laps/spun off	21
R	Nicola Larini	Sauber	Sauber-Petronas C16	24 laps/spun off	11
R	Jacques Villeneuve	Williams	Williams-Renault FW19	16 laps/spun off	3
R	Jean Alesi	Benetton	Benetton-Renault B197	16 laps/spun off	9
R	Ralf Schumacher	Jordan	Jordan-Peugeot 197	10 laps/spun off	6
R	Johnny Herbert	Sauber	Sauber-Petronas C16	9 laps/spun off	7
R	Jarno Trulli	Minardi	Minardi-Hart M197	7 laps/spun off	18
R	David Coulthard	McLaren	McLaren-Mercedes MP4-12	1 lap/spun off	5
R	Mika Hakkinen	McLaren	McLaren-Mercedes MP4-12	1 lap/collision	8
R	Damon Hill	Arrows	Arrows-Yamaha A18	1 lap/spun off	13
R	Pedro Diniz	Arrows	Arrows-Yamaha A18	0 laps/spun off	16

Pole: Frentzen, 1m18.216s, 96.265mph/154.924kph. Fastest lap: M Schumacher, 1m53.315s, 66.447mph/106.937kph on Lap 26. Race leaders: M Schumacher 1-62

PANIS BREAKS HIS LEGS

The pendulum of fortune swung the other way for 1996 race winner Olivier Panis when his run in the Canadian GP ended with a 145mph (233kph) collision with the wall that left him with two broken legs. This led to the race being red-flagged so that he could be extracted from his Prost. Schumacher went on to win for Ferrari.

SPANISH GRAND PRIX

BARCELONA-CATALUNYA • ROUND 6 • DATE: 25TH MAY 1997
Laps: 64 • Distance: 188.21miles/302.592km • Weather: Warm & bright

Pos	Driver	Team	Chassis-Engine	Result	Qual
1	Jacques Villeneuve	Williams	Williams-Renault FW19	1h30m35.896s	1
2	Olivier Panis	Prost	Prost-Mugen Honda JS45	1h30m41.700s	12
3	Jean Alesi	Benetton	Benetton-Renault B197	1h30m48.430s	4
4	Michael Schumacher	Ferrari	Ferrari F310B	1h30m53.875s	7
5	Johnny Herbert	Sauber	Sauber-Petronas C16	1h31m03.882s	10
6	David Coulthard	McLaren	McLaren-Mercedes MP4-12	1h31m05.640s	3
7	Mika Hakkinen	McLaren	McLaren-Mercedes MP4-12	1h31m24.681s	5

Pos	Driver	Team	Chassis-Engine	Result	Qual
8	Heinz-Harald Frentzen	Williams	Williams-Renault FW19	1h31m40.035s	2
9	Giancarlo Fisichella	Jordan	Jordan-Peugeot 197	1h31m40.663s	8
10	Gerhard Berger	Benetton	Benetton-Renault B197	1h31m41.566s	6
11	Jos Verstappen	Tyrrell	Tyrrell-Ford Cosworth 025	63 laps	19
12	Eddie Irvine	Ferrari	Ferrari F310B	63 laps	11
13	Jan Magnussen	Stewart	Stewart-Ford Cosworth SF1	63 laps	22
14	Gianni Morbidelli	Sauber	Sauber-Petronas C16	62 laps	13
15	Jarno Trulli	Minardi	Minardi-Hart M197	62 laps	18
R	Pedro Diniz	Arrows	Arrows-Yamaha A18	53 laps/engine	21
R	Ralf Schumacher	Jordan	Jordan-Peugeot 197	50 laps/engine	9
R	Rubens Barrichello	Stewart	Stewart-Ford Cosworth SF1	37 laps/engine	17
R	Mika Salo	Tyrrell	Tyrrell-Ford Cosworth 025	35 laps/puncture	14
R	Shinji Nakano	Prost	Prost-Mugen Honda JS45	34 laps/gearbox	16
R	Damon Hill	Arrows	Arrows-Yamaha A18	17 laps/engine	15
R	Ukyo Katayama	Minardi	Minardi-Hart M197	11 laps/gearbox	20

Pole: Villeneuve, 1m16.525s, 138.206mph/222.421kph. Fastest lap: Fisichella, 1m22.242s, 128.598mph/206.959kph on Lap 20. Race leaders: Villeneuve 1-20 & 22-45 & 47-64, Alesi 21, M Schumacher 46

CANADIAN GRAND PRIX

MONTREAL • ROUND 7 • DATE: 15TH JUNE 1997
Laps: 54 • Distance: 148.342miles/238.734km • Weather: Hot & bright

Pos	Driver	Team	Chassis-Engine	Result	Qual
1	Michael Schumacher	Ferrari	Ferrari F310B	1h17m40.646s	1
2	Jean Alesi	Benetton	Benetton-Renault B197	1h17m43.211s	8
3	Giancarlo Fisichella	Jordan	Jordan-Peugeot 197	1h17m43.865s	6
4	Heinz-Harald Frentzen	Williams	Williams-Renault FW19	1h17m44.414s	4
5	Johnny Herbert	Sauber	Sauber-Petronas C16	1h17m45.362s	13
6	Shinji Nakano	Prost	Prost-Mugen Honda JS45	1h18m17.347s	19
7	David Coulthard	McLaren	McLaren-Mercedes MP4-12	1h18m18.399s	5
8	Pedro Diniz	Arrows	Arrows-Yamaha A18	53 laps	16
9	Damon Hill	Arrows	Arrows-Yamaha A18	53 laps	15
10	Gianni Morbidelli	Sauber	Sauber-Petronas C16	53 laps	18
11	Olivier Panis	Prost	Prost-Mugen Honda JS45	51 laps/spun off	10
R	Mika Salo	Tyrrell	Tyrrell-Ford Cosworth 025	46 laps/engine	17
R	Jos Verstappen	Tyrrell	Tyrrell-Ford Cosworth 025	42 laps/gearbox	14
R	Alexander Wurz	Benetton	Benetton-Renault B197	35 laps/transmission	11
R	Rubens Barrichello	Stewart	Stewart-Ford Cosworth SF1	33 laps/gearbox	3
R	Jarno Trulli	Minardi	Minardi-Hart M197	32 laps/engine	20
R	Ralf Schumacher	Jordan	Jordan-Peugeot 197	14 laps/spun off	7
R	Ukyo Katayama	Minardi	Minardi-Hart M197	5 laps/spun off	22
R	Jacques Villeneuve	Williams	Williams-Renault FW19	1 lap/spun off	2
R	Mika Hakkinen	McLaren	McLaren-Mercedes MP4-12	0 laps/collision	9
R	Eddie Irvine	Ferrari	Ferrari F310B	0 laps/collision	12
R	Jan Magnussen	Stewart	Stewart-Ford Cosworth SF1	0 laps/spun off	21

Pole: M Schumacher, 1m18.095s, 126.634mph/203.797kph. Fastest lap: Coulthard, 1m19.635s, 124.185mph/199.856kph on Lap 37. Race leaders: M Schumacher 1-27 & 40-43 & 52-54, Coulthard 28-39 & 44-51

FRENCH GRAND PRIX

MAGNY-COURS • ROUND 8 • DATE: 29TH JUNE 1997
Laps: 72 • Distance: 190.139miles/306.0km • Weather: Warm but dull, rain later

Pos	Driver	Team	Chassis-Engine	Result	Qual
1	Michael Schumacher	Ferrari	Ferrari F310B	1h38m50.492s	1
2	Heinz-Harald Frentzen	Williams	Williams-Renault FW19	1h39m14.029s	2
3	Eddie Irvine	Ferrari	Ferrari F310B	1h40m05.293s	5
4	Jacques Villeneuve	Williams	Williams-Renault FW19	1h40m12.276s	4
5	Jean Alesi	Benetton	Benetton-Renault B197	1h40m13.227s	8
6	Ralf Schumacher	Jordan	Jordan-Peugeot 197	1h40m20.363s	3
7	David Coulthard	McLaren	McLaren-Mercedes MP4-12	71 laps/collision	9
8	Johnny Herbert	Sauber	Sauber-Petronas C16	71 laps	14
9	Giancarlo Fisichella	Jordan	Jordan-Peugeot 197	71 laps	11
10	Jarno Trulli	Prost	Prost-Mugen Honda JS45	70 laps	6
11	Ukyo Katayama	Minardi	Minardi-Hart M197	70 laps	21
12	Damon Hill	Arrows	Arrows-Yamaha A18	69 laps	17
R	Mika Salo	Tyrrell	Tyrrell-Ford Cosworth 025	61 laps/electrical	19
R	Alexander Wurz	Benetton	Benetton-Renault B197	60 laps/spun off	7
R	Pedro Diniz	Arrows	Arrows-Yamaha A18	58 laps/spun off	16
R	Norberto Fontana	Sauber	Sauber-Petronas C16	40 laps/spun off	20
R	Rubens Barrichello	Stewart	Stewart-Ford Cosworth SF1	36 laps/engine	13
R	Jan Magnussen	Stewart	Stewart-Ford Cosworth SF1	33 laps/brakes	15
R	Mika Hakkinen	McLaren	McLaren-Mercedes MP4-12	18 laps/engine	10
R	Jos Verstappen	Tyrrell	Tyrrell-Ford Cosworth 025	15 laps/spun off	18
R	Shinji Nakano	Prost	Prost-Mugen Honda JS45	7 laps/spun off	12
R	Tarso Marques	Minardi	Minardi-Hart M197	5 laps/engine	22

Pole: M Schumacher, 1m14.548s, 127.528mph/205.236kph. Fastest lap: M Schumacher, 1m17.910s, 122.025mph/196.380kph on Lap 37. Race leaders: M Schumacher 1-22 & 24-46 & 48-72, Frentzen 23 & 47

A 37-YEAR-OLD WINNER

Gerhard Berger won the German GP – his first F1 win since the same event in 1994 – and it was a surprise, as he arrived at Hockenheim after missing the previous three races with a sinus problem. The 37-year-old took pole and led all the way in his Benetton. It was to be the last of his 10 F1 wins and he retired at the end of the season.

ONE THAT GOT AWAY

In what would have been the biggest shock result for years, Damon Hill almost won the Hungarian GP for Arrows. The 1996 world champion seldom qualified well, but improved to finish sixth at Silverstone. He then qualified third in Hungary, passed Michael Schumacher to take lead, and led until a hydraulic problem let Villeneuve past on the last lap.

BRITISH GRAND PRIX

SILVERSTONE • ROUND 9 • DATE: 13TH JULY 1997
Laps: 59 • Distance: 188.291miles/303.26km • Weather: Hot & bright

Pos	Driver	Team	Chassis-Engine	Result	Qual
1	Jacques Villeneuve	Williams	Williams-Renault FW19	1h28m01.665s	1
2	Jean Alesi	Benetton	Benetton-Renault B197	1h28m11.870s	11
3	Alexander Wurz	Benetton	Benetton-Renault B197	1h28m12.961s	8
4	David Coulthard	McLaren	McLaren-Mercedes MP4-12	1h28m32.894s	6
5	Ralf Schumacher	Jordan	Jordan-Peugeot 197	1h28m33.545s	5
6	Damon Hill	Arrows	Arrows-Yamaha A18	1h29m15.217s	12
7	Giancarlo Fisichella	Jordan	Jordan-Peugeot 197	58 laps	10
8	Jarno Trulli	Prost	Prost-Mugen Honda JS45	58 laps	13
9	Norberto Fontana	Sauber	Sauber-Petronas C16	58 laps	22
10	Tarso Marques	Minardi	Minardi-Hart M197	58 laps	20
11	Shinji Nakano	Prost	Prost-Mugen Honda JS45	57 laps/engine	14
R	Mika Hakkinen	McLaren	McLaren-Mercedes MP4-12	52 laps/engine	3
R	Jan Magnussen	Stewart	Stewart-Ford Cosworth SF1	50 laps/engine	15
R	Jos Verstappen	Tyrrell	Tyrrell-Ford Cosworth 025	45 laps/engine	19
R	Eddie Irvine	Ferrari	Ferrari F310B	44 laps/halfshaft	7
R	Mika Salo	Tyrrell	Tyrrell-Ford Cosworth 025	44 laps/engine	17
R	Johnny Herbert	Sauber	Sauber-Petronas C16	42 laps/electrical	9
R	Michael Schumacher	Ferrari	Ferrari F310B	38 laps/wheel	4
R	Rubens Barrichello	Stewart	Stewart-Ford Cosworth SF1	37 laps/engine	21
R	Pedro Diniz	Arrows	Arrows-Yamaha A18	29 laps/engine	16
R	Heinz-Harald Frentzen	Williams	Williams-Renault FW19	0 laps/collision	2
R	Ukyo Katayama	Minardi	Minardi-Hart M197	0 laps/spun off	18

Pole: Villeneuve, 1m21.598s, 140.908mph/226.770kph. Fastest lap: M Schumacher, 1m24.475s, 136.109mph/219.047kph on Lap 34. Race leaders: Villeneuve 1-22 & 38-44 & 53-59, M Schumacher 23-37, Hakkinen 45-52

GERMAN GRAND PRIX

HOCKENHEIM • ROUND 10 • DATE: 27TH JULY 1997
Laps: 45 • Distance: 190.782miles/307.035km • Weather: Hot & bright

Pos	Driver	Team	Chassis-Engine	Result	Qual
1	Gerhard Berger	Benetton	Benetton-Renault B197	1h20m59.046s	1
2	Michael Schumacher	Ferrari	Ferrari F310B	1h21m16.573s	4
3	Mika Hakkinen	McLaren	McLaren-Mercedes MP4-12	1h21m23.816s	3
4	Jarno Trulli	Prost	Prost-Mugen Honda JS45	1h21m26.211s	11
5	Ralf Schumacher	Jordan	Jordan-Peugeot 197	1h21m29.041s	7
6	Jean Alesi	Benetton	Benetton-Renault B197	1h21m33.763s	6
7	Shinji Nakano	Prost	Prost-Mugen Honda JS45	1h22m18.768s	17
8	Damon Hill	Arrows	Arrows-Yamaha A18	44 laps	13
9	Norberto Fontana	Sauber	Sauber-Petronas C16	44 laps	18
10	Jos Verstappen	Tyrrell	Tyrrell-Ford Cosworth 025	44 laps	20
11	Giancarlo Fisichella	Jordan	Jordan-Peugeot 197	40 laps/tyre	2
R	Jacques Villeneuve	Williams	Williams-Renault FW19	33 laps/spun off	9
R	Rubens Barrichello	Stewart	Stewart-Ford Cosworth SF1	33 laps/engine	12
R	Mika Salo	Tyrrell	Tyrrell-Ford Cosworth 025	33 laps/clutch	19
R	Jan Magnussen	Stewart	Stewart-Ford Cosworth SF1	27 laps/engine	15
R	Ukyo Katayama	Minardi	Minardi-Hart M197	23 laps/out of fuel	22
R	Johnny Herbert	Sauber	Sauber-Petronas C16	8 laps/accident	14

Pos	Driver	Team	Chassis-Engine	Result	Qual
R	Pedro Diniz	Arrows	Arrows-Yamaha A18	8 laps/accident	16
R	Heinz-Harald Frentzen	Williams	Williams-Renault FW19	1 lap/collision	5
R	David Coulthard	McLaren	McLaren-Mercedes MP4-12	1 lap/transmission	8
R	Eddie Irvine	Ferrari	Ferrari F310B	1 lap/collision	10
R	Tarso Marques	Minardi	Minardi-Hart M197	0 laps/transmission	21

Pole: Berger, 1m41.873s, 149.820mph/241.111kph. Fastest lap: Berger, 1m45.747s, 144.331mph/232.278kph on Lap 9. Race leaders: Berger 1-17 & 25-45, Fisichella 18-24

HUNGARIAN GRAND PRIX

HUNGARORING • ROUND 11 • DATE: 10TH AUGUST 1997
Laps: 77 • Distance: 189.851miles/305.536km • Weather: Hot & bright

Pos	Driver	Team	Chassis-Engine	Result	Qual
1	Jacques Villeneuve	Williams	Williams-Renault FW19	1h45m47.149s	2
2	Damon Hill	Arrows	Arrows-Yamaha A18	1h45m56.228s	3
3	Johnny Herbert	Sauber	Sauber-Petronas C16	1h46m07.594s	10
4	Michael Schumacher	Ferrari	Ferrari F310B	1h46m17.650s	1
5	Ralf Schumacher	Jordan	Jordan-Peugeot 197	1h46m17.864s	14
6	Shinji Nakano	Prost	Prost-Mugen Honda JS45	1h46m28.661s	16
7	Jarno Trulli	Prost	Prost-Mugen Honda JS45	1h47m02.701s	12
8	Gerhard Berger	Benetton	Benetton-Renault B197	1h47m03.558s	7
9	Eddie Irvine	Ferrari	Ferrari F310B	76 laps/collision	5
10	Ukyo Katayama	Minardi	Minardi-Hart M197	76 laps	20
11	Jean Alesi	Benetton	Benetton-Renault B197	76 laps	9
12	Tarso Marques	Minardi	Minardi-Hart M197	75 laps	22
13	Mika Salo	Tyrrell	Tyrrell-Ford Cosworth 025	75 laps	21
R	David Coulthard	McLaren	McLaren-Mercedes MP4-12	65 laps/electrical	8
R	Jos Verstappen	Tyrrell	Tyrrell-Ford Cosworth 025	61 laps/gearbox	18
R	Pedro Diniz	Arrows	Arrows-Yamaha A18	53 laps/electrical	19
R	Giancarlo Fisichella	Jordan	Jordan-Peugeot 197	42 laps/spun off	13
R	Heinz-Harald Frentzen	Williams	Williams-Renault FW19	29 laps/oil leak	6
R	Rubens Barrichello	Stewart	Stewart-Ford Cosworth SF1	29 laps/engine	11
R	Mika Hakkinen	McLaren	McLaren-Mercedes MP4-12	12 laps/hydraulics	4
R	Gianni Morbidelli	Sauber	Sauber-Petronas C16	7 laps/engine	15
R	Jan Magnussen	Stewart	Stewart-Ford Cosworth SF1	5 laps/accident	17

Pole: M Schumacher, 1m14.672s, 118.868mph/191.300kph. Fastest lap: Frentzen, 1m18.372s, 113.256mph/182.269kph on Lap 25. Race leaders: M Schumacher 1-10, Hill 11-25 & 30-76, Frentzen 26-29, Villeneuve 77

A ONE-HIT BLUNDER

Lola's return to F1 was a disaster. The company had built F1 cars in the 1960s and mid-70s, and then again from 1986 to 1993, during which time it became the world's most successful builder of racing cars. Then, with little preparation, it turned up at the Australian GP with cars that were five seconds outside the 107 per cent qualifying cut-off point. They were never seen again.

BELGIAN GRAND PRIX

SPA-FRANCORCHAMPS • ROUND 12 • DATE: 24TH AUGUST 1997
Laps: 44 • Distance: 190.507miles/306.592km • Weather: Warm & wet, drying later

Pos	Driver	Team	Chassis-Engine	Result	Qual
1	Michael Schumacher	Ferrari	Ferrari F310B	1h33m46.717s	3
2	Giancarlo Fisichella	Jordan	Jordan-Peugeot 197	1h34m13.470s	4
3	Heinz-Harald Frentzen	Williams	Williams-Renault FW19	1h34m18.864s	7
4	Johnny Herbert	Sauber	Sauber-Petronas C16	1h34m25.742s	11
5	Jacques Villeneuve	Williams	Williams-Renault FW19	1h34m28.820s	1
6	Gerhard Berger	Benetton	Benetton-Renault B197	1h34m50.458s	15
7	Pedro Diniz	Arrows	Arrows-Yamaha A18	1h35m12.648s	8
8	Jean Alesi	Benetton	Benetton-Renault B197	1h35m28.725s	2
9	Gianni Morbidelli	Sauber	Sauber-Petronas C16	1h35m29.299s	13
10	Eddie Irvine	Ferrari	Ferrari F310B	43 laps/collision	17
11	Mika Salo	Tyrrell	Tyrrell-Ford Cosworth 025	43 laps	19
12	Jan Magnussen	Stewart	Stewart-Ford Cosworth SF1	43 laps	18
13	Damon Hill	Arrows	Arrows-Yamaha A18	42 laps/wheel	9
14	Ukyo Katayama	Minardi	Minardi-Hart M197	42 laps/engine	20
15	Jarno Trulli	Prost	Prost-Mugen Honda JS45	42 laps	14
DQ	Mika Hakkinen	McLaren	McLaren-Mercedes MP4-12	44 laps/fuel irregularities	5
R	Jos Verstappen	Tyrrell	Tyrrell-Ford Cosworth 025	25 laps/spun off	21
R	Ralf Schumacher	Jordan	Jordan-Peugeot 197	21 laps/spun off	6
R	David Coulthard	McLaren	McLaren-Mercedes MP4-12	19 laps/spun off	10
R	Tarso Marques	Minardi	Minardi-Hart M197	18 laps/spun off	22
R	Rubens Barrichello	Stewart	Stewart-Ford Cosworth SF1	8 laps/spun off	12
R	Shinji Nakano	Prost	Prost-Mugen Honda JS45	5 laps/spun off	16

Pole: Villeneuve, 1m49.450s, 142.411mph/229.189kph. Fastest lap: Villeneuve, 1m52.692s, 138.314mph/222.596kph on Lap 43. Race leaders: Villeneuve 1-4, M Schumacher 5-44

A QUALIFYING MIRACLE

The timekeepers at the final race of the year at Jerez could hardly believe it, but the three fastest drivers in qualifying ended up with identical times, at 1m 21.072s for the 2.751-mile (4.427km) Spanish circuit. Pole position went to Villeneuve, as he was the first of the trio to achieve that time, with Michael Schumacher and Frentzen next up.

ITALIAN GRAND PRIX

MONZA • ROUND 13 • DATE: 7TH SEPTEMBER 1997
Laps: 53 • Distance: 189.568miles/305.81km • Weather: Hot & bright

Pos	Driver	Team	Chassis-Engine	Result	Qual
1	David Coulthard	McLaren	McLaren-Mercedes MP4-12	1h17m04.609s	6
2	Jean Alesi	Benetton	Benetton-Renault B197	1h17m06.546s	1
3	Heinz-Harald Frentzen	Williams	Williams-Renault FW19	1h17m08.952s	2
4	Giancarlo Fisichella	Jordan	Jordan-Peugeot 197	1h17m10.480s	3
5	Jacques Villeneuve	Williams	Williams-Renault FW19	1h17m11.025s	4
6	Michael Schumacher	Ferrari	Ferrari F310B	1h17m16.090s	9
7	Gerhard Berger	Benetton	Benetton-Renault B197	1h17m17.080s	7

Pos	Driver	Team	Chassis-Engine	Result	Qual
8	Eddie Irvine	Ferrari	Ferrari F310B	1h17m22.248s	10
9	Mika Hakkinen	McLaren	McLaren-Mercedes MP4-12	1h17m53.982s	5
10	Jarno Trulli	Prost	Prost-Mugen Honda JS45	1h18m07.315s	16
11	Shinji Nakano	Prost	Prost-Mugen Honda JS45	1h18m07.936s	15
12	Gianni Morbidelli	Sauber	Sauber-Petronas C16	52 laps	18
13	Rubens Barrichello	Stewart	Stewart-Ford Cosworth SF1	52 laps	11
14	Tarso Marques	Minardi	Minardi-Hart M197	50 laps	22
R	Damon Hill	Arrows	Arrows-Yamaha A18	46 laps/engine	14
R	Ralf Schumacher	Jordan	Jordan-Peugeot 197	39 laps/collision	8
R	Johnny Herbert	Sauber	Sauber-Petronas C16	38 laps/collision	12
R	Mika Salo	Tyrrell	Tyrrell-Ford Cosworth 025	33 laps/engine	19
R	Jan Magnussen	Stewart	Stewart-Ford Cosworth SF1	31 laps/transmission	13
R	Jos Verstappen	Tyrrell	Tyrrell-Ford Cosworth 025	12 laps/gearbox	20
R	Ukyo Katayama	Minardi	Minardi-Hart M197	8 laps/spun off	21
R	Pedro Diniz	Arrows	Arrows-Yamaha A18	4 laps/suspension	17

Pole: Alesi, 1m22.990s, 155.526mph/250.295kph. Fastest lap: Hakkinen, 1m24.808s, 152.192mph/244.929kph on Lap 49. Race leaders: Alesi 1-31, Hakkinen 32-33, M Schumacher 34, Coulthard 35-53

NEW CIRCUITS

The much-loved Osterreichring, which had been dropped after the 1987 Austrian GP, made its return to the World Championship as the A1-Ring. Named after a mobile phone network, it was a safer version of the original, its lap losing much of the first half of the previous layout and cutting off the Bosch Kurve as it traversed the mountainside.

AUSTRIAN GRAND PRIX

A1-RING • ROUND 14 • DATE: 21ST SEPTEMBER 1997
Laps: 71 • Distance: 190.719miles/306.933km • Weather: Hot & bright

Pos	Driver	Team	Chassis-Engine	Result	Qual
1	Jacques Villeneuve	Williams	Williams-Renault FW19	1h27m35.999s	1
2	David Coulthard	McLaren	McLaren-Mercedes MP4-12	1h27m38.908s	10
3	Heinz-Harald Frentzen	Williams	Williams-Renault FW19	1h27m39.961s	4
4	Giancarlo Fisichella	Jordan	Jordan-Peugeot 197	1h27m48.126s	14
5	Ralf Schumacher	Jordan	Jordan-Peugeot 197	1h28m07.858s	11
6	Michael Schumacher	Ferrari	Ferrari F310B	1h28m09.409s	9
7	Damon Hill	Arrows	Arrows-Yamaha A18	1h28m13.206s	7
8	Johnny Herbert	Sauber	Sauber-Petronas C16	1h28m25.056s	12
9	Gianni Morbidelli	Sauber	Sauber-Petronas C16	1h28m42.454s	13
10	Gerhard Berger	Benetton	Benetton-Renault B197	70 laps	18
11	Ukyo Katayama	Minardi	Minardi-Hart M197	69 laps	19
12	Jos Verstappen	Tyrrell	Tyrrell-Ford Cosworth 025	69 laps	20
13	Pedro Diniz	Arrows	Arrows-Yamaha A18	67 laps/shock absorber	17
14	Rubens Barrichello	Stewart	Stewart-Ford Cosworth SF1	64 laps/spun off	5
R	Jarno Trulli	Prost	Prost-Mugen Honda JS45	58 laps/engine	3
R	Jan Magnussen	Stewart	Stewart-Ford Cosworth SF1	58 laps/engine	6

Pos	Driver	Team	Chassis-Engine	Result	Qual
R	Shinji Nakano	Prost	Prost-Mugen Honda JS45	57 laps/engine	16
R	Mika Salo	Tyrrell	Tyrrell-Ford Cosworth 025	48 laps/gearbox	21
R	Eddie Irvine	Ferrari	Ferrari F310B	38 laps/collision	8
R	Jean Alesi	Benetton	Benetton-Renault B197	37 laps/collision	15
R	Mika Hakkinen	McLaren	McLaren-Mercedes MP4-12	1 lap/engine	2
EX	Tarso Marques	Minardi	Minardi-Hart M197	car underweight	-

Pole: Villeneuve, 1m10.304s, 137.549mph/221.364kph. Fastest lap: Villeneuve, 1m11.814s, 134.657mph/216.709kph on Lap 36. Race leaders: Trulli 1-37, Villeneuve 38-40 & 44-71, M Schumacher 41-42, Coulthard 43

LUXEMBOURG GRAND PRIX

NURBURGRING • ROUND 15 • DATE: 28TH SEPTEMBER 1997
Laps: 67 • Distance: 189.674miles/305.252km • Weather: Warm & bright

Pos	Driver	Team	Chassis-Engine	Result	Qual
1	Jacques Villeneuve	Williams	Williams-Renault FW19	1h31m27.843s	2
2	Jean Alesi	Benetton	Benetton-Renault B197	1h31m39.613s	10
3	Heinz-Harald Frentzen	Williams	Williams-Renault FW19	1h31m41.323s	3
4	Gerhard Berger	Benetton	Benetton-Renault B197	1h31m44.259s	7
5	Pedro Diniz	Arrows	Arrows-Yamaha A18	1h32m10.990s	15
6	Olivier Panis	Prost	Prost-Mugen Honda JS45	1h32m11.593s	11
7	Johnny Herbert	Sauber	Sauber-Petronas C16	1h32m12.197s	16
8	Damon Hill	Arrows	Arrows-Yamaha A18	1h32m12.620s	13
9	Gianni Morbidelli	Sauber	Sauber-Petronas C16	66 laps	19
10	Mika Salo	Tyrrell	Tyrrell-Ford Cosworth 025	66 laps	20
R	Jos Verstappen	Tyrrell	Tyrrell-Ford Cosworth 025	50 laps/spun off	21
R	Mika Hakkinen	McLaren	McLaren-Mercedes MP4-12	43 laps/engine	1
R	Rubens Barrichello	Stewart	Stewart-Ford Cosworth SF1	43 laps/gearbox	9
R	David Coulthard	McLaren	McLaren-Mercedes MP4-12	42 laps/engine	6
R	Jan Magnussen	Stewart	Stewart-Ford Cosworth SF1	40 laps/halfshaft	12
R	Eddie Irvine	Ferrari	Ferrari F310B	22 laps/engine	14
R	Shinji Nakano	Prost	Prost-Mugen Honda JS45	16 laps/engine	17
R	Michael Schumacher	Ferrari	Ferrari F310B	2 laps/collision	5
R	Tarso Marques	Minardi	Minardi-Hart M197	1 lap/engine	18
R	Ukyo Katayama	Minardi	Minardi-Hart M197	1 lap/collision	22
R	Giancarlo Fisichella	Jordan	Jordan-Peugeot 197	0 laps/collision	4
R	Ralf Schumacher	Jordan	Jordan-Peugeot 197	0 laps/collision	8

Pole: Hakkinen, 1m16.602s, 133.044mph/214.114kph. Fastest lap: Frentzen, 1m18.805s, 129.325mph/208.128kph on Lap 32. Race leaders: Hakkinen 1-28 & 32-43, Coulthard 29-31, Villeneuve 44-67

NEW CONSTRUCTORS

In addition to Stewart GP, another team named after a former multiple world champion joined F1 in 1997. This was Alain Prost's team, and it showed enough promise for Panis to rank third, behind Villeneuve and Michael Schumacher before he broke his legs and, helped by stand-in Jarno Trulli coming fourth in Germany, the team that evolved from Ligier went on to finish sixth in the standings.

JAPANESE GRAND PRIX

SUZUKA • ROUND 16 • DATE: 12TH OCTOBER 1997
Laps: 53 • Distance: 193.117miles/310.792km • Weather: Hot & bright

Pos	Driver	Team	Chassis-Engine	Result	Qual
1	Michael Schumacher	Ferrari	Ferrari F310B	1h29m48.446s	2
2	Heinz-Harald Frentzen	Williams	Williams-Renault FW19	1h29m49.824s	6
3	Eddie Irvine	Ferrari	Ferrari F310B	1h30m14.830s	3
4	Mika Hakkinen	McLaren	McLaren-Mercedes MP4-12	1h30m15.575s	4
DQ	Jacques Villeneuve	Williams	Williams-Renault FW19	53 laps*	1
5	Jean Alesi	Benetton	Benetton-Renault B197	1h30m28.849s	7
6	Johnny Herbert	Sauber	Sauber-Petronas C16	1h30m30.076s	8
7	Giancarlo Fisichella	Jordan	Jordan-Peugeot 197	1h30m45.271s	9
8	Gerhard Berger	Benetton	Benetton-Renault B197	1h30m48.875s	5
9	Ralf Schumacher	Jordan	Jordan-Peugeot 197	1h31m10.482s	13
10	David Coulthard	McLaren	McLaren-Mercedes MP4-12	52 laps/engine	11
11	Damon Hill	Arrows	Arrows-Yamaha A18	52 laps	17
12	Pedro Diniz	Arrows	Arrows-Yamaha A18	52 laps	16
13	Jos Verstappen	Tyrrell	Tyrrell-Ford Cosworth 025	52 laps	21
R	Tarso Marques	Minardi	Minardi-Hart M197	46 laps/gearbox	20
R	Mika Salo	Tyrrell	Tyrrell-Ford Cosworth 025	46 laps/engine	22
R	Olivier Panis	Prost	Prost-Mugen Honda JS45	36 laps/engine	10
R	Shinji Nakano	Prost	Prost-Mugen Honda JS45	22 laps/wheel	15
R	Ukyo Katayama	Minardi	Minardi-Hart M197	8 laps/engine	19
R	Rubens Barrichello	Stewart	Stewart-Ford Cosworth SF1	6 laps/spun off	12
R	Jan Magnussen	Stewart	Stewart-Ford Cosworth SF1	3 laps/spun off	14
NS	Gianni Morbidelli	Sauber	Sauber-Petronas C16	Accident	18

*ignoring waved yellow flags in practice

Pole: Villeneuve, 1m36.071s, 136.538mph/219.737kph. Fastest lap: Frentzen, 1m38.942s, 132.576mph/213.361kph on Lap 48. Race leaders: Villeneuve 1-2 & 17-20, Irvine 3-16 & 22-24, Frentzen 21 & 34-37, M Schumacher 25-33 & 38-53

NEW DRIVERS

The best result achieved by the year's six rookies was third place. This was earned by Ralf Schumacher on his third outing for Jordan, which was then matched by Alexander Wurz at Silverstone on his third outing as a stand-in at Benetton for compatriot Berger. Trulli's fourth at Hockenheim also impressed, while Prost's Shinji Nakano was sixth in Canada.

EUROPEAN GRAND PRIX

JEREZ • ROUND 17 • DATE: 26TH OCTOBER 1997
Laps: 69 • Distance: 189.848miles/305.532km • Weather: Warm & bright

Pos	Driver	Team	Chassis-Engine	Result	Qual
1	Mika Hakkinen	McLaren	McLaren-Mercedes MP4-12	1h38m57.771s	5
2	David Coulthard	McLaren	McLaren-Mercedes MP4-12	1h38m59.425s	6
3	Jacques Villeneuve	Williams	Williams-Renault FW19	1h38m59.574s	1
4	Gerhard Berger	Benetton	Benetton-Renault B197	1h38m59.690s	8
5	Eddie Irvine	Ferrari	Ferrari F310B	1h39m01.560s	7
6	Heinz-Harald Frentzen	Williams	Williams-Renault FW19	1h39m02.308s	3

Pos	Driver	Team	Chassis-Engine	Result	Qual
7	Olivier Panis	Prost	Prost-Mugen Honda JS45	1h40m04.916s	9
8	Johnny Herbert	Sauber	Sauber-Petronas C16	1h40m10.732s	14
9	Jan Magnussen	Stewart	Stewart-Ford Cosworth SF1	1h40m15.258s	11
10	Shinji Nakano	Prost	Prost-Mugen Honda JS45	1h40m15.986s	15
11	Giancarlo Fisichella	Jordan	Jordan-Peugeot 197	68 laps	17
12	Mika Salo	Tyrrell	Tyrrell-Ford Cosworth 025	68 laps	21
13	Jean Alesi	Benetton	Benetton-Renault B197	68 laps	10
14	Norberto Fontana	Sauber	Sauber-Petronas C16	68 laps	18
15	Tarso Marques	Minardi	Minardi-Hart M197	68 laps	20
16	Jos Verstappen	Tyrrell	Tyrrell-Ford Cosworth 025	68 laps	22
17	Ukyo Katayama	Minardi	Minardi-Hart M197	68 laps	19
R	Michael Schumacher	Ferrari	Ferrari F310B	47 laps/collision	2
R	Damon Hill	Arrows	Arrows-Yamaha A18	47 laps/gearbox	4
R	Ralf Schumacher	Jordan	Jordan-Peugeot 197	44 laps/water leak	16
R	Rubens Barrichello	Stewart	Stewart-Ford Cosworth SF1	30 laps/gearbox	12
R	Pedro Diniz	Arrows	Arrows-Yamaha A18	11 laps/spun off	13

Pole: Villeneuve, 1m21.072s, 122.177mph/196.625kph. Fastest lap: Frentzen, 1m23.135s, 119.145mph/191.745kph on Lap 30. Race leaders: M Schumacher 1-21 & 28-42 & 45-47, Villeneuve 22 & 43-44 & 48-68, Frentzen 23-27, Hakkinen 69

WORLD DRIVERS' CHAMPIONSHIP FINAL RESULTS

Pos	Driver	Nat	Car-Engine	R1	R2	R3	R4	R5	R6
1	Jacques Villeneuve	CAN	Williams-Renault FW19	RP	1PF	1P	RP	R	1P
2	Heinz-Harald Frentzen	DEU	Williams-Renault FW19	8F	9	R	1F	RP	8
3	David Coulthard	GBR	McLaren-Mercedes MP4-12	1	10	R	R	R	6
4	Jean Alesi	FRA	Benetton-Renault B197	R	6	7	5	R	3
5	Gerhard Berger	AUT	Benetton-Renault B197	4	2	6F	R	9	10
6	Mika Hakkinen	FIN	McLaren-Mercedes MP4-12	3	4	5	6	R	7
7	Eddie Irvine	GBR	Ferrari F310B	R	16	2	3	3	12
8	Giancarlo Fisichella	ITA	Jordan-Peugeot 197	R	8	R	4	6	9F
9	Olivier Panis	FRA	Prost-Mugen Honda JS45	5	3	R	8	4	2
10	Johnny Herbert	GBR	Sauber-Petronas C16	R	7	4	R	R	5
11	Ralf Schumacher	DEU	Jordan-Peugeot 197	R	R	3	R	R	R
12	Damon Hill	GBR	Arrows-Yamaha A18	NS	17	R	R	R	R
13	Rubens Barrichello	BRA	Stewart-Ford Cosworth SF1	R	R	R	R	2	R
14	Alexander Wurz	AUT	Benetton-Renault B197	-	-	-	-	-	-
15	Jarno Trulli	ITA	Minardi-Hart M197	9	12	9	NS	R	15
			Prost-Mugen Honda JS45	-	-	-	-	-	-
16	Mika Salo	FIN	Tyrrell-Ford Cosworth 025	R	13	8	9	5	R
16	Pedro Diniz	BRA	Arrows-Yamaha A18	10	R	R	R	R	R
18	Shinji Nakano	JPN	Prost-Mugen Honda JS45	7	14	R	R	R	R
19	Nicola Larini	ITA	Sauber-Petronas C16	6	11	R	7	R	-
DQ	Michael Schumacher*	DEU	Ferrari F310B	2	5	R	2	1F	4

*Michael Schumacher scored 78 points but had them taken away for intentionally colliding with Villeneuve in the European GP.

Pos	Driver	R7	R8	R9	R10	R11	R12	R13	R14	R15	R16	R17	Total
1	Villeneuve	R	4	1P	R	1	5PF	5	1PF	1	DQP	3P	81
2	Frentzen	4	2	R	R	RF	3	3	3	3F	2F	6F	42
3	Coulthard	7F	7	4	R	R	R	1	2	R	10	2	36
4	Alesi	2	5	2	6	11	8	2P	R	2	5	13	36
5	Berger	-	-	-	1PF	8	6	7	10	4	8	4	27
6	Hakkinen	R	R	R	3	R	DQ	9F	R	RP	4	1	27

Pos	Driver	R7	R8	R9	R10	R11	R12	R13	R14	R15	R16	R17	Total
7	Irvine	R	3	R	R	9	10	8	R	R	3	5	24
8	Fisichella	3	9	7	11	R	2	4	4	R	7	11	20
9	Panis	11	-	-	-	-	-	-	-	6	R	7	16
10	Herbert	5	8	R	R	3	4	R	8	7	6	8	15
11	R Schumacher	R	6	5	5	5	R	R	5	R	9	R	13
12	Hill	9	12	6	8	2	13	R	7	8	11	R	7
13	Barrichello	R	R	R	R	R	R	13	14	R	R	R	6
14	Wurz	R	R	3	-	-	-	-	-	-	-	-	4
15	Trulli	R	-	-	-	-	-	-	-	-	-	-	3
		-	10	8	4	7	15	10	R	-	-	-	
16	Salo	R	R	R	R	13	11	R	R	10	R	12	2
16	Diniz	8	R	R	R	R	7	R	13	5	12	R	2
18	Nakano	6	R	11	7	6	R	11	R	R	R	10	2
19	Larini	-	-	-	-	-	-	-	-	-	-	-	1
DQ	M Schumacher*	1P	1PF	RF	2	4P	1	6	6	R	1	R	78

WORLD CONSTRUCTORS' CHAMPIONSHIP FINAL RESULTS

Pos	Team-Engine	R1	R2	R3	R4	R5	R6	R7	R8	R9
1	Williams-Renault	8/R	1/9	1/R	1/R	R/R	1/8	4/R	2/4	1/R
2	Ferrari	2/R	5/16	2/R	2/3	1/3	4/12	1/R	1/3	R/R
3	Benetton-Renault	4/R	2/6	6/7	5/R	9/R	3/10	2/R	5/R	2/3
4	McLaren-Mercedes	1/3	4/10	5/R	6/R	R/R	6/7	7/R	7/R	4/R
5	Jordan-Peugeot	R/R	8/R	3/R	4/R	6/R	9/R	3/R	6/9	5/7
6	Prost-Mugen Honda	5/7	3/14	R/R	8/R	4/R	2/R	6/11	10/R	8/11
7	Sauber-Petronas	6/R	7/11	4/R	7/R	R/R	5/14	5/10	8/R	9/R
8	Arrows-Yamaha	10/NS	17/R	R/R	R/R	R/R	R/R	8/9	12/R	6/R
9	Stewart-Ford	R/R	R/NS	10/R	R/R	2/7	13/R	R/R	R/R	R/R
10	Tyrrell-Ford	R/R	13/15	8/R	9/10	5/8	11/R	R/R	R/R	R/R

Pos	Team-Engine	R10	R11	R12	R13	R14	R15	R16	R17	Total
1	Williams-Renault	R/R	1/R	3/5	3/5	1/3	1/3	2/DQ	3/6	123
2	Ferrari	2/R	4/9	1/10	6/8	6/R	R/R	1/3	5/R	102
3	Benetton-Renault	1/6	8/11	6/8	2/7	10/R	2/4	5/8	4/13	67
4	McLaren-Mercedes	3/R	R/R	DQ/R	1/9	2/R	R/R	4/10	1/2	63
5	Jordan-Peugeot	5/11	5/R	2/R	4/R	4/5	R/R	7/9	11/R	33
6	Prost-Mugen Honda	4/7	6/7	15/R	10/11	R/R	6/R	R/R	7/10	21
7	Sauber-Petronas	9/R	3/R	4/9	12/R	8/9	7/9	6/NS	8/14	16
8	Arrows-Yamaha	8/R	2/R	7/13	R/R	7/13	5/8	11/12	R/R	9
9	Stewart-Ford	R/R	R/R	12/R	13/R	14/R	R/R	R/R	9/R	6
10	Tyrrell-Ford	10/R	13/R	11/R	R/R	12/R	10/R	13/R	12/16	2

SYMBOLS AND GRAND PRIX KEY

Round 1 Australian GP
Round 2 Brazilian GP
Round 3 Argentinian GP
Round 4 San Marino GP
Round 5 Monaco GP
Round 6 Spanish GP
Round 7 Canadian GP
Round 8 French GP
Round 9 British GP
Round 10 German GP
Round 11 Hungarian GP
Round 12 Belgian GP
Round 13 Italian GP
Round 14 Austrian GP
Round 15 Luxembourg GP
Round 16 Japanese GP
Round 17 European GP

SCORING

1st 10 points
2nd 6 points
3rd 4 points
4th 3 points
5th 2 points
6th 1 point

DNPQ DID NOT PRE-QUALIFY **DNQ** DID NOT QUALIFY **DQ** DISQUALIFIED **EX** EXCLUDED
F FASTEST LAP **NC** NOT CLASSIFIED **NS** NON-STARTER **P** POLE POSITION **R** RETIRED

1998

SEASON SUMMARY

After a promising conclusion to 1997, McLaren shifted up a gear to dominate in 1998, with Mika Hakkinen coming out on top, as he and team-mate David Coulthard controlled the season from the outset. Ferrari took a while to provide Michael Schumacher with a car with which to take on the McLaren-Mercedes, but he won at Monaco before adding four more as his Goodyear tyres found an edge over McLaren's Bridgestones, to end up just three points off Hakkinen. Williams failed to win a race for the first time in a decade and ranked a distant third, ending up only just ahead of first-time winners Jordan.

AUSTRALIAN GRAND PRIX

ALBERT PARK • ROUND 1 • DATE: 8TH MARCH 1998
Laps: 58 • Distance: 191.117miles/307.574km • Weather: Warm & bright

Pos	Driver	Team	Chassis-Engine	Result	Qual
1	Mika Hakkinen	McLaren	McLaren-Mercedes MP4-13	1h31m45.996s	1
2	David Coulthard	McLaren	McLaren-Mercedes MP4-13	1h31m46.698s	2
3	Heinz-Harald Frentzen	Williams	Williams-Mecachrome FW20	57 laps	6
4	Eddie Irvine	Ferrari	Ferrari F300	57 laps	8
5	Jacques Villeneuve	Williams	Williams-Mecachrome FW20	57 laps	4
6	Johnny Herbert	Sauber	Sauber-Petronas C17	57 laps	5
7	Alexander Wurz	Benetton	Benetton-Playlife B198	57 laps	11
8	Damon Hill	Jordan	Jordan-Mugen Honda 198	57 laps	10
9	Olivier Panis	Prost	Prost-Peugeot AP01	57 laps	21
R	Giancarlo Fisichella	Benetton	Benetton-Playlife B198	43 laps/wing	7
R	Jean Alesi	Sauber	Sauber-Petronas C17	41 laps/engine	12
R	Jarno Trulli	Prost	Prost-Peugeot AP01	26 laps/gearbox	15
R	Ricardo Rosset	Tyrrell	Tyrrell-Ford Cosworth 026	25 laps/gearbox	19
R	Mika Salo	Arrows	Arrows A19	23 laps/gearbox	16
R	Esteban Tuero	Minardi	Minardi-Ford Cosworth M198	22 laps/engine	17
R	Shinji Nakano	Minardi	Minardi-Ford Cosworth M198	8 laps/halfshaft	22
R	Michael Schumacher	Ferrari	Ferrari F300	5 laps/engine	3
R	Pedro Diniz	Arrows	Arrows A19	2 laps/gearbox	20
R	Ralf Schumacher	Jordan	Jordan-Mugen Honda 198	1 lap/collision	9
R	Toranosuke Takagi	Tyrrell	Tyrrell-Ford Cosworth 026	1 lap/spun off	13
R	Jan Magnussen	Stewart	Stewart-Ford Cosworth SF2	1 lap/collision	18
R	Rubens Barrichello	Stewart	Stewart-Ford Cosworth SF2	0 laps/gearbox	14

Pole: Hakkinen, 1m30.010s, 131.790mph/212.096kph. Fastest lap: Hakkinen, 1m31.649s, 129.433mph/208.303kph on Lap 39. Race leaders: Hakkinen 1-23 & 25-35 & 56-58, Coulthard 24 & 36-55

MAKING THE ENGINEERS WORK

For this season, the cars were narrowed by 20cm (7.9in) in order to reduce their speed. What made them look even more different was that their slicks were replaced by grooved tyres, to reduce their grip. The first test of this combination added six seconds to a lap time. But the engineers worked on this and the cars were almost as fast at the end of 1998 as they had been the season before.

BRAZILIAN GRAND PRIX

INTERLAGOS • ROUND 2 • DATE: 29TH MARCH 1998
Laps: 72 • Distance: 192.18miles/309.024km • Weather: Hot but dull

Pos	Driver	Team	Chassis-Engine	Result	Qual
1	Mika Hakkinen	McLaren	McLaren-Mercedes MP4-13	1h37m11.747s	1
2	David Coulthard	McLaren	McLaren-Mercedes MP4-13	1h37m12.849s	2
3	Michael Schumacher	Ferrari	Ferrari F300	1h38m12.297s	4
4	Alexander Wurz	Benetton	Benetton-Playlife B198	1h38m19.200s	5
5	Heinz-Harald Frentzen	Williams	Williams-Mecachrome FW20	71 laps	3
6	Giancarlo Fisichella	Benetton	Benetton-Playlife B198	71 laps	7
7	Jacques Villeneuve	Williams	Williams-Mecachrome FW20	71 laps	10
8	Eddie Irvine	Ferrari	Ferrari F300	71 laps	6
9	Jean Alesi	Sauber	Sauber-Petronas C17	71 laps	15
DQ	Damon Hill	Jordan	Jordan-Mugen Honda 198	70 laps/car underweight	11
10	Jan Magnussen	Stewart	Stewart-Ford Cosworth SF2	70 laps	16
11	Johnny Herbert	Sauber	Sauber-Petronas C17	67 laps/neck strain	14
R	Olivier Panis	Prost	Prost-Peugeot AP01	63 laps/engine	9
R	Rubens Barrichello	Stewart	Stewart-Ford Cosworth SF2	56 laps/gearbox	13
R	Ricardo Rosset	Tyrrell	Tyrrell-Ford Cosworth 026	52 laps/gearbox	21
R	Esteban Tuero	Minardi	Minardi-Ford Cosworth M198	44 laps/throttle	19
R	Pedro Diniz	Arrows	Arrows A19	26 laps/gearbox	22
R	Toranosuke Takagi	Tyrrell	Tyrrell-Ford Cosworth 026	19 laps/engine	17
R	Mika Salo	Arrows	Arrows A19	18 laps/engine	20
R	Jarno Trulli	Prost	Prost-Peugeot AP01	17 laps/fuel pump	12
R	Shinji Nakano	Minardi	Minardi-Ford Cosworth M198	3 laps/spun off	18
R	Ralf Schumacher	Jordan	Jordan-Mugen Honda 198	0 laps/spun off	8

Pole: Hakkinen, 1m17.092s, 124.538mph/200.425kph. Fastest lap: Hakkinen, 1m19.337s, 121.014mph/194.754kph on Lap 64. Race leaders: Hakkinen 1-72

ARGENTINIAN GRAND PRIX

BUENOS AIRES • ROUND 3 • DATE: 12TH APRIL 1998
Laps: 72 • Distance: 190.542miles/306.648km • Weather: Warm but dull

Pos	Driver	Team	Chassis-Engine	Result	Qual
1	Michael Schumacher	Ferrari	Ferrari F300	1h48m36.175s	2
2	Mika Hakkinen	McLaren	McLaren-Mercedes MP4-13	1h48m59.073s	3
3	Eddie Irvine	Ferrari	Ferrari F300	1h49m33.920s	4
4	Alexander Wurz	Benetton	Benetton-Playlife B198	1h49m44.309s	8
5	Jean Alesi	Sauber	Sauber-Petronas C17	1h49m54.461s	11
6	David Coulthard	McLaren	McLaren-Mercedes MP4-13	1h49m55.926s	1
7	Giancarlo Fisichella	Benetton	Benetton-Playlife B198	1h50m04.612s	10
8	Damon Hill	Jordan	Jordan-Mugen Honda 198	71 laps	9
9	Heinz-Harald Frentzen	Williams	Williams-Mecachrome FW20	71 laps	6
10	Rubens Barrichello	Stewart	Stewart-Ford Cosworth SF2	70 laps	14
11	Jarno Trulli	Prost	Prost-Peugeot AP01	70 laps	16
12	Toranosuke Takagi	Tyrrell	Tyrrell-Ford Cosworth 026	70 laps	13
13	Shinji Nakano	Minardi	Minardi-Ford Cosworth M198	69 laps	19
14	Ricardo Rosset	Tyrrell	Tyrrell-Ford Cosworth 026	68 laps	21
15	Olivier Panis	Prost	Prost-Peugeot AP01	65 laps/engine	15
R	Esteban Tuero	Minardi	Minardi-Ford Cosworth M198	63 laps/spun off	20
R	Jacques Villeneuve	Williams	Williams-Mecachrome FW20	52 laps/collision	7

Pos	Driver	Team	Chassis-Engine	Result	Qual
R	Johnny Herbert	Sauber	Sauber-Petronas C17	46 laps/collision	12
R	Ralf Schumacher	Jordan	Jordan-Mugen Honda 198	22 laps/suspension	5
R	Mika Salo	Arrows	Arrows A19	18 laps/gearbox	17
R	Jan Magnussen	Stewart	Stewart-Ford Cosworth SF2	17 laps/transmission	22
R	Pedro Diniz	Arrows	Arrows A19	13 laps/gearbox	18

Pole: Coulthard, 1m25.852s, 110.971mph/178.591kph. Fastest lap: Wurz, 1m28.179s, 108.042mph/173.878kph on Lap 39. Race leaders: Coulthard 1-4, M Schumacher 5-28 & 43-72, Hakkinen 29-42

SAN MARINO GRAND PRIX

IMOLA • ROUND 4 • DATE: 26TH APRIL 1998
Laps: 62 • Distance: 189.559miles/305.66km • Weather: Warm & bright

Pos	Driver	Team	Chassis-Engine	Result	Qual
1	David Coulthard	McLaren	McLaren-Mercedes MP4-13	1h34m24.593s	1
2	Michael Schumacher	Ferrari	Ferrari F300	1h34m29.147s	3
3	Eddie Irvine	Ferrari	Ferrari F300	1h35m16.368s	4
4	Jacques Villeneuve	Williams	Williams-Mecachrome FW20	1h35m19.183s	6
5	Heinz-Harald Frentzen	Williams	Williams-Mecachrome FW20	1h35m42.069s	8
6	Jean Alesi	Sauber	Sauber-Petronas C17	61 laps	12
7	Ralf Schumacher	Jordan	Jordan-Mugen Honda 198	60 laps	9
8	Esteban Tuero	Minardi	Minardi-Ford Cosworth M198	60 laps	19
9	Mika Salo	Arrows	Arrows A19	60 laps	14
10	Damon Hill	Jordan	Jordan-Mugen Honda 198	57 laps/hydraulics	7
11	Olivier Panis	Prost	Prost-Peugeot AP01	56 laps/engine	13
R	Ricardo Rosset	Tyrrell	Tyrrell-Ford Cosworth 026	48 laps/engine	22
R	Toranosuke Takagi	Tyrrell	Tyrrell-Ford Cosworth 026	40 laps/engine	15
R	Jarno Trulli	Prost	Prost-Peugeot AP01	34 laps/throttle	16
R	Shinji Nakano	Minardi	Minardi-Ford Cosworth M198	27 laps/engine	21
R	Pedro Diniz	Arrows	Arrows A19	18 laps/engine	18
R	Mika Hakkinen	McLaren	McLaren-Mercedes MP4-13	17 laps/gearbox	2
R	Alexander Wurz	Benetton	Benetton-Playlife B198	17 laps/engine	5
R	Giancarlo Fisichella	Benetton	Benetton-Playlife B198	17 laps/spun off	10
R	Johnny Herbert	Sauber	Sauber-Petronas C17	12 laps/puncture	11
R	Jan Magnussen	Stewart	Stewart-Ford Cosworth SF2	8 laps/transmission	20
R	Rubens Barrichello	Stewart	Stewart-Ford Cosworth SF2	0 laps/spun off	17

Pole: Coulthard, 1m25.973s, 128.273mph/206.436kph. Fastest lap: M Schumacher, 1m29.345s, 123.432mph/198.645kph on Lap 48. Race leaders: Coulthard 1-62

A MAN OF HIS WORD

David Coulthard handed victory in the Australian GP back to Mika Hakkinen because of a pre-race deal. They agreed that as the MP4-13 was so dominant that they should avoid squandering a maximum points haul. Whoever led into Turn 1 should win. This was Hakkinen, but he misheard a radio call and pitted early, only to be waved through.

ALESI ATTRACTS TROUBLE

Alex Wurz grabbed the headlines when he rolled his Benetton at the start of the Canadian GP in Montreal. This happened when the field packed together tightly on the approach to the first corner. The Austrian tried to dive inside Jean Alesi's Sauber, but clipped it and rolled. At the restart, Alesi ended up with Jarno Trulli's Prost on top of him…

SPANISH GRAND PRIX

BARCELONA-CATALUNYA • ROUND 5 • DATE: 10TH MAY 1998
Laps: 65 • Distance: 190.780miles/307.32km • Weather: Hot & bright

Pos	Driver	Team	Chassis-Engine	Result	Qual
1	Mika Hakkinen	McLaren	McLaren-Mercedes MP4-13	1h33m37.621s	1
2	David Coulthard	McLaren	McLaren-Mercedes MP4-13	1h33m47.060s	2
3	Michael Schumacher	Ferrari	Ferrari F300	1h34m24.716s	3
4	Alexander Wurz	Benetton	Benetton-Playlife B198	1h34m40.159s	5
5	Rubens Barrichello	Stewart	Stewart-Ford Cosworth SF2	64 laps	9
6	Jacques Villeneuve	Williams	Williams-Mecachrome FW20	64 laps	10
7	Johnny Herbert	Sauber	Sauber-Petronas C17	64 laps	7
8	Heinz-Harald Frentzen	Williams	Williams-Mecachrome FW20	63 laps	13
9	Jarno Trulli	Prost	Prost-Peugeot AP01	63 laps	16
10	Jean Alesi	Sauber	Sauber-Petronas C17	63 laps	14
11	Ralf Schumacher	Jordan	Jordan-Mugen Honda 198	63 laps	11
12	Jan Magnussen	Stewart	Stewart-Ford Cosworth SF2	63 laps	18
13	Toranosuke Takagi	Tyrrell	Tyrrell-Ford Cosworth 026	63 laps	21
14	Shinji Nakano	Minardi	Minardi-Ford Cosworth M198	63 laps	20
15	Esteban Tuero	Minardi	Minardi-Ford Cosworth M198	63 laps	19
16	Olivier Panis	Prost	Prost-Peugeot AP01	60 laps/hydraulics	12
R	Damon Hill	Jordan	Jordan-Mugen Honda 198	46 laps/engine	8
R	Giancarlo Fisichella	Benetton	Benetton-Playlife B198	28 laps/collision	4
R	Eddie Irvine	Ferrari	Ferrari F300	28 laps/collision	6
R	Mika Salo	Arrows	Arrows A19	21 laps/engine	17
R	Pedro Diniz	Arrows	Arrows A19	20 laps/engine	15
DNQ	Ricardo Rosset	Tyrrell	Tyrrell-Ford Cosworth 026	-	22

Pole: Hakkinen, 1m20.262s, 131.771mph/212.065kph. Fastest lap: Hakkinen, 1m24.275s, 125.496mph/201.967kph on Lap 25. Race leaders: Hakkinen 1-26 & 28-45 & 47-65, Coulthard 27 & 46

MONACO GRAND PRIX

MONTE CARLO • ROUND 6 • DATE: 24TH MAY 1998
Laps: 78 • Distance: 163.188miles/262.626km • Weather: Hot & bright

Pos	Driver	Team	Chassis-Engine	Result	Qual
1	Mika Hakkinen	McLaren	McLaren-Mercedes MP4-13	1h51m23.595s	1
2	Giancarlo Fisichella	Benetton	Benetton-Playlife B198	1h51m35.070s	3
3	Eddie Irvine	Ferrari	Ferrari F300	1h52m04.973s	7
4	Mika Salo	Arrows	Arrows A19	1h52m23.958s	8
5	Jacques Villeneuve	Williams	Williams-Mecachrome FW20	77 laps	13

Pos	Driver	Team	Chassis-Engine	Result	Qual
6	Pedro Diniz	Arrows	Arrows A19	77 laps	12
7	Johnny Herbert	Sauber	Sauber-Petronas C17	77 laps	9
8	Damon Hill	Jordan	Jordan-Mugen Honda 198	76 laps	15
9	Shinji Nakano	Minardi	Minardi-Ford Cosworth M198	76 laps	19
10	Michael Schumacher	Ferrari	Ferrari F300	76 laps	4
11	Toranosuke Takagi	Tyrrell	Tyrrell-Ford Cosworth 026	76 laps	20
12	Jean Alesi	Sauber	Sauber-Petronas C17	72 laps/gearbox	11
R	Jarno Trulli	Prost	Prost-Peugeot AP01	56 laps/gearbox	10
R	Olivier Panis	Prost	Prost-Peugeot AP01	49 laps/wheel	18
R	Ralf Schumacher	Jordan	Jordan-Mugen Honda 198	44 laps/suspension	16
R	Alexander Wurz	Benetton	Benetton-Playlife B198	42 laps/spun off	6
R	Jan Magnussen	Stewart	Stewart-Ford Cosworth SF2	30 laps/suspension	17
R	David Coulthard	McLaren	McLaren-Mercedes MP4-13	17 laps/engine	2
R	Rubens Barrichello	Stewart	Stewart-Ford Cosworth SF2	11 laps/suspension	14
R	Heinz-Harald Frentzen	Williams	Williams-Mecachrome FW20	9 laps/collision	5
R	Esteban Tuero	Minardi	Minardi-Ford Cosworth M198	0 laps/spun off	21
DNQ	Ricardo Rosset	Tyrrell	Tyrrell-Ford Cosworth 026	-	22

Pole: Hakkinen, 1m19.798s, 94.385mph/151.898kph. Fastest lap: Hakkinen, 1m22.948s, 90.801mph/146.130kph on Lap 29. Race leaders: Hakkinen 1-78

CANADIAN GRAND PRIX

MONTREAL • ROUND 7 • DATE: 7TH JUNE 1998
Laps: 69 • Distance: 189.548miles/305.049km • Weather: Cool & dull

Pos	Driver	Team	Chassis-Engine	Result	Qual
1	Michael Schumacher	Ferrari	Ferrari F300	1h40m57.355s	3
2	Giancarlo Fisichella	Benetton	Benetton-Playlife B198	1h41m14.017s	4
3	Eddie Irvine	Ferrari	Ferrari F300	1h41m57.414s	8
4	Alexander Wurz	Benetton	Benetton-Playlife B198	1h42m00.587s	11
5	Rubens Barrichello	Stewart	Stewart-Ford Cosworth SF2	1h42m18.868s	13
6	Jan Magnussen	Stewart	Stewart-Ford Cosworth SF2	68 laps	20
7	Shinji Nakano	Minardi	Minardi-Ford Cosworth M198	68 laps	18
8	Ricardo Rosset	Tyrrell	Tyrrell-Ford Cosworth 026	68 laps	22
9	Pedro Diniz	Arrows	Arrows A19	68 laps	19
10	Jacques Villeneuve	Williams	Williams-Mecachrome FW20	63 laps	6
R	Esteban Tuero	Minardi	Minardi-Ford Cosworth M198	53 laps/electrical	21
R	Damon Hill	Jordan	Jordan-Mugen Honda 198	42 laps/electrical	10
R	Olivier Panis	Prost	Prost-Peugeot AP01	39 laps/spun off	15
R	Heinz-Harald Frentzen	Williams	Williams-Mecachrome FW20	20 laps/spun off	7
R	David Coulthard	McLaren	McLaren-Mercedes MP4-13	18 laps/throttle	1
R	Johnny Herbert	Sauber	Sauber-Petronas C17	18 laps/spun off	12
R	Mika Salo	Arrows	Arrows A19	18 laps/spun off	17
R	Mika Hakkinen	McLaren	McLaren-Mercedes MP4-13	0 laps/gearbox	2
R	Ralf Schumacher	Jordan	Jordan-Mugen Honda 198	0 laps/gearbox	5
R	Jean Alesi	Sauber	Sauber-Petronas C17	0 laps/collision	9
R	Jarno Trulli	Prost	Prost-Peugeot AP01	0 laps/collision	14
R	Toranosuke Takagi	Tyrrell	Tyrrell-Ford Cosworth 026	0 laps/transmission	16

Pole: Coulthard, 1m18.213s, 126.443mph/203.490kph. Fastest lap: M Schumacher, 1m19.379s, 124.585mph/200.501kph on Lap 48. Race leaders: Coulthard 1-18, M Schumacher 19 & 44-69, Fisichella 20-43

FRENCH GRAND PRIX

MAGNY-COURS • ROUND 8 • DATE: 28TH JUNE 1998
Laps: 71 • Distance: 187.79miles/301.75km • Weather: Hot & bright

Pos	Driver	Team	Chassis-Engine	Result	Qual
1	Michael Schumacher	Ferrari	Ferrari F300	1h34m45.026s	2
2	Eddie Irvine	Ferrari	Ferrari F300	1h35m04.601s	4
3	Mika Hakkinen	McLaren	McLaren-Mercedes MP4-13	1h35m04.773s	1
4	Jacques Villeneuve	Williams	Williams-Mecachrome FW20	1h35m51.991s	5
5	Alexander Wurz	Benetton	Benetton-Playlife B198	70 laps	10
6	David Coulthard	McLaren	McLaren-Mercedes MP4-13	70 laps	3
7	Jean Alesi	Sauber	Sauber-Petronas C17	70 laps	11
8	Johnny Herbert	Sauber	Sauber-Petronas C17	70 laps	13
9	Giancarlo Fisichella	Benetton	Benetton-Playlife B198	70 laps	9
10	Rubens Barrichello	Stewart	Stewart-Ford Cosworth SF2	69 laps	14
11	Olivier Panis	Prost	Prost-Peugeot AP01	69 laps	16
12	Jos Verstappen	Stewart	Stewart-Ford Cosworth SF2	69 laps	15
13	Mika Salo	Arrows	Arrows A19	69 laps	19
14	Pedro Diniz	Arrows	Arrows A19	69 laps	17
15	Heinz-Harald Frentzen	Williams	Williams-Mecachrome FW20	68 laps/steering	8
16	Ralf Schumacher	Jordan	Jordan-Mugen Honda 198	68 laps	6
17	Shinji Nakano	Minardi	Minardi-Ford Cosworth M198	65 laps/engine	21
R	Toranosuke Takagi	Tyrrell	Tyrrell-Ford Cosworth 026	60 laps/engine	20
R	Jarno Trulli	Prost	Prost-Peugeot AP01	55 laps/spun off	12
R	Esteban Tuero	Minardi	Minardi-Ford Cosworth M198	41 laps/gearbox	22
R	Damon Hill	Jordan	Jordan-Mugen Honda 198	19 laps/hydraulics	7
R	Ricardo Rosset	Tyrrell	Tyrrell-Ford Cosworth 026	16 laps/hydraulics	18

Pole: Hakkinen, 1m14.929s, 126.879mph/204.193kph. Fastest lap: Coulthard, 1m17.523s, 122.634mph/197.360kph on Lap 59. Race leaders: M Schumacher 1-22 & 24-71, Irvine 23

DANCING AN IRISH JIG
Eddie Jordan had every reason to dance a jig at the Belgian GP, as his team scored its first win in its eighth year. Four cars were eliminated in a chaotic start, then three more at the second attempt, before Damon Hill took the lead when Michael Schumacher hit David Coulthard. Hill was chased home by team-mate Ralf Schumacher.

BRITISH GRAND PRIX

SILVERSTONE • ROUND 9 • DATE: 12TH JULY 1998
Laps: 60 • Distance: 191.384miles/308.4km • Weather: Warm but dull

Pos	Driver	Team	Chassis-Engine	Result	Qual
1	Michael Schumacher	Ferrari	Ferrari F300	1h47m02.450s	2
2	Mika Hakkinen	McLaren	McLaren-Mercedes MP4-13	1h47m24.915s	1
3	Eddie Irvine	Ferrari	Ferrari F300	1h47m31.649s	5
4	Alexander Wurz	Benetton	Benetton-Playlife B198	59 laps	11
5	Giancarlo Fisichella	Benetton	Benetton-Playlife B198	59 laps	10
6	Ralf Schumacher	Jordan	Jordan-Mugen Honda 198	59 laps	21
7	Jacques Villeneuve	Williams	Williams-Mecachrome FW20	59 laps	3

Pos	Driver	Team	Chassis-Engine	Result	Qual
8	Shinji Nakano	Minardi	Minardi-Ford Cosworth M198	58 laps	19
9	Toranosuke Takagi	Tyrrell	Tyrrell-Ford Cosworth 026	56 laps	17
R	Jean Alesi	Sauber	Sauber-Petronas C17	53 laps/electrical	8
R	Pedro Diniz	Arrows	Arrows A19	45 laps/spun off	12
R	Olivier Panis	Prost	Prost-Peugeot AP01	40 laps/spun off	22
R	Rubens Barrichello	Stewart	Stewart-Ford Cosworth SF2	39 laps/spun off	16
R	Jos Verstappen	Stewart	Stewart-Ford Cosworth SF2	38 laps/engine	15
R	David Coulthard	McLaren	McLaren-Mercedes MP4-13	37 laps/spun off	4
R	Jarno Trulli	Prost	Prost-Peugeot AP01	37 laps/spun off	14
R	Esteban Tuero	Minardi	Minardi-Ford Cosworth M198	29 laps/spun off	18
R	Ricardo Rosset	Tyrrell	Tyrrell-Ford Cosworth 026	29 laps/spun off	20
R	Johnny Herbert	Sauber	Sauber-Petronas C17	27 laps/spun off	9
R	Mika Salo	Arrows	Arrows A19	27 laps/throttle	13
R	Heinz-Harald Frentzen	Williams	Williams-Mecachrome FW20	15 laps/spun off	6
R	Damon Hill	Jordan	Jordan-Mugen Honda 198	13 laps/spun off	7

Pole: Hakkinen, 1m23.271s, 138.077mph/222.214kph. Fastest lap: M Schumacher, 1m35.704s, 120.139mph/193.346kph on Lap 12. Race leaders: Hakkinen 1-50, M Schumacher 51-60

WILLIAMS IN RETREAT

The dominant team in the mid-1990s, Williams, went into decline in 1998, discovering that life without a works engine deal can be tough. Despite the best efforts of Jacques Villeneuve and Heinz-Harald Frentzen with Mecachrome engines, it failed to register a win and fell to third. Worse than that, it scored just 38 points to McLaren's 156 and Ferrari's 133.

AUSTRIAN GRAND PRIX

A1-RING • ROUND 10 • DATE: 26TH JULY 1998
Laps: 71 • Distance: 190.542miles/306.649km • Weather: Hot & bright

Pos	Driver	Team	Chassis-Engine	Result	Qual
1	Mika Hakkinen	McLaren	McLaren-Mercedes MP4-13	1h30m44.086s	3
2	David Coulthard	McLaren	McLaren-Mercedes MP4-13	1h30m49.375s	14
3	Michael Schumacher	Ferrari	Ferrari F300	1h31m23.178s	4
4	Eddie Irvine	Ferrari	Ferrari F300	1h31m28.062s	8
5	Ralf Schumacher	Jordan	Jordan-Mugen Honda 198	1h31m34.740s	9
6	Jacques Villeneuve	Williams	Williams-Mecachrome FW20	1h31m37.288s	11
7	Damon Hill	Jordan	Jordan-Mugen Honda 198	1h31m57.710s	15
8	Johnny Herbert	Sauber	Sauber-Petronas C17	70 laps	18
9	Alexander Wurz	Benetton	Benetton-Playlife B198	70 laps	17
10	Jarno Trulli	Prost	Prost-Peugeot AP01	70 laps	16
11	Shinji Nakano	Minardi	Minardi-Ford Cosworth M198	70 laps	21
12	Ricardo Rosset	Tyrrell	Tyrrell-Ford Cosworth 026	69 laps	22
R	Jos Verstappen	Stewart	Stewart-Ford Cosworth SF2	51 laps/engine	12
R	Esteban Tuero	Minardi	Minardi-Ford Cosworth M198	30 laps/spun off	19
R	Giancarlo Fisichella	Benetton	Benetton-Playlife B198	21 laps/collision	1
R	Jean Alesi	Sauber	Sauber-Petronas C17	21 laps/collision	2
R	Heinz-Harald Frentzen	Williams	Williams-Mecachrome FW20	16 laps/engine	7

Pos	Driver	Team	Chassis-Engine	Result	Qual
R	Rubens Barrichello	Stewart	Stewart-Ford Cosworth SF2	8 laps/brakes	5
R	Pedro Diniz	Arrows	Arrows A19	3 laps/collision	13
R	Mika Salo	Arrows	Arrows A19	1 lap/collision	6
R	Olivier Panis	Prost	Prost-Peugeot AP01	0 laps/clutch	10
R	Toranosuke Takagi	Tyrrell	Tyrrell-Ford Cosworth 026	0 laps/collision	20

Pole: Fisichella, 1m29.598s, 107.829mph/173.535kph. Fastest lap: Coulthard, 1m12.878s, 132.568mph/213.348kph on Lap 30. Race leaders: Hakkinen 1-34 & 37-71, Coulthard 35-36

GERMAN GRAND PRIX

HOCKENHEIM • ROUND 11 • DATE: 2ND AUGUST 1998
Laps: 45 • Distance: 190.782miles/307.035km • Weather: Hot & bright

Pos	Driver	Team	Chassis-Engine	Result	Qual
1	Mika Hakkinen	McLaren	McLaren-Mercedes MP4-13	1h20m47.984s	1
2	David Coulthard	McLaren	McLaren-Mercedes MP4-13	1h20m48.410s	2
3	Jacques Villeneuve	Williams	Williams-Mecachrome FW20	1h20m50.561s	3
4	Damon Hill	Jordan	Jordan-Mugen Honda 198	1h20m55.169s	5
5	Michael Schumacher	Ferrari	Ferrari F300	1h21m00.597s	9
6	Ralf Schumacher	Jordan	Jordan-Mugen Honda 198	1h21m17.722s	4
7	Giancarlo Fisichella	Benetton	Benetton-Playlife B198	1h21m19.010s	8
8	Eddie Irvine	Ferrari	Ferrari F300	1h21m19.633s	6
9	Heinz-Harald Frentzen	Williams	Williams-Mecachrome FW20	1h21m20.768s	10
10	Jean Alesi	Sauber	Sauber-Petronas C17	1h21m36.355s	11
11	Alexander Wurz	Benetton	Benetton-Playlife B198	1h21m45.978s	7
12	Jarno Trulli	Prost	Prost-Peugeot AP01	44 laps	14
13	Toranosuke Takagi	Tyrrell	Tyrrell-Ford Cosworth 026	44 laps	15
14	Mika Salo	Arrows	Arrows A19	44 laps	17
15	Olivier Panis	Prost	Prost-Peugeot AP01	44 laps	16
16	Esteban Tuero	Minardi	Minardi-Ford Cosworth M198	43 laps	21
R	Johnny Herbert	Sauber	Sauber-Petronas C17	37 laps/gearbox	12
R	Shinji Nakano	Minardi	Minardi-Ford Cosworth M198	36 laps/gearbox	20
R	Rubens Barrichello	Stewart	Stewart-Ford Cosworth SF2	27 laps/gearbox	13
R	Jos Verstappen	Stewart	Stewart-Ford Cosworth SF2	24 laps/gearbox	19
R	Pedro Diniz	Arrows	Arrows A19	2 laps/throttle	18
DNQ	Ricardo Rosset	Tyrrell	Tyrrell-Ford Cosworth 026	-	-

Pole: Hakkinen, 1m41.838s, 149.871mph/241.194kph. Fastest lap: Coulthard, 1m46.116s, 143.829mph/231.471kph on Lap 17. Race leaders: Hakkinen 1-25 & 28-45, Coulthard 26-27

THE WORLD'S FASTEST TAXI

The thrill of driving an F1 car is something experienced only by the chosen few. Anxious to let others get a taste, McLaren built a two-seater F1 car with a stretched chassis that accommodated a passenger behind the driver. The MP4-98T was used at grand prix meetings to show sponsors and guests just how dynamic F1 cars really are.

HUNGARIAN GRAND PRIX

HUNGARORING • ROUND 12 • DATE: 16TH AUGUST 1998
Laps: 77 • Distance: 190.42miles/305.844km • Weather: Hot & bright

Pos	Driver	Team	Chassis-Engine	Result	Qual
1	Michael Schumacher	Ferrari	Ferrari F300	1h45m25.550s	3
2	David Coulthard	McLaren	McLaren-Mercedes MP4-13	1h45m34.983s	2
3	Jacques Villeneuve	Williams	Williams-Mecachrome FW20	1h46m09.994s	6
4	Damon Hill	Jordan	Jordan-Mugen Honda 198	1h46m20.626s	4
5	Heinz-Harald Frentzen	Williams	Williams-Mecachrome FW20	1h46m22.060s	7
6	Mika Hakkinen	McLaren	McLaren-Mercedes MP4-13	76 laps	1
7	Jean Alesi	Sauber	Sauber-Petronas C17	76 laps	11
8	Giancarlo Fisichella	Benetton	Benetton-Playlife B198	76 laps	8
9	Ralf Schumacher	Jordan	Jordan-Mugen Honda 198	76 laps	10
10	Johnny Herbert	Sauber	Sauber-Petronas C17	76 laps	15
11	Pedro Diniz	Arrows	Arrows A19	74 laps	12
12	Olivier Panis	Prost	Prost-Peugeot AP01	74 laps	20
13	Jos Verstappen	Stewart	Stewart-Ford Cosworth SF2	74 laps	17
14	Toranosuke Takagi	Tyrrell	Tyrrell-Ford Cosworth 026	74 laps	18
15	Shinji Nakano	Minardi	Minardi-Ford Cosworth M198	74 laps	19
16	Alexander Wurz	Benetton	Benetton-Playlife B198	69 laps/gearbox	9
R	Rubens Barrichello	Stewart	Stewart-Ford Cosworth SF2	54 laps/gearbox	14
R	Jarno Trulli	Prost	Prost-Peugeot AP01	28 laps/engine	16
R	Mika Salo	Arrows	Arrows A19	18 laps/gearbox	13
R	Eddie Irvine	Ferrari	Ferrari F300	13 laps/gearbox	5
R	Esteban Tuero	Minardi	Minardi-Ford Cosworth M198	13 laps/engine	21
DNQ	Ricardo Rosset	Tyrrell	Tyrrell-Ford Cosworth 026	-	-

Pole: Hakkinen, 1m16.973s, 115.431mph/185.769kph. Fastest lap: M Schumacher, 1m19.286s, 112.064mph/180.349kph on Lap 60. Race leaders: Hakkinen 1-46, M Schumacher 47-77

A PROPER TYRE WAR
The World Championship had been run as a one-supplier tyre formula from 1992 to 1996, but 1998 was spicier, as Goodyear gave its rubber an extra push in the company's final season before bowing out of F1. This helped Ferrari take the challenge to Bridgestone-shod McLaren. From 1999, all tyres were Bridgestone-only.

BELGIAN GRAND PRIX

SPA-FRANCORCHAMPS • ROUND 13 • DATE: 30TH AUGUST 1998
Laps: 44 • Distance: 190.507miles/306.592km • Weather: Cool with heavy rain

Pos	Driver	Team	Chassis-Engine	Result	Qual
1	Damon Hill	Jordan	Jordan-Mugen Honda 198	1h43m47.407s	3
2	Ralf Schumacher	Jordan	Jordan-Mugen Honda 198	1h43m48.339s	8
3	Jean Alesi	Sauber	Sauber-Petronas C17	1h43m54.647s	10
4	Heinz-Harald Frentzen	Williams	Williams-Mecachrome FW20	1h44m19.650s	9
5	Pedro Diniz	Arrows	Arrows A19	1h44m39.089s	16
6	Jarno Trulli	Prost	Prost-Peugeot AP01	42 laps	13
7	David Coulthard	McLaren	McLaren-Mercedes MP4-13	39 laps	2

Pos	Driver	Team	Chassis-Engine	Result	Qual
8	Shinji Nakano	Minardi	Minardi-Ford Cosworth M198	39 laps	21
R	Giancarlo Fisichella	Benetton	Benetton-Playlife B198	26 laps/collision	7
R	Michael Schumacher	Ferrari	Ferrari F300	25 laps/collision	4
R	Eddie Irvine	Ferrari	Ferrari F300	25 laps/spun off	5
R	Esteban Tuero	Minardi	Minardi-Ford Cosworth M198	17 laps/gearbox	22
R	Jacques Villeneuve	Williams	Williams-Mecachrome FW20	16 laps/spun off	6
R	Toranosuke Takagi	Tyrrell	Tyrrell-Ford Cosworth 026	10 laps/spun off	19
R	Jos Verstappen	Stewart	Stewart-Ford Cosworth SF2	8 laps/engine	17
R	Mika Hakkinen	McLaren	McLaren-Mercedes MP4-13	0 laps/collision	1
R	Alexander Wurz	Benetton	Benetton-Playlife B198	0 laps/collision	11
R	Johnny Herbert	Sauber	Sauber-Petronas C17	0 laps/collision	12
R	Rubens Barrichello	Stewart	Stewart-Ford Cosworth SF2	0 laps/collision	14
R	Olivier Panis	Prost	Prost-Peugeot AP01	0 laps/collision	15
R	Mika Salo	Arrows	Arrows A19	0 laps/collision	18
R	Ricardo Rosset	Tyrrell	Tyrrell-Ford Cosworth 026	0 laps/collision	20

Pole: Hakkinen, 1m48.682s, 146.106mph/235.136kph. Fastest lap: M Schumacher, 2m03.766s, 125.939mph/202.679kph on Lap 9. Race leaders: Hill 1-7 & 26-44, M Schumacher 8-25

ITALIAN GRAND PRIX

MONZA • ROUND 14 • DATE: 13TH SEPTEMBER 1998
Laps: 53 • Distance: 189.568miles/305.81km • Weather: Warm & bright

Pos	Driver	Team	Chassis-Engine	Result	Qual
1	Michael Schumacher	Ferrari	Ferrari F300	1h17m09.672s	1
2	Eddie Irvine	Ferrari	Ferrari F300	1h17m47.649s	5
3	Ralf Schumacher	Jordan	Jordan-Mugen Honda 198	1h17m50.824s	6
4	Mika Hakkinen	McLaren	McLaren-Mercedes MP4-13	1h18m05.343s	3
5	Jean Alesi	Sauber	Sauber-Petronas C17	1h18m11.544s	8
6	Damon Hill	Jordan	Jordan-Mugen Honda 198	1h18m16.360s	14
7	Heinz-Harald Frentzen	Williams	Williams-Mecachrome FW20	52 laps	12
8	Giancarlo Fisichella	Benetton	Benetton-Playlife B198	52 laps	11
9	Toranosuke Takagi	Tyrrell	Tyrrell-Ford Cosworth 026	52 laps	19
10	Rubens Barrichello	Stewart	Stewart-Ford Cosworth SF2	52 laps	13
11	Esteban Tuero	Minardi	Minardi-Ford Cosworth M198	51 laps	22
12	Ricardo Rosset	Tyrrell	Tyrrell-Ford Cosworth 026	51 laps	18
13	Jarno Trulli	Prost	Prost-Peugeot AP01	50 laps	10
R	Jos Verstappen	Stewart	Stewart-Ford Cosworth SF2	39 laps/gearbox	17
R	Jacques Villeneuve	Williams	Williams-Mecachrome FW20	37 laps/spun off	2
R	Mika Salo	Arrows	Arrows A19	32 laps/throttle	16
R	Alexander Wurz	Benetton	Benetton-Playlife B198	24 laps/gearbox	7
R	David Coulthard	McLaren	McLaren-Mercedes MP4-13	16 laps/engine	4
R	Olivier Panis	Prost	Prost-Peugeot AP01	15 laps/vibrations	9
R	Shinji Nakano	Minardi	Minardi-Ford Cosworth M198	13 laps/engine	21
R	Johnny Herbert	Sauber	Sauber-Petronas C17	12 laps/spun off	15
R	Pedro Diniz	Arrows	Arrows A19	10 laps/spun off	20

Pole: M Schumacher, 1m25.289s, 151.333mph/243.548kph. Fastest lap: Hakkinen, 1m25.139s, 151.600mph/243.977kph on Lap 45. Race leaders: Hakkinen 1-7 & 32-34, Coulthard 8-16, M Schumacher 17-31 & 35-53

NEW DRIVERS

There were just two new F1 drivers in 1998: Toranosuke Takagi and Esteban Tuero. Takagi was the faster of the two; he set good lap times for Tyrrell and was ninth twice, but made a string of mistakes. Tuero was simply not ready for F1 when he joined Minardi, but the 20-year-old Argentinian claimed eighth at Imola when only nine cars finished.

LUXEMBOURG GRAND PRIX

NURBURGRING • ROUND 15 • DATE: 27TH SEPTEMBER 1998
Laps: 67 • Distance: 189.674miles/305.252km • Weather: Cool & dull

Pos	Driver	Team	Chassis-Engine	Result	Qual
1	Mika Hakkinen	McLaren	McLaren-Mercedes MP4-13	1h32m14.789s	3
2	Michael Schumacher	Ferrari	Ferrari F300	1h32m17.000s	1
3	David Coulthard	McLaren	McLaren-Mercedes MP4-13	1h32m48.952s	5
4	Eddie Irvine	Ferrari	Ferrari F300	1h33m12.971s	2
5	Heinz-Harald Frentzen	Williams	Williams-Mecachrome FW20	1h33m15.036s	7
6	Giancarlo Fisichella	Benetton	Benetton-Playlife B198	1h33m16.148s	4
7	Alexander Wurz	Benetton	Benetton-Playlife B198	1h33m19.578s	8
8	Jacques Villeneuve	Williams	Williams-Mecachrome FW20	66 laps	9
9	Damon Hill	Jordan	Jordan-Mugen Honda 198	66 laps	10
10	Jean Alesi	Sauber	Sauber-Petronas C17	66 laps	11
11	Rubens Barrichello	Stewart	Stewart-Ford Cosworth SF2	65 laps	12
12	Olivier Panis	Prost	Prost-Peugeot AP01	65 laps	15
13	Jos Verstappen	Stewart	Stewart-Ford Cosworth SF2	65 laps	18
14	Mika Salo	Arrows	Arrows A19	65 laps	16
15	Shinji Nakano	Minardi	Minardi-Ford Cosworth M198	65 laps	20
16	Toranosuke Takagi	Tyrrell	Tyrrell-Ford Cosworth 026	65 laps	19
R	Esteban Tuero	Minardi	Minardi-Ford Cosworth M198	56 laps/engine	21
R	Ralf Schumacher	Jordan	Jordan-Mugen Honda 198	53 laps/brakes	6
R	Johnny Herbert	Sauber	Sauber-Petronas C17	37 laps/engine	13
R	Ricardo Rosset	Tyrrell	Tyrrell-Ford Cosworth 026	36 laps/engine	22
R	Jarno Trulli	Prost	Prost-Peugeot AP01	6 laps/transmission	14
R	Pedro Diniz	Arrows	Arrows A19	6 laps/hydraulics	17

Pole: M Schumacher, 1m18.561s, 129.726mph/208.775kph. Fastest lap: Hakkinen, 1m20.450s, 126.680mph/203.873kph on Lap 25. Race leaders: M Schumacher 1-24, Hakkinen 25-67

JAPANESE GRAND PRIX

SUZUKA • ROUND 16 • DATE: 1ST NOVEMBER 1998
Laps: 51 • Distance: 185.829miles/299.064km • Weather: Warm & bright

Pos	Driver	Team	Chassis-Engine	Result	Qual
1	Mika Hakkinen	McLaren	McLaren-Mercedes MP4-13	1h27m22.535s	2
2	Eddie Irvine	Ferrari	Ferrari F300	1h27m29.026s	4
3	David Coulthard	McLaren	McLaren-Mercedes MP4-13	1h27m50.197s	3
4	Damon Hill	Jordan	Jordan-Mugen Honda 198	1h28m36.026s	8
5	Heinz-Harald Frentzen	Williams	Williams-Mecachrome FW20	1h28m36.392s	5
6	Jacques Villeneuve	Williams	Williams-Mecachrome FW20	1h28m38.402s	6
7	Jean Alesi	Sauber	Sauber-Petronas C17	1h28m58.588s	12

Pos	Driver	Team	Chassis-Engine	Result	Qual
8	Giancarlo Fisichella	Benetton	Benetton-Playlife B198	1h29m03.837s	10
9	Alexander Wurz	Benetton	Benetton-Playlife B198	50 laps	9
10	Johnny Herbert	Sauber	Sauber-Petronas C17	50 laps	11
11	Olivier Panis	Prost	Prost-Peugeot AP01	50 laps	13
12	Jarno Trulli	Prost	Prost-Peugeot AP01	48 laps/engine	14
R	Shinji Nakano	Minardi	Minardi-Ford Cosworth M198	40 laps/throttle	20
R	Michael Schumacher	Ferrari	Ferrari F300	31 laps/tyre	1
R	Toranosuke Takagi	Tyrrell	Tyrrell-Ford Cosworth 026	28 laps/collision	17
R	Esteban Tuero	Minardi	Minardi-Ford Cosworth M198	28 laps/collision	21
R	Rubens Barrichello	Stewart	Stewart-Ford Cosworth SF2	25 laps/hydraulics	16
R	Jos Verstappen	Stewart	Stewart-Ford Cosworth SF2	21 laps/gearbox	19
R	Mika Salo	Arrows	Arrows A19	14 laps/hydraulics	15
R	Ralf Schumacher	Jordan	Jordan-Mugen Honda 198	13 laps/engine	7
R	Pedro Diniz	Arrows	Arrows A19	2 laps/spun off	18
DNQ	Ricardo Rosset	Tyrrell	Tyrrell-Ford Cosworth 026	-	22

Pole: M Schumacher, 1m36.293s, 136.223mph/219.230kph. Fastest lap: M Schumacher, 1m40.190s, 130.925mph/210.703kph on Lap 19. Race leaders: Hakkinen 1-51

CLASSIC CAR: McLAREN MP4-13

The second McLaren to race in the silver hues of cigarette company West, after decades of the red-and-white Marlboro livery, was a brilliant car. This was the first McLaren with design input from Adrian Newey, and he and Neil Oatley mastered the changing rules to make the most of the Mercedes V10 and new Bridgestone tyres. At the start of the season, the low-nose car's advantage was huge, shown by Hakkinen and Coulthard lapping the field at the first race and going on to win five of the first six rounds. Michael Schumacher and Ferrari did close in, but Hakkinen's eight wins earned him the title.

WORLD DRIVERS' CHAMPIONSHIP FINAL RESULTS

Pos	Driver	Nat	Car-Engine	R1	R2	R3	R4	R5	R6
1	Mika Hakkinen	FIN	McLaren-Mercedes MP4-13	1PF	1PF	2	R	1PF	1PF
2	Michael Schumacher	DEU	Ferrari F300	R	3	1	2F	3	10
3	David Coulthard	GBR	McLaren-Mercedes MP4-13	2	2	6P	1P	2	R
4	Eddie Irvine	GBR	Ferrari F300	4	8	3	3	R	3
5	Jacques Villeneuve	CAN	Williams-Mecachrome FW20	5	7	R	4	6	5
6	Damon Hill	GBR	Jordan-Mugen Honda 198	8	DQ	8	10	R	8
7	Heinz-Harald Frentzen	DEU	Williams-Mecachrome FW20	3	5	9	5	8	R
8	Alexander Wurz	AUT	Benetton-Playlife B198	7	4	4F	R	4	R
9	Giancarlo Fisichella	ITA	Benetton-Playlife B198	R	6	7	R	R	2
10	Ralf Schumacher	DEU	Jordan-Mugen Honda 198	R	R	R	7	11	R
11	Jean Alesi	FRA	Sauber-Petronas C17	R	9	5	6	10	12
12	Rubens Barrichello	BRA	Stewart-Ford Cosworth SF2	R	R	10	R	5	R
13	Mika Salo	FIN	Arrows A19	R	R	R	9	R	4
14	Pedro Diniz	BRA	Arrows A19	R	R	R	R	R	6
15	Johnny Herbert	GBR	Sauber-Petronas C17	6	11	R	R	7	7
16	Jan Magnussen	DNK	Stewart-Ford Cosworth SF2	R	10	R	R	12	R
17	Jarno Trulli	ITA	Prost-Peugeot AP01	R	R	11	R	9	R

Pos	Driver	R7	R8	R9	R10	R11	R12	R13	R14	R15	R16	Total
1	Hakkinen	R	3P	2P	1	1P	6P	RP	4F	1F	1	100
2	M Schumacher	1F	1	1F	3	5	1F	RF	1P	2P	RPF	86
3	Coulthard	RP	6F	R	2F	2F	2	7	R	3	3	56
4	Irvine	3	2	3	4	8	R	R	2	4	2	47
5	Villeneuve	10	4	7	6	3	3	R	R	8	6	21
6	Hill	R	R	R	7	4	4	1	6	9	4	20
7	Frentzen	R	15	R	R	9	5	4	7	5	5	17
8	Wurz	4	5	4	9	11	16	R	R	7	9	17
9	Fisichella	2	9	5	RP	7	8	R	8	6	8	16
10	R Schumacher	R	16	6	5	6	9	2	3	R	R	14
11	Alesi	R	7	R	R	10	7	3	5	10	7	9
12	Barrichello	5	10	R	R	R	R	R	10	11	R	4
13	Salo	R	13	R	R	14	R	R	R	14	R	3
14	Diniz	9	14	R	R	R	11	5	R	R	R	3
15	Herbert	R	8	R	8	R	10	R	R	R	10	1
16	Magnussen	6	-	-	-	-	-	-	-	-	-	1
17	Trulli	R	R	R	10	12	R	6	13	R	12	1

WORLD CONSTRUCTORS' CHAMPIONSHIP FINAL RESULTS

Pos	Team-Engine	R1	R2	R3	R4	R5	R6	R7	R8
1	McLaren-Mercedes	1/2	1/2	2/6	1/R	1/2	1/R	R/R	3/6
2	Ferrari	4/R	3/8	1/3	2/3	3/R	3/10	1/3	1/2
3	Williams-Mecachrome	3/5	5/7	9/R	4/5	6/8	5/R	10/R	4/15
4	Jordan-Mugen Honda	8/R	DQ/R	8/R	7/10	11/R	8/R	R/R	16/R
5	Benetton-Playlife	7/R	4/6	4/7	R/R	4/R	2/R	2/4	5/9
6	Sauber-Petronas	6/R	9/11	5/R	6/R	7/10	7/12	R/R	7/8
7	Arrows	R/R	R/R	R/R	9/R	R/R	4/6	9/R	13/14
8	Stewart-Ford	R/R	10/R	10/R	R/R	5/12	R/R	5/6	10/12
9	Prost-Peugeot	9/R	R/R	11/15	11/R	9/16	R/R	R/R	11/R

Pos	Team-Engine	R9	R10	R11	R12	R13	R14	R15	R16	Total
1	McLaren-Mercedes	2/R	1/2	1/2	2/6	7/R	4/R	1/3	1/3	156
2	Ferrari	1/3	3/4	5/8	1/R	R/R	1/2	2/4	2/R	133
3	Williams-Mecachrome	7/R	6/R	3/9	3/5	4/R	7/R	5/8	5/6	38
4	Jordan-Mugen Honda	6/R	5/7	4/6	4/9	1/2	3/6	9/R	4/R	34
5	Benetton-Playlife	4/5	9/R	7/11	8/16	R/R	8/R	6/7	8/9	33
6	Sauber-Petronas	R/R	8/R	10/R	7/10	3/R	5/R	10/R	7/10	10
7	Arrows	R/R	R/R	14/R	11/R	5/R	R/R	14/R	R/R	6
8	Stewart-Ford	R/R	R/R	R/R	13/R	R/R	10/R	11/13	R/R	5
9	Prost-Peugeot	R/R	10/R	12/15	12/R	6/R	13/R	12/R	11/12	1

SYMBOLS AND GRAND PRIX KEY

Round 1	Australian GP
Round 2	Brazilian GP
Round 3	Argentinian GP
Round 4	San Marino GP
Round 5	Spanish GP
Round 6	Monaco GP
Round 7	Canadian GP
Round 8	French GP
Round 9	British GP
Round 10	Austrian GP
Round 11	German GP
Round 12	Hungarian GP
Round 13	Belgian GP
Round 14	Italian GP
Round 15	Luxembourg GP
Round 16	Japanese GP

SCORING

1st	10 points
2nd	6 points
3rd	4 points
4th	3 points
5th	2 points
6th	1 point

DNPQ DID NOT PRE-QUALIFY **DNQ** DID NOT QUALIFY **DQ** DISQUALIFIED **EX** EXCLUDED
F FASTEST LAP **NC** NOT CLASSIFIED **NS** NON-STARTER **P** POLE POSITION **R** RETIRED

1999

SEASON SUMMARY

Mika Hakkinen took his second title in a row, profiting from Michael Schumacher's leg-breaking accident at the British GP that forced him to miss the next six races. There was still a challenge from Ferrari, in the form of Eddie Irvine, but this came up short even with help from the returning Schumacher, with Hakkinen clinching the title by winning the final round. In a year in which the number of grooves in the front tyres was increased from three to four, Jordan advanced to become the best of the rest, with Heinz-Harald Frentzen winning twice to end the year ranked third overall.

AUSTRALIAN GRAND PRIX

ALBERT PARK • ROUND 1 • DATE: 7TH MARCH 1999
Laps: 57 • Distance: 187.822miles/302.271km • Weather: Warm & bright

Pos	Driver	Team	Chassis-Engine	Result	Qual
1	Eddie Irvine	Ferrari	Ferrari F399	1h35m01.659s	6
2	Heinz-Harald Frentzen	Jordan	Jordan-Mugen Honda 199	1h35m02.686s	5
3	Ralf Schumacher	Williams	Williams-Supertec FW21	1h35m08.671s	8
4	Giancarlo Fisichella	Benetton	Benetton-Playlife B199	1h35m35.077s	7
5	Rubens Barrichello	Stewart	Stewart-Ford Cosworth SF3	1h35m56.357s	4
6	Pedro de la Rosa	Arrows	Arrows A20	1h36m25.976s	18
7	Toranosuke Takagi	Arrows	Arrows A20	1h36m27.947s	17
8	Michael Schumacher	Ferrari	Ferrari F399	56 laps	3
R	Ricardo Zonta	BAR	BAR-Supertec 01	48 laps/gearbox	19
R	Luca Badoer	Minardi	Minardi-Ford Cosworth M01	42 laps/gearbox	21
R	Alexander Wurz	Benetton	Benetton-Playlife B199	28 laps/suspension	10
R	Pedro Diniz	Sauber	Sauber-Petronas C18	27 laps/transmission	14
R	Jarno Trulli	Prost	Prost-Peugeot AP02	25 laps/collision	12
R	Marc Gene	Minardi	Minardi-Ford Cosworth M01	25 laps/collision	22
R	Olivier Panis	Prost	Prost-Peugeot AP02	23 laps/wheel	20
R	Mika Hakkinen	McLaren	McLaren-Mercedes MP4-14	21 laps/throttle	1
R	Alessandro Zanardi	Williams	Williams-Supertec FW21	20 laps/spun off	15
R	David Coulthard	McLaren	McLaren-Mercedes MP4-14	13 laps/hydraulics	2
R	Jacques Villeneuve	BAR	BAR-Supertec 01	13 laps/wing	11
R	Damon Hill	Jordan	Jordan-Mugen Honda 199	0 laps/collision	9
R	Jean Alesi	Sauber	Sauber-Petronas C18	0 laps/gearbox	16
R	Johnny Herbert	Stewart	Stewart-Ford Cosworth SF3	0 laps/oil leak	13

Pole: Hakkinen, 1m30.462s, 131.132mph/211.036kph. Fastest lap: M Schumacher, 1m32.112s, 128.783mph/207.256kph on Lap 55. Race leaders: Hakkinen 1-17, Irvine 18-57

STAND-IN HANDS OVER

Ferrari called up Mika Salo to drive its second car after Michael Schumacher broke his leg and the Finn – an F3 rival of compatriot Mika Hakkinen – ought to have become a grand prix winner at the German GP. He was comfortably in command at Hockenheim when he got the call to slow down and allow stand-in team leader Eddie Irvine to pass him for the win.

BRAZILIAN GRAND PRIX

INTERLAGOS • ROUND 2 • DATE: 11TH APRIL 1999
Laps: 72 • Distance: 192.18miles/309.024km • Weather: Hot & bright

Pos	Driver	Team	Chassis-Engine	Result	Qual
1	Mika Hakkinen	McLaren	McLaren-Mercedes MP4-14	1h36m03.785s	1
2	Michael Schumacher	Ferrari	Ferrari F399	1h36m08.710s	4
3	Heinz-Harald Frentzen	Jordan	Jordan-Mugen Honda 199	71 laps/out of fuel	8
4	Ralf Schumacher	Williams	Williams-Supertec FW21	71 laps	11
5	Eddie Irvine	Ferrari	Ferrari F399	71 laps	6
6	Olivier Panis	Prost	Prost-Peugeot AP02	71 laps	12
7	Alexander Wurz	Benetton	Benetton-Playlife B199	70 laps	9
8	Toranosuke Takagi	Arrows	Arrows A20	69 laps	19
9	Marc Gene	Minardi	Minardi-Ford Cosworth M01	69 laps	20
R	Pedro de la Rosa	Arrows	Arrows A20	52 laps/hydraulics	18
R	Jacques Villeneuve	BAR	BAR-Supertec 01	49 laps/hydraulics	21
R	Alessandro Zanardi	Williams	Williams-Supertec FW21	43 laps/gearbox	16
R	Rubens Barrichello	Stewart	Stewart-Ford Cosworth SF3	42 laps/engine	3
R	Pedro Diniz	Sauber	Sauber-Petronas C18	42 laps/collision	15
R	Giancarlo Fisichella	Benetton	Benetton-Playlife B199	38 laps/clutch	5
R	Stephane Sarrazin	Minardi	Minardi-Ford Cosworth M01	31 laps/spun off	17
R	Jean Alesi	Sauber	Sauber-Petronas C18	27 laps/gearbox	14
R	David Coulthard	McLaren	McLaren-Mercedes MP4-14	22 laps/gearbox	2
R	Jarno Trulli	Prost	Prost-Peugeot AP02	21 laps/gearbox	13
R	Johnny Herbert	Stewart	Stewart-Ford Cosworth SF3	15 laps/hydraulics	10
R	Damon Hill	Jordan	Jordan-Mugen Honda 199	10 laps/collision	7
NS	Ricardo Zonta	BAR	BAR-Supertec 01	accident	-

Pole: Hakkinen, 1m16.568s, 125.390mph/201.797kph. Fastest lap: Hakkinen, 1m18.448s, 122.385mph/196.961kph on Lap 70. Race leaders: Hakkinen 1-3 & 38-72, Barrichello 4-26, M Schumacher 27-37

STEWART'S DAY OF DAYS

Stewart GP's lone win was achieved in a peculiar wet/dry European GP at the Nurburgring that had David Coulthard spin out of the lead. Then Ralf Schumacher was in control, but his Williams had a puncture and so Johnny Herbert hit the front. Team-mate Rubens Barrichello finished third.

SAN MARINO GRAND PRIX

IMOLA • ROUND 3 • DATE: 2ND MAY 1999
Laps: 62 • Distance: 189.559miles/305.66km • Weather: Hot & bright

Pos	Driver	Team	Chassis-Engine	Result	Qual
1	Michael Schumacher	Ferrari	Ferrari F399	1h33m44.792s	3
2	David Coulthard	McLaren	McLaren-Mercedes MP4-14	1h33m49.057s	2
3	Rubens Barrichello	Stewart	Stewart-Ford Cosworth SF3	61 laps	6
4	Damon Hill	Jordan	Jordan-Mugen Honda 199	61 laps	8
5	Giancarlo Fisichella	Benetton	Benetton-Playlife B199	61 laps	16
6	Jean Alesi	Sauber	Sauber-Petronas C18	61 laps	13
7	Mika Salo	BAR	BAR-Supertec 01	59 laps/electrical	19

Pos	Driver	Team	Chassis-Engine	Result	Qual
8	Luca Badoer	Minardi	Minardi-Ford Cosworth M01	59 laps	22
9	Marc Gene	Minardi	Minardi-Ford Cosworth M01	59 laps	21
10	Johnny Herbert	Stewart	Stewart-Ford Cosworth SF3	58 laps/engine	12
11	Alessandro Zanardi	Williams	Williams-Supertec FW21	58 laps/spun off	10
R	Pedro Diniz	Sauber	Sauber-Petronas C18	49 laps/spun off	15
R	Olivier Panis	Prost	Prost-Peugeot AP02	48 laps/throttle	11
R	Eddie Irvine	Ferrari	Ferrari F399	46 laps/engine	4
R	Heinz-Harald Frentzen	Jordan	Jordan-Mugen Honda 199	46 laps/spun off	7
R	Toranosuke Takagi	Arrows	Arrows A20	29 laps/fuel pressure	20
R	Ralf Schumacher	Williams	Williams-Supertec FW21	28 laps/throttle	9
R	Mika Hakkinen	McLaren	McLaren-Mercedes MP4-14	17 laps/spun off	1
R	Alexander Wurz	Benetton	Benetton-Playlife B199	5 laps/spun off	17
R	Pedro de la Rosa	Arrows	Arrows A20	5 laps/spun off	18
R	Jacques Villeneuve	BAR	BAR-Supertec 01	0 laps/gearbox	5
R	Jarno Trulli	Prost	Prost-Peugeot AP02	0 laps/spun off	14

Pole: Hakkinen, 1m26.362s, 127.696mph/205.507kph. Fastest lap: M Schumacher, 1m28.547s, 124.545mph/200.435kph on Lap 45. Race leaders: Hakkinen 1-17, Coulthard 18-35, M Schumacher 36-62

DENNIS'S DRIVEN DESIRE

That McLaren was setting the pace was of great pride to team principal Ron Dennis as the partnership with Mercedes was finally yielding the kind of performance that could win titles again. When Dennis took over the team in 1980, it was in poor form, but his drive and organisation then led to the constructors' titles in 1984, 1985, 1988, 1989, 1990, 1991 and 1998.

MONACO GRAND PRIX

MONTE CARLO • ROUND 4 • DATE: 16TH MAY 1999
Laps: 78 • Distance: 163.188miles/262.626km • Weather: Hot & bright

Pos	Driver	Team	Chassis-Engine	Result	Qual
1	Michael Schumacher	Ferrari	Ferrari F399	1h49m31.812s	2
2	Eddie Irvine	Ferrari	Ferrari F399	1h50m02.288s	4
3	Mika Hakkinen	McLaren	McLaren-Mercedes MP4-14	1h50m09.295s	1
4	Heinz-Harald Frentzen	Jordan	Jordan-Mugen Honda 199	1h50m25.821s	6
5	Giancarlo Fisichella	Benetton	Benetton-Playlife B199	77 laps	9
6	Alexander Wurz	Benetton	Benetton-Playlife B199	77 laps	10
7	Jarno Trulli	Prost	Prost-Peugeot AP02	77 laps	7
8	Alessandro Zanardi	Williams	Williams-Supertec FW21	76 laps	11
9	Rubens Barrichello	Stewart	Stewart-Ford Cosworth SF3	71 laps/suspension	5
R	Ralf Schumacher	Williams	Williams-Supertec FW21	54 laps/spun off	16
R	Jean Alesi	Sauber	Sauber-Petronas C18	50 laps/suspension	14
R	Pedro Diniz	Sauber	Sauber-Petronas C18	49 laps/suspension	15
R	Olivier Panis	Prost	Prost-Peugeot AP02	40 laps/engine	18
R	David Coulthard	McLaren	McLaren-Mercedes MP4-14	36 laps/gearbox	3
R	Mika Salo	BAR	BAR-Supertec 01	36 laps/brakes	12
R	Toranosuke Takagi	Arrows	Arrows A20	36 laps/engine	19
R	Jacques Villeneuve	BAR	BAR-Supertec 01	32 laps/oil leak	8

Pos	Driver	Team	Chassis-Engine	Result	Qual
R	Johnny Herbert	Stewart	Stewart-Ford Cosworth SF3	32 laps/suspension	13
R	Pedro de la Rosa	Arrows	Arrows A20	30 laps/gearbox	21
R	Marc Gene	Minardi	Minardi-Ford Cosworth M01	24 laps/spun off	22
R	Luca Badoer	Minardi	Minardi-Ford Cosworth M01	10 laps/gearbox	20
R	Damon Hill	Jordan	Jordan-Mugen Honda 199	3 laps/collision	17

Pole: Hakkinen, 1m20.547s, 93.507mph/150.486kph. Fastest lap: Hakkinen, 1m22.259s, 91.561mph/147.354kph on Lap 67. Race leaders: M Schumacher 1-78

SPANISH GRAND PRIX

BARCELONA-CATALUNYA • ROUND 5 • DATE: 30TH MAY 1999
Laps: 65 • Distance: 190.780miles/307.32km • Weather: Hot & bright

Pos	Driver	Team	Chassis-Engine	Result	Qual
1	Mika Hakkinen	McLaren	McLaren-Mercedes MP4-14	1h34m13.665s	1
2	David Coulthard	McLaren	McLaren-Mercedes MP4-14	1h34m19.903s	3
3	Michael Schumacher	Ferrari	Ferrari F399	1h34m24.510s	4
4	Eddie Irvine	Ferrari	Ferrari F399	1h34m43.847s	2
5	Ralf Schumacher	Williams	Williams-Supertec FW21	1h35m40.873s	10
6	Jarno Trulli	Prost	Prost-Peugeot AP02	64 laps	9
7	Damon Hill	Jordan	Jordan-Mugen Honda 199	64 laps	11
DQ	Rubens Barrichello	Stewart	Stewart-Ford Cosworth SF3	64 laps/illegal undertray	7
8	Mika Salo	BAR	BAR-Supertec 01	64 laps	16
9	Giancarlo Fisichella	Benetton	Benetton-Playlife B199	64 laps	13
10	Alexander Wurz	Benetton	Benetton-Playlife B199	64 laps	18
11	Pedro de la Rosa	Arrows	Arrows A20	63 laps	19
12	Toranosuke Takagi	Arrows	Arrows A20	62 laps	20
R	Luca Badoer	Minardi	Minardi-Ford Cosworth M01	50 laps/spun off	22
R	Jacques Villeneuve	BAR	BAR-Supertec 01	40 laps/gearbox	6
R	Pedro Diniz	Sauber	Sauber-Petronas C18	40 laps/transmission	12
R	Johnny Herbert	Stewart	Stewart-Ford Cosworth SF3	40 laps/transmission	14
R	Heinz-Harald Frentzen	Jordan	Jordan-Mugen Honda 199	35 laps/halfshaft	8
R	Jean Alesi	Sauber	Sauber-Petronas C18	27 laps/transmission	5
R	Olivier Panis	Prost	Prost-Peugeot AP02	24 laps/gearbox	15
R	Alessandro Zanardi	Williams	Williams-Supertec FW21	24 laps/gearbox	17
R	Marc Gene	Minardi	Minardi-Ford Cosworth M01	0 laps/gearbox	21

Pole: Hakkinen, 1m22.088s, 128.840mph/207.348kph. Fastest lap: M Schumacher, 1m24.982s, 124.452mph/200.287kph on Lap 29. Race leaders: Hakkinen 1-23 & 27-44 & 46-65, Coulthard 24-26 & 45

CANADIAN GRAND PRIX

MONTREAL • ROUND 6 • DATE: 13TH JUNE 1999
Laps: 69 • Distance: 189.548miles/305.049km • Weather: Very hot & bright

Pos	Driver	Team	Chassis-Engine	Result	Qual
1	Mika Hakkinen	McLaren	McLaren-Mercedes MP4-14	1h41m35.727s	2
2	Giancarlo Fisichella	Benetton	Benetton-Playlife B199	1h41m36.509s	7
3	Eddie Irvine	Ferrari	Ferrari F399	1h41m37.524s	3
4	Ralf Schumacher	Williams	Williams-Supertec FW21	1h41m38.119s	13
5	Johnny Herbert	Stewart	Stewart-Ford Cosworth SF3	1h41m38.532s	10

Pos	Driver	Team	Chassis-Engine	Result	Qual
6	Pedro Diniz	Sauber	Sauber-Petronas C18	1h41m39.438s	18
7	David Coulthard	McLaren	McLaren-Mercedes MP4-14	1h41m40.731s	4
8	Marc Gene	Minardi	Minardi-Ford Cosworth M01	68 laps	22
9	Olivier Panis	Prost	Prost-Peugeot AP02	68 laps	15
10	Luca Badoer	Minardi	Minardi-Ford Cosworth M01	67 laps	21
11	Heinz-Harald Frentzen	Jordan	Jordan-Mugen Honda 199	65 laps/brakes	6
R	Alessandro Zanardi	Williams	Williams-Supertec FW21	50 laps/brakes	12
R	Toranosuke Takagi	Arrows	Arrows A20	41 laps/transmission	19
R	Jacques Villeneuve	BAR	BAR-Supertec 01	34 laps/spun off	16
R	Michael Schumacher	Ferrari	Ferrari F399	29 laps/spun off	1
R	Pedro de la Rosa	Arrows	Arrows A20	22 laps/transmission	20
R	Rubens Barrichello	Stewart	Stewart-Ford Cosworth SF3	14 laps/steering	5
R	Damon Hill	Jordan	Jordan-Mugen Honda 199	14 laps/spun off	14
R	Ricardo Zonta	BAR	BAR-Supertec 01	2 laps/spun off	17
R	Jean Alesi	Sauber	Sauber-Petronas C18	0 laps/collision	8
R	Jarno Trulli	Prost	Prost-Peugeot AP02	0 laps/collision	9
R	Alexander Wurz	Benetton	Benetton-Playlife B199	0 laps/transmission	11

Pole: M Schumacher, 1m19.298s, 124.713mph/200.706kph. Fastest lap: Irvine, 1m20.382s, 123.031mph/197.999kph on Lap 62. Race leaders: M Schumacher 1-29, Hakkinen 30-69

A POOR CAREER MOVE

World champion at his second attempt in 1997, Jacques Villeneuve's decision to leave Williams and move to all-new BAR was seen by many as career suicide. However, Williams had lost ground when it lost its Renault engines, and since he was friends with BAR principal Craig Pollock, he thought a switch would be fun. Alas, he failed to score a single point.

FRENCH GRAND PRIX

MAGNY-COURS • ROUND 7 • DATE: 27TH JUNE 1999
Laps: 72 • Distance: 190.139miles/306.0km • Weather: Warm & dull, rain later

Pos	Driver	Team	Chassis-Engine	Result	Qual
1	Heinz-Harald Frentzen	Jordan	Jordan-Mugen Honda 199	1h58m24.343s	5
2	Mika Hakkinen	McLaren	McLaren-Mercedes MP4-14	1h58m35.435s	14
3	Rubens Barrichello	Stewart	Stewart-Ford Cosworth SF3	1h59m07.775s	1
4	Ralf Schumacher	Williams	Williams-Supertec FW21	1h59m09.818s	16
5	Michael Schumacher	Ferrari	Ferrari F399	1h59m12.224s	6
6	Eddie Irvine	Ferrari	Ferrari F399	1h59m13.244s	17
7	Jarno Trulli	Prost	Prost-Peugeot AP02	1h59m22.114s	8
8	Olivier Panis	Prost	Prost-Peugeot AP02	1h59m22.874s	3
9	Ricardo Zonta	BAR	BAR-Supertec 01	1h59m53.107s	10
10	Luca Badoer	Minardi	Minardi-Ford Cosworth M01	71 laps	21
DQ	Toranosuke Takagi	Arrows	Arrows A20	71 laps/illegal tyres	20
11	Pedro de la Rosa	Arrows	Arrows A20	71 laps	19
R	Giancarlo Fisichella	Benetton	Benetton-Playlife B199	42 laps/spun off	7
R	Damon Hill	Jordan	Jordan-Mugen Honda 199	31 laps/electrical	18
R	Alessandro Zanardi	Williams	Williams-Supertec FW21	26 laps/engine	15
R	Jacques Villeneuve	BAR	BAR-Supertec 01	25 laps/spun off	12

Pos	Driver	Team	Chassis-Engine	Result	Qual
R	Alexander Wurz	Benetton	Benetton-Playlife B199	25 laps/spun off	13
R	Marc Gene	Minardi	Minardi-Ford Cosworth M01	25 laps/spun off	22
R	Jean Alesi	Sauber	Sauber-Petronas C18	24 laps/spun off	2
R	David Coulthard	McLaren	McLaren-Mercedes MP4-14	9 laps/electrical	4
R	Pedro Diniz	Sauber	Sauber-Petronas C18	6 laps/transmission	11
R	Johnny Herbert	Stewart	Stewart-Ford Cosworth SF3	4 laps/gearbox	9

Pole: Barrichello, 1m38.441s, 96.575mph/155.423kph. Fastest lap: Coulthard, 1m19.227s, 119.996mph/193.115kph on Lap 8. Race leaders: Barrichello 1-5 & 10-43 & 55-59, Coulthard 6-9, M Schumacher 44-54, Hakkinen 60-65, Frentzen 66-72

BRITISH GRAND PRIX

SILVERSTONE • ROUND 8 • DATE: 11TH JULY 1999
Laps: 60 • Distance: 191.384miles/308.4km • Weather: Hot & bright

Pos	Driver	Team	Chassis-Engine	Result	Qual
1	David Coulthard	McLaren	McLaren-Mercedes MP4-14	1h32m30.144s	3
2	Eddie Irvine	Ferrari	Ferrari F399	1h32m31.973s	4
3	Ralf Schumacher	Williams	Williams-Supertec FW21	1h32m57.555s	8
4	Heinz-Harald Frentzen	Jordan	Jordan-Mugen Honda 199	1h32m57.933s	5
5	Damon Hill	Jordan	Jordan-Mugen Honda 199	1h33m08.750s	6
6	Pedro Diniz	Sauber	Sauber-Petronas C18	1h33m23.787s	12
7	Giancarlo Fisichella	Benetton	Benetton-Playlife B199	1h33m24.758s	17
8	Rubens Barrichello	Stewart	Stewart-Ford Cosworth SF3	1h33m38.734s	7
9	Jarno Trulli	Prost	Prost-Peugeot AP02	1h33m42.189s	14
10	Alexander Wurz	Benetton	Benetton-Playlife B199	1h33m42.267s	18
11	Alessandro Zanardi	Williams	Williams-Supertec FW21	1h33m47.268s	13
12	Johnny Herbert	Stewart	Stewart-Ford Cosworth SF3	1h33m47.853s	11
13	Olivier Panis	Prost	Prost-Peugeot AP02	1h33m50.636s	15
14	Jean Alesi	Sauber	Sauber-Petronas C18	59 laps	10
15	Marc Gene	Minardi	Minardi-Ford Cosworth M01	58 laps	22
16	Toranosuke Takagi	Arrows	Arrows A20	58 laps	19
R	Ricardo Zonta	BAR	BAR-Supertec 01	41 laps/suspension	16
R	Mika Hakkinen	McLaren	McLaren-Mercedes MP4-14	35 laps/wheel	1
R	Jacques Villeneuve	BAR	BAR-Supertec 01	29 laps/halfshaft	9
R	Luca Badoer	Minardi	Minardi-Ford Cosworth M01	6 laps/gearbox	21
R	Pedro de la Rosa	Arrows	Arrows A20	0 laps/gearbox	20
R	Michael Schumacher	Ferrari	Ferrari F399	0 laps/broken leg	2

Pole: Hakkinen, 1m24.804s, 135.581mph/218.197kph. Fastest lap: Hakkinen, 1m28.309s, 130.200mph/209.536kph on Lap 28. Race leaders: Hakkinen 1-24, Irvine 25-26, Coulthard 27-42 & 46-60, Frentzen 43-44, Hill 45

FRENTZEN FINDS FORM

Like Villeneuve, Heinz-Harald Frentzen elected to leave Williams after its poor 1998 campaign, and his decision to join Jordan paid off. This was shown by finishing second at the opening round and third in the second. He won at Magny-Cours and Monza and would have won at the Nurburgring too, but for electrical failure.

ZANARDI'S SCANT REWARD

Having been IndyCar champion in 1997 and 1998, Alessandro Zanardi's return to F1 with Williams was no triumph. Although the team had won the constructors' title in 1997, its engine deal with Supertec was not competitive and the Italian peaked with seventh place, and so failed to score a single point. Meanwhile, team-mate Ralf Schumacher scored 35.

AUSTRIAN GRAND PRIX

A1-RING • ROUND 9 • DATE: 25TH JULY 1999
Laps: 71 • Distance: 190.542miles/306.649km • Weather: Warm but dull

Pos	Driver	Team	Chassis-Engine	Result	Qual
1	Eddie Irvine	Ferrari	Ferrari F399	1h28m12.438s	3
2	David Coulthard	McLaren	McLaren-Mercedes MP4-14	1h28m12.751s	2
3	Mika Hakkinen	McLaren	McLaren-Mercedes MP4-14	1h28m34.720s	1
4	Heinz-Harald Frentzen	Jordan	Jordan-Mugen Honda 199	1h29m05.241s	4
5	Alexander Wurz	Benetton	Benetton-Playlife B199	1h29m18.796s	10
6	Pedro Diniz	Sauber	Sauber-Petronas C18	1h29m23.371s	16
7	Jarno Trulli	Prost	Prost-Peugeot AP02	70 laps	13
8	Damon Hill	Jordan	Jordan-Mugen Honda 199	70 laps	11
9	Mika Salo	Ferrari	Ferrari F399	70 laps	7
10	Olivier Panis	Prost	Prost-Peugeot AP02	70 laps	18
11	Marc Gene	Minardi	Minardi-Ford Cosworth M01	70 laps	22
12	Giancarlo Fisichella	Benetton	Benetton-Playlife B199	68 laps/engine	12
13	Luca Badoer	Minardi	Minardi-Ford Cosworth M01	68 laps	19
14	Johnny Herbert	Stewart	Stewart-Ford Cosworth SF3	67 laps	6
15	Ricardo Zonta	BAR	BAR-Supertec 01	63 laps/clutch	15
R	Rubens Barrichello	Stewart	Stewart-Ford Cosworth SF3	55 laps/engine	5
R	Jean Alesi	Sauber	Sauber-Petronas C18	49 laps/out of fuel	17
R	Pedro de la Rosa	Arrows	Arrows A20	38 laps/spun off	21
R	Alessandro Zanardi	Williams	Williams-Supertec FW21	35 laps/out of fuel	14
R	Jacques Villeneuve	BAR	BAR-Supertec 01	34 laps/halfshaft	9
R	Toranosuke Takagi	Arrows	Arrows A20	25 laps/engine	20
R	Ralf Schumacher	Williams	Williams-Supertec FW21	8 laps/spun off	8

Pole: Hakkinen, 1m10.954s, 136.163mph/219.133kph. Fastest lap: Hakkinen, 1m12.107s, 133.985mph/215.629kph on Lap 39. Race leaders: Coulthard 1-39, Irvine 40-71

GERMAN GRAND PRIX

HOCKENHEIM • ROUND 10 • DATE: 1ST AUGUST 1999
Laps: 45 • Distance: 190.782miles/307.035km • Weather: Hot & bright

Pos	Driver	Team	Chassis-Engine	Result	Qual
1	Eddie Irvine	Ferrari	Ferrari F399	1h21m58.594s	5
2	Mika Salo	Ferrari	Ferrari F399	1h21m59.601s	4
3	Heinz-Harald Frentzen	Jordan	Jordan-Mugen Honda 199	1h22m03.789s	2
4	Ralf Schumacher	Williams	Williams-Supertec FW21	1h22m11.403s	11
5	David Coulthard	McLaren	McLaren-Mercedes MP4-14	1h22m15.417s	3
6	Olivier Panis	Prost	Prost-Peugeot AP02	1h22m28.473s	7
7	Alexander Wurz	Benetton	Benetton-Playlife B199	1h22m31.927s	13

Pos	Driver	Team	Chassis-Engine	Result	Qual
8	Jean Alesi	Sauber	Sauber-Petronas C18	1h23m09.885s	21
9	Marc Gene	Minardi	Minardi-Ford Cosworth M01	1h23m46.912s	15
10	Luca Badoer	Minardi	Minardi-Ford Cosworth M01	44 laps	19
11	Johnny Herbert	Stewart	Stewart-Ford Cosworth SF3	40 laps/gearbox	17
R	Pedro de la Rosa	Arrows	Arrows A20	37 laps/spun off	20
R	Mika Hakkinen	McLaren	McLaren-Mercedes MP4-14	25 laps/tyre	1
R	Alessandro Zanardi	Williams	Williams-Supertec FW21	21 laps/differential	14
R	Ricardo Zonta	BAR	BAR-Supertec 01	20 laps/engine	18
R	Toranosuke Takagi	Arrows	Arrows A20	15 laps/engine	22
R	Damon Hill	Jordan	Jordan-Mugen Honda 199	13 laps/brakes	8
R	Jarno Trulli	Prost	Prost-Peugeot AP02	10 laps/engine	9
R	Giancarlo Fisichella	Benetton	Benetton-Playlife B199	7 laps/suspension	10
R	Rubens Barrichello	Stewart	Stewart-Ford Cosworth SF3	6 laps/hydraulics	6
R	Jacques Villeneuve	BAR	BAR-Supertec 01	0 laps/collision	12
R	Pedro Diniz	Sauber	Sauber-Petronas C18	0 laps/collision	16

Pole: Hakkinen, 1m42.950s, 148.252mph/238.589kph. Fastest lap: Coulthard, 1m45.270s, 144.985mph/233.331kph on Lap 43. Race leaders: Hakkinen 1-24, Salo 25, Irvine 26-45

NEW CIRCUITS

The World Championship broke new ground when Malaysia hosted a grand prix for the first time in 1999 to broaden the sport's appeal in South-east Asia. The Sepang circuit was built 30 miles (50km) south of capital Kuala Lumpur, out near the airport. Designed by Hermann Tilke, it provided a great mix of corners and a double-sided grandstand.

HUNGARIAN GRAND PRIX

HUNGARORING • ROUND 11 • DATE: 15TH AUGUST 1999
Laps: 77 • Distance: 190.90miles/305.921km • Weather: Hot & bright

Pos	Driver	Team	Chassis-Engine	Result	Qual
1	Mika Hakkinen	McLaren	McLaren-Mercedes MP4-14	1h46m23.536s	1
2	David Coulthard	McLaren	McLaren-Mercedes MP4-14	1h46m33.242s	3
3	Eddie Irvine	Ferrari	Ferrari F399	1h46m50.764s	2
4	Heinz-Harald Frentzen	Jordan	Jordan-Mugen Honda 199	1h46m55.351s	5
5	Rubens Barrichello	Stewart	Stewart-Ford Cosworth SF3	1h47m07.344s	8
6	Damon Hill	Jordan	Jordan-Mugen Honda 199	1h47m19.262s	6
7	Alexander Wurz	Benetton	Benetton-Playlife B199	1h47m24.548s	7
8	Jarno Trulli	Prost	Prost-Peugeot AP02	76 laps	13
9	Ralf Schumacher	Williams	Williams-Supertec FW21	76 laps	16
10	Olivier Panis	Prost	Prost-Peugeot AP02	76 laps	14
11	Johnny Herbert	Stewart	Stewart-Ford Cosworth SF3	76 laps	10
12	Mika Salo	Ferrari	Ferrari F399	75 laps	18
13	Ricardo Zonta	BAR	BAR-Supertec 01	75 laps	17
14	Luca Badoer	Minardi	Minardi-Ford Cosworth M01	75 laps	19
15	Pedro de la Rosa	Arrows	Arrows A20	75 laps	20
16	Jean Alesi	Sauber	Sauber-Petronas C18	74 laps/fuel pressure	11
17	Marc Gene	Minardi	Minardi-Ford Cosworth M01	74 laps	22
R	Jacques Villeneuve	BAR	BAR-Supertec 01	60 laps/clutch	9

Pos	Driver	Team	Chassis-Engine	Result	Qual
R	Giancarlo Fisichella	Benetton	Benetton-Playlife B199	52 laps/engine	4
R	Toranosuke Takagi	Arrows	Arrows A20	26 laps/transmission	21
R	Pedro Diniz	Sauber	Sauber-Petronas C18	19 laps/spun off	12
R	Alessandro Zanardi	Williams	Williams-Supertec FW21	10 laps/differential	15

Pole: Hakkinen, 1m18.156s, 113.712mph/183.003kph. Fastest lap: Coulthard, 1m20.699s, 110.129mph/177.236kph on Lap 69. Race leaders: Hakkinen 1-77

NEW CONSTRUCTORS

British American Racing, known as BAR for short, entered F1 by taking over Tyrrell's entry in 1998, but 1999 was its first full season. It had a large budget and established a base at Brackley, near Silverstone. However, its Supertec-engined 01s were fragile and it took until the 12th round before team leader Villeneuve even finished a grand prix.

BELGIAN GRAND PRIX

SPA-FRANCORCHAMPS • ROUND 12 • DATE: 29TH AUGUST 1999
Laps: 44 • Distance: 190.507miles/306.592km • Weather: Hot & bright

Pos	Driver	Team	Chassis-Engine	Result	Qual
1	David Coulthard	McLaren	McLaren-Mercedes MP4-14	1h25m43.057s	2
2	Mika Hakkinen	McLaren	McLaren-Mercedes MP4-14	1h25m53.526s	1
3	Heinz-Harald Frentzen	Jordan	Jordan-Mugen Honda 199	1h26m16.490s	3
4	Eddie Irvine	Ferrari	Ferrari F399	1h26m28.005s	6
5	Ralf Schumacher	Williams	Williams-Supertec FW21	1h26m31.124s	5
6	Damon Hill	Jordan	Jordan-Mugen Honda 199	1h26m37.973s	4
7	Mika Salo	Ferrari	Ferrari F399	1h26m39.306s	9
8	Alessandro Zanardi	Williams	Williams-Supertec FW21	1h26m50.079s	8
9	Jean Alesi	Sauber	Sauber-Petronas C18	1h26m56.905s	16
10	Rubens Barrichello	Stewart	Stewart-Ford Cosworth SF3	1h27m03.799s	7
11	Giancarlo Fisichella	Benetton	Benetton-Playlife B199	1h27m15.252s	13
12	Jarno Trulli	Prost	Prost-Peugeot AP02	1h27m19.211s	12
13	Olivier Panis	Prost	Prost-Peugeot AP02	1h27m24.600s	17
14	Alexander Wurz	Benetton	Benetton-Playlife B199	1h27m40.802s	15
15	Jacques Villeneuve	BAR	BAR-Supertec 01	43 laps	11
16	Marc Gene	Minardi	Minardi-Ford Cosworth M01	43 laps	21
R	Pedro de la Rosa	Arrows	Arrows A20	35 laps/transmission	22
R	Ricardo Zonta	BAR	BAR-Supertec 01	33 laps/gearbox	14
R	Luca Badoer	Minardi	Minardi-Ford Cosworth M01	33 laps/suspension	20
R	Johnny Herbert	Stewart	Stewart-Ford Cosworth SF3	27 laps/brakes	10
R	Pedro Diniz	Sauber	Sauber-Petronas C18	19 laps/spun off	18
R	Toranosuke Takagi	Arrows	Arrows A20	0 laps/clutch	19

Pole: Hakkinen, 1m50.329s, 141.277mph/227.363kph. Fastest lap: Hakkinen, 1m53.955s, 136.781mph/220.128kph on Lap 23. Race leaders: Coulthard 1-44

NEW DRIVERS

Pedro de la Rosa came sixth on his debut for Arrows, and this made him the most successful of the newcomers. Marc Gene matched that finishing position later in the year for Minardi at the Nurburgring. Meanwhile, former F3000 champion Ricardo Zonta peaked with eighth for BAR, and Stephane Sarrazin was flying before a broken suspension pitched him into a wall in a one-off outing for Minardi in Brazil.

ITALIAN GRAND PRIX

MONZA • ROUND 13 • DATE: 12TH SEPTEMBER 1999
Laps: 53 • Distance: 189.568miles/305.81km • Weather: Hot & bright

Pos	Driver	Team	Chassis-Engine	Result	Qual
1	Heinz-Harald Frentzen	Jordan	Jordan-Mugen Honda 199	1h17m02.923s	2
2	Ralf Schumacher	Williams	Williams-Supertec FW21	1h17m06.195s	5
3	Mika Salo	Ferrari	Ferrari F399	1h17m14.855s	6
4	Rubens Barrichello	Stewart	Stewart-Ford Cosworth SF3	1h17m20.553s	7
5	David Coulthard	McLaren	McLaren-Mercedes MP4-14	1h17m21.065s	3
6	Eddie Irvine	Ferrari	Ferrari F399	1h17m30.325s	8
7	Alessandro Zanardi	Williams	Williams-Supertec FW21	1h17m30.970s	4
8	Jacques Villeneuve	BAR	BAR-Supertec 01	1h17m44.720s	11
9	Jean Alesi	Sauber	Sauber-Petronas C18	1h17m45.121s	13
10	Damon Hill	Jordan	Jordan-Mugen Honda 199	1h17m59.182s	9
11	Olivier Panis	Prost	Prost-Peugeot AP02	52 laps/engine	10
R	Johnny Herbert	Stewart	Stewart-Ford Cosworth SF3	40 laps/clutch	15
R	Pedro de la Rosa	Arrows	Arrows A20	35 laps/collision	21
R	Toranosuke Takagi	Arrows	Arrows A20	35 laps/spun off	22
R	Mika Hakkinen	McLaren	McLaren-Mercedes MP4-14	29 laps/spun off	1
R	Jarno Trulli	Prost	Prost-Peugeot AP02	29 laps/overheating	12
R	Ricardo Zonta	BAR	BAR-Supertec 01	25 laps/wheel	18
R	Luca Badoer	Minardi	Minardi-Ford Cosworth M01	23 laps/collision	19
R	Alexander Wurz	Benetton	Benetton-Playlife B199	11 laps/electrical	14
R	Pedro Diniz	Sauber	Sauber-Petronas C18	1 lap/spun off	16
R	Giancarlo Fisichella	Benetton	Benetton-Playlife B199	1 lap/spun off	17
R	Marc Gene	Minardi	Minardi-Ford Cosworth M01	0 laps/collision	20

Pole: Hakkinen, 1m22.432s, 156.579mph/251.989kph. Fastest lap: R Schumacher, 1m25.579s, 150.821mph/242.723kph on Lap 48. Race leaders: Hakkinen 1-29, Frentzen 30-35 & 37-53, Salo 36

EUROPEAN GRAND PRIX

NURBURGRING • ROUND 14 • DATE: 26TH SEPTEMBER 1999
Laps: 66 • Distance: 186.843miles/300.696km • Weather: Warm & dull, rain later

Pos	Driver	Team	Chassis-Engine	Result	Qual
1	Johnny Herbert	Stewart	Stewart-Ford Cosworth SF3	1h41m54.314s	14
2	Jarno Trulli	Prost	Prost-Peugeot AP02	1h42m16.933s	10
3	Rubens Barrichello	Stewart	Stewart-Ford Cosworth SF3	1h42m17.180s	15
4	Ralf Schumacher	Williams	Williams-Supertec FW21	1h42m33.822s	4
5	Mika Hakkinen	McLaren	McLaren-Mercedes MP4-14	1h42m57.264s	3

Pos	Driver	Team	Chassis-Engine	Result	Qual
6	Marc Gene	Minardi	Minardi-Ford Cosworth M01	1h42m59.468s	20
7	Eddie Irvine	Ferrari	Ferrari F399	1h43m00.997s	9
8	Ricardo Zonta	BAR	BAR-Supertec 01	65 laps	17
9	Olivier Panis	Prost	Prost-Peugeot AP02	65 laps	5
10	Jacques Villeneuve	BAR	BAR-Supertec 01	61 laps/clutch	8
R	Luca Badoer	Minardi	Minardi-Ford Cosworth M01	53 laps/gearbox	19
R	Pedro de la Rosa	Arrows	Arrows A20	52 laps/gearbox	22
R	Giancarlo Fisichella	Benetton	Benetton-Playlife B199	48 laps/spun off	6
R	Mika Salo	Ferrari	Ferrari F399	44 laps/brakes	12
R	Toranosuke Takagi	Arrows	Arrows A20	42 laps/spun off	21
R	David Coulthard	McLaren	McLaren-Mercedes MP4-14	37 laps/spun off	2
R	Jean Alesi	Sauber	Sauber-Petronas C18	35 laps/halfshaft	16
R	Heinz-Harald Frentzen	Jordan	Jordan-Mugen Honda 199	32 laps/electrical	1
R	Alessandro Zanardi	Williams	Williams-Supertec FW21	10 laps/collision	18
R	Damon Hill	Jordan	Jordan-Mugen Honda 199	0 laps/electrical	7
R	Alexander Wurz	Benetton	Benetton-Playlife B199	0 laps/collision	11
R	Pedro Diniz	Sauber	Sauber-Petronas C18	0 laps/collision	13

Pole: Frentzen, 1m19.910s, 127.537mph/205.250kph. Fastest lap: Hakkinen, 1m21.282s, 125.384mph/201.786kph on Lap 64. Race leaders: Frentzen 1-32, Coulthard 33-37, R Schumacher 38-44 & 49, Fisichella 45-48, Herbert 50-66

MALAYSIAN GRAND PRIX

SEPANG • ROUND 15 • DATE: 17TH OCTOBER 1999
Laps: 56 • Distance: 192.843miles/310.352km • Weather: Hot & bright

Pos	Driver	Team	Chassis-Engine	Result	Qual
1	Eddie Irvine	Ferrari	Ferrari F399	1h36m38.494s	2
2	Michael Schumacher	Ferrari	Ferrari F399	1h36m39.534s	1
3	Mika Hakkinen	McLaren	McLaren-Mercedes MP4-14	1h36m48.237s	4
4	Johnny Herbert	Stewart	Stewart-Ford Cosworth SF3	1h36m56.032s	5
5	Rubens Barrichello	Stewart	Stewart-Ford Cosworth SF3	1h37m10.790s	6
6	Heinz-Harald Frentzen	Jordan	Jordan-Mugen Honda 199	1h37m13.378s	14
7	Jean Alesi	Sauber	Sauber-Petronas C18	1h37m32.902s	15
8	Alexander Wurz	Benetton	Benetton-Playlife B199	1h37m39.428s	7
9	Marc Gene	Minardi	Minardi-Ford Cosworth M01	55 laps	19
10	Alessandro Zanardi	Williams	Williams-Supertec FW21	55 laps	16
11	Giancarlo Fisichella	Benetton	Benetton-Playlife B199	52 laps	11
R	Jacques Villeneuve	BAR	BAR-Supertec 01	48 laps/hydraulics	10
R	Pedro Diniz	Sauber	Sauber-Petronas C18	44 laps/spun off	17
R	Pedro de la Rosa	Arrows	Arrows A20	30 laps/engine	20
R	Luca Badoer	Minardi	Minardi-Ford Cosworth M01	15 laps/overheating	21
R	David Coulthard	McLaren	McLaren-Mercedes MP4-14	14 laps/fuel pressure	3
R	Ralf Schumacher	Williams	Williams-Supertec FW21	7 laps/spun off	8
R	Toranosuke Takagi	Arrows	Arrows A20	7 laps/transmission	22
R	Ricardo Zonta	BAR	BAR-Supertec 01	6 laps/engine	13
R	Olivier Panis	Prost	Prost-Peugeot AP02	5 laps/engine	12
R	Damon Hill	Jordan	Jordan-Mugen Honda 199	0 laps/collision	9
NS	Jarno Trulli	Prost	Prost-Peugeot AP02	Engine	18

Pole: M Schumacher, 1m39.688s, 124.359mph/200.136kph. Fastest lap: M Schumacher, 1m40.267s, 123.640mph/198.980kph on Lap 25. Race leaders: M Schumacher 1-3 & 26-28 & 42-52, Irvine 4-25 & 29-41 & 53-56

JAPANESE GRAND PRIX

SUZUKA • ROUND 16 • DATE: 31ST OCTOBER 1999
Laps: 53 • Distance: 193.117miles/310.792km • Weather: Warm & bright

Pos	Driver	Team	Chassis-Engine	Result	Qual
1	Mika Hakkinen	McLaren	McLaren-Mercedes MP4-14	1h31m18.785s	2
2	Michael Schumacher	Ferrari	Ferrari F399	1h31m23.800s	1
3	Eddie Irvine	Ferrari	Ferrari F399	1h32m54.473s	5
4	Heinz-Harald Frentzen	Jordan	Jordan-Mugen Honda 199	1h32m57.420s	4
5	Ralf Schumacher	Williams	Williams-Supertec FW21	1h32m58.279s	9
6	Jean Alesi	Sauber	Sauber-Petronas C18	52 laps	10
7	Johnny Herbert	Stewart	Stewart-Ford Cosworth SF3	52 laps	8
8	Rubens Barrichello	Stewart	Stewart-Ford Cosworth SF3	52 laps	13
9	Jacques Villeneuve	BAR	BAR-Supertec 01	52 laps	11
10	Alexander Wurz	Benetton	Benetton-Playlife B199	52 laps	15
11	Pedro Diniz	Sauber	Sauber-Petronas C18	52 laps	17
12	Ricardo Zonta	BAR	BAR-Supertec 01	52 laps	18
13	Pedro de la Rosa	Arrows	Arrows A20	51 laps	21
14	Giancarlo Fisichella	Benetton	Benetton-Playlife B199	47 laps/engine	14
R	Toranosuke Takagi	Arrows	Arrows A20	43 laps/gearbox	19
R	Luca Badoer	Minardi	Minardi-Ford Cosworth M01	43 laps/engine	22
R	David Coulthard	McLaren	McLaren-Mercedes MP4-14	39 laps/hydraulics	3
R	Marc Gene	Minardi	Minardi-Ford Cosworth M01	31 laps/gearbox	20
R	Damon Hill	Jordan	Jordan-Mugen Honda 199	21 laps/withdrawn	12
R	Olivier Panis	Prost	Prost-Peugeot AP02	19 laps/alternator	6
R	Jarno Trulli	Prost	Prost-Peugeot AP02	3 laps/engine	7
R	Alessandro Zanardi	Williams	Williams-Supertec FW21	0 laps/electrical	16

Pole: M Schumacher, 1m37.470s, 134.578mph/216.583kph. Fastest lap: M Schumacher, 1m41.319s, 129.466mph/208.355kph on Lap 31. Race leaders: Hakkinen 1-19 & 23-53, M Schumacher 20-22

IN MEMORIAM

Harvey Postlethwaite, one of F1's leading designers, died of a heart attack aged 55. He made his name with Hesketh, but then achieved greater success with Wolf, as his car won first time out in 1977. He helped Ferrari to the 1982 constructors' title, then introduced high-nose designs at Tyrrell. At the time of his death, Postlethwaite was developing a works Honda team.

WORLD DRIVERS' CHAMPIONSHIP FINAL RESULTS

Pos	Driver	Nat	Car-Engine	R1	R2	R3	R4	R5	R6
1	Mika Hakkinen	FIN	McLaren-Mercedes MP4-14	RP	1PF	RP	3PF	1P	1
2	Eddie Irvine	GBR	Ferrari F399	1	5	R	2	4	3F
3	Heinz-Harald Frentzen	DEU	Jordan-Mugen Honda 199	2	3	R	4	R	11
4	David Coulthard	GBR	McLaren-Mercedes MP4-14	R	R	2	R	2	7
5	Michael Schumacher	DEU	Ferrari F399	8F	2	1F	1	3F	RP
6	Ralf Schumacher	DEU	Williams-Supertec FW21	3	4	R	R	5	4
7	Rubens Barrichello	BRA	Stewart-Ford Cosworth SF3	5	R	3	9	DQ	R
8	Johnny Herbert	GBR	Stewart-Ford Cosworth SF3	R	R	10	R	R	5
9	Giancarlo Fisichella	ITA	Benetton-Playlife B199	4	R	5	5	9	2

Pos	Driver	Nat	Car-Engine	R1	R2	R3	R4	R5	R6
10	Mika Salo	FIN	BAR-Supertec 01	-	-	7	R	8	-
			Ferrari F399	-	-	-	-	-	-
11	Jarno Trulli	ITA	Prost-Peugeot AP02	R	R	R	7	6	R
12	Damon Hill	GBR	Jordan-Mugen Honda 199	R	R	4	R	7	R
13	Alexander Wurz	AUT	Benetton-Playlife B199	R	7	R	6	10	R
14	Pedro Diniz	BRA	Sauber-Petronas C18	R	R	R	R	R	6
15	Olivier Panis	FRA	Prost-Peugeot AP02	R	6	R	R	R	9
16	Jean Alesi	FRA	Sauber-Petronas C18	R	R	6	R	R	R
17	Pedro de la Rosa	ESP	Arrows A20	6	R	R	R	11	R
18	Marc Gene	ESP	Minardi-Ford Cosworth M01	R	9	9	R	R	8

Pos	Driver	R7	R8	R9	R10	R11	R12	R13	R14	R15	R16	Total
1	Hakkinen	2	RPF	3PF	RP	1P	2PF	RP	5F	3	1	76
2	Irvine	6	2	1	1	3	4	6	7	1	3	74
3	Frentzen	1	4	4	3	4	3	1	RP	6	4	54
4	Coulthard	RF	1	2	5F	2F	1	5	R	R	R	48
5	M Schumacher	5	R	-	-	-	-	-	-	2PF	2PF	44
6	R Schumacher	4	3	R	4	9	5	2F	4	R	5	35
7	Barrichello	3P	8	R	R	5	10	4	3	5	8	21
8	Herbert	R	12	14	11	11	R	R	1	4	7	15
9	Fisichella	R	7	12	R	R	11	R	R	11	14	13
10	Salo	-	-	-	-	-	-	-	-	-	-	10
		-	-	9	2	12	7	3	R	-	-	
11	Trulli	7	9	7	R	8	12	R	2	NS	R	7
12	Hill	R	5	8	R	6	6	10	R	R	R	7
13	Wurz	R	10	5	7	7	14	R	R	8	10	3
14	Diniz	R	6	6	R	R	R	R	R	R	11	3
15	Panis	8	13	10	6	10	13	11	9	R	R	2
16	Alesi	R	14	R	8	16	9	9	R	7	6	2
17	de la Rosa	11	R	R	R	15	R	R	R	R	13	1
18	Gene	R	15	11	9	17	16	R	6	9	R	1

SYMBOLS AND GRAND PRIX KEY

Round 1 Australian GP
Round 2 Brazilian GP
Round 3 San Marino GP
Round 4 Monaco GP
Round 5 Spanish GP
Round 6 Canadian GP
Round 7 French GP
Round 8 British GP
Round 9 Austrian GP
Round 10 German GP
Round 11 Hungarian GP
Round 12 Belgian GP
Round 13 Italian GP
Round 14 European GP
Round 15 Malaysian GP
Round 16 Japanese GP

DNPQ DID NOT PRE-QUALIFY **DNQ** DID NOT QUALIFY **DQ** DISQUALIFIED **EX** EXCLUDED
F FASTEST LAP **NC** NOT CLASSIFIED **NS** NON-STARTER **P** POLE POSITION **R** RETIRED

SCORING

1st 10 points
2nd 6 points
3rd 4 points
4th 3 points
5th 2 points
6th 1 point

WORLD CONSTRUCTORS' CHAMPIONSHIP FINAL RESULTS

Pos	Team-Engine	R1	R2	R3	R4	R5	R6	R7	R8
1	Ferrari	1/8	2/5	1/R	1/2	3/4	3/R	5/6	2/NS
2	McLaren-Mercedes	R/R	1/R	2/R	3/R	1/2	1/7	2/R	1/R
3	Jordan-Mugen Honda	2/R	3/R	4/R	4/R	7/R	11/R	1/R	4/5
4	Stewart-Ford	5/NS	R/R	3/10	9/R	DQ/R	5/R	3/R	8/12
5	Williams-Supertec	3/R	4/R	11/R	8/R	5/R	4/R	4/R	3/11
6	Benetton-Playlife	4/R	7/R	5/R	5/6	9/10	2/R	R/R	7/10
7	Prost-Peugeot	R/R	6/R	R/R	7/R	6/R	9/R	7/8	9/13

Pos	Team-Engine	R1	R2	R3	R4	R5	R6	R7	R8
8	Sauber-Petronas	R/R	R/R	6/R	R/R	R/R	6/R	R/R	6/14
9	Arrows	6/7	8/R	R/R	R/R	11/12	R/R	11/DQ	16/R
9	Minardi-Ford	R/R	9/R	8/9	R/R	R/R	8/10	10/R	15/R

Pos	Team-Engine	R9	R10	R11	R12	R13	R14	R15	R16	Total
1	Ferrari	1/9	1/2	3/12	4/7	3/6	7/R	1/2	2/3	128
2	McLaren-Mercedes	2/3	5/R	1/2	1/2	5/R	5/R	3/R	1/R	124
3	Jordan-Mugen Honda	4/8	3/R	4/6	3/6	1/10	R/R	6/R	4/R	61
4	Stewart-Ford	14/R	11/R	5/11	10/R	4/R	1/3	4/5	7/8	36
5	Williams-Supertec	R/R	4/R	9/R	5/8	2/7	4/R	10/R	5/R	35
6	Benetton-Playlife	5/12	7/R	7/R	11/14	R/R	R/R	8/11	10/14	16
7	Prost-Peugeot	7/10	6/R	8/10	12/13	11/R	2/9	R/NS	R/R	9
8	Sauber-Petronas	6/R	8/R	16/R	9/R	9/R	R/R	7/R	6/11	5
9	Arrows	R/R	R/R	15/R	R/R	R/R	R/R	R/R	13/R	1
9	Minardi-Ford	11/13	9/10	14/17	16/R	R/R	6/R	9/R	R/R	1

THE 2000s

SEASON SUMMARY

Michael Schumacher gave Ferrari its first drivers' title since 1979 by winning the championship with a round still left to run after an intense struggle with McLaren's Mika Hakkinen. While the top two teams finished well clear of the rest, there were signs of promise at Williams as it enjoyed its new involvement with BMW, with Ralf Schumacher going well and rookie Jenson Button impressing. Jordan looked strong, too, with Mugen-Honda power, but was held back by poor reliability, while Honda power advanced BAR's cause after its woeful first year in F1 in 1999. Giancarlo Fisichella shone for Benetton.

AUSTRALIAN GRAND PRIX

ALBERT PARK • ROUND 1 • DATE: 12TH MARCH 2000
Laps: 58 • Distance: 191.117miles/307.574km • Weather: Hot & bright

Pos	Driver	Team	Chassis-Engine	Result	Qual
1	Michael Schumacher	Ferrari	Ferrari F1-2000	1h34m01.987s	3
2	Rubens Barrichello	Ferrari	Ferrari F1-2000	1h34m13.402s	4
3	Ralf Schumacher	Williams	Williams-BMW FW22	1h34m21.996s	11
4	Jacques Villeneuve	BAR	BAR-Honda 002	1h34m46.434s	8
5	Giancarlo Fisichella	Benetton	Benetton-Playlife B200	1h34m47.152s	9
DQ	Mika Salo	Sauber	Sauber-Petronas C19	58 laps/illegal front wing	10
6	Ricardo Zonta	BAR	BAR-Honda 002	1h34m48.455s	16
7	Alexander Wurz	Benetton	Benetton-Playlife B200	1h34m48.902s	14
8	Marc Gene	Minardi	Minardi-Fondmetal M02	57 laps	18
9	Nick Heidfeld	Prost	Prost-Peugeot AP03	56 laps	15
R	Jenson Button	Williams	Williams-BMW FW22	46 laps/engine	21
R	Pedro Diniz	Sauber	Sauber-Petronas C19	41 laps/transmission	19
R	Gaston Mazzacane	Minardi	Minardi-Fondmetal M02	40 laps/gearbox	22
R	Heinz-Harald Frentzen	Jordan	Jordan-Mugen Honda EJ10	39 laps/hydraulics	5
R	Jarno Trulli	Jordan	Jordan-Mugen Honda EJ10	35 laps/engine	6
R	Jean Alesi	Prost	Prost-Peugeot AP03	27 laps/hydraulics	17
R	Mika Hakkinen	McLaren	McLaren-Mercedes MP4-15	18 laps/engine	1
R	Jos Verstappen	Arrows	Arrows-Supertec A21	16 laps/suspension	13
R	David Coulthard	McLaren	McLaren-Mercedes MP4-15	11 laps/engine	2
R	Eddie Irvine	Jaguar	Jaguar-Cosworth R1	6 laps/spun off	7
R	Pedro de la Rosa	Arrows	Arrows-Supertec A21	6 laps/suspension	12
R	Johnny Herbert	Jaguar	Jaguar-Cosworth R1	1 lap/clutch	20

Pole: Hakkinen, 1m30.556s, 130.995mph/210.817kph. Fastest lap: Barrichello, 1m31.481s, 129.671mph/208.685kph on Lap 41. Race leaders: Hakkinen 1-18, M Schumacher 19-29 & 36-44 & 46-58, Frentzen 30-35, Barrichello 45

FAREWELL TO 12 CYLINDERS

Although engine size was kept at 3000cc, the maximum number of cylinders was reduced to 10, meaning the end of the V12 in F1. Actually, the last time a V12 had been used was by Ferrari in 1994, but this fuel-hungry – but glorious-sounding – format was now simply not welcome back as the sport aimed for better fuel economy.

FERRARI'S 21-YEAR WAIT

When Jody Scheckter beat Gilles Villeneuve to the drivers' title in 1979, to take Ferrari's third title in three years, no one would have believed that it would take two decades for another Ferrari driver to be crowned. Indeed, Michael Schumacher might not have joined the team from Benetton if he had known that it would take him five years to grab that title.

BRAZILIAN GRAND PRIX

INTERLAGOS • ROUND 2 • DATE: 26TH MARCH 2000
Laps: 71 • Distance: 190.101miles/305.939km • Weather: Hot but dull

Pos	Driver	Team	Chassis-Engine	Result	Qual
1	Michael Schumacher	Ferrari	Ferrari F1-2000	1h31m35.271s	3
DQ	David Coulthard	McLaren	McLaren-Mercedes MP4-15	71 laps/illegal front wing	2
2	Giancarlo Fisichella	Benetton	Benetton-Playlife B200	1h32m15.169s	5
3	Heinz-Harald Frentzen	Jordan	Jordan-Mugen Honda EJ10	1h32m17.539s	7
4	Jarno Trulli	Jordan	Jordan-Mugen Honda EJ10	1h32m48.051s	12
5	Ralf Schumacher	Williams	Williams-BMW FW22	70 laps	11
6	Jenson Button	Williams	Williams-BMW FW22	70 laps	9
7	Jos Verstappen	Arrows	Arrows-Supertec A21	70 laps	14
8	Pedro de la Rosa	Arrows	Arrows-Supertec A21	70 laps	16
9	Ricardo Zonta	BAR	BAR-Honda 002	69 laps	8
10	Gaston Mazzacane	Minardi	Minardi-Fondmetal M02	69 laps	20
R	Johnny Herbert	Jaguar	Jaguar-Cosworth R1	51 laps/gearbox	17
R	Marc Gene	Minardi	Minardi-Fondmetal M02	31 laps/engine	18
R	Mika Hakkinen	McLaren	McLaren-Mercedes MP4-15	30 laps/fuel pressure	1
R	Rubens Barrichello	Ferrari	Ferrari F1-2000	27 laps/hydraulics	4
R	Eddie Irvine	Jaguar	Jaguar-Cosworth R1	20 laps/spun off	6
R	Jacques Villeneuve	BAR	BAR-Honda 002	16 laps/gearbox	10
R	Jean Alesi	Prost	Prost-Peugeot AP03	11 laps/electrical	15
R	Nick Heidfeld	Prost	Prost-Peugeot AP03	9 laps/engine	19
R	Alexander Wurz	Benetton	Benetton-Playlife B200	6 laps/engine	13
NS	Pedro Diniz	Sauber	Sauber-Petronas C19	rear wing	20
NS	Mika Salo	Sauber	Sauber-Petronas C19	rear wing	22

Pole: Hakkinen, 1m14.111s, 130.061mph/209.313kph. Fastest lap: M Schumacher, 1m14.755s, 128.940mph/207.509kph on Lap 48. Race leaders: Hakkinen 1 & 23-29, M Schumacher 2-20 & 30-71, Barrichello 21-22

SAN MARINO GRAND PRIX

IMOLA • ROUND 3 • DATE: 9TH APRIL 2000
Laps: 62 • Distance: 190.43miles/305.846km • Weather: Warm but dull

Pos	Driver	Team	Chassis-Engine	Result	Qual
1	Michael Schumacher	Ferrari	Ferrari F1-2000	1h31m39.776s	2
2	Mika Hakkinen	McLaren	McLaren-Mercedes MP4-15	1h31m40.944s	1
3	David Coulthard	McLaren	McLaren-Mercedes MP4-15	1h32m30.784s	3
4	Rubens Barrichello	Ferrari	Ferrari F1-2000	1h33m09.052s	4
5	Jacques Villeneuve	BAR	BAR-Honda 002	61 laps	9
6	Mika Salo	Sauber	Sauber-Petronas C19	61 laps	12

Pos	Driver	Team	Chassis-Engine	Result	Qual
7	Eddie Irvine	Jaguar	Jaguar-Cosworth R1	61 laps	7
8	Pedro Diniz	Sauber	Sauber-Petronas C19	61 laps	10
9	Alexander Wurz	Benetton	Benetton-Playlife B200	61 laps	11
10	Johnny Herbert	Jaguar	Jaguar-Cosworth R1	61 laps	17
11	Giancarlo Fisichella	Benetton	Benetton-Playlife B200	61 laps	19
12	Ricardo Zonta	BAR	BAR-Honda 002	61 laps	14
13	Gaston Mazzacane	Minardi	Minardi-Fondmetal M02	60 laps	20
14	Jos Verstappen	Arrows	Arrows-Supertec A21	59 laps	16
15	Jarno Trulli	Jordan	Jordan-Mugen Honda EJ10	58 laps/gearbox	8
R	Pedro de la Rosa	Arrows	Arrows-Supertec A21	49 laps/spun off	13
R	Ralf Schumacher	Williams	Williams-BMW FW22	45 laps/fuel system	5
R	Jean Alesi	Prost	Prost-Peugeot AP03	25 laps/hydraulics	15
R	Nick Heidfeld	Prost	Prost-Peugeot AP03	22 laps/hydraulics	22
R	Jenson Button	Williams	Williams-BMW FW22	5 laps/engine	18
R	Marc Gene	Minardi	Minardi-Fondmetal M02	5 laps/spun off	21
R	Heinz-Harald Frentzen	Jordan	Jordan-Mugen Honda EJ10	4 laps/gearbox	6

Pole: Hakkinen, 1m24.714s, 130.259mph/209.632kph. Fastest lap: Hakkinen, 1m26.523s, 127.536mph/205.249kph on Lap 60. Race leaders: Hakkinen 1-44, M Schumacher 45-62

BRITISH GRAND PRIX

SILVERSTONE • ROUND 4 • DATE: 23RD APRIL 2000
Laps: 60 • Distance: 191.410miles/308.46km • Weather: Warm & bright

Pos	Driver	Team	Chassis-Engine	Result	Qual
1	David Coulthard	McLaren	McLaren-Mercedes MP4-15	1h28m50.108s	4
2	Mika Hakkinen	McLaren	McLaren-Mercedes MP4-15	1h28m51.585s	3
3	Michael Schumacher	Ferrari	Ferrari F1-2000	1h29m10.025s	5
4	Ralf Schumacher	Williams	Williams-BMW FW22	1h29m31.420s	7
5	Jenson Button	Williams	Williams-BMW FW22	1h29m47.867s	6
6	Jarno Trulli	Jordan	Jordan-Mugen Honda EJ10	1h30m09.381s	11
7	Giancarlo Fisichella	Benetton	Benetton-Playlife B200	59 laps	12
8	Mika Salo	Sauber	Sauber-Petronas C19	59 laps	18
9	Alexander Wurz	Benetton	Benetton-Playlife B200	59 laps	20
10	Jean Alesi	Prost	Prost-Peugeot AP03	59 laps	15
11	Pedro Diniz	Sauber	Sauber-Petronas C19	59 laps	13
12	Johnny Herbert	Jaguar	Jaguar-Cosworth R1	59 laps	14
13	Eddie Irvine	Jaguar	Jaguar-Cosworth R1	59 laps	9
14	Marc Gene	Minardi	Minardi-Fondmetal M02	59 laps	21
15	Gaston Mazzacane	Minardi	Minardi-Fondmetal M02	59 laps	22
16	Jacques Villeneuve	BAR	BAR-Honda 002	56 laps/gearbox	10
17	Heinz-Harald Frentzen	Jordan	Jordan-Mugen Honda EJ10	54 laps/gearbox	2
R	Nick Heidfeld	Prost	Prost-Peugeot AP03	51 laps/engine	17
R	Ricardo Zonta	BAR	BAR-Honda 002	36 laps/spun off	16
R	Rubens Barrichello	Ferrari	Ferrari F1-2000	35 laps/hydraulics	1
R	Pedro de la Rosa	Arrows	Arrows-Supertec A21	26 laps/electronics	19
R	Jos Verstappen	Arrows	Arrows-Supertec A21	20 laps/electronics	8

Pole: Barrichello, 1m25.703s, 134.185mph/215.950kph. Fastest lap: Hakkinen, 1m26.217s, 133.385mph/214.663kph on Lap 56. Race leaders: Barrichello 1-30 & 33-35, Coulthard 31-32 & 42-60, M Schumacher 36-38, Frentzen 39-41

SPANISH GRAND PRIX

BARCELONA-CATALUNYA • ROUND 5 • DATE: 7TH MAY 2000
Laps: 65 • Distance: 190.788miles/307.45km • Weather: Warm & bright

Pos	Driver	Team	Chassis-Engine	Result	Qual
1	Mika Hakkinen	McLaren	McLaren-Mercedes MP4-15	1h33m55.390s	2
2	David Coulthard	McLaren	McLaren-Mercedes MP4-15	1h34m11.456s	4
3	Rubens Barrichello	Ferrari	Ferrari F1-2000	1h34m24.502s	3
4	Ralf Schumacher	Williams	Williams-BMW FW22	1h34m32.701s	5
5	Michael Schumacher	Ferrari	Ferrari F1-2000	1h34m43.373s	1
6	Heinz-Harald Frentzen	Jordan	Jordan-Mugen Honda EJ10	1h35m17.315s	8
7	Mika Salo	Sauber	Sauber-Petronas C19	64 laps	12
8	Ricardo Zonta	BAR	BAR-Honda 002	64 laps	16
9	Giancarlo Fisichella	Benetton	Benetton-Playlife B200	64 laps	13
10	Alexander Wurz	Benetton	Benetton-Playlife B200	64 laps	18
11	Eddie Irvine	Jaguar	Jaguar-Cosworth R1	64 laps	9
12	Jarno Trulli	Jordan	Jordan-Mugen Honda EJ10	64 laps	7
13	Johnny Herbert	Jaguar	Jaguar-Cosworth R1	64 laps	14
14	Marc Gene	Minardi	Minardi-Fondmetal M02	63 laps	20
15	Gaston Mazzacane	Minardi	Minardi-Fondmetal M02	63 laps	21
16	Nick Heidfeld	Prost	Prost-Peugeot AP03	62 laps	19
17	Jenson Button	Williams	Williams-BMW FW22	61 laps/engine	10
R	Jos Verstappen	Arrows	Arrows-Supertec A21	25 laps/gearbox	11
R	Jacques Villeneuve	BAR	BAR-Honda 002	21 laps/hydraulics	6
R	Jean Alesi	Prost	Prost-Peugeot AP03	1 lap/collision	17
R	Pedro de la Rosa	Arrows	Arrows-Supertec A21	1 lap/collision	22
R	Pedro Diniz	Sauber	Sauber-Petronas C19	0 laps/spun off	15

Pole: M Schumacher, 1m20.974s, 130.667mph/210.289kph. Fastest lap: Hakkinen, 1m24.470s, 125.259mph/201.586kph on Lap 28. Race leaders: M Schumacher 1-23 & 27-41, Hakkinen 24-26 & 42-65

A NEW FACE AT FERRARI

Rubens Barrichello joined Ferrari and the highlight of his year was his maiden F1 win, this coming in an extraordinary race at Hockenheim in which he advanced from 18th on the grid. His push to the front was boosted when a spectator got onto the track, resulting in a safety car period, then rain wrecked the McLaren challenge.

EUROPEAN GRAND PRIX

NURBURGRING • ROUND 6 • DATE: 21ST MAY 2000
Laps: 67 • Distance: 189.674miles/305.252km • Weather: Cool & dull, rain later

Pos	Driver	Team	Chassis-Engine	Result	Qual
1	Michael Schumacher	Ferrari	Ferrari F1-2000	1h42m00.307s	2
2	Mika Hakkinen	McLaren	McLaren-Mercedes MP4-15	1h42m14.129s	3
3	David Coulthard	McLaren	McLaren-Mercedes MP4-15	66 laps	1
4	Rubens Barrichello	Ferrari	Ferrari F1-2000	66 laps	4
5	Giancarlo Fisichella	Benetton	Benetton-Playlife B200	66 laps	7
6	Pedro de la Rosa	Arrows	Arrows-Supertec A21	66 laps	12

Pos	Driver	Team	Chassis-Engine	Result	Qual
7	Pedro Diniz	Sauber	Sauber-Petronas C19	65 laps	15
8	Gaston Mazzacane	Minardi	Minardi-Fondmetal M02	65 laps	21
9	Jean Alesi	Prost	Prost-Peugeot AP03	65 laps	17
10	Jenson Button	Williams	Williams-BMW FW22	62 laps/electrical	11
11	Johnny Herbert	Jaguar	Jaguar-Cosworth R1	61 laps/collision	16
12	Alexander Wurz	Benetton	Benetton-Playlife B200	61 laps/collision	14
R	Ricardo Zonta	BAR	BAR-Honda 002	51 laps/spun off	18
R	Marc Gene	Minardi	Minardi-Fondmetal M02	47 laps/throttle	20
R	Jacques Villeneuve	BAR	BAR-Honda 002	46 laps/engine	9
R	Ralf Schumacher	Williams	Williams-BMW FW22	29 laps/collision	5
R	Eddie Irvine	Jaguar	Jaguar-Cosworth R1	29 laps/collision	8
R	Jos Verstappen	Arrows	Arrows-Supertec A21	29 laps/spun off	13
R	Mika Salo	Sauber	Sauber-Petronas C19	27 laps/halfshaft	19
R	Heinz-Harald Frentzen	Jordan	Jordan-Mugen Honda EJ10	2 laps/engine	10
R	Jarno Trulli	Jordan	Jordan-Mugen Honda EJ10	0 laps/collision	6
EX	Nick Heidfeld	Prost	Prost-Peugeot AP03	car underweight	-

Pole: Coulthard, 1m17.529s, 131.453mph/211.554kph. Fastest lap: M Schumacher, 1m22.269s, 123.879mph/199.365kph on Lap 8. Race leaders: Hakkinen 1-10 & 36-45, M Schumacher 11-15 & 17-35 & 46-67, Barrichello 16

MONACO GRAND PRIX

MONTE CARLO • ROUND 7 • DATE: 4TH JUNE 2000
Laps: 78 • Distance: 162.852miles/262.86km • Weather: Hot & bright

Pos	Driver	Team	Chassis-Engine	Result	Qual
1	David Coulthard	McLaren	McLaren-Mercedes MP4-15	1h49m28.213s	3
2	Rubens Barrichello	Ferrari	Ferrari F1-2000	1h49m44.102s	6
3	Giancarlo Fisichella	Benetton	Benetton-Playlife B200	1h49m46.735s	8
4	Eddie Irvine	Jaguar	Jaguar-Cosworth R1	1h50m34.137s	10
5	Mika Salo	Sauber	Sauber-Petronas C19	1h50m48.988s	13
6	Mika Hakkinen	McLaren	McLaren-Mercedes MP4-15	77 laps	5
7	Jacques Villeneuve	BAR	BAR-Honda 002	77 laps	17
8	Nick Heidfeld	Prost	Prost-Peugeot AP03	77 laps	18
9	Johnny Herbert	Jaguar	Jaguar-Cosworth R1	76 laps	11
10	Heinz-Harald Frentzen	Jordan	Jordan-Mugen Honda EJ10	70 laps/spun off	4
R	Jos Verstappen	Arrows	Arrows-Supertec A21	60 laps/spun off	15
R	Michael Schumacher	Ferrari	Ferrari F1-2000	55 laps/suspension	1
R	Ricardo Zonta	BAR	BAR-Honda 002	48 laps/spun off	20
R	Ralf Schumacher	Williams	Williams-BMW FW22	37 laps/spun off	9
R	Jarno Trulli	Jordan	Jordan-Mugen Honda EJ10	36 laps/gearbox	2
R	Pedro Diniz	Sauber	Sauber-Petronas C19	30 laps/spun off	19
R	Jean Alesi	Prost	Prost-Peugeot AP03	29 laps/transmission	7
R	Gaston Mazzacane	Minardi	Minardi-Fondmetal M02	22 laps/spun off	22
R	Marc Gene	Minardi	Minardi-Fondmetal M02	21 laps/gearbox	21
R	Alexander Wurz	Benetton	Benetton-Playlife B200	18 laps/spun off	12
R	Jenson Button	Williams	Williams-BMW FW22	16 laps/engine	14
NS	Pedro de la Rosa	Arrows	Arrows-Supertec A21	collision damage	16

Pole: M Schumacher, 1m19.475s, 94.853mph/152.651kph. Fastest lap: Hakkinen, 1m21.571s, 92.416mph/148.729kph on Lap 57. Race leaders: M Schumacher 1-55, Coulthard 56-78

HAKKINEN PUSHED HARD

The difference between Michael Schumacher and Mika Hakkinen was 19 points at the end of the year. The Finn must have regretted his McLaren's failures in the first two races, in Australia and Brazil: on both occasions he retired from the lead, not just costing him 20 points, but also adding eight to Schumacher's pot as the German was elevated to both wins.

CANADIAN GRAND PRIX

MONTREAL • ROUND 8 • DATE: 18TH JUNE 2000
Laps: 69 • Distance: 189.548miles/305.049km • Weather: Cool & dull, rain later

Pos	Driver	Team	Chassis-Engine	Result	Qual
1	Michael Schumacher	Ferrari	Ferrari F1-2000	1h41m12.313s	1
2	Rubens Barrichello	Ferrari	Ferrari F1-2000	1h41m12.487s	3
3	Giancarlo Fisichella	Benetton	Benetton-Playlife B200	1h41m27.678s	10
4	Mika Hakkinen	McLaren	McLaren-Mercedes MP4-15	1h41m30.874s	4
5	Jos Verstappen	Arrows	Arrows-Supertec A21	1h42m04.521s	13
6	Jarno Trulli	Jordan	Jordan-Mugen Honda EJ10	1h42m14.000s	7
7	David Coulthard	McLaren	McLaren-Mercedes MP4-15	1h42m14.529s	2
8	Ricardo Zonta	BAR	BAR-Honda 002	1h42m22.768s	8
9	Alexander Wurz	Benetton	Benetton-Playlife B200	1h42m32.212s	14
10	Pedro Diniz	Sauber	Sauber-Petronas C19	1h43m06.857s	19
11	Jenson Button	Williams	Williams-BMW FW22	68 laps	18
12	Gaston Mazzacane	Minardi	Minardi-Fondmetal M02	68 laps	22
13	Eddie Irvine	Jaguar	Jaguar-Cosworth R1	66 laps	16
14	Ralf Schumacher	Williams	Williams-BMW FW22	64 laps/collision	12
15	Jacques Villeneuve	BAR	BAR-Honda 002	64 laps/collision	6
16	Marc Gene	Minardi	Minardi-Fondmetal M02	64 laps/spun off	20
R	Pedro de la Rosa	Arrows	Arrows-Supertec A21	48 laps/collision	9
R	Mika Salo	Sauber	Sauber-Petronas C19	42 laps/electrical	15
R	Jean Alesi	Prost	Prost-Peugeot AP03	38 laps/electrical	17
R	Nick Heidfeld	Prost	Prost-Peugeot AP03	34 laps/engine	21
R	Heinz-Harald Frentzen	Jordan	Jordan-Mugen Honda EJ10	32 laps/brakes	5
R	Johnny Herbert	Jaguar	Jaguar-Cosworth R1	14 laps/gearbox	11

Pole: M Schumacher, 1m18.439s, 126.078mph/202.904kph. Fastest lap: Hakkinen, 1m19.049s, 125.105mph/201.338kph on Lap 37. Race leaders: M Schumacher 1-34 & 43-69, Barrichello 35-42

FRENCH GRAND PRIX

MAGNY-COURS • ROUND 9 • DATE: 2ND JULY 2000
Laps: 72 • Distance: 190.184miles/306.072km • Weather: Hot & bright

Pos	Driver	Team	Chassis-Engine	Result	Qual
1	David Coulthard	McLaren	McLaren-Mercedes MP4-15	1h38m05.538s	2
2	Mika Hakkinen	McLaren	McLaren-Mercedes MP4-15	1h38m20.286s	4
3	Rubens Barrichello	Ferrari	Ferrari F1-2000	1h38m37.947s	3
4	Jacques Villeneuve	BAR	BAR-Honda 002	1h39m06.860s	7
5	Ralf Schumacher	Williams	Williams-BMW FW22	1h39m09.519s	5
6	Jarno Trulli	Jordan	Jordan-Mugen Honda EJ10	1h39m21.143s	9
7	Heinz-Harald Frentzen	Jordan	Jordan-Mugen Honda EJ10	71 laps	8

Pos	Driver	Team	Chassis-Engine	Result	Qual
8	Jenson Button	Williams	Williams-BMW FW22	71 laps	10
9	Giancarlo Fisichella	Benetton	Benetton-Playlife B200	71 laps	14
10	Mika Salo	Sauber	Sauber-Petronas C19	71 laps	12
11	Pedro Diniz	Sauber	Sauber-Petronas C19	71 laps	15
12	Nick Heidfeld	Prost	Prost-Peugeot AP03	71 laps	16
13	Eddie Irvine	Jaguar	Jaguar-Cosworth R1	70 laps	6
14	Jean Alesi	Prost	Prost-Peugeot AP03	70 laps	18
15	Marc Gene	Minardi	Minardi-Fondmetal M02	70 laps	21
R	Michael Schumacher	Ferrari	Ferrari F1-2000	58 laps/engine	1
R	Pedro de la Rosa	Arrows	Arrows-Supertec A21	45 laps/transmission	13
R	Alexander Wurz	Benetton	Benetton-Playlife B200	34 laps/spun off	17
R	Gaston Mazzacane	Minardi	Minardi-Fondmetal M02	31 laps/spun off	22
R	Jos Verstappen	Arrows	Arrows-Supertec A21	25 laps/transmission	20
R	Johnny Herbert	Jaguar	Jaguar-Cosworth R1	20 laps/gearbox	11
R	Ricardo Zonta	BAR	BAR-Honda 002	16 laps/spun off	19

Pole: M Schumacher, 1m15.632s, 125.730mph/202.342kph. Fastest lap: Coulthard, 1m19.479s, 119.644mph/192.548kph on Lap 28. Race leaders: M Schumacher 1-24 & 26-39, Coulthard 25 & 40-72

COULTHARD'S LUCKY ESCAPE

David Coulthard survived a light aircraft crash in the week leading up to the Spanish GP when the private jet he and his girlfriend were travelling in crashed at Lyon airport, killing the pilot and co-pilot. Showing remarkable resilience, the Scot fought through to second place behind McLaren team-mate Hakkinen in the race.

AUSTRIAN GRAND PRIX

A1-RING • ROUND 10 • DATE: 16TH JULY 2000
Laps: 71 • Distance: 190.851miles/307.146km • Weather: Hot & bright

Pos	Driver	Team	Chassis-Engine	Result	Qual
1	Mika Hakkinen	McLaren	McLaren-Mercedes MP4-15	1h28m15.818s	1
2	David Coulthard	McLaren	McLaren-Mercedes MP4-15	1h28m28.353s	2
3	Rubens Barrichello	Ferrari	Ferrari F1-2000	1h28m46.613s	3
4	Jacques Villeneuve	BAR	BAR-Honda 002	70 laps	7
5	Jenson Button	Williams	Williams-BMW FW22	70 laps	18
6	Mika Salo	Sauber	Sauber-Petronas C19	70 laps	9
7	Johnny Herbert	Jaguar	Jaguar-Cosworth R1	70 laps	16
8	Marc Gene	Minardi	Minardi-Fondmetal M02	70 laps	20
9	Pedro Diniz	Sauber	Sauber-Petronas C19	70 laps	11
10	Alexander Wurz	Benetton	Benetton-Playlife B200	70 laps	14
11	Luciano Burti	Jaguar	Jaguar-Cosworth R1	69 laps	21
12	Gaston Mazzacane	Minardi	Minardi-Fondmetal M02	68 laps	22
R	Ricardo Zonta	BAR	BAR-Honda 002	58 laps/engine	6
R	Ralf Schumacher	Williams	Williams-BMW FW22	52 laps/brakes	19
R	Nick Heidfeld	Prost	Prost-Peugeot AP03	41 laps/collision	13
R	Jean Alesi	Prost	Prost-Peugeot AP03	41 laps/collision	17
R	Pedro de la Rosa	Arrows	Arrows-Supertec A21	32 laps/gearbox	12
R	Jos Verstappen	Arrows	Arrows-Supertec A21	14 laps/engine	10

Pos	Driver	Team	Chassis-Engine	Result	Qual
R	Heinz-Harald Frentzen	Jordan	Jordan-Mugen Honda EJ10	4 laps/oil leak	15
R	Michael Schumacher	Ferrari	Ferrari F1-2000	0 laps/collision	4
R	Jarno Trulli	Jordan	Jordan-Mugen Honda EJ10	0 laps/collision	5
R	Giancarlo Fisichella	Benetton	Benetton-Playlife B200	0 laps/collision	8
NS	Eddie Irvine	Jaguar	Jaguar-Cosworth R1	driver unwell	-

Pole: Hakkinen, 1m10.410s, 137.437mph/221.184kph. Fastest lap: Coulthard, 1m11.783s, 134.808mph/216.953kph on Lap 67. Race leaders: Hakkinen 1-38 & 43-71, Coulthard 39-42

GERMAN GRAND PRIX

HOCKENHEIM • ROUND 11 • DATE: 30TH JULY 2000
Laps: 45 • Distance: 190.838miles/307.125km • Weather: Warm & dull, rain later

Pos	Driver	Team	Chassis-Engine	Result	Qual
1	Rubens Barrichello	Ferrari	Ferrari F1-2000	1h25m34.418s	18
2	Mika Hakkinen	McLaren	McLaren-Mercedes MP4-15	1h25m41.870s	4
3	David Coulthard	McLaren	McLaren-Mercedes MP4-15	1h25m55.586s	1
4	Jenson Button	Williams	Williams-BMW FW22	1h25m57.103s	16
5	Mika Salo	Sauber	Sauber-Petronas C19	1h26m01.530s	15
6	Pedro de la Rosa	Arrows	Arrows-Supertec A21	1h26m03.498s	5
7	Ralf Schumacher	Williams	Williams-BMW FW22	1h26m05.316s	14
8	Jacques Villeneuve	BAR	BAR-Honda 002	1h26m21.955s	9
9	Jarno Trulli	Jordan	Jordan-Mugen Honda EJ10B	1h26m25.319s	6
10	Eddie Irvine	Jaguar	Jaguar-Cosworth R1	1h26m54.082s	10
11	Gaston Mazzacane	Minardi	Minardi-Fondmetal M02	1h27m03.922s	21
12	Nick Heidfeld	Prost	Prost-Peugeot AP03	40 laps/alternator	13
R	Jos Verstappen	Arrows	Arrows-Supertec A21	39 laps/spun off	11
R	Heinz-Harald Frentzen	Jordan	Jordan-Mugen Honda EJ10B	39 laps/gearbox	17
R	Ricardo Zonta	BAR	BAR-Honda 002	37 laps/spun off	12
R	Marc Gene	Minardi	Minardi-Fondmetal M02	33 laps/engine	22
R	Alexander Wurz	Benetton	Benetton-Playlife B200	31 laps/electrical	7
R	Pedro Diniz	Sauber	Sauber-Petronas C19	29 laps/collision	19
R	Jean Alesi	Prost	Prost-Peugeot AP03	29 laps/collision	20
R	Johnny Herbert	Jaguar	Jaguar-Cosworth R1	12 laps/gearbox	8
R	Michael Schumacher	Ferrari	Ferrari F1-2000	0 laps/collision	2
R	Giancarlo Fisichella	Benetton	Benetton-Playlife B200	0 laps/collision	3

Pole: Coulthard, 1m45.697s, 144.442mph/232.456kph. Fastest lap: Barrichello, 1m44.300s, 146.376mph/235.570kph on Lap 20. Race leaders: Hakkinen 1-25 & 28-35, Coulthard 26-27, Barrichello 36-45

TURNING THE FANS AWAY

The moving of the British GP to a date in April, rather than its traditional slot in July, in a powerplay between the sport's governing body and the circuit was a disaster. Continuous rain in the lead-up to the event left Silverstone's parking areas flooded, forcing officials to turn fans away when they arrived to watch Saturday qualifying.

A TWO-WAY CONTEST

This World Championship was a two-horse race between Ferrari and McLaren, initially between Schumacher, Hakkinen and Coulthard before the Scot's challenge faded. It was the first time since 1988 that only two teams took race wins. Back then, it was the same two teams, albeit with McLaren winning all but the Italian GP.

HUNGARIAN GRAND PRIX

HUNGARORING • ROUND 12 • DATE: 13TH AUGUST 2000
Laps: 77 • Distance: 190.186miles/306.075km • Weather: Hot & bright

Pos	Driver	Team	Chassis-Engine	Result	Qual
1	Mika Hakkinen	McLaren	McLaren-Mercedes MP4-15	1h45m33.869s	3
2	Michael Schumacher	Ferrari	Ferrari F1-2000	1h45m41.786s	1
3	David Coulthard	McLaren	McLaren-Mercedes MP4-15	1h45m42.324s	2
4	Rubens Barrichello	Ferrari	Ferrari F1-2000	1h46m18.026s	5
5	Ralf Schumacher	Williams	Williams-BMW FW22	1h46m24.306s	4
6	Heinz-Harald Frentzen	Jordan	Jordan-Mugen Honda EJ10B	1h46m41.968s	6
7	Jarno Trulli	Jordan	Jordan-Mugen Honda EJ10B	76 laps	12
8	Eddie Irvine	Jaguar	Jaguar-Cosworth R1	76 laps	10
9	Jenson Button	Williams	Williams-BMW FW22	76 laps	8
10	Mika Salo	Sauber	Sauber-Petronas C19	76 laps	9
11	Alexander Wurz	Benetton	Benetton-Playlife B200	76 laps	11
12	Jacques Villeneuve	BAR	BAR-Honda 002	75 laps	16
13	Jos Verstappen	Arrows	Arrows-Supertec A21	75 laps	20
14	Ricardo Zonta	BAR	BAR-Honda 002	75 laps	18
15	Marc Gene	Minardi	Minardi-Fondmetal M02	74 laps	21
16	Pedro de la Rosa	Arrows	Arrows-Supertec A21	73 laps	15
R	Gaston Mazzacane	Minardi	Minardi-Fondmetal M02	68 laps/engine	22
R	Johnny Herbert	Jaguar	Jaguar-Cosworth R1	67 laps/gearbox	17
R	Pedro Diniz	Sauber	Sauber-Petronas C19	62 laps/transmission	13
R	Giancarlo Fisichella	Benetton	Benetton-Playlife B200	31 laps/brakes	7
R	Nick Heidfeld	Prost	Prost-Peugeot AP03	22 laps/electrical	19
R	Jean Alesi	Prost	Prost-Peugeot AP03	11 laps/suspension	14

Pole: M Schumacher, 1m17.514s, 114.712mph/184.611kph. Fastest lap: Hakkinen, 1m20.028s, 111.108mph/178.812kph on Lap 33. Race leaders: Hakkinen 1-31 & 33-77, Coulthard 32

BELGIAN GRAND PRIX

SPA-FRANCORCHAMPS • ROUND 13 • DATE: 27TH AUGUST 2000
Laps: 44 • Distance: 190.507miles/306.592km • Weather: Warm & wet, drying later

Pos	Driver	Team	Chassis-Engine	Result	Qual
1	Mika Hakkinen	McLaren	McLaren-Mercedes MP4-15	1h28m14.494s	1
2	Michael Schumacher	Ferrari	Ferrari F1-2000	1h28m15.598s	4
3	Ralf Schumacher	Williams	Williams-BMW FW22	1h28m52.590s	6
4	David Coulthard	McLaren	McLaren-Mercedes MP4-15	1h28m57.775s	5
5	Jenson Button	Williams	Williams-BMW FW22	1h29m04.408s	3
6	Heinz-Harald Frentzen	Jordan	Jordan-Mugen Honda EJ10B	1h29m10.478s	8
7	Jacques Villeneuve	BAR	BAR-Honda 002	1h29m26.874s	7

Pos	Driver	Team	Chassis-Engine	Result	Qual
8	Johnny Herbert	Jaguar	Jaguar-Cosworth R1	1h29m42.302s	9
9	Mika Salo	Sauber	Sauber-Petronas C19	1h29m43.164s	18
10	Eddie Irvine	Jaguar	Jaguar-Cosworth R1	1h29m46.049s	12
11	Pedro Diniz	Sauber	Sauber-Petronas C19	1h29m48.617s	15
12	Ricardo Zonta	BAR	BAR-Honda 002	43 laps	13
13	Alexander Wurz	Benetton	Benetton-Playlife B200	43 laps	19
14	Marc Gene	Minardi	Minardi-Fondmetal M02	43 laps	21
15	Jos Verstappen	Arrows	Arrows-Supertec A21	43 laps	20
16	Pedro de la Rosa	Arrows	Arrows-Supertec A21	42 laps	16
17	Gaston Mazzacane	Minardi	Minardi-Fondmetal M02	42 laps	22
R	Rubens Barrichello	Ferrari	Ferrari F1-2000	32 laps/fuel pressure	10
R	Jean Alesi	Prost	Prost-Peugeot AP03	32 laps/fuel pressure	17
R	Nick Heidfeld	Prost	Prost-Peugeot AP03	12 laps/engine	14
R	Giancarlo Fisichella	Benetton	Benetton-Playlife B200	8 laps/electrical	11
R	Jarno Trulli	Jordan	Jordan-Mugen Honda EJ10B	4 laps/collision	2

Pole: Hakkinen, 1m50.646s, 140.872mph/226.712kph. Fastest lap: Barrichello, 1m53.803s, 136.964mph/220.423kph on Lap 30. Race leaders: Hakkinen 1-12 & 23-27 & 41-44, M Schumacher 13-22 & 28-40

NEW CIRCUITS

The season marked the return of the Indianapolis Motor Speedway to the World Championship for the first time since 1960, when the Indy 500 counted for points. For its first F1 race, a reverse direction infield course was used, along with a stretch of the banking from Turn 2 back to Turn 1. Another change was the modification of Monza's first two chicanes.

ITALIAN GRAND PRIX

MONZA • ROUND 14 • DATE: 10TH SEPTEMBER 2000
Laps: 53 • Distance: 190.778miles/307.029km • Weather: Hot & bright

Pos	Driver	Team	Chassis-Engine	Result	Qual
1	Michael Schumacher	Ferrari	Ferrari F1-2000	1h27m31.638s	1
2	Mika Hakkinen	McLaren	McLaren-Mercedes MP4-15	1h27m35.448s	3
3	Ralf Schumacher	Williams	Williams-BMW FW22	1h28m24.070s	7
4	Jos Verstappen	Arrows	Arrows-Supertec A21	1h28m31.576s	11
5	Alexander Wurz	Benetton	Benetton-Playlife B200	1h28m39.064s	13
6	Ricardo Zonta	BAR	BAR-Honda 002	1h28m40.931s	17
7	Mika Salo	Sauber	Sauber-Petronas C19	52 laps	15
8	Pedro Diniz	Sauber	Sauber-Petronas C19	52 laps	16
9	Marc Gene	Minardi	Minardi-Fondmetal M02	52 laps	21
10	Gaston Mazzacane	Minardi	Minardi-Fondmetal M02	52 laps	22
11	Giancarlo Fisichella	Benetton	Benetton-Playlife B200	52 laps	9
12	Jean Alesi	Prost	Prost-Peugeot AP03	51 laps	19
R	Nick Heidfeld	Prost	Prost-Peugeot AP03	15 laps/spun off	20
R	Jacques Villeneuve	BAR	BAR-Honda 002	14 laps/electrical	4
R	Jenson Button	Williams	Williams-BMW FW22	10 laps/spun off	12
R	Johnny Herbert	Jaguar	Jaguar-Cosworth R1	1 lap/spun off	18
R	Rubens Barrichello	Ferrari	Ferrari F1-2000	0 laps/collision	2

Pos	Driver	Team	Chassis-Engine	Result	Qual
R	David Coulthard	McLaren	McLaren-Mercedes MP4-15	0 laps/collision	5
R	Jarno Trulli	Jordan	Jordan-Mugen Honda EJ10B	0 laps/collision	6
R	Heinz-Harald Frentzen	Jordan	Jordan-Mugen Honda EJ10B	0 laps/collision	8
R	Pedro de la Rosa	Arrows	Arrows-Supertec A21	0 laps/collision	10
R	Eddie Irvine	Jaguar	Jaguar-Cosworth R1	0 laps/spun off	14

Pole: M Schumacher, 1m23.770s, 154.692mph/248.953kph. Fastest lap: Hakkinen, 1m25.595s, 151.394mph/243.645kph on Lap 50. Race leaders: M Schumacher 1-39 & 43-53, Hakkinen 40-42

NEW CONSTRUCTORS

Jaguar became part of F1 for the first time with the British marque, synonymous with sports car success, entering F1 via its parent company, Ford, taking over Stewart Grand Prix. The team had two main problems. The first was management interference from the manufacturer itself. The second was the fact that its car, the R1, wasn't competitive.

UNITED STATES GRAND PRIX

INDIANAPOLIS MOTOR SPEEDWAY • ROUND 15 • DATE: 24TH SEPTEMBER 2000
Laps: 73 • Distance: 190.149miles/306.016km • Weather: Cool & damp, drying later

Pos	Driver	Team	Chassis-Engine	Result	Qual
1	Michael Schumacher	Ferrari	Ferrari F1-2000	1h36m30.883s	1
2	Rubens Barrichello	Ferrari	Ferrari F1-2000	1h36m43.001s	4
3	Heinz-Harald Frentzen	Jordan	Jordan-Mugen Honda EJ10B	1h36m48.251s	7
4	Jacques Villeneuve	BAR	BAR-Honda 002	1h36m48.819s	8
5	David Coulthard	McLaren	McLaren-Mercedes MP4-15	1h36m59.696s	2
6	Ricardo Zonta	BAR	BAR-Honda 002	1h37m22.577s	12
7	Eddie Irvine	Jaguar	Jaguar-Cosworth R1	1h37m41.998s	17
8	Pedro Diniz	Sauber	Sauber-Petronas C19	72 laps	9
9	Nick Heidfeld	Prost	Prost-Peugeot AP03	72 laps	16
10	Alexander Wurz	Benetton	Benetton-Playlife B200	72 laps	11
11	Johnny Herbert	Jaguar	Jaguar-Cosworth R1	72 laps	19
12	Marc Gene	Minardi	Minardi-Fondmetal M02	72 laps	22
R	Jean Alesi	Prost	Prost-Peugeot AP03	64 laps/engine	20
R	Gaston Mazzacane	Minardi	Minardi-Fondmetal M02	59 laps/engine	21
R	Ralf Schumacher	Williams	Williams-BMW FW22	58 laps/engine	10
R	Pedro de la Rosa	Arrows	Arrows-Supertec A21	45 laps/gearbox	18
R	Giancarlo Fisichella	Benetton	Benetton-Playlife B200	44 laps/engine	15
R	Jos Verstappen	Arrows	Arrows-Supertec A21	34 laps/brakes	13
R	Mika Hakkinen	McLaren	McLaren-Mercedes MP4-15	25 laps/engine	3
R	Mika Salo	Sauber	Sauber-Petronas C19	18 laps/spun off	14
R	Jenson Button	Williams	Williams-BMW FW22	14 laps/engine	6
R	Jarno Trulli	Jordan	Jordan-Mugen Honda EJ10B	12 laps/collision	5

Pole: M Schumacher, 1m14.266s, 126.265mph/203.204kph. Fastest lap: Coulthard, 1m14.711s, 125.513mph/201.994kph on Lap 40. Race leaders: Coulthard 1-6, M Schumacher 7-73

JAPANESE GRAND PRIX

SUZUKA • ROUND 16 • DATE: 8TH OCTOBER 2000
Laps: 53 • Distance: 193.117miles/310.792km • Weather: Cool & dull, rain later

Pos	Driver	Team	Chassis-Engine	Result	Qual
1	Michael Schumacher	Ferrari	Ferrari F1-2000	1h29m53.435s	1
2	Mika Hakkinen	McLaren	McLaren-Mercedes MP4-15	1h29m55.272s	2
3	David Coulthard	McLaren	McLaren-Mercedes MP4-15	1h31m03.349s	3
4	Rubens Barrichello	Ferrari	Ferrari F1-2000	1h31m12.626s	4
5	Jenson Button	Williams	Williams-BMW FW22	1h31m19.129s	5
6	Jacques Villeneuve	BAR	BAR-Honda 002	52 laps	9
7	Johnny Herbert	Jaguar	Jaguar-Cosworth R1	52 laps	10
8	Eddie Irvine	Jaguar	Jaguar-Cosworth R1	52 laps	7
9	Ricardo Zonta	BAR	BAR-Honda 002	52 laps	18
10	Mika Salo	Sauber	Sauber-Petronas C19	52 laps	19
11	Pedro Diniz	Sauber	Sauber-Petronas C19	52 laps	20
12	Pedro de la Rosa	Arrows	Arrows-Supertec A21	52 laps	13
13	Jarno Trulli	Jordan	Jordan-Mugen Honda EJ10B	52 laps	15
14	Giancarlo Fisichella	Benetton	Benetton-Playlife B200	52 laps	12
15	Gaston Mazzacane	Minardi	Minardi-Fondmetal M02	51 laps	22
R	Marc Gene	Minardi	Minardi-Fondmetal M02	46 laps/engine	21
R	Ralf Schumacher	Williams	Williams-BMW FW22	41 laps/spun off	6
R	Nick Heidfeld	Prost	Prost-Peugeot AP03	41 laps/suspension	16
R	Alexander Wurz	Benetton	Benetton-Playlife B200	37 laps/spun off	11
R	Heinz-Harald Frentzen	Jordan	Jordan-Mugen Honda EJ10B	29 laps/hydraulics	8
R	Jean Alesi	Prost	Prost-Peugeot AP03	19 laps/engine	17
R	Jos Verstappen	Arrows	Arrows-Supertec A21	9 laps/electrical	14

Pole: M Schumacher, 1m35.825s, 136.889mph/220.301kph. Fastest lap: Hakkinen, 1m39.189s, 132.246mph/212.830kph on Lap 26. Race leaders: Hakkinen 1-21 & 25-36, M Schumacher 22-23 & 37-53, Coulthard 24

NEW DRIVERS

Jenson Button was the best of the four rookies, ranking eighth overall for Williams with half the points tally of team-mate Ralf Schumacher, peaking with fourth at Hockenheim. Nick Heidfeld took an eighth place for Sauber, while Gaston Mazzacane matched that in his Minardi at the Nurburgring. Luciano Burti was 11th in his one race for Jaguar.

MALAYSIAN GRAND PRIX

SEPANG • ROUND 17 • DATE: 22ND OCTOBER 2000
Laps: 56 • Distance: 192.878miles/310.408km • Weather: Hot & bright

Pos	Driver	Team	Chassis-Engine	Result	Qual
1	Michael Schumacher	Ferrari	Ferrari F1-2000	1h35m54.235s	1
2	David Coulthard	McLaren	McLaren-Mercedes MP4-15	1h35m54.967s	3
3	Rubens Barrichello	Ferrari	Ferrari F1-2000	1h36m12.679s	4
4	Mika Hakkinen	McLaren	McLaren-Mercedes MP4-15	1h36m29.504s	2
5	Jacques Villeneuve	BAR	BAR-Honda 002	1h37m04.927s	6

Pos	Driver	Team	Chassis-Engine	Result	Qual
6	Eddie Irvine	Jaguar	Jaguar-Cosworth R1	1h37m06.803s	7
7	Alexander Wurz	Benetton	Benetton-Playlife B200	1h37m23.549s	5
8	Mika Salo	Sauber	Sauber-Petronas C19	55 laps	17
9	Giancarlo Fisichella	Benetton	Benetton-Playlife B200	55 laps	13
10	Jos Verstappen	Arrows	Arrows-Supertec A21	55 laps	15
11	Jean Alesi	Prost	Prost-Peugeot AP03	55 laps	18
12	Jarno Trulli	Jordan	Jordan-Mugen Honda EJ10B	55 laps	9
13	Gaston Mazzacane	Minardi	Minardi-Fondmetal M02	50 laps/engine	22
R	Johnny Herbert	Jaguar	Jaguar-Cosworth R1	48 laps/suspension	12
R	Ricardo Zonta	BAR	BAR-Honda 002	46 laps/engine	11
R	Ralf Schumacher	Williams	Williams-BMW FW22	43 laps/engine	8
R	Marc Gene	Minardi	Minardi-Fondmetal M02	36 laps/wheel	21
R	Jenson Button	Williams	Williams-BMW FW22	18 laps/engine	16
R	Heinz-Harald Frentzen	Jordan	Jordan-Mugen Honda EJ10B	7 laps/electrical	10
R	Pedro de la Rosa	Arrows	Arrows-Supertec A21	0 laps/collision	14
R	Nick Heidfeld	Prost	Prost-Peugeot AP03	0 laps/collision	19
R	Pedro Diniz	Sauber	Sauber-Petronas C19	0 laps/collision	20

Pole: M Schumacher, 1m37.397s, 127.307mph/204.881kph. Fastest lap: Hakkinen, 1m38.543s, 125.826mph/202.498kph on Lap 34. Race leaders: Hakkinen 1-2, Coulthard 3-17, M Schumacher 18-24 & 26-39 & 42-56, Barrichello 25 & 40-41

WORLD DRIVERS' CHAMPIONSHIP FINAL RESULTS

Pos	Driver	Nat	Car-Engine	R1	R2	R3	R4	R5	R6
1	Michael Schumacher	DEU	Ferrari F1-2000	1	1F	1	3	5P	1F
2	Mika Hakkinen	FIN	McLaren-Mercedes MP4-15	RP	RP	2PF	2F	1F	2
3	David Coulthard	GBR	McLaren-Mercedes MP4-15	R	DQ	3	1	2	3P
4	Rubens Barrichello	BRA	Ferrari F1-2000	2F	R	4	RP	3	4
5	Ralf Schumacher	DEU	Williams-BMW FW22	3	5	R	4	4	R
6	Giancarlo Fisichella	ITA	Benetton-Playlife B200	5	2	11	7	9	5
7	Jacques Villeneuve	CAN	BAR-Honda 002	4	R	5	16	R	R
8	Jenson Button	GBR	Williams-BMW FW22	R	6	R	5	17	10
9	Heinz-Harald Frentzen	DEU	Jordan-Mugen Honda EJ10	R	3	R	17	6	R
			Jordan-Mugen Honda EJ10B	-	-	-	-	-	-
10	Jarno Trulli	ITA	Jordan-Mugen Honda EJ10	R	4	15	6	12	R
			Jordan-Mugen Honda EJ10B	-	-	-	-	-	-
11	Mika Salo	FIN	Sauber-Petronas C19	DQ	NS	6	8	7	R
12	Jos Verstappen	NLD	Arrows-Supertec A21	R	7	14	R	R	R
13	Eddie Irvine	GBR	Jaguar Cosworth R1	R	R	7	13	11	R
14	Ricardo Zonta	BRA	BAR-Honda 002	6	9	12	R	8	R
15	Alexander Wurz	AUT	Benetton-Playlife B200	7	R	9	9	10	12
16	Pedro de la Rosa	ESP	Arrows-Supertec A21	R	8	R	R	R	6
17	Johnny Herbert	GBR	Jaguar-Cosworth R1	R	R	10	12	13	11
18	Pedro Diniz	BRA	Sauber-Petronas C19	R	NS	8	11	R	7
19	Marc Gene	ESP	Minardi-Fondmetal M02	8	R	R	14	14	R
20	Nick Heidfeld	DEU	Prost-Peugeot AP03	9	R	R	R	16	DNQ
21	Gaston Mazzacane	ARG	Minardi-Fondmetal M02	R	10	13	15	15	8
22	Jean Alesi	FRA	Prost-Peugeot AP03	R	R	R	10	R	9
23	Luciano Burti	BRA	Jaguar-Cosworth R1	-	-	-	-	-	-

Pos	Driver	R7	R8	R9	R10	R11	R12	R13	R14	R15	R16	R17	Total
1	M Schumacher	RP	1P	RP	R	R	2P	2	1P	1P	1P	1P	108
2	Hakkinen	6F	4F	2	1P	2	1F	1P	2F	R	2F	4F	89
3	Coulthard	1	7	1F	2F	3P	3	4	R	5F	3	2	73
4	Barrichello	2	2	3	3	1F	4	RF	R	2	4	3	62
5	R Schumacher	R	14	5	R	7	5	3	3	R	R	R	24
6	Fisichella	3	3	9	R	R	R	R	11	R	14	9	18
7	Villeneuve	7	15	4	4	8	12	7	R	4	6	5	17
8	Button	R	11	8	5	4	9	5	R	R	5	R	12
9	Frentzen	10	R	7	R	-	-	-	-	-	-	-	11
		-	-	-	-	R	6	6	R	3	R	R	
10	Trulli	R	6	6	R	-	-	-	-	-	-	-	6
		-	-	-	-	9	7	R	R	R	13	12	
11	Salo	5	R	10	6	5	10	9	7	R	10	8	6
12	Verstappen	R	5	R	R	R	13	15	4	R	R	10	5
13	Irvine	4	13	13	NS	10	8	10	R	7	8	6	4
14	Zonta	R	8	R	R	R	14	12	6	6	9	R	3
15	Wurz	R	9	R	10	R	11	13	5	10	R	7	2
16	de la Rosa	NS	R	R	R	6	16	16	R	R	12	R	2
17	Herbert	9	R	R	7	R	R	8	R	11	7	R	0
18	Diniz	R	10	11	9	R	R	11	8	8	11	R	0
19	Gene	R	16	15	8	R	15	14	9	12	R	R	0
20	Heidfeld	8	R	12	R	12	R	R	R	9	R	R	0
21	Mazzacane	R	12	R	12	11	R	17	10	R	15	13	0
22	Alesi	R	R	14	R	R	R	R	12	R	R	11	0
23	Burti	-	-	-	11	-	-	-	-	-	-	-	0

SYMBOLS AND GRAND PRIX KEY

Round 1 **Australian GP**
Round 2 **Brazilian GP**
Round 3 **San Marino GP**
Round 4 **British GP**
Round 5 **Spanish GP**
Round 6 **European GP**
Round 7 **Monaco GP**
Round 8 **Canadian GP**
Round 9 **French GP**
Round 10 **Austrian GP**
Round 11 **German GP**
Round 12 **Hungarian GP**
Round 13 **Belgian GP**
Round 14 **Italian GP**
Round 15 **United States GP**
Round 16 **Japanese GP**
Round 17 **Malaysian GP**

SCORING

1st **10 points**
2nd **6 points**
3rd **4 points**
4th **3 points**
5th **2 points**
6th **1 point**

DNPQ DID NOT PRE-QUALIFY **DNQ DID NOT QUALIFY** **DQ DISQUALIFIED** **EX EXCLUDED**
F FASTEST LAP **NC NOT CLASSIFIED** **NS NON-STARTER** **P POLE POSITION** **R RETIRED**

WORLD CONSTRUCTORS' CHAMPIONSHIP FINAL RESULTS

Pos	Team-Engine	R1	R2	R3	R4	R5	R6	R7	R8	R9
1	Ferrari	1/2	1/R	1/4	3/R	3/5	1/4	2/R	1/2	3/R
2	McLaren-Mercedes	R/R	DQ/R	2/3	1/2	1/2	2/3	1/6	4/7	1/2
3	Williams-BMW	3/R	5/6	R/R	4/5	4/17	10/R	R/R	11/14	5/8
4	Benetton-Playlife	5/7	2/R	9/11	7/9	9/10	5/12	3/R	3/9	9/R
5	BAR-Honda	4/6	9/R	5/12	16/R	8/R	R/R	7/R	8/15	4/R
6	Jordan-Mugen Honda	R/R	3/4	15/R	6/17	6/12	R/R	10/R	6/R	6/7
7	Arrows-Supertec	R/R	7/8	14/R	R/R	R/R	6/R	R/NS	5/R	R/R
8	Sauber-Petronas	DQ/R	NS/NS	6/8	8/11	7/R	7/R	5/R	10/R	10/11
9	Jaguar-Cosworth	R/R	R/R	7/10	12/13	11/13	11/R	4/9	13/R	13/R
10	Minardi-Fondmetal	8/R	10/R	13/R	14/15	14/15	8/R	R/R	12/16	15/R
11	Prost-Peugeot	9/R	R/R	R/R	10/R	16/R	9/DNQ	8/R	R/R	12/14

Pos	Team-Engine	R10	R11	R12	R13	R14	R15	R16	R17	Total
1	Ferrari	3/R	1/R	2/4	2/R	1/R	1/2	1/4	1/3	170
2	McLaren-Mercedes	1/2	2/3	1/3	1/4	2/R	5/R	2/3	2/4	152
3	Williams-BMW	5/R	4/7	5/9	3/5	3/R	R/R	5/R	R/R	36
4	Benetton-Playlife	10/R	R/R	11/R	13/R	5/11	10/R	14/R	7/9	20
5	BAR-Honda	4/R	8/R	12/14	7/12	6/R	4/6	6/9	5/R	20
6	Jordan-Mugen Honda	R/R	9/R	6/7	6/R	R/R	3/R	13/R	12/R	17
7	Arrows-Supertec	R/R	6/R	13/16	15/16	4/R	R/R	12/R	10/R	7
8	Sauber-Petronas	6/9	5/R	10/R	9/11	7/8	8/R	10/11	8/R	6
9	Jaguar-Cosworth	7/11	10/R	8/R	8/10	R/R	7/11	7/8	6/R	4
10	Minardi-Fondmetal	8/12	11/R	15/R	14/17	9/10	12/R	15/R	13/R	0
11	Prost-Peugeot	R/R	12/R	R/R	R/R	12/R	9/R	R/R	11/R	0

2001

SEASON SUMMARY

Michael Schumacher came back hungry for another F1 title and was able to achieve that with ease, as Ferrari raised its game to give him a superior car. On his way to equalling Alain Prost's tally of four world titles, he passed Prost's record of 51 F1 wins and scored more points in a season – 123 – than anyone had before, also taking his career points tally to a new record. The best of the rest, McLaren's David Coulthard, scored only just more than half his tally in a year in which team-mate Mika Hakkinen faded and announced a plan to take a year out.

AUSTRALIAN GRAND PRIX

ALBERT PARK • ROUND 1 • DATE: 4TH MARCH 2001
Laps: 58 • Distance: 191.117miles/307.574km • Weather: Hot & bright

Pos	Driver	Team	Chassis-Engine	Result	Qual
1	Michael Schumacher	Ferrari	Ferrari F2001	1h38m26.533s	1
2	David Coulthard	McLaren	McLaren-Mercedes MP4-16	1h38m28.251s	6
3	Rubens Barrichello	Ferrari	Ferrari F2001	1h39m00.024s	2
4	Nick Heidfeld	Sauber	Sauber-Petronas C20	1h39m38.012s	10
5	Heinz-Harald Frentzen	Jordan	Jordan-Honda EJ11	1h39m39.340s	4
6	Kimi Raikkonen	Sauber	Sauber-Petronas C20	1h39m50.676s	13
7	Olivier Panis *	BAR	BAR-Honda 003	1h39m53.583s	9
8	Luciano Burti	Jaguar	Jaguar-Cosworth R2	57 laps	21
9	Jean Alesi	Prost	Prost-Acer AP04	57 laps	14
10	Jos Verstappen *	Arrows	Arrows-Asiatech A22	57 laps	15
11	Eddie Irvine	Jaguar	Jaguar-Cosworth R2	57 laps	12
12	Fernando Alonso	Minardi	Minardi-European PS01	56 laps	19
13	Giancarlo Fisichella	Benetton	Benetton-Renault B201	55 laps	17
14	Jenson Button	Benetton	Benetton-Renault B201	52 laps/exhaust	16
R	Juan Pablo Montoya	Williams	Williams-BMW FW23	40 laps/engine	11
R	Jarno Trulli	Jordan	Jordan-Honda EJ11	38 laps/engine	7
R	Mika Hakkinen	McLaren	McLaren-Mercedes MP4-16	25 laps/suspension	3
R	Ralf Schumacher	Williams	Williams-BMW FW23	4 laps/collision	5
R	Jacques Villeneuve	BAR	BAR-Honda 003	4 laps/collision	8
R	Tarso Marques	Minardi	Minardi-European PS01	3 laps/battery	22
R	Enrique Bernoldi	Arrows	Arrows-Asiatech A22	2 laps/spun off	18
R	Gaston Mazzacane	Prost	Prost-Acer AP04	0 laps/brakes	20

Pole: M Schumacher, 1m26.892s, 136.519mph/219.707kph. Fastest lap: M Schumacher, 1m28.214s, 134.473mph/216.414kph on Lap 34. Race leaders: M Schumacher 1-36 & 41-58, Coulthard 37-40

* 25s penalty for yellow flag infringement

HELP IS AT HAND

From the Spanish GP onwards, electronic driver aids were permitted in F1 again. This meant launch control, traction control and fully automated gear-change mechanisms were back for the first time since 1993. And these, combined with an escalating tyre war between Bridgestone and Michelin, led to lap times tumbling by as much as three seconds per lap.

MALAYSIAN GRAND PRIX

SEPANG • ROUND 2 • DATE: 18TH MARCH 2001
Laps: 55 • Distance: 189.434miles/304.865km • Weather: Hot & bright, rain later

Pos	Driver	Team	Chassis-Engine	Result	Qual
1	Michael Schumacher	Ferrari	Ferrari F2001	1h47m34.801s	1
2	Rubens Barrichello	Ferrari	Ferrari F2001	1h47m58.461s	2
3	David Coulthard	McLaren	McLaren-Mercedes MP4-16	1h48m03.356s	8
4	Heinz-Harald Frentzen	Jordan	Jordan-Honda EJ11	1h48m21.344s	9
5	Ralf Schumacher	Williams	Williams-BMW FW23	1h48m23.034s	3
6	Mika Hakkinen	McLaren	McLaren-Mercedes MP4-16	1h48m23.407s	4
7	Jos Verstappen	Arrows	Arrows-Asiatech A22	1h48m56.361s	18
8	Jarno Trulli	Jordan	Jordan-Honda EJ11	54 laps	5
9	Jean Alesi	Prost	Prost-Acer AP04	54 laps	13
10	Luciano Burti	Jaguar	Jaguar-Cosworth R2	54 laps	15
11	Jenson Button	Benetton	Benetton-Renault B201	53 laps	17
12	Gaston Mazzacane	Prost	Prost-Acer AP04	53 laps	19
13	Fernando Alonso	Minardi	Minardi-European PS01	52 laps	21
14	Tarso Marques	Minardi	Minardi-European PS01	51 laps	20
R	Giancarlo Fisichella	Benetton	Benetton-Renault B201	31 laps/fuel pressure	16
R	Juan Pablo Montoya	Williams	Williams-BMW FW23	3 laps/spun off	6
R	Jacques Villeneuve	BAR	BAR-Honda 003	3 laps/spun off	7
R	Nick Heidfeld	Sauber	Sauber-Petronas C20	3 laps/spun off	11
R	Eddie Irvine	Jaguar	Jaguar-Cosworth R2	3 laps/water leak	12
R	Enrique Bernoldi	Arrows	Arrows-Asiatech A22	3 laps/spun off	22
R	Olivier Panis	BAR	BAR-Honda 003	1 lap/oil leak	10
R	Kimi Raikkonen	Sauber	Sauber-Petronas C20	0 laps/transmission	14

Pole: M Schumacher, 1m35.220s, 130.217mph/209.565kph. Fastest lap: Hakkinen, 1m40.962s, 122.811mph/197.646kph on Lap 48. Race leaders: M Schumacher 1-2 & 16-55, Trulli 3, Coulthard 4-15

YOUNGER BROTHER, TOO

Ralf Schumacher showed in 2001 that there were two Schumacher brothers who could be grand prix winners, rather than just Michael. Racing in F1 for a fifth season, his third for Williams, he won the fourth round at Imola and then took further victories in the Canadian and German GPs to end the year ranking fourth overall.

BRAZILIAN GRAND PRIX

INTERLAGOS • ROUND 3 • DATE: 1ST APRIL 2001
Laps: 71 • Distance: 190.101miles/305.939km • Weather: Hot & bright

Pos	Driver	Team	Chassis-Engine	Result	Qual
1	David Coulthard	McLaren	McLaren-Mercedes MP4-16	1h39m00.834s	5
2	Michael Schumacher	Ferrari	Ferrari F2001	1h39m16.998s	1
3	Nick Heidfeld	Sauber	Sauber-Petronas C20	70 laps	9
4	Olivier Panis	BAR	BAR-Honda 003	70 laps	11
5	Jarno Trulli	Jordan	Jordan-Honda EJ11	70 laps	7
6	Giancarlo Fisichella	Benetton	Benetton-Renault B201	70 laps	18

Pos	Driver	Team	Chassis-Engine	Result	Qual
7	Jacques Villeneuve	BAR	BAR-Honda 003	70 laps	12
8	Jean Alesi	Prost	Prost-Acer AP04	70 laps	15
9	Tarso Marques	Minardi	Minardi-European PS01	68 laps	22
10	Jenson Button	Benetton	Benetton-Renault B201	64 laps	20
11	Heinz-Harald Frentzen	Jordan	Jordan-Honda EJ11	63 laps/electrical	8
R	Kimi Raikkonen	Sauber	Sauber-Petronas C20	55 laps/spun off	10
R	Ralf Schumacher	Williams	Williams-BMW FW23	54 laps/spun off	2
R	Gaston Mazzacane	Prost	Prost-Acer AP04	54 laps/clutch	21
R	Eddie Irvine	Jaguar	Jaguar-Cosworth R2	52 laps/spun off	13
R	Juan Pablo Montoya	Williams	Williams-BMW FW23	38 laps/collision	4
R	Jos Verstappen	Arrows	Arrows-Asiatech A22	37 laps/collision	17
R	Luciano Burti	Jaguar	Jaguar-Cosworth R2	30 laps/engine	14
R	Fernando Alonso	Minardi	Minardi-European PS01	25 laps/throttle	19
R	Enrique Bernoldi	Arrows	Arrows-Asiatech A22	15 laps/hydraulics	16
R	Rubens Barrichello	Ferrari	Ferrari F2001	2 laps/collision	6
R	Mika Hakkinen	McLaren	McLaren-Mercedes MP4-16	0 laps/engine	3

Pole: M Schumacher, 1m13.780s, 130.644mph/210.252kph. Fastest lap: R Schumacher, 1m15.693s, 127.342mph/204.938kph on Lap 38. Race leaders: M Schumacher 1-2 & 48-49, Montoya 3-38, Coulthard 39-47 & 50-71

SAN MARINO GRAND PRIX

IMOLA • ROUND 4 • DATE: 15TH APRIL 2001
Laps: 62 • Distance: 190.43miles/305.846km • Weather: Warm & bright

Pos	Driver	Team	Chassis-Engine	Result	Qual
1	Ralf Schumacher	Williams	Williams-BMW FW23	1h30m44.817s	3
2	David Coulthard	McLaren	McLaren-Mercedes MP4-16	1h30m49.169s	1
3	Rubens Barrichello	Ferrari	Ferrari F2001	1h31m19.583s	6
4	Mika Hakkinen	McLaren	McLaren-Mercedes MP4-16	1h31m21.132s	2
5	Jarno Trulli	Jordan	Jordan-Honda EJ11	1h32m10.375s	5
6	Heinz-Harald Frentzen	Jordan	Jordan-Honda EJ11	61 laps	9
7	Nick Heidfeld	Sauber	Sauber-Petronas C20	61 laps	12
8	Olivier Panis	BAR	BAR-Honda 003	61 laps	8
9	Jean Alesi	Prost	Prost-Acer AP04	61 laps	14
10	Enrique Bernoldi	Arrows	Arrows-Asiatech A22	60 laps	16
11	Luciano Burti	Jaguar	Jaguar-Cosworth R2	60 laps	15
12	Jenson Button	Benetton	Benetton-Renault B201	60 laps	21
R	Tarso Marques	Minardi	Minardi-European PS01	50 laps/engine	22
R	Juan Pablo Montoya	Williams	Williams-BMW FW23	48 laps/clutch	7
R	Eddie Irvine	Jaguar	Jaguar-Cosworth R2	42 laps/engine	13
R	Giancarlo Fisichella	Benetton	Benetton-Renault B201	31 laps/engine	19
R	Jacques Villeneuve	BAR	BAR-Honda 003	30 laps/engine	11
R	Gaston Mazzacane	Prost	Prost-Acer AP04	28 laps/engine	20
R	Michael Schumacher	Ferrari	Ferrari F2001	24 laps/suspension	4
R	Kimi Raikkonen	Sauber	Sauber-Petronas C20	17 laps/steering	10
R	Jos Verstappen	Arrows	Arrows-Asiatech A22	6 laps/exhaust	17
R	Fernando Alonso	Minardi	Minardi-European PS01	5 laps/spun off	18

Pole: Coulthard, 1m23.054s, 132.863mph/213.822kph. Fastest lap: R Schumacher, 1m25.524s, 129.025mph/207.646kph on Lap 27. Race leaders: R Schumacher 1-62

RAIKKONEN SCORES ON DEBUT
Kimi Raikkonen scored points on his F1 debut in Melbourne for Sauber. The Finn, who had reached F1 after just 23 single-seater races – all below F3 – since graduating from karts, was a natural and his sixth place was just two places and 12 seconds behind team-mate Nick Heidfeld. Before the year was out, he had been signed by McLaren.

SPANISH GRAND PRIX

BARCELONA-CATALUNYA • ROUND 5 • DATE: 29TH APRIL 2001
Laps: 65 • Distance: 190.788miles/307.45km • Weather: Warm & bright

Pos	Driver	Team	Chassis-Engine	Result	Qual
1	Michael Schumacher	Ferrari	Ferrari F2001	1h31m03.305s	1
2	Juan Pablo Montoya	Williams	Williams-BMW FW23	1h31m44.042s	12
3	Jacques Villeneuve	BAR	BAR-Honda 003	1h31m52.930s	7
4	Jarno Trulli	Jordan	Jordan-Honda EJ11	1h31m54.557s	6
5	David Coulthard	McLaren	McLaren-Mercedes MP4-16	1h31m54.920s	3
6	Nick Heidfeld	Sauber	Sauber-Petronas C20	1h32m05.197s	10
7	Olivier Panis	BAR	BAR-Honda 003	1h32m08.281s	11
8	Kimi Raikkonen	Sauber	Sauber-Petronas C20	1h32m23.112s	9
9	Mika Hakkinen	McLaren	McLaren-Mercedes MP4-16	64 laps/clutch	2
10	Jean Alesi	Prost	Prost-Acer AP04	64 laps	15
11	Luciano Burti	Prost	Prost-Acer AP04	64 laps	14
12	Jos Verstappen	Arrows	Arrows-Asiatech A22	63 laps	17
13	Fernando Alonso	Minardi	Minardi-European PS01	63 laps	18
14	Giancarlo Fisichella	Benetton	Benetton-Renault B201	63 laps	19
15	Jenson Button	Benetton	Benetton-Renault B201	62 laps	21
16	Tarso Marques	Minardi	Minardi-European PS01	62 laps	22
R	Rubens Barrichello	Ferrari	Ferrari F2001	49 laps/suspension	4
R	Eddie Irvine	Jaguar	Jaguar-Cosworth R2	48 laps/engine	13
R	Ralf Schumacher	Williams	Williams-BMW FW23	20 laps/brakes	5
R	Enrique Bernoldi	Arrows	Arrows-Asiatech A22	8 laps/fuel pressure	16
R	Heinz-Harald Frentzen	Jordan	Jordan-Honda EJ11	5 laps/collision	8
R	Pedro de la Rosa	Jaguar	Jaguar-Cosworth R2	5 laps/collision	20

Pole: M Schumacher, 1m18.201s, 135.301mph/217.746kph. Fastest lap: M Schumacher, 1m21.151s, 130.382mph/209.831kph on Lap 25. Race leaders: M Schumacher 1-22 & 28-43 & 65, Hakkinen 23-27 & 44-64

AUSTRIAN GRAND PRIX

A1-RING • ROUND 6 • DATE: 13TH MAY 2001
Laps: 71 • Distance: 190.851miles/307.146km • Weather: Warm & bright

Pos	Driver	Team	Chassis-Engine	Result	Qual
1	David Coulthard	McLaren	McLaren-Mercedes MP4-16	1h27m45.927s	7
2	Michael Schumacher	Ferrari	Ferrari F2001	1h27m48.117s	1
3	Rubens Barrichello	Ferrari	Ferrari F2001	1h27m48.454s	4
4	Kimi Raikkonen	Sauber	Sauber-Petronas C20	1h28m27.520s	9
5	Olivier Panis	BAR	BAR-Honda 003	1h28m39.702s	10
6	Jos Verstappen	Arrows	Arrows-Asiatech A22	70 laps	16

Pos	Driver	Team	Chassis-Engine	Result	Qual
7	Eddie Irvine	Jaguar	Jaguar-Cosworth R2	70 laps	13
8	Jacques Villeneuve	BAR	BAR-Honda 003	70 laps	12
9	Nick Heidfeld	Sauber	Sauber-Petronas C20	69 laps	6
10	Jean Alesi	Prost	Prost-Acer AP04	69 laps	20
11	Luciano Burti	Prost	Prost-Acer AP04	69 laps	17
R	Jenson Button	Benetton	Benetton-Renault B201	60 laps/engine	21
R	Pedro de la Rosa	Jaguar	Jaguar-Cosworth R2	48 laps/transmission	14
R	Juan Pablo Montoya	Williams	Williams-BMW FW23	41 laps/hydraulics	2
R	Fernando Alonso	Minardi	Minardi-European PS01	38 laps/gearbox	18
R	Tarso Marques	Minardi	Minardi-European PS01	25 laps/gearbox	22
R	Enrique Bernoldi	Arrows	Arrows-Asiatech A22	17 laps/hydraulics	15
DQ	Jarno Trulli	Jordan	Jordan-Honda EJ11	14 laps/pit lane offence	5
R	Ralf Schumacher	Williams	Williams-BMW FW23	10 laps/brakes	3
R	Giancarlo Fisichella	Benetton	Benetton-Renault B201	3 laps/engine	19
R	Mika Hakkinen	McLaren	McLaren-Mercedes MP4-16	1 lap/electronics	8
R	Heinz-Harald Frentzen	Jordan	Jordan-Honda EJ11	0 laps/gearbox	11

Pole: M Schumacher, 1m09.562s, 139.113mph/223.880kph. Fastest lap: Coulthard, 1m10.843s, 136.597mph/219.832kph on Lap 48. Race leaders: Montoya 1-15, Barrichello 16-46, Coulthard 47-71

MONTOYA QUICK TO TAKE A WIN

Ralf Schumacher wasn't the only driver to win for the BMW Williams F1 Team in 2001, as rookie team-mate Juan Pablo Montoya won at Monza after coming second at Barcelona and the Nurburgring. The Colombian initially couldn't find a ride in F1 after winning the 1998 F3000 crown, but arrived after winning the IndyCar title and the Indy 500.

MONACO GRAND PRIX

MONTE CARLO • ROUND 7 • DATE: 27TH MAY 2001
Laps: 78 • Distance: 162.852miles/262.86km • Weather: Hot & bright

Pos	Driver	Team	Chassis-Engine	Result	Qual
1	Michael Schumacher	Ferrari	Ferrari F2001	1h47m22.561s	2
2	Rubens Barrichello	Ferrari	Ferrari F2001	1h47m22.992s	4
3	Eddie Irvine	Jaguar	Jaguar-Cosworth R2	1h47m53.259s	6
4	Jacques Villeneuve	BAR	BAR-Honda 003	1h47m55.015s	9
5	David Coulthard	McLaren	McLaren-Mercedes MP4-16	77 laps	1
6	Jean Alesi	Prost	Prost-Acer AP04	77 laps	11
7	Jenson Button	Benetton	Benetton-Renault B201	77 laps	17
8	Jos Verstappen	Arrows	Arrows-Asiatech A22	77 laps	19
9	Enrique Bernoldi	Arrows	Arrows-Asiatech A22	76 laps	20
10	Kimi Raikkonen	Sauber	Sauber-Petronas C20	73 laps	15
R	Ralf Schumacher	Williams	Williams-BMW FW23	57 laps/electrical	5
R	Tarso Marques	Minardi	Minardi-European PS01	56 laps/transmission	22
R	Fernando Alonso	Minardi	Minardi-European PS01	54 laps/gearbox	18
R	Heinz-Harald Frentzen	Jordan	Jordan-Honda EJ11	49 laps/spun off	13
R	Giancarlo Fisichella	Benetton	Benetton-Renault B201	43 laps/gearbox	10
R	Jarno Trulli	Jordan	Jordan-Honda EJ11	30 laps/hydraulics	8
R	Luciano Burti	Prost	Prost-Acer AP04	24 laps/gearbox	21

Pos	Driver	Team	Chassis-Engine	Result	Qual
R	Pedro de la Rosa	Jaguar	Jaguar-Cosworth R2	18 laps/hydraulics	14
R	Mika Hakkinen	McLaren	McLaren-Mercedes MP4-16	15 laps/steering	3
R	Olivier Panis	BAR	BAR-Honda 003	13 laps/steering	12
R	Juan Pablo Montoya	Williams	Williams-BMW FW23	2 laps/spun off	7
R	Nick Heidfeld	Sauber	Sauber-Petronas C20	0 laps/collision	16

Pole: Coulthard, 1m17.430s, 97.358mph/156.683kph. Fastest lap: Coulthard, 1m19.424s, 94.914mph/152.749kph on Lap 68. Race leaders: M Schumacher 1-54 & 60-78, Barrichello 55-59

CANADIAN GRAND PRIX

MONTREAL • ROUND 8 • DATE: 10TH JUNE 2001
Laps: 69 • Distance: 189.548miles/305.049km • Weather: Hot & bright

Pos	Driver	Team	Chassis-Engine	Result	Qual
1	Ralf Schumacher	Williams	Williams-BMW FW23	1h34m31.522s	2
2	Michael Schumacher	Ferrari	Ferrari F2001	1h34m51.757s	1
3	Mika Hakkinen	McLaren	McLaren-Mercedes MP4-16	1h35m12.194s	8
4	Kimi Raikkonen	Sauber	Sauber-Petronas C20	1h35m39.638s	7
5	Jean Alesi	Prost	Prost-Acer AP04	1h35m41.957s	16
6	Pedro de la Rosa	Jaguar	Jaguar-Cosworth R2	68 laps	14
7	Ricardo Zonta	Jordan	Jordan-Honda EJ11	68 laps	12
8	Luciano Burti	Prost	Prost-Acer AP04	68 laps	19
9	Tarso Marques	Minardi	Minardi-European PS01	66 laps	21
10	Jos Verstappen	Arrows	Arrows-Asiatech A22	65 laps/brakes	13
11	Jarno Trulli	Jordan	Jordan-Honda EJ11	63 laps/brakes	4
R	David Coulthard	McLaren	McLaren-Mercedes MP4-16	54 laps/engine	3
R	Olivier Panis	BAR	BAR-Honda 003	38 laps/brakes	6
R	Jacques Villeneuve	BAR	BAR-Honda 003	34 laps/halfshaft	9
R	Enrique Bernoldi	Arrows	Arrows-Asiatech A22	24 laps/overheating	17
R	Rubens Barrichello	Ferrari	Ferrari F2001	19 laps/spun off	5
R	Juan Pablo Montoya	Williams	Williams-BMW FW23	19 laps/spun off	10
R	Jenson Button	Benetton	Benetton-Renault B201	17 laps/oil leak	20
R	Fernando Alonso	Minardi	Minardi-European PS01	7 laps/transmission	22
R	Nick Heidfeld	Sauber	Sauber-Petronas C20	1 lap/collision	11
R	Eddie Irvine	Jaguar	Jaguar-Cosworth R2	1 lap/collision	15
R	Giancarlo Fisichella	Benetton	Benetton-Renault B201	0 laps/collision	18
NS	Heinz-Harald Frentzen	Jordan	Jordan-Honda EJ11	driver injury	-

Pole: M Schumacher, 1m15.782s, 130.499mph/210.018kph. Fastest lap: R Schumacher, 1m17.205s, 128.093mph/206.147kph on Lap 50. Race leaders: M Schumacher 1-45, R Schumacher 46-69

BENETTON BOWS OUT

The changing of team names can be confusing, but the 16th year of Benetton – now Alpine – deserves marking before it raced as Renault in 2002, as its achievements were noteworthy. Having been a rebranding of Toleman, it became a force and landed the 1994 and 1995 drivers' titles with Michael Schumacher, also winning the 1995 constructors' title.

AERIAL ACCIDENTS

F1 cars were safer than ever before in 2001, and this was shown when Jacques Villeneuve's BAR rode over Ralf Schumacher's Williams in Melbourne. Both were fine, but a wheel went through a slot in the fence and killed a marshal. At Hockenheim, Luciano Burti's Prost cartwheeled after hitting Michael Schumacher's Ferrari, but Burti was able to walk away.

EUROPEAN GRAND PRIX

NURBURGRING • ROUND 9 • DATE: 24TH JUNE 2001
Laps: 67 • Distance: 189.674miles/305.252km • Weather: Hot & bright

Pos	Driver	Team	Chassis-Engine	Result	Qual
1	Michael Schumacher	Ferrari	Ferrari F2001	1h29m42.724s	1
2	Juan Pablo Montoya	Williams	Williams-BMW FW23	1h29m46.941s	3
3	David Coulthard	McLaren	McLaren-Mercedes MP4-16	1h30m07.717s	5
4	Ralf Schumacher	Williams	Williams-BMW FW23	1h30m16.069s	2
5	Rubens Barrichello	Ferrari	Ferrari F2001	1h30m28.219s	4
6	Mika Hakkinen	McLaren	McLaren-Mercedes MP4-16	1h30m47.592s	6
7	Eddie Irvine	Jaguar	Jaguar-Cosworth R2	1h30m48.922s	12
8	Pedro de la Rosa	Jaguar	Jaguar-Cosworth R2	66 laps	16
9	Jacques Villeneuve	BAR	BAR-Honda 003	66 laps	11
10	Kimi Raikkonen	Sauber	Sauber-Petronas C20	66 laps	9
11	Giancarlo Fisichella	Benetton	Benetton-Renault B201	66 laps	15
12	Luciano Burti	Prost	Prost-Acer AP04	65 laps	17
13	Jenson Button	Benetton	Benetton-Renault B201	65 laps	20
14	Fernando Alonso	Minardi	Minardi-European PS01	65 laps	21
15	Jean Alesi	Prost	Prost-Acer AP04	64 laps/spun off	14
R	Jos Verstappen	Arrows	Arrows-Asiatech A22	58 laps/engine	19
R	Nick Heidfeld	Sauber	Sauber-Petronas C20	54 laps/halfshaft	10
R	Heinz-Harald Frentzen	Jordan	Jordan-Honda EJ11	48 laps/spun off	8
R	Jarno Trulli	Jordan	Jordan-Honda EJ11	44 laps/clutch	7
R	Enrique Bernoldi	Arrows	Arrows-Asiatech A22	29 laps/gearbox	18
R	Olivier Panis	BAR	BAR-Honda 003	23 laps/electrical	13
R	Tarso Marques	Minardi	Minardi-European PS01	7 laps/electrical	22

Pole: M Schumacher, 1m14.960s, 135.958mph/218.804kph. Fastest lap: Montoya, 1m18.354s, 130.069mph/209.326kph on Lap 27. Race leaders: M Schumacher 1-28 & 30-67, Montoya 29

FRENCH GRAND PRIX

MAGNY-COURS • ROUND 10 • DATE: 1ST JULY 2001
Laps: 72 • Distance: 190.184miles/306.072km • Weather: Hot & bright

Pos	Driver	Team	Chassis-Engine	Result	Qual
1	Michael Schumacher	Ferrari	Ferrari F2001	1h33m35.636s	2
2	Ralf Schumacher	Williams	Williams-BMW FW23	1h33m46.035s	1
3	Rubens Barrichello	Ferrari	Ferrari F2001	1h33m52.017s	8
4	David Coulthard	McLaren	McLaren-Mercedes MP4-16	1h33m52.742s	3
5	Jarno Trulli	Jordan	Jordan-Honda EJ11	1h34m43.921s	5
6	Nick Heidfeld	Sauber	Sauber-Petronas C20	71 laps	9
7	Kimi Raikkonen	Sauber	Sauber-Petronas C20	71 laps	13

Pos	Driver	Team	Chassis-Engine	Result	Qual
8	Heinz-Harald Frentzen	Jordan	Jordan-Honda EJ11	71 laps	7
9	Olivier Panis	BAR	BAR-Honda 003	71 laps	11
10	Luciano Burti	Prost	Prost-Acer AP04	71 laps	15
11	Giancarlo Fisichella	Benetton	Benetton-Renault B201	71 laps	16
12	Jean Alesi	Prost	Prost-Acer AP04	70 laps	19
13	Jos Verstappen	Arrows	Arrows-Asiatech A22	70 laps	18
14	Pedro de la Rosa	Jaguar	Jaguar-Cosworth R2	70 laps	14
15	Tarso Marques	Minardi	Minardi-European PS01	69 laps	22
16	Jenson Button	Benetton	Benetton-Renault B201	68 laps/fuel pressure	17
17	Fernando Alonso	Minardi	Minardi-European PS01	65 laps/engine	21
R	Eddie Irvine	Jaguar	Jaguar-Cosworth R2	54 laps/engine	12
R	Juan Pablo Montoya	Williams	Williams-BMW FW23	52 laps/engine	6
R	Enrique Bernoldi	Arrows	Arrows-Asiatech A22	17 laps/engine	20
R	Jacques Villeneuve	BAR	BAR-Honda 003	5 laps/engine	10
NS	Mika Hakkinen	McLaren	McLaren-Mercedes MP4-16	gearbox	4

Pole: R Schumacher, 1m12.989s, 130.282mph/209.669kph. Fastest lap: Coulthard, 1m16.088s, 124.976mph/201.130kph on Lap 53. Race leaders: R Schumacher 1-23, M Schumacher 24-25 & 31-45 & 51-72, Coulthard 26, Montoya 27-30 & 46-50

BRITISH GRAND PRIX

SILVERSTONE • ROUND 11 • DATE: 15TH JULY 2001
Laps: 60 • Distance: 191.410miles/308.46km • Weather: Warm but dull

Pos	Driver	Team	Chassis-Engine	Result	Qual
1	Mika Hakkinen	McLaren	McLaren-Mercedes MP4-16	1h25m33.770s	2
2	Michael Schumacher	Ferrari	Ferrari F2001	1h26m07.416s	1
3	Rubens Barrichello	Ferrari	Ferrari F2001	1h26m33.051s	6
4	Juan Pablo Montoya	Williams	Williams-BMW FW23	1h26m42.542s	8
5	Kimi Raikkonen	Sauber	Sauber-Petronas C20	59 laps	7
6	Nick Heidfeld	Sauber	Sauber-Petronas C20	59 laps	9
7	Heinz-Harald Frentzen	Jordan	Jordan-Honda EJ11	59 laps	5
8	Jacques Villeneuve	BAR	BAR-Honda 003	59 laps	12
9	Eddie Irvine	Jaguar	Jaguar-Cosworth R2	59 laps	15
10	Jos Verstappen	Arrows	Arrows-Asiatech A22	58 laps	17
11	Jean Alesi	Prost	Prost-Acer AP04	58 laps	14
12	Pedro de la Rosa	Jaguar	Jaguar-Cosworth R2	58 laps	13
13	Giancarlo Fisichella	Benetton	Benetton-Renault B201	58 laps	19
14	Enrique Bernoldi	Arrows	Arrows-Asiatech A22	58 laps	20
15	Jenson Button	Benetton	Benetton-Renault B201	58 laps	18
16	Fernando Alonso	Minardi	Minardi-European PS01	57 laps	21
R	Ralf Schumacher	Williams	Williams-BMW FW23	36 laps/engine	10
R	Luciano Burti	Prost	Prost-Acer AP04	6 laps/engine	16
R	David Coulthard	McLaren	McLaren-Mercedes MP4-16	2 laps/suspension	3
R	Jarno Trulli	Jordan	Jordan-Honda EJ11	0 laps/collision	4
R	Olivier Panis	BAR	BAR-Honda 003	0 laps/collision	11
DNQ	Tarso Marques	Minardi	Minardi-European PS01	-	22

Pole: M Schumacher, 1m20.447s, 142.952mph/230.059kph. Fastest lap: Hakkinen, 1m23.405s, 137.882mph/221.900kph on Lap 34. Race leaders: M Schumacher 1-4, Hakkinen 5-21 & 25-60, Montoya 22-24

GERMAN GRAND PRIX

HOCKENHEIM • ROUND 12 • DATE: 29TH JULY 2001
Laps: 45 • Distance: 190.838miles/307.125km • Weather: Very hot & bright

Pos	Driver	Team	Chassis-Engine	Result	Qual
1	Ralf Schumacher	Williams	Williams-BMW FW23	1h18m17.873s	2
2	Rubens Barrichello	Ferrari	Ferrari F2001	1h19m03.990s	6
3	Jacques Villeneuve	BAR	BAR-Honda 003	1h19m20.679s	12
4	Giancarlo Fisichella	Benetton	Benetton-Renault B201	1h19m21.350s	17
5	Jenson Button	Benetton	Benetton-Renault B201	1h19m23.327s	18
6	Jean Alesi	Prost	Prost-Acer AP04	1h19m23.823s	14
7	Olivier Panis	BAR	BAR-Honda 003	1h19m35.400s	13
8	Enrique Bernoldi	Arrows	Arrows-Asiatech A22	44 laps	19
9	Jos Verstappen	Arrows	Arrows-Asiatech A22	44 laps	20
10	Fernando Alonso	Minardi	Minardi-European PS01	44 laps	21
R	Jarno Trulli	Jordan	Jordan-Honda EJ11	34 laps/hydraulics	10
R	David Coulthard	McLaren	McLaren-Mercedes MP4-16	27 laps/engine	5
R	Tarso Marques	Minardi	Minardi-European PS01	26 laps/gearbox	22
R	Juan Pablo Montoya	Williams	Williams-BMW FW23	24 laps/engine	1
R	Michael Schumacher	Ferrari	Ferrari F2001	23 laps/fuel pressure	4
R	Luciano Burti	Prost	Prost-Acer AP04	23 laps/spun off	16
R	Kimi Raikkonen	Sauber	Sauber-Petronas C20	16 laps/halfshaft	8
R	Eddie Irvine	Jaguar	Jaguar-Cosworth R2	16 laps/fuel pressure	11
R	Mika Hakkinen	McLaren	McLaren-Mercedes MP4-16	13 laps/engine	3
R	Ricardo Zonta	Jordan	Jordan-Honda EJ11	7 laps/collision	15
R	Nick Heidfeld	Sauber	Sauber-Petronas C20	0 laps/collision	7
R	Pedro de la Rosa	Jaguar	Jaguar-Cosworth R2	0 laps/collision	9

Pole: Montoya, 1m38.117s, 155.600mph/250.415kph. Fastest lap: Montoya, 1m41.808s, 149.959mph/241.336kph on Lap 20. Race leaders: Montoya 1-22, R Schumacher 23-45

201 AND OUT

Jean Alesi was one of F1's enigmas: quick, but seldom rewarded. At the end of 2001, after 201 grands prix but just one win, the French ace retired. He started the year with Prost, but jumped ship to Jordan for the final five races after Heinz-Harald Frentzen was dropped. However, he wasn't offered a deal for 2002, so he retired.

HUNGARIAN GRAND PRIX

HUNGARORING • ROUND 13 • DATE: 19TH AUGUST 2001
Laps: 77 • Distance: 190.186miles/306.075km • Weather: Very hot & bright

Pos	Driver	Team	Chassis-Engine	Result	Qual
1	Michael Schumacher	Ferrari	Ferrari F2001	1h41m49.675s	1
2	Rubens Barrichello	Ferrari	Ferrari F2001	1h41m53.038s	3
3	David Coulthard	McLaren	McLaren-Mercedes MP4-16	1h41m53.615s	2
4	Ralf Schumacher	Williams	Williams-BMW FW23	1h42m39.362s	4
5	Mika Hakkinen	McLaren	McLaren-Mercedes MP4-16	1h42m59.968s	6
6	Nick Heidfeld	Sauber	Sauber-Petronas C20	76 laps	7
7	Kimi Raikkonen	Sauber	Sauber-Petronas C20	76 laps	9

Pos	Driver	Team	Chassis-Engine	Result	Qual
8	Juan Pablo Montoya	Williams	Williams-BMW FW23	76 laps	8
9	Jacques Villeneuve	BAR	BAR-Honda 003	75 laps	10
10	Jean Alesi	Jordan	Jordan-Honda EJ11	75 laps	12
11	Pedro de la Rosa	Jaguar	Jaguar-Cosworth R2	75 laps	13
12	Jos Verstappen	Arrows	Arrows-Asiatech A22	74 laps	21
R	Giancarlo Fisichella	Benetton	Benetton-Renault B201	67 laps/engine	15
R	Heinz-Harald Frentzen	Prost	Prost-Acer AP04	63 laps/spun off	16
R	Tarso Marques	Minardi	Minardi-European PS01B	63 laps/fuel pressure	22
R	Olivier Panis	BAR	BAR-Honda 003	58 laps/electrical	11
R	Jarno Trulli	Jordan	Jordan-Honda EJ11	53 laps/hydraulics	5
R	Fernando Alonso	Minardi	Minardi-European PS01	37 laps/brakes	18
R	Jenson Button	Benetton	Benetton-Renault B201	34 laps/spun off	17
R	Enrique Bernoldi	Arrows	Arrows-Asiatech A22	11 laps/spun off	20
R	Luciano Burti	Prost	Prost-Acer AP04	8 laps/spun off	19
R	Eddie Irvine	Jaguar	Jaguar-Cosworth R2	0 laps/spun off	14

Pole: M Schumacher, 1m14.059s, 120.064mph/193.224kph. Fastest lap: Hakkinen, 1m16.723s, 115.895mph/186.515kph on Lap 51. Race leaders: M Schumacher 1-28 & 33-52 & 55-77, Barrichello 29-30, Coulthard 31-32 & 53-54

A HONDA ENGINE BATTLE

With the costs of running a team soaring, a works engine deal became ever more vital. In 2001, Honda supplied both Jordan and BAR. In the end, Jordan came out ahead, but only by two points. In fact, it only did so two weeks after the season was over when Jarno Trulli's disqualification from fourth in the US GP was overturned.

BELGIAN GRAND PRIX

SPA-FRANCORCHAMPS • ROUND 14 • DATE: 2ND SEPTEMBER 2001
Laps: 36 • Distance: 155.869miles/250.848km • Weather: Warm but dull

Pos	Driver	Team	Chassis-Engine	Result	Qual
1	Michael Schumacher	Ferrari	Ferrari F2001	1h08m05.002s	3
2	David Coulthard	McLaren	McLaren-Mercedes MP4-16	1h08m15.100s	9
3	Giancarlo Fisichella	Benetton	Benetton-Renault B201	1h08m32.744s	8
4	Mika Hakkinen	McLaren	McLaren-Mercedes MP4-16	1h08m41.089s	7
5	Rubens Barrichello	Ferrari	Ferrari F2001	1h08m59.523s	5
6	Jean Alesi	Jordan	Jordan-Honda EJ11	1h09m04.686s	13
7	Ralf Schumacher	Williams	Williams-BMW FW23	1h09m04.988s	2
8	Jacques Villeneuve	BAR	BAR-Honda 003	1h09m09.972s	6
9	Heinz-Harald Frentzen	Prost	Prost-Acer AP04	35 laps	4
10	Jos Verstappen	Arrows	Arrows-Asiatech A22	35 laps	19
11	Olivier Panis	BAR	BAR-Honda 003	35 laps	11
12	Enrique Bernoldi	Arrows	Arrows-Asiatech A22	35 laps	21
13	Tarso Marques	Minardi	Minardi-European PS01B	32 laps	22
R	Jarno Trulli	Jordan	Jordan-Honda EJ11	31 laps/engine	16
R	Jenson Button	Benetton	Benetton-Renault B201	17 laps/spun off	15
R	Juan Pablo Montoya	Williams	Williams-BMW FW23	1 lap/engine	1
R	Pedro de la Rosa	Jaguar	Jaguar-Cosworth R2	1 lap/suspension	10

Pos	Driver	Team	Chassis-Engine	Result	Qual
R	Nick Heidfeld	Sauber	Sauber-Petronas C20	0 laps/suspension	14
R	Kimi Raikkonen	Sauber	Sauber-Petronas C20	Transmission	12
R	Eddie Irvine	Jaguar	Jaguar-Cosworth R2	Accident damage	17
R	Luciano Burti	Prost	Prost-Acer AP04	Accident damage	18
R	Fernando Alonso	Minardi	Minardi-European PS01B	Gearbox	20

Pole: Montoya, 1m52.072s, 139.079mph/223.827kph. Fastest lap: M Schumacher, 1m49.758s, 142.012mph/228.546kph on Lap 3. Race leaders: M Schumacher 1-36

ITALIAN GRAND PRIX

MONZA • ROUND 15 • DATE: 16TH SEPTEMBER 2001
Laps: 53 • Distance: 190.778miles/307.029km • Weather: Warm & bright

Pos	Driver	Team	Chassis-Engine	Result	Qual
1	Juan Pablo Montoya	Williams	Williams-BMW FW23	1h16m58.493s	1
2	Rubens Barrichello	Ferrari	Ferrari F2001	1h17m03.668s	2
3	Ralf Schumacher	Williams	Williams-BMW FW23	1h17m15.828s	4
4	Michael Schumacher	Ferrari	Ferrari F2001	1h17m23.484s	3
5	Pedro de la Rosa	Jaguar	Jaguar-Cosworth R2	1h18m13.477s	10
6	Jacques Villeneuve	BAR	BAR-Honda 003	1h18m20.962s	15
7	Kimi Raikkonen	Sauber	Sauber-Petronas C20	1h18m21.600s	9
8	Jean Alesi	Jordan	Jordan-Honda EJ11	52 laps	16
9	Olivier Panis	BAR	BAR-Honda 003	52 laps	17
10	Giancarlo Fisichella	Benetton	Benetton-Renault B201	52 laps	14
11	Nick Heidfeld	Sauber	Sauber-Petronas C20	52 laps	8
12	Tomas Enge	Prost	Prost-Acer AP04	52 laps	20
13	Fernando Alonso	Minardi	Minardi-European PS01B	51 laps	21
R	Enrique Bernoldi	Arrows	Arrows-Asiatech A22	46 laps/engine	18
R	Alex Yoong	Minardi	Minardi-European PS01B	44 laps/spun off	22
R	Heinz-Harald Frentzen	Prost	Prost-Acer AP04	28 laps/transmission	12
R	Jos Verstappen	Arrows	Arrows-Asiatech A22	25 laps/fuel pressure	19
R	Mika Hakkinen	McLaren	McLaren-Mercedes MP4-16	19 laps/gearbox	7
R	Eddie Irvine	Jaguar	Jaguar-Cosworth R2	14 laps/engine	13
R	David Coulthard	McLaren	McLaren-Mercedes MP4-16	6 laps/engine	6
R	Jenson Button	Benetton	Benetton-Renault B201	4 laps/engine	11
R	Jarno Trulli	Jordan	Jordan-Honda EJ11	0 laps/collision	5

Pole: Montoya, 1m22.216s, 157.616mph/253.658kph. Fastest lap: R Schumacher, 1m25.073s, 152.322mph/245.140kph on Lap 39. Race leaders: Montoya 1-8 & 20-28 & 42-53, Barrichello 9-19 & 36-41, R Schumacher 29-35

STILL NO SECOND FANGIOS

Juan Manuel Fangio bestrode the 1950s like a colossus. Carlos Reutemann promised great things in the late 1970s. Yet, since then, Argentina fans had no one of note to cheer. Ricardo Zunino took two sevenths for Brabham, Esteban Tuero was eighth at Imola in 1998 for Minardi, but Gaston Mazzacane could only take a 12th for Prost in 2001 before being dropped.

UNITED STATES GRAND PRIX

INDIANAPOLIS MOTOR SPEEDWAY • ROUND 16 • DATE: 30TH SEPTEMBER 2001
Laps: 73 • Distance: 190.149miles/306.016km • Weather: Warm & bright

Pos	Driver	Team	Chassis-Engine	Result	Qual
1	Mika Hakkinen	McLaren	McLaren-Mercedes MP4-16	1h32m42.840s	4
2	Michael Schumacher	Ferrari	Ferrari F2001	1h32m53.886s	1
3	David Coulthard	McLaren	McLaren-Mercedes MP4-16	1h32m54.883s	7
4	Jarno Trulli	Jordan	Jordan-Honda EJ11	1h33m40.263s	8
5	Eddie Irvine	Jaguar	Jaguar-Cosworth R2	1h33m55.274s	14
6	Nick Heidfeld	Sauber	Sauber-Petronas C20	1h33m55.836s	6
7	Jean Alesi	Jordan	Jordan-Honda EJ11	72 laps	9
8	Giancarlo Fisichella	Benetton	Benetton-Renault B201	72 laps	12
9	Jenson Button	Benetton	Benetton-Renault B201	72 laps	10
10	Heinz-Harald Frentzen	Prost	Prost-Acer AP04	72 laps	15
11	Olivier Panis	BAR	BAR-Honda 003	72 laps	13
12	Pedro de la Rosa	Jaguar	Jaguar-Cosworth R2	72 laps	16
13	Enrique Bernoldi	Arrows	Arrows-Asiatech A22	72 laps	19
14	Tomas Enge	Prost	Prost-Acer AP04	72 laps	21
15	Rubens Barrichello	Ferrari	Ferrari F2001	71 laps/engine	5
R	Jacques Villeneuve	BAR	BAR-Honda 003	45 laps/suspension	18
R	Jos Verstappen	Arrows	Arrows-Asiatech A22	44 laps/engine	20
R	Juan Pablo Montoya	Williams	Williams-BMW FW23	38 laps/hydraulics	3
R	Alex Yoong	Minardi	Minardi-European PS01B	38 laps/gearbox	22
R	Ralf Schumacher	Williams	Williams-BMW FW23	36 laps/spun off	2
R	Fernando Alonso	Minardi	Minardi-European PS01B	36 laps/halfshaft	17
R	Kimi Raikkonen	Sauber	Sauber-Petronas C20	2 laps/halfshaft	11

Pole: M Schumacher, 1m11.708s, 130.769mph/210.453kph. Fastest lap: Montoya, 1m14.448s, 125.956mph/202.707kph on Lap 35. Race leaders: M Schumacher 1-4 & 27-33 & 36-38, Barrichello 5-26 & 46-49, Montoya 34-35, Hakkinen 39-45 & 50-73

NEW DRIVERS

Juan Pablo Montoya was easily the best of 2001's new F1 drivers, with his Italian GP win helping him rank sixth. Of the other five, Kimi Raikkonen achieved the best result, coming fourth for Sauber at the A1-Ring and Montreal, while Enrique Bernoldi took an eighth for Arrows. Future F1 champion Fernando Alonso could rank only 23rd in the final standings in his Minardi.

JAPANESE GRAND PRIX

SUZUKA • ROUND 17 • DATE: 14TH OCTOBER 2001
Laps: 53 • Distance: 192.952miles/310.527km • Weather: Warm & bright

Pos	Driver	Team	Chassis-Engine	Result	Qual
1	Michael Schumacher	Ferrari	Ferrari F2001	1h27m33.298s	1
2	Juan Pablo Montoya	Williams	Williams-BMW FW23	1h27m36.452s	2
3	David Coulthard	McLaren	McLaren-Mercedes MP4-16	1h27m56.560s	7
4	Mika Hakkinen	McLaren	McLaren-Mercedes MP4-16	1h28m08.837s	5
5	Rubens Barrichello	Ferrari	Ferrari F2001	1h28m09.842s	4
6	Ralf Schumacher	Williams	Williams-BMW FW23	1h28m10.420s	3

Pos	Driver	Team	Chassis-Engine	Result	Qual
7	Jenson Button	Benetton	Benetton-Renault B201	1h29m10.400s	9
8	Jarno Trulli	Jordan	Jordan-Honda EJ11	52 laps	8
9	Nick Heidfeld	Sauber	Sauber-Petronas C20	52 laps	10
10	Jacques Villeneuve	BAR	BAR-Honda 003	52 laps	14
11	Fernando Alonso	Minardi	Minardi-European PS01B	52 laps	18
12	Heinz-Harald Frentzen	Prost	Prost-Acer AP04	52 laps	15
13	Olivier Panis	BAR	BAR-Honda 003	51 laps	17
14	Enrique Bernoldi	Arrows	Arrows-Asiatech A22	51 laps	20
15	Jos Verstappen	Arrows	Arrows-Asiatech A22	51 laps	21
16	Alex Yoong	Minardi	Minardi-European PS01B	50 laps	22
17	Giancarlo Fisichella	Benetton	Benetton-Renault B201	47 laps/gearbox	6
R	Pedro de la Rosa	Jaguar	Jaguar-Cosworth R2	45 laps/oil leak	16
R	Tomas Enge	Prost	Prost-Acer AP04	42 laps/brakes	19
R	Eddie Irvine	Jaguar	Jaguar-Cosworth R2	24 laps/out of fuel	13
R	Jean Alesi	Jordan	Jordan-Honda EJ11	5 laps/collision	11
R	Kimi Raikkonen	Sauber	Sauber-Petronas C20	5 laps/spun off	12

Pole: M Schumacher, 1m32.484s, 141.713mph/228.065kph. Fastest lap: R Schumacher, 1m36.944s, 135.193mph/217.573kph on Lap 46. Race leaders: M Schumacher 1-18 & 24-36 & 39-53, Montoya 19-21 & 37-38, R Schumacher 22-23

WORLD DRIVERS' CHAMPIONSHIP FINAL RESULTS

Pos	Driver	Nat	Car-Engine	R1	R2	R3	R4	R5	R6
1	Michael Schumacher	DEU	Ferrari F2001	1PF	1P	2P	R	1PF	2P
2	David Coulthard	GBR	McLaren-Mercedes MP4-16	2	3	1	2P	5	1F
3	Rubens Barrichello	BRA	Ferrari F2001	3	2	R	3	R	3
4	Ralf Schumacher	DEU	Williams-BMW FW23	R	5	RF	1F	R	R
5	Mika Hakkinen	FIN	McLaren-Mercedes MP4-16	R	6F	R	4	9	R
6	Juan Pablo Montoya	COL	Williams-BMW FW23	R	R	R	R	2	R
7	Jacques Villeneuve	CAN	BAR-Honda 003	R	R	7	R	3	8
8	Nick Heidfeld	DEU	Sauber-Petronas C20	4	R	3	7	6	9
9	Jarno Trulli	ITA	Jordan-Honda EJ11	R	8	5	5	4	DQ
10	Kimi Raikkonen	FIN	Sauber-Petronas C20	6	R	R	R	8	4
11	Giancarlo Fisichella	ITA	Benetton-Renault B201	13	R	6	R	14	R
12	Eddie Irvine	GBR	Jaguar-Cosworth R2	11	R	R	R	R	7
13	Heinz-Harald Frentzen	DEU	Jordan-Honda EJ11	5	4	11	6	R	R
			Prost-Acer AP04	-	-	-	-	-	-
14	Olivier Panis	FRA	BAR-Honda 003	7	R	4	8	7	5
15	Jean Alesi	FRA	Prost-Acer AP04	9	9	8	9	10	10
			Jordan-Honda EJ11	-	-	-	-	-	-
16	Pedro de la Rosa	ESP	Jaguar-Cosworth R2	-	-	-	-	R	R
17	Jenson Button	GBR	Benetton-Renault B201	14	11	10	12	15	R
18	Jos Verstappen	NLD	Arrows-Asiatech A22	10	7	R	R	12	6
19	Ricardo Zonta	BRA	Jordan-Honda EJ11	-	-	-	-	-	-
20	Luciano Burti	BRA	Jaguar-Cosworth R2	8	10	R	11	-	-
			Prost-Acer AP04	-	-	-	-	11	11
21	Enrique Bernoldi	BRA	Arrows-Asiatech A22	R	R	R	10	R	R
22	Tarso Marques	BRA	Minardi-European PS01	R	14	9	R	16	R
			Minardi-European PS01B	-	-	-	-	-	-
23	Fernando Alonso	ESP	Minardi-European PS01	12	13	R	R	13	R
			Minardi-European PS01B	-	-	-	-	-	-
24	Tomas Enge	CZE	Prost-Acer AP04	-	-	-	-	-	-
25	Gaston Mazzacane	ARG	Prost-Acer AP04	R	12	R	R	-	-
26	Alex Yoong	MYS	Minardi-European PS01B	-	-	-	-	-	-

Pos	Driver	R7	R8	R9	R10	R11	R12	R13	R14	R15	R16	R17	Total
1	M Schumacher	1	2P	1P	1	2P	R	1P	1F	4	2P	1P	123
2	Coulthard	5PF	R	3	4F	R	R	3	2	R	3	3	65
3	Barrichello	2	R	5	3	3	2	2	5	2	15	5	56
4	R Schumacher	R	1F	4	2P	R	1	4	7	3F	R	6F	49
5	Hakkinen	R	3	6	NS	1F	R	5F	4	R	1	4	37
6	Montoya	R	R	2F	R	4	RPF	8	RP	1P	RF	2	31
7	Villeneuve	4	R	9	R	8	3	9	8	6	R	10	12
8	Heidfeld	R	R	R	6	6	R	6	R	11	6	9	12
9	Trulli	R	11	R	5	R	R	R	R	R	4	8	12
10	Raikkonen	10	4	10	7	5	R	7	R	7	R	R	9
11	Fisichella	R	R	11	11	13	4	R	3	10	8	17	8
12	Irvine	3	R	7	R	9	R	R	R	R	5	R	6
13	Frentzen	R	NS	R	8	7	-	-	-	-	-	-	6
		-	-	-	-	-	-	R	9	R	10	12	
14	Panis	R	R	R	9	R	7	R	11	9	11	13	5
15	Alesi	6	5	15	12	11	6	-	-	-	-	-	5
		-	-	-	-	-	-	10	6	8	7	R	
16	de la Rosa	R	6	8	14	12	R	11	R	5	12	R	3
17	Button	7	R	13	16	15	5	R	R	R	9	7	2
18	Verstappen	8	10	R	13	10	9	12	10	R	R	15	1
19	Zonta	-	7	-	-	-	R	-	-	-	-	-	0
20	Burti	-	-	-	-	-	-	-	-	-	-	-	0
		R	8	12	10	R	R	R	R	-	-	-	
21	Bernoldi	9	R	R	R	14	8	R	12	R	13	14	0
22	Marques	R	9	R	15	DNQ	R	-	-	-	-	-	0
		-	-	-	-	-	-	R	13	-	-	-	
23	Alonso	R	R	14	17	16	10	R	-	-	-	-	0
		-	-	-	-	-	-	-	R	13	R	11	
24	Enge	-	-	-	-	-	-	-	-	12	14	R	0
25	Mazzacane	-	-	-	-	-	-	-	-	-	-	-	0
26	Yoong	-	-	-	-	-	-	-	-	R	R	16	0

WORLD CONSTRUCTORS' CHAMPIONSHIP FINAL RESULTS

Pos	Team-Engine	R1	R2	R3	R4	R5	R6	R7	R8	R9
1	Ferrari	1/3	1/2	2/R	3/R	1/R	2/3	1/2	2/R	1/5
2	McLaren-Mercedes	2/R	3/6	1/R	2/4	5/9	1/R	5/R	3/R	3/6
3	Williams-BMW	R/R	5/R	R/R	1/R	2/R	R/R	R/R	1/R	2/4
4	Sauber-Petronas	4/6	R/R	3/R	7/R	6/8	4/9	10/R	4/R	10/R
5	Jordan-Honda	5/R	4/8	5/11	5/6	4/R	DQ/R	R/R	7/11	R/R
6	BAR-Honda	7/R	R/R	4/7	8/R	3/7	5/8	4/R	R/R	9/R
7	Benetton-Renault	13/14	11/R	6/10	12/R	14/15	R/R	7/R	R/R	11/13
8	Jaguar-Cosworth	8/11	10/R	R/R	11/R	R/R	7/R	3/R	6/R	7/8
9	Prost-Acer	9/R	9/12	8/R	9/R	10/11	10/11	6/R	5/8	12/15
10	Arrows-Asiatech	10/R	7/R	R/R	10/R	12/R	6/R	8/9	10/R	R/R
11	Minardi-European	12/R	13/14	9/R	R/R	13/16	R/R	R/R	9/R	14/R

Pos	Team-Engine	R10	R11	R12	R13	R14	R15	R16	R17	Total
1	Ferrari	1/3	2/3	2/R	1/2	1/5	2/4	2/15	1/5	179
2	McLaren-Mercedes	4/NS	1/R	R/R	3/5	2/4	R/R	1/3	3/4	102
3	Williams-BMW	2/R	4/R	1/R	4/8	7/R	1/3	R/R	2/6	80
4	Sauber-Petronas	6/7	5/6	R/R	6/7	R/R	7/11	6/R	9/R	21

Pos	Team-Engine	R10	R11	R12	R13	R14	R15	R16	R17	Total
5	Jordan-Honda	5/8	7/R	R/R	10/R	6/R	8/R	4/7	8/R	19
6	BAR-Honda	9/R	8/R	3/7	9/R	8/11	6/9	11/R	10/13	17
7	Benetton-Renault	11/16	13/15	4/5	R/R	3/R	10/R	8/9	7/17	10
8	Jaguar-Cosworth	14/R	9/12	R/R	11/R	R/R	5/R	5/12	R/R	9
9	Prost-Acer	10/12	11/R	6/R	R/R	9/R	12/R	10/14	12/R	4
10	Arrows-Asiatech	13/R	10/14	8/9	12/R	10/12	R/R	13/R	14/15	1
11	Minardi-European	15/17	16/DNQ	10/R	R/R	13/R	13/R	R/R	11/16	0

SYMBOLS AND GRAND PRIX KEY

Round 1 **Australian GP**
Round 2 **Malaysian GP**
Round 3 **Brazilian GP**
Round 4 **San Marino GP**
Round 5 **Spanish GP**
Round 6 **Austrian GP**
Round 7 **Monaco GP**
Round 8 **Canadian GP**
Round 9 **European GP**
Round 10 **French GP**
Round 11 **British GP**
Round 12 **German GP**
Round 13 **Hungarian GP**
Round 14 **Belgian GP**
Round 15 **Italian GP**
Round 16 **United States GP**
Round 17 **Japanese GP**

SCORING

1st **10 points**
2nd **6 points**
3rd **4 points**
4th **3 points**
5th **2 points**
6th **1 point**

DNPQ DID NOT PRE-QUALIFY **DNQ DID NOT QUALIFY** **DQ DISQUALIFIED** **EX EXCLUDED**
F FASTEST LAP **NC NOT CLASSIFIED** **NS NON-STARTER** **P POLE POSITION** **R RETIRED**

2002

SEASON SUMMARY

Michael Schumacher assumed near-total control, winning 11 of the 17 grands prix and completing every single lap as he finished every race on the podium. It was a display of domination almost unparalleled in F1 history, which was fitting for a driver who matched Juan Manuel Fangio's record of five F1 titles. His Ferrari team-mate Rubens Barrichello was a distant second, but still easily clear of Williams's Juan Pablo Montoya in Ferrari's year of years. But Ferrari angered fans for issuing team orders as early as the sixth round despite their domination, telling Barrichello to relinquish victory in Austria.

AUSTRALIAN GRAND PRIX

ALBERT PARK • ROUND 1 • DATE: 3RD MARCH 2002
Laps: 58 • Distance: 191.117miles/307.574km • Weather: Warm but dull

Pos	Driver	Team	Chassis-Engine	Result	Qual
1	Michael Schumacher	Ferrari	Ferrari F2001	1h35m36.792s	2
2	Juan Pablo Montoya	Williams	Williams-BMW FW24	1h35m55.419s	6
3	Kimi Raikkonen	McLaren	McLaren-Mercedes MP4-17	1h36m01.858s	5
4	Eddie Irvine	Jaguar	Jaguar-Cosworth R3	57 laps	19
5	Mark Webber	Minardi	Minardi-Asiatech PS02	56 laps	18
6	Mika Salo	Toyota	Toyota TF102	56 laps	14
7	Alex Yoong	Minardi	Minardi-Asiatech PS02	55 laps	21
8	Pedro de la Rosa	Jaguar	Jaguar-Cosworth R3	53 laps	20
R	David Coulthard	McLaren	McLaren-Mercedes MP4-17	33 laps/gearbox	4
R	Jacques Villeneuve	BAR	BAR-Honda 004	27 laps/accident	13
DQ	Heinz-Harald Frentzen	Arrows	Arrows-Cosworth A23	16 laps/ignoring red light	15
DQ	Enrique Bernoldi	Arrows	Arrows-Cosworth A23	15 laps/using spare car	17
R	Takuma Sato	Jordan	Jordan-Honda EJ12	12 laps/electrical	22
R	Jarno Trulli	Renault F1	Renault R202	8 laps/spun off	7
R	Rubens Barrichello	Ferrari	Ferrari F2001	0 laps/collision	1
R	Ralf Schumacher	Williams	Williams-BMW FW24	0 laps/collision	3
R	Giancarlo Fisichella	Jordan	Jordan-Honda EJ12	0 laps/collision	8
R	Felipe Massa	Sauber	Sauber-Petronas C21	0 laps/collision	9
R	Nick Heidfeld	Sauber	Sauber-Petronas C21	0 laps/collision	10
R	Jenson Button	Renault F1	Renault R202	0 laps/collision	11
R	Olivier Panis	BAR	BAR-Honda 004	0 laps/collision	12
R	Allan McNish	Toyota	Toyota TF102	0 laps/collision	16

Pole: Barrichello, 1m25.843s, 138.188mph/222.392kph. Fastest lap: Raikkonen, 1m28.541s, 133.977mph/215.615kph on Lap 37. Race leaders: Coulthard 1-10, M Schumacher 11 & 17-58, Montoya 12-16

SWAPPING FINNS

With Mika Hakkinen taking a sabbatical to recharge his batteries, fellow Finn Kimi Raikkonen was drafted in to replace him at McLaren. Despite it being only his second year in F1, Raikkonen scored 24 points to team-mate David Coulthard's 41, peaking with second at Silverstone, as they ranked sixth and fifth respectively. Hakkinen never did return to F1.

MALAYSIAN GRAND PRIX

SEPANG • ROUND 2 • DATE: 17TH MARCH 2002
Laps: 56 • Distance: 192.878miles/310.408km • Weather: Very hot & sunny

Pos	Driver	Team	Chassis-Engine	Result	Qual
1	Ralf Schumacher	Williams	Williams-BMW FW24	1h34m12.912s	4
2	Juan Pablo Montoya	Williams	Williams-BMW FW24	1h34m52.611s	2
3	Michael Schumacher	Ferrari	Ferrari F2001	1h35m14.706s	1
4	Jenson Button	Renault F1	Renault R202	1h35m22.678s	8
5	Nick Heidfeld	Sauber	Sauber-Petronas C21	55 laps	7
6	Felipe Massa	Sauber	Sauber-Petronas C21	55 laps	14
7	Allan McNish	Toyota	Toyota TF102	55 laps	19
8	Jacques Villeneuve	BAR	BAR-Honda 004	55 laps	13
9	Takuma Sato	Jordan	Jordan-Honda EJ12	54 laps	15
10	Pedro de la Rosa	Jaguar	Jaguar-Cosworth R3	54 laps	17
11	Heinz-Harald Frentzen	Arrows	Arrows-Cosworth A23	54 laps	11
12	Mika Salo	Toyota	Toyota TF102	53 laps	10
13	Giancarlo Fisichella	Jordan	Jordan-Honda EJ12	53 laps	9
R	Rubens Barrichello	Ferrari	Ferrari F2001	39 laps/engine	3
R	Mark Webber	Minardi	Minardi-Asiatech PS02	34 laps/electrical	21
R	Eddie Irvine	Jaguar	Jaguar-Cosworth R3	30 laps/hydraulics	20
R	Alex Yoong	Minardi	Minardi-Asiatech PS02	29 laps/gearbox	22
R	Kimi Raikkonen	McLaren	McLaren-Mercedes MP4-17	24 laps/engine	5
R	Enrique Bernoldi	Arrows	Arrows-Cosworth A23	20 laps/fuel pressure	16
R	David Coulthard	McLaren	McLaren-Mercedes MP4-17	15 laps/engine	6
R	Jarno Trulli	Renault F1	Renault R202	9 laps/overheating	12
R	Olivier Panis	BAR	BAR-Honda 004	9 laps/clutch	18

Pole: M Schumacher, 1m35.266s, 130.154mph/209.464kph. Fastest lap: Montoya, 1m38.049s, 126.460mph/203.518kph on Lap 38. Race leaders: Barrichello 1-21 & 32-35, R Schumacher 22-31 & 36-56

QUICK AS A FLASH

Juan Pablo Montoya set the fastest F1 pole lap of 161.422mph (259.776kph) at Monza when he lapped the 3.599-mile (5.792km) circuit in 1m 20.264s in his BMW-powered Williams FW24. This beat the previous best of 160.925mph (258.976kph) set by Keke Rosberg in a Williams-Honda at Silverstone in 1985. However, Williams's pace through a race distance wasn't as competitive, so Montoya couldn't turn any of his seven poles into wins.

BRAZILIAN GRAND PRIX

INTERLAGOS • ROUND 3 • DATE: 31ST MARCH 2002
Laps: 71 • Distance: 190.101miles/305.939km • Weather: Very hot & bright

Pos	Driver	Team	Chassis-Engine	Result	Qual
1	Michael Schumacher	Ferrari	Ferrari F2002	1h31m43.663s	2
2	Ralf Schumacher	Williams	Williams-BMW FW24	1h31m44.251s	3
3	David Coulthard	McLaren	McLaren-Mercedes MP4-17	1h32m42.773s	4
4	Jenson Button	Renault F1	Renault R202	1h32m50.546s	7
5	Juan Pablo Montoya	Williams	Williams-BMW FW24	1h32m51.226s	1

Pos	Driver	Team	Chassis-Engine	Result	Qual
6	Mika Salo	Toyota	Toyota TF102	70 laps	10
7	Eddie Irvine	Jaguar	Jaguar-Cosworth R3	70 laps	13
8	Pedro de la Rosa	Jaguar	Jaguar-Cosworth R3	70 laps	11
9	Takuma Sato	Jordan	Jordan-Honda EJ12	69 laps	19
10	Jacques Villeneuve	BAR	BAR-Honda 004	68 laps/engine	15
11	Mark Webber	Minardi	Minardi-Asiatech PS02	68 laps	20
12	Kimi Raikkonen	McLaren	McLaren-Mercedes MP4-17	67 laps/wheel	5
13	Alex Yoong	Minardi	Minardi-Asiatech PS02	67 laps	22
R	Nick Heidfeld	Sauber	Sauber-Petronas C21	61 laps/brakes	9
R	Jarno Trulli	Renault F1	Renault R202	60 laps/engine	6
R	Felipe Massa	Sauber	Sauber-Petronas C21	41 laps/collision	12
R	Allan McNish	Toyota	Toyota TF102	40 laps/spun off	16
R	Olivier Panis	BAR	BAR-Honda 004	25 laps/gearbox	17
R	Heinz-Harald Frentzen	Arrows	Arrows-Cosworth A23	25 laps/suspension	18
R	Enrique Bernoldi	Arrows	Arrows-Cosworth A23	19 laps/suspension	21
R	Rubens Barrichello	Ferrari	Ferrari F2001	16 laps/hydraulics	8
R	Giancarlo Fisichella	Jordan	Jordan-Honda EJ12	6 laps/engine	14

Pole: Montoya, 1m13.114s, 131.834mph/212.167kph. Fastest lap: Montoya, 1m16.079s, 126.696mph/203.898kph on Lap 60. Race leaders: M Schumacher 1-13 & 17-39 & 45-71, Barrichello 14-16, R Schumacher 40-44

SAN MARINO GRAND PRIX

IMOLA • ROUND 4 • DATE: 14TH APRIL 2002
Laps: 62 • Distance: 190.43miles/305.846km • Weather: Warm but dull

Pos	Driver	Team	Chassis-Engine	Result	Qual
1	Michael Schumacher	Ferrari	Ferrari F2002	1h29m10.789s	1
2	Rubens Barrichello	Ferrari	Ferrari F2002	1h29m28.696s	2
3	Ralf Schumacher	Williams	Williams-BMW FW24	1h29m30.544s	3
4	Juan Pablo Montoya	Williams	Williams-BMW FW24	1h29m55.514s	4
5	Jenson Button	Renault F1	Renault R202	1h30m34.184s	9
6	David Coulthard	McLaren	McLaren-Mercedes MP4-17	61 laps	6
7	Jacques Villeneuve	BAR	BAR-Honda 004	61 laps	10
8	Felipe Massa	Sauber	Sauber-Petronas C21	61 laps	11
9	Jarno Trulli	Renault F1	Renault R202	61 laps	8
10	Nick Heidfeld	Sauber	Sauber-Petronas C21	61 laps	7
11	Mark Webber	Minardi	Minardi-Asiatech PS02	60 laps	19
R	Enrique Bernoldi	Arrows	Arrows-Cosworth A23	50 laps/engine	20
R	Eddie Irvine	Jaguar	Jaguar-Cosworth R3	45 laps/halfshaft	18
R	Kimi Raikkonen	McLaren	McLaren-Mercedes MP4-17	44 laps/exhaust	5
R	Olivier Panis	BAR	BAR-Honda 004	44 laps/throttle	12
R	Pedro de la Rosa	Jaguar	Jaguar-Cosworth R3	30 laps/halfshaft	21
R	Mika Salo	Toyota	Toyota TF102	26 laps/gearbox	16
R	Heinz-Harald Frentzen	Arrows	Arrows-Cosworth A23	25 laps/fuel pressure	13
R	Giancarlo Fisichella	Jordan	Jordan-Honda EJ12	19 laps/hydraulics	15
R	Takuma Sato	Jordan	Jordan-Honda EJ12	5 laps/gearbox	14
R	Allan McNish	Toyota	Toyota TF102	0 laps/transmission	17
DNQ	Alex Yoong	Minardi	Minardi-Asiatech PS02	-	22

Pole: M Schumacher, 1m21.091s, 136.079mph/218.998kph. Fastest lap: Barrichello, 1m24.170s, 131.101mph/210.987kph on Lap 38. Race leaders: M Schumacher 1-31 & 33-46 & 48-62, Barrichello 32 & 47

POINTS PAY PRIZES

Minardi started the 2002 season in style when debutant Mark Webber came fifth in Melbourne. This was a huge result for Paul Stoddart's team and all the better, as it came on home soil for both the team owner and driver. They were the only points the team scored but were enough for it to rank ninth with Arrows and Toyota, thus earning more prize money.

SPANISH GRAND PRIX

BARCELONA-CATALUNYA • ROUND 5 • DATE: 28TH APRIL 2002
Laps: 65 • Distance: 190.788miles/307.45km • Weather: Warm but dull

Pos	Driver	Team	Chassis-Engine	Result	Qual
1	Michael Schumacher	Ferrari	Ferrari F2002	1h30m29.981s	1
2	Juan Pablo Montoya	Williams	Williams-BMW FW24	1h31m05.610s	4
3	David Coulthard	McLaren	McLaren-Mercedes MP4-17	1h31m12.604s	7
4	Nick Heidfeld	Sauber	Sauber-Petronas C21	1h31m36.677s	8
5	Felipe Massa	Sauber	Sauber-Petronas C21	1h31m48.954s	11
6	Heinz-Harald Frentzen	Arrows	Arrows-Cosworth A23	1h31m50.410s	10
7	Jacques Villeneuve	BAR	BAR-Honda 004	64 laps	15
8	Allan McNish	Toyota	Toyota TF102	64 laps	19
9	Mika Salo	Toyota	Toyota TF102	64 laps	17
10	Jarno Trulli	Renault F1	Renault R202	63 laps/engine	9
11	Ralf Schumacher	Williams	Williams-BMW FW24	63 laps/engine	3
12	Jenson Button	Renault F1	Renault R202	60 laps/hydraulics	6
R	Olivier Panis	BAR	BAR-Honda 004	43 laps/exhaust	13
R	Eddie Irvine	Jaguar	Jaguar-Cosworth R3	41 laps/hydraulics	22
R	Enrique Bernoldi	Arrows	Arrows-Cosworth A23	40 laps/hydraulics	14
R	Takuma Sato	Jordan	Jordan-Honda EJ12	10 laps/spun off	18
R	Giancarlo Fisichella	Jordan	Jordan-Honda EJ12	5 laps/hydraulics	12
R	Kimi Raikkonen	McLaren	McLaren-Mercedes MP4-17	4 laps/wing	5
R	Pedro de la Rosa	Jaguar	Jaguar-Cosworth R3	2 laps/spun off	16
NS	Rubens Barrichello	Ferrari	Ferrari F2002	gearbox	2
W	Mark Webber	Minardi	Minardi-Asiatech PS02	rear wing failure	20
W	Alex Yoong	Minardi	Minardi-Asiatech PS02	-	21

Pole: M Schumacher, 1m16.364s, 138.556mph/222.984kph. Fastest lap: M Schumacher, 1m20.355s, 131.674mph/211.909kph on Lap 49. Race leaders: M Schumacher 1-65

NEW YEAR, NEW HUES

The multi-coloured hues that adorned the Benetton cars for years were replaced in 2002 by the plainer yellow and blue livery of Renault after the team's rebranding. Still based at Enstone in Oxfordshire, the team had its cars driven by Jenson Button and Jarno Trulli, to rankings of seventh and eighth respectively, with each driver coming fourth twice.

AUSTRIAN GRAND PRIX

A1-RING • ROUND 6 • DATE: 12TH MAY 2002
Laps: 71 • Distance: 190.851miles/307.146km • Weather: Warm but dull

Pos	Driver	Team	Chassis-Engine	Result	Qual
1	Michael Schumacher	Ferrari	Ferrari F2002	1h33m51.562s	3
2	Rubens Barrichello	Ferrari	Ferrari F2002	1h33m51.744s	1
3	Juan Pablo Montoya	Williams	Williams-BMW FW24	1h34m09.292s	4
4	Ralf Schumacher	Williams	Williams-BMW FW24	1h34m10.010s	2
5	Giancarlo Fisichella	Jordan	Jordan-Honda EJ12	1h34m41.527s	15
6	David Coulthard	McLaren	McLaren-Mercedes MP4-17	1h34m42.234s	8
7	Jenson Button	Renault F1	Renault R202	1h34m42.791s	13
8	Mika Salo	Toyota	Toyota TF102	1h35m00.987s	10
9	Allan McNish	Toyota	Toyota TF102	1h35m01.281s	14
10	Jacques Villeneuve	BAR	BAR-Honda 004	70 laps/engine	17
11	Heinz-Harald Frentzen	Arrows	Arrows-Cosworth A23	69 laps	11
12	Mark Webber	Minardi	Minardi-Asiatech PS02	69 laps	21
R	Jarno Trulli	Renault F1	Renault R202	44 laps/fuel pressure	16
R	Alex Yoong	Minardi	Minardi-Asiatech PS02	42 laps/engine	22
R	Eddie Irvine	Jaguar	Jaguar-Cosworth R3	38 laps/hydraulics	20
R	Nick Heidfeld	Sauber	Sauber-Petronas C21	27 laps/collision	5
R	Takuma Sato	Jordan	Jordan-Honda EJ12	26 laps/collision	18
R	Olivier Panis	BAR	BAR-Honda 004	22 laps/engine	9
R	Felipe Massa	Sauber	Sauber-Petronas C21	7 laps/suspension	7
R	Kimi Raikkonen	McLaren	McLaren-Mercedes MP4-17	5 laps/engine	6
R	Enrique Bernoldi	Arrows	Arrows-Cosworth A23	2 laps/collision	12
R	Pedro de la Rosa	Jaguar	Jaguar-Cosworth R3	0 laps/throttle	19

Pole: Barrichello, 1m08.082s, 142.137mph/228.747kph. Fastest lap: M Schumacher, 1m09.298s, 139.643mph/224.733kph on Lap 68. Race leaders: Barrichello 1-61 & 63-70, M Schumacher 62 & 71

OVER THE BARRIERS

Allan McNish didn't get to start the Japanese GP at Suzuka after failing a medical inspection, but was fortunate just to survive a huge crash at the track's feared 130R bend in qualifying. His Toyota ended up on the far side of the barriers at this 190mph (305kph) corner and it took considerable repair work for the race to be televised after he also split the TV cables.

MONACO GRAND PRIX

MONTE CARLO • ROUND 7 • DATE: 26TH MAY 2002
Laps: 78 • Distance: 162.852miles/262.86km • Weather: Warm & bright

Pos	Driver	Team	Chassis-Engine	Result	Qual
1	David Coulthard	McLaren	McLaren-Mercedes MP4-17	1h45m39.055s	2
2	Michael Schumacher	Ferrari	Ferrari F2002	1h45m40.104s	3
3	Ralf Schumacher	Williams	Williams-BMW FW24	1h46m56.504s	4
4	Jarno Trulli	Renault F1	Renault R202	77 laps	7
5	Giancarlo Fisichella	Jordan	Jordan-Honda EJ12	77 laps	11

Pos	Driver	Team	Chassis-Engine	Result	Qual
6	Heinz-Harald Frentzen	Arrows	Arrows-Cosworth A23	77 laps	12
7	Rubens Barrichello	Ferrari	Ferrari F2002	77 laps	5
8	Nick Heidfeld	Sauber	Sauber-Petronas C21	76 laps	17
9	Eddie Irvine	Jaguar	Jaguar-Cosworth R3	76 laps	21
10	Pedro de la Rosa	Jaguar	Jaguar-Cosworth R3	76 laps	20
11	Mark Webber	Minardi	Minardi-Asiatech PS02	76 laps	19
12	Enrique Bernoldi	Arrows	Arrows-Cosworth A23	76 laps	15
R	Mika Salo	Toyota	Toyota TF102	69 laps/brakes	9
R	Felipe Massa	Sauber	Sauber-Petronas C21	63 laps/spun off	13
R	Jenson Button	Renault F1	Renault R202	51 laps/collision	8
R	Olivier Panis	BAR	BAR-Honda 004	51 laps/collision	18
R	Juan Pablo Montoya	Williams	Williams-BMW FW24	46 laps/engine	1
R	Jacques Villeneuve	BAR	BAR-Honda 004	44 laps/engine	14
R	Kimi Raikkonen	McLaren	McLaren-Mercedes MP4-17	41 laps/collision	6
R	Alex Yoong	Minardi	Minardi-Asiatech PS02	29 laps/spun off	22
R	Takuma Sato	Jordan	Jordan-Honda EJ12	22 laps/spun off	16
R	Allan McNish	Toyota	Toyota TF102	15 laps/spun off	10

Pole: Montoya, 1m16.676s, 98.315mph/158.224kph. Fastest lap: Barrichello, 1m18.023s, 96.618mph/155.492kph on Lap 68. Race leaders: Coulthard 1-78

CANADIAN GRAND PRIX

MONTREAL • ROUND 8 • DATE: 9TH JUNE 2002
Laps: 70 • Distance: 189.534miles/305.27km • Weather: Hot but dull

Pos	Driver	Team	Chassis-Engine	Result	Qual
1	Michael Schumacher	Ferrari	Ferrari F2002	1h33m36.111s	2
2	David Coulthard	McLaren	McLaren-Mercedes MP4-17	1h33m37.243s	8
3	Rubens Barrichello	Ferrari	Ferrari F2002	1h33m43.193s	3
4	Kimi Raikkonen	McLaren	McLaren-Mercedes MP4-17	1h34m13.674s	5
5	Giancarlo Fisichella	Jordan	Jordan-Honda EJ12	1h34m18.923s	6
6	Jarno Trulli	Renault F1	Renault R202	1h34m25.059s	10
7	Ralf Schumacher	Williams	Williams-BMW FW24	1h34m27.629s	4
8	Olivier Panis	BAR	BAR-Honda 004	69 laps	11
9	Felipe Massa	Sauber	Sauber-Petronas C21	69 laps	12
10	Takuma Sato	Jordan	Jordan-Honda EJ12	69 laps	15
11	Mark Webber	Minardi	Minardi-Asiatech PS02	69 laps	21
12	Nick Heidfeld	Sauber	Sauber-Petronas C21	69 laps	7
13	Heinz-Harald Frentzen	Arrows	Arrows-Cosworth A23	69 laps	19
14	Alex Yoong	Minardi	Minardi-Asiatech PS02	68 laps	22
15	Jenson Button	Renault F1	Renault R202	65 laps/engine	13
R	Juan Pablo Montoya	Williams	Williams-BMW FW24	56 laps/engine	1
R	Allan McNish	Toyota	Toyota TF102	45 laps/spun off	20
R	Eddie Irvine	Jaguar	Jaguar-Cosworth R3	41 laps/overheating	14
R	Mika Salo	Toyota	Toyota TF102	41 laps/brakes	18
R	Pedro de la Rosa	Jaguar	Jaguar-Cosworth R3	29 laps/gearbox	16
R	Enrique Bernoldi	Arrows	Arrows-Cosworth A23	16 laps/vibrations	17
R	Jacques Villeneuve	BAR	BAR-Honda 004	8 laps/fuel pressure	9

Pole: Montoya, 1m12.836s, 133.934mph/215.547kph. Fastest lap: Montoya, 1m15.960s, 128.426mph/206.682kph on Lap 50. Race leaders: Barrichello 1-25, M Schumacher 26-37 & 51-70, Montoya 38-50

EUROPEAN GRAND PRIX

NURBURGRING • ROUND 9 • DATE: 23RD JUNE 2002
Laps: 60 • Distance: 191.429miles/308.76km • Weather: Warm but dull

Pos	Driver	Team	Chassis-Engine	Result	Qual
1	Rubens Barrichello	Ferrari	Ferrari F2002	1h35m07.426s	4
2	Michael Schumacher	Ferrari	Ferrari F2002	1h35m07.720s	3
3	Kimi Raikkonen	McLaren	McLaren-Mercedes MP4-17	1h35m53.861s	6
4	Ralf Schumacher	Williams	Williams-BMW FW24	1h36m14.389s	2
5	Jenson Button	Renault F1	Renault R202	1h36m24.370s	8
6	Felipe Massa	Sauber	Sauber-Petronas C21	59 laps	11
7	Nick Heidfeld	Sauber	Sauber-Petronas C21	59 laps	9
8	Jarno Trulli	Renault F1	Renault R202	59 laps	7
9	Olivier Panis	BAR	BAR-Honda 004	59 laps	12
10	Enrique Bernoldi	Arrows	Arrows-Cosworth A23	59 laps	21
11	Pedro de la Rosa	Jaguar	Jaguar-Cosworth R3	59 laps	16
12	Jacques Villeneuve	BAR	BAR-Honda 004	59 laps	19
13	Heinz-Harald Frentzen	Arrows	Arrows-Cosworth A23	59 laps	15
14	Allan McNish	Toyota	Toyota TF102	59 laps	13
15	Mark Webber	Minardi	Minardi-Asiatech PS02	58 laps	20
16	Takuma Sato	Jordan	Jordan-Honda EJ12	58 laps	14
R	Mika Salo	Toyota	Toyota TF102	51 laps/gearbox	10
R	Alex Yoong	Minardi	Minardi-Asiatech PS02	48 laps/hydraulics	22
R	Eddie Irvine	Jaguar	Jaguar-Cosworth R3	41 laps/hydraulics	17
R	Juan Pablo Montoya	Williams	Williams-BMW FW24	27 laps/collision	1
R	David Coulthard	McLaren	McLaren-Mercedes MP4-17	27 laps/collision	5
R	Giancarlo Fisichella	Jordan	Jordan-Honda EJ12	26 laps/collision	18

Pole: Montoya, 1m29.906s, 128.036mph/206.055kph. Fastest lap: M Schumacher, 1m32.226s, 124.815mph/200.871kph on Lap 26. Race leaders: Barrichello 1-60

GERMAN TRACK MODS

Hockenheim circuit was a given an overhaul to bring the cars past the grandstands more often during a grand prix. The long run through the forest was cut off and the lap reduced from 4.239 to 2.842 miles (6.821 to 4.573km). Conversely, the Nurburgring, also in Germany, was lengthened by the addition of a four-corner loop out of Turn 1.

BRITISH GRAND PRIX

SILVERSTONE • ROUND 10 • DATE: 7TH JULY 2002
Laps: 60 • Distance: 191.410miles/308.46km • Weather: Warm but dull, rain later

Pos	Driver	Team	Chassis-Engine	Result	Qual
1	Michael Schumacher	Ferrari	Ferrari F2002	1h31m45.015s	3
2	Rubens Barrichello	Ferrari	Ferrari F2002	1h31m59.593s	2
3	Juan Pablo Montoya	Williams	Williams-BMW FW24	1h32m16.676s	1
4	Jacques Villeneuve	BAR	BAR-Honda 004	59 laps	9
5	Olivier Panis	BAR	BAR-Honda 004	59 laps	13
6	Nick Heidfeld	Sauber	Sauber-Petronas C21	59 laps	10
7	Giancarlo Fisichella	Jordan	Jordan-Honda EJ12	59 laps	17

Pos	Driver	Team	Chassis-Engine	Result	Qual
8	Ralf Schumacher	Williams	Williams-BMW FW24	59 laps	4
9	Felipe Massa	Sauber	Sauber-Petronas C21	59 laps	11
10	David Coulthard	McLaren	McLaren-Mercedes MP4-17	58 laps	6
11	Pedro de la Rosa	Jaguar	Jaguar-Cosworth R3	58 laps	21
12	Jenson Button	Renault F1	Renault R202	54 laps/wheel	12
R	Takuma Sato	Jordan	Jordan-Honda EJ12	50 laps/engine	14
R	Kimi Raikkonen	McLaren	McLaren-Mercedes MP4-17	44 laps/engine	5
R	Jarno Trulli	Renault F1	Renault R202	29 laps/electrical	7
R	Enrique Bernoldi	Arrows	Arrows-Cosworth A23	28 laps/halfshaft	18
R	Eddie Irvine	Jaguar	Jaguar-Cosworth R3	23 laps/spun off	19
R	Heinz-Harald Frentzen	Arrows	Arrows-Cosworth A23	20 laps/engine	16
R	Mika Salo	Toyota	Toyota TF102	15 laps/transmission	8
R	Mark Webber	Minardi	Minardi-Asiatech PS02	9 laps/spun off	20
R	Allan McNish	Toyota	Toyota TF102	0 laps/clutch	15
DNQ	Alex Yoong	Minardi	Minardi-Asiatech PS02	-	22

Pole: Montoya, 1m18.998s, 145.574mph/234.279kph. Fastest lap: Barrichello, 1m23.083s, 138.416mph/222.760kph on Lap 58. Race leaders: Montoya 1-15, M Schumacher 16-60

NEW CONSTRUCTORS

The world's largest automobile manufacturer, Toyota, entered F1, running its team out of its motorsport facility in Cologne from where it had had such great success in rallying. It ran a pair of cars for Allan McNish and Mika Salo, with the latter scoring its only points for sixth place finishes in early-season races in Australia and Brazil.

FRENCH GRAND PRIX

MAGNY-COURS • ROUND 11 • DATE: 21ST JULY 2002
Laps: 72 • Distance: 190.184miles/306.072km • Weather: Hot but dull

Pos	Driver	Team	Chassis-Engine	Result	Qual
1	Michael Schumacher	Ferrari	Ferrari F2002	1h32m09.837s	2
2	Kimi Raikkonen	McLaren	McLaren-Mercedes MP4-17	1h32m10.941s	4
3	David Coulthard	McLaren	McLaren-Mercedes MP4-17	1h32m41.812s	6
4	Juan Pablo Montoya	Williams	Williams-BMW FW24	1h32m50.512s	1
5	Ralf Schumacher	Williams	Williams-BMW FW24	1h32m51.609s	5
6	Jenson Button	Renault F1	Renault R202	71 laps	7
7	Nick Heidfeld	Sauber	Sauber-Petronas C21	71 laps	10
8	Mark Webber	Minardi	Minardi-Asiatech PS02	71 laps	18
9	Pedro de la Rosa	Jaguar	Jaguar-Cosworth R3	70 laps	15
10	Alex Yoong	Minardi	Minardi-Asiatech PS02	68 laps	19
11	Allan McNish	Toyota	Toyota TF102	65 laps/engine	17
R	Eddie Irvine	Jaguar	Jaguar-Cosworth R3	52 laps/wing	9
R	Jarno Trulli	Renault F1	Renault R202	49 laps/engine	8
R	Felipe Massa	Sauber	Sauber-Petronas C21	48 laps/transmission	12
R	Mika Salo	Toyota	Toyota TF102	48 laps/engine	16
R	Jacques Villeneuve	BAR	BAR-Honda 004	35 laps/engine	13
R	Olivier Panis	BAR	BAR-Honda 004	29 laps/vibrations	11
R	Takuma Sato	Jordan	Jordan-Honda EJ12	23 laps/spun off	14

Pos	Driver	Team	Chassis-Engine	Result	Qual
NS	Rubens Barrichello	Ferrari	Ferrari F2002	electrics	3
DNQ	Heinz-Harald Frentzen	Arrows	Arrows-Cosworth A23	-	20
DNQ	Enrique Bernoldi	Arrows	Arrows-Cosworth A23	-	21
NS	Giancarlo Fisichella	Jordan	Jordan-Honda EJ12	driver injury	-

Pole: Montoya, 1m11.985s, 132.099mph/212.594kph. Fastest lap: Coulthard, 1m15.045s, 126.713mph/203.925kph on Lap 62. Race leaders: Montoya 1-23 & 36-42, M Schumacher 24-25 & 29-35 & 68-72, Raikkonen 26 & 43-49 & 55-67, Coulthard 27-28 & 50-54

GERMAN GRAND PRIX

HOCKENHEIM • ROUND 12 • DATE: 28TH JULY 2002
Laps: 67 • Distance: 190.424miles/306.458km • Weather: Hot & bright

Pos	Driver	Team	Chassis-Engine	Result	Qual
1	Michael Schumacher	Ferrari	Ferrari F2002	1h27m52.078s	1
2	Juan Pablo Montoya	Williams	Williams-BMW FW24	1h28m02.581s	4
3	Ralf Schumacher	Williams	Williams-BMW FW24	1h28m06.544s	2
4	Rubens Barrichello	Ferrari	Ferrari F2002	1h28m15.273s	3
5	David Coulthard	McLaren	McLaren-Mercedes MP4-17	66 laps	9
6	Nick Heidfeld	Sauber	Sauber-Petronas C21	66 laps	10
7	Felipe Massa	Sauber	Sauber-Petronas C21	66 laps	14
8	Takuma Sato	Jordan	Jordan-Honda EJ12	66 laps	12
9	Mika Salo	Toyota	Toyota TF102	66 laps	19
R	Kimi Raikkonen	McLaren	McLaren-Mercedes MP4-17	59 laps/spun off	5
R	Giancarlo Fisichella	Jordan	Jordan-Honda EJ12	59 laps/engine	6
R	Eddie Irvine	Jaguar	Jaguar-Cosworth R3	57 laps/brakes	16
R	Enrique Bernoldi	Arrows	Arrows-Cosworth A23	48 laps/engine	18
R	Olivier Panis	BAR	BAR-Honda 004	39 laps/engine	7
R	Jarno Trulli	Renault F1	Renault R202	36 laps/spun off	8
R	Jacques Villeneuve	BAR	BAR-Honda 004	27 laps/gearbox	11
R	Jenson Button	Renault F1	Renault R202	24 laps/engine	13
R	Allan McNish	Toyota	Toyota TF102	23 laps/engine	17
R	Mark Webber	Minardi	Minardi-Asiatech PS02	23 laps/hydraulics	21
R	Heinz-Harald Frentzen	Arrows	Arrows-Cosworth A23	18 laps/hydraulics	15
R	Pedro de la Rosa	Jaguar	Jaguar-Cosworth R3	0 laps/transmission	20
DNQ	Alex Yoong	Minardi	Minardi-Asiatech PS02	-	22

Pole: M Schumacher, 1m14.389s, 137.543mph/221.355kph. Fastest lap: M Schumacher, 1m16.462s, 133.814mph/215.354kph on Lap 44. Race leaders: M Schumacher 1-26 & 31-47 & 49-67, R Schumacher 27-29 & 48, Montoya 30

HUNGARIAN GRAND PRIX

HUNGARORING • ROUND 13 • DATE: 18TH AUGUST 2002
Laps: 77 • Distance: 190.186miles/306.075km • Weather: Very hot & bright

Pos	Driver	Team	Chassis-Engine	Result	Qual
1	Rubens Barrichello	Ferrari	Ferrari F2002	1h41m49.001s	1
2	Michael Schumacher	Ferrari	Ferrari F2002	1h41m49.435s	2
3	Ralf Schumacher	Williams	Williams-BMW FW24	1h42m02.357s	3
4	Kimi Raikkonen	McLaren	McLaren-Mercedes MP4-17	1h42m18.480s	11
5	David Coulthard	McLaren	McLaren-Mercedes MP4-17	1h42m26.801s	10
6	Giancarlo Fisichella	Jordan	Jordan-Honda EJ12	1h42m57.805s	5

Pos	Driver	Team	Chassis-Engine	Result	Qual
7	Felipe Massa	Sauber	Sauber-Petronas C21	1h43m02.613s	7
8	Jarno Trulli	Renault F1	Renault R202	76 laps	6
9	Nick Heidfeld	Sauber	Sauber-Petronas C21	76 laps	8
10	Takuma Sato	Jordan	Jordan-Honda EJ12	76 laps	14
11	Juan Pablo Montoya	Williams	Williams-BMW FW24	76 laps	4
12	Olivier Panis	BAR	BAR-Honda 004	76 laps	12
13	Pedro de la Rosa	Jaguar	Jaguar-Cosworth R3	75 laps	15
14	Allan McNish	Toyota	Toyota TF102	75 laps	18
15	Mika Salo *	Toyota	Toyota TF102	75 laps	17
16	Mark Webber	Minardi	Minardi-Asiatech PS02	75 laps	19
R	Anthony Davidson	Minardi	Minardi-Asiatech PS02	58 laps/spun off	20
R	Jenson Button	Renault F1	Renault R202	30 laps/spun off	9
R	Eddie Irvine	Jaguar	Jaguar-Cosworth R3	23 laps/engine	16
R	Jacques Villeneuve	BAR	BAR-Honda 004	20 laps/transmission	13

Pole: Barrichello, 1m13.333s, 121.252mph/195.137kph. Fastest lap: M Schumacher, 1m16.207s, 116.679mph/187.778kph on Lap 72. Race leaders: Barrichello 1-32 & 34-77, R Schumacher 33

* 25s penalty for impeding de la Rosa in the pit lane

CLASSIC CAR: FERRARI F2002

Created by a design team led by Ross Brawn that included Rory Byrne, Aldo Costa and Nikolas Tombazis, plus an engine group led by Paolo Martinelli, the F2002 was one of the greatest cars in F1 history and was easily the class of the field. It wasn't ready for the first two races, but then this V10-powered beauty was given a winning debut in the third round in Brazil, where it worked effectively on its Bridgestone rubber and handled better due to its shorter, lighter gearbox. By the end of the year, it had won 14 times from 15 starts.

BELGIAN GRAND PRIX

SPA-FRANCORCHAMPS • ROUND 14 • DATE: 1ST SEPTEMBER 2002
Laps: 44 • Distance: 190.370miles/306.372km • Weather: Cool but bright

Pos	Driver	Team	Chassis-Engine	Result	Qual
1	Michael Schumacher	Ferrari	Ferrari F2002	1h21m20.634s	1
2	Rubens Barrichello	Ferrari	Ferrari F2002	1h21m22.611s	3
3	Juan Pablo Montoya	Williams	Williams-BMW FW24	1h21m39.079s	5
4	David Coulthard	McLaren	McLaren-Mercedes MP4-17	1h21m39.992s	6
5	Ralf Schumacher	Williams	Williams-BMW FW24	1h22m17.074s	4
6	Eddie Irvine	Jaguar	Jaguar-Cosworth R3	1h22m38.004s	8
7	Mika Salo	Toyota	Toyota TF102	1h22m38.443s	9
8	Jacques Villeneuve	BAR	BAR-Honda 004	1h22m40.489s	12
9	Allan McNish	Toyota	Toyota TF102	43 laps	13
10	Nick Heidfeld	Sauber	Sauber-Petronas C21	43 laps	18
11	Takuma Sato	Jordan	Jordan-Honda EJ12	43 laps	16
12	Olivier Panis	BAR	BAR-Honda 004	39 laps/engine	15
R	Giancarlo Fisichella	Jordan	Jordan-Honda EJ12	38 laps/engine	14
R	Pedro de la Rosa	Jaguar	Jaguar-Cosworth R3	37 laps/suspension	11

Pos	Driver	Team	Chassis-Engine	Result	Qual
R	Felipe Massa	Sauber	Sauber-Petronas C21	37 laps/engine	17
R	Kimi Raikkonen	McLaren	McLaren-Mercedes MP4-17	35 laps/engine	2
R	Jarno Trulli	Renault F1	Renault R202	35 laps/engine	7
R	Anthony Davidson	Minardi	Minardi-Asiatech PS02	17 laps/spun off	20
R	Jenson Button	Renault F1	Renault R202	10 laps/engine	10
R	Mark Webber	Minardi	Minardi-Asiatech PS02	4 laps/gearbox	19

Pole: M Schumacher, 1m43.726s, 150.162mph/241.663kph. Fastest lap: M Schumacher, 1m47.176s, 145.329mph/233.884kph on Lap 15. Race leaders: M Schumacher 1-16 & 18-44, Barrichello 17

ITALIAN GRAND PRIX

MONZA • ROUND 15 • DATE: 15TH SEPTEMBER 2002
Laps: 53 • Distance: 190.778miles/307.029km • Weather: Hot & bright

Pos	Driver	Team	Chassis-Engine	Result	Qual
1	Rubens Barrichello	Ferrari	Ferrari F2002	1h16m19.982s	4
2	Michael Schumacher	Ferrari	Ferrari F2002	1h16m20.237s	2
3	Eddie Irvine	Jaguar	Jaguar-Cosworth R3	1h17m12.561s	5
4	Jarno Trulli	Renault F1	Renault R202	1h17m18.201s	11
5	Jenson Button	Renault F1	Renault R202	1h17m27.752s	17
6	Olivier Panis	BAR	BAR-Honda 004	1h17m28.473s	16
7	David Coulthard	McLaren	McLaren-Mercedes MP4-17	1h17m29.030s	7
8	Giancarlo Fisichella	Jordan	Jordan-Honda EJ12	1h17m30.874s	12
9	Jacques Villeneuve	BAR	BAR-Honda 004	1h17m41.051s	9
10	Nick Heidfeld	Sauber	Sauber-Petronas C21	1h17m42.028s	15
11	Mika Salo	Toyota	Toyota TF102	52 laps	10
12	Takuma Sato	Jordan	Jordan-Honda EJ12	52 laps	18
13	Alex Yoong	Minardi	Minardi-Asiatech PS02	47 laps	20
R	Juan Pablo Montoya	Williams	Williams-BMW FW24	33 laps/chassis	1
R	Kimi Raikkonen	McLaren	McLaren-Mercedes MP4-17	29 laps/engine	6
R	Mark Webber	Minardi	Minardi-Asiatech PS02	20 laps/electrical	19
R	Felipe Massa	Sauber	Sauber-Petronas C21	16 laps/collision	14
R	Pedro de la Rosa	Jaguar	Jaguar-Cosworth R3	15 laps/collision	8
R	Allan McNish	Toyota	Toyota TF102	13 laps/suspension	13
R	Ralf Schumacher	Williams	Williams-BMW FW24	4 laps/engine	3

Pole: Montoya, 1m20.264s, 161.449mph/259.827kph. Fastest lap: Barrichello, 1m23.657s, 154.901mph/249.289kph on Lap 15. Race leaders: R Schumacher 1-3, Montoya 4, Barrichello 5-19 & 29-53, M Schumacher 20-28

UNITED STATES GRAND PRIX

INDIANAPOLIS MOTOR SPEEDWAY • ROUND 16 • DATE: 29TH SEPTEMBER 2002
Laps: 73 • Distance: 190.149miles/306.016km • Weather: Warm & bright

Pos	Driver	Team	Chassis-Engine	Result	Qual
1	Rubens Barrichello	Ferrari	Ferrari F2002	1h31m07.934s	2
2	Michael Schumacher	Ferrari	Ferrari F2002	1h31m07.945s	1
3	David Coulthard	McLaren	McLaren-Mercedes MP4-17	1h31m15.733s	3
4	Juan Pablo Montoya	Williams	Williams-BMW FW24	1h31m17.845s	4
5	Jarno Trulli	Renault F1	Renault R202	1h32m04.781s	8
6	Jacques Villeneuve	BAR	BAR-Honda 004	1h32m06.146s	7
7	Giancarlo Fisichella	Jordan	Jordan-Honda EJ12	72 laps	9
8	Jenson Button	Renault F1	Renault R202	72 laps	14

Pos	Driver	Team	Chassis-Engine	Result	Qual
9	Nick Heidfeld	Sauber	Sauber-Petronas C21	72 laps	10
10	Eddie Irvine	Jaguar	Jaguar-Cosworth R3	72 laps	13
11	Takuma Sato	Jordan	Jordan-Honda EJ12	72 laps	15
12	Olivier Panis	BAR	BAR-Honda 004	72 laps	12
13	Heinz-Harald Frentzen	Sauber	Sauber-Petronas C21	71 laps	11
14	Mika Salo	Toyota	Toyota TF102	71 laps	19
15	Allan McNish	Toyota	Toyota TF102	71 laps	16
16	Ralf Schumacher	Williams	Williams-BMW FW24	71 laps	5
R	Kimi Raikkonen	McLaren	McLaren-Mercedes MP4-17	50 laps/engine	6
R	Alex Yoong	Minardi	Minardi-Asiatech PS02	46 laps/engine	20
R	Mark Webber	Minardi	Minardi-Asiatech PS02	38 laps/steering	18
R	Pedro de la Rosa	Jaguar	Jaguar-Cosworth R3	27 laps/transmission	17

Pole: M Schumacher, 1m10.790s, 132.465mph/213.182kph. Fastest lap: Barrichello, 1m12.738s, 128.917mph/207.473kph on Lap 27. Race leaders: M Schumacher 1-26 & 29-48 & 51-72, Barrichello 27-28 & 49-50 & 73

JAPANESE GRAND PRIX

SUZUKA • ROUND 17 • DATE: 13TH OCTOBER 2002
Laps: 53 • Distance: 191.701miles/308.513km • Weather: Hot & bright

Pos	Driver	Team	Chassis-Engine	Result	Qual
1	Michael Schumacher	Ferrari	Ferrari F2002	1h26m59.698s	1
2	Rubens Barrichello	Ferrari	Ferrari F2002	1h27m00.205s	2
3	Kimi Raikkonen	McLaren	McLaren-Mercedes MP4-17	1h27m22.990s	4
4	Juan Pablo Montoya	Williams	Williams-BMW FW24	1h27m35.973s	6
5	Takuma Sato	Jordan	Jordan-Honda EJ12	1h28m22.392s	7
6	Jenson Button	Renault F1	Renault R202	52 laps	10
7	Nick Heidfeld	Sauber	Sauber-Petronas C21	52 laps	12
8	Mika Salo	Toyota	Toyota TF102	52 laps	13
9	Eddie Irvine	Jaguar	Jaguar-Cosworth R3	52 laps	14
10	Mark Webber	Minardi	Minardi-Asiatech PS02	51 laps	19
11	Ralf Schumacher	Williams	Williams-BMW FW24	48 laps/engine	5
R	Pedro de la Rosa	Jaguar	Jaguar-Cosworth R3	39 laps/transmission	17
R	Giancarlo Fisichella	Jordan	Jordan-Honda EJ12	37 laps/engine	8
R	Jarno Trulli	Renault F1	Renault R202	32 laps/engine	11
R	Jacques Villeneuve	BAR	BAR-Honda 004	27 laps/engine	9
R	Alex Yoong	Minardi	Minardi-Asiatech PS02	14 laps/spun off	20
R	Olivier Panis	BAR	BAR-Honda 004	8 laps/throttle	16
R	David Coulthard	McLaren	McLaren-Mercedes MP4-17	7 laps/throttle	3
R	Felipe Massa	Sauber	Sauber-Petronas C21	3 laps/spun off	15
NS	Allan McNish	Toyota	Toyota TF102	driver injured	18

Pole: M Schumacher, 1m31.317s, 142.593mph/229.481kph. Fastest lap: M Schumacher, 1m36.125s, 135.461mph/218.003kph on Lap 15. Race leaders: M Schumacher 1-20 & 22-53, Barrichello 21

NEW DRIVERS

Felipe Massa did well enough in his first year with Sauber to rank 13th, peaking with fifth in Spain. Mark Webber had already taken a fifth in Australia, but would not score again, while Jordan's Takuma Sato waited until the final round to match that. Allan McNish (Toyota) and Anthony Davidson (Minardi) were the other rookies.

WORLD DRIVERS' CHAMPIONSHIP FINAL RESULTS

Pos	Driver	Nat	Car-Engine	R1	R2	R3	R4	R5	R6
1	Michael Schumacher	DEU	Ferrari F2001	1	3P	-	-	-	-
			Ferrari F2002	-	-	1	1P	1PF	1F
2	Rubens Barrichello	BRA	Ferrari F2001	RP	R	R	-	-	-
			Ferrari F2002	-	-	-	2F	NS	2P
3	Juan Pablo Montoya	COL	Williams-BMW FW24	2	2F	5PF	4	2	3
4	Ralf Schumacher	DEU	Williams-BMW FW24	R	1	2	3	11	4
5	David Coulthard	GBR	McLaren-Mercedes MP4-17	R	R	3	6	3	6
6	Kimi Raikkonen	FIN	McLaren-Mercedes MP4-17	3F	R	12	R	R	R
7	Jenson Button	GBR	Renault R202	R	4	4	5	12	7
8	Jarno Trulli	ITA	Renault R202	R	R	R	9	10	R
9	Eddie Irvine	GBR	Jaguar-Cosworth R3	4	R	7	R	R	R
10	Nick Heidfeld	DEU	Sauber-Petronas C21	R	5	R	10	4	R
11	Giancarlo Fisichella	ITA	Jordan-Honda EJ12	R	13	R	R	R	5
12	Jacques Villeneuve	CAN	BAR-Honda 004	R	8	10	7	7	10
13	Felipe Massa	BRA	Sauber-Petronas C21	R	6	R	8	5	R
14	Olivier Panis	FRA	BAR-Honda 004	R	R	R	R	R	R
15	Takuma Sato	JPN	Jordan-Honda EJ12	R	9	9	R	R	R
16	Mark Webber	AUS	Minardi-Asiatech PS02	5	R	11	11	NS	12
17	Mika Salo	FIN	Toyota TF102	6	12	6	R	9	8
18	Heinz-Harald Frentzen	DEU	Arrows-Cosworth A23	DQ	11	R	R	6	11
			Sauber-Petronas C21	-	-	-	-	-	-
19	Allan McNish	GBR	Toyota TF102	R	7	R	R	8	9
20	Alex Yoong	MYS	Minardi-Asiatech PS02	7	R	13	DNQ	NS	R
21	Pedro de la Rosa	ESP	Jaguar-Cosworth R3	8	10	8	R	R	R
22	Enrique Bernoldi	BRA	Arrows-Cosworth A23	DQ	R	R	R	R	R
23	Anthony Davidson	GBR	Minardi-Asiatech PS02	-	-	-	-	-	-

Pos	Driver	R7	R8	R9	R10	R11	R12	R13	R14	R15	R16	R17	Total
1	M Schumacher	-	-	-	-	-	-	-	-	-	-	-	144
		2	1	2F	1	1	1PF	2F	1PF	2	2P	1PF	
2	Barrichello	-	-	-	-	-	-	-	-	-	-	-	77
		7F	3	1	2F	NS	4	1P	2	1F	1F	2	
3	Montoya	RP	RPF	RP	3P	4P	2	11	3	RP	4	4	50
4	R Schumacher	3	7	4	8	5	3	3	5	R	16	11	42
5	Coulthard	1	2	R	10	3F	5	5	4	7	3	R	41
6	Raikkonen	R	4	3	R	2	R	4	R	R	R	3	24
7	Button	R	15	5	12	6	R	R	R	5	8	6	14
8	Trulli	4	6	8	R	R	R	8	R	4	5	R	9
9	Irvine	9	R	R	R	R	R	R	6	3	10	9	8
10	Heidfeld	8	12	7	6	7	6	9	10	10	9	7	7
11	Fisichella	5	5	R	7	NS	R	6	R	8	7	R	7
12	Villeneuve	R	R	12	4	R	R	R	8	9	6	R	4
13	Massa	R	9	6	9	R	7	7	R	R	-	R	4
14	Panis	R	8	9	5	R	R	12	12	6	12	R	3
15	Sato	R	10	16	R	R	8	10	11	12	11	5	2
16	Webber	11	11	15	R	8	R	16	R	R	R	10	2
17	Salo	R	R	R	R	R	9	15	7	11	14	8	2
18	Frentzen	6	13	13	R	DNQ	R	-	-	-	-	-	2
		-	-	-	-	-	-	-	-	-	13	-	
19	McNish	R	R	14	R	11	R	14	9	R	15	NS	0
20	Yoong	R	14	R	DNQ	10	DNQ	-	-	13	R	R	0
21	de la Rosa	10	R	11	11	9	R	13	R	R	R	R	0
22	Bernoldi	12	R	10	R	DNQ	R	-	-	-	-	-	0
23	Davidson	-	-	-	-	-	-	R	R	-	-	-	0

WORLD CONSTRUCTORS' CHAMPIONSHIP FINAL RESULTS

Pos	Team-Engine	R1	R2	R3	R4	R5	R6	R7	R8	R9
1	Ferrari	1/R	3/R	1/R	1/2	1/NS	1/2	2/7	1/3	1/2
2	Williams-BMW	2/R	1/2	2/5	3/4	2/11	3/4	3/R	7/R	4/R
3	McLaren-Mercedes	3/R	R/R	3/12	6/R	3/R	6/R	1/R	2/4	3/R
4	Renault F1	R/R	4/R	4/R	5/9	10/12	7/R	4/R	6/15	5/8
5	Sauber-Petronas	R/R	5/6	R/R	8/10	4/5	R/R	8/R	9/12	6/7
6	Jordan-Honda	R/R	9/13	9/R	R/R	R/R	5/R	5/R	5/10	16/R
7	Jaguar-Cosworth	4/8	10/R	7/8	R/R	R/R	R/R	9/10	R/R	11/R
8	BAR-Honda	R/R	8/R	10/R	7/R	7/R	10/R	R/R	8/R	9/12
9	Minardi-Asiatech	5/7	R/R	11/13	11/DNQ	NS/NS	12/R	11/R	11/14	15/R
10	Toyota	6/R	7/12	6/R	R/R	8/9	8/9	R/R	R/R	14/R
11	Arrows-Cosworth	DQ/DQ	11/R	R/R	R/R	6/R	11/R	6/12	13/R	10/13

Pos	Team-Engine	R10	R11	R12	R13	R14	R15	R16	R17	Total
1	Ferrari	1/2	1/NS	1/4	1/2	1/2	1/2	1/2	1/2	221
2	Williams-BMW	3/8	4/5	2/3	3/11	3/5	R/R	4/16	4/11	92
3	McLaren-Mercedes	10/R	2/3	5/R	4/5	4/R	7/R	3/R	3/R	65
4	Renault F1	12/R	6/R	R/R	8/R	R/R	4/5	5/8	6/R	23
5	Sauber-Petronas	6/9	7/R	6/7	7/9	10/R	10/R	9/13	7/R	11
6	Jordan-Honda	7/R	R	8/R	6/10	11/R	8/12	7/11	5/R	9
7	Jaguar-Cosworth	11/R	9/R	R/R	13/R	6/R	3/R	10/R	9/R	8
8	BAR-Honda	4/5	R/R	R/R	12/R	8/12	6/9	6/12	R/R	7
9	Minardi-Asiatech	R/DNQ	8/10	R/DNQ	16/R	R/R	13/R	R/R	10/R	2
10	Toyota	R/R	11/R	9/R	14/15	7/9	11/R	14/15	8/NS	2
11	Arrows-Cosworth	R/R	DNQ/DNQ	R/R	-	-	-	-	-	2

SYMBOLS AND GRAND PRIX KEY

Round 1 Australian GP
Round 2 Malaysian GP
Round 3 Brazilian GP
Round 4 San Marino GP
Round 5 Spanish GP
Round 6 Austrian GP
Round 7 Monaco GP
Round 8 Canadian GP
Round 9 European GP
Round 10 British GP
Round 11 French GP
Round 12 German GP
Round 13 Hungarian GP
Round 14 Belgian GP
Round 15 Italian GP
Round 16 United States GP
Round 17 Japanese GP

SCORING

1st 10 points
2nd 6 points
3rd 4 points
4th 3 points
5th 2 points
6th 1 point

DNPQ DID NOT PRE-QUALIFY **DNQ** DID NOT QUALIFY **DQ** DISQUALIFIED **EX** EXCLUDED
F FASTEST LAP **NC** NOT CLASSIFIED **NS** NON-STARTER **P** POLE POSITION **R** RETIRED

SEASON SUMMARY

Michael Schumacher claimed his fourth F1 title in a row, bringing his tally to a record-breaking sixth F1 crown. However, this was nothing like his utter dominance in 2002. This time, Schumacher had to pip McLaren's Kimi Raikkonen to become champion and did so by only two points across 16 grands prix. Not only did McLaren step up to push Ferrari, but BMW-powered Williams was right in the mix, too, and its lead driver, Juan Pablo Montoya, was an outside bet until the penultimate round. Renault also raised its game, with Fernando Alonso taking his first win to help it pull clear of the midfield pack.

AUSTRALIAN GRAND PRIX

ALBERT PARK • ROUND 1 • DATE: 9TH MARCH 2003
Laps: 58 • Distance: 191.117miles/307.574km • Weather: Warm & wet, drying later

Pos	Driver	Team	Chassis-Engine	Result	Qual
1	David Coulthard	McLaren	McLaren-Mercedes MP4-17D	1h34m42.124s	11
2	Juan Pablo Montoya	Williams	Williams-BMW FW25	1h34m50.799s	3
3	Kimi Raikkonen	McLaren	McLaren-Mercedes MP4-17D	1h34m51.316s	15
4	Michael Schumacher	Ferrari	Ferrari F2002	1h34m51.606s	1
5	Jarno Trulli	Renault F1	Renault R23	1h35m20.925s	12
6	Heinz-Harald Frentzen	Sauber	Sauber-Petronas C22	1h35m26.052s	4
7	Fernando Alonso	Renault F1	Renault R23	1h35m27.198s	10
8	Ralf Schumacher	Williams	Williams-BMW FW25	1h35m27.869s	9
9	Jacques Villeneuve	BAR	BAR-Honda 005	1h35m47.660s	6
10	Jenson Button	BAR	BAR-Honda 005	1h35m48.098s	8
11	Jos Verstappen	Minardi	Minardi-Cosworth PS03	57 laps	19
12	Giancarlo Fisichella	Jordan	Jordan-Ford EJ13	52 laps/gearbox	13
13	Antonio Pizzonia	Jaguar	Jaguar-Cosworth R4	52 laps/halfshaft	18
R	Olivier Panis	Toyota	Toyota TF103	31 laps/fuel pump	5
R	Nick Heidfeld	Sauber	Sauber-Petronas C22	20 laps/suspension	7
R	Justin Wilson	Minardi	Minardi-Cosworth PS03	16 laps/radiator damage	20
R	Mark Webber	Jaguar	Jaguar-Cosworth R4	15 laps/halfshaft	14
R	Cristiano da Matta	Toyota	Toyota TF103	7 laps/spun off	16
R	Ralph Firman	Jordan	Jordan-Ford EJ13	6 laps/spun off	17
R	Rubens Barrichello	Ferrari	Ferrari F2002	5 laps/spun off	2

Pole: M Schumacher, 1m27.173s, 136.079mph/218.999kph. Fastest lap: Raikkonen, 1m27.724s, 135.224mph/217.623kph on Lap 32. Race leaders: M Schumacher 1-6 & 42-45, Montoya 7-16 & 33-41 & 46-47, Raikkonen 17-32, Coulthard 48-58

A NEW QUALIFYING SHOW

Qualifying was given a major shake-up, as it adopted a one-at-a-time format in place of the former free-for-all, with the express aim of making it clearer for the fans. Another major change was to the points system, with the 10-6-4-3-2-1 allocation of points for the top six finishers being replaced by 10-8-6-5-4-3-2-1 allocation for the top eight.

TAKING TURNS TO LEAD

An extraordinary statistic was achieved in 2003 when all but one of the 10 teams led a lap during the 16 grands prix. The only team not to take a turn at the front was Minardi. The final tally of laps led was Ferrari (393), Williams (308), McLaren (177), Renault (111), Toyota (18), BAR (8), Jaguar (2), Jordan (1) and Sauber (1).

MALAYSIAN GRAND PRIX

SEPANG • ROUND 2 • DATE: 23RD MARCH 2003
Laps: 56 • Distance: 192.878miles/310.408km • Weather: Hot & bright

Pos	Driver	Team	Chassis-Engine	Result	Qual
1	Kimi Raikkonen	McLaren	McLaren-Mercedes MP4-17D	1h32m22.195s	7
2	Rubens Barrichello	Ferrari	Ferrari F2002	1h33m01.481s	5
3	Fernando Alonso	Renault F1	Renault R23	1h33m26.202s	1
4	Ralf Schumacher	Williams	Williams-BMW FW25	1h33m50.221s	17
5	Jarno Trulli	Renault F1	Renault R23	55 laps	2
6	Michael Schumacher	Ferrari	Ferrari F2002	55 laps	3
7	Jenson Button	BAR	BAR-Honda 005	55 laps	9
8	Nick Heidfeld	Sauber	Sauber-Petronas C22	55 laps	6
9	Heinz-Harald Frentzen	Sauber	Sauber-Petronas C22	55 laps	13
10	Ralph Firman	Jordan	Jordan-Ford EJ13	55 laps	20
11	Cristiano da Matta	Toyota	Toyota TF103	55 laps	11
12	Juan Pablo Montoya	Williams	Williams-BMW FW25	53 laps	8
13	Jos Verstappen	Minardi	Minardi-Cosworth PS03	52 laps	18
R	Antonio Pizzonia	Jaguar	Jaguar-Cosworth R4	42 laps/brakes	15
R	Justin Wilson	Minardi	Minardi-Cosworth PS03	41 laps/physical	19
R	Mark Webber	Jaguar	Jaguar-Cosworth R4	35 laps/engine	16
R	Olivier Panis	Toyota	Toyota TF103	12 laps/fuel pressure	10
R	David Coulthard	McLaren	McLaren-Mercedes MP4-17D	2 laps/electrical	4
R	Giancarlo Fisichella	Jordan	Jordan-Ford EJ13	0 laps/clutch	14
NS	Jacques Villeneuve	BAR	BAR-Honda 005	gearbox electronics	12

Pole: Alonso, 1m37.044s, 127.770mph/205.626kph. Fastest lap: M Schumacher, 1m36.412s, 128.607mph/206.974kph on Lap 45. Race leaders: Alonso 1-13, Raikkonen 14-19 & 23-56, Barrichello 20-22

BRAZILIAN GRAND PRIX

INTERLAGOS • ROUND 3 • DATE: 6TH APRIL 2003
Laps: 54 • Distance: 144.584miles/232.686km • Weather: Warm & wet, drying later

Pos	Driver	Team	Chassis-Engine	Result	Qual
1	Giancarlo Fisichella	Jordan	Jordan-Ford EJ13	1h31m17.748s	8
2	Kimi Raikkonen	McLaren	McLaren-Mercedes MP4-17D	1h31m18.693s	4
3	Fernando Alonso	Renault F1	Renault R23	1h31m24.096s	10
4	David Coulthard	McLaren	McLaren-Mercedes MP4-17D	1h31m25.844s	2
5	Heinz-Harald Frentzen	Sauber	Sauber-Petronas C22	1h31m26.390s	14
6	Jacques Villeneuve	BAR	BAR-Honda 005	1h31m33.802s	13
7	Ralf Schumacher	Williams	Williams-BMW FW25	1h31m56.274s	6
8	Jarno Trulli	Renault F1	Renault R23	1h32m03.675s	5
9	Mark Webber	Jaguar	Jaguar-Cosworth R4	53 laps/accident	3

Pos	Driver	Team	Chassis-Engine	Result	Qual
10	Cristiano da Matta	Toyota	Toyota TF103	53 laps	18
R	Rubens Barrichello	Ferrari	Ferrari F2002	46 laps/out of fuel	1
R	Jenson Button	BAR	BAR-Honda 005	32 laps/spun off	11
R	Jos Verstappen	Minardi	Minardi-Cosworth PS03	30 laps/spun off	19
R	Michael Schumacher	Ferrari	Ferrari F2002	26 laps/spun off	7
R	Juan Pablo Montoya	Williams	Williams-BMW FW25	24 laps/spun off	9
R	Antonio Pizzonia	Jaguar	Jaguar-Cosworth R4	24 laps/spun off	17
R	Olivier Panis	Toyota	Toyota TF103	17 laps/collision	15
R	Ralph Firman	Jordan	Jordan-Ford EJ13	17 laps/suspension	16
R	Justin Wilson	Minardi	Minardi-Cosworth PS03	15 laps/spun off	20
R	Nick Heidfeld	Sauber	Sauber-Petronas C22	8 laps/engine	12

Pole: Barrichello, 1m13.807s, 130.596mph/210.175kph. Fastest lap: Barrichello, 1m22.032s, 117.502mph/189.101kph on Lap 46. Race leaders: Barrichello 1-8 & 45-46, Coulthard 9-10 & 27-44 & 47-52, Raikkonen 11-26 & 53, Fisichella 54

SAN MARINO GRAND PRIX

IMOLA • ROUND 4 • DATE: 20TH APRIL 2003
Laps: 62 • Distance: 190.43miles/305.846km • Weather: Warm but dull

Pos	Driver	Team	Chassis-Engine	Result	Qual
1	Michael Schumacher	Ferrari	Ferrari F2002	1h28m12.058s	1
2	Kimi Raikkonen	McLaren	McLaren-Mercedes MP4-17D	1h28m13.940s	6
3	Rubens Barrichello	Ferrari	Ferrari F2002	1h28m14.349s	3
4	Ralf Schumacher	Williams	Williams-BMW FW25	1h28m20.861s	2
5	David Coulthard	McLaren	McLaren-Mercedes MP4-17D	1h28m21.469s	12
6	Fernando Alonso	Renault F1	Renault R23	1h28m55.747s	8
7	Juan Pablo Montoya	Williams	Williams-BMW FW25	1h28m57.329s	4
8	Jenson Button	BAR	BAR-Honda 005	61 laps	9
9	Olivier Panis	Toyota	Toyota TF103	61 laps	10
10	Nick Heidfeld	Sauber	Sauber-Petronas C22	61 laps	11
11	Heinz-Harald Frentzen	Sauber	Sauber-Petronas C22	61 laps	14
12	Cristiano da Matta	Toyota	Toyota TF103	61 laps	13
13	Jarno Trulli	Renault F1	Renault R23	61 laps	16
14	Antonio Pizzonia	Jaguar	Jaguar-Cosworth R4	60 laps	15
15	Giancarlo Fisichella	Jordan	Jordan-Ford EJ13	57 laps/engine	17
R	Mark Webber	Jaguar	Jaguar-Cosworth R4	54 laps/halfshaft	5
R	Ralph Firman	Jordan	Jordan-Ford EJ13	51 laps/engine	19
R	Jos Verstappen	Minardi	Minardi-Cosworth PS03	38 laps/electrical	20
R	Justin Wilson	Minardi	Minardi-Cosworth PS03	23 laps	18
R	Jacques Villeneuve	BAR	BAR-Honda 005	19 laps/hydraulics	7

Pole: M Schumacher, 1m22.327s, 134.036mph/215.710kph. Fastest lap: M Schumacher, 1m22.491s, 133.769mph/215.281kph on Lap 17. Race leaders: R Schumacher 1-15, M Schumacher 16-18 & 23-49 & 51-62, Raikkonen 19-22, Barrichello 50

MICHELIN MAKES ITS MARK

Michelin made great strides to take the battle to Bridgestone. The French tyres used by Williams, McLaren, Renault, Jaguar and Toyota seemed to be at their best in hot conditions and managed to win seven of the season's 16 grands prix. Ferrari said that the Michelins had tread that was too wide when worn, but this was rejected.

SPANISH GRAND PRIX

BARCELONA-CATALUNYA • ROUND 5 • DATE: 4TH MAY 2003
Laps: 65 • Distance: 190.788miles/307.45km • Weather: Hot & bright

Pos	Driver	Team	Chassis-Engine	Result	Qual
1	Michael Schumacher	Ferrari	Ferrari F2003-GA	1h33m46.933s	1
2	Fernando Alonso	Renault F1	Renault R23	1h33m52.649s	3
3	Rubens Barrichello	Ferrari	Ferrari F2003-GA	1h34m04.934s	2
4	Juan Pablo Montoya	Williams	Williams-BMW FW25	1h34m48.955s	9
5	Ralf Schumacher	Williams	Williams-BMW FW25	64 laps	7
6	Cristiano da Matta	Toyota	Toyota TF103	64 laps	13
7	Mark Webber	Jaguar	Jaguar-Cosworth R4	64 laps	12
8	Ralph Firman	Jordan	Jordan-Ford EJ13	63 laps	15
9	Jenson Button	BAR	BAR-Honda 005	63 laps	5
10	Nick Heidfeld	Sauber	Sauber-Petronas C22	63 laps	14
11	Justin Wilson	Minardi	Minardi-Cosworth PS03	63 laps	18
12	Jos Verstappen	Minardi	Minardi-Cosworth PS03	62 laps	19
R	Giancarlo Fisichella	Jordan	Jordan-Ford EJ13	43 laps/engine	17
R	Olivier Panis	Toyota	Toyota TF103	41 laps/gearbox	6
R	Heinz-Harald Frentzen	Sauber	Sauber-Petronas C22	38 laps/suspension	10
R	David Coulthard	McLaren	McLaren-Mercedes MP4-17D	17 laps/collision	8
R	Jacques Villeneuve	BAR	BAR-Honda 005	12 laps/fire	11
R	Jarno Trulli	Renault F1	Renault R23	0 laps/collision	4
R	Antonio Pizzonia	Jaguar	Jaguar-Cosworth R4	0 laps/collision	16
R	Kimi Raikkonen	McLaren	McLaren-Mercedes MP4-17D	0 laps/collision	20

Pole: M Schumacher, 1m17.762s, 136.065mph/218.975kph. Fastest lap: Barrichello, 1m20.143s, 132.022mph/212.470kph on Lap 52. Race leaders: M Schumacher 1-18 & 21-35 & 38-49 & 51-65, Barrichello 19-20, Alonso 36-37 & 50

KIMI'S FIRST VICTORY

Kimi Raikkonen served notice of his talent by finishing sixth on his F1 debut in 2001, and he struck early in 2003, taking the first of his 21 F1 victories when his McLaren was first to the finish at the second round in Sepang. He was helped by Michael Schumacher hitting Jarno Trulli's Renault at Turn 2, which scattered the field.

AUSTRIAN GRAND PRIX

A1-RING • ROUND 6 • DATE: 18TH MAY 2003
Laps: 69 • Distance: 185.475miles/298.494km • Weather: Warm with light showers

Pos	Driver	Team	Chassis-Engine	Result	Qual
1	Michael Schumacher	Ferrari	Ferrari F2003-GA	1h24m04.888s	1
2	Kimi Raikkonen	McLaren	McLaren-Mercedes MP4-17D	1h24m08.250s	2
3	Rubens Barrichello	Ferrari	Ferrari F2003-GA	1h24m08.839s	5
4	Jenson Button	BAR	BAR-Honda 005	1h24m47.131s	7
5	David Coulthard	McLaren	McLaren-Mercedes MP4-17D	1h25m04.628s	14
6	Ralf Schumacher	Williams	Williams-BMW FW25	68 laps	10
7	Mark Webber	Jaguar	Jaguar-Cosworth R4	68 laps	17
8	Jarno Trulli	Renault F1	Renault R23	68 laps	6
9	Antonio Pizzonia	Jaguar	Jaguar-Cosworth R4	68 laps	8

Pos	Driver	Team	Chassis-Engine	Result	Qual
10	Cristiano da Matta	Toyota	Toyota TF103	68 laps	13
11	Ralph Firman	Jordan	Jordan-Ford EJ13	68 laps	16
12	Jacques Villeneuve	BAR	BAR-Honda 005	68 laps	12
13	Justin Wilson	Minardi	Minardi-Cosworth PS03	67 laps	18
R	Giancarlo Fisichella	Jordan	Jordan-Ford EJ13	60 laps/fuel system	9
R	Nick Heidfeld	Sauber	Sauber-Petronas C22	46 laps/engine	4
R	Fernando Alonso	Renault F1	Renault R23	44 laps/engine	19
R	Juan Pablo Montoya	Williams	Williams-BMW FW25	32 laps/water leak	3
R	Olivier Panis	Toyota	Toyota TF103	6 laps/suspension	11
R	Jos Verstappen	Minardi	Minardi-Cosworth PS03	0 laps/launch control	20
R	Heinz-Harald Frentzen	Sauber	Sauber-Petronas C22	0 laps/clutch	15

Pole: M Schumacher, 1m09.150s, 139.941mph/225.214kph. Fastest lap: M Schumacher, 1m08.337s, 141.606mph/227.894kph on Lap 41. Race leaders: M Schumacher 1-23 & 32-42 & 51-69, Montoya 24-31, Raikkonen 43-49, Barrichello 50

MONACO GRAND PRIX

MONTE CARLO • ROUND 7 • DATE: 1ST JUNE 2003
Laps: 78 • Distance: 161.588miles/260.52km • Weather: Hot & bright

Pos	Driver	Team	Chassis-Engine	Result	Qual
1	Juan Pablo Montoya	Williams	Williams-BMW FW25	1h42m19.010s	3
2	Kimi Raikkonen	McLaren	McLaren-Mercedes MP4-17D	1h42m19.612s	2
3	Michael Schumacher	Ferrari	Ferrari F2003-GA	1h42m20.730s	5
4	Ralf Schumacher	Williams	Williams-BMW FW25	1h42m47.528s	1
5	Fernando Alonso	Renault F1	Renault R23	1h42m55.261s	8
6	Jarno Trulli	Renault F1	Renault R23	1h42m59.982s	4
7	David Coulthard	McLaren	McLaren-Mercedes MP4-17D	1h43m00.237s	6
8	Rubens Barrichello	Ferrari	Ferrari F2003-GA	1h43m12.276s	7
9	Cristiano da Matta	Toyota	Toyota TF103	77 laps	10
10	Giancarlo Fisichella	Jordan	Jordan-Ford EJ13	77 laps	12
11	Nick Heidfeld	Sauber	Sauber-Petronas C22	76 laps	14
12	Ralph Firman	Jordan	Jordan-Ford EJ13	76 laps	16
13	Olivier Panis	Toyota	Toyota TF103	74 laps	17
R	Jacques Villeneuve	BAR	BAR-Honda 005	63 laps/engine	11
R	Justin Wilson	Minardi	Minardi-Cosworth PS03	29 laps/fuel system	19
R	Jos Verstappen	Minardi	Minardi-Cosworth PS03	28 laps/fuel system	18
R	Mark Webber	Jaguar	Jaguar-Cosworth R4	16 laps/engine	9
R	Antonio Pizzonia	Jaguar	Jaguar-Cosworth R4	10 laps/electrical	13
R	Heinz-Harald Frentzen	Sauber	Sauber-Petronas C22	0 laps/spun off	15
NS	Jenson Button	BAR	BAR-Honda 005	driver injured	-

Pole: R Schumacher, 1m15.259s, 99.275mph/159.768kph. Fastest lap: Raikkonen, 1m14.545s, 100.226mph/161.298kph on Lap 49. Race leaders: R Schumacher 1-20, Montoya 21-22 & 31-48 & 59-78, Raikkonen 23-24 & 49-52, Trulli 25-26, M Schumacher 27-30 & 53-58

JORDAN MADE TO WAIT

Jordan was given victory in the Brazilian GP five days after the race. Giancarlo Fisichella had taken the lead from Kimi Raikkonen just before the wet race was stopped following Mark Webber's huge accident in his Jaguar. On countback, the Finn was given the win, but it was proved that Fisichella had started a further lap, so the win was his.

CANADIAN GRAND PRIX

MONTREAL • ROUND 8 • DATE: 15TH JUNE 2003
Laps: 70 • Distance: 189.534miles/305.27km • Weather: Hot but dull

Pos	Driver	Team	Chassis-Engine	Result	Qual
1	Michael Schumacher	Ferrari	Ferrari F2003-GA	1h31m13.591s	3
2	Ralf Schumacher	Williams	Williams-BMW FW25	1h31m14.375s	1
3	Juan Pablo Montoya	Williams	Williams-BMW FW25	1h31m14.946s	2
4	Fernando Alonso	Renault F1	Renault R23	1h31m18.072s	4
5	Rubens Barrichello	Ferrari	Ferrari F2003-GA	1h32m17.852s	5
6	Kimi Raikkonen	McLaren	McLaren-Mercedes MP4-17D	1h32m24.093s	20
7	Mark Webber	Jaguar	Jaguar-Cosworth R4	69 laps	6
8	Olivier Panis	Toyota	Toyota TF103	69 laps	7
9	Jos Verstappen	Minardi	Minardi-Cosworth PS03	68 laps	15
10	Antonio Pizzonia	Jaguar	Jaguar-Cosworth R4	66 laps/brakes	13
11	Cristiano da Matta	Toyota	Toyota TF103	64 laps/suspension	9
R	Justin Wilson	Minardi	Minardi-Cosworth PS03	60 laps/gearbox	18
R	Jenson Button	BAR	BAR-Honda 005	51 laps/gearbox	17
R	David Coulthard	McLaren	McLaren-Mercedes MP4-17D	47 laps/gearbox	11
R	Nick Heidfeld	Sauber	Sauber-Petronas C22	47 laps/engine	12
R	Jarno Trulli	Renault F1	Renault R23	22 laps/collision	8
R	Giancarlo Fisichella	Jordan	Jordan-Ford EJ13	20 laps/gearbox	16
R	Ralph Firman	Jordan	Jordan-Ford EJ13	20 laps/oil leak	19
R	Jacques Villeneuve	BAR	BAR-Honda 005	14 laps/brakes	14
R	Heinz-Harald Frentzen	Sauber	Sauber-Petronas C22	6 laps/electrical	10

Pole: R Schumacher, 1m15.529s, 129.159mph/207.861kph. Fastest lap: Alonso, 1m16.040s, 128.291mph/206.465kph on Lap 53. Race leaders: R Schumacher 1-19, M Schumacher 20 & 26-48 & 55-70, Alonso 21-25 & 49-54

ALONSO IS YOUNGEST WINNER

Fernando Alonso demonstrated that a year out testing for the Renault team after his maiden season with Minardi in 2001 did him no harm. After taking pole for the second round, he became the then-youngest grand prix winner in the 13th round when he triumphed in Hungary at the age of 22 years and 26 days.

EUROPEAN GRAND PRIX

NURBURGRING • ROUND 9 • DATE: 29TH JUNE 2003
Laps: 60 • Distance: 191.437miles/308.88km • Weather: Hot but dull

Pos	Driver	Team	Chassis-Engine	Result	Qual
1	Ralf Schumacher	Williams	Williams-BMW FW25	1h34m43.622s	3
2	Juan Pablo Montoya	Williams	Williams-BMW FW25	1h35m00.443s	4
3	Rubens Barrichello	Ferrari	Ferrari F2003-GA	1h35m23.295s	5
4	Fernando Alonso	Renault F1	Renault R23	1h35m49.353s	8
5	Michael Schumacher	Ferrari	Ferrari F2003-GA	1h35m49.784s	2
6	Mark Webber	Jaguar	Jaguar-Cosworth R4	59 laps	11
7	Jenson Button	BAR	BAR-Honda 005	59 laps	12
8	Nick Heidfeld	Sauber	Sauber-Petronas C22	59 laps	20

Pos	Driver	Team	Chassis-Engine	Result	Qual
9	Heinz-Harald Frentzen	Sauber	Sauber-Petronas C22	59 laps	15
10	Antonio Pizzonia	Jaguar	Jaguar-Cosworth R4	59 laps	16
11	Ralph Firman	Jordan	Jordan-Ford EJ13	58 laps	14
12	Giancarlo Fisichella	Jordan	Jordan-Ford EJ13	58 laps	13
13	Justin Wilson	Minardi	Minardi-Cosworth PS03	58 laps	19
14	Jos Verstappen	Minardi	Minardi-Cosworth PS03	57 laps	18
15	David Coulthard	McLaren	McLaren-Mercedes MP4-17D	56 laps/spun off	9
R	Cristiano da Matta	Toyota	Toyota TF103	53 laps/engine	10
R	Jacques Villeneuve	BAR	BAR-Honda 005	51 laps/gearbox	17
R	Jarno Trulli	Renault F1	Renault R23	37 laps/fuel pump	6
R	Olivier Panis	Toyota	Toyota TF103	37 laps/brakes	7
R	Kimi Raikkonen	McLaren	McLaren-Mercedes MP4-17D	25 laps/engine	1

Pole: Raikkonen, 1m31.523s, 125.823mph/202.493kph. Fastest lap: Raikkonen, 1m32.621s, 124.331mph/200.092kph on Lap 14. Race leaders: Raikkonen 1-16 & 22-25, R Schumacher 17-21 & 26-60

FRENCH GRAND PRIX

MAGNY-COURS • ROUND 10 • DATE: 6TH JULY 2003
Laps: 70 • Distance: 191.430miles/308.77km • Weather: Hot & bright

Pos	Driver	Team	Chassis-Engine	Result	Qual
1	Ralf Schumacher	Williams	Williams-BMW FW25	1h30m49.213s	1
2	Juan Pablo Montoya	Williams	Williams-BMW FW25	1h31m03.026s	2
3	Michael Schumacher	Ferrari	Ferrari F2003-GA	1h31m08.781s	3
4	Kimi Raikkonen	McLaren	McLaren-Mercedes MP4-17D	1h31m27.260s	4
5	David Coulthard	McLaren	McLaren-Mercedes MP4-17D	1h31m29.502s	5
6	Mark Webber	Jaguar	Jaguar-Cosworth R4	1h31m55.593s	9
7	Rubens Barrichello	Ferrari	Ferrari F2003-GA	69 laps	8
8	Olivier Panis	Toyota	Toyota TF103	69 laps	10
9	Jacques Villeneuve	BAR	BAR-Honda 005	69 laps	12
10	Antonio Pizzonia	Jaguar	Jaguar-Cosworth R4	69 laps	11
11	Cristiano da Matta	Toyota	Toyota TF103	69 laps	13
12	Heinz-Harald Frentzen	Sauber	Sauber-Petronas C22	68 laps	16
13	Nick Heidfeld	Sauber	Sauber-Petronas C22	68 laps	15
14	Justin Wilson	Minardi	Minardi-Cosworth PS03	67 laps	20
15	Ralph Firman	Jordan	Jordan-Ford EJ13	67 laps	18
16	Jos Verstappen	Minardi	Minardi-Cosworth PS03	66 laps	19
R	Jarno Trulli	Renault F1	Renault R23	45 laps/engine	6
R	Fernando Alonso	Renault F1	Renault R23	43 laps/engine	7
R	Giancarlo Fisichella	Jordan	Jordan-Ford EJ13	42 laps/engine	17
R	Jenson Button	BAR	BAR-Honda 005	21 laps/out of fuel	14

Pole: R Schumacher, 1m15.019s, 131.528mph/211.674kph. Fastest lap: Montoya, 1m15.512s, 130.669mph/210.292kph on Lap 36. Race leaders: R Schumacher 1-70

NEVER QUITE READY

The McLaren MP4-18 became one of F1's many anomalies when its race debut was delayed, and then delayed again, as the radical new design that pushed new boundaries in the team's attempt to tackle dominant Ferrari never appeared quite ready to go racing. Instead, the interim MP4-17D was kept on all the way through to the end of the year.

BRITISH GRAND PRIX

SILVERSTONE • ROUND 11 • DATE: 20TH JULY 2003
Laps: 60 • Distance: 191.410miles/308.46km • Weather: Warm & bright

Pos	Driver	Team	Chassis-Engine	Result	Qual
1	Rubens Barrichello	Ferrari	Ferrari F2003-GA	1h28m37.554s	1
2	Juan Pablo Montoya	Williams	Williams-BMW FW25	1h28m43.016s	7
3	Kimi Raikkonen	McLaren	McLaren-Mercedes MP4-17D	1h28m48.210s	3
4	Michael Schumacher	Ferrari	Ferrari F2003-GA	1h29m03.202s	5
5	David Coulthard	McLaren	McLaren-Mercedes MP4-17D	1h29m14.381s	12
6	Jarno Trulli	Renault F1	Renault R23B	1h29m20.621s	2
7	Cristiano da Matta	Toyota	Toyota TF103	1h29m22.639s	6
8	Jenson Button	BAR	BAR-Honda 005	1h29m23.032s	20
9	Ralf Schumacher	Williams	Williams-BMW FW25	1h29m35.586s	4
10	Jacques Villeneuve	BAR	BAR-Honda 005	1h29m41.123s	9
11	Olivier Panis	Toyota	Toyota TF103	1h29m42.761s	13
12	Heinz-Harald Frentzen	Sauber	Sauber-Petronas C22	1h29m43.118s	14
13	Ralph Firman	Jordan	Jordan-Ford EJ13	59 laps	17
14	Mark Webber	Jaguar	Jaguar-Cosworth R4	59 laps	11
15	Jos Verstappen	Minardi	Minardi-Cosworth PS03	58 laps	19
16	Justin Wilson	Minardi	Minardi-Cosworth PS03	58 laps	18
17	Nick Heidfeld	Sauber	Sauber-Petronas C22	58 laps	16
R	Fernando Alonso	Renault F1	Renault R23B	52 laps/gearbox	8
R	Giancarlo Fisichella	Jordan	Jordan-Ford EJ13	44 laps/suspension	15
R	Antonio Pizzonia	Jaguar	Jaguar-Cosworth R4	32 laps/engine	10

Pole: Barrichello, 1m21.209s, 141.611mph/227.900kph. Fastest lap: Barrichello, 1m22.236s, 139.842mph/225.054kph on Lap 38. Race leaders: Trulli 1-12, da Matta 13-29, Raikkonen 30-35 & 40-41, Barrichello 36-39 & 42-60

A SECOND HUNGARIAN

The first grand prix, the French GP of 1906 at Le Mans, was won by a Hungarian driver, Ferenc Szisz, but Hungary fans had to wait 97 years for another to come along. This was tail-end F3000 driver Zsolt Baumgartner, who was given his chance for Jordan when Ralph Firman was injured, fittingly at Baumgartner's home race.

GERMAN GRAND PRIX

HOCKENHEIM • ROUND 12 • DATE: 3RD AUGUST 2003
Laps: 67 • Distance: 190.424miles/306.458km • Weather: Very hot & bright

Pos	Driver	Team	Chassis-Engine	Result	Qual
1	Juan Pablo Montoya	Williams	Williams-BMW FW25	1h28m48.769s	1
2	David Coulthard	McLaren	McLaren-Mercedes MP4-17D	1h29m54.228s	10
3	Jarno Trulli	Renault F1	Renault R23B	1h29m57.829s	4
4	Fernando Alonso	Renault F1	Renault R23B	1h29m58.113s	8
5	Olivier Panis	Toyota	Toyota TF103	66 laps	7
6	Cristiano da Matta	Toyota	Toyota TF103	66 laps	9
7	Michael Schumacher	Ferrari	Ferrari F2003-GA	66 laps	6
8	Jenson Button	BAR	BAR-Honda 005	66 laps	17
9	Jacques Villeneuve	BAR	BAR-Honda 005	65 laps	13
10	Nick Heidfeld	Sauber	Sauber-Petronas C22	65 laps	15

Pos	Driver	Team	Chassis-Engine	Result	Qual
11	Mark Webber	Jaguar	Jaguar-Cosworth R4	64 laps/spun off	11
12	Nicolas Kiesa	Minardi	Minardi-Cosworth PS03	62 laps	20
13	Giancarlo Fisichella	Jordan	Jordan-Ford EJ13	60 laps/water leak	12
R	Jos Verstappen	Minardi	Minardi-Cosworth PS03	23 laps/hydraulics	19
R	Justin Wilson	Jaguar	Jaguar-Cosworth R4	6 laps/gearbox	16
R	Ralf Schumacher	Williams	Williams-BMW FW25	1 lap/collision	2
R	Heinz-Harald Frentzen	Sauber	Sauber-Petronas C22	1 lap/collision	14
R	Rubens Barrichello	Ferrari	Ferrari F2003-GA	0 laps/collision	3
R	Kimi Raikkonen	McLaren	McLaren-Mercedes MP4-17D	0 laps/collision	5
R	Ralph Firman	Jordan	Jordan-Ford EJ13	0 laps/collision	18

Pole: Montoya, 1m15.167s, 136.120mph/219.064kph. Fastest lap: Montoya, 1m14.917s, 136.574mph/219.795kph on Lap 14. Race leaders: Montoya 1-17 & 19-67, Alonso 18

NEW CIRCUITS

No new circuits were introduced, but there were notable changes. The first of these was Magny-Cours being given a final corner complex that extended further down the slope before joining the start/finish straight through a chicane. At the Hungaroring, the straight after Turn 11 was extended and the hairpin behind the paddock tightened.

HUNGARIAN GRAND PRIX

HUNGARORING • ROUND 13 • DATE: 24TH AUGUST 2003
Laps: 70 • Distance: 190.181miles/306.67km • Weather: Very hot & bright

Pos	Driver	Team	Chassis-Engine	Result	Qual
1	Fernando Alonso	Renault F1	Renault R23B	1h39m01.460s	1
2	Kimi Raikkonen	McLaren	McLaren-Mercedes MP4-17D	1h39m18.228s	7
3	Juan Pablo Montoya	Williams	Williams-BMW FW25	1h39m35.997s	4
4	Ralf Schumacher	Williams	Williams-BMW FW25	1h39m37.080s	2
5	David Coulthard	McLaren	McLaren-Mercedes MP4-17D	1h39m57.995s	9
6	Mark Webber	Jaguar	Jaguar-Cosworth R4	1h40m14.103s	3
7	Jarno Trulli	Renault F1	Renault R23B	69 laps	6
8	Michael Schumacher	Ferrari	Ferrari F2003-GA	69 laps	8
9	Nick Heidfeld	Sauber	Sauber-Petronas C22	69 laps	11
10	Jenson Button	BAR	BAR-Honda 005	69 laps	14
11	Cristiano da Matta	Toyota	Toyota TF103	68 laps	15
12	Jos Verstappen	Minardi	Minardi-Cosworth PS03	67 laps	18
13	Nicolas Kiesa	Minardi	Minardi-Cosworth PS03	66 laps	20
R	Heinz-Harald Frentzen	Sauber	Sauber-Petronas C22	47 laps/out of fuel	17
R	Justin Wilson	Jaguar	Jaguar-Cosworth R4	42 laps/engine	12
R	Zsolt Baumgartner	Jordan	Jordan-Ford EJ13	34 laps/engine	19
R	Olivier Panis	Toyota	Toyota TF103	33 laps/gearbox	10
R	Giancarlo Fisichella	Jordan	Jordan-Ford EJ13	28 laps/engine	13
R	Rubens Barrichello	Ferrari	Ferrari F2003-GA	19 laps/suspension	5
R	Jacques Villeneuve	BAR	BAR-Honda 005	14 laps/hydraulics	16
NS	Ralph Firman	Jordan	Jordan-Ford EJ13	driver injured	-

Pole: Alonso, 1m21.688s, 119.968mph/193.071kph. Fastest lap: Montoya, 1m22.095s, 119.374mph/192.114kph on Lap 37. Race leaders: Alonso 1-13 & 15-70, Raikkonen 14

NEW DRIVERS

Cristiano da Matta was the best of the six newcomers. Not only did he lead 17 laps of the British GP for Toyota, but he also claimed two other sixth places. British novices Ralph Firman and Justin Wilson took an eighth place finish apiece for Jordan and Jaguar respectively, with Antonio Pizzonia managing a ninth for Jaguar.

ITALIAN GRAND PRIX

MONZA • ROUND 14 • DATE: 14TH SEPTEMBER 2003
Laps: 53 • Distance: 190.778miles/307.029km • Weather: Hot & bright

Pos	Driver	Team	Chassis-Engine	Result	Qual
1	Michael Schumacher	Ferrari	Ferrari F2003-GA	1h14m19.838s	1
2	Juan Pablo Montoya	Williams	Williams-BMW FW25	1h14m25.132s	2
3	Rubens Barrichello	Ferrari	Ferrari F2003-GA	1h14m31.673s	3
4	Kimi Raikkonen	McLaren	McLaren-Mercedes MP4-17D	1h14m32.672s	4
5	Marc Gene	Williams	Williams-BMW FW25	1h14m47.729s	5
6	Jacques Villeneuve	BAR	BAR-Honda 005	52 laps	10
7	Mark Webber	Jaguar	Jaguar-Cosworth R4	52 laps	11
8	Fernando Alonso	Renault F1	Renault R23B	52 laps	20
9	Nick Heidfeld	Sauber	Sauber-Petronas C22	52 laps	16
10	Giancarlo Fisichella	Jordan	Jordan-Ford EJ13	52 laps	13
11	Zsolt Baumgartner	Jordan	Jordan-Ford EJ13	51 laps	18
12	Nicolas Kiesa	Minardi	Minardi-Cosworth PS03	51 laps	19
13	Heinz-Harald Frentzen	Sauber	Sauber-Petronas C22	50 laps/transmission	14
R	David Coulthard	McLaren	McLaren-Mercedes MP4-17D	45 laps/fuel pressure	8
R	Olivier Panis	Toyota	Toyota TF103	35 laps/brakes	9
R	Jos Verstappen	Minardi	Minardi-Cosworth PS03	27 laps/oil leak	17
R	Jenson Button	BAR	BAR-Honda 005	24 laps/gearbox	7
R	Cristiano da Matta	Toyota	Toyota TF103	3 laps/puncture	12
R	Justin Wilson	Jaguar	Jaguar-Cosworth R4	2 laps/transmission	15
R	Jarno Trulli	Renault F1	Renault R23B	0 laps/hydraulics	6
NS	Ralf Schumacher	Williams	Williams-BMW FW25	driver injured	-

Pole: M Schumacher, 1m20.963s, 160.055mph/257.584kph. Fastest lap: M Schumacher, 1m21.832s, 158.355mph/254.848kph on Lap 14. Race leaders: M Schumacher 1-15 & 17-53, Montoya 16

UNITED STATES GRAND PRIX

INDIANAPOLIS MOTOR SPEEDWAY • ROUND 15 • DATE: 28TH SEPTEMBER 2003
Laps: 73 • Distance: 190.149miles/306.016km • Weather: Warm but dull, rain later

Pos	Driver	Team	Chassis-Engine	Result	Qual
1	Michael Schumacher	Ferrari	Ferrari F2003-GA	1h33m35.997s	7
2	Kimi Raikkonen	McLaren	McLaren-Mercedes MP4-17D	1h33m54.255s	1
3	Heinz-Harald Frentzen	Sauber	Sauber-Petronas C22	1h34m13.961s	15
4	Jarno Trulli	Renault F1	Renault R23B	1h34m24.326s	10
5	Nick Heidfeld	Sauber	Sauber-Petronas C22	1h34m32.400s	13
6	Juan Pablo Montoya	Williams	Williams-BMW FW25	72 laps	4
7	Giancarlo Fisichella	Jordan	Jordan-Ford EJ13	72 laps	17
8	Justin Wilson	Jaguar	Jaguar-Cosworth R4	71 laps	16

Pos	Driver	Team	Chassis-Engine	Result	Qual
9	Cristiano da Matta	Toyota	Toyota TF103	71 laps	9
10	Jos Verstappen	Minardi	Minardi-Cosworth PS03	69 laps	19
11	Nicolas Kiesa	Minardi	Minardi-Cosworth PS03	69 laps	20
R	Jacques Villeneuve	BAR	BAR-Honda 005	63 laps/engine	12
R	Ralph Firman	Jordan	Jordan-Ford EJ13	48 laps/spun off	18
R	David Coulthard	McLaren	McLaren-Mercedes MP4-17D	45 laps/gearbox	8
R	Fernando Alonso	Renault F1	Renault R23B	44 laps/engine	6
R	Jenson Button	BAR	BAR-Honda 005	41 laps/engine	11
R	Olivier Panis	Toyota	Toyota TF103	27 laps/spun off	3
R	Ralf Schumacher	Williams	Williams-BMW FW25	21 laps/spun off	5
R	Mark Webber	Jaguar	Jaguar-Cosworth R4	21 laps/spun off	14
R	Rubens Barrichello	Ferrari	Ferrari F2003-GA	2 laps/collision	2

Pole: Raikkonen, 1m11.670s, 130.839mph/210.565kph. Fastest lap: M Schumacher, 1m11.473s, 131.199mph/211.145kph on Lap 13. Race leaders: Raikkonen 1-18, M Schumacher 19 & 38-47 & 49-73, Webber 20-21, Coulthard 22, Button 23-37, Frentzen 48

JAPANESE GRAND PRIX

SUZUKA • ROUND 16 • DATE: 12TH OCTOBER 2003
Laps: 53 • Distance: 191.240miles/307.771km • Weather: Warm but dull, rain later

Pos	Driver	Team	Chassis-Engine	Result	Qual
1	Rubens Barrichello	Ferrari	Ferrari F2003-GA	1h25m11.743s	1
2	Kimi Raikkonen	McLaren	McLaren-Mercedes MP4-17D	1h25m22.828s	8
3	David Coulthard	McLaren	McLaren-Mercedes MP4-17D	1h25m23.357s	7
4	Jenson Button	BAR	BAR-Honda 005	1h25m44.849s	9
5	Jarno Trulli	Renault F1	Renault R23B	1h25m46.012s	19
6	Takuma Sato	BAR	BAR-Honda 005	1h26m03.435s	13
7	Cristiano da Matta	Toyota	Toyota TF103	1h26m08.537s	3
8	Michael Schumacher	Ferrari	Ferrari F2003-GA	1h26m11.230s	14
9	Nick Heidfeld	Sauber	Sauber-Petronas C22	1h26m11.902s	11
10	Olivier Panis	Toyota	Toyota TF103	1h26m13.587s	4
11	Mark Webber	Jaguar	Jaguar-Cosworth R4	1h26m22.748s	6
12	Ralf Schumacher	Williams	Williams-BMW FW25	52 laps	20
13	Justin Wilson	Jaguar	Jaguar-Cosworth R4	52 laps	10
14	Ralph Firman	Jordan	Jordan-Ford EJ13	51 laps	15
15	Jos Verstappen	Minardi	Minardi-Cosworth PS03	51 laps	17
16	Nicolas Kiesa	Minardi	Minardi-Cosworth PS03	50 laps	18
R	Giancarlo Fisichella	Jordan	Jordan-Ford EJ13	33 laps/out of fuel	16
R	Fernando Alonso	Renault F1	Renault R23B	17 laps/engine	5
R	Juan Pablo Montoya	Williams	Williams-BMW FW25	9 laps/hydraulics	2
R	Heinz-Harald Frentzen	Sauber	Sauber-Petronas C22	9 laps/engine	12
W	Jacques Villeneuve	BAR	BAR-Honda 005	driver quit	-

Pole: Barrichello, 1m31.713s, 141.636mph/227.941kph. Fastest lap: R Schumacher, 1m33.408s, 139.066mph/223.805kph on Lap 43. Race leaders: Montoya 1-8, Barrichello 9-12 & 17-40 & 42-53, Raikkonen 13, Button 14-16, Coulthard 41

WORLD DRIVERS' CHAMPIONSHIP FINAL RESULTS

Pos	Driver	Nat	Car-Engine	R1	R2	R3	R4	R5	R6
1	Michael Schumacher	DEU	Ferrari F2002	4P	6F	R	1PF	-	-
			Ferrari F2003-GA	-	-	-	-	1P	1PF
2	Kimi Raikkonen	FIN	McLaren-Mercedes MP4-17D	3F	1	2	2	R	2
3	Juan Pablo Montoya	COL	Williams-BMW FW25	2	12	R	7	4	R
4	Rubens Barrichello	BRA	Ferrari F2002	R	2	RPF	3	-	-
			Ferrari F2003-GA	-	-	-	-	3F	3
5	Ralf Schumacher	DEU	Williams-BMW FW25	8	4	7	4	5	6
6	Fernando Alonso	ESP	Renault R23	7	3P	3	6	2	R
			Renault R23B	-	-	-	-	-	-
7	David Coulthard	GBR	McLaren-Mercedes MP4-17D	1	R	4	5	R	5
8	Jarno Trulli	ITA	Renault R23	5	5	8	13	R	8
			Renault R23B	-	-	-	-	-	-
9	Jenson Button	GBR	BAR-Honda 005	10	7	R	8	9	4
10	Mark Webber	AUS	Jaguar-Cosworth R4	R	R	9	R	7	7
11	Heinz-Harald Frentzen	DEU	Sauber-Petronas C22	6	9	5	11	R	R
12	Giancarlo Fisichella	ITA	Jordan-Ford EJ13	12	R	1	15	R	R
13	Cristiano da Matta	BRA	Toyota TF103	R	11	10	12	6	10
14	Nick Heidfeld	DEU	Sauber-Petronas C22	R	8	R	10	10	R
15	Olivier Panis	FRA	Toyota TF103	R	R	R	9	R	R
16	Jacques Villeneuve	CAN	BAR-Honda 005	9	NS	6	R	R	12
17	Marc Gene	ESP	Williams-BMW FW25	-	-	-	-	-	-
18	Takuma Sato	JPN	BAR-Honda 005	-	-	-	-	-	-
19	Ralph Firman	GBR	Jordan-Ford EJ13	R	10	R	R	8	11
20	Justin Wilson	GBR	Minardi-Cosworth PS03	R	R	R	R	11	13
			Jaguar-Cosworth R4	-	-	-	-	-	-
21	Antonio Pizzonia	BRA	Jaguar-Cosworth R4	13	R	R	14	R	9
22	Jos Verstappen	NLD	Minardi-Cosworth PS03	11	13	R	R	12	R
23	Nicolas Kiesa	DNK	Minardi-Cosworth PS03	-	-	-	-	-	-
24	Zsolt Baumgartner	HUN	Jordan-Ford EJ13	-	-	-	-	-	-

Pos	Driver	R7	R8	R9	R10	R11	R12	R13	R14	R15	R16	Total
1	M Schumacher	-	-	-	-	-	-	-	-	-	-	93
		3	1	5	3	4	7	8	1PF	1F	8	
2	Raikkonen	2F	6	RPF	4	3	R	2	4	2P	2	91
3	Montoya	1	3	2	2F	2	1PF	3F	2	6	R	82
4	Barrichello	-	-	-	-	-	-	-	-	-	-	65
		8	5	3	7	1PF	R	R	3	R	1P	
5	R Schumacher	4P	2P	1	1P	9	R	4	NS	R	12F	58
6	Alonso	5	4F	4	R	-	-	-	-	-	-	55
		-	-	-	-	R	4	1P	8	R	R	
7	Coulthard	7	R	15	5	5	2	5	R	R	3	51
8	Trulli	6	R	R	R	-	-	-	-	-	-	33
		-	-	-	-	6	3	7	R	4	5	
9	Button	NS	R	7	R	8	8	10	R	R	4	17
10	Webber	R	7	6	6	14	11	6	7	R	11	17
11	Frentzen	R	R	9	12	12	R	R	13	3	R	13
12	Fisichella	10	R	12	R	R	13	R	10	7	R	12
13	da Matta	9	11	R	11	7	6	11	R	9	7	10
14	Heidfeld	11	R	8	13	17	10	9	9	5	9	6
15	Panis	13	8	R	8	11	5	R	R	R	10	6
16	Villeneuve	R	R	R	9	10	9	R	6	R	-	6
17	Gene	-	-	-	-	-	-	-	5	-	-	4
18	Sato	-	-	-	-	-	-	-	-	-	6	3

Pos	Driver	R7	R8	R9	R10	R11	R12	R13	R14	R15	R16	Total
19	Firman	12	R	11	15	13	R	NS	-	R	14	1
20	Wilson	R	R	13	14	16	-	-	-	-	-	1
		-	-	-	-	-	R	R	R	8	13	
21	Pizzonia	R	10	10	10	R	-	-	-	-	-	0
22	Verstappen	R	9	14	16	15	R	12	R	10	15	0
23	Kiesa	-	-	-	-	-	12	13	12	11	16	0
24	Baumgartner	-	-	-	-	-	T	R	11	-	-	0

WORLD CONSTRUCTORS' CHAMPIONSHIP FINAL RESULTS

Pos	Team-Engine	R1	R2	R3	R4	R5	R6	R7	R8	R9
1	Ferrari	4/R	2/6	R/R	1/3	1/3	1/3	3/8	1/5	3/5
2	Williams-BMW	2/8	4/12	7/R	4/7	4/5	6/R	1/4	2/3	1/2
3	McLaren-Mercedes	1/3	1/R	2/4	2/5	R/R	2/5	2/7	6/R	15/R
4	Renault F1	5/7	3/5	3/8	6/13	2/R	8/R	5/6	4/R	4/R
5	BAR-Honda	9/10	7/NS	6/R	8/R	9/R	4/12	R/NS	R/R	7/R
6	Sauber-Petronas	6/R	8/9	5/R	10/11	10/R	R/NS	11/R	R/R	8/9
7	Jaguar-Cosworth	13/R	R/R	9/R	14/R	7/R	7/9	R/R	7/10	6/10
8	Toyota	R/R	11/R	10/R	9/12	6/R	10/R	9/13	8/11	R/R
9	Jordan-Ford	12/R	10/R	1/R	15/R	8/R	11/R	10/12	R/R	11/12
10	Minardi-Cosworth	11/R	13/R	R/R	R/R	11/12	13/R	R/R	9/R	13/14

Pos	Team-Engine	R10	R11	R12	R13	R14	R15	R16	Total
1	Ferrari	3/7	1/4	7/R	8/R	1/3	1/R	1/8	158
2	Williams-BMW	1/2	2/9	1/R	3/4	2/5	6/R	12/R	144
3	McLaren-Mercedes	4/5	3/5	2/R	2/5	4/R	2/R	2/3	142
4	Renault F1	R/R	6/R	3/4	1/7	8/R	4/R	5/R	88
5	BAR-Honda	9/R	8/10	8/9	10/R	6/R	R/R	4/6	26
6	Sauber-Petronas	12/13	12/17	10/R	9/R	9/13	3/5	9/R	19
7	Jaguar-Cosworth	6/10	14/R	11/R	6/R	7/R	8/R	11/13	18
8	Toyota	8/11	7/11	5/6	11/R	R/R	9/R	7/10	16
9	Jordan-Ford	15/R	13/R	13/R	R/R	10/11	7/R	14/R	13
10	Minardi-Cosworth	14/16	15/16	12/R	12/13	12/R	10/11	15/16	0

SYMBOLS AND GRAND PRIX KEY

Round 1	Australian GP
Round 2	Malaysian GP
Round 3	Brazilian GP
Round 4	San Marino GP
Round 5	Spanish GP
Round 6	Austrian GP
Round 7	Monaco GP
Round 8	Canadian GP
Round 9	European GP
Round 10	French GP
Round 11	British GP
Round 12	German GP
Round 13	Hungarian GP
Round 14	Italian GP
Round 15	United States GP
Round 16	Japanese GP

SCORING

1st	10 points
2nd	8 points
3rd	6 points
4th	5 points
5th	4 points
6th	3 points
7th	2 points
8th	1 point

DNPQ DID NOT PRE-QUALIFY   DNQ DID NOT QUALIFY   DQ DISQUALIFIED   EX EXCLUDED
F FASTEST LAP   NC NOT CLASSIFIED   NS NON-STARTER   P POLE POSITION   R RETIRED

SEASON SUMMARY

Michael Schumacher won a record seventh F1 title in a year in which tyre supplier Bridgestone raised its game to give his Ferrari a performance edge over Michelin-shod Williams and McLaren. Surprisingly, after their strong challenges in 2003, these two teams fell behind BAR as this much newer team had its best-ever year to end up second overall. Its lead driver, Jenson Button, pushed Schumacher and Rubens Barrichello the most often, albeit never finishing higher than second. Williams and McLaren were inconsistent in their challenge, but at least they were strong at the end of the year – unlike Renault, which faded.

AUSTRALIAN GRAND PRIX

ALBERT PARK • ROUND 1 • DATE: 7TH MARCH 2004
Laps: 58 • Distance: 191.117miles/307.574km • Weather: Warm & bright

Pos	Driver	Team	Chassis-Engine	Result	Qual
1	Michael Schumacher	Ferrari	Ferrari F2004	1h24m15.757s	1
2	Rubens Barrichello	Ferrari	Ferrari F2004	1h24m29.362s	2
3	Fernando Alonso	Renault F1	Renault R24	1h24m50.430s	5
4	Ralf Schumacher	Williams	Williams-BMW FW26	1h25m16.180s	8
5	Juan Pablo Montoya	Williams	Williams-BMW FW26	1h25m24.293s	3
6	Jenson Button	BAR	BAR-Honda 006	1h25m26.355s	4
7	Jarno Trulli	Renault F1	Renault R24	57 laps	9
8	David Coulthard	McLaren	McLaren-Mercedes MP4-19	57 laps	12
9	Takuma Sato	BAR	BAR-Honda 006	57 laps	7
10	Giancarlo Fisichella	Sauber	Sauber-Petronas C23	57 laps	14
11	Christian Klien	Jaguar	Jaguar-Cosworth R5	56 laps	19
12	Cristiano da Matta	Toyota	Toyota TF104	56 laps	13
13	Olivier Panis	Toyota	Toyota TF104	56 laps	18
14	Giorgio Pantano	Jordan	Jordan-Ford EJ14	55 laps	16
R	Felipe Massa	Sauber	Sauber-Petronas C23	44 laps/engine	11
R	Nick Heidfeld	Jordan	Jordan-Ford EJ14	43 laps/clutch	15
NC	Gianmaria Bruni	Minardi	Minardi-Cosworth PS04B	43 laps	20
R	Mark Webber	Jaguar	Jaguar-Cosworth R5	29 laps/gearbox	6
R	Zsolt Baumgartner	Minardi	Minardi-Cosworth PS04B	13 laps/engine	17
R	Kimi Raikkonen	McLaren	McLaren-Mercedes MP4-19	9 laps/engine	10

Pole: M Schumacher, 1m24.408s, 140.537mph/226.172kph. Fastest lap: M Schumacher, 1m24.125s, 141.010mph/226.933kph on Lap 29. Race leaders: M Schumacher 1-58

A NEW FORMAT

The format of a grand prix meeting was changed. Fridays had two one-hour practice sessions before Saturday offered two 45-minute practices followed by two one-hour qualifying sessions separated by a break of just two minutes. The starting order for qualifying was determined by a driver's finishing position in the previous race for the first session, then by a reversal of the session one order for the second.

MALAYSIAN GRAND PRIX

SEPANG • ROUND 2 • DATE: 21ST MARCH 2004
Laps: 56 • Distance: 192.878miles/310.408km • Weather: Very hot but dull

Pos	Driver	Team	Chassis-Engine	Result	Qual
1	Michael Schumacher	Ferrari	Ferrari F2004	1h31m07.490s	1
2	Juan Pablo Montoya	Williams	Williams-BMW FW26	1h31m12.512s	4
3	Jenson Button	BAR	BAR-Honda 006	1h31m19.058s	6
4	Rubens Barrichello	Ferrari	Ferrari F2004	1h31m21.106s	3
5	Jarno Trulli	Renault F1	Renault R24	1h31m44.850s	8
6	David Coulthard	McLaren	McLaren-Mercedes MP4-19	1h32m00.588s	9
7	Fernando Alonso	Renault F1	Renault R24	1h32m15.367s	19
8	Felipe Massa	Sauber	Sauber-Petronas C23	55 laps	11
9	Cristiano da Matta	Toyota	Toyota TF104	55 laps	10
10	Christian Klien	Jaguar	Jaguar-Cosworth R5	55 laps	13
11	Giancarlo Fisichella	Sauber	Sauber-Petronas C23	55 laps	12
12	Olivier Panis	Toyota	Toyota TF104	55 laps	14
13	Giorgio Pantano *	Jordan	Jordan-Ford EJ14	54 laps	18
14	Gianmaria Bruni	Minardi	Minardi-Cosworth PS04B	53 laps	16
15	Takuma Sato	BAR	BAR-Honda 006	52 laps/engine	20
16	Zsolt Baumgartner	Minardi	Minardi-Cosworth PS04B	52 laps	17
R	Kimi Raikkonen	McLaren	McLaren-Mercedes MP4-19	40 laps/transmission	5
R	Nick Heidfeld	Jordan	Jordan-Ford EJ14	34 laps/gearbox	15
R	Ralf Schumacher	Williams	Williams-BMW FW26	27 laps/engine	7
R	Mark Webber	Jaguar	Jaguar-Cosworth R5	23 laps/spun off	2

Pole: M Schumacher, 1m33.074s, 133.220mph/214.397kph. Fastest lap: Montoya, 1m34.223s, 131.595mph/211.782kph on Lap 28. Race leaders: M Schumacher 1-9 & 13-26 & 28-56, Montoya 10-12, Barrichello 27

* 1-place grid penalty for switching to spare car

UNLUCKY 13

Ralf Schumacher's season was interrupted by a high-impact shunt at the Indianapolis Motor Speedway. He lost control of his Williams on the way into the final corner of the anticlockwise circuit, the banked Turn 13. Schumacher missed the next six races while he recovered from two cracked vertebrae, and was replaced by Marc Gene, then Antonio Pizzonia.

BAHRAIN GRAND PRIX

SAKHIR • ROUND 3 • DATE: 4TH APRIL 2004
Laps: 57 • Distance: 191.860miles/308.769km • Weather: Very hot but dull, light rain

Pos	Driver	Team	Chassis-Engine	Result	Qual
1	Michael Schumacher	Ferrari	Ferrari F2004	1h28m34.875s	1
2	Rubens Barrichello	Ferrari	Ferrari F2004	1h28m36.242s	2
3	Jenson Button	BAR	BAR-Honda 006	1h29m01.562s	6
4	Jarno Trulli	Renault F1	Renault R24	1h29m07.089s	7
5	Takuma Sato	BAR	BAR-Honda 006	1h29m27.335s	5
6	Fernando Alonso	Renault F1	Renault R24	1h29m28.031s	16
7	Ralf Schumacher	Williams	Williams-BMW FW26	1h29m33.030s	4
8	Mark Webber	Jaguar	Jaguar-Cosworth R5	56 laps	14
9	Olivier Panis	Toyota	Toyota TF104	56 laps	8
10	Cristiano da Matta	Toyota	Toyota TF104	56 laps	9

Pos	Driver	Team	Chassis-Engine	Result	Qual
11	Giancarlo Fisichella	Sauber	Sauber-Petronas C23	56 laps	11
12	Felipe Massa	Sauber	Sauber-Petronas C23	56 laps	13
13	Juan Pablo Montoya	Williams	Williams-BMW FW26	56 laps	3
14	Christian Klien	Jaguar	Jaguar-Cosworth R5	56 laps	12
15	Nick Heidfeld *	Jordan	Jordan-Ford EJ14	56 laps	18
16	Giorgio Pantano	Jordan	Jordan-Ford EJ14	55 laps	15
17	Gianmaria Bruni	Minardi	Minardi-Cosworth PS04B	52 laps	17
R	David Coulthard	McLaren	McLaren-Mercedes MP4-19	50 laps/engine	10
R	Zsolt Baumgartner *	Minardi	Minardi-Cosworth PS04B	44 laps/engine	20
R	Kimi Raikkonen *	McLaren	McLaren-Mercedes MP4-19	7 laps/engine	19

Pole: M Schumacher, 1m30.139s, 134.431mph/216.345kph. Fastest lap: M Schumacher, 1m30.252s, 134.262mph/216.074kph on Lap 7. Race leaders: M Schumacher 1-9 & 12-24 & 28-41 & 44-57, Barrichello 10 & 25-27 & 42-43, Button 11

* 10-place grid penalty for engine change

ALL BAR A VICTORY

BAR had its greatest year as it advanced from fifth overall with a tally of 26 points in 2003 to second overall with 119 points in 2004. Jenson Button claimed 10 podium visits to help it along the way. One of the key factors in this burgeoning form was Honda making progress with the engines it supplied to the team.

SAN MARINO GRAND PRIX

IMOLA • ROUND 4 • DATE: 25TH APRIL 2004

Laps: 62 • Distance: 190.43miles/305.846km • Weather: Hot & bright

Pos	Driver	Team	Chassis-Engine	Result	Qual
1	Michael Schumacher	Ferrari	Ferrari F2004	1h26m19.670s	2
2	Jenson Button	BAR	BAR-Honda 006	1h26m29.372s	1
3	Juan Pablo Montoya	Williams	Williams-BMW FW26	1h26m41.287s	3
4	Fernando Alonso	Renault F1	Renault R24	1h26m43.324s	6
5	Jarno Trulli	Renault F1	Renault R24	1h26m55.886s	9
6	Rubens Barrichello	Ferrari	Ferrari F2004	1h26m56.353s	4
7	Ralf Schumacher	Williams	Williams-BMW FW26	1h27m15.400s	5
8	Kimi Raikkonen *	McLaren	McLaren-Mercedes MP4-19	61 laps	20
9	Giancarlo Fisichella	Sauber	Sauber-Petronas C23	61 laps	18
10	Felipe Massa	Sauber	Sauber-Petronas C23	61 laps	12
11	Olivier Panis	Toyota	Toyota TF104	61 laps	13
12	David Coulthard	McLaren	McLaren-Mercedes MP4-19	61 laps	11
13	Mark Webber	Jaguar	Jaguar-Cosworth R5	61 laps	8
14	Christian Klien	Jaguar	Jaguar-Cosworth R5	60 laps	14
15	Zsolt Baumgartner *	Minardi	Minardi-Cosworth PS04B	58 laps	19
16	Takuma Sato	BAR	BAR-Honda 006	56 laps/engine	7
R	Nick Heidfeld	Jordan	Jordan-Ford EJ14	48 laps/transmission	16
R	Cristiano da Matta	Toyota	Toyota TF104	32 laps/spun off	10
R	Gianmaria Bruni	Minardi	Minardi-Cosworth PS04B	22 laps/brakes	17
R	Giorgio Pantano	Jordan	Jordan-Ford EJ14	6 laps/hydraulics	15

Pole: Button, 1m19.753s, 138.362mph/222.672kph. Fastest lap: M Schumacher, 1m20.411s, 137.230mph/220.850kph on Lap 10. Race leaders: Button 1-8, M Schumacher 9-62

* 10-place grid penalty for engine change

SPANISH GRAND PRIX

BARCELONA-CATALUNYA • ROUND 5 • DATE: 9TH MAY 2004
Laps: 66 • Distance: 189.755miles/305.382km • Weather: Warm & bright

Pos	Driver	Team	Chassis-Engine	Result	Qual
1	Michael Schumacher	Ferrari	Ferrari F2004	1h27m32.841s	1
2	Rubens Barrichello	Ferrari	Ferrari F2004	1h27m46.131s	5
3	Jarno Trulli	Renault F1	Renault R24	1h28m05.135s	4
4	Fernando Alonso	Renault F1	Renault R24	1h28m05.793s	8
5	Takuma Sato	BAR	BAR-Honda 006	1h28m15.168s	3
6	Ralf Schumacher	Williams	Williams-BMW FW26	1h28m46.645s	6
7	Giancarlo Fisichella	Sauber	Sauber-Petronas C23	1h28m49.949s	12
8	Jenson Button	BAR	BAR-Honda 006	65 laps	14
9	Felipe Massa	Sauber	Sauber-Petronas C23	65 laps	17
10	David Coulthard	McLaren	McLaren-Mercedes MP4-19	65 laps	10
11	Kimi Raikkonen	McLaren	McLaren-Mercedes MP4-19	65 laps	13
12	Mark Webber	Jaguar	Jaguar-Cosworth R5	65 laps	9
13	Cristiano da Matta	Toyota	Toyota TF104	65 laps	11
R	Giorgio Pantano	Jordan	Jordan-Ford EJ14	51 laps/hydraulics	19
R	Juan Pablo Montoya	Williams	Williams-BMW FW26	46 laps/brakes	2
R	Christian Klien	Jaguar	Jaguar-Cosworth R5	43 laps/throttle	16
R	Olivier Panis	Toyota	Toyota TF104	33 laps/hydraulics	7
R	Nick Heidfeld	Jordan	Jordan-Ford EJ14	33 laps/hydraulics	15
R	Gianmaria Bruni	Minardi	Minardi-Cosworth PS04B	31 laps/brakes	18
R	Zsolt Baumgartner	Minardi	Minardi-Cosworth PS04B	17 laps/spun off	20

Pole: M Schumacher, 1m15.022s, 137.963mph/222.030kph. Fastest lap: M Schumacher, 1m17.450s, 133.638mph/215.070kph on Lap 12. Race leaders: Trulli 1-8, M Schumacher 9-10 & 18-66, Barrichello 11-17

TRULLI WINS, GETS FIRED

Jarno Trulli gave the Renault F1 Team reason to smile when he won the Monaco GP. However, the team went off the boil in the second half of the season and slipped back to an eventual third-place ranking in the constructors' championship. By then, Trulli had been fired with three races to go and was replaced by Jacques Villeneuve, who disappointed.

MONACO GRAND PRIX

MONTE CARLO • ROUND 6 • DATE: 23RD MAY 2004
Laps: 77 • Distance: 159.703miles/257.18km • Weather: Warm & bright

Pos	Driver	Team	Chassis-Engine	Result	Qual
1	Jarno Trulli	Renault F1	Renault R24	1h45m46.601s	1
2	Jenson Button	BAR	BAR-Honda 006	1h45m47.098s	2
3	Rubens Barrichello	Ferrari	Ferrari F2004	1h47m02.367s	6
4	Juan Pablo Montoya	Williams	Williams-BMW FW26	76 laps	9
5	Felipe Massa	Sauber	Sauber-Petronas C23	76 laps	16
6	Cristiano da Matta	Toyota	Toyota TF104	76 laps	15
7	Nick Heidfeld	Jordan	Jordan-Ford EJ14	75 laps	17
8	Olivier Panis	Toyota	Toyota TF104	74 laps	13
9	Zsolt Baumgartner	Minardi	Minardi-Cosworth PS04B	71 laps	19
10	Ralf Schumacher *	Williams	Williams-BMW FW26	69 laps/gearbox	12
R	Michael Schumacher	Ferrari	Ferrari F2004	45 laps/collision	4

Pos	Driver	Team	Chassis-Engine	Result	Qual
R	Fernando Alonso	Renault F1	Renault R24	41 laps/accident	3
R	Kimi Raikkonen	McLaren	McLaren-Mercedes MP4-19	27 laps/engine	5
R	Gianmaria Bruni	Minardi	Minardi-Cosworth PS04B	15 laps/gearbox	20
R	Giorgio Pantano	Jordan	Jordan-Ford EJ14	12 laps/transmission	18
R	Mark Webber	Jaguar	Jaguar-Cosworth R5	11 laps/transmission	11
R	Takuma Sato	BAR	BAR-Honda 006	2 laps/engine	7
R	David Coulthard	McLaren	McLaren-Mercedes MP4-19	2 laps/collision	8
R	Giancarlo Fisichella	Sauber	Sauber-Petronas C23	2 laps/collision	10
R	Christian Klien	Jaguar	Jaguar-Cosworth R5	0 laps/collision	14

Pole: Trulli, 1m13.985s, 100.984mph/162.519kph. Fastest lap: M Schumacher, 1m14.439s, 100.368mph/161.528kph on Lap 23. Race leaders: Trulli 1-23 & 26-42 & 46-77, Alonso 24, M Schumacher 25 & 43-45

* 10-place grid penalty for engine change

EUROPEAN GRAND PRIX

NURBURGRING • ROUND 7 • DATE: 30TH MAY 2004
Laps: 60 • Distance: 191.437miles/308.88km • Weather: Warm & bright

Pos	Driver	Team	Chassis-Engine	Result	Qual
1	Michael Schumacher	Ferrari	Ferrari F2004	1h32m35.101s	1
2	Rubens Barrichello	Ferrari	Ferrari F2004	1h32m53.090s	7
3	Jenson Button	BAR	BAR-Honda 006	1h32m57.634s	5
4	Jarno Trulli	Renault F1	Renault R24	1h33m28.774s	3
5	Fernando Alonso	Renault F1	Renault R24	1h33m36.088s	6
6	Giancarlo Fisichella *	Sauber	Sauber-Petronas C23	1h33m48.549s	18
7	Mark Webber	Jaguar	Jaguar-Cosworth R5	1h33m51.307s	14
8	Juan Pablo Montoya	Williams	Williams-BMW FW26	59 laps	8
9	Felipe Massa	Sauber	Sauber-Petronas C23	59 laps	16
10	Nick Heidfeld	Jordan	Jordan-Ford EJ14	59 laps	13
11	Olivier Panis	Toyota	Toyota TF104	59 laps	10
12	Christian Klien	Jaguar	Jaguar-Cosworth R5	59 laps	12
13	Giorgio Pantano	Jordan	Jordan-Ford EJ14	58 laps	15
14	Gianmaria Bruni *	Minardi	Minardi-Cosworth PS04B	57 laps	19
15	Zsolt Baumgartner *	Minardi	Minardi-Cosworth PS04B	57 laps	17
R	Takuma Sato	BAR	BAR-Honda 006	47 laps/engine	2
R	David Coulthard	McLaren	McLaren-Mercedes MP4-19	25 laps/engine	20
R	Kimi Raikkonen	McLaren	McLaren-Mercedes MP4-19	9 laps/engine	4
R	Ralf Schumacher	Williams	Williams-BMW FW26	0 laps/collision	9
R	Cristiano da Matta	Toyota	Toyota TF104	0 laps/collision	11

Pole: M Schumacher, 1m28.351s, 130.340mph/209.763kph. Fastest lap: M Schumacher, 1m29.468s, 128.713mph/207.144kph on Lap 7. Race leaders: M Schumacher 1-8 & 16-60, Alonso 9, Sato 10-11, Barrichello 12-15

* 10-place grid penalty for engine change

DIFFERENT ISN'T BEST

Williams's FW26 stood out from the crowd, with its unusually-shaped "walrus" nose designed by Antonia Terzi a real talking point. Unfortunately, it won only once, at the final round at Interlagos, with Juan Pablo Montoya driving – and a more standard nose had been fitted by that point. Long before that win, Patrick Head handed the reins of the design team to Sam Michael, ending an era.

CANADIAN GRAND PRIX

MONTREAL • ROUND 8 • DATE: 13TH JUNE 2004
Laps: 70 • Distance: 189.534miles/305.27km • Weather: Warm & bright

Pos	Driver	Team	Chassis-Engine	Result	Qual
1	Michael Schumacher	Ferrari	Ferrari F2004	1h28m24.803s	6
DQ	Ralf Schumacher	Williams	Williams-BMW FW26	Illegal brake ducts	1
2	Rubens Barrichello	Ferrari	Ferrari F2004	1h28m29.911s	7
3	Jenson Button	BAR	BAR-Honda 006	1h28m45.212s	2
DQ	Juan Pablo Montoya	Williams	Williams-BMW FW26	Illegal brake ducts	4
4	Giancarlo Fisichella	Sauber	Sauber-Petronas C23	69 laps	11
5	Kimi Raikkonen	McLaren	McLaren-Mercedes MP4-19	69 laps	8
DQ	Cristiano da Matta	Toyota	Toyota TF104	Illegal brake ducts	12
6	David Coulthard	McLaren	McLaren-Mercedes MP4-19	69 laps	9
DQ	Olivier Panis	Toyota	Toyota TF104	Illegal brake ducts	13
7	Timo Glock	Jordan	Jordan-Ford EJ14	68 laps	16
8	Nick Heidfeld	Jordan	Jordan-Ford EJ14	68 laps	15
9	Christian Klien	Jaguar	Jaguar-Cosworth R5	67 laps	10
10	Zsolt Baumgartner *	Minardi	Minardi-Cosworth PS04B	66 laps	18
R	Felipe Massa	Sauber	Sauber-Petronas C23	62 laps/spun off	17
R	Takuma Sato !	BAR	BAR-Honda 006	48 laps/engine	20
R	Fernando Alonso	Renault F1	Renault R24	44 laps/halfshaft	5
R	Gianmaria Bruni *	Minardi	Minardi-Cosworth PS04B	30 laps/gearbox	19
R	Mark Webber	Jaguar	Jaguar-Cosworth R5	6 laps/collision	14
R	Jarno Trulli	Renault F1	Renault R24	0 laps/suspension	3
NS	Giorgio Pantano	Jordan	Jordan-Ford EJ14	-	-

Pole: R Schumacher, 1m12.275s, 134.974mph/217.220kph. Fastest lap: Barrichello, 1m13.622s, 132.504mph/213.246kph on Lap 68. Race leaders: R Schumacher 1-14 & 19-32 & 47, Alonso 15-16, M Schumacher 17-18 & 33-46 & 48-70

* 10-place grid penalty for engine change • ! made to start from the pit lane, car modified in parc ferme

UNITED STATES GRAND PRIX

INDIANAPOLIS MOTOR SPEEDWAY • ROUND 9 • DATE: 20TH JUNE 2004
Laps: 73 • Distance: 190.149miles/306.016km • Weather: Hot & bright

Pos	Driver	Team	Chassis-Engine	Result	Qual
1	Michael Schumacher	Ferrari	Ferrari F2004	1h40m29.914s	2
2	Rubens Barrichello	Ferrari	Ferrari F2004	1h40m32.864s	1
3	Takuma Sato	BAR	BAR-Honda 006	1h40m51.950s	3
4	Jarno Trulli	Renault F1	Renault R24	1h41m04.458s	20
5	Olivier Panis	Toyota	Toyota TF104	1h41m07.448s	8
6	Kimi Raikkonen	McLaren	McLaren-Mercedes MP4-19	72 laps	7
7	David Coulthard	McLaren	McLaren-Mercedes MP4-19	72 laps	12
8	Zsolt Baumgartner	Minardi	Minardi-Cosworth PS04B	70 laps	19
9	Giancarlo Fisichella	Sauber	Sauber-Petronas C23	65 laps/hydraulics	14
R	Mark Webber	Jaguar	Jaguar-Cosworth R5	60 laps/oil leak	10
DQ	Juan Pablo Montoya	Williams	Williams-BMW FW26	57 laps/grid error	5
R	Nick Heidfeld	Jordan	Jordan-Ford EJ14	43 laps/engine	16
R	Jenson Button	BAR	BAR-Honda 006	26 laps/gearbox	4
R	Cristiano da Matta	Toyota	Toyota TF104	17 laps/gearbox	11
R	Ralf Schumacher	Williams	Williams-BMW FW26	9 laps/accident	6
R	Fernando Alonso	Renault F1	Renault R24	8 laps/accident	9
R	Christian Klien	Jaguar	Jaguar-Cosworth R5	0 laps/collision	13

Pos	Driver	Team	Chassis-Engine	Result	Qual
R	Felipe Massa	Sauber	Sauber-Petronas C23	0 laps/collision	15
R	Giorgio Pantano	Jordan	Jordan-Ford EJ14	0 laps/collision	17
R	Gianmaria Bruni	Minardi	Minardi-Cosworth PS04B	0 laps/collision	18

Pole: Barrichello, 1m10.223s, 133.535mph/214.903kph. Fastest lap: Barrichello, 1m10.399s, 133.201mph/214.366kph on Lap 7. Race leaders: Barrichello 1-5 & 42-50, M Schumacher 6-41 & 51-73

FRENCH GRAND PRIX

MAGNY-COURS • ROUND 10 • DATE: 4TH JULY 2004
Laps: 70 • Distance: 191.430miles/308.77km • Weather: Hot & bright

Pos	Driver	Team	Chassis-Engine	Result	Qual
1	Michael Schumacher	Ferrari	Ferrari F2004	1h30m18.133s	2
2	Fernando Alonso	Renault F1	Renault R24	1h30m26.462s	1
3	Rubens Barrichello	Ferrari	Ferrari F2004	1h30m49.755s	10
4	Jarno Trulli	Renault F1	Renault R24	1h30m50.215s	5
5	Jenson Button	BAR	BAR-Honda 006	1h30m50.617s	4
6	David Coulthard	McLaren	McLaren-Mercedes MP4-19B	1h30m53.653s	3
7	Kimi Raikkonen	McLaren	McLaren-Mercedes MP4-19B	1h30m54.363s	9
8	Juan Pablo Montoya	Williams	Williams-BMW FW26	1h31m01.552s	6
9	Mark Webber	Jaguar	Jaguar-Cosworth R5	1h31m10.527s	12
10	Marc Gene	Williams	Williams-BMW FW26	1h31m16.299s	8
11	Christian Klien	Jaguar	Jaguar-Cosworth R5	69 laps	13
12	Giancarlo Fisichella	Sauber	Sauber-Petronas C23	69 laps	15
13	Felipe Massa	Sauber	Sauber-Petronas C23	69 laps	16
14	Cristiano da Matta	Toyota	Toyota TF104	69 laps	11
15	Olivier Panis	Toyota	Toyota TF104	68 laps	14
16	Nick Heidfeld	Jordan	Jordan-Ford EJ14	68 laps	17
17	Giorgio Pantano	Jordan	Jordan-Ford EJ14	67 laps	18
18	Gianmaria Bruni	Minardi	Minardi-Cosworth PS04B	65 laps/gearbox	19
R	Zsolt Baumgartner	Minardi	Minardi-Cosworth PS04B	31 laps/spun off	20
R	Takuma Sato	BAR	BAR-Honda 006	15 laps/engine	7

Pole: Alonso, 1m13.698s, 133.885mph/215.468kph. Fastest lap: M Schumacher, 1m15.377s, 130.903mph/210.669kph on Lap 32. Race leaders: Alonso 1-32 & 43-46, M Schumacher 33-42 & 47-70

ONE FOR JAPAN

Japanese podium visitors have been rare in F1. Aguri Suzuki was the first to reach one, fittingly at the Japanese GP in 1990. However, Takuma Sato matched that in the US GP at the Indianapolis Motor Speedway. It was a race marked by a crash-strewn opening lap, but Sato avoided the carnage to finish third of the eight finishers for BAR.

BRITISH GRAND PRIX

SILVERSTONE • ROUND 11 • DATE: 11TH JULY 2004
Laps: 60 • Distance: 191.410miles/308.46km • Weather: Warm but dull

Pos	Driver	Team	Chassis-Engine	Result	Qual
1	Michael Schumacher	Ferrari	Ferrari F2004	1h24m42.700s	4
2	Kimi Raikkonen	McLaren	McLaren-Mercedes MP4-19B	1h24m44.830s	1
3	Rubens Barrichello	Ferrari	Ferrari F2004	1h24m45.814s	2
4	Jenson Button	BAR	BAR-Honda 006	1h24m53.383s	3
5	Juan Pablo Montoya	Williams	Williams-BMW FW26	1h24m54.873s	7
6	Giancarlo Fisichella *	Sauber	Sauber-Petronas C23	1h24m55.588s	20
7	David Coulthard	McLaren	McLaren-Mercedes MP4-19B	1h25m02.368s	6
8	Mark Webber	Jaguar	Jaguar-Cosworth R5	1h25m06.401s	9
9	Felipe Massa	Sauber	Sauber-Petronas C23	1h25m06.723s	10
10	Fernando Alonso *	Renault F1	Renault R24	1h25m07.535s	16
11	Takuma Sato	BAR	BAR-Honda 006	1h25m16.436s	8
12	Marc Gene	Williams	Williams-BMW FW26	1h25m17.003s	11
13	Cristiano da Matta	Toyota	Toyota TF104	59 laps	12
14	Christian Klien	Jaguar	Jaguar-Cosworth R5	59 laps	13
15	Nick Heidfeld	Jordan	Jordan-Ford EJ14	59 laps	15
16	Gianmaria Bruni *	Minardi	Minardi-Cosworth PS04B	56 laps	18
R	Giorgio Pantano	Jordan	Jordan-Ford EJ14	47 laps/spun off	14
R	Jarno Trulli	Renault F1	Renault R24	39 laps/spun off	5
R	Zsolt Baumgartner *	Minardi	Minardi-Cosworth PS04B	29 laps/engine	19
R	Olivier Panis !	Toyota	Toyota TF104	16 laps/fire extinguisher	17

Pole: Raikkonen, 1m18.233s, 146.997mph/236.570kph. Fastest lap: M Schumacher, 1m18.739s, 146.053mph/235.049kph on Lap 14. Race leaders: Raikkonen 1-11, M Schumacher 12-60

* 10-place grid penalty for engine change • ! 5-place grid penalty for baulking another driver

NEW CIRCUITS

Two new F1 circuits made their debuts in 2004. The first was Sakhir, hosting the Bahrain GP early in the season. The second was three races from the end, with the spectacular, money-no-object Shanghai International Circuit, built to a scale new to F1. Michael Schumacher won the first of these, Ferrari team-mate Rubens Barrichello the second.

GERMAN GRAND PRIX

HOCKENHEIM • ROUND 12 • DATE: 25TH JULY 2004
Laps: 66 • Distance: 187.582miles/301.884km • Weather: Hot & bright

Pos	Driver	Team	Chassis-Engine	Result	Qual
1	Michael Schumacher	Ferrari	Ferrari F2004	1h23m54.848s	1
2	Jenson Button *	BAR	BAR-Honda 006	1h24m03.236s	13
3	Fernando Alonso	Renault F1	Renault R24	1h24m11.199s	5
4	David Coulthard	McLaren	McLaren-Mercedes MP4-19B	1h24m14.079s	4
5	Juan Pablo Montoya	Williams	Williams-BMW FW26	1h24m17.903s	2
6	Mark Webber	Jaguar	Jaguar-Cosworth R5	1h24m35.956s	11
7	Antonio Pizzonia	Williams	Williams-BMW FW26	1h24m36.804s	10

Pos	Driver	Team	Chassis-Engine	Result	Qual
8	Takuma Sato	BAR	BAR-Honda 006	1h24m41.690s	8
9	Giancarlo Fisichella	Sauber	Sauber-Petronas C23	1h25m01.950s	14
10	Christian Klien	Jaguar	Jaguar-Cosworth R5	1h25m03.426s	12
11	Jarno Trulli	Renault F1	Renault R24	1h25m05.106s	6
12	Rubens Barrichello	Ferrari	Ferrari F2004	1h25m08.100s	7
13	Felipe Massa	Sauber	Sauber-Petronas C23	65 laps	16
14	Olivier Panis	Toyota	Toyota TF104B	65 laps	9
15	Giorgio Pantano	Jordan	Jordan-Ford EJ14	63 laps	17
16	Zsolt Baumgartner	Minardi	Minardi-Cosworth PS04B	62 laps	20
17	Gianmaria Bruni	Minardi	Minardi-Cosworth PS04B	62 laps	19
R	Nick Heidfeld	Jordan	Jordan-Ford EJ14	42 laps/handling	18
R	Cristiano da Matta	Toyota	Toyota TF104B	38 laps/puncture	15
R	Kimi Raikkonen	McLaren	McLaren-Mercedes MP4-19B	13 laps/wing	3

Pole: M Schumacher, 1m13.306s, 139.575mph/224.625kph. Fastest lap: Raikkonen, 1m13.780s, 138.679mph/223.182kph on Lap 10. Race leaders: M Schumacher 1-10 & 15-28 & 35-47 & 51-66, Raikkonen 11, Button 12-14 & 30-34 & 48-50, Alonso 29

* 10-place grid penalty for engine change

HUNGARIAN GRAND PRIX

HUNGARORING • ROUND 13 • DATE: 15TH AUGUST 2004
Laps: 70 • Distance: 190.181miles/306.67km • Weather: Hot & bright

Pos	Driver	Team	Chassis-Engine	Result	Qual
1	Michael Schumacher	Ferrari	Ferrari F2004	1h35m26.131s	1
2	Rubens Barrichello	Ferrari	Ferrari F2004	1h35m30.827s	2
3	Fernando Alonso	Renault F1	Renault R24	1h36m10.730s	5
4	Juan Pablo Montoya	Williams	Williams-BMW FW26	1h36m28.744s	7
5	Jenson Button	BAR	BAR-Honda 006	1h36m33.570s	4
6	Takuma Sato	BAR	BAR-Honda 006	69 laps	3
7	Antonio Pizzonia	Williams	Williams-BMW FW26	69 laps	6
8	Giancarlo Fisichella	Sauber	Sauber-Petronas C23	69 laps	8
9	David Coulthard	McLaren	McLaren-Mercedes MP4-19B	69 laps	12
10	Mark Webber	Jaguar	Jaguar-Cosworth R5	69 laps	11
11	Olivier Panis	Toyota	Toyota TF104B	69 laps	13
12	Nick Heidfeld	Jordan	Jordan-Ford EJ14	68 laps	16
13	Christian Klien	Jaguar	Jaguar-Cosworth R5	68 laps	14
14	Gianmaria Bruni	Minardi	Minardi-Cosworth PS04B	66 laps	19
15	Zsolt Baumgartner	Minardi	Minardi-Cosworth PS04B	65 laps	18
R	Giorgio Pantano	Jordan	Jordan-Ford EJ14	48 laps/gearbox	17
R	Jarno Trulli	Renault F1	Renault R24	41 laps/engine	9
R	Ricardo Zonta	Toyota	Toyota TF104B	31 laps/electrical	15
R	Felipe Massa *	Sauber	Sauber-Petronas C23	21 laps/brakes	20
R	Kimi Raikkonen	McLaren	McLaren-Mercedes MP4-19B	13 laps/electrical	10

Pole: M Schumacher, 1m19.146s, 123.822mph/199.272kph. Fastest lap: M Schumacher, 1m19.071s, 123.939mph/199.461kph on Lap 29. Race leaders: M Schumacher 1-70

* 10-place grid penalty for engine change

BELGIAN GRAND PRIX

SPA-FRANCORCHAMPS • ROUND 14 • DATE: 29TH AUGUST 2004
Laps: 44 • Distance: 190.726miles/306.944km • Weather: Warm but dull

Pos	Driver	Team	Chassis-Engine	Result	Qual
1	Kimi Raikkonen	McLaren	McLaren-Mercedes MP4-19B	1h32m35.274s	10
2	Michael Schumacher	Ferrari	Ferrari F2004	1h32m38.406s	2
3	Rubens Barrichello	Ferrari	Ferrari F2004	1h32m39.645s	6
4	Felipe Massa	Sauber	Sauber-Petronas C23	1h32m47.778s	8
5	Giancarlo Fisichella	Sauber	Sauber-Petronas C23	1h32m49.378s	5
6	Christian Klien	Jaguar	Jaguar-Cosworth R5	1h32m49.888s	13
7	David Coulthard	McLaren	McLaren-Mercedes MP4-19B	1h32m53.244s	4
8	Olivier Panis	Toyota	Toyota TF104B	1h32m53.967s	9
9	Jarno Trulli	Renault F1	Renault R24	1h32m57.389s	1
10	Ricardo Zonta	Toyota	Toyota TF104B	41 laps/engine	20
11	Nick Heidfeld	Jordan	Jordan-Ford EJ14	40 laps	16
R	Juan Pablo Montoya	Williams	Williams-BMW FW26	37 laps/tyre	11
R	Antonio Pizzonia	Williams	Williams-BMW FW26	31 laps/gearbox	14
R	Jenson Button	BAR	BAR-Honda 006	29 laps/tyre	12
R	Zsolt Baumgartner	Minardi	Minardi-Cosworth PS04B	28 laps/collision	18
R	Fernando Alonso	Renault F1	Renault R24	11 laps/oil leak	3
R	Mark Webber	Jaguar	Jaguar-Cosworth R5	0 laps/collision	7
R	Takuma Sato	BAR	BAR-Honda 006	0 laps/collision	15
R	Gianmaria Bruni	Minardi	Minardi-Cosworth PS04B	0 laps/collision	17
R	Giorgio Pantano	Jordan	Jordan-Ford EJ14	0 laps/collision	19

Pole: Trulli, 1m56.232s, 134.256mph/216.064kph. Fastest lap: Raikkonen, 1m45.108s, 148.465mph/238.931kph on Lap 42. Race leaders: Trulli 1-9, Alonso 10-11, Raikkonen 12-13 & 17-29 & 31-44, Montoya 14, M Schumacher 15 & 30, Pizzonia 16

NEW DRIVERS

Jordan gave F1 debuts to both Timo Glock and Giorgio Pantano, with German racer Glock doing better, coming seventh in Canada, while the Italian could finish no higher than 13th in the second round at Sepang. The third newcomer was Christian Klien, who outperformed both by coming home sixth for Jaguar Racing at Spa-Francorchamps.

ITALIAN GRAND PRIX

MONZA • ROUND 15 • DATE: 12TH SEPTEMBER 2004
Laps: 53 • Distance: 190.778miles/307.029km • Weather: Hot & wet, drying later

Pos	Driver	Team	Chassis-Engine	Result	Qual
1	Rubens Barrichello	Ferrari	Ferrari F2004	1h15m18.448s	1
2	Michael Schumacher	Ferrari	Ferrari F2004	1h15m19.795s	3
3	Jenson Button	BAR	BAR-Honda 006	1h15m28.645s	6
4	Takuma Sato	BAR	BAR-Honda 006	1h15m33.818s	5
5	Juan Pablo Montoya	Williams	Williams-BMW FW26	1h15m50.800s	2
6	David Coulthard	McLaren	McLaren-Mercedes MP4-19B	1h15m51.887s	10
7	Antonio Pizzonia	Williams	Williams-BMW FW26	1h15m52.200s	8
8	Giancarlo Fisichella	Sauber	Sauber-Petronas C23	1h15m53.879s	15

Pos	Driver	Team	Chassis-Engine	Result	Qual
9	Mark Webber	Jaguar	Jaguar-Cosworth R5	1h16m15.209s	12
10	Jarno Trulli	Renault F1	Renault R24	1h16m24.764s	9
11	Ricardo Zonta	Toyota	Toyota TF104B	1h16m40.979s	11
12	Felipe Massa	Sauber	Sauber-Petronas C23	52 laps	16
13	Christian Klien	Jaguar	Jaguar-Cosworth R5	52 laps	14
14	Nick Heidfeld *	Jordan	Jordan-Ford EJ14	52 laps	20
15	Zsolt Baumgartner ^	Minardi	Minardi-Cosworth PS04B	50 laps	19
R	Fernando Alonso	Renault F1	Renault R24	40 laps/spun off	4
R	Giorgio Pantano	Jordan	Jordan-Ford EJ14	33 laps/spun off	17
R	Gianmaria Bruni	Minardi	Minardi-Cosworth PS04B	29 laps/fire	18
R	Kimi Raikkonen	McLaren	McLaren-Mercedes MP4-19B	13 laps/water leak	7
R	Olivier Panis	Toyota	Toyota TF104B	0 laps/collision	13

Pole: Barrichello, 1m20.089s, 161.802mph/260.395kph. Fastest lap: Barrichello, 1m21.046s, 159.891mph/257.320kph on Lap 41. Race leaders: Barrichello 1-4 & 37-53, Alonso 5-10, Button 11-34, M Schumacher 35-36

* 10-place grid penalty for engine change • ^ 1s grid penalty for missing chicane

CHINESE GRAND PRIX

SHANGHAI INTERNATIONAL CIRCUIT • ROUND 16 • DATE: 26TH SEPTEMBER 2004
Laps: 56 • Distance: 189.677miles/305.256km • Weather: Hot but dull

Pos	Driver	Team	Chassis-Engine	Result	Qual
1	Rubens Barrichello	Ferrari	Ferrari F2004	1h29m12.420s	1
2	Jenson Button	BAR	BAR-Honda 006	1h29m13.455s	3
3	Kimi Raikkonen	McLaren	McLaren-Mercedes MP4-19B	1h29m13.889s	2
4	Fernando Alonso	Renault F1	Renault R24	1h29m44.930s	6
5	Juan Pablo Montoya	Williams	Williams-BMW FW26	1h29m57.613s	10
6	Takuma Sato *	BAR	BAR-Honda 006	1h30m07.211s	18
7	Giancarlo Fisichella	Sauber	Sauber-Petronas C23	1h30m17.884s	7
8	Felipe Massa	Sauber	Sauber-Petronas C23	1h30m32.500s	4
9	David Coulthard	McLaren	McLaren-Mercedes MP4-19B	1h30m33.039s	9
10	Mark Webber	Jaguar	Jaguar-Cosworth R5	55 laps	11
11	Jacques Villeneuve	Renault F1	Renault R24	55 laps	12
12	Michael Schumacher *	Ferrari	Ferrari F2004	55 laps	20
13	Nick Heidfeld	Jordan	Jordan-Ford EJ14	55 laps	14
14	Olivier Panis	Toyota	Toyota TF104B	55 laps	8
15	Timo Glock	Jordan	Jordan-Ford EJ14	55 laps	16
16	Zsolt Baumgartner *	Minardi	Minardi-Cosworth PS04B	53 laps	19
R	Gianmaria Bruni	Minardi	Minardi-Cosworth PS04B	38 laps/wheel	17
R	Ralf Schumacher	Williams	Williams-BMW FW26	37 laps/puncture	5
R	Ricardo Zonta	Toyota	Toyota TF104B	35 laps/gearbox	13
R	Christian Klien	Jaguar	Jaguar-Cosworth R5	11 laps/collision	15

Pole: Barrichello, 1m34.012s, 129.701mph/208.735kph. Fastest lap: M Schumacher, 1m32.238s, 132.196mph/212.749kph on Lap 55. Race leaders: Barrichello 1-12 & 16-29 & 36-56, Button 13-14 & 30-35, R Schumacher 15

* 10-place grid penalty for engine change

JAPANESE GRAND PRIX

SUZUKA • ROUND 17 • DATE: 10TH OCTOBER 2004
Laps: 53 • Distance: 191.240miles/307.771km • Weather: Hot & bright

Pos	Driver	Team	Chassis-Engine	Result	Qual
1	Michael Schumacher	Ferrari	Ferrari F2004	1h24m26.985s	1
2	Ralf Schumacher	Williams	Williams-BMW FW26	1h24m41.083s	2
3	Jenson Button	BAR	BAR-Honda 006	1h24m46.647s	5
4	Takuma Sato	BAR	BAR-Honda 006	1h24m58.766s	4
5	Fernando Alonso	Renault F1	Renault R24	1h25m04.752s	11
6	Kimi Raikkonen	McLaren	McLaren-Mercedes MP4-19B	1h25m06.347s	12
7	Juan Pablo Montoya	Williams	Williams-BMW FW26	1h25m22.332s	13
8	Giancarlo Fisichella	Sauber	Sauber-Petronas C23	1h25m23.261s	7
9	Felipe Massa	Sauber	Sauber-Petronas C23	1h25m56.641s	19
10	Jacques Villeneuve	Renault F1	Renault R24	52 laps	9
11	Jarno Trulli	Toyota	Toyota TF104B	52 laps	6
12	Christian Klien	Jaguar	Jaguar-Cosworth R5	52 laps	14
13	Nick Heidfeld	Jordan	Jordan-Ford EJ14	52 laps	16
14	Olivier Panis	Toyota	Toyota TF104B	51 laps	10
15	Timo Glock	Jordan	Jordan-Ford EJ14	51 laps	17
16	Gianmaria Bruni	Minardi	Minardi-Cosworth PS04B	50 laps	18
R	Zsolt Baumgartner *	Minardi	Minardi-Cosworth PS04B	41 laps/spun off	20
R	David Coulthard	McLaren	McLaren-Mercedes MP4-19B	38 laps/collision	8
R	Rubens Barrichello	Ferrari	Ferrari F2004	38 laps/collision	15
R	Mark Webber	Jaguar	Jaguar-Cosworth R5	20 laps/overheating	3

Pole: M Schumacher, 1m33.542s, 138.866mph/223.484kph. Fastest lap: Barrichello, 1m32.730s, 140.082mph/225.441kph on Lap 30. Race leaders: M Schumacher 1-53

* 10-place grid penalty for engine change

CLASSIC CAR: FERRARI F2004

Michael Schumacher was the best driver of his time, but he had been run close in 2003 after Ferrari had a slow start to the season. This certainly wasn't the case in 2004, as he used his F2004 to good effect to win the first five races before crashing at Monaco. He then won the next seven and would add one more in the remaining five rounds when team-mate Rubens Barrichello won twice. Created by a design team led by Ross Brawn and including Rory Byrne and Aldo Costa, plus an engine division under Paolo Martinelli, the F2004 was the pick of the pack.

BRAZILIAN GRAND PRIX

INTERLAGOS • ROUND 18 • DATE: 24TH OCTOBER 2004
Laps: 71 • Distance: 190.101miles/305.939km • Weather: Hot & damp, drying later

Pos	Driver	Team	Chassis-Engine	Result	Qual
1	Juan Pablo Montoya	Williams	Williams-BMW FW26	1h28m01.451s	2
2	Kimi Raikkonen	McLaren	McLaren-Mercedes MP4-19B	1h28m02.473s	3
3	Rubens Barrichello	Ferrari	Ferrari F2004	1h28m25.550s	1
4	Fernando Alonso	Renault F1	Renault R24	1h28m50.359s	8
5	Ralf Schumacher	Williams	Williams-BMW FW26	1h28m51.191s	7

Pos	Driver	Team	Chassis-Engine	Result	Qual
6	Takuma Sato	BAR	BAR-Honda 006	1h28m51.699s	6
7	Michael Schumacher *	Ferrari	Ferrari F2004	1h28m52.077s	18
8	Felipe Massa	Sauber	Sauber-Petronas C23	1h29m03.761s	4
9	Giancarlo Fisichella	Sauber	Sauber-Petronas C23	1h29m05.293s	10
10	Jacques Villeneuve	Renault F1	Renault R24	70 laps	13
11	David Coulthard	McLaren	McLaren-Mercedes MP4-19B	70 laps	12
12	Jarno Trulli	Toyota	Toyota TF104B	70 laps	9
13	Ricardo Zonta	Toyota	Toyota TF104B	70 laps	14
14	Christian Klien	Jaguar	Jaguar-Cosworth R5	69 laps	15
15	Timo Glock	Jordan	Jordan-Ford EJ14	69 laps	17
16	Zsolt Baumgartner *	Minardi	Minardi-Cosworth PS04B	67 laps	20
17	Gianmaria Bruni *	Minardi	Minardi-Cosworth PS04B	67 laps	19
R	Mark Webber	Jaguar	Jaguar-Cosworth R5	23 laps/collision	11
R	Nick Heidfeld	Jordan	Jordan-Ford EJ14	15 laps/clutch	16
R	Jenson Button	BAR	BAR-Honda 006	3 laps/engine	5

Pole: Barrichello, 1m10.646s, 136.440mph/219.579kph. Fastest lap: Montoya, 1m11.473s, 134.861mph/217.038kph on Lap 49. Race leaders: Raikkonen 1-3 & 29 & 51-55, Barrichello 4-5, Massa 6-7, Alonso 8-18, Montoya 19-28 & 30-50 & 56-71

* 10-place grid penalty for engine change

WORLD DRIVERS' CHAMPIONSHIP FINAL RESULTS

Pos	Driver	Nat	Car-Engine	R1	R2	R3	R4	R5	R6	R7
1	Michael Schumacher	DEU	Ferrari F2004	1PF	1P	1PF	1F	1PF	RF	1PF
2	Rubens Barrichello	BRA	Ferrari F2004	2	4	2	6	2	3	2
3	Jenson Button	GBR	BAR-Honda 006	6	3	3	2P	8	2	3
4	Fernando Alonso	ESP	Renault R24	3	7	6	4	4	R	5
5	Juan Pablo Montoya	COL	Williams-BMW FW26	5	2F	13	3	R	4	8
6	Jarno Trulli	ITA	Renault R24	7	5	4	5	3	1P	4
			Toyota TF104B	-	-	-	-	-	-	-
7	Kimi Raikkonen	FIN	McLaren-Mercedes MP4-19	R	R	R	8	11	R	R
			McLaren-Mercedes MP4-19B	-	-	-	-	-	-	-
8	Takuma Sato	JPN	BAR-Honda 006	9	15	5	16	5	R	R
9	Ralf Schumacher	DEU	Williams-BMW FW26	4	R	7	7	6	10	R
10	David Coulthard	GBR	McLaren-Mercedes MP4-19	8	6	R	12	10	R	R
			McLaren-Mercedes MP4-19B	-	-	-	-	-	-	-
11	Giancarlo Fisichella	ITA	Sauber-Petronas C23	10	11	11	9	7	R	6
12	Felipe Massa	BRA	Sauber-Petronas C23	R	8	12	10	9	5	9
13	Mark Webber	AUS	Jaguar-Cosworth R5	R	R	8	13	12	R	7
14	Olivier Panis	FRA	Toyota TF104	13	12	9	11	R	8	11
			Toyota TF104B	-	-	-	-	-	-	-
15	Antonio Pizzonia	BRA	Williams-BMW FW26	-	-	-	-	-	-	-
16	Christian Klien	AUT	Jaguar-Cosworth R5	11	10	14	14	R	R	12
17	Cristiano da Matta	BRA	Toyota TF104	12	9	10	R	13	6	R
			Toyota TF104B	-	-	-	-	-	-	-
18	Nick Heidfeld	DEU	Jordan-Ford EJ14	R	R	15	R	R	7	10
19	Timo Glock	DEU	Jordan-Ford EJ14	T	T	T	T	T	T	T
20	Zsolt Baumgartner	HUN	Minardi-Cosworth PS04B	R	16	R	15	R	9	15
21	Jacques Villeneuve	CAN	Renault R24	-	-	-	-	-	-	-
22	Ricardo Zonta	BRA	Toyota TF104	T	T	T	T	T	T	T
			Toyota TF104B	-	-	-	-	-	-	-
23	Marc Gene	ESP	Williams-BMW FW26	-	-	-	-	-	-	-
24	Giorgio Pantano	ITA	Jordan-Ford EJ14	14	13	16	R	R	R	13
25	Gianmaria Bruni	ITA	Minardi-Cosworth PS04B	NC	14	17	R	R	R	14

Pos	Driver	R8	R9	R10	R11	R12	R13	R14	R15	R16	R17	R18	Total
1	M Schumacher	1	1	1F	1F	1P	1PF	2	2	12F	1P	7	148
2	Barrichello	2F	2PF	3	3	12	2	3	1PF	1P	RF	3P	114
3	Button	3	R	5	4	2	5	R	3	2	3	R	85
4	Alonso	R	R	2P	10	3	3	R	R	4	5	4	59
5	Montoya	DQ	DQ	8	5	5	4	R	5	5	7	1F	58
6	Trulli	R	4	4	R	11	R	9P	10	-	-	-	46
		-	-	-	-	-	-	-	-	-	11	12	
7	Raikkonen	5	6	-	-	-	-	-	-	-	-	-	45
		-	-	7	2P	RF	R	1F	R	3	6	2	
8	Sato	R	3	R	11	8	6	R	4	6	4	6	34
9	R Schumacher	DQP	R	-	-	-	-	-	-	R	2	5	24
10	Coulthard	6	7	-	-	-	-	-	-	-	-	-	24
		-	-	6	7	4	9	7	6	9	R	11	
11	Fisichella	4	9	12	6	9	8	5	8	7	8	9	22
12	Massa	R	R	13	9	13	R	4	12	8	9	8	12
13	Webber	R	R	9	8	6	10	R	9	10	R	R	7
14	Panis	DQ	5	15	R	-	-	-	-	-	-	-	6
		-	-	-	-	14	11	8	R	14	14	-	
15	Pizzonia	-	-	-	-	7	7	R	7	-	-	-	6
16	Klien	9	R	11	14	10	13	6	13	R	12	14	3
17	da Matta	DQ	R	14	13	-	-	-	-	-	-	-	3
		-	-	-	-	R	-	-	-	-	-	-	
18	Heidfeld	8	R	16	15	R	12	11	14	13	13	R	3
19	Glock	7	T	T	T	T	T	T	T	15	15	15	2
20	Baumgartner	10	8	R	R	16	15	R	15	16	R	16	1
21	Villeneuve	-	-	-	-	-	-	-	-	11	10	10	0
22	Zonta	T	T	T	T	-	-	-	-	-	-	-	0
		-	-	-	-	T	R	10	11	R	-	13	0
23	Gene	-	-	10	12	-	-	-	-	-	-	-	0
24	Pantano	NS	R	17	R	15	R	R	R	-	-	-	0
25	Bruni	R	R	18	16	17	14	R	R	R	16	17	0

SYMBOLS AND GRAND PRIX KEY

Round 1 Australian GP
Round 2 Malaysian GP
Round 3 Bahrain GP
Round 4 San Marino GP
Round 5 Spanish GP
Round 6 Monaco GP
Round 7 European GP
Round 8 Canadian GP
Round 9 United States GP
Round 10 French GP
Round 11 British GP
Round 12 German GP
Round 13 Hungarian GP
Round 14 Belgian GP
Round 15 Italian GP
Round 16 Chinese GP
Round 17 Japanese GP
Round 18 Brazilian GP

SCORING

1st 10 points
2nd 8 points
3rd 6 points
4th 5 points
5th 4 points
6th 3 points
7th 2 points
8th 1 point

DNPQ DID NOT PRE-QUALIFY **DNQ** DID NOT QUALIFY **DQ** DISQUALIFIED **EX** EXCLUDED
F FASTEST LAP **NC** NOT CLASSIFIED **NS** NON-STARTER **P** POLE POSITION **R** RETIRED

WORLD CONSTRUCTORS' CHAMPIONSHIP FINAL RESULTS

Pos	Team-Engine	R1	R2	R3	R4	R5	R6	R7	R8	R9
1	Ferrari	1/2	1/4	1/2	1/6	1/2	3/R	1/2	1/2	1/2
2	BAR-Honda	6/9	3/15	3/5	2/16	5/8	2/R	3/R	3/R	3/R
3	Renault F1	3/7	5/7	4/6	4/5	3/4	1/R	4/5	R/R	4/R
4	Williams-BMW	4/5	2/R	7/13	3/7	6/R	4/10	8/R	DQ/DQ	DQ/R
5	McLaren-Mercedes	8/R	6/R	R/R	8/12	10/11	R/R	R/R	5/6	6/7
6	Sauber-Petronas	10/R	8/11	11/12	9/10	7/9	5/R	6/9	4/R	9/R
7	Jaguar-Cosworth	11/R	10/R	8/14	13/14	12/R	R/R	7/12	9/R	R/R
8	Toyota	12/13	9/12	9/10	11/R	13/R	6/8	11/R	DQ/DQ	5/R
9	Jordan-Ford	14/R	13/R	15/16	R/R	R/R	7/R	10/13	7/8	R/R
10	Minardi-Cosworth	NC/R	14/16	17/R	15/R	R/R	9/R	14/15	10/R	8/R

Pos	Team-Engine	R10	R11	R12	R13	R14	R15	R16	R17	R18	Total
1	Ferrari	1/3	1/3	1/12	1/2	2/3	1/2	1/12	1/R	3/7	262
2	BAR-Honda	5/R	4/11	2/8	5/6	R/R	3/4	2/6	3/4	6/R	119
3	Renault F1	2/4	10/R	3/11	3/R	9/R	10/R	4/11	5/10	4/10	105
4	Williams-BMW	8/10	5/12	5/7	4/7	R/R	5/7	5/R	2/7	1/5	88
5	McLaren-Mercedes	6/7	2/7	4/R	9/R	1/7	6/R	3/9	6/R	2/11	69
6	Sauber-Petronas	12/13	6/9	9/13	8/R	4/5	8/12	7/8	8/9	8/9	34
7	Jaguar-Cosworth	9/11	8/14	6/10	10/13	6/R	9/13	10/R	12/R	14/R	10
8	Toyota	14/15	13/R	14/R	11/R	8/10	11/R	14/R	11/14	12/13	9
9	Jordan-Ford	16/17	15/R	15/R	12/R	11/R	14/R	13/15	13/15	15/R	5
10	Minardi-Cosworth	18/R	16/R	16/17	14/15	R/R	15/R	16/R	16/R	16/17	1

2005

SEASON SUMMARY

Michael Schumacher's five-year reign came to an end when Fernando Alonso struck for Renault. The Spaniard won seven of the record 19 rounds and his strong start to the year gave him a cushion that he maintained for the rest of the campaign as Kimi Raikkonen came on strong for McLaren. Ferrari's struggle was clear when Schumacher ended up with less than half of Alonso's points tally to only just pip McLaren's second driver, Juan Pablo Montoya, to rank third. Landing the title at 24 years and 58 days, Alonso beat Emerson Fittipaldi's 33-year record to become the youngest world champion to that date.

AUSTRALIAN GRAND PRIX

ALBERT PARK • ROUND 1 • DATE: 6TH MARCH 2005
Laps: 57 • Distance: 187.822miles/302.271km • Weather: Warm but dull

Pos	Driver	Team	Chassis-Engine	Result	Qual
1	Giancarlo Fisichella	Renault F1	Renault R25	1h24m17.336s	1
2	Rubens Barrichello	Ferrari	Ferrari F2004M	1h24m22.889s	11
3	Fernando Alonso	Renault F1	Renault R25	1h24m24.048s	13
4	David Coulthard	Red Bull Racing	Red Bull-Cosworth RB1	1h24m33.467s	5
5	Mark Webber	Williams	Williams-BMW FW27	1h24m34.244s	3
6	Juan Pablo Montoya	McLaren	McLaren-Mercedes MP4-20	1h24m52.369s	9
7	Christian Klien	Red Bull Racing	Red Bull-Cosworth RB1	1h24m56.333s	6
8	Kimi Raikkonen	McLaren	McLaren-Mercedes MP4-20	1h24m56.969s	10
9	Jarno Trulli	Toyota	Toyota TF105	1h25m20.444s	2
10	Felipe Massa	Sauber	Sauber-Petronas C24	1h25m21.729s	18
11	Jenson Button	BAR	BAR-Honda 007	56 laps/engine	8
12	Ralf Schumacher	Toyota	Toyota TF105	56 laps	15
13	Jacques Villeneuve	Sauber	Sauber-Petronas C24	56 laps	4
14	Takuma Sato *	BAR	BAR-Honda 007	55 laps/engine	20
15	Narain Karthikeyan	Jordan	Jordan-Toyota EJ15	55 laps	12
16	Tiago Monteiro	Jordan	Jordan-Toyota EJ15	55 laps	14
17	Patrick Friesacher	Minardi	Minardi-Cosworth PS04B	53 laps	16
R	Nick Heidfeld	Williams	Williams-BMW FW27	42 laps/collision	7
R	Michael Schumacher *	Ferrari	Ferrari F2004M	42 laps/collision	19
R	Christijan Albers	Minardi	Minardi-Cosworth PS04B	16 laps/gearbox	17

Aggregate pole: Fisichella, 3m01.460s, 65.371mph/105.206kph. Fastest lap: Alonso, 1m25.683s, 138.446mph/222.807kph on Lap 24. Race leaders: Fisichella 1-23 & 25-42 & 45-57, Barrichello 24, Alonso 43-44

* 10-place grid penalty for engine change

SLOWING THE CARS

The FIA wanted to slow the cars after they had taken three seconds off most lap records in 2004. So, with a view to cutting both horsepower and costs, engines had to last for not one grand prix meeting but two. Downforce was slashed by raising the front wing and bringing the rear wing forward, while a set of tyres had to last through qualifying and the race.

MALAYSIAN GRAND PRIX

SEPANG • ROUND 2 • DATE: 20TH MARCH 2005
Laps: 56 • Distance: 192.878miles/310.408km • Weather: Very hot & bright

Pos	Driver	Team	Chassis-Engine	Result	Qual
1	Fernando Alonso	Renault F1	Renault R25	1h31m33.736s	1
2	Jarno Trulli	Toyota	Toyota TF105	1h31m58.063s	2
3	Nick Heidfeld	Williams	Williams-BMW FW27	1h32m05.924s	10
4	Juan Pablo Montoya	McLaren	McLaren-Mercedes MP4-20	1h32m15.367s	11
5	Ralf Schumacher	Toyota	Toyota TF105	1h32m25.590s	5
6	David Coulthard	Red Bull Racing	Red Bull-Cosworth RB1	1h32m46.279s	8
7	Michael Schumacher	Ferrari	Ferrari F2004M	1h32m53.724s	13
8	Christian Klien	Red Bull Racing	Red Bull-Cosworth RB1	1h32m54.571s	7
9	Kimi Raikkonen	McLaren	McLaren-Mercedes MP4-20	1h32m55.316s	6
10	Felipe Massa	Sauber	Sauber-Petronas C24	55 laps	14
11	Narain Karthikeyan	Jordan	Jordan-Toyota EJ15	54 laps	17
12	Tiago Monteiro	Jordan	Jordan-Toyota EJ15	53 laps	18
13	Christijan Albers	Minardi	Minardi-Cosworth PS04B	52 laps	19
R	Rubens Barrichello	Ferrari	Ferrari F2004M	49 laps/withdrawn	12
R	Giancarlo Fisichella	Renault F1	Renault R25	36 laps/collision	3
R	Mark Webber	Williams	Williams-BMW FW27	36 laps/collision	4
R	Jacques Villeneuve	Sauber	Sauber-Petronas C24	26 laps/spun off	16
R	Jenson Button	BAR	BAR-Honda 007	2 laps/engine	9
R	Anthony Davidson	BAR	BAR-Honda 007	2 laps/engine	15
R	Patrick Friesacher *	Minardi	Minardi-Cosworth PS04B	2 laps/spun off	20
NS	Takuma Sato	BAR	BAR-Honda 007	-	-

Aggregate pole: Alonso, 3m07.672s, 66.069mph/106.328kph. Fastest lap: Raikkonen, 1m35.483s, 129.859mph/208.987kph on Lap 23. Race leaders: Alonso 1-21 & 25-40 & 43-56, Fisichella 22, Raikkonen 23-24, Trulli 41-42

* 10-place grid penalty for engine change

FERRARI NEEDS NEW RUBBER

The new tyre rules meant that there would be no tyre changes at pit stops, just refuelling, and this hit Ferrari harder than its rivals – its tyre supplier Bridgestone simply couldn't build a tyre that could last through both qualifying and a race as well as Michelin did. This dropped it to third in the final ranking, keeping it ahead of Toyota only because of its US GP 1-2.

BAHRAIN GRAND PRIX

SAKHIR • ROUND 3 • DATE: 3RD APRIL 2005
Laps: 57 • Distance: 191.683miles/308.484km • Weather: Very hot & bright

Pos	Driver	Team	Chassis-Engine	Result	Qual
1	Fernando Alonso	Renault F1	Renault R25	1h29m18.531s	1
2	Jarno Trulli	Toyota	Toyota TF105	1h29m31.940s	3
3	Kimi Raikkonen	McLaren	McLaren-Mercedes MP4-20	1h29m50.594s	9
4	Ralf Schumacher	Toyota	Toyota TF105	1h30m11.803s	6
5	Pedro de la Rosa	McLaren	McLaren-Mercedes MP4-20	1h30m23.519s	8
6	Mark Webber	Williams	Williams-BMW FW27	1h30m33.232s	5
7	Felipe Massa	Sauber	Sauber-Petronas C24	56 laps	12

Pos	Driver	Team	Chassis-Engine	Result	Qual
8	David Coulthard	Red Bull Racing	Red Bull-Cosworth RB1	56 laps	14
9	Rubens Barrichello *	Ferrari	Ferrari F2005	56 laps	20
10	Tiago Monteiro	Jordan	Jordan-Toyota EJ15	55 laps	16
11	Jacques Villeneuve	Sauber	Sauber-Petronas C24	54 laps/collision	15
12	Patrick Friesacher *	Minardi	Minardi-Cosworth PS04B	54 laps	19
13	Christijan Albers *	Minardi	Minardi-Cosworth PS04B	53 laps	18
R	Jenson Button	BAR	BAR-Honda 007	46 laps/clutch	11
R	Takuma Sato	BAR	BAR-Honda 007	27 laps/brakes	13
R	Nick Heidfeld	Williams	Williams-BMW FW27	25 laps/engine	4
R	Michael Schumacher	Ferrari	Ferrari F2005	12 laps/hydraulics	2
R	Giancarlo Fisichella	Renault F1	Renault R25	4 laps/engine	10
R	Narain Karthikeyan	Jordan	Jordan-Toyota EJ15	2 laps/electrical	17
NS	Christian Klien	Red Bull Racing	Red Bull-Cosworth RB1	electrics	7

Aggregate pole: Alonso, 3m01.902s, 66.553mph/107.108kph. Fastest lap: de la Rosa, 1m31.447s, 132.385mph/213.054kph on Lap 43. Race leaders: Alonso 1-20 & 22-41 & 43-57, Trulli 21 & 42

* 10-place grid penalty for engine change

SAN MARINO GRAND PRIX

IMOLA • ROUND 4 • DATE: 24TH APRIL 2005
Laps: 62 • Distance: 190.43miles/305.846km • Weather: Warm but dull

Pos	Driver	Team	Chassis-Engine	Result	Qual
1	Fernando Alonso	Renault F1	Renault R25	1h27m41.921s	2
2	Michael Schumacher	Ferrari	Ferrari F2005	1h27m42.136s	13
DQ	Jenson Button	BAR	BAR-Honda 007	underweight	3
3	Alexander Wurz	McLaren	McLaren-Mercedes MP4-20	1h28m09.475s	7
DQ	Takuma Sato	BAR	BAR-Honda 007	underweight	6
4	Jacques Villeneuve	Sauber	Sauber-Petronas C24	1h28m46.363s	11
5	Jarno Trulli	Toyota	Toyota TF105	1h28m52.179s	5
6	Nick Heidfeld	Williams	Williams-BMW FW27	1h28m53.203s	8
7	Mark Webber	Williams	Williams-BMW FW27	1h29m05.218s	4
8	Vitantonio Liuzzi	Red Bull Racing	Red Bull-Cosworth RB1	1h29m05.685s	15
9	Ralf Schumacher !	Toyota	Toyota TF105	1h29m17.762s	10
10	Felipe Massa *	Sauber	Sauber-Petronas C24	61 laps	18
11	David Coulthard	Red Bull Racing	Red Bull-Cosworth RB1	61 laps	14
12	Narain Karthikeyan	Jordan	Jordan-Toyota EJ15	61 laps	16
13	Tiago Monteiro	Jordan	Jordan-Toyota EJ15	60 laps	17
R	Christijan Albers *	Minardi	Minardi-Cosworth PS05	20 laps/gearbox	20
R	Rubens Barrichello	Ferrari	Ferrari F2005	18 laps/electrical	9
R	Kimi Raikkonen	McLaren	McLaren-Mercedes MP4-20	9 laps/halfshaft	1
R	Patrick Friesacher *	Minardi	Minardi-Cosworth PS05	8 laps/clutch	19
R	Giancarlo Fisichella	Renault F1	Renault R25	5 laps/spun off	12

Aggregate pole: Raikkonen, 2m42.880s, 67.748mph/109.029kph. Fastest lap: M Schumacher, 1m21.858s, 134.804mph/216.946kph on Lap 48. Race leaders: Raikkonen 1-8, Alonso 9-23 & 25-42 & 50-62, Button 24 & 43-46, M Schumacher 47-49

! 25s penalty for dangerous driving • * 10-place grid penalty for engine change

SPANISH GRAND PRIX

BARCELONA-CATALUNYA • ROUND 5 • DATE: 8TH MAY 2005
Laps: 66 • Distance: 189.755miles/305.382km • Weather: Hot & bright

Pos	Driver	Team	Chassis-Engine	Result	Qual
1	Kimi Raikkonen	McLaren	McLaren-Mercedes MP4-20	1h27m16.830s	1
2	Fernando Alonso	Renault F1	Renault R25	1h27m44.482s	3
3	Jarno Trulli	Toyota	Toyota TF105	1h28m02.777s	5
4	Ralf Schumacher	Toyota	Toyota TF105	1h28m03.549s	4
5	Giancarlo Fisichella	Renault F1	Renault R25	1h28m14.766s	6
6	Mark Webber	Williams	Williams-BMW FW27	1h28m25.372s	2
7	Juan Pablo Montoya	McLaren	McLaren-Mercedes MP4-20	65 laps	7
8	David Coulthard	Red Bull Racing	Red Bull-Cosworth RB1	65 laps	9
9	Rubens Barrichello *	Ferrari	Ferrari F2005	65 laps	16
10	Nick Heidfeld *	Williams	Williams-BMW FW27	65 laps	17
11	Felipe Massa	Sauber	Sauber-Petronas C24	63 laps/wheel	10
12	Tiago Monteiro *	Jordan	Jordan-Toyota EJ15	63 laps	18
13	Narain Karthikeyan	Jordan	Jordan-Toyota EJ15	63 laps	13
R	Jacques Villeneuve	Sauber	Sauber-Petronas C24	51 laps/water leak	12
R	Michael Schumacher	Ferrari	Ferrari F2005	46 laps/puncture	8
R	Christijan Albers	Minardi	Minardi-Cosworth PS05	19 laps/gearbox	14
R	Patrick Friesacher	Minardi	Minardi-Cosworth PS05	11 laps/spun off	15
R	Vitantonio Liuzzi	Red Bull Racing	Red Bull-Cosworth RB1	9 laps/spun off	11

Aggregate pole: Raikkonen, 2m31.421s, 68.354mph/110.005kph. Fastest lap: Fisichella, 1m15.641s, 136.834mph/220.213kph on Lap 66. Race leaders: Raikkonen 1-66

* 10-place grid penalty for engine change

ENTER RED BULL

A new team appeared on the grid, but as is often the case, it was simply a rebrand of an existing team. The metallic green hues of Jaguar Racing were no more, after parent company Ford decided to pull the plug. The cars were now in Red Bull Racing's dark blue livery, driven by David Coulthard and Christian Klien.

MONACO GRAND PRIX

MONTE CARLO • ROUND 6 • DATE: 22ND MAY 2005
Laps: 78 • Distance: 161.588miles/260.52km • Weather: Warm & bright

Pos	Driver	Team	Chassis-Engine	Result	Qual
1	Kimi Raikkonen	McLaren	McLaren-Mercedes MP4-20	1h45m15.556s	1
2	Nick Heidfeld	Williams	Williams-BMW FW27	1h45m29.433s	6
3	Mark Webber	Williams	Williams-BMW FW27	1h45m34.040s	3
4	Fernando Alonso	Renault F1	Renault R25	1h45m52.043s	2
5	Juan Pablo Montoya !	McLaren	McLaren-Mercedes MP4-20	1h45m52.203s	16
6	Ralf Schumacher *	Toyota	Toyota TF105	1h45m52.733s	18
7	Michael Schumacher	Ferrari	Ferrari F2005	1h45m52.779s	8
8	Rubens Barrichello	Ferrari	Ferrari F2005	1h45m53.126s	10
9	Felipe Massa	Sauber	Sauber-Petronas C24	77 laps	11

Pos	Driver	Team	Chassis-Engine	Result	Qual
10	Jarno Trulli	Toyota	Toyota TF105	77 laps	5
11	Jacques Villeneuve	Sauber	Sauber-Petronas C24	77 laps	9
12	Giancarlo Fisichella	Renault F1	Renault R25	77 laps	4
13	Tiago Monteiro	Jordan	Jordan-Toyota EJ15	75 laps	15
14	Christijan Albers	Minardi	Minardi-Cosworth PS05	73 laps	14
R	Vitantonio Liuzzi	Red Bull Racing	Red Bull-Cosworth RB1	59 laps/collision	12
R	Patrick Friesacher	Minardi	Minardi-Cosworth PS05	29 laps/spun off	13
R	David Coulthard	Red Bull Racing	Red Bull-Cosworth RB1	23 laps/collision	7
R	Narain Karthikeyan *	Jordan	Jordan-Toyota EJ15	18 laps/collision	17

Aggregate pole: Raikkonen, 2m30.323s, 49.702mph/79.987kph. Fastest lap: M Schumacher, 1m15.842s, 98.512mph/158.540kph on Lap 40. Race leaders: Raikkonen 1-78

! sent to back of grid for impeding another driver • * 10-place grid penalty for engine change

EUROPEAN GRAND PRIX

NURBURGRING • ROUND 7 • DATE: 29TH MAY 2005
Laps: 59 • Distance: 188.730miles/303.732km • Weather: Hot & bright

Pos	Driver	Team	Chassis-Engine	Result	Qual
1	Fernando Alonso	Renault F1	Renault R25	1h31m46.648s	6
2	Nick Heidfeld	Williams	Williams-BMW FW27	1h32m03.215s	1
3	Rubens Barrichello	Ferrari	Ferrari F2005	1h32m05.197s	7
4	David Coulthard	Red Bull Racing	Red Bull-Cosworth RB1	1h32m18.236s	12
5	Michael Schumacher	Ferrari	Ferrari F2005	1h32m37.093s	10
6	Giancarlo Fisichella	Renault F1	Renault R25	1h32m38.580s	9
7	Juan Pablo Montoya	McLaren	McLaren-Mercedes MP4-20	1h32m44.821s	5
8	Jarno Trulli	Toyota	Toyota TF105	1h32m57.739s	4
9	Vitantonio Liuzzi	Red Bull Racing	Red Bull-Cosworth RB1	1h32m58.177s	14
10	Jenson Button	BAR	BAR-Honda 007	1h33m22.434s	13
11	Kimi Raikkonen	McLaren	McLaren-Mercedes MP4-20	58 laps/suspension	2
12	Takuma Sato	BAR	BAR-Honda 007	58 laps	16
13	Jacques Villeneuve	Sauber	Sauber-Petronas C24	58 laps	15
14	Felipe Massa	Sauber	Sauber-Petronas C24	58 laps	11
15	Tiago Monteiro	Jordan	Jordan-Toyota EJ15	58 laps	17
16	Narain Karthikeyan	Jordan	Jordan-Toyota EJ15	58 laps	19
17	Christijan Albers	Minardi	Minardi-Cosworth PS05	57 laps	20
18	Patrick Friesacher	Minardi	Minardi-Cosworth PS05	56 laps	18
R	Ralf Schumacher	Toyota	Toyota TF105	33 laps/spun off	8
R	Mark Webber	Williams	Williams-BMW FW27	0 laps/collision	3

Pole: Heidfeld, 1m30.081s, 127.837mph/205.734kph. Fastest lap: Alonso, 1m30.711s, 126.949mph/204.305kph on Lap 44. Race leaders: Raikkonen 1-18 & 24-29 & 31-43 & 48-58, Coulthard 19, Alonso 20-23 & 44-47 & 59, Heidfeld 30

TOYOTA STEPS UP

Toyota needed its fourth year in F1 to be good, as the company's investment had been considerable, for little reward. The team had its strongest driver line-up in the shape of Ralf Schumacher and Jarno Trulli, and they got the TF105 to fly, ranking sixth and seventh to propel Toyota to fourth overall, just 12 points behind Ferrari.

CANADIAN GRAND PRIX

MONTREAL • ROUND 8 • DATE: 12TH JUNE 2005
Laps: 70 • Distance: 189.534miles/305.27km • Weather: Hot but dull

Pos	Driver	Team	Chassis-Engine	Result	Qual
1	Kimi Raikkonen	McLaren	McLaren-Mercedes MP4-20	1h32m09.290s	7
2	Michael Schumacher	Ferrari	Ferrari F2005	1h32m10.427s	2
3	Rubens Barrichello	Ferrari	Ferrari F2005	1h32m49.773s	20
4	Felipe Massa	Sauber	Sauber-Petronas C24	1h33m04.429s	11
5	Mark Webber	Williams	Williams-BMW FW27	1h33m05.069s	14
6	Ralf Schumacher	Toyota	Toyota TF105	69 laps	10
7	David Coulthard	Red Bull Racing	Red Bull-Cosworth RB1	69 laps	12
8	Christian Klien	Red Bull Racing	Red Bull-Cosworth RB1	69 laps	16
9	Jacques Villeneuve	Sauber	Sauber-Petronas C24	69 laps	8
10	Tiago Monteiro	Jordan	Jordan-Toyota EJ15	67 laps	18
11	Christijan Albers	Minardi	Minardi-Cosworth PS05	67 laps	15
R	Jarno Trulli	Toyota	Toyota TF105	62 laps/brakes	9
DQ	Juan Pablo Montoya	McLaren	McLaren-Mercedes MP4-20	52 laps/red light	5
R	Jenson Button	BAR	BAR-Honda 007	46 laps/spun off	1
R	Nick Heidfeld	Williams	Williams-BMW FW27	43 laps/engine	13
R	Takuma Sato	BAR	BAR-Honda 007	40 laps/brakes	6
R	Patrick Friesacher	Minardi	Minardi-Cosworth PS05	39 laps/hydraulics	19
R	Fernando Alonso	Renault F1	Renault R25	38 laps/collision	3
R	Giancarlo Fisichella	Renault F1	Renault R25	32 laps/hydraulics	4
R	Narain Karthikeyan	Jordan	Jordan-Toyota EJ15	24 laps/collision	17

Pole: Button, 1m15.217s, 129.695mph/208.724kph. Fastest lap: Raikkonen, 1m14.384s, 131.147mph/211.061kph on Lap 23. Race leaders: Fisichella 1-32, Alonso 33-38, Montoya 39-48, Raikkonen 49-70

SCHUMACHER ONLY THIRD

It had seemed that Michael Schumacher might go on winning forever, but the new technical and sporting rules hit Ferrari harder than most. As a result, Schumacher's five titles on the trot were followed by merely a third-place ranking in 2005 after winning just one race, and that was in the depleted field of six cars that started the United States GP.

UNITED STATES GRAND PRIX

INDIANAPOLIS MOTOR SPEEDWAY • ROUND 9 • DATE: 19TH JUNE 2005
Laps: 73 • Distance: 190.149miles/306.016km • Weather: Hot but dull

Pos	Driver	Team	Chassis-Engine	Result	Qual
1	Michael Schumacher	Ferrari	Ferrari F2005	1h29m43.181s	5
2	Rubens Barrichello	Ferrari	Ferrari F2005	1h29m44.703s	7
3	Tiago Monteiro	Jordan	Jordan-Toyota EJ15	72 laps	17
4	Narain Karthikeyan	Jordan	Jordan-Toyota EJ15	72 laps	19
5	Christijan Albers	Minardi	Minardi-Cosworth PS05	71 laps	18
6	Patrick Friesacher	Minardi	Minardi-Cosworth PS05	71 laps	20
NS	Jarno Trulli	Toyota	Toyota TF105	tyre concerns	1
NS	Kimi Raikkonen	McLaren	McLaren-Mercedes MP4-20	tyre concerns	2

Pos	Driver	Team	Chassis-Engine	Result	Qual
NS	Jenson Button	BAR	BAR-Honda 007	tyre concerns	3
NS	Giancarlo Fisichella	Renault F1	Renault R25	tyre concerns	4
NS	Fernando Alonso	Renault F1	Renault R25	tyre concerns	6
NS	Takuma Sato	BAR	BAR-Honda 007	tyre concerns	8
NS	Mark Webber	Williams	Williams-BMW FW27	tyre concerns	9
NS	Felipe Massa	Sauber	Sauber-Petronas C24	tyre concerns	10
NS	Juan Pablo Montoya	McLaren	McLaren-Mercedes MP4-20	tyre concerns	11
NS	Jacques Villeneuve	Sauber	Sauber-Petronas C24	tyre concerns	12
NS	Ricardo Zonta	Toyota	Toyota TF105	tyre concerns	13
NS	Christian Klien	Red Bull Racing	Red Bull-Cosworth RB1	tyre concerns	14
NS	Nick Heidfeld	Williams	Williams-BMW FW27	tyre concerns	15
NS	David Coulthard	Red Bull Racing	Red Bull-Cosworth RB1	tyre concerns	16
NS	Ralf Schumacher	Toyota	Toyota TF105	-	-

Pole: Trulli, 1m10.625s, 132.774mph/213.680kph. Fastest lap: M Schumacher, 1m11.497s, 131.155mph/211.074kph on Lap 48. Race leaders: M Schumacher 1-26 & 49-73, Barrichello 27-48

A BOYCOTT AT INDIANAPOLIS

A tyre failure for Toyota's Ralf Schumacher pitched him into the Turn 13 wall at Indianapolis for the second year running, and this led to the six other teams using Michelin tyres to pull out of the event after voicing concerns following several rear tyre failures. This left just Ferrari, Jordan and Minardi to start the race, a record low for F1.

LEAVING IT LATE

Kimi Raikkonen pulled off one of the moves of the decade at the Japanese GP when he passed Giancarlo Fisichella for the lead at Turn 1 on the final lap. After making a better exit from the final corner, he got alongside past the pits and simply drove his McLaren around the outside of the Italian driver's Renault in a stunning show of bravado.

FRENCH GRAND PRIX

MAGNY-COURS • ROUND 10 • DATE: 3RD JULY 2005
Laps: 70 • Distance: 191.430miles/308.77km • Weather: Hot & bright

Pos	Driver	Team	Chassis-Engine	Result	Qual
1	Fernando Alonso	Renault F1	Renault R25	1h31m22.233s	1
2	Kimi Raikkonen *	McLaren	McLaren-Mercedes MP4-20	1h31m34.038s	13
3	Michael Schumacher	Ferrari	Ferrari F2005	1h32m44.147s	3
4	Jenson Button	BAR	BAR-Honda 007	69 laps	7
5	Jarno Trulli	Toyota	Toyota TF105	69 laps	2
6	Giancarlo Fisichella	Renault F1	Renault R25	69 laps	6
7	Ralf Schumacher	Toyota	Toyota TF105	69 laps	11
8	Jacques Villeneuve	Sauber	Sauber-Petronas C24	69 laps	10
9	Rubens Barrichello	Ferrari	Ferrari F2005	69 laps	5
10	David Coulthard	Red Bull Racing	Red Bull-Cosworth RB1	69 laps	15
11	Takuma Sato	BAR	BAR-Honda 007	69 laps	4

Pos	Driver	Team	Chassis-Engine	Result	Qual
12	Mark Webber	Williams	Williams-BMW FW27	68 laps	12
13	Tiago Monteiro	Jordan	Jordan-Toyota EJ15	67 laps	19
14	Nick Heidfeld	Williams	Williams-BMW FW27	66 laps	14
15	Narain Karthikeyan	Jordan	Jordan-Toyota EJ15	66 laps	17
R	Juan Pablo Montoya	McLaren	McLaren-Mercedes MP4-20	46 laps/hydraulics	8
R	Christijan Albers	Minardi	Minardi-Cosworth PS05	37 laps/tyre	20
R	Patrick Friesacher	Minardi	Minardi-Cosworth PS05	33 laps/tyre	18
R	Felipe Massa	Sauber	Sauber-Petronas C24	30 laps/hydraulics	9
R	Christian Klien	Red Bull Racing	Red Bull-Cosworth RB1	1 lap/fuel pressure	16

Pole: Alonso, 1m14m.412s, 132.595mph/213.392kph. Fastest lap: Raikkonen, 1m16.423s, 129.111mph/207.785kph on Lap 25. Race leaders: Alonso 1-70

* 10-place grid penalty for engine change

BRITISH GRAND PRIX

SILVERSTONE • ROUND 11 • DATE: 10TH JULY 2005
Laps: 60 • Distance: 191.410miles/308.46km • Weather: Warm & bright

Pos	Driver	Team	Chassis-Engine	Result	Qual
1	Juan Pablo Montoya	McLaren	McLaren-Mercedes MP4-20	1h24m29.588s	3
2	Fernando Alonso	Renault F1	Renault R25	1h24m32.327s	1
3	Kimi Raikkonen *	McLaren	McLaren-Mercedes MP4-20	1h24m44.024s	12
4	Giancarlo Fisichella	Renault F1	Renault R25	1h24m47.502s	6
5	Jenson Button	BAR	BAR-Honda 007	1h25m09.852s	2
6	Michael Schumacher	Ferrari	Ferrari F2005	1h25m44.910s	9
7	Rubens Barrichello	Ferrari	Ferrari F2005	1h25m46.155s	5
8	Ralf Schumacher	Toyota	Toyota TF105	1h25m48.800s	8
9	Jarno Trulli	Toyota	Toyota TF105	1h25m50.439s	4
10	Felipe Massa	Sauber	Sauber-Petronas C24	59 laps	16
11	Mark Webber	Williams	Williams-BMW FW27	59 laps	11
12	Nick Heidfeld	Williams	Williams-BMW FW27	59 laps	14
13	David Coulthard	Red Bull Racing	Red Bull-Cosworth RB1	59 laps	13
14	Jacques Villeneuve	Sauber	Sauber-Petronas C24	59 laps	10
15	Christian Klien	Red Bull Racing	Red Bull-Cosworth RB1	59 laps	15
16	Takuma Sato	BAR	BAR-Honda 007	58 laps	7
17	Tiago Monteiro *	Jordan	Jordan-Toyota EJ15	58 laps	20
18	Christijan Albers	Minardi	Minardi-Cosworth PS05	57 laps	18
19	Patrick Friesacher	Minardi	Minardi-Cosworth PS05	56 laps	19
R	Narain Karthikeyan	Jordan	Jordan-Toyota EJ15	10 laps/electrical	17

Pole: Alonso, 1m19.905s, 143.922mph/231.620kph. Fastest lap: Raikkonen, 1m20.502s, 142.854mph/229.902kph on Lap 60. Race leaders: Montoya 1-21 & 26-44 & 50-60, Alonso 22-23 & 45-49, Fisichella 24-25

* 10-place grid penalty for engine change

GERMAN GRAND PRIX

HOCKENHEIM • ROUND 12 • DATE: 24TH JULY 2005
Laps: 67 • Distance: 190.424miles/306.458km • Weather: Warm but dull

Pos	Driver	Team	Chassis-Engine	Result	Qual
1	Fernando Alonso	Renault F1	Renault R25	1h26m28.599s	3
2	Juan Pablo Montoya *	McLaren	McLaren-Mercedes MP4-20	1h26m51.168s	20

Pos	Driver	Team	Chassis-Engine	Result	Qual
3	Jenson Button	BAR	BAR-Honda 007	1h26m53.021s	2
4	Giancarlo Fisichella	Renault F1	Renault R25	1h27m19.186s	4
5	Michael Schumacher	Ferrari	Ferrari F2005	1h27m20.289s	5
6	Ralf Schumacher	Toyota	Toyota TF105	1h27m20.841s	12
7	David Coulthard	Red Bull Racing	Red Bull-Cosworth RB1	1h27m21.299s	11
8	Felipe Massa	Sauber	Sauber-Petronas C24	1h27m25.169s	13
9	Christian Klien	Red Bull Racing	Red Bull-Cosworth RB1	1h27m38.417s	10
10	Rubens Barrichello	Ferrari	Ferrari F2005	66 laps	15
11	Nick Heidfeld	Williams	Williams-BMW FW27	66 laps	7
12	Takuma Sato	BAR	BAR-Honda 007	66 laps	8
13	Christijan Albers	Minardi	Minardi-Cosworth PS05	65 laps	16
14	Jarno Trulli	Toyota	Toyota TF105	64 laps/engine	9
15	Jacques Villeneuve	Sauber	Sauber-Petronas C24	64 laps	14
16	Narain Karthikeyan	Jordan	Jordan-Toyota EJ15	64 laps	19
17	Tiago Monteiro	Jordan	Jordan-Toyota EJ15	64 laps	18
18	Robert Doornbos	Minardi	Minardi-Cosworth PS05	63 laps	17
NC	Mark Webber	Williams	Williams-BMW FW27	55 laps	6
R	Kimi Raikkonen	McLaren	McLaren-Mercedes MP4-20	35 laps/hydraulics	1

Pole: Raikkonen, 1m14.320s, 137.671mph/221.560kph. Fastest lap: Raikkonen, 1m14.873s, 136.654mph/219.924kph on Lap 24. Race leaders: Raikkonen 1-35, Alonso 36-67

* 10-place grid penalty for engine change

HUNGARIAN GRAND PRIX

HUNGARORING • ROUND 13 • DATE: 31ST JULY 2005
Laps: 70 • Distance: 190.181miles/306.67km • Weather: Very hot & bright

Pos	Driver	Team	Chassis-Engine	Result	Qual
1	Kimi Raikkonen	McLaren	McLaren-Mercedes MP4-20	1h37m25.552s	4
2	Michael Schumacher	Ferrari	Ferrari F2005	1h38m01.133s	1
3	Ralf Schumacher	Toyota	Toyota TF105	1h38m01.681s	5
4	Jarno Trulli	Toyota	Toyota TF105	1h38m19.773s	3
5	Jenson Button	BAR	BAR-Honda 007	1h38m24.384s	8
6	Nick Heidfeld	Williams	Williams-BMW FW27	1h38m33.927s	12
7	Mark Webber	Williams	Williams-BMW FW27	69 laps	16
8	Takuma Sato	BAR	BAR-Honda 007	69 laps	10
9	Giancarlo Fisichella	Renault F1	Renault R25	69 laps	9
10	Rubens Barrichello	Ferrari	Ferrari F2005	69 laps	7
11	Fernando Alonso	Renault F1	Renault R25	69 laps	6
12	Narain Karthikeyan	Jordan	Jordan-Toyota EJ15	67 laps	18
13	Tiago Monteiro *	Jordan	Jordan-Toyota EJ15	66 laps	20
14	Felipe Massa	Sauber	Sauber-Petronas C24	63 laps	14
NC	Christijan Albers	Minardi	Minardi-Cosworth PS05	59 laps	17
R	Jacques Villeneuve	Sauber	Sauber-Petronas C24	56 laps/overheating	15
R	Juan Pablo Montoya	McLaren	McLaren-Mercedes MP4-20	41 laps/halfshaft	2
R	Robert Doornbos	Minardi	Minardi-Cosworth PS05	26 laps/hydraulics	19
R	Christian Klien	Red Bull Racing	Red Bull-Cosworth RB1	0 laps/collision	11
R	David Coulthard	Red Bull Racing	Red Bull-Cosworth RB1	0 laps/collision	13

Pole: M Schumacher, 1m19.882s, 122.681mph/197.436kph. Fastest lap: Raikkonen, 1m21.219s, 120.661mph/194.186kph on Lap 40. Race leaders: M Schumacher 1-15 & 23-35, Montoya 16-22 & 38-40, Raikkonen 36-37 & 41-70

* 10-place grid penalty for engine change

TURKISH GRAND PRIX

ISTANBUL PARK • ROUND 14 • DATE: 21ST AUGUST 2005
Laps: 58 • Distance: 192.379miles/309.604km • Weather: Hot & bright

Pos	Driver	Team	Chassis-Engine	Result	Qual
1	Kimi Raikkonen	McLaren	McLaren-Mercedes MP4-20	1h24m34.454s	1
2	Fernando Alonso	Renault F1	Renault R25	1h24m53.063s	3
3	Juan Pablo Montoya	McLaren	McLaren-Mercedes MP4-20	1h24m54.089s	4
4	Giancarlo Fisichella	Renault F1	Renault R25	1h25m12.427s	2
5	Jenson Button	BAR	BAR-Honda 007	1h25m13.758s	13
6	Jarno Trulli	Toyota	Toyota TF105	1h25m29.874s	5
7	David Coulthard	Red Bull Racing	Red Bull-Cosworth RB1	1h25m43.750s	12
8	Christian Klien	Red Bull Racing	Red Bull-Cosworth RB1	1h25m46.076s	10
9	Takuma Sato !	BAR	BAR-Honda 007	1h26m24.441s	20
10	Rubens Barrichello	Ferrari	Ferrari F2005	57 laps	11
11	Jacques Villeneuve	Sauber	Sauber-Petronas C24	57 laps	16
12	Ralf Schumacher	Toyota	Toyota TF105	57 laps	9
13	Robert Doornbos	Minardi	Minardi-Cosworth PS05	55 laps	17
14	Narain Karthikeyan *	Jordan	Jordan-Toyota EJ15	55 laps	18
15	Tiago Monteiro	Jordan	Jordan-Toyota EJ15	55 laps	14
R	Christijan Albers	Minardi	Minardi-Cosworth PS05	48 laps/hydraulics	15
R	Michael Schumacher *	Ferrari	Ferrari F2005	32 laps/accident damage	19
R	Nick Heidfeld	Williams	Williams-BMW FW27	29 laps/tyre	6
R	Felipe Massa	Sauber	Sauber-Petronas C24	28 laps/engine	8
R	Mark Webber	Williams	Williams-BMW FW27	20 laps/tyre	7

Pole: Raikkonen, 1m26.797s, 137.571mph/221.399kph. Fastest lap: Montoya, 1m24.770s, 140.860mph/226.693kph on Lap 39. Race leaders: Raikkonen 1-58

! qualifying time disallowed for impeding Webber • * 10-place grid penalty for engine change

> **BAR SELECTS REVERSE**
> After its surprise rise to second in 2004, BAR had a major loss of form in 2005. After being disqualified for having secondary fuel tanks at Imola, the team were banned from the next two races and didn't score any points until the 10th round. Jenson Button took two thirds, but a final ranking of seventh showed how BAR hadn't adapted well to the new rules.

ITALIAN GRAND PRIX

MONZA • ROUND 15 • DATE: 4TH SEPTEMBER 2005
Laps: 53 • Distance: 190.778miles/307.029km • Weather: Hot & bright

Pos	Driver	Team	Chassis-Engine	Result	Qual
1	Juan Pablo Montoya	McLaren	McLaren-Mercedes MP4-20	1h14m28.659s	1
2	Fernando Alonso	Renault F1	Renault R25	1h14m31.138s	2
3	Giancarlo Fisichella	Renault F1	Renault R25	1h14m46.634s	8
4	Kimi Raikkonen *	McLaren	McLaren-Mercedes MP4-20	1h14m51.434s	11
5	Jarno Trulli	Toyota	Toyota TF105	1h15m02.445s	5
6	Ralf Schumacher	Toyota	Toyota TF105	1h15m12.584s	9
7	Antonio Pizzonia	Williams	Williams-BMW FW27	1h15m13.302s	16

Pos	Driver	Team	Chassis-Engine	Result	Qual
8	Jenson Button	BAR	BAR-Honda 007	1h15m32.294s	3
9	Felipe Massa	Sauber	Sauber-Petronas C24	1h15m44.072s	15
10	Michael Schumacher	Ferrari	Ferrari F2005	1h16m04.729s	6
11	Jacques Villeneuve	Sauber	Sauber-Petronas C24	52 laps	12
12	Rubens Barrichello	Ferrari	Ferrari F2005	52 laps	7
13	Christian Klien	Red Bull Racing	Red Bull-Cosworth RB1	52 laps	13
14	Mark Webber	Williams	Williams-BMW FW27	52 laps	14
15	David Coulthard	Red Bull Racing	Red Bull-Cosworth RB1	52 laps	10
16	Takuma Sato	BAR	BAR-Honda 007	52 laps	4
17	Tiago Monteiro	Jordan	Jordan-Toyota EJ15	51 laps	17
18	Robert Doornbos	Minardi	Minardi-Cosworth PS05	51 laps	18
19	Christijan Albers	Minardi	Minardi-Cosworth PS05	51 laps	20
20	Narain Karthikeyan	Jordan	Jordan-Toyota EJ15	50 laps	19
NS	Nick Heidfeld	Williams	Williams-BMW FW27	-	-

Pole: Montoya, 1m21.054s, 159.875mph/257.295kph. Fastest lap: Raikkonen, 1m21.504s, 158.993mph/255.874kph on Lap 51. Race leaders: Montoya 1-53

* 10-place grid penalty for engine change

BELGIAN GRAND PRIX

SPA-FRANCORCHAMPS • ROUND 16 • DATE: 11TH SEPTEMBER 2005
Laps: 44 • Distance: 190.726miles/306.944km • Weather: Warm but damp

Pos	Driver	Team	Chassis-Engine	Result	Qual
1	Kimi Raikkonen	McLaren	McLaren-Mercedes MP4-20	1h30m01.295s	2
2	Fernando Alonso	Renault F1	Renault R25	1h30m29.689s	4
3	Jenson Button	BAR	BAR-Honda 007	1h30m33.372s	8
4	Mark Webber	Williams	Williams-BMW FW27	1h31m10.462s	9
5	Rubens Barrichello	Ferrari	Ferrari F2005	1h31m19.431s	12
6	Jacques Villeneuve	Sauber	Sauber-Petronas C24	1h31m28.730s	14
7	Ralf Schumacher	Toyota	Toyota TF105	1h31m28.869s	5
8	Tiago Monteiro	Jordan	Jordan-Toyota EJ15	43 laps	19
9	Christian Klien	Red Bull Racing	Red Bull-Cosworth RB1	43 laps	16
10	Felipe Massa	Sauber	Sauber-Petronas C24	43 laps	7
11	Narain Karthikeyan	Jordan	Jordan-Toyota EJ15	43 laps	20
12	Christijan Albers	Minardi	Minardi-Cosworth PS05	42 laps	18
13	Robert Doornbos	Minardi	Minardi-Cosworth PS05	41 laps	17
14	Juan Pablo Montoya	McLaren	McLaren-Mercedes MP4-20	40 laps/collision	1
15	Antonio Pizzonia	Williams	Williams-BMW FW27	39 laps/collision	15
R	Jarno Trulli	Toyota	Toyota TF105	34 laps/collision	3
R	David Coulthard	Red Bull Racing	Red Bull-Cosworth RB1	18 laps/engine	11
R	Michael Schumacher	Ferrari	Ferrari F2005	13 laps/collision	6
R	Takuma Sato	BAR	BAR-Honda 007	13 laps/collision	10
R	Giancarlo Fisichella *	Renault F1	Renault R25	10 laps/spun off	13

Pole: Montoya, 1m46.391s, 146.674mph/236.050kph. Fastest lap: R Schumacher, 1m51.453s, 140.012mph/225.329kph on Lap 43. Race leaders: Montoya 1-32, Raikkonen 33-44

* 10-place grid penalty for engine change

BRAZILIAN GRAND PRIX

INTERLAGOS • ROUND 17 • DATE: 25TH SEPTEMBER 2005
Laps: 71 • Distance: 190.101miles/305.939km • Weather: Warm with light rain

Pos	Driver	Team	Chassis-Engine	Result	Qual
1	Juan Pablo Montoya	McLaren	McLaren-Mercedes MP4-20	1h29m20.574s	2
2	Kimi Raikkonen	McLaren	McLaren-Mercedes MP4-20	1h29m23.101s	5
3	Fernando Alonso	Renault F1	Renault R25	1h29m45.414s	1
4	Michael Schumacher	Ferrari	Ferrari F2005	1h29m56.242s	7
5	Giancarlo Fisichella	Renault F1	Renault R25	1h30m00.792s	3
6	Rubens Barrichello	Ferrari	Ferrari F2005	1h30m29.747s	9
7	Jenson Button	BAR	BAR-Honda 007	70 laps	4
8	Ralf Schumacher	Toyota	Toyota TF105	70 laps	10
9	Christian Klien	Red Bull Racing	Red Bull-Cosworth RB1	70 laps	6
10	Takuma Sato */^	BAR	BAR-Honda 007	70 laps	19
11	Felipe Massa	Sauber	Sauber-Petronas C24	70 laps	8
12	Jacques Villeneuve !	Sauber	Sauber-Petronas C24	70 laps	20
13	Jarno Trulli *	Toyota	Toyota TF105	69 laps	17
14	Christijan Albers	Minardi	Minardi-Cosworth PS05	69 laps	16
15	Narain Karthikeyan	Jordan	Jordan-Toyota EJ15	68 laps	15
R	Tiago Monteiro	Jordan	Jordan-Toyota EJ15	55 laps/engine	11
NC	Mark Webber	Williams	Williams-BMW FW27	45 laps	12
R	Robert Doornbos	Minardi	Minardi-Cosworth PS05	34 laps/oil pipe	18
R	Antonio Pizzonia	Williams	Williams-BMW FW27	0 laps/collision	13
R	David Coulthard	Red Bull Racing	Red Bull-Cosworth RB1	0 laps/collision	14

Pole: Alonso, 1m11.988s, 133.896mph/215.485kph. Fastest lap: Raikkonen, 1m12.268s, 133.377mph/214.651kph on Lap 29. Race leaders: Alonso 1-2, Montoya 3-28 & 32-54 & 60-71, Raikkonen 29-31 & 55-59

* 10-place grid penalty for engine change • ^ 10-place grid penalty for causing a collision at the Belgian GP • ! back of grid for car being modified in parc ferme

NEW CIRCUITS

Some circuits take a while to grow on the drivers, but Turkey's first foray into F1, with its all-new Istanbul Park circuit, was an instant hit. Designed by Hermann Tilke, its 14-turn lap provided the drivers with some serious challenges, notably the twisting sequence from Turn 3 to Turn 6, and the seemingly endless Turn 8 left-hander.

JAPANESE GRAND PRIX

SUZUKA • ROUND 18 • DATE: 9TH OCTOBER 2005
Laps: 53 • Distance: 191.240miles/307.771km • Weather: Hot & bright

Pos	Driver	Team	Chassis-Engine	Result	Qual
1	Kimi Raikkonen *	McLaren	McLaren-Mercedes MP4-20	1h29m02.212s	17
2	Giancarlo Fisichella	Renault F1	Renault R25	1h29m03.845s	3
3	Fernando Alonso	Renault F1	Renault R25	1h29m19.668s	16
4	Mark Webber	Williams	Williams-BMW FW27	1h29m24.486s	7
5	Jenson Button	BAR	BAR-Honda 007	1h29m31.719s	2

Pos	Driver	Team	Chassis-Engine	Result	Qual
6	David Coulthard	Red Bull Racing	Red Bull-Cosworth RB1	1h29m33.813s	6
7	Michael Schumacher	Ferrari	Ferrari F2005	1h29m36.091s	14
8	Ralf Schumacher	Toyota	Toyota TF105B	1h29m51.760s	1
9	Christian Klien	Red Bull Racing	Red Bull-Cosworth RB1	1h29m54.137s	4
10	Felipe Massa	Sauber	Sauber-Petronas C24	1h29m59.721s	10
11	Rubens Barrichello	Ferrari	Ferrari F2005	1h30m02.845s	9
12	Jacques Villeneuve !	Sauber	Sauber-Petronas C24	1h30m25.433s	8
DQ	Takuma Sato	BAR	BAR-Honda 007	aggressive driving	5
13	Tiago Monteiro	Jordan	Jordan-Toyota EJ15	52 laps	20
14	Robert Doornbos	Minardi	Minardi-Cosworth PS05	51 laps	15
15	Narain Karthikeyan	Jordan	Jordan-Toyota EJ15	51 laps	11
16	Christijan Albers	Minardi	Minardi-Cosworth PS05	49 laps	13
R	Antonio Pizzonia	Williams	Williams-BMW FW27	9 laps/spun off	12
R	Jarno Trulli	Toyota	Toyota TF105B	9 laps/collision	19
R	Juan Pablo Montoya	McLaren	McLaren-Mercedes MP4-20	0 laps/spun off	18

Pole: R Schumacher, 1m46.106s, 122.423mph/197.021kph. Fastest lap: Raikkonen, 1m31.540s, 141.903mph/228.372kph on Lap 44. Race leaders: R Schumacher 1-12, Fisichella 13-20 & 27-38 & 46-52, Button 21-22 & 39-40, Coulthard 23, M Schumacher 24-26, Raikkonen 41-45 & 53

* 10-place grid penalty for engine change • ! 25s penalty for aggressive driving

CHINESE GRAND PRIX

SHANGHAI INTERNATIONAL CIRCUIT • ROUND 19 • DATE: 16TH OCTOBER 2005
Laps: 56 • Distance: 189.677miles/305.256km • Weather: Warm & bright

Pos	Driver	Team	Chassis-Engine	Result	Qual
1	Fernando Alonso	Renault F1	Renault R25	1h39m53.618s	1
2	Kimi Raikkonen	McLaren	McLaren-Mercedes MP4-20	1h39m57.633s	3
3	Ralf Schumacher	Toyota	Toyota TF105B	1h40m18.994s	9
4	Giancarlo Fisichella	Renault F1	Renault R25	1h40m19.732s	2
5	Christian Klien	Red Bull Racing	Red Bull-Cosworth RB1	1h40m25.457s	14
6	Felipe Massa	Sauber	Sauber-Petronas C24	1h40m30.018s	11
7	Mark Webber	Williams	Williams-BMW FW27	1h40m30.460s	10
8	Jenson Button	BAR	BAR-Honda 007	1h40m34.867s	4
9	David Coulthard	Red Bull Racing	Red Bull-Cosworth RB1	1h40m37.865s	7
10	Jacques Villeneuve	Sauber	Sauber-Petronas C24	1h40m53.595s	16
11	Tiago Monteiro	Jordan	Jordan-Toyota EJ15	1h41m18.266s	19
12	Rubens Barrichello	Ferrari	Ferrari F2005	1h41m26.430s	8
13	Antonio Pizzonia	Williams	Williams-BMW FW27	55 laps/puncture	13
14	Robert Doornbos	Minardi	Minardi-Cosworth PS05	55 laps	20
15	Jarno Trulli	Toyota	Toyota TF105B	55 laps	12
16	Christijan Albers	Minardi	Minardi-Cosworth PS05	51 laps/wheel	18
R	Takuma Sato	BAR	BAR-Honda 007	34 laps/gearbox	17
R	Narain Karthikeyan	Jordan	Jordan-Toyota EJ15	28 laps/spun off	15
R	Juan Pablo Montoya	McLaren	McLaren-Mercedes MP4-20	24 laps/engine	5
R	Michael Schumacher	Ferrari	Ferrari F2005	22 laps/spun off	6

Pole: Alonso, 1m34.080s, 129.608mph/208.584kph. Fastest lap: Raikkonen, 1m33.242s, 130.773mph/210.458kph on Lap 56. Race leaders: Alonso 1-56

WORLD DRIVERS' CHAMPIONSHIP FINAL RESULTS

Pos	Driver	Nat	Car-Engine	R1	R2	R3	R4	R5	R6	R7
1	Fernando Alonso	ESP	Renault R25	3F	1P	1P	1	2	4	1F
2	Kimi Raikkonen	FIN	McLaren-Mercedes MP4-20	8	9F	3	RP	1P	1P	11
3	Michael Schumacher	DEU	Ferrari F2004M	R	7	-	-	-	-	-
			Ferrari F2005	-	-	R	2F	R	7F	5
4	Juan Pablo Montoya	COL	McLaren-Mercedes MP4-20	6	4	-	-	7	5	7
5	Giancarlo Fisichella	ITA	Renault R25	1P	R	R	R	5F	12	6
6	Ralf Schumacher	DEU	Toyota TF105	12	5	4	9	4	6	R
			Toyota TF105B	-	-	-	-	-	-	-
7	Jarno Trulli	ITA	Toyota TF105	9	2	2	5	3	10	8
			Toyota TF105B	-	-	-	-	-	-	-
8	Rubens Barrichello	BRA	Ferrari F2004M	2	R	-	-	-	-	-
			Ferrari F2005	-	-	9	R	9	8	3
9	Jenson Button	GBR	BAR-Honda 007	11	R	R	DQ	-	-	10
10	Mark Webber	AUS	Williams-BMW FW27	5	R	6	7	6	3	R
11	Nick Heidfeld	DEU	Williams-BMW FW27	R	3	R	6	10	2	2P
12	David Coulthard	GBR	Red Bull-Cosworth RB1	4	6	8	11	8	R	4
13	Felipe Massa	BRA	Sauber-Petronas C24	10	10	7	10	11	9	14
14	Jacques Villeneuve	CAN	Sauber-Petronas C24	13	R	11	4	R	11	13
15	Christian Klien	AUT	Red Bull-Cosworth RB1	7	8	NS	T	T	T	T
16	Tiago Monteiro	PRT	Jordan-Toyota EJ15	16	12	10	13	12	13	15
17	Alexander Wurz	AUT	McLaren-Mercedes MP4-20	-	-	T	3	-	T	T
18	Narain Karthikeyan	IND	Jordan-Toyota EJ15	15	11	R	12	13	R	16
19	Christijan Albers	NLD	Minardi-Cosworth PS04B	R	13	13	-	-	-	-
			Minardi-Cosworth PS05	-	-	-	R	R	14	17
20	Pedro de la Rosa	ESP	McLaren-Mercedes MP4-20	T	T	5F	T	T	-	-
21	Patrick Friesacher	AUT	Minardi-Cosworth PS04B	17	R	12	-	-	-	-
			Minardi-Cosworth PS05	-	-	-	R	R	R	18
22	Antonio Pizzonia	BRA	Williams-BMW FW27	-	-	-	-	-	-	-
23	Takuma Sato	JPN	BAR-Honda 007	14	NS	R	DQ	-	-	12
24	Vitantonio Liuzzi	ITA	Red Bull-Cosworth RB1	T	T	T	8	R	R	9
25	Robert Doornbos	NLD	Minardi-Cosworth PS05	-	-	-	-	-	-	-
			Jordan-Toyota EJ15	T	T	T	T	T	T	-

Pos	Driver	R8	R9	R10	R11	R12	R13	R14	R15	R16	R17	R18	R19	Total
1	Alonso	R	NS	1P	2P	1	11	2	2	2	3P	3	1P	133
2	Raikkonen	1F	NS	2F	3F	RPF	1F	1P	4F	1	2F	1F	2F	112
3	M Schumacher	-	-	-	-	-	-	-	-	-	-	-	-	62
		2	1F	3	6	5	2P	R	10	R	4	7	R	
4	Montoya	DQ	NS	R	1	2	R	3F	1P	14P	1	R	R	60
5	Fisichella	R	NS	6	4	4	9	4	3	R	5	2	4	58
6	R Schumacher	6	NS	7	8	6	3	12	6	7F	8	-	-	45
		-	-	-	-	-	-	-	-	-	-	8P	3	
7	Trulli	R	NSP	5	9	14	4	6	5	R	13	-	-	43
		-	-	-	-	-	-	-	-	-	-	R	15	
8	Barrichello	-	-	-	-	-	-	-	-	-	-	-	-	38
		3	2	9	7	10	10	10	12	5	6	11	12	
9	Button	RP	NS	4	5	3	5	5	8	3	7	5	8	37
10	Webber	5	NS	12	11	NC	7	R	14	4	NC	4	7	36
11	Heidfeld	R	NS	14	12	11	6	R	-	-	-	-	-	28
12	Coulthard	7	NS	10	13	7	R	7	15	R	R	6	9	24
13	Massa	4	NS	R	10	8	14	R	9	10	11	10	6	11
14	Villeneuve	9	NS	8	14	15	R	11	11	6	12	12	10	9
15	Klien	8	NS	R	15	9	R	8	13	9	9	9	5	9

Pos	Driver	R8	R9	R10	R11	R12	R13	R14	R15	R16	R17	R18	R19	Total
16	Monteiro	10	3	13	17	17	13	15	17	8	R	13	11	7
17	Wurz	-	-	-	-	T	T	-	-	T	T	T	-	6
18	Karthikeyan	R	4	15	R	16	12	14	20	11	15	15	R	5
19	Albers	-	-	-	-	-	-	-	-	-	-	-	-	4
		11	5	R	18	13	NC	R	19	12	14	16	16	
20	de la Rosa	T	T	T	T	-	-	T	T	-	-	T	T	4
21	Friesacher	-	-	-	-	-	-	-	-	-	-	-	-	3
		R	6	R	19	-	-	-	-	-	-	-	-	
22	Pizzonia	-	-	-	-	-	-	-	7	15	R	R	13	2
23	Sato	R	NS	11	16	12	8	9	16	R	10	DQ	R	1
24	Liuzzi	-	-	T	T	T	T	T	T	T	T	T	T	1
25	Doornbos	-	-	-	-	18	R	13	18	13	R	14	14	0

WORLD CONSTRUCTORS' CHAMPIONSHIP FINAL RESULTS

Pos	Team-Engine	R1	R2	R3	R4	R5	R6	R7	R8	R9	R10
1	Renault F1	1/3	1/R	1/R	1/R	2/5	4/12	1/6	R/R	NS/NS	1/6
2	McLaren-Mercedes	6/8	4/9	3/5	3/R	1/7	1/5	7/11	1/DQ	NS/NS	2/R
3	Ferrari	2/R	7/R	9/R	2/R	9/R	7/8	3/5	2/3	1/2	3/9
4	Toyota	9/12	2/5	2/4	5/9	3/4	6/10	8/R	6/R	NS/NS	5/7
5	Williams-BMW	5/R	3/R	6/R	6/7	6/10	2/3	2/R	5/R	NS/NS	12/14
6	BAR-Honda	11/14	R/R	R/R	DQ/DQ	-	-	10/12	R/R	NS/NS	4/11
7	Red Bull-Cosworth	4/7	6/8	8/NS	8/11	8/R	R/R	4/9	7/8	NS/NS	10/R
8	Sauber-Petronas	10/13	10/R	7/11	4/10	11/R	9/11	13/14	4/9	NS/NS	8/R
9	Jordan-Toyota	15/16	11/12	10/R	12/13	12/13	13/R	15/16	10/R	3/4	13/15
10	Minardi-Cosworth	17/R	13/R	12/13	R/R	R/R	14/R	17/18	11/R	5/6	R/R

Pos	Team-Engine	R11	R12	R13	R14	R15	R16	R17	R18	R19	Total
1	Renault F1	2/4	1/4	9/11	2/4	2/3	2/R	3/5	2/3	1/4	191
2	McLaren-Mercedes	1/3	2/R	1/R	1/3	1/4	1/14	1/2	1/R	2/R	182
3	Ferrari	6/7	5/10	2/10	10/R	10/12	5/R	4/6	7/11	12/R	100
4	Toyota	8/9	6/14	3/4	6/12	5/6	7/R	8/13	8/R	3/15	88
5	Williams-BMW	11/12	11/NC	6/7	R/R	7/14	4/15	NC/R	4/R	7/13	66
6	BAR-Honda	5/16	3/12	5/8	5/9	8/16	3/R	7/10	5/DQ	8/R	38
7	Red Bull-Cosworth	13/15	7/9	R/R	7/8	13/15	9/R	9/R	6/9	5/9	34
8	Sauber-Petronas	10/14	8/15	14/R	11/R	9/11	6/10	11/12	10/12	6/10	20
9	Jordan-Toyota	17/R	16/17	12/13	14/15	17/20	8/11	15/R	13/15	11/R	12
10	Minardi-Cosworth	18/19	13/18	NC/R	13/R	18/19	12/13	14/R	14/16	14/16	7

SYMBOLS AND GRAND PRIX KEY

Round 1	**Australian GP**	**Round 11**	**British GP**
Round 2	**Malaysian GP**	**Round 12**	**German GP**
Round 3	**Bahrain GP**	**Round 13**	**Hungarian GP**
Round 4	**San Marino GP**	**Round 14**	**Turkish GP**
Round 5	**Spanish GP**	**Round 15**	**Italian GP**
Round 6	**Monaco GP**	**Round 16**	**Belgian GP**
Round 7	**European GP**	**Round 17**	**Brazilian GP**
Round 8	**Canadian GP**	**Round 18**	**Japanese GP**
Round 9	**United States GP**	**Round 19**	**Chinese GP**
Round 10	**French GP**		

SCORING

1st	**10 points**
2nd	**8 points**
3rd	**6 points**
4th	**5 points**
5th	**4 points**
6th	**3 points**
7th	**2 points**
8th	**1 point**

DNPQ DID NOT PRE-QUALIFY   DNQ DID NOT QUALIFY   DQ DISQUALIFIED   EX EXCLUDED
F FASTEST LAP   NC NOT CLASSIFIED   NS NON-STARTER   P POLE POSITION   R RETIRED

2006

SEASON SUMMARY

Fernando Alonso edged out Michael Schumacher to make it two world titles in a row with Renault in a year of great racing but messy politics. The banning of Renault's mass damping system midway through the year cost the team its edge, but Alonso and team-mate Giancarlo Fisichella kept going to ensure that the Spaniard took the title – and the team the constructors' championship, just ahead of Ferrari, for whom Felipe Massa won twice in his first year with the team. Late in the year, after he won the Italian GP, it was announced that Schumacher was retiring, so it really was the end of an era.

BAHRAIN GRAND PRIX

SAKHIR • ROUND 1 • DATE: 12TH MARCH 2006
Laps: 57 • Distance: 191.683miles/308.484km • Weather: Very hot & bright

Pos	Driver	Team	Chassis-Engine	Result	Qual
1	Fernando Alonso	Renault F1	Renault R26	1h29m46.205s	4
2	Michael Schumacher	Ferrari	Ferrari 248 F1	1h29m47.451s	1
3	Kimi Raikkonen	McLaren	McLaren-Mercedes MP4-21	1h30m05.565s	22
4	Jenson Button	Honda Racing	Honda RA106	1h30m06.197s	3
5	Juan Pablo Montoya	McLaren	McLaren-Mercedes MP4-21	1h30m23.253s	5
6	Mark Webber	Williams	Williams-Cosworth FW28	1h30m28.137s	7
7	Nico Rosberg	Williams	Williams-Cosworth FW28	1h30m49.248s	12
8	Christian Klien	Red Bull Racing	Red Bull-Ferrari RB2	1h30m52.976s	8
9	Felipe Massa	Ferrari	Ferrari 248 F1	1h30m56.112s	2
10	David Coulthard	Red Bull Racing	Red Bull-Ferrari RB2	1h31m01.746s	13
11	Vitantonio Liuzzi	Toro Rosso	Toro Rosso-Cosworth STR01	1h31m12.202s	15
12	Nick Heidfeld	BMW Sauber	BMW Sauber F1.06	56 laps	10
13	Scott Speed	Toro Rosso	Toro Rosso-Cosworth STR01	56 laps	16
14	Ralf Schumacher	Toyota	Toyota TF106	56 laps	17
15	Rubens Barrichello	Honda Racing	Honda RA106	56 laps	6
16	Jarno Trulli	Toyota	Toyota TF106	56 laps	14
17	Tiago Monteiro	Midland	Midland-Toyota M16	55 laps	19
18	Takuma Sato	Super Aguri	Super Aguri-Honda SA05	53 laps	20
R	Yuji Ide	Super Aguri	Super Aguri-Honda SA05	35 laps/engine	21
R	Jacques Villeneuve	BMW Sauber	BMW Sauber F1.06	29 laps/engine	11
R	Giancarlo Fisichella	Renault F1	Renault R26	21 laps/hydraulics	9
R	Christijan Albers	Midland	Midland-Toyota M16	0 laps/halfshaft	18

Pole: M Schumacher, 1m31.431s, 132.409mph/213.091kph. Fastest lap: Rosberg, 1m32.408s, 131.009mph/210.838kph on Lap 42. Race leaders: M Schumacher 1-15 & 24-35, Alonso 16-19 & 36-39 & 41-57, Montoya 20-23, Button 40

V10s OUT, V8s IN

V10 engines were consigned to history at the end of 2005 and replaced in 2006 by V8s that were 600cc smaller, at 2.4 litres. A loss of performance was countered by better fuel economy and superior reliability, vital now that they had to last two races. Another change was that qualifying was given an elimination format run across three sessions.

MALAYSIAN GRAND PRIX

SEPANG • ROUND 2 • DATE: 19TH MARCH 2006
Laps: 56 • Distance: 192.878miles/310.408km • Weather: Hot but dull

Pos	Driver	Team	Chassis-Engine	Result	Qual
1	Giancarlo Fisichella	Renault F1	Renault R26	1h30m40.529s	1
2	Fernando Alonso	Renault F1	Renault R26	1h30m45.114s	7
3	Jenson Button	Honda Racing	Honda RA106	1h30m50.160s	2
4	Juan Pablo Montoya	McLaren	McLaren-Mercedes MP4-21	1h31m19.880s	5
5	Felipe Massa *	Ferrari	Ferrari 248 F1	1h31m23.783s	21
6	Michael Schumacher *	Ferrari	Ferrari 248 F1	1h31m24.383s	14
7	Jacques Villeneuve	BMW Sauber	BMW Sauber F1.06	1h32m00.990s	10
8	Ralf Schumacher *	Toyota	Toyota TF106	1h32m01.817s	22
9	Jarno Trulli	Toyota	Toyota TF106	55 laps	9
10	Rubens Barrichello *	Honda Racing	Honda RA106	55 laps	20
11	Vitantonio Liuzzi	Toro Rosso	Toro Rosso-Cosworth STR01	54 laps	13
12	Christijan Albers	Midland	Midland-Toyota M16	54 laps	15
13	Tiago Monteiro	Midland	Midland-Toyota M16	54 laps	16
14	Takuma Sato	Super Aguri	Super Aguri-Honda SA05	53 laps	17
R	Nick Heidfeld	BMW Sauber	BMW Sauber F1.06	48 laps/engine	11
R	Scott Speed	Toro Rosso	Toro Rosso-Cosworth STR01	41 laps/clutch	12
R	Yuji Ide	Super Aguri	Super Aguri-Honda SA05	33 laps/engine	18
R	Christian Klien	Red Bull Racing	Red Bull-Ferrari RB2	26 laps/hydraulics	8
R	Mark Webber	Williams	Williams-Cosworth FW28	15 laps/hydraulics	4
R	David Coulthard *	Red Bull Racing	Red Bull-Ferrari RB2	10 laps/hydraulics	19
R	Nico Rosberg	Williams	Williams-Cosworth FW28	6 laps/engine	3
R	Kimi Raikkonen	McLaren	McLaren-Mercedes MP4-21	0 laps/collision	6

Pole: Fisichella, 1m33.840s, 132.132mph/212.647kph. Fastest lap: Alonso, 1m34.803s, 130.790mph/210.487kph on Lap 45. Race leaders: Fisichella 1-17 & 27-38 & 44-56, Button 18-19, Alonso 20-26 & 39-43

* 10-place grid penalty for engine change

AUSTRALIAN GRAND PRIX

ALBERT PARK • ROUND 3 • DATE: 2ND APRIL 2006
Laps: 57 • Distance: 187.822miles/302.271km • Weather: Warm & bright

Pos	Driver	Team	Chassis-Engine	Result	Qual
1	Fernando Alonso	Renault F1	Renault R26	1h34m27.870s	3
2	Kimi Raikkonen	McLaren	McLaren-Mercedes MP4-21	1h34m29.699s	4
3	Ralf Schumacher	Toyota	Toyota TF106	1h34m52.694s	6
4	Nick Heidfeld	BMW Sauber	BMW Sauber F1.06	1h34m58.902s	8
5	Giancarlo Fisichella	Renault F1	Renault R26	1h35m06.291s	2
6	Jacques Villeneuve *	BMW Sauber	BMW Sauber F1.06	1h35m17.424s	19
7	Rubens Barrichello	Honda Racing	Honda RA106	1h35m19.774s	16
8	David Coulthard	Red Bull Racing	Red Bull-Ferrari RB2	1h35m21.853s	11
9	Scott Speed !	Toro Rosso	Toro Rosso-Cosworth STR01	1h35m46.687s	18
10	Jenson Button	Honda Racing	Honda RA106	56 laps/engine	1
11	Christijan Albers	Midland	Midland-Toyota M16	56 laps	17
12	Takuma Sato	Super Aguri	Super Aguri-Honda SA05	55 laps	21
13	Yuji Ide	Super Aguri	Super Aguri-Honda SA05	54 laps	22
R	Juan Pablo Montoya	McLaren	McLaren-Mercedes MP4-21	45 laps/spun off	5
R	Tiago Monteiro	Midland	Midland-Toyota M16	39 laps/hydraulics	20
R	Vitantonio Liuzzi	Toro Rosso	Toro Rosso-Cosworth STR01	37 laps/spun off	12
R	Michael Schumacher	Ferrari	Ferrari 248 F1	32 laps/spun off	10

Pos	Driver	Team	Chassis-Engine	Result	Qual
R	Mark Webber	Williams	Williams-Cosworth FW28	22 laps/gearbox	7
R	Christian Klien	Red Bull Racing	Red Bull-Ferrari RB2	4 laps/spun off	13
R	Jarno Trulli	Toyota	Toyota TF106	0 laps/collision	9
R	Nico Rosberg	Williams	Williams-Cosworth FW28	0 laps/collision	14
R	Felipe Massa	Ferrari	Ferrari 248 F1	0 laps/collision	15

Pole: Button, 1m25.229s, 139.183mph/223.994kph. Fastest lap: Raikkonen, 1m26.045s, 137.863mph/221.869kph on Lap 57. Race leaders: Button 1-3, Alonso 4-19 & 23-57, Raikkonen 20, Webber 21-22

* 10-place grid penalty for engine change • ! 25s penalty for overtaking under yellow flag

SAN MARINO GRAND PRIX

IMOLA • ROUND 4 • DATE: 23RD APRIL 2006
Laps: 62 • Distance: 191.45miles/307.458km • Weather: Warm & bright

Pos	Driver	Team	Chassis-Engine	Result	Qual
1	Michael Schumacher	Ferrari	Ferrari 248 F1	1h31m06.486s	1
2	Fernando Alonso	Renault F1	Renault R26	1h31m08.582s	5
3	Juan Pablo Montoya	McLaren	McLaren-Mercedes MP4-21	1h31m22.354s	7
4	Felipe Massa	Ferrari	Ferrari 248 F1	1h31m23.582s	4
5	Kimi Raikkonen	McLaren	McLaren-Mercedes MP4-21	1h31m24.010s	8
6	Mark Webber	Williams	Williams-Cosworth FW28	1h31m44.225s	10
7	Jenson Button	Honda Racing	Honda RA106	1h31m46.121s	2
8	Giancarlo Fisichella	Renault F1	Renault R26	1h31m46.686s	11
9	Ralf Schumacher	Toyota	Toyota TF106	1h31m51.997s	6
10	Rubens Barrichello	Honda Racing	Honda RA106	1h32m24.337s	3
11	Nico Rosberg	Williams	Williams-Cosworth FW28	1h32m26.161s	13
12	Jacques Villeneuve	BMW Sauber	BMW Sauber F1.06	1h32m28.856s	12
13	Nick Heidfeld	BMW Sauber	BMW Sauber F1.06	61 laps	15
14	Vitantonio Liuzzi	Toro Rosso	Toro Rosso-Cosworth STR01	61 laps	16
15	Scott Speed	Toro Rosso	Toro Rosso-Cosworth STR01	61 laps	18
16	Tiago Monteiro	Midland	Midland-Toyota M16	60 laps	19
R	David Coulthard	Red Bull Racing	Red Bull-Ferrari RB2	47 laps/halfshaft	14
R	Takuma Sato	Super Aguri	Super Aguri-Honda SA05	44 laps/spun off	21
R	Christian Klien	Red Bull Racing	Red Bull-Ferrari RB2	40 laps/hydraulics	17
R	Yuji Ide	Super Aguri	Super Aguri-Honda SA05	23 laps/suspension	22
R	Jarno Trulli	Toyota	Toyota TF106	5 laps/steering	9
R	Christijan Albers	Midland	Midland-Toyota M16	0 laps/collision	20

Pole: M Schumacher, 1m22.795s, 133.981mph/215.621kph. Fastest lap: Alonso, 1m24.569s, 131.170mph/211.098kph on Lap 23. Race leaders: M Schumacher 1-20 & 26-42 & 45-62, Alonso 21-25, Montoya 43-44

EUROPEAN GRAND PRIX

NURBURGRING • ROUND 5 • DATE: 7TH MAY 2006
Laps: 60 • Distance: 191.437miles/308.88km • Weather: Warm & bright

Pos	Driver	Team	Chassis-Engine	Result	Qual
1	Michael Schumacher	Ferrari	Ferrari 248 F1	1h35m58.765s	2
2	Fernando Alonso	Renault F1	Renault R26	1h36m02.516s	1
3	Felipe Massa	Ferrari	Ferrari 248 F1	1h36m03.212s	3
4	Kimi Raikkonen	McLaren	McLaren-Mercedes MP4-21	1h36m03.644s	5

Pos	Driver	Team	Chassis-Engine	Result	Qual
5	Rubens Barrichello	Honda Racing	Honda RA106	1h37m11.351s	4
6	Giancarlo Fisichella	Renault F1	Renault R26	1h37m12.881s	11
7	Nico Rosberg *	Williams	Williams-Cosworth FW28	1h37m13.330s	22
8	Jacques Villeneuve !	BMW Sauber	BMW Sauber F1.06	1h37m28.129s	9
9	Jarno Trulli	Toyota	Toyota TF106	59 laps	7
10	Nick Heidfeld	BMW Sauber	BMW Sauber F1.06	59 laps	13
11	Scott Speed	Toro Rosso	Toro Rosso-Cosworth STR01	59 laps	17
12	Tiago Monteiro	Midland	Midland-Toyota M16	59 laps	18
13	Christijan Albers	Midland	Midland-Toyota M16	59 laps	16
R	Juan Pablo Montoya	McLaren	McLaren-Mercedes MP4-21	52 laps/engine	8
R	Ralf Schumacher	Toyota	Toyota TF106	52 laps/engine	10
R	Takuma Sato	Super Aguri	Super Aguri-Honda SA05	45 laps/hydraulics	20
R	Franck Montagny	Super Aguri	Super Aguri-Honda SA05	29 laps/hydraulics	21
R	Jenson Button	Honda Racing	Honda RA106	28 laps/engine	6
R	Christian Klien	Red Bull Racing	Red Bull-Ferrari RB2	28 laps/transmission	15
R	Mark Webber *	Williams	Williams-Cosworth FW28	12 laps/hydraulics	19
R	David Coulthard	Red Bull Racing	Red Bull-Ferrari RB2	2 laps/collision	12
R	Vitantonio Liuzzi	Toro Rosso	Toro Rosso-Cosworth STR01	0 laps/collision	14

Pole: Alonso, 1m29.819s, 128.210mph/206.334kph. Fastest lap: M Schumacher, 1m32.099s, 125.036mph/201.226kph on Lap 39. Race leaders: Alonso 1-16 & 24-37, M Schumacher 17-18 & 38-41 & 45-60, Raikkonen 19-23 & 42-44

* 10-place grid penalty for engine change • ! 5-place grid penalty for baulking another driver

NOT VERY SPORTING

Michael Schumacher had shown in the 1994 finale that he would fight dirty if it suited him. In 2006, he did it again, in qualifying at Monaco. Realising that his time was the fastest, but others behind him were going faster still on their final laps, he deliberately hit the barriers at Rascasse to stop the session, stepping over the boundary into unsporting behaviour.

SPANISH GRAND PRIX

BARCELONA-CATALUNYA • ROUND 6 • DATE: 14TH MAY 2006
Laps: 66 • Distance: 189.755miles/305.382km • Weather: Hot & bright

Pos	Driver	Team	Chassis-Engine	Result	Qual
1	Fernando Alonso	Renault F1	Renault R26	1h26m21.759s	1
2	Michael Schumacher	Ferrari	Ferrari 248 F1	1h26m40.261s	3
3	Giancarlo Fisichella	Renault F1	Renault R26	1h26m45.710s	2
4	Felipe Massa	Ferrari	Ferrari 248 F1	1h26m51.618s	4
5	Kimi Raikkonen	McLaren	McLaren-Mercedes MP4-21	1h27m18.634s	9
6	Jenson Button	Honda Racing	Honda RA106	1h27m20.106s	8
7	Rubens Barrichello	Honda Racing	Honda RA106	65 laps	5
8	Nick Heidfeld	BMW Sauber	BMW Sauber F1.06	65 laps	10
9	Mark Webber	Williams	Williams-Cosworth FW28	65 laps	11
10	Jarno Trulli	Toyota	Toyota TF106	65 laps	7
11	Nico Rosberg	Williams	Williams-Cosworth FW28	65 laps	13
12	Jacques Villeneuve *	BMW Sauber	BMW Sauber F1.06	65 laps	22

Pos	Driver	Team	Chassis-Engine	Result	Qual
13	Christian Klien	Red Bull Racing	Red Bull-Ferrari RB2	65 laps	14
14	David Coulthard	Red Bull Racing	Red Bull-Ferrari RB2	65 laps	21
15	Vitantonio Liuzzi	Toro Rosso	Toro Rosso-Cosworth STR01	63 laps/hydraulics	15
16	Tiago Monteiro	Midland	Midland-Toyota M16	63 laps	17
17	Takuma Sato	Super Aguri	Super Aguri-Honda SA05	62 laps	19
R	Christijan Albers	Midland	Midland-Toyota M16	48 laps/wing	18
R	Scott Speed	Toro Rosso	Toro Rosso-Cosworth STR01	47 laps/engine	16
R	Ralf Schumacher	Toyota	Toyota TF106	31 laps/electrical	6
R	Juan Pablo Montoya	McLaren	McLaren-Mercedes MP4-21	17 laps/spun off	12
R	Franck Montagny	Super Aguri	Super Aguri-Honda SA05	10 laps/halfshaft	20

Pole: Alonso, 1m14.648s, 138.654mph/223.143kph. Fastest lap: Massa, 1m16.648s, 135.036mph/217.320kph on Lap 42. Race leaders: Alonso 1-17 & 24-40 & 47-66, Fisichella 18, M Schumacher 19-23 & 41-46

* 10-place grid penalty for engine change

MONACO GRAND PRIX

MONTE CARLO • ROUND 7 • DATE: 28TH MAY 2006
Laps: 78 • Distance: 161.588miles/260.52km • Weather: Warm & bright

Pos	Driver	Team	Chassis-Engine	Result	Qual
1	Fernando Alonso	Renault F1	Renault R26	1h43m43.116s	1
2	Juan Pablo Montoya	McLaren	McLaren-Mercedes MP4-21	1h43m57.683s	4
3	David Coulthard	Red Bull Racing	Red Bull-Ferrari RB2	1h44m35.414s	7
4	Rubens Barrichello	Honda Racing	Honda RA106	1h44m36.453s	5
5	Michael Schumacher *	Ferrari	Ferrari 248 F1	1h44m36.946s	22
6	Giancarlo Fisichella !	Renault F1	Renault R26	1h44m45.188s	9
7	Nick Heidfeld	BMW Sauber	BMW Sauber F1.06	77 laps	15
8	Ralf Schumacher	Toyota	Toyota TF106	77 laps	10
9	Felipe Massa ^	Ferrari	Ferrari 248 F1	77 laps	21
10	Vitantonio Liuzzi	Toro Rosso	Toro Rosso-Cosworth STR01	77 laps	12
11	Jenson Button	Honda Racing	Honda RA106	77 laps	13
12	Christijan Albers	Midland	Midland-Toyota M16	77 laps	16
13	Scott Speed	Toro Rosso	Toro Rosso-Cosworth STR01	77 laps	18
14	Jacques Villeneuve	BMW Sauber	BMW Sauber F1.06	77 laps	14
15	Tiago Monteiro	Midland	Midland-Toyota M16	76 laps	17
16	Franck Montagny	Super Aguri	Super Aguri-Honda SA05	75 laps	20
17	Jarno Trulli	Toyota	Toyota TF106	72 laps/hydraulics	6
R	Christian Klien	Red Bull Racing	Red Bull-Ferrari RB2	56 laps/transmission	11
R	Nico Rosberg	Williams	Williams-Cosworth FW28	51 laps/exhaust	8
R	Kimi Raikkonen	McLaren	McLaren-Mercedes MP4-21	50 laps/fire	3
R	Mark Webber	Williams	Williams-Cosworth FW28	48 laps/exhaust	2
R	Takuma Sato	Super Aguri	Super Aguri-Honda SA05	46 laps/electrical	19

Pole: Alonso, 1m13.962s, 101.016mph/162.569kph. Fastest lap: M Schumacher, 1m15.143s, 99.428mph/160.014kph on Lap 74. Race leaders: Alonso 1-23 & 25-78, Webber 24

* all laps deleted for blocking track in qualifying • ! best 3 qualifying times deleted for impeding Coulthard • ^ made to start from the back of the grid for engine change

BRITISH GRAND PRIX

SILVERSTONE • ROUND 8 • DATE: 11TH JUNE 2006
Laps: 60 • Distance: 191.410miles/308.46km • Weather: Warm & bright

Pos	Driver	Team	Chassis-Engine	Result	Qual
1	Fernando Alonso	Renault F1	Renault R26	1h25m51.927s	1
2	Michael Schumacher	Ferrari	Ferrari 248 F1	1h26m05.878s	3
3	Kimi Raikkonen	McLaren	McLaren-Mercedes MP4-21	1h26m10.599s	2
4	Giancarlo Fisichella	Renault F1	Renault R26	1h26m11.903s	5
5	Felipe Massa	Ferrari	Ferrari 248 F1	1h26m23.486s	4
6	Juan Pablo Montoya	McLaren	McLaren-Mercedes MP4-21	1h26m56.696s	8
7	Nick Heidfeld	BMW Sauber	BMW Sauber F1.06	1h27m03.521s	9
8	Jacques Villeneuve	BMW Sauber	BMW Sauber F1.06	1h27m10.226s	10
9	Nico Rosberg	Williams	Williams-Cosworth FW28	1h27m10.935s	12
10	Rubens Barrichello	Honda Racing	Honda RA106	59 laps	6
11	Jarno Trulli !	Toyota	Toyota TF106	59 laps	22
12	David Coulthard	Red Bull Racing	Red Bull-Ferrari RB2	59 laps	11
13	Vitantonio Liuzzi	Toro Rosso	Toro Rosso-Cosworth STR01	59 laps	13
14	Christian Klien	Red Bull Racing	Red Bull-Ferrari RB2	59 laps	14
15	Christijan Albers	Midland	Midland-Toyota M16	59 laps	18
16	Tiago Monteiro	Midland	Midland-Toyota M16	58 laps	16
17	Takuma Sato *	Super Aguri	Super Aguri-Honda SA05	57 laps	21
18	Franck Montagny	Super Aguri	Super Aguri-Honda SA05	57 laps	20
R	Jenson Button	Honda Racing	Honda RA106	8 laps/engine	19
R	Scott Speed	Toro Rosso	Toro Rosso-Cosworth STR01	1 lap/collision	15
R	Ralf Schumacher	Toyota	Toyota TF106	0 laps/collision	7
R	Mark Webber	Williams	Williams-Cosworth FW28	0 laps/collision	17

Pole: Alonso, 1m20.253s, 143.297mph/230.615kph. Fastest lap: Alonso, 1m21.599s, 140.934mph/226.811kph on Lap 21. Race leaders: Alonso 1-44 & 46-60, Fisichella 45

* 10-place grid penalty for engine change • ! made to start from back of the grid for engine change

BUTTON WINS IN THE WET

Jenson Button broke his F1 duck at the 114th attempt to give the Honda Racing team victory in its debut year after the team morphed from BAR. His win came at the Hungarian GP when he mastered wet/dry conditions to advance from 14th on the grid to take a lead that ought to have been Fernando Alonso's, but a wheel fell off his Renault after a pit stop.

MONTOYA MOVES ON

Seven-time grand prix winner Juan Pablo Montoya seemed to be dispirited that his McLaren was unlikely to win in 2006 and so elected to quit the team midway through the season to take up a NASCAR drive for 2007. He was replaced by Pedro de la Rosa, but apart from second place in the unusual Hungarian GP, the Spaniard failed to impress.

CANADIAN GRAND PRIX

MONTREAL • ROUND 9 • DATE: 25TH JUNE 2006
Laps: 70 • Distance: 189.534miles/305.27km • Weather: Hot & bright

Pos	Driver	Team	Chassis-Engine	Result	Qual
1	Fernando Alonso	Renault F1	Renault R26	1h34m37.308s	1
2	Michael Schumacher	Ferrari	Ferrari 248 F1	1h34m39.419s	5
3	Kimi Raikkonen	McLaren	McLaren-Mercedes MP4-21	1h34m46.121s	3
4	Giancarlo Fisichella	Renault F1	Renault R26	1h34m52.987s	2
5	Felipe Massa	Ferrari	Ferrari 248 F1	1h35m02.480s	10
6	Jarno Trulli	Toyota	Toyota TF106	69 laps	4
7	Nick Heidfeld	BMW Sauber	BMW Sauber F1.06	69 laps	13
8	David Coulthard *	Red Bull Racing	Red Bull-Ferrari RB2	69 laps	22
9	Jenson Button	Honda Racing	Honda RA106	69 laps	8
10	Scott Speed	Toro Rosso	Toro Rosso-Cosworth STR01	69 laps	17
11	Christian Klien	Red Bull Racing	Red Bull-Ferrari RB2	69 laps	12
12	Mark Webber	Williams	Williams-Cosworth FW28	69 laps	16
13	Vitantonio Liuzzi	Toro Rosso	Toro Rosso-Cosworth STR01	68 laps	15
14	Tiago Monteiro	Midland	Midland-Toyota M16	66 laps	18
15	Takuma Sato	Super Aguri	Super Aguri-Honda SA05	64 laps/spun off	20
R	Jacques Villeneuve	BMW Sauber	BMW Sauber F1.06	58 laps/spun off	11
R	Ralf Schumacher	Toyota	Toyota TF106	58 laps/handling	14
R	Juan Pablo Montoya	McLaren	McLaren-Mercedes MP4-21	13 laps/spun off	7
R	Rubens Barrichello	Honda Racing	Honda RA106	11 laps/engine	9
R	Franck Montagny	Super Aguri	Super Aguri-Honda SA05	2 laps/engine	21
R	Nico Rosberg	Williams	Williams-Cosworth FW28	1 lap/collision	6
R	Christijan Albers	Midland	Midland-Toyota M16	0 laps/collision	19

Pole: Alonso, 1m14.942s, 130.171mph/209.490kph. Fastest lap: Raikkonen, 1m15.841s, 128.628mph/207.006kph on Lap 22. Race leaders: Alonso 1-22 & 25-49 & 53-70, Raikkonen 23-24 & 50-52

* 10-place grid penalty for engine change

UNITED STATES GRAND PRIX

INDIANAPOLIS MOTOR SPEEDWAY • ROUND 10 • DATE: 2ND JULY 2006
Laps: 73 • Distance: 190.149miles/306.016km • Weather: Hot & bright

Pos	Driver	Team	Chassis-Engine	Result	Qual
1	Michael Schumacher	Ferrari	Ferrari 248 F1	1h34m35.199s	1
2	Felipe Massa	Ferrari	Ferrari 248 F1	1h34m43.183s	2
3	Giancarlo Fisichella	Renault F1	Renault R26	1h34m51.794s	3
4	Jarno Trulli ^	Toyota	Toyota TF106	1h34m58.803s	22
5	Fernando Alonso	Renault F1	Renault R26	1h35m03.609s	5
6	Rubens Barrichello	Honda Racing	Honda RA106	1h35m11.715s	4
7	David Coulthard	Red Bull Racing	Red Bull-Ferrari RB2	72 laps	17
8	Vitantonio Liuzzi *	Toro Rosso	Toro Rosso-Cosworth STR01	72 laps	20
9	Nico Rosberg !	Williams	Williams-Cosworth FW28	72 laps	21
R	Ralf Schumacher	Toyota	Toyota TF106	62 laps/wheel	8
R	Christijan Albers	Midland	Midland-Toyota M16	37 laps/transmission	14
R	Jacques Villeneuve	BMW Sauber	BMW Sauber F1.06	23 laps/engine	6
R	Tiago Monteiro	Midland	Midland-Toyota M16	9 laps/collision	15
R	Takuma Sato	Super Aguri	Super Aguri-Honda SA05	6 laps/collision	18
R	Jenson Button	Honda Racing	Honda RA106	3 laps/collision	7
R	Kimi Raikkonen	McLaren	McLaren-Mercedes MP4-21	0 laps/collision	9
R	Nick Heidfeld	BMW Sauber	BMW Sauber F1.06	0 laps/collision	10

Pos	Driver	Team	Chassis-Engine	Result	Qual
R	Juan Pablo Montoya	McLaren	McLaren-Mercedes MP4-21	0 laps/collision	11
R	Mark Webber	Williams	Williams-Cosworth FW28	0 laps/collision	12
R	Scott Speed	Toro Rosso	Toro Rosso-Cosworth STR01	0 laps/collision	13
R	Christian Klien	Red Bull Racing	Red Bull-Ferrari RB2	0 laps/collision	16
R	Franck Montagny	Super Aguri	Super Aguri-Honda SA05	0 laps/collision	19

Pole: M Schumacher, 1m10.832s, 132.387mph/213.056kph. Fastest lap: M Schumacher, 1m12.719s, 128.951mph/207.527kph on Lap 56. Race leaders: Massa 1-29, Alonso 30, M Schumacher 31-73

* 10-place grid penalty for engine change • ! sent to back of grid for missing weigh-in • ^ made to start from the back of the grid for working on the car in parc ferme

FRENCH GRAND PRIX

MAGNY-COURS • ROUND 11 • DATE: 16TH JULY 2006
Laps: 70 • Distance: 191.430miles/308.77km • Weather: Hot & bright

Pos	Driver	Team	Chassis-Engine	Result	Qual
1	Michael Schumacher	Ferrari	Ferrari 248 F1	1h32m07.803s	1
2	Fernando Alonso	Renault F1	Renault R26	1h32m17.934s	3
3	Felipe Massa	Ferrari	Ferrari 248 F1	1h32m30.349s	2
4	Ralf Schumacher	Toyota	Toyota TF106	1h32m35.015s	5
5	Kimi Raikkonen	McLaren	McLaren-Mercedes MP4-21	1h32m40.809s	6
6	Giancarlo Fisichella	Renault F1	Renault R26	1h32m53.068s	7
7	Pedro de la Rosa	McLaren	McLaren-Mercedes MP4-21	1h32m57.210s	8
8	Nick Heidfeld	BMW Sauber	BMW Sauber F1.06	69 laps	11
9	David Coulthard	Red Bull Racing	Red Bull-Ferrari RB2	69 laps	9
10	Scott Speed	Toro Rosso	Toro Rosso-Cosworth STR01	69 laps	14
11	Jacques Villeneuve	BMW Sauber	BMW Sauber F1.06	69 laps	16
12	Christian Klien	Red Bull Racing	Red Bull-Ferrari RB2	69 laps	12
13	Vitantonio Liuzzi *	Toro Rosso	Toro Rosso-Cosworth STR01	69 laps	22
14	Nico Rosberg *	Williams	Williams-Cosworth FW28	68 laps	19
15	Christijan Albers	Midland	Midland-Toyota M16	68 laps	15
16	Franck Montagny	Super Aguri	Super Aguri-Honda SA05	67 laps	20
R	Jenson Button	Honda Racing	Honda RA106	61 laps/engine	17
R	Mark Webber	Williams	Williams-Cosworth FW28	53 laps/tyre	10
R	Jarno Trulli	Toyota	Toyota TF106	39 laps/brakes	4
R	Rubens Barrichello	Honda Racing	Honda RA106	18 laps/engine	13
R	Tiago Monteiro	Midland	Midland-Toyota M16	11 laps/mechanical	18
R	Takuma Sato	Super Aguri	Super Aguri-Honda SA05	0 laps/clutch	21

Pole: M Schumacher, 1m15.493s, 130.702mph/210.345kph. Fastest lap: M Schumacher, 1m17.111s, 127.960mph/205.931kph on Lap 46. Race leaders: M Schumacher 1-18 & 23-38 & 42-70, Trulli 19-20, R Schumacher 21-22, Alonso 39-41

* 10-place grid penalty for engine change

BMW BOOSTS SAUBER

A financial injection from BMW propelled the usually underfunded Sauber team up the order. Nick Heidfeld took an early fourth place, then came third in Hungary. However, Robert Kubica matched that in only his third race with the team, at Monza, after replacing Jacques Villeneuve, who quit F1 with six races to go.

GERMAN GRAND PRIX

HOCKENHEIM • ROUND 12 • DATE: 30TH JULY 2006
Laps: 67 • Distance: 190.424miles/306.458km • Weather: Hot & bright

Pos	Driver	Team	Chassis-Engine	Result	Qual
1	Michael Schumacher	Ferrari	Ferrari 248 F1	1h27m51.693s	2
2	Felipe Massa	Ferrari	Ferrari 248 F1	1h27m52.413s	3
3	Kimi Raikkonen	McLaren	McLaren-Mercedes MP4-21	1h28m04.899s	1
4	Jenson Button	Honda Racing	Honda RA106	1h28m10.591s	4
5	Fernando Alonso	Renault F1	Renault R26	1h28m15.400s	7
6	Giancarlo Fisichella	Renault F1	Renault R26	1h28m16.507s	5
7	Jarno Trulli *	Toyota	Toyota TF106	1h28m18.237s	20
8	Christian Klien	Red Bull Racing	Red Bull-Ferrari RB2	1h28m39.824s	12
9	Ralf Schumacher	Toyota	Toyota TF106	1h28m52.044s	8
10	Vitantonio Liuzzi	Toro Rosso	Toro Rosso-Cosworth STR01	66 laps	16
11	David Coulthard	Red Bull Racing	Red Bull-Ferrari RB2	66 laps	10
12	Scott Speed	Toro Rosso	Toro Rosso-Cosworth STR01	66 laps	19
DQ	Christijan Albers !	Midland	Midland-Toyota M16	66 laps/rear wing	21
DQ	Tiago Monteiro	Midland	Midland-Toyota M16	65 laps/rear wing	18
R	Mark Webber	Williams	Williams-Cosworth FW28	59 laps/engine	11
R	Takuma Sato	Super Aguri	Super Aguri-Honda SA06	38 laps/oil leak	17
R	Jacques Villeneuve	BMW Sauber	BMW Sauber F1.06	30 laps/spun off	13
R	Rubens Barrichello	Honda Racing	Honda RA106	18 laps/engine	6
R	Nick Heidfeld	BMW Sauber	BMW Sauber F1.06	9 laps/brakes	15
R	Pedro de la Rosa	McLaren	McLaren-Mercedes MP4-21	2 laps/fuel pump	9
R	Sakon Yamamoto *	Super Aguri	Super Aguri-Honda SA06	1 lap/halfshaft	22
R	Nico Rosberg	Williams	Williams-Cosworth FW28	0 laps/spun off	14

Pole: Raikkonen, 1m14.070s, 138.136mph/222.308kph. Fastest lap: M Schumacher, 1m16.357s, 133.998mph/215.650kph on Lap 17. Race leaders: Raikkonen 1-9, M Schumacher 10-67

* 10-place grid penalty for engine change • ! best 3 laps taken away for impeding a rival

HIRE 'EM AND FIRE 'EM

Former F1 driver Helmut Marko created a scholarship scheme to identify and sign the best young talent to feed into Red Bull Racing and, by the team's second year, it was clear that he was a hard taskmaster. Christian Klien was the first to get fired for not meeting his expectations after scoring only two eighth-place finishes in the first 15 races.

HUNGARIAN GRAND PRIX

HUNGARORING • ROUND 13 • DATE: 6TH AUGUST 2006
Laps: 70 • Distance: 190.181miles/306.67km • Weather: Warm & wet, drying later

Pos	Driver	Team	Chassis-Engine	Result	Qual
1	Jenson Button *	Honda Racing	Honda RA106	1h52m20.941s	14
2	Pedro de la Rosa	McLaren	McLaren-Mercedes MP4-21	1h52m51.778s	4
3	Nick Heidfeld	BMW Sauber	BMW Sauber F1.06	1h53m04.763s	10
4	Rubens Barrichello	Honda Racing	Honda RA106	1h53m06.146s	3
5	David Coulthard	Red Bull Racing	Red Bull-Ferrari RB2	69 laps	12
6	Ralf Schumacher	Toyota	Toyota TF106	69 laps	6

Pos	Driver	Team	Chassis-Engine	Result	Qual
DQ	Robert Kubica ^	BMW Sauber	BMW Sauber F1.06	69 laps/underweight	9
7	Felipe Massa	Ferrari	Ferrari 248 F1	69 laps	2
8	Michael Schumacher !	Ferrari	Ferrari 248 F1	67 laps/collision	11
9	Tiago Monteiro	Midland	Midland-Toyota M16	67 laps	16
10	Christijan Albers *	Midland	Midland-Toyota M16	67 laps	22
11	Scott Speed ^	Toro Rosso	Toro Rosso-Cosworth STR01	66 laps	20
12	Jarno Trulli	Toyota	Toyota TF106	65 laps/engine	8
13	Takuma Sato	Super Aguri	Super Aguri-Honda SA06	65 laps	19
R	Fernando Alonso !	Renault F1	Renault R26	51 laps/wheel	15
R	Kimi Raikkonen	McLaren	McLaren-Mercedes MP4-21	25 laps/collision	1
R	Vitantonio Liuzzi	Toro Rosso	Toro Rosso-Cosworth STR01	25 laps/collision	17
R	Nico Rosberg	Williams	Williams-Cosworth FW28	19 laps/electrical	18
R	Giancarlo Fisichella	Renault F1	Renault R26	18 laps/spun off	7
R	Christian Klien	Red Bull Racing	Red Bull-Ferrari RB2	6 laps/spun off	13
R	Mark Webber	Williams	Williams-Cosworth FW28	1 lap/spun off	5
R	Sakon Yamamoto	Super Aguri	Super Aguri-Honda SA06	0 laps/spun off	21

Pole: Raikkonen, 1m19.599s, 123.117mph/198.138kph. Fastest lap: Massa, 1m23.516s, 117.343mph/188.845kph on Lap 65. Race leaders: Raikkonen 1-17, Alonso 18-51, Button 52-70

* 10-place grid penalty for engine change • ! 2s added to qualifying time for passing under red flag conditions in practice • ^ best 3 laps disallowed for impeding a rival

TURKISH GRAND PRIX

ISTANBUL PARK • ROUND 14 • DATE: 27TH AUGUST 2006
Laps: 58 • Distance: 192.379miles/309.604km • Weather: Hot & bright

Pos	Driver	Team	Chassis-Engine	Result	Qual
1	Felipe Massa	Ferrari	Ferrari 248 F1	1h28m51.082s	1
2	Fernando Alonso	Renault F1	Renault R26	1h28m56.657s	3
3	Michael Schumacher	Ferrari	Ferrari 248 F1	1h28m56.738s	2
4	Jenson Button	Honda Racing	Honda RA106	1h29m03.416s	6
5	Pedro de la Rosa	McLaren	McLaren-Mercedes MP4-21	1h29m36.990s	11
6	Giancarlo Fisichella	Renault F1	Renault R26	1h29m37.676s	4
7	Ralf Schumacher *	Toyota	Toyota TF106	1h29m50.419s	15
8	Rubens Barrichello	Honda Racing	Honda RA106	1h29m51.116s	13
9	Jarno Trulli	Toyota	Toyota TF106	57 laps	12
10	Mark Webber	Williams	Williams-Cosworth FW28	57 laps	9
11	Christian Klien	Red Bull Racing	Red Bull-Ferrari RB2	57 laps	10
12	Robert Kubica	BMW Sauber	BMW Sauber F1.06	57 laps	8
13	Scott Speed	Toro Rosso	Toro Rosso-Cosworth STR01	57 laps	17
14	Nick Heidfeld	BMW Sauber	BMW Sauber F1.06	56 laps	5
15	David Coulthard	Red Bull Racing	Red Bull-Ferrari RB2	55 laps/gearbox	16
R	Christijan Albers *	Midland	Midland-Toyota M16	46 laps/spun off	22
NC	Takuma Sato	Super Aguri	Super Aguri-Honda SA06	41 laps	21
R	Nico Rosberg	Williams	Williams-Cosworth FW28	25 laps/water leak	14
R	Sakon Yamamoto	Super Aguri	Super Aguri-Honda SA06	23 laps/spun off	20
R	Vitantonio Liuzzi	Toro Rosso	Toro Rosso-Cosworth STR01	12 laps/spun off	18
R	Kimi Raikkonen	McLaren	McLaren-Mercedes MP4-21	1 lap/spun off	7
R	Tiago Monteiro	Midland	Midland-Toyota M16	0 laps/collision	19

Pole: Massa, 1m26.907s, 137.397mph/221.119kph. Fastest lap: M Schumacher, 1m28.005s, 135.682mph/218.360kph on Lap 55. Race leaders: Massa 1-39 & 44-58, M Schumacher 40-43

* 10-place grid penalty for engine change

ITALIAN GRAND PRIX

MONZA • ROUND 15 • DATE: 10TH SEPTEMBER 2006
Laps: 53 • Distance: 190.778miles/307.029km • Weather: Hot & bright

Pos	Driver	Team	Chassis-Engine	Result	Qual
1	Michael Schumacher	Ferrari	Ferrari 248 F1	1h14m51.975s	2
2	Kimi Raikkonen	McLaren	McLaren-Mercedes MP4-21	1h15m00.021s	1
3	Robert Kubica	BMW Sauber	BMW Sauber F1.06	1h15m18.389s	6
4	Giancarlo Fisichella	Renault F1	Renault R26	1h15m24.020s	9
5	Jenson Button	Honda Racing	Honda RA106	1h15m24.660s	5
6	Rubens Barrichello	Honda Racing	Honda RA106	1h15m34.384s	8
7	Jarno Trulli	Toyota	Toyota TF106	1h15m36.637s	11
8	Nick Heidfeld	BMW Sauber	BMW Sauber F1.06	1h15m37.284s	3
9	Felipe Massa	Ferrari	Ferrari 248 F1	1h15m37.930s	4
10	Mark Webber	Williams	Williams-Cosworth FW28	1h16m04.577s	19
11	Christian Klien	Red Bull Racing	Red Bull-Ferrari RB2	52 laps	16
12	David Coulthard	Red Bull Racing	Red Bull-Ferrari RB2	52 laps	14
13	Scott Speed	Toro Rosso	Toro Rosso-Cosworth STR01	52 laps	15
14	Vitantonio Liuzzi	Toro Rosso	Toro Rosso-Cosworth STR01	52 laps	17
15	Ralf Schumacher	Toyota	Toyota TF106	52 laps	13
16	Takuma Sato	Super Aguri	Super Aguri-Honda SA06	51 laps	21
17	Christijan Albers	Midland	Midland-Toyota M16	51 laps	18
R	Tiago Monteiro	Midland	Midland-Toyota M16	44 laps/brakes	20
R	Fernando Alonso *	Renault F1	Renault R26	43 laps/engine	10
R	Pedro de la Rosa	McLaren	McLaren-Mercedes MP4-21	20 laps/engine	7
R	Sakon Yamamoto	Super Aguri	Super Aguri-Honda SA06	18 laps/hydraulics	22
R	Nico Rosberg	Williams	Williams-Cosworth FW28	9 laps/halfshaft	12

Pole: Raikkonen, 1m21.484s, 159.032mph/255.937kph. Fastest lap: Raikkonen, 1m22.559s, 156.961mph/252.604kph on Lap 13. Race leaders: Raikkonen 1-14, M Schumacher 15-17 & 23-53, Kubica 18-22

* best 3 laps annulled for impeding Massa

CHINESE GRAND PRIX

SHANGHAI INTERNATIONAL CIRCUIT • ROUND 16 • DATE: 1ST OCTOBER 2006
Laps: 56 • Distance: 189.677miles/305.256km • Weather: Warm but wet

Pos	Driver	Team	Chassis-Engine	Result	Qual
1	Michael Schumacher	Ferrari	Ferrari 248 F1	1h37m32.747s	6
2	Fernando Alonso	Renault F1	Renault R26	1h37m35.868s	1
3	Giancarlo Fisichella	Renault F1	Renault R26	1h38m16.944s	2
4	Jenson Button	Honda Racing	Honda RA106	1h38m44.803s	4
5	Pedro de la Rosa	McLaren	McLaren-Mercedes MP4-21	1h38m49.884s	7
6	Rubens Barrichello	Honda Racing	Honda RA106	1h38m51.878s	3
7	Nick Heidfeld	BMW Sauber	BMW Sauber F1.06	1h39m04.726s	8
8	Mark Webber	Williams	Williams-Cosworth FW28	1h39m16.335s	14
9	David Coulthard	Red Bull Racing	Red Bull-Ferrari RB2	1h39m16.543s	12
10	Vitantonio Liuzzi	Toro Rosso	Toro Rosso-Cosworth STR01	55 laps	13
11	Nico Rosberg	Williams	Williams-Cosworth FW28	55 laps	15
12	Robert Doornbos	Red Bull Racing	Red Bull-Ferrari RB2	55 laps	10
13	Robert Kubica	BMW Sauber	BMW Sauber F1.06	55 laps	9
DQ	Takuma Sato *	Super Aguri	Super Aguri-Honda SA06	55 laps/impeding rival	21
14	Scott Speed	Toro Rosso	Toro Rosso-Cosworth STR01	55 laps	11
15	Christijan Albers !	Midland	Midland-Toyota M16	53 laps	22
16	Sakon Yamamoto	Super Aguri	Super Aguri-Honda SA06	52 laps	19

Pos	Driver	Team	Chassis-Engine	Result	Qual
R	Ralf Schumacher	Toyota	Toyota TF106	49 laps/fuel pressure	16
R	Felipe Massa *	Ferrari	Ferrari 248 F1	44 laps/collision	20
R	Jarno Trulli	Toyota	Toyota TF106	38 laps/engine	17
R	Tiago Monteiro	Midland	Midland-Toyota M16	37 laps/spun off	18
R	Kimi Raikkonen	McLaren	McLaren-Mercedes MP4-21	18 laps/throttle	5

Pole: Alonso, 1m44.360s, 116.841mph/188.037kph. Fastest lap: Alonso, 1m37.586s, 124.951mph/201.090kph on Lap 49. Race leaders: Alonso 1-22 & 24-29, Fisichella 23 & 30-41, M Schumacher 42-56

* 10-place grid penalty for engine change • ! times disallowed for missing weight check

NEW CONSTRUCTORS

Super Aguri was F1's first new team in years and it was financed by Honda to assuage the guilt it felt at dropping Takuma Sato. The team wasn't the only change: the Minardi team was bought by Red Bull's Dietrich Mateschitz and turned into Scuderia Toro Rosso, while Jordan was also under a new name, competing as Midland.

JAPANESE GRAND PRIX

SUZUKA • ROUND 17 • DATE: 8TH OCTOBER 2006
Laps: 53 • Distance: 191.240miles/307.771km • Weather: Warm & bright

Pos	Driver	Team	Chassis-Engine	Result	Qual
1	Fernando Alonso	Renault F1	Renault R26	1h23m53.413s	5
2	Felipe Massa	Ferrari	Ferrari 248 F1	1h24m09.564s	1
3	Giancarlo Fisichella	Renault F1	Renault R26	1h24m17.366s	6
4	Jenson Button	Honda Racing	Honda RA106	1h24m27.514s	7
5	Kimi Raikkonen	McLaren	McLaren-Mercedes MP4-21	1h24m37.009s	11
6	Jarno Trulli	Toyota	Toyota TF106	1h24m40.130s	4
7	Ralf Schumacher	Toyota	Toyota TF106	1h24m42.282s	3
8	Nick Heidfeld	BMW Sauber	BMW Sauber F1.06	1h25m09.508s	9
9	Robert Kubica	BMW Sauber	BMW Sauber F1.06	1h25m10.345s	12
10	Nico Rosberg	Williams	Williams-Cosworth FW28	52 laps	10
11	Pedro de la Rosa	McLaren	McLaren-Mercedes MP4-21	52 laps	13
12	Rubens Barrichello	Honda Racing	Honda RA106	52 laps	8
13	Robert Doornbos	Red Bull Racing	Red Bull-Ferrari RB2	52 laps	18
14	Vitantonio Liuzzi	Toro Rosso	Toro Rosso-Cosworth STR01	52 laps	15
15	Takuma Sato	Super Aguri	Super Aguri-Honda SA06	52 laps	20
16	Tiago Monteiro	Midland	Midland-Toyota M16	51 laps	21
17	Sakon Yamamoto	Super Aguri	Super Aguri-Honda SA06	50 laps	22
18	Scott Speed	Toro Rosso	Toro Rosso-Cosworth STR01	48 laps/steering	19
R	Mark Webber	Williams	Williams-Cosworth FW28	39 laps/spun off	14
R	Michael Schumacher	Ferrari	Ferrari 248 F1	36 laps/engine	2
R	David Coulthard	Red Bull Racing	Red Bull-Ferrari RB2	35 laps/gearbox	17
R	Christijan Albers	Midland	Midland-Toyota M16	20 laps/suspension	16

Pole: Massa, 1m29.599s, 144.978mph/233.319kph. Fastest lap: Alonso, 1m32.676s, 140.164mph/225.572kph on Lap 14. Race leaders: Massa 1-2, M Schumacher 3-36, Alonso 37-53

BRAZILIAN GRAND PRIX

INTERLAGOS • ROUND 18 • DATE: 22ND OCTOBER 2006
Laps: 71 • Distance: 190.101miles/305.939km • Weather: Warm & bright

Pos	Driver	Team	Chassis-Engine	Result	Qual
1	Felipe Massa	Ferrari	Ferrari 248 F1	1h31m53.751s	1
2	Fernando Alonso	Renault F1	Renault R26	1h32m12.409s	4
3	Jenson Button	Honda Racing	Honda RA106	1h32m13.145s	14
4	Michael Schumacher	Ferrari	Ferrari 248 F1	1h32m17.845s	10
5	Kimi Raikkonen	McLaren	McLaren-Mercedes MP4-21	1h32m22.254s	2
6	Giancarlo Fisichella	Renault F1	Renault R26	1h32m24.038s	6
7	Rubens Barrichello	Honda Racing	Honda RA106	1h32m34.045s	5
8	Pedro de la Rosa	McLaren	McLaren-Mercedes MP4-21	1h32m45.819s	12
9	Robert Kubica	BMW Sauber	BMW Sauber F1.06	1h33m01.393s	9
10	Takuma Sato	Super Aguri	Super Aguri-Honda SA06	70 laps	19
11	Scott Speed	Toro Rosso	Toro Rosso-Cosworth STR01	70 laps	16
12	Robert Doornbos *	Red Bull Racing	Red Bull-Ferrari RB2	70 laps	22
13	Vitantonio Liuzzi	Toro Rosso	Toro Rosso-Cosworth STR01	70 laps	15
14	Christijan Albers	Midland	Midland-Toyota M16	70 laps	17
15	Tiago Monteiro	Midland	Midland-Toyota M16	69 laps	21
16	Sakon Yamamoto	Super Aguri	Super Aguri-Honda SA06	69 laps	20
17	Nick Heidfeld	BMW Sauber	BMW Sauber F1.06	63 laps/suspension	8
R	David Coulthard	Red Bull Racing	Red Bull-Ferrari RB2	14 laps/gearbox	18
R	Jarno Trulli	Toyota	Toyota TF106	10 laps/suspension	3
R	Ralf Schumacher	Toyota	Toyota TF106	9 laps/suspension	7
R	Mark Webber	Williams	Williams-Cosworth FW28	1 lap/collision	11
R	Nico Rosberg	Williams	Williams-Cosworth FW28	0 laps/spun off	13

Pole: Massa, 1m10.680s, 136.374mph/219.473kph. Fastest lap: M Schumacher, 1m12.162s, 133.573mph/214.966kph on Lap 70. Race leaders: Massa 1-24 & 27-71, Alonso 25-26

* 10-place grid penalty for engine change

NEW DRIVERS

Robert Kubica was the outstanding rookie in 2006, thanks to his third for BMW Sauber in Italy. Of the four other rookies, future world champion Nico Rosberg was easily the best, taking a pair of sevenths for Williams, while Robert Doornbos drove well in three races for Red Bull, coming 12th twice and 13th. Both Yuji Ide and Sakon Yamamoto had point-free outings for Super Aguri.

CLASSIC DRIVER: MICHAEL SCHUMACHER

Michael Schumacher retired at the end of 2006 and, after 15 full seasons in F1, he left with a slew of records to his name. His remarkable tally included seven drivers' titles, two more than Juan Manuel Fangio's haul in the 1950s, and 91 grand prix wins, fully 40 more than the next most prolific winner, Alain Prost. The 37-year-old German also had the most grands prix won in a year (13 in 2004), the most pole positions (68 to Ayrton Senna's 65), the highest number of fastest laps (75 to Prost's 41) and the most points (1369 to Prost's 798.5). He was the ultimate winning machine.

WORLD DRIVERS' CHAMPIONSHIP FINAL RESULTS

Pos	Driver	Nat	Car-Engine	R1	R2	R3	R4	R5	R6	R7
1	Fernando Alonso	ESP	Renault R26	1	2F	1	2F	2P	1P	1P
2	Michael Schumacher	DEU	Ferrari 248 F1	2P	6	R	1P	1F	2	5F
3	Felipe Massa	BRA	Ferrari 248 F1	9	5	R	4	3	4F	9
4	Giancarlo Fisichella	ITA	Renault R26	R	1P	5	8	6	3	6
5	Kimi Raikkonen	FIN	McLaren-Mercedes MP4-21	3	R	2F	5	4	5	R
6	Jenson Button	GBR	Honda RA106	4	3	10P	7	R	6	11
7	Rubens Barrichello	BRA	Honda RA106	15	10	7	10	5	7	4
8	Juan Pablo Montoya	COL	McLaren-Mercedes MP4-21	5	4	R	3	R	R	2
9	Nick Heidfeld	DEU	BMW Sauber F1.06	12	R	4	13	10	8	7
10	Ralf Schumacher	DEU	Toyota TF106	14	8	3	9	R	R	8
11	Pedro de la Rosa	ESP	McLaren-Mercedes MP4-21	-	-	-	-	-	-	-
12	Jarno Trulli	ITA	Toyota TF106	16	9	R	R	9	10	17
13	David Coulthard	GBR	Red Bull-Ferrari RB2	10	R	8	R	R	14	3
14	Mark Webber	AUS	Williams-Cosworth FW28	6	R	R	6	R	9	R
15	Jacques Villeneuve	CAN	BMW Sauber F1.06	R	7	6	12	8	12	14
16	Robert Kubica	POL	BMW Sauber F1.06	-	-	-	-	-	-	-
17	Nico Rosberg	DEU	Williams-Cosworth FW28	7F	R	R	11	7	11	R
18	Christian Klien	AUT	Red Bull-Ferrari RB2	8	R	R	R	R	13	R
19	Vitantonio Liuzzi	ITA	Toro Rosso-Cosworth STR01	11	11	R	14	R	15	10
20	Scott Speed	USA	Toro Rosso-Cosworth STR01	13	R	9	15	11	R	13
21	Tiago Monteiro	PRT	Midland-Toyota M16	17	13	R	16	12	16	15
22	Christijan Albers	NLD	Midland-Toyota M16	R	12	11	R	13	R	12
23	Takuma Sato	JPN	Super Aguri-Honda SA05	18	14	12	R	R	17	R
			Super Aguri-Honda SA06	-	-	-	-	-	-	-
24	Robert Doornbos	NLD	Red Bull-Ferrari RB2	T	T	T	T	T	T	T
25	Yuji Ide	JPN	Super Aguri-Honda SA05	R	R	13	R	-	-	-
26	Sakon Yamamoto	JPN	Super Aguri-Honda SA05	-	-	-	-	-	-	-
			Super Aguri-Honda SA06	-	-	-	-	-	-	-
27	Franck Montagny	FRA	Super Aguri-Honda SA05	-	-	-	-	R	R	16
			Super Aguri-Honda SA06	-	-	-	-	-	-	-

Pos	Driver	R8	R9	R10	R11	R12	R13	R14	R15	R16	R17	R18	Total
1	Alonso	1PF	1P	5	2	5	R	2	R	2PF	1F	2	134
2	M Schumacher	2	2	1PF	1PF	1F	8	3F	1	1	R	4F	121
3	Massa	5	5	2	3	2	7F	1P	9	R	2P	1P	80
4	Fisichella	4	4	3	6	6	R	6	4	3	3	6	72
5	Raikkonen	3	3F	R	5	3P	RP	R	2PF	R	5	5	65
6	Button	R	9	R	R	4	1	4	5	4	4	3	56
7	Barrichello	10	R	6	R	R	4	8	6	6	12	7	30
8	Montoya	6	R	R	-	-	-	-	-	-	-	-	26
9	Heidfeld	7	7	R	8	R	3	14	8	7	8	17	23
10	R Schumacher	R	R	R	4	9	6	7	15	R	7	R	20
11	de la Rosa	-	-	-	7	R	2	5	R	5	11	8	19
12	Trulli	11	6	4	R	7	12	9	7	R	6	R	15
13	Coulthard	12	8	7	9	11	5	15	12	9	R	R	14
14	Webber	R	12	R	R	R	R	10	10	8	R	R	7
15	Villeneuve	8	R	R	11	R	-	-	-	-	-	-	7
16	Kubica	-	-	-	-	-	DQ	12	3	13	9	9	6
17	Rosberg	9	R	9	14	R	R	R	R	11	10	R	4
18	Klien	14	11	R	12	8	R	11	11	-	-	-	2
19	Liuzzi	13	13	8	13	10	R	R	14	10	14	13	1
20	Speed	R	10	R	10	12	11	13	13	14	18	11	0
21	Monteiro	16	14	R	R	DQ	9	R	R	R	16	15	0
22	Albers	15	R	R	15	DQ	10	R	17	15	R	14	0

Pos	Driver	R8	R9	R10	R11	R12	R13	R14	R15	R16	R17	R18	Total
23	Sato	17	15	R	R	-	-	-	-	-	-	-	0
		-	-	-	-	R	13	NC	16	DQ	15	10	
24	Doornbos	T	T	T	T	T	T	T	T	12	13	12	0
25	Ide	-	-	-	-	-	-	-	-	-	-	-	0
26	Yamamoto	-	-	-	-	R	R	R	R	16	17	16	
		-	-	-	-	-	-	-	-	-	-	-	0
27	Montagny	18	R	R	16	-	-	-	-	-	-	-	0
		-	-	-	-	-	-	T	T	T	T	T	

WORLD CONSTRUCTORS' CHAMPIONSHIP FINAL RESULTS

Pos	Team-Engine	R1	R2	R3	R4	R5	R6	R7	R8	R9
1	Renault F1	1/R	1/2	1/5	2/8	2/6	1/3	1/6	1/4	1/4
2	Ferrari	2/9	5/6	R/R	1/4	1/3	2/4	5/9	2/5	2/5
3	McLaren-Mercedes	3/5	4/R	2/R	3/5	4/R	5/R	2/R	3/6	3/R
4	Honda Racing	4/15	3/10	7/10	7/10	5/R	6/7	4/11	10/R	9/R
5	BMW Sauber	12/R	7/R	4/6	12/13	8/10	8/12	7/14	7/8	7/R
6	Toyota	14/16	8/9	3/R	9/R	9/R	10/R	8/17	11/R	6/R
7	Red Bull-Ferrari	8/10	R/R	8/R	R/R	R/R	13/14	3/R	12/14	8/11
8	Williams-Cosworth	6/7	R/R	R/R	6/11	7/R	9/11	R/R	9/R	12/R
9	Toro Rosso-Cosworth	11/13	11/R	9/R	14/15	11/R	15/R	10/13	13/R	10/13
10	Midland-Toyota	17/R	12/13	11/R	16/R	12/13	16/R	12/15	15/16	14/R
11	Super Aguri-Honda	18/R	14/R	12/13	R/R	R/R	17/R	16/R	17/18	15/R

Pos	Team-Engine	R10	R11	R12	R13	R14	R15	R16	R17	R18	Total
1	Renault F1	3/5	2/6	5/6	R/R	2/6	4/R	2/3	1/3	2/6	206
2	Ferrari	1/2	1/3	1/2	7/8	1/3	1/9	1/R	2/R	1/4	201
3	McLaren-Mercedes	R/R	5/7	3/R	2/R	5/R	2/R	5/R	5/11	5/8	110
4	Honda Racing	6/R	R/R	4/R	1/4	4/8	5/6	4/6	4/12	3/7	86
5	BMW Sauber	R/R	8/11	R/R	3/DQ	12/14	3/8	7/13	8/9	9/17	36
6	Toyota	4/R	4/R	7/9	6/12	7/9	7/15	R/R	6/7	R/R	35
7	Red Bull-Ferrari	7/R	9/12	8/11	5/R	11/15	11/12	9/12	13/R	12/R	16
8	Williams-Cosworth	9/R	14/R	R/R	R/R	10/R	10/R	8/11	10/R	R/R	11
9	Toro Rosso-Cosworth	8/R	10/13	10/12	11/R	13/R	13/14	10/14	14/18	11/13	1
10	Midland-Toyota	R/R	15/R	DQ/DQ	9/10	R/R	17/R	15/R	16/R	14/15	0
11	Super Aguri-Honda	R/R	16/R	R/R	13/R	NC/R	16/R	16/DQ	15/17	10/16	0

SYMBOLS AND GRAND PRIX KEY

Round 1	**Bahrain GP**	**Round 11**	**French GP**
Round 2	**Malaysian GP**	**Round 12**	**German GP**
Round 3	**Australian GP**	**Round 13**	**Hungarian GP**
Round 4	**San Marino GP**	**Round 14**	**Turkish GP**
Round 5	**European GP**	**Round 15**	**Italian GP**
Round 6	**Spanish GP**	**Round 16**	**Chinese GP**
Round 7	**Monaco GP**	**Round 17**	**Japanese GP**
Round 8	**British GP**	**Round 18**	**Brazilian GP**
Round 9	**Canadian GP**		
Round 10	**United States GP**		

SCORING

1st	**10 points**
2nd	**8 points**
3rd	**6 points**
4th	**5 points**
5th	**4 points**
6th	**3 points**
7th	**2 points**
8th	**1 point**

DNPQ DID NOT PRE-QUALIFY **DNQ** DID NOT QUALIFY **DQ** DISQUALIFIED **EX** EXCLUDED
F FASTEST LAP **NC** NOT CLASSIFIED **NS** NON-STARTER **P** POLE POSITION **R** RETIRED

2007

SEASON SUMMARY

Kimi Raikkonen became champion in his first year with Ferrari, but the result could not have been closer, as his victory in the final round at Interlagos was enough to pip McLaren's Fernando Alonso and Lewis Hamilton by a point, 110 to their 109. Hamilton was a remarkable rookie who showed from his first race that he aimed to win, and did so by the middle of the year. This caused internal strife at McLaren, as he challenged the double world champion's position. Then McLaren had all its points removed because one of its design team was found with Ferrari documents, and was hit with a $100m (£75m) fine.

AUSTRALIAN GRAND PRIX

ALBERT PARK • ROUND 1 • DATE: 18TH MARCH 2007
Laps: 58 • Distance: 191.117miles/307.574km • Weather: Warm & bright

Pos	Driver	Team	Chassis-Engine	Result	Qual
1	Kimi Raikkonen	Ferrari	Ferrari F2007	1h25m28.770s	1
2	Fernando Alonso	McLaren	McLaren-Mercedes MP4-22	1h25m36.012s	2
3	Lewis Hamilton	McLaren	McLaren-Mercedes MP4-22	1h25m47.365s	4
4	Nick Heidfeld	BMW Sauber	BMW Sauber F1.07	1h26m07.533s	3
5	Giancarlo Fisichella	Renault F1	Renault R27	1h26m35.239s	6
6	Felipe Massa *	Ferrari	Ferrari F2007	1h26m35.575s	22
7	Nico Rosberg	Williams	Williams-Toyota FW29	57 laps	12
8	Ralf Schumacher	Toyota	Toyota TF107	57 laps	9
9	Jarno Trulli	Toyota	Toyota TF107	57 laps	8
10	Heikki Kovalainen	Renault F1	Renault R27	57 laps	13
11	Rubens Barrichello	Honda Racing	Honda RA107	57 laps	16
12	Takuma Sato	Super Aguri	Super Aguri-Honda SA07	57 laps	10
13	Mark Webber	Red Bull Racing	Red Bull-Renault RB3	57 laps	7
14	Vitantonio Liuzzi	Toro Rosso	Toro Rosso-Ferrari STR02	57 laps	19
15	Jenson Button	Honda Racing	Honda RA107	57 laps	14
16	Anthony Davidson	Super Aguri	Super Aguri-Honda SA07	56 laps	11
17	Adrian Sutil	Spyker	Spyker-Ferrari F8-VII	56 laps	20
R	Alexander Wurz	Williams	Williams-Toyota FW29	48 laps/collision	15
R	David Coulthard	Red Bull Racing	Red Bull-Renault RB3	48 laps/collision	18
R	Robert Kubica	BMW Sauber	BMW Sauber F1.07	36 laps/gearbox	5
R	Scott Speed	Toro Rosso	Toro Rosso-Ferrari STR02	28 laps/puncture	17
R	Christijan Albers	Spyker	Spyker-Ferrari F8-VII	10 laps/spun off	21

Pole: Raikkonen, 1m26.072s, 137.820mph/221.800kph. Fastest lap: Raikkonen, 1m25.235s, 139.173mph/223.978kph on Lap 41. Race leaders: Raikkonen 1-18 & 23-42 & 45-58, Hamilton 19-22, Alonso 43-44

* 10-place grid penalty for engine change

MALAYSIAN GRAND PRIX

SEPANG • ROUND 2 • DATE: 8TH APRIL 2007
Laps: 56 • Distance: 192.878miles/310.408km • Weather: Very hot & bright

Pos	Driver	Team	Chassis-Engine	Result	Qual
1	Fernando Alonso	McLaren	McLaren-Mercedes MP4-22	1h32m14.930s	2
2	Lewis Hamilton	McLaren	McLaren-Mercedes MP4-22	1h32m32.487s	4
3	Kimi Raikkonen	Ferrari	Ferrari F2007	1h32m33.269s	3
4	Nick Heidfeld	BMW Sauber	BMW Sauber F1.07	1h32m48.707s	5
5	Felipe Massa	Ferrari	Ferrari F2007	1h32m51.635s	1
6	Giancarlo Fisichella	Renault F1	Renault R27	1h33m20.568s	12
7	Jarno Trulli	Toyota	Toyota TF107	1h33m25.062s	8
8	Heikki Kovalainen	Renault F1	Renault R27	1h33m26.945s	11
9	Alexander Wurz	Williams	Williams-Toyota FW29	1h33m44.854s	19
10	Mark Webber	Red Bull Racing	Red Bull-Renault RB3	1h33m48.486s	10
11	Rubens Barrichello *	Honda Racing	Honda RA107	55 laps	22
12	Jenson Button	Honda Racing	Honda RA107	55 laps	15
13	Takuma Sato	Super Aguri	Super Aguri-Honda SA07	55 laps	14
14	Scott Speed	Toro Rosso	Toro Rosso-Ferrari STR02	55 laps	17
15	Ralf Schumacher	Toyota	Toyota TF107	55 laps	9
16	Anthony Davidson	Super Aguri	Super Aguri-Honda SA07	55 laps	18
17	Vitantonio Liuzzi	Toro Rosso	Toro Rosso-Ferrari STR02	55 laps	16
18	Robert Kubica	BMW Sauber	BMW Sauber F1.07	55 laps	7
R	Nico Rosberg	Williams	Williams-Toyota FW29	42 laps/water leak	6
R	David Coulthard	Red Bull Racing	Red Bull-Renault RB3	36 laps/brakes	13
R	Christijan Albers	Spyker	Spyker-Ferrari F8-VII	7 laps/engine	20
R	Adrian Sutil	Spyker	Spyker-Ferrari F8-VII	0 laps/accident	21

Pole: Massa, 1m35.043s, 130.460mph/209.955kph. Fastest lap: Hamilton, 1m36.701s, 128.223mph/206.355kph on Lap 22. Race leaders: Alonso 1-18 & 22-40 & 42-56, Hamilton 19-20, Heidfeld 21, Raikkonen 41

* 10-place grid penalty for engine change

TWO NUMBER ONES?

When Juan Pablo Montoya heard in 2006 that Fernando Alonso would be joining McLaren in 2007, he quit. However, Alonso didn't end up being the undisputed number one, as rookie Lewis Hamilton was almost immediately onto his pace. This led to trouble in Hungary, when Alonso delayed his departure from the pits to ensure that Hamilton wouldn't get a final run in qualifying.

ANOTHER NEW NAME

It was a case of another year, another name, for the team that had entered F1 in 1991 as Jordan. After just one year as MF1 Racing, or Midland, it went racing in 2007 as Spyker MF1 Racing, or Spyker for short. The team changed from Toyota power to use Ferrari customer engines for the first time, but only advanced from no points to one.

BAHRAIN GRAND PRIX

SAKHIR • ROUND 3 • DATE: 15TH APRIL 2007
Laps: 57 • Distance: 191.683miles/308.484km • Weather: Very hot & bright

Pos	Driver	Team	Chassis-Engine	Result	Qual
1	Felipe Massa	Ferrari	Ferrari F2007	1h33m27.515s	1
2	Lewis Hamilton	McLaren	McLaren-Mercedes MP4-22	1h33m29.875s	2
3	Kimi Raikkonen	Ferrari	Ferrari F2007	1h33m38.354s	3
4	Nick Heidfeld	BMW Sauber	BMW Sauber F1.07	1h33m41.346s	5
5	Fernando Alonso	McLaren	McLaren-Mercedes MP4-22	1h33m41.941s	4
6	Robert Kubica	BMW Sauber	BMW Sauber F1.07	1h34m13.044s	6
7	Jarno Trulli	Toyota	Toyota TF107	1h34m48.886s	9
8	Giancarlo Fisichella	Renault F1	Renault R27	1h34m49.216s	7
9	Heikki Kovalainen	Renault F1	Renault R27	1h34m56.926s	12
10	Nico Rosberg	Williams	Williams-Toyota FW29	1h34m57.431s	10
11	Alexander Wurz	Williams	Williams-Toyota FW29	56 laps	11
12	Ralf Schumacher	Toyota	Toyota TF107	56 laps	14
13	Rubens Barrichello	Honda Racing	Honda RA107	56 laps	15
14	Christijan Albers	Spyker	Spyker-Ferrari F8-VII	55 laps	22
15	Adrian Sutil	Spyker	Spyker-Ferrari F8-VII	53 laps	20
16	Anthony Davidson	Super Aguri	Super Aguri-Honda SA07	51 laps/engine	13
R	Mark Webber	Red Bull Racing	Red Bull-Renault RB3	41 laps/gearbox	8
R	David Coulthard	Red Bull Racing	Red Bull-Renault RB3	36 laps/halfshaft	21
R	Takuma Sato	Super Aguri	Super Aguri-Honda SA07	34 laps/engine	17
R	Vitantonio Liuzzi	Toro Rosso	Toro Rosso-Ferrari STR02	26 laps/hydraulics	18
R	Jenson Button	Honda Racing	Honda RA107	0 laps/collision	16
R	Scott Speed	Toro Rosso	Toro Rosso-Ferrari STR02	0 laps/collision	19

Pole: Massa, 1m32.652s, 130.664mph/210.283kph. Fastest lap: Massa, 1m34.067s, 128.698mph/207.120kph on Lap 42. Race leaders: Massa 1-21 & 24-40 & 45-57, Raikkonen 22-23, Hamilton 41-44

SPANISH GRAND PRIX

BARCELONA-CATALUNYA • ROUND 4 • DATE: 13TH MAY 2007
Laps: 65 • Distance: 188.11miles/302.575km • Weather: Hot & bright

Pos	Driver	Team	Chassis-Engine	Result	Qual
1	Felipe Massa	Ferrari	Ferrari F2007	1h31m36.230s	1
2	Lewis Hamilton	McLaren	McLaren-Mercedes MP4-22	1h31m43.020s	4
3	Fernando Alonso	McLaren	McLaren-Mercedes MP4-22	1h31m53.686s	2
4	Robert Kubica	BMW Sauber	BMW Sauber F1.07	1h32m07.845s	5
5	David Coulthard	Red Bull Racing	Red Bull-Renault RB3	1h32m34.561s	9
6	Nico Rosberg	Williams	Williams-Toyota FW29	1h32m35.768s	11
7	Heikki Kovalainen	Renault F1	Renault R27	1h32m38.358s	8
8	Takuma Sato	Super Aguri	Super Aguri-Honda SA07	64 laps	13
9	Giancarlo Fisichella	Renault F1	Renault R27	64 laps	10
10	Rubens Barrichello	Honda Racing	Honda RA107	64 laps	12
11	Anthony Davidson	Super Aguri	Super Aguri-Honda SA07	64 laps	15
12	Jenson Button	Honda Racing	Honda RA107	64 laps	14
13	Adrian Sutil	Spyker	Spyker-Ferrari F8-VII	63 laps	20
14	Christijan Albers	Spyker	Spyker-Ferrari F8-VII	63 laps	21
R	Nick Heidfeld	BMW Sauber	BMW Sauber F1.07	46 laps/gearbox	7
R	Ralf Schumacher	Toyota	Toyota TF107	44 laps/crash damage	17
R	Vitantonio Liuzzi	Toro Rosso	Toro Rosso-Ferrari STR02	19 laps/hydraulics	16

Pos	Driver	Team	Chassis-Engine	Result	Qual
R	Kimi Raikkonen	Ferrari	Ferrari F2007	9 laps/electrical	3
R	Scott Speed	Toro Rosso	Toro Rosso-Ferrari STR02	9 laps/tyre	22
R	Jarno Trulli	Toyota	Toyota TF107	8 laps/fuel pressure	6
R	Mark Webber	Red Bull Racing	Red Bull-Renault RB3	7 laps/hydraulics	19
R	Alexander Wurz	Williams	Williams-Toyota FW29	1 lap/collision	18

Pole: Massa, 1m21.421s, 127.890mph/205.819kph. Fastest lap: Massa, 1m22.680s, 125.942mph/202.685kph on Lap 14. Race leaders: Massa 1-19 & 25-42 & 48-65, Hamilton 20-22 & 43-47, Heidfeld 23-24

MONACO GRAND PRIX

MONTE CARLO • ROUND 5 • DATE: 27TH MAY 2007
Laps: 78 • Distance: 161.588miles/260.52km • Weather: Warm & bright

Pos	Driver	Team	Chassis-Engine	Result	Qual
1	Fernando Alonso	McLaren	McLaren-Mercedes MP4-22	1h40m29.329s	1
2	Lewis Hamilton	McLaren	McLaren-Mercedes MP4-22	1h40m33.424s	2
3	Felipe Massa	Ferrari	Ferrari F2007	1h41m38.443s	3
4	Giancarlo Fisichella	Renault F1	Renault R27	77 laps	4
5	Robert Kubica	BMW Sauber	BMW Sauber F1.07	77 laps	8
6	Nick Heidfeld	BMW Sauber	BMW Sauber F1.07	77 laps	7
7	Alexander Wurz	Williams	Williams-Toyota FW29	77 laps	11
8	Kimi Raikkonen	Ferrari	Ferrari F2007	77 laps	16
9	Scott Speed	Toro Rosso	Toro Rosso-Ferrari STR02	77 laps	18
10	Rubens Barrichello	Honda Racing	Honda RA107	77 laps	9
11	Jenson Button	Honda Racing	Honda RA107	77 laps	10
12	Nico Rosberg	Williams	Williams-Toyota FW29	77 laps	5
13	Heikki Kovalainen	Renault F1	Renault R27	76 laps/engine	15
14	David Coulthard *	Red Bull Racing	Red Bull-Renault RB3	76 laps	13
15	Jarno Trulli	Toyota	Toyota TF107	76 laps	14
16	Ralf Schumacher	Toyota	Toyota TF107	76 laps	20
17	Takuma Sato	Super Aguri	Super Aguri-Honda SA07	76 laps	21
18	Anthony Davidson	Super Aguri	Super Aguri-Honda SA07	76 laps	17
19	Christijan Albers	Spyker	Spyker-Ferrari F8-VII	70 laps/halfshaft	22
R	Adrian Sutil	Spyker	Spyker-Ferrari F8-VII	53 laps/spun off	19
R	Mark Webber	Red Bull Racing	Red Bull-Renault RB3	17 laps/misfire	6
R	Vitantonio Liuzzi	Toro Rosso	Toro Rosso-Ferrari STR02	1 lap/spun off	12

Pole: Alonso, 1m15.726s, 98.663mph/158.782kph. Fastest lap: Alonso, 1m15.284s, 99.242mph/159.715kph on Lap 44. Race leaders: Alonso 1-25 & 29-50 & 53-78, Hamilton 26-28 & 51-52

* 2-place grid penalty for impeding Kovalainen

MARKO KEEPS ON FIRING

Being given financial help to take a tilt at getting to F1 is what drew many drivers to the Red Bull driver scholarship, but its reputation for dropping drivers was growing. In 2007, it was the turn of the wonderfully named Scott Speed to be dropped from Toro Rosso by Helmut Marko, and be replaced by Sebastian Vettel.

STARTING IN THE POINTS

Becoming a test driver for an F1 team tended to give laps in the car, but little hope of a race seat. However, Sebastian Vettel's role with BMW Sauber yielded a race seat when Robert Kubica was injured. Impressively, he finished eighth on his debut in the US GP. Later in the year, he was invited to replace Scott Speed at Scuderia Toro Rosso.

CANADIAN GRAND PRIX

MONTREAL • ROUND 6 • DATE: 10TH JUNE 2007
Laps: 70 • Distance: 189.534miles/305.27km • Weather: Warm & bright

Pos	Driver	Team	Chassis-Engine	Result	Qual
1	Lewis Hamilton	McLaren	McLaren-Mercedes MP4-22	1h44m11.292s	1
2	Nick Heidfeld	BMW Sauber	BMW Sauber F1.07	1h44m15.635s	3
3	Alexander Wurz	Williams	Williams-Toyota FW29	1h44m16.617s	19
4	Heikki Kovalainen *	Renault F1	Renault R27	1h44m18.021s	22
5	Kimi Raikkonen	Ferrari	Ferrari F2007	1h44m24.299s	4
6	Takuma Sato	Super Aguri	Super Aguri-Honda SA07	1h44m27.990s	11
7	Fernando Alonso	McLaren	McLaren-Mercedes MP4-22	1h44m33.228s	2
8	Ralf Schumacher	Toyota	Toyota TF107	1h44m34.180s	18
9	Mark Webber	Red Bull Racing	Red Bull-Renault RB3	1h44m34.252s	6
10	Nico Rosberg	Williams	Williams-Toyota FW29	1h44m35.276s	7
11	Anthony Davidson	Super Aguri	Super Aguri-Honda SA07	1h44m35.610s	17
12	Rubens Barrichello	Honda Racing	Honda RA107	1h44m41.731s	13
R	Jarno Trulli	Toyota	Toyota TF107	58 laps/spun off	10
R	Vitantonio Liuzzi	Toro Rosso	Toro Rosso-Ferrari STR02	54 laps/spun off	12
DQ	Felipe Massa	Ferrari	Ferrari F2007	51 laps/red light	5
DQ	Giancarlo Fisichella	Renault F1	Renault R27	51 laps/red light	9
R	Christijan Albers	Spyker	Spyker-Ferrari F8-VII	47 laps/spun off	21
R	David Coulthard	Red Bull Racing	Red Bull-Renault RB3	36 laps/gearbox	14
R	Robert Kubica	BMW Sauber	BMW Sauber F1.07	26 laps/spun off	8
R	Adrian Sutil	Spyker	Spyker-Ferrari F8-VII	21 laps/spun off	20
R	Scott Speed	Toro Rosso	Toro Rosso-Ferrari STR02	8 laps/collision	16
R	Jenson Button	Honda Racing	Honda RA107	0 laps/transmission	15

Pole: Hamilton, 1m15.707s, 128.855mph/207.373kph. Fastest lap: Alonso, 1m16.367s, 127.742mph/205.580kph on Lap 46. Race leaders: Hamilton 1-21 & 25-70, Massa 22-24

* 10-place grid penalty for engine change

RED BULL FRAGILITY

Red Bull Racing added speed to its repertoire in its third year in F1, but it was hurt by a poor reliability record. Mark Webber and David Coulthard were denied points on numerous occasions by assorted failures that really cost them. Their best day was coming third and fifth, Webber ahead of Coulthard, at the European GP.

UNITED STATES GRAND PRIX

INDIANAPOLIS MOTOR SPEEDWAY • ROUND 7 • DATE: 17TH JUNE 2007
Laps: 73 • Distance: 190.149miles/306.016km • Weather: Warm & bright

Pos	Driver	Team	Chassis-Engine	Result	Qual
1	Lewis Hamilton	McLaren	McLaren-Mercedes MP4-22	1h31m09.965s	1
2	Fernando Alonso	McLaren	McLaren-Mercedes MP4-22	1h31m11.483s	2
3	Felipe Massa	Ferrari	Ferrari F2007	1h31m22.807s	3
4	Kimi Raikkonen	Ferrari	Ferrari F2007	1h31m25.387s	4
5	Heikki Kovalainen	Renault F1	Renault R27	1h31m51.367s	6
6	Jarno Trulli	Toyota	Toyota TF107	1h32m16.668s	8
7	Mark Webber	Red Bull Racing	Red Bull-Renault RB3	1h32m17.296s	9
8	Sebastian Vettel	BMW Sauber	BMW Sauber F1.07	1h32m17.748s	7
9	Giancarlo Fisichella	Renault F1	Renault R27	72 laps	10
10	Alexander Wurz	Williams	Williams-Toyota FW29	72 laps	17
11	Anthony Davidson	Super Aguri	Super Aguri-Honda SA07	72 laps	16
12	Jenson Button	Honda Racing	Honda RA107	72 laps	13
13	Scott Speed	Toro Rosso	Toro Rosso-Ferrari STR02	71 laps	20
14	Adrian Sutil	Spyker	Spyker-Ferrari F8-VII	71 laps	21
15	Christijan Albers	Spyker	Spyker-Ferrari F8-VII	70 laps	22
16	Nico Rosberg	Williams	Williams-Toyota FW29	68 laps/oil leak	14
17	Vitantonio Liuzzi	Toro Rosso	Toro Rosso-Ferrari STR02	68 laps/water leak	19
R	Nick Heidfeld	BMW Sauber	BMW Sauber F1.07	55 laps/hydraulics	5
R	Takuma Sato	Super Aguri	Super Aguri-Honda SA07	13 laps/spun off	18
R	David Coulthard	Red Bull Racing	Red Bull-Renault RB3	0 laps/collision	11
R	Ralf Schumacher	Toyota	Toyota TF107	0 laps/collision	12
R	Rubens Barrichello	Honda Racing	Honda RA107	0 laps/collision	15

Pole: Hamilton, 1m12.331s, 129.643mph/208.640kph. Fastest lap: Raikkonen, 1m13.117s, 128.249mph/206.397kph on Lap 49. Race leaders: Hamilton 1-20 & 27-50 & 52-73, Alonso 21, Kovalainen 22-26, Massa 51

FRENCH GRAND PRIX

MAGNY-COURS • ROUND 8 • DATE: 1ST JULY 2007
Laps: 70 • Distance: 191.430miles/308.77km • Weather: Warm but dull

Pos	Driver	Team	Chassis-Engine	Result	Qual
1	Kimi Raikkonen	Ferrari	Ferrari F2007	1h30m54.200s	3
2	Felipe Massa	Ferrari	Ferrari F2007	1h30m56.614s	1
3	Lewis Hamilton	McLaren	McLaren-Mercedes MP4-22	1h31m26.353s	2
4	Robert Kubica	BMW Sauber	BMW Sauber F1.07	1h31m35.927s	4
5	Nick Heidfeld	BMW Sauber	BMW Sauber F1.07	1h31m43.001s	7
6	Giancarlo Fisichella	Renault F1	Renault R27	1h31m46.410s	5
7	Fernando Alonso	McLaren	McLaren-Mercedes MP4-22	1h31m50.716s	10
8	Jenson Button	Honda Racing	Honda RA107	1h31m53.085s	12
9	Nico Rosberg	Williams	Williams-Toyota FW29	1h32m02.705s	9
10	Ralf Schumacher	Toyota	Toyota TF107	69 laps	11
11	Rubens Barrichello	Honda Racing	Honda RA107	69 laps	13
12	Mark Webber	Red Bull Racing	Red Bull-Renault RB3	69 laps	14
13	David Coulthard	Red Bull Racing	Red Bull-Renault RB3	69 laps	16
14	Alexander Wurz	Williams	Williams-Toyota FW29	69 laps	18
15	Heikki Kovalainen	Renault F1	Renault R27	69 laps	6
16	Takuma Sato *	Super Aguri	Super Aguri-Honda SA07	68 laps	22
17	Adrian Sutil	Spyker	Spyker-Ferrari F8-VII	68 laps	21

Pos	Driver	Team	Chassis-Engine	Result	Qual
R	Scott Speed	Toro Rosso	Toro Rosso-Ferrari STR02	55 laps/gearbox	15
R	Christijan Albers	Spyker	Spyker-Ferrari F8-VII	28 laps	20
R	Jarno Trulli	Toyota	Toyota TF107	1 lap/collision	8
R	Anthony Davidson	Super Aguri	Super Aguri-Honda SA07	1 lap/collision	19
R	Vitantonio Liuzzi	Toro Rosso	Toro Rosso-Ferrari STR02	0 laps/collision	17

Pole: Massa, 1m15.034s, 131.502mph/211.632kph. Fastest lap: Massa, 1m16.099s, 129.661mph/208.670kph on Lap 42. Race leaders: Massa 1-19 & 23-43, Raikkonen 20-22 & 44-70

* 10-place grid penalty for overtaking under waved yellow flags in US GP

GUESSING CORRECTLY

Markus Winkelhock can make the extraordinary claim of leading the only grand prix he contested. This was the European GP at the Nurburgring and, despite starting last, he hit the front for Spyker on lap two. He had started the race on intermediate tyres, guessing correctly that rain was coming. When it did on lap one, his rivals dived for the pits.

BRITISH GRAND PRIX

SILVERSTONE • ROUND 9 • DATE: 8TH JULY 2007

Laps: 59 • Distance: 188.473miles/303.319km • Weather: Warm & bright

Pos	Driver	Team	Chassis-Engine	Result	Qual
1	Kimi Raikkonen	Ferrari	Ferrari F2007	1h21m43.074s	2
2	Fernando Alonso	McLaren	McLaren-Mercedes MP4-22	1h21m45.533s	3
3	Lewis Hamilton	McLaren	McLaren-Mercedes MP4-22	1h22m22.447s	1
4	Robert Kubica	BMW Sauber	BMW Sauber F1.07	1h22m36.393s	5
5	Felipe Massa	Ferrari	Ferrari F2007	1h22m37.137s	4
6	Nick Heidfeld	BMW Sauber	BMW Sauber F1.07	1h22m39.410s	9
7	Heikki Kovalainen	Renault F1	Renault R27	58 laps	7
8	Giancarlo Fisichella	Renault F1	Renault R27	58 laps	8
9	Rubens Barrichello	Honda Racing	Honda RA107	58 laps	14
10	Jenson Button	Honda Racing	Honda RA107	58 laps	18
11	David Coulthard	Red Bull Racing	Red Bull-Renault RB3	58 laps	12
12	Nico Rosberg	Williams	Williams-Toyota FW29	58 laps	17
13	Alexander Wurz	Williams	Williams-Toyota FW29	58 laps	13
14	Takuma Sato	Super Aguri	Super Aguri-Honda SA07	57 laps	22
15	Christijan Albers	Spyker	Spyker-Ferrari F8-VII	57 laps	21
16	Vitantonio Liuzzi	Toro Rosso	Toro Rosso-Ferrari STR02	53 laps/gearbox	16
R	Jarno Trulli	Toyota	Toyota TF107	43 laps/handling	10
R	Anthony Davidson	Super Aguri	Super Aguri-Honda SA07	35 laps/handling	19
R	Scott Speed	Toro Rosso	Toro Rosso-Ferrari STR02	29 laps/collision	15
R	Ralf Schumacher	Toyota	Toyota TF107	22 laps/wheel	6
R	Adrian Sutil	Spyker	Spyker-Ferrari F8-VII	16 laps/engine	20
R	Mark Webber	Red Bull Racing	Red Bull-Renault RB3	8 laps/differential	11

Pole: Hamilton, 1m19.997s, 143.756mph/231.353kph. Fastest lap: Raikkonen, 1m20.638s, 142.613mph/229.514kph on Lap 17. Race leaders: Hamilton 1-15, Raikkonen 16-17 & 38-59, Alonso 18-37

EUROPEAN GRAND PRIX

NURBURGRING • ROUND 10 • DATE: 22ND JULY 2007
Laps: 60 • Distance: 191.437miles/308.88km • Weather: Warm & dull, rain later

Pos	Driver	Team	Chassis-Engine	Result	Qual
1	Fernando Alonso	McLaren	McLaren-Mercedes MP4-22	2h06m26.358s	2
2	Felipe Massa	Ferrari	Ferrari F2007	2h06m34.513s	3
3	Mark Webber	Red Bull Racing	Red Bull-Renault RB3	2h07m32.032s	6
4	Alexander Wurz	Williams	Williams-Toyota FW29	2h07m32.295s	12
5	David Coulthard	Red Bull Racing	Red Bull-Renault RB3	2h07m40.014s	20
6	Nick Heidfeld	BMW Sauber	BMW Sauber F1.07	2h07m46.656s	4
7	Robert Kubica	BMW Sauber	BMW Sauber F1.07	2h07m48.773s	5
8	Heikki Kovalainen	Renault F1	Renault R27	59 laps	7
9	Lewis Hamilton	McLaren	McLaren-Mercedes MP4-22	59 laps	10
10	Giancarlo Fisichella	Renault F1	Renault R27	59 laps	13
11	Rubens Barrichello	Honda Racing	Honda RA107	59 laps	14
12	Anthony Davidson	Super Aguri	Super Aguri-Honda SA07	59 laps	15
13	Jarno Trulli	Toyota	Toyota TF107	59 laps	8
R	Kimi Raikkonen	Ferrari	Ferrari F2007	34 laps/hydraulics	1
R	Takuma Sato	Super Aguri	Super Aguri-Honda SA07	19 laps/hydraulics	16
R	Ralf Schumacher	Toyota	Toyota TF107	18 laps/collision	9
R	Markus Winkelhock	Spyker	Spyker-Ferrari F8-VII	13 laps/hydraulics	22
R	Nico Rosberg	Williams	Williams-Toyota FW29	2 laps/spun off	11
R	Jenson Button	Honda Racing	Honda RA107	2 laps/spun off	17
R	Scott Speed	Toro Rosso	Toro Rosso-Ferrari STR02	2 laps/spun off	18
R	Vitantonio Liuzzi	Toro Rosso	Toro Rosso-Ferrari STR02	2 laps/spun off	19
R	Adrian Sutil	Spyker	Spyker-Ferrari F8-VII	2 laps/spun off	21

Pole: Raikkonen, 1m31.450s, 125.923mph/202.655kph. Fastest lap: Massa, 1m32.853s, 124.021mph/199.592kph on Lap 34. Race leaders: Raikkonen 1, Winkelhock 2-7, Massa 8-12 & 14-55, Coulthard 13, Alonso 56-60

HUNGARIAN GRAND PRIX

HUNGARORING • ROUND 11 • DATE: 5TH AUGUST 2007
Laps: 70 • Distance: 190.181miles/306.67km • Weather: Hot & bright

Pos	Driver	Team	Chassis-Engine	Result	Qual
1	Lewis Hamilton	McLaren	McLaren-Mercedes MP4-22	1h35m52.991s	1
2	Kimi Raikkonen	Ferrari	Ferrari F2007	1h35m53.706s	3
3	Nick Heidfeld	BMW Sauber	BMW Sauber F1.07	1h36m36.120s	2
4	Fernando Alonso *	McLaren	McLaren-Mercedes MP4-22	1h36m37.849s	6
5	Robert Kubica	BMW Sauber	BMW Sauber F1.07	1h36m40.607s	7
6	Ralf Schumacher	Toyota	Toyota TF107	1h36m43.660s	5
7	Nico Rosberg	Williams	Williams-Toyota FW29	1h36m52.130s	4
8	Heikki Kovalainen	Renault F1	Renault R27	1h37m01.095s	11
9	Mark Webber	Red Bull Racing	Red Bull-Renault RB3	1h37m09.322s	9
10	Jarno Trulli	Toyota	Toyota TF107	69 laps	8
11	David Coulthard	Red Bull Racing	Red Bull-Renault RB3	69 laps	10
12	Giancarlo Fisichella !	Renault F1	Renault R27	69 laps	13
13	Felipe Massa	Ferrari	Ferrari F2007	69 laps	14
14	Alexander Wurz	Williams	Williams-Toyota FW29	69 laps	12
15	Takuma Sato	Super Aguri	Super Aguri-Honda SA07	69 laps	19
16	Sebastian Vettel	Toro Rosso	Toro Rosso-Ferrari STR02	69 laps	20
17	Adrian Sutil	Spyker	Spyker-Ferrari F8-VII	68 laps	21

Pos	Driver	Team	Chassis-Engine	Result	Qual
18	Rubens Barrichello	Honda Racing	Honda RA107	68 laps	18
R	Vitantonio Liuzzi	Toro Rosso	Toro Rosso-Ferrari STR02	42 laps/electrical	16
R	Anthony Davidson	Super Aguri	Super Aguri-Honda SA07	41 laps/collision	15
R	Jenson Button	Honda Racing	Honda RA107	35 laps/throttle	17
R	Sakon Yamamoto	Spyker	Spyker-Ferrari F8-VIIB	4 laps/spun off	22

Pole: Hamilton, 1m19.781s, 122.836mph/197.686kph. Fastest lap: Raikkonen, 1m20.047s, 122.428mph/197.029kph on Lap 70. Race leaders: Hamilton 1-70

* 5-place grid penalty for delaying Hamilton in the pits • ! 5-place grid penalty for impeding Yamamoto

TURKISH GRAND PRIX

ISTANBUL PARK • ROUND 12 • DATE: 26TH AUGUST 2007
Laps: 58 • Distance: 192.379miles/309.604km • Weather: Hot & bright

Pos	Driver	Team	Chassis-Engine	Result	Qual
1	Felipe Massa	Ferrari	Ferrari F2007	1h26m42.161s	1
2	Kimi Raikkonen	Ferrari	Ferrari F2007	1h26m44.436s	3
3	Fernando Alonso	McLaren	McLaren-Mercedes MP4-22	1h27m08.342s	4
4	Nick Heidfeld	BMW Sauber	BMW Sauber F1.07	1h27m21.835s	6
5	Lewis Hamilton	McLaren	McLaren-Mercedes MP4-22	1h27m27.246s	2
6	Heikki Kovalainen	Renault F1	Renault R27	1h27m28.330s	7
7	Nico Rosberg	Williams	Williams-Toyota FW29	1h27m37.939s	8
8	Robert Kubica	BMW Sauber	BMW Sauber F1.07	1h27m38.868s	5
9	Giancarlo Fisichella	Renault F1	Renault R27	1h27m41.652s	10
10	David Coulthard	Red Bull Racing	Red Bull-Renault RB3	1h27m53.170s	13
11	Alexander Wurz	Williams	Williams-Toyota FW29	1h28m01.789s	14
12	Ralf Schumacher	Toyota	Toyota TF107	57 laps	16
13	Jenson Button *	Honda Racing	Honda RA107	57 laps	21
14	Anthony Davidson	Super Aguri	Super Aguri-Honda SA07	57 laps	11
15	Vitantonio Liuzzi	Toro Rosso	Toro Rosso-Ferrari STR02	57 laps	15
16	Jarno Trulli	Toyota	Toyota TF107	57 laps	9
17	Rubens Barrichello *	Honda Racing	Honda RA107	57 laps	22
18	Takuma Sato	Super Aguri	Super Aguri-Honda SA07	57 laps	17
19	Sebastian Vettel	Toro Rosso	Toro Rosso-Ferrari STR02	57 laps	18
20	Sakon Yamamoto	Spyker	Spyker-Ferrari F8-VIIB	56 laps	20
21	Adrian Sutil	Spyker	Spyker-Ferrari F8-VII	53 laps/fuel pressure	19
R	Mark Webber	Red Bull Racing	Red Bull-Renault RB3	9 laps/differential	12

Pole: Massa, 1m27.329s, 136.733mph/220.050kph. Fastest lap: Raikkonen, 1m27.295s, 136.786mph/220.136kph on Lap 57. Race leaders: Massa 1-19 & 22-42 & 44-58, Hamilton 20, Kovalainen 21, Alonso 43

* 10-place grid penalty for engine change

HONDA LOSES ITS FORM

Honda engaged reverse in 2007. Having been fourth in 2006 with 86 points, Jenson Button and Rubens Barrichello struggled in 2007, collecting just six points and ending the year ninth out of the 11 teams, largely thanks to Button's fifth place in China, before being promoted to eighth when McLaren's points were removed.

HOW NOT TO IMPRESS
Sebastian Vettel was obviously a rare young talent, but what he did in the extremely wet Japanese GP at Fuji was not what the doctor ordered. Not only did he crash his Toro Rosso out of the race and throw away an impressive third place, but he collected Mark Webber, who was running second for Red Bull's senior team. Oops.

ITALIAN GRAND PRIX

MONZA • ROUND 13 • DATE: 9TH SEPTEMBER 2007
Laps: 53 • Distance: 190.778miles/307.029km • Weather: Warm & bright

Pos	Driver	Team	Chassis-Engine	Result	Qual
1	Fernando Alonso	McLaren	McLaren-Mercedes MP4-22	1h18m37.806s	1
2	Lewis Hamilton	McLaren	McLaren-Mercedes MP4-22	1h18m43.868s	2
3	Kimi Raikkonen	Ferrari	Ferrari F2007	1h19m05.131s	5
4	Nick Heidfeld	BMW Sauber	BMW Sauber F1.07	1h19m34.368s	4
5	Robert Kubica	BMW Sauber	BMW Sauber F1.07	1h19m38.364s	6
6	Nico Rosberg	Williams	Williams-Toyota FW29	1h19m43.616s	8
7	Heikki Kovalainen	Renault F1	Renault R27	1h19m44.557s	7
8	Jenson Button	Honda Racing	Honda RA107	1h19m49.974s	10
9	Mark Webber	Red Bull Racing	Red Bull-Renault RB3	1h19m53.685s	11
10	Rubens Barrichello	Honda Racing	Honda RA107	1h19m54.764s	12
11	Jarno Trulli	Toyota	Toyota TF107	1h19m55.542s	9
12	Giancarlo Fisichella	Renault F1	Renault R27	52 laps	15
13	Alexander Wurz	Williams	Williams-Toyota FW29	52 laps	13
14	Anthony Davidson	Super Aguri	Super Aguri-Honda SA07	52 laps	14
15	Ralf Schumacher	Toyota	Toyota TF107	52 laps	18
16	Takuma Sato	Super Aguri	Super Aguri-Honda SA07	52 laps	17
17	Vitantonio Liuzzi	Toro Rosso	Toro Rosso-Ferrari STR02	52 laps	19
18	Sebastian Vettel	Toro Rosso	Toro Rosso-Ferrari STR02	52 laps	16
19	Adrian Sutil	Spyker	Spyker-Ferrari F8-VIIB	52 laps	21
20	Sakon Yamamoto	Spyker	Spyker-Ferrari F8-VIIB	52 laps	22
R	Felipe Massa	Ferrari	Ferrari F2007	10 laps/suspension	3
R	David Coulthard	Red Bull Racing	Red Bull-Renault RB3	1 lap/collision	20

Pole: Alonso, 1m21.997s, 158.037mph/254.336kph. Fastest lap: Alonso, 1m22.871s, 156.370mph/251.653kph on Lap 15. Race leaders: Alonso 1-20 & 26-53, Raikkonen 21-25

BELGIAN GRAND PRIX

SPA-FRANCORCHAMPS • ROUND 14 • DATE: 16TH SEPTEMBER 2007
Laps: 44 • Distance: 191.491miles/308.176km • Weather: Warm & bright

Pos	Driver	Team	Chassis-Engine	Result	Qual
1	Kimi Raikkonen	Ferrari	Ferrari F2007	1h20m39.066s	1
2	Felipe Massa	Ferrari	Ferrari F2007	1h20m43.761s	2
3	Fernando Alonso	McLaren	McLaren-Mercedes MP4-22	1h20m53.409s	3
4	Lewis Hamilton	McLaren	McLaren-Mercedes MP4-22	1h21m02.681s	4
5	Nick Heidfeld	BMW Sauber	BMW Sauber F1.07	1h21m30.945s	6
6	Nico Rosberg	Williams	Williams-Toyota FW29	1h21m55.942s	5
7	Mark Webber	Red Bull Racing	Red Bull-Renault RB3	1h21m59.705s	7

Pos	Driver	Team	Chassis-Engine	Result	Qual
8	Heikki Kovalainen	Renault F1	Renault R27	1h22m04.172s	9
9	Robert Kubica *	BMW Sauber	BMW Sauber F1.07	1h22m04.727s	14
10	Ralf Schumacher	Toyota	Toyota TF107	1h22m07.640s	10
11	Jarno Trulli	Toyota	Toyota TF107	1h22m22.719s	8
12	Vitantonio Liuzzi	Toro Rosso	Toro Rosso-Ferrari STR02	43 laps	13
13	Rubens Barrichello	Honda Racing	Honda RA107	43 laps	17
14	Adrian Sutil	Spyker	Spyker-Ferrari F8-VIIB	43 laps	19
15	Takuma Sato	Super Aguri	Super Aguri-Honda SA07	43 laps	18
16	Anthony Davidson	Super Aguri	Super Aguri-Honda SA07	43 laps	20
17	Sakon Yamamoto	Spyker	Spyker-Ferrari F8-VIIB	43 laps	21
R	Jenson Button	Honda Racing	Honda RA107	36 laps/hydraulics	12
R	Alexander Wurz	Williams	Williams-Toyota FW29	34 laps/fuel pressure	15
R	David Coulthard	Red Bull Racing	Red Bull-Renault RB3	29 laps/hydraulics	11
R	Sebastian Vettel	Toro Rosso	Toro Rosso-Ferrari STR02	8 laps/steering	16
R	Giancarlo Fisichella *	Renault F1	Renault R27	1 lap/spun off	22

Pole: Raikkonen, 1m45.994s, 147.814mph/237.885kph. Fastest lap: Massa, 1m48.036s, 145.021mph/233.388kph on Lap 34. Race leaders: Raikkonen 1-15 & 17-31 & 33-44, Massa 16 & 32

* 10-place grid penalty for engine change

JAPANESE GRAND PRIX

FUJI SPEEDWAY • ROUND 15 • DATE: 30TH SEPTEMBER 2007
Laps: 67 • Distance: 189.966miles/305.721km • Weather: Warm but very wet

Pos	Driver	Team	Chassis-Engine	Result	Qual
1	Lewis Hamilton	McLaren	McLaren-Mercedes MP4-22	2h00m34.579s	1
2	Heikki Kovalainen	Renault F1	Renault R27	2h00m42.956s	11
3	Kimi Raikkonen	Ferrari	Ferrari F2007	2h00m44.057s	3
4	David Coulthard	Red Bull Racing	Red Bull-Renault RB3	2h00m54.876s	12
5	Giancarlo Fisichella	Renault F1	Renault R27	2h01m13.443s	10
6	Felipe Massa	Ferrari	Ferrari F2007	2h01m23.621s	4
7	Robert Kubica	BMW Sauber	BMW Sauber F1.07	2h01m23.864s	9
8	Adrian Sutil	Spyker	Spyker-Ferrari F8-VIIB	2h01m34.708s	20
9	Vitantonio Liuzzi !	Toro Rosso	Toro Rosso-Ferrari STR02	2h01m55.201s	14
10	Rubens Barrichello	Honda Racing	Honda RA107	2h02m02.921s	17
11	Jenson Button	Honda Racing	Honda RA107	66 laps/suspension	6
12	Sakon Yamamoto	Spyker	Spyker-Ferrari F8-VIIB	66 laps	22
13	Jarno Trulli	Toyota	Toyota TF107	66 laps	13
14	Nick Heidfeld	BMW Sauber	BMW Sauber F1.07	65 laps/accident damage	5
15	Takuma Sato	Super Aguri	Super Aguri-Honda SA07	65 laps/collision	21
R	Ralf Schumacher	Toyota	Toyota TF107	55 laps/puncture	15
R	Anthony Davidson	Super Aguri	Super Aguri-Honda SA07	54 laps/throttle	19
R	Nico Rosberg *	Williams	Williams-Toyota FW29	49 laps/electrical	16
R	Sebastian Vettel	Toro Rosso	Toro Rosso-Ferrari STR02	46 laps/collision	8
R	Mark Webber	Red Bull Racing	Red Bull-Renault RB3	45 laps/collision	7
R	Fernando Alonso	McLaren	McLaren-Mercedes MP4-22	41 laps/spun off	2
R	Alexander Wurz	Williams	Williams-Toyota FW29	19 laps/collision	18

Pole: Hamilton, 1m25.368s, 119.566mph/192.423kph. Fastest lap: Hamilton, 1m28.193s, 115.736mph/186.259kph on Lap 27. Race leaders: Hamilton 1-28 & 41-67, Vettel 29-31, Webber 32-36, Kovalainen 37-39, Fisichella 40

* 10-place grid penalty for engine change • ! 25s penalty for overtaking under yellow flags

CHINESE GRAND PRIX

SHANGHAI INTERNATIONAL CIRCUIT • ROUND 16 • DATE: 7TH OCTOBER 2007
Laps: 56 • Distance: 189.677miles/305.256km • Weather: Warm & wet, drying later

Pos	Driver	Team	Chassis-Engine	Result	Qual
1	Kimi Raikkonen	Ferrari	Ferrari F2007	1h37m58.395s	2
2	Fernando Alonso	McLaren	McLaren-Mercedes MP4-22	1h38m08.201s	4
3	Felipe Massa	Ferrari	Ferrari F2007	1h38m11.286s	3
4	Sebastian Vettel *	Toro Rosso	Toro Rosso-Ferrari STR02	1h38m51.904s	17
5	Jenson Button	Honda Racing	Honda RA107	1h39m07.061s	10
6	Vitantonio Liuzzi	Toro Rosso	Toro Rosso-Ferrari STR02	1h39m12.068s	11
7	Nick Heidfeld	BMW Sauber	BMW Sauber F1.07	1h39m12.619s	8
8	David Coulthard	Red Bull Racing	Red Bull-Renault RB3	1h39m19.145s	5
9	Heikki Kovalainen	Renault F1	Renault R27	1h39m19.581s	13
10	Mark Webber	Red Bull Racing	Red Bull-Renault RB3	1h39m23.080s	7
11	Giancarlo Fisichella	Renault F1	Renault R27	1h39m25.078s	18
12	Alexander Wurz	Williams	Williams-Toyota FW29	55 laps	19
13	Jarno Trulli	Toyota	Toyota TF107	55 laps	12
14	Takuma Sato	Super Aguri	Super Aguri-Honda SA07	55 laps	20
15	Rubens Barrichello	Honda Racing	Honda RA107	55 laps	16
16	Nico Rosberg	Williams	Williams-Toyota FW29	54 laps	15
17	Sakon Yamamoto	Spyker	Spyker-Ferrari F8-VIIB	53 laps	22
R	Robert Kubica	BMW Sauber	BMW Sauber F1.07	33 laps/hydraulics	9
R	Lewis Hamilton	McLaren	McLaren-Mercedes MP4-22	30 laps/spun off	1
R	Ralf Schumacher	Toyota	Toyota TF107	25 laps/spun off	6
R	Adrian Sutil	Spyker	Spyker-Ferrari F8-VIIB	24 laps/spun off	21
R	Anthony Davidson	Super Aguri	Super Aguri-Honda SA07	11 laps/brakes	14

Pole: Hamilton, 1m35.908s, 127.137mph/204.608kph. Fastest lap: Massa, 1m37.454s, 125.120mph/201.362kph on Lap 56. Race leaders: Hamilton 1-15 & 20-28, Raikkonen 16-19 & 29-32 & 34-56, Kubica 33

* 5-place grid penalty for impeding Kovalainen

CHANGING SHAPES

Fuji Speedway hosted the Japanese GP in 1976 and 1977, but had been transformed for its return in 2007. The revisions were to the end of the lap, with the final section being given a chicane, then an esse and a slow loop as it climbed the hill. Meanwhile the Circuit de Catalunya ruined its sweeping final corner by inserting a chicane.

BRAZILIAN GRAND PRIX

INTERLAGOS • ROUND 17 • DATE: 21ST OCTOBER 2007
Laps: 71 • Distance: 190.101miles/305.939km • Weather: Hot & bright

Pos	Driver	Team	Chassis-Engine	Result	Qual
1	Kimi Raikkonen	Ferrari	Ferrari F2007	1h28m15.270s	3
2	Felipe Massa	Ferrari	Ferrari F2007	1h28m16.763s	1
3	Fernando Alonso	McLaren	McLaren-Mercedes MP4-22	1h29m12.289s	4
4	Nico Rosberg	Williams	Williams-Toyota FW29	1h29m18.118s	10
5	Robert Kubica	BMW Sauber	BMW Sauber F1.07	1h29m26.227s	7

Pos	Driver	Team	Chassis-Engine	Result	Qual
6	Nick Heidfeld	BMW Sauber	BMW Sauber F1.07	1h29m26.587s	6
7	Lewis Hamilton	McLaren	McLaren-Mercedes MP4-22	70 laps	2
8	Jarno Trulli	Toyota	Toyota TF107	70 laps	8
9	David Coulthard	Red Bull Racing	Red Bull-Renault RB3	70 laps	9
10	Kazuki Nakajima	Williams	Williams-Toyota FW29	70 laps	19
11	Ralf Schumacher	Toyota	Toyota TF107	70 laps	15
12	Takuma Sato	Super Aguri	Super Aguri-Honda SA07	69 laps	18
13	Vitantonio Liuzzi	Toro Rosso	Toro Rosso-Ferrari STR02	69 laps	14
14	Anthony Davidson	Super Aguri	Super Aguri-Honda SA07	68 laps	20
R	Adrian Sutil	Spyker	Spyker-Ferrari F8-VIIB	43 laps/brakes	21
R	Rubens Barrichello	Honda Racing	Honda RA107	40 laps/engine	11
R	Heikki Kovalainen	Renault F1	Renault R27	35 laps/spun off	17
R	Sebastian Vettel	Toro Rosso	Toro Rosso-Ferrari STR02	34 laps/hydraulics	13
R	Jenson Button	Honda Racing	Honda RA107	20 laps/engine	16
R	Mark Webber	Red Bull Racing	Red Bull-Renault RB3	14 laps/transmission	5
R	Giancarlo Fisichella	Renault F1	Renault R27	2 laps/collision	12
R	Sakon Yamamoto	Spyker	Spyker-Ferrari F8-VIIB	2 laps/collision	22

Pole: Massa, 1m11.931s, 134.002mph/215.656kph. Fastest lap: Raikkonen, 1m12.445s, 133.052mph/214.126kph on Lap 66. Race leaders: Massa 1-19 & 23-49, Raikkonen 20-21 & 50-71, Alonso 22

NEW DRIVERS

Lewis Hamilton was easily the best of the five newcomers, his four wins coming within two points of making him the first rookie world champion. Remarkably, Renault's Finnish rookie Heikki Kovalainen raced to second in Japan, while Sebastian Vettel finished fourth for Toro Rosso in another wet race at the following round in China.

WORLD DRIVERS' CHAMPIONSHIP FINAL RESULTS

Pos	Driver	Nat	Car-Engine	R1	R2	R3	R4	R5	R6	R7
1	Kimi Raikkonen	FIN	Ferrari F2007	1PF	3	3	R	8	5	4F
2	Lewis Hamilton	GBR	McLaren-Mercedes MP4-22	3	2F	2	2	2	1P	1P
3	Fernando Alonso	ESP	McLaren-Mercedes MP4-22	2	1	5	3	1PF	7F	2
4	Felipe Massa	BRA	Ferrari F2007	6	5P	1PF	1PF	3	DQ	3
5	Nick Heidfeld	DEU	BMW Sauber F1.07	4	4	4	R	6	2	R
6	Robert Kubica	POL	BMW Sauber F1.07	R	18	6	4	5	R	-
7	Heikki Kovalainen	FIN	Renault R27	10	8	9	7	13	4	5
8	Giancarlo Fisichella	ITA	Renault R27	5	6	8	9	4	DQ	9
9	Nico Rosberg	DEU	Williams-Toyota FW29	7	R	10	6	12	10	16
10	David Coulthard	GBR	Red Bull-Renault RB3	R	R	R	5	14	R	R
11	Alexander Wurz	AUT	Williams-Toyota FW29	R	9	11	R	7	3	10
12	Mark Webber	AUS	Red Bull-Renault RB3	13	10	R	R	R	9	7
13	Jarno Trulli	ITA	Toyota TF107	9	7	7	R	15	R	6
14	Sebastian Vettel	DEU	BMW Sauber F1.07	T	T	-	-	-	-	8
			Toro Rosso-Ferrari STR02	-	-	-	-	-	-	-
15	Jenson Button	GBR	Honda RA107	15	12	R	12	11	R	12
16	Ralf Schumacher	DEU	Toyota TF107	8	15	12	R	16	8	R
17	Takuma Sato	JPN	Super Aguri-Honda SA07	12	13	R	8	17	6	R

Pos	Driver	Nat	Car-Engine	R1	R2	R3	R4	R5	R6	R7
18	Vitantonio Liuzzi	ITA	Toro Rosso-Ferrari STR02	14	17	R	R	R	R	17
19	Adrian Sutil	DEU	Spyker-Ferrari F8-VII	17	R	15	13	R	R	14
			Spyker-Ferrari F8-VIIB	-	-	-	-	-	-	-
20	Rubens Barrichello	BRA	Honda RA107	11	11	13	10	10	12	R
21	Scott Speed	USA	Toro Rosso-Ferrari STR02	R	14	R	R	9	R	13
22	Kazuki Nakajima	JPN	Williams-Toyota FW29	T	T	-	-	-	-	T
23	Anthony Davidson	GBR	Super Aguri-Honda SA07	16	16	16	11	18	11	11
24	Sakon Yamamoto	JPN	Spyker-Ferrari V8-VII	-	-	-	-	-	-	-
			Spyker-Ferrari F8-VIIB	-	-	-	-	-	-	-
25	Christijan Albers	NLD	Spyker-Ferrari F8-VII	R	R	14	14	19	R	15

Pos	Driver	R8	R9	R10	R11	R12	R13	R14	R15	R16	R17	Total
1	Raikkonen	1	1F	RP	2F	2F	3	1P	3	1	1F	110
2	Hamilton	3	3P	9	1P	5	2	4	1PF	RP	7	109
3	Alonso	7	2	1	4	3	1PF	3	R	2	3	109
4	Massa	2PF	5	2F	13	1P	R	2F	6	3F	2P	94
5	Heidfeld	5	6	6	3	4	4	5	14	7	6	61
6	Kubica	4	4	7	5	8	5	9	7	R	5	39
7	Kovalainen	15	7	8	8	6	7	8	2	9	R	30
8	Fisichella	6	8	10	12	9	12	R	5	11	R	21
9	Rosberg	9	12	R	7	7	6	6	R	16	4	20
10	Coulthard	13	11	5	11	10	R	R	4	8	9	14
11	Wurz	14	13	4	14	11	13	R	R	12	-	13
12	Webber	12	R	3	9	R	9	7	R	10	R	10
13	Trulli	R	R	13	10	16	11	11	13	13	8	8
14	Vettel	-	-	-	-	-	-	-	-	-	-	6
		-	-	-	16	19	18	R	R	4	R	
15	Button	8	10	R	R	13	8	R	11	5	R	6
16	R Schumacher	10	R	R	6	12	15	10	R	R	11	5
17	Sato	16	14	R	15	18	16	15	15	14	12	4
18	Liuzzi	R	16	R	R	15	17	12	9	6	13	3
19	Sutil	17	R	R	17	21	-	-	-	-	-	1
		-	-	-	-	-	19	14	8	R	R	
20	Barrichello	11	9	11	18	17	10	13	10	15	R	0
21	Speed	R	R	R	-	-	-	-	-	-	-	0
22	Nakajima	-	-	-	-	-	-	-	-	-	10	0
23	Davidson	R	R	12	R	14	14	16	R	R	14	0
24	Yamamoto	-	-	-	R	20	-	-	-	-	-	0
		-	-	-	-	-	20	17	12	17	R	
25	Albers	R	15	-	-	-	-	-	-	-	-	0

SYMBOLS AND GRAND PRIX KEY

Round 1 Australian GP
Round 2 Malaysian GP
Round 3 Bahrain GP
Round 4 Spanish GP
Round 5 Monaco GP
Round 6 Canadian GP
Round 7 United States GP
Round 8 French GP
Round 9 British GP
Round 10 European GP
Round 11 Hungarian GP
Round 12 Turkish GP
Round 13 Italian GP
Round 14 Belgian GP
Round 15 Japanese GP
Round 16 Chinese GP
Round 17 Brazilian GP

SCORING

1st 10 points
2nd 8 points
3rd 6 points
4th 5 points
5th 4 points
6th 3 points
7th 2 points
8th 1 point

DNPQ DID NOT PRE-QUALIFY **DNQ** DID NOT QUALIFY **DQ** DISQUALIFIED **EX** EXCLUDED
F FASTEST LAP **NC** NOT CLASSIFIED **NS** NON-STARTER **P** POLE POSITION **R** RETIRED

WORLD CONSTRUCTORS' CHAMPIONSHIP FINAL RESULTS

Pos	Team-Engine	R1	R2	R3	R4	R5	R6	R7	R8	R9
1	Ferrari	1/6	3/5	1/3	1/R	3/8	5/DQ	3/4	1/2	1/5
2	BMW Sauber	4/R	4/18	4/6	4/R	5/6	2/R	8/R	4/5	4/6
3	Renault F1	5/10	6/8	8/9	7/9	4/13	4/DQ	5/9	6/15	7/8
4	Williams-Toyota	7/R	9/R	10/11	6/R	7/12	3/10	10/16	9/14	12/13
5	Red Bull-Renault	13/R	10/R	R/R	5/R	14/R	9/R	7/R	12/13	11/R
6	Toyota	8/9	7/15	7/12	R/R	15/16	8/R	6/R	10/R	R/R
7	Toro Rosso-Ferrari	14/R	14/17	R/R	R/R	9/R	R/R	13/17	R/R	16/R
8	Honda Racing	11/15	11/12	13/R	10/12	10/11	12/R	12/R	8/11	9/10
9	Super Aguri-Honda	12/16	13/16	16/R	8/11	17/18	6/11	11/R	16/R	14/R
10	Spyker-Ferrari	17/R	R/R	14/15	13/14	19/R	R/R	14/15	17/R	15/R
11	McLaren-Mercedes	2/3	1/2	2/5	2/3	1/2	1/7	1/2	3/7	2/3

Pos	Team-Engine	R10	R11	R12	R13	R14	R15	R16	R17	Total
1	Ferrari	2/R	2/13	1/2	3/R	1/2	3/6	1/3	1/2	204
2	BMW Sauber	6/7	3/5	4/8	4/5	5/9	7/14	7/R	5/6	101
3	Renault F1	8/10	8/12	6/9	7/12	8/R	2/5	9/11	R/R	51
4	Williams-Toyota	4/R	7/14	7/11	6/13	6/R	R/R	12/16	4/10	33
5	Red Bull-Renault	3/5	9/11	10/R	9/R	7/R	4/R	8/10	9/R	24
6	Toyota	13/R	6/10	12/16	11/15	10/11	13/R	13/R	8/11	13
7	Toro Rosso-Ferrari	R/R	16/R	15/19	17/18	12/R	9/R	4/6	13/R	8
8	Honda Racing	11/R	18/R	13/17	8/10	13/R	10/11	5/15	R/R	6
9	Super Aguri-Honda	12/R	15/R	14/18	14/16	15/16	15/R	14/R	12/14	4
10	Spyker-Ferrari	R/R	17/R	20/21	19/20	14/17	8/12	17/R	R/R	1
11	McLaren-Mercedes *	1/9	1/4	3/5	1/2	3/4	1/R	2/R	3/7	0*

* McLaren's points were annulled for one of their employees being found in possession of Ferrari documentation

2008

SEASON SUMMARY

Lewis Hamilton laid down a marker by winning the opening round in Australia, and then added four more to take the first of his F1 titles in his second year with McLaren, beating Alonso's record to become the youngest champion at 23 years, 9 months and 26 days. However, it was unbelievably close in the final round, where he edged out Ferrari's Felipe Massa on the final lap of the season. Robert Kubica starred as BMW Sauber claimed its first win, while Fernando Alonso had to make do with fifth overall after quitting McLaren to return to Renault. With Red Bull Racing still pushing for a first win, there was a major surprise when its junior team, Scuderia Toro Rosso, beat it to that goal – thanks to Sebastian Vettel.

AUSTRALIAN GRAND PRIX

ALBERT PARK • ROUND 1 • DATE: 16TH MARCH 2008
Laps: 58 • Distance: 191.117miles/307.574km • Weather: Hot & bright

Pos	Driver	Team	Chassis-Engine	Result	Qual
1	Lewis Hamilton	McLaren	McLaren-Mercedes MP4-23	1h34m50.616s	1
2	Nick Heidfeld	BMW Sauber	BMW Sauber F1.08	1h34m56.094s	5
3	Nico Rosberg	Williams	Williams-Toyota FW30	1h34m58.779s	7
4	Fernando Alonso	Renault F1	Renault R28	1h35m07.797s	11
5	Heikki Kovalainen	McLaren	McLaren-Mercedes MP4-23	1h35m08.630s	3
DQ	Rubens Barrichello ^	Honda Racing	Honda RA108	pit infringement	10
6	Kazuki Nakajima	Williams	Williams-Toyota FW30	57 laps	13
7	Sebastien Bourdais	Toro Rosso	Toro Rosso-Ferrari STR02B	55 laps/transmission	17
8	Kimi Raikkonen	Ferrari	Ferrari F2008	53 laps/engine	15
R	Robert Kubica	BMW Sauber	BMW Sauber F1.08	47 laps/collision	2
R	Timo Glock */!	Toyota	Toyota TF108	43 laps/spun off	18
R	Takuma Sato	Super Aguri	Super Aguri-Honda SA08A	32 laps/transmission	19
R	Nelson Piquet Jr.	Renault F1	Renault R28	30 laps/collision	20
R	Felipe Massa	Ferrari	Ferrari F2008	29 laps/engine	4
R	David Coulthard	Red Bull Racing	Red Bull-Renault RB4	25 laps/collision	8
R	Jarno Trulli	Toyota	Toyota TF108	19 laps/battery	6
R	Adrian Sutil #	Force India	Force India-Ferrari VJM01	8 laps/hydraulics	22
R	Sebastian Vettel	Toro Rosso	Toro Rosso-Ferrari STR02B	0 laps/collision	9
R	Jenson Button	Honda Racing	Honda RA108	0 laps/collision	12
R	Mark Webber	Red Bull Racing	Red Bull-Renault RB4	0 laps/collision	14
R	Giancarlo Fisichella	Force India	Force India-Ferrari VJM01	0 laps/collision	16
R	Anthony Davidson	Super Aguri	Super Aguri-Honda SA08A	0 laps/collision	21

Pole: Hamilton, 1m26.714s, 136.799mph/220.158kph. Fastest lap: Kovalainen, 1m27.418s, 135.698mph/218.385kph on Lap 43. Race leaders: Hamilton 1-17 & 22-42 & 47-58, Kovalainen 18-21 & 43-46

* 5-place grid penalty for gearbox change • ! 5-place grid penalty for impeding Webber • ^ disqualified for pit lane infringement
• # made to start from the pit lane for replacing survival cell

THREE YEARS, THREE NAMES
The team that was once Jordan had its third name change in three years. Thanks to money from Indian drinks tycoon Vijay Mallya, the team was renamed Force India Racing, a name that would stick around for more than a decade. Its first year was no triumph, as neither Giancarlo Fisichella nor Adrian Sutil scored a point.

MALAYSIAN GRAND PRIX

SEPANG • ROUND 2 • DATE: 23RD MARCH 2008
Laps: 56 • Distance: 192.878miles/310.408km • Weather: Very hot & bright

Pos	Driver	Team	Chassis-Engine	Result	Qual
1	Kimi Raikkonen	Ferrari	Ferrari F2008	1h31m18.555s	2
2	Robert Kubica	BMW Sauber	BMW Sauber F1.08	1h31m38.125s	4
3	Heikki Kovalainen *	McLaren	McLaren-Mercedes MP4-23	1h31m57.005s	8
4	Jarno Trulli	Toyota	Toyota TF108	1h32m04.387s	3
5	Lewis Hamilton ^	McLaren	McLaren-Mercedes MP4-23	1h32m05.103s	9
6	Nick Heidfeld	BMW Sauber	BMW Sauber F1.08	1h32m08.388s	5
7	Mark Webber	Red Bull Racing	Red Bull-Renault RB4	1h32m26.685s	6
8	Fernando Alonso	Renault F1	Renault R28	1h32m28.596s	7
9	David Coulthard	Red Bull Racing	Red Bull-Renault RB4	1h32m34.775s	12
10	Jenson Button	Honda Racing	Honda RA108	1h32m44.769s	11
11	Nelson Piquet Jr.	Renault F1	Renault R28	1h32m50.757s	13
12	Giancarlo Fisichella	Force India	Force India-Ferrari VJM01	55 laps	17
13	Rubens Barrichello	Honda Racing	Honda RA108	55 laps	14
14	Nico Rosberg	Williams	Williams-Toyota FW30	55 laps	16
15	Anthony Davidson	Super Aguri	Super Aguri-Honda SA08A	55 laps	21
16	Takuma Sato	Super Aguri	Super Aguri-Honda SA08A	54 laps	19
17	Kazuki Nakajima !	Williams	Williams-Toyota FW30	54 laps	22
R	Sebastian Vettel	Toro Rosso	Toro Rosso-Ferrari STR02B	39 laps/engine	15
R	Felipe Massa	Ferrari	Ferrari F2008	30 laps/spun off	1
R	Adrian Sutil	Force India	Force India-Ferrari VJM01	5 laps/hydraulics	20
R	Timo Glock	Toyota	Toyota TF108	1 lap/collision	10
R	Sebastien Bourdais	Toro Rosso	Toro Rosso-Ferrari STR02B	0 laps/spun off	18

Pole: Massa, 1m35.748s, 129.499mph/208.409kph. Fastest lap: Heidfeld, 1m35.366s, 130.018mph/209.244kph on Lap 55. Race leaders: Massa 1-16, Raikkonen 17-18 & 22-38 & 44-56, Kubica 19-21 & 39-43

* 5-place grid penalty for impeding Alonso & Heidfeld • ! 10-place grid penalty for causing a collision in Australian GP • ^ 5-place penalty for impeding Heidfeld

BAHRAIN GRAND PRIX

SAKHIR • ROUND 3 • DATE: 6TH APRIL 2008
Laps: 57 • Distance: 191.683miles/308.484km • Weather: Very hot & bright

Pos	Driver	Team	Chassis-Engine	Result	Qual
1	Felipe Massa	Ferrari	Ferrari F2008	1h31m06.970s	2
2	Kimi Raikkonen	Ferrari	Ferrari F2008	1h31m10.309s	4
3	Robert Kubica	BMW Sauber	BMW Sauber F1.08	1h31m11.968s	1
4	Nick Heidfeld	BMW Sauber	BMW Sauber F1.08	1h31m15.379s	6
5	Heikki Kovalainen	McLaren	McLaren-Mercedes MP4-23	1h31m33.759s	5

Pos	Driver	Team	Chassis-Engine	Result	Qual
6	Jarno Trulli	Toyota	Toyota TF108	1h31m48.284s	7
7	Mark Webber	Red Bull Racing	Red Bull-Renault RB4	1h31m52.443s	11
8	Nico Rosberg	Williams	Williams-Toyota FW30	1h32m02.859s	8
9	Timo Glock	Toyota	Toyota TF108	1h32m16.470s	13
10	Fernando Alonso	Renault F1	Renault R28	1h32m24.151s	10
11	Rubens Barrichello	Honda Racing	Honda RA108	1h32m24.832s	12
12	Giancarlo Fisichella	Force India	Force India-Ferrari VJM01	56 laps	18
13	Lewis Hamilton	McLaren	McLaren-Mercedes MP4-23	56 laps	3
14	Kazuki Nakajima	Williams	Williams-Toyota FW30	56 laps	16
15	Sebastien Bourdais	Toro Rosso	Toro Rosso-Ferrari STR02B	56 laps	15
16	Anthony Davidson	Super Aguri	Super Aguri-Honda SA08A	56 laps	21
17	Takuma Sato	Super Aguri	Super Aguri-Honda SA08A	56 laps	22
18	David Coulthard	Red Bull Racing	Red Bull-Renault RB4	56 laps	17
19	Adrian Sutil	Force India	Force India-Ferrari VJM01	55 laps	20
R	Nelson Piquet Jr.	Renault F1	Renault R28	40 laps/gearbox	14
R	Jenson Button	Honda Racing	Honda RA108	19 laps/collision	9
R	Sebastian Vettel	Toro Rosso	Toro Rosso-Ferrari STR02B	0 laps/collision	19

Pole: Kubica, 1m33.096s, 130.041mph/209.280kph. Fastest lap: Kovalainen, 1m33.193s, 129.905mph/209.062kph on Lap 49. Race leaders: Massa 1-39 & 46-57, Kubica 40-41, Heidfeld 42-45

SO CLOSE, AND YET...

Felipe Massa became world champion, but only for a few seconds. He did all he could and won the final race to trigger celebrations for the home fans in the grandstands and in the Ferrari garage. However, Lewis Hamilton was able to catch and pass Timo Glock's Toyota top move from sixth to fifth and so overhaul Massa's points tally.

SPANISH GRAND PRIX

BARCELONA-CATALUNYA • ROUND 4 • DATE: 27TH APRIL 2008
Laps: 66 • Distance: 190.775miles/307.23km • Weather: Warm & bright

Pos	Driver	Team	Chassis-Engine	Result	Qual
1	Kimi Raikkonen	Ferrari	Ferrari F2008	1h38m19.051s	1
2	Felipe Massa	Ferrari	Ferrari F2008	1h38m22.279s	3
3	Lewis Hamilton	McLaren	McLaren-Mercedes MP4-23	1h38m23.238s	5
4	Robert Kubica	BMW Sauber	BMW Sauber F1.08	1h38m24.745s	4
5	Mark Webber	Red Bull Racing	Red Bull-Renault RB4	1h38m54.989s	7
6	Jenson Button	Honda Racing	Honda RA108	1h39m12.061s	13
7	Kazuki Nakajima	Williams	Williams-Toyota FW30	1h39m17.295s	12
8	Jarno Trulli	Toyota	Toyota TF108	1h39m18.486s	8
9	Nick Heidfeld	BMW Sauber	BMW Sauber F1.08	1h39m22.124s	9
10	Giancarlo Fisichella	Force India	Force India-Ferrari VJM01	65 laps	19
11	Timo Glock	Toyota	Toyota TF108	65 laps	14
12	David Coulthard	Red Bull Racing	Red Bull-Renault RB4	65 laps	17
13	Takuma Sato	Super Aguri	Super Aguri-Honda SA08A	65 laps	22
R	Nico Rosberg	Williams	Williams-Toyota FW30	41 laps/engine	15
R	Fernando Alonso	Renault F1	Renault R28	34 laps/engine	2
R	Rubens Barrichello	Honda Racing	Honda RA108	34 laps/collision	11
R	Heikki Kovalainen	McLaren	McLaren-Mercedes MP4-23	21 laps/wheel	6

Pos	Driver	Team	Chassis-Engine	Result	Qual
R	Anthony Davidson	Super Aguri	Super Aguri-Honda SA08A	8 laps/radiator	21
R	Sebastien Bourdais	Toro Rosso	Toro Rosso-Ferrari STR02B	7 laps/collision	16
R	Nelson Piquet Jr.	Renault F1	Renault R28	6 laps/collision	10
R	Sebastian Vettel	Toro Rosso	Toro Rosso-Ferrari STR02B	0 laps/collision	18
R	Adrian Sutil	Force India	Force India-Ferrari VJM01	0 laps/collision	20

Pole: Raikkonen, 1m21.813s, 127.277mph/204.832kph. Fastest lap: Raikkonen, 1m21.670s, 127.500mph/205.191kph on Lap 46. Race leaders: Raikkonen 1-20 & 25-66, Hamilton 21, Heidfeld 22-24

TURKISH GRAND PRIX

ISTANBUL PARK • ROUND 5 • DATE: 11TH MAY 2008
Laps: 58 • Distance: 192.379miles/309.604km • Weather: Warm & bright

Pos	Driver	Team	Chassis-Engine	Result	Qual
1	Felipe Massa	Ferrari	Ferrari F2008	1h26m49.451s	1
2	Lewis Hamilton	McLaren	McLaren-Mercedes MP4-23	1h26m53.230s	3
3	Kimi Raikkonen	Ferrari	Ferrari F2008	1h26m53.722s	4
4	Robert Kubica	BMW Sauber	BMW Sauber F1.08	1h27m11.396s	5
5	Nick Heidfeld	BMW Sauber	BMW Sauber F1.08	1h27m28.192s	9
6	Fernando Alonso	Renault F1	Renault R28	1h27m43.175s	7
7	Mark Webber	Red Bull Racing	Red Bull-Renault RB4	1h27m53.680s	6
8	Nico Rosberg	Williams	Williams-Toyota FW30	1h28m00.857s	11
9	David Coulthard	Red Bull Racing	Red Bull-Renault RB4	1h28m04.721s	10
10	Jarno Trulli	Toyota	Toyota TF108	1h28m05.795s	8
11	Jenson Button	Honda Racing	Honda RA108	57 laps	13
12	Heikki Kovalainen	McLaren	McLaren-Mercedes MP4-23	57 laps	2
13	Timo Glock	Toyota	Toyota TF108	57 laps	15
14	Rubens Barrichello	Honda Racing	Honda RA108	57 laps	12
15	Nelson Piquet Jr.	Renault F1	Renault R28	57 laps	17
16	Adrian Sutil	Force India	Force India-Ferrari VJM01	57 laps	19
17	Sebastian Vettel	Toro Rosso	Toro Rosso-Ferrari STR02B	57 laps	14
R	Sebastien Bourdais	Toro Rosso	Toro Rosso-Ferrari STR02B	24 laps/spun/brakes	18
R	Kazuki Nakajima	Williams	Williams-Toyota FW30	1 lap/collision	16
R	Giancarlo Fisichella *	Force India	Force India-Ferrari VJM01	0 laps/collision	20

Pole: Massa, 1m27.617s, 136.283mph/219.327kph. Fastest lap: Raikkonen, 1m26.506s, 138.033mph/222.144kph on Lap 20. Race leaders: Massa 1-19 & 22-23 & 33-40 & 46-58, Raikkonen 20-21 & 41-43, Hamilton 24-32 & 44-45

* 3-place grid penalty for pit lane infringement

NOT ALL IT SEEMED

Fernando Alonso's Singapore GP win was unlikely when he qualified 15th after his Renault broke. However, the timing of a safety car that was triggered when team-mate Nelson Piquet Jr hit the wall gave him a huge help, as he had just pitted. When the others came in, he vaulted into the lead and stayed there. There would be ramifications for Renault when it was revealed in 2009 that Piquet had gone off intentionally.

MONACO GRAND PRIX

MONTE CARLO • ROUND 6 • DATE: 25TH MAY 2008
Laps: 76 • Distance: 157.259miles/253.84km • Weather: Warm & wet, drying later

Pos	Driver	Team	Chassis-Engine	Result	Qual
1	Lewis Hamilton	McLaren	McLaren-Mercedes MP4-23	2h00m42.742s	3
2	Robert Kubica	BMW Sauber	BMW Sauber F1.08	2h00m45.806s	5
3	Felipe Massa	Ferrari	Ferrari F2008	2h00m47.553s	1
4	Mark Webber	Red Bull Racing	Red Bull-Renault RB4	2h01m02.037s	9
5	Sebastian Vettel *	Toro Rosso	Toro Rosso-Ferrari STR03	2h01m07.399s	19
6	Rubens Barrichello	Honda Racing	Honda RA108	2h01m11.150s	14
7	Kazuki Nakajima	Williams	Williams-Toyota FW30	2h01m12.922s	13
8	Heikki Kovalainen	McLaren	McLaren-Mercedes MP4-23	2h01m15.933s	4
9	Kimi Raikkonen	Ferrari	Ferrari F2008	2h01m16.534s	2
10	Fernando Alonso	Renault F1	Renault R28	75 laps	7
11	Jenson Button	Honda Racing	Honda RA108	75 laps	11
12	Timo Glock	Toyota	Toyota TF108	75 laps	10
13	Jarno Trulli	Toyota	Toyota TF108	75 laps	8
14	Nick Heidfeld	BMW Sauber	BMW Sauber F1.08	72 laps	12
R	Adrian Sutil	Force India	Force India-Ferrari VJM01	67 laps/collision	18
R	Nico Rosberg	Williams	Williams-Toyota FW30	59 laps/spun off	6
R	Nelson Piquet Jr.	Renault F1	Renault R28	47 laps/spun off	17
R	Giancarlo Fisichella *	Force India	Force India-Ferrari VJM01	36 laps/gearbox	20
R	David Coulthard *	Red Bull Racing	Red Bull-Renault RB4	7 laps/spun off	15
R	Sebastien Bourdais	Toro Rosso	Toro Rosso-Ferrari STR03	7 laps/collision	16

Pole: Massa, 1m15.787s, 98.583mph/158.655kph. Fastest lap: Raikkonen, 1m16.689s, 97.424mph/156.789kph on Lap 74. Race leaders: Massa 1-15 & 26-32, Kubica 16-25, Hamilton 33-76

* 5-place grid penalty for gearbox change

SAUBER'S DAY OF DAYS

BMW's financial injection into Sauber was rewarded when not only did Robert Kubica win the Canadian GP, but was also followed home by team-mate Nick Heidfeld for a one-two. It had been a race that looked set to be won by Lewis Hamilton, but he was caught out by a red light at the pit exit and hit Kimi Raikkonen's Ferrari.

CANADIAN GRAND PRIX

MONTREAL • ROUND 7 • DATE: 8TH JUNE 2008
Laps: 70 • Distance: 189.534miles/305.27km • Weather: Hot & bright

Pos	Driver	Team	Chassis-Engine	Result	Qual
1	Robert Kubica	BMW Sauber	BMW Sauber F1.08	1h36m24.447s	2
2	Nick Heidfeld	BMW Sauber	BMW Sauber F1.08	1h36m40.942s	8
3	David Coulthard	Red Bull Racing	Red Bull-Renault RB4	1h36m47.799s	13
4	Timo Glock	Toyota	Toyota TF108	1h37m07.074s	11
5	Felipe Massa	Ferrari	Ferrari F2008	1h37m08.381s	6
6	Jarno Trulli	Toyota	Toyota TF108	1h37m12.222s	14
7	Rubens Barrichello	Honda Racing	Honda RA108	1h37m18.044s	9
8	Sebastian Vettel !	Toro Rosso	Toro Rosso-Ferrari STR03	1h37m18.567s	19
9	Heikki Kovalainen	McLaren	McLaren-Mercedes MP4-23	1h37m18.880s	7
10	Nico Rosberg	Williams	Williams-Toyota FW30	1h37m22.196s	5

Pos	Driver	Team	Chassis-Engine	Result	Qual
11	Jenson Button *	Honda Racing	Honda RA108	1h37m31.987s	20
12	Mark Webber	Red Bull Racing	Red Bull-Renault RB4	1h37m35.676s	10
13	Sebastien Bourdais *	Toro Rosso	Toro Rosso-Ferrari STR03	69 laps	18
R	Giancarlo Fisichella	Force India	Force India-Ferrari VJM01	51 laps/spun off	17
R	Kazuki Nakajima	Williams	Williams-Toyota FW30	46 laps/collision	12
R	Fernando Alonso	Renault F1	Renault R28	44 laps/spun off	4
R	Nelson Piquet Jr.	Renault F1	Renault R28	39 laps/brakes	15
R	Lewis Hamilton	McLaren	McLaren-Mercedes MP4-23	19 laps/collision	1
R	Kimi Raikkonen	Ferrari	Ferrari F2008	19 laps/collision	3
R	Adrian Sutil	Force India	Force India-Ferrari VJM01	13 laps/gearbox	16

Pole: Hamilton, 1m17.886s, 125.250mph/201.571kph. Fastest lap: Raikkonen, 1m17.387s, 126.058mph/202.871kph on Lap 14. Race leaders: Hamilton 1-18, Heidfeld 19-28, Barrichello 29-35, Coulthard 36, Trulli 37-38, Glock 39-41, Kubica 42-70

* 5-place grid penalty for gearbox change • ! made to start from the pit lane for modifying car in parc ferme

FRENCH GRAND PRIX

MAGNY-COURS • ROUND 8 • DATE: 22ND JUNE 2008
Laps: 70 • Distance: 191.430miles/308.77km • Weather: Warm but damp, wet later

Pos	Driver	Team	Chassis-Engine	Result	Qual
1	Felipe Massa	Ferrari	Ferrari F2008	1h31m50.245s	2
2	Kimi Raikkonen	Ferrari	Ferrari F2008	1h32m08.229s	1
3	Jarno Trulli	Toyota	Toyota TF108	1h32m18.495s	4
4	Heikki Kovalainen *	McLaren	McLaren-Mercedes MP4-23	1h32m19.174s	10
5	Robert Kubica	BMW Sauber	BMW Sauber F1.08	1h32m20.757s	5
6	Mark Webber	Red Bull Racing	Red Bull-Renault RB4	1h32m30.549s	6
7	Nelson Piquet Jr.	Renault F1	Renault R28	1h32m31.278s	9
8	Fernando Alonso	Renault F1	Renault R28	1h32m33.617s	3
9	David Coulthard	Red Bull Racing	Red Bull-Renault RB4	1h32m41.317s	7
10	Lewis Hamilton !	McLaren	McLaren-Mercedes MP4-23	1h32m44.766s	13
11	Timo Glock	Toyota	Toyota TF108	1h32m47.983s	8
12	Sebastian Vettel	Toro Rosso	Toro Rosso-Ferrari STR03	1h32m48.310s	12
13	Nick Heidfeld	BMW Sauber	BMW Sauber F1.08	1h32m52.324s	11
14	Rubens Barrichello ^	Honda Racing	Honda RA108	69 laps	20
15	Kazuki Nakajima	Williams	Williams-Toyota FW30	69 laps	15
16	Nico Rosberg !	Williams	Williams-Toyota FW30	69 laps	19
17	Sebastien Bourdais	Toro Rosso	Toro Rosso-Ferrari STR03	69 laps	14
18	Giancarlo Fisichella	Force India	Force India-Ferrari VJM01	69 laps	17
19	Adrian Sutil	Force India	Force India-Ferrari VJM01	69 laps	18
R	Jenson Button	Honda Racing	Honda RA108	16 laps/collision	16

Pole: Raikkonen, 1m16.449s, 129.068mph/207.714kph. Fastest lap: Raikkonen, 1m16.630s, 128.763mph/207.224kph on Lap 16. Race leaders: Raikkonen 1-21 & 24-38, Massa 22-23 & 39-70

* 5-place grid penalty for impeding Webber • ! 10-place grid penalty for pit lane accident in Canadian GP • ^ 5-place grid penalty for gearbox change

THE YOUNGEST WINNER

Sebastian Vettel excelled in wet conditions not only to qualify on pole, but also to go on to win the Italian GP for Toro Rosso. He had already been the youngest F1 starter and the youngest point scorer, but at Monza he beat Alonso's record to become the youngest pole qualifier and then the youngest winner, at 21 years and 73 days.

BRITISH GRAND PRIX

SILVERSTONE • ROUND 9 • DATE: 6TH JULY 2008
Laps: 60 • Distance: 191.410miles/308.46km • Weather: Warm but wet

Pos	Driver	Team	Chassis-Engine	Result	Qual
1	Lewis Hamilton	McLaren	McLaren-Mercedes MP4-23	1h39m09.440s	4
2	Nick Heidfeld	BMW Sauber	BMW Sauber F1.08	1h40m18.017s	5
3	Rubens Barrichello	Honda Racing	Honda RA108	1h40m31.713s	16
4	Kimi Raikkonen	Ferrari	Ferrari F2008	59 laps	3
5	Heikki Kovalainen	McLaren	McLaren-Mercedes MP4-23	59 laps	1
6	Fernando Alonso	Renault F1	Renault R28	59 laps	6
7	Jarno Trulli	Toyota	Toyota TF108	59 laps	14
8	Kazuki Nakajima	Williams	Williams-Toyota FW30	59 laps	15
9	Nico Rosberg *	Williams	Williams-Toyota FW30	59 laps	20
10	Mark Webber	Red Bull Racing	Red Bull-Renault RB4	59 laps	2
11	Sebastien Bourdais	Toro Rosso	Toro Rosso-Ferrari STR03	59 laps	13
12	Timo Glock	Toyota	Toyota TF108	59 laps	12
13	Felipe Massa	Ferrari	Ferrari F2008	58 laps	9
R	Robert Kubica	BMW Sauber	BMW Sauber F1.08	39 laps/spun off	10
R	Jenson Button	Honda Racing	Honda RA108	38 laps/spun off	17
R	Nelson Piquet Jr.	Renault F1	Renault R28	35 laps/spun off	7
R	Giancarlo Fisichella	Force India	Force India-Ferrari VJM01	26 laps/spun off	19
R	Adrian Sutil	Force India	Force India-Ferrari VJM01	10 laps/spun off	18
R	Sebastian Vettel	Toro Rosso	Toro Rosso-Ferrari STR03	0 laps/spun off	8
R	David Coulthard	Red Bull Racing	Red Bull-Renault RB4	0 laps/spun off	11

Pole: Kovalainen, 1m21.049s, 141.890mph/228.350kph. Fastest lap: Raikkonen, 1m32.150s, 124.797mph/200.842kph on Lap 18. Race leaders: Kovalainen 1-4, Hamilton 5-21 & 23-60, Heidfeld 22

* made to start from the pit lane for modifying car in parc ferme

KOVALAINEN'S ONE WIN

Heikki Kovalainen's drive swap with Fernando Alonso meant that he joined McLaren from Renault, and, although he was no match for clear number one Lewis Hamilton, he was able to take one win. This came in Hungary, on a day when Felipe Massa lost out with engine failure and Hamilton had a puncture. It was to remain this second-year driver's only win.

GERMAN GRAND PRIX

HOCKENHEIM • ROUND 10 • DATE: 20TH JULY 2008
Laps: 67 • Distance: 190.424miles/306.458km • Weather: Warm but dull

Pos	Driver	Team	Chassis-Engine	Result	Qual
1	Lewis Hamilton	McLaren	McLaren-Mercedes MP4-23	1h31m20.874s	1
2	Nelson Piquet Jr.	Renault F1	Renault R28	1h31m26.460s	17
3	Felipe Massa	Ferrari	Ferrari F2008	1h31m30.213s	2
4	Nick Heidfeld	BMW Sauber	BMW Sauber F1.08	1h31m30.699s	12
5	Heikki Kovalainen	McLaren	McLaren-Mercedes MP4-23	1h31m33.285s	3
6	Kimi Raikkonen	Ferrari	Ferrari F2008	1h31m35.357s	6
7	Robert Kubica	BMW Sauber	BMW Sauber F1.08	1h31m43.477s	7
8	Sebastian Vettel	Toro Rosso	Toro Rosso-Ferrari STR03	1h31m54.156s	9

Pos	Driver	Team	Chassis-Engine	Result	Qual
9	Jarno Trulli	Toyota	Toyota TF108	1h31m58.073s	4
10	Nico Rosberg	Williams	Williams-Toyota FW30	1h31m58.532s	13
11	Fernando Alonso	Renault F1	Renault R28	1h31m59.499s	5
12	Sebastien Bourdais	Toro Rosso	Toro Rosso-Ferrari STR03	1h31m59.985s	15
13	David Coulthard	Red Bull Racing	Red Bull-Renault RB4	1h32m15.845s	10
14	Kazuki Nakajima	Williams	Williams-Toyota FW30	1h32m20.877s	16
15	Adrian Sutil	Force India	Force India-Ferrari VJM01	1h32m30.362s	19
16	Giancarlo Fisichella *	Force India	Force India-Ferrari VJM01	1h32m44.967s	20
17	Jenson Button	Honda Racing	Honda RA108	66 laps	14
R	Rubens Barrichello	Honda Racing	Honda RA108	50 laps/collision	18
R	Mark Webber	Red Bull Racing	Red Bull-Renault RB4	40 laps/oil leak	8
R	Timo Glock	Toyota	Toyota TF108	35 laps/suspension	11

Pole: Hamilton, 1m15.666s, 135.222mph/217.619kph. Fastest lap: Heidfeld, 1m15.987s, 134.651mph/216.700kph on Lap 52. Race leaders: Hamilton 1-18 & 22-37 & 39-50 & 60-67, Massa 19-20 & 38, Kovalainen 21, Heidfeld 51-53, Piquet Jr 54-59

* 25s penalty for safety car infringement

HUNGARIAN GRAND PRIX

HUNGARORING • ROUND 11 • DATE: 3RD AUGUST 2008
Laps: 70 • Distance: 190.181miles/306.67km • Weather: Hot & bright

Pos	Driver	Team	Chassis-Engine	Result	Qual
1	Heikki Kovalainen	McLaren	McLaren-Mercedes MP4-23	1h37m27.067s	2
2	Timo Glock	Toyota	Toyota TF108	1h37m38.128s	5
3	Kimi Raikkonen	Ferrari	Ferrari F2008	1h37m43.923s	6
4	Fernando Alonso	Renault F1	Renault R28	1h37m48.681s	7
5	Lewis Hamilton	McLaren	McLaren-Mercedes MP4-23	1h37m50.115s	1
6	Nelson Piquet Jr.	Renault F1	Renault R28	1h37m59.365s	10
7	Jarno Trulli	Toyota	Toyota TF108	1h38m03.516s	9
8	Robert Kubica	BMW Sauber	BMW Sauber F1.08	1h38m15.388s	4
9	Mark Webber	Red Bull Racing	Red Bull-Renault RB4	1h38m25.901s	8
10	Nick Heidfeld	BMW Sauber	BMW Sauber F1.08	1h38m34.776s	15
11	David Coulthard	Red Bull Racing	Red Bull-Renault RB4	1h38m37.474s	13
12	Jenson Button	Honda Racing	Honda RA108	69 laps	12
13	Kazuki Nakajima	Williams	Williams-Toyota FW30	69 laps	16
14	Nico Rosberg	Williams	Williams-Toyota FW30	69 laps	14
15	Giancarlo Fisichella	Force India	Force India-Ferrari VJM01	69 laps	18
16	Rubens Barrichello	Honda Racing	Honda RA108	68 laps	17
17	Felipe Massa	Ferrari	Ferrari F2008	67 laps/engine	3
18	Sebastien Bourdais *	Toro Rosso	Toro Rosso-Ferrari STR03	67 laps	19
R	Adrian Sutil	Force India	Force India-Ferrari VJM01	62 laps/puncture	20
R	Sebastian Vettel	Toro Rosso	Toro Rosso-Ferrari STR03	22 laps/overheating	11

Pole: Hamilton, 1m20.899s, 121.138mph/194.954kph. Fastest lap: Raikkonen, 1m21.195s, 120.697mph/194.243kph on Lap 61. Race leaders: Massa 1-18 & 22-44 & 49-67, Hamilton 19, Kovalainen 20-21 & 45-48 & 68-70

* 5-place grid penalty for impeding Heidfeld

EUROPEAN GRAND PRIX

VALENCIA STREET CIRCUIT • ROUND 12 • DATE: 24TH AUGUST 2008
Laps: 57 • Distance: 191.931miles/308.883km • Weather: Hot & bright

Pos	Driver	Team	Chassis-Engine	Result	Qual
1	Felipe Massa	Ferrari	Ferrari F2008	1h35m32.339s	1
2	Lewis Hamilton	McLaren	McLaren-Mercedes MP4-23	1h35m37.950s	2
3	Robert Kubica	BMW Sauber	BMW Sauber F1.08	1h36m09.692s	3
4	Heikki Kovalainen	McLaren	McLaren-Mercedes MP4-23	1h36m12.042s	5
5	Jarno Trulli	Toyota	Toyota TF108	1h36m23.023s	7
6	Sebastian Vettel	Toro Rosso	Toro Rosso-Ferrari STR03	1h36m24.964s	6
7	Timo Glock	Toyota	Toyota TF108	1h36m40.329s	13
8	Nico Rosberg	Williams	Williams-Toyota FW30	1h36m43.796s	9
9	Nick Heidfeld	BMW Sauber	BMW Sauber F1.08	1h36m54.516s	8
10	Sebastien Bourdais	Toro Rosso	Toro Rosso-Ferrari STR03	1h37m02.133s	10
11	Nelson Piquet Jr.	Renault F1	Renault R28	1h37m05.056s	15
12	Mark Webber	Red Bull Racing	Red Bull-Renault RB4	56 laps	14
13	Jenson Button	Honda Racing	Honda RA108	56 laps	16
14	Giancarlo Fisichella	Force India	Force India-Ferrari VJM01	56 laps	18
15	Kazuki Nakajima	Williams	Williams-Toyota FW30	56 laps	11
16	Rubens Barrichello *	Honda Racing	Honda RA108	56 laps	19
17	David Coulthard	Red Bull Racing	Red Bull-Renault RB4	56 laps	17
R	Kimi Raikkonen	Ferrari	Ferrari F2008	45 laps/engine	4
R	Adrian Sutil *	Force India	Force India-Ferrari VJM01	41 laps/spun off	20
R	Fernando Alonso	Renault F1	Renault R28	0 laps/collision	12

Pole: Massa, 1m38.989s, 122.457mph/197.076kph. Fastest lap: Massa, 1m38.708s, 122.806mph/197.637kph on Lap 36. Race leaders: Massa 1-14 & 20-36 & 39-57, Hamilton 15-16 & 37-38, Kubica 17, Kovalainen 18-19

* made to start from the pit lane for modifying car in parc ferme

NEW CIRCUITS

Singapore's first time hosting the World Championship was a triumph: not only did it provide something different – a night race run under floodlights – but it also answered sponsors' needs by taking F1 into the middle of a global business hub. The other street circuit used for the first time was in Valencia, with a track laid out around its port area.

BELGIAN GRAND PRIX

SPA-FRANCORCHAMPS • ROUND 13 • DATE: 7TH SEPTEMBER 2008
Laps: 44 • Distance: 191.491miles/308.176km • Weather: Warm, damp later

Pos	Driver	Team	Chassis-Engine	Result	Qual
1	Felipe Massa	Ferrari	Ferrari F2008	1h22m59.394s	2
2	Nick Heidfeld	BMW Sauber	BMW Sauber F1.08	1h23m08.777s	5
3	Lewis Hamilton *	McLaren	McLaren-Mercedes MP4-23	1h23m09.933s	1
4	Fernando Alonso	Renault F1	Renault R28	1h23m13.872s	6
5	Sebastian Vettel	Toro Rosso	Toro Rosso-Ferrari STR03	1h23m13.970s	10
6	Robert Kubica	BMW Sauber	BMW Sauber F1.08	1h23m14.431s	8

Pos	Driver	Team	Chassis-Engine	Result	Qual
7	Sebastien Bourdais	Toro Rosso	Toro Rosso-Ferrari STR03	1h23m16.129s	9
8	Mark Webber	Red Bull Racing	Red Bull-Renault RB4	1h23m42.170s	7
9	Timo Glock !	Toyota	Toyota TF108	1h24m06.439s	13
10	Heikki Kovalainen	McLaren	McLaren-Mercedes MP4-23	43 laps/gearbox	3
11	David Coulthard	Red Bull Racing	Red Bull-Renault RB4	43 laps	14
12	Nico Rosberg	Williams	Williams-Toyota FW30	43 laps	15
13	Adrian Sutil	Force India	Force India-Ferrari VJM01	43 laps	18
14	Kazuki Nakajima	Williams	Williams-Toyota FW30	43 laps	19
15	Jenson Button	Honda Racing	Honda RA108	43 laps	17
16	Jarno Trulli	Toyota	Toyota TF108	43 laps	11
17	Giancarlo Fisichella	Force India	Force India-Ferrari VJM01	43 laps	20
18	Kimi Raikkonen	Ferrari	Ferrari F2008	42 laps/spun off	4
R	Rubens Barrichello	Honda Racing	Honda RA108	19 laps/gearbox	16
R	Nelson Piquet Jr.	Renault F1	Renault R28	13 laps/spun off	12

Pole: Hamilton, 1m47.338s, 145.964mph/234.906kph. Fastest lap: Raikkonen, 1m47.930s, 145.163mph/233.618kph on Lap 24. Race leaders: Hamilton 1 & 43-44, Raikkonen 2-12 & 14-25 & 29-42, Massa 13 & 26-28

* 25s penalty for cutting the chicane • ! 25s penalty for ignoring yellow flags

ITALIAN GRAND PRIX

MONZA • ROUND 14 • DATE: 14TH SEPTEMBER 2008
Laps: 53 • Distance: 190.778miles/307.029km • Weather: Warm & wet, drying later

Pos	Driver	Team	Chassis-Engine	Result	Qual
1	Sebastian Vettel	Toro Rosso	Toro Rosso-Ferrari STR03	1h26m47.494s	1
2	Heikki Kovalainen	McLaren	McLaren-Mercedes MP4-23	1h27m00.006s	2
3	Robert Kubica	BMW Sauber	BMW Sauber F1.08	1h27m07.965s	11
4	Fernando Alonso	Renault F1	Renault R28	1h27m11.397s	8
5	Nick Heidfeld	BMW Sauber	BMW Sauber F1.08	1h27m15.242s	10
6	Felipe Massa	Ferrari	Ferrari F2008	1h27m16.310s	6
7	Lewis Hamilton	McLaren	McLaren-Mercedes MP4-23	1h27m17.406s	15
8	Mark Webber	Red Bull Racing	Red Bull-Renault RB4	1h27m19.542s	3
9	Kimi Raikkonen	Ferrari	Ferrari F2008	1h27m26.962s	14
10	Nelson Piquet Jr.	Renault F1	Renault R28	1h27m41.939s	17
11	Timo Glock	Toyota	Toyota TF108	1h27m46.382s	9
12	Kazuki Nakajima	Williams	Williams-Toyota FW30	1h27m49.509s	18
13	Jarno Trulli	Toyota	Toyota TF108	1h27m53.448s	7
14	Nico Rosberg	Williams	Williams-Toyota FW30	1h27m56.129s	5
15	Jenson Button	Honda Racing	Honda RA108	1h28m00.864s	19
16	David Coulthard	Red Bull Racing	Red Bull-Renault RB4	52 laps	13
17	Rubens Barrichello	Honda Racing	Honda RA108	52 laps	16
18	Sebastien Bourdais	Toro Rosso	Toro Rosso-Ferrari STR03	52 laps	4
19	Adrian Sutil	Force India	Force India-Ferrari VJM01	51 laps	20
R	Giancarlo Fisichella	Force India	Force India-Ferrari VJM01	11 laps/collision	12

Pole: Vettel, 1m37.555s, 132.833mph/213.774kph. Fastest lap: Raikkonen, 1m28.047s, 147.177mph/236.859kph on Lap 53. Race leaders: Vettel 1-18 & 23-53, Kovalainen 19-22

NEW DRIVERS

Second-generation F1 racer Nelson Piquet Jr had a mixed year with Renault, ranging from coming second at Hockenheim to crashing out in Singapore. The other rookie in 2008 was Sebastien Bourdais, who scored on his debut in Melbourne for Scuderia Toro Rosso by finishing seventh, a result he matched in the Belgian GP.

SINGAPORE GRAND PRIX

MARINA BAY CIRCUIT • ROUND 15 • DATE: 28TH SEPTEMBER 2008
Laps: 61 • Distance: 192.57miles/309.087km • Weather: Hot & humid

Pos	Driver	Team	Chassis-Engine	Result	Qual
1	Fernando Alonso	Renault F1	Renault R28	1h57m16.304s	15
2	Nico Rosberg	Williams	Williams-Toyota FW30	1h57m19.261s	8
3	Lewis Hamilton	McLaren	McLaren-Mercedes MP4-23	1h57m22.221s	2
4	Timo Glock	Toyota	Toyota TF108	1h57m24.459s	7
5	Sebastian Vettel	Toro Rosso	Toro Rosso-Ferrari STR03	1h57m26.572s	6
6	Nick Heidfeld *	BMW Sauber	BMW Sauber F1.08	1h57m27.405s	9
7	David Coulthard	Red Bull Racing	Red Bull-Renault RB4	1h57m32.691s	14
8	Kazuki Nakajima	Williams	Williams-Toyota FW30	1h57m34.793s	10
9	Jenson Button	Honda Racing	Honda RA108	1h57m36.189s	12
10	Heikki Kovalainen	McLaren	McLaren-Mercedes MP4-23	1h57m43.206s	5
11	Robert Kubica	BMW Sauber	BMW Sauber F1.08	1h57m44.279s	4
12	Sebastien Bourdais	Toro Rosso	Toro Rosso-Ferrari STR03	1h57m45.736s	17
13	Felipe Massa	Ferrari	Ferrari F2008	1h57m51.474s	1
14	Giancarlo Fisichella	Force India	Force India-Ferrari VJM01	1h57m59.875s	20
15	Kimi Raikkonen	Ferrari	Ferrari F2008	57 laps/spun off	3
R	Jarno Trulli	Toyota	Toyota TF108	50 laps/hydraulics	11
R	Adrian Sutil	Force India	Force India-Ferrari VJM01	49 laps/spun off	19
R	Mark Webber	Red Bull Racing	Red Bull-Renault RB4	29 laps/gearbox	13
R	Rubens Barrichello	Honda Racing	Honda RA108	14 laps/electrical	18
R	Nelson Piquet Jr.	Renault F1	Renault R28	13 laps/spun off	16

Pole: Massa, 1m44.801s, 108.153mph/174.055kph. Fastest lap: Raikkonen, 1m45.599s, 107.335mph/172.740kph on Lap 14. Race leaders: Massa 1-17, Rosberg 18-28, Trulli 29-33, Alonso 34-61

* 3-place grid penalty for impeding Barrichello

JAPANESE GRAND PRIX

FUJI SPEEDWAY • ROUND 16 • DATE: 12TH OCTOBER 2008
Laps: 67 • Distance: 189.966miles/305.721km • Weather: Cool & dull

Pos	Driver	Team	Chassis-Engine	Result	Qual
1	Fernando Alonso	Renault F1	Renault R28	1h30m21.892s	4
2	Robert Kubica	BMW Sauber	BMW Sauber F1.08	1h30m27.175s	6
3	Kimi Raikkonen	Ferrari	Ferrari F2008	1h30m28.292s	2
4	Nelson Piquet Jr.	Renault F1	Renault R28	1h30m42.462s	12
5	Jarno Trulli	Toyota	Toyota TF108	1h30m45.659s	7
6	Sebastian Vettel	Toro Rosso	Toro Rosso-Ferrari STR03	1h31m01.099s	9
7	Felipe Massa	Ferrari	Ferrari F2008	1h31m08.050s	5

Pos	Driver	Team	Chassis-Engine	Result	Qual
8	Mark Webber	Red Bull Racing	Red Bull-Renault RB4	1h31m12.703s	13
9	Nick Heidfeld	BMW Sauber	BMW Sauber F1.08	1h31m16.012s	16
10	Sebastien Bourdais *	Toro Rosso	Toro Rosso-Ferrari STR03	1h31m20.977s	10
11	Nico Rosberg	Williams	Williams-Toyota FW30	1h31m23.988s	15
12	Lewis Hamilton	McLaren	McLaren-Mercedes MP4-23	1h31m40.792s	1
13	Rubens Barrichello	Honda Racing	Honda RA108	66 laps	17
14	Jenson Button	Honda Racing	Honda RA108	66 laps	18
15	Kazuki Nakajima	Williams	Williams-Toyota FW30	66 laps	14
R	Giancarlo Fisichella	Force India	Force India-Ferrari VJM01	21 laps/gearbox	20
R	Heikki Kovalainen	McLaren	McLaren-Mercedes MP4-23	16 laps/engine	3
R	Adrian Sutil	Force India	Force India-Ferrari VJM01	8 laps/puncture	19
R	Timo Glock	Toyota	Toyota TF108	6 laps/accident	8
R	David Coulthard	Red Bull Racing	Red Bull-Renault RB4	0 laps/collision	11

Pole: Hamilton, 1m18.404s, 130.186mph/209.514kph. Fastest lap: Massa, 1m18.426s, 130.149mph/209.456kph on Lap 55. Race leaders: Kubica 1-16 & 44-45, Alonso 17-18 & 29-43 & 53-67, Trulli 19-21 & 49, Bourdais 22-24, Piquet Jr. 25-28 & 50-52, Raikkonen 46-48

* 25s penalty for incident with Massa when leaving pits

CLASSIC CAR: McLAREN MP4-23

This McLaren has a special place in Lewis Hamilton's affections, as it helped him to his first F1 title. Designed by a team led by engineering director Paddy Lowe, it was very much a refined version of the previous year's car, with a focus on getting the most out of its Bridgestone tyres, plus improving aerodynamic efficiency and saving weight. The car's supple nature helped it to get heat into its tyres more quickly than the Ferrari F2008 did, making the MP4-23 extra effective in qualifying, as shown by the team's eight poles. Lowe reckoned the car improved by one second per lap throughout the season.

CHINESE GRAND PRIX

SHANGHAI INTERNATIONAL CIRCUIT • ROUND 17 • DATE: 19TH OCTOBER 2008
Laps: 56 • Distance: 189.677miles/305.256km • Weather: Warm but dull

Pos	Driver	Team	Chassis-Engine	Result	Qual
1	Lewis Hamilton	McLaren	McLaren-Mercedes MP4-23	1h31m57.403s	1
2	Felipe Massa	Ferrari	Ferrari F2008	1h32m12.328s	3
3	Kimi Raikkonen	Ferrari	Ferrari F2008	1h32m13.848s	2
4	Fernando Alonso	Renault F1	Renault R28	1h32m15.773s	4
5	Nick Heidfeld *	BMW Sauber	BMW Sauber F1.08	1h32m26.326s	9
6	Robert Kubica	BMW Sauber	BMW Sauber F1.08	1h32m30.622s	11
7	Timo Glock	Toyota	Toyota TF108	1h32m39.125s	12
8	Nelson Piquet Jr.	Renault F1	Renault R28	1h32m54.048s	10
9	Sebastian Vettel	Toro Rosso	Toro Rosso-Ferrari STR03	1h33m01.742s	6
10	David Coulthard	Red Bull Racing	Red Bull-Renault RB4	1h33m12.245s	15
11	Rubens Barrichello	Honda Racing	Honda RA108	1h33m22.464s	13
12	Kazuki Nakajima	Williams	Williams-Toyota FW30	1h33m28.250s	17
13	Sebastien Bourdais	Toro Rosso	Toro Rosso-Ferrari STR03	1h33m28.860s	8
14	Mark Webber !	Red Bull Racing	Red Bull-Renault RB4	1h33m29.825s	16

Pos	Driver	Team	Chassis-Engine	Result	Qual
15	Nico Rosberg	Williams	Williams-Toyota FW30	55 laps	14
16	Jenson Button	Honda Racing	Honda RA108	55 laps	18
17	Giancarlo Fisichella	Force India	Force India-Ferrari VJM01	55 laps	20
R	Heikki Kovalainen	McLaren	McLaren-Mercedes MP4-23	49 laps/hydraulics	5
R	Adrian Sutil	Force India	Force India-Ferrari VJM01	13 laps/gearbox	19
R	Jarno Trulli	Toyota	Toyota TF108	2 laps/collision	7

Pole: Hamilton, 1m36.303s, 126.616mph/203.769kph. Fastest lap: Hamilton, 1m36.325s, 126.587mph/203.722kph on Lap 13. Race leaders: Hamilton 1-15 & 19-56, Kovalainen 16-18

* 3-place grid penalty for impeding Coulthard • ! 10-place grid penalty for engine change

BRAZILIAN GRAND PRIX

INTERLAGOS • ROUND 18 • DATE: 2ND NOVEMBER 2008
Laps: 71 • Distance: 190.101miles/305.939km • Weather: Warm & wet

Pos	Driver	Team	Chassis-Engine	Result	Qual
1	Felipe Massa	Ferrari	Ferrari F2008	1h34m11.435s	1
2	Fernando Alonso	Renault F1	Renault R28	1h34m24.733s	6
3	Kimi Raikkonen	Ferrari	Ferrari F2008	1h34m27.670s	3
4	Sebastian Vettel	Toro Rosso	Toro Rosso-Ferrari STR03	1h34m49.446s	7
5	Lewis Hamilton	McLaren	McLaren-Mercedes MP4-23	1h34m50.342s	4
6	Timo Glock	Toyota	Toyota TF108	1h34m55.803s	10
7	Heikki Kovalainen	McLaren	McLaren-Mercedes MP4-23	1h35m06.509s	5
8	Jarno Trulli	Toyota	Toyota TF108	1h35m19.898s	2
9	Mark Webber	Red Bull Racing	Red Bull-Renault RB4	1h35m31.101s	12
10	Nick Heidfeld	BMW Sauber	BMW Sauber F1.08	70 laps	8
11	Robert Kubica	BMW Sauber	BMW Sauber F1.08	70 laps	13
12	Nico Rosberg	Williams	Williams-Toyota FW30	70 laps	18
13	Jenson Button	Honda Racing	Honda RA108	70 laps	17
14	Sebastien Bourdais	Toro Rosso	Toro Rosso-Ferrari STR03	70 laps	9
15	Rubens Barrichello	Honda Racing	Honda RA108	70 laps	15
16	Adrian Sutil	Force India	Force India-Ferrari VJM01	69 laps	20
17	Kazuki Nakajima	Williams	Williams-Toyota FW30	69 laps	16
18	Giancarlo Fisichella	Force India	Force India-Ferrari VJM01	69 laps	19
R	Nelson Piquet Jr.	Renault F1	Renault R28	0 laps/accident	11
R	David Coulthard	Red Bull Racing	Red Bull-Renault RB4	0 laps/collision	14

Pole: Massa, 1m12.368s, 133.193mph/214.354kph. Fastest lap: Massa, 1m13.736s, 130.722mph/210.377kph on Lap 36. Race leaders: Massa 1-9 & 12-38 & 44-71, Trulli 10-11, Alonso 39-40, Raikkonen 41-43

WORLD DRIVERS' CHAMPIONSHIP FINAL RESULTS

Pos	Driver	Nat	Car-Engine	R1	R2	R3	R4	R5	R6	R7
1	Lewis Hamilton	GBR	McLaren-Mercedes MP4-23	1P	5	13	3	2	1	RP
2	Felipe Massa	BRA	Ferrari F2008	R	RP	1	2	1P	3P	5
3	Kimi Raikkonen	FIN	Ferrari F2008	8	1	2	1PF	3F	9F	RF
4	Robert Kubica	POL	BMW Sauber F1.08	R	2	3P	4	4	2	1
5	Fernando Alonso	ESP	Renault R28	4	8	10	R	6	10	R
6	Nick Heidfeld	DEU	BMW Sauber F1.08	2	6F	4	9	5	14	2
7	Heikki Kovalainen	FIN	McLaren-Mercedes MP4-23	5F	3	5F	R	12	8	9
8	Sebastian Vettel	DEU	Toro Rosso-Ferrari STR02B	R	R	R	R	17	-	-
			Toro Rosso-Ferrari STR03	-	-	-	-	-	5	8

Pos	Driver	Nat	Car-Engine	R1	R2	R3	R4	R5	R6	R7
9	Jarno Trulli	ITA	Toyota TF108	R	4	6	8	10	13	6
10	Timo Glock	DEU	Toyota TF108	R	R	9	11	13	12	4
11	Mark Webber	AUS	Red Bull-Renault RB4	R	7	7	5	7	4	12
12	Nelson Piquet Jr.	BRA	Renault R28	R	11	R	R	15	R	R
13	Nico Rosberg	DEU	Williams-Toyota FW30	3	14	8	R	8	R	10
14	Rubens Barrichello	BRA	Honda RA108	DQ	13	11	R	14	6	7
15	Kazuki Nakajima	JPN	Williams-Toyota FW30	6	17	14	7	R	7	R
16	David Coulthard	GBR	Red Bull-Renault RB4	R	9	18	12	9	R	3
17	Sebastien Bourdais	FRA	Toro Rosso-Ferrari STR02B	7	R	15	R	R	-	-
			Toro Rosso-Ferrari STR03	-	-	-	-	-	R	13
18	Jenson Button	GBR	Honda RA108	R	10	R	6	11	11	11
19	Giancarlo Fisichella	ITA	Force India-Ferrari VJM01	R	12	12	10	R	R	R
20	Adrian Sutil	DEU	Force India-Ferrari VJM01	R	R	19	R	16	R	R
21	Takuma Sato	JPN	Super Aguri-Honda SA08A	R	16	17	13	-	-	-
22	Anthony Davidson	GBR	Super Aguri-Honda SA08A	R	15	16	R	-	-	-

Pos	Driver	R8	R9	R10	R11	R12	R13	R14	R15	R16	R17	R18	Total
1	Hamilton	10	1	1P	5P	2	3P	7	3	12P	1PF	5	98
2	Massa	1	13	3	17	1PF	1	6	13P	7F	2	1PF	97
3	Raikkonen	2PF	4F	6	3F	R	18F	9F	15F	3	3	3	75
4	Kubica	5	R	7	8	3	6	3	11	2	6	11	75
5	Alonso	8	6	11	4	R	4	4	1	1	4	2	61
6	Heidfeld	13	2	4F	10	9	2	5	6	9	5	10	60
7	Kovalainen	4	5P	5	1	4	10	2	10	R	R	7	53
8	Vettel	-	-	-	-	-	-	-	-	-	-	-	35
		12	R	8	R	6	5	1P	5	6	9	4	
9	Trulli	3	7	9	7	5	16	13	R	5	R	8	31
10	Glock	11	12	R	2	7	9	11	4	R	7	6	25
11	Webber	6	10	R	9	12	8	8	R	8	14	9	21
12	Piquet Jr.	7	R	2	6	11	R	10	R	4	8	R	19
13	Rosberg	16	9	10	14	8	12	14	2	11	15	12	17
14	Barrichello	14	3	R	16	16	R	17	R	13	11	15	11
15	Nakajima	15	8	14	13	15	14	12	8	15	12	17	9
16	Coulthard	9	R	13	11	17	11	16	7	R	10	R	8
17	Bourdais	-	-	-	-	-	-	-	-	-	-	-	4
		17	11	12	18	10	7	18	12	10	13	14	
18	Button	R	R	17	12	13	15	15	9	14	16	13	3
19	Fisichella	18	R	16	15	14	17	R	14	R	17	18	0
20	Sutil	19	R	15	R	R	13	19	R	R	R	16	0
21	Sato	-	-	-	-	-	-	-	-	-	-	-	0
22	Davidson	-	-	-	-	-	-	-	-	-		-	0

SYMBOLS AND GRAND PRIX KEY

Round 1 Australian GP
Round 2 Malaysian GP
Round 3 Bahrain GP
Round 4 Spanish GP
Round 5 Turkish GP
Round 6 Monaco GP
Round 7 Canadian GP
Round 8 French GP
Round 9 British GP
Round 10 German GP
Round 11 Hungarian GP
Round 12 European GP
Round 13 Belgian GP
Round 14 Italian GP
Round 15 Singapore GP
Round 16 Japanese GP
Round 17 Chinese GP
Round 18 Brazilian GP

SCORING

1st 10 points
2nd 8 points
3rd 6 points
4th 5 points
5th 4 points
6th 3 points
7th 2 points
8th 1 point

DNPQ DID NOT PRE-QUALIFY **DNQ** DID NOT QUALIFY **DQ** DISQUALIFIED **EX** EXCLUDED
F FASTEST LAP **NC** NOT CLASSIFIED **NS** NON-STARTER **P** POLE POSITION **R** RETIRED

WORLD CONSTRUCTORS' CHAMPIONSHIP FINAL RESULTS

Pos	Team-Engine	R1	R2	R3	R4	R5	R6	R7	R8	R9	R10
1	Ferrari	8/R	1/R	1/2	1/2	1/3	3/9	5/R	1/2	4/13	3/6
2	McLaren-Mercedes	1/5	3/5	5/13	3/R	2/12	1/8	9/R	4/10	1/5	1/5
3	BMW Sauber	2/R	2/6	3/4	4/9	4/5	2/14	1/2	5/13	2/R	4/7
4	Renault F1	4/R	8/11	10/R	R/R	6/15	10/R	R/R	7/8	6/R	2/11
5	Toyota	R/R	4/R	6/9	8/11	10/13	12/13	4/6	3/11	7/12	9/R
6	Toro Rosso-Ferrari	7/R	R/R	15/R	R/R	17/R	5/R	8/13	12/17	11/R	8/12
7	Red Bull-Renault	R/R	7/9	7/18	5/12	7/9	4/R	3/12	6/9	10/R	13/R
8	Williams-Toyota	3/6	14/17	8/14	7/R	8/R	7/R	10/R	15/16	8/9	10/14
9	Honda Racing	DQ/R	10/13	11/R	6/R	11/14	6/11	7/11	14/R	3/R	17/R
10	Force India-Ferrari	R/R	12/R	12/19	10/R	16/R	R/R	R/R	18/19	R/R	15/16
11	Super Aguri-Honda	R/R	15/16	16/17	13/R	-	-	-	-	-	-

Pos	Team-Engine	R11	R12	R13	R14	R15	R16	R17	R18	Total
1	Ferrari	3/17	1/R	1/18	6/9	13/15	3/7	2/3	1/3	172
2	McLaren-Mercedes	1/5	2/4	3/10	2/7	3/10	12/R	1/R	5/7	151
3	BMW Sauber	8/10	3/9	2/6	3/5	6/11	2/9	5/6	10/11	135
4	Renault F1	4/6	11/R	4/R	4/10	1/R	1/4	4/8	2/R	80
5	Toyota	2/7	5/7	9/16	11/13	4/R	5/R	7/R	6/8	56
6	Toro Rosso-Ferrari	18/R	6/10	5/7	1/18	5/12	6/10	9/13	4/14	39
7	Red Bull-Renault	9/11	12/17	8/11	8/16	7/R	8/R	10/14	9/R	29
8	Williams-Toyota	13/14	8/15	12/14	12/14	2/8	11/15	12/15	12/17	26
9	Honda Racing	12/16	13/16	15/R	15/17	9/R	13/14	11/16	13/15	14
10	Force India-Ferrari	15/R	14/R	13/17	19/R	14/R	R/R	17/R	16/18	0
11	Super Aguri-Honda	-	-	-	-	-	-	-	-	0

SEASON SUMMARY

Ross Brawn saved the Honda Racing team from folding, called it Brawn GP and pulled off one of the biggest shocks in F1 history, as Jenson Button gathered wins for fun and then held on to take the drivers' title, after the other teams responded to the clever double-decked diffusers that gave Brawn such an early-season advantage. Red Bull Racing came on strong and Sebastian Vettel pulled ahead of Brawn GP's second driver Rubens Barrichello, with Mark Webber not far behind. Neither 2008 champions McLaren, nor Ferrari, reacted to the rule changes as well as Brawn GP, and they ended up scrapping over third in the constructors' championship.

AUSTRALIAN GRAND PRIX

ALBERT PARK • ROUND 1 • DATE: 29TH MARCH 2009
Laps: 58 • Distance: 191.117miles/307.574km • Weather: Hot & bright

Pos	Driver	Team	Chassis-Engine	Result	Qual
1	Jenson Button	Brawn	Brawn-Mercedes BGP 001	1h34m15.784s	1
2	Rubens Barrichello	Brawn	Brawn-Mercedes BGP 001	1h34m16.591s	2
3	Jarno Trulli !	Toyota	Toyota TF109	1h34m17.388s	19
DQ	Lewis Hamilton */!	McLaren	McLaren-Mercedes MP4-24	misleading stewards	18
4	Timo Glock !	Toyota	Toyota TF109	1h34m20.219s	20
5	Fernando Alonso	Renault F1	Renault R29	1h34m20.663s	10
6	Nico Rosberg	Williams	Williams-Toyota FW31	1h34m21.506s	5
7	Sebastien Buemi	Toro Rosso	Toro Rosso-Ferrari STR04	1h34m21.788s	13
8	Sebastien Bourdais	Toro Rosso	Toro Rosso-Ferrari STR04	1h34m22.082s	17
9	Adrian Sutil	Force India	Force India-Mercedes VJM02	1h34m22.119s	16
10	Nick Heidfeld	BMW Sauber	BMW Sauber F1.09	1h34m22.869s	9
11	Giancarlo Fisichella	Force India	Force India-Mercedes VJM02	1h34m23.158s	15
12	Mark Webber	Red Bull Racing	Red Bull-Renault RB5	57 laps	8
13	Sebastian Vettel	Red Bull Racing	Red Bull-Renault RB5	56 laps/collision	3
14	Robert Kubica	BMW Sauber	BMW Sauber F1.09	55 laps/collision	4
15	Kimi Raikkonen	Ferrari	Ferrari F60	55 laps/differential	7
R	Felipe Massa	Ferrari	Ferrari F60	45 laps/suspension	6
R	Nelson Piquet Jr.	Renault F1	Renault R29	24 laps/spun off	14
R	Kazuki Nakajima	Williams	Williams-Toyota FW31	17 laps/spun off	11
R	Heikki Kovalainen	McLaren	McLaren-Mercedes MP4-24	0 laps/collision	12

Pole: Button, 1m26.202s, 137.612mph/221.465kph. Fastest lap: Rosberg, 1m27.706s, 135.252mph/217.668kph on Lap 48. Race leaders: Button 1-58

* 5-place grid penalty for gearbox change • ^ made to start from the pit lane for modifying car in parc ferme. • ! disqualified for misleading the race stewards • ! made to start from back of grid for using an illegal rear wing

SLICK TYRES RETURN

There was a return to slick tyres after 11 years on grooved rubber, plus a major reduction in downforce, achieved by banning bargeboards along the flanks, shortening diffusers and narrowing the rear wing. Kinetic Energy Recovery Systems (KERS) were introduced to harness energy created by heavy braking and turn it into electrical boost.

MALAYSIAN GRAND PRIX

SEPANG • ROUND 2 • DATE: 5TH APRIL 2009
Laps: 31 • Distance: 106.772miles/171.833km • Weather: Hot but dull, heavy rain later

Pos	Driver	Team	Chassis-Engine	Result	Qual
1	Jenson Button	Brawn	Brawn-Mercedes BGP 001	55m30.622s	1
2	Nick Heidfeld	BMW Sauber	BMW Sauber F1.09	55m53.344s	10
3	Timo Glock	Toyota	Toyota TF109	55m54.135s	3
4	Jarno Trulli	Toyota	Toyota TF109	56m16.795s	2
5	Rubens Barrichello *	Brawn	Brawn-Mercedes BGP 001	56m17.982s	8
6	Mark Webber	Red Bull Racing	Red Bull-Renault RB5	56m22.955s	5
7	Lewis Hamilton	McLaren	McLaren-Mercedes MP4-24	56m31.355s	12
8	Nico Rosberg	Williams	Williams-Toyota FW31	56m42.198s	4
9	Felipe Massa	Ferrari	Ferrari F60	56m47.554s	16
10	Sebastien Bourdais	Toro Rosso	Toro Rosso-Ferrari STR04	57m12.786s	15
11	Fernando Alonso	Renault F1	Renault R29	57m20.044s	9
12	Kazuki Nakajima	Williams	Williams-Toyota FW31	57m26.752s	11
13	Nelson Piquet Jr.	Renault F1	Renault R29	57m27.335s	17
14	Kimi Raikkonen	Ferrari	Ferrari F60	57m53.463s	7
15	Sebastian Vettel !	Red Bull Racing	Red Bull-Renault RB5	30 laps/spun off	13
16	Sebastien Buemi	Toro Rosso	Toro Rosso-Ferrari STR04	30 laps/spun off	20
17	Adrian Sutil	Force India	Force India-Mercedes VJM02	30 laps	19
18	Giancarlo Fisichella	Force India	Force India-Mercedes VJM02	29 laps/spun off	18
R	Robert Kubica	BMW Sauber	BMW Sauber F1.09	1 lap/engine	6
R	Heikki Kovalainen	McLaren	McLaren-Mercedes MP4-24	0 laps/spun off	14

Pole: Button, 1m35.181s, 130.271mph/209.651kph. Fastest lap: Button, 1m36.641s, 128.303mph/206.483kph on Lap 18. Race leaders: Rosberg 1-15, Trulli 16, Button 17-19 & 21-31, Barrichello 20

* 5-place grid penalty for gearbox change • ! 10-place grid penalty for causing an accident in Australian GP

GOOD YEAR, BAD YEAR

McLaren may have started as champions but also found themselves in front of the stewards in Melbourne to explain why Lewis Hamilton had passed a rival while the safety car was out, telling them one thing, the press another. Hamilton threatened to quit, team manager Davey Ryan was fired and team principal Ron Dennis stepped down to leave Martin Whitmarsh in control.

CHINESE GRAND PRIX

SHANGHAI INTERNATIONAL CIRCUIT • ROUND 3 • DATE: 19TH APRIL 2009
Laps: 56 • Distance: 189.677miles/305.256km • Weather: Warm & very wet

Pos	Driver	Team	Chassis-Engine	Result	Qual
1	Sebastian Vettel	Red Bull Racing	Red Bull-Renault RB5	1h57m43.485s	1
2	Mark Webber	Red Bull Racing	Red Bull-Renault RB5	1h57m54.455s	3
3	Jenson Button	Brawn	Brawn-Mercedes BGP 001	1h58m28.460s	5
4	Rubens Barrichello	Brawn	Brawn-Mercedes BGP 001	1h58m47.189s	4
5	Heikki Kovalainen	McLaren	McLaren-Mercedes MP4-24	1h58m48.587s	12
6	Lewis Hamilton	McLaren	McLaren-Mercedes MP4-24	1h58m55.351s	9
7	Timo Glock *	Toyota	Toyota TF109	1h58m57.961s	19

Pos	Driver	Team	Chassis-Engine	Result	Qual
8	Sebastien Buemi	Toro Rosso	Toro Rosso-Ferrari STR04	1h58m59.924s	10
9	Fernando Alonso	Renault F1	Renault R29	1h59m07.794s	2
10	Kimi Raikkonen	Ferrari	Ferrari F60	1h59m15.235s	8
11	Sebastien Bourdais	Toro Rosso	Toro Rosso-Ferrari STR04	1h59m17.641s	15
12	Nick Heidfeld	BMW Sauber	BMW Sauber F1.09	1h59m19.319s	11
13	Robert Kubica	BMW Sauber	BMW Sauber F1.09	1h59m30.338s	17
14	Giancarlo Fisichella	Force India	Force India-Mercedes VJM02	55 laps	20
15	Nico Rosberg	Williams	Williams-Toyota FW31	55 laps	7
16	Nelson Piquet Jr.	Renault F1	Renault R29	54 laps	16
17	Adrian Sutil	Force India	Force India-Mercedes VJM02	50 laps/spun off	18
R	Kazuki Nakajima	Williams	Williams-Toyota FW31	43 laps/transmission	14
R	Felipe Massa	Ferrari	Ferrari F60	20 laps/electrical	13
R	Jarno Trulli	Toyota	Toyota TF109	18 laps/collision	6

Pole: Vettel, 1m36.184s, 126.773mph/204.021kph. Fastest lap: Barrichello, 1m52.592s, 108.298mph/174.289kph on Lap 42. Race leaders: Vettel 1-15 & 20-37 & 41-56, Button 16-19 & 40, Webber 38-39

* 5-place grid penalty for gearbox change

BAHRAIN GRAND PRIX

SAKHIR • ROUND 4 • DATE: 26TH APRIL 2009
Laps: 57 • Distance: 191.683miles/308.484km • Weather: Hot & bright

Pos	Driver	Team	Chassis-Engine	Result	Qual
1	Jenson Button	Brawn	Brawn-Mercedes BGP 001	1h31m48.182s	4
2	Sebastian Vettel	Red Bull Racing	Red Bull-Renault RB5	1h31m55.369s	3
3	Jarno Trulli	Toyota	Toyota TF109	1h31m57.352s	1
4	Lewis Hamilton	McLaren	McLaren-Mercedes MP4-24	1h32m10.278s	5
5	Rubens Barrichello	Brawn	Brawn-Mercedes BGP 001	1h32m25.961s	6
6	Kimi Raikkonen	Ferrari	Ferrari F60	1h32m30.239s	10
7	Timo Glock	Toyota	Toyota TF109	1h32m31.062s	2
8	Fernando Alonso	Renault F1	Renault R29	1h32m40.957s	7
9	Nico Rosberg	Williams	Williams-Toyota FW31	1h32m46.380s	9
10	Nelson Piquet Jr.	Renault F1	Renault R29	1h32m53.331s	15
11	Mark Webber	Red Bull Racing	Red Bull-Renault RB5	1h32m55.823s	18
12	Heikki Kovalainen	McLaren	McLaren-Mercedes MP4-24	1h33m06.006s	11
13	Sebastien Bourdais	Toro Rosso	Toro Rosso-Ferrari STR04	1h33m06.987s	20
14	Felipe Massa	Ferrari	Ferrari F60	56 laps	8
15	Giancarlo Fisichella	Force India	Force India-Mercedes VJM02	56 laps	17
16	Adrian Sutil *	Force India	Force India-Mercedes VJM02	56 laps	19
17	Sebastien Buemi	Toro Rosso	Toro Rosso-Ferrari STR04	56 laps	16
18	Robert Kubica	BMW Sauber	BMW Sauber F1.09	56 laps	13
19	Nick Heidfeld	BMW Sauber	BMW Sauber F1.09	56 laps	14
R	Kazuki Nakajima	Williams	Williams-Toyota FW31	48 laps/fuel pressure	12

Pole: Trulli, 1m33.431s, 129.574mph/208.530kph. Fastest lap: Trulli, 1m34.556s, 128.033mph/206.049kph on Lap 10. Race leaders: Glock 1-10, Trulli 11-12, Button 13-15 & 22-37 & 41-57, Vettel 16-19 & 38-40, Raikkonen 20-21

* 3-place grid penalty for impeding Webber

RENAULT CAUGHT OUT

The "Crashgate" saga from the 2008 Singapore GP was uncovered when Nelson Piquet Jr was fired after the Hungarian GP and admitted that he had been asked to crash to bring out a safety car to help Fernando Alonso win. This led to major ramifications for the Renault team, with Flavio Briatore and Pat Symonds being banned for two years.

SPANISH GRAND PRIX

BARCELONA-CATALUNYA • ROUND 5 • DATE: 10TH MAY 2009
Laps: 66 • Distance: 190.775miles/307.23km • Weather: Warm & bright

Pos	Driver	Team	Chassis-Engine	Result	Qual
1	Jenson Button	Brawn	Brawn-Mercedes BGP 001	1h37m19.202s	1
2	Rubens Barrichello	Brawn	Brawn-Mercedes BGP 001	1h37m32.258s	3
3	Mark Webber	Red Bull Racing	Red Bull-Renault RB5	1h37m33.126s	5
4	Sebastian Vettel	Red Bull Racing	Red Bull-Renault RB5	1h37m38.143s	2
5	Fernando Alonso	Renault F1	Renault R29	1h38m02.368s	8
6	Felipe Massa	Ferrari	Ferrari F60	1h38m10.029s	4
7	Nick Heidfeld	BMW Sauber	BMW Sauber F1.09	1h38m11.514s	13
8	Nico Rosberg	Williams	Williams-Toyota FW31	1h38m24.413s	9
9	Lewis Hamilton	McLaren	McLaren-Mercedes MP4-24	65 laps	14
10	Timo Glock	Toyota	Toyota TF109	65 laps	6
11	Robert Kubica	BMW Sauber	BMW Sauber F1.09	65 laps	10
12	Nelson Piquet Jr.	Renault F1	Renault R29	65 laps	12
13	Kazuki Nakajima	Williams	Williams-Toyota FW31	65 laps	11
14	Giancarlo Fisichella	Force India	Force India-Mercedes VJM02	65 laps	20
R	Kimi Raikkonen	Ferrari	Ferrari F60	17 laps/hydraulics	16
R	Heikki Kovalainen	McLaren	McLaren-Mercedes MP4-24	7 laps/gearbox	18
R	Jarno Trulli	Toyota	Toyota TF109	0 laps/collision	7
R	Sebastien Buemi	Toro Rosso	Toro Rosso-Ferrari STR04	0 laps/collision	15
R	Sebastien Bourdais	Toro Rosso	Toro Rosso-Ferrari STR04	0 laps/collision	17
R	Adrian Sutil	Force India	Force India-Mercedes VJM02	0 laps/collision	19

Pole: Button, 1m20.527s, 129.309mph/208.104kph. Fastest lap: Barrichello, 1m22.762s, 125.817mph/202.484kph on Lap 28. Race leaders: Barrichello 1-19 & 21-31 & 49-50, Massa 20, Button 32-48 & 51-66

MONACO GRAND PRIX

MONTE CARLO • ROUND 6 • DATE: 24TH MAY 2009
Laps: 78 • Distance: 161.588miles/260.52km • Weather: Warm & bright

Pos	Driver	Team	Chassis-Engine	Result	Qual
1	Jenson Button	Brawn	Brawn-Mercedes BGP 001	1h40m44.282s	1
2	Rubens Barrichello	Brawn	Brawn-Mercedes BGP 001	1h40m51.948s	3
3	Kimi Raikkonen	Ferrari	Ferrari F60	1h40m57.724s	2
4	Felipe Massa	Ferrari	Ferrari F60	1h40m59.392s	5
5	Mark Webber	Red Bull Racing	Red Bull-Renault RB5	1h41m00.012s	8
6	Nico Rosberg	Williams	Williams-Toyota FW31	1h41m17.868s	6
7	Fernando Alonso	Renault F1	Renault R29	1h41m22.121s	9
8	Sebastien Bourdais	Toro Rosso	Toro Rosso-Ferrari STR04	1h41m47.424s	14
9	Giancarlo Fisichella	Force India	Force India-Mercedes VJM02	1h41m49.322s	13

Pos	Driver	Team	Chassis-Engine	Result	Qual
10	Timo Glock !	Toyota	Toyota TF109	77 laps	20
11	Nick Heidfeld	BMW Sauber	BMW Sauber F1.09	77 laps	16
12	Lewis Hamilton *	McLaren	McLaren-Mercedes MP4-24	77 laps	19
13	Jarno Trulli	Toyota	Toyota TF109	77 laps	18
14	Adrian Sutil	Force India	Force India-Mercedes VJM02	77 laps	15
15	Kazuki Nakajima	Williams	Williams-Toyota FW31	76 laps/spun off	10
R	Heikki Kovalainen	McLaren	McLaren-Mercedes MP4-24	51 laps/spun off	7
R	Robert Kubica	BMW Sauber	BMW Sauber F1.09	28 laps/brakes	17
R	Sebastian Vettel	Red Bull Racing	Red Bull-Renault RB5	15 laps/spun off	4
R	Sebastien Buemi	Toro Rosso	Toro Rosso-Ferrari STR04	10 laps/collision	11
R	Nelson Piquet Jr.	Renault F1	Renault R29	10 laps/collision	12

Pole: Button, 1m14.902s, 99.748mph/160.529kph. Fastest lap: Massa, 1m15.154s, 99.414mph/159.991kph on Lap 50. Race leaders: Button 1-51 & 53-78, Raikkonen 52

* 5-place grid penalty for gearbox change • ! made to start from the pit lane for working on car in parc ferme

TURKISH GRAND PRIX

ISTANBUL PARK • ROUND 7 • DATE: 7TH JUNE 2009
Laps: 58 • Distance: 192.379miles/309.604km • Weather: Very hot & bright

Pos	Driver	Team	Chassis-Engine	Result	Qual
1	Jenson Button	Brawn	Brawn-Mercedes BGP 001	1h26m24.848s	2
2	Mark Webber	Red Bull Racing	Red Bull-Renault RB5	1h26m31.562s	4
3	Sebastian Vettel	Red Bull Racing	Red Bull-Renault RB5	1h26m32.309s	1
4	Jarno Trulli	Toyota	Toyota TF109	1h26m52.691s	5
5	Nico Rosberg	Williams	Williams-Toyota FW31	1h26m56.387s	9
6	Felipe Massa	Ferrari	Ferrari F60	1h27m04.844s	7
7	Robert Kubica	BMW Sauber	BMW Sauber F1.09	1h27m11.095s	10
8	Timo Glock	Toyota	Toyota TF109	1h27m11.807s	13
9	Kimi Raikkonen	Ferrari	Ferrari F60	1h27m15.094s	6
10	Fernando Alonso	Renault F1	Renault R29	1h27m27.268s	8
11	Nick Heidfeld	BMW Sauber	BMW Sauber F1.09	1h27m29.175s	11
12	Kazuki Nakajima	Williams	Williams-Toyota FW31	1h27m31.224s	12
13	Lewis Hamilton	McLaren	McLaren-Mercedes MP4-24	1h27m45.302s	16
14	Heikki Kovalainen	McLaren	McLaren-Mercedes MP4-24	57 laps	14
15	Sebastien Buemi	Toro Rosso	Toro Rosso-Ferrari STR04	57 laps	18
16	Nelson Piquet Jr.	Renault F1	Renault R29	57 laps	17
17	Adrian Sutil	Force India	Force India-Mercedes VJM02	57 laps	15
18	Sebastien Bourdais	Toro Rosso	Toro Rosso-Ferrari STR04	57 laps	20
R	Rubens Barrichello	Brawn	Brawn-Mercedes BGP 001	47 laps/gearbox	3
R	Giancarlo Fisichella	Force India	Force India-Mercedes VJM02	4 laps/brakes	19

Pole: Vettel, 1m28.316s, 135.205mph/217.591kph. Fastest lap: Button, 1m27.579s, 136.342mph/219.422kph on Lap 40. Race leaders: Button 1-17 & 19-58, Webber 18

A BLOW TO THE HEAD

The most frightening moment of the year came in qualifying for the Hungarian GP, when Felipe Massa was hit on the helmet by a spring flipped up by Rubens Barrichello's Brawn and crashed his Ferrari into a tyre wall. The Brazilian suffered a fractured skull but luckily not the loss of sight in his left eye, which had been a concern.

BRITISH GRAND PRIX

SILVERSTONE • ROUND 8 • DATE: 21ST JUNE 2009
Laps: 60 • Distance: 191.410miles/308.46km • Weather: Warm & bright

Pos	Driver	Team	Chassis-Engine	Result	Qual
1	Sebastian Vettel	Red Bull Racing	Red Bull-Renault RB5	1h22m49.328s	1
2	Mark Webber	Red Bull Racing	Red Bull-Renault RB5	1h23m04.516s	3
3	Rubens Barrichello	Brawn	Brawn-Mercedes BGP 001	1h23m30.503s	2
4	Felipe Massa	Ferrari	Ferrari F60	1h23m34.371s	11
5	Nico Rosberg	Williams	Williams-Toyota FW31	1h23m35.243s	7
6	Jenson Button	Brawn	Brawn-Mercedes BGP 001	1h23m35.613s	6
7	Jarno Trulli	Toyota	Toyota TF109	1h23m57.635s	4
8	Kimi Raikkonen	Ferrari	Ferrari F60	1h23m58.950s	9
9	Timo Glock	Toyota	Toyota TF109	1h23m59.151s	8
10	Giancarlo Fisichella	Force India	Force India-Mercedes VJM02	1h24m00.850s	16
11	Kazuki Nakajima	Williams	Williams-Toyota FW31	1h24m03.351s	5
12	Nelson Piquet Jr.	Renault F1	Renault R29	59 laps	14
13	Robert Kubica	BMW Sauber	BMW Sauber F1.09	59 laps	12
14	Fernando Alonso	Renault F1	Renault R29	59 laps	10
15	Nick Heidfeld	BMW Sauber	BMW Sauber F1.09	59 laps	15
16	Lewis Hamilton	McLaren	McLaren-Mercedes MP4-24	59 laps	18
17	Adrian Sutil *	Force India	Force India-Mercedes VJM02	59 laps	20
18	Sebastien Buemi	Toro Rosso	Toro Rosso-Ferrari STR04	59 laps	19
R	Sebastien Bourdais	Toro Rosso	Toro Rosso-Ferrari STR04	37 laps/collision	17
R	Heikki Kovalainen	McLaren	McLaren-Mercedes MP4-24	36 laps/collision	13

Pole: Vettel, 1m19.509s, 144.638mph/232.773kph. Fastest lap: Vettel, 1m20.735s, 142.442mph/229.238kph on Lap 16. Race leaders: Vettel 1-44 & 48-60, Webber 45-47

* made to start from the pit lane for changing chassis

TOYOTA FLUFFS IT

Toyota had been disappointing since entering F1, but they were competitive enough at the start of 2009, courtesy of a double-decked diffuser, to have a shot at landing a first win. This came at round four in Bahrain, with Jarno Trulli and Timo Glock filling the front row, but their tyre choice was wrong and they couldn't keep Button and Vettel back.

GERMAN GRAND PRIX

NURBURGRING • ROUND 9 • DATE: 12TH JULY 2009
Laps: 60 • Distance: 191.437miles/308.88km • Weather: Cool but bright

Pos	Driver	Team	Chassis-Engine	Result	Qual
1	Mark Webber	Red Bull Racing	Red Bull-Renault RB5	1h36m43.310s	1
2	Sebastian Vettel	Red Bull Racing	Red Bull-Renault RB5	1h36m52.562s	4
3	Felipe Massa	Ferrari	Ferrari F60	1h36m59.216s	8
4	Nico Rosberg	Williams	Williams-Toyota FW31	1h37m04.409s	15
5	Jenson Button	Brawn	Brawn-Mercedes BGP 001	1h37m06.919s	3
6	Rubens Barrichello	Brawn	Brawn-Mercedes BGP 001	1h37m07.778s	2
7	Fernando Alonso	Renault F1	Renault R29	1h37m08.198s	12
8	Heikki Kovalainen	McLaren	McLaren-Mercedes MP4-24	1h37m42.002s	6

Pos	Driver	Team	Chassis-Engine	Result	Qual
9	Timo Glock *	Toyota	Toyota TF109	1h37m44.767s	20
10	Nick Heidfeld	BMW Sauber	BMW Sauber F1.09	1h37m45.235s	11
11	Giancarlo Fisichella	Force India	Force India-Mercedes VJM02	1h37m45.637s	18
12	Kazuki Nakajima	Williams	Williams-Toyota FW31	1h37m46.186s	13
13	Nelson Piquet Jr.	Renault F1	Renault R29	1h37m51.638s	10
14	Robert Kubica	BMW Sauber	BMW Sauber F1.09	1h37m52.865s	16
15	Adrian Sutil	Force India	Force India-Mercedes VJM02	1h37m55.251s	7
16	Sebastien Buemi	Toro Rosso	Toro Rosso-Ferrari STR04	1h38m13.535s	17
17	Jarno Trulli	Toyota	Toyota TF109	1h38m14.280s	14
18	Lewis Hamilton	McLaren	McLaren-Mercedes MP4-24	59 laps	5
R	Kimi Raikkonen	Ferrari	Ferrari F60	34 laps/radiator	9
R	Sebastien Bourdais	Toro Rosso	Toro Rosso-Ferrari STR04	18 laps/hydraulics	19

Pole: Webber, 1m32.230s, 124.859mph/200.941kph. Fastest lap: Alonso, 1m33.365s, 123.341mph/198.498kph on Lap 49. Race leaders: Barrichello 1-14 & 25-31, Webber 15-19 & 32-43 & 45-60, Massa 20-24, Vettel 44

* 3-place grid penalty for impeding Alonso

NEW CIRCUIT

Few circuits have made more of an impact on their World Championship debut than Abu Dhabi's Yas Marina venue. Part of a sports complex including a golf course and a theme park, the track also ran alongside a marina and underneath a wing of a hotel. It impressed the teams for the money-no-object standard of its facilities.

HUNGARIAN GRAND PRIX

HUNGARORING • ROUND 10 • DATE: 26TH JULY 2009
Laps: 70 • Distance: 190.181miles/306.67km • Weather: Hot & bright

Pos	Driver	Team	Chassis-Engine	Result	Qual
1	Lewis Hamilton	McLaren	McLaren-Mercedes MP4-24	1h38m23.876s	4
2	Kimi Raikkonen	Ferrari	Ferrari F60	1h38m35.405s	7
3	Mark Webber	Red Bull Racing	Red Bull-Renault RB5	1h38m40.762s	3
4	Nico Rosberg	Williams	Williams-Toyota FW31	1h38m50.843s	5
5	Heikki Kovalainen	McLaren	McLaren-Mercedes MP4-24	1h38m58.268s	14
6	Timo Glock	Toyota	Toyota TF109	1h38m59.113s	13
7	Jenson Button	Brawn	Brawn-Mercedes BGP 001	1h39m18.964s	8
8	Jarno Trulli	Toyota	Toyota TF109	1h39m32.048s	12
9	Kazuki Nakajima	Williams	Williams-Toyota FW31	1h39m32.650s	9
10	Rubens Barrichello	Brawn	Brawn-Mercedes BGP 001	1h39m33.132s	13
11	Nick Heidfeld	BMW Sauber	BMW Sauber F1.09	1h39m34.488s	16
12	Nelson Piquet Jr.	Renault F1	Renault R29	1h39m35.388s	15
13	Robert Kubica	BMW Sauber	BMW Sauber F1.09	1h39m37.922s	19
14	Giancarlo Fisichella	Force India	Force India-Mercedes VJM02	69 laps	17
15	Jaime Alguersuari	Toro Rosso	Toro Rosso-Ferrari STR04	69 laps	20
16	Sebastien Buemi	Toro Rosso	Toro Rosso-Ferrari STR04	69 laps	11
R	Sebastian Vettel	Red Bull Racing	Red Bull-Renault RB5	29 laps/suspension	2

Pos	Driver	Team	Chassis-Engine	Result	Qual
R	Fernando Alonso	Renault F1	Renault R29	15 laps/fuel pump	1
R	Adrian Sutil	Force India	Force India-Mercedes VJM02	1 lap/overheating	18
NS	Felipe Massa	Ferrari	Ferrari F60	driver injured	10

Pole: Alonso, 1m21.569s, 120.143mph/193.352kph. Fastest lap: Webber, 1m21.931s, 119.613mph/192.498kph on Lap 65. Race leaders: Alonso 1-11, Hamilton 12-20 & 22-70, Kovalainen 21

EUROPEAN GRAND PRIX

VALENCIA STREET CIRCUIT • ROUND 11 • DATE: 23RD AUGUST 2009
Laps: 57 • Distance: 191.931miles/308.883km • Weather: Very hot & bright

Pos	Driver	Team	Chassis-Engine	Result	Qual
1	Rubens Barrichello	Brawn	Brawn-Mercedes BGP 001	1h35m51.289s	3
2	Lewis Hamilton	McLaren	McLaren-Mercedes MP4-24	1h35m53.647s	1
3	Kimi Raikkonen	Ferrari	Ferrari F60	1h36m07.283s	6
4	Heikki Kovalainen	McLaren	McLaren-Mercedes MP4-24	1h36m11.321s	2
5	Nico Rosberg	Williams	Williams-Toyota FW31	1h36m12.159s	7
6	Fernando Alonso	Renault F1	Renault R29	1h36m19.033s	8
7	Jenson Button	Brawn	Brawn-Mercedes BGP 001	1h36m26.202s	5
8	Robert Kubica	BMW Sauber	BMW Sauber F1.09	1h36m27.956s	10
9	Mark Webber	Red Bull Racing	Red Bull-Renault RB5	1h36m36.199s	9
10	Adrian Sutil	Force India	Force India-Mercedes VJM02	1h36m39.224s	12
11	Nick Heidfeld	BMW Sauber	BMW Sauber F1.09	1h36m40.111s	11
12	Giancarlo Fisichella	Force India	Force India-Mercedes VJM02	1h36m54.903s	16
13	Jarno Trulli	Toyota	Toyota TF109	1h36m55.816s	18
14	Timo Glock	Toyota	Toyota TF109	1h37m17.808s	13
15	Romain Grosjean	Renault F1	Renault R29	1h37m23.063s	14
16	Jaime Alguersuari	Toro Rosso	Toro Rosso-Ferrari STR04	56 laps	19
17	Luca Badoer	Ferrari	Ferrari F60	56 laps	20
18	Kazuki Nakajima	Williams	Williams-Toyota FW31	54 laps/suspension	17
R	Sebastien Buemi	Toro Rosso	Toro Rosso-Ferrari STR04	41 laps/brakes	15
R	Sebastian Vettel	Red Bull Racing	Red Bull-Renault RB5	23 laps/engine	4

Pole: Hamilton, 1m39.498s, 121.831mph/196.068kph. Fastest lap: Glock, 1m38.683s, 122.837mph/197.687kph on Lap 55. Race leaders: Hamilton 1-15 & 21-36, Kovalainen 16, Barrichello 17-20 & 37-57

BELGIAN GRAND PRIX

SPA-FRANCORCHAMPS • ROUND 12 • DATE: 30TH AUGUST 2009
Laps: 44 • Distance: 191.491miles/308.176km • Weather: Warm & bright

Pos	Driver	Team	Chassis-Engine	Result	Qual
1	Kimi Raikkonen	Ferrari	Ferrari F60	1h23m50.995s	6
2	Giancarlo Fisichella	Force India	Force India-Mercedes VJM02	1h23m51.934s	1
3	Sebastian Vettel	Red Bull Racing	Red Bull-Renault RB5	1h23m54.870s	8
4	Robert Kubica	BMW Sauber	BMW Sauber F1.09	1h24m00.961s	5
5	Nick Heidfeld	BMW Sauber	BMW Sauber F1.09	1h24m02.271s	3
6	Heikki Kovalainen	McLaren	McLaren-Mercedes MP4-24	1h24m23.758s	15
7	Rubens Barrichello	Brawn	Brawn-Mercedes BGP 001	1h24m26.456s	4
8	Nico Rosberg	Williams	Williams-Toyota FW31	1h24m27.203s	10
9	Mark Webber	Red Bull Racing	Red Bull-Renault RB5	1h24m27.954s	9
10	Timo Glock	Toyota	Toyota TF109	1h24m32.485s	7

Pos	Driver	Team	Chassis-Engine	Result	Qual
11	Adrian Sutil	Force India	Force India-Mercedes VJM02	1h24m33.631s	11
12	Sebastien Buemi	Toro Rosso	Toro Rosso-Ferrari STR04	1h24m37.101s	16
13	Kazuki Nakajima	Williams	Williams-Toyota FW31	1h24m45.236s	18
14	Luca Badoer	Ferrari	Ferrari F60	1h25m33.172s	20
R	Fernando Alonso	Renault F1	Renault R29	26 laps/wheel	13
R	Jarno Trulli	Toyota	Toyota TF109	21 laps/brakes	2
R	Lewis Hamilton	McLaren	McLaren-Mercedes MP4-24	0 laps/collision	12
R	Jenson Button	Brawn	Brawn-Mercedes BGP 001	0 laps/collision	14
R	Jaime Alguersuari	Toro Rosso	Toro Rosso-Ferrari STR04	0 laps/collision	17
R	Romain Grosjean	Renault F1	Renault R29	0 laps/collision	19

Pole: Fisichella, 1m46.308s, 147.378mph/237.182kph. Fastest lap: Vettel, 1m47.263s, 146.066mph/235.070kph on Lap 38. Race leaders: Fisichella 1-4, Raikkonen 5-14 & 18-31 & 36-44, Vettel 15-16 & 32-35, Rosberg 17

ITALIAN GRAND PRIX

MONZA • ROUND 13 • DATE: 13TH SEPTEMBER 2009
Laps: 53 • Distance: 190.778miles/307.029km • Weather: Hot & bright

Pos	Driver	Team	Chassis-Engine	Result	Qual
1	Rubens Barrichello	Brawn	Brawn-Mercedes BGP 001	1h16m21.706s	5
2	Jenson Button	Brawn	Brawn-Mercedes BGP 001	1h16m24.572s	6
3	Kimi Raikkonen	Ferrari	Ferrari F60	1h16m52.370s	3
4	Adrian Sutil	Force India	Force India-Mercedes VJM02	1h16m52.837s	2
5	Fernando Alonso	Renault F1	Renault R29	1h17m20.888s	8
6	Heikki Kovalainen	McLaren	McLaren-Mercedes MP4-24	1h17m22.399s	4
7	Nick Heidfeld	BMW Sauber	BMW Sauber F1.09	1h17m44.118s	15
8	Sebastian Vettel	Red Bull Racing	Red Bull-Renault RB5	1h17m47.113s	9
9	Giancarlo Fisichella	Ferrari	Ferrari F60	1h17m48.562s	14
10	Kazuki Nakajima	Williams	Williams-Toyota FW31	1h19m03.869s	17
11	Timo Glock	Toyota	Toyota TF109	1h19m05.631s	16
12	Lewis Hamilton	McLaren	McLaren-Mercedes MP4-24	52 laps/spun off	1
13	Sebastien Buemi	Toro Rosso	Toro Rosso-Ferrari STR04	52 laps	19
14	Jarno Trulli	Toyota	Toyota TF109	52 laps	11
15	Romain Grosjean	Renault F1	Renault R29	52 laps	12
16	Nico Rosberg	Williams	Williams-Toyota FW31	51 laps	18
R	Vitantonio Liuzzi	Force India	Force India-Mercedes VJM02	22 laps/transmission	7
R	Jaime Alguersuari *	Toro Rosso	Toro Rosso-Ferrari STR04	19 laps/gearbox	20
R	Robert Kubica	BMW Sauber	BMW Sauber F1.09	15 laps/oil leak	13
R	Mark Webber	Red Bull Racing	Red Bull-Renault RB5	0 laps/collision	10

Pole: Hamilton, 1m24.066s, 154.147mph/248.076kph. Fastest lap: Sutil, 1m24.739s, 152.923mph/246.106kph on Lap 36. Race leaders: Hamilton 1-15 & 30-34, Raikkonen 16-19 & 35-37, Barrichello 20-29 & 38-53

* made to start from pit lane for working on car in parc ferme

NEW CONSTRUCTORS

The global economic slump in 2008 made manufacturers consider their expenditure on F1, and Honda pulled the plug on Honda Racing. This came as a shock, but team principal Ross Brawn and CEO Nick Fry said they would try to find a buyer, then took it on themselves and renamed it Brawn GP. Taking both titles was their reward for their incredible endeavour.

SINGAPORE GRAND PRIX

MARINA BAY CIRCUIT • ROUND 14 • DATE: 27TH SEPTEMBER 2009
Laps: 61 • Distance: 192.285miles/309.453km • Weather: Hot & humid

Pos	Driver	Team	Chassis-Engine	Result	Qual
1	Lewis Hamilton	McLaren	McLaren-Mercedes MP4-24	1h56m06.337s	1
2	Timo Glock	Toyota	Toyota TF109	1h56m15.971s	6
3	Fernando Alonso	Renault F1	Renault R29	1h56m22.961s	5
4	Sebastian Vettel	Red Bull Racing	Red Bull-Renault RB5	1h56m26.598s	2
5	Jenson Button	Brawn	Brawn-Mercedes BGP 001	1h56m36.352s	11
6	Rubens Barrichello *	Brawn	Brawn-Mercedes BGP 001	1h56m38.195s	9
7	Heikki Kovalainen	McLaren	McLaren-Mercedes MP4-24	1h56m42.494s	8
8	Robert Kubica	BMW Sauber	BMW Sauber F1.09	1h57m01.391s	7
9	Kazuki Nakajima	Williams	Williams-Toyota FW31	1h57m02.391s	10
10	Kimi Raikkonen	Ferrari	Ferrari F60	1h57m05.229s	12
11	Nico Rosberg	Williams	Williams-Toyota FW31	1h57m06.114s	3
12	Jarno Trulli	Toyota	Toyota TF109	1h57m19.346s	14
13	Giancarlo Fisichella	Ferrari	Ferrari F60	1h57m26.227s	17
14	Vitantonio Liuzzi	Force India	Force India-Mercedes VJM02	1h57m39.839s	19
R	Sebastien Buemi	Toro Rosso	Toro Rosso-Ferrari STR04	47 laps/gearbox	13
R	Jaime Alguersuari	Toro Rosso	Toro Rosso-Ferrari STR04	47 laps/brakes	16
R	Mark Webber	Red Bull Racing	Red Bull-Renault RB5	45 laps/brakes	4
R	Adrian Sutil	Force India	Force India-Mercedes VJM02	23 laps/brakes	15
R	Nick Heidfeld !	BMW Sauber	BMW Sauber F1.09	19 laps/collision	20
R	Romain Grosjean	Renault F1	Renault R29	3 laps/brakes	18

Pole: Hamilton, 1m47.891s, 105.180mph/169.270kph. Fastest lap: Alonso, 1m48.240s, 104.840mph/168.725kph on Lap 53. Race leaders: Hamilton 1-46 & 51-61, Alonso 47-50

* 5-place grid penalty for gearbox change • ! made to start from the pit lane as car underweight

NEW DRIVERS

Kamui Kobayashi made his mark when Toyota ran him in the final two races, and he came sixth in Abu Dhabi. Scuderia Toro Rosso also had impressive rookies, with Sebastien Buemi taking two seventh places and Jaime Alguersuari joining in the second half of the year. The fourth rookie was Romain Grosjean who joined Renault after Piquet Jr was dropped.

JAPANESE GRAND PRIX

SUZUKA • ROUND 15 • DATE: 4TH OCTOBER 2009
Laps: 53 • Distance: 191.240miles/307.771km • Weather: Warm & bright

Pos	Driver	Team	Chassis-Engine	Result	Qual
1	Sebastian Vettel	Red Bull Racing	Red Bull-Renault RB5	1h28m20.443s	1
2	Jarno Trulli	Toyota	Toyota TF109	1h28m25.320s	2
3	Lewis Hamilton	McLaren	McLaren-Mercedes MP4-24	1h28m26.915s	3
4	Kimi Raikkonen	Ferrari	Ferrari F60	1h28m28.383s	5
5	Nico Rosberg	Williams	Williams-Toyota FW31	1h28m29.236s	7
6	Nick Heidfeld	BMW Sauber	BMW Sauber F1.09	1h28m29.952s	4
7	Rubens Barrichello *	Brawn	Brawn-Mercedes BGP 001	1h28m31.084s	6
8	Jenson Button *	Brawn	Brawn-Mercedes BGP 001	1h28m31.917s	10

Pos	Driver	Team	Chassis-Engine	Result	Qual
9	Robert Kubica	BMW Sauber	BMW Sauber F1.09	1h28m32.220s	9
10	Fernando Alonso *	Renault F1	Renault R29	1h28m33.508s	16
11	Heikki Kovalainen ^	McLaren	McLaren-Mercedes MP4-24	1h28m34.178s	11
12	Giancarlo Fisichella	Ferrari	Ferrari F60	1h28m35.039s	14
13	Adrian Sutil !	Force India	Force India-Mercedes VJM02	1h28m35.402s	8
14	Vitantonio Liuzzi ^	Force India	Force India-Mercedes VJM02	1h28m36.177s	18
15	Kazuki Nakajima	Williams	Williams-Toyota FW31	1h28m38.416s	15
16	Romain Grosjean	Renault F1	Renault R29	52 laps	17
17	Mark Webber †	Red Bull Racing	Red Bull-Renault RB5	51 laps	19
R	Jaime Alguersuari	Toro Rosso	Toro Rosso-Ferrari STR04	43 laps/spun off	12
R	Sebastien Buemi #	Toro Rosso	Toro Rosso-Ferrari STR04	11 laps/clutch	13
NS	Timo Glock	Toyota	Toyota TF109	-	-
NS	Kamui Kobayashi	Toyota	Toyota TF109	-	-

Pole: Vettel, 1m32.160s, 140.949mph/226.835kph. Fastest lap: Webber, 1m32.569s, 140.326mph/225.833kph on Lap 50. Race leaders: Vettel 1-53

* 3-place grid penalty for not slowing under yellow flags • ! 5-place grid penalty for not slowing under yellow flags • ^ 5-place grid penalty for gearbox change • † made to start from pit lane for chassis change • # 5-place grid penalty for impeding another driver

CLASSIC CAR: BRAWN BGP 001

This was a car designed by Loic Bigois and Craig Wilson, but with major input from Ben Wood, who had been tasked with getting on with understanding the scope of the technical rule changes for 2009 after working at Super Aguri. The design trick that gave Brawn GP its performance advantage was a twin diffuser. The way that this worked was by identifying that an extra layer within the diffuser could be used to direct air over the top of the diffuser tunnel onto the sloped base of a crash structure to boost downforce. It was a clever interpretation that left their rivals playing catch-up.

BRAZILIAN GRAND PRIX

INTERLAGOS • ROUND 16 • DATE: 18TH OCTOBER 2009
Laps: 71 • Distance: 190.101miles/305.939km • Weather: Warm but dull

Pos	Driver	Team	Chassis-Engine	Result	Qual
1	Mark Webber	Red Bull Racing	Red Bull-Renault RB5	1h32m23.001s	2
2	Robert Kubica	BMW Sauber	BMW Sauber F1.09	1h32m30.707s	8
3	Lewis Hamilton	McLaren	McLaren-Mercedes MP4-24	1h32m42.025s	17
4	Sebastian Vettel	Red Bull Racing	Red Bull-Renault RB5	1h32m42.733s	15
5	Jenson Button	Brawn	Brawn-Mercedes BGP 001	1h32m52.086s	14
6	Kimi Raikkonen	Ferrari	Ferrari F60	1h32m56.421s	5
7	Sebastien Buemi	Toro Rosso	Toro Rosso-Ferrari STR04	1h32m59.072s	6
8	Rubens Barrichello	Brawn	Brawn-Mercedes BGP 001	1h33m08.535s	1
9	Kamui Kobayashi	Toyota	Toyota TF109	1h33m26.405s	11
10	Giancarlo Fisichella	Ferrari	Ferrari F60	1h33m33.746s	19
11	Vitantonio Liuzzi *	Force India	Force India-Mercedes VJM02	1h33m34.469s	20
12	Heikki Kovalainen !	McLaren	McLaren-Mercedes MP4-24	1h33m36.580s	16
13	Romain Grosjean	Renault F1	Renault R29	70 laps	13
14	Jaime Alguersuari	Toro Rosso	Toro Rosso-Ferrari STR04	70 laps	12
R	Kazuki Nakajima	Williams	Williams-Toyota FW31	30 laps/accident	9
R	Nico Rosberg	Williams	Williams-Toyota FW31	27 laps/gearbox	7

Pos	Driver	Team	Chassis-Engine	Result	Qual
R	Nick Heidfeld	BMW Sauber	BMW Sauber F1.09	21 laps/out of fuel	18
R	Adrian Sutil	Force India	Force India-Mercedes VJM02	0 laps/collision	3
R	Jarno Trulli	Toyota	Toyota TF109	0 laps/collision	4
R	Fernando Alonso	Renault F1	Renault R29	0 laps/collision	10

Pole: Barrichello, 1m19.576s, 121.128mph/194.938kph. Fastest lap: Webber, 1m13.733s, 130.727mph/210.386kph on Lap 25. Race leaders: Barrichello 1-20, Webber 21-71

* 5-place grid penalty for gearbox change • ! 25s penalty for unsafe release from pit stop

ABU DHABI GRAND PRIX

YAS MARINA CIRCUIT • ROUND 17 • DATE: 1ST NOVEMBER 2009
Laps: 55 • Distance: 189.547miles/305.47km • Weather: Very hot & bright

Pos	Driver	Team	Chassis-Engine	Result	Qual
1	Sebastian Vettel	Red Bull Racing	Red Bull-Renault RB5	1h34m03.414s	2
2	Mark Webber	Red Bull Racing	Red Bull-Renault RB5	1h34m21.271s	3
3	Jenson Button	Brawn	Brawn-Mercedes BGP 001	1h34m21.881s	5
4	Rubens Barrichello	Brawn	Brawn-Mercedes BGP 001	1h34m26.149s	4
5	Nick Heidfeld	BMW Sauber	BMW Sauber F1.09	1h34m29.667s	8
6	Kamui Kobayashi	Toyota	Toyota TF109	1h34m31.757s	12
7	Jarno Trulli	Toyota	Toyota TF109	1h34m37.780s	6
8	Sebastien Buemi	Toro Rosso	Toro Rosso-Ferrari STR04	1h34m44.708s	10
9	Nico Rosberg	Williams	Williams-Toyota FW31	1h34m49.355s	9
10	Robert Kubica	BMW Sauber	BMW Sauber F1.09	1h34m51.594s	7
11	Heikki Kovalainen *	McLaren	McLaren-Mercedes MP4-24	1h34m56.212s	18
12	Kimi Raikkonen	Ferrari	Ferrari F60	1h34m57.731s	11
13	Kazuki Nakajima	Williams	Williams-Toyota FW31	1h35m03.253s	13
14	Fernando Alonso	Renault F1	Renault R29	1h35m13.101s	15
15	Vitantonio Liuzzi	Force India	Force India-Mercedes VJM02	1h35m37.864s	16
16	Giancarlo Fisichella	Ferrari	Ferrari F60	54 laps	20
17	Adrian Sutil	Force India	Force India-Mercedes VJM02	54 laps	17
18	Romain Grosjean	Renault F1	Renault R29	54 laps	19
R	Lewis Hamilton	McLaren	McLaren-Mercedes MP4-24	20 laps/brakes	1
R	Jaime Alguersuari	Toro Rosso	Toro Rosso-Ferrari STR04	18 laps/gearbox	14

Pole: Hamilton, 1m40.948s, 123.072mph/198.066kph. Fastest lap: Vettel, 1m40.279s, 123.893mph/199.387kph on Lap 54. Race leaders: Hamilton 1-16, Vettel 17-55

* 5-place grid penalty for gearbox change

WORLD DRIVERS' CHAMPIONSHIP FINAL RESULTS

Pos	Driver	Nat	Car-Engine	R1	R2	R3	R4	R5	R6
1	Jenson Button	GBR	Brawn-Mercedes BGP 001	1P	1PF	3	1	1P	1P
2	Sebastian Vettel	DEU	Red Bull-Renault RB5	13	15	1P	2	4	R
3	Rubens Barrichello	BRA	Brawn-Mercedes BGP 001	2	5	4F	5	2F	2
4	Mark Webber	AUS	Red Bull-Renault RB5	12	6	2	11	3	5
5	Lewis Hamilton	GBR	McLaren-Mercedes MP4-24	DQ	7	6	4	9	12
6	Kimi Raikkonen	FIN	Ferrari F60	15	14	10	6	R	3
7	Nico Rosberg	DEU	Williams-Toyota FW31	6F	8	15	9	8	6
8	Jarno Trulli	ITA	Toyota TF109	3	4	R	3PF	R	13
9	Fernando Alonso	ESP	Renault R29	5	11	9	8	5	7
10	Timo Glock	DEU	Toyota TF109	4	3	7	7	10	10

Pos	Driver	Nat	Car-Engine	R1	R2	R3	R4	R5	R6
11	Felipe Massa	BRA	Ferrari F60	R	9	R	14	6	4F
12	Heikki Kovalainen	FIN	McLaren-Mercedes MP4-24	R	R	5	12	R	R
13	Nick Heidfeld	DEU	BMW Sauber F1.09	10	2	12	19	7	11
14	Robert Kubica	POL	BMW Sauber F1.09	14	R	13	18	11	R
15	Giancarlo Fisichella	ITA	Force India-Mercedes VJM02	11	18	14	15	14	9
			Ferrari F60	-	-	-	-	-	-
16	Sebastien Buemi	CHE	Toro Rosso-Ferrari STR04	7	16	8	17	R	R
17	Adrian Sutil	DEU	Force India-Mercedes VJM02	9	17	17	16	R	14
18	Kamui Kobayashi	JPN	Toyota TF109	-	-	-	-	-	-
19	Sebastien Bourdais	FRA	Toro Rosso-Ferrari STR04	8	10	11	13	R	8
20	Kazuki Nakajima	JPN	Williams-Toyota FW31	R	12	R	R	13	15
21	Nelson Piquet Jr.	BRA	Renault R29	R	13	16	10	12	R
22	Vitantonio Liuzzi	ITA	Force India-Mercedes VJM02	-	-	-	-	-	-
23	Romain Grosjean	FRA	Renault R29	-	-	-	-	-	-
24	Jaime Alguersuari	ESP	Toro Rosso-Ferrari STR04	-	-	-	-	-	-
25	Luca Badoer	ITA	Ferrari F60	-	-	-	-	-	-

Pos	Driver	R7	R8	R9	R10	R11	R12	R13	R14	R15	R16	R17	Total
1	Button	1F	6	5	7	7	R	2	5	8	5	3	95
2	Vettel	3P	1PF	2	R	R	3F	8	4	1P	4	1F	84
3	Barrichello	R	3	6	10	1	7	1	6	7	8P	4	77
4	Webber	2	2	1P	3F	9	9	R	R	17F	1F	2	69.5
5	Hamilton	13	16	18	1	2P	R	12P	1P	3	3	RP	49
6	Raikkonen	9	8	R	2	3	1	3	10	4	6	12	48
7	Rosberg	5	5	4	4	5	8	16	11	5	R	9	34.5
8	Trulli	4	7	17	8	13	R	14	12	2	R	7	32.5
9	Alonso	10	14	7F	RP	6	R	5	3F	10	R	14	26
10	Glock	8	9	9	6	14F	10	11	2	NS	-	-	24
11	Massa	6	4	3	NS	-	-	-	-	-	-	-	22
12	Kovalainen	14	R	8	5	4	6	6	7	11	12	11	22
13	Heidfeld	11	15	10	11	11	5	7	R	6	R	5	19
14	Kubica	7	13	14	13	8	4	R	8	9	2	10	17
15	Fisichella	R	10	11	14	12	2P	-	-	-	-	-	8
		-	-	-	-	-	-	9	13	12	10	16	
16	Buemi	15	18	16	16	R	12	13	R	R	7	8	6
17	Sutil	17	17	15	R	10	11	4F	R	13	R	17	5
18	Kobayashi	-	-	-	-	-	-	-	-	NS	9	6	3
19	Bourdais	18	R	R	-	-	-	-	-	-	-	-	2
20	Nakajima	12	11	12	9	18	13	10	9	15	R	13	0
21	Piquet Jr.	16	12	13	12	-	-	-	-	-	-	-	0
22	Liuzzi	-	-	-	-	-	-	R	14	14	11	15	0
23	Grosjean	-	-	-	-	15	R	15	R	16	13	18	0
24	Alguersuari	-	-	-	15	16	R	R	R	R	14	R	0
25	Badoer	-	-	-	-	17	14	-	-	-	-	-	0

SYMBOLS AND GRAND PRIX KEY

Round 1	**Australian GP**	**Round 10**	**Hungarian GP**
Round 2	**Malaysian GP**	**Round 11**	**European GP**
Round 3	**Chinese GP**	**Round 12**	**Belgian GP**
Round 4	**Bahrain GP**	**Round 13**	**Italian GP**
Round 5	**Spanish GP**	**Round 14**	**Singapore GP**
Round 6	**Monaco GP**	**Round 15**	**Japanese GP**
Round 7	**Turkish GP**	**Round 16**	**Brazilian GP**
Round 8	**British GP**	**Round 17**	**Abu Dhabi GP**
Round 9	**German GP**		

SCORING

1st	**10 points**
2nd	**8 points**
3rd	**6 points**
4th	**5 points**
5th	**4 points**
6th	**3 points**
7th	**2 points**
8th	**1 point**

DNPQ DID NOT PRE-QUALIFY **DNQ** DID NOT QUALIFY **DQ** DISQUALIFIED **EX** EXCLUDED
F FASTEST LAP **NC** NOT CLASSIFIED **NS** NON-STARTER **P** POLE POSITION **R** RETIRED

WORLD CONSTRUCTORS' CHAMPIONSHIP FINAL RESULTS

Pos	Team-Engine	R1	R2	R3	R4	R5	R6	R7	R8	R9
1	Brawn-Mercedes	1/2	1/5	3/4	1/5	1/2	1/2	1/R	3/6	5/6
2	Red Bull-Renault	12/13	6/15	1/2	2/11	3/4	5/R	2/3	1/2	1/2
3	McLaren-Mercedes	DQ/R	7/R	5/6	4/12	9/R	12/R	13/14	16/R	8/18
4	Ferrari	15/R	9/14	10/R	6/14	6/R	3/4	6/9	4/8	3/R
5	Toyota	3/4	3/4	7/R	3/7	10/R	10/13	4/8	7/9	9/17
6	BMW Sauber	10/14	2/R	12/13	18/19	7/11	11/R	7/11	13/15	10/14
7	Williams-Toyota	6/R	8/12	15/R	9/R	8/13	6/15	5/12	5/11	4/12
8	Renault F1	5/R	11/13	9/16	8/10	5/12	7/R	10/16	12/14	7/13
9	Force India-Mercedes	9/11	17/18	14/17	15/16	14/R	9/14	17/R	10/17	11/15
10	Toro Rosso-Ferrari	7/8	10/16	8/11	13/17	R/R	8/R	15/18	18/R	16/R

Pos	Team-Engine	R10	R11	R12	R13	R14	R15	R16	R17	Total
1	Brawn-Mercedes	7/10	1/7	7/R	1/2	5/6	7/8	5/8	3/4	172
2	Red Bull-Renault	3/R	9/R	3/9	8/R	4/R	1/17	1/4	1/2	153.5
3	McLaren-Mercedes	1/5	2/4	6/R	6/12	1/7	3/11	3/12	11/R	71
4	Ferrari	2/NS	3/17	1/14	3/9	10/13	4/12	6/10	12/16	70
5	Toyota	6/8	13/14	10/R	11/14	2/12	2/NS	9/R	6/7	59.5
6	BMW Sauber	11/13	8/11	4/5	7/R	8/R	6/9	2/R	5/10	36
7	Williams-Toyota	4/9	5/18	8/13	10/16	9/11	5/15	R/R	9/13	34.5
8	Renault F1	12/R	6/15	R/R	5/15	3/R	10/16	13/R	14/18	26
9	Force India-Mercedes	14/R	10/12	2/11	4/R	14/R	13/14	11/R	15/17	13
10	Toro Rosso-Ferrari	15/16	16/R	12/R	13/R	R/R	R/R	7/14	8/R	8

THE 2010s

2010

SEASON SUMMARY

Red Bull Racing enjoyed its breakthrough season when Sebastian Vettel came through to take the title in a four-way shoot-out at the final round in Abu Dhabi. That the four contenders were spread across three teams was fantastic for F1. The title fight was enthralling as these teams had form that ebbed and flowed through the season's 19 grands prix. At 23 years, 4 months and 11 days, Vettel became the youngest world champion. With Mark Webber also performing strongly for the team, Red Bull Racing landed the constructors' title as well, comfortably clear of McLaren, with Ferrari back in third place overall. There were three new teams, but not one of them scored.

BAHRAIN GRAND PRIX

SAKHIR • ROUND 1 • DATE: 14TH MARCH 2010
Laps: 49 • Distance: 191.786miles/308.651km • Weather: Hot & bright

Pos	Driver	Team	Chassis-Engine	Result	Qual
1	Fernando Alonso	Ferrari	Ferrari F10	1h39m20.396s	3
2	Felipe Massa	Ferrari	Ferrari F10	1h39m36.495s	2
3	Lewis Hamilton	McLaren	McLaren-Mercedes MP4-25	1h39m43.578s	4
4	Sebastian Vettel	Red Bull Racing	Red Bull-Renault RB6	1h39m59.195s	1
5	Nico Rosberg	Mercedes AMG	Mercedes MGP W01	1h40m00.609s	5
6	Michael Schumacher	Mercedes AMG	Mercedes MGP W01	1h40m04.559s	7
7	Jenson Button	McLaren	McLaren-Mercedes MP4-25	1h40m05.676s	8
8	Mark Webber	Red Bull Racing	Red Bull-Renault RB6	1h40m06.756s	6
9	Vitantonio Liuzzi	Force India	Force India-Mercedes VJM03	1h40m13.404s	12
10	Rubens Barrichello	Williams	Williams-Cosworth FW32	1h40m22.885s	11
11	Robert Kubica	Renault F1	Renault R30	1h40m29.489s	9
12	Adrian Sutil	Force India	Force India-Mercedes VJM03	1h40m43.354s	10
13	Jaime Alguersuari	Toro Rosso	Toro Rosso-Ferrari STR5	1h40m53.052s	18
14	Nico Hulkenberg	Williams	Williams-Cosworth FW32	48 laps	13
15	Heikki Kovalainen	Lotus Racing	Lotus-Cosworth T127	47 laps	21
16	Sebastien Buemi	Toro Rosso	Toro Rosso-Ferrari STR5	46 laps/electrical	15
17	Jarno Trulli	Lotus Racing	Lotus-Cosworth T127	46 laps/hydraulics	20
R	Pedro de la Rosa	BMW Sauber	BMW Sauber-Ferrari C29	28 laps/hydraulics	14
R	Bruno Senna	HRT	HRT-Cosworth F110	17 laps/overheating	23
R	Timo Glock	Virgin Racing	Virgin-Cosworth VR-01	16 laps/gearbox	19
R	Vitaly Petrov	Renault F1	Renault R30	13 laps/suspension	17
R	Kamui Kobayashi	BMW Sauber	BMW Sauber-Ferrari C29	11 laps/hydraulics	16
R	Lucas di Grassi	Virgin Racing	Virgin-Cosworth VR-01	2 laps/hydraulics	22
R	Karun Chandhok	HRT	HRT-Cosworth F110	1 lap/spun off	24

Pole: Vettel, 1m54.101s, 123.491mph/198.739kph. Fastest lap: Alonso, 1m58.287s, 119.120mph/191.706kph on Lap 45. Race leaders: Vettel 1-33, Alonso 34-49

MERCEDES' RETURN

Brawn GP disappeared immediately after taking its surprise titles in 2009, as the team was bought by Mercedes and the cars went racing in a silver livery, echoing the cars that the works team ran in 1954 and 1955. After three years away, Michael Schumacher was brought out of retirement to lead Mercedes AMG's attack, alongside Nico Rosberg.

RED BULL RUCTIONS

Bad feeling surfaced at Red Bull Racing during the Turkish GP when the team instructed Mark Webber to turn his engine down as fuel consumption was high. He agreed, but then came under attack from team-mate Sebastian Vettel and they clashed. Webber was doubly furious when team adviser Helmut Marko then blamed him for the contact.

AUSTRALIAN GRAND PRIX

ALBERT PARK • ROUND 2 • DATE: 28TH MARCH 2010
Laps: 58 • Distance: 191.117miles/307.574km • Weather: Warm with drizzle

Pos	Driver	Team	Chassis-Engine	Result	Qual
1	Jenson Button	McLaren	McLaren-Mercedes MP4-25	1h33m36.531s	4
2	Robert Kubica	Renault F1	Renault R30	1h33m48.565s	9
3	Felipe Massa	Ferrari	Ferrari F10	1h33m51.019s	5
4	Fernando Alonso	Ferrari	Ferrari F10	1h33m52.835s	3
5	Nico Rosberg	Mercedes AMG	Mercedes MGP W01	1h33m53.214s	6
6	Lewis Hamilton	McLaren	McLaren-Mercedes MP4-25	1h34m06.429s	11
7	Vitantonio Liuzzi	Force India	Force India-Mercedes VJM03	1h34m36.378s	13
8	Rubens Barrichello	Williams	Williams-Cosworth FW32	1h34m37.067s	8
9	Mark Webber	Red Bull Racing	Red Bull-Renault RB6	1h34m43.850s	2
10	Michael Schumacher	Mercedes AMG	Mercedes MGP W01	1h34m45.922s	7
11	Jaime Alguersuari	Toro Rosso	Toro Rosso-Ferrari STR5	1h34m47.832s	17
12	Pedro de la Rosa	BMW Sauber	BMW Sauber-Ferrari C29	1h34m50.615s	14
13	Heikki Kovalainen	Lotus Racing	Lotus-Cosworth T127	56 laps	19
14	Karun Chandhok	HRT	HRT-Cosworth F110	53 laps	24
R	Timo Glock	Virgin Racing	Virgin-Cosworth VR-01	41 laps/suspension	21
R	Lucas di Grassi	Virgin Racing	Virgin-Cosworth VR-01	26 laps/hydraulics	22
R	Sebastian Vettel	Red Bull Racing	Red Bull-Renault RB6	25 laps/wheel	1
R	Adrian Sutil	Force India	Force India-Mercedes VJM03	9 laps/engine	10
R	Vitaly Petrov	Renault F1	Renault R30	9 laps/spun off	18
R	Bruno Senna	HRT	HRT-Cosworth F110	4 laps/hydraulics	23
R	Sebastien Buemi	Toro Rosso	Toro Rosso-Ferrari STR5	0 laps/collision	12
R	Nico Hulkenberg	Williams	Williams-Cosworth FW32	0 laps/collision	15
R	Kamui Kobayashi	BMW Sauber	BMW Sauber-Ferrari C29	0 laps/collision	16
NS	Jarno Trulli	Lotus Racing	Lotus-Cosworth T127	hydraulics	20

Pole: Vettel, 1m23.919s, 141.356mph/227.490kph. Fastest lap: Webber, 1m28.358s, 134.254mph/216.061kph on Lap 47. Race leaders: Vettel 1-8 & 11-25, Webber 9-10, Button 26-58

MALAYSIAN GRAND PRIX

SEPANG • ROUND 3 • DATE: 4TH APRIL 2010
Laps: 56 • Distance: 192.878miles/310.408km • Weather: Hot & bright

Pos	Driver	Team	Chassis-Engine	Result	Qual
1	Sebastian Vettel	Red Bull Racing	Red Bull-Renault RB6	1h33m48.412s	3
2	Mark Webber	Red Bull Racing	Red Bull-Renault RB6	1h33m53.261s	1
3	Nico Rosberg	Mercedes AMG	Mercedes MGP W01	1h34m01.916s	2
4	Robert Kubica	Renault F1	Renault R30	1h34m07.001s	6
5	Adrian Sutil	Force India	Force India-Mercedes VJM03	1h34m09.471s	4

Pos	Driver	Team	Chassis-Engine	Result	Qual
6	Lewis Hamilton	McLaren	McLaren-Mercedes MP4-25	1h34m11.883s	20
7	Felipe Massa	Ferrari	Ferrari F10	1h34m15.480s	21
8	Jenson Button	McLaren	McLaren-Mercedes MP4-25	1h34m26.330s	17
9	Jaime Alguersuari	Toro Rosso	Toro Rosso-Ferrari STR5	1h34m59.014s	14
10	Nico Hulkenberg	Williams	Williams-Cosworth FW32	1h35m01.811s	5
11	Sebastien Buemi	Toro Rosso	Toro Rosso-Ferrari STR5	1h35m07.350s	13
12	Rubens Barrichello	Williams	Williams-Cosworth FW32	55 laps	7
13	Fernando Alonso	Ferrari	Ferrari F10	54 laps/engine	19
14	Lucas di Grassi	Virgin Racing	Virgin-Cosworth VR-01	53 laps	24
15	Karun Chandhok	HRT	HRT-Cosworth F110	53 laps	22
16	Bruno Senna	HRT	HRT-Cosworth F110	52 laps	23
17	Jarno Trulli	Lotus Racing	Lotus-Cosworth T127	51 laps	18
NC	Heikki Kovalainen	Lotus Racing	Lotus-Cosworth T127	46 laps	15
R	Vitaly Petrov	Renault F1	Renault R30	32 laps/gearbox	11
R	Vitantonio Liuzzi	Force India	Force India-Mercedes VJM03	12 laps/throttle	10
R	Michael Schumacher	Mercedes AMG	Mercedes MGP W01	9 laps/wheel nut	8
R	Kamui Kobayashi	BMW Sauber	BMW Sauber-Ferrari C29	8 laps/engine	9
R	Timo Glock	Virgin Racing	Virgin-Cosworth VR-01	2 laps/collision	16
NS	Pedro de la Rosa	BMW Sauber	BMW Sauber-Ferrari C29	engine	12

Pole: Webber, 1m49.327s, 113.415mph/182.523kph. Fastest lap: Webber, 1m37.054s, 127.757mph/205.605kph on Lap 53. Race leaders: Vettel 1-22 & 25-56, Webber 23-24

TEAM ORDERS

A Ferrari one-two is a cause for celebration for the Tifosi, but their one-two at the German GP left a bad taste in their mouth as Felipe Massa had been told to pull over and let team-mate Fernando Alonso through to win. The Brazilian later regretted agreeing to the request. As team orders were not allowed, Ferrari was fined $100,000 (£75,000).

CHINESE GRAND PRIX

SHANGHAI INTERNATIONAL CIRCUIT • ROUND 4 • DATE: 18TH APRIL 2010
Laps: 56 • Distance: 189.677miles/305.256km • Weather: Warm but dull, rain later

Pos	Driver	Team	Chassis-Engine	Result	Qual
1	Jenson Button	McLaren	McLaren-Mercedes MP4-25	1h46m42.163s	5
2	Lewis Hamilton	McLaren	McLaren-Mercedes MP4-25	1h46m43.693s	6
3	Nico Rosberg	Mercedes AMG	Mercedes MGP W01	1h46m51.647s	4
4	Fernando Alonso	Ferrari	Ferrari F10	1h46m54.032s	3
5	Robert Kubica	Renault F1	Renault R30	1h47m04.376s	8
6	Sebastian Vettel	Red Bull Racing	Red Bull-Renault RB6	1h47m15.473s	1
7	Vitaly Petrov	Renault F1	Renault R30	1h47m29.763s	14
8	Mark Webber	Red Bull Racing	Red Bull-Renault RB6	1h47m34.335s	2
9	Felipe Massa	Ferrari	Ferrari F10	1h47m39.959s	7
10	Michael Schumacher	Mercedes AMG	Mercedes MGP W01	1h47m43.912s	9
11	Adrian Sutil	Force India	Force India-Mercedes VJM03	1h47m45.037s	10
12	Rubens Barrichello	Williams	Williams-Cosworth FW32	1h47m45.828s	11
13	Jaime Alguersuari	Toro Rosso	Toro Rosso-Ferrari STR5	1h47m53.579s	12

Pos	Driver	Team	Chassis-Engine	Result	Qual
14	Heikki Kovalainen	Lotus Racing	Lotus-Cosworth T127	55 laps	21
15	Nico Hulkenberg	Williams	Williams-Cosworth FW32	55 laps	16
16	Bruno Senna	HRT	HRT-Cosworth F110	54 laps	23
17	Karun Chandhok	HRT	HRT-Cosworth F110	52 laps	24
R	Jarno Trulli	Lotus Racing	Lotus-Cosworth T127	26 laps/hydraulics	20
R	Lucas di Grassi	Virgin Racing	Virgin-Cosworth VR-01	8 laps/clutch	22
R	Pedro de la Rosa	BMW Sauber	BMW Sauber-Ferrari C29	7 laps/engine	17
R	Sebastien Buemi	Toro Rosso	Toro Rosso-Ferrari STR5	0 laps/collision	13
R	Kamui Kobayashi	BMW Sauber	BMW Sauber-Ferrari C29	0 laps/collision	15
R	Vitantonio Liuzzi	Force India	Force India-Mercedes VJM03	0 laps/collision	18
NS	Timo Glock	Virgin Racing	Virgin-Cosworth VR-01	engine	19

Pole: Vettel, 1m34.558s, 128.953mph/207.529kph. Fastest lap: Hamilton, 1m42.061s, 119.473mph/192.273kph on Lap 13. Race leaders: Alonso 1-2, Rosberg 3-18, Button 19-56

SPANISH GRAND PRIX

BARCELONA-CATALUNYA • ROUND 5 • DATE: 9TH MAY 2010
Laps: 66 • Distance: 190.775miles/307.23km • Weather: Warm & bright

Pos	Driver	Team	Chassis-Engine	Result	Qual
1	Mark Webber	Red Bull Racing	Red Bull-Renault RB6	1h35m44.101s	1
2	Fernando Alonso	Ferrari	Ferrari F10	1h36m08.166s	4
3	Sebastian Vettel	Red Bull Racing	Red Bull-Renault RB6	1h36m35.439s	2
4	Michael Schumacher	Mercedes AMG	Mercedes MGP W01	1h36m46.296s	6
5	Jenson Button	McLaren	McLaren-Mercedes MP4-25	1h36m47.829s	5
6	Felipe Massa	Ferrari	Ferrari F10	1h36m49.868s	9
7	Adrian Sutil	Force India	Force India-Mercedes VJM03	1h36m57.042s	11
8	Robert Kubica	Renault F1	Renault R30	1h36m57.778s	7
9	Rubens Barrichello	Williams	Williams-Cosworth FW32	65 laps	17
10	Jaime Alguersuari	Toro Rosso	Toro Rosso-Ferrari STR5	65 laps	15
11	Vitaly Petrov *	Renault F1	Renault R30	65 laps	19
12	Kamui Kobayashi	BMW Sauber	BMW Sauber-Ferrari C29	65 laps	10
13	Nico Rosberg	Mercedes AMG	Mercedes MGP W01	65 laps	8
14	Lewis Hamilton	McLaren	McLaren-Mercedes MP4-25	64 laps/wheel	3
15	Vitantonio Liuzzi	Force India	Force India-Mercedes VJM03	64 laps/engine	16
16	Nico Hulkenberg	Williams	Williams-Cosworth FW32	64 laps	13
17	Jarno Trulli	Lotus Racing	Lotus-Cosworth T127	63 laps	18
18	Timo Glock *	Virgin Racing	Virgin-Cosworth VR-01	63 laps	22
19	Lucas di Grassi *	Virgin Racing	Virgin-Cosworth VR-01	62 laps	23
R	Sebastien Buemi	Toro Rosso	Toro Rosso-Ferrari STR5	42 laps/hydraulics	14
R	Karun Chandhok *	HRT	HRT-Cosworth F110	27 laps/collision	24
R	Pedro de la Rosa	BMW Sauber	BMW Sauber-Ferrari C29	18 laps/collision	12
R	Bruno Senna	HRT	HRT-Cosworth F110	0 laps/spun off	21
NS	Heikki Kovalainen	Lotus Racing	Lotus-Cosworth T127	gearbox software	20

Pole: Webber, 1m19.995s, 130.169mph/209.488kph. Fastest lap: Hamilton, 1m24.357s, 123.438mph/198.655kph on Lap 59. Race leaders: Webber 1-66

* 5-place grid penalty for gearbox change

AN ADVANTAGE LOST

Scuderia Toro Rosso had to build its own cars for the first time since the team was created from Minardi for 2006. In the intervening four years, Toro Rosso had run lightly adapted chassis built by parent team, Red Bull Racing. For 2010, their cars were built at their Faenza base, with their best result Sebastian Buemi's eighth place, one lap down, in Canada.

MONACO GRAND PRIX

MONTE CARLO • ROUND 6 • DATE: 16TH MAY 2010
Laps: 78 • Distance: 161.588miles/260.52km • Weather: Warm & bright

Pos	Driver	Team	Chassis-Engine	Result	Qual
1	Mark Webber	Red Bull Racing	Red Bull-Renault RB6	1h50m13.355s	1
2	Sebastian Vettel	Red Bull Racing	Red Bull-Renault RB6	1h50m13.803s	3
3	Robert Kubica	Renault F1	Renault R30	1h50m15.030s	2
4	Felipe Massa	Ferrari	Ferrari F10	1h50m16.021s	4
5	Lewis Hamilton	McLaren	McLaren-Mercedes MP4-25	1h50m17.718s	5
6	Fernando Alonso	Ferrari	Ferrari F10	1h50m19.696s	24
7	Nico Rosberg	Mercedes AMG	Mercedes MGP W01	1h50m20.006s	6
8	Adrian Sutil	Force India	Force India-Mercedes VJM03	1h50m20.325s	12
9	Vitantonio Liuzzi	Force India	Force India-Mercedes VJM03	1h50m20.660s	10
10	Sebastien Buemi	Toro Rosso	Toro Rosso-Ferrari STR5	1h50m21.554s	13
11	Jaime Alguersuari	Toro Rosso	Toro Rosso-Ferrari STR5	1h50m22.490s	17
12	Michael Schumacher *	Mercedes AMG	Mercedes MGP W01	1h50m39.067s	7
13	Vitaly Petrov	Renault F1	Renault R30	73 laps/suspension	14
14	Karun Chandhok	HRT	HRT-Cosworth F110	70 laps/collision	23
15	Jarno Trulli	Lotus Racing	Lotus-Cosworth T127	70 laps/collision	19
R	Heikki Kovalainen	Lotus Racing	Lotus-Cosworth T127	58 laps/steering	18
R	Bruno Senna	HRT	HRT-Cosworth F110	58 laps/hydraulics	22
R	Rubens Barrichello	Williams	Williams-Cosworth FW32	30 laps/suspension	9
R	Kamui Kobayashi	BMW Sauber	BMW Sauber-Ferrari C29	26 laps/gearbox	16
R	Lucas di Grassi	Virgin Racing	Virgin-Cosworth VR-01	25 laps/wheel	21
R	Timo Glock	Virgin Racing	Virgin-Cosworth VR-01	22 laps/suspension	20
R	Pedro de la Rosa	BMW Sauber	BMW Sauber-Ferrari C29	21 laps/hydraulics	15
R	Jenson Button	McLaren	McLaren-Mercedes MP4-25	2 laps/overheating	8
R	Nico Hulkenberg	Williams	Williams-Cosworth FW32	0 laps/collision	11

Pole: Webber, 1m13.826s, 101.202mph/162.869kph. Fastest lap: Vettel, 1m15.192s, 99.363mph/159.910kph on Lap 71. Race leaders: Webber 1-78

* 20s penalty for passing Alonso in safety car period

TURKISH GRAND PRIX

ISTANBUL PARK • ROUND 7 • DATE: 30TH MAY 2010
Laps: 58 • Distance: 192.379miles/309.604km • Weather: Hot & bright

Pos	Driver	Team	Chassis-Engine	Result	Qual
1	Lewis Hamilton	McLaren	McLaren-Mercedes MP4-25	1h28m47.620s	2
2	Jenson Button	McLaren	McLaren-Mercedes MP4-25	1h28m50.265s	4
3	Mark Webber	Red Bull Racing	Red Bull-Renault RB6	1h29m11.905s	1
4	Michael Schumacher	Mercedes AMG	Mercedes MGP W01	1h29m18.730s	5

Pos	Driver	Team	Chassis-Engine	Result	Qual
5	Nico Rosberg	Mercedes AMG	Mercedes MGP W01	1h29m19.886s	6
6	Robert Kubica	Renault F1	Renault R30	1h29m20.444s	7
7	Felipe Massa	Ferrari	Ferrari F10	1h29m24.255s	8
8	Fernando Alonso	Ferrari	Ferrari F10	1h29m34.164s	12
9	Adrian Sutil	Force India	Force India-Mercedes VJM03	1h29m36.649s	11
10	Kamui Kobayashi	BMW Sauber	BMW Sauber-Ferrari C29	1h29m53.270s	10
11	Pedro de la Rosa	BMW Sauber	BMW Sauber-Ferrari C29	1h29m53.564s	13
12	Jaime Alguersuari	Toro Rosso	Toro Rosso-Ferrari STR5	1h29m55.420s	16
13	Vitantonio Liuzzi	Force India	Force India-Mercedes VJM03	57 laps	18
14	Rubens Barrichello	Williams	Williams-Cosworth FW32	57 laps	15
15	Vitaly Petrov	Renault F1	Renault R30	57 laps	9
16	Sebastien Buemi	Toro Rosso	Toro Rosso-Ferrari STR5	57 laps	14
17	Nico Hulkenberg	Williams	Williams-Cosworth FW32	57 laps	17
18	Timo Glock	Virgin Racing	Virgin-Cosworth VR-01	55 laps	21
19	Lucas di Grassi	Virgin Racing	Virgin-Cosworth VR-01	55 laps	23
20	Karun Chandhok	HRT	HRT-Cosworth F110	52 laps/fuel system	24
R	Bruno Senna	HRT	HRT-Cosworth F110	46 laps/fuel pressure	22
R	Sebastian Vettel	Red Bull Racing	Red Bull-Renault RB6	39 laps/collision	3
R	Heikki Kovalainen	Lotus Racing	Lotus-Cosworth T127	33 laps/hydraulics	20
R	Jarno Trulli	Lotus Racing	Lotus-Cosworth T127	32 laps/hydraulics	19

Pole: Webber, 1m26.295s, 138.371mph/222.687kph. Fastest lap: Petrov, 1m29.165s, 133.917mph/215.519kph on Lap 57. Race leaders: Webber 1-15 & 18-39, Button 16-17 & 48, Hamilton 40-47 & 49-58

SAFETY CAR AFFECTS FINALE

Alonso held an eight-point lead over Webber going into the finale in Abu Dhabi, with Vettel seven points further back, but Alonso's hopes of a third F1 title were thwarted when the safety car was deployed. He was fourth, which was enough to become champion, but three cars that had been behind him came out in front when the safety car arrived and so Vettel took the title.

CANADIAN GRAND PRIX

MONTREAL • ROUND 8 • DATE: 13TH JUNE 2010
Laps: 70 • Distance: 189.534miles/305.27km • Weather: Hot & bright

Pos	Driver	Team	Chassis-Engine	Result	Qual
1	Lewis Hamilton	McLaren	McLaren-Mercedes MP4-25	1h33m53.456s	1
2	Jenson Button	McLaren	McLaren-Mercedes MP4-25	1h33m55.710s	4
3	Fernando Alonso	Ferrari	Ferrari F10	1h34m02.670s	3
4	Sebastian Vettel	Red Bull Racing	Red Bull-Renault RB6	1h34m31.273s	2
5	Mark Webber *	Red Bull Racing	Red Bull-Renault RB6	1h34m32.747s	7
6	Nico Rosberg	Mercedes AMG	Mercedes MGP W01	1h34m49.540s	10
7	Robert Kubica	Renault F1	Renault R30	1h34m50.756s	8
8	Sebastien Buemi	Toro Rosso	Toro Rosso-Ferrari STR5	69 laps	15
9	Vitantonio Liuzzi	Force India	Force India-Mercedes VJM03	69 laps	5
10	Adrian Sutil	Force India	Force India-Mercedes VJM03	69 laps	9
11	Michael Schumacher	Mercedes AMG	Mercedes MGP W01	69 laps	13
12	Jaime Alguersuari	Toro Rosso	Toro Rosso-Ferrari STR5	69 laps	16

Pos	Driver	Team	Chassis-Engine	Result	Qual
13	Nico Hulkenberg	Williams	Williams-Cosworth FW32	69 laps	12
14	Rubens Barrichello	Williams	Williams-Cosworth FW32	69 laps	11
15	Felipe Massa !	Ferrari	Ferrari F10	69 laps	6
16	Heikki Kovalainen	Lotus Racing	Lotus-Cosworth T127	68 laps	19
17	Vitaly Petrov	Renault F1	Renault R30	68 laps	14
18	Karun Chandhok *	HRT	HRT-Cosworth F110	66 laps	24
19	Lucas di Grassi	Virgin Racing	Virgin-Cosworth VR-01	65 laps	23
R	Timo Glock	Virgin Racing	Virgin-Cosworth VR-01	50 laps/steering	21
R	Jarno Trulli	Lotus Racing	Lotus-Cosworth T127	42 laps/vibrations	20
R	Pedro de la Rosa	BMW Sauber	BMW Sauber-Ferrari C29	30 laps/engine	17
R	Bruno Senna	HRT	HRT-Cosworth F110	13 laps/gearbox	22
R	Kamui Kobayashi	BMW Sauber	BMW Sauber-Ferrari C29	1 laps/spun off	18

Pole: Hamilton, 1m15.105s, 129.888mph/209.035kph. Fastest lap: Kubica, 1m16.972s, 126.738mph/203.965kph on Lap 67. Race leaders: Hamilton 1-6 & 15-25 & 50-70, Vettel 7-13, Buemi 14, Alonso 26-27, Webber 28-49

* 5-place grid penalty for gearbox change • ! 20s penalty for speeding in the pit lane

EUROPEAN GRAND PRIX

VALENCIA STREET CIRCUIT • ROUND 9 • DATE: 27TH JUNE 2010
Laps: 57 • Distance: 191.931miles/308.883km • Weather: Hot & bright

Pos	Driver	Team	Chassis-Engine	Result	Qual
1	Sebastian Vettel	Red Bull Racing	Red Bull-Renault RB6	1h40m29.571s	1
2	Lewis Hamilton	McLaren	McLaren-Mercedes MP4-25	1h40m34.613s	3
3	Jenson Button!	McLaren	McLaren-Mercedes MP4-25	1h40m42.229s	7
4	Rubens Barrichello!	Williams	Williams-Cosworth FW32	1h40m55.198s	9
5	Robert Kubica!	Renault F1	Renault R30	1h40m56.693s	6
6	Adrian Sutil!	Force India	Force India-Mercedes VJM03	1h40m59.739s	13
7	Kamui Kobayashi	BMW Sauber	BMW Sauber-Ferrari C29	1h41m00.536s	18
8	Fernando Alonso	Ferrari	Ferrari F10	1h41m02.380s	4
9	Sebastien Buemi!	Toro Rosso	Toro Rosso-Ferrari STR5	1h41m05.870s	11
10	Nico Rosberg	Mercedes AMG	Mercedes MGP W01	1h41m13.953s	12
11	Felipe Massa	Ferrari	Ferrari F10	1h41m16.192s	5
12	Pedro de la Rosa!	BMW Sauber	BMW Sauber-Ferrari C29	1h41m16.985s	16
13	Jaime Alguersuari	Toro Rosso	Toro Rosso-Ferrari STR5	1h41m17.810s	17
14	Vitaly Petrov!	Renault F1	Renault R30	1h41m17.858s	10
15	Michael Schumacher	Mercedes AMG	Mercedes MGP W01	1h41m18.397s	15
16	Vitantonio Liuzzi!	Force India	Force India-Mercedes VJM03	1h41m20.461s	14
17	Lucas di Grassi	Virgin Racing	Virgin-Cosworth VR-01	56 laps	21
18	Karun Chandhok	HRT	HRT-Cosworth F110	55 laps	23
19	Timo Glock *	Virgin Racing	Virgin-Cosworth VR-01	55 laps	22
20	Bruno Senna	HRT	HRT-Cosworth F110	55 laps	24
21	Jarno Trulli	Lotus Racing	Lotus-Cosworth T127	53 laps	19
R	Nico Hulkenberg !	Williams	Williams-Cosworth FW32	49 laps/exhaust	8
R	Mark Webber	Red Bull Racing	Red Bull-Renault RB6	8 laps/collision	2
R	Heikki Kovalainen	Lotus Racing	Lotus-Cosworth T127	8 laps/collision	20

Pole: Vettel, 1m37.587s, 124.216mph/199.907kph. Fastest lap: Button, 1m38.766s, 122.734mph/197.521kph on Lap 54. Race leaders: Vettel 1-57

* 20s penalty for ignoring blue flags • ! 5s penalty for driving too far behind safety car

BRITISH GRAND PRIX

SILVERSTONE • ROUND 10 • DATE: 11TH JULY 2010
Laps: 52 • Distance: 190.345miles/306.332km • Weather: Warm & bright

Pos	Driver	Team	Chassis-Engine	Result	Qual
1	Mark Webber	Red Bull Racing	Red Bull-Renault RB6	1h24m38.200s	2
2	Lewis Hamilton	McLaren	McLaren-Mercedes MP4-25	1h24m39.560s	4
3	Nico Rosberg	Mercedes AMG	Mercedes MGP W01	1h24m59.507s	5
4	Jenson Button	McLaren	McLaren-Mercedes MP4-25	1h25m00.186s	14
5	Rubens Barrichello	Williams	Williams-Cosworth FW32	1h25m09.656s	8
6	Kamui Kobayashi	BMW Sauber	BMW Sauber-Ferrari C29	1h25m10.371s	12
7	Sebastian Vettel	Red Bull Racing	Red Bull-Renault RB6	1h25m14.934s	1
8	Adrian Sutil	Force India	Force India-Mercedes VJM03	1h25m19.132s	11
9	Michael Schumacher	Mercedes AMG	Mercedes MGP W01	1h25m19.799s	10
10	Nico Hulkenberg	Williams	Williams-Cosworth FW32	1h25m20.212s	13
11	Vitantonio Liuzzi *	Force India	Force India-Mercedes VJM03	1h25m20.659s	20
12	Sebastien Buemi	Toro Rosso	Toro Rosso-Ferrari STR5	1h25m25.827s	16
13	Vitaly Petrov	Renault F1	Renault R30	1h25m37.574s	15
14	Fernando Alonso	Ferrari	Ferrari F10	1h25m40.585s	3
15	Felipe Massa	Ferrari	Ferrari F10	1h25m45.689s	7
16	Jarno Trulli	Lotus Racing	Lotus-Cosworth T127	51 laps	21
17	Heikki Kovalainen	Lotus Racing	Lotus-Cosworth T127	51 laps	18
18	Timo Glock	Virgin Racing	Virgin-Cosworth VR-01	50 laps	19
19	Karun Chandhok	HRT	HRT-Cosworth F110	50 laps	23
20	Sakon Yamamoto	HRT	HRT-Cosworth F110	50 laps	24
R	Jaime Alguersuari	Toro Rosso	Toro Rosso-Ferrari STR5	44 laps/brakes	17
R	Pedro de la Rosa	BMW Sauber	BMW Sauber-Ferrari C29	29 laps/collision	9
R	Robert Kubica	Renault F1	Renault R30	19 laps/halfshaft	6
R	Lucas di Grassi	Virgin Racing	Virgin-Cosworth VR-01	9 laps/hydraulics	22

Pole: Vettel, 1m29.615s, 147.048mph/236.652kph. Fastest lap: Alonso, 1m30.874s, 145.011mph/233.373kph on Lap 52. Race leaders: Webber 1-52

* 5s grid penalty for impeding Hulkenberg

A STAND-OUT LAP

One of the surprises of 2010 came at the penultimate round when Nico Hulkenberg took pole at Interlagos for Williams by using slicks on a drying track. The rookie's best result in the previous 17 races had been sixth in Hungary, but hopes that pole would lead to anything better were quashed when he dropped to eighth by the finish.

A NEW-LOOK SILVERSTONE

Silverstone is a circuit that has been nipped and tucked over the decades, but its transformation for 2010 was way beyond that. The pits and startline were moved to between Club and Abbey, which was a righthander that led onto a new infield loop, before returning to the old track at Brooklands.

GERMAN GRAND PRIX

HOCKENHEIM • ROUND 11 • DATE: 25TH JULY 2010
Laps: 67 • Distance: 190.424miles/306.458km • Weather: Warm & bright

Pos	Driver	Team	Chassis-Engine	Result	Qual
1	Fernando Alonso	Ferrari	Ferrari F10	1h27m38.864s	2
2	Felipe Massa	Ferrari	Ferrari F10	1h27m43.060s	3
3	Sebastian Vettel	Red Bull Racing	Red Bull-Renault RB6	1h27m43.985s	1
4	Lewis Hamilton	McLaren	McLaren-Mercedes MP4-25	1h28m05.760s	6
5	Jenson Button	McLaren	McLaren-Mercedes MP4-25	1h28m08.346s	5
6	Mark Webber	Red Bull Racing	Red Bull-Renault RB6	1h28m22.470s	4
7	Robert Kubica	Renault F1	Renault R30	66 laps	7
8	Nico Rosberg	Mercedes AMG	Mercedes MGP W01	66 laps	9
9	Michael Schumacher	Mercedes AMG	Mercedes MGP W01	66 laps	11
10	Vitaly Petrov	Renault F1	Renault R30	66 laps	13
11	Kamui Kobayashi	BMW Sauber	BMW Sauber-Ferrari C29	66 laps	12
12	Rubens Barrichello	Williams	Williams-Cosworth FW32	66 laps	8
13	Nico Hulkenberg	Williams	Williams-Cosworth FW32	66 laps	10
14	Pedro de la Rosa	BMW Sauber	BMW Sauber-Ferrari C29	66 laps	14
15	Jaime Alguersuari	Toro Rosso	Toro Rosso-Ferrari STR5	66 laps	15
16	Vitantonio Liuzzi	Force India	Force India-Mercedes VJM03	65 laps	21
17	Adrian Sutil *	Force India	Force India-Mercedes VJM03	65 laps	19
18	Timo Glock *	Virgin Racing	Virgin-Cosworth VR-01	64 laps	23
19	Bruno Senna	HRT	HRT-Cosworth F110	63 laps	20
R	Heikki Kovalainen	Lotus Racing	Lotus-Cosworth T127	56 laps/collision	18
R	Lucas di Grassi *	Virgin Racing	Virgin-Cosworth VR-01	50 laps/spun off	24
R	Sakon Yamamoto	HRT	HRT-Cosworth F110	19 laps/gearbox	22
R	Jarno Trulli	Lotus Racing	Lotus-Cosworth T127	3 laps/gearbox	17
R	Sebastien Buemi	Toro Rosso	Toro Rosso-Ferrari STR5	1 laps/collision	16

Pole: Vettel, 1m13.791s, 138.658mph/223.149kph. Fastest lap: Vettel, 1m15.824s, 134.940mph/217.166kph on Lap 67. Race leaders: Massa 1-14 & 23-48, Button 15-22, Alonso 49-67

* 5-place grid penalty for gearbox change

NEW CIRCUIT

The World Championship broke yet more new ground in South-East Asia with South Korea joining the F1 roadshow. The race was not held near capital Seoul but near Mokpo in the south-west corner of the country. The Yeongam circuit was still being completed when the teams arrived, but the drivers approved of the challenge it provided.

HUNGARIAN GRAND PRIX

HUNGARORING • ROUND 12 • DATE: 1ST AUGUST 2010
Laps: 70 • Distance: 190.181miles/306.67km • Weather: Hot & bright

Pos	Driver	Team	Chassis-Engine	Result	Qual
1	Mark Webber	Red Bull Racing	Red Bull-Renault RB6	1h41m05.571s	2
2	Fernando Alonso	Ferrari	Ferrari F10	1h41m23.392s	3
3	Sebastian Vettel	Red Bull Racing	Red Bull-Renault RB6	1h41m24.823s	1
4	Felipe Massa	Ferrari	Ferrari F10	1h41m33.045s	4

Pos	Driver	Team	Chassis-Engine	Result	Qual
5	Vitaly Petrov	Renault F1	Renault R30	1h42m18.763s	7
6	Nico Hulkenberg	Williams	Williams-Cosworth FW32	1h42m22.294s	10
7	Pedro de la Rosa	BMW Sauber	BMW Sauber-Ferrari C29	69 laps	9
8	Jenson Button	McLaren	McLaren-Mercedes MP4-25	69 laps	11
9	Kamui Kobayashi *	BMW Sauber	BMW Sauber-Ferrari C29	69 laps	23
10	Rubens Barrichello	Williams	Williams-Cosworth FW32	69 laps	12
11	Michael Schumacher	Mercedes AMG	Mercedes MGP W01	69 laps	14
12	Sebastien Buemi	Toro Rosso	Toro Rosso-Ferrari STR5	69 laps	15
13	Vitantonio Liuzzi	Force India	Force India-Mercedes VJM03	69 laps	16
14	Heikki Kovalainen	Lotus Racing	Lotus-Cosworth T127	67 laps	19
15	Jarno Trulli	Lotus Racing	Lotus-Cosworth T127	67 laps	20
16	Timo Glock	Virgin Racing	Virgin-Cosworth VR-01	67 laps	18
17	Bruno Senna	HRT	HRT-Cosworth F110	67 laps	22
18	Lucas di Grassi	Virgin Racing	Virgin-Cosworth VR-01	66 laps	21
19	Sakon Yamamoto	HRT	HRT-Cosworth F110	66 laps	24
R	Lewis Hamilton	McLaren	McLaren-Mercedes MP4-25	23 laps/gearbox	5
R	Robert Kubica	Renault F1	Renault R30	23 laps/collision	8
R	Nico Rosberg	Mercedes AMG	Mercedes MGP W01	15 laps/wheel	6
R	Adrian Sutil	Force India	Force India-Mercedes VJM03	15 laps/collision	13
R	Jaime Alguersuari	Toro Rosso	Toro Rosso-Ferrari STR5	1 laps/engine	17

Pole: Vettel, 1m18.773s, 124.408mph/200.215kph. Fastest lap: Vettel, 1m22.362s, 118.987mph/191.491kph on Lap 70. Race leaders: Vettel 1-15, Webber 16-70

* 5-place grid penalty for failing to stop for weight check

NEW CONSTRUCTORS

F1 opened its door to four new teams. US F1 failed to come to`z fruition, but the other three reached the grid. HRT was created by former F1 driver Adrian Campos but handed over to Jose Ramon Carabante, while Lotus Racing was a team started by Tony Fernandes, with no link to the original Lotus, and Virgin Racing was built from Formula 3 outfit Manor Motorsport.

BELGIAN GRAND PRIX

SPA-FRANCORCHAMPS • ROUND 13 • DATE: 29TH AUGUST 2010
Laps: 44 • Distance: 191.491miles/308.176km • Weather: Warm with showers

Pos	Driver	Team	Chassis-Engine	Result	Qual
1	Lewis Hamilton	McLaren	McLaren-Mercedes MP4-25	1h29m04.268s	2
2	Mark Webber	Red Bull Racing	Red Bull-Renault RB6	1h29m05.839s	1
3	Robert Kubica	Renault F1	Renault R30	1h29m07.761s	3
4	Felipe Massa	Ferrari	Ferrari F10	1h29m12.532s	6
5	Adrian Sutil	Force India	Force India-Mercedes VJM03	1h29m13.362s	8
6	Nico Rosberg *	Mercedes AMG	Mercedes MGP W01	1h29m16.627s	14
7	Michael Schumacher †	Mercedes AMG	Mercedes MGP W01	1h29m19.816s	21
8	Kamui Kobayashi	BMW Sauber	BMW Sauber-Ferrari C29	1h29m20.946s	17
9	Vitaly Petrov	Renault F1	Renault R30	1h29m28.119s	23
10	Vitantonio Liuzzi	Force India	Force India-Mercedes VJM03	1h29m39.099s	12
11	Pedro de la Rosa ‡	BMW Sauber	BMW Sauber-Ferrari C29	1h29m40.287s	24
12	Sebastien Buemi !	Toro Rosso	Toro Rosso-Ferrari STR5	1h29m44.163s	16

Pos	Driver	Team	Chassis-Engine	Result	Qual
13	Jaime Alguersuari ¶	Toro Rosso	Toro Rosso-Ferrari STR5	1h29m53.725s	11
14	Nico Hulkenberg	Williams	Williams-Cosworth FW32	43 laps	9
15	Sebastian Vettel	Red Bull Racing	Red Bull-Renault RB6	43 laps	4
16	Heikki Kovalainen	Lotus Racing	Lotus-Cosworth T127	43 laps	13
17	Lucas di Grassi	Virgin Racing	Virgin-Cosworth VR-01	43 laps	22
18	Timo Glock ^	Virgin Racing	Virgin-Cosworth VR-01	43 laps	20
19	Jarno Trulli	Lotus Racing	Lotus-Cosworth T127	43 laps	15
20	Sakon Yamamoto	HRT	HRT-Cosworth F110	42 laps	19
R	Fernando Alonso	Ferrari	Ferrari F10	37 laps/spun off	10
R	Jenson Button	McLaren	McLaren-Mercedes MP4-25	15 laps/collision	5
R	Bruno Senna	HRT	HRT-Cosworth F110	5 laps/suspension	18
R	Rubens Barrichello	Williams	Williams-Cosworth FW32	0 laps/collision	7

Pole: Webber, 1m45.778s, 148.116mph/238.370kph. Fastest lap: Hamilton, 1m49.069s, 143.647mph/231.178kph on Lap 32. Race leaders: Hamilton 1-44

* 5-place penalty for gearbox change • ! 3-place grid penalty for impeding Rosberg • ^ 5-place grid penalty for impeding Yamamoto • † 10-place grid penalty for impeding Barrichello in Hungarian GP • ‡ 10-place grid penalty for engine change • ¶ 20sec penalty for leaving the track and gaining an advantage

ITALIAN GRAND PRIX

MONZA • ROUND 14 • DATE: 12TH SEPTEMBER 2010
Laps: 53 • Distance: 190.778miles/307.029km • Weather: Hot & bright

Pos	Driver	Team	Chassis-Engine	Result	Qual
1	Fernando Alonso	Ferrari	Ferrari F10	1h16m24.572s	1
2	Jenson Button	McLaren	McLaren-Mercedes MP4-25	1h16m27.510s	2
3	Felipe Massa	Ferrari	Ferrari F10	1h16m28.795s	3
4	Sebastian Vettel	Red Bull Racing	Red Bull-Renault RB6	1h16m52.768s	6
5	Nico Rosberg	Mercedes AMG	Mercedes MGP W01	1h16m54.514s	7
6	Mark Webber	Red Bull Racing	Red Bull-Renault RB6	1h16m55.848s	4
7	Nico Hulkenberg	Williams	Williams-Cosworth FW32	1h16m57.384s	8
8	Robert Kubica	Renault F1	Renault R30	1h16m58.600s	9
9	Michael Schumacher	Mercedes AMG	Mercedes MGP W01	1h17m09.520s	12
10	Rubens Barrichello	Williams	Williams-Cosworth FW32	1h17m28.785s	10
11	Sebastien Buemi	Toro Rosso	Toro Rosso-Ferrari STR5	1h17m29.628s	14
12	Vitantonio Liuzzi	Force India	Force India-Mercedes VJM03	1h17m30.678s	19
13	Vitaly Petrov!	Renault F1	Renault R30	1h17m43.491s	20
14	Pedro de la Rosa	BMW Sauber	BMW Sauber-Ferrari C29	52 laps	16
15	Jaime Alguersuari	Toro Rosso	Toro Rosso-Ferrari STR5	52 laps	15
16	Adrian Sutil	Force India	Force India-Mercedes VJM03	52 laps	11
17	Timo Glock *	Virgin Racing	Virgin-Cosworth VR-01	51 laps	24
18	Heikki Kovalainen	Lotus Racing	Lotus-Cosworth T127	51 laps	18
19	Sakon Yamamoto	HRT	HRT-Cosworth F110	51 laps	23
20	Lucas di Grassi	Virgin Racing	Virgin-Cosworth VR-01	50 laps/suspension	21
R	Jarno Trulli	Lotus Racing	Lotus-Cosworth T127	46 laps/gearbox	17
R	Bruno Senna	HRT	HRT-Cosworth F110	11 laps/hydraulics	22
R	Lewis Hamilton	McLaren	McLaren-Mercedes MP4-25	0 laps/collision	5
R	Kamui Kobayashi	BMW Sauber	BMW Sauber-Ferrari C29	0 laps/gearbox	13

Pole: Alonso, 1m21.962s, 158.104mph/254.444kph. Fastest lap: Alonso, 1m24.139s, 154.013mph/247.861kph on Lap 52. Race leaders: Button 1-35, Alonso 36 & 39-53, Massa 37-38

* 5-place grid penalty for gearbox change • ! 5-place grid penalty for impeding Glock

SINGAPORE GRAND PRIX

MARINA BAY CIRCUIT • ROUND 15 • DATE: 26TH SEPTEMBER 2010
Laps: 61 • Distance: 192.285miles/309.453km • Weather: Very hot & humid

Pos	Driver	Team	Chassis-Engine	Result	Qual
1	Fernando Alonso	Ferrari	Ferrari F10	1h57m53.579s	1
2	Sebastian Vettel	Red Bull Racing	Red Bull-Renault RB6	1h57m53.872s	2
3	Mark Webber	Red Bull Racing	Red Bull-Renault RB6	1h58m22.720s	5
4	Jenson Button	McLaren	McLaren-Mercedes MP4-25	1h58m23.963s	4
5	Nico Rosberg	Mercedes AMG	Mercedes MGP W01	1h58m42.973s	7
6	Rubens Barrichello	Williams	Williams-Cosworth FW32	1h58m49.680s	6
7	Robert Kubica	Renault F1	Renault R30	1h59m20.138s	8
8	Felipe Massa *	Ferrari	Ferrari F10	1h59m46.876s	24
9	Adrian Sutil !	Force India	Force India-Mercedes VJM03	2h00m05.995s	15
10	Nico Hulkenberg */!	Williams	Williams-Cosworth FW32	2h00m06.370s	17
11	Vitaly Petrov	Renault F1	Renault R30	60 laps	12
12	Jaime Alguersuari	Toro Rosso	Toro Rosso-Ferrari STR5	60 laps	11
13	Michael Schumacher	Mercedes AMG	Mercedes MGP W01	60 laps	9
14	Sebastien Buemi	Toro Rosso	Toro Rosso-Ferrari STR5	60 laps	13
15	Lucas di Grassi	Virgin Racing	Virgin-Cosworth VR-01	59 laps	20
16	Heikki Kovalainen	Lotus Racing	Lotus-Cosworth T127	58 laps/fire	19
R	Timo Glock	Virgin Racing	Virgin-Cosworth VR-01	49 laps/hydraulics	18
R	Nick Heidfeld	BMW Sauber	BMW Sauber-Ferrari C29	36 laps/collision	14
R	Lewis Hamilton	McLaren	McLaren-Mercedes MP4-25	35 laps/collision	3
R	Christian Klien	HRT	HRT-Cosworth F110	31 laps/hydraulics	22
R	Kamui Kobayashi	BMW Sauber	BMW Sauber-Ferrari C29	30 laps/spun off	10
R	Bruno Senna	HRT	HRT-Cosworth F110	29 laps/collision	23
R	Jarno Trulli	Lotus Racing	Lotus-Cosworth T127	27 laps/hydraulics	21
R	Vitantonio Liuzzi	Force India	Force India-Mercedes VJM03	1 laps/collision	16

Pole: Alonso, 1m45.390s, 107.676mph/173.287kph. Fastest lap: Alonso, 1m47.976s, 105.097mph/169.137kph on Lap 58. Race leaders: Alonso 1-61

* 5-place grid penalty for gearbox change • ! 20s penalty for leaving the track and gaining an advantage

JAPANESE GRAND PRIX

SUZUKA • ROUND 16 • DATE: 10TH OCTOBER 2010
Laps: 53 • Distance: 191.240miles/307.771km • Weather: Warm & bright

Pos	Driver	Team	Chassis-Engine	Result	Qual
1	Sebastian Vettel	Red Bull Racing	Red Bull-Renault RB6	1h30m27.323s	1
2	Mark Webber	Red Bull Racing	Red Bull-Renault RB6	1h30m28.228s	2
3	Fernando Alonso	Ferrari	Ferrari F10	1h30m30.044s	4
4	Jenson Button	McLaren	McLaren-Mercedes MP4-25	1h30m40.845s	5
5	Lewis Hamilton *	McLaren	McLaren-Mercedes MP4-25	1h31m06.918s	8
6	Michael Schumacher	Mercedes AMG	Mercedes MGP W01	1h31m27.256s	10
7	Kamui Kobayashi	BMW Sauber	BMW Sauber-Ferrari C29	1h31m31.361s	14
8	Nick Heidfeld	BMW Sauber	BMW Sauber-Ferrari C29	1h31m36.971s	11
9	Rubens Barrichello	Williams	Williams-Cosworth FW32	1h31m38.169s	7
10	Sebastien Buemi	Toro Rosso	Toro Rosso-Ferrari STR5	1h31m40.129s	18
11	Jaime Alguersuari	Toro Rosso	Toro Rosso-Ferrari STR5	52 laps	16
12	Heikki Kovalainen	Lotus Racing	Lotus-Cosworth T127	52 laps	20
13	Jarno Trulli	Lotus Racing	Lotus-Cosworth T127	51 laps	19
14	Timo Glock	Virgin Racing	Virgin-Cosworth VR-01	51 laps	22
15	Bruno Senna	HRT	HRT-Cosworth F110	51 laps	23
16	Sakon Yamamoto	HRT	HRT-Cosworth F110	50 laps	24

Pos	Driver	Team	Chassis-Engine	Result	Qual
17	Nico Rosberg	Mercedes AMG	Mercedes MGP W01	47 laps/wheel	6
R	Adrian Sutil	Force India	Force India-Mercedes VJM03	44 laps/oil leak	15
R	Robert Kubica	Renault F1	Renault R30	2 laps/wheel	3
R	Nico Hulkenberg	Williams	Williams-Cosworth FW32	0 laps/collision	9
R	Felipe Massa	Ferrari	Ferrari F10	0 laps/collision	12
R	Vitaly Petrov	Renault F1	Renault R30	0 laps/collision	13
R	Vitantonio Liuzzi	Force India	Force India-Mercedes VJM03	0 laps/collision	17
NS	Lucas di Grassi	Virgin Racing	Virgin-Cosworth VR-01	-	21

Pole: Vettel, 1m30.785s, 143.084mph/230.271kph. Fastest lap: Webber, 1m33.474s, 138.967mph/223.647kph on Lap 53. Race leaders: Vettel 1-24 & 39-53, Webber 25, Button 26-38

* 5-place grid penalty for gearbox change

KOREAN GRAND PRIX

KOREA INTERNATIONAL CIRCUIT • ROUND 17 • DATE: 24TH OCTOBER 2010
Laps: 55 • Distance: 191.894miles/308.825km • Weather: Warm with heavy rain

Pos	Driver	Team	Chassis-Engine	Result	Qual
1	Fernando Alonso	Ferrari	Ferrari F10	2h48m20.810s	3
2	Lewis Hamilton	McLaren	McLaren-Mercedes MP4-25	2h48m35.809s	4
3	Felipe Massa	Ferrari	Ferrari F10	2h48m51.678s	6
4	Michael Schumacher	Mercedes AMG	Mercedes MGP W01	2h49m00.498s	9
5	Robert Kubica	Renault F1	Renault R30	2h49m08.544s	8
6	Vitantonio Liuzzi	Force India	Force India-Mercedes VJM03	2h49m14.381s	17
7	Rubens Barrichello	Williams	Williams-Cosworth FW32	2h49m30.067s	10
8	Kamui Kobayashi	BMW Sauber	BMW Sauber-Ferrari C29	2h49m38.699s	12
9	Nick Heidfeld	BMW Sauber	BMW Sauber-Ferrari C29	2h49m40.917s	13
10	Nico Hulkenberg	Williams	Williams-Cosworth FW32	2h49m41.661s	11
11	Jaime Alguersuari	Toro Rosso	Toro Rosso-Ferrari STR5	2h49m44.956s	15
12	Jenson Button	McLaren	McLaren-Mercedes MP4-25	2h49m50.749s	7
13	Heikki Kovalainen	Lotus Racing	Lotus-Cosworth T127	54 laps	21
14	Bruno Senna	HRT	HRT-Cosworth F110	53 laps	24
15	Sakon Yamamoto	HRT	HRT-Cosworth F110	53 laps	23
R	Adrian Sutil	Force India	Force India-Mercedes VJM03	46 laps/collision	14
R	Sebastian Vettel	Red Bull Racing	Red Bull-Renault RB6	45 laps/engine	1
R	Vitaly Petrov *	Renault F1	Renault R30	39 laps/spun off	20
R	Timo Glock	Virgin Racing	Virgin-Cosworth VR-01	31 laps/collision	19
R	Sebastien Buemi	Toro Rosso	Toro Rosso-Ferrari STR5	30 laps/collision	16
R	Jarno Trulli	Lotus Racing	Lotus-Cosworth T127	25 laps/hydraulics	18
R	Lucas di Grassi	Virgin Racing	Virgin-Cosworth VR-01	25 laps/spun off	22
R	Mark Webber	Red Bull Racing	Red Bull-Renault RB6	18 laps/spun off	2
R	Nico Rosberg	Mercedes AMG	Mercedes MGP W01	18 laps/collision	5

Pole: Vettel, 1m35.585s, 131.405mph/211.476kph. Fastest lap: Alonso, 1m50.257s, 113.919mph/183.335kph on Lap 42. Race leaders: Vettel 1-45, Alonso 46-55

* 5-place grid penalty for causing an avoidable accident at Japanese GP

BRAZILIAN GRAND PRIX

INTERLAGOS • ROUND 18 • DATE: 7TH NOVEMBER 2010
Laps: 71 • Distance: 190.101miles/305.939km • Weather: Hot & bright

Pos	Driver	Team	Chassis-Engine	Result	Qual
1	Sebastian Vettel	Red Bull Racing	Red Bull-Renault RB6	1h33m11.803s	2
2	Mark Webber	Red Bull Racing	Red Bull-Renault RB6	1h33m16.046s	3
3	Fernando Alonso	Ferrari	Ferrari F10	1h33m18.610s	5
4	Lewis Hamilton	McLaren	McLaren-Mercedes MP4-25	1h33m26.437s	4
5	Jenson Button	McLaren	McLaren-Mercedes MP4-25	1h33m27.396s	11
6	Nico Rosberg	Mercedes AMG	Mercedes MGP W01	1h33m47.123s	13
7	Michael Schumacher	Mercedes AMG	Mercedes MGP W01	1h33m55.259s	8
8	Nico Hulkenberg	Williams	Williams-Cosworth FW32	70 laps	1
9	Robert Kubica	Renault F1	Renault R30	70 laps	7
10	Kamui Kobayashi	BMW Sauber	BMW Sauber-Ferrari C29	70 laps	12
11	Jaime Alguersuari	Toro Rosso	Toro Rosso-Ferrari STR5	70 laps	14
12	Adrian Sutil *	Force India	Force India-Mercedes VJM03	70 laps	22
13	Sebastien Buemi *	Toro Rosso	Toro Rosso-Ferrari STR5	70 laps	19
14	Rubens Barrichello	Williams	Williams-Cosworth FW32	70 laps	6
15	Felipe Massa	Ferrari	Ferrari F10	70 laps	9
16	Vitaly Petrov	Renault F1	Renault R30	70 laps	10
17	Nick Heidfeld	BMW Sauber	BMW Sauber-Ferrari C29	70 laps	15
18	Heikki Kovalainen	Lotus Racing	Lotus-Cosworth T127	69 laps	20
19	Jarno Trulli	Lotus Racing	Lotus-Cosworth T127	69 laps	18
20	Timo Glock	Virgin Racing	Virgin-Cosworth VR-01	69 laps	17
21	Bruno Senna!	HRT	HRT-Cosworth F110	69 laps	24
22	Christian Klien	HRT	HRT-Cosworth F110	65 laps	23
NC	Lucas di Grassi	Virgin Racing	Virgin-Cosworth VR-01	62 laps	21
R	Vitantonio Liuzzi	Force India	Force India-Mercedes VJM03	49 laps/spun off	16

Pole: Hulkenberg, 1m14.470s, 129.434mph/208.304kph. Fastest lap: Hamilton, 1m13.851s, 130.518mph/210.049kph on Lap 66. Race leaders: Vettel 1-24 & 27-71, Webber 25-26

* 5-place grid penalty for avoidable crash at Korean GP • ! 5-place grid penalty for gearbox change

ABU DHABI GRAND PRIX

YAS MARINA CIRCUIT • ROUND 19 • DATE: 14TH NOVEMBER 2010
Laps: 55 • Distance: 189.547miles/305.47km • Weather: Hot & bright

Pos	Driver	Team	Chassis-Engine	Result	Qual
1	Sebastian Vettel	Red Bull Racing	Red Bull-Renault RB6	1h39m36.837s	1
2	Lewis Hamilton	McLaren	McLaren-Mercedes MP4-25	1h39m46.999s	2
3	Jenson Button	McLaren	McLaren-Mercedes MP4-25	1h39m47.884s	4
4	Nico Rosberg	Mercedes AMG	Mercedes MGP W01	1h40m07.584s	9
5	Robert Kubica	Renault F1	Renault R30	1h40m15.863s	11
6	Vitaly Petrov	Renault F1	Renault R30	1h40m20.357s	10
7	Fernando Alonso	Ferrari	Ferrari F10	1h40m20.634s	3
8	Mark Webber	Red Bull Racing	Red Bull-Renault RB6	1h40m21.080s	5
9	Jaime Alguersuari	Toro Rosso	Toro Rosso-Ferrari STR5	1h40m27.038s	17
10	Felipe Massa	Ferrari	Ferrari F10	1h40m27.705s	6
11	Nick Heidfeld	BMW Sauber	BMW Sauber-Ferrari C29	1h40m28.388s	14
12	Rubens Barrichello	Williams	Williams-Cosworth FW32	1h40m34.523s	7
13	Adrian Sutil	Force India	Force India-Mercedes VJM03	1h40m35.162s	13
14	Kamui Kobayashi	BMW Sauber	BMW Sauber-Ferrari C29	1h40m36.395s	12
15	Sebastien Buemi	Toro Rosso	Toro Rosso-Ferrari STR5	1h40m40.015s	18
16	Nico Hulkenberg	Williams	Williams-Cosworth FW32	1h40m41.600s	15

Pos	Driver	Team	Chassis-Engine	Result	Qual
17	Heikki Kovalainen	Lotus Racing	Lotus-Cosworth T127	54 laps	20
18	Lucas di Grassi	Virgin Racing	Virgin-Cosworth VR-01	53 laps	22
19	Bruno Senna	HRT	HRT-Cosworth F110	53 laps	23
20	Christian Klien	HRT	HRT-Cosworth F110	53 laps	24
21	Jarno Trulli	Lotus Racing	Lotus-Cosworth T127	51 laps/wing	19
R	Timo Glock	Virgin Racing	Virgin-Cosworth VR-01	43 laps/gearbox	21
R	Michael Schumacher	Mercedes AMG	Mercedes MGP W01	0 laps/collision	8
R	Vitantonio Liuzzi	Force India	Force India-Mercedes VJM03	0 laps/collision	16

Pole: Vettel, 1m39.394s, 124.996mph/201.163kph. Fastest lap: Hamilton, 1m41.274s, 122.676mph/197.428kph on Lap 47. Race leaders: Vettel 1-24 & 40-55, Button 25-39

NEW DRIVERS

Vitaly Petrov achieved the best result of the season's crop of new drivers, coming home fifth for Renault in Hungary. Hulkenberg was next best with sixth in the same race for Williams and they ranked 13th and 14th at year's end. The other three – Karun Chandhok and Bruno Senna for HRT, and Lucas di Grassi for Virgin – all peaked with a 14th-place finish.

WORLD DRIVERS' CHAMPIONSHIP FINAL RESULTS

Pos	Driver	Nat	Car-Engine	R1	R2	R3	R4	R5	R6	R7	R8
1	Sebastian Vettel	DEU	Red Bull-Renault RB6	4P	RP	1	6P	3	2F	R	4
2	Fernando Alonso	ESP	Ferrari F10	1F	4	13	4	2	6	8	3
3	Mark Webber	AUS	Red Bull-Renault RB6	8	9F	2PF	8	1P	1P	3P	5
4	Lewis Hamilton	GBR	McLaren-Mercedes MP4-25	3	6	6	2F	14F	5	1	1P
5	Jenson Button	GBR	McLaren-Mercedes MP4-25	7	1	8	1	5	R	2	2
6	Felipe Massa	BRA	Ferrari F10	2	3	7	9	6	4	7	15
7	Nico Rosberg	DEU	Mercedes MGP W01	5	5	3	3	13	7	5	6
8	Robert Kubica	POL	Renault R30	11	2	4	5	8	3	6	7F
9	Michael Schumacher	DEU	Mercedes MGP W01	6	10	R	10	4	12	4	11
10	Rubens Barrichello	BRA	Williams-Cosworth FW32	10	8	12	12	9	R	14	14
11	Adrian Sutil	DEU	Force India-Mercedes VJM03	12	R	5	11	7	8	9	10
12	Kamui Kobayashi	JPN	BMW Sauber-Ferrari C29	R	R	R	R	12	R	10	R
13	Vitaly Petrov	RUS	Renault R30	R	R	R	7	11	13	15F	17
14	Nico Hulkenberg	DEU	Williams-Cosworth FW32	14	R	10	15	16	R	17	13
15	Vitantonio Liuzzi	ITA	Force India-Mercedes VJM03	9	7	R	R	15	9	13	9
16	Sebastien Buemi	CHE	Toro Rosso-Ferrari STR5	16	R	11	R	R	10	16	8
17	Pedro de la Rosa	ESP	BMW Sauber-Ferrari C29	R	12	NS	R	R	R	11	R
18	Nick Heidfeld	DEU	BMW Sauber-Ferrari C29	-	-	-	-	-	-	-	-
19	Jaime Alguersuari	ESP	Toro Rosso-Ferrari STR5	13	11	9	13	10	11	12	12
20	Heikki Kovalainen	FIN	Lotus-Cosworth T127	15	13	NC	14	NS	R	R	16
21	Jarno Trulli	ITA	Lotus-Cosworth T127	17	NS	17	R	17	15	R	R
22	Karun Chandhok	IND	HRT-Cosworth F110	R	14	15	17	R	14	20	18
23	Bruno Senna	BRA	HRT-Cosworth F110	R	R	16	16	R	R	R	R
24	Lucas di Grassi	BRA	Virgin-Cosworth VR-01	R	R	14	R	19	R	19	19
25	Timo Glock	DEU	Virgin-Cosworth VR-01	R	R	R	NS	18	R	18	R
26	Sakon Yamamoto	JPN	HRT-Cosworth F110	-	-	-	-	-	-	T	-
27	Christian Klien	AUT	HRT-Cosworth F110	-	-	-	-	T	-	-	-

Pos	Driver	R9	R10	R11	R12	R13	R14	R15	R16	R17	R18	R19	Total
1	Vettel	1P	7P	3PF	3PF	15	4	2	1P	RP	1	1P	256
2	Alonso	8	14F	1	2	R	1PF	1PF	3	1F	3	7	252
3	Webber	R	1	6	1	2P	6	3	2F	R	2	8	242
4	Hamilton	2	2	4	R	1F	R	R	5	2	4F	2F	240
5	Button	3F	4	5	8	R	2	4	4	12	5	3	214
6	Massa	11	15	2	4	4	3	8	R	3	15	10	144
7	Rosberg	10	3	8	R	6	5	5	17	R	6	4	142
8	Kubica	5	R	7	R	3	8	7	R	5	9	5	136
9	Schumacher	15	9	9	11	7	9	13	6	4	7	R	72
10	Barrichello	4	5	12	10	R	10	6	9	7	14	12	47
11	Sutil	6	8	17	R	5	16	9	R	R	12	13	47
12	Kobayashi	7	6	11	9	8	R	R	7	8	10	14	32
13	Petrov	14	13	10	5	9	13	11	R	R	16	6	27
14	Hulkenberg	R	10	13	6	14	7	10	R	10	8P	16	22
15	Liuzzi	16	11	16	13	10	12	R	R	6	R	R	21
16	Buemi	9	12	R	12	12	11	14	10	R	13	15	8
17	de la Rosa	12	R	14	7	11	14	-	-	-	-	-	6
18	Heidfeld	-	-	-	-	-	-	R	8	9	17	11	6
19	Alguersuari	13	R	15	R	13	15	12	11	11	11	9	5
20	Kovalainen	R	17	R	14	16	18	16	12	13	18	17	0
21	Trulli	21	16	R	15	19	R	R	13	R	19	21	0
22	Chandhok	18	19	-	-	-	-	-	-	-	-	-	0
23	Senna	20	-	19	17	R	R	R	15	14	21	19	0
24	di Grassi	17	R	R	18	17	20	15	NS	R	NC	18	0
25	Glock	19	18	18	16	18	17	R	14	R	20	R	0
26	Yamamoto	-	20	R	19	20	19	-	16	15	-	-	0
27	Klien	T	-	-	-	-	-	R	-	-	22	20	0

SYMBOLS AND GRAND PRIX KEY

Round 1 **Bahrain GP**
Round 2 **Australian GP**
Round 3 **Malaysian GP**
Round 4 **Chinese GP**
Round 5 **Spanish GP**
Round 6 **Monaco GP**
Round 7 **Turkish GP**
Round 8 **Canadian GP**
Round 9 **European GP**
Round 10 **British GP**
Round 11 **German GP**
Round 12 **Hungarian GP**
Round 13 **Belgian GP**
Round 14 **Italian GP**
Round 15 **Singapore GP**
Round 16 **Japanese GP**
Round 17 **Korean GP**
Round 18 **Brazilian GP**
Round 19 **Abu Dhabi GP**

SCORING

1st **25 points**
2nd **18 points**
3rd **15 points**
4th **12 points**
5th **10 points**
6th **8 points**
7th **6 points**
8th **4 points**
9th **2 points**
10th **1 point**

DNPQ DID NOT PRE-QUALIFY **DNQ DID NOT QUALIFY** **DQ DISQUALIFIED** **EX EXCLUDED**
F FASTEST LAP **NC NOT CLASSIFIED** **NS NON-STARTER** **P POLE POSITION** **R RETIRED**

WORLD CONSTRUCTORS' CHAMPIONSHIP FINAL RESULTS

Pos	Team-Engine	R1	R2	R3	R4	R5	R6	R7	R8	R9	R10
1	Red Bull-Renault	4/8	9/R	1/2	6/8	1/3	1/2	3/R	4/5	1/R	1/7
2	McLaren-Mercedes	3/7	1/6	6/8	1/2	5/14	5/R	1/2	1/2	2/3	2/4
3	Ferrari	1/2	3/4	7/13	4/9	2/6	4/6	7/8	3/15	8/11	14/15
4	Mercedes AMG	5/6	5/10	3/R	3/10	4/13	7/12	4/5	6/11	10/15	3/9
5	Renault F1	11/R	2/R	4/R	5/7	8/11	3/13	6/15	7/17	5/14	13/R
6	Williams-Cosworth	10/14	8/R	10/12	12/15	9/16	R/R	14/17	13/14	4/R	5/10
7	Force India-Mercedes	9/12	7/R	5/R	11/R	7/15	8/9	9/13	9/10	6/16	8/11
8	BMW Sauber-Ferrari	R/R	12/R	R/NS	R/R	12/R	R/R	10/11	R/R	7/12	6/R
9	Toro Rosso-Ferrari	13/16	11/R	9/11	13/R	10/R	10/11	12/16	8/12	9/13	12/R
10	Lotus-Cosworth	15/17	13/NS	17/NC	14/R	17/NS	15/R	R/R	16/R	21/R	16/17

Pos	Team-Engine	R1	R2	R3	R4	R5	R6	R7	R8	R9	R10
11	HRT-Cosworth	R/R	14/R	15/16	16/17	R/R	14/R	20/R	18/R	18/20	19/20
12	Virgin-Cosworth	R/R	R/R	14/R	R/NS	18/19	R/R	18/19	19/R	17/19	18/R

Pos	Team-Engine	R11	R12	R13	R14	R15	R16	R17	R18	R19	Total
1	Red Bull-Renault	3/6	1/3	2/15	4/6	2/3	1/2	R/R	1/2	1/8	498
2	McLaren-Mercedes	4/5	8/R	1/R	2/R	4/R	4/5	2/12	4/5	2/3	454
3	Ferrari	1/2	2/4	4/R	1/3	1/8	3/R	1/3	3/15	7/10	396
4	Mercedes AMG	8/9	11/R	6/7	5/9	5/13	6/17	4/R	6/7	4/R	214
5	Renault F1	7/10	5/R	3/9	8/13	7/11	R/R	5/R	9/16	5/6	163
6	Williams-Cosworth	12/13	6/10	14/R	7/10	6/10	9/R	7/10	8/14	12/16	69
7	Force India-Mercedes	16/17	13/R	5/10	12/16	9/R	R/R	6/R	12/R	13/R	68
8	BMW Sauber-Ferrari	11/14	7/9	8/11	14/R	R/R	7/8	8/9	10/17	11/14	44
9	Toro Rosso-Ferrari	15/R	12/R	12/13	11/15	12/14	10/11	11/R	11/13	9/15	13
10	Lotus-Cosworth	R/R	14/15	16/19	18/R	16/R	12/13	13/R	18/19	17/21	0
11	HRT-Cosworth	19/R	17/19	20/R	19/R	R/R	15/16	14/15	21/22	19/20	0
12	Virgin-Cosworth	18/R	16/18	17/18	17/20	15/R	14/NS	R/R	20/NC	18/R	0

SEASON SUMMARY

Red Bull Racing's Sebastian Vettel did it again, to add a second F1 title. Having become the youngest world champion in 2010 at 23 years and 134 days, eclipsing Lewis Hamilton's record from 2008 by 165 days, he duly became the youngest-ever double world champion. And he did it by a margin, wrapping it up with four rounds remaining, with the team landing the constructors' crown at the following round. McLaren put up a fight to rank second after coming out on top of another scrap with Ferrari, with runner-up Jenson Button really impressing as he outpaced team-mate Lewis Hamilton.

AUSTRALIAN GRAND PRIX

ALBERT PARK • ROUND 1 • DATE: 27TH MARCH 2011
Laps: 58 • Distance: 191.117miles/307.574km • Weather: Hot & bright

Pos	Driver	Team	Chassis-Engine	Result	Qual
1	Sebastian Vettel	Red Bull Racing	Red Bull-Renault RB7	1h29m30.259s	1
2	Lewis Hamilton	McLaren	McLaren-Mercedes MP4-26	1h29m52.556s	2
3	Vitaly Petrov	Renault F1	Renault R31	1h30m00.819s	6
4	Fernando Alonso	Ferrari	Ferrari F150 Italia	1h30m02.031s	5
5	Mark Webber	Red Bull Racing	Red Bull-Renault RB7	1h30m08.430s	3
6	Jenson Button	McLaren	McLaren-Mercedes MP4-26	1h30m24.563s	4
7	Felipe Massa	Ferrari	Ferrari F150 Italia	1h30m55.445s	8
8	Sebastien Buemi	Toro Rosso	Toro Rosso-Ferrari STR6	57 laps	10
9	Adrian Sutil	Force India	Force India-Mercedes VJM04	57 laps	16
10	Paul di Resta	Force India	Force India-Mercedes VJM04	57 laps	14
11	Jaime Alguersuari	Toro Rosso	Toro Rosso-Ferrari STR6	57 laps	12
12	Nick Heidfeld	Renault F1	Renault R31	57 laps	18
13	Jarno Trulli	Lotus Racing	Lotus-Renault T128	56 laps	20
14	Jerome d'Ambrosio	Virgin Racing	Virgin-Cosworth MVR-02	54 laps	22
DQ	Kamui Kobayashi	Sauber	Sauber-Ferrari C30	58 laps	9
DQ	Sergio Perez	Sauber	Sauber-Ferrari C30	58 laps	13
NC	Timo Glock	Virgin Racing	Virgin-Cosworth MVR-02	49 laps	21
R	Rubens Barrichello	Williams	Williams-Cosworth FW33	48 laps/transmission	17
R	Nico Rosberg	Mercedes AMG	Mercedes MGP W02	22 laps/collision	7
R	Michael Schumacher	Mercedes AMG	Mercedes MGP W02	19 laps/collision	11
R	Heikki Kovalainen	Lotus Racing	Lotus-Renault T128	19 laps/water leak	19
R	Pastor Maldonado	Williams	Williams-Cosworth FW33	9 laps/transmission	15
DNQ	Narain Karthikeyan	HRT	HRT-Cosworth F111	-	24
DNQ	Vitantonio Liuzzi	HRT	HRT-Cosworth F111	-	23

Pole: Vettel, 1m23.529s, 142.016mph/228.552kph. Fastest lap: Massa, 1m28.947s, 133.365mph/214.631kph on Lap 55. Race leaders: Vettel 1-13 & 17-58, Hamilton 14-16

LARGER POINT SCORES

There was a new points system for 2011, with points awarded not just to the first eight finishers, but to the first 10, with the 10-8-6-5-4-3-2-1 allocation replaced by 25-18-15-12-10-8-6-4-2-1. This generosity would clearly have an effect on the record books, with early F1 drivers suffering by comparison.

MALAYSIAN GRAND PRIX

SEPANG • ROUND 2 • DATE: 10TH APRIL 2011
Laps: 56 • Distance: 192.878miles/310.408km • Weather: Very hot & bright

Pos	Driver	Team	Chassis-Engine	Result	Qual
1	Sebastian Vettel	Red Bull Racing	Red Bull-Renault RB7	1h37m39.832s	1
2	Jenson Button	McLaren	McLaren-Mercedes MP4-26	1h37m43.093s	4
3	Nick Heidfeld	Renault F1	Renault R31	1h38m04.907s	6
4	Mark Webber	Red Bull Racing	Red Bull-Renault RB7	1h38m06.216s	3
5	Felipe Massa	Ferrari	Ferrari F150 Italia	1h38m16.790s	7
6	Fernando Alonso *	Ferrari	Ferrari F150 Italia	1h38m37.080s	5
7	Kamui Kobayashi	Sauber	Sauber-Ferrari C30	1h38m46.271s	10
8	Lewis Hamilton !	McLaren	McLaren-Mercedes MP4-26	1h38m49.789s	2
9	Michael Schumacher	Mercedes AMG	Mercedes MGP W02	1h39m04.728s	11
10	Paul di Resta	Force India	Force India-Mercedes VJM04	1h39m11.395s	14
11	Adrian Sutil	Force India	Force India-Mercedes VJM04	1h39m21.211s	17
12	Nico Rosberg	Mercedes AMG	Mercedes MGP W02	55 laps	9
13	Sebastien Buemi	Toro Rosso	Toro Rosso-Ferrari STR6	55 laps	12
14	Jaime Alguersuari	Toro Rosso	Toro Rosso-Ferrari STR6	55 laps	13
15	Heikki Kovalainen	Lotus Racing	Lotus-Renault T128	55 laps	19
16	Timo Glock	Virgin Racing	Virgin-Cosworth MVR-02	54 laps	21
17	Vitaly Petrov	Renault F1	Renault R31	52 laps/spun off	8
R	Vitantonio Liuzzi	HRT	HRT-Cosworth F111	46 laps/wing	23
R	Jerome d'Ambrosio	Virgin Racing	Virgin-Cosworth MVR-02	42 laps/spun off	22
R	Jarno Trulli	Lotus Racing	Lotus-Renault T128	31 laps/clutch	20
R	Sergio Perez	Sauber	Sauber-Ferrari C30	23 laps/collision	16
R	Rubens Barrichello	Williams	Williams-Cosworth FW33	22 laps/hydraulics	15
R	Narain Karthikeyan	HRT	HRT-Cosworth F111	14 laps/overheating	24
R	Pastor Maldonado	Williams	Williams-Cosworth FW33	8 laps/electrical	18

Pole: Vettel, 1m34.870s, 130.698mph/210.338kph. Fastest lap: Webber, 1m40.571s, 123.289mph/198.415kph on Lap 46. Race leaders: Vettel 1-13 & 15-25 & 27-56, Alonso 14 & 26

* 20s penalty for causing a collision with Hamilton • ! 20s penalty for more than one change of direction

CHINESE GRAND PRIX

SHANGHAI INTERNATIONAL CIRCUIT • ROUND 3 • DATE: 17TH APRIL 2011
Laps: 56 • Distance: 189.677miles/305.256km • Weather: Warm but dull

Pos	Driver	Team	Chassis-Engine	Result	Qual
1	Lewis Hamilton	McLaren	McLaren-Mercedes MP4-26	1h36m58.226s	3
2	Sebastian Vettel	Red Bull Racing	Red Bull-Renault RB7	1h37m03.424s	1
3	Mark Webber	Red Bull Racing	Red Bull-Renault RB7	1h37m05.781s	18
4	Jenson Button	McLaren	McLaren-Mercedes MP4-26	1h37m08.226s	2
5	Nico Rosberg	Mercedes AMG	Mercedes MGP W02	1h37m11.674s	4
6	Felipe Massa	Ferrari	Ferrari F150 Italia	1h37m14.066s	6
7	Fernando Alonso	Ferrari	Ferrari F150 Italia	1h37m28.848s	5
8	Michael Schumacher	Mercedes AMG	Mercedes MGP W02	1h37m29.252s	14
9	Vitaly Petrov	Renault F1	Renault R31	1h37m55.630s	10
10	Kamui Kobayashi	Sauber	Sauber-Ferrari C30	1h38m01.499s	13
11	Paul di Resta	Force India	Force India-Mercedes VJM04	1h38m06.983s	8
12	Nick Heidfeld	Renault F1	Renault R31	1h38m10.965s	16
13	Rubens Barrichello	Williams	Williams-Cosworth FW33	1h38m28.415s	15
14	Sebastien Buemi	Toro Rosso	Toro Rosso-Ferrari STR6	1h38m28.897s	9
15	Adrian Sutil	Force India	Force India-Mercedes VJM04	55 laps	11
16	Heikki Kovalainen	Lotus Racing	Lotus-Renault T128	55 laps	19
17	Sergio Perez	Sauber	Sauber-Ferrari C30	55 laps	12

Pos	Driver	Team	Chassis-Engine	Result	Qual
18	Pastor Maldonado	Williams	Williams-Cosworth FW33	55 laps	17
19	Jarno Trulli	Lotus Racing	Lotus-Renault T128	55 laps	20
20	Jerome d'Ambrosio	Virgin Racing	Virgin-Cosworth MVR-02	54 laps	21
21	Timo Glock	Virgin Racing	Virgin-Cosworth MVR-02	54 laps	22
22	Vitantonio Liuzzi	HRT	HRT-Cosworth F111	54 laps	23
23	Narain Karthikeyan	HRT	HRT-Cosworth F111	54 laps	24
R	Jaime Alguersuari	Toro Rosso	Toro Rosso-Ferrari STR6	9 laps/wheel	7

Pole: Vettel, 1m33.706s, 130.125mph/209.416kph. Fastest lap: Webber, 1m38.993s, 123.175mph/198.232kph on Lap 42. Race leaders: Button 1-13, Hamilton 14 & 52-56, Alonso 15-16, Rosberg 17-24 & 34-39, Vettel 25-30 & 40-51, Massa 31-335-16, Rosberg 17-24 & 34-39, Vettel 25-30 & 40-51, Massa 31-33

TURKISH GRAND PRIX

ISTANBUL PARK • ROUND 4 • DATE: 8TH MAY 2011
Laps: 58 • Distance: 192.379miles/309.604km • Weather: Warm but bright

Pos	Driver	Team	Chassis-Engine	Result	Qual
1	Sebastian Vettel	Red Bull Racing	Red Bull-Renault RB7	1h30m17.558s	1
2	Mark Webber	Red Bull Racing	Red Bull-Renault RB7	1h30m26.365s	2
3	Fernando Alonso	Ferrari	Ferrari F150 Italia	1h30m27.633s	5
4	Lewis Hamilton	McLaren	McLaren-Mercedes MP4-26	1h30m57.790s	4
5	Nico Rosberg	Mercedes AMG	Mercedes MGP W02	1h31m05.097s	3
6	Jenson Button	McLaren	McLaren-Mercedes MP4-26	1h31m16.989s	6
7	Nick Heidfeld	Renault F1	Renault R31	1h31m18.415s	9
8	Vitaly Petrov	Renault F1	Renault R31	1h31m25.726s	7
9	Sebastien Buemi	Toro Rosso	Toro Rosso-Ferrari STR6	1h31m26.952s	16
10	Kamui Kobayashi	Sauber	Sauber-Ferrari C30	1h31m35.579s	24
11	Felipe Massa	Ferrari	Ferrari F150 Italia	1h31m37.381s	10
12	Michael Schumacher	Mercedes AMG	Mercedes MGP W02	1h31m43.002s	8
13	Adrian Sutil	Force India	Force India-Mercedes VJM04	57 laps	12
14	Sergio Perez	Sauber	Sauber-Ferrari C30	57 laps	15
15	Rubens Barrichello	Williams	Williams-Cosworth FW33	57 laps	11
16	Jaime Alguersuari	Toro Rosso	Toro Rosso-Ferrari STR6	57 laps	17
17	Pastor Maldonado	Williams	Williams-Cosworth FW33	57 laps	14
18	Jarno Trulli	Lotus	Lotus-Renault T128	57 laps	19
19	Heikki Kovalainen	Lotus	Lotus-Renault T128	56 laps	18
20	Jerome d'Ambrosio *	Virgin Racing	Virgin-Cosworth MVR-02	56 laps	23
21	Narain Karthikeyan	HRT	HRT-Cosworth F111	55 laps	22
22	Vitantonio Liuzzi	HRT	HRT-Cosworth F111	53 laps	20
R	Paul di Resta	Force India	Force India-Mercedes VJM04	44 laps/wheel	13
NS	Timo Glock	Virgin Racing	Virgin-Cosworth MVR-02	-	21

Pole: Vettel, 1m25.049s, 140.398mph/225.949kph. Fastest lap: Webber, 1m29.703s, 133.114mph/214.226kph on Lap 48. Race leaders: Vettel 1-11 & 13-58, Button 12

* 5-place grid penalty for ignoring yellow flags

A LONG TIME COMING

Jenson Button won a Canadian GP that ran for fully 4h 04m 40s. There were spins galore on a wet track and Button fell to last after a drive-through penalty, but then attacked on intermediates until the race was stopped for two hours due to standing water. He got onto Vettel's tail on the last lap and the German slid wide, so last became first for the McLaren driver.

SPANISH GRAND PRIX

BARCELONA-CATALUNYA • ROUND 5 • DATE: 22ND MAY 2011
Laps: 66 • Distance: 190.775miles/307.23km • Weather: Warm & bright

Pos	Driver	Team	Chassis-Engine	Result	Qual
1	Sebastian Vettel	Red Bull Racing	Red Bull-Renault RB7	1h39m03.301s	2
2	Lewis Hamilton	McLaren	McLaren-Mercedes MP4-26	1h39m03.931s	3
3	Jenson Button	McLaren	McLaren-Mercedes MP4-26	1h39m38.998s	5
4	Mark Webber	Red Bull Racing	Red Bull-Renault RB7	1h39m51.267s	1
5	Fernando Alonso	Ferrari	Ferrari F150 Italia	65 laps	4
6	Michael Schumacher	Mercedes AMG	Mercedes MGP W02	65 laps	10
7	Nico Rosberg	Mercedes AMG	Mercedes MGP W02	65 laps	7
8	Nick Heidfeld	Renault F1	Renault R31	65 laps	24
9	Sergio Perez	Sauber	Sauber-Ferrari C30	65 laps	12
10	Kamui Kobayashi	Sauber	Sauber-Ferrari C30	65 laps	14
11	Vitaly Petrov	Renault F1	Renault R31	65 laps	6
12	Paul di Resta	Force India	Force India-Mercedes VJM04	65 laps	16
13	Adrian Sutil	Force India	Force India-Mercedes VJM04	65 laps	17
14	Sebastien Buemi	Toro Rosso	Toro Rosso-Ferrari STR6	65 laps	11
15	Pastor Maldonado	Williams	Williams-Cosworth FW33	65 laps	9
16	Jaime Alguersuari	Toro Rosso	Toro Rosso-Ferrari STR6	64 laps	13
17	Rubens Barrichello	Williams	Williams-Cosworth FW33	64 laps	19
18	Jarno Trulli	Lotus Racing	Lotus-Renault T128	64 laps	18
19	Timo Glock	Virgin Racing	Virgin-Cosworth MVR-02	63 laps	20
20	Jerome d'Ambrosio	Virgin Racing	Virgin-Cosworth MVR-02	62 laps	23
21	Narain Karthikeyan	HRT	HRT-Cosworth F111	61 laps	22
R	Felipe Massa	Ferrari	Ferrari F150 Italia	57 laps/gearbox	8
R	Heikki Kovalainen	Lotus Racing	Lotus-Renault T128	47 laps/spun off	15
R	Vitantonio Liuzzi	HRT	HRT-Cosworth F111	27 laps/gearbox	21

Pole: Webber, 1m20.981s, 128.584mph/206.937kph. Fastest lap: Hamilton, 1m26.727s, 120.065mph/193.227kph on Lap 52. Race leaders: Alonso 1-10 & 12-18, Hamilton 11 & 19-23 & 34-35 & 48-49, Vettel 24-33 & 36-47 & 50-66

RUBENS GOES TOP

Rubens Barrichello brought his F1 career to an end with a record number of grand prix starts: 325. The Williams driver passed Riccardo Patrese's long-standing record of 256 grands prix at the 2008 Austrian GP. The Brazilian's spell in F1 lasted 19 years, just two more than Patrese, but seasons typically had more races in them by 2011.

MONACO GRAND PRIX

MONTE CARLO • ROUND 6 • DATE: 29TH MAY 2011
Laps: 78 • Distance: 161.588miles/260.52km • Weather: Warm & bright

Pos	Driver	Team	Chassis-Engine	Result	Qual
1	Sebastian Vettel	Red Bull Racing	Red Bull-Renault RB7	2h09m38.373s	1
2	Fernando Alonso	Ferrari	Ferrari F150 Italia	2h09m39.511s	4
3	Jenson Button	McLaren	McLaren-Mercedes MP4-26	2h09m40.751s	2
4	Mark Webber	Red Bull Racing	Red Bull-Renault RB7	2h10m01.474s	3

Pos	Driver	Team	Chassis-Engine	Result	Qual
5	Kamui Kobayashi	Sauber	Sauber-Ferrari C30	2h10m05.289s	12
6	Lewis Hamilton *	McLaren	McLaren-Mercedes MP4-26	2h10m25.583s	9
7	Adrian Sutil	Force India	Force India-Mercedes VJM04	77 laps	14
8	Nick Heidfeld	Renault F1	Renault R31	77 laps	15
9	Rubens Barrichello	Williams	Williams-Cosworth FW33	77 laps	11
10	Sebastien Buemi	Toro Rosso	Toro Rosso-Ferrari STR6	77 laps	16
11	Nico Rosberg	Mercedes AMG	Mercedes MGP W02	76 laps	7
12	Paul di Resta	Force India	Force India-Mercedes VJM04	76 laps	13
13	Jarno Trulli	Lotus Racing	Lotus-Renault T128	76 laps	18
14	Heikki Kovalainen	Lotus Racing	Lotus-Renault T128	76 laps	17
15	Jerome d'Ambrosio	Virgin Racing	Virgin-Cosworth MVR-02	75 laps	21
16	Vitantonio Liuzzi	HRT	HRT-Cosworth F111	75 laps	23
17	Narain Karthikeyan	HRT	HRT-Cosworth F111	74 laps	22
18	Pastor Maldonado	Williams	Williams-Cosworth FW33	73 laps/collision	8
R	Vitaly Petrov	Renault F1	Renault R31	67 laps/collision	10
R	Jaime Alguersuari	Toro Rosso	Toro Rosso-Ferrari STR6	66 laps/collision	19
R	Michael Schumacher	Mercedes AMG	Mercedes MGP W02	32 laps/fire	5
R	Felipe Massa	Ferrari	Ferrari F150 Italia	32 laps/spun off	6
R	Timo Glock	Virgin Racing	Virgin-Cosworth MVR-02	30 laps/suspension	20
NS	Sergio Perez	Sauber	Sauber-Ferrari C30	driver injured	10

Pole: Vettel, 1m13.556s, 101.573mph/163.467kph. Fastest lap: Webber, 1m16.234s, 98.005mph/157.724kph on Lap 78. Race leaders: Vettel 1-15 & 33-78, Alonso 16, Button 17-32

* 20s penalty for causing avoidable crash

SCHUMACHER STRUGGLES

The Mercedes team's relative lack of pace meant that Michael Schumacher had to grow accustomed to life in the midfield in his second year back in F1. He and team-mate Nico Rosberg pushed hard but neither was able to break into the top three, with the seven-time world champion's fourth place in Montreal their best result.

CANADIAN GRAND PRIX

MONTREAL • ROUND 7 • DATE: 12TH JUNE 2011
Laps: 70 • Distance: 189.534miles/305.27km • Weather: Warm & wet, drying later

Pos	Driver	Team	Chassis-Engine	Result	Qual
1	Jenson Button	McLaren	McLaren-Mercedes MP4-26	4h04m39.537s	7
2	Sebastian Vettel	Red Bull Racing	Red Bull-Renault RB7	4h04m42.246s	1
3	Mark Webber	Red Bull Racing	Red Bull-Renault RB7	4h04m53.365s	4
4	Michael Schumacher	Mercedes AMG	Mercedes MGP W02	4h04m53.756s	8
5	Vitaly Petrov	Renault F1	Renault R31	4h04m59.932s	10
6	Felipe Massa	Ferrari	Ferrari F150 Italia	4h05m12.762s	3
7	Kamui Kobayashi	Sauber	Sauber-Ferrari C30	4h05m12.807s	13
8	Jaime Alguersuari	Toro Rosso	Toro Rosso-Ferrari STR6	4h05m15.501s	18
9	Rubens Barrichello	Williams	Williams-Cosworth FW33	4h05m24.654s	16
10	Sebastien Buemi	Toro Rosso	Toro Rosso-Ferrari STR6	4h05m26.593s	15
11	Nico Rosberg	Mercedes AMG	Mercedes MGP W02	4h05m29.991s	6
12	Pedro de la Rosa	Sauber	Sauber-Ferrari C30	4h05m43.144s	17
13	Vitantonio Liuzzi	HRT	HRT-Cosworth F111	69 laps	20

Pos	Driver	Team	Chassis-Engine	Result	Qual
14	Jerome d'Ambrosio	Virgin Racing	Virgin-Cosworth MVR-02	69 laps	23
15	Timo Glock	Virgin Racing	Virgin-Cosworth MVR-02	69 laps	21
16	Jarno Trulli	Lotus Racing	Lotus-Renault T128	69 laps	18
17	Narain Karthikeyan*	HRT	HRT-Cosworth F111	69 laps	22
18	Paul di Resta	Force India	Force India-Mercedes VJM04	67 laps/spun off	11
R	Pastor Maldonado	Williams	Williams-Cosworth FW33	61 laps/spun off	12
R	Nick Heidfeld	Renault F1	Renault R31	55 laps/collision	9
R	Adrian Sutil	Force India	Force India-Mercedes VJM04	49 laps/spun off	14
R	Fernando Alonso	Ferrari	Ferrari F150 Italia	36 laps/collision	2
R	Heikki Kovalainen	Lotus Racing	Lotus-Renault T128	28 laps/transmission	19
R	Lewis Hamilton	McLaren	McLaren-Mercedes MP4-26	7 laps/collision	5
NS	Sergio Perez	Sauber	Sauber-Ferrari C30	driver injured	-

Pole: Vettel, 1m13.014s, 133.608mph/215.021kph. Fastest lap: Button, 1m16.956s, 126.764mph/204.007kph on Lap 69. Race leaders: Vettel 1-19 & 21-69, Massa 20, Button 70

*20s penalty for leaving the track and gaining an advantage

EUROPEAN GRAND PRIX

VALENCIA STREET CIRCUIT • ROUND 8 • DATE: 26TH JUNE 2011
Laps: 57 • Distance: 191.931miles/308.883km • Weather: Hot & bright

Pos	Driver	Team	Chassis-Engine	Result	Qual
1	Sebastian Vettel	Red Bull Racing	Red Bull-Renault RB7	1h39m36.169s	1
2	Fernando Alonso	Ferrari	Ferrari F150 Italia	1h39m47.060s	4
3	Mark Webber	Red Bull Racing	Red Bull-Renault RB7	1h40m03.424s	2
4	Lewis Hamilton	McLaren	McLaren-Mercedes MP4-26	1h40m22.359s	3
5	Felipe Massa	Ferrari	Ferrari F150 Italia	1h40m27.874s	5
6	Jenson Button	McLaren	McLaren-Mercedes MP4-26	1h40m36.234s	6
7	Nico Rosberg	Mercedes AMG	Mercedes MGP W02	1h41m14.259s	7
8	Jaime Alguersuari	Toro Rosso	Toro Rosso-Ferrari STR6	56 laps	18
9	Adrian Sutil	Force India	Force India-Mercedes VJM04	56 laps	10
10	Nick Heidfeld	Renault F1	Renault R31	56 laps	9
11	Sergio Perez	Sauber	Sauber-Ferrari C30	56 laps	16
12	Rubens Barrichello	Williams	Williams-Cosworth FW33	56 laps	13
13	Sebastien Buemi	Toro Rosso	Toro Rosso-Ferrari STR6	56 laps	17
14	Paul di Resta	Force India	Force India-Mercedes VJM04	56 laps	12
15	Vitaly Petrov	Renault F1	Renault R31	56 laps	11
16	Kamui Kobayashi	Sauber	Sauber-Ferrari C30	56 laps	14
17	Michael Schumacher	Mercedes AMG	Mercedes MGP W02	56 laps	8
18	Pastor Maldonado	Williams	Williams-Cosworth FW33	56 laps	15
19	Heikki Kovalainen	Lotus Racing	Lotus-Renault T128	55 laps	19
20	Jarno Trulli	Lotus Racing	Lotus-Renault T128	55 laps	20
21	Timo Glock	Virgin Racing	Virgin-Cosworth MVR-02	55 laps	21
22	Jerome d'Ambrosio	Virgin Racing	Virgin-Cosworth MVR-02	55 laps	23
23	Vitantonio Liuzzi	HRT	HRT-Cosworth F111	54 laps	22
24	Narain Karthikeyan	HRT	HRT-Cosworth F111	54 laps	24

Pole: Vettel, 1m36.975s, 125.000mph/201.169kph. Fastest lap: Vettel, 1m41.852s, 119.014mph/191.536kph on Lap 53. Race leaders: Vettel 1-13 & 15-57, Massa 14

BRITISH GRAND PRIX

SILVERSTONE • ROUND 9 • DATE: 10TH JULY 2011
Laps: 52 • Distance: 190.345miles/306.332km • Weather: Warm & wet, drying later

Pos	Driver	Team	Chassis-Engine	Result	Qual
1	Fernando Alonso	Ferrari	Ferrari F150 Italia	1h28m41.194s	3
2	Sebastian Vettel	Red Bull Racing	Red Bull-Renault RB7	1h28m57.705s	2
3	Mark Webber	Red Bull Racing	Red Bull-Renault RB7	1h28m58.141s	1
4	Lewis Hamilton	McLaren	McLaren-Mercedes MP4-26	1h29m10.180s	10
5	Felipe Massa	Ferrari	Ferrari F150 Italia	1h29m10.204s	4
6	Nico Rosberg	Mercedes AMG	Mercedes MGP W02	1h29m41.849s	9
7	Sergio Perez	Sauber	Sauber-Ferrari C30	1h29m46.784s	12
8	Nick Heidfeld	Renault F1	Renault R31	1h29m56.736s	16
9	Michael Schumacher	Mercedes AMG	Mercedes MGP W02	1h29m59.106s	13
10	Jaime Alguersuari	Toro Rosso	Toro Rosso-Ferrari STR6	1h30m00.302s	18
11	Adrian Sutil	Force India	Force India-Mercedes VJM04	1h30m00.906s	11
12	Vitaly Petrov	Renault F1	Renault R31	1h30m01.875s	14
13	Rubens Barrichello	Williams	Williams-Cosworth FW33	51 laps	15
14	Pastor Maldonado	Williams	Williams-Cosworth FW33	51 laps	7
15	Paul di Resta	Force India	Force India-Mercedes VJM04	51 laps	6
16	Timo Glock	Virgin Racing	Virgin-Cosworth MVR-02	50 laps	20
17	Jerome d'Ambrosio	Virgin Racing	Virgin-Cosworth MVR-02	50 laps	22
18	Vitantonio Liuzzi	HRT	HRT-Cosworth F111	50 laps	23
19	Daniel Ricciardo	HRT	HRT-Cosworth F111	49 laps	24
R	Jenson Button	McLaren	McLaren-Mercedes MP4-26	39 laps/wheel	5
R	Sebastien Buemi	Toro Rosso	Toro Rosso-Ferrari STR6	25 laps/collision	19
R	Kamui Kobayashi	Sauber	Sauber-Ferrari C30	23 laps/oil leak	8
R	Jarno Trulli	Lotus Racing	Lotus-Renault T128	10 laps/oil leak	21
R	Heikki Kovalainen	Lotus Racing	Lotus-Renault T128	2 laps/gearbox	17

Pole: Webber, 1m30.399s, 145.773mph/234.599kph. Fastest lap: Alonso, 1m34.908s, 138.847mph/223.454kph on Lap 41. Race leaders: Vettel 1-27, Alonso 28-52

KUBICA'S TERRIBLE INJURIES

Robert Kubica's desire for competition cost him his F1 ride with Renault for 2011, as a rally accident in the close-season left him with terrible arm injuries. It took him until 2019 to return to F1. Nick Heidfeld filled the seat and stood on the podium at Sepang as he generally outran Vitaly Petrov, but was later replaced by Bruno Senna.

GERMAN GRAND PRIX

NURBURGRING • ROUND 10 • DATE: 24TH JULY 2011
Laps: 60 • Distance: 191.437miles/308.88km • Weather: Warm but dull

Pos	Driver	Team	Chassis-Engine	Result	Qual
1	Lewis Hamilton	McLaren	McLaren-Mercedes MP4-26	1h37m30.344s	2
2	Fernando Alonso	Ferrari	Ferrari F150 Italia	1h37m34.324s	4
3	Mark Webber	Red Bull Racing	Red Bull-Renault RB7	1h37m40.132s	1
4	Sebastian Vettel	Red Bull Racing	Red Bull-Renault RB7	1h38m18.265s	3

Pos	Driver	Team	Chassis-Engine	Result	Qual
5	Felipe Massa	Ferrari	Ferrari F150 Italia	1h38m22.596s	5
6	Adrian Sutil	Force India	Force India-Mercedes VJM04	1h38m56.552s	8
7	Nico Rosberg	Mercedes AMG	Mercedes MGP W02	59 laps	6
8	Michael Schumacher	Mercedes AMG	Mercedes MGP W02	59 laps	10
9	Kamui Kobayashi	Sauber	Sauber-Ferrari C30	59 laps	17
10	Vitaly Petrov	Renault F1	Renault R31	59 laps	9
11	Sergio Perez	Sauber	Sauber-Ferrari C30	59 laps	15
12	Jaime Alguersuari	Toro Rosso	Toro Rosso-Ferrari STR6	59 laps	16
13	Paul di Resta	Force India	Force India-Mercedes VJM04	59 laps	12
14	Pastor Maldonado	Williams	Williams-Cosworth FW33	59 laps	13
15	Sebastien Buemi	Toro Rosso	Toro Rosso-Ferrari STR6	59 laps	24
16	Heikki Kovalainen	Lotus Racing	Lotus-Renault T128	58 laps	18
17	Timo Glock	Virgin Racing	Virgin-Cosworth MVR-02	57 laps	19
18	Jerome d'Ambrosio	Virgin Racing	Virgin-Cosworth MVR-02	57 laps	21
19	Daniel Ricciardo	HRT	HRT-Cosworth F111	57 laps	22
20	Karun Chandhok	Lotus Racing	Lotus-Renault T128	56 laps	20
R	Vitantonio Liuzzi *	HRT	HRT-Cosworth F111	37 laps/electrical	23
R	Jenson Button	McLaren	McLaren-Mercedes MP4-26	35 laps/hydraulics	7
R	Rubens Barrichello	Williams	Williams-Cosworth FW33	16 laps/oil leak	14
R	Nick Heidfeld	Renault F1	Renault R31	9 laps/collision	11

Pole: Webber, 1m30.079s, 127.840mph/205.739kph. Fastest lap: Hamilton, 1m34.302s, 122.115mph/196.526kph on Lap 59. Race leaders: Hamilton 1-11 & 13-16 & 30 & 33-50 & 57-60, Webber 12 & 17-29 & 54-56, Alonso 31-32 & 51-53

* 5-place grid penalty for gearbox change

WILLIAMS IN FREEFALL

From sixth overall in 2010 to ninth in 2011, ahead only of the three teams that were new to F1 in 2010, the plight of Williams was becoming a concern for F1 fans as this once great team faded rapidly. Even lead driver Rubens Barrichello could do little to keep up with the pack and had to make do with a pair of ninth-place finishes.

HUNGARIAN GRAND PRIX

HUNGARORING • ROUND 11 • DATE: 31ST JULY 2011
Laps: 70 • Distance: 190.181miles/306.67km • Weather: Warm & wet, drying later

Pos	Driver	Team	Chassis-Engine	Result	Qual
1	Jenson Button	McLaren	McLaren-Mercedes MP4-26	1h46m42.337s	3
2	Sebastian Vettel	Red Bull Racing	Red Bull-Renault RB7	1h46m45.925s	1
3	Fernando Alonso	Ferrari	Ferrari F150 Italia	1h47m02.156s	5
4	Lewis Hamilton	McLaren	McLaren-Mercedes MP4-26	1h47m30.675s	2
5	Mark Webber	Red Bull Racing	Red Bull-Renault RB7	1h47m32.079s	6
6	Felipe Massa	Ferrari	Ferrari F150 Italia	1h48m05.513s	4
7	Paul di Resta	Force India	Force India-Mercedes VJM04	69 laps	11
8	Sebastien Buemi *	Toro Rosso	Toro Rosso-Ferrari STR6	69 laps	23
9	Nico Rosberg	Mercedes AMG	Mercedes MGP W02	69 laps	7
10	Jaime Alguersuari	Toro Rosso	Toro Rosso-Ferrari STR6	69 laps	16
11	Kamui Kobayashi	Sauber	Sauber-Ferrari C30	69 laps	13
12	Vitaly Petrov	Renault F1	Renault R31	69 laps	12

Pos	Driver	Team	Chassis-Engine	Result	Qual
13	Rubens Barrichello	Williams	Williams-Cosworth FW33	68 laps	15
14	Adrian Sutil	Force India	Force India-Mercedes VJM04	68 laps	8
15	Sergio Perez	Sauber	Sauber-Ferrari C30	68 laps	10
16	Pastor Maldonado	Williams	Williams-Cosworth FW33	68 laps	17
17	Timo Glock	Virgin Racing	Virgin-Cosworth MVR-02	66 laps	20
18	Daniel Ricciardo	HRT	HRT-Cosworth F111	66 laps	22
19	Jerome d'Ambrosio	Virgin Racing	Virgin-Cosworth MVR-02	65 laps	24
20	Vitantonio Liuzzi	HRT	HRT-Cosworth F111	65 laps	21
R	Heikki Kovalainen	Lotus Racing	Lotus-Renault T128	55 laps/water leak	18
R	Michael Schumacher	Mercedes AMG	Mercedes MGP W02	26 laps/gearbox	9
R	Nick Heidfeld	Renault F1	Renault R31	23 laps/fire	14
R	Jarno Trulli	Lotus Racing	Lotus-Renault T128	17 laps/oil leak	19

Pole: Vettel, 1m19.815s, 122.784mph/197.601kph. Fastest lap: Massa, 1m23.415s, 117.484mph/189.073kph on Lap 61. Race leaders: Vettel 1-4 & 28, Hamilton 5-26 & 29-40 & 43-46 & 51, Button 27 & 41-42 & 47-50 & 52-70

* 5-place grid penalty for causing avoidable crash in German GP

BELGIAN GRAND PRIX

SPA-FRANCORCHAMPS • ROUND 12 • DATE: 28TH AUGUST 2011
Laps: 44 • Distance: 191.491miles/308.176km • Weather: Cool & dull

Pos	Driver	Team	Chassis-Engine	Result	Qual
1	Sebastian Vettel	Red Bull Racing	Red Bull-Renault RB7	1h26m44.893s	1
2	Mark Webber	Red Bull Racing	Red Bull-Renault RB7	1h26m48.634s	3
3	Jenson Button	McLaren	McLaren-Mercedes MP4-26	1h26m54.562s	13
4	Fernando Alonso	Ferrari	Ferrari F150 Italia	1h26m57.915s	8
5	Michael Schumacher	Mercedes AMG	Mercedes MGP W02	1h27m32.357s	24
6	Nico Rosberg	Mercedes AMG	Mercedes MGP W02	1h27m33.567s	5
7	Adrian Sutil	Force India	Force India-Mercedes VJM04	1h27m44.606s	15
8	Felipe Massa	Ferrari	Ferrari F150 Italia	1h27m51.599s	4
9	Vitaly Petrov	Renault F1	Renault R31	1h27m56.810s	10
10	Pastor Maldonado *	Williams	Williams-Cosworth FW33	1h28m02.508s	21
11	Paul di Resta	Force India	Force India-Mercedes VJM04	1h28m08.887s	17
12	Kamui Kobayashi	Sauber	Sauber-Ferrari C30	1h28m16.869s	12
13	Bruno Senna	Renault F1	Renault R31	1h28m17.878s	7
14	Jarno Trulli	Lotus Racing	Lotus-Renault T128	43 laps	18
15	Heikki Kovalainen	Lotus Racing	Lotus-Renault T128	43 laps	16
16	Rubens Barrichello	Williams	Williams-Cosworth FW33	43 laps	14
17	Jerome d'Ambrosio	Virgin Racing	Virgin-Cosworth MVR-02	43 laps	20
18	Timo Glock	Virgin Racing	Virgin-Cosworth MVR-02	43 laps	19
19	Vitantonio Liuzzi	HRT	HRT-Cosworth F111	43 laps	22
R	Sergio Perez	Sauber	Sauber-Ferrari C30	27 laps/collision	9
R	Daniel Ricciardo	HRT	HRT-Cosworth F111	13 laps/chassis	23
R	Lewis Hamilton	McLaren	McLaren-Mercedes MP4-26	12 laps/collision	2
R	Sebastien Buemi	Toro Rosso	Toro Rosso-Ferrari STR6	6 laps/collision	11
R	Jaime Alguersuari	Toro Rosso	Toro Rosso-Ferrari STR6	0 laps/collision	6

Pole: Vettel, 1m48.298s, 144.670mph/232.824kph. Fastest lap: Webber, 1m49.883s, 142.582mph/229.465kph on Lap 33. Race leaders: Rosberg 1-2 & 6, Vettel 3-5 & 11-13 & 18-30 & 32-44, Alonso 7 & 14-17, Hamilton 8-10, Button 31

* 5-place grid penalty for causing avoidable accident in qualifying

ITALIAN GRAND PRIX

MONZA • ROUND 13 • DATE: 11TH SEPTEMBER 2011
Laps: 53 • Distance: 190.778miles/307.029km • Weather: Warm & bright

Pos	Driver	Team	Chassis-Engine	Result	Qual
1	Sebastian Vettel	Red Bull Racing	Red Bull-Renault RB7	1h20m46.172s	1
2	Jenson Button	McLaren	McLaren-Mercedes MP4-26	1h20m55.762s	3
3	Fernando Alonso	Ferrari	Ferrari F150 Italia	1h21m03.081s	4
4	Lewis Hamilton	McLaren	McLaren-Mercedes MP4-26	1h21m03.589s	2
5	Michael Schumacher	Mercedes AMG	Mercedes MGP W02	1h21m18.849s	8
6	Felipe Massa	Ferrari	Ferrari F150 Italia	1h21m29.165s	6
7	Jaime Alguersuari	Toro Rosso	Toro Rosso-Ferrari STR6	52 laps	18
8	Paul di Resta	Force India	Force India-Mercedes VJM04	52 laps	11
9	Bruno Senna	Renault F1	Renault R31	52 laps	10
10	Sebastien Buemi	Toro Rosso	Toro Rosso-Ferrari STR6	52 laps	16
11	Pastor Maldonado	Williams	Williams-Cosworth FW33	52 laps	14
12	Rubens Barrichello	Williams	Williams-Cosworth FW33	52 laps	13
13	Heikki Kovalainen	Lotus Racing	Lotus-Renault T128	51 laps	20
14	Jarno Trulli	Lotus Racing	Lotus-Renault T128	51 laps	19
15	Timo Glock	Virgin Racing	Virgin-Cosworth MVR-02	51 laps	21
NC	Daniel Ricciardo	HRT	HRT-Cosworth F111	39 laps	23
R	Sergio Perez	Sauber	Sauber-Ferrari C30	32 laps/gearbox	15
R	Kamui Kobayashi	Sauber	Sauber-Ferrari C30	21 laps/gearbox	17
R	Adrian Sutil	Force India	Force India-Mercedes VJM04	9 laps/hydraulics	12
R	Mark Webber	Red Bull Racing	Red Bull-Renault RB7	4 laps/collision	5
R	Jerome d'Ambrosio	Virgin Racing	Virgin-Cosworth MVR-02	1 laps/gearbox	22
R	Vitaly Petrov	Renault F1	Renault R31	0 laps/collision	7
R	Nico Rosberg	Mercedes AMG	Mercedes MGP W02	0 laps/collision	9
R	Vitantonio Liuzzi	HRT	HRT-Cosworth F111	0 laps/collision	24

Pole: Vettel, 1m22.275s, 157.503mph/253.476kph. Fastest lap: Hamilton, 1m26.187s, 150.353mph/241.971kph on Lap 52. Race leaders: Alonso 1-4, Vettel 5-53

SINGAPORE GRAND PRIX

MARINA BAY CIRCUIT • ROUND 14 • DATE: 25TH SEPTEMBER 2011
Laps: 61 • Distance: 192.285miles/309.453km • Weather: Very hot & humid

Pos	Driver	Team	Chassis-Engine	Result	Qual
1	Sebastian Vettel	Red Bull Racing	Red Bull-Renault RB7	1h59m06.757s	1
2	Jenson Button	McLaren	McLaren-Mercedes MP4-26	1h59m08.494s	3
3	Mark Webber	Red Bull Racing	Red Bull-Renault RB7	1h59m36.036s	2
4	Fernando Alonso	Ferrari	Ferrari F150 Italia	2h00m02.206s	5
5	Lewis Hamilton	McLaren	McLaren-Mercedes MP4-26	2h00m14.523s	4
6	Paul di Resta	Force India	Force India-Mercedes VJM04	2h00m57.824s	10
7	Nico Rosberg	Mercedes AMG	Mercedes MGP W02	60 laps	7
8	Adrian Sutil	Force India	Force India-Mercedes VJM04	60 laps	9
9	Felipe Massa	Ferrari	Ferrari F150 Italia	60 laps	6
10	Sergio Perez	Sauber	Sauber-Ferrari C30	60 laps	11
11	Pastor Maldonado	Williams	Williams-Cosworth FW33	60 laps	13
12	Sebastien Buemi	Toro Rosso	Toro Rosso-Ferrari STR6	60 laps	14
13	Rubens Barrichello	Williams	Williams-Cosworth FW33	60 laps	12
14	Kamui Kobayashi	Sauber	Sauber-Ferrari C30	59 laps	17
15	Bruno Senna	Renault F1	Renault R31	59 laps	15
16	Heikki Kovalainen	Lotus Racing	Lotus-Renault T128	59 laps	19
17	Vitaly Petrov	Renault F1	Renault R31	59 laps	18
18	Jerome d'Ambrosio	Virgin Racing	Virgin-Cosworth MVR-02	59 laps	22

Pos	Driver	Team	Chassis-Engine	Result	Qual
19	Daniel Ricciardo	HRT	HRT-Cosworth F111	57 laps	23
20	Vitantonio Liuzzi *	HRT	HRT-Cosworth F111	57 laps	24
21	Jaime Alguersuari	Toro Rosso	Toro Rosso-Ferrari STR6	56 laps/spun off	16
R	Jarno Trulli	Lotus Racing	Lotus-Renault T128	47 laps/gearbox	20
R	Michael Schumacher	Mercedes AMG	Mercedes MGP W02	28 laps/collision	8
R	Timo Glock	Virgin Racing	Virgin-Cosworth MVR-02	9 laps/spun off	21

Pole: Vettel, 1m44.381s, 108.716mph/174.962kph. Fastest lap: Button, 1m48.454s, 104.633mph/168.392kph on Lap 54. Race leaders: Vettel 1-61

* 5-place grid penalty for causing avoidable accident at the Italian GP

JAPANESE GRAND PRIX

SUZUKA • ROUND 15 • DATE: 9TH OCTOBER 2011
Laps: 53 • Distance: 191.240miles/307.771km • Weather: Warm & bright

Pos	Driver	Team	Chassis-Engine	Result	Qual
1	Jenson Button	McLaren	McLaren-Mercedes MP4-26	1h30m53.427s	2
2	Fernando Alonso	Ferrari	Ferrari F150 Italia	1h30m54.587s	5
3	Sebastian Vettel	Red Bull Racing	Red Bull-Renault RB7	1h30m55.433s	1
4	Mark Webber	Red Bull Racing	Red Bull-Renault RB7	1h31m01.498s	6
5	Lewis Hamilton	McLaren	McLaren-Mercedes MP4-26	1h31m17.695s	3
6	Michael Schumacher	Mercedes AMG	Mercedes MGP W02	1h31m20.547s	8
7	Felipe Massa	Ferrari	Ferrari F150 Italia	1h31m21.667s	4
8	Sergio Perez	Sauber	Sauber-Ferrari C30	1h31m32.804s	17
9	Vitaly Petrov	Renault F1	Renault R31	1h31m36.034s	10
10	Nico Rosberg	Mercedes AMG	Mercedes MGP W02	1h31m37.749s	23
11	Adrian Sutil	Force India	Force India-Mercedes VJM04	1h31m47.874s	11
12	Paul di Resta	Force India	Force India-Mercedes VJM04	1h31m55.753s	12
13	Kamui Kobayashi	Sauber	Sauber-Ferrari C30	1h31m57.132s	7
14	Pastor Maldonado	Williams	Williams-Cosworth FW33	1h31m57.621s	14
15	Jaime Alguersuari	Toro Rosso	Toro Rosso-Ferrari STR6	1h32m00.050s	16
16	Bruno Senna	Renault F1	Renault R31	1h32m06.055s	9
17	Rubens Barrichello	Williams	Williams-Cosworth FW33	1h32m07.618s	13
18	Heikki Kovalainen	Lotus Racing	Lotus-Renault T128	1h32m21.251s	18
19	Jarno Trulli	Lotus Racing	Lotus-Renault T128	1h32m29.567s	19
20	Timo Glock	Virgin Racing	Virgin-Cosworth MVR-02	51 laps	21
21	Jerome d'Ambrosio	Virgin Racing	Virgin-Cosworth MVR-02	51 laps	20
22	Daniel Ricciardo	HRT	HRT-Cosworth F111	51 laps	22
23	Vitantonio Liuzzi	HRT	HRT-Cosworth F111	50 laps	24
R	Sebastien Buemi	Toro Rosso	Toro Rosso-Ferrari STR6	11 laps/wheel	15

Pole: Vettel, 1m30.466s, 143.588mph/231.083kph. Fastest lap: Button, 1m36.568s, 134.515mph/216.481kph on Lap 52. Race leaders: Vettel 1-9 & 12-18, Button 10 & 19-20 & 23-36 & 41-53, Massa 11 & 22, Alonso 21 & 37, Schumacher 38-40

KOREAN GRAND PRIX

KOREA INTERNATIONAL CIRCUIT • ROUND 16 • DATE: 16TH OCTOBER 2011
Laps: 55 • Distance: 191.894miles/308.825km • Weather: Warm but dull

Pos	Driver	Team	Chassis-Engine	Result	Qual
1	Sebastian Vettel	Red Bull Racing	Red Bull-Renault RB7	1h38m01.994s	2
2	Lewis Hamilton	McLaren	McLaren-Mercedes MP4-26	1h38m14.013s	1
3	Mark Webber	Red Bull Racing	Red Bull-Renault RB7	1h38m14.471s	4
4	Jenson Button	McLaren	McLaren-Mercedes MP4-26	1h38m16.688s	3

Pos	Driver	Team	Chassis-Engine	Result	Qual
5	Fernando Alonso	Ferrari	Ferrari F150 Italia	1h38m17.683s	6
6	Felipe Massa	Ferrari	Ferrari F150 Italia	1h38m27.127s	5
7	Jaime Alguersuari	Toro Rosso	Toro Rosso-Ferrari STR6	1h38m51.532s	11
8	Nico Rosberg	Mercedes AMG	Mercedes MGP W02	1h38m56.047s	7
9	Sebastien Buemi	Toro Rosso	Toro Rosso-Ferrari STR6	1h39m04.756s	13
10	Paul di Resta	Force India	Force India-Mercedes VJM04	1h39m05.596s	9
11	Adrian Sutil	Force India	Force India-Mercedes VJM04	1h39m13.223s	10
12	Rubens Barrichello	Williams	Williams-Cosworth FW33	1h39m35.062s	18
13	Bruno Senna	Renault F1	Renault R31	54 laps	15
14	Heikki Kovalainen	Lotus Racing	Lotus-Renault T128	54 laps	19
15	Kamui Kobayashi	Sauber	Sauber-Ferrari C30	54 laps	14
16	Sergio Perez	Sauber	Sauber-Ferrari C30	54 laps	17
17	Jarno Trulli	Lotus Racing	Lotus-Renault T128	54 laps	20
18	Timo Glock	Virgin Racing	Virgin-Cosworth MVR-02	54 laps	21
19	Daniel Ricciardo	HRT	HRT-Cosworth F111	54 laps	24
20	Jerome d'Ambrosio	Virgin Racing	Virgin-Cosworth MVR-02	54 laps	22
21	Vitantonio Liuzzi	HRT	HRT-Cosworth F111	52 laps	23
R	Pastor Maldonado	Williams	Williams-Cosworth FW33	30 laps/engine	16
R	Vitaly Petrov	Renault F1	Renault R31	16 laps/collision	8
R	Michael Schumacher	Mercedes AMG	Mercedes MGP W02	15 laps/collision	12

Pole: Hamilton, 1m35.820s, 131.083mph/210.958kph. Fastest lap: Vettel, 1m39.605s, 126.101mph/202.941kph on Lap 55. Race leaders: Vettel 1-34 & 37-55, Alonso 35-36

NEW CIRCUITS

India entered the World Championship, with its grand prix held at the all-new Buddh International Circuit outside New Delhi. The circuit had a great flow to it and made the most of a good degree of gradient change. Back in England, following the completion of Silverstone's Wing Building and its pit complex, the start line was moved to between Club and Abbey.

INDIAN GRAND PRIX

BUDDH INTERNATIONAL CIRCUIT • ROUND 17 • DATE: 30TH OCTOBER 2011
Laps: 60 • Distance: 190.764miles/307.5km • Weather: Hot but hazy

Pos	Driver	Team	Chassis-Engine	Result	Qual
1	Sebastian Vettel	Red Bull Racing	Red Bull-Renault RB7	1h30m35.002s	1
2	Jenson Button	McLaren	McLaren-Mercedes MP4-26	1h30m43.435s	4
3	Fernando Alonso	Ferrari	Ferrari F150 Italia	1h30m59.303s	3
4	Mark Webber	Red Bull Racing	Red Bull-Renault RB7	1h31m00.531s	2
5	Michael Schumacher	Mercedes AMG	Mercedes MGP W02	1h31m40.423s	11
6	Nico Rosberg	Mercedes AMG	Mercedes MGP W02	1h31m41.853s	7
7	Lewis Hamilton *	McLaren	McLaren-Mercedes MP4-26	1h31m59.185s	5
8	Jaime Alguersuari	Toro Rosso	Toro Rosso-Ferrari STR6	59 laps	10
9	Adrian Sutil	Force India	Force India-Mercedes VJM04	59 laps	8
10	Sergio Perez *	Sauber	Sauber-Ferrari C30	59 laps	20
11	Vitaly Petrov !	Renault F1	Renault R31	59 laps	16
12	Bruno Senna	Renault F1	Renault R31	59 laps	14

Pos	Driver	Team	Chassis-Engine	Result	Qual
13	Paul di Resta	Force India	Force India-Mercedes VJM04	59 laps	12
14	Heikki Kovalainen	Lotus Racing	Lotus-Renault T128	58 laps	18
15	Rubens Barrichello	Williams	Williams-Cosworth FW33	58 laps	15
16	Jerome d'Ambrosio	Virgin Racing	Virgin-Cosworth MVR-02	57 laps	21
17	Narain Karthikeyan ^	HRT	HRT-Cosworth F111	57 laps	24
18	Daniel Ricciardo †	HRT	HRT-Cosworth F111	57 laps	23
19	Jarno Trulli	Lotus Racing	Lotus-Renault T128	55 laps	19
R	Felipe Massa	Ferrari	Ferrari F150 Italia	32 laps/suspension	6
R	Sebastien Buemi	Toro Rosso	Toro Rosso-Ferrari STR6	24 laps/engine	9
R	Pastor Maldonado	Williams	Williams-Cosworth FW33	12 laps/gearbox	13
R	Timo Glock	Virgin Racing	Virgin-Cosworth MVR-02	2 laps/collision	22
R	Kamui Kobayashi	Sauber	Sauber-Ferrari C30	0 laps/collision	17

Pole: Vettel, 1m24.178s, 136.191mph/219.178kph. Fastest lap: Vettel, 1m27.249s, 131.397mph/211.463kph on Lap 60. Race leaders: Vettel 1-60

* 3-place grid penalty for ignoring yellow flags • ! 5-place grid penalty for causing avoidable accident at Korean GP • ^ 5-place grid penalty for impeding Schumacher • † 5-place grid penalty for gearbox change

ABU DHABI GRAND PRIX

YAS MARINA CIRCUIT • ROUND 18 • DATE: 13TH NOVEMBER 2011
Laps: 55 • Distance: 189.547miles/305.47km • Weather: Hot & bright

Pos	Driver	Team	Chassis-Engine	Result	Qual
1	Lewis Hamilton	McLaren	McLaren-Mercedes MP4-26	1h37m11.886s	2
2	Fernando Alonso	Ferrari	Ferrari F150 Italia	1h37m20.343s	5
3	Jenson Button	McLaren	McLaren-Mercedes MP4-26	1h37m37.757s	3
4	Mark Webber	Red Bull Racing	Red Bull-Renault RB7	1h37m47.670s	4
5	Felipe Massa	Ferrari	Ferrari F150 Italia	1h38m02.464s	6
6	Nico Rosberg	Mercedes AMG	Mercedes MGP W02	1h38m04.203s	7
7	Michael Schumacher	Mercedes AMG	Mercedes MGP W02	1h38m27.850s	8
8	Adrian Sutil	Force India	Force India-Mercedes VJM04	1h38m29.008s	9
9	Paul di Resta	Force India	Force India-Mercedes VJM04	1h38m52.973s	10
10	Kamui Kobayashi	Sauber	Sauber-Ferrari C30	54 laps	16
11	Sergio Perez	Sauber	Sauber-Ferrari C30	54 laps	11
12	Rubens Barrichello	Williams	Williams-Cosworth FW33	54 laps	24
13	Vitaly Petrov	Renault F1	Renault R31	54 laps	12
14	Pastor Maldonado */^	Williams	Williams-Cosworth FW33	54 laps	23
15	Jaime Alguersuari !	Toro Rosso	Toro Rosso-Ferrari STR6	54 laps	15
16	Bruno Senna	Renault F1	Renault R31	54 laps	14
17	Heikki Kovalainen	Lotus Racing	Lotus-Renault T128	54 laps	17
18	Jarno Trulli	Lotus Racing	Lotus-Renault T128	53 laps	18
19	Timo Glock	Virgin Racing	Virgin-Cosworth MVR-02	53 laps	19
20	Vitantonio Liuzzi	HRT	HRT-Cosworth F111	53 laps	22
R	Daniel Ricciardo	HRT	HRT-Cosworth F111	48 laps/alternator	20
R	Sebastien Buemi	Toro Rosso	Toro Rosso-Ferrari STR6	19 laps/hydraulics	13
R	Jerome d'Ambrosio	Virgin Racing	Virgin-Cosworth MVR-02	18 laps/brakes	21
R	Sebastian Vettel	Red Bull Racing	Red Bull-Renault RB7	1 lap/puncture	1

Pole: Vettel, 1m38.481s, 126.155mph/203.027kph. Fastest lap: Webber, 1m42.612s, 121.076mph/194.854kph on Lap 51. Race leaders: Hamilton 1-16 & 18-40 & 44-55, Webber 17, Alonso 41-43

* 10-place grid penalty for engine change • ! 20s penalty for ignoring waved blue flags • ^ 30s penalty for ignoring waved blue flags

BRAZILIAN GRAND PRIX

INTERLAGOS • ROUND 19 • DATE: 27TH NOVEMBER 2011
Laps: 71 • Distance: 190.101miles/305.939km • Weather: Hot & bright

Pos	Driver	Team	Chassis-Engine	Result	Qual
1	Mark Webber	Red Bull Racing	Red Bull-Renault RB7	1h32m17.464s	2
2	Sebastian Vettel	Red Bull Racing	Red Bull-Renault RB7	1h32m34.447s	1
3	Jenson Button	McLaren	McLaren-Mercedes MP4-26	1h32m45.102s	3
4	Fernando Alonso	Ferrari	Ferrari F150 Italia	1h32m52.512s	5
5	Felipe Massa	Ferrari	Ferrari F150 Italia	1h33m24.197s	7
6	Adrian Sutil	Force India	Force India-Mercedes VJM04	70 laps	8
7	Nico Rosberg	Mercedes AMG	Mercedes MGP W02	70 laps	6
8	Paul di Resta	Force India	Force India-Mercedes VJM04	70 laps	11
9	Kamui Kobayashi	Sauber	Sauber-Ferrari C30	70 laps	16
10	Vitaly Petrov	Renault F1	Renault R31	70 laps	15
11	Jaime Alguersuari	Toro Rosso	Toro Rosso-Ferrari STR6	70 laps	13
12	Sebastien Buemi	Toro Rosso	Toro Rosso-Ferrari STR6	70 laps	14
13	Sergio Perez	Sauber	Sauber-Ferrari C30	70 laps	17
14	Rubens Barrichello	Williams	Williams-Cosworth FW33	70 laps	12
15	Michael Schumacher	Mercedes AMG	Mercedes MGP W02	70 laps	10
16	Heikki Kovalainen	Lotus Racing	Lotus-Renault T128	69 laps	19
17	Bruno Senna	Renault F1	Renault R31	69 laps	9
18	Jarno Trulli	Lotus Racing	Lotus-Renault T128	69 laps	20
19	Jerome d'Ambrosio	Virgin Racing	Virgin-Cosworth MVR-02	68 laps	23
20	Daniel Ricciardo	HRT	HRT-Cosworth F111	68 laps	22
R	Vitantonio Liuzzi	HRT	HRT-Cosworth F111	61 laps/alternator	21
R	Lewis Hamilton	McLaren	McLaren-Mercedes MP4-26	46 laps/gearbox	4
R	Pastor Maldonado	Williams	Williams-Cosworth FW33	26 laps/spun off	18
R	Timo Glock	Virgin Racing	Virgin-Cosworth MVR-02	21 laps/wheel	24

Pole: Vettel, 1m11.918s, 134.027mph/215.695kph. Fastest lap: Webber, 1m15.324s, 127.966mph/205.942kph on Lap 71. Race leaders: Vettel 1-16 & 21-29 & 38-39 & 59, Webber 17-18 & 30-37 & 40-58 & 60-71, Massa 19-20

NEW DRIVERS

Paul di Resta was the most successful of the year's five newcomers, racing to sixth in Singapore for Force India. Sergio Perez also went well, finishing seventh for Sauber at Silverstone, where Daniel Ricciardo kicked off with HRT. Pastor Maldonado controlled his raw speed at Williams and Jerome d'Ambrosio gave his all for Virgin.

CLASSIC CAR: RED BULL RB7

If Red Bull's success in 2010 was hard-won, life was easier for Sebastian Vettel in 2011 as he galloped clear of the field to make it two titles in a row. His mount, the Renault-powered Red Bull RB7 was produced by chief technical officer Adrian Newey, chief designer Rob Marshall and head of aerodynamics, Peter Prodromou. Its greatest strength was its speed in qualifying, taking pole for every race bar one. After 19 rounds, its tally was 12 wins, 11 to Vettel and one to Mark Webber at the final round. However, the margins often weren't huge, as the Pirelli tyres degraded more than in 2010.

WORLD DRIVERS' CHAMPIONSHIP FINAL RESULTS

Pos	Driver	Nat	Car-Engine	R1	R2	R3	R4	R5	R6	R7	R8
1	Sebastian Vettel	DEU	Red Bull-Renault RB7	1P	1P	2P	1P	1	1P	2P	1PF
2	Jenson Button	GBR	McLaren-Mercedes MP4-26	6	2	4	6	3	3	1F	6
3	Mark Webber	AUS	Red Bull-Renault RB7	5	4F	3F	2F	4P	4F	3	3
4	Fernando Alonso	ESP	Ferrari F150 Italia	4	6	7	3	5	2	R	2
5	Lewis Hamilton	GBR	McLaren-Mercedes MP4-26	2	8	1	4	2F	6	R	4
6	Felipe Massa	BRA	Ferrari F150 Italia	7F	5	6	11	R	R	6	5
7	Nico Rosberg	DEU	Mercedes MGP W02	R	12	5	5	7	11	11	7
8	Michael Schumacher	DEU	Mercedes MGP W02	R	9	8	12	6	R	4	17
9	Adrian Sutil	DEU	Force India-Mercedes VJM04	9	11	15	13	13	7	R	9
10	Vitaly Petrov	RUS	Renault R31	3	17	9	8	11	R	5	15
11	Nick Heidfeld	DEU	Renault R31	12	3	12	7	8	8	R	10
12	Kamui Kobayashi	JPN	Sauber-Ferrari C30	DQ	7	10	10	10	5	7	16
13	Paul di Resta	GBR	Force India-Mercedes VJM04	10	10	11	R	12	12	18	14
14	Jaime Alguersuari	ESP	Toro Rosso-Ferrari STR6	11	14	R	16	16	R	8	8
15	Sebastien Buemi	CHE	Toro Rosso-Ferrari STR6	8	13	14	9	14	10	10	13
16	Sergio Perez	MEX	Sauber-Ferrari C30	DQ	R	17	14	9	NS	NS	11
17	Rubens Barrichello	BRA	Williams-Cosworth FW33	R	R	13	15	17	9	9	12
18	Bruno Senna	BRA	Renault R31	-	-	-	-	-	-	-	-
19	Pastor Maldonado	VEN	Williams-Cosworth FW33	R	R	18	17	15	18	R	18
20	Pedro de la Rosa	ESP	Sauber-Ferrari C30	-	-	-	-	-	-	12	-
21	Jarno Trulli	ITA	Lotus-Renault T128	13	R	19	18	18	13	16	20
22	Heikki Kovalainen	FIN	Lotus-Renault T128	R	15	16	19	R	14	R	19
23	Vitantonio Liuzzi	ITA	HRT-Cosworth F111	DNQ	R	22	22	R	16	13	23
24	Jerome d'Ambrosio	BEL	Virgin-Cosworth MVR-02	14	R	20	20	20	15	14	22
25	Timo Glock	DEU	Virgin-Cosworth MVR-02	NC	16	21	NS	19	R	15	21
26	Narain Karthikeyan	IND	HRT-Cosworth F111	DNQ	R	23	21	21	17	17	24
27	Daniel Ricciardo	AUS	Toro Rosso-Ferrari STR6	T	T	T	T	T	T	T	T
			FRT-Cosworth F111	-	-	-	-	-	-	-	-
28	Karun Chandhok	IND	Lotus-Renault T128	T	-	-	T	-	-	-	T

Pos	Driver	R9	R10	R11	R12	R13	R14	R15	R16	R17	R18	R19	Total
1	Vettel	2	4	2P	1P	1P	1P	3P	1F	1PF	RP	2P	392
2	Button	R	R	1	3	2	2F	1F	4	2	3	3	270
3	Webber	3P	3P	5	2F	R	3	4	3	4	4F	1F	258
4	Alonso	1F	2	3	4	3	4	2	5	3	2	4	257
5	Hamilton	4	1F	4	R	4F	5	5	2P	7	1	R	227
6	Massa	5	5	6F	8	6	9	7	6	R	5	5	118
7	Rosberg	6	7	9	6	R	7	10	8	6	6	7	89
8	Schumacher	9	8	R	5	5	R	6	R	5	7	15	76
9	Sutil	11	6	14	7	R	8	11	11	9	8	6	42
10	Petrov	12	10	12	9	R	17	9	R	11	13	10	37
11	Heidfeld	8	R	R	-	-	-	-	-	-	-	-	34
12	Kobayashi	R	9	11	12	R	14	13	15	R	10	9	30
13	di Resta	15	13	7	11	8	6	12	10	13	9	8	27
14	Alguersuari	10	12	10	R	7	21	15	7	8	15	11	26
15	Buemi	R	15	8	R	10	12	R	9	R	R	12	15
16	Perez	7	11	15	R	R	10	8	16	10	11	13	14
17	Barrichello	13	R	13	16	12	13	17	12	15	12	14	4
18	Senna	-	-	T	13	9	15	16	13	12	16	17	2
19	Maldonado	14	14	16	10	11	11	14	R	R	14	R	1
20	de la Rosa	-	-	-	-	-	-	-	-	-	-	-	0
21	Trulli	R	-	R	14	14	R	19	17	19	18	18	0
22	Kovalainen	R	16	R	15	13	16	18	14	14	17	16	0
23	Liuzzi	18	R	20	19	R	20	23	21	-	20	R	0

Pos	Driver	R9	R10	R11	R12	R13	R14	R15	R16	R17	R18	R19	Total
24	d'Ambrosio	17	18	19	17	R	18	21	20	16	R	19	0
25	Glock	16	17	17	18	15	R	20	18	R	19	R	0
26	Karthikeyan	-	T	-	-	-	T	T	T	17	-	-	0
27	Ricciardo	-	-	-	-	-	-	-	-	-	-	-	0
		19	19	18	R	NC	19	22	19	18	R	20	
28	Chandhok	T	20	-	T	T	-	T	T	T	-	-	0

WORLD CONSTRUCTORS' CHAMPIONSHIP FINAL RESULTS

Pos	Team-Engine	R1	R2	R3	R4	R5	R6	R7	R8	R9	R10
1	Red Bull-Renault	1/5	1/4	2/3	1/2	1/4	1/4	2/3	1/3	2/3	3/4
2	McLaren-Mercedes	2/6	2/8	1/4	4/6	2/3	3/6	R/1	4/6	R/4	R/1
3	Ferrari	4/7	5/6	6/7	3/11	R/5	R/2	R/6	2/5	1/5	2/5
4	Mercedes AMG	R/R	9/12	5/8	5/12	6/7	R/11	4/11	7/17	6/9	7/8
5	Renault F1	3/12	3/17	9/12	7/8	8/11	R/8	R/5	10/15	8/12	R/10
6	Force India-Mercedes	9/10	10/11	11/15	13/R	12/13	7/12	R/18	9/14	11/15	6/13
7	Sauber-Ferrari	DQ/DQ	R/7	10/17	10/14	9/10	5	7/12	11/16	R/7	9/11
8	Toro Rosso-Ferrari	8/11	13/14	R/14	9/16	14/16	R/10	8/10	8/13	R/10	12/15
9	Williams-Cosworth	R/R	R/R	13/18	15/17	15/17	9/18	R/9	12/18	13/14	R/14
10	Lotus-Renault	R/13	R/15	16/19	18/19	R/18	13/14	R/16	19/20	R/R	16/20
11	HRT-Cosworth	DNQ/DNQ	R/R	22/23	21/22	R/21	16/17	13/17	23/24	18/19	R/19
12	Virgin-Cosworth	14/NC	R/16	20/21	20/NS	19/20	R/15	14/15	21/22	16/17	17/18

Pos	Team-Engine	R11	R12	R13	R14	R15	R16	R17	R18	R19	Total
1	Red Bull-Renault	2/5	1/2	R/1	1/3	3/4	1/3	1/4	R/4	1/2	650
2	McLaren-Mercedes	1/4	R/3	2/4	2/5	1/5	2/4	2/7	1/3	R/3	497
3	Ferrari	3/6	4/8	3/6	4/9	2/7	5/6	R/3	2/5	4/5	375
4	Mercedes AMG	R/9	5/6	R/5	R/7	6/10	R/8	5/6	6/7	7/15	165
5	Renault F1	R/12	9/13	R/9	15/17	9/16	R/13	11/12	13/16	10/17	73
6	Force India-Mercedes	7/14	7/11	R/8	6/8	11/12	10/11	9/13	8/9	6/8	69
7	Sauber-Ferrari	11/15	R/12	R/R	10/14	8/13	15/16	R/10	10/11	9/13	44
8	Toro Rosso-Ferrari	8/10	R/R	7/10	12/21	R/15	7/9	R/8	R/15	11/12	41
9	Williams-Cosworth	13/16	10/16	11/12	11/13	14/17	R/12	R/15	12/14	R/14	5
10	Lotus-Renault	R/R	14/15	13/14	R/16	18/19	14/17	14/19	17/18	16/18	0
11	HRT-Cosworth	18/20	R/19	R/NC	19/20	22/23	19/21	17/18	R/20	R/20	0
12	Virgin-Cosworth	17/19	17/18	R/15	R/18	20/21	18/20	R/16	R/19	R/19	0

SYMBOLS AND GRAND PRIX KEY

Round 1 Australian GP
Round 2 Malaysian GP
Round 3 Chinese GP
Round 4 Turkish GP
Round 5 Spanish GP
Round 6 Monaco GP
Round 7 Canadian GP
Round 8 European GP
Round 9 British GP
Round 10 German GP
Round 11 Hungarian GP
Round 12 Belgian GP
Round 13 Italian GP
Round 14 Singapore GP
Round 15 Japanese GP
Round 16 Korean GP
Round 17 Indian GP
Round 18 Abu Dhabi GP
Round 19 Brazilian GP

SCORING

1st 25 points
2nd 18 points
3rd 15 points
4th 12 points
5th 10 points
6th 8 points
7th 6 points
8th 4 points
9th 2 points
10th 1 point

DNPQ DID NOT PRE-QUALIFY **DNQ** DID NOT QUALIFY **DQ** DISQUALIFIED **EX** EXCLUDED
F FASTEST LAP **NC** NOT CLASSIFIED **NS** NON-STARTER **P** POLE POSITION **R** RETIRED

SEASON SUMMARY

Eight drivers won grands prix in 2012 and the title race took a while to settle down but, from mid-season, was only ever between two of them. Red Bull Racing's Sebastian Vettel had to fight hard to resist Fernando Alonso's Ferrari challenge to make it three in a row. In landing the title, Vettel became only the third driver to win three consecutive titles along with Juan Manuel Fangio and Michael Schumacher. The early races had the teams struggling to get to grips with the latest Pirelli tyres and it was noticeable how McLaren hit the best form of all at the final two rounds.

AUSTRALIAN GRAND PRIX

ALBERT PARK • ROUND 1 • DATE: 18TH MARCH 2012
Laps: 58 • Distance: 191.117miles/307.574km • Weather: Warm & bright

Pos	Driver	Team	Chassis-Engine	Result	Qual
1	Jenson Button	McLaren	McLaren-Mercedes MP4-27	1h34m09.565s	2
2	Sebastian Vettel	Red Bull Racing	Red Bull-Renault RB8	1h34m11.704s	6
3	Lewis Hamilton	McLaren	McLaren-Mercedes MP4-27	1h34m13.640s	1
4	Mark Webber	Red Bull Racing	Red Bull-Renault RB8	1h34m14.112s	5
5	Fernando Alonso	Ferrari	Ferrari F2012	1h34m31.130s	12
6	Kamui Kobayashi	Sauber	Sauber-Ferrari C31	1h34m46.331s	13
7	Kimi Raikkonen	Lotus F1	Lotus-Renault E20	1h34m47.579s	17
8	Sergio Perez *	Sauber	Sauber-Ferrari C31	1h34m49.023s	22
9	Daniel Ricciardo	Toro Rosso	Toro Rosso-Ferrari STR7	1h34m49.121s	10
10	Paul di Resta	Force India	Force India-Mercedes VJM05	1h34m49.302s	15
11	Jean-Eric Vergne	Toro Rosso	Toro Rosso-Ferrari STR7	1h34m49.413s	11
12	Nico Rosberg	Mercedes AMG	Mercedes F1 W03	1h35m07.207s	7
13	Pastor Maldonado	Williams	Williams-Renault FW34	57 laps/spun off	8
14	Timo Glock	Marussia	Marussia-Cosworth MR01	57 laps	20
15	Charles Pic	Marussia	Marussia-Cosworth MR01	53 laps/fuel pressure	21
16	Bruno Senna	Williams	Williams-Renault FW34	52 laps/collision	14
R	Felipe Massa	Ferrari	Ferrari F2012	46 laps/collision	16
R	Heikki Kovalainen	Caterham	Caterham-Renault CT01	38 laps/suspension	18
R	Vitaly Petrov	Caterham	Caterham-Renault CT01	34 laps/steering	19
R	Michael Schumacher	Mercedes AMG	Mercedes F1 W03	10 laps/gearbox	4
R	Romain Grosjean	Lotus F1	Lotus-Renault E20	1 laps/collision	3
R	Nico Hulkenberg	Force India	Force India-Mercedes VJM05	0 laps/collision	9
DNQ	Narain Karthikeyan	HRT	HRT-Cosworth F112	-	24
DNQ	Pedro de la Rosa	HRT	HRT-Cosworth F112	-	23

Pole: Hamilton, 1m24.922s, 139.686mph/224.803kph. Fastest lap: Button, 1m29.187s, 133.006mph/214.053kph on Lap 56. Race leaders: Button 1-15 & 17-35 & 37-58, Hamilton 16, Vettel 36

* 5-place grid penalty for gearbox change

THIRD TIME LUCKY

In the team's third year since taking over Brawn GP, Nico Rosberg gave Mercedes its first win. His victory in the Chinese GP came as a surprise, as they had taken only a 10th place in the first two races. However, Mercedes filled the front row in Shanghai and Rosberg survived a challenge by McLaren's Jenson Button to triumph.

MALAYSIAN GRAND PRIX

SEPANG • ROUND 2 • DATE: 25TH MARCH 2012
Laps: 56 • Distance: 192.878miles/310.408km • Weather: Hot & damp, wet later

Pos	Driver	Team	Chassis-Engine	Result	Qual
1	Fernando Alonso	Ferrari	Ferrari F2012	2h44m51.812s	8
2	Sergio Perez	Sauber	Sauber-Ferrari C31	2h44m54.075s	9
3	Lewis Hamilton	McLaren	McLaren-Mercedes MP4-27	2h45m06.403s	1
4	Mark Webber	Red Bull Racing	Red Bull-Renault RB8	2h45m09.500s	4
5	Kimi Raikkonen *	Lotus F1	Lotus-Renault E20	2h45m21.268s	10
6	Bruno Senna	Williams	Williams-Renault FW34	2h45m29.479s	13
7	Paul di Resta	Force India	Force India-Mercedes VJM05	2h45m36.224s	14
8	Jean-Eric Vergne	Toro Rosso	Toro Rosso-Ferrari STR7	2h45m38.797s	18
9	Nico Hulkenberg	Force India	Force India-Mercedes VJM05	2h45m39.704s	16
10	Michael Schumacher	Mercedes AMG	Mercedes F1 W03	2h45m41.808s	3
11	Sebastian Vettel	Red Bull Racing	Red Bull-Renault RB8	2h46m07.339s	5
12	Daniel Ricciardo	Toro Rosso	Toro Rosso-Ferrari STR7	2h46m08.640s	15
13	Nico Rosberg	Mercedes AMG	Mercedes F1 W03	2h46m10.405s	7
14	Jenson Button	McLaren	McLaren-Mercedes MP4-27	2h46m11.531s	2
15	Felipe Massa	Ferrari	Ferrari F2012	2h46m29.131s	12
16	Vitaly Petrov	Caterham	Caterham-Renault CT01	55 laps	19
17	Timo Glock	Marussia	Marussia-Cosworth MR01	55 laps	20
18	Heikki Kovalainen !	Caterham	Caterham-Renault CT01	55 laps	24
19	Pastor Maldonado	Williams	Williams-Renault FW34	54 laps/engine	11
20	Charles Pic	Marussia	Marussia-Cosworth MR01	54 laps	21
21	Pedro de la Rosa	HRT	HRT-Cosworth F112	54 laps	22
22	Narain Karthikeyan ^	HRT	HRT-Cosworth F112	54 laps	23
R	Kamui Kobayashi	Sauber	Sauber-Ferrari C31	46 laps/brakes	17
R	Romain Grosjean	Lotus F1	Lotus-Renault E20	3 laps/spun off	6

Pole: Hamilton, 1m36.219s, 128.865mph/207.389kph. Fastest lap: Raikkonen, 1m40.722s, 123.104mph/198.117kph on Lap 53. Race leaders: Hamilton 1-13, Perez 14-15 & 40-41, Alonso 16-39 & 42-56

* 5-place grid penalty for gearbox change • ! 5-place penalty for overtaking in unsafe conditions at Australian GP • ^ 20s penalty for causing an avoidable accident

CHINESE GRAND PRIX

SHANGHAI INTERNATIONAL CIRCUIT • ROUND 3 • DATE: 15TH APRIL 2012
Laps: 56 • Distance: 189.677miles/305.256km • Weather: Warm but dull

Pos	Driver	Team	Chassis-Engine	Result	Qual
1	Nico Rosberg	Mercedes AMG	Mercedes F1 W03	1h36m26.929s	1
2	Jenson Button	McLaren	McLaren-Mercedes MP4-27	1h36m47.555s	5
3	Lewis Hamilton *	McLaren	McLaren-Mercedes MP4-27	1h36m52.941s	7
4	Mark Webber	Red Bull Racing	Red Bull-Renault RB8	1h36m54.853s	6
5	Sebastian Vettel	Red Bull Racing	Red Bull-Renault RB8	1h36m57.412s	11
6	Romain Grosjean	Lotus F1	Lotus-Renault E20	1h36m58.420s	10
7	Bruno Senna	Williams	Williams-Renault FW34	1h37m01.526s	14
8	Pastor Maldonado	Williams	Williams-Renault FW34	1h37m02.572s	13
9	Fernando Alonso	Ferrari	Ferrari F2012	1h37m04.185s	9
10	Kamui Kobayashi	Sauber	Sauber-Ferrari C31	1h37m05.649s	3
11	Sergio Perez	Sauber	Sauber-Ferrari C31	1h37m07.995s	8
12	Paul di Resta	Force India	Force India-Mercedes VJM05	1h37m09.202s	15
13	Felipe Massa	Ferrari	Ferrari F2012	1h37m09.708s	12

Pos	Driver	Team	Chassis-Engine	Result	Qual
14	Kimi Raikkonen	Lotus F1	Lotus-Renault E20	1h37m17.502s	4
15	Nico Hulkenberg	Force India	Force India-Mercedes VJM05	1h37m18.142s	16
16	Jean-Eric Vergne!	Toro Rosso	Toro Rosso-Ferrari STR7	1h37m18.685s	24
17	Daniel Ricciardo	Toro Rosso	Toro Rosso-Ferrari STR7	1h37m30.085s	17
18	Vitaly Petrov	Caterham	Caterham-Renault CT01	55 laps	19
19	Timo Glock	Marussia	Marussia-Cosworth MR01	55 laps	20
20	Charles Pic	Marussia	Marussia-Cosworth MR01	55 laps	21
21	Pedro de la Rosa	HRT	HRT-Cosworth F112	55 laps	22
22	Narain Karthikeyan	HRT	HRT-Cosworth F112	54 laps	23
23	Heikki Kovalainen	Caterham	Caterham-Renault CT01	53 laps	18
R	Michael Schumacher	Mercedes AMG	Mercedes F1 W03	12 laps/wheel	2

Pole: Rosberg, 1m35.121s, 128.189mph/206.301kph. Fastest lap: Kobayashi, 1m39.960s, 121.984mph/196.314kph on Lap 40. Race leaders: Rosberg 1-13 & 17-34 & 40-56, Perez 14-16, Button 35-39

* 5-place grid penalty for gearbox change • ! Required to start from pit lane for modifying car under parc ferme conditions

THREE NEW LIVERIES

It looked as though there were three new teams on the grid in 2012, but these were rebrands. The Renault F1 team from Enstone became the Lotus F1 Team, while Tony Fernandes' team that had been racing as Lotus in 2011 had to be renamed as Caterham. Virgin Racing came back as Marussia, also moving away from its original Sheffield base to Banbury.

BAHRAIN GRAND PRIX

SAKHIR • ROUND 4 • DATE: 22ND APRIL 2012

Laps: 57 • Distance: 191.683miles/308.484km • Weather: Hot but dull

Pos	Driver	Team	Chassis-Engine	Result	Qual
1	Sebastian Vettel	Red Bull Racing	Red Bull-Renault RB8	1h35m10.990s	1
2	Kimi Raikkonen	Lotus F1	Lotus-Renault E20	1h35m14.323s	11
3	Romain Grosjean	Lotus F1	Lotus-Renault E20	1h35m21.184s	7
4	Mark Webber	Red Bull Racing	Red Bull-Renault RB8	1h35m49.778s	3
5	Nico Rosberg	Mercedes AMG	Mercedes F1 W03	1h36m06.450s	5
6	Paul di Resta	Force India	Force India-Mercedes VJM05	1h36m08.533s	10
7	Fernando Alonso	Ferrari	Ferrari F2012	1h36m08.793s	9
8	Lewis Hamilton	McLaren	McLaren-Mercedes MP4-27	1h36m09.974s	2
9	Felipe Massa	Ferrari	Ferrari F2012	1h36m15.989s	14
10	Michael Schumacher *	Mercedes AMG	Mercedes F1 W03	1h36m22.480s	22
11	Sergio Perez	Sauber	Sauber-Ferrari C31	1h36m23.692s	8
12	Nico Hulkenberg	Force India	Force India-Mercedes VJM05	1h36m27.529s	13
13	Kamui Kobayashi	Sauber	Sauber-Ferrari C31	1h36m41.324s	12
14	Jean-Eric Vergne	Toro Rosso	Toro Rosso-Ferrari STR7	1h36m44.713s	17
15	Daniel Ricciardo	Toro Rosso	Toro Rosso-Ferrari STR7	56 laps	6
16	Vitaly Petrov	Caterham	Caterham-Renault CT01	56 laps	18
17	Heikki Kovalainen	Caterham	Caterham-Renault CT01	56 laps	16
18	Jenson Button	McLaren	McLaren-Mercedes MP4-27	55 laps/differential	4
19	Timo Glock	Marussia	Marussia-Cosworth MR01	55 laps	23
20	Pedro de la Rosa	HRT	HRT-Cosworth F112	55 laps	20

Pos	Driver	Team	Chassis-Engine	Result	Qual
21	Narain Karthikeyan	HRT	HRT-Cosworth F112	55 laps	24
22	Bruno Senna	Williams	Williams-Renault FW34	54 laps/handling	15
R	Pastor Maldonado *	Williams	Williams-Renault FW34	25 laps/puncture	21
R	Charles Pic	Marussia	Marussia-Cosworth MR01	24 laps/engine	19

Pole: Vettel, 1m32.422s, 130.989mph/210.806kph. Fastest lap: Vettel, 1m36.379s, 125.611mph/202.151kph on Lap 41. Race leaders: Vettel 1-11 & 13-39 & 41-57, di Resta 12, Grosjean 40

* 5-place grid penalty for gearbox change

OUT OF THE BLUE

After only managing points for an eighth place in the first four rounds, Pastor Maldonado scored a shock result for Williams when he won the Spanish GP. The Venezuelan stuck his Renault-engined FW34 on pole and, unusually, didn't make a single mistake as his speed took him to victory from Alonso's Ferrari by 3s. The benefits were huge for the team's survival.

SPANISH GRAND PRIX

BARCELONA-CATALUNYA • ROUND 5 • DATE: 13TH MAY 2012
Laps: 66 • Distance: 190.775miles/307.23km • Weather: Hot & bright

Pos	Driver	Team	Chassis-Engine	Result	Qual
1	Pastor Maldonado	Williams	Williams-Renault FW34	1h39m09.145s	1
2	Fernando Alonso	Ferrari	Ferrari F2012	1h39m12.340s	2
3	Kimi Raikkonen	Lotus F1	Lotus-Renault E20	1h39m13.029s	4
4	Romain Grosjean	Lotus F1	Lotus-Renault E20	1h39m23.944s	3
5	Kamui Kobayashi	Sauber	Sauber-Ferrari C31	1h40m13.786s	9
6	Sebastian Vettel	Red Bull Racing	Red Bull-Renault RB8	1h40m16.721s	7
7	Nico Rosberg	Mercedes AMG	Mercedes F1 W03	1h40m27.064s	6
8	Lewis Hamilton *	McLaren	McLaren-Mercedes MP4-27	1h40m27.285s	24
9	Jenson Button	McLaren	McLaren-Mercedes MP4-27	1h40m34.391s	10
10	Nico Hulkenberg	Force India	Force India-Mercedes VJM05	65 laps	13
11	Mark Webber	Red Bull Racing	Red Bull-Renault RB8	65 laps	11
12	Jean-Eric Vergne	Toro Rosso	Toro Rosso-Ferrari STR7	65 laps	14
13	Daniel Ricciardo	Toro Rosso	Toro Rosso-Ferrari STR7	65 laps	15
14	Paul di Resta	Force India	Force India-Mercedes VJM05	65 laps	12
15	Felipe Massa	Ferrari	Ferrari F2012	65 laps	16
16	Heikki Kovalainen	Caterham	Caterham-Renault CT01	65 laps	19
17	Vitaly Petrov	Caterham	Caterham-Renault CT01	65 laps	18
18	Timo Glock	Marussia	Marussia-Cosworth MR01	64 laps	21
19	Pedro de la Rosa	HRT	HRT-Cosworth F112	63 laps	22
R	Sergio Perez	Sauber	Sauber-Ferrari C31	37 laps/transmission	5
R	Charles Pic	Marussia	Marussia-Cosworth MR01	35 laps/halfshaft	20
R	Narain Karthikeyan	HRT	HRT-Cosworth F112	22 laps/wheel	23
R	Michael Schumacher	Mercedes AMG	Mercedes F1 W03	12 laps/collision	8
R	Bruno Senna	Williams	Williams-Renault FW34	12 laps/collision	17

Pole: Maldonado, 1m22.285s, 126.547mph/203.658kph. Fastest lap: Grosjean, 1m26.250s, 120.729mph/194.295kph on Lap 53. Race leaders: Alonso 1-9 & 12-26 & 42-44, Maldonado 10-11 & 27-41 & 47-66, Raikkonen 45-46

* excluded from qualifying for not having enough fuel for a sample

MONACO GRAND PRIX

MONTE CARLO • ROUND 6 • DATE: 27TH MAY 2012
Laps: 78 • Distance: 161.588miles/260.52km • Weather: Warm but dull, damp later

Pos	Driver	Team	Chassis-Engine	Result	Qual
1	Mark Webber	Red Bull Racing	Red Bull-Renault RB8	1h46m06.557s	1
2	Nico Rosberg	Mercedes AMG	Mercedes F1 W03	1h46m07.200s	2
3	Fernando Alonso	Ferrari	Ferrari F2012	1h46m07.504s	5
4	Sebastian Vettel	Red Bull Racing	Red Bull-Renault RB8	1h46m07.900s	9
5	Lewis Hamilton	McLaren	McLaren-Mercedes MP4-27	1h46m10.658s	3
6	Felipe Massa	Ferrari	Ferrari F2012	1h46m12.752s	7
7	Paul di Resta	Force India	Force India-Mercedes VJM05	1h46m48.094s	14
8	Nico Hulkenberg	Force India	Force India-Mercedes VJM05	1h46m49.119s	10
9	Kimi Raikkonen	Lotus F1	Lotus-Renault E20	1h46m50.593s	8
10	Bruno Senna	Williams	Williams-Renault FW34	1h46m51.073s	13
11	Sergio Perez !	Sauber	Sauber-Ferrari C31	77 laps	23
12	Jean-Eric Vergne	Toro Rosso	Toro Rosso-Ferrari STR7	77 laps	16
13	Heikki Kovalainen	Caterham	Caterham-Renault CT01	77 laps	17
14	Timo Glock	Marussia	Marussia-Cosworth MR01	77 laps	19
15	Narain Karthikeyan	HRT	HRT-Cosworth F112	76 laps	22
16	Jenson Button	McLaren	McLaren-Mercedes MP4-27	70 laps/puncture	12
R	Daniel Ricciardo	Toro Rosso	Toro Rosso-Ferrari STR7	65 laps/steering	15
R	Charles Pic	Marussia	Marussia-Cosworth MR01	64 laps/electrical	21
R	Michael Schumacher *	Mercedes AMG	Mercedes F1 W03	63 laps/fuel pressure	6
R	Vitaly Petrov	Caterham	Caterham-Renault CT01	15 laps/electrical	18
R	Kamui Kobayashi	Sauber	Sauber-Ferrari C31	5 laps/collision	11
R	Romain Grosjean	Lotus F1	Lotus-Renault E20	0 laps/collision	4
R	Pedro de la Rosa	HRT	HRT-Cosworth F112	0 laps/collision	20
R	Pastor Maldonado !/^	Williams	Williams-Renault FW34	0 laps/collision	24

Pole: Webber, 1m14.381s, 100.447mph/161.654kph. Fastest lap: Perez, 1m17.296s, 96.659mph/155.557kph on Lap 49. Race leaders: Webber 1-28 & 46-78, Alonso 29, Massa 30, Vettel 31-45

* 5-place grid penalty for causing crash in Spanish GP • ! 5-place grid penalty for gearbox change • ^ 10-place grid penalty for causing collision

CANADIAN GRAND PRIX

MONTREAL • ROUND 7 • DATE: 10TH JUNE 2012
Laps: 70 • Distance: 189.534miles/305.27km • Weather: Hot & bright

Pos	Driver	Team	Chassis-Engine	Result	Qual
1	Lewis Hamilton	McLaren	McLaren-Mercedes MP4-27	1h32m29.586s	2
2	Romain Grosjean	Lotus F1	Lotus-Renault E20	1h32m32.099s	7
3	Sergio Perez	Sauber	Sauber-Ferrari C31	1h32m34.846s	15
4	Sebastian Vettel	Red Bull Racing	Red Bull-Renault RB8	1h32m36.881s	1
5	Fernando Alonso	Ferrari	Ferrari F2012	1h32m42.997s	3
6	Nico Rosberg	Mercedes AMG	Mercedes F1 W03	1h32m43.428s	5
7	Mark Webber	Red Bull Racing	Red Bull-Renault RB8	1h32m44.671s	4
8	Kimi Raikkonen	Lotus F1	Lotus-Renault E20	1h32m45.153s	12
9	Kamui Kobayashi	Sauber	Sauber-Ferrari C31	1h32m54.018s	11
10	Felipe Massa	Ferrari	Ferrari F2012	1h32m54.858s	6
11	Paul di Resta	Force India	Force India-Mercedes VJM05	1h33m07.279s	8
12	Nico Hulkenberg	Force India	Force India-Mercedes VJM05	1h33m15.822s	13
13	Pastor Maldonado *	Williams	Williams-Renault FW34	1h33m16.638s	22
14	Daniel Ricciardo	Toro Rosso	Toro Rosso-Ferrari STR7	1h33m34.061s	14

Pos	Driver	Team	Chassis-Engine	Result	Qual
15	Jean-Eric Vergne	Toro Rosso	Toro Rosso-Ferrari STR7	69 laps	19
16	Jenson Button	McLaren	McLaren-Mercedes MP4-27	69 laps	10
17	Bruno Senna	Williams	Williams-Renault FW34	69 laps	16
18	Heikki Kovalainen	Caterham	Caterham-Renault CT01	69 laps	17
19	Vitaly Petrov	Caterham	Caterham-Renault CT01	69 laps	18
20	Charles Pic	Marussia	Marussia-Cosworth MR01	67 laps	23
R	Timo Glock	Marussia	Marussia-Cosworth MR01	56 laps/brakes	21
R	Michael Schumacher	Mercedes AMG	Mercedes F1 W03	43 laps/hydraulics	9
R	Pedro de la Rosa	HRT	HRT-Cosworth F112	24 laps/brakes	20
R	Narain Karthikeyan	HRT	HRT-Cosworth F112	22 laps/brakes	24

Pole: Vettel, 1m13.784s, 132.214mph/212.777kph. Fastest lap: Vettel, 1m15.752s, 128.779mph/207.249kph on Lap 70. Race leaders: Vettel 1-15, Hamilton 16 & 21-49 & 64-70, Alonso 17-19 & 50-63, Grosjean 20

* 5-place grid penalty for gearbox change

RAIKKONEN RETURNS

Kimi Raikkonen loved racing but never liked the rest of F1, especially speaking to the press. So, he took two years out before returning with Lotus F1 Team after a sabbatical spent in the less PR-busy World Rally Championship and even in NASCAR. Not only did he win in Abu Dhabi on his return, but he scored consistently enough to rank third at year's end.

EUROPEAN GRAND PRIX

VALENCIA STREET CIRCUIT • ROUND 8 • DATE: 24TH JUNE 2012
Laps: 57 • Distance: 191.931miles/308.883km • Weather: Hot & bright

Pos	Driver	Team	Chassis-Engine	Result	Qual
1	Fernando Alonso	Ferrari	Ferrari F2012	1h44m16.649s	11
2	Kimi Raikkonen	Lotus F1	Lotus-Renault E20	1h44m23.070s	5
3	Michael Schumacher	Mercedes AMG	Mercedes F1 W03	1h44m29.288s	12
4	Mark Webber	Red Bull Racing	Red Bull-Renault RB8	1h44m30.277s	19
5	Nico Hulkenberg	Force India	Force India-Mercedes VJM05	1h44m36.642s	8
6	Nico Rosberg	Mercedes AMG	Mercedes F1 W03	1h44m37.825s	6
7	Paul di Resta	Force India	Force India-Mercedes VJM05	1h44m39.515s	10
8	Jenson Button	McLaren	McLaren-Mercedes MP4-27	1h44m41.302s	9
9	Sergio Perez	Sauber	Sauber-Ferrari C31	1h44m44.426s	15
10	Bruno Senna	Williams	Williams-Renault FW34	1h44m52.610s	14
11	Daniel Ricciardo	Toro Rosso	Toro Rosso-Ferrari STR7	1h44m53.690s	17
12	Pastor Maldonado *	Williams	Williams-Renault FW34	1h45m11.279s	3
13	Vitaly Petrov	Caterham	Caterham-Renault CT01	1h45m32.520s	20
14	Heikki Kovalainen	Caterham	Caterham-Renault CT01	1h45m51.303s	16
15	Charles Pic	Marussia	Marussia-Cosworth MR01	1h45m53.200s	23
16	Felipe Massa	Ferrari	Ferrari F2012	56 laps	13
17	Pedro de la Rosa	HRT	HRT-Cosworth F112	56 laps	21
18	Narain Karthikeyan	HRT	HRT-Cosworth F112	56 laps	22
19	Lewis Hamilton	McLaren	McLaren-Mercedes MP4-27	55 laps/collision	2
R	Romain Grosjean	Lotus F1	Lotus-Renault E20	40 laps/alternator	4
R	Sebastian Vettel	Red Bull Racing	Red Bull-Renault RB8	33 laps/alternator	1
R	Kamui Kobayashi	Sauber	Sauber-Ferrari C31	33 laps/collision	7

Pos	Driver	Team	Chassis-Engine	Result	Qual
R	Jean-Eric Vergne	Toro Rosso	Toro Rosso-Ferrari STR7	26 laps/collision	18
NS	Timo Glock	Marussia	Marussia-Cosworth MR01	driver unwell	20

Pole: Vettel, 1m38.086s, 123.584mph/198.890kph. Fastest lap: Rosberg, 1m42.163s, 118.653mph/190.953kph on Lap 54. Race leaders: Vettel 1-33, Alonso 34-57

* 20s penalty for causing a collision

FIGHTING OVER SCRAPS

Teams fighting at the top of F1 are fighting for wins. For those at the rear, it's about fighting for survival, knowing that just one place gained, even outside the top 10, could make a difference of millions in end-of-season prize money. This is why Caterham celebrated at the Yas Marina finale as Vitaly Petrov's 11th place moved it ahead of Marussia.

BRITISH GRAND PRIX

SILVERSTONE • ROUND 9 • DATE: 8TH JULY 2012
Laps: 52 • Distance: 190.345miles/306.332km • Weather: Warm & bright

Pos	Driver	Team	Chassis-Engine	Result	Qual
1	Mark Webber	Red Bull Racing	Red Bull-Renault RB8	1h25m11.288s	2
2	Fernando Alonso	Ferrari	Ferrari F2012	1h25m14.348s	1
3	Sebastian Vettel	Red Bull Racing	Red Bull-Renault RB8	1h25m16.124s	4
4	Felipe Massa	Ferrari	Ferrari F2012	1h25m20.807s	5
5	Kimi Raikkonen	Lotus F1	Lotus-Renault E20	1h25m21.602s	6
6	Romain Grosjean	Lotus F1	Lotus-Renault E20	1h25m28.389s	9
7	Michael Schumacher	Mercedes AMG	Mercedes F1 W03	1h25m40.441s	3
8	Lewis Hamilton	McLaren	McLaren-Mercedes MP4-27	1h25m47.751s	8
9	Bruno Senna	Williams	Williams-Renault FW34	1h25m54.635s	13
10	Jenson Button	McLaren	McLaren-Mercedes MP4-27	1h25m55.732s	16
11	Kamui Kobayashi !	Sauber	Sauber-Ferrari C31	1h25m56.658s	17
12	Nico Hulkenberg *	Force India	Force India-Mercedes VJM05	1h25m59.144s	14
13	Daniel Ricciardo	Toro Rosso	Toro Rosso-Ferrari STR7	1h26m02.529s	12
14	Jean-Eric Vergne ^	Toro Rosso	Toro Rosso-Ferrari STR7	1h26m04.601s	23
15	Nico Rosberg	Mercedes AMG	Mercedes F1 W03	1h26m08.682s	11
16	Pastor Maldonado	Williams	Williams-Renault FW34	51 laps	7
17	Heikki Kovalainen	Caterham	Caterham-Renault CT01	51 laps	19
18	Timo Glock	Marussia	Marussia-Cosworth MR01	51 laps	20
19	Charles Pic *	Marussia	Marussia-Cosworth MR01	51 laps	24
20	Pedro de la Rosa	HRT	HRT-Cosworth F112	50 laps	21
21	Narain Karthikeyan	HRT	HRT-Cosworth F112	50 laps	22
R	Sergio Perez	Sauber	Sauber-Ferrari C31	11 laps/collision	15
R	Paul di Resta	Force India	Force India-Mercedes VJM05	2 laps/collision	10
NS	Vitaly Petrov	Caterham	Caterham-Renault CT01	engine	18

Pole: Alonso, 1m51.746s, 117.926mph/189.783kph. Fastest lap: Raikkonen, 1m34.661s, 139.210mph/224.037kph on Lap 50. Race leaders: Alonso 1-15 & 19-47, Hamilton 16-18, Webber 48-52

* 5-place grid penalty for gearbox change • ! 5-place grid penalty for causing crash in European GP • ^ 10-place grid penalty for causing crash in European GP

GERMAN GRAND PRIX

HOCKENHEIM • ROUND 10 • DATE: 22ND JULY 2012
Laps: 67 • Distance: 190.424miles/306.458km • Weather: Warm & bright

Pos	Driver	Team	Chassis-Engine	Result	Qual
1	Fernando Alonso	Ferrari	Ferrari F2012	1h31m05.862s	1
2	Jenson Button	McLaren	McLaren-Mercedes MP4-27	1h31m12.793s	6
3	Kimi Raikkonen	Lotus F1	Lotus-Renault E20	1h31m22.271s	10
4	Kamui Kobayashi	Sauber	Sauber-Ferrari C31	1h31m27.787s	12
5	Sebastian Vettel ^	Red Bull Racing	Red Bull-Renault RB8	1h31m29.594s	2
6	Sergio Perez !	Sauber	Sauber-Ferrari C31	1h31m33.758s	17
7	Michael Schumacher	Mercedes AMG	Mercedes F1 W03	1h31m34.832s	3
8	Mark Webber *	Red Bull Racing	Red Bull-Renault RB8	1h31m52.803s	8
9	Nico Hulkenberg	Force India	Force India-Mercedes VJM05	1h31m54.024s	4
10	Nico Rosberg *	Mercedes AMG	Mercedes F1 W03	1h31m54.751s	21
11	Paul di Resta	Force India	Force India-Mercedes VJM05	1h32m05.089s	9
12	Felipe Massa	Ferrari	Ferrari F2012	1h32m17.290s	13
13	Daniel Ricciardo	Toro Rosso	Toro Rosso-Ferrari STR7	1h32m22.691s	11
14	Jean-Eric Vergne	Toro Rosso	Toro Rosso-Ferrari STR7	1h32m22.827s	15
15	Pastor Maldonado	Williams	Williams-Renault FW34	66 laps	5
16	Vitaly Petrov	Caterham	Caterham-Renault CT01	66 laps	18
17	Bruno Senna	Williams	Williams-Renault FW34	66 laps	14
18	Romain Grosjean *	Lotus F1	Lotus-Renault E20	66 laps	19
19	Heikki Kovalainen	Caterham	Caterham-Renault CT01	65 laps	16
20	Charles Pic	Marussia	Marussia-Cosworth MR01	65 laps	20
21	Pedro de la Rosa	HRT	HRT-Cosworth F112	64 laps	23
22	Timo Glock	Marussia	Marussia-Cosworth MR01	64 laps	22
23	Narain Karthikeyan	HRT	HRT-Cosworth F112	64 laps	24
R	Lewis Hamilton	McLaren	McLaren-Mercedes MP4-27	56 laps/puncture	7

Pole: Alonso, 1m40.621s, 101.685mph/163.647kph. Fastest lap: Schumacher, 1m18.725s, 129.968mph/209.163kph on Lap 57. Race leaders: Alonso 1-17 & 21-67, Vettel 18-20

* 5-place grid penalty for gearbox change • ! 5-place grid penalty for impeding • ^ 20s penalty for gaining an advantage by leaving the track

HUNGARIAN GRAND PRIX

HUNGARORING • ROUND 11 • DATE: 29TH JULY 2012
Laps: 69 • Distance: 187.833miles/302.289km • Weather: Hot & bright

Pos	Driver	Team	Chassis-Engine	Result	Qual
1	Lewis Hamilton	McLaren	McLaren-Mercedes MP4-27	1h41m05.503s	1
2	Kimi Raikkonen	Lotus F1	Lotus-Renault E20	1h41m06.535s	5
3	Romain Grosjean	Lotus F1	Lotus-Renault E20	1h41m16.021s	2
4	Sebastian Vettel	Red Bull Racing	Red Bull-Renault RB8	1h41m17.117s	3
5	Fernando Alonso	Ferrari	Ferrari F2012	1h41m32.156s	6
6	Jenson Button	McLaren	McLaren-Mercedes MP4-27	1h41m35.746s	4
7	Bruno Senna	Williams	Williams-Renault FW34	1h41m39.402s	9
8	Mark Webber	Red Bull Racing	Red Bull-Renault RB8	1h41m39.961s	11
9	Felipe Massa	Ferrari	Ferrari F2012	1h41m43.853s	7
10	Nico Rosberg	Mercedes AMG	Mercedes F1 W03	1h41m56.737s	13
11	Nico Hulkenberg	Force India	Force India-Mercedes VJM05	1h42m02.786s	10
12	Paul di Resta	Force India	Force India-Mercedes VJM05	1h42m08.390s	12
13	Pastor Maldonado	Williams	Williams-Renault FW34	1h42m09.109s	8
14	Sergio Perez	Sauber	Sauber-Ferrari C31	1h42m09.997s	14
15	Daniel Ricciardo	Toro Rosso	Toro Rosso-Ferrari STR7	68 laps	18
16	Jean-Eric Vergne	Toro Rosso	Toro Rosso-Ferrari STR7	68 laps	16

Pos	Driver	Team	Chassis-Engine	Result	Qual
17	Heikki Kovalainen	Caterham	Caterham-Renault CT01	68 laps	19
18	Kamui Kobayashi	Sauber	Sauber-Ferrari C31	67 laps/hydraulics	15
19	Vitaly Petrov	Caterham	Caterham-Renault CT01	67 laps	20
20	Charles Pic	Marussia	Marussia-Cosworth MR01	67 laps	21
21	Timo Glock	Marussia	Marussia-Cosworth MR01	66 laps	22
22	Pedro de la Rosa	HRT	HRT-Cosworth F112	66 laps	23
R	Narain Karthikeyan	HRT	HRT-Cosworth F112	60 laps/steering	24
R	Michael Schumacher	Mercedes AMG	Mercedes F1 W03	58 laps/overheating	17

Pole: Hamilton, 1m20.953s, 121.058mph/194.824kph. Fastest lap: Vettel, 1m24.136s, 116.478mph/187.453kph on Lap 68. Race leaders: Hamilton 1-17 & 21-40 & 46-69, Grosjean 18-19, Raikkonen 20 & 41-45

BELGIAN GRAND PRIX

SPA-FRANCORCHAMPS • ROUND 12 • DATE: 2ND SEPTEMBER 2012
Laps: 44 • Distance: 191.491miles/308.176km • Weather: Warm & bright

Pos	Driver	Team	Chassis-Engine	Result	Qual
1	Jenson Button	McLaren	McLaren-Mercedes MP4-27	1h29m08.530s	1
2	Sebastian Vettel	Red Bull Racing	Red Bull-Renault RB8	1h29m22.154s	10
3	Kimi Raikkonen	Lotus F1	Lotus-Renault E20	1h29m33.864s	3
4	Nico Hulkenberg	Force India	Force India-Mercedes VJM05	1h29m36.373s	11
5	Felipe Massa	Ferrari	Ferrari F2012	1h29m38.375s	14
6	Mark Webber !	Red Bull Racing	Red Bull-Renault RB8	1h29m39.774s	12
7	Michael Schumacher	Mercedes AMG	Mercedes F1 W03	1h30m01.904s	13
8	Jean-Eric Vergne	Toro Rosso	Toro Rosso-Ferrari STR7	1h30m07.395s	15
9	Daniel Ricciardo	Toro Rosso	Toro Rosso-Ferrari STR7	1h30m11.512s	16
10	Paul di Resta	Force India	Force India-Mercedes VJM05	1h30m12.313s	9
11	Nico Rosberg !	Mercedes AMG	Mercedes F1 W03	1h30m13.641s	23
12	Bruno Senna	Williams	Williams-Renault FW34	1h30m20.059s	17
13	Kamui Kobayashi	Sauber	Sauber-Ferrari C31	1h31m04.649s	2
14	Vitaly Petrov	Caterham	Caterham-Renault CT01	43 laps	19
15	Timo Glock	Marussia	Marussia-Cosworth MR01	43 laps	20
16	Charles Pic	Marussia	Marussia-Cosworth MR01	43 laps	22
17	Heikki Kovalainen	Caterham	Caterham-Renault CT01	43 laps	18
18	Pedro de la Rosa	HRT	HRT-Cosworth F112	43 laps	21
R	Narain Karthikeyan	HRT	HRT-Cosworth F112	30 laps/wheel	24
R	Pastor Maldonado *	Williams	Williams-Renault FW34	5 laps/collision	6
R	Sergio Perez	Sauber	Sauber-Ferrari C31	0 laps/collision	4
R	Fernando Alonso	Ferrari	Ferrari F2012	0 laps/collision	5
R	Lewis Hamilton	McLaren	McLaren-Mercedes MP4-27	0 laps/collision	7
R	Romain Grosjean	Lotus F1	Lotus-Renault E20	0 laps/collision	8

Pole: Button, 1m47.573s, 145.645mph/234.393kph. Fastest lap: Senna, 1m52.822s, 138.869mph/223.488kph on Lap 43. Race leaders: Button 1-44

* 3-place grid penalty for impeding • ! 5-place grid penalty for gearbox change

ITALIAN GRAND PRIX

MONZA • ROUND 13 • DATE: 9TH SEPTEMBER 2012
Laps: 53 • Distance: 190.778miles/307.029km • Weather: Warm & bright

Pos	Driver	Team	Chassis-Engine	Result	Qual
1	Lewis Hamilton	McLaren	McLaren-Mercedes MP4-27	1h19m41.221s	1
2	Sergio Perez	Sauber	Sauber-Ferrari C31	1h19m45.577s	12

Pos	Driver	Team	Chassis-Engine	Result	Qual
3	Fernando Alonso	Ferrari	Ferrari F2012	1h20m01.815s	10
4	Felipe Massa	Ferrari	Ferrari F2012	1h20m10.888s	3
5	Kimi Raikkonen	Lotus F1	Lotus-Renault E20	1h20m12.102s	7
6	Michael Schumacher	Mercedes AMG	Mercedes F1 W03	1h20m12.480s	4
7	Nico Rosberg	Mercedes AMG	Mercedes F1 W03	1h20m14.771s	6
8	Paul di Resta *	Force India	Force India-Mercedes VJM05	1h20m22.278s	9
9	Kamui Kobayashi	Sauber	Sauber-Ferrari C31	1h20m25.119s	8
10	Bruno Senna	Williams	Williams-Renault FW34	1h20m29.365s	13
11	Pastor Maldonado !/^	Williams	Williams-Renault FW34	1h20m29.903s	22
12	Daniel Ricciardo	Toro Rosso	Toro Rosso-Ferrari STR7	1h20m31.537s	14
13	Jerome d'Ambrosio	Lotus F1	Lotus-Renault E20	1h20m57.082s	15
14	Heikki Kovalainen	Caterham	Caterham-Renault CT01	52 laps	17
15	Vitaly Petrov	Caterham	Caterham-Renault CT01	52 laps	18
16	Charles Pic	Marussia	Marussia-Cosworth MR01	52 laps	20
17	Timo Glock	Marussia	Marussia-Cosworth MR01	52 laps	19
18	Pedro de la Rosa	HRT	HRT-Cosworth F112	52 laps	23
19	Narain Karthikeyan	HRT	HRT-Cosworth F112	52 laps	21
20	Mark Webber	Red Bull Racing	Red Bull-Renault RB8	51 laps/spun off	11
21	Nico Hulkenberg	Force India	Force India-Mercedes VJM05	50 laps/brakes	24
22	Sebastian Vettel	Red Bull Racing	Red Bull-Renault RB8	47 laps/alternator	5
R	Jenson Button	McLaren	McLaren-Mercedes MP4-27	32 laps/fuel pump	2
R	Jean-Eric Vergne	Toro Rosso	Toro Rosso-Ferrari STR7	8 laps/suspension	16

Pole: Hamilton, 1m24.010s, 154.250mph/248.241kph. Fastest lap: Rosberg, 1m27.239s, 148.541mph/239.053kph on Lap 53. Race leaders: Hamilton 1-23 & 29-53, Perez 24-28

* 5-place grid penalty for gearbox change • ! 5-place grid penalty for jumping start of Belgian GP • ^ 5-place grid penalty for causing a crash in Belgian GP

SINGAPORE GRAND PRIX

MARINA BAY CIRCUIT • ROUND 14 • DATE: 23RD SEPTEMBER 2012
Laps: 59 • Distance: 185.980miles/299.307km • Weather: Hot & humid

Pos	Driver	Team	Chassis-Engine	Result	Qual
1	Sebastian Vettel	Red Bull Racing	Red Bull-Renault RB8	2h00m26.144s	3
2	Jenson Button	McLaren	McLaren-Mercedes MP4-27	2h00m35.103s	4
3	Fernando Alonso	Ferrari	Ferrari F2012	2h00m41.371s	5
4	Paul di Resta	Force India	Force India-Mercedes VJM05	2h00m45.207s	6
5	Nico Rosberg	Mercedes AMG	Mercedes F1 W03	2h01m00.928s	10
6	Kimi Raikkonen	Lotus F1	Lotus-Renault E20	2h01m01.903s	12
7	Romain Grosjean	Lotus F1	Lotus-Renault E20	2h01m02.042s	8
8	Felipe Massa	Ferrari	Ferrari F2012	2h01m08.973s	13
9	Daniel Ricciardo	Toro Rosso	Toro Rosso-Ferrari STR7	2h01m11.964s	15
10	Sergio Perez	Sauber	Sauber-Ferrari C31	2h01m16.763s	14
11	Mark Webber !	Red Bull Racing	Red Bull-Renault RB8	2h01m33.319s	7
12	Timo Glock	Marussia	Marussia-Cosworth MR01	2h01m58.062s	20
13	Kamui Kobayashi	Sauber	Sauber-Ferrari C31	2h02m03.285s	17
14	Nico Hulkenberg	Force India	Force India-Mercedes VJM05	2h02m05.557s	11
15	Heikki Kovalainen	Caterham	Caterham-Renault CT01	2h02m13.611s	19
16	Charles Pic ^	Marussia	Marussia-Cosworth MR01	2h00m26.144s	21
17	Pedro de la Rosa *	HRT	HRT-Cosworth F112	58 laps	24
18	Bruno Senna *	Williams	Williams-Renault FW34	57 laps/engine	22
19	Vitaly Petrov	Caterham	Caterham-Renault CT01	57 laps	18
R	Michael Schumacher	Mercedes AMG	Mercedes F1 W03	39 laps/collision	9
R	Jean-Eric Vergne	Toro Rosso	Toro Rosso-Ferrari STR7	39 laps/collision	16
R	Pastor Maldonado	Williams	Williams-Renault FW34	36 laps/hydraulics	2

Pos	Driver	Team	Chassis-Engine	Result	Qual
R	Narain Karthikeyan	HRT	HRT-Cosworth F112	30 laps/spun off	23
R	Lewis Hamilton	McLaren	McLaren-Mercedes MP4-27	22 laps/gearbox	1

Pole: Hamilton, 1m46.362s, 106.692mph/171.704kph. Fastest lap: Hulkenberg, 1m51.033s, 102.203mph/164.480kph on Lap 52. Race leaders: Hamilton 1-11 & 15-22, Button 12-14, Vettel 23-59

* 5-place grid penalty for changing gearbox • ! 20s penalty for gaining an advantage by leaving the track • ^ 20s penalty for overtaking under red flags in practice

JAPANESE GRAND PRIX

SUZUKA • ROUND 15 • DATE: 7TH OCTOBER 2012
Laps: 53 • Distance: 191.240miles/307.771km • Weather: Warm & bright

Pos	Driver	Team	Chassis-Engine	Result	Qual
1	Sebastian Vettel	Red Bull Racing	Red Bull-Renault RB8	1h28m56.242s	1
2	Felipe Massa	Ferrari	Ferrari F2012	1h29m16.874s	10
3	Kamui Kobayashi	Sauber	Sauber-Ferrari C31	1h29m20.780s	3
4	Jenson Button !	McLaren	McLaren-Mercedes MP4-27	1h29m21.340s	8
5	Lewis Hamilton	McLaren	McLaren-Mercedes MP4-27	1h29m42.732s	9
6	Kimi Raikkonen	Lotus F1	Lotus-Renault E20	1h29m46.666s	7
7	Nico Hulkenberg !	Force India	Force India-Mercedes VJM05	1h29m47.401s	15
8	Pastor Maldonado	Williams	Williams-Renault FW34	1h29m48.606s	12
9	Mark Webber	Red Bull Racing	Red Bull-Renault RB8	1h29m50.917s	2
10	Daniel Ricciardo	Toro Rosso	Toro Rosso-Ferrari STR7	1h30m03.161s	14
11	Michael Schumacher ^	Mercedes AMG	Mercedes F1 W03	1h30m04.011s	23
12	Paul di Resta	Force India	Force India-Mercedes VJM05	1h30m19.702s	11
13	Jean-Eric Vergne *	Toro Rosso	Toro Rosso-Ferrari STR7	1h30m24.887s	19
14	Bruno Senna	Williams	Williams-Renault FW34	1h30m24.951s	16
15	Heikki Kovalainen	Caterham	Caterham-Renault CT01	52 laps	17
16	Timo Glock	Marussia	Marussia-Cosworth MR01	52 laps	18
17	Vitaly Petrov	Caterham	Caterham-Renault CT01	52 laps	22
18	Pedro de la Rosa	HRT	HRT-Cosworth F112	52 laps	20
19	Romain Grosjean	Lotus F1	Lotus-Renault E20	51 laps/tyres	4
R	Charles Pic	Marussia	Marussia-Cosworth MR01	36 laps/engine	21
R	Narain Karthikeyan	HRT	HRT-Cosworth F112	32 laps/chassis	24
R	Sergio Perez	Sauber	Sauber-Ferrari C31	19 laps/spun off	5
R	Fernando Alonso	Ferrari	Ferrari F2012	0 laps/collision	6
R	Nico Rosberg	Mercedes AMG	Mercedes F1 W03	0 laps/collision	13

Pole: Vettel, 1m30.839s, 142.999mph/230.134kph. Fastest lap: Vettel, 1m35.774s, 135.630mph/218.276kph on Lap 52. Race leaders: Vettel 1-53

* 3-place grid penalty for impeding Senna • ! 5-place grid penalty for gearbox change • ^ 10-place grid penalty for causing crash in Singapore GP

SCHUMACHER RETIRES AGAIN

Michael Schumacher made his second and final retirement from F1. His second spell failed to bring another win to add to his 91 triumphs. Indeed, he scored only 49 points to team-mate Nico Rosberg's 93 across three seasons, but he bowed out after 308 grands prix with the most titles, the most wins, the most poles, the most fastest laps and the most points.

KOREAN GRAND PRIX

KOREA INTERNATIONAL CIRCUIT • ROUND 16 • DATE: 14TH OCTOBER 2012
Laps: 55 • Distance: 191.894miles/308.825km • Weather: Warm but dull

Pos	Driver	Team	Chassis-Engine	Result	Qual
1	Sebastian Vettel	Red Bull Racing	Red Bull-Renault RB8	1h36m28.651s	2
2	Mark Webber	Red Bull Racing	Red Bull-Renault RB8	1h36m36.882s	1
3	Fernando Alonso	Ferrari	Ferrari F2012	1h36m42.595s	4
4	Felipe Massa	Ferrari	Ferrari F2012	1h36m48.819s	6
5	Kimi Raikkonen	Lotus F1	Lotus-Renault E20	1h37m05.390s	5
6	Nico Hulkenberg	Force India	Force India-Mercedes VJM05	1h37m13.952s	8
7	Romain Grosjean	Lotus F1	Lotus-Renault E20	1h37m23.463s	7
8	Jean-Eric Vergne	Toro Rosso	Toro Rosso-Ferrari STR7	1h37m38.240s	16
9	Daniel Ricciardo *	Toro Rosso	Toro Rosso-Ferrari STR7	1h37m40.438s	21
10	Lewis Hamilton	McLaren	McLaren-Mercedes MP4-27	1h37m48.343s	3
11	Sergio Perez	Sauber	Sauber-Ferrari C31	1h37m48.713s	12
12	Paul di Resta	Force India	Force India-Mercedes VJM05	1h37m53.099s	14
13	Michael Schumacher	Mercedes AMG	Mercedes F1 W03	1h37m57.892s	10
14	Pastor Maldonado	Williams	Williams-Renault FW34	1h38m03.575s	15
15	Bruno Senna	Williams	Williams-Renault FW34	1h38m05.553s	17
16	Vitaly Petrov	Caterham	Caterham-Renault CT01	54 laps	18
17	Heikki Kovalainen	Caterham	Caterham-Renault CT01	54 laps	19
18	Timo Glock	Marussia	Marussia-Cosworth MR01	54 laps	20
19	Charles Pic !	Marussia	Marussia-Cosworth MR01	53 laps	24
20	Narain Karthikeyan	HRT	HRT-Cosworth F112	53 laps	23
R	Kamui Kobayashi	Sauber	Sauber-Ferrari C31	16 laps/collision	13
R	Pedro de la Rosa	HRT	HRT-Cosworth F112	16 laps/throttle	22
R	Nico Rosberg	Mercedes AMG	Mercedes F1 W03	1 laps/collision	9
R	Jenson Button	McLaren	McLaren-Mercedes MP4-27	0 laps/collision	11

Pole: Webber, 1m37.242s, 129.166mph/207.873kph. Fastest lap: Webber, 1m42.037s, 123.096mph/198.104kph on Lap 54. Race leaders: Vettel 1-55

* 5-place grid penalty for gearbox change • ! 10-place grid penalty for engine change

INDIAN GRAND PRIX

BUDDH INTERNATIONAL CIRCUIT • ROUND 17 • DATE: 28TH OCTOBER 2012
Laps: 60 • Distance: 190.764miles/307.5km • Weather: Warm but dull

Pos	Driver	Team	Chassis-Engine	Result	Qual
1	Sebastian Vettel	Red Bull Racing	Red Bull-Renault RB8	1h31m10.744s	1
2	Fernando Alonso	Ferrari	Ferrari F2012	1h31m20.181s	5
3	Mark Webber	Red Bull Racing	Red Bull-Renault RB8	1h31m23.961s	2
4	Lewis Hamilton	McLaren	McLaren-Mercedes MP4-27	1h31m24.653s	3
5	Jenson Button	McLaren	McLaren-Mercedes MP4-27	1h31m37.010s	4
6	Felipe Massa	Ferrari	Ferrari F2012	1h31m55.418s	6
7	Kimi Raikkonen	Lotus F1	Lotus-Renault E20	1h31m55.971s	7
8	Nico Hulkenberg	Force India	Force India-Mercedes VJM05	1h32m05.742s	12
9	Romain Grosjean	Lotus F1	Lotus-Renault E20	1h32m06.847s	11
10	Bruno Senna	Williams	Williams-Renault FW34	1h32m25.719s	13
11	Nico Rosberg	Mercedes AMG	Mercedes F1 W03	1h32m32.438s	10
12	Paul di Resta	Force India	Force India-Mercedes VJM05	1h32m33.559s	16
13	Daniel Ricciardo	Toro Rosso	Toro Rosso-Ferrari STR7	1h32m36.808s	15
14	Kamui Kobayashi	Sauber	Sauber-Ferrari C31	1h32m37.239s	17
15	Jean-Eric Vergne	Toro Rosso	Toro Rosso-Ferrari STR7	59 laps	18
16	Pastor Maldonado	Williams	Williams-Renault FW34	59 laps	9

Pos	Driver	Team	Chassis-Engine	Result	Qual
17	Vitaly Petrov	Caterham	Caterham-Renault CT01	59 laps	19
18	Heikki Kovalainen	Caterham	Caterham-Renault CT01	59 laps	20
19	Charles Pic	Marussia	Marussia-Cosworth MR01	59 laps	24
20	Timo Glock	Marussia	Marussia-Cosworth MR01	58 laps	21
21	Narain Karthikeyan	HRT	HRT-Cosworth F112	58 laps	23
22	Michael Schumacher	Mercedes AMG	Mercedes F1 W03	55 laps/gearbox	14
R	Pedro de la Rosa	HRT	HRT-Cosworth F112	43 laps/brakes	22
R	Sergio Perez	Sauber	Sauber-Ferrari C31	21 laps/collision	8

Pole: Vettel, 1m25.283s, 134.426mph/216.338kph. Fastest lap: Button, 1m28.203s, 129.976mph/209.176kph on Lap 60. Race leaders: Vettel 1-60

NEW CIRCUIT

Modelled on some of the best corners and sections of the world's leading circuits, the new home of the United States GP outside Austin in Texas was an instant hit. The Circuit of the Americas offered considerable gradient change, starting with the run from the grid up a hill to the first corner, and an amazing sequence of esses.

NEW DRIVERS

French pride swelled when the country provided both of the year's new intake. Competing for Scuderia Toro Rosso, Formula Renault 3.5 runner-up Jean-Eric Vergne impressed by collecting a quartet of eight places and outscoring team-mate Daniel Ricciardo. Occasional GP2 winner Charles Pic never finished higher than 15th for tail-end Marussia.

ABU DHABI GRAND PRIX

YAS MARINA CIRCUIT • ROUND 18 • DATE: 4TH NOVEMBER 2012
Laps: 55 • Distance: 189.547miles/305.47km • Weather: Hot & bright

Pos	Driver	Team	Chassis-Engine	Result	Qual
1	Kimi Raikkonen	Lotus F1	Lotus-Renault E20	1h45m58.667s	4
2	Fernando Alonso	Ferrari	Ferrari F2012	1h45m59.519s	6
3	Sebastian Vettel *	Red Bull Racing	Red Bull-Renault RB8	1h46m02.830s	24
4	Jenson Button	McLaren	McLaren-Mercedes MP4-27	1h46m06.454s	5
5	Pastor Maldonado	Williams	Williams-Renault FW34	1h46m11.674s	3
6	Kamui Kobayashi	Sauber	Sauber-Ferrari C31	1h46m18.743s	15
7	Felipe Massa	Ferrari	Ferrari F2012	1h46m21.563s	8
8	Bruno Senna	Williams	Williams-Renault FW34	1h46m22.209s	14
9	Paul di Resta	Force India	Force India-Mercedes VJM05	1h46m22.827s	12
10	Daniel Ricciardo	Toro Rosso	Toro Rosso-Ferrari STR7	1h46m26.130s	16
11	Michael Schumacher	Mercedes AMG	Mercedes F1 W03	1h46m26.742s	13
12	Jean-Eric Vergne	Toro Rosso	Toro Rosso-Ferrari STR7	1h46m33.573s	17
13	Heikki Kovalainen	Caterham	Caterham-Renault CT01	1h46m46.431s	18
14	Timo Glock	Marussia	Marussia-Cosworth MR01	1h46m55.140s	21
15	Sergio Perez	Sauber	Sauber-Ferrari C31	1h46m55.435s	11

Pos	Driver	Team	Chassis-Engine	Result	Qual
16	Vitaly Petrov	Caterham	Caterham-Renault CT01	1h47m03.262s	20
17	Pedro de la Rosa	HRT	HRT-Cosworth F112	1h47m10.445s	22
R	Charles Pic	Marussia	Marussia-Cosworth MR01	41 laps/engine	19
R	Mark Webber	Red Bull Racing	Red Bull-Renault RB8	37 laps/collision	2
R	Romain Grosjean	Lotus F1	Lotus-Renault E20	37 laps/collision	9
R	Lewis Hamilton	McLaren	McLaren-Mercedes MP4-27	19 laps/fuel pressure	1
R	Nico Rosberg	Mercedes AMG	Mercedes F1 W03	7 laps/collision	7
R	Narain Karthikeyan	HRT	HRT-Cosworth F112	7 laps/hydraulics	23
R	Nico Hulkenberg	Force India	Force India-Mercedes VJM05	0 laps/collision	10

Pole: Hamilton, 1m40.630s, 123.461mph/198.692kph. Fastest lap: Vettel, 1m43.964s, 119.502mph/192.320kph on Lap 54. Race leaders: Hamilton 1-19, Raikkonen 20-55

* excluded from qualifying for not having enough fuel for a sample

UNITED STATES GRAND PRIX

CIRCUIT OF THE AMERICAS • ROUND 19 • DATE: 18TH NOVEMBER 2012
Laps: 56 • Distance: 191.834miles/308.728km • Weather: Warm & bright

Pos	Driver	Team	Chassis-Engine	Result	Qual
1	Lewis Hamilton	McLaren	McLaren-Mercedes MP4-27	1h35m55.269s	2
2	Sebastian Vettel	Red Bull Racing	Red Bull-Renault RB8	1h35m55.944s	1
3	Fernando Alonso	Ferrari	Ferrari F2012	1h36m34.498s	7
4	Felipe Massa *	Ferrari	Ferrari F2012	1h36m41.282s	11
5	Jenson Button	McLaren	McLaren-Mercedes MP4-27	1h36m51.701s	12
6	Kimi Raikkonen	Lotus F1	Lotus-Renault E20	1h36m59.694s	4
7	Romain Grosjean *	Lotus F1	Lotus-Renault E20	1h37m05.582s	8
8	Nico Hulkenberg	Force India	Force India-Mercedes VJM05	1h37m09.061s	6
9	Pastor Maldonado	Williams	Williams-Renault FW34	1h37m09.794s	9
10	Bruno Senna	Williams	Williams-Renault FW34	1h37m10.402s	11
11	Sergio Perez	Sauber	Sauber-Ferrari C31	1h37m19.610s	15
12	Daniel Ricciardo	Toro Rosso	Toro Rosso-Ferrari STR7	1h37m20.140s	18
13	Nico Rosberg	Mercedes AMG	Mercedes F1 W03	1h37m20.779s	17
14	Kamui Kobayashi	Sauber	Sauber-Ferrari C31	55 laps	16
15	Paul di Resta	Force India	Force India-Mercedes VJM05	55 laps	13
16	Michael Schumacher	Mercedes AMG	Mercedes F1 W03	55 laps	5
17	Vitaly Petrov	Caterham	Caterham-Renault CT01	55 laps	21
18	Heikki Kovalainen	Caterham	Caterham-Renault CT01	55 laps	22
19	Timo Glock	Marussia	Marussia-Cosworth MR01	55 laps	19
20	Charles Pic	Marussia	Marussia-Cosworth MR01	54 laps	20
21	Pedro de la Rosa	HRT	HRT-Cosworth F112	54 laps	23
22	Narain Karthikeyan	HRT	HRT-Cosworth F112	54 laps	24
R	Mark Webber	Red Bull Racing	Red Bull-Renault RB8	16 laps/alternator	3
R	Jean-Eric Vergne	Toro Rosso	Toro Rosso-Ferrari STR7	14 laps/suspension	14

Pole: Vettel, 1m35.657s, 128.921mph/207.478kph. Fastest lap: Vettel, 1m39.347s, 124.133mph/199.772kph on Lap 56. Race leaders: Vettel 1-41, Hamilton 42-56

* 5-place grid penalty for gearbox change

BRAZILIAN GRAND PRIX

INTERLAGOS • ROUND 20 • DATE: 25TH NOVEMBER 2012
Laps: 71 • Distance: 190.101miles/305.939km • Weather: Hot with drizzle then rain

Pos	Driver	Team	Chassis-Engine	Result	Qual
1	Jenson Button	McLaren	McLaren-Mercedes MP4-27	1h45m22.656s	2
2	Fernando Alonso	Ferrari	Ferrari F2012	1h45m25.390s	7
3	Felipe Massa	Ferrari	Ferrari F2012	1h45m26.271s	5
4	Mark Webber	Red Bull Racing	Red Bull-Renault RB8	1h45m27.592s	3
5	Nico Hulkenberg	Force India	Force India-Mercedes VJM05	1h45m28.364s	6
6	Sebastian Vettel	Red Bull Racing	Red Bull-Renault RB8	1h45m32.109s	4
7	Michael Schumacher	Mercedes AMG	Mercedes F1 W03	1h45m34.563s	13
8	Jean-Eric Vergne	Toro Rosso	Toro Rosso-Ferrari STR7	1h45m51.309s	17
9	Kamui Kobayashi	Sauber	Sauber-Ferrari C31	1h45m53.906s	14
10	Kimi Raikkonen	Lotus F1	Lotus-Renault E20	70 laps	8
11	Vitaly Petrov	Caterham	Caterham-Renault CT01	70 laps	19
12	Charles Pic	Marussia	Marussia-Cosworth MR01	70 laps	22
13	Daniel Ricciardo	Toro Rosso	Toro Rosso-Ferrari STR7	70 laps	15
14	Heikki Kovalainen	Caterham	Caterham-Renault CT01	70 laps	20
15	Nico Rosberg	Mercedes AMG	Mercedes F1 W03	70 laps	9
16	Timo Glock	Marussia	Marussia-Cosworth MR01	70 laps	21
17	Pedro de la Rosa *	HRT	HRT-Cosworth F112	69 laps	24
18	Narain Karthikeyan	HRT	HRT-Cosworth F112	69 laps	23
19	Paul di Resta	Force India	Force India-Mercedes VJM05	68 laps/spun off	10
R	Lewis Hamilton	McLaren	McLaren-Mercedes MP4-27	54 laps/collision	1
R	Romain Grosjean	Lotus F1	Lotus-Renault E20	5 laps/spun off	18
R	Pastor Maldonado !	Williams	Williams-Renault FW34	1 lap/spun off	16
R	Bruno Senna	Williams	Williams-Renault FW34	0 laps/collision	11
R	Sergio Perez	Sauber	Sauber-Ferrari C31	0 laps/collision	12

Pole: Hamilton, 1m12.458s, 133.028mph/214.088kph. Fastest lap: Hamilton, 1m18.069s, 123.467mph/198.701kph on Lap 38. Race leaders: Hamilton 1-5 & 7 & 48-54, Button 6 & 8-17 & 55-71, Hulkenberg 18-47

* 5-place grid penalty for gearbox change • ! 10-place grid penalty for failing to stop for weight check

KEY PERSON: ADRIAN NEWEY

With three F1 titles in a row with Red Bull Racing, Newey was the hottest property in the F1 paddock. After qualifying in aeronautics, he joined F1 with Fittipaldi in 1980, then spread his wings with March in sports cars, and IndyCar, too. Newey made his mark with Williams in the 1990s, starting with his dominant FW14B in 1992, with three more titles won before he moved again. Success came quickly at McLaren, where Mika Hakkinen won two in a row with his cars. Red Bull Racing wanted to win like that, so he moved there and the titles started to flow. He was far from finished.

WORLD DRIVERS' CHAMPIONSHIP FINAL RESULTS

Pos	Driver	Nat	Car-Engine	R1	R2	R3	R4	R5	R6	R7	R8
1	Sebastian Vettel	DEU	Red Bull-Renault RB8	2	11	5	1PF	6	4	4PF	RP
2	Fernando Alonso	ESP	Ferrari F2012	5	1	9	7	2	3	5	1
3	Kimi Raikkonen	FIN	Lotus-Renault E20	7	5F	14	2	3	9	8	2
4	Lewis Hamilton	GBR	McLaren-Mercedes MP4-27	3P	3P	3	8	8	5	1	19
5	Jenson Button	GBR	McLaren-Mercedes MP4-27	1F	14	2	18	9	16	16	8
6	Mark Webber	AUS	Red Bull-Renault RB8	4	4	4	4	11	1P	7	4
7	Felipe Massa	BRA	Ferrari F2012	R	15	13	9	15	6	10	16
8	Romain Grosjean	FRA	Lotus-Renault E20	R	R	6	3	4F	R	2	R
9	Nico Rosberg	DEU	Mercedes F1 W03	12	13	1P	5	7	2	6	6F
10	Sergio Perez	MEX	Sauber-Ferrari C31	8	2	11	11	R	11F	3	9
11	Nico Hulkenberg	DEU	Force India-Mercedes VJM05	R	9	15	12	10	8	12	5
12	Kamui Kobayashi	JPN	Sauber-Ferrari C31	6	R	10F	13	5	R	9	R
13	Michael Schumacher	DEU	Mercedes F1 W03	R	10	R	10	R	R	R	3
14	Paul di Resta	GBR	Force India-Mercedes VJM05	10	7	12	6	14	7	11	7
15	Pastor Maldonado	VEN	Williams-Renault FW34	13	19	8	R	1P	R	13	12
16	Bruno Senna	BRA	Williams-Renault FW34	16	6	7	22	R	10	17	10
17	Jean-Eric Vergne	FRA	Toro Rosso-Ferrari STR7	11	8	16	14	12	12	15	R
18	Daniel Ricciardo	AUS	Toro Rosso-Ferrari STR7	9	12	17	15	13	R	14	11
19	Vitaly Petrov	RUS	Caterham-Renault CT01	R	16	18	16	17	R	19	13
20	Timo Glock	DEU	Marussia-Cosworth MR01	14	17	19	19	18	14	R	NS
21	Charles Pic	FRA	Marussia-Cosworth MR01	15	20	20	R	R	R	20	15
22	Heikki Kovalainen	FIN	Caterham-Renault CT01	R	18	23	17	16	13	18	14
23	Jerome d'Ambrosio	BEL	Lotus-Renault E20	-	-	-	-	-	-	-	-
24	Narain Karthikeyan	IND	HRT-Cosworth F112	DNQ	22	22	21	R	15	R	18
25	Pedro de la Rosa	ESP	HRT-Cosworth F112	DNQ	21	21	20	19	R	R	17

Pos	Driver	R9	R10	R11	R12	R13	R14	R15	R16	R17	R18	R19	R20	Total
1	Vettel	3	5	4F	2	22	1	1PF	1	1P	3F	2PF	6	281
2	Alonso	2P	1P	5	R	3	3	R	3	2	2	3	2	278
3	Raikkonen	5F	3	2	3	5	6	6	5	7	1	6	10	207
4	Hamilton	8	R	1P	R	1P	RP	5	10	4	RP	1	RPF	190
5	Button	10	2	6	1P	R	2	4	R	5F	4	5	1	188
6	Webber	1	8	8	6	20	11	9	2PF	3	R	R	4	179
7	Massa	4	12	9	5	4	8	2	4	6	7	4	3	122
8	Grosjean	6	18	3	R	-	7	19	7	9	R	7	R	96
9	Rosberg	15	10	10	11	7F	5	R	R	11	R	13	15	93
10	Perez	R	6	14	R	2	10	R	11	R	15	11	R	66
11	Hulkenberg	12	9	11	4	21	14F	7	6	8	R	8	5	63
12	Kobayashi	11	4	18	13	9	13	3	R	14	6	14	9	60
13	Schumacher	7	7F	R	7	6	R	11	13	22	11	16	7	49
14	di Resta	R	11	12	10	8	4	12	12	12	9	15	19	46
15	Maldonado	16	15	13	R	11	R	8	14	16	5	9	R	45
16	Senna	9	17	7	12F	10	18	14	15	10	8	10	R	31
17	Vergne	14	14	16	8	R	R	13	8	15	12	R	8	16
18	Ricciardo	13	13	15	9	12	9	10	9	13	10	12	13	10
19	Petrov	NS	16	19	14	15	19	17	16	17	16	17	11	0
20	Glock	18	22	21	15	17	12	16	18	20	14	19	16	0
21	Pic	19	20	20	16	16	16	R	19	19	R	20	12	0
22	Kovalainen	17	19	17	17	14	15	15	17	18	13	18	14	0
23	d'Ambrosio	-	-	-	-	13	-	-	-	-	-	-	-	0
24	Karthikeyan	21	23	R	R	19	R	R	20	21	R	22	18	0
25	de la Rosa	20	21	22	18	18	17	18	R	R	17	21	17	0

WORLD CONSTRUCTORS' CHAMPIONSHIP FINAL RESULTS

Pos	Team-Engine	R1	R2	R3	R4	R5	R6	R7	R8	R9	R10
1	Red Bull-Renault	2/4	4/11	4/5	1/4	6/11	1/4	4/7	4/R	1/3	5/8
2	Ferrari	5/R	1/15	9/13	7/9	2/15	3/6	5/10	1/16	2/4	1/12
3	McLaren-Mercedes	1/3	3/14	2/3	8/18	8/9	5/16	1/16	8/19	8/10	2/R
4	Lotus-Renault	7/R	5/R	6/14	2/3	3/4	9/R	2/8	2/R	5/6	3/18
5	Mercedes AMG	12/R	10/13	1/R	5/10	7/R	2/R	6/R	3/6	7/15	7/10
6	Sauber-Ferrari	6/8	2/R	10/11	11/13	5/R	11/R	3/9	9/R	11/R	4/6
7	Force India-Mercedes	10/R	7/9	12/15	6/12	10/14	7/8	11/12	5/7	12/R	9/11
8	Williams-Renault	13/16	6/19	7/8	22/R	1/R	10/R	13/17	10/12	9/16	15/17
9	Toro Rosso-Ferrari	9/11	8/12	16/17	14/15	12/13	12/R	14/15	11/R	13/14	13/14
10	Caterham-Renault	R/R	16/18	18/23	16/17	16/17	13/R	18/19	13/14	17/NS	16/19
11	Marussia-Cosworth	14/15	17/20	19/20	19/R	18/R	14/R	20/R	15/NS	18/19	20/22
12	HRT-Cosworth	DNQ/DNQ	21/22	21/22	20/21	19/R	15/R	R/R	17/18	20/21	21/23

Pos	Team-Engine	R11	R12	R13	R14	R15	R16	R17	R18	R19	R20	Total
1	Red Bull-Renault	4/8	2/6	20/22	1/11	1/9	1/2	1/3	3/R	2/R	4/6	460
2	Ferrari	5/9	5/R	3/4	3/8	2/R	3/4	2/6	2/7	3/4	2/3	400
3	McLaren-Mercedes	1/6	1/R	1/R	2/R	4/5	10/R	4/5	4/R	1/5	1/R	378
4	Lotus-Renault	2/3	3/R	5/13	6/7	6/19	5/7	7/9	1/R	6/7	10/R	303
5	Mercedes AMG	10/R	7/11	6/7	5/R	11/R	13/R	11/22	11/R	13/16	7/15	142
6	Sauber-Ferrari	14/18	13/R	2/9	10/13	3/R	11/R	14/R	6/15	11/14	9/R	126
7	Force India-Mercedes	11/12	4/10	8/21	4/14	7/12	6/12	8/12	9/R	8/15	5/19	109
8	Williams-Renault	7/13	12/R	10/11	18/R	8/14	14/15	10/16	5/8	9/10	R/R	76
9	Toro Rosso-Ferrari	15/16	8/9	12/R	9/R	10/13	8/9	13/15	10/12	12/R	8/13	26
10	Caterham-Renault	17/19	14/17	14/15	15/19	15/17	16/17	17/18	13/16	17/18	11/14	0
11	Marussia-Cosworth	20/21	15/16	16/17	12/16	16/R	18/19	19/20	14/R	19/20	12/16	0
12	HRT-Cosworth	22/R	18/R	18/19	17/R	18/R	20/R	21/R	17/R	21/22	17/18	0

SYMBOLS AND GRAND PRIX KEY

Round 1 **Australian GP**
Round 2 **Malaysian GP**
Round 3 **Chinese GP**
Round 4 **Bahrain GP**
Round 5 **Spanish GP**
Round 6 **Monaco GP**
Round 7 **Canadian GP**
Round 8 **European GP**
Round 9 **British GP**
Round 10 **German GP**
Round 11 **Hungarian GP**
Round 12 **Belgian GP**
Round 13 **Italian GP**
Round 14 **Singapore GP**
Round 15 **Japanese GP**
Round 16 **Korean GP**
Round 17 **Indian GP**
Round 18 **Abu Dhabi GP**
Round 19 **United States GP**
Round 20 **Brazilian GP**

SCORING

1st **25 points**
2nd **18 points**
3rd **15 points**
4th **12 points**
5th **10 points**
6th **8 points**
7th **6 points**
8th **4 points**
9th **2 points**
10th **1 point**

DNPQ DID NOT PRE-QUALIFY **DNQ DID NOT QUALIFY** **DQ DISQUALIFIED** **EX EXCLUDED**
F FASTEST LAP **NC NOT CLASSIFIED** **NS NON-STARTER** **P POLE POSITION** **R RETIRED**

2013

SEASON SUMMARY

Sebastian Vettel was in a class of his own as he took his fourth F1 title with Red Bull Racing. Fernando Alonso was a contender in the battle for honours for Ferrari until the second half of the season when Pirelli reacted to a series of blow-outs and reverted to their 2012 compounds. This suited Red Bull nicely. Mark Webber was usually in the mix in the second Red Bull but failed to win a race, compared to Vettel's 13 victories, which equalled Michael Schumacher's record tally from 2004. Mercedes was great in qualifying, with Lewis Hamilton's five podium finishes including victory in Hungary.

AUSTRALIAN GRAND PRIX

ALBERT PARK • ROUND 1 • DATE: 17TH MARCH 2013
Laps: 58 • Distance: 191.117miles/307.574km • Weather: Warm & damp, drying later

Pos	Driver	Team	Chassis-Engine	Result	Qual
1	Kimi Raikkonen	Lotus F1	Lotus-Renault E21	1h30m03.225s	7
2	Fernando Alonso	Ferrari	Ferrari F138	1h30m15.676s	5
3	Sebastian Vettel	Red Bull Racing	Red Bull-Renault RB9	1h30m25.571s	1
4	Felipe Massa	Ferrari	Ferrari F138	1h30m36.802s	4
5	Lewis Hamilton	Mercedes AMG	Mercedes F1 W04	1h30m48.786s	3
6	Mark Webber	Red Bull Racing	Red Bull-Renault RB9	1h30m50.025s	2
7	Adrian Sutil	Force India	Force India-Mercedes VJM06	1h31m08.293s	12
8	Paul di Resta	Force India	Force India-Mercedes VJM06	1h31m11.674s	9
9	Jenson Button	McLaren	McLaren-Mercedes MP4-28	1h31m24.855s	10
10	Romain Grosjean	Lotus F1	Lotus-Renault E21	1h31m25.984s	8
11	Sergio Perez	McLaren	McLaren-Mercedes MP4-28	1h31m26.592s	15
12	Jean-Eric Vergne	Toro Rosso	Toro Rosso-Ferrari STR8	1h31m27.082s	13
13	Esteban Gutierrez	Sauber	Sauber-Ferrari C32	57 laps	18
14	Valtteri Bottas	Williams	Williams-Renault FW35	57 laps	16
15	Jules Bianchi	Marussia	Marussia-Cosworth MR02	57 laps	19
16	Charles Pic	Caterham	Caterham-Renault CT03	56 laps	22
17	Max Chilton	Marussia	Marussia-Cosworth MR02	56 laps	20
18	Giedo van der Garde	Caterham	Caterham-Renault CT03	56 laps	21
R	Daniel Ricciardo	Toro Rosso	Toro Rosso-Ferrari STR8	39 laps/exhaust	14
R	Nico Rosberg	Mercedes AMG	Mercedes F1 W04	26 laps/electrical	6
R	Pastor Maldonado	Williams	Williams-Renault FW35	24 laps/spun off	17
NS	Nico Hulkenberg	Sauber	Sauber-Ferrari C32	fuel leak	11

Pole: Vettel, 1m27.407s, 135.715mph/218.412kph. Fastest lap: Raikkonen, 1m29.274s, 132.877mph/213.845kph on Lap 56. Race leaders: Vettel 1-6, Massa 7 & 21-22, Alonso 8 & 34-38, Hamilton 9-12, Rosberg 13, Sutil 14-20 & 39-42, Raikkonen 23-33 & 43-58

RAIKKONEN STARTS WELL

A win and three second places in the first five grands prix suggested that Kimi Raikkonen might be in with a title shot in his second year back with Lotus. However, this was a false dawn as Red Bull, Ferrari and Mercedes all became more competitive. Had he not missed the last two races to have back surgery, Raikkonen might have ranked third.

MALAYSIAN GRAND PRIX

SEPANG • ROUND 2 • DATE: 24TH MARCH 2013
Laps: 56 • Distance: 192.878miles/310.408km • Weather: Hot & damp, drying later

Pos	Driver	Team	Chassis-Engine	Result	Qual
1	Sebastian Vettel	Red Bull Racing	Red Bull-Renault RB9	1h38m56.681s	1
2	Mark Webber	Red Bull Racing	Red Bull-Renault RB9	1h39m00.979s	5
3	Lewis Hamilton	Mercedes AMG	Mercedes F1 W04	1h39m08.862s	4
4	Nico Rosberg	Mercedes AMG	Mercedes F1 W04	1h39m09.321s	6
5	Felipe Massa	Ferrari	Ferrari F138	1h39m22.329s	2
6	Romain Grosjean	Lotus F1	Lotus-Renault E21	1h39m32.245s	11
7	Kimi Raikkonen *	Lotus F1	Lotus-Renault E21	1h39m45.160s	10
8	Nico Hulkenberg	Sauber	Sauber-Ferrari C32	1h39m49.725s	12
9	Sergio Perez	McLaren	McLaren-Mercedes MP4-28	1h40m09.038s	9
10	Jean-Eric Vergne	Toro Rosso	Toro Rosso-Ferrari STR8	1h40m23.805s	17
11	Valtteri Bottas	Williams	Williams-Renault FW35	1h40m25.291s	18
12	Esteban Gutierrez	Sauber	Sauber-Ferrari C32	55 laps	14
13	Jules Bianchi	Marussia	Marussia-Cosworth MR02	55 laps	19
14	Charles Pic	Caterham	Caterham-Renault CT03	55 laps	20
15	Giedo van der Garde	Caterham	Caterham-Renault CT03	55 laps	22
16	Max Chilton	Marussia	Marussia-Cosworth MR02	54 laps	21
17	Jenson Button	McLaren	McLaren-Mercedes MP4-28	53 laps/vibrations	7
18	Daniel Ricciardo	Toro Rosso	Toro Rosso-Ferrari STR8	51 laps/exhaust	13
R	Pastor Maldonado	Williams	Williams-Renault FW35	45 laps/kers	16
R	Adrian Sutil	Force India	Force India-Mercedes VJM06	27 laps/wheel nut	8
R	Paul di Resta	Force India	Force India-Mercedes VJM06	22 laps/wheel nut	15
R	Fernando Alonso	Ferrari	Ferrari F138	1 lap/collision	3

Pole: Vettel, 1m49.674s, 113.056mph/181.946kph. Fastest lap: Perez, 1m39.199s, 124.994mph/201.159kph on Lap 56. Race leaders: Vettel 1-4 & 19-22 & 31-32 & 46-56, Webber 5-7 & 9-18 & 23-30 & 35-45, Rosberg 8, Button 33-34

* 3-place grid penalty for impeding Rosberg

MAKING HIS MARK

A grand prix winner nine times but never quite a world champion, Mark Webber quit F1 at the end of 2013. The Australian left Red Bull Racing after seven years with the team, during which time his best ranking was third in 2010, 2011 and 2013. He then turned to sports cars, going on to win the 2015 WEC title for Porsche.

CHINESE GRAND PRIX

SHANGHAI INTERNATIONAL CIRCUIT • ROUND 3 • DATE: 14TH APRIL 2013
Laps: 56 • Distance: 189.677miles/305.256km • Weather: Warm & bright

Pos	Driver	Team	Chassis-Engine	Result	Qual
1	Fernando Alonso	Ferrari	Ferrari F138	1h36m26.945s	3
2	Kimi Raikkonen	Lotus F1	Lotus-Renault E21	1h36m37.113s	2
3	Lewis Hamilton	Mercedes AMG	Mercedes F1 W04	1h36m39.267s	1
4	Sebastian Vettel	Red Bull Racing	Red Bull-Renault RB9	1h36m39.470s	9
5	Jenson Button	McLaren	McLaren-Mercedes MP4-28	1h37m02.230s	8
6	Felipe Massa	Ferrari	Ferrari F138	1h37m07.772s	5

Pos	Driver	Team	Chassis-Engine	Result	Qual
7	Daniel Ricciardo	Toro Rosso	Toro Rosso-Ferrari STR8	1h37m09.636s	7
8	Paul di Resta	Force India	Force India-Mercedes VJM06	1h37m18.029s	11
9	Romain Grosjean	Lotus F1	Lotus-Renault E21	1h37m20.368s	6
10	Nico Hulkenberg	Sauber	Sauber-Ferrari C32	1h37m23.543s	10
11	Sergio Perez	McLaren	McLaren-Mercedes MP4-28	1h37m30.805s	12
12	Jean-Eric Vergne	Toro Rosso	Toro Rosso-Ferrari STR8	1h37m39.549s	15
13	Valtteri Bottas	Williams	Williams-Renault FW35	1h38m00.806s	16
14	Pastor Maldonado	Williams	Williams-Renault FW35	1h38m02.398s	14
15	Jules Bianchi	Marussia	Marussia-Cosworth MR02	55 laps	18
16	Charles Pic	Caterham	Caterham-Renault CT03	55 laps	20
17	Max Chilton	Marussia	Marussia-Cosworth MR02	55 laps	19
18	Giedo van der Garde	Caterham	Caterham-Renault CT03	55 laps	21
R	Nico Rosberg	Mercedes AMG	Mercedes F1 W04	21 laps/suspension	4
R	Mark Webber *	Red Bull Racing	Red Bull-Renault RB9	15 laps/wheel nut	22
R	Adrian Sutil	Force India	Force India-Mercedes VJM06	5 laps/collision	13
R	Esteban Gutierrez	Sauber	Sauber-Ferrari C32	4 laps/collision	17

Pole: Hamilton, 1m34.484s, 129.054mph/207.692kph. Fastest lap: Vettel, 1m36.808s, 125.955mph/202.706kph on Lap 53. Race leaders: Hamilton 1-4, Alonso 5 & 21-23 & 29-41 & 43-56, Massa 6, Hulkenberg 7-14, Button 15-20, Vettel 24-28 & 42

* excluded from qualifying for not having enough fuel for a sample

NINE IN A ROW

Sebastian Vettel was on a real roll in the second half of the season, winning the final nine rounds. This stunning sequence finally equalled the record for consecutive wins set by Antonio Ascari in a run that started in 1952 and carried on into 1953 as the Italian won everything for Ferrari, to make it two titles in a row.

BAHRAIN GRAND PRIX

SAKHIR • ROUND 4 • DATE: 21ST APRIL 2013
Laps: 57 • Distance: 191.683miles/308.484km • Weather: Hot & bright

Pos	Driver	Team	Chassis-Engine	Result	Qual
1	Sebastian Vettel	Red Bull Racing	Red Bull-Renault RB9	1h36m00.498s	2
2	Kimi Raikkonen	Lotus F1	Lotus-Renault E21	1h36m09.609s	8
3	Romain Grosjean	Lotus F1	Lotus-Renault E21	1h36m20.005s	11
4	Paul di Resta	Force India	Force India-Mercedes VJM06	1h36m22.225s	5
5	Lewis Hamilton ^	Mercedes AMG	Mercedes F1 W04	1h36m35.728s	9
6	Sergio Perez	McLaren	McLaren-Mercedes MP4-28	1h36m36.496s	12
7	Mark Webber *	Red Bull Racing	Red Bull-Renault RB9	1h36m37.742s	7
8	Fernando Alonso	Ferrari	Ferrari F138	1h36m38.072s	3
9	Nico Rosberg	Mercedes AMG	Mercedes F1 W04	1h36m41.624s	1
10	Jenson Button	McLaren	McLaren-Mercedes MP4-28	1h36m47.129s	10
11	Pastor Maldonado	Williams	Williams-Renault FW35	1h37m06.948s	17
12	Nico Hulkenberg	Sauber	Sauber-Ferrari C32	1h37m13.431s	14
13	Adrian Sutil	Force India	Force India-Mercedes VJM06	1h37m17.217s	6

Pos	Driver	Team	Chassis-Engine	Result	Qual
14	Valtteri Bottas	Williams	Williams-Renault FW35	1h37m22.009s	15
15	Felipe Massa	Ferrari	Ferrari F138	1h37m26.862s	4
16	Daniel Ricciardo	Toro Rosso	Toro Rosso-Ferrari STR8	56 laps	13
17	Charles Pic	Caterham	Caterham-Renault CT03	56 laps	18
18	Esteban Gutierrez !	Sauber	Sauber-Ferrari C32	56 laps	22
19	Jules Bianchi	Marussia	Marussia-Cosworth MR02	56 laps	19
20	Max Chilton	Marussia	Marussia-Cosworth MR02	56 laps	21
21	Giedo van der Garde	Caterham	Caterham-Renault CT03	55 laps	20
R	Jean-Eric Vergne	Toro Rosso	Toro Rosso-Ferrari STR8	16 laps/collision	16

Pole: Rosberg, 1m32.330s, 131.119mph/211.017kph. Fastest lap: Vettel, 1m36.961s, 124.857mph/200.938kph on Lap 55. Race leaders: Rosberg 1-2, Vettel 3-10 & 15-57, di Resta 11-13, Raikkonen 14

* 3-place grid penalty for causing a crash in Chinese GP • ! 5-place grid penalty for causing a crash in Chinese GP • ^ 5-place grid penalty for gearbox change

SPANISH GRAND PRIX

BARCELONA-CATALUNYA • ROUND 5 • DATE: 12TH MAY 2013
Laps: 66 • Distance: 190.775miles/307.23km • Weather: Warm & bright

Pos	Driver	Team	Chassis-Engine	Result	Qual
1	Fernando Alonso	Ferrari	Ferrari F138	1h39m16.596s	5
2	Kimi Raikkonen	Lotus F1	Lotus-Renault E21	1h39m25.934s	4
3	Felipe Massa *	Ferrari	Ferrari F138	1h39m42.645s	9
4	Sebastian Vettel	Red Bull Racing	Red Bull-Renault RB9	1h39m54.869s	3
5	Mark Webber	Red Bull Racing	Red Bull-Renault RB9	1h40m04.559s	7
6	Nico Rosberg	Mercedes AMG	Mercedes F1 W04	1h40m24.616s	1
7	Paul di Resta	Force India	Force India-Mercedes VJM06	1h40m25.584s	10
8	Jenson Button	McLaren	McLaren-Mercedes MP4-28	1h40m36.102s	14
9	Sergio Perez	McLaren	McLaren-Mercedes MP4-28	1h40m38.334s	8
10	Daniel Ricciardo	Toro Rosso	Toro Rosso-Ferrari STR8	65 laps	11
11	Esteban Gutierrez !	Sauber	Sauber-Ferrari C32	65 laps	19
12	Lewis Hamilton	Mercedes AMG	Mercedes F1 W04	65 laps	2
13	Adrian Sutil	Force India	Force India-Mercedes VJM06	65 laps	13
14	Pastor Maldonado	Williams	Williams-Renault FW35	65 laps	17
15	Nico Hulkenberg	Sauber	Sauber-Ferrari C32	65 laps	15
16	Valtteri Bottas	Williams	Williams-Renault FW35	65 laps	16
17	Charles Pic	Caterham	Caterham-Renault CT03	65 laps	22
18	Jules Bianchi	Marussia	Marussia-Cosworth MR02	64 laps	20
19	Max Chilton	Marussia	Marussia-Cosworth MR02	64 laps	21
R	Jean-Eric Vergne	Toro Rosso	Toro Rosso-Ferrari STR8	52 laps/collision	12
R	Giedo van der Garde	Caterham	Caterham-Renault CT03	21 laps/wheel	18
R	Romain Grosjean	Lotus F1	Lotus-Renault E21	8 laps/suspension	6

Pole: Rosberg, 1m20.718s, 129.003mph/207.611kph. Fastest lap: Gutierrez, 1m26.217s, 120.775mph/194.370kph on Lap 56. Race leaders: Rosberg 1-10, Gutierrez 11-12, Alonso 13-21 & 26-36 & 39-66, Vettel 22-23, Raikkonen 24-25 & 37-38

* 3-place grid penalty for impeding Webber • ! 3-place grid penalty for impeding Raikkonen

MONACO GRAND PRIX

MONTE CARLO • ROUND 6 • DATE: 26TH MAY 2013
Laps: 78 • Distance: 161.588miles/260.52km • Weather: Warm & bright

Pos	Driver	Team	Chassis-Engine	Result	Qual
1	Nico Rosberg	Mercedes AMG	Mercedes F1 W04	2h17m52.056s	1
2	Sebastian Vettel	Red Bull Racing	Red Bull-Renault RB9	2h17m55.944s	3
3	Mark Webber	Red Bull Racing	Red Bull-Renault RB9	2h17m58.370s	4
4	Lewis Hamilton	Mercedes AMG	Mercedes F1 W04	2h18m05.950s	2
5	Adrian Sutil	Force India	Force India-Mercedes VJM06	2h18m13.533s	8
6	Jenson Button	McLaren	McLaren-Mercedes MP4-28	2h18m15.159s	9
7	Fernando Alonso	Ferrari	Ferrari F138	2h18m18.790s	6
8	Jean-Eric Vergne	Toro Rosso	Toro Rosso-Ferrari STR8	2h18m19.279s	10
9	Paul di Resta	Force India	Force India-Mercedes VJM06	2h18m19.664s	17
10	Kimi Raikkonen	Lotus F1	Lotus-Renault E21	2h18m28.638s	5
11	Nico Hulkenberg	Sauber	Sauber-Ferrari C32	2h18m34.628s	11
12	Valtteri Bottas	Williams	Williams-Renault FW35	2h18m34.747s	14
13	Esteban Gutierrez	Sauber	Sauber-Ferrari C32	2h18m35.268s	19
14	Max Chilton *	Marussia	Marussia-Cosworth MR02	2h18m41.941s	22
15	Giedo van der Garde	Caterham	Caterham-Renault CT03	2h18m54.646s	15
16	Sergio Perez	McLaren	McLaren-Mercedes MP4-28	72 laps/brakes	7
R	Romain Grosjean	Lotus F1	Lotus-Renault E21	63 laps/collision	13
R	Daniel Ricciardo	Toro Rosso	Toro Rosso-Ferrari STR8	61 laps/collision	12
R	Jules Bianchi	Marussia	Marussia-Cosworth MR02	58 laps/brakes	20
R	Pastor Maldonado	Williams	Williams-Renault FW35	44 laps/collision	16
R	Felipe Massa *	Ferrari	Ferrari F138	28 laps/suspension	21
R	Charles Pic	Caterham	Caterham-Renault CT03	7 laps/gearbox	18

Pole: Rosberg, 1m13.876s, 101.133mph/162.759kph. Fastest lap: Vettel, 1m16.577s, 97.566mph/157.018kph on Lap 77. Race leaders: Rosberg 1-78

* 5-place grid penalty for gearbox change

ALONSO'S FRUSTRATION

Angered by Red Bull Racing's superiority, Fernando Alonso spoke out against Ferrari. He was in a good position to do so, as he was leading their attack while team-mate Felipe Massa languished some distance behind. Ferrari's management didn't like this criticism, though, and so Kimi Raikkonen was signed to push Alonso in 2014.

CANADIAN GRAND PRIX

MONTREAL • ROUND 7 • DATE: 9TH JUNE 2013
Laps: 70 • Distance: 189.534miles/305.27km • Weather: Warm & bright

Pos	Driver	Team	Chassis-Engine	Result	Qual
1	Sebastian Vettel	Red Bull Racing	Red Bull-Renault RB9	1h32m09.143s	1
2	Fernando Alonso	Ferrari	Ferrari F138	1h32m23.551s	6
3	Lewis Hamilton	Mercedes AMG	Mercedes F1 W04	1h32m25.085s	2
4	Mark Webber	Red Bull Racing	Red Bull-Renault RB9	1h32m34.874s	5
5	Nico Rosberg	Mercedes AMG	Mercedes F1 W04	1h33m18.868s	4
6	Jean-Eric Vergne	Toro Rosso	Toro Rosso-Ferrari STR8	69 laps	7

Pos	Driver	Team	Chassis-Engine	Result	Qual
7	Paul di Resta	Force India	Force India-Mercedes VJM06	69 laps	17
8	Felipe Massa	Ferrari	Ferrari F138	69 laps	16
9	Kimi Raikkonen *	Lotus F1	Lotus-Renault E21	69 laps	10
10	Adrian Sutil	Force India	Force India-Mercedes VJM06	69 laps	8
11	Sergio Perez	McLaren	McLaren-Mercedes MP4-28	69 laps	12
12	Jenson Button	McLaren	McLaren-Mercedes MP4-28	69 laps	14
13	Romain Grosjean !	Lotus F1	Lotus-Renault E21	69 laps	22
14	Valtteri Bottas	Williams	Williams-Renault FW35	69 laps	3
15	Daniel Ricciardo *	Toro Rosso	Toro Rosso-Ferrari STR8	68 laps	11
16	Pastor Maldonado	Williams	Williams-Renault FW35	68 laps	13
17	Jules Bianchi	Marussia	Marussia-Cosworth MR02	68 laps	19
18	Charles Pic	Caterham	Caterham-Renault CT03	67 laps	18
19	Max Chilton	Marussia	Marussia-Cosworth MR02	67 laps	20
20	Esteban Gutierrez	Sauber	Sauber-Ferrari C32	63 laps/spun off	15
R	Nico Hulkenberg	Sauber	Sauber-Ferrari C32	45 laps/collision	9
R	Giedo van der Garde	Caterham	Caterham-Renault CT03	43 laps/collision	21

Pole: Vettel, 1m25.425s, 114.197mph/183.782kph. Fastest lap: Webber, 1m16.182s, 128.052mph/206.080kph on Lap 69. Race leaders: Vettel 1-15 & 19-70, Hamilton 16-18

* 2-place grid penalty for jumping pit lane queue • ! 10-place grid penalty for causing a crash in Monaco GP

BRITISH GRAND PRIX

SILVERSTONE • ROUND 8 • DATE: 30TH JUNE 2013
Laps: 52 • Distance: 190.345miles/306.332km • Weather: Warm & bright

Pos	Driver	Team	Chassis-Engine	Result	Qual
1	Nico Rosberg	Mercedes AMG	Mercedes F1 W04	1h32m59.456s	2
2	Mark Webber	Red Bull Racing	Red Bull-Renault RB9	1h33m00.221s	4
3	Fernando Alonso	Ferrari	Ferrari F138	1h33m06.580s	9
4	Lewis Hamilton	Mercedes AMG	Mercedes F1 W04	1h33m07.212s	1
5	Kimi Raikkonen	Lotus F1	Lotus-Renault E21	1h33m10.713s	8
6	Felipe Massa	Ferrari	Ferrari F138	1h33m14.029s	11
7	Adrian Sutil	Force India	Force India-Mercedes VJM06	1h33m15.791s	6
8	Daniel Ricciardo	Toro Rosso	Toro Rosso-Ferrari STR8	1h33m15.999s	5
9	Paul di Resta *	Force India	Force India-Mercedes VJM06	1h33m17.399s	21
10	Nico Hulkenberg	Sauber	Sauber-Ferrari C32	1h33m19.165s	14
11	Pastor Maldonado	Williams	Williams-Renault FW35	1h33m20.591s	15
12	Valtteri Bottas	Williams	Williams-Renault FW35	1h33m24.550s	16
13	Jenson Button	McLaren	McLaren-Mercedes MP4-28	1h33m25.425s	10
14	Esteban Gutierrez	Sauber	Sauber-Ferrari C32	1h33m25.741s	17
15	Charles Pic	Caterham	Caterham-Renault CT03	1h33m31.069s	18
16	Jules Bianchi	Marussia	Marussia-Cosworth MR02	1h33m35.553s	19
17	Max Chilton	Marussia	Marussia-Cosworth MR02	1h34m07.116s	20
18	Giedo van der Garde !/^	Caterham	Caterham-Renault CT03	1h34m07.215s	22
19	Romain Grosjean	Lotus F1	Lotus-Renault E21	51 laps/wing	7
20	Sergio Perez	McLaren	McLaren-Mercedes MP4-28	46 laps/puncture	13
R	Sebastian Vettel	Red Bull Racing	Red Bull-Renault RB9	41 laps/gearbox	3
R	Jean-Eric Vergne	Toro Rosso	Toro Rosso-Ferrari STR8	35 laps/puncture	12

Pole: Hamilton, 1m29.607s, 147.062mph/236.673kph. Fastest lap: Webber, 1m33.401s, 141.087mph/227.059kph on Lap 52. Race leaders: Hamilton 1-7, Vettel 8-40, Rosberg 41-52

* excluded from qualifying for being underweight • ! 5-place grid penalty for ignoring blue flags in Canadian GP • ^ 5-place grid penalty for gearbox change

GOING BACK A YEAR

The first few grands prix of 2013 were confusing for the teams, as the drivers couldn't get on with Pirelli's tyres, describing their performance as suddenly "dropping off a cliff" as they wore down. After consideration, Pirelli reverted to its 2012 compounds and so, from the ninth round onwards, the drivers went out on tyres that they understood.

GERMAN GRAND PRIX

NURBURGRING • ROUND 9 • DATE: 7TH JULY 2013
Laps: 60 • Distance: 191.437miles/308.88km • Weather: Warm & bright

Pos	Driver	Team	Chassis-Engine	Result	Qual
1	Sebastian Vettel	Red Bull Racing	Red Bull-Renault RB9	1h41m14.711s	2
2	Kimi Raikkonen	Lotus F1	Lotus-Renault E21	1h41m15.719s	4
3	Romain Grosjean	Lotus F1	Lotus-Renault E21	1h41m20.541s	5
4	Fernando Alonso	Ferrari	Ferrari F138	1h41m22.432s	8
5	Lewis Hamilton	Mercedes AMG	Mercedes F1 W04	1h41m41.638s	1
6	Jenson Button	McLaren	McLaren-Mercedes MP4-28	1h41m42.707s	9
7	Mark Webber	Red Bull Racing	Red Bull-Renault RB9	1h41m52.273s	3
8	Sergio Perez	McLaren	McLaren-Mercedes MP4-28	1h41m53.017s	13
9	Nico Rosberg	Mercedes AMG	Mercedes F1 W04	1h42m01.532s	11
10	Nico Hulkenberg	Sauber	Sauber-Ferrari C32	1h42m04.603s	10
11	Paul di Resta	Force India	Force India-Mercedes VJM06	1h42m08.482s	12
12	Daniel Ricciardo	Toro Rosso	Toro Rosso-Ferrari STR8	1h42m11.686s	6
13	Adrian Sutil	Force India	Force India-Mercedes VJM06	1h42m12.449s	15
14	Esteban Gutierrez	Sauber	Sauber-Ferrari C32	1h42m14.871s	14
15	Pastor Maldonado	Williams	Williams-Renault FW35	1h42m16.640s	18
16	Valtteri Bottas	Williams	Williams-Renault FW35	59 laps	17
17	Charles Pic *	Caterham	Caterham-Renault CT03	59 laps	22
18	Giedo van der Garde	Caterham	Caterham-Renault CT03	59 laps	20
19	Max Chilton	Marussia	Marussia-Cosworth MR02	59 laps	21
R	Jean-Eric Vergne	Toro Rosso	Toro Rosso-Ferrari STR8	22 laps/hydraulics	16
R	Jules Bianchi	Marussia	Marussia-Cosworth MR02	21 laps/engine	19
R	Felipe Massa	Ferrari	Ferrari F138	3 laps/spun off	7

Pole: Hamilton, 1m29.398s, 128.814mph/207.306kph. Fastest lap: Alonso, 1m33.468s, 123.204mph/198.279kph on Lap 51. Race leaders: Vettel 1-6 & 14-40 & 50-60, Webber 7-8, Grosjean 9-13, Raikkonen 41-49

* 5-place grid penalty for gearbox change

SILVERSTONE TYRE FAILURES

Having a tyre explode would be scary in a road car, let alone on a circuit like Silverstone where drivers top 200mph (320kph). Lewis Hamilton suffered one when leading, Fernando Alonso and team-mate Felipe Massa followed suit, then Jean-Eric Vergne had the same fate. In response, Pirelli reverted to its 2012-spec tyres from the next race.

HUNGARIAN GRAND PRIX

HUNGARORING • ROUND 10 • DATE: 28TH JULY 2013
Laps: 70 • Distance: 190.181miles/306.67km • Weather: Hot & bright

Pos	Driver	Team	Chassis-Engine	Result	Qual
1	Lewis Hamilton	Mercedes AMG	Mercedes F1 W04	1h42m29.445s	1
2	Kimi Raikkonen	Lotus F1	Lotus-Renault E21	1h42m40.383s	6
3	Sebastian Vettel	Red Bull Racing	Red Bull-Renault RB9	1h42m41.904s	2
4	Mark Webber	Red Bull Racing	Red Bull-Renault RB9	1h42m47.489s	10
5	Fernando Alonso	Ferrari	Ferrari F138	1h43m00.856s	5
6	Romain Grosjean *	Lotus F1	Lotus-Renault E21	1h43m01.740s	3
7	Jenson Button	McLaren	McLaren-Mercedes MP4-28	1h43m23.264s	13
8	Felipe Massa	Ferrari	Ferrari F138	1h43m25.892s	7
9	Sergio Perez	McLaren	McLaren-Mercedes MP4-28	69 laps	9
10	Pastor Maldonado	Williams	Williams-Renault FW35	69 laps	15
11	Nico Hulkenberg	Sauber	Sauber-Ferrari C32	69 laps	12
12	Jean-Eric Vergne	Toro Rosso	Toro Rosso-Ferrari STR8	69 laps	14
13	Daniel Ricciardo	Toro Rosso	Toro Rosso-Ferrari STR8	69 laps	8
14	Giedo van der Garde	Caterham	Caterham-Renault CT03	68 laps	20
15	Charles Pic	Caterham	Caterham-Renault CT03	68 laps	19
16	Jules Bianchi	Marussia	Marussia-Cosworth MR02	67 laps	21
17	Max Chilton	Marussia	Marussia-Cosworth MR02	67 laps	22
18	Paul di Resta	Force India	Force India-Mercedes VJM06	66 laps/hydraulics	18
19	Nico Rosberg	Mercedes AMG	Mercedes F1 W04	64 laps/engine	4
R	Valtteri Bottas	Williams	Williams-Renault FW35	42 laps/hydraulics	16
R	Esteban Gutierrez	Sauber	Sauber-Ferrari C32	28 laps/gearbox	17
R	Adrian Sutil	Force India	Force India-Mercedes VJM06	19 laps/hydraulics	11

Pole: Hamilton, 1m19.388s, 123.444mph/198.664kph. Fastest lap: Webber, 1m24.069s, 116.571mph/187.603kph on Lap 61. Race leaders: Hamilton 1-8 & 23-31 & 35-50 & 56-70, Vettel 9-10 & 32-34 & 51-55, Grosjean 11-13, Webber 14-22

* 20s penalty for causing a collision

BELGIAN GRAND PRIX

SPA-FRANCORCHAMPS • ROUND 11 • DATE: 25TH AUGUST 2013
Laps: 44 • Distance: 191.491miles/308.176km • Weather: Warm & bright

Pos	Driver	Team	Chassis-Engine	Result	Qual
1	Sebastian Vettel	Red Bull Racing	Red Bull-Renault RB9	1h23m42.196s	2
2	Fernando Alonso	Ferrari	Ferrari F138	1h23m59.065s	9
3	Lewis Hamilton	Mercedes AMG	Mercedes F1 W04	1h24m09.930s	1
4	Nico Rosberg	Mercedes AMG	Mercedes F1 W04	1h24m12.068s	4
5	Mark Webber	Red Bull Racing	Red Bull-Renault RB9	1h24m16.041s	3
6	Jenson Button	McLaren	McLaren-Mercedes MP4-28	1h24m22.990s	6
7	Felipe Massa	Ferrari	Ferrari F138	1h24m36.118s	10
8	Romain Grosjean	Lotus F1	Lotus-Renault E21	1h24m38.042s	7
9	Adrian Sutil	Force India	Force India-Mercedes VJM06	1h24m51.743s	12
10	Daniel Ricciardo	Toro Rosso	Toro Rosso-Ferrari STR8	1h24m55.666s	19
11	Sergio Perez	McLaren	McLaren-Mercedes MP4-28	1h25m04.132s	13
12	Jean-Eric Vergne	Toro Rosso	Toro Rosso-Ferrari STR8	1h25m08.936s	18
13	Nico Hulkenberg	Sauber	Sauber-Ferrari C32	1h25m10.454s	11
14	Esteban Gutierrez	Sauber	Sauber-Ferrari C32	1h25m22.632s	21
15	Valtteri Bottas	Williams	Williams-Renault FW35	1h25m29.652s	20
16	Giedo van der Garde	Caterham	Caterham-Renault CT03	43 laps	14
17	Pastor Maldonado	Williams	Williams-Renault FW35	43 laps	17

Pos	Driver	Team	Chassis-Engine	Result	Qual
18	Jules Bianchi	Marussia	Marussia-Cosworth MR02	43 laps	15
19	Max Chilton	Marussia	Marussia-Cosworth MR02	42 laps	16
R	Paul di Resta	Force India	Force India-Mercedes VJM06	26 laps/collision	5
R	Kimi Raikkonen	Lotus F1	Lotus-Renault E21	25 laps/brakes	8
R	Charles Pic	Caterham	Caterham-Renault CT03	8 laps/oil leak	22

Pole: Hamilton, 2m01.012s, 129.470mph/208.362kph. Fastest lap: Vettel, 1m50.756s, 141.459mph/227.657kph on Lap 40. Race leaders: Vettel 1-44

ITALIAN GRAND PRIX

MONZA • ROUND 12 • DATE: 8TH SEPTEMBER 2013
Laps: 53 • Distance: 190.778miles/307.029km • Weather: Warm but dull

Pos	Driver	Team	Chassis-Engine	Result	Qual
1	Sebastian Vettel	Red Bull Racing	Red Bull-Renault RB9	1h18m33.352s	1
2	Fernando Alonso	Ferrari	Ferrari F138	1h18m38.819s	5
3	Mark Webber	Red Bull Racing	Red Bull-Renault RB9	1h18m39.702s	2
4	Felipe Massa	Ferrari	Ferrari F138	1h18m42.713s	4
5	Nico Hulkenberg	Sauber	Sauber-Ferrari C32	1h18m43.707s	3
6	Nico Rosberg	Mercedes AMG	Mercedes F1 W04	1h18m44.351s	6
7	Daniel Ricciardo	Toro Rosso	Toro Rosso-Ferrari STR8	1h19m05.681s	7
8	Romain Grosjean	Lotus F1	Lotus-Renault E21	1h19m06.482s	13
9	Lewis Hamilton	Mercedes AMG	Mercedes F1 W04	1h19m06.879s	12
10	Jenson Button	McLaren	McLaren-Mercedes MP4-28	1h19m11.679s	9
11	Kimi Raikkonen	Lotus F1	Lotus-Renault E21	1h19m12.047s	11
12	Sergio Perez	McLaren	McLaren-Mercedes MP4-28	1h19m13.117s	8
13	Esteban Gutierrez	Sauber	Sauber-Ferrari C32	1h19m14.232s	16
14	Pastor Maldonado	Williams	Williams-Renault FW35	1h19m22.437s	14
15	Valtteri Bottas	Williams	Williams-Renault FW35	1h19m30.179s	18
16	Adrian Sutil *	Force India	Force India-Mercedes VJM06	52 laps/brakes	17
17	Charles Pic	Caterham	Caterham-Renault CT03	52 laps	20
18	Giedo van der Garde	Caterham	Caterham-Renault CT03	52 laps	19
19	Jules Bianchi	Marussia	Marussia-Cosworth MR02	52 laps	21
20	Max Chilton	Marussia	Marussia-Cosworth MR02	52 laps	22
R	Jean-Eric Vergne	Toro Rosso	Toro Rosso-Ferrari STR8	14 laps/transmission	10
R	Paul di Resta	Force India	Force India-Mercedes VJM06	0 laps/collision	15

Pole: Vettel, 1m23.755s, 154.719mph/248.997kph. Fastest lap: Hamilton, 1m25.849s, 150.946mph/242.924kph on Lap 51. Race leaders: Vettel 1-23 & 28-53, Alonso 24-27

* 3-place grid penalty for impeding Hamilton

McLAREN IN REVERSE

McLaren struggled in 2013, failing to achieve a single podium placing, as they dropped from a ranking of third overall in 2012 to a distant fifth as Jenson Button and Sergio Pérez struggled with the MP4-28. Team Principal Martin Whitmarsh said they had been overambitious technically and the fall-out was swift as technical director Paddy Lowe quit to join Mercedes.

SINGAPORE GRAND PRIX

MARINA BAY CIRCUIT • ROUND 13 • DATE: 22ND SEPTEMBER 2013
Laps: 61 • Distance: 191.981miles/308.965km • Weather: Very hot & humid

Pos	Driver	Team	Chassis-Engine	Result	Qual
1	Sebastian Vettel	Red Bull Racing	Red Bull-Renault RB9	1h59m13.132s	1
2	Fernando Alonso	Ferrari	Ferrari F138	1h59m45.759s	7
3	Kimi Raikkonen	Lotus F1	Lotus-Renault E21	1h59m57.052s	13
4	Nico Rosberg	Mercedes AMG	Mercedes F1 W04	2h00m04.287s	2
5	Lewis Hamilton	Mercedes AMG	Mercedes F1 W04	2h00m06.291s	5
6	Felipe Massa	Ferrari	Ferrari F138	2h00m17.009s	6
7	Jenson Button	McLaren	McLaren-Mercedes MP4-28	2h00m36.486s	8
8	Sergio Perez	McLaren	McLaren-Mercedes MP4-28	2h00m36.952s	14
9	Nico Hulkenberg	Sauber	Sauber-Ferrari C32	2h00m37.393s	11
10	Adrian Sutil	Force India	Force India-Mercedes VJM06	2h00m37.800s	15
11	Pastor Maldonado	Williams	Williams-Renault FW35	2h00m41.611s	18
12	Esteban Gutierrez	Sauber	Sauber-Ferrari C32	2h00m51.026s	10
13	Valtteri Bottas	Williams	Williams-Renault FW35	2h00m58.293s	16
14	Jean-Eric Vergne	Toro Rosso	Toro Rosso-Ferrari STR8	2h01m06.644s	12
15	Mark Webber	Red Bull Racing	Red Bull-Renault RB9	60 laps/water leak	4
16	Giedo van der Garde	Caterham	Caterham-Renault CT03	60 laps	20
17	Max Chilton	Marussia	Marussia-Cosworth MR02	60 laps	22
18	Jules Bianchi	Marussia	Marussia-Cosworth MR02	60 laps	21
19	Charles Pic	Caterham	Caterham-Renault CT03	60 laps	19
20	Paul di Resta	Force India	Force India-Mercedes VJM06	54 laps/spun off	17
R	Romain Grosjean	Lotus F1	Lotus-Renault E21	37 laps/engine	3
R	Daniel Ricciardo	Toro Rosso	Toro Rosso-Ferrari STR8	23 laps/spun off	9

Pole: Vettel, 1m42.841s, 110.170mph/177.302kph. Fastest lap: Vettel, 1m48.574s, 104.353mph/167.940kph on Lap 46. Race leaders: Vettel 1-61

KOREAN GRAND PRIX

KOREA INTERNATIONAL CIRCUIT • ROUND 14 • DATE: 6TH OCTOBER 2013
Laps: 55 • Distance: 191.894miles/308.825km • Weather: Hot but dull

Pos	Driver	Team	Chassis-Engine	Result	Qual
1	Sebastian Vettel	Red Bull Racing	Red Bull-Renault RB9	1h43m13.701s	1
2	Kimi Raikkonen	Lotus F1	Lotus-Renault E21	1h43m17.925s	9
3	Romain Grosjean	Lotus F1	Lotus-Renault E21	1h43m18.628s	3
4	Nico Hulkenberg	Sauber	Sauber-Ferrari C32	1h43m37.815s	7
5	Lewis Hamilton	Mercedes AMG	Mercedes F1 W04	1h43m38.956s	2
6	Fernando Alonso	Ferrari	Ferrari F138	1h43m39.890s	5
7	Nico Rosberg	Mercedes AMG	Mercedes F1 W04	1h43m40.399s	4
8	Jenson Button	McLaren	McLaren-Mercedes MP4-28	1h43m45.963s	11
9	Felipe Massa	Ferrari	Ferrari F138	1h43m48.091s	6
10	Sergio Perez	McLaren	McLaren-Mercedes MP4-28	1h43m48.856s	10
11	Esteban Gutierrez	Sauber	Sauber-Ferrari C32	1h43m49.691s	8
12	Valtteri Bottas	Williams	Williams-Renault FW35	1h44m00.750s	17
13	Pastor Maldonado	Williams	Williams-Renault FW35	1h44m03.714s	18
14	Charles Pic	Caterham	Caterham-Renault CT03	1h44m17.279s	19
15	Giedo van der Garde	Caterham	Caterham-Renault CT03	1h44m18.202s	20
16	Jules Bianchi *	Marussia	Marussia-Cosworth MR02	1h44m21.671s	22
17	Max Chilton	Marussia	Marussia-Cosworth MR02	1h44m26.599s	21
18	Jean-Eric Vergne	Toro Rosso	Toro Rosso-Ferrari STR8	53 laps/brakes	16

Pos	Driver	Team	Chassis-Engine	Result	Qual
19	Daniel Ricciardo	Toro Rosso	Toro Rosso-Ferrari STR8	52 laps/brakes	12
20	Adrian Sutil	Force India	Force India-Mercedes VJM06	50 laps/collision	14
R	Mark Webber !	Red Bull Racing	Red Bull-Renault RB9	36 laps/collision	13
R	Paul di Resta	Force India	Force India-Mercedes VJM06	24 laps/spun off	15

Pole: Vettel, 1m37.202s, 129.219mph/207.958kph. Fastest lap: Vettel, 1m41.380s, 123.894mph/199.388kph on Lap 53. Race leaders: Vettel 1-55

* 3-place grid penalty for impeding di Resta • ! 10-place grid penalty for receiving 3 reprimands

JAPANESE GRAND PRIX

SUZUKA • ROUND 15 • DATE: 13TH OCTOBER 2013
Laps: 53 • Distance: 191.240miles/307.771km • Weather: Warm & bright

Pos	Driver	Team	Chassis-Engine	Result	Qual
1	Sebastian Vettel	Red Bull Racing	Red Bull-Renault RB9	1h26m49.301s	2
2	Mark Webber	Red Bull Racing	Red Bull-Renault RB9	1h26m56.430s	1
3	Romain Grosjean	Lotus F1	Lotus-Renault E21	1h26m59.211s	4
4	Fernando Alonso	Ferrari	Ferrari F138	1h27m34.906s	8
5	Kimi Raikkonen	Lotus F1	Lotus-Renault E21	1h27m36.626s	9
6	Nico Hulkenberg	Sauber	Sauber-Ferrari C32	1h27m40.916s	7
7	Esteban Gutierrez	Sauber	Sauber-Ferrari C32	1h28m00.931s	14
8	Nico Rosberg	Mercedes AMG	Mercedes F1 W04	1h28m01.324s	6
9	Jenson Button	McLaren	McLaren-Mercedes MP4-28	1h28m10.122s	10
10	Felipe Massa	Ferrari	Ferrari F138	1h28m18.564s	5
11	Paul di Resta	Force India	Force India-Mercedes VJM06	1h28m27.873s	12
12	Jean-Eric Vergne	Toro Rosso	Toro Rosso-Ferrari STR8	52 laps	17
13	Daniel Ricciardo	Toro Rosso	Toro Rosso-Ferrari STR8	52 laps	16
14	Adrian Sutil *	Force India	Force India-Mercedes VJM06	52 laps	22
15	Sergio Perez	McLaren	McLaren-Mercedes MP4-28	52 laps	11
16	Pastor Maldonado	Williams	Williams-Renault FW35	52 laps	15
17	Valtteri Bottas	Williams	Williams-Renault FW35	52 laps	13
18	Charles Pic !	Caterham	Caterham-Renault CT03	52 laps	20
19	Max Chilton	Marussia	Marussia-Cosworth MR02	52 laps	18
R	Lewis Hamilton	Mercedes AMG	Mercedes F1 W04	7 laps/collision	3
R	Giedo van der Garde	Caterham	Caterham-Renault CT03	0 laps/collision	19
R	Jules Bianchi !	Marussia	Marussia-Cosworth MR02	0 laps/collision	21

Pole: Webber, 1m30.915s, 142.879mph/229.942kph. Fastest lap: Webber, 1m34.587s, 137.332mph/221.015kph on Lap 44. Race leaders: Grosjean 1-12 & 15-28, Vettel 13-14 & 29-37 & 43-53, Webber 38-42

* 5-place grid penalty for gearbox change • ! 10-place grid penalty for receiving 3 reprimands

HARD TO PLEASE

Nico Hulkenberg drove his heart out for Sauber, a team that ranked only seventh, yet still did well enough to rank 10th in the drivers' points table. This was thanks to a fourth-place finish in Korea and a fifth at Monza, where he impressed by qualifying behind only the Red Bulls for the Swiss team. His reward? He was dropped.

INDIAN GRAND PRIX

BUDDH INTERNATIONAL CIRCUIT • ROUND 16 • DATE: 27TH OCTOBER 2013
Laps: 60 • Distance: 190.764miles/307.5km • Weather: Hot but dull

Pos	Driver	Team	Chassis-Engine	Result	Qual
1	Sebastian Vettel	Red Bull Racing	Red Bull-Renault RB9	1h31m12.187s	1
2	Nico Rosberg	Mercedes AMG	Mercedes F1 W04	1h31m42.010s	2
3	Romain Grosjean	Lotus F1	Lotus-Renault E21	1h31m52.079s	17
4	Felipe Massa	Ferrari	Ferrari F138	1h31m53.879s	5
5	Sergio Perez	McLaren	McLaren-Mercedes MP4-28	1h31m56.016s	9
6	Lewis Hamilton	Mercedes AMG	Mercedes F1 W04	1h32m04.662s	3
7	Kimi Raikkonen	Lotus F1	Lotus-Renault E21	1h32m20.175s	6
8	Paul di Resta	Force India	Force India-Mercedes VJM06	1h32m25.055s	12
9	Adrian Sutil	Force India	Force India-Mercedes VJM06	1h32m26.921s	13
10	Daniel Ricciardo	Toro Rosso	Toro Rosso-Ferrari STR8	1h32m28.424s	11
11	Fernando Alonso	Ferrari	Ferrari F138	1h32m30.484s	8
12	Pastor Maldonado	Williams	Williams-Renault FW35	1h32m31.138s	18
13	Jean-Eric Vergne	Toro Rosso	Toro Rosso-Ferrari STR8	59 laps	14
14	Jenson Button	McLaren	McLaren-Mercedes MP4-28	59 laps	10
15	Esteban Gutierrez	Sauber	Sauber-Ferrari C32	59 laps	16
16	Valtteri Bottas	Williams	Williams-Renault FW35	59 laps	15
17	Max Chilton	Marussia	Marussia-Cosworth MR02	58 laps	22
18	Jules Bianchi	Marussia	Marussia-Cosworth MR02	58 laps	19
19	Nico Hulkenberg	Sauber	Sauber-Ferrari C32	54 laps/brakes	7
R	Mark Webber	Red Bull Racing	Red Bull-Renault RB9	39 laps/alternator	4
R	Charles Pic	Caterham	Caterham-Renault CT03	35 laps/hydraulics	21
R	Giedo van der Garde	Caterham	Caterham-Renault CT03	1 lap/collision	20

Pole: Vettel, 1m24.119s, 136.286mph/219.332kph. Fastest lap: Raikkonen, 1m27.679s, 130.753mph/210.426kph on Lap 60. Race leaders: Vettel 1-2 & 29-31 & 33-60, Massa 3-8, Webber 9-28 & 32

SEEKING PROMOTION

Both the Scuderia Toro Rosso drivers knew that if they had a good season they might earn promotion to Red Bull Racing, as Mark Webber would be retiring at the end of the season. There was little to separate Daniel Ricciardo and Jean-Eric Vergne, but the Australian got picked for his superior pace in qualifying.

ABU DHABI GRAND PRIX

YAS MARINA CIRCUIT • ROUND 17 • DATE: 3RD NOVEMBER 2013
Laps: 55 • Distance: 189.547miles/305.47km • Weather: Hot & bright

Pos	Driver	Team	Chassis-Engine	Result	Qual
1	Sebastian Vettel	Red Bull Racing	Red Bull-Renault RB9	1h38m06.106s	2
2	Mark Webber	Red Bull Racing	Red Bull-Renault RB9	1h38m36.935s	1
3	Nico Rosberg	Mercedes AMG	Mercedes F1 W04	1h38m39.756s	3
4	Romain Grosjean	Lotus F1	Lotus-Renault E21	1h38m40.908s	6
5	Fernando Alonso	Ferrari	Ferrari F138	1h39m13.287s	10
6	Paul di Resta	Force India	Force India-Mercedes VJM06	1h39m24.280s	11

Pos	Driver	Team	Chassis-Engine	Result	Qual
7	Lewis Hamilton	Mercedes AMG	Mercedes F1 W04	1h39m25.373s	4
8	Felipe Massa	Ferrari	Ferrari F138	1h39m28.992s	7
9	Sergio Perez	McLaren	McLaren-Mercedes MP4-28	1h39m37.304s	8
10	Adrian Sutil	Force India	Force India-Mercedes VJM06	1h39m39.363s	17
11	Pastor Maldonado	Williams	Williams-Renault FW35	1h39m42.095s	14
12	Jenson Button	McLaren	McLaren-Mercedes MP4-28	1h39m49.873s	12
13	Esteban Gutierrez	Sauber	Sauber-Ferrari C32	1h39m50.401s	16
14	Nico Hulkenberg	Sauber	Sauber-Ferrari C32	54 laps	5
15	Valtteri Bottas	Williams	Williams-Renault FW35	54 laps	15
16	Daniel Ricciardo	Toro Rosso	Toro Rosso-Ferrari STR8	54 laps	9
17	Jean-Eric Vergne	Toro Rosso	Toro Rosso-Ferrari STR8	54 laps	13
18	Giedo van der Garde	Caterham	Caterham-Renault CT03	54 laps	18
19	Charles Pic	Caterham	Caterham-Renault CT03	54 laps	19
20	Jules Bianchi *	Marussia	Marussia-Cosworth MR02	53 laps	21
21	Max Chilton	Marussia	Marussia-Cosworth MR02	53 laps	20
R	Kimi Raikkonen !	Lotus F1	Lotus-Renault E21	0 laps/collision	22

Pole: Webber, 1m39.957s, 124.292mph/200.030kph. Fastest lap: Alonso, 1m43.434s, 120.114mph/193.305kph on Lap 55. Race leaders: Vettel 1-55

* 5-place grid penalty for gearbox change • ! excluded from qualifying for failing floor flexibility test

NEW DRIVERS

Esteban Gutierrez and Valtteri Bottas were the only two of the five rookies to score points. The Mexican finished seventh at Suzuka for Sauber, the Finn eighth in the penultimate round at Circuit of the Americas for Williams. Jules Bianchi took a 13th with Marussia team-mate Max Chilton claiming a 14th, a result equalled by Caterham's Giedo van der Garde.

UNITED STATES GRAND PRIX

CIRCUIT OF THE AMERICAS • ROUND 18 • DATE: 17TH NOVEMBER 2013
Laps: 56 • Distance: 191.834miles/308.728km • Weather: Hot & bright

Pos	Driver	Team	Chassis-Engine	Result	Qual
1	Sebastian Vettel	Red Bull Racing	Red Bull-Renault RB9	1h39m17.148s	1
2	Romain Grosjean	Lotus F1	Lotus-Renault E21	1h39m23.432s	3
3	Mark Webber	Red Bull Racing	Red Bull-Renault RB9	1h39m25.544s	2
4	Lewis Hamilton	Mercedes AMG	Mercedes F1 W04	1h39m44.506s	5
5	Fernando Alonso	Ferrari	Ferrari F138	1h39m46.740s	6
6	Nico Hulkenberg	Sauber	Sauber-Ferrari C32	1h39m47.548s	4
7	Sergio Perez	McLaren	McLaren-Mercedes MP4-28	1h40m03.840s	7
8	Valtteri Bottas	Williams	Williams-Renault FW35	1h40m11.657s	9
9	Nico Rosberg	Mercedes AMG	Mercedes F1 W04	1h40m16.289s	12
10	Jenson Button *	McLaren	McLaren-Mercedes MP4-28	1h40m34.426s	15
11	Daniel Ricciardo	Toro Rosso	Toro Rosso-Ferrari STR8	1h40m38.152s	10
12	Felipe Massa	Ferrari	Ferrari F138	1h40m44.062s	13
13	Esteban Gutierrez	Sauber	Sauber-Ferrari C32	1h40m48.855s	20
14	Heikki Kovalainen	Lotus F1	Lotus-Renault E21	1h40m52.211s	8
15	Paul di Resta	Force India	Force India-Mercedes VJM06	1h40m54.001s	11

Pos	Driver	Team	Chassis-Engine	Result	Qual
16	Jean-Eric Vergne	Toro Rosso	Toro Rosso-Ferrari STR8	1h41m01.722s	14
17	Pastor Maldonado	Williams	Williams-Renault FW35	55 laps	17
18	Jules Bianchi	Marussia	Marussia-Cosworth MR02	55 laps	19
19	Giedo van der Garde	Caterham	Caterham-Renault CT03	55 laps	18
20	Charles Pic ^	Caterham	Caterham-Renault CT03	55 laps	22
21	Max Chilton	Marussia	Marussia-Cosworth MR02	54 laps	21
R	Adrian Sutil	Force India	Force India-Mercedes VJM06	0 laps/collision	16

Pole: Vettel, 1m36.338s, 128.010mph/206.012kph. Fastest lap: Vettel, 1m39.856s, 123.500mph/198.754kph on Lap 54. Race leaders: Vettel 1-27 & 30-56, Grosjean 28-29

* 3-place grid penalty for overtaking under red flags • ! 10-place grid penalty for impeding Maldonado • ^ 5-place grid penalty for gearbox change

BRAZILIAN GRAND PRIX

INTERLAGOS • ROUND 19 • DATE: 24TH NOVEMBER 2013
Laps: 71 • Distance: 190.101miles/305.939km • Weather: Hot but dull, rain later

Pos	Driver	Team	Chassis-Engine	Result	Qual
1	Sebastian Vettel	Red Bull Racing	Red Bull-Renault RB9	1h32m36.300s	1
2	Mark Webber	Red Bull Racing	Red Bull-Renault RB9	1h32m46.752s	4
3	Fernando Alonso	Ferrari	Ferrari F138	1h32m55.213s	3
4	Jenson Button	McLaren	McLaren-Mercedes MP4-28	1h33m13.660s	14
5	Nico Rosberg	Mercedes AMG	Mercedes F1 W04	1h33m15.348s	2
6	Sergio Perez *	McLaren	McLaren-Mercedes MP4-28	1h33m20.351s	19
7	Felipe Massa	Ferrari	Ferrari F138	1h33m25.410s	9
8	Nico Hulkenberg	Sauber	Sauber-Ferrari C32	1h33m40.552s	10
9	Lewis Hamilton	Mercedes AMG	Mercedes F1 W04	1h33m49.203s	5
10	Daniel Ricciardo	Toro Rosso	Toro Rosso-Ferrari STR8	70 laps	7
11	Paul di Resta	Force India	Force India-Mercedes VJM06	70 laps	12
12	Esteban Gutierrez	Sauber	Sauber-Ferrari C32	70 laps	17
13	Adrian Sutil	Force India	Force India-Mercedes VJM06	70 laps	15
14	Heikki Kovalainen	Lotus F1	Lotus-Renault E21	70 laps	11
15	Jean-Eric Vergne	Toro Rosso	Toro Rosso-Ferrari STR8	70 laps	8
16	Pastor Maldonado	Williams	Williams-Renault FW35	70 laps	16
17	Jules Bianchi	Marussia	Marussia-Cosworth MR02	69 laps	21
18	Giedo van der Garde	Caterham	Caterham-Renault CT03	69 laps	20
19	Max Chilton	Marussia	Marussia-Cosworth MR02	69 laps	22
R	Charles Pic	Caterham	Caterham-Renault CT03	58 laps/suspension	18
R	Valtteri Bottas	Williams	Williams-Renault FW35	45 laps/collision	13
R	Romain Grosjean	Lotus F1	Lotus-Renault E21	2 laps/engine	6

Pole: Vettel, 1m26.479s, 111.460mph/179.377kph. Fastest lap: Webber, 1m15.436s, 127.776mph/205.636kph on Lap 51. Race leaders: Vettel 1-71

* 5-place grid penalty for gearbox change

WORLD DRIVERS' CHAMPIONSHIP FINAL RESULTS

Pos	Driver	Nat	Car-Engine	R1	R2	R3	R4	R5	R6	R7	R8
1	Sebastian Vettel	DEU	Red Bull-Renault RB9	3P	1P	4F	1F	4	2F	1P	R
2	Fernando Alonso	ESP	Ferrari F138	2	R	1	8	1	7	2	3
3	Mark Webber	AUS	Red Bull-Renault RB9	6	2	R	7	5	3	4F	2F
4	Lewis Hamilton	GBR	Mercedes F1 W04	5	3	3P	5	12	4	3	4P
5	Kimi Raikkonen	FIN	Lotus-Renault E21	1F	7	2	2	2	10	9	5
6	Nico Rosberg	DEU	Mercedes F1 W04	R	4	R	9P	6P	1P	5	1
7	Romain Grosjean	FRA	Lotus-Renault E21	10	6	9	3	R	R	13	19
8	Felipe Massa	BRA	Ferrari F138	4	5	6	15	3	R	8	6
9	Jenson Button	GBR	McLaren-Mercedes MP4-28	9	17	5	10	8	6	12	13
10	Nico Hulkenberg	DEU	Sauber-Ferrari C32	NS	8	10	12	15	11	R	10
11	Sergio Perez	MEX	McLaren-Mercedes MP4-28	11	9F	11	6	9	16	11	20
12	Paul di Resta	GBR	Force India-Mercedes VJM06	8	R	8	4	7	9	7	9
13	Adrian Sutil	DEU	Force India-Mercedes VJM06	7	R	R	13	13	5	10	7
14	Daniel Ricciardo	AUS	Toro Rosso-Ferrari STR8	R	18	7	16	10	R	15	8
15	Jean-Eric Vergne	FRA	Toro Rosso-Ferrari STR8	12	10	12	R	R	8	6	R
16	Esteban Gutierrez	MEX	Sauber-Ferrari C32	13	12	R	18	11F	13	20	14
17	Valtteri Bottas	FIN	Williams-Renault FW35	14	11	13	14	16	12	14	12
18	Pastor Maldonado	VEN	Williams-Renault FW35	R	R	14	11	14	R	16	11
19	Jules Bianchi	FRA	Marussia-Cosworth MR02	15	13	15	19	18	R	17	16
20	Charles Pic	FRA	Caterham-Renault CT03	16	14	16	17	17	R	18	15
21	Heikki Kovalainen	FIN	Lotus-Renault E21	-	-	-	T	T	-	-	-
22	Giedo van der Garde	NLD	Caterham-Renault CT03	18	15	18	21	R	15	R	18
23	Max Chilton	GBR	Marussia-Cosworth MR02	17	16	17	20	19	14	19	17

Pos	Driver	R9	R10	R11	R12	R13	R14	R15	R16	R17	R18	R19	Total
1	Vettel	1	3	1F	1P	1PF	1PF	1	1P	1	1PF	1P	397
2	Alonso	4F	5	2	2	2	6	4	11	5F	5	3	242
3	Webber	7	4F	5	3	15	R	2PF	R	2P	3	2F	199
4	Hamilton	5P	1P	3P	9F	5	5	R	6	7	4	9	189
5	Raikkonen	2	2	R	11	3	2	5	7F	R	-	-	183
6	Rosberg	9	19	4	6	4	7	8	2	3	9	5	171
7	Grosjean	3	6	8	8	R	3	3	3	4	2	R	132
8	Massa	R	8	7	4	6	9	10	4	8	12	7	112
9	Button	6	7	6	10	7	8	9	14	12	10	4	73
10	Hulkenberg	10	11	13	5	9	4	6	19	14	6	8	51
11	Perez	8	9	11	12	8	10	15	5	9	7	6	49
12	di Resta	11	18	R	R	20	R	11	8	6	15	11	48
13	Sutil	13	R	9	16	10	20	14	9	10	R	13	29
14	Ricciardo	12	13	10	7	R	19	13	10	16	11	10	20
15	Vergne	R	12	12	R	14	18	12	13	17	16	15	13
16	Gutierrez	14	R	14	13	12	11	7	15	13	13	12	6
17	Bottas	16	R	15	15	13	12	17	16	15	8	R	4
18	Maldonado	15	10	17	14	11	13	16	12	11	17	16	1
19	Bianchi	R	16	18	19	18	16	R	18	20	18	17	0
20	Pic	17	15	R	17	19	14	18	R	19	20	R	0
21	Kovalainen	-	-	T	T	-	-	T	-	T	14	14	0
22	van der Garde	18	14	16	18	16	15	R	R	18	19	18	0
23	Chilton	19	17	19	20	17	17	19	17	21	21	19	0

WORLD CONSTRUCTORS' CHAMPIONSHIP FINAL RESULTS

Pos	Team-Engine	R1	R2	R3	R4	R5	R6	R7	R8	R9	R10
1	Red Bull-Renault	3/6	1/2	4/R	1/7	4/5	2/3	1/4	2/R	1/7	3/4
2	Mercedes AMG	5/R	3/4	3/R	5/9	6/12	1/4	3/5	1/4	5/9	1/19
3	Ferrari	2/4	5/R	1/6	8/15	1/3	7/R	2/8	3/6	4/R	5/8
4	Lotus-Renault	1/10	6/7	2/9	2/3	2/R	10/R	9/13	5/19	2/3	2/6
5	McLaren-Mercedes	9/11	9/17	5/11	6/10	8/9	6/16	11/12	13/20	6/8	7/9
6	Force India-Mercedes	7/8	R/R	8/R	4/13	7/13	5/9	7/10	7/9	11/13	18/R
7	Sauber-Ferrari	13/NS	8/12	10/R	12/18	11/15	11/13	20/R	10/14	10/14	11/R
8	Toro Rosso-Ferrari	12/R	10/18	7/12	16/R	10/R	8/R	6/15	8/R	12/R	12/13
9	Williams-Renault	14/R	11/R	13/14	11/14	14/16	12/R	14/16	11/12	15/16	10/R
10	Marussia-Cosworth	15/17	13/16	15/17	19/20	18/19	14/R	17/19	16/17	19/R	16/17
11	Caterham-Renault	16/18	14/15	16/18	17/21	17/R	15/R	18/R	15/18	17/18	14/15

Pos	Team-Engine	R11	R12	R13	R14	R15	R16	R17	R18	R19	Total
1	Red Bull-Renault	1/5	1/3	1/15	1/R	1/2	1/R	1/2	1/3	1/2	596
2	Mercedes AMG	3/4	6/9	4/5	5/7	8/R	2/6	3/7	4/9	5/9	360
3	Ferrari	2/7	2/4	2/6	6/9	4/10	4/11	5/8	5/12	3/7	354
4	Lotus-Renault	8/R	8/11	3/R	2/3	3/5	3/7	4/R	2/14	14/R	315
5	McLaren-Mercedes	6/11	10/12	7/8	8/10	9/15	5/14	9/12	7/10	4/6	122
6	Force India-Mercedes	9/R	16/R	10/20	20/R	11/14	8/9	6/10	15/R	11/13	77
7	Sauber-Ferrari	13/14	5/13	9/12	4/11	6/7	15/19	13/14	6/13	8/12	57
8	Toro Rosso-Ferrari	10/12	7/R	14/R	18/19	12/13	10/13	16/17	11/16	10/15	33
9	Williams-Renault	15/17	14/15	11/13	12/13	16/17	12/16	11/15	8/17	16/R	5
10	Marussia-Cosworth	18/19	19/20	17/18	16/17	19/R	17/18	20/21	18/21	17/19	0
11	Caterham-Renault	16/R	17/18	16/19	14/15	18/R	R/R	18/19	19/20	18/R	0

SYMBOLS AND GRAND PRIX KEY

Round 1 Australian GP
Round 2 Malaysian GP
Round 3 Chinese GP
Round 4 Bahrain GP
Round 5 Spanish GP
Round 6 Monaco GP
Round 7 Canadian GP
Round 8 British GP
Round 9 German GP
Round 10 Hungarian GP
Round 11 Belgian GP
Round 12 Italian GP
Round 13 Singapore GP
Round 14 Korean GP
Round 15 Japanese GP
Round 16 Indian GP
Round 17 Abu Dhabi GP
Round 18 United States GP
Round 19 Brazilian GP

SCORING

1st 25 points
2nd 18 points
3rd 15 points
4th 12 points
5th 10 points
6th 8 points
7th 6 points
8th 4 points
9th 2 points
10th 1 point

DNPQ DID NOT PRE-QUALIFY **DNQ** DID NOT QUALIFY **DQ** DISQUALIFIED **EX** EXCLUDED
F FASTEST LAP **NC** NOT CLASSIFIED **NS** NON-STARTER **P** POLE POSITION **R** RETIRED

2014

SEASON SUMMARY

This was the year in which Mercedes made its breakthrough and became the champion team for the first time in its second-generation guise. Few knew in the second round at Sepang, when Lewis Hamilton led a Mercedes championship one-two ahead of Nico Rosberg, that this was the start of a remarkable run of titles for the team from Brackley. In a year that had a comprehensive rule change with the introduction of state-of-the-art turbo hybrid engines, not one of the 10 rival teams was able to get close, and second-placed team Red Bull Racing could score only 405 points to Mercedes's 701. It was a rout.

AUSTRALIAN GRAND PRIX

ALBERT PARK • ROUND 1 • DATE: 16TH MARCH 2014
Laps: 57 • Distance: 187.822miles/302.271km • Weather: Warm but dull

Pos	Driver	Team	Chassis-Engine	Result	Qual
1	Nico Rosberg	Mercedes AMG	Mercedes F1 W05	1h32m58.710s	3
DQ	Daniel Ricciardo ^	Red Bull Racing	Red Bull-Renault RB10	1h33m23.235s	2
2	Kevin Magnussen	McLaren	McLaren-Mercedes MP4-29	1h33m25.487s	4
3	Jenson Button	McLaren	McLaren-Mercedes MP4-29	1h33m28.737s	10
4	Fernando Alonso	Ferrari	Ferrari F14 T	1h33m33.994s	5
5	Valtteri Bottas *	Williams	Williams-Mercedes FW36	1h33m46.349s	15
6	Nico Hulkenberg	Force India	Force India-Mercedes VJM07	1h33m49.428s	7
7	Kimi Raikkonen	Ferrari	Ferrari F14 T	1h33m56.385s	11
8	Jean-Eric Vergne	Toro Rosso	Toro Rosso-Renault STR9	1h33m59.151s	6
9	Daniil Kvyat	Toro Rosso	Toro Rosso-Renault STR9	1h34m02.295s	8
10	Sergio Perez	Force India	Force India-Mercedes VJM07	1h34m24.626s	16
11	Adrian Sutil	Sauber	Sauber-Ferrari C33	56 laps	13
12	Esteban Gutierrez *	Sauber	Sauber-Ferrari C33	56 laps	20
13	Max Chilton	Marussia	Marussia-Ferrari MR03	55 laps	17
NC	Jules Bianchi	Marussia	Marussia-Ferrari MR03	49 laps	18
R	Romain Grosjean !	Lotus F1	Lotus-Renault E22	43 laps/power unit	22
R	Pastor Maldonado	Lotus F1	Lotus-Renault E22	29 laps/power unit	21
R	Marcus Ericsson	Caterham	Caterham-Renault CT05	27 laps/fuel pressure	19
R	Sebastian Vettel	Red Bull Racing	Red Bull-Renault RB10	3 laps/engine	12
R	Lewis Hamilton	Mercedes AMG	Mercedes F1 W05	2 laps/engine	1
R	Felipe Massa	Williams	Williams-Mercedes FW36	0 laps/collision	9
R	Kamui Kobayashi	Caterham	Caterham-Renault CT05	0 laps/brakes	14

Pole: Hamilton, 1m44.231s, 113.809mph/183.158kph. Fastest lap: Rosberg, 1m32.478s, 128.273mph/206.436kph on Lap 19. Race leaders: Rosberg 1-57

* 5-place grid penalty for gearbox change • ! Put to back of grid as car modified in parc ferme • ^ excluded for fuel flow exceeding 100kg per hour

TURBO ENGINES RETURN

It was all change in the engine regulations, and the 2.4-litre V8 engines were replaced by turbocharged 1.6-litre units. These had to produce some of their power from energy recovery systems as F1 aligned itself more with the road car industry. Mercedes did it best, with customer teams Williams, McLaren and Force India ranking 3rd, 5th and 6th.

MALAYSIAN GRAND PRIX

SEPANG • ROUND 2 • DATE: 30TH MARCH 2014
Laps: 56 • Distance: 192.878miles/310.408km • Weather: Very hot & bright

Pos	Driver	Team	Chassis-Engine	Result	Qual
1	Lewis Hamilton	Mercedes AMG	Mercedes F1 W05	1h40m25.974s	1
2	Nico Rosberg	Mercedes AMG	Mercedes F1 W05	1h40m43.287s	3
3	Sebastian Vettel	Red Bull Racing	Red Bull-Renault RB10	1h40m50.508s	2
4	Fernando Alonso	Ferrari	Ferrari F14 T	1h41m01.966s	4
5	Nico Hulkenberg	Force India	Force India-Mercedes VJM07	1h41m13.173s	7
6	Jenson Button	McLaren	McLaren-Mercedes MP4-29	1h41m49.665s	10
7	Felipe Massa	Williams	Williams-Mercedes FW36	1h41m51.050s	13
8	Valtteri Bottas *	Williams	Williams-Mercedes FW36	1h41m51.511s	18
9	Kevin Magnussen	McLaren	McLaren-Mercedes MP4-29	55 laps	8
10	Daniil Kvyat	Toro Rosso	Toro Rosso-Renault STR9	55 laps	11
11	Romain Grosjean	Lotus F1	Lotus-Renault E22	55 laps	15
12	Kimi Raikkonen	Ferrari	Ferrari F14 T	55 laps	6
13	Kamui Kobayashi	Caterham	Caterham-Renault CT05	55 laps	20
14	Marcus Ericsson	Caterham	Caterham-Renault CT05	54 laps	22
15	Max Chilton	Marussia	Marussia-Ferrari MR03	54 laps	21
R	Daniel Ricciardo	Red Bull Racing	Red Bull-Renault RB10	49 laps/wing	5
R	Esteban Gutierrez	Sauber	Sauber-Ferrari C33	35 laps/gearbox	12
R	Adrian Sutil	Sauber	Sauber-Ferrari C33	32 laps/power unit	17
R	Jean-Eric Vergne	Toro Rosso	Toro Rosso-Renault STR9	18 laps/turbo	9
R	Jules Bianchi	Marussia	Marussia-Ferrari MR03	8 laps/collision	19
R	Pastor Maldonado	Lotus F1	Lotus-Renault E22	7 laps/power unit	16
NS	Sergio Perez	Force India	Force India-Mercedes VJM07	gearbox	14

Pole: Hamilton, 1m59.431s, 103.820mph/167.082kph. Fastest lap: Hamilton, 1m43.066s, 120.304mph/193.611kph on Lap 53. Race leaders: Hamilton 1-56

* 3-place grid penalty for impeding Ricciardo

LEARNING TO DRIVE

This first year with hybrid power in F1 made it a real case of learning how to drive in a new fashion, as the drivers had to understand both how and when to harness the extra power available from their cars' energy recovery systems and then, going into the slowest corners, how to handle their cars under heavy braking.

BAHRAIN GRAND PRIX

SAKHIR • ROUND 3 • DATE: 6TH APRIL 2014
Laps: 57 • Distance: 191.683miles/308.484km • Weather: Hot & dry

Pos	Driver	Team	Chassis-Engine	Result	Qual
1	Lewis Hamilton	Mercedes AMG	Mercedes F1 W05	1h39m42.743s	2
2	Nico Rosberg	Mercedes AMG	Mercedes F1 W05	1h39m43.828s	1
3	Sergio Perez	Force India	Force India-Mercedes VJM07	1h40m06.810s	4
4	Daniel Ricciardo !	Red Bull Racing	Red Bull-Renault RB10	1h40m07.232s	13
5	Nico Hulkenberg	Force India	Force India-Mercedes VJM07	1h40m11.397s	11
6	Sebastian Vettel	Red Bull Racing	Red Bull-Renault RB10	1h40m12.622s	10

Pos	Driver	Team	Chassis-Engine	Result	Qual
7	Felipe Massa	Williams	Williams-Mercedes FW36	1h40m14.008s	7
8	Valtteri Bottas	Williams	Williams-Mercedes FW36	1h40m14.619s	3
9	Fernando Alonso	Ferrari	Ferrari F14 T	1h40m15.338s	9
10	Kimi Raikkonen	Ferrari	Ferrari F14 T	1h40m16.205s	5
11	Daniil Kvyat	Toro Rosso	Toro Rosso-Renault STR9	1h40m24.085s	12
12	Romain Grosjean	Lotus F1	Lotus-Renault E22	1h40m25.886s	16
13	Max Chilton	Marussia	Marussia-Ferrari MR03	1h40m42.652s	21
14	Pastor Maldonado	Lotus F1	Lotus-Renault E22	1h40m45.546s	17
15	Kamui Kobayashi	Caterham	Caterham-Renault CT05	1h41m10.643s	18
16	Jules Bianchi	Marussia	Marussia-Ferrari MR03	56 laps	19
17	Jenson Button	McLaren	McLaren-Mercedes MP4-29	55 laps/clutch	6
R	Kevin Magnussen	McLaren	McLaren-Mercedes MP4-29	40 laps/clutch	8
R	Esteban Gutierrez	Sauber	Sauber-Ferrari C33	39 laps/collision	15
R	Marcus Ericsson	Caterham	Caterham-Renault CT05	33 laps/oil leak	20
R	Jean-Eric Vergne	Toro Rosso	Toro Rosso-Renault STR9	18 laps/collision	14
R	Adrian Sutil *	Sauber	Sauber-Ferrari C33	17 laps/collision	22

Pole: Rosberg, 1m33.185s, 129.916mph/209.080kph. Fastest lap: Rosberg, 1m37.020s, 124.781mph/200.816kph on Lap 49. Race leaders: Hamilton 1-18 & 22-57, Rosberg 19-21

* 5-place grid penalty for forcing Grosjean off • ! 10-place grid penalty for unsafe release in Malaysian GP

CHINESE GRAND PRIX

SHANGHAI INTERNATIONAL CIRCUIT • ROUND 4 • DATE: 20TH APRIL 2014
Laps: 54 • Distance: 182.903miles/294.354km • Weather: Warm but dull

Pos	Driver	Team	Chassis-Engine	Result	Qual
1	Lewis Hamilton	Mercedes AMG	Mercedes F1 W05	1h33m28.338s	1
2	Nico Rosberg	Mercedes AMG	Mercedes F1 W05	1h33m46.400s	4
3	Fernando Alonso	Ferrari	Ferrari F14 T	1h33m51.942s	5
4	Daniel Ricciardo	Red Bull Racing	Red Bull-Renault RB10	1h33m55.474s	2
5	Sebastian Vettel	Red Bull Racing	Red Bull-Renault RB10	1h34m16.116s	3
6	Nico Hulkenberg	Force India	Force India-Mercedes VJM07	1h34m22.633s	8
7	Valtteri Bottas	Williams	Williams-Mercedes FW36	1h34m24.035s	7
8	Kimi Raikkonen	Ferrari	Ferrari F14 T	1h34m44.673s	11
9	Sergio Perez	Force India	Force India-Mercedes VJM07	1h34m50.985s	16
10	Daniil Kvyat	Toro Rosso	Toro Rosso-Renault STR9	53 laps	13
11	Jenson Button	McLaren	McLaren-Mercedes MP4-29	53 laps	12
12	Jean-Eric Vergne	Toro Rosso	Toro Rosso-Renault STR9	53 laps	9
13	Kevin Magnussen	McLaren	McLaren-Mercedes MP4-29	53 laps	15
14	Pastor Maldonado *	Lotus F1	Lotus-Renault E22	53 laps	22
15	Felipe Massa	Williams	Williams-Mercedes FW36	53 laps	6
16	Esteban Gutierrez	Sauber	Sauber-Ferrari C33	53 laps	17
17	Jules Bianchi	Marussia	Marussia-Ferrari MR03	53 laps	19
18	Kamui Kobayashi	Caterham	Caterham-Renault CT05	53 laps	18
19	Max Chilton	Marussia	Marussia-Ferrari MR03	52 laps	21
20	Marcus Ericsson	Caterham	Caterham-Renault CT05	52 laps	20
R	Romain Grosjean	Lotus F1	Lotus-Renault E22	28 laps/gearbox	10
R	Adrian Sutil	Sauber	Sauber-Ferrari C33	5 laps/engine	14

Pole: Hamilton, 1m53.860s, 107.092mph/172.348kph. Fastest lap: Rosberg, 1m40.402s, 121.447mph/195.450kph on Lap 39. Race leaders: Hamilton 1-54

* 5-place grid penalty for causing accident at Bahrain GP

SPANISH GRAND PRIX

BARCELONA-CATALUNYA • ROUND 5 • DATE: 11TH MAY 2014
Laps: 66 • Distance: 190.775miles/307.23km • Weather: Warm & bright

Pos	Driver	Team	Chassis-Engine	Result	Qual
1	Lewis Hamilton	Mercedes AMG	Mercedes F1 W05	1h41m05.155s	1
2	Nico Rosberg	Mercedes AMG	Mercedes F1 W05	1h41m05.791s	2
3	Daniel Ricciardo	Red Bull Racing	Red Bull-Renault RB10	1h41m54.169s	3
4	Sebastian Vettel *	Red Bull Racing	Red Bull-Renault RB10	1h42m21.857s	15
5	Valtteri Bottas	Williams	Williams-Mercedes FW36	1h42m24.448s	4
6	Fernando Alonso	Ferrari	Ferrari F14 T	1h42m32.898s	7
7	Kimi Raikkonen	Ferrari	Ferrari F14 T	65 laps	6
8	Romain Grosjean	Lotus F1	Lotus-Renault E22	65 laps	5
9	Sergio Perez	Force India	Force India-Mercedes VJM07	65 laps	11
10	Nico Hulkenberg	Force India	Force India-Mercedes VJM07	65 laps	10
11	Jenson Button	McLaren	McLaren-Mercedes MP4-29	65 laps	8
12	Kevin Magnussen	McLaren	McLaren-Mercedes MP4-29	65 laps	14
13	Felipe Massa	Williams	Williams-Mercedes FW36	65 laps	9
14	Daniil Kvyat	Toro Rosso	Toro Rosso-Renault STR9	65 laps	12
15	Pastor Maldonado	Lotus F1	Lotus-Renault E22	65 laps	22
16	Esteban Gutierrez	Sauber	Sauber-Ferrari C33	65 laps	13
17	Adrian Sutil	Sauber	Sauber-Ferrari C33	65 laps	16
18	Jules Bianchi	Marussia	Marussia-Ferrari MR03	64 laps	18
19	Max Chilton	Marussia	Marussia-Ferrari MR03	64 laps	17
20	Marcus Ericsson	Caterham	Caterham-Renault CT05	64 laps	19
R	Kamui Kobayashi	Caterham	Caterham-Renault CT05	34 laps/brakes	20
R	Jean-Eric Vergne !	Toro Rosso	Toro Rosso-Renault STR9	24 laps/exhaust	21

Pole: Hamilton, 1m25.232s, 122.171mph/196.616kph. Fastest lap: Vettel, 1m28.918s, 117.107mph/188.465kph on Lap 55. Race leaders: Hamilton 1-17 & 22-43 & 46-66, Rosberg 18-21 & 44-45

* 5-place grid penalty for gearbox change • ! 10-place grid penalty for unsafe release

NEAR DOMINANCE

Mercedes's tally in landing its first world championships, for drivers and for constructors, was 17 poles, 12 fastest laps, 16 wins and 701 points across the season's 19 rounds. Also emphasising their grip on this new-look F1, Lewis Hamilton and Nico Rosberg shared 11 one-two finishes, usually with Hamilton in front.

CHANGING THE GUARD

With four world titles to his name, Sebastian Vettel was royalty at Red Bull Racing. However, he had a rude awakening when he was made to play second fiddle by incoming team-mate Daniel Ricciardo, who took his first win in Canada and added two more in Hungary and Belgium to rank third overall, with Vettel not tasting victory all year.

MONACO GRAND PRIX

MONTE CARLO • ROUND 6 • DATE: 25TH MAY 2014
Laps: 78 • Distance: 161.588miles/260.52km • Weather: Warm & bright

Pos	Driver	Team	Chassis-Engine	Result	Qual
1	Nico Rosberg	Mercedes AMG	Mercedes F1 W05	1h49m27.661s	1
2	Lewis Hamilton	Mercedes AMG	Mercedes F1 W05	1h49m36.871s	2
3	Daniel Ricciardo	Red Bull Racing	Red Bull-Renault RB10	1h49m37.275s	3
4	Fernando Alonso	Ferrari	Ferrari F14 T	1h50m00.113s	5
5	Nico Hulkenberg	Force India	Force India-Mercedes VJM07	77 laps	11
6	Jenson Button	McLaren	McLaren-Mercedes MP4-29	77 laps	12
7	Felipe Massa	Williams	Williams-Mercedes FW36	77 laps	16
8	Romain Grosjean	Lotus F1	Lotus-Renault E22	77 laps	14
9	Jules Bianchi *	Marussia	Marussia-Ferrari MR03	77 laps	21
10	Kevin Magnussen	McLaren	McLaren-Mercedes MP4-29	77 laps	8
11	Marcus Ericsson !	Caterham	Caterham-Renault CT05	77 laps	22
12	Kimi Raikkonen	Ferrari	Ferrari F14 T	77 laps	6
13	Kamui Kobayashi	Caterham	Caterham-Renault CT05	75 laps	20
14	Max Chilton	Marussia	Marussia-Ferrari MR03	75 laps	19
R	Esteban Gutierrez	Sauber	Sauber-Ferrari C33	59 laps/spun off	17
R	Valtteri Bottas	Williams	Williams-Mercedes FW36	55 laps/engine	13
R	Jean-Eric Vergne	Toro Rosso	Toro Rosso-Renault STR9	50 laps/engine	7
R	Adrian Sutil	Sauber	Sauber-Ferrari C33	23 laps/spun off	18
R	Daniil Kvyat	Toro Rosso	Toro Rosso-Renault STR9	10 laps/engine	9
R	Sebastian Vettel	Red Bull Racing	Red Bull-Renault RB10	5 laps/turbo	4
R	Sergio Perez	Force India	Force India-Mercedes VJM07	0 laps/collision	10
NS	Pastor Maldonado	Lotus F1	Lotus-Renault E22	fuel supply	15

Pole: Rosberg, 1m15.989s, 98.321mph/158.233kph. Fastest lap: Raikkonen, 1m18.479s, 95.202mph/153.212kph on Lap 75. Race leaders: Rosberg 1-78

* - 5-place grid penalty for gearbox change • ! required to start from the pit lane for causing a crash

STARTING WITH SILVER

Kevin Magnussen had a most remarkable debut year with McLaren, but it never lived up to his result in the opening race in Australia, where he finished second. He was actually third at the chequered flag behind Nico Rosberg and Daniel Ricciardo, but the Australian's Red Bull was disqualified for exceeding the maximum permissible fuel flow.

CANADIAN GRAND PRIX

MONTREAL • ROUND 7 • DATE: 8TH JUNE 2014
Laps: 70 • Distance: 189.534miles/305.27km • Weather: Hot & bright

Pos	Driver	Team	Chassis-Engine	Result	Qual
1	Daniel Ricciardo	Red Bull Racing	Red Bull-Renault RB10	1h39m12.830s	6
2	Nico Rosberg	Mercedes AMG	Mercedes F1 W05	1h39m17.066s	1
3	Sebastian Vettel	Red Bull Racing	Red Bull-Renault RB10	1h39m18.077s	3
4	Jenson Button	McLaren	McLaren-Mercedes MP4-29	1h39m24.585s	9
5	Nico Hulkenberg	Force India	Force India-Mercedes VJM07	1h39m25.673s	11
6	Fernando Alonso	Ferrari	Ferrari F14 T	1h39m27.699s	7
7	Valtteri Bottas	Williams	Williams-Mercedes FW36	1h39m36.408s	4

Pos	Driver	Team	Chassis-Engine	Result	Qual
8	Jean-Eric Vergne	Toro Rosso	Toro Rosso-Renault STR9	1h39m40.856s	8
9	Kevin Magnussen	McLaren	McLaren-Mercedes MP4-29	1h39m42.084s	12
10	Kimi Raikkonen	Ferrari	Ferrari F14 T	1h40m06.508s	10
11	Sergio Perez	Force India	Force India-Mercedes VJM07	69 laps/collision	13
12	Felipe Massa	Williams	Williams-Mercedes FW36	69 laps/collision	5
13	Adrian Sutil	Sauber	Sauber-Ferrari C33	69 laps	16
14	Esteban Gutierrez !	Sauber	Sauber-Ferrari C33	64 laps/power unit	22
R	Romain Grosjean	Lotus F1	Lotus-Renault E22	59 laps/wing	14
R	Daniil Kvyat	Toro Rosso	Toro Rosso-Renault STR9	47 laps/transmission	15
R	Lewis Hamilton	Mercedes AMG	Mercedes F1 W05	46 laps/brakes	2
R	Kamui Kobayashi *	Caterham	Caterham-Renault CT05	23 laps/suspension	21
R	Pastor Maldonado	Lotus F1	Lotus-Renault E22	21 laps/power unit	17
R	Marcus Ericsson	Caterham	Caterham-Renault CT05	7 laps/power unit	20
R	Max Chilton	Marussia	Marussia-Ferrari MR03	0 laps/collision	18
R	Jules Bianchi	Marussia	Marussia-Ferrari MR03	0 laps/collision	19

Pole: Rosberg, 1m14.874s, 130.289mph/209.680kph. Fastest lap: Massa, 1m18.504s, 124.264mph/199.984kph on Lap 58. Race leaders: Rosberg 1-17 & 19-43 & 48-67, Hamilton 18 & 44-45, Massa 46-47, Ricciardo 68-70

* 5-place grid penalty for gearbox change • ! required to start from the pit lane as car modified in parc ferme

AUSTRIAN GRAND PRIX

RED BULL RING • ROUND 8 • DATE: 22ND JUNE 2014
Laps: 71 • Distance: 190.851miles/307.146km • Weather: Warm & bright

Pos	Driver	Team	Chassis-Engine	Result	Qual
1	Nico Rosberg	Mercedes AMG	Mercedes F1 W05	1h27m54.976s	3
2	Lewis Hamilton	Mercedes AMG	Mercedes F1 W05	1h27m56.908s	9
3	Valtteri Bottas	Williams	Williams-Mercedes FW36	1h28m03.148s	2
4	Felipe Massa	Williams	Williams-Mercedes FW36	1h28m12.334s	1
5	Fernando Alonso	Ferrari	Ferrari F14 T	1h28m13.529s	4
6	Sergio Perez !	Force India	Force India-Mercedes VJM07	1h28m23.522s	15
7	Kevin Magnussen	McLaren	McLaren-Mercedes MP4-29	1h28m27.007s	6
8	Daniel Ricciardo	Red Bull Racing	Red Bull-Renault RB10	1h28m38.498s	5
9	Nico Hulkenberg	Force India	Force India-Mercedes VJM07	1h28m39.113s	10
10	Kimi Raikkonen	Ferrari	Ferrari F14 T	1h28m42.753s	8
11	Jenson Button	McLaren	McLaren-Mercedes MP4-29	1h28m45.942s	11
12	Pastor Maldonado	Lotus F1	Lotus-Renault E22	70 laps	13
13	Adrian Sutil	Sauber	Sauber-Ferrari C33	70 laps	16
14	Romain Grosjean ^	Lotus F1	Lotus-Renault E22	70 laps	22
15	Jules Bianchi	Marussia	Marussia-Ferrari MR03	69 laps	18
16	Kamui Kobayashi	Caterham	Caterham-Renault CT05	69 laps	19
17	Max Chilton *	Marussia	Marussia-Ferrari MR03	69 laps	21
18	Marcus Ericsson	Caterham	Caterham-Renault CT05	69 laps	20
19	Esteban Gutierrez	Sauber	Sauber-Ferrari C33	69 laps	17
R	Jean-Eric Vergne	Toro Rosso	Toro Rosso-Renault STR9	59 laps/brakes	14
R	Sebastian Vettel	Red Bull Racing	Red Bull-Renault RB10	34 laps/withdrawn	12
R	Daniil Kvyat	Toro Rosso	Toro Rosso-Renault STR9	24 laps/suspension	7

Pole: Massa, 1m08.759s, 140.737mph/226.495kph. Fastest lap: Perez, 1m12.142s, 134.138mph/215.874kph on Lap 59. Race leaders: Massa 1-13 & 42, Bottas 14-15 & 41, Perez 16-26, Rosberg 27-40 & 48-71, Alonso 43-47

* 3-place grid penalty for causing crash in Canadian GP • ! 5-place grid penalty for causing crash in Canadian GP • ^ made to start from pit lane for modifying car in parc ferme

BRITISH GRAND PRIX

SILVERSTONE • ROUND 9 • DATE: 6TH JULY 2014
Laps: 52 • Distance: 190.345miles/306.332km • Weather: Warm & bright

Pos	Driver	Team	Chassis-Engine	Result	Qual
1	Lewis Hamilton	Mercedes AMG	Mercedes F1 W05	2h26m52.094s	6
2	Valtteri Bottas	Williams	Williams-Mercedes FW36	2h27m22.229s	14
3	Daniel Ricciardo	Red Bull Racing	Red Bull-Renault RB10	2h27m38.589s	8
4	Jenson Button	McLaren	McLaren-Mercedes MP4-29	2h27m39.484s	3
5	Sebastian Vettel	Red Bull Racing	Red Bull-Renault RB10	2h27m45.958s	2
6	Fernando Alonso	Ferrari	Ferrari F14 T	2h27m52.040s	16
7	Kevin Magnussen	McLaren	McLaren-Mercedes MP4-29	2h27m54.657s	5
8	Nico Hulkenberg	Force India	Force India-Mercedes VJM07	2h28m20.786s	4
9	Daniil Kvyat	Toro Rosso	Toro Rosso-Renault STR9	2h28m21.434s	9
10	Jean-Eric Vergne	Toro Rosso	Toro Rosso-Renault STR9	51 laps	10
11	Sergio Perez	Force India	Force India-Mercedes VJM07	51 laps	7
12	Romain Grosjean	Lotus F1	Lotus-Renault E22	51 laps	11
13	Adrian Sutil	Sauber	Sauber-Ferrari C33	51 laps	13
14	Jules Bianchi	Marussia	Marussia-Ferrari MR03	51 laps	12
15	Kamui Kobayashi	Caterham	Caterham-Renault CT05	50 laps	22
16	Max Chilton *	Marussia	Marussia-Ferrari MR03	50 laps	17
17	Pastor Maldonado ^	Lotus F1	Lotus-Renault E22	49 laps/exhaust	20
R	Nico Rosberg	Mercedes AMG	Mercedes F1 W05	28 laps/gearbox	1
R	Marcus Ericsson	Caterham	Caterham-Renault CT05	11 laps/suspension	21
R	Esteban Gutierrez */!	Sauber	Sauber-Ferrari C33	9 laps/collision	19
R	Felipe Massa	Williams	Williams-Mercedes FW36	0 laps/collision	15
R	Kimi Raikkonen	Ferrari	Ferrari F14 T	0 laps/spun off	18

Pole: Rosberg, 1m35.766s, 137.604mph/221.452kph. Fastest lap: Hamilton, 1m37.176s, 135.607mph/218.239kph on Lap 26. Race leaders: Rosberg 1-18 & 25-28, Hamilton 19-24 & 29-52

* 5-place grid penalty for gearbox change • ! 10-place grid penalty for unsafe release in Austrian GP • ^ excluded from qualifying for not supplying fuel sample

GERMAN GRAND PRIX

HOCKENHEIM • ROUND 10 • DATE: 20TH JULY 2014
Laps: 67 • Distance: 190.424miles/306.458km • Weather: Warm but dull

Pos	Driver	Team	Chassis-Engine	Result	Qual
1	Nico Rosberg	Mercedes AMG	Mercedes F1 W05	1h33m42.914s	1
2	Valtteri Bottas	Williams	Williams-Mercedes FW36	1h34m03.703s	2
3	Lewis Hamilton *	Mercedes AMG	Mercedes F1 W05	1h34m05.444s	20
4	Sebastian Vettel	Red Bull Racing	Red Bull-Renault RB10	1h34m26.928s	6
5	Fernando Alonso	Ferrari	Ferrari F14 T	1h34m35.381s	7
6	Daniel Ricciardo	Red Bull Racing	Red Bull-Renault RB10	1h34m35.463s	5
7	Nico Hulkenberg	Force India	Force India-Mercedes VJM07	1h34m47.092s	9
8	Jenson Button	McLaren	McLaren-Mercedes MP4-29	1h35m07.625s	11
9	Kevin Magnussen	McLaren	McLaren-Mercedes MP4-29	66 laps	4
10	Sergio Perez	Force India	Force India-Mercedes VJM07	66 laps	10
11	Kimi Raikkonen	Ferrari	Ferrari F14 T	66 laps	12
12	Pastor Maldonado	Lotus F1	Lotus-Renault E22	66 laps	18
13	Jean-Eric Vergne	Toro Rosso	Toro Rosso-Renault STR9	66 laps	13
14	Esteban Gutierrez !	Sauber	Sauber-Ferrari C33	66 laps	16
15	Jules Bianchi	Marussia	Marussia-Ferrari MR03	66 laps	17
16	Kamui Kobayashi	Caterham	Caterham-Renault CT05	65 laps	19
17	Max Chilton	Marussia	Marussia-Ferrari MR03	65 laps	21

Pos	Driver	Team	Chassis-Engine	Result	Qual
18	Marcus Ericsson ^	Caterham	Caterham-Renault CT05	65 laps	22
R	Adrian Sutil	Sauber	Sauber-Ferrari C33	47 laps/spun off	15
R	Daniil Kvyat	Toro Rosso	Toro Rosso-Renault STR9	44 laps/ignition	8
R	Romain Grosjean	Lotus F1	Lotus-Renault E22	26 laps/overheating	14
R	Felipe Massa	Williams	Williams-Mercedes FW36	0 laps/collision	3

Pole: Rosberg, 1m16.540s, 133.678mph/215.134kph. Fastest lap: Hamilton, 1m19.908s, 128.044mph/206.066kph on Lap 53. Race leaders: Rosberg 1-67

* 5-place grid penalty for gearbox change • ! 3-place grid penalty for causing a crash at British GP • ^ made to start from rear of grid as car modified in parc ferme

COMING ON STRONG

Making the most of its Mercedes engines, Williams improved through the course of the season and so made huge strides after finishing ninth overall in 2013 to end 2014 third overall. Valtteri Bottas led its attack and twice came home second, while Felipe Massa finished with a third followed by a second in the Abu Dhabi finale.

HUNGARIAN GRAND PRIX

HUNGARORING • ROUND 11 • DATE: 27TH JULY 2014
Laps: 70 • Distance: 190.181miles/306.67km • Weather: Warm & wet, drying later

Pos	Driver	Team	Chassis-Engine	Result	Qual
1	Daniel Ricciardo	Red Bull Racing	Red Bull-Renault RB10	1h53m05.058s	4
2	Fernando Alonso	Ferrari	Ferrari F14 T	1h53m10.283s	5
3	Lewis Hamilton !	Mercedes AMG	Mercedes F1 W05	1h53m10.915s	22
4	Nico Rosberg	Mercedes AMG	Mercedes F1 W05	1h53m11.419s	1
5	Felipe Massa	Williams	Williams-Mercedes FW36	1h53m34.899s	6
6	Kimi Raikkonen	Ferrari	Ferrari F14 T	1h53m36.549s	16
7	Sebastian Vettel	Red Bull Racing	Red Bull-Renault RB10	1h53m46.022s	2
8	Valtteri Bottas	Williams	Williams-Mercedes FW36	1h53m46.402s	3
9	Jean-Eric Vergne	Toro Rosso	Toro Rosso-Renault STR9	1h54m03.585s	8
10	Jenson Button	McLaren	McLaren-Mercedes MP4-29	1h54m12.338s	7
11	Adrian Sutil	Sauber	Sauber-Ferrari C33	1h54m13.227s	11
12	Kevin Magnussen !	McLaren	McLaren-Mercedes MP4-29	1h54m23.523s	21
13	Pastor Maldonado *	Lotus F1	Lotus-Renault E22	1h54m29.082s	20
14	Daniil Kvyat	Toro Rosso	Toro Rosso-Renault STR9	69 laps	10
15	Jules Bianchi	Marussia	Marussia-Ferrari MR03	69 laps	15
16	Max Chilton	Marussia	Marussia-Ferrari MR03	69 laps	18
R	Esteban Gutierrez	Sauber	Sauber-Ferrari C33	32 laps/power unit	13
R	Kamui Kobayashi	Caterham	Caterham-Renault CT05	24 laps/fuel system	17
R	Sergio Perez	Force India	Force India-Mercedes VJM07	22 laps/spun off	12
R	Nico Hulkenberg	Force India	Force India-Mercedes VJM07	14 laps/collision	9
R	Romain Grosjean	Lotus F1	Lotus-Renault E22	10 laps/spun off	14
R	Marcus Ericsson	Caterham	Caterham-Renault CT05	7 laps/spun off	19

Pole: Rosberg, 1m22.715s, 118.479mph/190.674kph. Fastest lap: Rosberg, 1m25.724s, 114.320mph/183.981kph on Lap 64. Race leaders: Rosberg 1-9, Ricciardo 10-13 & 15-23 & 39-54 & 68-70, Button 14, Alonso 24-37 & 55-67, Hamilton 38

* 5-place grid penalty for gearbox change • ! made to start from the pit lane as car modified in parc ferme

BELGIAN GRAND PRIX

SPA-FRANCORCHAMPS • ROUND 12 • DATE: 24TH AUGUST 2014
Laps: 44 • Distance: 191.491miles/308.176km • Weather: Hot & bright

Pos	Driver	Team	Chassis-Engine	Result	Qual
1	Daniel Ricciardo	Red Bull Racing	Red Bull-Renault RB10	1h24m36.556s	5
2	Nico Rosberg	Mercedes AMG	Mercedes F1 W05	1h24m39.939s	1
3	Valtteri Bottas	Williams	Williams-Mercedes FW36	1h25m04.588s	6
4	Kimi Raikkonen	Ferrari	Ferrari F14 T	1h25m13.371s	8
5	Sebastian Vettel	Red Bull Racing	Red Bull-Renault RB10	1h25m28.752s	3
6	Jenson Button	McLaren	McLaren-Mercedes MP4-29	1h25m31.136s	10
7	Fernando Alonso	Ferrari	Ferrari F14 T	1h25m37.718s	4
8	Sergio Perez	Force India	Force India-Mercedes VJM07	1h25m40.849s	13
9	Daniil Kvyat	Toro Rosso	Toro Rosso-Renault STR9	1h25m41.903s	11
10	Nico Hulkenberg	Force India	Force India-Mercedes VJM07	1h25m42.253s	18
11	Jean-Eric Vergne	Toro Rosso	Toro Rosso-Renault STR9	1h25m48.476s	12
12	Kevin Magnussen *	McLaren	McLaren-Mercedes MP4-29	1h25m50.818s	7
13	Felipe Massa	Williams	Williams-Mercedes FW36	1h25m52.531s	9
14	Adrian Sutil	Sauber	Sauber-Ferrari C33	1h25m59.003s	14
15	Esteban Gutierrez	Sauber	Sauber-Ferrari C33	1h26m07.381s	20
16	Max Chilton	Marussia	Marussia-Ferrari MR03	43 laps	19
17	Marcus Ericsson	Caterham	Caterham-Renault CT05	43 laps	22
18	Jules Bianchi	Marussia	Marussia-Ferrari MR03	39 laps/gearbox	16
R	Lewis Hamilton	Mercedes AMG	Mercedes F1 W05	38 laps/handling	2
R	Romain Grosjean	Lotus F1	Lotus-Renault E22	33 laps/handling	15
R	Pastor Maldonado	Lotus F1	Lotus-Renault E22	1 laps/exhaust	17
R	Andre Lotterer	Caterham	Caterham-Renault CT05	1 laps/power unit	21

Pole: Rosberg, 2m05.591s, 124.750mph/200.765kph. Fastest lap: Rosberg, 1m50.511s, 141.773mph/228.161kph on Lap 36. Race leaders: Hamilton 1, Rosberg 2-7, Ricciardo 8-11 & 13-44, Bottas 12

* 20s penalty for forcing Alonso off track

FERRARI ONLY FOURTH

The Ferrari camp was not a happy one in 2014 as the team failed to achieve the best results from its new 1.6-litre engines while Mercedes dominated. Fernando Alonso ended up sixth overall, with second place in Hungary his best showing. Team-mate Kimi Raikkonen never finished higher than fourth and didn't even rank in the top 10.

ITALIAN GRAND PRIX

MONZA • ROUND 13 • DATE: 7TH SEPTEMBER 2014
Laps: 53 • Distance: 190.778miles/307.029km • Weather: Hot & bright

Pos	Driver	Team	Chassis-Engine	Result	Qual
1	Lewis Hamilton	Mercedes AMG	Mercedes F1 W05	1h19m10.236s	1
2	Nico Rosberg	Mercedes AMG	Mercedes F1 W05	1h19m13.411s	2
3	Felipe Massa	Williams	Williams-Mercedes FW36	1h19m35.262s	4
4	Valtteri Bottas	Williams	Williams-Mercedes FW36	1h19m51.022s	3
5	Daniel Ricciardo	Red Bull Racing	Red Bull-Renault RB10	1h20m00.545s	9
6	Sebastian Vettel	Red Bull Racing	Red Bull-Renault RB10	1h20m10.201s	8

Pos	Driver	Team	Chassis-Engine	Result	Qual
7	Sergio Perez	Force India	Force India-Mercedes VJM07	1h20m12.754s	10
8	Jenson Button	McLaren	McLaren-Mercedes MP4-29	1h20m13.299s	6
9	Kimi Raikkonen	Ferrari	Ferrari F14 T	1h20m13.771s	11
10	Kevin Magnussen ^	McLaren	McLaren-Mercedes MP4-29	1h20m16.407s	5
11	Daniil Kvyat *	Toro Rosso	Toro Rosso-Renault STR9	1h20m21.420s	21
12	Nico Hulkenberg	Force India	Force India-Mercedes VJM07	1h20m22.842s	13
13	Jean-Eric Vergne	Toro Rosso	Toro Rosso-Renault STR9	1h20m23.329s	12
14	Pastor Maldonado	Lotus F1	Lotus-Renault E22	52 laps	16
15	Adrian Sutil	Sauber	Sauber-Ferrari C33	52 laps	14
16	Romain Grosjean	Lotus F1	Lotus-Renault E22	52 laps	17
17	Kamui Kobayashi	Caterham	Caterham-Renault CT05	52 laps	18
18	Jules Bianchi	Marussia	Marussia-Ferrari MR03	52 laps	19
19	Marcus Ericsson !	Caterham	Caterham-Renault CT05	51 laps	22
20	Esteban Gutierrez #	Sauber	Sauber-Ferrari C33	51 laps	15
R	Fernando Alonso	Ferrari	Ferrari F14 T	28 laps/power unit	7
R	Max Chilton	Marussia	Marussia-Ferrari MR03	5 laps/spun off	20

Pole: Hamilton, 1m24.109s, 154.068mph/247.949kph. Fastest lap: Hamilton, 1m28.004s, 147.249mph/236.975kph on Lap 29. Race leaders: Rosberg 1-23 & 26-28, Hamilton 24-25 & 29-53

* 10-place grid penalty for using 6th engine • ! Made to start from the pit lane for ignoring waved yellow flags • ^ 5s penalty for forcing Bottas off track • # 20s penalty for causing an accident with Grosjean

SINGAPORE GRAND PRIX

MARINA BAY CIRCUIT • ROUND 14 • DATE: 21ST SEPTEMBER 2014
Laps: 60 • Distance: 188.281miles/303.9km • Weather: Very hot & humid

Pos	Driver	Team	Chassis-Engine	Result	Qual
1	Lewis Hamilton	Mercedes AMG	Mercedes F1 W05	2h00m04.795s	1
2	Sebastian Vettel	Red Bull Racing	Red Bull-Renault RB10	2h00m18.329s	4
3	Daniel Ricciardo	Red Bull Racing	Red Bull-Renault RB10	2h00m19.068s	3
4	Fernando Alonso	Ferrari	Ferrari F14 T	2h00m20.184s	5
5	Felipe Massa	Williams	Williams-Mercedes FW36	2h00m46.956s	6
6	Jean-Eric Vergne *	Toro Rosso	Toro Rosso-Renault STR9	2h01m01.596s	12
7	Sergio Perez	Force India	Force India-Mercedes VJM07	2h01m03.833s	15
8	Kimi Raikkonen	Ferrari	Ferrari F14 T	2h01m05.436s	7
9	Nico Hulkenberg	Force India	Force India-Mercedes VJM07	2h01m06.456s	13
10	Kevin Magnussen	McLaren	McLaren-Mercedes MP4-29	2h01m07.025s	9
11	Valtteri Bottas	Williams	Williams-Mercedes FW36	2h01m09.860s	8
12	Pastor Maldonado	Lotus F1	Lotus-Renault E22	2h01m11.710s	18
13	Romain Grosjean	Lotus F1	Lotus-Renault E22	2h01m12.824s	16
14	Daniil Kvyat	Toro Rosso	Toro Rosso-Renault STR9	2h01m16.803s	10
15	Marcus Ericsson	Caterham	Caterham-Renault CT05	2h01m38.983s	22
16	Jules Bianchi	Marussia	Marussia-Ferrari MR03	2h01m39.338s	19
17	Max Chilton	Marussia	Marussia-Ferrari MR03	59 laps	21
R	Jenson Button	McLaren	McLaren-Mercedes MP4-29	52 laps/electrical	11
R	Adrian Sutil	Sauber	Sauber-Ferrari C33	40 laps/water leak	17
R	Esteban Gutierrez	Sauber	Sauber-Ferrari C33	17 laps/electrical	14
R	Nico Rosberg	Mercedes AMG	Mercedes F1 W05	13 laps/steering	2
NS	Kamui Kobayashi	Caterham	Caterham-Renault CT05	-	20

Pole: Hamilton, 1m45.681s, 107.210mph/172.538kph. Fastest lap: Hamilton, 1m50.417s, 102.611mph/165.137kph on Lap 39. Race leaders: Hamilton 1-26 & 28-52 & 54-60, Ricciardo 27, Vettel 53

* 5s penalty for exceeding track limits

A TRAGIC INJURY

Marussia beat Sauber and Caterham in their bottom of the table clash thanks to Jules Bianchi's ninth place at Monaco. Sadly, the French ace crashed in the wet at Suzuka and hit a recovery vehicle. This left him with severe head trauma. Put into an induced coma, he would live for another nine months before succumbing to his injuries.

JAPANESE GRAND PRIX

SUZUKA • ROUND 15 • DATE: 5TH OCTOBER 2014
Laps: 44 • Distance: 158.765miles/255.508km • Weather: Warm with heavy rain

Pos	Driver	Team	Chassis-Engine	Result	Qual
1	Lewis Hamilton	Mercedes AMG	Mercedes F1 W05	1h51m43.021s	2
2	Nico Rosberg	Mercedes AMG	Mercedes F1 W05	1h51m52.201s	1
3	Sebastian Vettel	Red Bull Racing	Red Bull-Renault RB10	1h52m12.143s	9
4	Daniel Ricciardo	Red Bull Racing	Red Bull-Renault RB10	1h52m21.839s	6
5	Jenson Button	McLaren	McLaren-Mercedes MP4-29	1h52m50.571s	8
6	Valtteri Bottas	Williams	Williams-Mercedes FW36	1h53m36.794s	3
7	Felipe Massa	Williams	Williams-Mercedes FW36	1h53m38.147s	4
8	Nico Hulkenberg	Force India	Force India-Mercedes VJM07	1h53m38.969s	13
9	Jean-Eric Vergne *	Toro Rosso	Toro Rosso-Renault STR9	1h53m50.659s	20
10	Sergio Perez	Force India	Force India-Mercedes VJM07	43 laps	11
11	Daniil Kvyat	Toro Rosso	Toro Rosso-Renault STR9	43 laps	12
12	Kimi Raikkonen	Ferrari	Ferrari F14 T	43 laps	10
13	Esteban Gutierrez	Sauber	Sauber-Ferrari C33	43 laps	15
14	Kevin Magnussen	McLaren	McLaren-Mercedes MP4-29	43 laps	7
15	Romain Grosjean	Lotus F1	Lotus-Renault E22	43 laps	16
16	Pastor Maldonado */!	Lotus F1	Lotus-Renault E22	43 laps	22
17	Marcus Ericsson	Caterham	Caterham-Renault CT05	43 laps	17
18	Max Chilton	Marussia	Marussia-Ferrari MR03	43 laps	21
19	Kamui Kobayashi	Caterham	Caterham-Renault CT05	43 laps	19
20	Jules Bianchi	Marussia	Marussia-Ferrari MR03	41 laps/spun off	18
21	Adrian Sutil	Sauber	Sauber-Ferrari C33	40 laps/spun off	14
R	Fernando Alonso	Ferrari	Ferrari F14 T	2 laps/electrical	5

Pole: Rosberg, 1m32.506s, 140.422mph/225.987kph. Fastest lap: Hamilton, 1m51.600s, 116.396mph/187.322kph on Lap 39. Race leaders: Rosberg 1-12 & 15-28, Hamilton 13-14 & 29-44

* 10-place grid penalty for using 6th engine • ! 20s penalty for speeding in the pit lane

RUSSIAN GRAND PRIX

SOCHI • ROUND 16 • DATE: 12TH OCTOBER 2014
Laps: 53 • Distance: 192.590miles/309.944km • Weather: Warm & bright

Pos	Driver	Team	Chassis-Engine	Result	Qual
1	Lewis Hamilton	Mercedes AMG	Mercedes F1 W05	1h31m50.744s	1
2	Nico Rosberg	Mercedes AMG	Mercedes F1 W05	1h32m04.401s	2
3	Valtteri Bottas	Williams	Williams-Mercedes FW36	1h32m08.169s	3
4	Jenson Button	McLaren	McLaren-Mercedes MP4-29	1h32m20.978s	4
5	Kevin Magnussen *	McLaren	McLaren-Mercedes MP4-29	1h32m44.360s	11
6	Fernando Alonso	Ferrari	Ferrari F14 T	1h32m50.760s	7

Pos	Driver	Team	Chassis-Engine	Result	Qual
7	Daniel Ricciardo	Red Bull Racing	Red Bull-Renault RB10	1h32m52.556s	6
8	Sebastian Vettel	Red Bull Racing	Red Bull-Renault RB10	1h32m56.929s	10
9	Kimi Raikkonen	Ferrari	Ferrari F14 T	1h33m09.621s	8
10	Sergio Perez	Force India	Force India-Mercedes VJM07	1h33m10.811s	12
11	Felipe Massa	Williams	Williams-Mercedes FW36	1h33m11.621s	18
12	Nico Hulkenberg *	Force India	Force India-Mercedes VJM07	1h33m12.053s	17
13	Jean-Eric Vergne	Toro Rosso	Toro Rosso-Renault STR9	1h33m28.039s	9
14	Daniil Kvyat	Toro Rosso	Toro Rosso-Renault STR9	52 laps	5
15	Esteban Gutierrez	Sauber	Sauber-Ferrari C33	52 laps	13
16	Adrian Sutil	Sauber	Sauber-Ferrari C33	52 laps	14
17	Romain Grosjean ^	Lotus F1	Lotus-Renault E22	52 laps	15
18	Pastor Maldonado */!	Lotus F1	Lotus-Renault E22	52 laps	21
19	Marcus Ericsson	Caterham	Caterham-Renault CT05	51 laps	16
R	Kamui Kobayashi	Caterham	Caterham-Renault CT05	21 laps/brakes	19
R	Max Chilton *	Marussia	Marussia-Ferrari MR03	9 laps/suspension	20

Pole: Hamilton, 1m38.513s, 132.790mph/213.705kph. Fastest lap: Bottas, 1m40.896s, 129.654mph/208.658kph on Lap 53. Race leaders: Hamilton 1-53

* 5-place grid penalty for gearbox change • ! 5-place grid penalty for using 6th engine • ^ 5s penalty for causing an accident

UNITED STATES GRAND PRIX

CIRCUIT OF THE AMERICAS • ROUND 17 • DATE: 2ND NOVEMBER 2014
Laps: 56 • Distance: 191.834miles/308.728km • Weather: Warm & bright

Pos	Driver	Team	Chassis-Engine	Result	Qual
1	Lewis Hamilton	Mercedes AMG	Mercedes F1 W05	1h40m04.785s	2
2	Nico Rosberg	Mercedes AMG	Mercedes F1 W05	1h40m09.099s	1
3	Daniel Ricciardo	Red Bull Racing	Red Bull-Renault RB10	1h40m30.345s	5
4	Felipe Massa	Williams	Williams-Mercedes FW36	1h40m31.709s	4
5	Valtteri Bottas	Williams	Williams-Mercedes FW36	1h40m35.777s	3
6	Fernando Alonso	Ferrari	Ferrari F14 T	1h41m40.016s	6
7	Sebastian Vettel ^	Red Bull Racing	Red Bull-Renault RB10	1h41m40.519s	18
8	Kevin Magnussen	McLaren	McLaren-Mercedes MP4-29	1h41m45.467s	7
9	Pastor Maldonado #	Lotus F1	Lotus-Renault E22	1h41m52.655s	10
10	Jean-Eric Vergne @	Toro Rosso	Toro Rosso-Renault STR9	1h41m53.648s	14
11	Romain Grosjean	Lotus F1	Lotus-Renault E22	55 laps	16
12	Jenson Button *	McLaren	McLaren-Mercedes MP4-29	55 laps	12
13	Kimi Raikkonen	Ferrari	Ferrari F14 T	55 laps	8
14	Esteban Gutierrez	Sauber	Sauber-Ferrari C33	55 laps	15
15	Daniil Kvyat !	Toro Rosso	Toro Rosso-Renault STR9	55 laps	17
R	Nico Hulkenberg	Force India	Force India-Mercedes VJM07	16 laps/power unit	13
R	Sergio Perez	Force India	Force India-Mercedes VJM07	1 laps/collision	11
R	Adrian Sutil	Sauber	Sauber-Ferrari C33	0 laps/collision	9

Pole: Rosberg, 1m36.067s, 128.371mph/206.593kph. Fastest lap: Vettel, 1m41.379s, 121.644mph/195.768kph on Lap 50. Race leaders: Rosberg 1-15 & 17-23 & 34, Hamilton 16 & 24-33 & 35-56

* 5-place grid penalty for gearbox change • ! 10-place penalty for using 7th power unit • ^ made to start from the pit lane for taking 6th complete power unit • # 5s penalty for speeding in the pit lane. • @ 5s penalty for forcing Grosjean off the track

NEW CIRCUIT
After years of coming up with ideas about where to host a grand prix, Russia finally got on the F1 map thanks to the creation of a circuit in the Black Sea resort of Sochi. A temporary layout was built in the town in an area that had hosted some of the events for the 2014 Winter Olympic Games. The track was a mixture of fast and slow corners.

BRAZILIAN GRAND PRIX

INTERLAGOS • ROUND 18 • DATE: 9TH NOVEMBER 2014
Laps: 71 • Distance: 190.101miles/305.939km • Weather: Hot & humid

Pos	Driver	Team	Chassis-Engine	Result	Qual
1	Nico Rosberg	Mercedes AMG	Mercedes F1 W05	1h30m02.555s	1
2	Lewis Hamilton	Mercedes AMG	Mercedes F1 W05	1h30m04.012s	2
3	Felipe Massa	Williams	Williams-Mercedes FW36	1h30m43.586s	3
4	Jenson Button	McLaren	McLaren-Mercedes MP4-29	1h30m51.213s	5
5	Sebastian Vettel	Red Bull Racing	Red Bull-Renault RB10	1h30m53.975s	6
6	Fernando Alonso	Ferrari	Ferrari F14 T	1h31m04.461s	8
7	Kimi Raikkonen	Ferrari	Ferrari F14 T	1h31m06.285s	10
8	Nico Hulkenberg	Force India	Force India-Mercedes VJM07	1h31m06.489s	12
9	Kevin Magnussen	McLaren	McLaren-Mercedes MP4-29	1h31m12.640s	7
10	Valtteri Bottas	Williams	Williams-Mercedes FW36	70 laps	4
11	Daniil Kvyat *	Toro Rosso	Toro Rosso-Renault STR9	70 laps	17
12	Pastor Maldonado	Lotus F1	Lotus-Renault E22	70 laps	16
13	Jean-Eric Vergne	Toro Rosso	Toro Rosso-Renault STR9	70 laps	15
14	Esteban Gutierrez	Sauber	Sauber-Ferrari C33	70 laps	11
15	Sergio Perez !	Force India	Force India-Mercedes VJM07	70 laps	18
16	Adrian Sutil	Sauber	Sauber-Ferrari C33	70 laps	13
17	Romain Grosjean	Lotus F1	Lotus-Renault E22	63 laps/power unit	14
R	Daniel Ricciardo	Red Bull Racing	Red Bull-Renault RB10	39 laps/suspension	9

Pole: Rosberg, 1m10.023s, 137.654mph/221.532kph. Fastest lap: Hamilton, 1m13.555s, 131.044mph/210.895kph on Lap 62. Race leaders: Rosberg 1-6 & 14-25 & 29-49 & 52-71, Hamilton 7-8 & 26-28 & 50-51, Hulkenberg 9-13

* 7-place grid penalty for using 6th engine • ! 7-place grid penalty for causing an accident in US GP

ABU DHABI GRAND PRIX

YAS MARINA CIRCUIT • ROUND 19 • DATE: 23RD NOVEMBER 2014
Laps: 55 • Distance: 189.547miles/305.47km • Weather: Hot & bright

Pos	Driver	Team	Chassis-Engine	Result	Qual
1	Lewis Hamilton	Mercedes AMG	Mercedes F1 W05	1h39m02.619s	2
2	Felipe Massa	Williams	Williams-Mercedes FW36	1h39m05.195s	4
3	Valtteri Bottas	Williams	Williams-Mercedes FW36	1h39m31.499s	3
4	Daniel Ricciardo !	Red Bull Racing	Red Bull-Renault RB10	1h39m39.856s	20
5	Jenson Button	McLaren	McLaren-Mercedes MP4-29	1h40m02.953s	6
6	Nico Hulkenberg	Force India	Force India-Mercedes VJM07	1h40m04.767s	12
7	Sergio Perez	Force India	Force India-Mercedes VJM07	1h40m13.679s	11
8	Sebastian Vettel !	Red Bull Racing	Red Bull-Renault RB10	1h40m14.664s	19
9	Fernando Alonso	Ferrari	Ferrari F14 T	1h40m28.432s	8
10	Kimi Raikkonen	Ferrari	Ferrari F14 T	1h40m30.439s	7

Pos	Driver	Team	Chassis-Engine	Result	Qual
11	Kevin Magnussen	McLaren	McLaren-Mercedes MP4-29	1h40m32.995s	9
12	Jean-Eric Vergne	Toro Rosso	Toro Rosso-Renault STR9	1h40m34.566s	10
13	Romain Grosjean *	Lotus F1	Lotus-Renault E22	54 laps	18
14	Nico Rosberg	Mercedes AMG	Mercedes F1 W05	54 laps	1
15	Esteban Gutierrez	Sauber	Sauber-Ferrari C33	54 laps	14
16	Adrian Sutil	Sauber	Sauber-Ferrari C33	54 laps	13
17	Will Stevens	Caterham	Caterham-Renault CT05	54 laps	17
R	Kamui Kobayashi	Caterham	Caterham-Renault CT05	42 laps/vibrations	16
R	Pastor Maldonado	Lotus F1	Lotus-Renault E22	26 laps/engine	15
R	Daniil Kvyat	Toro Rosso	Toro Rosso-Renault STR9	14 laps/ignition	5

Pole: Rosberg, 1m40.480s, 123.645mph/198.988kph. Fastest lap: Ricciardo, 1m44.496s, 118.893mph/191.341kph on Lap 50. Race leaders: Hamilton 1-10 & 14-31 & 44-55, Rosberg 11, Massa 12-13 & 32-43

* 20-place grid penalty for using 6th power unit • ! excluded from qualifying for excess front wing deflection

NEW DRIVERS

The four other rookies suffered in comparison to Kevin Magnussen, but Daniil Kvyat did well to not only take a ninth place for Toro Rosso but then to match that twice. The best of the rest, all Caterham drivers, was Marcus Ericsson who was 11th at Monaco – Andre Lotterer lasted only a lap at Spa and Will Stevens was 17th in Abu Dhabi.

WORLD DRIVERS' CHAMPIONSHIP FINAL RESULTS

Pos	Driver	Nat	Car-Engine	R1	R2	R3	R4	R5	R6	R7	R8
1	Lewis Hamilton	GBR	Mercedes F1 W05	RP	1PF	1	1P	1P	2	R	2
2	Nico Rosberg	DEU	Mercedes F1 W05	1F	2	2PF	2F	2	1P	2P	1
3	Daniel Ricciardo	AUS	Red Bull-Renault RB10	DQ	R	4	4	3	3	1	8
4	Valtteri Bottas	FIN	Williams-Mercedes FW36	5	8	8	7	5	R	7	3
5	Sebastian Vettel	DEU	Red Bull-Renault RB10	R	3	6	5	4F	R	3	R
6	Fernando Alonso	ESP	Ferrari F14 T	4	4	9	3	6	4	6	5
7	Felipe Massa	BRA	Williams-Mercedes FW36	R	7	7	15	13	7	12F	4P
8	Jenson Button	GBR	McLaren-Mercedes MP4-29	3	6	17	11	11	6	4	11
9	Nico Hulkenberg	DEU	Force India-Mercedes VJM07	6	5	5	6	10	5	5	9
10	Sergio Perez	MEX	Force India-Mercedes VJM07	10	NS	3	9	9	R	11	6F
11	Kevin Magnussen	DNK	McLaren-Mercedes MP4-29	2	9	R	13	12	10	9	7
12	Kimi Raikkonen	FIN	Ferrari F14 T	7	12	10	8	7	12F	10	10
13	Jean-Eric Vergne	FRA	Toro Rosso-Renault STR9	8	R	R	12	R	R	8	R
14	Romain Grosjean	FRA	Lotus-Renault E22	R	11	12	R	8	8	R	14
15	Daniil Kvyat	RUS	Toro Rosso-Renault STR9	9	10	11	10	14	R	R	R
16	Pastor Maldonado	VEN	Lotus-Renault E22	R	R	14	14	15	NS	R	12
17	Jules Bianchi	FRA	Marussia-Ferrari MR03	NC	R	16	17	18	9	R	15
18	Adrian Sutil	DEU	Sauber-Ferrari C33	11	R	R	R	17	R	13	13
19	Marcus Ericsson	SWE	Caterham-Renault CT05	R	14	R	20	20	11	R	18
20	Esteban Gutierrez	MEX	Sauber-Ferrari C33	12	R	R	16	16	R	14	19
21	Max Chilton	GBR	Marussia-Ferrari MR03	13	15	13	19	19	14	R	17
22	Kamui Kobayashi	JPN	Caterham-Renault CT05	R	13	15	18	R	13	R	16
23	Will Stevens	GBR	Caterham-Renault CT05	-	-	-	-	-	-	-	-
24	Andre Lotterer	DEU	Caterham-Renault CT05	-	-	-	-	-	-	-	-

Pos	Driver	R9	R10	R11	R12	R13	R14	R15	R16	R17	R18	R19	Total
1	Hamilton	1F	3F	3	R	1PF	1PF	1F	1P	1	2F	1	384
2	Rosberg	RP	1P	4PF	2PF	2	R	2P	2	2P	1P	14P	317
3	Ricciardo	3	6	1	1	5	3	4	7	3	R	4F	238
4	Bottas	2	2	8	3	4	11	6	3F	5	10	3	186
5	Vettel	5	4	7	5	6	2	3	8	7F	5	8	167
6	Alonso	6	5	2	7	R	4	R	6	6	6	9	161
7	Massa	R	R	5	13	3	5	7	11	4	3	2	134
8	Button	4	8	10	6	8	R	5	4	12	4	5	126
9	Hulkenberg	8	7	R	10	12	9	8	12	R	8	6	96
10	Perez	11	10	R	8	7	7	10	10	R	15	7	59
11	Magnussen	7	9	12	12	10	10	14	5	8	9	11	55
12	Raikkonen	R	11	6	4	9	8	12	9	13	7	10	55
13	Vergne	10	13	9	11	13	6	9	13	10	13	12	22
14	Grosjean	12	R	R	R	16	13	15	17	11	17	13	8
15	Kvyat	9	R	14	9	11	14	11	14	15	11	R	8
16	Maldonado	17	12	13	R	14	12	16	18	9	12	R	2
17	Bianchi	14	15	15	18	18	16	20	-	-	-	-	2
18	Sutil	13	R	11	14	15	R	21	16	R	16	16	0
19	Ericsson	R	18	R	17	19	15	17	19	-	-	-	0
20	Gutierrez	R	14	R	15	20	R	13	15	14	14	15	0
21	Chilton	16	17	16	16	R	17	18	R	-	-	-	0
22	Kobayashi	15	16	R	-	17	NS	19	R	-	-	R	0
23	Stevens	-	-	-	-	-	-	-	-	-	-	17	0
24	Lotterer	-	-	-	R	-	-	-	-	-	-	-	0

SYMBOLS AND GRAND PRIX KEY

Round 1 Australian GP
Round 2 Malaysian GP
Round 3 Bahrain GP
Round 4 Chinese GP
Round 5 Spanish GP
Round 6 Monaco GP
Round 7 Canadian GP
Round 8 Austrian GP
Round 9 British GP
Round 10 German GP
Round 11 Hungarian GP
Round 12 Belgian GP
Round 13 Italian GP
Round 14 Singapore GP
Round 15 Japanese GP
Round 16 Russian GP
Round 17 United States GP
Round 18 Brazilian GP
Round 19 Abu Dhabi GP

SCORING

1st 25 points
2nd 18 points
3rd 15 points
4th 12 points
5th 10 points
6th 8 points
7th 6 points
8th 4 points
9th 2 points
10th 1 point

DNPQ DID NOT PRE-QUALIFY **DNQ** DID NOT QUALIFY **DQ** DISQUALIFIED **EX** EXCLUDED
F FASTEST LAP **NC** NOT CLASSIFIED **NS** NON-STARTER **P** POLE POSITION **R** RETIRED

WORLD CONSTRUCTORS' CHAMPIONSHIP FINAL RESULTS

Pos	Team-Engine	R1	R2	R3	R4	R5	R6	R7	R8	R9	R10
1	Mercedes AMG	1/R	1/2	1/2	1/2	1/2	1/2	2/R	1/2	1/R	1/3
2	Red Bull-Renault	DQ/R	3/R	4/6	4/5	3/4	3/R	1/3	8/R	3/5	4/6
3	Williams-Mercedes	5/R	7/8	7/8	7/15	5/13	7/R	7/12	3/4	2/R	2/R
4	Ferrari	4/7	4/12	9/10	3/8	6/7	4/12	6/10	5/10	6/R	5/11
5	McLaren-Mercedes	2/3	6/9	17/R	11/13	11/12	6/10	4/9	7/11	4/7	8/9
6	Force India-Mercedes	6/10	5/NS	3/5	6/9	9/10	5/R	5/11	6/9	8/11	7/10
7	Toro Rosso-Renault	8/9	10/R	11/R	10/12	14/R	R/R	8/R	R/R	9/10	13/R
8	Lotus-Renault	R/R	11/R	12/14	14/R	8/15	8/NS	R/R	12/14	12/17	12/R
9	Marussia-Ferrari	13/NC	15/R	13/16	17/19	18/19	9/14	R/R	15/17	14/16	15/17
10	Sauber-Ferrari	11/12	R/R	R/R	16/R	16/17	R/R	13/14	13/19	13/R	14/R
11	Caterham-Renault	R/R	13/14	15/R	18/20	20/R	11/13	R/R	16/18	15/R	16/18

Pos	Team-Engine	R11	R12	R13	R14	R15	R16	R17	R18	R19	Total
1	Mercedes AMG	3/4	2/R	1/2	1/R	1/2	1/2	1/2	1/2	1/14	701
2	Red Bull-Renault	1/7	1/5	5/6	2/3	3/4	7/8	3/7	5/R	4/8	405
3	Williams-Mercedes	5/8	3/13	3/4	5/11	6/7	3/11	4/5	3/10	2/3	320
4	Ferrari	2/6	4/7	9/R	4/8	12/R	6/9	6/13	6/7	9/10	216
5	McLaren-Mercedes	10/12	6/12	8/10	10/R	5/14	4/5	8/12	4/9	5/11	181
6	Force India-Mercedes	R/R	8/10	7/12	7/9	8/10	10/12	R/R	8/15	6/7	155
7	Toro Rosso-Renault	9/14	9/11	11/13	6/14	9/11	13/14	10/15	11/13	12/R	30
8	Lotus-Renault	13/R	R/R	14/16	12/13	15/16	17/18	9/11	12/17	13/R	10
9	Marussia-Ferrari	15/16	16/18	18/R	16/17	18/20	R	-	-	-	2
10	Sauber-Ferrari	11/R	14/15	15/20	R/R	13/21	15/16	14/R	14/16	15/16	0
11	Caterham-Renault	R/R	17/R	17/19	15/NS	17/19	19/R	-	-	17/R	0

2015

SEASON SUMMARY

Lewis Hamilton added a third F1 title to his CV, his second in succession for Mercedes in a second year in which none of the other drivers could get close to the pace of the Mercedes. This intensified the battle between Hamilton and team-mate Nico Rosberg and it became a little bitter at times. Ferrari's Sebastian Vettel and Kimi Raikkonen tried their best to keep Mercedes in sight. Red Bull Racing, though, went in the opposite direction, falling to fourth overall, but nowhere near as calamitously as McLaren, which had a truly disastrous year after changing from Mercedes to Honda engines.

AUSTRALIAN GRAND PRIX

ALBERT PARK • ROUND 1 • DATE: 15TH MARCH 2015
Laps: 58 • Distance: 191.117miles/307.574km • Weather: Warm & bright

Pos	Driver	Team	Chassis-Engine	Result	Qual
1	Lewis Hamilton	Mercedes AMG	Mercedes F1 W06	1h31m54.067s	1
2	Nico Rosberg	Mercedes AMG	Mercedes F1 W06	1h31m55.427s	2
3	Sebastian Vettel	Ferrari	Ferrari SF15-T	1h32m28.590s	4
4	Felipe Massa	Williams	Williams-Mercedes FW37	1h32m32.263s	3
5	Felipe Nasr	Sauber	Sauber-Ferrari C34	1h33m29.216s	10
6	Daniel Ricciardo	Red Bull Racing	Red Bull-Renault RB11	57 laps	6
7	Nico Hulkenberg	Force India	Force India-Mercedes VJM08	57 laps	13
8	Marcus Ericsson	Sauber	Sauber-Ferrari C34	57 laps	15
9	Carlos Sainz	Toro Rosso	Toro Rosso-Renault STR10	57 laps	7
10	Sergio Perez	Force India	Force India-Mercedes VJM08	57 laps	14
11	Jenson Button	McLaren	McLaren-Honda MP4-30	56 laps	16
R	Kimi Raikkonen	Ferrari	Ferrari SF15-T	40 laps/wheel	5
R	Max Verstappen	Toro Rosso	Toro Rosso-Renault STR10	32 laps/power unit	11
R	Romain Grosjean	Lotus F1	Lotus-Mercedes E23 Hybrid	0 laps/power unit	8
R	Pastor Maldonado	Lotus F1	Lotus-Mercedes E23 Hybrid	0 laps/collision	9
NS	Valtteri Bottas	Williams	Williams-Mercedes FW37	driver injured	6
NS	Daniil Kvyat	Red Bull Racing	Red Bull-Renault RB11	gearbox	12
NS	Kevin Magnussen	McLaren	McLaren-Honda MP4-30	power unit	17
NS	Roberto Merhi	Marussia	Marussia-Ferrari MR03B	car not ready	-
NS	Will Stevens	Marussia	Marussia-Ferrari MR03B	car not ready	-

Pole: Hamilton, 1m26.327s, 137.413mph/221.145kph. Fastest lap: Hamilton, 1m30.945s, 130.435mph/209.915kph on Lap 50. Race leaders: Hamilton 1-24 & 27-58, Rosberg 25-26

MALAYSIAN GRAND PRIX

SEPANG • ROUND 2 • DATE: 29TH MARCH 2015
Laps: 56 • Distance: 192.878miles/310.408km • Weather: Very hot & bright

Pos	Driver	Team	Chassis-Engine	Result	Qual
1	Sebastian Vettel	Ferrari	Ferrari SF15-T	1h41m05.793s	2
2	Lewis Hamilton	Mercedes AMG	Mercedes F1 W06	1h41m14.362s	1
3	Nico Rosberg	Mercedes AMG	Mercedes F1 W06	1h41m18.103s	3
4	Kimi Raikkonen	Ferrari	Ferrari SF15-T	1h41m59.615s	11
5	Valtteri Bottas	Williams	Williams-Mercedes FW37	1h42m16.202s	8

Pos	Driver	Team	Chassis-Engine	Result	Qual
6	Felipe Massa	Williams	Williams-Mercedes FW37	1h42m19.379s	7
7	Max Verstappen	Toro Rosso	Toro Rosso-Renault STR10	1h42m43.555s	6
8	Carlos Sainz	Toro Rosso	Toro Rosso-Renault STR10	55 laps	15
9	Daniil Kvyat	Red Bull Racing	Red Bull-Renault RB11	55 laps	5
10	Daniel Ricciardo	Red Bull Racing	Red Bull-Renault RB11	55 laps	4
11	Romain Grosjean *	Lotus F1	Lotus-Mercedes E23 Hybrid	55 laps	10
12	Felipe Nasr	Sauber	Sauber-Ferrari C34	55 laps	16
13	Sergio Perez	Force India	Force India-Mercedes VJM08	55 laps	14
14	Nico Hulkenberg	Force India	Force India-Mercedes VJM08	55 laps	13
15	Roberto Merhi	Marussia	Marussia-Ferrari MR03B	53 laps	19
R	Pastor Maldonado	Lotus F1	Lotus-Mercedes E23 Hybrid	47 laps/brakes	12
R	Jenson Button	McLaren	McLaren-Honda MP4-30	41 laps/power unit	17
R	Fernando Alonso	McLaren	McLaren-Honda MP4-30	21 laps/power unit	18
R	Marcus Ericsson	Sauber	Sauber-Ferrari C34	3 laps/spun off	9
NS	Will Stevens	Marussia	Marussia-Ferrari MR03B	fuel system	20

Pole: Hamilton, 1m49.834s, 112.891mph/181.681kph. Fastest lap: Rosberg, 1m42.062s, 121.488mph/195.516kph on Lap 43. Race leaders: Hamilton 1-3 & 18-23 & 38, Vettel 4-17 & 24-37 & 39-56

* 2-place grid penalty for leaving pit lane out of order

CHINESE GRAND PRIX

SHANGHAI INTERNATIONAL CIRCUIT • ROUND 3 • DATE: 12TH APRIL 2015
Laps: 56 • Distance: 189.677miles/305.256km • Weather: Warm & bright

Pos	Driver	Team	Chassis-Engine	Result	Qual
1	Lewis Hamilton	Mercedes AMG	Mercedes F1 W06	1h39m42.008s	1
2	Nico Rosberg	Mercedes AMG	Mercedes F1 W06	1h39m42.722s	2
3	Sebastian Vettel	Ferrari	Ferrari SF15-T	1h39m44.996s	3
4	Kimi Raikkonen	Ferrari	Ferrari SF15-T	1h39m45.843s	6
5	Felipe Massa	Williams	Williams-Mercedes FW37	1h39m50.552s	4
6	Valtteri Bottas	Williams	Williams-Mercedes FW37	1h39m51.893s	5
7	Romain Grosjean	Lotus F1	Lotus-Mercedes E23 Hybrid	1h40m01.016s	8
8	Felipe Nasr	Sauber	Sauber-Ferrari C34	1h40m04.633s	9
9	Daniel Ricciardo	Red Bull Racing	Red Bull-Renault RB11	1h40m14.125s	7
10	Marcus Ericsson	Sauber	Sauber-Ferrari C34	55 laps	10
11	Sergio Perez	Force India	Force India-Mercedes VJM08	55 laps	15
12	Fernando Alonso	McLaren	McLaren-Honda MP4-30	55 laps	18
13	Carlos Sainz	Toro Rosso	Toro Rosso-Renault STR10	55 laps	14
14	Jenson Button *	McLaren	McLaren-Honda MP4-30	55 laps	17
15	Will Stevens	Marussia	Marussia-Ferrari MR03B	54 laps	19
16	Roberto Merhi !	Marussia	Marussia-Ferrari MR03B	54 laps	20
17	Max Verstappen	Toro Rosso	Toro Rosso-Renault STR10	52 laps/engine	13
R	Pastor Maldonado	Lotus F1	Lotus-Mercedes E23 Hybrid	49 laps/collision	11
R	Daniil Kvyat	Red Bull Racing	Red Bull-Renault RB11	15 laps/engine	12
R	Nico Hulkenberg	Force India	Force India-Mercedes VJM08	9 laps	16

Pole: Hamilton, 1m35.782s, 127.305mph/204.877kph. Fastest lap: Hamilton, 1m42.208s, 119.301mph/191.996kph on Lap 31. Race leaders: Hamilton 1-13 & 16-33 & 35-56, Rosberg 14-15, Raikkonen 34

* 5s penalty for causing a collision • ! 5s penalty for speeding in a safety car period

VETTEL SETTLES IN

Sebastian Vettel joined Ferrari as its lead driver after Fernando Alonso's departure to McLaren and spent the season being the best of the rest behind Mercedes' Hamilton and Rosberg. Impressively, he was able to win on his second start for the sport's most famous team, in Malaysia, but then only twice more, in Hungary and Singapore.

BAHRAIN GRAND PRIX

SAKHIR • ROUND 4 • DATE: 19TH APRIL 2015
Laps: 57 • Distance: 191.683miles/308.484km • Weather: Hot & dry

Pos	Driver	Team	Chassis-Engine	Result	Qual
1	Lewis Hamilton	Mercedes AMG	Mercedes F1 W06	1h35m05.809s	1
2	Kimi Raikkonen	Ferrari	Ferrari SF15-T	1h35m09.189s	4
3	Nico Rosberg	Mercedes AMG	Mercedes F1 W06	1h35m11.842s	3
4	Valtteri Bottas	Williams	Williams-Mercedes FW37	1h35m48.766s	5
5	Sebastian Vettel	Ferrari	Ferrari SF15-T	1h35m49.798s	2
6	Daniel Ricciardo	Red Bull Racing	Red Bull-Renault RB11	1h36m07.560s	7
7	Romain Grosjean	Lotus F1	Lotus-Mercedes E23 Hybrid	1h36m30.572s	10
8	Sergio Perez	Force India	Force India-Mercedes VJM08	56 laps	11
9	Daniil Kvyat	Red Bull Racing	Red Bull-Renault RB11	56 laps	17
10	Felipe Massa	Williams	Williams-Mercedes FW37	56 laps	6
11	Fernando Alonso	McLaren	McLaren-Honda MP4-30	56 laps	14
12	Felipe Nasr	Sauber	Sauber-Ferrari C34	56 laps	12
13	Nico Hulkenberg	Force India	Force India-Mercedes VJM08	56 laps	8
14	Marcus Ericsson	Sauber	Sauber-Ferrari C34	56 laps	13
15	Pastor Maldonado	Lotus F1	Lotus-Mercedes E23 Hybrid	56 laps	16
16	Will Stevens	Marussia	Marussia-Ferrari MR03B	55 laps	18
17	Roberto Merhi	Marussia	Marussia-Ferrari MR03B	54 laps	19
R	Max Verstappen	Toro Rosso	Toro Rosso-Renault STR10	34 laps/electrical	15
R	Carlos Sainz	Toro Rosso	Toro Rosso-Renault STR10	29 laps/wheel	9
NS	Jenson Button	McLaren	McLaren-Honda MP4-30	electrics	20

Pole: Hamilton, 1m32.571s, 130.778mph/210.467kph. Fastest lap: Raikkonen, 1m36.311s, 125.700mph/202.294kph on Lap 42. Race leaders: Hamilton 1-15 & 18-33 & 40-57, Raikkonen 16-17 & 35-39, Rosberg 34

SPANISH GRAND PRIX

BARCELONA-CATALUNYA • ROUND 5 • DATE: 10TH MAY 2015
Laps: 66 • Distance: 190.775miles/307.23km • Weather: Hot & bright

Pos	Driver	Team	Chassis-Engine	Result	Qual
1	Nico Rosberg	Mercedes AMG	Mercedes F1 W06	1h41m12.555s	1
2	Lewis Hamilton	Mercedes AMG	Mercedes F1 W06	1h41m30.106s	2
3	Sebastian Vettel	Ferrari	Ferrari SF15-T	1h41m57.897s	3
4	Valtteri Bottas	Williams	Williams-Mercedes FW37	1h42m11.772s	4
5	Kimi Raikkonen	Ferrari	Ferrari SF15-T	1h42m12.557s	7
6	Felipe Massa	Williams	Williams-Mercedes FW37	1h42m33.869s	9
7	Daniel Ricciardo	Red Bull Racing	Red Bull-Renault RB11	65 laps	10
8	Romain Grosjean	Lotus F1	Lotus-Mercedes E23 Hybrid	65 laps	11
9	Carlos Sainz	Toro Rosso	Toro Rosso-Renault STR10	65 laps	5

Pos	Driver	Team	Chassis-Engine	Result	Qual
10	Daniil Kvyat	Red Bull Racing	Red Bull-Renault RB11	65 laps	8
11	Max Verstappen	Toro Rosso	Toro Rosso-Renault STR10	65 laps	6
12	Felipe Nasr	Sauber	Sauber-Ferrari C34	65 laps	15
13	Sergio Perez	Force India	Force India-Mercedes VJM08	65 laps	18
14	Marcus Ericsson	Sauber	Sauber-Ferrari C34	65 laps	16
15	Nico Hulkenberg	Force India	Force India-Mercedes VJM08	65 laps	17
16	Jenson Button	McLaren	McLaren-Honda MP4-30	65 laps	14
17	Will Stevens	Marussia	Marussia-Ferrari MR03B	63 laps	19
18	Roberto Merhi	Marussia	Marussia-Ferrari MR03B	62 laps	20
R	Pastor Maldonado	Lotus F1	Lotus-Mercedes E23 Hybrid	45 laps/accident	12
R	Fernando Alonso	McLaren	McLaren-Honda MP4-30	26 laps/brakes	13

Pole: Rosberg, 1m24.681s, 122.966mph/197.895kph. Fastest lap: Hamilton, 1m28.270s, 117.966mph/189.849kph on Lap 54. Race leaders: Rosberg 1-15 & 17-45 & 51-66, Raikkonen 16, Hamilton 46-50

MONACO GRAND PRIX

MONTE CARLO • ROUND 6 • DATE: 24TH MAY 2015
Laps: 78 • Distance: 161.734miles/260.286km • Weather: Warm & bright

Pos	Driver	Team	Chassis-Engine	Result	Qual
1	Nico Rosberg	Mercedes AMG	Mercedes F1 W06	1h49m18.420s	2
2	Sebastian Vettel	Ferrari	Ferrari SF15-T	1h49m22.906s	3
3	Lewis Hamilton	Mercedes AMG	Mercedes F1 W06	1h49m24.473s	1
4	Daniil Kvyat	Red Bull Racing	Red Bull-Renault RB11	1h49m30.385s	5
5	Daniel Ricciardo	Red Bull Racing	Red Bull-Renault RB11	1h49m32.028s	4
6	Kimi Raikkonen	Ferrari	Ferrari SF15-T	1h49m32.765s	6
7	Sergio Perez	Force India	Force India-Mercedes VJM08	1h49m33.433s	7
8	Jenson Button	McLaren	McLaren-Honda MP4-30	1h49m34.483s	10
9	Felipe Nasr	Sauber	Sauber-Ferrari C34	1h49m42.046s	14
10	Carlos Sainz *	Toro Rosso	Toro Rosso-Renault STR10	1h49m43.476s	20
11	Nico Hulkenberg	Force India	Force India-Mercedes VJM08	1h49m44.652s	11
12	Romain Grosjean !	Lotus F1	Lotus-Mercedes E23 Hybrid	1h49m46.835s	15
13	Marcus Ericsson	Sauber	Sauber-Ferrari C34	1h49m49.579s	17
14	Valtteri Bottas	Williams	Williams-Mercedes FW37	1h50m04.209s	16
15	Felipe Massa	Williams	Williams-Mercedes FW37	77 laps	12
16	Roberto Merhi	Marussia	Marussia-Ferrari MR03B	76 laps	19
17	Will Stevens	Marussia	Marussia-Ferrari MR03B	76 laps	18
R	Max Verstappen	Toro Rosso	Toro Rosso-Renault STR10	62 laps/collision	9
R	Fernando Alonso	McLaren	McLaren-Honda MP4-30	41 laps/overheating	13
R	Pastor Maldonado	Lotus F1	Lotus-Mercedes E23 Hybrid	5 laps/brakes	8

Pole: Hamilton, 1m15.098s, 99.398mph/159.966kph. Fastest lap: Ricciardo, 1m18.063s, 95.623mph/153.891kph on Lap 74. Race leaders: Hamilton 1-64, Rosberg 65-78

* required to start from pit lane for failing to stop for weight check • ! 5-place grid penalty for gearbox change

NO RETURN TO GLORY

McLaren's glory days in the late 1980s and early 1990s came with Honda power in a melding of two companies focused on engineering excellence. However, McLaren-Honda's second coming didn't start with any such success. In fact, McLaren went into freefall after its change from Mercedes engines and scored just 27 points across the 19 races, to rank only ahead of Marussia.

THE YOUNGEST STARTER

Max Verstappen broke Jaime Alguersuari's record by a year and 324 days to become F1's youngest ever driver when he made his debut at the Australian GP for Scuderia Toro Rosso after just one season of car racing. He was 17 years 166 days and was scared of no one. Guided by his F1 racer father Jos, he immediately showed raw pace.

CANADIAN GRAND PRIX

MONTREAL • ROUND 7 • DATE: 7TH JUNE 2015
Laps: 70 • Distance: 189.534miles/305.27km • Weather: Warm but dull

Pos	Driver	Team	Chassis-Engine	Result	Qual
1	Lewis Hamilton	Mercedes AMG	Mercedes F1 W06	1h31m53.145s	1
2	Nico Rosberg	Mercedes AMG	Mercedes F1 W06	1h31m55.430s	2
3	Valtteri Bottas	Williams	Williams-Mercedes FW37	1h32m33.811s	4
4	Kimi Raikkonen	Ferrari	Ferrari SF15-T	1h32m38.770s	3
5	Sebastian Vettel *	Ferrari	Ferrari SF15-T	1h32m43.048s	18
6	Felipe Massa	Williams	Williams-Mercedes FW37	1h32m49.526s	15
7	Pastor Maldonado	Lotus F1	Lotus-Mercedes E23 Hybrid	1h32m59.809s	6
8	Nico Hulkenberg	Force India	Force India-Mercedes VJM08	69 laps	7
9	Daniil Kvyat	Red Bull Racing	Red Bull-Renault RB11	69 laps	8
10	Romain Grosjean †	Lotus F1	Lotus-Mercedes E23 Hybrid	69 laps	5
11	Sergio Perez	Force India	Force India-Mercedes VJM08	69 laps	10
12	Carlos Sainz	Toro Rosso	Toro Rosso-Renault STR10	69 laps	11
13	Daniel Ricciardo	Red Bull Racing	Red Bull-Renault RB11	69 laps	9
14	Marcus Ericsson	Sauber	Sauber-Ferrari C34	69 laps	12
15	Max Verstappen !/^	Toro Rosso	Toro Rosso-Renault STR10	69 laps	19
16	Felipe Nasr	Sauber	Sauber-Ferrari C34	68 laps	14
17	Will Stevens	Marussia	Marussia-Ferrari MR03B	66 laps	17
R	Roberto Merhi	Marussia	Marussia-Ferrari MR03B	57 laps/halfshaft	16
R	Jenson Button ^	McLaren	McLaren-Honda MP4-30	54 laps/exhaust	20
R	Fernando Alonso	McLaren	McLaren-Honda MP4-30	44 laps/exhaust	13

Pole: Hamilton, 1m14.393s, 131.131mph/211.035kph. Fastest lap: Raikkonen, 1m16.987s, 126.713mph/203.925kph on Lap 42. Race leaders: Hamilton 1-28 & 30-70, Rosberg 29

* 5-place grid penalty for overtaking under red flags • ! 5-place grid penalty for causing crash in Monaco GP • ^ 10-place grid penalty for using additional power unit elements • † 5s penalty for causing a collision

AUSTRIAN GRAND PRIX

RED BULL RING • ROUND 8 • DATE: 21ST JUNE 2015
Laps: 71 • Distance: 190.851miles/307.146km • Weather: Cool & dull

Pos	Driver	Team	Chassis-Engine	Result	Qual
1	Nico Rosberg	Mercedes AMG	Mercedes F1 W06	1h30m16.930s	2
2	Lewis Hamilton †	Mercedes AMG	Mercedes F1 W06	1h30m25.730s	1
3	Felipe Massa	Williams	Williams-Mercedes FW37	1h30m34.503s	4
4	Sebastian Vettel	Ferrari	Ferrari SF15-T	1h30m35.111s	3
5	Valtteri Bottas	Williams	Williams-Mercedes FW37	1h31m10.534s	6
6	Nico Hulkenberg	Force India	Force India-Mercedes VJM08	1h31m21.005s	5
7	Pastor Maldonado	Lotus F1	Lotus-Mercedes E23 Hybrid	70 laps	10

Pos	Driver	Team	Chassis-Engine	Result	Qual
8	Max Verstappen	Toro Rosso	Toro Rosso-Renault STR10	70 laps	7
9	Sergio Perez	Force India	Force India-Mercedes VJM08	70 laps	13
10	Daniel Ricciardo *	Red Bull Racing	Red Bull-Renault RB11	70 laps	18
11	Felipe Nasr	Sauber	Sauber-Ferrari C34	70 laps	8
12	Daniil Kvyat *	Red Bull Racing	Red Bull-Renault RB11	70 laps	15
13	Marcus Ericsson	Sauber	Sauber-Ferrari C34	69 laps	11
14	Roberto Merhi	Marussia	Marussia-Ferrari MR03B	68 laps	16
R	Romain Grosjean	Lotus F1	Lotus-Mercedes E23 Hybrid	35 laps/gearbox	9
R	Carlos Sainz ‡	Toro Rosso	Toro Rosso-Renault STR10	35 laps/power unit	12
R	Jenson Button !	McLaren	McLaren-Honda MP4-30	8 laps/electrical	20
R	Will Stevens	Marussia	Marussia-Ferrari MR03B	1 laps/oil leak	17
R	Kimi Raikkonen	Ferrari	Ferrari SF15-T	0 laps/collision	14
R	Fernando Alonso ^	McLaren	McLaren-Honda MP4-30	0 laps/collision	19

Pole: Hamilton, 1m08.455s, 141.362mph/227.501kph. Fastest lap: Rosberg, 1m11.235s, 135.845mph/218.622kph on Lap 35. Race leaders: Rosberg 1-32 & 37-71, Hamilton 33-35, Vettel 36

* 10-place grid penalty for using additional power unit elements • ! 25-place grid penalty for using additional power unit elements • ^ 25-place grid penalty for using additional power unit elements & gearbox change • † 5s penalty for crossing line at pit exit • ‡ 5s penalty for speeding in the pit lane

BRITISH GRAND PRIX

SILVERSTONE • ROUND 9 • DATE: 5TH JULY 2015
Laps: 52 • Distance: 190.345miles/306.332km • Weather: Warm & bright, rain later

Pos	Driver	Team	Chassis-Engine	Result	Qual
1	Lewis Hamilton	Mercedes AMG	Mercedes F1 W06	1h31m27.729s	1
2	Nico Rosberg	Mercedes AMG	Mercedes F1 W06	1h31m38.685s	2
3	Sebastian Vettel	Ferrari	Ferrari SF15-T	1h31m53.172s	6
4	Felipe Massa	Williams	Williams-Mercedes FW37	1h32m04.568s	3
5	Valtteri Bottas	Williams	Williams-Mercedes FW37	1h32m30.923s	4
6	Daniil Kvyat	Red Bull Racing	Red Bull-Renault RB11	1h32m31.684s	7
7	Nico Hulkenberg	Force India	Force India-Mercedes VJM08	1h32m46.473s	9
8	Kimi Raikkonen	Ferrari	Ferrari SF15-T	51 laps	5
9	Sergio Perez	Force India	Force India-Mercedes VJM08	51 laps	11
10	Fernando Alonso	McLaren	McLaren-Honda MP4-30	51 laps	17
11	Marcus Ericsson	Sauber	Sauber-Ferrari C34	51 laps	15
12	Roberto Merhi	Marussia	Marussia-Ferrari MR03B	49 laps	20
13	Will Stevens	Marussia	Marussia-Ferrari MR03B	49 laps	19
R	Carlos Sainz	Toro Rosso	Toro Rosso-Renault STR10	31 laps/electrical	8
R	Daniel Ricciardo	Red Bull Racing	Red Bull-Renault RB11	21 laps/electrical	10
R	Max Verstappen	Toro Rosso	Toro Rosso-Renault STR10	3 laps/spun off	13
R	Romain Grosjean	Lotus F1	Lotus-Mercedes E23 Hybrid	0 laps/collision	12
R	Pastor Maldonado	Lotus F1	Lotus-Mercedes E23 Hybrid	0 laps/collision	14
R	Jenson Button	McLaren	McLaren-Honda MP4-30	0 laps/collision	18
NS	Felipe Nasr	Sauber	Sauber-Ferrari C34	Gearbox	16

Pole: Hamilton, 1m32.248s, 142.851mph/229.897kph. Fastest lap: Hamilton, 1m37.093s, 135.723mph/218.425kph on Lap 29. Race leaders: Massa 1-18 & 20, Hamilton 19 & 22-43 & 45-52, Bottas 21, Rosberg 44

BACK FROM THE BRINK

It took an 11th hour rescue mounted by energy tycoon Stephen Fitzpatrick to save the Marussia team that had gone into receivership and had to miss the final three races of the 2014 season. When the British team appeared for the opening race in Australia, it had been rebranded as Manor. Unluckily, its factory had been sold and many of its staff had left.

HUNGARIAN GRAND PRIX

HUNGARORING • ROUND 10 • DATE: 26TH JULY 2015
Laps: 69 • Distance: 187.833miles/302.289km • Weather: Warm & bright

Pos	Driver	Team	Chassis-Engine	Result	Qual
1	Sebastian Vettel	Ferrari	Ferrari SF15-T	1h46m09.985s	3
2	Daniil Kvyat *	Red Bull Racing	Red Bull-Renault RB11	1h46m25.733s	7
3	Daniel Ricciardo	Red Bull Racing	Red Bull-Renault RB11	1h46m35.069s	4
4	Max Verstappen	Toro Rosso	Toro Rosso-Renault STR10	1h46m54.236s	9
5	Fernando Alonso	McLaren	McLaren-Honda MP4-30	1h46m59.064s	15
6	Lewis Hamilton	Mercedes AMG	Mercedes F1 W06	1h47m02.010s	1
7	Romain Grosjean	Lotus F1	Lotus-Mercedes E23 Hybrid	1h47m08.563s	10
8	Nico Rosberg	Mercedes AMG	Mercedes F1 W06	1h47m08.861s	2
9	Jenson Button	McLaren	McLaren-Honda MP4-30	1h47m17.013s	16
10	Marcus Ericsson	Sauber	Sauber-Ferrari C34	1h47m19.115s	17
11	Felipe Nasr	Sauber	Sauber-Ferrari C34	1h47m23.443s	18
12	Felipe Massa	Williams	Williams-Mercedes FW37	1h47m24.263s	8
13	Valtteri Bottas	Williams	Williams-Mercedes FW37	1h47m30.213s	6
14	Pastor Maldonado ^	Lotus F1	Lotus-Mercedes E23 Hybrid	1h47m35.127s	14
15	Roberto Merhi	Marussia	Marussia-Ferrari MR03B	67 laps	19
16	Will Stevens	Marussia	Marussia-Ferrari MR03B	65 laps/vibrations	20
R	Carlos Sainz	Toro Rosso	Toro Rosso-Renault STR10	60 laps/power unit	12
R	Kimi Raikkonen †	Ferrari	Ferrari SF15-T	55 laps/power unit	5
R	Sergio Perez	Force India	Force India-Mercedes VJM08	53 laps/brakes	13
R	Nico Hulkenberg	Force India	Force India-Mercedes VJM08	41 laps/wing	11

Pole: Hamilton, 1m22.020s, 119.483mph/192.289kph. Fastest lap: Ricciardo, 1m24.821s, 115.537mph/185.939kph on Lap 68. Race leaders: Vettel 1-21 & 23-69, Raikkonen 22

* 10s penalty for gaining advantage by exceeding track limits • ^ 10s penalty for overtaking in safety car period • † 5s penalty for speeding in pit lane

BELGIAN GRAND PRIX

SPA-FRANCORCHAMPS • ROUND 11 • DATE: 23RD AUGUST 2015
Laps: 43 • Distance: 187.139miles/301.172km • Weather: Warm & bright

Pos	Driver	Team	Chassis-Engine	Result	Qual
1	Lewis Hamilton	Mercedes AMG	Mercedes F1 W06	1h23m40.387s	1
2	Nico Rosberg	Mercedes AMG	Mercedes F1 W06	1h23m42.445s	2
3	Romain Grosjean *	Lotus F1	Lotus-Mercedes E23 Hybrid	1h24m18.375s	9
4	Daniil Kvyat	Red Bull Racing	Red Bull-Renault RB11	1h24m26.079s	12
5	Sergio Perez	Force India	Force India-Mercedes VJM08	1h24m34.384s	4
6	Felipe Massa	Williams	Williams-Mercedes FW37	1h24m35.670s	6
7	Kimi Raikkonen *	Ferrari	Ferrari SF15-T	1h24m36.090s	16

Pos	Driver	Team	Chassis-Engine	Result	Qual
8	Max Verstappen !	Toro Rosso	Toro Rosso-Renault STR10	1h24m36.463s	18
9	Valtteri Bottas	Williams	Williams-Mercedes FW37	1h24m41.427s	3
10	Marcus Ericsson	Sauber	Sauber-Ferrari C34	1h25m11.621s	13
11	Felipe Nasr	Sauber	Sauber-Ferrari C34	1h25m22.698s	14
12	Sebastian Vettel	Ferrari	Ferrari SF15-T	42 laps/tyre	8
13	Fernando Alonso †	McLaren	McLaren-Honda MP4-30	42 laps	20
14	Jenson Button ^	McLaren	McLaren-Honda MP4-30	42 laps	19
15	Roberto Merhi	Marussia	Marussia-Ferrari MR03B	42 laps	17
16	Will Stevens	Marussia	Marussia-Ferrari MR03B	42 laps	15
R	Carlos Sainz	Toro Rosso	Toro Rosso-Renault STR10	32 laps/power unit	10
R	Daniel Ricciardo	Red Bull Racing	Red Bull-Renault RB11	19 laps/electrical	5
R	Pastor Maldonado	Lotus F1	Lotus-Mercedes E23 Hybrid	2 laps/transmission	7
NS	Nico Hulkenberg	Force India	Force India-Mercedes VJM08	Power unit	11

Pole: Hamilton, 1m47.197s, 146.156mph/235.215kph. Fastest lap: Rosberg, 1m52.416s, 139.370mph/224.295kph on Lap 34. Race leaders: Hamilton 1-30 & 32-43, Rosberg 31

* 5-place grid penalty for gearbox change • ! 10-place grid penalty for using additional power unit elements • ^ 50-place grid penalty for using additional power unit elements • † 55-place grid penalty for using additional power unit elements

ITALIAN GRAND PRIX

MONZA • ROUND 12 • DATE: 6TH SEPTEMBER 2015
Laps: 53 • Distance: 190.778miles/307.029km • Weather: Warm & bright

Pos	Driver	Team	Chassis-Engine	Result	Qual
1	Lewis Hamilton	Mercedes AMG	Mercedes F1 W06	1h18m00.688s	1
2	Sebastian Vettel	Ferrari	Ferrari SF15-T	1h18m25.730s	3
3	Felipe Massa	Williams	Williams-Mercedes FW37	1h18m48.323s	5
4	Valtteri Bottas	Williams	Williams-Mercedes FW37	1h18m48.684s	6
5	Kimi Raikkonen	Ferrari	Ferrari SF15-T	1h19m09.548s	2
6	Sergio Perez	Force India	Force India-Mercedes VJM08	1h19m13.471s	7
7	Nico Hulkenberg	Force India	Force India-Mercedes VJM08	52 laps	9
8	Daniel Ricciardo ¶	Red Bull Racing	Red Bull-Renault RB11	52 laps	19
9	Marcus Ericsson *	Sauber	Sauber-Ferrari C34	52 laps	12
10	Daniil Kvyat §	Red Bull Racing	Red Bull-Renault RB11	52 laps	18
11	Carlos Sainz ‡	Toro Rosso	Toro Rosso-Renault STR10	52 laps	17
12	Max Verstappen †	Toro Rosso	Toro Rosso-Renault STR10	52 laps	20
13	Felipe Nasr	Sauber	Sauber-Ferrari C34	52 laps	11
14	Jenson Button !	McLaren	McLaren-Honda MP4-30	52 laps	15
15	Will Stevens	Marussia	Marussia-Ferrari MR03B	51 laps	13
16	Roberto Merhi	Marussia	Marussia-Ferrari MR03B	51 laps	14
17	Nico Rosberg	Mercedes AMG	Mercedes F1 W06	50 laps/engine	4
18	Fernando Alonso ^	McLaren	McLaren-Honda MP4-30	47 laps/electrical	16
R	Romain Grosjean	Lotus F1	Lotus-Mercedes E23 Hybrid	1 lap/collision	8
R	Pastor Maldonado	Lotus F1	Lotus-Mercedes E23 Hybrid	1 lap/collision	10

Pole: Hamilton, 1m23.397s, 155.384mph/250.066kph. Fastest lap: Hamilton, 1m26.672s, 149.512mph/240.617kph on Lap 48. Race leaders: Hamilton 1-53

* 3-place grid penalty for impeding Hulkenberg • ! 5-place grid penalty for using additional power unit elements • ^ 10-place grid penalty for using additional power unit elements • † 30-place grid penalty for using additional power unit elements • ‡ 35-place grid penalty for using additional power unit elements • § 35-place grid penalty for using additional power unit elements & gearbox change • ¶ 50-place grid penalty for using additional power unit elements

ONE DRIVER TOO MANY

Three drivers turned up at the season-opening race in Melbourne expecting to drive for Sauber. These were Marcus Ericsson, Felipe Nasr and Giedo van der Garde. Neither of the team's two cars went out in first practice while lawyers wrangled. The eventual outcome was that van der Garde's contract was found not to be valid, and so ended his 32-race F1 career.

SINGAPORE GRAND PRIX

MARINA BAY CIRCUIT • ROUND 13 • DATE: 20TH SEPTEMBER 2015
Laps: 61 • Distance: 191.981miles/308.965km • Weather: Hot & humid

Pos	Driver	Team	Chassis-Engine	Result	Qual
1	Sebastian Vettel	Ferrari	Ferrari SF15-T	2h01m22.118s	1
2	Daniel Ricciardo	Red Bull Racing	Red Bull-Renault RB11	2h01m23.596s	2
3	Kimi Raikkonen	Ferrari	Ferrari SF15-T	2h01m39.272s	3
4	Nico Rosberg	Mercedes AMG	Mercedes F1 W06	2h01m46.838s	6
5	Valtteri Bottas	Williams	Williams-Mercedes FW37	2h01m56.322s	7
6	Daniil Kvyat	Red Bull Racing	Red Bull-Renault RB11	2h01m57.626s	4
7	Sergio Perez	Force India	Force India-Mercedes VJM08	2h02m12.954s	13
8	Max Verstappen	Toro Rosso	Toro Rosso-Renault STR10	2h02m13.568s	8
9	Carlos Sainz	Toro Rosso	Toro Rosso-Renault STR10	2h02m14.978s	14
10	Felipe Nasr	Sauber	Sauber-Ferrari C34	2h02m52.163s	16
11	Marcus Ericsson	Sauber	Sauber-Ferrari C34	2h02m59.625s	17
12	Pastor Maldonado	Lotus F1	Lotus-Mercedes E23 Hybrid	2h02m59.836s	18
13	Romain Grosjean	Lotus F1	Lotus-Mercedes E23 Hybrid	59 laps/gearbox	10
14	Alexander Rossi *	Marussia	Marussia-Ferrari MR03B	59 laps	20
15	Will Stevens *	Marussia	Marussia-Ferrari MR03B	59 laps	19
R	Jenson Button	McLaren	McLaren-Honda MP4-30	52 laps/gearbox	15
R	Fernando Alonso	McLaren	McLaren-Honda MP4-30	33 laps/gearbox	12
R	Lewis Hamilton	Mercedes AMG	Mercedes F1 W06	32 laps/power unit	5
R	Felipe Massa	Williams	Williams-Mercedes FW37	30 laps/power unit	9
R	Nico Hulkenberg	Force India	Force India-Mercedes VJM08	12 laps/collision	11

Pole: Vettel, 1m43.885s, 109.063mph/175.521kph. Fastest lap: Ricciardo, 1m50.041s, 102.962mph/165.701kph on Lap 52. Race leaders: Vettel 1-61

* 5-place grid penalty for gearbox change

JAPANESE GRAND PRIX

SUZUKA • ROUND 14 • DATE: 27TH SEPTEMBER 2015
Laps: 53 • Distance: 191.240miles/307.771km • Weather: Hot but dull

Pos	Driver	Team	Chassis-Engine	Result	Qual
1	Lewis Hamilton	Mercedes AMG	Mercedes F1 W06	1h28m06.508s	2
2	Nico Rosberg	Mercedes AMG	Mercedes F1 W06	1h28m25.472s	1
3	Sebastian Vettel	Ferrari	Ferrari SF15-T	1h28m27.358s	4
4	Kimi Raikkonen	Ferrari	Ferrari SF15-T	1h28m40.276s	6
5	Valtteri Bottas	Williams	Williams-Mercedes FW37	1h28m43.254s	3
6	Nico Hulkenberg *	Force India	Force India-Mercedes VJM08	1h29m02.067s	13
7	Romain Grosjean	Lotus F1	Lotus-Mercedes E23 Hybrid	1h29m18.806s	8
8	Pastor Maldonado	Lotus F1	Lotus-Mercedes E23 Hybrid	1h29m20.083s	11

Pos	Driver	Team	Chassis-Engine	Result	Qual
9	Max Verstappen !	Toro Rosso	Toro Rosso-Renault STR10	1h29m41.823s	17
10	Carlos Sainz	Toro Rosso	Toro Rosso-Renault STR10	52 laps	10
11	Fernando Alonso	McLaren	McLaren-Honda MP4-30	52 laps	12
12	Sergio Perez	Force India	Force India-Mercedes VJM08	52 laps	9
13	Daniil Kvyat ^	Red Bull Racing	Red Bull-Renault RB11	52 laps	20
14	Marcus Ericsson	Sauber	Sauber-Ferrari C34	52 laps	15
15	Daniel Ricciardo	Red Bull Racing	Red Bull-Renault RB11	52 laps	7
16	Jenson Button	McLaren	McLaren-Honda MP4-30	52 laps	14
17	Felipe Massa	Williams	Williams-Mercedes FW37	51 laps	5
18	Alexander Rossi	Marussia	Marussia-Ferrari MR03B	51 laps	19
19	Will Stevens	Marussia	Marussia-Ferrari MR03B	50 laps	18
20	Felipe Nasr	Sauber	Sauber-Ferrari C34	49 laps/steering	16

Pole: Rosberg, 1m32.584s, 140.303mph/225.797kph. Fastest lap: Hamilton, 1m36.145s, 135.107mph/217.434kph on Lap 33. Race leaders: Hamilton 1-53

* 3-place grid penalty for causing a crash in Singapore GP • ! 3-place grid penalty for stopping on the racing line • ^ made to start from pit lane for car modification

KEEPING ON GOING

With the cost of competing in F1 going ever upwards, several teams were financially on the brink. One of them, Lotus F1 Team, as the team from Enstone was called from 2012 to 2015, was getting backing on a race-by-race basis as funds were slow to arrive. Romain Grosjean's third place in the Belgian GP bought the team time as the bailiffs closed in.

MEXICO'S F1 RETURN

After hosting grands prix from 1963 to 1970 and then 1986 to 1992, there was a welcome return to the Autodromo Hermanos Rodriguez in Mexico City. There had been major revisions since the 1992 visit, notably with the long, lightly banked final corner – Peraltada – now joined only halfway around after a slow section through a baseball arena.

RUSSIAN GRAND PRIX

SOCHI • ROUND 15 • DATE: 11TH OCTOBER 2015
Laps: 53 • Distance: 192.590miles/309.944km • Weather: Warm but dull

Pos	Driver	Team	Chassis-Engine	Result	Qual
1	Lewis Hamilton	Mercedes AMG	Mercedes F1 W06	1h37m11.024s	2
2	Sebastian Vettel	Ferrari	Ferrari SF15-T	1h37m16.977s	4
3	Sergio Perez	Force India	Force India-Mercedes VJM08	1h37m39.942s	7
4	Felipe Massa	Williams	Williams-Mercedes FW37	1h37m49.855s	15
5	Daniil Kvyat	Red Bull Racing	Red Bull-Renault RB11	1h37m58.590s	11
6	Felipe Nasr	Sauber	Sauber-Ferrari C34	1h38m07.532s	12
7	Pastor Maldonado	Lotus F1	Lotus-Mercedes E23 Hybrid	1h38m12.112s	14
8	Kimi Raikkonen ‡	Ferrari	Ferrari SF15-T	1h38m23.382s	5
9	Jenson Button	McLaren	McLaren-Honda MP4-30	1h38m30.491s	13

Pos	Driver	Team	Chassis-Engine	Result	Qual
10	Max Verstappen	Toro Rosso	Toro Rosso-Renault STR10	1h38m39.448s	9
11	Fernando Alonso !/†	McLaren	McLaren-Honda MP4-30	1h38m42.234s	19
12	Valtteri Bottas	Williams	Williams-Mercedes FW37	52 laps/collision	3
13	Roberto Merhi *	Marussia	Marussia-Ferrari MR03B	52 laps	18
14	Will Stevens	Marussia	Marussia-Ferrari MR03B	51 laps	17
15	Daniel Ricciardo	Red Bull Racing	Red Bull-Renault RB11	47 laps/suspension	10
R	Carlos Sainz */^	Toro Rosso	Toro Rosso-Renault STR10	45 laps/brakes	20
R	Romain Grosjean	Lotus F1	Lotus-Mercedes E23 Hybrid	11 laps/spun off	8
R	Nico Rosberg	Mercedes AMG	Mercedes F1 W06	7 laps/throttle	1
R	Nico Hulkenberg	Force India	Force India-Mercedes VJM08	0 laps/collision	6
R	Marcus Ericsson	Sauber	Sauber-Ferrari C34	0 laps/collision	16

Pole: Rosberg, 1m37.113s, 134.704mph/216.786kph. Fastest lap: Vettel, 1m40.071s, 130.723mph/210.378kph on Lap 51. Race leaders: Rosberg 1-6, Hamilton 7-53

* 20-place grid penalty for using additional power unit elements • ! 35-place grid penalty for excess power unit element use • ^ 5s penalty for crossing line at pit entry • † 5s penalty for exceeding track limits • ‡ 30s penalty for causing crash with Bottas

THROUGH THE NIGHT

Nico Hulkenberg became the first contemporary F1 driver since Yannick Dalmas in 1994 to win the Le Mans 24 Hours. Sharing a works Porsche with Earl Bamber and Nick Tandy, he led a Porsche one-two from the sister car of Mark Webber, Timo Bernhard and Brendon Hartley. Nico then earned kudos when he brought the trophy to the next grand prix.

NEW DRIVERS

Felipe Nasr started his F1 career by finishing fifth on his debut for Sauber in Australia. It was to be the Brazilian's best result. This was bettered, though, by Max Verstappen, who retired from his first race for Toro Rosso, but went on to take two fourths, with team-mate Carlos Sainz Jr the best of the other three rookies, taking a seventh.

UNITED STATES GRAND PRIX

CIRCUIT OF THE AMERICAS • ROUND 16 • DATE: 25TH OCTOBER 2015
Laps: 56 • Distance: 191.834miles/308.728km • Weather: Warm & wet, drying later

Pos	Driver	Team	Chassis-Engine	Result	Qual
1	Lewis Hamilton	Mercedes AMG	Mercedes F1 W06	1h50m52.703s	2
2	Nico Rosberg	Mercedes AMG	Mercedes F1 W06	1h50m55.553s	1
3	Sebastian Vettel !	Ferrari	Ferrari SF15-T	1h50m56.084s	13
4	Max Verstappen	Toro Rosso	Toro Rosso-Renault STR10	1h51m15.062s	8
5	Sergio Perez	Force India	Force India-Mercedes VJM08	1h51m17.116s	5
6	Jenson Button	McLaren	McLaren-Honda MP4-30	1h51m20.761s	11
7	Carlos Sainz †	Toro Rosso	Toro Rosso-Renault STR10	1h51m23.322s	20
8	Pastor Maldonado	Lotus F1	Lotus-Mercedes E23 Hybrid	1h51m24.976s	12

Pos	Driver	Team	Chassis-Engine	Result	Qual
9	Felipe Nasr	Sauber	Sauber-Ferrari C34	1h51m32.960s	15
10	Daniel Ricciardo	Red Bull Racing	Red Bull-Renault RB11	1h51m46.074s	3
11	Fernando Alonso	McLaren	McLaren-Honda MP4-30	1h51m47.519s	9
12	Alexander Rossi	Marussia	Marussia-Ferrari MR03B	1h52m07.980s	17
R	Daniil Kvyat	Red Bull Racing	Red Bull-Renault RB11	41 laps/spun off	4
R	Nico Hulkenberg	Force India	Force India-Mercedes VJM08	35 laps/collision	6
R	Marcus Ericsson	Sauber	Sauber-Ferrari C34	25 laps/electrical	14
R	Kimi Raikkonen !	Ferrari	Ferrari SF15-T	25 laps/spun off	18
R	Felipe Massa	Williams	Williams-Mercedes FW37	23 laps/suspension	7
R	Romain Grosjean	Lotus F1	Lotus-Mercedes E23 Hybrid	10 laps/collision	10
R	Valtteri Bottas *	Williams	Williams-Mercedes FW37	5 laps/suspension	16
R	Will Stevens ^	Marussia	Marussia-Ferrari MR03B	1 laps/collision	19

Pole: Rosberg, 1m56.824s, 105.562mph/169.886kph. Fastest lap: Rosberg, 1m40.666s, 122.506mph/197.154kph on Lap 49. Race leaders: Hamilton 1-14 & 39-43 & 48-56, Ricciardo 15-21, Rosberg 22-38 & 44-47

* 5-place grid penalty for gearbox change • ! 10-place grid penalty for using additional power unit elements • ^ 20-place grid penalty for using additional power unit elements • † 5s penalty for speeding in the pit lane

MEXICAN GRAND PRIX

MEXICO CITY • ROUND 17 • DATE: 1ST NOVEMBER 2015
Laps: 71 • Distance: 189.881miles/305.584km • Weather: Warm & bright

Pos	Driver	Team	Chassis-Engine	Result	Qual
1	Nico Rosberg	Mercedes AMG	Mercedes F1 W06	1h42m35.038s	1
2	Lewis Hamilton	Mercedes AMG	Mercedes F1 W06	1h42m36.992s	2
3	Valtteri Bottas	Williams	Williams-Mercedes FW37	1h42m49.630s	6
4	Daniil Kvyat	Red Bull Racing	Red Bull-Renault RB11	1h42m51.610s	4
5	Daniel Ricciardo	Red Bull Racing	Red Bull-Renault RB11	1h42m54.720s	5
6	Felipe Massa	Williams	Williams-Mercedes FW37	1h42m56.531s	7
7	Nico Hulkenberg	Force India	Force India-Mercedes VJM08	1h43m00.898s	10
8	Sergio Perez	Force India	Force India-Mercedes VJM08	1h43m09.381s	9
9	Max Verstappen	Toro Rosso	Toro Rosso-Renault STR10	1h43m10.267s	8
10	Romain Grosjean	Lotus F1	Lotus-Mercedes E23 Hybrid	1h43m12.972s	12
11	Pastor Maldonado	Lotus F1	Lotus-Mercedes E23 Hybrid	1h43m13.576s	13
12	Marcus Ericsson	Sauber	Sauber-Ferrari C34	1h43m15.218s	14
13	Carlos Sainz	Toro Rosso	Toro Rosso-Renault STR10	1h43m23.810s	11
14	Jenson Button ^	McLaren	McLaren-Honda MP4-30	1h43m24.252s	20
15	Alexander Rossi	Marussia	Marussia-Ferrari MR03B	69 laps	16
16	Will Stevens	Marussia	Marussia-Ferrari MR03B	69 laps	17
R	Felipe Nasr	Sauber	Sauber-Ferrari C34	57 laps/brakes	15
R	Sebastian Vettel	Ferrari	Ferrari SF15-T	50 laps/spun off	3
R	Kimi Raikkonen !	Ferrari	Ferrari SF15-T	21 laps/collision	19
R	Fernando Alonso *	McLaren	McLaren-Honda MP4-30	1 laps/power unit	18

Pole: Rosberg, 1m19.480s, 121.134mph/194.947kph. Fastest lap: Rosberg, 1m20.521s, 119.568mph/192.426kph on Lap 67. Race leaders: Rosberg 1-25 & 29-45 & 49-71, Hamilton 26-28 & 46-48

* 15-place grid penalty for gearbox change & using additional power unit elements • ! 35-place grid penalty for gearbox change & using additional power unit elements • ^ 70-place grid penalty for using additional power unit elements

BRAZILIAN GRAND PRIX

INTERLAGOS • ROUND 18 • DATE: 15TH NOVEMBER 2015
Laps: 71 • Distance: 190.101miles/305.939km • Weather: Hot & humid

Pos	Driver	Team	Chassis-Engine	Result	Qual
1	Nico Rosberg	Mercedes AMG	Mercedes F1 W06	1h31m09.090s	1
2	Lewis Hamilton	Mercedes AMG	Mercedes F1 W06	1h31m16.846s	2
3	Sebastian Vettel	Ferrari	Ferrari SF15-T	1h31m23.334s	3
4	Kimi Raikkonen	Ferrari	Ferrari SF15-T	1h31m56.633s	4
5	Valtteri Bottas *	Williams	Williams-Mercedes FW37	70 laps	7
6	Nico Hulkenberg	Force India	Force India-Mercedes VJM08	70 laps	5
7	Daniil Kvyat	Red Bull Racing	Red Bull-Renault RB11	70 laps	6
DQ	Felipe Massa ‡	Williams	Williams-Mercedes FW37	Tyre temperature	8
8	Romain Grosjean	Lotus F1	Lotus-Mercedes E23 Hybrid	70 laps	14
9	Max Verstappen	Toro Rosso	Toro Rosso-Renault STR10	70 laps	9
10	Pastor Maldonado	Lotus F1	Lotus-Mercedes E23 Hybrid	70 laps	15
11	Daniel Ricciardo ^	Red Bull Racing	Red Bull-Renault RB11	70 laps	19
12	Sergio Perez	Force India	Force India-Mercedes VJM08	70 laps	11
13	Felipe Nasr !	Sauber	Sauber-Ferrari C34	70 laps	13
14	Jenson Button	McLaren	McLaren-Honda MP4-30	70 laps	16
15	Fernando Alonso †	McLaren	McLaren-Honda MP4-30	70 laps	20
16	Marcus Ericsson	Sauber	Sauber-Ferrari C34	69 laps	12
17	Will Stevens	Marussia	Marussia-Ferrari MR03B	67 laps	18
18	Alexander Rossi	Marussia	Marussia-Ferrari MR03B	67 laps	17
R	Carlos Sainz	Toro Rosso	Toro Rosso-Renault STR10	0 laps/electrical	10

Pole: Rosberg, 1m11.282s, 135.222mph/217.620kph. Fastest lap: Hamilton, 1m14.832s, 128.807mph/207.296kph on Lap 51. Race leaders: Rosberg 1-12 & 15-32 & 35-47 & 50-71, Hamilton 13-14 & 33-34 & 48-49

* 3-place grid penalty for overtaking under red flags • ! 3-place grid penalty for impeding Massa • ^ 20-place grid penalty for using additional power unit elements • † 25-place grid penalty for using additional power unit elements • ‡ disqualified for tyre being heated above limit pre-race

IN MEMORIAM

Head injuries suffered in the 2014 Japanese GP finally led to the death of Marussia driver Jules Bianchi in the July of 2015. The 25-year-old French driver had been a champion in the French Formula Renault and European Formula 3 series, and runner-up in Formula Renault 3.5. He had been marked for great things.

ABU DHABI GRAND PRIX

YAS MARINA CIRCUIT • ROUND 19 • DATE: 29TH NOVEMBER 2015
Laps: 55 • Distance: 189.547miles/305.47km • Weather: Hot & bright

Pos	Driver	Team	Chassis-Engine	Result	Qual
1	Nico Rosberg	Mercedes AMG	Mercedes F1 W06	1h38m30.175s	1
2	Lewis Hamilton	Mercedes AMG	Mercedes F1 W06	1h38m38.446s	2
3	Kimi Raikkonen	Ferrari	Ferrari SF15-T	1h38m49.605s	3
4	Sebastian Vettel	Ferrari	Ferrari SF15-T	1h39m13.910s	15
5	Sergio Perez	Force India	Force India-Mercedes VJM08	1h39m34.127s	4
6	Daniel Ricciardo	Red Bull Racing	Red Bull-Renault RB11	1h39m35.185s	5

Pos	Driver	Team	Chassis-Engine	Result	Qual
7	Nico Hulkenberg	Force India	Force India-Mercedes VJM08	1h40m03.793s	7
8	Felipe Massa	Williams	Williams-Mercedes FW37	1h40m07.926s	8
9	Romain Grosjean *	Lotus F1	Lotus-Mercedes E23 Hybrid	1h40m08.376s	18
10	Daniil Kvyat	Red Bull Racing	Red Bull-Renault RB11	1h40m12.546s	9
11	Carlos Sainz	Toro Rosso	Toro Rosso-Renault STR10	1h40m13.700s	10
12	Jenson Button	McLaren	McLaren-Honda MP4-30	54 laps	12
13	Valtteri Bottas	Williams	Williams-Mercedes FW37	54 laps	6
14	Marcus Ericsson	Sauber	Sauber-Ferrari C34	54 laps	17
15	Felipe Nasr	Sauber	Sauber-Ferrari C34	54 laps	14
16	Max Verstappen †/‡	Toro Rosso	Toro Rosso-Renault STR10	54 laps	11
17	Fernando Alonso	McLaren	McLaren-Honda MP4-30	53 laps	16
18	Will Stevens !	Marussia	Marussia-Ferrari MR03B	53 laps	19
19	Roberto Merhi ^	Marussia	Marussia-Ferrari MR03B	52 laps	20
R	Pastor Maldonado	Lotus F1	Lotus-Mercedes E23 Hybrid	0 laps/collision	13

Pole: Rosberg, 1m40.237s, 123.945mph/199.471kph. Fastest lap: Hamilton, 1m44.517s, 118.870mph/191.302kph on Lap 44. Race leaders: Rosberg 1-10 & 12-30 & 42-55, Hamilton 11 & 31-41

* 5-place grid penalty for gearbox change • ! 5-place grid penalty for using additional power unit elements • ^ made to start from pit lane for car modification in parc ferme • † 5s penalty for exceeding track limits • ‡ 20s penalty for ignoring blue flags

WORLD DRIVERS' CHAMPIONSHIP FINAL RESULTS

Pos	Driver	Nat	Car-Engine	R1	R2	R3	R4	R5	R6	R7	R8
1	Lewis Hamilton	GBR	Mercedes F1 W06	1PF	2P	1PF	1P	2F	3P	1P	2P
2	Nico Rosberg	DEU	Mercedes F1 W06	2	3F	2	3	1P	1	2	1F
3	Sebastian Vettel	DEU	Ferrari SF15-T	3	1	3	5	3	2	5	4
4	Kimi Raikkonen	FIN	Ferrari SF15-T	R	4	4	2F	5	6	4F	R
5	Valtteri Bottas	FIN	Williams-Mercedes FW37	NS	5	6	4	4	14	3	5
6	Felipe Massa	BRA	Williams-Mercedes FW37	4	6	5	10	6	15	6	3
7	Daniil Kvyat	RUS	Red Bull-Renault RB11	NS	9	R	9	10	4	9	12
8	Daniel Ricciardo	AUS	Red Bull-Renault RB11	6	10	9	6	7	5F	13	10
9	Sergio Perez	MEX	Force India-Mercedes VJM08	10	13	11	8	13	7	11	9
10	Nico Hulkenberg	DEU	Force India-Mercedes VJM08	7	14	R	13	15	11	8	6
11	Romain Grosjean	FRA	Lotus-Mercedes E23 Hybrid	R	11	7	7	8	12	10	R
12	Max Verstappen	NLD	Toro Rosso-Renault STR10	R	7	17	R	11	R	15	8
13	Felipe Nasr	BRA	Sauber-Ferrari C34	5	12	8	12	12	9	16	11
14	Pastor Maldonado	VEN	Lotus-Mercedes E23 Hybrid	R	R	R	15	R	R	7	7
15	Carlos Sainz	ESP	Toro Rosso-Renault STR10	9	8	13	R	9	10	12	R
16	Jenson Button	GBR	McLaren-Honda MP4-30	11	R	14	NS	16	8	R	R
17	Fernando Alonso	ESP	McLaren-Honda MP4-30	-	R	12	11	R	R	R	R
18	Marcus Ericsson	SWE	Sauber-Ferrari C34	8	R	10	14	14	13	14	13
19	Roberto Merhi	ESP	Marussia-Ferrari MR03B	NS	15	16	17	18	16	R	14
20	Alexander Rossi	USA	Marussia-Ferrari MR03B	-	-	-	-	-	-	-	-
21	Will Stevens	GBR	Marussia-Ferrari MR03B	NS	NS	15	16	17	17	17	R

Pos	Driver	R9	R10	R11	R12	R13	R14	R15	R16	R17	R18	R19	Total
1	Hamilton	1PF	6P	1P	1PF	R	1F	1	1	2	2F	2F	381
2	Rosberg	2	8	2F	17	4	2P	RP	2PF	1PF	1P	1P	322
3	Vettel	3	1	12	2	1P	3	2F	3	R	3	4	278
4	Raikkonen	8	R	7	5	3	4	8	R	R	4	3	150
5	Bottas	5	13	9	4	5	5	12	R	3	5	13	136
6	Massa	4	12	6	3	R	17	4	R	6	DQ	8	121
7	Kvyat	6	2	4	10	6	13	5	R	4	7	10	95
8	Ricciardo	R	3F	R	8	2F	15	15	10	5	11	6	92

Pos	Driver	R9	R10	R11	R12	R13	R14	R15	R16	R17	R18	R19	Total
9	Perez	9	R	5	6	7	12	3	5	8	12	5	78
10	Hulkenberg	7	R	NS	7	R	6	R	R	7	6	7	58
11	Grosjean	R	7	3	R	13	7	R	R	10	8	9	51
12	Verstappen	R	4	8	12	8	9	10	4	9	9	16	49
13	Nasr	NS	11	11	13	10	20	6	9	R	13	15	27
14	Maldonado	R	14	R	R	12	8	7	8	11	10	R	27
15	Sainz	R	R	R	11	9	10	R	7	13	R	11	18
16	Button	R	9	14	14	R	16	9	6	14	14	12	16
17	Alonso	10	5	13	18	R	11	11	11	R	15	17	11
18	Ericsson	11	10	10	9	11	14	R	R	12	16	14	9
19	Merhi	12	15	15	16	-	-	13	-	-	-	19	0
20	Rossi	-	-	-	-	14	18	-	12	15	18	-	0
21	Stevens	13	16	16	15	15	19	14	R	16	17	18	0

WORLD CONSTRUCTORS' CHAMPIONSHIP FINAL RESULTS

Pos	Team-Engine	R1	R2	R3	R4	R5	R6	R7	R8	R9	R10
1	Mercedes AMG	1/2	2/3	1/2	1/3	1/2	1/3	1/2	1/2	1/2	6/8
2	Ferrari	3/R	1/4	3/4	2/5	3/5	2/6	4/5	4/R	3/8	1/R
3	Williams-Mercedes	4/NS	5/6	5/6	4/10	4/6	14/15	3/6	3/5	4/5	12/13
4	Red Bull-Renault	6/NS	9/10	9/R	6/9	7/10	4/5	9/13	10/12	6/R	2/3
5	Force India-Mercedes	7/10	13/14	11/R	8/13	13/15	7/11	8/11	6/9	7/9	R/R
6	Lotus-Mercedes	R/R	11/R	7/R	7/15	8/R	12/R	7/10	7/R	R/R	7/14
7	Toro Rosso-Renault	9/R	7/8	13/17	R/R	9/11	10/R	12/15	8/R	R/R	4/R
8	Sauber-Ferrari	5/8	12/R	8/10	12/14	12/14	9/13	14/16	11/13	11/NS	10/11
9	McLaren-Honda	11/NS	R/R	12/14	11/NS	16/R	8/R	R/R	R/R	10/R	5/9
10	Marussia-Ferrari	NS/NS	15/NS	15/16	16/17	17/18	16/17	17/R	14/R	12/13	15/16

Pos	Team-Engine	R11	R12	R13	R14	R15	R16	R17	R18	R19	Total
1	Mercedes AMG	1/2	1/17	4/R	1/2	1/R	1/2	1/2	1/2	1/2	703
2	Ferrari	7/12	2/5	1/3	3/4	2/8	3/R	R/R	3/4	3/4	428
3	Williams-Mercedes	6/9	3/4	5/R	5/17	4/12	R/R	3/6	5/DQ	8/13	257
4	Red Bull-Renault	4/R	8/10	2/6	13/15	5/15	10/R	4/5	7/11	6/10	187
5	Force India-Mercedes	5/NS	6/7	7/R	6/12	3/R	5/R	7/8	6/12	5/7	136
6	Lotus-Mercedes	3/R	R/R	12/13	7/8	7/R	8/R	10/11	8/10	9/R	78
7	Toro Rosso-Renault	8/R	11/12	8/9	9/10	10/R	4/7	9/13	9/R	11/16	67
8	Sauber-Ferrari	10/11	9/13	10/11	14/20	6/R	9/R	12/R	13/16	14/15	36
9	McLaren-Honda	13/14	14/18	R/R	11/16	9/11	6/11	14/R	14/15	12/17	27
10	Marussia-Ferrari	15/16	15/16	14/15	18/19	13/14	12/R	15/16	17/18	18/19	0

SYMBOLS AND GRAND PRIX KEY

Round 1 Australian GP
Round 2 Malaysian GP
Round 3 Chinese GP
Round 4 Bahrain GP
Round 5 Spanish GP
Round 6 Monaco GP
Round 7 Canadian GP
Round 8 Austrian GP
Round 9 British GP
Round 10 Hungarian GP
Round 11 Belgian GP
Round 12 Italian GP
Round 13 Singapore GP
Round 14 Japanese GP
Round 15 Russian GP
Round 16 United States GP
Round 17 Mexican GP
Round 18 Brazilian GP
Round 19 Abu Dhabi GP

SCORING

1st 25 points
2nd 18 points
3rd 15 points
4th 12 points
5th 10 points
6th 8 points
7th 6 points
8th 4 points
9th 2 points
10th 1 point

DNPQ DID NOT PRE-QUALIFY **DNQ** DID NOT QUALIFY **DQ** DISQUALIFIED **EX** EXCLUDED
F FASTEST LAP **NC** NOT CLASSIFIED **NS** NON-STARTER **P** POLE POSITION **R** RETIRED

2016

SEASON SUMMARY

It was another year of Mercedes domination, and this time Nico Rosberg broke Lewis Hamilton's run to become the second second-generation champion after Damon Hill in 1996. The title battle went down to the last lap of the final round and second place was enough for the German to take the title by five points. Then, surprisingly, he decided to stop racing just days later. Daniel Ricciardo ended up third in the rankings for Red Bull Racing, which had a slight upper hand over Ferrari, and the team was inspired when Max Verstappen joined them in the fifth round and promptly became F1's youngest-ever winner.

AUSTRALIAN GRAND PRIX

ALBERT PARK • ROUND 1 • DATE: 20TH MARCH 2016
Laps: 57 • Distance: 187.822miles/302.271km • Weather: Warm & bright

Pos	Driver	Team	Chassis-Engine	Result	Qual
1	Nico Rosberg	Mercedes AMG	Mercedes F1 W07	1h48m15.565s	2
2	Lewis Hamilton	Mercedes AMG	Mercedes F1 W07	1h48m23.625s	1
3	Sebastian Vettel	Ferrari	Ferrari SF16-H	1h48m25.208s	3
4	Daniel Ricciardo	Red Bull Racing	Red Bull-TAG Heuer RB12	1h48m39.895s	8
5	Felipe Massa	Williams	Williams-Mercedes FW38	1h49m14.544s	6
6	Romain Grosjean	Haas	Haas-Ferrari VF-16	1h49m27.646s	19
7	Nico Hulkenberg	Force India	Force India-Mercedes VJM09	1h49m29.764s	10
8	Valtteri Bottas !	Williams	Williams-Mercedes FW38	1h49m30.718s	16
9	Carlos Sainz	Toro Rosso	Toro Rosso-Ferrari STR11	1h49m31.245s	7
10	Max Verstappen	Toro Rosso	Toro Rosso-Ferrari STR11	1h49m32.398s	5
11	Jolyon Palmer	Renault F1	Renault RS16	1h49m38.964s	13
12	Kevin Magnussen	Renault F1	Renault RS16	1h49m41.171s	14
13	Sergio Perez	Force India	Force India-Mercedes VJM09	1h49m47.264s	9
14	Jenson Button	McLaren	McLaren-Honda MP4-31	56 laps	12
15	Felipe Nasr	Sauber	Sauber-Ferrari C35	56 laps	17
16	Pascal Wehrlein	Manor Racing	Manor-Mercedes MRT05	56 laps	21
R	Marcus Ericsson	Sauber	Sauber-Ferrari C35	38 laps/tyre	15
R	Kimi Raikkonen	Ferrari	Ferrari SF16-H	21 laps/fire	4
R	Rio Haryanto *	Manor Racing	Manor-Mercedes MRT05	17 laps/transmission	22
R	Fernando Alonso	McLaren	McLaren-Honda MP4-31	16 laps/collision	11
R	Esteban Gutierrez	Haas	Haas-Ferrari VF-16	16 laps/collision	20
NS	Daniil Kvyat	Red Bull Racing	Red Bull-TAG Heuer RB12	Power unit	18

Pole: Hamilton, 1m23.837s, 141.494mph/227.713kph. Fastest lap: Ricciardo, 1m28.997s, 133.290mph/214.510kph on Lap 49. Race leaders: Vettel 1-12 & 16-34, Raikkonen 13-15, Rosberg 35-57

* 3-place grid penalty for causing a crash in pit lane • ! 5-place grid penalty for gearbox change

ANOTHER AMERICAN THRUST

It sometimes seems that it has been the World Championship's eternal quest to be popular in the USA. So it was with pleasure that F1 greeted a new American team as a sign of the sport's growing acceptance in the US. Haas F1 joined a short list that started with Scarab and went on to include race-winning outfits Eagle, Penske and Shadow.

BAHRAIN GRAND PRIX

SAKHIR • ROUND 2 • DATE: 3RD APRIL 2016
Laps: 57 • Distance: 191.683miles/308.484km • Weather: Warm & bright

Pos	Driver	Team	Chassis-Engine	Result	Qual
1	Nico Rosberg	Mercedes AMG	Mercedes F1 W07	1h33m34.696s	2
2	Kimi Raikkonen	Ferrari	Ferrari SF16-H	1h33m44.978s	4
3	Lewis Hamilton	Mercedes AMG	Mercedes F1 W07	1h34m04.844s	1
4	Daniel Ricciardo	Red Bull Racing	Red Bull-TAG Heuer RB12	1h34m37.190s	5
5	Romain Grosjean	Haas	Haas-Ferrari VF-16	1h34m52.995s	9
6	Max Verstappen	Toro Rosso	Toro Rosso-Ferrari STR11	1h34m55.625s	10
7	Daniil Kvyat	Red Bull Racing	Red Bull-TAG Heuer RB12	56 laps	15
8	Felipe Massa	Williams	Williams-Mercedes FW38	56 laps	7
9	Valtteri Bottas	Williams	Williams-Mercedes FW38	56 laps	6
10	Stoffel Vandoorne	McLaren	McLaren-Honda MP4-31	56 laps	12
11	Kevin Magnussen *	Renault F1	Renault RS16	56 laps	22
12	Marcus Ericsson	Sauber	Sauber-Ferrari C35	56 laps	17
13	Pascal Wehrlein	Manor Racing	Manor-Mercedes MRT05	56 laps	16
14	Felipe Nasr	Sauber	Sauber-Ferrari C35	56 laps	21
15	Nico Hulkenberg	Force India	Force India-Mercedes VJM09	56 laps	8
16	Sergio Perez	Force India	Force India-Mercedes VJM09	56 laps	18
17	Rio Haryanto	Manor Racing	Manor-Mercedes MRT05	56 laps	20
R	Carlos Sainz	Toro Rosso	Toro Rosso-Ferrari STR11	29 laps/collision	11
R	Esteban Gutierrez	Haas	Haas-Ferrari VF-16	9 laps/brakes	13
R	Jenson Button	McLaren	McLaren-Honda MP4-31	6 laps/power unit	14
NS	Sebastian Vettel	Ferrari	Ferrari SF16-H	Power unit	3
NS	Jolyon Palmer	Renault F1	Renault RS16	Hydraulics	19

Pole: Hamilton, 1m29.493s, 135.276mph/217.706kph. Fastest lap: Rosberg, 1m34.482s, 128.133mph/206.210kph on Lap 41. Race leaders: Rosberg 1-39 & 41-57, Hamilton 40

* made to start from pit lane for failing to stop for weight check

NOTHING STANDS STILL

After being plagued by financial problems, the four-time world championship title-winning team from Enstone changed its name again, reverting from Lotus to go racing as the Renault Sport F1 Team. The French manufacturer bought Lotus back from Genii Capital and struggled without Mercedes engines, but at least put the name back on a firm footing.

CHINESE GRAND PRIX

SHANGHAI INTERNATIONAL CIRCUIT • ROUND 3 • DATE: 17TH APRIL 2016
Laps: 56 • Distance: 189.677miles/305.256km • Weather: Warm & bright

Pos	Driver	Team	Chassis-Engine	Result	Qual
1	Nico Rosberg	Mercedes AMG	Mercedes F1 W07	1h38m53.891s	1
2	Sebastian Vettel	Ferrari	Ferrari SF16-H	1h39m31.667s	4
3	Daniil Kvyat	Red Bull Racing	Red Bull-TAG Heuer RB12	1h39m39.827s	6
4	Daniel Ricciardo	Red Bull Racing	Red Bull-TAG Heuer RB12	1h39m46.579s	2
5	Kimi Raikkonen	Ferrari	Ferrari SF16-H	1h39m59.763s	3
6	Felipe Massa	Williams	Williams-Mercedes FW38	1h40m09.402s	10

Pos	Driver	Team	Chassis-Engine	Result	Qual
7	Lewis Hamilton !	Mercedes AMG	Mercedes F1 W07	1h40m12.121s	22
8	Max Verstappen	Toro Rosso	Toro Rosso-Ferrari STR11	1h40m13.159s	9
9	Carlos Sainz	Toro Rosso	Toro Rosso-Ferrari STR11	1h40m18.018s	8
10	Valtteri Bottas	Williams	Williams-Mercedes FW38	1h40m20.083s	5
11	Sergio Perez	Force India	Force India-Mercedes VJM09	1h40m28.174s	7
12	Fernando Alonso	McLaren	McLaren-Honda MP4-31	1h40m31.144s	11
13	Jenson Button	McLaren	McLaren-Honda MP4-31	1h40m35.881s	12
14	Esteban Gutierrez	Haas	Haas-Ferrari VF-16	55 laps	18
15	Nico Hulkenberg *	Force India	Force India-Mercedes VJM09	55 laps	13
16	Marcus Ericsson	Sauber	Sauber-Ferrari C35	55 laps	15
17	Kevin Magnussen	Renault F1	Renault RS16	55 laps	17
18	Pascal Wehrlein	Manor Racing	Manor-Mercedes MRT05	55 laps	21
19	Romain Grosjean	Haas	Haas-Ferrari VF-16	55 laps	14
20	Felipe Nasr	Sauber	Sauber-Ferrari C35	55 laps	16
21	Rio Haryanto	Manor Racing	Manor-Mercedes MRT05	55 laps	20
22	Jolyon Palmer	Renault F1	Renault RS16	55 laps	19

Pole: Rosberg, 1m35.402s, 127.812mph/205.693kph. Fastest lap: Hulkenberg, 1m39.824s, 122.150mph/196.581kph on Lap 48. Race leaders: Ricciardo 1-2, Rosberg 3-56

* 3-place grid penalty for unsafe release • ! 5-place grid penalty for gearbox change

RUSSIAN GRAND PRIX

SOCHI • ROUND 4 • DATE: 1ST MAY 2016
Laps: 53 • Distance: 192.590miles/309.944km • Weather: Warm & bright

Pos	Driver	Team	Chassis-Engine	Result	Qual
1	Nico Rosberg	Mercedes AMG	Mercedes F1 W07	1h32m41.997s	1
2	Lewis Hamilton	Mercedes AMG	Mercedes F1 W07	1h33m07.019s	10
3	Kimi Raikkonen	Ferrari	Ferrari SF16-H	1h33m13.995s	3
4	Valtteri Bottas	Williams	Williams-Mercedes FW38	1h33m32.214s	2
5	Felipe Massa	Williams	Williams-Mercedes FW38	1h33m56.424s	4
6	Fernando Alonso	McLaren	McLaren-Honda MP4-31	52 laps	14
7	Kevin Magnussen	Renault F1	Renault RS16	52 laps	17
8	Romain Grosjean	Haas	Haas-Ferrari VF-16	52 laps	15
9	Sergio Perez	Force India	Force India-Mercedes VJM09	52 laps	6
10	Jenson Button	McLaren	McLaren-Honda MP4-31	52 laps	12
11	Daniel Ricciardo	Red Bull Racing	Red Bull-TAG Heuer RB12	52 laps	5
12	Carlos Sainz !	Toro Rosso	Toro Rosso-Ferrari STR11	52 laps	11
13	Jolyon Palmer	Renault F1	Renault RS16	52 laps	18
14	Marcus Ericsson	Sauber	Sauber-Ferrari C35	52 laps	22
15	Daniil Kvyat	Red Bull Racing	Red Bull-TAG Heuer RB12	52 laps	8
16	Felipe Nasr ^	Sauber	Sauber-Ferrari C35	52 laps	19
17	Esteban Gutierrez	Haas	Haas-Ferrari VF-16	52 laps	16
18	Pascal Wehrlein	Manor Racing	Manor-Mercedes MRT05	51 laps	20
R	Max Verstappen	Toro Rosso	Toro Rosso-Ferrari STR11	33 laps/power unit	9
R	Sebastian Vettel *	Ferrari	Ferrari SF16-H	0 laps/collision	7
R	Nico Hulkenberg	Force India	Force India-Mercedes VJM09	0 laps/collision	13
R	Rio Haryanto	Manor Racing	Manor-Mercedes MRT05	0 laps/collision	21

Pole: Rosberg, 1m35.417s, 137.099mph/220.639kph. Fastest lap: Rosberg, 1m39.094s, 132.012mph/212.452kph on Lap 52. Race leaders: Rosberg 1-53

* 5-place grid penalty for gearbox change • ! 10s penalty for forcing another driver off the track • ^ 5s penalty for not responding to race director's instructions

SPANISH GRAND PRIX

BARCELONA-CATALUNYA • ROUND 5 • DATE: 15TH MAY 2016
Laps: 66 • Distance: 190.775miles/307.23km • Weather: Warm & bright

Pos	Driver	Team	Chassis-Engine	Result	Qual
1	Max Verstappen	Red Bull Racing	Red Bull-TAG Heuer RB12	1h41m40.017s	4
2	Kimi Raikkonen	Ferrari	Ferrari SF16-H	1h41m40.633s	5
3	Sebastian Vettel	Ferrari	Ferrari SF16-H	1h41m45.598s	6
4	Daniel Ricciardo	Red Bull Racing	Red Bull-TAG Heuer RB12	1h42m23.967s	3
5	Valtteri Bottas	Williams	Williams-Mercedes FW38	1h42m25.288s	7
6	Carlos Sainz	Toro Rosso	Toro Rosso-Ferrari STR11	1h42m41.412s	8
7	Sergio Perez	Force India	Force India-Mercedes VJM09	1h42m59.555s	9
8	Felipe Massa	Williams	Williams-Mercedes FW38	1h43m00.724s	18
9	Jenson Button	McLaren	McLaren-Honda MP4-31	65 laps	12
10	Daniil Kvyat	Toro Rosso	Toro Rosso-Ferrari STR11	65 laps	13
11	Esteban Gutierrez	Haas	Haas-Ferrari VF-16	65 laps	16
12	Marcus Ericsson	Sauber	Sauber-Ferrari C35	65 laps	19
13	Jolyon Palmer	Renault F1	Renault RS16	65 laps	17
14	Felipe Nasr	Sauber	Sauber-Ferrari C35	65 laps	20
15	Kevin Magnussen *	Renault F1	Renault RS16	65 laps	15
16	Pascal Wehrlein	Manor Racing	Manor-Mercedes MRT05	65 laps	21
17	Rio Haryanto	Manor Racing	Manor-Mercedes MRT05	65 laps	22
R	Romain Grosjean	Haas	Haas-Ferrari VF-16	56 laps/brakes	14
R	Fernando Alonso	McLaren	McLaren-Honda MP4-31	45 laps/power unit	10
R	Nico Hulkenberg	Force India	Force India-Mercedes VJM09	20 laps/oil leak	11
R	Lewis Hamilton	Mercedes AMG	Mercedes F1 W07	0 laps/collision	1
R	Nico Rosberg	Mercedes AMG	Mercedes F1 W07	0 laps/collision	2

Pole: Hamilton, 1m22.000s, 126.987mph/204.365kph. Fastest lap: Kvyat, 1m26.948s, 119.760mph/192.735kph on Lap 53. Race leaders: Ricciardo 1-10 & 16-27 & 36-43, Verstappen 11 & 28-33 & 44-66, Vettel 12-15, Raikkonen 34-35

* 10s penalty for causing an accident

PLEASING THE BOSS

Haas F1's entry to the top of the single-seater tree could hardly have got off to a better or more unexpected start as Romain Grosjean finished sixth in Melbourne. After improving to fifth in the second round at Sepang, life became harder, but this outstanding start helped him to score 29 points, while team-mate Esteban Gutierrez scored none.

MONACO GRAND PRIX

MONTE CARLO • ROUND 6 • DATE: 29TH MAY 2016
Laps: 78 • Distance: 161.734miles/260.286km • Weather: Warm & wet, drying later

Pos	Driver	Team	Chassis-Engine	Result	Qual
1	Lewis Hamilton	Mercedes AMG	Mercedes F1 W07	1h59m29.133s	3
2	Daniel Ricciardo	Red Bull Racing	Red Bull-TAG Heuer RB12	1h59m36.385s	1
3	Sergio Perez	Force India	Force India-Mercedes VJM09	1h59m42.958s	7
4	Sebastian Vettel	Ferrari	Ferrari SF16-H	1h59m44.979s	4
5	Fernando Alonso	McLaren	McLaren-Honda MP4-31	2h00m54.209s	9

Pos	Driver	Team	Chassis-Engine	Result	Qual
6	Nico Hulkenberg	Force India	Force India-Mercedes VJM09	2h01m02.132s	5
7	Nico Rosberg	Mercedes AMG	Mercedes F1 W07	2h01m02.423s	2
8	Carlos Sainz	Toro Rosso	Toro Rosso-Ferrari STR11	77 laps	6
9	Jenson Button	McLaren	McLaren-Honda MP4-31	77 laps	13
10	Felipe Massa	Williams	Williams-Mercedes FW38	77 laps	14
11	Esteban Gutierrez	Haas	Haas-Ferrari VF-16	77 laps	12
12	Valtteri Bottas †	Williams	Williams-Mercedes FW38	77 laps	10
13	Romain Grosjean	Haas	Haas-Ferrari VF-16	76 laps	15
14	Pascal Wehrlein ‡/§	Manor Racing	Manor-Mercedes MRT05	76 laps	20
15	Rio Haryanto	Manor Racing	Manor-Mercedes MRT05	74 laps	19
R	Marcus Ericsson	Sauber	Sauber-Ferrari C35	51 laps/collision	17
R	Felipe Nasr ^	Sauber	Sauber-Ferrari C35	48 laps/collision	22
R	Max Verstappen !	Red Bull Racing	Red Bull-TAG Heuer RB12	34 laps/spun off	21
R	Kevin Magnussen	Renault F1	Renault RS16	32 laps/spun off	16
R	Daniil Kvyat	Toro Rosso	Toro Rosso-Ferrari STR11	18 laps/collision	8
R	Kimi Raikkonen *	Ferrari	Ferrari SF16-H	10 laps/spun off	11
R	Jolyon Palmer	Renault F1	Renault RS16	7 laps/spun off	18

Pole: Ricciardo, 1m13.622s, 101.391mph/163.174kph. Fastest lap: Hamilton, 1m17.939s, 95.775mph/154.135kph on Lap 71. Race leaders: Ricciardo 1-22 & 31-32, Hamilton 23-30 & 33-78

* 5-place grid penalty for gearbox change • ! made to start from pit lane for change of survival cell • ^ made to start from pit lane for car being modified in parc ferme • † 10s penalty for causing an accident • ‡ 10s penalty for not staying above minimum speed under VSC • § 10s penalty for ignoring blue flags

NEW-STYLE QUALIFYING

There was a new qualifying format in which each of the three sessions reached a point after which the slowest driver would be eliminated every 90 seconds. The sessions lasted 16 minutes, 15 minutes and 14 minutes, with elimination kicking in every 90 seconds from the seven-, six- and five-minute marks respectively. This was dropped after the second round.

CANADIAN GRAND PRIX

MONTREAL • ROUND 7 • DATE: 12TH JUNE 2016
Laps: 70 • Distance: 189.534miles/305.27km • Weather: Cool & dull

Pos	Driver	Team	Chassis-Engine	Result	Qual
1	Lewis Hamilton	Mercedes AMG	Mercedes F1 W07	1h31m05.296s	1
2	Sebastian Vettel	Ferrari	Ferrari SF16-H	1h31m10.307s	3
3	Valtteri Bottas	Williams	Williams-Mercedes FW38	1h31m51.718s	7
4	Max Verstappen	Red Bull Racing	Red Bull-TAG Heuer RB12	1h31m58.316s	5
5	Nico Rosberg	Mercedes AMG	Mercedes F1 W07	1h32m07.389s	2
6	Kimi Raikkonen	Ferrari	Ferrari SF16-H	1h32m08.313s	6
7	Daniel Ricciardo	Red Bull Racing	Red Bull-TAG Heuer RB12	1h32m08.930s	4
8	Nico Hulkenberg	Force India	Force India-Mercedes VJM09	69 laps	9
9	Carlos Sainz !	Toro Rosso	Toro Rosso-Ferrari STR11	69 laps	20
10	Sergio Perez	Force India	Force India-Mercedes VJM09	69 laps	11
11	Fernando Alonso	McLaren	McLaren-Honda MP4-31	69 laps	10
12	Daniil Kvyat *	Toro Rosso	Toro Rosso-Ferrari STR11	69 laps	15
13	Esteban Gutierrez	Haas	Haas-Ferrari VF-16	68 laps	13
14	Romain Grosjean	Haas	Haas-Ferrari VF-16	68 laps	14
15	Marcus Ericsson *	Sauber	Sauber-Ferrari C35	68 laps	21

Pos	Driver	Team	Chassis-Engine	Result	Qual
16	Kevin Magnussen !	Renault F1	Renault RS16	68 laps	22
17	Pascal Wehrlein	Manor Racing	Manor-Mercedes MRT05	68 laps	17
18	Felipe Nasr	Sauber	Sauber-Ferrari C35	68 laps	18
19	Rio Haryanto	Manor Racing	Manor-Mercedes MRT05	68 laps	19
R	Felipe Massa	Williams	Williams-Mercedes FW38	35 laps/overheating	8
R	Jolyon Palmer	Renault F1	Renault RS16	16 laps/water leak	16
R	Jenson Button	McLaren	McLaren-Honda MP4-31	9 laps/gearbox	12

Pole: Hamilton, 1m12.812s, 133.979mph/215.618kph. Fastest lap: Rosberg, 1m15.599s, 129.039mph/207.669kph on Lap 60. Race leaders: Vettel 1-10 & 24-36, Hamilton 11-23 & 37-70

* 3-place grid penalty for causing a crash in Monaco GP • ! 5-place grid penalty for gearbox change

EUROPEAN GRAND PRIX

BAKU CITY CIRCUIT • ROUND 8 • DATE: 19TH JUNE 2016
Laps: 51 • Distance: 190.234miles/306.153km • Weather: Hot & bright

Pos	Driver	Team	Chassis-Engine	Result	Qual
1	Nico Rosberg	Mercedes AMG	Mercedes F1 W07	1h32m52.366s	1
2	Sebastian Vettel	Ferrari	Ferrari SF16-H	1h33m09.062s	3
3	Sergio Perez *	Force India	Force India-Mercedes VJM09	1h33m17.607s	7
4	Kimi Raikkonen !	Ferrari	Ferrari SF16-H	1h33m25.468s	4
5	Lewis Hamilton	Mercedes AMG	Mercedes F1 W07	1h33m48.701s	10
6	Valtteri Bottas	Williams	Williams-Mercedes FW38	1h33m53.252s	8
7	Daniel Ricciardo	Red Bull Racing	Red Bull-TAG Heuer RB12	1h34m01.595s	2
8	Max Verstappen	Red Bull Racing	Red Bull-TAG Heuer RB12	1h34m03.062s	9
9	Nico Hulkenberg	Force India	Force India-Mercedes VJM09	1h34m10.074s	12
10	Felipe Massa	Williams	Williams-Mercedes FW38	1h34m17.741s	5
11	Jenson Button	McLaren	McLaren-Honda MP4-31	1h34m37.183s	19
12	Felipe Nasr	Sauber	Sauber-Ferrari C35	50 laps	15
13	Romain Grosjean	Haas	Haas-Ferrari VF-16	50 laps	11
14	Kevin Magnussen *	Renault F1	Renault RS16	50 laps	22
15	Jolyon Palmer	Renault F1	Renault RS16	50 laps	21
16	Esteban Gutierrez	Haas	Haas-Ferrari VF-16	50 laps	14
17	Marcus Ericsson	Sauber	Sauber-Ferrari C35	50 laps	20
18	Rio Haryanto	Manor Racing	Manor-Mercedes MRT05	49 laps	16
R	Fernando Alonso	McLaren	McLaren-Honda MP4-31	42 laps/gearbox	13
R	Pascal Wehrlein	Manor Racing	Manor-Mercedes MRT05	39 laps/brakes	17
R	Carlos Sainz *	Toro Rosso	Toro Rosso-Ferrari STR11	31 laps/suspension	18
R	Daniil Kvyat	Toro Rosso	Toro Rosso-Ferrari STR11	6 laps/suspension	6

Pole: Rosberg, 1m42.758s, 130.679mph/210.307kph. Fastest lap: Rosberg, 1m46.485s, 126.105mph/202.946kph on Lap 48. Race leaders: Rosberg 1-51

* 5-place grid penalty for gearbox change • ! 5s penalty for crossing white line at pit entry

A WINNER AT 18

Max Verstappen was settling into his second year in F1 with Scuderia Toro Rosso, but then Red Bull's adviser Helmut Marko made him swap rides with Red Bull Racing's Daniil Kvyat after four races. He immediately won the Spanish GP after the Mercedes collided on lap one, and so became F1's youngest winner at 18 years and 228 days.

SELF-INFLICTED GLITCHES

The only two of the 21 grands prix that Mercedes failed to win came after the team tripped itself up. The first of these was in Spain when Hamilton and Rosberg crashed out at the fourth corner of the opening lap. The second race that got away was in Malaysia where Hamilton's engine blew and Rosberg was spun around on lap 1.

AUSTRIAN GRAND PRIX

RED BULL RING • ROUND 9 • DATE: 3RD JULY 2016
Laps: 71 • Distance: 190.851miles/307.146km • Weather: Warm & bright

Pos	Driver	Team	Chassis-Engine	Result	Qual
1	Lewis Hamilton	Mercedes AMG	Mercedes F1 W07	1h27m38.107s	1
2	Max Verstappen	Red Bull Racing	Red Bull-TAG Heuer RB12	1h27m43.826s	8
3	Kimi Raikkonen	Ferrari	Ferrari SF16-H	1h27m44.131s	4
4	Nico Rosberg !/†	Mercedes AMG	Mercedes F1 W07	1h28m04.817s	6
5	Daniel Ricciardo	Red Bull Racing	Red Bull-TAG Heuer RB12	1h28m09.088s	5
6	Jenson Button	McLaren	McLaren-Honda MP4-31	1h28m15.813s	3
7	Romain Grosjean ‡	Haas	Haas-Ferrari VF-16	1h28m22.775s	13
8	Carlos Sainz	Toro Rosso	Toro Rosso-Ferrari STR11	1h28m25.507s	15
9	Valtteri Bottas	Williams	Williams-Mercedes FW38	70 laps	7
10	Pascal Wehrlein	Manor Racing	Manor-Mercedes MRT05	70 laps	12
11	Esteban Gutierrez	Haas	Haas-Ferrari VF-16	70 laps	11
12	Jolyon Palmer *	Renault F1	Renault RS16	70 laps	19
13	Felipe Nasr *	Sauber	Sauber-Ferrari C35	70 laps	21
14	Kevin Magnussen	Renault F1	Renault RS16	70 laps	17
15	Marcus Ericsson	Sauber	Sauber-Ferrari C35	70 laps	18
16	Rio Haryanto *	Manor Racing	Manor-Mercedes MRT05	70 laps	20
17	Sergio Perez	Force India	Force India-Mercedes VJM09	69 laps/brakes	16
18	Fernando Alonso	McLaren	McLaren-Honda MP4-31	64 laps/power unit	14
19	Nico Hulkenberg	Force India	Force India-Mercedes VJM09	64 laps/brakes	2
20	Felipe Massa	Williams	Williams-Mercedes FW38	63 laps/brakes	10
R	Sebastian Vettel !	Ferrari	Ferrari SF16-H	26 laps/tyre	9
R	Daniil Kvyat ^	Toro Rosso	Toro Rosso-Ferrari STR11	2 laps/mechanical	22

Pole: Hamilton, 1m07.922s, 142.472mph/229.286kph. Fastest lap: Hamilton, 1m08.411s, 141.453mph/227.647kph on Lap 67. Race leaders: Hamilton 1-21 & 71, Raikkonen 22, Vettel 23-26, Rosberg 27-55 & 61-70, Verstappen 56-60

* 3-place grid penalty for failing to slow for yellow flags • ! 5-place grid penalty for gearbox change • ^ made to start from pit lane for change of survival cell • † 10s penalty for causing an accident • ‡ 5s penalty for speeding in the pit lane

BRITISH GRAND PRIX

SILVERSTONE • ROUND 10 • DATE: 10TH JULY 2016
Laps: 52 • Distance: 190.345miles/306.332km • Weather: Warm with showers

Pos	Driver	Team	Chassis-Engine	Result	Qual
1	Lewis Hamilton	Mercedes AMG	Mercedes F1 W07	1h34m55.831s	1
2	Max Verstappen	Red Bull Racing	Red Bull-TAG Heuer RB12	1h35m04.081s	3
3	Nico Rosberg ^	Mercedes AMG	Mercedes F1 W07	1h35m12.742s	2
4	Daniel Ricciardo	Red Bull Racing	Red Bull-TAG Heuer RB12	1h35m22.042s	4

Pos	Driver	Team	Chassis-Engine	Result	Qual
5	Kimi Raikkonen	Ferrari	Ferrari SF16-H	1h36m05.574s	5
6	Sergio Perez	Force India	Force India-Mercedes VJM09	1h36m12.772s	10
7	Nico Hulkenberg	Force India	Force India-Mercedes VJM09	1h36m13.543s	8
8	Carlos Sainz	Toro Rosso	Toro Rosso-Ferrari STR11	1h36m21.689s	7
9	Sebastian Vettel */†	Ferrari	Ferrari SF16-H	1h36m27.485s	11
10	Daniil Kvyat	Toro Rosso	Toro Rosso-Ferrari STR11	1h36m28.431s	15
11	Felipe Massa	Williams	Williams-Mercedes FW38	51 laps	12
12	Jenson Button	McLaren	McLaren-Honda MP4-31	51 laps	17
13	Fernando Alonso	McLaren	McLaren-Honda MP4-31	51 laps	9
14	Valtteri Bottas	Williams	Williams-Mercedes FW38	51 laps	6
15	Felipe Nasr	Sauber	Sauber-Ferrari C35	51 laps	21
16	Esteban Gutierrez	Haas	Haas-Ferrari VF-16	51 laps	14
17	Kevin Magnussen	Renault F1	Renault RS16	49 laps/gearbox	16
R	Jolyon Palmer	Renault F1	Renault RS16	37 laps/gearbox	18
R	Rio Haryanto	Manor Racing	Manor-Mercedes MRT05	24 laps/spun off	19
R	Romain Grosjean	Haas	Haas-Ferrari VF-16	17 laps/transmission	13
R	Marcus Ericsson !	Sauber	Sauber-Ferrari C35	11 laps/electrical	22
R	Pascal Wehrlein	Manor Racing	Manor-Mercedes MRT05	6 laps/spun off	20

Pole: Hamilton, 1m29.287s, 147.589mph/237.521kph. Fastest lap: Rosberg, 1m35.548s, 137.918mph/221.957kph on Lap 44. Race leaders: Hamilton 1-17 & 19-52, Verstappen 18

* 5-place grid penalty for gearbox change • ! made to start from pit lane for change of survival cell • ^ 10s penalty for receiving unlawful radio communication • † 5s penalty for forcing another driver off track

CUTTING THE TIES

For decades, Ron Dennis had been McLaren, making the team great after taking it over from Teddy Mayer, building up the road car side of the business, and masterminding its move to its astonishing headquarters outside Woking. By the end of 2016, after 35 years, he was no longer involved after losing a boardroom battle to take back control from leading shareholder Mansour Ojjeh and a Bahriani investment fund.

HUNGARIAN GRAND PRIX

HUNGARORING • ROUND 11 • DATE: 24TH JULY 2016
Laps: 70 • Distance: 190.181miles/306.67km • Weather: Hot & bright

Pos	Driver	Team	Chassis-Engine	Result	Qual
1	Lewis Hamilton	Mercedes AMG	Mercedes F1 W07	1h40m30.115s	2
2	Nico Rosberg	Mercedes AMG	Mercedes F1 W07	1h40m32.092s	1
3	Daniel Ricciardo	Red Bull Racing	Red Bull-TAG Heuer RB12	1h40m57.654s	3
4	Sebastian Vettel	Ferrari	Ferrari SF16-H	1h40m58.328s	5
5	Max Verstappen	Red Bull Racing	Red Bull-TAG Heuer RB12	1h41m18.774s	4
6	Kimi Raikkonen	Ferrari	Ferrari SF16-H	1h41m19.159s	14
7	Fernando Alonso	McLaren	McLaren-Honda MP4-31	69 laps	7
8	Carlos Sainz	Toro Rosso	Toro Rosso-Ferrari STR11	69 laps	6
9	Valtteri Bottas	Williams	Williams-Mercedes FW38	69 laps	10
10	Nico Hulkenberg	Force India	Force India-Mercedes VJM09	69 laps	9
11	Sergio Perez	Force India	Force India-Mercedes VJM09	69 laps	13
12	Jolyon Palmer	Renault F1	Renault RS16	69 laps	17

Pos	Driver	Team	Chassis-Engine	Result	Qual
13	Esteban Gutierrez ^	Haas	Haas-Ferrari VF-16	69 laps	15
14	Romain Grosjean	Haas	Haas-Ferrari VF-16	69 laps	11
15	Kevin Magnussen	Renault F1	Renault RS16	69 laps	19
16	Daniil Kvyat	Toro Rosso	Toro Rosso-Ferrari STR11	69 laps	12
17	Felipe Nasr	Sauber	Sauber-Ferrari C35	69 laps	16
18	Felipe Massa	Williams	Williams-Mercedes FW38	68 laps	18
19	Pascal Wehrlein	Manor Racing	Manor-Mercedes MRT05	68 laps	20
20	Marcus Ericsson !	Sauber	Sauber-Ferrari C35	68 laps	22
21	Rio Haryanto *	Manor Racing	Manor-Mercedes MRT05	68 laps	21
R	Jenson Button	McLaren	McLaren-Honda MP4-31	60 laps/oil leak	8

Pole: Rosberg, 1m19.965s, 122.553mph/197.231kph. Fastest lap: Raikkonen, 1m23.086s, 117.950mph/189.822kph on Lap 52. Race leaders: Hamilton 1-15 & 18-40 & 43-70, Rosberg 16-17 & 41-42

* 5-place grid penalty for gearbox change • ! made to start from pit lane for change of survival cell • ^ 5s penalty for ignoring blue flags

GERMAN GRAND PRIX

HOCKENHEIM • ROUND 12 • DATE: 31ST JULY 2016
Laps: 67 • Distance: 190.424miles/306.458km • Weather: Warm but dull

Pos	Driver	Team	Chassis-Engine	Result	Qual
1	Lewis Hamilton	Mercedes AMG	Mercedes F1 W07	1h30m44.200s	2
2	Daniel Ricciardo	Red Bull Racing	Red Bull-TAG Heuer RB12	1h30m51.196s	3
3	Max Verstappen	Red Bull Racing	Red Bull-TAG Heuer RB12	1h30m57.613s	4
4	Nico Rosberg	Mercedes AMG	Mercedes F1 W07	1h31m00.045s	1
5	Sebastian Vettel	Ferrari	Ferrari SF16-H	1h31m16.770s	6
6	Kimi Raikkonen	Ferrari	Ferrari SF16-H	1h31m21.223s	5
7	Nico Hulkenberg *	Force India	Force India-Mercedes VJM09	1h31m54.249s	8
8	Jenson Button	McLaren	McLaren-Honda MP4-31	66 laps	12
9	Valtteri Bottas	Williams	Williams-Mercedes FW38	66 laps	7
10	Sergio Perez	Force India	Force India-Mercedes VJM09	66 laps	9
11	Esteban Gutierrez	Haas	Haas-Ferrari VF-16	66 laps	11
12	Fernando Alonso	McLaren	McLaren-Honda MP4-31	66 laps	13
13	Romain Grosjean ^	Haas	Haas-Ferrari VF-16	66 laps	20
14	Carlos Sainz !	Toro Rosso	Toro Rosso-Ferrari STR11	66 laps	15
15	Daniil Kvyat	Toro Rosso	Toro Rosso-Ferrari STR11	66 laps	18
16	Kevin Magnussen	Renault F1	Renault RS16	66 laps	16
17	Pascal Wehrlein	Manor Racing	Manor-Mercedes MRT05	65 laps	17
18	Marcus Ericsson	Sauber	Sauber-Ferrari C35	65 laps	22
19	Jolyon Palmer	Renault F1	Renault RS16	65 laps	14
20	Rio Haryanto	Manor Racing	Manor-Mercedes MRT05	65 laps	19
R	Felipe Nasr	Sauber	Sauber-Ferrari C35	57 laps/power unit	21
R	Felipe Massa	Williams	Williams-Mercedes FW38	36 laps/collision	10

Pole: Rosberg, 1m14.363s, 137.591mph/221.432kph. Fastest lap: Ricciardo, 1m18.442s, 130.437mph/209.918kph on Lap 48. Race leaders: Hamilton 1-67

* 1-place grid penalty for using tyres without appropriate identification • ! 3-place grid penalty for impeding Massa • ^ 5-place grid penalty for gearbox change

BELGIAN GRAND PRIX

SPA-FRANCORCHAMPS • ROUND 13 • DATE: 28TH AUGUST 2016
Laps: 44 • Distance: 191.491miles/308.176km • Weather: Hot & bright

Pos	Driver	Team	Chassis-Engine	Result	Qual
1	Nico Rosberg	Mercedes AMG	Mercedes F1 W07	1h44m51.058s	1
2	Daniel Ricciardo	Red Bull Racing	Red Bull-TAG Heuer RB12	1h45m05.171s	5
3	Lewis Hamilton ^/#	Mercedes AMG	Mercedes F1 W07	1h45m18.692s	21
4	Nico Hulkenberg	Force India	Force India-Mercedes VJM09	1h45m26.965s	7
5	Sergio Perez	Force India	Force India-Mercedes VJM09	1h45m31.718s	6
6	Sebastian Vettel	Ferrari	Ferrari SF16-H	1h45m36.452s	4
7	Fernando Alonso @	McLaren	McLaren-Honda MP4-31	1h45m50.503s	22
8	Valtteri Bottas	Williams	Williams-Mercedes FW38	1h45m51.209s	8
9	Kimi Raikkonen	Ferrari	Ferrari SF16-H	1h45m52.167s	3
10	Felipe Massa	Williams	Williams-Mercedes FW38	1h45m56.931s	10
11	Max Verstappen	Red Bull Racing	Red Bull-TAG Heuer RB12	1h46m02.196s	2
12	Esteban Gutierrez *	Haas	Haas-Ferrari VF-16	1h46m04.935s	18
13	Romain Grosjean	Haas	Haas-Ferrari VF-16	1h46m07.532s	11
14	Daniil Kvyat	Toro Rosso	Toro Rosso-Ferrari STR11	1h46m18.155s	19
15	Jolyon Palmer	Renault F1	Renault RS16	1h46m24.223s	13
16	Esteban Ocon	Manor Racing	Manor-Mercedes MRT05	43 laps	17
17	Felipe Nasr	Sauber	Sauber-Ferrari C35	43 laps	16
R	Kevin Magnussen	Renault F1	Renault RS16	5 laps/spun off	12
R	Marcus Ericsson !	Sauber	Sauber-Ferrari C35	3 laps/gearbox	20
R	Jenson Button	McLaren	McLaren-Honda MP4-31	1 lap/collision	9
R	Carlos Sainz	Toro Rosso	Toro Rosso-Ferrari STR11	1 lap/tyre	14
R	Pascal Wehrlein	Manor Racing	Manor-Mercedes MRT05	0 laps/collision	15

Pole: Rosberg, 1m46.744s, 146.776mph/236.213kph. Fastest lap: Hamilton, 1m51.583s, 140.411mph/225.969kph on Lap 40. Race leaders: Rosberg 1-44

* 5-place grid penalty for impeding. • ! 10-place grid penalty for changing power-unit elements • ^ 55-place grid penalty for changing power-unit elements. • # 5-place grid penalty for changing gearbox • @ 60-place grid penalty for changing power-unit elements

ITALIAN GRAND PRIX

MONZA • ROUND 14 • DATE: 4TH SEPTEMBER 2016
Laps: 53 • Distance: 190.778miles/307.029km • Weather: Hot & bright

Pos	Driver	Team	Chassis-Engine	Result	Qual
1	Nico Rosberg	Mercedes AMG	Mercedes F1 W07	1h17m28.089s	2
2	Lewis Hamilton	Mercedes AMG	Mercedes F1 W07	1h17m43.159s	1
3	Sebastian Vettel	Ferrari	Ferrari SF16-H	1h17m49.079s	3
4	Kimi Raikkonen	Ferrari	Ferrari SF16-H	1h17m55.650s	4
5	Daniel Ricciardo	Red Bull Racing	Red Bull-TAG Heuer RB12	1h18m13.384s	6
6	Valtteri Bottas	Williams	Williams-Mercedes FW38	1h18m19.104s	5
7	Max Verstappen	Red Bull Racing	Red Bull-TAG Heuer RB12	1h18m22.325s	7
8	Sergio Perez	Force India	Force India-Mercedes VJM09	1h18m33.043s	8
9	Felipe Massa	Williams	Williams-Mercedes FW38	1h18m33.706s	11
10	Nico Hulkenberg	Force India	Force India-Mercedes VJM09	1h18m46.745s	9
11	Romain Grosjean *	Haas	Haas-Ferrari VF-16	52 laps	17
12	Jenson Button	McLaren	McLaren-Honda MP4-31	52 laps	14
13	Esteban Gutierrez	Haas	Haas-Ferrari VF-16	52 laps	10
14	Fernando Alonso	McLaren	McLaren-Honda MP4-31	52 laps	12
15	Carlos Sainz	Toro Rosso	Toro Rosso-Ferrari STR11	52 laps	15
16	Marcus Ericsson	Sauber	Sauber-Ferrari C35	52 laps	19
17	Kevin Magnussen	Renault F1	Renault RS16	52 laps	21

Pos	Driver	Team	Chassis-Engine	Result	Qual
18	Esteban Ocon *	Manor Racing	Manor-Mercedes MRT05	51 laps	22
R	Daniil Kvyat	Toro Rosso	Toro Rosso-Ferrari STR11	36 laps/battery	16
R	Pascal Wehrlein	Manor Racing	Manor-Mercedes MRT05	26 laps/fuel pressure	13
R	Jolyon Palmer	Renault F1	Renault RS16	7 laps/collision	20
R	Felipe Nasr	Sauber	Sauber-Ferrari C35	6 laps/collision	18

Pole: Hamilton, 1m21.135s, 159.716mph/257.038kph. Fastest lap: Alonso, 1m25.340s, 151.846mph/244.373kph on Lap 51. Race leaders: Rosberg 1-24 & 26-53, Hamilton 25

* 5-place grid penalty for gearbox change

SINGAPORE GRAND PRIX

MARINA BAY CIRCUIT • ROUND 15 • DATE: 18TH SEPTEMBER 2016
Laps: 61 • Distance: 191.981miles/308.965km • Weather: Hot & humid

Pos	Driver	Team	Chassis-Engine	Result	Qual
1	Nico Rosberg	Mercedes AMG	Mercedes F1 W07	1h55m48.950s	1
2	Daniel Ricciardo	Red Bull Racing	Red Bull-TAG Heuer RB12	1h55m49.438s	2
3	Lewis Hamilton	Mercedes AMG	Mercedes F1 W07	1h55m56.988s	3
4	Kimi Raikkonen	Ferrari	Ferrari SF16-H	1h55m59.169s	5
5	Sebastian Vettel ^/†	Ferrari	Ferrari SF16-H	1h56m16.644s	22
6	Max Verstappen	Red Bull Racing	Red Bull-TAG Heuer RB12	1h57m00.147s	4
7	Fernando Alonso	McLaren	McLaren-Honda MP4-31	1h57m18.148s	9
8	Sergio Perez */!	Force India	Force India-Mercedes VJM09	1h57m40.012s	17
9	Daniil Kvyat	Toro Rosso	Toro Rosso-Ferrari STR11	1h57m40.507s	7
10	Kevin Magnussen	Renault F1	Renault RS16	1h57m48.902s	15
11	Esteban Gutierrez	Haas	Haas-Ferrari VF-16	60 laps	13
12	Felipe Massa	Williams	Williams-Mercedes FW38	60 laps	11
13	Felipe Nasr	Sauber	Sauber-Ferrari C35	60 laps	16
14	Carlos Sainz	Toro Rosso	Toro Rosso-Ferrari STR11	60 laps	6
15	Jolyon Palmer	Renault F1	Renault RS16	60 laps	18
16	Pascal Wehrlein	Manor Racing	Manor-Mercedes MRT05	60 laps	19
17	Marcus Ericsson	Sauber	Sauber-Ferrari C35	60 laps	14
18	Esteban Ocon	Manor Racing	Manor-Mercedes MRT05	59 laps	21
R	Jenson Button	McLaren	McLaren-Honda MP4-31	43 laps/brakes	12
R	Valtteri Bottas	Williams	Williams-Mercedes FW38	35 laps/engine	10
R	Nico Hulkenberg	Force India	Force India-Mercedes VJM09	0 laps/collision	8
NS	Romain Grosjean ^	Haas	Haas-Ferrari VF-16	-	20

Pole: Rosberg, 1m42.584s, 110.446mph/177.747kph. Fastest lap: Ricciardo, 1m47.187s, 105.703mph/170.113kph on Lap 49. Race leaders: Rosberg 1-16 & 18-33 & 35-61, Raikkonen 17, Hamilton 34

* 3-place grid penalty for overtaking under yellow flags • ! 5-place grid penalty for ignoring yellow flags • ^ 5-place grid penalty for gearbox change • † 20-place grid penalty for using additional power unit elements

NEW CIRCUIT

As the World Championship looked to continue spreading its wings, it probably hadn't pinpointed Azerbaijan as a likely host country, but this oil-rich nation agreed a long-term contract with the sport. F1's newest race was put on a street circuit around the capital, Baku, with a lap that included a run around the citadel's walls and past its grandest buildings.

MALAYSIAN GRAND PRIX

SEPANG • ROUND 16 • DATE: 2ND OCTOBER 2016
Laps: 56 • Distance: 192.878miles/310.408km • Weather: Hot & bright

Pos	Driver	Team	Chassis-Engine	Result	Qual
1	Daniel Ricciardo	Red Bull Racing	Red Bull-TAG Heuer RB12	1h37m12.776s	4
2	Max Verstappen	Red Bull Racing	Red Bull-TAG Heuer RB12	1h37m15.219s	3
3	Nico Rosberg !	Mercedes AMG	Mercedes F1 W07	1h37m38.292s	2
4	Kimi Raikkonen	Ferrari	Ferrari SF16-H	1h37m41.561s	6
5	Valtteri Bottas	Williams	Williams-Mercedes FW38	1h38m14.358s	11
6	Sergio Perez	Force India	Force India-Mercedes VJM09	1h38m16.570s	7
7	Fernando Alonso *	McLaren	McLaren-Honda MP4-31	1h38m17.981s	22
8	Nico Hulkenberg	Force India	Force India-Mercedes VJM09	1h38m26.838s	8
9	Jenson Button	McLaren	McLaren-Honda MP4-31	1h38m34.592s	9
10	Jolyon Palmer	Renault F1	Renault RS16	1h38m48.242s	19
11	Carlos Sainz	Toro Rosso	Toro Rosso-Ferrari STR11	1h38m51.654s	16
12	Marcus Ericsson	Sauber	Sauber-Ferrari C35	55 laps	17
13	Felipe Massa	Williams	Williams-Mercedes FW38	55 laps	10
14	Daniil Kvyat	Toro Rosso	Toro Rosso-Ferrari STR11	55 laps	15
15	Pascal Wehrlein	Manor Racing	Manor-Mercedes MRT05	55 laps	21
16	Esteban Ocon ^	Manor Racing	Manor-Mercedes MRT05	55 laps	20
R	Felipe Nasr	Sauber	Sauber-Ferrari C35	46 laps/brakes	18
R	Lewis Hamilton	Mercedes AMG	Mercedes F1 W07	40 laps/engine	1
R	Esteban Gutierrez	Haas	Haas-Ferrari VF-16	39 laps/wheel	13
R	Kevin Magnussen	Renault F1	Renault RS16	17 laps/brakes	14
R	Romain Grosjean	Haas	Haas-Ferrari VF-16	7 laps/brakes	12
R	Sebastian Vettel	Ferrari	Ferrari SF16-H	0 laps/collision	5

Pole: Hamilton, 1m32.850s, 133.541mph/214.914kph. Fastest lap: Rosberg, 1m36.424s, 128.591mph/206.948kph on Lap 44. Race leaders: Hamilton 1-20 & 28-40, Ricciardo 21 & 41-56, Verstappen 22-27

* 45-place grid penalty for using additional power unit elements • ! 10s penalty for causing an accident • ^ 5s penalty for speeding in the pit lane

JAPANESE GRAND PRIX

SUZUKA • ROUND 17 • DATE: 9TH OCTOBER 2016
Laps: 53 • Distance: 191.240miles/307.771km • Weather: Warm but dull

Pos	Driver	Team	Chassis-Engine	Result	Qual
1	Nico Rosberg	Mercedes AMG	Mercedes F1 W07	1h26m43.333s	1
2	Max Verstappen	Red Bull Racing	Red Bull-TAG Heuer RB12	1h26m48.311s	3
3	Lewis Hamilton	Mercedes AMG	Mercedes F1 W07	1h26m49.109s	2
4	Sebastian Vettel *	Ferrari	Ferrari SF16-H	1h27m03.602s	6
5	Kimi Raikkonen !	Ferrari	Ferrari SF16-H	1h27m11.703s	8
6	Daniel Ricciardo	Red Bull Racing	Red Bull-TAG Heuer RB12	1h27m17.274s	4
7	Sergio Perez	Force India	Force India-Mercedes VJM09	1h27m40.828s	5
8	Nico Hulkenberg	Force India	Force India-Mercedes VJM09	1h27m42.510s	9
9	Felipe Massa	Williams	Williams-Mercedes FW38	1h28m21.096s	12
10	Valtteri Bottas	Williams	Williams-Mercedes FW38	1h28m21.656s	11
11	Romain Grosjean	Haas	Haas-Ferrari VF-16	1h28m22.587s	7
12	Jolyon Palmer	Renault F1	Renault RS16	52 laps	16
13	Daniil Kvyat	Toro Rosso	Toro Rosso-Ferrari STR11	52 laps	13
14	Kevin Magnussen	Renault F1	Renault RS16	52 laps	17
15	Marcus Ericsson	Sauber	Sauber-Ferrari C35	52 laps	18
16	Fernando Alonso	McLaren	McLaren-Honda MP4-31	52 laps	15
17	Carlos Sainz	Toro Rosso	Toro Rosso-Ferrari STR11	52 laps	14
18	Jenson Button ^	McLaren	McLaren-Honda MP4-31	52 laps	22

Pos	Driver	Team	Chassis-Engine	Result	Qual
19	Felipe Nasr	Sauber	Sauber-Ferrari C35	52 laps	19
20	Esteban Gutierrez	Haas	Haas-Ferrari VF-16	52 laps	10
21	Esteban Ocon	Manor Racing	Manor-Mercedes MRT05	52 laps	20
22	Pascal Wehrlein !	Manor Racing	Manor-Mercedes MRT05	52 laps	21

Pole: Rosberg, 1m30.647s, 143.301mph/230.622kph. Fastest lap: Vettel, 1m35.118s, 136.566mph/219.781kph on Lap 36. Race leaders: Rosberg 1-29 & 35-53, Vettel 30-34

* 3-place grid penalty for causing an accident in Malaysian GP • ! 5-place grid penalty for gearbox change • ^ 35-place grid penalty for using additional power unit elements

UNITED STATES GRAND PRIX

CIRCUIT OF THE AMERICAS • ROUND 18 • DATE: 23RD OCTOBER 2016
Laps: 56 • Distance: 191.834miles/308.728km • Weather: Hot & bright

Pos	Driver	Team	Chassis-Engine	Result	Qual
1	Lewis Hamilton	Mercedes AMG	Mercedes F1 W07	1h38m12.618s	1
2	Nico Rosberg	Mercedes AMG	Mercedes F1 W07	1h38m17.138s	2
3	Daniel Ricciardo	Red Bull Racing	Red Bull-TAG Heuer RB12	1h38m32.310s	3
4	Sebastian Vettel	Ferrari	Ferrari SF16-H	1h38m55.752s	6
5	Fernando Alonso	McLaren	McLaren-Honda MP4-31	1h39m46.571s	12
6	Carlos Sainz	Toro Rosso	Toro Rosso-Ferrari STR11	1h39m48.742s	10
7	Felipe Massa	Williams	Williams-Mercedes FW38	55 laps	9
8	Sergio Perez	Force India	Force India-Mercedes VJM09	55 laps	11
9	Jenson Button	McLaren	McLaren-Honda MP4-31	55 laps	19
10	Romain Grosjean	Haas	Haas-Ferrari VF-16	55 laps	17
11	Daniil Kvyat	Toro Rosso	Toro Rosso-Ferrari STR11	55 laps	13
12	Kevin Magnussen *	Renault F1	Renault RS16	55 laps	18
13	Jolyon Palmer	Renault F1	Renault RS16	55 laps	15
14	Marcus Ericsson	Sauber	Sauber-Ferrari C35	55 laps	16
15	Felipe Nasr	Sauber	Sauber-Ferrari C35	55 laps	21
16	Valtteri Bottas	Williams	Williams-Mercedes FW38	55 laps	8
17	Pascal Wehrlein	Manor Racing	Manor-Mercedes MRT05	55 laps	20
18	Esteban Ocon	Manor Racing	Manor-Mercedes MRT05	54 laps	22
R	Kimi Raikkonen	Ferrari	Ferrari SF16-H	38 laps/wheel	5
R	Max Verstappen	Red Bull Racing	Red Bull-TAG Heuer RB12	28 laps/gearbox	4
R	Esteban Gutierrez	Haas	Haas-Ferrari VF-16	16 laps/brakes	14
R	Nico Hulkenberg	Force India	Force India-Mercedes VJM09	1 lap/collision	7

Pole: Hamilton, 1m34.999s, 129.814mph/208.915kph. Fastest lap: Vettel, 1m39.877s, 123.474mph/198.712kph on Lap 55. Race leaders: Hamilton 1-11 & 15-56, Vettel 12-14

* 5s penalty for gaining advantage by leaving the track

MEXICAN GRAND PRIX

MEXICO CITY • ROUND 19 • DATE: 30TH OCTOBER 2016
Laps: 71 • Distance: 189.881miles/305.584km • Weather: Warm & bright

Pos	Driver	Team	Chassis-Engine	Result	Qual
1	Lewis Hamilton	Mercedes AMG	Mercedes F1 W07	1h40m31.402s	1
2	Nico Rosberg	Mercedes AMG	Mercedes F1 W07	1h40m39.756s	2
3	Daniel Ricciardo	Red Bull Racing	Red Bull-TAG Heuer RB12	1h40m52.260s	4
4	Max Verstappen !	Red Bull Racing	Red Bull-TAG Heuer RB12	1h40m52.725s	3
5	Sebastian Vettel ^	Ferrari	Ferrari SF16-H	1h40m58.715s	7
6	Kimi Raikkonen	Ferrari	Ferrari SF16-H	1h41m20.778s	6

Pos	Driver	Team	Chassis-Engine	Result	Qual
7	Nico Hulkenberg	Force India	Force India-Mercedes VJM09	1h41m30.293s	5
8	Valtteri Bottas	Williams	Williams-Mercedes FW38	1h41m37.014s	8
9	Felipe Massa	Williams	Williams-Mercedes FW38	1h41m47.608s	9
10	Sergio Perez	Force India	Force India-Mercedes VJM09	1h41m48.200s	12
11	Marcus Ericsson	Sauber	Sauber-Ferrari C35	70 laps	15
12	Jenson Button	McLaren	McLaren-Honda MP4-31	70 laps	13
13	Fernando Alonso	McLaren	McLaren-Honda MP4-31	70 laps	11
14	Jolyon Palmer	Renault F1	Renault RS16	70 laps	21
15	Felipe Nasr	Sauber	Sauber-Ferrari C35	70 laps	19
16	Carlos Sainz †	Toro Rosso	Toro Rosso-Ferrari STR11	70 laps	10
17	Kevin Magnussen	Renault F1	Renault RS16	70 laps	14
18	Daniil Kvyat !	Toro Rosso	Toro Rosso-Ferrari STR11	70 laps	18
19	Esteban Gutierrez	Haas	Haas-Ferrari VF-16	70 laps	17
20	Romain Grosjean *	Haas	Haas-Ferrari VF-16	70 laps	22
21	Esteban Ocon	Manor Racing	Manor-Mercedes MRT05	69 laps	20
R	Pascal Wehrlein	Manor Racing	Manor-Mercedes MRT05	0 laps/collision	16

Pole: Hamilton, 1m18.704s, 122.328mph/196.869kph. Fastest lap: Ricciardo, 1m21.134s, 118.665mph/190.972kph on Lap 53. Race leaders: Hamilton 1-17 & 33-71, Rosberg 18-20, Vettel 21-32

* made to start from pit lane for car being modified in parc ferme • ! 5s penalty for gaining advantage by leaving the track • ^ 10s penalty for illegal defending under braking • † 5s penalty for forcing a car off the track

NEW CONSTRUCTOR

Milling machine tycoon Gene Haas promoted his brand by owning a NASCAR team. This was a success, and he wanted to go global, so he decided to start an F1 team of his own. Haas F1 was based alongside the NASCAR outfit in North Carolina, but wisely had a base in England to make life easier for the rounds held in Europe.

BRAZILIAN GRAND PRIX

INTERLAGOS • ROUND 20 • DATE: 13TH NOVEMBER 2016
Laps: 71 • Distance: 190.101miles/305.939km • Weather: Warm but wet

Pos	Driver	Team	Chassis-Engine	Result	Qual
1	Lewis Hamilton	Mercedes AMG	Mercedes F1 W07	3h01m01.335s	1
2	Nico Rosberg	Mercedes AMG	Mercedes F1 W07	3h01m12.790s	2
3	Max Verstappen	Red Bull Racing	Red Bull-TAG Heuer RB12	3h01m22.816s	4
4	Sergio Perez	Force India	Force India-Mercedes VJM09	3h01m26.681s	9
5	Sebastian Vettel	Ferrari	Ferrari SF16-H	3h01m27.669s	5
6	Carlos Sainz	Toro Rosso	Toro Rosso-Ferrari STR11	3h01m30.495s	15
7	Nico Hulkenberg	Force India	Force India-Mercedes VJM09	3h01m31.162s	8
8	Daniel Ricciardo	Red Bull Racing	Red Bull-TAG Heuer RB12	3h01m31.821s	6
9	Felipe Nasr	Sauber	Sauber-Ferrari C35	3h01m43.955s	21
10	Fernando Alonso	McLaren	McLaren-Honda MP4-31	3h01m45.767s	10
11	Valtteri Bottas	Williams	Williams-Mercedes FW38	3h01m46.627s	11
12	Esteban Ocon *	Manor Racing	Manor-Mercedes MRT05	3h01m47.144s	22
13	Daniil Kvyat	Toro Rosso	Toro Rosso-Ferrari STR11	3h01m52.527s	14
14	Kevin Magnussen	Renault F1	Renault RS16	3h01m52.890s	18
15	Pascal Wehrlein	Manor Racing	Manor-Mercedes MRT05	3h02m01.833s	19
16	Jenson Button	McLaren	McLaren-Honda MP4-31	3h02m23.329s	17

Pos	Driver	Team	Chassis-Engine	Result	Qual
R	Esteban Gutierrez	Haas	Haas-Ferrari VF-16	60 laps/electrical	12
R	Felipe Massa	Williams	Williams-Mercedes FW38	46 laps/spun off	13
R	Jolyon Palmer	Renault F1	Renault RS16	20 laps/collision	16
R	Kimi Raikkonen	Ferrari	Ferrari SF16-H	19 laps/spun off	3
R	Marcus Ericsson	Sauber	Sauber-Ferrari C35	11 laps/spun off	20
NS	Romain Grosjean	Haas	Haas-Ferrari VF-16	Accident	7

Pole: Hamilton, 1m10.736s, 136.266mph/219.299kph. Fastest lap: Verstappen, 1m25.305s, 112.994mph/181.846kph on Lap 67. Race leaders: Hamilton 1-71

* 3-place grid penalty for impeding Palmer

NEW DRIVERS

Three of 2016's five rookies claimed a 10th place finish. The first was Stoffel Vandoorne on his only outing that season for McLaren, when he stood in for Fernando Alonso at Sakhir. The second was Pascal Wehrlein for Manor in Austria, and the third was Jolyon Palmer for Renault at Sepang. Esteban Ocon and Rio Haryanto shared a ride for Manor.

ABU DHABI GRAND PRIX

YAS MARINA CIRCUIT • ROUND 21 • DATE: 27TH NOVEMBER 2016
Laps: 55 • Distance: 189.547miles/305.47km • Weather: Warm & bright

Pos	Driver	Team	Chassis-Engine	Result	Qual
1	Lewis Hamilton	Mercedes AMG	Mercedes F1 W07	1h38m04.013s	1
2	Nico Rosberg	Mercedes AMG	Mercedes F1 W07	1h38m04.452s	2
3	Sebastian Vettel	Ferrari	Ferrari SF16-H	1h38m04.856s	5
4	Max Verstappen	Red Bull Racing	Red Bull-TAG Heuer RB12	1h38m05.698s	6
5	Daniel Ricciardo	Red Bull Racing	Red Bull-TAG Heuer RB12	1h38m09.328s	3
6	Kimi Raikkonen	Ferrari	Ferrari SF16-H	1h38m22.829s	4
7	Nico Hulkenberg	Force India	Force India-Mercedes VJM09	1h38m54.127s	7
8	Sergio Perez	Force India	Force India-Mercedes VJM09	1h39m02.789s	8
9	Felipe Massa	Williams	Williams-Mercedes FW38	1h39m03.449s	10
10	Fernando Alonso	McLaren	McLaren-Honda MP4-31	1h39m03.909s	9
11	Romain Grosjean	Haas	Haas-Ferrari VF-16	1h39m20.790s	14
12	Esteban Gutierrez	Haas	Haas-Ferrari VF-16	1h39m39.126s	13
13	Esteban Ocon	Manor Racing	Manor-Mercedes MRT05	54 laps	20
14	Pascal Wehrlein	Manor Racing	Manor-Mercedes MRT05	54 laps	16
15	Marcus Ericsson	Sauber	Sauber-Ferrari C35	54 laps	22
16	Felipe Nasr	Sauber	Sauber-Ferrari C35	54 laps	19
17	Jolyon Palmer	Renault F1	Renault RS16	54 laps	15
R	Carlos Sainz	Toro Rosso	Toro Rosso-Ferrari STR11	41 laps/collision	21
R	Daniil Kvyat	Toro Rosso	Toro Rosso-Ferrari STR11	14 laps/gearbox	17
R	Jenson Button	McLaren	McLaren-Honda MP4-31	12 laps/suspension	12
R	Valtteri Bottas	Williams	Williams-Mercedes FW38	6 laps/suspension	11
R	Kevin Magnussen	Renault F1	Renault RS16	5 laps/collision	18

Pole: Hamilton, 1m38.755s, 125.805mph/202.464kph. Fastest lap: Vettel, 1m43.729s, 119.773mph/192.756kph on Lap 43. Race leaders: Hamilton 1-6 & 10-28 & 38-55, Rosberg 7-8 & 29, Ricciardo 9, Vettel 30-37

WORLD DRIVERS' CHAMPIONSHIP FINAL RESULTS

Pos	Driver	Nat	Car-Engine	R1	R2	R3	R4	R5	R6	R7	R8	R9
1	Nico Rosberg	DEU	Mercedes F1 W07	1	1F	1P	1PF	R	7	5F	1PF	4
2	Lewis Hamilton	GBR	Mercedes F1 W07	2P	3P	7	2	RP	1F	1P	5	1PF
3	Daniel Ricciardo	AUS	Red Bull-TAG Heuer RB12	4F	4	4	11	4	2P	7	7	5
4	Sebastian Vettel	DEU	Ferrari SF16-H	3	NS	2	R	3	4	2	2	R
5	Max Verstappen	NLD	Toro Rosso-Ferrari STR11	10	6	8	R	-	-	-	-	-
			Red Bull-TAG Heuer RB12	-	-	-	-	1	R	4	8	2
6	Kimi Raikkonen	FIN	Ferrari SF16-H	R	2	5	3	2	R	6	4	3
7	Sergio Perez	MEX	Force India-Mercedes VJM09	13	16	11	9	7	3	10	3	17
8	Valtteri Bottas	FIN	Williams-Mercedes FW38	8	9	10	4	5	12	3	6	9
9	Nico Hulkenberg	DEU	Force India-Mercedes VJM09	7	15	15F	R	R	6	8	9	19
10	Fernando Alonso	ESP	McLaren-Honda MP4-31	R	-	12	6	R	5	11	R	18
11	Felipe Massa	BRA	Williams-Mercedes FW38	5	8	6	5	8	10	R	10	20
12	Carlos Sainz	ESP	Toro Rosso-Ferrari STR11	9	R	9	12	6	8	9	R	8
13	Romain Grosjean	FRA	Haas-Ferrari VF-16	6	5	19	8	R	13	14	13	7
14	Daniil Kvyat	RUS	Red Bull-TAG Heuer RB12	NS	7	3	15	-	-	-	-	-
			Toro Rosso-Ferrari STR11	-	-	-	-	10F	R	12	R	R
15	Jenson Button	GBR	McLaren-Honda MP4-31	14	R	13	10	9	9	R	11	6
16	Kevin Magnussen	DNK	Renault RS16	12	11	17	7	15	R	16	14	14
17	Felipe Nasr	BRA	Sauber-Ferrari C35	15	14	20	16	14	R	18	12	13
18	Jolyon Palmer	GBR	Renault RS16	11	NS	22	13	13	R	R	15	12
19	Pascal Wehrlein	DEU	Manor-Mercedes MRT05	16	13	18	18	16	14	17	R	10
20	Stoffel Vandoorne	BEL	McLaren-Honda MP4-31	-	10	-	-	-	-	-	-	-
21	Esteban Gutierrez	MEX	Haas-Ferrari VF-16	R	R	14	17	11	11	13	16	11
22	Marcus Ericsson	SWE	Sauber-Ferrari C35	R	12	16	14	12	R	15	17	15
23	Esteban Ocon	FRA	Manor-Mercedes MRT05	-	-	-	-	-	-	-	-	-
			Renault RS16	-	-	-	-	T	-	-	-	-
24	Rio Haryanto	IDN	Manor-Mercedes MRT05	R	17	21	R	17	15	19	18	16

Pos	Driver	R10	R11	R12	R13	R14	R15	R16	R17	R18	R19	R20	R21	Total
1	Rosberg	3F	2P	4P	1P	1	1P	3F	1P	2	2	2	2	385
2	Hamilton	1P	1	1	3F	2P	3	RP	3	1P	1P	1P	1P	380
3	Ricciardo	4	3	2F	2	5	2F	1	6	3	3F	8	5	256
4	Vettel	9	4	5	6	3	5	R	4F	4F	5	5	3F	212
5	Verstappen	-	-	-	-	-	-	-	-	-	-	-	-	204
		2	5	3	11	7	6	2	2	R	4	3F	4	
6	Raikkonen	5	6F	6	9	4	4	4	5	R	6	R	6	186
7	Perez	6	11	10	5	8	8	6	7	8	10	4	8	101
8	Bottas	14	9	9	8	6	R	5	10	16	8	11	R	85
9	Hulkenberg	7	10	7	4	10	R	8	8	R	7	7	7	72
10	Alonso	13	7	12	7	14F	7	7	16	5	13	10	10	54
11	Massa	11	18	R	10	9	12	13	9	7	9	R	9	53
12	Sainz	8	8	14	R	15	14	11	17	6	16	6	R	46
13	Grosjean	R	14	13	13	11	NS	R	11	10	20	NS	11	29
14	Kvyat	-	-	-	-	-	-	-	-	-	-	-	-	25
		10	16	15	14	R	9	14	13	11	18	13	R	
15	Button	12	R	8	R	12	R	9	18	9	12	16	R	21
16	Magnussen	17	15	16	R	17	10	R	14	12	17	14	R	7
17	Nasr	15	17	R	17	R	13	R	19	15	15	9	16	2
18	Palmer	R	12	19	15	R	15	10	12	13	14	R	17	1
19	Wehrlein	R	19	17	R	R	16	15	22	17	R	15	14	1
20	Vandoorne	-	-	-	-	-	-	-	-	-	-	-	-	1
21	Gutierrez	16	13	11	12	13	11	R	20	R	19	R	12	0
22	Ericsson	R	20	18	R	16	17	12	15	14	11	R	15	0
23	Ocon	-	-	-	16	18	18	16	21	18	21	12	13	0
		T	T	T	-	-	-	-	-	-	-	-	-	
24	Haryanto	R	21	20	-	-	-	-	-	-	-	-	-	0

WORLD CONSTRUCTORS' CHAMPIONSHIP FINAL RESULTS

Pos	Team-Engine	R1	R2	R3	R4	R5	R6	R7	R8	R9	R10	R11
1	Mercedes AMG	1/2	1/3	1/7	1/2	R/R	1/7	1/5	1/5	1/4	1/3	1/2
2	Red Bull-TAG Heuer	4/NS	4/7	3/4	11/15	1/4	2/R	4/7	7/8	2/5	2/4	3/5
3	Ferrari	3/R	2/NS	2/5	3/R	2/3	4/R	2/6	2/4	3/R	5/9	4/6
4	Force India-Mercedes	7/13	15/16	11/15	9/R	7/R	3/6	8/10	3/9	17/19	6/7	10/11
5	Williams-Mercedes	5/8	8/9	6/10	4/5	5/8	10/12	3/R	6/10	9/20	11/14	9/18
6	McLaren-Honda	14/R	10/R	12/13	6/10	9/R	5/9	11/R	11/R	6/18	12/13	7/R
7	Toro Rosso-Ferrari	9/10	6/R	8/9	12/R	6/10	8/R	9/12	R/R	8/R	8/10	8/16
8	Haas-Ferrari	6/R	5/R	14/19	8/17	11/R	11/13	13/14	13/16	7/11	16/R	13/14
9	Renault F1	11/12	11/NS	17/22	7/13	13/15	R/R	16/R	14/15	12/14	17/R	12/15
10	Sauber-Ferrari	15/R	12/14	16/20	14/16	12/14	R/R	15/18	12/17	13/15	15/R	17/20
11	Manor-Mercedes	16/R	13/17	18/21	18/R	16/17	14/15	17/19	18/R	10/16	R/R	19/21

Pos	Team-Engine	R12	R13	R14	R15	R16	R17	R18	R19	R20	R21	Total
1	Mercedes AMG	1/4	1/3	1/2	1/3	3/R	1/3	1/2	1/2	1/2	1/2	765
2	Red Bull-TAG Heuer	2/3	2/11	5/7	2/6	1/2	2/6	3/R	3/4	3/8	4/5	468
3	Ferrari	5/6	6/9	3/4	4/5	4/R	4/5	4/R	5/6	5/R	3/6	398
4	Force India-Mercedes	7/10	4/5	8/10	8/R	6/8	7/8	8/R	7/10	4/7	7/8	173
5	Williams-Mercedes	9/R	8/10	6/9	12/R	5/13	9/10	7/16	8/9	11/R	9/R	138
6	McLaren-Honda	8/12	7/R	12/14	7/R	7/9	16/18	5/9	12/13	10/16	10/R	76
7	Toro Rosso-Ferrari	14/15	14/R	15/R	9/14	11/14	13/17	6/11	16/18	6/13	R/R	63
8	Haas-Ferrari	11/13	12/13	11/13	11/NS	R/R	11/20	10/R	19/20	R/NS	11/12	29
9	Renault F1	16/19	15/R	17/R	10/15	10/R	12/14	12/13	14/17	14/R	17/R	8
10	Sauber-Ferrari	18/R	17/R	16/R	13/17	12/R	15/19	14/15	11/15	9/R	15/16	2
11	Manor-Mercedes	17/20	16/R	18/R	16/18	15/16	21/22	17/18	21/R	12/15	13/14	1

SYMBOLS AND GRAND PRIX KEY

Round 1 **Australian GP**
Round 2 **Bahrain GP**
Round 3 **Chinese GP**
Round 4 **Russian GP**
Round 5 **Spanish GP**
Round 6 **Monaco GP**
Round 7 **Canadian GP**
Round 8 **European GP**
Round 9 **Austrian GP**
Round 10 **British GP**
Round 11 **Hungarian GP**
Round 12 **German GP**
Round 13 **Belgian GP**
Round 14 **Italian GP**
Round 15 **Singapore GP**
Round 16 **Malaysian GP**
Round 17 **Japanese GP**
Round 18 **United States GP**
Round 19 **Mexican GP**
Round 20 **Brazilian GP**
Round 21 **Abu Dhabi GP**

SCORING

1st **25 points**
2nd **18 points**
3rd **15 points**
4th **12 points**
5th **10 points**
6th **8 points**
7th **6 points**
8th **4 points**
9th **2 points**
10th **1 point**

DNPQ DID NOT PRE-QUALIFY DNQ DID NOT QUALIFY DQ DISQUALIFIED EX EXCLUDED
F FASTEST LAP NC NOT CLASSIFIED NS NON-STARTER P POLE POSITION R RETIRED

SEASON SUMMARY

Mercedes mastered the latest rule changes best to give Lewis Hamilton a helping hand in landing his fourth world title. He was joined at Mercedes by Valtteri Bottas, who adapted well and ranked third. The interloper in Mercedes' party was Ferrari's Sebastian Vettel, who played his hand early on by finishing either first or second in the first six races and would lead the title race until the Italian GP. However, Mercedes then really got into its stride and pulled away. Red Bull Racing gradually found form, too, enabling Daniel Ricciardo to inherit victory in Baku and Max Verstappen to win in Malaysia and Mexico.

AUSTRALIAN GRAND PRIX

ALBERT PARK • ROUND 1 • DATE: 26TH MARCH 2017
Laps: 57 • Distance: 187.822miles/302.271km • Weather: Warm & bright

Pos	Driver	Team	Chassis-Engine	Result	Qual
1	Sebastian Vettel	Ferrari	Ferrari SF70H	1h24m11.672s	2
2	Lewis Hamilton	Mercedes AMG	Mercedes F1 W08	1h24m21.647s	1
3	Valtteri Bottas	Mercedes AMG	Mercedes F1 W08	1h24m22.922s	3
4	Kimi Raikkonen	Ferrari	Ferrari SF70H	1h24m34.065s	4
5	Max Verstappen	Red Bull Racing	Red Bull-TAG Heuer RB13	1h24m40.499s	5
6	Felipe Massa	Williams	Williams-Mercedes FW40	1h25m35.058s	7
7	Sergio Perez	Force India	Force India-Mercedes VJM10	56 laps	10
8	Carlos Sainz	Toro Rosso	Toro Rosso-Renault STR12	56 laps	8
9	Daniil Kvyat	Toro Rosso	Toro Rosso-Renault STR12	56 laps	9
10	Esteban Ocon	Force India	Force India-Mercedes VJM10	56 laps	13
11	Nico Hulkenberg	Renault F1	Renault RS17	56 laps	11
12	Antonio Giovinazzi	Sauber	Sauber-Ferrari C36	55 laps	16
13	Stoffel Vandoorne	McLaren	McLaren-Honda MCL32	55 laps	18
R	Fernando Alonso	McLaren	McLaren-Honda MCL32	50 laps/floor	12
R	Kevin Magnussen	Haas	Haas-Ferrari VF-17	46 laps/puncture	17
R	Lance Stroll	Williams	Williams-Mercedes FW40	40 laps/brakes	20
R	Daniel Ricciardo *	Red Bull Racing	Red Bull-TAG Heuer RB13	25 laps/power unit	15
R	Marcus Ericsson	Sauber	Sauber-Ferrari C36	21 laps/collision	14
R	Jolyon Palmer	Renault F1	Renault RS17	15 laps/brakes	19
R	Romain Grosjean	Haas	Haas-Ferrari VF-17	13 laps/water leak	6
NS	Pascal Wehrlein	Sauber	Sauber-Ferrari C36	Back injury	

Pole: Hamilton, 1m22.188s, 144.333mph/232.282kph. Fastest lap: Raikkonen, 1m26.538s, 137.078mph/220.605kph on Lap 56. Race leaders: Hamilton 1-16, Vettel 17-22 & 26-57, Bottas 23-24, Raikkonen 25

* 5-place grid penalty for gearbox change

MAKING THE CARS FASTER

A major set of rule changes was introduced for 2017 with the aim of facilitating more overtaking, to make F1 more exciting and draw in a new crop of fans. Wider tyres and wider front and rear wings, plus larger bargeboards and a longer diffuser, were the key ingredients to make the cars faster and more spectacular.

CHINESE GRAND PRIX

SHANGHAI INTERNATIONAL CIRCUIT • ROUND 2 • DATE: 9TH APRIL 2017
Laps: 56 • Distance: 189.677miles/305.256km • Weather: Cool & dull

Pos	Driver	Team	Chassis-Engine	Result	Qual
1	Lewis Hamilton	Mercedes AMG	Mercedes F1 W08	1h37m36.158s	1
2	Sebastian Vettel	Ferrari	Ferrari SF70H	1h37m42.408s	2
3	Max Verstappen	Red Bull Racing	Red Bull-TAG Heuer RB13	1h38m21.350s	16
4	Daniel Ricciardo	Red Bull Racing	Red Bull-TAG Heuer RB13	1h38m22.193s	5
5	Kimi Raikkonen	Ferrari	Ferrari SF70H	1h38m24.234s	4
6	Valtteri Bottas	Mercedes AMG	Mercedes F1 W08	1h38m24.966s	3
7	Carlos Sainz	Toro Rosso	Toro Rosso-Renault STR12	1h38m49.051s	11
8	Kevin Magnussen	Haas	Haas-Ferrari VF-17	55 laps	12
9	Sergio Perez	Force India	Force India-Mercedes VJM10	55 laps	8
10	Esteban Ocon	Force India	Force India-Mercedes VJM10	55 laps	17
11	Romain Grosjean !	Haas	Haas-Ferrari VF-17	55 laps	19
12	Nico Hulkenberg	Renault F1	Renault RS17	55 laps	7
13	Jolyon Palmer !	Renault F1	Renault RS17	55 laps	20
14	Felipe Massa	Williams	Williams-Mercedes FW40	55 laps	6
15	Marcus Ericsson	Sauber	Sauber-Ferrari C36	55 laps	14
R	Fernando Alonso	McLaren	McLaren-Honda MCL32	33 laps/halfshaft	13
R	Daniil Kvyat	Toro Rosso	Toro Rosso-Renault STR12	18 laps/hydraulics	9
R	Stoffel Vandoorne	McLaren	McLaren-Honda MCL32	17 laps/fuel pressure	15
R	Antonio Giovinazzi *	Sauber	Sauber-Ferrari C36	3 laps/spun off	18
R	Lance Stroll	Williams	Williams-Mercedes FW40	0 laps/collision	10

Pole: Hamilton, 1m31.678s, 133.003mph/214.049kph. Fastest lap: Hamilton, 1m35.378s, 127.844mph/205.745kph on Lap 44. Race leaders: Hamilton 1-56

* 5-place grid penalty for gearbox change • ! 5-place grid penalty for failing to slow for double waved yellow flags

MERCEDES' VACANT SEAT

When Nico Rosberg decided five days after he had won the world title that he would stop racing, it left Mercedes with a dilemma, as almost all the top drivers it might have wanted had contracts with other teams. So Valtteri Bottas got his break, released to take the drive by Williams, alongside Felipe Massa.

BAHRAIN GRAND PRIX

SAKHIR • ROUND 3 • DATE: 16TH APRIL 2017
Laps: 57 • Distance: 191.683miles/308.484km • Weather: Warm & dry

Pos	Driver	Team	Chassis-Engine	Result	Qual
1	Sebastian Vettel	Ferrari	Ferrari SF70H	1h33m53.374s	3
2	Lewis Hamilton	Mercedes AMG	Mercedes F1 W08	1h34m00.034s	2
3	Valtteri Bottas	Mercedes AMG	Mercedes F1 W08	1h34m13.771s	1
4	Kimi Raikkonen	Ferrari	Ferrari SF70H	1h34m15.849s	5
5	Daniel Ricciardo	Red Bull Racing	Red Bull-TAG Heuer RB13	1h34m32.720s	4
6	Felipe Massa	Williams	Williams-Mercedes FW40	1h34m47.700s	8
7	Sergio Perez	Force India	Force India-Mercedes VJM10	1h34m55.980s	18
8	Romain Grosjean	Haas	Haas-Ferrari VF-17	1h35m08.239s	9
9	Nico Hulkenberg	Renault F1	Renault RS17	1h35m13.562s	7

Pos	Driver	Team	Chassis-Engine	Result	Qual
10	Esteban Ocon	Force India	Force India-Mercedes VJM10	1h35m29.085s	14
11	Pascal Wehrlein	Sauber	Sauber-Ferrari C36	56 laps	13
12	Daniil Kvyat	Toro Rosso	Toro Rosso-Renault STR12	56 laps	11
13	Jolyon Palmer	Renault F1	Renault RS17	56 laps	10
14	Fernando Alonso	McLaren	McLaren-Honda MCL32	54 laps/power unit	15
R	Marcus Ericsson	Sauber	Sauber-Ferrari C36	50 laps/gearbox	19
R	Lance Stroll	Williams	Williams-Mercedes FW40	12 laps/collision	12
R	Carlos Sainz	Toro Rosso	Toro Rosso-Renault STR12	12 laps/collision	16
R	Max Verstappen	Red Bull Racing	Red Bull-TAG Heuer RB13	11 laps/brakes	6
R	Kevin Magnussen	Haas	Haas-Ferrari VF-17	8 laps/electrical	20
NS	Stoffel Vandoorne	McLaren	McLaren-Honda MCL32	water pressure	17

Pole: Bottas, 1m28.769s, 136.379mph/219.482kph. Fastest lap: Hamilton, 1m32.798s, 130.458mph/209.952kph on Lap 46. Race leaders: Bottas 1-13, Vettel 14-33 & 42-57, Hamilton 34-41

UNBECOMING BEHAVIOUR

Sebastian Vettel displayed a few chinks in his armour in the heat of the title battle. The first came in Baku when, bizarrely, he clashed with Lewis Hamilton's Mercedes as they ran behind the safety car. Caught out by Hamilton not accelerating when he expected him to, they touched, but then Vettel jinked to one side and swerved into the Mercedes.

RUSSIAN GRAND PRIX

SOCHI • ROUND 4 • DATE: 30TH APRIL 2017
Laps: 52 • Distance: 188.956miles/304.096km • Weather: Warm & bright

Pos	Driver	Team	Chassis-Engine	Result	Qual
1	Valtteri Bottas	Mercedes AMG	Mercedes F1 W08	1h28m08.743s	3
2	Sebastian Vettel	Ferrari	Ferrari SF70H	1h28m09.360s	1
3	Kimi Raikkonen	Ferrari	Ferrari SF70H	1h28m19.743s	2
4	Lewis Hamilton	Mercedes AMG	Mercedes F1 W08	1h28m45.063s	4
5	Max Verstappen	Red Bull Racing	Red Bull-TAG Heuer RB13	1h29m09.159s	7
6	Sergio Perez	Force India	Force India-Mercedes VJM10	1h29m35.531s	9
7	Esteban Ocon	Force India	Force India-Mercedes VJM10	1h29m43.747s	10
8	Nico Hulkenberg	Renault F1	Renault RS17	1h29m44.931s	8
9	Felipe Massa	Williams	Williams-Mercedes FW40	51 laps	6
10	Carlos Sainz *	Toro Rosso	Toro Rosso-Renault STR12	51 laps	14
11	Lance Stroll	Williams	Williams-Mercedes FW40	51 laps	11
12	Daniil Kvyat	Toro Rosso	Toro Rosso-Renault STR12	51 laps	12
13	Kevin Magnussen	Haas	Haas-Ferrari VF-17	51 laps	13
14	Stoffel Vandoorne !	McLaren	McLaren-Honda MCL32	51 laps	20
15	Marcus Ericsson	Sauber	Sauber-Ferrari C36	51 laps	18
16	Pascal Wehrlein	Sauber	Sauber-Ferrari C36	50 laps	17
R	Daniel Ricciardo	Red Bull Racing	Red Bull-TAG Heuer RB13	5 laps/brakes	5
R	Jolyon Palmer	Renault F1	Renault RS17	0 laps/collision	16
R	Romain Grosjean	Haas	Haas-Ferrari VF-17	0 laps/collision	19
NS	Fernando Alonso	McLaren	McLaren-Honda MCL32	engine software	15

Pole: Vettel, 1m33.194s, 140.369mph/225.902kph. Fastest lap: Raikkonen, 1m36.844s, 135.079mph/217.388kph on Lap 49. Race leaders: Bottas 1-26 & 35-52, Vettel 27-34

* 3-place grid penalty for causing crash in Bahrain GP • ! 15-place grid penalty for using additional power unit elements

SINGAPORE FLING

Hamilton led Vettel by just three points when they got to Singapore, the 14th of 20 rounds, so it was all to play for. However, Vettel made a poor start from pole and team-mate Kimi Raikkonen made a great one from fourth, meaning that they were line abreast with Max Verstappen as they approached Turn 1. Vettel moved across and all three were eliminated.

SPANISH GRAND PRIX

BARCELONA-CATALUNYA • ROUND 5 • DATE: 14TH MAY 2017
Laps: 66 • Distance: 190.775miles/307.23km • Weather: Hot & bright

Pos	Driver	Team	Chassis-Engine	Result	Qual
1	Lewis Hamilton	Mercedes AMG	Mercedes F1 W08	1h35m56.497s	1
2	Sebastian Vettel	Ferrari	Ferrari SF70H	1h35m59.987s	2
3	Daniel Ricciardo	Red Bull Racing	Red Bull-TAG Heuer RB13	1h37m12.317s	6
4	Sergio Perez	Force India	Force India-Mercedes VJM10	65 laps	8
5	Esteban Ocon	Force India	Force India-Mercedes VJM10	65 laps	10
6	Nico Hulkenberg	Renault F1	Renault RS17	65 laps	13
7	Carlos Sainz	Toro Rosso	Toro Rosso-Renault STR12	65 laps	12
8	Pascal Wehrlein !	Sauber	Sauber-Ferrari C36	65 laps	15
9	Daniil Kvyat	Toro Rosso	Toro Rosso-Renault STR12	65 laps	19
10	Romain Grosjean	Haas	Haas-Ferrari VF-17	65 laps	14
11	Marcus Ericsson	Sauber	Sauber-Ferrari C36	64 laps	16
12	Fernando Alonso	McLaren	McLaren-Honda MCL32	64 laps	7
13	Felipe Massa	Williams	Williams-Mercedes FW40	64 laps	9
14	Kevin Magnussen	Haas	Haas-Ferrari VF-17	64 laps	11
15	Jolyon Palmer	Renault F1	Renault RS17	64 laps	17
16	Lance Stroll	Williams	Williams-Mercedes FW40	64 laps	18
R	Valtteri Bottas	Mercedes AMG	Mercedes F1 W08	38 laps/power unit	3
R	Stoffel Vandoorne *	McLaren	McLaren-Honda MCL32	32 laps/collision	20
R	Max Verstappen	Red Bull Racing	Red Bull-TAG Heuer RB13	1 lap/collision	5
R	Kimi Raikkonen	Ferrari	Ferrari SF70H	0 laps/collision	4

Pole: Hamilton, 1m19.149s, 131.561mph/211.727kph. Fastest lap: Hamilton, 1m23.593s, 124.566mph/200.471kph on Lap 64. Race leaders: Vettel 1-13 & 25-43, Hamilton 14-21 & 44-66, Bottas 22-24

* 10-place grid penalty for using additional power unit elements • ! 5s penalty for failing to keep to the right of pit entry bollard

MONACO GRAND PRIX

MONTE CARLO • ROUND 6 • DATE: 28TH MAY 2017
Laps: 78 • Distance: 161.734miles/260.286km • Weather: Hot & bright

Pos	Driver	Team	Chassis-Engine	Result	Qual
1	Sebastian Vettel	Ferrari	Ferrari SF70H	1h44m44.340s	2
2	Kimi Raikkonen	Ferrari	Ferrari SF70H	1h44m47.485s	1
3	Daniel Ricciardo	Red Bull Racing	Red Bull-TAG Heuer RB13	1h44m48.085s	5
4	Valtteri Bottas	Mercedes AMG	Mercedes F1 W08	1h44m49.857s	3
5	Max Verstappen	Red Bull Racing	Red Bull-TAG Heuer RB13	1h44m50.539s	4
6	Carlos Sainz	Toro Rosso	Toro Rosso-Renault STR12	1h44m56.378s	6
7	Lewis Hamilton	Mercedes AMG	Mercedes F1 W08	1h45m00.141s	13

Pos	Driver	Team	Chassis-Engine	Result	Qual
8	Romain Grosjean	Haas	Haas-Ferrari VF-17	1h45m02.490s	8
9	Felipe Massa	Williams	Williams-Mercedes FW40	1h45m03.785s	14
10	Kevin Magnussen	Haas	Haas-Ferrari VF-17	1h45m05.783s	11
11	Jolyon Palmer	Renault F1	Renault RS17	1h45m07.077s	16
12	Esteban Ocon	Force India	Force India-Mercedes VJM10	1h45m08.065s	15
13	Sergio Perez †	Force India	Force India-Mercedes VJM10	1h45m33.429s	7
14	Daniil Kvyat	Toro Rosso	Toro Rosso-Renault STR12	71 laps/collision	9
15	Lance Stroll	Williams	Williams-Mercedes FW40	71 laps/brakes	17
R	Stoffel Vandoorne *	McLaren	McLaren-Honda MCL32	66 laps/spun off	12
R	Marcus Ericsson !	Sauber	Sauber-Ferrari C36	63 laps/spun off	19
R	Pascal Wehrlein ‡	Sauber	Sauber-Ferrari C36	57 laps/collision	18
R	Jenson Button ^	McLaren	McLaren-Honda MCL32	57 laps/collision	20
R	Nico Hulkenberg	Renault F1	Renault RS17	15 laps/gearbox	10

Pole: Raikkonen, 1m12.178s, 103.420mph/166.438kph. Fastest lap: Perez, 1m14.820s, 99.767mph/160.561kph on Lap 76. Race leaders: Raikkonen 1-33, Vettel 34-78

* 3-place grid penalty for causing crash in Spanish GP • ! 5-place grid penalty for gearbox change • ^ 15-place grid penalty for using additional power unit elements & made to start from pit lane for car being modified in parc ferme • † 10s penalty for causing a crash with Kvyat • ‡ 5s penalty for unsafe release

CANADIAN GRAND PRIX

MONTREAL • ROUND 7 • DATE: 11TH JUNE 2017
Laps: 70 • Distance: 189.534miles/305.27km • Weather: Hot & bright

Pos	Driver	Team	Chassis-Engine	Result	Qual
1	Lewis Hamilton	Mercedes AMG	Mercedes F1 W08	1h33m05.154s	1
2	Valtteri Bottas	Mercedes AMG	Mercedes F1 W08	1h33m24.937s	3
3	Daniel Ricciardo	Red Bull Racing	Red Bull-TAG Heuer RB13	1h33m40.451s	6
4	Sebastian Vettel	Ferrari	Ferrari SF70H	1h33m41.061s	2
5	Sergio Perez	Force India	Force India-Mercedes VJM10	1h33m45.630s	8
6	Esteban Ocon	Force India	Force India-Mercedes VJM10	1h33m45.870s	9
7	Kimi Raikkonen	Ferrari	Ferrari SF70H	1h34m03.786s	4
8	Nico Hulkenberg	Renault F1	Renault RS17	1h34m05.528s	10
9	Lance Stroll	Williams	Williams-Mercedes FW40	69 laps	17
10	Romain Grosjean	Haas	Haas-Ferrari VF-17	69 laps	14
11	Jolyon Palmer	Renault F1	Renault RS17	69 laps	15
12	Kevin Magnussen	Haas	Haas-Ferrari VF-17	69 laps	18
13	Marcus Ericsson	Sauber	Sauber-Ferrari C36	69 laps	19
14	Stoffel Vandoorne	McLaren	McLaren-Honda MCL32	69 laps	16
15	Pascal Wehrlein *	Sauber	Sauber-Ferrari C36	68 laps	20
16	Fernando Alonso	McLaren	McLaren-Honda MCL32	66 laps/engine	12
R	Daniil Kvyat	Toro Rosso	Toro Rosso-Renault STR12	54 laps/wheel	11
R	Max Verstappen	Red Bull Racing	Red Bull-TAG Heuer RB13	10 laps/battery	5
R	Felipe Massa	Williams	Williams-Mercedes FW40	0 laps/collision	7
R	Carlos Sainz	Toro Rosso	Toro Rosso-Renault STR12	0 laps/collision	13

Pole: Hamilton, 1m11.459s, 136.515mph/219.700kph. Fastest lap: Hamilton, 1m14.551s, 130.853mph/210.588kph on Lap 64. Race leaders: Hamilton 1-70

* 5-place grid penalty for gearbox change & made to start from pit lane for car being modified in parc ferme

AZERBAIJAN GRAND PRIX

BAKU CITY CIRCUIT • ROUND 8 • DATE: 25TH JUNE 2017
Laps: 51 • Distance: 190.234miles/306.153km • Weather: Hot & bright

Pos	Driver	Team	Chassis-Engine	Result	Qual
1	Daniel Ricciardo	Red Bull Racing	Red Bull-TAG Heuer RB13	2h03m55.573s	10
2	Valtteri Bottas	Mercedes AMG	Mercedes F1 W08	2h03m59.477s	2
3	Lance Stroll	Williams	Williams-Mercedes FW40	2h03m59.582s	8
4	Sebastian Vettel	Ferrari	Ferrari SF70H	2h04m01.549s	4
5	Lewis Hamilton	Mercedes AMG	Mercedes F1 W08	2h04m01.761s	1
6	Esteban Ocon	Force India	Force India-Mercedes VJM10	2h04m25.871s	7
7	Kevin Magnussen	Haas	Haas-Ferrari VF-17	2h04m37.326s	12
8	Carlos Sainz *	Toro Rosso	Toro Rosso-Renault STR12	2h04m44.973s	15
9	Fernando Alonso †	McLaren	McLaren-Honda MCL32	2h04m55.124s	19
10	Pascal Wehrlein	Sauber	Sauber-Ferrari C36	2h05m24.666s	14
11	Marcus Ericsson	Sauber	Sauber-Ferrari C36	2h05m27.367s	17
12	Stoffel Vandoorne !/^	McLaren	McLaren-Honda MCL32	2h05m27.733s	18
13	Romain Grosjean	Haas	Haas-Ferrari VF-17	50 laps	16
14	Kimi Raikkonen	Ferrari	Ferrari SF70H	46 laps/floor	3
R	Sergio Perez	Force India	Force India-Mercedes VJM10	39 laps/collision	6
R	Felipe Massa	Williams	Williams-Mercedes FW40	25 laps/suspension	9
R	Nico Hulkenberg	Renault F1	Renault RS17	24 laps/accident	13
R	Max Verstappen	Red Bull Racing	Red Bull-TAG Heuer RB13	12 laps/engine	5
R	Daniil Kvyat	Toro Rosso	Toro Rosso-Renault STR12	9 laps/electrical	11
R	Jolyon Palmer	Renault F1	Renault RS17	7 laps/ignition	20

Pole: Hamilton, 1m40.593s, 133.491mph/214.834kph. Fastest lap: Vettel, 1m43.441s, 129.816mph/208.919kph on Lap 47. Race leaders: Hamilton 1-30, Vettel 31-33, Ricciardo 34-51

* 3-place grid penalty for causing a crash in Canadian GP • ! 30-place grid penalty for using additional power unit elements • ^ 5-place grid penalty for gearbox change • † 40-place grid penalty for using additional power unit elements

GIVING IT TO THE MAX

With Max Verstappen hitting a rich vein of form in the final third of the season, Red Bull Racing increasingly looked to him rather than to Daniel Ricciardo as their driver of choice. This became clear at the United States GP when the young Dutchman was given the team's development engine and Ricciardo wasn't even told.

AUSTRIAN GRAND PRIX

RED BULL RING • ROUND 9 • DATE: 9TH JULY 2017
Laps: 71 • Distance: 190.498miles/306.578km • Weather: Hot & bright

Pos	Driver	Team	Chassis-Engine	Result	Qual
1	Valtteri Bottas	Mercedes AMG	Mercedes F1 W08	1h21m48.523s	1
2	Sebastian Vettel	Ferrari	Ferrari SF70H	1h21m49.181s	2
3	Daniel Ricciardo	Red Bull Racing	Red Bull-TAG Heuer RB13	1h21m54.535s	4
4	Lewis Hamilton *	Mercedes AMG	Mercedes F1 W08	1h21m55.953s	8
5	Kimi Raikkonen	Ferrari	Ferrari SF70H	1h22m08.893s	3
6	Romain Grosjean	Haas	Haas-Ferrari VF-17	1h23m01.683s	6

Pos	Driver	Team	Chassis-Engine	Result	Qual
7	Sergio Perez	Force India	Force India-Mercedes VJM10	70 laps	7
8	Esteban Ocon	Force India	Force India-Mercedes VJM10	70 laps	9
9	Felipe Massa	Williams	Williams-Mercedes FW40	70 laps	17
10	Lance Stroll	Williams	Williams-Mercedes FW40	70 laps	18
11	Jolyon Palmer	Renault F1	Renault RS17	70 laps	16
12	Stoffel Vandoorne	McLaren	McLaren-Honda MCL32	70 laps	13
13	Nico Hulkenberg	Renault F1	Renault RS17	70 laps	11
14	Pascal Wehrlein !	Sauber	Sauber-Ferrari C36	70 laps	20
15	Marcus Ericsson	Sauber	Sauber-Ferrari C36	69 laps	19
16	Daniil Kvyat	Toro Rosso	Toro Rosso-Renault STR12	68 laps	14
R	Carlos Sainz	Toro Rosso	Toro Rosso-Renault STR12	44 laps/engine	10
R	Kevin Magnussen	Haas	Haas-Ferrari VF-17	29 laps/hydraulics	15
R	Fernando Alonso	McLaren	McLaren-Honda MCL32	1 lap/collision	12
R	Max Verstappen	Red Bull Racing	Red Bull-TAG Heuer RB13	0 laps/collision	5

Pole: Bottas, 1m04.251s, 150.333mph/241.938kph. Fastest lap: Hamilton, 1m07.411s, 143.286mph/230.597kph on Lap 69. Race leaders: Bottas 1-41 & 44-71, Raikkonen 42-43

* 5-place grid penalty for gearbox change • ! made to start from pit lane for car being modified in parc ferme

MASSA WALKS AWAY

Felipe Massa brought his 270-race F1 career to a close at the end of what was a disappointing season with Williams. Brought back as a result of Nico Rosberg's decision to quit Mercedes, and with Bottas moving on, he didn't come close to adding to his 11 wins. Although the Williams was never going to be a race-winning car, he only just outscored team-mate Lance Stroll.

A FORCE WITHIN

The Force India camp was a lively place to be in 2017 as Sergio Perez settled into his fourth season in a row with the team and found himself coming under increasing pressure from new team-mate Esteban Ocon. Their best day together produced fourth and fifth in Spain, but there were moments when their pink cars clashed.

BRITISH GRAND PRIX

SILVERSTONE • ROUND 10 • DATE: 16TH JULY 2017
Laps: 51 • Distance: 186.685miles/300.441km • Weather: Warm but dull

Pos	Driver	Team	Chassis-Engine	Result	Qual
1	Lewis Hamilton	Mercedes AMG	Mercedes F1 W08	1h21m27.430s	1
2	Valtteri Bottas *	Mercedes AMG	Mercedes F1 W08	1h21m41.493s	9
3	Kimi Raikkonen	Ferrari	Ferrari SF70H	1h22m04.000s	2
4	Max Verstappen	Red Bull Racing	Red Bull-TAG Heuer RB13	1h22m19.555s	4
5	Daniel Ricciardo */!	Red Bull Racing	Red Bull-TAG Heuer RB13	1h22m33.385s	19
6	Nico Hulkenberg	Renault F1	Renault RS17	1h22m35.539s	5
7	Sebastian Vettel	Ferrari	Ferrari SF70H	1h23m01.419s	3

Pos	Driver	Team	Chassis-Engine	Result	Qual
8	Esteban Ocon	Force India	Force India-Mercedes VJM10	50 laps	7
9	Sergio Perez	Force India	Force India-Mercedes VJM10	50 laps	6
10	Felipe Massa	Williams	Williams-Mercedes FW40	50 laps	14
11	Stoffel Vandoorne	McLaren	McLaren-Honda MCL32	50 laps	8
12	Kevin Magnussen	Haas	Haas-Ferrari VF-17	50 laps	16
13	Romain Grosjean	Haas	Haas-Ferrari VF-17	50 laps	10
14	Marcus Ericsson	Sauber	Sauber-Ferrari C36	50 laps	18
15	Daniil Kvyat	Toro Rosso	Toro Rosso-Renault STR12	50 laps	12
16	Lance Stroll	Williams	Williams-Mercedes FW40	50 laps	15
17	Pascal Wehrlein	Sauber	Sauber-Ferrari C36	50 laps	17
R	Fernando Alonso ^	McLaren	McLaren-Honda MCL32	32 laps/fuel pump	20
R	Carlos Sainz	Toro Rosso	Toro Rosso-Renault STR12	0 laps/collision	13
NS	Jolyon Palmer	Renault F1	Renault RS17	-	11

Pole: Hamilton, 1m26.600s, 152.168mph/244.891kph. Fastest lap: Hamilton, 1m30.621s, 145.416mph/234.025kph on Lap 48. Race leaders: Hamilton 1-51

* 5-place grid penalty for gearbox change • ! 10-place grid penalty for using additional power unit elements • ^ 30-place grid penalty for using additional power unit elements

HUNGARIAN GRAND PRIX

HUNGARORING • ROUND 11 • DATE: 30TH JULY 2017
Laps: 70 • Distance: 190.181miles/306.67km • Weather: Hot & bright

Pos	Driver	Team	Chassis-Engine	Result	Qual
1	Sebastian Vettel	Ferrari	Ferrari SF70H	1h39m46.713s	1
2	Kimi Raikkonen	Ferrari	Ferrari SF70H	1h39m47.621s	2
3	Valtteri Bottas	Mercedes AMG	Mercedes F1 W08	1h39m59.175s	3
4	Lewis Hamilton	Mercedes AMG	Mercedes F1 W08	1h39m59.598s	4
5	Max Verstappen	Red Bull Racing	Red Bull-TAG Heuer RB13	1h39m59.989s	5
6	Fernando Alonso	McLaren	McLaren-Honda MCL32	1h40m57.936s	7
7	Carlos Sainz	Toro Rosso	Toro Rosso-Renault STR12	69 laps	9
8	Sergio Perez	Force India	Force India-Mercedes VJM10	69 laps	13
9	Esteban Ocon	Force India	Force India-Mercedes VJM10	69 laps	11
10	Stoffel Vandoorne	McLaren	McLaren-Honda MCL32	69 laps	8
11	Daniil Kvyat !	Toro Rosso	Toro Rosso-Renault STR12	69 laps	16
12	Jolyon Palmer	Renault F1	Renault RS17	69 laps	10
13	Kevin Magnussen ^	Haas	Haas-Ferrari VF-17	69 laps	15
14	Lance Stroll	Williams	Williams-Mercedes FW40	69 laps	17
15	Pascal Wehrlein	Sauber	Sauber-Ferrari C36	68 laps	18
16	Marcus Ericsson	Sauber	Sauber-Ferrari C36	68 laps	20
17	Nico Hulkenberg *	Renault F1	Renault RS17	67 laps/collision	12
R	Paul di Resta	Williams	Williams-Mercedes FW40	60 laps/oil leak	19
R	Romain Grosjean	Haas	Haas-Ferrari VF-17	20 laps/wheel	14
R	Daniel Ricciardo	Red Bull Racing	Red Bull-TAG Heuer RB13	0 laps/collision	6
NS	Felipe Massa	Williams	Williams-Mercedes FW40	driver unwell	-

Pole: Vettel, 1m16.276s, 128.481mph/206.770kph. Fastest lap: Alonso, 1m20.182s, 122.221mph/196.697kph on Lap 69. Race leaders: Vettel 1-31 & 43-70, Raikkonen 32-33, Verstappen 34-42

* 5-pace grid penalty for gearbox change • ! 3-place grid penalty for impeding Ericsson • ^ 5s penalty for forcing Hulkenberg off track

McLAREN'S WOES CONTINUE

Honda was a year behind the other engine suppliers when it introduced its 1.6-litre hybrid engine and it never really caught up. So there was nothing that the once-great McLaren could do. Double world champion Fernando Alonso and Stoffel Vandoorne collected just 30 points between them, peaking with sixth in Hungary, as the team ranked ninth out of the 10 teams.

BELGIAN GRAND PRIX

SPA-FRANCORCHAMPS • ROUND 12 • DATE: 27TH AUGUST 2017
Laps: 44 • Distance: 191.491miles/308.176km • Weather: Warm & bright

Pos	Driver	Team	Chassis-Engine	Result	Qual
1	Lewis Hamilton	Mercedes AMG	Mercedes F1 W08	1h24m42.820s	1
2	Sebastian Vettel	Ferrari	Ferrari SF70H	1h24m45.178s	2
3	Daniel Ricciardo	Red Bull Racing	Red Bull-TAG Heuer RB13	1h24m53.611s	6
4	Kimi Raikkonen	Ferrari	Ferrari SF70H	1h24m57.291s	4
5	Valtteri Bottas	Mercedes AMG	Mercedes F1 W08	1h24m59.276s	3
6	Nico Hulkenberg	Renault F1	Renault RS17	1h25m10.907s	7
7	Romain Grosjean	Haas	Haas-Ferrari VF-17	1h25m14.373s	11
8	Felipe Massa !	Williams	Williams-Mercedes FW40	1h25m19.469s	16
9	Esteban Ocon	Force India	Force India-Mercedes VJM10	1h25m20.974s	9
10	Carlos Sainz	Toro Rosso	Toro Rosso-Renault STR12	1h25m22.267s	13
11	Lance Stroll	Williams	Williams-Mercedes FW40	1h25m31.819s	15
12	Daniil Kvyat ^	Toro Rosso	Toro Rosso-Renault STR12	1h25m32.760s	19
13	Jolyon Palmer *	Renault F1	Renault RS17	1h25m36.059s	14
14	Stoffel Vandoorne */†	McLaren	McLaren-Honda MCL32	1h25m39.898s	20
15	Kevin Magnussen	Haas	Haas-Ferrari VF-17	1h25m50.082s	12
16	Marcus Ericsson *	Sauber	Sauber-Ferrari C36	1h25m52.531s	17
17	Sergio Perez	Force India	Force India-Mercedes VJM10	42 laps/accident	8
R	Fernando Alonso	McLaren	McLaren-Honda MCL32	25 laps/engine	10
R	Max Verstappen	Red Bull Racing	Red Bull-TAG Heuer RB13	7 laps/engine	5
R	Pascal Wehrlein *	Sauber	Sauber-Ferrari C36	2 laps/suspension	18

Pole: Hamilton, 1m42.553s, 152.774mph/245.867kph. Fastest lap: Vettel, 1m46.577s, 147.006mph/236.583kph on Lap 41. Race leaders: Hamilton 1-11 & 15-44, Vettel 12-14

* 5-place grid penalty for gearbox change • ! 5-place grid penalty for failing to slow for yellow flags • ^ 20-place grid penalty for using additional power unit elements • † 60-place grid penalty for using additional power unit elements

ITALIAN GRAND PRIX

MONZA • ROUND 13 • DATE: 3RD SEPTEMBER 2017
Laps: 53 • Distance: 190.778miles/307.029km • Weather: Hot & bright

Pos	Driver	Team	Chassis-Engine	Result	Qual
1	Lewis Hamilton	Mercedes AMG	Mercedes F1 W08	1h15m32.312s	1
2	Valtteri Bottas	Mercedes AMG	Mercedes F1 W08	1h15m36.783s	4
3	Sebastian Vettel	Ferrari	Ferrari SF70H	1h16m08.629s	6
4	Daniel Ricciardo */†	Red Bull Racing	Red Bull-TAG Heuer RB13	1h16m12.647s	16
5	Kimi Raikkonen	Ferrari	Ferrari SF70H	1h16m32.394s	5
6	Esteban Ocon	Force India	Force India-Mercedes VJM10	1h16m43.840s	3
7	Lance Stroll	Williams	Williams-Mercedes FW40	1h16m46.468s	2

Pos	Driver	Team	Chassis-Engine	Result	Qual
8	Felipe Massa	Williams	Williams-Mercedes FW40	1h16m47.146s	7
9	Sergio Perez *	Force India	Force India-Mercedes VJM10	1h16m47.588s	10
10	Max Verstappen †	Red Bull Racing	Red Bull-TAG Heuer RB13	52 laps	13
11	Kevin Magnussen	Haas	Haas-Ferrari VF-17	52 laps	9
12	Daniil Kvyat	Toro Rosso	Toro Rosso-Renault STR12	52 laps	8
13	Nico Hulkenberg !	Renault F1	Renault RS17	52 laps	14
14	Carlos Sainz !	Toro Rosso	Toro Rosso-Renault STR12	52 laps	15
15	Romain Grosjean *	Haas	Haas-Ferrari VF-17	52 laps	20
16	Pascal Wehrlein	Sauber	Sauber-Ferrari C36	51 laps	12
17	Fernando Alonso §	McLaren	McLaren-Honda MCL32	50 laps/gearbox	19
18	Marcus Ericsson	Sauber	Sauber-Ferrari C36	49 laps/accident	11
R	Stoffel Vandoorne ‡	McLaren	McLaren-Honda MCL32	33 laps/power unit	18
R	Jolyon Palmer ^	Renault F1	Renault RS17	29 laps/transmission	17

Pole: Hamilton, 1m35.554s, 135.615mph/218.251kph. Fastest lap: Ricciardo, 1m23.361s, 155.450mph/250.174kph on Lap 49. Race leaders: Hamilton 1-31 & 34-53, Bottas 32-33

* 5-place grid penalty for gearbox change • ! 10-place grid penalty for using additional power unit elements • ^ 15-place grid penalty for using additional power unit elements • † 20-place grid penalty for using additional power unit elements • ‡ 25-place grid penalty for using additional power unit elements • § 35-place grid penalty for using additional power unit elements

LOOKING FOR TALENT

The Red Bull drinks company went into F1 for publicity. Its policy for sourcing talent was to spread its net wide, pay for a few seasons of racing for the rising stars identified by Helmut Marko, pick the best and discard the rest. It then introduced them to F1 via its junior team, Scuderia Toro Rosso, and, if they were good enough, put them in the Red Bull Racing senior team.

SINGAPORE GRAND PRIX

MARINA BAY CIRCUIT • ROUND 14 • DATE: 17TH SEPTEMBER 2017
Laps: 58 • Distance: 182.109miles/293.77km • Weather: Hot & wet, drying later

Pos	Driver	Team	Chassis-Engine	Result	Qual
1	Lewis Hamilton	Mercedes AMG	Mercedes F1 W08	2h03m23.544s	5
2	Daniel Ricciardo	Red Bull Racing	Red Bull-TAG Heuer RB13	2h03m28.051s	3
3	Valtteri Bottas	Mercedes AMG	Mercedes F1 W08	2h03m32.344s	6
4	Carlos Sainz	Toro Rosso	Toro Rosso-Renault STR12	2h03m46.366s	10
5	Sergio Perez	Force India	Force India-Mercedes VJM10	2h03m48.903s	12
6	Jolyon Palmer	Renault F1	Renault RS17	2h03m50.803s	11
7	Stoffel Vandoorne	McLaren	McLaren-Honda MCL32	2h03m53.932s	9
8	Lance Stroll	Williams	Williams-Mercedes FW40	2h04m05.240s	18
9	Romain Grosjean	Haas	Haas-Ferrari VF-17	2h04m06.826s	15
10	Esteban Ocon	Force India	Force India-Mercedes VJM10	2h04m08.339s	14
11	Felipe Massa	Williams	Williams-Mercedes FW40	2h04m10.080s	17
12	Pascal Wehrlein	Sauber	Sauber-Ferrari C36	56 laps	19
R	Kevin Magnussen	Haas	Haas-Ferrari VF-17	50 laps/power unit	16
R	Nico Hulkenberg	Renault F1	Renault RS17	48 laps/oil leak	7
R	Marcus Ericsson *	Sauber	Sauber-Ferrari C36	35 laps/spun off	20
R	Daniil Kvyat	Toro Rosso	Toro Rosso-Renault STR12	10 laps/spun off	13

Pos	Driver	Team	Chassis-Engine	Result	Qual
R	Fernando Alonso	McLaren	McLaren-Honda MCL32	8 laps/collision	8
R	Sebastian Vettel	Ferrari	Ferrari SF70H	0 laps/collision	1
R	Max Verstappen	Red Bull Racing	Red Bull-TAG Heuer RB13	0 laps/collision	2
R	Kimi Raikkonen	Ferrari	Ferrari SF70H	0 laps/collision	4

Pole: Vettel, 1m39.491s, 113.880mph/183.272kph. Fastest lap: Hamilton, 1m45.008s, 107.896mph/173.643kph on Lap 55. Race leaders: Hamilton 1-58

* 5-place grid penalty for gearbox change

MALAYSIAN GRAND PRIX

SEPANG • ROUND 15 • DATE: 1ST OCTOBER 2017
Laps: 56 • Distance: 192.878miles/310.408km • Weather: Hot but dull

Pos	Driver	Team	Chassis-Engine	Result	Qual
1	Max Verstappen	Red Bull Racing	Red Bull-TAG Heuer RB13	1h30m01.290s	3
2	Lewis Hamilton	Mercedes AMG	Mercedes F1 W08	1h30m14.060s	1
3	Daniel Ricciardo	Red Bull Racing	Red Bull-TAG Heuer RB13	1h30m23.809s	4
4	Sebastian Vettel *	Ferrari	Ferrari SF70H	1h30m38.652s	20
5	Valtteri Bottas	Mercedes AMG	Mercedes F1 W08	1h30m57.311s	5
6	Sergio Perez	Force India	Force India-Mercedes VJM10	1h31m19.920s	9
7	Stoffel Vandoorne	McLaren	McLaren-Honda MCL32	55 laps	7
8	Lance Stroll	Williams	Williams-Mercedes FW40	55 laps	13
9	Felipe Massa	Williams	Williams-Mercedes FW40	55 laps	11
10	Esteban Ocon	Force India	Force India-Mercedes VJM10	55 laps	6
11	Fernando Alonso	McLaren	McLaren-Honda MCL32	55 laps	10
12	Kevin Magnussen	Haas	Haas-Ferrari VF-17	55 laps	17
13	Romain Grosjean	Haas	Haas-Ferrari VF-17	55 laps	16
14	Pierre Gasly	Toro Rosso	Toro Rosso-Renault STR12	55 laps	15
15	Jolyon Palmer	Renault F1	Renault RS17	55 laps	12
16	Nico Hulkenberg	Renault F1	Renault RS17	55 laps	8
17	Pascal Wehrlein	Sauber	Sauber-Ferrari C36	55 laps	18
18	Marcus Ericsson	Sauber	Sauber-Ferrari C36	54 laps	19
R	Carlos Sainz	Toro Rosso	Toro Rosso-Renault STR12	29 laps/electrical	14
NS	Kimi Raikkonen	Ferrari	Ferrari SF70H	power unit	2

Pole: Hamilton, 1m30.076s, 137.654mph/221.532kph. Fastest lap: Vettel, 1m34.080s, 131.795mph/212.104kph on Lap 41. Race leaders: Hamilton 1-3, Verstappen 4-27 & 30-56, Ricciardo 28-29

* 20-place grid penalty for using additional power unit elements

JAPANESE GRAND PRIX

SUZUKA • ROUND 16 • DATE: 8TH OCTOBER 2017
Laps: 53 • Distance: 191.240miles/307.771km • Weather: Warm & bright

Pos	Driver	Team	Chassis-Engine	Result	Qual
1	Lewis Hamilton	Mercedes AMG	Mercedes F1 W08	1h27m31.194s	1
2	Max Verstappen	Red Bull Racing	Red Bull-TAG Heuer RB13	1h27m32.405s	4
3	Daniel Ricciardo	Red Bull Racing	Red Bull-TAG Heuer RB13	1h27m40.873s	3
4	Valtteri Bottas *	Mercedes AMG	Mercedes F1 W08	1h27m41.774s	6
5	Kimi Raikkonen *	Ferrari	Ferrari SF70H	1h28m03.816s	10
6	Esteban Ocon	Force India	Force India-Mercedes VJM10	1h28m38.982s	5
7	Sergio Perez	Force India	Force India-Mercedes VJM10	1h28m42.618s	7

Pos	Driver	Team	Chassis-Engine	Result	Qual
8	Kevin Magnussen	Haas	Haas-Ferrari VF-17	1h29m00.147s	12
9	Romain Grosjean	Haas	Haas-Ferrari VF-17	1h29m01.077s	13
10	Felipe Massa	Williams	Williams-Mercedes FW40	52 laps	8
11	Fernando Alonso ^	McLaren	McLaren-Honda MCL32	52 laps	20
12	Jolyon Palmer !	Renault F1	Renault RS17	52 laps	18
13	Pierre Gasly	Toro Rosso	Toro Rosso-Renault STR12	52 laps	14
14	Stoffel Vandoorne	McLaren	McLaren-Honda MCL32	52 laps	9
15	Pascal Wehrlein	Sauber	Sauber-Ferrari C36	51 laps	17
R	Lance Stroll	Williams	Williams-Mercedes FW40	45 laps/suspension	15
R	Nico Hulkenberg	Renault F1	Renault RS17	40 laps/mechanical	11
R	Marcus Ericsson	Sauber	Sauber-Ferrari C36	7 laps/spun off	16
R	Sebastian Vettel	Ferrari	Ferrari SF70H	4 laps/mechanical	2
R	Carlos Sainz !	Toro Rosso	Toro Rosso-Renault STR12	0 laps/spun off	19

Pole: Hamilton, 1m27.319s, 148.763mph/239.411kph. Fastest lap: Bottas, 1m33.144s, 139.459mph/224.439kph on Lap 50. Race leaders: Hamilton 1-22 & 28-53, Ricciardo 23-25, Bottas 26-27

* 5-place grid penalty for gearbox change • ! 20-place grid penalty for using additional power unit elements • ^ 35-place grid penalty for using additional power unit elements

UNITED STATES GRAND PRIX

CIRCUIT OF THE AMERICAS • ROUND 17 • DATE: 22ND OCTOBER 2017
Laps: 56 • Distance: 191.834miles/308.728km • Weather: Warm & bright

Pos	Driver	Team	Chassis-Engine	Result	Qual
1	Lewis Hamilton	Mercedes AMG	Mercedes F1 W08	1h33m50.991s	1
2	Sebastian Vettel	Ferrari	Ferrari SF70H	1h34m01.134s	2
3	Kimi Raikkonen	Ferrari	Ferrari SF70H	1h34m06.770s	5
4	Max Verstappen ^/¶	Red Bull Racing	Red Bull-TAG Heuer RB13	1h34m07.759s	16
5	Valtteri Bottas	Mercedes AMG	Mercedes F1 W08	1h34m25.958s	3
6	Esteban Ocon	Force India	Force India-Mercedes VJM10	1h35m21.971s	6
7	Carlos Sainz	Renault F1	Renault RS17	1h35m23.935s	7
8	Sergio Perez	Force India	Force India-Mercedes VJM10	55 laps	9
9	Felipe Massa	Williams	Williams-Mercedes FW40	55 laps	10
10	Daniil Kvyat	Toro Rosso	Toro Rosso-Renault STR12	55 laps	11
11	Lance Stroll *	Williams	Williams-Mercedes FW40	55 laps	15
12	Stoffel Vandoorne §	McLaren	McLaren-Honda MCL32	55 laps	20
13	Brendon Hartley ‡	Toro Rosso	Toro Rosso-Renault STR12	55 laps	19
14	Romain Grosjean	Haas	Haas-Ferrari VF-17	55 laps	12
15	Marcus Ericsson **	Sauber	Sauber-Ferrari C36	55 laps	13
16	Kevin Magnussen !	Haas	Haas-Ferrari VF-17	55 laps	17
R	Fernando Alonso	McLaren	McLaren-Honda MCL32	24 laps/engine	8
R	Daniel Ricciardo	Red Bull Racing	Red Bull-TAG Heuer RB13	14 laps/engine	4
R	Pascal Wehrlein	Sauber	Sauber-Ferrari C36	5 laps/accident	14
R	Nico Hulkenberg †	Renault F1	Renault RS17	3 laps/fuel pressure	18

Pole: Hamilton, 1m33.108s, 132.450mph/213.158kph. Fastest lap: Vettel, 1m37.766s, 126.140mph/203.003kph on Lap 51. Race leaders: Vettel 1-5, Hamilton 6-19 & 23-56, Raikkonen 20, Verstappen 21-22

* 3-place grid penalty for impeding Grosjean • ! 3-place grid penalty for impeding Perez • ^ 15-place grid penalty for using additional power unit elements • † 20-place grid penalty for using additional power unit elements • ‡ 25-place grid penalty for using additional power unit elements • § 30-place grid penalty for using additional power unit elements • ¶ 5s penalty for gaining an advantage by leaving the track • ** 5s penalty for causing an accident

MEXICAN GRAND PRIX

MEXICO CITY • ROUND 18 • DATE: 29TH OCTOBER 2017
Laps: 71 • Distance: 189.881miles/305.584km • Weather: Warm but dull

Pos	Driver	Team	Chassis-Engine	Result	Qual
1	Max Verstappen	Red Bull Racing	Red Bull-TAG Heuer RB13	1h36m26.552s	2
2	Valtteri Bottas	Mercedes AMG	Mercedes F1 W08	1h36m46.230s	4
3	Kimi Raikkonen	Ferrari	Ferrari SF70H	1h37m20.559s	5
4	Sebastian Vettel	Ferrari	Ferrari SF70H	1h37m36.630s	1
5	Esteban Ocon	Force India	Force India-Mercedes VJM10	70 laps	6
6	Lance Stroll	Williams	Williams-Mercedes FW40	70 laps	11
7	Sergio Perez	Force India	Force India-Mercedes VJM10	70 laps	9
8	Kevin Magnussen	Haas	Haas-Ferrari VF-17	70 laps	14
9	Lewis Hamilton	Mercedes AMG	Mercedes F1 W08	70 laps	3
10	Fernando Alonso *	McLaren	McLaren-Honda MCL32	70 laps	18
11	Felipe Massa	Williams	Williams-Mercedes FW40	70 laps	10
12	Stoffel Vandoorne !	McLaren	McLaren-Honda MCL32	70 laps	19
13	Pierre Gasly *	Toro Rosso	Toro Rosso-Renault STR12	70 laps	20
14	Pascal Wehrlein	Sauber	Sauber-Ferrari C36	69 laps	13
15	Romain Grosjean	Haas	Haas-Ferrari VF-17	69 laps	15
R	Carlos Sainz	Renault F1	Renault RS17	59 laps/steering	8
R	Marcus Ericsson	Sauber	Sauber-Ferrari C36	55 laps/suspension	12
R	Brendon Hartley *	Toro Rosso	Toro Rosso-Renault STR12	30 laps/power unit	17
R	Nico Hulkenberg	Renault F1	Renault RS17	24 laps/power unit	7
R	Daniel Ricciardo *	Red Bull Racing	Red Bull-TAG Heuer RB13	5 laps/turbo	16

Pole: Vettel, 1m16.488s, 125.872mph/202.572kph. Fastest lap: Vettel, 1m18.785s, 122.203mph/196.666kph on Lap 68. Race leaders: Verstappen 1-71

* 20-place grid penalty for using additional power unit elements • ! 35-place grid penalty for using additional power unit elements

NEW DRIVERS

A podium finish in even a driver's second year in F1 is good going, so 18-year-old Canadian Lance Stroll sported a huge grin when he came third in Baku for Williams. Antonio Giovinazzi did the first two races for Sauber as Pascal Wehrlein was injured, and took a 12th place, a result matched by Pierre Gasly for Toro Rosso. Brendon Hartley took a 13th for the same team.

BRAZILIAN GRAND PRIX

INTERLAGOS • ROUND 19 • DATE: 12TH NOVEMBER 2017
Laps: 71 • Distance: 190.101miles/305.939km • Weather: Hot & bright

Pos	Driver	Team	Chassis-Engine	Result	Qual
1	Sebastian Vettel	Ferrari	Ferrari SF70H	1h31m26.262s	2
2	Valtteri Bottas	Mercedes AMG	Mercedes F1 W08	1h31m29.024s	1
3	Kimi Raikkonen	Ferrari	Ferrari SF70H	1h31m30.862s	3
4	Lewis Hamilton †	Mercedes AMG	Mercedes F1 W08	1h31m31.730s	20
5	Max Verstappen	Red Bull Racing	Red Bull-TAG Heuer RB13	1h31m59.202s	4
6	Daniel Ricciardo !	Red Bull Racing	Red Bull-TAG Heuer RB13	1h32m14.953s	14
7	Felipe Massa	Williams	Williams-Mercedes FW40	1h32m35.144s	9
8	Fernando Alonso	McLaren	McLaren-Honda MCL32	1h32m35.625s	6

Pos	Driver	Team	Chassis-Engine	Result	Qual
9	Sergio Perez	Force India	Force India-Mercedes VJM10	1h32m35.762s	5
10	Nico Hulkenberg	Renault F1	Renault RS17	70 laps	7
11	Carlos Sainz	Renault F1	Renault RS17	70 laps	8
12	Pierre Gasly ^	Toro Rosso	Toro Rosso-Renault STR12	70 laps	19
13	Marcus Ericsson *	Sauber	Sauber-Ferrari C36	70 laps	17
14	Pascal Wehrlein	Sauber	Sauber-Ferrari C36	70 laps	15
15	Romain Grosjean	Haas	Haas-Ferrari VF-17	69 laps	11
16	Lance Stroll *	Williams	Williams-Mercedes FW40	69 laps	16
R	Brendon Hartley !	Toro Rosso	Toro Rosso-Renault STR12	40 laps/engine	18
R	Esteban Ocon	Force India	Force India-Mercedes VJM10	0 laps/collision	10
R	Stoffel Vandoorne	McLaren	McLaren-Honda MCL32	0 laps/collision	12
R	Kevin Magnussen	Haas	Haas-Ferrari VF-17	0 laps/collision	13

Pole: Bottas, 1m08.322s, 141.081mph/227.048kph. Fastest lap: Verstappen, 1m11.044s, 135.675mph/218.349kph on Lap 64. Race leaders: Vettel 1-28 & 43-71, Raikkonen 29, Hamilton 30-42

* 5-place grid penalty for gearbox change • ! 10-place grid penalty for using additional power unit elements • ^ 25-place grid penalty for using additional power unit elements • † made to start from pit lane for car being modified in parc ferme

ABU DHABI GRAND PRIX

YAS MARINA CIRCUIT • ROUND 20 • DATE: 26TH NOVEMBER 2017
Laps: 55 • Distance: 189.547miles/305.47km • Weather: Hot & dry

Pos	Driver	Team	Chassis-Engine	Result	Qual
1	Valtteri Bottas	Mercedes AMG	Mercedes F1 W08	1h34m14.062s	1
2	Lewis Hamilton	Mercedes AMG	Mercedes F1 W08	1h34m17.961s	2
3	Sebastian Vettel	Ferrari	Ferrari SF70H	1h34m33.392s	3
4	Kimi Raikkonen	Ferrari	Ferrari SF70H	1h34m59.448s	5
5	Max Verstappen	Red Bull Racing	Red Bull-TAG Heuer RB13	1h35m00.331s	6
6	Nico Hulkenberg	Renault F1	Renault RS17	1h35m39.775s	7
7	Sergio Perez	Force India	Force India-Mercedes VJM10	1h35m46.124s	8
8	Esteban Ocon	Force India	Force India-Mercedes VJM10	1h35m52.973s	9
9	Fernando Alonso	McLaren	McLaren-Honda MCL32	54 laps	11
10	Felipe Massa	Williams	Williams-Mercedes FW40	54 laps	10
11	Romain Grosjean	Haas	Haas-Ferrari VF-17	54 laps	16
12	Stoffel Vandoorne	McLaren	McLaren-Honda MCL32	54 laps	13
13	Kevin Magnussen	Haas	Haas-Ferrari VF-17	54 laps	14
14	Pascal Wehrlein	Sauber	Sauber-Ferrari C36	54 laps	18
15	Brendon Hartley *	Toro Rosso	Toro Rosso-Renault STR12	54 laps	20
16	Pierre Gasly	Toro Rosso	Toro Rosso-Renault STR12	54 laps	17
17	Marcus Ericsson	Sauber	Sauber-Ferrari C36	54 laps	19
18	Lance Stroll	Williams	Williams-Mercedes FW40	54 laps	15
R	Carlos Sainz	Renault F1	Renault RS17	31 laps/wheel	12
R	Daniel Ricciardo	Red Bull Racing	Red Bull-TAG Heuer RB13	20 laps/hydraulics	4

Pole: Bottas, 1m36.231s, 129.105mph/207.775kph. Fastest lap: Bottas, 1m40.650s, 123.437mph/198.652kph on Lap 52. Race leaders: Bottas 1-21 & 25-55, Hamilton 22-24

* 10-place grid penalty for using additional power unit elements

WORLD DRIVERS' CHAMPIONSHIP FINAL RESULTS

Pos	Driver	Nat	Car-Engine	R1	R2	R3	R4	R5	R6	R7	R8
1	Lewis Hamilton	GBR	Mercedes F1 W08	2P	1PF	2F	4	1PF	7	1PF	5P
2	Sebastian Vettel	DEU	Ferrari SF70H	1	2	1	2P	2	1	4	4F
3	Valtteri Bottas	FIN	Mercedes F1 W08	3	6	3P	1	R	4	2	2
4	Kimi Raikkonen	FIN	Ferrari SF70H	4F	5	4	3F	R	2P	7	14
5	Daniel Ricciardo	AUS	Red Bull-TAG Heuer RB13	R	4	5	R	3	3	3	1
6	Max Verstappen	NLD	Red Bull-TAG Heuer RB13	5	3	R	5	R	5	R	R
7	Sergio Perez	MEX	Force India-Mercedes VJM10	7	9	7	6	4	13F	5	R
8	Esteban Ocon	FRA	Force India-Mercedes VJM10	10	10	10	7	5	12	6	6
9	Carlos Sainz	ESP	Toro Rosso-Renault STR12	8	7	R	10	7	6	R	8
			Renault RS17	-	-	-	-	-	-	-	-
10	Nico Hulkenberg	DEU	Renault RS17	11	12	9	8	6	R	8	R
11	Felipe Massa	BRA	Williams-Mercedes FW40	6	14	6	9	13	9	R	R
12	Lance Stroll	CAN	Williams-Mercedes FW40	R	R	R	11	16	15	9	3
13	Romain Grosjean	FRA	Haas-Ferrari VF-17	R	11	8	R	10	8	10	13
14	Kevin Magnussen	DNK	Haas-Ferrari VF-17	R	8	R	13	14	10	12	7
15	Fernando Alonso	ESP	McLaren-Honda MCL32	R	R	14	NS	12	-	16	9
16	Stoffel Vandoorne	BEL	McLaren-Honda MCL32	13	R	NS	14	R	R	14	12
17	Jolyon Palmer	GBR	Renault RS17	R	13	13	R	15	11	11	R
18	Pascal Wehrlein	DEU	Sauber-Ferrari C36	NS	-	11	16	8	R	15	10
19	Daniil Kvyat	RUS	Toro Rosso-Renault STR12	9	R	12	12	9	14	R	R
20	Marcus Ericsson	SWE	Sauber-Ferrari C36	R	15	R	15	11	R	13	11
21	Pierre Gasly	FRA	Toro Rosso-Renault STR12	-	-	-	-	-	-	-	-
22	Antonio Giovinazzi	ITA	Sauber-Ferrari C36	12	R	-	-	-	-	-	-
			Haas-Ferrari VF-17	-	-	-	-	-	-	-	-
23	Brendon Hartley	NZL	Toro Rosso-Renault STR12	-	-	-	-	-	-	-	-

Pos	Driver	R9	R10	R11	R12	R13	R14	R15	R16	R17	R18	R19	R20	Total
1	Hamilton	4F	1PF	4	1P	1P	1F	2P	1P	1P	9	4	2	363
2	Vettel	2	7	1P	2F	3	RP	4F	R	2F	4PF	1	3	317
3	Bottas	1P	2	3	5	2	3	5	4F	5	2	2P	1PF	305
4	Raikkonen	5	3	2	4	5	R	NS	5	3	3	3	4	205
5	Ricciardo	3	5	R	3	4F	2	3	3	R	R	6	R	200
6	Verstappen	R	4	5	R	10	R	1	2	4	1	5F	5	168
7	Perez	7	9	8	17	9	5	6	7	8	7	9	7	100
8	Ocon	8	8	9	9	6	10	10	6	6	5	R	8	87
9	Sainz	R	R	7	10	14	4	R	R	-	-	-	-	54
		-	-	-	-	-	-	-	-	7	R	11	R	
10	Hulkenberg	13	6	17	6	13	R	16	R	R	R	10	6	43
11	Massa	9	10	NS	8	8	11	9	10	9	11	7	10	43
12	Stroll	10	16	14	11	7	8	8	R	11	6	16	18	40
13	Grosjean	6	13	R	7	15	9	13	9	14	15	15	11	28
14	Magnussen	R	12	13	15	11	R	12	8	16	8	R	13	19
15	Alonso	R	R	6F	R	17	R	11	11	R	10	8	9	17
16	Vandoorne	12	11	10	14	R	7	7	14	12	12	R	12	13
17	Palmer	11	NS	12	13	R	6	15	12	-	-	-	-	8
18	Wehrlein	14	17	15	R	16	12	17	15	R	14	14	14	5
19	Kvyat	16	15	11	12	12	R	-	-	10	-	-	-	5
20	Ericsson	15	14	16	16	18	R	18	R	15	R	13	17	0
21	Gasly	-	-	-	-	-	-	14	13	-	13	12	16	0
22	Giovinazzi	-	-	-	-	-	-	-	-	-	-	-	-	0
		-	T	T	-	-	T	T	-	-	T	T	T	
23	Hartley	-	-	-	-	-	-	-	-	13	R	R	15	0

WORLD CONSTRUCTORS' CHAMPIONSHIP FINAL RESULTS

Pos	Team-Engine	R1	R2	R3	R4	R5	R6	R7	R8	R9	R10	R11
1	Mercedes AMG	2/3	1/6	2/3	1/4	1/R	4/7	1/2	2/5	1/4	1/2	3/4
2	Ferrari	1/4	2/5	1/4	2/3	2/R	1/2	4/7	4/14	2/5	3/7	1/2
3	Red Bull-TAG Heuer	5/R	3/4	5/R	5/R	3/R	3/5	3/R	1/R	3/R	4/5	5/R
4	Force India-Mercedes	7/10	9/10	7/10	6/7	4/5	12/13	5/6	6/R	7/8	8/9	8/9
5	Williams-Mercedes	6/R	14/R	6/R	9/11	13/16	9/15	9/R	3/R	9/10	10/16	14
6	Renault F1	11/R	12/13	9/13	8/R	6/15	11/R	8/11	R/R	11/13	6/NS	12/17
7	Toro Rosso-Renault	8/9	7/R	12/R	10/12	7/9	6/14	R/R	8/R	16/R	15/R	7/11
8	Haas-Ferrari	R/R	8/11	8/R	13/R	10/14	8/10	10/12	7/13	6/R	12/13	13/R
9	McLaren-Honda	13/R	R/R	14/NS	14/NS	12/R	R/R	14/16	9/12	12/R	11/R	6/10
10	Sauber-Ferrari	R	15	11/R	15/16	8/11	R/R	13/15	10/11	14/15	14/17	15/16

Pos	Team-Engine	R11	R12	R13	R14	R15	R16	R17	R18	R19	R20	Total
1	Mercedes AMG	3/4	1/5	1/2	1/3	2/5	1/4	1/5	2/9	2/4	1/2	668
2	Ferrari	1/2	2/4	3/5	R/R	4/NS	5/NC	2/3	3/4	1/3	3/4	522
3	Red Bull-TAG Heuer	5/R	3/R	4/10	2/R	1/3	2/3	4/NC	1/R	5/6	5/R	368
4	Force India-Mercedes	8/9	9/17	6/9	5/10	6/10	6/7	6/8	5/7	9/NC	7/8	187
5	Williams-Mercedes	14	8/11	7/8	8/11	8/9	10/NC	9/11	6/11	7/16	10/18	83
6	Renault F1	12/17	6/13	13/R	6/R	15/16	12/NC	7/NC	R/R	10/11	6/R	57
7	Toro Rosso-Renault	7/11	10/12	12/14	4/R	14/R	13/NC	10/13	13/R	12/NC	15/16	53
8	Haas-Ferrari	13/R	7/15	11/15	9/R	12/13	8/9	14/16	8/15	15/NC	11/13	47
9	McLaren-Honda	6/10	14/R	17/R	7/R	7/11	11/14	12/NC	10/12	8/NC	9/12	30
10	Sauber-Ferrari	15/16	16/R	16/18	12/R	17/18	15/NC	15/NC	14/R	13/14	14/17	5

SYMBOLS AND GRAND PRIX KEY

Round 1 Australian GP
Round 2 Chinese GP
Round 3 Bahrain GP
Round 4 Russian GP
Round 5 Spanish GP
Round 6 Monaco GP
Round 7 Canadian GP
Round 8 Azerbaijan GP
Round 9 Austrian GP
Round 10 British GP
Round 11 Hungarian GP
Round 12 Belgian GP
Round 13 Italian GP
Round 14 Singapore GP
Round 15 Malaysian GP
Round 16 Japanese GP
Round 17 United States GP
Round 18 Mexican GP
Round 19 Brazilian GP
Round 20 Abu Dhabi GP

SCORING

1st 25 points
2nd 18 points
3rd 15 points
4th 12 points
5th 10 points
6th 8 points
7th 6 points
8th 4 points
9th 2 points
10th 1 point

DNPQ DID NOT PRE-QUALIFY **DNQ** DID NOT QUALIFY **DQ** DISQUALIFIED **EX** EXCLUDED
F FASTEST LAP **NC** NOT CLASSIFIED **NS** NON-STARTER **P** POLE POSITION **R** RETIRED

2018

SEASON SUMMARY

Lewis Hamilton rode out Ferrari's early challenge in 2018 and came out on top for Mercedes again to claim his fifth F1 title, thus matching Juan Manuel Fangio's tally from the 1950s. What pleased his fans most, though, was how Hamilton seemed to rise to new heights to ensure that the title was his as he weathered all that Sebastian Vettel could throw at him. As in 2017, Red Bull Racing, and Max Verstappen in particular, went better in the later races when it was he, rather than the Ferrari drivers, who pushed Hamilton hardest. Behind them, Renault led the midfield pack.

AUSTRALIAN GRAND PRIX

ALBERT PARK • ROUND 1 • DATE: 25TH MARCH 2018
Laps: 58 • Distance: 191.117miles/307.574km • Weather: Warm & bright

Pos	Driver	Team	Chassis-Engine	Result	Qual
1	Sebastian Vettel	Ferrari	Ferrari SF71H	1h29m33.283s	3
2	Lewis Hamilton	Mercedes AMG	Mercedes F1 W09	1h29m38.319s	1
3	Kimi Raikkonen	Ferrari	Ferrari SF71H	1h29m39.592s	2
4	Daniel Ricciardo *	Red Bull Racing	Red Bull-TAG Heuer RB14	1h29m40.352s	8
5	Fernando Alonso	McLaren	McLaren-Renault MCL33	1h30m01.169s	10
6	Max Verstappen	Red Bull Racing	Red Bull-TAG Heuer RB14	1h30m02.228s	4
7	Nico Hulkenberg	Renault F1	Renault RS18	1h30m05.954s	7
8	Valtteri Bottas !	Mercedes AMG	Mercedes F1 W09	1h30m07.622s	15
9	Stoffel Vandoorne	McLaren	McLaren-Renault MCL33	1h30m08.204s	11
10	Carlos Sainz	Renault F1	Renault RS18	1h30m19.005s	9
11	Sergio Perez	Force India	Force India-Mercedes VJM11	1h30m20.100s	12
12	Esteban Ocon	Force India	Force India-Mercedes VJM11	1h30m33.561s	14
13	Charles Leclerc	Sauber	Sauber-Ferrari C37	1h30m49.042s	18
14	Lance Stroll	Williams	Williams-Mercedes FW41	1h30m51.571s	13
15	Brendon Hartley	Toro Rosso	Toro Rosso-Honda STR13	57 laps	16
R	Romain Grosjean	Haas	Haas-Ferrari VF-18	24 laps/wheel nut	6
R	Kevin Magnussen	Haas	Haas-Ferrari VF-18	22 laps/wheel nut	5
R	Pierre Gasly	Toro Rosso	Toro Rosso-Honda STR13	13 laps/power unit	20
R	Marcus Ericsson	Sauber	Sauber-Ferrari C37	5 laps/hydraulics	17
R	Sergey Sirotkin	Williams	Williams-Mercedes FW41	4 laps/brakes	19

Pole: Hamilton, 1m21.164s, 146.153mph/235.212kph. Fastest lap: Ricciardo, 1m25.945s, 138.024mph/222.128kph on Lap 54. Race leaders: Hamilton 1-18, Vettel 19-58

* 3-place grid penalty for excessive speed under red flags • ! 5-place grid penalty for gearbox change

HEAD PROTECTION

In the 1950s, drivers appeared to sit on their F1 cars rather than in them. Roll hoops made them safer in the 1960s, but the arrival in 2018 of "halo" head protection was a huge advance. Triggered by former F1 racer Justin Wilson being killed by an errant wheel in an IndyCar race, F1 made this wishbone-like bodywork above the driver's head mandatory.

BAHRAIN GRAND PRIX

SAKHIR • ROUND 2 • DATE: 8TH APRIL 2018
Laps: 57 • Distance: 191.683miles/308.484km • Weather: Hot & bright

Pos	Driver	Team	Chassis-Engine	Result	Qual
1	Sebastian Vettel	Ferrari	Ferrari SF71H	1h32m01.940s	1
2	Valtteri Bottas	Mercedes AMG	Mercedes F1 W09	1h32m02.639s	3
3	Lewis Hamilton	Mercedes AMG	Mercedes F1 W09	1h32m08.452s	9
4	Pierre Gasly	Toro Rosso	Toro Rosso-Honda STR13	1h33m04.174s	5
5	Kevin Magnussen	Haas	Haas-Ferrari VF-18	1h33m16.986s	6
6	Nico Hulkenberg	Renault F1	Renault RS18	1h33m40.964s	7
7	Fernando Alonso	McLaren	McLaren-Renault MCL33	56 laps	13
8	Stoffel Vandoorne	McLaren	McLaren-Renault MCL33	56 laps	14
9	Marcus Ericsson	Sauber	Sauber-Ferrari C37	56 laps	17
10	Esteban Ocon	Force India	Force India-Mercedes VJM11	56 laps	8
11	Carlos Sainz	Renault F1	Renault RS18	56 laps	10
12	Charles Leclerc	Sauber	Sauber-Ferrari C37	56 laps	19
13	Romain Grosjean	Haas	Haas-Ferrari VF-18	56 laps	16
14	Lance Stroll	Williams	Williams-Mercedes FW41	56 laps	20
15	Sergey Sirotkin	Williams	Williams-Mercedes FW41	56 laps	18
16	Sergio Perez *	Force India	Force India-Mercedes VJM11	56 laps	12
17	Brendon Hartley !	Toro Rosso	Toro Rosso-Honda STR13	56 laps	11
R	Kimi Raikkonen	Ferrari	Ferrari SF71H	35 laps/wheel	2
R	Max Verstappen	Red Bull Racing	Red Bull-TAG Heuer RB14	3 laps/collision	15
R	Daniel Ricciardo	Red Bull Racing	Red Bull-TAG Heuer RB14	1 lap/electrical	4

Pole: Vettel, 1m27.958s, 137.636mph/221.505kph. Fastest lap: Bottas, 1m33.740s, 129.147mph/207.842kph on Lap 22. Race leaders: Vettel 1-17 & 26-57, Bottas 18-20, Hamilton 21-25

* 30s penalty for overtaking on the formation lap • ! 30s penalty for failing to re-establish original start order

A CLUMSY SWAP

Valtteri Bottas knew that Lewis Hamilton was invariably the faster of the Mercedes drivers. However, it rankled with him on days when he had the upper hand to be told to let Hamilton through. This was handled poorly at the Russian GP when the Finn was told to pull aside and settle for second, meaning that his first win of the year would have to wait.

A RISING STAR

Charles Leclerc made a serious impression with some stunning performances that made him look like anything other than a rookie. The reigning F2 champion slotted in alongside Marcus Ericsson at Sauber and was soon the team leader, thanks to his outstanding ability to put the car where it didn't deserve to be, and finishing sixth in Baku.

CHINESE GRAND PRIX

SHANGHAI INTERNATIONAL CIRCUIT • ROUND 3 • DATE: 15TH APRIL 2018
Laps: 56 • Distance: 189.677miles/305.256km • Weather: Warm & bright

Pos	Driver	Team	Chassis-Engine	Result	Qual
1	Daniel Ricciardo	Red Bull Racing	Red Bull-TAG Heuer RB14	1h35m36.380s	6
2	Valtteri Bottas	Mercedes AMG	Mercedes F1 W09	1h35m45.274s	3
3	Kimi Raikkonen	Ferrari	Ferrari SF71H	1h35m46.017s	2
4	Lewis Hamilton	Mercedes AMG	Mercedes F1 W09	1h35m53.365s	4
5	Max Verstappen !	Red Bull Racing	Red Bull-TAG Heuer RB14	1h35m56.816s	5
6	Nico Hulkenberg	Renault F1	Renault RS18	1h35m57.432s	7
7	Fernando Alonso	McLaren	McLaren-Renault MCL33	1h36m07.019s	13
8	Sebastian Vettel	Ferrari	Ferrari SF71H	1h36m11.666s	1
9	Carlos Sainz	Renault F1	Renault RS18	1h36m12.143s	9
10	Kevin Magnussen	Haas	Haas-Ferrari VF-18	1h36m15.974s	11
11	Esteban Ocon	Force India	Force India-Mercedes VJM11	1h36m20.430s	12
12	Sergio Perez	Force India	Force India-Mercedes VJM11	1h36m21.105s	8
13	Stoffel Vandoorne	McLaren	McLaren-Renault MCL33	1h36m25.753s	14
14	Lance Stroll	Williams	Williams-Mercedes FW41	1h36m31.870s	18
15	Sergey Sirotkin	Williams	Williams-Mercedes FW41	1h36m34.621s	16
16	Marcus Ericsson *	Sauber	Sauber-Ferrari C37	1h36m38.984s	20
17	Romain Grosjean	Haas	Haas-Ferrari VF-18	1h36m41.676s	10
18	Pierre Gasly !	Toro Rosso	Toro Rosso-Honda STR13	1h36m42.710s	17
19	Charles Leclerc	Sauber	Sauber-Ferrari C37	1h36m58.955s	19
20	Brendon Hartley	Toro Rosso	Toro Rosso-Honda STR13	51 laps/gearbox	15

Pole: Vettel, 1m31.095s, 133.855mph/215.419kph. Fastest lap: Ricciardo, 1m35.785s, 127.301mph/204.871kph on Lap 55. Race leaders: Vettel 1-20, Raikkonen 21-26, Bottas 27-44, Ricciardo 45-56

* 5-place grid penalty for failing to slow for double waved yellow flags • ! 10s penalty for causing an accident

AZERBAIJAN GRAND PRIX

BAKU CITY CIRCUIT • ROUND 4 • DATE: 29TH APRIL 2018
Laps: 51 • Distance: 190.234miles/306.153km • Weather: Warm but dull

Pos	Driver	Team	Chassis-Engine	Result	Qual
1	Lewis Hamilton	Mercedes AMG	Mercedes F1 W09	1h43m44.291s	2
2	Kimi Raikkonen	Ferrari	Ferrari SF71H	1h43m46.751s	6
3	Sergio Perez	Force India	Force India-Mercedes VJM11	1h43m48.315s	8
4	Sebastian Vettel	Ferrari	Ferrari SF71H	1h43m49.620s	1
5	Carlos Sainz	Renault F1	Renault RS18	1h43m51.806s	9
6	Charles Leclerc	Sauber	Sauber-Ferrari C37	1h43m53.449s	13
7	Fernando Alonso	McLaren	McLaren-Renault MCL33	1h43m55.222s	12
8	Lance Stroll	Williams	Williams-Mercedes FW41	1h43m56.837s	10
9	Stoffel Vandoorne	McLaren	McLaren-Renault MCL33	1h43m58.443s	16
10	Brendon Hartley	Toro Rosso	Toro Rosso-Honda STR13	1h44m02.321s	19
11	Marcus Ericsson	Sauber	Sauber-Ferrari C37	1h44m02.803s	18
12	Pierre Gasly	Toro Rosso	Toro Rosso-Honda STR13	1h44m09.011s	17
13	Kevin Magnussen !	Haas	Haas-Ferrari VF-18	1h44m24.954s	15
14	Valtteri Bottas	Mercedes AMG	Mercedes F1 W09	48 laps/tyre	3
R	Romain Grosjean *	Haas	Haas-Ferrari VF-18	42 laps/spun off	20
R	Daniel Ricciardo	Red Bull Racing	Red Bull-TAG Heuer RB14	39 laps/collision	4
R	Max Verstappen	Red Bull Racing	Red Bull-TAG Heuer RB14	39 laps/collision	5

Pos	Driver	Team	Chassis-Engine	Result	Qual
R	Nico Hulkenberg *	Renault F1	Renault RS18	10 laps/spun off	14
R	Esteban Ocon	Force India	Force India-Mercedes VJM11	0 laps/collision	7
R	Sergey Sirotkin	Williams	Williams-Mercedes FW41	0 laps/collision	11

Pole: Vettel, 1m41.498s, 132.301mph/212.918kph. Fastest lap: Bottas, 1m45.149s, 127.707mph/205.525kph on Lap 37. Race leaders: Vettel 1-30, Bottas 31-48, Hamilton 49-51

* 5-place grid penalty for gearbox change • ! 10s penalty for causing a crash with Gasly

SPANISH GRAND PRIX

BARCELONA-CATALUNYA • ROUND 5 • DATE: 13TH MAY 2018
Laps: 66 • Distance: 190.775miles/307.23km • Weather: Warm & bright

Pos	Driver	Team	Chassis-Engine	Result	Qual
1	Lewis Hamilton	Mercedes AMG	Mercedes F1 W09	1h35m29.972s	1
2	Valtteri Bottas	Mercedes AMG	Mercedes F1 W09	1h35m50.565s	2
3	Max Verstappen	Red Bull Racing	Red Bull-TAG Heuer RB14	1h35m56.845s	5
4	Sebastian Vettel	Ferrari	Ferrari SF71H	1h35m57.556s	3
5	Daniel Ricciardo	Red Bull Racing	Red Bull-TAG Heuer RB14	1h36m20.030s	6
6	Kevin Magnussen	Haas	Haas-Ferrari VF-18	65 laps	7
7	Carlos Sainz	Renault F1	Renault RS18	65 laps	9
8	Fernando Alonso	McLaren	McLaren-Renault MCL33	65 laps	8
9	Sergio Perez	Force India	Force India-Mercedes VJM11	64 laps	15
10	Charles Leclerc	Sauber	Sauber-Ferrari C37	64 laps	14
11	Lance Stroll	Williams	Williams-Mercedes FW41	64 laps	18
12	Brendon Hartley !	Toro Rosso	Toro Rosso-Honda STR13	64 laps	20
13	Marcus Ericsson	Sauber	Sauber-Ferrari C37	64 laps	17
14	Sergey Sirotkin *	Williams	Williams-Mercedes FW41	63 laps	19
R	Stoffel Vandoorne	McLaren	McLaren-Renault MCL33	45 laps/gearbox	11
R	Esteban Ocon	Force India	Force India-Mercedes VJM11	38 laps/oil leak	13
R	Kimi Raikkonen	Ferrari	Ferrari SF71H	25 laps/power unit	4
R	Romain Grosjean	Haas	Haas-Ferrari VF-18	0 laps/collision	10
R	Pierre Gasly	Toro Rosso	Toro Rosso-Honda STR13	0 laps/collision	12
R	Nico Hulkenberg	Renault F1	Renault RS18	0 laps/collision	16

Pole: Hamilton, 1n16.173s, 136.609mph/219.851kph. Fastest lap: Ricciardo, 1m18.441s, 132.748mph/213.638kph on Lap 61. Race leaders: Hamilton 1-25 & 34-66, Verstappen 26-33

* 3-place grid penalty for causing a crash in Azerbaijan GP • ! 5-place grid penalty for gearbox change

MONACO GRAND PRIX

MONTE CARLO • ROUND 6 • DATE: 27TH MAY 2018
Laps: 78 • Distance: 161.734miles/260.286km • Weather: Hot & bright

Pos	Driver	Team	Chassis-Engine	Result	Qual
1	Daniel Ricciardo	Red Bull Racing	Red Bull-TAG Heuer RB14	1h42m54.807s	1
2	Sebastian Vettel	Ferrari	Ferrari SF71H	1h43m02.143s	2
3	Lewis Hamilton	Mercedes AMG	Mercedes F1 W09	1h43m11.820s	3
4	Kimi Raikkonen	Ferrari	Ferrari SF71H	1h43m12.934s	4
5	Valtteri Bottas	Mercedes AMG	Mercedes F1 W09	1h43m13.629s	5
6	Esteban Ocon	Force India	Force India-Mercedes VJM11	1h43m18.474s	6
7	Pierre Gasly	Toro Rosso	Toro Rosso-Honda STR13	1h43m19.138s	10
8	Nico Hulkenberg	Renault F1	Renault RS18	1h43m19.646s	11
9	Max Verstappen !/^	Red Bull Racing	Red Bull-TAG Heuer RB14	1h43m20.124s	20
10	Carlos Sainz	Renault F1	Renault RS18	1h44m03.820s	8

Pos	Driver	Team	Chassis-Engine	Result	Qual
11	Marcus Ericsson	Sauber	Sauber-Ferrari C37	1h44m04.671s	16
12	Sergio Perez	Force India	Force India-Mercedes VJM11	1h44m05.268s	9
13	Kevin Magnussen	Haas	Haas-Ferrari VF-18	1h44m09.630s	19
14	Stoffel Vandoorne	McLaren	McLaren-Renault MCL33	77 laps	12
15	Romain Grosjean *	Haas	Haas-Ferrari VF-18	77 laps	18
16	Sergey Sirotkin	Williams	Williams-Mercedes FW41	77 laps	13
17	Lance Stroll	Williams	Williams-Mercedes FW41	76 laps	17
18	Charles Leclerc	Sauber	Sauber-Ferrari C37	70 laps/brakes	14
19	Brendon Hartley †	Toro Rosso	Toro Rosso-Honda STR13	70 laps/collision	15
R	Fernando Alonso	McLaren	McLaren-Renault MCL33	52 laps/gearbox	7

Pole: Ricciardo, 1m10.810s, 105.418mph/169.654kph. Fastest lap: Verstappen, 1m14.260s, 100.520mph/161.772kph on Lap 60. Race leaders: Ricciardo 1-78

* 3-place grid penalty for causing a crash in Spanish GP • ! 5-place grid penalty for gearbox change • ^ 10-place grid penalty for using additional power unit elements • † 5s penalty for speeding in the pit lane

CANADIAN GRAND PRIX

MONTREAL • ROUND 7 • DATE: 10TH JUNE 2018
Laps: 68 • Distance: 184.266miles/296.548km • Weather: Warm & bright

Pos	Driver	Team	Chassis-Engine	Result	Qual
1	Sebastian Vettel	Ferrari	Ferrari SF71H	1h28m31.377s	1
2	Valtteri Bottas	Mercedes AMG	Mercedes F1 W09	1h28m38.753s	2
3	Max Verstappen	Red Bull Racing	Red Bull-TAG Heuer RB14	1h28m39.737s	3
4	Daniel Ricciardo	Red Bull Racing	Red Bull-TAG Heuer RB14	1h28m52.269s	6
5	Lewis Hamilton	Mercedes AMG	Mercedes F1 W09	1h28m52.936s	4
6	Kimi Raikkonen	Ferrari	Ferrari SF71H	1h28m58.561s	5
7	Nico Hulkenberg	Renault F1	Renault RS18	67 laps	7
8	Carlos Sainz	Renault F1	Renault RS18	67 laps	9
9	Esteban Ocon	Force India	Force India-Mercedes VJM11	67 laps	8
10	Charles Leclerc	Sauber	Sauber-Ferrari C37	67 laps	13
11	Pierre Gasly *	Toro Rosso	Toro Rosso-Honda STR13	67 laps	19
12	Romain Grosjean	Haas	Haas-Ferrari VF-18	67 laps	20
13	Kevin Magnussen	Haas	Haas-Ferrari VF-18	67 laps	11
14	Sergio Perez	Force India	Force India-Mercedes VJM11	67 laps	10
15	Marcus Ericsson	Sauber	Sauber-Ferrari C37	66 laps	18
16	Stoffel Vandoorne	McLaren	McLaren-Renault MCL33	66 laps	15
17	Sergey Sirotkin	Williams	Williams-Mercedes FW41	66 laps	17
R	Fernando Alonso	McLaren	McLaren-Renault MCL33	40 laps/exhaust	14
R	Brendon Hartley	Toro Rosso	Toro Rosso-Honda STR13	0 laps/collision	12
R	Lance Stroll	Williams	Williams-Mercedes FW41	0 laps/collision	16

Pole: Vettel, 1m10.764s, 137.856mph/221.858kph. Fastest lap: Verstappen, 1m13.864s, 132.070mph/212.547kph on Lap 65. Race leaders: Vettel 1-68

* made to start from rear of grid for using additional power unit elements

VETTEL'S COSTLY ERRORS

Sebastian Vettel led the World Championship through the first half of the season. However, he dropped the ball by crashing at the first corner of the French GP, dropping him down the order, then slid out of the lead and into the gravel trap in the wet at Hockenheim, helping Hamilton to win.

FRENCH GRAND PRIX

CIRCUIT PAUL RICARD • ROUND 8 • DATE: 24TH JUNE 2018
Laps: 53 • Distance: 192.392miles/309.626km • Weather: Hot & bright

Pos	Driver	Team	Chassis-Engine	Result	Qual
1	Lewis Hamilton	Mercedes AMG	Mercedes F1 W09	1h30m11.385s	1
2	Max Verstappen	Red Bull Racing	Red Bull-TAG Heuer RB14	1h30m18.475s	4
3	Kimi Raikkonen	Ferrari	Ferrari SF71H	1h30m37.273s	6
4	Daniel Ricciardo	Red Bull Racing	Red Bull-TAG Heuer RB14	1h30m46.121s	5
5	Sebastian Vettel	Ferrari	Ferrari SF71H	1h31m13.320s	3
6	Kevin Magnussen	Haas	Haas-Ferrari VF-18	1h31m30.749s	9
7	Valtteri Bottas	Mercedes AMG	Mercedes F1 W09	1h31m32.017s	2
8	Carlos Sainz	Renault F1	Renault RS18	1h31m38.569s	7
9	Nico Hulkenberg	Renault F1	Renault RS18	1h31m43.374s	12
10	Charles Leclerc	Sauber	Sauber-Ferrari C37	1h31m45.258s	8
11	Romain Grosjean	Haas	Haas-Ferrari VF-18	52 laps	10
12	Stoffel Vandoorne	McLaren	McLaren-Renault MCL33	52 laps	17
13	Marcus Ericsson	Sauber	Sauber-Ferrari C37	52 laps	15
14	Brendon Hartley *	Toro Rosso	Toro Rosso-Honda STR13	52 laps	20
15	Sergey Sirotkin !	Williams	Williams-Mercedes FW41	52 laps	18
16	Fernando Alonso	McLaren	McLaren-Renault MCL33	50 laps/suspension	16
17	Lance Stroll	Williams	Williams-Mercedes FW41	48 laps/tyre	19
R	Sergio Perez	Force India	Force India-Mercedes VJM11	27 laps/power unit	13
R	Esteban Ocon	Force India	Force India-Mercedes VJM11	0 laps/collision	11
R	Pierre Gasly	Toro Rosso	Toro Rosso-Honda STR13	0 laps/collision	14

Pole: Hamilton, 1m30.029s, 145.154mph/233.604kph. Fastest lap: Bottas, 1m34.225s, 138.691mph/223.201kph on Lap 41. Race leaders: Hamilton 1-32 & 34-53, Raikkonen 33

* made to start from rear of grid for using additional power unit elements • ! 5s penalty for driving too slowly behind safety car

CHANGE AT A PRICE

Force India ended up ranked only seventh ion the constructors' championship as it had to forfeit the 59 points that it had scored before the Belgian GP in order to enable it to change its name to Racing Point. Had it been able to keep them, the team from Silverstone would have ended the year fifth overall, just 11 points behind Renault.

AUSTRIAN GRAND PRIX

RED BULL RING • ROUND 9 • DATE: 1ST JULY 2018
Laps: 71 • Distance: 190.498miles/306.578km • Weather: Warm & bright

Pos	Driver	Team	Chassis-Engine	Result	Qual
1	Max Verstappen	Red Bull Racing	Red Bull-TAG Heuer RB14	1h21m56.024s	4
2	Kimi Raikkonen	Ferrari	Ferrari SF71H	1h21m57.528s	3
3	Sebastian Vettel *	Ferrari	Ferrari SF71H	1h21m59.205s	6
4	Romain Grosjean	Haas	Haas-Ferrari VF-18	70 laps	5
5	Kevin Magnussen	Haas	Haas-Ferrari VF-18	70 laps	8
6	Esteban Ocon	Force India	Force India-Mercedes VJM11	70 laps	11
7	Sergio Perez	Force India	Force India-Mercedes VJM11	70 laps	15
8	Fernando Alonso †	McLaren	McLaren-Renault MCL33	70 laps	20

Pos	Driver	Team	Chassis-Engine	Result	Qual
9	Charles Leclerc !	Sauber	Sauber-Ferrari C37	70 laps	17
10	Marcus Ericsson	Sauber	Sauber-Ferrari C37	70 laps	18
11	Pierre Gasly	Toro Rosso	Toro Rosso-Honda STR13	70 laps	12
12	Carlos Sainz	Renault F1	Renault RS18	70 laps	9
13	Sergey Sirotkin	Williams	Williams-Mercedes FW41	69 laps	16
14	Lance Stroll ‡	Williams	Williams-Mercedes FW41	69 laps	13
15	Stoffel Vandoorne	McLaren	McLaren-Renault MCL33	65 laps/gearbox	14
R	Lewis Hamilton	Mercedes AMG	Mercedes F1 W09	62 laps/fuel pressure	2
R	Brendon Hartley ^	Toro Rosso	Toro Rosso-Honda STR13	54 laps/mechanical	19
R	Daniel Ricciardo	Red Bull Racing	Red Bull-TAG Heuer RB14	53 laps/exhaust	7
R	Valtteri Bottas	Mercedes AMG	Mercedes F1 W09	13 laps/hydraulics	1
R	Nico Hulkenberg	Renault F1	Renault RS18	11 laps/turbo	10

Pole: Bottas, 1m03.130s, 153.002mph/246.234kph. Fastest lap: Raikkonen, 1m06.957s, 144.258mph/232.160kph on Lap 71. Race leaders: Hamilton 1-25, Verstappen 26-71

* 3-place grid penalty for impeding Sainz • ! 5-place grid penalty for gearbox change • ^ made to start from rear of grid for using additional power unit elements • † made to start from pit lane for car being modified in parc ferme • ‡ 10s penalty for ignoring blue flags

DANGER AT TURN 1

The perils of Spa-Francorchamps' first corner, the La Source hairpin, were made clear yet again on the opening lap of the Belgian GP. Fernando Alonso's McLaren had been hit from behind by Nico Hulkenberg's Renault when the German left his braking too late and launched the Spaniard onto and then over Charles Leclerc's Sauber.

BRITISH GRAND PRIX

SILVERSTONE • ROUND 10 • DATE: 8TH JULY 2018
Laps: 52 • Distance: 190.345miles/306.332km • Weather: Hot & bright

Pos	Driver	Team	Chassis-Engine	Result	Qual
1	Sebastian Vettel	Ferrari	Ferrari SF71H	1h27m29.784s	2
2	Lewis Hamilton	Mercedes AMG	Mercedes F1 W09	1h27m32.048s	1
3	Kimi Raikkonen	Ferrari	Ferrari SF71H	1h27m33.436s	3
4	Valtteri Bottas	Mercedes AMG	Mercedes F1 W09	1h27m38.667s	4
5	Daniel Ricciardo	Red Bull Racing	Red Bull-TAG Heuer RB14	1h27m39.284s	6
6	Nico Hulkenberg	Renault F1	Renault RS18	1h27m58.004s	11
7	Esteban Ocon	Force India	Force India-Mercedes VJM11	1h27m59.714s	10
8	Fernando Alonso	McLaren	McLaren-Renault MCL33	1h28m00.899s	13
9	Kevin Magnussen	Haas	Haas-Ferrari VF-18	1h28m02.972s	7
10	Sergio Perez	Force India	Force India-Mercedes VJM11	1h28m04.492s	12
11	Stoffel Vandoorne	McLaren	McLaren-Renault MCL33	1h28m05.558s	17
12	Lance Stroll *	Williams	Williams-Mercedes FW41	1h28m07.890s	19
13	Pierre Gasly ^	Toro Rosso	Toro Rosso-Honda STR13	1h28m08.913s	14
14	Sergey Sirotkin *	Williams	Williams-Mercedes FW41	1h28m17.897s	18
15	Max Verstappen	Red Bull Racing	Red Bull-TAG Heuer RB14	46 laps/brakes	5
R	Romain Grosjean	Haas	Haas-Ferrari VF-18	37 laps/collision	8
R	Carlos Sainz	Renault F1	Renault RS18	37 laps/collision	16

Pos	Driver	Team	Chassis-Engine	Result	Qual
R	Marcus Ericsson	Sauber	Sauber-Ferrari C37	31 laps/spun off	15
R	Charles Leclerc	Sauber	Sauber-Ferrari C37	18 laps/wheel	9
R	Brendon Hartley !	Toro Rosso	Toro Rosso-Honda STR13	1 lap/power unit	20

Pole: Hamilton, 1m25.892s, 153.422mph/246.910kph. Fastest lap: Vettel, 1m30.696s, 145.296mph/233.831kph on Lap 47. Race leaders: Vettel 1-20 & 22-33 & 47-52, Bottas 21 & 34-46

* made to start from pit lane for car being modified in parc ferme • ! made to start from pit lane for new survival cell being fitted & for using additional power unit elements • ^ 5s penalty for causing an accident

GERMAN GRAND PRIX

HOCKENHEIM • ROUND 11 • DATE: 22ND JULY 2018
Laps: 67 • Distance: 190.424miles/306.458km • Weather: Rain showers

Pos	Driver	Team	Chassis-Engine	Result	Qual
1	Lewis Hamilton	Mercedes AMG	Mercedes F1 W09	1h32m29.845s	14
2	Valtteri Bottas	Mercedes AMG	Mercedes F1 W09	1h32m34.380s	2
3	Kimi Raikkonen	Ferrari	Ferrari SF71H	1h32m36.577s	3
4	Max Verstappen	Red Bull Racing	Red Bull-TAG Heuer RB14	1h32m37.499s	4
5	Nico Hulkenberg	Renault F1	Renault RS18	1h32m56.454s	7
6	Romain Grosjean	Haas	Haas-Ferrari VF-18	1h32m58.716s	6
7	Sergio Perez	Force India	Force India-Mercedes VJM11	1h33m00.401s	10
8	Esteban Ocon	Force India	Force India-Mercedes VJM11	1h33m01.595s	15
9	Marcus Ericsson	Sauber	Sauber-Ferrari C37	1h33m02.207s	13
10	Brendon Hartley	Toro Rosso	Toro Rosso-Honda STR13	1h33m04.042s	16
11	Kevin Magnussen	Haas	Haas-Ferrari VF-18	1h33m04.764s	5
12	Carlos Sainz !	Renault F1	Renault RS18	1h33m12.914s	8
13	Stoffel Vandoorne	McLaren	McLaren-Renault MCL33	1h33m16.462s	18
14	Pierre Gasly *	Toro Rosso	Toro Rosso-Honda STR13	66 laps	20
15	Charles Leclerc	Sauber	Sauber-Ferrari C37	66 laps	9
16	Fernando Alonso	McLaren	McLaren-Renault MCL33	65 laps/gearbox	11
R	Lance Stroll	Williams	Williams-Mercedes FW41	53 laps/brakes	17
R	Sebastian Vettel	Ferrari	Ferrari SF71H	51 laps/spun off	1
R	Sergey Sirotkin	Williams	Williams-Mercedes FW41	51 laps/oil leak	12
R	Daniel Ricciardo	Red Bull Racing	Red Bull-TAG Heuer RB14	27 laps/power unit	19

Pole: Vettel, 1m11.212s, 143.679mph/231.230kph. Fastest lap: Hamilton, 1m15.545s, 135.439mph/217.968kph on Lap 66. Race leaders: Vettel 1-25 & 39-51, Bottas 26-28 & 52, Raikkonen 29-38, Hamilton 53-67

* made to start from rear of grid for using additional power unit elements • ! 10s penalty for overtaking under safety car conditions

HUNGARIAN GRAND PRIX

HUNGARORING • ROUND 12 • DATE: 29TH JULY 2018
Laps: 70 • Distance: 190.181miles/306.67km • Weather: Very hot & bright

Pos	Driver	Team	Chassis-Engine	Result	Qual
1	Lewis Hamilton	Mercedes AMG	Mercedes F1 W09	1h37m16.427s	1
2	Sebastian Vettel	Ferrari	Ferrari SF71H	1h37m33.550s	4
3	Kimi Raikkonen	Ferrari	Ferrari SF71H	1h37m36.528s	3
4	Daniel Ricciardo	Red Bull Racing	Red Bull-TAG Heuer RB14	1h38m02.846s	12
5	Valtteri Bottas !	Mercedes AMG	Mercedes F1 W09	1h38m16.427s	2
6	Pierre Gasly	Toro Rosso	Toro Rosso-Honda STR13	1h38m29.700s	6

Pos	Driver	Team	Chassis-Engine	Result	Qual
7	Kevin Magnussen	Haas	Haas-Ferrari VF-18	69 laps	9
8	Fernando Alonso	McLaren	McLaren-Renault MCL33	69 laps	11
9	Carlos Sainz	Renault F1	Renault RS18	69 laps	5
10	Romain Grosjean	Haas	Haas-Ferrari VF-18	69 laps	10
11	Brendon Hartley	Toro Rosso	Toro Rosso-Honda STR13	69 laps	8
12	Nico Hulkenberg	Renault F1	Renault RS18	69 laps	13
13	Esteban Ocon	Force India	Force India-Mercedes VJM11	69 laps	17
14	Sergio Perez	Force India	Force India-Mercedes VJM11	69 laps	18
15	Marcus Ericsson	Sauber	Sauber-Ferrari C37	68 laps	14
16	Sergey Sirotkin	Williams	Williams-Mercedes FW41	68 laps	19
17	Lance Stroll *	Williams	Williams-Mercedes FW41	68 laps	20
R	Stoffel Vandoorne	McLaren	McLaren-Renault MCL33	49 laps/gearbox	15
R	Max Verstappen	Red Bull Racing	Red Bull-TAG Heuer RB14	5 laps/power unit	7
R	Charles Leclerc	Sauber	Sauber-Ferrari C37	0 laps/collision	16

Pole: Hamilton, 1m35.658s, 102.447mph/164.874kph. Fastest lap: Ricciardo, 1m20.012s, 122.481mph/197.115kph on Lap 46. Race leaders: Hamilton 1-25 & 40-70, Vettel 26-39

* made to start from rear of grid for car being modified in parc ferme • ! 10s penalty for causing an accident

BELGIAN GRAND PRIX

SPA-FRANCORCHAMPS • ROUND 13 • DATE: 26TH AUGUST 2018
Laps: 44 • Distance: 191.491miles/308.176km • Weather: Warm & bright

Pos	Driver	Team	Chassis-Engine	Result	Qual
1	Sebastian Vettel	Ferrari	Ferrari SF71H	1h23m34.476s	2
2	Lewis Hamilton	Mercedes AMG	Mercedes F1 W09	1h23m45.537s	1
3	Max Verstappen	Red Bull Racing	Red Bull-TAG Heuer RB14	1h24m05.848s	7
4	Valtteri Bottas */!	Mercedes AMG	Mercedes F1 W09	1h24m43.081s	17
5	Sergio Perez	Force India	Force India-Mercedes VJM11	1h24m45.499s	4
6	Esteban Ocon	Force India	Force India-Mercedes VJM11	1h24m53.996s	3
7	Romain Grosjean	Haas	Haas-Ferrari VF-18	1h25m00.429s	5
8	Kevin Magnussen	Haas	Haas-Ferrari VF-18	1h25m02.115s	9
9	Pierre Gasly	Toro Rosso	Toro Rosso-Honda STR13	1h25m20.368s	10
10	Marcus Ericsson	Sauber	Sauber-Ferrari C37	43 laps	13
11	Carlos Sainz *	Renault F1	Renault RS18	43 laps	19
12	Sergey Sirotkin	Williams	Williams-Mercedes FW41	43 laps	15
13	Lance Stroll	Williams	Williams-Mercedes FW41	43 laps	16
14	Brendon Hartley	Toro Rosso	Toro Rosso-Honda STR13	43 laps	11
15	Stoffel Vandoorne *	McLaren	McLaren-Renault MCL33	43 laps	20
R	Daniel Ricciardo	Red Bull Racing	Red Bull-TAG Heuer RB14	28 laps/accident	8
R	Kimi Raikkonen	Ferrari	Ferrari SF71H	8 laps/accident	6
R	Charles Leclerc	Sauber	Sauber-Ferrari C37	0 laps/collision	12
R	Fernando Alonso	McLaren	McLaren-Renault MCL33	0 laps/collision	14
R	Nico Hulkenberg *	Renault F1	Renault RS18	0 laps/collision	18

Pole: Hamilton, 1m58.179s, 132.573mph/213.357kph. Fastest lap: Bottas, 1m46.286s, 147.408mph/237.231kph on Lap 32. Race leaders: Vettel 1-44

* made to start from rear of grid for using additional power unit elements • ! 5s penalty for causing an accident

ITALIAN GRAND PRIX

MONZA • ROUND 14 • DATE: 2ND SEPTEMBER 2018
Laps: 53 • Distance: 190.778miles/307.029km • Weather: Hot & bright

Pos	Driver	Team	Chassis-Engine	Result	Qual
1	Lewis Hamilton	Mercedes AMG	Mercedes F1 W09	1h16m54.484s	3
2	Kimi Raikkonen	Ferrari	Ferrari SF71H	1h17m03.189s	1
3	Valtteri Bottas	Mercedes AMG	Mercedes F1 W09	1h17m08.550s	4
4	Sebastian Vettel	Ferrari	Ferrari SF71H	1h17m10.635s	2
5	Max Verstappen †	Red Bull Racing	Red Bull-TAG Heuer RB14	1h17m12.692s	5
DQ	Romain Grosjean	Haas	Haas-Ferrari VF-18	53 laps/Illegal bodywork	6
6	Esteban Ocon *	Force India	Force India-Mercedes VJM11	1h17m52.245s	8
7	Sergio Perez	Force India	Force India-Mercedes VJM11	1h17m53.162s	14
8	Carlos Sainz	Renault F1	Renault RS18	1h18m12.624s	7
9	Lance Stroll	Williams	Williams-Mercedes FW41	52 laps	10
10	Sergey Sirotkin	Williams	Williams-Mercedes FW41	52 laps	12
11	Charles Leclerc	Sauber	Sauber-Ferrari C37	52 laps	15
12	Stoffel Vandoorne	McLaren	McLaren-Renault MCL33	52 laps	17
13	Nico Hulkenberg !/^	Renault F1	Renault RS18	52 laps	20
14	Pierre Gasly	Toro Rosso	Toro Rosso-Honda STR13	52 laps	9
15	Marcus Ericsson *	Sauber	Sauber-Ferrari C37	52 laps	18
16	Kevin Magnussen	Haas	Haas-Ferrari VF-18	52 laps	11
R	Daniel Ricciardo !	Red Bull Racing	Red Bull-TAG Heuer RB14	23 laps/clutch	19
R	Fernando Alonso	McLaren	McLaren-Renault MCL33	9 laps/electrical	13
R	Brendon Hartley	Toro Rosso	Toro Rosso-Honda STR13	0 laps/collision	16

Pole: Raikkonen, 1m19.119s, 163.785mph/263.587kph. Fastest lap: Hamilton, 1m22.497s, 157.079mph/252.794kph on Lap 30. Race leaders: Raikkonen 1-19 & 36-44, Hamilton 20-28 & 45-53, Bottas 29-35

* 10-place grid penalty for using additional power unit elements • ! made to start from rear of grid for using additional power unit elements • ^ 10-pace grid penalty for causing a crash in Belgian GP • † 5s penalty for causing an accident

AN UNUSUAL ERROR

It's a rare thing in F1 history that a driver unlapping himself takes a potential winner out of a grand prix. This is what happened, though, in the Brazilian GP. Esteban Ocon was on fresh tyres after a pitstop and decided to use this brief performance advantage to pass leader Max Verstappen. They clashed in the Senna S and both spun.

SINGAPORE GRAND PRIX

MARINA BAY CIRCUIT • ROUND 15 • DATE: 16TH SEPTEMBER 2018
Laps: 61 • Distance: 191.906miles/308.843km • Weather: Very hot & humid

Pos	Driver	Team	Chassis-Engine	Result	Qual
1	Lewis Hamilton	Mercedes AMG	Mercedes F1 W09	1h51m11.611s	1
2	Max Verstappen	Red Bull Racing	Red Bull-TAG Heuer RB14	1h51m20.572s	2
3	Sebastian Vettel	Ferrari	Ferrari SF71H	1h51m51.556s	3
4	Valtteri Bottas	Mercedes AMG	Mercedes F1 W09	1h52m03.541s	4
5	Kimi Raikkonen	Ferrari	Ferrari SF71H	1h52m04.612s	5
6	Daniel Ricciardo	Red Bull Racing	Red Bull-TAG Heuer RB14	1h52m05.593s	6
7	Fernando Alonso	McLaren	McLaren-Renault MCL33	1h52m54.622s	11

Pos	Driver	Team	Chassis-Engine	Result	Qual
8	Carlos Sainz	Renault F1	Renault RS18	60 laps	12
9	Charles Leclerc	Sauber	Sauber-Ferrari C37	60 laps	13
10	Nico Hulkenberg	Renault F1	Renault RS18	60 laps	10
11	Marcus Ericsson	Sauber	Sauber-Ferrari C37	60 laps	14
12	Stoffel Vandoorne	McLaren	McLaren-Renault MCL33	60 laps	18
13	Pierre Gasly	Toro Rosso	Toro Rosso-Honda STR13	60 laps	15
14	Lance Stroll	Williams	Williams-Mercedes FW41	60 laps	20
15	Romain Grosjean *	Haas	Haas-Ferrari VF-18	60 laps	8
16	Sergio Perez	Force India	Force India-Mercedes VJM11	60 laps	7
17	Brendon Hartley	Toro Rosso	Toro Rosso-Honda STR13	60 laps	17
18	Kevin Magnussen	Haas	Haas-Ferrari VF-18	59 laps	16
19	Sergey Sirotkin	Williams	Williams-Mercedes FW41	59 laps	19
R	Esteban Ocon	Force India	Force India-Mercedes VJM11	0 laps/collision	9

Pole: Hamilton, 1m36.015s, 117.956mph/189.832kph. Fastest lap: Magnussen, 1m41.905s, 111.138mph/178.860kph on Lap 50. Race leaders: Hamilton 1-14 & 27-61, Verstappen 15-17, Raikkonen 18-21, Ricciardo 22-26

* 5s penalty for ignoring blue flags

ALONSO HEADS WEST

Life in the midfield wasn't satisfying enough for Fernando Alonso, so he announced that he would be leaving F1 for new challenges. Having already raced at Indianapolis in 2017, and won the Le Mans 24 Hours in 2018, with Toyota, he said that he fancied another shot at winning the Indianapolis 500 in order to achieve a rare motor racing triple crown.

RUSSIAN GRAND PRIX

SOCHI • ROUND 16 • DATE: 30TH SEPTEMBER 2018
Laps: 53 • Distance: 192.590miles/309.944km • Weather: Hot & bright

Pos	Driver	Team	Chassis-Engine	Result	Qual
1	Lewis Hamilton	Mercedes AMG	Mercedes F1 W09	1h27m25.181s	2
2	Valtteri Bottas	Mercedes AMG	Mercedes F1 W09	1h27m27.726s	1
3	Sebastian Vettel	Ferrari	Ferrari SF71H	1h27m32.668s	3
4	Kimi Raikkonen	Ferrari	Ferrari SF71H	1h27m41.724s	4
5	Max Verstappen */!/^	Red Bull Racing	Red Bull-TAG Heuer RB14	1h27m56.197s	19
6	Daniel Ricciardo !/^	Red Bull Racing	Red Bull-TAG Heuer RB14	1h28m45.632s	18
7	Charles Leclerc	Sauber	Sauber-Ferrari C37	1h29m03.571s	7
8	Kevin Magnussen	Haas	Haas-Ferrari VF-18	52 laps	5
9	Esteban Ocon	Force India	Force India-Mercedes VJM11	52 laps	6
10	Sergio Perez	Force India	Force India-Mercedes VJM11	52 laps	8
11	Romain Grosjean	Haas	Haas-Ferrari VF-18	52 laps	9
12	Nico Hulkenberg	Renault F1	Renault RS18	52 laps	12
13	Marcus Ericsson	Sauber	Sauber-Ferrari C37	52 laps	10
14	Fernando Alonso ^	McLaren	McLaren-Renault MCL33	52 laps	16
15	Lance Stroll	Williams	Williams-Mercedes FW41	52 laps	14
16	Stoffel Vandoorne !	McLaren	McLaren-Renault MCL33	51 laps	15
17	Carlos Sainz	Renault F1	Renault RS18	51 laps	11

Pos	Driver	Team	Chassis-Engine	Result	Qual
18	Sergey Sirotkin	Williams	Williams-Mercedes FW41	51 laps	13
R	Pierre Gasly ^	Toro Rosso	Toro Rosso-Honda STR13	4 laps/brakes	17
R	Brendon Hartley ^	Toro Rosso	Toro Rosso-Honda STR13	4 laps/brakes	20

Pole: Bottas, 1m31.387s, 143.144mph/230.369kph. Fastest lap: Bottas, 1m35.861s, 136.464mph/219.617kph on Lap 50. Race leaders: Bottas 1-11, Hamilton 12-14 & 43-53, Raikkonen 15-18, Verstappen 19-42

* 3-place grid penalty for failing to slow for waved yellow flags • ! 5-place grid penalty for gearbox change • ^ made to start from rear of grid for using additional power unit elements

JAPANESE GRAND PRIX

SUZUKA • ROUND 17 • DATE: 7TH OCTOBER 2018
Laps: 53 • Distance: 191.240miles/307.771km • Weather: Hot but dull

Pos	Driver	Team	Chassis-Engine	Result	Qual
1	Lewis Hamilton	Mercedes AMG	Mercedes F1 W09	1h27m17.062s	1
2	Valtteri Bottas	Mercedes AMG	Mercedes F1 W09	1h27m29.981s	2
3	Max Verstappen	Red Bull Racing	Red Bull-TAG Heuer RB14	1h27m31.357s	3
4	Daniel Ricciardo	Red Bull Racing	Red Bull-TAG Heuer RB14	1h27m36.557s	15
5	Kimi Raikkonen	Ferrari	Ferrari SF71H	1h28m08.060s	4
6	Sebastian Vettel	Ferrari	Ferrari SF71H	1h28m26.935s	8
7	Sergio Perez	Force India	Force India-Mercedes VJM11	1h28m36.441s	9
8	Romain Grosjean	Haas	Haas-Ferrari VF-18	1h28m44.260s	5
9	Esteban Ocon *	Force India	Force India-Mercedes VJM11	1h28m45.117s	11
10	Carlos Sainz	Renault F1	Renault RS18	52 laps	13
11	Pierre Gasly	Toro Rosso	Toro Rosso-Honda STR13	52 laps	7
12	Marcus Ericsson !	Sauber	Sauber-Ferrari C37	52 laps	20
13	Brendon Hartley	Toro Rosso	Toro Rosso-Honda STR13	52 laps	6
14	Fernando Alonso	McLaren	McLaren-Renault MCL33	52 laps	18
15	Stoffel Vandoorne	McLaren	McLaren-Renault MCL33	52 laps	19
16	Sergey Sirotkin	Williams	Williams-Mercedes FW41	52 laps	17
17	Lance Stroll	Williams	Williams-Mercedes FW41	52 laps	14
R	Charles Leclerc	Sauber	Sauber-Ferrari C37	38 laps/mechanical	10
R	Nico Hulkenberg	Renault F1	Renault RS18	37 laps/rear end	16
R	Kevin Magnussen	Haas	Haas-Ferrari VF-18	8 laps/accident	12

Pole: Hamilton, 1m27.760s, 148.015mph/238.208kph. Fastest lap: Vettel, 1m32.318s, 140.708mph/226.447kph on Lap 53. Race leaders: Hamilton 1-53

* 3-place grid penalty for failing to slow for red flags • ! 15-place grid penalty for using additional power unit elements & for gearbox change

NEW CIRCUIT

After a break of 28 years, Circuit Paul Ricard made a return to the World Championship to host the French GP. The track that had been the most modern in F1 when introduced in 1971 had been updated extensively with huge areas of run-off at all points, with blue-painted bands of increasingly abrasive tarmac to slow errant cars.

UNITED STATES GRAND PRIX

CIRCUIT OF THE AMERICAS • ROUND 18 • DATE: 21ST OCTOBER 2018
Laps: 56 • Distance: 191.834miles/308.728km • Weather: Warm & bright

Pos	Driver	Team	Chassis-Engine	Result	Qual
1	Kimi Raikkonen	Ferrari	Ferrari SF71H	1h34m18.643s	2
2	Max Verstappen !	Red Bull Racing	Red Bull-TAG Heuer RB14	1h34m19.924s	18
3	Lewis Hamilton	Mercedes AMG	Mercedes F1 W09	1h34m20.985s	1
4	Sebastian Vettel *	Ferrari	Ferrari SF71H	1h34m36.865s	5
5	Valtteri Bottas	Mercedes AMG	Mercedes F1 W09	1h34m43.387s	3
6	Nico Hulkenberg	Renault F1	Renault RS18	1h35m45.853s	7
7	Carlos Sainz	Renault F1	Renault RS18	1h35m53.637s	11
DQ	Esteban Ocon	Force India	Force India-Mercedes VJM11	fuel mass flow	6
DQ	Kevin Magnussen	Haas	Haas-Ferrari VF-18	excess fuel	12
8	Sergio Perez	Force India	Force India-Mercedes VJM11	1h35m59.723s	10
9	Brendon Hartley ^	Toro Rosso	Toro Rosso-Honda STR13	55 laps	20
10	Marcus Ericsson	Sauber	Sauber-Ferrari C37	55 laps	16
11	Stoffel Vandoorne	McLaren	McLaren-Renault MCL33	55 laps	17
12	Pierre Gasly ^	Toro Rosso	Toro Rosso-Honda STR13	55 laps	19
13	Sergey Sirotkin	Williams	Williams-Mercedes FW41	55 laps	14
14	Lance Stroll	Williams	Williams-Mercedes FW41	54 laps	15
R	Charles Leclerc	Sauber	Sauber-Ferrari C37	31 laps/collision	9
R	Daniel Ricciardo	Red Bull Racing	Red Bull-TAG Heuer RB14	8 laps/electrical	4
R	Romain Grosjean	Haas	Haas-Ferrari VF-18	2 laps/collision	8
R	Fernando Alonso	McLaren	McLaren-Renault MCL33	1 lap/collision	13

Pole: Hamilton, 1m32.237s, 133.701mph/215.171kph. Fastest lap: Hamilton, 1m37.392s, 126.624mph/203.782kph on Lap 40. Race leaders: Raikkonen 1-10 & 12-21 & 38-56, Hamilton 11 & 22-37

* 3-place grid penalty for not slowing enough during a red flag period • ! 5-place grid penalty for gearbox change • ^ 10-place grid penalty for using additional power unit elements, required to start from the back of the grid

MEXICAN GRAND PRIX

MEXICO CITY • ROUND 19 • DATE: 28TH OCTOBER 2018
Laps: 71 • Distance: 189.881miles/305.584km • Weather: Warm but dull

Pos	Driver	Team	Chassis-Engine	Result	Qual
1	Max Verstappen	Red Bull Racing	Red Bull-TAG Heuer RB14	1h38m28.851s	2
2	Sebastian Vettel	Ferrari	Ferrari SF71H	1h38m46.167s	4
3	Kimi Raikkonen	Ferrari	Ferrari SF71H	1h39m18.765s	6
4	Lewis Hamilton	Mercedes AMG	Mercedes F1 W09	1h39m47.589s	3
5	Valtteri Bottas	Mercedes AMG	Mercedes F1 W09	70 laps	5
6	Nico Hulkenberg	Renault F1	Renault RS18	69 laps	7
7	Charles Leclerc	Sauber	Sauber-Ferrari C37	69 laps	9
8	Stoffel Vandoorne	McLaren	McLaren-Renault MCL33	69 laps	15
9	Marcus Ericsson	Sauber	Sauber-Ferrari C37	69 laps	10
10	Pierre Gasly !/^	Toro Rosso	Toro Rosso-Honda STR13	69 laps	20
11	Esteban Ocon	Force India	Force India-Mercedes VJM11	69 laps	11
12	Lance Stroll	Williams	Williams-Mercedes FW41	69 laps	17
13	Sergey Sirotkin	Williams	Williams-Mercedes FW41	69 laps	19
14	Brendon Hartley †	Toro Rosso	Toro Rosso-Honda STR13	69 laps	14
15	Kevin Magnussen	Haas	Haas-Ferrari VF-18	69 laps	16
16	Romain Grosjean *	Haas	Haas-Ferrari VF-18	68 laps	18

Pos	Driver	Team	Chassis-Engine	Result	Qual
R	Daniel Ricciardo	Red Bull Racing	Red Bull-TAG Heuer RB14	61 laps/hydraulics	1
R	Sergio Perez	Force India	Force India-Mercedes VJM11	38 laps/brakes	13
R	Carlos Sainz	Renault F1	Renault RS18	28 laps/electrical	8
R	Fernando Alonso	McLaren	McLaren-Renault MCL33	3 laps/accident	12

Pole: Ricciardo, 1m14.759s, 128.783mph/207.257kph. Fastest lap: Bottas, 1m18.741s, 122.271mph/196.776kph on Lap 65. Race leaders: Verstappen 1-13 & 18-71, Vettel 14-17

* 3-place grid penalty for causing a crash in United States GP • ! 5-place grid penalty for gearbox change • ^ 15-place grid penalty for using additional power unit elements • † 5s penalty for causing an accident

BRAZILIAN GRAND PRIX

INTERLAGOS • ROUND 20 • DATE: 11TH NOVEMBER 2018
Laps: 71 • Distance: 190.101miles/305.939km • Weather: Warm & bright

Pos	Driver	Team	Chassis-Engine	Result	Qual
1	Lewis Hamilton	Mercedes AMG	Mercedes F1 W09	1h27m09.066s	1
2	Max Verstappen	Red Bull Racing	Red Bull-TAG Heuer RB14	1h27m10.535s	5
3	Kimi Raikkonen	Ferrari	Ferrari SF71H	1h27m13.830s	4
4	Daniel Ricciardo *	Red Bull Racing	Red Bull-TAG Heuer RB14	1h27m14.259s	11
5	Valtteri Bottas	Mercedes AMG	Mercedes F1 W09	1h27m32.009s	3
6	Sebastian Vettel	Ferrari	Ferrari SF71H	1h27m36.063s	2
7	Charles Leclerc	Sauber	Sauber-Ferrari C37	1h27m53.265s	7
8	Romain Grosjean	Haas	Haas-Ferrari VF-18	1h28m00.296s	8
9	Kevin Magnussen	Haas	Haas-Ferrari VF-18	1h28m01.923s	10
10	Sergio Perez	Force India	Force India-Mercedes VJM11	70 laps	12
11	Brendon Hartley	Toro Rosso	Toro Rosso-Honda STR13	70 laps	16
12	Carlos Sainz	Renault F1	Renault RS18	70 laps	15
13	Pierre Gasly	Toro Rosso	Toro Rosso-Honda STR13	70 laps	9
14	Esteban Ocon !	Force India	Force India-Mercedes VJM11	70 laps	18
15	Stoffel Vandoorne ^	McLaren	McLaren-Renault MCL33	70 laps	20
16	Sergey Sirotkin	Williams	Williams-Mercedes FW41	69 laps	14
17	Fernando Alonso ^	McLaren	McLaren-Renault MCL33	69 laps	17
18	Lance Stroll	Williams	Williams-Mercedes FW41	69 laps	19
R	Nico Hulkenberg	Renault F1	Renault RS18	32 laps/overheating	13
R	Marcus Ericsson	Sauber	Sauber-Ferrari C37	20 laps/accident	6

Pole: Hamilton, 1m07.281s, 143.263mph/230.561kph. Fastest lap: Bottas, 1m10.540s, 136.645mph/219.909kph on Lap 65. Race leaders: Hamilton 1-18 & 44-71, Verstappen 19-35 & 40-43, Ricciardo 36-39

* 5-place grid penalty for using 6th turbocharger • ! 5-place grid penalty for gearbox change • ^ 5s penalty for ignoring blue flags

ABU DHABI GRAND PRIX

YAS MARINA CIRCUIT • ROUND 21 • DATE: 25TH NOVEMBER 2018
Laps: 55 • Distance: 189.547miles/305.47km • Weather: Hot & dry

Pos	Driver	Team	Chassis-Engine	Result	Qual
1	Lewis Hamilton	Mercedes AMG	Mercedes F1 W09	1h39m40.382s	1
2	Sebastian Vettel	Ferrari	Ferrari SF71H	1h39m42.963s	3
3	Max Verstappen	Red Bull Racing	Red Bull-TAG Heuer RB14	1h39m53.088s	6
4	Daniel Ricciardo	Red Bull Racing	Red Bull-TAG Heuer RB14	1h39m55.761s	5
5	Valtteri Bottas	Mercedes AMG	Mercedes F1 W09	1h40m28.339s	2
6	Carlos Sainz	Renault F1	Renault RS18	1h40m52.930s	11
7	Charles Leclerc	Sauber	Sauber-Ferrari C37	1h41m11.171s	8
8	Sergio Perez	Force India	Force India-Mercedes VJM11	1h41m11.657s	14
9	Romain Grosjean	Haas	Haas-Ferrari VF-18	54 laps	7
10	Kevin Magnussen	Haas	Haas-Ferrari VF-18	54 laps	13
11	Fernando Alonso *	McLaren	McLaren-Renault MCL33	54 laps	15
12	Brendon Hartley	Toro Rosso	Toro Rosso-Honda STR13	54 laps	16
13	Lance Stroll	Williams	Williams-Mercedes FW41	54 laps	20
14	Stoffel Vandoorne	McLaren	McLaren-Renault MCL33	54 laps	18
15	Sergey Sirotkin	Williams	Williams-Mercedes FW41	54 laps	19
R	Pierre Gasly	Toro Rosso	Toro Rosso-Honda STR13	46 laps/oil leak	17
R	Esteban Ocon !	Force India	Force India-Mercedes VJM11	44 laps/oil leak	9
R	Marcus Ericsson	Sauber	Sauber-Ferrari C37	24 laps	12
R	Kimi Raikkonen	Ferrari	Ferrari SF71H	6 laps/electrical	4
R	Nico Hulkenberg	Renault F1	Renault RS18	0 laps/collision	10

Pole: Hamilton, 1m34.794s, 131.062mph/210.924kph. Fastest lap: Vettel, 1m40.867s, 123.171mph/198.225kph on Lap 54. Race leaders: Hamilton 1-7 & 34-55, Bottas 8-16, Ricciardo 17-33

* three 5s penalties for gaining an advantage by leaving the track • ! 5s penalty for gaining an advantage by leaving the track

NEW DRIVERS

In addition to the sparkling debut season for Charles Leclerc, Sergey Sirotkin was the other rookie in 2018. The Russian joined Williams to race alongside Lance Stroll and pretty much matched the sophomore Canadian for pace, with a best result of 10th at Monza, but both had little chance as the team had lost direction.

WORLD DRIVERS' CHAMPIONSHIP FINAL RESULTS

Pos	Driver	Nat	Car-Engine	R1	R2	R3	R4	R5	R6	R7	R8	R9
1	Lewis Hamilton	GBR	Mercedes F1 W09	2P	3	4	1	1P	3	5	1P	R
2	Sebastian Vettel	DEU	Ferrari SF71H	1	1P	8P	4P	4	2	1P	5	3
3	Kimi Raikkonen	FIN	Ferrari SF71H	3	R	3	2	R	4	6	3	2F
4	Max Verstappen	NLD	Red Bull-TAG Heuer RB14	6	R	5	R	3	9F	3F	2	1
5	Valtteri Bottas	FIN	Mercedes F1 W09	8	2F	2	14F	2	5	2	7F	RP
6	Daniel Ricciardo	AUS	Red Bull-TAG Heuer RB14	4F	R	1F	R	5F	1P	4	4	R
7	Nico Hulkenberg	DEU	Renault RS18	7	6	6	R	R	8	7	9	R
8	Sergio Perez	MEX	Force India-Mercedes VJM11	11	16	12	3	9	12	14	R	7

Pos	Driver	Nat	Car-Engine	R1	R2	R3	R4	R5	R6	R7	R8	R9
9	Kevin Magnussen	DNK	Haas-Ferrari VF-18	R	5	10	13	6	13	13	6	5
10	Carlos Sainz	ESP	Renault RS18	10	11	9	5	7	10	8	8	12
11	Fernando Alonso	ESP	McLaren-Renault MCL33	5	7	7	7	8	R	R	16	8
12	Esteban Ocon	FRA	Force India-Mercedes VJM11	12	10	11	R	R	6	9	R	6
13	Charles Leclerc	MCO	Sauber-Ferrari C37	13	12	19	6	10	18	10	10	9
14	Romain Grosjean	FRA	Haas-Ferrari VF-18	R	13	17	R	R	15	12	11	4
15	Pierre Gasly	FRA	Toro Rosso-Honda STR13	R	4	18	12	R	7	11	R	11
16	Stoffel Vandoorne	BEL	McLaren-Renault MCL33	9	8	13	9	R	14	16	12	15
17	Marcus Ericsson	SWE	Sauber-Ferrari C37	R	9	16	11	13	11	15	13	10
18	Lance Stroll	CAN	Williams-Mercedes FW41	14	14	14	8	11	17	R	17	14
19	Brendon Hartley	NZL	Toro Rosso-Honda STR13	15	17	20	10	12	19	R	14	R
20	Sergey Sirotkin	RUS	Williams-Mercedes FW41	R	15	15	R	14	16	17	15	13

Pos	Driver	R10	R11	R12	R13	R14	R15	R16	R17	R18	R19	R20	R21	Total
1	Hamilton	2P	1F	1P	2P	1F	1P	1	1P	3PF	4	1P	1P	408
2	Vettel	1F	RP	2	1	4	3	3	6F	4	2	6	2F	320
3	Raikkonen	3	3	3	R	2P	5	4	5	1	3	3	R	251
4	Verstappen	15	4	R	3	5	2	5	3	2	1	2	3	249
5	Bottas	4	2	5	4F	3	4	2PF	2	5	5F	5F	5	247
6	Ricciardo	5	R	4F	R	R	6	6	4	R	RP	4	4	170
7	Hulkenberg	6	5	12	R	13	10	12	R	6	6	R	R	69
8	Perez	10	7	14	5	7	16	10	7	8	R	10	8	62
9	Magnussen	9	11	7	8	16	18F	8	R	DQ	15	9	10	56
10	Sainz	R	12	9	11	8	8	17	10	7	R	12	6	53
11	Alonso	8	16	8	R	R	7	14	14	R	R	17	11	50
12	Ocon	7	8	13	6	6	R	9	9	DQ	11	14	R	49
13	Leclerc	R	15	R	R	11	9	7	R	R	7	7	7	39
14	Grosjean	R	6	10	7	DQ	15	11	8	R	16	8	9	37
15	Gasly	13	14	6	9	14	13	R	11	12	10	13	R	29
16	Vandoorne	11	13	R	15	12	12	16	15	11	8	15	14	12
17	Ericsson	R	9	15	10	15	11	13	12	10	9	R	R	9
18	Stroll	12	R	17	13	9	14	15	17	14	12	18	13	6
19	Hartley	R	10	11	14	R	17	R	13	9	14	11	12	4
20	Sirotkin	14	R	16	12	10	19	18	16	13	13	16	15	1

SYMBOLS AND GRAND PRIX KEY

Round 1	**Australian GP**
Round 2	**Bahrain GP**
Round 3	**Chinese GP**
Round 4	**Azerbaijan GP**
Round 5	**Spanish GP**
Round 6	**Monaco GP**
Round 7	**Canadian GP**
Round 8	**French GP**
Round 9	**Austrian GP**
Round 10	**British GP**
Round 11	**German GP**
Round 12	**Hungarian GP**
Round 13	**Belgian GP**
Round 14	**Italian GP**
Round 15	**Singapore GP**
Round 16	**Russian GP**
Round 17	**Japanese GP**
Round 18	**United States GP**
Round 19	**Mexican GP**
Round 20	**Brazilian GP**
Round 21	**Abu Dhabi GP**

SCORING

1st	**25 points**
2nd	**18 points**
3rd	**15 points**
4th	**12 points**
5th	**10 points**
6th	**8 points**
7th	**6 points**
8th	**4 points**
9th	**2 points**
10th	**1 point**

DNPQ DID NOT PRE-QUALIFY DNQ DID NOT QUALIFY DQ DISQUALIFIED EX EXCLUDED
F FASTEST LAP NC NOT CLASSIFIED NS NON-STARTER P POLE POSITION R RETIRED

WORLD CONSTRUCTORS' CHAMPIONSHIP FINAL RESULTS

Pos	Team-Engine	R1	R2	R3	R4	R5	R6	R7	R8	R9	R10	R11
1	Mercedes AMG	2/8	2/3	2/4	1/14	1/2	3/5	2/5	1/7	R/R	2/4	1/2
2	Ferrari	1/3	1/R	3/8	2/4	4/R	2/4	1/6	3/5	2/3	1/3	3/R
3	Red Bull-TAG Heuer	4/6	R/R	1/5	R/R	3/5	1/9	3/4	2/4	1/R	5/15	4/R
4	Renault F1	7/10	6/11	6/9	5/R	7/R	8/10	7/8	8/9	12/R	6/R	5/12
5	Haas-Ferrari	R/R	5/13	10/17	13/R	6/R	13/15	12/13	6/11	4/5	9/R	6/11
6	McLaren-Renault	5/9	7/8	7/13	7/9	8/R	14/R	16/R	12/16	8/15	8/11	13/16
7	Force India-Mercedes	11/12	10/16	11/12	3/R	9/R	6/12	9/14	R/R	6/7	7/10	7/8
8	Sauber-Ferrari	13/R	9/12	16/19	6/11	10/13	11/18	10/15	10/13	9/10	R/R	9/15
9	Toro Rosso-Honda	15/R	4/17	18/20	10/12	12/R	7/19	11/R	14/R	11/R	13/R	10/14
10	Williams-Mercedes	14/R	14/15	14/15	8/R	11/14	16/17	17/R	15/17	13/14	12/14	R/R

Pos	Team-Engine	R12	R13	R14	R15	R16	R17	R18	R19	R20	R21	Total
1	Mercedes AMG	1/5	2/4	1/3	1/4	1/2	1/2	3/5	4/5	1/5	1/5	655
2	Ferrari	2/3	1/R	2/4	3/5	3/4	5/6	1/4	2/3	3/6	2/R	571
3	Red Bull-TAG Heuer	4/R	3/R	5/R	2/6	5/6	3/4	2/R	1/R	2/4	3/4	419
4	Renault F1	9/12	11/R	8/13	8/10	12/17	10/R	6/7	6/R	12/R	6/R	122
5	Haas-Ferrari	7/10	7/8	16/DQ	15/18	8/11	8/R	DQ/R	15/16	8/9	9/10	93
6	McLaren-Renault	8/R	15/R	12/R	7/12	14/16	14/15	11/R	8/R	15/17	11/14	62
7	Force India-Mercedes	13/14	5/6	6/7	16/R	9/10	7/9	8/DQ	11/R	10/14	8/R	52
8	Sauber-Ferrari	15/R	10/R	11/15	9/11	7/13	12/R	10/R	7/9	7/R	7/R	48
9	Toro Rosso-Honda	6/11	9/14	14/R	13/17	R/R	11/13	9/12	10/14	11/13	12/R	33
10	Williams-Mercedes	16/17	12/13	9/10	14/19	15/18	16/17	13/14	12/13	16/18	13/15	7

2019

SEASON SUMMARY

Lewis Hamilton claimed his sixth F1 title as Valtteri Bottas played the role of wingman again at Mercedes. For the sake of competition, it was great news that there were times during the season that Mercedes didn't have the fastest car, with both Ferrari and Red Bull Racing enjoying moments when they were superior. Ferrari new boy Charles Leclerc could have won the second race, in Bahrain, but a technical glitch denied him, while a penalty cost Sebastian Vettel in Canada. McLaren began to rediscover form under the guidance of team principal Andreas Seidl and rose from sixth in 2018 to fourth.

AUSTRALIAN GRAND PRIX

ALBERT PARK • ROUND 1 • DATE: 17TH MARCH 2019
Laps: 58 • Distance: 191.117miles/307.574km • Weather: Warm & bright

Pos	Driver	Team	Chassis-Engine	Result	Qual
1	Valtteri Bottas	Mercedes AMG	Mercedes F1 W10	1h25m27.325s	2
2	Lewis Hamilton	Mercedes AMG	Mercedes F1 W10	1h25m48.211s	1
3	Max Verstappen	Red Bull Racing	Red Bull-Honda RB15	1h25m49.845s	4
4	Sebastian Vettel	Ferrari	Ferrari SF90	1h26m24.434s	3
5	Charles Leclerc	Ferrari	Ferrari SF90	1h26m25.555s	5
6	Kevin Magnussen	Haas	Haas-Ferrari VF-19	1h26m54.481s	7
7	Nico Hulkenberg	Renault F1	Renault RS19	57 laps	11
8	Kimi Raikkonen	Alfa Romeo Racing	Alfa Romeo-Ferrari C38	57 laps	9
9	Lance Stroll	Racing Point	Racing Point-Mercedes RP19	57 laps	16
10	Daniil Kvyat	Toro Rosso	Toro Rosso-Honda STR14	57 laps	15
11	Pierre Gasly	Red Bull Racing	Red Bull-Honda RB15	57 laps	17
12	Lando Norris	McLaren	McLaren-Renault MCL34	57 laps	8
13	Sergio Perez	Racing Point	Racing Point-Mercedes RP19	57 laps	10
14	Alexander Albon	Toro Rosso	Toro Rosso-Honda STR14	57 laps	13
15	Antonio Giovinazzi	Alfa Romeo Racing	Alfa Romeo-Ferrari C38	57 laps	14
16	George Russell	Williams	Williams-Mercedes FW42	56 laps	19
17	Robert Kubica	Williams	Williams-Mercedes FW42	55 laps	20
R	Romain Grosjean	Haas	Haas-Ferrari VF-19	29 laps/wheel	6
R	Daniel Ricciardo	Renault F1	Renault RS19	28 laps/accident	12
R	Carlos Sainz	McLaren	McLaren-Renault MCL34	9 laps/power unit	18

Pole: Hamilton, 1m20.486s, 147.385mph/237.194kph. Fastest lap: Bottas, 1m25.580s, 138.612mph/223.075kph on Lap 57. Race leaders: Bottas 1-22 & 25-58, Verstappen 23-24

LESS OF A DRAG

Ask F1 fans what they want and the answer tends to be more overtaking. In order to try to give them this, F1's rule-makers changed the technical regulations so that the front and rear wings produced less turbulence for the following car, and made the slot in the rear wing larger to enhance the DRS drag reduction system.

ALFA ROMEO IS BACK

Following Force India's transformation into Racing Point during the 2018 season, Sauber followed suit and emerged as Alfa Romeo. Again, this was just a rebranding exercise, as the team continued under the same management from its base at Hinwil in Switzerland. It brought in Kimi Raikkonen and Antonio Giovinazzi to drive.

BAHRAIN GRAND PRIX

SAKHIR • ROUND 2 • DATE: 31ST MARCH 2019
Laps: 57 • Distance: 191.683miles/308.484km • Weather: Hot & bright

Pos	Driver	Team	Chassis-Engine	Result	Qual
1	Lewis Hamilton	Mercedes AMG	Mercedes F1 W10	1h34m21.295s	3
2	Valtteri Bottas	Mercedes AMG	Mercedes F1 W10	1h34m24.275s	4
3	Charles Leclerc	Ferrari	Ferrari SF90	1h34m27.426s	1
4	Max Verstappen	Red Bull Racing	Red Bull-Honda RB15	1h34m27.703s	5
5	Sebastian Vettel	Ferrari	Ferrari SF90	1h34m57.363s	2
6	Lando Norris	McLaren	McLaren-Renault MCL34	1h35m07.049s	9
7	Kimi Raikkonen	Alfa Romeo Racing	Alfa Romeo-Ferrari C38	1h35m08.765s	8
8	Pierre Gasly	Red Bull Racing	Red Bull-Honda RB15	1h35m19.389s	13
9	Alexander Albon	Toro Rosso	Toro Rosso-Honda STR14	1h35m23.992s	12
10	Sergio Perez	Racing Point	Racing Point-Mercedes RP19	1h35m24.991s	14
11	Antonio Giovinazzi	Alfa Romeo Racing	Alfa Romeo-Ferrari C38	1h35m25.894s	16
12	Daniil Kvyat !	Toro Rosso	Toro Rosso-Honda STR14	56 laps	15
13	Kevin Magnussen	Haas	Haas-Ferrari VF-19	56 laps	6
14	Lance Stroll	Racing Point	Racing Point-Mercedes RP19	56 laps	18
15	George Russell	Williams	Williams-Mercedes FW42	56 laps	19
16	Robert Kubica	Williams	Williams-Mercedes FW42	55 laps	20
17	Nico Hulkenberg	Renault F1	Renault RS19	53 laps/engine	17
18	Daniel Ricciardo	Renault F1	Renault RS19	53 laps/power unit	10
19	Carlos Sainz	McLaren	McLaren-Renault MCL34	53 laps/gearbox	7
R	Romain Grosjean *	Haas	Haas-Ferrari VF-19	16 laps/accident	11

Pole: Leclerc, 1m27.866s, 137.780mph/221.737kph. Fastest lap: Leclerc, 1m33.411s, 129.602mph/208.575kph on Lap 38. Race leaders: Vettel 1-5 & 14, Leclerc 6-13 & 15-47, Hamilton 48-57

* 3-place grid penalty for impeding Norris • ! 5s penalty for speeding in the pit lane

CHINESE GRAND PRIX

SHANGHAI INTERNATIONAL CIRCUIT • ROUND 3 • DATE: 14TH APRIL 2019
Laps: 56 • Distance: 189.677miles/305.256km • Weather: Warm but dull

Pos	Driver	Team	Chassis-Engine	Result	Qual
1	Lewis Hamilton	Mercedes AMG	Mercedes F1 W10	1h32m06.350s	2
2	Valtteri Bottas	Mercedes AMG	Mercedes F1 W10	1h32m12.902s	1
3	Sebastian Vettel	Ferrari	Ferrari SF90	1h32m20.094s	3
4	Max Verstappen	Red Bull Racing	Red Bull-Honda RB15	1h32m33.977s	5
5	Charles Leclerc	Ferrari	Ferrari SF90	1h32m37.626s	4
6	Pierre Gasly	Red Bull Racing	Red Bull-Honda RB15	1h33m35.657s	6
7	Daniel Ricciardo	Renault F1	Renault RS19	55 laps	7

Pos	Driver	Team	Chassis-Engine	Result	Qual
8	Sergio Perez	Racing Point	Racing Point-Mercedes RP19	55 laps	12
9	Kimi Raikkonen	Alfa Romeo Racing	Alfa Romeo-Ferrari C38	55 laps	13
10	Alexander Albon */!	Toro Rosso	Toro Rosso-Honda STR14	55 laps	20
11	Romain Grosjean	Haas	Haas-Ferrari VF-19	55 laps	10
12	Lance Stroll	Racing Point	Racing Point-Mercedes RP19	55 laps	16
13	Kevin Magnussen	Haas	Haas-Ferrari VF-19	55 laps	9
14	Carlos Sainz	McLaren	McLaren-Renault MCL34	55 laps	14
15	Antonio Giovinazzi	Alfa Romeo Racing	Alfa Romeo-Ferrari C38	55 laps	19
16	George Russell	Williams	Williams-Mercedes FW42	54 laps	17
17	Robert Kubica	Williams	Williams-Mercedes FW42	54 laps	18
18	Lando Norris	McLaren	McLaren-Renault MCL34	50 laps/accident	15
R	Daniil Kvyat ^	Toro Rosso	Toro Rosso-Honda STR14	41 laps/withdrawn	11
R	Nico Hulkenberg	Renault F1	Renault RS19	16 laps/power unit	8

Pole: Bottas, 1m31.547s, 133.194mph/214.355kph. Fastest lap: Gasly, 1m34.742s, 128.702mph/207.126kph on Lap 55. Race leaders: Hamilton 1-56

* 5-place grid penalty for gearbox change • ! made to start from pit lane for changing survival cell • ^ drivethrough penalty for causing a crash with Norris & Sainz

AZERBAIJAN GRAND PRIX

BAKU CITY CIRCUIT • ROUND 4 • DATE: 28TH APRIL 2019
Laps: 51 • Distance: 190.234miles/306.153km • Weather: Warm & bright

Pos	Driver	Team	Chassis-Engine	Result	Qual
1	Valtteri Bottas	Mercedes AMG	Mercedes F1 W10	1h31m52.942s	1
2	Lewis Hamilton	Mercedes AMG	Mercedes F1 W10	1h31m54.466s	2
3	Sebastian Vettel	Ferrari	Ferrari SF90	1h32m04.681s	3
4	Max Verstappen	Red Bull Racing	Red Bull-Honda RB15	1h32m10.435s	4
5	Charles Leclerc	Ferrari	Ferrari SF90	1h33m02.049s	8
6	Sergio Perez	Racing Point	Racing Point-Mercedes RP19	1h33m09.358s	5
7	Carlos Sainz	McLaren	McLaren-Renault MCL34	1h33m16.768s	9
8	Lando Norris	McLaren	McLaren-Renault MCL34	1h33m33.210s	7
9	Lance Stroll	Racing Point	Racing Point-Mercedes RP19	1h33m36.758s	13
10	Kimi Raikkonen ^	Alfa Romeo Racing	Alfa Romeo-Ferrari C38	50 laps	19
11	Alexander Albon	Toro Rosso	Toro Rosso-Honda STR14	50 laps	11
12	Antonio Giovinazzi *	Alfa Romeo Racing	Alfa Romeo-Ferrari C38	50 laps	17
13	Kevin Magnussen	Haas	Haas-Ferrari VF-19	50 laps	12
14	Nico Hulkenberg	Renault F1	Renault RS19	50 laps	15
15	George Russell	Williams	Williams-Mercedes FW42	49 laps	16
16	Robert Kubica !/§	Williams	Williams-Mercedes FW42	49 laps	18
R	Romain Grosjean	Haas	Haas-Ferrari VF-19	38 laps/brakes	14
R	Pierre Gasly †/‡	Red Bull Racing	Red Bull-Honda RB15	38 laps/driveshaft	20
R	Daniil Kvyat	Toro Rosso	Toro Rosso-Honda STR14	33 laps/accident	6
R	Daniel Ricciardo	Renault F1	Renault RS19	31 laps/accident	10

Pole: Bottas, 1m40.495s, 133.621mph/215.043kph. Fastest lap: Leclerc, 1m43.009s, 130.360mph/209.795kph on Lap 50. Race leaders: Bottas 1-11 & 32-51, Hamilton 12, Leclerc 13-31

* 10-place grid penalty for using additional power unit elements • ! made to start from rear of grid for car being modified in parc ferme • ^ made to start from pit lane for changing front wing adjuster hooks • † 5-place grid penalty for gearbox change • ‡ made to start from pit lane for failing to stop for weight check & for car being modified in parc ferme • § drivethrough penalty for leaving pit garage when not permitted to do so

SPANISH GRAND PRIX

BARCELONA-CATALUNYA • ROUND 5 • DATE: 12TH MAY 2019
Laps: 66 • Distance: 190.775miles/307.23km • Weather: Warm & bright

Pos	Driver	Team	Chassis-Engine	Result	Qual
1	Lewis Hamilton	Mercedes AMG	Mercedes F1 W10	1h35m50.443s	2
2	Valtteri Bottas	Mercedes AMG	Mercedes F1 W10	1h35m54.517s	1
3	Max Verstappen	Red Bull Racing	Red Bull-Honda RB15	1h35m58.122s	4
4	Sebastian Vettel	Ferrari	Ferrari SF90	1h35m59.610s	3
5	Charles Leclerc	Ferrari	Ferrari SF90	1h36m03.804s	5
6	Pierre Gasly	Red Bull Racing	Red Bull-Honda RB15	1h36m10.019s	6
7	Kevin Magnussen	Haas	Haas-Ferrari VF-19	1h36m18.602s	8
8	Carlos Sainz	McLaren	McLaren-Renault MCL34	1h36m22.785s	12
9	Daniil Kvyat	Toro Rosso	Toro Rosso-Honda STR14	1h36m23.499s	9
10	Romain Grosjean	Haas	Haas-Ferrari VF-19	1h36m25.084s	7
11	Alexander Albon	Toro Rosso	Toro Rosso-Honda STR14	1h36m25.888s	11
12	Daniel Ricciardo *	Renault F1	Renault RS19	1h36m27.201s	13
13	Nico Hulkenberg ^	Renault F1	Renault RS19	1h36m29.684s	20
14	Kimi Raikkonen	Alfa Romeo Racing	Alfa Romeo-Ferrari C38	1h36m32.246s	14
15	Sergio Perez	Racing Point	Racing Point-Mercedes RP19	1h36m37.320s	15
16	Antonio Giovinazzi !	Alfa Romeo Racing	Alfa Romeo-Ferrari C38	1h36m38.134s	18
17	George Russell !	Williams	Williams-Mercedes FW42	65 laps	19
18	Robert Kubica	Williams	Williams-Mercedes FW42	65 laps	17
R	Lando Norris	McLaren	McLaren-Renault MCL34	44 laps/collision	10
R	Lance Stroll	Racing Point	Racing Point-Mercedes RP19	44 laps/collision	16

Pole: Bottas, 1m15.406s, 138.091mph/222.236kph. Fastest lap: Hamilton, 1m18.492s, 132.662mph/213.499kph on Lap 54. Race leaders: Hamilton 1-66

* 3-place grid penalty for reversing into Kvyat in Azerbaijan GP • ! 5-place grid penalty for gearbox change • ^ made to start from pit lane for car being modified in parc ferme & for using additional power unit elements

LECLERC DENIED FIRST WIN

Charles Leclerc had impressed in his rookie year with Sauber and looked to be the real deal in only his second race with Ferrari. He qualified on pole at Sakhir by 0.3 seconds from team-mate Sebastian Vettel, made up places after a poor first few laps and led by lap six. He was cruising to victory when his engine management system stuttered and both Mercedes cars got by.

MONACO GRAND PRIX

MONTE CARLO • ROUND 6 • DATE: 26TH MAY 2019
Laps: 78 • Distance: 161.734miles/260.286km • Weather: Warm but dull

Pos	Driver	Team	Chassis-Engine	Result	Qual
1	Lewis Hamilton	Mercedes AMG	Mercedes F1 W10	1h43m28.437s	1
2	Sebastian Vettel	Ferrari	Ferrari SF90	1h43m31.039s	4
3	Valtteri Bottas	Mercedes AMG	Mercedes F1 W10	1h43m31.599s	2
4	Max Verstappen ^	Red Bull Racing	Red Bull-Honda RB15	1h43m33.974s	3
5	Pierre Gasly *	Red Bull Racing	Red Bull-Honda RB15	1h43m38.383s	8
6	Carlos Sainz	McLaren	McLaren-Renault MCL34	1h44m21.891s	9
7	Daniil Kvyat	Toro Rosso	Toro Rosso-Honda STR14	1h44m23.011s	7

Pos	Driver	Team	Chassis-Engine	Result	Qual
8	Alexander Albon	Toro Rosso	Toro Rosso-Honda STR14	1h44m23.637s	10
9	Daniel Ricciardo	Renault F1	Renault RS19	1h44m29.331s	6
10	Romain Grosjean †	Haas	Haas-Ferrari VF-19	1h44m29.471s	13
11	Lando Norris	McLaren	McLaren-Renault MCL34	1h44m35.238s	12
12	Sergio Perez	Racing Point	Racing Point-Mercedes RP19	77 laps	16
13	Nico Hulkenberg	Renault F1	Renault RS19	77 laps	11
14	Kevin Magnussen ‡	Haas	Haas-Ferrari VF-19	77 laps	5
15	George Russell	Williams	Williams-Mercedes FW42	77 laps	19
16	Lance Stroll ‡	Racing Point	Racing Point-Mercedes RP19	77 laps	17
17	Kimi Raikkonen	Alfa Romeo Racing	Alfa Romeo-Ferrari C38	77 laps	14
18	Robert Kubica	Williams	Williams-Mercedes FW42	77 laps	20
19	Antonio Giovinazzi !/§	Alfa Romeo Racing	Alfa Romeo-Ferrari C38	76 laps	18
R	Charles Leclerc	Ferrari	Ferrari SF90	16 laps/accident	15

Pole: Hamilton, 1m10.166s, 106.385mph/171.211kph. Fastest lap: Gasly, 1m14.279s, 100.494mph/161.730kph on Lap 72. Race leaders: Hamilton 1-78

* 3-place grid penalty for impeding Grosjean • ! 3-place grid penalty for impeding Hulkenberg • ^ 5s penalty for unsafe release from pitstop • † 5s penalty for crossing the line at pit exit • ‡ 5s penalty for gaining an advantage by leaving the track • § 10s penalty for causing a crash with Kubica

FERRARI STEPS UP

Ferrari was the most competitive it had been in years and was faster than Mercedes on occasion in the second half of the year. But it was able to rank only second as its SF90s started the year with an aero shortfall that made it uncompetitive at high-downforce tracks. Its run of wins in Belgium, Italy and Singapore showed what could have been.

CANADIAN GRAND PRIX

MONTREAL • ROUND 7 • DATE: 9TH JUNE 2019
Laps: 70 • Distance: 189.534miles/305.27km • Weather: Hot & bright

Pos	Driver	Team	Chassis-Engine	Result	Qual
1	Lewis Hamilton	Mercedes AMG	Mercedes F1 W10	1h29m07.084s	2
2	Sebastian Vettel ^	Ferrari	Ferrari SF90	1h29m10.742s	1
3	Charles Leclerc	Ferrari	Ferrari SF90	1h29m11.780s	3
4	Valtteri Bottas	Mercedes AMG	Mercedes F1 W10	1h29m58.127s	6
5	Max Verstappen	Red Bull Racing	Red Bull-Honda RB15	1h30m04.739s	9
6	Daniel Ricciardo	Renault F1	Renault RS19	69 laps	4
7	Nico Hulkenberg	Renault F1	Renault RS19	69 laps	7
8	Pierre Gasly	Red Bull Racing	Red Bull-Honda RB15	69 laps	5
9	Lance Stroll	Racing Point	Racing Point-Mercedes RP19	69 laps	17
10	Daniil Kvyat	Toro Rosso	Toro Rosso-Honda STR14	69 laps	10
11	Carlos Sainz *	McLaren	McLaren-Renault MCL34	69 laps	11
12	Sergio Perez	Racing Point	Racing Point-Mercedes RP19	69 laps	15
13	Antonio Giovinazzi	Alfa Romeo Racing	Alfa Romeo-Ferrari C38	69 laps	12
14	Romain Grosjean	Haas	Haas-Ferrari VF-19	69 laps	14
15	Kimi Raikkonen	Alfa Romeo Racing	Alfa Romeo-Ferrari C38	69 laps	16
16	George Russell	Williams	Williams-Mercedes FW42	68 laps	18
17	Kevin Magnussen !	Haas	Haas-Ferrari VF-19	68 laps	20

Pos	Driver	Team	Chassis-Engine	Result	Qual
18	Robert Kubica	Williams	Williams-Mercedes FW42	67 laps	19
R	Alexander Albon	Toro Rosso	Toro Rosso-Honda STR14	59 laps/withdrawn	13
R	Lando Norris	McLaren	McLaren-Renault MCL34	8 laps/brakes	8

Pole: Vettel, 1m10.240s, 138.884mph/223.513kph. Fastest lap: Bottas, 1m13.078s, 133.491mph/214.833kph on Lap 69. Race leaders: Vettel 1-25 & 33-70, Hamilton 26-27, Leclerc 28-32

* 3-place grid penalty for impeding Albon • ! made to start from pit lane for changing survival cell & gearbox & for using additional power unit elements • ^ 5s penalty for leaving track & failing to rejoin safely, forcing Hamilton off

FRENCH GRAND PRIX

CIRCUIT PAUL RICARD • ROUND 8 • DATE: 23RD JUNE 2019
Laps: 53 • Distance: 192.392miles/309.626km • Weather: Hot & bright

Pos	Driver	Team	Chassis-Engine	Result	Qual
1	Lewis Hamilton	Mercedes AMG	Mercedes F1 W10	1h24m31.198s	1
2	Valtteri Bottas	Mercedes AMG	Mercedes F1 W10	1h24m49.254s	2
3	Charles Leclerc	Ferrari	Ferrari SF90	1h24m50.183s	3
4	Max Verstappen	Red Bull Racing	Red Bull-Honda RB15	1h25m06.103s	4
5	Sebastian Vettel	Ferrari	Ferrari SF90	1h25m33.994s	7
6	Carlos Sainz	McLaren	McLaren-Renault MCL34	1h26m06.660s	6
7	Kimi Raikkonen	Alfa Romeo Racing	Alfa Romeo-Ferrari C38	52 laps	12
8	Nico Hulkenberg	Renault F1	Renault RS19	52 laps	13
9	Lando Norris	McLaren	McLaren-Renault MCL34	52 laps	5
10	Pierre Gasly	Red Bull Racing	Red Bull-Honda RB15	52 laps	9
11	Daniel Ricciardo ^/†	Renault F1	Renault RS19	52 laps	8
12	Sergio Perez †	Racing Point	Racing Point-Mercedes RP19	52 laps	14
13	Lance Stroll	Racing Point	Racing Point-Mercedes RP19	52 laps	17
14	Daniil Kvyat *	Toro Rosso	Toro Rosso-Honda STR14	52 laps	19
15	Alexander Albon	Toro Rosso	Toro Rosso-Honda STR14	52 laps	11
16	Antonio Giovinazzi	Alfa Romeo Racing	Alfa Romeo-Ferrari C38	52 laps	10
17	Kevin Magnussen	Haas	Haas-Ferrari VF-19	52 laps	15
18	Robert Kubica	Williams	Williams-Mercedes FW42	51 laps	18
19	George Russell !	Williams	Williams-Mercedes FW42	51 laps	20
R	Romain Grosjean	Haas	Haas-Ferrari VF-19	44 laps/withdrawn	16

Pole: Hamilton, 1m28.319s, 147.965mph/238.127kph. Fastest lap: Vettel, 1m32.740s, 140.912mph/226.775kph on Lap 53. Race leaders: Hamilton 1-53

* made to start from rear of grid for using additional power unit elements • ! made to start from rear of grid for using additional power unit elements • ^ 5s penalty for failing to rejoin track safely • † 5s penalty for gaining an advantage by leaving track

WILLIAMS SLOWEST OF ALL

Williams hit rock bottom. The team knew that it was in trouble when its FW42 wasn't ready for winter testing and chief technical officer Paddy Lowe was fired. The car was always short of downforce, leaving drivers Robert Kubica and George Russell not just at the back of the grid but adrift on lap times. Twenty-one races returned just one point.

AUSTRIAN GRAND PRIX

RED BULL RING • ROUND 9 • DATE: 30TH JUNE 2019
Laps: 71 • Distance: 190.498miles/306.578km • Weather: Very hot & bright

Pos	Driver	Team	Chassis-Engine	Result	Qual
1	Max Verstappen	Red Bull Racing	Red Bull-Honda RB15	1h22m01.822s	2
2	Charles Leclerc	Ferrari	Ferrari SF90	1h22m04.546s	1
3	Valtteri Bottas	Mercedes AMG	Mercedes F1 W10	1h22m20.782s	3
4	Sebastian Vettel	Ferrari	Ferrari SF90	1h22m21.432s	9
5	Lewis Hamilton *	Mercedes AMG	Mercedes F1 W10	1h22m24.627s	4
6	Lando Norris	McLaren	McLaren-Renault MCL34	70 laps	5
7	Pierre Gasly	Red Bull Racing	Red Bull-Honda RB15	70 laps	8
8	Carlos Sainz ^	McLaren	McLaren-Renault MCL34	70 laps	19
9	Kimi Raikkonen	Alfa Romeo Racing	Alfa Romeo-Ferrari C38	70 laps	6
10	Antonio Giovinazzi	Alfa Romeo Racing	Alfa Romeo-Ferrari C38	70 laps	7
11	Sergio Perez	Racing Point	Racing Point-Mercedes RP19	70 laps	13
12	Daniel Ricciardo	Renault F1	Renault RS19	70 laps	12
13	Nico Hulkenberg !	Renault F1	Renault RS19	70 laps	15
14	Lance Stroll	Racing Point	Racing Point-Mercedes RP19	70 laps	14
15	Alexander Albon ^	Toro Rosso	Toro Rosso-Honda STR14	70 laps	18
16	Romain Grosjean	Haas	Haas-Ferrari VF-19	70 laps	11
17	Daniil Kvyat	Toro Rosso	Toro Rosso-Honda STR14	70 laps	16
18	George Russell †/‡	Williams	Williams-Mercedes FW42	69 laps	20
19	Kevin Magnussen §	Haas	Haas-Ferrari VF-19	69 laps	10
20	Robert Kubica	Williams	Williams-Mercedes FW42	68 laps	17

Pole: Leclerc, 1m03.003s, 153.311mph/246.731kph. Fastest lap: Verstappen, 1m07.475s, 143.150mph/230.378kph on Lap 60. Race leaders: Leclerc 1-22 & 32-68, Hamilton 23-30, Verstappen 31 & 69-71

* 3-place grid penalty for impeding Raikkonen • ! 5-place grid penalty for using additional power unit elements • ^ made to start from rear of grid for using additional power unit elements • † 3-place grid penalty for impeding Kvyat • ‡ made to start from rear of grid for car being modified in parc ferme • § drivethrough penalty for moving before the start signal

BRITISH GRAND PRIX

SILVERSTONE • ROUND 10 • DATE: 14TH JULY 2019
Laps: 52 • Distance: 190.262miles/306.198km • Weather: Warm but dull

Pos	Driver	Team	Chassis-Engine	Result	Qual
1	Lewis Hamilton	Mercedes AMG	Mercedes F1 W10	1h21m08.452s	2
2	Valtteri Bottas	Mercedes AMG	Mercedes F1 W10	1h21m33.380s	1
3	Charles Leclerc	Ferrari	Ferrari SF90	1h21m38.569s	3
4	Pierre Gasly	Red Bull Racing	Red Bull-Honda RB15	1h21m43.144s	5
5	Max Verstappen	Red Bull Racing	Red Bull-Honda RB15	1h21m47.910s	4
6	Carlos Sainz	McLaren	McLaren-Renault MCL34	1h22m02.091s	13
7	Daniel Ricciardo	Renault F1	Renault RS19	1h22m02.853s	7
8	Kimi Raikkonen	Alfa Romeo Racing	Alfa Romeo-Ferrari C38	1h22m13.992s	12
9	Daniil Kvyat	Toro Rosso	Toro Rosso-Honda STR14	1h22m15.172s	17
10	Nico Hulkenberg	Renault F1	Renault RS19	1h22m21.185s	10
11	Lando Norris	McLaren	McLaren-Renault MCL34	1h22m22.733s	8
12	Alexander Albon	Toro Rosso	Toro Rosso-Honda STR14	1h22m24.069s	9
13	Lance Stroll	Racing Point	Racing Point-Mercedes RP19	1h22m29.538s	18
14	George Russell	Williams	Williams-Mercedes FW42	51 laps	19
15	Robert Kubica	Williams	Williams-Mercedes FW42	51 laps	20
16	Sebastian Vettel *	Ferrari	Ferrari SF90	51 laps	6

Pos	Driver	Team	Chassis-Engine	Result	Qual
17	Sergio Perez	Racing Point	Racing Point-Mercedes RP19	51 laps	15
R	Antonio Giovinazzi	Alfa Romeo Racing	Alfa Romeo-Ferrari C38	18 laps/spun off	11
R	Romain Grosjean	Haas	Haas-Ferrari VF-19	9 laps/accident	14
R	Kevin Magnussen	Haas	Haas-Ferrari VF-19	6 laps/accident	16

Pole: Bottas, 1m25.093s, 154.863mph/249.228kph. Fastest lap: Hamilton, 1m27.369s, 150.829mph/242.735kph on Lap 52. Race leaders: Bottas 1-16, Hamilton 17-52

* 10s penalty for causing a crash with Verstappen

GERMAN GRAND PRIX

HOCKENHEIM • ROUND 11 • DATE: 28TH JULY 2019
Laps: 64 • Distance: 181.897miles/292.736km • Weather: Hot & wet

Pos	Driver	Team	Chassis-Engine	Result	Qual
1	Max Verstappen	Red Bull Racing	Red Bull-Honda RB15	1h44m31.275s	2
2	Sebastian Vettel !	Ferrari	Ferrari SF90	1h44m38.608s	20
3	Daniil Kvyat	Toro Rosso	Toro Rosso-Honda STR14	1h44m39.580s	14
4	Lance Stroll	Racing Point	Racing Point-Mercedes RP19	1h44m40.241s	15
5	Carlos Sainz	McLaren	McLaren-Renault MCL34	1h44m40.858s	7
6	Alexander Albon	Toro Rosso	Toro Rosso-Honda STR14	1h44m41.327s	16
7	Romain Grosjean	Haas	Haas-Ferrari VF-19	1h44m48.113s	6
8	Kevin Magnussen	Haas	Haas-Ferrari VF-19	1h44m50.040s	12
9	Lewis Hamilton ^	Mercedes AMG	Mercedes F1 W10	1h44m50.942s	1
10	Robert Kubica	Williams	Williams-Mercedes FW42	1h44m56.262s	18
11	George Russell	Williams	Williams-Mercedes FW42	1h44m57.679s	17
12	Kimi Raikkonen †	Alfa Romeo Racing	Alfa Romeo-Ferrari C38	1h45m13.489s	5
13	Antonio Giovinazzi †	Alfa Romeo Racing	Alfa Romeo-Ferrari C38	1h45m15.124s	11
14	Pierre Gasly	Red Bull Racing	Red Bull-Honda RB15	61 laps/collision	4
R	Valtteri Bottas	Mercedes AMG	Mercedes F1 W10	56 laps/spun off	3
R	Nico Hulkenberg	Renault F1	Renault RS19	39 laps/spun off	9
R	Charles Leclerc	Ferrari	Ferrari SF90	27 laps/spun off	10
R	Lando Norris *	McLaren	McLaren-Renault MCL34	25 laps/power unit	19
R	Daniel Ricciardo	Renault F1	Renault RS19	13 laps/exhaust	13
R	Sergio Perez	Racing Point	Racing Point-Mercedes RP19	1 laps/spun off	8

Pole: Hamilton, 1m11.767s, 142.568mph/229.442kph. Fastest lap: Verstappen, 1m16.645s, 133.495mph/214.839kph on Lap 61. Race leaders: Hamilton 1-29 & 47, Verstappen 30-46 & 48-64

* made to start from rear of grid for using additional power unit elements • ! 10-place grid penalty for using additional power unit elements • ^ 5s penalty for entering pit lane on wrong side of bollard • † 30s penalty for using driver aids under safety car conditions

HUNGARIAN GRAND PRIX

HUNGARORING • ROUND 12 • DATE: 4TH AUGUST 2019
Laps: 70 • Distance: 190.181miles/306.67km • Weather: Hot & bright

Pos	Driver	Team	Chassis-Engine	Result	Qual
1	Lewis Hamilton	Mercedes AMG	Mercedes F1 W10	1h35m03.796s	3
2	Max Verstappen	Red Bull Racing	Red Bull-Honda RB15	1h35m21.592s	1
3	Sebastian Vettel	Ferrari	Ferrari SF90	1h36m05.229s	5
4	Charles Leclerc	Ferrari	Ferrari SF90	1h36m09.046s	4
5	Carlos Sainz	McLaren	McLaren-Renault MCL34	69 laps	8
6	Pierre Gasly	Red Bull Racing	Red Bull-Honda RB15	69 laps	6

Pos	Driver	Team	Chassis-Engine	Result	Qual
7	Kimi Raikkonen	Alfa Romeo Racing	Alfa Romeo-Ferrari C38	69 laps	10
8	Valtteri Bottas	Mercedes AMG	Mercedes F1 W10	69 laps	2
9	Lando Norris	McLaren	McLaren-Renault MCL34	69 laps	7
10	Alexander Albon	Toro Rosso	Toro Rosso-Honda STR14	69 laps	12
11	Sergio Perez	Racing Point	Racing Point-Mercedes RP19	69 laps	16
12	Nico Hulkenberg	Renault F1	Renault RS19	69 laps	11
13	Kevin Magnussen	Haas	Haas-Ferrari VF-19	69 laps	14
14	Daniel Ricciardo !	Renault F1	Renault RS19	69 laps	20
15	Daniil Kvyat	Toro Rosso	Toro Rosso-Honda STR14	68 laps	13
16	George Russell	Williams	Williams-Mercedes FW42	68 laps	15
17	Lance Stroll	Racing Point	Racing Point-Mercedes RP19	68 laps	18
18	Antonio Giovinazzi *	Alfa Romeo Racing	Alfa Romeo-Ferrari C38	68 laps	17
19	Robert Kubica	Williams	Williams-Mercedes FW42	67 laps	19
R	Romain Grosjean	Haas	Haas-Ferrari VF-19	49 laps/water leak	9

Pole: Verstappen, 1m14.572s, 131.416mph/211.494kph. Fastest lap: Verstappen, 1m17.103s, 127.102mph/204.552kph on Lap 69. Race leaders: Verstappen 1-24 & 32-66, Hamilton 25-31 & 67-70

* 3-place grid penalty for impeding Stroll • ! made to start from rear of grid for using additional power unit elements

BELGIAN GRAND PRIX

SPA-FRANCORCHAMPS • ROUND 13 • DATE: 1ST SEPTEMBER 2019
Laps: 44 • Distance: 191.491miles/308.176km • Weather: Warm but dull

Pos	Driver	Team	Chassis-Engine	Result	Qual
1	Charles Leclerc	Ferrari	Ferrari SF90	1h23m45.710s	1
2	Lewis Hamilton	Mercedes AMG	Mercedes F1 W10	1h23m46.691s	3
3	Valtteri Bottas	Mercedes AMG	Mercedes F1 W10	1h23m58.295s	4
4	Sebastian Vettel	Ferrari	Ferrari SF90	1h24m12.132s	2
5	Alexander Albon ^	Red Bull Racing	Red Bull-Honda RB15	1h25m07.035s	17
6	Sergio Perez	Racing Point	Racing Point-Mercedes RP19	1h25m10.158s	7
7	Daniil Kvyat ^/†	Toro Rosso	Toro Rosso-Honda STR14	1h25m15.367s	19
8	Nico Hulkenberg *	Renault F1	Renault RS19	1h25m32.349s	12
9	Pierre Gasly	Toro Rosso	Toro Rosso-Honda STR14	1h25m34.878s	13
10	Lance Stroll ^	Racing Point	Racing Point-Mercedes RP19	1h25m35.548s	16
11	Lando Norris	McLaren	McLaren-Renault MCL34	43 laps/power unit	11
12	Kevin Magnussen	Haas	Haas-Ferrari VF-19	43 laps	8
13	Romain Grosjean	Haas	Haas-Ferrari VF-19	43 laps	9
14	Daniel Ricciardo *	Renault F1	Renault RS19	43 laps	10
15	George Russell	Williams	Williams-Mercedes FW42	43 laps	14
16	Kimi Raikkonen	Alfa Romeo Racing	Alfa Romeo-Ferrari C38	43 laps	6
17	Robert Kubica †/‡	Williams	Williams-Mercedes FW42	43 laps	20
18	Antonio Giovinazzi ^/†	Alfa Romeo Racing	Alfa Romeo-Ferrari C38	42 laps/spun off	18
R	Carlos Sainz !	McLaren	McLaren-Renault MCL34	1 laps/power unit	15
R	Max Verstappen	Red Bull Racing	Red Bull-Honda RB15	0 laps/collision	5

Pole: Leclerc, 1m42.519s, 152.825mph/245.948kph. Fastest lap: Vettel, 1m46.409s, 147.238mph/236.957kph on Lap 36. Race leaders: Leclerc 1-20 & 27-44, Hamilton 21-22, Vettel 23-26

* 5-place grid penalty for using additional power unit elements • ! 15-place grid penalty for using additional power unit elements • ^ made to start from rear of grid for using additional power unit elements • † 5-place grid penalty foe gearbox change • ‡ made to start from rear of grid for car being modified in parc ferme

ITALIAN GRAND PRIX

MONZA • ROUND 14 • DATE: 8TH SEPTEMBER 2019
Laps: 53 • Distance: 190.778miles/307.029km • Weather: Warm & bright

Pos	Driver	Team	Chassis-Engine	Result	Qual
1	Charles Leclerc	Ferrari	Ferrari SF90	1h15m26.665s	1
2	Valtteri Bottas	Mercedes AMG	Mercedes F1 W10	1h15m27.500s	3
3	Lewis Hamilton	Mercedes AMG	Mercedes F1 W10	1h16m01.864s	2
4	Daniel Ricciardo	Renault F1	Renault RS19	1h16m12.180s	5
5	Nico Hulkenberg	Renault F1	Renault RS19	1h16m24.830s	6
6	Alexander Albon ^	Red Bull Racing	Red Bull-Honda RB15	1h16m25.980s	8
7	Sergio Perez *	Racing Point	Racing Point-Mercedes RP19	1h16m40.467s	18
8	Max Verstappen *	Red Bull Racing	Red Bull-Honda RB15	1h16m41.157s	19
9	Antonio Giovinazzi	Alfa Romeo Racing	Alfa Romeo-Ferrari C38	52 laps	10
10	Lando Norris *	McLaren	McLaren-Renault MCL34	52 laps	16
11	Pierre Gasly *	Toro Rosso	Toro Rosso-Honda STR14	52 laps	17
12	Lance Stroll †	Racing Point	Racing Point-Mercedes RP19	52 laps	9
13	Sebastian Vettel ‡	Ferrari	Ferrari SF90	52 laps	4
14	George Russell	Williams	Williams-Mercedes FW42	52 laps	14
15	Kimi Raikkonen !/§	Alfa Romeo Racing	Alfa Romeo-Ferrari C38	52 laps	20
16	Romain Grosjean	Haas	Haas-Ferrari VF-19	52 laps	13
17	Robert Kubica	Williams	Williams-Mercedes FW42	51 laps	15
R	Kevin Magnussen	Haas	Haas-Ferrari VF-19	43 laps/hydraulics	11
R	Daniil Kvyat	Toro Rosso	Toro Rosso-Honda STR14	29 laps/oil leak	12
R	Carlos Sainz	McLaren	McLaren-Renault MCL34	27 laps/wheel	7

Pole: Leclerc, 1m19.307s, 163.397mph/262.962kph. Fastest lap: Hamilton, 1m21.779s, 158.458mph/255.014kph on Lap 51. Race leaders: Leclerc 1-19 & 28-53, Bottas 20-27

* made to start from rear of grid for using additional power unit elements • ! 5-place grid penalty for gearbox change & made to start from pit lane for car being modified in parc ferme • ^ 5s penalty for gaining an advantage by leaving track • † drivethrough penalty for failing to rejoin track safely • ‡ 10s stop/go penalty for failing to rejoin track safely • § 10s stop/go penalty for starting race on tyres not used for his fastest lap in Q2

HOCKENHEIM BEDLAM

In the 1950s, it was not unusual for half of the field to retire, but by 2019 it was not unique for races to have all cars finish. This is why the German GP was unusual, as just 14 of the 20 starters made it. Rain blowing in and out led to cars spinning, five pit stops for winner Max Verstappen, and Sebastian Vettel rising from 20th to second.

SINGAPORE GRAND PRIX

MARINA BAY CIRCUIT • ROUND 15 • DATE: 22ND SEPTEMBER 2019
Laps: 61 • Distance: 191.906miles/308.843km • Weather: Hot & humid

Pos	Driver	Team	Chassis-Engine	Result	Qual
1	Sebastian Vettel	Ferrari	Ferrari SF90	1h58m33.667s	3
2	Charles Leclerc	Ferrari	Ferrari SF90	1h58m36.308s	1
3	Max Verstappen	Red Bull Racing	Red Bull-Honda RB15	1h58m37.488s	4
4	Lewis Hamilton	Mercedes AMG	Mercedes F1 W10	1h58m38.275s	2
5	Valtteri Bottas	Mercedes AMG	Mercedes F1 W10	1h58m39.786s	5

Pos	Driver	Team	Chassis-Engine	Result	Qual
6	Alexander Albon	Red Bull Racing	Red Bull-Honda RB15	1h58m45.330s	6
7	Lando Norris	McLaren	McLaren-Renault MCL34	1h58m48.436s	9
8	Pierre Gasly	Toro Rosso	Toro Rosso-Honda STR14	1h58m49.214s	11
9	Nico Hulkenberg	Renault F1	Renault RS19	1h58m50.385s	8
10	Antonio Giovinazzi ^	Alfa Romeo Racing	Alfa Romeo-Ferrari C38	1h59m01.522s	10
11	Romain Grosjean	Haas	Haas-Ferrari VF-19	1h59m09.103s	17
12	Carlos Sainz	McLaren	McLaren-Renault MCL34	1h59m09.641s	7
13	Lance Stroll	Racing Point	Racing Point-Mercedes RP19	1h59m10.086s	16
14	Daniel Ricciardo !	Renault F1	Renault RS19	1h59m11.327s	20
15	Daniil Kvyat	Toro Rosso	Toro Rosso-Honda STR14	1h59m11.845s	14
16	Robert Kubica	Williams	Williams-Mercedes FW42	1h59m20.691s	19
17	Kevin Magnussen	Haas	Haas-Ferrari VF-19	2h00m00.189s	13
R	Kimi Raikkonen	Alfa Romeo Racing	Alfa Romeo-Ferrari C38	49 laps/collision	12
R	Sergio Perez *	Racing Point	Racing Point-Mercedes RP19	42 laps/oil leak	15
R	George Russell	Williams	Williams-Mercedes FW42	34 laps/collision	18

Pole: Leclerc, 1m36.217s, 117.708mph/189.434kph. Fastest lap: Magnussen, 1m42.301s, 110.708mph/178.168kph on Lap 58. Race leaders: Leclerc 1-19, Hamilton 20-26, Giovinazzi 27-30, Vettel 31-61

* 5-place grid penalty for gearbox change • ! 10-place grid penalty for using additional power unit elements • ^ 10s penalty for failing to follow race director's instructions in safety car period

RUSSIAN GRAND PRIX

SOCHI • ROUND 16 • DATE: 29TH SEPTEMBER 2019
Laps: 53 • Distance: 192.590miles/309.944km • Weather: Warm & bright

Pos	Driver	Team	Chassis-Engine	Result	Qual
1	Lewis Hamilton	Mercedes AMG	Mercedes F1 W10	1h33m38.992s	2
2	Valtteri Bottas	Mercedes AMG	Mercedes F1 W10	1h33m42.821s	4
3	Charles Leclerc	Ferrari	Ferrari SF90	1h33m44.204s	1
4	Max Verstappen *	Red Bull Racing	Red Bull-Honda RB15	1h33m53.202s	9
5	Alexander Albon ^	Red Bull Racing	Red Bull-Honda RB15	1h34m17.340s	20
6	Carlos Sainz	McLaren	McLaren-Renault MCL34	1h34m24.881s	5
7	Sergio Perez	Racing Point	Racing Point-Mercedes RP19	1h34m27.720s	11
8	Lando Norris	McLaren	McLaren-Renault MCL34	1h34m36.741s	7
9	Kevin Magnussen †	Haas	Haas-Ferrari VF-19	1h34m37.771s	13
10	Nico Hulkenberg	Renault F1	Renault RS19	1h34m38.833s	6
11	Lance Stroll	Racing Point	Racing Point-Mercedes RP19	1h34m39.813s	14
12	Daniil Kvyat !	Toro Rosso	Toro Rosso-Honda STR14	1h34m41.488s	19
13	Kimi Raikkonen ‡	Alfa Romeo Racing	Alfa Romeo-Ferrari C38	1h34m47.902s	15
14	Pierre Gasly *	Toro Rosso	Toro Rosso-Honda STR14	1h34m49.068s	16
15	Antonio Giovinazzi	Alfa Romeo Racing	Alfa Romeo-Ferrari C38	1h34m52.338s	12
R	Robert Kubica !	Williams	Williams-Mercedes FW42	28 laps/withdrawn	18
R	George Russell	Williams	Williams-Mercedes FW42	27 laps/accident	17
R	Sebastian Vettel	Ferrari	Ferrari SF90	26 laps/power unit	3
R	Daniel Ricciardo	Renault F1	Renault RS19	24 laps/accident	10
R	Romain Grosjean	Haas	Haas-Ferrari VF-19	0 laps/collision	8

Pole: Leclerc, 1m31.628s, 142.768mph/229.763kph. Fastest lap: Hamilton, 1m35.761s, 136.606mph/219.847kph on Lap 51. Race leaders: Vettel 1-25, Hamilton 26-53

* 5-place grid penalty for using additional power unit elements • ! made to start from rear of grid for using additional power unit elements • ^ made to start from pit lane for car being modified in parc ferme & for using additional power unit elements & for gearbox change • † 5s penalty for gaining an advantage by leaving track • ‡ drivethrough penalty for moving before the start signal

A BONUS POINT

A new element was introduced in the chase for World Championship points: a point for the race's fastest lap, if achieved by a driver finishing in the top 10. This didn't prove enough to change the order in either the drivers' or the constructors' championships, as no battle was that tight, but for the record Mercedes claimed the most, nine, to Ferrari's six.

JAPANESE GRAND PRIX

SUZUKA • ROUND 17 • DATE: 13TH OCTOBER 2019
Laps: 52 • Distance: 187.631miles/301.964km • Weather: Warm & bright

Pos	Driver	Team	Chassis-Engine	Result	Qual
1	Valtteri Bottas	Mercedes AMG	Mercedes F1 W10	1h21m46.755s	3
2	Sebastian Vettel	Ferrari	Ferrari SF90	1h22m00.098s	1
3	Lewis Hamilton	Mercedes AMG	Mercedes F1 W10	1h22m00.613s	4
4	Alexander Albon	Red Bull Racing	Red Bull-Honda RB15	1h22m46.292s	6
5	Carlos Sainz	McLaren	McLaren-Renault MCL34	1h22m55.856s	7
DQ	Nico Hulkenberg	Renault F1	Renault RS19	51 laps/brake bias system	15
6	Charles Leclerc ^/†	Ferrari	Ferrari SF90	51 laps	2
7	Pierre Gasly	Toro Rosso	Toro Rosso-Honda STR14	51 laps	9
8	Sergio Perez	Racing Point	Racing Point-Mercedes RP19	51 laps	17
DQ	Daniel Ricciardo	Renault F1	Renault RS19	51 laps/brake bias system	16
9	Lance Stroll	Racing Point	Racing Point-Mercedes RP19	51 laps	12
10	Daniil Kvyat	Toro Rosso	Toro Rosso-Honda STR14	51 laps	14
11	Lando Norris	McLaren	McLaren-Renault MCL34	51 laps	8
12	Kimi Raikkonen	Alfa Romeo Racing	Alfa Romeo-Ferrari C38	51 laps	13
13	Romain Grosjean	Haas	Haas-Ferrari VF-19	51 laps	10
14	Antonio Giovinazzi	Alfa Romeo Racing	Alfa Romeo-Ferrari C38	51 laps	11
15	Kevin Magnussen *	Haas	Haas-Ferrari VF-19	51 laps	19
16	George Russell	Williams	Williams-Mercedes FW42	50 laps	18
17	Robert Kubica */!	Williams	Williams-Mercedes FW42	50 laps	20
R	Max Verstappen	Red Bull Racing	Red Bull-Honda RB15	14 laps/accident	5

Pole: Vettel, 1m27.064s, 149.199mph/240.113kph. Fastest lap: Hamilton, 1m30.983s, 142.772mph/229.770kph on Lap 45. Race leaders: Bottas 1-17 & 21-36 & 43-52, Hamilton 18-20 & 37-42

* 5-place grid penalty for gearbox change • ! made to start from rear of grid for changing survival cell • ^ 5s penalty for causing crash with Verstappen • † 10s penalty for continuing to drive car in unsafe condition

MEXICAN GRAND PRIX

MEXICO CITY • ROUND 18 • DATE: 27TH OCTOBER 2019
Laps: 71 • Distance: 189.881miles/305.584km • Weather: Warm & bright

Pos	Driver	Team	Chassis-Engine	Result	Qual
1	Lewis Hamilton	Mercedes AMG	Mercedes F1 W10	1h36m48.904s	3
2	Sebastian Vettel	Ferrari	Ferrari SF90	1h36m50.670s	2
3	Valtteri Bottas	Mercedes AMG	Mercedes F1 W10	1h36m52.457s	6
4	Charles Leclerc	Ferrari	Ferrari SF90	1h36m55.272s	1
5	Alexander Albon	Red Bull Racing	Red Bull-Honda RB15	1h37m10.303s	5

Pos	Driver	Team	Chassis-Engine	Result	Qual
6	Max Verstappen *	Red Bull Racing	Red Bull-Honda RB15	1h37m57.711s	4
7	Sergio Perez	Racing Point	Racing Point-Mercedes RP19	1h38m02.723s	11
8	Daniel Ricciardo	Renault F1	Renault RS19	1h38m03.828s	13
9	Pierre Gasly	Toro Rosso	Toro Rosso-Honda STR14	70 laps	10
10	Nico Hulkenberg	Renault F1	Renault RS19	70 laps	12
11	Daniil Kvyat !	Toro Rosso	Toro Rosso-Honda STR14	70 laps	9
12	Lance Stroll	Racing Point	Racing Point-Mercedes RP19	70 laps	16
13	Carlos Sainz	McLaren	McLaren-Renault MCL34	70 laps	7
14	Antonio Giovinazzi	Alfa Romeo Racing	Alfa Romeo-Ferrari C38	70 laps	15
15	Kevin Magnussen	Haas	Haas-Ferrari VF-19	69 laps	17
16	George Russell	Williams	Williams-Mercedes FW42	69 laps	19
17	Romain Grosjean	Haas	Haas-Ferrari VF-19	69 laps	18
18	Robert Kubica	Williams	Williams-Mercedes FW42	69 laps	20
R	Kimi Raikkonen	Alfa Romeo Racing	Alfa Romeo-Ferrari C38	58 laps/overheating	14
R	Lando Norris	McLaren	McLaren-Renault MCL34	48 laps/withdrawn	8

Pole: Leclerc, 1m15.024s, 128.328mph/206.525kph. Fastest lap: Leclerc, 1m19.232s, 121.513mph/195.557kph on Lap 53. Race leaders: Leclerc 1-14 & 38-43, Vettel 15-37, Hamilton 44-71

* 3-place grid penalty for failing to slow for yellow flags • ! 10s penalty for causing a crash with Hulkenberg

CLASSIC CAR: MERCEDES F1 W10

With a tally of 15 wins from 21 starts to help it dominate a record sixth successive constructors' championship, the 2019 Mercedes was a massive success. Produced by a design team overseen by James Allison and led by John Owen, the F1 W10 was shaped so that it sought more downforce from the rear in response to the latest mandated aero changes. Andy Cowell's engine division continued to make the hybrid power unit more efficient. And the car was right on the money from the start, with Hamilton leading Bottas in a one-two finish in the opening race in Melbourne.

UNITED STATES GRAND PRIX

CIRCUIT OF THE AMERICAS • ROUND 19 • DATE: 3RD NOVEMBER 2019
Laps: 56 • Distance: 191.834miles/308.728km • Weather: Warm & bright

Pos	Driver	Team	Chassis-Engine	Result	Qual
1	Valtteri Bottas	Mercedes AMG	Mercedes F1 W10	1h33m55.653s	1
2	Lewis Hamilton	Mercedes AMG	Mercedes F1 W10	1h33m59.801s	5
3	Max Verstappen	Red Bull Racing	Red Bull-Honda RB15	1h34m00.655s	3
4	Charles Leclerc	Ferrari	Ferrari SF90	1h34m47.892s	4
5	Alexander Albon	Red Bull Racing	Red Bull-Honda RB15	1h35m13.691s	6
6	Daniel Ricciardo	Renault F1	Renault RS19	1h35m26.019s	9
7	Lando Norris	McLaren	McLaren-Renault MCL34	1h35m26.417s	8
8	Carlos Sainz	McLaren	McLaren-Renault MCL34	55 laps	7
9	Nico Hulkenberg	Renault F1	Renault RS19	55 laps	11
10	Sergio Perez *	Racing Point	Racing Point-Mercedes RP19	55 laps	20
11	Kimi Raikkonen	Alfa Romeo Racing	Alfa Romeo-Ferrari C38	55 laps	17

Pos	Driver	Team	Chassis-Engine	Result	Qual
12	Daniil Kvyat !	Toro Rosso	Toro Rosso-Honda STR14	55 laps	13
13	Lance Stroll	Racing Point	Racing Point-Mercedes RP19	55 laps	14
14	Antonio Giovinazzi	Alfa Romeo Racing	Alfa Romeo-Ferrari C38	55 laps	16
15	Romain Grosjean	Haas	Haas-Ferrari VF-19	55 laps	15
16	Pierre Gasly	Toro Rosso	Toro Rosso-Honda STR14	54 laps/accident	10
17	George Russell	Williams	Williams-Mercedes FW42	54 laps	18
18	Kevin Magnussen	Haas	Haas-Ferrari VF-19	52 laps/brakes	12
R	Robert Kubica	Williams	Williams-Mercedes FW42	31 laps/hydraulics	19
R	Sebastian Vettel	Ferrari	Ferrari SF90	7 laps/suspension	2

Pole: Bottas, 1m32.029s, 134.003mph/215.658kph. Fastest lap: Leclerc, 1m36.169s, 128.234mph/206.374kph on Lap 44. Race leaders: Bottas 1-14 & 24-35 & 52-56, Hamilton 15-23 & 36-51

* made to start from rear of grid for failing to stop for weight check & for using additional power unit elements • ! 5s penalty for causing crash with Perez

BRAZILIAN GRAND PRIX

INTERLAGOS • ROUND 20 • DATE: 17TH NOVEMBER 2019
Laps: 71 • Distance: 190.83miles/305.909km • Weather: Warm & bright

Pos	Driver	Team	Chassis-Engine	Result	Qual
1	Max Verstappen	Red Bull Racing	Red Bull-Honda RB15	1h33m14.678s	1
2	Pierre Gasly	Toro Rosso	Toro Rosso-Honda STR14	1h33m20.755s	6
3	Carlos Sainz !	McLaren	McLaren-Renault MCL34	1h33m23.574s	20
4	Kimi Raikkonen	Alfa Romeo Racing	Alfa Romeo-Ferrari C38	1h33m24.130s	8
5	Antonio Giovinazzi	Alfa Romeo Racing	Alfa Romeo-Ferrari C38	1h33m24.879s	12
6	Daniel Ricciardo §	Renault F1	Renault RS19	1h33m25.219s	11
7	Lewis Hamilton ^	Mercedes AMG	Mercedes F1 W10	1h33m25.817s	3
8	Lando Norris	McLaren	McLaren-Renault MCL34	1h33m25.882s	10
9	Sergio Perez	Racing Point	Racing Point-Mercedes RP19	1h33m26.207s	15
10	Daniil Kvyat	Toro Rosso	Toro Rosso-Honda STR14	1h33m26.609s	16
11	Kevin Magnussen	Haas	Haas-Ferrari VF-19	1h33m27.410s	9
12	George Russell	Williams	Williams-Mercedes FW42	1h33m28.277s	18
13	Romain Grosjean	Haas	Haas-Ferrari VF-19	1h33m28.925s	7
14	Alexander Albon	Red Bull Racing	Red Bull-Honda RB15	1h33m29.605s	5
15	Nico Hulkenberg †	Renault F1	Renault RS19	1h33m32.737s	13
16	Robert Kubica ‡	Williams	Williams-Mercedes FW42	70 laps	19
17	Sebastian Vettel	Ferrari	Ferrari SF90	65 laps/collision	2
18	Charles Leclerc *	Ferrari	Ferrari SF90	65 laps/collision	14
19	Lance Stroll	Racing Point	Racing Point-Mercedes RP19	65 laps/accident	17
R	Valtteri Bottas	Mercedes AMG	Mercedes F1 W10	51 laps/power unit	4

Pole: Verstappen, 1m07.508s, 142.782mph/229.786kph. Fastest lap: Bottas, 1m10.698s, 136.339mph/219.417kph on Lap 43. Race leaders: Verstappen 1-21 & 26-44 & 49-53 & 60-71, Vettel 22-25 & 45-48, Hamilton 54-59

* 10-place grid penalty for using additional power unit elements • ! made to start from rear of grid for using additional power unit elements • ^ 5s penalty for causing a crash with Albon • † 5s penalty for overtaking under safety car conditions • ‡ 5s penalty for unsafe release from a pitstop • § 5s penalty for causing a crash with Magnussen

ABU DHABI GRAND PRIX

YAS MARINA CIRCUIT • ROUND 21 • DATE: 1ST DECEMBER 2019
Laps: 55 • Distance: 189.738miles/305.355km • Weather: Warm & dry

Pos	Driver	Team	Chassis-Engine	Result	Qual
1	Lewis Hamilton	Mercedes AMG	Mercedes F1 W10	1h34m05.715s	1
2	Max Verstappen	Red Bull Racing	Red Bull-Honda RB15	1h34m22.487s	2
3	Charles Leclerc	Ferrari	Ferrari SF90	1h34m49.150s	3
4	Valtteri Bottas *	Mercedes AMG	Mercedes F1 W10	1h34m50.094s	20
5	Sebastian Vettel	Ferrari	Ferrari SF90	1h35m10.072s	4
6	Alexander Albon	Red Bull Racing	Red Bull-Honda RB15	1h35m14.920s	5
7	Sergio Perez	Racing Point	Racing Point-Mercedes RP19	54 laps	10
8	Lando Norris	McLaren	McLaren-Renault MCL34	54 laps	6
9	Daniil Kvyat	Toro Rosso	Toro Rosso-Honda STR14	54 laps	13
10	Carlos Sainz	McLaren	McLaren-Renault MCL34	54 laps	8
11	Daniel Ricciardo	Renault F1	Renault RS19	54 laps	7
12	Nico Hulkenberg	Renault F1	Renault RS19	54 laps	9
13	Kimi Raikkonen	Alfa Romeo Racing	Alfa Romeo-Ferrari C38	54 laps	17
14	Kevin Magnussen	Haas	Haas-Ferrari VF-19	54 laps	14
15	Romain Grosjean	Haas	Haas-Ferrari VF-19	54 laps	15
16	Antonio Giovinazzi	Alfa Romeo Racing	Alfa Romeo-Ferrari C38	54 laps	16
17	George Russell	Williams	Williams-Mercedes FW42	54 laps	18
18	Pierre Gasly	Toro Rosso	Toro Rosso-Honda STR14	53 laps	11
19	Robert Kubica	Williams	Williams-Mercedes FW42	53 laps	19
R	Lance Stroll	Racing Point	Racing Point-Mercedes RP19	45 laps/brakes	12

Pole: Hamilton, 1m34.779s, 131.083mph/210.958kph. Fastest lap: Hamilton, 1m39.283s, 125.136mph/201.387kph on Lap 53. Race leaders: Hamilton 1-55

* made to start from rear of grid for using additional power unit elements

NEW DRIVERS

All three rookies were British, with George Russell, Lando Norris and Alex Albon having finished 1-2-3 in F2 in 2018. Albon scored the best result, fourth, after a mid-season promotion from Toro Rosso to Red Bull Racing. Norris grabbed a pair of sixths for McLaren, while Russell could get his recalcitrant Williams no higher than 11th.

WORLD DRIVERS' CHAMPIONSHIP FINAL RESULTS

Pos	Driver	Nat	Car-Engine	R1	R2	R3	R4	R5	R6	R7	R8
1	Lewis Hamilton	GBR	Mercedes F1 W10	2P	1	1	2	1F	1P	1	1P
2	Valtteri Bottas	FIN	Mercedes F1 W10	1F	2	2P	1P	2P	3	4F	2
3	Max Verstappen	NLD	Red Bull-Honda RB15	3	4	4	4	3	4	5	4
4	Charles Leclerc	MCO	Ferrari SF90	5	3PF	5	5F	5	R	3	3
5	Sebastian Vettel	DEU	Ferrari SF90	4	5	3	3	4	2	2P	5F
6	Carlos Sainz	ESP	McLaren-Renault MCL34	R	19	14	7	8	6	11	6
7	Pierre Gasly	FRA	Red Bull-Honda RB15	11	8	6F	R	6	5F	8	10
			Toro Rosso-Honda STR14	-	-	-	-	-	-	-	-
8	Alexander Albon	THA	Toro Rosso-Honda STR14	14	9	10	11	11	8	R	15
			Red Bull-Honda RB15	-	-	-	-	-	-	-	-

Pos	Driver	Nat	Car-Engine	R1	R2	R3	R4	R5	R6	R7	R8
9	Daniel Ricciardo	AUS	Renault RS19	R	18	7	R	12	9	6	11
10	Sergio Perez	MEX	Racing Point-Mercedes RP19	13	10	8	6	15	12	12	12
11	Lando Norris	GBR	McLaren-Renault MCL34	12	6	18	8	R	11	R	9
12	Kimi Raikkonen	FIN	Alfa Romeo-Ferrari C38	8	7	9	10	14	17	15	7
13	Daniil Kvyat	RUS	Toro Rosso-Honda STR14	10	12	R	R	9	7	10	14
14	Nico Hulkenberg	DEU	Renault RS19	7	17	R	14	13	13	7	8
15	Lance Stroll	CAN	Racing Point-Mercedes RP19	9	14	12	9	R	16	9	13
16	Kevin Magnussen	DNK	Haas-Ferrari VF-19	6	13	13	13	7	14	17	17
17	Antonio Giovinazzi	ITA	Alfa Romeo-Ferrari C38	15	11	15	12	16	19	13	16
18	Romain Grosjean	FRA	Haas-Ferrari VF-19	R	R	11	R	10	10	14	R
19	Robert Kubica	POL	Williams-Mercedes FW42	17	16	17	16	18	18	18	18
20	George Russell	GBR	Williams-Mercedes FW42	16	15	16	15	17	15	16	19

Pos	Driver	R9	R10	R11	R12	R13	R14	R15	R16	R17	R18	R19	R20	R21	Total
1	Hamilton	5	1F	9P	1	2	3F	4	1F	3F	1	2	7	1PF	413
2	Bottas	3	2P	R	8	3	2	5	2	1	3	1P	RF	4	326
3	Verstappen	1F	5	1F	2PF	R	8	3	4	R	6	3	1P	2	278
4	Leclerc	2P	3	R	4	1P	1P	2P	3P	6	4PF	4F	18	3	264
5	Vettel	4	16	2	3	4F	13	1	R	2P	2	R	17	5	240
6	Sainz	8	6	5	5	R	R	12	6	5	13	8	3	10	96
7	Gasly	7	4	14	6	-	-	-	-	-	-	-	-	-	95
		-	-	-	-	9	11	8	14	7	9	16	2	18	
8	Albon	15	12	6	10	-	-	-	-	-	-	-	-	-	92
		-	-	-	-	5	6	6	5	4	5	5	14	6	
9	Ricciardo	12	7	R	14	14	4	14	R	DQ	8	6	6	11	54
10	Perez	11	17	R	11	6	7	R	7	8	7	10	9	7	52
11	Norris	6	11	R	9	11	10	7	8	11	R	7	8	8	49
12	Raikkonen	9	8	12	7	16	15	R	13	12	R	11	4	13	43
13	Kvyat	17	9	3	15	7	R	15	12	10	11	12	10	9	37
14	Hulkenberg	13	10	R	12	8	5	9	10	DQ	10	9	15	12	37
15	Stroll	14	13	4	17	10	12	13	11	9	12	13	19	R	21
16	Magnussen	19	R	8	13	12	R	17F	9	15	15	18	11	14	20
17	Giovinazzi	10	R	13	18	18	9	10	15	14	14	14	5	16	14
18	Grosjean	16	R	7	R	13	16	11	R	13	17	15	13	15	8
19	Kubica	20	15	10	19	17	17	16	R	17	18	R	16	19	1
20	Russell	18	14	11	16	15	14	R	R	16	16	17	12	17	0

SYMBOLS AND GRAND PRIX KEY

Round 1 Australian GP
Round 2 Bahrain GP
Round 3 Chinese GP
Round 4 Azerbaijan GP
Round 5 Spanish GP
Round 6 Monaco GP
Round 7 Canadian GP
Round 8 French GP
Round 9 Austrian GP
Round 10 British GP
Round 11 German GP
Round 12 Hungarian GP
Round 13 Belgian GP
Round 14 Italian GP
Round 15 Singapore GP
Round 16 Russian GP
Round 17 Japanese GP
Round 18 Mexican GP
Round 19 United States GP
Round 20 Brazilian GP
Round 21 Abu Dhabi GP

SCORING

1st	25 points
2nd	18 points
3rd	15 points
4th	12 points
5th	10 points
6th	8 points
7th	6 points
8th	4 points
9th	2 points
10th	1 point
Fastest lap (in top 10)	1 point

DNPQ DID NOT PRE-QUALIFY **DNQ** DID NOT QUALIFY **DQ** DISQUALIFIED **EX** EXCLUDED
F FASTEST LAP **NC** NOT CLASSIFIED **NS** NON-STARTER **P** POLE POSITION **R** RETIRED

WORLD CONSTRUCTORS' CHAMPIONSHIP FINAL RESULTS

Pos	Team-Engine	R1	R2	R3	R4	R5	R6	R7	R8	R9	R10	R11
1	Mercedes AMG	1/2	1/2	1/2	1/2	1/2	1/3	1/4	1/2	3/5	1/2	9/R
2	Ferrari	4/5	3/5	3/5	3/5	4/5	2/R	2/3	3/5	2/4	3/16	2/R
3	Red Bull-Honda	3/11	4/8	4/6	4/R	3/6	4/5	5/8	4/10	1/7	4/5	1/14
4	McLaren-Renault	12/R	6/19	14/18	7/8	8/R	6/11	11/R	6/9	6/8	6/11	5/R
5	Renault F1	7/R	17/18	7/R	14/R	12/13	9/13	6/7	8/11	12/13	7/10	R/R
6	Toro Rosso-Honda	10/14	9/12	10/R	11/R	9/11	7/8	10/R	14/15	15/17	9/12	3/6
7	Racing Point-Mercedes	9/13	10/14	8/12	6/9	15/R	12/16	9/12	12/13	11/14	13/17	4/R
8	Alfa Romeo-Ferrari	8/15	7/11	9/15	10/12	14/16	17/19	13/15	7/16	9/10	8/R	12/13
9	Haas-Ferrari	6/R	13/R	11/13	13/R	7/10	10/14	14/17	17/R	16/19	R/R	7/8
10	Williams-Mercedes	16/17	15/16	16/17	15/16	17/18	15/18	16/18	18/19	18/20	14/15	10/11

Pos	Team-Engine	R12	R13	R14	R15	R16	R17	R18	R19	R20	R21	Total
1	Mercedes AMG	1/8	2/3	2/3	4/5	1/2	1/3	1/3	1/2	7/R	1/4	739
2	Ferrari	3/4	1/4	1/13	1/2	3/R	2/6	2/4	4/R	17/18	3/5	504
3	Red Bull-Honda	2/6	5/R	6/8	3/6	4/5	4/R	5/6	3/5	1/14	2/6	417
4	McLaren-Renault	5/9	11/R	10/R	7/12	6/8	5/11	13/R	7/8	3/8	8/10	145
5	Renault F1	12/14	8/14	4/5	9/14	10/R	DQ/DQ	8/10	6/9	6/15	11/12	91
6	Toro Rosso-Honda	10/15	7/9	11/R	8/15	12/14	7/10	9/11	12/16	2/10	9/18	85
7	Racing Point-Mercedes	11/17	6/10	7/12	13/R	7/11	8/9	7/12	10/13	9/19	7/R	73
8	Alfa Romeo-Ferrari	7/18	16/18	9/15	10/R	13/15	12/14	14/R	11/14	4/5	13/16	57
9	Haas-Ferrari	13/R	12/13	16/R	11/17	9/R	13/15	15/17	15/18	11/13	14/15	28
10	Williams-Mercedes	16/19	15/17	14/17	16/R	R/R	16/17	16/18	17/R	12/16	17/19	1

THE 2020s

SEASON SUMMARY

It was an extraordinary year as the COVID pandemic led to the season being delayed and then crammed into the second half of the year. There were no spectators present, two circuits were used twice in a row, two were revisited and two had their first shot at F1. Yet, for all this, the outcome was the same as it had been for years, as Lewis Hamilton was crowned champion for a seventh time. His Mercedes team-mate Valtteri Bottas was a distant second, Max Verstappen was the best of the rest for Red Bull Racing, and Sergio Perez was a winner for Racing Point.

AUSTRIAN GRAND PRIX

RED BULL RING • ROUND 1 • DATE: 5TH JULY 2020
Laps: 71 • Distance: 190.762miles/307.02km • Weather: Hot & bright

Pos	Driver	Team	Chassis-Engine	Result	Qual
1	Valtteri Bottas	Mercedes AMG	Mercedes F1 W11	1h30m55.739s	1
2	Charles Leclerc	Ferrari	Ferrari SF1000	1h30m58.439s	7
3	Lando Norris	McLaren	McLaren-Renault MCL35	1h31m01.230s	3
4	Lewis Hamilton */!	Mercedes AMG	Mercedes F1 W11	1h31m01.428s	5
5	Carlos Sainz	McLaren	McLaren-Renault MCL35	1h31m04.642s	8
6	Sergio Perez ^	Racing Point	Racing Point-Mercedes RP20	1h31m10.831s	6
7	Pierre Gasly	AlphaTauri	AlphaTauri-Honda AT01	1h31m12.421s	12
8	Esteban Ocon	Renault F1	Renault R.S.20	1h31m13.195s	14
9	Antonio Giovinazzi	Alfa Romeo Racing	Alfa Romeo-Ferrari C39	1h31m16.885s	18
10	Sebastian Vettel	Ferrari	Ferrari SF1000	1h31m20.284s	11
11	Nicholas Latifi	Williams	Williams-Mercedes FW43	1h31m27.389s	20
12	Daniil Kvyat	AlphaTauri	AlphaTauri-Honda AT01	69 laps/suspension	13
13	Alexander Albon	Red Bull Racing	Red Bull-Honda RB16	67 laps/power unit	4
R	Kimi Raikkonen	Alfa Romeo Racing	Alfa Romeo-Ferrari C39	53 laps/wheel	19
R	Romain Grosjean	Haas	Haas-Ferrari VF-20	49 laps/brakes	15
R	George Russell	Williams	Williams-Mercedes FW43	49 laps/fuel pressure	17
R	Kevin Magnussen	Haas	Haas-Ferrari VF-20	24 laps/brakes	16
R	Lance Stroll	Racing Point	Racing Point-Mercedes RP20	20 laps/power unit	9
R	Daniel Ricciardo	Renault F1	Renault R.S.20	17 laps/overheating	10
R	Max Verstappen	Red Bull Racing	Red Bull-Honda RB16	11 laps/power unit	2

Pole: Bottas, 1m02.939s, 153.466mph/246.981kph. Fastest lap: Norris, 1m07.475s, 143.150mph/230.378kph on Lap 71. Race leaders: Bottas 1-71

* 3-place grid penalty for failing to slow for waved yellow flag • ! 5s penalty for causing a crash with Albon • ^ 5s penalty for speeding in pit lane

2020'S FALSE START

The teams will remember their visit to the Australian GP, but it was the race that never was and so won't feature in the record books. A few positive COV-ID tests were registered in the paddock and the opening race of the season was scrapped two hours before the cars had been due out on the track for the first time. It would be almost four months until the first round happened, in Austria.

THE MOST F1 WINS

Lewis Hamilton equalled Michael Schumacher's seven F1 titles in 2020. He had yet to equal Schumacher's record of 13 wins in a season, with 2020 his third in a row of taking 11 wins. Yet, after 266 races, he had the most wins (95, four more than Schumacher), the most poles (98) and the most points (3,778), but still not the most fastest laps, (53 to Schumacher's 77).

STYRIAN GRAND PRIX

RED BULL RING • ROUND 2 • DATE: 12TH JULY 2020
Laps: 71 • Distance: 190.762miles/307.02km • Weather: Hot & bright

Pos	Driver	Team	Chassis-Engine	Result	Qual
1	Lewis Hamilton	Mercedes AMG	Mercedes F1 W11	1h22m50.683s	1
2	Valtteri Bottas	Mercedes AMG	Mercedes F1 W11	1h23m04.402s	4
3	Max Verstappen	Red Bull Racing	Red Bull-Honda RB16	1h23m24.381s	2
4	Alexander Albon	Red Bull Racing	Red Bull-Honda RB16	1h23m35.083s	6
5	Lando Norris *	McLaren	McLaren-Renault MCL35	1h23m52.153s	9
6	Sergio Perez	Racing Point	Racing Point-Mercedes RP20	1h23m53.070s	17
7	Lance Stroll	Racing Point	Racing Point-Mercedes RP20	1h23m53.136s	12
8	Daniel Ricciardo	Renault F1	Renault R.S.20	1h23m53.274s	8
9	Carlos Sainz	McLaren	McLaren-Renault MCL35	70 laps	3
10	Daniil Kvyat	AlphaTauri	AlphaTauri-Honda AT01	70 laps	13
11	Kimi Raikkonen	Alfa Romeo Racing	Alfa Romeo-Ferrari C39	70 laps	16
12	Kevin Magnussen	Haas	Haas-Ferrari VF-20	70 laps	15
13	Romain Grosjean †	Haas	Haas-Ferrari VF-20	70 laps	20
14	Antonio Giovinazzi ^	Alfa Romeo Racing	Alfa Romeo-Ferrari C39	70 laps	19
15	Pierre Gasly	AlphaTauri	AlphaTauri-Honda AT01	70 laps	7
16	George Russell	Williams	Williams-Mercedes FW43	69 laps	11
17	Nicholas Latifi	Williams	Williams-Mercedes FW43	69 laps	18
R	Esteban Ocon	Renault F1	Renault R.S.20	25 laps/overheating	5
R	Charles Leclerc !	Ferrari	Ferrari SF1000	4 laps/accident	14
R	Sebastian Vettel	Ferrari	Ferrari SF1000	1 lap/collision	10

Pole: Hamilton, 1m19.273s, 121.845mph/196.091kph. Fastest lap: Sainz, 1m05.619s, 147.199mph/236.894kph on Lap 68. Race leaders: Hamilton 1-27 & 35-71, Bottas 28-34

* 3-place grid penalty for overtaking under yellow flags • ! 3-place grid penalty for impeding Kvyat • ^ 5-place grid penalty for changing gearbox • † made to start from pit lane for car being modified in parc ferme

HUNGARIAN GRAND PRIX

HUNGARORING • ROUND 3 • DATE: 19TH JULY 2020
Laps: 70 • Distance: 190.178miles/306.63km • Weather: Warm but dull

Pos	Driver	Team	Chassis-Engine	Result	Qual
1	Lewis Hamilton	Mercedes AMG	Mercedes F1 W11	1h36m12.473s	1
2	Max Verstappen	Red Bull Racing	Red Bull-Honda RB16	1h36m21.175s	7
3	Valtteri Bottas	Mercedes AMG	Mercedes F1 W11	1h36m21.925s	2
4	Lance Stroll	Racing Point	Racing Point-Mercedes RP20	1h37m10.052s	3
5	Alexander Albon	Red Bull Racing	Red Bull-Honda RB16	1h37m30.789s	13
6	Sebastian Vettel	Ferrari	Ferrari SF1000	69 laps	5
7	Sergio Perez	Racing Point	Racing Point-Mercedes RP20	69 laps	4

Pos	Driver	Team	Chassis-Engine	Result	Qual
8	Daniel Ricciardo	Renault F1	Renault R.S.20	69 laps	11
9	Carlos Sainz	McLaren	McLaren-Renault MCL35	69 laps	9
10	Kevin Magnussen *	Haas	Haas-Ferrari VF-20	69 laps	16
11	Charles Leclerc	Ferrari	Ferrari SF1000	69 laps	6
12	Daniil Kvyat	AlphaTauri	AlphaTauri-Honda AT01	69 laps	17
13	Lando Norris	McLaren	McLaren-Renault MCL35	69 laps	8
14	Esteban Ocon	Renault F1	Renault R.S.20	69 laps	14
15	Kimi Raikkonen ^	Alfa Romeo Racing	Alfa Romeo-Ferrari C39	69 laps	20
16	Romain Grosjean *	Haas	Haas-Ferrari VF-20	69 laps	18
17	Antonio Giovinazzi	Alfa Romeo Racing	Alfa Romeo-Ferrari C39	69 laps	19
18	George Russell	Williams	Williams-Mercedes FW43	69 laps	12
19	Nicholas Latifi !	Williams	Williams-Mercedes FW43	65 laps	15
R	Pierre Gasly	AlphaTauri	AlphaTauri-Honda AT01	15 laps/gearbox	10

Pole: Hamilton, 1m13.447s, 133.429mph/214.734kph. Fastest lap: Hamilton, 1m16.627s, 127.892mph/205.823kph on Lap 70. Race leaders: Hamilton 1-3 & 5-70, Verstappen 4

* 10s penalty for use of radio communication on formation lap • ! 5s penalty for unsafe release from pitstop • ^ 5s penalty for being out of position at start

BRITISH GRAND PRIX

SILVERSTONE • ROUND 4 • DATE: 2ND AUGUST 2020
Laps: 52 • Distance: 190.262miles/306.198km • Weather: Warm & bright

Pos	Driver	Team	Chassis-Engine	Result	Qual
1	Lewis Hamilton	Mercedes AMG	Mercedes F1 W11	1h28m01.283s	1
2	Max Verstappen	Red Bull Racing	Red Bull-Honda RB16	1h28m07.139s	3
3	Charles Leclerc	Ferrari	Ferrari SF1000	1h28m19.757s	4
4	Daniel Ricciardo	Renault F1	Renault R.S.20	1h28m20.933s	8
5	Lando Norris	McLaren	McLaren-Renault MCL35	1h28m23.560s	5
6	Esteban Ocon	Renault F1	Renault R.S.20	1h28m28.220s	9
7	Pierre Gasly	AlphaTauri	AlphaTauri-Honda AT01	1h28m32.471s	11
8	Alexander Albon ^	Red Bull Racing	Red Bull-Honda RB16	1h28m33.953s	12
9	Lance Stroll	Racing Point	Racing Point-Mercedes RP20	1h28m38.594s	6
10	Sebastian Vettel	Ferrari	Ferrari SF1000	1h28m43.140s	10
11	Valtteri Bottas	Mercedes AMG	Mercedes F1 W11	1h28m43.450s	2
12	George Russell !	Williams	Williams-Mercedes FW43	1h28m53.287s	20
13	Carlos Sainz	McLaren	McLaren-Renault MCL35	1h28m54.653s	7
14	Antonio Giovinazzi †	Alfa Romeo Racing	Alfa Romeo-Ferrari C39	1h28m55.488s	15
15	Nicholas Latifi	Williams	Williams-Mercedes FW43	1h28m55.832s	18
16	Romain Grosjean	Haas	Haas-Ferrari VF-20	1h28m56.333s	17
17	Kimi Raikkonen	Alfa Romeo Racing	Alfa Romeo-Ferrari C39	51 laps	16
R	Daniil Kvyat *	AlphaTauri	AlphaTauri-Honda AT01	11 laps/puncture	19
R	Kevin Magnussen	Haas	Haas-Ferrari VF-20	1 lap/collision	14
NS	Nico Hulkenberg	Racing Point	Racing Point-Mercedes RP20	clutch	13
NS	Sergio Perez	Racing Point	Racing Point-Mercedes RP20	driver unwell	-

Pole: Hamilton, 1m24.303s, 156.314mph/251.564kph. Fastest lap: Verstappen, 1m27.097s, 151.300mph/243.494kph on Lap 52. Race leaders: Hamilton 1-52

* 5-place grid penalty for gearbox change • ! 5-place grid penalty for failing to respect double yellow flags • ^ 5s penalty for causing a crash with Magnussen • † 5s penalty for failure to slow under safety car

70TH ANNIVERSARY GRAND PRIX

SILVERSTONE • ROUND 5 • DATE: 9TH AUGUST 2020
Laps: 52 • Distance: 190.262miles/306.198km • Weather: Hot & bright

Pos	Driver	Team	Chassis-Engine	Result	Qual
1	Max Verstappen	Red Bull Racing	Red Bull-Honda RB16	1h19m41.993s	4
2	Lewis Hamilton	Mercedes AMG	Mercedes F1 W11	1h19m53.319s	2
3	Valtteri Bottas	Mercedes AMG	Mercedes F1 W11	1h20m01.224s	1
4	Charles Leclerc	Ferrari	Ferrari SF1000	1h20m11.282s	8
5	Alexander Albon	Red Bull Racing	Red Bull-Honda RB16	1h20m21.139s	9
6	Lance Stroll	Racing Point	Racing Point-Mercedes RP20	1h20m24.531s	6
7	Nico Hulkenberg	Racing Point	Racing Point-Mercedes RP20	1h20m37.944s	3
8	Esteban Ocon *	Renault F1	Renault R.S.20	1h20m46.766s	14
9	Lando Norris	McLaren	McLaren-Renault MCL35	1h20m47.537s	10
10	Daniil Kvyat	AlphaTauri	AlphaTauri-Honda AT01	1h20m51.662s	16
11	Pierre Gasly	AlphaTauri	AlphaTauri-Honda AT01	1h20m52.635s	7
12	Sebastian Vettel	Ferrari	Ferrari SF1000	1h20m55.363s	11
13	Carlos Sainz	McLaren	McLaren-Renault MCL35	1h20m56.063s	12
14	Daniel Ricciardo	Renault F1	Renault R.S.20	51 laps	5
15	Kimi Raikkonen	Alfa Romeo Racing	Alfa Romeo-Ferrari C39	51 laps	20
16	Romain Grosjean	Haas	Haas-Ferrari VF-20	51 laps	13
17	Antonio Giovinazzi	Alfa Romeo Racing	Alfa Romeo-Ferrari C39	51 laps	19
18	George Russell	Williams	Williams-Mercedes FW43	51 laps	15
19	Nicholas Latifi	Williams	Williams-Mercedes FW43	51 laps	18
R	Kevin Magnussen !	Haas	Haas-Ferrari VF-20	43 laps/tyre	17

Pole: Bottas, 1m25.154s, 154.751mph/249.049kph. Fastest lap: Hamilton, 1m28.451s, 148.984mph/239.766kph on Lap 43. Race leaders: Bottas 1-13, Hamilton 14 & 33-41, Verstappen 15-32 & 42-52

* 3-place grid penalty for impeding Russell • ! 5s penalty for failing to rejoin track safely

CHANGING THE CALENDAR

The F1 calendar had to be rejigged considerably to skirt COVID travel restrictions as they arose. One casualty was the Vietnamese GP, which had been scheduled to hold its inaugural grand prix on a temporary circuit in Hanoi in April. But this never got to happen and the project collapsed. In the end, 17 of the planned 22 grands prix were held.

THE END OF AN ERA

The Williams' family involvement in its own team ended at the Italian GP when the reins were handed over to Dorilton Capital. After two years of finishing last, it was time for fresh financial input. The team's impressive legacy was nine constructors' titles, second only to Ferrari, seven drivers' titles, 114 wins, 128 pole positions and 133 fastest laps.

SPANISH GRAND PRIX

BARCELONA-CATALUNYA • ROUND 6 • DATE: 16TH AUGUST 2020
Laps: 66 • Distance: 190.825miles/307.104km • Weather: Hot & bright

Pos	Driver	Team	Chassis-Engine	Result	Qual
1	Lewis Hamilton	Mercedes AMG	Mercedes F1 W11	1h31m45.279s	1
2	Max Verstappen	Red Bull Racing	Red Bull-Honda RB16	1h32m09.456s	3
3	Valtteri Bottas	Mercedes AMG	Mercedes F1 W11	1h32m30.031s	2
4	Lance Stroll	Racing Point	Racing Point-Mercedes RP20	65 laps	5
5	Sergio Perez *	Racing Point	Racing Point-Mercedes RP20	65 laps	4
6	Carlos Sainz	McLaren	McLaren-Renault MCL35	65 laps	7
7	Sebastian Vettel	Ferrari	Ferrari SF1000	65 laps	11
8	Alexander Albon	Red Bull Racing	Red Bull-Honda RB16	65 laps	6
9	Pierre Gasly	AlphaTauri	AlphaTauri-Honda AT01	65 laps	10
10	Lando Norris	McLaren	McLaren-Renault MCL35	65 laps	8
11	Daniel Ricciardo	Renault F1	Renault R.S.20	65 laps	13
12	Daniil Kvyat *	AlphaTauri	AlphaTauri-Honda AT01	65 laps	12
13	Esteban Ocon	Renault F1	Renault R.S.20	65 laps	15
14	Kimi Raikkonen	Alfa Romeo Racing	Alfa Romeo-Ferrari C39	65 laps	14
15	Kevin Magnussen	Haas	Haas-Ferrari VF-20	65 laps	16
16	Antonio Giovinazzi	Alfa Romeo Racing	Alfa Romeo-Ferrari C39	65 laps	20
17	George Russell	Williams	Williams-Mercedes FW43	65 laps	18
18	Nicholas Latifi	Williams	Williams-Mercedes FW43	64 laps	19
19	Romain Grosjean	Haas	Haas-Ferrari VF-20	64 laps	17
R	Charles Leclerc	Ferrari	Ferrari SF1000	38 laps/electrical	9

Pole: Hamilton, 1m15.584s, 137.766mph/221.713kph. Fastest lap: Bottas, 1m18.183s, 133.186mph/214.343kph on Lap 66. Race leaders: Hamilton 1-66

* 5s penalty for ignoring blue flags

WELCOME ALPHATAURI

There was a new name on a trophy in 2020: Scuderia AlphaTauri. This was a rebranding of Red Bull's junior team, Toro Rosso. That it took a win was down to Pierre Gasly producing a great drive from 10th at Monza that was looking good for a podium until leader Lewis Hamilton was penalised for entering the pits when they were closed, handing the lead to Gasly in the closing stages of the race.

BELGIAN GRAND PRIX

SPA-FRANCORCHAMPS • ROUND 7 • DATE: 30TH AUGUST 2020
Laps: 44 • Distance: 191.414miles/308.052km • Weather: Warm but dull

Pos	Driver	Team	Chassis-Engine	Result	Qual
1	Lewis Hamilton	Mercedes AMG	Mercedes F1 W11	1h24m08.761s	1
2	Valtteri Bottas	Mercedes AMG	Mercedes F1 W11	1h24m17.209s	2
3	Max Verstappen	Red Bull Racing	Red Bull-Honda RB16	1h24m24.216s	3
4	Daniel Ricciardo	Renault F1	Renault R.S.20	1h24m27.638s	4
5	Esteban Ocon	Renault F1	Renault R.S.20	1h24m49.411s	6

Pos	Driver	Team	Chassis-Engine	Result	Qual
6	Alexander Albon	Red Bull Racing	Red Bull-Honda RB16	1h24m51.473s	5
7	Lando Norris	McLaren	McLaren-Renault MCL35	1h24m52.535s	10
8	Pierre Gasly	AlphaTauri	AlphaTauri-Honda AT01	1h24m56.132s	12
9	Lance Stroll	Racing Point	Racing Point-Mercedes RP20	1h25m01.364s	9
10	Sergio Perez	Racing Point	Racing Point-Mercedes RP20	1h25m01.940s	8
11	Daniil Kvyat	AlphaTauri	AlphaTauri-Honda AT01	1h25m18.961s	11
12	Kimi Raikkonen	Alfa Romeo Racing	Alfa Romeo-Ferrari C39	1h25m20.265s	16
13	Sebastian Vettel	Ferrari	Ferrari SF1000	1h25m21.655s	14
14	Charles Leclerc	Ferrari	Ferrari SF1000	1h25m23.681s	13
15	Romain Grosjean	Haas	Haas-Ferrari VF-20	1h25m25.554s	17
16	Nicholas Latifi	Williams	Williams-Mercedes FW43	1h25m26.556s	19
17	Kevin Magnussen	Haas	Haas-Ferrari VF-20	1h25m34.301s	20
R	George Russell	Williams	Williams-Mercedes FW43	9 laps/collision	15
R	Antonio Giovinazzi	Alfa Romeo Racing	Alfa Romeo-Ferrari C39	9 laps/spun off	18
NS	Carlos Sainz	McLaren	McLaren-Renault MCL35	exhaust	7

Pole: Hamilton, 1m41.252s, 154.737mph/249.026kph. Fastest lap: Ricciardo, 1m47.483s, 145.767mph/234.589kph on Lap 44. Race leaders: Hamilton 1-44

ITALIAN GRAND PRIX

MONZA • ROUND 8 • DATE: 6TH SEPTEMBER 2020
Laps: 53 • Distance: 193.18miles/310.633km • Weather: Warm & bright

Pos	Driver	Team	Chassis-Engine	Result	Qual
1	Pierre Gasly	AlphaTauri	AlphaTauri-Honda AT01	1h47m06.056s	10
2	Carlos Sainz	McLaren	McLaren-Renault MCL35	1h47m06.471s	3
3	Lance Stroll	Racing Point	Racing Point-Mercedes RP20	1h47m09.414s	8
4	Lando Norris	McLaren	McLaren-Renault MCL35	1h47m12.056s	6
5	Valtteri Bottas	Mercedes AMG	Mercedes F1 W11	1h47m13.164s	2
6	Daniel Ricciardo	Renault F1	Renault R.S.20	1h47m14.447s	7
7	Lewis Hamilton *	Mercedes AMG	Mercedes F1 W11	1h47m23.301s	1
8	Esteban Ocon	Renault F1	Renault R.S.20	1h47m24.747s	12
9	Daniil Kvyat	AlphaTauri	AlphaTauri-Honda AT01	1h47m28.264s	11
10	Sergio Perez	Racing Point	Racing Point-Mercedes RP20	1h47m29.280s	4
11	Nicholas Latifi	Williams	Williams-Mercedes FW43	1h47m38.932s	20
12	Romain Grosjean	Haas	Haas-Ferrari VF-20	1h47m41.220s	16
13	Kimi Raikkonen	Alfa Romeo Racing	Alfa Romeo-Ferrari C39	1h47m42.368s	14
14	George Russell	Williams	Williams-Mercedes FW43	1h47m42.649s	19
15	Alexander Albon !	Red Bull Racing	Red Bull-Honda RB16	1h47m43.589s	9
16	Antonio Giovinazzi *	Alfa Romeo Racing	Alfa Romeo-Ferrari C39	1h48m01.255s	18
R	Max Verstappen	Red Bull Racing	Red Bull-Honda RB16	30 laps/power unit	5
R	Charles Leclerc	Ferrari	Ferrari SF1000	23 laps/spun off	13
R	Kevin Magnussen	Haas	Haas-Ferrari VF-20	17 laps/power unit	15
R	Sebastian Vettel	Ferrari	Ferrari SF1000	6 laps/brakes	17

Pole: Hamilton, 1m18.887s, 164.266mph/264.362kph. Fastest lap: Hamilton, 1m22.746s, 156.606mph/252.034kph on Lap 34. Race leaders: Hamilton 1-20 & 22-27, Sainz 21, Gasly 28-53

* 10s stop/go penalty for entering pit lane when it was closed • ! 5s penalty for not leaving one car width when moving back to racing line

CALL IN THE RESERVES

Despite entry to F1 paddocks being extremely restricted and the teams having to operate in bubbles, it was inevitable that positive COVID cases would occur. Both Sergio Perez and Lance Stroll had to be substituted at Racing Point at different times by Nico Hulkenberg, and George Russell shifted up from Williams to Mercedes at Sakhir when Lewis Hamilton was unwell.

TUSCAN GRAND PRIX

MUGELLO • ROUND 9 • DATE: 13TH SEPTEMBER 2020
Laps: • Distance: • Weather: Hot & bright

Pos	Driver	Team	Chassis-Engine	Result	Qual
1	Lewis Hamilton	Mercedes AMG	Mercedes F1 W11	2h19m35.060s	1
2	Valtteri Bottas	Mercedes AMG	Mercedes F1 W11	2h19m39.940s	2
3	Alexander Albon	Red Bull Racing	Red Bull-Honda RB16	2h19m43.124s	4
4	Daniel Ricciardo	Renault F1	Renault R.S.20	2h19m45.477s	8
5	Sergio Perez *	Racing Point	Racing Point-Mercedes RP20	2h19m50.710s	7
6	Lando Norris	McLaren	McLaren-Renault MCL35	2h19m53.943s	11
7	Daniil Kvyat	AlphaTauri	AlphaTauri-Honda AT01	2h19m56.816s	12
8	Charles Leclerc	Ferrari	Ferrari SF1000	2h20m03.405s	5
9	Kimi Raikkonen !	Alfa Romeo Racing	Alfa Romeo-Ferrari C39	2h20m04.830s	13
10	Sebastian Vettel	Ferrari	Ferrari SF1000	2h20m05.043s	14
11	George Russell	Williams	Williams-Mercedes FW43	2h20m07.464s	18
12	Romain Grosjean	Haas	Haas-Ferrari VF-20	2h20m17.096s	15
R	Lance Stroll	Racing Point	Racing Point-Mercedes RP20	42 laps/puncture	6
R	Esteban Ocon	Renault F1	Renault R.S.20	7 laps/brakes	10
R	Nicholas Latifi	Williams	Williams-Mercedes FW43	6 laps/collision	19
R	Carlos Sainz	McLaren	McLaren-Renault MCL35	5 laps/collision	9
R	Antonio Giovinazzi	Alfa Romeo Racing	Alfa Romeo-Ferrari C39	5 laps/collision	17
R	Kevin Magnussen	Haas	Haas-Ferrari VF-20	5 laps/collision	20
R	Max Verstappen	Red Bull Racing	Red Bull-Honda RB16	0 laps/collision	3
R	Pierre Gasly	AlphaTauri	AlphaTauri-Honda AT01	0 laps/collision	16

Pole: Hamilton, 1m15.144s, 156.136mph/251.277kph. Fastest lap: Hamilton, 1m18.833s, 148.830mph/239.519kph on Lap 58. Race leaders: Bottas 1-9, Hamilton 10-59

* 1-place grid penalty for causing crash with Raikkonen • ! 5s penalty for crossing the pit entry line

THE MOST F1 STARTS

Alfa Romeo's Kimi Raikkonen became the most experienced driver in F1 history mid-way through the season when he surpassed Rubens Barrichello's tally of 325 grand prix starts and then motored on to 332 by year's end. He would continue in F1 for one further season before retiring with a tally of 352 grands prix to his name.

RUSSIAN GRAND PRIX

SOCHI • ROUND 10 • DATE: 27TH SEPTEMBER 2020
Laps: 53 • Distance: 192.466miles/309.745km • Weather: Hot & bright

Pos	Driver	Team	Chassis-Engine	Result	Qual
1	Valtteri Bottas	Mercedes AMG	Mercedes F1 W11	1h34m00.364s	3
2	Max Verstappen	Red Bull Racing	Red Bull-Honda RB16	1h34m08.093s	2
3	Lewis Hamilton !	Mercedes AMG	Mercedes F1 W11	1h34m23.093s	1
4	Sergio Perez	Racing Point	Racing Point-Mercedes RP20	1h34m30.922s	4
5	Daniel Ricciardo ^	Renault F1	Renault R.S.20	1h34m52.429s	5
6	Charles Leclerc	Ferrari	Ferrari SF1000	1h35m02.550s	10
7	Esteban Ocon	Renault F1	Renault R.S.20	1h35m08.370s	7
8	Daniil Kvyat	AlphaTauri	AlphaTauri-Honda AT01	1h35m09.104s	11
9	Pierre Gasly	AlphaTauri	AlphaTauri-Honda AT01	1h35m30.130s	9
10	Alexander Albon */^	Red Bull Racing	Red Bull-Honda RB16	1h35m38.224s	15
11	Antonio Giovinazzi	Alfa Romeo Racing	Alfa Romeo-Ferrari C39	52 laps	17
12	Kevin Magnussen	Haas	Haas-Ferrari VF-20	52 laps	18
13	Sebastian Vettel	Ferrari	Ferrari SF1000	52 laps	14
14	Kimi Raikkonen	Alfa Romeo Racing	Alfa Romeo-Ferrari C39	52 laps	19
15	Lando Norris	McLaren	McLaren-Renault MCL35	52 laps	8
16	Nicholas Latifi *	Williams	Williams-Mercedes FW43	52 laps	20
17	Romain Grosjean	Haas	Haas-Ferrari VF-20	52 laps	16
18	George Russell	Williams	Williams-Mercedes FW43	52 laps	13
R	Carlos Sainz	McLaren	McLaren-Renault MCL35	0 laps/collision	6
R	Lance Stroll	Racing Point	Racing Point-Mercedes RP20	0 laps/collision	12

Pole: Hamilton, 1m31.304s, 143.275mph/230.579kph. Fastest lap: Bottas, 1m37.030s, 134.820mph/216.972kph on Lap 51. Race leaders: Hamilton 1-15, Bottas 16-53

* 5-place grid penalty for gearbox change • ! 10s penalty for two practice start violations • ^ 5s penalty for failing to follow race director's instructions

EIFEL GRAND PRIX

NURBURGRING • ROUND 11 • DATE: 11TH OCTOBER 2020
Laps: • Distance: • Weather: Cool & bright

Pos	Driver	Team	Chassis-Engine	Result	Qual
1	Lewis Hamilton	Mercedes AMG	Mercedes F1 W11	1h35m49.641s	2
2	Max Verstappen	Red Bull Racing	Red Bull-Honda RB16	1h35m54.111s	3
3	Daniel Ricciardo	Renault F1	Renault R.S.20	1h36m04.254s	6
4	Sergio Perez	Racing Point	Racing Point-Mercedes RP20	1h36m05.711s	9
5	Carlos Sainz	McLaren	McLaren-Renault MCL35	1h36m11.546s	10
6	Pierre Gasly	AlphaTauri	AlphaTauri-Honda AT01	1h36m12.407s	12
7	Charles Leclerc	Ferrari	Ferrari SF1000	1h36m20.455s	4
8	Nico Hulkenberg	Racing Point	Racing Point-Mercedes RP20	1h36m22.237s	20
9	Romain Grosjean	Haas	Haas-Ferrari VF-20	1h36m28.722s	16
10	Antonio Giovinazzi	Alfa Romeo Racing	Alfa Romeo-Ferrari C39	1h36m29.676s	14
11	Sebastian Vettel	Ferrari	Ferrari SF1000	1h36m30.451s	11
12	Kimi Raikkonen *	Alfa Romeo Racing	Alfa Romeo-Ferrari C39	1h36m31.117s	19
13	Kevin Magnussen	Haas	Haas-Ferrari VF-20	1h36m39.226s	15
14	Nicholas Latifi	Williams	Williams-Mercedes FW43	1h36m44.090s	18
15	Daniil Kvyat	AlphaTauri	AlphaTauri-Honda AT01	1h36m45.229s	13
R	Lando Norris	McLaren	McLaren-Renault MCL35	42 laps/power unit	8
R	Alexander Albon !	Red Bull Racing	Red Bull-Honda RB16	23 laps/radiator	5

Pos	Driver	Team	Chassis-Engine	Result	Qual
R	Esteban Ocon	Renault F1	Renault R.S.20	22 laps/hydraulics	7
R	Valtteri Bottas	Mercedes AMG	Mercedes F1 W11	18 laps/power unit	1
R	George Russell	Williams	Williams-Mercedes FW43	12 laps/collision	17
NS	Lance Stroll	Racing Point	Racing Point-Mercedes RP20	-	-

Pole: Bottas, 1m25.269s, 135.051mph/217.345kph. Fastest lap: Verstappen, 1m28.139s, 130.654mph/210.268kph on Lap 60. Race leaders: Bottas 1-12, Hamilton 13-60

* 10s penalty for causing a crash with Russell • ! 5s penalty for causing a crash with Kvyat

PORTUGUESE GRAND PRIX

ALGARVE INTERNATIONAL CIRCUIT • ROUND 12 • DATE: 25TH OCTOBER 2020
Laps: • Distance: • Weather: Warm with drizzle, drying later

Pos	Driver	Team	Chassis-Engine	Result	Qual
1	Lewis Hamilton	Mercedes AMG	Mercedes F1 W11	1h29m56.828s	1
2	Valtteri Bottas	Mercedes AMG	Mercedes F1 W11	1h30m22.420s	2
3	Max Verstappen	Red Bull Racing	Red Bull-Honda RB16	1h30m31.336s	3
4	Charles Leclerc	Ferrari	Ferrari SF1000	1h31m02.140s	4
5	Pierre Gasly	AlphaTauri	AlphaTauri-Honda AT01	65 laps	9
6	Carlos Sainz	McLaren	McLaren-Renault MCL35	65 laps	7
7	Sergio Perez	Racing Point	Racing Point-Mercedes RP20	65 laps	5
8	Esteban Ocon	Renault F1	Renault R.S.20	65 laps	11
9	Daniel Ricciardo	Renault F1	Renault R.S.20	65 laps	10
10	Sebastian Vettel	Ferrari	Ferrari SF1000	65 laps	15
11	Kimi Raikkonen	Alfa Romeo Racing	Alfa Romeo-Ferrari C39	65 laps	16
12	Alexander Albon	Red Bull Racing	Red Bull-Honda RB16	65 laps	6
13	Lando Norris	McLaren	McLaren-Renault MCL35	65 laps	8
14	George Russell	Williams	Williams-Mercedes FW43	65 laps	14
15	Antonio Giovinazzi	Alfa Romeo Racing	Alfa Romeo-Ferrari C39	65 laps	17
16	Kevin Magnussen	Haas	Haas-Ferrari VF-20	65 laps	19
17	Romain Grosjean *	Haas	Haas-Ferrari VF-20	65 laps	18
18	Nicholas Latifi	Williams	Williams-Mercedes FW43	64 laps	20
19	Daniil Kvyat *	AlphaTauri	AlphaTauri-Honda AT01	64 laps	13
R	Lance Stroll */!	Racing Point	Racing Point-Mercedes RP20	51 laps/accident	12

Pole: Hamilton, 1m16.652s, 135.788mph/218.530kph. Fastest lap: Hamilton, 1m18.750s, 133.051mph/214.126kph on Lap 63. Race leaders: Bottas 1 & 6-19 & 41, Sainz 2-5, Hamilton 20-40 & 42-66

* 5s penalty for exceeding track limits • ! 5s penalty for causing a crash with Norris

EMILIA ROMAGNA GRAND PRIX

IMOLA • ROUND 13 • DATE: 1ST NOVEMBER 2020
Laps: • Distance: • Weather: Warm but dull

Pos	Driver	Team	Chassis-Engine	Result	Qual
1	Lewis Hamilton	Mercedes AMG	Mercedes F1 W11	1h28m32.430s	2
2	Valtteri Bottas	Mercedes AMG	Mercedes F1 W11	1h28m38.213s	1
3	Daniel Ricciardo	Renault F1	Renault R.S.20	1h28m46.750s	5
4	Daniil Kvyat	AlphaTauri	AlphaTauri-Honda AT01	1h28m47.571s	8
5	Charles Leclerc	Ferrari	Ferrari SF1000	1h28m51.541s	7
6	Sergio Perez	Racing Point	Racing Point-Mercedes RP20	1h28m52.082s	11

Pos	Driver	Team	Chassis-Engine	Result	Qual
7	Carlos Sainz	McLaren	McLaren-Renault MCL35	1h28m52.660s	10
8	Lando Norris	McLaren	McLaren-Renault MCL35	1h28m53.561s	9
9	Kimi Raikkonen	Alfa Romeo Racing	Alfa Romeo-Ferrari C39	1h28m54.654s	18
10	Antonio Giovinazzi	Alfa Romeo Racing	Alfa Romeo-Ferrari C39	1h28m58.828s	20
11	Nicholas Latifi	Williams	Williams-Mercedes FW43	1h28m59.565s	19
12	Sebastian Vettel	Ferrari	Ferrari SF1000	1h29m00.883s	14
13	Lance Stroll	Racing Point	Racing Point-Mercedes RP20	1h29m01.593s	15
14	Romain Grosjean *	Haas	Haas-Ferrari VF-20	1h29m05.365s	16
15	Alexander Albon	Red Bull Racing	Red Bull-Honda RB16	1h29m29.714s	6
R	George Russell	Williams	Williams-Mercedes FW43	51 laps/spun off	13
R	Max Verstappen	Red Bull Racing	Red Bull-Honda RB16	50 laps/puncture	3
R	Kevin Magnussen	Haas	Haas-Ferrari VF-20	47 laps/gearbox	17
R	Esteban Ocon	Renault F1	Renault R.S.20	27 laps/clutch	12
R	Pierre Gasly	AlphaTauri	AlphaTauri-Honda AT01	8 laps/radiator	4

Pole: Bottas, 1m13.609s, 149.181mph/240.084kph. Fastest lap: Hamilton, 1m15.484s, 145.476mph/234.121kph on Lap 63. Race leaders: Bottas 1-18, Hamilton 19-63

* 5s penalty for leaving the track multiple times

GROSJEAN'S FIERY ESCAPE

Romain Grosjean was hugely fortunate to escape an accident at Sakhir that split his Haas in two and left him in an inferno for 30 seconds. He'd swerved in avoidance of team-mate Kevin Magnussen, pivoted across the nose of Daniil Kvyat's AlphaTauri and speared into the barriers at Turn 3, the front half of the car piercing the barriers with him in it.

TURKISH GRAND PRIX

ISTANBUL PARK • ROUND 14 • DATE: 15TH NOVEMBER 2020
Laps: • Distance: • Weather: Cool & wet

Pos	Driver	Team	Chassis-Engine	Result	Qual
1	Lewis Hamilton	Mercedes AMG	Mercedes F1 W11	1h42m19.313s	6
2	Sergio Perez	Racing Point	Racing Point-Mercedes RP20	1h42m50.946s	3
3	Sebastian Vettel	Ferrari	Ferrari SF1000	1h42m51.273s	11
4	Charles Leclerc	Ferrari	Ferrari SF1000	1h42m53.171s	12
5	Carlos Sainz *	McLaren	McLaren-Renault MCL35	1h42m53.676s	15
6	Max Verstappen	Red Bull Racing	Red Bull-Honda RB16	1h43m04.186s	2
7	Alexander Albon	Red Bull Racing	Red Bull-Honda RB16	1h43m05.797s	4
8	Lando Norris !	McLaren	McLaren-Renault MCL35	1h43m20.572s	14
9	Lance Stroll	Racing Point	Racing Point-Mercedes RP20	1h43m31.666s	1
10	Daniel Ricciardo	Renault F1	Renault R.S.20	1h43m54.773s	5
11	Esteban Ocon	Renault F1	Renault R.S.20	57 laps	7
12	Daniil Kvyat	AlphaTauri	AlphaTauri-Honda AT01	57 laps	16
13	Pierre Gasly ^	AlphaTauri	AlphaTauri-Honda AT01	57 laps	19
14	Valtteri Bottas	Mercedes AMG	Mercedes F1 W11	57 laps	9
15	Kimi Raikkonen	Alfa Romeo Racing	Alfa Romeo-Ferrari C39	57 laps	8
16	George Russell !/^	Williams	Williams-Mercedes FW43	57 laps	20

Pos	Driver	Team	Chassis-Engine	Result	Qual
17	Kevin Magnussen	Haas	Haas-Ferrari VF-20	55 laps/withdrawn	13
R	Romain Grosjean	Haas	Haas-Ferrari VF-20	49 laps/accident	17
R	Nicholas Latifi	Williams	Williams-Mercedes FW43	39 laps/accident	18
R	Antonio Giovinazzi	Alfa Romeo Racing	Alfa Romeo-Ferrari C39	11 laps/gearbox	10

Pole: Stroll, 1m47.765s, 110.803mph/178.321kph. Fastest lap: Norris, 1m36.806s, 123.347mph/198.508kph on Lap 58. Race leaders: Stroll 1-9 & 13-35, Perez 10 & 36, Verstappen 11, Albon 12, Hamilton 37-58

* 3-place grid penalty for impeding Perez • ! 5-place grid penalty for not respecting yellow flags • ^ made to start from rear of grid for using additional power unit elements

BAHRAIN GRAND PRIX

SAKHIR • ROUND 15 • DATE: 29TH NOVEMBER 2020
Laps: 57 • Distance: 191.530miles/308.238km • Weather: Warm & dry

Pos	Driver	Team	Chassis-Engine	Result	Qual
1	Lewis Hamilton	Mercedes AMG	Mercedes F1 W11	2h59m47.515s	1
2	Max Verstappen	Red Bull Racing	Red Bull-Honda RB16	2h59m48.769s	3
3	Alexander Albon	Red Bull Racing	Red Bull-Honda RB16	2h59m55.520s	4
4	Lando Norris	McLaren	McLaren-Renault MCL35	2h59m58.852s	9
5	Carlos Sainz	McLaren	McLaren-Renault MCL35	2h59m59.302s	15
6	Pierre Gasly	AlphaTauri	AlphaTauri-Honda AT01	2h59m59.457s	8
7	Daniel Ricciardo	Renault F1	Renault R.S.20	3h00m06.883s	6
8	Valtteri Bottas	Mercedes AMG	Mercedes F1 W11	3h00m07.195s	2
9	Esteban Ocon	Renault F1	Renault R.S.20	3h00m10.318s	7
10	Charles Leclerc	Ferrari	Ferrari SF1000	56 laps	12
11	Daniil Kvyat *	AlphaTauri	AlphaTauri-Honda AT01	56 laps	10
12	George Russell	Williams	Williams-Mercedes FW43	56 laps	14
13	Sebastian Vettel	Ferrari	Ferrari SF1000	56 laps	11
14	Nicholas Latifi	Williams	Williams-Mercedes FW43	56 laps	20
15	Kimi Raikkonen	Alfa Romeo Racing	Alfa Romeo-Ferrari C39	56 laps	17
16	Antonio Giovinazzi	Alfa Romeo Racing	Alfa Romeo-Ferrari C39	56 laps	16
17	Kevin Magnussen	Haas	Haas-Ferrari VF-20	56 laps	18
18	Sergio Perez	Racing Point	Racing Point-Mercedes RP20	53 laps/power unit	5
R	Lance Stroll	Racing Point	Racing Point-Mercedes RP20	2 laps/accident	13
R	Romain Grosjean	Haas	Haas-Ferrari VF-20	0 laps/accident	19

Pole: Hamilton, 1m27.264s, 138.731mph/223.267kph. Fastest lap: Verstappen, 1m32.014s, 131.570mph/211.742kph on Lap 48. Race leaders: Hamilton 1-19 & 21-57, Verstappen 20

* 10s penalty for causing a crash with Stroll

NEW CIRCUITS

The near-total reshaping of the F1 calendar due to COVID led to first visits to Mugello and the Algarve International Circuit. The first of these was built in the Tuscan hills in Italy in 1974 and held F2 and national races before being bought by Ferrari as a testing facility in 1988. Just inland from the Portuguese city of Portimao, also in rolling hills, the Algarve International Circuit offered fabulous gradient changes.

SAKHIR GRAND PRIX

SAKHIR • ROUND 16 • DATE: 6TH DECEMBER 2020
Laps: 87 • Distance: 191.379miles/307.995km • Weather: Warm & dry

Pos	Driver	Team	Chassis-Engine	Result	Qual
1	Sergio Perez	Racing Point	Racing Point-Mercedes RP20	1h31m15.114s	5
2	Esteban Ocon	Renault F1	Renault R.S.20	1h31m25.632s	11
3	Lance Stroll	Racing Point	Racing Point-Mercedes RP20	1h31m26.983s	10
4	Carlos Sainz	McLaren	McLaren-Renault MCL35	1h31m27.694s	8
5	Daniel Ricciardo	Renault F1	Renault R.S.20	1h31m28.444s	7
6	Alexander Albon	Red Bull Racing	Red Bull-Honda RB16	1h31m28.956s	12
7	Daniil Kvyat	AlphaTauri	AlphaTauri-Honda AT01	1h31m29.648s	6
8	Valtteri Bottas	Mercedes AMG	Mercedes F1 W11	1h31m30.503s	1
9	George Russell	Mercedes AMG	Mercedes F1 W11	1h31m33.670s	2
10	Lando Norris *	McLaren	McLaren-Renault MCL35	1h31m34.655s	19
11	Pierre Gasly	AlphaTauri	AlphaTauri-Honda AT01	1h31m35.641s	9
12	Sebastian Vettel	Ferrari	Ferrari SF1000	1h31m37.725s	13
13	Antonio Giovinazzi	Alfa Romeo Racing	Alfa Romeo-Ferrari C39	1h31m39.225s	14
14	Kimi Raikkonen	Alfa Romeo Racing	Alfa Romeo-Ferrari C39	1h31m41.267s	18
15	Kevin Magnussen	Haas	Haas-Ferrari VF-20	1h31m47.484s	15
16	Jack Aitken	Williams	Williams-Mercedes FW43	1h31m48.788s	17
17	Pietro Fittipaldi *	Haas	Haas-Ferrari VF-20	1h31m51.972s	20
R	Nicholas Latifi	Williams	Williams-Mercedes FW43	52 laps/oil leak	16
R	Max Verstappen	Red Bull Racing	Red Bull-Honda RB16	0 laps/accident	3
R	Charles Leclerc	Ferrari	Ferrari SF1000	0 laps/collision	4

Pole: Bottas, 53.377s, 148.480mph/238.956kph. Fastest lap: Russell, 55.404s, 143.048mph/230.214kph on Lap 80. Race leaders: Russell 1-45 & 50-63, Bottas 46-49, Perez 64-87

* made to start from rear of grid for using additional power unit elements

NEW DRIVERS

There were no rich pickings, or even points, for the season's three newcomers. Nicolas Latifi came closest, missing out by one place on three occasions when he finished 11th for Williams. Jack Aitken came 16th on his one outing for Williams, which was one position higher than Pietro Fittipaldi managed in his two races for Haas.

ABU DHABI GRAND PRIX

YAS MARINA CIRCUIT • ROUND 17 • DATE: 13TH DECEMBER 2020
Laps: 55 • Distance: 189.738miles/305.355km • Weather: Warm & dry

Pos	Driver	Team	Chassis-Engine	Result	Qual
1	Max Verstappen	Red Bull Racing	Red Bull-Honda RB16	1h36m28.645s	1
2	Valtteri Bottas	Mercedes AMG	Mercedes F1 W11	1h36m44.621s	2
3	Lewis Hamilton	Mercedes AMG	Mercedes F1 W11	1h36m47.060s	3
4	Alexander Albon	Red Bull Racing	Red Bull-Honda RB16	1h36m48.632s	5
5	Lando Norris	McLaren	McLaren-Renault MCL35	1h37m29.374s	4
6	Carlos Sainz	McLaren	McLaren-Renault MCL35	1h37m34.307s	6
7	Daniel Ricciardo	Renault F1	Renault R.S.20	1h37m42.393s	11

Pos	Driver	Team	Chassis-Engine	Result	Qual
8	Pierre Gasly	AlphaTauri	AlphaTauri-Honda AT01	1h37m58.363s	9
9	Esteban Ocon	Renault F1	Renault R.S.20	1h38m09.714s	10
10	Lance Stroll	Racing Point	Racing Point-Mercedes RP20	1h38m11.383s	8
11	Daniil Kvyat	AlphaTauri	AlphaTauri-Honda AT01	54 laps	7
12	Kimi Raikkonen	Alfa Romeo Racing	Alfa Romeo-Ferrari C39	54 laps	15
13	Charles Leclerc *	Ferrari	Ferrari SF1000	54 laps	12
14	Sebastian Vettel	Ferrari	Ferrari SF1000	54 laps	13
15	George Russell	Williams	Williams-Mercedes FW43	54 laps	16
16	Antonio Giovinazzi	Alfa Romeo Racing	Alfa Romeo-Ferrari C39	54 laps	14
17	Nicholas Latifi	Williams	Williams-Mercedes FW43	54 laps	18
18	Kevin Magnussen !	Haas	Haas-Ferrari VF-20	54 laps	20
19	Pietro Fittipaldi	Haas	Haas-Ferrari VF-20	53 laps	17
R	Sergio Perez !	Racing Point	Racing Point-Mercedes RP20	8 laps/power unit	19

Pole: Verstappen, 1m35.246s, 130.440mph/209.923kph. Fastest lap: Ricciardo, 1m40.926s, 123.099mph/198.110kph on Lap 55. Race leaders: Verstappen 1-55

* 3-place grid penalty for causing a crash at Sakhir GP • ! made to start from rear of grid for using additional power unit elements

WORLD DRIVERS' CHAMPIONSHIP FINAL RESULTS

Pos	Driver	Nat	Car-Engine	R1	R2	R3	R4	R5	R6
1	Lewis Hamilton	GBR	Mercedes F1 W11	4	1P	1PF	1P	2F	1P
2	Valtteri Bottas	FIN	Mercedes F1 W11	1P	2	3	11	3P	3F
3	Max Verstappen	NLD	Red Bull-Honda RB16	R	3	2	2F	1	2
4	Sergio Perez	MEX	Racing Point-Mercedes RP20	6	6	7	-	-	5
5	Daniel Ricciardo	AUS	Renault R.S.20	R	8	8	4	14	11
6	Carlos Sainz	ESP	McLaren-Renault MCL35	5	9F	9	13	13	6
7	Alexander Albon	THA	Red Bull-Honda RB16	13	4	5	8	5	8
8	Charles Leclerc	MCO	Ferrari SF1000	2	R	11	3	4	R
9	Lando Norris	GBR	McLaren-Renault MCL35	3F	5	13	5	9	10
10	Pierre Gasly	FRA	AlphaTauri-Honda AT01	7	15	R	7	11	9
11	Lance Stroll	CAN	Racing Point-Mercedes RP20	R	7	4	9	6	4
12	Esteban Ocon	FRA	Renault R.S.20	8	R	14	6	8	13
13	Sebastian Vettel	DEU	Ferrari SF1000	10	R	6	10	12	7
14	Daniil Kvyat	RUS	AlphaTauri-Honda AT01	12	10	12	R	10	12
15	Nico Hulkenberg	DEU	Racing Point-Mercedes RP20	-	-	-	NS	7	-
16	Kimi Raikkonen	FIN	Alfa Romeo-Ferrari C39	R	11	15	17	15	14
17	Antonio Giovinazzi	ITA	Alfa Romeo-Ferrari C39	9	14	17	14	17	16
18	George Russell	GBR	Williams-Mercedes FW43	R	16	18	12	18	17
			Mercedes F1 W11	-	-	-	-	-	-
19	Romain Grosjean	FRA	Haas-Ferrari VF-20	R	13	16	16	16	19
20	Kevin Magnussen	DNK	Haas-Ferrari VF-20	R	12	10	R	R	15
21	Nicholas Latifi	CAN	Williams-Mercedes FW43	11	17	19	15	19	18
22	Jack Aitken	GBR	Williams-Mercedes FW43	-	T	-	-	-	-
23	Pietro Fittipaldi	BRA	Haas-Ferrari VF-20	-	-	-	-	-	-

Pos	Driver	R7	R8	R9	R10	R11	R12	R13	R14	R15	R16	R17	Total
1	Hamilton	1P	7PF	1PF	3P	1	1PF	1F	1	1P	-	3	347
2	Bottas	2	5	2	1F	RP	2	2P	14	8	8P	2	223
3	Verstappen	3	R	R	2	2F	3	R	6	2F	R	1P	214
4	Perez	10	10	5	4	4	7	6	2	18	1	R	125
5	Ricciardo	4F	6	4	5	3	9	3	10	7	5	7F	119
6	Sainz	NS	2	R	R	5	6	7	5	5	4	6	105

Pos	Driver	R7	R8	R9	R10	R11	R12	R13	R14	R15	R16	R17	Total
7	Albon	6	15	3	10	R	12	15	7	3	6	4	105
8	Leclerc	14	R	8	6	7	4	5	4	10	R	13	98
9	Norris	7	4	6	15	R	13	8	8F	4	10	5	97
10	Gasly	8	1	R	9	6	5	R	13	6	11	8	75
11	Stroll	9	3	R	R	NS	R	13	9P	R	3	10	75
12	Ocon	5	8	R	7	R	8	R	11	9	2	9	62
13	Vettel	13	R	10	13	11	10	12	3	13	12	14	33
14	Kvyat	11	9	7	8	15	19	4	12	11	7	11	32
15	Hulkenberg	-	-	-	-	8	-	-	-	-	-	-	10
16	Raikkonen	12	13	9	14	12	11	9	15	15	14	12	4
17	Giovinazzi	R	16	R	11	10	15	10	R	16	13	16	4
18	Russell	R	14	11	18	R	14	R	16	12	-	15	3
		-	-	-	-	-	-	-	-	-	9F	-	
19	Grosjean	15	12	12	17	9	17	14	R	R	-	-	2
20	Magnussen	17	R	R	12	13	16	R	17	17	15	18	1
21	Latifi	16	11	R	16	14	18	11	R	14	R	17	0
22	Aitken	-	-	-	-	-	-	-	-	-	16	-	0
23	Fittipaldi	-	-	-	-	-	-	-	-	-	17	19	0

SYMBOLS AND GRAND PRIX KEY

Round 1 Austrian GP
Round 2 Styrian GP
Round 3 Hungarian GP
Round 4 British GP
Round 5 70th Anniversary GP
Round 6 Spanish GP
Round 7 Belgian GP
Round 8 Italian GP
Round 9 Tuscany GP
Round 10 Russian GP
Round 11 Eifel GP
Round 12 Portuguese GP
Round 13 Emilia Romagna GP
Round 14 Turkish GP
Round 15 Bahrain GP
Round 16 Sakhir GP
Round 17 Abu Dhabi GP

SCORING

1st	25 points
2nd	18 points
3rd	15 points
4th	12 points
5th	10 points
6th	8 points
7th	6 points
8th	4 points
9th	2 points
10th	1 point
Fastest lap (in top 10)	1 point

DNPQ DID NOT PRE-QUALIFY **DNQ** DID NOT QUALIFY **DQ** DISQUALIFIED **EX** EXCLUDED
F FASTEST LAP **NC** NOT CLASSIFIED **NS** NON-STARTER **P** POLE POSITION **R** RETIRED

WORLD CONSTRUCTORS' CHAMPIONSHIP FINAL RESULTS

Pos	Team-Engine	R1	R2	R3	R4	R5	R6	R7	R8	R9
1	Mercedes AMG	1/4	1/2	1/3	1/11	2/3	1/3	1/2	5/7	1/2
2	Red Bull-Honda	13/R	3/4	2/5	2/8	1/5	2/8	3/6	15/R	3/R
3	McLaren-Renault	3/5	5/9	9/13	5/13	9/13	6/10	7/NS	2/4	6/R
4	Racing Point-Mercedes	6/R	6/7	4/7	9/NS	6/7	4/5	9/10	3/10	5/R
5	Renault F1	8/R	8/R	8/14	4/6	8/14	11/13	4/5	6/8	4/R
6	Ferrari	2/10	R/R	6/11	3/10	4/12	7/R	13/14	R/R	8/10
7	Alpha Tauri-Honda	7/12	10/15	12/R	7/R	10/11	9/12	8/11	1/9	7/R
8	Alfa Romeo-Ferrari	9/R	11/14	15/17	14/17	15/17	14/16	12/R	13/16	9/R
9	Haas-Ferrari	R/R	12/13	10/16	16/R	16/R	15/19	15/17	12/R	12/R
10	Williams-Mercedes	11/R	16/17	18/19	12/15	18/19	17/18	16/R	11/14	11/R

Pos	Team-Engine	R10	R11	R12	R13	R14	R15	R16	R17	Total
1	Mercedes AMG	1/3	1/R	1/2	1/2	1/14	1/8	8/9	2/3	573
2	Red Bull-Honda	2/10	2/R	3/12	15/R	6/7	2/3	6/R	1/4	319
3	McLaren-Renault	15/R	5/R	6/13	7/8	5/8	4/5	4/10	5/6	202

Pos	Team-Engine	R10	R11	R12	R13	R14	R15	R16	R17	Total
4	Racing Point-Mercedes	4/R	4/8	7/R	6/13	2/9	18/R	1/3	10/R	195*
5	Renault F1	5/7	3/R	8/9	3/R	10/11	7/9	2/5	7/9	181
6	Ferrari	6/13	7/11	4/10	5/12	3/4	10/13	12/R	13/14	131
7	AlphaTauri-Honda	8/9	6/15	5/19	4/R	12/13	6/11	7/11	8/11	107
8	Alfa Romeo-Ferrari	11/14	10/12	11/15	9/10	15/R	15/16	13/14	12/16	8
9	Haas-Ferrari	12/17	9/13	16/17	14/R	17/R	17/R	15/17	18/19	3
10	Williams-Mercedes	16/18	14/R	14/18	11/R	16/R	12/14	16/R	15/17	0

* Racing Point were given a 15-point penalty for copying Mercedes' 2019 rear brake ducts

SEASON SUMMARY

Lewis Hamilton scrapped with Max Verstappen for the title in a season that became increasingly acrimonious between both drivers and their teams as contact on the track was backed up by squabbling off it. It certainly boosted the TV ratings, but didn't always show F1 in the best light. Just when Hamilton appeared to have the final round in the bag, a safety car period gave Verstappen a slim hope. They were left with a one-lap sprint to the flag and Verstappen, on newer tyres, went past to win race and title. Ferrari gained pace to overhaul McLaren, while Alpine (formerly Renault) got back to winning ways in its latest guise.

BAHRAIN GRAND PRIX

SAKHIR • ROUND 1 • DATE: 28TH MARCH 2021
Laps: 57 • Distance: 191.530miles/308.238km • Weather: Warm & dry

Pos	Driver	Team	Chassis-Engine	Result	Qual
1	Lewis Hamilton	Mercedes AMG	Mercedes F1 W12	1h32m03.897s	2
2	Max Verstappen	Red Bull Racing	Red Bull-Honda RB16B	1h32m04.642s	1
3	Valtteri Bottas	Mercedes AMG	Mercedes F1 W12	1h32m41.280s	3
4	Lando Norris	McLaren	McLaren-Mercedes MCL35M	1h32m50.363s	7
5	Sergio Perez	Red Bull Racing	Red Bull-Honda RB16B	1h32m55.944s	11
6	Charles Leclerc	Ferrari	Ferrari SF21	1h33m02.987s	4
7	Daniel Ricciardo	McLaren	McLaren-Mercedes MCL35M	1h33m09.901s	6
8	Carlos Sainz	Ferrari	Ferrari SF21	1h33m10.997s	8
9	Yuki Tsunoda	AlphaTauri	AlphaTauri-Honda AT02	1h33m29.589s	13
10	Lance Stroll	Aston Martin F1	Aston Martin-Mercedes AMR21	1h33m30.610s	10
11	Kimi Raikkonen	Alfa Romeo Racing	Alfa Romeo-Ferrari C41	1h33m32.761s	14
12	Antonio Giovinazzi	Alfa Romeo Racing	Alfa Romeo-Ferrari C41	55 laps	12
13	Esteban Ocon	Alpine	Alpine-Renault A521	55 laps	16
14	George Russell	Williams	Williams-Mercedes FW43B	55 laps	15
15	Sebastian Vettel */!	Aston Martin F1	Aston Martin-Mercedes AMR21	55 laps	20
16	Mick Schumacher	Haas	Haas-Ferrari VF-21	55 laps	18
17	Pierre Gasly	AlphaTauri	AlphaTauri-Honda AT02	52 laps/accident damage	5
18	Nicholas Latifi	Williams	Williams-Mercedes FW43B	51 laps/power unit	17
R	Fernando Alonso	Alpine	Alpine-Renault A521	32 laps/brakes	9
R	Nikita Mazepin	Haas	Haas-Ferrari VF-21		19

Pole: Verstappen, 1m28.997s, 136.029mph/218.919kph. Fastest lap: Bottas, 1m32.090s, 131.461mph/211.567kph on Lap 56. Race leaders: Verstappen 1-17 & 28-39, Hamilton 18-27 & 40-56

* 5-place grid penalty for failing to respect double yellow flags • ! 10s penalty for causing a crash with Ocon

A MAN WITH F1 HISTORY

Stefano Domenicali took the over the helm of F1 from Chase Carey as the CEO of the Formula One Group. This was a popular appointment as he had been a respected team principal at Ferrari from 2008 to 2014 before going off to become CEO of Lamborghini and brought a considered approach to the shape that F1 was taking.

EMILIA ROMAGNA GRAND PRIX

IMOLA • ROUND 2 • DATE: 18TH APRIL 2021
Laps: • Distance: • Weather: Cool & damp

Pos	Driver	Team	Chassis-Engine	Result	Qual
1	Max Verstappen	Red Bull Racing	Red Bull-Honda RB16B	2h02m34.598s	3
2	Lewis Hamilton	Mercedes AMG	Mercedes F1 W12	2h02m56.598s	1
3	Lando Norris	McLaren	McLaren-Mercedes MCL35M	2h02m58.300s	7
4	Charles Leclerc	Ferrari	Ferrari SF21	2h03m00.177s	4
5	Carlos Sainz	Ferrari	Ferrari SF21	2h03m01.634s	11
6	Daniel Ricciardo	McLaren	McLaren-Mercedes MCL35M	2h03m25.818s	6
7	Pierre Gasly	AlphaTauri	AlphaTauri-Honda AT02	2h03m27.416s	5
8	Lance Stroll ^	Aston Martin F1	Aston Martin-Mercedes AMR21	2h03m31.507s	10
9	Esteban Ocon	Alpine	Alpine-Renault A521	2h03m40.302s	9
10	Fernando Alonso	Alpine	Alpine-Renault A521	2h03m41.159s	15
11	Sergio Perez !	Red Bull Racing	Red Bull-Honda RB16B	2h03m41.749s	2
12	Yuki Tsunoda */‡	AlphaTauri	AlphaTauri-Honda AT02	2h03m47.782s	20
13	Kimi Raikkonen †	Alfa Romeo Racing	Alfa Romeo-Ferrari C41	2h04m09.371s	16
14	Antonio Giovinazzi	Alfa Romeo Racing	Alfa Romeo-Ferrari C41	62 laps	17
15	Sebastian Vettel §	Aston Martin F1	Aston Martin-Mercedes AMR21	61 laps/gearbox	13
16	Mick Schumacher	Haas	Haas-Ferrari VF-21	61 laps	18
17	Nikita Mazepin	Haas	Haas-Ferrari VF-21	61 laps	19
R	Valtteri Bottas	Mercedes AMG	Mercedes F1 W12	30 laps/collision	8
R	George Russell	Williams	Williams-Mercedes FW43B	30 laps/collision	12
R	Nicholas Latifi	Williams	Williams-Mercedes FW43B	0 laps/spun off	14

Pole: Hamilton, 1m14.411s, 147.573mph/237.497kph. Fastest lap: Hamilton, 1m16.702s, 143.165mph/230.403kph on Lap 60. Race leaders: Verstappen 1-26 & 29-63, Hamilton 27-28

* 5-place grid penalty for changing gearbox & made to start from rear of grid for using additional power unit elements • ! 10s stop/go penalty for overtaking in a safety car period • ^ 5s penalty for gaining an advantage by leaving track • † 10s stop/go penalty turned into 30s penalty for failing to enter pit lane for restart • ‡ 5s penalty for leaving track multiple times • § 10s stop/go penalty for rear wheels not fitted at 5-minute signal

NEW YEAR, NEW NAMES

The Renault Sport livery of yellow and black was replaced by a more patriotic French blue for Alpine as the company promoted its sports car arm. The team that had competed as Racing Point for just two years came out in a new metallic green racing livery as it changed its name again to the Aston Martin F1 Team.

PORTUGUESE GRAND PRIX

ALGARVE INTERNATIONAL CIRCUIT • ROUND 3 • DATE: 2ND MAY 2021
Laps: • Distance: • Weather: Warm & bright

Pos	Driver	Team	Chassis-Engine	Result	Qual
1	Lewis Hamilton	Mercedes AMG	Mercedes F1 W12	1h34m31.421s	2
2	Max Verstappen	Red Bull Racing	Red Bull-Honda RB16B	1h35m00.569s	3
3	Valtteri Bottas	Mercedes AMG	Mercedes F1 W12	1h35m04.951s	1
4	Sergio Perez	Red Bull Racing	Red Bull-Honda RB16B	1h35m11.156s	4

Pos	Driver	Team	Chassis-Engine	Result	Qual
5	Lando Norris	McLaren	McLaren-Mercedes MCL35M	1h35m22.790s	7
6	Charles Leclerc	Ferrari	Ferrari SF21	1h35m27.202s	8
7	Esteban Ocon	Alpine	Alpine-Renault A521	1h35m35.170s	6
8	Fernando Alonso	Alpine	Alpine-Renault A521	1h35m36.229s	13
9	Daniel Ricciardo	McLaren	McLaren-Mercedes MCL35M	1h35m46.790s	16
10	Pierre Gasly	AlphaTauri	AlphaTauri-Honda AT02	1h35m47.884s	9
11	Carlos Sainz	Ferrari	Ferrari SF21	1h35m50.376s	5
12	Antonio Giovinazzi	Alfa Romeo Racing	Alfa Romeo-Ferrari C41	65 laps	12
13	Sebastian Vettel	Aston Martin F1	Aston Martin-Mercedes AMR21	65 laps	10
14	Lance Stroll	Aston Martin F1	Aston Martin-Mercedes AMR21	65 laps	17
15	Yuki Tsunoda	AlphaTauri	AlphaTauri-Honda AT02	65 laps	14
16	George Russell	Williams	Williams-Mercedes FW43B	65 laps	11
17	Mick Schumacher	Haas	Haas-Ferrari VF-21	64 laps	19
18	Nicholas Latifi	Williams	Williams-Mercedes FW43B	64 laps	18
19	Nikita Mazepin *	Haas	Haas-Ferrari VF-21	64 laps	20
R	Kimi Raikkonen	Alfa Romeo Racing	Alfa Romeo-Ferrari C41	1 lap/collision	15

Pole: Bottas, 1m18.348s, 132.848mph/213.799kph. Fastest lap: Bottas, 1m19.865s, 130.325mph/209.739kph on Lap 65. Race leaders: Bottas 1-19, Hamilton 20-37 & 51-66, Perez 38-50

* 5s penalty for ignoring blue flags

SPANISH GRAND PRIX

BARCELONA-CATALUNYA • ROUND 4 • DATE: 9TH MAY 2021
Laps: 66 • Distance: 190.825miles/307.104km • Weather: Hot & bright

Pos	Driver	Team	Chassis-Engine	Result	Qual
1	Lewis Hamilton	Mercedes AMG	Mercedes F1 W12	1h33m07.680s	1
2	Max Verstappen	Red Bull Racing	Red Bull-Honda RB16B	1h33m23.521s	2
3	Valtteri Bottas	Mercedes AMG	Mercedes F1 W12	1h33m34.290s	3
4	Charles Leclerc	Ferrari	Ferrari SF21	1h34m02.296s	4
5	Sergio Perez	Red Bull Racing	Red Bull-Honda RB16B	1h34m11.351s	8
6	Daniel Ricciardo	McLaren	McLaren-Mercedes MCL35M	1h34m21.448s	7
7	Carlos Sainz	Ferrari	Ferrari SF21	1h34m22.350s	6
8	Lando Norris	McLaren	McLaren-Mercedes MCL35M	65 laps	9
9	Esteban Ocon	Alpine	Alpine-Renault A521	65 laps	5
10	Pierre Gasly !	AlphaTauri	AlphaTauri-Honda AT02	65 laps	12
11	Lance Stroll	Aston Martin F1	Aston Martin-Mercedes AMR21	65 laps	11
12	Kimi Raikkonen	Alfa Romeo Racing	Alfa Romeo-Ferrari C41	65 laps	17
13	Sebastian Vettel	Aston Martin F1	Aston Martin-Mercedes AMR21	65 laps	13
14	George Russell	Williams	Williams-Mercedes FW43B	65 laps	15
15	Antonio Giovinazzi	Alfa Romeo Racing	Alfa Romeo-Ferrari C41	65 laps	14
16	Nicholas Latifi	Williams	Williams-Mercedes FW43B	65 laps	19
17	Fernando Alonso	Alpine	Alpine-Renault A521	65 laps	10
18	Mick Schumacher	Haas	Haas-Ferrari VF-21	64 laps	18
19	Nikita Mazepin *	Haas	Haas-Ferrari VF-21	64 laps	20
R	Yuki Tsunoda	AlphaTauri	AlphaTauri-Honda AT02	6 laps/fuel pressure	16

Pole: Hamilton, 1m16.741s, 136.272mph/219.309kph. Fastest lap: Verstappen, 1m18.149s, 133.244mph/214.437kph on Lap 62. Race leaders: Verstappen 1-23 & 29-59, Hamilton 24-28 & 60-66

* 5-place grid penalty for impeding Norris • ! 5s penalty for being out of position at start

A YEAR OF CONTACT

There were a series of clashes between Hamilton and Verstappen as they scrapped for the title. The most violent was at Silverstone where a collision fired the Red Bull into the barriers. Another at Monza left Verstappen's car sitting on top of the Mercedes. More followed in Brazil and Saudi Arabia but they kept it clean in the Abu Dhabi finale.

MONACO GRAND PRIX

MONTE CARLO • ROUND 5 • DATE: 23RD MAY 2021
Laps: 78 • Distance: 161.734miles/260.286km • Weather: Warm & bright

Pos	Driver	Team	Chassis-Engine	Result	Qual
1	Max Verstappen	Red Bull Racing	Red Bull-Honda RB16B	1h38m56.820s	2
2	Carlos Sainz	Ferrari	Ferrari SF21	1h39m05.788s	4
3	Lando Norris	McLaren	McLaren-Mercedes MCL35M	1h39m16.247s	5
4	Sergio Perez	Red Bull Racing	Red Bull-Honda RB16B	1h39m17.310s	9
5	Sebastian Vettel	Aston Martin F1	Aston Martin-Mercedes AMR21	1h39m49.411s	8
6	Pierre Gasly	AlphaTauri	AlphaTauri-Honda AT02	1h39m50.716s	6
7	Lewis Hamilton	Mercedes AMG	Mercedes F1 W12	1h40m05.051s	7
8	Lance Stroll	Aston Martin F1	Aston Martin-Mercedes AMR21	77 laps	13
9	Esteban Ocon	Alpine	Alpine-Renault A521	77 laps	11
10	Antonio Giovinazzi	Alfa Romeo Racing	Alfa Romeo-Ferrari C41	77 laps	10
11	Kimi Raikkonen	Alfa Romeo Racing	Alfa Romeo-Ferrari C41	77 laps	14
12	Daniel Ricciardo	McLaren	McLaren-Mercedes MCL35M	77 laps	12
13	Fernando Alonso	Alpine	Alpine-Renault A521	77 laps	17
14	George Russell	Williams	Williams-Mercedes FW43B	77 laps	15
15	Nicholas Latifi	Williams	Williams-Mercedes FW43B	77 laps	18
16	Yuki Tsunoda	AlphaTauri	AlphaTauri-Honda AT02	77 laps	16
17	Nikita Mazepin	Haas	Haas-Ferrari VF-21	75 laps	19
18	Mick Schumacher *	Haas	Haas-Ferrari VF-21	75 laps	20
R	Valtteri Bottas	Mercedes AMG	Mercedes F1 W12	29 laps/wheel nut	3
NS	Charles Leclerc	Ferrari	Ferrari SF21	driveshaft hub	1

Pole: Leclerc, 1m10.346s, 106.113mph/170.773kph. Fastest lap: Hamilton, 1m12.909s, 102.383mph/164.770kph on Lap 69. Race leaders: Verstappen 1-78

* 5-place grid penalty for gearbox change

AZERBAIJAN GRAND PRIX

BAKU CITY CIRCUIT • ROUND 6 • DATE: 6TH JUNE 2021
Laps: 51 • Distance: 190.170miles/306.049km • Weather: Hot & bright

Pos	Driver	Team	Chassis-Engine	Result	Qual
1	Sergio Perez	Red Bull Racing	Red Bull-Honda RB16B	2h13m36.410s	6
2	Sebastian Vettel	Aston Martin F1	Aston Martin-Mercedes AMR21	2h13m37.795s	11
3	Pierre Gasly	AlphaTauri	AlphaTauri-Honda AT02	2h13m39.172s	4
4	Charles Leclerc	Ferrari	Ferrari SF21	2h13m40.238s	1
5	Lando Norris *	McLaren	McLaren-Mercedes MCL35M	2h13m41.164s	9
6	Fernando Alonso	Alpine	Alpine-Renault A521	2h13m42.792s	8
7	Yuki Tsunoda	AlphaTauri	AlphaTauri-Honda AT02	2h13m43.034s	7
8	Carlos Sainz	Ferrari	Ferrari SF21	2h13m44.119s	5

Pos	Driver	Team	Chassis-Engine	Result	Qual
9	Daniel Ricciardo	McLaren	McLaren-Mercedes MCL35M	2h13m45.284s	13
10	Kimi Raikkonen	Alfa Romeo Racing	Alfa Romeo-Ferrari C41	2h13m45.986s	14
11	Antonio Giovinazzi	Alfa Romeo Racing	Alfa Romeo-Ferrari C41	2h13m46.664s	20
12	Valtteri Bottas	Mercedes AMG	Mercedes F1 W12	2h13m47.674s	10
13	Mick Schumacher	Haas	Haas-Ferrari VF-21	2h13m50.651s	17
14	Nikita Mazepin	Haas	Haas-Ferrari VF-21	2h13m50.725s	18
15	Lewis Hamilton	Mercedes AMG	Mercedes F1 W12	2h13m54.078s	2
16	Nicholas Latifi !	Williams	Williams-Mercedes FW43B	2h14m18.789s	16
17	George Russell	Williams	Williams-Mercedes FW43B	48 laps/gearbox	15
18	Max Verstappen	Red Bull Racing	Red Bull-Honda RB16B	45 laps/tyre	3
R	Lance Stroll	Aston Martin F1	Aston Martin-Mercedes AMR21	29 laps/tyre	19
R	Esteban Ocon	Alpine	Alpine-Renault A521	3 laps/power unit	12

Pole: Leclerc, 1m41.218s, 132.667mph/213.507kph. Fastest lap: Verstappen, 1m44.481s, 128.524mph/206.840kph on Lap 44. Race leaders: Leclerc 1, Hamilton 2-10, Verstappen 11 & 18-45, Perez 12-13 & 46-51, Vettel 14-17

* 3-place grid penalty for failing to enter pit lane during red flag period • ! 10s stop/go penalty turned into 30s penalty for failing to enter pit lane in safety car period

ALONSO'S THIRD SPELL

Fernando Alonso returned to F1 after a two-year break, rejoining Alpine, a team that he had raced for from 2003 to 2006, then 2008 and 2009, when it was branded Renault. The former world champion took a while to adapt alongside Esteban Ocon, but went better and better to first help Ocon win in Hungary, and then to finish a delighted third in Qatar.

FRENCH GRAND PRIX

CIRCUIT PAUL RICARD • ROUND 7 • DATE: 20TH JUNE 2021
Laps: 53 • Distance: 192.392miles/309.626km • Weather: Hot & bright

Pos	Driver	Team	Chassis-Engine	Result	Qual
1	Max Verstappen	Red Bull Racing	Red Bull-Honda RB16B	1h27m25.770s	1
2	Lewis Hamilton	Mercedes AMG	Mercedes F1 W12	1h27m28.674s	2
3	Sergio Perez	Red Bull Racing	Red Bull-Honda RB16B	1h27m34.581s	4
4	Valtteri Bottas	Mercedes AMG	Mercedes F1 W12	1h27m40.388s	3
5	Lando Norris	McLaren	McLaren-Mercedes MCL35M	1h28m29.802s	8
6	Daniel Ricciardo	McLaren	McLaren-Mercedes MCL35M	1h28m41.627s	10
7	Pierre Gasly	AlphaTauri	AlphaTauri-Honda AT02	1h28m42.366s	6
8	Fernando Alonso	Alpine	Alpine-Renault A521	1h28m43.465s	9
9	Sebastian Vettel	Aston Martin F1	Aston Martin-Mercedes AMR21	1h28m45.436s	12
10	Lance Stroll	Aston Martin F1	Aston Martin-Mercedes AMR21	1h28m57.716s	19
11	Carlos Sainz	Ferrari	Ferrari SF21	1h29m05.107s	5
12	George Russell	Williams	Williams-Mercedes FW43B	52 laps	14
13	Yuki Tsunoda *	AlphaTauri	AlphaTauri-Honda AT02	52 laps	20
14	Esteban Ocon	Alpine	Alpine-Renault A521	52 laps	11
15	Antonio Giovinazzi	Alfa Romeo Racing	Alfa Romeo-Ferrari C41	52 laps	13
16	Charles Leclerc	Ferrari	Ferrari SF21	52 laps	7
17	Kimi Raikkonen	Alfa Romeo Racing	Alfa Romeo-Ferrari C41	52 laps	17

Pos	Driver	Team	Chassis-Engine	Result	Qual
18	Nicholas Latifi	Williams	Williams-Mercedes FW43B	52 laps	16
19	Mick Schumacher	Haas	Haas-Ferrari VF-21	52 laps	15
20	Nikita Mazepin	Haas	Haas-Ferrari VF-21	52 laps	18

Pole: Verstappen, 1m29.990s, 145.217mph/233.705kph. Fastest lap: Verstappen, 1m36.404s, 135.556mph/218.157kph on Lap 35. Race leaders: Hamilton 1-18 & 32-51, Perez 19-23, Verstappen 24-31 & 52-53

* 5-place grid penalty for gearbox change & made to start from rear of grid for car being modified in parc ferme

THE RIGHT TYRES

The Hungarian GP has long been a race that has produced unexpected winners and Esteban Ocon became the latest when he won for Alpine. A first corner accident on a wet track took out four cars and stopped the race. Lewis Hamilton returned to the grid on intermediates, but the others pitted for slick tyres. These were way faster and Ocon sprinted clear to win.

STYRIAN GRAND PRIX

RED BULL RING • ROUND 8 • DATE: 27TH JUNE 2021
Laps: 71 • Distance: 190.498miles/306.578km • Weather: Hot & bright

Pos	Driver	Team	Chassis-Engine	Result	Qual
1	Max Verstappen	Red Bull Racing	Red Bull-Honda RB16B	1h22m18.925s	1
2	Lewis Hamilton	Mercedes AMG	Mercedes F1 W12	1h22m54.668s	2
3	Valtteri Bottas *	Mercedes AMG	Mercedes F1 W12	1h23m05.832s	5
4	Sergio Perez	Red Bull Racing	Red Bull-Honda RB16B	1h23m06.359s	4
5	Lando Norris	McLaren	McLaren-Mercedes MCL35M	70 laps	3
6	Carlos Sainz	Ferrari	Ferrari SF21	70 laps	12
7	Charles Leclerc	Ferrari	Ferrari SF21	70 laps	7
8	Lance Stroll	Aston Martin F1	Aston Martin-Mercedes AMR21	70 laps	9
9	Fernando Alonso	Alpine	Alpine-Renault A521	70 laps	8
10	Yuki Tsunoda !	AlphaTauri	AlphaTauri-Honda AT02	70 laps	11
11	Kimi Raikkonen	Alfa Romeo Racing	Alfa Romeo-Ferrari C41	70 laps	18
12	Sebastian Vettel	Aston Martin F1	Aston Martin-Mercedes AMR21	70 laps	14
13	Daniel Ricciardo	McLaren	McLaren-Mercedes MCL35M	70 laps	13
14	Esteban Ocon	Alpine	Alpine-Renault A521	70 laps	17
15	Antonio Giovinazzi	Alfa Romeo Racing	Alfa Romeo-Ferrari C41	70 laps	15
16	Mick Schumacher	Haas	Haas-Ferrari VF-21	69 laps	19
17	Nicholas Latifi	Williams	Williams-Mercedes FW43B	68 laps	16
18	Nikita Mazepin	Haas	Haas-Ferrari VF-21	68 laps	20
R	George Russell	Williams	Williams-Mercedes FW43B	36 laps/power unit	10
R	Pierre Gasly	AlphaTauri	AlphaTauri-Honda AT02	1 lap/collision	6

Pole: Verstappen, 1m03.841s, 151.298mph/243.492kph. Fastest lap: Hamilton, 1m07.058s, 144.040mph/231.811kph on Lap 71. Race leaders: Verstappen 1-71

* 3-place grid penalty for dangerous driving in pit lane • ! 3-place grid penalty for impeding Bottas

AUSTRIAN GRAND PRIX

RED BULL RING • ROUND 9 • DATE: 4TH JULY 2021
Laps: 71 • Distance: 190.498miles/306.578km • Weather: Warm & bright

Pos	Driver	Team	Chassis-Engine	Result	Qual
1	Max Verstappen	Red Bull Racing	Red Bull-Honda RB16B	1h23m54.543s	1
2	Valtteri Bottas	Mercedes AMG	Mercedes F1 W12	1h24m12.516s	5
3	Lando Norris !	McLaren	McLaren-Mercedes MCL35M	1h24m14.562s	2
4	Lewis Hamilton	Mercedes AMG	Mercedes F1 W12	1h24m40.995s	4
5	Carlos Sainz	Ferrari	Ferrari SF21	1h24m51.687s	10
6	Sergio Perez ^	Red Bull Racing	Red Bull-Honda RB16B	1h24m52.458s	3
7	Daniel Ricciardo	McLaren	McLaren-Mercedes MCL35M	1h24m54.938s	13
8	Charles Leclerc	Ferrari	Ferrari SF21	1h24m55.738s	12
9	Pierre Gasly	AlphaTauri	AlphaTauri-Honda AT02	1h24m56.387s	6
10	Fernando Alonso	Alpine	Alpine-Renault A521	70 laps	14
11	George Russell	Williams	Williams-Mercedes FW43B	70 laps	8
12	Yuki Tsunoda **	AlphaTauri	AlphaTauri-Honda AT02	70 laps	7
13	Lance Stroll †	Aston Martin F1	Aston Martin-Mercedes AMR21	70 laps	9
14	Antonio Giovinazzi ¶	Alfa Romeo Racing	Alfa Romeo-Ferrari C41	70 laps	15
15	Kimi Raikkonen ‡	Alfa Romeo Racing	Alfa Romeo-Ferrari C41	70 laps	16
16	Nicholas Latifi §	Williams	Williams-Mercedes FW43B	70 laps	18
17	Sebastian Vettel *	Aston Martin F1	Aston Martin-Mercedes AMR21	69 laps/accident	11
18	Mick Schumacher	Haas	Haas-Ferrari VF-21	69 laps	19
19	Nikita Mazepin §	Haas	Haas-Ferrari VF-21	69 laps	20
R	Esteban Ocon	Alpine	Alpine-Renault A521	0 laps/collision	17

Pole: Verstappen, 1m03.720s, 151.585mph/243.954kph. Fastest lap: Verstappen, 1m06.200s, 145.907mph/234.816kph on Lap 62. Race leaders: Verstappen 1-71

* 3-place grid penalty for impeding Alonso • ! 5s penalty for forcing Perez off the track • ^ 10s penalty for twice forcing Leclerc off the track • † 5s penalty for speeding in pit lane • ‡ drivethrough penalty turned into 20s penalty for causing a crash with Vettel • § 10s stop/go penalty turned into 30s penalty for failing to respect double yellow flags • ¶ 5s penalty for overtaking in a safety car period • ** 2 5s penalties for crossing white line at pit entry

BRITISH GRAND PRIX

SILVERSTONE • ROUND 10 • DATE: 18TH JULY 2021
Laps: 52 • Distance: 190.262miles/306.198km • Weather: Hot & bright

Pos	Driver	Team	Chassis-Engine	Result	Qual
1	Lewis Hamilton ^	Mercedes AMG	Mercedes F1 W12	1h58m23.284s	2
2	Charles Leclerc	Ferrari	Ferrari SF21	1h58m27.155s	4
3	Valtteri Bottas	Mercedes AMG	Mercedes F1 W12	1h58m34.409s	3
4	Lando Norris	McLaren	McLaren-Mercedes MCL35M	1h58m51.857s	5
5	Daniel Ricciardo	McLaren	McLaren-Mercedes MCL35M	1h59m05.908s	6
6	Carlos Sainz	Ferrari	Ferrari SF21	1h59m06.738s	10
7	Fernando Alonso	Alpine	Alpine-Renault A521	1h59m35.377s	7
8	Lance Stroll	Aston Martin F1	Aston Martin-Mercedes AMR21	1h59m37.573s	14
9	Esteban Ocon	Alpine	Alpine-Renault A521	1h59m39.446s	9
10	Yuki Tsunoda	AlphaTauri	AlphaTauri-Honda AT02	1h59m45.349s	16
11	Pierre Gasly	AlphaTauri	AlphaTauri-Honda AT02	1h59m48.611s	11
12	George Russell *	Williams	Williams-Mercedes FW43B	51 laps	12
13	Antonio Giovinazzi	Alfa Romeo Racing	Alfa Romeo-Ferrari C41	51 laps	15
14	Nicholas Latifi	Williams	Williams-Mercedes FW43B	51 laps	17
15	Kimi Raikkonen	Alfa Romeo Racing	Alfa Romeo-Ferrari C41	51 laps	13
16	Sergio Perez !	Red Bull Racing	Red Bull-Honda RB16B	51 laps	20
17	Nikita Mazepin	Haas	Haas-Ferrari VF-21	51 laps	19

Pos	Driver	Team	Chassis-Engine	Result	Qual
18	Mick Schumacher	Haas	Haas-Ferrari VF-21	51 laps	18
R	Sebastian Vettel	Aston Martin F1	Aston Martin-Mercedes AMR21	40 laps/overheating	8
R	Max Verstappen	Red Bull Racing	Red Bull-Honda RB16B	0 laps/collision	1

Pole: Verstappen, 1m26.209s, 152.858mph/246.002kph. Fastest lap: Perez, 1m28.617s, 148.705mph/239.318kph on Lap 50. Race leaders: Leclerc 1-49, Hamilton 50-52

* 3-place grid penalty for causing a crash with Sainz • ! made to start from pit lane for using for using additional power unit elements & for car being modified in parc ferme • ^ 10s penalty for causing a crash with Verstappen

HUNGARIAN GRAND PRIX

HUNGARORING • ROUND 11 • DATE: 1ST AUGUST 2021
Laps: 70 • Distance: 190.181miles/306.67km • Weather: Hot & wet, drying later

Pos	Driver	Team	Chassis-Engine	Result	Qual
1	Esteban Ocon	Alpine	Alpine-Renault A521	2h04m43.199s	8
DQ	Sebastian Vettel !	Aston Martin F1	Aston Martin-Mercedes AMR21	70 laps/fuel sample	10
2	Lewis Hamilton	Mercedes AMG	Mercedes F1 W12	2h04m45.935s	1
3	Carlos Sainz	Ferrari	Ferrari SF21	2h04m58.217s	15
4	Fernando Alonso	Alpine	Alpine-Renault A521	2h04m58.850s	9
5	Pierre Gasly	AlphaTauri	AlphaTauri-Honda AT02	2h05m46.813s	5
6	Yuki Tsunoda	AlphaTauri	AlphaTauri-Honda AT02	2h05m59.002s	16
7	Nicholas Latifi	Williams	Williams-Mercedes FW43B	2h06m01.109s	18
8	George Russell	Williams	Williams-Mercedes FW43B	2h06m02.293s	17
9	Max Verstappen	Red Bull Racing	Red Bull-Honda RB16B	2h06m03.443s	3
10	Kimi Raikkonen †	Alfa Romeo Racing	Alfa Romeo-Ferrari C41	69 laps	13
11	Daniel Ricciardo	McLaren	McLaren-Mercedes MCL35M	69 laps	11
12	Mick Schumacher *	Haas	Haas-Ferrari VF-21	69 laps	20
13	Antonio Giovinazzi ^	Alfa Romeo Racing	Alfa Romeo-Ferrari C41	69 laps	14
R	Nikita Mazepin	Haas	Haas-Ferrari VF-21	3 laps/collision	19
R	Lando Norris	McLaren	McLaren-Mercedes MCL35M	2 laps/accident	6
R	Valtteri Bottas	Mercedes AMG	Mercedes F1 W12	0 laps/collision	2
R	Sergio Perez	Red Bull Racing	Red Bull-Honda RB16B	0 laps/collision	4
R	Charles Leclerc	Ferrari	Ferrari SF21	0 laps/collision	7
R	Lance Stroll	Aston Martin F1	Aston Martin-Mercedes AMR21	0 laps/collision	12

Pole: Hamilton, 1m15.419s, 129.940mph/209.119kph. Fastest lap: Gasly, 1m18.394s, 125.009mph/201.184kph on Lap 70. Race leaders: Hamilton 1-2 & 4, Ocon 3 & 5-37 & 40-70, Alonso 38-39

* 5-place grid penalty for gearbox change • ! disqualified for not being able to provide 1-litre fuel sample • ^ 10s stop/go penalty for speeding in pit lane • † 10s penalty for unsafe release from pitstop

SILVER FOR RUSSELL

Excessive rain led to the Belgian GP being started behind the safety car. It ran for two laps before stopping for three hours then trying again also behind the safety car. This time they did one 'race' lap before a result was declared, meaning that Max Verstappen was first and George Russell second, a reward for Russell for a brave decision to go out late in qualifying on intermediates.

BELGIAN GRAND PRIX

SPA-FRANCORCHAMPS • ROUND 12 • DATE: 29TH AUGUST 2021
Laps: 1 • Distance: 4.352 miles/6.880km • Weather: Cool & exceptionally wet

Pos	Driver	Team	Chassis-Engine	Result	Qual
1	Max Verstappen	Red Bull Racing	Red Bull-Honda RB16B	3m27.071s	1
2	George Russell	Williams	Williams-Mercedes FW43B	3m29.066s	2
3	Lewis Hamilton	Mercedes AMG	Mercedes F1 W12	3m29.672s	3
4	Daniel Ricciardo	McLaren	McLaren-Mercedes MCL35M	3m31.567s	4
5	Sebastian Vettel	Aston Martin F1	Aston Martin-Mercedes AMR21	3m34.550s	5
6	Pierre Gasly	AlphaTauri	AlphaTauri-Honda AT02	3m37.248s	6
7	Esteban Ocon	Alpine	Alpine-Renault A521	3m38.650s	8
8	Charles Leclerc	Ferrari	Ferrari SF21	3m39.679s	9
9	Nicholas Latifi	Williams	Williams-Mercedes FW43B	3m42.555s	10
10	Carlos Sainz	Ferrari	Ferrari SF21	3m43.237s	11
11	Fernando Alonso	Alpine	Alpine-Renault A521	3m47.661s	12
12	Valtteri Bottas *	Mercedes AMG	Mercedes F1 W12	3m49.485s	13
13	Antonio Giovinazzi	Alfa Romeo Racing	Alfa Romeo-Ferrari C41	3m51.234s	14
14	Lando Norris #	McLaren	McLaren-Mercedes MCL35M	3m54.180s	15
15	Yuki Tsunoda	AlphaTauri	AlphaTauri-Honda AT02	3m55.400s	16
16	Mick Schumacher	Haas	Haas-Ferrari VF-21	3m56.578s	17
17	Nikita Mazepin	Haas	Haas-Ferrari VF-21	3m59.064s	18
18	Kimi Raikkonen ^	Alfa Romeo Racing	Alfa Romeo-Ferrari C41	4m03.125s	20
19	Sergio Perez	Red Bull Racing	Red Bull-Honda RB16B	4m05.276s	7
20	Lance Stroll !/†	Aston Martin F1	Aston Martin-Mercedes AMR21	4m11.179s	19

Pole: Verstappen, 1m59.765s, 130.818mph/210.532kph. Fastest lap: not awarded. Race leaders: Verstappen 1

* 5-place grid penalty for causing a crash with Norris at Hungarian GP • # 5-place grid penalty for gearbox change • ! 5-place grid penalty for causing a crash with Leclerc at Hungarian GP • ^ made to start from pit lane for car being modified in parc ferme • † 10s penalty for car being modified during temporary race stoppage

NEW CIRCUIT

A new circuit built on Jeddah's corniche made its debut and was undoubtedly fast and spectacular, if not a little scary if anyone should crash or slow through its sequence of esses, as there was little room for error. Zandvoort was also back for the first time since 1985 and had been revamped by adding slight banking to both the Hugenholtzbocht and the final corner.

DUTCH GRAND PRIX

ZANDVOORT • ROUND 13 • DATE: 5TH SEPTEMBER 2021
Laps: 72 • Distance: 190.542miles/306.648km • Weather: Warm & bright

Pos	Driver	Team	Chassis-Engine	Result	Qual
1	Max Verstappen	Red Bull Racing	Red Bull-Honda RB16B	1h30m05.395s	1
2	Lewis Hamilton	Mercedes AMG	Mercedes F1 W12	1h30m26.327s	2
3	Valtteri Bottas	Mercedes AMG	Mercedes F1 W12	1h31m01.855s	3
4	Pierre Gasly	AlphaTauri	AlphaTauri-Honda AT02	71 laps	4
5	Charles Leclerc	Ferrari	Ferrari SF21	71 laps	5
6	Fernando Alonso	Alpine	Alpine-Renault A521	71 laps	9
7	Carlos Sainz	Ferrari	Ferrari SF21	71 laps	6

Pos	Driver	Team	Chassis-Engine	Result	Qual
8	Sergio Perez ^	Red Bull Racing	Red Bull-Honda RB16B	71 laps	20
9	Esteban Ocon	Alpine	Alpine-Renault A521	71 laps	8
10	Lando Norris	McLaren	McLaren-Mercedes MCL35M	71 laps	13
11	Daniel Ricciardo	McLaren	McLaren-Mercedes MCL35M	71 laps	10
12	Lance Stroll	Aston Martin F1	Aston Martin-Mercedes AMR21	70 laps	12
13	Sebastian Vettel	Aston Martin F1	Aston Martin-Mercedes AMR21	70 laps	15
14	Antonio Giovinazzi	Alfa Romeo Racing	Alfa Romeo-Ferrari C41	70 laps	7
15	Robert Kubica	Alfa Romeo Racing	Alfa Romeo-Ferrari C41	70 laps	16
16	Nicholas Latifi */!	Williams	Williams-Mercedes FW43B	70 laps	19
17	George Russell †	Williams	Williams-Mercedes FW43B	69 laps/gearbox	11
18	Mick Schumacher	Haas	Haas-Ferrari VF-21	69 laps	17
R	Yuki Tsunoda	AlphaTauri	AlphaTauri-Honda AT02	48 laps/transmission	14
R	Nikita Mazepin	Haas	Haas-Ferrari VF-21	41 laps/hydraulics	18
NS	Kimi Raikkonen	Alfa Romeo Racing	Alfa Romeo-Ferrari C41	driver unwell	-

Pole: Verstappen, 1m08.885s, 138.304mph/222.579kph. Fastest lap: Hamilton, 1m11.097s, 134.001mph/215.655kph on Lap 72. Race leaders: Verstappen 1-21 & 30-72, Bottas 22-29

* 5-place grid penalty for gearbox change • ! made to start from pit lane for being modified in parc ferme • ^ made to start from pit lane for using additional power unit elements & for car being modified in parc ferme • † 5s penalty for speeding in pit lane

ITALIAN GRAND PRIX

MONZA • ROUND 14 • DATE: 12TH SEPTEMBER 2021
Laps: 53 • Distance: 190.778miles/307.029km • Weather: Hot & bright

Pos	Driver	Team	Chassis-Engine	Result	Qual
1	Daniel Ricciardo	McLaren	McLaren-Mercedes MCL35M	1h21m54.365s	2
2	Lando Norris	McLaren	McLaren-Mercedes MCL35M	1h21m56.112s	3
3	Valtteri Bottas *	Mercedes AMG	Mercedes F1 W12	1h21m59.286s	19
4	Charles Leclerc	Ferrari	Ferrari SF21	1h22m01.674s	5
5	Sergio Perez §	Red Bull Racing	Red Bull-Honda RB16B	1h22m03.088s	8
6	Carlos Sainz	Ferrari	Ferrari SF21	1h22m04.900s	6
7	Lance Stroll	Aston Martin F1	Aston Martin-Mercedes AMR21	1h22m10.169s	9
8	Fernando Alonso	Alpine	Alpine-Renault A521	1h22m11.566s	10
9	George Russell	Williams	Williams-Mercedes FW43B	1h22m14.107s	14
10	Esteban Ocon ‡	Alpine	Alpine-Renault A521	1h22m15.233s	12
11	Nicholas Latifi	Williams	Williams-Mercedes FW43B	1h22m18.108s	13
12	Sebastian Vettel	Aston Martin F1	Aston Martin-Mercedes AMR21	1h22m18.986s	11
13	Antonio Giovinazzi ^	Alfa Romeo Racing	Alfa Romeo-Ferrari C41	1h22m21.581s	7
14	Robert Kubica	Alfa Romeo Racing	Alfa Romeo-Ferrari C41	1h22m24.134s	17
15	Mick Schumacher	Haas	Haas-Ferrari VF-21	1h22m45.453s	18
R	Nikita Mazepin †	Haas	Haas-Ferrari VF-21	41 laps/power unit	16
R	Max Verstappen	Red Bull Racing	Red Bull-Honda RB16B	25 laps/collision	1
R	Lewis Hamilton	Mercedes AMG	Mercedes F1 W12	25 laps/collision	4
R	Pierre Gasly !	AlphaTauri	AlphaTauri-Honda AT02	3 laps/power unit	20
NS	Yuki Tsunoda	AlphaTauri	AlphaTauri-Honda AT02	brakes	15

Pole: Verstappen, 1m19.966s, 162.050mph/260.795kph. Fastest lap: Ricciardo, 1m24.812s, 152.791mph/245.894kph on Lap 53. Race leaders: Ricciardo 1-21 & 27-53, Verstappen 22, Norris 23, Hamilton 24-25, Leclerc 26

* made to start from rear of grid for using additional power unit elements • ! 5-place grid penalty for gearbox change & made to start from pit lane for car being modified in parc ferme • ^ 5s penalty for rejoining the track in unsafe manner • † 5s penalty for causing a crash with Schumacher • ‡ 5s penalty for causing a crash with Vettel • § 5s penalty for gaining an advantage by leaving track

RUSSIAN GRAND PRIX

SOCHI • ROUND 15 • DATE: 26TH SEPTEMBER 2021
Laps: 53 • Distance: 192.590miles/309.944km • Weather: Warm but dull, rain later

Pos	Driver	Team	Chassis-Engine	Result	Qual
1	Lewis Hamilton	Mercedes AMG	Mercedes F1 W12	1h30m41.001s	4
2	Max Verstappen ^/†	Red Bull Racing	Red Bull-Honda RB16B	1h31m34.272s	20
3	Carlos Sainz	Ferrari	Ferrari SF21	1h31m43.476s	2
4	Daniel Ricciardo	McLaren	McLaren-Mercedes MCL35M	1h31m46.608s	5
5	Valtteri Bottas *	Mercedes AMG	Mercedes F1 W12	1h31m48.534s	16
6	Fernando Alonso	Alpine	Alpine-Renault A521	1h32m02.322s	6
7	Lando Norris	McLaren	McLaren-Mercedes MCL35M	1h32m08.225s	1
8	Kimi Raikkonen	Alfa Romeo Racing	Alfa Romeo-Ferrari C41	1h32m09.956s	13
9	Sergio Perez	Red Bull Racing	Red Bull-Honda RB16B	1h32m11.077s	8
10	George Russell	Williams	Williams-Mercedes FW43B	1h32m21.552s	3
11	Lance Stroll ‡	Aston Martin F1	Aston Martin-Mercedes AMR21	1h32m37.199s	7
12	Sebastian Vettel	Aston Martin F1	Aston Martin-Mercedes AMR21	52 laps	10
13	Pierre Gasly	AlphaTauri	AlphaTauri-Honda AT02	52 laps	11
14	Esteban Ocon	Alpine	Alpine-Renault A521	52 laps	9
15	Charles Leclerc ^	Ferrari	Ferrari SF21	52 laps	19
16	Antonio Giovinazzi !	Alfa Romeo Racing	Alfa Romeo-Ferrari C41	52 laps	17
17	Yuki Tsunoda	AlphaTauri	AlphaTauri-Honda AT02	52 laps	12
18	Nikita Mazepin	Haas	Haas-Ferrari VF-21	51 laps	15
19	Nicholas Latifi ^	Williams	Williams-Mercedes FW43B	47 laps/accident	18
R	Mick Schumacher	Haas	Haas-Ferrari VF-21	32 laps/hydraulics	14

Pole: Norris, 1m41.993s, 128.259mph/206.414kph. Fastest lap: Norris, 1m37.423s, 134.276mph/216.097kph on Lap 39. Race leaders: Sainz 1-12, Norris 13-28 & 37-50, Perez 29-36, Hamilton 51-53

* 15-place grid penalty for using additional power unit elements • ! 5-place grid penalty for gearbox change • ^ made to start from rear of grid for using additional power unit elements • † 3-place grid penalty for causing a crash at Italian GP • ‡ 10s penalty for causing a crash with Gasly

TURKISH GRAND PRIX

ISTANBUL PARK • ROUND 16 • DATE: 10TH OCTOBER 2021
Laps: 58 • Distance: 199.586miles/321.204km • Weather: Warm with drizzle

Pos	Driver	Team	Chassis-Engine	Result	Qual
1	Valtteri Bottas	Mercedes AMG	Mercedes F1 W12	1h31m04.103s	1
2	Max Verstappen	Red Bull Racing	Red Bull-Honda RB16B	1h31m18.687s	2
3	Sergio Perez	Red Bull Racing	Red Bull-Honda RB16B	1h31m37.574s	6
4	Charles Leclerc	Ferrari	Ferrari SF21	1h31m41.917s	3
5	Lewis Hamilton *	Mercedes AMG	Mercedes F1 W12	1h31m45.915s	11
6	Pierre Gasly †	AlphaTauri	AlphaTauri-Honda AT02	1h31m48.395s	4
7	Lando Norris	McLaren	McLaren-Mercedes MCL35M	1h31m51.316s	7
8	Carlos Sainz !	Ferrari	Ferrari SF21	1h31m55.629s	19
9	Lance Stroll	Aston Martin F1	Aston Martin-Mercedes AMR21	1h32m26.121s	8
10	Esteban Ocon	Alpine	Alpine-Renault A521	57 laps	12
11	Antonio Giovinazzi	Alfa Romeo Racing	Alfa Romeo-Ferrari C41	57 laps	16
12	Kimi Raikkonen	Alfa Romeo Racing	Alfa Romeo-Ferrari C41	57 laps	17
13	Daniel Ricciardo !	McLaren	McLaren-Mercedes MCL35M	57 laps	20
14	Yuki Tsunoda	AlphaTauri	AlphaTauri-Honda AT02	57 laps	9
15	George Russell	Williams	Williams-Mercedes FW43B	57 laps	13
16	Fernando Alonso ^	Alpine	Alpine-Renault A521	57 laps	5

Pos	Driver	Team	Chassis-Engine	Result	Qual
17	Nicholas Latifi	Williams	Williams-Mercedes FW43B	57 laps	15
18	Sebastian Vettel	Aston Martin F1	Aston Martin-Mercedes AMR21	57 laps	10
19	Mick Schumacher	Haas	Haas-Ferrari VF-21	56 laps	14
20	Nikita Mazepin	Haas	Haas-Ferrari VF-21	56 laps	18

Pole: Bottas, 1m22.998s, 143.867mph/231.533kph. Fastest lap: Bottas, 1m30.432s, 132.041mph/212.500kph on Lap 58. Race leaders: Bottas 1-37 & 47-58, Leclerc 38-46

* 10-place grid penalty for using additional power unit elements • ! made to start from rear of grid for using additional power unit elements • ^ 5s penalty for causing a crash with Schumacher • † 5s penalty for causing a crash with Alonso

UNITED STATES GRAND PRIX

CIRCUIT OF THE AMERICAS • ROUND 17 • DATE: 24TH OCTOBER 2021
Laps: 56 • Distance: 191.834miles/308.728km • Weather: Hot & bright

Pos	Driver	Team	Chassis-Engine	Result	Qual
1	Max Verstappen	Red Bull Racing	Red Bull-Honda RB16B	1h34m36.552s	1
2	Lewis Hamilton	Mercedes AMG	Mercedes F1 W12	1h34m37.885s	2
3	Sergio Perez	Red Bull Racing	Red Bull-Honda RB16B	1h35m18.775s	3
4	Charles Leclerc	Ferrari	Ferrari SF21	1h35m28.798s	4
5	Daniel Ricciardo	McLaren	McLaren-Mercedes MCL35M	1h35m53.406s	6
6	Valtteri Bottas *	Mercedes AMG	Mercedes F1 W12	1h35m56.680s	9
7	Carlos Sainz	Ferrari	Ferrari SF21	1h36m00.097s	5
8	Lando Norris	McLaren	McLaren-Mercedes MCL35M	1h36m00.947s	7
9	Yuki Tsunoda	AlphaTauri	AlphaTauri-Honda AT02	55 laps	10
10	Sebastian Vettel !	Aston Martin F1	Aston Martin-Mercedes AMR21	55 laps	18
11	Antonio Giovinazzi	Alfa Romeo Racing	Alfa Romeo-Ferrari C41	55 laps	12
12	Lance Stroll	Aston Martin F1	Aston Martin-Mercedes AMR21	55 laps	13
13	Kimi Raikkonen	Alfa Romeo Racing	Alfa Romeo-Ferrari C41	55 laps	15
14	George Russell !	Williams	Williams-Mercedes FW43B	55 laps	20
15	Nicholas Latifi	Williams	Williams-Mercedes FW43B	55 laps	14
16	Mick Schumacher	Haas	Haas-Ferrari VF-21	54 laps	16
17	Nikita Mazepin	Haas	Haas-Ferrari VF-21	54 laps	17
R	Fernando Alonso !	Alpine	Alpine-Renault A521	49 laps/wing	19
R	Esteban Ocon	Alpine	Alpine-Renault A521	40 laps/mechanical	11
R	Pierre Gasly	AlphaTauri	AlphaTauri-Honda AT02	14 laps/suspension	8

Pole: Verstappen, 1m32.910s, 132.732mph/213.613kph. Fastest lap: Hamilton, 1m38.485s, 125.219mph/201.521kph on Lap 41. Race leaders: Hamilton 1-13 & 30-37, Verstappen 14-29 & 38-56

* 5-place grid penalty for using additional power unit elements • ! made to start from rear of grid for using additional power unit elements

MEXICO CITY GRAND PRIX

MEXICO CITY • ROUND 18 • DATE: 7TH NOVEMBER 2021
Laps: 71 • Distance: 189.881miles/305.584km • Weather: Warm & bright

Pos	Driver	Team	Chassis-Engine	Result	Qual
1	Max Verstappen	Red Bull Racing	Red Bull-Honda RB16B	1h38m39.086s	3
2	Lewis Hamilton	Mercedes AMG	Mercedes F1 W12	1h38m55.641s	2
3	Sergio Perez	Red Bull Racing	Red Bull-Honda RB16B	1h38m56.838s	4
4	Pierre Gasly	AlphaTauri	AlphaTauri-Honda AT02	1h39m42.931s	5
5	Charles Leclerc	Ferrari	Ferrari SF21	1h40m00.123s	8

Pos	Driver	Team	Chassis-Engine	Result	Qual
6	Carlos Sainz	Ferrari	Ferrari SF21	70 laps	6
7	Sebastian Vettel	Aston Martin F1	Aston Martin-Mercedes AMR21	70 laps	9
8	Kimi Raikkonen	Alfa Romeo Racing	Alfa Romeo-Ferrari C41	70 laps	10
9	Fernando Alonso	Alpine	Alpine-Renault A521	70 laps	12
10	Lando Norris !	McLaren	McLaren-Mercedes MCL35M	70 laps	18
11	Antonio Giovinazzi	Alfa Romeo Racing	Alfa Romeo-Ferrari C41	70 laps	11
12	Daniel Ricciardo	McLaren	McLaren-Mercedes MCL35M	70 laps	7
13	Esteban Ocon !	Alpine	Alpine-Renault A521	70 laps	19
14	Lance Stroll */!	Aston Martin F1	Aston Martin-Mercedes AMR21	69 laps	20
15	Valtteri Bottas	Mercedes AMG	Mercedes F1 W12	69 laps	1
16	George Russell *	Williams	Williams-Mercedes FW43B	69 laps	16
17	Nicholas Latifi	Williams	Williams-Mercedes FW43B	69 laps	13
18	Nikita Mazepin	Haas	Haas-Ferrari VF-21	68 laps	15
R	Mick Schumacher	Haas	Haas-Ferrari VF-21	0 laps/collision	14
R	Yuki Tsunoda !	AlphaTauri	AlphaTauri-Honda AT02	0 laps/collision	17

Pole: Bottas, 1m15.875s, 126.889mph/204.209kph. Fastest lap: Bottas, 1m17.774s, 123.791mph/199.223kph on Lap 69. Race leaders: Verstappen 1-33 & 40-71, Perez 34-39

* 5-place grid penalty for gearbox change • ! made to start rom rear of grid for using additional power unit elements

SAO PAULO GRAND PRIX

INTERLAGOS • ROUND 19 • DATE: 14TH NOVEMBER 2021
Laps: 71 • Distance: 190.101miles/305.939km • Weather: Hot & bright

Pos	Driver	Team	Chassis-Engine	Result	Qual
1	Lewis Hamilton *	Mercedes AMG	Mercedes F1 W12	1h32m22.851s	10
2	Max Verstappen	Red Bull Racing	Red Bull-Honda RB16B	1h32m33.347s	2
3	Valtteri Bottas	Mercedes AMG	Mercedes F1 W12	1h32m36.427s	1
4	Sergio Perez	Red Bull Racing	Red Bull-Honda RB16B	1h33m02.791s	4
5	Charles Leclerc	Ferrari	Ferrari SF21	1h33m12.368s	6
6	Carlos Sainz	Ferrari	Ferrari SF21	1h33m14.671s	3
7	Pierre Gasly	AlphaTauri	AlphaTauri-Honda AT02	70 laps	7
8	Esteban Ocon	Alpine	Alpine-Renault A521	70 laps	8
9	Fernando Alonso	Alpine	Alpine-Renault A521	70 laps	12
10	Lando Norris	McLaren	McLaren-Mercedes MCL35M	70 laps	5
11	Sebastian Vettel	Aston Martin F1	Aston Martin-Mercedes AMR21	70 laps	9
12	Kimi Raikkonen !	Alfa Romeo Racing	Alfa Romeo-Ferrari C41	70 laps	20
13	George Russell	Williams	Williams-Mercedes FW43B	70 laps	17
14	Antonio Giovinazzi	Alfa Romeo Racing	Alfa Romeo-Ferrari C41	70 laps	13
15	Yuki Tsunoda ^	AlphaTauri	AlphaTauri-Honda AT02	70 laps	15
16	Nicholas Latifi	Williams	Williams-Mercedes FW43B	70 laps	16
17	Nikita Mazepin	Haas	Haas-Ferrari VF-21	69 laps	19
18	Mick Schumacher	Haas	Haas-Ferrari VF-21	69 laps	18
R	Daniel Ricciardo	McLaren	McLaren-Mercedes MCL35M	49 laps/chassis	11
R	Lance Stroll	Aston Martin F1	Aston Martin-Mercedes AMR21	47 laps/accident	14

Pole: Bottas, 1m08.469s, 140.777mph/226.560kph. Fastest lap: Perez, 1m11.010s, 135.741mph/218.454kph on Lap 71. Race leaders: Verstappen 1-27 & 31-39 & 44-58, Bottas 28-30, Hamilton 40-43 & 59-71

* 5-place grid penalty for using additional power unit element • ! made to start from pit lane for car being modified in parc ferme • ^ 10s penalty for causing a crash with Stroll

QATAR GRAND PRIX

LOSAIL INTERNATIONAL CIRCUIT • ROUND 20 • DATE: 21ST NOVEMBER 2021
Laps: 57 • Distance: 190.180miles/306.66km • Weather: Warm & dry

Pos	Driver	Team	Chassis-Engine	Result	Qual
1	Lewis Hamilton	Mercedes AMG	Mercedes F1 W12	1h24m28.471s	1
2	Max Verstappen !	Red Bull Racing	Red Bull-Honda RB16B	1h24m54.214s	7
3	Fernando Alonso	Alpine	Alpine-Renault A521	1h25m27.928s	3
4	Sergio Perez	Red Bull Racing	Red Bull-Honda RB16B	1h25m30.777s	11
5	Esteban Ocon	Alpine	Alpine-Renault A521	1h25m49.041s	9
6	Lance Stroll	Aston Martin F1	Aston Martin-Mercedes AMR21	1h25m49.745s	12
7	Carlos Sainz	Ferrari	Ferrari SF21	1h25m50.382s	5
8	Charles Leclerc	Ferrari	Ferrari SF21	1h25m51.597s	13
9	Lando Norris	McLaren	McLaren-Mercedes MCL35M	56 laps	4
10	Sebastian Vettel	Aston Martin F1	Aston Martin-Mercedes AMR21	56 laps	10
11	Pierre Gasly	AlphaTauri	AlphaTauri-Honda AT02	56 laps	2
12	Daniel Ricciardo	McLaren	McLaren-Mercedes MCL35M	56 laps	14
13	Yuki Tsunoda	AlphaTauri	AlphaTauri-Honda AT02	56 laps	8
14	Kimi Raikkonen	Alfa Romeo Racing	Alfa Romeo-Ferrari C41	56 laps	16
15	Antonio Giovinazzi	Alfa Romeo Racing	Alfa Romeo-Ferrari C41	56 laps	18
16	Mick Schumacher	Haas	Haas-Ferrari VF-21	56 laps	19
17	George Russell	Williams	Williams-Mercedes FW43B	55 laps	15
18	Nikita Mazepin	Haas	Haas-Ferrari VF-21	55 laps	20
R	Nicholas Latifi	Williams	Williams-Mercedes FW43B	50 laps/puncture	17
R	Valtteri Bottas *	Mercedes AMG	Mercedes F1 W12	48 laps/puncture	6

Pole: Hamilton, 1m20.827s, 148.894mph/239.622kph. Fastest lap: Verstappen, 1m23.196s, 144.655mph/232.800kph on Lap 57. Race leaders: Hamilton 1-57

* 3-place grid penalty for failing to respect a yellow flag • ! 5-place grid penalty for failing to respect double yellow flags

NEW DRIVERS

Yuki Tsunoda made an instant impact for Scuderia AlphaTauri by coming ninth in the opening round, then fourth in the final race. Haas F1 ran two rookies in Mick Schumacher and Nikita Mazepin, with the son of the seven-time world champion peaking with 13th, and Mazepin 14th, both in the Azerbaijan GP.

SAUDI ARABIAN GRAND PRIX

JEDDAH CORNICHE CIRCUIT • ROUND 21 • DATE: 5TH DECEMBER 2021
Laps: 50 • Distance: 191.386miles/308.7km • Weather: Warm & dry

Pos	Driver	Team	Chassis-Engine	Result	Qual
1	Lewis Hamilton	Mercedes AMG	Mercedes F1 W12	2h06m15.118s	1
2	Max Verstappen !/^	Red Bull Racing	Red Bull-Honda RB16B	2h06m36.943s	3
3	Valtteri Bottas	Mercedes AMG	Mercedes F1 W12	2h06m42.649s	2
4	Esteban Ocon	Alpine	Alpine-Renault A521	2h06m42.751s	9
5	Daniel Ricciardo	McLaren	McLaren-Mercedes MCL35M	2h06m55.239s	11
6	Pierre Gasly	AlphaTauri	AlphaTauri-Honda AT02	2h06m56.731s	6
7	Charles Leclerc	Ferrari	Ferrari SF21	2h06m59.593s	4
8	Carlos Sainz	Ferrari	Ferrari SF21	2h07m01.724s	15

Pos	Driver	Team	Chassis-Engine	Result	Qual
9	Antonio Giovinazzi	Alfa Romeo Racing	Alfa Romeo-Ferrari C41	2h07m13.623s	10
10	Lando Norris	McLaren	McLaren-Mercedes MCL35M	2h07m16.476s	7
11	Lance Stroll	Aston Martin F1	Aston Martin-Mercedes AMR21	2h07m32.330s	18
12	Nicholas Latifi	Williams	Williams-Mercedes FW43B	2h07m38.367s	16
13	Fernando Alonso	Alpine	Alpine-Renault A521	49 laps	13
14	Yuki Tsunoda *	AlphaTauri	AlphaTauri-Honda AT02	49 laps	8
15	Kimi Raikkonen	Alfa Romeo Racing	Alfa Romeo-Ferrari C41	49 laps	12
R	Sebastian Vettel	Aston Martin F1	Aston Martin-Mercedes AMR21	44 laps/accident	17
R	Sergio Perez	Red Bull Racing	Red Bull-Honda RB16B	14 laps/collision	5
R	George Russell	Williams	Williams-Mercedes FW43B	14 laps/collision	14
R	Nikita Mazepin	Haas	Haas-Ferrari VF-21	14 laps/collision	20
R	Mick Schumacher	Haas	Haas-Ferrari VF-21	8 laps/accident	19

Pole: Hamilton, 1m27.511s, 157.818mph/253.984kph. Fastest lap: Hamilton, 1m30.734s, 152.212mph/244.962kph on Lap 47. Race leaders: Hamilton 1-10 & 43-50, Verstappen 11-15 & 17-42, Ocon 16

* 5s penalty for causing a crash with Vettel • ! 5s penalty for gaining an advantage by leaving track • ^ 10s penalty for causing a crash with Hamilton

KEY PERSON: SIR FRANK WILLIAMS

The death of Sir Frank Williams in November 2021 at the age of 79 left F1 without one of its great achievers. Williams raced in F3 but turned to running cars for others. His involvement with F1 dated back to 1969 when he fielded a car for Piers Courage, which was followed by almost a decade of trying to run a team capable of winning a grand prix. This finally happened at the 1979 British GP and Alan Jones provided the team's first world title in 1980. Williams were title winners with Honda later that decade before a golden age with Renault power produced five constructors' titles in six years from 1992.

ABU DHABI GRAND PRIX

YAS MARINA CIRCUIT • ROUND 22 • DATE: 12TH DECEMBER 2021
Laps: 58 • Distance: 190.324miles/306.298km • Weather: Warm & dry

Pos	Driver	Team	Chassis-Engine	Result	Qual
1	Max Verstappen	Red Bull Racing	Red Bull-Honda RB16B	1h30m17.345s	1
2	Lewis Hamilton	Mercedes AMG	Mercedes F1 W12	1h30m19.601s	2
3	Carlos Sainz	Ferrari	Ferrari SF21	1h30m22.518s	5
4	Yuki Tsunoda	AlphaTauri	AlphaTauri-Honda AT02	1h30m23.037s	8
5	Pierre Gasly	AlphaTauri	AlphaTauri-Honda AT02	1h30m23.876s	12
6	Valtteri Bottas	Mercedes AMG	Mercedes F1 W12	1h30m24.808s	6
7	Lando Norris	McLaren	McLaren-Mercedes MCL35M	1h31m16.545s	3
8	Fernando Alonso	Alpine	Alpine-Renault A521	1h31m19.053s	11
9	Esteban Ocon	Alpine	Alpine-Renault A521	1h31m21.371s	9
10	Charles Leclerc	Ferrari	Ferrari SF21	1h31m23.402s	7
11	Sebastian Vettel	Aston Martin F1	Aston Martin-Mercedes AMR21	1h31m24.872s	15
12	Daniel Ricciardo	McLaren	McLaren-Mercedes MCL35M	57 laps	10
13	Lance Stroll	Aston Martin F1	Aston Martin-Mercedes AMR21	57 laps	13

Pos	Driver	Team	Chassis-Engine	Result	Qual
14	Mick Schumacher	Haas	Haas-Ferrari VF-21	57 laps	19
15	Sergio Perez	Red Bull Racing	Red Bull-Honda RB16B	55 laps/engine	4
R	Nicholas Latifi	Williams	Williams-Mercedes FW43B	50 laps/accident	16
R	Antonio Giovinazzi	Alfa Romeo Racing	Alfa Romeo-Ferrari C41	33 laps/gearbox	14
R	George Russell	Williams	Williams-Mercedes FW43B	26 laps/gearbox	17
R	Kimi Raikkonen	Alfa Romeo Racing	Alfa Romeo-Ferrari C41	25 laps/wheel nut	18
NS	Nikita Mazepin	Haas	Haas-Ferrari VF-21	-	20

Pole: Verstappen, 1m22.109s, 143.872mph/231.541kph. Fastest lap: Verstappen, 1m26.103s, 137.199mph/220.800kph on Lap 39. Race leaders: Hamilton 1-14 & 21-57, Perez 15-20, Verstappen 58

WORLD DRIVERS' CHAMPIONSHIP FINAL RESULTS

Pos	Driver	Nat	Car-Engine	R1	R2	R3	R4	R5	R6	R7	R8
1	Max Verstappen	NLD	Red Bull-Honda RB16B	2P	1	2	2F	1	18F	1PF	1P
2	Lewis Hamilton	GBR	Mercedes F1 W12	1	2PF	1	1P	7F	15	2	2F
3	Valtteri Bottas	FIN	Mercedes F1 W12	3F	R	3PF	3	R	12	4	3
4	Sergio Perez	MEX	Red Bull-Honda RB16B	5	11	4	5	4	1	3	4
5	Carlos Sainz	ESP	Ferrari SF21	8	5	11	7	2	8	11	6
6	Lando Norris	GBR	McLaren-Mercedes MCL35M	4	3	5	8	3	5	5	5
7	Charles Leclerc	MCO	Ferrari SF21	6	4	6	4	NSP	4P	16	7
8	Daniel Ricciardo	AUS	McLaren-Mercedes MCL35M	7	6	9	6	12	9	6	13
9	Pierre Gasly	FRA	AlphaTauri-Honda AT02	17	7	10	10	6	3	7	R
10	Fernando Alonso	ESP	Alpine-Renault A521	R	10	8	17	13	6	8	9
11	Esteban Ocon	FRA	Alpine-Renault A521	13	9	7	9	9	R	14	14
12	Sebastian Vettel	DEU	Aston Martin-Mercedes AMR21	15	15	13	13	5	2	9	12
13	Lance Stroll	CAN	Aston Martin-Mercedes AMR21	10	8	14	11	8	R	10	8
14	Yuki Tsunoda	JPN	AlphaTauri-Honda AT02	9	12	15	R	16	7	13	10
15	George Russell	GBR	Williams-Mercedes FW43B	14	R	16	14	14	17	12	R
16	Kimi Raikkonen	FIN	Alfa Romeo-Ferrari C41	11	13	R	12	11	10	17	11
17	Nicholas Latifi	CAN	Williams-Mercedes FW43B	18	R	18	16	15	16	18	17
18	Antonio Giovinazzi	ITA	Alfa Romeo-Ferrari C41	12	14	12	15	10	11	15	15
19	Mick Schumacher	DEU	Haas-Ferrari VF-21	16	16	17	18	18	13	19	16
20	Robert Kubica	POL	Alfa Romeo-Ferrari C41	-	-	-	T	-	-	-	T
21	Nikita Mazepin	RAF	Haas-Ferrari VF-21	R	17	19	19	17	14	20	18

Pos	Driver	R9	R10	R11	R12	R13	R14	R15	R16	R17	R18	R19	R20	R21	R22	Total
1	Verstappen	1PF	RP	9	1P	1P	RP	2	2	1P	1	2	2F	2	1PF	395.5
2	Hamilton	4	1	2P	3	2F	R	1	5	2F	2	1	1P	1PF	2	387.5
3	Bottas	2	3	R	12	3	3	5	1PF	6	15PF	3P	R	3	6	226
4	Perez	6	16F	R	19	8	5	9	3	3	3	4F	4	R	15	190
5	Sainz	5	6	3	10	7	6	3	8	7	6	6	7	8	3	164.5
6	Norris	3	4	R	14	10	2	7PF	7	8	10	10	9	10	7	160
7	Leclerc	8	2	R	8	5	4	15	4	4	5	5	8	7	10	159
8	Ricciardo	7	5	11	4	11	1F	4	13	5	12	R	12	5	12	115
9	Gasly	9	11	5F	6	4	R	13	6	R	4	7	11	6	5	110
10	Alonso	10	7	4	11	6	8	6	16	R	9	9	3	13	8	81
11	Ocon	R	9	1	7	9	10	14	10	R	13	8	5	4	9	74
12	Vettel	17	R	DQ	5	13	12	12	18	10	7	11	10	R	11	43
13	Stroll	13	8	R	20	12	7	11	9	12	14	R	6	11	13	34
14	Tsunoda	12	10	6	15	R	NS	17	14	9	R	15	13	14	4	32
15	Russell	11	12	8	2	17	9	10	15	14	16	13	17	R	R	16

Pos	Driver	R9	R10	R11	R12	R13	R14	R15	R16	R17	R18	R19	R20	R21	R22	Total
16	Raikkonen	15	15	10	18	NS	-	8	12	13	8	12	14	15	R	10
17	Latifi	16	14	7	9	16	11	19	17	15	17	16	R	12	R	7
18	Giovinazzi	14	13	13	13	14	13	16	11	11	11	14	15	9	R	3
19	Schumacher	18	18	12	16	18	15	R	19	16	R	18	16	R	14	0
20	Kubica	-	-	T	-	15	14	-	-	-	-	-	-	-	-	0
21	Mazepin	19	17	R	17	R	R	18	20	17	18	17	18	R	NS	0

WORLD CONSTRUCTORS' CHAMPIONSHIP FINAL RESULTS

Pos	Team-Engine	R1	R2	R3	R4	R5	R6	R7	R8	R9	R10	R11	R12
1	Mercedes AMG	1/3	2/R	1/3	1/3	7/R	12/15	2/4	2/3	2/4	1/3	2/R	3/12
2	Red Bull-Honda	2/5	1/11	2/4	2/5	1/4	1/18	1/3	1/4	1/6	16/R	9/R	1/19
3	Ferrari	6/8	4/5	6/11	4/7	2/NS	4/8	11/16	6/7	5/8	2/6	3/R	8/10
4	McLaren-Mercedes	4/7	3/6	5/9	6/8	3/12	5/9	5/6	5/13	3/7	4/5	11/R	4/14
5	Alpine-Renault	13/R	9/10	7/8	9/17	9/13	6/R	8/14	9/14	10/R	7/9	1/4	7/11
6	Alpha Tauri-Honda	9/17	7/12	10/15	10/R	6/16	3/7	7/13	10/R	9/12	10/11	5/6	6/15
7	Aston Martin-Mercedes	10/15	8/15	13/14	11/13	5/8	2/R	9/10	8/12	13/17	8/R	DQ/R	5/20
8	Williams-Mercedes	14/18	R/R	16/18	14/16	14/15	16/17	12/18	17/R	11/16	12/14	7/8	2/9
9	Alfa Romeo-Ferrari	11/12	13/14	12/R	12/15	10/11	10/11	15/17	11/15	14/15	13/15	10/13	13/18
10	Haas-Ferrari	16/R	16/17	17/19	18/19	17/18	13/14	19/20	16/18	18/19	17/18	12/R	16/17

Pos	Team-Engine	R13	R14	R15	R16	R17	R18	R19	R20	R21	R22	Total
1	Mercedes AMG	2/3	3/R	1/5	1/5	2/6	2/15	1/3	1/R	1/3	2/6	613.5
2	Red Bull-Honda	1/8	5/R	2/9	2/3	1/3	1/3	2/4	2/4	2/R	1/15	585.5
3	Ferrari	5/7	4/6	3/15	4/8	4/7	5/6	5/6	7/8	7/8	3/10	323.5
4	McLaren-Mercedes	10/11	1/2	4/7	7/13	5/8	10/12	10/R	9/12	5/10	7/12	275
5	Alpine-Renault	6/9	8/10	6/14	10/16	R/R	9/13	8/9	3/5	4/13	8/9	155
6	Alpha Tauri-Honda	4/R	R/NS	13/17	6/14	9/R	4/R	7/15	11/13	6/14	4/5	142
7	Aston Martin-Mercedes	12/13	7/12	11/12	9/18	10/12	7/14	11/R	6/10	11/R	11/13	77
8	Williams-Mercedes	16/17	9/11	10/19	15/17	14/15	16/17	13/16	17/R	12/R	R/R	23
9	Alfa Romeo-Ferrari	14/15	13/14	8/16	11/12	11/13	8/11	12/14	14/15	9/15	R/R	13
10	Haas-Ferrari	18/R	15/R	18/R	19/20	16/17	18/R	17/18	16/18	R/R	14	0

SYMBOLS AND GRAND PRIX KEY

Round 1 Bahrain GP
Round 2 Emilia Romana GP
Round 3 Portuguese GP
Round 4 Spanish GP
Round 5 Monaco GP
Round 6 Azerbaijan GP
Round 7 French GP
Round 8 Styrian GP
Round 9 Austrian GP
Round 10 British GP
Round 11 Hungarian GP
Round 12 Belgian GP
Round 13 Dutch GP
Round 14 Italian GP
Round 15 Russian GP
Round 16 Turkish GP
Round 17 United States GP
Round 18 Mexican GP
Round 19 Brazilian GP
Round 20 Qatar GP
Round 21 Saudi Arabian GP
Round 22 Abu Dhabi GP

SCORING

1st 25 points
2nd 18 points
3rd 15 points
4th 12 points
5th 10 points
6th 8 points
7th 6 points
8th 4 points
9th 2 points
10th 1 point
Fastest lap (in top 10) 1 point

DNPQ DID NOT PRE-QUALIFY **DNQ** DID NOT QUALIFY **DQ** DISQUALIFIED **EX** EXCLUDED
F FASTEST LAP **NC** NOT CLASSIFIED **NS** NON-STARTER **P** POLE POSITION **R** RETIRED

SEASON SUMMARY

Max Verstappen raced to a second F1 title in a season in which a new set of technical regulations reshaped the order. Long dominant Mercedes produced a car that porpoised, making the drivers both uncomfortable and off the pace, wrecking Lewis Hamilton's chances of an eighth title. Indeed, he didn't win all season. Ferrari started best, but their race strategies were poor and so Verstappen overhauled Charles Leclerc and pulled away as Red Bull developed its RB17s into the pick of the pack, landing the title with four races to spare. Team-mate Sergio Perez was pipped by Leclerc in their battle to be second overall while Carlos Sainz and George Russell both scored breakthrough victories.

BAHRAIN GRAND PRIX

SAKHIR • ROUND 1 • DATE: 20TH MARCH 2022
Laps: 57 • Distance: 191.683miles/308.484km • Weather: Warm & bright

Pos	Driver	Team	Chassis-Engine	Result	Qual
1	Charles Leclerc	Ferrari	Ferrari F1-75	1h37m33.584s	1
2	Carlos Sainz	Ferrari	Ferrari F1-75	1h37m39.182s	3
3	Lewis Hamilton	Mercedes AMG	Mercedes F1 W13	1h37m43.259s	5
4	George Russell	Mercedes AMG	Mercedes F1 W13	1h37m44.795s	9
5	Kevin Magnussen	Haas	Haas-Ferrari VF-22	1h37m48.338s	7
6	Valtteri Bottas	Alfa Romeo Racing	Alfa Romeo-Ferrari C42	1h37m49.703s	6
7	Esteban Ocon*	Alpine	Alpine-Renault A522	1h37m53.007s	11
8	Yuki Tsunoda	AlphaTauri	AlphaTauri-Red Bull AT03	1h37m53.970s	16
9	Fernando Alonso	Alpine	Alpine-Renault A522	1h37m55.974s	8
10	Guanyu Zhou	Alfa Romeo Racing	Alfa Romeo-Ferrari C42	1h37m56.648s	15
11	Mick Schumacher	Haas	Haas-Ferrari VF-22	1h38m06.158s	12
12	Lance Stroll	Aston Martin F1	Aston Martin-Mercedes AMR22	1h38m19.457s	19
13	Alexander Albon	Williams	Williams-Mercedes FW44	1h38m27.516s	14
14	Daniel Ricciardo	McLaren	McLaren-Mercedes MCL36	1h38m28.559s	18
15	Lando Norris	McLaren	McLaren-Mercedes MCL36	1h38m29.919s	13
16	Nicholas Latifi	Williams	Williams-Mercedes FW44	1h38m35.379s	20
17	Nico Hulkenberg	Aston Martin F1	Aston Martin-Mercedes AMR22	1h38m37.413s	17
18	Sergio Perez	Red Bull Racing	Red Bull RB18	56 laps/fuel system	4
19	Max Verstappen	Red Bull Racing	Red Bull RB18	54 laps/fuel system	2
R	Pierre Gasly	AlphaTauri	AlphaTauri-Red Bull AT03	44 laps/power unit	10

Pole: Leclerc, 1m30.558s, 133.685mph/215.146kph. Fastest lap: Leclerc, 1m34.570s, 128.014mph/206.019kph on Lap 51. Race leaders: Leclerc 1-31 & 34-57, Sainz 32-33

* 5s penalty for causing a collision with Schumacher

MOST WINS IN A SEASON

Two retirements in the first three races wasn't great, but then the wins flowed for Max Verstappen as Red Bull outperformed Ferrari, and he was able to pass the record of 13 wins in a season held by Michael Schumacher and Sebastian Vettel, and go on to 15 wins from 22 races.

THE ENEMY WITHIN

Sergio Perez and Max Verstappen had a bust-up after the penultimate race, when Verstappen, already crowned champion, refused to yield a position to Perez to help the Mexican's quest to end the year as runner-up. It was unseemly and suggested that all is not sweetness and light at Red Bull Racing.

SAUDI ARABIAN GRAND PRIX

JEDDAH CORNICHE CIRCUIT • ROUND 2 • DATE: 27TH MARCH 2022
Laps: 50 • Distance: 191.386miles/308.7km • Weather: Hot & bright

Pos	Driver	Team	Chassis-Engine	Result	Qual
1	Max Verstappen	Red Bull Racing	Red Bull RB18	1h24m19.293s	4
2	Charles Leclerc	Ferrari	Ferrari F1-75	1h24m19.842s	2
3	Carlos Sainz	Ferrari	Ferrari F1-75	1h24m27.390s	3
4	Sergio Perez	Red Bull Racing	Red Bull RB18	1h24m30.093s	1
5	George Russell	Mercedes AMG	Mercedes F1 W13	1h24m52.025s	6
6	Esteban Ocon	Alpine	Alpine-Renault A522	1h25m15.310s	5
7	Lando Norris	McLaren	McLaren-Mercedes MCL36	1h25m15.417s	11
8	Pierre Gasly	AlphaTauri	AlphaTauri-Red Bull AT03	1h25m22.239s	9
9	Kevin Magnussen	Haas	Haas-Ferrari VF-22	1h25m23.601s	10
10	Lewis Hamilton	Mercedes AMG	Mercedes F1 W13	1h25m33.241s	15
11	Guanyu Zhou	Alfa Romeo Racing	Alfa Romeo-Ferrari C42	1h25m41.508s	12
12	Nico Hulkenberg	Aston Martin F1	Aston Martin-Mercedes AMR22	1h25m51.035s	17
13	Lance Stroll	Aston Martin F1	Aston Martin-Mercedes AMR22	49 laps	13
14	Alexander Albon	Williams	Williams-Mercedes FW44	47 laps/collision	16
R	Valtteri Bottas	Alfa Romeo Racing	Alfa Romeo-Ferrari C42	36 laps/overheating	8
R	Fernando Alonso	Alpine	Alpine-Renault A522	35 laps/mechanical	7
R	Daniel Ricciardo *	McLaren	McLaren-Mercedes MCL36	35 laps/mechanical	14
R	Nicholas Latifi	Williams	Williams-Mercedes FW44	14 laps/spun off	18
NS	Mick Schumacher	Haas	Haas-Ferrari VF-22	-	-
NS	Yuki Tsunoda	AlphaTauri	AlphaTauri-Red Bull AT03	-	19

Pole: Perez, 1m28.200s, 156.585mph/252.000kph. Fastest lap: Leclerc, 1m31.634s, 150.717mph/242.556kph on Lap 48. Race leaders: Perez 1-14, Leclerc 15-41 & 43-45, Verstappen 42 & 46-50

* 3-place grid penalty for impeding Ocon

AUSTRALIAN GRAND PRIX

ALBERT PARK • ROUND 3 • DATE: 10TH APRIL 2022
Laps: 58 • Distance: 190.252miles/306.182km • Weather: Hot & bright

Pos	Driver	Team	Chassis-Engine	Result	Qual
1	Charles Leclerc	Ferrari	Ferrari F1-75	1h27m46.548s	1
2	Sergio Perez	Red Bull Racing	Red Bull RB18	1h28m07.072s	3
3	George Russell	Mercedes AMG	Mercedes F1 W13	1h28m12.141s	6
4	Lewis Hamilton	Mercedes AMG	Mercedes F1 W13	1h28m15.091s	5
5	Lando Norris	McLaren	McLaren-Mercedes MCL36	1h28m39.851s	4
6	Daniel Ricciardo	McLaren	McLaren-Mercedes MCL36	1h28m40.285s	7
7	Esteban Ocon	Alpine	Alpine-Renault A522	1h28m48.231s	8
8	Valtteri Bottas	Alfa Romeo Racing	Alfa Romeo-Ferrari C42	1h28m54.987s	12

Pos	Driver	Team	Chassis-Engine	Result	Qual
9	Pierre Gasly	AlphaTauri	AlphaTauri-Red Bull AT03	1h29m02.769s	11
10	Alexander Albon !/^	Williams	Williams-Mercedes FW44	1h29m05.930s	20
11	Guanyu Zhou	Alfa Romeo Racing	Alfa Romeo-Ferrari C42	1h29m08.243s	14
12	Lance Stroll */†	Aston Martin F1	Aston Martin-Mercedes AMR22	1h29m15.146s	19
13	Mick Schumacher	Haas	Haas-Ferrari VF-22	57 laps	15
14	Kevin Magnussen	Haas	Haas-Ferrari VF-22	57 laps	16
15	Yuki Tsunoda	AlphaTauri	AlphaTauri-Red Bull AT03	57 laps	13
16	Nicholas Latifi	Williams	Williams-Mercedes FW44	57 laps	18
17	Fernando Alonso	Alpine	Alpine-Renault A522	57 laps	10
R	Max Verstappen	Red Bull Racing	Red Bull RB18	38 laps/fuel system	2
R	Sebastian Vettel	Aston Martin F1	Aston Martin-Mercedes AMR22	22 laps/spun off	17
R	Carlos Sainz	Ferrari	Ferrari F1-75	1 laps/spun off	9

Pole: Leclerc, 1m17.868s, 151.622mph/244.012kph. Fastest lap: Leclerc, 1m20.260s, 147.104mph/236.741kph on Lap 58. Race leaders: Leclerc 1-58

* 3-place grid penalty for causing a collision • ! 3-place grid penalty for causing a crash in Saudi Arabian GP • ^ excluded from qualifying for inability to supply a fuel sample • † 5s penalty for weaving

EMILIA ROMAGNA GRAND PRIX

IMOLA • ROUND 4 • DATE: 24TH APRIL 2022
Laps: 63 • Distance: 192.169miles/309.267km • Weather: Warm but damp

Pos	Driver	Team	Chassis-Engine	Result	Qual
1	Max Verstappen	Red Bull Racing	Red Bull RB18	1h32m07.986s	1
2	Sergio Perez	Red Bull Racing	Red Bull RB18	1h32m24.513s	3
3	Lando Norris	McLaren	McLaren-Mercedes MCL36	1h32m42.820s	5
4	George Russell	Mercedes AMG	Mercedes F1 W13	1h32m50.492s	11
5	Valtteri Bottas	Alfa Romeo Racing	Alfa Romeo-Ferrari C42	1h32m51.167s	7
6	Charles Leclerc	Ferrari	Ferrari F1-75	1h33m04.058s	2
7	Yuki Tsunoda	AlphaTauri	AlphaTauri-Red Bull AT03	1h33m09.096s	12
8	Sebastian Vettel	Aston Martin F1	Aston Martin-Mercedes AMR22	1h33m18.878s	13
9	Kevin Magnussen	Haas	Haas-Ferrari VF-22	1h33m23.246s	8
10	Lance Stroll	Aston Martin F1	Aston Martin-Mercedes AMR22	62 laps	15
11	Alexander Albon	Williams	Williams-Mercedes FW44	62 laps	18
12	Pierre Gasly	AlphaTauri	AlphaTauri-Red Bull AT03	62 laps	17
13	Lewis Hamilton	Mercedes AMG	Mercedes F1 W13	62 laps	14
14	Esteban Ocon !	Alpine	Alpine-Renault A522	62 laps	16
15	Guanyu Zhou *	Alfa Romeo Racing	Alfa Romeo-Ferrari C42	62 laps	20
16	Nicholas Latifi	Williams	Williams-Mercedes FW44	62 laps	19
17	Mick Schumacher	Haas	Haas-Ferrari VF-22	62 laps	10
18	Daniel Ricciardo	McLaren	McLaren-Mercedes MCL36	62 laps	6
R	Fernando Alonso	Alpine	Alpine-Renault A522	6 laps/accident	9
R	Carlos Sainz	Ferrari	Ferrari F1-75	0 laps/accident	4

Pole: Verstappen, 1m27.999s, 124.786mph/200.825kph. Fastest lap: Verstappen, 1m18.446s, 139.983mph/225.281kph on Lap 55. Race leaders: Verstappen 1-63

* made to start from pit lane for car being modified in parc ferme • ! 5s penalty for unsafe release

MIAMI GRAND PRIX

MIAMI INTERNATIONAL AUTODROME • ROUND 5 • DATE: 8TH MAY 2022
Laps: 57 • Distance: 191.405miles/308.37km • Weather: Hot & bright

Pos	Driver	Team	Chassis-Engine	Result	Qual
1	Max Verstappen	Red Bull Racing	Red Bull RB18	1h34m24.258s	3
2	Charles Leclerc	Ferrari	Ferrari F1-75	1h34m28.044s	1
3	Carlos Sainz	Ferrari	Ferrari F1-75	1h34m32.487s	2
4	Sergio Perez	Red Bull Racing	Red Bull RB18	1h34m34.896s	4
5	George Russell	Mercedes AMG	Mercedes F1 W13	1h34m42.840s	12
6	Lewis Hamilton	Mercedes AMG	Mercedes F1 W13	1h34m45.626s	6
7	Valtteri Bottas	Alfa Romeo Racing	Alfa Romeo-Ferrari C42	1h34m49.331s	5
8	Esteban Ocon	Alpine	Alpine-Renault A522	1h34m52.644s	20
9	Alexander Albon	Williams	Williams-Mercedes FW44	1h34m56.623s	18
10	Lance Stroll	Aston Martin F1	Aston Martin-Mercedes AMR22	1h35m01.284s	10
11	Fernando Alonso */!	Alpine	Alpine-Renault A522	1h35m01.386s	11
12	Yuki Tsunoda	AlphaTauri	AlphaTauri-Red Bull AT03	1h35m04.404s	9
13	Daniel Ricciardo !	McLaren	McLaren-Mercedes MCL36	1h35m05.160s	14
14	Nicholas Latifi	Williams	Williams-Mercedes FW44	1h35m14.194s	19
15	Mick Schumacher	Haas	Haas-Ferrari VF-22	1h35m37.563s	15
16	Kevin Magnussen ^	Haas	Haas-Ferrari VF-22	56 laps/accident	16
17	Sebastian Vettel	Aston Martin F1	Aston Martin-Mercedes AMR22	54 laps/accident	13
R	Pierre Gasly	AlphaTauri	AlphaTauri-Red Bull AT03	45 laps/accident	7
R	Lando Norris	McLaren	McLaren-Mercedes MCL36	39 laps/collision	8
R	Guanyu Zhou	Alfa Romeo Racing	Alfa Romeo-Ferrari C42	6 laps/mechanical	17

Pole: Leclerc, 1m28.796s, 136.338mph/219.415kph. Fastest lap: Verstappen, 1m31.361s, 132.510mph/213.255kph on Lap 54. Race leaders: Leclerc 1-8, Verstappen 9-26 & 28-57, Sainz 27

* 5s penalty for causing a collision with Gasly • ! 5s penalty for gaining an advantage by leaving track • ^ 5s penalty for causing a collision with Stroll

MAGNUSSEN'S MAGNIFICENT RETURN

After a year out of F1, when he raced sportscars in the United States, Kevin Magnussen was given a reprieve when sanctions against Russian businesses meant that Nikita Mazepin's father couldn't pay for his ride at Haas, so the team welcomed Kevin back and he took a surprise fifth in the first round.

SPANISH GRAND PRIX

BARCELONA-CATALUNYA • ROUND 6 • DATE: 22ND MAY 2022
Laps: 66 • Distance: 191.416miles/308.55km • Weather: Very hot & bright

Pos	Driver	Team	Chassis-Engine	Result	Qual
1	Max Verstappen	Red Bull Racing	Red Bull RB18	1h37m20.475s	2
2	Sergio Perez	Red Bull Racing	Red Bull RB18	1h37m33.547s	5
3	George Russell	Mercedes AMG	Mercedes F1 W13	1h37m53.402s	4
4	Carlos Sainz	Ferrari	Ferrari F1-75	1h38m05.683s	3
5	Lewis Hamilton	Mercedes AMG	Mercedes F1 W13	1h38m15.009s	6
6	Valtteri Bottas	Alfa Romeo Racing	Alfa Romeo-Ferrari C42	1h38m20.451s	7
7	Esteban Ocon	Alpine	Alpine-Renault A522	1h38m35.872s	12
8	Lando Norris	McLaren	McLaren-Mercedes MCL36	1h38m43.710s	11

Pos	Driver	Team	Chassis-Engine	Result	Qual
9	Fernando Alonso *	Alpine	Alpine-Renault A522	65 laps	20
10	Yuki Tsunoda	AlphaTauri	AlphaTauri-Red Bull AT03	65 laps	13
11	Sebastian Vettel	Aston Martin F1	Aston Martin-Mercedes AMR22	65 laps	16
12	Daniel Ricciardo	McLaren	McLaren-Mercedes MCL36	65 laps	9
13	Pierre Gasly ^	AlphaTauri	AlphaTauri-Red Bull AT03	65 laps	14
14	Mick Schumacher	Haas	Haas-Ferrari VF-22	65 laps	10
15	Lance Stroll	Aston Martin F1	Aston Martin-Mercedes AMR22	65 laps	17
16	Nicholas Latifi	Williams	Williams-Mercedes FW44	64 laps	19
17	Kevin Magnussen	Haas	Haas-Ferrari VF-22	64 laps	8
18	Alexander Albon !	Williams	Williams-Mercedes FW44	64 laps	18
R	Guanyu Zhou	Alfa Romeo Racing	Alfa Romeo-Ferrari C42	28 laps/power unit	15
R	Charles Leclerc	Ferrari	Ferrari F1-75	27 laps/power unit	1

Pole: Leclerc, 1m18.750s, 132.795mph/213.714kph. Fastest lap: Perez, 1m24.108s, 123.804mph/199.244kph on Lap 55. Race leaders: Leclerc 1-26, Russell 27-30, Perez 31-37 & 45-48, Verstappen 38-44 & 49-66

* made to start from rear of grid for using additional power unit elements • ! 5s penalty for exceeding track limits • ^ 5s penalty for causing a collision with Stroll

MONACO GRAND PRIX

MONTE CARLO • ROUND 7 • DATE: 29TH MAY 2022
Laps: 64 • Distance: 132.705 miles/213.568km • Weather: Warm but dull

Pos	Driver	Team	Chassis-Engine	Result	Qual
1	Sergio Perez	Red Bull Racing	Red Bull RB18	1h56m30.265s	3
2	Carlos Sainz	Ferrari	Ferrari F1-75	1h56m31.419s	2
3	Max Verstappen	Red Bull Racing	Red Bull RB18	1h56m31.756s	4
4	Charles Leclerc	Ferrari	Ferrari F1-75	1h56m33.187s	1
5	George Russell	Mercedes AMG	Mercedes F1 W13	1h56m42.233s	6
6	Lando Norris	McLaren	McLaren-Mercedes MCL36	1h56m42.496s	5
7	Fernando Alonso	Alpine	Alpine-Renault A522	1h57m16.623s	7
8	Lewis Hamilton	Mercedes AMG	Mercedes F1 W13	1h57m20.653s	8
9	Valtteri Bottas	Alfa Romeo Racing	Alfa Romeo-Ferrari C42	1h57m22.790s	12
10	Sebastian Vettel	Aston Martin F1	Aston Martin-Mercedes AMR22	1h57m23.801s	9
11	Pierre Gasly	AlphaTauri	AlphaTauri-Red Bull AT03	1h57m24.554s	17
12	Esteban Ocon *	Alpine	Alpine-Renault A522	1h57m25.909s	10
13	Daniel Ricciardo	McLaren	McLaren-Mercedes MCL36	1h57m27.900s	14
14	Lance Stroll	Aston Martin F1	Aston Martin-Mercedes AMR22	1h57m31.067s	18
15	Nicholas Latifi	Williams	Williams-Mercedes FW44	63 laps	19
16	Guanyu Zhou	Alfa Romeo Racing	Alfa Romeo-Ferrari C42	63 laps	20
17	Yuki Tsunoda	AlphaTauri	AlphaTauri-Red Bull AT03	63 laps	11
R	Alexander Albon !	Williams	Williams-Mercedes FW44	48 laps/handling	16
R	Mick Schumacher	Haas	Haas-Ferrari VF-22	24 laps/accident	15
R	Kevin Magnussen	Haas	Haas-Ferrari VF-22	19 laps/power unit	13

Pole: Leclerc, 1m11.376s, 104.581mph/168.308kph. Fastest lap: Norris, 1m14.693s, 99.937mph/160.834kph on Lap 55. Race leaders: Leclerc 1-17, Sainz 18-20, Perez 21-64

* 5s penalty for causing a collision with Hamilton • ! 5s penalty for gaining an advantage by leaving track

AZERBAIJAN GRAND PRIX

BAKU CITY CIRCUIT • ROUND 8 • DATE: 12TH JUNE 2022
Laps: 51 • Distance: 190.234miles/306.153km • Weather: Hot & bright

Pos	Driver	Team	Chassis-Engine	Result	Qual
1	Max Verstappen	Red Bull Racing	Red Bull RB18	1h34m05.941s	3
2	Sergio Perez	Red Bull Racing	Red Bull RB18	1h34m26.764s	2
3	George Russell	Mercedes AMG	Mercedes F1 W13	1h34m51.936s	5
4	Lewis Hamilton	Mercedes AMG	Mercedes F1 W13	1h35m17.620s	7
5	Pierre Gasly	AlphaTauri	AlphaTauri-Red Bull AT03	1h35m23.240s	6
6	Sebastian Vettel	Aston Martin F1	Aston Martin-Mercedes AMR22	1h35m30.040s	9
7	Fernando Alonso	Alpine	Alpine-Renault A522	1h35m34.537s	10
8	Daniel Ricciardo	McLaren	McLaren-Mercedes MCL36	1h35m38.148s	12
9	Lando Norris	McLaren	McLaren-Mercedes MCL36	1h35m38.497s	11
10	Esteban Ocon	Alpine	Alpine-Renault A522	1h35m54.125s	13
11	Valtteri Bottas	Alfa Romeo Racing	Alfa Romeo-Ferrari C42	50 laps	15
12	Alexander Albon	Williams	Williams-Mercedes FW44	50 laps	17
13	Yuki Tsunoda	AlphaTauri	AlphaTauri-Red Bull AT03	50 laps	8
14	Mick Schumacher	Haas	Haas-Ferrari VF-22	50 laps	20
15	Nicholas Latifi *	Williams	Williams-Mercedes FW44	50 laps	18
16	Lance Stroll	Aston Martin F1	Aston Martin-Mercedes AMR22	46 laps/vibrations	19
R	Kevin Magnussen	Haas	Haas-Ferrari VF-22	31 laps/power unit	16
R	Guanyu Zhou	Alfa Romeo Racing	Alfa Romeo-Ferrari C42	23 laps/hydraulics	14
R	Charles Leclerc	Ferrari	Ferrari F1-75	21 laps/power unit	1
R	Carlos Sainz	Ferrari	Ferrari F1-75	8 laps/hydraulics	4

Pole: Leclerc, 1m41.359s, 132.482mph/213.210kph. Fastest lap: Perez, 1m46.046s, 126.627mph/203.787kph on Lap 36. Race leaders: Perez 1-14, Verstappen 15-18 & 20-51, Leclerc 19

* 5s penalty for ignoring blue flags

ZHOU'S LUCKY ESCAPE

Guanyu Zhou was fortunate to survive the most spectacular F1 accident in many years. His Alfa Romeo collided with George Russell's Mercedes going into the first corner at the British GP at Silverstone, skidded across a gravel bed, then hit the tyre wall and got launched over it, landing inverted on the other side. Fortunately, he was uninjured.

CANADIAN GRAND PRIX

MONTREAL • ROUND 9 • DATE: 19TH JUNE 2022
Laps: 70 • Distance: 189.534miles/305.27km • Weather: Warm & bright

Pos	Driver	Team	Chassis-Engine	Result	Qual
1	Max Verstappen	Red Bull Racing	Red Bull RB18	1h36m21.757s	1
2	Carlos Sainz	Ferrari	Ferrari F1-75	1h36m22.750s	3
3	Lewis Hamilton	Mercedes AMG	Mercedes F1 W13	1h36m28.763s	4
4	George Russell	Mercedes AMG	Mercedes F1 W13	1h36m34.070s	8
5	Charles Leclerc */!	Ferrari	Ferrari F1-75	1h36m36.925s	19
6	Esteban Ocon	Alpine	Alpine-Renault A522	1h36m45.647s	7
7	Valtteri Bottas	Alfa Romeo Racing	Alfa Romeo-Ferrari C42	1h36m47.004s	11

Pos	Driver	Team	Chassis-Engine	Result	Qual
8	Guanyu Zhou	Alfa Romeo Racing	Alfa Romeo-Ferrari C42	1h36m48.709s	10
9	Fernando Alonso ^	Alpine	Alpine-Renault A522	1h36m51.702s	2
10	Lance Stroll	Aston Martin F1	Aston Martin-Mercedes AMR22	1h36m59.979s	17
11	Daniel Ricciardo	McLaren	McLaren-Mercedes MCL36	1h37m04.804s	9
12	Sebastian Vettel	Aston Martin F1	Aston Martin-Mercedes AMR22	1h37m06.002s	16
13	Alexander Albon	Williams	Williams-Mercedes FW44	1h37m06.650s	12
14	Pierre Gasly	AlphaTauri	AlphaTauri-Red Bull AT03	1h37m06.940s	15
15	Lando Norris †	McLaren	McLaren-Mercedes MCL36	1h37m13.902s	14
16	Nicholas Latifi	Williams	Williams-Mercedes FW44	1h37m21.735s	18
17	Kevin Magnussen	Haas	Haas-Ferrari VF-22	1h37m29.937s	5
R	Yuki Tsunoda !	AlphaTauri	AlphaTauri-Red Bull AT03	47 laps/spun off	20
R	Mick Schumacher	Haas	Haas-Ferrari VF-22	18 laps/hydraulics	6
R	Sergio Perez	Red Bull Racing	Red Bull RB18	7 laps/hydraulics	13

Pole: Verstappen, 1m21.299s, 119.992mph/193.109kph. Fastest lap: Sainz, 1m15.749s, 128.784mph/207.258kph on Lap 63. Race leaders: Verstappen 1-8 & 20-42 & 49-70, Sainz 9-19 & 43-48

* 10-place grid penalty for using additional power unit element • ! made to start from rear of grid for using additional power unit elements • ^ 5s penalty for more than one change of direction • † 5s penalty for speeding in pit lane

BRITISH GRAND PRIX

SILVERSTONE • ROUND 10 • DATE: 3RD JULY 2022
Laps: 52 • Distance: 190.345miles/306.332km • Weather: Warm & bright

Pos	Driver	Team	Chassis-Engine	Result	Qual
1	Carlos Sainz	Ferrari	Ferrari F1-75	2h17m50.311s	1
2	Sergio Perez	Red Bull Racing	Red Bull RB18	2h17m54.090s	4
3	Lewis Hamilton	Mercedes AMG	Mercedes F1 W13	2h17m56.536s	5
4	Charles Leclerc	Ferrari	Ferrari F1-75	2h17m58.857s	3
5	Fernando Alonso	Alpine	Alpine-Renault A522	2h17m59.882s	7
6	Lando Norris	McLaren	McLaren-Mercedes MCL36	2h18m02.254s	6
7	Max Verstappen	Red Bull Racing	Red Bull RB18	2h18m09.088s	2
8	Mick Schumacher	Haas	Haas-Ferrari VF-22	2h18m09.306s	19
9	Sebastian Vettel	Aston Martin F1	Aston Martin-Mercedes AMR22	2h18m12.666s	18
10	Kevin Magnussen	Haas	Haas-Ferrari VF-22	2h18m14.901s	17
11	Lance Stroll	Aston Martin F1	Aston Martin-Mercedes AMR22	2h18m16.458s	20
12	Nicholas Latifi	Williams	Williams-Mercedes FW44	2h18m22.822s	10
13	Daniel Ricciardo	McLaren	McLaren-Mercedes MCL36	2h18m23.128s	14
14	Yuki Tsunoda *	AlphaTauri	AlphaTauri-Red Bull AT03	2h18m31.221s	13
R	Esteban Ocon	Alpine	Alpine-Renault A522	37 laps/fuel pump	15
R	Pierre Gasly	AlphaTauri	AlphaTauri-Red Bull AT03	26 laps/accident	11
R	Valtteri Bottas	Alfa Romeo Racing	Alfa Romeo-Ferrari C42	20 laps/gearbox	12
R	George Russell	Mercedes AMG	Mercedes F1 W13	0 laps/collision	8
R	Guanyu Zhou	Alfa Romeo Racing	Alfa Romeo-Ferrari C42	0 laps/collision	9
R	Alexander Albon	Williams	Williams-Mercedes FW44	0 laps/collision	16

Pole: Sainz, 1m40.983s, 130.494mph/210.011kph. Fastest lap: Hamilton, 1m30.510s, 145.594mph/234.312kph on Lap 52. Race leaders: Verstappen 1 & 10-12, Sainz 2-9 & 13-20 & 39 & 43-52, Leclerc 21-25 & 34-38 & 40-42, Hamilton 26-33

* 5s penalty for causing a collision with Gasly

RACING ALL AROUND THE GLOBE

The 2022 World Championship was made up of a record-equalling 22 grands prix. There had actually been 23 grands prix on the provisional calendar, which would have outstripped the 2021 race tally, but Russia's invasion of Ukraine at the start of the year led to its race at Sochi being dropped.

AUSTRIAN GRAND PRIX

RED BULL RING • ROUND 11 • DATE: 10TH JULY 2022
Laps: 71 • Distance: 190.498miles/306.578km • Weather: Hot & bright

Pos	Driver	Team	Chassis-Engine	Result	Qual
1	Charles Leclerc	Ferrari	Ferrari F1-75	1h24m24.312s	2
2	Max Verstappen	Red Bull Racing	Red Bull RB18	1h24m25.844s	1
3	Lewis Hamilton	Mercedes AMG	Mercedes F1 W13	1h25m05.529s	8
4	George Russell #	Mercedes AMG	Mercedes F1 W13	1h25m23.284s	4
5	Esteban Ocon	Alpine	Alpine-Renault A522	1h25m32.748s	6
6	Mick Schumacher	Haas	Haas-Ferrari VF-22	70 laps	9
7	Lando Norris †	McLaren	McLaren-Mercedes MCL36	70 laps	10
8	Kevin Magnussen	Haas	Haas-Ferrari VF-22	70 laps	7
9	Daniel Ricciardo	McLaren	McLaren-Mercedes MCL36	70 laps	11
10	Fernando Alonso *	Alpine	Alpine-Renault A522	70 laps	19
11	Valtteri Bottas */!	Alfa Romeo Racing	Alfa Romeo-Ferrari C42	70 laps	20
12	Alexander Albon	Williams	Williams-Mercedes FW44	70 laps	15
13	Lance Stroll	Aston Martin F1	Aston Martin-Mercedes AMR22	70 laps	12
14	Zhou Guanyu †	Alfa Romeo Racing	Alfa Romeo-Ferrari C42	70 laps	13
15	Pierre Gasly ^/†	AlphaTauri	AlphaTauri-Red Bull AT03	70 laps	14
16	Yuki Tsunoda	AlphaTauri	AlphaTauri-Red Bull AT03	70 laps	16
17	Sebastian Vettel †	Aston Martin F1	Aston Martin-Mercedes AMR22	70 laps	18
R	Carlos Sainz	Ferrari	Ferrari F1-75	56 laps/engine	3
R	Nicholas Latifi	Williams	Williams-Mercedes FW44	48 laps/floor	17
R	Sergio Perez	Red Bull Racing	Red Bull RB18	24 laps/accident	5

Pole: Verstappen, 1m04.984s, 148.637mph/239.209kph. Fastest lap: Verstappen, 1m07.275s, 143.576mph/231.064kph on Lap 62. Race leaders: Verstappen 1-11 & 28-32 & 51-52, Leclerc 12-26 & 33-49 & 53-71, Sainz 27 & 50

5s penalty for causing a collision with Perez • * made to start from rear of grid for using additional power unit elements • ! made to start from pit lane for car being modified in parc ferme • ^ 5s penalty for causing a collision • † 5s penalty for exceeding track limits

FRENCH GRAND PRIX

CIRCUIT PAUL RICARD • ROUND 12 • DATE: 24TH JULY 2022
Laps: 53 • Distance: 192.392miles/309.626km • Weather: Very hot & bright

Pos	Driver	Team	Chassis-Engine	Result	Qual
1	Max Verstappen	Red Bull Racing	Red Bull RB18	1h30m02.112s	2
2	Lewis Hamilton	Mercedes AMG	Mercedes F1 W13	1h30m12.699s	4
3	George Russell	Mercedes AMG	Mercedes F1 W13	1h30m18.607s	6
4	Sergio Perez	Red Bull Racing	Red Bull RB18	1h30m19.422s	3
5	Carlos Sainz */!/~	Ferrari	Ferrari F1-75	1h30m30.984s	19
6	Fernando Alonso	Alpine	Alpine-Renault A522	1h30m44.991s	7
7	Lando Norris	McLaren	McLaren-Mercedes MCL36	1h30m54.138s	5

Pos	Driver	Team	Chassis-Engine	Result	Qual
8	Esteban Ocon #	Alpine	Alpine-Renault A522	1h30m59.071s	10
9	Daniel Ricciardo	McLaren	McLaren-Mercedes MCL36	1h31m02.484s	9
10	Lance Stroll	Aston Martin F1	Aston Martin-Mercedes AMR22	1h31m04.661s	15
11	Sebastian Vettel	Aston Martin F1	Aston Martin-Mercedes AMR22	1h31m06.606s	12
12	Pierre Gasly	AlphaTauri	AlphaTauri-Red Bull AT03	1h31m07.560s	14
13	Alexander Albon	Williams	Williams-Mercedes FW44	1h31m10.677s	13
14	Valtteri Bottas	Alfa Romeo Racing	Alfa Romeo-Ferrari C42	1h31m18.778s	11
15	Mick Schumacher	Haas	Haas-Ferrari VF-22	1h31m22.506s	17
16	Zhou Guanyu ^	Alfa Romeo Racing	Alfa Romeo-Ferrari C42	47 laps/power unit	16
R	Nicholas Latifi	Williams	Williams-Mercedes FW44	40 laps/accident	18
R	Kevin Magnussen !	Haas	Haas-Ferrari VF-22	37 laps/accident	20
R	Charles Leclerc	Ferrari	Ferrari F1-75	17 laps/spun off	1
R	Yuki Tsunoda	AlphaTauri	AlphaTauri-Red Bull AT03	17 laps/accident	8

Pole: Leclerc, 1m30.872s, 143.808mph/231.437kph. Fastest lap: Sainz, 1m35.781s, 136.438mph/219.576kph on Lap 51. Race leaders: Leclerc 1-17, Hamilton 18, Verstappen 19-53

* 10-place grid penalty for using additional power unit elements • ! made to start from rear of grid for using additional power unit elements • ~ 5s penalty for unsafe release • ^ 5s penalty for causing a collision with Schumacher • # 5s penalty for causing a collision with Tsunoda

HUNGARIAN GRAND PRIX

HUNGARORING • ROUND 13 • DATE: 31ST JULY 2022
Laps: 70 • Distance: 190.181miles/306.67km • Weather: Hot but dull

Pos	Driver	Team	Chassis-Engine	Result	Qual
1	Max Verstappen	Red Bull Racing	Red Bull RB18	1h39m35.912s	10
2	Lewis Hamilton	Mercedes AMG	Mercedes F1 W13	1h39m43.746s	7
3	George Russell	Mercedes AMG	Mercedes F1 W13	1h39m48.249s	1
4	Carlos Sainz	Ferrari	Ferrari F1-75	1h39m50.491s	2
5	Sergio Perez	Red Bull Racing	Red Bull RB18	1h39m51.600s	11
6	Charles Leclerc	Ferrari	Ferrari F1-75	1h39m51.959s	3
7	Lando Norris	McLaren	McLaren-Mercedes MCL36	1h40m54.212s	4
8	Fernando Alonso	Alpine	Alpine-Renault A522	69 laps	6
9	Esteban Ocon	Alpine	Alpine-Renault A522	69 laps	5
10	Sebastian Vettel	Aston Martin F1	Aston Martin-Mercedes AMR22	69 laps	18
11	Lance Stroll	Aston Martin F1	Aston Martin-Mercedes AMR22	69 laps	14
12	Pierre Gasly *	AlphaTauri	AlphaTauri-Red Bull AT03	69 laps	20
13	Zhou Guanyu	Alfa Romeo Racing	Alfa Romeo-Ferrari C42	69 laps	12
14	Mick Schumacher	Haas	Haas-Ferrari VF-22	69 laps	15
15	Daniel Ricciardo !	McLaren	McLaren-Mercedes MCL36	69 laps	9
16	Kevin Magnussen	Haas	Haas-Ferrari VF-22	69 laps	13
17	Alexander Albon	Williams	Williams-Mercedes FW44	69 laps	17
18	Nicholas Latifi	Williams	Williams-Mercedes FW44	69 laps	19
19	Yuki Tsunoda	AlphaTauri	AlphaTauri-Red Bull AT03	68 laps	16
20	Valtteri Bottas	Alfa Romeo Racing	Alfa Romeo-Ferrari C42	65 laps/power unit	8

Pole: Russell, 1m17.377s, 126.652mph/203.828kph. Fastest lap: Hamilton, 1m21.386s, 120.414mph/193.788kph on Lap 57. Race leaders: Russell 1-15 & 22-30, Sainz 16 & 40-46, Leclerc 17-21 & 31-39, Hamilton 47-50, Verstappen 51-70

* made to start from pit lane for car being modified in parc ferme & for using additional power unit elements • ! 5s penalty for causing a collision with Stroll

BELGIAN GRAND PRIX

SPA-FRANCORCHAMPS • ROUND 14 • DATE: 28TH AUGUST 2022
Laps: 44 • Distance: 191.491miles/308.176km • Weather: Hot & bright

Pos	Driver	Team	Chassis-Engine	Result	Qual
1	Max Verstappen !/‡	Red Bull Racing	Red Bull RB18	1h25m52.894s	14
2	Sergio Perez	Red Bull Racing	Red Bull RB18	1h26m10.735s	2
3	Carlos Sainz	Ferrari	Ferrari F1-75	1h26m19.780s	1
4	George Russell	Mercedes AMG	Mercedes F1 W13	1h26m22.034s	5
5	Fernando Alonso	Alpine	Alpine-Renault A522	1h27m06.150s	3
6	Charles Leclerc †/‡/¶	Ferrari	Ferrari F1-75	1h27m07.830s	15
7	Esteban Ocon ‡	Alpine	Alpine-Renault A522	1h27m08.534s	16
8	Sebastian Vettel	Aston Martin F1	Aston Martin-Mercedes AMR22	1h27m11.001s	10
9	Pierre Gasly	AlphaTauri	AlphaTauri-Red Bull AT03	1h27m25.075s	8
10	Alexander Albon	Williams	Williams-Mercedes FW44	1h27m34.794s	6
11	Lance Stroll	Aston Martin F1	Aston Martin-Mercedes AMR22	1h27m35.972s	9
12	Lando Norris ‡	McLaren	McLaren-Mercedes MCL36	1h27m37.633s	17
13	Yuki Tsunoda ‡/§	AlphaTauri	AlphaTauri-Red Bull AT03	1h27m38.111s	20
14	Zhou Guanyu ^/‡	Alfa Romeo Racing	Alfa Romeo-Ferrari C42	1h27m39.146s	18
15	Daniel Ricciardo	McLaren	McLaren-Mercedes MCL36	1h27m40.057s	7
16	Kevin Magnussen	Haas	Haas-Ferrari VF-22	43 laps	12
17	Mick Schumacher ^/†/‡	Haas	Haas-Ferrari VF-22	43 laps	19
18	Nicholas Latifi	Williams	Williams-Mercedes FW44	43 laps	11
R	Valtteri Bottas */!	Alfa Romeo Racing	Alfa Romeo-Ferrari C42	1 lap/accident	13
R	Lewis Hamilton	Mercedes AMG	Mercedes F1 W13	0 laps/accident	4

Pole: Sainz, 1m44.297s, 150.219mph/241.755kph. Fastest lap: Verstappen, 1m49.354s, 143.273mph/230.576kph on Lap 32. Race leaders: Sainz 1-10 & 16-17, Perez 11, Verstappen 12-15 & 18-44

* 15-place grid penalty for using additional power unit elements • ! 5-place grid penalty for using additional restricted number components • ^ 10-place grid penalty for using additional restricted number units • † 10-place grid penalty for using additional power unit elements • ‡ made to start from rear of grid for using additional power unit elements • § made to start from pit lane for car being modified in parc ferme • ¶ 5s penalty for speeding in pit lane

THE END OF AN ERA

Sebastian Vettel brought his illustrious F1 career to a close when he stepped down at the end of his 16th season. In that time, he gave Scuderia Toro Rosso its first win, Red Bull Racing its first F1 title (and second, third and fourth) on the way to racking up 53 wins from his 299 starts.

A FIRST TIME WINNER

Carlos Sainz Jr came very close to taking his first F1 win when he raced for McLaren and was pipped by AlphaTauri's Pierre Gasly in the 2020 Italian GP. However, the Spaniard got everything right when he triumphed in the British GP at Silverstone after Verstappen's Red Bull suffered a puncture.

DUTCH GRAND PRIX

ZANDVOORT • ROUND 15 • DATE: 4TH SEPTEMBER 2022
Laps: 72 • Distance: 190.542miles/306.648km • Weather: Warm & bright

Pos	Driver	Team	Chassis-Engine	Result	Qual
1	Max Verstappen	Red Bull Racing	Red Bull RB18	1h36m42.773s	1
2	George Russell	Mercedes AMG	Mercedes F1 W13	1h36m46.844s	6
3	Charles Leclerc	Ferrari	Ferrari F1-75	1h36m53.702s	2
4	Lewis Hamilton	Mercedes AMG	Mercedes F1 W13	1h36m55.789s	4
5	Sergio Perez	Red Bull Racing	Red Bull RB18	1h37m00.941s	5
6	Fernando Alonso	Alpine	Alpine-Renault A522	1h37m01.527s	13
7	Lando Norris	McLaren	McLaren-Mercedes MCL36	1h37m02.079s	7
8	Carlos Sainz *	Ferrari	Ferrari F1-75	1h37m03.689s	3
9	Esteban Ocon	Alpine	Alpine-Renault A522	1h37m03.890s	12
10	Lance Stroll	Aston Martin F1	Aston Martin-Mercedes AMR22	1h37m05.232s	10
11	Pierre Gasly	AlphaTauri	AlphaTauri-Red Bull AT03	1h37m09.782s	11
12	Alexander Albon	Williams	Williams-Mercedes FW44	1h37m13.163s	15
13	Mick Schumacher	Haas	Haas-Ferrari VF-22	1h37m15.768s	8
14	Sebastian Vettel !	Aston Martin F1	Aston Martin-Mercedes AMR22	1h37m18.780s	19
15	Kevin Magnussen	Haas	Haas-Ferrari VF-22	1h37m19.642s	18
16	Zhou Guanyu #	Alfa Romeo Racing	Alfa Romeo-Ferrari C42	1h37m20.093s	14
17	Daniel Ricciardo	McLaren	McLaren-Mercedes MCL36	1h37m20.537s	17
18	Nicholas Latifi	Williams	Williams-Mercedes FW44	71 laps	20
R	Valtteri Bottas	Alfa Romeo Racing	Alfa Romeo-Ferrari C42	53 laps/fuel system	16
R	Yuki Tsunoda	AlphaTauri	AlphaTauri-Red Bull AT03	43 laps/differential	9

Pole: Verstappen, 1m10.342s, 135.439mph/217.969kph. Fastest lap: Verstappen, 1m13.652s, 129.353mph/208.174kph on Lap 62. Race leaders: Verstappen 1-18 & 29-56 & 61-72, Hamilton 19-28 & 57-60

* 5s penalty for unsafe release • ! 5s penalty for ignoring blue flags • # 5s penalty for speeding in the pit lane

ITALIAN GRAND PRIX

MONZA • ROUND 16 • DATE: 11TH SEPTEMBER 2022
Laps: 53 • Distance: 190.778miles/307.029km • Weather: Warm & bright

Pos	Driver	Team	Chassis-Engine	Result	Qual
1	Max Verstappen !	Red Bull Racing	Red Bull RB18	1h20m27.511s	7
2	Charles Leclerc **	Ferrari	Ferrari F1-75	1h20m29.957s	1
3	George Russell	Mercedes AMG	Mercedes F1 W13	1h20m30.916s	2
4	Carlos Sainz ‡/!!	Ferrari	Ferrari F1-75	1h20m32.572s	18
5	Lewis Hamilton !!	Mercedes AMG	Mercedes F1 W13	1h20m32.891s	19
6	Sergio Perez †	Red Bull Racing	Red Bull RB18	1h20m33.602s	13
7	Lando Norris	McLaren	McLaren-Mercedes MCL36	1h20m33.718s	3
8	Pierre Gasly	AlphaTauri*	AlphaTauri-Red Bull AT03	1h20m33.907s	5
9	Nyck de Vries	Williams	Williams-Mercedes FW44	1h20m34.633s	8
10	Zhou Guanyu **	Alfa Romeo Racing	Alfa Romeo-Ferrari C42	1h20m35.421s	9
11	Esteban Ocon !	Alpine	Alpine-Renault A522	1h20m35.834s	14
12	Mick Schumacher !/^/‡/**	Haas	Haas-Ferrari VF-22	1h20m36.060s	17
13	Valtteri Bottas ¶	Alfa Romeo Racing	Alfa Romeo-Ferrari C42	52 laps	15
14	Yuki Tsunoda */§/!!	AlphaTauri*	AlphaTauri-Red Bull AT03	52 laps	20
15	Nicholas Latifi	Williams	Williams-Mercedes FW44	52 laps	10
16	Kevin Magnussen ¶/#	Haas	Haas-Ferrari VF-22	52 laps	16
R	Daniel Ricciardo	McLaren	McLaren-Mercedes MCL36	45 laps/oil leak	4
R	Lance Stroll	Aston Martin F1	Aston Martin-Mercedes AMR22	39 laps/withdrawn	12

Pos	Driver	Team	Chassis-Engine	Result	Qual
R	Fernando Alonso	Alpine	Alpine-Renault A522	31 laps/mechanical	6
R	Sebastian Vettel	Aston Martin F1	Aston Martin-Mercedes AMR22	10 laps/power unit	11
NS	Alexander Albon	Williams	Williams-Mercedes FW44	-	-

Pole: Leclerc, 1m20.161s, 161.656mph/260.161kph. Fastest lap: Perez, 1m24.030s, 154.213mph/248.183kph on Lap 46. Race leaders: Leclerc 1-11 & 26-33, Verstappen 12-25 & 34-53

* 3-place grid penalty for failing to slow for yellow flags • ! 5-place grid penalty for using additional power unit element • ^ 10-place grid penalty for using additional power unit elements • † 10-place grid penalty for using additional power unit element • ‡ 10-place grid penalty for using additional restricted number components • § 10-place grid penalty for accumulation of 5 reprimands • ¶ 15-place grid penalty for additional power unit elements • # 5s penalty for leaving the track and gaining an advantage • ** 10-place grid penalty for using additional power unit elements • !! made to start from rear of grid for using additional power unit elements

SINGAPORE GRAND PRIX

MARINA BAY CIRCUIT • ROUND 17 • DATE: 2ND OCTOBER 2022
Laps: 61 • Distance: 191.906miles/308.843km • Weather: Very hot & humid

Pos	Driver	Team	Chassis-Engine	Result	Qual
1	Sergio Perez !	Red Bull Racing	Red Bull RB18	2h02m20.238s	2
2	Charles Leclerc	Ferrari	Ferrari F1-75	2h02m22.833s	1
3	Carlos Sainz	Ferrari	Ferrari F1-75	2h02m30.543s	4
4	Lando Norris	McLaren	McLaren-Mercedes MCL36	2h02m41.371s	6
5	Daniel Ricciardo	McLaren	McLaren-Mercedes MCL36	2h03m13.520s	16
6	Lance Stroll	Aston Martin F1	Aston Martin-Mercedes AMR22	2h03m16.568s	11
7	Max Verstappen	Red Bull Racing	Red Bull RB18	2h03m19.063s	8
8	Sebastian Vettel	Aston Martin F1	Aston Martin-Mercedes AMR22	2h03m20.270s	13
9	Lewis Hamilton	Mercedes AMG	Mercedes F1 W13	2h03m21.753s	3
10	Pierre Gasly	AlphaTauri	AlphaTauri-Red Bull AT03	2h03m29.814s	7
11	Valtteri Bottas	Alfa Romeo Racing	Alfa Romeo-Ferrari C42	2h03m49.082s	15
12	Kevin Magnussen	Haas	Haas-Ferrari VF-22	2h03m52.848s	9
13	Mick Schumacher	Haas	Haas-Ferrari VF-22	58 laps	12
14	George Russell *	Mercedes AMG	Mercedes F1 W13	57 laps/withdrawn	20
R	Yuki Tsunoda	AlphaTauri	AlphaTauri-Red Bull AT03	34 laps/accident	10
R	Esteban Ocon	Alpine	Alpine-Renault A522	26 laps/power unit	17
R	Alexander Albon	Williams	Williams-Mercedes FW44	25 laps/accident	18
R	Fernando Alonso	Alpine	Alpine-Renault A522	20 laps/power unit	5
R	Nicholas Latifi	Williams	Williams-Mercedes FW44	7 laps/accident	19
R	Zhou Guanyu	Alfa Romeo Racing	Alfa Romeo-Ferrari C42	6 laps/collision	14

Pole: Leclerc, 1m49.412s, 103.512mph/166.588kph. Fastest lap: Russell, 1m46.458s, 106.385mph/171.211kph on Lap 54. Race leaders: Perez 1-59

* made to start from pit lane for car being modified in parc ferme • ! 5s penalty for safety car infringement

ANOTHER FIRST-TIME WINNER

After spending the first three years of his F1 career with tail-end Williams, George Russell joined Mercedes just as it produced its worst car in years. However, not only did he claim his first win, in Brazil, he also outscored his illustrious team-mate, seven-time world champion Lewis Hamilton.

JAPANESE GRAND PRIX

SUZUKA • ROUND 18 • DATE: 9TH OCTOBER 2022
Laps: 28 • Distance: 100.846 miles/162.296km • Weather: Warm & wet

Pos	Driver	Team	Chassis-Engine	Result	Qual
1	Max Verstappen	Red Bull Racing	Red Bull RB18	3h01m44.004s	1
2	Sergio Perez	Red Bull Racing	Red Bull RB18	3h02m11.070s	4
3	Charles Leclerc ^	Ferrari	Ferrari F1-75	3h02m15.767s	2
4	Esteban Ocon	Alpine	Alpine-Renault A522	3h02m23.689s	5
5	Lewis Hamilton	Mercedes AMG	Mercedes F1 W13	3h02m24.330s	6
6	Sebastian Vettel	Aston Martin F1	Aston Martin-Mercedes AMR22	3h02m30.362s	9
7	Fernando Alonso	Alpine	Alpine-Renault A522	3h02m30.373s	7
8	George Russell	Mercedes AMG	Mercedes F1 W13	3h02m31.665s	8
9	Nicholas Latifi *	Williams	Williams-Mercedes FW44	3h02m54.147s	19
10	Lando Norris	McLaren	McLaren-Mercedes MCL36	3h02m54.786s	10
11	Daniel Ricciardo	McLaren	McLaren-Mercedes MCL36	3h02m56.881s	11
12	Lance Stroll	Aston Martin F1	Aston Martin-Mercedes AMR22	3h02m57.908s	18
13	Yuki Tsunoda	AlphaTauri	AlphaTauri-Red Bull AT03	3h02m59.603s	13
14	Kevin Magnussen	Haas	Haas-Ferrari VF-22	3h03m10.020s	17
15	Valtteri Bottas	Alfa Romeo Racing	Alfa Romeo-Ferrari C42	3h03m10.500s	12
16	Zhou Guanyu	Alfa Romeo Racing	Alfa Romeo-Ferrari C42	3h03m11.047s	14
17	Mick Schumacher	Haas	Haas-Ferrari VF-22	3h03m16.527s	15
18	Pierre Gasly !/†	AlphaTauri	AlphaTauri-Red Bull AT03	3h03m32.095s	20
R	Carlos Sainz	Ferrari	Ferrari F1-75	0 laps/accident	3
R	Alexander Albon	Williams	Williams-Mercedes FW44	0 laps/accident	16

Pole: Verstappen, 1m29.304s, 145.456mph/234.090kph. Fastest lap: Zhou, 1m44.411s, 124.411mph/200.220kph on Lap 20. Race leaders: Verstappen 1-7 & 9-28, Alonso 8

* 5-place grid penalty for causing a crash in Singapore GP • ! made to start from pit lane for car being modified in parc ferme • ^ 5s penalty for gaining an advantage by leaving track • † drivethrough penalty turned into 20s penalty for speeding under red flag conditions

UNITED STATES GRAND PRIX

CIRCUIT OF THE AMERICAS • ROUND 19 • DATE: 23RD OCTOBER 2022
Laps: 56 • Distance: 191.834miles/308.728km • Weather: Warm & bright

Pos	Driver	Team	Chassis-Engine	Result	Qual
1	Max Verstappen	Red Bull Racing	Red Bull RB18	1h42m11.687s	2
2	Lewis Hamilton	Mercedes AMG	Mercedes F1 W13	1h42m16.710s	3
3	Charles Leclerc ^	Ferrari	Ferrari F1-75	1h42m19.188s	12
4	Sergio Perez *	Red Bull Racing	Red Bull RB18	1h42m19.980s	9
5	George Russell #	Mercedes AMG	Mercedes F1 W13	1h42m56.502s	4
6	Lando Norris	McLaren	McLaren-Mercedes MCL36	1h43m05.472s	6
7	Fernando Alonso *	Alpine	Alpine-Renault A522	1h43m06.765s	14
8	Sebastian Vettel	Aston Martin F1	Aston Martin-Mercedes AMR22	1h43m17.041s	10
9	Kevin Magnussen	Haas	Haas-Ferrari VF-22	1h43m17.521s	13
10	Yuki Tsunoda !	AlphaTauri	AlphaTauri-Red Bull AT03	1h43m22.606s	19
11	Esteban Ocon †	Alpine	Alpine-Renault A522	1h43m24.562s	20
12	Zhou Guanyu *	Alfa Romeo Racing	Alfa Romeo-Ferrari C42	1h43m27.851s	18
13	Alexander Albon ‡	Williams	Williams-Mercedes FW44	1h43m31.744s	8
14	Pierre Gasly **	AlphaTauri	AlphaTauri-Red Bull AT03	1h43m33.450s	11
15	Mick Schumacher §	Haas	Haas-Ferrari VF-22	1h43m36.177s	16
16	Daniel Ricciardo	McLaren	McLaren-Mercedes MCL36	1h43m42.174s	15
17	Nicholas Latifi ¶	Williams	Williams-Mercedes FW44	1h43m55.275s	17

Pos	Driver	Team	Chassis-Engine	Result	Qual
R	Lance Stroll	Aston Martin F1	Aston Martin-Mercedes AMR22	21 laps/accident	5
R	Valtteri Bottas	Alfa Romeo Racing	Alfa Romeo-Ferrari C42	16 laps/spun off	7
R	Carlos Sainz	Ferrari	Ferrari F1-75	1 lap/accident	1

Pole: Sainz, 1m34.356s, 130.698mph/210.339kph. Fastest lap: Russell, 1m38.788s, 124.835mph/200.903kph on Lap 56. Race leaders: Verstappen 1-13 & 15-17 & 19-35 & 50-56, Perez 14 & 36-38, Leclerc 18, Vettel 39-40, Hamilton 41-49

* 5-place grid penalty for using additional power unit element • ! 5-place grid penalty for using additional restricted number components • ^ 10-place grid penalty for using additional power unit elements • # 5s penalty for causing a collision with Sainz • † made to start from pit lane for car being modified in parc ferme & for using additional power unit elements • ‡ 5s penalty for gaining an advantage by leaving track • § 5s penalty for exceeding track limits • ¶ 5s penalty for causing a collision with Schumacher • ** 10s penalty for not serving safety car infringement penalty correctly

MEXICO CITY GRAND PRIX

MEXICO CITY • ROUND 20 • DATE: 30TH OCTOBER 2022
Laps: 71 • Distance: 189.881miles/305.584km • Weather: Warm & bright

Pos	Driver	Team	Chassis-Engine	Result	Qual
1	Max Verstappen	Red Bull Racing	Red Bull RB18	1h38m36.729s	1
2	Lewis Hamilton	Mercedes AMG	Mercedes F1 W13	1h38m51.915s	3
3	Sergio Perez	Red Bull Racing	Red Bull RB18	1h38m54.826s	4
4	George Russell	Mercedes AMG	Mercedes F1 W13	1h39m26.160s	2
5	Carlos Sainz	Ferrari	Ferrari F1-75	1h39m34.852s	5
6	Charles Leclerc	Ferrari	Ferrari F1-75	1h39m45.503s	7
7	Daniel Ricciardo ^	McLaren	McLaren-Mercedes MCL36	70 laps	11
8	Esteban Ocon	Alpine	Alpine-Renault A522	70 laps	10
9	Lando Norris	McLaren	McLaren-Mercedes MCL36	70 laps	8
10	Valtteri Bottas	Alfa Romeo Racing	Alfa Romeo-Ferrari C42	70 laps	6
11	Pierre Gasly #	AlphaTauri	AlphaTauri-Red Bull AT03	70 laps	14
12	Alexander Albon	Williams	Williams-Mercedes FW44	70 laps	17
13	Zhou Guanyu	Alfa Romeo Racing	Alfa Romeo-Ferrari C42	70 laps	12
14	Sebastian Vettel	Aston Martin F1	Aston Martin-Mercedes AMR22	70 laps	16
15	Lance Stroll *	Aston Martin F1	Aston Martin-Mercedes AMR22	70 laps	20
16	Mick Schumacher	Haas	Haas-Ferrari VF-22	70 laps	15
17	Kevin Magnussen !	Haas	Haas-Ferrari VF-22	70 laps	19
18	Nicholas Latifi	Williams	Williams-Mercedes FW44	69 laps	18
19	Fernando Alonso	Alpine	Alpine-Renault A522	63 laps/power unit	9
R	Yuki Tsunoda	AlphaTauri	AlphaTauri-Red Bull AT03	50 laps/accident	13

Pole: Verstappen, 1m17.775s, 123.789mph/199.220kph. Fastest lap: Russell, 1m20.153s, 120.117mph/193.310kph on Lap 71. Race leaders: Verstappen 1-24 & 35-71, Hamilton 25-29, Russell 30-34

* 3-place grid penalty for causing crash with Alonso in United States GP • ! 5-place grid penalty for using additional power unit element • ^ 10s penalty for causing a crash with Tsunoda • # 5s penalty for leaving the track and gaining an advantage

NEW CIRCUITS

America's surge in interest in F1, propelled by the Netflix *Drive to Survive* series, was the reason for Miami achieving its decades-long ambition to land a grand prix. The venue was a temporary circuit in the parking lot of the Hard Rock Stadium, the home ground for the Miami Dolphins NFL team.

SAO PAULO GRAND PRIX

INTERLAGOS • ROUND 21 • DATE: 13TH NOVEMBER 2022
Laps: 71 • Distance: 190.101miles/305.939km • Weather: Warm & bright

Pos	Driver	Team	Chassis-Engine	Result	Qual
1	George Russell	Mercedes AMG	Mercedes F1 W13	1h38m34.044s	1
2	Lewis Hamilton	Mercedes AMG	Mercedes F1 W13	1h38m35.573s	2
3	Carlos Sainz *	Ferrari	Ferrari F1-75	1h38m38.095s	7
4	Charles Leclerc	Ferrari	Ferrari F1-75	1h38m42.485s	5
5	Fernando Alonso	Alpine	Alpine-Renault A522	1h38m43.605s	17
6	Max Verstappen #	Red Bull Racing	Red Bull RB18	1h38m44.100s	3
7	Sergio Perez	Red Bull Racing	Red Bull RB18	1h38m48.124s	4
8	Esteban Ocon	Alpine	Alpine-Renault A522	1h38m52.734s	16
9	Valtteri Bottas	Alfa Romeo Racing	Alfa Romeo-Ferrari C42	1h38m56.596s	14
10	Lance Stroll	Aston Martin F1	Aston Martin-Mercedes AMR22	1h38m57.596s	15
11	Sebastian Vettel	Aston Martin F1	Aston Martin-Mercedes AMR22	1h39m00.227s	9
12	Zhou Guanyu	Alfa Romeo Racing	Alfa Romeo-Ferrari C42	1h39m03.369s	13
13	Mick Schumacher	Haas	Haas-Ferrari VF-22	1h39m03.943s	12
14	Pierre Gasly ^	AlphaTauri	AlphaTauri-Red Bull AT03	1h39m05.911s	10
15	Alexander Albon	Williams	Williams-Mercedes FW44	1h39m10.060s	19
16	Nicholas Latifi	Williams	Williams-Mercedes FW44	1h39m11.082s	18
17	Yuki Tsunoda !	AlphaTauri	AlphaTauri-Red Bull AT03	70 laps	20
R	Lando Norris †	McLaren	McLaren-Mercedes MCL36	50 laps/electrical	6
R	Kevin Magnussen	Haas	Haas-Ferrari VF-22	0 laps/collision	8
R	Daniel Ricciardo	McLaren	McLaren-Mercedes MCL36	0 laps/collision	11

Pole: Russell, 1m12.059s, 133.764mph/215.273kph. Fastest lap: Russell, 1m13.785s, 130.635mph/210.238kph on Lap 61. Race leaders: Russell 1-24 & 30-71, Hamilton 25-29

* 5-place grid penalty for using additional power unit element • # 5s penalty for causing a collision with Hamilton • ! made to start from pit lane for car being modified in parc ferme • ^ 5s penalty for speeding in pit lane • † 5s penalty for causing a collision with Leclerc

NEW DRIVERS

Only one of the drivers starting the season was new to F1. This was China's first grand prix starter, Guanyu Zhou, who finished 10th on his debut for Alfa Romeo. Dutch racer Nyck de Vries made his F1 bow when he subbed for Alex Albon at Williams at Monza and grabbed a ninth place.

ABU DHABI GRAND PRIX

YAS MARINA CIRCUIT • ROUND 22 • DATE: 20TH NOVEMBER 2022
Laps: 58 • Distance: 190.324miles/306.298km • Weather: warm & dry

Pos	Driver	Team	Chassis-Engine	Result	Qual
1	Max Verstappen	Red Bull Racing	Red Bull RB18	1h27m45.914s	1
2	Charles Leclerc	Ferrari	Ferrari F1-75	1h27m54.685s	3
3	Sergio Perez	Red Bull Racing	Red Bull RB18	1h27m56.007s	2
4	Carlos Sainz	Ferrari	Ferrari F1-75	1h28m10.806s	4
5	George Russell ^	Mercedes AMG	Mercedes F1 W13	1h28m21.802s	6
6	Lando Norris	McLaren	McLaren-Mercedes MCL36	1h28m42.148s	7
7	Esteban Ocon	Alpine	Alpine-Renault A522	1h28m43.154s	8
8	Lance Stroll	Aston Martin F1	Aston Martin-Mercedes AMR22	1h29m02.845s	14

Pos	Driver	Team	Chassis-Engine	Result	Qual
9	Daniel Ricciardo *	McLaren	McLaren-Mercedes MCL36	1h29m09.182s	13
10	Sebastian Vettel	Aston Martin F1	Aston Martin-Mercedes AMR22	1h29m09.812s	9
11	Yuki Tsunoda	AlphaTauri	AlphaTauri-Red Bull AT03	1h29m15.285s	11
12	Zhou Guanyu	Alfa Romeo Racing	Alfa Romeo-Ferrari C42	57 laps	15
13	Alexander Albon	Williams	Williams-Mercedes FW44	57 laps	19
14	Pierre Gasly	AlphaTauri	AlphaTauri-Red Bull AT03	57 laps	17
15	Valtteri Bottas	Alfa Romeo Racing	Alfa Romeo-Ferrari C42	57 laps	18
16	Mick Schumacher !	Haas	Haas-Ferrari VF-22	57 laps	12
17	Kevin Magnussen	Haas	Haas-Ferrari VF-22	57 laps	16
18	Lewis Hamilton	Mercedes AMG	Mercedes F1 W13	55 laps/hydraulics	5
19	Nicholas Latifi	Williams	Williams-Mercedes FW44	55 laps/electrical	20
R	Fernando Alonso	Alpine	Alpine-Renault A522	27 laps/water leak	10

Pole: Verstappen, 1m23.824s, 140.928mph/226.803kph. Fastest lap: Norris, 1m28.391s, 133.647mph/215.085kph on Lap 44. Race leaders: Verstappen 1-20 & 22-58, Leclerc 21

* 3-place grid penalty for causing crash with Magnussen in Brazilian GP • ! 5s penalty for causing a collision with Latifi • ^ 5s penalty for unsafe release

WORLD DRIVERS' CHAMPIONSHIP FINAL RESULTS

Pos	Driver	Nat	Car-Engine	R1	R2	R3	R4	R5	R6	R7	R8
1	Max Verstappen	NLD	Red Bull RB18	19	1	R	1PF	1F	1	3	1
2	Charles Leclerc	MCO	Ferrari F1-75	1PF	2F	1PF	6	2P	RP	4P	RP
3	Sergio Perez	MEX	Red Bull RB18	18	4P	2	2	4	2F	1	2F
4	George Russell	GBR	Mercedes F1 W13	4	5	3	4	5	3	5	3
5	Carlos Sainz	ESP	Ferrari F1-75	2	3	R	R	3	4	2	R
6	Lewis Hamilton	GBR	Mercedes F1 W13	3	10	4	13	6	5	8	4
7	Lando Norris	GBR	McLaren-Mercedes MCL36	15	7	5	3	R	8	6F	9
8	Esteban Ocon	FRA	Alpine-Renault A522	7	6	7	14	8	7	12	10
9	Fernando Alonso	ESP	Alpine-Renault A522	9	R	17	R	11	9	7	7
10	Valtteri Bottas	FIN	Alfa Romeo-Ferrari C42	6	R	8	5	7	6	9	11
11	Daniel Ricciardo	AUS	McLaren-Mercedes MCL36	14	R	6	18	13	12	13	8
12	Sebastian Vettel	DEU	Aston Martin-Mercedes AMR22	-	-	R	8	17	11	10	6
13	Kevin Magnussen	DNK	Haas-Ferrari VF-22	5	9	14	9	16	17	R	R
14	Pierre Gasly	FRA	AlphaTauri-Red Bull AT03	R	8	9	12	R	13	11	5
15	Lance Stroll	CAN	Aston Martin-Mercedes AMR22	12	13	12	10	10	15	14	16
16	Mick Schumacher	DEU	Haas-Ferrari VF-22	11	NS	13	17	15	14	R	14
17	Yuki Tsunoda	JPN	AlphaTauri-Red Bull AT03	8	NS	15	7	12	10	17	13
18	Guanyu Zhou	CHN	Alfa Romeo-Ferrari C42	10	11	11	15	R	R	16	R
19	Alexander Albon	THA	Williams-Mercedes FW44	13	14	10	11	9	18	R	12
20	Nicholas Latifi	CAN	Williams-Mercedes FW44	16	R	16	16	14	16	15	15
21	Nyck de Vries	NLD	Williams-Mercedes FW44	-	-	-	-	-	-	-	-
			Mercedes F1 W13	-	-	-	-	-	-	-	-
			Aston Martin-Mercedes AMR22	-	-	-	-	-	-	-	-
22	Nico Hulkenberg	DEU	Aston Martin-Mercedes AMR22	17	12	-	-	-	-	-	-

Pos	Driver	R9	R10	R11	R12	R13	R14	R15	R16	R17	R18	R19	R20	R21	R22	Total
1	Verstappen	1P	7	2PF	1	1	1F	1PF	1	7	1P	1	1P	6	1P	454
2	Leclerc	5	4	1	RP	6	6	3	2P	2P	3	3	6	4	2	308
3	Perez	R	2	R	4	5	2	5	6F	1	2	4	3	7	3	305
4	Russell	4	R	4	3	3P	4	2	3	14F	8	5F	4F	1PF	5	275
5	Sainz	2F	1P	R	5F	4	3P	8	4	3	R	RP	5	3	4	246
6	Hamilton	3	3F	3	2	2F	R	4	5	9	5	2	2	2	18	240
7	Norris	15	6	7	7	7	12	7	7	4	10	6	9	R	6F	122

Pos	Driver	R9	R10	R11	R12	R13	R14	R15	R16	R17	R18	R19	R20	R21	R22	Total
8	Ocon	6	R	5	8	9	7	9	11	R	4	11	8	8	7	92
9	Alonso	9	5	10	6	8	5	6	R	R	7	7	19	5	R	81
10	Bottas	7	R	11	14	20	R	R	13	11	15	R	10	9	15	49
11	Ricciardo	11	13	9	9	15	15	17	R	5	11	16	7	R	9	37
12	Vettel	12	9	17	11	10	8	14	R	8	6	8	14	11	10	37
13	Magnussen	17	10	8	R	16	16	15	16	12	14	9	17	R	17	25
14	Gasly	14	R	15	12	12	9	11	8	10	18	14	11	T	14	23
15	Stroll	10	11	13	10	11	11	10	R	6	12	R	15	10	8	18
16	Schumacher	R	8	6	15	14	17	13	12	13	17	15	16	13	16	12
17	Tsunoda	R	14	16	R	19	13	R	14	R	13	10	R	17	11	12
18	Zhou	8	R	14	16	13	14	16	10	R	16F	12	13	12	12	6
19	Albon	13	R	12	13	17	10	12	NS	R	R	13	12	15	13	4
20	Latifi	16	12	R	R	18	18	18	15	R	9	17	18	16	19	2
21	de Vries	-	-	-	-	-	-	-	9	-	-	-	-	-	-	2
		-	-	-	T	-	-	-	-	-	-	-	T	-	-	-
		-	-	-	-	-	-	-	T	-	-	-	-	-	-	-
22	Hulkenberg	-	-	-	-	-	-	-	-	-	-	-	-	-	-	0

SYMBOLS AND GRAND PRIX KEY

Round 1 Bahrain GP
Round 2 Saudi Arabian GP
Round 3 Australian GP
Round 4 Emilia Romagna GP
Round 5 Miami GP
Round 6 Spanish GP
Round 7 Monaco GP
Round 8 Azerbaijan
Round 9 Canadian GP
Round 10 British GP
Round 11 Austrian GP
Round 12 French GP
Round 13 Hungarian GP
Round 14 Belgian GP
Round 15 Dutch GP
Round 16 Italian GP
Round 17 Singapore GP
Round 18 Japanese GP
Round 19 United States GP
Round 20 Mexican GP
Round 21 Brazilian GP
Round 22 Abu Dhabi GP

SCORING

1st	25 points
2nd	18 points
3rd	15 points
4th	12 points
5th	10 points
6th	8 points
7th	6 points
8th	4 points
9th	2 points
10th	1 point
Fastest lap (in top 10)	1 point

DNPQ DID NOT PRE-QUALIFY **DNQ** DID NOT QUALIFY **DQ** DISQUALIFIED **EX** EXCLUDED
F FASTEST LAP **NC** NOT CLASSIFIED **NS** NON-STARTER **P** POLE POSITION **R** RETIRED

WORLD CONSTRUCTORS' CHAMPIONSHIP FINAL RESULTS

Pos	Team-Engine	R1	R2	R3	R4	R5	R6	R7	R8	R9	R10	R11	R12
1	Red Bull	18/19	1/4	2/R	1/2	1/4	1/2	1/3	1/2	1/R	2/7	2/R	1/4
2	Ferrari	1/2	2/3	1/R	6/R	2/3	4/R	2/4	R/R	2/5	1/4	1/R	5/R
3	Mercedes AMG	3/4	5/10	3/4	4/13	5/6	3/5	5/8	3/4	3/4	3/R	3/4	2/3
4	Alpine-Renault	7/9	6/R	7/17	14/R	8/11	7/9	7/12	7/10	6/9	5/R	5/10	6/8
5	McLaren-Mercedes	14/15	7/R	5/6	3/18	13/R	8/12	6/13	8/9	11/15	6/13	7/9	7/9
6	Alfa Romeo-Ferrari	6/10	11/R	8/11	5/15	7/R	6/R	9/16	11/R	7/8	R/R	11/14	14/16
7	Aston Martin-Mercedes	12/17	12/13	12/R	8/10	10/17	11/15	10/14	6/16	10/12	9/11	13/17	10/11
8	Haas-Ferrari	5/11	9	13/14	9/17	15/16	14/17	R/R	14/R	17/R	8/10	6/8	15/R
9	AlphaTauri-Red Bull	8/R	8/NS	9/15	7/12	12/R	10/13	11/17	5/13	14/R	14/R	15/16	12/R
10	Williams-Mercedes	13/16	14/R	10/16	11/16	9/14	16/18	15/R	12/15	13/16	12/R	12/R	13/R

Pos	Team-Engine	R13	R14	R15	R16	R17	R18	R19	R20	R21	R22	Total
1	Red Bull	1/5	1/2	1/5	1/6	1/7	1/2	1/4	1/3	6/7	1/3	759
2	Ferrari	4/6	3/6	3/8	2/4	2/3	3/R	3/R	5/6	3/4	2/4	554
3	Mercedes AMG	2/3	4/R	2/4	3/5	9/14	5/8	2/5	2/4	1/2	5/18	515
4	Alpine-Renault	8/9	5/7	6/9	11/R	R/R	4/7	7/11	8/19	5/8	7/R	173
5	McLaren-Mercedes	7/15	12/15	7/17	7/R	4/5	10/11	6/16	7/9	R/R	6/9	159
6	Alfa Romeo-Ferrari	13/20	14/R	16/R	10/13	11/R	15/16	12/R	10/13	9/12	12/15	55
7	Aston Martin-Mercedes	10/11	8/11	10/14	R/R	6/8	6/12	8/R	14/15	10/11	8/10	55
8	Haas-Ferrari	14/16	16/17	13/15	12/16	12/13	14/17	9/15	16/17	13/R	16/17	37
9	AlphaTauri-Red Bull	12/19	9/13	11/R	8/14	10/R	13/18	10/14	11/R	14/17	11/14	35
10	Williams-Mercedes	17/18	10/18	12/18	9/15	R/R	9/R	13/17	12/18	15/16	13/19	8

THE DRIVERS

*** The German GP admitted F2 cars to bolster the grid in 1957, 1958, 1966, 1967 & 1969. The F2 drivers weren't able to score points though, meaning that if a driver in an F1 car finished 5th behind an F2 driver in 4th, then they would take the points for 4th.**

	Nationality	Debut date	Debut GP	Last date
George Abecassis	GBR	27 May 1951	Swiss GP	18 May 1952
Kenny Acheson	GBR	16 Jul 1983	British GP	8 Sep 1985
Philippe Adams	BEL	28 Aug 1994	Belgian GP	25 Sep 1994
Kurt Adolff	DEU	2 Aug 1953	German GP	2 Aug 1953
Kurt Ahrens	DEU	7 Aug 1966	German GP	3 Aug 1969
Jack Aitken	GBR	6 Dec 2020	Sakhir GP	6 Dec 2020
Christijan Albers	NED	6 Mar 2005	Australian GP	8 Jul 2007
Alexander Albon	GBR/THA	17 Mar 2019	Australian GP	20 Nov 2022
Michele Alboreto	ITA	3 May 1981	San Marino GP	13 Nov 1994
Jean Alesi	FRA	9 Jul 1989	French GP	14 Oct 2001
Jaime Alguersuari	ESP	26 Jul 2009	Hungarian GP	27 Nov 2011
Philippe Alliot	FRA	25 Mar 1984	Brazilian GP	28 Aug 1994
Cliff Allison	GBR	18 May 1958	Monaco GP	18 Jun 1961
Fernando Alonso	ESP	4 Mar 2001	Australian GP	20 Nov 2022
Giovanna Amati	ITA	1 Mar 1992	South African GP	5 Apr 1992
Chris Amon	NZL	26 May 1963	Monaco GP	3 Oct 1976
Bob Anderson	GBR	20 Jul 1963	British GP	15 Jul 1967
Conny Andersson	SWE	29 Aug 1976	Dutch GP	3 Jul 1977
Mario Andretti	USA	8 Sep 1968	Italian GP	25 Sep 1982
Michael Andretti	USA	14 Mar 1993	South African GP	12 Sep 1993
Marco Apicella	ITA	12 Sep 1993	Italian GP	12 Sep 1993
Rene Arnoux	FRA	4 Mar 1978	South African GP	5 Nov 1989
Peter Arundell	GBR	30 Jun 1963	French GP	23 Oct 1966
Alberto Ascari	ITA	21 May 1950	Monaco GP	22 May 1955
Peter Ashdown	GBR	18 Jul 1959	British GP	18 Jul 1959
Ian Ashley	GBR	4 Aug 1974	German GP	9 Oct 1977
Gerry Ashmore	GBR	15 Jul 1961	British GP	16 Sep 1962
Bill Aston	GBR	19 Jul 1952	British GP	7 Sep 1952

Last GP	GPs entered	GPs started	Wins/best finish	Pole positions	Fastest laps	Total Points	Titles
Swiss GP	2	2	0	0	0	0	0
Italian GP	10	3	12th	0	0	0	0
Portuguese GP	2	2	16th	0	0	0	0
German GP	1	1	0	0	0	0	0
German GP	4	4	7th*	0	0	0	0
Sakhir GP	1	1	16th	0	0	0	0
British GP	46	46	5th	0	0	4	0
Abu Dhabi GP	59	59	3rd	0	0	201	0
Australian GP	215	194	5	2s	5	186.5	0
Japanese GP	202	201	1	2	4	241	0
Brazilian GP	46	46	7th	0	0	31	0
Belgian GP	116	109	5th	0	0	7	0
Belgian GP	18	16	2nd	0	0	11	0
Abu Dhabi GP	358	356	32	22	23	2061	2
Brazilian GP	3	0	0	0	0	0	0
Canadian GP	108	96	2nd	5	4	83	0
British GP	29	25	3rd	0	0	8	0
French GP	5	1	0	0	0	0	0
Caesars Palace GP	131	128	12	18	10	180	1
Italian GP	13	13	3rd	0	0	7	0
Italian GP	1	1	0	0	0	0	0
Australian GP	164	149	7	18	12	181	0
Mexican GP	13	11	3rd	0	0	12	0
Monaco GP	31	31	13	14	12	140.64	2
British GP	1	1	12th	0	0	0	0
Canadian GP	11	4	14th	0	0	0	0
Italian GP	4	3	16th	0	0	0	0
Italian GP	3	1	0	0	0	0	0

	Nationality	Debut date	Debut GP	Last date
Richard Attwood	GBR	11 Jul 1964	British GP	3 Aug 1969
Luca Badoer	ITA	14 Mar 1993	South African GP	30 Aug 2009
Giancarlo Baghetti	ITA	2 Jul 1961	French GP	10 Sep 1967
Julian Bailey	GBR	3 Apr 1988	Brazilian GP	12 May 1991
Mauro Baldi	ITA	23 Jan 1982	South African GP	5 May 1985
Marcel Balsa	FRA	3 Aug 1952	German GP	3 Aug 1952
Lorenzo Bandini	ITA	18 Jun 1961	Belgian GP	7 May 1967
Fabrizio Barbazza	ITA	28 Apr 1991	San Marino GP	4 Jul 1993
John Barber	GBR	18 Jan 1953	Argentinian GP	18 Jan 1953
Skip Barber	USA	23 May 1971	Monaco GP	8 Oct 1972
Paolo Barilla	ITA	22 Oct 1989	Japanese GP	30 Sep 1990
Rubens Barrichello	BRA	14 Mar 1993	South African GP	27 Nov 2011
Michael Bartels	DEU	28 Jul 1991	German GP	29 Sep 1991
Edgar Barth	DEU	2 Aug 1953	German GP	2 Aug 1964
Giorgio Bassi	ITA	12 Sep 1965	Italian GP	12 Sep 1965
Erwin Bauer	DEU	2 Aug 1953	German GP	2 Aug 1953
Zsolt Baumgartner	HUN	24 Aug 2003	Hungarian GP	24 Oct 2004
Azdrubal Bayardo	URY	5 Jul 1959	French GP	5 Jul 1959
Elie Bayol	FRA	7 Sep 1952	Italian GP	13 May 1956
Don Beauman	GBR	17 Jul 1954	British GP	17 Jul 1954
Gunther Bechem (aka Bernd Nacke)	DEU	3 Aug 1952	German GP	2 Aug 1953
Jean Behra	FRA	18 May 1952	Swiss GP	2 Aug 1959
Derek Bell	GBR	8 Sep 1968	Italian GP	22 Sep 1974
Stefan Bellof	DEU	25 Mar 1984	Brazilian GP	25 Aug 1985
Paul Belmondo	FRA	1 Mar 1992	South African GP	13 Nov 1994
Tom Belsø	DNK	17 Jun 1973	Swedish GP	20 Jul 1974
Jean-Pierre Beltoise	FRA	7 Aug 1966	German GP	6 Oct 1974
Olivier Beretta	MCO	27 Mar 1994	Brazilian GP	14 Aug 1994
Allen Berg	CAN	22 Jun 1986	Detroit GP	26 Oct 1986
Georges Berger	BEL	21 Jun 1953	Belgian GP	4 Jul 1954
Gerhard Berger	AUT	19 Aug 1984	Austrian GP	26 Oct 1997

Last GP	GPs entered	GPs started	Wins/best finish	Pole positions	Fastest laps	Total Points	Titles
German GP	18	17	2nd	0	1	11	0
Belgian GP	58	51	7th	0	0	0	0
Italian GP	21	21	1	0	1	14	0
Monaco GP	20	7	6th	0	0	1	0
San Marino GP	41	36	5th	0	0	5	0
German GP	1	1	0	0	0	0	0
Monaco GP	42	42	1	1	2	58	0
French GP	20	8	6th	0	0	2	0
Argentinian GP	1	1	8th	0	0	0	0
United States GP	6	5	16th	0	0	0	0
Spanish GP	15	9	11th	0	0	0	0
Brazilian GP	326	323	11	14	17	658	0
Spanish GP	4	0	0	0	0	0	0
German GP	5	5	6th*	0	0	0	0
Italian GP	1	1	0	0	0	0	0
German GP	1	1	0	0	0	0	0
Brazilian GP	20	20	8th	0	0	1	0
French GP	1	0	0	0	0	0	0
Monaco GP	8	7	5th	0	0	2	0
British GP	1	1	11th	0	0	0	0
German GP	2	2	0	0	0	0	0
German GP	53	52	2nd	0	1	51.14	0
Canadian GP	16	9	6th	0	0	1	0
Dutch GP	22	20	4th	0	0	4	0
Australian GP	27	7	9th	0	0	0	0
British GP	5	2	8th	0	0	0	0
United States GP	88	86	1	0	4	77	0
Hungarian GP	10	9	7th	0	0	0	0
Australian GP	9	9	12th	0	0	0	0
French GP	2	2	0	0	0	0	0
European GP	210	210	10	12	21	385	0

	Nationality	Debut date	Debut GP	Last date
Eric Bernard	FRA	9 Jul 1989	French GP	16 Oct 1994
Enrique Bernoldi	BRA	4 Mar 2001	Australian GP	28 Jul 2002
Enrico Bertaggia	ITA	27 Aug 1989	Belgian GP	1 Mar 1992
Mike Beuttler	GBR	17 Jul 1971	British GP	7 Oct 1973
Jules Bianchi	FRA	17 Mar 2013	Australian GP	5 Oct 2014
Lucien Bianchi	BEL	10 May 1959	Monaco GP	3 Nov 1968
Gino Bianco	BRA	19 Jul 1952	British GP	7 Sep 1952
Hans Binder	AUT	15 Aug 1976	Austrian GP	13 Aug 1978
Clemente Biondetti	ITA	3 Sep 1950	Italian GP	3 Sep 1950
'B Bira'	THA	13 May 1950	British GP	24 Oct 1954
Pablo Birger	ARG	18 Jan 1953	Argentinian GP	16 Jan 1955
Harry Blanchard	USA	12 Dec 1959	United States GP	12 Dec 1959
Michael Bleekemolen	NED	28 Aug 1977	Dutch GP	8 Oct 1978
Trevor Blokdyk	ZAF	28 Dec 1963	South African GP	1 Jan 1965
Mark Blundell	GBR	10 Mar 1991	United States GP	12 Nov 1995
Raul Boesel	BRA	23 Jan 1982	South African GP	15 Oct 1983
Bob Bondurant	USA	3 Oct 1965	United States GP	23 Oct 1966
Felice Bonetto	ITA	4 Jun 1950	Swiss GP	13 Sep 1953
Jo Bonnier	SWE	2 Sep 1956	Italian GP	3 Oct 1971
Roberto Bonomi	ARG	7 Feb 1960	Argentinian GP	7 Feb 1960
Juan Manuel Bordeu	ARG	2 Jul 1961	French GP	2 Jul 1961
Slim Borgudd	SWE	3 May 1981	San Marino GP	4 Apr 1982
Luki Botha	ZAF	2 Jan 1967	South African GP	2 Jan 1967
Valtteri Bottas	FIN	25 Mar 2012	Malaysian GP	20 Nov 2022
Jean-Christophe Boullion	FRA	28 May 1995	Monaco GP	22 Oct 1995
Sebastien Bourdais	FRA	16 Mar 2008	Australian GP	12 Jul 2009
Thierry Boutsen	BEL	22 May 1983	Belgian GP	29 Aug 1993
David Brabham	AUS	13 May 1990	San Marino GP	13 Nov 1994
Gary Brabham	AUS	11 Mar 1990	United States GP	25 Mar 1990
Jack Brabham	AUS	16 Jul 1955	British GP	25 Oct 1970
Bill Brack	CAN	22 Sep 1968	Canadian GP	24 Sep 1972

Last GP	GPs entered	GPs started	Wins/best finish	Pole positions	Fastest laps	Total Points	Titles
European GP	47	45	3rd	0	0	10	0
German GP	29	28	8th	0	0	0	0
South African GP	7	0	0	0	0	0	0
United States GP	29	28	7th	0	0	0	0
Japanese GP	34	34	9th	0	0	2	0
Mexican GP	19	17	3rd	0	0	6	0
Italian GP	4	4	18th	0	0	0	0
Austrian GP	15	13	8th	0	0	0	0
Italian GP	1	1	0	0	0	0	0
Spanish GP	19	19	4th	0	0	8	0
Argentinian GP	2	2	0	0	0	0	0
United States GP	1	1	7th	0	0	0	0
Canadian GP	5	1	0	0	0	0	0
South African GP	2	1	12th	0	0	0	0
Australian GP	63	61	3rd	0	0	32	0
South African GP	30	23	7th	0	0	0	0
Mexican GP	9	9	4th	0	0	3	0
Italian GP	16	15	3rd	0	0	17.5	0
United States GP	109	104	1	1	0	39	0
Argentinian GP	1	1	11th	0	0	0	0
French GP	1	0	0	0	0	0	0
United States GP West	15	10	6th	0	0	1	0
South African GP	1	1	0	0	0	0	0
Abu Dhabi GP	200	200	10	20	19	1787	0
Pacific GP	11	11	5th	0	0	3	0
German GP	27	27	7th	0	0	6	0
Belgian GP	164	163	3	1	1	132	0
Australian GP	30	24	10th	0	0	0	0
Brazilian GP	2	0	0	0	0	0	0
Mexican GP	128	126	14	13	12	253	3
Canadian GP	3	3	0	0	0	0	0

	Nationality	Debut date	Debut GP	Last date
Ernesto Brambilla	ITA	8 Sep 1963	Italian GP	7 Sep 1969
Vittorio Brambilla	ITA	30 Mar 1974	South African GP	14 Sep 1980
Toni Branca	CHE	4 Jun 1950	Swiss GP	29 Jul 1951
Gianfranco Brancatelli	ITA	29 Apr 1979	Spanish GP	27 May 1979
Eric Brandon	GBR	18 May 1952	Swiss GP	17 Jul 1954
Tommy Bridger	GBR	19 Oct 1958	Moroccan GP	19 Oct 1958
Tony Brise	GBR	27 Apr 1975	Spanish GP	5 Oct 1975
Chris Bristow	GBR	18 Jul 1959	British GP	19 Jun 1960
Peter Broeker	CAN	6 Oct 1963	United States GP	6 Oct 1963
Tony Brooks	GBR	13 May 1956	Monaco GP	8 Oct 1961
Alan Brown	GBR	18 May 1952	Swiss GP	17 Jul 1954
Warwick Brown	AUS	10 Oct 1976	United States GP	10 Oct 1976
Adolf Brudes	DEU	3 Aug 1952	German GP	3 Aug 1952
Martin Brundle	GBR	25 Mar 1984	Brazilian GP	13 Oct 1996
Gianmaria Bruni	ITA	7 Mar 2004	Australian GP	24 Oct 2004
Clemar Bucci	ARG	17 Jul 1954	British GP	16 Jan 1955
Ronnie Bucknum	USA	2 Aug 1964	German GP	23 Oct 1966
Ivor Bueb	GBR	19 May 1957	Monaco GP	18 Jul 1959
Sebastien Buemi	CHE	29 Mar 2009	Australian GP	27 Nov 2011
Luiz Bueno	BRA	11 Feb 1973	Brazilian GP	11 Feb 1973
Ian Burgess	GBR	19 Jul 1958	British GP	4 Aug 1963
Luciano Burti	BRA	16 Jul 2000	Austrian GP	2 Sep 2001
Roberto Bussinello	ITA	10 Sep 1961	Italian GP	12 Sep 1965
Jenson Button	GBR	12 Mar 2000	Australian GP	28 May 2017
Tommy Byrne	IRL	8 Aug 1982	German GP	25 Sep 1982
Giulio Cabianca	ITA	18 May 1958	Monaco GP	4 Sep 1960
Mario Cabral	PRT	23 Aug 1959	Portuguese GP	6 Sep 1964
Phil Cade	USA	12 Dec 1959	United States GP	12 Dec 1959
Alex Caffi	ITA	7 Sep 1986	Italian GP	3 Nov 1991
John Campbell-Jones	GBR	17 Jun 1962	Belgian GP	20 Jul 1963
Adrian Campos	ESP	12 Apr 1987	Brazilian GP	12 Jun 1988

Last GP	GPs entered	GPs started	Wins/best finish	Pole positions	Fastest laps	Total Points	Titles
Italian GP	2	0	0	0	0	0	0
Italian GP	79	74	1	1	1	15.5	0
German GP	3	3	10th	0	0	0	0
Monaco GP	3	0	0	0	0	0	0
British GP	5	5	8th	0	0	0	0
Moroccan GP	1	1	0	0	0	0	0
United States GP	10	10	6th	0	0	1	0
Belgian GP	4	4	10th	0	0	0	0
United States GP	1	1	7th	0	0	0	0
United States GP	39	38	6	3	3	75	0
British GP	9	8	5th	0	0	2	0
United States GP	1	1	14th	0	0	0	0
German GP	1	1	0	0	0	0	0
Japanese GP	165	158	2nd	0	0	98	0
Brazilian GP	18	18	14th	0	0	0	0
Argentinian GP	5	5	0	0	0	0	0
Mexican GP	11	11	5th	0	0	2	0
British GP	6	5	8th	0	0	0	0
Brazilian GP	55	55	7th	0	0	29	0
Brazilian GP	1	1	12th	0	0	0	0
German GP	20	16	6th	0	0	0	0
Belgian GP	15	15	8th	0	0	0	0
Italian GP	3	2	13th	0	0	0	0
Monaco GP	309	306	15	8	8	1235	1
Caesars Palace GP	5	2	0	0	0	0	0
Italian GP	4	3	4th	0	0	3	0
Italian GP	5	4	9th	0	0	0	0
United States GP	1	0	0	0	0	0	0
Australian GP	75	56	4th	0	0	6	0
British GP	2	2	11th	0	0	0	0
Canadian GP	21	17	10th	0	0	0	0

	Nationality	Debut date	Debut GP	Last date
John Cannon	CAN	3 Oct 1971	United States GP	3 Oct 1971
Eitel Cantoni	URY	19 Jul 1952	British GP	7 Sep 1952
Ivan Capelli	ITA	6 Oct 1985	European GP	28 Mar 1993
Piero Carini	ITA	6 Jul 1952	French GP	13 Sep 1953
Eugenio Castellotti	ITA	16 Jan 1955	Argentinian GP	13 Jan 1957
Johnny Cecotto	VEN	13 Mar 1983	Brazilian GP	22 Jul 1984
Francois Cevert	FRA	3 Aug 1969	German GP	7 Oct 1973
Eugene Chaboud	FRA	18 Jun 1950	Belgian GP	1 Jul 1951
Jay Chamberlain	USA	21 Jul 1962	British GP	16 Sep 1962
Karun Chandhok	IND	14 Mar 2010	Bahrain GP	30 Oct 2011
Colin Chapman	GBR	1 Jul 1956	French GP	1 Jul 1956
Dave Charlton	ZAF	1 Jan 1965	South African GP	1 Mar 1975
Pedro Chaves	PRT	10 Mar 1991	United States GP	22 Sep 1991
Eddie Cheever	USA	15 Jan 1978	Argentinian GP	5 Nov 1989
Andrea Chiesa	CHE	1 Mar 1992	South African GP	26 Jul 1992
Max Chilton	GBR	4 Nov 2012	Abu Dhabi GP	12 Oct 2014
Ettore Chimeri	VEN	7 Feb 1960	Argentinian GP	7 Feb 1960
Louis Chiron	MCO	13 May 1950	British GP	18 May 1958
Johnny Claes	BEL	13 May 1950	British GP	19 Jun 1955
Jim Clark	GBR	6 Jun 1960	Dutch GP	1 Jan 1968
Kevin Cogan	USA	28 Sep 1980	Canadian GP	15 Mar 1981
Peter Collins	GBR	18 May 1952	Swiss GP	3 Aug 1958
Bernard Collomb	FRA	2 Jul 1961	French GP	10 May 1964
Alberto Colombo	ITA	21 May 1978	Belgian GP	10 Sep 1978
Erik Comas	FRA	10 Mar 1991	United States GP	6 Nov 1994
Franco Comotti	ITA	3 Sep 1950	Italian GP	6 Jul 1952
George Constantine	USA	12 Dec 1959	United States GP	12 Dec 1959
John Cordts	CAN	20 Sep 1969	Canadian GP	20 Sep 1969
David Coulthard	GBR	29 May 1994	Spanish GP	2 Nov 2008
Piers Courage	GBR	7 Aug 1966	German GP	21 Jun 1970
Chris Craft	GBR	19 Sep 1971	Canadian GP	3 Oct 1971

Last GP	GPs entered	GPs started	Wins/best finish	Pole positions	Fastest laps	Total Points	Titles
United States GP	1	1	14th	0	0	0	0
Italian GP	3	3	11th	0	0	0	0
Brazilian GP	98	93	2nd	0	0	31	0
Italian GP	3	3	0	0	0	0	0
Argentinian GP	14	14	2nd	3	0	19.5	0
British GP	23	18	6th	0	0	1	0
United States GP	48	47	1	0	2	89	0
French GP	3	3	5th	0	0	1	0
Italian GP	3	1	15th	0	0	0	0
Indian GP	20	11	14th	0	0	0	0
French GP	1	0	0	0	0	0	0
South African GP	13	11	12th	0	0	0	0
Portuguese GP	13	0	0	0	0	0	0
Australian GP	143	132	2nd	0	0	70	0
German GP	10	3	0	0	0	0	0
Russian GP	35	35	13th	0	0	0	0
Argentinian GP	1	1	0	0	0	0	0
Monaco GP	19	15	3rd	0	0	4	0
Dutch GP	25	23	7th	0	0	0	0
South African GP	73	72	25	32	27	255	2
United States GP West	2	0	0	0	0	0	0
German GP	35	32	3	0	1	47	0
Monaco GP	6	4	10th	0	0	0	0
Italian GP	3	0	0	0	0	0	0
Japanese GP	63	59	5th	0	0	7	0
French GP	2	2	12th	0	0	0	0
United States GP	1	1	0	0	0	0	0
Canadian GP	1	1	0	0	0	0	0
Brazilian GP	247	246	13	12	18	535	0
Dutch GP	30	28	2nd	0	0	20	0
United States GP	2	1	24th	0	0	0	0

	Nationality	Debut date	Debut GP	Last date
Jim Crawford	GBR	19 Jul 1975	British GP	7 Sep 1975
Alberto Crespo	ARG	7 Sep 1952	Italian GP	7 Sep 1952
Antonio Creus	ESP	7 Feb 1960	Argentinian GP	7 Feb 1960
Tony Crook	GBR	19 Jul 1952	British GP	18 Jul 1953
Geoff Crossley	GBR	13 May 1950	British GP	18 Jun 1950
Cristiano da Matta	BRA	9 Mar 2003	Australian GP	25 Jul 2004
Nano da Silva Ramos	BRA/FRA	19 Jun 1955	Dutch GP	2 Sep 1956
Chuck Daigh	USA	29 May 1960	Monaco GP	20 Nov 1960
Yannick Dalmas	FRA	18 Oct 1987	Mexican GP	25 Sep 1994
Derek Daly	IRL	2 Apr 1978	United States GP West	25 Sep 1982
Christian Danner	DEU	15 Sep 1985	Belgian GP	24 Sep 1989
Jorge Daponte	ARG	17 Jan 1954	Argentinian GP	5 Sep 1954
Anthony Davidson	GBR	18 Aug 2002	Hungarian GP	27 Apr 2008
Colin Davis	GBR	5 Jul 1959	French GP	13 Sep 1959
Andrea de Adamich	ITA	1 Jan 1968	South African GP	14 Jul 1973
Elio de Angelis	ITA	21 Jan 1979	Argentinian GP	11 May 1986
Carel Godin de Beaufort	NED	4 Aug 1957	German GP	2 Aug 1964
Andrea de Cesaris	ITA	28 Sep 1980	Canadian GP	16 Oct 1994
Alain de Changy	BEL	10 May 1959	Monaco GP	10 May 1959
Bernard de Dryver	BEL	5 Jun 1977	Belgian GP	21 May 1978
Maria Teresa de Filippis	ITA	18 May 1958	Monaco GP	10 May 1959
Emmanuel de Graffenried	CHE	13 May 1950	British GP	2 Sep 1956
Peter de Klerk	ZAF	28 Dec 1963	South African GP	7 Mar 1970
Pedro de la Rosa	ESP	7 Mar 1999	Australian GP	25 Nov 2012
Alfonso de Portago	ESP	1 Jul 1956	French GP	13 Jan 1957
Giovanni de Riu	ITA	5 Sep 1954	Italian GP	24 Oct 1954
Max de Terra	CHE	18 May 1952	Swiss GP	23 Aug 1953
Alessandro de Tomaso	ARG	13 Jan 1957	Argentinian GP	12 Dec 1959
Charles de Tornaco	BEL	22 Jun 1952	Belgian GP	21 Jun 1953
Emilio de Villota	ESP	2 May 1976	Spanish GP	3 Jul 1982
Nyck de Vries	NED	11 Sep 2022	Italian GP	11 Sep 2022

Last GP	GPs entered	GPs started	Wins/best finish	Pole positions	Fastest laps	Total Points	Titles
Italian GP	2	2	13th	0	0	0	0
Italian GP	1	0	0	0	0	0	0
Argentinian GP	1	1	0	0	0	0	0
British GP	2	2	21st	0	0	0	0
Belgian GP	2	2	9th	0	0	0	0
German GP	28	28	6th	0	0	13	0
Italian GP	7	7	5th	0	0	2	0
United States GP	6	3	10th	0	0	0	0
Portuguese GP	50	23	5th	0	0	0	0
Caesars Palace GP	64	49	4th	0	0	15	0
Portuguese GP	47	36	4th	0	0	4	0
Italian GP	2	2	11th	0	0	0	0
Spanish GP	24	24	11th	0	0	0	0
Italian GP	2	2	11th	0	0	0	0
British GP	36	30	4th	0	0	6	0
Monaco GP	109	108	2	3	0	122	0
German GP	31	28	6th	0	0	4	0
European GP	214	208	2nd	1	1	59	0
Monaco GP	1	0	0	0	0	0	0
Belgian GP	2	0	0	0	0	0	0
Monaco GP	5	3	10th	0	0	0	0
Italian GP	23	22	4th	0	0	9	0
South African GP	4	4	10th	0	0	0	0
Brazilian GP	107	105	2nd	0	1	35	0
Argentinian GP	5	5	2nd	0	0	4	0
Spanish GP	2	0	0	0	0	0	0
Swiss GP	2	2	8th	0	0	0	0
United States GP	2	2	9th	0	0	0	0
Belgian GP	4	2	7th	0	0	0	0
Dutch GP	14	2	13th	0	0	0	0
Italian GP	1	1	9th	0	0	2	0

	Nationality	Debut date	Debut GP	Last date
Jean-Denis Deletraz	CHE	13 Nov 1994	Australian GP	1 Oct 1995
Patrick Depailler	FRA	2 Jul 1972	French GP	13 Jul 1980
Lucas di Grassi	BRA	14 Mar 2010	Bahrain GP	14 Nov 2010
Paul di Resta	GBR	28 Mar 2010	Australian GP	30 Jul 2017
Pedro Diniz	BRA	26 Mar 1995	Brazilian GP	22 Oct 2000
Frank Dochnal	USA	27 Oct 1963	Mexican GP	27 Oct 1963
Jose Dolhem	FRA	7 Jul 1974	French GP	6 Oct 1974
Martin Donnelly	GBR	9 Jul 1989	French GP	30 Sep 1990
Mark Donohue	USA	19 Sep 1971	Canadian GP	17 Aug 1975
Robert Doornbos	NED	24 Jul 2005	German GP	22 Oct 2006
Ken Downing	GBR	19 Jul 1952	British GP	17 Aug 1952
Bob Drake	USA	20 Nov 1960	United States GP	20 Nov 1960
Paddy Driver	ZAF	28 Dec 1963	South African GP	30 Mar 1974
Piero Drogo	ITA	4 Sep 1960	Italian GP	4 Sep 1960
Johnny Dumfries	GBR	23 Mar 1986	Brazilian GP	26 Oct 1986
Piero Dusio	ITA	7 Sep 1952	Italian GP	7 Sep 1952
Jerome d'Ambrosio	BEL	27 Mar 2011	Australian GP	9 Sep 2012
Fritz d'Orey	BRA	5 Jul 1959	French GP	12 Dec 1959
George Eaton	CAN	5 Oct 1969	United States GP	19 Sep 1971
Bernie Ecclestone	GBR	18 May 1958	Monaco GP	19 Jul 1958
Guy Edwards	GBR	13 Jan 1974	Argentinian GP	16 Jul 1977
Vic Elford	GBR	7 Jul 1968	French GP	1 Aug 1971
Paul Emery	GBR	14 Jul 1956	British GP	18 May 1958
Tomas Enge	CZE	16 Sep 2001	Italian GP	14 Oct 2001
Paul England	AUS	4 Aug 1957	German GP	4 Aug 1957
Marcus Ericsson	SWE	16 Mar 2014	Australian GP	25 Nov 2018
Harald Ertl	AUT	3 Aug 1975	German GP	10 Aug 1980
Nasif Estefano	ARG	7 Feb 1960	Argentinian GP	16 Sep 1962
Philippe Etancelin	FRA	13 May 1950	British GP	6 Jul 1952
Bob Evans	GBR	1 Mar 1975	South African GP	18 Jul 1976
Corrado Fabi	ITA	13 Mar 1983	Brazilian GP	8 Jul 1984

Last GP	GPs entered	GPs started	Wins/best finish	Pole positions	Fastest laps	Total Points	Titles
European GP	3	3	15th	0	0	0	0
British GP	95	95	2	1	4	139	0
Abu Dhabi GP	19	18	14th	0	0	0	0
Hungarian GP	67	59	4th	0	0	121	0
Malaysian GP	99	98	5th	0	0	10	0
Mexican GP	1	0	0	0	0	0	0
United States GP	3	1	0	0	0	0	0
Spanish GP	15	13	7th	0	0	0	0
Austrian GP	16	14	3rd	0	0	8	0
Brazilian GP	11	11	12th	0	0	0	0
Dutch GP	2	2	9th	0	0	0	0
United States GP	1	1	13th	0	0	0	0
South African GP	2	1	25th	0	0	0	0
Italian GP	1	1	8th	0	0	0	0
Australian GP	16	15	5th	0	0	3	0
Italian GP	1	0	0	0	0	0	0
Italian GP	20	20	13th	0	0	0	0
United States GP	3	3	10th	0	0	0	0
Canadian GP	13	11	10th	0	0	0	0
British GP	2	0	0	0	0	0	0
British GP	17	11	7th	0	0	0	0
German GP	13	13	4th	0	0	8	0
Monaco GP	2	1	0	0	0	0	0
Japanese GP	3	3	12th	0	0	0	0
German GP	1	1	0	0	0	0	0
Abu Dhabi GP	97	97	8th	0	0	18	0
German GP	28	19	7th	0	0	0	0
Italian GP	2	1	14th	0	0	0	0
French GP	12	12	5th	0	0	3	0
British GP	12	10	9th	0	0	0	0
Dallas GP	18	12	7th	0	0	0	0

	Nationality	Debut date	Debut GP	Last date
Teo Fabi	ITA	23 Jan 1982	South African GP	15 Nov 1987
Pascal Fabre	FRA	12 Apr 1987	Brazilian GP	18 Oct 1987
Carlo Facetti	ITA	8 Sep 1974	Italian GP	8 Sep 1974
Luigi Fagioli	ITA	13 May 1950	British GP	1 Jul 1951
Jack Fairman	GBR	18 Jul 1953	British GP	10 Sep 1961
Juan Manuel Fangio	ARG	13 May 1950	British GP	6 Jul 1958
Giuseppe Farina	ITA	13 May 1950	British GP	11 Sep 1955
William Ferguson	ZAF	4 Mar 1972	South African GP	4 Mar 1972
Ralph Firman	GBR	9 Mar 2003	Australian GP	12 Oct 2003
Ludwig Fischer	DEU	3 Aug 1952	German GP	3 Aug 1952
Rudi Fischer	CHE	27 May 1951	Swiss GP	7 Sep 1952
Mike Fisher	USA	27 Aug 1967	Canadian GP	22 Oct 1967
Giancarlo Fisichella	ITA	10 Mar 1996	Australian GP	1 Nov 2009
John Fitch	USA	13 Sep 1953	Italian GP	11 Sep 1955
Christian Fittipaldi	BRA	1 Mar 1992	South African GP	13 Nov 1994
Emerson Fittipaldi	BRA	18 Jul 1970	British GP	5 Oct 1980
Pietro Fittipaldi	BRA	6 Dec 2020	Sakhir GP	13 Dec 2020
Wilson Fittipaldi	BRA	1 May 1972	Spanish GP	5 Oct 1975
Theo Fitzau	DEU	2 Aug 1953	German GP	2 Aug 1953
Jan Flinterman	NED	17 Aug 1952	Dutch GP	17 Aug 1952
Ron Flockhart	GBR	17 Jul 1954	British GP	20 Nov 1960
Gregor Foitek	CHE	26 Mar 1989	Brazilian GP	12 Aug 1990
George Follmer	USA	3 Mar 1973	South African GP	7 Oct 1973
Norberto Fontana	ARG	29 Jun 1997	French GP	26 Oct 1997
Franco Forini	CHE	6 Sep 1987	Italian GP	27 Sep 1987
Philip Fotheringham-Parker	GBR	14 Jul 1951	British GP	14 Jul 1951
Giorgio Francia	ITA	11 Sep 1977	Italian GP	21 Jun 1981
Heinz-Harald Frentzen	DEU	27 Mar 1994	Brazilian GP	12 Oct 2003
Paul Frere	BEL	22 Jun 1952	Belgian GP	3 Jun 1956
Patrick Friesacher	AUT	6 Mar 2005	Australian GP	10 Jul 2005
Joe Fry	GBR	13 May 1950	British GP	13 May 1950

Last GP	GPs entered	GPs started	Wins/best finish	Pole positions	Fastest laps	Total Points	Titles
Australian GP	71	64	3rd	3	2	23	0
Mexican GP	14	11	9th	0	0	0	0
Italian GP	1	0	0	0	0	0	0
French GP	7	7	1	0	0	28	0
Italian GP	13	12	4th	0	0	5	0
French GP	51	51	24	29	23	245	5
Italian GP	36	33	5	6	5	115.33	1
South African GP	1	0	0	0	0	0	0
Japanese GP	16	14	8th	0	0	1	0
German GP	1	0	0	0	0	0	0
Italian GP	8	7	2nd	0	0	10	0
Mexican GP	2	1	11th	0	0	0	0
Abu Dhabi GP	231	229	3	4	2	275	0
Italian GP	2	2	9th	0	0	0	0
Australian GP	43	40	4th	0	0	12	0
United States GP	149	144	14	6	6	281	2
Abu Dhabi GP	2	2	17th	0	0	0	0
United States GP	38	36	5th	0	0	3	0
German GP	1	1	0	0	0	0	0
Dutch GP	1	1	9th	0	0	0	0
United States GP	14	13	3rd	0	0	5	0
Hungarian GP	22	7	7th	0	0	0	0
United States GP	13	12	3rd	0	0	5	0
European GP	4	4	9th	0	0	0	0
Spanish GP	3	2	18th	0	0	0	0
British GP	1	1	0	0	0	0	0
Spanish GP	2	0	0	0	0	0	0
Japanese GP	160	157	3	2	6	174	0
Belgian GP	11	11	2nd	0	0	11	0
British GP	11	11	6th	0	0	3	0
British GP	1	1	10th	0	0	0	0

	Nationality	Debut date	Debut GP	Last date
Hiroshi Fushida	JPN	22 Jun 1975	Dutch GP	19 Jul 1975
Beppe Gabbiani	ITA	1 Oct 1978	United States GP	17 Oct 1981
Bertrand Gachot	BEL/FRA	26 Mar 1989	Brazilian GP	12 Nov 1995
Patrick Gaillard	FRA	1 Jul 1979	French GP	26 Aug 1979
Divina Galica	GBR	18 Jul 1976	British GP	29 Jan 1978
Nanni Galli	ITA	6 Sep 1970	Italian GP	3 Jun 1973
Oscar Galvez	ARG	18 Jan 1953	Argentinian GP	18 Jan 1953
Fred Gamble	USA	4 Sep 1960	Italian GP	4 Sep 1960
Howden Ganley	NZL	6 Mar 1971	South African GP	4 Aug 1974
Frank Gardner	AUS	11 Jul 1964	British GP	8 Sep 1968
Jo Gartner	AUT	6 May 1984	San Marino GP	21 Oct 1984
Pierre Gasly	FRA	1 Oct 2017	Malaysian GP	20 Nov 2022
Tony Gaze	AUS	22 Jun 1952	Belgian GP	7 Sep 1952
'Geki' (Giacomo Russo)	ITA	6 Sep 1964	Italian GP	4 Sep 1966
Olivier Gendebien	BEL	22 Jan 1956	Argentinian GP	8 Oct 1961
Marc Gene	ESP	7 Mar 1999	Australian GP	11 Jul 2004
Bob Gerard	GBR	13 May 1950	British GP	20 Jul 1957
Gerino Gerini	ITA	22 Jan 1956	Argentinian GP	19 Oct 1958
Peter Gethin	GBR	21 Jun 1970	Dutch GP	20 Jul 1974
Piercarlo Ghinzani	ITA	17 May 1981	Belgian GP	5 Nov 1989
Bruno Giacomelli	ITA	11 Sep 1977	Italian GP	30 Sep 1990
Dick Gibson	GBR	4 Aug 1957	German GP	3 Aug 1958
'Gimax' (aka Carlo Franchi)	ITA	10 Sep 1978	Italian GP	10 Sep 1978
Richie Ginther	USA	29 May 1960	Monaco GP	7 May 1967
Antonio Giovinazzi	ITA	26 Mar 2017	Australian GP	23 Oct 2022
Yves Giraud-Cabantous	FRA	13 May 1950	British GP	13 Sep 1953
Ignazio Giunti	ITA	7 Jun 1970	Belgian GP	6 Sep 1970
Timo Glock	DEU	13 Jun 2004	Canadian GP	25 Nov 2012
Helm Glockler	DEU	2 Aug 1953	German GP	2 Aug 1953
Francesco Godia	ESP	28 Oct 1951	Spanish GP	6 Jul 1958
Christian Goethals	BEL	3 Aug 1958	German GP	3 Aug 1958

Last GP	GPs entered	GPs started	Wins/best finish	Pole positions	Fastest laps	Total Points	Titles
British GP	2	0	0	0	0	0	0
Caesars Palace GP	17	3	0	0	0	0	0
Australian GP	84	47	5th	0	1	5	0
Dutch GP	5	2	13th	0	0	0	0
Brazilian GP	3	0	0	0	0	0	0
Monaco GP	20	17	9th	0	0	0	0
Argentinian GP	1	1	5th	0	0	2	0
Italian GP	1	1	10th	0	0	0	0
German GP	41	35	4th	0	0	10	0
Italian GP	9	8	8th	0	0	0	0
Portuguese GP	8	8	5th	0	0	0	0
Abu Dhabi GP	108	108	1	0	3	332	0
Italian GP	4	3	15th	0	0	0	0
Italian GP	3	2	9th	0	0	0	0
United States GP	15	14	2nd	0	0	18	0
British GP	36	36	5th	0	0	5	0
British GP	8	8	6th	0	0	0	0
Moroccan GP	7	6	4th	0	0	1.5	0
British GP	31	30	1	0	0	11	0
Australian GP	111	76	5th	0	0	2	0
Spanish GP	82	69	3rd	1	0	14	0
German GP	2	2	0	0	0	0	0
Italian GP	1	0	0	0	0	0	0
Monaco GP	54	52	1	0	3	102	0
United States GP	62	62	5th	0	0	21	0
Italian GP	13	13	4th	0	0	5	0
Italian GP	4	4	4th	0	0	3	0
Brazilian GP	95	91	2nd	0	1	51	0
German GP	1	0	0	0	0	0	0
French GP	14	13	4th	0	0	6	0
German GP	1	1	0	0	0	0	0

	Nationality	Debut date	Debut GP	Last date
Jose Froilan Gonzalez	ARG	21 May 1950	Monaco GP	7 Feb 1960
Oscar Gonzalez	URY	22 Jan 1956	Argentinian GP	22 Jan 1956
Aldo Gordini	FRA	1 Jul 1951	French GP	1 Jul 1951
Horace Gould	GBR	17 Jul 1954	British GP	4 Sep 1960
Jean-Marc Gounon	FRA	24 Oct 1993	Japanese GP	25 Sep 1994
Keith Greene	GBR	18 Jul 1959	British GP	16 Sep 1962
Masten Gregory	USA	19 May 1957	Monaco GP	12 Sep 1965
Georges Grignard	FRA	28 Oct 1951	Spanish GP	28 Oct 1951
Romain Grosjean	FRA	23 Aug 2009	European GP	29 Nov 2020
Olivier Grouillard	FRA	26 Mar 1989	Brazilian GP	8 Nov 1992
Brian Gubby	GBR	10 Jul 1965	British GP	10 Jul 1965
Andre Guelfi	FRA	19 Oct 1958	Moroccan GP	19 Oct 1958
Miguel Angel Guerra	ARG	15 Mar 1981	United States GP West	3 May 1981
Roberto Guerrero	COL	23 Jan 1982	South African GP	25 Sep 1983
Maurício Gugelmin	BRA	3 Apr 1988	Brazilian GP	8 Nov 1992
Dan Gurney	USA	5 Jul 1959	French GP	18 Jul 1970
Esteban Gutierrez	MEX	28 Oct 2012	Indian GP	27 Nov 2016
Hubert Hahne	DEU	7 Aug 1966	German GP	2 Aug 1970
Mike Hailwood	GBR	20 Jul 1963	British GP	4 Aug 1974
Mika Hakkinen	FIN	10 Mar 1991	United States GP	14 Oct 2001
Bruce Halford	GBR	14 Jul 1956	British GP	3 Jul 1960
Jim Hall	USA	20 Nov 1960	United States GP	27 Oct 1963
Duncan Hamilton	GBR	14 Jul 1951	British GP	18 Jul 1953
Lewis Hamilton	GBR	18 Mar 2007	Australian GP	20 Nov 2022
David Hampshire	GBR	13 May 1950	British GP	2 Jul 1950
Walt Hansgen	USA	8 Oct 1961	United States GP	4 Oct 1964
Mike Harris	ZMB	29 Dec 1962	South African GP	29 Dec 1962
Cuth Harrison	GBR	13 May 1950	British GP	3 Sep 1950
Brian Hart	GBR	6 Aug 1967	German GP	6 Aug 1967
Brendon Hartley	NZL	22 Oct 2017	United States GP	25 Nov 2018
Rio Haryanto	INA	20 Mar 2016	Australian GP	31 Jul 2016

Last GP	GPs entered	GPs started	Wins/best finish	Pole positions	Fastest laps	Total Points	Titles
Argentinian GP	26	26	2	3	6	72.14	0
Argentinian GP	1	1	6th	0	0	0	0
French GP	1	1	0	0	0	0	0
Italian GP	18	14	5th	0	0	2	0
Portuguese GP	9	9	9th	0	0	0	0
Italian GP	6	3	15th	0	0	0	0
Italian GP	43	38	2nd	0	0	21	0
Spanish GP	1	1	0	0	0	0	0
Bahrain GP	181	179	2nd	0	2	391	0
Australian GP	62	41	6th	0	0	1	0
British GP	1	0	0	0	0	0	0
Moroccan GP	1	1	0	0	0	0	0
San Marino GP	4	1	0	0	0	0	0
European GP	29	21	8th	0	0	0	0
Australian GP	80	74	3rd	0	1	10	0
British GP	87	86	4	3	6	133	0
Abu Dhabi GP	60	59	7th	0	1	6	0
German GP	5	3	9th	0	0	0	0
German GP	50	50	2nd	0	1	29	0
Japanese GP	165	161	20	26	25	420	2
French GP	9	8	8th	0	0	0	0
Mexican GP	12	11	5th	0	0	3	0
British GP	5	5	7th	0	0	0	0
Abu Dhabi GP	310	310	103	103	61	4405.5	7
French GP	2	2	9th	0	0	0	0
United States GP	2	2	5th	0	0	2	0
South African GP	1	1	0	0	0	0	0
Italian GP	3	3	7th	0	0	0	0
German GP	1	1	12th	0	0	0	0
Abu Dhabi GP	25	25	9th	0	0	4	0
German GP	12	12	15th	0	0	0	0

	Nationality	Debut date	Debut GP	Last date
Masahiro Hasemi	JPN	24 Oct 1976	Japanese GP	24 Oct 1976
Naoki Hattori	JPN	20 Oct 1991	Japanese GP	3 Nov 1991
Paul Hawkins	AUS	1 Jan 1965	South African GP	1 Aug 1965
Mike Hawthorn	GBR	22 Jun 1952	Belgian GP	19 Oct 1958
Boy Hayje	NED	29 Aug 1976	Dutch GP	28 Aug 1977
Willi Heeks	DEU	3 Aug 1952	German GP	2 Aug 1953
Nick Heidfeld	DEU	12 Mar 2000	Australian GP	31 Jul 2011
Theo Helfrich	DEU	3 Aug 1952	German GP	1 Aug 1954
Brian Henton	GBR	19 Jul 1975	British GP	25 Sep 1982
Johnny Herbert	GBR	26 Mar 1989	Brazilian GP	22 Oct 2000
Hans Herrmann	DEU	2 Aug 1953	German GP	3 Aug 1969
Francois Hesnault	FRA	25 Mar 1984	Brazilian GP	4 Aug 1985
Hans Heyer	DEU	31 Jul 1977	German GP	31 Jul 1977
Damon Hill	GBR	3 May 1992	Spanish GP	31 Oct 1999
Graham Hill	GBR	18 May 1958	Monaco GP	11 May 1975
Phil Hill	USA	6 Jul 1958	French GP	4 Sep 1966
Peter Hirt	CHE	27 May 1951	Swiss GP	23 Aug 1953
David Hobbs	GBR	15 Jul 1967	British GP	8 Sep 1974
Ingo Hoffmann	BRA	25 Jan 1976	Brazilian GP	23 Jan 1977
Kazuyoshi Hoshino	JPN	24 Oct 1976	Japanese GP	23 Oct 1977
Nico Hulkenberg	DEU	14 Mar 2010	Bahrain GP	27 Mar 2022
Denny Hulme	NZL	30 May 1965	Monaco GP	6 Oct 1974
James Hunt	GBR	3 Jun 1973	Monaco GP	27 May 1979
Gus Hutchison	USA	4 Oct 1970	United States GP	4 Oct 1970
Jacky Ickx	BEL	7 Aug 1966	German GP	7 Oct 1979
Yuji Ide	JPN	12 Mar 2006	Bahrain GP	23 Apr 2006
Jesus Iglesias	ARG	16 Jan 1955	Argentinian GP	16 Jan 1955
Taki Inoue	JPN	6 Nov 1994	Japanese GP	12 Nov 1995
Innes Ireland	GBR	31 May 1959	Dutch GP	23 Oct 1966
Eddie Irvine	GBR	24 Oct 1993	Japanese GP	13 Oct 2002
Chris Irwin	GBR	16 Jul 1966	British GP	22 Oct 1967

Last GP	GPs entered	GPs started	Wins/best finish	Pole positions	Fastest laps	Total Points	Titles
Japanese GP	1	1	11th	0	1	0	0
Australian GP	2	0	0	0	0	0	0
German GP	3	3	9th	0	0	0	0
Moroccan GP	47	45	3	4	6	112.64	1
Dutch GP	7	3	15th	0	0	0	0
German GP	2	2	0	0	0	0	0
Hungarian GP	186	183	2nd	1	2	259	0
German GP	3	3	12th	0	0	0	0
Caesars Palace GP	37	19	7th	0	1	0	0
Malaysian GP	165	162	3	0	0	98	0
German GP	21	18	3rd	0	1	10	0
German GP	21	19	7th	0	0	0	0
German GP	1	1	0	0	0	0	0
Japanese GP	122	115	22	20	19	360	1
Monaco GP	179	176	14	13	10	270	2
Italian GP	51	48	3	6	6	94	1
Swiss GP	5	5	7th	0	0	0	0
Italian GP	7	7	7th	0	0	0	0
Brazilian GP	6	3	7th	0	0	0	0
Japanese GP	2	2	11th	0	0	0	0
Saudi Arabian GP	181	181	4th	1	2	521	0
United States GP	112	112	8	1	9	248	1
Monaco GP	93	92	10	14	9	179	1
United States GP	1	1	0	0	0	0	0
United States GP	122	116	8	13	14	181	0
San Marino GP	4	4	13th	0	0	0	0
Argentinian GP	1	1	0	0	0	0	0
Australian GP	18	18	8th	0	0	0	0
Mexican GP	53	50	1	0	1	47	0
Japanese GP	148	146	4	0	1	191	0
Mexican GP	10	10	5th	0	0	2	0

	Nationality	Debut date	Debut GP	Last date
Jean-Pierre Jabouille	FRA	7 Jul 1974	French GP	21 Jun 1981
John James	GBR	14 Jul 1951	British GP	14 Jul 1951
Jean-Pierre Jarier	FRA	5 Sep 1971	Italian GP	15 Oct 1983
Max Jean	FRA	4 Jul 1971	French GP	4 Jul 1971
Stefan Johansson	SWE	13 Jan 1980	Argentinian GP	14 Jul 1991
Leslie Johnson	GBR	13 May 1950	British GP	13 May 1950
Bruce Johnstone	ZAF	29 Dec 1962	South African GP	29 Dec 1962
Alan Jones	AUS	27 Apr 1975	Spanish GP	26 Oct 1986
Tom Jones	USA	27 Aug 1967	Canadian GP	27 Aug 1967
Juan Jover	ESP	28 Oct 1951	Spanish GP	28 Oct 1951
Oswald Karch	DEU	2 Aug 1953	German GP	2 Aug 1953
Narain Karthikeyan	IND	6 Mar 2005	Australian GP	25 Nov 2012
Ukyo Katayama	JPN	1 Mar 1992	South African GP	26 Oct 1997
Ken Kavanagh	AUS	18 May 1958	Monaco GP	15 Jun 1958
Rupert Keegan	GBR	8 May 1977	Spanish GP	25 Sep 1982
Eddie Keizan	ZAF	3 Mar 1973	South African GP	1 Mar 1975
Joe Kelly	IRL	13 May 1950	British GP	14 Jul 1951
David Kennedy	IRL	13 Jan 1980	Argentinian GP	29 Jun 1980
Loris Kessel	CHE	2 May 1976	Spanish GP	11 Sep 1977
Bruce Kessler	USA	18 May 1958	Monaco GP	18 May 1958
Nicolas Kiesa	DNK	3 Aug 2003	German GP	16 Oct 2005
Leo Kinnunen	FIN	12 May 1974	Belgian GP	8 Sep 1974
Hans Klenk	DEU	3 Aug 1952	German GP	3 Aug 1952
Christian Klien	AUT	7 Mar 2004	Australian GP	14 Nov 2010
Karl Kling	DEU	4 Jul 1954	French GP	11 Sep 1955
Ernst Klodwig	DEU	3 Aug 1952	German GP	2 Aug 1953
Kamui Kobayashi	JPN	4 Oct 2009	Japanese GP	23 Nov 2014
Helmuth Koinigg	AUT	18 Aug 1974	Austrian GP	6 Oct 1974
Heikki Kovalainen	FIN	18 Mar 2007	Australian GP	24 Nov 2013
Mikko Kozarowitzky	FIN	19 Jun 1977	Swedish GP	16 Jul 1977
Willi Krakau	DEU	3 Aug 1952	German GP	3 Aug 1952

Last GP	GPs entered	GPs started	Wins/best finish	Pole positions	Fastest laps	Total Points	Titles
Spanish GP	56	49	2	6	0	21	0
British GP	1	1	0	0	0	0	0
South African GP	143	134	3rd	2	3	31.5	0
French GP	1	1	0	0	0	0	0
British GP	103	79	2nd	0	0	88	0
British GP	1	1	0	0	0	0	0
South African GP	1	1	9th	0	0	0	0
Australian GP	117	116	12	6	13	199	1
Canadian GP	1	0	0	0	0	0	0
Spanish GP	1	0	0	0	0	0	0
German GP	1	1	0	0	0	0	0
Brazilian GP	52	46	4th	0	1	5	0
European GP	97	95	5th	0	0	5	0
Belgian GP	2	0	0	0	0	0	0
Caesars Palace GP	37	25	7th	0	0	0	0
South African GP	3	3	13th	0	0	0	0
British GP	2	2	0	0	0	0	0
French GP	7	0	0	0	0	0	0
Italian GP	6	3	12th	0	0	0	0
Monaco GP	1	0	0	0	0	0	0
Chinese GP	5	5	11th	0	0	0	0
Italian GP	6	1	0	0	0	0	0
German GP	1	1	11th	0	0	0	0
Abu Dhabi GP	51	49	5th	0	0	14	0
Italian GP	11	11	2nd	0	1	17	0
German GP	2	2	12th	0	0	0	0
Abu Dhabi GP	77	75	3rd	0	1	125	0
United States GP	3	2	10th	0	0	0	0
Brazilian GP	112	111	1	1	2	105	0
British GP	2	0	0	0	0	0	0
German GP	1	0	0	0	0	0	0

	Nationality	Debut date	Debut GP	Last date
Rudolf Krause	DEU	3 Aug 1952	German GP	2 Aug 1953
Robert Kubica	POL	12 Mar 2006	Bahrain GP	20 Nov 2022
Kurt Kuhnke	DEU	4 Aug 1963	German GP	4 Aug 1963
Masami Kuwashima	JPN	24 Oct 1976	Japanese GP	24 Oct 1976
Daniil Kvyat	RUS	17 Nov 2013	United States GP	13 Dec 2020
Robert La Caze	FRA/MAR	19 Oct 1958	Moroccan GP	19 Oct 1958
Jacques Laffite	FRA	4 Aug 1974	German GP	13 Jul 1986
Franck Lagorce	FRA	6 Nov 1994	Japanese GP	13 Nov 1994
Jan Lammers	NED	21 Jan 1979	Argentinian GP	8 Nov 1992
Pedro Lamy	PRT	12 Sep 1993	Italian GP	13 Oct 1996
Chico Landi	BRA	16 Sep 1951	Italian GP	22 Jan 1956
Hermann Lang	DEU	23 Aug 1953	Swiss GP	1 Aug 1954
Claudio Langes	ITA	11 Mar 1990	United States GP	30 Sep 1990
Nicola Larini	ITA	6 Sep 1987	Italian GP	11 May 1997
Oscar Larrauri	ARG	3 Apr 1988	Brazilian GP	5 Nov 1989
Alberto Rodriguez Larreta	ARG	7 Feb 1960	Argentinian GP	7 Feb 1960
Gerard Larrousse	FRA	12 May 1974	Belgian GP	7 Jul 1974
Nicholas Latifi	CAN	5 Jul 2020	Austrian GP	20 Nov 2022
Niki Lauda	AUT	15 Aug 1971	Austrian GP	3 Nov 1985
Roger Laurent	BEL	22 Jun 1952	Belgian GP	3 Aug 1952
Giovanni Lavaggi	ITA	30 Jul 1995	German GP	13 Oct 1996
Chris Lawrence	GBR	16 Jul 1966	British GP	7 Aug 1966
Charles Leclerc	MCO	25 Mar 2018	Australian GP	20 Nov 2022
Michel Leclere	FRA	5 Oct 1975	United States GP	4 Jul 1976
Neville Lederle	ZAF	29 Dec 1962	South African GP	1 Jan 1965
Geoff Lees	GBR	16 Jul 1978	British GP	25 Jul 1982
Arthur Legat	BEL	22 Jun 1952	Belgian GP	21 Jun 1953
JJ Lehto	FIN	24 Sep 1989	Portuguese GP	13 Nov 1994
Lamberto Leoni	ITA	11 Sep 1977	Italian GP	2 Apr 1978
Les Leston	GBR	2 Sep 1956	Italian GP	20 Jul 1957
'Pierre Levegh'	FRA	18 Jun 1950	Belgian GP	16 Sep 1951

Last GP	GPs entered	GPs started	Wins/best finish	Pole positions	Fastest laps	Total Points	Titles
German GP	2	2	14th	0	0	0	0
Abu Dhabi GP	126	99	1	1	1	274	0
German GP	1	0	0	0	0	0	0
Japanese GP	1	0	0	0	0	0	0
Abu Dhabi GP	114	110	2nd	0	1	202	0
Moroccan GP	1	1	14th	0	0	0	0
British GP	180	175	6	7	7	228	0
Australian GP	2	2	11th	0	0	0	0
Australian GP	42	23	9th	0	0	0	0
Japanese GP	32	32	6th	0	0	1	0
Argentinian GP	6	6	4th	0	0	1.5	0
German GP	2	2	5th	0	0	2	0
Spanish GP	14	0	0	0	0	0	0
Monaco GP	75	49	2nd	0	0	7	0
Australian GP	21	7	13th	0	0	0	0
Argentinian GP	1	1	9th	0	0	0	0
French GP	2	1	0	0	0	0	0
Abu Dhabi GP	61	61	7th	0	0	9	0
Australian GP	177	171	25	24	23	420.5	3
German GP	2	2	6th	0	0	0	0
Japanese GP	10	7	10th	0	0	0	0
German GP	2	2	11th	0	0	0	0
Abu Dhabi GP	103	102	5	18	7	868	0
French GP	8	7	10th	0	0	0	0
South African GP	2	1	6th	0	0	1	0
French GP	12	5	7th	0	0	0	0
Belgian GP	2	2	13th	0	0	0	0
Australian GP	70	62	3rd	0	0	10	0
United States GP West	5	1	0	0	0	0	0
British GP	3	2	0	0	0	0	0
Italian GP	6	6	7th	0	0	0	0

	Nationality	Debut date	Debut GP	Last date
Jack Lewis	GBR	18 Jun 1961	Belgian GP	5 Aug 1962
Stuart Lewis-Evans	GBR	19 May 1957	Monaco GP	19 Oct 1958
Guy Ligier	FRA	22 May 1966	Monaco GP	22 Oct 1967
Roberto Lippi	ITA	10 Sep 1961	Italian GP	8 Sep 1963
Vitantonio Liuzzi	ITA	24 Apr 2005	San Marino GP	27 Nov 2011
Lella Lombardi	ITA	20 Jul 1974	British GP	15 Aug 1976
Ricardo Londono-Bridge	COL	29 Mar 1981	Brazilian GP	29 Mar 1981
Ernst Loof	DEU	2 Aug 1953	German GP	2 Aug 1953
Andre Lotterer	DEU	24 Aug 2014	Belgian GP	24 Aug 2014
Henri Louveau	FRA	3 Sep 1950	Italian GP	27 May 1951
John Love	ZWE	29 Dec 1962	South African GP	4 Mar 1972
Pete Lovely	USA	10 May 1959	Monaco GP	3 Oct 1971
Roger Loyer	FRA	17 Jan 1954	Argentinian GP	17 Jan 1954
Jean Lucas	FRA	11 Sep 1955	Italian GP	11 Sep 1955
Jean Lucienbonnet	FRA	10 May 1959	Monaco GP	10 May 1959
Brett Lunger	USA	17 Aug 1975	Austrian GP	1 Oct 1978
Mike MacDowel	GBR	7 Jul 1957	French GP	7 Jul 1957
Herbert MacKay-Fraser	USA	7 Jul 1957	French GP	7 Jul 1957
Lance Macklin	GBR	18 May 1952	Swiss GP	16 Jul 1955
Damien Magee	GBR	8 Jun 1975	Swedish GP	4 Jul 1976
Tony Maggs	ZAF	15 Jul 1961	British GP	1 Jan 1965
Umberto Maglioli	ITA	13 Sep 1953	Italian GP	4 Aug 1957
Jan Magnussen	DNK	22 Oct 1995	Pacific GP	7 Jun 1998
Kevin Magnussen	DNK	16 Mar 2014	Australian GP	20 Nov 2022
Guy Mairesse	FRA	3 Sep 1950	Italian GP	1 Jul 1951
Willy Mairesse	BEL	19 Jun 1960	Belgian GP	13 Jun 1965
Pastor Maldonado	VEN	27 Mar 2011	Australian GP	29 Nov 2015
Nigel Mansell	GBR	17 Aug 1980	Austrian GP	14 May 1995
Sergio Mantovani	ITA	13 Sep 1953	Italian GP	16 Jan 1955
Robert Manzon	FRA	21 May 1950	Monaco GP	2 Sep 1956
Onofre Marimon	ARG	1 Jul 1951	French GP	1 Aug 1954

Last GP	GPs entered	GPs started	Wins/best finish	Pole positions	Fastest laps	Total Points	Titles
German GP	11	9	4th	0	0	3	0
Moroccan GP	14	14	3rd	2	0	16	0
Mexican GP	13	12	6th	0	0	1	0
Italian GP	3	1	0	0	0	0	0
Brazilian GP	82	80	6th	0	0	26	0
Austrian GP	17	12	6th	0	0	0.5	0
Brazilian GP	1	0	0	0	0	0	0
German GP	1	1	0	0	0	0	0
Belgian GP	1	1	0	0	0	0	0
Swiss GP	2	2	0	0	0	0	0
South African GP	10	9	2nd	0	0	6	0
United States GP	11	7	7th	0	0	0	0
Argentinian GP	1	1	0	0	0	0	0
Italian GP	1	1	0	0	0	0	0
Monaco GP	1	0	0	0	0	0	0
United States GP	43	34	7th	0	0	0	0
French GP	1	1	7th	0	0	0	0
French GP	1	1	0	0	0	0	0
British GP	15	13	8th	0	0	0	0
French GP	2	1	14th	0	0	0	0
South African GP	27	25	2nd	0	0	26	0
German GP	10	10	3rd	0	0	3.33	0
Canadian GP	25	25	6th	0	0	1	0
Abu Dhabi GP	142	142	2nd	1	2	183	0
French GP	3	3	9th	0	0	0	0
Belgian GP	13	12	3rd	0	0	7	0
Abu Dhabi GP	96	95	1	1	0	76	0
Spanish GP	192	187	31	32	30	480	1
Argentinian GP	8	7	5th	0	0	4	0
Italian GP	29	28	3rd	0	0	16	0
German GP	12	11	3rd	0	1	8.14	0

	Nationality	Debut date	Debut GP	Last date
Helmut Marko	AUT	1 Aug 1971	German GP	2 Jul 1972
Tarso Marques	BRA	31 Mar 1996	Brazilian GP	2 Sep 2001
Leslie Marr	GBR	17 Jul 1954	British GP	16 Jul 1955
Tony Marsh	GBR	4 Aug 1957	German GP	6 Aug 1961
Eugene Martin	FRA	13 May 1950	British GP	4 Jun 1950
Pierluigi Martini	ITA	9 Sep 1984	Italian GP	30 Jul 1995
Jochen Mass	DEU	14 Jul 1973	British GP	25 Jul 1982
Felipe Massa	BRA	3 Mar 2002	Australian GP	26 Nov 2017
Michael May	CHE	14 May 1961	Monaco GP	10 Sep 1961
Timmy Mayer	USA	7 Oct 1962	United States GP	7 Oct 1962
Nikita Mazepin	RUS	28 Mar 2021	Bahrain GP	12 Dec 2021
Francois Mazet	FRA	4 Jul 1971	French GP	4 Jul 1971
Gaston Mazzacane	ARG	12 Mar 2000	Australian GP	15 Apr 2001
Kenneth McAlpine	GBR	19 Jul 1952	British GP	16 Jul 1955
Perry McCarthy	GBR	3 May 1992	Spanish GP	30 Aug 1992
Brian McGuire	AUS	16 Jul 1977	British GP	16 Jul 1977
Bruce McLaren	NZL	3 Aug 1958	German GP	10 May 1970
Allan McNish	GBR	3 Mar 2002	Australian GP	13 Oct 2002
Graham McRae	NZL	14 Jul 1973	British GP	14 Jul 1973
Carlos Menditeguy	ARG	18 Jan 1953	Argentinian GP	7 Feb 1960
Roberto Merhi	ESP	7 Sep 2014	Italian GP	29 Nov 2015
Harry Merkel	DEU	3 Aug 1952	German GP	3 Aug 1952
Arturo Merzario	ITA	15 Jul 1972	British GP	7 Oct 1979
Roberto Mieres	ARG	7 Jun 1953	Dutch GP	11 Sep 1955
Francois Migault	FRA	15 Jul 1972	British GP	6 Jul 1975
John Miles	GBR	6 Jul 1969	French GP	6 Sep 1970
Andre Milhoux	BEL	5 Aug 1956	German GP	5 Aug 1956
Gerhard Mitter	DEU	23 Jun 1963	Dutch GP	3 Aug 1969
Stefano Modena	ITA	15 Nov 1987	Australian GP	8 Nov 1992
Franck Montagny	FRA	29 May 2005	European GP	16 Jul 2006
Tiago Monteiro	PRT	6 Mar 2005	Australian GP	22 Oct 2006

Last GP	GPs entered	GPs started	Wins/best finish	Pole positions	Fastest laps	Total Points	Titles
French GP	10	9	8th	0	0	0	0
Belgian GP	26	24	9th	0	0	0	0
British GP	2	2	13th	0	0	0	0
German GP	5	4	8th	0	0	0	0
Swiss GP	2	2	0	0	0	0	0
German GP	124	118	4th	0	0	18	0
French GP	114	105	1	0	2	71	0
Abu Dhabi GP	272	269	11	16	15	1167	0
Italian GP	3	2	11th	0	0	0	0
United States GP	1	1	0	0	0	0	0
Abu Dhabi GP	22	21	14th	0	0	0	0
French GP	1	1	13th	0	0	0	0
San Marino GP	21	21	8th	0	0	0	0
British GP	7	7	13th	0	0	0	0
Belgian GP	7	0	0	0	0	0	0
British GP	1	0	0	0	0	0	0
Monaco GP	104	100	4	0	3	188.5	0
Japanese GP	17	16	7th	0	0	0	0
British GP	1	1	0	0	0	0	0
Argentinian GP	11	10	3rd	0	0	9	0
Abu Dhabi GP	14	13	12th	0	0	0	0
German GP	1	0	0	0	0	0	0
United States GP	84	57	4th	0	0	11	0
Italian GP	17	17	4th	0	1	13	0
French GP	16	13	14th	0	0	0	0
Italian GP	15	12	5th	0	0	2	0
German GP	1	1	0	0	0	0	0
German GP	7	5	4th	0	0	3	0
Australian GP	81	70	2nd	0	0	17	0
French GP	7	7	16th	0	0	0	0
Brazilian GP	37	37	3rd	0	0	7	0

	Nationality	Debut date	Debut GP	Last date
Andrea Montermini	ITA	29 May 1994	Spanish GP	14 Jul 1996
Robin Montgomerie-Charrington	GBR	22 Jun 1952	Belgian GP	22 Jun 1952
Juan Pablo Montoya	COL	4 Mar 2001	Australian GP	2 Jul 2006
Gianni Morbidelli	ITA	11 Mar 1990	United States GP	12 Oct 1997
Roberto Moreno	BRA	3 Jul 1982	Dutch GP	12 Nov 1995
Dave Morgan	GBR	19 Jul 1975	British GP	19 Jul 1975
Silvio Moser	CHE	15 Jul 1967	British GP	5 Sep 1971
Bill Moss	GBR	18 Jul 1959	British GP	18 Jul 1959
Stirling Moss	GBR	27 May 1951	Swiss GP	8 Oct 1961
Gino Munaron	ITA	7 Feb 1960	Argentinian GP	4 Sep 1960
David Murray	GBR	13 May 1950	British GP	19 Jul 1952
Luigi Musso	ITA	13 Sep 1953	Italian GP	6 Jul 1958
Bernd Nacke (see Gunther Bechem)				
Kazuki Nakajima	JPN	18 Mar 2007	Australian GP	1 Nov 2009
Satoru Nakajima	JPN	12 Apr 1987	Brazilian GP	3 Nov 1991
Shinji Nakano	JPN	9 Mar 1997	Australian GP	1 Nov 1998
Alessandro Nannini	ITA	23 Mar 1986	Brazilian GP	30 Sep 1990
Emanuele Naspetti	ITA	30 Aug 1992	Belgian GP	26 Sep 1993
Felipe Nasr	BRA	6 Apr 2014	Bahrain GP	27 Nov 2016
Massimo Natili	ITA	15 Jul 1961	British GP	15 Jul 1961
Brian Naylor	GBR	4 Aug 1957	German GP	10 Sep 1961
Tiff Needell	GBR	4 May 1980	Belgian GP	18 May 1980
Jac Nelleman	DNK	13 Jun 1976	Swedish GP	13 Jun 1976
Patrick Neve	BEL	16 May 1976	Belgian GP	9 Oct 1977
John Nicholson	NZL	20 Jul 1974	British GP	19 Jul 1975
Helmut Niedermayr	DEU	3 Aug 1952	German GP	3 Aug 1952
Brausch Niemann	ZAF	28 Dec 1963	South African GP	1 Jan 1965
Gunnar Nilsson	SWE	6 Mar 1976	South African GP	23 Oct 1977
Hideki Noda	JPN	16 Oct 1994	European GP	13 Nov 1994
Lando Norris	GBR	17 Mar 2019	Australian GP	20 Nov 2022
Rodney Nuckey	GBR	2 Aug 1953	German GP	17 Jul 1954

Last GP	GPs entered	GPs started	Wins/best finish	Pole positions	Fastest laps	Total Points	Titles
British GP	28	20	8th	0	0	0	0
Belgian GP	1	1	0	0	0	0	0
United States GP	95	94	7	13	12	307	0
Japanese GP	70	67	3rd	0	0	8.5	0
Australian GP	75	42	2nd	0	1	15	0
British GP	1	1	18th	0	0	0	0
Italian GP	20	12	5th	0	0	3	0
British GP	1	0	0	0	0	0	0
United States GP	67	66	16	16	19	185.64	0
Italian GP	5	4	13th	0	0	0	0
British GP	5	4	0	0	0	0	0
French GP	25	24	1	0	2	44	0
Abu Dhabi GP	36	36	6th	0	0	9	0
Australian GP	80	74	4th	0	1	16	0
Japanese GP	33	33	6th	0	0	2	0
Spanish GP	78	76	1	0	2	65	0
Portuguese GP	6	6	11th	0	0	0	0
Abu Dhabi GP	45	39	5th	0	0	29	0
British GP	1	1	0	0	0	0	0
Italian GP	8	7	13th	0	0	0	0
Monaco GP	2	1	0	0	0	0	0
Swedish GP	1	0	0	0	0	0	0
Canadian GP	13	10	7th	0	0	0	0
British GP	2	1	17th	0	0	0	0
German GP	1	1	9th	0	0	0	0
South African GP	2	1	14th	0	0	0	0
Japanese GP	32	31	1	0	1	31	0
Australian GP	3	3	23rd	0	0	0	0
Abu Dhabi GP	82	82	2nd	1	5	428	0
British GP	2	1	11th	0	0	0	0

	Nationality	Debut date	Debut GP	Last date
Esteban Ocon	FRA	28 Aug 2016	Belgian GP	20 Nov 2022
Jackie Oliver	GBR	6 Aug 1967	German GP	19 Jun 1977
Danny Ongais	USA	2 Oct 1977	United States GP	27 Aug 1978
Arthur Owen	GBR	4 Sep 1960	Italian GP	4 Sep 1960
Robert O'Brien	USA	22 Jun 1952	Belgian GP	22 Jun 1952
Carlos Pace	BRA	4 Mar 1972	South African GP	5 Mar 1977
Nello Pagani	ITA	4 Jun 1950	Swiss GP	4 Jun 1950
Riccardo Paletti	ITA	23 Jan 1982	South African GP	13 Jun 1982
Torsten Palm	SWE	11 May 1975	Monaco GP	8 Jun 1975
Jolyon Palmer	GBR	20 Mar 2016	Australian GP	8 Oct 2017
Jonathan Palmer	GBR	25 Sep 1983	European GP	5 Nov 1989
Olivier Panis	FRA	27 Mar 1994	Brazilian GP	3 Jul 2005
Giorgio Pantano	ITA	7 Mar 2004	Australian GP	12 Sep 2004
Massimiliano Papis	ITA	16 Jul 1995	British GP	1 Oct 1995
Mike Parkes	GBR	18 Jul 1959	British GP	18 Jun 1967
Reg Parnell	GBR	13 May 1950	British GP	17 Jul 1954
Tim Parnell	GBR	18 Jul 1959	British GP	4 Aug 1963
Riccardo Patrese	ITA	22 May 1977	Monaco GP	7 Nov 1993
Al Pease	CAN	27 Aug 1967	Canadian GP	20 Sep 1969
Roger Penske	USA	8 Oct 1961	United States GP	7 Oct 1962
Cesare Perdisa	ITA	22 May 1955	Monaco GP	13 Jan 1957
Sergio Perez	MEX	27 Mar 2011	Australian GP	20 Nov 2022
Luis Perez Sala	ESP	3 Apr 1988	Brazilian GP	5 Nov 1989
Larry Perkins	AUS	4 Aug 1974	German GP	3 Jul 1977
Xavier Perrot	SUI	3 Aug 1969	German GP	3 Aug 1969
Henri Pescarolo	FRA	22 Sep 1968	Canadian GP	10 Oct 1976
Alessandro Pesenti-Rossi	ITA	1 Aug 1976	German GP	12 Sep 1976
Josef Peters	DEU	3 Aug 1952	German GP	3 Aug 1952
Ronnie Peterson	SWE	10 May 1970	Monaco GP	10 Sep 1978
Vitaly Petrov	RUS	14 Mar 2010	Bahrain GP	25 Nov 2012
Alfredo Pian	ARG	21 May 1950	Monaco GP	21 May 1950

Last GP	GPs entered	GPs started	Wins/best finish	Pole positions	Fastest laps	Total Points	Titles
Abu Dhabi GP	111	111	1	0	0	364	0
Swedish GP	52	50	3rd	0	1	13	0
Dutch GP	6	4	7th	0	0	0	0
Italian GP	1	1	0	0	0	0	0
Belgian GP	1	1	14th	0	0	0	0
South African GP	73	72	1	1	5	58	0
Swiss GP	1	1	7th	0	0	0	0
Canadian GP	8	2	0	0	0	0	0
Swedish GP	2	1	10th	0	0	0	0
Japanese GP	37	35	6th	0	0	9	0
Australian GP	88	83	4th	0	1	14	0
French GP	159	158	1	0	0	76	0
Italian GP	14	14	13th	0	0	0	0
European GP	7	7	7th	0	0	0	0
Belgian GP	7	6	2nd	1	0	14	0
British GP	7	6	3rd	0	0	9	0
German GP	4	2	10th	0	0	0	0
Australian GP	257	256	6	8	13	281	0
Canadian GP	3	2	0	0	0	0	0
United States GP	2	2	8th	0	0	0	0
Argentinian GP	8	7	3rd	0	1	5	0
Abu Dhabi GP	239	235	4	1	9	1201	0
Australian GP	32	26	6th	0	0	1	0
French GP	15	11	8th	0	0	0	0
German GP	1	1	10th	0	0	0	0
United States GP	65	57	3rd	0	1	12	0
Italian GP	4	3	11th	0	0	0	0
German GP	1	1	0	0	0	0	0
Italian GP	123	123	10	14	9	206	0
Brazilian GP	58	57	3rd	0	1	64	0
Monaco GP	1	0	0	0	0	0	0

	Nationality	Debut date	Debut GP	Last date
Charles Pic	FRA	18 Mar 2012	Australian GP	24 Nov 2013
Francois Picard	FRA	19 Oct 1958	Moroccan GP	19 Oct 1958
Ernie Pieterse	ZAF	29 Dec 1962	South African GP	1 Jan 1965
Paul Pietsch	DEU	3 Sep 1950	Italian GP	3 Aug 1952
Andre Pilette	BEL	17 Jun 1951	Belgian GP	2 Aug 1964
Teddy Pilette	BEL	12 May 1974	Belgian GP	11 Sep 1977
Luigi Piotti	ITA	11 Sep 1955	Italian GP	18 May 1958
David Piper	GBR	18 Jul 1959	British GP	16 Jul 1960
Nelson Piquet	BRA	30 Jul 1978	German GP	3 Nov 1991
Nelson Piquet Jr.	BRA	16 Mar 2008	Australian GP	26 Jul 2009
Renato Pirocchi	ITA	10 Sep 1961	Italian GP	10 Sep 1961
Didier Pironi	FRA	15 Jan 1978	Argentinian GP	8 Aug 1982
Emanuele Pirro	ITA	9 Jul 1989	French GP	3 Nov 1991
Antonio Pizzonia	BRA	9 Mar 2003	Australian GP	16 Oct 2005
Jacques Pollet	FRA	4 Jul 1954	French GP	11 Sep 1955
Ben Pon	NED	20 May 1962	Dutch GP	20 May 1962
Dennis Poore	GBR	19 Jul 1952	British GP	7 Sep 1952
Sam Posey	USA	3 Oct 1971	United States GP	8 Oct 1972
Charles Pozzi	FRA	2 Jul 1950	French GP	2 Jul 1950
Jackie Pretorius	ZAF	1 Jan 1965	South African GP	3 Mar 1973
Ernesto Prinoth	ITA	16 Sep 1962	Italian GP	16 Sep 1962
David Prophet	GBR	28 Dec 1963	South African GP	1 Jan 1965
Alain Prost	FRA	13 Jan 1980	Argentinian GP	7 Nov 1993
Tom Pryce	GBR	12 May 1974	Belgian GP	5 Mar 1977
David Purley	GBR	3 Jun 1973	Monaco GP	16 Jul 1977
Clive Puzey	ZWE	1 Jan 1965	South African GP	1 Jan 1965
Dieter Quester	AUT	18 Aug 1974	Austrian GP	18 Aug 1974
Ian Raby	GBR	20 Jul 1963	British GP	1 Aug 1965
Bobby Rahal	USA	1 Oct 1978	United States GP	8 Oct 1978
Kimi Raikkonen	FIN	4 Mar 2001	Australian GP	12 Dec 2021
Pierre-Henri Raphanel	FRA	13 Nov 1988	Australian GP	5 Nov 1989

Last GP	GPs entered	GPs started	Wins/best finish	Pole positions	Fastest laps	Total Points	Titles
Brazilian GP	39	39	12th	0	1	0	0
Moroccan GP	1	1	0	0	0	0	0
South African GP	3	2	10th	0	0	0	0
German GP	3	3	0	0	0	0	0
German GP	14	9	5th	0	0	2	0
Italian GP	4	1	17th	0	0	0	0
Monaco GP	9	5	6th	0	0	0	0
British GP	3	2	12th	0	0	0	0
Australian GP	207	204	23	24	23	481.5	3
Hungarian GP	28	28	2nd	0	0	19	0
Italian GP	1	1	12th	0	0	0	0
German GP	72	70	3	3	5	101	0
Australian GP	40	37	5th	0	0	3	0
Chinese GP	20	20	7th	0	0	8	0
Italian GP	5	5	7th	0	0	0	0
Dutch GP	1	1	0	0	0	0	0
Italian GP	2	2	4th	0	0	3	0
United States GP	2	2	12th	0	0	0	0
French GP	1	1	6th	0	0	0	0
South African GP	4	3	0	0	0	0	0
Italian GP	1	0	0	0	0	0	0
South African GP	2	2	14th	0	0	0	0
Australian GP	202	199	51	33	41	768.5	4
South African GP	42	42	3rd	1	0	19	0
British GP	11	7	9th	0	0	0	0
South African GP	1	0	0	0	0	0	0
Austrian GP	2	1	9th	0	0	0	0
German GP	7	3	11th	0	0	0	0
Canadian GP	2	2	12th	0	0	0	0
Abu Dhabi GP	353	350	21	18	46	1873	1
Australian GP	17	1	0	0	0	0	0

	Nationality	Debut date	Debut GP	Last date
Roland Ratzenberger	AUT	27 Mar 1994	Brazilian GP	1 May 1994
Hector Rebaque	MEX	5 Jun 1977	Belgian GP	17 Oct 1981
Brian Redman	GBR	6 Aug 1967	German GP	26 May 1974
Alan Rees	GBR	7 Aug 1966	German GP	6 Aug 1967
Clay Regazzoni	CHE	21 Jun 1970	Dutch GP	30 Mar 1980
Carlos Reutemann	ARG	23 Jan 1972	Argentinian GP	21 Mar 1982
Lance Reventlow	USA	29 May 1960	Monaco GP	16 Jul 1960
Peter Revson	USA	10 May 1964	Monaco GP	27 Jan 1974
John Rhodes	GBR	10 Jul 1965	British GP	10 Jul 1965
Alex Ribeiro	BRA	10 Oct 1976	United States GP	7 Oct 1979
Daniel Ricciardo	AUS	10 Jul 2011	British GP	20 Nov 2022
Ken Richardson	GBR	16 Sep 1951	Italian GP	16 Sep 1951
Fritz Riess	DEU	3 Aug 1952	German GP	3 Aug 1952
Jochen Rindt	AUT	23 Aug 1964	Austrian GP	6 Sep 1970
John Riseley-Prichard	GBR	17 Jul 1954	British GP	17 Jul 1954
Richard Robarts	GBR	13 Jan 1974	Argentinian GP	9 Jun 1974
Pedro Rodriguez	MEX	6 Oct 1963	United States GP	4 Jul 1971
Ricardo Rodriguez	MEX	10 Sep 1961	Italian GP	16 Sep 1962
Franco Rol	ITA	21 May 1950	Monaco GP	7 Sep 1952
Alan Rollinson	GBR	10 Jul 1965	British GP	10 Jul 1965
Tony Rolt	GBR	13 May 1950	British GP	16 Jul 1955
Bertil Roos	SWE	9 Jun 1974	Swedish GP	9 Jun 1974
Keke Rosberg	FIN	4 Mar 1978	South African GP	26 Oct 1986
Nico Rosberg	DEU	12 Mar 2006	Bahrain GP	27 Nov 2016
Louis Rosier	FRA	13 May 1950	British GP	5 Aug 1956
Ricardo Rosset	BRA	10 Mar 1996	Australian GP	1 Nov 1998
Alexander Rossi	USA	20 Sep 2015	Singapore GP	15 Nov 2015
Huub Rothengatter	NED	17 Jun 1984	Canadian GP	26 Oct 1986
Lloyd Ruby	USA	8 Oct 1961	United States GP	8 Oct 1961
Jean-Claude Rudaz	CHE	6 Sep 1964	Italian GP	6 Sep 1964
George Russell	GBR	17 Mar 2019	Australian GP	20 Nov 2022

Last GP	GPs entered	GPs started	Wins/best finish	Pole positions	Fastest laps	Total Points	Titles
San Marino GP	3	1	11th	0	0	0	0
Caesars Palace GP	58	41	4th	0	0	13	0
Monaco GP	15	13	3rd	0	0	8	0
German GP	3	3	7th	0	0	0	0
United States GP West	139	132	5	5	15	209	0
Brazilian GP	146	146	12	6	6	298	0
British GP	4	1	0	0	0	0	0
Brazilian GP	32	30	2	1	0	61	0
British GP	1	1	0	0	0	0	0
United States GP	20	10	8th	0	0	0	0
Abu Dhabi GP	232	232	8	3	16	1311	0
Italian GP	1	0	0	0	0	0	0
German GP	1	1	7th	0	0	0	0
Italian GP	62	60	6	10	3	107	1
British GP	1	1	0	0	0	0	0
Swedish GP	4	3	15th	0	0	0	0
French GP	55	55	2	0	1	71	0
Italian GP	6	5	4th	0	0	4	0
Italian GP	5	5	9th	0	0	0	0
British GP	1	0	0	0	0	0	0
British GP	3	3	0	0	0	0	0
Swedish GP	1	1	0	0	0	0	0
Australian GP	128	114	5	5	3	159.5	1
Abu Dhabi GP	206	206	23	30	20	1594.5	1
German GP	38	38	3rd	0	0	18	0
Japanese GP	33	27	8th	0	0	0	0
Brazilian GP	5	5	12th	0	0	0	0
Australian GP	30	25	7th	0	0	0	0
United States GP	1	1	0	0	0	0	0
Italian GP	1	0	0	0	0	0	0
Abu Dhabi GP	83	82	1	1	5	294	0

	Nationality	Debut date	Debut GP	Last date
Troy Ruttman	USA	6 Jul 1958	French GP	3 Aug 1958
Peter Ryan	CAN	8 Oct 1961	United States GP	8 Oct 1961
Bob Said	USA	12 Dec 1959	United States GP	12 Dec 1959
Carlos Sainz	ESP	15 Mar 2015	Australian GP	20 Nov 2022
Eliseo Salazar	RCH	15 Mar 1981	United States GP West	22 May 1983
Mika Salo	FIN	6 Nov 1994	Japanese GP	13 Oct 2002
Roy Salvadori	GBR	19 Jul 1952	British GP	29 Dec 1962
Consalvo Sanesi	ITA	3 Sep 1950	Italian GP	14 Jul 1951
Stephane Sarrazin	FRA	11 Apr 1999	Brazilian GP	11 Apr 1999
Takuma Sato	JPN	3 Mar 2002	Australian GP	27 Apr 2008
Ludovico Scarfiotti	ITA	23 Jun 1963	Dutch GP	26 May 1968
Giorgio Scarlatti	ITA	13 May 1956	Monaco GP	2 Jul 1961
Ian Scheckter	ZAF	30 Mar 1974	South African GP	9 Oct 1977
Jody Scheckter	ZAF	8 Oct 1972	United States GP	5 Oct 1980
Harry Schell	USA	21 May 1950	Monaco GP	7 Feb 1960
Tim Schenken	AUS	16 Aug 1970	Austrian GP	6 Oct 1974
Albert Scherrer	CHE	23 Aug 1953	Swiss GP	23 Aug 1953
Domenico Schiattarella	ITA	16 Oct 1994	European GP	28 May 1995
Heinz Schiller	CHE	17 Jun 1962	Belgian GP	5 Aug 1962
Jean-Louis Schlesser	FRA	17 Apr 1983	French GP	11 Sep 1988
Jo Schlesser	FRA	7 Aug 1966	German GP	7 Jul 1968
Bernd Schneider	DEU	3 Apr 1988	Brazilian GP	30 Sep 1990
Rudolf Schoeller	CHE	3 Aug 1952	German GP	3 Aug 1952
Rob Schroeder	USA	7 Oct 1962	United States GP	7 Oct 1962
Michael Schumacher	DEU	25 Aug 1991	Belgian GP	25 Nov 2012
Mick Schumacher	DEU	28 Mar 2021	Bahrain GP	20 Nov 2022
Ralf Schumacher	DEU	9 Mar 1997	Australian GP	21 Oct 2007
Vern Schuppan	AUS	4 Jun 1972	Belgian GP	28 Aug 1977
Adolfo Schwelm Cruz	ARG	18 Jan 1953	Argentinian GP	18 Jan 1953
Archie Scott-Brown	GBR	14 Jul 1956	British GP	14 Jul 1956
Piero Scotti	ITA	3 Jun 1956	Belgian GP	3 Jun 1956

Last GP	GPs entered	GPs started	Wins/best finish	Pole positions	Fastest laps	Total Points	Titles
German GP	2	1	10th	0	0	9.5	0
United States GP	1	1	9th	0	0	0	0
United States GP	1	1	0	0	0	0	0
Abu Dhabi GP	163	162	1	3	3	782.5	0
Belgian GP	37	24	5th	0	0	3	0
Japanese GP	111	110	2nd	0	0	33	0
South African GP	50	47	2nd	0	0	19	0
British GP	5	5	4th	0	0	3	0
Brazilian GP	1	1	0	0	0	0	0
Spanish GP	92	90	3rd	0	0	44	0
Monaco GP	12	10	1	0	1	17	0
French GP	15	12	5th	0	0	1	0
Canadian GP	20	18	10th	0	0	0	0
United States GP	113	112	10	3	5	246	1
Argentinian GP	57	56	2nd	0	0	32	0
United States GP	36	34	3rd	0	0	7	0
Swiss GP	1	1	9th	0	0	0	0
Monaco GP	7	7	9th	0	0	0	0
German GP	2	1	0	0	0	0	0
Italian GP	2	1	11th	0	0	0	0
French GP	3	3	10th	0	0	0	0
Spanish GP	34	9	12th	0	0	0	0
German GP	1	1	0	0	0	0	0
United States GP	1	1	10th	0	0	0	0
Brazilian GP	308	307	91	67	77	1566	7
Abu Dhabi GP	44	43	6th	0	0	12	0
Brazilian GP	182	180	6	6	8	329	0
Dutch GP	13	9	7th	0	0	0	0
Argentinian GP	1	1	0	0	0	0	0
British GP	1	1	0	0	0	0	0
Belgian GP	1	1	0	0	0	0	0

	Nationality	Debut date	Debut GP	Last date
Wolfgang Seidel	DEU	2 Aug 1953	German GP	5 Aug 1962
Gunther Seiffert	DEU	5 Aug 1962	German GP	5 Aug 1962
Ayrton Senna	BRA	25 Mar 1984	Brazilian GP	1 May 1994
Bruno Senna	BRA	14 Mar 2010	Bahrain GP	25 Nov 2012
Dorino Serafini	ITA	3 Sep 1950	Italian GP	3 Sep 1950
Chico Serra	BRA	15 Mar 1981	United States GP West	15 May 1983
Doug Serrurier	ZAF	29 Dec 1962	South African GP	1 Jan 1965
Johnny Servoz-Gavin	FRA	7 May 1967	Monaco GP	10 May 1970
Tony Settember	USA	21 Jul 1962	British GP	8 Sep 1963
Hap Sharp	USA	8 Oct 1961	United States GP	25 Oct 1964
Brian Shawe-Taylor	GBR/IRL	13 May 1950	British GP	14 Jul 1951
Carroll Shelby	USA	6 Jul 1958	French GP	13 Sep 1959
Tony Shelly	NZL	21 Jul 1962	British GP	16 Sep 1962
Jo Siffert	CHE	3 Jun 1962	Monaco GP	3 Oct 1971
Andre Simon	FRA	1 Jul 1951	French GP	8 Sep 1957
Sergey Sirotkin	RUS	25 Mar 2018	Australian GP	25 Nov 2018
Moises Solana	MEX	27 Oct 1963	Mexican GP	3 Nov 1968
Alex Soler-Roig	ESP	19 Apr 1970	Spanish GP	1 May 1972
Raymond Sommer	FRA	21 May 1950	Monaco GP	3 Sep 1950
Vincenzo Sospiri	ITA	9 Mar 1997	Australian GP	9 Mar 1997
Stephen South	GBR	30 Mar 1980	United States GP West	30 Mar 1980
'Mike Sparken'	FRA	16 Jul 1955	British GP	16 Jul 1955
Scott Speed	USA	12 Mar 2006	Bahrain GP	22 Jul 2007
Mike Spence	GBR	8 Sep 1963	Italian GP	1 Jan 1968
Alan Stacey	GBR	19 Jul 1958	British GP	19 Jun 1960
Gaetano Starrabba	ITA	10 Sep 1961	Italian GP	10 Sep 1961
Will Stevens	GBR	23 Nov 2014	Abu Dhabi GP	29 Nov 2015
Ian Stewart	GBR	18 Jul 1953	British GP	18 Jul 1953
Jackie Stewart	GBR	1 Jan 1965	South African GP	7 Oct 1973
Jimmy Stewart	GBR	18 Jul 1953	British GP	18 Jul 1953
Siegfried Stohr	ITA	15 Mar 1981	United States GP West	13 Sep 1981

Last GP	GPs entered	GPs started	Wins/best finish	Pole positions	Fastest laps	Total Points	Titles
German GP	12	10	9th	0	0	0	0
German GP	1	0	0	0	0	0	0
San Marino GP	162	161	41	65	19	610	3
Brazilian GP	47	46	6th	0	1	33	0
Italian GP	1	1	2nd	0	0	3	0
Monaco GP	33	18	6th	0	0	1	0
South African GP	3	2	11th	0	0	0	0
Monaco GP	13	12	2nd	0	0	9	0
Italian GP	7	6	8th	0	0	0	0
Mexican GP	6	6	7th	0	0	0	0
British GP	2	2	8th	0	0	0	0
Italian GP	8	8	4th	0	0	0	0
Italian GP	3	1	0	0	0	0	0
United States GP	101	96	2	2	4	68	0
Italian GP	12	11	6th	0	0	0	0
Abu Dhabi GP	21	21	10th	0	0	1	0
Mexican GP	8	8	10th	0	0	0	0
Spanish GP	10	6	16th	0	0	0	0
Italian GP	5	5	4th	0	0	3	0
Australian GP	1	0	0	0	0	0	0
United States GP West	1	0	0	0	0	0	0
British GP	1	1	7th	0	0	0	0
European GP	28	28	9th	0	0	0	0
South African GP	37	36	3rd	0	0	27	0
Belgian GP	7	7	8th	0	0	0	0
Italian GP	1	1	0	0	0	0	0
Abu Dhabi GP	20	18	13th	0	0	0	0
British GP	1	1	0	0	0	0	0
United States GP	100	99	27	17	15	359	3
British GP	1	1	0	0	0	0	0
Italian GP	13	9	7th	0	0	0	0

	Nationality	Debut date	Debut GP	Last date
Rolf Stommelen	DEU	3 Aug 1969	German GP	8 Oct 1978
Philippe Streiff	FRA	21 Oct 1984	Portuguese GP	13 Nov 1988
Lance Stroll	CAN	26 Mar 2017	Australian GP	20 Nov 2022
Hans Stuck	DEU	16 Sep 1951	Italian GP	13 Sep 1953
Hans-Joachim Stuck	DEU	13 Jan 1974	Argentinian GP	7 Oct 1979
Otto Stuppacher	AUT	12 Sep 1976	Italian GP	10 Oct 1976
Danny Sullivan	USA	13 Mar 1983	Brazilian GP	15 Oct 1983
Marc Surer	CHE	9 Sep 1979	Italian GP	25 May 1986
John Surtees	GBR	29 May 1960	Monaco GP	8 Oct 1972
Andy Sutcliffe	GBR	16 Jul 1977	British GP	16 Jul 1977
Adrian Sutil	DEU	7 May 2006	European GP	23 Nov 2014
Aguri Suzuki	JPN	30 Oct 1988	Japanese GP	29 Oct 1995
Toshio Suzuki	JPN	24 Oct 1993	Japanese GP	7 Nov 1993
Jacques Swaters	BEL	29 Jul 1951	German GP	24 Oct 1954
Toranosuke Takagi	JPN	8 Mar 1998	Australian GP	31 Oct 1999
Noritake Takahara	JPN	24 Oct 1976	Japanese GP	23 Oct 1977
Kunimitsu Takahashi	JPN	23 Oct 1977	Japanese GP	23 Oct 1977
Patrick Tambay	FRA	3 Jul 1977	French GP	26 Oct 1986
Luigi Taramazzo	ITA	18 May 1958	Monaco GP	18 May 1958
Gabriele Tarquini	ITA	3 May 1987	San Marino GP	1 Oct 1995
Piero Taruffi	ITA	3 Sep 1950	Italian GP	2 Sep 1956
Dennis Taylor	GBR	18 Jul 1959	British GP	18 Jul 1959
Henry Taylor	GBR	18 Jul 1959	British GP	10 Sep 1961
John Taylor	GBR	11 Jul 1964	British GP	7 Aug 1966
Mike Taylor	GBR	18 Jul 1959	British GP	19 Jun 1960
Trevor Taylor	GBR	18 Jul 1959	British GP	16 Jul 1966
Andre Testut	MCO/FRA	18 May 1958	Monaco GP	10 May 1959
Mike Thackwell	NZL	31 Aug 1980	Dutch GP	5 Aug 1984
Alfonso Thiele	ITA	4 Sep 1960	Italian GP	4 Sep 1960
Eric Thompson	GBR	19 Jul 1952	British GP	19 Jul 1952
Leslie Thorne	GBR	17 Jul 1954	British GP	17 Jul 1954

Last GP	GPs entered	GPs started	Wins/best finish	Pole positions	Fastest laps	Total Points	Titles
Canadian GP	63	54	3rd	0	0	14	0
Australian GP	54	53	3rd	0	0	11	0
Abu Dhabi GP	122	122	3rd	1	0	194	0
Italian GP	5	3	14th	0	0	0	0
United States GP	81	74	3rd	0	0	29	0
United States GP	3	0	0	0	0	0	0
South African GP	15	15	5th	0	0	2	0
Belgian GP	88	81	4th	0	1	17	0
United States GP	113	111	6	8	10	180	1
British GP	1	0	0	0	0	0	0
Abu Dhabi GP	130	128	4th	0	1	124	0
Japanese GP	88	64	3rd	0	0	8	0
Australian GP	2	2	12th	0	0	0	0
Spanish GP	8	7	7th	0	0	0	0
Japanese GP	32	32	7th	0	0	0	0
Japanese GP	2	2	9th	0	0	0	0
Japanese GP	1	1	9th	0	0	0	0
Australian GP	123	114	2	5	2	103	0
Monaco GP	1	0	0	0	0	0	0
European GP	78	38	6th	0	0	1	0
Italian GP	18	18	1	0	1	41	0
British GP	1	0	0	0	0	0	0
Italian GP	11	8	4th	0	0	3	0
German GP	5	5	6th	0	0	1	0
Belgian GP	2	1	0	0	0	0	0
British GP	29	27	2nd	0	0	8	0
Monaco GP	2	0	0	0	0	0	0
German GP	5	2	0	0	0	0	0
Italian GP	1	1	0	0	0	0	0
British GP	1	1	5th	0	0	2	0
British GP	1	1	14th	0	0	0	0

	Nationality	Debut date	Debut GP	Last date
Sam Tingle	ZWE	28 Dec 1963	South African GP	1 Mar 1969
Desmond Titterington	GBR	14 Jul 1956	British GP	14 Jul 1956
Tony Trimmer	GBR	3 Aug 1975	German GP	16 Jul 1978
Maurice Trintignant	FRA	21 May 1950	Monaco GP	6 Sep 1964
Jarno Trulli	ITA	9 Mar 1997	Australian GP	27 Nov 2011
Yuki Tsunoda	JPN	28 Mar 2021	Bahrain GP	20 Nov 2022
Esteban Tuero	ARG	8 Mar 1998	Australian GP	1 Nov 1998
Guy Tunmer	ZAF	1 Mar 1975	South African GP	1 Mar 1975
Toni Ulmen	DEU	18 May 1952	Swiss GP	3 Aug 1952
Bobby Unser	USA	8 Sep 1968	Italian GP	6 Oct 1968
Alberto Uria	URY	16 Jan 1955	Argentinian GP	22 Jan 1956
Nino Vaccarella	ITA	10 Sep 1961	Italian GP	12 Sep 1965
Eric van de Poele	BEL	10 Mar 1991	United States GP	13 Sep 1992
Giedo van der Garde	NED	17 Mar 2013	Australian GP	23 Nov 2013
Dries van der Lof	NED	17 Aug 1952	Dutch GP	17 Aug 1952
Gijs van Lennep	NED	20 Jun 1971	Dutch GP	3 Aug 1975
Basil van Rooyen	ZAF	1 Jan 1968	South African GP	1 Mar 1969
Stoffel Vandoorne	BEL	3 Apr 2016	Bahrain GP	25 Nov 2018
Jean-Eric Vergne	FRA	18 Mar 2012	Australian GP	23 Nov 2014
Jos Verstappen	NED	27 Mar 1994	Brazilian GP	12 Oct 2003
Max Verstappen	NED	15 Mar 2015	Australian GP	20 Nov 2022
Sebastian Vettel	DEU	17 Jun 2007	United States GP	20 Nov 2022
Gilles Villeneuve	CAN	16 Jul 1977	British GP	9 May 1982
Jacques Villeneuve	CAN	10 Mar 1996	Australian GP	30 Jul 2006
Jacques Villeneuve Sr.	CAN	27 Sep 1981	Canadian GP	12 Jun 1983
Luigi Villoresi	ITA	21 May 1950	Monaco GP	2 Sep 1956
Ottorino Volonterio	CHE	24 Oct 1954	Spanish GP	8 Sep 1957
Rikky von Opel	LIE	1 Jul 1973	French GP	7 Jul 1974
Wolfgang von Trips	DEU	2 Sep 1956	Italian GP	10 Sep 1961
Jo Vonlanthen	CHE	17 Aug 1975	Austrian GP	17 Aug 1975
Fred Wacker	USA	7 Jun 1953	Dutch GP	24 Oct 1954

Last GP	GPs entered	GPs started	Wins/best finish	Pole positions	Fastest laps	Total Points	Titles
South African GP	5	5	8th	0	0	0	0
British GP	1	1	0	0	0	0	0
British GP	6	0	0	0	0	0	0
Italian GP	85	82	2	0	1	72.33	0
Brazilian GP	256	252	1	3	1	246.5	0
Abu Dhabi GP	43	43	4th	0	0	44	0
Japanese GP	16	16	8th	0	0	0	0
South African GP	1	1	11th	0	0	0	0
German GP	2	2	8th	0	0	0	0
United States GP	2	1	0	0	0	0	0
Argentinian GP	2	2	6th	0	0	0	0
Italian GP	5	4	9th	0	0	0	0
Italian GP	29	5	9th	0	0	0	0
Brazilian GP	19	19	14th	0	0	0	0
Dutch GP	1	1	0	0	0	0	0
German GP	10	8	6th	0	0	2	0
South African GP	2	2	0	0	0	0	0
Abu Dhabi GP	42	41	7th	0	0	26	0
Abu Dhabi GP	58	58	6th	0	0	51	0
Japanese GP	107	107	3rd	0	0	17	0
Abu Dhabi GP	163	163	35	20	21	2011.5	2
Abu Dhabi GP	301	299	53	57	38	3098	4
Belgian GP	68	67	6	2	8	101	0
German GP	166	163	11	13	9	235	1
Canadian GP	3	0	0	0	0	0	0
Italian GP	33	31	2nd	0	1	46	0
Italian GP	3	3	11th	0	0	0	0
French GP	14	10	9th	0	0	0	0
Italian GP	29	27	2	1	0	56	0
Austrian GP	1	1	0	0	0	0	0
Spanish GP	5	3	6th	0	0	0	0

	Nationality	Debut date	Debut GP	Last date
Dave Walker	AUS	20 Jun 1971	Dutch GP	8 Oct 1972
Peter Walker	GBR	13 May 1950	British GP	16 Jul 1955
Heini Walter	CHE	5 Aug 1962	German GP	5 Aug 1962
Rodger Ward	USA	12 Dec 1959	United States GP	6 Oct 1963
Derek Warwick	GBR	3 May 1981	San Marino GP	7 Nov 1993
John Watson	GBR	14 Jul 1973	British GP	6 Oct 1985
Mark Webber	AUS	3 Mar 2002	Australian GP	24 Nov 2013
Pascal Wehrlein	DEU	20 Mar 2016	Australian GP	26 Nov 2017
Volker Weidler	DEU	26 Mar 1989	Brazilian GP	13 Aug 1989
Karl Wendlinger	AUT	20 Oct 1991	Japanese GP	12 Nov 1995
Peter Westbury	GBR	3 Aug 1969	German GP	4 Oct 1970
Ken Wharton	GBR	18 May 1952	Swiss GP	11 Sep 1955
Ted Whiteaway	GBR	22 May 1955	Monaco GP	22 May 1955
Graham Whitehead	GBR	19 Jul 1952	British GP	19 Jul 1952
Peter Whitehead	GBR	21 May 1950	Monaco GP	17 Jul 1954
Bill Whitehouse	GBR	17 Jul 1954	British GP	17 Jul 1954
Robin Widdows	GBR	20 Jul 1968	British GP	20 Jul 1968
Eppie Wietzes	CAN	27 Aug 1967	Canadian GP	22 Sep 1974
Mike Wilds	GBR	20 Jul 1974	British GP	18 Jul 1976
Jonathan Williams	GBR	22 Oct 1967	Mexican GP	22 Oct 1967
Roger Williamson	GBR	14 Jul 1973	British GP	29 Jul 1973
Desire Wilson	ZAF	13 Jul 1980	British GP	13 Jul 1980
Justin Wilson	GBR	9 Mar 2003	Australian GP	12 Oct 2003
Vic Wilson	GBR	4 Sep 1960	Italian GP	12 Jun 1966
Joachim Winkelhock	DEU	26 Mar 1989	Brazilian GP	9 Jul 1989
Manfred Winkelhock	DEU	14 Sep 1980	Italian GP	4 Aug 1985
Markus Winkelhock	DEU	22 Jul 2007	European GP	22 Jul 2007
Reine Wisell	SWE	4 Oct 1970	United States GP	9 Jun 1974
Roelof Wunderink	NED	27 Apr 1975	Spanish GP	5 Oct 1975
Alexander Wurz	AUT	15 Jun 1997	Canadian GP	7 Oct 2007
Sakon Yamamoto	JPN	30 Jul 2006	German GP	24 Oct 2010

Last GP	GPs entered	GPs started	Wins/best finish	Pole positions	Fastest laps	Total Points	Titles
United States GP	11	11	9th	0	0	0	0
British GP	4	4	7th	0	0	0	0
German GP	1	1	14th	0	0	0	0
United States GP	2	2	0	0	0	14	0
Australian GP	162	146	2nd	0	2	71	0
European GP	154	152	5	2	5	169	0
Brazilian GP	217	215	9	13	19	1047.5	0
Abu Dhabi GP	39	39	8th	0	0	6	0
Hungarian GP	10	0	0	0	0	0	0
Australian GP	42	41	4th	0	0	14	0
United States GP	2	1	9th	0	0	0	0
Italian GP	16	15	4th	0	0	3	0
Monaco GP	1	0	0	0	0	0	0
British GP	1	1	12th	0	0	0	0
British GP	12	10	3rd	0	0	4	0
British GP	1	1	0	0	0	0	0
British GP	1	1	0	0	0	0	0
Canadian GP	2	2	0	0	0	0	0
British GP	8	3	0	0	0	0	0
Mexican GP	1	1	8th	0	0	0	0
Dutch GP	2	2	0	0	0	0	0
British GP	1	0	0	0	0	0	0
Japanese GP	16	16	8th	0	0	1	0
Belgian GP	2	1	0	0	0	0	0
French GP	7	0	0	0	0	0	0
German GP	56	47	5th	0	0	2	0
European GP	1	1	0	0	0	0	0
Swedish GP	23	22	3rd	0	0	13	0
United States GP	6	3	0	0	0	0	0
Chinese GP	69	69	3rd	0	1	45	0
Korean GP	21	21	12th	0	0	0	0

	Nationality	Debut date	Debut GP	Last date
Alex Yoong	MYS	16 Sep 2001	Italian GP	13 Oct 2002
Alessandro Zanardi	ITA	29 Sep 1991	Spanish GP	31 Oct 1999
Emilio Zapico	ESP	2 May 1976	Spanish GP	2 May 1976
Guanyu Zhou	CHN	4 Jul 2021	Austrian GP	20 Nov 2022
Ricardo Zonta	BRA	7 Mar 1999	Australian GP	24 Oct 2004
Renzo Zorzi	ITA	7 Sep 1975	Italian GP	8 May 1977
Ricardo Zunino	ARG	30 Sep 1979	Canadian GP	12 Apr 1981

Last GP	GPs entered	GPs started	Wins/best finish	Pole positions	Fastest laps	Total Points	Titles
Japanese GP	18	14	7th	0	0	0	0
Japanese GP	44	41	6th	0	0	1	0
Spanish GP	1	0	0	0	0	0	0
Abu Dhabi GP	22	22	8th	0	1	6	0
Brazilian GP	37	36	6th	0	0	3	0
Spanish GP	7	7	6th	0	0	1	0
Argentinian GP	11	10	7th	0	0	0	0

THE TEAMS

Teams didn't score points until 1958 when the first championship for constructors was held and privateer teams using proprietary chassis had their points attributed to the chassis constructor, but only if they finished higher up the order than the works cars.

*** Several teams have changed names, notably Jordan becoming Midland, Spyker, Force India, Racing Point and, most recently, Aston Martin. This is the second iteration of Aston Martin in F1 and, as with Alfa Romeo, Lotus and Renault, the later version is marked with an asterisk.**

	Debut GP	Location	Last GP
AAW Racing	1974 Belgian GP	Nivelles	1974 Italian GP
ACE Garage (Rotherham)	1959 British GP	Aintree	1959 British GP
Adolf Brudes (von Breslau)	1952 German GP	Nurburgring	1952 German GP
AFM	1952 Swiss GP	Bremgarten	1952 Swiss GP
AGS (Automobiles Gonfaronaise Sportive)	1986 Italian GP	Monza	1991 Spanish GP
Ahrens Racing	1969 German GP	Nurburgring	1969 German GP
Alan Brown Equipe	1959 British GP	Aintree	1959 British GP
Alberto Uria	1955 Argentinian GP	Buenos Aires	1956 Argentinian GP
Alfa Romeo	1950 British GP	Silverstone	1985 Australian GP
Alfa Romeo*	2019 Australian GP	Melbourne	-
Alfred Dattner	1952 Swiss GP	Bremgarten	1952 Swiss GP
Allied Polymer Group (*see* John Goldie Racing)			
AlphaTauri	2020 Austrian GP	Red Bull Ring	-
Alpine	2021 Bahrain GP	Sakhir	-
Andre Guelfi	1958 Moroccan GP	Ain-Diab	1958 Moroccan GP
Andre Pilette	1963 Italian GP	Monza	1963 Italian GP
Andre Simon	1956 French GP	Reims	1956 French GP
Andre Testut	1958 Monaco GP	Monte Carlo	1958 Monaco GP
Andrea Moda	1992 Brazilian GP	Interlagos	1992 Italian GP
Anglo-American Equipe	1962 British GP	Aintree	1962 Italian GP
Anglo American Racers	1966 Belgian GP	Spa-Francorchamps	1968 Mexican GP
Anglo-Suisse Racing (*see* Joakim Bonnier Racing Team)			

Location	GPs entered	GPs started	Wins/best finish	Pole positions	Fastest laps	Points	Drivers' titles	Constructors' titles
Monza	6	1	0	0	0	0	0	0
Aintree	1	0	0	0	0	0	0	0
Nurburgring	1	1	0	0	0	0	0	0
Bremgarten	1	1	0	0	0	0	0	0
Catalunya	80	46	6th	0	0	1	0	0
Nurburgring	1	1	7th	0	0	0	0	0
Aintree	1	1	12th	0	0	0	0	0
Buenos Aires	2	2	6th	0	0	0	0	0
Adelaide	112	112	10	12	14	214	2	0
-	82	82	4th	0	0	133	0	0
Bremgarten	1	1	0	0	0	0	0	0
-	61	61	1	0	1	284	0	0
-	44	44	1	0	0	328	0	0
Ain-Diab	1	1	15th	0	0	0	0	0
Monza	1	0	0	0	0	0	0	0
Reims	1	1	0	0	0	0	0	0
Monte Carlo	1	0	0	0	0	0	0	0
Monza	11	1	0	0	0	0	0	0
Monza	3	2	11th	0	0	0	0	0
Mexico City	28	28	1	0	0	17	0	0

	Debut GP	Location	Last GP
Antique Automobiles Racing (*see* Colin Crabbe Racing)			
Antonio Creus	1960 Argentinian GP	Buenos Aires	1960 Argentinian GP
Archie Bryde	1952 French GP	Rouen-les-Essarts	1952 British GP
Arrows (including Footwork)	1978 Brazilian GP	Jacarepagua	2002 German GP
Arthur Legat	1952 Belgian GP	Spa-Francorchamps	1953 Belgian GP
Arthur Owen	1960 Italian GP	Monza	1960 Italian GP
Aston Martin	1959 Dutch GP	Zandvoort	1960 British GP
Aston Martin*	2021 Bahrain GP	Sakhir	-
Atlantic Stable	1953 British GP	Silverstone	1953 British GP
ATS (Automobili Turismo e Sport)	1963 Belgian GP	Spa-Francorchamps	1963 Mexican GP
ATS Wheels	1977 United States GP West	Long Beach	1984 Portuguese GP
Autodelta (*see* Alfa Romeo)			
'B Bira'	1951 Spanish GP	Pedralbes	1954 Spanish GP
BAR (British American Racing, then Honda Racing)	1999 Australian GP	Melbourne	2005 Chinese GP
BC Ecclestone	1958 Monaco GP	Monte Carlo	1958 British GP
Benetton (then Renault*)	1986 Brazilian GP	Jacarepagua	2001 Japanese GP
Bernard Collomb	1961 French GP	Reims	1964 Monaco GP
Bernard de Dryver	1978 Belgian GP	Zolder	1978 Belgian GP
Bernard White Racing	1966 United States GP	Watkins Glen	1968 Italian GP
Bill Whitehouse	1954 British GP	Silverstone	1954 British GP
Blanchard Automobiles	1959 United States GP	Sebring	1959 United States GP
Blignaut Racing	1973 South African GP	Kyalami	1974 South African GP
BMS Scuderia Italia	1988 Brazilian GP	Jacarepagua	1993 Portuguese GP
BMW (Bayerische Motoren Werke)	1967 German GP	Nurburgring	1969 German GP
BMW Sauber (*see* Sauber)			
Bob Gerard Racing	1950 British GP	Silverstone	1965 British GP

Location	GPs entered	GPs started	Wins/best finish	Pole positions	Fastest laps	Points	Drivers' titles	Constructors' titles
Buenos Aires	1	1	0	0	0	0	0	0
Silverstone	2	2	7th	0	0	0	0	0
Hockenheim	393	382	2nd	1	0	167	0	0
Spa-Francorchamps	2	2	0	0	0	0	0	0
Monza	1	1	0	0	0	0	0	0
Silverstone	6	5	6th	0	0	0	0	0
-	44	44	2nd	0	0	132	0	0
Silverstone	1	1	9th	0	0	0	0	0
Mexico City	5	5	11th	0	0	0	0	0
Estoril	118	101	5th	0	0	8	0	0
Pedralbes	7	7	4th	0	0	3	0	0
Shanghai	118	117	2nd	2	0	227	0	0
Silverstone	2	1	0	0	0	0	0	0
Suzuka	260	260	27	15	36	861.5	2	1
Monte Carlo	6	4	10th	0	0	0	0	0
Zolder	1	0	0	0	0	0	0	0
Monza	5	4	8th	0	0	0	0	0
Silverstone	1	1	0	0	0	0	0	0
Sebring	1	1	7th	0	0	0	0	0
Kyalami	2	2	14th	0	0	0	0	0
Estoril	94	92	3rd	0	0	15	0	0
Nurburgring	3	2	10th	0	0	0	0	0
Silverstone	10	10	6th	0	0	0	0	0

	Debut GP	Location	Last GP
Boro (*see* HB Bewaking)			
Bowmaker Racing Team	1962 Dutch GP	Zandvoort	1962 South African GP
Brabham	1962 German GP	Nurburgring	1992 Hungarian GP
Brands Hatch Racing (*see* RAM Racing)			
Brawn GP (then Mercedes AMG)	2009 Australian GP	Melbourne	2009 Abu Dhabi GP
Brian Gubby	1965 British GP	Silverstone	1965 British GP
Brian McGuire	1976 Spanish GP	Jarama	1977 British GP
Brian Shawe-Taylor	1951 British GP	Silverstone	1951 British GP
British Formula 1 Racing Team	1977 Spanish GP	Jarama	1977 Austrian GP
BRP (British Racing Partnership)	1958 Moroccan GP	Casablanca	1964 Mexican GP
BRM (British Racing Motors)	1951 British GP	Silverstone	1977 Italian GP
Bruce Halford	1956 British GP	Silverstone	1957 Italian GP
BS Fabrications	1976 Monaco GP	Monaco	1978 Italian GP
Bugatti	1956 French GP	Reims	1956 French GP
Caltex Racing	1966 German GP	Nurburgring	1968 German GP
Camoradi International	1959 United States GP	Sebring	1961 German GP
Canadian Stebro Racing	1963 United States GP	Watkins Glen	1963 United States GP
Castrol Oils Ltd	1967 Canadian GP	Mosport Park	1968 Canadian GP
Caterham	2010 Bahrain GP	Sakhir	2014 Abu Dhabi GP
Centro Aseguredor F1	1978 Spanish GP	Jarama	1978 Spanish GP
Champcarr Inc	1972 United States GP	Watkins Glen	1972 United States GP
Charles Pozzi	1950 French GP	Reims	1950 French GP
Charles Vogele Racing	1967 British GP	Silverstone	1968 Italian GP
Chequered Flag/ Richard Oaten	1974 Canadian GP	Mosport Park	1974 United States GP
Chesterfield Racing (*see* BS Fabrications)			

Location	GPs entered	GPs started	Wins/best finish	Pole positions	Fastest laps	Points	Drivers' titles	Constructors' titles
East London	9	9	2nd	1	0	19	0	0
Hungaroring	407	399	35	39	41	983	4	2
Yas Marina	17	17	8	5	4	172	1	1
Silverstone	1	0	0	0	0	0	0	0
Silverstone	3	0	0	0	0	0	0	0
Silverstone	1	1	8th	0	0	0	0	0
Osterreichring	3	0	0	0	0	0	0	0
Mexico City	22	21	2nd	0	2	20	0	0
Monza	205	197	17	11	13	513	1	1
Monza	6	6	11th	0	0	0	0	0
Monza	36	27	7th	0	0	0	0	0
Reims	1	1	0	0	0	0	0	0
Nurburgring	2	2	12th	0	0	0	0	0
Nurburgring	9	7	10th	0	0	0	0	0
Watkins Glen	1	1	7th	0	0	0	0	0
Mosport Park	2	1	0	0	0	0	0	0
Yas Marina	56	56	11th	0	0	0	0	0
Jarama	1	0	0	0	0	0	0	0
Watkins Glen	1	1	0	0	0	0	0	0
Reims	1	1	6th	0	0	0	0	0
Monza	6	3	5th	0	0	2	0	0
Watkins Glen	2	0	0	0	0	0	0	0

	Debut GP	Location	Last GP
Chris Amon Racing	1966 French GP	Reims	1974 Italian GP
Clarke-Mordaunt-Guthrie-Durlacher Racing	1971 British GP	Silverstone	1973 United States GP
Clemente Biondetti	1950 Italian GP	Monza	1950 Italian GP
Clive Puzey Motors	1965 South African GP	East London	1965 South African GP
Colin Crabbe Racing	1969 Monaco GP	Monte Carlo	1970 United States GP
Coloni (then Andrea Moda)	1987 Italian GP	Monza	1991 Australian GP
Comstock Racing	1967 Canadian GP	Mosport Park	1967 Canadian GP
Connaught	1952 British GP	Silverstone	1957 Monaco GP
Connew	1972 British GP	Brands Hatch	1972 Austrian GP
Cooper	1953 Argentinian GP	Buenos Aires	1968 Mexican GP
CT Atkins	1960 British GP	Silverstone	1960 British GP
Cuth Harrison	1950 British GP	Silverstone	1950 Italian GP
David Bridges	1966 French GP	Reims	1967 German GP
David Fry	1959 British GP	Aintree	1959 British GP
David Prophet Racing	1963 South African GP	East London	1965 South African GP
Dempster International Racing Team	1974 British GP	Brands Hatch	1974 British GP
Dennis Taylor	1959 British GP	Aintree	1959 British GP
Derrington-Francis	1964 Italian GP	Monza	1964 Italian GP
De Tomaso	1961 Italian GP	Monza	1962 Italian GP
Dick Gibson	1957 German GP	Nurburgring	1958 German GP
Dora Greifzu	1953 German GP	Nurburgring	1953 German GP
Dorchester Service Station	1959 British GP	Aintree	1959 British GP
Duncan Hamilton	1951 British GP	Silverstone	1951 German GP
Dupont Team Zerex	1962 United States GP	Watkins Glen	1962 United States GP
DW Racing Enterprises	1963 British GP	Silverstone	1967 British GP
Ecurie Belge	1950 British GP	Silverstone	1953 Italian GP
Ecurie Belgique (then Ecurie Francorchamps)	1951 Belgian GP	Spa-Francorchamps	1951 Italian GP
Ecurie Bleue	1950 Swiss GP	Bremgarten	1960 Argentinian GP

Location	GPs entered	GPs started	Wins/best finish	Pole positions	Fastest laps	Points	Drivers' titles	Constructors' titles
Monza	5	1	0	0	0	0	0	0
Watkins Glen	29	28	7th	0	0	0	0	0
Monza	1	1	0	0	0	0	0	0
East London	1	0	0	0	0	0	0	0
Watkins Glen	14	14	5th	0	0	3	0	0
Adelaide	65	13	8th	0	0	0	0	0
Mosport Park	1	1	0	0	0	0	0	
Monte Carlo	11	11	3rd	0	0	0	0	0
Osterreichring	1	1	0	0	0	0	0	0
Mexico City	115	113	12	6	10	364	2	2
Silverstone	1	1	0	0	0	0	0	0
Monza	3	3	7th	0	0	0	0	0
Nurburgring	5	4	6th	0	0	0	0	0
Aintree	1	0	0	0	0	0	0	0
East London	2	2	14th	0	0	0	0	0
Brands Hatch	1	0	0	0	0	0	0	0
Aintree	1	0	0	0	0	0	0	0
Monza	1	1	0	0	0	0	0	0
Monza	2	1	0	0	0	0	0	0
Nurburgring	2	2	0	0	0	0	0	0
Nurburgring	1	1	14th	0	0	0	0	0
Aintree	1	1	0	0	0	0	0	
Nurburgring	2	2	12th	0	0	0	0	0
Watkins Glen	1	1	9th	0	0	0	0	0
Silverstone	29	26	3rd	0	0	8	0	0
Monza	21	21	7th	0	0	0	0	0
Monza	3	3	6th	0	0	0	0	0
Buenos Aires	3	3	8th	0	0	0	0	0

	Debut GP	Location	Last GP
Ecurie Demi-Litre	1958 German GP	Nurburgring	1958 German GP
Ecurie Ecosse	1952 British GP	Silverstone	1954 British GP
Ecurie Eperon D'Or	1958 German GP	Nurburgring	1958 German GP
Ecurie Espadon	1951 Swiss GP	Bremgarten	1953 Swiss GP
Ecurie Evergreen	1971 Canadian GP	Mosport Park	1971 United States GP
Ecurie Excelsior	1962 British GP	Aintree	1962 Italian GP
Ecurie Filipinetti	1962 Belgian GP	Spa-Francorchamps	1963 French GP
Ecurie Ford France	1967 German GP	Nurburgring	1967 German GP
Ecurie Francorchamps	1952 Belgian GP	Spa-Francorchamps	1954 Spanish GP
Ecurie Galloise	1962 Dutch GP	Zandvoort	1962 German GP
Ecurie Leutitia	1950 Belgian GP	Spa-Francorchamps	1950 French GP
Ecurie Maarsbergen	1957 German GP	Nurburgring	1964 German GP
Ecurie Nationale Suisse	1962 Monaco GP	Monte Carlo	1962 Monaco GP
Ecurie Richmond	1952 Swiss GP	Bremgarten	1954 British GP
Ecurie Rosier	1950 Monaco GP	Monte Carlo	1956 German GP
Ecurie Tomahawk	1965 South African GP	East London	1965 South African GP
Eifelland	1972 South African GP	Kyalami	1972 Austrian GP
Elie Bayol	1952 Italian GP	Monza	1953 Swiss GP
Embassy Racing	1973 Spanish GP	Montjuich Park	1975 United States GP
Emeryson	1956 British GP	Silverstone	1962 Italian GP
Emmanuel de Graffenried	1950 British GP	Silverstone	1954 Spanish GP
EMW (Eisenacher Motoren Werke)	1953 German GP	Nurburgring	1953 German GP
Enrico Plate	1950 British GP	Silverstone	1952 Italian GP
Ensign	1973 French GP	Paul Ricard	1982 Caesars Palace GP
Equipe Anglaise	1953 German GP	Nurburgring	1954 British GP
Equipe Banco Occidental (*see* RAM Racing)			
Equipe Moss/AE Moss/Stirling Moss Auto Racing Team	1954 Belgian GP	Spa-Francorchamps	1955 Italian GP
ENB (Equipe Nationale Belge)	1955 Dutch GP	Zandvoort	1962 German GP

Location	GPs entered	GPs started	Wins/best finish	Pole positions	Fastest laps	Points	Drivers' titles	Constructors' titles
Nurburgring	1	1	0	0	0	0	0	0
Silverstone	3	3	14th	0	0	0	0	0
Nurburgring	1	1	0	0	0	0	0	0
Bremgarten	10	9	2nd	0	0	10	0	0
Watkins Glen	2	1	0	0	0	0	0	0
Monza	3	1	15th	0	0	0	0	0
Reims	5	4	10th	0	0	0	0	0
Nurburgring	1	1	0	0	0	0	0	0
Pedralbes	12	8	6th	0	0	0	0	0
Nurburgring	5	4	8th	0	0	0	0	0
Reims	2	1	0	0	0	0	0	0
Nurburgring	30	25	4th	0	0	7	0	0
Monte Carlo	1	0	0	0	0	0	0	0
Silverstone	5	5	5th	0	0	2	0	0
Nurburgring	34	34	3rd	0	0	15	0	0
East London	1	0	0	0	0	0	0	0
Osterreichring	8	8	10th	0	0	0	0	0
Bremgarten	3	2	0	0	0	0	0	0
Watkins Glen	41	40	5th	0	0	4	0	0
Monza	4	4	11th	0	0	0	0	0
Pedralbes	14	14	4th	0	0	0	0	0
Nurburgring	1	1	0	0	0	0	0	0
Monza	11	10	4th	0	0	5	0	0
Caesars Palace	134	97	4th	0	1	14	0	0
Silverstone	3	2	12th	0	0	0	0	0
Monza	8	6	3rd	0	1	4	0	0
Nurburgring	7	4	6th	0	0	1	0	0

	Debut GP	Location	Last GP
Equipe Prideaux/Dick Gibson	1960 Italian GP	Monza	1960 Italian GP
Equipe Scirocco Belge	1964 Belgian GP	Spa-Francorchamps	1964 German GP
ERA (English Racing Automobiles)	1952 Belgian GP	Spa-Francorchamps	1952 Dutch GP
Ernest Pieterse	1962 South African GP	East London	1962 South African GP
Ernst Klodwig	1952 German GP	Nurburgring	1953 German GP
Ernst Loof	1953 German GP	Nurburgring	1953 German GP
Erwin Bauer	1953 German GP	Nurburgring	1953 German GP
Escuderia Bandeirantes	1952 French GP	Rouen-les-Essarts	1953 Swiss GP
Ettore Chimeri	1960 Argentinian GP	Buenos Aires	1960 Argentinian GP
Eugene Chaboud	1951 French GP	Reims	1951 French GP
EuroBrun	1988 Brazilian GP	Jacarepagua	1990 Spanish GP
Fabre Urbain	1964 Italian GP	Monza	1964 Italian GP
Felday Engineering	1969 German GP	Nurburgring	1969 German GP
Ferrari	1950 Monaco GP	Monte Carlo	-
FISA (Federazione Italiane Scuderie Automobilistiche)	1961 French GP	Reims	1961 French GP
Fittipaldi	1975 Argentinian GP	Buenos Aires	1982 Caesars Palace GP
Fondmetal	1991 United States GP	Phoenix	1992 Italian GP
Footwork (*see* Arrows)			
Force India (then Racing Point)	2008 Australian GP	Melbourne	2018 Abu Dhabi GP
Forti	1995 Brazilian GP	Interlagos	1996 British GP
Francesco Godia-Sales	1957 German GP	Nurburgring	1958 French GP
Francisco Landi	1951 Italian GP	Monza	1951 Italian GP
Frank J Dochnal	1963 Mexican GP	Mexico City	1963 Mexican GP
Frank Williams Racing Cars (then Wolf & Williams)	1969 Spanish GP	Montjuich Park	1976 Japanese GP
Fred Armbruster	1960 United States GP	Riverside	1960 United States GP
Fred Tuck Cars	1960 Monaco GP	Monte Carlo	1961 Italian GP

Location	GPs entered	GPs started	Wins/best finish	Pole positions	Fastest laps	Points	Drivers' titles	Constructors' titles
Monza	1	1	0	0	0	0	0	0
Nurburgring	2	1	0	0	0	0	0	0
Zandvoort	3	3	0	0	0	0	0	0
East London	1	1	10th	0	0	0	0	0
Nurburgring	2	2	0	0	0	0	0	0
Nurburgring	1	1	0	0	0	0	0	0
Nurburgring	1	1	0	0	0	0	0	0
Bremgarten	6	6	8th	0	0	0	0	0
Buenos Aires	1	1	0	0	0	0	0	0
Reims	1	1	8th	0	0	0	0	0
Jerez	46	14	11th	0	0	0	0	0
Monza	1	0	0	0	0	0	0	0
Nurburgring	1	1	9th	0	0	0	0	0
-	1053	1051	243	243	261	10123.42	15	16
Reims	1	1	1	0	0	9	0	0
Caesars Palace	120	103	2nd	0	0	44	0	0
Monza	29	19	10th	0	0	0	0	0
Yas Marina	212	212	2nd	1	5	1098	0	0
Silverstone	27	23	7th	0	0	0	0	0
Reims	7	6	8th	0	0	0	0	0
Monza	1	1	0	0	0	0	0	0
Mexico City	1	0	0	0	0	0	0	0
Fuji	104	95	2nd	0	1	35	0	0
Riverside	1	1	11th	0	0	0	0	0
Monza	4	3	0	0	0	0	0	0

	Debut GP	Location	Last GP
Fritz Riess	1952 German GP	Nurburgring	1952 German GP
F&S Properties (*see* Goldie Hexagon Racing)			
Gene Mason Racing	1971 Monaco GP	Monte Carlo	1972 United States GP
Geoffrey Crossley	1950 British GP	Silverstone	1950 Belgian GP
Georges Berger	1953 Belgian GP	Spa-Francorchamps	1954 French GP
Georges Grignard	1951 Spanish GP	Pedralbes	1951 Spanish GP
Gerhard Mitter	1967 German GP	Nurburgring	1967 German GP
Gerry Ashmore	1961 British GP	Aintree	1962 Italian GP
Giacomo Caprara	1952 British GP	Silverstone	1952 British GP
Gilby Engineering	1954 French GP	Reims	1962 Italian GP
Gino Munaron	1960 Argentinian GP	Buenos Aires	1960 Argentinian GP
Giorgio Scarlatti	1956 Monaco GP	Monte Carlo	1960 Argentinian GP
Giovanni de Riu	1954 Italian GP	Monza	1954 Spanish GP
Goldie Hexagon Racing	1974 Argentinian GP	Buenos Aires	1976 Dutch GP
Gordini	1950 Monaco GP	Monte Carlo	1956 Italian GP
Graham Whitehead	1951 French GP	Reims	1951 French GP
Gunther Bechem	1952 German GP	Nurburgring	1953 German GP
Gus Hutchison	1970 United States GP	Watkins Glen	1970 United States GP
Guy Ligier	1966 Monaco GP	Monte Carlo	1967 Mexican GP
Guy Mairesse	1951 Swiss GP	Bremgarten	1951 French GP
H & L Motors	1961 Belgian GP	Spa-Francorchamps	1961 Italian GP
Haas F1	2016 Australian GP	Melbourne	-
Hans Herrmann	1953 German GP	Nurburgring	1953 German GP
Hans Klenk	1952 German GP	Nurburgring	1954 German GP
Hans Stuck	1953 German GP	Nurburgring	1953 Italian GP
Hap Sharp	1961 United States GP	Watkins Glen	1962 United States GP
Harry Schell	1954 Argentinian GP	Buenos Aires	1954 Spanish GP
Harry Stiller Racing	1975 Spanish GP	Montjuich Park	1975 Swedish GP
HB Bewaking (including Boro)	1976 Spanish GP	Jarama	1976 Italian GP
Helmut Niedermayr	1952 German GP	Nurburgring	1953 German GP
Heros Racing	1976 Japanese GP	Fuji	1977 Japanese GP
Hesketh	1973 Monaco GP	Monte Carlo	1978 Belgian GP

Location	GPs entered	GPs started	Wins/best finish	Pole positions	Fastest laps	Points	Drivers' titles	Constructors' titles
Nurburgring	1	1	7th	0	0	0	0	0
Watkins Glen	6	5	16th	0	0	0	0	0
Spa-Francorchamps	2	2	9th	0	0	0	0	0
Reims	2	2	0	0	0	0	0	0
Pedralbes	1	1	0	0	0	0	0	0
Nurburgring	1	1	0	0	0	0	0	0
Monza	4	3	16th	0	0	0	0	0
Silverstone	1	1	8th	0	0	0	0	0
Monza	11	9	15th	0	0	0	0	0
Buenos Aires	1	1	13th	0	0	0	0	0
Buenos Aires	5	4	8th	0	0	0	0	0
Pedralbes	1	0	0	0	0	0	0	0
Zandvoort	17	16	4th	0	0	6	0	0
Monza	40	40	3rd	0	1	28	0	0
Reims	1	1	0	0	0	0	0	0
Nurburgring	2	2	0	0	0	0	0	0
Watkins Glen	1	1	0	0	0	0	0	0
Mexico City	13	12	6th	0	0	1	0	0
Reims	2	2	9th	0	0	0	0	0
Monza	5	5	4th	0	0	3	0	0
-	144	144	4th	1	2	237	0	0
Nurburgring	1	1	9th	0	0	0	0	0
Nurburgring	2	2	0	0	0	0	0	0
Monza	2	2	0	0	0	0	0	0
Watkins Glen	2	2	10th	0	0	0	0	0
Pedralbes	5	5	6th	0	0	0	0	0
Anderstorp	4	4	11th	0	0	0	0	0
Monza	6	5	8th	0	0	0	0	0
Nurburgring	2	2	0	0	0	0	0	0
Fuji	2	2	11th	0	0	0	0	0
Zolder	70	61	1	0	3	62	0	0

	Debut GP	Location	Last GP
High Efficiency Motors	1958 German GP	Nurburgring	1960 United States GP
Honda	1964 German GP	Nurburgring	1968 Mexican GP
Honda Racing (then Brawn GP)	2006 Bahrain GP	Sakhir	2008 Brazilian GP
Horace Gould	1954 British GP	Silverstone	1960 Italian GP
Horschell Racing Corporation	1950 Monaco GP	Monte Carlo	1950 Monaco GP
HRT (Hispania Racing Team)	2010 Bahrain GP	Sakhir	2012 Brazilian GP
Hubert Hahne	1970 German GP	Hockenheim	1970 German GP
HWM (Hersham & Walton Motors)	1951 Swiss GP	Bremgarten	1954 French GP
Ian Raby Racing	1963 British GP	Silverstone	1965 German GP
Iberia Airlines (then Centro Aseguredor F1)	1977 Spanish GP	Jarama	1977 Italian GP
Interscope Racing	1977 United States GP	Watkins Glen	1978 Dutch GP
J Frank Harrison	1961 United States GP	Watkins Glen	1961 United States GP
J Wheeler Autosport	1961 United States GP	Watkins Glen	1961 United States GP
Jack Brabham	1956 British GP	Silverstone	1956 British GP
Jack Holme	1969 South African GP	Kyalami	1969 South African GP
Jackie Pretorius	1965 South African GP	East London	1965 South African GP
Jaguar (then Red Bull Racing)	2000 Australian GP	Melbourne	2004 Brazilian GP
JB Naylor	1957 German GP	Nurburgring	1961 Italian GP
Jean Behra	1959 German GP	AVUS	1959 German GP
'Jean Lucienbonnet'	1959 Monaco GP	Monte Carlo	1959 Monaco GP
Jim Hall	1960 United States GP	Riverside	1962 United States GP
Joakim Bonnier Racing Team (including Anglo-Suisse Racing Team)	1957 British GP	Aintree	1971 United States GP
Joe Fry	1950 British GP	Silverstone	1950 British GP
Joe Kelly	1950 British GP	Silverstone	1951 British GP
Joe Lubin	1960 United States GP	Riverside	1960 United States GP
John Dalton	1962 British GP	Aintree	1962 Italian GP

Location	GPs entered	GPs started	Wins/best finish	Pole positions	Fastest laps	Points	Drivers' titles	Constructors' titles
Riverside	8	7	7th	0	0	0	0	0
Mexico City	35	35	1	1	2	50	0	0
Interlagos	53	53	1	1	1	106	0	0
Monza	16	14	5th	0	0	2	0	0
Monte Carlo	1	1	0	0	0	0	0	0
Interlagos	58	56	13th	0	0	0	0	0
Hockenheim	1	0	0	0	0	0	0	0
Reims	15	14	5th	0	0	2	0	0
Nurburgring	7	3	11th	0	0	0	0	0
Monza	7	2	13th	0	0	0	0	0
Zandvoort	4	2	7th	0	0	0	0	0
Watkins Glen	1	1	0	0	0	0	0	0
Watkins Glen	1	1	9th	0	0	0	0	0
Silverstone	1	1	0	0	0	0	0	0
Kyalami	1	1	0	0	0	0	0	0
East London	1	0	0	0	0	0	0	0
Interlagos	85	85	3rd	0	0	49	0	0
Monza	8	7	13th	0	0	0	0	0
AVUS	1	0	0	0	0	0	0	0
Monte Carlo	1	0	0	0	0	0	0	0
Watkins Glen	3	2	7th	0	0	0	0	0
Watkins Glen	43	37	5th	7	0	0	0	0
Silverstone	1	1	10th	0	0	0	0	0
Silverstone	2	2	0	0	0	0	0	0
Riverside	1	1	13th	0	0	0	0	0
Monza	3	1	0	0	0	0	0	0

	Debut GP	Location	Last GP
John Fisher Equipe	1959 Monaco GP	Monte Carlo	1959 Monaco GP
John Heath	1953 British GP	Silverstone	1953 British GP
John James	1951 British GP	Silverstone	1951 British GP
John Love	1962 South African GP	East London	1968 South African GP
John Maryon	1969 Canadian GP	Mosport Park	1969 Canadian GP
John Mecom	1962 United States GP	Watkins Glen	1962 United States GP
John M Wyatt III	1961 United States GP	Watkins Glen	1961 United States GP
John Willment Automobiles	1964 British GP	Brands Hatch	1965 Italian GP
Jolly Club of Switzerland	1971 Italian GP	Monza	1977 Italian GP
Jordan (then Midland)	1991 United States GP	Phoenix	2005 Chinese GP
Jorge Daponte	1954 Argentinian GP	Buenos Aires	1954 Italian GP
Jose Froilan Gonzalez	1951 Swiss GP	Bremgarten	1951 Swiss GP
Josef Peters	1952 German GP	Nurburgring	1952 German GP
Juan Manuel Fangio	1958 French GP	Reims	1958 French GP
Kauhsen	1979 Spanish GP	Jarama	1979 Belgian GP
Ken Kavanagh	1958 Argentinian GP	Buenos Aires	1958 Belgian GP
Ken Tyrrell Racing	1966 German GP	Nurburgring	1967 German GP
Ken Wharton	1953 Dutch GP	Zandvoort	1953 Italian GP
Kenneth Downing	1952 Dutch GP	Zandvoort	1952 Dutch GP
Kojima	1976 Japanese GP	Fuji	1977 Japanese GP
Kurt Kuhnke	1963 German GP	Nurburgring	1963 German GP
Lancia	1954 Spanish GP	Pedralbes	1955 Belgian GP
Larrousse	1987 San Marino GP	Imola	1994 Australian GP
Lawson Organisation/Team Lawson	1963 South African GP	East London	1969 South African GP
LBT Team March (*see* RAM Racing)			
Leader Cars Incorporated	1959 United States GP	Sebring	1959 United States GP
LEC	1973 Monaco GP	Monte Carlo	1977 British GP
Leslie Hawthorn	1952 Belgian GP	Spa-Francorchamps	1952 Italian GP
Leslie Marr	1954 British GP	Silverstone	1955 British GP
Lexington Racing	1975 South African GP	Kyalami	1976 South African GP

Location	GPs entered	GPs started	Wins/best finish	Pole positions	Fastest laps	Points	Drivers' titles	Constructors' titles
Monte Carlo	1	1	0	0	0	0	0	0
Silverstone	1	1	0	0	0	0	0	0
Silverstone	1	1	0	0	0	0	0	0
Kyalami	5	5	2nd	0	0	6	0	0
Mosport Park	1	1	0	0	0	0	0	0
Watkins Glen	1	1	10th	0	0	0	0	0
Watkins Glen	1	1	8th	0	0	0	0	0
Monza	8	8	8th	0	0	0	0	0
Monza	1	0	0	0	0	0	0	0
Shanghai	250	250	4	2	2	291	0	0
Monza	2	2	0	0	0	0	0	0
Bremgarten	1	1	0	0	0	0	0	0
Nurburgring	1	1	0	0	0	0	0	0
Reims	1	1	4th	0	0	3	0	0
Zolder	2	0	0	0	0	0	0	0
Spa-Francorchamps	3	1	5th	0	0	2	0	0
Nurburgring	2	2	9th	0	0	0	0	0
Monza	5	5	7th	0	0	0	0	0
Zandvoort	1	1	0	0	0	0	0	0
Fuji	2	2	11th	0	1	0	0	0
Nurburgring	1	0	0	0	0	0	0	0
Spa-Francorchamps	4	4	2nd	2	1	9	0	0
Adelaide	127	126	3rd	0	0	23	0	0
Kyalami	3	2	0	0	0	0	0	0
Sebring	1	1	0	0	0	0	0	0
Silverstone	10	7	9th	0	0	0	0	0
Monza	4	4	3rd	0	0	10	0	0
Silverstone	2	2	13th	0	0	0	0	0
Kyalami	2	2	0	0	0	0	0	0

	Debut GP	Location	Last GP
Leyton House (then March again)	1990 United States GP	Phoenix	1991 Australian GP
Life	1990 United States GP	Phoenix	1990 Spanish GP
Ligier	1976 Brazilian GP	Interlagos	1996 Japanese GP
Lola	1967 German GP	Nurburgring	1997 Australian GP
Lotus	1958 Monaco GP	Monte Carlo	1994 Australian GP
Lotus* (then Renault*)	2012 Australian GP	Melbourne	2015 Abu Dhabi GP
Lotus Components	1967 German GP	Nurburgring	1967 German GP
Lotus F1 Racing (then Caterham)	2010 Bahrain GP	Sakhir	2011 Brazilian GP
Louis Chiron	1953 French GP	Reims	1953 Italian GP
Louise Bryden-Brown	1961 British GP	Aintree	1961 German GP
Lucky Strike Racing	1975 South African GP	Kyalami	1975 South African GP
Ludwig Fischer	1952 German GP	Nurburgring	1952 German GP
Luigi Piotti	1956 French GP	Reims	1957 Italian GP
Luki Botha	1967 South African GP	Kyalami	1967 South African GP
Lyncar	1974 British GP	Brands Hatch	1975 British GP
Maki	1974 British GP	Brands Hatch	1976 Japanese GP
Manor	2016 Australian GP	Melbourne	2016 Abu Dhabi GP
Mapfre-Williams (*see* Brian McGuire)			
Marcel Balsa	1952 German GP	Nurburgring	1952 German GP
March	1970 South African GP	Kyalami	1992 Australian GP
Maria Teresa de Filippis	1958 Monaco GP	Monte Carlo	1958 Italian GP
Mario Deliotti Racing	1978 British GP	Brands Hatch	1978 British GP
Martini	1978 South African GP	Kyalami	1978 Dutch GP
Martini Racing Team	1972 French GP	Clermont-Ferrand	1973 Austrian GP
Marussia (then Manor)	2012 Australian GP	Melbourne	2015 Abu Dhabi GP
Maserati	1950 British GP	Silverstone	1957 Italian GP
Matra	1966 German GP	Nurburgring	1972 United States GP
Maurice Trintignant	1964 Monaco GP	Monte Carlo	1964 Italian GP
McLaren	1966 Monaco GP	Monte Carlo	-
Meiritsu Racing Team	1977 Japanese GP	Fuji	1977 Japanese GP
Melchester Racing	1977 British GP	Silverstone	1978 British GP

Location	GPs entered	GPs started	Wins/best finish	Pole positions	Fastest laps	Points	Drivers' titles	Constructors' titles
Adelaide	32	30	2nd	0	0	8	0	0
Jerez	14	0	0	0	0	0	0	0
Suzuka	330	326	9	9	10	388	0	0
Melbourne	2	1	0	0	0	0	0	0
Adelaide	492	491	79	107	71	1514	5	7
Yas Marina	77	77	2	0	4	706	0	0
Nurburgring	1	1	5th	0	0	0	0	0
Interlagos	38	38	12th	0	0	0	0	0
Monza	4	2	10th	0	0	0	0	0
Nurburgring	2	2	11th	0	0	0	0	0
Kyalami	1	1	14th	0	0	0	0	0
Nurburgring	1	0	0	0	0	0	0	0
Monza	8	7	6th	0	0	0	0	0
Kyalami	1	1	0	0	0	0	0	0
Silverstone	2	1	17th	0	0	0	0	0
Fuji	8	0	0	0	0	0	0	0
Yas Marina	21	21	10th	0	0	1	0	0
Nurburgring	1	1	0	0	0	0	0	0
Adelaide	205	194	2	2	4	130	0	0
Monza	3	2	10th	0	0	0	0	0
Brands Hatch	1	0	0	0	0	0	0	0
Zandvoort	7	4	9th	0	0	0	0	0
Osterreichring	10	6	6th	0	0	1	0	0
Yas Marina	74	73	9th	0	0	2	0	0
Monza	43	43	9	9	16	214.5	2	0
Watkins Glen	64	62	9	4	12	184	1	1
Monza	5	4	5th	0	0	2	0	0
-	928	924	183	156	162	6301.5	12	8
Fuji	1	1	9th	0	0	0	0	0
Brands Hatch	2	0	0	0	0	0	0	0

	Debut GP	Location	Last GP
Mercedes AMG	2010 Bahrain GP	Sakhir	-
Mercedes-Benz	1954 French GP	Reims	1955 Italian GP
Merzario	1977 Spanish GP	Jarama	1979 United States GP
Midland (then Spyker)	2006 Bahrain GP	Sakhir	2006 Brazilian GP
Mike Fisher	1967 Canadian GP	Mosport Park	1967 Mexican GP
Mike Harris	1962 South African GP	East London	1962 South African GP
Mike Taylor	1959 United States GP	Sebring	1959 United States GP
Minardi (then Toro Rosso)	1985 Brazilian GP	Jacarepagua	2005 Chinese GP
Modena Team	1991 United States GP	Phoenix	1991 Australian GP
Momo Corporation	1961 United States GP	Watkins Glen	1961 United States GP
Monte Carlo Auto Sport	1959 Monaco GP	Monte Carlo	1959 Monaco GP
Motor Presse Verlag	1952 German GP	Nurburgring	1952 German GP
Neville Lederle	1962 South African GP	East London	1962 South African GP
North American Racing Team (*see* Ferrari)			
OASC Racing Team	1976 Italian GP	Monza	1976 United States GP
Onofre Marimon	1954 Argentinian GP	Buenos Aires	1954 Argentinian GP
Onyx (including Monteverdi)	1989 Brazilian GP	Jacarepagua	1990 Hungarian GP
OSCA	1951 Italian GP	Monza	1959 United States GP
Osella (then Fondmetal)	1980 Argentinian GP	Buenos Aires	1990 Australian GP
Oswald Karch	1953 German GP	Nurburgring	1953 German GP
Otelle Nucci	1962 South African GP	East London	1965 South African GP
Ottorino Volonterio	1956 German GP	Nurburgring	1959 Italian GP
Owen Racing Organisation (*see* BRM)			
Pacific	1994 Brazilian GP	Interlagos	1995 Australian GP
Parnelli	1974 Canadian GP	Mosport Park	1976 United States GP West
Patrick Neve	1978 Belgian GP	Zolder	1978 Belgian GP
Paul Emery	1959 United States GP	Sebring	1959 United States GP
Paul Pietsch	1950 Italian GP	Monza	1950 Italian GP

Location	GPs entered	GPs started	Wins/best finish	Pole positions	Fastest laps	Points	Drivers' titles	Constructors' titles
-	259	259	116	129	96	6796.5	9	9
Monza	12	12	9	8	9	139.14	1	0
Watkins Glen	38	15	14th	0	0	0	0	0
Interlagos	18	18	9th	0	0	0	0	0
Mexico City	2	1	11th	0	0	0	0	0
East London	1	1	0	0	0	0	0	0
Sebring	1	1	0	0	0	0	0	0
Shanghai	346	340	4th	0	0	38	0	0
Adelaide	16	6	7th	0	0	0	0	0
Watkins Glen	1	1	0	0	0	0	0	0
Monte Carlo	1	0	0	0	0	0	0	0
Nurburgring	1	1	0	0	0	0	0	0
East London	1	1	6th	0	0	1	0	0
Watkins Glen	3	0	0	0	0	0	0	0
Buenos Aires	1	0	0	0	0	0	0	0
Hungaroring	26	17	3rd	0	0	6	0	0
Sebring	3	3	9th	0	0	0	0	0
Adelaide	172	133	4th	0	0	5	0	0
Nurburgring	1	1	0	0	0	0	0	0
East London	3	3	10th	0	0	0	0	0
Monza	3	3	11th	0	0	0	0	0
Adelaide	33	22	8th	0	0	0	0	0
Long Beach	16	16	4th	0	1	6	0	0
Zolder	1	0	0	0	0	0	0	0
Sebring	1	1	0	0	0	0	0	0
Monza	1	1	0	0	0	0	0	0

	Debut GP	Location	Last GP
Paul Seitz	1969 Canadian GP	Mosport Park	1969 Canadian GP
Penske (including Penske-White Racing)	1971 Canadian GP	Mosport Park	1976 Japanese GP
Pescara Racing Club	1961 Italian GP	Monza	1961 Italian GP
Pete Lovely Volkswagen Inc	1969 Canadian GP	Mosport Park	1971 United States GP
Peter Walker	1950 British GP	Silverstone	1950 British GP
Peter Whitehead	1952 Monaco GP	Monte Carlo	1954 British GP
Phil Cade	1959 United States GP	Sebring	1959 United States GP
Phil Hill	1966 Monaco GP	Monte Carlo	1966 Belgian GP
Philip Fotheringham-Parker	1951 British GP	Silverstone	1951 British GP
Philippe Etancelin	1950 Monaco GP	Monte Carlo	1951 Spanish GP
Piero Dusio	1952 Italian GP	Monza	1952 Italian GP
Piero Scotti	1956 Belgian GP	Spa-Francorchamps	1956 Belgian GP
'Pierre Levegh'	1950 Belgian GP	Spa-Francorchamps	1951 Italian GP
Pinch Plant (*see* Lyncar)			
Polar Caravans (*see* Hesketh)			
Porsche	1957 German GP	Nurburgring	1962 United States GP
Prince Gaetano Starrabba	1961 Italian GP	Monza	1961 Italian GP
Prost	1997 Australian GP	Melbourne	2001 Japanese GP
Racing Point (then Aston Martin*)	2019 Australian GP`	Melbourne	2020 Abu Dhabi GP
RAM Racing (including Brands Hatch Racing, Equipe Banco Occidental & LBT Team March)	1976 Spanish GP	Jarama	1985 European GP
Raymond Sommer	1950 Belgian GP	Spa-Francorchamps	1951 Italian GP
Rebaque	1978 Argentinian GP	Buenos Aires	1979 United States GP
Red Bull Racing	2005 Australian GP	Melbourne	-
Reg Parnell Racing	1959 British GP	Aintree	1969 Monaco GP
Renault	1977 British GP	Silverstone	1985 Australian GP

Location	GPs entered	GPs started	Wins/best finish	Pole positions	Fastest laps	Points	Drivers' titles	Constructors' titles
Mosport Park	1	1	0	0	0	0	0	0
Fuji	33	32	1	0	0	28	0	0
Monza	1	1	12th	0	0	0	0	0
Watkins Glen	9	6	7th	0	0	0	0	0
Silverstone	1	1	0	0	0	0	0	0
Silverstone	8	6	3rd	0	0	4	0	0
Sebring	1	0	0	0	0	0	0	0
Spa-Francorchamps	2	0	0	0	0	0	0	0
Silverstone	1	1	0	0	0	0	0	0
Pedralbes	10	10	5th	0	0	3	0	0
Monza	1	0	0	0	0	0	0	0
Spa-Francorchamps	1	1	0	0	0	0	0	0
Monza	6	6	7th	0	0	0	0	0
Watkins Glen	21	17	1	1	0	43	0	0
Monza	1	1	0	0	0	0	0	0
Suzuka	83	83	2nd	0	0	35	0	0
Yas Marina	38	38	1	0	0	268	0	0
Brands Hatch	65	41	8th	0	0	0	0	0
Monza	2	2	0	0	0	0	0	0
Watkins Glen	30	19	6th	0	0	1	0	0
-	348	347	92	81	84	6338	6	5
Monte Carlo	81	75	2nd	1	0	32	0	0
Adelaide	125	122	16	31	18	312	0	0

	Debut GP	Location	Last GP
Renault* (then Lotus* & then Alpine)	2002 Australian GP	Melbourne	2020 Abu Dhabi GP
Reventlow Automobiles	1960 Monaco GP	Monte Carlo	1960 United States GP
Revson Racing (America)	1964 Monaco GP	Monte Carlo	1964 Italian GP
Rial	1988 Brazilian GP	Jacarepagua	1989 Australian GP
Ridgeway Management	1957 German GP	Nurburgring	1957 German GP
RJ Chase	1953 British GP	Silverstone	1953 British GP
Rob Walker Racing	1953 British GP	Silverstone	1970 Mexican GP
Robert Bodle	1960 French GP	Reims	1960 British GP
Robert la Caze	1958 Moroccan GP	Ain-Diab	1958 Moroccan GP
Robert O'Brien	1952 Belgian GP	Spa-Francorchamps	1952 Belgian GP
Roberto Mieres	1954 Argentinian GP	Buenos Aires	1954 German GP
Robin Montgomerie-Charrington	1952 Belgian GP	Spa-Francorchamps	1952 Belgian GP
Rodney Nuckey	1953 German GP	Nurburgring	1953 German GP
Ron Harris	1966 German GP	Nurburgring	1967 German GP
Roy Winkelmann Racing	1966 German GP	Nurburgring	1969 German GP
Rudolf Krause	1952 German GP	Nurburgring	1952 German GP
Sam Tingle	1963 South African GP	East London	1967 South African GP
Sauber (including BMW Sauber then Alfa Romeo*)	1993 South African GP	Kyalami	2018 Abu Dhabi GP
Scirocco-Powell Racing	1963 Belgian GP	Spa-Francorchamps	1964 German GP
Scuderia Achille Varzi	1950 Monaco GP	Monte Carlo	1950 French GP
Scuderia Ambrosiana	1950 British GP	Silverstone	1954 British GP
Scuderia Castellotti	1960 Monaco GP	Monte Carlo	1960 Italian GP
Scuderia Centro Sud	1956 Monaco GP	Monte Carlo	1965 Italian GP
Scuderia Colonia	1960 Italian GP	Monza	1961 Italian GP
Scuderia Finotto	1974 Belgian GP	Nivelles	1974 Italian GP
Scuderia Franera	1952 Swiss GP	Bremgarten	1952 Italian GP
Scuderia Guastalla	1956 Italian GP	Monza	1956 Italian GP
Scuderia Gulf Rondini	1976 German GP	Nurburgring	1976 Italian GP

Location	GPs entered	GPs started	Wins/best finish	Pole positions	Fastest laps	Points	Drivers' titles	Constructors' titles
Yas Marina	278	278	19	20	15	1465	2	2
Riverside	5	2	10th	0	0	0	0	0
Monza	4	3	13th	0	0	0	0	0
Adelaide	32	20	4th	0	0	6	0	0
Nurburgring	1	1	15th	0	0	0	0	0
Silverstone	1	1	0	0	0	0	0	0
Mexico City	124	120	9	10	9	158	0	0
Silverstone	2	1	12th	0	0	0	0	0
Ain-Diab	1	1	14th	0	0	0	0	0
Spa-Francorchamps	1	1	0	0	0	0	0	0
Nurburgring	5	5	6th	0	0	0	0	0
Spa-Francorchamps	1	1	0	0	0	0	0	0
Nurburgring	1	1	11th	0	0	0	0	0
Nurburgring	2	2	12th	0	0	0	0	0
Nurburgring	3	3	7th	0	0	0	0	0
Nurburgring	1	1	0	0	0	0	0	0
Kyalami	3	3	13th	0	0	0	0	0
Yas Marina	465	462	1	1	5	865	0	0
Nurburgring	8	5	8th	0	0	0	0	0
Reims	3	3	7th	0	0	0	0	0
Silverstone	6	5	9th	0	0	0	0	0
Monza	4	3	4th	0	0	3	0	0
Monza	49	47	3rd	0	0	24	0	0
Monza	7	6	8th	0	0	0	0	0
Monza	4	1	0	0	0	0	0	0
Monza	4	4	4th	0	0	3	0	0
Monza	1	1	10th	0	0	0	0	0
Monza	4	3	11th	0	0	0	0	0

	Debut GP	Location	Last GP
Scuderia Jolly Club	1962 Italian GP	Monza	1962 Italian GP
Scuderia Lupini	1963 South African GP	East London	1963 South African GP
Scuderia Marzotto	1952 French GP	Rouen-les-Essarts	1952 German GP
Scuderia Milano	1950 Swiss GP	Bremgarten	1953 Italian GP
Scuderia Sant Ambroeus	1961 British GP	Aintree	1961 Italian GP
Scuderia Scribante	1965 South African GP	East London	1974 South African GP
Scuderia Serenissima	1961 Monaco GP	Monte Carlo	1961 Italian GP
Scuderia Settecolli	1961 Italian GP	Monza	1963 Italian GP
Scuderia SSS Republica di Venezia	1962 Monaco GP	Monte Carlo	1962 Italian GP
Scuderia Sud Americana	1958 Argentinian GP	Buenos Aires	1958 Argentinian GP
Scuderia Ugolini	1959 Monaco GP	Monte Carlo	1959 French GP
Selby Auto Spares	1963 South African GP	East London	1963 South African GP
Shadow	1973 South African GP	Kyalami	1980 French GP
Shannon	1966 British GP	Brands Hatch	1966 British GP
Shell Arnold	1971 Italian GP	Monza	1971 Italian GP
Shellsport/Whiting	1976 British GP	Brands Hatch	1976 British GP
Siffert Racing Team	1963 Monaco GP	Monte Carlo	1971 French GP
Silvio Moser	1969 Monaco GP	Monte Carlo	1970 Italian GP
Simtek	1994 Brazilian GP	Interlagos	1995 Monaco GP
Sir Jeremy Boles	1954 British GP	Silverstone	1954 British GP
Spirit	1983 British GP	Silverstone	1985 San Marino GP
Sports Cars Of Austria	1976 Austrian GP	Osterreichring	1976 Austrian GP
Spyker (then Force India)	2007 Australian GP	Melbourne	2007 Brazilian GP
Squadra Tartaruga	1969 German GP	Nurburgring	1969 German GP
Stewart (then Jaguar)	1997 Australian GP	Melbourne	1999 Japanese GP
Stichting Autoraces Nederland	1971 Dutch GP	Zandvoort	1971 Dutch GP
STP Corporation	1970 South African GP	Kyalami	1970 Austrian GP
Super Aguri	2006 Bahrain GP	Sakhir	2008 Spanish GP
Surtees	1970 South African GP	Kyalami	1978 Canadian GP
TAD Crook	1952 British GP	Silverstone	1953 British GP

Location	GPs entered	GPs started	Wins/best finish	Pole positions	Fastest laps	Points	Drivers' titles	Constructors' titles
Monza	1	0	0	0	0	0	0	0
East London	1	1	12th	0	0	0	0	0
Nurburgring	2	2	12th	0	0	0	0	0
Monza	6	6	5th	0	0	2	0	0
Monza	2	2	0	0	1	0	0	0
Kyalami	10	8	12th	0	0	0	0	0
Monza	5	5	7th	0	0	0	0	0
Monza	3	1	0	0	0	0	0	0
Monza	3	2	9th	0	0	0	0	0
Buenos Aires	1	1	4th	1	0	3	0	0
Reims	2	1	8th	0	0	0	0	0
East London	1	0	0	0	0	0	0	0
Paul Ricard	112	103	1	3	2	68.5	0	0
Brands Hatch	1	1	0	0	0	0	0	0
Monza	1	1	12th	0	0	0	0	0
Brands Hatch	1	0	0	0	0	0	0	0
Paul Ricard	18	18	4th	0	0	4	0	0
Monza	12	8	6th	0	0	1	0	0
Monte Carlo	21	21	9th	0	0	0	0	0
Silverstone	1	1	11th	0	0	0	0	0
Imola	25	23	7th	0	0	0	0	0
Osterreichring	1	0	0	0	0	0	0	0
Interlagos	17	17	8th	0	0	1	0	0
Nurburgring	1	1	10th	0	0	0	0	0
Suzuka	49	49	1	1	0	47	0	0
Zandvoort	1	1	8th	0	0	0	0	0
Osterreichring	5	5	3rd	0	0	4	0	0
Barcelona	39	39	8th	0	0	4	0	0
Montreal	122	121	2nd	0	3	54	0	0
Silverstone	2	2	0	0	0	0	0	0

	Debut GP	Location	Last GP
Talbot-Darracq	1950 British GP	Silverstone	1950 French GP
TASO Mathieson	1950 British GP	Silverstone	1950 British GP
Taylor-Crawley Racing Team	1960 Belgian GP	Spa-Francorchamps	1960 Belgian GP
Team Canada Formula 1	1974 Canadian GP	Mosport Park	1974 Canadian GP
Team Chamaco Collect	1966 Monaco GP	Monte Carlo	1966 Italian GP
Team Gunston	1968 South African GP	Kyalami	1975 South African GP
Team Haas (USA)	1985 Italian GP	Monza	1986 Australian GP
Team Pierre Robert	1973 Swedish GP	Anderstorp	1973 Swedish GP
Team PR Reilly	1976 British GP	Brands Hatch	1976 British GP
Team Pretoria	1968 South African GP	Kyalami	1968 South African GP
Tecno	1969 German GP	Nurburgring	1969 German GP
Ted Lanfear	1963 South African GP	East London	1965 South African GP
Ted Whiteaway	1955 Monaco GP	Monte Carlo	1955 Monaco GP
Temple Buell	1958 Portuguese GP	Oporto	1958 Moroccan GP
Theo Helfrich	1952 German GP	Nurburgring	1953 German GP
Theodore	1977 British GP	Silverstone	1983 European GP
Tim Parnell	1961 British GP	Aintree	1963 Italian GP
Token	1974 Belgian GP	Nivelles	1974 Austrian GP
Toleman (then Benetton)	1981 San Marino GP	Imola	1985 Australian GP
Tom Jones	1967 Canadian GP	Mosport Park	1967 Canadian GP
Tom Wheatcroft Racing	1970 Belgian GP	Spa-Francorchamps	1970 Belgian GP
Toni Branca	1950 Swiss GP	Bremgarten	1951 German GP
Toni Ulmen	1952 Swiss GP	Bremgarten	1952 German GP
Tony Gaze	1952 Belgian GP	Spa-Francorchamps	1952 Italian GP
Tony Marsh	1958 German GP	Nurburgring	1961 German GP
Toro Rosso (then AlphaTauri)	2006 Bahrain GP	Sakhir	2019 Abu Dhabi GP
Toyota	2002 Australian GP	Melbourne	2009 Abu Dhabi GP
Trevor Blokdyk	1965 South African GP	East London	1965 South African GP
Trojan-Tauranac Racing	1974 Spanish GP	Jarama	1974 Italian GP
Tyrrell	1970 South African GP	Kyalami	1998 Japanese GP

Location	GPs entered	GPs started	Wins/best finish	Pole positions	Fastest laps	Points	Drivers' titles	Constructors' titles
Reims	4	4	3rd	0	0	8	0	0
Silverstone	1	1	0	0	0	0	0	0
Spa-Francorchamps	1	0	0	0	0	0	0	0
Mosport Park	1	1	0	0	0	0	0	0
Monza	5	5	4th	0	0	3	0	0
Kyalami	7	7	8th	0	0	0	0	0
Adelaide	20	19	4th	0	0	6	0	0
Anderstorp	1	0	0	0	0	0	0	0
Brands Hatch	1	0	0	0	0	0	0	0
Kyalami	1	1	0	0	0	0	0	0
Nurburgring	1	1	0	0	0	0	0	0
East London	2	1	14th	0	0	0	0	0
Monte Carlo	1	0	0	0	0	0	0	0
Casablanca	3	3	6th	0	0	0	0	0
Nurburgring	2	2	12th	0	0	0	0	0
Brands Hatch	63	44	5th	0	0	7	0	0
Monza	6	5	10th	0	0	0	0	0
Osterreichring	4	3	0	0	0	0	0	0
Adelaide	70	57	2nd	1	2	26	0	0
Mosport Park	1	0	0	0	0	0	0	0
Spa-Francorchamps	1	1	0	0	0	0	0	0
Nurburgring	2	2	10th	0	0	0	0	0
Nurburgring	2	2	8th	0	0	0	0	0
Monza	4	3	15th	0	0	0	0	0
Nurburgring	4	3	8th	0	0	0	0	0
Yas Marina	268	268	1	1	1	500	0	0
Yas Marina	140	139	2nd	2	3	278.5	0	0
East London	1	0	0	0	0	0	0	0
Monza	8	6	10th	0	0	0	0	0
Suzuka	430	430	23	14	22	617	2	1

	Debut GP	Location	Last GP
UDT Laystall Racing Team	1961 Monaco GP	Monte Carlo	1962 South African GP
United Racing Stable	1959 British GP	Aintree	1959 British GP
Vandervell Products	1951 French GP	Reims	1960 French GP
Vickomtesse de Walckiers	1952 Italian GP	Monza	1952 Italian GP
Virgin (then Marussia)	2010 Bahrain GP	Sakhir	2011 Brazilian GP
Volpini	1955 Italian GP	Monza	1955 Italian GP
Warsteiner Racing	1975 German GP	Nurburgring	1975 Italian GP
Williams (also see Frank Williams Racing Cars)	1977 Spanish GP	Jarama	-
Willi Heeks	1952 German GP	Nurburgring	1953 German GP
Willi Krakau	1952 German GP	Nurburgring	1952 German GP
Wolf	1977 Argentinian GP	Buenos Aires	1979 United States GP
Wolfgang Seidel	1953 German GP	Nurburgring	1962 Italian GP
World Wide Racing (*see* Lotus)			
WS Aston	1952 British GP	Silverstone	1952 Italian GP
Yeoman Credit Racing Team (then Bowmaker Racing Team)	1960 Monaco GP	Monte Carlo	1961 United States GP
Yves Giraud-Cabantous	1951 Swiss GP	Bremgarten	1951 Spanish GP
Zakspeed	1985 Portuguese GP	Estoril	1989 Australian GP

Location	GPs entered	GPs started	Wins/best finish	Pole positions	Fastest laps	Points	Drivers' titles	Constructors' titles
East London	14	7	5th	0	0	3	0	0
Aintree	1	0	0	0	0	0	0	0
Reims	32	30	9	7	6	108	0	1
Monza	1	0	0	0	0	0	0	0
Interlagos	38	38	14th	0	0	0	0	0
Monza	1	0	0	0	0	0	0	0
Monza	3	3	8th	0	0	0	0	0
-	792	788	114	128	134	3592	7	9
Nurburgring	2	2	0	0	0	0	0	0
Nurburgring	1	0	0	0	0	0	0	0
Watkins Glen	48	47	3	1	2	79	0	0
Monza	4	3	9th	0	0	0	0	0
Monza	3	1	0	0	0	0	0	0
Watkins Glen	15	15	2nd	0	0	27	0	0
Pedralbes	6	6	5th	0	0	2	0	0
Adelaide	74	53	5th	0	0	2	0	0

THE CIRCUITs

	GP Name	Debut date	Last date
A1 Ring/Red Bull Ring	Austrian/Styrian GP	21 September 1997	Present
Adelaide	Australian GP	3 November 1985	12 November 1995
Ain-Diab	Moroccan GP	19 October 1958	19 October 1958
Aintree	British GP	16 July 1955	21 July 1962
Albert Park	Australian GP	10 March 1996	Present
Algarve International Circuit	Portuguese GP	25 October 2020	2 May 2021
Anderstorp	Swedish GP	17 June 1973	17 June 1978
AVUS	German GP	2 August 1959	2 August 1959
Baku City Circuit	European/Azerbaijan GP	19 June 2016	Present
Barcelona-Catalunya	Spanish GP	29 September 1991	Present
Brands Hatch	British GP	11 July 1964	13 July 1986
Bremgarten	Swiss GP	4 June 1950	22 August 1954
Buddh International Circuit	Indian GP	30 October 2011	27 October 2013
Buenos Aires	Argentinian GP	18 January 1953	12 April 1998
Caesars Palace	Las Vegas GP	17 October 1981	25 September 1982
Circuit of the Americas	United States GP	18 November 2012	Present
Clermont-Ferrand	French GP	27 June 1965	2 July 1972
Detroit	Detroit GP	6 June 1982	19 June 1988
Dijon-Prenois	French/Swiss GP	7 July 1974	20 May 1984
Donington Park	European GP	11 April 1993	11 April 1993
East London	South African GP	29 December 1962	1 January 1965
Estoril	Portuguese GP	21 October 1984	22 September 1996
Fair Park	Dallas GP	8 July 1984	8 July 1984
Fuji Speedway	Japanese GP	24 October 1976	12 October 2008
Hockenheim	German GP	2 August 1970	28 July 2019
Hungaroring	Hungarian GP	10 August 1986	Present

GPs hosted	Highest average winning speed	Most successful driver	Wins	Most successful team	Wins
18	139.706mph/224.787kph	Max Verstappen	4	Mercedes	6
11	107.530mph/173.015kph	Gerhard Berger/ Alain Prost/Ayrton Senna	2	McLaren	5
1	116.227mph/187.009kph	Stirling Moss	1	Vanwall	1
5	92.247mph/148.425kph	Stirling Moss	2	Cooper/Ferrari/Lotus/ Mercedes/Vanwall	1
24	136.082mph/218.955kph	Michael Schumacher	4	Ferrari	9
2	127.166mph/204.610kph	Lewis Hamilton	2	Mercedes	2
6	104.158mph/167.590kph	Niki Lauda/Jody Scheckter	2	Tyrrell	2
1	143.331mph/230.620kph	Tony Brooks	1	Ferrari	1
6	124.246mph/199.912kph	Valtteri Bottas/ Lewis Hamilton/ Sergio Perez/ Daniel Ricciardo/ Nico Rosberg/Max Verstappen	1	Mercedes/Red Bull	3
32	131.774mph/212.024kph	Lewis Hamilton/ Michael Schumacher	6	Ferrari	8
14	129.756mph/208.777kph	Niki Lauda	3	Lotus/Williams	3
5	99.211mph/159.631kph	Juan Manuel Fangio	2	Ferrari/Alfa Romeo	2
3	126.476mph/203.500kph	Sebastian Vettel	3	Red Bull Racing	3
20	124.751mph/200.724kph	Juan Manuel Fangio	4	Williams	4
2	100.110mph/161.077kph	Michele Alboreto/ Alan Jones	1	Tyrrell/Williams	1
10	122.529mph/197.149kph	Lewis Hamilton	5	Mercedes	5
4	101.563mph/163.414kph	Jackie Stewart	2	Lotus/Tyrrell	2
7	85.697mph/137.886kph	Ayrton Senna	3	Lotus/McLaren	2
6	122.711mph/197.442kph	Mario Andretti/ Jean-Pierre Jabouille/Niki Lauda/Ronnie Peterson/Alain Prost/Keke Rosberg	1	Lotus/Renault	2
1	102.387mph/164.741kph	Ayrton Senna	1	McLaren	1
3	98.004mph/157.688kph	Jim Clark	2	Lotus	2
13	124.119mph/199.708kph	Nigel Mansell/Alain Prost	3	Williams	6
1	80.283mph/129.175kph	Keke Rosberg	1	Williams	1
4	129.167mph/207.829kph	Fernando Alonso/ Mario Andretti/ Lewis Hamilton/ James Hunt	1	McLaren	2
37	146.176mph/235.198kph	Michael Schumacher	4	Ferrari	11
37	120.245mph/193.475kph	Lewis Hamilton	8	McLaren	11

	GP Name	Debut date	Last date
Imola	Italian/San Marino/ Emilia Romagna GP	14 September 1980	Present
Indianapolis Motor Speedway	United States GP	24 September 2000	17 June 2007
Interlagos	Brazilian/Sao Paulo GP	11 February 1973	Present
Istanbul Park	Turkish GP	21 August 2005	10 October 2021
Jacarepagua	Brazilian GP	29 January 1978	26 March 1989
Jarama	Spanish GP	12 May 1968	21 June 1981
Jeddah Corniche Circuit	Saudi Arabian GP	5 December 2021	Present
Jerez	Spanish/European GP	13 April 1986	26 October 1997
Korea International Circuit	Korean GP	24 October 2010	6 October 2013
Kyalami	South African GP	2 January 1967	14 March 1993
Le Mans Bugatti Circuit	French GP	2 July 1967	2 July 1967
Long Beach	United States GP West	28 March 1976	27 March 1983
Losail International Circuit	Qatar GP	21 November 2021	21 November 2021
Magny-Cours	French GP	7 July 1991	22 June 2008
Marina Bay Circuit	Singapore GP	28 September 2008	Present
Mexico City	Mexican/Mexico City GP	27 October 1963	Present
Miami International Autodrome	Miami GP	8 May 2022	Present
Monsanto	Portuguese GP	23 August 1959	23 August 1959
Monte Carlo	Monaco GP	21 May 1950	Present
Montjuich Park	Spanish GP	4 May 1969	27 April 1975
Montreal	Canadian GP	8 October 1978	Present
Monza	Italian GP	3 September 1950	Present
Mosport Park	Canadian GP	27 August 1967	9 October 1977
Mugello	Tuscany GP	13 September 2020	13 September 2020
Nivelles	Belgian GP	4 June 1972	12 May 1974
Nurburgring	German/European/ Luxembourg/Eifel GP	29 July 1951	11 October 2020

GPs hosted	Highest average winning speed	Most successful driver	Wins	Most successful team	Wins
30	131.930mph/212.276kph	Michael Schumacher	7	Ferrari/Williams	8
8	127.173mph/204.621kph	Michael Schumacher	5	Ferrari	6
39	130.840mph/210.522kph	Michael Schumacher	4	Ferrari	9
9	136.394mph/219.458kph	Felipe Massa	3	Ferrari	3
10	117.086mph/188.391kph	Alain Prost	5	McLaren	4
9	95.922mph/154.339kph	Mario Andretti	2	Lotus	4
2	136.367mph/219.415kph	Lewis Hamilton/Max Verstappen	1	Mercedes/Red Bull Racing	1
7	115.127mph/185.239kph	Alain Prost/Ayrton Senna	2	McLaren	3
4	119.266mph/191.898kph	Sebastian Vettel	3	Red Bull Racing	3
20	129.835mph/208.905kph	Mario Andretti/Alan Jones/Niki Lauda/ Nelson Piquet/Clay Regazzoni/Carlos Reutemann/Gilles Villeneuve/John Watson	3	Ferrari	4
1	98.912mph/159.149kph	Jack Brabham	1	Brabham	1
8	88.448mph/142.312kph	Mario Andretti/Alan Jones/Niki Lauda/ Nelson Piquet/Clay Regazzoni/Carlos Reutemann/Gilles Villeneuve/John Watson	1	Ferrari	3
1	135.343mph/217.767kph	Lewis Hamilton	1	Mercedes	1
18	128.107mph/206.124kph	Michael Schumacher	8	Ferrari	8
13	103.507mph/166.542kph	Sebastian Vettel	5	Mercedes/Red Bull Racing	4
22	123.759mph/199.128kph	Max Verstappen	4	Red Bull Racing	4
1	121.770mph/195.927kph	Max Verstappen	1	Red Bull Racing	1
1	95.310mph/153.353kph	Stirling Moss	1	Rob Walker Racing Team	1
68	98.096mph/157.837kph	Ayrton Senna	6	McLaren	15
4	97.843mph/157.429kph	Jackie Stewart	2	Tyrrell	2
41	128.689mph/207.060kph	Lewis Hamilton/ Michael Schumacher	7	Ferrari	11
72	153.817mph/247.491kph	Lewis Hamilton/ Michael Schumacher	5	Ferrari	19
8	118.032mph/189.913kph	Jackie Stewart	2	McLaren	3
1	82.640mph/132.968kph	Lewis Hamilton	1	Mercedes	1
2	113.353mph/182.385kph	Emerson Fittipaldi	2	Lotus/McLaren	1
41	126.850mph/204.101kph	Michael Schumacher	5	Ferrari	14

	GP Name	Debut date	Last date
Oporto	Portuguese GP	24 August 1958	14 August 1960
Osterreichring	Austrian GP	16 August 1970	16 August 1987
Paul Ricard	French GP	4 July 1971	Present
Pedralbes	Spanish GP	28 October 1951	24 October 1954
Pescara	Pescara GP	18 August 1957	18 August 1957
Phoenix	United States GP	4 June 1989	10 March 1991
Reims	French GP	2 July 1950	3 July 1966
Riverside	United States GP	20 November 1960	20 November 1960
Rouen-les-Essarts	French GP	6 July 1952	7 July 1968
Sakhir	Bahrain/Sakhir GP	4 April 2004	Present
Sebring	United States GP	12 December 1959	12 December 1959
Sepang	Malaysian GP	17 October 1999	1 October 2017
Shanghai International Circuit	Chinese GP	26 September 2004	14 April 2019
Silverstone	British/70th Anniversary GP	13 May 1950	Present
Sochi	Russian GP	12 October 2014	26 September 2021
Spa-Francorchamps	Belgian GP	18 June 1950	Present
St Jovite	Canadian GP	22 September 1968	20 September 1970
Suzuka	Japanese GP	1 November 1987	Present
TI Circuit	Pacific GP	17 April 1994	22 October 1995
Valencia Street Circuit	European GP	24 August 2008	24 June 2012
Watkins Glen	United States GP	8 October 1961	5 October 1980
Yas Marina Circuit	Abu Dhabi GP	1 November 2009	Present
Zandvoort	Dutch GP	17 August 1952	Present
Zeltweg	Austrian GP	23 August 1964	23 August 1964
Zolder	Belgian GP	20 May 1973	29 April 1984

GPs hosted	Highest average winning speed	Most successful driver	Wins	Most successful team	Wins
2	109.279mph/175.831kph	Jack Brabham/ Stirling Moss	1	Cooper/Vanwall	1
18	146.277mph/235.359kph	Alain Prost	3	Lotus	4
18	136.604mph/219.796kph	Alain Prost	4	McLaren/Williams	3
2	98.771mph/158.922kph	Juan Manuel Fangio/ Mike Hawthorn	1	Alfa Romeo/Ferrari	1
1	96.525mph/155.309kph	Stirling Moss	1	Vanwall	1
3	93.018mph/149.666kph	Ayrton Senna	2	McLaren	3
11	136.885mph/220.249kph	Juan Manuel Fangio	3	Ferrari	4
1	98.996mph/159.284kph	Stirling Moss	1	Rob Walker Racing Team	1
5	108.766mph/175.005kph	Dan Gurney	2	Ferrari	2
19	129.853mph/208.933kph	Lewis Hamilton	5	Ferrari	7
1	98.827mph/159.013kph	Bruce McLaren	1	Cooper	1
19	128.545mph/206.829kph	Sebastian Vettel	4	Ferrari	7
16	127.493mph/205.136kph	Lewis Hamilton	6	Mercedes	6
57	146.274mph/235.355kph	Lewis Hamilton	8	Ferrari	15
8	132.288mph/212.851kph	Lewis Hamilton	5	Mercedes	8
55	149.936mph/241.247kph	Michael Schumacher	6	Ferrari	14
2	101.269mph/162.942kph	Denny Hulme/Jacky Ickx	1	McLaren	1
32	137.514mph/221.260kph	Michael Schumacher	6	Ferrari/McLaren	7
2	108.075mph/173.892kph	Michael Schumacher	2	Benetton	2
5	120.528mph/193.930kph	Sebastian Vettel	2	Ferrari/Red Bull Racing	2
20	129.549mph/208.444kph	Jim Clark/Graham Hill	3	Lotus	7
14	130.047mph/209.246kph	Lewis Hamilton	5	Mercedes/Red Bull Racing	6
32	126.881mph/204.152kph	Jim Clark	4	Ferrari	8
1	99.161mph/159.550kph	Lorenzo Bandini	1	Ferrari	1
10	116.213mph/186.987kph	Niki Lauda	2	Ferrari	4